DARK HOURS

South Carolina Soldiers, Sailors and Citizens Who Were Held in Federal Prisons during the War for Southern Independence, 1861–1865

RANDOLPH W. KIRKLAND, JR.

FOR THE SOUTH CAROLINA HISTORICAL SOCIETY

The University of South Carolina Press

© 2002 South Carolina Historical Society

Cloth edition published by the South Carolina Historical Society, 2002
Paperback edition published in Columbia, South Carolina,
by the University of South Carolina Press, 2012

www.sc.edu/uscpress

Manufactured in the United States of America

21 20 19 18 17 16 15 14 13 12
10 9 8 7 6 5 4 3 2 1

ISBN 978-1-61117-144-0 (pbk)

DEDICATION

Sergeant Berry Greenwood Benson
Image courtesy of the South Carolina Historical Society

This compilation of South Carolinians held by the United States as prisoners of war, 1861-1865, is dedicated to the memory of Sergeant Berry Greenwood Benson, Company H, 1st South Carolina Volunteer Infantry, (Gregg's) McGowan's Brigade, Wilcox's Division, A.P. Hill's Corps, Army of Northern Virginia. A cheerful comrade in adversity, a lethal soldier and intrepid scout, who was captured behind enemy lines while scouting at Spotsylvania and sent to Point Lookout. He escaped two days later and swam the Potomac but was recaptured and sent to Elmira. He escaped from there by tunnel and walked back to rejoin his regiment at Petersburg, VA. He refused to surrender at Appomattox, evaded enemy sentries and walked home with his arms. His service confirms the adage that a good soldier makes a very bad prisoner.

INSCRIPTION ON THE CONFEDERATE MONUMENT AT COLUMBIA, S.C.

To South Carolina's Dead
1861   of the   1865
Confederate Army
Erected by the Women of South Carolina

This Monument
Perpetuates the Memory
Of Those Who
True to the Instincts of Their Birth,
Faithful to the Teaching of Their Fathers,
Constant in Their Love for the State,
Died in the Performance of Their Duty,
Who
Have Glorified a Fallen Cause
By the Simple Manhood of Their Lives,
The Patient Endurance of Suffering
And the Heroism of Death
And Who
In the Dark Hours of Imprisonment,
And the Hopelessness of the Hospital.
In the Short, Sharp Agony of the Field,
Found Support and Consolation
In the Belief
That at Home They Would not be Forgotten.
Let the Stranger
Who May in Future Times
Read This Inscription
Recognize That These Were Men
Whom Power Could Not Corrupt,
Whom Death Could Not Terrify,
Whom Defeat Could Not Dishonor,
And Let Their Virtue Plead
For Just Judgment
Of the Cause For Which They Perished;
Let the South Carolinian
Of Another Generation
Remember
That the State Taught Them
How to Live and How to Die,
And That From Her Broken Fortunes
She Has Preserved For Her Children
The Priceless Treasure of Their Memories;
Teaching All Who May Claim
The Same Birthright
That Truth, Courage, and Patriotism
Endureth Forever.

William Henry Trescott

CONTENTS

Preface • i

Acknowledgments • ii

Introduction • iii

Alphabetical lists of soldiers, sailors and citizens held in captivity:

A • 1	J • 237	S • 404
B • 14	K • 254	T • 448
C • 68	L • 267	U • 466
D • 111	M • 289	V • 467
E • 135	N • 339	W • 470
F • 145	O • 346	Y • 507
G • 164	P • 352	Z • 510
H • 191	Q • 376	
I • 235	R • 378	

Appendices:

Source Codes and Abbreviations • 512

Extracts from the *Official Records* Concerning Prisoners of War • 524

Statistical Summaries • 536

PREFACE

All cultures have honored their warriors in story and song. The epic literature of ancient Greece and India, Norse sagas and the *Torah* celebrate the exploits and honor the deaths in combat of their national heroes. Hector, Odysseus, Lord Rama, Joshua and Beowulf epitomize the warrior values of bravery, camaraderie and sacrifice, which give higher meaning to the brutal facts of war. The events of the American Civil War have entered modern historical consciousness as subjects worthy of epic literary treatment. The *casus belli* were of the highest political and social consequence. Combatants on both sides were warriors of great renown or great infamy, and the defeat of the Confederacy in 1865 transformed both North and South in profound ways. Since Appomattox, writers and historians, some of whom were combatants, have labored to transform the true facts of the war into literature–to elevate the war and its warriors to heroic status. Ulysses S. Grant's *Memoirs*, Herman Melville's *Battle Pieces*, Shelby Foote's *Civil War: A Narrative* and Gordon Rhea's magnificent battle histories are among the works succeeding in this endeavor. However, epic writers and Civil War mythmakers depend upon other scholars in very important ways. The Civil War was a true event that took place in a modern era of mass communication, fast-traveling news and widespread literacy. Accounts of the war are myriad and must be considered by every writer on the subject. In order to create literature that rings true, writers must get the facts straight. They must know with certainty the true dates and locations of events and accurate names of participants. Without truth, Civil War literature fails, and histories sink into irrelevance.

Randolph Kirkland's books are the foundations upon which South Carolina's Civil War literature is built. His *Broken Fortunes*, published in 1995 by the South Carolina Historical Society, listed South Carolina's Civil War casualties. It gave names, families and homes to the state's fallen soldiers. That work is the authoritative source of information on the state's Civil War casualties. Now, in his companion work *Dark Hours*, Mr. Kirkland has expanded his research to identify those South Carolinians who suffered capture and imprisonment as prisoners of war in Union prison camps. These warriors call to be named. Their families, friends and neighbors endured their going to war. They shared the uncertainty and fears that were part of their loved ones' absence, and celebrated the prisoners' return. Mr. Kirkland has opened a new door to our understanding; not only of the Civil War in South Carolina, but also into the aftermath of that war. He has introduced us to unfamiliar sites of the Civil War, such as Elmira, New York; Johnson's Island, Ohio; Rock Island, Illinois; and Camp Morton, Indiana. Most importantly, he has given us the names of 11,238 fallen South Carolina warriors.

The men of *Dark Hours* came back home after the war. Those immortalized in *Broken Fortunes* did not. Some of the men of *Dark Hours* returned to their old lives. Others took up new professions, new families and new lives. Mr. Kirkland has given scholars an important research tool for inquiry into the history of postwar South Carolina. Did the former prisoners of war become the state's leaders? Did they and their sons reconcile with their former enemies? If so, how and under what terms was that reconciliation achieved?

In addition to building the future, the returning prisoners began to create the literary epic of the Civil War. They remembered in writing and in fireside stories the events they had witnessed and the lives of their fallen comrades in arms. Those thousands who emerged from Union prisons linked the Old and New South through their personal experiences. They helped to reunite an American society that they had previously sought to sunder.

Historians have used *Broken Fortunes* with great success. They will find *Dark Hours* equally, if not more, provocative. The stories are the stuff of legend. The tellers speak as witnesses.

Alexander Moore
University of South Carolina Press

ACKNOWLEDGMENTS

This compilation of South Carolina prisoners of war from 1861-1865 has been prepared almost entirely from National Archive microfilm records or published sources. There is little glamour in the grinding weariness of captivity, and the descendants of prisoners who survived have not been inclined to volunteer family stories and papers. The structured and tedious work of transcribing data from seemingly endless rolls of microfilm was such that it was not practical to seek or accept help from those not thoroughly familiar with computer database programs and South Carolina military organizations.

There was a small band of interested and involved people who volunteered their time, talent and knowledge in certain details. Dr. Alexander Moore, as always considerate and generous, provided the preface to this work and the link to the previous book in this series, *Broken Fortunes*. Others include:

W. Eric Emerson
Editor in Chief, South Carolina Historical Society

Stephen G. Hoffius
Former Director of Publications, South Carolina Historical Society

James B. Clary
Author, Manuscript History of the 15th SCVI
Cary, NC

J.R. Fisher, Jr.
Florence Stockade Museum Records
Florence, SC

Mary C. Cunningham
An incident involving an arranged POW exchange
Liberty Hill, SC

Retta Sanders
Details of the prison death and family history of a Stateburg, SC member of the Charleston Light Dragoons
Sumter, SC

INTRODUCTION

This volume is a compilation of the names and prison circumstances of those South Carolinians–soldiers, sailors and citizens–who were held in Federal military prisons during the War for Southern Independence. It is not a study of the Northern prison system, policies or practices. However, some description of the Federal prison structure and the prisoner exchange procedure is included in this introduction, so that those who have not studied the subject can better understand the movement of the individual prisoners into, through, and out of the system.

The entire subject of the handling, and mishandling, of prisoners, both by the North and the South, is very complicated and rich in acrimony and prejudice. The basic facts of this aspect of the war are contained in the eight volumes in Series II of the *Official Records of the War of the Rebellion*.

Other facts and actions involving the capture of individuals and their disposition are scattered throughout the rest of the *Official Records* in the reports and correspondence. The records in these lists are based primarily on microfilmed copies of the surviving prisoner rolls and records kept at the Northern prisons. These are assembled in the M598 series microfilm publications relating to Confederate Prisoners of War 1861-1865 from the National Archives. There are 145 rolls in this series, which reproduce 427 bound volumes of records. There is great variation in the completeness of the rolls and lists kept at the many camps and prisons, and there is considerable duplication. A number of the pages and entries in the records are illegible due to fading and/or poor handwriting. All of the records are in script that is not always easy to read even in well-preserved documents. Fortunately, there is duplication of information in the lists made up for prisoners to be transferred, which often provided means to correct the spelling of names and the identification of units. The records in this volume are thus not always an exact rendering of the basic prison record. The spelling of names and the unit identifications have been corrected in many cases. Care has been taken to avoid the creation of phantom individuals and to eliminate those detected. This editing is important for genealogical and statistical uses of the material. Instances were found in which one individual became four separate individuals due to variations in spelling and unit identity.

THE COMPILED SERVICE RECORDS

It was realized, upon completion of the research into the Federal prison camp records, that the Compiled Service Records, or CSR's, would have to be included in this study. The Compiled Service Records of Confederate Soldiers Who Served in Organizations from the State of South Carolina are available in the M267 Series of National Archives microfilm in 392 rolls. These rolls are organized by units, and names appear in alphabetical order within each regiment, battalion or independent company unit. The War Department created the Compiled Service Records beginning in the early 1900s. It was a tedious and complicated project. Forms were designed and printed for each unit, prison or hospital. An envelope was opened for each man. Federal and Confederate records were examined for details of each man whose name was found on a report, list or muster roll. The details were entered into an appropriate form and the form put into the named man's envelope. The work was done by hand since typewriters were not in common use. These compiled records were kept in the archives in Washington and were difficult to access until 1954 when the Confederate CSRs were microfilmed and became much more accessible. The CSRs are a valuable source for prisoner of war records because they provide details of captures before a prisoner entered the formal prison system. The CSRs also record captures in which the prisoner was paroled in the field and released without being sent to a prison. The CSRs are certainly the single best source for details of Confederate service records. They are, however, not infallible. Names are misspelled, the records for men with similar names are often misfiled. Many of the original records used for the foundation of the CSRs were missing or incomplete. By 1954 it also was apparent that some of the documents created fifty odd years before had aged badly.

THE ORGANIZATION OF THE ALPHABETIC LISTS

There are one or more records for each man identified in this volume. Each record, or line, covers a stopover point in the movements of a man through the Federal prison system from capture to death, exchange or release. A full record includes the name, rank, company, unit, place of capture, date of capture, place held, date of movement, destination, the disposition of the man and a coded listing of the sources supporting the records. These sources do not necessarily agree or provide all of the details in the records but do agree on the identity and existence of the man.

The first or single line in each entry provides the full identity of the man and his time and place of capture plus his first known holding point or disposition. Subsequent lines or records omit the information that is common to all records in order to more easily read the man's complete prison history.

The source codes listed at the end of each record will often include entries that begin with the letter "P" followed by a number. The number is the microfilm roll in the prison system M598 series. Additional sources are listed using a code identity such as 'KEB' which identifies "The History of Kershaw's Brigade" by D. Augustus Dickert. These source entries do not necessarily indicate that additional data might be found in that source but do represent that the individual's name and unit have been confirmed by rolls in that source. The source code entry "CSR" indicates that a record was derived from or confirmed by the Compiled Service Records. A fuller description of the sources related to these codes is to be found in the appendix. The user of this compilation should finally be aware that there are many errors in the original records. The Prisoners often lied to their captors. Some prisoners took the names of dead or departed prisoners for reasons unexplained. As a result, some records that show a man as having both died and been exchanged. The dates given for the same event often do not match.

It must be recognized also that all of the records are based on handwritten lists of people, places and plans. Many of the lists were lists made with the intent to ship selected prisoners from one place to another. Any number of prisoners on the list may not have gone. The practice of selecting the most feeble for exchange guaranteed that some would die or be too ill to be moved. Last minute decisions and actions could effect the accuracy of a transport list. One little known incident illustrates this. Towards the end of 1864, the burden of holding and caring for prisoners of war became intolerable for the Confederate authorities. Until then, exchanges had been made man for man at a mutually agreed upon time and place. This trickle exchange of debilitated prisoners, plus General Grant's relentless attacks, produced a massive increase in the prison population of both sides.

In desperation, the Confederate Commissioner of Exchange, Colonel Robert Oulds, informed the Federal authorities that he intended to unilaterally release 14,000 prisoners near Savannah, GA. The place chosen for the release was Venus Pt. on the Savannah River, near the Federal stronghold on Hilton Head. This resulted in a hurried decision by the Federal authorities to load some 3500 prisoners on a ship bound for Venus Pt., GA. Many of these prisoners were diverted from shipments bound for exchange at Aikens Ldg., VA. The unequal exchange took place on November 15, 1864. The records for these diverted prisoners thus shows transfers for exchange to both Aikens Ldg., VA and Venus Pt., GA.

In this compilation no attempt has been made to eliminate conflicting entries. The conflicts themselves may be of value to a researcher interested in prisoner administration. In those cases where a record is incomplete, it is recommended that the more complete records of a man captured and processed at the same time and place be assumed as the most probable material for filling in gaps. This is a practical solution for the individual case, because prisoners were transferred in large groups and seldom if ever singly.

NORTHERN PRISONS

When the war started neither the United States nor Confederate States had made provision for the holding, care and transportation of prisoners. In the North, existing forts and jails were initially used. These quickly became overcrowded, as the war settled into an unexpected ferocity. Additional camps were established, often in great haste, so that accommodations of one sort or another were provided for the thousands of guests who arrived in unplanned waves. A number of hospitals were also required, but these were either attached to the prison camps or were facilities also used by the Federal army. An exception ito this occured following the battle of Gettysburg. The Confederate casualties left behind after that battle were so numerous that special hospitals for Confederate soldiers were established at Davids Island, NY, Bedloes Island, NY and Chester, PA. The Prisons used in the North, in order of establishment:

PRISON	OPEN	CLOSED	CAPACITY
Ft. Warren, Boston MA	/ /61	09/ /65	333
Ft. Columbus, NY	/ /61	04/ /65	486
Ft. Lafayette, NY	/ /61	03/ /66	128
Ft. McHenry, MD	03/ /63	09/ /65	1195
Gratiot St., St. Louis, MO	/ /61	07/ /65	747
Old Capitol, Washington	10/ /62	10/ /65	1009
Camp Chase, Columbus, OH	11/15/61	07/ /65	9045
Alton, IL Penitentiary	02/01/62	07/ /65	1351
Camp Douglas, Chicago IL	02/15/62	07/ /65	11702
Camp Morton, Indianapolis	02/22/62	07/ /65	490
Camp Butler, Springfield IL	02/23/62	12/ /63	2186
Johnson's Island, Sandusky	02/24/62	09/ /65	3209
Ft. Delaware, DE	04/15/62	01/ /66	9174
Pt. Lookout, MD	07/15/63	07/ /65	19786
Rock Island, IL	12/15/63	07/ /65	8398
New Orleans, LA	12/ /63	06/ /65	1691
Elmira, NY	07/15/64	07/ /65	9480
Ship Island, MS	10/ /64	06/ /65	4070
Hart's Island, NY	04/ /65	07/ /65	3413
Newport News, VA	04/ /65	07/ /65	3434

(From Gen. Hoffman's final summary report, O.R. S2, V8)

Most early prisoners from the eastern theater were initially sent to Fort Warren, in Boston Harbor, and to Forts Lafayette and Columbus in New York Harbor. Fort Warren was later reserved for captured general officers. Johnson's Island, Sandusky, OH, was set aside as a prison for officers on or about May 1, 1862. Naval prisoners appear to have also been sent there. A survey of the records would indicate that in the last two years of the war, officers who were captured in the east were usually sent to Fort Delaware.

Federal prison management was a responsibility of Montgomery Meigs, the Quartermaster General. On October 7th, 1861 General Meigs appointed Lieutenant Colonel William Hoffman as Commissary General of prisoners. Colonel Hoffman assumed responsibility for the housing, feeding, clothing and discipline of all prisoners in Federal military prisons. He had little control over the nature or quantity of the prisoners turned over to him. His office probably had little control over the terms governing the release or exchange of prisoners. There are hints within the prisoner rolls that suggest that prison authorities exercised some control over the selection of individuals to be included in a release or exchange contingent. There is a note attached to the Fort Delaware prison entry for Captain Edward J. Dean of Company C, 22nd South Carolina Volunteer Infantry, captured at the Petersburg Crater, July 30, 1864, that reads, "Is a bitter and uncompromising rebel–a dangerous man to be released." Captain Dean was held to the very end and was released with permanently injured health. Colonel Hoffman's office could and did transfer prisoners within the system to relieve crowding and to segregate hard case rebels. The sociology of the prisons is beyond the scope of this work, but it should be noted that the military prison system also had to confine a large number of suspected disloyal citizens and occasionally hold paroled U.S. soldiers awaiting exchange.

All evidence suggests that Colonel Hoffman tried to be a fair and efficient manager. Deficiencies were due to indifferent provisions of clothing, food and fuel and the varying effectiveness of local prison administrators. He initiated a system of inspections that reported fairly on bad conditions at the various camps.

The U.S. military prison system was under a centralized control. The excellent railroad network in the north and the well established telegraph communication system was such that the movement of prisoners was directed and controlled by logic and plan rather than by local expediency.

EXCHANGE AND RELEASE

No examination of the handling of prisoners can avoid the very messy and confusing matter of paroles. A parole is the release of a prisoner upon his oath or promise to not take up arms against the captor side until properly exchanged. It was common practice in the early stages of the war to parole captives in the field at the site of surrender. General Grant paroled the garrison of Vicksburg in 1863 and General Lee paroled the garrison of Harper's Ferry in 1862. The problems created by the mass paroling of prisoners are not obvious, but they were real and constantly interfered with the periodic exchange and release of prisoners. The subject is outside the scope of this document, but some knowledge will help the reader to understand the erratic decisions affecting the exchanges of prisoners. The problems caused by field paroles included the administrative mess in documenting and accounting for individuals. The man and his paper record were separated. Who kept track of paroled and released prisoners? Those who were simply set free were apt to avoid later service. What duties could parolees perform to pay for their keep that would not violate the spirit of their parole? The concern over these problems was such that the Federal government turned against the use of field paroles and, with certain exceptions, largely sent captives physically into the prison system.

An informal exchange of prisoners existed early in the war. This was usually done under a flag of truce between opposing commanders and involved a one-for-one exchange, though the unilateral release of badly wounded individuals was not uncommon. The accumulation of large blocks of prisoners as the war became more serious created a desire on both sides for a more orderly system. Special exchanges continued but were hampered by Federal reluctance to enter into any sort of agreement that might constitute recognition of the Confederacy. The matter of special exchanges was irksome and inefficient in an age of pen and paper. The following extract from the *Official Records* of one transaction illustrates the involvement of important people in minor details:

DEPARTMENT. ADJUTANT-GENERAL'S OFFICE
Washington, May 30, 1862

Brig. Gen. WADSWORTH
Commanding, &c, Military Governor District of Columbia.

Sir: The Secretary of War directs that First Lieut. J.B. Fellers, South Carolina Volunteers, a prisoner taken in arms against the United States, now in the Old Capitol, be transferred to Major-General Wool at Fort Monroe to be exchanged for First Lieut. A.M. Underhill, Eleventh New York Volunteers, a prisoner of war at Richmond.

I am, sir, & c.,
L. THOMAS
Adjutant-General

ADJUTANT-GENERAL's OFFICE,
Washington, May 30, 1862

Maj. Gen. John E. Wool, U.S. Army,
Commanding Department of Virginia, Fort Monroe, Va.

Sir: Brigadier-General Wadsworth has been directed to send from this city First Lieut. J.B. Fellers, South Carolina volunteers and Colonel Dimick has been ordered to send from Fort Warren Lieut. Col. James Jackson, Twenty-seventh Alabama volunteers, to Fort Monroe to report to you to be exchanged for First Lieut. A.J. Underhill, Eleventh New York Volunteers and Lieut. Col. G.W. Neff, Second Kentucky Volunteers. The Secretary of War directs that on their arrival at Fort Monroe you inform the nearest rebel officer that they are to be exchanged as above indicated, and that they be released whenever Lieutenant Underhill and Colonel Neff may be given up.

I am, sir, & c.,
L. THOMAS
Adjutant-General

HEADQUARTERS ARMY OF THE POTOMAC,
June 14, 1862

General R.E. Lee,
Commanding Army of Northern Virginia, Richmond Sir: Lieutenant Fellers, Company G, Thirteenth Regiment of South Carolina Infantry, is now at Fortress Monroe waiting to be exchanged, according to the information I have from the War Department, for Lieutenant Underhill, of the Eleventh Regiment of New York Volunteers, who is said to be a prisoner at Richmond. I am prepared to send Lieutenant Fellers within your lines at City Point upon an intimation from you that Lieutenant Underhill has been released.

I am, sir, very respectfully, your obedient servant,
GEO. B. McClellan
Major General, Commanding
[Endorsement]

General Lee:

No arrangement of the sort has been made and individual exchanges are declined. We will exchange generally or according to some principle, but not by arbitrary selections.

G.W. RANDOLPH
Secretary of War

The Confederate authorities continued to press for a general exchange agreement. On February 23, 1862 General

Howell Cobb, C.S.A., met with General John E. Wool, U.S.A., Commander of the Department of Virginia at Fort Monroe, and they discussed the terms of a general exchange cartel. They agreed that it would be based on a similar cartel that had been developed between the United States and Great Britain during the War of 1812. This agreement provided for a scale of values assigned to various ranks. The side which had an excess of prisoners over those offered by the opposing side would deliver these excess prisoners to that side on parole.

These negotiations were stalled by U.S. Secretary of War Stanton, who preferred a continuance of the special exchanges, since the Ft. Donelson surrender suddenly gave the North a preponderance of prisoners. However, the Peninsula campaign began to result in a growing number of Federal prisoners, and the pressure upon President Lincoln to secure their safety resulted in a resumption in negotiations. C.S.A. General D.H. Hill and U.S. General John A. Dix, Commanding at Fort Monroe, began discussions on July 18, 1862 and formally signed a cartel governing the general exchange of prisoners. The cartel established the equivalent values of prisoners of different ranks and identified the individuals who were entitled to be treated as bona-fide prisoners of war, which also then settled the treatment of captured privateers and blockade runners. Under the terms of the cartel each side was to appoint two agents of exchange. Aiken's Landing on the James River was the agreed upon exchange point in the east; Vicksburg was to be that for the west.

The Confederacy appointed Judge Robert Ould, acting Judge Advocate of the Confederate Army, as agent for the east. The United States initially named Generals Dix and Franklin as their agents for exchange. The Confederacy appointed Major N.G. Watts agent for the west, to act under the direction of Judge Oulds.

A report by U.S. Colonel Hoffman, shown below, gives an estimate of the Confederate prisoners held at the beginning of the general exchange:

OFFICE COMMISSARY-GENERAL of PRISONERS
Washington, D.C., July 24, 1862
Hon. E. M. Stanton, Secretary of War.

Sir: I have the honor to submit the following as the approximate number of prisoners of war held at the several prison stations:

Fort Warren, Boston.................................	500
Fort Delaware, Del.................................	1,000
Fort McHenry, MD.................................	500
Fort Monroe, VA.................................	1,000
Depot at Sandusky, Ohio.................................	1,300
Camp Chase, Columbus, Ohio.................................	1,500
Camp Morton, Indianapolis.................................	4,000
Camp Douglas, Chicago.................................	7,800
Camp Butler, Springfield.................................	2,000
Military Prison, Alton.................................	500
Military Prison, Saint Louis.................................	<u>400</u>
	20,500

Very respectfully, your obedient servant,
W. HOFFMAN
Colonel Third Infantry, Commissary- General of Prisoners.

On July 27, 1862 U.S. Adjutant General Lorenzo Thomas was appointed agent for the exchange of prisoners, replacing General Dix. General Franklin was ill and unable to act as exchange agent in the west, and he was replaced by Captains H.M. Lazelle and H.W. Freedley. They were directed to take the prisoners from Camp Morton, Camp Chase, Sandusky Depot, Camp Douglas, Camp Butler and Alton, Illinois, totaling some 12,000 men, to Vicksburg. They were to be moved by rail to Cairo, there to be put on steamers for Vicksburg under flag of truce.

On or about August 3, 1862 some 3,500 Confederate prisoners from Fort Warren and Fort Delaware were exchanged

at Aiken's Landing. Exchanges continued such that by November 1, 1862 all Confederate prisoners from regular organizations who did not refuse exchange had been returned to Confederate control.

Sometime in October or November 1862 U.S. Lieutenant Colonel W.H. Ludlow, Inspector General of the 7th Corps, was appointed Agent of Exchange to replace Lorenzo Thomas. It is clear that this position was not a popular one.

In December President Davis issued a proclamation declaring General Benjamin Butler a felon and outlaw for the illegal execution in New Orleans of a citizen, William B. Mumford, for hauling down a U.S. flag upon the occupation of that city by the Federals. Davis's proclamation directed that no commissioned officers of the Federal army would be released on parole prior to exchange until General Benjamin Butler was punished for his actions in New Orleans. The federal authorities retaliated by suspending the exchange of officers. The place of exchange was shifted about this time to City Point, VA.

On March 6, 1863 the Confederate congress passed a resolution requiring the return of any captured former slaves in Federal service to their former owners, which later had serious repercussions. The Federal authorities were forced to hold back the exchange of prisoners in order to hold hostages to ensure proper treatment for their enrolled black soldiers. The Confederacy was forced to yield on this matter.

On July 23, 1863 U.S. Brigadier General S.A. Meredith was detailed as Agent of Exchange replacing Lieutenant Colonel Ludlow. On the same day U.S. Major John E. Mulford, in charge of flag-of-truce boats, was detailed to assist General Meredith. Major Mulford was to serve to the end with the final rank of Brevet Brigadier General.

On July 23, 1863 orders were issued by federal authorities to send all wounded prisoners of Gettysburg to City Point for exchange or parole. A summary report by U.S. Colonel Hoffman listing the prison circumstances up through November 1, 1863 showed that 92,027 officers, men and civilians had been exchanged, 14,830 had died, escaped or been released, 15,260 were out on parole and 30,609 were still in prison.

This traffic in prisoners is dry reading today, but any movement of humanity is sure to have its antic occasions. The following extract from the *Official Records* illustrates one such affair involving the transfer of certain civilians:

Col. W. HOFFMAN, Commissary-General of Prisoners

COLONEL: I enclose to you a letter just received from Mr. Ould. The character of these women was of course not known to you, and they were probably sent by some mistake on a flag-of truce boat instead of to a penitentiary.

I am, very respectfully, your obedient servant,
WM H. LUDLOW
Lieutenant-Colonel and Agent for the Exchange of Prisoners

P.S. The Description of these women as given by Mr. Ould is fully sustained by the officer in charge of them.

W. H. L.
CITY POINT, VA., May 14, 1863
Lieutenant-Colonel LUDLOW, Agent of Exchange.

Sir: I send back to you two strumpets who were landed at this place yesterday in company with honorable and virtuous women. If after arriving here they had behaved themselves I should have stood the transaction, though with hard thoughts. A state of war even does not allow any outrage to be perpetrated upon the sanctity of a pure woman's character and last of all where a flag of truce is the vehicle. We are husbands and fathers and brothers and no form of war should stifle or subdue the holy feelings that spring from those relations. If I did not believe you were imposed upon I would be justified in taking this matter as a personal affront. These women since their arrival at City Point have descended to a depth of infamy that I hardly thought could be reached by the sex. They have delighted themselves with the foulest billingsgate that ever disgraced a fish-woman, courting prostitution at every turn and making themselves loud-mouthed in their denunciation of everything cherished and beloved by our people. Their conduct for one night has been so outrageous as to attract the attention of the press and engage the gossip of the streets. Though I cannot charge myself with blame in the affair I feel a deep sense of mortification that so infamous a proceeding should have had the countenance of the purity of a flag of truce. I have written strongly about this matter not only because every sensibility of my nature has been aroused but because of the further reason that I have a jealous regard for a flag whose honor and purity it is our special mission to uphold.

Very respectfully, your obedient servant,
R.O. Ould,
Agent of Exchange

As stated before on December 17, 1863 General Benjamin F. Butler was appointed Agent of Exchange at his own request. This appointment was odious to the Southern authorities, who had declared him a war criminal, but U.S. Major Mulford continued to work amicably with Judge Oulds, by-passing Butler. The exchange of sick and disabled prisoners continued but General Grant suspended exchanges of other prisoners in April 1864.

The exchange situation became even more interesting when the former neutral area at City Point was captured by the U.S. Army. General Grant ordered the release of the Confederate personnel left there by Judge Oulds. The exchange of sick and disabled continued but was shifted largely south to Fort Pulaski, GA, Savannah, GA and Charleston, SC, as most federal prisoners had been sent south. General exchanges were resumed in February 1865 but the end was near. On April 9, 1865 Judge Oulds presented himself and his records to General Grant. A final report by General Hoffman indicated that as of October 20, 1865 there remained in federal prisons but two captains, one non-com, three privates and nine civilians.

PRISONER TRANSPORT

The prisoner lists, in some cases, show that there was a considerable shifting of prison populations. This was done to relieve overcrowding in the camps nearest the battle zones and to segregate the officers from the enlisted men. Unwounded individuals captured in the course of battle would be herded to the rear to a collecting point, where they would be held under guard until their captors got around to considering their futures. They would be interrogated at this stage and enrolled and counted. They might be used for messy tasks such as burial of the dead. Wounded prisoners would be cared for by their own surgeons in their own field hospitals or they would be collected and put into Federal field hospitals. General Lee left his wounded in the care of Confederate field hospitals, with assigned surgeons and nurses. (The opposing forces had agreed early in the war that surgeons and chaplains would not be imprisoned.) Seriously wounded prisoners would be sent along to regular or specially established general hospitals. Any prisoner could expect to be searched and to lose any possession of value. Prisoners would be moved under charge of the army Provost Marshal to a railhead or embarkation point. In the east in the later months a prisoner could expect to go first to Point Lookout. Officers held there would be sent to Fort Delaware; the men to either Camp Chase or Elmira Prison. The flow would be reversed when returning for exchange. In the west the prisoners seem to have been moved through Louisville to Camp Chase, Camp Douglas or Alton Prison. Toward the end most prisoners in the east went directly to Point Lookout and stayed there until exchanged or released. These movements, by rail or steamship, could not have been pleasant; prisoners did not have priority. Cooked rations of a vile sort would have been distributed at the start of the trip. Sanitary facilities and bedding for trips of many days are not even mentioned. It should not be supposed that this low priority traffic went smoothly. Two documents in the *Official Records* illustrate the vexations of those in charge:

Camp Chase April 28, 1862

Dear Sir:

I have to report that in pursuance of Special Order I proceeded to Sandusky in charge of Prisoners of War with an escort consisting of the remainder of Captain McGrourty's Co. numbering twenty two men together with a detail of thirty men from Captain Crouse's Company. The entire escort under command of Lieut. Bending of the 61st Reg't. According to my own counting, that of Lieutenant Bending and also that of Mr. Patterson, the Sup't of the R. Road over which we were transported, I delivered on the Island 230 Prisoners of War. The names of the prisoners were called off from the Roll furnished me by Lieut. Teams of Capt. McGroarty's Company and as they answered they were counted by one of Major Pearson's officers, who returned but 228 - I demanded a recounting before they were turned into the yard.

Accordingly two corporals were stationed at the gate and the prisoners were let in one at a time, and each corporal returned 230 as the number he had counted. Major Pearson however declined giving his receipt for more than the number reported to him by his officer of the day. I accepted his receipts under protest - averring that I had delivered two more than stated in the receipt. The receipt also mentions 12 prisoners on parole of or about whom I had no

instructions and did not consider them under my charge. According to my receipt which you hold I started with 234 prisoners - Of course I have now no right to question the correctness of your list in regard to numbers - I lost two prisoners after leaving Columbus, each of whom jumped out of the car window when we were going at the rate of about 25 miles per hour - One of them was again taken and returned to Camp Chase - the other escaped. If I lost any more it must have occurred at the Depot in Columbus - My escort was not sufficiently large to keep off the crowd of Citizens, in addition to which the balance of Capt McGroarty's Co. were permitted by Lieut. Teams to start out of camp with almost every canteen filled with whiskey.

The Lieutenant himself whilst at the Depot in Columbus was more occupied in parting with his acquaintances than in attending to his guard. In regard to Lieut. Bending permit me to state that you will find him trustworthy and efficient in the discharge of his duty at all times. Capt. McGroarty's men remained on the Island - Lieut Bending with the detail of 30 men returned to Camp Chase arriving here at 1/2 past 2 Sunday morning.

In conclusion permit me to suggest the propriety when you again send off a lot of Prisoners of sending a full Company at least 1/2 an hour before starting your prisoners with orders to clear the Depot and not allow a single citizen to enter until after the train starts.

I am very respectfully
Your obt. servt.
H. B. Hunter

To G. Moody
Col Comdg.

I desire to include in the foregoing Report the following statement - On arriving at the Island and calling over the list of prisoners furnished me I found that I had several whose names were not included in the list - viz. E. K. Palmer, W. F. Ellison, Alex McCallahan, R. N. Crow and J. M. Dockey. There was also mention on the list names of individuals some of whom I am satisfied were not in my charge - a statement of which I here to annex.

Viz: N. B. Dyer - reported in prison hospital

G. M. Ewing   "   " "   " #2 mess 3

Es   P. Haynes Missing & supposed to have escaped

M. Kelly - In prison No 2 mess 3 J. Mass - "   "   " 3 " 56

Es   F. Manney "   "   " 1 " 14

M. G. Merley " "   " 3 " 23

Es   Y. G. Napier Captain 49 Tennessee

Poindexter in Prison No 3 Mess 32

T. D. Overton Escaped and was retaken and brought back to Camp Chase.

Very Respectfully
H. B. Hunter
Lt. Col.

OFFICE COMMISSARY-GENERAL OF PRISONERS

Washington, D.C., November 27, 1863

Col. C. THOMAS,

Acting Quartermaster-General, Washington, D.C.

COLONEL: I would respectfully call your attention to the fact that in transferring prisoners of war from place to place on railroads the arrangements are often so carelessly made or so badly carried out that much delay and much embarrassment are experienced and numerous escapes occur in consequence. Recently, when about 150 rebel officers were *to leave the city, arrangements were made for them to take the 8:30 train, but on their reaching the depot there were no cars to receive them, and they were in consequence obliged to return to the Old Capitol to wait for another train. On the 5th instant sixty prisoners were put on two freight cars of a freight train at Louisville at 8 p.m. to go to Indianapolis. No lights were put in the cars, and it was, of course, impossible that the guard could see the prisoners in their charge. By an accident the train was delayed three hours, and during this time, or somewhere on the route, three prisoners escaped. The journey, though a short one, was not completed till 2 p.m. the following day. Other cases have been reported to me, the particulars of which I cannot recite. I have therefore respectfully to request you will direct the quartermasters at places from which prisoners are most frequently sent to require in their contracts for transportation that suitable cars be furnished, provided with lights for night travel; that the time in which the journey is to be made may be stipulated, and that a vessel of water of proper size be placed in each car where the number of prisoners is sufficiently large to require one or more cars. The following are places from which are most frequently for warded by rail. Washington; Baltimore; Camp Chase, Columbus, Ohio; Sandusky, Ohio; Cincinnati, Ohio; Louisville, Ky.; Camp Morton, Indianapolis, Ind.; Camp Douglas, Chicago, Ill.; Camp Butler, Springfield, Ill.; Alton,Ill.; Rock Island, Ill.; Cairo, Ill.; Saint Louis, Mo.*

W. HOFFMAN
Colonel Third Infantry and
Commissary General of Prisoners

Still, the movements were made and the system worked reasonably well. There is report of only one serious railroad accident during the war. This occurred during the transport of 833 prisoners from Point Lookout, MD to Elmira, NY. The prisoners left under guard of 129 officers and men of the 11th Regiment, Veterans Reserve. They moved from Point Lookout to Jersey City by steamer and proceeded from there on the Erie Railway. At 3:00 PM on July 15,1864 their train collided with a coal train near Shohola, PA. Seventeen of the guard and forty-eight of the prisoners were killed. Sixteen of the guard and ninety-three of the prisoners were wounded.

A review of the M598 prison rolls suggests the fate of those Confederate soldiers and citizens who were captured during General Sherman's great raid through the Carolinas after leaving Savannah; they trudged along with the Yankee army. They do not seem to have been turned over to the prison system until Sherman's army joined the other federal army from the coast at Goldsboro on March 23, 1865. The sick and wounded prisoners were put into the federal general hospital in New Berne, the others were sent north through Moorehead City or Wilmington.

It should finally be noted that those Confederates unfortunate enough to become prisoners of war even a day before the surrender and parole of their respective armies were doomed to be held for months longer than those who were formally surrendered. Those above the rank of Colonel were held even longer.

DESERTERS AND DEFECTORS

Not all South Carolinians were dedicated heroes, though the state had the lowest desertion rate among the Confederate forces. Some defections should be be expected in a state that required virtually every man to serve. The Federal prisoner of war system was also a factor in any consideration of desertion and defection by Confederate servicemen for two reasons:

1) Deserters who crossed the lines and surrendered to the enemy were quickly processed through the prison system and set free. This process was known and was an inducement for desertion.

2) Prisoners captured in normal conflict were encouraged to take the oath and reject Confederate loyalty. Late in the war this even involved active recruiting to get prisoners to join U.S. forces.

It is not a purpose of this study to isolate or to judge the character of those prisoners who resisted return to active service. Many were men of Northern or foreign origin with no ties to the Confederacy. It might be noted, for those who care, that desertion to the enemy was considered to be a particularly odious act of treachery because the deserter carries information of more value to his captors than his personal worth as a prize.

The Federal government early in the war issued instructions that deserters or prisoners who did not want to be exchanged would not be forced to do so. This policy does not appear to have been well explained or understood, for the records contain many questions on the matter from officers in the field and involved in the prison system. In any case it appears that it was practice and policy not to force any prisoner to be exchanged. It is not clear as to the disposition of those

prisoners who were willing to take the oath and ostensibly return to loyal citizen status. The obvious action would have been to simply release them in some safe place, the catch being that many, if not most, would have no place to go and would be subject to the draft into Federal service. In practice it seems that many such oath takers were allowed to remain in the prisons. General Grant issued an interesting order on January 4, 1865 that specifically protected Rebel deserters and defectors from being impressed into military service and also guaranteed them employment in the Quartermaster Corps as civilian employees. There are occasional notes in the prison records indicating that an individual deserted into Federal lines. The records do not comment as to whether or not a man refused to be exchanged, they do record those who took the oath. It is possible that any Confederate prisoner captured before January 1863, who was still in prison after that date, wanted to be there or, at least, did not want to return to Confederate service.

Late in the war manpower problems led the Federal authorities to consider the recruitment of Confederate prisoners into the U. S. Army. As late as April 1863 the announced policy still did not permit such enlistment. Some prisoners were enlisted into U. S. regiments by obstinate or careless officers, though the number was small. General Benjamin F. Butler began to press for the recruitment of prisoners late in December 1863. He had political clout. President Lincoln thereupon agreed that recruiting could begin but under very controlled methods. Lincoln required that each prisoner answer four questions in privacy and sign his name in a ledger with the answers. The questions were:

1. Do you desire to be sent South as a prisoner of war for exchange?
2. Do you desire to take the oath of allegiance and parole, and enlist in the army or Navy of the U.S., and if so which?
3. Do you desire to take the oath and parole and be sent North to work on public works, under penalty of death if found in the South before the end of the war?
4. Do you desire to take the oath of allegiance and to go to your home within the lines of the U. S. Army, under like penalty if found South beyond those lines during the war?

Ultimately, sufficient recruits were found to man six infantry regiments. These "Galvanized Yankees" were sent west to protect the frontier against Indians. A number of South Carolinians were among those who enlisted in the U.S. forces. Their motives are unknown. It is interesting, though, to note that a curiously large number of these were among the men who were captured during the defense and evacuation of Morris Island in 1863.

AN EXAMPLE HISTORY OF CAPTURE AND EXCHANGE

2nd Lt. Samuel S. Sarvis, Company A, 9th SCVIBn, from Horry District was captured at the battle of Secessionville, SC on June 16, 1862. He was held in the enemy Surgeon's tent that night and sent to Hilton Head the following morning. He was held in the guard house at Hilton Head until August. He was then shipped to Ft. Columbus on Governors Island, New York. He was held with no bedding or blankets. On August 23, 1862 he was brought over to New York and shipped by rail to Philadelphia. There were about 30 prisoners in the shipment. They were loaded on a steamer and taken to Ft. Delaware. Sometime in October, Lt. Sarvis and the other prisoners were paroled for exchange but kept in Ft. Delaware because of Confederate action involving the incarceration of some Federal officer prisoners as hostages because of General Pope's behavior in Virginia. On October 6, 1862 Lt. Sarvis and a number of other prisoners were put on the truce boat *City of New York* and sent to Aikens Ldg. on the James River, VA. There was no food provided on the boat nor was there food supplied at the landing. The Confederate prisoners were exchanged at Aikens Ldg. and simply released to make there own way to Richmond. Aikens Ldg. was about 12 miles from Richmond and Lt. Sarvis gave out about half way and crept up on a nearby porch to sleep. The next morning he walked into Richmond and managed to talk his way into a boarding house even though he was filthy and penniless. After a few days on the cuff of rehabilitation, Lt. Jarvis went to the War Department to seek his back pay. The Clerks could not find any record of him or the 9th SCVIBn. He then told them that Captain Smart had been his company commander and Lt. Col. Smith commanded his battalion. This made a connection and he learned that his old battalion had been consolidated with the 6th SCVIBn and was now a part of the 26th SCVI, and that the regiment was in South Carolina. He drew his back pay and began to enjoy life in Richmond. Lt. Sarvis stayed in Richmond for three more weeks, reporting every day to the War Department. He had talked his way out of reporting to Camp Lee, the camp for paroled officers and men awaiting formal exchange. He then became ill and was given a 20-day furlough to recover. He made his way home to Socastee near Conway, SC. He recovered his health and remained at home until notified that he had been formally exchanged and to report for duty with the 26th SCVI at Church Flats, SC. Lt. Jarvis survived the war, and died on December 16, 1931 at age 88.

THE END

The end of the war was not a sudden affair for the men in Federal prisons. There were around 4500 South Carolinians remaining in prison at the end. Those who had taken the oath before the fall of Richmond were released first under General Order #85. Those who took the oath after the fall of Richmond were released a few weeks later under General Order #109. It took time to administer the oaths and to organize transportation to points near their homes. Transportation was provided. Men who were ill or disabled were kept in camp hospitals until they were able to travel. By October 1865 only eight prisoners of war remained; all were gone by the end of November. The shooting war was over but at least two tortured men had more to endure. President Jefferson Davis was in chains in Fts. Monroe. He remained in shackles under the charge of the malignant Major General Nelson A. Miles. He was held in chains until November 1865 and not released on bail until May 13, 1867. The other man was Private John P. Allen, a Galvanized Yankee of the 1st U.S. Volunteer regiment at Fort Rice in what is now North Dakota. He had been court martialed in May 1865 for sleeping on sentry duty and sentenced to 18 months imprisonment. John P. Allen had been a very young volunteer in Company E, 7th SCVIBn from Kershaw District, South Carolina. He had been captured on Morris Island, SC, July 10, 1863. He was recruited into the U.S. Army at Point Lookout on February 17, 1864. No further record of his service has yet been found, but no great search has been made either.

SOUTH CAROLINA SOLDIERS, SAILORS AND  CITIZENS HELD IN U.S. PRISONS 1861-1865

NAME	RANK	REGIMENT	CAPTURED AT	WHEN	PRISON	MOVED	DISPOSITION	SOURCES
Abbott, Andrew J.	Pvt	C Hol.Leg.	Petersburg, VA	03/25/65	City Pt., VA	03/28/65	Pt. Lookout, MD	CSR
					Pt. Lookout, MD	06/22/65	Rlsd. G.O. #109	P114,P117
Abbott, George W.	Pvt	F Orr's Ri.	Petersburg, VA	04/03/65	City Pt., VA	04/11/65	Hart's Island, NY	CSR
					Hart's Island, NY	06/16/65	Rlsd. G.O. #109	P79,CSR
Abbott, J.G.	Pvt	C Hol.Leg.	Petersburg, VA	10/27/64	Pt. Lookout, MD	03/17/65	Exchanged	P114,P117,P124
					Rchmd. Hospitals	03/28/65	Furlghd. 60 days	CSR
Abbott, J.W.	Pvt	C 7th SCVIBn	Weldon RR, VA	08/21/64	City Pt., VA	08/24/64	Pt. Lookout, MD	CSR
					Pt. Lookout, MD	05/12/65	Rlsd. G.O. #85	P117,P124,CSR
Abbott, John P.	Pvt	C 1st SCVIG	Gettysburg, PA	07/03/63	David's Island, NY	09/05/63	City Pt., VA Xc	P1,SA1,CSR
					City Pt., VA	04/21/65	Pt. Lookout, MD	CSR
					Pt. Lookout, MD	06/23/65	Rlsd. G.O. #109	P114,P118,SA1,CSR
Abbott, Simeon	Pvt	C 26th SCVI	Five Forks, VA	04/02/65	City Pt., VA	04/05/65	Pt. Lookout, MD	CSR
					Pt. Lookout, MD	06/23/65	Rlsd. G.O. #109	P114,HMC,CSR
Abbott, Waddy T.	Pvt	F Orr's Ri.	Petersburg, VA	04/03/65	City Pt., VA	04/11/65	Hart's Island, NY	CSR
					Hart's Island, NY	06/16/65	Rlsd. G.O. #109	P79,CDC,CSR
Abel, Ashley B.	Pvt	A 3rd SCVC	Dallas, GA	05/28/64	Nashville, TN	06/04/64	Louisville, KY	P3
					Louisville, KY	06/07/64	Rock Island, IL	P88,P91,P93
					Rock Island, IL	05/20/65	Rlsd. G.O. 5/9/65	P131
Abercrombie, A.	Pvt	B 1st SCVC	Madison Co., VA	09/22/63	Ft. McHenry, MD	09/26/63	Pt. Lookout, MD	P110,CSR
					Pt. Lookout, MD	01/29/64	Died Ch. Diarrhea	P5,P113,P116,CSR
Abercrombie, Calvin	Pvt	C 14th SCVI	Richmond, VA Hos.	04/03/65	Libby Prison Rchmd	04/23/65	Newport News, VA	CSR
					Newport News, VA	06/26/65	Rlsd. G.O. #109	CSR
Abercrombie, Haynes	Pvt	E 2nd SCVIRi	Chattanooga, TN	10/29/63	Nashville, TN	11/07/63	Louisville, KY	P39,CSR
					Louisville, KY	11/09/63	Camp Morton, IN	P89,CSR
					Camp Morton, IN	01/22/64	Died, Pneumonia	P5,P100,CSR, FPH
					Camp Morton, IN	02/19/65	Pt. Lookout to Xc	P101,CSR
Abercrombie, Orwell	Pvt	E 2nd SCVIRi	Chattanooga, TN	10/29/63	Nashville, TN	11/07/63	Louisville, KY	P39,CSR
					Louisville, KY	11/07/63	Camp Morton, IN	P89,CSR
					Camp Morton, IN	02/26/65	City Pt., VA Xc	P100,CSR
Abernathy, C.P.	2Lt	D 3rd SCVI	Sharpsburg, MD	09/17/62	Sharpsburg, MD	09/17/62	Died of wounds	P12,SA2,H3,CSR
Able, Carson	Pvt	F 5th SCVC	Augusta, GA	05/19/65	Augusta, GA	05/19/65	Paroled	CSR
Able, Jefferson	Pvt	G 27th SCVI	Augusta, GA	05/22/65	Augusta, GA	05/22/65	Paroled	CSR
Ables, Newton	Pvt	G 27th SCVI	Weldon RR, VA	08/22/64	Fts. Monroe, VA	08/24/64	Pt. Lookout, MD	CSR,HAG
					Pt. Lookout, MD	03/14/65	Aikens Ldg., VA Xc	P113,P117,P124
Abney, John B.	Sgt	E 27th SCVI	Weldon RR, VA	08/21/64	City Pt., VA	08/24/64	Pt. Lookout, MD	CSR,HAG
					Pt. Lookout, MD	10/30/64	Venus Pt., GA Xc	P113,P117,P123,CSR
Abraham, I.	Pvt	B 21st SCVI	Petersburg, VA	06/24/64	Pt. Lookout, MD	08/11/64	Elmira, NY	P113,P117
					Elmira, NY	10/11/64	Tfd. for exchange	P65,HAG
Abrams, G.W.	Sgt	A 13th SCVI	Petersburg, VA	04/03/65	City Pt.,VA	03/31/65	Hart's Island, NY	CSR
					Hart's Island, NY	06/15/65	Rlsd. G.O. #109	P79,CSR
Abrams, James E.	Pvt	G Hol.Leg.	Five Forks, VA	04/01/65	City Pt., VA	04/05/65	Pt. Lookout, MD	CSR
					Pt. Lookout, MD	06/22/65	Rlsd. G.O. #109	P114,P118,ANY,CSR
Abrams, Joseph F.	Pvt	B 1st SCVIG	Gettysburg, PA	07/04/63	David's Island, NY	08/24/63	City Pt., VA Xc	P1,SA1,CSR
					Newport News, VA	06/27/65	Rlsd. G.O. #109	P107,SA1,CSR
Abrams, W.L.	Pvt	G 15th SCVI	Gettysburg, PA	07/02/63	Ft. McHenry, MD	07/15/63	Ft. Delaware, DE	CSR
					Ft. Delaware, DE	05/15/65	Hos. 5/15-5/26/65	P47,CTA
					Ft. Delaware, DE	06/10/65	Rlsd. G.O. #109	P40,P43,P44,P45
Abrams, William J.	Pvt	H 1st SCVIR	Morris Island, SC	07/10/63	Hilton Head, SC	09/05/63	Ft. Columbus, NY	CSR
					Ft. Columbus, NY	09/23/63	Rlsd. on oath	P1,CSR

A

SOUTH CAROLINA SOLDIERS, SAILORS AND CITIZENS HELD IN U.S. PRISONS 1861-1865

NAME	RANK	REGIMENT	CAPTURED AT	WHEN	PRISON	MOVED	DISPOSITION	SOURCES
Acker, Elihu H.	Pvt	D Ham.Leg.MI	Richmond, VA Hos.	04/14/65	Richmond, VA	04/14/65	Provost Marshal	CSR
					Libby Prison,Rchmd	04/23/65	Newport News, VA	CSR
					Newport News, VA	07/03/65	Rlsd. G.O. #109	CSR
					At home	07/22/65	Died	ACC
Acker, Peter G.	Pvt	G 1st SCSSBn	Warrenton, VA	09/29/62	Warrenton, VA	09/29/62	Paroled	CSR
Ackis, James S.	Cpl	Brooks LA	Cashtown, PA	07/05/63	Cashtown, PA	08/17/63	Chester, PA USGH	CSR
					Chester, PA USGH	08/17/63	City Pt., VA Xc	CSR
					Williamsburg, VA H	09/02/63	Returned to duty	CSR
Ackis, James S.	Cpl	Brooks LA	Harper's Farm, VA	04/11/65	City Pt., VA	04/14/65	Pt. Lookout, MD	P114,CSR
					Pt. Lookout, MD	06/22/65	Rlsd. G.O. #109	P114,CSR
Acock, R.J.	Pvt	I 23rd SCVI	Farmville, VA	04/11/65	Farmville, VA	04/11/65	paroled	CSR
Acton, William J.	Pvt	F 7th SCVI	Cedar Creek, VA	10/19/64	Harpers Ferry, WV	10/24/64	Pt. Lookout, MD	CSR
					Pt. Lookout, MD	02/11/65	Coxes Ldg., VA Xc	P114,P117,P123,CSR
Adair, A.O.	Pvt	D 22nd SCVI	Petersburg, VA	04/03/65	City Pt., VA	04/11/65	Hart's Island, NY	CSR
					Hart's Island, NY	06/20/65	Rlsd. G.O. #109	CSR
Adair, James W.	Sgt	I 3rd SCVI	Strasburg, VA	10/19/64	Harper's Ferry, WV	10/24/64	Pt. Lookout, MD	H3,CSR
					Pt. Lookout, MD	03/28/65	Aikens Ldg., VA Xc	P124,KEB,SA2,CSR
Adair, L.L.	Pvt	A 13th SCVI	Gettysburg, PA	07/02/63	Harrisburg, PA	07/07/63	Philadelphia, PA	CSR
					Philadelphia, PA		Ft. Delaware, DE	CSR
					Ft. Delaware, DE	06/08/64	Hos. 6/8-7/8/64	P47
					Ft. Delaware, DE	06/10/65	Released	P42,P44,P45,CSR
Adams, A.	Pvt	H 25th SCVI	Ft. Fisher, NC	01/15/65	New York, NY	01/30/65	Elmira, NY	CSR,HAG
					Elmira, NY	02/17/65	Died, Diarrhea	P6,P12,P65,P66,FPH
Adams, A. Melvin	Pvt	G Hol.Leg.	Five Forks, VA	04/01/65	Pt. Lookout, MD	06/22/65	Rlsd. G.O. #109	P114.ANY
Adams, A.B.	Pvt	K 14th SCVI	Gettysburg, PA	07/03/63	David's Island, NY	08/05/63	Died of wounds	P1,P6,P12,FPH
Adams, Aaron	Pvt	E 22nd SCVI	Five Forks, VA	04/01/65	Pt. of Rocks Hos.	05/14/65	Fts. Monroe, VA GH	CSR,LAN
					Fts. Monroe, VA	07/22/65	Rlsd. G.O. #109	CSR
Adams, Benjamin C.	Pvt	Beaufort A	Port Royal, SC	09/24/62	New York, NY P.M.	11/06/62	Ft. Columbus, NY	CSR
					Ft. Columbus, NY	11/21/62	Ft. Delaware, DE	CSR
					Ft. Delaware, DE	12/15/62	Fts. Monroe, VA Xc	CSR
Adams, Calvin B.	Pvt	E 3rd SCVI	Gettysburg, PA	07/04/63	Gettysburg, PA USG	07/21/63	Prov. Marshal N.Y	CSR
					David's Island, NY	09/23/63	City Pt., VA Xc	P1,SA2,ANY,H3,CSR
Adams, David L.	Cpl	I 12th SCVI	Gettysburg, PA	07/04/63	David's Island, NY	09/05/63	City Pt., VA Xc	P1,LAN,CSR
Adams, Elijah	Sgt	G 8th SCVI	Gettysburg, PA		Letterman G.H. Gbg		Died, undated	P1,P12,KEB
Adams, Henry M.	Pvt	G Hol.Leg.	Five Forks, VA	04/01/65	City Pt., VA	04/05/65	Pt. Lookout, MD	CSR
					Pt. Lookout, MD	06/22/65	Rlsd. G.O. #109	P118,CSR
Adams, Ira P.	Pvt	C 15th SCVI	Maryland		Sandy Hook, MD		Died of wounds	P12,KEB,H15
Adams, J. Calhoun	Pvt	A 4th SCVC	Stony Creek, VA	12/01/64	City Pt., VA	12/03/64	Pt. Lookout, MD	CSR
					Pt. Lookout, MD	06/22/65	Rlsd. G.O. #109	P114,CSR
Adams, J.L.	Pvt	G 7th SCVC	Wakefield, VA	05/06/64	Elmira, NY	10/11/64	Tfd. for exchange	P65
Adams, James	Pvt	C 8th SCVI	Gettysburg, PA	07/04/63	David's Island, NY	09/12/63	City Pt., VA Xc	P1,P4,KEB
Adams, James	Pvt	K 6th SCVI	Farmville, VA	04/11/65	Farmville, VA	04/21/65	Paroled	CSR
Adams, James Z.	Pvt	C 15th SCVI	Charlestown, WV	08/16/64	Harper's Ferry, WV	09/02/64	Camp Chase, OH	CSR
					Camp Chase, OH	03/18/65	Pt. Lookout, MD	P22,KEB,H15,CSR
					Pt. Lookout, MD	03/18/65	Boulwares Wh. Xc	CSR
Adams, John	Pvt	D 1st SCVIR	Bennettsville, SC	03/06/65	Fts. Monroe, VA	04/02/65	Washington, DC	CSR
					Washington, DC	04/04/65	Memphis, TN/oath	CSR
Adams, John Tyler	Pvt	G 8th SCVI	Gettysburg, PA	07/05/63	Ft. McHenry, MD	07/14/63	Ft. Delaware, DE	CSR
Adams, John Tyler	Pvt	G 8th SCVI	Gettysburg, PA	07/05/63	Ft. Delaware, DE	06/10/65	Rlsd. G.O. #109	P43,P44,P45,P144
Adams, Jonathan S.	Pvt	A 3rd SCVI	Leesburg, VA Hos.	10/02/62	Leesburg, VA	10/02/62	Paroled	H3,CSR
					W. Bldg. Balt., MD	02/16/65	Pt. Lookout, MD Xc	P1,SA2,KEB
					Richmond, VA Hos.	03/06/65	Furloughed 30 days	H3,CSR

SOUTH CAROLINA SOLDIERS, SAILORS AND **A** CITIZENS HELD IN U.S. PRISONS 1861-1865

NAME	RANK	REGIMENT	CAPTURED AT	WHEN	PRISON	MOVED	DISPOSITION	SOURCES
Adams, Joseph Manning	2Lt	H 2nd SCVIRi	Wauhatchie, TN	10/29/63	Nashville, TN	04/27/64	Louisville, KY	P2,CSR
					Louisville, KY	05/12/64	Johnson's Isl., OH	P88,P91,P93,CSR
					Johnson's Isl., OH	06/11/65	Rlsd. G.O. #109	P82,CSR
Adams, Joshua M.	Pvt	I 6th SCVI	Highbridge, VA	04/06/65	City Pt., VA	04/14/65	Newport News, VA	CSR
					Newport News, VA	06/27/65	Rlsd. G.O. #109	P107,HHC,CSR
Adams, Lawrence A.	Pvt	B 7th SCVC	Talahassee, FL	05/10/65	Talahassee, FL	05/12/65	Paroled	CSR
Adams, M.S.	Pvt	Beaufort A	Port Royal, SC	09/24/62	New York, NY P.M.	11/06/62	Ft. Columbus, NY	CSR
					Ft. Columbus, NY	11/21/62	Ft. Delaware, DE	CSR
					Ft. Delaware, DE	12/16/62	Fts. Monroe, VA Xc	CSR
Adams, Preston Lewis	Pvt	F 24th SCVI	Taylors Ridge, GA	10/16/64	Louisville, KY	10/27/64	Camp Douglas, IL	P88,P91,P94
					Camp Douglas, IL	06/17/65	Rlsd. G.O.#109	P55,EFW
Adams, Richard L.	Pvt	C 2nd SCVIRi	Richmond, VA Hos.	04/03/65	Richmond, VA Hos.	04/14/65	Richmond, VA P.M.	CSR
					Libby Prison Rchmd	04/23/65	Newport News, VA	CSR
					Newport News, VA	06/26/65	Rlsd. G.O. #109	CSR
Adams, Robert	Cpl	K 4th SCVC	Old Church, VA	05/30/64	Lincoln G.H., DC	06/13/64	Old Capitol, DC	CSR
					Old Capitol, DC	07/23/64	Elmira, NY	CSR
					Ft. McHenry, MD	07/23/64	Elmira, NY	P110,HHC
					Elmira, NY	02/13/65	James R., VA Xc	P65,CSR
Adams, Robert W.	Pvt	B 4th SCVC	Hawe's Shop, VA	05/28/64	Pt. Lookout, MD	07/08/64	Elmira, NY	P117,P120,HHC,CSR
					Elmira, NY	01/03/65	Died, Pneumonia	P12,P65,FPH,CSR
Adams, T.	Pvt	6th SCResB	Cheraw, SC	03/05/65	Cheraw, SC	03/05/65	Paroled	CSR
Adams, T.L.	Pvt	B 7th SCVC	Augusta, GA	05/20/65	Augusta, GA	05/20/65	Paroled	CSR
Adams, Thomas H.	Pvt	G Hol.Leg.	Petersburg, VA	04/03/65	City Pt., VA	04/11/65	Hart's Island, NY	CSR
					Hart's Island, NY	06/16/65	Rlsd. G.O. #109	P79,ANY
Adams, Thomas S.	Pvt	K 2nd SCVC	Augusta, GA	05/31/65	Augusta, GA	05/31/65	Paroled on oath	CSR
Adams, W.A.	Pvt	A 6th SCVC	Louisa C.H., VA	06/11/64	Fts. Monroe, VA	06/20/64	Pt. Lookout, MD	CSR
					Pt. Lookout, MD	01/25/65	U.S. Gen. Hospital	P113,CSR
Adams, W.A.	Pvt				Pt. Lookout, MD	02/10/65	Aikens Ldg., VA Xc	P116,P121,P123,CSR
Adams, W.H.W.	Pvt	K 14th SCVI	Gettysburg, PA	07/04/63	David's Island, NY	09/12/63	City Pt., VA Xc	P1,UD6,CSR
					Williamsburg, VA H	09/24/63	Furloughed	CSR
Adams, William	Pvt	SC Militia	Lynch's Creek, SC	02/25/65	Hart's Island, NY	06/16/65	Rlsd. G.O. #109	P79
Adams, William	Pvt	A 4th SCVC	Fayetteville, NC	03/14/65	New Berne, NC	03/30/65	Pt. Lookout, MD	CSR
Adams, William	Pvt	A 4th SCVC	Fayetteville, NC	03/14/65	Pt. Lookout, MD	06/05/65	Rlsd. G.O. #85	P114,P117,CSR
Adams, William	Pvt	A 17th SCVI	Amelia C.H., VA	04/04/65	City Pt., VA	04/13/65	Pt. Lookout, MD	CSR
Adams, William	Pvt	A 17th SCVI	Amelia C.H., VA	04/04/65	Pt. Lookout, MD	06/22/65	Rlsd. G.O. #109	P114,P118,HHC,CSR
Adams, William F.	Pvt	F 21st SCVI	Ft. Fisher, NC	01/15/65	Hammond G.H., MD	03/31/65	Pt. Lookout, MD	CSR
					Pt. Lookout, MD	06/23/65	Rlsd. G.O. #109	P117,CSR
Adamson, William H.	Pvt	H 19th SCVI	Pulaski, TN	12/25/64	Nashville, TN	02/14/65	Louisville, KY	P3,P39
					Louisville, KY	02/17/65	Camp Chase, OH	P92,P94
					Camp Chase, OH	03/26/65	Pt. Lookout, MD	P22,P26
					Pt. Lookout, MD	06/06/65	Rlsd. G.O. #109	P114,CSR
Addis, James	Pvt	H 15th SCVI	Gettysburg, PA	07/04/63	Gettysburg G.H.	07/12/63	Ft. Delawre, DE	P4,KEB,UD5
					Ft. McHenry, MD	07/07/63	Ft. Delaware, DE	CSR
					Ft. Delaware, DE	07/30/63	City Pt., VA Xc	P40,P44,P144,CSR
Addis, William	Pvt	H 15th SCVI	Gettysburg, PA	07/04/63	Baltimore, MD USGH	11/12/63	City Pt., VA Xc	P1,KEB,UD5,CSR
Addison, George B.	Pvt	I 2nd SCVC	Augusta, GA	05/19/65	Augusta, GA	05/19/65	Paroled on oath	CSR
Addison, J.	Pvt	B 27th SCVI	Petersburg, VA	06/24/64	Pt. Lookout, MD	08/16/64	Elmira, NY	P120,HAG
					Elmira, NY	10/11/64	Pt. Lookout, MD	P66
Addison, J.M.	Pvt	B 1st SCVIR	Albany, GA	05/11/65	Albany, GA	05/18/65	Paroled	CSR
Addison, W.S.	Pvt	B 14th SCVI	Spotsylvania, VA	05/17/64	Pt. Lookout, MD	10/30/64	Died, Diarrhea	P6,P114,P117,FPH
Addy, Levi W.	Pvt	B 14th SCVI	Gettysburg, PA	07/02/63	Ft. Delaware, DE	02/09/64	Hos. 2/19-2/23/64	P47,HOE
					Ft. Delaware, DE	09/18/64	Aikens Ldg., VA Xc	P42,HOE,CSR

SOUTH CAROLINA SOLDIERS, SAILORS AND  CITIZENS HELD IN U.S. PRISONS 1861-1865

NAME	RANK	REGIMENT	CAPTURED AT	WHEN	PRISON	MOVED	DISPOSITION	SOURCES
Addy, R.J.	Pvt	F 1st SCVIR	Bentonville, NC	03/22/65	New Berne, NC	04/10/65	Hart's Island, NY	CSR
					Hart's Island, NY	06/16/65	Rlsd. G.O. #109	P79,CSR
Adisekis, John W.	Pvt	C German A	Charleston, SC	03/21/65	Charleston, SC	03/21/65	Released on oath	CSR
Adkins, W.	Pvt	C 23rd SCVI	Deserted/enemy	11/04/64	Washington, DC	11/25/64	New York, NY/oath	CSR
Adkins, William	Pvt	H 1st SCVC	Gettysburg, PA	07/05/63	W. Bldg. Balt., MD	11/12/63	City Pt., VA Xc	CSR
Adkins, William C.	Pvt	H 2nd SCVI	Gettysburg, PA	07/05/63	Letterman G.H. Gbg.	07/20/63	Provost Marshal	P1,LAN,KEB,CSR
					David's Island, NY	08/23/63	City Pt., VA Xc	P1,LAN,CSR
Adkinson, Darling	Pvt	Mathewes A	Charleston, SC	02/18/65	Charleston, SC	03/03/65	Released on oath	CSR
Agen, Thomas	Pvt	H 27th SCVI	Town Creek, NC	02/20/65	Ft. Anderson, NC	02/28/65	Pt. Lookout, MD	CSR
					Pt. Lookout, MD	05/12/65	Released on oath	CSR
Agerton, John	Pvt	C 5th SCResB	Chesterfield, SC	03/02/65	Pt. Lookout, MD	06/23/65	Rlsd. G.O. #109	P122
Agnew, Elijah	Pvt	A 16th SCVI	Franklin, TN	12/17/64	Nashville, TN	12/31/64	Louisville, KY	CSR
					Louisville, KY	01/02/65	Camp Chase, OH	CSR
					Camp Chase, OH	05/19/65	Died, Pharyngitis	P6,P22,P27,FPH
Aiken, D. Wyatt	Col	7th SCVI	Sharpsburg, MD	09/17/62	Aikens Ldg., VA	11/08/62	Paroled	CSR
Aiken, Hugh W.	Pvt	G 3rd SCVIBn	Frederick, MD	09/13/62	Ft. Delaware, DE	10/02/62	Aikens Ldg., VA Xc	CSR
Aikens, James	Pvt	I 1st SCVA	Morris Island, SC	07/10/63	Hilton Head, SC	08/31/63	Ft. Columbus, NY	CSR
					Ft. Columbus, NY	09/23/63	Took the oath	P1
					Ft. Columbus, NY	09/30/63	Pt. Lookout MD	CSR
					Pt. Lookout, MD	07/13/64	Released on oath	P119
					Pt. Lookout, MD	07/13/64	Escaped	P113,CSR
Albers, Henry J.	Pvt	A 24th SCVI	Jackson, MS	05/14/63	Demopolis, AL	06/05/63	Paroled	EFW,CSR
Albertson, J.C.	Pvt	A Orr's Ri.			Aikens Ldg., VA Xc	09/27/62	Paroled	CSR,CDC
Albrecht, Emil	Cpl	C German A	Charleston, SC	02/18/65	Charleston, SC	02/18/65	Released on oath	CSR
Album, P.A.	Pvt	E 8th SCVI	Cedar Creek, VA	10/19/64	Harper's Ferry, WV	10/23/64	Pt. Lookout, MD	CSR
					Pt. Lookout, MD	06/23/65	Rlsd. G.O. #109	CSR
Alderman, John E.	Pvt	B 1st SCVIR	Bentonville, SC	03/19/65	New Berne, NC	03/30/65	Pt. Lookout, MD	CSR
					Pt. Lookout, MD	06/23/65	Rlsd. G.O. #109	P114,P117,CSR
Alexander, A.A.	Pvt	E 1st SCVIR	Cheraw, SC	02/28/65	Provost Marshal			CSR
Alexander, A.N.	Pvt	E 18th SCVI	Richmd/Pbg. Area	05/20/64	Pt. Lookout, MD	03/14/65	Aikens Ldg., VA Xc	P113,P116,P124
Alexander, Ansel	Pvt	D Hol.Leg.	Five Forks, VA	04/01/65	City Pt., VA	04/05/65	Pt. Lookout, MD	CSR
					Pt. Lookout, MD	06/22/65	Rlsd. G.O. #109	P114,P118,CSR
Alexander, D.W.	Pvt	A 14th SCVI	Pickett's Fm., VA	07/21/64	Curls Neck, VA	07/21/64	Bermuda Hundred, VA	CSR
					Bermuda Hundred, VA	07/24/64	Camp Hamilton, VA	CSR
					Camp Hamilton, VA	08/11/64	Pt. Lookout, MD	CSR
					Pt. Lookout, MD	08/16/64	Elmira, NY	P113,P117,P120
					Elmira, NY	03/14/65	James R., VA Xc	P65,CSR
Alexander, F.T.	Pvt	H 1st SCVC	Ellis Ford, VA	01/01/63	Old Capitol, DC	03/29/63	City Pt. VA Xc	CSR
Alexander, G.W.	Pvt	C 18th SCVI	Deserted/enemy	03/02/65	Washington, DC	03/06/65	New York, NY/ oath	CSR
Alexander, H.F.	Pvt	A 18th SCVAB	Charleston, SC	03/18/65	Charleston, SC	03/18/65	Released on oath	CSR
Alexander, Isaac N.	Sgt	E Orr's Ri.	Warrenton, VA	09/29/62	Warrenton, VA	09/29/62	Paroled	CSR
Alexander, J.C.	Pvt	K 17th SCVI	Five Forks, VA	04/01/65	City Pt., VA	04/06/65	Pt. Lookout, MD	CSR
					Pt. Lookout, MD	06/23/65	Rlsd. G.O. #109	P114,P118,YEB,CSR
Alexander, Jacob B.	Pvt	G 12th SCVI	Falling Waters, MD	07/14/63	Old Capitol, DC	08/08/63	Pt. Lookout, MD	CSR
					Ft. McHenry, MD	08/08/63	Pt. Lookout, MD	P110
					Pt. Lookout, MD Xc	03/03/64	City Pt., VA Xc	P116,P123,P124,CSR
					Chattanooga, TN	06/11/64	Took oath, Sent N.	P8,CSR
					Louisville, KY	06/14/64	Released to north	P8,P92
Alexander, John E.	Sgt	E 19th SCVI	Chickamauga, GA	09/20/63	Nashville, TN	09/30/63	Louisville, KY	P38,CSR
					Louisville, KY	10/02/63	Camp Douglas, IL	P89,CSR
					Camp Douglas, IL		No record of disp.	P55,P57,CSR
Alexander, Joseph	Pvt	E 1st SCVIR	Cheraw, SC	02/28/65	Provost Marshal			CSR

A

SOUTH CAROLINA SOLDIERS, SAILORS AND CITIZENS HELD IN U.S. PRISONS 1861-1865

NAME	RANK	REGIMENT	CAPTURED AT	WHEN	PRISON	MOVED	DISPOSITION	SOURCES
Alexander, Joseph C.	Pvt	B 16th SCVI	Franklin, TN	11/30/64	Nashville, TN	12/02/64	Louisville, KY	CSR
					Louisville, KY	12/05/64	Camp Douglas, IL	P91,P94,16R
					Camp Douglas, IL	06/18/65	Rlsd. G.O. #109	P55,CSR
Alexander, Joseph G.	Pvt	F 22nd SCVI	Kinston, NC	12/14/62	Kinston, NC	12/14/62	Paroled POW	CSR
Alexander, Joseph G.	Pvt	F 22nd SCVI	Petersburg, VA	03/25/65	City Pt., VA	03/28/65	Pt. Lookout, MD	CSR
					Pt. Lookout, MD	06/05/65	Rlsd. G.O. #109	P114,P117
Alexander, Thomas	Pvt	B 16th SCVI	Ringgold, GA	11/26/63	Nashville, TN	01/10/64	Louisville, KY	P39,16R,CSR
					Louisville, KY	01/17/64	Rock Island, IL	P88,P93
					Rock Island, IL	03/02/65	Pt. Lookout, MD Xc	P131,CSR
Alexander, W.E.	Pvt	B 2nd SCVIRi	Deserted/enemy	03/03/65	Bermuda Hundred, VA	03/07/65	Washington, DC P.M.	CSR
					Washington, DC P.M.	03/08/65	Columbus, OH/oath	CSR
Alexander, W.W.	Pvt	G 18th SCVI	Bermuda Hundred, VA	05/22/64	Fts. Monroe, VA	05/23/64	Pt. Lookout, MD	CSR
					Pt. Lookout, MD	03/14/65	Aikens Ldg., VA Xc	P124,CSR
Alexander, William	Pvt	E 18th SCVI	Petersburg, VA	05/20/64	Bermuda Hundred, VA	05/22/64	Fts. Monroe, VA	CSR
					Fts. Monroe, VA	05/23/64	Pt. Lookout, MD	CSR
					Pt. Lookout, MD	03/14/65	Exchanged	CSR
Alford, Arnold B.	Cpl	E 26th SCVI	Amelia C.H., VA	04/03/65	City Pt., VA	04/13/65	Pt. Lookout, MD	CSR
					Pt. Lookout, MD	06/22/65	Rlsd. G.O. #109	P114,P118
Alford, Ashley L.	Pvt	E 26th SCVI	Farmville, VA	04/06/65	City Pt., VA	04/14/65	Newport News, VA	CSR
					Newport News, VA	06/24/65	Rlsd. G.O. #109	P107,CEN,CSR
Alford, Joel	Pvt	2 10/19 SCVI	Missionary Ridge, TN	11/25/63	Nashville, TN	12/06/63	Louisville, KY	P39,RAS,CSR
					Louisville, KY	12/07/63	Rock Island, IL	P88,P89
					Rock Island, IL	10/17/64	Jd. US Army F.S.	CSR
Alford, M. M.	1Sg	K 8th SCVI	Loudon, TN	12/03/63	Nashville, TN G.H.	06/14/64		P2,KEB,CSR
					Chattanooga, TN G.H.	06/15/64	Louisville, KY	P1,KEB,CSR
					Louisville, KY	06/22/64	Rock Island, IL	P88,P91,P93,CSR
					Rock Island, IL	02/15/65	Pt. Lookout, MD Xc	P131,CSR
Alford, N.T.	Sgt	K 8th SCVI	Opequan Creek, VA	09/18/64	Harper's Ferry, WV	09/19/64	Camp Chase, OH	CSR
					Camp Chase, OH	06/13/65	Rlsd. G.O. #109	P22,KEB,HOM,CSR
Alford, Silvius	Pvt	B 10th SCVI	Chattahootchie, GA	07/05/64	Louisville, KY	07/13/64	Camp Morton, IN	P91,RAS,CSR
					Camp Morton, IN	02/26/65	City Pt., VA Xc	P100,P101,CSR
Alford, W.H.	Pvt	B 18th SCVAB	Charleston, SC	02/20/65	Charleston, SC	03/11/65	Released on oath	CSR
Alford, Walter	Pvt	D 7th SCVI	Charleston, SC Hos.	02/18/65	Charleston, SC P.M.	03/27/65	Released on oath	CSR
Alford, William McD.	Pvt	L 8th SCVI	Winchester, VA	09/09/64	Harper's Ferry, WV	09/19/64	Camp Chase, OH	CSR
					Camp Chase, OH	05/02/65	New Orleans, LA	P22,P26,KEB,CSR
					New Orleans, LA	05/15/65	Vicksburg, MS Xc	CSR
Algary, Wesley C.	Pvt	F Hol.Leg.	Five Forks, VA	04/01/65	Pt. Lookout, MD			P114,P118,UD3
Algary, William S.	Pvt	D 22nd SCVI	Deserted/enemy	02/25/65	City Pt., VA	03/11/65	Washington, DC PM	CSR
					Washington, DC P.M.	03/11/65	Salem, IL on oath	CSR
Allen, Alfred	Pvt	G 1st SCVA	Kinston, NC	03/10/65	New Berne, NC	03/30/65	Pt. Lookout, MD	CSR
					Pt. Lookout, MD	06/23/65	Rlsd. G.O. #109	P114,P117,CSR
Allen, B.B.	Pvt	A Ham.Leg.	Warrenton, VA	09/29/62	Warrenton, VA	09/29/62	Paroled in Hos.	CSR
Allen, Charles H.	Pvt	A 17th SCVI	Petersburg, VA	03/25/65	City Pt., VA		Pt. Lookout, MD	CSR
					Pt. Lookout, MD	06/22/65	Rlsd. G.O. #109	P117,HHC,CSR
Allen, Charles L.	Pvt	MacBeth LA			Nashville, TN	05/08/65	Released on oath	P8,CSR
Allen, Charles T.	Pvt	B 15th SCVAB	Averysboro, NC	03/16/65	New Berne, NC	03/30/65	Pt. Lookout, MD	CSR
					Pt. Lookout, MD	06/22/65	Rlsd. G.O. #109	P121,CSR
Allen, Drury A.	Pvt	C 25th SCVI	Ft. Fisher, NC	01/15/65	New York, NY	01/30/65	Elmira, NY	CSR, CTA
					Elmira, NY	02/20/65	Died, Pneumonia	P6,P12,P65,P66,FPH
Allen, George W.	Pvt	K 1st SCVIG	P.M. Army of Pot.	02/17/65	City Pt., VA	02/17/65	Washington, DC	CSR
					Washington, DC	02/18/65	Nashville, TN/oath	CSR

A

SOUTH CAROLINA SOLDIERS, SAILORS AND CITIZENS HELD IN U.S. PRISONS 1861-1865

NAME	RANK	REGIMENT	CAPTURED AT	WHEN	PRISON	MOVED	DISPOSITION	SOURCES
Allen, H.P.	Pvt	K 22nd SCVI	Richmond, VA Hos.	04/03/65	Libby Prison Rchmd	04/23/65	Newport News, VA	CSR
					Newport News, VA	06/16/65	Rlsd. G.O. #109	CSR
Allen, Hardy M.	Pvt	F 26th SCVI	Petersburg, VA	03/25/65	City Pt., VA	03/28/65	Pt. Lookout, MD	CSR
Allen, Hardy M.	Pvt	F 26th SCVI	Petersburg, VA	03/25/65	Pt. Lookout, MD	06/22/65	Rlsd. G.O. #109	P114,CSR
Allen, Henry H.	Pvt	F 26th SCVI	Southside RR, VA	04/01/65	Pt. Lookout, MD	06/25/65	Rlsd. G.O. #109	P114,CSR
Allen, J.D.	Pvt	D 18th SCVI	Farmville, VA	04/06/65	City Pt., VA	04/14/65	Newport News, VA	CSR
					Newport News, VA	06/26/65	Rlsd. G.O. #109	P107,UD2,CSR
Allen, James A.	Pvt	E 7th SCVIBn	Morris Island, SC	07/10/63	Ft. Columbus, NY	09/25/63	Rlsd. on oath	P1,HAG,HIC
Allen, James W.	Pvt	H 23rd SCVI	Five Forks, VA	04/01/65	City Pt., VA	04/06/65	Pt. Lookout, MD	CSR
					Pt. Lookout, MD	06/22/65	Rlsd. G.O. #109	CSR
Allen, John	Pvt	B Hol.Leg.	Deserted/enemy	02/14/65	City Pt., VA	02/18/65	Washington, DC	CSR
					Washington, DC	02/21/65	Newark, NJ/oath	CSR
Allen, John P.	Pvt	E 7th SCVIBn	Morris Island, SC	07/10/63	Hilton Head, SC		Ft. Columbus, NY	CSR, HAG,GAY,HIC
					Ft. Columbus, NY	09/26/63	Pt. Lookout, MD	CSR
					Pt. Lookout, MD	02/17/64	Joined U.S. Army	P113,P125,
Allen, John Z.	Pvt	E 17th SCVI	Petersburg, VA	03/25/65	City Pt., VA		Pt. Lookout, MD	CSR
					Pt. Lookout, MD	06/23/65	Rlsd. G.O. #109	P114,P117,YEB,CSR
Allen, Joseph T.	Pvt	M 7th SCVI	Wren Mills, VA	04/14/64	Pt. Lookout, MD	10/30/64	Aikens Ldg., VA Xc	P116
Allen, Joseph W.	Pvt	A 23rd SCVI	Five Forks, VA	04/01/65	Pt. Lookout, MD	06/22/65	Rlsd. G.O. #109	P114,P118
Allen, M.P.	Pvt	D 18th SCVI	Canton, MS	07/08/63	Camp Morton, IN	03/19/64	Ft. Delaware, DE	P100,P101,UD2,CSR
					Ft. Delaware, DE	09/18/64	Aikens Ldg., VA Xc	P42,UD2,CSR
Allen, W.	Pvt	A 7th SCVI	Richmond, VA Hos.	04/03/65	Newport News, VA	06/16/65	Rlsd. G.O. #109	CSR
Allen, W.G.	Pvt	A 3rd SCVABn	High Pt., NC	05/02/65	High Pt., NC	05/02/65	Paroled on oath	CSR
Allen, Wade	3Lt	D 3rd SCVI	Knoxville, TN	12/04/63	Nashville, TN	02/11/64	Louisville, KY	P39,KEB,SA2,H3,CSR
					Louisville, KY	02/13/64	Camp Chase, OH	P88,P91,P93,CSR
					Camp Chase, OH	03/25/64	Ft. Delaware, DE	P22,P26,CSR
					Ft. Delaware, DE	05/06/64	Died, Lung Inflam	P5,P42,P44,P47,FPH,H
Allen, Washington	Pvt	A 23rd SCVI	Petersburg, VA	04/02/65	City Pt., VA	04/04/65	Pt. Lookout, MD	CSR
					Pt. Lookout, MD	06/23/65	Rlsd. G.O. #109	P114,P118
Allen, Wesley	Pvt	E 12th SCVI	Deserted/enemy	01/16/65	City Pt., VA	01/20/65	Pittsburg, PA	P8,CSR
Allen, Wiley H.C.	Pvt	F 26th SCVI	Southside RR, VA	04/01/65	City Pt., VA	04/05/65	Pt. Lookout, MD	CSR
					Pt. Lookout, MD	06/04/65	Released	P118,CSR
Allen, William	Pvt	I 18th SCVI	Petersburg, VA	04/02/65	City Pt., VA	04/04/65	Pt. Lookout, MD	P114,P118,CSR
					Pt. Lookout, MD	06/22/65	Rlsd.G.O. #109	P114,P118,CSR
Allen, William D.	Pvt	A 1st SCVIH	Richmond, VA Hos.	04/03/65	Richmond, VA Hos.	04/14/65	Richmond, VA P.M.	CSR
					Libby Prison Rchmd	04/23/65	Newport News, VA	CSR
					Newport News, VA			CSR
Allenburg, John	Pvt	C 19th SCVI	Nashville, TN	12/16/64	Nashville, TN	12/31/64	Louisville, KY	CSR
					Louisville, KY	01/02/65	Camp Chase, OH	CSR
					Camp Chase, OH	05/02/65	New Orleans, LA Xc	CSR
					New Orleans, LA	05/12/65	Vicksburg, MS Xc	CSR
Allgood, Joel T.	Pvt	Brooks LA	Gettysburg, PA	07/05/63	Chester, PA USGH	10/03/63	Pt. Lookout, MD	P1,CSR
					Pt. Lookout, MD	10/04/63	Hammond G.H., MD	CSR
					Hammond G.H., MD	03/17/64	City Pt., VA Xc	P116,CSR
Allis, F.B.	Pvt	F 12th SCVI	Kershaw, SC	02/28/65	17th AC Pro. Marsh	03/17/65	17th AC P.M.	CSR
Allis, Samuel	Pvt	B 23rd SCVI	Petersburg, VA	06/17/64	Pt. Lookout, MD	07/27/64	Elmira, NY	P113,P117,P120
					Elmira, NY	01/24/65	Died, Diarrhea	P65,P66
Allison, Andrew J.	Pvt	D 16th SCVI	Nashville, KY	12/16/64	Nashville, TN	12/19/64	Louisville, KY	CSR
					Louisville, KY	12/21/64	Camp Douglas, IL	P90,P91,P94,CSR
					Camp Douglas, IL	04/06/65	Jd. 5th USVI.	P55,CSR
Allison, Hugh J.	2Lt	F 5th SCVI	Sharpsburg, MD	09/17/62	Aikens Ldg., VA	11/08/62	Paroled & Xc	CSR

A

SOUTH CAROLINA SOLDIERS, SAILORS AND CITIZENS HELD IN U.S. PRISONS 1861-1865

NAME	RANK	REGIMENT	CAPTURED AT	WHEN	PRISON	MOVED	DISPOSITION	SOURCES
Allison, Thomas P.	Pvt	H 12th SCVI	Spotsylvania, VA	05/12/64	Ft. Delaware, DE		Hos. 7/22-9/18/64	P47,UD6
					Belle Plain, VA	05/21/64	Ft. Delaware, DE	CSR
					Ft. Delaware, DE	09/18/64	Aikens Ldg., VA Xc	P41,P42,CWC,CSR
					Richmond, VA Hos.	09/25/64	Furloughed 30 days	P41,P42,CSR
Allison, William S.	1Sg	A 24th SCVI	Jackson, MS	05/14/63	Demopolis, AL	06/05/63	Paroled	CSR
Allison, William S.	1Sg	A 24th SCVI	Franklin, TN	12/17/64	Nashville, TN	12/20/64	Louisville, KY	P3,CSR
					Louisville, KY	01/02/65	Camp Chase, OH	CSR
					Camp Chase, OH	06/12/65	Rlsd. G.O. #109	P22,EFW
Allsbrooks, William W.	Pvt	D 2nd SCVI	Gettysburg, PA	07/05/63	Gettysburg, PA G.H.	12/02/63	Provost Marshal	P4,SA2,H2,CSR
Allston, Thomas Blythe	Cpt	F 27th SCVI	Town Creek, NC	02/20/65	Ft. Anderson, NC	02/25/65	Pt. Lookout, MD	CSR,HAG
					Pt. Lookout, MD	02/28/65	Washington, DC	P114,P120,HAG
					Old Capitol, DC	03/02/65	Ft. Delaware, DE	CSR
					Ft. McHenry, MD	03/24/65	Ft. Delaware, DE	P110
					Ft. Delaware, DE	06/17/65	Rlsd. G.O. #109	P43,P45,P46,CSR
Altee, Thomas M.	Pvt	A 2nd SCVI	Gettysburg, PA	07/05/63	Gettysburg G.H.		Provost Marshal	P4,H2
					David's Island, NY	09/08/63	City Pt., VA Xc	P1,SA2,KEB,CSR
Altman, James P.	Pvt	A 21st SCVI	Petersburg, VA	06/16/64	Pt. Lookout, MD	07/09/64	Elmira, NY	P113,P117,P120
					Elmira, NY	03/29/65	Died, Diarrhea	P12,P65,HAG
Altman, L.C.	Pvt	G 15th SCVI	South Mtn., MD	09/14/62	New York, NY		Ft. Delaware, DE	CSR
					Ft. Delaware, DE	10/02/62	Aikens Ldg., VA Xc	H15,CSR
Altman, Owen	Pvt	D 11th SCVI	Ft. Fisher, NC	01/15/65	Elmira, NY	03/14/65	Pt. Lookout, MD Xc	P65,P66,CSR
Altman, Samuel S.	Pvt	I 21st SCVI	Ft. Fisher, NC	01/15/65	Elmira, NY	03/02/65	Pt. Lookout, MD Xc	P65,P66,HAG
Altman, Thomas	Cpl	E 10th SCVI	Macon, GA	04/20/65	Macon, GA	04/20/65	Paroled	CSR
Altman, W.B.	Pvt	A German LA	Augusta, GA	05/23/65	Augusta, GA	05/23/65	Paroled	CSR
Alverson, Benjamin F.	Pvt	F 13th SCVI	Deserted/enemy	02/24/65	City Pt.,VA	02/27/65	Springfield, IL	CSR
Alverson, Franklin	Pvt	E 16th SCVI	Talladega, AL	06/20/65	Talladega, AL	06/20/65	Paroled on oath	CSR
Alverson, Madison	Pvt	F 13th SCVI	Deserted/enemy	02/24/65	City Pt., VA	02/27/65	Springfield, IL	CSR
Alverson, William C.	Pvt	F 13th SCVI	Deserted/enemy	02/24/65	City Pt., VA	02/27/65	Springfield, IL	CSR
Amadei, Antonio	Pvt	G 1st SCVA	Averysboro, NC	09/16/65	New Berne, NC	03/31/65	Hart's Island, NY	CSR
					Hart's Island, NY	06/16/65	Rlsd. G.O. #109	P79,CSR
Amaker, J.E.	Pvt	B 7th SCVC	Augusta, GA	05/18/65	Augusta, GA	05/18/65	Paroled	CSR
Amaker, R.D.	Pvt	K 14th SCVI	Sutherland Stn., VA	04/02/65	City Pt., VA	04/07/65	Hart's Island, NY	CSR
					Hart's Island, NY	06/16/65	Rlsd. G.O. #109	P79,CSR
Amick, Drayton J.	Pvt	I 15th SCVI	Williamsport, MD	07/14/63	Hagerstown, MD	07/22/63	DOW, Arm Amptd.	P12,KEB,H15,CSR
Amick, Elijah R.	Pvt	C 15th SCVI	Gettysburg, PA	07/02/63	Gettysburg, PA G.H.		Provost Marshal	P4,KEB,H15
					Gettysburg, PA	09/06/63	Died of wounds	P1,P5,CSR
Amick, Henry Luther	Sgt	I 15th SCVI	South Mtn., MD	09/14/62	Ft. Delaware, DE	10/02/62	Aikens Ldg., VA Xc	CSR
Amick, James Joshua	Pvt	I 15th SCVI	Halltown, WV	08/26/64	Harper's Ferry, WV	08/29/64	Camp Chase, OH	CSR,KEB,H15
					Camp Chase, OH	03/26/65	Pt. Lookout, MD	P22,P26,CSR
					Pt. Lookout, MD	06/20/65	Died, Scurvy	P12,P119,FPH,CSR
Amick, Solomon D.W.	Pvt	I 15th SCVI	Boonesboro, MD	09/14/62	Frederick, MD G.H.	09/27/62	Died of wounds	CSR
Amick, Thomas B.	Pvt	L 1st SCVIG	Southside RR, VA	04/03/65	Hart's Island, NY	06/16/65	Rlsd. G.O. #109	P79,CSR
Ammons, Alcien M.	Pvt	E 7th SCVIBn	Town Creek, NC	02/20/65	Ft. Anderson, NC	02/28/65	Pt. Lookout, MD	CSR
					Pt. Lookout, MD	06/22/65	Rlsd. G.O. #109	P114,P121,HAG,CSR
Ammons, J.	Pvt	E 7th SCVIBn	Charlotte, NC Hos.	05/15/65	Charlotte, NC	05/15/65	Paroled	CSR
Ammons, J. Duncan	Pvt	L 8th SCVI	Opequan Creek, VA	09/13/64	Harper's Ferry, WV	09/19/64	Camp Chase, OH	CSR
					Camp Chase, OH	06/11/65	Rlsd. G.O. #109	CSR
Amos, James	Pvt	K 18th SCVI	Sutherland Stn., VA	04/02/65	City Pt., VA	04/13/65	Pt. Lookout, MD	CSR
					Pt. Lookout, MD	06/12/65	Died, Dysentery	P6,P118,P119,CSR
Ancrum, William	Pvt	A 2nd SCVC	Warrenton, VA	06/13/63	P.M. Alexandria, VA	06/16/63	Old Capitol, DC	CSR
					Old Capitol, DC	06/25/63	City Pt., VA to Xc	CSR
					Ft. McHenry, MD	06/25/63	City Pt., VA Xc	P110

SOUTH CAROLINA SOLDIERS, SAILORS AND  CITIZENS HELD IN U.S. PRISONS 1861-1865

NAME	RANK	REGIMENT	CAPTURED AT	WHEN	PRISON	MOVED	DISPOSITION	SOURCES
Anderson, Abijah	Pvt	F 19th SCVI	Atlanta, GA	07/22/64	Nashville, TN	07/29/64	Louisville, KY	CSR
					Louisville, KY	07/31/64	Camp Chase, OH	P88,P91,P93
					Camp Chase, OH	02/11/65	Died, Pneumonia	P6,P22,P27,FPH,CSR
Anderson, Augustus	Pvt	B 16th SCVI	Graysville, GA	11/26/63	Nashville, TN	12/09/63	Louisville, KY	P39,CSR
					Louisville, KY	12/11/63	Rock Island, IL	P88,P89,CSR
					Rock Island, IL	12/11/63	Vicksburg, MS Xc	P131
Anderson, B.M.	Pvt	K 2nd SCVI	Raleigh, NC	05/10/65	Raleigh, NC	05/10/65	Paroled	CSR
Anderson, D.G.	Pvt	K 1st SCVA	Bennettsville, SC	03/08/65	Pt. Lookout, MD	06/06/65	Released on oath	P114,P118,CSR
Anderson, F.J.	Pvt	K 1st SCVC	Bennettsville, SC	03/06/65	New Berne, NC	04/03/65	Pt. Lookout, MD	CSR
					Pt. Lookout, MD	06/06/65	Rlsd. G.O. #109	CSR
Anderson, J.F.	Pvt	E 8th SCVI	Winchester, VA	09/13/64	Camp Chase, OH	05/02/65	New Orleans, LA	P22,KEB
Anderson, J.H.	Pvt	G Ham.Leg.MI	Augusta, GA	05/20/65	Augusta, GA	05/20/65	Paroled	CSR
Anderson, J.M.	Pvt	E 8th SCVI	Opequan Creek, VA	09/13/64	Harper's Ferry, WV	09/19/64	Camp Chase, OH	CSR
					Camp Chase, OH	05/12/65	Rlsd. G.O. #85	P22,KEB,CSR
Anderson, J.R.	Pvt	F 14th SCVI	Spotsylvania, VA	05/12/64	Belle Plain, VA	05/20/64	Ft. Delaware, DE	CSR
					Ft. Delaware, DE	09/15/64	Hos. 9/15-9/18/64	P47
					Ft. Delaware, DE	10/12/64	Hos. 10/12-10/21/64	P47
					Ft. Delaware, DE	02/11/65	Hos. 2/11-2/14/65	P47
					Ft. Delaware, DE	03/28/65	Hos. 3/28-4/6/65	P47
					Ft. Delaware, DE	06/10/65	Rlsd. G.O. #109	P41,P43,P45,CSR
Anderson, J.S.	Sgt	C 3rd SCVIBn	South Mtn., MD	09/14/62	Ft. Delaware, DE	12/15/62	Fts. Monroe, VA	CSR
					Fts. Monroe, VA	12/18/62	City Pt., VA Xc	KEB,CSR
Anderson, J.S.	Pvt	E 7th SCVC	Richmond, VA Hos.	04/03/65	Richmond, VA Hos.	04/14/65	Richmond, VA P.M.	CSR
					Libby Prison Rchmd	05/04/65	Newport News, VA	CSR
					Newport News, VA	06/26/65	Rlsd. G.O. #109	CSR
Anderson, James	Pvt	A 15th SCVI	Deserted/enemy	02/18/65	Charleston, SC	03/22/65	New York, NY/oath	CSR
Anderson, James A.	Pvt	G 16th SCVI	Missionary Ridge, TN	11/25/63	Nashville, TN	12/05/63	Louisville, KY	P39,16R,CSR
					Louisville, KY	12/06/63	Rock Island, IL	P88,P89,CSR
					Rock Island, IL	10/11/64	Rlsd., Recapd12/3/64	P131,CSR
Anderson, James A.	Pvt	I 1st SCVIR	Raleigh, NC Hos.	04/13/65	Raleigh, NC	04/13/65	Paroled	SA1,CSR
Anderson, James E.	Pvt	G Ham.Leg.MI	Deep Bottom, VA	08/17/64	Pt. Lookout, MD	09/30/64	City Pt., VA Xc	P113,P117,P125
					Richmond, VA Hos.	10/13/64	Died, Ch. Diarrhea	CSR
Anderson, John	Pvt	I 1st SCVIG	Petersburg, VA	04/02/65	City Pt., VA	04/04/65	Pt. Lookout, MD	CSR
					Pt. Lookout, MD	06/25/65	Rlsd. G.O. #109	P114,P118,SA1,CSR
Anderson, Lucian B.	Pvt	C 15th SCVI	Knoxville, TN	12/18/63	Louisville, KY	01/25/64	Rock Island, IL	P88,P93,H15,CSR
					Rock Island, IL	10/13/64	Jd. US Army Fr. Ser	P131,CSR
Anderson, M.J.	Pvt	A 2nd SCVI	Gettysburg, PA	07/03/63	Baltimore, MD Jail	08/05/63	Rlsd. on oath	CSR
Anderson, Richard S.	Pvt	G Hol.Leg.	Five Forks, VA	04/01/65	City Pt., VA	04/01/65	Pt. Lookout, VA	CSR,ANY
					Pt. Lookout, MD	06/22/65	Rlsd. G.O. #109	P114,P118
Anderson, Robert	Pvt	K 1st SCVIG	Gettysburg, PA	07/02/63	Ft. Delaware, DE	09/15/63	Jd. US 3rd MD Cav.	P42,SA1,CSR
Anderson, Robert	Pvt	F Hol.Leg.	Five Forks, VA	04/01/65	City Pt., VA	04/03/65	Pt. Lookout, MD	CSR
					Pt. Lookout, MD	06/05/65	Rlsd. G.O. #85	P114,P118
Anderson, S.	Pvt	B 1st SCV			Ft. Monroe, VA	04/24/65	Died, Typhoid	P12,TOD
Anderson, S. Pinckney	Pvt	K 21st SCVI	Ft. Fisher, NC	01/15/65	Ft. Delaware, DE	03/02/65	Hos. 3/2-3/14/65	P47,HAG
					Ft. Delaware, DE	06/16/65	Rlsd. G.O. #109	P41,P42,P43,P45

SOUTH CAROLINA SOLDIERS, SAILORS AND  CITIZENS HELD IN U.S. PRISONS 1861-1865

NAME	RANK	REGIMENT	CAPTURED AT	WHEN	PRISON	MOVED	DISPOSITION	SOURCES
Anderson, Samuel T.	2Lt	D 1st SCVC	Martinsburg, WV	07/19/63	Wheeling, WV	10/22/63	Camp Chase, OH	P1,P24,CSR
					Camp Chase, OH	11/14/63	Johnsons Isl., OH	P22,P26,CSR
					Johnsons Isl., OH	02/14/64	Pt. Lookout, MD	P82,CSR
					Pt. Lookout, MD	06/23/64	Ft. Delaware, DE	P113,P117,P120,CSR
					Ft. Delaware, DE	08/20/64	Hilton Head, SC	P42,CSR
					Ft. Pulaski, GA	10/20/64		CSR
					Hilton Head, SC	03/12/65	Ft. Delaware, DE	CSR
					Ft. Delaware, DE	06/12/65	Rlsd. G.O. #109	P43,P44,P45,CSR
Anderson, T.D.	Pvt	E 8th SCVI	Winchester, VA	09/13/64	Camp Chase, OH	05/02/65	New Orleans, LA	P26,CSR
					New Orleans, LA	05/02/65	Vicksburg, MS Xc	P26,CSR
Anderson, Thomas W.	Sgt	I 17th SCVI	Petersburg, VA	03/25/65	City Pt., VA	03/27/65	Pt. Lookout, MD	CSR
					Pt. Lookout, MD	06/07/65	Rlsd. G.O. #109	P117,LAN,CSR
Anderson, W.H.	Pvt	E 8th SCVI	Winchester, VA	09/13/64	Harper's Ferry, WV	09/19/64	Camp Chase, OH	P22,KEB,CSR
					Camp Chase, OH	06/10/65	Rlsd. G.O. #109	P22,KEB,CSR
Anderson, W.H.	2Lt	A 3rd SCVABn	High Pt., NC	05/02/65	High Pt., NC	05/02/65	Paroled on oath	CSR
Anderson, W.J.	Pvt	C Ham.Leg.MI	Greensboro, NC	05/01/65	Greensboro, NC	05/01/65	Paroled	CSR
Anderson, William C.	Cpl	B 15th SCVI	Deserted/enemy	04/03/65	Charleston, SC	04/03/65	Rlsd. on oath	CSR
Anderson, William H.	Pvt	A 2nd SCVC	Hedgeville, VA	07/17/63	Wheeling, WV	07/22/63	Camp Chase, OH	P1
					Camp Chase, OH		Refused exchange	P25
					Camp Chase, OH	01/17/64	Rock Island, IL	P22,P26,CSR
					Rock Island, IL	06/16/65	Rlsd. G.O. #109	CSR
Anderson, William W.	Pvt	1st SCVA	Williamsburg, VA		Fts. Monroe, VA	09/23/64	Took oath	P8,CSR
Andre, George	Pvt	A 2nd SCVI	Staunton, VA	10/01/64	Harper's Ferry, WV	10/12/64	Pt. Lookout, MD	CSR
					Pt. Lookout, MD	05/12/65	Rlsd. G.O. #85	P114,P117,H2,CSR
Andrews, Frederick W.	1Lt	K 24th SCVI	Franklin, TN	12/18/64	Nashville, TN P.H.	01/04/65	Louisville, KY	P2
					Louisville, KY	03/03/65	Camp Chase, OH	P92,P93,HOE
					Camp Chase, OH	03/18/65	Pt. Lookout, MD Xc	P22,P26,CSR
					Stuart Hos. Rchmd.	03/29/65	Furloughed 30 days	CSR
Andrews, H.A.	Pvt	B 3rd SCVI	Savage Stn., VA	06/28/62	Harrison's Ldg.,VA	07/08/62	Ft. Columbus, NY	H3,CSR
					Ft. Columbus, NY	07/09/62	Ft. Delaware, DE	H3,CSR
					Ft. Delaware, DE	08/05/62	Aikens Ldg., VA Xc	H3,CSR
Andrews, John E.	Pvt	A 14th SCVI	Gettysburg, PA	07/03/63	Chester, PA Hosp.	09/21/63	City Pt., VA Xc	P1,CSR
Andrews, Leonard P.	Pvt	G 1st SCVIG	Gettysburg, PA	07/06/63	Ft. Delaware, DE	06/10/65	Rlsd. G.O. #109	P43,P44,P144,SA1
Andrews, Milton A.	Pvt	C 24th SCVI	Fayetteville, NC	03/18/65	New Berne, NC	03/30/65	Pt. Lookout, MD	CSR
					Pt. Lookout, MD	06/09/65	Rlsd. G.O. #109	P114,P117,EFW,CSR
Andrews, W.L.	Pvt	G 27th SCVI	Petersburg, VA	06/24/64	Fts. Monroe, VA	06/27/64	Pt. Lookout, MD	CSR
					Pt. Lookout, MD	08/11/64	Elmira, NY	P113,P117,P120
					Elmira, NY	06/14/65	Rlsd. G.O. #109	P65,P66,HAG
Andrews, William W.	Pvt	C 3rd SCVIBn	Gettysburg, PA	07/04/63	Letterman G.H. Gbg	09/10/63	Provost Marshal	P1,CSR
					Baltimore, MD USGH	09/25/63	City Pt., VA Xc	P1,KEB,CSR
Antibus, George	Pvt	Brooks LA	Lynchburg, VA	04/13/65	Lynchburg, VA	04/13/65	Paroled	CSR
Antilly, J.B.	Pvt	H 25th SCVI	Ft. Fisher, NC	01/15/65	Str. Champion	01/17/65	Fts. Monroe, VA	CSR
					Fts. Monroe, VA	02/01/65	Pt. Lookout, MD	CSR
					Pt. Lookout, MD	02/14/65	Cox's Ldg., VA Xc	CSR
Antilly, M. Furman	Pvt	G 25th SCVI	Ft. Fisher, NC	01/15/65	New York, NY	01/30/65	Elmira, NY	CSR
					Elmira, NY	06/27/65	Rlsd. G.O. #109	P65,P66,HAG
Anton, J.A.	Pvt	H Hol.Leg.	Petersburg, VA	10/27/64	City Pt., VA	10/31/64	Pt. Lookout, MD	CSR
					Pt. Lookout, MD	03/17/65	Aikens Ldg., VA Xc	P114,P117,P124,CSR
Appleby, A.W.	Sgt	H 11th SCVI	Weldon RR, VA	08/21/64	Pt. Lookout, MD	03/17/65	Aikens Ldg., VA Xc	P113,P124,CSR

SOUTH CAROLINA SOLDIERS, SAILORS AND CITIZENS HELD IN U.S. PRISONS 1861-1865

NAME	RANK	REGIMENT	CAPTURED AT	WHEN	PRISON	MOVED	DISPOSITION	SOURCES
Appleby, Franklin B.	Pvt	F 6th SCVC	Johns Island, SC	02/09/64	Hilton Head, SC	04/03/64	Ft. Lafayette, NY	CSR
					Ft. Lafayette, NY	04/19/64	Ft. Delaware, DE	CSR
					Ft. Delaware, DE	06/11/64	To hospital	P47
					Ft. Delaware, DE	09/18/64	Aikens Ldg., VA Xc	P41,P42,CSR
Appleton, William L.	Pvt	A 20th SCVI	Cedar Creek, VA	10/19/64	Harper's Ferry, WV	10/25/64	Pt. Lookout, MD	CSR
					Pt. Lookout, MD	03/28/65	Aikens Ldg., VA Xc	P114,P117,P124,CSR
Arant, James H.	Pvt	G 25th SCVI	Ft. Fisher, NC	01/15/65	Elmira, NY	03/02/65	Pt.Lookout, MD Xc	P65,P66,HAG
Arant, John W.	Pvt	A 5th SCVC	Stony Creek, VA	12/01/64	City Pt., VA	12/05/64	Pt. Lookout, MD	CSR
					Pt. Lookout, MD	02/22/65	Died, Pneumonia	P114,P119,FPH,CSR
Archer, C.M.	Pvt	C 17th SCVI	Petersburg, VA	02/23/65	City Pt., VA P.M.	02/23/65	Washington, DC	CSR
					Washington, DC	02/24/65	Boston, MA on oath	CSR
Ard, Benjamin R.	Cpl	K 25th SCVI	Ft. Fisher, NC	01/15/65	New York, NY	01/30/65	Elmira, NY	CSR, HAG
					Elmira, NY	06/01/65	Died, Pneumonia	P6,P12,P65,P66,FPH
Ard, Edward G.	Pvt	C 25th SCVI	Ft. Fisher, NC	01/15/65	New York, NY	01/30/65	Elmira, NY	CSR
					Elmira, NY	07/26/65	Rlsd. G.O. #109	P65,P66,HAG
Ard, Elias Franklin	Pvt	G 15th SCVI	Sharpsburg, MD	09/17/62	Frederick, MD Hos.	02/25/63	Died of wounds	P6,P12,FPH,H15,CSR
Ard, Elihu B.	Pvt	K 25th SCVI	Petersburg, VA	05/09/64	Fts. Monroe, VA	11/24/64	Pt. Lookout, MD	CSR,CTA
					Pt. Lookout, MD	02/19/65	Cox's Ldg., VA Xc	P123,P124,HAG,CSR
					Jackson Hos. Rchmd.	02/21/65	Furloughed home	CSR
Ard, Emanuel H.	Pvt	K 21st SCVI	Drury's Bluff, VA	05/16/64	Pt. Lookout, MD	08/15/64	Elmira, NY	P113,P116,P120,HAG
					Elmira, NY	09/20/64	Died, Ch. Diarrhea	P6,P12,FPH
Ard, General	Pvt	McQueen LA	Richmond, VA	04/03/65	Richmond, VA Hos.	04/14/65	Richmond, VA P.M.	CSR
					Libby Prison Rchmd	04/23/65	Newport News, VA	CSR
					Newport News, VA	06/14/65	Rlsd. G.O. #109	CSR
Ard, James	Pvt	C 25th SCVI	Town Creek, NC	02/20/65	Ft. Anderson, NC	02/28/65	Pt. Lookout, MD	CSR
					Pt. Lookout, MD	06/22/65	Rlsd. G.O. #109	P114,HAG
Ard, John J.	Pvt	G 15th SCVI	Gettysburg, PA	07/02/63	Ft. McHenry, MD	07/06/63	Ft. Delaware, DE	CSR, KEB
					Ft. Delaware, DE	11/28/63	Died, Smallpox	P5,P40,P42,P47,FPH
Ard, S. Reuben	Pvt	C 25th SCVI	Ft. Fisher, NC	01/15/65	New York, NY	01/30/65	Elmira, NY	CSR
					Elmira, NY	07/26/65	Rlsd. G.O. #109	P65,P66,HAG
Ardis, Abraham J.	Pvt	C 3rd SCVABn	Ft. Gaines, AL	08/08/64	New Orleans, LA	08/24/64	St. Louis, MO USGH	CSR
					St. Louis, MO USGH	09/24/64	New Orleans, LA	CSR
					New Orleans, LA	10/24/64	Ship Island, MS	CSR
					Ship Island, MS	01/04/65	Exchanged	CSR
Ardis, Abraham J.	Pvt	C 3rd SCVABn	Blakely, AL	04/09/65	Ship Island, MS	05/01/65	Vicksburg, MS Xc	P136,CSR
Ardis, J.L.	Pvt	C 3rd SCVABn	Ft. Gaines, AL	08/08/64	New Orleans, LA	10/25/64	Ship Island, MS	CSR
					Ship Island, MS	01/04/65	Exchanged	CSR
Ardis, J.L.	Pvt	C 3rd SCVABn	Ft. Tyler, GA	04/16/65	P.M 1st Cav. Div.	04/26/65	Macon, GA Prison	CSR
					Macon, GA Prison		Paroled	CSR
Ardis, J.W.	Pvt	C 3rd SCVABn	Blakely, AL	04/09/65	Ship Island, MS	05/01/65	Vicksburg, MS Prld	P136,CSR
Ardis, W.J.	Pvt	C 3rd SCVABn	Ft. Gaines, AL	08/08/64	New Orleans, LA	10/25/64	Ship Island, MS	CSR
					Ship Island, MS	01/04/65	Exchanged	CSR
Ardis, W.J.	Pvt	C 3rd SCVABn	Blakely, AL	04/09/65	Ship Island, MS	05/01/65	Vicksburg, MS Prld	CSR
Ardis, William	Pvt	C 3rd SCVABn	Macon, GA	04/20/65	Macon, GA	04/20/65	Paroled	CSR
Arebutt, H.N.	Cit	Lexington	Lexington, SC	02/25/65	Hart's Island, NY	06/20/65	Rlsd. G.O. #109	P79
Arledge, Jeptha R.	Pvt	I Ham.Leg.MI	Richmond, VA	04/03/65	Richmond, VA	04/14/65	Provost Marshal	CSR
					Libby Prsn., Rchmd	04/23/65	Newport News, VA	CSR
					Newport News, VA	06/26/65	Rlsd. G.O. #109	CSR
Arledge, Thomas W.	Sgt	I 25th SCVI	Town Creek, NC	02/20/65	Ft. Anderson, NC	02/28/65	Pt. Lookout, MD	CSR
					Pt. Lookout, MD	05/18/65	Rlsd. G.O. #85	P114,HAG,CSR
Arms, Edward S.	Pvt	E 5th SCVI	Williamsburg, VA	04/30/62	Fts. Monroe, VA		Washington, DC Hos.	CSR,CDC,TSE
Arms, Edward S.	Pvt	E 5th SCVI	Williamsburg, VA	05/05/62	Cliffburn GH, DC	05/22/62	Died of wounds	P6,P12,ROH,CSR

SOUTH CAROLINA SOLDIERS, SAILORS AND  CITIZENS HELD IN U.S. PRISONS 1861-1865

NAME	RANK	REGIMENT	CAPTURED AT	WHEN	PRISON	MOVED	DISPOSITION	SOURCES
Armstrong, James	Cpt	K 1st SCVIG	Southside RR, VA	04/01/65	City Pt., VA Hosp.	04/12/65	Washington, DC Hos	CSR
					Old Capitol, DC			P110,SA1
Armstrong, John W.	Pvt	E 1st SCVIG	Gettysburg, PA	07/05/63	Ft. McHenry, MD	07/18/63	Ft. Delaware, DE	CSR
					Ft. Delaware, DE	03/19/64	Hos. 3/19/-3/23/64	P47,SA1
					Ft. Delaware, DE	03/24/64	Hos. 3/24-3/28/64	P47
					Ft. Delaware, DE	09/20/64	Hos. 9/20-9/21/64	P47
					Ft. Delaware, DE	06/10/65	Released	P42,P44,P45,CSR
Armstrong, William	Pvt	H 1st SCVA	Charleston, SC	02/18/65	Charleston, SC	03/13/65	Taken oath & disch	CSR
Armstrong, William F.	Pvt	G 18th SCVI	Crater,Pbg., VA	07/30/64	Pt. Lookout, MD	08/08/64	Elmira, NY	P113,P117,P125,CSR
					Elmira, NY	10/11/64	Pt. Lookout, MD	P65
					Pt. Lookout, MD	10/29/64	Venus Pt., GA Xc	P114,P117,P123,CSR
Armstrong, William F.	Pvt	G 18th SCVI	Petersburg, VA	03/25/65	Pt. Lookout, MD	06/22/65	Rlsd G.O. #109	P114,P117,CSR
Arnhart, M.R.	Cit		Orangeburg, SC		Pt. Lookout, MD	06/19/65	Released	P121
Arnold, George William	Pvt	A 24th SCVI	Marietta, GA	07/03/64	Nashville, TN	07/14/64	Louisville, KY	CSR
					Louisville, KY	07/16/64	Camp Douglas, IL	P88,P91,CDC
					Camp Douglas, IL	01/13/65	Released on oath	P7,P53,P58,EFW
Arnold, J.H.	Pvt	A 1st SCVIR	Cheraw, SC	03/05/65	Cheraw, SC	03/05/65	Paroled	CSR
Arnold, John W.	Cpl	B 27th SCVI	Town Creek, NC	02/20/65	Ft. Anderson, NC	02/28/65	Pt. Lookout, MD	CSR,HAG
					Pt. Lookout, MD	06/22/65	Rlsd. G.O. #109	P114
Arnold, Preston	Pvt	G 19th SCVI	Nashville, TN	12/16/64	Louisville, KY	01/16/65	Camp Chase, OH	P94,CSR
					Camp Chase, OH	05/02/65	New Orleans Xc	P22,P26,CSR
					New Orleans, LA Xc	05/12/65	Vicksburg, MS Xc	CSR
Arnold, T.J.	Pvt	F Hol.Leg.	Petersburg, VA	04/02/65	City Point, VA	04/07/65	Hart's Island, NY	CSR
					Hart's Island, NY	06/18/65	Rlsd. G.O.# 109	P79,CSR
Arnold, W.B.	Pvt	B 23rd SCVI	Deserted/enemy	12/02/64	City Point, VA	12/05/64	Phila., PA/ oath	P8,CSR
Arnold, W.J.	Pvt	F Hol.Leg.	Jarratts Stn., VA	05/08/64	Fts. Monroe, VA	05/13/64	Pt. Lookout, MD	CSR
					Pt. Lookout, MD	08/15/64	Elmira, NY	P113,CSR
					Elmira, NY	10/14/64	Tfd. for exchange	P65,P66,CSR
					Pt. Lookout, MD	10/29/64	Venus Pt., GA Xc	P114,P117,CSR
Arnold, W.J.	Pvt	F Hol.Leg.	Five Forks, VA	04/01/65	City Pt., VA	04/05/65	Pt. Lookout, MD	CSR
					Pt. Lookout, MD	06/22/65	Rlsd. G.O. #109	P114,P118,CSR
Arnold, William	Pvt	K 5th SCVC	Chester, SC	05/05/65	Chester, SC	05/05/65	Paroled	CSR
Arrowood, James R.	Pvt	B 12th SCVI	Manassas, VA	08/27/62	Fts. Monroe, VA	09/07/62	Aikens Ldg., VA Xc	CSR
Arrowood, James R.	Pvt	B 12th SCVI	Manassas, VA	04/13/65	Lynchburg, VA	04/13/65	Paroled	CSR
Arthur, J.	Pvt	K 7th SCVC	Wh. Oak Swamp, VA	08/14/64	City Pt., VA	08/22/64	Pt. Lookout, MD	CSR
					Pt. Lookout, MD	02/18/65	Aikens ldg., VA Xt	P117,P124,P125,CSR
Arthur, J.T.	Pvt	F 27th SCVI	Town Creek, NC	02/20/65	Ft. Anderson, NC	02/28/65	Pt. Lookout, MD	CSR
					Pt. Lookout, MD	06/05/65	Rlsd. G.O. #109	P114,P117,CSR,HAG
Asbell, G.W.	Pvt	E 15th SCVI	Augusta, GA	05/25/65	Augusta, GA	05/25/65	Paroled	H15,CSR
Ash, Robert E.	Pvt	K 17th SCVI	South Mtn., MD	09/14/62	Philadelphia, PA	09/27/62	Ft. Delaware, DE	CSR
					Ft. Delaware, DE	03/28/63	Fts. Monroe, VA Xc	CSR
Ashbey, W.E.	Sgt	D 19th SCVCB	Augusta, GA	05/25/65	Augusta, GA	05/25/65	Paroled on oath	CSR
Ashcraft, Joseph G.	Pvt	H 19th SCVI	Marietta, GA	07/03/64	Louisville, KY	07/13/64	Camp Morton, IN	P88,P91,CSR
Ashcraft, Joseph G.	Pvt	H 19th SCVI	Marietta, GA	07/05/64	Camp Morton, IN	03/15/65	Pt. Lookout, MD Xc	P100,P101,CSR
					Jackson Hos. Rchmd	03/28/65	Furloughed 60 days	CSR
Ashe, Andrew F.	Pvt	K 17th SCVI	Five Forks, VA	04/01/65	City Pt., VA	04/06/65	Pt. Lookout, MD	CSR
					Pt. Lookout, MD	06/23/65	Rlsd. G.O. #109	P114,P118,YEB,CSR
Ashe, John J.	Pvt	K 17th SCVI	Petersburg, VA	03/25/65	City Pt., VA	03/28/65	Pt. Lookout, MD	CSR
					Pt. Lookout, MD	06/22/65	Rlsd. G.O. #109	P114,P117,YEB,CSR

SOUTH CAROLINA SOLDIERS, SAILORS AND CITIZENS HELD IN U.S. PRISONS 1861-1865

NAME	RANK	REGIMENT	CAPTURED AT	WHEN	PRISON	MOVED	DISPOSITION	SOURCES
Ashley, J.S.	Pvt	G 2nd SCVC	Burke's Stn., VA	10/28/63	Alexandria, VA USG	12/21/63	U.S. Gen. Hos.	CSR
					Lincoln G.H., DC	01/11/64	Washington, DC PM	CSR
					Old Capitol, DC	02/03/64	Pt. Lookout, MD	CSR
					Ft. McHenry, MD	02/03/64	Pt. Lookout, MD	P110
					Pt. Lookout, MD	05/03/64	City Pt., VA Xc	P113,P116,P124,CSR
					Richmond, VA Hos.	05/19/64	Furloughed 30 days	CSR
Ashley, L.A.	Pvt	G 2nd SCVA	James Island, SC	02/10/65	Durham's Stn., NC	05/29/65	Paroled	CSR
Ashley, Richard S.	Pvt	G Orr's Ri.	Falling Waters, MD	07/14/63	Baltimore, MD	08/16/63	Pt. Lookout, MD	CSR
					Pt. Lookout, MD	08/24/64	Died, Dysentery	P5,P113,P116
Ashley, Wilson Augustus	Pvt	G Orr's Ri.	Petersburg, VA	04/03/65	City Pt., VA	04/11/65	Hart's Island, NY	CSR
					Hart's Island, NY	06/16/65	Rlsd. G.O. #109	P79,CSR
Ashton, William	Cit	Charleston	Potomac River, VA	02/07/63	Ft. McHenry, MD	05/02/63	City Pt., VA Xc	P110
Askew, M.	Pvt	G 7th SCVC	Richmond, VA Hos.	04/03/65	Richmond, VA Hos.	04/29/65	Died, Scurvy	P12,CSR
Askins, John A.J.	Pvt	E 8th SCVI	Winchester, VA	09/13/64	Harper's Ferry, WV	09/19/64	Camp Chase, OH	CSR
					Camp Chase, OH	05/26/65	Died, Pneumonia	P12,P22,P27,FPH,KEB,CSR
Asplin, John	Pvt	C 15th SCVAB	Columbia, SC	02/17/65	New Berne, NC	04/10/65	Hart's Island, NY	CSR
					Hart's Island, NY	06/16/65	Rlsd. G.O. #109	CSR
Astle, John S.	Pvt	B 5th SCVC	Stony Creek, VA	12/01/64	City Pt., VA	12/05/64	Pt. Lookout, MD	P114,CSR
					Pt. Lookout, MD	06/22/65	Rlsd. G.O. #109	P114,CSR
Astle, William B.	Pvt	A 24th SCVI	Franklin, TN	12/17/64	Nashville, TN	12/20/64	Louisville, KY	CSR
					Louisville, KY	01/05/65	Camp Chase, OH	P94,EFW
					Camp Chase, OH	06/12/65	Rlsd. G.O. #109	P22,EFW
Atcheson, Robert	Pvt	A 13th SCVI	Amelia C.H., VA	04/05/65	City Pt., VA	04/13/65	Pt. Lookout, MD	CSR
					Pt. Lookout, MD	06/22/65	Rlsd. G.O. #109	P114,P118
Atkins, Alexander	Pvt	K 14th SCVI	Deep Creek, VA	04/03/65	City Pt., VA	04/13/65	Pt. Lookout, MD	CSR
					Pt. Lookout, MD	06/22/65	Rlsd. G.O. #109	P114,P118,CSR
Atkins, Henry R.	Pvt	K 14th SCVI	Petersburg, VA	04/03/65	City Pt., VA	04/11/65	Hart's Island, NY	CSR
					Hart's Island, NY	06/16/65	Rlsd. G.O. #109	P79,CSR
Atkins, John P.	Pvt	B 22nd SCVI	Kinston, NC	12/15/62	Kinston, NC	12/15/62	Paroled POW	CSR
Atkins, N. Jasper	Pvt	B 22nd SCVI	Kinston, NC	12/15/62	Kinston, NC	12/15/62	Paroled POW	CSR
Atkins, Oliver	Pvt	K 14th SCVI	Augusta, GA	05/23/65	Augusta, GA	05/23/65	Paroled	CSR
Atkins, William	Pvt	H 1st SCVC	Gettysburg, PA	07/04/63	Baltimore, MD Hos.	11/12/63	City Pt., VA Xc	P1,CSR
Atkinson, C.H.	Sgt	13th SCVI	Deserted/enemy	02/24/65	Washington D.C.	02/27/65	Dubuque, OH oath	CSR
Atkinson, Charles M.	Sgt	E 7th SCVIBn	Weldon RR, VA	08/21/64	City Pt., VA 5th U	09/06/64	Died of wounds	P12,ROH,HAG,CSR
Atkinson, J.	Pvt	C 3rd SCVABn	Blakely, AL	04/09/65	Ship Island, MS	05/01/65	Vicksburg, MS Prld	P136,CSR
Atkinson, J.C.	Pvt	F 2nd SCVC	Stephensburg, VA	06/09/63	P.M. Army of Potomac	06/11/63	Old Capitol, DC	CSR
					Old Capitol, DC	06/23/63	City Pt., VA to Xc	CSR
					Ft. McHenry, MD	06/25/63	City Pt., VA Xc	P110
Atkinson, J.S.	Pvt	C 3rd SCVABn	Augusta, GA	05/20/65	Augusta, GA	05/20/65	Paroled on oath	CSR
Atkinson, J.W.	Pvt	G 20th SCVI	Cedar Creek, VA	10/19/64	Harper's Ferry, WV	10/28/64	Pt. Lookout, MD	CSR
					Pt. Lookout, MD	03/28/65	Aikens Ldg., VA Xc	P114,P117,P124,CSR
Atkinson, J.W.	Pvt	F 4th SCVC	Stony Creek, VA	12/01/64	City Pt., VA	12/05/64	Pt. Lookout, MD	CSR
					Pt. Lookout, MD	02/13/65	Exchanged	P114,CSR
Atkinson, James W.	Pvt	A 14th SCVI	Falling Waters, MD	07/14/63	Old Capitol, DC	08/08/63	Pt. Lookout, MD	CSR
					Ft. McHenry, MD	08/08/63	Pt. Lookout, MD	P110,CSR
					Pt. Lookout, MD	03/03/64	City Pt., VA Xc	P116,P123,P124,CSR
Atkinson, James W.	Pvt	A 14th SCVI	Hatchers Run, VA	04/02/65	City Pt., VA	04/07/65	Hart's Island, NY	CSR
					Hart's Island, NY	06/16/65	Rlsd. G.O. #109	P79,CSR
Atkinson, Peter W.	2Lt	H 21st SCVI	Weldon RR, VA	08/21/64	Ft. McHenry, MD	08/27/64	Ft. Delaware, DE	P110,HAG
					Old Capitol, DC	08/27/64	Ft. Delaware, DE	CSR
					Ft. Delaware, DE	06/21/65	Rlsd. G.O. #109	P45,P46,CSR

SOUTH CAROLINA SOLDIERS, SAILORS AND **A** CITIZENS HELD IN U.S. PRISONS 1861-1865

NAME	RANK	REGIMENT	CAPTURED AT	WHEN	PRISON	MOVED	DISPOSITION	SOURCES
Atkinson, S.S.	Pvt	H 5th SCVI	Spotsylvania, VA	05/12/64	Belle Plain, VA	05/21/64	Ft. Delaware, DE	P47,CSR
					Ft. Delaware, DE	01/27/65	Hos. 1/27-1/28/65	P47
					Ft. Delaware, DE	03/12/65	To Hos. 3/12/65	P47
					Ft. Delaware, DE	03/19/65	Died, Lung Infl.	P12,P42,FPH,CSR
Atkinson, Solomon	Pvt	C 3rd SCVABn	Blakely, AL	04/09/65	Ship Island, MS	05/01/65	Vicksburg, MS Xc	P136,CSR
Atkinson, T.	Pvt	G 3rd SCVABn	Augusta, GA	05/20/65	Augusta, GA	05/20/65	Paroled on oath	CSR
Atkinson, Thomas	Pvt	G 21st SCVI	Ft. Fisher, NC	01/15/65	Elmira, NY	04/06/65	Died, Diarrhea	P12,P65,P66,FPH
Atkinson, William	Pvt	D 21st SCVI	Morris Island, SC	07/18/63	Hilton Head, SC	08/08/63	Died, Diarrhea	P12,ROH,HAG,CSR
Attaway, Charles	Pvt	B 7th SCVC	Burkville, VA	04/06/65	City Pt., VA	04/14/65	Pt. Lookout, MD	CSR
					Pt. Lookout, MD	06/22/65	Rlsd. G.O. #109	P114,CSR
Attaway, J. Simon	Pvt	G 1st SCVIG	Gettysburg, PA	07/01/63	Gettysburg, PA	08/13/63	Died of wounds	P1,P5,SA1,CSR
Attaway, Simon	Pvt	K 15th SCVI	Gettysburg, PA	07/04/63	5th Sec. GBG. Gen H.	08/13/63	Died of wounds	P5,P12
Attaway, T.G.	Pvt	F 27th SCVI	Town Creek, NC	02/20/65	Ft. Anderson, NC	02/28/65	Pt. Lookout, MD	CSR
					Pt. Lookout, MD	06/18/65	Died, Diarrhea	P12,P114,FPH,CSR
Atteberry, D.D.	Pvt	I 5th SCVC	Augusta, GA	05/20/65	Augusta, GA	05/20/65	Paroled	CSR
Attenburg, John	Pvt	C 19th SCVI	Nashville, TN	12/16/64	Camp Chase, OH	06/12/65	Rlsd G.O. #109	P22
Atterberry, William	Pvt	H 17th SCVI	Warrenton, VA	09/29/62	Warrenton, VA	09/29/62	Paroled	CSR
Atwood, John L.	Cpl	Palmetto LA	Amelia C.H., VA	04/05/65	City Pt., VA	04/13/65	Pt. Lookout, MD	CSR
					Pt. Lookout, MD	06/22/65	Rlsd. G.O. #109	P114,CSR
Augley, J.W.	Pvt	G 17th SCVI	Augusta, GA	05/22/65	Augusta, GA	05/22/65	Paroled	CSR
Augustine, F.J.A.	Pvt	H 2nd SCVC	Vienna Stn., VA	10/02/63	Old Capitol, DC	02/03/64	Pt. Lookout, MD	CSR
					Ft. McHenry, MD	02/03/64	Pt. Lookout, MD	P110
					Pt. Lookout, MD	10/30/64	Aikens Ldg., VA Xc	P113,P116,P124
Augustine, James A.	Pvt	D Ham.Leg. MI	Alexandria, VA	02/17/65	Alexandria, VA	02/17/65	Dead on arrival	CSR
Augustine, William	Pvt	I 24th SCVI	Franklin, TN	12/17/64	Nashville, TN	01/04/65	Louisville, KY	CSR
					Louisville, KY	01/09/65	Camp Chase, OH	P92,P94,EFW
					Camp Chase, OH	05/02/65	New Orleans, LA Xc	P22,P26,EFW
Augustine, William	Pvt	I 24th SCVI	Franklin, TN	12/17/64	New Orleans, LA Xc	05/12/65	Vicksburg, MS Xc	CSR
Auld, G.M.	Sgt	F 14th SCVI	Gettysburg, PA	07/05/63	David's Island, NY	09/05/63	City Pt., VA Xc	P1,CSR
Aultman, Thomas	Pvt	F 27th SCVI	Weldon RR, VA	08/21/64	City Pt., VA	08/24/64	Pt. Lookout, MD	CSR,HAG
					Pt. Lookout, MD	03/14/65	Exchanged	P117,P124,P125
Aulton, R.	Pvt	A 3rd SCVABn	High Pt., NC	05/02/65	High Pt., NC	05/02/65	Paroled on oath	CSR
Austin, Daniel	Pvt	B 3rd SCVC	Deserted/enemy	06/12/63	Washington, DC	06/24/63	Released on oath	CSR
Austin, Nathaniel	2Lt	E 14th SCVI	Gettysburg, PA	07/05/63	Letterman G.H. Gbg	07/14/63	Provost Marshal	P1,CSR
					Letterman G.H., PA	08/22/63	Died of wounds	CSR,UD3
Austin, Samuel	Pvt	D 27th SCVI	Town Creek, NC	02/20/65	Ft. Anderson, NC	02/28/65	Pt. Lookout, MD	CSR,HOS
					Pt. Lookout, MD	06/23/65	Rlsd. G.O. #109	CSR
Austin, Samuel	Pvt	C Hol.Leg.	Hatchers Run, VA	03/29/65	City Pt., VA	04/02/65	Pt. Lookout, MD	CSR
					Pt. Lookout, MD	06/10/65	Rlsd. G.O. #109	P114,P117
Austin, William H.	Pvt	E 16th SCVI	Egypt Stn., MS	12/28/64	Memphis, TN	01/17/65	Alton, IL	CSR
					Alton, IL	02/28/65	Pt. Lookout, MD Xc	P13,P14,16R,CSR
Avant, James	Pvt	C 25th SCVI	Ft. Fisher, NC	01/15/65	New York, NY	01/30/65	Elmira, NY	CSR
					Elmira, NY	03/02/65	James R., VA for Xc	CSR
Avant, Jerry R.	Sgt	A 21st SCVI	Weldon RR, VA	08/21/64	Pt. Lookout, MD	01/15/65	Died, Dropsy	P6,P113,P124
Avant, M.	Pvt	F 1st SCVA	Charleston, SC	02/24/65	Charleston, SC	03/02/65	Will take oath	CSR
Avant, O.R.	Pvt	I 21st SCVI	Ft. Fisher, NC	01/15/65	Elmira, NY	07/11/65	Rlsd. G.O. #109	P65,P66,HAG
Avant, Samuel	Sgt	A 21st SCVI	Petersburg, VA	06/24/64	Pt. Lookout, MD	08/16/64	Elmira, NY	P113,P120,HAG
					Elmira, NY	09/26/64	Died, Diarrhea	P6,P12,P65,FPH
Avery, John W.	Maj	17th SCVI	Petersburg, VA	04/11/65	24th AC Field Hos.	04/13/65	US Gen. Hos.	LC,CSR
Avery, Samuel J.	Pvt	C 14th SCVI	N. Anna River, VA	05/23/64	Pt. Lookout, MD	11/01/64	Aikens Ldg., VA Xc	P116,P123,P124,UD6
Avin, James R.	Pvt	C 3rd SCVABn	Ft. Gaines, AL	08/08/64	New Orleans, LA	10/25/64	Ship Island, MS	CSR
					Ship Island, MS	01/04/65	Exchanged	CSR

SOUTH CAROLINA SOLDIERS, SAILORS AND **A** CITIZENS HELD IN U.S. PRISONS 1861-1865

NAME	RANK	REGIMENT	CAPTURED AT	WHEN	PRISON	MOVED	DISPOSITION	SOURCES
Avin, James R.	Pvt	C 3rd SCVABn	Citronelle, AL	05/04/65	Meridian, MS	05/10/65	Paroled	CSR
Avinger, A.P.	Sgt	E 25th SCVI	Ft. Fisher, NC	01/15/65	New York, NY	01/30/65	Elmira, NY	CSR
					Elmira, NY	06/07/65	Rlsd. G.O. #109	P65,P66,HAG
Avinger, G.W.	Pvt	D 2nd SCVC	Wilmington, NC	03/01/65	Wilmington, NC	04/17/65	Baltimore, MD oath	CSR
Axum, James	Pvt	C 8th SCVI	Gettysburg, PA	07/01/63	David's Island, NY	08/24/63	City Pt., VA Xc	CSR
					Harper's Ferry, WV	09/19/64	Camp Chase, OH	CSR
Axum, James	Pvt	C 8th SCVI	Winchester, VA	09/13/64	Camp Chase, OH	06/10/65	Rlsd. G.O. #109	P22,CSR
Ayer, F.C.	Pvt	A 19th SCVCB	Augusta, GA	05/26/65	Augusta, GA	05/25/65	Paroled on oath	CSR
Ayers, Alfred M.	1Lt	G 2nd SCVIRi	Deep Bottom, VA	08/14/64	Bermuda Hundred, VA	08/15/64	Fts. Monroe, VA	CSR
					Fts. Monroe, VA	08/16/64	Pt. Lookout, MD	CSR
					Pt. Lookout, MD	08/18/64	Washington, DC	P113,P120,P125,CSR
					Old Capitol, DC	08/27/64	Ft. Delaware, DE	CSR
Ayers, Alfred M.	1Lt	G 2nd SCVIRi	Deep Bottom, VA	08/14/64	Ft. Delaware, DE	06/17/65	Rlsd. G.O. #109	P43,P45,P46,CSR
Ayers, Jefferson	Pvt	K 17th SCVI	Richmond, VA Hos.	04/03/65	USS Thomas Powell	05/06/65	Pt. Lookout, MD GH	CSR
					Pt. Lookout G.H.	07/02/65	Died, Diarrhea	P6,FPH,CSR
Ayers, Nathaniel H.	Pvt	L 2nd SCVIRi	Chattanooga, TN	10/29/63	Nashville, TN	11/07/63	Louisville, KY	P39,CSR
					Louisville, KY	11/09/63	Camp Morton, IN	P89,CSR
					Camp Morton, IN	02/26/65	City Pt., VA Xc	P100,P101,CSR

B

SOUTH CAROLINA SOLDIERS, SAILORS AND CITIZENS HELD IN U.S. PRISONS 1861-1865

NAME	RANK	REGIMENT	CAPTURED AT	WHEN	PRISON	MOVED	DISPOSITION	SOURCES
Babb, Barnett	Pvt	A 6th SCVC	Stony Creek, VA	12/01/64	City Pt., VA	12/05/64	Pt. Lookout, MD	CSR
					Pt. Lookout, MD	02/13/65	Aikens Ldg., VA Xc	P118,P121,P124,CSR
Babb, Joseph	Pvt	D 3rd SCVIBn	Knoxville, TN	12/06/63	Nashville, TN	02/11/64	Louisville, KY	P39,KEB,CSR
					Louisville, KY	02/15/64	Rock Island, IL	P90,P91,P94,CSR
Babb, Joseph	Pvt	D 3rd SCVIBn	Knoxville, TN	12/26/63	Rock Island, IL	03/02/65	Pt.Lookout, MD Xc	P131,CSR
Babba, W.B.	Pvt	17th SCVI	Athens, GA	05/08/65	Athens, GA	05/08/65	Paroled	CSR
Bachman, Henry	Cit	LN Dist SC	Lexington, SC	02/16/65	Pt. Lookout, MD	06/05/65	Released	P114,P118
Bacon, Augustus	Pvt	B 2nd SCVI	Gettysburg, PA	07/03/63	Letterman G.H. Gbg.	09/23/63	Provost Marshal	P1,P4,KEB,CSR
					W. Bldg. Balt., MD	09/25/63	City Pt., VA Xc	P1,KEB,H2,CSR
Bacon, Randolph	Pvt	B 2nd SCVI	Gettysburg, PA	07/03/63	W. Bldg. Balt., MD	09/25/63	City Pt., VA Xc	P1,KEB,H2,CSR
Badenhoff, H.	Pvt	A German LA	Macon, GA	04/30/65	Macon, GA	04/30/65	Paroled	CSR
Badger, D.E.	Pvt	I 27th SCVI	Hilton Head, SC	05/25/65	Hilton Head, SC	05/25/65	Paroled on oath	CSR,HAG
Baggett, James H.	Cit	Marlboro D	Washington, DC	01/30/64	Pt. Lookout, MD	03/14/65	Aikens Ldg., VA Xc	P121
Baggett, N.W.	Sgt	I 23rd SCVI	Five Forks, VA	04/01/65	City Pt., VA	04/04/65	Hart's Island, NY	CSR
					Hart's Island, NY	06/16/65	Rlsd. G.O. #109	P79,HCL,CSR
Bagginetta, John	Pvt	Ferguson's A	Ringgold, GA	11/26/63	Nashville, TN	12/09/63	Louisville, KY	P39,CSR
					Louisville, KY	12/11/63	Rock Island, IL	CSR
					Rock Island, IL	10/28/64	Released on oath	CSR
					Rock Island, IL	10/28/64	Vol. for U.S. Serv.	CSR
Bagley, James D.	Sgt	D 2nd SCVI	Halltown, WV	08/26/64	Harpers Ferry, WV	08/29/63	Camp Chase, OH	CSR
					Camp Chase, OH	06/10/65	Rlsd. G.O. #109	P23,SA2,H2,CSR
Bagley, Lee	Pvt	E 15th SCVI	Sharpsburg, MD	09/28/62	Ft. McHenry, MD	11/06/62	Aikens Ldg., VA Xc	CSR
Bagley, Thomas R.	Pvt	H 24th SCVI	Jackson, MS	05/14/64	Mobile, AL US Hos.	05/16/64	Paroled	CSR
Bagnal, J. Moultrie	Sgt	I 25th SCVI	Ft. Fisher, NC	01/15/65	New York, NY	01/30/65	Elmira, NY	CSR
					Elmira, NY	06/27/65	Rlsd. G.O. #109	P65,P66,HAG,CSR
Bagnall, John C.	Pvt	C Ham.Leg.	Fair Oaks, VA	05/31/62	Fts. Monroe, VA	06/05/62	Ft. Delaware, DE	CSR
					Ft. Delaware, DE	08/05/62	Aikens Ldg., VA Xc	CSR
Bagwell, Berry J.	Cpl	E 16th SCVI	Ringgold, GA	11/27/63	Nashville, TN	12/07/63	Louisville, KY	P39,CSR
					Louisville, KY	12/11/63	Rock Island, IL	P88,P89,CSR
					Rock Island, IL	06/19/65	Released G.O. #109	P131,CSR
Bagwell, John B.	Pvt	C 14th SCVI	Gettysburg, PA	07/04/63	W. Bldg. Balt., MD	07/30/63	Baltimore, MD Jail	P1
					Baltimore, MD jail	08/20/63	Pt. Lookout, MD	CSR
					Pt. Lookout, MD	02/18/65	Aikens Ldg., VA Xc	P113,P116,P124,CSR
Bagwell, John J.	Pvt	I 13th SCVI	Petersburg, VA Hos.	04/03/65	Ft. Monroe, VA Hos.	05/06/65		CSR
Bagwell, W.A.	Pvt	E Ham.Leg.	Fair Oaks, VA	06/01/62	Fts. Monroe, VA	07/15/62	Ft. Delaware, DE	CSR
					Richmond, VA Hos.	09/04/62	Furloughed 30 days	CSR
Bagwell, William W.	Pvt	G 7th SCVI	Halltown, WV	08/21/64	Washington, DC	09/02/64	Camp Chase, OH	CSR
					Camp Chase, OH	02/19/65	Died, pneumonia	P6,P12,P23,P27,CSR
Bahr, L.N.	Pvt	C 23rd SCVI	Deserted/enemy	03/30/65	Washington, DC	04/04/65	Charleston, SC	CSR
Bailey, A.W.	Sur	1st SCVIH	Augusta, GA	05/26/65	Augusta, GA	05/26/65	Paroled	CSR
Bailey, Charles M.	Pvt	G 25th SCVI	Ft. Fisher, NC	01/15/65	New York, NY	01/30/65	Elmira, NY	CSR
					Elmira, NY	04/14/65	Died, Typhoid	P6,P65,P66,FPH
Bailey, D.B.	Pvt	K 18th SCVI	Crater, Pbg., VA	07/30/64	City Pt., VA	08/05/64	Pt. Lookout, MD	CSR
					Pt. Lookout, MD	08/08/64	Elmira, NY	P117,P120,P125,CSR
					Elmira, NY	06/14/65	Rlsd. G.O.#109	P65,CSR
Bailey, Daniel	Pvt	D 7th SCVIBn	Weldon RR, VA	08/19/64	City Pt., VA 5th A	08/23/64	USHS Atlantic	CSR
					White Hall, PA USG	12/23/64	Phila., PA USGH	CSR
					W. Bldg. Balt., MD		Pt. Lookout, MD US	P4,HAG,CSR
					Pt. Lookout, MD	01/28/65	U.S. Gen. Hosp.	P114,HAG,CSR
					Pt. Lookout, MD	06/04/65	Released	P121,CSR
Bailey, E.B.	Pvt	C 18th SCVI	Deserted/enemy	03/02/65	Washington, DC	03/06/65	New York, NY/oath	CSR

B

SOUTH CAROLINA SOLDIERS, SAILORS AND CITIZENS HELD IN U.S. PRISONS 1861-1865

NAME	RANK	REGIMENT	CAPTURED AT	WHEN	PRISON	MOVED	DISPOSITION	SOURCES
Bailey, F.M.	Cpl	I 3rd SCVC	Edisto Island, SC	04/09/63	Ft. Norfolk, VA	06/29/63	Paroled	CSR
Bailey, Henry L.	Pvt	G 25th SCVI	Ft. Fisher, NC	01/15/65	New York, NY	01/30/65	Elmira, NY	CSR
					Elmira, NY	03/13/65	Died, Diarrhea	P6,P12,P65,P66,HAG
Bailey, J.F.	Pvt	C 18th SCVI	Sharpsburg, MD	09/17/62	Ft. McHenry, MD	07/28/62	Fts. Monroe, VA Xc	CSR
Bailey, J.G.	Sgt	H 15th SCVI	Gettysburg, PA	07/05/63	Ft. Delaware, DE	05/28/64	Dis. Hos. 5/28/64	P47,KEB
					Pt. Lookout, MD	10/31/64	Aikens Ldg., VA Xc	P42,P114,P118
					Ft. Delaware, DE	10/31/64	Venus Pt., GA Xc	P40,P44,CSR
Bailey, John	Pvt	A 23rd SCVI	Boonesboro, MD	09/14/62	Fts. Monroe, VA	10/10/62	Aikens Ldg., VA Xc	CSR
Bailey, John B.	Pvt	I 11th SCVI	Drury's Bluff, VA	05/16/64	Bermuda Hundred, VA	05/16/64	Fts. Monroe, VA	CSR
					Pt. Lookout, MD	08/15/64	Elmira, NY	P117,P120,CSR
					Elmira, NY	03/19/65	Died, Diarrhea	P6,P65,HAG,FPH
Bailey, M.J.	Pvt	A 10th SCVI	Montgomery, AL	06/12/65	Montgomery, AL	06/12/65	Paroled	CSR,RAS
Bailey, Newell	Pvt	D 2nd SCVIRi	Anderson, SC	05/23/65	Anderson, SC	05/23/65	Paroled	CSR
Bailey, R.W.	Pvt	C 18th SCVI	Petersburg, VA	02/07/65	City Pt., VA	02/09/65	To Indiana on oath	P8,CSR
Bailey, Rix	Pvt	H 4th SCVC	Hawe's Shop, VA	05/25/64	3rd Div. 5th A.C.	05/31/64	Died of wounds	CSR
Bailey, Thomas J.	Pvt	Brooks LA	Harpers Farm, VA	04/06/65	City Pt., VA	04/14/65	Pt. Lookout, MD	CSR
					Pt. Lookout, MD	06/23/65	Rlsd. G.O. #109	CSR
Bailey, W.G.	Pvt	D 1st SCVIH	Frederick, MD	09/12/62	Frederick, MD USGH	09/18/62	Ft. Delaware, DE	CSR
					Ft. Delaware, DE	10/02/62	Aikens Ldg., VA Xc	CSR
Bailey, Wesley	Pvt	L 21st SCVI	Morris Island, SC	07/12/63	Hilton Head, SC	07/23/63	Exchanged	P2,HAG,CSR
Bailey, Wesley	Pvt	L 21st SCVI	Petersburg, VA	05/09/64	Bermuda Hundred, VA	05/11/64	Fts. Monroe, VA	CSR
					Fts. Monroe, VA	05/15/64	Pt. Lookout, MD	CSR
					Pt. Lookout, MD	03/14/65	Aikens Ldg., VA Xc	P113,P117,P124,CSR
Bailey, Wiley M.	Pvt	D Hol.Leg.	Petersburg, VA	03/25/65	City Pt., VA	03/27/65	Pt. Lookout, MD	CSR
					Pt. Lookout, MD	06/24/65	Rlsd. G.O. #109	P114,P118,P123,CSR
Bailey, William	Pvt	C 3rd SCVABn	Blakely, AL	04/09/65	Ship Island, MS	05/01/65	Vicksburg, MS Prld	P136,CSR
Bailey, William	Pvt	C 3rd SCVABn	Augusta, GA	05/26/65	Augusta, GA	05/26/65	Paroled on oath	CSR
Bailey, William A.	Pvt	E 3rd SCVI	Maryland Hts., MD	09/16/62	Sandy Hook, MD	09/22/62	Released on parole	H3,CSR
Bailey, William F.	2Lt	F 3rd SCVI	Winchester, VA	09/19/64	W. Bldg. Balt., MD	10/25/64	Pt. Lookout, MD	P3,SA2,H3,CSR
					Pt. Lookout, MD	11/02/64	Washington, DC	P114,P117,P120,CSR
					Old Capitol, DC	12/16/64	Ft. Delaware, DE	P110,H3,CSR
					Ft. McHenry, MD	12/16/64	Ft. Delaware, DE	P110
					Ft. Delaware, DE	06/17/65	Rlsd. G.O. #109	P45,P46,H3,CSR
Bailey, William F.	Pvt	B 15th SCVAB	Deserted/enemy	03/18/65	Charleston, SC	03/18/65	Taken oath & disch.	CSR
Bailey, William W.	Pvt	I 24th SCVI	Missionary Ridge, TN	11/25/63	Nashville, TN	12/07/63	Louisville, KY	P39
					Louisville, KY	12/08/63	Rock Island, IL	P88,P89
					Rock Island, IL	01/25/64	Enlstd., US Navy	P131,CSR,EFW
Bailey, Zacharia R.	Pvt	Brooks LA	Harpers Farm, VA	04/06/65	City Pt., VA	04/14/65	Pt. Lookout, MD	CSR
					Pt. Lookout, MD	06/24/65	Rlsd. G.O. #109	CSR
Baine, Michael	Pvt	E 25th SCVI	Charleston, SC	02/18/65	Charleston, SC	03/13/65	Released on oath	HAG,CSR
Baker, Albert T.	Pvt	I 14th SCVI	Sutherland Stn., VA	04/02/65	City Pt., VA	04/07/65	Hart's Island, NY	CSR
					Hart's Island, NY	06/16/65	Rlsd. G.O. #109	P79,CSR
Baker, Bernard E.	Pvt	A 27th SCVI	Weldon RR, VA	08/21/64	City Pt., VA	08/24/64	Pt. Lookout, MD	CSR
					Pt. Lookout, MD	10/11/64	Aikens Ldg., VA Xc	P113,P117,P123,HAG
					Richmond, VA Hos.	10/22/64	Died of disease	CSR,HAG
Baker, D.D.	Pvt	B 15th SCVAB	Deserted/enemy	03/18/65	Charleston, SC	03/18/65	Taken oath & disch	CSR
Baker, Ellis J.	Pvt	A 14th SCVI	Appomattox R., VA	04/03/65	City Pt., VA	04/11/65	Hart's Island, NY	CSR
					Hart's Island, NY	06/21/65	Rlsd. G.O. #109	P79,CSR
Baker, G.W.	Pvt	C 5th SCResB	Cheraw, SC	03/03/65	New Berne, NC	03/30/65	Pt. Lookout, MD	CSR
					Pt. Lookout, MD	06/24/65	Rlsd. G.O. #109	P114,P123,CSR
Baker, George S.	Cpl	B 25th SCVI	Ft. Fisher, NC	01/15/65	New York, NY	01/30/65	Elmira, NY	CSR
					Elmira, NY	02/11/65	Released S.O.	P65,P66,HAG

SOUTH CAROLINA SOLDIERS, SAILORS AND  CITIZENS HELD IN U.S. PRISONS 1861-1865

NAME	RANK	REGIMENT	CAPTURED AT	WHEN	PRISON	MOVED	DISPOSITION	SOURCES
Baker, Henry H.	Sgt	A 27th SCVI	Town Creek, NC	02/20/65	Ft. Anderson, NC	02/28/65	Pt. Lookout, MD	CSR,HAG
					Pt. Lookout, MD		No other data	P114,CSR
Baker, J.A.	Pvt	E 1st SCVIG	N. Anna River, VA	05/23/64	Front Royal, VA	05/30/64	Pt. Lookout, MD	CSR
					Pt. Lookout, MD	03/15/65	Aikens Ldg., VA Xc	P113,P117,P124,CSR
Baker, James J. Melton	Pvt	A 1st SCVIR	Morris Island, SC	09/07/63	Ft. Columbus, NY	10/09/63	Johnson's Isl., OH	P1
					Pt. Lookout, MD	03/02/64	Ft. Delaware, DE	P113,P120,SA1
					Pt. Lookout, MD		Took the Oath	P124
					Fts. Monroe, VA	03/03/64	Rlsd. on oath	P8,SA1,CSR
Baker, James S.	Pvt	F 26th SCVI	Deserted/enemy	01/22/65	City Pt., VA	01/23/65	Washington, DC	P8,CSR
					Washington, DC	01/26/65	Phila., PA on oath	CSR
Baker, John	Pvt	K 6th SCVC	Gloucester Co., VA	03/10/64	Pt. Lookout, MD			P113,P116
Baker, John G.	Pvt	B 10th SCVI	Chattahootchie, GA	07/05/64	Louisville, KY	07/13/64	Camp Morton, IN	P90,P91,P94,CSR
					Camp Morton, IN	03/04/65	City Pt., VA Xc	P100,P101,CSR
Baker, Major R.D.	Cpl	C 25th SCVI	Ft. Fisher, NC	01/15/65	New York, NY	01/30/65	Elmira, NY	CSR
					Elmira, NY	03/31/65	Died, Diarrhea	P6,P65,P66,HAG,FPH
Baker, Oscar H.	Sgt	G 19th SCVI	Bentonville, NC	03/09/65	New Berne, NC	04/05/65	Pt. Lookout, MD	CSR,HOL
					Pt. Lookout, MD	06/09/65	Released	P118,CSR,HOL
Baker, Thomas Herrison	Mtr	P. *Savannah*	Off Charleston	06/03/61	Tombs Prison NYC		Ft. Lafayette, NY	OR
Baker, Wellington	Cpl	D 6th SCVC	Chesterfield, SC	03/02/65	Pt. Lookout, MD	06/24/65	Rlsd. G.O. #109	P114,P118,P123,CSR
Baker, William	Pvt	B 15th SCMil	SC or NC	03/31/65	Foster G.H. Newbern	04/01/65	Died, Diarrhea	P1,P6,P12
Baker, William	Pvt	C 1st SCVIR	Bentonville, NC	03/22/65	New Berne, NC G.H.	04/10/65	Hart's Island, NY	CSR
					Hart's Island, NY	06/16/65	Rlsd. G.O. #109	P79,SA1,CSR
Baker, William Alexander	Pvt	G 21st SCVI	Morris Island, SC	07/10/63	Morris Island, SC	07/11/63	Hilton Head, SC	CSR
					Hilton Head, SC	09/22/63	Ft. Columbus, NY	P2,CSR
					Pt. Lookout, MD	05/03/64	City Pt., VA Xc	P116,P123
					Ft. Anderson, NC	02/28/65	Pt. Lookout, MD	CSR
					Pt. Lookout, MD	06/24/65	Rlsd. G.O. #109	P114,P123,P124,CSR
Baker, William C.	Cpt	L 21st SCVI	Ft. Fisher, NC	01/15/65	Ft. Columbus, NY	03/01/65	City Pt., VA Xc	P2,HAG
Baker, William M.	Pvt	K 23rd SCVI	Amelia C.H., VA	04/02/65	City Pt., VA	04/13/65	Pt. Lookout, MD	CSR
					Pt. Lookout, MD	06/24/65	Rlsd. G.O. #109	P114,P123,CSR
Baldwin, D.H.	Pvt	C 3rd SCVIBn	N. Anna River, VA	05/22/64	Port Royal, VA	05/30/64	Pt. Lookout, MD	CSR, KEB
					Pt. Lookout, MD	05/12/65	Rlsd. G.O. #85	P113,P117,P124,FPH
Baldwin, D.W.	Pvt	B 1st SCVIR	Raleigh, NC Hos.	04/13/65	Raleigh, NC	04/13/65	Paroled	SA1,CSR
Baldwin, James	Pvt	C 3rd SCVIBn	Boonesboro, MD	09/14/62	Old Capitol, DC	10/31/62	Fts. Monroe, VA Xc	CSR
					Fts. Monroe, VA	11/02/62	Aikens Ldg., VA Xc	CSR
Baldwin, Marcus L.	Pvt	14th SCMil	Beer's Bridge, SC	02/10/65	Pt. Lookout, MD	06/19/65	Rlsd. G.O. #109	P118,P121
Baldwin, R.J.	Pvt	17th SCVI	Athens, GA	05/08/65	Athens, GA	05/08/65	Paroled	CSR
Baldwin, W.A.J.	Pvt	F 2nd SCVC	Charlotte, NC	05/25/65	Charlotte, NC	05/25/65	Paroled on oath	CSR
Bale, William F.	Pvt	I 27th SCVI	Petersburg, VA	06/24/64	Fts. Monroe, VA	06/27/64	Pt. Lookout, MD	CSR,HAG
					Pt. Lookout, MD	08/16/64	Elmira, NY	P113,P117,P120
					Elmira, NY	07/03/65	Rlsd. G.O. #109	P65
Ball, Adam	Pvt	F 2nd SCVIRi	Cold Harbor, VA	06/01/64	White House, VA	06/11/64	Pt. Lookout, MD	CSR
					Pt. Lookout, MD	07/12/64	Elmira, NY	P113.P117,P120,CSR
					Elmira, NY, parole	03/10/65	Boulwares Wh., VA	P65,P66,CSR
Ball, J.J.	Pvt	D 27th SCVI	Weldon RR, VA	08/21/64	City Pt., VA	08/24/64	Pt. Lookout, MD	CSR,HAG
					Pt. Lookout, MD	12/11/64	Died, Dysentery	P5,P117,P119
Ball, T.	Pvt	C 3rd SCVABn	Blakely, AL	04/09/65	Ship Island, MS	05/01/65	Vicksburg, MS Prld	P136

SOUTH CAROLINA SOLDIERS, SAILORS AND  CITIZENS HELD IN U.S. PRISONS 1861-1865

NAME	RANK	REGIMENT	CAPTURED AT	WHEN	PRISON	MOVED	DISPOSITION	SOURCES
Ball, William H.	Pvt	G 3rd SCVI	Harpers Ferry, WV	07/17/63	Sandy Hook, MD	09/22/62	Released on Parole	H3,CSR
					Washington, DC P.M.		Baltimore, MD	CSR
					Baltimore, MD	08/20/63	Pt. Lookout, MD	CSR
					Pt. Lookout, MD	01/27/65	Hammond G.H., MD	P113,P121,CSR
					Hammond G.H., MD	04/08/65	Pt. Lookout, MD	CSR
					Pt. Lookout, MD	06/23/65	Rlsd. G.O. #109	P121,P122,P124,CSR
Ballard, Hugh	Pvt	A 15th SCVAB	Smith's Ford, NC	03/16/65	New Berne, NC	03/30/65	Pt. Lookout, MD	CSR
					Pt. Lookout, MD	06/24/65	Rlsd. G.O. #109	P118,P121,P123,CSR
Ballenger, Adam W.	Lt	E 13th SCVI	Richmond, VA Hos.	04/03/65	Pt. Lookout, MD	05/02/65		CSR
Ballenger, Dillingham	1Sg	B 22nd SCVI	Kinston, NC	12/15/62	Kinston, NC	12/15/62	Paroled POW	CSR
Ballenger, Jabez W.	Cpl	I Hol.Leg.	Kinston, NC	12/15/62	Kinston, NC	12/15/62	Paroled POW	CSR
Ballenger, Jabez W.	Cpl	I Hol.Leg.	Stony Creek, VA	05/07/64	Fts. Monroe, VA	05/13/64	Pt. Lookout, MD	CSR
					Pt. Lookout, MD	08/15/64	Elmira, NY	CSR
					Elmira, NY	06/19/65	Rlsd. G.O. #109	CSR,HOS
Ballentine, Albert	Pvt	E 1st SCVIR	Cheraw, SC	03/05/65	Cheraw, SC	03/05/65	Released on oath	CSR
Ballentine, D.O.S.	Pvt	D 4th SCVC	Louisa C.H., VA	06/11/64	Fts. Monroe, VA	06/20/64	Pt. Lookout, MD	CSR
					Pt. Lookout, MD	07/22/64	Died	P6,P117,FPH
Ballentine, David F.	Pvt	C 14th SCVI	Farmville, VA	04/02/65	Farmville, VA G.H.	04/02/65	Paroled	CSR
Ballentine, Thomas M.	Pvt	C 5th SCVC	Stony Creek, VA	12/01/64	City Pt., VA	12/05/64	Pt. Lookout, MD	CSR
					Pt. Lookout, MD	01/27/65	Aikens Ldg., VA Xc	P118,P124,CSR
Ballew, David	Pvt	D 16th SCVI	Marietta, GA	06/16/64	Nashville, TN	06/20/64	Louisville, KY	P3,16R
Ballew, David	Pvt	D 16th SCVI	Marietta, GA	06/15/64	Louisville, KY	06/22/64	Rock Island, IL	P91,P94,CSR
Ballew, David	Pvt	D 16th SCVI	Marietta, GA	06/16/64	Rock Island, IL	07/06/64	Joined US Navy	P131,CSR
Ballew, Isaac A.	Pvt	D 16th SCVI	Missionary Ridge, TN	11/25/63	Nashville, TN	12/07/63	Louisville, KY	P39,16R,CSR
					Louisville, KY	12/08/63	Rock Island, IL	P88,P89,16R,CSR
					Rock Island, IL	06/20/65	Rlsd. G.O. #109	P131,CSR
Ballew, Kinian	Pvt	D 16th SCVI	Missionary Ridge, TN	11/25/63	Nashville, TN	12/07/63	Louisville, KY	P39,16R,CSR
					Louisville, KY	12/08/63	Rock Island, IL	P88,P89,CSR
					Rock Island, IL	06/20/65	Rlsd. G.O. #109	P131,CSR
Ballinger, Joel	Pvt	C 13th SCVI	Ruffles, VA	07/28/64	City Pt., VA Hos.	08/16/64	Died of wounds	CSR
Ballinger, Peyton	Pvt	H 6th SCVC	Stony Creek, VA	12/01/64	City Pt., VA	12/05/64	Pt. Lookout, MD	CSR
					Pt. Lookout, MD	06/10/65	Rlsd. G.O. #109	P118,CSR
Ballis, Jeremiah F.	Pvt	H 1st SCVC	Malvern Hill, VA	07/28/64	Camp Chase, OH		Old Capitol, DC	P23
					Old Capitol, DC	10/26/64	Elmira, NY	P110
Balls, James	Pvt	G 24th SCVI	Jackson, MS	05/14/63	Demopolis, AL	06/05/63	Paroled	CSR
Balls, James	Pvt	G 24th SCVI	Covington, GA	07/22/64	Louisville, KY	08/03/64	Camp Chase, OH	P90,P91,P94,EFW
					Camp Chase, OH	01/31/65	Died	P6,P12,P23,P27,FPH
Ban___, Samuel	Plt		Off Charleston	10/24/62	Ft. Lafayette, NY	04/15/63	Ft. Delaware, DE	P144
Bane, Boswell F.	Pvt	I 1st SCVI	Richmond, VA Hos.	04/03/65	Libby Prison, VA	04/23/65	Newport News, VA	CSR
					Newport News, VA	06/14/65	Rlsd. G.O. #109	CSR
Bane, David L.	Pvt	H 16th SCVI	Chattahootchie, GA	07/04/64	Nashville, TN	07/12/64	Louisville, KY	CSR
					Louisville, KY	07/13/64	Camp Morton, IN	P90,P94,16R,CSR
					Camp Morton, IN	05/18/65	Released G.O. #85	P100,P101,CSR
Bangs, J.C.	Pvt	A Hol.Leg.	Hatchers Run, VA	03/25/65	City Pt., VA	04/02/65	Pt. Lookout, MD	CSR
					Pt. Lookout, MD	06/25/65	Rlsd. G.O. #109	CSR
Bangs, R.	Pvt	B Hol.Leg.	Burkeville, VA	04/17/65	Burkeville, VA	04/17/65	Paroled in Hos.	CSR
Banister, J.L.	Pvt	E 7th SCVI	Cedar Creek, VA	10/19/64	Pt. Lookout, MD	03/17/65	Exchanged	P114
					Pt. Lookout, MD	06/24/65	Rlsd. G.O. #109	P118
Banister, John H.	Pvt	E 20th SCVI	Cedar Creek, VA	10/19/64	Harpers Ferry, VA	10/24/64	Pt. Lookout, MD	CSR
					Pt. Lookout, MD	06/24/65	Rlsd. G.O. #109	P123,CSR
Banknight, Martin J.	Pvt	F 5th SCVC	Augusta, GA	05/24/65	Augusta, GA	05/24/65	Paroled	CSR

SOUTH CAROLINA SOLDIERS, SAILORS AND  CITIZENS HELD IN U.S. PRISONS 1861-1865

NAME	RANK	REGIMENT	CAPTURED AT	WHEN	PRISON	MOVED	DISPOSITION	SOURCES
Banks, Amos O.	1Lt	C 3rd SCVC	Cuthbert House, SC	10/22/62	Hilton Head, SC		Fort Columbus, NY	CSR
					Ft Columbus, NY	11/21/62	Ft. Delaware, DE	CSR
					Ft. Delaware, DE	12/15/62	Fts. Monroe, VA Xc	CSR
Banks, G.W.	Pvt	I 1st SCVA	Morris Island, SC	07/10/63	Hilton Head, SC	08/31/63	Ft. Columbus, NY	CSR
					Ft. Columbus, NY	09/23/63	Took the oath	P1
Banks, John F.	1Lt	G 13th SCVI	Gettysburg, PA	07/01/63	Chester, PA Hosp.	10/02/63	Pt. Lookout, MD	P1,CSR
					Pt. Lookout, MD	12/05/63	Johnson's Isl., OH	P116,CSR
					Johnson's Isl., OH	02/24/65	City Pt., VA Xc	P81,P82,CSR
Banks, S.Q.	Pvt	B 15th SCVI	Halltown, WV	08/21/64	Harpers Ferry, WV	08/29/64	Camp Chase, OH	CSR
					Camp Chase, OH	03/18/65	Pt. Lookout, MD	P23,P26,CSR
					Pt. Lookout, MD	03/27/65	Boulware's Wh. Xc	CSR
Banks, Thomas	Pvt	C 6th SCVI	Deserted/enemy	02/28/65	Bermuda Hundred, VA	03/01/65	City Pt., VA P.M.	CSR,KCS
					City Pt., VA P.M.	03/03/65	Washington, DC P.M.	CSR
					Washington, DC	03/06/65	Troy, PA on oath	CSR
Banks, Thomas C.	Pvt	D 14th SCVI	Burkeville, VA	04/14/65	Burkeville, VA	04/14/65	Paroled	CSR
Bannister, Rousum	Pvt	D 2nd SCVC	Hagerstown, MD	07/12/63	Baltimore, MD	08/20/63	Pt. Lookout, MD	CSR
					Pt. Lookout, MD	03/16/64	City Pt., VA Xc	P113,P116,P124,CSR
Bannon, Patrick	Pvt	E 1st SCVA	Morris Island, SC	07/10/63	Hilton Head, SC	09/05/63	Has taken oath	CSR
Barber, G.D.	Pvt	F 25th SCVI	Ft. Fisher, NC	09/15/65	New York, NY	01/30/65	Elmira, NY	CSR, HAG
Barber, G.D.	Pvt	F 25th SCVI	Ft. Fisher, NC	01/15/65	Elmira, NY	06/26/65	Died, Diarrhea	P6,P12,P65,P66,HAG,FPH
Barber, Hilliard A.	Pvt	F 6th SCVI	Williamsburg, VA	05/05/62	Cliffburn U.S.G.H.	05/25/62	Died of wounds	P6,HHC,CSR
Barber, John A.	Pvt	G 27th SCVI	Weldon RR, VA	08/21/64	City Pt., VA	08/24/64	Pt. Lookout, MD	CSR,HAG
					Pt. Lookout, MD	01/17/65	Aikens Ldg., VA Xc	P113,P117,P124
Barber, John A.	Pvt	G 27th SCVI	Richmond, VA Hos.	04/03/65	Pt. Lookout, MD	07/25/65	Rlsd. G.O. #109	CSR
Barber, Nathaniel C.	Pvt	B 7th SCVIBn	Deserted/enemy		Fts. Monroe, VA	04/02/65	Washington, DC P.M.	CSR
					Washington, DC P.M.	04/05/65	Charleston, SC	CSR
Barber, William	Pvt	L 10th SCVI	Franklin, TN	12/17/64	Louisville, KY	12/20/64	Camp Douglas, IL	P90,P91,P95,RAS,CSR
					Camp Douglas, IL	04/02/65	Jd. US 6th USVI	P55,CSR, RAS
Barber, William	Pvt	C 11th SCVI	Town Creek, NC	02/20/65	Ft. Anderson, NC	02/28/65	Pt. Lookout, MD	CSR, RAS
					Pt. Lookout, MD	06/24/65	Rlsd. G.O. #109	P114,P123,HAG,CSR
Barber, William	Pvt	G 18th SCVI	Petersburg, VA	04/02/65	City Pt., VA	03/05/65	Pt. Lookout, MD	CSR
					Pt. Lookout, MD	06/24/65	Rlsd. G.O. #109	P114,P118,CSR
Barber, William A.	Sgt	E 17th SCVI	Five Forks, VA	04/01/65	City Pt., VA	04/06/65	Pt. Lookout, MD	CSR
					Pt. Lookout, MD	06/23/65	Rlsd. G.O. #109	P114,P118,CSR
Barclay, James B.	Pvt	A 1st SCVIBn	James Island, SC	06/08/62	Ft. Columbus, NY	08/23/62	Ft. Delaware, DE	P37
Barefield, Alfred	Cpl	C 1st SCVIG	Gettysburg, PA	07/03/63	David's Island, NY		Not given	P1,SA1
Barfield, Harlee	Pvt	E 1st SCVIG	Gettysburg, PA	07/04/63	David's Island, NY	09/05/63	City Pt., VA Xc	SA1,P1
Barfield, Morgan	Pvt	F 27th SCVI	Weldon RR, VA	08/21/64	City Pt., VA	08/24/64	Baltimore, MD	CSR
					W. Bldg. Balt, MD	02/16/65	Ft. McHenry, MD	P4,HAG
					Baltimore, MD	02/28/65	Died of wounds	CSR
Barfield, W.H.	Pvt	G Hol.Leg.	Hatchers Run, VA	03/27/65	Pt. Lookout, MD	06/24/65	Rlsd. G.O. #109	P123
Barfield, William H.	Pvt	F 27th SCVI	Town Creek, NC	02/20/65	Pt. Lookout, MD	06/26/65	Rlsd. G.O. #109	P114,HAG,CSR
Barineau, E.G.	Pvt	C 25th SCVI	Town Creek, NC	02/20/65	Pt. Lookout, MD	06/24/65	Rlsd. G.O. #109	P114,HAG
Barker, G.W.	Sgt	D 1st SCVA	Marlboro Dis., SC	03/06/65	New Berne, NC	03/31/65	Hart's Island, NY	CSR
					Hart's Island, NY	06/16/65	Rlsd. G.O. #109	P79,CSR
Barker, J.G.	Pvt	G 2nd SCVA	James Island, SC	01/12/65	Morris Island, SC			CSR
Barker, J.H.	Pvt	B German LA	Georgetown, SC	10/01/64	Hilton Head, SC	10/13/64	Sent North on oath	P8,CSR
Barker, James H.	Pvt	E 1st SCVC	Barnwell, SC	02/05/65	New Berne, NC	03/30/65	Pt. Lookout, MD	CSR
					Pt.Lookout, MD	06/24/65	Rlsd. G.O. #109	P114,P118,P123,CSR
Barker, James M.	Pvt	D 22nd SCVI	Sharpsburg, MD	09/17/62	Frederick, MD G.H.	09/21/62	Died of wounds	P6,FPH,P12,CSR

SOUTH CAROLINA SOLDIERS, SAILORS AND  CITIZENS HELD IN U.S. PRISONS 1861-1865

NAME	RANK	REGIMENT	CAPTURED AT	WHEN	PRISON	MOVED	DISPOSITION	SOURCES
Barker, Joshua	Pvt	A Orr's Ri.	Spotsylvania, VA	05/12/64	Fredericksburg, VA	08/05/64	Old Capitol, DC	P1, CSR
					Ft. McHenry, MD		Lincoln G.H., DC	P110
					Old Capitol, DC	08/27/64	Elmira, NY	P110
					Elmira, NY	02/09/65	Died, Pneumonia	P6,P65,P12, FPH
Barker, R.M.	Pvt	A 14th SCMil	Lynch's Creek, SC	02/25/65	Hart's Island, NY	06/21/65	Rlsd. G.O. #109	P79
Barker, Samuel C.	Pvt	E 15th SCVI	Knoxville, TN	12/13/63	Louisville, KY	12/31/63	Rock Island, IL	P88,P89,P93,CSR
					Rock Island, IL	06/18/65	Rlsd. G.O. #109	CSR, KEB
Barker, William J.	Pvt	E 15th SCVI	Knoxville, TN	12/03/63	Louisville, KY	12/31/63	Rock Island, IL	P88,P89,P93,CSR
					Rock Island, IL	12/31/64	Died, Pthiasis	P5,P12,P132,CSR
Barker, William J.	Pvt	C Orr's Ri.	Petersburg, VA	04/03/65	City Pt., VA	04/11/65	Hart's Island, NY	CSR, KEB
					Hart's Island, NY	06/18/65	Rlsd. G.O. #109	P79,CSR
Barksdale, H.W.	Pvt	G Hol.Leg.	Hatchers Run, VA	03/25/65	City Pt., VA	04/02/65	Pt. Lookout, MD	CSR
Barksdale, H.W.	Pvt	G Hol.Leg.	Hatchers Run, VA	03/31/65	Pt. Lookout, MD	06/24/65	Rlsd. G.O. #109	P114,P118,P123,CSR
Barksdale, Thomas W.	Pvt	C 7th SCVI	Gettysburg, PA	07/02/63	David's Island, NY	09/05/63	City Pt., VA Xc	P1,KEB,CSR,P4
Barnes, A.L.	Pvt	G 3rd SCVABn	Camden, SC	04/18/65	Charleston, SC			CSR
Barnes, Francis H.	Pvt	I 25th SCVI	Ft. Fisher, NC	01/15/65	New York, NY	01/30/65	Elmira, NY	CSR, HAG
					Elmira, NY	04/01/65	Died, Diarrhea	P6,P12,P65,P66,FPH
Barnes, H.A.	Pvt	C 6th SCVI	Boonesboro, MD	09/15/62	Ft. Delaware, DE	11/10/62	Aikens Ldg., VA Xc	CSR
Barnes, J.B.	Pvt	E 2nd SCVI	Bean's Stn., TN	12/14/63	Louisville, KY	02/05/64	Sent North on oath	P90,P92,P94,H2,CSR
Barnes, J.R.	Pvt	F Orr's Ri.	Petersburg, VA	04/03/65	Hart's Island, NY	06/16/65	Rlsd. G.O. #109	P79,CSR
Barnes, James R.	Pvt	I 25th SCVI	Morris Island, SC	09/07/63	Hilton Head, SC	10/06/63	Ft. Columbus, NY	CSR
					Ft. Columbus, NY	10/09/63	Pt. Lookout, MD	P1,HAG,CSR
					Pt. Lookout, MD	02/24/65	Aikens Ldg.,VA Xc	P113,P124,CSR
Barnes, Nickerson	Pvt	H 24th SCVI	Jonesboro, GA	09/02/64	Nashville, TN	10/24/64	Louisville, KY	CSR
					Louisville, KY	10/29/64	Camp Douglas, IL	P91,P95,EFW,CSR
					Camp Douglas, IL	11/16/64	Died, Brain Fever	P6,P53,P55,FPH,CSR
Barnes, O.B.	Pvt	A 19th SCVCB	Augusta, GA	05/25/65	Augusta, GA	05/25/65	Paroled on oath	CSR
Barnes, W.A.	Pvt	A 12th SCVI	Spotsylvania, VA	05/12/64	Ft. McHenry, MD	06/15/64	Ft. Delaware, DE	P110
					Ft. Delaware, DE	06/08/65	Released	P43
Barnes, William	Pvt	B 21st SCVI	Ft. Fisher, NC	01/15/65	Pt. Lookout, MD	02/02/65	Hammond G.H., MD	P114,P118,P121,CSR
					Hammond G.H., MD	02/06/65	Died	P12,CSR
Barnett, Alonzo M.	Pvt	B 15th SCVI	Petersburg, VA	07/27/64	City Pt., VA	08/05/64	Pt. Lookout, MD	CSR
					Pt. Lookout, MD	08/08/64	Elmira, NY	P117,CSR
					Elmira, NY	07/07/65	Rlsd. G.O. #109	CSR
Barnett, Charles	Pvt	K 5th SCVC	Chester, SC	05/05/65	Chester, SC	05/05/65	Paroled	CSR
Barnett, Daniel D.	Pvt	D 25th SCVI	Ft. Fisher, NC	01/15/65	New York, NY	01/30/65	Elmira, NY	CSR,HMC,HAG
					Elmira, NY	02/20/65	Pt. Lookout, MD Xc	P65,P66
					Richmond Hos. #8	03/07/65	Died, Ch. Diarrhea	CSR
Barnett, John S.	Pvt	C 27th SCVI	Petersburg, VA	06/24/64	Bermuda Hundred, VA	06/25/64	Fts. Monroe, VA	CSR
					Fts. Monroe, VA	06/26/64	Pt. Lookout, MD	CSR, HAG
					Pt. Lookout, MD	08/16/64	Elmira, NY	P113,P117,P118,P120,CSR
					Elmira, NY	10/11/64	Tfd. for exchange	P65
					Pt. Lookout, MD	10/29/64	Venus Pt., GA Xc	P114,P123,CSR
Barnhardt, C.M.	Pvt	C 1st SCVIR	Raleigh, NC Hos.	04/13/65	Raleigh, NC	04/13/65	Paroled	SA1,CSR
Barnwell, G.H.	Pvt	E 3rd SCVC	Adams Run, SC	07/11/63	Pt. Lookout, MD		Exchanged	P124,CSR
Barnwell, Nathaniel B.	Pvt	B 7th SCVC	Dabneys Ferry, VA	05/27/64	White House, VA	06/08/64	Pt. Lookout, MD	CSR
					Pt. Lookout, MD	09/18/64	Aikens Ldg., VA Xc	P113,P117,P123,CSR
Barr, James C.	Pvt	B 11th SCVI	Town Creek, NC	02/20/65	Ft. Anderson, NC	02/28/65	Pt. Lookout, MD	CSR
					Pt. Lookout, MD	06/24/65	Rlsd. G.O. #109	P123,CSR
Barr, James D	Pvt	E 15th SCMil	Lancaster, SC	02/27/65	Pt. Lookout, MD	06/24/65	Rlsd. G.O. #109	P114,P118,P123
Barr, W.F.	Pvt	G 7th SCVC	Richmond, VA Hos.	04/03/65	Richmond, VA P.M.	08/26/65	Released on Parole	CSR
					Richmond, VA Hos.	04/19/65	Richmond, VA P.M.	CSR

SOUTH CAROLINA SOLDIERS, SAILORS AND **B** CITIZENS HELD IN U.S. PRISONS 1861-1865

NAME	RANK	REGIMENT	CAPTURED AT	WHEN	PRISON	MOVED	DISPOSITION	SOURCES
Barre, John P.	Pvt	D 13th SCVI	Gettysburg, PA	07/05/63	David's Island, NY	09/05/63	City Pt., VA Xc	P1,CSR
Barrentine, G.	Pvt	B 24th SCVI	Jonesboro, GA	08/31/64	Rough & Ready, GA	09/22/64	Paroled	CSR
Barrett, David	Pvt	H 1st SCVA	Knoxville, TN	06/20/64	Jeffersonville, IN	06/24/64	Rlsd. on oath	CSR
Barrett, J.W.	Pvt	A P.S.S.	Richmond, VA Hos.	04/03/65	Richmond, VA Hos.	04/29/65	Paroled	CSR,TSE
Barrett, John	Pvt	Ferguson's	Brandon, MS	07/18/63	Snyders Bluff, MS	08/07/63	Camp Morton, IN	CSR
					Camp Morton, IN	03/19/64	Ft. Delaware, DE	CSR
					Ft. Delaware, DE	10/30/64	Pt. Lookout, MD	CSR
					Pt. Lookout, MD	10/31/64	Exchanged	P123,CSR
Barrett, John	Pvt	F 1st SCVA	Bentonville, NC	03/15/65	New Berne, NC	03/31/65	Hart's Island, NY	CSR
					Hart's Island, NY	06/16/65	Rlsd. G.O. #109	P79,CSR
Barrett, Thomas P.	Pvt	D Ham.Leg.			Fts. Monroe, VA	08/31/62	Aikens Ldg., VA Xc	CSR
Barrett, William J.	Sgt	K 10th SCVI	Jonesboro, GA	09/01/64	Louisville, KY	10/29/64	Camp Douglas, IL	P90,P91,RAS,CSR
					Camp Douglas, IL	05/12/65	Rlsd. G.O. #85	P7,P53,P55,CSR
Barrineau, Benjamin L.	Pvt	I 4th SCVC	Fairfield, SC	02/20/65	New Berne, NC	02/20/65	Pt. Lookout, MD	CSR
					Pt. Lookout, MD	06/23/65	Rlsd. G.O. #109	P114,P123,CSR
Barrineau, Ebbin G.	Pvt	C 25th SCVI	Town Creek, NC	02/20/65	Ft. Anderson, NC	02/28/65	Pt. Lookout, MD	CSR,HAG
					Pt. Lookout, MD	06/24/65	Rlsd. G.O. #109	CSR,CTA
Barrineau, Edwin M.	Pvt	C 25th SCVI	Ft. Fisher, NC	01/15/65	New York, NY	01/30/65	Elmira, NY	CSR,CTA
					Elmira, NY	07/11/65	Rlsd. G.O. #109	P65,P66,HAG,CTA
Barrineau, J.E.	Pvt	I 4th SCVC	Stony Creek, VA	12/01/64	City Pt., VA	12/05/64	Pt. Lookout, MD	CSR
					Pt. Lookout, MD	01/27/65	Aikens Ldg., VA Xc	P118,P123,P124,CSR
Barrineau, J.G.	Pvt	C 25th SCVI	Ft. Anderson, NC	02/20/65	Pt. Lookout, MD	06/24/65	Rlsd. G.O. #109	P123,CTA
Barrineau, John J.	Pvt	E 15th SCVI	South Mtn., MD	09/14/62	Ft. Delaware, DE	10/02/62	Aikens Ldg., VA Xc	CSR
Barrineau, R. Henry	Pvt	C 25th SCVI	Ft. Fisher, NC	01/15/65	New York, NY	01/30/65	Elmira, NY	CSR
					Elmira, NY	03/02/65	Tfd. for exchange	P65,P66,HAG,CTA,CSR
Barrington, Alexander H	Pvt	D 26th SCVI	Petersburg, VA	03/25/65	Washington, DC	03/30/65	Pt. Lookout, MD	CSR,HOM
					Pt. Lookout, MD	05/14/65	Rlsd. G.O. #85	CSR
Barrington, Eben W.	Pvt	D 26th SCVI	Petersburg, VA	03/25/65	City Pt., VA	04/05/65	Pt. Lookout, MD	CSR,HOM
Barrington, Eben W.	Pvt	D 26th SCVI	Southside RR, VA	04/01/65	Pt. Lookout, MD	06/24/65	Rlsd. G.O. #109	P114,P118,P123,CSR
Barron, Benjamin Pressle	Pvt	I 4th SCVC	Louisa C.H., VA	06/11/64	Fts. Monroe, VA	06/20/64	Pt. Lookout, MD	CSR
					Pt. Lookout, MD	07/25/64	Elmira, NY	P113,P117,CSR
					Elmira, NY	02/20/65	James R., VA Xc	P65,CSR
Barron, J.F.	Pvt	B 6th SCVI	Frederick, MD	09/12/62	Frederick, MD USFH	09/18/62	Ft. Delaware, DE	CSR
					Ft. Delaware, DE	10/02/62	Aikens Ldg.,VA Xc	CSR
					Richmond, VA Hos.	10/18/62	Camp Winder, VA	CSR
Barron, S.D.	Pvt	Lafayette A	Pocotaligo, SC	01/18/65	Hilton Head, SC	02/01/65	Pt. Lookout, MD	CSR
					Pt. Lookout, MD	06/23/65	Rlsd. G.O. #109	CSR
Barron, W.R.	ASr	5th SCVI	Richmond, VA Hos.	04/03/65	Richmond, VA	05/12/65	Paroled	CSR
Barrow, J.	Pvt	G 2nd SCVC	Augusta, GA	05/19/65	Augusta, GA	05/19/65	Paroled on oath	CSR
Barrow, John L.	Pvt	B 24th SCVI	Ringgold, GA	11/25/63	Nashville, TN	12/05/63	Louisville, KY	P39,CSR,EFW
					Louisville, KY	12/06/63	Rock Island, IL	P88,P89,CSR
					Rock Island, IL	06/14/64	Died, Ch. Diarrhea	P5,P131,P132,FPH
Barrow, S.P.	Cpl	A Orr's Ri.	Petersburg, VA	04/03/65	City Pt., VA	04/11/65	Hart's Island, NY	CSR
					Hart's Island, NY	06/16/65	Rlsd. G.O. #109	P79,CSR
Barrs, J.V.	Pvt	K 1st SCVIH	Warrenton, VA	09/29/62	Warrenton, VA	09/29/62	Paroled	CSR
Barrs, J.V.	Pvt	K 1st SCVIH	Augusta, GA	05/21/65	Augusta, GA	05/21/65	Paroled	CSR
Barry, W.L.	Pvt	C 27th SCVI	Virginia				MIA in enemy hands	CSR,HAG
Bartee, William V.	Pvt	D 14th SCVI	Petersburg, VA	07/29/64	Pt. Lookout, MD	08/08/64	Elmira, NY	P113,P117,P118,P125
					Elmira, NY	10/11/64	Tfd. for exchange	P65
					Pt. Lookout, MD	10/29/64	Fts. Monroe, VA	P114,P123,HOE,CSR
					Fts. Monroe, VA	11/01/64	Died	CSR
Bartell, Michael	Pvt	C German LA	Charleston, SC	03/21/65	Charleston, SC	03/21/65	Released on oath	CSR

B

SOUTH CAROLINA SOLDIERS, SAILORS AND CITIZENS HELD IN U.S. PRISONS 1861-1865

NAME	RANK	REGIMENT	CAPTURED AT	WHEN	PRISON	MOVED	DISPOSITION	SOURCES
Bartless, William H.	Cpt	H 25th SCVI	Town Creek, NC	02/20/65	Ft. Anderson, NC	02/28/65	Washington, DC	CSR,HAG
					Pt. Lookout, MD	02/28/65	Washington, DC	P114,P117,P120
					Ft. McHenry, MD	03/24/65	Ft. Delaware, DE	P110
					Ft. Delaware, DE	06/16/65	Rlsd. G.O. #109	P43,P45,P47,CSR
Bartless, William H.,Jr.	Sgt	H 8th SCResB	Town Creek, NC	02/20/65	Pt. Lookout, MD		Old Capitol, SC	CSR
					Old Capitol, DC		Ft. Delaware, DE	CSR
					Ft. Delaware, DE	06/10/65	Released	CSR
Bartlett, J.W.	Pvt	I 23rd SCVI	Five Forks, VA	04/01/65	City Pt., VA	04/12/65	Hart's Island, NY	CSR
					Hart's Island, NY	06/16/65	Rlsd. G.O. #109	P79,CSR
Bartlett, Richard S.	Pvt	G Ham.Leg.MI	Petersburg, VA	07/26/64	City Pt., VA	08/05/64	Pt. Lookout, MD	CSR
Bartlett, Richard S.	Pvt	G Ham.Leg.MI	Petersburg, VA	06/26/64	Pt. Lookout, MD	08/08/64	Elmira, NY	P113,P117,P120,CSR
Bartlett, Richard S.	Pvt	G Ham.Leg.MI	Petersburg, VA	07/29/64	Elmira, NY	03/14/65	James R., VA Xc	P65,CSR
Bartlett, Robert C.	Pvt	A Hol.Leg.C	Hickory Neck, VA	01/23/63	Yorktown, VA	01/24/63	Fts. Monroe, VA	CSR
					Fts. Monroe, VA	02/22/63	Pt. Lookout, MD	CSR
					Pt. Lookout, MD	03/14/65	Aikens Ldg., VA Xc	P113,P124,CSR
Bartlett, William	Pvt	G 11th SCVI	Deserted/enemy	10/02/62	Ft. McHenry, MD	10/08/62	Released on oath	CSR
Bartley, E.	Pvt	H 8th SCVI	Winchester, VA	09/13/64	Harpers Ferry, WV	09/19/64	Camp Chase, OH	CSR
					Camp Chase, OH	06/11/65	Rlsd. G.O. #109	P23,KEB,CSR
Bartley, Milledge L.	Pvt	D 14th SCVI	Gettysburg, PA	07/04/63	David's Island, NY	09/05/63	City Pt., VA Xc	P1,CSR
Bartley, Thomas H.	Pvt	I 7th SCVI	Spotsylvania, VA	05/07/64	Belle Plain, VA	05/21/64	Ft. Delaware, DE	CSR
					Ft. Delaware, DE	06/10/65	Released	P41,P43,CSR
Bartley, Wesley	Pvt	B 14th SCVI	Warrenton, VA	09/29/62	Warrenton, VA	09/29/62	Paroled	CSR
Barton, Albert	Pvt	D 16th SCVI	Missionary Ridge, TN	11/26/63	Nashville, TN	12/07/63	Louisville, KY	P39,16R
					Louisville, KY	12/08/63	Rock Island, IL	P88,16R,CSR
Barton, Andrew	Pvt	H 1st SCVIG	Deserted/enemy	02/02/65	Washington, DC	02/10/65	Savannah, GA oath	CSR
Barton, Charles T.	Pvt	E 19th SCVI	Atlanta, GA	07/22/64	Nashville, TN	07/24/64	Louisville, KY	CSR
					Louisville, KY	07/31/64	Camp Chase, OH	P90,P91
					Camp Chase, OH	03/04/65	City Pt., VA Xc	P26,CSR
Barton, Francis J..	Pvt	D 16th SCVI	Missionary Ridge, TN	11/25/63	Nashville, TN	01/26/64	Pest House Hos.	CSR
					Pest House H. Nash	02/07/64	Died of Smallpox	P2,P5,16R,CSR
Barton, Francis M.	Cpl	K 22nd SCVI	Kinston, NC	12/15/62	Kinston, NC	12/15/62	Paroled POW	CSR
Barton, Francis M.	Sgt	K 22nd SCVI	Hatchers Run, VA	04/01/65	City Pt., VA	04/04/65	Pt. Lookout, MD	CSR
					Pt. Lookout, MD	06/24/65	Rlsd. G.O. #109	P114,P118,P123
Barton, Franklin	Pvt	H 22nd SCVI	Richmond, VA Hos.	04/03/65	Libby Prison Rchmd	04/23/65	Newport News, VA	CSR
					Newport News, VA		Release not given	CSR
Barton, H.M.	Pvt	F 1st SCVIH	Deep Bottom, VA	08/14/64	Bermuda Hundred, VA	08/15/64	Fts. Monroe, VA	CSR
					Fts. Monroe, VA		Pt. Lookout, MD	CSR,SA1
					Pt. Lookout, MD	03/14/65	Aikens Ldg., VA Xc	P113,P117,P124,CSR
Barton, Jefferson	Pvt	B 11th SCVI	Ft. Fisher, NC	01/15/65	Pt. Lookout, MD	06/24/65	Rlsd. G.O. #109	P114,P121,P123,CSR
Barton, John J.	Pvt	A 19th SCVI	Chattahootchee, GA	07/03/64	Louisville, KY	07/13/64	Camp Morton, IN	P90,P91,P94
					Camp Morton, IN	03/04/65	City Pt., VA Xc	P100,P101
Barton, John J.	Pvt	A 19th SCVI	Augusta, GA	05/29/65	Augusta, GA	05/29/65	Paroled	CSR
Barton, Joseph	Pvt	K Ham.Leg.MI	Nine Mile Rd., VA	10/27/64	City Pt., VA	10/31/64	Pt Lookout, MD	CSR
					Pt. Lookout, MD	03/13/65	Died, Diarrhea	P6,P114,P118,FPH
Barton, P.P.	Pvt	H 22nd SCVI	Kinston, NC	12/15/62	Kinston, NC	12/15/62	Paroled POW	CSR
Barton, S.F.	Pvt	H 22nd SCVI	Richmond, VA	04/03/65	Newport News, VA	06/26/65	Rlsd. G.O. #109	P107,CSR
Barton, S.W.	Pvt	K Ham.Leg.MI	Newton, NC	04/19/65	Newton, NC	04/19/65	Paroled	CSR
Barton, William J.N.	Pvt	I P.S.S.			Ft. McHenry, MD	11/13/62	Fts. Monroe, VA Xc	P145
Baruch, Simon	ASr	3rd SCVIBn	Gettysburg, PA	07/03/63	Pro. Marshal			CSR
Barwick, Andrew J.	Pvt	H 5th SCVC	US Dept. of South	03/21/65	Charleston, SC	04/01/65	Relsd. on oath	CSR
Barwick, Edward W.C.	Pvt	G 14th SCVI	Sutherland Stn. VA	04/02/65	City Pt., VA	04/07/65	Hart's Island, NY	CSR
					Hart's Island, NY	04/23/65	Died, Pneumonia	P6,P12,P79,CSR

SOUTH CAROLINA SOLDIERS, SAILORS AND CITIZENS HELD IN U.S. PRISONS 1861-1865

NAME	RANK	REGIMENT	CAPTURED AT	WHEN	PRISON	MOVED	DISPOSITION	SOURCES
Barwick, George W.	Pvt	I 25th SCVI	Ft. Fisher, NC	01/15/65	New York, NY	01/30/65	Elmira, NY	CSR
					Elmira, NY	02/20/65	Pt. Lookout, MD Xc	P65,HAG,P66
					Richmond, VA Hos.	03/10/65	Died, Frost bite	CSR
Barwick, John	Pvt	G 14th SCVI	Malvern Hill, VA	07/28/64	Alexandria, VA	09/12/64	Washington, DC	P1
					Old Capitol, DC	10/24/64	Elmira, NY	P110,CSR
					Elmira, NY	02/20/65	James R., VA Xc	P65,CSR
					Richmond, VA Hos.	03/08/65	Furloughed	CSR
Barwick, John H.	Pvt	H 6th SCVI	Sharpsburg, MD	09/19/62	Sharpsburg, MD Hos.	09/27/62	Paroled	CSR
Bason, M.	Pvt	F 22nd SCVI	Bermuda Hundred, VA	06/02/64	Pt. Lookout, MD	07/03/64	Died	P113,P117
Bass, J.	Pvt	F 2nd SCVI	Gettysburg, PA	07/05/63	Gettysburg, PA USG	10/01/63	U.S. Provost Marsh.	P4,CSR
Bass, J.C.	Pvt	M 8th SCVI	Williamsport, MD	07/13/63	Chester, PA G.H.	10/03/63	Pt. Lookout, MD	P1,CSR
Bass, J.C.	Pvt	M 8th SCVI	Williamsport, MD	07/14/63	Pt. Lookout, MD	03/17/64	City Pt., VA Xc	P116,P124
Bass, J.C.	Pvt	M 8th SCVI	Winchester, VA	09/13/64	Harpers Ferry, WV	09/19/64	Camp Chase, OH	CSR
					Camp Chase, OH	05/02/65	New Orleans, LA	P23,P26,CSR
					New Orleans, LA	05/12/65	Released	CSR
Bass, Jesse	Pvt	A 14th SCVI	Gettysburg, PA	07/05/63	David's Island, NY	09/05/63	City Pt., VA Xc	P1,CSR
					Williamsburg, VA H.	09/13/63	Furloughed	CSR
Bass, John C.	Cpl	H 23rd SCVI	Deserted/enemy	03/14/65	City Pt., VA P.M.	03/15/65	Washington, DC	CSR,HMC
					Washington, DC	03/18/65	Wilmington, NC	CSR,HMC
Bass, John N.	Pvt	A 3rd SCVI	Deep Bottom, VA	07/28/64	City Pt. VA US Fld	12/05/64	US Str Connecticut	P12,H3,CSR
					US Str. Connecticut	12/06/64	Armory Sq. Hos., D	CSR
					Armory Sq. Hos., D	12/28/64	Lincoln G.H., DC	CSR
					Lincoln G.H., DC	01/27/65	Old Capitol, DC	CSR
					Old Capitol, DC	02/03/65	Elmira, NY	CSR
					Elmira, NY	02/09/65	James River, VA Xc	CSR
					Richmond, VA Hos.	03/17/65	Furloughed 60 days	CSR
Bass, W.J.C.	Pvt	C 6th SCVI	Richmond, VA	05/16/62	Cliffbourne G.H., DC	06/27/62	Old Capitol, DC	CSR,HIC
					US Str. CoatsColoo	05/06/62	Williamsburg, VA H	CSR
Bass, W.J.C.	Pvt	C 6th SCVI	Farmville, VA	04/06/65	City Pt., VA	04/17/65	Pt. Lookout, MD	CSR
					Pt. Lookout, MD	06/24/65	Rlsd. G.O. #109	P114,P119,P123,CSR
Bass, W.M.	Pvt	D 11th SCVI	Fort Fisher, NC	01/15/65	Elmira NY	03/02/65	James R., VA Xc	P65,CSR
Bass, Wade H.	Pvt	E 4th SCVC	Marlboro Dis., SC	03/01/65	New Berne, NC	04/10/65	Hart's Island, NY	CSR
					Hart's Island, NY	06/17/65	Rlsd. G.O. #109	P79,CSR
Bassett, J.J.	Pvt	G 1st SCVIH	Warrenton, VA	09/29/62	Warrenton, VA	09/29/62	Paroled	CSR
Baswell, Thomas A.	Pvt	B 13th SCVI	Petersburg, VA	04/02/65	City Pt., VA	04/04/65	Pt. Lookout, MD	CSR,HOS
					Pt. Lookout, MD	06/24/65	Rlsd. G.O. #109	P114,P118,P123,CSR
Bateman, D.O.	Pvt	C 1st SCVC	Madison C.H., VA	09/22/63	Ft. McHenry, MD	09/25/63	Pt. Lookout, MD	P110
					Old Capitol, DC	09/26/63	Pt Lookout, MD	CSR
					Pt. Lookout, MD	08/16/64	Elmira, NY	P113,P116,P120,CSR
					Elmira, NY	03/10/65	James R., VA Xc	CSR,P65
Bateman, Henry E.	Pvt	I 23rd SCVI	Petersburg, VA	04/01/65	City Pt. VA	04/04/65	Pt. Lookout MD	CSR
					Pt. Lookout, MD	06/04/65	Released	P114,P118,CSR
Bates, Aaron	Pvt	L 1st SCVIG	Deserted/enemy	04/18/65	City Pt., VA	04/21/65	Blainsville, PA	SA1,CSR
Bates, E. Henry	1Lt	B Hol.Leg.	Five Forks, VA	04/01/65	City Pt., VA	04/04/65	Old Capitol, DC	CSR
					Old Capitol, DC	04/09/65	Johnson's Isl., OH	CSR
					Johnson's Isl., OH	06/18/65	Rlsd. G.O. #109	P81,P83,CSR
Bates, George W.	Pvt	K 21st SCVI	Morris Island, SC	07/10/63	Hilton Head, SC	09/09/63	Ft. Columbus, NY	CSR
					Ft. Columbus, NY	09/23/63	Paroled on oath	P1,HAG
					Ft. Columbus, NY	09/26/63	Pt. Lookout, MD	CSR
					Pt. Lookout, MD	08/16/64	Elmira, NY	P113,P120,P124
					Elmira, NY	03/10/65	James R., VA Xc	P65,CSR

B

SOUTH CAROLINA SOLDIERS, SAILORS AND CITIZENS HELD IN U.S. PRISONS 1861-1865

NAME	RANK	REGIMENT	CAPTURED AT	WHEN	PRISON	MOVED	DISPOSITION	SOURCES
Bates, Greenbury B.	Pvt	K 16th SCVI	Missionary Ridge, TN	11/25/63	Nashville, TN	12/07/63	Louisville, KY	P39,CSR
					Louisville, KY	12/08/63	Rock Island, IL	P88,P89,CSR
					Rock Island, IL	06/19/65	Rlsd. G.O. #109	P131,CSR
Bates, Henry H.	Pvt	B 27th SCVI	Wilmington, NC	02/22/65	Pt. Lookout, MD	06/24/65	Rlsd. G.O. #109	P114,P118,P123,CSR
Bates, Lucius B.	Pvt	F 2nd SCVA	James Island, SC	05/12/64	Port Royal Fy., SC	08/16/64	Exchanged	CSR
Bates, W.P.	Pvt	C 19th SCVCB	Augusta, GA	05/19/65	Augusta, GA	05/19/65	Paroled on oath	CSR
Bates, W.T.	Pvt	B 11th SCVI	Fort Fisher, NC	01/15/65	Pt. Lookout, MD	06/05/65	Rlsd. on oath	P114,CSR
Bates, William T.	Pvt	G 2nd SCVA	3rd Div. 20 AC Hos.	03/08/65	New Berne, NC P.M.	03/13/65	Foster G.H., NC	CSR
					New Berne, NC USGH	05/05/65	New Berne, NC	CSR
Bath, Thomas	Sgt	A 21st SCVI	Petersburg, VA	06/24/64	City Pt., VA USFH	09/11/64	Fts. Monroe, VA	P114,HAG
					Fts. Monroe, VA	09/29/64	Pt. Lookout, MD	CSR
					Pt. Lookout, MD	02/27/65	Aikens Ldg., VA Xc	P114,P118,P123,P124
Batson, Baylis E.	Sgt	I Ham.Leg.MI	Burkeville, VA	04/06/65	Pt. Lookout, MD	06/23/65	Rlsd. G.O. #109	P114,SA2
Batson, Ervin	Cpl	C 16th SCVI	Jonesboro, GA	09/02/64	Rough & Ready, GA	09/19/64	Exchanged	CSR
Batson, Ervin	Cpl	K 16th SCVI	Franklin, TN	12/17/64	Nashville, TN	01/11/65	Louisville, KY	P4,CSR
					Louisville, KY	01/14/65	Camp Chase, OH	P92,P95,CSR,16R
					Camp Chase, OH	03/13/65	Died	P6,P23,P27,FPH,CSR
Batson, J.A.	Pvt	A 3rd SCVABn	High Pt., NC	05/02/65	High Pt., NC	05/02/65	Paroled on oath	CSR
Batson, John	Cpl	G 16th SCVI	Franklin, TN	12/17/64	Nashville, TN	03/01/65	Louisville, KY	P4,P39,16R,CSR
					Louisville, KY	03/10/65	Camp Chase, OH	P92,P95,CSR
					Camp Chase, OH	03/26/65	Pt. Lookout, MD	P23,P26,CSR
Batson, John	Cpl	G 16th SCVI	Franklin, TN	12/08/64	Pt. Lookout, MD	06/05/65	Released	P114,CSR
Batson, Smith	Pvt	K 16th SCVI	Jonesboro, GA	09/01/64	Rough & Ready, GA	09/19/64	Exchanged	CSR
Battle, R.R.	Pvt	C 3rd SCVABn	Spanish Fort, AL	04/09/65	Spanish Fort, AL	04/10/65	P.M. West Mississi	CSR
Baucom, Aaron	Pvt	E 20th SCVI	Santee River, SC	02/14/65	New Berne, NC	04/03/65	Pt. Lookout, MD	CSR,KEB
					Pt. Lookout, MD	05/17/65	Died, Diarrhea	P6,P118,P119,CSR
Baugh, Lemuel	Pvt	H 25th SCVI	Ft. Fisher, NC	01/15/65	Pt. Lookout, MD	02/02/65	Hammond G.H., MD	P114,P121,HAG,CSR
					Pt. Lookout, MD	06/26/65	Rlsd. G.O. #109	P118,CSR
Baugh, P.	Pvt	H 25th SCVI	Ft. Fisher, NC	01/15/65	New York, NY	01/30/65	Elmira, NY	CSR
					Elmira, NY	07/11/65	Rlsd. G.O. #109	CSR
Baughman, Charles W.	Pvt	C 1st SCVIG	Gettysburg, PA	07/05/63	Ft. Delaware, DE	10/24/63	Pt. Lookout, MD	P40,P42,P44,CSR
					Pt. Lookout, MD	03/16/64	City Pt. VA for Xc	P113,P123,P124,CSR
Baughman, Charles W.	Pvt	C 1st SCVIG	Petersburg, VA	04/03/65	Hart's Island, NY	06/16/65	Rlsd. G.O. #109	P79,CSR,SA1
Baughman, Eli	Pvt	E 6th SCVI	Augusta, GA	05/29/65	Augusta, GA	05/29/65	Paroled	CSR
Baughman, Francis M.	2Lt	C 1st SCVIG	N. Anna River, VA	05/23/64	Old Capitol, DC	06/17/64	Ft. Delaware, DE	P110,CSR
					Ft. Delaware, DE		Rlsd O.O. Secy/War	P44
					Ft. Delaware, DE	08/20/64	Hilton Head, SC	P43,CSR
					Beaufort, SC	08/28/64	(From Ft.Delaware)	P1,SA1
					Charleston Harbor	12/15/64	Paroled	CSR
					Beaufort, SC	01/01/65	Charleston, SC	P1
Baughman, Harmom	Cpl	G Ham.Leg.MI	Lexington, SC	02/14/65	New Berne, NC	03/30/65	Pt. Lookout, MD	CSR
					Pt. Lookout, MD	06/05/65	Released	P114,P118,CSR
Baughman, Henry L.	Pvt	C 1st SCVIG	Gettysburg, PA	07/04/63	David's Island, NY	08/24/63	City Pt., Xc	P1,SA1,CSR
					City Pt., VA	04/11/65	Hart's Island, NY	CSR
Baughman, Henry L.	Pvt	C 1st SCVIG	Petersburg, VA	04/03/65	Hart's Island, NY	05/21/65	Died, Typhoid	P6,P12,P79,CSR,FPH
Baughman, R.H.	Pvt	G Ham.Leg.MI	Deserted/enemy	04/05/65	Bermuda Hundred, VA	04/08/65	City Pt., VA P.M.	CSR
Baughman, William	Pvt	D Hol.Leg.	Farmville, VA	04/11/65	Farmville, VA	04/11/65	Paroled	CSR
Baughn, Henry C.	Pvt	C 3rd SCVI	Cedar Creek, VA	10/19/64	W. Bldg. Balt, MD	10/25/64	Pt. Lookout, MD	P4,KEB,SA2,H3,CSR
					Pt. Lookout, MD	10/30/64	Aikens Ldg., VA Xc	P114,P118,ANY,CSR
Baught, M.	Pvt	Waccamaw A	Eagletown Hbr., SC	02/27/63	Ft. Lafayette, NY	04/07/63	Fts. Monroe, VA	P144,145
Baum, Charles	Pvt	G 27th SCVI	Town Creek, NC	02/20/65	Ft. Anderson, NC	03/28/65	Pt. Lookout, MD	CSR
					Pt. Lookout, MD	05/15/65	Rlsd. G.O. #85	P7,P114,HAG,CSR

B

SOUTH CAROLINA SOLDIERS, SAILORS AND CITIZENS HELD IN U.S. PRISONS 1861-1865

NAME	RANK	REGIMENT	CAPTURED AT	WHEN	PRISON	MOVED	DISPOSITION	SOURCES
Bauman, Charles		11th SCVI	Deserted	10/08/63	Provost Army of Pot.			CSR
Baumguard, James C.	Pvt	G 18th SCVI	Petersburg, VA	03/25/65	City Pt., VA	03/26/65	Pt. Lookout, MD	CSR
					Pt. Lookout, MD	06/24/65	Rlsd. G.O. #109	P114,P118,CSR
Baxley, W.M.	Cpl	A 1st SCVIH	Richmond, VA Hos.	04/03/65	Richmond, VA Hos.	05/12/65	Paroled	CSR
Baxley, Willis	Pvt	2 10/19 SCVI	Missionary Ridge, TN	11/25/63	Louisville, KY	12/11/63	Rock Island, IL	P88,P89,RAS,CSR
					Rock Island, IL	06/21/65	Rlsd. G.O. #109	P131,CSR
Baxter, J.C.	Pvt	F 2nd SCVA	James Island, SC	05/12/64	Hilton Head, SC	08/16/64	Port Royal Fy., SC	CSR
					Port Royal Fy., SC	08/16/64	Exchanged	CSR
Baxter, J.W.	Pvt	B 15th SCVI	Augusta, GA	05/24/65	Augusta, GA	05/24/65	Paroled	H15,CSR
Baxter, Joseph D.	Pvt	D 1st SCVA	Orangeburg, SC	02/10/65	New Berne, NC	05/01/65	Fts. Monroe, VA	CSR
					Fts. Monroe, VA	05/01/65	Newport News, VA	CSR
					Newport News, VA	06/26/65	Rlsd. G.O. # 109	P107,CSR
Baylor, Lewis	Pvt	I 23rd SCVI	Petersburg, VA	03/25/65	Pt. Lookout, MD	06/24/65	Rlsd. G.O. #109	P118,P123
Baylor, Wainwright	Pvt	I 23rd SCVI	Petersburg, VA	03/25/65	City Pt., VA	03/28/65	Pt. Lookout, MD	CSR
					Pt. Lookout, MD	06/24/65	Rlsd. G.O. #109	P114,P118,P123,CSR
Baynard, W.G.	Pvt	I 3rd SCVC	Edisto Island, SC	04/09/63	Ft. Norfolk, VA	06/29/63		CSR
Bayne, John	Pvt	B 6th SCVI	Farmville, VA	04/06/65	City Pt., VA	04/14/65	Newport News, VA	CSR
					Newport News, VA	06/26/65	Rlsd. G.O. #109	P107,YEB,CSR
Bazin, John W.	Pvt	B Orr's Ri.	Petersburg, VA	04/03/63	City Pt., VA	04/11/65	Hart's Island, NY	CSR
					Hart's Island, NY	06/16/65	Rlsd.G.O.# 109	P79,CSR
Bazzell, R.T.	Pvt	I 17th SCVI	Petersburg, VA Hos.	04/03/65	Petersburg, VA G.H	07/18/65	Rlsd. on parole	CSR
Beach, Eli	Pvt	E 1st SCVIR	Raleigh, NC Hos.	04/13/65	Raleigh, NC	04/13/65	Paroled	SA1,CSR
Beacham, Thomas L.D.	Pvt	B P.S.S.	Knoxville, TN	12/03/63	Louisville, KY	12/31/63	Rock Island, IL	P88,P89,P93,CSR
					Rock Island, IL	06/17/65	Rlsd. G.O. #109	P123,P131,CSR
Beadle, B. August	Pvt	D 27th SCVI	Town Creek, NC	02/20/65	Ft. Anderson, NC	02/28/65	Pt. Lookout, MD	CSR
					Pt. Lookout, MD	06/17/65	Rlsd. G.O. #109	P114,P122,HAG,CSR
Beal, T.F.	Pvt	A 2nd SCVIRi	Spotsylvania, VA	05/06/64	Ft. Delaware, DE	02/27/65	Exchanged	P41
Beale, John W.	1Sg	A 1st SCVA	Deserted/enemy	03/23/65	Charleston, SC	03/23/65	Released on oath	CSR
Beam, George	Pvt	B 17th SCVI	Hatchers Run, VA	04/01/65	City Pt., VA	04/06/65	Pt. Lookout, MD	CSR
					Pt. Lookout, MD	06/24/65	Rlsd. G.O. #109	P121,P123,CSR
Beamer, John C.	Pgr	Str. Calypso		06/11/63	Ft. Warren, MA			P137
Beamguard, Samuel	Pvt	E 17th SCVI	Amelia C.H., VA	04/03/65	City Pt., VA	04/13/65	Pt. Lookout, MD	CSR
					Pt. Lookout, MD	06/24/65	Rlsd. G.O. #109	P114,P119,CSR
Beard, Caswell	Pvt	G 13th SCVI	Falling Waters, MD	07/14/63	Baltimore, MD	08/20/63	Pt. Lookout, MD	CSR,ANY
					Pt. Lookout, MD	03/16/64	City Pt., VA Xc	P116,P123,P124
Beard, F.W.	Pvt	C 1st SCVIG	Gettysburg, PA	07/05/63	Ft. Delaware, DE	06/30/64	City Pt., VA Xc	P44
Beard, H.D.	Pvt	A 19th SCVCB	Augusta, GA	05/20/65	Augusta, GA	05/20/65	Paroled on oath	CSR
Beard, J.M.	Pvt	G 18th SCVI	Gettysburg, PA	07/04/63	Gettysburg G.H.	07/14/63	Provost Marshal	P4,CSR
Beard, James O.	Pvt	A Orr's Ri.	Petersburg, VA	04/03/65	City Pt., VA	04/11/65	Hart's Island, NY	CSR
					Hart's Island, NY	05/23/65	Died, Heart Dis.	P6,P12,P79,FPH,CSR
Beard, John	Pvt	A 14th SCMil	Lynch's Creek, SC	02/25/65	New Berne, NC	04/10/65	Hart's Island, NY	CSR
					Hart's Island, NY	06/16/65	Rlsd. G.O. #109	P79,CSR
Beard, Samuel N.	Pvt	G 13th SCVI	Cashtown, PA	07/05/63	Ft. McHenry, MD	07/12/63	Ft. Delaware, DE	CSR,ANY
					Ft. Delaware, DE	08/30/63	Joined 1st CT Cav.	P40,P42,P44,CSR
Beard, William A.	Pvt	C 1st SCVIG	Gettysburg, PA	07/05/63	Ft. Delaware, DE	07/30/63	City Pt., Xc	P40,P42,CSR
Beard, William A.	Pvt	C 1st SCVIG	Petersburg, VA	04/03/65	Hart's Island, NY	06/16/65	Rlsd. G.O. #109	P79,CSR
Bearden, Columbus C.	Pvt	C 13th SCVI	Burkeville, VA	04/06/65	City Pt., VA	04/14/65	Pt. Lookout, MD	CSR
					Pt. Lookout, MD	06/24/65	Rlsd. G.O. #109	P123,CSR
Bearden, J.C.	Pvt	H 1st SCVIH	Farmville, VA	04/11/65	Farmville, VA	04/21/65	Paroled	CSR
Bearden, O.P.	Pvt	H 1st SCVIH	Richmond, VA Hos.	04/03/65	Richmond, VA	06/19/65	Died, Ch. Diarrhea	P12,SA1,CSR
Bearden, William T.	Cpl	H Orr's Ri.	N. Anna River, VA	05/23/64	Port Royal, VA	05/30/64	Pt. Lookout, MD	CSR,CDC
					Pt. Lookout, MD	03/14/65	Aikens Ldg., VA Xc	P113,P117,P123,CSR

SOUTH CAROLINA SOLDIERS, SAILORS AND  CITIZENS HELD IN U.S. PRISONS 1861-1865

NAME	RANK	REGIMENT	CAPTURED AT	WHEN	PRISON	MOVED	DISPOSITION	SOURCES
Beasinger, G.W.	Pvt	F 3rd SCVC	South Newport, GA	08/17/64	Philadelphia, PA	01/10/65	Ft. Delaware, DE	CSR
					Ft. Delaware, DE	02/27/65	City Pt., VA Xc	P41,P43,CSR
Beasley, J.J.R.	Pvt	F Hol.Leg.	Petersburg, VA	11/05/64	City Pt., VA	11/11/64	Washington, DC	CSR
					Pt. Lookout, MD	02/18/65	Aikens Ldg., VA Xc	P118,P123,P124,CSR
					Rchmd. Hospitals	02/27/65	Cmp Lee, Prld POW	CSR
Beasley, M.	Pvt	A 7th SCST	Darlington, SC	03/03/65	New Berne, NC	04/10/65	Hart's Island, NY	CSR
					Hart's Island, NY	06/16/65	Rlsd. G.O. #109	P79,CSR
Beatty, Benjamin	Pvt	5 10/19 SCVI	Missionary Ridge, TN	11/25/63	Nashville, TN	12/07/63	Louisville, KY	P39,RAS,CSR
					Louisville, KY	12/09/63	Rock Island, IL	P88,P89,CSR
					Rock Island, IL	10/04/64	Joined US Army	P131,CSR
Beatty, Christopher L.	Cpt	A P.S.S.	Richmond, VA	08/14/64	US 3rd Div. Corps Hqs.	08/15/64	Died of wounds	P10,TSE,CSR
Beatty, R.R.	Cpl	D Orr's Ri.	Petersburg, VA	04/03/65	City Pt., VA	04/11/65	Hart's Island, NY	CSR
					Hart's Island, NY	06/16/65	Rlsd. G.O. #109	P79,CDC,CSR
Beaty, Alexander	Pvt	D 17th SCVI	Crater, Pbg., VA	07/30/64	City Pt., VA	08/05/64	Pt. Lookout, MD	CSR
					Pt. Lookout, MD	08/08/64	Elmira, NY	P113,P117,P120,CSR
					Elmira, NY	10/11/64	Pt. Lookout, MD Xc	P65,HHC,CSR
					Pt. Lookout, MD	10/29/64	Venus Pt., GA Xc	P114,P118,P123,CSR
Beaver, Anderson	Pvt	C 1st SCVIR	Bentonville, NC	03/22/65	New Berne, NC	04/10/65	Hart's Island, NY	CSR
					Hart's Island, NY	06/16/65	Rlsd. G.O. #109	P79,LAN,SA1,CSR
Beaver, John R.	Pvt	E 2nd SCVI	Williamsburg, VA	05/05/62	Fts. Monroe, VA	08/05/62	Aikens Ldg., VA Xc	CSR
Beaver, John R.	Pvt	E 2nd SCVI	Gettysburg, PA	07/05/63	Ft. McHenry, MD	07/12/63	Ft. Delaware, DE	CSR
					Ft. Delaware, DE	09/13/63	Joined. US 3rd MD	P40,P42,P44,H2,CSR
Bechley, J.T.	Cit	Blockade R	Off Charleston	03/15/63	Ft. Lafayette, NY	06/10/63	Washington, DC	P144
Beck, Charles J.	Sgt	C 2nd SCVI	Gettysburg, PA	07/05/63	Gettysburg G.H.	12/02/63	Provost Marshal	P4,KEB,H2,CSR
					Provost Marshal	04/30/64	Escaped	CSR,H2
Beck, Elijah J.	2Lt	B 14th SCVI	Richmond, VA	04/03/65	Fts. Monroe, VA	05/01/65	Newport News, VA	CSR
					Newport News, VA	06/14/65	Rlsd. G.O. #109	CSR
					Newport News, VA	06/15/65	Fts. Monroe, VA	CSR
					Fts. Monroe, VA	07/09/65	Died, Ch. Diarrhea	P107
Beck, John	Pvt	E 27th SCVI	Town Creek, NC	02/20/65	Pt. Lookout, MD	06/24/65	Rlsd. G.O. #109	P114,P121,P123,HAG
Beck, Josiah	Pvt	I 2nd SCVC	Cedar Run, VA	04/13/63	P.M. Army of Potom.	04/18/63	Washington, DC	CSR
					Old Capitol, DC	05/10/63	City Pt., VA Xc	CSR
Beck, M.J.	Pvt	E 27th SCVI	Town Creek, NC	02/20/65	Ft. Anderson, NC	02/28/65	Pt. Lookout, MD	CSR,HAG
Beckham, Bolivar S.	Pvt	F 1st SCVA	Lancaster, SC	04/03/65	City Pt., VA	04/14/65	Newport News, VA	CSR
					Newport News, VA	04/14/65	Camp Hamilton, VA	CSR
					Camp Hamilton, VA	05/03/65	Newport News, VA	CSR
					Newport News, VA	05/06/65	Died, Ch. Diarrhea	P6,P107,PP,CSR
Becknell, J.D.	Pvt	H 1st SCVIR	Bentonville, NC	03/22/65	New Berne, NC	04/10/65	Hart's Island, NY	CSR
					Hart's Island, NY	06/17/65	Rlsd. G.O. #109	P79,CSR
Beckwith, George W.	Pvt	K 2nd SCVA	Prob Averysboro, NC		Fts. Monroe, VA	05/02/65	Fts. Monroe, VA G.H.	CSR
					Fts. Monroe, VA GH	05/14/65	Discharged on oath	CSR
Becot, A.B.	Pvt	H 14th SCVI	Petersburg, VA	04/02/65	City Pt., VA	04/07/65	Hart's Island, NY	CSR
					Hart's Island, NY	06/16/65	Rlsd. G.O. #109	P79,CSR
Becot, M.R.	Pvt	H 14th SCVI	Petersburg, VA	04/02/65	Hart's Island, NY	06/16/65	Rlsd. G.O. #109	CSR
Bedell, Allen	Pvt	A 15th SCVI	Washington, GA	06/09/65	Washington, GA	06/09/65	Paroled	H15,CSR
Bedell, Charles A.	Pvt	A 15th SCVI	Washington, GA	06/09/65	Washington, GA	06/05/65	Paroled	H15,CSR
Bedenbaugh, J.T.	Pvt	M 7th SCVI	Gettysburg, PA	07/05/63	David's Island, NY	09/05/63	City Pt., VA Xc	P1,KEB,CSR
Bedenbaugh, Jacob A.	Pvt	H Hol.Leg.	Kinston, NC	12/15/62	Kinston, NC	12/15/62	Paroled POW	CSR
Bedenbaugh, Jacob A.	Pvt	H Hol.Leg.	Petersburg, VA	11/05/64	City Pt., VA	11/11/64	Pt. Lookout, MD	CSR
Bedenbaugh, Jacob A.	Pvt	H Hol.Leg.	Petersburg, VA	11/06/64	Pt. Lookout, MD	06/24/65	Rlsd. G.O. #109	P118,P123,CSR
Bedenbaugh, John A.	Pvt	H Hol.Leg.	Kinston, NC	12/14/62	Kinston, NC	12/14/62	Paroled POW	CSR8

SOUTH CAROLINA SOLDIERS, SAILORS AND **B** CITIZENS HELD IN U.S. PRISONS 1861-1865

NAME	RANK	REGIMENT	CAPTURED AT	WHEN	PRISON	MOVED	DISPOSITION	SOURCES
Bedenbaugh, John A.	Pvt	H Hol.Leg.	Five Forks, VA	04/01/65	City Pt., VA	04/05/65	Pt. Lookout, MD	CSR
					Pt. Lookout, MD	06/23/65	Rlsd. G.O. #109	P114,P118,CSR
Bedenbaugh, William J.	Pvt	H Hol.Leg.	Richmond, VA Hos	04/03/65	Richmond Hospital	05/09/65	Pt. Lookout, MD	CSR
					Pt. Lookout, MD	07/07/65	Rlsd. G.O. #109	ANY,CSR
Bee, James Ladson	Pvt	K 4th SCVC	Old Church, VA	05/30/64	Ft. McHenry, MD	06/04/64	Lincoln G.H., DC	P110,CSR
Bee, James Ladson.	Pvt	K 4th SCVC	Old Church, VA	12/30/63	Washington, DC	07/08/64	Died of wounds	P5,P12,CSR
Bee, John Price	Pvt	I 27th SCVI	Petersburg, VA	06/18/64	City Pt., VA	06/24/64	Pt. Lookout, MD	CSR
					Pt. Lookout, MD	02/13/65	Aikens Ldg., VA Xc	P113,P117,P121,P123
Bee, John S.	Lt	I 1st SCVA	Morris Island, SC	07/10/63	Hilton Head, SC G.H.	07/18/63	Died of wounds	P12,P2,SCA,CSR
Beesom, William A.	PMr	*Huntress*	Off Charleston	01/18/63	Ft. Lafayette, NY	04/15/63	Ft. Delaware, DE	P144
Beggles, Elijah B.	Pvt	G 14th SCVI	Gettysburg, PA	07/02/63	David's Island, NY	08/24/63	City Pt., VA Xc	CSR
					Williamsburg, VA Hos.	09/04/63	Furloughed	CSR
Beheler, F.A.	Pvt	F 17th SCVI	Crater, Pbg., VA	07/30/64	Pt. Lookout, MD	08/08/64	Elmira, NY	P125,CSR
					Elmira, NY	09/01/64	Died	FPH,CSR
Beheler, William T.	Pvt	F 17th SCVI	Petersburg, VA	03/25/65	City Pt., VA	03/28/65	Pt. Lookout, MD	CSR
					Pt. Lookout, MD	06/23/65	Rlsd. G.O. #109	P118,CSR
Behling, Henry	Pvt	C 24th SCVI	Nashville, TN	12/16/64	Louisville, KY	01/05/65	Camp Chase, OH	P95,EFW
					Camp Chase, OH	03/28/65	Pt. Lookout, MD	P23
					Pt. Lookout, MD	06/04/65	Released G.O. #85	P114,P119,CSR
Behrmann, H.	Pvt	A German LA	Savannah, GA	03/31/65	Savannah, GA	03/31/65	Released on oath	CSR
Bein, Daniel	Sgt	I 5th SCVC	Bentonville, NC	03/21/65	New Berne, NC	04/10/65	Hart's Island, NY	CSR
					Hart's Island, NY	06/16/65	Rlsd. G.O. #109	P79,CSR
Belcher, H.C.	Pvt	A 1st SCVC	Johns Island, SC	07/02/64	Hilton Head, SC	08/01/64	Port Royal Fy., SC	CSR
					Port Royal Fy., SC	08/16/64	Exchanged	CSR
Belitzer, Jacob	Pvt	B Wash'n LA	Spotsylvania, VA	05/09/64	Bermuda Hundred, VA	05/15/64	Fts. Monroe, VA	CSR
					Fts. Monroe, VA	05/16/64	Pt. Lookout, MD	CSR
					Pt. Lookout, MD		Elmira, NY	P113,CSR
					Elmira, NY	02/25/65	James R., VA Xc	CSR
Belk, D.D.A.	Sgt	H 4th SCVC	Charlotte, NC	05/03/65	Charlotte, NC	05/03/65	Paroled	CSR
Belk, J.M.	Pvt	K 6th SCVC	Stony Creek, VA	12/01/64	City Pt., VA	12/05/64	Pt. Lookout, MD	CSR
					Pt. Lookout, MD	06/23/65	Rlsd. G.O. #109	P118,CSR
Belk, J.M.	Pvt	G 3rd SCVABn	High Pt., NC	05/01/65	High Pt., NC	05/01/65	Paroled on oath	CSR
Belk, Joseph A.	Pvt	E 7th SCVIBn	Weldon RR, VA	08/21/64	City Pt., VA	08/24/64	Pt. Lookout, MD	CSR,HAG
					Pt. Lookout, MD	03/14/65	Aikens Ldg., VA Xc	P113,P117,P124,CSR
Belk, Joseph A.	Pvt	E 7th SCVIBn	Weldon RR, VA	08/21/64	Richmond, VA Hos.	03/20/65	Camp Lee, VA Prld.	CSR
Belk, William C.	Pvt	19th SCVI	Booneville, MS	06/02/62	Alton, IL	07/31/62	Died	CSR
Bell, Andrew J.	Pvt	H 12th SCVI	N. Anna River, VA	05/24/64	Pt. Lookout, MD		Took the Oath	P124
					Pt. Lookout, MD	03/06/65	Died, Scurvy	P6,P119,P121,CSR
Bell, Andrew James	Pvt	A Orr's Ri.	Hatchers Run, VA	03/27/65	Pt. Lookout, MD	06/23/65	Rlsd. G.O.#109	CSR
Bell, Benjamin	Pvt	D 3rd SCVABn	Cheraw, SC	03/05/65	Cheraw, SC	03/05/65	Paroled on oath	CSR
Bell, C.J.	Pvt	B 4th SCVC	Louisa C.H., VA	06/11/64	Fts. Monroe, VA	06/20/64	Pt. Lookout, MD	CSR
					Pt. Lookout, MD	07/25/64	Elmira, NY	P113,P117,CSR
					Elmira, NY	03/14/65	James R., VA Xc	P65,CSR
Bell, Charles W.	Pvt	K 2nd SCVI	Gettysburg, PA		Gettysburg G.H.		Provost Marshal	P4
Bell, Charles W.	Pvt	K 2nd SCVI	Gettysburg, PA	07/05/63	Letterman G.H. Gbg.	07/15/65	Died of wounds	P1,P12,KEB,H2,CSR
Bell, Henry C.	Pvt	D 23rd SCVI	Deserted/enemy	03/14/65	Charleston, SC	03/14/65	Rlsd. on oath	CSR
Bell, J.B.	Pvt	Beaufort L	Salisbury, NC	05/02/65	Salisbury, NC	05/02/65	Paroled	CSR
Bell, James	Pvt	D 23rd SCVI	Deserted/enemy	02/18/65	Charleston SC	03/14/65	released on oath	CSR
Bell, James M.	Pvt	I 25th SCVI	Town Creek, NC	02/20/65	Ft. Anderson, NC	02/28/65	Pt. Lookout, MD	CSR
					Pt. Lookout, MD	06/24/65	Rlsd. G.O. #109	P114,P123,HAG,CSR
Bell, James W.	Pvt	A Orr's Ri.	Hatchers Run, VA	03/27/65	Pt. Lookout, MD	06/23/65	Rlsd. G.O. #109	P114,P118
Bell, John	Pvt	H 24th SCVI	Jonesboro, GA	09/01/64	Camp Douglas, IL	04/03/65	Joined US Army	P53

B

SOUTH CAROLINA SOLDIERS, SAILORS AND CITIZENS HELD IN U.S. PRISONS 1861-1865

NAME	RANK	REGIMENT	CAPTURED AT	WHEN	PRISON	MOVED	DISPOSITION	SOURCES
Bell, John F.	Pvt	C 13th SCVI	Petersburg, VA	04/03/65	City Pt., VA	04/07/65	Hart's Island, NY	CSR
					Hart's Island, NY	06/15/65	Rlsd. G.O. #109	P79,CSR
Bell, John H.	Pvt	A Orr's Ri.	Spotsylvania, VA	05/12/64	Belle Plain, VA	05/21/64	Ft. Delaware, DE	CSR
					Ft. Delaware, DE	06/02/64	Hos. 6/2-7/4/64	P47
					Ft. Delaware, DE	06/10/65	Released	P41,P43,P45
Bell, Joseph	Pvt	D Hol.Leg.C	Williamsburg, VA	11/22/62	Fts. Monroe, VA	11/27/62	City Pt., VA Xc	CSR
Bell, Joseph	Pvt	C 7th SCVC	Not given	04/09/65	Fts. Monroe, VA	04/24/64	Camp Hamilton, VA	CSR
Bell, Leander C.	Pvt	D 7th SCVIBn	Weldon RR, VA	08/21/64	City Pt., VA	08/24/64	Pt. Lookout, MD	CSR
					Pt. Lookout, MD	03/17/65	Aikens Ldg., VA Xc	P117,P124,P125,CSR
Bell, Manning A.	Pvt	I 25th SCVI	Ft. Fisher, NC	01/15/65	New York, NY	01/30/65	Elmira, NY	CSR
					Elmira, NY	07/03/65	Rlsd. G.O. #109	P65,P66,CSR
Bell, Nathaniel E.	Sgt	B Orr's Ri.	Spotsylvania, VA	05/12/64	Belle Plain, VA	05/21/64	Ft. Delaware, DE	CSR
					Ft. Delaware, DE	09/13/64	Hos.9/13- 9/30/64	P47
					Ft. Delaware, DE	09/28/64	Truce Boat	CSR
					Ft. Delaware, DE	09/30/64	Aikens Ldg., VA Xc	P41,P43,CDC
					Truce Boat	10/02/64	died on boat	CSR
Bell, Sanders W.	Pvt	A 1st SCVIG	N. Anna River, VA	05/23/64	Front Royal, VA	05/30/64	Pt. Lookout, MD	CSR
					Pt. Lookout, MD	06/18/64	Died, Ch. Diarrhea	P6,P12,P113,P117,SA1
Bell, W.V.	Pvt	F Hol.Leg.	Jarratts Stn., VA	05/08/64	Fts. Monroe, VA	05/13/64	Pt. Lookout, MD	CSR
					Pt. Lookout, MD	08/13/64	Elmira, NY	P113,P117,P120,CSR
					Elmira, NY	06/19/65	Rlsd. G.O. #109	P65,CSR
Bell, William	Pvt	K 4th SCVC	Old Church, VA	05/30/64	Ft. McHenry, MD	06/05/64	Lincoln G.H., DC	CSR
					Lincoln G.H., DC	07/30/64	Old Capitol, DC	CSR
					Old Capitol, DC	08/12/64	Elmira, NY	P110,CSR
					Elmira, NY	10/11/64	Tfd. for exchange	P65,CSR
					Pt. Lookout, MD	10/29/64	Aikens Ldg., VA Xc	P114,P118,CSR
Bell, William D.F.	Cpl	A 1st SCVIG	Farmville, VA	04/07/65	Pt. Lookout, MD	06/04/65	Released	P114,P119,SA1,CSR
Bell, William H.	Pvt	H 7th SCVIBn	Drury's Bluff, VA	05/16/64	Bermuda Hundred VA	05/17/64	Fts. Monroe, VA	CSR
					Fts. Monroe, VA	05/19/64	Pt. Lookout, MD	CSR
					Pt. Lookout, MD	07/25/64	Died	P6,P117,FPH
Bellamy, Abraham M.	Pvt	B 10th SCVI	Atlanta, GA	07/22/64	Nashville, TN	07/29/64	Louisville, KY	CSR,RAS
					Louisville, KY	07/30/64	Camp Douglas, IL	P90,P91,P94,CSR
					Camp Douglas, IL	06/16/65	Rlsd. G.O. #109	P53,P55,CSR
Bellamy, Francis K.	Pvt	6 10/19 SCVI	Missionary Ridge, TN	11/25/63	Nashville, TN	12/07/63	Louisville, KY	P39,CSR,RAS
					Louisville, KY	12/09/63	Rock Island, IL	P88,P89,CSR
					Rock Island, IL	06/20/65	Rlsd. G.O. #109	P131,CSR
Bellflower, Samuel	Pvt	McQueen LA	Farmville, VA	04/11/65	Farmville, VA	04/21/65	Paroled	CSR
Bellinger, C.C.P.	Pvt	I 2nd SCVI	Gettysburg, PA	07/04/63	Gettysburg G.H.	07/20/63	Provost Marshal	P4,KEB,CSR
					David's Island, NY	08/24/63	City Pt., VA Xc	P1,KEB,CSR
Bellott, Ebenezer J.	Sgt	H 19th SCVI	Murfreesboro, TN	01/05/63	Nashville, TN	04/21/63	Louisville, KY	P38,CSR
					Louisville, KY	04/27/63	City Pt., VA Xc	P88,P93,CSR
Bellotte, John D.	Pvt	C 4th SCVC	Hawe's Shop, VA	05/28/64	3rd Div. 5th A.C.			CSR
					Ft. McHenry, MD			P110
					Old Capitol, DC	12/16/64	Elmira, NY	CSR
					Elmira, NY	03/16/65	Died, Diarrhea	P12,P65,P66,CSR
Bellotte, T.D.	1Lt	C 4th SCVC	Hawe's Shop, VA	05/28/64	No other dara			CSR
Benbow, Henry Laurens	Col	23rd SCVI	Five Forks, VA	04/01/65	City Pt., VA	05/02/65	Lincoln G.H., DC	CSR,LC
					Lincoln G.H., DC	06/14/65	Released	P7,LC,CSR
Benedikt, Edward	Pvt	A German LA	Deserted/enemy	12/21/64	Savannah, GA	03/31/65	Work in Q.M. Dept.	P8,CSR
Benjamin, Samuel	Pvt	F 22nd SCVI	Bermuda Hundred VA	06/02/64	Fts. Monroe, VA	06/04/64	Pt. Lookout, MD	CSR
					Pt. Lookout, MD	03/15/65	Aikens Ldg., VA Xc	P113,P117,P124
Benjes, F.	Pvt	B German LA	Deserted/enemy	10/01/64	Hilton Head, SC D.	10/13/64	Sent North on oath	P8,CSR

SOUTH CAROLINA SOLDIERS, SAILORS AND **B** CITIZENS HELD IN U.S. PRISONS 1861-1865

NAME	RANK	REGIMENT	CAPTURED AT	WHEN	PRISON	MOVED	DISPOSITION	SOURCES
Bennefield, John	Pvt	Ferguson's A	Franklin, TN	12/17/64	Nashville, TN	12/31/64	Louisville, KY	CSR
Bennefield, John	Pvt	Ferguson's A	Nashville, TN	12/16/64	Louisville, KY	01/02/65	Camp Chase, OH	P95,CSR
					Camp Chase, OH	01/07/65	Died, Ch. Diarrhea	P6,P23,P27,FPH,CSR
Bennett, C.E.	Pvt	G 7th SCVC	Athens, GA	05/08/65	Athens, GA	05/08/65	Paroled	CSR
Bennett, Charles E.	Pvt	C 1st SCVIG	Petersburg, VA	03/25/65	Pt. Lookout, MD	06/05/65	Released	P114,P118,SA1,CSR
Bennett, Franklin	Pvt	F 21st SCVI	Morris Island, SC	07/10/63	Hilton Head, SC	09/19/63	Ft. Columbus, NY	CSR
					Ft. Columbus, NY	09/23/63	took the oath	P1,HAG
					Ft.Columbus, NY	09/26/63	Pt. Lookout, MD	CSR
					Pt. Lookout, MD	02/25/64	Jd. U.S. Army	P113,P116,P125
Bennett, H.J.	Pvt	K 3rd SCVC	Pocotaligo, SC	01/16/65	Pt. Lookout, MD	06/24/65	Rlsd. G.O. #109	P114,P118,P121,CSR
Bennett, John	Pvt	E 24th SCVI	Marietta, GA	07/03/64	Nashvuille, TN	07/13/64	Louisville, KY	CSR
					Louisville, KY	07/16/64	Camp Douglas, IL	P90,P91,P94,CSR
					Camp Douglas, IL	02/21/65	Pt.Lookout, MD Xc	P53,CSR
Bennett, T.J.	Pvt	E 11th SCVI	Petersburg, VA	06/24/64	Fts. Monroe, VA	06/25/64	Pt. Lookout, MD	CSR
					Pt. Lookout, MD	09/18/64	Aikens Ldg., VA Xc	P113,P117,P123,CSR
Bennett, Thomas	Pvt	F 21st SCVI	Morris Island, SC	07/10/63	Hilton Head, SC	09/09/63	Ft. Columbus, NY	CSR
					Ft. Columbus, NY	09/23/63	Took the oath	P1,HAG
					Ft. Columbus, NY	09/26/63	Pt. Lookout, MD	CSR
					Pt. Lookout, MD	02/25/64	Joined U.S. Army	P113,P116,P125,HAG
Bennett, Thomas Benton	Cpl	D Ham Leg.	Gaines' Mill, VA	06/08//62	Fts. Monroe, VA	08/31/62	Aikens Ldg., VA Xc	CSR
Bennett, William H.	Pvt	C German LA	Augusta, GA	05/18/65	Augusta, GA	05/18/65	Paroled	CSR
Bensch, William J.	Pvt	G 3rd SCVC	Deserted/enemy	02/03/65	Savannah, GA	02/18/65	New York, NY	CSR
Benson, A.J.	Pvt	C 15th SCVAB	Fayetteville, NC	03/13/65	New Berne, NC	03/13/65	Hart's Island, NY	CSR
					Hart's Island, NY	06/17/65	Rlsd. G.O. #109	P79,CSR
Benson, Berry G.	Sgt	H 1st SCVIG	Spotsylvania, VA	05/14/64	Ft. McHenry, MD	07/23/64	Elmira, NY	P110,CSR
					Elmira, NY	10/17/64	Escaped by tunnel	P65,P113,SA1,CSR
Benson, Joseph F.	Pvt	A 2nd SCVIRi	Warrenton, VA	09/29/62	Warrenton, VA	09/29/62	Paroled	CSR
Benson, Robert T.	2Lt	G 16th SCVI	Pulaski, TN	12/25/64	Nashville, TN	03/01/65	Louisville, KY	P3,P39,16RCSR
					Louisville, KY	03/10/65	Camp Chase, OH	P92,P95,16R,CSR
					Camp Chase, OH	03/18/65	Pt. Lookout, MD Xc	P26,16R,CSR
					Pt. Lookout, MD	03/27/65	Boulwares Wh,VA X	CSR
Benson, Thomas H.	Pvt	K 16th SCVI	Lookout Mtn., TN	12/08/63	Nashville, TN	03/10/64	Died, Ch. Diarrhea	P2,P5,P12,CSR
Bentley, A. Griffin	Sgt	F 18th SCVI	Ft. Steadman, VA	03/25/65	Old Capitol, DC	06/06/65	Released on oath	CSR
Bentley, W.H.	Pvt	B Orr's Ri.		09/13/62	Old Capitol, DC	09/27/62	Aikens Ldg., VA Xc	CSR
Benton, E.J.	Pvt	G 11th SCVI	Deserted/enemy	04/05/65	Hilton Head, SC PM		New York, NY oath	CSR
Benton, Henry E.	Pvt	E 24th SCVI	Nashville, TN	12/16/64	Nashville, TN	12/31/64	Louisville, KY	CSR
					Louisville, KY	01/03/65	Camp Chase, OH	P95,EFW
					Camp Chase, OH	02/24/65	Died, Pneumonia	P6,P12,P23,P27,FPH
Benton, James W.	Pvt	G 25th SCVI	Town Creek, NC	02/20/65	Ft. Anderson, NC	02/28/65	Pt. Lookout, MD	CSR
					Pt. Lookout, MD	06/24/65	Rlsd. G.O. #109	P114,P123,HAG
Benton, John M.	Pvt	G 1st SCVA	Waynesboro, NC	03/17/65	New Berne, NC	03/30/65	Pt. Lookout, MD	CSR
					Pt. Lookout, MD	04/17/65	Died	P6,P114,P121,FPH
					Pt. Lookout, MD	05/12/65	Released G.O. #85	P114,P118,CSR
Benton, Joshua	Pvt	I 11th SCVI	Petersburg, VA	04/24/64	Bermuda Hundred VA	06/25/64	Fts. Monroe, VA	CSR, HAG
					Fts. Monroe, VA	06/26/64	Pt. Lookout, MD	CSR
					Pt. Lookout, MD	08/16/64	Elmira, NY	P113,P117,P120
					Elmira, NY	10/01/64	Died, Diarrhea	P6,P12,P65,CSR
Benton, Louis	Pvt	C 3rd SCVABn	Blakely, AL	04/09/65	Ship Island, MS	05/01/65	Vicksburg, MS Prld	CSR
Benton, Louis	Pvt	C 3rd SCVABn	Augusta, GA	05/20/65	Augusta, GA	05/20/65	Paroled on oath	CSR
Benton, Mischack	Pvt	C 1st SCVIR	Deserted/enemy	02/28/65	Charleston, SC	03/15/65	taken oath & disch	SA1,CSR
Benton, S.	Pvt	K 1st SCVIR	Deserted/enemy	02/28/65	Charleston, SC	03/15/65	Taken oath & disch	SA1,CSR
Benton, Samuel M.	Pvt	C 3rd SCVABn	Blakely, AL	04/09/65	Ship Island, MS	05/01/65	Vicksburg, MS Prld	P136,CSR

SOUTH CAROLINA SOLDIERS, SAILORS AND  CITIZENS HELD IN U.S. PRISONS 1861-1865

NAME	RANK	REGIMENT	CAPTURED AT	WHEN	PRISON	MOVED	DISPOSITION	SOURCES
Berdine, R.H.	Pvt	I P.S.S.	Williamsburg, VA	05/05/62	Site unknown	05/31/62	Died of wounds	CSR,TSE
Bergmann, Ambrose	Pvt	I 1st SCVIG	Petersburg, VA	07/29/64	City Pt., VA	08/05/64	Pt. Lookout, MD	CSR
					Pt. Lookout, MD	08/08/64	Elmira, NY	P113,P117,P120,CSR
					Elmira, NY	05/15/65	Rlsd. G.O. #85	P65,SA1,CSR
Bernard, Louis	Smn	CSS *Chicora*	Morris Island, SC	09/07/63	Pt. Lookout, MD	01/21/64	Joined U.S. Army	P125
Berry, Commodore P.	Pvt	I Ham.Leg.MI	Richmond, VA Hos.	04/03/65	Richmond, VA Hos.	04/14/65	Provost Marshal	CSR
					Libby Prsn.,Rchmd	04/23/65	Newport News, VA	CSR
					Newport News, VA	06/15/65	Rlsd. G.O. #109	P107,CSR
Berry, D.S.	Pvt	E Ham.Leg.MI	24th AC Fld.Hos.	04/11/65	24thy AC Fld. Hos	04/13/65	General Hospital	CSR
Berry, J.W.	Pvt	D 5th SCVI	Deserted/enemy	03/21/65	Charleston, SC	03/21/65	Released on oath	CSR
Berry, J.W..	Pvt	C 3rd SCVABn	Blakely, AL	04/09/65	Ship Island, MS	05/01/65	Vicksburg, MS Prld	P136,CSR
Berry, John	Pvt	D 5th SCVI	Richmond, VA Hos.	04/03/65	Libby Prison, VA	04/23/65	Newport News, VA	CSR
					Newport News, VA	06/15/65	Rlsd. G.O. #109	CSR
Berry, John	Pvt	G 17th SCVI	Augusta, GA	05/24/65	Augusta, GA	05/24/65	Paroled	CSR
Berry, Lenwood	Sgt	E 23rd SCVI	Five Forks, VA	04/01/65	City Pt., VA	04/06/65	Pt. Lookout, MD	CSR
					Pt. Lookout, MD	06/24/65	Rlsd. G.O. #109	P114,P118,P123,CSR
Berry, R.S.	Pvt	E P.S.S.	Petersburg, VA	04/03/65	Hart's Island, NY	06/16/65	Rlsd. G.O. #109	P79,TSE,CSR
Berry, Samuel Obediah	Pvt	7 10/19 SCVI	Missionary Ridge, TN	11/25/63	Nashville, TN	01/20/64	Louisville, KY	P39,CSR
					Louisville, KY	01/22/64	#5 Smallpox Hos.	CSR
					Louisville, KY	02/09/64	Died, Variola	P5,P12,CSR
Berry, W.S.	Pvt	G 7th SCVI	Gettysburg, PA	07/06/63	Chester, PA G.H.	07/25/63	Died, Erysipelas	P4,P6,P12,FPH,CSR
Besinger, Adam	Pvt	A 1st SCVIH	Deserted/enemy	03/23/65	City Pt., VA P.M..	03/27/65	Washington, DC P.M	CSR
					Washington, DC	03/27/65	Charleston, SC	CSR
Besinger, J.A.	Pvt	G 1st SCVIH	Richmond Hos. VA	04/03/65	Richmond, VA Hos.		Pt. Lookout, MD US	CSR
					Pt. Lookout, MD	06/26/65	Rlsd. G.O. #109	P119,SA1,CSR
Besinger, John	Pvt	G 3rd SCVABn	High Pt., NC	05/01/65	High Pt., NC	05/01/65	Paroled on oath	CSR
Bessellieu, Henry T.	Cpl	B 2nd SCVC	Brandy Stn., VA	08/01/63	Ft.McHenry, MD			P110
					Douglas Hos., DC	10/24/63	Lincoln G.H., DC	CSR
					Lincoln G.H., DC	11/24/63	Old Capitol, DC	CSR
					Old Capitol, DC	09/19/64	Ft. Delawre, DE	CSR
					Ft. Delaware, DE	10/13/64	Hos 10/13-11/9/64	P47
					Ft. Delaware, DE	06/10/65	Rlsd. G.O. #109	P41,P43,P45,CSR
Best, James P.	Pvt	H 21st SCVI	Morris Island, SC	07/10/63	Hilton Head, SC	09/14/63	Ft. Columbus, NY	CSR
					Ft. Columbus, NY	09/23/63	Prld. on oath	P1,HAG
					Ft. Columbus, NY	09/26/63	Pt. Lookout, MD	CSR
					Pt. Lookout, MD	08/16/64	Elmira, NY	P113,P116,P120
					Elmira, NY	02/20/65	James R., VA Xc	P65,P124
Best, John J.	2Lt	E 26th SCVI	Dinwiddie C.H., VA	04/01/65	Old Capitol, DC	04/09/65	Johnson's Isl., VA	P110,CSR
					Johnsons Isl., OH	06/18/65	Rlsd. G.O. #109	P81,P83,CSR
Best, William	Sgt	F 1st SCVA	Deserted/enemy	02/18/65	Charleston, SC	03/13/65	Taken oath & disch	CSR
Best, William	Pvt	H 21st SCVI	Town Creek, NC	02/20/65	Pt. Lookout, MD	06/24/65	Rlsd. G.O. #109	P114,P123,HAG
Best, William T.	Pvt	E 1st SCVIH	Sharpsburg, MD	09/19/62	Ft. McHenry, MD	10/14/62	Aikens Ldg., VA Xc	JRH,CSR
Betenbaugh, John J.	Pvt	F 15th SCVI	Gettysburg, PA	07/03/63	Gettysburg G.H.		Provost Marshal	P4,KEB
Betenbaugh, John J.	Pvt	F 15th SCVI	Gettysburg, PA	07/03/63	W. Bldg. Balt., MD	07/30/63	Baltimore Jail	P1
Betenbaugh, John J.	Pvt	F 15th SCVI	Gettysburg, PA	07/12/63	Pt. Lookout, MD	03/24/65	Died	P6,P113,FPH
Betenbaugh, Joseph	Pvt	F 15th SCVI	Gettysburg, PA	07/12/63	Pt. Lookout, MD	03/14/65	Aikens Ldg., VA Xc	P121,P124,UD5,CSR
Bethea, Henry P.	Pvt	L 8th SCVI	Winchester, VA	09/13/64	Harpers Ferry, WV	09/19/64	Camp Chase, OH	CSR,KEB
					Camp Chase, OH	02/15/65	Died,debility	P12,P23,P27,CSR
Bethea, Holden W.	Pvt	I 1st SCVIH	Knoxville, TN	01/05/64	Nashville, TN	01/17/64	Louisville, KY	P39,SA1
					Louisville, KY	01/23/64	Rock Island, IL	P88,P93,P94,CSR
					Rock Island, IL	03/02/65	Pt. Lookout, MD Xc	P131,CSR

SOUTH CAROLINA SOLDIERS, SAILORS AND CITIZENS HELD IN U.S. PRISONS 1861-1865

NAME	RANK	REGIMENT	CAPTURED AT	WHEN	PRISON	MOVED	DISPOSITION	SOURCES
Bethea, Phillip W.	Pvt	G 23rd SCVI	Five Forks, VA	04/01/65	City Pt., VA	04/06/65	Pt. Lookout MD	CSR,HOM
					Pt. Lookout, MD	06/24/65	Rlsd. G.O. #109	P114,P118,P123,CSR
Bethea, Redden R.	Pvt	H Orr's Ri.	Richmond, VA Hos.	04/03/65	Richmond, VA Hos.	05/15/65	Paroled	CSR
Bethune, Henry	Pvt	D 1st SCVIR	Charleston, SC Bar	03/21/63	Ft. Lafayette, NY	06/29/63	Ft. Delaware, DE	P40,P42,P144,SA1
Bethune, Malcolm	Pvt	D 1st SCVIR	Charleston, SC Bar	03/24/63	Fort Lafayette, NY	06/29/63	Ft. Delaware, DE	CSR
					Ft. Delaware, DE	06/29/63	paroled	CSR
Bethune, Malcolm	Pvt	D 1st SCVIR	Salisbury, NC	05/12/65	Nashville, TN	04/29/65	Louisville, KY	P39,SA1,CSR
Bethune, Malcolm	Pvt	D 1st SCVIR	Salisbury, NC	04/12/65	Louisville, KY	05/02/65	Camp Chase, OH	P92,P95,SA1,CSR
					Camp Chase, OH	06/13/65	Rlsd. G.O. #109	P23,SA1,CSR
Betsell, Henry G.	Pvt	I 27th SCVI	Town Creek, NC	02/20/65	Fts. Monroe, VA	02/26/65	Pt. Lookout, MD	CSR,HAG
					Pt. Lookout, MD	06/24/65	Rlsd. G.O. #109	P114,P123,CSR
Betts, John	Pvt	Palmetto L	Nine Mile Rd., VA	10/27/64	City Pt., VA	10/31/64	Pt. Lookout, MD	CSR
					Pt. Lookout, MD	03/28/65	Aikens Ldg., VA Xc	P114,P124,CSR
Beverly, John	Pvt	D 25th SCVI	Ft. Fisher, NC	01/15/65	New York, NY	01/30/65	Elmira, NY	CSR
					Elmira, NY	02/27/65	Died, Variola	P6,P65,P66,FPH,CSR
Beverly, John B.	Pvt	K 11th SCVI	Town Creek, NC	02/20/65	Ft. Anderson, NC	02/28/65	Pt. Lookout, MD	CSR,HAG
					Pt. Lookout, MD	04/22/65	Died, Lung Inflam.	P6,P12,FPH
Beverly, John B.	Pvt	K 11th SCVI	Town Creek, NC	02/20/65	Pt. Lookout, MD	06/24/65	Rlsd. G.O. #109	P114
Bevill, James	Pvt	H 1st SCVIR	Bentonville, NC	03/19/65	New Berne, NC	04/03/65	Pt. Lookout, MD	CSR
					Pt. Lookout, MD		Assumed other name	P118,SA1,CSR
Bevill, W.H.	Pvt	H 15th SCVI	Gettysburg, PA	07/02/63	Baltimore, MD	08/20/63	Pt. Lookout, MD	CSR
					Pt. Lookout, MD	02/18/65	Exchanged	P113,P123,P124,KEB
Bewley, W.C.	Pvt	B 2nd SCVC	Anderson, SC	05/03/65	Anderson, SC	05/03/65	Paroled on oath	CSR
Bexley, John	Pvt	C 11th SCVI	Town Creek, NC	02/20/65	Ft. Anderson, NC	02/28/65	Pt. Lookout, MD	CSR
					Pt. Lookout, MD	06/24/65	Rlsd. G.O. #109	P123,HAG,CSR
Bibb, B.F.	Pvt	C 4th SCVC	Anderson, SC	05/03/65	Anderson, SC	05/03/65	Paroled on oath	CSR
Bibb, Samuel R.	Pvt	B P.S.S.	Richmond, VA	10/07/64	Richmond, VA	10/17/64	Died of wounds	P12,TSE,CSR
Bickley, Jefferson J.	Pvt	I 15th SCVI	Halltown, WV	08/21/64	Halltown, WV	08/26/64	Washington, DC	CSR,KEB,H15
					Washington, DC	08/29/64	Camp Chase, OH	CSR
					Camp Chase, OH	03/26/65	Pt. Lookout, MD	P23,P26,CSR
					Pt. Lookout, MD	07/17/65	Died, Ch. Diarrhea	P12
Bickley, Joseph H.	Pvt	I 15th SCVI	Halltown, WV	08/26/64	Halltown, WV	08/26/64	Washington, DC	P125,CSR,KEB
					Washington, DC	08/29/64	Pt. Lookout, MD	CSR
					Pt. Lookout, MD	06/24/65	Rlsd. G.O. #109	P119,P121,P123
Bigby, John W.	Pvt	K Orr's Ri.	Appomattox R., VA	04/02/65	City Pt., VA	04/07/65	Hart's Island, NY	CSR
					Hart's Island, NY	06/15/65	Rlsd. G.O. #109	CSR,P79
Biggers, Amzi	Pvt	F 5th SCVI	Deserted/enemy	03/02/65	Washington, DC	03/07/65	Indianapolis, IN	CSR
Bigham, Elijah	Pvt	A 17th SCVI	Amelia C.H., VA	04/04/65	City Pt., VA	04/13/65	Pt. Lookout, MD	CSR,HHC
					Pt. Lookout, MD	05/26/65	Died	P6,P114,P119,FPH
Bigham, James W.	Pvt	H 24th SCVI	Nashville, TN	12/16/64	Nashville, TN	01/01/65	Louisville, KY	CSR
					Louisville, KY	01/04/65	Camp Chase, OH	P92,P95
					Camp Chase, OH	06/12/65	Released	P23,EFW,HHC
Bigham, Joseph H.	Pvt	A 17th SCVI	Farmville, VA	04/06/65	City Pt., VA	04/14/65	Newport News, VA	CSR
					Newport News, VA	06/15/65	Rlsd. G.O. #109	P107,CSR
					Fts. Monroe, VA GH	06/27/65	Died, after Rls.	P12
Bigham, Joseph T.	Pvt	B 12th SCVI	Warrenton, VA	09/29/62	Warrenton, VA	09/29/62	Paroled	CSR
Bigham, William J.	Pvt	A 17th SCVI	Five Forks, VA	04/01/65	City Pt., VA	04/04/65	Pt. Lookout, MD	CSR
					Pt. Lookout, MD	06/24/65	Rlsd. G.O. #109	P118,P121,P123
Bigler, J.	Pvt	H 1st SCVC	Wilderness, VA	05/06/64	Ft. Delaware, DE	09/28/64	Died, Typhoid	P5,P12,P47,FPH
Billing, E.W.	Pvt	C 1st SCVIH	Augusta, GA	05/25/65	Augusta, GA	05/25/65	Paroled	CSR
Billings, Constantine T.	Pvt	D 7th SCVIBn	Morris Island, SC	07/10/64	Morris Island, SC	07/13/64	Hilton Head, SC US	P2,HAG,CSR
					Hilton Head, SC G.H.	07/23/64	Xchgd. CN Harbor	P2,HAG,CSR

SOUTH CAROLINA SOLDIERS, SAILORS AND  CITIZENS HELD IN U.S. PRISONS 1861-1865

NAME	RANK	REGIMENT	CAPTURED AT	WHEN	PRISON	MOVED	DISPOSITION	SOURCES
Bilton, Jacob J.	Pvt	E 25th SCVI	Ft. Fisher, NC	01/15/65	New York, NY	01/30/65	Elmira, NY	CSR
					Elmira, NY	05/17/65	Rlsd. G.O. #85	P65,P66,HAG,CSR
					New York, NY	01/30/65	Elmira, NY	CSR
Bilton, William H.	Pvt	E 25th SCVI	Ft. Fisher, NC	01/15/65	Elmira, NY	02/20/65	Pt.Lookout, MD Xc	P65,P66,HAG,CSR
					Richmond, VA Hos.	03/20/65	Died	CSR
Birch, J. Douglass	Pvt	G 1st SCVIR	Cheraw, SC	03/16/65	New Berne, NC	04/10/65	Hart's Island, NY	CSR
					Hart's Island, NY	05/29/65	Released O.O. Pres	P79,SA1,CSR
Birch, James C.	Pvt	A 4th SCMil	Lynch's Creek, SC	02/25/65	Hart's Island, NY	06/16/65	Rlsd. G.O. #109	P79
Bircher, Henry	Pvt	B German LA	Gettysburg, PA	07/06/63	Chambersburg, PA	07/28/63	Harrisburg, PA	CSR
					Harrisburg, PA	07/29/63	Philadelphia, PA	CSR
					Philadelphia, PA	07/30/63	Ft. Delaware, DE	CSR
					Ft. Delaware, DE	09/15/63	Jd. US 3rd MD Cav	P40,P42,CSR
Birchfield, Eli C.	Pvt	Ferguson's	Ringgold, GA	11/26/63	Nashville, TN	12/09/63	Louisville, KY	P39,CSR
					Louisville, KY	12/11/63	Rock Island, IL	P88,CSR
Bird, Daniel	Pvt	K 15th SCVI	Halltown, WV	08/26/64	Harpers Ferry, WV	08/02/64	Camp Chase, OH	CSR,KEB
					Camp Chase, OH	02/07/65	Died	P6,P12,P23,P27,FPH
Bird, George W.	Pvt	B 1st SCVC	Cassville, GA	05/24/64	Louisville, KY			P4,CSR
Bird, Holloway J.	Cpt	K 15th SCVI	Halltown, WV	08/26/64	Harpers Ferry, WV	08/30/64	Ft. Delaware, DE	CSR
					Ft. Delaware, DE	10/06/64	Pt. Lookout, MD	P43,CSR
					Pt. Lookout, MD	10/11/64	Exchanged	P114,P123,KEB,CSR
Bird, L.G.	Pvt	E 3rd SCMil	Darlington, SC	03/03/65	Hart's Island, NY	06/16/65	Rlsd. G.O. #109	P79
Bird, M.B.	Cpl	K 15th SCVI	Halltown, WV	08/26/64	Halltown, WV		Washington, DC	CSR
					Washington, DC		Camp Chase, OH	CSR
Bird, M.B.	Cpl	K 15th SCVI	Halltown, WV	08/26/64	Harpers Ferry, WV	08/29/64	Camp Chase, OH	CSR
					Camp Chase, OH	03/18/65	Pt. Lookout, MD Xc	P23,P26,KEB,CSR
Bird, Richard W.	Pvt	G 12th SCVI	Petersburg, VA	04/03/65	City Pt., VA	04/07/65	Hart's Island, NY	CSR
					Hart's Island, NY	06/15/65	Rlsd. G.O. #109	P79,CSR
Bird, Samuel A.	Pvt	G 12th SCVI	Gettysburg, PA	07/05/63	Letterman G.H. Gbg	09/25/63	Provost Marshal	P1,CSR
					W. Bldg. Balt., MD	11/12/63	City Pt., VA Xc	P1,CSR
Bird, Stephen	Sgt	2 10/19 SCVI	Missionary Ridge, TN	11/25/63	Nashville, TN	12/07/63	Louisville, KY	P39,RAS,CSR
				11/25/63	Louisville, KY	12/07/63	Rock Island, IL	P88,RAS,CSR
				11/25/63	Rock Island, IL	03/02/65	Trfd. for Xc	CSR
Bird, W. Cooper	Pvt	A 25th SCVI	Ft. Fisher, NC	01/15/65	New York, NY	01/30/65	Elmira, NY	CSR,HAG
					Elmira, NY	07/07/65	Rlsd. G.O. #109	P65,P66,HAG
Bird, W.L.	Pvt	G 2nd SCVI	Gettysburg, PA	07/01/63	Gettysburg, G.H.	08/25/63	Provost Marshal	P4,CSR,SA2,H2
Bird, W.L.	Pvt	G 2nd SCVI	Gettysburg, PA	07/04/63	David's Island, NY	08/29/63	Died of wounds	P1,P5,FPH,CSR
Bird, Wiley	Pvt	G 21st SCVI	Ft. Fisher, NC	01/15/65	Elmira, NY	06/28/65	Rlsd. G.O. #109	P66Gettysburg G.H.
Birke, J. T.	Pvt	H 1st SCVIR	Ft. Fisher, NC	01/15/65	Pt. Lookout, MD	05/15/65	Rlsd. G.O. #85	CSR
Birt, William B.	Pvt	H 17th SCVI	Crater, Pbg., VA	07/30/64	City Pt., VA	08/05/64	Pt. Lookout, MD	CSR
					Pt. Lookout, MD	08/08/64	Elmira, NY	P117,P120,P125,CSR
					Elmira, NY	08/30/64	Died, Typhoid	P5,P12,P65,FPH,CSR
Bishop, A.J.	Pvt	I 5th SCVI	Warrenton, VA	09/29/62	Warrenton, VA	09/29/62	Paroled	CSR
Bishop, A.J.	Pvt	I 5th SCVI	Richmond, VA Hos	04/03/65	Richmond, VA Hos	04/22/65	Paroled	CSR
Bishop, Aaron	Pvt	F 1st SCVIH	Deserted/enemy	03/22/65	City Pt., VA P.M.	03/27/65	Washington, DC P.M	CSR
					Washington, DC P.M	03/29/65	Phila., PA on oath	CSR
Bishop, Adam	Pvt	G 17th SCVI	Petersburg, VA	03/25/65	City Pt., VA	03/28/65	Pt. Lookout, MD	CSR
					Pt. Lookout, MD	06/24/65	Rlsd. G.O. #109	P114,P118,P123,CSR
Bishop, Andrew J.	Pvt	D 16th SCVI	Ringgold, GA	11/27/63	Nashville, TN	12/07/63	Louisville, KY	P39,16R,CSR
					Louisville, KY	12/11/63	Rock Island, IL	P88,P89,CSR
					Rock Island, IL	02/25/65	Pt.Lookout, MD Xc	P131,CSR
					Richmond, VA Hos.	03/08/65	Furloughed 30 days	CSR

SOUTH CAROLINA SOLDIERS, SAILORS AND  CITIZENS HELD IN U.S. PRISONS 1861-1865

NAME	RANK	REGIMENT	CAPTURED AT	WHEN	PRISON	MOVED	DISPOSITION	SOURCES
Bishop, Cornelius M.	Pvt	D 16th SCVI	Missionary Ridge, TN	11/25/63	Nashville, TN	12/04/63	Louisville, KY	CSR
					Louisville, KY	12/09/63	Rock Island, IL	P88,16R,CSR
Bishop, Cornelius M.	Pvt	D 16th SCVI	Missionary Ridge, TN	10/25/64	Rock Island, IL	02/15/65	Pt. Lookout, MD Xc	P131,CSR
					Richmond, VA Hos.	03/20/65	Furloughed 60 days	CSR
Bishop, D.P.	Pvt	A 3rd SCVABn	High Pt., NC	05/02/65	High Pt., NC	05/02/65	Paroled on oath	CSR
Bishop, E.M.	Pvt	C Hol.Leg.	Boonesboro, MD	09/16/62	Ft. Delaware, DE	10/02/62	Aikens Ldg., VA Xc	CSR
Bishop, E.M.	Pvt	C Hol.Leg.	Petersburg, VA	10/27/64	City Pt., VA	10/31/64	Pt. Lookout, MD	CSR
					Pt. Lookout, MD	03/28/65	Aikens Ldg., VA Xc	P124,CSR
Bishop, Elisha A.	Pvt	E 16th SCVI	Missionary Ridge, TN	11/25/63	Nashville, TN	12/05/63	Louisville, KY	P39,16R,CSR
					Louisville, KY	12/06/63	Rock Island, IL	P88,CSR
					Rock Island, IL	02/15/65	Pt. Lookout, MD Xc	P131,CSR
Bishop, G.W.	Pvt	A 19th SCVCB	Augusta, GA	05/26/65	Augusta, GA	05/26/65	Paroled on oath	CSR
Bishop, George W.	Pvt	I Hol.Leg.	Kinston, NC	12/15/62	Kinston, NC	12/15/62	Paroled POW	CSR
Bishop, George W.	Pvt	I Hol.Leg.	Stony Creek, VA	05/07/64	Fts. Monroe, VA	08/03/64	Pt. Lookout, MD	CSR
					Pt. Lookout, MD	08/15/64	Elmira, NY	P113,P117,P120,CSR
					Elmira, NY	06/23/65	Rlsd. G.O. #109	P65,CSR
Bishop, Henry M.	Pvt	B 11th SCVI	Deserted/enemy	03/10/65	Charleston, SC	03/10/65	Released on oath	CSR
Bishop, Isaac C.	Pvt	D Ham.Leg.MI	Deep Bottom, VA	08/17/64	City Pt., VA	08/22/64	Pt. Lookout, MD	CSR
					Pt. Lookout, MD	11/01/64	Exchanged	P113,P117,P124,CSR
Bishop, Isaac C.	Pvt	G Ham.Leg.MI	Richmond, VA Hos	04/03/65	Richmond, VA Hos.	05/15/65	Paroled	CSR
Bishop, J.I.	Pvt	A 19th SCVCB	Augusta, GA	05/26/65	Augusta, GA	05/26/65	Paroled on oath	CSR
Bishop, J.W.	Pvt	A 19th SCVCB	Augusta, GA	05/26/65	Augusta, GA	05/26/65	Paroled on oath	CSR
Bishop, James	Pvt	D 17th SCVI	Crater, Pbg., VA	07/30/64	City Pt., VA	08/05/64	Pt. Lookout, MD	CSR
					Pt. Lookout, MD	08/08/64	Elmira, NY	P117,P120,P125,CSR
					Elmira, NY	11/09/64	Died, Ch. Diarrhea	P6,P65,FPH
Bishop, James T.	Sgt	D 5th SCVI	Wilderness, VA	05/06/64	Belle Plain, VA	05/21/64	Ft. Delaware, DE	CSR
					Ft. Delaware, DE			P41,P45,SA2
					Ft. Delaware, DE	06/10/65	Released	P43,SA3,CSR
Bishop, Joel	Pvt	F 1st SCVIH	Deserted/enemy	03/23/65	City Pt., VA P.M.	03/27/65	Washington, DC P.M	CSR
					Washington, DC P.M	03/29/65	Phila., PA on oath	CSR
Bishop, L.G.	Sgt	C 18th SCVI	Five Forks, VA	04/01/65	City Pt., VA	04/06/65	Pt. Lookout, MD	CSR
					Pt. Lookout, MD	06/24/65	Rlsd. G.O. #109	P114,P118,P123,CSR
Bishop, O.	Pvt	B 19th SCVCB	Augusta, GA	05/26/65	Augusta, GA	05/26/65	Paroled on oath	CSR
Bishop, S..	Pvt	A 3rd SCVABn	High Pt., NC	05/02/65	High Pt., NC	05/02/65	Paroled on oath	CSR
Bishop, Simpson B.	Pvt	F 13th SCVI	Petersburg, VA	04/02/65	City Pt., VA	04/04/65	Pt. Lookout, MD	CSR
					Pt. Lookout, MD	06/24/65	Rlsd. G.O. #109	P114,P118,P123,CSR
Bishop, T..	Pvt	A 3rd SCVABn	High Pt., NC	05/02/65	High Pt., NC	05/02/65	Paroled on oath	CSR
Bishop, W.	Pvt	A 3rd SCVABn	High Pt., NC	05/02/65	High Pt., NC	05/02/65	Paroled on oath	CSR
Bishop, W.J.	Pvt	C 19th SCVCB	Augusta, GA	05/26/65	Augusta, GA	05/26/65	Paroled on oath	CSR
Bishop, William C.	Pvt	I 27th SCVI	Petersburg, VA	06/18/64	Fts. Monroe, VA	07/25/64	Died of wounds	P12,ROH,CSR
Bishop, William J.	Pvt	G 17th SCVI	Five Forks, VA	04/01/65	City Pt., VA	04/06/65	Pt. Lookout, MD	CSR
					Pt. Lookout, MD	06/24/65	Rlsd. G.O. #109	P114,P118,P123,CSR
Bissell, William Swinton	2Lt	I 2nd SCVI	Gettysburg, PA	07/04/63	Letterman G.H. Gbg	10/15/63	Baltimore, MD	P1,SA2,CSR
Bissell, William Swinton	2Lt	I 2nd SCVI	Gettysburg, PA	07/05/63	W. Bldg. Balt., MD	03/02/64	Ft. McHenry, MD	P1,P7,SA2,CSR
Bissell, William Swinton	2Lt	I 2nd SCVI	Gettysburg, PA	07/03/63	Ft. McHenry, MD	06/15/64	Ft. Delaware, DE	P96,H2,CSR
					Ft. Delaware, DE	08/20/64	Hilton Head, SC	P43,P44,CSR
Bissell, William Swinton	2Lt	I 2nd SCVI	Gettysburg, PA	07/03/63	Fort Pulaski, GA	11/19/64	Hilton Head, SC	CSR
					Charleston Hbr. SC	12/15/64	Paroled	H2,CSR
Biter, John	Pvt	C 22nd SCVI	Crater, Pbg., VA	07/30/64	City Pt., VA	08/05/64	Pt. Lookout, MD	CSR
					Pt. Lookout, MD	08/08/64	Elmira, NY	P120
					Elmira, NY	10/10/64	Died	P6,P12,P65,FPH

B

SOUTH CAROLINA SOLDIERS, SAILORS AND CITIZENS HELD IN U.S. PRISONS 1861-1865

NAME	RANK	REGIMENT	CAPTURED AT	WHEN	PRISON	MOVED	DISPOSITION	SOURCES
Biter, Willis	Pvt	C 22nd SCVI	Bermuda Hundred, VA	06/02/64	Fts. Monroe, VA	06/04/64	Pt. Lookout, MD	CSR
					Pt. Lookout, MD	06/06/64	Elmira, NY	P117,CSR
					Elmira, NY	07/01/64	Died, Ch, Diarrhea	P12
Biven, E.R..	Pvt	C 3rd SCVABn	Blakely, AL	04/09/65	Ship Island, MS	05/01/65	Vicksburg, MS Prld	CSR
Bivins, Joseph	Pvt	I 3rd SCVC	Deserted/enemy	03/06/65	Charleston, SC	03/15/65	Rlsd. on oath	CSR
Black, Abraham	Pvt	B 16th SCVI	Ringgold, GA	11/27/63	Nashville, TN	12/07/63	Louisville, KY	P39,16R,CSR
					Louisville, KY	12/11/63	Rock Island, IL	P88,P89,CSR
					Rock Island, IL	03/02/65	Pt.Lookout, MD Xc	P131,CSR
Black, Calvin	Pvt	C 1st SCVA	Smiths Ford, NC	03/16/65	New Berne, NC	04/03/65	Pt. Lookout, MD	CSR
					Pt. Lookout, MD	06/24/65	Rlsd. G.O. #109	P114,P118,CSR
Black, Clarendon	Pvt	H 17th SCVI	Deserted/enemy	11/17/64	Provost Marshal A.	11/20/64	City Pt., VA	CSR
					City Pt., VA	11/23/64	Washington, DC	CSR
					Washington, DC	03/14/65	Charleston, SC	CSR
Black, Cornelius T.	Cpl	A 25th SCVI	Weldon RR, VA	08/21/64	City Pt., VA	08/24/64	Pt. Lookout, MD	CSR,HAG
					Pt. Lookout, MD	03/15/65	Aikens Ldg., VA Xc	P117,P124,P125
Black, Daniel L.	Pvt.	G 7th SCVC	Cypress Bridge, VA	05/07/64	Pt. Lookout, MD	08/15/64	Elmira, NY	P113,P116,P120
					Elmira, nY	09/26/64	Died, Diarrhea	P5,P12,P65,P66,FPH
Black, David	Sgt	D 17th SCVI	Crater, Pbg., VA	07/30/64	Pt. Lookout, MD	08/08/64	Elmira, NY	P117,P120,P125,CSR
					Elmira, NY	02/09/65	Tfd. for exchange	P65,CSR
Black, David W.	Pvt	C 1st SCVA	Smiths Ford, NC	03/16/64	New Berne, NC	04/03/65	Pt. Lookout, MD	CSR
					Pt. Lookout, MD	06/24/65	Rlsd. G.O. #109	P114,P118,P123,CSR
Black, E.T.	2Of	Huntress	Off Charleston	01/18/63	Ft. Lafayette, NY	05/08/63	Rlsd. OO Secy/Navy	P144
Black, G.W.	Pvt	G Orr's Ri.	Appomattox R., VA	04/02/65	Hart's Island, NY	06/15/65	Rlsd. G.O. #109	P79,CSR
Black, Gaines	Pvt	I 6th SCVI	Williamsport, MD	09/15/62	Ft. Delaware, DE	10/02/62	Aikens Ldg., VA Xc	CSR
Black, H.P.	Pvt	A 3rd SCVABn	High Pt., NC	05/02/65	High Pt., NC	05/02/65	Paroled on oath	CSR
Black, Isaac	Pvt	B 16th SCVI	Franklin, TN	11/30/64	Nashville, TN	12/02/64	Louisville, KY	CSR
					Louisville, KY	12/03/64	Camp Douglas, IL	P90,P95,16R,CSR
					Camp Douglas, IL	06/18/65	Rlsd. G.O. #109	P55,CSR
Black, J.R.	Pvt	K 20th SCVI	Cedar Creek, VA	10/19/64	W. Bldg. Balt., MD	11/22/64	Hammond G.H., MD	P4,CSR,KEB
					Pt. Lookout, MD	01/25/65	Hammond G.H., MD	P114,P121,CSR
					Hammond G.H., MD	02/09/65	Pt. Lookout, MD	CSR
					Pt. Lookout, MD	02/10/65	Aikens Ldg., VA Xc	P118,P121,P124,CSR
Black, James	Pvt	L 1st SCVIG	Petersburg, VA	04/02/65	City Pt., VA	04/02/65	Hart's Island, NY	CSR
					Hart's Island, NY	06/16/65	Rlsd. G.O. #109	P79,CSR
Black, John R.	Pvt	G 12th SCVI	Southside RR, VA	04/03/65	City Pt., VA	04/07/65	Hart's Island, NY	CSR
					Hart's Island, NY	06/15/65	Rlsd. G.O. #109	P79
Black, Michael	Pvt	I 1st SCVA	Morris Island, SC	07/10/63	Hilton Head, SC	09/05/63	Ft. Columbus, NY	CSR
					Ft. Columbus, NY	09/23/63	Took the oath	P1,CSR
Black, N.L.	Pvt	C 20th SCVI	Cedar Creek, VA	10/19/64	Harpers Ferry, WV	10/28/64	Pt. Lookout, MD	CSR,KEB
					Pt. Lookout, MD	03/28/65	Aikens Ldg., VA Xc	P118,P123,P124
Black, Orlando	Pvt	C 1st SCVA	Deserted/enemy	02/20/65	Charleston, SC	03/02/65	will take oath	CSR
Black, Paul	Pvt	E 7th SCVI	Cedar Creek, VA	10/19/64	Harpers Ferry, WV	10/24/64	Pt. Lookout, MD	CSR
					Pt. Lookout, MD	03/28/65	Aikens Ldg., VA Xc	P114,P118,P124,HOE
Black, Robert J.	Cpl	F 24th SCVI	Ringgold, GA	11/25/63	Nashville, TN	12/05/63	Louisville, KY	P39
					Louisville, KY	12/06/63	Rock Island, IL	P88
					Rock Island, IL	05/19/65	Released G.O. #85	P131,CSR
Black, S.F.	Pvt	G 7th SCVC	Cypress Bridge, VA	05/07/64	Pt. Lookout, MD	08/15/64	Elmira, NY	P113,P116,P120
					Elmira, NY	02/13/65	Tfd. for exchange	P65
Black, S.L.	Pvt	C 15th SCVI	Cedar Creek, VA	10/19/64	Harpers Ferry, WV	10/24/64	Pt. Lookout, MD	CSR
					Pt. Lookout, MD	03/28/65	Aikens Ldg., VA Xc	P118,P123,P124,CSR
Black, W.E.	Pvt	C 20th SCVI	Cedar Creek, VA	10/19/64	Harpers Ferry, WV	10/28/64	Pt. Lookout, MD	CSR,KEB
					Pt. Lookout, MD	03/17/65	Aikens Ldg., VA Xc	P114,P118,P124,CSR

SOUTH CAROLINA SOLDIERS, SAILORS AND  CITIZENS HELD IN U.S. PRISONS 1861-1865

NAME	RANK	REGIMENT	CAPTURED AT	WHEN	PRISON	MOVED	DISPOSITION	SOURCES
Black, Wash	Pvt	A 2nd SCVA	Fayettville, NC	03/16/65	Pt. Lookout, MD	05/12/65	Released on oath	CSR
Black, William	Mtr	Str. *Calypso*	Blockade Runner		Ft. Lafayette, NY	07/03/63	Ft. Warren, MS	P144
				06/11/63	Ft. Warren, MA			P137
Black, William A.	Pvt	A 2nd SCVC	Martinsburg, WV	07/17/63	Wheeling, WV	07/22/63	Camp Chase, OH	P1,CSR
					Camp Chase, OH	02/29/64	Ft. Delaware, DE	P22,P25,P26,CSR
					Ft. Delaware, DE		(DTE)	P41,P42
Black, William S.	Pvt	A 2nd SCVA	Bentonville, NC	03/16/65	New Berne, NC	03/30/65	Pt. Lookout, MD	CSR
					Pt. Lookout, MD	05/12/65	Released G.O. #85	P114,P118,CSR
Blackburn, J.H.	Pvt	G 7th SCVC			Pt. Lookout, MD	03/08/65	Died, Ch. Diarrhea	P12,FPH
Blackburn, John	Pvt	K 1st SCVA	Deserted/enemy	02/18/65	Charleston, SC	03/02/65	Will take oath	CSR
Blackman, Henry	Pvt	H 14th SCVI	Petersburg, VA	04/02/65	City Pt., VA	04/05/65	Pt. Lookout, MD	CSR
					Pt. Lookout, MD	06/24/65	Rlsd. G.O. #109	P114,P118,P123,CSR
Blackman, Hugh G.	Pvt	F 4th SCVC	Old Church, VA	05/30/64	Pt. Lookout, MD	08/19/64	Died	P5,P117,P119,CSR
Blackman, James	Pvt	B 21st SCVI	Petersburg, VA	06/24/64	Pt. Lookout, MD	08/16/64	Elmira, NY	P113,P120
					Elmira, NY	03/06/65	Died, Diarrhea	P6,P12,P65
Blackmon, Enoch	Pvt	H 12th SCVI	Charlotte, NC	05/23/65	Charlotte, NC	05/23/65	Paroled	CSR
Blackmon, John C.	Pvt	E 12th SCVI	Lancaster, SC	02/27/65	New Berne, NC	03/30/65	Pt. Lookout, MD	P114,P118,LAN,CSR
					Pt. Lookout, MD	06/23/65	Rlsd. G.O. #109	P114,P118,CSR
Blackmon, John E.	Sgt	E 12th SCVI	Spotsylvania, VA	05/12/64	Ft. Delaware, DE	06/16/64	Hos 6/16-6/22/64	P47,LAN
					Ft. Delaware, DE	07/27/64	Hospital, d:8/3/64	P47
					Ft. Delaware, DE	08/03/64	Exchanged	P41
					Ft. Delaware, DE	08/03/64	Died, Typhoid	P5,P12,P43,FPH,CSR
Blackmon, Wesley	Pvt	I 12th SCVI	Gettysburg, PA	07/04/63	David's Island, NY	09/12/63	City Pt., VA Xc	P1,LAN
Blackmon, Wesley	Pvt	I 12th SCVI	Southside RR, VA	04/02/65	Hart's Island, NY	06/15/65	Rlsd. G.O. #109	P79
Blackmon, William J.	Pvt	E 12th SCVI	Funkstown, MD	07/10/63	Frederick, MD USGH	08/07/63	W. Bldg. Balt., MD	P1,CSR
					Hagerstown, MD GH	08/07/63	Baltimore, MD USGH	P2,CSR
					W. Bldg. Balt., MD	08/23/63	City Pt., VA Xc	P1,CSR
					Williamsburg, VA H	09/09/63	Furloughed, Wdd	CSR
Blackwell, A.	Pvt	C 5th SCResB	Kershaw, SC	02/25/65	Hart's Island, NY	06/16/65	Rlsd. G.O. #109	P79
Blackwell, Andrew J.	Pvt	H 1st SCVA	Morris Island, SC		Hilton Head, SC	09/05/63	Ft. Columbus, NY	CSR
					Ft. Columbus, NY	09/23/63	Took the oath	P1,CSR
Blackwell, B.F.	Pvt	K 12th SCVI	Falling Waters, MD	07/14/63	Baltimore, MD	08/16/63	Pt. Lookout, MD Xc	CSR
					Pt. Lookout, MD		Joined US Army	P113,P116,P125,CSR
Blackwell, George	Pvt	H 1st SCVIR	Chesterfield, SC	02/25/65	New Berne, NC	04/10/65	Hart's Island, NY	CSR
					Hart's Island, NY	06/16/65	Rlsd. G.O. #109	P79,SA1,CSR
Blackwell, J.D.	Pvt	K Hol.Leg.	Five Forks, VA	04/01/65	City Pt., VA	04/05/65	Pt. Lookout, MD	CSR
					Pt. Lookout, MD	06/23/65	Rlsd. G.O. #109	P114,P118,P123,CSR
Blackwell, John	Pvt	K 1st SCVA	Smiths Ford, NC	03/16/65	New Berne, NC	04/03/65	Pt. Lookout, MD	CSR
					Pt. Lookout, MD	06/23/65	Rlsd. G.O. #109	P114,P118,CSR
Blackwell, John C.	Sgt	A 2nd SCVC	Florence, SC	03/05/65	New Berne, NC	04/03/65	Pt. Lookout, MD	CSR
					Pt. Lookout, MD	06/24/65	Rlsd. G.O. #109	P114,P118,P123,CSR
Blackwell, M.C.	Pvt	K Hol.Leg.	Stony Creek, VA	05/07/64	Fts. Monroe, VA	05/13/64	Pt. Lookout, MD	CSR
					Pt. Lookout, MD	08/15/64	Elmira, NY	P113,P116,P120,CSR
					Elmira, NY	06/23/65	Rlsd. G.O. #109	P65,CSR
Blackwell, Robert	Pvt	G 12th SCVI	Petersburg, VA	03/25/65	City Pt., VA	03/28/65	Pt. Lookout, MD	CSR
					Pt. Lookout, MD	06/24/65	Rlsd. G.O. #109	P114,P118,P123
Blackwell, Samuel	Pvt	B 6th SCVC	Louisa C.H., VA	06/12/64	Pt. Lookout, MD	07/25/64	Elmira, NY	P113,P117,FPH,CSR
					Elmira, NY	02/03/65	Died, Diarrhea	P6,P12,P65,CSR
Blackwell, Simpson	Sgt	K Hol.Leg.	Five Forks, VA	04/01/65	City Pt., VA	04/05/65	Pt. Lookout, MD	CSR
					Pt. Lookout, MD	06/24/65	Rlsd. G.O. #109	CSR

SOUTH CAROLINA SOLDIERS, SAILORS AND  CITIZENS HELD IN U.S. PRISONS 1861-1865

NAME	RANK	REGIMENT	CAPTURED AT	WHEN	PRISON	MOVED	DISPOSITION	SOURCES
Blackwell, Uriah A.	Pvt	B 7th SCVIBn	Weldon RR, VA	08/21/64	City Pt., VA USFH	08/24/64	Washington, DC USG	CSR
					Alexandria, VA USG	08/27/64	Washington, DC USG	P1,CSR
					Lincoln G.H., DC	12/04/64	Old Capitol, DC	CSR
					Old Capitol, DC	12/16/64	Elmira, NY	P110,CSR
					Elmira, NY	03/10/65	James R., VA Xc	P65,P66,HAG,CSR
Blackwell, Wiley	Pvt	B 26th SCVI	Hatchers Run, VA	03/29/65	City Pt. VA	04/02/65	Pt. Lookout, MD	CSR
					Pt. Lookout, MD	06/24/65	Rlsd. G.O. #109	P114,P118,P123,CSR
Blackwell, William B.	Pvt	B 1st SCVA	Smith's Farm, NC	03/16/65	Smith's Farm, NC	03/16/65	paroled	CSR
Blackwood, F.A.	Pvt	G 17th SCVI	Richmond, VA	04/03/65	Richmond, VA	04/14/65	Libby Prison, P.M.	CSR
					Libby Prison, Rchm	04/23/65	Newport News, VA	CSR
					Newport News, VA	06/27/65	Rlsd. G.O. #109	P107,CSR
Blackwood, G. Gibbes	Cpl	A 25th SCVI	Ft. Fisher, NC	01/15/65	New York, NY	01/30/65	Elmira, NY	CSR,HAG
					Elmira, NY	07/26/65	Rlsd. G.O. #109	P65,P66,CSR
Blackwood, James	Pvt	K Hol.Leg.	Warrenton, VA	09/29/62	Warrenton, VA	09/29/62	Paroled/ Hospital	CSR
Blackwood, John K.	Pvt	K Hol.Leg.	Stony Creek, VA	05/07/64	Fts. Monroe, VA	05/13/64	Pt. Lookout, MD	CSR
					Pt. Lookout, MD	08/15/64	Elmira, NY	P113,P116,P120,CSR
					Elmira, NY	12/15/64	Died	P6,P12,P65,FPH,CSR
Blackwood, Marcus	Pvt	F 13th SCVI	N. Anna River, VA	05/23/64	Port Royal, VA	05/20/64	Pt. Lookout, MD	CSR
					Pt. Lookout, MD	10/30/64	Aikens Ldg., VA Xc	P113,P117,P124,CSR
Blain, J.	Pvt	B 20th SCVI	Cedar Creek, VA	10/19/64	Pt. Lookout, MD	06/06/65	Rlsd. on oath	CSR
Blain, James M.	Pvt	H 6th SCVI	Fair Oaks, VA	05/31/62	Fts. Monroe, VA	06/05/62	Ft. Delaware, DE	CSR
					Ft. Delaware, DE	08/06/62	Aikens Ldg., VA Xc	CSR
Blair, David	Pvt	E Hol.Leg.	Warrenton, VA	09/29/62	Warrenton, VA	09/29/62	Paroled/Hospital	CSR
Blair, Irvin	Pvt	F 6th SCVI	Richmond, VA	10/07/64	Dutch Gap Canal, VA	10/21/64	Pt. Lookout, MD	CSR
					Pt. Lookout, MD	10/29/64	City Pt., VA Xc	P114,CSR
					City Pt., VA	02/10/65	Exchanged	CSR
Blake, Charles G.	Pvt	C 27th SCVI	Deserted/enemy	05/31/64	Bermuda Hundred, VA	06/01/64	Fts. Monroe, VA	CSR
					Fts. Monroe, VA	06/11/64	New York, NY oath	P8,HAG,CSR
Blake, Francis D.	Cpt	A 1st SCVA	Bentonville, NC	03/22/65	New Berne, NC	04/10/65	Hart's Island, NY	CSR
					Hart's Island, NY	04/15/65	Ft. Delaware, DE	P79,CSR
					Ft. Delaware, DE	06/17/65	Rlsd. G.O. #109	P43,P45,P47,CSR
Blake, Julias Augustus	LtC	27th SCVI	Weldon RR, VA	08/21/64	Ft. McHenry, MD	08/27/64	Ft. Delaware, DE	P110,HAG
					Washington, DC	08/29/64	Ft. Delaware, DE	CSR,LC,HAG
					Ft. Delaware, DE	10/30/64	Pt. Lookout, MD	P43
					Pt. Lookout, MD	10/31/64	Exchanged	P114,HAG
Blake, William	Pvt	C 12th SCVI	Falling Waters, MD	07/14/63	Frederick, MD USGH	08/07/63	Baltimore, MD USGH	CSR
					W. Bldg. Balt., MD	09/25/63	City Pt., VA Xc	CSR
					Richmond, VA Hos.	10/03/63	Clothing issued	CSR
Blake, William	Pvt	C 12th SCVI	Spotsylvania, VA	05/12/64	Belle Plain, VA	05/20/64	Ft. Delaware, DE	CSR
					Ft. Delaware, DE	06/10/65	Released	P41,P43,P45
Blakeley, Harvey W.	Pvt	E 10th SCVI	Murfreesboro, TN	01/01/63	Nashville, TN	04/17/63	Louisville, KY	P38,RAS,CSR
					Louisville, KY	04/27/63	City Pt., VA Xc	P88,P93,CSR
					Petersburg, VA	06/12/63	Furloughed 40 days	CSR
Blakeley, Harvey W.	Pvt	5 10/19 SCVI	Missionary Ridge, TN	11/25/63	Nashville, TN	12/07/63	Louisville, KY	P39,CSR
					Louisville, KY	12/09/63	Rock Island, IL	P88,P89,CSR
					Rock Island, IL	06/20/65	Rlsd. G.O. #109	P131,CSR
Blakely, Henry P.	Pvt	F 14th SCVI	Gettysburg, VA	07/04/63	David's Island, NY	09/08/63	City Pt., VA Xc	CSR
					Richmond, VA Hos.	09/16/63	Furloughed 60 days	CSR

SOUTH CAROLINA SOLDIERS, SAILORS AND **B** CITIZENS HELD IN U.S. PRISONS 1861-1865

NAME	RANK	REGIMENT	CAPTURED AT	WHEN	PRISON	MOVED	DISPOSITION	SOURCES
Blakely, J.K.	Pvt	G 27th SCVI	Petersburg, VA	06/24/64	Bermuda Hundred, VA	06/25/64	Fts. Monroe, VA	CSR,HAG
					Fts. Monroe, VA	06/26/64	Pt. Lookout, MD	CSR
					Pt. Lookout, MD	08/16/64	Elmira, NY	P117,P118,P120,CSR
					Elmira, NY	10/11/64	Pt.Lookout to Xc	P65
					Pt. Lookout, MD	10/29/64	Venus Pt., GA Xc	P114,P123
Blakely, J.W.	Pvt	I 14th SCVI	Petersburg, VA	04/02/65	City Pt., VA	04/07/65	Hart's Island, NY	CSR
					Hart's Island, NY	06/15/65	Rlsd. G.O. #109	P79,CSR
Blakely, Madison P.	Pvt	F 14th SCVI	Petersburg, VA	07/28/64	City Pt., VA	08/05/64	Pt. Lookout, MD	CSR
					Pt. Lookout, MD	08/08/64	Elmira, NY	P113,P117,P120
					Elmira, NY	03/14/65	James R., VA Xc	P65,CSR
Blakely, Rutherford R.	Cpl	F 14th SCVI	Gettysburg, PA	07/05/63	Chester, PA G.H.	10/03/63	Pt. Lookout, MD	P1,CSR
					Pt. Lookout, MD	03/03/64	City Pt., VA Xc	P116,CSR
					Richmond, VA Hos.	03/16/64	Furloughed 30 days	CSR
Blakeney, George W.	Pvt	A 1st SCVIR	Morris Island, SC	09/07/63	Ft. Columbus, NY	10/09/63	Pt. Lookout, MD	CSR,SA1
					Pt. Lookout, MD	02/13/65	Aikens Ldg., VA Xc	P113,P121,P124,CSR
Blanchard, Oscar	Pvt	Ferguson's	Graysville, GA	11/27/63	Nashville, TN	12/11/63	Louisville, KY	CSR
					Louisville, KY	12/12/63	Rock Island, IL	P89,CSR
					Rock Island, IL	10/11/64	Vol. USA/rejected	P131,CSR
Bland, Lawrence W.	Pvt	A 7th SCVI	Bentonville, NC	03/19/65	New Berne, NC	03/31/65	Pt. Lookout, MD	CSR
					Pt. Lookout, MD	06/23/65	Rlsd. G.O. #109	P114,P118,CSR
Blanding, H.W.	ASr	1st SCV	Gillisonville, SC	01/16/65	Ft. Delaware, DE	04/03/65		P43,P47
					Ft. Delaware, DE	06/17/65	Rlsd. G.O. #109	P43
Blanton, Ambrose	Pvt	F 15th SCVI	Sharpsburg, MD	09/17/62	Frederick, MD G.H.	10/01/62	Died, Typhoid	P1,P6,KEB,FPH,CSR
Blanton, J.L.	Pvt	K Hol.Leg.	Stony Creek, VA	05/07/64	Fts. Monroe, VA	05/13/64	Pt. Lookout, MD	CSR
					Pt. Lookout, MD	08/15/64	Elmira, NY	P113,P116,P120
					Elmira, NY	10/11/64	Pt. Lookout, MD Xc	P65
					Pt. Lookout, MD	10/29/64	Aikens Ldg., VA Xc	P114,P118
Blanton, John	Pvt	M P.S.S.	Deserted/enemy	03/05/65	Bermuda Hundred, VA	03/07/65	City Pt., VA	CSR
					City Pt., VA	03/07/65	Washington, DC	CSR
					Washington, DC	03/08/65	Nashville, TN oath	CSR,TSE
Blanton, Joseph	Pvt	M P.S.S.	Virginia	04/09/65	City Pt., VA GH	04/21/65	Steamer St/Maine	CSR
					Steamer St/Maine	05/01/65	Wash.D.C./dead	CSR,TSE
					Washington, DC	05/02/65	Died, Typhoid	P12
Blanton, Lewis L.	Pvt	D 27th SCVI	Wilmington, NC	02/20/65	Pt. Lookout, MD	06/24/65	Rlsd. G.O. #109	P121,P123
Blanton, William H.	Pvt	M P.S.S.	Richmond, VA Hos.	04/03/65	Libby Prsn. Rchmd.	04/08/65	Pt. Lookout, MD	CSR
					Pt. Lookout, MD	06/05/65	Released	P114,P119,CSR
Blanton, William M.	Pvt	K Hol.Leg.	Stony Creek, VA	05/07/64	Fts. Monroe, VA	05/13/64	Pt. Lookout, MD	CSR
					Pt. Lookout, MD	08/15/64	Elmira, NY	P113,P117,P120,CSR
					Elmira, NY	10/11/64	Pt. Lookout, MD Xc	P65,CSR
					Pt. Lookout, MD	10/29/64	Aikens Ldg., VA Xc	P114,P118,P123,CSR
Blassingame, Thomas	Pvt	K 5th SCVC	Stony Creek, VA	12/01/64	City Pt., VA	12/05/64	Pt. Lookout, MD	CSR
					Pt. Lookout, MD	06/24/65	Rlsd. G.O. #109	P123,CSR
Blassingham, H.	Pvt	A 3rd SCVABn	High Pt., NC	05/02/65	High Pt., NC	05/02/65	Paroled on oath	CSR
Blichington, James W.	Pvt	G 1st SCVIH	Richmond, VA Hos.	04/03/65	Libby Prison Rchmd	04/14/65	Pt. Lookout, MD	CSR
					Pt. Lookout, MD	06/23/65	Rlsd. G.O. #109	P114,P119,SA1,CSR
Blizzard, Darling A.	Pvt	B 7th SCVIBn	Weldon RR, VA	08/21/64	City Pt., VA	08/24/64	Pt. Lookout, MD	CSR,HAG
					Pt. Lookout, MD	10/11/64	Coxes Wh., VA Xc	P113,P117,P123,CSR
					Richmond, VA Hos.	10/24/64	Furloughed 30 days	CSR
Blizzard, E.W.	Pvt	B 3rd SCVABn	Ft. Tyler, GA	04/16/65	Ft. Tyler, GA	04/23/65	Macon, GA Prison	CSR
Blizzard, James T.	Pvt	B 7th SCVIBn	Weldon RR, VA	08/21/64	City Pt., VA USFH	08/26/64	Alexandria, VA USG	CSR
					Alexandria, VA USG	08/28/64	Washington, DC USG	P1,HAG,CSR
					Lincoln G.H., DC	10/29/64	Died, of wounds	P5,P110,CSR

SOUTH CAROLINA SOLDIERS, SAILORS AND  CITIZENS HELD IN U.S. PRISONS 1861-1865

NAME	RANK	REGIMENT	CAPTURED AT	WHEN	PRISON	MOVED	DISPOSITION	SOURCES
Blizzard, James William	Pvt	B 3rd SCVABn	Ft. Tyler, GA	04/16/65	Ft. Tyler, GA	04/23/65	Macon, GA Prison	CSR
Blizzard, William	Pvt	B 1st SCVA	Deserted/enemy	02/18/65	Fts. Monroe, VA	04/02/65	Washington, DC	CSR
					Washington, DC	04/05/65	Charleston, SC	CSR
Blocker, T.J.	Pvt	K 1st SCVIR	Waynesboro, NC	03/16/65	New Berne, NC	03/30/65	Pt. Lookout, MD	SA1,CSR
					Pt. Lookout, MD	05/26/65	Died, Lung Inflam.	P6,P114,P118,P119
Bloodworth, Samuel	Pvt	F 19th SCVI	Augusta, GA	05/23/65	Augusta, GA	05/23/65	Paroled	CSR
Bloom, John	Pvt	H 17th SCVI	Warrenton, VA	09/29/62	Warrenton, VA	09/29/62	Paroled	CSR
Bloomingburg, D.B.	Pvt	B 11th SCVI	Deserted/enemy	03/13/65	Charleston, SC	03/13/65	Released on oath	CSR
Blue, William	Pvt	I 1st SCVIH	Frederick, MD	09/12/62	Ft. Delaware, DE	10/02/62	Aikens Ldg., VA Xc	CSR
Blum, Otto	Pvt	B 1st SCVA	Smith's Farm, NC	03/16/65	New Berne, NC	03/31/65	Hart's Island, NY	CSR
					Hart's Island, NY	06/16/65	Rlsd. G.O. #109	P79,CSR
Blume, C.C.	Pvt	K 2nd SCVI	Staunton, VA	05/10/65	Staunton, VA	05/10/65	Paroled	SA2,H2,CSR
Blume, John H.	Pvt	A 14th SCVI	NC or SC	03/29/65	New Berne, NC USGH	04/09/65	Died, Pleurisy	P1,P6,P12,CSR
Boag, John T.	Pvt	D 1st SCVA	Black River, SC	03/16/65	Pt. Lookout, MD	05/14/65	Released G.O. #85	P118
Boag, William	Pvt	E 18th SCVAB	Deserted/enemy	02/18/65	Hilton Head, SC	04/07/65	P.M. New York, NY	CSR
Boan, Archer E.	Cpl	E 21st SCVI	Petersburg, VA	06/24/64	Bermuda Hundred VA	06/25/64	Fts. Monroe, VA	CSR,HAG
					Fts. Monroe, VA	06/26/64	Pt. Lookout, MD	CSR
					Pt. Lookout, MD	08/16/64	Elmira, NY	P113,P117,P120
					Elmira, NY	10/11/64	Pt.Lookout , MD Xc	P65
					Pt. Lookout, MD	10/29/64	Venus Pt., GA Xc	P114,P118,P123
Boan, Archer E.	Cpl	E 21st SCVI	Black Creek, SC	03/01/65	New Berne, NC	04/03/65	Pt. Lookout, MD	CSR
					Pt. Lookout, MD	06/24/65	Rlsd. G.O. #109	P118,P121,P123
					Washington, DC	06/26/65	Wheeling, WV	CSR
Boan, B.F.	Pvt	C 23rd SCVI	Five Forks, VA	04/01/65	City Pt., VA	04/06/65	Pt. Lookout, MD	CSR,HOM
					Pt. Lookout, MD	06/24/65	Rlsd. G.O. #109	P114,P118,P123,CSR
Boan, Daniel	Pvt	E 21st SCVI	Morris Island, SC	07/10/63	Hilton Head, SC	07/23/63	Morris Island, SC Xc	P2,HAG,CSR
Boan, Daniel	Pvt	E 21st SCVI	Cheraw, SC	03/05/65	Cheraw, SC	03/05/65	Paroled on oath	CSR
Boan, John S.	Pvt	I 1st SCVA	Black Creek, SC	03/01/65	New Berne, NC	04/03/65	Pt. lookout MD	CSR
					Pt. Lookout, MD	06/24/65	Rlsd. G.O. #109	P114,P121,CSR
Boan, Richard J.	Pvt	E 21st SCVI	Morris Island, SC	07/10/63	Hilton Head, SC	07/23/63	Morris Island, SC Xc	P2,HAG,CSR
					Hilton Head, SC	07/23/63	Morris Island, SC Xc	P2,HAG,CSR
Boatwright, Azariah J.	Pvt	K 13th SCVI	Gettysburg, PA	07/05/63	David's Island, NY	09/08/63	City Pt. VA, Xc	CSR
Boatwright, Azariah J.	Pvt	K 13th SCVI	Hatcher's Run, VA	03/31/65	City Pt., VA	04/02/65	Pt. Lookout, MD	CSR
					Pt. Lookout, MD	06/24/65	Rlsd. G.O.#109	CSR
Boatwright, Isaiah	Pvt	D 1st SCVA	Rockingham, NC	03/05/65	New Berne, NC	03/31/65	Hart's Island, NY	CSR
					Hart's Island, NY	07/01/65	David's Island, NY	P79,CSR
Boatwright, Isaiah	Pvt	D 1st SCVA	Rockingham, NC	03/05/65	David's Island, NY	10/19/66	Died, consumption	P1,CSR
Boatwright, Sumter	Pvt	B Ham.Leg.MI	Augusta, GA	05/22/65	Augusta, GA	05/22/65	Paroled	CSR
Boatwright, Thomas	Pvt	C 6th SCResB	Augusta, GA	05/18/65	Augusta, GA	05/18/65	Paroled	CSR
Boazman, L.J.	3Lt	F 3rd SCVI	Sharpsburg, MD	09/17/62	Sharpsburg, MD	10/17/62	Died of wounds	P12,SA2,H3,CSR
Boazman, W.M.	Pvt	G 2nd SCVC	Culpepper, VA	09/13/63	Old Capital, DC	09/16/63	Pt. Lookout, MD	CSR
					Ft. McHenry, VA	09/26/63	Pt. Lookout, MD	P110
					Pt. Lookout, MD	08/16/64	Elmira, NY	P116,P118,P120,CSR
					Elmira, NY	10/11/64	Pt. Lookout, MD Xc	P65,CSR
					Pt. Lookout, MD	10/29/64	Exchanged	P114,P123,P124
					Pt. Lookout, MD	10/29/64	Venus Pt., GA Xc	CSR
Bobb, Francis	Pvt	H Hol.Leg.	Petersburg, VA	11/06/64	City Pt., VA	11/11/64	Washington, DC	CSR,ANY
					Pt. Lookout, MD	06/22/65	Rlsd. G.O. #109	P114,P118,CSR
Bobo, Barham	1Sg	B 15th SCVI	Halltown, WV	08/21/64	Harpers Ferry, WV	08/29/64	Camp Chase, OH	CSR
					Camp Chase, OH	03/18/65	Pt. Lookout, MD	P23,P26,KEB,CSR
					Pt. lookout, MD	03/27/65	Boulwares Wh., VA	H15,CSR
Bobo, Charles B.	Sgt	C 18th SCVI	Hatchers Run, VA	03/29/65	Pt. Lookout, MD	06/24/65	Rlsd. G.O. #109	P114,P118,P123,CSR

SOUTH CAROLINA SOLDIERS, SAILORS AND  CITIZENS HELD IN U.S. PRISONS 1861-1865

NAME	RANK	REGIMENT	CAPTURED AT	WHEN	PRISON	MOVED	DISPOSITION	SOURCES
Bobo, Edwin H.	1Lt	E Hol.Leg.	Five Forks, VA	04/01/65	City Pt., VA	04/04/65	Old Capitol, DC	CSR
					Old Capitol, DC	04/09/65	Johnson's Isl., OH	CSR
					Johnson's Isl., OH	06/11/65	Released	P81,P83,CSR
Bobo, James E.	Pvt	E Hol.Leg.	Hatchers Run, VA	03/29/65	City Pt., VA	04/09/65	Lincoln G.H., DC	CSR
					Old Capitol, DC	06/12/65	Released	P110
Bobo, Jason	Pvt	B 15th SCVI	Halltown, WV	08/21/64	Harpers Ferry, WV	08/29/64	Camp Chase, OH	CSR
					Camp Chase, OH	03/26/65	Pt. Lookout, MD	P23,P26,KEB,CSR
Bobo, Jason	Pvt	B 15th SCVI	Halltown, WV	08/20/64	Pt. Lookout, MD	06/24/65	Rlsd. G.O. #109	P114,P119,P123,CSR
Boesch, John J.	Cpl	C 27th SCVI	Town Creek, NC	02/20/65	Ft. Anderson, NC	02/28/65	Pt. Lookout, MD	CSR,HAG
Boesch, John J.	Pvt	C 27th SCVI	Town Creek, NC	02/20/65	Pt. Lookout, MD	06/24/65	Rlsd. G.O. #109	P114,P121,P123,HAG
Bogan, Benjamin G.	Pvt	H 1st SCVIG	Petersburg, VA	07/29/64	City Pt., VA	08/05/64	Pt. Lookout, MD	CSR
					Pt. Lookout, MD	08/08/64	Elmira, NY	P113,P117,P120,CSR
					Elmira, NY	12/09/64	Died, Heart Dis.	P6,P12,P65,FPH,CSR
Bogan, John C.	Pvt	A Hol.Leg.	Five Forks, VA	04/01/65	City Pt., VA	04/05/65	Pt. Lookout, MD	CSR
					Pt. Lookout, MD	06/24/65	Rlsd. G.O. #109	P114,P118,P123,CSR
Bogan, Robert F.	Pvt	H 1st SCVIH	Warrenton, VA	09/29/62	Warrenton, VA	09/29/62	Paroled	CSR
Bogan, Robert F.	Pvt	H 1st SCVIH	Deserted/enemy	08/25/64	Bermuda Hundred, VA	08/28/64	North on oath	CSR
Boggs, J. Thomas	Pvt	I P.S.S.	Deserted/enemy	03/18/65	Bermuda Hundred, VA	03/22/65	City Pt., VA P.M.	CSR
					City Pt., VA P.M.	03/24/65	Washington, DC	CSR
Boggs, J. Thomas	Pvt	I P.S.S.	Deserted/enemy	03/18/65	Washington, DC	03/25/65	Franklin Cty., IL	CSR
Boggs, J.A.	Pvt	D Ham.Leg.MI	Richmond, VA Hos.	04/03/65	Richmond, VA Hos.	04/14/65	Provost Marshal	CSR
					Libby Prsn. Rchmd.	04/23/65	Newport News, VA	CSR
					Newport News, VA	07/01/65	Rlsd. G.O. #109	P107,CSR
Boggs, J.H.	Pvt	G 1st SCVIR	Bentonville, NC	03/22/65	New Berne, NC	04/10/65	Hart's Island, NY	CSR
					Hart's Island, NY	06/16/65	Rlsd. G.O. #109	SA1,P79,CSR
Boland, James	Pvt	B 1st SCVIR	Morris Island, SC	09/01/64	Hilton Head, SC	10/03/64	On oath, at QM work	CSR
Boland, James M.	Pvt	H Hol.Leg.	Five Forks, VA	04/01/65	City Pt., VA	04/05/65	Pt. Lookout, MD	CSR
					Pt. Lookout, MD	06/23/65	Rlsd. G.O. #109	P114,P118,ANY
Bolding, James H.	Pvt	F Orr's Ri.	Petersburg, VA	04/03/65	City Pt., VA	04/11/65	Hart's Island, NY	CSR
					Hart's Island, NY	06/16/65	Rlsd. G.O. #109	CSR, P79
Boldt, J.D.	Pvt	F 11th SCVI	Ft. Fisher, NC	01/15/65	Pt. Lookout, MD	02/02/65	Hammond G.H., MD	P121
					Pt. Lookout, MD	07/19/65	Rlsd. G.O. #109	P118,CSR
Bolen, J.	Pvt	B 20th SCVI	Cedar Creek, VA	10/19/64	Harpers Ferry, WV	10/25/64	Pt. Lookout, MD	CSR
					Pt. Lookout, MD	06/06/65	Rlsd. G.O. #85	P114,KEB,CSR
Bolin, Louis	Pvt	B 12th SCVI	Spotsylvania, VA	05/12/64	Belle Plain, VA	05/21/64	Ft. Delaware, DE	CSR,YEB
					Ft. Delaware, DE	08/16/64	Hos 8/16-8/26/64	P47
					Ft. Delaware, DE	06/08/65	Released	P41,P43,P45,CSR
Bolin, Thomas	Pvt	K Ham.Leg.	Lookout Mtn., TN	10/29/63	Nashville, TN	02/28/64	Louisville, KY	CSR
					Louisville, KY	02/29/64	Ft. Delaware, DE	P90,P91,P94,CSR
					Ft. Delaware, DE	03/23/64	Hos 3/23-4/6/64	P47,CSR
					Ft. Delaware, DE	07/20/64	To Hos 7/20/64	P47
					Ft. Delaware, DE	07/28/64	Died, Typhoid	P5,P41,P43,P47,CSR
Bolivar, George	2Lt	I 2nd SCVA	Deserted/enemy	02/23/65	Hilton Head, SC	03/22/65	New York, NY/ oath	CSR
Bolon, Edward	Pvt	C 1st SCVIR	Smith's Ford, NC	03/16/65	New Berne, NC	04/03/65	Pt. Lookout, MD	SA1,CSR
					Pt. Lookout, MD	06/09/65	Rlsd. on oath	P114,P118,SA1,CSR
Bolt, Abraham	Pvt	G 22nd SCVI	Farmville, VA	04/06/65	City Pt., VA	04/14/65	Newport News, VA	CSR
					Newport News, VA	06/26/65	Rlsd. G.O. #109	CSR
Bolt, Dorah	Pvt	C 14th SCVI	Petersburg, VA	07/29/64	City Pt., VA	08/05/64	Pt. Lookout, MD	CSR
					Pt. Lookout, MD	08/08/64	Elmira, NY	P113,P117,P120,CSR
					Elmira, NY	06/21/65	Rlsd. G.O. #109	P65,CSR
Bolt, James B.	Pvt	C 14th SCVI	Sutherland Stn., VA	04/02/65	City Pt., VA	04/07/65	Hart's Island, NY	CSR
					Hart's Island, NY	06/16/65	Rlsd. G.O. #109	P79,CSR

B

SOUTH CAROLINA SOLDIERS, SAILORS AND CITIZENS HELD IN U.S. PRISONS 1861-1865

NAME	RANK	REGIMENT	CAPTURED AT	WHEN	PRISON	MOVED	DISPOSITION	SOURCES
Bolt, W.	Pvt	C 14th SCVI	Farmville, VA	04/11/65	Farmville, VA	04/21/65	Paroled	CSR
Bolt, W. Pinckney	Pvt	A 3rd SCVI	Gettysburg, PA	07/04/63	Gettysburg G.H.	07/21/63	Provost Marshal	P4,KEB,,SA2,H3,CSR
					David's Island, NY	08/24/63	City Pt., VA Xc	P1,CSR
Bolt, William L.	Cpl	G 22nd SCVI	South Mtn., MD	09/14/62	Frederick, MD Hos.	01/15/63	Baltimore, MD Hos.	CSR
					Camden St. Balt H	02/14/63	Ft. McHenry, MD	CSR
					Ft. McHenry, MD	02/18/63	City Pt., VA Xc	CSR
Bolt, William L.	Pvt	G 22nd SCVI	Petersburg, VA	04/03/65	Farmville, VA	04/21/65	Pt.of Rocks G.H.VA	CSR
Bolton, Moses S.	Pvt	Brooks LA	Harpers Farm, VA	04/06/65	City Pt., VA	04/14/65	Pt. Lookout, MD	CSR
					Pt. Lookout, MD	06/24/65	Rlsd. G.O. #109	P119,P121,P123,CSR
Bolton, William S.	Pvt	G 5th SCVI	Wilderness, VA	05/06/64	Belle Plain, VA	05/21/64	Ft. Delaware, DE	CSR
					Ft. Delaware, DE	03/28/65	Hos.3/28-4/3/65	P47
					Ft. Delaware, DE	06/10/65	Released	P41,P43,P45,SA3
Bolton, J.H.	Pvt	B 20th SCVI	Deserted/enemy	02/11/65	Fts. Monroe, VA	04/02/65	Washington, DC	CSR
					Washington, DC	04/05/65	Charleston, SC	CSR
Bomar, George W.	Pvt	B 25th SCVI	Ft. Fisher, NC	01/15/65	New York, NY	01/30/65	Elmira, NY	CSR,HAG
					Elmira, NY	06/16/65	Rlsd. G.O. #109	P65,P66,CSR
Bomar, J.E.	Pvt	C 27th SCVI	Petersburg, VA	06/24/64	Fts. Monroe, VA	06/26/64	Pt. Lookout, MD	CSR,HAG
					Pt. Lookout, MD	09/18/64	Aikens Ldg., VA Xc	P113,P117,P123,CSR
Bomar, W.M.	Pvt	F 13th SCVI	Petersburg, VA	04/02/65	City Pt., VA	04/04/65	Pt. Lookout, MD	CSR
					Pt. Lookout, MD	06/24/65	Rlsd. G.O. #109	P114,P118,CSR
Bomar, William B.	Pvt	C 27th SCVI	Town Creek, NC	02/20/65	Ft. Anderson, NC	02/28/65	Pt. Lookout, MD	CSR,HAG
					Pt. Lookout, MD	06/24/65	Rlsd. G.O. #109	P114,P123,CSR
Bonamire, Henry	Pvt	F 4th SCVI	1st Manassas, VA	07/21/61	Ft. McHenry, MD	11/13/62	Fts. Monroe, VA Xc	P145,SA2,CSR
Bond, William	Pvt	C 1st SCVA	Ft. Moultrie, SC	06/10/64	Morris Island, SC	09/01/64	Hilton Head, SC	CSR
Bone, William	Pvt	C 14th SCVI	Falling Waters, MD	07/14/63	Baltimore, MD	08/17/63	Pt. Lookout, MD	CSR
					Pt. Lookout, MD	03/03/64	City Pt., VA Xc	P116,P123,P124,CSR
Bone, William W.	Pvt	F 7th SCVIBn	Weldon RR, VA	08/21/64	City Pt., VA	08/24/64	Pt. Lookout, MD	CSR,HAG
					Pt. Lookout, MD	01/27/65	Aikens Ldg., VA Xc	P113,P118,P124,CSR
Bonham, C.C.	Pvt	E 13th SCVI	Burkeville, VA	04/06/65	Pt. Lookout, MD	06/24/65	Rlsd. G.O. #109	P114,HOS
Bonham, W.C.	Pvt	E 13th SCVI	Gettysburg, PA	07/05/63	College House Hos	07/19/63	Ft. McHenry, MD	CSR
					Ft. McHenry, MD	07/31/63	Ft. Delaware, DE	CSR
					Ft. Delaware, DE	09/18/63	Died, typhoid	P5,P40,P47,FPH,CSR
Boniface, Louis	Pvt	D 23rd SCVI	Richmond, VA Hos.	04/09/65	Provost Marshal	04/11/65	Baltimore, MD/oath	CSR
Bonner, Wiley	Pvt	A 24th SCVI	Marietta, GA	06/19/64	Nashville, TN	06/24/64	Louisville, KY	P3
					Louisville, KY	06/27/64	Camp Morton, IN	P91
					Camp Morton, IN	02/13/65	Died, Lung Inflam.	P6,EFW
Bonnet, C.	Pvt	C 18th SCVI	Deserted/enemy	03/01/65	Washingon, DC	03/06/65	New York, NY	CSR
Bonneval, H.	Pvt	D 18th SCVAB	Salisbury, NC	04/12/65	Louisville, KY	04/26/65	Camp Chase, OH	CSR
					Camp Chase, OH	06/13/65	Rlsd. G.O. #109	CSR
Bonney, Usher P.	1Lt	H 7th SCVC	Old Church, VA	05/30/64	White House, VA	06/08/64	Pt. Lookout, MD	CSR
					Pt. Lookout, MD	06/23/64	Ft. Delaware, DE	P46,P113,P117,P120
					Ft. Delaware, DE	06/16/65	Rlsd. G.O. #109	P43,P44,P45,CSR
Bookman, O.H.	Pvt	F 12th SCVI	Gettysburg, PA	07/03/63	W. Bldg. Balt, MD	09/25/63	City Pt., VA Xc	P1,HFC,CSR
Boone, John	Pvt	G 2nd SCVI	Gettysburg, PA	07/03/63	Ft. McHenry, MD	07/12/63	Ft. Delaware, DE	CSR
					Ft. Delaware, DE		Hos 12/20-12/22/64	P47
					Ft. Delaware, DE	06/10/65	Rlsd. G.O. #109	P40,P42,P45,SA2,H2,CSR
Boone, Llewellen P.	Pvt	G 1st SCVIG	Gettysburg, PA	07/05/63	Ft. McHenry, MD	07/30/63	Ft. Delaware, DE	CSR,SA1
					Ft. Delaware, DE	02/29/64	Hos 2/29-3/14/64	P47
					Ft. Delaware, DE	05/03/64	Hos 5/3-5/27/64	P47
					Ft. Delaware, DE	09/20/64	Hos 9/20-10/30/64	P47
					Ft. Delaware, DE	10/30/64	Pt.Lookout to Xc	P40,P42,P44,CSR
					Pt. Lookout, MD	10/31/64	Aikens Ldg. Xc	P114,P118,P123

SOUTH CAROLINA SOLDIERS, SAILORS AND B CITIZENS HELD IN U.S. PRISONS 1861-1865

NAME	RANK	REGIMENT	CAPTURED AT	WHEN	PRISON	MOVED	DISPOSITION	SOURCES
Boone, Llewellen P.	Pvt	G 1st SCVIG	Petersburg, VA	04/02/65	Pt. Lookout, MD	06/24/65	Rlsd. G.O. #109	P114,P118,P123
Boone, W.H.	Pvt	E 1st SCVC	Bennettsville, SC	03/05/65	Pt. Lookout, MD	06/14/65	Rlsd. G.O. #109	P114
Booth, G.G.	Cpl	Brooks LA	South Mtn., MD	07/04/63	Ft. Delaware, DE	07/30/63	City Pt., VA Xc	P40,P42
Boothe, Benjamin W.	Pvt	A 19th SCVI	Atlanta, GA	07/22/64	Nashville, TN	07/24/64	Louisville, KY	CSR
					Louisville, KY	07/31/64	Camp Chase, OH	P90,P91,HOE
					Camp Chase, OH	03/04/65	City Pt., VA Xc	P26,CSR
Boothe, James E.	Pvt	H 19th SCVI	Dalton, GA	10/17/64	Nashville, TN	10/23/64	Louisville, KY	CSR
					Louisville, KY	10/26/64	Camp Douglas, IL	P90,P91,P95,HOE
					Camp Douglas, IL	04/14/65	Jd. 5th USVI	P55,CSR
Boozer, Thomas N.	Pvt	G 13th SCVI	Farmville, VA	04/12/65	Farmville, VA	04/14/65	Paroled	CSR
Boozer, Cornelius P	Pvt	C 3rd SCVI	Knoxville, TN	12/04/63	Nashville, TN	02/28/64	Louisville, KY	P39,KEB,SA2,H3,CSR
					Louisville, KY	02/29/64	Ft. Delaware, DE	P90,P91,P94,CSR
					Ft. Delaware, DE	08/18/64	Exchanged	P41,CSR
					Richmond, VA Hos.	08/25/64	Furloughed 60 days	CSR
Boozer, Frederick A.	Pvt	H Hol.Leg.	Petersburg, VA	11/06/64	City Pt., VA	11/11/64	Pt. Lookout, MD	CSR
					Pt. Lookout, MD	02/10/65	Aikens Ldg., VA Xc	P114,P118,ANY
					Jackson Hos. Rchmd.	02/21/65	Furloughed 60 days	CSR
Boozer, Frederick S.	Sgt	K 5th SCVC	Pamunkey River, VA	05/28/64	Alexandria, VA US	06/10/64	Lincoln G.H., DC	P1,CSR,CDC,UD5
					Lincoln G.H., DC	07/21/64	Died of wounds	P6,P110,CSR
Boozer, H.D.	Cpl	C Hol.Leg.C	James Gate, VA	11/22/62	Fts. Monroe, VA	11/29/62	Exchanged	CSR
Boozer, Henry S.	Cpt	H Hol.Leg.	Five Forks, VA	04/01/65	Old Capitol, DC	04/09/65	Johnsons Isl., OH	CSR
					Johnson's Isl., OH	06/18/65	Rlsd. G.O. #109	P81,P83,CSR
Boozer, John C.	Pvt	G Hol.Leg.	Five Forks, VA	04/02/65	City Pt., VA	04/05/65	Pt. Lookout, MD	CSR
					Pt. Lookout, MD	06/04/65	Released, sick list	P114,P118,ANY
Boozer, Simon P.	Pvt	F 2nd SCVI	Gettysburg, PA	07/05/63	Letterman G.H. Gbg	10/01/63	Provost Marshal	P1,KEB,H2,CSR
					W. Bldg. Balt., MD	11/12/63	City Pt., VA Xc	SA2,P1,CSR
Boozer, William G.	Sgt	F 2nd SCVI	Gettysburg, PA	07/04/63	Gettysburg, PA G.H.	10/01/63	Provost Marshal	P4,KEB,H2,CSR
					W. Bldg. Balt., MD	11/12/63	City Pt., VA Xc	SA2,P1,CSR
Boren, Manchester	Pvt	F 22nd SCVI	Bermuda Hundred, VA	06/02/64	Fts. Monroe, VA	06/04/64	Pt. Lookout, MD	CSR
					Pt. Lookout, MD	07/05/64	Died, Dysentery	P12,P119,CSR
Boren, William	Pvt	F 22nd SCVI	Bermuda Hundred, VA	06/02/64	Fts. Monroe, VA	06/04/64	Pt. Lookout, MD	CSR
					Pt. Lookout, MD	02/18/65	Aikens Ldg., VA Xc	P117,P123,P124,CSR
					Aikens Ldg., VA	02/23/65	Richmond, VA Hos.	CSR
					Richmond, VA Hos.	03/17/65	60 days Furlough	CSR
Boscheen, Charles	Pvt	A 15th SCVI	Cold Harbor, VA	06/07/64	White House, VA	06/15/64	Pt. Lookout, MD	P7,KEB,CSR
					Pt. Lookout, MD	05/10/65	Rlsd. on Oath	P113,P122,P124,CSR
Bosdell, S.A.	Pvt	C 7th SCVI	Gettysburg, PA	07/04/63	David's Island, NY	08/24/63	City Pt., VA Xc	P1,CSR
Bosse, C. Lewis	Sgt	C Hol.Leg.	Richmond Hos., VA	04/09/65	Pt. Lookout, MD	06/26/65	Rlsd. G.O. #109	P119,HOS
Bostick, James N.	Cpl	6 10/19 SCVI	Missionary Ridge, TN	11/25/63	Nashville, TN	12/07/63	Louisville, KY	P39,RAS,CSR
					Louisville, KY	12/07/63	Rock Island, IL	P88,P89,CSR
					Rock Island, IL	03/02/65	Pt.Lookout to Xc	P131,CSR
Bostick, Joseph H.	Pvt	McQueen LA	Petersburg, VA	04/02/65	City Pt., VA	04/04/65	Pt. Lookout, MD	P114,P118,CSR
					Pt. Lookout, MD	06/24/65	Rlsd. G.O. #109	P114,P118,CSR
Bostick, L.R.	Sgt	K 4th SCVC	Old Church, VA	05/30/64	Pt. Lookout, MD	03/14/65	Aikens Ldg., VA Xc	P113,P117,P124,CSR
Boswell, B.	Pvt	Pee Dee LA	Fountain Dale, PA	06/28/63	Ft. McHenry, MD	07/06/63	Ft. Delaware, DE	CSR
					Ft. Delaware, DE	10/26/63	Pt. Lookout, MD	CSR
					Pt. Lookout, MD	02/18/65	Exchanged	P124,PDL,CSR
Boswell, J.P.	Cpl	G 3rd SCVABn	High Pt., NC	05/01/65	High Pt., NC	05/01/65	Paroled on oath	CSR
Bott, J.B.	Pvt	2nd SCVI	Deserted/enemy	03/03/65	City Pt., VA P.M	03/05/65	Washington, D.C.	CSR
					Washington, DC P.M	03/08/65	Ohio on oath	CSR
Bottger, Diedr	Pvt	C German LA	Deserted/enemy	07/06/63	Pennsylvania			CSR

SOUTH CAROLINA SOLDIERS, SAILORS AND  CITIZENS HELD IN U.S. PRISONS 1861-1865

NAME	RANK	REGIMENT	CAPTURED AT	WHEN	PRISON	MOVED	DISPOSITION	SOURCES
Botts, Charles A.	Pvt	G Orr's Ri.	Falling Waters, MD	07/14/63	Baltimore, MD	08/16/63	Pt. Lookout, MD	CSR,CDC
					Pt. Lookout, MD	08/16/64	Elmira, NY	P113,P116,P120
					Elmira, NY	03/10/65	Pt.Lookout, MD Xc	P65,P124,CSR
Botts, F.A.	Pvt	F Hol.Leg.	Jarratts Stn., VA	05/08/64	Fts. Monroe, VA	05/13/64	Elmira, NY	CSR
					Pt. Lookout, MD	08/13/64	Elmira, NY	P117,P120
					Elmira, NY	05/14/64	Died, Ch. Diarrhea	P6,P12,P65,FPH,CSR
Botts, J.G.	Cpl	F Hol.Leg.	Jarratts Stn., VA	05/08/64	Fts. Monroe, VA	05/08/64	Pt. Lookout, MD	CSR
					Pt. Lookout, MD	05/13/64	Elmira, NY	P117,P120
					Elmira, NY	03/14/65	James R., VA Xc	P65,CSR
Bouchelle, J.N.	Chp	13th SCVI	Gettysburg, PA	07/05/63	Ft. McHenry, MD	07/14/63	Ft. Delaware, DE	CSR
					Ft. Delaware, DE	07/27/63	Johnson's Isl., OH	P42,P44,CSR
					Johnson's Isl., OH	10/14/63	City Pt., VA Xc	CSR
Bouknight, Asaiah J.	Pvt	K 13th SCVI	Gettysburg, PA	07/05/63	David's Island, NY	09/05/63	City Pt., VA Xc	P1,CSR
Bouknight, Asaiah J.	Pvt	K 13th SCVI	Hatchers Run, VA	03/31/65	Pt. Lookout, MD	06/24/65	Rlsd. G.O. #109	P114,P118,P123,CSR
Bouknight, Daniel P.	Pvt	B Ham.Leg.MI	Newton, NC	04/19/65	Newton, NC	04/19/65	Paroled	CSR
Bouknight, S.J.	Pvt	M 7th SCVI	Gettysburg, PA	07/05/63	Letterman G.H., Gbg	09/25/63	Provost Marshal	P1,CSR
					W. Bldg. Balt., MD	11/12/63	City Pt., VA Xc	P1,KEB,CSR
Boulware, B.F.	Pvt	B 4th SCVC	Old Church, VA	05/30/64	White House, VA	06/08/64	Pt. Lookout, MD	CSR,HHC
					Pt. Lookout, MD	06/22/64	Elmira, NY	P117,P120,CSR
					Elmira, NY	06/14/65	Rlsd. G.O. #109	P65,UD2,CSR
Boulware, Daniel P.	Pvt	B 17th SCVI	Warrenton, VA	09/29/82	Warrenton, VA	09/29/62	Paroled	CSR
Boulware, J.H.	Pvt	G 7th SCVI	Charlotte, NC	05/15/65	Charlotte, NC	05/15/65	Paroled	CSR
Boulware, J.R.	ASr	6th SCVI	Knoxville, TN	01/26/64	Knoxville, TN	02/12/64	U.S. Medical Direc	P84,CSR
Bounds, Leonard Rush	Cpl	C 1st SCVIR	Deserted/enemy	09/30/64	Chattanooga, TN	09/27/64	took oath of amnesty	CSR,SA1
					Louisville, KY	10/14/64	Remain N. of Ohio R.	P8,P92,CSR
Bouschette, A.R.	Pvt	Santee LA	Pratt Bluff, SC	04/08/65	Charleston, SC			CSR
Boutet, A.M.	Pvt	B 7th SCVC	Old Church, VA	05/30/64	White House, VA	06/08/64	Pt. Lookout, MD	CSR
					Pt. Lookout, MD	07/25/64	Elmira, NY	P113,P117,P120,CSR
					Elmira, NY	03/10/65	James R., VA Xc	P65,CSR
Boutet, A.M.	Pvt	B 7th SCVC	Albany, GA	05/10/65	Albany, GA	05/22/65	Paroled	CSR
Bowden, Reuben	Pvt	B 1st SCResB	Salisbury, NC	04/12/65	Nashville, TN	04/29/65	Louisville, KY	P39,P95
					Louisville, KY	05/02/65	Camp Chase, OH	P92
					Camp Chase, OH	06/13/65	Released GO #109	P23
Bowen, A. Cornelius	Pvt	G Orr's Ri.	Cashtown, PA	07/06/63	Chester, PA G.H.	07/27/63	Died, Diarrhea	P1,P6,P12,CSR,FPH
Bowen, Charles	Pvt	F 21st SCVI	Richmond, VA Hos.	04/03/65	Newport News, VA	06/24/65	Rlsd. G.O. #109	P107,HAG
Bowen, D.P.	Pvt	I 1st SCVIR	Raleigh, NC Hos.	04/13/65	Raleigh, NC	04/13/65	Paroled	SA1,CSR
Bowen, Elijah M.	Pvt	H 1st SCVA	Morris Island, SC	07/10/63	Hilton Head, SC	09/19/63	Ft. Columbus, NY	CSR
					Ft. Columbus, NY	09/23/63	took the oath	P1,CSR
Bowen, John	Pvt	B 1st SCVIR	Cheraw, SC	03/04/65	New Berne, NC	04/10/65	Hart's Island, NY	CSR
					Hart's Island, NY	06/16/65	Rlsd. G.O. #109	CSR
Bowen, John H.	Cpt	K Ham.Leg.	Chattanooga, TN	10/29/63	Nashville, TN	11/07/63	Louisville, KY	P39,CSR
					Louisville, KY	11/09/63	Camp Chase, OH	P89,P93,SA2,CSR
					Johnson's Isl., OH	10/04/64	Pt. Lookout, MD	P82,CSR
					Pt. Lookout, MD	10/11/64	Aikens Ldg., VA Xc	P117,P123,CSR
Bowen, Jonathan	Pvt	B 1st SCRes	Cheraw, SC	03/04/65	Hart's Island, NY	06/16/65	Rlsd. G.O. #109	P79
Bowen, N.J.N.	Cpl	Lafayette, LA	Gillisonville, SC	01/16/65	Hilton Head, SC	02/01/65	Pt. Lookout, MD	CSR
					Pt. Lookout, MD	02/18/65	Exchanged	P124,CSR
Bowen, N.J.N.	Cpl	Lafayette, LA	Chester, SC	05/05/65	Chester, SC	05/05/65	Paroled	CSR
Bowers, Andrew M.	1Lt	D 13th SCVI	Gettysburg, PA	07/05/63	Chester, PA Hos.	10/04/63	Pt. Lookout, MD GH	P1,CSR
					Pt. Lookout, MD	10/20/63	Johnson's Isl., OH	P120,P121,CSR
					Johnson's Isl., OH	02/10/64	Pt. Lookout, MD	P80,P82,CSR
					Pt. Lookout, MD	04/27/64	City Pt., VA Xc	P113,P117,P123,CSR

SOUTH CAROLINA SOLDIERS, SAILORS AND CITIZENS HELD IN U.S. PRISONS 1861-1865

NAME	RANK	REGIMENT	CAPTURED AT	WHEN	PRISON	MOVED	DISPOSITION	SOURCES
Bowers, Anthony B.	Sgt	H 22nd SCVI	Kinston, NC	12/15/62	Kinston, NC	12/15/62	Paroled POW	CSR
Bowers, Anthony B.	Sgt	H 22nd SCVI	Crater, Pbg., VA	07/30/64	City Pt., VA	08/05/64	Pt. Lookout, MD	CSR
					Pt. Lookout, MD	08/08/64	Elmira, NY	P113,P117,P120,CSR
					Elmira, NY	03/07/65	Died, Ch. Diarrhea	P6,P12,P65,FPH,CSR
Bowers, Charles E.	Sgt	D 24th SCVI	Nashville, TN	12/16/64	Nashville, TN	12/31/64	Louisville, KY	CSR
					Louisville, KY	01/05/65	Camp Chase, OH	P95,EFW
					Camp Chase, OH	01/13/65	Died, Pneumonia	P6,P23,P27,FPH
Bowers, Godfrey C.	2Lt	A 2nd SCVIRi	Knoxville, TN	04/10/65	Nashville, TN	05/14/65	Louisville, KY	P39,CSR
					Louisville, KY	06/16/65	Rlsd. G.O. #109	P92,P95,CSR
Bowers, J.W.	Pvt	F 1st SCVIR	Deserted/enemy	03/22/65	Charleston, SC	03/22/65	Paroled on oath	SA1,CSR
Bowers, J.W.	Pvt	A 19th SCVCB	Augusta, GA	05/29/65	Augusta, GA	05/29/65	Paroled on oath	CSR
Bowers, Jacob Andrew	Pvt	I 15th SCVI	South Mtn., MD	09/14/62	Frederick, MD	10/10/62	Died	P6,FPH,KEB
Bowers, James F.	Pvt	C Ham.Leg.	Knoxville, TN	12/05/63	Louisville, KY	12/29/63	Smallpox Hos. Lvle	CSR
					Smallpox Hos.Lvle	03/07/64	Louisville, KY GH	CSR
					Louisville, KY	03/09/64	Camp Chase, OH	P90,P94,CSR
					Camp Chase, OH	02/15/65	Died, Pneumonia	P6,P27,FPH,CSR,P22
					Camp Chase, OH	02/25/65	City Pt., VA Xc	CSR
Bowers, James Smiley	Cpl	H Hol.Leg.	Five Forks, VA	04/02/65	City Pt., VA MD	04/05/65	Pt. Lookout, MD	CSR
					Pt. Lookout, MD	06/03/65	Died, Dysentery	P6,P118,P119,FPH
Bowers, John	Pvt	H Hol.Leg.	Petersburg, VA	04/03/65	Fair Gds. Hos Pbg.	04/10/65	Died of wounds	P6,P12,ANY,CSR
Bowers, John S.	1Lt	G 13th SCVI	Farmville, VA	04/07/65	Farmville, VA	05/03/65	Died of wounds	P6,P12,R47,CSR
Bowers, Malcolm	Pvt	I 1st SCVIH	Warrenton, VA	09/29/62	Warrenton, VA	09/29/62	Paroled	CSR
Bowers, N.T.	Pvt	C Ham.Leg.MI			master rolls 9 &10, '64		In enemy hands, '64	CSR
Bowers, Robert	Pvt	C 1st SCVC	Deserted/enemy	03/22/65	Charleston, SC	03/23/65	Released on oath	CSR
Bowers, Samuel J.	Pvt	D 1st SCVIH	Lancaster, SC	03/01/65	New Berne, NC	03/30/65	Pt. Lookout, MD	CSR
					Pt. Lookout, MD	06/23/65	Rlsd. G.O. #109	P114,P118,SA1,CSR
Bowers, William J.	Pvt	H 2nd SCVI	Bentonville, NC	03/19/65	New Berne, NC	03/30/65	Pt. Lookout, MD	CSR,SA2,H2
					Pt. Lookout, MD	06/23/65	Rlsd. G.O. #109	P114,P118,CSR
Bowick, Joseph	Pvt	H 19th SCVI	Atlanta, GA	07/22/64	Nashville, TN	07/29/64	Louisville, KY	CSR
					Louisville, KY	07/31/64	Camp Chase, OH	P90,P91
					Camp Chase, OH	03/04/65	City Pt., VA Xc	CSR
Bowie, Alexander	Pvt	A 18th SCVAB	James Island, SC	02/10/65				CSR,STR
Bowie, Augustus L.	Pvt	F Hol.Leg.	Five Forks, VA	04/01/65	City Pt., VA	04/05/65	Pt. Lookout, MD	CSR
					Pt. Lookout, MD	06/24/65	Rlsd. G.O. #109	P114,P118,P123,CSR
Bowie, F.E.	1Lt	F Hol.Leg.	Jarratts Stn., VA	05/08/64	Fts. Monroe, VA	05/13/64	Pt. Lookout, MD	CSR
					Pt. Lookout, MD	06/23/64	Ft. Delaware, DE	P113,P117,P120
					Ft. Delaware, DE	06/16/65	Rlsd. G.O. #109	P43,P45,P46
Bowie, Henry B.	Pvt	F Hol.Leg.	Five Forks, VA	04/01/65	City Pt., VA	04/05/65	Pt. Lookout, MD	CSR
					Pt. Lookout, MD	06/24/65	Rlsd. G.O. #109	P114,P118,P123,CSR
Bowie, Jacob H.	Pvt	F Hol.Leg.	Five Forks, VA	04/01/65	City Pt., VA	04/05/65	Pt. Lookout, MD	CSR
					Pt. Lookout, MD	06/24/65	Rlsd. G.O. #109	P114,P118,P123,CSR
Bowie, James A.	Pvt	A 18th SCVAB	James Island, SC	02/10/65				CSR,STR
Bowie, James A.	Pvt	A 2nd SCVIRi	Burkeville, VA	04/14/65	Burkeville, VA	04/17/65	Paroled	CSR
Bowie, Thomas J.M.	Pvt	F Hol.Leg.	Five Forks, VA	04/01/65	City Pt., VA	04/05/65	Pt. Lookout, MD	CSR
					Pt. Lookout, MD	06/24/65	Rlsd. G.O. #109	P114,P118,CSR
Bowles, Peter	2Lt	G 21st SCVI	Weldon RR, VA	08/21/64	Ft. McHenry, MD	08/27/64	Ft. Delaware, DE	P110,HAG
					Ft. Delaware, DE	03/07/65	Dschgd. Hospital	P46,P47
					Ft. Delaware, DE	05/16/65	Rlsd. G.O. #85	P43
Bowlin, William N.	Sgt	G 12th SCVI	Appomattox R., VA	04/03/65	City Pt., VA	04/13/65	Pt. Lookout, MD	CSR
					Pt. Lookout, MD	06/24/65	Rlsd. G.O. #109	P114,P119,P123,CSR
Bowling, Berry	Pvt	I P.S.S.	Deserted/enemy	03/18/65	Bermuda Hundred, VA	03/25/65	Washington, DC	CSR
Bowling, C.B.	Pvt	F 13th SCVI	Deserted/enemy	02/27/65	Washington, DC	02/27/65	Springfield, IL	CSR

B

SOUTH CAROLINA SOLDIERS, SAILORS AND CITIZENS HELD IN U.S. PRISONS 1861-1865

NAME	RANK	REGIMENT	CAPTURED AT	WHEN	PRISON	MOVED	DISPOSITION	SOURCES
Bowman, D.R.	CSg	H 11th SCVI	Petersburg, VA	08/22/64	Died	08/23/64		P12,CSR
Bowman, H.W.G.	1Lt	B 11th SCVI	Weldon RR, VA	08/21/64	Old Capitol, DC	08/27/64	Ft. Delaware, DE	CSR
					Ft. McHenry, MD	08/27/64	Ft. Delaware, DE	P110,HAG
					Ft. Delaware, DE	05/19/65	Disch. hospital	P46,P47
					Ft. Delaware, DE	06/21/65	Releasd G.O.#109	CSR
Bowman, N.	Pvt	A 23rd SCVI	Kinston, NC	12/14/62	Kinston, NC	12/31/62	paroled	CSR
Bowman, N.	Pvt	A 23rd SCVI	Deserted/enemy	05/15/63	Charleston, SC		No other data	CSR
Bowman, N.	Pvt	B 11th SCVI	Deserted/enemy	03/14/65	Charleston, SC	03/14/65	Released on oath	CSR
Bowman, Samuel John	Cpl	D 2nd SCVI	Gettysburg, PA	07/03/63	W. Bldg. Balt., MD	07/30/63	Baltimore, MD Jail	P1,KEB,H2,CSR
					Baltimore, MD	08/21/63	Pt. Lookout, MD	SA2,CSR
					Pt. Lookout, MD	03/17/64	City Pt., VA Xc	P116,P123,P124
Bowman, W.	Pvt	B 11th SCVI	Deserted/enemy	03/11/65	Charleston, SC	03/11/65	Released on oath	CSR
Boyce, J.E.	Cpl	C 23rd SCVI	Deserted/enemy	02/18/65	Charleston, SC	02/18/65	Rlsd. on oath	CSR
Boyce, Jerry I.	Pvt	A 25th SCVI	Deserted/enemy	03/29/65	Charleston, SC	03/29/65	Released on oath	CSR
Boyce, John	Pvt	E 25th SCVI	Ft. Fisher, NC	01/15/65	New York, NY	01/30/65	Elmira, NY	CSR
					Elmira, NY	05/15/65	Released on oath	CSR
Boyce, S.P.	Pvt	A 3rd SCVABn	High Pt., NC	05/02/65	High Pt., NC	05/02/65	Paroled on oath	CSR
Boyd, B.	Pvt	D Hol.Leg.	Petersburg, VA	04/03/65	Pt. Lookout, MD	06/24/65	Rlsd. G.O. #109	P123
Boyd, Benjamin	Pvt	Brooks LA	Richmond, VA	04/03/65	Richmond, VA Hos.	04/05/65	Libby Prison Rchmd	CSR
					Libby Prison Rchmd	04/13/65	City Pt., VA	CSR
					City Pt., VA	04/14/65	Pt. Lookout, MD	CSR
					Pt. Lookout, MD	06/24/65	Rlsd. G.O. #109	CSR
Boyd, Calhoun Fair	Sgt	E 3rd SCVI	Cedar Creek, VA	10/19/64	Winchester, VA USF	10/17/64	Baltimore, MD USGH	H3,CSR
					W. Bldg. Balt., MD	01/07/65	Pt. Lookout, MD	P4,KEB
					Pt. Lookout, MD	01/25/65	Hammond G.H., MD	P114,CSR
					Hammond G.H., MD	07/27/65	Rlsd. G.O. #109	CSR
Boyd, Daniel	Cpl	D 7th SCVI	Gettysburg, PA	07/04/63	Gettysburg G.H.		Provost Marshal	P4
					David's Island, NY	08/24/63	City Pt., VA Xc	P1,KEB,CSR
Boyd, E.B.	Pvt	H 6th SCVI	Augusta, GA	05/20/65	Augusta, GA	05/20/65	Paroled	CSR
Boyd, Isaac	Pvt	E 2nd SCVA	Deserted/enemy	02/21/65	Charleston, SC	02/21/65	Released on oath	CSR
Boyd, J.H.	Pvt	C 14th SCVI	Petersburg, VA	04/03/65	City Pt., VA	04/11/65	Hart's Island, NY	CSR
					Hart's Island, NY	06/21/65	Rlsd. G.O. #109	P79,CSR
Boyd, J.H.	Pvt	E 25th SCVI	Ft. Fisher, NC	01/15/65	Pt. Lookout, MD	06/24/65	Rlsd. G.O. #109	P123,CSR
Boyd, J.S.	Pvt	E Ham.Leg.MI	Farmville, VA	04/11/65	Farmville, VA	04/11/65	Paroled	CSR
Boyd, James A.	Pvt	D 13th SCVI	Gettysburg, PA	07/01/63	Baltimore, MD Hos	07/20/63	Died, of wounds	CSR
Boyd, James Brown	Sgt	I 2nd SCVI	Sharpsburg, MD	09/17/62	Sharpsburg, MD	09/17/62	Died of wounds	SA2,P12,H2,CSR
Boyd, Jesse	Sgt	G 10th SCVI	Murfreesboro, TN	01/01/63	Nashville, TN			P38,CSR
					Murfreesboro, TN	01/10/63	Died of wounds	P12,CSR,RAS
Boyd, Julius F.	Pvt	Palmetto, L A	Coldfield, VA	04/07/65	City Pt., VA	04/14/65	Pt. Lookout, MD	CSR
					Pt. Lookout, MD	06/24/65	Rlsd. G.O. #109	CSR
Boyd, L.D.	Pvt	D 13th SCVI	Petersburg, VA	04/02/65	City Pt., VA	04/13/65	Pt. Lookout, MD	CSR
					Pt. Lookout, MD	06/24/65	Rlsd. G.O. #109	CSR
Boyd, Patrick	Pvt	3rd SCVC	Deserted/enemy	03/25/65	Charleston, SC	03/25/65	Taken oath & disch	CSR
Boyd, R.J.	Pvt	B 2nd SCVC	Beverly Ford, VA	06/09/63	Old Capitol, DC	06/25/63	City Pt., VA Xc	CSR
					Ft. McHenry, MD	06/25/63	City Pt., VA Xc	P110
Boyd, Samuel D.	Pvt	D 13th SCVI	Hatcher's Run, VA	04/02/65	City Pt., VA	04/13/65	Pt. Lookout, MD	CSR,ANY
					Pt. Lookout, MD	06/24/65	Rlsd. G.O. #109	P114,P119,P123,CSR
Boyd, T.W.	Pvt	G 3rd SCVIBn	South Mtn., MD	09/14/62	Ft. Delaware, DE	10/02/62	Aikens Ldg., VA Xc	CSR
Boyett, Benjamin	Pvt	I 2nd SCVI	Sharpsburg, MD	09/17/62	Frederick, MD USGH	12/29/62	Ft. McHenry, MD	CSR
					Ft. McHenry, MD	05/17/63	Ft. Monroe, VA Xc	SA2,H2,CSR
Boykin, Henry T.	Pvt	H 7th SCVIBn	Weldon RR, VA	08/21/64	City Pt., VA	08/24/64	Pt. Lookout, MD	CSR,HAG
					Pt. Lookout, MD	09/30/64	City Pt., VA Xc	P113,P117,P124,CSR

SOUTH CAROLINA SOLDIERS, SAILORS AND  CITIZENS HELD IN U.S. PRISONS 1861-1865

NAME	RANK	REGIMENT	CAPTURED AT	WHEN	PRISON	MOVED	DISPOSITION	SOURCES
Boykin, James F.	Pvt	E 2nd SCVI	Gettysburg, PA	07/05/63	Harrisburg, PA	07/07/63	Philadelphia, PA	CSR
					Ft. Delaware, DE	06/08/65	Rlsd. G.O. #109	SA2,P40,P42,P44,H2,CSR
Boykin, John	Pvt	A 2nd SCVC	Martinsburg, WV	07/17/63	Wheeling, WV	07/22/63	Camp Chase, OH	P1,CSR
					Camp Chase, OH	02/29/64	Ft. Delaware, DE	P22,P25,P26,CSR
					Ft. Delaware, DE	03/23/64	Died	P5,P41,P47,FPH
Boykin, Manley H.	Pvt	G 20th SCVI	Cedar Creek, VA	10/19/64	W. Bldg. Balt, MD	01/07/65	Pt. Lookout, MD	P4,KEB,CSR
					Pt. Lookout, MD	01/25/65	Hammond G.H., MD	P114
					Pt. Lookout, MD	02/10/65	Aikens Ldg., VA Xc	P118,P123
					Pt. Lookout, MD	06/24/65	Rlsd. G.O. #109	CSR
Boykin, Samuel	Pvt	A 2nd SCVC	Martinsburg, WV	07/13/63	Wheeling, WV	07/23/63	Camp Chase, OH	P1,CSR
					Camp Chase,OH	02/29/64	Ft. Delaware, DE	P22,P25,P26,CSR
					Ft. Delaware, DE	06/10/65	Rlsd. G.O. #109	P41,P42,P45,CSR
Boykin, Stephen Madison	Col	20th SCVI	Cedar Creek, VA	10/19/64	Ft. Delaware, DE	04/09/65	Dschgd Frm. Hos.	P45,P46,P47
					Ft. Delaware, DE	07/24/65	Rlsd. G.O. #109	P43,LC,CSR
Boyle, George	Pvt	A Orr's Ri.	Fairfax Co., VA	06/01/64	Old Capitol, DC	07/23/64	Elmira, NY	CSR
					Ft. McHenry, MD	07/23/64	Elmira, NY	P110
					Elmira, NY	05/15/65	Released	P65,CDC,CSR
Boyle, James	Pvt	D 23rd SCVI	Petersburg, VA	03/25/65	Washington, DC	03/30/65	Pt. Lookout, MD	CSR
					Pt. Lookout, MD	05/12/65	Rlsd. G.O. #85	P114,P118,CSR
Boyle, John C.	2Lt	G 21st SCVI	Weldon RR, VA	08/21/64	Old Capitol, DC	08/27/64	Ft. Delaware, DE	CSR
					Ft. McHenry, MD	08/27/64	Ft. Delaware, DE	P110,HAG
					Ft. Delaware, DE	03/07/65		P7,HAG
					Ft. Delaware, DE	03/20/65	Rlsd Secy of War	P43,P45,CSR
Boyle, Patrick	Pvt	Col.Post G	Columbia, SC	02/19/65	Hart's Island, NY	06/22/65	Rlsd. G.O. #109	P79
Boyles, E.B.	Pvt	C 14th SCVI	Gettysburg, PA	07/04/63	David's Island, NY	08/24/63	City Pt., VA Xc	P1
Boyles, J.R.	2Lt	C 12th SCVI	Gettysburg, PA	07/03/63	Bedloes Island, NY	10/24/63	Johnson's Isl., OH	P2,CSR
					David's Island, NY	10/29/63	Johnson's Isl., OH	P1,CSR
					Johnson's Isl., OH	02/09/64	Baltimore, MD	P80,CSR
Boyles, J.R.	2Lt	C 12th SCVI	Gettysburg, PA	07/05/63	Johnson's Isl., OH	02/10/64	Pt. Lookout, MD	P82
					Pt. Lookout, MD	03/03/64	City Pt., VA Xc	P113,P117,P123,CSR
Boynton, James B.	1Lt	H 17th SCVI	Petersburg, VA	03/25/65	Old Capitol, DC	03/30/65	Ft. Delaware, DE	P110,CSR
					Ft. Delaware, DE	06/17/65	Rlsd. G.O. #109	P43,P45,CSR
Boynton, William R.	Pvt	H 17th SCVI	Petersburg, VA	03/25/65	City Pt., VA	03/28/65	Pt. Lookout, MD	CSR
					Pt. Lookout, MD	06/24/65	Rlsd. G.O. #109	P114,P118,P123,CSR
Boys, A.S.	Pvt	17th SCVI	Athens, GA	05/08/65	Athens, GA	05/08/65	Paroled	CSR
Bozard, David T.	Pvt	G 25th SCVI	Ft. Fisher, NC	01/15/65	New York, NY	01/31/65	Elmira, NY	CSR
					Elmira, NY	07/07/65	Rlsd. G.O. #109	P65,P66,HAG,CSR
Bozard, J.D.	Pvt	B 20th SCVI	Cedar Creek, VA	10/19/64	W. Bldg. Balt, MD	11/22/64	Pt. Lookout, MD	P4,KEB,CSR
					Pt. Lookout, MD	01/28/65	Hammond G.H., MD	P114,P121,P123,CSR
					Pt. Lookout, MD	07/25/65	Rlsd. G.O. #109	P118,CSR
Bozard, Jacob C.	Pvt	G 25th SCVI	Town Creek, NC	02/20/65	Ft. Anderson, NC	02/28/65	Pt. Lookout, MD	P123,CSR
					Pt. Lookout, MD	06/24/65	Rlsd. G.O. #109	P114,HAG
Bozeman, Henry	Pvt	F 8th SCVI	Gettysburg, PA	07/04/63	Letterman G.H. Gbg	09/25/63	W. Bldg. Balt, MD	P1,KEB,CSR
Bozeman, Henry	Pvt	F 8th SCVI	Gettysburg, PA	07/03/63	W. Bldg. Balt, MD	09/25/63	City Pt., VA Xc	P1,CSR
Bozeman, Peter W.	Pvt	F 8th SCVI	Sharpsburg, MD	09/17/62	Sharpsburg, MD	10/02/62	Died of wounds	P12,KEB,CSR
Brabham, John M.	1Lt	C 19th SCVCB	Augusta, GA	05/24/65	Augusta, GA	05/24/65	Paroled on oath	CSR
Bracey, J.W.	1Lt	G Ham.Leg.MI	Farmville, VA	04/11/65	Farmville, VA	04/11/65	Paroled	CSR
Bradberry, Anderson	Sgt	D 2nd SCVIRi	Knoxville, TN	12/03/63	Louisville, KY	12/31/63	Rock Island, IL	P88,P89,P93,CSR
					Rock Island, IL	03/02/65	Pt. Lookout, MD Xc	P131,CSR

B

SOUTH CAROLINA SOLDIERS, SAILORS AND CITIZENS HELD IN U.S. PRISONS 1861-1865

NAME	RANK	REGIMENT	CAPTURED AT	WHEN	PRISON	MOVED	DISPOSITION	SOURCES
Braddock, Frank	Pvt	D 21st SCVI	Morris Island, SC	07/10/63	Ft. Columbus, NY	09/23/63	took the oath	P1,HAG
					Pt. Lookout, MD	08/16/64	Elmira, NY	P113,P118,P120
					Elmira, NY	10/11/64	Pt.Lookout, MD Xc	P65
					Pt. Lookout, MD	10/29/64	Exchanged	P114,P123,P124
Braddock, John	Pvt	D 21st SCVI	Petersburg, VA	06/18/64	City Pt., VA	06/24/64	Pt. Lookout, MD	CSR
					Pt. Lookout, MD	07/27/64	Elmira, NY	P113,P117,P120
					Elmira, NY	03/04/65	James R., VA Xc	P65,HAG,CSR
Braddock, Ralph	Pvt	D 21st SCVI	Ft. Fisher, NC	01/15/65	New York, NY	01/30/65	Elmira, NY	CSR
					Elmira, NY	02/20/65	Pt.Lookout, MD Xc	P65,P66,HAG
Braddock, Thomas	Pvt	D 21st SCVI	Ft. Fisher, NC	01/15/65	Elmira, NY	07/07/65	Rlsd. G.O. #109	P65,P66,HAG
Braddy, Derril	Pvt	F 25th SCVI	Weldon RR, VA	08/21/64	Ft. McHenry, MD	02/20/65	Pt. Lookout, MD Xc	CSR
					Howards Grove Hos.	03/02/65	Camp Lee on parole	CSR
Braddy, Edward	Pvt	F 25th SCVI	Town Creek, NC	02/20/65	Ft. Anderson, NC	02/28/65	Pt. Lookout, MD	CSR,HAG
					Pt. Lookout, MD	06/24/65	Rlsd. G.O. #109	P114,P123,CSR
Bradford, George P.	Pvt	L 1st SCVIG	Hatchers Run, VA	04/03/65	City Point, VA	04/07/65	Hart's Island, NY	CSR
					Hart's Island, NY	06/16/65	Rlsd. G.O. #109	P79,SA1,CSR
Bradford, Walter A.	Pvt	A 3rd SCVI	Gettysburg, PA	07/05/63	Gettysburg, PA G.H	07/28/63	Provost Marshal	P4,KEB,CSR,H3
					W. Bldg. Balt, MD	07/30/63	Baltimore, MD Jail	P1
					Baltimore, MD	08/20/63	Pt. Lookout, MD	CSR
					Pt. Lookout, MD	02/18/64	Died, Diarrhea	P5,P113,P116,P119
Bradham, Julius A.	Pvt	C 25th SCVI	Drury's Bluff, VA	05/14/64	Fts. Monroe, VA	09/29/64	Pt. Lookout, MD	CSR,HAG
					Pt. Lookout, MD	11/12/64	Venus Pt., GA Xc	CSR
					Pt. Lookout, MD	11/15/64	Aikens Ldg., VA Xc	P114,P118,P124,CSR
Bradham, L.S.	Pvt	I 23rd SCVI	Petersburg, VA Hos	04/03/65	Pt. of Rocks, VA H	04/12/65	Fts. Monroe, VA H.	CSR
					Fts. Monroe, VA H.	05/30/65		CSR
Bradham, S.H.	Pvt	D 4th SCVC	Stony Creek, VA	12/01/64	City Pt., VA	12/05/64	Pt. Lookout, MD	CSR
					Pt. Lookout, MD	06/24/65	Rlsd. G.O. #109	P118,P123,CSR
Bradham, T.A.	Cpl	D 4th SCVC	Old Church, VA	05/30/64	White House, VA	06/08/64	Pt. Lookout, MD	CSR
					Pt. Lookout, MD	07/08/64	Elmira, NY	P113,P117,P120,CSR
					Elmira, NY	06/16/65	Rlsd. G.O. #109	P65,CSR
Bradham, William J.	Pvt	D 4th SCVC	Stony Creek, VA	12/01/64	City Pt., VA	12/05/64	Pt. Lookout, MD	CSR
					Pt. Lookout, MD	06/24/65	Rlsd. G.O. #109	P118,P123,CSR
Bradley, A.	Pvt	A 3rd SCVABn	High Pt., NC	05/02/65	High Pt., NC	05/02/65	Paroled on oath	CSR
Bradley, B.J.E.	Pvt	I Ham.Leg.	Chattanooga, TN	10/29/63	Nashville, TN	11/07/63	Louisville, KY	P39,CSR
					Louisville, KY	11/09/63	Camp Morton, IN	P88,P89,P93,CSR
					Camp Morton, IN	05/18/65	Released on oath	P100,CSR
Bradley, E.P.	Pvt	I 4th SCVC	Stony Creek, VA	12/01/64	City Pt., VA	12/05/64	Pt. Lookout, MD	CSR
					Pt. Lookout, MD	01/17/65	Aikens Ldg., VA Xc	P118,P123,P124,CSR
Bradley, Henry M.	Pvt	B 1st SCVIG	Petersburg, VA	04/03/65	City Point, VA	04/07/65	Hart's Island, NY	CSR
					Hart's Island, NY	06/15/65	Rlsd. G.O. #109	P79,SA1,CSR
Bradley, J.H.	Pvt	F 7th SCVC	Petersburg, VA	06/09/64	Pt. Lookout, MD	07/28/64	Died	P6,P119,FPH
Bradley, Robert	Pvt	E 2nd SCST	Augusta, GA	05/22/65	Augusta, GA	05/22/65	Paroled	CSR
Bradley, W.A.	Pvt	A 3rd SCVABn	High Pt., NC	05/02/65	High Pt., NC	05/02/65	Paroled on oath	CSR
Bradley, W.H.	Pvt	D 17th SCVI	Farmville, VA	04/11/65	Farmville, VA	04/21/65	Paroled	HHC,CSR
Bradley, Wiley.	Sgt	G 3rd SCVABn	High Pt., NC	05/01/65	High Pt., NC	05/01/65	Paroled on oath	CSR
Bradshaw, Elijah M.	Pvt	A 8th SCVI	Winchester, VA	09/13/64	Harpers Ferry, WV	09/19/64	Camp Chase, OH	CSR
					Camp Chase, OH	02/07/65	Died	P6,P23,P27,FPH,CSR
Bradshaw, William H.	Pvt	F 24th SCVI	Jackson, MS	05/16/64	Hospital in MS	05/16/63	Paroled	CSR
Bragan, A.H.	Pvt	B CN.Arsenal	Savannah, GA	12/09/64	Ft. Delaware, DE	06/16/65	Rlsd. G.O. #109	P43
Bragdon, J.J.	Pvt	H 8th SCVI	Winchester, VA	09/13/64	Harpers Ferry, WV	09/19/64	Camp Chase, OH	CSR
					Camp Chase, OH	05/02/65	New Orleans, LA	P23,P26,KEB,CSR
					New Orleans, LA	05/12/65	Vicksburg, MS Exc	CSR

SOUTH CAROLINA SOLDIERS, SAILORS AND  CITIZENS HELD IN U.S. PRISONS 1861-1865

NAME	RANK	REGIMENT	CAPTURED AT	WHEN	PRISON	MOVED	DISPOSITION	SOURCES
Bragg, J.B.	Pvt	E Hol.Leg.	Petersburg, VA	03/25/65	City Pt., VA	03/30/65	Pt. Lookout, MD	CSR
					Pt. Lookout, MD	06/24/65	Rlsd. G.O. #109	P114,P118,P123,CSR
Bragg, William P.	Pvt	E Hol.Leg.	Petersburg, VA	03/25/65	City Pt., VA	03/28/65	Pt. Lookout, MD	CSR
					Pt. Lookout, MD	06/16/65	Rlsd. G.O. #109	P114,P188,P122,CSR
Brailsford, A. Moultrie	Sgt	I 2nd SCVI	Gettysburg, PA	07/02/63	Gettysburg G.H.	07/20/63	Provost Marshal	P4,KEB,CSR
					W. Bldg. Balt., MD	07/30/63	Baltimore, MD Jail	SA2,H2,P1,CSR
					Baltimore, MD	12/21/63	Pt. Lookout, MD	CSR
					Pt. Lookout, MD	03/17/64	City Pt., VA Xc	P116,P123,P124,CSR
Brailsford, William R.	Pvt	H 3rd SCVC	Salisbury, NC	04/12/65	Nashville, TN	06/14/65	to Gen'l Hosp.	P4,CSR
Bramblett, John L.	Pvt	C 14th SCVI	Gettysburg, PA	07/04/63	David's Island, NY	09/08/63	City Pt., VA Xc	CSR
					Williamsburg, VA H	09/13/63	Furloughed	CSR
Bramlett, A.W.	Pvt	D 13th SCVI	Wilderness, VA	05/06/64	Belle Plain, VA	05/21/64	Ft. Delaware, DE	CSR
					Ft. Delaware, DE	01/02/65	Hos 1/2-1/13/65	P47
					Ft. Delaware, DE	03/30/65	Hos 3/30-4/3/65	P47
					Ft. Delaware, DE	06/10/65	Released	P41,P43,P45,CSR
Bramllett, James H.	Pvt	C 14th SCVI	Sutherland Stn. VA	04/03/65	City Pt., VA	04/13/65	Pt. Lookout, MD	CSR
					Pt. Lookout, MD	06/24/65	Rlsd. G.O. #109	P1109,P123,CSR
Bramlett, John L.	Pvt	E 3rd SCVIBn	Bean's Stn., TN	12/13/63	Knoxville, TN	12/18/63	Louisville, KY	CSR
					Louisville, KY	01/23/64	Rock Island, IL	P88,P93,KEB,CSR
					Rock Island, IL	04/22/64	Died, Erysipelas	P5,P131,P132,FPH
Bramlett, Joseph N.	Pvt	B 2nd SCVI	Cedar Creek, VA	10/19/64	Pt. Lookout, MD	01/17/65	Aikens Ldg., VA Xc	P118,P124,KEB,H2
Bramlett, L.R.	Pvt	E 3rd SCVIBn	South Mtn., MD	09/14/62	Ft. Delaware, DE	10/02/62	Aikens Ldg., VA Xc	CSR
Bramlett, W.J.O.	Pvt	A 3rd SCVABn	High Pt., NC	05/02/65	High Pt., NC	05/02/65	Paroled on oath	CSR
Branch, T.J.	Pvt	A 19th SCVCB	Lancaster, SC	04/03/65	Newport News, VA	06/14/65	Released	P107
Branch, William J.	Pvt	A 19th SCVCB	Pocotaligo, SC	01/31/65	New Berne, NC	04/25/65	Fts. Monroe, VA	CSR
					Fts. Monroe, VA	05/01/65	Newport News, VA	CSR
					Newport News, VA	06/14/65	Rlsd. G.O. #109	CSR
Brandes, Henry	Pvt	H Ham.Leg.MI	Deserted/enemy	10/02/64	Bermuda Hundred, VA	10/02/64	Philadelphia, PA	CSR
Brandon, Hugh	Pvt	H 18th SCVI	Crater, Pbg., VA	07/30/64	City Pt., VA	08/05/64	Pt. Lookout, MD	CSR,YEB
					Pt. Lookout, MD	08/08/64	Elmira, NY	P113,P117,P120,CSR
					Elmira, NY	09/07/64	Died, Diarrhea	P5,P12,P65,CSR
Brandon, Reuben	Pvt	B 1st SCRes	Salisbury, NC	04/12/65	Louisville, KY	05/02/65	Camp Chase, OH	P95
Brandon, Thomas W.	Pvt	I 27th SCVI	Deserted/enemy	03/21/65	Camp Hamilton, VA	03/21/65	Bermuda Hundred VA	CSR
					Bermuda Hundred, VA	03/22/65	Washington, DC	CSR
					Washington, DC	03/25/65	Bridgeport, CN	CSR
Brandon, William	Pvt	C 7th SCVC	Deserted/enemy	02/22/65	Bermuda Hundred, VA	02/22/65	City Pt., VA P.M.	CSR
					City Pt., VA P.M.	02/23/65	Washington, DC	CSR
					Washington, DC	02/24/65	Savannah, GA/ oath	CSR
Brandt, John F.	Pvt	C 19th SCVCB	Florence, SC	03/05/65	New Berne, NC	04/03/65	Pt. Lookout, MD	CSR
					Pt. Lookout, MD	05/31/65	Died	P6,P118,P119,CSR
Branigan, James	Pvt	H 1st SCVIR	Deserted/enemy	07/18/63	Hilton Head, SC	07/21/63	took oath	CSR
Brannan, Luke	Pvt	F 1st SVIR	Smith's Ford, NC	03/01/65	New Berne, Nc	04/03/65	Pt. Lookout, MD	CSR
					Pt. Lookout, MD	05/15/65	Rlsd. G.O. #85	SA1,CSR
Brannon, Augustus G.	Pvt	C Hol.Leg.	Boonesboro, MD	09/14/62	Ft. McHenry, MD	10/17/62	Fts. Monroe, VA Xc	CSR,HOS
Brannon, Columbus L.	Pvt	C Hol.Leg.	Five Forks, VA	04/01/65	City Pt., VA	04/05/65	Pt. Lookout, MD	CSR,HOS
					Pt. Lookout, MD	06/24/65	Rlsd. G.O. #109	P114,P118,P123,CSR
Brannon, David	Pvt	D 15th SCVI	Gettysburg, PA	07/04/63	Ft. McHenry, MD	07/15/63	Ft. Delaware, DE	CSR
					Ft. Delaware, DE			P40,P44,P45
					Ft. Delaware, DE	05/01/62	Hos 5/1-5/22/65	P47,HIC
					Ft. Delaware, DE	06/10/65	Released on oath	P40,P42,P45,CSR
Brannon, James J.	Cpl	K 27th SCVI	Town Creek, NC	02/20/65	Ft. Anderson, NC	02/28/65	Pt. Lookout, MD	CSR,HAG
					Pt. Lookout, MD	06/24/65	Rlsd. G.O. #109	P114,P123,CSR

B

SOUTH CAROLINA SOLDIERS, SAILORS AND CITIZENS HELD IN U.S. PRISONS 1861-1865

NAME	RANK	REGIMENT	CAPTURED AT	WHEN	PRISON	MOVED	DISPOSITION	SOURCES
Brannon, Joseph M.	Pvt	B 13th SCVI	Gettysburg, PA	07/04/63	David's Island, NY	08/24/63	City Pt., VA Xc	P1,CSR
Brannon, L.	Pvt	F 1st SCVA	Smiths Ford, NC	03/16/65	Pt. Lookout, MD	05/15/65	Released	P114,P118
Brannon, Patrick	Pvt	E 1st SCVA	Morris Island, SC	07/10/63	Hilton Head, SC		Ft. Columbus,NY	CSR
					Ft. Columbus, NY		Took the oath	P1,CSR
Brannon, Pressley B.	Pvt	L 1st SCVIG	Petersburg, VA	04/02/65	City Pt., VA	04/04/65	Pt. Lookout, MD	CSR,SA1
					Pt. Lookout, MD	06/24/65	Rlsd. G.O. #109	P114,P118,P123,SA1,CSR
Brannon, Reuben	Pvt	C Hol.Leg.	Five Forks, VA	04/01/65	City Pt., VA	04/05/65	Pt. Lookout, MD	CSR,HOS
					Pt. Lookout, MD	06/04/65	Rlsd., sick list	P114,P118,CSR
Brannon, William, Jr.	Cpl	D 15th SCVI	Gettysburg, PA	07/04/63	Gettysburg G.H.		David's Island, NY	P4,KEB,HIC
					David's Island, NY	09/08/63	City Pt., VA Xc	H15,CSR
Brannon, Willis	Pvt	F 6th SCVC	Johns Island, SC	02/10/64	Hilton Head, SC GH	10/21/64	Ft. Pulaski, GA	P2,CAG,CSR
Branson, Eli	Pvt	G 1st SCVIG	Gettysburg, PA	07/04/63	Chester, PA Hos.	08/17/63	City Pt., VA Xc	P1,SA1
Brant, George M.	Pvt	G 17th SCVI	Petersburg, VA	03/25/65	City Pt., VA	03/28/65	Pt. Lookout, MD	CSR
					Pt. Lookout, MD	06/24/65	Rlsd. G.O. #109	P114,P118,P123,CSR
Brant, Giles	Cit	Barnwell	Bufords Bridge, SC	02/04/65	Hart's Island, NY	07/01/65	David's Island, NY	P79
Brant, L.R.	Pvt	B 19th SCVCB	Barnwell, SC	02/04/65	New Berne, NC	04/10/65	Hart's Island, NY	CSR
					Hart's Island, NY	06/17/65	Rlsd. G.O. #109	P79,CSR
Brantley, Francis M.	Pvt	A 4th SCVC	Raleigh, NC Hos.	04/13/65	Greensboro, NC	06/26/65	Died of wounds	P12,ROH,PP,CSR
Branton, Richard	Pvt	B 11th SCVI	Deserted/enemy	03/06/65	Charleston, SC	03/06/65	Released on oath	CSR
Branyan, R.P.	Cpl	F 24th SCVI	Nashville, TN	12/16/64	Nashville, TN	12/31/64	Louisville, KY	CSR
					Louisville, KY	01/04/65	Camp Chase, OH	CSR
					Camp Chase, OH	08/17/65	Died, Pneumonia	P6,P23,FPH,EFW
Branyon, Samuel Thompson	Pvt	I 19th SCVI	Danville, KY	10/10/62	Berryville, KY	01/06/63	Lexington, KY	CSR
					Lexington, KY	01/07/63	Louisville, KY	CSR
					Louisville, KY	01/14/63	Vicksburg, MS	P88,CSR
					Vicksburg, MS		St. Louis, MO Hos.	CSR
					St. Louis, MO Hos.	03/05/63	Died	P12,FPH,CSR
Brasington, George C.	2Lt	H 2nd SCVI	Gettysburg, PA	07/04/63	Letterman G.H. Gbg	07/06/63	Died of wounds	P12,KEB,SA2,H2,CSR
Brassell, William C.	Pvt	4 10/19 SCVI	Missionary Ridge, TN	11/25/63	Nashville, TN	12/07/63	Louisville, KY	P39,RAS,CSR
					Louisville, KY	12/09/63	Rock Island, IL	P88,P89,RAS,CSR
					Rock Island, IL	10/06/64	Jd. US Army F.S.	CSR
Braswell, James R.	Sgt	E 23rd SCVI	Five Forks, VA	04/01/65	City Pt. VA	04/06/65	Pt. Lookout, MD	CSR
					Pt. Lookout, MD	06/24/65	Rlsd. G.O. #109	P114,P123,HMC,CSR
Bratcher, Henry	Pvt	K 1st SCVIG	Sutherland Stn., VA	04/02/65	City Point, VA	04/07/65	Hart's Island, NY	CSR
					Hart's Island, NY	06/16/65	Rlsd. G.O. #109	P79,SA1,CSR
Brattie, J.E.	Pvt	A 3rd SCVABn	High Pt., NC	05/02/65	High Pt., NC	05/02/65	Paroled on oath	CSR
Bratton, N.B.	Sgt	E 5th SCVI	Williamsburg, VA	05/05/62	Cliffburn USGH, DC		Exchanged	CSR
Bratton, R.G.	Pvt	K 17th SCVI	Five Forks, VA	04/01/65	City Pt., VA	04/11/65	Hart's Island, NY	CSR
					Hart's Island, NY	06/18/65	Rlsd. G.O. #109	P79,CSR
Brauer, H.	Pvt	C 27th SCVI	Petersburg, VA	06/24/64	Camp Hamilton, VA	06/26/64	Fts. Monroe, VA	CSR,HAG
					Fts. Monroe, VA	03/02/65	Pt. Lookout, MD	CSR
					Pt. Lookout, MD	05/12/65	Rlsd. G.O. #85	CSR
Braun, Herman	Cpl	Brooks LA	Gettysburg, PA	07/04/63	Davids I., NY G.H.	10/24/63	Bedloes Island, NY	P1,CSR
					Bedloes Island, NY	12/17/63	Pt. Lookout, MD	P2
					Pt. Lookout, MD	01/29/64	Joined U.S. Army	P113,P116,P125,CSR
Braveboy, Morris M.	Pvt	3 10/19 SCVI	Missionary Ridge, TN	11/25/63	Nashville, TN	12/07/63	Louisville, KY	P39,RAS,CSR
					Louisville, KY	12/09/63	Rock Island, IL	P88,P89,RAS,CSR
					Rock Island, IL	05/26/65	Released G.O. #85	P131,CSR
Brawley, J.B.	Sgt	K Hol.Leg.	Stony Creek, VA	05/07/64	Pt. Lookout, MD	08/15/64	Elmira, NY	P113,P116,P120
					Fts.. Monroe, VA	08/15/64	Elmira, NY	CSR
					Elmira, NY	10/11/64	Pt.Lookout to Xc	P65
					Pt. Lookout, MD	10/29/64	Aikens Ldg., VA Xc	P114,P118

B

SOUTH CAROLINA SOLDIERS, SAILORS AND CITIZENS HELD IN U.S. PRISONS 1861-1865

NAME	RANK	REGIMENT	CAPTURED AT	WHEN	PRISON	MOVED	DISPOSITION	SOURCES
Braxton, J.J.	Pvt	B 2nd SCVC	Augusta, GA	05/18/65	Augusta, GA	05/18/65	Paroled on oath	CSR
Braxton, J.W.	Pvt	I 7th SCVI	Spotsylvania, VA	05/07/64	Belle Plain, VA	05/20/64	Ft. Delaware, DE	CSR
					Ft. Delaware, DE	05/11/65	Rlsd. G.O. #85	P41,P43,P46,CSR
Bray, John T.	Pvt	D 1st SCVA	Black River, NC	03/16/65	New Berne, NC	03/30/65	Pt. Lookout, MD	CSR
					Pt. Lookout, MD	05/12/65	Rlsd. G.O. #85	P114,CSR
Brayman, Alex	Msc	1st SCVA	Deserted/enemy	02/19/65	Charleston, SC	03/02/65	Released on oath	CSR
Brazel, Richard V.	Pvt	C 12th SCVI	Deep Bottom, VA	07/28/64	City Pt., VA JSH	08/01/64	Old Capitol, DC	CSR
					Armory Sq.Hos., DC	12/12/64	Lincoln G.H., DC	CSR
					Lincoln G.H., DC	01/27/65	Old Capitol, DC	CSR
					Old Capitol, DC	02/03/65	Elmira, NY	P110,HFC,CSR
					Elmira, NY	02/13/65	James R., VA Xc	CSR
					Richmond, VA Hos.	02/27/65	Parole Camp Lee	CSR
Brazell, H.	Pvt	D 12th SCVI	Spotsylvania, VA	05/12/64	Belle Plain, VA	05/21/64	Ft. Delaware, DE	CSR
					Ft. Delaware, DE	07/01/64	Died, Bowel Infl.	P5,P43,P47,FPH,CSR
Brazell, Joel	Pvt	D 12th SCVI	Spotsylvania, VA	05/12/64	Belle Plain, VA	05/20/64	Ft. Delaware, DE	CSR
					Ft. Delaware, DE	06/09/64	Hos 6/9-6/26/64	P47
					Ft. Delaware, DE	06/29/64	Hos 6/29-7/17/64	P47
					Ft. Delaware, DE	08/30/64	Died, Dropsy	P5,P12,P47,FPH,CSR
Brazell, Joseph	Pvt	D 12th SCVI	Spotsylvania, VA	05/12/64	Belle Plain, VA	05/21/64	Ft. Delaware, DE	CSR
					Ft. Delaware, DE	05/10/65	Released on oath	P41,P43,CSR
Brazell, William	Pvt	G 1st SCVIH	Farmville, VA	04/09/65	City Pt., VA	04/24/65	Newport News, VA	CSR
					Newport News, VA	06/26/65	Rlsd. G.O. #109	CSR
Breakfield, George W.	Pvt	E 6th SCVI	Dranesville, VA	12/20/61	Field Hos. Army of	12/30/61	Died of wounds	CSR
Breland, Isaiah B.	Pvt	D 24th SCVI	Taylors Ridge, GA	10/16/64	Nashville, TN	10/23/64	Louisville, KY	CSR
					Louisville, KY	10/27/64	Camp Douglas, IL	P90,P91,P95,EFW
					Camp Douglas, IL	02/21/65	Died, Scurvy	P6,P12,P55,FPH
Breland, Josiah W.	Pvt	E 24th SCVI	Pulaski, TN	12/25/64	Nashville, TN	02/14/65	Louisville, KY	P4,P39
					Louisville, KY	02/17/65	Camp Chase, OH	P92,P95,COT
					Camp Chase, OH	06/13/65	Released, GO #109	P23
Breland, W.E.	1Sg	C 1st SCVIH	Richmond, VA Hos.	04/03/65	Richmond, VA	04/24/65	Newport News, VA	CSR
					Newport News, VA	06/26/65	Rlsd. G.O. #109	CSR
Bremond, H.D.	Cap	*Huntress*	Off Charleston	01/18/63	Ft. Lafayette, NY	04/15/63	Ft. Delaware, DE	P144
Brereton, Daniel	Cpl	K 1st SCVIG	Gettysburg, PA	07/05/63	Ft. McHenry, MD	07/30/63	Ft. Delaware, DE	CSR
					Ft. Delaware, DE	09/13/63	Jd. US 1st CN Cav.	P7,P40,P42,P44,CSR
Bressenham, Timothy	Sgt	A 15th SCVAB	Fayetteville, NC	04/22/65	Wilmington, NC	04/26/65	Rlsd. on oath	CSR
Brewer, Daniel W.	Pvt	C 1st SCVIG	Chaffin's Farm, VA	10/02/64	City Pt., VA	10/04/64	Pt. Lookout, MD	CSR,SA1
Brewer, George B.	Pvt	F 26th SCVI	Petersburg, VA	03/25/65	City Pt., VA	03/28/65	Pt. Lookout, MD	P118
					Pt. Lookout, MD	06/24/65	Rlsd. G.O. #109	P114,P118
Brewer, J.S.	Pvt	A 20th SCVI	Cedar Creek, VA	10/19/64	Winchester, VA USH	11/08/64	Died, of wounds	P12,CSR
Brewton, L.C.	Pvt	A Hol.Leg.	Hatchers Run, VA	03/31/65	Pt. Lookout, MD	06/25/65	Rlsd. G.O. #109	P114,P118
Briant, Alfred T.	Pvt	G 18th SCVI	Petersburg, VA	07/30/64	City Pt., VA	08/08/64	Pt. Lookout, MD	CSR,HOS
					Pt. Lookout, MD	08/08/64	Elmira, NY	P113,P117,P120,CSR
					Elmira, NY	12/16/64	Died, Typhoid	P6,P12,P65,FPH,CSR
Briant, Mitchell	Pvt	H 16th SCVI	Marietta, GA	07/03/64	Nashville, TN	07/12/64	Louisville, KY	CSR
					Louisville, KY	07/13/64	Camp Morton, IN	P90,P91,P94,CSR
					Camp Morton, IN	03/15/65	Pt.Lookout, MD Xc	P101,CSR
					Richmond, VA Hos.	03/31/65	Furlougheed 60 day	CSR
					Nashville, TN	07/12/64	Louisville, KY	CSR
Briant, William	Pvt	H 16th SCVI	Marietta, GA	07/03/64	Louisville, KY	07/13/64	Camp Morton, IN	P90,P91,P94,CSR
					Camp Morton, IN	03/15/65	Pt. Lookout, MD Xc	P100,P101,CSR

B

SOUTH CAROLINA SOLDIERS, SAILORS AND CITIZENS HELD IN U.S. PRISONS 1861-1865

NAME	RANK	REGIMENT	CAPTURED AT	WHEN	PRISON	MOVED	DISPOSITION	SOURCES
Brice, David P.	Pvt	K 3rd SCVI	Berryville, VA	09/03/64	Harpers Ferry, WV	09/11/64	Camp Chase, OH	CSR,SA2,H3
					Camp Chase, OH		(DES)	P23
					Camp Chase, OH	04/20/65	Joined U.S. Army	P23,P26,H3,CSR
Brice, J. Yongue	Sgt	F 12th SCVI	Spotsylvania, VA	05/12/64	Ft. Delaware, DE	12/23/64	Hos12/23/64-2/8/65	P47
					Ft. Delaware, DE	04/10/65	Hos. 4/10-5/23/65	P47
					Ft. Delaware, DE	06/10/65	Released	P41,P43,P45,CSR
Brice, J.M.	1Lt	G 6th SCVI	Frederick, MD	09/12/62	Baltimore, MD	10/11/62	Fts. Monroe, VA Xc	CSR
					Fts. Monroe, VA	10/12/62	Aikens Ldg., VA Xc	CSR
Brice, James A.	Pvt	H 6th SCVI	Seven Pines, VA	05/31/62	Fts. Monroe, VA	07/15/62	Ft. Delaware, DE	CSR
					Ft. Delaware, DE	08/05/62	Str. *Karskill*	CSR
Brice, Thomas K.	Pvt	F 1st SCVIH	Deep Bottom, VA	08/14/64	Fts. Monroe, VA	08/16/64	Pt. Lookout, MD	CSR,SA1
					Pt. Lookout, MD	02/24/65	Died	P113,P124,P125,CSR
Brice, Walter W.	Pvt	F 12th SCVI	Petersburg, VA	03/25/65	Pt. Lookout, MD	06/23/65	Rlsd. G.O. #109	P114,P118,CSR
Bridgeforth, J.V.	Pvt	A 1st SCVIR	Greenville, SC	05/24/65	Nashville, TN	06/27/65	Released on oath	SA1,CSR
Bridges, Alexander	Pvt	A Hol.Leg.	Five Forks, VA	04/01/65	City Pt., VA	04/05/65	Pt. Lookout, MD	CSR,HOS
					Pt. Lookout, MD	06/04/65	Rlsd. sick list	P118,P121,P123,CSR
Bridges, Edmund H.	Pvt	F 17th SCVI	Petersburg, VA	03/25/65	City Pt., VA	03/28/65	Pt. Lookout, MD	CSR
					Pt. Lookout, MD	06/23/65	Rlsd. G.O. #109	P114,P118,CSR
Bridges, Fletcher H.	Pvt	F 17th SCVI	Petersburg, VA	03/25/65	City Pt., VA	03/28/65	Pt. Lookout, MD	CSR
					Pt. Lookout, MD	06/23/65	Rlsd. G.O. #109	P114,P118,CSR
Bridges, G.H.	Pvt	K 27th SCVI	Petersburg, VA	06/18/64	City Pt., VA	06/24/64	Pt. Lookout, MD	CSR,HAG
					Pt. Lookout, MD	07/26/64	Died	P6,P113,P117,P119
Bridges, J.G.	Pvt	C 17th SCVI	Athens, GA	05/08/65	Athens, GA	05/08/65	Paroled	CSR
Bridges, James	Pvt	C 17th SCVI	Petersburg, VA	03/25/65	City Pt., VA	03/28/65	Pt. Lookout, MD	CSR
					Pt. Lookout, MD	06/23/65	Rlsd. G.O. #109	P114,P118,CSR
Bridges, William M.	Cpl	K 18th SCVI	Five Forks, VA	04/01/65	City Pt., VA	04/06/65	Pt. Lookout, MD	CSR
					Pt. Lookout, MD	06/24/65	Rlsd. G.O. #109	P118,P121,P123,CSR
Bridwell, Joseph C.	Pvt	B 13th SCVI	Petersburg, VA	04/02/65	Hart's Island, NY	06/16/65	Rlsd. G.O. #109	P79,HOS,CSR
Bridwell, William W.	Pvt	H 16th SCVI	Marietta, GA	07/03/64	Nashville, TN	07/12/64	Louisville, KY	CSR
					Louisville, KY	07/13/64	Camp Morton, IN	P90,P91,P94,CSR
					Camp Morton, IN	03/10/65	Pt. Lookout, MD Xc	P101,CSR
					Richmond, VA Hos.	03/28/65	Furloughed 60 days	CSR
Briggs, J.	Pvt	C 7th SCVC	Columbia, VA	03/11/65	Fts. Monroe, VA	03/24/65	Pt. Lookout, MD	CSR
					Pt. Lookout, MD	06/24/65	Rlsd. G.O. #109	P114,P118,CSR
Briggs, John	Pvt	F 26th SCVI	Cheraw, SC	03/06/65	New Berne, NC	04/25/65	Camp Hamilton, VA	CSR
					Camp Hamilton, VA	05/03/65	Newport News, VA	CSR
					Newport News, VA	06/16/65	Rlsd. G.O. #109	P107,CSR
Briggs, Lafayette	Pvt	C 7th SCVC	Goochland C.H., VA	03/11/65	Pt. Lookout, MD	06/24/65	Rlsd. G.O. #109	P123,CSR
Briggs, W.H.	Pvt	B 6th SCVC	Bennett's Pt., SC	06/28/63	Pt. Lookout, MD		Camp Lee 2/17/64	P124,CSR
					Augusta, GA	05/19/65	Paroled	CSR
Bright, Andrew J.	Pvt	C 22nd SCVI	Kinston, NC	12/15/62	Kinston, NC	12/15/62	Paroled POW	CSR
Bright, Andrew J.	Pvt	C 22nd SCVI	Crater, Pbg., VA	07/30/64	City Pt., VA	08/05/64	Pt. Lookout, MD	CSR
					Pt. Lookout, MD	08/08/64	Elmira, NY	P113,P117
					Elmira, NY	07/03/65	Rlsd. G.O. #109	P65,HOS
Bright, Manley F.	Pvt	B 13th SCVI	Richmond, VA Hos.	04/03/65	Richmond, VA	05/04/65	paroled	CSR
Bright, Robert B.	Pvt	H 22nd SCVI	Crater, Pbg., VA	07/30/64	City Pt., VA	08/05/64	Pt. Lookout, MD	CSR
					Pt. Lookout, MD	08/08/64	Elmira, NY	CSR
					Elmira, NY	09/13/64	Died, Typhoid Fev.	P5,P12,FPH,CSR
Bright, Thomas B.	Pvt	K P.S.S.	Deserted/enemy	03/14/65	Bermuda Hundred, VA	03/15/65	City Pt. VA P.M.	CSR
					City Pt., VA	03/18/65	Washington, DC	CSR
Bright, Tobias	Pvt	C Hol.Leg.	Five Forks, VA	04/01/65	City Pt., VA	04/05/65	Pt. Lookout, MD	CSR
					Pt. Lookout, MD	06/24/65	Rlsd. G.O. #109	P114,P118,P123,CSR,HOS

SOUTH CAROLINA SOLDIERS, SAILORS AND **B** CITIZENS HELD IN U.S. PRISONS 1861-1865

NAME	RANK	REGIMENT	CAPTURED AT	WHEN	PRISON	MOVED	DISPOSITION	SOURCES
Bright, W.J.	Pvt	A 3rd SCVI	N. Anna River, VA	05/23/64	Port Royal, VA	05/30/64	Pt. Lookout, MD	CSR
					Pt. Lookout, MD	11/01/64	Aikens Ldg., VA Xc	P117,P124,H3,CSR
Bright, William A.	Pvt	B 13th SCVI	Deserted/enemy	02/24/65	Washington, DC	02/26/65	Springfield, IL	CSR
Bright, William J.	Pvt	C 22nd SCVI	Crater, Pbg., VA	07/30/64	City Pt., VA	08/05/64	Pt. Lookout, MD	CSR
					Pt. Lookout, MD	08/08/64	Elmira, NY	P117,P120,P125,CSR
					Elmira, NY	09/23/64	Died, Pneumonia	P5,P12,P65,FPH,HOS
Brigman, Arthur P.	Pvt	I 1st SCVIH	Deserted/enemy	02/28/65	Washington, DC P.M	03/06/65	Wilmington, NC	CSR
					City Pt., VA	03/06/65	Washington, DC P.M	CSR
Brigman, Henry	Pvt	D 26th SCVI	Cheraw, SC	03/06/65	New Berne, NC	04/10/65	Hart's Island, NY	CSR
					Hart's Island, NY	06/17/65	Rlsd. G.O. #109	P79,HOM,CSR
Brigman, Robert	Pvt	B 26th SCVI	Crater, Pbrg., VA	07/30/64	City Pt., VA	08/05/64	Pt. Lookout, MD	CSR
					Pt. Lookout, MD	08/08/64	Elmira, NY	P113,P120,P125,CSR
					Elmira, NY	10/14/64	Pt.Lookout to Xc	P65,P117,CSR
					Pt. Lookout, MD	10/29/64	Venus Pt., GA Xc	P114,P118,P123,CSR
Brigman, William	Pvt	D 26th SCVI	NC or SC		New Berne, NC G.H.	04/18/65	Died, Lung Infl.	P6,P12
Brinson, T.W.	Pvt	G 10th SCVI	Warrenton, VA	09/29/62	Warrenton, VA	09/29/62	Paroled	CSR
Brissey, J.A.	Pvt	B 16th SCVI	Greenville, SC	05/23/65	Greenville, SC	05/23/65	Paroled on oath	16R,CSR
Bristow, Chesley D.	Pvt	G 8th SCVI			Pt. Lookout, MD		Exchanged	P124,KEB,HOM
Bristow, Columbus C.	HSd	E 8th SCVI	Gettysburg, PA	07/02/63	Gettysburg G.H.		Baltimore, MD	P4,KEB,CSR
					Baltimore, MD	08/17/63	Pt. Lookout, MD	CSR
					Pt. Lookout, MD	03/06/64	City Pt., VA Xc	P113,P116,P123,CSR
Bristow, David M.	Pvt	F 21st SCVI	Ft. Fisher, NC	01/15/65	Elmira, NY	03/03/65	Died, Pneumonia	P6,P12,P65,P66,HAG
Bristow, John M.	Pvt	Ferguson's	Salisbury, NC	05/12/65	Nashville, TN	04/29/65	Louisville, KY	P39,CSR
					Louisville, KY	05/02/65	Camp Chase, OH	P95,CSR
					Camp Chase, OH	06/13/65	Rlsd. G.O. #109	CSR
Bristow, Robert N.	Pvt	F 21st SCVI	Ft. Fisher, NC	01/15/65	Elmira, NY	03/18/65	Died, Typhoid	P6,P12,P65,P66,HAG
Britt, Arick	Pvt	H 24th SCVI	Jonesboro, GA	09/02/64	Nashville, TN	10/27/64	Louisville, KY	CSR
					Louisville, KY	10/29/64	Camp Douglas, IL	P90,P91,P95
					Camp Douglas, IL	04/03/65	Jd. 6th US Inf.	P55,EFW
Britt, John	Pvt	F 19th SCVI	Atlanta, GA	07/22/64	Louisville, KY	07/31/64	Camp Chase, OH	P90,P91,HOE,CSR
					Camp Chase, OH	02/05/65	Died	P6,P12,P27,FPH,CSR
Britt, William	Pvt	D 6th SCResB	Augusta, GA	05/22/65	Augusta, GA	05/22/65	Paroled	CSR
Britton, John Francis	Cpl	A 27th SCVI	Petersburg, VA	06/24/64	Fts. Monroe, VA	06/26/64	Pt. Lookout, MD	CSR,HAG
					Pt. Lookout, MD	08/16/64	Elmira, NY	P117,P118,P120
					Elmira, NY	10/11/64	Pt.Lookout, MD to Xc	P65
					Pt. Lookout, MD	10/29/64	Venus Pt., GA Xc	P114,P123
Britton, John Francis	Cpl	A 27th SCVI	Town Creek, NC	02/20/65	Ft. Anderson, NC	02/28/65	Pt. Lookout, MD	CSR
					Pt. Lookout, MD	06/24/65	Rlsd. G.O. #109	P114,P121
Britton, Richard A.	Cpl	A 27th SCVI	Town Creek, NC	02/20/65	Ft. Anderson, NC	02/28/65	Pt. Lookout, MD	CSR,HAG
					Pt. Lookout, MD	06/24/65	Rlsd. G.O. #109	P114,P123
Britton, Thomas F.	Pvt	Brooks LA	Harper's Farm, VA	04/06/65	City Pt., VA	04/14/65	Pt. Lookout, MD	CSR
					Pt. Lookout, MD	06/24/65	Rlsd. G.O. #109	P114,P123,CSR
Britton, Thomas G.	Pvt	I 4th SCVC	Hawe's Shop, VA	05/28/64	3rd Div.5th A.C. H	06/12/64	Stanton G.H., DC	CSR
					Stanton, G.H., DC	07/16/64	Old Capitol, DC	CSR
					Old Capitol, DC	07/23/64	Elmira, NY	CSR
					Elmira, NY	06/30/65	Rlsd. G.O. #109	P65,CTA,CSR
Broach, John E.	Pvt	G 26th SCVI	Five Forks, VA	04/01/65	City Pt., VA	04/05/65	Pt. Lookout, MD	CSR
					Pt. Lookout, MD	06/24/65	Rlsd. G.O. #109	P114,P118,P123,CSR
Broach, Robert	Pvt	C 23rd SCVI	Five Forks, VA	04/01/65	City Pt., VA	04/06/65	Pt. Lookout, MD	CSR
					Pt. Lookout, MD	06/07/65	Rlsd. G.O. #85	P114,P118,CSR
Broadwater, George M.	Pvt	D 14th SCVI	Deep Bottom, VA	08/17/64	Pt. Lookout, MD	11/01/64	Aikens Ldg., VA Xc	P113,P117,HOE,CSR
					Pt. Lookout, MD	11/01/64	Venus Pt., GA Xc	CSR

B

SOUTH CAROLINA SOLDIERS, SAILORS AND CITIZENS HELD IN U.S. PRISONS 1861-1865

NAME	RANK	REGIMENT	CAPTURED AT	WHEN	PRISON	MOVED	DISPOSITION	SOURCES
Broadwater, George M.	Pvt	D 14th SCVI	Sutherland Stn. VA	04/03/65	City Pt., VA	04/13/65	Pt. Lookout, MD	CSR
					Pt. Lookout, MD	06/24/65	Rlsd. G.O. #109	P119,P123,P124
Broadwater, N.L.	Pvt	I 7th SCVI	Sharpsburg, MD Hos	09/30/62	Fredericksburg, US	10/13/62	Ft. McHenry, MD	CSR
					Ft. McHenry, MD	10/30/62	Aikens Ldg., VA Xc	CSR
Brock, Calvin	Pvt	B 8th SCVI	Winchester, VA	09/13/64	Harpers Ferry, WV	09/19/64	Camp Chase, OH	CSR,KEB
					Camp Chase, OH	02/09/65	Died	P6,P12,P23,P27,FPH
Brock, George W.	Pvt	G 27th SCVI	Petersburg, VA	06/24/64	Bermuda Hundred, VA	06/25/64	Fts. Monroe, VA	CSR,HAG
					Fts. Monroe, VA	06/26/64	Pt. Lookout, MD	CSR
					Pt. Lookout, MD	08/16/64	Elmira, NY	P113,P120
					Elmira, NY	10/11/64	Pt. Lookout, MD Xc	P65
					Pt. Lookout, MD	10/29/64	Venus Pt., GA Xc	P114,P118,P123
Brock, H.	Cit		Chesterfield, SC	03/01/65	Pt. Lookout, MD	06/12/65	Died, Lung Infl.	P6,P114,P118,FPH
Brock, J.T.	Pvt	K 1st SCVA	Bentonville, NC	03/16/65	Hart's Island, NY	07/08/65	Rlsd. G.O. #109	P79
Brock, Jacob H.	Cpl	Ch'fld LA	South Carolina	04/12/64	Hilton Head, SC	05/17/64	Ft. Lafayette, NY	CSR
					Ft. Lafayette, NY	03/13/65	Ft. Delaware, DE	CSR
					Ft. Delaware, DE		Not given	CSR
Brock, James	Cpl	F 1st SCVA	Deserted/enemy	03/15/65	Charleston, SC	03/15/65	Released on oath	CSR
Brock, James	Pvt	E 1st SCVIR	Bentonville, NC	03/22/65	New Berne, NC	04/10/65	Hart's Island, NY	CSR
					Hart's Island, NY	06/17/65	Rlsd. G.O. #109	SA1,P79,CSR
Brock, James L.	Sgt	E 20th SCVI	Cedar Creek, VA	10/19/64	Harpers Ferry, WV	10/23/64	Pt. Lookout, MD	CSR,KEB
					Pt. Lookout, MD	06/24/65	Rlsd. G.O. #109	P114,P118,P123,CSR
Brockland, William E.	Pvt	C 1st SCVIG	Richmond ,VA Hos.	04/03/65	Libby Prison, VA	04/23/65	Newport News, VA	CSR
Brogan, Martin	Pvt	C 1st SCVC	Fredericksburg, VA	12/13/62	Falmouth, VA	12/17/62	Exchanged	CSR
Bronson, John	Pvt	I 1st SCVA	Deserted/enemy	02/21/65	Charleston, SC	09/21/65	Released on oath	CSR
Bronson, Marion D.	Pvt	G 25th SCVI	Town Creek, NC	02/20/65	Ft. Anderson, NC	02/28/65	Pt. Lookout, MD	CSR,HAG
					Pt. Lookout, MD	06/24/65	Rlsd. G.O. #109	P114,P123
Brookbanks, William	Pvt	Brooks LA	Harpers Farm, VA	04/06/65	City Pt., VA	04/14/65	Pt. Lookout, MD	CSR
					Pt. Lookout, MD	06/24/65	Rlsd. G.O. #109	P123,CSR
Brookbanks, William	Pvt	I 1st SCVA	Morris Island, SC	07/10/63	Hilton Head, SC	09/05/63	Ft. Columbus, NY	CSR
					Ft. Columbus, NY	09/23/63	took the oath	P1,CSR
Brooker, E.	1Lt	I 5th SCVC	Cheraw, SC	03/05/65	Cheraw, SC	03/05/65	Paroled	CSR
Brooker, John R.	Pvt	E 11th SCVI	Petersburg, VA	06/24/64	Fts. Monroe, VA	09/10/64	Died of wounds	HAG,P12
Brooks, Andrew P.	Pvt	G Orr's Ri.	Falling Waters, MD	07/14/63	Baltimore, MD	08/16/63	Pt. Lookout, MD	CSR
					Pt. Lookout, MD	08/16/64	Elmira, NY	P113,P116,P120,CSR
					Elmira, NY	06/15/65	Died, Ch. Diarrhea	P12,FPH
Brooks, Charles Elisha.	Sgt	F 2nd SCVI	Halltown, WV	08/21/64	Harpers Ferry, WV	09/02/64	Camp Chase, OH	CSR,KEB,H2
					Camp Chase, OH	01/23/65	Died	SA2,P23,FPH,H2,CSR
Brooks, E.A.	Pvt	G 2nd SCVC	South River, NC	03/19/65	New Berne, NC	04/10/65	Hart's Island, NY	CSR
					Hart's Island, NY	06/06/65	Rlsd. G.O. #109	CSR
Brooks, James	Pvt	C 3rd SCVIBn	Frederick, MD	09/12/62	Ft. Delaware, DE	10/02/62	Aikens Ldg., VA Xc	CSR
Brooks, L.W.	Pvt	K 2nd SCVC	Greenville, SC	05/25/65	Greenville, SC	05/25/65	Paroled on oath	CSR
Brooks, Robert	Pvt	F 2nd SCVIRi	Farmville, VA	04/11/65	Farmville, VA	04/21/65	Paroled	CSR
Brooks, Whitfield	HSd	16th SCVI	Franklin, TN	12/17/64	Nashville, TN	01/04/65	Louisville, KY	P4,P39,CSR
					Louisville, KY	01/09/65	Camp Chase, OH	P92,P95,CSR
					Camp Chase, OH	06/13/65	Rlsd. G.O. #109	P23,CSR
Brookshire, David	Pvt	F 1st SCVIH	Deserted/enemy	01/06/64	Knoxville, TN		Took the oath	HAG,CSR
Broom, James	Pvt	D Hol.Leg.	Amelia C.H., VA	04/06/65	Pt. Lookout, MD	06/24/65	Rlsd. G.O. #109	P123
Brostols, George	Pvt	B 15th SCVAB	Cheraw, SC	03/05/65	Cheraw, SC	03/05/65	Released on oath	CSR
Broughton, Julius J.	Pvt	E 23rd SCVI	South Mtn., MD	09/14/62	Ft. McHenry, MD	11/06/62	Prld. to Exchange	CSR
Broundell, J.L.	Pvt	C 14th SCVI	Gettysburg, PA	07/04/63	David's Island, NY	09/05/63	City Pt., VA Xc	P1
Browder, Benjamin R.	Pvt	K 25th SCVI	Ft. Fisher, NC	01/15/65	New York, NY	01/31/65	Elmira, NY	CSR
					Elmira, NY	07/11/65	Rlsd. G.O. #109	P65,P66,HAG,CTA

SOUTH CAROLINA SOLDIERS, SAILORS AND  CITIZENS HELD IN U.S. PRISONS 1861-1865

NAME	RANK	REGIMENT	CAPTURED AT	WHEN	PRISON	MOVED	DISPOSITION	SOURCES
Browder, G.W.	Pvt	K 25th SCVI	Ft. Fisher, NC	01/15/65	Elmira, NY	06/23/65	Rlsd. G.O. #109	P65,P66,HAG
Browder, John J.	Pvt	G 21st SCVI	Ft. Fisher, NC	01/15/65	Elmira, NY	07/07/65	Rlsd. G.O. #109	P65,P66,HAG
Browder, Samuel Warren	Pvt	C 25th SCVI	Ft. Darling, VA	05/14/64	Fts. Monroe, VA	05/17/64	Pt. Lookout, MD	CSR
					Pt. Lookout, MD	08/15/64	Elmira, NY	P113,P120,HAG
					Elmira, NY	05/17/65	Died, Rheumatism	P6,P65,FPH,CTA
Browder, William T.	Pvt	K 25th SCVI	Ft. Fisher, NC	01/15/65	New York, NY	01/30/65	Elmira, NY	CSR
					Elmira, NY	07/13/65	Elmira, NY USGH	P65,HAG
					Elmira, NY	07/19/65	Rlsd. G.O. #109	P66,CTA
Brower, Wiley	Pvt	A 24th SCVI	Marietta, GA	06/19/64	Louisville, KY	06/27/64	Camp Morton, IN	P94
					Camp Morton, IN	02/13/65	Died	P100,P101
Brown, A.F.	Pvt	G 17th SCVI	Amelia C.H., VA	04/06/65	Pt. Lookout, MD	06/24/65	Rlsd. G.O. #109	P123
Brown, Adolphus W.	Cpt	A Hol.Leg.	Five Forks, VA	04/01/65	City Pt., VA	04/04/65	Old Capitol, DC	CSR
					Old Capitol, DC	04/19/65	Johnson's Isl., OH	CSR
					Johnson's Isl., OH	06/18/65	Rlsd. G.O.#109	P81,P82,P83,CSR
Brown, Alexander E.	Pvt	L Orr's Ri.	Spotsylvania, VA	05/12/64	Belle Plain, VA	05/21/64	Ft. Delaware, DE	CSR
					Ft. Delaware, DE		Hos 7/21-7/26/64	P47
					Ft. Delaware, DE	06/10/65	Rlsd. G.O. #109	P41,P43,P45,CSR
Brown, Alfred B.	Pvt	E 17th SCVI	Petersburg, VA	03/25/65	City Pt., VA	03/28/65	Pt. Lookout, MD	CSR
					Pt. Lookout, MD	06/23/65	Rlsd. G.O. #109	P114,CSR
Brown, Alwyn H.	Pvt	L 1st SCVIG	Falling Waters, MD	07/14/63	Ft. McHenry, MD	08/06/63	Pt. Lookout, MD	P110,SA1
					Old Capitol, DC	08/08/63	Pt. Lookout, MD	CSR
					Pt. Lookout, MD	03/14/65	Exchanged	P113,P124,CSR
					Pt. Lookout, MD	06/05/66	Died, Diarrhea	P6,P116,P119,FPH
Brown, Ambrose P.	Pvt	F 24th SCVI	Atlanta, GA	09/02/64	Nashville, TN	10/27/64	Louisville, KY	CSR
					Louisville, KY	10/29/64	Camp Douglas, IL	P90,P91,P95,CSR
					Camp Douglas, IL	04/15/65	Jd. 5th US Vol.	P53,EFW,CSR
Brown, Andrew C.	Pvt	G 14th SCVI	Spotsylvania, VA	05/12/64	Belle Plain, VA	05/21/64	Ft. Delaware, DE	CSR
					Ft. Delaware, DE	06/10/65	Released	P41,P45,CSR
Brown, Andrew J.	Pvt	B Wash'n LA	Culpepper, VA	11/10/63	Old Capitol, DC	03/18/64	Philadelphia, PA	CSR
Brown, Andrew J.	Pvt	D 27th SCVI	Town Creek, NC	02/20/65	Ft. Anderson, NC	02/28/65	Pt. Lookout, MD	CSR,HAG
Brown, Andrew J.	Pvt	D 27th SCVI	Town Creek, NC	02/20/65	Pt. Lookout, MD	06/27/65	Rlsd. G.O. #109	P114,HAG
Brown, Andrew J.	Pvt	A 18th SCVI	Hatchers Run, VA	03/29/65	City Pt., VA	03/29/65	Pt. Lookout, MD	CSR
					Pt. Lookout, MD	06/24/65	Rlsd. G.O. #109	P123
Brown, Angus P.	Cpt	K 1st SCVC	Upperville, VA	06/21/63	Old Capitol, DC	08/08/63	Johnson's Isl., OH	CSR
					Ft.McHenry, MD	08/08/63	Johnson's Isl., OH	P110
					Johnson's Isl., OH	02/09/64	Pt. Lookout, MD	P80,P82,CSR
					Pt. Lookout, MD	03/10/65	City Pt., VA Xc	P113,P117,P123,CSR
Brown, Asa	Pvt	F 4th SCVC	Louisa, C.H., VA	06/12/64	Fts. Monroe, VA	06/20/64	Pt. Lookout, MD	CSR
					Pt. Lookout, MD	07/25/64	Elmira, NY	P117,HMC,CSR
					Elmira, NY	10/10/64	Died, Diarrhea	P6,P12,P65,FPH,CSR
Brown, B.S.	Pvt	D Hol.Leg.	Petersburg, VA	04/03/65	City Pt., VA	04/11/65	Hart's Island, NY	CSR
					Hart's Island, NY	06/16/65	Rlsd. G.O. #109	P79,CSR
Brown, Breaker	Pvt	E 19th SCVI	Chattahoochee, GA	07/10/64	Nashville, TN	07/26/64	Louisville, KY	CSR
					Louisville, KY	07/26/64	Camp Douglas, IL	P90,P91,P94,CSR
					Camp Douglas, IL	04/06/65	Jd. 6th US Inf.	P7,P53,P55,CSR
Brown, Burnett	Pvt	A Ham.Leg.MI	Deserted/enemy	01/31/65	Bermuda Hundred, VA	02/01/65	City Pt., VA P.M.	CSR
					City Pt., VA	02/01/65	Washington, DC	CSR
					Washington, DC	02/04/65	Troy, NY on oath	CSR
Brown, Burrell	Pvt	8 10/19 SCVI	Missionary Ridge, TN	11/25/63	Nashville, TN	12/07/63	Louisville, KY	P39
					Louisville, KY	12/09/63	Rock Island, IL	P88,P89
					Rock Island, IL	10/27/64	Released on oath	P131,CSR
Brown, Burrell J.	Pvt	E 19th SCVI	Munfordville, KY H	09/23/62	Munfordville, KY H	12/23/62	Paroled	CSR

SOUTH CAROLINA SOLDIERS, SAILORS AND  CITIZENS HELD IN U.S. PRISONS 1861-1865

NAME	RANK	REGIMENT	CAPTURED AT	WHEN	PRISON	MOVED	DISPOSITION	SOURCES
Brown, Burrell J.	Pvt	E 19th SCVI	Missionary Ridge, TN	11/25/63	Nashville, TN	12/07/63	Louisville, KY	CSR
					Louisville, KY	12/11/63	Rock Island, IL	CSR
					Rock Island, IL	10/27/64	Released on oath	CSR
Brown, C.K.	Sgt	G 17th SCVI	Petersburg, VA Hos	04/09/65	Pt. O Rocks US Hos	04/12/65	Fts. Monroe, VA GH	CSR
					Fts. Monroe G.H.	06/11/65	Camp Hamilton, MD	CSR
					Camp Hamilton, VA	06/18/65	Rlsd. G.O. #109	CSR
Brown, Calvin F.	Pvt	F 18th SCVI	Petersburg, VA	07/30/64	City Pt., VA	08/08/64	Pt. Lookout, MD	CSR
					Pt. Lookout, MD	08/08/64	Elmira, NY	P117,P120,CSR
					Elmira, NY	03/14/65	James R., VA Xc	P65,CSR
Brown, Charles	Pvt	D 14th SCVI	Greensboro, NC	05/09/65	Greensboro, NC	05/09/65	Paroled	CSR
Brown, Charles	Pvt	D 14th SCVI	Alexandria, VA	05/14/65	Alexandria, VA	05/14/65	Amnesty	CSR
Brown, Charles A.	Pvt	Ferguson's LA	Salisbury, NC	05/12/65	Nashville, TN	04/29/65	Louisville, KY	P39,CSR
					Louisville, KY	05/02/65	Camp Chase, OH	P95,CSR
					Camp Chase, OH	06/13/65	Rlsd. G.O. #109	CSR
Brown, Cornelius J.H.	1Sg	A 24th SCVI	Taylors Ridge, GA	10/16/64	Nashville, TN	10/23/64	Louisville, KY	CSR
					Louisville, KY	10/27/64	Camp Douglas, IL	P90,P91,P95,CSR
					Camp Douglas, IL	06/17/65	Rlsd. G.O. #109	CSR
Brown, Cyrus W.	Pvt	1st SCVIG	Richmond, VA Hos.	04/18/65	Richmond, VA	04/18/65	Paroled	CSR
Brown, D.W.	Pvt	C 3rd SCVABn	Ft. Gaines, AL	08/08/64	New Orleans, LA	08/21/64	St. Louis, MO G.H.	CSR
					St. Louis, MO G,H,	08/30/64	New Orleans, LA	CSR
					New Orleans, LA	09/05/64	St. Louis, MO. G.H	CSR
					St. Louis, MO.G.H.	09/20/64	New Orleans, LA	CSR
					New Orleans, LA	10/23/64	Ship Island, MS	P3,CSR
					Ship Island, MS	01/04/65	Exchanged	CSR
Brown, Daniel Edward	1LA	14th SCVI	Spotsylvania, VA	05/12/64	Judiciary Sq.H, DC	05/25/64	Died	P6,CGS,CSR
Brown, David	Pvt	G 25th SCVI	Town Creek, NC	02/20/65	Ft. Anderson, NC	02/28/65	Pt. Lookout, MD	CSR,HAG
					Pt. Lookout, MD	05/08/65	Died	P6,P114,P119,FPH
Brown, David J.	Pvt	B 1st SCVIG	Wilderness, VA	05/06/64	Belle Plain, VA	05/21/64	Ft. Delaware, DE	CSR
					Ft. Delaware, DE	11/28/64	Hos 11/28-12/15/64	P47
					Ft. Delaware, DE	06/10/65	Released	P41,P43,P45,SA1,CSR
Brown, E.	Pvt	A 26th SCVI	Hatcher's Run, VA	03/31/65	City Pt., VA	04/02/65	Pt. Lookout, MD	CSR
					Pt. Lookout, MD	06/24/65	Rlsd. G.O. #109	P114,P118,P123,CSR
Brown, Edmond T.	Cpl	A 27th SCVI	Ft. Anderson, NC	02/19/65	Ft. Anderson, NC	02/28/65	Pt. Lookout, MD	CSR,HAG
					Pt. Lookout, MD	06/24/65	Rlsd. G.O. #109	P114,P121,P123
Brown, Edward	Pvt	K 3rd SCVI	Middletown, VA	07/12/63	Ft. McHenry, MD	07/15/63	Ft. Delaware, DE	CSR
					Ft. Delaware, DE	08/30/63	Jd. 3rd MD Cav. U.	P40,CSR
Brown, Edward	Pvt	E 11th SCVI	Petersburg, VA	06/24/64	Bermuda Hundred, VA	06/25/64	Fts. Monroe, VA	CSR
					Fts. Monroe, VA	06/26/64	Pt. Lookout, MD	CSR
					Pt. Lookout, MD	08/16/64	Elmira, NY	P113,P117,P120,CSR
					Elmira, NY	01/23/65	Died, Pneumonia	P6,P12,P65,HAG,CSR
Brown, Edward	Pvt	F 18th SCVI	Farmville, VA	04/06/65	City Pt., VA	04/07/63	Pt. Lookout, MD	CSR
					Pt. Lookout, MD	06/20/65	Rlsd. G.O. #109	P119,P121,P122,CSR
Brown, Edward P.	Pvt	B 5th SCVC	Deserted/enemy	03/18/65	Charleston, SC	04/01/65	Released on oath	CSR
Brown, Edwin	Pvt	I 27th SCVI	Town Creek, NC	02/20/65	Ft. Anderson, NC	02/28/65	Pt. Lookout, MD	CSR
					Pt. Lookout, MD	05/28/65	Rlsd. G.O. #85	P114,HAG
Brown, Elias	Pvt	8 10/19 SCVI	Missionary Ridge, TN	11/25/63	Nashville, TN	12/07/63	Louisville, KY	P39,CSR
					Louisville, KY	12/09/63	Rock Island, IL	P88,P89,CSR
					Rock Island, IL	10/16/64	Jd. US Army, F.S.	P131
					Rock Island, IL	06/20/65	Rlsd. G.O. #109	CSR
Brown, F.W.	Pvt	D 20th SCVI	Cedar Creek, VA	10/19/64	Harpers Ferry, WV	10/28/64	Pt. Lookout, MD	CSR
					Pt. Lookout, MD	01/27/65	Hammond G.H., MD	P114,P121,KEB,CSR
					Pt. Lookout, MD	05/11/65	Died, Lithiasis	P6,P118,FPH,CSR

SOUTH CAROLINA SOLDIERS, SAILORS AND  CITIZENS HELD IN U.S. PRISONS 1861-1865

NAME	RANK	REGIMENT	CAPTURED AT	WHEN	PRISON	MOVED	DISPOSITION	SOURCES
Brown, G.A.	Pvt	A 6th SCVI	Richmond, VA Hos.	04/03/65	Libby Prison Rchmd	04/23/65	Newport News, VA	CSR
					Newport News, VA	06/16/65	Rlsd. G.O. #109	P107,CSR
Brown, G.M.	Pvt	C 3rd SCVABn	Ft. Gaines, AL	08/08/64	St. Louis, MO G.H.	11/02/64	New Orleans, LA	CSR
					Ship Island, MS	01/05/65	Exchanged	CSR
Brown, G.W.	Pvt	G Ham.Leg.MI	Deserted/enemy	02/27/65	Bermuda Hundred, VA	02/28/65	City Pt., VA P.M.	CSR
					City Pt., VA	03/01/65	Washington, DC	CSR
					Washington, DC	03/02/65	Charleston, SC	CSR
Brown, G.W.	Pvt	I 18th SCVI	Farmville, VA	04/06/65	City Pt., VA	04/14/65	Newport News, VA	CSR
					Newport News, VA	06/16/65	Rlsd. G.O. #109	P107,CSR
Brown, George	Pvt	G 3rd SCVABn	High Pt., NC	05/01/65	High Pt., NC	05/01/65	Paroled on oath	CSR
Brown, H.B.	1Lt	C 17th SCVI	Crater, Pbg., VA	07/30/64	Old Capitol, DC	08/11/64	Ft. Delaware, DE	CSR
					Ft. Delaware, DE	06/17/65	Rlsd. G.O. #109	P43,P45,CSR
Brown, Harvey E.	Pvt	H 26th SCVI	Southside RR, VA	04/01/65	City Pt., VA	04/05/65	Pt. Lookout, MD	CSR
					Pt. Lookout, MD	06/24/65	Rlsd. G.O. #109	P114,P118,P123
Brown, Harvey J.	Pvt	C 25th SCVI	Ft. Fisher, NC	01/15/65	New York, NY	01/30/65	Elmira, NY	CSR
					Elmira, NY	06/23/65	Rlsd. G.O. #109	P65,P66,HAG,CTA
Brown, Henry J.	Pvt	Brooks LA	Harpers Farm, VA	04/06/65	City Pt., VA	04/14/65	Pt. Lookout, MD	CSR
					Pt. Lookout, MD	06/23/65	Rlsd. G.O. #109	CSR
Brown, Henry J.	Pvt	D 2nd SCVI	Wilderness, VA	05/06/64	Belle Plain, VA	05/21/64	Ft. Delaware, DE	CSR,SA2,H2
					Ft. Delaware, DE	11/26/64	Hos 11/26-12/23/64	P47
					Ft. Delaware, DE	03/06/65	Hos 3/6-4/5/65	P47
					Ft. Delaware, DE	04/24/65	Hos 4/24-4/29/65	P47
					Ft. Delaware, DE	05/11/65	Rlsd. G.O. #85	P41,P43,P46,CSR
Brown, Henry M.	Pvt	G 25th SCVI	Town Creek, NC	02/20/65	Ft. Anderson, NC	02/24/65	Pt. Lookout, MD	CSR
					Pt. lookout, MD	06/24/65	Rlsd. G.O. #109	P114,P123,HAG
Brown, Herrington E.	Pvt	B 13th SCVI	Gettysburg, PA	07/04/63	David's Island, NY	10/12/63	Died, of wounds	P1,P6,FPH,HOS,CSR
Brown, Hiram	Pvt	H 22nd SCVI	Crater, Pbg., VA	07/30/64	City Pt., VA	08/05/64	Pt. Lookout, MD	CSR
					Pt. Lookout, MD	08/08/64	Elmira, NY	P113,P117,P120,CSR
					Elmira, NY	03/11/65	Died, Diarrhea	P6,P12,P65,FPH,CSR
Brown, Ira B.	Pvt	A 15th SCVI	Deserted/enemy	07/27/63	Ft. Mifflin, PA	11/14/63	Released on oath	P2,KEB,CSR
Brown, J.A.	Pvt	B P.S.S.	Ft. Harrison, VA	10/07/64	Newport News, VA	06/14/65	Rlsd. G.O. #109	CSR
Brown, J.A.	Pvt	H 23rd SCVI	Richmond Hos., VA	04/09/65	Pt. Lookout, MD	07/25/65	Rlsd. G.O. #109	P119,CSR
Brown, J.D.	Pvt	K 1st SCVIH	Richmond, VA Hos.	04/03/65	Libby Prison Rchmd		No release data	CSR
Brown, J.D.	Pvt	H Ham.Leg.MI	Farmville, VA	04/11/65	Farmville, VA	04/11/65	Paroled	CSR
Brown, J.E.	Pvt	K 1st SCVIH	Richmond, VA	04/02/65	Richmond, VA P.M.	04/15/65	South Carolina	CSR
Brown, J.E.	Pvt	A 14th SCMil	Lynch's Creek, SC	02/25/65	Hart's Island, NY	06/14/65	Released	P79
Brown, J.F.	Pvt	I 5th SCVI	Deep Bottom, VA	08/14/64	Bermuda Hundred, VA	08/15/64	Fts. Monroe, VA	CSR,SA3
					Fts. Monroe, VA	08/16/64	Pt. Lookout, MD	CSR
					Pt. Lookout, MD	02/10/65	Aikens Ldg. Xc	P117,P124,P125
Brown, J.J.	Pvt	I 6th SCVC			New Bern, NC	04/09/65	Hart's Island, NY	CSR
					Hart's Island, NY	04/15/65	David's Island, NY	P1,CSR
					David's Island, NY	05/05/65	Died	P6,FPH
Brown, J.L.	Pvt	C 17th SCVI	Deserted/enemy	02/24/65	City Pt., VA	02/26/65	Washington, DC	CSR
					Washington, DC	02/27/65	Jacksonville, FL	CSR
Brown, J.M.	Pvt	D 27th SCVI	Weldon RR, VA	08/21/64	Pt. Lookout, MD	12/11/64	Died	P117
Brown, J.M.	Pvt	B 14th SCVI	Augusta, GA	05/19/65	Augusta, GA	05/19/65	Paroled	CSR
Brown, J.S.	Pvt	A 27th SCVI	Petersburg, VA	06/24/64	Pt. Lookout, MD	03/14/65	Aikens Ldg., VA Xc	P117
Brown, J.T.	Cpl	B 12th SCVI	Gettysburg, PA	07/05/63	Chester, PA G.H.	07/18/63	Died, Debility	P1,P6,P12,FPH,CSR
Brown, James	Pvt	B 22nd SCVI	Kinston, NC	12/15/62	Kinston, NC	12/15/62	Paroled POW	CSR
Brown, James	Pvt	H 1st SCVA	Morris Island, SC	07/10/63	Hilton Head, SC	08/31/63	Ft. Columbus, NY	CSR
					Ft. Columbus, NY	09/23/63	Took the oath	P1,CSR

SOUTH CAROLINA SOLDIERS, SAILORS AND  CITIZENS HELD IN U.S. PRISONS 1861-1865

NAME	RANK	REGIMENT	CAPTURED AT	WHEN	PRISON	MOVED	DISPOSITION	SOURCES
Brown, James	Pvt	8 10/19 SCVI	Missionary Ridge, TN	11/25/63	Nashville, TN	12/07/63	Louisville, KY	P39,CSR
					Louisville, KY	12/07/63	Rock Island, IL	P88,P89,CSR
					Rock Island, IL	02/10/64	Died, Variola	P5,P131,P132,FPH,CSR
Brown, James	Pvt	K 1st SCVIG	Deserted/enemy	03/10/65	Charleston, SC	03/15/65	Rlsd. on oath	SA1,CSR
Brown, James	Pvt	D Hol.Leg.	Amelia C.H., VA	04/06/65	City Pt., VA	04/13/65	Pt. Lookout, MD	CSR
					Pt. Lookout, MD	06/24/65	Rlsd. G.O. #109	P114,P119,CSR
Brown, James C.	Pvt	E 3rd SCVIBn	Gettysburg, PA	07/05/63	Letterman Hosp., P	09/28/63	Baltimore, MD USGH	P1,CSR
					W. Bldg. Balt., MD	01/10/64	City Pt, VA Xc	P1,CSR
					Pt. Lookout, MD	03/17/64	City Pt., Xc	P116,P124,CSR
Brown, James H.	Pvt	B 25th SCVI	Weldon RR, VA	08/21/64	City Pt., VA	08/24/64	Pt. Lookout, MD	CSR,HAG
					Pt. Lookout, MD	02/10/65	Aikens Ldg., VA Xc	P113,P117,P124,HAG
Brown, James M.	Pvt	A 2nd SCVC	Martinsburg, WV	07/13/63	Wheeling, WV	07/22/63	Camp Chase, OH	P1,CSR
					Camp Chase, OH	02/29/64	Ft. Delaware, DE	P22,P25,CSR
					Ft. Delaware, DE	06/10/65	Rlsd. G.O. #109	P41,P42,P45,CSR
Brown, James M.	Pvt	C 25th SCVI	Weldon RR, VA	08/21/64	City Pt., VA	08/24/64	Pt. Lookout, MD	CSR
					Pt. Lookout, MD	10/11/64	Exchanged	P113,P123,CTA
Brown, James T.	Sgt	C Hol.Leg.	Five Forks, VA	04/01/65	City Pt., VA	04/05/65	Pt. Lookout, MD	CSR
					Pt. Lookout, MD	06/07/65	Rlsd. sick list	P114,P118,CSR
Brown, James W.	Pvt	3 10/19 SCVI	Missionary Ridge, TN	11/25/63	Nashville, TN	12/07/63	Louisville, KY	P39,CSR
					Louisville, KY	12/07/63	Rock Island, IL	P88,P89,RAS,CSR
Brown, Jesse	Cpl	E 2nd SCVC	Brandy Stn., VA	08/01/63	Old Capitol, DC	08/23/63	Pt. Lookout, MD	CSR
					Pt. Lookout, MD	11/12/63	U.S. Gen. Hospital	P113
					Pt. Lookout, MD	11/13/63	Died	P5,P116,FPH,CSR
Brown, Jesse	Pvt	B 14th SCVI	Augusta, GA	05/19/65	Augusta, GA	05/19/65	Paroled	CSR
Brown, Jesse J.	Pvt	L 1st SCVIG	Hanover Jctn., VA	05/25/64	Pt. Lookout, MD	07/08/64	Elmira, NY	P117,P120,SA1,CSR
					Elmira, NY	04/29/65	Died, Diarrhea	P6,P12,P65,FPH,CSR
Brown, Jesse T.	Pvt	A 2nd SCVI	Gettysburg, PA	07/02/63	Gettysburg G.H.	12/02/63	Provost Marshal	P4,KEB,SA2,CSR
					Pt. Lookout, MD	03/17/64	City Pt., VA Xc	P113,P116,P123,H2
Brown, John	Pvt	B 1st SCVA	Deserted/enemy	08/06/64	Philadelphia, PA	08/06/64	Not given	CSR
Brown, John	Pvt	H 19th SCVI	Pulaski, TN	12/25/64	Nashville, TN	02/14/65	Louisville, KY	P4,P39,CSR
					Louisville, KY	02/17/65	Camp Chase, OH	P92,P95,CSR
					Camp Chase, OH	03/28/65	Pt. Lookout, MD	P23,CSR
					Pt. Lookout, MD	06/06/65	Released G.O. #85	P114,P119,CSR
Brown, John	Pvt	D 24th SCVI	Fayetteville, NC	03/10/65	Pt. Lookout, MD	06/09/65	Released	P114,P118,EFW
Brown, John A.	Pvt	F 7th SCVI	Cass Stn., GA	06/03/64	Nashville, TN	06/13/64	Louisville, KY	P3,CSR
					Louisville, KY	06/14/64	Rock Island, IL	P90,P91,P94,CSR
					Rock Island, IL	07/06/64	Joined US Navy	P131
Brown, John M.	Pvt	K 15th SCVI	Halltown, WV	08/21/64	Harpers Ferry, WV	08/29/64	Camp Chase, OH	CSR
					Camp Chase, OH	12/08/64	Died, Smallpox	P6,P12,P23,P27,CSR
					Camp Chase, OH	03/18/65	Camp Lookout, MD	P26
Brown, John O.	Pvt	L 21st SCVI	Ft. Fisher, NC	01/15/65	Pt. Lookout, MD	02/13/65	Aikens Ldg., VA Xc	P114,P121,P124,HAG
Brown, John T.	Pvt	8 10/19 SCVI	Missionary Ridge, TN	11/25/63	Nashville, TN	12/07/63	Louisville, KY	P39,CSR
					Louisville, KY	12/09/63	Rock Island, IL	P88,P89,CSR
					Rock Island, IL	02/25/65	Pt. Lookout, MD Xc	P131
					Ft. Columbus, NY	03/06/65	Boulwares Wh. Xc	CSR
Brown, Joseph	Pvt	6 10/19 SCVI	Missionary Ridge, TN	11/25/63	Nashville, TN	12/07/63	Louisville, KY	P39,CSR
					Louisville, KY	12/09/63	Rock Island, IL	P88,P89,RAS,CSR
					Rock Island, IL	04/21/64	Released	P131,CSR
Brown, Joseph	Pvt	B 22nd SCVI	Petersburg, VA	02/05/65	City Pt., VA	02/09/65	Pt. Lookout, MD	CSR
					Pt. Lookout, MD	06/23/65	Rlsd. G.O. #109	CSR
Brown, Joseph M.	Pvt	B 13th SCVI	Gettysburg, PA	07/04/63	David's Island, NY	08/24/63	City Pt., VA Xc	P1,CSR

SOUTH CAROLINA SOLDIERS, SAILORS AND  CITIZENS HELD IN U.S. PRISONS 1861-1865

NAME	RANK	REGIMENT	CAPTURED AT	WHEN	PRISON	MOVED	DISPOSITION	SOURCES
Brown, Joseph Newton	Col	14th SCVI	N. Anna River, VA	05/23/64	Old Capitol, DC	06/15/64	Ft. Delaware, DE	P44,CSR
					Ft. Delaware, DE	06/25/64	Hilton Head, SC Xc	P43
Brown, Joseph Newton	Col	14th SCVI	Southside RR, VA	04/02/65	City Pt., VA	04/05/65	Old Capitol, DC	CSR
					Old Capitol, DC	04/09/65	Johnson's Isl., OH	CSR
					Johnson's Isl., OH	07/25/65	Rlsd. G.O. #109	P81,P83,LC,CSR
Brown, Joseph T.	Pvt	E 19th SCVI	Nashville, TN	12/15/64	Louisville, KY	12/20/64	Camp Douglas, IL	P90,P91,P95,CSR
					Camp Douglas, IL	04/06/65	Jd. US 6th NJVI	P55,CSR
Brown, Joshua	Pvt	K 15th SCVI	Halltown, WV	08/26/64	Harpers Ferry, WV	08/29/63	Camp Chase, OH	CSR
					Washington, DC	09/02/64	Camp Chase, OH	CSR
					Camp Chase, OH	03/18/65	Pt. Lookout, MD Xc	P23,KEB,CSR
					Pt. Lookout, MD	03/27/65	Boulware's Wh. Xc	H15,CSR
Brown, Joshua	Pvt	K 15th SCVI	Richmond, VA Hos.	04/03/65	Libby Prison Rchmd	04/24/65	Paroled	CSR
Brown, Josiah	Pvt	E 27th SCVI	Petersburg, VA	06/18/64	City Pt., VA	06/24/64	Pt. Lookout, MD	CSR,HAG
					Pt. Lookout, MD	07/27/64	Elmira, NY	P113,P117,P120
					Elmira, NY	03/14/65	Pt.Lookout, MD Xc	P65
Brown, Josiah S.	Pvt	A 27th SCVI	Petersburg, VA	06/24/64	Bermuda Hundred, VA	06/25/64	Fts. Monroe, VA	CSR,HAG
					Fts. Monroe, VA	06/26/64	Pt. Lookout, MD	CSR
					Pt. Lookout, MD	03/14/65	Exchanged	P113,P124
Brown, L.S.	Pvt	B 1st SCVIH	Warrenton, VA	09/29/62	Warrenton, VA	09/29/62	Paroled	CSR
Brown, M.	Pvt	F 1st SCVIH	Hartwell, GA	05/17/65	Hartwell, GA	05/17/65	Paroled	CSR
Brown, Malcolm M.	Pvt	B Ham.Leg.	Warrenton, VA	09/29/62	Warrenton, VA	09/29/62	Paroled	CSR
Brown, Malcolm M.	Pvt	K 15th SCVI	Halltown, WV	08/26/64	Harpers Ferry, WV	08/29/64	Camp Chase, OH	CSR
					Camp Chase, OH	03/18/65	Pt. Lookout, MD	CSR
					Pt. Lookout, MD	03/27/65	Boulwares Wh. Xc	CSR
Brown, Marcus	Pvt	C Hol.Leg.	Richmond Hos. VA	04/09/65	Pt. Lookout, MD	06/26/65	Rlsd. G.O. #109	P119
Brown, Micajah C.	Pvt	G 14th SCVI	Five Forks, VA	04/01/65	City Pt., VA	04/05/65	Pt. Lookout, MD	CSR
					Pt. Lookout, MD	06/24/65	Rlsd. G.O. #109	P114,P118,P123,CSR
Brown, N.D.	Pvt	D Orr's Ri.	Falling Waters, MD	07/14/63	Baltimore, MD	08/16/63	Pt. Lookout, MD	CSR,CDC
					Pt. Lookout, MD	08/16/64	Elmira, NY	P113,P116,P120
					Elmira, NY	03/02/65	Pt.Lookout, MD Xc	P65,CSR
					Pt. Lookout, MD		Exchanged	P124
Brown, Perry W.	Cpl	D 24th SCVI	Nashville, TN	12/16/64	Nashville, TN	12/31/64	Louisville, KY	CSR
					Louisville, KY	01/02/65	Camp Chase, OH	CSR
					Camp Chase, OH	06/12/65	Rlsd. G.O. #109	P23,EFW,CSR
Brown, Peter	Pvt	G 6th SCVI	Ft. Harrison, VA	09/30/64	Fld. Hos.18th AC A	10/01/64	U.S. Gnl. Hospital	CSR
Brown, Peter	Pvt	17th SCVI	Tallahassee, FL	05/10/65	Tallahassee, FL	05/10/65	Paroled	CSR
Brown, Phillip	Sgt	A 16th SCVI	Yazoo City, MS Hos	07/13/63	Yazoo City, MS Hos	07/13/63	Paroled on oath	CSR
Brown, Pierce B.	Pvt	E 16th SCVI	Franklin, TN	11/30/64	Nashville, TN	12/03/64	Louisville, KY	CSR
					Louisville, KY	12/04/64	Camp Douglas, IL	P90,P91,P95,CSR
					Camp Douglas, IL	07/31/65	Camp Douglas Hos.	P53,16R,CSR
					Camp Douglas Hos.	08/20/65	Sent home	CSR
Brown, Pressley	Cpt	A 15th SCVI	Halltown, WV	08/26/64	Harpers Ferry, WV	08/31/64	Ft. Delaware, DE	CSR
					Ft. Delaware, DE	06/17/65	Rlsd. G.O. #109	P43,P45,KEB,CSR
Brown, R.M.	Pvt	K 2nd SCVI	Sharpsburg, MD	09/10/62	Frederick, MD USGH	11/07/62	Died of wounds	SA2,P6,P12,FPH,H2
Brown, R.S.	Pvt	K 7th SCVC	Farmville, VA	04/11/65	Farmville, VA	04/21/65	Paroled	CSR
Brown, Richard	Pvt	F 7th SCVC	Richmond, VA	04/03/65	Richmond, VA Hos.	04/21/65	P.M. Richmond, VA	CSR
					P.M. Richmond, VA	04/24/65	Newport News, VA	CSR
					Newport News, VA	06/15/65	Fts. Monroe, VA	CSR
					Fts. Monroe, VA	07/15/65	Died	P6,CSR

B

SOUTH CAROLINA SOLDIERS, SAILORS AND CITIZENS HELD IN U.S. PRISONS 1861-1865

NAME	RANK	REGIMENT	CAPTURED AT	WHEN	PRISON	MOVED	DISPOSITION	SOURCES
Brown, Richard Evander	Pvt	I 21st SCVI	Petersburg, VA	05/09/64	Bermuda Hundred, VA	05/11/64	Camp Hamilton, VA	CSR,HAG
					Camp Hamilton, VA	05/13/64	Pt. Lookout, MD	CSR
					Pt. Lookout, MD	08/16/64	Elmira, NY	P113,P117,CSR
					Elmira, NY	10/01/64	Died	P6,P12,FPH
Brown, Samuel S.	Pvt	A 15th SCVAB	Smith's Farm, NC	04/28/65	Paroled		Left behind in hosp.	CSR
Brown, Simon	Pvt	E 7th SCVIBn	Weldon RR, VA	08/21/64	City Pt., VA	08/24/64	Pt. Lookout, MD	CSR
					Pt. Lookout, MD	03/18/65	Aikens Ldg., VA Xc	P117,CSR
Brown, Stephen	Pvt	McQueen LA	Petersburg, VA	04/02/65	City Pt., VA	04/04/65	Pt. Lookout, MD	CSR
					Pt. Lookout, MD	06/28/65	Rlsd. G.O. #109	P114,P118,CSR
Brown, Sylvester	Sgt	K 20th SCVI	Winchester, VA	09/19/64	W. Bldg. Balt., MD	11/22/64	Pt. Lookout, MD	P4,KEB,CSR
					Pt. Lookout, MD	01/28/65	Hammond G.H., MD	P114,CSR
					Pt. Lookout, MD	07/25/65	Rlsd. G.O. #109	P118,CSR
Brown, Thomas	Pvt	15th SCVI	Deserted/enemy		Chattanooga, TN	05/26/65		P8,CSR
Brown, Thomas E.	Sgt	E 1st SCVA	Deserted/enemy	02/18/65	Charleston, SC	03/15/65	Taken oath & disch.	CSR
Brown, Thomas H.	Sgt	H 25th SCVI	Deserted/enemy	08/06/64	Provost Marshal		Phila., PA on oath	CSR
Brown, Thomas R.	Pvt	C 3rd SCVABn	Blakely, AL	04/09/65	Ship Island, MS	05/01/65	Vicksburg, MS Prld	CSR
Brown, Timothy C.	Cpl	F 12th SCVI	Waynesboro, VA	02/21/65	Pt. Lookout, MD	06/24/65	Rlsd. G.O. #109	P114,P118,P123,CSR
Brown, W.	Pvt	A 16th SCVI	Greenville, SC	05/23/65	Greenville, SC	05/23/65	Paroled on oath	CSR
Brown, W.M.	Pvt	K 15th SCVI	Halltown, WV	08/21/64	Camp Chase, OH	03/18/65	Pt. Lookout, MD Xc	P23,P26,KEB,CSR
Brown, Willam F.	Pvt	G 17th SCVI	Appomattox Co., VA	04/07/65	Libby Prison, Rchm	04/07/65	City Pt., VA	CSR
					City Pt., VA	04/14/65	Pt. Lookout, MD	CSR
					Pt. Lookout, MD	06/24/65	Rlsd. G.O. #109	P114,P119,CSR
Brown, William	Pvt	H 21st SCVI	Morris Island, SC	07/10/63	Hilton Head, SC	07/23/63	Morris Island, SC Xc	P2,HAG,CSR
Brown, William	Pvt	B 2nd SCVIRi	Knoxville, TN	12/18/63	Louisville, KY	01/23/64	Rock Island, IL	P88,P93,CSR
					Rock Island, IL	05/03/65	New Orleans, LA Xc	P131
					New Orleans, LA	05/23/65	Exchanged	P4,CSR
Brown, William	Pvt	B 1st SCVIH	Deserted/enemy	03/01/65	City Pt., VA	03/05/65	Washington, DC P.M	CSR
					Washington, DC P.M	03/07/65	Phila., PA on oath	CSR
Brown, William	Pvt	F 27th SCVI	Ft. Anderson, NC	02/17/65	Ft. Anderson, NC	02/28/65	Pt. Lookout, MD	CSR,HAG
					Pt. Lookout, MD	06/24/65	Rlsd. G.O. #109	P123,P124,CSR
Brown, William D.	Pvt	K 23rd SCVI	Hatchers Run, VA	04/01/65	City Pt., VA	04/05/65	Pt. Lookout, MD	CSR
					Pt. Lookout, MD	06/24/65	Rlsd. G.O. #109	P114,P118,P123,CSR
Brown, William H.	Sgt	D 12th SCVI	Spotsylvania, VA	05/12/64	Belle Plain, VA	05/21/64	Ft. Delaware, DE	CSR
					Ft. Delaware, DE	05/25/64	Hos 5/25-6/6/64	P47
					Ft. Delaware, DE	05/10/65	Rlsd., War Dept.	P41,P43,P45,CSR
Brown, William J.	Pvt	I 21st SCVI	Morris Island, SC	07/10/63	Ft. Columbus, NY	09/23/63	Took the oath	P1,HAG
					Pt. Lookout, MD	05/03/64	City Pt., VA Xc	P116,P123,P124
Brown, William R.	Cpl	E 7th SCVIBn	Weldon RR, VA	08/21/64	City Pt., VA	08/24/64	Pt. Lookout, MD	CSR,HAG
					Pt. Lookout, MD	03/14/65	Boulwares W., VA X	P113,P124,CSR
Brown, William Theodore	Cpl	A Hol.Leg.	Five Forks, VA	04/01/65	City Pt., VA	04/05/65	Pt. Lookout, MD	CSR,HOS
					Pt. Lookout, MD	06/24/65	Rlsd. G.O. #109	P114,P118,P123,CSR
Browning, Arnold A.	Pvt	D 2nd SCVC	Deserted/enemy	03/01/65	Wilmington, NC	04/09/65	Baltimore, MD oath	CSR
Browning, Henry	Cpl	Brooks L.A	Gettysburg, PA	07/04/63	David's Island, NY	08/24/63	City Pt., VA Xc	P1,CSR
					Williamsburg, VA H	09/07/63	Rtd. to duty	CSR
Browning, James H.	Pvt	D 18th SCVI	Five Forks, VA	04/01/65	City Pt., VA	04/04/65	Pt. Lookout, MD	CSR
					Pt. Lookout, MD	06/05/65	Rlsd. G.O. #85	P114,P118,UD2,CSR
Browning, John	Pvt	D 18th SCVI	Five Forks, VA	04/01/65	City Pt., VA	04/04/65	Pt. Lookout, MD	CSR
					Pt. Lookout, MD	06/23/65	Rlsd. G.O. #109	P114,P118,CSR
Browning, John H.	Pvt	D 2nd SC VC	Raleigh, NC	04/13/65	Raleigh, NC	04/13/65	Released on oath	CSR
Browning, W.F.	Pvt	D 2nd SCVIRi	Darbytown Rd., VA	12/12/64	Bermuda Hundred, VA	01/15/64	City Pt., VA	CSR
					City Pt., VA	12/15/64	Pt. Lookout, MD	CSR
					Pt. Lookout, MD	01/17/65	Aikens Ldg., VA Xc	P118,P123,P124,CSR

B

SOUTH CAROLINA SOLDIERS, SAILORS AND CITIZENS HELD IN U.S. PRISONS 1861-1865

NAME	RANK	REGIMENT	CAPTURED AT	WHEN	PRISON	MOVED	DISPOSITION	SOURCES
Brownlee, E.J.	Pvt	G 11th SCVI	Petersburg, VA	06/18/64	City Pt., VA	06/24/64	Pt. Lookout, MD	CSR,HAG
					Pt. Lookout, MD	07/27/64	Elmira, NY	P113,P117,P120
					Elmira, NY	07/07/65	Rlsd. G.O. #109	P65,CSR
Brownlee, F.L.	Pvt	G 11th SCVI	Drury's Bluff, VA	05/16/64	Fts. Monroe, VA	05/17/64	Pt. Lookout, MD	CSR,HAG
					Pt. Lookout, MD	08/15/64	Elmira, NY	P117,P120
					Elmira, NY	05/16/65	Died, Pneumonia	P6,P65,CSR
Brownlee, George W.	Sgt	8 10/19 SCVI	Missionary Ridge, TN	11/25/63	Nashville, TN	12/05/63	Louisville, KY	P39,CSR
					Louisville, KY	12/06/63	Rock Island, IL	P88,P89,CSR
					Rock Island, IL	03/01/65	Pt.lookout, MD Xc	P131,CSR
					Richmond, VA Hos.	06/10/65	Died, Ch. Diarrhea	P12,CSR
Brownlee, George W.	Sgt	8 10/19 SCVI	Richmond, VA Hos.	04/03/65	Richmond, VA Hos.	06/10/65	Paroled on oath	CSR
Brownlee, J.R.	Pvt	D 3rd SCVIBn	Sharpsburg, MD	10/06/62	Frederick, MD USFH	01/17/63	Ft. McHenry, MD	CSR
					Ft. McHenry, MD	01/31/63	City Pt., VA Xc	CSR
Brownlee, T.W.	Pvt	G 11th SCVI	Weldon RR, VA	08/21/64	David's Island, NY	10/09/64	Elmira, NY	CSR
					Elmira, NY	03/14/65	Boulware's Wh., VA	P65,CSR
Bruce, J.J.	Sgt	C 22nd SCVI	Kinston, NC	12/15/62	Kinston, NC	12/15/62	Paroled POW	CSR
Bruce, John B.	Pvt	D 7th SCVC	Deserted/enemy	10/13/64	Yorktown, VA	10/13/64	Fts. Monroe, VA	CSR
					Fts. Monroe, VA	10/15/64	New York, NY oath	CSR
Bruce, Joseph D.	Cpl	K 8th SCVI	Greencastle, PA	07/05/63	Ft. Delaware, DE	02/27/64	Hos 2/27-3/20/64	P47,HOM
					Ft. Delaware, DE	06/10/65	Rlsd. on oath	P40,P44,P45,CSR
Brumby, John S.	Pvt	D 2nd SCVI	Halltown, WV	08/26/64	Harpers Ferry, WV	09/02/64	Camp Chase, OH	SA2,CSR,KEB,H2
					Camp Chase, OH	03/26/65	Pt. Lookout, MD	P23,P26,CSR
					Pt. Lookout, MD	06/24/65	Rlsd. G.O. #109	P114,P119,P123
Brunson, G.W.	Cpl	A 19th SCVCB	Augusta, GA	05/25/65	Augusta, GA	05/25/65	Paroled on oath	CSR
Brunson, James Oscar	Pvt	D 14th SCVI	Sutherland Stn. VA	04/03/65	City Pt., VA	04/13/65	Pt. Lookout, MD	CSR,HOE
					Pt. Lookout, MD	06/24/65	Rlsd. G.O. #109	P114,P119,P123,HOE,CSR
Brunson, John H.	Pvt	K 26th SCVI	Petersburg, VA	03/25/65	City Pt., VA	03/27/65	Pt. Lookout, MD	CSR
					Pt. Lookout, MD	06/24/65	Rlsd. G.O. #109	P114,P123,P118,CSR
Brunson, W.E.	Pvt	E P.S.S.	Ft. Harrison, VA	09/30/64	Richmond, VA	10/12/64	Died of wounds	P12,CSR,TSE
Brunson, W.W.	Cpl	F 3rd SCVC	South Newport, GA	08/17/64	Philadelphia, PA	01/10/65	Ft. Delaware, DE	CSR
					Ft. Delaware, DE	02/02/65	Hos 2/2-2/12/65	P47
					Ft. Delaware, DE	06/10/65	Released	P41,P43,P45,CSR
Bruorton, Henty W.	Pvt	A 7th SCVC	Richmond, VA Hos	04/03/65	Richmond, VA Hos.	04/14/65	P.M. Richmond, VA	CSR
					Libby Prison Rchmd	04/23/65	Newport News, VA	CSR
					Newport News, VA	05/16/65	Died	P6,P12,P107,CSR
Bryan, J.M.	Pvt	Brooks LA	Richmond, VA	04/03/65	Richmond, VA Hos.	04/14/65	Provost Marshal	CSR
					Newport News, VA	06/14/65	Rlsd. G.O. #109	CSR
					Newport News, VA	06/16/65	Fts. Monroe, VA G.	CSR
					Fts. Monroe, VA GH	06/18/65	Disharged frm Hos	CSR
Bryan, J.T.	Pvt	9th SCVIH	Hilton Head, SC	10/07/61	Ft. Delaware, DE	08/01/62	Aikens Ldg., VA Xc	CSR
Bryan, James	Pvt	13th SCVI	Deserted/enemy	12/21/64	Washington, DC	12/21/64	New York, NY/oath	CSR
Bryan, James P.	Pvt	I 2nd SCVC	Stephenburg, VA	06/09/63	P.M. Army of Potom.	06/12/63	Old Capitol, DC	CSR
					Old Capitol, DC	06/25/63	City Pt., VA Xc	CSR
					Ft. McHenry, MD	06/25/63	City Pt., VA Xc	P110,UD2
Bryan, John	Pvt	E 1st SCVA	Deserted/enemy	02/24/65	Charleston, SC	03/12/65	Taken oath & disch.	CSR
Bryan, L.T.	Pvt	I 9th SCVIB	Chaplin Hills, KY	10/08/62	Danville, KY	11/04/62	Died	P12,FPH,CSR
Bryan, Lorenzo M.	Pvt	F 7th SCVC	Farmville, VA	04/06/65	City Pt., VA	04/15/64	Pt. Lookout, MD	CSR
					Pt. Lookout, MD	06/24/65	Rlsd. G.O. #109	P114,P119,P123,CSR
Bryan, Paul W.A.	Pvt	E 24th SCVI	Nashville, TN	12/16/64	Nashville, TN	01/01/65	Louisville, KY	P39
					Louisville, KY	01/03/65	Camp Chase, OH	P95
					Camp Chase, OH	06/12/65	Rlsd. G.O. #109	P23,CSR
Bryan, Robert S.	Pvt	A 22nd SCVI	Boonesboro, MD	09/14/62	Ft. Delaware, DE	10/02/62	Aikens Ldg., VA Xc	CSR

B

SOUTH CAROLINA SOLDIERS, SAILORS AND CITIZENS HELD IN U.S. PRISONS 1861-1865

NAME	RANK	REGIMENT	CAPTURED AT	WHEN	PRISON	MOVED	DISPOSITION	SOURCES
Bryan, Robert S.	Pvt	A 22nd SCVI	Kinston, NC	12/15/62	Kinston, NC	12/15/62	Paroled POW	CSR
Bryan, Robert S.	Pvt	A 22nd SCVI	Bermuda Hundred, VA	06/02/64	Fts. Monroe, VA	06/04/64	Pt. Lookout, MD	CSR
					Pt. Lookout, MD	07/28/64	Elmira, NY	P113,CSR
					Elmira, NY	11/28/64	Died	P12,FPH
Bryant, A.B.	Cpl	H Orr's Ri.	Richmond, VA Hos.	04/03/65	Richmond, VA Hos.	05/12/65	Paroled	CSR
Bryant, Bert R.	Sgt	D 18th SCVI	Petersburg, VA	03/25/65	City Pt., VA	03/28/65	Pt. Lookout, MD	CSR
					Pt. Lookout, MD	06/24/65	Rlsd. G.O. #109	P114,P118,P123,CSR
Bryant, Charles	Pvt	11th SCVI	Fredericksburg, VA	12/13/62	Fredericksburg, VA	12/17/62	Paroled to exch.	CSR
Bryant, David	Pvt	B Hol.Leg.	Petersburg, VA	03/25/65	City Pt., VA	03/28/65	Pt. Lookout, MD	CSR,HOS
					Pt. Lookout, MD	06/24/65	Rlsd. G.O. #109	P114,P118,P123
Bryant, H.	Pvt	A 19th SCVCB	Bufords Bridge, SC	02/04/65	Hart's Island, NY	06/16/65	Rlsd. G.O. #109	P79
Bryant, J.C.	Pvt	H 23rd SCVI	Farmville, VA	04/06/65	Newport News, VA	06/26/65	Rlsd. G.O. # 109	CSR
Bryant, J.J.	Pvt	B 18th SCVAB	Rockingham, NC	03/08/65	New Berne, NC	04/01/65	Hart's Island, NY	CSR
					Hart's Island, NY	06/21/65	Rlsd. G.O. #109	P79,CSR
Bryant, Jackson G.	Pvt	H 14th SCVI	Petersburg, VA	04/02/65	City Pt., VA	04/05/65	Pt. Lookout, MD	CSR,UD2
					Pt. Lookout, MD	06/24/65	Rlsd. G.O. #109	P114,P118,P123,CSR
Bryant, Jackson W.	Pvt	G 1st SCVIG	Petersburg, VA	07/29/64	City Pt., VA	08/05/64	Pt. Lookout, MD	CSR,SA1
					Pt. Lookout, MD	08/08/64	Elmira, NY	P113,P117,P120,CSR
					Elmira, NY	07/03/65	Rlsd. G.O. #109	P65,P66,CSR
Bryant, Jacob M.	Pvt	D 18th SCVI	Petersburg, VA	03/25/65	Pt. Lookout, MD	06/24/65	Rlsd. G.O. #109	P114,P118,P123,CSR
Bryant, James R.	Pvt	E 13th SCVI	Gettysburg, PA	07/05/63	Ft. McHenry, MD	07/14/63	Ft. Delaware, DE	CSR
					Ft. Delaware, DE	08/10/63	Chester, PA G.H.	P40,P42,P44,CSR
					Chester, PA G.H.	08/10/63	City Pt., VA Xc	CSR
Bryant, Jesse	Pvt	B 21st SCVI	Ft. Fisher, NC	01/15/65	Ft. Delaware, DE	03/13/65	Hos 3/13-3/27/65	P47,HAG
					Ft. Delaware, DE	06/10/65	Released	P41,P43,P45
Bryant, John R.	Pvt	A 22nd SCVI	Farmville, VA	04/06/65	City Pt., VA	04/14/65	Newport News, VA	CSR
					Newport News, VA	06/26/65	Rlsd. G.O. #109	P107,CSR
Bryant, John T.	Pvt	F 27th SCVI	Town Creek, NC	02/20/65	Ft. Anderson, NC	02/28/65	Pt. Lookout, MD	CSR,HAG
					Pt. Lookout, MD	06/24/65	Rlsd. G.O. #109	P114,P123,CSR
Bryant, John W.	Pvt	E 3rd SCVIBn	Sharpsburg, MD	09/14/62	Ft. McHenry, MD	10/17/62	Fts. Monroe, VA Xc	CSR
					Fts. Monroe, VA	10/19/62	Aikens Ldg., VA Xc	CSR
Bryant, Martin	Pvt	G 3rd SCVI	N. Anna River, VA	05/23/64	Port Royal, VA	05/30/64	Pt. Lookout, MD	CSR
					Pt. Lookout, MD	10/17/64	Joined U.S. Army	P117,P122,P124
Bryant, Richard A.	2Lt	E 1st SCVIH	Farmville, VA	04/11/65	Farmville, VA	04/21/65	Paroled	CSR
Bryant, Solomon	Cpl	McQueen LA	Petersburg, VA	04/02/65	City Pt., VA	04/04/65	Pt. Lookout, MD	CSR
					Pt. Lookout, MD	06/24/65	Rlsd. G.O. #109	P114,P118,P123,CSR
Bryant, William H.	Pvt	4 10/19 SCVI	Missionary Ridge, TN	11/25/63	Nashville, TN	12/07/63	Louisville, KY	P39,RAS,CSR
					Louisville, KY	12/09/63	Rock Island, IL	P88,P89,CSR
					Rock Island, IL	03/03/64	Died, Variola	P12,P132,FPH,CSR
Bryant, William N.	Sgt	D 18th SCVI	Crater, Pbg., VA	07/30/64	City Pt., VA	08/05/64	Pt. Lookout, MD	CSR
					Pt. Lookout, MD	08/08/64	Elmira, NY	P113,P117,P120,CSR
					Elmira, NY	01/28/65	Died, Diarrhea	P6,P12,P65,FPH,CSR
Bryant, William T.	Pvt	D 18th SCVI	Petersburg, VA	03/25/65	Pt. Lookout, MD	06/24/65	Rlsd. G.O. #109	P121,P123,UD2,CSR
Bryson, H.C.	Pvt	C 5th SCVI	Chattanooga, TN	10/29/63	Nashville, TN	11/07/63	Louisville, KY	P39,SA2,CSR
					Louisville, KY	11/09/63	Camp Morton, IN	P88,P89,P93,SA2,CSR
Bryson, H.C.	Pvt	C 5th SCVI	Chattanooga, TN	10/29/63	Camp Morton, IN	03/04/65	Tfd. for Xc	P100,CSR
					Ft. Delaware, DE	03/10/65	Cox's Wharf, VA, Xc	CSR
Bryson, W.L.	Pvt	L 2nd SCVIRi	N. Anna River, VA	05/23/64	Pt. Lookout, MD	03/14/64	Aikens Ldg., VA Xc	P117

SOUTH CAROLINA SOLDIERS, SAILORS AND  CITIZENS HELD IN U.S. PRISONS 1861-1865

NAME	RANK	REGIMENT	CAPTURED AT	WHEN	PRISON	MOVED	DISPOSITION	SOURCES
Bryson, Wesley	Pvt	G 27th SCVI	Petersburg, VA	06/24/64	Bermuda Hundred, VA	06/25/64	Fts. Monroe, VA	CSR,HAG
					Fts. Monroe, VA	06/26/64	Pt. Lookout, MD	CSR,HAG
					Pt. Lookout, MD	08/16/64	Elmira, NY	P113,P117,P120
					Elmira, NY	10/11/64	Pt. Lookout, MD Xc	P65
					Pt. Lookout, MD	10/29/64	Venus Pt., GA Xc	P114,P123,CSR
Bryson, William L.	Pvt	L 2nd SCVIRi	N. Anna River, VA	05/23/64	Port Royal, VA	05/30/64	Pt. Lookout, MD	CSR
					Pt. Lookout, MD	03/14/65	Aikens Ldg., VA Xc	P117,P124,CSR
Buchanan, Gabriel D.	Pvt	B Orr's Ri.	Petersburg, VA	04/03/65	City Pt., VA	04/11/65	Hart's Island, NY	CSR
					Hart's Island, NY	06/16/65	Rlsd. G.O. #109	P79,CDC,CSR
Buchanan, George G.	Pvt	A P.S.S.	Deep Bottom, VA	08/14/64	Bermuda Hundred, VA	08/15/64	Fts. Monroe, VA	CSR,TSE
					Fts. Monroe, VA	09/12/64	Pt. Lookout, MD	CSR
Buchanan, George G.	Pvt	A P.S.S.	Deep Bottom, VA	08/14/64	Pt. Lookout, MD	06/24/65	Rlsd. G.O. #109	P113,P123,P124
Buchanan, Hugh	Cit				Ft. Delaware, DE	05/07/64		P7
Buchanan, J.D.	Pvt	K 11th SCVI	Weldon RR, VA	08/21/64	City Pt., VA	08/24/64	Pt. Lookout, MD	CSR
					Pt. Lookout, MD	03/14/65	Aikens Ldg., VA Xc	P113,P118,P124,CSR
Buchanan, John S.	Pvt	K 11th SCVI	Weldon RR, VA	08/21/64	City Pt., Va	08/24/64	Str. State/Maine	CSR
					Str. State/Maine	08/25/64	Alexandria, VA Hos	CSR
					Alexandria, VA Hos	11/19/64	Washington, DC	P1,CSR
					Lincoln G.H., DC	12/30/64	Old Capitol, DC	CSR
					Old Capitol, DC	03/25/65	Elmira, NY	P110,CSR
					Elmira, NY	06/27/65	Rlsd. G.O. #109	P65,HAG
Buchanan, William P.	Pvt	A 13th SCVI	Gettysburg, PA	07/05/63	W. Bldg. Balt., MD	07/30/63	Baltimore, MD Jail	P1,CSR
					Baltimore, MD	08/20/63	Pt. Lookout, MD	CSR
					Pt. Lookout, MD	02/18/65	Aikens Ldg., VA Xc	P113,P116,P124,CSR
Buchanan, William P.	Pvt	A 13th SCVI	Lancaster, SC	04/03/65	Newport News, VA	06/26/65	Rlsd. G.O. #109	P107
Buche, A.A.	Pvt	F 3rd SCVC	South Newport, GA	08/17/64	Philadelphia, PA	01/10/65	Ft. Delaware, DE	CSR
					Ft. Delaware, DE	06/10/65	Released	P41,P43,P45,CSR
Buck, Henry L.	Cpt	A 26th SCVI	Petersburg, VA	03/25/65	Old Capitol, DC	03/30/65	Ft. Delaware, DE	P110,CSR
					Ft. Delaware, DE	06/17/65	Rlsd. G.O. #109	P43,P45,CSR
Buck, William	Pvt	I 1st SCVA	Deserted/enemy	02/19/65	Charleston, SC	03/02/65	Released on oath	CSR
Buckhalter, Andrew J.	Pvt	H 14th SCVI	Deserted/enemy	10/08/64	City Pt., VA	10/10/64	Washington, DC	P8,UD2,CSR
					Washington, DC	10/12/64	Pittsburg, PA oath	CSR
Buckhalter, John M.	Pvt	G Ham.Leg.MI	Augusta, GA	05/23/65	Augusta, GA	05/23/65	Paroled	CSR
Buckheister, William C.	Cpl	B 27th SCVI	Weldon RR, VA	08/21/64	Pt. Lookout, MD	09/30/64	Aikens Ldg., VA Xc	P118,P123,HAG,CSR
Buckner, P.F.	1Lt	B 5th SCVC	Augusta, GA	05/25/65	Augusta, GA	05/25/65	Paroled	CSR
Buckster, Joel R.	Pvt	A Orr's Ri.	Deserted/enemy	02/26/65	City Pt., VA	02/26/65	Washington D.C.	CSR
					Washington, D.C.	03/01/65	Peru, IN on oath	CSR
Buff, George	Cpl	D 15th SCVI	Lynch's Creek, SC	02/27/65				CSR
Buff, H.J.	Pvt	C 20th SCVI	Columbia, SC	02/18/65	New Berne, NC	04/10/65	Hart's Island, NY	CSR
					Hart's Island, NY	06/16/65	Rlsd. G.O. #109	P79,CSR
Buff, W.J.	Pvt	C 20th SCVI	Richland Dis., SC	02/16/65	New Berne, NC	04/10/65	Hart's Island, NY	CSR
					Hart's Island, NY	06/16/65	Rlsd. G.O. # 109	CSR
Buffkin, Albert J.	Pvt	K 26th SCVI	Southside RR, VA	04/01/65	City Pt., VA	04/05/65	Pt. Lookout, MD	CSR,CEN
					Pt. Lookout, MD	06/24/65	Rlsd. G.O. #109	P114,P118,CSR
Buffkin, Redding R.	Pvt	K 26th SCVI	Southside RR, VA	04/01/65	City Pt., VA	04/05/65	Pt. Lookout, MD	CSR
					Pt. Lookout, MD	06/24/65	Rlsd. G.O. #109	P114,P118,P123,CSR
Buford, R.W.	Pvt	F 3rd SCVC	South Newport, GA	08/17/64	Philadelphia, PA	01/10/65	Ft. Delaware, DE	CSR
					Ft. Delaware, DE	01/14/65	Hos 1/14-2/14/65	P47
					Ft. Delaware, DE	02/23/65	Hos 2/23-3/7/65	P47
					Ft. Delaware, DE	03/11/65	Hos 3/25-4/17/65	P47
					Ft. Delaware, DE	03/25/65	Hos 3/11-3/19/65	P47
					Ft. Delaware, DE	06/22/65	Rlsd. G.O. #109	P41,P43,P45,CSR

SOUTH CAROLINA SOLDIERS, SAILORS AND  CITIZENS HELD IN U.S. PRISONS 1861-1865

NAME	RANK	REGIMENT	CAPTURED AT	WHEN	PRISON	MOVED	DISPOSITION	SOURCES
Buist, Henry	Cpt	G 27th SCVI	Petersburg, VA	06/24/64	Bermuda Hundred, VA	06/25/64	Washington, DC	CSR,HAG
					Pt. Lookout, MD	06/25/64	Ft. Delaware, DE	P113,P117
					Pt. Lookout, MD	06/29/64	Washington, DC	P120
					Old Capitol, DC	07/22/64	Ft. Delaware, DE	P110,CSR
					Ft. Delaware, DE	08/20/64	Hilton Head, SC	P43,P44,CSR
Bulger, John	Pvt	D 24th SCVI	Marietta, GA	12/16/64	Nashville, TN	12/31/64	Louisville, KY	CSR
					Louisville, KY	01/02/65	Camp Chase, OH	CSR
					Camp Chase, OH	06/12/65	Rlsd. G.O. #109	CSR
Bull, J.D.	Pvt	A 3rd SCVABn	High Pt., NC	05/02/65	High Pt., NC	05/02/65	Paroled on oath	CSR
Bull, J.P.	Pvt	F 2nd SCVA	James Island, SC	05/12/64	Port Royal Fy., SC	08/16/64	Exchanged	CSR
Bull, J.T.	Pvt	K 18th SCVI	Funkstown, MD	07/12/63	Pt. Lookout, MD	03/17/64	City Pt., Xc	P113,P116
Bull, W.S.	Pvt	A 3rd SCVABn	High Pt., NC	05/02/65	High Pt., NC	05/02/65	Paroled on oath	CSR
Bullard, Henry H.	Pvt	G 8th SCVI	Gettysburg, PA	07/05/63	Ft. Delaware, DE	09/13/63	Jd. US 3rd MD Cav.	P40,P42,KEB,CSR
Bullard, P.B.D.	Pvt	D 25th SCVI	Town Creek, NC	02/20/65	Ft. Anderson, NC	02/28/65	Pt. Lookout, MD	CSR,HAG,HMC
					Pt. Lookout, MD	06/27/65	Rlsd. G.O. #109	P114,P123
Bullington, David G.	Pvt	I 27th SCVI	Town Creek, NC	02/20/65	Ft. Anderson, NC	02/28/65	Pt. Lookout, MD	CSR
					Pt. lookout, MD	06/24/65	Rlsd. G.O. #109	P114,P123,CSR
Bullington, R.	Pvt	F 13th SCVI	Falling Waters, MD	07/14/63	Baltimore, MD	08/16/63	Pt. Lookout, MD	CSR
					Pt. Lookout, MD	09/18/64	Aikens Ldg., VA Xc	P113,P116,P124,CSR
Bullman, James L.	Pvt	I Hol.Leg.	Stony Creek, VA	05/07/64	Fts. Monroe, VA	05/13/64	Pt. Lookout, MD	CSR,HOS
					Pt. Lookout, MD	08/15/64	Elmira, NY	P113,P116,P120,CSR
					Elmira, NY	02/04/65	Died, Variola	P6,P12,P65,FPH
Bullock, Hugh Giles	Sgt	F 1st SCVIG	Wilderness, VA	05/06/64	Belle Plain, VA	05/21/64	Ft. Delaware, DE	CSR,SA1
					Ft. Delaware, DE	06/10/65	Released	P41,P43,P45,SA1,CSR
Bullock, W.E.	Pvt	F 1st SCVIG	Sharpsburg, MD	09/17/62	Ft. Delaware, DE	10/02/62	Aikens Ldg., VA Xc	CSR
					Aikens Ldg., VA c	11/10/62	Exchanged	CSR
Bullock, William P.	Pvt	F 1st SCVIG	Gettysburg, PA	07/04/63	David's Island, NY	09/16/63	paroled	P1,SA1,CSR
Bullock, William P.	Pvt	F 1st SCVIG	Petersburg, VA	03/25/65	City Pt., VA	03/28/65	Pt. Lookout, MD	CSR
					Pt. Lookout, MD	06/24/65	Rlsd. G.O. #109	P114,P118,P123
Bullwinkle, G.H.	Pvt	B German LA	Deserted/enemy	03/30/65	Charleston, SC	03/30/65	Rele4ased on oath	CSR
Bunch, E.C.	Pvt	D 6th SCVC	Louisa C.H., VA	06/11/64	Fts. Monroe, VA	06/20/64	Pt. Lookout, MD	CSR
					Pt. Lookout, MD	07/25/64	Elmira, NY	P113,P117
					Elmira, NY	06/11/65	Rlsd. G.O. #109	P65,CSR
Bunch, Henry	Pvt	C 11th SCVI	Town Creek, NC	02/20/65	Ft. Anderson, NC	02/28/65	Pt. Lookout, MD	CSR,HAG
					Pt. Lookout, MD	06/24/65	Rlsd. G.O. #109	P114,P123,CSR
Bunch, J.C.	Pvt	A 4th SCMil	Lynch's Creek, SC	02/25/65	Hart's Island, NY	06/16/65	Rlsd. G.O. #109	P79
Bunch, J.W.	Pvt	G 27th SCVI	Petersburg, VA	06/24/64	Pt. Lookout, MD	08/16/64	Elmira, NY	P117
Bunch, Samuel F.	Pvt	C 1st SCVIG	Spotsylvania, VA	05/12/64	Ft. McHenry, MD	06/15/64	Ft. Delaware, DE	P110,SA1,CSR
					Ft. Delaware, DE	06/10/65	Released	P41,P43,P45,SA1,CSR
Bunch, W.M.	Pvt	C 11th SCVI	Petersburg, VA	06/24/64	Fts. Monroe, VA	06/26/64	Pt. Lookout, MD	CSR
					Pt. Lookout, MD	10/30/64	Aikens Ldg., VA Xc	P113,P117,P123,CSR
Bunch, William	Pvt	C 15th SCMil	Lynch's Creek, SC	02/25/65	Foster G.H., Newbern	04/17/65	Died	P1,P6,P12
Bunch, William M.	Pvt	C 11th SCVI	Darbytown Rd., VA	10/07/64	Bermuda Hundred, VA	10/30/64	City Pt., VA	CSR
					City Point VA		Point Lookout MD	CSR
					Pt. Lookout, MD	02/10/65	Exchanged	P114,P124,HAG,CSR
Bunch, William W.	Cpl	L 1st SCVIG	Petersburg, VA	04/03/65	City Pt., VA	04/13/65	Pt. Lookout, MD	CSR,SA1
					Pt. Lookout, MD	06/24/65	Rlsd. G.O. #109	P114,P119,P123,CSR
Bundrick, Arthur H.	Pvt	H 13th SCVI	Petersburg, VA	04/03/65	City Pt., VA	04/13/65	Pt. Lookout, MD	CSR
					Pt. Lookout, MD	06/24/65	Rlsd. G.O. #109	P114,P119,P123,CSR
Bundy, G. Washington	Pvt	F 21st SCVI	Ft. Fisher, NC	01/15/65	Elmira, NY	03/05/65	Died, Diarrhea	P65,P66,HAG,FPH
Burbridge, James	Pvt	G 1st SCVIR	Deserted/enemy	03/31/65	Charleston, SC	03/31/65	Taken oath & disch	CSR
Burbridge, Paul	Pvt	G 1st SCVIR	Deserted/enemy	03/31/65	Charleston, SC	03/31/65	Taken oath & disch	CSR

SOUTH CAROLINA SOLDIERS, SAILORS AND  CITIZENS HELD IN U.S. PRISONS 1861-1865

NAME	RANK	REGIMENT	CAPTURED AT	WHEN	PRISON	MOVED	DISPOSITION	SOURCES
Burch, James C.	Pvt	A 4th SCVC	Lynch's Creek, SC	02/25/65	New Berne, NC	04/10/65	Hart's Island, NY	CSR
					Hart's Island, NY	06/16/65	Rlsd. G.O. #109	CSR
Burch, James F.	Pvt	H 7th SCVC	Burkeville, VA	04/06/65	City Pt., VA	04/15/65	Pt. Lookout, MD	CSR
					Pt. Lookout, MD	06/24/65	Rlsd. G.O. #109	P114,P123,P125,CSR
Burch, Thomas C.	Pvt	H 1st SCVA	Deserted/enemy	03/15/65	Charleston, SC	03/15/65	Released on oath	CSR
Burck, John	Pvt	B 1st SCVA	Hoopers Island, MD	04/01/65	Ft. McHenry, MD	05/26/65	Escaped	CSR
Burckhalter, D. Claude	Pvt	A 1st SCVIG	Gettysburg, PA	07/05/63	Ft. Delaware, DE	12/30/63	Died, Ch. Diarrhea	P12,P40,P42,FPH
Burcomb, C.R.	Pvt	C 14th SCVI	Richmond, VA Hos	04/03/65	Provost Marshal	04/14/65	Paroled	CSR
Burdashaw, S.S.	Pvt	H 2nd SCVC	Augusta, GA	05/29/65	Augusta, GA	05/29/65	Paroled on oath	CSR
Burdell, W.L.	Pvt	I 14th SCVI	Petersburg, VA	04/03/65	City Pt., VA	04/11/65	Hart's Island, NY	CSR
					Hart's Island, NY	06/16/65	Rlsd. G.O. #109	P79,CSR
Burden, J.D.	Pvt	I 4th SCVI	Deserted/enemy	12/14/63	Kentucky	12/16/63	Released on oath	CSR
Burden, J.N.	Pvt	G 1st SCVC	Greenville, SC	05/23/65	Greenville, SC	05/23/65	Paroled	CSR
Burdet, Samuel	Pvt	F 24th SCVI	Jackson, MS	05/14/63	Jackson, MS	05/16/63	Paroled	CSR
Burdett, David W.	Pvt	I 16th SCVI	Franklin, TN	12/18/64	Nashville, TN	01/17/65	Louisville, KY	P4,P39,16R,CSR
					Louisville, KY	01/18/65	Camp Chase, OH	P92,CSR
					Camp Chase, OH	03/26/65	Pt. Lookout, MD	P23,P26
					Pt. Lookout, MD	06/09/65	Rlsd. G.O. #109	P114,P119,CSR
Burdett, Frederick H.	Pvt	E 14th SCVI	Fords Depot, VA	04/08/65	City Pt., VA	04/14/65	Pt. Lookout, MD	CSR
					Pt. Lookout, MD	06/23/65	Rlsd. G.O. #109	P114,P119,CSR
Burdett, Henry A.	Pvt	F 1st SCVIG	Petersburg, VA	03/25/65	City Pt., VA	03/28/65	Pt. Lookout, MD	CSR
					Pt. Lookout, MD	06/24/65	Rlsd. G.O. #109	P114,P118,P123,CSR
Burdett, J.W.	Pvt	F 1st SCVIH	Warrenton, VA	09/29/62	Warrenton, VA	09/29/62	Paroled	CSR
Burdine, J.W.	Pvt	D Ham.Leg.	Richmond, VA Hos	04/03/65	Libby Prsn. Rchmd.	04/23/65	Newport News, VA	CSR
					Newport News, VA	06/13/65	Released	P107
Burdine, James H.	Pvt	D Ham.Leg.	Shell Mound, AL	11/01/63	Bridgeport, AL Hos	11/05/63	Nashville, TN	CSR
					Nashville, TN	12/13/63	Louisville, KY	P39,CSR
					Louisville, KY	12/16/63	Rock Island, IL	P88,P89,UD5,CSR
Burdine, James H.	Pvt	D Ham.Leg.	Lookout Mtn., TN	11/28/63	Rock Island, IL	03/02/65	Pt.Lookout, MD Xc	P131,CSR
Burgess, A.W.	Pvt	I 25th SCVI	Weldon RR, VA	08/21/64	Bristol, PA Hos.	09/12/64	Died of wounds	CSR
Burgess, Franklin M.	Pvt	H 15th SCVI	Gettysburg, PA	07/03/63	Letterman G.H. Gbg	07/16/63	Died of wounds	P1,P12,KEB,ROH,CSR
Burgess, J. Calvin	Pvt	I 25th SCVI	Ft. Fisher, NC	01/15/65	New York, NY	01/30/65	Elmira, NY	CSR,HAG
					Elmira, NY	07/10/65	Died, Diarrhea	P6,P12,P65,P66
Burgess, John A.	Pvt	I 25th SCVI	Ft. Fisher, NC	01/15/65	New York, NY	01/30/65	Elmira, NY	CSR
					Elmira, NY	07/26/65	Rlsd. G.O. #109	HAG,CSR
Burgess, John H.	Pvt	D 7th SCVC	Saylers Creek, VA	04/06/65	Elmira, NY	06/23/65	Rlsd. G.O. #109	CSR
Burgess, Joseph	Pvt	B 18th SCVI	Petersburg, VA	07/30/64	City Pt., VA	08/05/64	Pt. Lookout, MD	CSR
					Pt. Lookout, MD	08/08/64	Elmira, NY	P113,P117,P120,CSR
					Elmira, NY	02/20/65	Died, Diarrhea	P12,P65,CSR
Burgess, N.F.	Pvt	K 2nd SCVC	Greenville, SC	05/23/65	Greenville, SC	05/23/65	Paroled on oath	CSR
Burgess, P.W.	Pvt	C 14th SCVI	Petersburg, VA	04/03/65	City Pt., VA	04/07/65	Hart's Island, NY	CSR
					Hart's Island, NY	06/15/65	Rlsd. G.O. #109	P79,CSR
Burgess, Robert B.	Pvt	I 25th SCVI	Morris Island, SC	09/07/63	Hilton Head, SC	09/15/63	Ft. Columbus, NY	CSR,HAG
					Ft. Columbus, NY	09/26/63	Johnson's Isl., OH	P1,CSR
					Pt. Lookout, MD	09/30/64	Exchanged	P113,P123,CSR
					Jackson Hos., Rchmd	10/10/64	Furloughed	CSR
Burgess, S.H.	Cpl	I 25th SCVI	Ft. Fisher, NC	01/15/65	New York, NY	01/30/65	Elmira, NY	CSR
					Elmira, NY	03/02/65	Pt. Lookout, MD Xc	P65,P66,HAG
					Jackson Hos., Rchmd	03/09/65	Furloughed	CSR
Burgess, Samuel W.	Pvt	D 18th SCVI	Petersburg, VA	04/01/65	City Pt., VA	04/04/65	Pt. Lookout, MD	CSR,UD2
					Pt. Lookout, MD	06/24/65	Rlsd. G.O. #109	P114,P118,P123,UD2,CSR

SOUTH CAROLINA SOLDIERS, SAILORS AND  CITIZENS HELD IN U.S. PRISONS 1861-1865

NAME	RANK	REGIMENT	CAPTURED AT	WHEN	PRISON	MOVED	DISPOSITION	SOURCES
Burgess, Thomas L.	Pvt	B 18th SCVI	Five Forks, VA	04/01/65	City Pt., VA	04/06/64	Pt. Lookout, MD	CSR
					Pt. Lookout, MD	06/24/65	Rlsd. G.O. #109	P114,P118,P123,CSR
Burgess, William	Pvt	E 26th SCVI	Hatchers Run, VA	03/29/65	City Pt., VA	04/02/65	Pt. Lookout, MD	CSR
					Pt. Lookout, MD	06/24/65	Rlsd. G.O. #109	P114,P118,P123,CSR
Burgess, William	Pvt	A 18th SCVI	Richmond, VA Hos	04/03/65	Libby Prison Rchmd	04/23/65	Newport News, VA	CSR
					Newport News, VA	06/28/65	Died, Ch. Diarrhea	P12,PP,CSR
Burgess, William H.	Sgt	D 1st SCVIR	Morris Island, SC	07/10/63	Hilton Head, SC	09/19/63	Ft. Columbus, NY	CSR
					Ft. Columbus, NY	09/23/63	took the oath	P1,SA1,CSR
Burk, Daniel	Pvt	E 1st SCVA	Morris Island, SC	07/10/63	Hilton Head, SC	09/05/63	Ft. Columbus, NY	CSR
					Ft. Columbus, NY	09/23/63	Took the oath	P1,CSR
Burk, James Henry	Pvt	B 15th SCVAB	Charlotte, NC Hosp	04/30/65	Paroled			CSR
Burk, John F.	Pvt	E 3rd SCVC	Summerhouse Mills	04/18/64	Louisville, KY	04/22/64	Camp Morton, IN	P90,P91,CSR
					Camp Morton, IN	02/26/65	Pt. Lookout, MD Xc	P100,P101,CSR
Burk, William	Smn	9th SCVIH	Teresa	05/10/61	Ft. Delaware, DE	08/05/62	Aikens Ldg., VA Xc	CSR
Burke, I.J.	Cpl	G 27th SCVI	Petersburg, VA	06/24/64	Bermuda Hundred, VA	06/25/64	Fts. Monroe, VA	CSR,HAG
					Fts. Monroe, VA	06/26/64	Pt. Lookout, MD	CSR,HAG
					Pt. Lookout, MD	08/16/64	Elmira, NY	P113,P117,P120,HAG
					Elmira, NY	04/11/65	Died	P6,P12,P65,FPH,HAG
Burke, J.	Pvt	C 14th SCMil	Lynch's Creek, SC	03/01/65	Hart's Island, NY	06/16/65	Rlsd. G.O. #109	P79
Burke, J.E.	Pvt	D 1st SCVIG	Newton, VA	05/24/64	White House, VA	06/08/64	Pt. Lookout, MD	CSR
					Pt. Lookout, MD	09/30/64	City Pt., VA Xc	P113,P117,CSR
Burke, M.P.	1Sg	D 1st SCVIR	Charleston Bar	03/21/63	Ft. Lafayette, NY	06/29/63	Ft. Delaware, DE	CSR,SA1
					Ft. Delaware, DE	07/31/63	City Pt., VA Xc	P40,P42,P44,CSR
Burke, Thomas	Pvt	K 1st SCVA	Deserted/Enemy	03/27/65	Charleston, SC	03/27/65	Released on oath	CSR
Burke, William	Pvt	C Hol.Leg.	Deserted/Enemy	12/31/64	City Pt., VA	01/02/65	Washington, DC	CSR
					Washington, DC	01/04/65	Phila., PA /oath	P8,CSR
Burkett, Charles M.	Pvt	K 2nd SCVIRi	Burkeville, VA	04/14/65	Burkesville, VA	04/17/65	Paroled	CSR
Burkett, G.W.	Pvt	C 2nd SCVIRi	Deserted/enemy	03/04/65	Bermuda Hundred, VA	03/04/65	City Pt., VA P.M.	CSR
					City Pt., VA	03/05/65	Washington, DC P.M	CSR
					Washington, DC P.M	03/08/65	Columbus, OH/ oath	CSR
Burkett, Thomas H.	Pvt	D 2nd SCVI	Gettysburg, PA	07/05/63	Letterman G.H. Gbg	10/06/63	Provost Marshal	P1,KEB,SA2,CSR
					W. Bldg. Balt., MD	11/12/63	City Pt., VA Xc	P1,H2,CSR
Burkett, Thomas P.	Pvt	C 2nd SCVIRi	Deserted/enemy	03/04/65	Bermuda Hundred, VA	03/05/65	City Pt., VA P.M.	CSR
					City Pt., VA P.M.	03/07/65	Washington, DC P.M	CSR
Burkett, Thomas P.	Pvt	C 2nd SCVIRi	Deserted/enemy	03/04/65	Washington, DC P.M	03/08/65	Columbus, OH/ oath	CSR
Burkett, Thomas W.	Pvt	C 6th SCResB	Augusta, GA	05/18/65	Augusta, GA	05/18/65	Paroled	CSR
Burkett, W.E.	Pvt	M P.S.S.	Richmond, VA Hos.	04/03/65	Newport News, VA	06/15/65	Rlsd. G.O. #109	P107,TSE,CSR
Burkett, William H.	Pvt	G 27th SCVI	Town Creek, NC	02/20/65	Ft. Anderson, NC	02/28/65	Pt. Lookout, MD	CSR
					Pt. Lookout, MD	05/12/65	Rlsd. G.O. #85	P114,HAG,CSR
Burley, Noah A.	Cpt	B 17th SCVI	Petersburg, VA	03/25/65	Old Capitol, DC	03/30/65	Ft. Delaware, DE	P110,CSR
					Ft. Delaware, DE	06/17/65	Rlsd. G.O. #109	P43,P45,HFC,P47,CSR
Burley, William	Pvt	A 1st SCVA	Deserted/enemy	02/18/65	Charleston, SC	03/02/65	Will take oath	CSR
Burn, Henry C.	Pvt	B 2nd SCVI	Knoxville, TN	12/18/63	Louisville, KY	01/23/64	Rock Island, IL	CSR,SA2,H2
					Rock Island, IL	06/20/65	Rlsd. G.O. #109	P88,P93,SR
Burn, Robert H.	Pvt	K 6th SCVC	Reams Station, VA	08/24/64	City Pt. VA	09/09/64	Old Capitol, DC	CSR
					Old Capitol, DC	10/27/64	Elmira, NY	CSR
					Old Capitol, DC	11/28/64	St. Louis, MO oath	P8,CSR
Burnell, J.	Pvt	C 16th SCVI	Greenville, SC	05/23/65	Greenville, SC	05/23/65	Paroled on oath	CSR
Burnes, J.	Pvt	A Naval Bn.	Amelia C.H., VA	04/06/65	Pt. Lookout, MD	06/24/65	Rlsd. G.O. #109	P123
Burnett, Alfred	Pvt	C 5th SCVC	Deserted/enemy	02/18/65	Charleston, SC	03/15/65	Released on oath	CSR
Burnett, Alvin M.	Pvt	B 13th SCVI	Gettysburg, PA	07/04/63	David's Island, NY	09/12/63	City Pt., VA Xc	P1,HOS,CSR

SOUTH CAROLINA SOLDIERS, SAILORS AND  CITIZENS HELD IN U.S. PRISONS 1861-1865

NAME	RANK	REGIMENT	CAPTURED AT	WHEN	PRISON	MOVED	DISPOSITION	SOURCES
Burnett, Alvin M.	Pvt	B 13th SCVI	Petersburg, VA	07/27/64	Pt. Lookout, MD	08/08/64	Elmira, NY	P113,P120,P125
					Elmira, NY	07/01/65	Rlsd. G.O. #109	P65
Burnett, Bury	Pvt	I 2nd SCVC	Augusta, GA	05/18/65	Augusta, GA	05/18/65	Released on oath	CSR
Burnett, D.S.	Sgt	E Hol.Leg.	Burkeville, VA	04/15/65	Burkesville, VA	04/15/65	Paroled in Hos.	CSR
Burnett, G.W.	Pvt	C 3rd SCVABn	Blakely, AL	04/09/65	Ship Island, MS	05/01/65	Vicksburg, MS Prld	P136,CSR
Burnett, H.	Pvt	G 7th SCVI	Gettysburg, PA	07/04/63	David's Island, NY	08/24/64	City Pt., VA Xc	P1,P4,KEB,HOE,CSR
Burnett, J.D.	Cpl	B 7th SCVC	Cypress Bridge, VA	05/06/64	Pt. Lookout, MD	08/15/64	Elmira, NY	P113,P120
					Elmira, NY	10/11/64	Tfd. for exchange	P65
Burnett, J.L.	Pvt	G 7th SCVI	Gettysburg, PA	07/04/63	Gettysburg G.H.		Provost Marshal	P4,KEB
Burnett, James D.	Pvt	B 13th SCVI	Burkeville, VA	04/06/65	W. Bldg. Balt., MD	05/09/65	Ft. McHenry, MD	P4,P96,HOS,CSR
					Ft. McHenry, MD	06/09/65	Rlsd. G.O. #109	CSR
Burnett, John	Cpl	I 1st SCVIH	Charlotte, NC	05/15/65	Charlotte, NC	05/15/65	Paroled	CSR
Burnett, John E.	Pvt	C 22nd SCVI	Crater, Pbg., VA	07/30/64	City Pt., VA	08/05/64	Pt. Lookout, MD	CSR
					Pt. Lookout, MD	08/08/64	Elmira, NY	P117,P120
					Elmira, NY	12/07/64	Died	P6,P12,P65,FPH
Burnett, John W.	Pvt	C 13th SCVI	Petersburg, VA	04/02/65	Pt. Lookout, MD	06/24/65	Rlsd. G.O. #109	P114,P118,HOS,CSR
Burnett, Matthew	Pvt	E 13th SCVI	Petersburg, VA	03/25/65	Pt. Lookout, MD	06/24/65	Rlsd. G.O. #109	P114,P118,P123,CSR
Burnett, P.A.	Pvt	B 7th SCVC	Deserted/enemy		Williamsburg, VA		Fts. Monroe, VA	CSR
					Fts. Monroe, VA	02/28/65	Released on oath	P8,CSR
Burnett, William N.	Pvt	I 2nd SCVC	Augusta, GA	06/02/65	Augusta, GA	06/02/65	Released on oath	CSR
Burnett, William P.	Pvt	C Hol.Leg.	Deserted/Enemy	11/27/64	City Pt., VA	11/28/64	Washington, DC	CSR
Burnett, William T.	Pvt	E 13th SCVI	Southside RR, VA	04/02/65	Hart's Island, NY	05/11/65	Died	P6,P12,P79,FPH,CSR
Burnham, H.J.L.	Pvt	C 14th SCVI	Petersburg, VA	04/03/65	Fair Gds. Hos Pbg	04/05/65	Died, Remit. Fever	P6,P12,CSR
Burnham, Porter B.	2Lt	K 16th SCVI	Nashville, TN	11/25/63	Nashville, TN	12/04/63	Louisville, KY	P39,CSR,16R
Burnham, Porter B.	2Lt	K 16th SCVI	Missionary Ridge, TN	11/25/63	Louisville, KY	12/05/63	Johnson's Isl., OH	P88,P89,P93,CSR
					Johnsons Isl., OH	06/12/65	Rlsd. G.O. #109	P80,P81,CSR
Burns, B. Clenny	Pvt	B 22nd SCVI	Deserted/Enemy	10/20/64	City Point, VA	10/23/64	Camp Hamilton, VA	P8,CSR,HOS
					Camp Hamilton, VA	11/12/64	Ogden City, IL	CSR
Burns, J.A.	Pvt	F 13th SCVI	Deserted/enemy	02/24/65	Washington, DC	02/27/65	Springfield, IL	CSR
Burns, James	Sgt	A 1st SCVA	Bentonville, NC	03/19/65	New Berne, NC		Pt. Lookout, MD	CSR
					Pt. Lookout, MD	05/12/65	Rlsd. G.O. #85	P114,P118,CSR
Burns, James	Pvt	B 6th SCVI	Richmond, VA Hos.	04/03/65	Richmond, VA P.M.	05/12/65	Paroled	CSR
Burns, James R.	Pvt	F Orr's Ri.	Petersburg, VA	04/03/65	City Pt., VA	04/11/65	Hart's Island, NY	CSR
					Hart's Island, NY	06/06/65	Rlsd. G.O. #109	CSR
Burns, John	Pvt	B 1st SCVA	Deserted/enemy	02/18/65	Charleston, SC	03/13/65	Taken oath & disch	CSR
Burns, John	Pvt	C 22nd SCVI	Deserted/enemy	02/28/65	Hilton Head, SC	03/22/65	New York City	CSR
Burns, Robert	Pvt	E 17th SCVI	Richmond, VA Hos.	04/03/65	@ Jackson Hos. 5/2	07/05/65	Discharged on oath	CSR
Burns, Samuel	Pvt	E 1st SCVA	Savannah, GA	12/20/64	Hilton Head, SC	01/25/65	New York, NY	CSR
Burns, W.H.	Pvt	E 1st SCVC	Bennettesville, SC	03/08/65	Pt. Lookout, MD	06/04/65	Rlsd. G.O. #109	P118,CSR
Burns, W.L.	Pvt	D 27th SCVI	Weldon RR, VA	08/21/64	City Pt., VA	08/24/64	Pt. Lookout, MD	CSR
					Pt. Lookout, MD	09/18/64	Aikens Ldg., VA Xc	P113,P118,CSR
Burns, William A.	Pvt	A 12th SCVI	Gettsburg, PA	07/05/63	Chester, PA G.H.	08/17/63	City Pt., VA Xc	CSR
Burns, William A.	Pvt	A 12th SCVI	Spotsylvania, VA	05/12/64	Old Capitol, DC	06/13/64	Ft. Delaware, DE	CSR
					Ft. Delaware, DE	02/22/65	Hos 2/22-3/20/65	P47
					Ft. Delaware, DE	03/25/65	Hos 3/25-4/3/65	P47
					Ft. Delaware, DE	04/07/65	Hos 4/7-4/11/65	P47
					Ft. Delaware, DE	05/10/65	To Hos. 5/10/65-?	P45,P47,YEB
					Ft. Delaware, DE	06/07/65	Released	CSR
Burns, William H..	Pvt	E 1st SCVC	Cheraw, SC	03/14/65	Pt. Lookout, MD	06/04/65	Rlsd. Instr. 5/30/65	P121
Burns, William J.	Pvt	B 17th SCVI	Five Forks, VA	04/01/65	City Pt., VA	04/06/65	Pt. Lookout, MD	CSR
					Pt. Lookout, MD	06/24/65	Rlsd. G.O. #109	P114,P121,P123,CSR

SOUTH CAROLINA SOLDIERS, SAILORS AND  CITIZENS HELD IN U.S. PRISONS 1861-1865

NAME	RANK	REGIMENT	CAPTURED AT	WHEN	PRISON	MOVED	DISPOSITION	SOURCES
Burrell, A.	Pvt	H 22nd SCVI	Deserted/Enemy	01/12/65	City Pt., VA P.M.	02/17/65	Old Capitol, DC	CSR
					Old Capitol, DC	02/20/65	Ducktown, TN/oath	CSR
Burress, John F.	Cpt	K 7th SCVI	Sharpsburg, MD	09/17/62	Frederick, MD USGH	10/13/62	Ft. McHenry, MD	CSR
					Ft. McHenry, MD	10/14/62	Aikens Ldg., VA Xc	CSR,YEB
Burris, George W.	SMj	17th SCVI	Petersburg, VA	07/30/64	City Pt., VA	08/05/64	Pt. Lookout, MD	CSR
					Pt. Lookout, MD	08/08/64	Elmira, NY	P113,P117,P120,CSR
Burris, George W.	SMj	17th SCVI	Petersburg, VA	07/30/64	Elmira, NY	07/13/65	Tfd. for exchange	P65,YEB,CSR
Burris, James N.	Pvt	F 24th SCVI	Taylor's Ridge, GA	12/16/64	Nashville, TN	10/23/64	Louisville, KY	CSR
					Louisville, KY	10/27/64	Camp Douglas, IL	P90,P91,EFW,CSR
					Camp Douglas, IL	02/20/65	Pt. Lookout, MD Xc	P55,CSR
Burrough, H.C.	Pvt	C 7th SCVC	Appomattox, VA	04/09/65	Fld. Hos. 24th A.C	04/14/65	City Pt., VA USGH	CSR
					6th AC Hos. City P	04/24/65	Baltimore, MD	CSR
					W. Bldg. Balt., MD	05/09/65	Ft. McHenry, MD	P4, CSR
					Ft. McHenry, MD	05/17/65	Died, of wounds	P6,FPH,CSR
Burroughs, Franklin G.	Pvt	B 10th SCVI	Nashville, TN	12/15/64	Louisville, KY	12/20/64	Camp Douglas, IL	P90,P91,P95,CSR
					Camp Douglas, IL	06/18/65	Rlsd. G.O. #109	P55,CSR
Burrow, Saltus	Cit	Charleston	SS Brittania	06/24/63	Ft. Lafayette, NY	04/15/64	Sent ? for exchang	P144
Burrows, Francis A.	Sgt	K 2nd SCVI	Cedar Creek, VA	10/19/64	Harper's Ferry, WV	10/25/64	Pt. Lookout, MD	CSR,SA2,KEB,H2
					Pt. Lookout, MD	05/12/65	Rlsd. G.O. #85	P114,CSR
Burrows, Samuel	Plt		Bulls Bay, SC	10/24/62	Ft. Delaware, DE			P47
					Ft. Warren, MA		US War Dept.	
Burrows, Thomas James	Cpl	G 15th SCVI	Gettysburg, PA	07/05/63	Gettysburg G.H.	07/21/63	Provost Marshal	P4,KEB,CSR,CTA
					David's Island, NY	10/24/63	Bedloes Island, NY	P1,CSR
					Bedloes Island, NY	01/06/64	Ft. Delaware, DE	P2,CSR
					Ft. Delaware, DE	09/14/64	Aikens Ldg., VA Xc	CSR
Burt, Augustus W.	1Lt	A 7th SCVI	Gettysburg, PA	07/02/63	Chambersburg, PA H	08/17/63	Harrisburg, PA Hos	P1,CSR
					Harrisburg, PA GH	09/26/63	Cotton Ftry. Hos.	P2,CSR
					Cotton Ftry. Hos.	11/06/63	W. Walnut St. Hos.	P2,CSR
					Harrisburg, PA Hos	03/01/64	Ft. McHenry, MD	CSR
					W. Bldg. Balt., MD	03/02/64	Ft. McHenry, MD	P1
					Ft. McHenry, MD	06/01/64	Ft. Delaware, DE	CSR,P96
					Ft. Delaware, DE	08/20/64	Hilton Head, SC	P43,P44,CSR
					Beaufort, SC	08/28/64	(From Ft. Delaware)	P1,CSR
					Beaufort, SC	12/15/64	Charleston, SC Xc	CSR
Burton, Joseph	Pvt	H 1st SCVA	Deserted/enemy	02/21/65	Charleston, SC	02/21/65	Released on oath	CSR
Burton, J.M.	Pvt	C 1st SCVA	Smiths Ford, NC	03/16/65	New Berne, NC	04/17/65	Pt. Lookout, MD	CSR,P118
					Pt. Lookout, MD	04/17/65	Died, inmt. fever	CSR,P12
Burton, Joseph	Pvt	B 19th SCVI	Augusta, GA	05/19/65	Augusta, GA	05/19/65	Paroled	CSR
Burton, Nathan M.	Pvt	B 14th SCVI	Southside RR, VA	04/02/65	City Pt., VA	04/07/65	Hart's Island, NY	CSR
					Hart's Island, NY	06/16/65	Rlsd. G.O. #109	P79,CSR
Burton, Peter M.J.	Pvt	Ferguson's	Triune, TN	12/19/64	Nashville, TN	01/04/65	Louisville, KY	CSR
					Louisville, KY	01/09/65	Camp Chase, OH	P92,P95,CSR
					Camp Chase, OH	06/11/65	Rlsd. G.O. #109	P23,CSR
Burton, Toliver J.	Pvt	C Orr's Ri.	Southside RR, VA	04/03/65	City Pt., VA	04/05/65	Hart's Island, NY	CSR
					Hart's Island, NY	06/06/65	Rlsd. G.O. #109	P79,CSR
Burton, William J.N.	Pvt	I 4th SCVI	1st Manassas, VA	08/07/61	Ft. McHenry, MD	11/13/61	Fts. Monroe, VA Xc	CSR
Burzack, Malone D.	Pvt	H 22nd SCVI	Petersburg, VA	03/25/65	City Pt., VA	03/28/65	Pt. Lookout, MD	CSR
					Pt. Lookout, MD	06/24/65	Rlsd. G.O. #109	P114,P118,CSR
Busbee, Allen	Pvt	K 19th SCVI	Nashville, TN	12/15/64	Nashville, TN USGH	12/19/64	Died of wounds	P4,P6,P12,HOE,CSR
Busby, Benjamin	Pvt	K 14th SCVI	Richmond, VA Hos	04/03/65	Provost Marshal	04/21/65	Paroled	CSR
Busby, John Thomas	Pvt	F 19th SCVI	Franklin, TN	12/18/64	Nashville, TN	05/06/65	Louisville, KY	P4,P39,CSR
					Louisville, KY	06/16/65	Rlsd. G.O. #109	P92,P95,HOE,CSR

SOUTH CAROLINA SOLDIERS, SAILORS AND  CITIZENS HELD IN U.S. PRISONS 1861-1865

NAME	RANK	REGIMENT	CAPTURED AT	WHEN	PRISON	MOVED	DISPOSITION	SOURCES
Busby, W.	Pvt	A 22nd SCVI	Burkeville, VA	04/06/65	City Pt., VA	04/21/65	Baltimore, MD G.H.	CSR
					W.Bldg. Balt, MD	05/09/65	Ft. McHenry, MD	P4,CSR
					Ft. McHenry, MD	06/24/65	Rlsd. G.O. #109	CSR
Busby, W. Tillman	Pvt	I 15th SCVI	Sharpsburg, MD	09/17/62	Ft. McHenry, MD	10/17/62	Fts. Monroe, VA Xc	CSR,H15
Busby, Wade A.	Cpl	H 3rd SCVI	Deserted/enemy	01/07/65	City Pt., VA P.M.	01/10/65	Washington, DC P.M	CSR
					Washington, DC P.M	01/11/65	Baltimore on oath	SA2,H3,CSR
Bush, Augustus M.	Pvt	C 19th SCVCB	Augusta, GA	05/19/65	Augusta, GA	05/18/65	Paroled on oath	CSR
Bush, Cornelius	Pvt	I Hol.Leg.	Stony Creek, VA	05/07/64	Fts. Monroe, VA	05/13/64	Pt. Lookout, MD	CSR
					Pt. Lookout, MD	06/17/64	Joined US Army	P117,P121,P125,CSR
Bush, Dionicius W.	Cpl	A 1st SCVIG	N. Anna River, VA	05/23/64	Port Royal, VA	05/30/64	Pt. Lookout, MD	CSR
					Pt. Lookout, MD	08/17/64	Elmira, NY	SA1,CSR
					Elmira, NY	03/14/65	Tfd. for exchange	P65,SA1,CSR
					Pt. Lookout, MD	03/14/65	Aikens Ldg., VA Xc	P113,P117,SA1,CSR
Bush, H.D.	Pvt	C 19th SCVCB	Augusta, GA	05/18/65	Augusta, GA	05/18/65	Paroled on oath	CSR
Bush, J.M.	Pvt	K 5th SCVI	Deserted/enemy	03/14/65	Washington, DC	03/24/65	Cleveland, OH/oath	CSR
Bush, J.W.	Pvt	G 3rd SCVABn	High Pt., NC	05/01/65	High Pt., NC	05/01/65	Paroled on oath	CSR
Bush, John E.	Pvt	I 24th SCVI	Jonesboro, GA	08/31/64	Rough & Ready, GA	09/22/64	Exchanged	CSR
Bush, Thomas J.	Rfg		Hilton Head, SC		Hilton Head, SC	03/05/64	Died	P6
Bush, William D.	Cpt	A 1st SCVIG	Deep Bottom, VA	07/28/64	Old Capitol, DC n	08/12/64	Ft. Delaware, DE	CSR
					Ft. Delaware, DE	01/22/65	Discharged Hos.	P47
					Ft. Delaware, DE	06/17/65	Rlsd. G.O. #109	P43,P45,CSR
Bushardt, Samuel	Pvt	C 2nd SCVI	Hanover Jctn. VA	05/24/64	Pt. Lookout, MD	07/08/64	Elmira, NY	P113,P117,H2,CSR
					Elmira, NY	10/11/64	Pt.Lookout, MD Xc	P65,SA2,KEB,CSR
					Pt. Lookout, MD	10/29/64	Aikens Ldg., VA Xc	P114,P118,P120
Bushart, J.L.	Pvt	G 3rd SCVABn	High Pt., NC	05/01/65	High Pt., NC	05/01/65	Paroled on oath	CSR
Bussey, Thomas J.	Pvt	K 15th SCVI	Halltown, WV	08/26/64	Harper's Ferry, WV	09/02/64	Camp Chase, OH	CSR
					Camp Chase, OH	03/18/65	Pt. Lookout, MD Xc	P22,P26,KEB,CSR
					Pt. Lookout, MD	03/27/65	Boulware's Wh. Xc	CSR
Bussy, J.	Pvt	E 6th SCVI	Augusta, GA	05/18/65	Augusta, GA	05/18/65	Paroled	CSR
Butler, A.	Pvt	B 6th SCVI	Goldsboro, NC	05/30/65	Goldsboro, NC	05/30/65	Paroled	CSR
Butler, A.P.	Pvt	G 7th SCVC			Fld. Hos. 24th A.C	04/14/65	City Pt., VA USGH	CSR
Butler, Augustus M.	Pvt	A 13th SCVI	Petersburg, VA	04/02/65	City Pt., VA	04/04/65	Pt. Lookout, MD	CSR
					Pt. Lookout, MD	06/24/65	Rlsd. G.O. #109	P114,P118,P123,CSR
Butler, Ballis A.	Pvt	I 1st SCVA	Goldsboro, NC	03/16/65	Pt. lookout, MD	06/23/65	Rlsd. G.O. #109	P114,P118,P122
Butler, D.P.	Pvt	K 14th SCVI	Augusta, GA	05/25/65	Augusta, GA	05/25/65	Paroled	CSR
Butler, G.T.	Pvt	D 2nd SCVC	Augusta, GA	05/25/65	Augusta, GA	05/25/65	Paroled on oath	CSR
Butler, J.P.	1Lt	Donovant S			Ft. Delaware, DE	02/22/65	Discharged	P47
Butler, Jeremiah F.	Pvt	H 1st SCVIG	Deep Bottom, VA	07/28/64	Old Capitol, DC	10/24/64	Elmira, NY	CSR
					Elmira, NY	02/13/65	Pt.Lookout, MD Xc	P66,CSR
					W. Bldg. Balt, MD	05/09/65	Ft. McHenry, MD	P4,SA1,CSR
Butler, Pierce M.	1Lt	I 2nd SCVC	Augusta, GA	05/20/65	Augusta, GA	05/20/65	Paroled on oath	CSR
Butler, R.P.	Pvt	B 3rd SCVIBn	N. Anna River, VA	05/23/64	Port Royal, VA	05/30/64	Pt. Lookout, MD	CSR,KEB
					Pt. Lookout, MD	11/01/64	Aikens Ldg., VA Xc	P117,P121,P124,CSR
Butler, R.S.	ASr	A 3rd SCVABn	High Pt., NC	05/02/65	High Pt., NC	05/02/65	Paroleed on oath	CSR
Butler, W.H.	Pvt	E Orr's Ri.	Petersburg, VA	04/03/65	City Pt., VA	04/05/65	Hart's Island, NY	CSR
					Hart's Island, NY	06/16/65	Rlsd. G.O. #109	P79,CSR
Butler, W.W.	Sgt	D 2nd SCVIRi	Combahee Fy., SC	01/29/65	New Berne, NC	04/10/65	Hart's Island, NY	CSR
					Hart's Island, NY	06/17/65	Rlsd. G.O. #109	CSR,P79
Butts, C.H.	Pvt	A 24th SCVI	Jackson, MS	05/14/63	Demopolis, AL	06/05/63	Paroled	CSR,CDC
Buzhardt, Abner M.	Pvt	K 14th SCVI	Malvern Hill, VA	07/28/64	City Pt.,VA 2AC H.	08/09/64	Alexandria, VA GH	CSR
					Alexandria, VA	09/08/64	Died, of wounds	P6,P12,CV,UD6

SOUTH CAROLINA SOLDIERS, SAILORS AND  CITIZENS HELD IN U.S. PRISONS 1861-1865

NAME	RANK	REGIMENT	CAPTURED AT	WHEN	PRISON	MOVED	DISPOSITION	SOURCES
Buzhardt, D.P.	Cpl	D 13th SCVI	Southside RR, VA	04/02/65	City Pt., VA	04/07/65	Hart's Island, NY	CSR
					Hart's Island, NY	06/16/65	Rlsd. G.O. #109	CSR
Buzzard, J.C.	Sgt	K 14th SCVI	Gettysburg, PA	07/05/63	David's Island, NY	09/27/63	City Pt., VA Xc	P1,CSR
Buzzard, Michael H.	Pvt	H Hol.Leg.	Five Forks, VA	04/01/65	City Pt., VA	04/05/65	Pt. Lookout, MD	CSR
					Pt. Lookout, MD	06/23/65	Rlsd. G.O. #109	P114,P118
Buzzard, Walton J.	Pvt	F 20th SCVI	Cedar Creek, VA	10/19/64	Harper's Ferry, WV	10/23/64	Pt. Lookout, MD	CSR
					Pt. Lookout, MD	03/28/65	Aikens Ldg., VA Xc	P114,P124,P118,CSR
Byars, Nathan N.	Pvt	D 27th SCVI	Ft. Anderson, NC	02/19/65	Ft. Anderson, NC	02/28/65	Pt. Lookout, MD	CSR,HAG
					Pt. Lookout, MD	06/24/65	Rlsd. G.O. #109	P114,P123,CSR
Byars, Robert	Pvt	E 13th SCVI	Hatchers Run, VA	03/31/65	City Pt., VA	04/02/65	Pt. Lookout, MD	CSR
					Pt. Lookout, MD	06/07/65	Released	P114,P118,CSR
Byers, Samuel R.	Pvt	C 1st SCVIG	Fredericksburg, VA	12/13/62	Paroled for Xch	12/17/62		CSR,SA1
Byers, Samuel R.	Pvt	C 1st SCVIG	N. Anna River, VA	05/23/64	Port Royal, VA	05/30/64	Pt. Lookout, MD	CSR
					Pt. Lookout, MD	07/25/64	Elmira, NY	P113,P117,P120,CSR
					Elmira, NY	06/19/65	Rlsd. G.O. #109	P65,CSR
Byrd, Alexander F.	Pvt	E 6th SCVI	Sharpsburg, MD	09/18/62	Sharpsburg, MD	09/18/62	Died of wounds	P12,CSR
Byrd, D.M.	Cpl	M 8th SCVI	Gettysburg, PA		Gettysburg G.H.	09/25/63	Provost Marshal	P4,KEB
Byrd, D.M.	Cpl	M 8th SCVI	Gettysburg, PA	07/05/63	W. Bldg. Balt, MD	11/12/63	City Pt., VA Xc	P1,KEB,CSR
Byrd, D.M.	Sgt	H 8th SCVI	Cedar Creek, VA	10/19/64	W. Bldg. Balt, MD	10/25/64	Pt. Lookout, MD	P4,KEB
Byrd, D.M.	Sgt	H 8th SCVI	Winchester, VA	09/19/64	W. Bldg. Balt, MD	12/09/64	Ft. McHenry, MD	CSR
					Ft. McHenry, MD	01/03/65	Pt. Lookout, MD	P144,CSR
					Pt. Lookout, MD	02/10/65	Aikens Ldg., VA Xc	P114,P118,CSR
Byrd, J.F.	Pvt	G 22nd SCVI	Deserted/Enemy	02/23/65	City Pt., VA	02/24/65	Washington, DC	CSR
Byrd, John B.	Cpl	C 15th SCVAB	Smith's Ford, NC	03/16/65	New Berne, NC	04/03/65	Pt. Lookout, MD	CSR
					Pt. Lookout, MD	06/24/65	Rlsd. G.O. #109	P114,P118,P121,CSR
Byrd, John F.	Pvt	G 21st SCVI	Town Creek, NC	02/20/65	Pt. Lookout, MD	06/24/65	Rlsd. G.O. #109	P114,P123,HAG
Byrd, Matthew	Pvt	G 21st SCVI	Morris Island, SC	07/13/63	Hilton Head, SC	07/23/63	Morris Island, SC Xc	P2,HAG
Byrd, Matthew	Pvt	G 21st SCVI	Ft. Fisher, NC	01/15/65	New York, NY	03/27/65	Elmira, NY	P66,CSR
					Elmira, NY	03/28/65	Died, Diarrhea	P6,P12,P65,FPH
Byrd, Michael	Pvt	K 1st SCVIG	Gettysburg, PA	07/04/63	Ft. Delaware, DE		SA1=deserted	P40,P44,SA1,CSR
Byrd, Samuel	Pvt	F 2nd SCVA	Raleigh, NC Hos.	04/13/65	Raleigh, NC	04/13/65	Paroled	CSR
Byrd, T.P.	Pvt	G 21st SCVI	Weldon RR, VA	08/21/64	W. Bldg. Balt, MD	10/17/64	Pt. Lookout, MD	P1
					Pt. Lookout, MD	10/31/64	Aikens Ldg., VA Xc	P118
Byrd, William F.	Pvt	M 8th SCVI	Knoxville, TN	12/18/63	Louisville, KY	01/23/64	Rock Island, IL	P88,P93,CSR
					Rock Island, IL	02/12/64	Died, Smallpox	P5,P132,FPH,CSR

SOUTH CAROLINA SOLDIERS, SAILORS AND  CITIZENS HELD IN U.S. PRISONS 1861-1865

NAME	RANK	REGIMENT	CAPTURED AT	WHEN	PRISON	MOVED	DISPOSITION	SOURCES
Caddin, R.	Pvt	B 11th SCVI	Deserted/enemy	02/22/65	Charleston, SC	02/22/65	Released on oath	CSR
Caddin, William	Pvt	E 11th SCVI	Deserted/enemy	02/18/65	Charleston, SC	03/13/65	Released on oath	CSR
Cade, H.L.	Pvt	Unassigned	Columbia, SC	02/19/65	Hart's Island, NY	06/21/65	Rlsd. G.O. #109	P79
Cade, John L.	Sgt	K 21st SCVI	Ft. Fisher, NC	01/15/65	Elmira, NY	07/16/65	Rlsd. G.O. #109	P65,HAG
Cade, Robert J.Y.	Pvt	I 4th SCVC	Louisa C.H., VA	06/11/64	Fts. Monroe, VA	06/11/64	Pt. Lookout, MD	CTA,CSR
					Pt. Lookout, MD	07/25/64	Elmira, NY	P113,P117,P120,CSR
					Elmira, NY	06/30/65	Rlsd. G.O. #109	P65,P66,CSR
Caffy, Thomas	Pvt	C 23rd SCVI	Petersburg, VA	03/25/65	Pt. Lookout, MD	05/15/65	Rlsd. G.O. #85	P114,P118
Cahill, John	Cpl	B 3rd SCVABn	Ft. Tyler, GA	04/16/65	1st U.S. Cav. Div.	04/23/65	Macon, GA Prison	CSR
Cain, Eric	Pvt	3 10/19 SCVI	Missionary Ridge, TN	11/25/63	Nashville, TN	12/07/63	Louisville, KY	P39,CSR,RAS,CTA
					Louisville, KY	12/09/63	Rock Island, IL	P88,P89,CSR
					Rock Island, IL	06/19/65	Rlsd. G.O. #109	P131,CSR
Cain, James P.	ASr	27th SCVI	Town Creek, NC	02/20/65	Ft. Anderson, NC	02/28/65	Pt. Lookout, MD	CSR
					Pt. Lookout, MD	02/28/65	Washington, DC	P114,P117,P120,HAG,RAS
					Old Capitol, DC	03/20/65	Fts. Monroe, VA	CSR,HAG,RAS
					Camp Hamilton, VA	03/28/65	Pt. Lookout Xc	CSR
Cain, S.G.	Cpl	C 26th SCVI	Petersburg, VA	10/27/64	City Pt., VA	10/31/64	Pt. Lookout, MD	CSR,HMC
					Pt. Lookout, MD	03/16/65	Died, Bronchitis	P12,P114,FPH,CSR
Cainby, William	Pvt	C 23rd SCVI	Petersburg, VA	03/25/65	Pt. Lookout, MD	05/13/65	Rlsd. G.O. #85	P114
Calcutt, Charles	Mus	B 1st SCVA	Deserted/enemy	02/19/65	Charleston, SC	03/02/65	Released on oath	CSR
Calder, A.	Pvt	A 27th SCVI	Petersburg, VA	06/18/64	City Pt., VA	06/24/64	Pt. Lookout, MD	CSR
					Pt. Lookout, MD	07/27/64	Elmira, NY	P113,P117,P120
					Elmira, NY	10/11/64	Pt. Lookout, MD Xc	P65
					Pt. Lookout, MD	10/29/64	Venus Pt., GA Xc	P114,P118,CSR
Calder, Boswell	Pvt	G 23rd SCVI	Five Forks, VA	04/02/65	City Pt., VA	04/05/65	Pt. Lookout, MD	CSR,HOM
					Pt. Lookout, MD	06/24/65	Rlsd. G.O. #109	P114,P118,P121,CSR
Calder, Edward E.	Pvt	A 25th SCVI	Ft. Fisher, NC	01/15/65	New York, NY	01/30/65	Elmira, NY	CSR
					Elmira, NY	05/17/65	Rlsd. G.O. #85	P65,P66,HAG
Calder, R.	Pvt	C Ham.Leg.MI	Farmville, VA	04/11/65	Farmville, VA	04/11/65	Paroled	CSR
Calder, William	Pvt	F 27th SCVI	Petersburg, VA	08/21/64	Old Capitol, DC	02/03/65	Elmira, NY	P110,CSR
					Elmira, NY	07/11/65	Rlsd. G.O. #109	P66,CSR
Caldwell, Hugh T.	Sgt	K 17th SCVI	Five Forks, VA	04/01/65	City Pt., VA	04/06/65	Pt. Lookout, MD	CSR
					Pt. Lookout, MD	05/01/65	Died, Catarrh	P6,P118,P119,CSR
Caldwell, J.C.	Pvt	B 25th SCVI	Ft. Fisher, NC	01/15/65	Fts. Monroe, VA	02/27/65	Ft. Delaware, DE	CSR
Caldwell, J.J.	Pvt	C Hol.Leg.	Kinston, NC	12/15/62	Kinston, NC	12/15/62	Paroled POW	CSR,HOS
Caldwell, J.W.	Pvt	C Hol.Leg.	Kinston, NC	12/14/62	Kinston, NC	12/14/62	Paroled POW	CSR
Caldwell, J.W.	Pvt	C Hol.Leg.	Five Forks, VA	04/01/65	City Pt., VA	04/05/65	Pt. Lookout, MD	CSR
					Pt. Lookout, MD	06/26/65	Rlsd. G.O. #109	P114,P118,P123,CSR
Caldwell, James A.	Pvt	B Orr's Ri.	Richmond, VA Hos.	04/03/65	Provost Marshal	04/21/65	Paroled	CSR
Caldwell, James M.	Pvt	F 17th SCVI	Five Forks, VA	04/01/65	City Pt., VA	04/06/65	Pt. Lookout, MD	CSR
					Pt. Lookout, MD	06/26/65	Rlsd. G.O. #109	P114,P118,P122,CSR
Caldwell, James Shapter	Cpl	B 25th SCVI	Ft. Fisher, NC	01/15/65	Ft. Delaware, DE	06/03/65	Released on oath	P45,HAG,CSR
Caldwell, John P.	Sgt	C 14th SCVI	Dinwiddie C.H., VA	04/01/65	City Pt., VA	04/11/65	Hart's Island, NY	CSR
					Hart's Island, NY	06/21/65	Rlsd. G.O. #109	CSR
Caldwell, John W.	ASr	12th SCVI	Appomattox R., VA	04/03/65	Old Capitol, DC	05/01/65	Johnson's Isl., OH	P110
					Johnson's Isl., OH	06/18/65	Rlsd. G.O. #109	P81,P82,P83
Caldwell, L.J.	Pvt	B 4th SCResB	Hartwell, GA	05/19/65	Hartwell, GA	05/19/65	Paroled	CSR
Caldwell, Payne	Pvt	F 17th SCVI	Five Forks, VA	04/01/65	Pt. Lookout, MD	06/26/65	Rlsd. G.O. #109	P123
Caldwell, Robert A.	Pvt	D 17th SCVI	Dinwiddie C.H., VA	04/01/65	City Pt., VA	04/11/65	Hart's Island, NY	CSR
					Hart's Island, NY	06/21/65	Rlsd. G.O. #109	P79,CSR

SOUTH CAROLINA SOLDIERS, SAILORS AND  CITIZENS HELD IN U.S. PRISONS 1861-1865

NAME	RANK	REGIMENT	CAPTURED AT	WHEN	PRISON	MOVED	DISPOSITION	SOURCES
Caldwell, Robert P.	Pvt	F 17th SCVI	Crater, Pbg., VA	07/30/64	City Pt., VA MD	08/05/64	Pt. Lookout, MD	CSR
					Pt. Lookout, MD	08/08/64	Elmira, NY	P113,P120,CSR
					Elmira, NY	07/03/65	Rlsd. G.O. #109	P65,YEB,CSR
Caldwell, Samuel A.	Pvt	C 27th SCVI	Town Creek, NC	02/20/65	Ft. Anderson, NC	02/28/65	Pt. Lookout, MD	CSR,HAG
					Pt. Lookout, MD	06/24/65	Rlsd. G.O. #109	P114,P118,P121
Caldwell, W.A.	Pvt	A 27th SCVI	Town Creek, NC	02/20/65	Ft. Anderson, NC	02/28/65	Pt. Lookout, MD	CSR
					Pt. Lookout, MD	06/02/65	Rlsd. Instr. 5/30/65	P114,P122,HAG,CSR
Caldwell, W.R.	ASr	15th SCVAB	Morris Island, SC	07/10/63	USHS Cosmopolitan		Exchanged	CSR
Cale, Henry H.	Pvt	C 3rd SCVABn	Ft. Gaines, AL	08/08/64	New Orleans, LA	10/25/64	Ship Island, MS	P3,CSR
					Ship Island, MS	01/04/65	Exchanged	P136,CSR
Cale, James	Pvt	G 23rd SCVI	Petersburg, VA	06/17/64	City Pt., VA	06/24/64	Pt. Lookout, MD	CSR
					Pt. Lookout, MD	07/27/64	Elmira, NY	CSR
					Elmira, NY	02/13/65	James R., VA Xc	CSR
Calhoun, Archibald L.	Sgt	G 23rd SCVI	Five Forks, VA	04/01/65	City Pt., VA.	04/05/65	Pt. Lookout, MD	CSR,HOM
					Pt. Lookout, MD	06/24/65	Rlsd. G.O. #109	P114,P118,P121
Calhoun, J.S.	Pvt	K 3rd SCVC	Pocotaligo, SC	01/18/65	Hilton Head, SC		Ft. Delaware, DE	CSR
					Ft. Delaware, DE	06/10/65	Released	P41,P43,CSR
Calhoun, Nathan	Pvt	F Hol.Leg.	Jarratts Stn., VA	05/08/64	Fts. Monroe, VA	05/13/64	Pt. Lookout, MD	CSR
					Pt. Lookout, MD	08/15/64	Elmira, NY	P113,P116,P120,CSR
					Elmira, NY	09/14/64	Died, Typhoid	P5,P12,P65,CSR
Calhoun, T.H.	Pvt	B 3rd SCVIBn	South Mtn., MD	09/14/62	Ft. Delaware, DE	10/02/62	Aikens Ldg., VA Xc	CSR
Calhoun, Thomas W.	Pvt	C Orr's Ri.			Aikens Ldg., VA Xc	11/10/62	Exchanged	CSR,CDC
Calk, Alexander	Pvt	K 13th SCVI	Southside RR, VA	04/02/65	City Pt., VA	04/07/65	Hart's Island, NY	P79,CSR
					Hart's Island, NY	06/16/65	Rlsd. G.O. #109	P79,CSR
Calk, James A.	Pvt	K 13th SCVI	Gettysburg, PA	07/05/63	David's Island, NY	08/24/63	City Pt., VA Xc	P1,CSR
Call, J.W.	Cpl	B 3rd SCVABn	Ft. Tyler, GA	04/16/65	1st Div. Cavalry C	04/23/65	Macon, GA Prison	CSR
Callahan, Dennis	Pvt	H 1st SCVIR	Deserted/enemy	02/27/65	Charleston, SC	03/02/65	Will take oath	SA1,CSR
Callahan, Thomas	Pvt	E 25th SCVI	Ft. Fisher, NC	01/15/65	New York, NY	01/30/65	Elmira, NY	CSR
					Elmira, NY	07/13/65	Elmira, NY USGH	P65,CSR
					Elmira, NY	08/07/65	Rlsd. G.O. #109	CSR
Callen, Hugh	Pvt	A German LA	Deserted/enemy	03/01/65	Savannah, GA	03/01/65	Charleston on oath	CSR
Callis, John H.	Pvt	D 7th SCVC	Nottaway, VA	05/08/64	Elmira, NY	03/02/65	Tfd. for exchange	P65
Calton, G.W.	Pvt	E 2nd SCVIRi	Hartwell, GA	05/19/65	Hartwell, GA	05/19/65	Paroled	CSR
Calvert, Francis M.	Pvt	G Orr's Ri.	Petersburg, VA	04/03/65	City Pt., VA	04/11/65	Hart's Island, NY	CSR
					Hart's Island, NY	06/15/65	Rlsd. G.O. #109	P79,CDC,CSR
Calvert, James	Pvt	E 13th SCVI	N. Anna River, VA	05/23/64	Port Royal, VA	05/30/64	Pt. Lookout, MD	CSR
					Pt. Lookout, MD	06/26/65	Rlsd. G.O. # 109	P113,HOS,CSR
Calvert, James H.	Sgt	E Hol.Leg.	Petersburg, VA	03/25/65	City Pt., VA	03/28/65	Pt. Lookout, MD	CSR
					Pt. Lookout, MD	06/26/65	Rlsd. G.O. #109	P114,P118,P122
Calvert, John	Cit	Charleston	Columbia, SC	02/19/65	Hart's Island, NY	05/31/65	Died, Chr. Diarrhea	P6,P79
Calvin, A.D.	Pvt	H 17th SCVI	Sharpsburg, MD.	09/17/62	Frederick, MD G.H.	10/02/62	Died of wounds	P1,P6,P12
Camack, Andrew F.	Cpl	E 15th SCVI	Halltown, WV	08/26/64	Harpers Ferry, WV	09/02/64	Camp Chase, OH	CSR
					Camp Chase, OH	03/26/65	Pt. Lookout, MD	P23,P26,KEB,CSR
					Pt. Lookout, MD	05/22/65	Died, Diarrhea	P6,P114,FPH,CSR
Cambell, J.T.	Pvt	5th SCVI	Deserted/enemy	03/15/65	Washington, DC	03/18/65	New York, NY/oath	CSR
Camelford, William	Pvt	F 1st SCVIR	Deserted/enemy	02/20/65	Charleston, SC	03/01/65	Wife on Sullivan's	CSR
Cameron, Henry G.	Pvt	I 26th SCVI	Farmville, VA	04/06/65	Newport News, VA	06/14/65	Released	P107,CTA
Cameron, Isaiah	Pvt	F 23rd SCVI	Amelia C.H., VA	04/03/65	City Pt., VA	04/13/65	Pt. Lookout, MD	CSR
					Pt. Lookout, MD	06/26/65	Rlsd. G.O. #109	P114,P119,P122,CSR
Cameron, Joseph	Pvt	D 17th SCVI	Warrenton, VA	09/29/62	Warrenton, VA	09/29/62	Paroled	HHC,CSR

SOUTH CAROLINA SOLDIERS, SAILORS AND  CITIZENS HELD IN U.S. PRISONS 1861-1865

NAME	RANK	REGIMENT	CAPTURED AT	WHEN	PRISON	MOVED	DISPOSITION	SOURCES
Cameron, Robert F.	Pvt	B 4th SCVC	Hawe's Shop, VA	05/28/64	White House, VA	06/08/64	Pt. Lookout, MD	CSR,HHC
					Pt. Lookout, MD	07/08/64	Elmira, NY	P113,P117,CSR
					Elmira, NY	12/23/64	Died, Pneumonia	P5,P12,P65,FPH,CSR
Caminade, J.C.	Pvt	B P.S.S.	Richmond, VA area	05/30/62	Fts. Monroe, VA		Died	CSR,TSE
Camp, James M.	Pvt	I Hol. Leg.	Stony Creek, VA	05/07/64	Fts. Monroe, VA	05/13/64	Pt. Lookout, MD	CSR
					Pt. Lookout, MD	08/15/64	Elmira, NY	P113,P118,P120,CSR
					Elmira, NY	10/11/64	Pt. Lookout, MD Xc	P65,CSR
					Pt. Lookout, MD	10/29/64	Aikens Ldg., VA Xc	P114,P118,CSR
Camp, Matthew	Pvt	C 1st SCVIR	Deserted/enemy	02/19/65	17th US Army Corps	02/23/65	Rlsd. by Sp. order	CSR
Camp, Napoleon B.	Pvt	C Hol. Leg.	Petersburg, VA	11/06/64	City Pt., VA	11/11/64	Washington, DC	CSR
					Pt. Lookout, MD	02/13/65	Aikens Ldg., VA Xc	P114,P121,P124
Campbell, Alexander	Pvt	B 18th SCVI	Farmville, VA	04/06/65	Newport News, VA	06/03/65	Died	P107,PP,CSR
Campbell, Alexander L.	Pvt	D 16th SCVI	Graysville, GA	11/27/63	Nashville, TN	12/11/63	Louisville, KY	P39,16R,CSR
					Louisville, KY	12/12/63	Rock Island, IL	P88,P89,CSR
					Rock Island, IL	06/20/65	Rlsd. G.O. #109	P131,CSR
Campbell, Archibald	Pvt	F 1st SCVA	Deserted/enemy	12/01/64	Hilton Head, SC	12/25/64		P8,CSR
Campbell, Archibald E.	Pvt	F 1st SCVIG	Petersburg, VA	04/04/65	City Pt., VA USGH	04/06/65	Died of wounds	SA1,CSR
Campbell, Benjamin	Pvt	F 7th SCResB	Raleigh, NC Hos.	04/13/65	Raleigh, NC	04/13/65	Paroled	CSR
Campbell, D.B.	Pvt	I 1st SCVIH	Petersburg, VA	04/03/65	City Pt., VA	04/11/65	Hart's Island, NY	CSR
					Hart's Island, NY	06/16/65	Rlsd. G.O. #109	CSR
Campbell, Daniel	Sgt	I 1st SCVIH	Frederick, MD	09/12/62	Frederick, MD USGH	09/18/62	Ft. Delaware, DE	CSR
					Ft. Delaware, DE	10/02/62	Aikens Ldg., VA Xc	CSR
Campbell, Duncan B.	Pvt	F 1st SCVIG	Petersburg, VA	04/03/65	Hart's Island, NY	06/16/65	Released	P79,SA1,CSR
Campbell, E.	Pvt	A 14th SC Mil	Lynch's Creek, SC	02/25/65	Hart's Island, NY			P79
Campbell, George A.	Pvt	E 27th SCVI	Town Creek, NC	02/20/65	Ft. Anderson, NC	02/28/65	Pt. Lookout, MD	CSR
					Pt. Lookout, MD	06/24/65	Rlsd. G.O. #109	P114,P118,P121,CSR
Campbell, H.B.	Cpl	D 21st SCVI	Ft. Fisher, NC	01/15/65	Elmira, NY	07/11/65	Rlsd. G.O. #109	P65,HAG
Campbell, J.	Pvt	C 7th SCVI	Columbia, SC	02/19/65	Pt. Lookout, MD	06/06/65	Released	P114,P118
Campbell, J.A.	Pvt	B 2nd SCVA	Salisbury, NC Hos.	05/02/65	Salisbury, NC Hos.	05/20/65	US 2 Div 23 AC Hos.	CSR
Campbell, J.C.	1Sg	D 21st SCVI	Ft. Fisher, NC	01/15/65	Elmira, NY	07/11/65	Rlsd. G.O. #109	P65,HAG
Campbell, J.M.	Pvt	D 6th SCVC	Armstrong Mills, VA	12/10/64	City Pt., VA	12/12/64	Pt. Lookout, MD	CSR
					Pt. Lookout, MD	04/02/65	Died, Lung Infl.	P6,P114,P119,FPH
Campbell, J.T.	Pvt	A 3rd SCVABn	High Pt., NC	05/02/65	High Pt., NC	05/02/65	Paroled on oath	CSR
Campbell, James	Pvt	F 3rd SCVIBn	South Mtn., MD	09/14/62	Ft. Delaware, DE	10/02/62	Aikens Ldg., VA Xc	CSR
Campbell, James	1Lt	F 1st SCVIBn	Bty. Wagner, SC	07/18/63	Ft. Columbus, NY	10/09/63	Johnson's Isl., OH	P1,P80,CSR
Campbell, James	1Lt	F 1st SCVIBn	Bty. Wagner, SC	07/18/63	Ft. Delaware, DE	06/12/65	Released	P43,P45,HAG
Campbell, James	Pvt	K 1st SCVIG	Southside RR, VA	04/02/65	City Pt. VA	04/02/65	Hart's Island, NY	CSR
Campbell, James	Pvt	K 1st SCVIG	Southside RR, VA	04/02/65	Hart's Island, NY	06/20/65	Rlsd. G.O. #109	P79,SA1,CSR
Campbell, John	Pvt	C 1st SCVA	Deserted/enemy	05/31/64	Louisville, KY	06/13/64	Rlsd, stay N. of OH	P90,P94,CSR
Campbell, John	Pvt	C 7th SCVIBn	Columbia, SC	03/17/65	New Berne, NC	04/03/65	Pt. Lookout, MD	CSR
					Pt. Lookout, MD	06/06/65	Rlsd. Instr. 5/30/65	P121,CSR
Campbell, John	Pvt	B 18th SCVI	Petersburg, VA	04/03/65	Pt. Lookout, MD	06/26/65	Rlsd. G.O. #109	P122,P123,CSR
Campbell, John A.	Pvt	H 1st SCVA	Cheraw, SC	03/06/65	New Berne, NC	03/31/65	Hart's Island, NY	CSR
Campbell, John A.	Pvt	H 1st SCVA	Cheraw, SC	03/06/65	Hart's Island, NY	06/17/65	Rlsd. G.O. #109	P79,CSR
Campbell, John A.	Pvt	H 18th SCVI	Petersburg, VA	04/01/65	City Pt., VA	04/05/63	Pt. Lookout, MD	CSR
Campbell, John A.	Pvt	H 18th SCVI	Petersburg, VA	04/01/65	Pt. Lookout, MD	06/26/65	Rlsd. G.O. #109	P114,P118,YEB,CSR
Campbell, John C.	Pvt	E 17th SCVI	Petersburg, VA	03/25/65	City Pt., VA	03/28/65	Pt. Lookout, MD	CSR,YEB
					Pt. Lookout, MD	06/26/65	Rlsd. G.O. #109	P114,P118,P122,CSR
Campbell, John C.	Pvt	B 18th SCVI	Petersburg, VA	04/03/65	City Pt., VA	04/14/65	Pt. Lookout, MD	P119,CSR
					Pt. Lookout, MD	06/26/65	Rlsd. G.O.#109	P119,CSR

SOUTH CAROLINA SOLDIERS, SAILORS AND CITIZENS HELD IN U.S. PRISONS 1861-1865

NAME	RANK	REGIMENT	CAPTURED AT	WHEN	PRISON	MOVED	DISPOSITION	SOURCES
Campbell, Jonathan Boyd	Pvt	B 3rd SCVI	Gettysburg, PA	07/02/63	Harrisburg, PA	07/07/63	Philadelphia, PA	CSR.KEB,H3
					Ft. Delaware, DE	02/21/64	To hospital	P47
					Ft. Delaware, DE	06/10/65	Released	P42,P44,P45,CSR
					New York, NY Trans	06/17/65	Transport	CSR
Campbell, Leonard	Pvt	B 18th SCVI	Crater, Pbg., VA	07/30/64	City Pt., VA	08/05/64	Pt. Lookout, MD	CSR
					Pt. Lookout, MD	08/08/64	Elmira, NY	P113,P117,P120,CSR
					Elmira, NY	03/28/65	Died, Diarrhea	P6,P12,P65,FPH,CSR
Campbell, Levi	Pvt	D 3rd SCVI	Chester, SC	05/05/65	Chester, SC	05/05/65	Paroled	CSR
Campbell, Robert	Pvt	H 1st SCVIR	Bentonville, NC	03/22/65	New Berne, NC	04/10/65	Hart's Island, NY	CSR
					Hart's Island, NY	05/18/65	Died, Ch. Diarrhea	P6,P79,FPH,SA1,CSR
Campbell, Samuel H.	Pvt	C 14th SCVI	Petersburg, VA	06/30/64	City Pt., VA USFH	07/29/64	Died of wounds	CSR
Campbell, Samuel L.	1Lt	H 18th SCVI	South Mtn., MD	09/14/62	Ft. McHenry, MD	11/08/62	Aikens Ldg., VA Xc	CSR
Campbell, T.A.F.	Cpl	C P.S.S.	Darbytown Rd., VA	10/17/64	Fts. Monroe, VA	12/23/64	Pt. Lookout, MD	CSR,TSE
					Pt. Lookout, MD	06/05/65	Rlsd. Instr. 5/30/65	P114,P118,P122,CSR
Campbell, Terry T.	Pvt	B 22nd SCVI	Farmville, VA	04/06/65	City Pt., VA	04/14/65	Newport News, VA	CSR
					Newport News, VA	06/24/65	Rlsd. G.O. #109	P107,CSR
Campbell, Tyson	Pvt	D 12th SCVI	Spotsylvania, VA	05/12/64	Ft. Delaware, DE	09/18/64	Aikens Ldg., VA Xc	P41,P43,CSR
Campbell, W.L.	Cpt	I 11th SCVI	Petersburg, VA	05/09/64	Bermuda Hundred, VA	05/11/64	Fts. Monroe, VA	CSR
					Fts. Monroe, VA	05/13/64	Pt. Lookout, MD	CSR
					Pt. Lookout, MD	06/23/64	Ft. Delaware, DE	P113,P117,P120,CSR
					Ft. Delaware, DE	08/20/64	Hilton Head, SC	P43,CSR
					Hilton Head, SC	03/12/65	Ft. Delaware, DE	CSR
					Ft. Pulaski, GA			P4,CSR
					Ft. Delaware, DE	06/16/65	Rlsd. G.O. #109	P43,P44,P45,CSR
Campbell, W.M.	Cpl	A 3rd SCVABn	High Pt., NC	05/02/65	High Pt., NC	05/02/65	Paroled on oath	CSR
Campbell, William L.	Pvt	A 18th SCVAB	James Island, SC	02/10/65	Beaufort, SC USGH	05/09/65	Hilton Head, SC	STR
					Hilton Head, SC	05/10/65	Paroled & released	STR
Campbell, William Scott	Pvt	A 16th SCVI	Missionary Ridge, TN	11/25/63	Nashville, TN	12/07/63	Louisville, KY	P39,16R,CSR
					Louisville, KY	12/09/63	Rock Island, IL	CSR
					Rock Island, IL	01/05/64	Died, Rheumatism	P5,P131,P132,CSR
Campion, B. Franklin	Pvt	D 21st SCVI	Ft. Fisher, NC	01/15/65	Elmira, NY	05/29/65	Released	P65,HAG
Canaday, Lewis D	Pvt	H 11th SCVI	Deserted/enemy	10/18/64	Bermuda Hundred, VA		Wants to go north	CSR
Canady, J. Wesley	Pvt	I 3rd SCVI	Gettysburg, PA	07/02/63	Gettysburg, PA	07/23/63	Died of wounds	CSR
Canady, S.R.	Pvt	G Ham.Leg.MI	Farmville, VA	04/11/65	Farmville, VA	04/11/65	Paroled	CSR
Canby, William	Sgt	C 5th SCResB	Cheraw, SC	03/03/65	Pt. Lookout, MD			P118
Cane, S.C.	Pvt	B 2nd SCVC	Augusta, GA	05/20/65	Augusta, GA	05/20/65	Paroled on oath	CSR
Canley, James F.	Pvt	B P.S.S.	Deserted/enemy	03/04/65	Bermuda Hundred, VA	03/05/65	End of record	CSR,TSE
Canley, James W.	Pvt	B 1st SCVA	Bentonville, NC	03/31/65	New Berne, NC	03/31/00	Hart's Island, NY	CSR
					Hart's Island, NY	06/16/65	Rlsd. G.O. #109	P79,CSR
Cann, James G.	Pvt	I 14th SCVI	Gettysburg, PA	07/03/63	David's Island, NY	10/22/63	City Pt., VA Xc	P1,CSR
Cannaday, Caleb	Pvt	B 15th SCVI	Gettysburg, PA	07/05/63	Gettysburg, PA G.H.	08/15/63	Provost Marshal	CSR
					W. Bldg. Balt., MD	08/22/63	City Pt., VA Xc	P1,KEB
Cannaday, Caleb	Pvt	B 15th SCVI	Halltown, WV	08/26/64	Camp Chase, OH	03/25/65	Pt. Lookout, MD	P22,P26,P119,CSR
					Pt. Lookout, MD	06/26/65	Rlsd. G.O. #109	P114,P122,P123
Cannady, James A.	Pvt	H 11th SCVI	Town Creek, NC	02/20/65	Ft. Anderson, NC	02/28/65	Pt. Lookout, MD	CSR,HAG
					Pt. Lookout, MD	06/24/65	Rlsd. G.O. #109	P114,P121,CSR
Cannady, William	Pvt	E 2nd SCVA	Fayetteville, NC	03/16/65	New Berne, NC	03/30/65	Pt. Lookout, MD	CSR
					Pt. Lookout, MD	06/10/65	Rlsd. G.O. #109	P114,CSR
Cannon, C.T.	Pvt	A 3rd SCVIBn	South Mtn., MD	09/14/63	Baltimore, MD	11/28/62	Baltimore, MD Hos.	CSR
					Baltimore, MD Hos.	02/13/63	Ft. McHenry, MD	CSR
					Ft. McHenry, MD	02/18/63	City Pt., VA Xc	CSR

SOUTH CAROLINA SOLDIERS, SAILORS AND **C** CITIZENS HELD IN U.S. PRISONS 1861-1865

NAME	RANK	REGIMENT	CAPTURED AT	WHEN	PRISON	MOVED	DISPOSITION	SOURCES
Cannon, Caleb	Pvt	E 26th SCVI	Amelia C.H., VA	04/04/65	City Pt., VA	04/13/65	Pt. Lookout, MD	CSR,CEN
					Pt. Lookout, MD	06/26/65	Rlsd. G.O. #109	P119,P122,P123,CSR
Cannon, E.	Pvt	M 1st SCVIG	Spotsylvania, VA	05/12/64	Belle Plain, VA	05/14/64	Pt. Lookout, MD	CSR
					Pt. Lookout, MD	07/09/64	Elmira, NY	CSR
					Elmira, NY	10/11/64	Pt. Lookout, MD	CSR
					Pt. Lookout, MD	10/29/64	Venus Pt., GA Xc	CSR
Cannon, Elkana	Pvt	M P.S.S.	Deserted/enemy	03/22/65	Bermuda Hundred, VA	03/24/65	Washington, DC	CSR
					Washington, DC	03/25/65	Elmira, NY oath	CSR
Cannon, Enoch	Pvt	M P.S.S.	Spotsylvania, VA	05/12/64	Pt. Lookout, MD	07/09/64	Elmira, NY	P113,P117,P120
					Elmira, NY	10/11/64	Pt. Lookout, MD Xc	P65,TSE
					Pt. Lookout, MD	10/29/64	Aikens Ldg., VA Xc	P114,P118,P123
Cannon, Enoch	Pvt	B 13th SCVI	Deserted/enemy	11/12/64	Washington, DC	11/25/64	Elmira, NY on oath	CSR
Cannon, George E.	Pvt	C 13th SCVI	Petersburg, VA	04/02/65	City Pt., VA	04/04/65	Pt. Lookout, MD	CSR
					Pt. Lookout, MD	06/26/65	Rlsd. G.O. #109	P118,P122,CSR
Cannon, George S.	Pvt	G Hol.Leg.	Hatchers Run, VA	03/25/65	City Pt., VA	04/02/65	Pt. Lookout, MD	CSR,ANY
					Pt. Lookout, MD	06/26/65	Rlsd. G.O. #109	P118,P122,P123
Cannon, H.H.	Pvt	I 3rd SCVI	Maryland Hts., MD	09/15/62	Sandy Hook, MD	09/22/62	Paroled	CSR
					Brownsville, MD	09/25/62	Died of wounds	CSR
Cannon, Henry David	Pvt	C 3rd SCVI	N. Anna River, VA	05/23/64	Port Royal, VA	05/30/64	Pt. Lookout, MD	CSR,H3
					Pt. Lookout, MD	03/14/65	Aikens Ldg., VA Xc	P113,P117,P123,P124,CSR
Cannon, Jacob James	Pvt.	H 3rd SCVI	Gettysburg, PA	07/04/63	Gettysburg, PA G.H.	07/20/63	Provost Marshal	P4
Cannon, Jacob James	Pvt	H 3rd SCVI	Gettysburg, PA	07/04/63	Gettysburg, PA U.S.G.	07/21/63	Prov. Marshal N.Y	CSR
					David's Island, NY	09/12/63	City Pt., VA Xc	P1,SA2,KEB,H3,CSR
					Williamsburg, VA H.	09/24/63	Furloughed	CSR
Cannon, Lewis	Pvt	E 26th SCVI	Hatchers Run, VA	03/29/65	City Pt., VA	04/02/65	Pt. Lookout, MD	CSR
					Pt. Lookout, MD	06/26/65	Rlsd. G.O. #109	P118,P122,P123,CSR
Cannon, Nahum	Cpl	K P.S.S.	Deserted/enemy	03/20/65	Bermuda Hundred, VA	03/21/65	Washington, DC	CSR,TSE
					Washington, DC	03/24/65	Phila., PA/ oath	CSR
Cannon, Owen	Sgt	F P.S.S.	Chattanooga, TN	10/29/63	Louisville, KY	11/04/63	Camp Morton, IN	P88,P89,P93
Cannon, Owen	Sgt	F P.S.S.	Chattanooga, TN	10/28/63	Pt. Lookout, MD	10/31/64	Aikens Ldg., VA Xc	P114,P118,P123
Cannon, Owen	Sgt	F P.S.S.	Deserted/enemy	03/26/65	Bermuda Hundred, VA	03/29/65	Took oath	CSR,TSE
Cannon, R.J.	Pvt	K 25th SCVI	Ft. Fisher, NC	01/15/65	New York, NY	01/30/65	Elmira, NY	CSR,HAG,CTA
					Elmira, NY	03/09/65	Died, Diarrhea	P6,P12,P65,FPH
Cannon, Thomas A.	Pvt	Palmetto LA	Cheraw, SC	03/03/65	Fts. Monroe, VA	04/02/65	Washington, DC	CSR
					Washington, DC	04/02/65	Newville, PA/oath	CSR
Cannon, Thomas H.	Pvt	C 13th SCVI	Deserted/enemy	02/24/65	Washington, DC	02/27/65	Springfield, IL	CSR
Cannon, Vincent	Pvt	E 13th SCVI	Deserted/enemy	02/24/65	Washington, DC	02/27/65	Springfield, IL	CSR
Cannon, William H.	Pvt	D 27th SCVI	Town Creek, NC	02/20/65	Ft. Anderson, NC	02/28/65	Pt. Lookout, MD	CSR,HAG
					Pt. Lookout, MD	05/13/65	Rlsd. G.O. #85	P114,P118,P122,CSR
Cannon, William J.	Sgt	A 26th SCVI	Five Forks, VA	04/01/65	City Pt., VA	04/05/65	Pt. Lookout, MD	CSR
					Pt. Lookout, MD	06/26/65	Rlsd. G.O. #109	P118,P122,P123,CSR
Cantrell, Alfred	Pvt	I 5th SCVI	Deep Bottom, VA	08/14/64	Bermuda Hundred, VA	08/15/64	Fts. Monroe, VA	CSR,SAB
					Fts. Monroe, VA	08/16/64	Pt. Lookout, MD	CSR
					Pt. Lookout, MD	03/14/65	Aikens Ldg., VA Xc	P123,P124,P125,CSR
Cantrell, C.M.	Pvt	E 13th SCVI	Gettysburg, PA	07/05/63	David's Island, NY	09/12/63	City Pt., VA Xc	P1,CSR
Cantrell, J.H.	Pvt	K 7th SCVI	Knoxville, TN	01/30/64	Knoxville, TN	02/04/64	Died, Variola	P84,CSR
Cantrell, J.T.	Pvt	H P.S.S.	Richmond, VA Hos.	04/03/65	Libby Prison	04/23/65	Newport News, VA	CSR
					Newport News, VA	06/26/65	Rlsd. G.O. #109	P107,TSE,CSR
Cantrell, John	Pvt	K Hol.Leg.	Stony Creek, VA	05/07/64	Pt. Lookout, MD	06/25/64	Joined U.S. Army	P121,P125,CSR
Cantrell, John	Pvt	D 1st SCVIH	Fayetteville, NC	03/20/65	New Berne, NC	04/10/65	Hart's Island, NY	CSR
					Hart's Island, NY	07/08/65	Rlsd. O.of G.of POWs	P79,CSR

C

SOUTH CAROLINA SOLDIERS, SAILORS AND CITIZENS HELD IN U.S. PRISONS 1861-1865

NAME	RANK	REGIMENT	CAPTURED AT	WHEN	PRISON	MOVED	DISPOSITION	SOURCES
Cantrell, John T.	Cpl	G 12th SCVI	Appomattox R., VA	04/03/65	City Pt., VA	04/11/65	Hart's Island, NY	CSR
					Hart's Island, NY	06/15/65	Rlsd. G.O. #109	P79
Cantrell, L.A.	Pvt	I 5th SCVI	Deep Bottom, VA	08/08/64	Bermuda Hundred, VA	08/10/64	Fts. Monroe, VA	CSR,SA3
					Fts. Monroe, VA	08/10/64	Pt. Lookout, MD	CSR
					Pt. Lookout, MD	08/11/64	Elmira, NY	P113,P120,CSR
					Elmira, NY	05/17/65	Rlsd. G.O. #85	P65,CSR
Cantrell, T.B.	Pvt	E 13th SCVI	Deserted/enemy	02/24/65	Washington, DC	02/27/65	Released on oath	CSR
Canty, John J.	Pvt	H 26th SCVI	Five Forks, VA	04/02/65	City Pt., VA	04/05/65	Pt. Lookout, MD	P118,CSR
					Pt. Lookout, MD	06/26/65	Rlsd. G.O. #109	P118,P123,CSR
Capell, W.H.	Pvt	D 15th SCVI	South Mtn., MD	09/14/62	Frederick, MD		Ft. McHenry, MD	CSR
					Ft. McHenry, MD	10/25/62	Aikens Ldg., VA Xc	CSR
Capp, Robert A.	Pvt	B 24th SCVI	Taylors Ridge, GA	10/16/64	Louisville, KY	10/27/64	Camp Douglas, IL	P90,P91,P94
					Camp Douglas, IL	04/03/65	Jd. US 6th NJV	P55
Capps, Francis	Pvt	McQueen LA	Petersburg, VA	04/02/65	City Pt., VA	04/07/65	Hart's Island, NY	CSR
					Hart's Island, NY	06/16/65	Rlsd. G.O. #109	CSR
Capps, Greenberry B.	Pvt	G 16th SCVI	Missionary Ridge, TN	11/25/63	Nashville, TN	12/07/63	Louisville, KY	P39,CSR
					Louisville, KY	12/08/63	Rock Island, IL	P88,P89,16R,CSR
					Rock Island, IL	10/24/64	Rlsd. Vol US Rjctd	P131,CSR
Capps, John	Pvt	G 12th SCVI	Lynchburg, VA	04/13/65	Lynchburg, VA	04/13/65	Paroled	CSR
Capps, Richard	Pvt	McQueen LA	Petersburg, VA	04/02/65	City Pt., VA	04/07/65	Hart's Island, NY	CSR
					Hart's Island, NY	06/16/65	Rlsd. G.O. #109	CSR
Capps, Samuel R.	Pvt	H 18th SCVI	Five Forks, VA	04/02/65	City Pt., VA	04/05/65	Pt. Lookout, MD	CSR
					Pt. Lookout, MD	06/24/65	Rlsd. G.O. #109	P114,P118,P121,CSR
Caraway, J.J.	Pvt	H 26th SCVI	Deserted/enemy	02/18/65	City Pt., VA	02/27/65	Waterford, PA oath	CSR
Caraway, Jesse	Pvt	H 26th SCVI	Deserted/enemy	02/23/65	City Pt., VA	02/25/65	Washington, DC	CSR
					Washington, DC	02/27/65	Oil City, PA oath	CSR
Carbe, J.M.	Pvt	26th SCVI	Deserted/enemy	11/28/64	Washington, DC	02/18/64	Cincinnatti, OH	CSR
Carder, Harvey	Pvt	H 12th SCVI	Charlotte, NC	05/16/65	Charlotte, NC	05/16/65	Paroled	CSR
Carder, S.C.	Pvt	F 10th SCVI	Danville, KY	10/16/62	Louisville, KY	11/12/62	Vicksburg, MS Xc	P88,CSR
					Louisville, KY	12/09/63	Rock Island, IL	CSR
Carder, Samuel	Pvt	H 12th SCVI	Gettysburg, PA	07/04/63	David's Island, NY	08/24/63	City Pt., VA Xc	P1,YEB
					Williamsburg, VA H	09/03/63	Wounded furlough	P1,YEB,CSR
Carey, Thomas	Pvt	H 27th SCVI	Weldon RR, VA	08/21/64	City Pt., VA	08/24/64	Pt. Lookout, MD	CSR
					Pt. Lookout, MD	02/10/65	Aikens Ldg., VA Xc	P117,P123,P124,CSR
Cargill, Charles W.	Sgt	D 16th SCVI	Franklin, TN	12/17/64	Nashville, TN	01/20/65	Louisville, KY	P39,16R,CSR
					Louisville, KY	01/23/65	Camp Chase, OH	P92,P95,CSR
					Camp Chase, TN	06/12/65	Rlsd. G.O. #109	P23,CSR
Carlisle, A.R.	Pvt	A Ham.Leg.MI	Deserted/enemy	01/07/65	Bermuda Hundred, VA	01/08/65	City Pt., VA P.M.	CSR
					City Pt., VA	01/09/65	Washington, DC	CSR
					Washington, DC	01/11/65	Baltimore, MD	CSR
Carlisle, Thomas P.	1Lt	D 17th SCVI	Petersburg, VA	07/30/64	Old Capitol, DC	08/11/64	Ft. Delaware, DE	P110,HHC,CSR
					Ft. Delaware, DE	06/17/65	Rlsd. G.O. #109	P43,CSR
Carlton, Elias	Pvt	E Hol.Leg.	Frederick, MD	09/16/62	U.S. G.H. #1	10/15/62	Ft. Delaware, DE	CSR
					Ft. Delaware, DE	11/02/62	Aikens Ldg., VA Xc	CSR
Carlton, J.T.	Pvt	K 27th SCVI	Petersburg, VA	06/24/64	Pt. Lookout, MD	08/11/64	Elmira, NY	P113,HAG
Carman, Samuel E.	Pvt	G 3rd SCVIBn	Gettysburg, PA	07/04/63	David's Island, NY	08/24/63	City Pt., VA Xc	P1,KEB,CSR
Carmichael, Daniel M.	Pvt	L 21st SCVI	Town Creek, NC	02/20/65	Pt. Lookout, MD	06/26/65	Rlsd. G.O. #109	P118,P122,P123,HAG
Carmichael, Edward	Sgt	H 23rd SCVI	Petersburg, VA	03/25/65	City Pt., VA	03/28/65	Pt. Lookout, MD	CSR
					Pt. Lookout, MD	06/26/65	Rlsd. G.O. #109	P118,P122,P123,CSR
Carmichael, G.C.	Pvt	A 2nd SCVI	Warrenton, VA	09/29/62	Warrenton, VA	09/29/62	Paroled	CSR
Carmichael, J.C.	Pvt	I 1st SCVIH	Richmond, VA Hos.	04/03/65	Richmond, VA P.M.	05/12/65	Paroled	CSR

SOUTH CAROLINA SOLDIERS, SAILORS AND CITIZENS HELD IN U.S. PRISONS 1861-1865

NAME	RANK	REGIMENT	CAPTURED AT	WHEN	PRISON	MOVED	DISPOSITION	SOURCES
Carmichael, J.D.	Sgt	H Hol.Leg.	Petersburg, VA	11/05/64	City Pt., VA	11/11/64	Washington, DC	CSR
					Pt. Lookout, MD	06/24/65	Rlsd. G.O. #109	P114,P118,P121,CSR
Carmichael, Judson D.	Pvt	L 21st SCVI	Ft. Fisher, NC	01/15/65	Elmira, NY	03/30/65	Died, Pneumonia	P6,P12,P65,FPH,HAG
Carmon, W.T.	Pvt	H 26th SCVI	Deserted/enemy	02/26/65	City Pt., VA	02/28/65	Washington, DC	CSR
					Washington, DC	03/01/65	Charleston, SC	CSR
Carn, L.C.	Pvt	H Ham.Leg.MI	Gainesville, FL	06/15/65	Gainesville, FL	06/15/65	Paroled	CSR
Carnard, L.A.	Pvt	G 4th SCVC	Hawe's Shop, VA	05/28/64	Pt. Lookout, MD	07/08/64	Elmira, NY	P113,P117,P120
					Elmira, NY	10/11/64	Tfd. for exchange	P65
					Pt. Lookout, MD	10/29/64	Aikens Ldg., VA Xc	P118
Carnes, J.J.D.	Pvt	A 5th SCVI	Wilderness, VA	05/06/64	Belle Plain, VA	05/21/64	Ft. Delaware, DE	CSR,LAN
					Ft. Delaware, DE	06/10/65	Rlsd. G.O. #109	P41,P43,P45,CSR
Carnes, John	Pvt	G 1st SCVIR	Bennettsville, SC	03/08/65	New Berne, NC	04/03/65	Pt. Lookout, MD	CSR
					Pt. Lookout, MD	06/26/65	Rlsd. G.O. #109	P114,P118,SA1,CSR
Carnes, Jonas A.	Pvt	E 22nd SCVI	Kinston, NC	12/15/62	Kinston, NC	12/15/62	Paroled POW	CSR
Carnes, Jonas A.	Pvt	E 22nd SCVI	Petersburg, VA	07/29/64	Pt. Lookout, MD	08/04/64	Elmira, NY	P117,P120,LAN
					Elmira, NY	04/17/65	Died, Pneumonia	P12,P65,LAN,FPH
Carnes, N.	Pvt	E 22nd SCVI	Kinston, NC	12/15/62	Kinston, NC	12/15/62	Paroled POW	CSR
Carney, Robert	Msc	K 1st SCVA	Averysboro, NC	03/17/65	New Berne, NC	03/30/65	Pt. Lookout, MD	CSR
					Pt. Lookout, MD	05/13/65	Rlsd. G.O. #85	P114,P118,P122,CSR
Carnwell, E.	Pvt	A 14th SCMil	Lynch's Creek, SC	02/25/65	Hart's Island, NY	05/06/65	Died, Ch. Diarrhea	P6,P79,FPH
Carolan, A.M.	Pvt	Brooks LA	Gettysburg, PA	07/04/63	David's Island, NY	09/12/63	City Pt., VA Xc	P1,CSR
					Williamsburg, VA H	09/26/63	Rtd. to duty	CSR
Carothers, James F.	Pvt	E 17th SCVI	Petersburg, VA	03/25/65	City Pt., VA	03/28/65	Pt. Lookout, MD	CSR
					Pt. Lookout, MD	06/26/65	Rlsd. G.O. #109	P114,P118,P123,CSR
Carothers, T.M.	Pvt	E 17th SCVI	Richmond, VA Hos.	04/03/65	Richmond, VA Hos.	05/04/65	Escaped	CSR
Carpenter, A.E.	Pvt	I 23rd SCVI	Richmond, VA Hos.	04/03/65	Libby Prison	04/02/65	Newport News, VA	CSR
					Newport News, VA	06/14/65	Released	P107,CSR
Carpenter, Benjamin F.	Pvt	C Orr's Ri.	Petersburg, VA	04/03/65	City Pt., VA	04/11/65	Hart's Island, NY	CSR
					Hart's Island, NY	06/06/65	Rlsd. G.O. #109	P79,CSR
Carpenter, G.F.	Pvt	F Orr's Ri.	Petersburg, VA	04/03/65	City Pt., VA	04/11/65	Hart's Island, NY	CSR
					Hart's Island, NY	06/16/65	Rlsd. G.O. #109	P79,CSR
Carpenter, J.B.	Sgt	L 2nd SCVIRi	N. Anna River, VA	05/24/64	Port Royal, VA	05/30/64	Pt. Lookout, MD	CSR
					Pt. Lookout, MD	03/17/65	Aikens Ldg., VA Xc	P113,P117,P124,CSR
Carpenter, J.F.	Pvt	B 2nd SCVC	Hartwell, GA	05/18/65	Hartwell, GA	05/18/65	Paroled on oath	CSR
Carpenter, John C.	Pvt	G 2nd SCVIRi	Knoxville, TN	01/05/64	Nashville, TN	01/17/64	Louisville, KY	P39,CSR
					Louisville, KY	01/23/64	Rock Island, IL	P90,P93,CSR
					Rock Island, IL	10/06/64	Joined US Army	P131,CSR
Carpenter, Sydney J.	Pvt	B 2nd SCVI	Cedar Creek, VA	10/19/64	Harpers Ferry, WV	10/20/64	Pt. Lookout MD	SA2,CSR,H2
					Pt. Lookout, MD	02/18/65	Aikens Ldg., VA Xc	P114,P118,P124,CSR
Carr, C.E.	Pvt	D 5th SCVC	Augusta, GA	05/25/65	Augusta, GA	05/25/65	Paroled	CSR
Carraway, James Henry	Pvt	K 23rd SCVI	Petersburg, VA	06/15/64	Pt. Lookout, MD	07/25/64	Elmira, NY	P113,P120,CSR
					Elmira, NY	11/24/64	Died, Diarrhea	P5,P12,P65,FPH,CSR
Carraway, Pleasant T.	Pvt	D 2nd SCVI	Gettysburg, PA	07/02/63	Letterman G.H. Gbg	09/10/63	Provost Marshal	P1,P4,CSR
					W. Bldg. Balt., MD	09/25/63	City Pt., VA Xc	P1,KEB,SA2,H2,CSR
Carrell, Newel Pickens	Pvt	K Ham.Leg.MI	Deserted/enemy	12/10/64	Bermuda Hundred VA	12/15/64	Pt. Lookout, MD	CSR
					Pt. Lookout, MD	06/26/65	Rlsd. G.O. #109	P114,P118,P122,SA2
Carrick, John	Pvt	B German LA	Deserted/enemy	04/25/65	Savannah, GA P.M.	04/30/65	Wants to go north	CSR
Carrol, Silas E.	2Lt	B 5th SCVI	Sharpsburg, MD	10/01/62	Ft. McHenry, MD	10/20/62	Fts. Monroe, MD	CSR
					Fts. Monroe, VA	11/08/62	Aikens Ldg., VA Xc	SA3,CSR
Carroll, David A.	Pvt	L 2nd SCVIRi	Darbytown Rd., VA	12/12/64	City Pt., VA	12/15/64	Pt. Lookout, MD	CSR
					Pt. Lookout, MD	06/26/65	Rlsd. G.O. #109	P118,P122,P123,CSR

C

SOUTH CAROLINA SOLDIERS, SAILORS AND CITIZENS HELD IN U.S. PRISONS 1861-1865

NAME	RANK	REGIMENT	CAPTURED AT	WHEN	PRISON	MOVED	DISPOSITION	SOURCES
Carroll, Gustavus E.	Pvt	K 17th SCVI	Petersburg, VA	03/25/65	City Pt., VA	03/28/65	Pt. Lookout, MD	CSR,YEB
					Pt. Lookout, MD	06/26/65	Rlsd. G.O. #109	P118,P122,P123
Carroll, Jeremiah M.	Pvt	F 6th SCVI	Blackwater, VA	07/13/63	Fts. Monroe, VA	06/28/63	Baltimore, MD	CSR
					Baltimore, MD	06/30/63	Ft. McHenry, MD	CSR
					Ft. McHenry, MD	07/29/63	Ft. Delaware, DE	P96,HHC,CSR
					Ft. Delaware, DE	08/30/63	Jd. US 3rd MD Cav.	P40,CSR
Carroll, John	Cpl	C 2nd SCVI	Gettysburg, PA	07/05/63	Ft. Delaware, DE	07/19/63	Chester, PA Hos.	P40,P42,P44,KEB,H2
					Chester, PA G.H.	08/17/63	City Pt., VA Xc	SA2,P1,CSR
Carroll, John	Pvt	I 1st SCVA	Morris Island, SC	07/10/63	Hilton Head, SC	08/31/63	Ft. Columbus, NY	CSR
					Ft. Columbus, NY	08/16/64	Pt. Lookout, MD	CSR
					Pt. Lookout, MD	08/16/64	Elmira, NY	P113,P120,P116,CSR
					Elmira, NY	03/10/65	James R., VA Xc	P65,CSR
Carroll, John	1Lt	C 2nd SCVIRi	Richmond, VA	04/03/65	Old Capitol, DC	05/03/65	Johnson's Isl., OH	P110,CSR
					Johnsons Isl., OH	06/14/65	Rlsd. G.O. #109	P81,P82,CSR
Carroll, Michael	Pvt	1st SCVIR	Deserted/enemy	03/01/65	Charleston, SC	03/22/65	Sent north on oath	CSR
Carroll, Russell	Pvt	H 19th SCVI	Glasgow, KY		Glasgow, KY		Paroled	CSR
Carroll, Russell	Pvt	H 19th SCVI	Columbia, TN	12/18/64	Nashville, TN	01/03/65	Louisville, KY	P39
					Louisville, KY	01/09/65	Camp Chase, OH	P92,P95,CSR
					Camp Chase, OH	05/02/65	New Orleans, LA Xc	P23,P26
					New Orleans, LA	05/12/65	Vicksburg, MS Xc	CSR
Carroll, Thomas M.	Pvt	F 17th SCVI	Petersburg, VA	03/25/65	City Pt., VA	03/28/65	Pt. Lookout, MD	CSR
					Pt. Lookout, MD	06/26/65	Rlsd. G.O. #109	P118,P122,P123,CSR
Carroll, William	Cpl	A 24th SCVI	Jackson, MS	05/14/63	Demopolis, AL	06/05/63	Paroled	CSR
Carroll, William H.	Pvt	F 17th SCVI	Ft. Stedman, VA	03/25/65	Old Capitol, DC	05/01/65	Elmira, NY	P110,CSR
					Elmira, NY	07/07/65	Rlsd. on oath	P65,CSR
Carson, Andrew	Pvt	I 1st SCVA	Morris Island, SC	07/10/63	Hilton Head, SC		Ft. Columbus, NY	CSR
					Ft. Columbus, NY	09/23/63	Took the oath	P1
					Ft. Columbus, NY	09/26/63	Pt. Lookout, MD	CSR
					Pt. Lookout, MD	08/16/64	Elmira, NY	P113,P116,P120,CSR
					Elmira, NY	02/28/65	James R., VA Xc	P124,CSR
Carson, B.A.	Sgt	H Ham.Leg.MI	Newton, NC	04/19/65	Newton, NC	04/19/65	Paroled	CSR
Carson, Charles	Pvt	B 7th SCVC	Burkeville, VA	04/06/65	City Pt., VA	04/14/65	Pt. Lookout, MD	CSR
					Pt. Lookout, MD	06/26/65	Rlsd. G.O. #109	P114,P119,P123,CSR
Carson, E. Scott	2Lt	G Ham.Leg.MI	Farmville, VA	04/11/65	Farmville, VA	04/11/65	Paroled	CSR
Carson, I.P.	Pvt	K 4th SCVI	Greensboro, NC	05/02/65	Greensboro, NC	05/02/65	Paroled	CSR
Carson, James A.	Pvt	E 27th SCVI	Florence, SC	03/05/65	New Berne, NC	04/03/65	Pt. Lookout, MD	CSR,HAG
					Pt. Lookout, MD	06/26/65	Rlsd. G.O. #109	P114,P118,P122,HAG,CSR
Carson, James M.	Cpt	A 25th SCVI	Ft. Fisher, NC	01/15/65	Fts. Monroe, VA	02/09/65	Ft. Delaware, DE	CSR,HAG
					Ft. Delaware, DE	06/17/65	Rlsd. G.O. #109	P43,P45,CSR
Carson, John L.	Pvt	I 1st SCVA	Morris Island, SC	07/10/63	Hilton Head, SC	08/31/63	Ft. Columbus, NY	CSR
					Ft. Columbus, NY	09/23/63	Took the oath	P1
					Ft. Columbus, NY	09/23/63	Elmira, NY	CSR
					Elmira, NY	02/21/65	Died	P6,P12,P65,FPH,CSR
Carson, Joseph McDowell	Pvt	B 2nd SCVI	Gettysburg, PA	07/05/63	Gettysburg, PA G.H.	07/20/63	Provost Marshal	P4,KEB,SA2,CSR,H2
					Ft. Delaware, DE	07/21/63	Chester, PA Hos.	P40,P42,P44,CSR
					Chester, PA G.H.	08/17/63	City Pt., VA Xc	P1,CSR
Carson, Joseph McDowell	Pvt	B 2nd SCVI	Cedar Creek, VA	10/19/64	Harpers Ferry, WV	10/25/64	Pt. Lookout, MD	CSR
					Pt. Lookout, MD	03/28/65	Aikens Ldg., VA Xc	P118,P121,P123,CSR
Carson, Roland	Pvt	B 14th SCMil			New Berne, NC USGH	05/09/65	Died	P6,WAT
Carson, Thomas J.	Pvt	F 22nd SCVI	Hatchers Run, VA	04/01/65	Pt. Lookout, MD	06/26/65	Rlsd. G.O. #109	P114,P118

SOUTH CAROLINA SOLDIERS, SAILORS AND  CITIZENS HELD IN U.S. PRISONS 1861-1865

NAME	RANK	REGIMENT	CAPTURED AT	WHEN	PRISON	MOVED	DISPOSITION	SOURCES
Carson, W.B.	Chp	14th SCVI	Gettysburg, PA	07/05/63	Letterman G.H. Gbg	08/22/63	Baltimore, MD	P1,CSR
					Baltimore, MD	08/23/63	Ft. McHenry, MD	P96,P114,CSR
					Ft. McHenry, MD	10/05/63	Fts. Monroe, VA Xc	CSR
Carson, William C.	Pvt	G 12th SCVI	Wilderness, VA	05/06/64	Belle Plain, VA	05/20/64	Ft. Delaware, DE	CSR
					Ft. Delaware, DE	08/20/64	Died, Measles	P5,P41,P43,P45,P47
Carten, Charles J.	Sgt	K 1st SCVIG	Appomattox R., VA	04/03/65	Pt. Lookout, MD	06/24/65	Rlsd. G.O. #109	P119,P121,P122,SA1
Carter, Adam	Pvt	E 24th SCVI	Battery Isl., SC	05/21/62	Ft. Columbus, NY	08/23/62	Ft. Delaware, DE	P37
					Ft. Delaware, DE	10/02/62	Aikens Ldg., VA Xc	CSR
Carter, Adam	Pvt	E 24th SCVI	Nashville, TN	12/16/64	Nashville, TN	12/31/64	Louisville, KY	CSR
					Louisville, KY	01/04/65	Camp Chase, OH	P92,P95
					Camp Chase, OH	06/02/65	Died, Gv. #2013	P6,P23,P27,FPH
Carter, Albert J.	Pvt	C 12th SCVI	Gettysburg, PA	07/04/63	David's Island, NY	08/24/63	City Pt., VA Xc	P1,CSR
					Williamsburg, VA	09/07/63	Wounded furlough	CSR
Carter, Allex	Cpl	A 8th SCVI	Gettysburg, PA		Gettysburg, PA G.H.	07/12/63	Provost Marshal	P4,CSR
Carter, Charles J.	Sgt	K 1st SCVIH	Hatchers Run, VA	04/02/65	City Pt., VA	04/13/65	Pt. Lookout, MD	CSR
					Pt. Lookout, MD	06/13/65	Released	CSR
Carter, David L.	Cpl	C 12th SCVI	Gettysburg, PA	07/03/63	David's Island, NY	09/16/63	City Pt., VA Xc	P1,HFC,CSR
					Williamsburg, VA	09/25/63	Wounded furlough	CSR
Carter, David L.	Sgt	C 12th SCVI	Petersburg, VA	04/03/65	City Pt., VA	04/07/65	Hart's Island, NY	CSR
					Hart's Island, NY	06/16/65	Rlsd. G.O. #109	P79,CSR
Carter, Freeman W.	Pvt	A 15th SCVAB	Smith's Ford, NC	03/16/65	Pt. Lookout, MD	06/26/65	Released	P118,P122,P123,CSR
Carter, George	Pvt	B 21st SCVI	Morris Island, SC	07/10/63	Ft. Columbus, NY	09/23/63	Took the oath	P1
					Pt. Lookout, MD	02/27/64	Joined U.S. Army	P113,P125
Carter, George W.	Pvt	B 26th SCVI	Five Forks, VA	04/01/65	City Pt., VA	04/05/65	Pt. Lookout, MD	CSR
					Pt. Lookout, MD	06/26/65	Rlsd. G.O. #109	P118,P122,P123,CSR
Carter, Gilbert	Pvt	F 1st SCVIR	Chesterfield, SC	03/04/65	New Berne, NC	03/30/65	Pt. Lookout, MD	CSR,SA1
					Pt. Lookout, MD	06/26/65	Rlsd. G.O. # 109	P118,P122,123,CSR
Carter, Giles	Pvt	A 14th SCVI	Gettysburg, PA	07/13/63	David's Island, NY	09/12/63	City Pt., VA Xc	P1,CSR
					Williamsburg, VA H	09/21/63	Furloughed	CSR
Carter, H.M.	Pvt	E 8th SCVI	Winchester, VA	09/13/64	Harpers Ferry, WV	09/16/64	Camp Chase, OH	CSR
					Camp Chase, OH	05/02/65	New Orleans, LA	P23,P26,KEB,CSR
					New Orleans, LA	05/12/65	Vicksburg, MS Xc	CSR
Carter, Harvey L.	Pvt	A 7th SCVC	Richmond, VA Hos.	04/03/65	Libby Prsn. Rchmd, VA	04/13/65	Pt. Lookout, MD	CSR
					City Pt., VA	04/14/65	Pt. Lookout, MD	CSR
					Pt. Lookout, MD	06/06/65	Released	P114,P119,P121,CSR
Carter, Henry E.	Pvt	F 1st SCVIR	Fayettville, NC	03/16/65	New Berne, NC	04/10/65	Hart's Island, NY	CSR
					Hart's Island, NY	06/13/65	Rlsd. G.O. #109	P79,SA1,CSR
Carter, Isaac	Pvt	E 24th SCVI	Battery Isl., SC	05/21/62	Ft. Columbus, NY	08/23/62	Ft. Delaware, DE	P37,EFW
					Ft. Delaware, DE	10/02/62	Aikens Ldg., VA Xc	CSR
Carter, Isaac	Pvt	H 17th SCVI	Five Forks, VA	04/01/65	City Pt., VA	04/06/65	Pt. Lookout, MD	CSR
					Pt. Lookout, MD	06/26/65	Rlsd. G.O. #109	P118,P122,P123,CSR
Carter, Isham	Pvt	F 22nd SCVI	Deserted/enemy	02/16/65	City Pt., VA	02/18/65	Washington, DC	CSR
					Washington, DC	02/21/65	Savannah, GA/oath	CSR
Carter, J.	Pvt	E 22nd SCVI	Five Forks, VA	04/01/65	Pt. Lookout, MD	06/26/65	Rlsd. G.O. #109	P123
Carter, J.B.	Pvt	K 5th SCVI	Richmond, VA Hos.	04/03/65	Richmond, VA P.M.	03/21/65	Paroled	CSR
Carter, J.G.	Pvt	K 21st SCVI	Morris Island, SC	07/10/63	Ft. Columbus, NY	09/23/63	Took the oath	P1
					Pt. Lookout, MD	02/13/65	Exchanged	P113,P123,P124
Carter, J.J.	Pvt	21st SCVI	Deserted/enemy		Louisville, KY	01/29/64	DTE, sent north	P93
Carter, James	Msc	B 5th SCVI	Chester Stn., VA	04/03/65	Bermuda Hundred, VA	04/08/65	City Pt., VA	CSR
					City Pt., VA	04/11/65	Hart's Island, NY	CSR
					Hart's Island, NY	07/03/65	Rlsd. G.O. #109	P79,CSR
Carter, James C.	Pvt	C 5th SCVC	Deserted/enemy	03/14/65	Combahee Ferry, SC		Beaufort, SC P.M.	CSR

SOUTH CAROLINA SOLDIERS, SAILORS AND  CITIZENS HELD IN U.S. PRISONS 1861-1865

NAME	RANK	REGIMENT	CAPTURED AT	WHEN	PRISON	MOVED	DISPOSITION	SOURCES
Carter, James R.P.	Pvt	F 4th SCVC	Old Church, VA	05/30/64	White House, VA	06/08/64	Pt. Lookout, MD	CSR
					Pt. Lookout, MD	07/08/64	Elmira, NY	P113,P117,P129,CSR
					Elmira, NY	10/17/64	Died, Spinal Menin.	P5,P12,P65,CSR,FPH
Carter, John	Pvt	E 8th SCVI	Richmond, VA	04/09/65	Pt. Lookout, MD	07/25/65	Rlsd. G.O. #109	P119
Carter, John M.	Pvt	G 1st SCVIG	Petersburg, VA	04/02/65	City Pt., VA	04/04/65	Pt. Lookout, MD	CSR,SA1
					Pt. Lookout, MD	06/26/65	Rlsd. G.O. #109	P118,P122,P123,CSR
Carter, John W.	Pvt	H 23rd SCVI	Hagerstown, MD	09/16/62	Ft. Delaware, DE	10/02/62	Aikens Ldg., VA Xc	CSR
Carter, Joseph	Pvt	E 23rd SCVI	Five Forks, VA	04/01/65	City Pt., VA	04/06/65	Pt. Lookout, MD	CSR
					Pt. Lookout, MD	06/26/65	Rlsd. G.O. #109	P114,P118,P122,CSR
Carter, R.P.	Pvt	A 3rd SCVABn	High Pt., VA	05/02/65	High Pt., NC	05/02/65	Paroled on oath	CSR
Carter, Reuben	Pvt	I 11th SCVI	Petersburg, VA	06/24/64	USA Field Hospital			HAG,CSR
Carter, Samuel	Pvt	K 7th SCVC	Darbytown Rd., VA	10/07/64	Bermuda Hundred, VA	10/08/64	P.M. G.	CSR
Carter, Samuel B.	Pvt	E 8th SCVI	Gettysburg, PA	07/03/63	Ft. McHenry, MD	07/10/63	Ft. Delaware, DE	CSR
					Ft. Delaware, DE	04/03/65	Hos. 4/3-4/6/65	P47
					Ft. Delaware, DE	06/10/65	Rlsd. on oath	KEB,CSR
Carter, Thomas S.	Pvt	D 18th SCVI	Petersburg, VA	03/25/65	City Pt., VA	03/28/65	Pt. Lookout, MD	CSR
					Pt. Lookout, MD	06/24/65	Rlsd. G.O. #109	P118,P122,P123,CSR
Carter, Timothy	Pvt	H 1st SCVIR	Bentonville, NC	03/16/65	New Berne, NC	04/10/65	Hart's Island, NY	CSR,SA1
					Hart's Island, NY	05/19/65	Died, Typhoid	P6,P79,FPH,CSR
Carter, W.M.	Pvt	K 11th SCVI	Petersburg, VA	06/18/64	City Pt., VA	06/24/64	Pt. Lookout, MD	CSR,HAG
					Pt. Lookout, MD	07/27/64	Elmira, NY	P113,P117,P120,CSR
					Elmira, NY	07/03/65	Rlsd. G.O. #109	P65,CSR
Carter, W.R.	Cpl	A 8th SCVI	Gettysburg, PA	07/04/63	David's Island, NY	08/24/63	City Pt., VA Xc	P1,KEB,CSR
Carter, William	Pvt	G 15th SCVI	Pleasant Val., MD	10/15/62	Prld. on oath			H15,CSR
Carter, William G.	Pvt	I 21st SCVI	Morris Island, SC	07/10/63	Ft. Columbus, NY	09/23/63	Took the oath	P1
					Ft. Columbus, NY	09/26/63	Pt. Lookout, MD	CSR
					Pt. Lookout, MD	02/27/64	Joined U.S. Army	P113,P125,CSR
Carter, William James	Pvt	D 18th SCVI	Farmville, VA	04/06/65	City Pt., VA	04/14/65	Newport News, VA	CSR
					Newport News, VA	06/26/65	Rlsd. G.O. #109	P107,CSR
Carter, William P.	Cit		Barnwell, SC		Pt. Lookout, MD	06/19/65	Rlsd. Instr. 6/17/65	P121
Carter, Wilson O.	Pvt	K 11th SCVI	Town Creek, NC	02/20/65	Ft. Anderson, NC	02/28/65	Pt. Lookout, MD	CSR
					Pt. Lookout, MD	06/26/65	Rlsd. G.O. #109	P118,P122,P123,CSR
Carter, Zimri	Sgt	E 16th SCVI	Franklin, TN	12/18/64	Nashville, TN	01/04/65	Louisville, KY	P3,P39,16R,CSR
					Louisville, KY	01/09/65	Camp Chase, OH	P92,P95,CSR
					Camp Chase, OH	03/26/65	Pt. Lookout, MD	P23,P26,16R
					Pt. Lookout, MD	06/05/65	Released	P114,P119,16R,CSR
Cartin, C.C.	Pvt	C 18th SCVAB	Cheraw, SC	03/08/65	Hart's Island, NY	06/16/65	Rlsd. G.O. #109	P79
Cartin, W.H.	Sgt	E 26th SCVI	Hatchers Run, VA	03/27/65	Pt. Lookout, MD	06/24/65	Rlsd. G.O. #109	P123
Cartledge, James	Pvt	F 26th SCVI	Petersburg, VA	03/25/65	City Pt., VA	03/28/65	Pt. Lookout, MD	CSR
					Pt. Lookout, MD	06/26/65	Rlsd. G.O. #109	P118,P122,P123,CSR
Cartledge, W.	Pvt	I 2nd SCST	Augusta, GA	05/23/65	Augusta, GA	05/23/65	Paroled	CSR
Cartrett, Hezekiah	Pvt	I 10/19 SCVI	Missionary Ridge, TN	11/25/63	Nashville, TN	12/07/63	Louisville, KY	P39,CSR
					Louisville, KY	12/09/63	Rock Island, IL	P89,RAS,CEN
					Rock Island, IL	03/29/64	Died, Variola	P6,P12,FPH
Cartwright, J.P.	Pvt	A 22nd SCVI	Hatchers Run, VA	03/25/65	Pt. Lookout, MD	06/10/65	Released	P114
Cartwright, R.	Pvt	C 26th SCVI	Richmond, VA	04/09/65	Pt. Lookout, MD	06/26/65	Rlsd. G.O. #109	P119,CSR
Cartwright, Samuel L.	Pvt	A 21st SCVI	Petersburg, VA	06/18/64	Pt. Lookout, MD	03/14/65	Aikens Ldg., VA Xc	P117,P123,P124,CSR
Caruthers, John N.	Sgt	F 6th SCVI	Dranesville, VA	12/20/61	U.S. Field Hos.	12/27/61	Died of wounds	CSR
Carver, Fred	Pvt	A 1st SCVA	Smith's Ford, NC	03/16/65	Pt. Lookout, MD	06/26/65	Rlsd. G.O. #109	P114
Carver, J. Wise	Pvt	A 1st SCVA	Montgomery, AL	05/09/65	paroled on oath		No other data	CSR
Carver, John	Pvt	G 12th SCVI	Rapidan River, VA	08/11/62	Fts. Monroe, VA	09/01/62	Aikens Ldg., VA Xc	CSR
Carver, John	Pvt	G 12th SCVI	Spotsylvania, VA	05/12/64	No US records			CSR

SOUTH CAROLINA SOLDIERS, SAILORS AND C CITIZENS HELD IN U.S. PRISONS 1861-1865

NAME	RANK	REGIMENT	CAPTURED AT	WHEN	PRISON	MOVED	DISPOSITION	SOURCES
Carver, Terrill	Pvt	A 1st SCVIR	Smiths Ford, NC	03/16/65	New Berne, NC	04/09/65	Pt. Lookout, MD	CSR,SA1
					Pt. Lookout, MD	06/26/65	Rlsd. G.O. #109	P118,P122,P123,CSR
Case, Elijah H.	Cit		Chesterfield, SC	03/03/65	Pt. Lookout, MD	06/19/65	Rlsd. G.O. #109	P114,P118
Casey, Dennis	Pvt	H 1st SCVA	Fayetteville, NC	03/16/65	New Berne, NC	03/30/65	Pt. Lookout, MD	CSR
					Pt. Lookout, MD	05/14/65	Released on oath	P114,P118,CSR
Casey, James	Pvt	E 2nd SCVC	Greensboro, NC	04/26/65	Greensboro, NC	04/26/65	Paroled on oath	CSR
Casey, R.T.	Pvt	D 22nd SCVI	Goldsboro, NC	12/17/62	Goldsboro, NC	12/17/62	Paroled POW	CSR
Casey, S.G.	Pvt	K 22nd SCVI	Deserted/enemy	03/01/65	City Pt., VA	03/03/65	Washington, DC	CSR
					Washington, DC	03/06/65	Savannah, GA oath	CSR
Casey, Thomas	Pvt	D 27th SCVI	Pt. Walthal Jctn.,VA	05/07/64	Bermuda Hundred, VA	05/08/64	Fts. Monroe, VA	CSR,HAG
					Fts. Monroe, VA	05/13/64	Pt. Lookout, MD	CSR
					Pt. Lookout, MD	09/18/64	Aikens Ldg., VA Xc	P7,P113,P116,CSR
Casey, William	Pvt	B 3rd SCVABn	Ft. Tyler, GA	04/16/65	1st Div. Cavalry C	04/23/65	Macon, GA Prison	CSR
Cash, A.F.	Pvt	? P.S.S.	Deserted/enemy	03/03/65	Bermuda Hundred, VA	03/04/65	No further records	CSR,TSE
Cash, Andrew M.	Pvt	H P.S.S.	Fair Oaks, VA	05/31/62	Fts. Monroe, VA	06/22/62	Ft. Delaware, DE	CSR
					Ft. Delaware, DE	06/26/62	Aikens Ldg., VA Xc	CSR
Cash, Andrew M.	Pvt	H P.S.S.	Deserted/enemy	03/05/65	Bermuda Hundred, VA	03/08/65	Washington, DC	CSR
					Washington, DC	03/08/65	Boston, MA oath	CSR,TSE
Cash, Arthur	Pvt	E 13th SCVI	Gettysburg, PA	07/03/63	David's Island, NY	08/24/63	City Pt., VA Xc	CSR
Cash, C.M.	Pvt	H 1st SCVIG	Caroline Co, VA	05/25/64	Old Capitol, DC	06/10/64	Ft. Delaware, DE	P110,CSR
					Ft. Delaware, DE	10/07/64	To Hos. 10/7-10/10	P47,SA1
					Ft. Delaware, DE	10/13/64	To Hos. 10/13-10/27	P47,SA1
					Ft. Delaware, DE	05/03/65	Rlsd., Sec. of War	P41,P43,P46,SA1,CSR
Cash, Green	Sgt	E 13th SCVI	Deserted/enemy	02/24/65	Washington, DC	02/27/65	Springfield, IL	CSR
Cash, Marvel	Pvt	H P.S.S.	Deserted/enemy	03/03/65	Bermuda Hundred, VA	03/05/65	City Pt., VA P.M.	CSR
					City Pt., VA P.M.	03/07/65	Washington, DC	CSR
					Washington, DC	03/08/65	Pittsburgh, PA	CSR
Cash, Simpson M.	Pvt	E 13th SCVI	Petersburg, VA	03/25/65	City Pt., VA	03/28/65	Pt. Lookout, MD	CSR
					Pt. Lookout, MD	06/26/65	Rlsd. G.O. #109	P114,P118,HOS,CSR
Cash, Smith	Pvt	H P.S.S.	Deserted/enemy	03/03/65	Bermuda Hundred, VA	03/05/65	City Pt., VA P.M.	CSR
					City Pt., VA P.M.	03/07/65	Washington, DC	CSR
					Washington, DC	03/08/65	Pittsburgh, PA	CSR
Cash, Walter B.	Pvt	E 13th SCVI	Gettysburg, PA	07/04/63	David's Island, NY	08/24/63	City Pt., VA Xc	P1,HOS
Caskey, Jacob	Pvt	E 24th SCVI	Marietta, GA	07/04/64	Louisville, KY	07/13/64	Camp Morton, IN	P90
					Camp Morton, IN	05/18/65	Rlsd. G.O. #85	P101
Caskey, Jefferson J.	Cpl	D 1st SCVIH	Farmville, VA	04/11/65	Farmville, VA	04/12/65	Paroled	SA1,CSR
Caskey, Joseph S.	Pvt	H 24th SCVI	Franklin, TN	12/18/64	Nashville, TN	07/09/65	Rlsd. G.O. #109	P4,EFW
Cason, John A.	Pvt	K 17th SCVI	Petersburg, VA	03/25/65	City Pt., VA	03/28/65	Pt. Lookout, MD	CSR
					Pt. Lookout, MD	06/26/65	Rlsd. G.O. #109	P118,P122,P123,CSR
Cassels, Thomas M.	Pvt	G 3rd SCVABn	High Pt., NC	05/01/65	High Pt., NC	05/01/65	Paroled on oath	CSR
Cassidy, Andrew J.	Pvt	E 21st SCVI	Ft. Anderson, NC	02/20/65	Pt. Lookout, MD	06/26/65	Rlsd. G.G. #109	P118,P122,P123,HAG
Cassidy, Frank J.	1Lt	K 11th SCVI	Town Creek, NC	02/20/65	Ft. Anderson, NC	02/28/65	Washington, DC	CSR,HAG
					Pt. Lookout, MD	02/28/65	Washington, DC	P114,P117,P120,CSR
					Old Capitol, DC	03/24/65	Ft. Delaware, DE	P110,CSR
Casson, James H.	Pvt	A 2nd SCVI	Gettysburg, PA	07/05/63	Letterman G.H. Gbg	07/07/63	Died of wounds	P1,KEB,SA2,H2,CSR
Castleman, Jacob D.	Pvt	I 26th SCVI	Drury's Bluff, VA	05/19/64	Pt. Lookout, MD	06/17/64	Died	P6,P12,P117,P119
Castles, Dennis	Pvt	I 12th SCVI	Deserted/enemy	02/28/65	City Pt., VA P.M.	03/02/65	Washington, DC	CSR
					Washington, DC	03/02/65	Frankfort, KY oath	CSR
Castles, Hezekiah R.	Pvt	B 15th SCVAB	Averysboro, NC	03/16/65	New Berne, NC	03/30/65	Pt. Lookout, MD	CSR
					Pt. Lookout, MD	06/04/65	Released on oath	P114,P121,CSR

C

SOUTH CAROLINA SOLDIERS, SAILORS AND CITIZENS HELD IN U.S. PRISONS 1861-1865

NAME	RANK	REGIMENT	CAPTURED AT	WHEN	PRISON	MOVED	DISPOSITION	SOURCES
Castles, William P.	Pvt	C 6th SCVI	Sharpsburg, MD	09/18/62	Frederick, MD USGH	10/13/62	Baltimore, MD G.H.	CSR
					Ft. McHenry, MD	10/14/62	Aikens Ldg., VA Xc	CSR
					Richmond, VA Hos.	10/24/62	Furloughed 60 days	CSR
Caston, J.G.	Pvt	D 1st SCVIR	Bentonville, NC	03/22/65	New Berne, NC	04/10/65	Hart's Island, NY	CSR
					Hart's Island, NY	06/17/65	Rlsd. G.O. #109	P79,SA1,CSR
Cate, J.J.	Pvt	H Ham.Leg.MI	Richmond, VA	05/04/65	Richmond, VA	05/04/65	Paroled	CSR
Cater, James	Pvt	A 7th SCVIBn	Richmond, VA Hos.	04/03/65	Libby Prison, Rchmd	04/23/65	Newport News, VA	CSR
				04/03/65	Newport News, VA	06/26/65	Rlsd. G.O. #109	P107,CSR
Cathcart, Joseph H.	Pvt	E 17th SCVI	Petersburg, VA	03/25/65	City Pt., VA	03/28/65	Pt. Lookout, MD	CSR,YEB
					Pt. Lookout, MD	06/26/65	Rlsd. G.O. #109	P114,P118,P123,CSR
Catherine, William	Pvt	SC Res.	Barham, SC	02/03/65	Pt. Lookout, MD	06/19/65	Rlsd. G.O. #109	P114,P118
Cato, John	Pvt	G 3rd SCVABn	High Pt., NC	05/01/65	High Pt., NC	05/01/65	Paroled on oath	CSR
Caughman, Patrick H.	1Lt	F 5th SCVC	Bennettsville, SC	03/21/65	New Berne, NC	04/10/65	Hart's Island, NY	CSR
					Hart's Island, NY	04/15/65	Ft. Delaware, DE	P79,CSR
					Ft. Delaware, DE	06/14/65	Rlsd. G.O. #109	P43,P45,CSR
Causey, Asa G.	Pvt	A 26th SCVI	Southside RR, VA	04/01/65	City Pt., VA	04/05/65	Pt. Lookout, MD	CSR,CEN
					Pt. Lookout, MD	06/26/65	Rlsd. G.O. #109	P118,P122,P123,CSR
Causey, Frank	Pvt	K 26th SCVI	Richmond, VA Hos.	04/03/65	Newport News, VA	06/26/65	Rlsd. G.O. #109	CSR
Causey, H.L.	Pvt	D 4th SCVC	Stony Creek, VA	12/01/64	City Pt., VA	12/05/64	Pt. Lookout, MD	CSR
					Pt. Lookout, MD	02/13/65	Aikens Ldg., VA Xc	P118,P121,P124,CSR
Cauthen, John M.	Pvt	D 7th SCVIBn	Weldon RR, VA	08/21/64	City Pt., MD	08/24/64	Pt. Lookout, MD	HIC,CSR
					Pt. Lookout, MD	02/28/65	Died, Ch. Diarrhea	P6,P113,P117,CSR
Cauthen, William C.	Sgt	D 7th SCVIBn	Charlotte, NC Hos.	05/15/65	Charlotte, NC	05/15/65	Paroled	CSR
Cauthren, J.T.	Pvt	C 13th SCVI	Appomattox R., VA	04/03/65	City Pt., VA	04/11/65	Hart's Island, NY	CSR
					Hart's Island, NY	06/17/65	Rlsd. G.O. #109	P79,CSR
Cavanaugh, Thomas	Smn	CS Chlstn.	Deserted/enemy		Hilton Head, SC	12/25/64		P8
Cave, Jesse M.	Pvt	E 1st SCVIH	Richmond, VA	04/03/65	City Pt., VA	04/14/65	Pt. Lookout, MD	CSR,SA1
					Pt. Lookout, MD	06/26/65	Rlsd. G.O. #109	P119,P122,P123,CSR
Cave, William T.	Sgt	H 17th SCVI	Five Forks, VA	04/01/65	City Pt., VA	04/06/65	Pt. Lookout, MD	CSR
					Pt. Lookout, MD	06/26/65	Rlsd. G.O. #109	P118,P122,P123,CSR
Caveny, John P.	Pvt	F 17th SCVI	Sharpsburg, MD	09/17/62	Frederick, MD G.H.	10/14/62	Died of wounds	P1,P6,P12,FPH,CSR
Cavney, R.L.	Pvt	G 5th SCVI	Richmond, VA Hos.	04/03/65	Libby Pris., Rich., VA	04/23/65	Newport News, VA	CSR
					Newport News, VA	06/26/65	Released on oath	CSR
Cely, W.H.	Sgt	F 1st SCVIH	Deep Bottom, VA	08/14/64	Bermuda Hundred, VA	08/16/64	Fts. Monroe, VA	CSR
					Fts. Monroe, VA	08/17/64	Pt. Lookout, MD	CSR
					Pt. Lookout, MD	03/17/65	Aikens Ldg., VA Xc	P117,P123,P124,CSR
Centane, Edward S.	Smn	CS Navy	Fayetteville, NC	03/10/65	Pt. Lookout, MD	05/15/65	Rlsd. G.O. #85	P114
Centerfield, Stephen	Pvt	E 27th SCVI	Town Creek, NC	02/20/65	Ft. Anderson, NC	02/28/65	Pt. Lookout, MD	CSR,HAG
					Pt. Lookout, MD	06/19/65	Rlsd. G.O. #109	P115,P118,CSR
Chalk, T.G.	Pvt	4th SCResB	Cheraw, SC	03/05/65	Cheraw, SC	03/05/65	Paroled	CSR
Chamberlain, Henry A.	1Sg	B 27th SCVI	Town Creek, NC	02/20/65	Ft. Anderson, NC	02/28/65	Pt. Lookout, MD	CSR,HAG
					Pt. Lookout, MD	05/13/65	Rlsd. G.O. #85	P7,P118,P122,CSR
Chambers, Alexander M.	Pvt	B 1st SCVIG	Harrisburg, PA	07/22/63	Philadelphia, PA		ANY=Prob DIP	SA1,ANY,CSR
Chambers, E.R.	Pvt	C 2nd SCVI	Gettysburg, PA	07/02/63	Provost Marshal	07/21/63	David's Island, NY	CSR
					David's Island, NY	09/05/63	City Pt., VA Xc	P1,P4,KEB,SA2,CSR
Chambers, James W.	Pvt	C Orr's Ri.	Petersburg, VA	04/03/65	City Pt., VA	04/11/65	Hart's Island, NY	CSR
					Hart's Island, NY	06/16/65	Rlsd. G.O. #109	P79,CDC,CSR
Champion, H.M.	Pvt	A 3rd SCVABn	High Pt., NC	05/02/65	High Pt., NC	05/02/65	Paroled on oath	CSR
Chandler, Aaron	Pvt	G 1st SCVA	Deserted/enemy	02/08/64	Knoxville, TN	08/15/64	Pass to Jefferson	CSR
					Louisville, KY	08/15/64	Took the oath	P90
					Louisville, KY	08/19/64	North of Ohio R.	CSR

SOUTH CAROLINA SOLDIERS, SAILORS AND  CITIZENS HELD IN U.S. PRISONS 1861-1865

NAME	RANK	REGIMENT	CAPTURED AT	WHEN	PRISON	MOVED	DISPOSITION	SOURCES
Chandler, D.I.J.	Pvt	G Hol.Leg.	Petersburg, VA	11/05/64	City Pt., VA	11/11/64	Washington, DC	CSR
					Pt. Lookout, MD	06/24/65	Rlsd. G.O. #109	P114,P118,P121,CSR
Chandler, Daniel S.	Pvt	K 21st SCVI	Morris Island, SC	07/10/63	Ft. Columbus, NY	09/23/63	Took the oath	P1,HAG
					Pt. Lookout, MD	01/30/64	Joined U.S. Army	P113,P125
Chandler, Daniel S.	Pvt	H 26th SCVI	Farmville, VA	04/06/65	Newport News, VA	06/26/65	Rlsd. G.O. #109	P107,CSR
Chandler, G.W.	Pvt	D Hol.Leg.C.	New Kent C.H., VA	08/27/63	Fts. Monroe, VA	08/31/63	Pt. Lookout, MD	CSR
					Pt. Lookout, MD	09/16/64	Elmira, NY	P120
					Elmira, NY		Pt. Lookout, MD Xc	P65
					Pt. Lookout, MD	10/29/64	Aikens Ldg., VA Xc	P118,P123,P124
Chandler, J.A.B.	Pvt	F Hol.Leg.	Five Forks, VA	04/01/65	City Pt., VA	04/05/65	Pt. Lookout, MD	CSR
					Pt. Lookout, MD	06/05/65	Rlsd. Instr. 5/30/65	P114,P118,P122
Chandler, James Fleming	Pvt	K 6th SCVI	N. Anna River, VA	05/24/64	Port Royal, VA	05/30/64	Pt. Lookout, MD	CSR,CTA
					Pt. Lookout, MD	08/17/64	Elmira, NY	CSR
					Pt. Lookout, MD	03/17/65	Aikens Ldg., VA Xc	P113,P117,P124
					Elmira, NY	06/14/65	Rlsd. G.O. #109	P65,CTA,CSR
Chandler, John	Pvt	I Hol.Leg.	Petersburg, VA	10/27/64	Pt. Lookout, MD	06/04/65	Rlsd. Instr. 5/5/65	P121,CSR
Chandler, John J.	Pvt	D 27th SCVI	Town Creek, NC	02/20/65	Ft. Anderson, NC	02/28/65	Pt. Lookout, MD	CSR,HAG
					Pt. Lookout, MD	06/26/65	Rlsd. G.O. #109	P118,P122,P123,CSR
Chandler, M.M.	Pvt	A 7th SCVC	Augusta, GA	05/25/65	Augusta, GA	05/25/65	Paroled	CSR
Chandler, Samuel Thomas	Pvt	D Ham.Leg.	Fair Oaks, VA	05/31/62	Fts. Monroe, VA	06/26/62	Died of wounds	P12,ROH,CNM
Chandler, W.W.D.	Pvt	I 7th SCVC	Farmville, VA	04/11/65	Farmville, VA	04/21/65	Paroled	CSR
Chandler, William	Pvt	Ferguson's LA	Salisbury, NC	04/12/65	Nashville, TN	04/29/65	Louisville, KY	CSR
					Louisville, KY	05/02/65	Camp Chase, OH	P92,CSR
					Camp Chase, OH	06/13/65	Rlsd. G.O. #109	P23,CSR
Chandler, William A.	Sgt	K 16th SCVI	Ringgold, GA	11/26/63	Nashville, TN	12/09/63	Louisville, KY	P39,16R,CSR
					Louisville, KY	12/11/63	Rock Island, IL	P88,P89,CSR
					Rock Island, IL	06/18/65	Rlsd. G.O. #109	P131,CSR
Chaney, Jacob H.	Sgt	K 13th SCVI	Gettysburg, PA	07/04/63	Letterman G.H. Gbg	08/09/63	Died of wounds	P1,P5,P12,ROH,CSR
Chaney, James S.	Pvt	F 2nd SCVI	Halltown, WV	08/21/64	Harpers Ferry, WV	09/02/64	Camp Chase, OH	CSR
					Camp Chase, OH	03/26/65	Pt. Lookout, MD	P23,P26,P119,P122
					Pt. Lookout, MD	06/26/65	Rlsd. G.O. #109	CSR
Chaney, R. Elmore	Pvt	F 2nd SCVI	Gettysburg, PA	07/05/63	Letterman G.H. Gbg	10/15/63	Provost Marshal	P1,KEB,SA2,H2,CSR
					W. Bldg. Balt., MD	11/12/63	City Pt., VA Xc	P1
Chaney, R. Elmore	Cpl	F 2nd SCVI	Cedar Creek, VA	10/19/64	Pt. Lookout, MD	03/14/65	Aikens Ldg., VA Xc	P121
Chanons, Joseph L.	Pvt	I 22nd SCVI	Bermuda Hundred, VA	06/02/64	Pt. Lookout, MD	10/30/64	Aikens Ldg., VA Xc	P113,P117
Chaplin, D.J.	Pvt	D 5th SCVC	Louisa C.H., VA	06/11/64	Fts. Monroe, VA	06/20/64	Pt. Lookout, MD	CSR
					Pt. Lookout, MD	07/25/64	Elmira, NY	P113,P117,P120,CSR
					Elmira, NY	03/04/65	James R., VA Xc	P65,CSR
Chaplin, E.T.	Pvt	D 5th SCVC	State Road, SC	02/13/65	17th US A.C.		Probably paroled	CSR
Chaplin, Edward A.	Pvt	D 5th SCVC	Orangeburg, SC	02/13/65	New Berne, NC	04/03/65	Pt. Lookout, MD	CSR
					Pt. Lookout, MD	06/26/65	Rlsd. G.O. #109	P114,P118,P123,CSR
Chapman, A.A.	Pvt	I 18th SCVI	Crater, Pbg., VA	07/30/64	City Pt., VA	08/05/64	Pt. Lookout, MD	CSR
					Pt. Lookout, MD	08/08/64	Elmira, NY	P117,P120,P125,CSR
					Elmira, NY	04/06/65	Died, Ch. Diarrhea	P6,P12,P65,FPH,CSR
Chapman, Allen	Sgt	C 5th SCResB	Cheraw, SC	03/03/65	Pt. Lookout, MD	06/26/65	Rlsd. G.O. #109	P122,P123,CSR
Chapman, Burwell	Pvt	E Ham.Leg.MI	Amelia C.H., VA	04/05/65	Pt. Lookout, MD	06/26/65	Rlsd. G.O. #109	P114,P122
Chapman, Calvin E.	Pvt	D 21st SCVI	Morris Island, SC	07/10/63	Pt. Lookout, MD	04/27/64	City Pt., VA Xc	P116,P123,P124,CSR
Chapman, Cyrus	Pvt	A Orr's Ri.	Falling Waters, MD	07/14/63	Baltimore, MD	08/16/63	Pt. Lookout, MD	CSR
					Pt. Lookout, MD	12/25/63	City Pt., VA Xc	P113,P116,CSR
Chapman, David	Pvt	E 16th SCVI	Missionary Ridge, TN	11/25/63	Nashville, TN	12/09/63	Louisville, KY	P39,CSR
					Louisville, KY	12/11/63	Rock Island, IL	P88,P89,16R,CSR
					Rock Island, IL	02/01/65	Died, Ch. Diarrhea	P6,P132,FPH,CSR

C

SOUTH CAROLINA SOLDIERS, SAILORS AND CITIZENS HELD IN U.S. PRISONS 1861-1865

NAME	RANK	REGIMENT	CAPTURED AT	WHEN	PRISON	MOVED	DISPOSITION	SOURCES
Chapman, H.Z.	Pvt	F 20th SCVI	Cedar Creek, VA	10/19/64	W. Bldg. Balt., MD	11/10/64	Died of wounds	P3,FPH,KEB,ANY,CSR
Chapman, Henry H.	Pvt	H 3rd SCVI	N. Anna River, VA	05/23/64	Port Royal, VA	05/30/64	Pt. Lookout, MD	CSR,H3
					Pt. Lookout, MD	10/30/64	Aikens Ldg., VA Xc	P113,P117,P123,CSR
Chapman, Henson	Pvt	A Orr's Ri.	Falling Waters, MD	07/14/63	Ft. McHenry, MD	08/08/63	Ft. Delaware, DE	P110,CDC
					Old Capitol, DC	08/08/63	Pt. Lookout, MD	CSR
					Pt. Lookout, MD	03/17/64	City Pt., VA Xc	P116,P123,P124,CSR
Chapman, Henson	Pvt	A Orr's Ri.	Petersburg, VA	04/02/65	City Pt., VA	04/04/65	Pt. Lookout, MD	CSR
					Pt. Lookout, MD	06/24/65	Rlsd. G.O. #109	P118,P121,P123,CSR
Chapman, Hewlett P.	Pvt	E Ham.Leg.MI	Amelia C.H., VA	04/05/65	City Pt., VA	04/13/65	Pt. Lookout, MD	CSR
					Pt. Lookout, MD	06/26/65	Rlsd. G.O. #109	P119,P123,CSR,ACC
Chapman, Ira C.	Pvt	E Ham.Leg.	Chattanooga, TN	10/29/63	Nashville, TN	11/07/63	Louisville, KY	P39,CSR
					Louisville, KY	11/09/63	Camp Morton, IN	P89,CSR
					Camp Morton, IN	03/24/65	Jd. U.S. Forces	CSR
Chapman, James T.	Pvt	C 22nd SCVI	Crater, Pbg., VA	07/30/64	City Pt., VA	08/05/64	Pt. Lookout, MD	CSR,HOS
					Pt. Lookout, MD	08/08/64	Elmira, NY	P113,P117,P120,CSR
					Elmira, NY	02/20/65	James R., VA Xc	P65,CSR
Chapman, Joseph	Pvt	A Orr's Ri.	Richmond, VA Hos.	04/03/65	Libby Pris., Rich., VA	04/02/65	Newport News, VA	CSR
					Newport News, VA	06/30/65	Rlsd. G.O. #109	P107,CDC,CSR
Chapman, Marcus B.	Pvt	B 27th SCVI	Ft. Anderson, NC	02/19/65	Ft. Anderson, NC	02/28/65	Pt. Lookout, MD	CSR
					Pt. Lookout, MD	06/26/65	Rlsd. G.O. #109	P118,P122,P123,CSR
Chapman, N.D.	Pvt	F 1st SCVA	Bentonville, NC	03/22/65	New Berne, NC	03/31/65	Hart's Island, NY	CSR
					Hart's Island, NY	06/16/65	Rlsd. G.O. #109	P79,CSR
Chapman, Phillip	Cpl	A Orr's Ri.	Petersburg, VA	04/03/65	City Pt., VA	04/11/65	Hart's Island, NY	CSR
					Hart's Island, NY	06/16/65	Rlsd. G.O. #109	CSR
Chapman, Solomon D.	Pvt	E 16th SCVI	Ringgold, GA	11/26/63	Nashville, TN	12/09/63	Louisville, KY	P39,16R,CSR
					Louisville, KY	12/11/63	Rock Island, IL	P88,P89CSR
					Rock Island, IL	05/03/65	New Orleans, LA Xc	CSR
					New Orleans, LA	05/23/65	Exchanged	P4,16R,CSR
Chapman, Solomon D.	Pvt	E 16th SCVI	Shreveport, LA	05/26/65	Shreveport, LA	06/08/65	Paroled on oath	CSR
Chapman, Thomas H.	Pvt	E 2nd SCVIRi	Richmond, VA	06/28/62	Army of Potomac	07/03/62	Ft. Columbus, NY	CSR
					Ft. Columbus, NY	07/09/62	Ft. Delaware, DE	CSR
Chapman, Thomas J.	Pvt	E 16th SCVI	Franklin, TN	12/17/64	Nashville, TN	01/04/65	Louisville, KY	P4,P39,16R,CSR
					Louisville, KY	01/09/65	Camp Chase, OH	P92,P95,CSR
					Camp Chase, OH	06/12/65	Rlsd. G.O. #109	P23,16R,CSR
Chapman, William A.	Pvt	C Hol.Leg.	Petersburg, VA	11/05/64	City Pt., VA	11/11/64	Washington, DC	CSR
					Pt. Lookout, MD	06/04/65	Rlsd. Instr. 5/5/65	P114,P118,P121
Chapman, William M.	Pvt	I Ham.Leg.MI	Hartwell, GA	05/18/65	Hartwell, GA	05/18/65	Paroled	CSR
Chapman, William W.	Cpl	B 14th SCVI	Warrenton, VA H.	09/29/62	Warrenton, VA	09/29/62	Paroled	CSR
Chapman, William W.	Sgt	B 14th SCVI	Sutherland Stn., VA	04/02/65	City Pt., VA	04/07/65	Hart's Island, NY	CSR
					Hart's Island, NY	06/16/65	Rlsd. G.O. #109	P79,CSR
Chapman, Jackson J.	Pvt	B 14th SCVI	Warrenton, VA	09/29/62	Warrenton, VA	09/29/62	Paroled	CSR
Chappell, David H.	Cpl	F 12th SCVI	Gettysburg, PA	07/04/63	David's Island, NY	09/08/63	City Pt., VA Xc	CSR
					Williamsburg, VA H	09/13/63	Wounded furlough	CSR
Chappell, G.S.	Cpl	F 12th SCVI	Gettysburg, PA	07/04/63	David's Island, NY	09/05/63	City Pt., VA Xc	P1,CSR
Chappell, Oscar F.	Pvt	F 12th SCVI	Petersburg, VA	04/03/65	City Pt., VA	04/07/65	Hart's Island, NY	CSR
					Hart's Island, NY	06/16/65	Rlsd. G.O. #109	P79,HFC,CSR
Chappell, William T.	Pvt	A 3rd SCVI	Cedar Creek, VA	10/19/64	W. Bldg. Balt., MD	01/08/65	Pt. Lookout, MD	P3,KEB,SA2,H3,CSR
					Pt. Lookout, MD	01/28/65	Hammond G.H., MD	P114,P121,CSR
					Hammond G.H., MD	07/25/65	Rlsd. G.O. #109	P118,CSR
Charles, Frank E.	Pvt	I 1st SCVIG	Sutherland Stn., VA	04/03/65	City Pt., VA	04/13/65	Pt. Lookout, MD	CSR
					Pt. Lookout, MD	06/26/65	Rlsd. G.O. #109	P119,P122,P123,CSR

SOUTH CAROLINA SOLDIERS, SAILORS AND  CITIZENS HELD IN U.S. PRISONS 1861-1865

NAME	RANK	REGIMENT	CAPTURED AT	WHEN	PRISON	MOVED	DISPOSITION	SOURCES
Charles, Joel D.	1Lt	G Orr's Ri.	Falling Waters, MD	07/14/63	Baltimore, MD	08/02/63	Johnson's Isl., OH	CSR
					Johnson's Isl., OH	06/11/65	Released	P80,P83,CSR
Chasereau, John F.	Pvt	G 17th SCVI	Petersburg, VA	03/25/65	City Pt., VA	03/28/65	Pt. Lookout, MD	CSR
					Pt. Lookout, MD	06/19/65	Rlsd G.O. #109	P114,P118,CSR
Chassereau, M.E.	Pvt	A 19th SCVCB	Augusta, GA	05/27/65	Augusta, GA	05/27/65	Paroled on oath	CSR
Chastain, B.W.	Pvt	B 14th SCVI	Richmond, VA	04/03/65	Newport News, VA	06/14/65	Released	P107
Chastain, E.H.	Cpl	D 18th SCVI	Petersburg, VA	04/02/65	Pt. Lookout, MD	06/26/65	Rlsd. G.O. #109	P114
Chastain, George W., Sr.	Pvt	D 2nd SCVIRi	Knoxville, TN	12/03/63	Louisville, KY	01/17/64	Rock Island, IL	P90,CSR
					Rock Island, IL	02/12/65	Died, Consumption	P6,P131,FPH,CSR
Chastain, H.A.	Pvt	K 12th SCVI	Cedar Mtn., VA	08/15/62	Fts. Monroe, VA Xc	09/01/62	Exchanged 9/21	CSR
Chastain, H.A.	Pvt	K 12th SCVI	Petersburg, VA	04/03/65	City Pt., VA	04/07/65	Hart's Island, NY	CSR
					Hart's Island, NY	06/16/65	Rlsd. G.O. #109	P79,CSR
Chastain, William	Pvt	C 1st SCVA	DTE @ Ft. Johnson	04/11/63	Knoxville, TN	05/27/64	Sent north on oath	CSR
Chasteen, J.F.	Pvt	A 3rd SCVABn	High Pt., NC	05/02/65	High Pt., NC	05/02/65	Paroled on oath	CSR
Chatfield, James	Smn	CS Chicora	Morris Island, SC	09/07/63	Pt. Lookout, MD	01/24/64	Joined U.S. Army	P125
Chavis, Abner J.	Pvt	D 26th SCVI	Five Forks, VA	04/01/65	Pt. Lookout, MD	06/26/65	Rlsd. G.O. #109	P114,P118
Chavis, Calvin	Pvt	D 26th SCVI	Five Forks, VA	04/01/65	City Pt., VA	04/05/65	Pt. Lookout, MD	CSR,HOM
					Pt. Lookout, MD	06/26/65	Rlsd. G.O. #109	P122,P123,CSR
Chavis, Elia B.	Pvt	D 26th SCVI	Petersburg, VA	03/25/65	City Pt., VA	03/28/65	Pt. Lookout, MD	CSR,HOM
					Pt. Lookout, MD	06/26/65	Rlsd. G.O. #109	P114,P118,P123,CSR
Chavis, J. Calvin	Pvt	I 22nd SCVI	New Berne, NC	12/23/62	New Berne, NC	12/23/62	Paroled POW	CSR
Chavis, Josiah L.	Pvt	I 22nd SCVI	Bermuda Hundred, VA	06/03/64	Fts. Monroe, VA	06/04/64	Pt. Lookout, MD	CSR
					Pt. Lookout, MD	10/30/64	Venus Pt., GA Xc	CSR
Chavis, W.L.	Pvt	I 22nd SCVI	Sharpsburg, MD	09/15/62	Ft. Delaware, DE	10/02/62	Aikens Ldg., VA Xc	CSR
					City Pt., VA	02/24/65	Washington, DC	CSR
Chavis, W.L.	Pvt	I 22nd SCVI	Deserted/enemy	02/23/65	Washington, DC	02/24/64	Charleston, SC	CSR
Cheatham, John H.	Pvt	F 2nd SCVI	Knoxville, TN	12/05/63	Nashville, TN	02/11/64	Louisville, KY	P39,KEB,SA2,CSR
					Louisville, KY	02/15/64	Rock Island, IL	P90,P91,P94,CSR
					Rock Island, IL	02/15/65	Pt. Lookout, MD Xc	P131,H2,CSR
Cheatham, John H.	Pvt	D 14th SCVI	Augusta, GA	05/22/65	Augusta, GA	05/22/65	Paroled	CSR
Cheek, William	Pvt	E 4th SCResB	Salisbury, NC	05/02/65	Salisbury, NC	05/02/65	Paroled	CSR
Cheney, I.S.R.	Pvt	I 27th SCVI	Petersburg, VA	06/24/64	Bermuda Hundred, VA	06/25/64	Fts. Monroe, VA	CSR,HAG
					Fts. Monroe, VA	06/26/64	Pt. Lookout, MD	CSR
					Pt. Lookout, MD	08/11/64	Elmira, NY	P113,P117,P120,CSR
					Elmira, NY	09/28/64	Died, Pneumonia	P5,P12,P65,FPH,CSR
Chesney, William	Pvt	G 3rd SCVI	Cedar Creek, VA	10/19/64	Winchester, VA USF	12/20/64	Baltimore, MD G.H.	CSR
					W. Bldg. Balt., MD	01/07/65	Pt. Lookout, MD	P3,KEB,SA2,CSR
					Pt. Lookout, MD	01/28/65	Hammond G.H., MD	P114,P118,P121,CSR
					Hammomd G.H., MD	03/31/65	Pt. Lookout, MD	CSR
					Pt. Lookout, MD	06/06/65	Rlsd. Instr. 5/30/65	P121
Chesnut, D.H.	Pvt	G 10th SCVI	Kentucky	09/15/62	Kentucky	11/15/62	Returned on parole	RAS,CSR
Chesser, James F.	Pvt	A 12th SCVI	Sutherland Stn., VA	04/02/65	City Pt., VA	04/07/65	Hart's Island, NY	CSR
					Hart's Island, NY	06/16/65	Rlsd. G.O. #109	P79,YEB,CSR
Chew, David	Pvt	G 2nd SCVC	White's Bridge, VA	11/01/64	Pt. Lookout, MD	02/18/65	Aikens Ldg., VA Xc	P116
Chewning, G.W.	Pvt	I 23rd SCVI	Petersburg, VA	04/01/65	City Pt., VA	04/05/65	Pt. Lookout, MD	CSR,HCL
					Pt. Lookout, MD	06/13/65	Died	P6,P119,FPH,CSR
Child, William	Pvt	E 1st SCVA	Deserted/enemy	02/20/65	Charleston, SC	02/20/65	Released on oath	CSR
Childers, A. Crowell	Sgt	C 22nd SCVI	Crater, Pbg., VA	07/30/64	City Pt., VA	08/05/64	Pt. Lookout, MD	CSR
					Pt. Lookout, MD	08/08/64	Elmira, NY	P113,P117,P120,CSR
					Elmira, NY	07/03/65	Rlsd. G.O. #109	P65,CSR
Childers, A.L.	Pvt	A 3rd SCVABn	High Pt., NC	05/02/65	High Pt., NC	05/02/65	Paroled on oath	CSR
Childers, Eziekiel C.	Pvt	B 12th SCVI	Warrenton, VA	09/29/62	Warrenton, VA	09/29/62	Paroled	CSR

SOUTH CAROLINA SOLDIERS, SAILORS AND  CITIZENS HELD IN U.S. PRISONS 1861-1865

NAME	RANK	REGIMENT	CAPTURED AT	WHEN	PRISON	MOVED	DISPOSITION	SOURCES
Childers, Ezikiel C.	Pvt	B 12th SCVI	Lynchburg, VA Hos.	04/13/65	Lynchburg, VA	04/13/65	Paroled	CSR
Childers, J.R.	Pvt	A 3rd SCVABn	High Pt., NC	05/02/65	High Pt., NC	05/02/65	Paroled on oath	CSR
Childers, J.T.	Pvt	G 1st SCVIR	Bentonville, NC	03/19/65	New Berne, NC	04/09/65	Pt. Lookout, MD	CSR
					Pt. Lookout, MD	06/26/65	Rlsd. G.O. #109	P118,P122,P123,CSR
Childers, John L.	Pvt	C 17th SCVI	Petersburg, VA	04/02/65	City Pt., VA	04/05/65	Pt. Lookout, MD	CSR
					Pt. Lookout, MD	06/06/65	Released on oath	P118,CSR
Childers, Josiah	Pvt	B 12th SCVI	Appomattox R., VA	04/04/65	Bermuda Hundred, VA	04/11/65	Hart's Island, NY	CSR
					Hart's Island, NY	06/15/65	Rlsd. G.O. #109	P79,YEB,CSR
Childers, Sherod	Pvt	C 17th SCVI	Petersburg, VA	03/25/65	City Pt., VA	03/28/65	Pt. Lookout, MD	CSR,YEB
					Pt. Lookout, MD	06/26/65	Rlsd. G.O. #109	P114,P118,P123,CSR
Childers, Sherod	Pvt	B 12th SCVI	Appomattox R., VA	04/04/65	City Pt., VA	04/11/65	Hart's Island, NY	CSR
					Hart's Island, NY	06/15/65	Rlsd. G.O. #109	CSR
Childers, Tench	Pvt	E 13th SCVI	N. Anna River, VA	05/23/64	Port Royal, VA	05/30/64	Pt. Lookout, MD	CSR,HOS
					Pt. Lookout, MD	03/15/65	Aikens Ldg., VA Xc	P113,P117,P124,CSR
Childers, William	Pvt	B 15th SCVAB	Deserted/enemy	07/25/64	Louisville, KY	04/27/64	Oath, north of Ohio	CSR
Childers, William J.	Pvt	B 27th SCVI	Town Creek, NC	02/20/65	Ft. Anderson, NC	02/28/65	Pt. Lookout, MD	CSR
					Pt. Lookout, MD	05/14/65	Rlsd. G.O. #85	P114,P118,P121,CSR
Chiles, John H.	Pvt	G Orr's Ri.	Falling Waters, MD	07/14/63	Frederick, MD G.H.	08/07/63	W. Bldg. Balt, MD	P1,CDC
					W. Bldg. Balt., MD	08/24/63	City Pt., VA Xc	P1,CDC,CSR
Chiles, L.S.	Pvt	D 1st SCVIR	Averysboro, NC	03/16/65	New Berne, NC	04/10/65	Hart's Island, NY	CSR
					Hart's Island, NY	06/18/65	Rlsd. G.O. #109	P79,CSR
Chiles, O.B.	Pvt	A 3rd SCVABn	High Pt., NC	05/02/65	High Pt., NC	05/02/65	Paroled on oath	CSR
Chiles, W.T.	Pvt	A 3rd SCVABn	High Pt., NC	05/02/65	High Pt., NC	05/02/65	Paroled on oath	CSR
China, J. Randolph	2Lt	C 25th SCVI	Town Creek, NC	02/20/65	Ft. Anderson, NC	02/28/65	Pt. Lookout, MD	CSR,HAG,CTA
					Pt. Lookout, MD	02/28/65	Washington, DC	P114,P117,P120,CSR
					Old Capitol, DC	03/24/65	Ft. Delaware, DE	P110
					Ft. Delaware, DE	06/17/65	Rlsd. G.O. #109	P43,P45,CSR
Chipley, Thomas J.	Pvt	F 2nd SCVI	Gettysburg, PA	07/05/63	Letterman G.H. Gbg	11/10/63	Baltimore, MD G.H.	SA2,P1,H2,CSR,KEB
					W. Bldg. Balt., MD	01/10/64	City Pt., VA Xc	P1,P116,P124,CSR
Chisholm, J.C.	Pvt	F 6th SCVI	Richmond, VA Hos.	04/03/65	Richmond, VA Hos.	04/14/65	Richmond, VA P.M.	CSR
					Libby Pris., Rchmd.	04/23/65	Newport News, VA	CSR
					Newport News, VA	07/03/65	Rlsd. G.O. #109	P107,HHC,CSR
Chisholm, W.B.	Pvt	F 3rd SCVC	South Newport, GA	08/17/64	Philadelphia, PA	01/10/65	Ft. Delaware, DE	CSR
					Ft. Delaware, DE	06/10/65	Released	P41,P43,P45,CSR
Chistophel, M.	Pvt	E 25th SCVI	Deserted/enemy	02/18/65	Washington, DC		Rlsd. on oath	HAG,CSR
Chitty, Edward C.	Sgt	H 17th SCVI	Petersburg, VA	03/25/65	City Pt., VA	03/28/65	Pt. Lookout, MD	CSR
					Pt. Lookout, MD	06/26/65	Rlsd. G.O. #109	P114,P122,P123,CSR
Choate, Stephen McCorkle	Pvt	E 17th SCVI	Petersburg, VA	03/25/65	City Pt., VA	03/28/65	Pt. Lookout, MD	CSR,YEB
					Pt. Lookout, MD	06/26/65	Rlsd. G.O. #109	P114,P118,P123,CSR
Choate, William	Pvt	E 17th SCVI	Petersburg, VA	03/25/65	City Pt., VA	03/28/65	Pt. Lookout, MD	YEB,CSR
					Pt. Lookout, MD	06/26/65	Rlsd. G.O. #109	P114,P118,P123,CSR
Choisy, A. McD.	Pvt	Marion LA	Camden, SC	02/24/65	New Berne, NC	04/10/65	Hart's Island, NY	CSR
					Hart's Island, NY	05/08/65	Died, Ch. Diarrhea	P6,P79,FPH,CSR
Chresman, J.M.	Pvt	C 3rd SCVABn	Blakely, AL	04/09/65	Ship Island, MS	05/01/65	Vicksburg, MS Xc	P136,CSR
Christian, Beauford W.	Pvt	D 14th SCVI	Richmond, VA Hos.	04/03/65	Provost Marshal	04/21/65	Libby Prison, Rchmd.	CSR
					Libby Prison, Rchmd	04/23/65	Newport News, VA	CSR
Christian, Beauford W.	Pvt	D 14th SCVI	Richmond, VA	04/03/65	Newport News, VA	06/14/65	Rlsd. G.O. #109	CSR
Christian, Edward H.	Cpl	D 13th SCVI	Petersburg, VA	04/02/65	City Pt., VA	04/04/65	Pt. Lookout, MD	CSR,ANY
					Pt. Lookout, MD	06/26/65	Rlsd. G.O. #109	P118,P122,P123,CSR
Christian, J.W.	Pvt	H Hol. Leg.	Frederick, MD	09/12/62	Ft. Delaware, DE	10/02/62	Aikens Ldg., VA Xc	CSR
Christian, Josiah T.	Pvt	K 15th SCVI	Amelia C.H., VA	04/06/65	City Pt., VA	04/14/65	Pt. Lookout, MD	CSR,KEB
					Pt. Lookout, MD	06/24/65	Rlsd. G.O. #109	P114,P121,P123,CSR

SOUTH CAROLINA SOLDIERS, SAILORS AND *C* CITIZENS HELD IN U.S. PRISONS 1861-1865

NAME	RANK	REGIMENT	CAPTURED AT	WHEN	PRISON	MOVED	DISPOSITION	SOURCES
Christie, Mark A.	Pvt	D 14th SCVI	Sutherland Stn., VA	04/02/65	City Pt., VA	04/07/65	Hart's Island, NY	CSR
					Hart's Island, NY	06/16/65	Rlsd. G.O. #109	P79,HOE,CSR
Christmas, J.L.	Pvt	E 23rd SCVI	Hagerstown, MD	09/15/62	Ft. Delaware, DE	10/02/62	Aikens Ldg., VA Xc	HMC,CSR
Christopher, L.N.	Pvt	K Ham.Leg.MI	Farmville, VA	04/11/65	Farmville, VA	04/11/65	Paroled	CSR
Christopher, T.C.	Pvt	D 14th SCVI			Cliffham G.H., DC	05/24/62	Died	P6,CV,PP
Chumley, George W.	Pvt	K 3rd SCVI	Chickamauga, GA	09/20/63	Nashville, TN	10/01/63	Louisville, KY	P38,KEB,SA2,CSR
					Louisville, KY	10/02/63	Camp Douglas, IL	P88,P89,H3,CSR
					Camp Douglas, IL	07/27/64	Died, Pleurisy	P5,P12,P53,P55,FPH,CSR
Churchill, Michael	Pvt	B 1st SCVIR	Cheraw, SC	03/03/65	New Berne, NC	04/02/65	Camp Hamilton, VA	CSR
					Camp Hamilton, VA	04/02/65	Washington, DC	CSR
					Washington, DC	04/30/65	New York, NY oath	SA1,CSR
Claffey, Patrick	Pvt	F 3rd SCVIBn	Sharpsburg, MD	10/01/62	Ft. McHenry, MD	10/18/62	Fts. Monroe, VA	CSR
					Fts. Monroe, VA	10/25/62	Aikens Ldg., VA Xc	CSR
Clamp, David L.	Pvt	B 3rd SCVI	Falling Waters, MD	07/04/63	Ft. McHenry, MD	07/08/63	Ft. Delaware, DE	P96,H3,CSRSA2,KEB
					Ft. Delaware, DE	07/10/64	To Hos	P47
					Ft. Delaware, DE	07/19/63	Chester, PA Hos.	P40,P44,CSR
					Ft. Delaware, DE	06/10/65	Rlsd. G.O. #109	P42,P45,CSR
Clamp, Henry	Pvt	E 14th SCVI	South Carolina		New Berne, NC USGH	04/03/65	Died, Ch. Diarrhea	CSR
Clamp, Henry Carwile	Pvt	G 13th SCVI	Petersburg, VA	04/03/65	City Pt., VA	04/13/65	Pt. Lookout, MD	CSR
					Pt. Lookout, MD	06/26/65	Rlsd. G.O. #109	P119,P123,ANY,CSR
Clamp, Henry E.	Pvt	E 14th SCMil	NC or SC		New Berne, NC USGH	04/03/65	Died, Ch. Diarrhea	P6,P12,WAT
Clamp, J.B.	Pvt	G Orr's Ri.	Falling Waters, MD	07/14/63	Baltimore, MD	08/16/63	Pt. Lookout, MD	CSR
					Pt. Lookout, MD	08/16/64	Elmira, NY	P113,P120,CSR
					Elmira, NY	03/02/65	Pt. Lookout, MD Xc	P65,P124
					Elmira, NY	03/10/65	Boulwares Wh., VA	CSR
Clamp, John Thomas E.	Pvt	I 19th SCVI	Murfreesboro, TN	01/05/63	Nashville, TN		Louisville, KY	P38
					Louisville, KY	03/11/63	Camp Butler, IL	P88,CSR
Clamp, William J.	Pvt	K 13th SCVI	Gettysburg, PA	07/05/63	Gettysburg, PA	07/19/63	Chester, PA G.H.	CSR
					Chester, PA G.H.	08/17/63	City Pt., VA Xc	P1,CSR
					Ft. Delaware, DE	08/20/63	City Pt., VA Xc	CSR
Clamp, William J.	Pvt	K 13th SCVI	Richmond, VA Hos	04/03/65	Richmond Hospital	04/21/65	Provost Marshal	P107,CSR
					Provost Marshal	04/21/65	Libby Prison Rchmd	CSR
					Libby Prison Rchmd	04/23/65	Newport News, VA	CSR
					Newport News, VA	06/26/65	Rlsd. G.O. #109	CSR
Clampet, Henry C.	Pvt	G 23rd SCVI	Petersburg, VA	04/03/65	Pt. Lookout, MD	06/26/65	Rlsd. G.O. #109	P114
Clancy, Arthur R.	Cpl	C 1st SCVIG	Wilderness, VA	05/06/64	Old Capitol, DC	12/07/64	Elmira, NY	CSR
					Elmira, NY	06/19/65	Rlsd. G.O. #109	P65,SA1,CSR
Clantery, John	Smn	CS *Chlstn*	Deserted/enemy		Hilton Head, SC	10/31/64		P8
Clanton, B.R.	Pvt	A 1st SCVIR	Cheraw, SC	03/02/65	New Berne, NC	04/10/65	Hart's Island, NY	CSR
					Hart's Island, NY	06/16/65	Rlsd. G.O. #109	SA1,P79,CSR
Clanton, Ephraim	Pvt	A 1st SCVIR	Black Creek, NC	03/01/65	New Berne, NC	04/03/65	Pt. Lookout, MD	CSR,SA1
					Pt. Lookout, MD	06/10/65	Released	P114,P118,P122,CSR
Clardy, J.F.	Sgt	D 18th SCVI	Petersburg, VA	07/30/64	Pt. Lookout, MD	08/08/64	Elmira, NY	P117,P120,P125,CSR
					Elmira, NY	07/07/65	Rlsd. G.O. #109	P65,CSR
Clardy, William	Pvt	C 4th SCVC	Hartwell, GA	05/19/65	Hartwell, GA	05/19/65	Paroled	CSR
Clare, William	Pvt	I 1st SCVIR	Deserted/enemy	03/17/65	Hilton Head, SC	03/20/65	NY City/steamer	CSR
Clark, Alfred	Pvt	C Orr's Ri.			Aikens Landing, VA	09/27/62	Exchanged	CDC,CSR
Clark, Angus J.	Pvt	F 4th SCVC	Hawe's Shop, VA	05/28/64	3rd Div., 5th A.C.	06/04/64	Lincoln G.H., DC	CSR
					Lincoln G.H., DC	12/04/64	Old Capitol, DC	CSR
					Old Capitol, DC	12/16/64	Elmira, NY	P110,CSR
					Elmira, NY	02/20/65	James R., VA Xc	P65,CSR
					Richmond, VA Hos.	03/30/65	Died, Pneumonia	CSR

SOUTH CAROLINA SOLDIERS, SAILORS AND **C** CITIZENS HELD IN U.S. PRISONS 1861-1865

NAME	RANK	REGIMENT	CAPTURED AT	WHEN	PRISON	MOVED	DISPOSITION	SOURCES
Clark, Bird M.	Pvt	A 16th SCVI	Kennesaw Mtn., GA	07/03/64	Nashville, TN	07/12/64	Louisville, KY	CSR
					Louisville, KY	07/13/64	Camp Morton, IN	P90,P91,P94,CSR
					Camp Morton, IN	06/12/65	Rlsd. G.O. #109	P100, P101,CSR
Clark, Charles	Pvt	G 3rd SCVABn	High Pt., NC	05/01/65	High Pt., NC	05/01/65	Paroled on oath	CSR
Clark, Daniel	Pvt	G 23rd SCVI	Five Forks, VA	04/01/65	City Pt., VA	04/05/65	Pt. Lookout, MD	CSR
					Pt. Lookout, MD	06/26/65	Rlsd. G.O. #109	P114,CSR
Clark, David A.	Pvt	K 1st SCVIG	Petersburg, VA	04/14/65	City Pt. VA	04/28/65	Newport News, VA	CSR
					Newport News, VA	06/26/65	Released G.O.#109	P107,CSR
Clark, David Z.	Pvt	E 24th SCVI	Nashville, TN	12/16/64	Nashville, TN	12/18/64	Louisville, KY	CSR
					Louisville, KY	12/20/64	Camp Douglas, IL	P90,P91
					Camp Douglas, IL	06/18/65	Rlsd. G.O. #109	CSR
Clark, F.W.	Pvt	B 19th SCVI	Orangeburg, SC	02/12/65	New Berne, NC	04/10/65	Hart's Island, NY	CSR
					Hart's Island, NY	06/17/65	Rlsd. G.O. #109	P79,CSR
Clark, J.A.	Pvt	2nd SCVI	Deserted/enemy	03/04/65	Bermuda Hundred VA	03/05/65	City Pt., VA	CSR
					City Pt., VA	03/06/65	Washington,DC PM	CSR
					Washington, DC	03/08/65	Columbus, OH oath	CSR
Clark, J.D.	Pvt	H 20th SCVI	Columbia, SC	02/16/65	New Berne, NC	04/03/65	Pt. Lookout, MD	CSR,KEB
					Pt. Lookout, MD	06/26/65	Rlsd. G.O. #109	P114,P118,P122,CSR
Clark, J.M.	Pvt	H 13th SCVI	Falling Waters, MD	07/14/63	Pt. Lookout, MD	02/24/65	Aikens Ldg., VA Xc	P113,P116,P124,CSR
Clark, J.N.	Pvt	A 12th SCVI	Sharpsburg, MD	09/17/62	Army of Potomac P.	09/27/62	Paroled	CSR
Clark, James	Pvt	I 1st SCVC	Deserted/enemy	03/15/65	Charleston, SC	03/15/65	Released on oath	CSR
Clark, James A.	Pvt	B 4th SCVC	Hartwell, GA	05/19/65	Hartwell, GA	05/19/65	Paroled	CSR
Clark, James M.	Pvt	B 12th SCVI	N. Anna River, VA	05/23/64	Pt. Lookout, MD	06/20/64	Joined U.S. Army	P113,P117,P121,P125,YEB,
Clark, James R.	Pvt	Ferguson's LA	Salisbury, NC	04/12/65	Nashville, TN	04/29/65	Louisville, KY	CSR
					Louisville, KY	05/02/65	Camp Chase, OH	P92,CSR
					Camp Chase, OH	06/13/65	Rlsd. G.O. #109	CSR
Clark, John	Pvt	H Orr's Ri.	Spotsylvania, VA	05/12/64	Belle Plain, VA	05/20/64	Ft. Delaware, DE	CSR
					Ft. Delaware, DE	06/10/65	Released	P41,P43,P45,CDC
Clark, John C.	Pvt	B 24th SCVI	Nashville, TN	12/16/64	Nashville, TN	12/19/64	Louisville, KY	CSR
					Louisville, KY	12/21/64	Camp Douglas, IL	P90,P91,P95
					Camp Douglas, IL	04/06/65	Jd. US 6th NJ Vols	P55,EFW
Clark, John L.	Sgt	G 5th SCVC	Salem Church, VA	05/28/64	3rd Div. 5th A.C.	06/02/64	Stanton G.H., DC	P5,P12,CSR
					Stanton G.H., DC	06/18/64	Died of wounds	P5,P12,CSR
Clark, John W.	Pvt	G 23rd SCVI	Five Forks, VA	04/01/65	City Pt., VA	04/05/65	Pt. Lookout, MD	CSR
					Pt. Lookout, MD	06/24/65	Rlsd. G.O. #109	P118,P121,P123,CSR
Clark, Joshua C.	Pvt	D 1st SCVA	Black River, NC	03/16/65	New Berne, NC	03/30/65	Pt. Lookout, MD	CSR
					Pt. Lookout, MD	06/26/65	Rlsd. G.O. #109	P114,P118,P122,CSR
Clark, Robert E.	Pvt	A 16th SCVI	Missionary Ridge, TN	11/26/63	Nashville, TN	12/27/63	Louisville, KY	P39,CSR
					Louisville, KY	12/29/63	Rock Island, IL	P89,P90,P93,CSR
					Rock Island, IL	06/18/65	Rlsd. G.O. #109	P131,CSR
Clark, Thomas	Pvt	K 7th SCVI	Gettysburg, PA	07/04/63	Harrisburg, PA	07/04/63	Philadelphia, PA	CSR
					Philadelphia, PA	07/12/63	Ft. Delaware, DE	CSR
					Ft. Delaware, DE	07/15/63	Jd. US forces	P40,P42,P44
Clark, William		P. *Savannah*	Off Charleston	06/03/61	Tombs Prison, NY	02/15/62	Ft. Lafayette, NY	OR,TCP
					Ft. Lafayette, NY	06/06/62	City Pt., VA Xc	OR,TCP,CDC
Clark, William	Pvt	H 18th SCVI	Crater, Pbg., VA	07/30/64	City Pt., VA	08/05/64	Pt. Lookout, MD	CSR,YEB
					Pt. Lookout, MD	08/08/64	Elmira, NY	P113,P117,P120,CSR
Clarke, Starling	Pvt	D 1st SCVIR	Charleston Bar	03/21/63	Ft. Lafayette, NY	06/29/63	Ft. Delaware, DE	CSR
					Ft. Delaware, DE	08/30/63	Joined US Cavalry	P40,P42,P44,SA1,CSR
Clary, Asa W.	Pvt	K 18th SCVI	Richmond, VA Hos	04/03/65	Libby Prison Rchmd	04/23/65	Newport News, VA	CSR
					Newport News, VA	06/26/65	Rlsd. G.O. #109	P107,CSR

SOUTH CAROLINA SOLDIERS, SAILORS AND **C** CITIZENS HELD IN U.S. PRISONS 1861-1865

NAME	RANK	REGIMENT	CAPTURED AT	WHEN	PRISON	MOVED	DISPOSITION	SOURCES
Clary, G.B.	Pvt	F 15th SCVI	Gettysburg, PA	07/04/63	Gettysburg G.H.	07/12/63	Provost Marshal	P4,KEB
					David's Island, NY	08/24/63	City Pt., VA Xc	P1,CSR
Clary, J.W.	Pvt	F 1st SCVIH	Deep Bottom, VA	08/14/64	Bermuda Hundred, VA	08/15/64	Fts. Monroe, VA	CSR
					Fts. Monroe, VA	08/17/64	Pt. Lookout, MD	CSR
					Pt. Lookout, MD	03/14/65	Aikens Idg., VA Xc	P117,P123,P124,CSR
Clary, James B.	Pvt	G Hol.Leg.	Five Forks, VA	04/01/65	City Pt., VA	04/05/65	Pt. Lookout, MD	CSR,ANY
					Pt. Lookout, MD	06/26/65	Rlsd. G.O. #109	P118,P122,P123,CSR
Clary, John E.	1Lt	K 18th SCVI	Petersburg, VA	07/30/64	Old Capitol, DC	08/08/64	Ft. Delaware, DE	P110,CSR
					Ft. Delaware, DE	06/17/65	Rlsd. G.O. #109	P43,P45,CSR
Clary, M.J.	Pvt	C Ham.Leg.MI	Farmville, VA	04/11/65	Farmville, VA	04/11/65	Paroled	CSR
Clary, R.C.	Sgt	G 7th SCVI	Halltown, WV	08/21/64	Harpers Ferry, WV	09/02/62	Camp Chase, OH	CSR
					Camp Chase, OH	03/18/65	Pt. Lookout, MD	P23,P26,HOE,CSR
Clary, Singleton	Pvt	F 15th SCVI	Wilderness, VA	05/06/64	Ft. Delaware, DE		To Hos 7/25-8/20/6	P47
					Belle Plain, VA	05/20/64	Ft. Delaware, DE	CSR,KEB
					Ft. Delaware, DE	06/10/65	Released on oath	P41,P43,P45,CSR
Clawson, W.H.	Pvt	A 17th SCVI	Hatchers Run, VA	03/27/65	City Pt., VA P.M.	04/01/65	Pt. Lookout, MD	CSR
					Pt. Lookout, MD	06/26/65	Rlsd. G.O. #109	P118,P122,P123,CSR
Claxton, Lewis V.	Sgt	A 19th SCVI	Atlanta, GA	07/22/64	Louisville, GA	07/31/64	Camp Chase, OH	P90,P91,HOE,CSR
					Camp Chase, OH	03/04/65	City Pt,, VA Xc	P26,CSR
Clayton, C.R.	Cpl	G 1st SCVIH	Burkeville, VA	04/14/65	Burkeville, VA	04/17/65	Paroled	CSR
Clayton, D.J.	Pvt	F 25th SCVI	Ft. Fisher, NC	01/15/65	New York, NY	01/30/65	Elmira, NY	CSR
					Elmira, NY	03/02/65	Tfd. for exchange	P65,HAG
					Pt. Lookout, MD	07/19/65	Rlsd. G.O. #109	CSR
Clayton, Frank R.	Pvt	F 25th SCVI	Ft. Fisher, NC	01/15/65	New York, NY	01/30/65	Elmira, NY	CSR
					Elmira, NY	03/23/65	Died, Ch. Diarrhea	P6,P12,P65,FPH
Clayton, J.A.	Pvt	G 2nd SCVI	Cheraw, SC	03/05/65	Cheraw, SC	03/05/65	Paroled	CSR
Clayton, J.J.	Pvt	I 5th SCVC	Nashville, TN	07/21/65	Nashville, TN	07/21/65	Paroled	CSR
Clayton, Jesse J.	Pvt	A 1st SCVIH	Burkeville, VA	04/14/65	Burkeville, VA	04/17/65	Paroled	CSR
Clayton, John	Pvt	F 1st SCVA	Marlboro D., SC	04/06/65	New Berne, NC		Camp Hamilton, VA	CSR
					Camp Hamilton, VA	05/01/65	Newport News, VA	CSR
					Newport News, VA	05/13/65	Died	P6,P107,CSR
Clayton, Robert C.	Pvt	B 2nd SCVIRi	Burkeville, VA	04/14/65	Burkeville, VA	04/17/65	Paroled	CSR
Clayton, S.P.	Pvt	C 1st SCVA	Smith's Ford, NC	03/16/65	New Berne, Nc	03/31/65	Pt. Lookout MD	CSR
					Pt. Lookout, MD	06/26/65	Rlsd. G.O. #109	P118,P123,CSR
Clayton, W.H.	Pvt	A 25th SCVI	Deserted/enemy	03/23/65	Washington, DC		Rlsd. on oath	HAG,CSR
Clayton, W.W.	Pvt	F 25th SCVI	Ft. Fisher, NC	01/15/65	New York, NY	01/30/65	Elmira, NY	CSR
					Elmira, NY	02/21/65	Tfd. for exchange	P65,HAG
					Baltimore, MD G.H.	03/26/65	Died	CSR,FPH
Cleaper, Charles H.	Pvt	D 23rd SCVI	Deserted/enemy	02/17/65	Charleston, SC	02/17/65	Washington, DC	CSR
					Washington, DC	02/21/65	New York, NY/oath	CSR
Cleary, Dennis	Pvt	E 1st SCVIR	Morris Island, SC	09/08/64	Hilton Head, SC	10/03/64	Works at QM on oath	SA1,CSR
Cleary, William	Pvt	D 27th SCVI	Town Creek, NC	02/20/65	Ft. Anderson, NC	02/28/65	Pt. Lookout, MD	CSR,HAG
					Pt. Lookout, MD	06/26/65	Rlsd. G.O. #109	P118,P122,P123,CSR
Clegg, A.J.	Pvt	G 1st SCVIG	Petersburg, VA	04/02/65	City Pt. VA	04/07/65	Hart's Island, NY	CSR
					Hart's Island, NY	06/16/65	Rlsd. G.O. #109	P79,CSR
Cleland, Elihu H.	Pvt	G Hol.Leg.	Five Forks, VA	04/01/65	City Pt., VA	04/05/65	Pt. Lookout, MD	CSR
					Pt. Lookout, MD	06/24/65	Rlsd. G.O. #109	P114,P118,P121,CSR
Cleland, J.E.	Pvt	A 19th SCVCB	Augusta, GA	05/25/65	Augusta, GA	05/25/65	Paroled on oath	CSR
Cleland, M.E.	Pvt	A 19th SCVCB	Augusta, GA	05/24/65	Augusta, GA	05/24/65	Paroled on oath	CSR
Cleland, W.	Pvt	A 19th SCVCB	Augusta, GA	05/25/65	Augusta, GA	05/25/65	Paroled on oath	CSR
Clem, Roland A.	Pvt	G 14th SCVI	Petersburg, VA	07/29/64	Pt. Lookout, MD	08/08/64	Elmira, NY	P113,P117,P120,CSR
					Elmira, NY	07/03/65	Rlsd. G.O. #109	P65,CSR

SOUTH CAROLINA SOLDIERS, SAILORS AND  CITIZENS HELD IN U.S. PRISONS 1861-1865

NAME	RANK	REGIMENT	CAPTURED AT	WHEN	PRISON	MOVED	DISPOSITION	SOURCES
Clem, Simpson	Pvt	G 14th SCVI	Wilderness, VA	05/06/64	Belle Plain, VA	05/20/64	Ft. Delaware, DE	CSR
					Ft. Delaware, DE	06/10/65	Released	P41,P43,P45,CSR
Clem, William G.	Pvt	K 2nd SCVIRi	Deserted/enemy	12/16/63	Knoxville, TN	12/16/63	Released	P8,CSR
Clement, A.W.	SMj	11th SCVI	Town Creek, NC	02/20/65	Ft. Anderson, NC	02/28/65	Pt. Lookout, MD	CSR
					Pt. Lookout, MD	06/04/65	Rlsd. Instr. 5/5/65	P114,P118,P121,CSR
Clement, B.S.	Cpl	Ham.Leg.MI	Richmond, VA	04/21/65	Richmond, VA	04/21/65	Paroled	CSR
Clements, John C.	1Lt	B 21st SCVI	Petersburg, VA	06/24/64	Pt. Lookout, MD	06/29/64	Washington, DC	P120,HAG
					Ft. Delaware, DE	10/06/64	Pt. Lookout, MD Xc	P43,P44,P46
					Pt. Lookout, MD	10/11/64	Aikens Ldg., VA Xc	P114,P117,P123
					Ft. Columbus, NY	03/01/65	City Pt., VA Xc	P2
Cleveland, F.M.	Pvt	K 22nd SCVI	Deserted/Enemy	03/01/65	City Pt., VA	03/03/65	Washington, DC	CSR
					Washington, DC	03/06/65	New York, NY/oath	CSR
Cleveland, Louis C.	Msc	C 1st SCVA	Deserted/enemy	02/18/65	Charleston, SC	03/21/65	Taken oath & disch	CSR
Cleveland, Vannoy	Pvt	F Ham.Leg.	Warrenton, VA	09/29/62	Warrenton, VA	09/29/62	Paroled	CSR
Clifford, Samuel R.	Pvt	H Ham.Leg.MI	Deserted/enemy	11/04/64	Bermuda Hundred, VA	11/05/64	City Pt., VA	CSR
					City Pt., VA	11/06/64	Fts. Monroe, VA	CSR
					Fts. Monroe, VA	11/14/64	Carrollton, MD	CSR
Clifton, Henry J.	1Lt	K 21st SCVI	Petersburg, VA	06/17/64	Ft. Pulaski, GA			P4,HAG,ISH
					Ft. Delaware, DE	08/20/64	Hilton Head, SC	P43
					Ft. Delaware, DE	05/12/65	Discharged Hos.	P47
Clifton, Henry J.	1Lt	K 21st SCVI	Petersburg, VA	06/17/64	Ft. Delaware, DE	06/17/65	Rlsd. G.O. #109	P43,P44,P45
Clifton, Wesley H.	Pvt	B 15th SCVI	Gettysburg, PA	07/04/63	David's Island, NY	08/24/63	City Pt., VA Xc	P1,KEB,CSR
					Camp Chase, OH	03/26/65	Pt. Lookout, MD	P23,CSR
Clifton, Wesley H.	Pvt	B 15th SCVI	Halltown, WV	08/21/64	Pt. Lookout, MD	06/06/65	Rlsd. Instr. 5/30/65	P114,P119,P121,KEB,CSR
Cline, H.F.	Pvt	A 3rd SCVABn	High Pt., NC	05/02/65	High Pt., NC	05/02/65	Paroled on oath	CSR
Cline, M.P.	Pvt	G 2nd SCVC	Brandy Stn., VA	08/01/63	Ft. McHenry, MD		Hold for orders	P110
					Old Capitol, DC	11/23/63	Ft. Delaware, DE	P110,CSR
					Ft. Delaware, DE	06/10/65	Rlsd.G.O. #109	P41,P43,P45,CSR
Cline, Robert	Pvt	C 2nd SCVC	Gettysburg, PA	07/03/63	Harrisburg, PA	07/07/63	Philadelphia, PA	CSR
					Ft. Delaware, DE	04/06/65	To Hos 4/6-5/13/65	P47
					Ft. Delaware, DE	06/10/65	Rlsd. G.O. #109	P42,P44,P45,CSR
Clinkscales, C.L.	Pvt	B 4th SCResB	Hartwell, GA	05/19/65	Hartwell, GA	05/19/65	Paroled	CSR
Clopton, George W.	Pvt	D 27th SCVI	Town Creek, NC	02/20/65	Ft. Anderson, NC	02/28/65	Pt. Lookout, MD	CSR,HAG
					Pt. Lookout, MD	06/26/65	Rlsd. G.O. #109	P114,P123,CSR
Cloud, Thomas	Cpl	F 26th SCVI	Orangeburg, SC	02/12/65	Hart's Island, NY	06/14/65	Rlsd. G.O. #109	P79
Clyburn, Benjamin R.	Maj	2nd SCVI	Cedar Creek, VA	10/19/64	Frederick, MD G.H.	12/30/64	Baltimore, MD	P3,KEB,SA2,CSR
					W. Bldg. Balt., MD	01/10/65	Ft. Delaware, DE	P1,CSR
					Ft. Delaware, DE	02/27/65	City Pt., VA Xc	P43,P47,H2,CSR
Clyburn, Jesse	Pvt	D 1st SCVIH	Charlotte, NC	05/05/65	Charlotte, NC	05/05/65	Paroled	CSR
Clyburn, William C.	Cpt	G 7th SCVIBn	Morris Island, SC	07/10/63	Hilton Head, SC	10/06/63	Ft. Columbus, NY	CSR
					Ft. Columbus, NY	10/09/63	Johnson's Isl., OH	P1,HAG,CSR
					Johnsons Isl., OH	02/09/64	Baltimore, MD	P80,CSR
					Johnsons Isl., OH	02/10/64	Pt. Lookout, MD	P82
					Pt. Lookout, MD	03/03/65	Exchanged	P113,P123,CSR
Clyde, Joseph B.	Pvt	G 22nd SCVI	Richmond, VA Hos	04/03/65	Richmond, VA	04/21/65	Rlsd. on parole	CSR
Clyde, Samuel C.	1Sg	B 2nd SCVI	Cedar Creek, VA	10/19/64	W. Bldg. Balt., MD	10/25/64	Pt. Lookout, MD	P3,KEB,SA2,CSR
					Pt. Lookout, MD	10/30/64	Aikens Ldg., VA Xc	P114,P118,H2,CSR
Coachman, Edgar F.	Sgt	A Ham.Leg.	Williamsburg, VA	06/08/62	Fts. Monroe, VA H.	08/06/62	Died of wounds	P12,CSR
Coates, Drayton N.	Pvt	E 27th SCVI	Florence, SC	03/05/65	New Berne, NC	04/03/65	Pt. Lookout, MD	CSR,HAG
					Pt. Lookout, MD	06/26/65	Rlsd. G.O. #109	P118,P122,P123,CSR
Coates, Gabriel H.	Pvt	G 2nd SCVI	Cedar Creek, VA	10/19/64	Harpers Ferry, WV	10/24/64	Pt. Lookout, MD	CSR,SA2,H2,KEB
					Pt. Lookout, MD	03/25/65	Aikens Ldg., VA Xc	P121,P124,CSR

SOUTH CAROLINA SOLDIERS, SAILORS AND  CITIZENS HELD IN U.S. PRISONS 1861-1865

NAME	RANK	REGIMENT	CAPTURED AT	WHEN	PRISON	MOVED	DISPOSITION	SOURCES
Cobb, George W.	Pvt	B 12th SCVI	Warrenton, VA	09/29/62	Warrenton, VA	09/29/62	Paroled	CSR
Cobb, George W.	Pvt	B 12th SCVI	Falling Waters, MD	07/14/63	W. Bldg. Balt., MD	08/14/63	Ft. McHenry, MD	P1,CSR
					Ft. McHenry, MD	08/22/63	City Pt., VA	P96,P144,YEB,CSR
					City Pt., VA	08/22/63	Pt. Lookout, MD	CSR
					Pt. Lookout, MD	11/15/63	Hammond G.H., MD	P113,P121,P125,CSR
					Hammond G.H., MD	11/25/63	Died, Ch. Diarrhea	P5,P116,FPH,CSR
Cobb, J.A.	Pvt	B 12th SCVI	Sharpsburg, MD	09/17/62	Sharpsburg, MD	09/21/62	Paroled	CSR
Cobb, James M.	Pvt	B Orr's Ri.	Petersburg, VA	04/03/65	City Pt., VA	04/11/65	Hart's Island, NY	CSR
					Hart's Island, NY	04/29/65	David's Island, NY	CSR
					David's Island, NY	05/26/65	Hart's Island, NY	CSR
					Hart's Island, NY	06/16/65	Rlsd. G.O. #109	P79, CSR
Cobb, Robert A.	Pvt	K 12th SCVI	Falling Waters, MD	07/14/63	Old Capitol, DC	08/08/63	Pt. Lookout, MD	CSR
					Pt. Lookout, MD	04/22/64	Died, Ch. Diarrhea	P5,P13,P116,P119
Cobb, William H.	Pvt	F Hol.Leg.	Five Forks, VA	04/01/65	City Pt., VA	04/05/65	Pt. Lookout, MD	CSR
					Pt. Lookout, MD	06/26/65	Rlsd. G.O. #109	P114,P118,P123,CSR
Coburn, A.B..	Pvt	D 15th SCMil	Cheraw, SC	02/28/65	Pt. Lookout, MD	06/26/65	Rlsd. G.O. #109	P118,P122,P123,CSR
Cochran, A.W.	Pvt	I 25th SCVI	Ft. Fisher, NC	01/15/65	New York, NY	01/30/65	Elmira, NY	CSR
					Elmira, NY	03/08/65	Died, Ch. Diarrhea	P5,P12,P65
Cochran, J.F.	Pvt	H 1st SCVA	Morris Island, SC	07/10/63	Hilton Head, SC	09/05/63	Ft. Columbus, NY	CSR
					Ft. Columbus, NY	09/23/63	Took the oath	P1,CSR
Cochran, James J.	Pvt	D Hol.Leg.	Petersburg, VA	11/06/64	City Pt., VA	11/11/64	Pt. Lookout, MD	CSR
					Pt. Lookout, MD	06/10/65	Released	P114,P118,CSR
Cochran, Samuel H.	Pvt	A 2nd SCVIRi	Missionary Ridge, TN	11/25/63	Nashville, TN	02/28/64	Louisville, KY	P2,P39,CSR
					Louisville, KY	03/09/64	Camp Chase, OH	P90,P91,P94,CSR
					Camp Chase, OH	02/25/65	City Pt., VA Xc	P23,P26,CSR
					Richmond, VA Hos.	03/14/65	Furloughed 60 days	CSR
Cockcroft, George W.	Pvt	K 13th SCVI	Petersburg VA Hos	04/03/65	Camp Hamilton, VA	05/31/65	Released on oath	CSR
Cockcroft, Joseph P.	Pvt	A 22nd SCVI	Hatchers Run, VA	03/30/65	City Pt., VA	04/01/65	Pt. Lookout, MD	CSR
					Pt. Lookout, MD	06/10/65	Released	P122
Cockcroft, R.H.	Pvt	B 4th SCVC	Pocotaligo, SC	02/02/65	New Berne, NC	04/10/65	Hart's Island, NY	CSR
					Hart's Island, NY	06/16/65	Rlsd. G.O. #109	P79,CSR
Cockerell, G.F.	Pvt	F 27th SCVI	Weldon RR, VA	08/21/64	City Pt., VA	08/24/64	Pt. Lookout, MD	CSR
					Pt. Lookout, MD	01/27/65	Hammond G.H., MD	P113,P121
					Pt. Lookout, MD	06/26/65	Rlsd. G.O. #109	P117,CSR
Cockrell, John	Pvt	D 14th SCVI	Petersburg, VA	04/03/65	City Pt., VA	04/13/65	Pt. Lookout, MD	CSR
					Pt. Lookout, MD	06/26/65	Rlsd. G.O. #109	P122,P123,HOE,CSR
Cody, Martin M.	Pvt	H 21st SCVI	Morris Island, SC	07/10/63	Hilton Head, SC	07/23/63	Morris Island, SC Xc	P2,HAG,CSR
Coe, Theodore H.	1Lt	Enrol Offr	Gillisonville, SC	01/16/65	Hilton Head, SC	03/12/65	Ft. Delaware, DE	CSR
					Ft. Delaware, DE	06/17/65	Rlsd. G.O. #109	CSR
Coffee, Thomas	Pvt	D 23rd SCVI	Petersburg, VA	03/25/65	Pt. Lookout, MD	05/13/65	Rlsd. G.O. #85	P122,CSR
Coffee, Timothy	Pvt	Ferguson's	Ringgold, GA	11/26/63	Nashville, TN	12/11/63	Louisville, KY	P39,CSR
					Louisville, GA	12/12/63	Rock Island, IL	P88,P89,CSR
					Rock Island, IL	04/21/64	Rlsd. on oath	P131,CSR
Coffey, William	Pvt	D 23rd SCVI	Petersburg, VA	03/27/65	Washington, DC PM	03/30/65	Pt. Lookout, MD	CSR
					Pt. Lookout, MD		Rlsd. G.O. #85	CSR
Cogburn, Lawrence R.	Pvt	Mathewes A	Augusta, GA	05/17/65	Augusta, GA	05/19/65	Paroled	CSR
Cogburn, Simeon	2Lt	K 14th SCVI	Gettysburg, PA	07/03/63	Newton U. Balt. MD	07/18/63	Chester, PA G.H.	CSR
					Chester, PA G.H.	10/02/63	Hammond G.H., MD	P1,CSR
					Hammonmd G.H., MD	12/09/63	Johnson's Isl., OH	P80,P116,CSR
					Johnson's Isl., OH	02/24/65	City Pt., VA Xc	P82,CSR

SOUTH CAROLINA SOLDIERS, SAILORS AND  CITIZENS HELD IN U.S. PRISONS 1861-1865

NAME	RANK	REGIMENT	CAPTURED AT	WHEN	PRISON	MOVED	DISPOSITION	SOURCES
Cogburn, W.H.	Pvt	I 2nd SCVC	Brandy Stn., VA	08/01/63	Old Capitol, DC			CSR
					Ft. McHenry, MD			P110
					Pt. Lookout, MD	11/01/64	Aikens Ldg., VA Xc	P116,P121,P124,CSR
Cogburn, W.H.	Pvt	I 2nd SCVC	Augusta, GA	05/29/65	Augusta, GA	05/29/65	Paroled on oath	CSR
Cohen, Arthur M.	Pvt	C 3rd SCVABn	Blakely, AL	04/09/65	Ship Island, MS	05/01/65	Vicksburg, MS Prld	P136,CSR
Cohen, Arthur M.	Pvt	C 3rd SCVABn	Augusta, GA	05/20/65	Augusta, GA	05/20/65	Paroled on oath	CSR
Cohen, D.A.	Pvt	G 1st SCVIH	Deserted/enemy	12/22/64	City Pt., VA	01/02/65	Washington, DC PM	CSR
					Washington, DC	01/04/65	New York, NY/ oath	CSR
Cohen, David	Pvt	G 2nd SCVC	Whites Bridge, VA	11/26/63	Old Capitol, DC	02/03/64	Pt. Lookout, MD	CSR
					Pt. Lookout, MD	02/18/65	Exchanged	P113,P123,P124
Cohen, Joseph	Pvt	McQueen LA	Chester, SC	05/05/65	Chester, SC	05/05/65		CSR
Cohen, Morris	HSd	B 7th SCVIBn	Morris Island, SC	07/11/63	Hilton Head, SC	09/22/63	Ft. Columbus, NY	CSR
					Ft. Columbus, NY	09/26/63	Pt. Lookout, MD	P1,CSR
					Pt. Lookout, MD	04/22/64	Released on oath	P113P116,,P124,CSR
Cohen, Samuel	Pvt	G Hol.Leg.	Petersburg, VA	04/03/65	City Pt., VA	04/14/65	Pt. Lookout, MD	CSR
					Pt. Lookout, MD	06/10/65	Released	P114,P119,CSR
Cohen, Lawrence L., Sr.	Pvt	C 3rd SCVABn	Citronelle, AL	05/04/65	Meridian, MS	05/10/65	Paroled	CSR
Coit, Alexander??		P. Savannah	Off Charleston	06/03/61	Ft. Lafayette, NY	06/06/62	City Pt., VA Xc	TCP
					City Pt., VA	06/15/62	Died on transport	TCP
Coit, David Gardner	ASr	8th SCVI	Ft. Fisher, NC	01/15/65	Ft. Columbus, NY	03/01/65	City Pt., VA Xc	P2
Coker, Asa	Pvt	I 1st SCVA	Morris Island, SC	07/10/63	Hilton Head, SC	08/31/63	Ft. Columbus, NY	CSR
					Pt. Lookout, MD	08/16/64	Elmira, NY	P113,P116,P120
Coker, Asa	Pvt	I 1st SCVA	Morris Island, SC	07/10/63	Ft. Columbus, NY	08/18/64	Elmira, NY	CSR
					Elmira, NY	09/25/64	Died, Diarrhea	P5,P12,P65,FPH
Coker, Caleb	Pvt	I 18th SCVI	Southside RR, VA	04/02/65	City Pt., VA	04/07/65	Hart's Island, NY	CSR
					Hart's Island, NY	06/16/65	Rlsd. G.O. #109	P79,CSR
					Hart's Island, NY	06/18/65	Rlsd. G.O. #109	P79,HAG
Coker, Daniel C.	Sgt	E 6th SCVI	Fair Oaks, VA	06/01/62	Fts. Monroe, VA	06/05/62	Ft. Delaware, DE	CSR
					Ft. Delaware, DE	08/05/62	Aikens Ldg., VA Xc	CSR
Coker, J.	Pvt	D 21st SCVI	Southside RR, VA	04/02/65	City Pt., VA	04/07/65	Hart's Island, NY	CSR
					Hart's Island, NY	06/14/65	Rlsd. G.O. #109	P79,CSR
Coker, J.W.	Pvt	C 8th SCVI	Winchester, VA	09/13/64	Camp Chase, OH	05/02/65	New Orleans, LA Xc	P23
Coker, James Lide	Cpt	E 6th SCVI	Chattanooga, TN	11/24/63	Nashville, TN	04/20/64	Chattanooga, Paroled	P39
					Chattanooga, TN	05/10/64	Louisville, KY	CSR
					Louisville, KY	05/30/64	Ft. McHenry, MD	P90,P94,CSR
Coker, James Lide	Cpt	E 6th SCVI	Chattanooga, TN	11/24/63	Ft. McHenry, MD	06/16/64	Fts. Monroe, VA	CSR
					Fts. Monroe, VA	07/13/64	City Pt., VA Xc	CSR
					Fts. Monroe, VA	06/20/64	Pt. Lookout, MD	CSR,CTA
					Pt. Lookout, MD	07/25/64	Elmira, NY	P113,P117,P120,CSR
					Elmira, NY	12/10/64	Died, Diarrhea	P12,P65,FPH,CSR
Coker, M.Y.	Pvt	A 6th SCVC	Stony Creek, VA	12/01/64	Pt. Lookout, MD	06/10/65	Released	CSR
Coker, P.J.	Pvt	I 7th SCVI	Cedar Creek, VA	10/19/64	W. Bldg. Balt., MD	02/16/65	Ft. McHenry, MD Ex	P3,CSR
Coker, Sherry J.	Pvt	I 26th SCVI	Five Forks, VA	04/02/65	City Pt., VA MD	04/05/65	Pt. Lookout, MD	CSR,CTA
					Pt. Lookout, MD	06/26/65	Rlsd. G.O. #109	P114,P118,P123,CSR
Coker, Thomas L.	Pvt	D 21st SCVI	Ft. Fisher, NC	01/15/65	New York, NY	01/30/65	Elmira, NY	CSR
					Elmira, NY	02/20/65	James R., VA Xc	P65,HAG
Coker, William C.	Cpt	M 8th SCVI	Williamsport, MD	07/14/63	Frederick, MD G.H.	08/07/63	W. Bldg. Balt., MD	P1,KEB
					W. Bldg. Balt., MD	08/22/63	Johnson's Isl., OH	P1,CSR
					Johnson's Isl., OH	02/09/64	Baltimore, MD	P80
					Johnson's Isl., OH	02/10/64	Pt. Lookout, MD	P82,CSR
					Pt. Lookout, MD	06/23/64	Ft. Delaware, DE	P113,P117,P120,CSR
					Ft. Delaware, DE	03/07/65	City Pt., VA Xch	P43,P44,P46,KEB,CSR

SOUTH CAROLINA SOLDIERS, SAILORS AND C CITIZENS HELD IN U.S. PRISONS 1861-1865

NAME	RANK	REGIMENT	CAPTURED AT	WHEN	PRISON	MOVED	DISPOSITION	SOURCES
Coker, William C.	Pvt	A 4th SCVC	Hawe's Shop, VA	05/28/64	3rd Div. 5th A.C.	06/05/64	Lincoln G.H., DC	CSR
					Lincoln G.H., DC	06/19/64	Died of wounds	P6,P12,P110
Colbert, Augustus G.	Pvt	H P.S.S.	Fair Oaks, VA	05/31/62	Fts. Monroe, VA	06/03/62	Ft. Delaware, DE	CSR
Colburn, E.L.	Pvt	B 23rd SCVI	Petersburg, VA	04/02/65	City Pt., VA	04/04/65	Pt. Lookout, MD	CSR
					Pt. Lookout, MD	06/10/65	Rlsd. G.O. #109	P114,P118,P122,CSR
Colcock, Charles Jones	Cpl	I 2nd SCVI	Gettysburg, PA	07/02/63	Letterman G.H. Gbg	09/01/63	Provost Marshal	P1,KEB,H2,CSR
					W. Bldg. Balt., MD	09/25/63	City Pt., VA Xchg.	SA2,P1,CSR
Cole, A.B.	Pvt	I Hol.Leg.	Sharpsburg, MD	09/15/62	Ft. Delaware, DE	10/02/62	Aikens Ldg., VA Xc	CSR
Cole, Elijah W.	Pvt	I Hol.Leg.	Stony Creek, VA	05/07/64	Fts. Monroe, VA	05/13/64	Pt. Lookout, MD	CSR
					Pt. Lookout, MD	08/15/64	Elmira, NY	P113,P116,P120
					Elmira, NY	09/19/64	Died, Ch. Diarrhea	P5,P12,P65,FPH
Cole, F.M.	Pvt	K 2nd SCVI	Hartwell, GA	05/19/65	Hartwell, GA	05/19/65	Paroled on oath	CSR
Cole, Farrow	Pvt	E 13th SCVI	Deserted/enemy	02/24/65	City Pt., VA	02/26/65	Washington, DC	CSR
					Washington D.C.	02/27/65	Springfield, IL	CSR
Cole, J.D.	Pvt	Wash'n LA	Raleigh, NC	04/13/65	Raleigh, NC	05/05/65	Paroled	CSR
Cole, James	Pvt	G 23rd SCVI	Petersburg, VA	06/17/64	Pt. Lookout, MD	07/27/64	Elmira, NY	P113,P117,P120,HOM
					Elmira, NY	02/13/65	Tfd. for exchange	P65
Cole, John B.	Pvt	H 12th SCVI	Sutherland Stn., VA	04/03/65	City Pt., VA	04/07/65	Hart's Island, NY	CSR
					Hart's Island, NY	06/16/65	Rlsd. G.O. #109	P79,CSR
Cole, John S.	Pvt	F 7th SCVC	Farmville, VA	04/13/65	Farmville, VA	04/16/65	Paroled	CSR
Cole, L.A.	Pvt	Ferguson's LA	Hartwell, GA	05/19/65	Hartwell, GA	05/19/65		CSR
Cole, S. Rush	Cpl	D 2nd SCVI	Gettysburg, PA	07/05/63	Gettysburg G.H.	07/21/63	Provost Marshal	P4,KEB,CSR
					David's Island, NY	09/05/63	City Pt., VA Xc	P1,KEB,H2,CSR
Cole, Sidney F.	Pvt	C Ham.Leg.	Williamsburg, VA	06/08/62	Fts. Monroe, VA	08/31/62	Aikens Ldg., VA Xc	CSR
Cole, Sidney F.	Pvt	C Ham.Leg.MI	Deserted/enemy	03/25/65	Bermuda Hundred, VA	03/27/65	City Pt., VA P.M.	CSR
					City Pt., VA	03/27/65	Washington, DC	CSR
					Washington, DC	03/30/65	Philadelphia, PA	CSR
Cole, Thomas	Pvt	B German LA	Hartwell, GA	05/19/65	Hartwell, GA	05/19/65	Paroled	CSR
Cole, William	Pvt	D 26th SCVI	Deserted/enemy	12/11/64	Washington, DC		Released on oath	CSR
					City Point, VA	12/13/64	Washington, DC	P8,HOM,CSR
Cole, William H.	Cpl	I 23rd SCVI	Petersburg, VA	04/02/65	Pt. Lookout, MD	06/10/65	Released	P114,P118,HCL,CSR
Cole, William P.	Pvt	I 5th SCVI	Richmond, VA	04/03/65	Libby Prison, VA	04/08/65	City Pt., VA	CSR
					City Pt., VA	04/14/65	Pt. Lookout, MD	CSR
					Pt. Lookout, MD	06/26/65	Rlsd. G.O. #109	P119,P122,P123,CSR
Coleman, A.J.	Pvt	E 7th SCVC	Augusta, GA	06/02/65	Augusta, GA	06/02/65	Paroled	CSR
Coleman, B.C.	Sgt	H 15th SCVI	Gettysburg, PA	07/05/63	Gettysburg G.H.	07/12/63	Provost Marshal	P4,KEB,CSR
					Ft. McHenry, MD	07/12/63	Ft. Delaware, DE	CSR
					Ft. Delaware, DE	07/30/63	City Pt., VA Xc	P40,P42,P44,CSR
Coleman, David	Pvt	A 6th SCVC	Chaffins Farm, VA	10/02/64	City Pt., VA	10/03/64	Pt. Lookout, MD	CSR
					Pt. Lookout, MD	06/24/65	Rlsd. G.O. #109	P118,P122,P123,CSR
Coleman, G.W.	Pvt	I 4th SCVC	Hawe's Shop, VA	05/28/64	White House, VA	06/08/64	Pt. Lookout, MD	CSR
					Pt. Lookout, MD	07/08/64	Elmira, NY	P113,P117,P120,CSR
					Elmira, NY	03/02/65	James R., VA Xc	P65,CSR
					Richmond, VA Hos.	03/09/65	Furloughed 30 days	CSR
Coleman, George W.	Sgt	B 17th SCVI	Five Forks, VA	04/01/65	City Pt., VA	04/06/65	Pt. Lookout, MD	CSR
					Pt. Lookout, MD	06/26/65	Rlsd. G.O. #109	P118,P122,P123,CSR
Coleman, Henry J.	Pvt	B 17th SCVI	Petersburg, VA	03/25/65	City Pt., VA	03/28/65	Pt. Lookout, MD	CSR,HOF
					Pt. Lookout, MD	06/26/65	Rlsd. G.O. #109	P114,P118,P122,CSR
Coleman, Isaac M.	Pvt	C 22nd SCVI	Crater, Pbg., VA	07/30/64	City Pt., VA	08/05/64	Pt. Lookout, MD	CSR,HOS
					Pt. Lookout, MD	08/08/64	Elmira, NY	P117,P120,P125
					Elmira, NY	11/12/64	Died, Pneumonia	P5,P12,P65,FPH

SOUTH CAROLINA SOLDIERS, SAILORS AND  CITIZENS HELD IN U.S. PRISONS 1861-1865

NAME	RANK	REGIMENT	CAPTURED AT	WHEN	PRISON	MOVED	DISPOSITION	SOURCES
Coleman, J.P.	Pvt	F 4th SCVC	Stony Creek, VA	12/01/64	City Pt., VA	12/05/64	Pt. Lookout, MD	CSR
					Pt. Lookout, MD	06/08/65	Rlsd. G.O. #109	P114,P118,HMC,CSR
Coleman, J.W.	Pvt	C 6th SCVC	Stony Creek, VA	12/01/64	City Pt., VA	12/04/64	Pt. Lookout, MD	CSR
					Pt. Lookout, MD	02/13/65	Exchanged	P118,P121,P124,CSR
Coleman, James T.	Pvt	B 18th SCVI	Five Forks, VA	04/01/65	City Pt., VA	04/06/65	Pt. Lookout, MD	CSR
					Pt. Lookout, MD	06/26/65	Rlsd. G.O. #109	P118,P122,P123,CSR
Coleman, John E.	Pvt	6 10/19 SCVI	Missionary Ridge, TN	11/25/63	Nashville, TN	12/07/63	Louisville, KY	P39,CSR
					Louisville, KY	12/09/63	Rock Island, IL	P88,P89,RAS,CSR
					Rock Island, IL	10/13/64	Enlstd. US Front. S.	P131,CSR
Coleman, John L.	Pvt	I 24th SCVI	Covington, GA	07/22/64	Nashville, TN	08/02/64	Louisville, KY	CSR
					Louisville, KY	08/03/64	Camp Chase, OH	P90,P91,P94
					Camp Chase, OH	03/04/65	City Pt., VA Xc	P26,EFW,CSR
Coleman, John W.	Pvt	D 10th SCVI	Kentucky	09/15/62	Kentucky	11/15/62	Paroled	CSR
Coleman, Joseph H.	Pvt	G 16th SCVI	Atlanta, GA	07/22/64	Nashville, TN	07/29/64	Louisville, KY	CSR
					Louisville, KY	07/30/64	Camp Douglas, IL	P90,P91,16R,CSR
					Camp Douglas, IL	05/04/65	New Orleans, LA Xc	P53,P55,CSR
					New Orleans, LA	06/01/65	Rlsd. on parole	P4,CSR
Coleman, Robert L.	Pvt	B 17th SCVI	Five Forks, VA	04/01/65	City Pt., VA	04/06/65	Pt. Lookout, MD	CSR,HHC
					Pt. Lookout, MD	06/26/65	Rlsd. G.O. #109	P118,P122,P123,CSR
Coleman, S.J.	Sgt	F 21st SCVI	Ft. Fisher, NC	01/15/65	Pt. Lookout, MD	02/02/65	Hammond G.H., MD	P114,P118,P121
					Hammond G.H., MD	07/25/65	Rlsd. G.O. #109	CSR
Coleman, T.F.	Pvt	F 1st SCVA	Bentonville, NC	03/22/65	New Berne, NC	04/10/65	Hart's Island, NC	CSR
					Hart's Island, NY	06/16/65	Rlsd. G.O. #109	P79,CSR
Coleman, Thomas J.	Pvt	B 3rd SCVIBn	South Mtn., MD	09/14/62	Ft. Delaware, DE	09/20/62	died	CSR
Coleman, W.J.	Pvt	B 17th SCVI	Petersburg, VA	03/25/65	Pt. Lookout, MD	06/26/65	Rlsd. G.O. #109	P123
Coleman, William R.	Pvt	F 1st SCVA	Bentonville, NC	03/22/65	New Berne, NC	04/10/65	Hart's Island, NY	CSR
					Hart's Island, NY	06/16/65	Rlsd. G.O. #109	P79,CSR
Coley, R. Benjamin	Pvt	G 3rd SCVI	Jordan Springs, VA	07/26/63	Jordan Springs, VA	07/26/63	Paroled	P2,KEB,SA2,CSR
Colgan, John E.	Pvt	D 14th SCVI	Five Forks, VA	04/01/65	City Pt., VA	04/05/65	Pt. Lookout, MD	CSR
					Pt. Lookout, MD	06/26/65	Rlsd. G.O. #109	P118,P122,P123,CSR
Collar, W.S.	Cpl	A Orr's Ri.	Gettysburg, PA	07/05/63	Gettysburg, PA	07/09/63	Died of wounds	P1,P12
Colley, J.B.	Pvt	F Orr's Ri.	Petersburg, VA	04/03/65	City Pt., VA	04/11/65	Hart's Island, NY	CSR
					Hart's Island, NY	06/16/65	Rlsd. G.O. #109	P79,CSR
Collins, A.D.	Pvt	H 17th SCVI	South Mtn., MD	09/14/62	Frederick, MD US G	10/03/62	Died of wounds	CSR
Collins, Albert T.	Pvt	B 13th SCVI	Ni River, VA	05/12/64	Fredericksburg, VA	05/17/64	Died, of wounds	CSR
Collins, Andrew M.	Pvt	C 26th SCVI	Five Forks, VA	04/01/65	City Pt., VA	04/05/65	Pt. Lookout, MD	CSR
					Pt. Lookout, MD	06/26/65	Rlsd. G.O. #109	P114,P118,P122,P123,CSR
Collins, B.	Pvt	K 2nd SCVC	Farmvillle, VA	04/11/65	Farmville, VA	04/21/65	Paroled on oath	CSR
Collins, C.F.	Pvt	F 7th SCVC	Lynchburg, VA	04/14/65	Lynchburg, VA	04/14/65	Paroled	CSR
Collins, Calvin	Pvt	E 1st SCVA	Bentonville, NC	03/22/65	New Berne, NC	04/10/65	Hart's Island, NY	CSR
					Hart's Island, NY	06/17/65	Rlsd. G.O. #109	P79,CSR
Collins, E.O.	Pvt	F 1st SCVIH	Milford Stn., VA	05/21/64	Front Royal, VA	05/30/64	Pt. Lookout, MD	CSR
					Pt. Lookout, MD	09/12/64	Died, Scurvy	P6,P113,P117,CSR
Collins, Frank	Pvt	I 26th SCVI	Petersburg, VA	04/02/65	City Pt., VA	04/05/65	Pt. Lookout, MD	CSR,CTA
					Pt. Lookout, MD	06/26/65	Rlsd. G.O. #109	P114,P122,P123,CSR
Collins, Green B.	Pvt	H 12th SCVI	Petersburg, VA	04/02/65	City Pt., VA	04/04/65	Pt. Lookout, MD	CSR
					Pt. Lookout, MD	06/26/65	Rlsd. G.O. #109	P114,P118,P123,CSR
Collins, H.L.	Pvt	H 17th SCVI	Deserted/enemy	03/08/65	City Pt., VA	03/09/65	Washington, DC	CSR
					Washington, DC	03/10/65	Charleston, SC on	CSR
Collins, Henry	Pvt	I 26th SCVI	Five Forks, VA	04/01/65	City Pt., VA	04/05/65	Pt. Lookout, MD	CSR,CTA
					Pt. Lookout, MD	06/26/65	Rlsd. G.O. #109	P118,P122,P123,CSR

SOUTH CAROLINA SOLDIERS, SAILORS AND C CITIZENS HELD IN U.S. PRISONS 1861-1865

NAME	RANK	REGIMENT	CAPTURED AT	WHEN	PRISON	MOVED	DISPOSITION	SOURCES
Collins, J.B.	Pvt	F 17th SCVI	Deserted/enemy	02/20/65	City Pt., VAS	02/22/65	Washington, DC	CSR
					Washington, DC	02/24/65	Boston, MA on oath	CSR
Collins, James	Pvt	K 24th SCVI	Secessionville, SC	05/16/62	Ft. Columbus, NY	08/23/62	Ft. Delaware, DE	P37,EFW
Collins, James	Pvt	H 17th SCVI	Deserted/enemy	03/08/65	City Pt., VA	03/09/65	Washington, DC	CSR
					Washington, DC	03/13/65	Charleston, SC on	CSR
Collins, James W.	Pvt	H 12th SCVI	Petersburg, VA	04/02/65	City Pt., VA	04/04/65	Pt. Lookout, MD	CSR,YEB
					Pt. Lookout, MD	06/26/65	Rlsd. G.O. #109	P114,P118,P123,CSR
Collins, Joel B.	Pvt	L 21st SCVI	Morris Island, SC	07/10/63	Pt. Lookout, MD	08/16/64	Elmira, NY	P113,P120,HAG
					Elmira, NY	10/11/64	Pt.Lookout, MD Xch	P65
					Pt. Lookout, MD	10/29/64	Exchanged	P114,P124
Collins, Joseph B.	Cpl	C 8th SCVI	Winchester, VA	09/13/64	Harpers Ferry, WV	09/19/64	Camp Chase, OH	CSR
					Camp Chase, OH	05/02/65	New Orleans, LA	P23,P26,KEB,CSR
					New Orleans, LA	05/12/65	Vicksburg, MS Xch	CSR
Collins, L.C.	Pvt	K 12th SCVI			Aikens Ldg., VA	09/27/62	Exchanged	CSR
					Richmond, VA	10/01/62	Paroled POWs Paid	CSR
Collins, L.C.	Pvt	K 12th SCVI	Gettysburg, PA	07/06/63	Ft. Delaware, DE	06/08/65	Released	P42,P44,P45,CSR
Collins, P.A.	Pvt	C 4th SCVC	Hawe's Shop, VA	05/28/64	White House, VA	06/08/64	Pt. Lookout, MD	CSR
					Pt. Lookout, MD	07/08/64	Elmira, NY	P113,P117,P120,CSR
					Elmira, NY	04/11/65	Died, Remit. Fever	P6,P12,P65,FPH,CSR
Collins, Patrick	Pvt	Ferguson's	Ringgold, GA	11/26/63	Nashville, TN	12/09/63	Louisville, KY	P39,CSR
					Louisville, KY	12/11/63	Rock Island, IL	P88,P89,CSR
					Rock Island, IL	01/25/64	Joined US Navy	P131,CSR
Collins, Reuben	Pvt	K 7th SCVC	Farmville, VA	04/07/65	Farmville, VA	05/02/65	Died	HIC,P6,CSR
Collins, Richard H.	Pvt	L 21st SCVI	Ft. Fisher, NC	01/15/65	Elmira, NY	02/09/65	Died, Typhoid	P6,P12,P65,HAG,FPH
Collins, Robert	Pvt	5 10/19 SCVI	Missionary Ridge, TN	11/25/63	Nashville, TN	12/07/63	Louisville, KY	P39,RAS,CSR
					Louisville, KY	12/09/63	Rock Island, IL	P88,P89,CSR
					Rock Island, IL	03/02/65	Pt. Lookout, MD Xch	P131,CSR
Collins, S.H.	Pvt	A 1st SCVIBn		06/08/62	Ft. Columbus, NY	08/23/63	Ft. Delaware, DE	P37
Collins, Valentine	Pvt	I 21st SCVI	Petersburg, VA	05/09/64	Pt. Lookout, MD	03/14/65	Aikens Ldg., VA Xc	P113,P116,P123,P124
Collins, William	Pvt	D 1st SCVA	Deserted/enemy	02/18/65	Charleston, SC	03/16/65	Taken oath & disch	CSR
					Pt. Lookout, MD	06/10/65	Rlsd. G.O. #109	P122,CSR
Collum, Jesse M.	Pvt	D 14th SCVI	Richmond, VA Hos	04/03/65	Provost Marshal	04/21/65	Libby Prison Rchmd	CSR
					Libby Prison Rchmd	04/23/65	Newport News, VA	CSR
					Newport News, VA	06/26/65	Rlsd. G.O. #109	P107,CSR
Colson, Andrew C.	Cpl	D 27th SCVI	Town Creek, NC	02/20/65	Ft. Anderson, NC	02/28/65	Pt. Lookout, MD	CSR,HAG
					Pt. Lookout, MD	06/26/65	Rlsd. G.O. #109	P118,P122,P123,CSR
Colson, J.S.	Pvt	F 9th SCVIH	Ft. Walker, SC	11/07/61	Ft. Delaware, DE	08/05/62	Aikens Ldg., VA Xc	CSR
Colson, W.P.	Cpl	I 5th SCVC	Stony Creek, VA	12/01/64	City Pt., VA	12/05/64	Pt. Lookout, MD	CSR
					Pt. Lookout, MD	06/05/65	Rlsd. Instr. 5/30/65	P114,P118,P122,CSR
Colter, John Henry	Pvt	A 4th SCResB	Raleigh, NC	04/13/65	Raleigh, NC	04/13/65	Paroled	ANY,CSR
Colthorp, Henry T.	Pvt	B 6th SCVI	Richmond, VA	04/03/65	Richmond, VA Hos.	04/14/65	Richmond, VA P.M.	CSR
					Libby Prison Rchmd	04/23/65	Newport News, VA	CSR
					Newport News, VA	06/26/65	Rlsd. G.O. #109	P107,CSR
Colton, John	Pvt	E 1st SCVIR	Deserted/enemy	09/01/64	Hilton Head, SC	09/30/64	work for QM on oat	CSR
Colwell, J.P.	Sgt	C 14th SCVI	Dinwiddie C.H., VA	04/01/65	Hart's Island, NY	06/21/65	Rlsd. G.O. #109	P79
Compton, E.M.	Pvt	I 3rd SCVI	Malvern Hill, VA	07/29/64	Pt. Lookout, MD	08/04/64	Elmira, NY	P117,P120,P125,CSR
					Elmira, NY	05/29/65	Rlsd. G.O. #85	P65,KEB,SA2,H3,CSR
Compton, J.R.	Pvt	F 3rd SCVC	South Newport, GA	08/17/64	Philadelphia, PA	01/10/65	Ft. Delaware, DE	CSR
					Ft. Delaware, DE	03/02/65	Hos 3/2-3/5/65	P47
					Ft. Delaware, DE	04/15/65	Hos 4/15-4/30 D	P47
					Ft. Delaware, DE	04/29/65	Died, Typhoid	P6,P41,P43,P45,CSR

C

SOUTH CAROLINA SOLDIERS, SAILORS AND CITIZENS HELD IN U.S. PRISONS 1861-1865

NAME	RANK	REGIMENT	CAPTURED AT	WHEN	PRISON	MOVED	DISPOSITION	SOURCES
Compton, Wesley W.	Pvt	E 14th SCVI	Cox Road Pbg., VA	04/03/65	City Pt., VA	04/07/65	Hart's Island, NY	CSR
					Hart's Island, NY	06/15/65	Rlsd. G.O. #109	P79,CSR
Compton, William B.	Pvt	G 27th SCVI	Weldon RR, VA	08/21/64	City Pt., VA	08/24/64	Pt. Lookout, MD	CSR
					Pt. Lookout, MD	06/04/65	Released	P113,P117,P125,CSR
Comstreet, J.W.	Pvt	13th SCVI	Gettysburg, PA		Gettysburg G.H.	07/14/63	Provost Marshal	P4,CSR
Conart, J.W.	Pvt	P.S.S.	Deserted/enemy	03/03/65	Dept. of VA			CSR,TSE
Condon, Jerome F.	Pvt	F 11th SCVI	Drury's Bluff, VA	05/20/64	Pt. Lookout, MD	06/30/64	Died, of wounds	P5,P117,FPH,HAG
Condon, Thomas	Pvt	I 26th SCVI	Cheraw, SC	03/05/65	New Berne, NC	04/10/65	Hart's Island, NY	CSR
					Hart's Island, NY	07/08/65	Rlsd, O. Cmdg. Gen.	P79
Cone, J. Cooper	Pvt	E 11th SCVI	Petersburg, VA	06/21/64	Bermuda Hundred, VA	06/22/64	Fts. Monroe, VA	CSR,HAG
					Fts. Monroe, VA	06/23/64	Pt. Lookout, MD	CSR
					Pt. Lookout, MD	11/01/64	Aikens Ldg., VA Xc	P117,P121,P124
					Pt. Lookout, MD	11/01/64	Venus Pt., GA Xchg	CSR
Cone, Joseph Hamilton	Pvt	I 1st SCVC	Beverly Ford, VA	06/09/63			Alexandria, VA USH	P1
					Baltimore, MD	08/23/63	City Pt., VA Xchg.	CSR
Cone, Joseph Hamilton	Pvt	I 1st SCVC	Deserted/enemy	03/22/65	Charleston, SC	03/22/65	Released on oath	CSR
Cone, W.H.	Cpl	A 19th SCVCB	Augusta, GA	05/25/65	Augusta, GA	05/25/65	Paroled on oath	CSR
Conley, Littleton	Pvt	F 22nd SCVI	Bermuda Hundred, VA	06/02/64	Pt. Lookout, MD	03/14/65	Aikens Ldg., VA Xc	P113,P117,P123,P124
Conley, W.A.	Pvt	H 17th SCVI	Petersburg, VA	03/25/65	Pt. Lookout, MD	06/26/65	Rlsd. G.O. #109	P123
Conlin, J.B.	Pvt	K 27th SCVI	Petersburg, VA	06/24/64	Fts. Monroe, VA	06/26/64	Pt. Lookout, MD	CSR,HAG
					Pt. Lookout, MD	08/16/64	Elmira, NY	P117,P120,CSR
					Elmira, NY	09/22/64	Died, Ch. Diarrhea	P5,P65,FPH,CSR
Connell, John F.	Pvt	E 22nd SCVI	Kinston, NC	12/15/62	Kinston, NC	12/15/62	Paroled POW	CSR
Connelley, Charles B.	Cpl	C 11th SCVI	Town Creek, NC	02/20/65	Ft. Anderson, NC	02/28/65	Pt. Lookout, MD	CSR
					Pt. Lookout, MD	06/24/65	Rlsd. G.O. #109	P114,P118,P121,,HAG,CSR
Connelly, Daniel	Pvt	E 1st SCVIR	Averysboro, NC	03/16/65	New Berne, NC	03/30/65	Pt. Lookout, MD	SA1,CSR
					Pt. Lookout, MD	06/24/65	Rlsd.G.O. #109	CSR
Connelly, Michael	Pvt	B 1st SCVA	Deserted/enemy	02/18/65	Charleston, SC	04/04/65	New York, NY/ oath	CSR
Connely, Littleton C.	Cpl	F 22nd SCVI	Kinston, NC	12/14/62	Kinston, NC	12/14/62	Paroled POW	CSR
Connely, Littleton C.	Cpl	F 22nd SCVI	Bermuda Hundred, VA	06/02/64	Fts. Monroe, VA	06/04/64	Pt.. Lookout, MD	CSR
Connely, Littleton C.	Cpl	F 22nd SCVI	Bermuda Hundred, VA	06/02/64	Pt. Lookout, MD	03/14/65	Aikens Ldg., VA Xc	CSR
Conner, E.J.	Pvt	E 8th SCVI	Winchester, VA	09/13/64	Harpers Ferry, WV	09/19/64	Camp Chase, OH	CSR
					Camp Chase, OH	06/10/65	Released on oath	P23,KEB,CSR
Conner, H.M.	Pvt	E 7th SCVI	Cedar Creek, VA	10/19/64	W. Bldg. Balt., MD	11/22/64	Pt. Lookout, MD	P3
Conner, John	Pvt	C 7tth SCVC	Burkeville, VA	04/06/65	Burkeville, VA	04/25/65	Paroled	CSR
Connolly, David R.	Pvt	E 1st SCVA	Averysboro, NC	03/16/65	Pt. Lookout, MD	06/24/65	Rlsd. G.O. #109	P118,P121,P123
Connolly, Henry W.	Pvt	H 17th SCVI	Petersburg, VA	03/25/65	City Pt., VA	03/28/65	Pt. Lookout, MD	CSR
					Pt. Lookout, MD	06/26/65	Rlsd. G.O. #109	P118,P122,CSR
Connolly, P.	Sgt	C 27th SCVI	Petersburg, VA	06/24/64	Fts. Monroe, VA	06/26/64	Pt. Lookout, MD	CSR,HAG
					Pt. Lookout, MD	08/11/64	Elmira, NY	P113,P117,P120,CSR
					Elmira, NY	06/11/65	Released	P65
Connor, George W.	2Lt	F 2nd SCVI	Cedar Creek, VA	10/19/64	Harpers Ferry, VA	10/25/64	Ft. Delaware, DE	CSR,SA2,H2
					Ft. Delaware, DE	06/17/65	Rlsd. G.O. #109	P43,P45,P46,CSR
Connor, L.D.C.	Pvt	A 3rd SCVIBn	Frederick, MD	09/12/62	Ft. Delaware, DE	10/02/62	Aikens Ldg., VA Xc	CSR
Connor, Patrick	Pvt	C 1st SCVA	Fayetteville, NC	03/12/65	New Berne, NC	04/10/65	Hart's Island, NY	CSR
					Hart's Island, NY	04/27/65	Died	P6,P12,P79,CSR
Connors, Jasper	Pvt	I 23rd SCVI	Deserted/enemy	04/19/65	Charleston, SC	04/19/65	Paroled on oath	CSR
Conrad, Robert	Pvt	A 12th SCVI	Amelia C.H., VA	04/03/65	City Pt., VA	04/13/65	Pt. Lookout, MD	CSR
					Pt. Lookout, MD	06/26/65	Rlsd. G.O. #109	P119,YEB,CSR
Conrad, William R.	Pvt	A 12th SCVI	Petersburg, VA	04/03/65	City Pt. , VA	04/07/65	Hart's Island, NY	CSR
					Hart's Island, NY	06/16/65	Rlsd. G.O. #109	P79,YEB,CSR

SOUTH CAROLINA SOLDIERS, SAILORS AND  CITIZENS HELD IN U.S. PRISONS 1861-1865

NAME	RANK	REGIMENT	CAPTURED AT	WHEN	PRISON	MOVED	DISPOSITION	SOURCES
Conroy, John D.	Cpl	H 27th SCVI	Town Creek, NC	02/20/65	Ft. Anderson, NC	02/28/65	Pt. Lookout, MD	CSR,HAG
					Pt. Lookout, MD	05/13/65	Rlsd. G.O. #85	P114,P118,P122,CSR
Conroy, William	Pvt	D 1st SCVA	Deserted/enemy	06/11/64	South Carolina	09/01/64	Hilton Head, SC	CSR
Conroy, William	Pvt	A 15th SCVAB	Deserted/enemy	03/18/65	Charleston, SC	03/18/65	Taken oath & disch.	CSR
Constantine, Alex	Pvt	A 1st SCVA	Deserted/enemy	03/17/65	Charleston, SC	04/01/65	Taken oath & disch.	CSR
Conyers, Robert	Pvt	H 26th SCVI	Farmville, VA	04/06/65	Newport News, VA	06/26/65	Rlsd. G.O. #109	P107,CSR
Coogler, J.P.	Pvt	C 20th SCVI	Cedar Creek, VA	10/19/64	Harpers Ferry, WV	10/23/64	Pt. Lookout, MD	CSR
					Pt. Lookout, MD	06/26/65	Rlsd. G.O. #109	P118,P122,P123,CSR
Cook, A.	Pvt	G 26th SCVI	Appomattox R., VA	04/03/65	City Pt., VA	04/11/65	Hart's Island, NY	CSR
					Hart's Island, NY	06/16/65	Rlsd. G.O. #109	P79,CSR
Cook, A.J.	Pvt	Post Guard	Columbia, SC	02/17/65	Hart's Island, NY	06/16/65	Rlsd. G.O. #109	P79
Cook, Abram M.	Pvt	E 11th SCVI	Petersburg, VA	06/24/64	Bermuda Hundred, VA	06/25/64	Fts. Monroe, VA	CSR,HAG
					Fts. Monroe, VA	06/26/64	Pt. Lookout, MD	CSR
					Pt. Lookout, MD	08/16/64	Elmira, NY	P113,P117,P120,CSR
					Elmira, NY	02/13/65	Aikens Ldg., VA Xc	P65,CSR
Cook, Abram M.	Pvt	E 11th SCVI	Richmond, VA Hos.	04/03/65	Provost Marshal	04/14/65	Libby Prison	CSR
Cook, Abram M.	Cpl	E 11th SCVI	Richmond, VA Hos	04/03/65	Libby Prison, Rchmd.	04/24/65	Paroled	CSR
Cook, Alexander	Pvt	H 25th SCVI	Ft. Fisher, NC	01/15/65	New York, NY	01/30/65	Elmira, NY	CSR
					Elmira, NY	06/23/65	Rlsd. G.O. #109	P65,HAG
Cook, Constantine	Sgt	D 11th SCVI	Midway, SC	02/06/65	New Berne, NC	04/03/65	PT. Lookout, MD	CSR,HAG
					Pt. Lookout, MD	06/24/65	Rlsd. G.O. #109	P114,P118,P123,CSR
Cook, D.J.	Pvt	K 7th SCVC	Bottoms Bridge, VA	01/30/65	City Pt., VA	02/10/65	Pt. Lookout, MD	CSR,HIC
					Pt. Lookout, MD	06/04/65	Rlsd. Instr. 5/5/65	P114,P118,P121,CSR
Cook, Daniel	Pvt	D 3rd SCVABn	Deserted/enemy	02/22/65	Charleston, SC	03/15/65	Released on oath	CSR
Cook, Francis A.	Pvt	F 11th SCVI	Ft. Fisher, NC	01/15/65	Pt. Lookout, MD	06/26/65	Rlsd. G.O. #109	P114,P118,P123,HAG
Cook, Henry	Pvt	D 12th SCVI	Petersburg, VA	04/03/65	City Pt., VA	04/07/65	Hart's Island, NY	CSR
					Hart's Island, NY	06/16/65	Rlsd. G.O. #109	P79,CSR
Cook, Henry	Pvt	B 1st SC Eng	Fayetteville, NC	03/15/65	Pt. Lookout, MD	06/24/65	Rlsd. G.O. 3109	P118,P123
Cook, Henry H.	Pvt	A 3rd SCVIBn	Frederick, MD	10/08/62	Ft. McHenry, MD	12/04/62	City Pt., VA Exchg	CSR
Cook, Isaac B.	Pvt	A 10th SCVI	Murfreesboro, TN	12/28/62	St.Louis, MO	02/11/63	Died, Bronchitis	P5,P12,P38,RAS,CSR
Cook, J.W.	Pvt	B 1st SCVIR	Cheraw, SC	03/05/65	Cheraw, SC	03/05/65	Released on oath	SA1,CSR
Cook, James C.	Pvt	A 24th SCVI	Taylors Ridge, GA	10/16/64	Nashville, TN	10/23/64	Louisville, KY	CSR
					Louisville, KY	10/27/64	Camp Douglas, IL	P90,P91
					Camp Douglas, IL	06/17/65	Rlsd. G.O. #109	P55,EFW
Cook, James J.	Pvt	A 26th SCVI	Appomattox C.H., VA	04/09/65	Old Capitol, DC	06/12/65	Rlsd. G.O. #109	P110,CSR
Cook, James R.	Pvt	H 18th SCVI	Farmville, VA	04/06/65	City Pt., VA	04/14/65	Newport News, VA	CSR
					Newport News, VA	06/26/65	Rlsd. G.O. #109	P107,YEB,CSR
Cook, Jesse	Pvt	C 12th SCVI	Warrenton, VA	09/29/62	Warrenton, VA	09/29/62	Paroled	CSR
Cook, John C.	Pvt	B 3rd SCVABn	Augusta, GA	05/23/65	Bermuda Hundred, VA	06/25/64	Fts. Monroe, VA	CSR
					Augusta, GA	05/23/65	Paroled on oath	CSR
Cook, John C.	Pvt	E 11th SCVI	Petersburg, VA	06/24/64	Elmira, NY	07/11/65	Rlsd. G.O. #109	P65,HAG,CSR
					Pt. Lookout, MD	08/16/64	Elmira, NY	P113,P117,P120,CSR
Cook, Joseph K.	Pvt	F 12th SCVI	Deep Bottom, VA	08/16/64	City Pt., VA	08/22/64	Pt. Lookout, MD	HFC,CSR
					Pt. Lookout, MD	03/14/65	Aikens Ldg., VA Xc	P123,P124,HFC,CSR
					Richmond, VA Hos.	03/20/65	Furloughed 60 days	CSR
Cook, Micajah H.	Pvt	D Hol.Leg.	Five Forks, VA	04/01/65	City Pt., VA	04/05/65	Pt. Lookout, MD	CSR
					Pt. Lookout, MD	06/26/65	Rlsd. G.O. #109	P114,P118,P123
Cook, S.E.	Pvt	F 11th SCVI	Ft. Fisher, NC	01/15/65	Pt. Lookout, MD	06/26/65	Rlsd. G.O. #109	P114,P118,HAG,CSR
Cook, T. James	Pvt	C 25th SCVI	Ft. Fisher, NC	01/15/65	New York, NY	01/30/65	Elmira, NY	CSR,HAG
					Elmira, NY	03/02/65	Pt.Lookout, MD Xch	P65,P66,CTA
					Jackson Hos.Rchmd.	03/09/65	Furloughed	CSR

SOUTH CAROLINA SOLDIERS, SAILORS AND  CITIZENS HELD IN U.S. PRISONS 1861-1865

NAME	RANK	REGIMENT	CAPTURED AT	WHEN	PRISON	MOVED	DISPOSITION	SOURCES
Cook, Thomas J.	Pvt	E 8th SCVI	Winchester, VA	09/13/64	Harpers Ferry, WV	09/19/64	Camp Chase, OH	CSR
					Camp Chase, OH	06/11/65	Released on oath	P23,KEB,CSR
Cook, W. Dorsey	Pvt	C 25th SCVI	Ft. Fisher, NC	01/15/65	New York, NY	01/30/65	Elmira, NY	CSR,CTA
					Elmira, NY	03/29/65	Died, Pneumonia	P6,P12,P65,P66,FPH
Cook, W.E.	Pvt	A 3rd SCVIBn	N. Anna River, VA	05/23/64	Port Royal, VA	05/30/64	Pt. Lookout, MD	CSR
					Pt. Lookout, MD	02/18/65	Aikens Ldg., VA Xc	P113,P117,P123,CSR
Cook, W.J.	Pvt	C 15th SCVAB	Smith's Corner, NC	03/15/65	New Berne, NC	04/03/65	Pt. Lookout MD	CSR
					Pt. Lookout, MD	05/16/65	Died, lung Inflam.	P6,P118,FPH,CSR
Cook, William D.	2Lt	F 21st SCVI	Ft. Fisher, NC	01/15/65	Pt. Lookout, MD	02/02/65	Hammond G.H., MD	P114,P121,HAG
					Pt. Lookout, MD	04/29/65	Died of wounds	P6,P12,P117
Cook, William E.	Pvt	F 13th SCVI	Gettysburg, PA	07/05/63	David's Island, NY	09/05/63	City Pt., VA Xchg.	P1,HOS,CSR
Cook, William E.	Pvt	F 13th SCVI	Deserted/enemy	02/24/65	City Pt., VA	02/26/65	Washington, DC	CSR
					Washington, DC	02/27/65	Springfield, IL	CSR
Cook, William L.	Pvt	C 6th SCVI	Darbytown Rd., VA	10/07/64	Bermuda Hundred, VA	10/07/64	City Pt., VA P.M.	CSR,HIC
					City Pt., VA	12/29/64	Pt. Lookout, MD	CSR
					Pt. Lookout, MD	03/29/65	Aikens Ldg., VA Xc	P118,P121nP124,CSR
Cook, William W.	Cpl	C 12th SCVI	Petersburg, VA	04/02/65	City Pt., VA	04/07/65	Hart's Island, NY	CSR
					Hart's Island, NY	06/17/65	Rlsd. G.O. #109	P79,HFC,CSR
Cooksey, A.	Pvt	D 16th SCVI	Macon, GA	04/30/65	Macon, GA	04/30/65	Paroled	CSR
Cooler, Washington	Pvt	E 11th SCVI	Petersburg, VA	06/24/64	Fts. Monroe, VA	06/26/64	Pt. Lookout, MD	CSR
					Pt. Lookout, MD	08/11/64	Elmira, NY	P113,P117,P120
					Elmira, NY	10/11/64	Pt.Lookout, MD Xc	P65
					Elmira, NY	10/11/64	Venus Pt., GA Xc	CSR
					Pt. Lookout, MD	10/29/64	Aikens Ldg., VA Xc	P114,P118
Cooley, A.L.	Pvt	6th SCVI	Fair Oaks, VA	06/01/62	Ft. Delaware, DE	08/05/62	Aikens Ldg., VA Xc	CSR
Cooley, J.E.	Pvt	H P.S.S.	Deserted/enemy	03/03/65	Bermuda Hundred, VA	03/07/65	City Pt., VA P.M.	CSR
					City Pt., VA P.M.	03/08/65	Washington, DC	CSR
					Washington, DC	03/08/65	Columbus, OH	CSR,TSE
Cooley, J.N.	Pvt	C 13th SCVI	Petersburg, VA	04/03/64	City Pt., VA	04/07/64	Hart's Island, NY	CSR
					Hart's Island, NY	06/16/65	Rlsd. G.O. #109	CSR
Cooley, J.S.	Pvt	G 22nd SCVI	Petersburg, VA	06/21/64	City Pt., VA	06/30/64	Pt. Lookout, MD	CSR,UD3
					Pt. Lookout, MD	10/14/64	Jd. U.S. Army	P113,P117,P122,P125
Coon, Levi	Pvt	K 19th SCVI	Nashville, TN	12/17/64	Louisville, KY	01/05/65	Camp Chase, OH	P95,CSR
					Camp Chase, OH	06/12/65	Rlsd. G.O. #109	P23,CSR
Coon, S. Calvin	Pvt	G 2nd SCVI	Gettysburg, PA	07/05/63	Letterman G.H. Gbg	07/16/63	Died of wounds	P1,KEB,SA2,LAN,H2
Cooper, Andrew J.	Pvt	A 1st SCVIH	Chaffins Farm, VA	09/30/64	Fts. Monroe, VA	01/13/65	Pt. Lookout, MD	CSR
					Pt. Lookout, MD	02/18/65	Aikens Ldg., VA Xc	P118,P123,P124,CSR
Cooper, D.	Cit		Orangeburg, SC	03/12/65	Pt. Lookout, MD	06/19/65	Rlsd. G.O. #109	P114,P118
Cooper, Edward	Pvt	C 26th SCVI	Richmond, VA Hos	04/03/65	Pt. Lookout, MD	07/07/65	Rlsd. G.O. #109	CSR
Cooper, F.W.	Pvt	Palmetto LA	Nine Mile Rd., VA	10/27/64	City Pt., VA	10/31/64	Pt. Lookout, MD	CSR
					Pt. Lookout, MD	01/17/65	Tfd. for exchange	P124,CSR
					Richmond, VA Hos.	01/27/65	Furloughed 60 days	CSR
Cooper, Green Flavius	Sgt	A 2nd SCVI	Raleigh, NC Hos.	04/13/65	Raleigh, NC Hos.	04/13/65	Paroled	SA2,H2,CSR
Cooper, J.E.	Pvt	E Hol.Leg.	Boonesboro, MD	09/14/62	Ft. Delaware, DE	10/02/65	Aikens Ldg., VA Xc	CSR
Cooper, J.W.	Pvt	A 8th SCVI	Winchester, VA	09/13/64	Harpers Ferry, WV	09/19/64	Camp Chase, OH	CSR
					Camp Chase, OH	05/02/65	New Orleans, LA	P26,CSR
					New Orleans, LA	05/12/65	Vicksburg, MS Xch	CSR
Cooper, Joel P.	Sgt	G 7th SCVIBn	Weldon RR, VA	08/24/64	City Pt., VA USFH	08/27/64	Washington, DC	CSR
					Carver G.H., DC	10/18/64	Lincoln G.H., DC	CSR
					Lincoln G.H., DC	03/01/65	Old Capitol, DC	CSR
					Old Capitol, DC	03/27/65	Elmira, NY	P110,HAG,CSR
					Elmira, NY	06/30/65	Rlsd. G.O. #109	P65,CSR

SOUTH CAROLINA SOLDIERS, SAILORS AND CITIZENS HELD IN U.S. PRISONS 1861-1865

NAME	RANK	REGIMENT	CAPTURED AT	WHEN	PRISON	MOVED	DISPOSITION	SOURCES
Cooper, John H.	Cpt	K 23rd SCVI	Five Forks, VA	04/01/65	Old Capitol, DC	04/09/65	Johnsons Isl., OH	P110,CSR
					Johnsons Isl., OH	06/18/65	Rlsd. G.O. #109	P81,P83,CSR
Cooper, Joseph D.	1Sg	G 16th SCVI	Franklin, TN	12/17/64	Nashville, TN	01/08/65	Louisville, KY	P4,P39,16R,CSR
					Louisville, KY	01/14/65	Camp Chase, OH	P92,P95,CSR
					Camp Chase, OH	06/13/65	Rlsd. G.O. #109	P23,CSR
Cooper, L.S.	Cpl	L 7th SCVI	N. Anna River, VA	05/23/64	Port Royal, VA	05/30/64	Pt. Lookout, MD	CSR
					Pt. Lookout, MD	10/17/64	Joined US Army	P117,P122,P125,CSR
Cooper, Levi	Pvt	G 16th SCVI	Franklin, TN	12/17/64	Nashville, TN	01/11/65	Louisville, KY	P4,P39,16R
					Louisville, KY	01/14/65	Camp Chase, OH	P92,CSR
					Camp Chase, OH	05/02/65	New Orleans, LA Xc	P23,P26,CSR
					Vicksburg, MS USGH	05/23/65	Released	CSR
Cooper, S.H.	Pvt	A 26th SCVI	Petersburg, VA	04/02/65	City Pt., VA	04/05/65	Pt. Lookout, MD	CSR
					Pt. Lookout, MD	06/05/65	Released on oath	P118,P122,CSR
Cooper, T.B.	1Lt	L 7th SCVI	Cedar Creek, VA	10/19/64	No prison records		On a roster as POW	CSR
Cooper, Thomas M.	Pvt	L 1st SCVIG	Petersburg, VA	04/03/65	City Pt. VA	04/13/65	Pt. Lookout, MD	CSR
					Pt. Lookout, MD	06/26/65	Rlsd. G.O. #109	P119,P122,P123,CSR
Cooper, Thomas P.	Sgt	C 3rd SCVIBn	South Mtn., MD	09/14/62	Ft. Delaware, DE	10/02/62	Aikens Ldg., VA Xc	CSR
Cooper, W.W.	Cpl	D 12th SCVI	Petersburg, VA	04/02/65	Hart's Island, NY	06/18/65	Rlsd. G.O. #109	P79
Cooper, William D.	Pvt	E Hol.Leg.	Five Forks, VA	04/01/65	City Pt., VA	04/05/65	Pt. Lookout, MD	CSR,HOS
					Pt. Lookout, MD	06/26/65	Rlsd. G.O. #109	P118,P122,P123,CSR
Cooper, William H.	Sur	16th SCVI	Franklin, TN	12/17/64	Nashville, TN	01/10/65	Louisville, KY	P2,P39,16R,CSR
					Louisville, KY	01/14/65	Ft. Delaware, DE	P92,P95,CSR
					Ft. Delaware, DE	01/18/65	Fts.Monroe, VA Xch	P43
					Fts. Monroe, VA	01/21/65	Varina, VA Xchg.	CSR
Cooper, William J.	Cpl	B 7th SCVIBn	Drury's Bluff, VA	05/16/64	Bermuda Hundred, VA	05/17/64	Fts. Monroe, VA	CSR,HAG
					Fts. Monroe, VA	05/19/64	Pt. Lookout, MD	CSR
					Pt. Lookout, MD	08/15/64	Elmira, NY	P113,P117,P120,CSR
					Elmira, NY	11/05/64	Died, Ch. Diarrhea	P5,P12,P65,FPH,CSR
Cooper, William J.	Cpl	F 1st SCVA	Smith's Ford, NC	03/16/65	Pt. Lookout, MD	06/26/65	Rlsd. G.O. #109	P118,P122,P123,CSR
Cope, Daniel	Pvt	E 4th SCVC	Cold Harbor, VA	05/31/64	White House, VA	06/08/64	Pt. Lookout, MD	CSR
					Pt. Lookout, MD	07/08/64	Elmira, NY	P113,P117,P120,CSR
					Elmira, NY	10/11/64	Pt. Lookout, MD Xch	P65,CSR
					Pt. Lookout, MD	10/29/64	Venus Pt., GA Xchg	P114,CSR
Copeland, Elbert T.	QSg	14th SCVI	Amelia C.H., VA	04/03/65	City Pt., VA	04/13/65	Pt. Lookout, MD	CSR
					Pt. Lookout, MD	06/26/65	Rlsd. G.O. #109	P119,P122,P123,CSR
Copeland, Francis E.	Pvt	K 11th SCVI	Town Creek, NC	02/20/65	Ft. Anderson, NC	02/28/65	Pt. Lookout, MD	P118,P122,P123,HAG
					Pt. Lookout, MD	06/26/65	Rlsd. G.O. #109	P118,P122,P123,CSR
Copeland, George B.T.	Pvt	D 7th SCVIBn	Weldon RR, VA	08/21/64	City Pt., VA	08/24/64	Pt. Lookout, MD	CSR,HIC
					Pt. Lookout, MD	09/30/64	Aikens Ldg., VA Xc	P117,P123,P125,CSR
Copeland, J.L.	Pvt	C 19th SCVCB	Augusta, GA	05/26/65	Augusta, GA	05/26/65	Paroled on oath	CSR
Copeland, James L.	Pvt	C 2nd SCVI	Gettysburg, PA	07/05/63	Letterman G.H. Gbg	07/17/63	Died of Wounds	P1,P12,SA2,H2,CSR
Copeland, W.R.	Pvt	A 1st SCVIH	Farmville, VA	04/11/65	Farmville, VA	04/21/65	Paroled	CSR
Copeland, William A.	Pvt	K 11th SCVI	Town Creek, NC	02/20/65	Ft. Anderson, NC	02/28/65	Pt. Lookout, MD	CSR,HAG
					Pt. Lookout, MD	06/26/65	Rlsd. G.O. #109	P118,P122,P123,CSR
Coppock, Moses M.	Pvt	D 13th SCVI	Gettysburg, PA	07/05/63	Chester, PA G.H.	08/17/63	City Pt., VA Xchg.	P1,ANY,CSR
Corbett, John	Pvt	B 15th SCVAB	Raleigh, NC Hosp.	04/17/65	Raleigh, NC	04/20/65	Paroled	CSR
Corbett, M.F.	Pvt	I 22nd SCVI	Kinston, NC	12/14/62	Kinston, NC	12/14/62	Paroled POW	CSR
Corbin, Alexander	Pvt	K 2nd SCVIRi	Knoxville, TN	12/20/63	Knoxville, TN	01/17/64	Died of Pneumonia	P5,P12,CSR
Corbin, Charles	Pvt	D 11th SCVI	Ft. Fisher, NC	01/15/65	Elmira, NY	06/23/65	Rlsd. G.O. #109	P65,HAG,CSR
Corbin, Edward	Pvt	D 11th SCVI	Ft. Fisher, NC	01/15/65	Elmira, NY	05/23/65	Died, Variola	P6,P65,FPH,HAG,CSR

C

SOUTH CAROLINA SOLDIERS, SAILORS AND CITIZENS HELD IN U.S. PRISONS 1861-1865

NAME	RANK	REGIMENT	CAPTURED AT	WHEN	PRISON	MOVED	DISPOSITION	SOURCES
Corbin, William F.	Pvt	G 12th SCVI	Spotsylvania, VA	05/12/64	Belle Plain, VA	05/20/64	Ft. Delaware, DE	CSR
					Ft. Delaware, DE	01/04/65	To Hos 1/4-1/14/65	P47
					Ft. Delaware, DE	06/10/65	Released	P41,P43,P45,CSR
Corder, David A.	Pvt	D 17th SCVI	Petersburg, VA	07/30/64	City Pt., VA	08/05/64	Pt. Lookout, MD	CSR
					Pt. Lookout, MD	08/08/64	Elmira, NY	P113,P117,P120,CSR
					Elmira, NY	07/04/65	Died, Ch. Diarrhea	P6,P12,P65,FPH,CSR
Corder, John A.	Cpl	D 17th SCVI	Crater, Pbg., VA	07/30/64	City Pt., VA	08/08/64	Pt. Lookout, MD	CSR
					Pt. Lookout, MD	08/08/64	Elmira, NY	P113,P117,P120,CSR
					Elmira, NY	07/07/65	Rlsd. G.O. #109	P65,HHC,CSR
Corder, Samuel A.	Pvt	D 17th SCVI	Petersburg, VA	03/25/65	City Pt., VA	03/28/65	Pt. Lookout, MD	CSR,HHC
					Pt. Lookout, MD	06/26/65	Rlsd. G.O. #109	P114,P118,P123,CSR
Cordes, George	Pvt	B 11th SCVI	Petersburg, VA	06/24/64	Bermuda Hundred VA	06/25/64	Fts. Monroe, VA	CSR,HAG
					Fts. Monroe, VA	06/26/64	Pt. Lookout, MD	CSR
					Pt. Lookout, MD	07/25/64	Elmira, NY	P113,P117,P120,CSR
					Elmira, NY	06/30/65	Rlsd. G.O. #109	P65,CSR
Cordrey, John	Pvt	B 11th SCVI	Darbytown Rd., VA	10/07/64	Bermuda Hundred VA	10/08/64	City Pt., VA	CSR
					City Pt., VA	10/29/64	Pt. Lookout, MD	CSR,HAG
					Pt. Lookout, MD	02/10/65	Aikens Ldg., VA Xc	P114,P118,P124,CSR
Corley, Adam D.	Pvt	B 14th SCVI	Augusta, GA	05/19/65	Augusta, GA	05/19/65	Paroled	CSR
Corley, Baley	Pvt	D 14th SCVI	Gettysburg, PA	07/04/63	David's Island, NY	09/08/63	City Pt., VA Xchg.	P1,HOE,CSR
Corley, Daniel	Pvt	K 13th SCVI	Southside RR, VA	04/02/65	City Pt., VA	04/07/65	Hart's Island, NY	CSR
					Hart's Island, NY	06/14/65	Rlsd. G.O. #109	P79,CSR
Corley, Hezekiah F.	Pvt	B Ham.Leg.MI	Ft. Harrison, VA	09/29/64	Bermuda Hundred VA	09/30/64	City Pt., VA P.M.	CSR
					City Pt., VA	10/05/64	Pt. Lookout, MD	CSR
					Pt. Lookout, MD	03/17/65	Aikens Ldg., VA Xc	P118,P123,P124,CSR
Corley, Isaiah	Pvt	K 13th SCVI	Petersburg, VA	04/03/65	City Pt., VA	04/11/65	Hart's Island, NY	CSR
					Hart's Island, NY	06/16/65	Rlsd. G.O. #109	P79,CSR
Corley, J.A.	Pvt	K 15th SCVI	Halltown, WV	08/21/64	Harpers Ferry, WV	08/29/64	Camp Chase, OH	CSR,KEB
					Camp Chase, OH	02/07/65	Died, Pneumonia	P6,P23,P27,FPH,CSR
Corley, J.N.	Pvt	E 7th SCVI	Gettysburg, PA	07/04/63	Gettysburg G.H.	08/16/63	David's Island, NY	P4,CSR
					David's Island, NY	09/12/63	City Pt., VA Xchg.	P1,CNM,CSR
Corley, James A.	Cpl	C 7th SCVI	Gettysburg, PA	07/04/63	David's Island, NY	08/24/63	City Pt., VA Xchg.	P1,KEB,CNM,CSR
Corley, John L.	Pvt	K 13th SCVI	Southside RR, VA	04/02/65	City Pt., VA	04/07/65	Hart's Island, NY	CSR
					Hart's Island, NY	06/14/65	Rlsd. G.O. #109	P79,CSR
Corley, R.C.	Pvt	F 3rd SCVC	South Newport, GA	08/17/64	Philadelphia, PA	01/10/65	Ft. Delaware, DE	CSR
					Ft. Delaware, DE	03/02/65	Died, Ch. Diarrhea	P6,P41,P43,FPH,CSR
Corley, S. Wilson	Pvt	B Ham.Leg.	Fair Oaks, VA	05/30/62	Fts. Monroe, VA GH	07/15/62	Ft. Delaware, DE	CSR
Corley, S.J.	Pvt	H 16th SCVI	Augusta, GA	05/25/05	Augusta, GA	05/25/65	Paroled on oath	CSR
Corley, Simeon	Pvt	C 1st SCVIG	Petersburg, VA	04/02/65	City Pt., VA	04/18/65	Pt. Lookout, MD	CSR
					Pt. Lookout, MD	06/05/65	Rlsd.Instr.5/30/65	P114,P118,P122,SA1,CSR
Corley, T.F.	Pvt	I 22nd SCVI	Deserted/Enemy	01/02/65	City Pt., VA	01/05/65	Washington, DC	CSR
					Washington, DC	01/06/65	Vicksburg, MS oath	CSR
Corley, W.A.	Sgt	F 5th SCVC	Armstrong's Mill, VA	12/10/64	City Pt., VA	12/12/64	Pt. Lookout, MD	CSR
					Pt. Lookout, MD	06/26/65	Rlsd. G.O. #109	CSR
Corley, W.T.	Pvt	A 3rd SCVABn	High Pt., NC	05/02/65	High Pt., NC	05/02/65	Paroled on oath	CSR
Corley, William A.	Sgt	F 6th SCVC	Armstrong's Mill, VA	12/10/64	Pt. Lookout, MD	06/26/65	Rlsd. G.O. #109	P118,P122,P123
Corley, William H.	Pvt	D 19th SCVI	Marietta, GA	07/04/64	Nashville, TN	07/12/64	Louisville, KY	CSR
					Louisville, KY	07/13/64	Camp Morton, IN	P90,P94,HOE,CSR
					Camp Morton, IN	03/15/65	Pt.Lookout, MD Xch	P100,P101,CSR
Cornwall, Jerry	Smn	CS Navy	Fayetteville, NC	03/19/65	Pt. Lookout, MD	05/15/65	Rlsd. G.O. #85	P114

SOUTH CAROLINA SOLDIERS, SAILORS AND  CITIZENS HELD IN U.S. PRISONS 1861-1865

NAME	RANK	REGIMENT	CAPTURED AT	WHEN	PRISON	MOVED	DISPOSITION	SOURCES
Cornwell, R.D.	Pvt	A 6th SCVI	Deserted/enemy	03/04/65	Bermuda Hundred, VA	04/05/65	City Pt., VA P.M.	CSR
					City Pt., VA P.M.	04/07/65	Washington, DC	CSR
					Washington, DC P.M	04/08/65	Phila., PA on oath	CSR
Cornwell, William J.	Pvt	F 6th SCVI	Williamsburg, VA	05/06/62	Cliffbourne G.H., DC	07/26/62	Old Capitol, DC	CSR,HHC
					Old Capitol, DC	08/01/62	Fts. Monroe, VA	CSR
					Fts. Monroe, VA	08/05/62	Aikens Ldg., VA Xc	CSR
Cornwell, William J.	Pvt	F 6th SCVI	Farmville, VA	04/07/65	City Pt., VA P.M.	04/14/65	Pt. Lookout, MD	CSR
					Pt. Lookout, MD	06/26/65	Rlsd. G.O. #109	P119,P122,P123,CSR
Cosby, John W.	Pvt	G 19th SCVI	Nashville, TN	12/15/64	Nashville, TN	12/23/64	Died, Cumberland H.	P4,P6,CSR
Cotchett, W. Dana, Jr.	1Lt	A 25th SCVI	Ft. Fisher, NC	01/15/65	Fts. Monroe, VA	01/26/65	Ft. Columbus, NY	CSR
					Ft. Columbus, NY	03/01/65	City Pt., VA Xchg.	P2,HAG,CSR
Cotchett, W. Dana, Jr.	1Lt	A 25th SCVI	Augusta, GA	05/29/65	Augusta, GA	05/29/65	Paroled on oath	CSR
Cothran, Samuel A.	Pvt	G 14th SCVI	Augusta, GA	05/29/65	Augusta, GA	05/29/65	Paroled	CSR
Cothran, William J.	Pvt	E Orr's Ri.	Deserted/enemy	02/21/65	Army/Potomac	02/21/65	Washington D.C.	CSR
					Pt. Lookout, MD	02/24/65	Washington D.C.	CSR
					Washington D.C.	02/24/65	New York, NY/ oath	CSR
Coton, A.	Pvt	D 1st SCVIG	Charlotte, NC	05/17/65	Charlotte, NC	05/17/65	Paroled	CSR
Cottella, James	Pvt	B 1st SCVA	Deserted/enemy	02/18/65	Charleston, SC	03/22/65	to be sent to NYC	CSR
Cottingham, Jonathan	Pvt	B 19th SCVCB	Bennettsville, SC	03/05/65	New Berne, NC	04/03/65	Pt. Lookout, MD	CSR
					Pt. Lookout, MD	06/26/65	Rlsd. G.O. #109	P118,P122,P123,CSR
Cottingham, Stewart	Pvt	I 1st SCVIH	Warrenton, VA	09/29/62	Warrenton, VA	09/29/62	Paroled	CSR
Cottingham, T.F.	Pvt	E 23rd SCVI	Deserted/Enemy	12/02/64	City Pt., VA Xchg.	12/03/64	Phila., PA on oath	P8,HMC,CSR
Cottrell, Henry C.	Pvt	G 6th SCVC	Amelia C.H., VA	04/04/65	Pt. Lookout, MD	06/24/65	Rlsd. G.O. #109	P114
Couch, E.	Pvt	A 3rd SCVABn	High Pt., NC	05/02/65	High Pt., NC	05/02/65	Paroled on oath	CSR
Couch, J.	Pvt	A 3rd SCVABn	High Pt., NC	05/02/65	High Pt., NC	05/02/65	Paroled on oath	CSR
Couch, Jesse	Pvt	A 19th SCVI	Augusta, GA	05/19/65	Augusta, GA	05/19/65	Paroled	CSR
Couch, Jesse A.	Pvt	E 18th SCVI	Crater, Pbg., VA	07/30/64	City Pt., VA	08/05/64	Pt. Lookout, MD	CSR
					Pt. Lookout, MD	08/08/64	Elmira, NY	P117,P120,CSR
					Elmira, NY	02/12/65	Died, Diarrhea	P6,P12,P65,FPH,CSR
Couch, John	Pvt	G 12th SCVI	Gettysburg, PA	07/05/63	Ft. Delaware, DE	05/10/64	Urinated in Yard	P47
					Ft. Delaware, DE	07/06/64	To Hos 7/6-7/16/64	P47
					Ft. Delaware, DE	05/12/65	Rlsd. G.O. #85	P7,P42,P46,CSR
Couch, Tollivar R.	Pvt	E 18th SCVI	Crater, Pbg., VA	07/30/64	City Pt., VA	08/08/64	Pt. Lookout, MD	CSR
					Pt. Lookout, MD	08/08/64	Elmira, NY	P113,P117,P120,CSR
					Elmira, NY	05/29/65	Rlsd.G.O.#85	P65,CSR
Couchig, Thomas J.	Cpl	F 1st SCVA	Black River, NC	03/18/65	Pt. Lookout, MD	06/26/65	Rlsd. G.O. #109	P122,P123,CSR
Counts, H.H.	Pvt	G 3rd SCVABn	High Pt., NC	05/01/65	High Pt., NC	05/01/65	Paroled on oath	CSR
Counts, J.A.	Cpl	G 3rd SCVABn	High Pt., NC	05/01/65	High Pt., NC	05/01/65	Paroled on oath	CSR
Counts, O.B.	Pvt	G 3rd SCVABn	High Pt., NC	05/01/65	High Pt., NC	05/01/65	Paroled on oath	CSR
Courtney, Oliver	Pvt	B 8th SCVI	Charlotte, NC	04/26/65	Charlotte, NC	04/26/65	Paroled	KEB,CSR
Courtney, William A.	2Lt	B 8th SCVI	Winchester, VA	09/13/64	Harpers Ferry, WV	09/19/64	Johnson's Isl., OH	CSR
					Johnson's Isl., OH	06/16/65	Rlsd. G.O. #109	P81,P82,P83,CSR
Covar, Charles	Pvt	H 7th SCVI	Cedar Creek, VA	10/19/64	Harpers Ferry, WV	10/24/64	Pt. Lookout, MD	CSR
					Pt. Lookout, MD	02/14/65	Coxe's Ldg., VA Xc	CSR
Covin, Oscar W.	Pvt	K 15th SCVI	Gettysburg, PA	07/02/63	Gettysburg G.H.	07/12/63	Provost Marshal	P4,KEB,CSR
					Chester, PA G.H.	08/11/63	Died of wounds	P1,P6,P12,FPH,CSR
Covington, Alfred D.	Pvt	F 21st SCVI	Petersburg, VA	05/09/64	Bermuda Hundred, VA	05/11/64	Fts. Monroe, VA	CSR,HAG,HOM
					Fts. Monroe, VA	05/13/64	Pt. Lookout, MD	CSR
					Pt. Lookout, MD	01/21/65	Rlsd O./Sec. of War	P116
					Pt. Lookout, MD	02/13/65	Aikens Ldg., VA Xc	P113,P121,P124

SOUTH CAROLINA SOLDIERS, SAILORS AND  CITIZENS HELD IN U.S. PRISONS 1861-1865

NAME	RANK	REGIMENT	CAPTURED AT	WHEN	PRISON	MOVED	DISPOSITION	SOURCES
Covington, Elijah	Pvt	D 1st SCVA	Marlboro Dist., SC	03/06/65	New Berne, NC	04/10/65	Hart's Island, NY	CSR
					Hart's Island, NY	05/24/65	Died, Ch. Diarrhea	P6,P79,FPH,CSR
Covington, J.A.	Sgt	G 23rd SCVI	Petersburg, VA Hop	04/03/65	Fairground Hosp	07/03/65	Died	P6,CSR
Covington, J.R.	Cit	Charleston	Columbia, SC	02/19/65	Hart's Island, NY	06/20/65	Rlsd. G.O. #109	P79
Covington, W.W.	1Lt	C 23rd SCVI	Petersburg, VA	06/17/64	City Pt., VA	06/25/64	Ft. Delaware, DE	P45,CSR
					Ft. Delaware, DE	08/20/64	Hilton Head, SC	P2,CSR,ISH,CSR, P43
					Hilton Head, SC	08/20/64	Morris Island, SC	P2,CSR,CSR
					Morris Island, SC	10/20/64	Ft. Pulaski, GA	OR,CSR
					Ft. Pulaski, GA	03/12/65	Ft. Delaware, DE	P2,CSR
					Ft. Delaware, DE	06/17/65	Rlsd. G.O. #109	CSR
Cowan, William T.	Pvt	G Orr's Ri.	Falling Waters, MD	07/14/63	Old Capitol, DC	08/08/63	Pt. Lookout, MD	CSR
					Ft. McHenry, MD	08/08/63	Ft. Delaware, DE	P110
					Pt. Lookout, MD	03/03/64	City Pt., VA Xchg.	P116,P123,P124
Coward, D.A.	Pvt	F 2nd SCVC	Darbytown Rd., VA	12/12/64	Pt. Lookout, MD	06/26/65	Rlsd. G.O. #109	P114
Coward, Drayton E.	Pvt	H 10th SCVI	Franklin, TN	12/17/64	Nashville, TN	02/14/65	Louisville, KY	P4,P39,RAS,CTA,CSR
					Louisville, KY	02/17/65	Camp Chase, OH	P92,P95,CSR
					Camp Chase, OH	06/13/65	Rlsd. G.O. #109	P23,CSR
Coward, James A.	1Sg	C 3rd SCVABn	Ft. Gaines, AL	08/08/64	New Orleans, LA	10/25/64	Ship Island, MS	P3,CSR
					Ship Island, MS	01/04/65	Exchanged	P136,CTA,CSR
					Ship Island, MS	05/01/65	Vicksburg, MS Xchg	P136,CSR
Coward, James A.	1Sg	C 3rd SCVABn	Augusta, GA	05/20/65	Augusta, GA	05/20/65	Paroled on oath	CSR
Coward, James H.	Pvt	D 7th SCVIBn	Weldon RR, VA	08/21/64	City Pt., VA USFH	08/23/64	Washington, DC USG	P1,CSR,HIC,HAG
					Fts. Monroe, VA	08/26/64	USHS Metropolis	CSR
					Alexandria, VA USG	08/28/64	Washington, DC USG	CSR
					Old Capitol, DC	10/22/64	Elmira, NY	P110,CSR
					Elmira, NY	02/08/65	Pt.Lookout, MD Xch	P65,P66,CSR
					Pt. Lookout, MD	02/20/65	Coxe's Wh., VA Xch	CSR
Coward, Lewis M.	Pvt	E 4th SCVC	Hawe's Shop, VA	05/28/64	White House, VA	06/08/64	Pt. Lookout, MD	CSR
					Elmira, NY	10/11/64	Tfd. for Exchange	CSR
					Pt. Lookout, MD	10/29/64	Venus Pt., GA Xchg	P114,P123,CSR
Coward, N.M.	Pvt	B 14th SCMil	Lynch's Creek, SC	02/25/65	Hart's Island, NY	05/10/65	Died	P6,P79,FPH
Cowperthwait, William B.	Cpl	A 25th SCVI	Ft. Fisher, NC	01/15/65	New York, NY	01/30/65	Elmira, NY	CSR
					Elmira, NY	06/17/65	Rlsd. G.O. #109	P65,P66,HAG
Cox, A.F.	Pvt	C 8th SCVI	Gettysburg, PA	07/05/63	Ft. Delaware, DE			P42
Cox, A.P.	Pvt	C 1st SCVC	Rapidan R., VA	02/29/64	Old Capitol, DC	06/15/64	Ft. Delaware, DE	P110,CSR
					Ft. Delaware, DE	01/27/65	died, pneumonia	P110,CSR
Cox, Aaron C.	Pvt	C 22nd SCVI	Hatchers Run, VA	03/29/65	City Pt., VA	04/02/65	Pt. Lookout, MD	CSR
					Pt. Lookout, MD	06/26/65	Rlsd. G.O. #109	P118,P122,P123,CSR
Cox, Abraham	Pvt	A 16th SCVI	Nashville, TN	12/16/64	Louisville, KY	12/21/64	Camp Douglas, IL	P90,P91,P95,CSR
					Camp Douglas, IL	02/10/65	Died, Pneumonia	P58,FPH,CSR
Cox, Alexander W.	Pvt	E 26th SCVI	Five Forks, VA	04/01/65	City Pt., VA	04/05/65	Pt. Lookout, MD	CSR
					Pt. Lookout, MD	06/26/65	Released	P114,P118,P123
Cox, Andrew P.	Pvt	C Orr's Ri.	Spotsylvania, VA	05/12/64	Ft. Delaware, DE	11/28/64	Hos 11/28-12/20/64	P47,CDC
					Ft. Delaware, DE	01/24/65	Hos 1/24-1/27/65	P41,P47
Cox, Andrew P.	Pvt	C Orr's Ri.	Spotsylvania, VA	06/12/64	Ft. Delaware, DE	01/27/65	Died, Pneumonia	P5,P12,P43,P47,FPH
Cox, Benjamin B.	Sgt	B Wash'n LA	Raleigh, NC	04/13/65	Raleigh, NC	04/13/65	Paroled	CSR
Cox, Charles W.	Pvt	4 10/19 SCVI	Missionary Ridge, TN	11/25/63	Nashville, TN	12/07/63	Louisville, KY	P39,RAS,CSR
					Louisville, KY	12/07/63	Rock Island, IL	P88,P89,CSR
					Rock Island, IL	05/03/65	New Orleans Xchg.	P131,CSR
Cox, Charles W.	Pvt	4 10/19 SCVI	Missionary Ridge, TN	11/25/63	New Orleans, LA	05/23/65	Exchanged	P4,CSR

SOUTH CAROLINA SOLDIERS, SAILORS AND  CITIZENS HELD IN U.S. PRISONS 1861-1865

NAME	RANK	REGIMENT	CAPTURED AT	WHEN	PRISON	MOVED	DISPOSITION	SOURCES
Cox, D.M.	Pvt	D 4th SCVC	Louisa C.H., VA	07/11/64	Fts. Monroe, VA	06/20/64	Pt. Lookout, MD	CSR
					Pt. Lookout, MD	07/25/64	Elmira, NY	P113,P117,P120,CSR
					Elmira, NY	10/11/64	Trfd. for Xchg.	P65,CSR
					Pt. Lookout, MD	10/29/64	Venus Pt., GA Xc	P114,P118,P123,CSR
Cox, Edwin	Pvt	G 23rd SCVI	Farmville, VA	04/06/65	City Pt., VA	04/14/65	Newport News, VA	CSR
					Newport News, VA	07/01/65	Rlsd. G.O. #109	P107,CSR
Cox, Edwin M.	Pvt	H Ham.Leg.Ml	Richmond, VA	04/03/65	Libby Prsn. Rchmd	04/23/65	Newport News, VA	CSR
					Newport News, VA	06/23/65	Died	P107,PP,CSR
Cox, G.E.G.	Pvt	C 3rd SCVABn	Blakely, AL	04/09/65	Ship Island, MS	01/05/65	Vicksburg, MS Xc	P136,CSR
Cox, G.E.G.	Pvt	C 3rd SCVABn	Augusta, GA	05/20/65	Augusta, GA	05/20/65	Paroled on oath	CSR
Cox, G.W.	Pvt	A 1st SCVC	Beverly Ford, VA	06/09/63	Ft. McHenry, MD	06/25/63	City Pt., VA Xc	P110,CSR
Cox, George W.	Pvt	E 14th SCVI	Cox Rd.,Pbg., VA	04/03/65	City Pt., VA	04/07/65	Hart's Island, NY	CSR
					Hart's Island, NY	06/16/65	Rlsd. G.O. #109	P79,CSR
Cox, Henry	Pvt	C 22nd SCVI	Kinston, NC	12/15/62	Kinston, NC	12/15/62	Paroled POW	CSR
Cox, Isaiah	Pvt	6th SCVC	Deserted/enemy	11/25/64		11/25/64	N. of Ohio R, oath	CSR
Cox, James	Pvt	E 16th SCVI	Ringgold, GA	11/25/63	Nashville, TN	12/09/63	Louisville, KY	P39,16R,CSR
					Louisville, KY	12/11/63	Rock Island, IL	P88,P89,CSR
					Rock Island, IL	02/17/64	Died, Rubiola	P5,P131,P132,CSR
Cox, James	Pvt	C 22nd SCVI	Crater, Pbg., VA	07/30/64	City Pt., VA	08/05/64	Pt. Lookout, MD	CSR
					Pt. Lookout, MD	08/08/64	Elmira, NY	P113,P117,P120
					Elmira, NY	06/21/65	Rlsd. G.O. #109	P65
Cox, James G.	Pvt	B 10th SCVI	Atlanta, GA	07/22/64	Nashville, TN	12/09/64	Louisville, KY	P3,RAS,CSR
					Louisville, KY	12/15/64	Camp Douglas, IL	P91,RAS,CSR
					Camp Douglas, IL	02/20/65	Pt.Lookout, MD Xch	CSR
Cox, James G.	Pvt	B 10th SCVI	Atlanta, GA	07/22/64	Richmond, VA Hos.	03/17/65	Furloughed 60 days	CSR
Cox, John J.	Sgt	C 3rd SCVABn	Citronelle, AL	05/04/65	Meridian, MS	05/10/65	Paroled	CSR
Cox, Lorenzo D.	Pvt	2 10/19 SCVI	Missionary Ridge, TN	11/25/63	Nashville, TN	12/07/63	Louisville, KY	P39,CSR,RAS
					Louisville, KY	12/09/63	Rock Island, IL	P88,P89,CSR
					Rock Island, IL	01/07/64	Died, Pneumonia	P5,P132,FPH
Cox, M.L.	Pvt	A 1st SCVC	Gettysburg, PA	07/05/63	Ft. Delaware, DE	02/18/64	To Hos 2/18-4/12/6	P47
					Ft. Delaware, DE	06/30/64	Died	P5,P40,P42,P44,CSR
Cox, Samuel	Pvt	D 15th SCMil	Camden, SC	02/28/65	Pt. Lookout, MD	04/30/65	Died, Ch. Diarrhea	P6,P119,P121,FPH
Cox, Solomon C.	Pvt	6 10/19 SCVI	Missionary Ridge, TN	11/25/63	Nashville, TN	12/07/63	Louisville, KY	P39,RAS,CSR
					Louisville, KY	12/09/63	Rock Island, IL	P88,P89,CSR
					Rock Island, IL	01/21/64	Joined US Navy	P131,CSR
Cox, W.B.	Pvt	K Orr's Ri.	Petersburg, VA	04/03/65	City Pt., VA	04/11/65	Hart's Island, NY	P79,CSR
					Hart's Island, NY	06/16/65	Rlsd. G.O. #109	CSR
Cox, W.E.	Pvt	B 3rd SCVABn	Ft. Tyler, GA	04/16/65	1st Div. Cavalry C	04/23/65	Macon, GA Prison	CSR
Cox, W.G.	Pvt	B 15th SCVI	Gettysburg, PA	07/04/63	David's Island, NY	08/24/63	City Pt., VA Xc	P1,CSR
Cox, William	Pvt	7th SCVI	Sharpsburg, MD	09/17/62	Stone House Hos.	09/18/62	Died of wounds	P12,CSR
Cox, William J.	Pvt	C 3rd SCVC	River's Bridge, SC	02/02/65	US 17th A. C. F.H.	03/16/65	Died of wounds	CSR
Cox, William S.	Pvt	K Ham.Leg.Ml	Richmond, VA	04/03/65	On U.S. list			CSR
Cox, William W.	Pvt	E 16th SCVI	Ringgold, GA	11/24/63	Nashville, TN	12/09/63	Louisville, KY	P39,16R,CSR
					Louisville, KY	12/11/63	Rock Island, IL	P88,P89,CSR
					Rock Island, IL	03/06/64	Died, Jaundice	P5,P131,132,FPH
Coyle, Emor G.	Pvt	M P.S.S.	Spotsylvania, VA	05/13/64	Belle Plain, VA	05/21/64	Ft. Delaware, DE	CSR
					Ft. Delaware, DE	08/07/64	To Hos 8/7-8/20/64	P47
					Ft. Delaware, DE	05/03/65	Rlsd, Secy. of War	P43,P46,CSR

SOUTH CAROLINA SOLDIERS, SAILORS AND C CITIZENS HELD IN U.S. PRISONS 1861-1865

NAME	RANK	REGIMENT	CAPTURED AT	WHEN	PRISON	MOVED	DISPOSITION	SOURCES
Crabtree, George	Pvt	K 1st SCVIG	Wilderness, VA	05/06/64	Belle Plain, VA	05/21/64	Ft. Delaware, DE	CSR,SR1
					Ft. Delaware, DE	07/02/64	Hos 7/2-7/7/64	P47
					Ft. Delaware, DE	07/23/64	Hos 7/23-8/15/64	P47
					Ft. Delaware, DE	09/14/64	Hos 9/14-10/8/64	P47
					Ft. Delaware, DE	10/26/64	Hos 10/26-12/23/64	P47
					Ft. Delaware, DE	01/20/65	Hos 1/20-1/30/65	P47
					Ft. Delaware, DE	02/01/65	To Hos 2/1-2/21/65	P47
					Ft. Delaware, DE	02/27/65	City Point, VA Xc	P41,P43,CSR
					Pt. Lookout, MD	07/17/65	Died, Ch. Diarrhea	P12,CSR
Crabtree, T.	Pvt	1st SCVIG	Fredericksburg, VA	05/03/63	Washington, DC	05/10/63	City Pt., VA Xchg.	CSR
Craddock, Daniel F.	Pvt	B 3rd SCVI	Savage Stn., VA	06/28/62	Harrison's Ldg.,VA	07/03/62	Ft. Columbus, NY	CSR
					Ft. Columbus, NY	07/09/62	Ft. Delaware, DE	CSR
					Ft. Delaware, DE	08/05/62	Aikens Ldg., VA Xc	CSR
Craddock, William H.	Pvt	A 1st SCVIG	Petersburg, VA	04/02/65	City Pt., VA	04/04/65	Pt. Lookout, MD	CSR,SA1
					Pt. Lookout, MD	06/26/65	Rlsd. G.O. #109	P118,P122,P123
Craddock, William P.	Pvt	C 1st SCVIH	Warrenton, VA	09/29/62	Warrenton, VA	09/29/62	Paroled	CSR
Crady, William	Pvt	K 15th SCVI	Deserted/enemy	11/22/63	Louisville, KY	11/25/63	Sent north on oath	CSR
Craft, A.W.	Pvt	A 15th SCMil	Flat Rock, SC	02/26/65	Hart's Island, NY	06/17/65	Rlsd. G.O. #109	P79
Craft, James	Pvt	D 12th SCVI	Long Bridge, VA	07/28/64	City Pt., VA USFH	07/31/64	Died of wounds	CSR
Craft, Moses	Pvt	G 24th SCVI	Nashville, TN	12/16/64	Nashville, TN	01/01/65	Louisville, KY	P39
					Louisville, KY	01/05/65	Camp Chase, OH	P92,P95
					Camp Chase, OH	06/12/65	Rlsd. G.O. #109	P23,CSR
Craig, Alexander	Pvt	H 12th SCVI	Spotsylvania, VA	05/12/64	Belle Plain, VA	05/20/64	Ft. Delaware, DE	CSR,YEB
					Ft. Delaware, DE	09/03/64	Hos 9/3-10/15/64	P47
					Ft. Delaware, DE	05/18/65	Hos 5/18-6/4/65	P47
					Ft. Delaware, DE	06/10/65	Released	P41,P43,P45,YEB,CSR
Craig, Alexander P.	2Lt	E 21st SCVI	Morris Island, SC	07/10/63	Ft. Columbus, NY	10/09/63	Johnson's Isl., OH	P1,HAG
					Johnson's Isl., OH	03/21/65	Pt. Lookout, MD	P80,P81,P82
					Ft. Delaware, DE	06/12/65	Released	P43,P45
Craig, Hugh	2Lt	A 4th SCVC	Stony Creek, VA	12/01/64	P.M. Army of Potomac	12/04/64	Washington, DC	CSR
					Old Capitol, DC	12/17/64	Ft. Delaware, DE	P110,CSR
					Ft. Delaware, DE	06/17/65	Rlsd. G.O. #109	P43,P45,P46,CSR
Craig, J.P.	Pvt	E P.S.S.	Fair Oaks, VA	05/31/62	Aikens Ldg., VA Xc	06/26/62	Xchd.	CSR
Craig, J.T.B.	Pvt	I 17th SCVI	Warrenton, VA	09/29/62	Warrenton, VA	09/29/62	Paroled	CSR
Craig, J.T.B.	Cpl	I 17th SCVI	Crater, Pbg., VA	07/30/64	City Pt., VA	08/05/64	Pt. Lookout, MD	CSR
					Pt. Lookout, MD	08/08/64	Elmira, NY	P117,P120,P125,CSR
					Elmira, NY	07/03/65	Rlsd. G.O. #109	P65,CSR
Craig, James A.	2Lt	D 8th SCVI	Winchester, VA	09/13/64	Harpers Ferry, WV	09/19/64	Johnson's Isl., OH	CSR
					Johnson's Isl., OH	06/16/65	Rlsd. G.O. #109	P81,P82,P83,CSR
Craig, John P.	Pvt	C 8th SCVI	Gettysburg, PA	07/02/63	Ft. Delaware, DE	09/18/64	Aikens Ldg., VA Xc	KEB,P42
Craig, John P.	Pvt	C 8th SCVI	Winchester, VA	09/13/64	Harpers Ferry, WV	09/19/64	Camp Chase, OH	CSR
					Camp Chase, OH	05/15/65	Rlsd. G.O. #85	P23,P26,CSR
Craig, Thomas B.	Pvt	I 12th SCVI	Warrenton, VA	09/29/62	Warrenton, VA	09/29/62	Paroled	CSR
Craig, Thomas P.	Sgt	C 8th SCVI	Gettysburg, PA	07/03/63	Ft. Delaware, DE			P40,KEB
					Ft. Delaware, DE	01/26/64	Hos 12/6-12/17/64	P47
					Ft. Delaware, DE	06/10/65	Released	P43,P44,P45,CSR
Craig, W.J.	Sgt	F Signal Cps	Harpers Farm, VA	04/06/65	Pt. Lookout, MD	06/24/65	Rlsd. G.O. #109	P123
Craig, W.S.	Pvt		Brooks LA		Pt. Lookout, MD	06/24/65	Rlsd. G.O. #109	CSR
Crain, Dennis	Sgt	H 22nd SCVI	Kinston, NC	12/15/62	Kinston, NC	12/15/62	Paroled POW	CSR
Crain, S.J.	Pvt	F 3rd SCVI	Sharpsburg, MD	09/17/62	Sharpsburg, MD	09/17/62	Died of wounds	P12,SA2,ROH,JR
Crain, William D.	Pvt	D 16th SCVI	Kennesaw Mtn. GA	07/03/64	Louisville, KY	07/13/64	Camp Morton, IN	CSR
					Camp Morton, IN	06/12/65	Rlsd. G.O. #109	P7,P100,P101,CSR

SOUTH CAROLINA SOLDIERS, SAILORS AND  CITIZENS HELD IN U.S. PRISONS 1861-1865

NAME	RANK	REGIMENT	CAPTURED AT	WHEN	PRISON	MOVED	DISPOSITION	SOURCES
Craley, Samuel E.	Pvt	D 2nd SCVC	Brandy Stn., VA	08/24/63	Old Capital, DC	09/28/63		P7,CSR
					Ft. McHenry, MD	09/28/63	Phila., PA on oath	P110,CSR
Crane, Francis C.	Pvt	B 17th SCVI	Petersburg, VA	03/25/65	City Pt., VA	03/28/65	Pt. Lookout, MD	CSR,HOF
					Pt. Lookout, MD	06/26/65	Rlsd. G.O. #109	P118,P122,P123,HOF,
Crane, J.B.	Pvt	I P.S.S.	Deserted/enemy	03/18/65	Bermuda Hundred, VA	03/22/65	Washington, DC	CSR
					Washington, DC	03/25/65	Memphis, TN oath	CSR,TSE
Crane, Thuruston	Pvt	F Ham.Leg.	Sharpsburg, MD	09/17/62	Frederick, MD G.H.	09/24/62	Transferred	CSR
Crane, Warren L.	Pvt	K 12th SCVI	Gettysburg, PA	07/04/63	Wdd & left behind		No US records foun	CSR
Crane, Warren L.	Pvt	K 12th SCVI	Petersburg, VA	03/25/65	City Pt., VA	03/28/65	Pt. Lookout, MD	CSR
					Pt. Lookout, MD	06/26/65	Rlsd. G.O. #109	P118,P122,P123,CSR
Crapps, H.H.	Pvt	I 15th SCVI	Piedmont, VA	06/05/64	Camp Morton, IN	06/24/64	Jd. US Army	H15,CSR
Crapps, Paul Hamilton	Pvt	C 15th SCVI	Sharpsburg, MD	09/17/62	Ft. Mchenry, MD	10/18/62	Fts. Monroe, VA Xc	CSR,H15
Crapps, S.W.	Pvt	I 4th SCVC	Old Church, VA	05/29/64	U.S. Field Hosp.	05/29/64	Died of wounds	P12,ROH,CTA
Crapps, S.W.	Pvt	H Hol.Leg.	Petersburg, VA	11/06/64	City Pt., VA	11/11/64	Washington, DC	CSR
					Pt. Lookout, MD	02/13/65	Aikens Ldg., VA Xc	P116,P121,P124,CSR
Craps, William J.	Pvt	D 24th SCVI	Franklin, TN	12/18/64	Nashville, TN	03/11/65	Died, Ch. Diarrhea	P4,P12,EFW
Crapse, Henry T.	Pvt	E 11th SCVI	Barnwell, SC	02/08/65	New Berne, NC	03/30/65	Pt. Lookout, VA	CSR
					Pt. Lookout, MD	06/26/65	Rlsd. G.O. #109	P118,P122,P123,HAG
Crapse, Michael D.	Pvt	E 3rd SCVC	Florence, SC	03/05/65	New Berne, NC	04/03/65	Pt. Lookout, MD	CSR
					Pt. Lookout, MD	06/26/65	Rlsd. G.O. #109	P114,P118,P123,CSR
Craven, R. Martin	Pvt	I 11th SCVI	Drury's Bluff, VA	05/16/64	Pt. Lookout, MD	06/13/64	Joined U.S. Army	P117,P122,P125,HAG
Craven, Thomas	Pvt	I 11th SCVI	Petersburg, VA	06/24/64	Fts. Monroe, VA	06/26/64	Pt. Lookout MD	CSR,HAG
					Pt. Lookout, MD	08/11/64	Elmira, NY	P113,P117,P120,CSR
					Elmira, NY	12/04/64	Died, Ch. Diarrhea	P5,P12,P65,FPH,CSR
Crawford, Benjamin F.	Pvt	A 18th SCVI	Jackson, MS	07/15/63	Snyders Bluff, MS	08/07/63	Camp Morton, IN	CSR
					Camp Morton, IN	05/20/65	Rlsd. G.O. #85	P100,UD5,CSR
Crawford, D.W.	Pvt	Santee LA	Deserted/enemy	03/05/65	Charleston, SC	03/05/65	Released on oath	CSR
Crawford, Daniel	Sgt	G 1st SCVA	Deserted/enemy	02/18/65	Hilton Head, SC	04/04/65	To be sent to NYC	CSR
Crawford, Daniel A	Pvt	C 23rd SCVI	Five Forks, VA	04/01/65	City Pt., VA	04/04/65	Pt. Lookout, MD	CSR
					Pt. Lookout, MD	06/18/65	Died, gunshot Wd.	P6,P118,P119,FPH
Crawford, David	Pvt	G Orr's Ri.	Deep Bottom, VA	07/28/64	Old Capitol, DC	12/16/64	Elmira, NY	P110,CSR
					Elmira, NY	02/13/65	Tfd. for exchange	P65
					Baltimore, MD	05/09/65	Ft. McHenry, MD	P3,CSR
					Ft. McHenry, MD	06/09/65	Rlsd. G.O. #109	P96,CSR
Crawford, David H.	Pvt	M 10th SCVI	Kentucky	09/15/62	Kentucky	11/15/62	Paroled for Xchg.	CSR,RAS
Crawford, Elijah	Pvt	E 5th SCVC	Columbia, SC	02/17/65	New Berne, NC	04/10/65	Pt. Lookout, MD	CSR
					Hart's Island, NY	06/16/65	Rlsd. G.O. #109	P79,CSR
Crawford, J.D.	Cpl	C P.S.S.	Richmond, VA	10/07/64	Pt. Lookout, MD	03/28/65	Aikens Ldg., VA Xc	P118,P121,P123,CSR
Crawford, James	Pvt	K 15th SCVI	Deserted/enemy	03/05/65	Charleston, SC	03/05/65	Released on oath	CSR
Crawford, James Franklin	Pvt	8 10/19 SCVI	Missionary Ridge, TN	11/25/63	Nashville, TN	12/05/63	Louisville, KY	P39,CSR
					Louisville, KY	12/06/63	Rock Island, IL	P88,P89,CSR
					Rock Island, IL	05/08/64	Died, Diarrhea	P5,P132,FPH,CSR
Crawford, James M.	Pvt	H 1st SCVA	Rabon County, GA	05/25/64	Louisville, KY	05/19/64	Discharged on oath	P90,P92,P94,CSR
Crawford, John H.	3Lt	G Orr's Ri.	Falling Waters, MD	07/14/63	Old Capitol, DC	08/08/63	Johnson's Isl., OH	CSR
					Ft.McHenry, MD	08/08/63	Johnson's Isl., OH	P110,CDC
					Johnson's Isl., OH	06/24/65	Rlsd. G.O. #109	P7,P81,P83,CDC,CSR
Crawford, John M.	Pvt	A 18th SCVI	Crater, Pbg., VA	07/30/64	Pt. Lookout, MD	08/08/64	Elmira, NY	P113,P117,P120,CSR
					Elmira, NY	10/11/64	Pt.Lookout, MD Xc	P65,CSR
					Pt. Lookout, MD	10/29/64	Venus Pt., GA Xchg	P118,P123,P125,CSR
Crawford, John T.	Pvt	H 1st SCVA	Rabon County, GA	06/04/64	Louisville, KY	06/08/64	Sent north on oath	P94,CSR
Crawford, Levi	Pvt	E 5th SCVC	Deserted/enemy	03/13/65	Charleston, SC	03/15/65	Released on oath	CSR
Crawford, Peter C.	Pvt	G 1st SCVA	Deserted/enemy	03/13/65	Charleston, SC	03/14/65	Taken oath & disch	CSR

SOUTH CAROLINA SOLDIERS, SAILORS AND C CITIZENS HELD IN U.S. PRISONS 1861-1865

NAME	RANK	REGIMENT	CAPTURED AT	WHEN	PRISON	MOVED	DISPOSITION	SOURCES
Crawford, R.D.	Pvt	D 6th SCVI	Sharpsburg, MD	09/17/62	Sharpsburg, MD	09/17/62	Died of wounds	P12,ROH,BOD,YMD
Crawford, R.T.	Pvt	I 1st SCVIR	Deserted/enemy	02/21/65	Charleston, SC	02/21/65	Released on oath	SA1,CSR
Crawford, Robert Wesley	1Lt	I 19th SCVI	Pulaski, TN	12/25/64	Nashville, TN	02/14/65	Louisville, KY	CSR
					Louisville, KY	02/17/65	Camp Chase, OH	P92,P95,CSR
					Camp Chase, OH	03/01/85	Pt. Lookout, MD Xc	P23,P26,CSR
					Richmond, VA Hosp.	03/27/65	Furloughed home	CSR
Crawford, S.M.	2Lt	K 22nd SCVI	Kinston, NC	12/15/62	Kinston, NC	12/15/62	Paroled POW	CSR
Crawford, Samuel L.	Pvt	B 7th SCVIBn	Deserted/enemy	04/02/65	Fts. Monroe, VA	04/02/65	Washington, DC P.M.	CSR
					Washington, DC P.M	04/05/65	Charleston, SC	CSR
Crawford, Thomas	Pvt	B 7th SCVIBn	Bentonville, NC	03/19/65	New Berne, NC	04/10/65	Hart's Island, NY	CSR
					Hart's Island, NY	06/16/65	Rlsd. G.O. #109	CSR
Crawford, Thomas C.	Pvt	E 1st SCVIG	Petersburg, VA	04/02/65	Old Capitol, DC	05/01/65	Elmira, NY	P110,SA1,CSR
					Elmira, NY	07/07/65	Rlsd. G.O. #109	CSR
Crawford, W.G.	Pvt	A 18th SCVI	Jackson, MS	07/04/63	Camp Morton, IN	05/20/65	Rlsd. G.O. #85	P101
Crawford, W.M.	Pvt	G 7th SCVI	Sharpsburg, MD	09/17/62	Frederick, MD	09/30/62	Ft. McHenry, MD	CSR
					Ft. McHenry, MD	10/25/62	Aikens Ldg., VA Xc	CSR
Crawford, William Elias	Pvt	G 25th SCVI	Ft. Fisher, NC	01/15/65	New York, NY	01/30/65	Elmira, NY	CSR
					Elmira, NY	03/07/65	Died, Pneumonia	P6,P12,P65,FPH,HAG
Crawford, William H.	Pvt	B 24th SCVI	Nashville, TN	12/16/64	Nashville, TN	12/19/64	Louisville, KY	CSR
					Louisville, KY	12/21/64	Camp Douglas, IL	P90,P91,P95
					Camp Douglas, IL	04/02/65	Jd. US 6th NJV	P55
Crawford, William T.	Pvt	A 12th SCVI	Petersburg, VA	04/02/65	City Pt., VA	04/04/65	Pt. Lookout, MD	CSR,YEB
					Pt. Lookout, MD	06/06/65	Rlsd. Instr. 5/30/65	P114,P118,P121,CSR
Crawley, Thomas M.	Pvt	F 26th SCVI	Petersburg, VA	04/02/65	Pt. Lookout, MD	06/26/65	Rlsd. G.O. #109	P118,P122,P123
Creasey, T.M.	Pvt	I 23rd SCVI	Five Forks, VA	04/01/65	City Pt., VA	04/06/65	Hart's Island, NY	CSR
					Hart's Island, NY	06/15/65	Released	P79,CSR
Creech, David L.	Pvt	F 21st SCVI	Ft. Fisher, NC	01/15/65	Elmira, NY	06/03/65	Died, Diarrhea	P6,P65,HAG,FPH
Creech, George W.	Pvt	H 17th SCVI	Petersburg, VA	03/25/65	City Pt., VA	03/28/65	Pt. Lookout, MD	CSR
					Pt. Lookout, MD	06/26/65	Rlsd. G.O. #109	P114,P118,P123,CSR
Creech, James	Pvt	H 17th SCVI	Warrenton, VA	09/29/62	Warrenton, VA	09/29/62	Paroled	CSR
Creech, John J.	3Lt	H 17th SCVI	Petersburg, VA	03/25/65	City Pt., VA	03/26/65	Washington, DC	CSR
					Old Capitol, DC	03/30/65	Ft. Delaware, DE	CSR
					Ft. Delaware, DE	06/17/65	Rlsd. G.O. #109	P43,P45,CSR
Creech, Lewis B.	Pvt	H 17th SCVI	Warrenton, VA	09/29/62	Warrenton, VA	09/29/62	Paroled	CSR
Creech, Lewis B.	Pvt	H 17th SCVI	Five Forks, VA	04/01/65	City Pt., VA	04/06/65	Pt. Lookout, MD	CSR
					Pt. Lookout, MD	06/26/65	Rlsd. G.O. #109	P118,P122,P123,CSR
Creed, B.O.	Pvt	I 20th SCVI	Cedar Creek, VA	10/19/64	Harpers Ferry, WV	10/24/64	Pt. Lookout, MD	CSR,KEB
					Pt. Lookout, MD	05/10/65	Rlsd. G.O. #85	P114,P118,P122,CSR
Creel, Samuel E.	Pvt	McQueen LA	Charlotte, NC	05/15/65	Charlotte, NC	05/15/65	Paroled	CSR
Creighton, George W.	Pvt	I 12th SCVI	Richmond, VA Hos.	04/03/65	Escaped	05/06/65		CSR
Creighton, James D.	Pvt	C Ham.Leg.Ml	Farmville, VA	04/11/65	Farmville, VA	04/11/65	Paroled	CSR
Crenshaw, Hezekiah K.	Pvt	C Orr's Ri.	Petersburg, VA	04/03/65	City Pt., VA	04/11/65	Hart's Island, NY	CSR
					Hart's Island, NY	06/16/65	Rlsd. G.O. #109	P79,CDC,CSR
Crenshaw, Samuel	Pvt	C Orr's Ri.	Falling Waters, MD	07/14/63	Baltimore, MD	08/16/63	Pt. Lookout, MD	CSR
					Pt. Lookout, MD	08/16/64	Elmira, NY	P113,P120
					Elmira, NY	03/10/65	Pt. Lookout, MD Xc	P65,P124,CDC,CSR
Crenshaw, W.H.	Pvt	D Ham.Leg.Ml	Hartwell, GA		Hartwell, GA		Paroled	CSR
Crenshaw, Wilson	Pvt	I 12th SCVI	Gettysburg, PA	07/05/63	David's Island, NY	09/27/63	City Pt., VA Xchg.	P1,LAN,CSR
Creps, Wesley C.	Sgt	A 12th SCVI	Sharpsburg, VA	09/17/62	Frederick, MD USGH	10/16/62	Ft. McHenry, MD GH	CSR
					Ft. McHenry, MD	10/18/62	Fts. Monroe, VA Xc	CSR
					Richmond, VA Hos.	11/23/62	Died of wounds	CSR
Crew, J.C.	Pvt	H 1st SCVIG	Sharpsburg, MD	10/01/62	Ft. McHenry, MD	10/18/62	Fts. Monroe, VA Xc	CSR

SOUTH CAROLINA SOLDIERS, SAILORS AND **C** CITIZENS HELD IN U.S. PRISONS 1861-1865

NAME	RANK	REGIMENT	CAPTURED AT	WHEN	PRISON	MOVED	DISPOSITION	SOURCES
Crews, John	Pvt	D 9th SCVIH	Port Royal, SC	02/13/62	Ft. Lafayette, NY	03/15/62	Baltimore, MD	CSR
					Ft. Lafayette, NY	03/15/62	(date is rcd @ Pr)	P85
					Baltimore, MD	08/02/62	Fts. Monroe, VA	CSR
					Fts. Monroe, VA	08/05/62	Aikens Ldg., VA Ex	CSR
Crews, Marcus Aurelius	Pvt	F 2nd SCVI	Cold Harbor, VA	06/01/64	Armory Sq.G.H., DC	10/25/64	Died of wounds	P6,KEB,P2,H2,CSR
Crews, Moses	Pvt	D 24th SCVI	Marietta, GA	06/19/64	Nashville, TN	06/24/64	Louisville, KY	P3
					Louisville, KY	06/27/64	Camp Morton, IN	P90,P91,P94
					Camp Morton, IN	12/04/64	Died, Lung Infl.	P5,P100,P101,FPH
Crews, W.L.	Pvt	D 11th SCVI	Town Creek, NC	02/20/65	USA Hosp. Steamer	02/28/65	Wilmington, NC Hosp	CSR
					Wilmington NC Hosp	06/06/65	Died of wounds	CSR
Cribb, A. Jack	Pvt	A 21st SCVI	Ft. Fisher, NC	01/15/65	Elmira, NY	07/09/65	Rlsd. G.O. #109	P65,HAG
Cribb, David W.	Pvt	G 15th SCVI	Gettysburg, PA	07/04/63	Gettysburg G.H.	09/16/63	Provost Marshal	P4,KEB,CSR
					David's Island, NY	08/24/63	City Pt., VA Xc	P1,KEB,CTA,CSR
Cribb, Henry	Cpl	A 21st SCVI	Weldon RR, VA	08/21/64	Pt. Lookout, MD	03/14/65	Aikens Ldg., VA Xc	P117,P123,P124,HAG
Cribb, James Elijah C.	Pvt	G 15th SCVI	Cedar Creek, VA	10/19/64	Pt. Lookout, MD	03/17/65	Exchanged	P118,P123,P124,CSR
Cribb, William L.	Pvt	A 21st SCVI	Smithfield, NC	01/18/65	Pt. Lookout, MD	02/11/65	Hammond G.H., MD	P114,P118,HAG
					Pt. Lookout, MD	06/20/65	Rlsd. G.O. #109	P121
Crider, David H.	Pvt	K 1st SCVIH	Loudon, TN	12/03/63	Nashville, TN	12/31/63	Louisville, KY	P39,SA1,CSR
					Louisville, KY	01/27/64	Rock Island, IL	P89,P93,JRH,CSR
					Rock Island, IL	02/14/64	Died, Variola	P131,P132,FPH,SA1
Crider, George B.	Pvt	G 25th SCVI	Ream's Stn., VA	08/21/64	City Pt., VA	08/26/64	Philadelphia, PA	CSR
					McClellan GH Phila	09/01/64	Died of wounds	P6,P12,FPH,HAG
Crim, Daniel G.	Pvt	B 1st SCVIH	Jefferson Co., TN	01/22/65	Knoxville, TN	01/30/65	Hospital, as nurse	P84,SA1,CSR
					Nashville, TN	06/11/65	Louisville, KY	P39,SA1,CSR
					Louisville, KY	06/16/65	Released on oath	P92,CSR
Crim, Reuben F.	Pvt	C 15th SCVI	Halltown, WV	08/21/64	Camp Chase, OH	03/18/65	Pt. Lookout, MD	P23,P26,KEB,CSR
					Pt. Lookout, MD	03/27/65	Boulware's Wh. Xc	CSR,H15
Crim, S.	Cit		Lynch's Creek, SC	02/25/65	Hart's Island, NY	04/28/65	Died, Inter. fever	P6,P12,P79
Crimm, Jeter W.	Cpl	X 10/19 SCVI	Missionary Ridge, TN	11/25/63	Nashville, TN	12/07/63	Louisville, KY	P39,CSR
					Louisville, KY	12/09/63	Rock Island, IL	P88,CSR
					Rock Island, IL	06/20/65	Rlsd. G.O. #109	P131,CSR
					Nashville, TN	12/07/63	Louisville, KY	CSR
					Louisville, KY	12/09/63	Rock Island, IL	CSR
					Rock Island, IL	06/20/65	Rlsd. G.O. #109	CSR
Crimminger, Robert A.	Pvt	E 12th SCVI	Five Forks, VA	04/01/65	City Pt., VA	04/07/65	Hart's Island, NY	CSR
					Hart's Island, NY	06/16/65	Rlsd. G.O. #109	P79,LAN,CSR
Criswell, Thomas V.	Pvt	G 14th SCVI	Augusta, GA	05/25/65	Augusta, GA	05/25/65	Paroled	CSR
Crittenden, Rudolphus D.	Cit	Charleston	Brooklyn, NY	03/07/63	Ft. Lafayette, NY	07/02/63	Ft. Warren, MS	P144
					Ft. Warren, MA			P2
Crocker, A.T.	Sgt	B Hol.Leg.	Petersburg, VA	10/27/64	City Pt., VA	10/31/64	Pt. Lookout, MD	CSR
					Pt. Lookout, MD	03/28/65	Aikens Ldg., VA Xc	P121,P124,P118,CSR
Crocker, Alexander	Pvt	H P.S.S.	Deserted/enemy	03/03/65	Bermuda Hundred VA	03/04/65	Washington, DC	CSR
					Washington, DC	03/07/65	Columbus, OH/ oath	CSR
Crocker, James	Pvt	B Hol.Leg.	Newton, NC	04/19/65	Newton, NC	04/19/65	Paroled	CSR
Crocker, Mattison	Pvt	B Hol.Leg.	Deserted/Enemy	02/14/65	City Pt., VA	02/18/65	Washington, DC	CSR
					Washington, DC	02/21/65	Columbus, OH/ oath	CSR
Crocker, Thomas	Pvt	B Hol.Leg.	Deserted/Enemy	02/14/65	City Pt., VA	02/18/65	Washington, DC	CSR
					Washington, DC	02/21/65	Columbus, OH /oath	CSR
Crocker, W.H.	Pvt	B Hol.Leg.	Deserted/Enemy	02/14/65	City Pt., VA	02/18/65	Washington, DC	CSR
					Washington, DC	02/21/65	Columbus, OH /oath	CSR

SOUTH CAROLINA SOLDIERS, SAILORS AND C CITIZENS HELD IN U.S. PRISONS 1861-1865

NAME	RANK	REGIMENT	CAPTURED AT	WHEN	PRISON	MOVED	DISPOSITION	SOURCES
Crocker, William J.	2Lt	C 7th SCVC	Columbia, VA	03/11/65	Fts. Monroe, VA	03/24/65	Washington, DC	CSR
					Pt. Lookout, MD	03/25/65	Washington, DC	P114,P117,P120,CSR
					Old Capitol, DC	03/30/65	Ft. Delaware, DE	CSR
					Ft. Delaware, DE	06/16/65	Rlsd. G.O. #109	P43,P45,P47,CSR
Croft, H.J.	2Cl	H 17th SCVI	Petersburg, VA	03/09/65	City Pt., VA	03/11/65	Washington, DC	CSR
					Washington, DC	03/13/65	Charleston, SC	CSR
Croft, J.	Pvt	A 19th SCVCB	Augusta, GA	05/31/65	Augusta, GA	05/31/65	Paroled on oath	CSR
Croft, W.Y.	Pvt	D 18th SCVI	Petersburg, VA	07/30/64	City Pt., VA	08/08/64	Pt. Lookout, MD	CSR
					Pt. Lookout, MD	08/08/64	Elmira, NY	P113,P117,P120,CSR
					Elmira, NY	07/03/65	Rlsd. G.O. #109	P65,CSR
Croft, William	Pvt	G 20th SCVI	Cedar Creek, VA	10/19/64	Harpers Ferry, WV	10/24/64	Pt. Lookout, MD	CSR
					Pt. Lookout, MD	03/28/65	Exchanged	P118,P121,P124
Croft, William	Pvt	H 17th SCVI	Petersburg, VA	03/25/65	City Pt., VA	03/28/65	Pt. Lookout, MD	CSR
					Pt. Lookout, MD	06/26/65	Rlsd. G.O. #109	P114,P118,P123,CSR
Crofts, W.J.	Pvt	F 1st SCVIR	Deserted/enemy	02/27/65	Charleston, SC	03/01/65	will take oath	SA1,CSR
Cromer, Abraham Barron	Pvt	C 3rd SCVI	Cedar Creek, VA	10/19/64	Harpers Ferry, WV	10/24/64	Pt. Lookout, MD	CSR
					Pt. Lookout, MD	03/17/65	Aikens Ldg., VA Xc	P118,P123,P124,KEB
Cromer, Andrew J.	Pvt	A 22nd SCVI	Hatchers Run, VA	03/25/65	City Pt., VA	04/02/65	Pt. Lookout, MD	CSR
					Pt. Lookout, MD	06/26/65	Rlsd. G.O. #109	P118,P122,P123,CSR
Cromer, Daniel	Pvt	D 15th SCMil	Lynch's Creek, SC	02/27/65	New Berne, NC USGH	04/10/65	Died, Anemia	P6,P12,WAT,CSR
Cromer, G.A.	Pvt	K 12th SCVI	Gettysburg, PA	07/05/63	Ft. Delaware, DE	09/30/64	Aikens Ldg., VA Xc	P40,P42,P44
Cromer, G.H.	Pvt	D 13th SCVI	Gettysburg, PA	07/05/63	David's Island, NY	11/02/63	City Pt., VA Xchg.	CSR
Cromer, George A.	Pvt	K 12th SCVI	Gettysburg, PA	07/05/63	Gettysburg, PA	07/19/63	Ft. McHenry, MD	CSR
					Ft. McHenry, MD	08/15/63	Ft. Delaware, DE	CSR
					Ft. Delaware, DE	09/21/64	Hos 9/21-9/30/64	P47
					Ft. Delaware, DE	09/30/64	Aikens Ldg., VA Xc	CSR
Cromer, George C.	Pvt	G Hol.Leg.	Five Forks, VA	04/01/65	City Pt., VA	04/05/65	Pt. Lookout, MD	CSR
					Pt. Lookout, MD	06/26/65	Rlsd. G.O. #109	P118,P121,P123,ANY
Cromer, H.M.	Pvt	E 7th SCVI	Cedar Creek, VA	10/19/64	Winchester, VA USH	10/23/64	W. Bldg. Balt, MD	CSR
					W. Bldg. Balt, MD	11/23/64	Pt. Lookout, MD	CSR
					Pt. Lookout, MD	01/25/65	Hammond G.H., MD	P114,P118,P121,CSR
					Hammond G.H., MD	03/31/65	Pt. Lookout, MD	CSR
					Pt. Lookout, MD	06/26/65	Rlsd. G.O. #109	P122,P123,CSR
Cromer, Ivey	Pvt	G Hol.Leg.	Petersburg, VA	04/03/65	City Pt., VA	04/11/65	Hart's Island, NY	CSR
					Hart's Island, NY	06/17/65	Rlsd. G.O. #109	P79
Cromer, J. Franklin	Pvt	G Hol.Leg.	Kinston, NC	12/14/62	Kinston, NC	12/14/62	Paroled POW	CSR
Cromer, J. Franklin	Pvt	G Hol.Leg.	Petersburg, VA	04/03/65	City Pt., VA	04/13/65	Pt. Lookout, MD	CSR
Cromer, J. Franklin	Pvt	G Hol.Leg.	Five Forks, VA	04/02/65	Pt. Lookout, MD	06/26/65	Rlsd. G.O. #109	P118,P119,P123
Cromer, John	Pvt	G Hol.Leg.	Five Forks, VA	04/01/65	City Pt., VA	04/05/65	Pt. Lookout, MD	CSR
					Pt. Lookout, MD	06/26/65	Rlsd. G.O. #109	
Cromer, John L.	Pvt	F 20th SCVI	Cedar Creek, VA	10/19/64	Pt. Lookout, MD	12/21/64	Died, Typhoid Fever	P5,P118,P119,FPH
Cromer, Robert	Pvt	G Hol.Leg.	Five Forks, VA	04/01/65	City Pt., VA	04/05/65	Pt. Lookout, MD	CSR
					Pt. Lookout, MD	06/20/65	Rlsd. G.O. #109	P118,P121,P123,ANY
Cromer, T.L.	Pvt	D 2nd SCVIRi	Burkeville, VA	04/14/65	Burkesville, VA	04/17/65	Paroled	CSR
Crompton, William J.	Pvt	G 12th SCVI	Gettysburg, PA	07/05/63	Chester, PA G.H.	10/03/63	Pt. Lookout, MD	P1,CSR
					Pt. Lookout, MD	03/17/64	City Pt.,VA Xchg.	P116,P124,CSR
Cronan, Patrick	Pvt	K 1st SCVIG	N. Anna River, VA	05/23/64	Port Royal, VA	05/30/64	Pt. Lookout, MD	SA1,CSR
					Pt. Lookout, MD	06/24/65	Rlsd. G.O. #109	P7,P117,P122,P123
Crook, J.	Pvt	C 3rd SCVABn	Blakely, AL	04/09/65	Ship Island, MS	05/01/65	Vicksburg, MS Xchg	P136,CSR
Crook, Jacob W.	Cpl	H 11th SCVI	Town Creek, NC	02/20/65	Ft. Anderson, NC	02/28/65	Pt. Lookout MD	CSR
					Pt. Lookout, MD	06/26/65	Rlsd. G.O. #109	P118,P122,P123,CSR
Crook, Wiley	Pvt	D 6th SCVI	Burkeville, VA	04/14/65	Burkesville, VA	04/17/65	Paroled	CSR

SOUTH CAROLINA SOLDIERS, SAILORS AND  CITIZENS HELD IN U.S. PRISONS 1861-1865

NAME	RANK	REGIMENT	CAPTURED AT	WHEN	PRISON	MOVED	DISPOSITION	SOURCES
Crooks, John A.B.	Pvt	B 3rd SCVI	Gettysburg, PA	07/03/63	Ft. Delaware, DE	06/18/65	Released	P42,P47,H3,KEB,SA2
Crooks, T.W.	Pvt	C 4th SCVC	Pocotaligo, SC	11/28/63	Hilton Head, SC	01/13/64	Ft. Columbus, NY	CSR
					Ft. Columbus, NY	04/10/64	Ft. McHenry, MD	CSR
					Ft. McHenry, MD	07/21/64	Pt. Lookout, MD	P96,P144,CSR
					Pt. Lookout, MD	02/11/65	Coxes Ldg., VA Xc	P113,P117,CSR
Crosby, Abraham	Pvt	I 11th SCVI	Petersburg, VA	06/24/64	Bermuda Hundred, VA	06/25/64	Fts. Monroe, VA	CSR
					Fts. Monroe, VA	06/26/64	Pt. Lookout, MD	CSR
					Pt. Lookout, MD	08/11/64	Elmira, NY	P113,P117,P120,P121,HAG
					Elmira, NY	10/11/64	Pt. Lookout, MD Xc	P65,HAG
					Pt. Lookout, MD	10/29/64	Aikens Ldg., VA Xc	P114,P118
					Pt. Lookout, MD	10/29/64	Venus Pt., GA Xchg	CSR
					Venus Pt., GA Xchg	11/15/64	Exchanged	CSR
Crosby, Alexander W.	Sgt	E 11th SCVI	Petersburg, VA	06/16/64	Bermuda Hundred, VA	06/17/64	Fts. Monroe, VA	CSR
					Fts. Monroe, VA	06/18/64	Pt. Lookout, MD	CSR
					Pt. Lookout, MD	07/25/64	Elmira, NY	P117,P120,HAG,CSR
					Elmira, NY	03/10/65	Aikens Ldg., VA Xc	P65,HAG
Crosby, Daniel	Pvt	F 11th SCVI	Drury's Bluff, VA	05/16/64	Fts. Monroe, VA	05/24/64	Died of wounds	P12,ROH,PP
Crosby, Dennis F.	Pvt	I 6th SCVI	Deep Bottom, VA	09/30/64	Fts. Monroe, VA	01/13/65	Pt. Lookout, MD	CSR,HHC
					Pt. Lookout, MD	02/10/65	Aikens Ldg., VA Xc	P118,P123,P124,CSR
					Gordonsville, VA H	03/27/65	Rcd. no discharge	CSR
					Burkeville, VA H.	04/14/65	Paroled	CSR
Crosby, E.	Pvt	7th SCVI	Deserted/enemy		Savannah, GA		Fts. Monroe, VA	CSR
Crosby, E.	Pvt	F 11th SCVI	Deserted/enemy		Fts Monroe, VA	04/02/65	Washington, DC	CSR
Crosby, E.	Pvt	7th SCVI	Deserted/enemy		Washington, DC PM	04/05/65	Savannah, GA, oath	CSR
Crosby, George	1Lt	D 15th SCVI	Cedar Creek, VA	10/19/64	Harpers Ferry, WV	10/25/64	Ft. Delaware, DE	P45,P46,HIC,CSR
					Ft. Delaware, DE	06/17/65	Rlsd. G.O. #109	CSR
Crosby, J.A.	Pvt	K 11th SCVI	Town Creek, NC	02/20/65	Ft. Anderson, NC	02/28/65	Pt. Lookout, MD	CSR
					Pt. Lookout, MD	06/26/65	Rlsd. G.O. #109	P118,P122,P123,CSR
Crosby, Jacob C.	Pvt	E 24th SCVI	Marietta, GA	07/02/64	Nashville, TN	07/12/64	Louisville, KY	CSR
					Louisville, KY	07/13/64	Camp Morton, IN	P91,P94,COT
					Camp Morton, IN	05/18/65	Released on oath	P100
Crosby, James B.	Pvt	K 11th SCVI	Town Creek, NC	02/20/65	Ft. Anderson, NC	02/26/65	Pt. Lookout, MD	CSR
					Pt. Lookout, MD	06/26/65	Rlsd. G.O. #109	P114,P122,P123,CSR
Crosby, James D.	Pvt	K 11th SCVI	Town Creek, NC	02/20/65	Ft. Anderson, NC	02/28/65	Pt. Lookout, MD	CSR
					Pt. Lookout, MD	06/26/65	Rlsd. G.O. #109	P118,P122,P123
Crosby, John Daniel	Pvt	I 11th SCVI	Drury's Bluff, VA	05/16/64	Camp Hamilton, VA	05/25/64	Old Capitol, DC	CSR
					Old Capitol, DC	12/16/64	Elmira, NY	P110,HAG,CSR
					Elmira, NY	03/14/65	Boulwares Wh., VA	P65,CSR
Crosby, Richard L.	Pvt	H 1st SCVIG	Gettysburg, PA	07/05/63	Ft. McHenry, MD	07/30/63	Ft. Delaware, DE	CSR,SA1
					Ft. Delaware, DE	07/30/63	City Pt., VA Xchg.	P40,P42,P44,CSR
Crosby, Thomas Eli	Pvt	F 10th SCVI	Danville, KY	10/10/62	Louisville, KY	11/29/62	Vicksburg, MS Xchg	P88,RAS,CSR
Crosby, William	2Lt	E 5th SCVI	Shell Mound, TN	11/02/63	Bridgeport, AL Hos	11/05/63	Nashville, TN	P2,SA3,YEB,CSR
					Nashville, TN	12/13/63	Died, of wounds	CSR,P6,P12
Crosland, J.S.	Sgt	A 23rd SCVI	Five Forks, VA	04/01/65	City Pt., VA	04/05/65	Pt. Lookout, MD	CSR
					Pt. Lookout, MD	06/26/65	Rlsd. G.O. #109	P114,P118,P123,CSR
Crossland, Abraham	Pvt	E 15th SCVI	Gettysburg, PA	07/04/63	Letterman G.H. Gbg	09/16/63	Baltimore, MD G.H.	P1,P4,KEB,CSR
					W. Bldg. Balt, MD	09/25/63	City Pt., VA Xchg.	CSR
Crossland, J.D.	Pvt	C 12th SCVI	Sutherland Stn. VA	04/03/65	City Pt., VA	04/07/65	Hart's Island, NY	CSR
					Hart's Island, NY	06/16/65	Rlsd. G.O. #109	P79,CSR
Crossland, Samuel Y.	Pvt	C 12th SCVI	Shepherdstown, WV	09/19/63	Frederick, MD USGH	10/16/62	Ft. McHenry, MD GH	CSR
					Ft. McHenry, MD	10/18/62	Fts. Monroe, VA Xc	CSR

SOUTH CAROLINA SOLDIERS, SAILORS AND CITIZENS HELD IN U.S. PRISONS 1861-1865

C

NAME	RANK	REGIMENT	CAPTURED AT	WHEN	PRISON	MOVED	DISPOSITION	SOURCES
Crossland, Samuel Y.	Pvt	C 12th SCVI	Sutherland Stn. VA	04/03/65	City Pt., VA	04/07/65	Hart's Island, NY	CSR
					Hart's Island, NY	06/16/65	Rlsd. G.O. #109	P79,CSR
Crossland, William D.	Pvt	A Hol.Leg.	12 Mile Rd., VA	02/18/64	Pt. Lookout, MD	02/10/65	Aikens Ldg., VA Xc	P113,P116,P124
Crosson, H.S.N.	Pvt	C 3rd SCVI	Wilderness, VA	05/06/64	Belle Plain, VA	05/21/64	Ft. Delaware, DE	CSR,SA2,H3,KEB
					Ft. Delaware, DE	12/10/64	Hos 12/10/64-1/21/	P47
					Ft. Delaware, DE	04/08/65	Hos 4/8-4/20/65	P47
					Ft. Delaware, DE	06/08/65	Rlsd. G.O. #109	P41,P43,P45,CSR
Crosswell, A.L.	Pvt	K 25th SCVI	Ft. Fisher, NC	01/15/65	Pt. Lookout, MD	06/04/65	Rlsd.Instr. 5/30/65	P114,P121
Crosswell, David O.	Pvt	E 3rd SCVABn	Raleigh, NC Hos.	04/13/65	Not given			CSR
Croswell, William K.	Pvt	Palmetto LA	Richmond, VA	04/06/65	Libby Prison Rchmd	04/10/65	City Pt., VA	CSR
					City Pt., VA		Pt. Lookout, MD	CSR
					Pt. Lookout, MD	06/26/65	Rlsd. G.O. #109	P119,P123,CSR
Crotwell, John	Pvt	C 1st SCVA	Smith's Ford, NC	03/16/65	New Berne, NC	04/03/65	Pt. Lookout, MD	CSR
					Pt. Lookout, MD	06/28/65	Rlsd. G.O. #109	P114,P118,CSR
Crouch, Jacob W.	Pvt	B 14th SCVI	Deep Bottom, VA	08/14/64	Bermuda Hundred, VA	08/15/64	Fts. Monroe, VA	CSR
					Fts. Monroe, VA	08/16/64	Pt. Lookout, MD	P123,CSR
					Pt. Lookout, MD	10/11/64	Aikens Ldg., VA Xc	P117,P125,CSR
Crouch, R.H.	Pvt	E 22nd SCVI	Farmville, VA	04/11/65	Farmville, VA	04/21/65	Paroled	CSR
Crouch, T.B.	Pvt	E 7th SCVI	Sharpsburg, MD	08/02/62	Ft. McHenry, MD	10/14/62	Aikens Ldg., VA Xc	CNM,CSR
Crouch, Willis	Pvt	E 7th SCVI	Urbana, VA	09/26/62	Ft. McHenry, MD	10/17/62	Fts. Monroe, VA	CSR
					Fts. Monroe, VA	10/19/62	Aikens Ldg., VA Xc	CNM,CSR
Crouder, William	Pvt	A 15th SCVAB	Smith's Ford, NC	03/16/65	New Berne, NC	03/16/65	Hart's Island, NY	CSR
					Hart's Island, NY	05/11/65	Died, Pneumonia	P6,P10,P79,FPH,CSR
Crout, Wesley	Pvt	K 20th SCVI	Cedar Creek, VA	10/19/64	Pt. Lookout, MD	06/26/65	Rlsd. G.O. #109	P118,P122,P123,KEB
Crow, Francis M.	Pvt	G 12th SCVI	Appomattox R., VA	04/03/65	City Pt., VA	04/11/65	Hart's Island, NY	CSR
					Hart's Island, NY	06/16/65	Rlsd. G.O. #109	P79,CSR
Crow, H.B.	Pvt	F 1st SCVC	Upperville, VA	06/21/63	Ft. McHenry, MD	06/25/63	City Pt., VA Xc	P110,CSR
Crow, Milton P.	Pvt	F 17th SCVI	Five Forks, VA	04/01/65	City Pt., VA	04/05/65	Pt. Lookout, MD	CSR
					Pt. Lookout, MD	06/26/65	Rlsd. G.O. #109	P118,P122,P123,CSR
Crowder, T.A.	Pvt	B 17th SCVI	Richmond, VA Hos.	04/03/65	Richmond, VA Hos.	04/28/65	Paroled	CSR
Crowder, William J.	Pvt	B 17th SCVI	Petersburg, VA	03/25/65	City Pt., VA	03/28/65	Pt. Lookout, MD	CSR,HFC
					Pt. Lookout, MD	06/26/65	Rlsd. G.O. #109	P118,P122,P123
Crowley, Alexander L.	Pvt	E 6th SCVI	Fair Oaks, VA	06/01/62	Fts. Monroe, VA	06/05/62	Ft. Delaware, DE	CSR
					Ft. Delaware, DE		Tfd. for exchange	CSR
					Richmond, VA Hos.	10/14/62	Furloughed 30 days	CSR
Croxton, John Q.	Pvt	G 2nd SCVI	Gettysburg, PA	07/05/63	Letterman G.H. Gbg	07/20/63	Died, thigh wound	P1,KEB,SA2,H2,CSR
Crumby, John	Pvt	C 14th SCVI	Appomattox R., VA	04/03/65	City Pt., VA	04/11/65	Hart's Island, NY	CSR
					Hart's Island, NY	06/21/65	Rlsd. G.O. #109	P79,CSR
Crumpton, A.P.	Pvt	F Ham.Leg.	Warrenton, VA	09/29/62	Warrenton, VA	09/29/62	Paroled	CSR
Crumpton, F.M.	Pvt	A 3rd SCVABn	High Pt., NC	05/02/65	High Pt., NC	05/02/65	Paroled on oath	CSR
Cruzdel Cano, Joseph		P. *Savannah*	Off Charleston	06/03/61	Tombs Prison, NY	02/15/62	Ft. Lafayette, NY	OR,TCP
					Ft. Lafayette, NY	06/06/62	City Pt., VA Xc	OR,TCP,CDC
Cryan, Dominick	Ldm	CS Navy	Harpers Farm, VA	04/06/65	Pt. Lookout, MD	06/26/65	Rlsd. G.O #109	P123
Cudd, J.P.	Pvt	E 13th SCVI	Spotsylvania, VA	05/12/64	Belle Plain, VA	05/21/64	Ft. Delaware, DE	CSR
					Ft. Delaware, DE	08/08/64	Hos 8/8-9/18/64	P47
					Ft. Delaware, DE	09/18/64	Aikens Ldg., VA Xc	P41,P43,HOS,CSR
Cudworth, A.	Pvt	A 25th SCVI	Ft. Fisher, NC	01/15/65	New York, NY	01/30/65	Elmira, NY	CSR
					Elmira, NY	06/16/65	Rlsd. G.O. #109	P65,P66,HAG
Cudworth, Arthur G.	2Lt	I 27th SCVI	Town Creek, NC	02/20/65	Ft. Anderson, NC	02/28/65	Pt. Lookout, MD	CSR,HAG
					Pt. Lookout, MD	02/28/65	Washington, DC	P114,P120,CSR
					Old Capitol, DC	03/24/65	Ft. Delaware, DE	P110,CSR
					Ft. Delaware, DE	06/17/65	Rlsd. G.O. #109	P43,P45,CSR

C

SOUTH CAROLINA SOLDIERS, SAILORS AND CITIZENS HELD IN U.S. PRISONS 1861-1865

NAME	RANK	REGIMENT	CAPTURED AT	WHEN	PRISON	MOVED	DISPOSITION	SOURCES
Culbertson, A.	Pvt	C 14th SCVI	Farmville, VA	04/23/65	Farmville, VA		Paroled	CSR
Culbertson, George W.	Cpt	C 14th SCVI	Appomattox R., VA	04/03/65	Old Capitol, DC	04/19/65	Johnson's Isl., OH	P110,CSR
					Johnson's Isl., OH	06/18/65	Rlsd. G.O. #109	CSR
Culclasure, D.	Pvt	H Ham.Leg.	Frederick, MD	09/12/62	Ft. Delaware, DE	11/10/62	Aikens Ldg., VA Xc	CSR
Culclasure, J.F.	Pvt	H Ham.Leg.	Frederick, MD	09/12/62	Ft. Delaware, DE	11/10/62	Aikens Ldg., VA Xc	CSR
Culclasure, N.W.	Pvt	B 20th SCVI	Cedar Creek, VA	10/19/64	Harpers Ferry, WV	10/23/64	Pt. Lookout, MD	KEB,CSR
					Pt. Lookout, MD	03/17/65	Exchanged	P118,P123,P124,CSR
Culler, J.H.	Pvt	D 20th SCVI	Cedar Creek, VA	10/19/64	Harpers Ferry, WV	10/24/64	Pt. Lookout, MD	CSR
					Pt. Lookout, MD	03/17/65	Aikens Ldg., VA Xc	P118,P123,P124,CSR
Culler, L.H.	Sgt	G 25th SCVI	Town Creek, NC	02/20/65	Ft. Anderson, NC	02/28/65	Pt. Lookout, MD	CSR
					Pt. Lookout, MD	06/24/65	Rlsd. G.O. #109	P114,P118,HAG
Culleton, Patrick	Cpl	H 27th SCVI	Weldon RR, VA	08/21/64	City Pt., VA	08/24/64	Pt. Lookout, MD	CSR,HAG
					Pt. Lookout, MD	10/11/64	Aikens Ldg., VA Xc	P117,P123,P125,CSR
Cullum, William	Pvt	A 19th SCVI	Nashville, TN	12/15/64	Nashville, TN	01/17/65	Louisville, KY	P4,HOE,CSR
					Louisville, KY	01/18/65	Camp Chase, OH	P39,P92,P95,CSR
					Camp Chase, OH	02/15/65	Died, Pneumonia	P6,P12,P23,P27,FPH
Culp, James M.	Pvt	B 6th SCVI	Boonesboro, MD	09/15/62	Ft. Delaware, DE	10/02/62	Aikens Ldg., VA Xc	CSR
Culp, James M.	Pvt	B 6th SCVI	Charlotte, NC	05/20/65	Charlotte, NC	05/20/65	Paroled	CSR
Culp, John Ripley	LtC	17th SCVI	Five Forks, VA	04/01/65	City Pt., VA	04/05/65	Washington, DC	CSR
					Old Capitol, DC	04/09/65	Johnson's Isl., OH	CSR
					Johnson's Isl., OH	07/25/65	Released	P81,P83,LC,HHC,CSR
Culp, Joseph H.	Pvt	A 17th SCVI	Warrenton, VA	09/29/62	Warrenton, VA	09/29/62	Paroled	CSR
Culp, L.N.	Sgt	I 17th SCVI	Charlotte, NC	05/03/65	Charlotte, NC	05/03/65	Paroled	CSR
Culp, Minor M.	1Lt	I 17th SCVI	Petersburg, VA	03/25/65	City Pt., VA	03/26/65	Washington, DC	CSR
					Old Capitol, DC	03/30/65	Ft. Delaware, DE	CSR
					Ft. Delaware, DE	06/17/65	Rlsd. G.O. #109	P43,P45,LAN,CSR
Culp, Robert N.	Pvt	B 4th SCVC	Cold Harbour, VA	05/28/64	3rd Div. 5th A.C.	05/05/64	Washington, DC	CSR
					Lincoln G.H., DC	07/14/64	Old Capitol, DC	CSR
					Old Capitol, DC	07/23/64	Elmira, NY	P110,CSR
					Elmira, NY	10/11/64	Pt.Lookout to Xchg	P65,CSR
					Pt. Lookout, MD	10/29/64	Aikens Ldg., VA Xc	P114,P118,P123,CSR
Culp, Robert N.	Pvt	B 4th SCVC	Chester, SC	05/05/65	Chester, SC	05/05/65	Paroled	CSR
Culpepper, James F.	Cpt	C 3rd SCVABn	Ft. Gaines, AL	08/08/64	New Orleans, LA	11/25/64	Ship Island, MS	P3,CSR
					Ship Island, MS	01/04/65	Exchanged	P136,CSR
Culpepper, James F.	Cpt	C 3rd SCVABn	Blakely, AL	04/09/65	Ship Island, MS	04/28/65	Vicksburg, MS Xc	P3,CSR
Cumbee, Pinckney	Pvt	D 23rd SCVI	Five Forks, VA	04/01/65	City Pt., VA	04/05/65	Pt. Lookout, MD	CSR
					Pt. Lookout, MD	06/26/65	Rlsd. G.O. #109	P118,P122,P123,CSR
Cumbee, William	Pvt	D 23rd SCVI	Petersburg, VA	03/25/65	Washington, DC	03/30/65	Pt. Lookout, MD	CSR
					Pt. Lookout, MD	05/13/65	Rlsd. G.O. #85	P122,CSR
Cumbie, Daniel C.	Cpl	A 21st SCVI	Weldon RR, VA	08/21/64	Pt. Lookout, MD	01/27/65	Aikens Ldg., VA Xc	P117,P123,P124,HAG
Cumbie, Elias	Pvt	A 21st SCVI	Weldon RR, VA	08/21/64	Pt. Lookout, MD	06/05/65	Rlsd.Instr.5/30/65	P117,P122,P125,HAG
Cummerford, William	Pvt	F 1st SCVIR	Deserted/enemy	03/15/65	Charleston, SC	03/15/65	Released on oath	CSR
Cummings, Columbus C.	Pvt	E 20th SCVI	Salisbury, NC	04/12/65	Nashville, TN	04/29/65	Louisville, KY	P39,CSR
					Louisville, KY	05/01/65	Camp Chase, OH	P92,CSR
Cummings, Columbus C.	Pvt	E 20th SCVI	Salisbury, NC	04/12/65	Camp Chase, OH	06/13/65	Rlsd. G.O. #109	P23,KEB,CSR
Cummings, Elisha	Pvt	I 1st SCVIR	Morris Island, SC	07/10/63	Hilton Head, SC	09/19/63	Ft. Columbus, NY	CSR
					Ft. Columbus, NY	09/23/63	has taken oath	P1,CSR
Cummings, Henry A.	Pvt	E 20th SCVI	Salisbury, NC	04/12/65	Nashville, TN	04/29/65	Louisville, KY	P39,KEB,CSR
					Louisville, KY	05/01/65	Camp Chase, OH	P92,CSR
					Camp Chase, OH	06/13/65	Rlsd. G.O. #109	P23,CSR
Cummings, John	Pvt	K 11th SCVI	Town Creek, NC	02/20/65	Ft. Anderson, NC	02/28/65	Pt. Lookout, MD	CSR
					Pt. Lookout, MD	06/26/65	Rlsd. G.O. #109	P118,P122,P123,CSR

C

SOUTH CAROLINA SOLDIERS, SAILORS AND CITIZENS HELD IN U.S. PRISONS 1861-1865

NAME	RANK	REGIMENT	CAPTURED AT	WHEN	PRISON	MOVED	DISPOSITION	SOURCES
Cummings, Patrick	Pvt	E 1st SCVIR	Deserted/enemy	09/18/64	Hilton Head, SC	10/03/64	Work @ QM on oath	SA1,CSR
Cummings, Robert	Pvt	E 1st SCVIR	Deserted/enemy	09/01/64	Hilton Head, SC	09/03/64	Work @ QM oath	CSR
Cummings, William	Pvt	K 11th SCVI	Town Creek, NC	02/20/65	Ft. Anderson, NC	02/28/65	Pt. Lookout, MD	CSR,HAG
					Pt. Lookout, MD	06/26/65	Rlsd. G.O. #109	P118,P122,P123,CSR
Cunningham, Henry M.	Pvt	K 3rd SCVI	N. Anna River, VA	05/23/64	Port Royal, VA	05/30/64	Pt. Lookout, MD	CSR,H3,KEB
					Pt. Lookout, MD	01/08/65	Died, Lung Infl.	P6,P12,P117,P119,CSR
Cunningham, John	Cit	Charleston	SS *Brittania*	06/24/63	Ft. Lafayette, NY	09/04/63	Ft. Warren, MS	P144
Cunningham, S.D.	Pvt	F 22nd SCVI	Deserted/Enemy	02/25/65	City Pt., VA	02/28/65	Washington, DC	CSR
					Washington, DC	03/01/65	Hilton Head, SC	CSR
Cureton, Abner H.	Pvt	B 2nd SCVI	Russellville, TN	04/18/64	Knoxville, TN	05/24/64	Chattanooga, TN	CSR,KEB,H2
					Chattanooga, TN	05/31/64	Louisville, KY	CSR
					Nashville, TN	05/31/64	Louisville, KY	P3,CSR
					Louisville, KY	06/04/64	Rock Island, IL	P90,P91,P94,CSR
					Rock Island, IL	02/25/65	Pt.Lookout, MD Xc	P131,CSR
					Pt. Lookout, MD	03/05/65	Boulwares Wh., VA	CSR
Cureton, Everard B.	Pvt	A 2nd SCVC	Martinsburg, WV	07/17/63	Wheeling, WV	07/22/63	Camp Chase, OH	P1,CSR
					Camp Chase, OH	02/29/64	Ft. Delaware, DE	P22,P25,P26,CSR
					Ft. Delaware, DE	06/10/65	Rlsd. G.O. #109	P41,P42,P45,CSR
Cureton, J.D.	Cpt	G 6th SCVI	Boonesboro, MD	09/15/62	Baltimore, MD	10/11/62	Aikens Ldg., VA Xc	CSR
					Fts. Monroe, VA	10/12/62	Aikens Ldg., VA Xc	CSR
Cureton, Thomas J.	Cpl	F Ham.Leg.MI	Amelia C.H., VA	04/06/65	City Pt., VA	04/14/65	Pt. Lookout, MD	CSR
					Pt. Lookout, MD	06/24/65	Rlsd. G.O. #109	P114,P121,CSR
Curran, John	Pvt	K 1st SCVIG	Mechanics Town, PA	07/04/63	Ft. McHenry, MD	07/12/63	Ft. Delaware, MD	P96,SA1,CSR
					Ft. Delaware, DE	09/15/63	Jd. US 3rd MD Cav.	P42,CSR
Currence, D.A.	Pvt	F 17th SCVI	Five Forks, VA	04/01/65	City Pt., VA	04/05/65	Pt. Lookout, MD	CSR
					Pt. Lookout, MD	05/08/65	Died, Dysentery	P6,P118,FPH,CS
Currie, Neal R.	Pvt	F 21st SCVI	Ft. Fisher, NC	01/15/65	Elmira, NY	05/14/65	Died, Pneumonia	P6,P65,HAG
Curry, George W.	Pvt	6 10/19 SCVI	Missionary Ridge, TN	11/25/63	Nashville, TN	12/07/63	Louisville, KY	CSR
					Louisville, KY	12/09/63	Rock Island, IL	P89,RAS,CSR
Curry, H.L.	Pvt	G 3rd SCVIBn	Frederick, MD	09/19/62	Alexandria, VA G.H.	10/04/62	Old Capitol, DC	CSR
					Old Capitol, DC	10/31/62	Fts. Monroe, VA	CSR
					Fts. Monroe, VA	11/02/62	Aikens Ldg., VA Xc	CSR
Curry, John C.	Pvt	D 21st SCVI	Petersburg, VA	08/21/64	City Pt., VA	08/29/64	Died of wounds	P12,CSR
Curry, John D.	Pvt	D 17th SCVI	Five Forks, VA	04/01/65	City Pt., VA	04/06/65	Pt. Lookout, MD	CSR
					Pt. Lookout, MD	06/26/65	Rlsd. G.O. #109	P118,P122,P123,CSR
Curry, Joseph H.	Pvt	D 17th SCVI	Petersburg, VA	07/30/64	City Pt., VA	08/05/64	Pt. Lookout, MD	CSR,HHC
					Pt. Lookout, MD	08/08/64	Elmira, NY	P113,P117,P120,CSR
					Elmira, NY	07/07/65	Rlsd. G.O. #109	P65,CSR
Curry, Martin Y.	Pvt	A 6th SCVC	Stony Creek, VA	12/01/64	City Pt., VA	12/04/64	Pt. Lookout, MD	CSR
					Pt. Lookout, MD	06/26/65	Rlsd. G.O. #109	P114,P122,P123,CSR
Curry, N.B.	Pvt	A 6th SCVC	Stony Creek, VA	12/01/64	City Pt., VA	12/04/64	Pt. Lookout, MD	CSR
					Pt. Lookout, MD	06/26/65	Rlsd. G.O. #109	P118,P122,P123,CSR
Curry, Robert.H.	Cpl	F 12th SCVI	Spotsylvania, VA	05/12/64	Belle Plain, VA	05/20/64	Ft. Delaware, DE	CSR
					Ft. Delaware, DE	01/20/65	Fts. Monroe, VA Xc	P41,P43,HFC,CSR
					Fts. Monroe, VA	02/02/65	Truce Stmr, Xc	CSR
Curry, William D.	Pvt	G 2nd SCVC	Gloucester Co., VA	01/29/64	Yorktown, VA	02/03/64	Fts. Monroe, VA	CSR
					Fts. Monroe, VA	02/05/64	Ft. Norfolk, VA	CSR
					Ft. Norfolk, VA	02/27/64	Pt. Lookout, MD	CSR
					Pt. Lookout, MD	03/15/65	Aikens Ldg. Xc	P116,P123,P124,CSR
Curtin, John	Pvt	C 1st SCVIH	Deserted/enemy	03/26/65	Washington, DC P.M	03/30/65	New York, on oath	CSR
Curtis, George H.	Pvt	K 1st SCVIH	Frederick, MD	09/12/62	Frederick, MD P.M.	11/05/62	Aikens Ldg., VA Xc	CSR
Curtis, James M.	Pvt	H Ham.Leg.	Deserted/ Enemy	01/15/64	Louisville, KY	01/16/64	Sent North on oath	CSR

SOUTH CAROLINA SOLDIERS, SAILORS AND  CITIZENS HELD IN U.S. PRISONS 1861-1865

NAME	RANK	REGIMENT	CAPTURED AT	WHEN	PRISON	MOVED	DISPOSITION	SOURCES
Curtiss, John	Pvt	H 1st SCVA	Bentonville, NC	03/22/65	Hart's Island, NY	06/18/65	Rlsd. G.O. #109	P79,CSR
Cusack, Joseph B.	Pvt	H Orr's Ri.	Deserted/enemy	03/22/65	City Pt., VA	03/23/65	Washington D.C.	CSR
Cussack, S.O.	Sgt	I 8th SCVI	Winchester, VA	09/13/64	Harpers Ferry, WV	09/19/64	Camp Chase, OH	KEB,CSR
					Camp Chase, OH	05/02/65	New Orleans, LA	P23,P26,KEB,CSR
					New Orleans, LA	05/12/65	Vicksburg, MS Xc	CSR
Cushman, Jackson	Pvt	D 6th SCVI	Deserted/enemy	03/20/65	Bermuda Hundred, VA	03/20/65	City Pt., VA P.M.	CSR
					City Pt., VA P.M.	03/24/65	Washington, DC P.M	CSR
					Washington, DC P.M	03/25/65	Pittsburg, PA/oath	CSR
Cushman, James	Cpl	Mathewes LA	Augusta, GA	05/22/65	Augusta, GA	05/22/65	Paroled	CSR
Cusick, Patrick	Pvt	E 2nd SCVI	Cedar Creek, VA	10/19/64	Harpers Ferry, WV	10/23/64	Pt. Lookout, MD	CSR,SA2,H2,KEB
					Pt. Lookout, MD	03/28/65	Aikens Ldg., VA Xc	CSR
					Pt. Lookout, MD	03/28/65	Exchanged	P114,P118,P124
Cuthbert, T.F.	Pvt	Beaufort LA	Augusta, GA	05/20/65	Augusta, GA	05/20/65	Paroled	CSR
Cutt, Henry	Pvt	H 2nd SCVC	Martinsburg, WV	07/17/63	Wheeling, VA	07/22/63	Camp Chase	P1
					Camp Chase, OH	09/20/63	Escaped	P22,P25
Cutter, J.F.	Pvt	C Ham.Leg.MI	Richmond, VA Hos	04/03/65	Libby Prsn. Rchmd.	04/23/65	Newport News, VA	CSR
					Newport News, VA	06/15/65	Rlsd. G.O. #109	CSR
Cuttino, William H.	Pvt	C Ham.Leg.MI	Chester, SC G.H.	05/05/65	Chester, SC	05/05/65	Paroled	FLR,CSR
Cylvanus, Joseph	Pvt	H 1st SCVA	Deserted/enemy	03/21/65	Charleston, SC	04/01/65	Taken oath & disch	CSR

SOUTH CAROLINA SOLDIERS, SAILORS AND  CITIZENS HELD IN U.S. PRISONS 1861-1865

NAME	RANK	REGIMENT	CAPTURED AT	WHEN	PRISON	MOVED	DISPOSITION	SOURCES
Dalrymple, David	Pvt	A 13th SCVI	Falling Waters, MD	07/14/63	Frederick, MD G.H.	10/10/63	Baltimore, MD USGH	CSR
					W. Bldg. Balt., MD	11/12/63	City Pt., VA Xc	P1,CSR
Dalrymple, J.	Pvt	14th SCVI	Fredericksburg, VA	05/03/63	Ft. McHenry, MD	05/11/63	City Pt., VA Xc	P110
Dalrymple, John R.	Pvt	B 3rd SCVI	Knoxvillle, TN	12/05/63	Nashville, TN	02/28/64	Louisville, KY	P39,KEB,H3,ANY,CSR
					Louisville, KY	02/29/64	Ft. Delaware, DE	P88,P91,P93,CSR
					Ft. Delaware, DE	03/03/64	Hos. 3/5-6/3/64	P47,KEB
					Ft. Delaware, DE	09/18/64	Aikens Ldg., VA Xc	P41,P42,CSR
					Richmond, VA Hos.	09/25/64	Furloughed 30 days	CSR
Dalrymple, W.J.	Pvt	E 20th SCVI	Lexington Dist., SC	02/14/65	Hart's Island, NY	04/16/65	Released	P79,KEB
Dalton, Amos H.	Pvt	A Ham.Leg.	Chattanooga, TN	10/29/63	Nashville, TN		Louisville, KY	P39,CSR
					Louisville, KY	11/09/63	Camp Morton, IN	P89,P93,CSR
					Camp Morton, IN	03/23/64	Died	P100,P12,CSR
Dalton, Andrew J.	Cpl	F Orr's Ri.	Petersburg, VA	04/03/65	City Pt., VA	04/11/65	Hart's Island, NY	CSR
					Hart's Island, NY	06/16/65	Rlsd. G.O. #109	P79,CSR
Dalton, J.T.	Pvt	I 2nd SCVI	Harpers Ferry, WV	09/14/62	Sandy Hook, MD	09/22/62	Ft. McHenry, MD	CSR
					Ft. McHenry, MD	10/25/62	Aikens Ldg., VA Xc	SA2,CSR
Daly, J.R.	Pvt	A 2nd SCVC	Catlett's Stn., VA	03/30/63	Ft. McHenry, MD	04/13/63	City Pt., VA Xc	P110
Daly, Patrick		P. *Savannah*	Off Charleston	06/03/01	Tomb's Prison, NY	02/15/62	Ft. Lafayette, NY	OR,TCP
					Ft. Lafayette, NY	06/06/62	City Pt., VA Xc	OR,TCP
Daly, Thomas	Pvt	C 27th SCVI	Deserted/enemy	05/31/64	Bermuda Hundred, VA	06/01/64	Fts. Monroe, VA	CSR,HAG
					Fts. Monroe, VA	06/06/64	Released to Canada	CSR
Damp, Charles	Pvt	A German LA	Deserted/enemy	02/18/65	Charleston, SC	03/14/65	Released on oath	CSR
Dandey, Daniel L.	Pvt	H Ham.Leg.MI	Richmond, VA	04/03/65	Pt. Lookout, MD	06/26/65	Rlsd. G.O. #109	P114,P122
Dangerfield, Richard	Sgt	C 27th SCVI	Weldon RR, VA	08/21/64	City Pt., VA	08/28/64	Washington, DC	P1,HAG,CSR
					Old Capitol, DC	12/13/64	Ft. Delaware, DE	CSR
					Ft. McHenry, MD	12/15/64	Ft. Delaware, DE	P110,HAG
					Ft. Delaware, DE		Hos. 1/14-2/22/65	P47,HAG
					Ft. Delaware, DE	02/27/65	City Pt., VA Xc	P7,P42,HAG,CSR
Dangerfield, Thomas	Pvt	D 1st SCVIR	Deserted/enemy	03/31/65	Charleston, SC		Released on oath	SA1,CSR
Dangham, Lewis	Pvt	D 27th SCVI	Town Creek, NC	02/20/65	Ft. Anderson, NC	02/28/65	Pt. Lookout, MD	CSR
					Pt. Lookout, MD		No release data	P114,P118,CSR
Daniel, Dendy	Sgt	C Hol.Leg.C	Ridgeley's Shoals		W. Bldg. Balt., MD	10/14/64	Died	ANY,CSR
Daniel, Isham H.	Pvt	C Hol.Leg.	Five Forks, VA	04/01/65	City Pt., VA	04/05/65	Pt. Lookout, MD	CSR,HOS
					Pt. Lookout, MD	06/09/65	Died, Diarrhea	P6,P114,FPH,P118
Daniel, J.F.	Cpl	F 13th SCVI	Deserted/enemy	02/24/65	City Pt., VA	02/26/65	Washington, DC	CSR
					Washington, DC	02/27/65	Springfield, IL	CSR
Daniel, Robert M.	Pvt	C 14th SCVI	Falling Waters, MD	07/14/64	Pt. Lookout, MD	08/16/64	Elmira, NY	P120
Daniels, Benjamin	Pvt	D 1st SCVA	Raleigh, NC Hos.	04/13/65	Raleigh, NC	04/13/65	Released on oath	CSR
Daniels, Calvin J.	Sgt	K 18th SCVI	Jackson, MS	07/12/63	Snyders Bluff, MS	07/30/63	Camp Morton, IN	CSR
					Camp Morton, IN	03/04/65	City Pt., VA Xc	P100,P101,CSR
Daniels, Edmund G.	Cpl	G 7th SCVIBn	Weldon RR, VA	08/21/64	City Pt., VA	08/24/64	Pt. Lookout, MD	CSR
					Pt. Lookout, MD	04/19/65	Died, Scurvy	P6,P113,FPH,CSR
Daniels, Ferdinand	Pvt	C 1st SCVA	Deserted/enemy	02/25/65	Charleston, SC		Released on oath	CSR
Daniels, George W.	Pvt	A Ham.Leg.	Frederick, MD	09/12/62	Ft. Delaware, DE	11/10/62	Aikens Ldg., VA Xc	CSR
Daniels, George W.	Sgt	A Ham.Leg.MI	Burkeville, VA	04/06/65	City Pt., VA	04/14/65	Pt. Lookout, MD	CSR
					Pt. Lookout, MD	06/26/65	Rlsd. G.O. #109	P114,P119,CSR
Daniels, Henry	Pvt	A Ham.Leg.MI	Burkeville, VA	04/06/65	City Pt., VA	04/14/65	Pt. Lookout, MD	CSR
					Pt. Lookout, MD	06/26/65	Rlsd. G.O. #109	P114, P122

SOUTH CAROLINA SOLDIERS, SAILORS AND  CITIZENS HELD IN U.S. PRISONS 1861-1865

NAME	RANK	REGIMENT	CAPTURED AT	WHEN	PRISON	MOVED	DISPOSITION	SOURCES
Daniels, John M.	2Lt	C Hol.Leg.	Dinwiddie C.H., VA	04/01/65	City Pt., VA	04/04/65	Old Capitol, DC	CSR
					Old Capitol, DC	04/09/65	Johnson's Isl., OH	P110
					Johnson's Isl., OH	06/19/65	Rlsd. G.O. #109	P81,P82,P83
Daniels, Julius A.	Pvt	L P.S.S.	Darbytown Rd., VA	12/12/64	Bermuda Hundred, VA	12/15/64	City Pt., VA	CSR
					City Pt., VA	12/18/64	Pt. Lookout, MD	CSR
					Pt. Lookout, MD	05/13/65	Rlsd. G.O. #85	P114,P117,TSE,CSR
Daniels, L.	Pvt	B 15th SCVI			Elmira, NY	04/14/65	Died	P12,FPH
Daniels, Thomas	Pvt	A Ham.Leg.MI	Deserted/enemy	01/23/65	Bermuda Hundred, VA	02/02/65	Washington, DC	CSR
					Washington, DC	02/04/65	Troy, NY on oath	CSR
Daniels, William D.	Pvt	B 10th SCVI	Chattahootchie, GA	07/05/64	Louisville, KY	07/13/64	Camp Morton, IN	P90,P91,P94,CSR
					Camp Morton, IN	02/26/65	City Pt., VA Xc	P100,P101,CSR
Danner, John M.	Pvt	I 27th SCVI	Town Creek, NC	02/20/65	Ft. Anderson, NC	02/28/65	Pt. Lookout, MD	CSR,HAG
					Pt. Lookout, MD	06/08/65	Rlsd. G.O. #85	P114,P118,CSR
Dantzler, Arthur P.	Pvt	F 25th SCVI	Ft. Fisher, NC	01/15/65	New York, NY	01/30/65	Elmira, NY	CSR,HAG
					Elmira, NY	07/10/65	Rlsd. G.O. #109	CSR
Dantzler, Benjamin M.	Sgt	F 25th SCVI	Ft. Fisher, NC	01/15/65	New York, NY	01/30/65	Elmira, NY	CSR
					Elmira, NY	02/20/65	Died, Diarrhea	P6,P65,P66,HAG
Dantzler, D.B.	Pvt	E 14th SCMil	Lynch's Creek, SC	03/01/65	Hart's Island, NY	06/16/65	Rlsd. G.O. #109	P79,CSR
Dantzler, D.Z.	Pvt	E 14th SCVI	Lynch's Creek, SC	03/01/65	New Berne, NC	04/10/65	Hart's Island, NY	CSR
					Hart's Island, NY	06/16/65	Rlsd. G.O. #109	CSR
Dantzler, David W.	Pvt	G 25th SCVI	Ft. Fisher, NC	01/15/65	New York, NY	01/30/65	Elmira, NY	CSR
					Elmira, NY	04/01/65	Died, Pneumonia	P6,P12,P65,P66,FPH
Dantzler, Edward L.	Cpl	F 25th SCVI	Weldon RR, VA	08/21/64	City Pt., VA	08/24/64	Pt. Lookout, MD	CSR,HAG
					Pt. Lookout, MD	03/14/65	Aikens Ldg., VA Xc	P113,P117,CSR
Dantzler, Frederick W.	Pvt	F 25th SCVI	Weldon RR, VA	08/21/64	City Pt., VA	08/24/64	Pt. Lookout, MD	CSR
					Pt. Lookout, MD	10/30/64	Aikens Ldg., VA Xc	P113,P117,P125,HAG
Dantzler, Frederick W.	Pvt	F 25th SCVI	Ft. Fisher, NC	01/15/65	New York, NY	01/30/65	Elmira, NY	CSR
					Elmira, NY	07/07/65	Camp Gen. Hospital	CSR
					Elmira, NY	11/26/65	Released on oath	CSR
Dantzler, Henry F.	Pvt	F 25th SCVI	Ft. Fisher, NC	01/15/65	New York, NY	01/30/65	Elmira, NY	CSR
					Elmira, NY	07/07/65	Rlsd. G.O. #109	P65,P66,HAG
Dantzler, Irvin P.	Pvt	F 25th SCVI	Town Creek, NC	02/20/65	Ft. Anderson, NC	02/28/65	Pt. Lookout, MD	CSR,HAG
					Pt. Lookout, MD	06/26/65	Rlsd. G.O. #109	P114,P118,P122,CSR
Dantzler, Jacob S.	Pvt	C 24th SCVI	Franklin, TN	12/17/64	Louisville, KY	12/20/64	Camp Douglas, IL	P90,P91,P94,EFW
					Nashville, TN	12/17/64	Louisville, KY	CSR
					Camp Douglas, IL	05/16/65	Released on oath	CSR
Dantzler, Lewis W.	Pvt	F 25th SCVI	Town Creek, NC	02/20/65	Ft. Anderson, NC	02/28/65	Pt. Lookout, MD	CSR,HAG
					Pt. Lookout, MD	06/26/65	Rlsd. G.O. #109	P114,P122,P123,CSR
Dantzler, Peter A.	Pvt	A 5th SCVC	Cheraw, SC	03/05/65	Cheraw, SC	03/05/65	Paroled	CSR
Dantzler, Samuel D	Pvt	B 1st SCVIH	Mossy Creek, TN	01/22/64	Nashville, TN	02/11/64	Louisville, KY	P39,SA1,CSR
					Louisville, KY	02/15/64	Rock Island, IL	P88,P91,P93,CSR
					Rock Island, IL	06/17/65	Rlsd. G.O. #109	P131,CSR
Dantzler, W.H.	Pvt	F 25th SCVI	Ft. Fisher, NC	01/15/65	Elmira, NY	07/07/65	Rlsd. G.O. #109	P65,HAG
Darby, James	Pvt	I 19th SCVI	Marietta, GA	10/13/64	Marietta, GA	10/13/64	Atlanta, GA USGH	CSR
					Chattanooga G.H.	11/28/64	Nashville, TN	CSR
					Nashville, TN	12/29/64	Died, Typhoid	P3,P6,P12,CSR
Darby, John T.	Pvt	F 23rd SCVI	Petersburg, VA	03/25/65	Pt. Lookout, MD	06/26/65	Rlsd. G.O. #109	P114,P118,P122,CSR
Darby, Joseph	Pvt	E Orr's Ri.	Southside RR, VA	04/02/65	City Pt., VA	04/07/65	Hart's Island, NY	CSR
					Hart's Island, NY	06/15/65	Rlsd. G.O. #109	P79,CSR
Dare, A.	Pvt	D 22nd SCVI	Petersburg, VA	04/03/65	Hart's Island, NY	06/21/65	Rlsd. G.O. #109	P79
Dargan, W.E.	Pvt	D 2nd SCVA	Saluda, SC	02/16/65	Hart's Island, NY	04/16/65	Released	P79

SOUTH CAROLINA SOLDIERS, SAILORS AND **D** CITIZENS HELD IN U.S. PRISONS 1861-1865

NAME	RANK	REGIMENT	CAPTURED AT	WHEN	PRISON	MOVED	DISPOSITION	SOURCES
Daring, John Thomas	Pvt	E 11th SCVI	Petersburg, VA	06/18/64	City Pt., VA	06/24/64	Pt. Lookout, MD	CSR,HAG
					Pt. Lookout, MD	07/27/64	Elmira, NY	P113,P117,P120
					Elmira, NY	05/20/65	Died, Diarrhea	P6,P65,FPH,CSR
Darkin, Edward	Pvt	E 22nd SCVI	Deserted/enemy	02/18/65	Hilton Head, SC	03/22/65	New York, NY oath	CSR
Darlington, Edward	Pvt	F 1st SCVA	Deserted/enemy	02/19/65	Charleston, SC		Released on oath	CSR
Darnold, John W.	Pvt	C Hol.Leg.C	Deserted/enemy	10/29/63				CSR
Darr, Henry	Pvt	A 14th SCVI	Staunton, VA	05/17/65	Staunton, VA	05/17/65	Paroled	CSR
Darwin, Elzy S.	Pvt	B 12th SCVI	Warrenton, VA	09/29/62	Warrenton, VA	09/29/62	Paroled	CSR,YEB
					Old Capitol, DC	08/08/63	Pt. Lookout, MD	P110,CSR
					Ft. McHenry, MD	08/08/63	Pt. Lookout, MD	P110,CSR
					Pt. Lookout, MD	03/03/64	Exchanged	P113,P123,P124,CSR
Darwin, M.V.	1Lt	B 12th SCVI	Warrenton, VA	09/29/62	Warrenton, VA	09/29/62	Paroled	CSR
Darwin, R.R.	Pvt	B 12th SCVI	Warrenton, VA	09/29/62	Warrenton, VA	09/29/62	Paroled	CSR
Dash, L.W.	Pvt	D 15th SCMIL	Lynch's Creek, SC	02/27/65	Pt. Lookout, MD	06/19/65	Rlsd. G.O. #109	P114,P118
Dashill, Thomas J.	Sgt	A 23rd SCVI	Five Forks, VA	04/01/65	Pt. Lookout, MD			P118
Davenport, C.J.	Pvt	E Ham.Leg.MI	Westover Ch., VA	08/07/64	Bermuda Hundred, VA	08/22/64	Fts. Monroe, VA	CSR
					Fts. Monroe, VA	08/25/64	Pt. Lookout, MD	CSR
					Pt. Lookout, MD	03/17/65	Aikens Ldg., VA Xc	P113,P117,P123,CSR
Davenport, Francis M.	Pvt	R Ham.Leg.MI	Burkeville, VA	04/06/65	City Pt., VA	04/14/65	Pt. Lookout, MD	CSR
					Pt. Lookout, MD	06/26/65	Rlsd. G.O. #109	P114,P119,CSR
Davenport, H.W.	Pvt	E 27th SCVI	Petersburg, VA	06/24/64	Fts. Monroe, VA	06/26/64	Pt. Lookout, MD	CSR,HAG
					Pt. Lookout, MD	09/10/64	Died	P6,P113,FPH,CSR
Davenport, J.V.	Sgt	C 14th SCVI	Spotsylvania, VA	05/10/64	Belle Plain, VA	05/21/64	Ft. Delaware, DE	P41,P45,CSR
					Ft. Delaware, DE	02/28/65	Hos. 2/28-3/5/65	P47,CSR
					Ft. Delaware, DE	06/10/65	Released	CSR
Davenport, John N.	Pvt	E Ham.Leg.MI	Farmville, VA	04/11/65	Farmville, VA	04/11/65	Paroled	CSR
Davenport, T.J.	Pvt	G 2nd SCVC	Stephensburg, VA	06/09/63	Old Capitol, DC	06/25/63	City Pt., VA Xc	CSR
					Ft. McHenry, MD	06/25/63	City Pt., VA Xc	P110,CSR
Davenport, Thomas T.	Pvt	B 1st SCVIG	Southside RR, VA	04/03/65	City Pt., VA	04/07/65	Hart's Island, NY	CSR
					Hart's Island, NY	06/16/65	Rlsd. G.O. #109	P79,SA1,CSR
Davenport, William P.	Pvt	E 6th SCVC	Stony Creek, VA	12/01/64	City Pt., VA	12/04/64	Pt. Lookout, MD	CSR
					Pt. Lookout, MD	06/26/65	Rlsd. G.O. #109	CSR
David, Ephraim C.	Pvt	G 8th SCVI	Winchester, VA	09/13/64	Harpers Ferry, WV	09/19/64	Camp Chase, OH	CSR
					Camp Chase, OH	06/10/65	Rlsd. G.O. #109	P23,KEB,CSR
David, Henry	Pvt	C 3rd SCVABn	Blakely, AL	04/09/65	Ship Island, MS	05/01/65	Vicksburg, MS Xc	P136,CSR
David, J.H.	Sgt	G 8th SCVI	Winchester, VA	09/09/64	Camp Chase, OH	06/11/65	Released	P23,KEB
David, John	Pvt	K 25th SCVI	Ft. Fisher, NC	01/15/65	New York, NY	01/30/65	Elmira, NY	CSR
					Elmira, NY	03/02/65	James R., VA Xc	P65,P66,HAG,CSR
David, Joseph A.	Pvt	Ferguson's LA	Franklin, TN	12/17/64	Nashville, TN	02/08/65	Louisville, KY	P3,CSR
					Louisville, KY	03/10/65	Camp Chase, OH	P95,CSR
					Camp Chase, OH	06/11/65	Rlsd. G.O. #109	P23,CSR
David, Joseph H.	Sgt	G 8th SCVI	Winchester, VA	09/09/64	Harpers Ferry, WV	09/19/64	Camp Chase, OH	CSR
					Camp Chase, OH	06/11/65	Rlsd. G.O. #109	P23,KEB,CSR
David, Manly J.	Sgt	C 3rd SCVABn	Ft. Gaines, AL	08/08/64	New Orleans, LA	09/26/64	St. Louis Hos. N.O	CSR
					St. Louis Hos. N.O	09/30/64	New Orleans, LA	CSR
					New Orleans, LA	10/11/64	St. Louis USGH N.O.	CSR
					St. Louis USGH N.O.	10/15/64	New Orleans, LA	CSR
					New Orleans, LA	10/25/64	Ship Island, MS	P3,CSR
					Ship Island, MS	01/04/65	Exchanged	P136,CSR
David, Manly J.	Sgt	C 3rd SCVABn	Ocmulgee G.H. Macon	04/16/65	Ocmulgee G.H. Macon	04/29/65	1st Bgd. 2nd US Cav.	CSR
Davidson, F.	Pvt	K 17th SCVI	Farmville, VA US Hos.	04/07/65	Farmville, VA	04/23/65	Paroled	CSR
Davidson, H.B.	Pvt	K 17th SCVI	Farmville, VA Hos.	04/07/65	Farmville, VA Hos.	04/23/65	Paroled	CSR

SOUTH CAROLINA SOLDIERS, SAILORS AND  CITIZENS HELD IN U.S. PRISONS 1861-1865

NAME	RANK	REGIMENT	CAPTURED AT	WHEN	PRISON	MOVED	DISPOSITION	SOURCES
Davidson, John C.	Pvt	H P.S.S.	Campbells Stn., TN	12/05/63	Nashville, TN	02/28/64	Louisville, KY	P39,CSR,TSE,HOS
					Knoxville, TN	02/29/64	Louisville, KY	P91,CSR
					Louisville, KY	03/09/64	Camp Chase, OH	P88,P93,CSR
					Camp Chase, OH	02/25/65	City Pt., VA Xc	P22,P26,CSR
Davidson, Samuel T.	Pvt	H 18th SCVI	Crater, Pbg., VA	07/30/64	City Pt., VA	08/05/64	Pt. Lookout, MD	CSR
					Pt. Lookout, MD	08/08/64	Elmira, NY	P113,P117,P120,CSR
					Elmira, NY	03/14/65	Aikens Ldg., VA Xc	P65,YEB,CSR
Davis, A.W.	Cpl	G 3rd SCVABn	Sumter Dist., SC	02/26/65	Hart's Island, NY	06/17/65	Rlsd. G.O. #109	P79
Davis, Andrew	Pvt	A 3rd SCVIBn	Gettysburg, PA	07/05/63	Gettysburg G.H.		Provost Marshal	P4,KEB
					Gettysburg G.H.	07/20/63	David's Island, NY	P4,CSR
					David's Island, NY	09/05/63	City Pt., VA Xc	P1,CSR
Davis, Andrew C.	1Sg	F 3rd SCVIBn	Williamsport, MD	09/14/62	Ft. Delaware, DE	10/02/62	Aikens Ldg., VA Xc	CSR
Davis, Ashbury A.	Pvt	E 16th SCVI	Missionary Ridge, TN	11/25/63	Nashville, TN	12/09/63	Louisville, KY	P39,16R,CSR
					Louisville, KY	12/11/63	Rock Island, IL	P88,P89,16R,CSR
					Rock Island, IL	03/13/64	Died, Ch. Diarrhea	P6,P12,P131,FPH,CSR
Davis, B.F.	Pvt	H P.S.S.	Deserted/enemy	03/03/65	Bermuda Hundred, VA	03/05/65	City Pt., VA P.M.	CSR
					City Pt., VA P.M.	03/02/67	Washington, DC	CSR
					Washington, DC	03/08/65	Boston, MA oath	CSR
Davis, Benjamin F.	Pvt	F 7th SCVC	Fayetteville, NC	03/12/65	New Berne, NC	04/03/65	Pt. Lookout, MD	CSR
					Pt. Lookout, MD	06/26/65	Rlsd. G.O. #109	P114,P118,P123,CSR
Davis, C.C.	Pvt	A 1st SCVIH	Chattanooga, TN	10/29/63	Louisville, KY	11/09/63	Camp Morton, IN	P88,P89,P93,CSR
					Camp Morton, IN	03/02/65	Joined US Forces	P100,CSR
Davis, Charles	Pvt	E 1st SCVA	Deserted/enemy	12/20/64	Hilton Head, SC	01/25/65	North on oath	CSR
Davis, Charles C.	Pvt	A 5th SCVI	Lookout Valley, TN	10/29/63	Camp Morton, IN	03/14/65	Enlisted US Army	CSR
Davis, Columbus	Pvt	K 8th SCVI	Winchester, VA	09/13/64	Harpers Ferry, WV	09/19/64	Camp Chase, OH	CSR,KEB,HOM
					Camp Chase, OH	03/17/65	Died, Pneumonia	P6,P12,P23,P27,CSR
Davis, D.C.	1Sg	H 22nd SCVI	Kinston, NC	12/15/62	Kinston, NC	12/15/62	Paroled POW	CSR
Davis, D.C.	1Sg	H 22nd SCVI	Deserted/enemy	02/15/65	City Pt., VA	02/17/65	Old Capitol, DC	CSR
					Old Capitol, DC	02/20/65	Ducktown, TN oath	CSR
Davis, Daniel	Pvt	K 13th SCVI	Gettysburg, PA	07/05/63	Ft. McHenry, MD	10/02/63	Ft. Delaware, DE	CSR
					Ft. Delaware, DE	11/26/63	Died, Lung infl.	P5,P40,P42,FPH,CSR
Davis, Edward W.	Pvt	I 23rd SCVI	Petersburg, VA	04/02/65	City Pt., VA	04/05/65	Pt. Lookout, MD	CSR
					Pt. Lookout, MD	05/27/65	Died,Diarrhea	P6,P118,FPH,CSR
					Pt. Lookout, MD	06/12/65	Released	P114,P121,CSR
Davis, Edwin L.	Pvt	A 1st SCVA	Bentonville, NC	03/16/65	Pt. Lookout, MD	06/26/65	Rlsd. G.O. #109	P114
Davis, Elisha	Pvt	E 21st SCVI	Morris Island, SC	07/10/63	Hilton Head, SC	09/15/63	Ft. Columbus, NY	CSR
					Ft. Columbus, NY	09/23/63	Paroled on oath	P1,HAG
					Pt. Lookout, MD	05/03/64	City Pt., VA Xc	P116,P123,P124,CSR
Davis, F.M.	Pvt	C 26th SCVI	Petersburg, VA	10/27/64	City Pt., VA	10/31/64	Pt. Lookout, MD	CSR,HMC
					Pt. Lookout, MD	01/17/65	Exchanged	P114,P123,P124,CSR
Davis, Francis M.	Pvt	L 2nd SCVIRi	Loudon, TN	12/25/63	Knoxville, TN USGH	01/06/64	Died	P1,P5, P84,ROH,CSR
Davis, G.M.	Pvt	D 22nd SCVI	Deserted/enemy	03/24/65	City Pt., VA	03/26/65	Washington, DC	CSR
					Washington, DC	02/27/65	Savannah, GA oath	CSR
Davis, G.W.	Pvt	B 7th SCVC	Charlotte, NC	05/15/65	Charlotte, NC	05/15/65	Paroled patient	CSR
Davis, Gardner L.	Pvt	A 1st SCVA	Averysboro, NC	03/16/65	Pt. Lookout, MD	06/26/65	Rlsd. G.O. #109	P123,CSR
Davis, Garrison P.W.	Sgt	G 20th SCVI	Cold Harbor, VA	06/01/64	White House, VA	06/11/64	Pt. Lookout, MD	CSR,KEB
					Pt. Lookout, MD	07/12/64	Elmira, NY	P117,P120
					Elmira, NY	03/02/65	James R., VA Xc	P65,CSR
Davis, George W.	Pvt	I 19th SCVI	Marietta, GA	08/09/64	15th USAC Marietta	08/09/64	Died of wounds	P12,CSR
Davis, George W.	Pvt	E 16th SCVI	Franklin, TN	12/17/64	Nashville, TN		Louisville, KY	P3,P39,16R,CSR
					Louisville, KY	04/03/65	Camp Chase, OH	P92,P95,CSR
					Camp Chase, OH	06/13/65	Rlsd. G.O. #109	P23,CSR

SOUTH CAROLINA SOLDIERS, SAILORS AND  CITIZENS HELD IN U.S. PRISONS 1861-1865

NAME	RANK	REGIMENT	CAPTURED AT	WHEN	PRISON	MOVED	DISPOSITION	SOURCES
Davis, Gordon L.	Pvt	A 1st SCVA	Averysboro, NC	03/16/65	New Berne, NC	03/30/65	Pt. Lookout, MD	CSR
					Pt. Lookout, MD	06/26/65	Rlsd. G.O. #109	P118,P123,CSR
Davis, Henry	Sgt	H 2nd SCVC	Jacksonville, NC	03/08/65	Pt. Lookout, MD	06/26/65	Rlsd. G.O. #109	P114,P118,P122
Davis, Hiram M.	Cpl	C 2nd SCVI	Cedar Creek, VA	10/19/64	Harpers Ferry, WV	10/23/64	Pt. Lookout, MD	CSR
					Pt. Lookout, MD	06/06/65	Died, Typhoid	P6,P114,P117,FPH
Davis, Isaac Henry	Sgt	H 2nd SCVC	Jacksonville, NC	03/08/65	New Berne, NC	03/30/65	Pt. Lookout, MD	CSR
					Pt. Lookout, MD	06/26/65	Rlsd. G.O. #109	P114,P118,P122,CSR
Davis, J. Robertson	Pvt	E 6th SCVI	N. Anna River, VA	05/23/64	Fts. Monroe, VA	05/30/64	Pt. Lookout, MD	CSR
					Pt. Lookout, MD	09/16/64	Died, Diptheria	P6,P116,P117,FPH
Davis, J.A.	Pvt	Ferguson's LA	Franklin, TN	12/17/64	Camp Chase, OH	06/11/65	Released	P23
Davis, J.A.	Pvt	F 6th SCVC	Deserted/enemy	03/09/65	Charleston, SC	03/09/65	Taken oath & disch.	CSR
Davis, J.A.	Pvt	E 7th SCVC	Richmond, VA Hos.	04/03/65	Richmond, VA Hos.	04/19/65	Escaped	CSR
Davis, J.B.	Pvt	B 18th SCVI	Burkeville, VA	04/06/64	U.S. Gen'l Hosp. B	05/09/65	Ft. McHenry, MD	CSR
					Ft. McHenry, MD	06/10/65	Rlsd. G.O. #109	CSR
Davis, J.C.	Pvt	I 23rd SCVI	Petersburg, VA	06/30/65	Pt. Lookout, MD	06/12/65	Released	P114
Davis, J.L.	Cpl	A 12th SCVI	Petersburg, VA	04/03/65	City Pt., VA	04/07/65	Hart's Island, NY	CSR
					Hart's Island, NY	06/16/65	Rlsd. G.O. #109	P79,YEB,CSR
Davis, J.N.	Pvt	F 6th SCVC	Stony Creek, VA	12/01/64	Pt. Lookout, MD	06/26/65	Rlsd. G.O. #109	P123,P114
Davis, J.R.	Pvt	K 7th SCVC	Kershaw Dist., SC	02/25/65	City Pt., VA	04/07/65	Hart's Island, NY	CSR
					Hart's Island, NY	05/11/65	Died, Ch. Diarrhea	P6,P79,FPH,CSR
Davis, J.R.	Pvt	E 27th SCVI	Deserted/enemy	03/04/65	Fts. Monroe, VA	04/02/65	Washington, DC	CSR
					Washington, DC	04/02/65	Charleston, SC	CSR,HAG
Davis, J.T.	Pvt	E Ham.Leg.MI	Farmville, VA	04/11/65	Farmville, VA	04/11/65	Paroled	CSR
Davis, J.W.	Cit	Beaufort	SS Brittania	06/24/63	Ft. Lafayette, NY	09/06/63	Fts. Monroe, VA	P144
Davis, J.W.	Pvt	A 15th SCVI	Cedar Creek, VA	10/20/64	Pt. Lookout, MD	03/28/65	Aikens Ldg., VA Xc	P114,P123,P124,KEB
Davis, J.W.	Pvt	F 6th SCVC	Stony Creek, VA	12/01/64	City Pt., VA	12/04/64	Pt. Lookout, MD	CSR
					Pt. Lookout, MD	06/26/65	Rlsd. G.O. #109	P123,P114,CSR
Davis, James	Pvt	Ferguson's	Ringgold, GA	11/27/63	Nashville, TN	12/07/63	Louisville, KY	P39,CSR
					Louisville, KY	12/11/63	Rock Island, IL	P88,P89,CSR
					Rock Island, IL	02/15/65	Pt.Lookout, MD Xc	P131,CSR
Davis, James	Pvt	H 7th SCVI			Pt. Lookout, MD	06/07/65	Died, Lung Infl.	P6,P119,P121,FPH
Davis, James A.	Pvt	H 7th SCVC	Old Church, VA	05/30/64	Not given	06/07/64	Died, Pneumonia	CSR
Davis, James E.	Pvt	F 11th SCVI	Town Creek, NC	02/20/65	Ft. Anderson, NC	02/28/65	Pt. Lookout, MD	CSR,HAG
					Pt. Lookout, MD	06/21/65	Rlsd. G.O. #109	P114,P118,P122,CSR
Davis, James M.	Pvt	B 19th SCVI	Dalton, GA	05/19/64	Nashville, TN	05/29/64	Louisville, KY	P3,HOE,CSR
					Louisville, KY	06/14/64	Rock Island, IL	P88,P91,P94,CSR
					Rock Island, IL	10/17/64	Vol. US Army	CSR
					Rock Island, IL	06/22/65	Rlsd. G.O. #109	P131,CSR
Davis, Jasper T.	Pvt	L 2nd SCVIRi	Burkesville, VA	04/14/65	Burkesville, VA	04/17/65	Paroled	CSR
Davis, John	Pvt	F Hol.Leg.	Petersburg, VA	11/05/64	City Pt., VA	11/11/64	Washington, DC	CSR
					Pt. Lookout, MD	06/11/65	Released	P114,CSR
Davis, John P.	Pvt	K Hol.Leg.	Stony Creek, VA	05/07/64	Pt. Lookout, MD	06/06/64	Died	P6,P12,P113,P116,P119
Davis, John T.	Pvt	I 4th SCVC	Fairfield Dist., SC	02/26/65	New Berne, NC	03/30/65	Pt. Lookout, MD	CSR
					Pt. Lookout, MD	06/12/65	Released	P114,P118,P121,CTA,CSR
Davis, John T.	Pvt	I Hol.Leg.	Five Forks, VA	04/01/65	Pt. Lookout, MD	06/16/65	Rlsd. G.O. #109	P114,P118
					City Pt., VA	04/05/65	Pt. Lookout, MD	CSR
Davis, John W.	Pvt	E 21st SCVI	Morris Island, SC	07/10/63	Hilton Head, SC	07/23/63	Morris Island Xc	P2,HAG,CSR
Davis, Levi J.	Pvt	I 25th SCVI	Town Creek, NC	02/20/65	Ft. Anderson, NC	02/28/65	Pt. Lookout, MD	CSR
Davis, Levi J.	Pvt	I 25th SCVI	Ft. Anderson, NC	02/19/65	Pt. Lookout, MD		Not given	P114,P118,CSR
Davis, M.	Pvt	C 14th SCVI	Winchester, VA	12/04/62	Winchester, VA	12/04/62	Paroled patient	CSR

SOUTH CAROLINA SOLDIERS, SAILORS AND  CITIZENS HELD IN U.S. PRISONS 1861-1865

NAME	RANK	REGIMENT	CAPTURED AT	WHEN	PRISON	MOVED	DISPOSITION	SOURCES
Davis, M.T.	Pvt	F 6th SCVC	Lee's Mill, VA	07/30/64	Pt. Lookout, MD	08/08/64	Elmira, NY	P113,P117,P120,CSR
					City Pt., VA	08/04/64	Pt. Lookout, MD	CSR
					Elmira, NY	06/19/65	Rlsd. G.O. #109	P65,CSR
Davis, Mathew H.	Pvt	H 22nd SCVI	Crater, Pbg., VA	07/30/64	City Pt., VA	08/05/64	Pt. Lookout, MD	CSR
					Pt. Lookout, MD	08/08/64	Elmira, NY	CSR
					Elmira, NY	07/03/65	Rlsd. G.O. #109	CSR
Davis, Morgan A.	Pvt	F 25th SCVI	Petersburg, VA	06/16/64	City Pt., VA	06/24/64	Pt. Lookout, MD	CSR,HAG
					Pt. Lookout, MD	07/27/64	Elmira, NY	P117,P120
					Elmira, NY	07/03/65	Rlsd. G.O. #109	P65
Davis, Posey W.	Pvt	C 7th SCVI	Gettysburg, PA	07/02/63	Ft. McHenry, MD	07/06/63	Ft. Delaware, DE	CSR,KEB,CNM
					Ft. Delaware, DE	06/10/65	Released	P40,P44,P45,CSR
Davis, Pringle	Pvt	A 24th SCVI	Franklin, TN	12/17/64	Nashville, TN	12/20/64	Louisville, KY	CSR,CDC
					Louisville, KY	01/02/65	Camp Chase, OH	CSR
					Camp Chase, OH	01/15/65	Died, Pneumonia	P6,P12,P23,P27,FPH
Davis, R.S.	Pvt	I 25th SCVI	Ft. Fisher, NC	01/15/65	Fts. Monroe, VA		No further data	CSR
Davis, R.T.	Sgt	A P.S.S.	Deep Bottom, VA	08/14/64	Bermuda Hundred, VA	08/15/64	Fts. Monroe, VA	CSR,TSE
					Fts. Monroe, VA	08/17/64	Pt. Lookout, MD	CSR
					Pt. Lookout, MD	03/14/65	Aikens Ldg., VA Xc	P113,P123,P124,CSR
Davis, Robert W.	Pvt	C 7th SCVC	New Kent C.H., VA	04/28/64	Fts. Monroe, VA	05/02/65	Newport News, VA	CSR
					Newport News, VA	06/26/65	Rlsd. G.O. #109	P107,CSR
Davis, S.G.	1Lt	A 9th SCVIBn	James Island, SC	06/16/63	Ft. Columbus, NY	08/23/62	Ft. Delaware, DE	P37
Davis, Samuel C.	Pvt	1 10/19 SCVI	Missionary Ridge, TN	11/25/63	Nashville, TN	12/07/63	Louisville, KY	P39,RAS,CSR
					Louisville, KY	12/07/63	Rock Island, IL	P88,P89,CSR
					Rock Island, IL	03/21/64	Jd. USA front ser.	P131
					Rock Island, IL	05/03/65	New Orleans, LA Xc	CSR
					New Orleans, LA	05/23/65	Exchanged	P4,CSR
Davis, Samuel N.	Pvt	A 24th SCVI	Marietta, GA	07/03/64	Nashville, TN	07/03/64	Louisville, KY	CSR
					Louisville, KY	07/16/64	Camp Douglas, IL	P90,P94,EFW
					Camp Douglas, IL	03/29/65	Jd. 5th US Vol.	P53,CSR
Davis, Stephen	Pvt	D 1st SCVIR	Charleston Harbor	03/21/63	Ft. Lafayette, NY	06/29/63	Ft. Delaware, DE	CSR,SA1,OR
					Ft. Delaware, DE	11/02/64	Rlsd. on parole	P40,P42,P44,CSR
Davis, T.W.	Pvt	C 7th SCVI	Gettysburg, PA	07/03/63	Ft. Delaware, DE	10/15/63	Pt. Lookout, MD	P42
Davis, Thomas	Pvt	F 25th SCVI	Ft. Fisher, NC	01/15/65	Pt. Lookout, MD	02/02/65	U.S. Gen. Hospital	P114,P117,HAG
					Pt. Lookout, MD	02/14/65	Died, Pneumonia	P12
Davis, Thomas	Pvt	B 13th SCVI	Deserted/enemy	02/24/65	Washington, DC	02/27/65	Salem, OH on oath	CSR
					City Pt.,VA	02/26/65	Washington, DC	CSR
Davis, Thomas	Cpl	F 1st SCVA	Black River, NC	03/16/65	New Berne, NC	03/30/65	Pt. Lookout, MD	CSR
					Pt. Lookout, MD	06/11/65	Released	P114,P118,P122,CSR
Davis, Thomas E.	Pvt	E Ham.Leg.MI	Richmond, VA	04/18/65	Richmond, VA	04/18/65	Amnesty oath	CSR
Davis, Thomas F.	Pvt	E 21st SCVI	Petersburg, VA	06/24/64	Bermuda Hundred, VA	06/23/64	Fts. Monroe, VA	CSR
					Fts. Monroe, VA	06/24/64	Pt. Lookout, MD	CSR,HAG
					Pt. Lookout, MD	08/08/64	Elmira, NY	P117,P120,CSR
					Elmira, NY	03/02/65	Pt. Lookout, MD Xc	P65,P66
Davis, Thompson	Pvt	B 2nd SCVIRi	Middletown, MD	09/14/62	Frederick, MD USGH	09/25/62	Washington, DC	CSR
					Germantown, PA USG	02/04/63	Ft. Delaware, DE	CSR
					Ft. Delaware, DE	03/28/63	Fts. Monroe, VA Xc	CSR
Davis, W.A.H.	Pvt	C 3rd SCVABn	Ft. Gaines, AL	08/08/64	New Orleans, LA	10/25/64	Ship Island, MS	P3
					Ship Island, MS	01/04/65	Exchanged	CSR
Davis, W.A.H.	Pvt	C 3rd SCVABn	Citronelle, AL	05/04/65	Meridian, MS	05/10/65	Paroled	CSR
Davis, W.H.	Pvt	F Ham.Leg.MI	Greensboro, NC	05/01/65	Greensboro, NC	05/01/65	Paroled	CSR
Davis, W.R.	Smn	CS Navy	Morris Island, SC	09/07/63	Ft. Columbus, NY	09/26/63	Pt. Lookout, MD	CSR
					Pt. Lookout, MD	09/14/64	died of measles	P6,P121,CSR

SOUTH CAROLINA SOLDIERS, SAILORS AND **D** CITIZENS HELD IN U.S. PRISONS 1861-1865

NAME	RANK	REGIMENT	CAPTURED AT	WHEN	PRISON	MOVED	DISPOSITION	SOURCES
Davis, W.R.	Pvt	B 7th SCVC	Farmville, VA	04/11/65	Farmville, VA	04/21/65	Paroled patient	CSR
Davis, W.R.	Pvt	Wash'n LA	Charlotte, NC	05/01/65	Charlotte, NC	05/01/65	Paroled	CSR
Davis, W.W.	Pvt	I 12th SCVI	N. Anna River, VA	05/23/64	Pt. Lookout, MD	05/13/65	Released G.O. #85	P113,P117,P122,LAN
Davis, William	Pvt	H 22nd SCVI	Crater, Pbg., VA	07/30/64	Pt. Lookout, MD	08/08/64	Elmira, NY	P113,P117,P120
					Elmira, NY	07/03/65	Rlsd. G.O. #109	P65
Davis, William A.	Pvt	C 11th SCVI	Town Creek, NC	02/20/65	Ft. Anderson, NC	02/28/65	Pt. Lookout MD	CSR
					Pt. Lookout, MD	06/26/65	Rlsd. G.O. #109	P114,P118,CSR
Davis, William B.	Pvt	E 21st SCVI	Petersburg, VA	01/25/65	Pt. Lookout, MD	02/10/65	Aikens Ldg., VA Xc	P114,P117,HAG
Davis, Zimmerman	Col	5th SCVC	Augusta, GA	05/25/65	Augusta, GA	05/25/65	Paroled	CSR
Davison, Andrew	Pvt	C 1st SCVA	Goldsboro, NC	03/16/65	Pt. Lookout, MD	06/10/65	Released	P114,P122
Davy, George W.	Pvt	I 27th SCVI	Town Creek, NC	02/20/65	Ft. Anderson, NC	02/28/65	Pt. Lookout, MD	CSR,HAG
					Pt. Lookout, MD	05/13/65	Rlsd. G.O. #85	P114,P118,P122,CSR
Dawkins, John T.	Pvt	D 17th SCVI	Crater, Pbg., VA	07/30/64	City Pt., VA	08/05/64	Pt. Lookout, MD	CSR,HHC
					Pt. Lookout, MD	08/08/64	Elmira, NY	P113,P117,P120,CSR
					Elmira, NY	08/23/64	Died, Ch. Diarrhea	P6,P12,P65,CB,CSR
Dawkins, Levi B.	Pvt	E 27th SCVI	Florence, SC	03/05/65	New Berne, NC	04/03/65	Pt. Lookout, MD	CSR,HAG
					Pt. Lookout, MD	06/26/65	Rlsd. G.O. #109	P114,P118,P123,CSR
Dawkins, W.C.	Pvt	D 17th SCVI	Crater, Pbg., VA	07/30/64	City Pt., VA	08/05/64	Pt. Lookout, MD	CSR
					Pt. Lookout, MD	08/08/64	Elmira, NY	P113,P117,P120,CSR
					Elmira, NY	09/04/64	Died	P6,P65,FPH,CSR
Dawkins, William J.	Cpt	E 15th SCVI	Deep Bottom, VA	07/27/64	Ft. McHenry, MD	08/12/64	Ft. Delaware, DE	P110,KEB
					Ft. Delaware, DE	06/17/65	Rlsd. G.O. #109	P43,P45
Dawson, Francis	Pvt	7th SCVC	Deserted/enemy	08/25/64	Washington, DC	08/31/64	Phila., PA on oath	CSR
Day, A. Mansfield	Pvt	K 2nd SCVI	Talladega, AL	06/25/65	Talladega, AL	06/25/65	Paroled	SA2,H2,CSR
Day, Allen	Pvt	C 4th SCVC	Hawe's Shop, VA	05/28/64	White House, VA	06/08/64	Pt. Lookout, MD	CSR
					Pt. Lookout, MD	08/15/64	Died, Dysentery	P6,P113,P117,CSR
Day, Henry	Pvt	E 2nd SCVC	Augusta, GA	05/19/65	Augusta, GA	05/19/65	Paroled on oath	CSR
Day, J.E.	Pvt	I 19th SCVCB	Greenville, SC	05/24/65	Greenville, J.E.	05/24/65	Paroled on oath	CSR
Day, James	Pvt	H 14th SCVI	Augusta, GA	05/20/65	Augusta, GA	05/20/65	Paroled	CSR
Day, James S.	Pvt	B Ham.Leg.MI	Augusta, GA	05/18/65	Augusta, GA	05/18/65	Paroled	CSR
Day, John T.	Pvt	C 4th SCVC	Hawe's Shop, VA	05/28/64	3rd Div. 5th A.C.	06/02/64	Washington, DC	CSR
					Stanton G.H., DC	08/29/64	Lincoln G.H., DC	CSR
					Lincoln G.H., DC	10/14/64	Old Capitol, DC	CSR
					Old Capitol, DC	10/24/64	Elmira, NY	CSR
					Ft. McHenry, MD	10/24/64	Elmira, NY	P110
					Elmira, NY	02/13/65	Pt. Lookout, MD Xc	P65,P66,CSR
					Richmond, VA Hos.	03/17/65	Furloughed 60 days	CSR
Dayton, E.R.	Pvt	B 7th SCVC	Old Church, VA	05/30/64	Pt. Lookout, MD	09/18/64	Exchanged	P123
DeBerry, R.M.	Pvt	D 6th SCVC	Deserted/enemy	03/10/65	Georgetown, SC	03/10/65	Released on oath	CSR
DeLoach, Charles H.	Pvt	A 19th SCVCB	Florence, SC	03/05/65	New Berne, SC	04/03/65	Pt. Lookout, MD	CSR
					Pt. Lookout, MD	06/26/65	Rlsd. G.O. #109	P114,P118,P123,CSR
DeLoach, George	Cpl	F 27th SCVI	Weldon RR, VA	08/21/64	City Pt., VA	08/24/64	Pt. Lookout, MD	CSR,HAG
					Pt. Lookout, MD	03/15/65	Aikens Ldg., VA Xc	P113,P117,P124,CSR
DeLoach, James	Pvt	F 11th SCVI	Ft. Fisher, NC	01/15/65	Pt. Lookout, MD	02/02/65	U.S. Gen. Hospital	P114,HAG,CSR
					Pt. Lookout, MD	07/08/65	Died, Ch. Diarrhea	P6,P12,117,FPH,CSR
DeLoach, Jesse A.	Pvt	A 19th SCVCB	Florence, SC	03/05/65	New Berne, NC	04/03/65	Pt. Lookout, MD	CSR
					Pt. Lookout, MD	06/26/65	Rlsd. G.O. #109	P114,P118,P123,CSR
DeLoach, Nelson	Pvt	I 25th SCVI	Ft. Fisher, NC	01/15/65	New York, NY	01/30/65	Pt. Lookout, MD	CSR,HAG
					Elmira, NY	03/04/65	Died, Diarrhea	P6,P12,P65,P66,FPH
DeLoach, W.E.	Sgt	G 3rd SCVCBn	High Pt., NC	05/01/65	High Pt., NC	05/01/65	Paroled on oath	CSR
DeLorme, H.B.	Pvt	C 3rd SCVABn	Blakely, AL	04/09/65	Ship Island, MS	05/01/65	Vicksburg, MS Xc	P136,CSR
DeLorme, H.B.	Pvt	C 3rd SCVABn	Augusta, GA	05/20/65	Augusta, GA	05/20/65	Paroled on oath	CSR

SOUTH CAROLINA SOLDIERS, SAILORS AND  CITIZENS HELD IN U.S. PRISONS 1861-1865

NAME	RANK	REGIMENT	CAPTURED AT	WHEN	PRISON	MOVED	DISPOSITION	SOURCES
DePass, William Lambert	Cpt	G 3rd SCVABn	Kershaw Dist., SC	02/24/65	New Berne, NC	04/10/63	Hart's Island, NY	CSR,KCE,HIC
					Hart's Island, NY	04/15/65	Ft. Delaware, DE	P79,CSR
					Ft. Delaware, DE	06/16/65	Rlsd. G.O. #109	P43,P45,CSR
DeRackin, J.	Pvt	C 3rd SCVABn	Blakely, AL	04/09/65	Ship Island, MS	05/01/65	Vicksburg, MS Xc	P136,CSR
DeVeaux, Edward S.	Pvt	B 5th SCVC	Camden, SC	04/10/65	Charleston, SC		No release data	CSR
DeVeaux, William P.	Cpl	B 27th SCVI	Petersburg, VA	06/24/64	Bermuda Hundred, VA	06/25/64	Fts. Monroe, VA	CSR,HAG
					Fts. Monroe, VA	06/26/64	Pt. Lookout, MD	CSR
					Pt. Lookout, MD	08/16/64	Elmira, NY	P113,P117,P120
					Elmira, NY	06/21/65	Rlsd. G.O. #109	P65,P66,HAG
DeVoe, James H.	Pvt	B 25th SCVI	Ft. Fisher, NC	01/15/65	New York, NY	01/30/65	Elmira, NY	CSR
					Elmira, NY	03/29/65	Released S.O.	P65,P66
DeWitt, R.R.	Pvt	G 11th SCVI	Petersburg, VA	06/16/64	Bermuda Hundred, VA	06/17/64	Fts. Monroe, VA	CSR
					Fts. Monroe, VA	06/18/64	Pt. Lookout, MD	CSR
					Pt. Lookout, MD	07/25/64	Elmira, NY	P113,P117,P120,CSR
					Elmira, NY	06/21/65	Rlsd. G.O. #109	P65,CSR
Deacon, Perry	Pvt	Brooks LA	Hatchers Farm, VA	04/06/65	Pt. Lookout, MD	06/26/65	Rlsd. G.O. #109	P114
Deal, James	Pvt.	Mathewes A	Charlotte, NC	04/30/65	Charlotte, NC	05/03/65	Paroled	CSR
Deal, William	Pvt	Mathewes A	Greenville, SC	05/23/65	Greenville, SC	05/23/65	Paroled	CSR
Deal, William A.	Pvt	I 27th SCVI	Town Creek, NC	02/20/65	Ft. Anderson, NC	02/28/65	Pt. Lookout, MD	CSR,HAG
					Pt. Lookout, MD	05/13/65	Rlsd. G.O. #85	P114,P118,P122,CSR
Dean, Andrew R.	Pvt	E 11th SCVI	Petersburg, VA	06/24/64	Bermuda Hundred, VA	06/25/64	Fts. Monroe, VA	CSR,HAG
					Fts. Monroe, VA	06/26/64	Pt. Lookout, MD	CSR
					Pt. Lookout, MD	03/14/65	Aikens Ldg., VA Xc	P117,P123,P124,CSR
Dean, Edward J.	Cpt	C 22nd SCVI	Crater, Pbg., VA	07/30/64	Old Capitol, DC	08/11/64	Ft. Delaware, DE	CSR,HOS
					Ft. McHenry, MD	08/12/64	Ft. Delaware, DE	P110
					Ft. Delaware, DE	06/17/65	Rlsd. G.O. #109	P43,P45
Dean, George A.	Pvt	G 7th SCVIBn	Morris Island, SC	07/10/63	Hilton Head, SC	09/22/63	Ft. Columbus, NY	CSR,HAG
					Ft. Columbus, NY	09/23/63	Paroled	P1
					Pt. Lookout, MD	08/16/64	Elmira, NY	P113,P116,P120,CSR
					Elmira, NY	10/11/64	Pt.Lookout, MD Xc	P65,P66
					Elmira, NY	10/11/64	Venus Pt., GA Xc	P114,P117,P124
					Pt. Lookout, MD	10/29/64	Aikens Ldg., VA Xc	P114,P117,P124
Dean, H. Rufus	Cpt	C 19th SCVI	Franklin, TN	12/17/64	Louisville, KY	03/10/65	Camp Chase, OH	P92
					Camp Chase, OH	03/12/65	Pt. Lookout, MD Xc	CSR
					Richmond, VA Hos.	03/27/65	Furloughed home	CSR
Dean, J.D.	Pvt	E 8th SCResB	Coosawatchie, SC	02/27/65	Hilton Head, SC	03/03/65	Took the oath	CSR
Dean, J.F.	Pvt	C 3rd SCVABn	Blakely, AL	04/09/65	Ship Island, MS	05/01/65	Vicksburg, MS Xc	P136,CSR
Dean, James	Pvt	E 1st SCVA	Deserted/enemy	02/18/65	Charleston, SC	03/13/65	Taken oath & disch.	CSR
Dean, John L.	Pvt	G 21st SCVI	Ream's Stn., VA	08/20/64	Pt. Lookout, MD	01/17/65	Exchanged	P113,P117,P124,HAG
Dean, Robert F.	Pvt	K 15th SCVI	Halltown, WV	08/26/64	Camp Chase, OH	03/18/65	Pt. Lookout, MD Xc	P22,P26,KEB,CSR
Dean, Robert M.	Pvt	C Ham.Leg.MI	Ft. Harrison, VA	09/29/64	Bermuda Hundred, VA	09/30/64	City Pt., VA	CSR
					City Pt., VA	10/04/64	Pt. Lookout, MD	CSR
					Pt. Lookout, MD	03/17/65	Aikens Ldg., VA Xc	P114,P117,P124,CSR
Dean, Robert N.	Pvt	E 11th SCVI	Town Creek, NC	02/20/65	Ft. Anderson, NC	02/28/65	Pt. Lookout, MD	CSR,HAG
					Pt. Lookout, MD	05/13/65	Rlsd. G.O. #85	P114,P118,P122,CSR
Dean, Wiley J.	Pvt	A 3rd SCVABn	High Pt., NC	05/02/65	High Pt., NC	05/02/65	Paroled on oath	CSR
Deas, A.	Cpl	K 7th SCVC	Farmville, VA	04/06/65	City Pt., VA	04/16/65	Newport News, VA	CSR
					Newport News, VA	06/24/65	Rlsd. G.O. #109	P107,CSR
Deas, Caleb S.	Pvt	B 26th SCVI	Five Forks, VA	04/01/65	City Pt., VA	04/05/65	Pt. Lookout, MD	CSR
					Pt. Lookout, MD	06/26/65	Rlsd. G.O. #109	P114,P118,P123

SOUTH CAROLINA SOLDIERS, SAILORS AND  CITIZENS HELD IN U.S. PRISONS 1861-1865

NAME	RANK	REGIMENT	CAPTURED AT	WHEN	PRISON	MOVED	DISPOSITION	SOURCES
Deas, Frank	Pvt	I 17th SCVI	Petersburg, VA	07/30/64	City Pt., VA	08/05/64	Pt. Lookout, MD	CSR,LAN
					Pt. Lookout, MD	08/08/64	Elmira, NY	P113,P117,P120
					Elmira, NY	10/11/64	Pt.Lookout, MD Xc	P65,CSR
					Pt. Lookout, MD	10/29/64	Exchanged	P123,CSR
Deas, Henry Lynch	Pvt	F 7th SCVC	Old Church, VA	05/30/64	Lincoln G.H., DC	06/08/64	Old Capitol, DC	CSR
					Old Capitol, DC	07/23/64	Elmira, NY	CSR
					Ft. McHenry, MD	07/23/64	Elmira, NY	P110
					Elmira, NY	10/11/64	Pt. Lookout, MD Xc	P65,H2,CSR
					Pt. Lookout, MD	10/29/64	Aikens Ldg., VA Xc	P114,P117,P123,CSR
Deas, Henry Lynch	Pvt	F 7th SCVC	Saylers Ck., VA	04/06/65	City Pt., VA	04/16/65	Newport News, VA	CSR
					Newport News, VA	06/26/65	Rlsd. G.O. #109	CSR
Deas, James	Pvt	D 1st SCVIR	Cheraw, SC	03/05/65	New Bern, NC Hos.	04/03/65	Died, Typhoid	P1,P6,SA1,CSR
Deas, Lewis	Pvt	I 17th SCVI	Petersburg, VA	07/30/64	Pt. Lookout, MD	10/29/64	Aikens Ldg., VA Xc	P114,P117,LAN,CSR
Deas, Sanford	Pvt	D 1st SCVIH	Knoxville, TN	01/25/64	Knoxville, TN	02/04/64	Camp Chase, OH	P84,SA1,LAN,CSR
Deas, Thomas A.	Pvt	B 8th SCVI	Winchester, VA	09/13/64	Harpers Ferry, WV	09/19/64	Camp Chase, OH	CSR
					Camp Chase, OH	06/11/65	Rlsd. G.O. #109	P23,KEB,CSR
Deaton, Nathan	Pvt	C 2nd SCVIRi	Deserted/enemy	10/07/64	Bermuda Hundred, VA	10/22/64	City Pt., VA P.M.	CSR
					City Pt., VA	10/23/64	Washington, DC P.M.	CSR
					Camp Distribution	10/24/64	New York, NY oath	CSR
Deaver, Alexander	Pvt	L 10th SCVI	Murfreesboro, TN	01/05/63	Louisville, KY	04/27/63	City Pt., VA Xc	P88,P89,P93,CSR
					Nashville, TN	04/17/63	Louisville, KY	P38,RAS
					Confederate Hos.#2	04/17/63	Released	CSR
Debard, Lewis W.	Pvt	E 14th SCVI	Cox Rd. Pbg., VA	04/02/65	City Pt., VA	04/07/65	Hart's Island, NY	CSR
					Hart's Island, NY	06/01/65	Died, Pneumonia	CSR,FPH
Decker, James H.C.	Pvt	Ferguson's LA	Ringgold, GA	11/26/63	Nashville, TN	12/09/63	Louisville, KY	P39,CSR
					Louisville, KY	12/11/63	Rock, Island, IL	P88,CSR
					Rock Island, IL	01/23/64	Joined US Navy	P131,CSR
Deer, William P.	Pvt	E 1st SCVIG	Southside RR, VA	04/02/65	City Pt., VA	04/02/65	Hart's Island, NY	CSR
					Hart's Island, NY	06/16/65	Rlsd. G.O. #109	P79,SA1,HMC,CSR
Deery, Cornelius	Cpl	B 3rd ACVABn	Ft. Tyler, GA	04/16/65	1st Div. Cavalry C	04/23/65	Macon, GA prison	CSR
Dees, George W.	Pvt	E 17th SCVI	Petersburg, VA	03/25/65	City Pt., VA	03/28/65	Pt. Lookout, MD	CSR
					Pt. Lookout, MD	06/12/65	Rlsd. G.O. #109	P114,P118,P121,CSR
Dees, William.	Pvt	I 17th SCVI	Five Forks, VA	04/01/65	Pt. Lookout, MD	06/11/65	Rlsd. G.O. #109	P122,CSR
Defee, James W.	Sgt	B 1st SCVIR	Bentonville, SC	03/22/65	New Berne, NC	04/23/65	Fts. Monroe, VA	CSR
					Fts. Monroe, VA	05/08/65	Newport News, VA	CSR
					Newport News, VA	06/26/65	Rlsd. G.O. #109	SA1,CSR
Dehart, B.D.	Pvt	F 1st SCVA	Bentonville, NC	03/22/65	Hart's Island, NY	06/30/65	David's Island, NY	P79,CSR
Deighen, Perry	Pvt	Brooks LA	Harpers Farm, VA	04/06/65	City Pt., VA	04/14/65	Pt. Lookout, MD	CSR
					Pt. Lookout, MD	06/26/65	Rlsd. G.O. #109	CSR
Deizen, P.	Pvt	F Naval Bn.	Hagerstown, MD	04/06/65	Pt. Lookout, MD	06/26/65	Rlsd. G.O. #109	P123
Delaney, Michael	Cpl	I 1st SCVA	Rockingham, NC	03/06/65	New Berne, NC	04/10/65	Hart's Island, NY	CSR
					Hart's Island, NY	06/16/65	Rlsd. G.O. #109	P79,CSR
Delesline, J.E.	Pvt	B 23rd SCVI	Petersburg, VA	06/18/64	Fts. Monroe, VA	06/22/64	Pt. Lookout, MD	CSR
					Pt. Lookout, MD	10/14/64	Joined U.S. Army	P113,P117,P122,CSR
Delhvies, Dierick	Pvt	F 1st SCVIR	Deserted/enemy	03/15/65	Charleston, SC		Released on oath	SA1,CSR
Delk, R.T.	Pvt	I 5th SCVC	Augusta, GA	05/20/65	Augusta, GA	05/20/65	Paroled	CSR
Delleney, Jesse R.	Pvt	B 2nd SCVC	South Mtn., MD	09/28/62	Frederick, MD USGH	02/09/63	Baltimore, MD USGH	CSR
					Baltimore, MD USGH	02/15/63	Ft. McHenry, MD	CSR
					Ft. McHenry, MD	02/14/63	Fts. Monroe for Xc	P145,CSR
Dellinger, Valentine	Pvt	F 2nd SCVIRi	Deserted/enemy	05/10/63	Knoxville, TN	12/16/63	Released on oath	CSR
Dellister, E.	Pvt	B 23rd SCVI	Petersburg, VA	06/18/64	Pt. Lookout, MD	10/14/64	Jd. U.S. Army	P113,P117,P122

SOUTH CAROLINA SOLDIERS, SAILORS AND **D** CITIZENS HELD IN U.S. PRISONS 1861-1865

NAME	RANK	REGIMENT	CAPTURED AT	WHEN	PRISON	MOVED	DISPOSITION	SOURCES
Delph, Wallace I.	SMj	1st SCVIG	Appomattox R., VA	04/03/65	City Pt., VA	04/05/65	Pt. Lookout, MD	CSR,SA1
					Pt. Lookout, MD	06/26/65	Rlsd. G.O. #109	P114,P119,P122,CSR
Delph, Wallace Ivor	Cpt	I 1st SCVIG	Appomattox R., VA	04/03/65	Old Capitol, DC	04/17/65	Johnson's Isl., OH	P110,SA1,CSR
Delph, Wallace Ivor	Cpt	I 1st SCVIG	Petersburg, VA	04/03/65	Johnson's Isl., OH	06/17/65	Rlsd. G.O. #109	P81,P82,P83,CSR
Demford, John	Pvt	G 23rd SCVI	South Mtn., MD	09/14/62	Ft. Delaware, DE	10/02/62	Aikens Ldg., VA Xc	CSR
					Aikens Ldg., VA	11/10/62	Exchanged	CSR
Dempsey, D.R.	Pvt	D 3rd SCVC	Salkehatchie, SC	03/29/65			No other data	CSR
Dempsey, L.D.	Pvt	K 5th SCVI	Wilderness, VA	05/06/64	Belle Plain, VA	04/30/20	Ft. Delaware, DE	CSR
					Ft. Delaware, DE	03/21/65	Hos. 3/21-3/24/65	P47,SA3
					Ft. Delaware, DE	07/18/65	Rlsd. G.O. #109	P42,P45,CSR
Dempsey, Nathan	Pvt	K 5th SCVI	Deserted/enemy	02/15/64	Knoxville, TN	02/26/64		P8,SA3,CSR
Dendy, Daniel	Sgt	C 7th SCVC	Malvern Hill, VA	06/13/64	City Pt., VA	06/24/64	Pt. Lookout, MD	CSR
					Pt. Lookout, MD	07/27/64	Elmira, NY	P117,P120,CSR
					Elmira, NY	10/11/64	Pt. Lookout, MD Xc	P65,CSR
					W. Bldg. Balt., MD	10/14/64	Died, Ch. Diarrhea	P1,P6,P12,FPH,CSR
Deneaux, Edward	Pvt	Gist Gd HA	Deserted/enemy	02/18/65	Hilton Head, SC	04/07/65	P.M. New York, NY	CSR
Deneaux, William	Pvt	Gist Gd HA	Deserted/enemy		Hilton Head, SC	04/07/65	P.M. New York, NY	CSR
Dennis, Benjamin B.	Pvt	I 26th SCVI	Southside RR, VA	04/01/65	City Pt., VA	04/05/65	Pt. Lookout, MD	CSR,HOW,CTA
					Pt. Lookout, MD	06/26/65	Rlsd. G.O. #109	P114,P118,P123,CSR
Dennis, Jesse O.	Pvt	H 1st SCVIH			Knoxville, TN	01/06/64	Died, Typhoid fever	P5,P12,NCC,CSR
Dennis, John W.	Sgt	D 2nd SCVI	Cedar Creek, VA	10/19/64	W. Bldg. Balt., MD	10/27/64	Pt. Lookout, MD	P1,KEB,SA2,CSR,H2
					Pt. Lookout, MD	10/29/64	Aikens Ldg., VA Xc	P114,P117,P123,CSR
Dennis, W. Lawrence	Lt	E 19th SCVI	Thomasville, GA	05/22/65	Thomasville, GA	05/22/65	Paroled	CSR
Dennis, W.T.	Pvt	G 13th SCVI	Gettysburg, PA	07/06/63	Ft. McHenry, MD	07/12/63	Ft. Delaware, DE	P40,P44,P45,ANY,CSR
					Ft. Delaware, DE	01/29/65	Dis. Hos. 1/29/65	P47
					Ft. Delaware, DE	03/04/65	Hos. 3/4-3/20/65	P47
					Ft. Delaware, DE	07/16/65	Released	P42,ANY,CSR
Denny, J.O.	Pvt	E 7th SCVI	Gettysburg, PA		Gettysburg G.H.		Provost Marshal	P4,KEB
Denny, J.O.	Pvt	E 7th SCVI	Gettysburg, PA	07/04/63	David's Island, NY	10/22/63	Fts. Monroe, VA Xc	P1,P4,CSR
Denny, J.W.	Cpt	D 19th SCVI	Augusta, GA	05/22/65	Augusta, GA	05/22/65	Paroled	CSR
Dent, T. Frank	Pvt	F 23rd SCVI	Deserted/enemy	03/14/65	City Pt., VA	03/27/65	Washington, DC	CSR
Dent, William	Cpl	I 1st SCVA	Deserted/enemy	03/01/65	Charleston, SC	03/01/65	Taken the oath & disc.	CSR
Denton, Edward J.	Pvt	A 17th SCVI	Five Forks, VA	04/01/65	City Pt., VA	04/04/65	Pt. Lookout, MD	CSR
					Pt. Lookout, MD	06/06/65	Rlsd. Instr. 5/30/65	P114,P118,P121,HHC,CSR
Denton, Francis M.	Pvt	H 4th SCVC	Hawe's Shop, VA	05/28/64	3rd Div. 5th A.C.	06/05/64	Washington, DC	CSR
					Lincoln G.H. DC	11/19/03	Died of wounds	P6,P12,LAN,CSR
Denton, J.W.	Pvt	I 12th SCVI	Gettysburg, PA	07/04/63	David's Island, NY	08/24/63	City Pt., VA Xc	P1,LAN
Denver, C.P.	Cit	Charleston	Wilmington, NC	11/06/63	Ft. Warren, MA	06/15/65	Rlsd. G.O. #109	P137
Derackin, Samuel	Pvt	C Ham.Leg.	Richmond, VA area	05/31/62	Fts. Monroe, VA G.H.	08/05/62	Ft. Delaware, DE	CSR
					Richmond, VA Hos.	09/04/62	Furloughed 30 days	CSR
Derrer, Marcus	Pvt	F 17th SCVI	Petersburg, VA Hos.	04/03/65	Petersburg, VA US	04/30/65	Pt. O Rocks US G.H	CSR
					Pt. O Rocks US G.H	05/13/65	Died	CSR
Derrick, David Isaiah	Pvt	I 15th SCVI	Gettysburg, PA	07/05/63	Ft. Delaware, DE		Hos. 2/18-3/14/64	P47,KEB,HIS
					Ft. Delaware, DE	06/10/65	Released	P40,P42,P45,CSR
Derrick, F.W.	1Lt	I 15th SCVI	Halltown, WV	08/26/64	Ft. Delaware, DE	12/28/64	From Hospital	P47,KEB
					Ft. Delaware, DE	06/16/65	Rlsd. G.O. #109	P43,P45,P47,KEB
Derrick, Frederick Earl	Pvt	I 15th SCVI	Gettysburg, PA	07/05/63	Letterman G.H. Gbg	08/22/63	Died, Amptd. thigh	P1,P5,MAG,KEB,CSR
Derrick, George M.	Pvt	H 13th SCVI	Gettysburg, PA	07/05/63	Chester, PA G.H.	07/24/63	Died	P1,P6,P12,FPH,CSR
Derrick, John L.	Cpl	H Hol.Leg.	Five Forks, VA	04/01/65	City Pt., VA	04/05/65	Pt. Lookout, MD	CSR
					Pt. Lookout, MD	06/05/65	Rlsd. Instr. 5/3/65	P114,P122,CSR

SOUTH CAROLINA SOLDIERS, SAILORS AND  CITIZENS HELD IN U.S. PRISONS 1861-1865

NAME	RANK	REGIMENT	CAPTURED AT	WHEN	PRISON	MOVED	DISPOSITION	SOURCES
Derrick, John T.	Pvt	E 7th SCVI	Cedar Creek, VA	10/19/64	Harpers Ferry, WV	10/23/64	Pt. Lookout, MD	CSR
					Pt. Lookout, MD	03/28/65	Aikens Ldg., VA Xc	P114,P117,P121,CSR
Derrick, Joshua A.	1Lt	I 15th SCVI	Gettysburg, PA	07/03/63	Ft. Delaware, DE		Johnson's Isl., OH	P44,P144,H15
					Johnsons Isl., OH	02/24/65	City Pt., VA Xc	P80,P81,P82,CSR
Derrick, Rufus	Pvt	X 10/19 SCVI	Missionary Ridge, TN	11/25/63	Nashville, TN	12/07/63	Louisville, KY	P39,CSR
					Louisville, KY	12/09/63	Rock Island, IL	P88,P89,CSR
					Rock Island, IL	03/10/65	Pt. Lookout, MD Xc	P131
					Richmond Hospital	03/15/65	Furloughed home	CSR
Derrick, Rufus	Pvt	A 19th SCVI	Augusta, GA	05/19/65	Augusta, GA	05/19/65	Paroled	CSR
Desebrock, H.	Pvt	B German LA	Deserted/enemy	03/15/65	Charleston, SC	03/15/65	Released on oath	CSR
Desel, John B.	Pvt	K 4th SCVC	Old Church, VA	05/30/64	Lincoln G.H., DC	07/20/64	Old Capitol, DC	CSR,CLD
					Old Capitol, DC	08/12/64	Elmira, NY	CSR
					Elmira, NY	10/11/64	Pt.Lookout, MD Xch	P65,CSR
					Pt. Lookout, MD	10/29/64	Aikens Ldg., VA Xc	P114,P117,P123,CSR
Desmond, Humphrey	Pvt	E 1st SCVA	Morris Island, SC	07/10/63	Hilton Head, SC	09/18/63	Ft. Columbus, NY	CSR
					Ft. Columbus, NY	09/23/63	Took the oath	P1,CSR
Dever, Alexander	Pvt	L 10th SCVI	Murfreesboro, TN	12/31/62	Dept./Cumberland	04/17/63	Nashville, TN	P38,RAS
Devine, Martin	Pvt	E 1st SCVA	Deserted/enemy	02/20/65	Charleston, SC		member of 51 NY US	CSR
Devore, John W.	Cpl	C 19th SCVI	Resaca, GA	05/16/64	Nashville, TN		Louisville, KY	P39,CSR
					Louisville, KY	05/23/64	Alton, IL	P88,P91,P94,CSR
					Alton, IL	02/18/65	Pt. Lookout, MD Xc	P14,CSR
					Richmond, VA Hos.	03/09/65	Furloughed 30 days	CSR
Devore, John W.	Cpl	C 19th SCVI	Augusta, GA	05/18/65	Augusta, GA	05/18/65	Paroled	CSR
Dewberry, John	1Lt	E 13th SCVI	Gettysburg, PA	07/04/63	Chester, PA G.H.	08/30/63	Johnson's Isl., OH	P1,CSR
					Johnson's Isl., OH	02/09/64	Baltimore, MD	P80,CSR
					Johnson's Isl., OH	02/24/65	City Pt., VA Xc	P81,P82,HOS,CSR
Dewitt, W.J.	Pvt	F 7th SCVC	Deserted/enemy	04/04/65	Bermuda Hundred, VA	04/04/65	City Pt., VA	CSR
					City Pt., VA	04/06/65	Washington, DC	CSR
					Washington, DC	04/06/65	Wilmington, NC	CSR
Deyoung, Robert M.	Pvt	B 13th SCVI	N. Anna River, VA	05/23/64	Fts. Monroe, VA	05/30/64	Pt. Lookout, MD	CSR
					Pt. Lookout, MD	09/18/64	Aikens Ldg., VA Xc	CSR
Dial, Jacob	Pvt	F 21st SCVI	Ft. Fisher, NC	01/15/65	Elmira, NY	03/19/65	Died, Pneumonia	P6,P66,FPH,HAG,CSR
Dias, William J.	Pvt	G 1st SCVIH	Sharpsburg, MD	09/21/62	Sharpsburg, MD P.M	09/21/62	Paroled	CSR
Dias, William J.	Pvt	G 1st SCVIH	Deserted/enemy	02/28/65	City Pt., VA P.M.	03/03/65	Washington, DC P.M.	CSR
					Washington, DC P.M.	03/06/65	Phila., PA on oath	CSR
Dibble, Marion W.	Pvt	D 25th SCVI	Ft. Fisher, NC	01/15/65	New York, NY	01/30/65	Elmira, NY	CSR
					Elmira, NY	06/16/65	Rlsd. G.O. #109	P65,P66,HAG
Dibble, Samuel W.	1Lt	G 25th SCVI	Morris Island, SC	07/10/63	Hilton Head, SC		Ft. Columbus, NY	CSR,HAG
					Ft. Columbus, NY	10/09/63	Johnson's Isl., OH	P1,CSR
					Johnsons Isl., OH	02/09/64	Baltimore, MD	P80,P81
					Johnsons Isl., OH	10/06/64	Pt. Lookout, MD	P82
					Pt. Lookout, MD	10/11/64	Aikens Ldg., VA Xc	P114,P117,P123,CSR
Dibble, Samuel W.	1Lt	G 25th SCVI	Town Creek, NC	02/20/65	Ft. Anderson, NC	02/28/65	Pt. Lookout, MD	CSR
					Pt. Lookout, MD	02/28/65	Washington, DC	P114,P120
					Ft. Delaware, DE	06/17/65	Rlsd. G.O. #109	P43,P45,P46,CSR
					Old Capitol, DC	03/24/65	Ft. Delaware, DE	P110,CSR
Dickens, Lawrence B	Pvt	L Orr's Ri.	Deserted/enemy		City Pt., VA	04/12/65	Washington D.C.	CSR
					Washington, DC	04/12/65	New York, NY oath	CSR
Dickerson, John	Pvt	B 17th SCVI	Farmville, VA Hos.		Farmville, VA	04/27/65	Paroled	CSR
Dickerson, Marion	Pvt	B 17th SCVI	Five Forks, VA	04/01/65	City Pt., VA	04/06/65	Pt. Lookout, MD	CSR,HFC
					Pt. Lookout, MD	06/26/65	Rlsd. G.O. #109	P114,P118,P122,CSR

SOUTH CAROLINA SOLDIERS, SAILORS AND  CITIZENS HELD IN U.S. PRISONS 1861-1865

NAME	RANK	REGIMENT	CAPTURED AT	WHEN	PRISON	MOVED	DISPOSITION	SOURCES
Dickerson, Michael A.	Pvt	D 18th SCVI	Five Forks, VA	04/02/63	City Pt., VA	04/13/63	Pt. Lookout, MD	CSR
					Pt. Lookout, MD	06/26/65	Rlsd. G.O. #109	P114,P122,P123,CSR
Dickerson, W.A.	Pvt	B 37th VAVCB	Liberty, VA	06/19/64	Cumberland, MD	07/12/64	Wheeling, WV	CSR
					Wheeling, WV	08/11/64	Camp Chase, OH	CSR
					Camp Chase, OH	03/02/65	City Pt. VA	CSR
					City Pt., VA	03/10/65	Cox's Wh., VA Xc	CSR
Dickerson, William P.	Pvt	B 17th SCVI	Petersburg, VA	03/25/65	City Pt., VA	03/28/65	Pt. Lookout, MD	CSR
					Pt. Lookout, MD	06/26/65	Rlsd. G.O. #109	P114,P118,P123,CSR
Dickey, Peter	Pvt	D 17th SCVI	Petersburg, VA	03/25/65	City Pt., VA	03/28/65	Pt. Lookout, MD	CSR
					Pt. Lookout, MD	06/08/65	Rlsd. G.O. #85	P118,HHC,CSR
Dickinson, James H.	Sgt	A 25th SCVI	Ft. Fisher, NC	01/15/65	New York, NY	01/30/65	Elmira, NY	CSR
					Elmira, NY	03/02/65	James R., VA Xc	P65,P66,HAG
Dickinson, W.J.	Cpt	G 17th SCVI	Warrenton, VA	09/29/62	Warrenton, VA	09/29/62	Paroled	CSR
					Augusta, GA	05/19/65	Paroled	CSR
Dickinson, William M.	Pvt	D 18th SCVI	Crater, Pbg., VA	07/30/64	City Pt., VA	08/05/64	Pt. Lookout, MD	CSR
					Pt. Lookout, MD	08/08/64	Elmira, NY	P113,P120,P117,CSR
					Elmira, NY	12/18/64	Died, Pneumonia	P6,P12,P65,FPH,CSR
Dicks, Joseph	Pvt	A 1st SCVIG	Gettysburg, PA	07/05/63	David's Island, NY	09/12/63	City Pt., VA Xc	P1,SA1,CSR
Dicks, S.A.	Pvt	K 7th SCVI	Charlotte, NC	05/03/65	Charlotte, NC	05/03/65	Paroled	CSR
Dicks, William Sydney	Pvt	A 1st SCVIG	Petersburg, VA	04/02/65	City Pt., VA	04/04/65	Pt. Lookout, MD	CSR,SA1
					Pt. Lookout, MD	06/26/65	Rlsd. G.O. #109	P114,P118,P123,CSR
Dickson, David	Cpl	C Orr's Ri.	Falling Waters, MD	07/14/63	Old Capitol, DC	08/08/63	Pt. Lookout, MD	CSR
					Ft. McHenry, MD	08/08/63	Pt. Lookout, MD	P110,CDC
					Pt. Lookout, MD	04/03/64	Exchanged	P113,P123,P124,CSR
Dickson, George W.	Pvt	I 25th SCVI	Ft. Fisher, NC	01/15/65	New York, NY	01/30/65	Elmira, NY	CSR
					Elmira, NY	03/02/65	James R., VA Xc	HAG,CSR
Dickson, J.J.	1Sg	D 22nd SCVI	Deserted/enemy	02/24/65	City Pt., VA	02/26/65	Washington, DC	CSR
					Washington, DC	02/27/65	Salem, IL on oath	CSR
Dickson, James L.	Pvt	F 2nd SCVC	Cashtown, PA	07/03/63	Ft. Delaware, DE	08/01/63	City Pt., VA Xc	CSR
					Williamsburg, VA	08/24/63	Richmond, VA Pcamp	CSR
Dickson, James W.Y.	Pvt	F 17th SCVI	Five Forks, VA	04/01/65	City Pt., VA	04/06/65	Pt. Lookout, MD	CSR,YEB
					Pt. Lookout, MD	06/26/65	Rlsd. G.O. #109	P114,P118,P123
Dickson, John W.	Pvt	E 21st SCVI				08/23/64	Died	P12,HAG
Dickson, Marshal P.	Pvt	C Orr's Ri.	Sutherland Stn., VA	04/03/65	City Pt., VA	04/13/65	Pt. Lookout, MD	CSR,CDC
					Pt. Lookout, MD	06/06/65	Rlsd. Instr. 5/30/65	P114,P119,P121,CSR
Dickson, Thomas J.	Sgt.	D Ham.Leg.	Sharpsburg, MD	10/01/62	Ft. McHenry, MD	10/14/62	Aikens Ldg., VA Xc	CSR,UD5
Dickson, Thomas J.	1Sg	D Ham.Leg.	Chattanooga, TN	10/29/63	Nashville, TN		Louisville, KY	P39,CSR
					Louisville, KY	11/09/63	Camp Morton, IN	P89,P93,CSR
					Camp Morton, IN	12/18/63	Died, Pneumonia	P5,P12,P100,FPH,CSR
Dietriech, Adam	Pvt	E 1st SCVA	Deserted/enemy	04/17/65	Charleston, SC		Released on oath	CSR
Diggins, Eli	Msc	23rd SCVI	Fredericksburg, VA	11/25/62	Fredericksburg, VA	11/25/62	Paroled to Xc	CSR
Dill, Andrew	Pvt	D 16th SCVI	Missionary Ridge, TN	11/25/63	Nashville, TN	12/07/63	Louisville, KY	P39,16R,CSR
					Louisville, KY	12/08/63	Rock Island, IL	P88,P89,CSR
					Rock Island, IL	02/25/65	Pt. Lookout, MD Xc	P131,CSR
					Pt. Lookout, MD	03/05/65	Boulwares Wh., VA	CSR
Dill, Jesse E.	Pvt	D 16th SCVI	Missionary Ridge, TN	11/25/63	Nashville, TN	12/04/63	Louisville, KY	P39,16R,CSR
					Louisville, KY	12/08/63	Rock Island, IL	P88,P89,CSR
					Rock Island, IL	06/20/65	Rlsd. G.O. #109	P131,CSR
Dill, Joseph P.	Pvt	D 16th SCVI	Ringgold, GA	11/28/63	Nashville, TN	12/11/63	Louisville, KY	P39,16R,CSR
					Louisville, KY	12/12/63	Rock Island, IL	P89,CSR

D

SOUTH CAROLINA SOLDIERS, SAILORS AND  CITIZENS HELD IN U.S. PRISONS 1861-1865

NAME	RANK	REGIMENT	CAPTURED AT	WHEN	PRISON	MOVED	DISPOSITION	SOURCES
Dill, Milton P.	Pvt	D 16th SCVI	Marietta, GA	06/17/64	Nashville, TN	06/24/64	Louisville, KY	P3,16R,CSR
					Louisville, KY	06/27/64	Camp Morton, IN	P90,P91,P94CSR
					Camp Morton, IN	02/19/65	Pt. Lookout, MD Xc	P100,P101,CSR
					Richmond, VA Hos.	03/15/65	Furloughed 60 days	CSR
Dill, Thomas J.	Pvt	I 3rd SCVABn	High Pt., NC	05/01/65	High Pt., NC	05/01/65	Paroled on oath	CSR
Dillard, Edward	Pvt	C 26th SCVI	Southside RR, VA	04/01/65	City Pt., VA	04/05/65	Pt. Lookout, MD	CSR,HMC
					Pt. lookout, MD	06/26/65	Rlsd. G.O. #109	P114,P118,P123,CSR
Dillard, Harris	Pvt	A Orr's Ri.	Harper's Farm, VA	04/06/65	City Pt., VA	04/14/65	Pt. Lookout, MD	CSR,HMC
					Pt. Lookout, MD	06/26/65	Rlsd. G.O. #109	P114,P119,P123,CSR
Dillard, James P.	Pvt	F 14th SCVI	Petersburg, VA	07/29/64	Richmond, VA Hos.	03/24/65	Furloughed 60 days	CSR
					Elmira, NY	03/14/65	Tfd. for exchange	P65,CSR
Dillard, James P.	Pvt	F 14th SCVI	Gettysburg, PA	07/04/63	David's Island, NY	08/24/63	City Pt., VA Xc	P1,CSR
					Pt. Lookout, MD	08/08/64	Elmira, NY	P113,P117,P120,CSR
Dillard, John	Pvt	B Hol.Leg.	Deserted/enemy	02/14/65	City Pt., VA	02/18/65	Washington, DC	CSR
					Washington, DC	02/21/65	Columbus, OH, oath	CSR
Dillard, Lemuel G.	Pvt	F Ham.Leg.	Sharpsburg, MD	09/27/62	Ft. McHenry, MD	10/18/62	Fts. Monroe, VA Xc	CSR
					Richmond, VA Hos.	10/31/62	Furloughed 40 days	CSR
Dillard, S.J.	Pvt	A 13th SCVI	Petersburg, VA	04/03/65	City Pt., VA	04/07/65	Hart's Island, NY	CSR
					Hart's Island, NY	06/16/65	Rlsd. G.O. #109	P79,CSR
Dillard, William	Pvt	B 15th SCVI	Sharpsburg, MD	08/01/62	Frederick, MD USGH	02/13/63	Ft. McHenry, MD	CSR
					Ft. McHenry, MD	02/14/63	Fts. Monroe, VA	P96,CSR
					Fts. Monroe, VA	02/14/63	City Pt.,VA Xc	KEB,H15,CSR
Dillashaw, James	Pvt	G 14th SCVI	Sutherland Stn., VA	04/02/65	City Pt., VA	04/07/65	Hart's Island, NY	CSR
					Hart's Island, NY	06/14/65	Rlsd. G.O. #109	P79,CSR
Dillon, Edmond	Pvt	K 1st SCVIG	Mechanicstown, PA	07/04/63	Ft. McHenry, MD	07/12/63	Ft. Delaware, DE	P96,SA1,CSR
					Ft. Delaware, DE	09/15/63	Jd. US 3rd MD Cav.	P42,P44,CSR
Dillon, Thomas W.	Pvt	I 1st SCVA	Morris Island, SC	07/10/63	Hilton Head, SC	09/05/63	Ft. Columbus, NY	CSR
					Ft. Columbus, NY	09/23/63	Took the oath	P1,CSR
Dimary, James T.	Pvt	6 10/19 SCVI	Chickamauga, GA	09/20/63	Nashville, TN	09/30/63	Louisville, KY	P38,RAS,CSR
					Louisville, KY	10/02/63	Camp Douglas, IL	P88
					Camp Douglas, IL	06/12/65	Rlsd. G.O. #109	P53,P57,CSR
Dinan, Cornelius	Pvt	H 27th SCVI	Petersburg, VA	06/24/64	Bermuda Hundred, VA	06/25/64	Fts. Monroe, VA	CSR,HAG
					Fts. Monroe, VA	06/26/64	Pt. Lookout, MD	CSR,HAG
					Pt. Lookout, MD	07/23/64	Elmira, NY	P113,P117,P120,CSR
					Elmira, NY	08/14/64	Died, Diarrhea	P6,P12,P65,FPH,CSR
Dinitt, E.B.	Pvt	C 3rd SCVABn	Blakely, AL	04/09/65	Ship Island, MS	05/01/65	Vicksburg, MS Xc	P136
Dinkins, Charles M.	Pvt	B 19th SCVI	Murfreesboro, TN	12/31/62	Dept./Cumberland	02/16/63	Nashville, TN	P38,HOE,CSR
					Camp Morton, IN	04/22/63	City Pt., VA Xc	P101,CSR
Dinkins, Edward M.	Pvt	D 14th SCVI	Gettysburg, PA	07/04/63	Gettysburg, PA	07/18/63	Chester, PA G.H.	CSR
					Chester, PA G.H.	08/17/63	City Pt., VA Xc	P1,CSR
Diver, H.B.	Pvt	A 3rd SCVABn	High Pt., NC	05/02/65	High Pt., NC	05/02/65	Paroled on oath	CSR
Diver, Y.H.	Pvt	A 3rd SCVABn	High Pt., NC	05/02/65	High Pt., NC	05/02/65	Paroled on oath	CSR
Divine, John L.	Pvt	H 27th SCVI	Deserted/enemy	10/08/64	City Pt., VA	10/09/64	Washington, DC	CSR,HAG
					Washington, DC	10/11/64	New York, NY oath	CSR
Dixon, A.L.	Pvt	F 1st SCVIH	Wilderness, VA	05/06/64	Belle Plain, VA	05/20/64	Ft. Delaware, DE	CSR,SA1
					Ft. Delaware, DE		Hos. 8/8-9/24/64	P47
					Ft. Delaware, DE	09/30/64	Aikens Ldg., VA Xc	P41,P42,CSR
Dixon, A.L.	Pvt	F 1st SCVIH	Richmond, VA	04/03/65	Libby Prison Rchmd.	04/23/65	Newport News, VA	CSR
					Newport News, VA	06/26/65	Rlsd. G.O. #109	P107,CSR
Dixon, Charles N.	Pvt	D 21st SCVI	Morris Island, SC	07/10/63	Ft. Columbus, NY	09/23/63	Took the oath	P1,HAG
					Pt. Lookout, MD	06/02/64	Joined U.S. Army	P113,P116,P125

SOUTH CAROLINA SOLDIERS, SAILORS AND  CITIZENS HELD IN U.S. PRISONS 1861-1865

NAME	RANK	REGIMENT	CAPTURED AT	WHEN	PRISON	MOVED	DISPOSITION	SOURCES
Dixon, Daniel	Pvt	D 21st SCVI	Morris Island, SC	07/10/63	Morris Island, SC	07/13/63	Hilton Head, SC	CSR
					Hilton Head, SC GH	09/22/63	Ft. Columbus, NY	P2,HAG
					Ft.Columbus, NY	09/25/63	Pt. Lookout, MD	CSR
					Pt. Lookout, MD	11/06/63	Smallpox H. Pt. LO	CSR
					SmallPox H. Pt.LO	01/27/64	Pt. Lookout, MD	CSR
					Pt. Lookout, MD	02/02/64	Joined U.S. Army	P113,P116,P125,CSR
Dixon, Fleming B.	Pvt	G 14th SCVI	Deep Bottom, VA	07/28/64	City Pt., VA	08/22/64	Pt. Lookout, MD	CSR
					Pt. Lookout, MD	01/27/65	Died, Ch. Diarrhea	P12,P113,P117,FPH
Dixon, G.L.	Pvt	D 7th SCVIBn	Weldon RR, VA	08/21/64	City Pt., VA	08/24/64	Pt. Lookout, MD	CSR,HAG
					Pt. Lookout, MD	03/14/65	Aikens Ldg., VA Xc	P113,P117,P123,CSR
Dixon, Hugh	Pvt	F 2nd SCVC	Greencastle, PA	07/05/63	Ft. Delaware, DE	05/12/65	Released G.O. #85	P7,P42,P46,P47,CSR
Dixon, J.A.	Pvt	C 17th SCVI	Deserted/enemy	11/28/64	P.M. A. of the P.	11/29/64	City Pt., VA	CSR
					City Pt., VA	11/30/64	Washington, DC	CSR
					Washington, DC	11/30/64	Alexandria, VA oath	CSR
Dixon, James	Pvt	D 21st SCVI	Morris Island, SC	07/10/63	Ft. Columbus, NY	09/23/63	Took the oath	P1,HAG
					Pt. Lookout, MD	05/05/64	City Pt., VA Xc	P116,P123,P124,CSR
Dixon, Richard	Pvt	Palmetto L	Richmond, VA Hos.	04/03/65	Richmond, VA	04/20/65	Paroled	CSR
Dixon, Thomas E.	Pvt	E 24th SCVI	Jackson, MS	05/16/63	Jackson, MS	05/16/63	Paroled in Hos.	CSR
Dixon, Thomas E.	Pvt	A 24th SCVI	Jonesboro, GA	09/02/64	Nashville, TN	10/27/64	Louisville, KY	CSR
					Louisville, KY	10/29/64	Camp Douglas, IL	P90,P91,P94,CSR
					Camp Douglas, IL	03/29/65	Jd. 6th U.S. Vols.	CSR
Dixon, William	Pvt	G 18th SCVI	Petersburg, VA	07/29/64	City Pt., VA	08/08/64	Pt. Lookout, MD	CSR
					Pt. Lookout, MD	08/08/64	Elmira, NY	P113,CSR
					Elmira, NY	03/17/65	Died, Pneumonia	CSR
Dixon, William	Pvt	A 24th SCVI	Jonesboro, GA	09/01/64	Camp Douglas, IL	03/25/65	Jd. 6th US Vol.	P53
Dixon, William Henry	Pvt	E 19th SCVI	Sumter Dist., SC	02/26/65	City Pt., VA	04/07/65	Hart's Island, NY	CSR
					Hart's Island, NY	06/17/65	Rlsd. G.O. #109	P79,CSR
Dixon, William L.	1Sg	D Hol.Leg.	Five Forks, VA	04/01/65	City Pt., VA	04/05/65	Pt. Lookout, MD	CSR
					Pt. Lookout, MD	06/26/65	Rlsd. G.O. #109	P114,P118,P123,CSR
Doar, George W.	Pvt	E 17th SCVI	Petersburg, VA	03/25/65	Pt. Lookout, MD	06/12/65	Released	P114
Doar, Hugh R.	Pvt	D 2nd SCVC	Deserted/enemy	04/27/65	Charleston, SC	04/27/65	Released on oath	CSR
Dobbins, A.C.	Pvt	B 2nd SCVC	Greenville, SC	05/23/65	Greenville, SC	05/23/65	Paroled on oath	CSR
Dobbins, B.F.	Pvt	H 22nd SCVI	Deserted/enemy	02/26/65	Washington, DC	03/01/65	Oil City, PA oath	CSR
Dobbins, J.	Pvt	F 3rd SCVI	Sharpsburg, MD	09/20/62	Ft. McHenry, MD	10/13/62	Fts. Monroe, VA Xc	P96,SA2,H3,CSR
Dobbins, Thomas C.	Pvt	H 25th SCVI	Ft. Anderson, NC	02/19/65	Ft. Anderson, NC	02/28/65	Pt. Lookout, MD	CSR,HAG
					Pt. Lookout, MD	06/26/65	Rlsd. G.O. #109	P114,P118,P122,CSR
Dobson, Charles R.	Pvt	E 11th SCVI	Petersburg, VA	06/18/64	City Pt., VA	06/24/64	Pt. Lookout, MD	CSR,HAG
					Pt. Lookout, MD	07/24/64	Elmira, NY	P113,P117,P120,CSR
					Elmira, NY	01/03/65	Died, Pneumonia	P6,P12,P65,FPH,CSR
Dobson, J.C.	Pvt	D 22nd SCVI	Bermuda Hundred, VA	06/02/64	Fts. Monroe, VA	06/04/64	Pt. Lookout, MD	CSR,FPH
					Pt. Lookout, MD	03/06/65	Died, Scurvy	P6,P12,P113,P117,P119
Dobson, John S.	Pvt	E 11th SCVI	Petersburg, VA	06/24/64	Bermuda Hundred, VA	06/25/64	Fts. Monroe, VA	CSR,HAG
					Fts. Monroe, VA	06/26/64	Pt. Lookout, MD	CSR
					Pt. Lookout, MD	08/16/64	Elmira, NY	P117,P120
					Elmira, NY	10/11/64	Pt. Lookout to Xc	P65,P66,CSR
					Pt. Lookout, MD	10/29/64	Aikens Ldg. Xc	P114,P123,P117
					Pt. Lookout, MD	11/01/64	Died	CSR
Dobson, Joseph	Pvt	F 1st SCVIR	Fayetteville, NC	03/16/65	City Pt., VA	04/07/65	Hart's Island, NY	CSR,SA1
					Hart's Island, NY	06/19/65	Rlsd. G.O. #109	P79,CSR
Dobson, William A.	Pvt	Ferguson's LA	Nashville, TN	12/16/64	Nashville, TN	12/19/64	Louisville, KY	CSR
					Louisville, KY	12/21/64	Camp Douglas, IL	P90,P94
					Camp Douglas, IL	03/14/65	City Pt., VA Xc	CSR

SOUTH CAROLINA SOLDIERS, SAILORS AND  CITIZENS HELD IN U.S. PRISONS 1861-1865

NAME	RANK	REGIMENT	CAPTURED AT	WHEN	PRISON	MOVED	DISPOSITION	SOURCES
Dobson, William F.	Pvt	E 11th SCVI	Bufords Bridge, SC	02/08/65	New Berne, NC	03/30/65	Pt. Lookout, MD	CSR,HAG
					Pt. Lookout, MD	06/26/65	Rlsd. G.O. #109	P114,P118,P123,CSR
Doby, Joseph W.	Pvt	H 7th SCVC	Deep Bottom, VA	08/17/64	City Pt., VA	08/22/64	Pt. Lookout, MD	CSR
					Pt. Lookout, MD	01/29/65	Died, Erysipelas	P6,P113,P117,FPH
Dodd, Henry J.	Pvt	C Hol.Leg.	Kinston, NC	12/15/62	Kinston, NC	12/15/62	Paroled POW	CSR
Dodd, Henry J.	Pvt	C Hol.Leg.	Deserted/enemy	12/20/64	City Point, VA	12/24/64	Washington, DC	P8,CSR
					Washington, DC	12/27/64	Rlsd. on oath	CSR
Dodd, Levi D.	2Lt	C 18th SCVI	Dinwiddie C.H., VA	04/01/65	Old Capitol, DC	04/09/65	Johnson's Isl., OH	P110
					Johnsons Isl., OH	06/19/65	Rlsd. G.O. #109	P81,P83,CSR
Dodds, John W.	Pvt	I 6th SCVI	Williamsburg, VA	05/05/62	Fts. Monroe, VA	05/20/62	Died of wounds	P12,HHC,CSR
Dodgins, Henry	Pvt	G 12th SCVI	Falling Waters, MD	07/14/63	Old Capitol, DC	08/08/63	Pt. Lookout, MD	CSR
					Ft. McHenry, MD	08/08/63	Pt. Lookout, MD	P110
					Pt. Lookout, MD	03/03/64	Exchanged	P113,P123,CSR
Dodgins, Henry	Pvt	G 12th SCVI	Petersburg, VA	04/03/65	City Pt., VA	04/13/65	Pt. Lookout, MD	CSR
					Pt. Lookout, MD	06/26/65	Rlsd. G.O. #109	P114,P119,P124,CSR
Dodson, W.W.	Pvt	A 3rd SCVIBn	Hanover Jctn., VA	05/23/64	Port Royal, VA	05/30/64	Pt. Lookout, MD	CSR,KEB
					Pt. Lookout, MD	03/14/65	Aikens Ldg., VA Xc	P113,P117,P124,CSR
Doherty, Charles	Sgt	C 1st SCVIG	Deserted/enemy	11/28/64	Washington, DC PMG	12/01/64	New York, NY, oath	SA1,CSR
Doherty, Luke	Cpl	H 27th SCVI	Town Creek, NC	02/20/65	Pt. Lookout, MD	06/26/65	Rlsd. G.O. #109	P114,P118,P123,HAG
Dominick, A.B.C.	Pvt	G 13th SCVI	Fredericksburg, VA	05/11/62	Aikens Ldg., VA	08/05/62	exchanged	CSR
Dominick, Aaron M.	Pvt	H Hol.Leg.	Farmville, VA	04/06/65	City Pt., VA	04/14/65	Newport News, VA	CSR,ANY
					Newport News, VA	06/26/65	Rlsd. G.O. #109	CSR
Dominick, Andrew P.	Sgt	G 13th SCVI	Fredericksburg, VA	05/10/62	Aikens Ldg., VA	08/05/62	exchanged	CSR
Dominick, Benjamin L.	Sgt	H Hol.Leg.	Five Forks, VA	04/01/65	City Pt., VA	04/05/65	Pt. Lookout, MD	CSR
					Pt. Lookout, MD	06/26/65	Rlsd. G.O. #109	P114,P118,P123,CSR
Dominick, Henry M.	Pvt	H 3rd SCVI	N. Anna River, VA	05/23/64	Port Royal, VA	05/30/64	Pt. Lookout, MD	CSR,KEB,H3
					Pt. Lookout, MD	02/13/65	Aikens Ldg., VA Xc	P113,P117,P121,CSR
Dominick, Henry Wesley	Pvt	H Hol.Leg.	Five Forks, VA	04/01/65	City Pt., VA	04/05/65	Pt. Lookout, MD	CSR,ANY
					Pt. Lookout, MD	06/26/65	Rlsd. G.O. #109	P114,P118,P123,CSR
Dominsey, William	Pvt	C 12th SCVI	Sharpsburg, MD	10/01/62	Frederick, MD USGH	10/11/62	Ft. McHenry, MD GH	CSR
					Ft. McHenry, MD	10/13/62	Fts. Monroe, VA Xc	P96,CSR
Donahoe, Hugh	Pvt	H 1st SCVIR	Deserted/enemy	02/24/65	Charleston, SC	03/02/65	Will take oath	SA1,CSR
Donahoe, Joseph	Pvt	D 27th SCVI	Deserted/enemy	06/21/64	Knoxville, TN	06/24/64	Jeffersonville, IN	CSR
Donahue, J.D.	Pvt	B 17th SCVI	Southside RR, VA	04/02/65	City Pt., VA	04/07/65	Hart's Island, NY	CSR
					Hart's Island, NY	06/16/65	Rlsd. G.O. #109	P79,CSR
Donald, Robert D.G.	Sgt	F 7th SCVI	Cedar Creek, VA	10/19/64	Harpers Ferry, WV	10/24/64	Pt. Lookout, MD	CSR,KEB
					Pt. Lookout, MD	05/18/65	Released G.O. #85	P114,P117,P122,CSR
Donald, S.R.	Pvt	C 3rd SCVABn	Citronelle, AL	05/04/65	Meridian, MS	05/10/64	Paroled	CSR
Donlan, Peter	Pvt	E 1st SCVA	Deserted/enemy	02/18/65	Charleston, SC	03/13/65	Taken oath & disch.	CSR
Donnell, John	Pvt	C Hol.Leg.C	Deserted/enemy	10/27/63	Bottoms Bridge, VA	10/26/63	Fts. Monroe, VA	CSR
Donnell, John	Pvt	C Hol.Leg.C	Deserted/enemy	10/27/63	Fts. Monroe, VA	10/29/63	Yorktown, VA oath	CSR
Donnelly, Henry M.	Pvt	A 24th SCVI	Franklin, TN	12/17/64	Nashville, TN	12/20/64	Louisville, KY	CSR
					Louisville, KY	01/25/65	Camp Chase, OH	P95
					Camp Chase, OH	06/12/65	Rlsd. G.O. #109	P23,CSR
Donnelly, Patrick	Pvt	B 15th SCVAB	Deserted/enemy	04/19/65	Charleston, SC	04/19/65	Taken oath & disch.	CSR
Dooley, George W.	Sgt	K 19th SCVI	Augusta, GA	05/20/65	Augusta, GA	05/20/65	Paroled	CSR
Dooley, J.K.	Pvt	H 20th SCVI	Lexington, SC	02/15/65	Pt. Lookout, MD	05/14/65	Rlsd. G.O. #85	P121,KEB
Dooley, James L.	Pvt	H 20th SCVI	Cedar Creek, VA	10/19/64	Harpers Ferry, WV	10/24/64	Pt. Lookout, MD	CSR,KEB
					Pt. Lookout, MD	03/21/65	Died, Ch. Diarrhea	P12,ROH,CSR
Dooley, Jesse K.	Pvt	H 20th SCVI	Lexington, SC	03/18/65	New Berne, NC	03/30/65	Pt. Lookout, MD	CSR,KEB
					Pt. Lookout, MD	05/15/65	Released GO #85	P114,P118,CSR

D

SOUTH CAROLINA SOLDIERS, SAILORS AND CITIZENS HELD IN U.S. PRISONS 1861-1865

NAME	RANK	REGIMENT	CAPTURED AT	WHEN	PRISON	MOVED	DISPOSITION	SOURCES
Doolittle, Benjamin	Pvt	K 1st SCVIG	Deep Bottom, VA	07/29/64	City Pt., VA	08/05/64	Pt. Lookout, MD	CSR
					Pt. Lookout, MD	08/08/64	Elmira, NY	P113,P117,P120,CSR
					Elmira, NY	10/30/64	Died, Ch. Diarrhea	P6,P12,P65,FPH,CSR
Doolittle, C.A.	Sgt	B 7th SCVC	Albany, GA	06/01/65	Albany, GA	06/01/65	Paroled	CSR,SA1
Doolittle, Jesse E.	Pvt	K 15th SCVI	Halltown, WV	08/26/64	Camp Chase, OH	03/18/65	Pt. Lookout, MD Xc	P22,P26,KEB,CSR
Doolittle, W.S.	Pvt	K 15th SCVI	Halltown, WV	08/26/64	Camp Chase, OH	03/18/65	Pt. Lookout, MD Xc	P22,P26,KEB,CSR
Dopson, Isham W.	Pvt	K 11th SCVI	Town Creek, NC	02/20/65	Ft. Anderson, NC	02/28/65	Pt. Lookout, MD	CSR,HAG
					Pt. Lookout, MD	06/26/65	Rlsd. G.O. #109	P114,P118,P123,CSR
Doran, James	Pvt	Brooks LA	Falling Waters, MD	07/14/63	Old Capitol, DC	12/13/63	Sent north on oath	CSR
Doran, John	Pvt	E 1st SCVA	Deserted/enemy	07/31/64	Hilton Head, SC	08/25/64	New York on oath	CSR
Doran, Patrick	Pvt	F 12th SCVI	Deserted/enemy	01/10/65	Army of Potomac	01/08/65	City Pt., VA	P8,CSR
					City Pt., VA	01/14/65	Boston, MA on oath	CSR
Doran, Thomas	Pvt	E 1st SCVA	Deserted/enemy	12/21/64	Hilton Head, SC	04/07/65	P.M. New York, NY	CSR
Dority, James	Pvt	G 26th SCVI	Five Forks, VA	04/01/65	City Pt., VA	04/05/65	Pt. Lookout, MD	CSR
					Pt. Lookout, MD	06/17/65	Rlsd. G.O. #109	P114,P118,P122,CSR
Dorius, Lewis	Pvt	C 5th SCVC	Deserted/enemy	02/18/65	Charleston, SC	03/15/65	Released on oath	CSR
Dorman, Dennis D.	Pvt	F 27th SCVI	Town Creek, NC	02/20/65	Ft. Anderson, NC	02/28/65	Pt. Lookout, MD	CSR,HAG
					Pt. Lookout, MD	06/26/65	Rlsd. G.O. #109	P114,P118,P123,CSR
Dorn, Davis W.	Pvt	B Ham.Leg.	Frederick, MD	09/12/62	Frederick, MD	09/18/62	Aikens Ldg., VA Xc	CSR
Dorn, William R.	Sgt	B Ham.Leg.	Dandridge, TN	01/17/64	New Orleans, LA	05/23/65	Exchanged	P4,CSR
					Nashville, TN	01/24/64	Louisville, KY	P39,CSR
					Louisville, KY	01/27/64	Rock Island, IL	P88,P93,CSR
					Rock Island, IL	05/03/65	New Orleans Xc	P118,CSR
					New Orleans, LA	05/23/65	Exchanged	P4,CSR
Dorr, Charles W.	Pvt	K 22nd SCVI	Petersburg, VA	03/25/65	City Pt., VA	03/28/65	Pt. Lookout, MD	CSR
					Pt. Lookout, MD	06/26/65	Rlsd. G.O. #109	P114,P118,P123
Dorre, Charles F.	Pvt	B 25th SCVI	Ft. Anderson, NC	02/19/65	Ft. Anderson, NC	02/28/65	Pt. Lookout, MD	CSR
					Pt. Lookout, MD	05/13/65	Rlssd. G.O. #85	P114,P118,P122,CSR
Dorris, E.B.	Pvt	C 3rd SCVABn	Blakely, AL	04/09/65	Ship Island, MS	05/01/65	Vicksburg, MS Xc	CSR
Dorsey, Samuel	Pvt	H 1st SCVA	Smiths Ford, NC	03/16/65	Pt. Lookout, MD	05/13/65	Rlsd. G.O. #85	P122
					Washington, DC P.M.	05/15/65	Memphis TN on oath	CSR
Doscher, Henry	Pvt	B German LA			Washington, DC	03/15/64	Took oath	CSR
Doster, George S.	Pvt	A 12th SCVI	Sharpsburg, MD	10/02/62	Ft. McHenry, MD	11/06/62	Paroled	CSR,YEB
Doster, George S.	Pvt	A 12th SCVI	Gettysburg, PA	07/05/63	Ft. Delaware, DE	10/02/63	Died, Ch. Diarrhea	P5,P40,P44,P47,FPH
Doster, John W.	Pvt	A 12th SCVI	Gettysburg, PA	07/04/63	David's Island, NY	09/05/63	City Pt., VA Xc	P1,YEB,CSR
Dougherty, J.A.F.	Sgt	C Ham.Leg.	Middle Brook, TN	12/05/63	Knoxville, TN	01/08/64	Died	P1,P5,CSR
Dougherty, Joseph	Pvt	K 1st SCVIG	Richmond, VA	04/10/65	Hilton Head, SC	04/30/65	New York, NY oath	SA1,CSR
Dougherty, Luke	Pvt	H 27th SCVI	Town Creek, NC	02/20/65	Ft. Anderson, NC	02/28/65	Pt. Lookout, MD	CSR,HAG
					Pt. Lookout, MD	06/26/65	Rlsd. G.O. #109	CSR
Doughery, Edward	Pvt	F 1st SCVA	Deserted/enemy	02/19/65	Charleston, SC	03/12/65	Taken oath & disch.	CSR
Douglas, A.	Pvt	G 1st SCV	Sharpsburg, MD	09/17/62	Sharpsburg, MD	09/17/62	Died of wounds	P12
Douglas, Charles	Pvt	D 17th SCVI	Petersburg, VA	04/03/65	City Pt., VA	04/13/65	Pt. Lookout, MD	CSR,HHC
					Pt. Lookout, MD	06/26/65	Rlsd. G.O. #109	P114,P119,P122,CSR
Douglas, Charles M.	SMj	17th SCVI	Five Forks, VA	04/01/65	City Pt., VA	05/05/65	Pt. Lookout, MD	CSR
					Pt. Lookout, MD		Refused the oath	P118
					Pt. Lookout, MD	06/12/65	Released	P114,P121,CSR
Douglas, Edward	Pvt	A 7th SCVIBn	Ft. Anderson, NC	02/19/65	Ft. Anderson, NC	02/28/65	Pt. Lookout, MD	CSR,HAG
					Pt. Lookout, MD	06/26/65	Rlsd. G.O. #109	P114,P118,P122,CSR
Douglas, F.W.	Pvt	B 23rd SCVI	Petersburg, VA	04/02/65	City Pt., VA	04/04/65	Pt. Lookout, MD	CSR
					Pt. Lookout, MD	06/12/65	Rlsd. G.O. #109	P114,P118,P121,CSR
Douglas, Henry A.	Pvt	D 21st SCVI	Ft. Fisher, NC	01/15/65	Elmira, NY	04/02/65	Died, Epilepsy	P6,P12,P65,P66,FPH
Douglas, Solomon	Pvt	A 19th SCVI	Citronelle, AL	05/04/65	Meridian, MS	05/09/65	Paroled on oath	CSR

SOUTH CAROLINA SOLDIERS, SAILORS AND  CITIZENS HELD IN U.S. PRISONS 1861-1865

NAME	RANK	REGIMENT	CAPTURED AT	WHEN	PRISON	MOVED	DISPOSITION	SOURCES
Douglass, Campbell	Pvt	A 25th SCVI	Ft. Anderson, NC	02/20/65	Ft. Anderson, NC	02/28/65	Pt. Lookout, MD	CSR,HAG
					Pt. Lookout, MD	05/13/65	Released G.O. #85	P18,P114,P122,CSR
Douglass, George C.	Sgt	A 19th SCVCB	Florence, SC	03/05/65	New Berne, NC	04/03/65	Pt. Lookout, MD	CSR
					Pt. Lookout, MD	06/11/65	Released	P114,P118,P122,CSR
Douglass, J.B.	Pvt	B 8th SCVI	Wilderness, VA	05/08/64	Belle Plain, VA	07/18/64	Ft. Delaware, DE	CSR,KEB
					Ft. Delaware, DE	07/18/64	Released G.O.#109	P41,P42,P45,CSR
Douglass, John J.	Pvt	C 2nd SCVI	Strasburg, VA	10/23/64	Harpers Ferry, WV	10/23/64	Pt. Lookout, MD	SA2,H2,CSR
					Pt. Lookout, MD	03/28/65	Aikens Ldg., VA Xc	P114,P117,P121,CSR
Douglass, W.O.	Pvt	G 3rd SCVIBn	Saluda, SC	02/16/65	City Pt., VA	04/07/65	Hart's Island, NY	CSR
					Hart's Island, NY	06/16/65	Rlsd. G.O. #109	CSR
Douglass, William W.	Pvt	B Orr's Ri.	Falling Waters, MD	07/14/63	Baltimore, MD	08/16/65	Pt. Lookout, MD	CSR,CDC
					Pt. Lookout, MD	08/16/64	Elmira, NY	P113,P116,P120
					Pt. Lookout, MD		Exchanged	P124,CDC
Douglass, William W.	Pvt	B Orr's Ri.	Wilderness, VA	05/05/64	Elmira, NY	02/07/65	Died, Rem. fever	P6,P65,P66,FPH,CSR
Dove, A.B.C.	Pvt	C 3rd SCVABn	Blakely, AL	04/09/65	Ship Island, MS	05/01/65	Vicksburg, MS Xc	P136,CSR
Dove, A.B.C.	Pvt	C 3rd SCVABn	Citronelle, AL	05/04/65	Meridian, MS	05/20/65	Paroled	CSR
Dove, J.C.	Sgt	C 3rd SCVABn	Ft. Gaines, AL	08/08/64	St. Louis, MO USGH	10/15/64	New Orleans, LA	CSR
					New Orleans, LA	10/06/64	St. Louis, MO USGH	CSR
					New Orleans, LA	09/02/64	St. Louis, MO USGH	CSR
					St. Louis, MO USGH	08/29/64	New Orleans, LA	CSR
					New Orleans, LA	10/25/64	Ship Island, MS	P3,CSR
					Ship Island, MS	01/04/65	Exchanged	P136,CSR
Dove, J.L.S.	1Lt	C 3rd SCVABn	Ft. Gaines, AL	08/08/64	New Orleans, LA	11/25/64	Ship Island, MS	P3,CSR
					Ship Island, MS	01/04/65	Exchanged	P136
Dove, J.L.S.	1Lt	C 3rd SCVABn			Meridian, MS	05/10/65	Paroled	CSR
Dove, Richard	Pvt	B 17th SCVI	Amelia C.H., VA	04/04/65	City Pt., VA	04/13/65	Pt. Lookout, MD	CSR,HFC
					Pt. Lookout, MD	06/26/65	Rlsd. G.O. #109	P114,P119,P122,CSR
Dove, Samuel	Pvt	B 17th SCVI	Hatchers Run, VA	03/27/65	City Pt., VA	04/02/65	Pt. Lookout, MD	CSR
					Pt. Lookout, MD	06/26/65	Rlsd. G.O. #109	P114,P118,P123,CSR
Dover, Felix	Pvt	F 17th SCVI	Deserted/enemy	02/20/65	P.M. 9th AC A Of P	02/21/65	City Pt., VA P.M.	CSR
					City Pt., VA P.M.	02/22/65	Washington, DC	CSR
					Washington, DC	02/24/65	Boston, MA on oath	CSR
Dover, George W.	Pvt	G 5th SCVI	Chattanooga, TN	10/29/63	Nashville, TN	11/07/63	Louisville, KY	P39,SA3,CSR,YEB
					Louisville, KY	11/09/63	Camp Morton, IN	P88,P89,P93
					Camp Morton, IN	12/25/63	Died, Ch. Diarrhea	P5,P12,FPH,CSR
Dover, J.J.	Pvt	H Ham.Leg.	Deserted/enemy	09/18/62	Keedysville, MD	09/20/62	Paroled on oath	CSR
Dover, Willis	Pvt	A 12th SCVI	Petersburg, VA	04/02/65	City Pt., VA	04/04/65	Pt. Lookout, MD	CSR
					Pt. Lookout, MD	06/26/65	Rlsd. G.O. #109	P118,P123,YEB
Dowd, Owen	Cpl	D 1st SCVIR	Deserted/enemy	02/24/65	Charleston, SC	03/02/65	Will take oath	SA1,CSR
Dowdel, William	Pvt	C 1st SCVIR	Smith's Ford, NC	03/16/65	New Berne, NC	04/03/65	Pt. Lookout, MD	CSR,SA1
					Pt. Lookout, MD	06/12/65	Released G.O. #109	P114,P118,CSR
					Pt. Lookout, MD	06/12/65	Washington, D.C. PM	CSR
					Washington, D.C. PM	06/13/65	Walmouth Cty., WVA	CSR
Dowdle, John J.	Pvt	B 12th SCVI	Falling Waters, MD	07/14/63	Baltimore, MD	08/16/63	Pt. Lookout, MD	CSR,YEB
					Pt. Lookout, MD	03/17/65	Exchanged	P113,P121,P123,P124
Dowdle, William G.	Pvt	K 17th SCVI	Petersburg, VA	03/25/65	City Pt., VA	03/28/65	Pt. Lookout, MD	CSR,YEB
					Pt. Lookout, MD	06/21/65	Rlsd. G.O. #109	P114,P118,P122,CSR
Dowler, Alexander L.	Pvt	I 14th SCVI	Gettysburg, PA	07/03/63	Harrisburg, PA	07/07/63	Washington, DC	P40,P44,CSR
					Washington, DC	07/07/63	Rlsd on oath	CSR
Dowling, J.C.	Pvt	A 1st SCVIH	South Mtn., MD	09/14/62	Ft. McHenry, MD	10/17/62	Fts. Monroe, VA Xc	CSR

SOUTH CAROLINA SOLDIERS, SAILORS AND  CITIZENS HELD IN U.S. PRISONS 1861-1865

NAME	RANK	REGIMENT	CAPTURED AT	WHEN	PRISON	MOVED	DISPOSITION	SOURCES
Downing, E.J.	Pvt	F 17th SCVI	Crater, Pbg., VA	07/30/64	City Pt., VA	08/05/64	Pt. Lookout, MD	CSR
					Pt. Lookout, MD	08/08/64	Elmira, NY	P113,P117,P120,CSR
					Elmira, NY	06/12/65	Released	P65,CSR
Downy, John W.	Pvt	F 17th SCVI	Petersburg, VA	03/25/65	City Pt., VA	03/28/65	Pt. Lookout, MD	CSR
					Pt. Lookout, MD	06/12/65	Released G.O. #109	P114,P118,P121,CSR
Doyal, James	Pvt	I 1st SCVIR	Deserted/enemy	04/06/65	Charleston, SC	04/06/65	Released on oath	CSR
Doyle, Andrew	Pvt	B 1st SCVIBn	Morris Island, SC	09/07/63	Ft. Columbus, NY	09/23/63	Took the oath	P1
Doyle, Marion	Pvt	B 11th SCVI	Deserted/enemy	02/18/65	Charleston, SC		Released on oath	HAG,CSR
Doyle, Thomas	Pvt	B 11th SCVI	Deserted/enemy	02/18/65	Charleston, SC		Released on oath	CSR
Doyle, William E.	Pvt	G 7th SCVC	Darbytown Rd., VA	09/29/64	Bermuda Hundred, VA	10/01/64	City Pt., VA	CSR
					City Pt., VA	10/05/64	Pt. Lookout, MD	CSR
					Pt. Lookout, MD	03/17/65	Aikens Ldg., VA Xc	P124,CSR
Dozier, A.W.	1Lt	F 6th SCVC	Johns Island, SC	02/09/64	Ft. Lafayette, NY	04/23/64	Ft. Delaware, DE	P144,CSR
					Hilton Head, SC	04/03/64	Ft. Lafayette, NY	CSR
					Ft. Delaware, DE		Held as hostage	P42,P46
					Ft. Delaware, DE	01/20/65	Fts. Monroe, VA Xc	CSR
					Fts. Monroe, VA	01/26/65	Camp Hamilton, VA	CSR
					Camp Hamilton, VA	02/02/65	Paroled	CSR
Dozier, J. Valentine	Cpl	I 21st SCVI	Morris Island, SC	07/10/63	Hilton Head, SC	07/13/64	Died	P2,P5,HAG,BNC
Dozier, John F.	Pvt	I 21st SCVI	Morris Island, SC	07/10/63	Ft. Columbus, NY	09/23/63	Paroled on oath	P1,HAG,HMC
					Ft. Columbus, NY	09/25/63	Pt. Lookout, MD	CSR
					Pt. Lookout, MD	03/14/65	Aikens Ldg., VA Xc	P116,P124
Dozier, John Tully	Sgt	I 21st SCVI	Town Creek, NC	02/20/65	Pt. Lookout, MD	06/04/65	Rlsd. Instr. 5/30/65	P114,P118,P121,HMC
Dozier, John W.	Pvt	I 21st SCVI	Morris Island, SC	07/10/63	Pt. Lookout, MD	03/06/65	Exchanged	P113
Dozier, Peter C.	SMj	B 21st SCVI	Morris Island, SC	07/10/63	Hilton Head G.H.	07/23/64	Morris Island Xc	P2,R48,CTA,HAG
Dozier, Peter C.	1Lt	B 21st SCVI	Weldon RR, VA	08/21/64	City Pt., VA	08/24/64	Alexandria, VA	CSR
					Alexandria, VA	09/16/64	Lincoln G.H., DC	CSR
					Lincoln G.H., DC	09/21/64	Old Capitol, DC	CSR
					Old Capitol, DC	10/21/64	Ft. Delaware, DE	CSR
					Ft. Delaware, DE	06/17/65	Rlsd. G.O. #109	CSR
Draffin, Nathaniel T.	Pvt	I 17th SCVI	Petersburg, VA	03/25/65	City Pt., VA	03/27/65	Pt. Lookout, MD	CSR,LAN
					Pt. Lookout, MD	06/11/65	Released G.O.#109	P114,P118,P122,CSR
Draft, I.C.	Pvt	K 15th SCVI	Warrenton, VA	09/29/62	Warrenton, VA	09/29/62	Paroled	CSR
Drafts, Michael	Pvt	B 15th SCVI			New Berne, NC USGH	04/03/65	Died	CSR
Draper, Rufus	Pvt	D 26th SCVI	Richmond, VA Hos.	04/03/65	Libby Prison Rchmd.	04/23/65	Newport News, VA	CSR
					Newport News, VA	06/26/65	Rlsd. G.O. #109	P107,CSR
Drawdy, Daniel L.	Pvt	H Ham.Leg.MI	Richmond, VA Hos.	04/03/65	Richmond, VA Hos.	04/05/65	Provost Marshal	CSR
					Libby Prison Rchmd.	04/13/65	City Pt., VA	CSR
					City Pt., VA	04/14/65	Pt. Lookout, MD	CSR
					Pt. Lookout, MD	06/26/65	Rlsd. G.O. #109	P119,P123,CSR
Drawdy, R.A.	Pvt	B 3rd SCVC	Deserted/enemy	02/27/65	Charleston, SC	03/01/65	Hilton Head, SC	CSR
					Hilton Head, SC	04/04/65	New York, NY oath	CSR
Drayton, C.E.R.	Pvt	7th SCVC	Old Church, VA	05/30/64	White House, VA	06/08/64	Pt. Lookout, MD	CSR
					Pt. Lookout, MD	09/30/64	City Pt., VA Xc	P113,P117,P123,CSR
Dreher, E.J.	Pvt	F 5th SCVC	Fayetteville, NC	03/09/65	New Berne, NC	03/20/65	Pt. Lookout, MD	P118,CSR
					Pt. Lookout, MD	06/06/65	Released on oath	P118,CSR
Dreher, G.L.	Pvt	I 15th SCVI	Halltown, WV	08/21/64	Washington, D.C.	08/29/64	Camp Chase, OH	CSR
					Camp Chase, OH	03/26/65	Pt. Lookout, MD	P23,KEB,CSR
					Pt. Lookout, MD	06/05/65	Released on oath	CSR
Dreher, Jacob J.	Pvt	B German LA	Charlotte, NC	05/06/65	Charlotte, NC	05/06/65	Paroled	CSR
Dreifus, Solomon	Pvt	K 25th SCVI	Deserted/enemy	02/24/64	Suffolk, VA	02/24/64	Fts. Monroe, VA	CSR,CTA
					Fts. Monroe, VA	02/24/64	Phila., PA on oath	P8,CSR

SOUTH CAROLINA SOLDIERS, SAILORS AND  CITIZENS HELD IN U.S. PRISONS 1861-1865

NAME	RANK	REGIMENT	CAPTURED AT	WHEN	PRISON	MOVED	DISPOSITION	SOURCES
Drenan, Andrew	Pvt	C 1st SCVA	Goldsboro, NC	03/16/65	New Berne, NC	04/03/65	Pt. Lookout, MD	CSR
					Pt. Lookout, MD	06/11/65	Rlsd. G.O. #109	P114,P118,P122,CSR
Drennan, Samuel A.	Pvt	E 20th SCVI	Salisbury, NC	04/12/65	Nashville, TN		Louisville, KY	P39,KEB
					Louisville, KY	05/01/65	Hospital, Diarrhea	P95,CSR
					Louisville, KY	05/02/65	Camp Chase, OH	P92
					Camp Chase, OH	06/13/65	Rlsd. G.O. #109	P23,CSR
Drews, Samuel	Pvt	B 2nd SCVA	Deserted/enemy	02/25/65	Charleston, SC		Released on oath	CSR
Dreyer, Albert	Pvt	B German LA	Deserted/enemy	02/18/65	Charleston, SC	03/14/65	Released on oath	CSR
Driggers, D.F.	Pvt	I 1st SCVC	Deserted/enemy	03/13/65	Charleston, SC	03/13/65	Released on oath	CSR
Driggers, Joel	Pvt	C 11th SCVI	Town Creek, NC	02/25/65	Ft. Anderson, NC	02/28/65	Pt. Lookout, MD	CSR
					Pt. Lookout, MD	05/08/65	Died, Pneumonia	P6,P114,P118,FPH
Driggers, John	Pvt	B 8th SCVI	Winchester, VA	09/13/64	Camp Chase, OH	02/25/65	Died, Pneumonia	P6,P23,P27,KEB,FPH
Driggers, John W.	Pvt	B 11th SCVI	Deserted/enemy	03/06/65	Charleston, SC oath	03/06/65	Released on oath	HAG,CSR
Driggers, Mack	Pvt	C 11th SCVI	Town Creek, NC	02/20/65	Ft. Anderson, NC	02/28/65	Pt. Lookout, MD	CSR,HAG
					Pt. Lookout, MD	06/26/65	Rlsd. G.O. #109	P114,P122,P123,CSR
Driggers, Roberson	Pvt	C 11th SCVI	Town Creek, NC	02/20/65	Ft. Anderson, NC	02/28/65	Pt. Lookout, MD	CSR,HAG
					Pt. Lookout, MD	06/19/65	Died	P6,P114,P119,FPH
Driggers, Whitfield	Pvt	B 24th SCVI	Nashville, TN	12/16/64	Nashville, TN	12/16/64	Louisville, KY	CSR,HOM
					Louisville, KY	12/21/64	Camp Douglas, IL	P90,P91,P95,CSR
					Camp Douglas, IL	06/19/65	Rlsd. G.O. #109	CSR,P55
Driscoll, Timothy O.	Pvt	H 27th SCVI	Town Creek, NC	02/20/65	Ft. Anderson, NC	02/28/65	Pt. Lookout, MD	CSR,HAG
					Pt. Lookout, MD	05/13/65	Released G.O. #85	P114,P118,P122,CSR
Driver, G.B.	Pvt	A 1st SCVIG	Petersburg, VA	04/03/65	City Pt., VA	04/07/65	Hart's Island, NY	CSR
					Hart's Island, NY	06/15/65	Rlsd. G.O. #109	P79,CSR
Driver, John B.	Pvt	K Orr's Ri	Falling Waters, MD	07/14/63	Baltimore, MD	08/20/63	Pt. Lookout, MD	CSR
					Pt. Lookout, MD	03/17/64	City Pt., VA Xc	P116,P123,CDC,CSR
Drose, Joseph C.	Pvt	I 23rd SCVI	Petersburg, VA	04/01/65	City Pt., VA	04/05/65	Pt. Lookout, MD	CSR
					Pt. Lookout, MD	06/12/65	Released	P118,P121,CSR
Droze, John P.	Pvt	D 3rd SCVABn	Deserted/enemy	02/24/65	Charleston, SC	03/02/65	Will take the oath	CSR
Drum, S.P.	Pvt	E 5th SCVI	Lookout Valley, TN	10/28/64	Camp Morton, IN	03/04/65	City Pt., VA	CSR
					City Pt., VA	03/04/65	Ft. Delaware, DE	CSR
					Ft. Delaware, DE	03/10/65	Boulware's Wharf X	CSR
Drummand, J.A.	Pvt	G 1st SCVIH	Warrenton, VA	09/29/62	Warrenton, VA	09/29/62		CSR
Drummond, J.	Pvt	B 14th SCVI	Lynch's Creek, SC	02/25/65	New Berne, NC	05/21/65	Died, Ch. Diarrhea	CSR
Drummond, J.W.C.	Pvt	F Hol.Leg.	Warrenton, VA	09/29/62	Warrenton, VA	09/29/62	Paroled/ Hospital	CSR
Drummond, J.W.C.	Pvt	F Hol.Leg.	Jarratts Stn., VA	05/08/64	Fts. Monroe, VA	05/13/64	Pt. Lookout, MD	CSR
					Pt. Lookout, MD	08/15/64	Elmira, NY	P113,P116,P120,CSR
					Elmira, NY	06/21/65	Rlsd. G.O. #109	P65,P66,CSR
Drummond, James W.	Pvt	F Hol.Leg.	Kinston, NC	12/14/62	Kinston, NC	12/14/62	Paroled POW	CSR
Drummond, James W.	Pvt	F Hol.Leg.	Jarratts Stn., VA	05/08/64	Fts. Monroe, VA	05/13/64	Pt. Lookout, MD	CSR
					Pt. Lookout, MD	09/18/64	Exchanged	P113,P123
					Richmond Hospitals	09/25/64	Died	CSR
Drummond, James	Pvt	B 14th SCMil	Lynch's Creek, SC	02/25/65	Hart's Island, NY	05/21/65	Died	P6,P79,FPH
Drummond, John F.	Pvt	C 27th SCVI				08/22/64	Died	P12,HAG
Dryman, Leonard	Pvt	F 22nd SCVI	Kinston, NC	12/14/62	Kinston, NC	12/14/62	Paroled POW	CSR
DuBose, D.G.	Cpt	H 21st SCVI	Ft. Fisher, NC	01/15/65	Ft. Columbus, NY	03/01/65	City Pt., VA Xc	P2,HAG
DuBose, H.K.	Pvt	B 21st SCVI	Petersburg, VA	06/24/64	Pt. Lookout, MD	08/16/64	Elmira, NY	P113,P117,P120,HAG
					Elmira, NY	06/30/65	Rlsd. G.O. #109	P65,P66,CSR
DuBose, J.M.	Pvt	H 26th SCVI	Deserted/enemy	02/23/65	City Pt., VA	03/24/65	Washington, DC	CSR
					Washington, DC	03/27/65	Savannah, GA oath	CSR
DuBose, John W.	Cpl	A 14th SCVI	Petersburg, VA	04/02/65	City Pt., VA	04/05/65	Pt. Lookout, MD	CSR
					Pt. Lookout, MD	06/26/65	Rlsd. G.O. #109	P114,P118,P123,CSR

SOUTH CAROLINA SOLDIERS, SAILORS AND  CITIZENS HELD IN U.S. PRISONS 1861-1865

NAME	RANK	REGIMENT	CAPTURED AT	WHEN	PRISON	MOVED	DISPOSITION	SOURCES
DuBose, L.	Pvt	Mathewes A	Augusta, GA	05/29/65	Augusta, GA	05/29/65	Paroled	CSR
DuBose, Sewell W.	Pvt	A 14th SCVI	Five Forks, VA	04/01/65	City Pt., VA	04/05/65	Pt. Lookout, MD	CSR
					Pt. Lookout, MD	06/26/65	Rlsd. G.O. #109	P114,P118
DuBose, W.H.	Pvt	H 26th SCVI	Deserted/enemy	02/18/65	City Pt., VA	02/20/65	Washington, DC	CSR
					Washington, DC	02/21/65	Waterford, PA oath	CSR
DuBose, William P.	1Lt	Hol.Leg.	Boonesboro, MD	09/13/62	Ft. Delaware, DE	10/02/62	Aikens Ldg., VA Xc	CSR
DuPre, James C.	Pvt	B 27th SCVI	Town Creek, NC	02/20/65	Ft. Anderson, NC	02/28/65	Pt. Lookout, MD	CSR,HAG
					Pt. Lookout, MD	05/13/65	Released GO #85	P114,P118,P122
Dubard, L.W.	Pvt	E 14th SCVI	Cox Road, Pbg., VA	04/02/65	Hart's Island, NY	06/01/65	Died, Pneumonia	P6,P79,FPH
Duc, Virgil	2Lt	E 25th SCVI	Weldon RR, VA	08/21/64	Old Capitol, DC	08/27/64	Ft. Delaware, DE	CSR,HAG
					Ft. McHenry, MD	08/27/64	Ft. Delaware, DE	P110
					Ft. Delaware, DE	10/06/64	Pt. Lookout, MD	P43,CSR
Duc, Virgil	2Lt	E 25th SCVI	Petersburg, VA	08/22/64	Pt. Lookout, MD	10/11/64	Aikens Ldg., VA Xc	P114,P117,P123,CSR
Duckett, John W.	Pvt	B 37th VAVCB	Moorefield, VA	08/07/64	Wheeling, WV	08/11/64	Camp Chase, OH	CSR
					Camp Chase, OH	03/18/65	Pt. Lookout, MD	CSR
					Pt. Lookout, MD	03/28/65	Aikens Ldg., VA Xc	CSR
Duckett, Thomas J.	2Lt	I 3rd SCVI	Bentonville, NC	03/19/65	New Berne, NC	04/03/65	Pt. Lookout, MD	CSR,KEB,H3
					Pt. Lookout, MD	04/03/65	Washington, DC	P114,P120,CSR
					Old Capitol, DC	04/09/65	Johnson's Isl., OH	P110
					Johnson's Isl., OH	06/17/65	Rlsd. G.O. #109	P81,P83,CSR
Duff, Adam	Msc	25th SCVI	Deserted/enemy	03/24/65	Charleston, SC	03/24/65	Released on oath	CSR
Duffey, Henry B.	Pvt	I 6th SCVI	Savage Stn., VA	06/26/62	Harrisons Ldg., VA	07/03/62	Ft. Columbus, NY	CSR
					Ft. Columbus, NY	07/09/62	Ft. Delaware, DE	CSR
					Ft. Delaware, DE	08/05/62	Aikens Ldg., VA Xc	CSR
Duffey, Henry B.	Pvt	I 6th SCVI	Jetersville, VA	04/06/65	City Pt., VA	04/14/65	Newport News, VA	CSR
					Newport News, VA	06/15/65	Rlsd. G.O. #109	P107/CSR
Duffey, J.V.	Pvt	M 7th SCVI	Harrisonburg, VA	09/25/64	Pt. Lookout, MD	03/17/65	Exchanged	P114,P117,P124,KEB
Duffey, Michael	Pvt	K 1st SCVIG	Gettysburg, PA	07/05/63	Ft. Delaware, DE	07/19/63	Chester, PA Hos.	P40,P42,P44,SA1
					Chester, PA Hos.	10/04/63	Pt. Lookout, MD	CSR
					Pt. Lookout, MD	09/30/64	Exchanged	P121,P123,P124,CSR
Duffie, J.V.	Pvt	M 7th SCVI	Harrisonburg, VA	09/25/64	Harper's Ferry, WV	10/18/64	Pt. Lookout, MD	CNM,UD3,CSR,KEB
					Pt. Lookout, MD	03/17/65	Exchanged	P114,P117,P124,CSR
Duffus, George E.L.	Pvt	L 1st SCVIG	Gettysburg, PA	07/05/63	David's Island, NY	07/30/63	Died of wounds	P1,P6,SA1,FPH,CSR
Duffy, J.W.	Pvt	G 7th SCVI	Gettysburg, PA	07/02/63	Gettysburg G.H.		Provost Marshal	P4,KEB
					David's Island, NY	09/08/63	City Pt., VA Xc	CNM,P4,P1,CSR
Duffy, Lawrence	Sgt	A 17th SCVI	Warrenton, VA	09/29/62	Warrenton, VA	09/29/62	Paroled	CSR
Duffy, Reuben M.	Pvt	I 6tth SCVI	Fair Oaks, VA	05/31/62	Fts. Monroe, VA	06/21/62	Ft. Delaware, DE	CSR
					Ft. Delaware, DE	08/05/62	Aikens Ldg., VA Xc	CSR
Duggan, John A.	2Lt	6 10/19 SCVI	Missionary Ridge, TN	11/25/63	Nashville, TN	12/04/63	Louisville, KY	P39,RAS,CSR
					Louisville, KY	12/05/63	Johnsons Isl., OH	P88,P89
					Johnson's Isl., OH	06/13/65	Rlsd. G.O. #109	P81,P83,CSR
Duhme, Cord	Pvt	B German LA	Deserted/enemy	03/22/65	Charleston, SC	03/22/65	Released on oath	CSR
Duke, Benjamin F.	Pvt	C 25th SCVI	Drury's Bluff, VA	05/14/65	Fts. Monroe, VA	05/25/64	Died of wounds	CDC,CSR
Duke, Berry W.	Pvt	G 12th SCVI	Petersburg, VA Hos.	04/03/65	Petersburg, VA Hos.	04/17/65	Pt. O Rocks, VA Hos.	CSR
					Pt. O Rocks, VA Hos.	05/17/65	Camp Hamilton, VA	CSR
					Camp Hamilton, VA		Newport News, VA	CSR
					Newport News, VA	06/14/65	Rlsd. G.O. #109	CSR
Duke, G.R.	Pvt	K 22nd SCVI	Deserted/enemy	03/01/65	City Pt., VA	03/03/65	Washington, DC	CSR
					Washington, DC	03/06/65	New York, NY oath	CSR
Duke, J.J.	Pvt	E 1st SCVC	Catlett's Stn., VA	03/30/63	Ft. McHenry, MD	04/13/63	City Pt., VA Xc	P110

SOUTH CAROLINA SOLDIERS, SAILORS AND  CITIZENS HELD IN U.S. PRISONS 1861-1865

NAME	RANK	REGIMENT	CAPTURED AT	WHEN	PRISON	MOVED	DISPOSITION	SOURCES
Duke, John	Pvt	B 7th SCVC	Deserted/enemy	03/17/65	Bermuda Hundred, VA	03/21/65	City Pt., VA	CSR
					City Pt., VA	03/24/65	Washington, DC	CSR
					Washington, DC	03/24/65	Phila., PA on oath	CSR
Duke, Robert E.	Pvt	C 25th SCVI	Ft. Darling, VA	05/14/64	Bermuda Hundred, VA	05/16/64	Fts. Monroe, VA	CSR,HAG
					Fts. Monroe, VA	05/17/64	Pt. Lookout, MD	CSR
					Pt. Lookout, MD	08/15/64	Elmira, NY	P113,P116,P120
					Pt. Lookout, MD	06/19/65	Rlsd. G.O. #109	CSR
Duke, Russell	Pvt	F 1st SCVC	Upperville, VA	06/21/63	Ft. McHenry, MD	06/25/63	City Pt., VA Xc	P110,CSR
Duke, Thomas J.	Pvt	C 25th SCVI	Ft. Darling, VA	05/14/64	Bermuda Hundred, VA	05/16/64	Fts. Monroe, VA	CSR,HAG
					Fts. Monroe, VA	05/17/64	Pt. Lookout, MD	CSR
					Pt. Lookout, MD	08/15/64	Elmira, NY	P113,P116,P120
					Elmira, NY	06/19/65	Rlsd. G.O. #109	P65,P66
Duke, William A.	Cpl	G 12th SCVI	Appomattox R., VA	04/03/65	City Pt., VA	04/11/65	Hart's Island, NY	CSR
					Hart's Island, NY	06/16/65	Rlsd. G.O. #109	P79,CSR
Dukes, G.L.	Pvt	I 13th SCVI	Harpers Farm, VA	08/26/64	Pt. Lookout, MD	06/05/65	Rlsd. Instr. 5/30/65	P122
Dukes, George M.	Pvt	C 24th SCVI	Chickamauga, GA	09/20/63	Nashville, TN	09/30/63	Louisville, KY	P38,CSR
					Louisville, KY	10/02/63	Camp Douglas, IL	P88,P89,EFW,CSR
					Camp Douglas, IL	06/20/65	Rlsd. G.O. #109	P53,P55,P57,CSR
Dukes, J.J.	Pvt	E 1st SCVC	Brentsville, VA	03/31/63	Provost Marshal	04/03/63	Old Capitol, DC	CSR
					Old Capitol, DC	04/17/63	City Pt., VA Xc	CSR
					Ft. McHenry, MD	04/13/63	City Pt., VA Xc	P110
Dukes, Thomas J.	Pvt	D 18th SCVI	Farmville, VA	04/06/65	City Pt., VA	04/14/65	Newport News, VA	CSR
					Newport News, VA	06/13/65	Rlsd. G.O.#109	P107,CSR
Dulian, Traston	Smn	CS *Chicora*	Morris Island, SC	09/07/63	Ft. Columbus, NY	10/09/63	Johnson's Isl., OH	P1
Dulin, James R.	Pvt	A 2nd SCVC	Catletts Stn., VA	03/30/63	Old Capitol, DC	04/17/63	City Pt., VA Xc	CSR
Dulin, James R.	Pvt	A 2nd SCVC	Madison C.H., VA	09/22/63	Old Capitol, DC	09/26/63	Pt. Lookout, MD	P113,P116,CSR
					Ft. McHenry, MD	09/26/63	Pt. Lookout, MD	P110,P113,P116
					Pt. Lookout, MD		Exchanged	P124
Dumas, Edward	Pvt	H Ham.Leg.MI	Ashland, VA	06/01/65	Ashland, VA	06/01/65	Paroled on oath	CSR
Dunaho, Elisha	Pvt	F 26th SCVI	Petersburg, VA	03/25/65	City Pt., VA	03/28/65	Pt. Lookout, MD	CSR
					Pt. Lookout, MD	06/26/65	Rlsd. G.O. #109	P118,P122,CSR
Dunbar, J.H.	AEn	*Huntress*	High seas	01/18/63	Ft. Delaware, DE			P47
Dunbar, Robert J.	Cpt	D Hol.Leg.	Hatchers Run, VA	03/29/65	Old Capitol, DC	04/09/65	Johnson's Isl., OH	P110,CSR
					Johnson's Isl., OH	06/17/65	Rlsd. G.O. #109	P81,P82,P83,CSR
Duncan, Alexander	Pvt	C 27th SCVI	Deserted/enemy	02/18/65	Charleston, SC	04/04/65	New York, NY oath	CSR,HAG
Duncan, Alfred W.	CiO	Tax Coll'r	Cheraw, SC	03/05/65	Hart's Island, NY	04/15/65	Ft. Delaware, DE	P79
Duncan, David	Pvt	B 7th SCVI	Halltown, WV	08/26/64	Harpers Ferry, WV	09/02/64	Camp Chase, OH	CNM,CSR,KEB
					Camp Chase, OH	11/03/64	Died, Rem. fever	P12,P22,P27,FPH
Duncan, David	Pvt	L 2nd SCVIRi	Richmond, VA Hos.	04/03/65	Libby Prison Rchmd.	04/23/65	Newport News, VA	CSR
					Newport News, VA	06/26/65	Rlsd. G.O. #109	P107,CSR
Duncan, David R.	Maj	13th SCVI	Petersburg, VA	04/08/65	Old Capitol, DC	04/09/65	Johnson's Isl., OH	P110,LC,CSR
					Johnson's Isl., OH	05/18/65	Released on oath	P81,P82,CSR
Duncan, George W.	Cpl	F 7th SCVC	Jarratt's Stn., VA	05/08/64	Pt. Lookout, MD	08/15/64	Elmira, NY	P113,P116,P120
					Elmira, NY	01/14/65	Died, Heart Disease	P6,P12,P65,P66,FPH
Duncan, Hezekiah E.	Pvt	A 2nd SCVC	Whitehall, NC	03/18/65	New Berne, NC	03/30/65	Pt. Lookout, MD	CSR
					Pt. Lookout, MD	06/26/65	Rlsd. G.O. #109	P118,P122,CSR
Duncan, J.W.	Pvt	G 13th SCVI	Fredericksburg, VA	05/11/62	Steamer Coatzacoal		Prob. Aikens Ldg.	CSR

SOUTH CAROLINA SOLDIERS, SAILORS AND **D** CITIZENS HELD IN U.S. PRISONS 1861-1865

NAME	RANK	REGIMENT	CAPTURED AT	WHEN	PRISON	MOVED	DISPOSITION	SOURCES
Duncan, James	Pvt	E Hol.Leg. C	Winchester, VA	07/29/63	Hancock, MD	08/08/63	New Creek, WVA	CSR
					New Creek, WVA	08/09/63	Wheeling, WVA	CSR
					Wheeling, WVA	08/11/63	Camp Chase, OH	CSR
					Camp Chase, OH	03/17/64	Ft. Delaware, DE	CSR
					Ft. Delaware, DE	03/18/65	Hos. 3/18-4/15/65	P47
					Ft. Delaware, DE	06/11/65	Rlsd. G.O. #109	P43,CSR
Duncan, John	Pvt	I 24th SCVI	James Island, SC	05/16/62	Hilton Head, SC		Ft. Columbus, NY	CSR
					Ft. Columbus, NY	08/23/62	Ft. Delaware, DE	P37,CSR
					Ft. Delaware, DE	11/10/62	Aikens Ldg., VA Xc	CSR
Duncan, John	Pvt	I 14th SCVI	Deep Bottom, VA	07/28/64	City Pt., VA Hos.	07/28/65	Died of wounds	CSR
Duncan, John G.	Pvt	C Ham.Leg.MI	Manchester, VA	04/05/65	Manchester, VA	04/07/65	Provost Marshal	CSR
					Libby Prison Rchmd.	04/13/65	City Pt., VA	CSR
					City Pt., VA	04/14/65	Pt. Lookout, MD	CSR
					Pt. Lookout, MD	06/05/65	Rlsd. Instr. 5/30/65	P114,P119,P122,CSR
Duncan, Joseph	Pvt	K 16th SCVI	Macon, GA	04/30/65	Macon, GA	04/30/65	Paroled on oath	CSR
Duncan, Nathaniel	Pvt	K Ham.Leg.MI	Farmville, VA	04/11/65	Farmville, VA	04/11/65	Paroled	CSR
Duncan, Reuben T.	Pvt	F 7th SCVI	Society Hill, SC	03/02/65	New Berne, NC	03/26/65	Pt. Lookout, MD	CSR,KEB
					Pt. Lookout, MD	06/26/65	Rlsd. G.O. #109	P114,P118,P123
Duncan, Thomas	Pvt	E 1st SCVIR	Deserted/enemy	02/18/65	Charleston, SC		New York, NY oath	CSR
Duncan, Thomas J.	Pvt	I 12th SCVI	Spotsylvania, VA	05/12/64	Belle Plain, VA	05/20/64	Ft. Delaware, DE	CSR,LAN
					Ft. Delaware, DE	07/18/65	Rlsd. G.O. #109	P41,P42,P45,CSR
Duncan, William	Pvt	Ferguson's LA	Nashville, TN	12/16/64	Nashville, TN	12/19/64	Louisville, KY	CSR
					Louisville, KY	12/21/64	Camp Douglas, IL	P90,P94,CSR
Duncan, William M.	Pvt	K 2nd SCVI	Cedar Creek, VA	10/19/64	W. Bldg. Balt., MD	10/27/64	Pt. Lookout, MD	P1,KEB,SA2,H2,CSR
					Pt. Lookout, MD	10/29/64	Aikens Ldg., VA Xc	P114,P117,CSR
Dunham, W.S.	Pvt	C 4th SCVC	Deserted/enemy		City Pt., VA P.M.	04/12/65	Washington, DC	CSR
					Washington, DC	04/12/65	Columbus, OH oath	CSR
Dunlap, A.S.	Pvt	C 12th SCVI	Gettysburg, PA	07/05/63	Ft. Delaware, DE	10/02/63	Died, Typhoid	P5,P40,P44,P47,FPH
Dunlap, Edward B.	QSg	E 2nd SCVI	Amelia Springs, VA	04/05/65	City Pt, VA	04/09/65	Pt. Lookout, MD	H2,CSR,SA2
					Pt. Lookout, MD	06/26/65	Rlsd. G.O. #109	P114,P122,P123,CSR
Dunlap, J.H.	Pvt	F 13th SCVI	Deserted/enemy	02/24/65	City Pt., VA	02/26/65	Washington, DC	CSR
					Washington, DC	02/27/65	Springfield, IL	CSR
Dunlap, J.L.	Pvt	E 12th SCVI	Gettysburg, PA	07/04/63	David's Island, NY	09/06/63	Died	P1,P6,P12,FPH
Dunlap, Milton G.	Pvt	C 2nd SCVC	Hedgesville, VA	10/22/62	Ft. McHenry, MD	10/24/62	Aikens Ldg., VA Xc	CSR
Dunlap, R.A.	Pvt	A 17th SCVI	Crater, Pbg., VA	07/30/64	City Pt., VA	08/05/64	Pt. Lookout, MD	CSR
					Pt. Lookout, MD	08/08/64	Elmira, NY	P113,P117,P120,CSR
					Elmira, NY	10/11/64	Tfd. for exchange	P65,CSR
					Pt. Lookout, MD	10/29/64	Venus Pt., GA Xc	P114,P117,P123,CSR
Dunlap, Robert T.	Cpl	H 4th SCVC	Stony Creek, VA	12/01/64	City Pt., VA	12/05/64	Pt. Lookout, MD	CSR
					Pt. Lookout, MD	06/26/65	Rlsd. G.O. #109	P123,CSR
Dunlap, W.H.	Pvt	A 2nd SCVABn	Fayetteville, NC	03/07/65	Pt. Lookout, MD	05/18/65	Released G.O. #85	P114,P118
Dunlap, William D.	Pvt	E 17th SCVI	Petersburg, VA	03/25/65	City Pt., VA	03/28/65	Pt. Lookout, MD	CSR
					Pt. Lookout, MD	06/04/65	Rlsd. Instr. 5/30/65	P114,P121,P118,CSR
Dunlap, William F.	Pvt	E 20th SCVI	Lexington, SC	02/14/65	City Pt., VA	04/07/65	Hart's Island, NY	CSR
					Hart's Island NY	06/16/65	Rlsd. G.O. #109	CSR
Dunlap, William S.	Cpt	B 12th SCVI	Appomattox R., VA	04/03/65	Old Capitol, DC	04/20/65	Johnson' Isl., OH	P110,CSR
					Johnson' Isl., OH	06/18/65	Rlsd. G.O. #109	P81,CSR
Dunleavy, John	Pvt	K 1st SCVIG			Ft. Delaware, DE	08/05/62	Aikens Ldg., VA Xc	CSR
Dunlop, W.J.	Pvt	E 28th SCMil	Lexington Dist., SC	02/14/65	Hart's Island, NY	06/16/65	Rlsd. G.O. #109	P79
Dunn, A.M.	Cpl	G 3rd SCVABn	Sumter Dist., SC	02/26/65	New Berne, NC	04/10/62	Hart's Island, NY	CSR
					Hart's Island, NY	06/17/65	Rlsd. G.O. #109	P79,CSR
Dunn, Henry	Pvt	D 22nd SCVI	Kinston, NC	12/14/62	Kinston, NC	12/14/62	Paroled POW	CSR

SOUTH CAROLINA SOLDIERS, SAILORS AND D CITIZENS HELD IN U.S. PRISONS 1861-1865

NAME	RANK	REGIMENT	CAPTURED AT	WHEN	PRISON	MOVED	DISPOSITION	SOURCES
Dunn, Henry	Pvt	D 22nd SCVI	Hatchers Run, VA	03/29/65	City Pt., VA	04/02/65	Pt. Lookout, MD	CSR
					Pt. Lookout, MD	06/26/65	Rlsd. G.O. #109	P118,P122,P123
Dunn, James	Pvt	H 27th SCVI	Deserted/enemy	02/18/65	Charleston, SC	02/18/65	New York, NY oath	CSR,HAG
Dunn, John	Pvt	LafayetteA	Deserted/enemy	02/18/65	Charleston, SC	03/02/65	Taken the oath	CSR
Dunn, M.	Pvt	D 22nd SCVI	Kinston, NC	12/14/62	Kinston, NC	12/14/62	Paroled POW	CSR
Dunn, M.	Pvt	D 22nd SCVI	Hatchers Run, VA	04/03/65	City Pt., VA	04/07/65	Hart's Island, NY	CSR
					Hart's Island, NY	06/15/65	Rlsd. G.O. #109	P79
Dunn, Phillip	Pvt	E 19th SCVI	Sumter Dist., SC	02/26/65	City Pt., VA	04/07/65	Hart's Island, NY	CSR
					Hart's Island, NY	06/17/65	Rlsd. G.O. #109	P79,CSR
Dunn, Stephen	Pvt	C 6th SCVI	Boonesboro, MD	09/15/62	Ft. Delaware, DE	10/02/62	Aikens Ldg., VA	CSR
Dunn, Stephen	Pvt	G 3rd SCVABn	Sumter Dist., SC	02/26/65	Hart's Island, NY	06/17/65	Rlsd. G.O. #109	P79,CSR
Dunn, Thomas	Pvt	B 19th SCVI	Atlanta, GA	08/18/64	Nashville, TN	08/30/64	Louisville, KY	CSR
					Louisville, KY	09/02/64	Camp Chase, OH	P90,P91,P94
					Camp Chase, OH	01/28/65	Died, Pneumonia	P6,P12,P22,P27,FPH
Dunnahoo, James H.	Pvt	Ferguson's LA	Ringgold, GA	11/26/63	Nashville, TN	12/09/63	Louisville, KY	P39,CSR
					Louisville, KY	12/11/63	Rock Island, IL	P88,CSR
					Rock Island, IL	10/11/64	Jd. US Army/Rejctd.	CSR
Dunneman, Henry	Sgt	G 3rd SCVC	Deserted/enemy	02/19/65	Charleston, SC		Released on oath	CSR
Dunnevant, William T.	Pvt	Ferguson's LA	Jackson, MS	07/17/63	Jackson, MS	07/30/63	Snyder's Bluff, MS	CSR
					Snyder's Bluff, MS	08/07/63	Camp Morton, IN	CSR
					Camp Morton, IN	05/10/65	Rlsd. G.O. #85	CSR
Dupont, Daniel B.	Pvt	Wash'n LA	Augusta, GA	06/02/65	Augusta, GA	06/02/65	Paroled	CSR
Durant, Alexander W.	Pvt	K 23rd SCVI	Five Forks, VA	04/01/65	City Pt., VA	04/05/65	Pt. Lookout, MD	CSR
					Pt. Lookout, MD	06/26/65	Rlsd. G.O. #109	P114,P123,CSR
Durant, J.J.	Pvt	E 6th SCVI	Fair Oaks, VA	05/31/62	Fts. Monroe, VA	06/21/62	Ft. Delaware, DE	CSR
					Ft. Delaware, DE	08/05/62	Aikens Ldg., VA Xc	CSR
Durham, Benjamin D.	Pvt	F 1st SCVA	Bentonville, NC	03/22/65	City Pt., VA	04/07/65	Hart's Island, NY	CSR
					Hart's Island, NY	06/30/65	David's Island, NY	CSR
					David's Island, NY	07/03/65	Died, Ch. diarrhea	CSR
Durham, Perry E.	Pvt	Ferguson's LA	Knoxville, TN	01/07/65	Knoxville, TN	01/10/65	Chattanooga, TN	CSR
					Chattanooga, TN	01/21/65	Sent North on oath	P92,CSR
Durham, Richard W.	Cpl	G 1st SCVA	Fayettville, NC	03/10/65	New Berne, NC	03/30/65	Pt. Lookout, MD	CSR
					Pt. Lookout, MD	06/26/65	Rlsd. G.O. #109	P114,P118,P122,CSR
Durham, S.P.	Pvt	E 1st SCVIH	Chattanooga, TN	10/29/63	Nashville, TN		Louisville, KY	P39
					Louisville, KY	11/09/63	Camp Morton, IN	P88,P93
Durisoe, C.L.	Sgt	D 14th SCVI	Gettysburg, PA	07/04/63	David's Island, NY	07/23/63	Died of wounds	P1,P6,P12,FPH,CSR
Durn, Perry	Pvt	F 1st SCVA			David's Island, NY	07/03/65	Died, Ch. Diarrhea	P6,P12,FPH
Durr, John	Pvt	G 11th SCVI	Petersburg, VA	06/15/64	Fts. Monroe, VA	06/19/64	Pt. Lookout MD	CSR
					Pt. Lookout, MD	08/01/64	Died, Typhoid	P6,P113,P117,CSR
Durst, William	Pvt	K 14th SCVI	Appomattox R., VA	04/03/65	City Pt., VA	04/11/65	Pt. Lookout, MD	CSR
					Hart's Island, NY	06/14/65	Rlsd. G.O. #109	P79,CSR
Dusenberry, W.A.	Pvt	L 7th SCVI	Charlestowne, VA	10/16/62	Ft. McHenry, MD	10/25/62	Aikens Ldg., VA Xc	CSR
Dutton, Benjamin Z.	Pvt	E 2nd SCVI	Caroline Co., VA	05/24/64	Old Capitol, DC	06/16/64	Ft. Delaware, DE	CSR,KEB,SA2,H2,KCE
					Ft. Delaware, DE	07/14/64	Hos. 7/14-7/22/64	P47
					Ft. Delaware, DE	05/03/65	Released on oath	P42,CSR,P96
Dutton, J.D.	Pvt	H 22nd SCVI	Greenville, SC	05/24/65	Greenville, SC	05/24/65	Paroled POW	CSR
Dwyer, Henry	Sgt	C 1st SCVIR	Deserted/enemy	02/18/65	Charleston, SC	04/04/65	New York, NY	SA1,CSR
Dwyer, J.C.	Cpl	A 2nd SCVIRi	Chattanooga, TN	10/29/63	Louisville, KY	11/09/63	Camp Morton, IN	P88,P89,P93
					Camp Morton, IN	03/04/65	Tfd. for Xc	P100
Dye, John C.	Pvt	C 2nd SCVC	Raleigh, NC	04/13/65	Raleigh, NC	04/13/65	Paroled on oath	CSR
Dye, John L.	Pvt	B 17th SCVI	Petersburg, VA	03/25/65	City Pt., VA	03/28/65	Pt. Lookout, MD	CSR,HFC
					Pt. Lookout, MD	06/26/65	Rlsd. G.O. #109	P114,P123,CSR

SOUTH CAROLINA SOLDIERS, SAILORS AND  CITIZENS HELD IN U.S. PRISONS 1861-1865

NAME	RANK	REGIMENT	CAPTURED AT	WHEN	PRISON	MOVED	DISPOSITION	SOURCES
Dye, Thomas E.	Pvt	B 17th SCVI	Petersburg, VA	03/25/65	City Pt., VA	03/28/65	Pt. Lookout, MD	CSR
					Pt. Lookout, MD	06/26/65	Rlsd. G.O. #109	P118,P122,P123,CSR
Dye, William F.	Pvt	1st SCVIG		04/03/62	Fts. Monroe, VA	08/05/62	Aikens Ldg. for Xc	CSR
Dykes, E.	Pvt	A 14th SCMil	Lynch's Creek, SC	02/25/65	Hart's Island, NY	06/17/65	Rlsd. G.O. #109	P79
Dykes, G.A.	Pvt	A 14th SCMil	Lynch's Creek, SC	02/25/65	Hart's Island, NY	06/17/65	Rlsd. G.O. #109	P79
Dykes, Thomas	Pvt	D 1st SCVIR	Bentonville, NC	03/22/65	City Pt., VA	04/07/65	Hart's Island, NY	CSR
					Hart's Island, NY	06/17/65	Rlsd. G.O. #109	SA1,P79,CSR
Dykes, William R.	Pvt	H 17th SCVI	Petersburg, VA	04/02/65	City Pt., VA	04/13/65	Pt. Lookout, MD	CSR
					Pt. Lookout, MD	06/26/65	Rlsd. G.O. #109	P114,P119,P123,CSR
Dyson, Archibald S.	HSd	D 21st SCVI	Morris Island, SC	07/10/63	Hilton Head, SC	09/22/63	Ft. Columbus, NY	CSR,HAG
					Ft. Columbus, NY	09/23/63	Pt. Lookout, MD	P1,CSR
					Pt. Lookout, MD	10/15/63	Hammond G.H., MD	P113,P125,CSR
					Pt. Lookout, MD	12/23/63	Died, Typhoid	P5,P116,FPH,CSR

SOUTH CAROLINA SOLDIERS, SAILORS AND  CITIZENS HELD IN U.S. PRISONS 1861-1865

NAME	RANK	REGIMENT	CAPTURED AT	WHEN	PRISON	MOVED	DISPOSITION	SOURCES
Eades, Miles A.	Pvt	F 1st SCVC	Culpepper, VA	09/13/63	Ft. McHenry, MD	09/23/63	Pt. Lookout, MD	P110
					Old Capitol, DC	09/26/63	Pt. Lookout, MD	CSR
					Pt. Lookout, MD	01/13/65	US Smallpox Hos.	CSR
					Pt. Lookout, MD	04/27/64	City Pt., VA Xc	P116,P124,CSR
Eadon, John Legrand	Sgt	I 23rd SCVI	Petersburg, VA Hos.	04/03/65	Fair Gds. Hos. Pbg.	04/08/65	Died of wounds	P6,P12,HCL,CSR
Eagan, John	Pvt	E 1st SCVIR	Morris Island, SC	07/10/63	Hilton Head, SC	09/19/63	Ft. Columbus NY	SA1,CSR
Eagan, Michael	Pvt	K 1st SCVA	Fayetteville, NC	03/16/65	New Berne, NC	03/30/65	Pt. Lookout, MD	CSR
					Pt. Lookout, MD	05/13/65	Rlsd. G.O. #85	P114,P117,CSR
Eagerton, H.G.	CCp	H 8th SCVI	Winchester, VA	09/13/64	Harpers Ferry, WV	09/19/64	Camp Chase, OH	CSR
					Camp Chase, OH	06/11/65	Rlsd. G.O. #109	CSR
Eagerton, John	Pvt	C 5th SCVI	Black Creek, SC	03/04/65	New Berne, NC	04/03/65	Pt. Lookout, MD	CSR
					Pt. Lookout, MD	06/23/65	Rlsd. G.O.#109	CSR
Eakins, Benjamin H.	Pvt	F Hol.Leg.	Five Forks, VA	04/01/65	Pt. Lookout, MD	06/26/65	Rlsd. G.O. #109	P114,P122,CSR
Eakins, J.D.	Pvt	F Hol.Leg.	Jarratts Stn., VA	05/08/64	Fts. Monroe, VA	05/13/64	Pt. Lookout, MD	CSR
					Pt. Lookout, MD	08/15/64	Elmira, NY	P113,P116
					Elmira, NY	02/13/65	James R., VA Xc	P65,CSR
					Boulwares Wh., VA	02/22/65	Jackson Hos. Rchmd.	CSR
Eargle, George A.	Pvt	I 15th SCVI	Gettysburg, PA	07/03/63	Letterman G.H. Gbg	07/20/63	Provost Marshal	P1,KEB,H15
					David's Island, NY	10/22/63	Fts. Monroe, VA	P1
					Fts. Monroe, VA	10/28/63	City Pt., VA Xc	CSR
Eargle, J.A.	Sgt	I 15th SCVI	Halltown, VA	08/26/64	Washington, D.C.	08/29/64	Harpers Ferry, WV	CSR,KEB
					Harpers Ferry, WV	09/02/64	Camp Chase, OH	CSR
					Camp Chase, OH	03/18/65	Pt. Lookout, MD Xc	P22,P26,CSR
					Pt. Lookout, MD	03/27/65	Boulware's Wh., Xc	CSR
Eargle, William R.	Cpl	H 13th SCVI	Gettysburg, PA	07/01/63	David's Island, NY	09/12/63	City Pt., VA Xc	P1,CSR
Earl, Elijah	Pvt	E 4th SCVC	Bennettsville, SC	03/06/65	New Berne, NC	04/03/65	Pt. Lookout, MD	CSR
					Pt. Lookout, MD	06/26/65	Rlsd. G.O. #109	P114,P117,P122,CSR
Earle, B.J.	Pvt	A 3rd SCVABn	High Pt., NC	05/02/65	High Pt., NC	05/02/65	Paroled on oath	CSR
Earle, E.D.	Sgt	A 3rd SCVABn	High Pt., NC	05/02/65	High Pt., NC	05/02/65	Paroled on oath	CSR
Earle, J.H.	Cpl	A 3rd SCVABn	High Pt., NC	05/02/65	High Pt., NC	05/02/65	Paroled on oath	CSR
Earle, William E.	Cpt	A 3rd SCVABn	High Pt., NC	05/02/65	High Pt., NC	05/02/65	Paroled on oath	CSR
Earnhart, James B.	Pvt	K P.S.S.	Salisbury, NC	04/12/65	Nashville, TN	04/29/65	Louisville, KY	P39,CSR
					Louisville, KY	05/02/65	Camp Chase, OH	P92,P94,CSR
					Camp Chase, OH	05/09/65	Died, Ch. Diarrhea	P6,P12,P27,FPH,CSR
Easler, Henry C.	Pvt	C 23rd SCVI	Five Forks, VA	04/01/65	City Pt., VA	04/04/65	Pt. Lookout, MD	CSR
					Pt. Lookout, MD	06/12/65	Rlsd. G.O. #109	P114,P117,CSR
Easley, J.R.	Pvt	F 2nd SCVC	Anderson, SC	05/08/65	Anderson, SC	05/08/65	Paroled on oath	CSR
Easter, J.	Pvt	B 7th SCVI	Fts. Monroe, VA	04/02/65	Washington, DC P.M.	04/05/65	Charleston, SC	CSR
Easterling, A. Jackson	Pvt	F 21st SCVI	Ft. Fisher, NC	01/15/65	Elmira, NY	05/26/65	Died, Erysipelas	P6,P65,P66,FPH,HAG
Easterling, A.H.	Pvt	F 21st SCVI	Petersburg, VA	05/09/64	Pt. Lookout, MD	03/14/65	Aikens Ldg., VA Xc	P113,P116,P124
Easterling, Andrew B.	Sgt	F 21st SCVI	Weldon RR, VA	08/21/64	Ft. McHenry, MD	08/26/64	Washington, DC	P1,HAG
					Lincoln Hos., DC	09/20/64	Died of wounds	P5,P110
Easterling, C.D.	1Lt	B 24th SCVI	Marlboro, SC	03/05/65	Hart's Island, NY	04/15/65	Ft. Delaware, DE	P79,EFW
					Ft. Delaware, DE	06/17/65	Rlsd. G.O. #109	P43,P45,EFW
Easterling, Elijah	Pvt	G 8th SCVI	Bennettsville, SC	03/06/65	New Berne, NC	04/03/65	Pt. Lookout, MD	CSR
					Pt. Lookout, MD	06/26/65	Rlsd. G.O. #109	P114,P117,P122,CSR
Easterling, Enos	Pvt	F 1st SCVIG	Warrenton, VA	09/29/62	Warrenton, VA	09/29/62	Paroled	SA1,CSR
Easterling, George W.	Cpl	F 21st SCVI	Weldon RR, VA	08/21/64		08/26/64	Washington, DC	P1,HAG
					Pt. Lookout, MD	10/30/64	Aikens Ldg., VA Xc	P116,P121,P123
					Pt. Lookout, MD	03/14/65	Exchanged	P113
Easterling, George W.	Cpl	F 21st SCVI	Bennettsville, SC	03/06/65	Pt. Lookout, MD	06/04/65	Rlsd per Instr 5/	P121,P114,HAG

SOUTH CAROLINA SOLDIERS, SAILORS AND  CITIZENS HELD IN U.S. PRISONS 1861-1865

NAME	RANK	REGIMENT	CAPTURED AT	WHEN	PRISON	MOVED	DISPOSITION	SOURCES
Easterling, John N.	Pvt	B 24th SCVI	Jonesboro, GA	09/01/64	Nashville, TN	10/27/64	Louisville, KY	CSR
					Louisville, KY	10/29/64	Camp Douglas, IL	P90,P91,P93
					Camp Douglas, IL	04/14/65	Joined 5th US Vol.	P53,P55
Easterling, Nelson A.	1Lt	F 21st SCVI	Weldon RR, VA	08/21/64	Ft. McHenry, MD	08/27/64	Ft. Delaware, DE	P110,HAG
					Ft. Delaware, DE	12/03/64	Died, Typhoid	P5,P42,P46,P47,HAG
Easterling, Thomas	Sgt	G 8th SCVI	Gettysburg, PA	07/09/63	Baltimore, MD	08/16/63	Pt. Lookout, MD	CSR,KEB
					Pt. Lookout, MD	08/16/64	Elmira, NY	P113,P116,P120,CSR
					Elmira, NY	10/11/64	Pt. Lookout, MD	P65,CSR
					Pt. Lookout, MD	10/19/64	Aikens Ldg., VA Xc	P117
					Pt. Lookout, MD	10/29/64	Exchanged	P114,P123,P124
					Pt. Lookout, MD	10/29/64	Venus Pt., GA Xc	CSR
Easterling, Thomas W.	1Lt	G 5th SCVC	Louisa C.H., VA	06/12/64	Pt. Lookout, MD	06/25/64	Ft. Delaware, DE	P113,P116,P120,CSR
					Ft. Delaware, DE	08/20/64	Hilton Head, SC	P42,P44,ISH,CSR
					Hilton Head, SC		Ft. Pulaski, GA	CSR
					Ft. Pulaski, GA	12/15/64	Charleston to Xc	CSR
Easterling, W.T.	Pvt	F 21st SCVI	Ft. Fisher, NC	01/15/65	Elmira, NY	07/11/65	Rlsd. G.O. #109	P65,P66,HAG
Easterling, William B.	Sgt	B 24th SCVI	Franklin, TN	12/17/64	Nashville, TN	01/04/65	Louisville, KY	P3,HOM,EFW
					Louisville, KY	01/14/65	Camp Chase, OH	P92,P94
					Camp Chase, OH	06/13/65	Rlsd. G.O. #109	CSR
Easters, J. Samuel	Sgt	A 18th SCVI	Richmond, VA Hos.	04/03/65	Provost Marshal	05/12/65	Paroled	CSR
Easters, J.A.M.	Pvt	G 18th SCVI	Petersburg, VA A	05/20/64	Bermuda Hundred, VA	05/21/64	Fts. Monroe, VA	CSR
					Fts. Monroe, VA	05/23/64	Pt. Lookout, MD	CSR
					Pt. Lookout, MD	03/14/65	Aikens Ldg., VA Xc	P113,P124,CSR
Easters, William	Pvt	D 5th SCVI	Williamsburg, VA	05/05/62	Fts. Monroe, VA		SUR Appomattox	CSR
Eastridge, J.N.	Pvt	E 22nd SCVI	Crater, Pbg., VA	07/30/64	City Pt., VA	08/05/64	Pt. Lookout, MD	CSR,LAN
					Pt. Lookout, MD	08/08/64	Elmira, NY	P113,P116,P120
					Elmira, NY	03/02/65	James R., VA Xc	CSR
					James R., VA Xc	03/09/65	Richmond, VA Hos.	CSR
Eastridge, John W.	Pvt	E 22nd SCVI	Crater, Pbg., VA	07/30/64	City Pt., VA	08/05/64	Pt. Lookout, MD	CSR,LAN
					Pt. Lookout, MD	08/08/64	Elmira, NY	P113,P116,P120
					Elmira, NY	02/03/65	Died, Diarrhea	P6,P12,P65,FPH
Eastridge, W.M.	Pvt	E 22nd SCVI	Kinston, NC	12/15/62	Kinston, NC	12/15/62	Paroled POW	CSR,LAN
Eastridge, W.M.	Pvt	E 22nd SCVI	Crater, Pbg., VA	07/30/64	City Pt., VA	08/05/64	Pt. Lookout, MD	CSR
					Pt. Lookout, MD	08/08/64	Elmira, NY	P113,P116,P120
					Elmira, NY	06/11/65	Rlsd. G.O. #109	P65,CSR
Eaton, J.M.	Pvt	D 22nd SCVI	Deserted/enemy	02/25/65	City Pt., VA	02/28/65	Washington, DC	CSR
					Washington, DC	03/01/65	Salem, IL on oath	CSR
Eaton, Joseph L.	Cpl	D 1st SCVIR	Morris Island, SC	07/10/63	Hilton Head, SC G.H.	07/24/63	Paroled	P2,SA1,CSR
Eaves, J.	Pvt	K 17th SCVI	Richmond, VA Hos.	04/03/65	Richmond, VA	05/02/65	Pt. Lookout, MD	CSR
Eberhart, Jacob	Pvt	I 7th SCVI	Louisa C.H., VA	06/11/64	Fts. Monroe, VA	06/30/64	Pt. Lookout, MD	CSR
					Pt. Lookout, MD	07/25/64	Elmira, NY	P113,CSR
Eberhart, Malachi	Pvt	SC Home Gd	Orangeburg, SC	02/13/65	Pt. Lookout, MD			P117
Echols, John	Pvt	I 1st SCVA	Morris Island, SC	07/10/63	Hilton Head, SC	07/18/63	Ft. Columbus, NY	CSR
					Ft. Columbus, NY	09/20/63	Pt. Lookout, MD	CSR
					Ft. Columbus, NY	09/23/63	Took the oath	P1
					Pt. Lookout, MD	10/15/63	Hammond G.H., MD	P113,P125
					Pt. Lookout, MD	11/06/63	Died, Ch. Diarrhea	P5,P116,FPH,CSR
Echols, Martin B.	Pvt	E 3rd SCVC	Spring Place, GA	02/27/64	Louisville, KY	03/09/64	Camp Chase, OH	P88,P93
					Camp Chase, OH	09/13/64	Johnson's Isl.,OH	P22,P26
Edenfield, J.L.	Pvt	B 2nd SCVC	Augusta, GA	05/22/65	Augusta, GA	05/22/65	Paroled on oath	CSR

SOUTH CAROLINA SOLDIERS, SAILORS AND CITIZENS HELD IN U.S. PRISONS 1861-1865

NAME	RANK	REGIMENT	CAPTURED AT	WHEN	PRISON	MOVED	DISPOSITION	SOURCES
Edens, A.K.	Pvt	F 22nd SCVI	Petersburg, VA	06/18/64	City Pt., VA	06/24/64	Pt. Lookout, MD	CSR
					Pt. Lookout, MD	07/27/64	Elmira, NY	P116,P120
					Elmira, NY	03/14/65	James R., VA Xc	P65,CSR
Edens, Alexander	Pvt.	K Ham.Leg.MI	Deserted/enemy	02/27/65	Bermuda Hundred, VA	02/28/65	City Pt., VA P.M.	CSR
					City Pt., VA P.M.	03/01/65	Washington, DC	CSR
					Washington, DC	03/02/65	Springfield, IL	CSR
Edens, Samuel	Pvt	F 22nd SCVI	Petersburg, VA	03/25/65	City Pt., VA	03/28/65	Pt. Lookout, MD	CSR
					Pt. Lookout, MD	06/26/65	Rlsd. G.O. #109	P117,CSR
Edens, Warren D.	Pvt	K Ham.Leg.MI	Deserted/enemy	03/05/65	Bermuda Hundred, VA	03/05/65	City Pt., VA P.M.	CSR
					City Pt., VA P.M.	03/07/65	Washington, DC	CSR
					Washington, DC	03/07/65	Springfield, IL	CSR
Edes, G.W.	Pvt	C 1st SCVA	Deserted/enemy	02/28/65	Charleston, SC		Released on oath	CSR
Edge, B.F.P.	Pvt	E 14th SCVI	Wilderness, VA	05/06/64	Belle PLain, VA	05/21/64	Ft. Delaware, DE	CSR
					Ft. Delaware, DE	05/03/65	Released on oath	P41,P42,CSR
Edge, Daniel	Pvt	B 18th SCVAB	Charleston, SC	03/18/65	Charleston, SC	03/18/65	Released on oath	CSR
Edge, William L.	Pvt	G 10th SCVI	Murfreesboro, TN	12/31/62	Nashville, TN	04/22/63	Nashville, TN	P38,RAS,CSR
					Louisville, KY	05/06/63	City Pt., VA Xc	P88,P89,CSR
					Ft. McHenry, MD	05/10/63	Paroled to City Pt.	CSR
					Petersburg, VA SCH	06/16/63	Furloughed and DIS	CSR
Edgeworth, Oliver P.	Pvt	A 4th SCVC	Anson Co., NC	03/02/65	New Berne, NC	03/30/65	Pt. Lookout, MD	CSR
					Pt. Lookout, MD	05/13/65	Released G.O. #85	P117,P122,CSR
Edgins, W.G.	Pvt	D 1st SCVIR	Morris Island, SC	07/10/63	Hilton head, SC			SA1,CSR
Edings, Joseph	Pvt	I 3rd SCVC	Edisto Island, SC	04/09/63	Ft. Norfolk, VA	06/29/63	Paroled	CSR
Edlin, Peter	Pvt	I 1st SCVA	Morris Island,SC	07/10/63	Hilton Head, SC	09/05/63	Ft. Columbus, NY	CSR
					Ft. Columbus, NY	09/23/63	Took the oath	P1
					Ft. Columbus, NY	10/10/63	Released	CSR
Edmonds, Charles	Pvt	G 1st SCVIH	Richmond, VA	04/03/65	Richmond, VA P.M.	05/18/65	Paroled	CSR
Edmonds, James	Pvt	C 27th SCVI	Deserted/enemy	09/02/64	Morris Island, SC	09/10/64	Hilton Head, SC	CSR
					Hilton Head, SC	09/13/64	Sent north on oath	CSR
Edmonds, Richard L.	Pvt	H 1st SCVIG	Gettysburg, PA	07/05/63	Ft. Delaware, DE		Hos. 7/16/64	P46,P47,SA1
					Ft. Delaware, DE	05/11/65	Released G.O. #85	P40,P42,P45,CSR
Edmondson, Jesse	Cpl	C 11th SCVI	Town Creek, NC	02/20/65	Ft. Anderson, NC	02/28/65	Pt. Lookout, MD	CSR
					Pt. Lookout, MD	06/26/65	Released G.O. #109	P114,P117,P122,CSR
Edmonston, Edward	Pvt	A 24th SCVI	Marietta, GA	07/03/64	Nashville, TN	07/13/64	Louisville, KY	CSR
					Louisville, KY	07/16/64	Camp Douglas, IL	P88,P91,CDC,EFW
					Camp Douglas, IL	12/03/64	Died, Smallpox	P5,P53,P58,FPH
Edmunds, Thomas J.	Pvt	C 7th SCVI			Cumberland, MD USH	11/14/63	Died, Ch. Diarrhea	P12,KEB,ROH,CSR
Edwards, Alexander D.	Pvt	D 21st SCVI	Morris Island, SC	07/27/63	Hilton Head, SC	09/22/63	Ft. Columbus, NY	P2,HAG,CSR
					Ft. Columbus, NY	09/26/63	Pt. Lookout, MD	CSR
					Pt. Lookout, MD	08/16/64	Elmira, NY	P120
					Elmira, NY	03/14/65	Tfd. for Exchange	CSR
					Pt. Lookout, MD	03/17/65	Exchanged	P123,P124,CSR
Edwards, Alexander D.	Pvt	D 21st SCVI	Cheraw, SC	03/03/65	New Berne, NC	04/10/65	Harts Island, NY	CSR
					Hart's Island, NY	06/17/65	Rlsd. G.O. #109	P79
Edwards, Allen	Pvt	D 21st SCVI	Morris Island, SC	07/10/63	Ft. Columbus, NY	09/26/63	Pt. Lookout, MD	CSR,HAG
					Pt. Lookout, MD	08/16/64	Elmira, NY	P113,P116
					Elmira, NY	03/14/65	Tfd. for exchange	P65
Edwards, B.F.	Sgt	D 21st SCVI	Weldon RR, VA	08/21/64	Pt. Lookout, MD	09/18/64	Aikens Ldg., VA Xc	P113,P116,P123,HAG
Edwards, Edward	Pvt	D 21st SCVI	Morris Island, SC	07/10/63	Ft. Columbus, NY	09/23/63	Took the oath	P1,HAG
					Pt. Lookout, MD	04/27/64	City Pt., VA Xc	P113,P116,P124
Edwards, Euphrates L.	Pvt	E 14th SCVI	Petersburg, VA	04/02/65	City Pt., VA	04/04/65	Pt. Lookout, MD	CSR
					Pt. Lookout, MD	06/26/65	Released G.O. #109	P114,P117,P122,CSR

SOUTH CAROLINA SOLDIERS, SAILORS AND  CITIZENS HELD IN U.S. PRISONS 1861-1865

NAME	RANK	REGIMENT	CAPTURED AT	WHEN	PRISON	MOVED	DISPOSITION	SOURCES
Edwards, John	Pvt	H 27th SCVI	Weldon RR, VA	08/21/64	City Pt., VA	08/24/64	Pt. Lookout, MD	CSR,HAG
					Pt. Lookout, MD	05/13/65	Released G.O. #85	P113,P116,P122,CSR
Edwards, John	Pvt	G 1st SCVA	Fayetteville, NC	03/10/65	New Berne, NC	03/30/65	Pt. Lookout, MD	CSR
					Pt. Lookout, MD	06/26/65	Rlsd G.O. #109	P114,P117,P122,CSR
Edwards, John H.	Pvt	D 21st SCVI	Weldon RR, VA	08/21/64	No U.S. records Fd.			CSR,HAG
Edwards, John O.	Pvt	E 5th SCVC	Deserted/enemy	03/31/65	Charleston, SC	03/31/65	Released on oath	CSR
Edwards, Joseph C.	Pvt	D 21st SCVI	Weldon RR, VA	08/21/64	City Pt., VA	08/24/64	Pt. Lookout, MD	CSR,HAG
					Pt. Lookout, MD	03/14/65	Exchanged	P113,P124,CSR
Edwards, Levi H.	Pvt	E 1st SCVIG	Gettysburg, PA	07/03/63	David's Island, NY	09/05/63	City Pt., VA Xc	P1,SA1,CSR
Edwards, Manning	Pvt	G 3rd SCVI	Maryland Hts., MD	09/14/62	Sandy Hook, MD	09/22/62	Rlsd. on parole	SA2,H3,CSR
Edwards, Manning	Pvt	G 3rd SCVI	Harpers Ferry, VA	05/27/65	Harpers Ferry, VA	05/27/65	Amnesty oath	CSR
Edwards, Owen	Pvt	K 1st SCVIH	Loudon, TN	12/03/63	Pittsburg, TN Hos.	02/14/64	Exchanged	P1,SA1,CSR
Edwards, Reps	Pvt	A 18th SCVI	Richmond, VA Hos.	04/03/65	Not given			CSR
Edwards, Robert P.	1Lt	H 7th SCVC	Peebles Fm., VA	09/30/64	Ft.McHenry, MD	10/23/64	Ft. Delaware, DE	P110
					Ft. Delaware, DE	06/10/65	Released	P43,P45
Edwards, Samuel Thomas	Sgt	D 19th SCVI	Atlanta, GA	07/28/64	Nashville, TN	02/26/65	Louisville, KY	P3,P39,HOE,CSR
					Louisville, KY	03/03/65	Camp Chase, OH	P92,P94,CSR
					Camp Chase, OH	03/26/65	Pt. Lookout, MD	P22,P26
					Pt. Lookout, MD	06/05/65	Released	P117,P114,P122,CSR
Edwards, T.B.	Pvt	A 3rd SCVABn	High Pt., NC	05/02/65	High Pt., NC	05/02/65	Paroled on oath	CSR
Edwards, W.E.	Pvt	K 1st SC Eng	Richmond, VA	04/03/65	Newport News, VA	06/14/65	Released	P107
Edwards, W.H.	Cpt	A 17th SCVI	Farmville, VA	04/07/65	Farmville, VA US Hos.	05/10/65	Burkesville, VA US	CSR
Edwards, W.P.	Pvt	B 27th SCVI	Weldon RR, VA	08/21/64	City Pt., VA	08/24/64	Pt. Lookout, MD	CSR
					Pt. Lookout, MD	09/18/64	Aikens Ldg., VA Xc	P113,P116,P123,CSR
Edwards, William W.	Pvt	C 7th SCVI	Paynesville, VA	04/05/65	City Pt., VA	04/13/65	Pt. Lookout, MD	CSR,KEB
					Pt. Lookout, MD	06/11/65	Rlsd. G.O. #109	P114,P117,P122,CSR
Egan, Charles E.	Pvt	I 27th SCVI	Petersburg, VA	06/18/64	Bermuda Hundred, VA	06/21/64	Fts. Monroe, VA	CSR,HAG
					Fts. Monroe, VA	06/22/64	Pt. Lookout, MD	CSR
					Pt. Lookout, MD	03/14/65	Aikens Ldg., VA Xc	P113,P116,P124,CSR
Egan, John	Pvt	E 1st SCVA	Morris Island, SC	07/10/63	Ft. Columbus, NY	09/23/63	Took the oath	P1
Egan, Thomas	Pvt	H 27th SCVI	Town Creek, NC	02/20/65	Pt. Lookout, MD	05/12/65	Rlsd. G.O. #85	P114,HAG
Eggerking, Frederick W.	Pvt	C 27th SCVI	Town Creek, NC	02/20/65	Ft. Anderson, NC	02/28/65	Pt. Lookout, MD	CSR,HAG
					Pt. Lookout, MD	05/13/65	Released G.O. #85	P114,P117,P122,CSR
Eidson, James H.	Pvt	I 2nd SCVC	Augusta, GA	05/19/65	Augusta, GA	05/19/65	Paroled on oath	CSR
Eidson, John J.	Pvt	I 2nd SCVC	Augusta, GA	05/19/65	Augusta, GA	05/19/65	Paroled on oath	CSR
Eidson, Larkin	Pvt	G 7th SCVI	Cheraw, SC	03/05/65	Cheraw, SC	03/05/65	Paroled	KEB,CSR
Eidson, M.	Pvt	D 6th SCResB	Augusta, GA	05/25/65	Augusta, GA	05/25/65	Paroled	CSR
Eikenketter, John F.	Pvt	C Ham.Leg.	Frederick, MD	09/12/62	Frederick, MD	09/22/62	Ft. Delaware, DE	CSR
					Ft. Delaware, DE	10/02/62	Aikens Ldg., VA Xc	CSR
Elder, David H.	Pvt	B Hol.Leg.	Petersburg, VA	03/25/65	City Pt., VA	03/28/65	Pt. Lookout, MD	CSR
					Pt. Lookout, MD	06/26/65	Rlsd. G.O. #109	P114,P117,P122,CSR
Elder, John	Pvt	B Hol.Leg.	Petersburg, VA	03/25/65	City Pt., VA	03/28/65	Pt. Lookout, MD	CSR,HOS
					Pt. Lookout, MD	06/26/65	Rlsd. G.O. #109	P114,P117,CSR
Eleazer, Robert E.	Pvt	C 20th SCVI	Cedar Creek, VA	10/19/64	Harpers Ferry, WV	10/23/64	Pt. Lookout, MD	CSR,KEB
					Pt. Lookout, MD	06/26/65	Rlsd. G.O. #109	P114,P117,P122,CSR
Elkin, David R.	Pvt	H 6th SCVI	Lynch's Creek, SC	02/23/65	New Berne, NC	04/03/65	Pt. Lookout, MD	CSR,HFC
					Pt. Lookout, MD	06/11/65	Rlsd. G.O. #109	P114,P117,122,CSR
Elkins, John. P.	Pvt	K 6th SCVI	Darbytown Rd., VA	04/03/65	Libby Prison Rchmd.	04/08/65	City Pt., VA P.M.	CSR
					City Pt., VA	04/13/65	Pt. Lookout, MD	CSR
					Pt. Lookout, MD	06/11/65	Rlsd. G.O. #109	P114,P117,P122,CSR
Elkins, Lafayette T.	Pvt	A 17th SCVI	Petersburg, VA	04/02/65	City Pt., VA	04/04/65	Pt. Lookout, MD	CSR
					Pt. Lookout, MD	06/26/65	Rlsd. G.O. #109	P114,P117,P122,CSR

SOUTH CAROLINA SOLDIERS, SAILORS AND  CITIZENS HELD IN U.S. PRISONS 1861-1865

NAME	RANK	REGIMENT	CAPTURED AT	WHEN	PRISON	MOVED	DISPOSITION	SOURCES
Elkins, William	Pvt	G 14th SCVI	Gettysburg, PA	07/04/63	David's Island, NY	09/08/63	City Pt., VA Xc	P1,CSR
Elkins, William	Pvt	I 5th SCVI	Deep Bottom, VA	08/14/64	Bermuda Hundred, VA	08/15/64	Fts. Monroe, VA	CSR,SA3
					Pt. Lookout, MD	09/30/64	Exchanged	P125,CSR
Elkins, William	Pvt	I 5th SCVI	Richmond, VA Hos.	04/03/65	Libby Prison, VA	04/23/65	Newport News, VA	CSR
					Newport News, VA	05/20/65	Died	CSR
Elledge, R.Y.J.	Sgt	A 6th SCVC	Armstrong's Mill	12/09/64	City Pt., VA	12/12/64	Pt. Lookout, MD	CSR
					Pt. Lookout, MD	06/11/65	Rlsd. G.O. #109	P114,CSR
Ellenburg, John	Pvt	H 7th SCVIBn	Augusta, GA	05/31/65	Augusta, GA	05/31/65	Paroled	CSR
Ellenburg, John A.	Pvt	F 22nd SCVI	Kinston, NC	12/14/62	Kinston, NC	12/14/62	Paroled POW	CSR
Ellenburg, John A.	Pvt	F 22nd SCVI	Petersburg, VA	03/25/65	City Pt., VA	03/28/65	Pt. Lookout, MD	CSR
					Pt. Lookout, MD	06/26/65	Rlsd. G.O. #109	P114,P117,P122
Ellenburg, John H.	Pvt	C 19th SCVI	Nashville, TN	12/16/64	Louisville, KY	01/05/65	Camp Chase, OH	P94
					Camp Chase, OH	05/02/65	New Orleans, LA Xc	P26,UD3,HOE
Elliot, William H.	Pvt	H 1st SCVIG	Sharpsburg, MD	10/01/62	Ft. McHenry, MD	10/13/62	Fts. Monroe, VA Xc	P96,SA1,CSR
Elliott, Dred	Pvt	K 26th SCVI	Farmville, VA	04/06/65	City Pt., VA	04/14/65	Newport News, VA	CSR
					Newport News, VA	06/26/65	Rlsd. G.O. #109	P107,CSR
Elliott, H.G.	Pvt	K 26th SCVI	Farmville, VA	04/06/65	City Pt., VA	04/14/65	Newport News, VA	CSR
					Newport News, VA	06/26/65	Rlsd. G.O. #109	P107,CSR
Elliott, James M.	Pvt	G 10th SCVI	Atlanta, GA	07/22/64	Nashville, TN	07/29/64	Louisville, KY	CSR,RAS
					Louisville, KY	07/30/64	Camp Chase, OH	P88,P91,P93,CSR
					Camp Chase, OH	03/02/65	City Pt., VA Xc	P26,CSR
					Richmond, VA Hos.	03/17/65	Furloughed 60 days	CSR
					Camp Chase, OH	06/11/65	Released	P22
Elliott, L.M.	Pvt	H P.S.S.	Fair Oaks, VA	05/31/62	Fts. Monroe, VA	06/03/62	Ft. Delaware, DE	CSR
					Ft. Delaware, DE	08/05/62	Aikens Ldg., VA Xc	CSR,TSE
Elliott, L.T.	Pvt	F 1st SCVIR	Deserted/enemy	02/22/65	Charleston, SC	03/22/65	New York, NY	CSR
Elliott, Samuel	Pvt	K 26th SCVI	Petersburg, VA	04/02/65	City Pt., VA	04/05/65	Pt. Lookout, MD	CSR
					Pt. Lookout, MD		Released, no date	P114,P116,P117,CSR
Elliott, Thomas	Pvt	G Ham.Leg.MI	Deep Bottom, VA	08/14/64	Pt. Lookout, MD	11/01/64	Aikens Ldg., VA Xc	P113,P116,P121,CSR
Elliott, Washington F.	Pvt	A 21st SCVI	Petersburg, VA	06/24/64	Pt. Lookout, MD	08/16/64	Elmira, NY	P113,P116,P120,HAG
					Elmira, NY	07/03/65	Rlsd. G.O. #109	P65,HAG
Ellis, Wesley W.	Pvt	B 21st SCVI	Ft. Fisher, NC	01/15/65	Elmira, NY	03/06/65	Died, Diarrhea	P6,P12,P65,P66,HAG
Ellis, Amaziah Rice	Pvt	G Orr's Ri.	Amelia C.H., VA	04/05/65	City Pt., VA	04/13/65	Pt. Lookout, MD	CSR,CDC
					Pt. Lookout, MD	06/26/65	Rlsd. G.O. #109	P114,P117,P122,CSR
Ellis, Archibald B.	Cpl	F 2nd SCVI	Cedar Creek, VA	10/19/64	Harpers Ferry, WV	10/23/64	Pt. Lookout, MD	SA2,H2,CSR
					Pt. Lookout, MD	03/28/65	Aikens Ldg., VA Xc	P114,P117,P121,CSR
Ellis, Benjamin F.	Pvt	B Wash'n LA	Spotsylvania, VA	05/09/64	Bermuda Hundred, VA	05/15/64	Fts. Monroe, VA	CSR
					Fts. Monroe, VA	05/16/64	Pt. Lookout, MD	CSR
					Pt. Lookout, MD	08/15/64	Elmira, NY	P113,CSR
					Elmira, NY	06/21/65	Rlsd. G.O. #109	CSR
Ellis, Edward	Pvt	C 15th SCVAB	Deserted/enemy	02/18/65	Charleston, SC	03/18/65	New York, NY oath	CSR
Ellis, Ellie S.	Pvt	C 25th SCVI	Ft. Fisher, NC	01/15/65	New York, NY	01/30/65	Elmira, NY	CSR,CTA,HAG
					Elmira, NY	05/17/65	Died, Diarrhea	P6,P12,P65,P66,CSR
Ellis, Henry H.	Pvt	E 6th SCVI	Fair Oaks, VA	05/31/62	Fts. Monroe, VA	06/05/62	Ft. Delaware, DE	CSR
					Ft. Delaware, DE	08/05/62	Aikens Ldg., VA Xc	CSR
Ellis, Henry H.	Pvt	E 6th SCVI	Richmond, VA	04/03/65	Libby Prison Rchmd.	04/08/65	City Pt., VA P.M.	CSR
					City Pt., VA	04/14/65	Pt. Lookout, MD	CSR
					Pt. Lookout, MD	05/23/65	Died	P6,P114,P117,FPH
Ellis, J.M.	Pvt	M 7th SCVI	Morris Mills, VA	04/14/64	Pt. Lookout, MD	08/17/64	Died	P113,FPH
Ellis, James G.	Pvt	B 21st SCVI	Petersburg, VA	06/24/64	Pt. Lookout, MD	08/16/64	Elmira, NY	P113,P116,P120,HAG
					Elmira, NY	10/11/64	Tfd. for exchange	P65
					Pt. Lookout, MD	10/29/64	Aikens Ldg., VA Xc	P114,P116,P123

SOUTH CAROLINA SOLDIERS, SAILORS AND  CITIZENS HELD IN U.S. PRISONS 1861-1865

NAME	RANK	REGIMENT	CAPTURED AT	WHEN	PRISON	MOVED	DISPOSITION	SOURCES
Ellis, John W.	Pvt	E 2nd SCVIRi	Loudon, TN	12/03/63	Chattanooga G.H.	02/13/64	Nashville, TN USGH	P1,CSR
					Nashville, TN USGH	02/19/64	Nashville, TN P.M.	P1,CSR
					Nashville, TN	02/19/64	Louisville, KY	P39,CSR
					Louisville, KY	03/09/64	Ft. Delaware, DE	P88,P91,P93,CSR
					Camp Chase, OH	09/13/64	Johnson's Isl., OH	P22,P26,CSR
Ellis, John W.	Pvt	E 2nd SCVIRi	Loudon, TN	12/03/63	Johnsons Isl., OH	06/13/65	Released	P82,P83,CSR
Ellis, Oscar A.	Pvt	A 24th SCVI	Taylor's Ridge, GA	10/06/64	Nashville, TN	10/23/64	Louisville, KY	CSR,EFW
					Louisville, KY	10/26/64	Camp Douglas, IL	P90,P91,P93
					Camp Douglas, IL	02/20/65	Pt. Lookout, MD Xc	P55
Ellis, Oscar A.	Pvt	A 24th SCVI	Tallahassee, FL	10/06/64	Tallahassee, FL	05/10/65	Paroled	CSR
Ellis, Samuel	Pvt	B 23rd SCVI	Petersburg, VA	06/17/64	City Pt., VA	06/24/64	Pt. Lookout, MD	CSR
					Pt. Lookout, MD	07/27/64	Elmira, NY	CSR
					Elmira, NY	01/24/65	Died, Ch. Diarrhea	P6,P12,FPH,CSR
Ellis, W.J.	Sgt	I 1st SCVIG	Cox Road, VA	04/02/65	City Pt., VA	04/07/65	Hart's Island, NY	CSR
					Hart's Island, NY	06/15/65	Rlsd. G.O. #109	P79,CSR
Ellis, William D.	Pvt	4 10/19 SCVI	Missionary Ridge, TN	11/25/63	Nashville, TN	12/07/63	Louisville, KY	P39,RAS,CSR
					Louisville, KY	12/07/63	Rock Island, IL	P88,P89,RAS,CSR
					Rock Island, IL	06/18/65	Rlsd. G.O. #109	P131,CSR
Ellis, William D.	2Lt	B 11th SCVI	Town Creek, NC	02/20/65	Ft. Anderson, NC	02/28/65	Pt. Lookout, MD	CSR
					Pt. Lookout, MD	02/28/65	Washington, DC	P114,P116,P120,CSR
					Old Capitol, DC	03/24/65	Ft. Delaware, DE	CSR
					Ft. Delaware, DE	06/17/65	Rlsd. G.O. #109	P43,P45,HAG,CSR
Ellison, Azakiah E.	Pvt	D 27th SCVI	Town Creek, NC	02/20/65	Ft. Anderson, NC	02/28/65	Pt. Lookout, MD	CSR,HAG
					Pt. Lookout, MD	06/26/65	Rlsd. G.O. #109	P114,P117,P122,CSR
Ellison, Greenlee	Pvt	D 18th SCVI	Petersburg, VA Hos.	04/02/65	Camp Hamilton, VA	05/09/65	Newport News, VA	CSR
					Newport News, VA	06/26/65	Rlsd. G.O. #109	P107,CSR
Ellison, James	Pvt	E Ham.Leg.	Malvern Hill, VA	06/13/64	City Pt., VA	06/24/64	Pt. Lookout, MD	CSR
					Pt. Lookout, MD	07/27/64	Elmira, NY	P116,P120,CSR
					Elmira, NY	01/08/65	Died, Variola	P6,P12,P65,FPH
Ellrodd, Elijah W.	Pvt	H 7th SCVI	N. Anna River, VA	05/23/64	Port Royal, VA	05/30/64	Pt. Lookout, MD	CSR
					Pt. Lookout, MD	09/18/64	Aikens Ldg., VA Xc	P113,P123,P116,CSR
Elmore, Ellis	Pvt	H 21st SCVI	Petersburg, VA	05/09/64	Pt. Lookout, MD	05/14/65	Died, Ch. Diarrhea	P6,P113,P116,FPH
Elmore, J.A.	Pvt	H 13th SCVI	Chaffins Bluff, VA	08/15/64	Bermuda Hundred, VA	08/22/64	Camp Hamilton, VA	CSR
					Camp Hamilton, VA	08/24/64	Pt. Lookout, MD	CSR
					Pt. Lookout, MD	03/14/65	Aikens Ldg., VA Xc	P113,P116,P124,CSR
Elmore, W.R.	Pvt	I 13th SCVI	Petersburg, VA	04/02/65	City Pt., VA	04/04/65	Pt. Lookout, MD	CSR,HOS
					Pt. Lookout, MD	06/26/65	Rlsd. G.O. #109	P114,P117,P122,CSR
Elrod, Benjamin D.	Pvt	D 18th SCVI	Petersburg, VA	04/02/65	City Pt., VA	04/13/65	Pt. Lookout, MD	CSR
					Pt. Lookout, MD	06/26/65	Rlsd. G.O. #109	P114,P117,P122,CSR
Elrod, D.S.	Pvt	F 24th SCVI	Jackson, MS	05/16/63	Jackson, MS	05/16/63	Paroled in Hos.	CSR
Elrod, E.B.	Pvt	D 18th SCVI	Petersburg, VA	07/30/64	Pt. Lookout, MD	08/08/64	Elmira, NY	P113,P116,P120,CSR
					Elmira, NY	07/03/65	Rlsd. G.O. #109	P65,UD2,CSR
Elrod, Elias F.	Pvt	A 6th SCVC	Stony Creek, VA	12/01/64	City Pt., VA	12/04/64	Pt. Lookout, MD	CSR
					Pt. Lookout, MD	06/12/65	Released G.O. #109	P114,P121,CSR
Elrod, Everet	Pvt	D 18th SCVI	Petersburg, VA	07/30/64	City Pt., VA	08/05/64	Pt. Lookout, MD	CSR
					Pt. Lookout, MD	08/08/64	Elmira NY	CSR
					Elmira, NY	07/03/65	Rlsd. G.O. #109	CSR
Elsmore, John E.	Pvt	A 7th SCVI	Knoxville, TN	01/05/64	Nashville, TN	01/17/64	Louisville, KY	P39,CSR,CNM,KEB
					Louisville, KY	01/17/64	Rock Island, IL	P88,P93,CSR
					Rock Island, IL	10/31/64	Jd. USA, frontier S	P131,CSR
Elvington, David R.	Pvt	E 1st SCVIG	Deep Bottom, VA	07/28/64	City Pt., VA Hos.	07/31/64	Died of wounds	P12,SA1,HMC,CSR
Elvington, John H.	Pvt	E 1st SCVIG	Warrenton, VA	09/29/62	Warrenton, VA	09/29/62	Paroled	CSR

SOUTH CAROLINA SOLDIERS, SAILORS AND  CITIZENS HELD IN U.S. PRISONS 1861-1865

NAME	RANK	REGIMENT	CAPTURED AT	WHEN	PRISON	MOVED	DISPOSITION	SOURCES
Elvington, Nathan T.	Pvt	E 1st SCVIG	Petersburg, VA	07/29/64	Pt. Lookout, MD	08/08/64	Elmira, NY	P113,P116,P120,P125,SA1
Elvington, Nathan T.	Pvt	E 1st SCVIG	Deep Bottom, VA	07/28/64	Elmira, NY	02/13/65	James R., VA Xc	P65,SA1,CSR
Emanuel, Charles L.	Pvt	E 4th SCVC	Hawe's Shop, VA	05/28/64	White House, VA	06/08/64	Pt. Lookout, MD	CSR
					Pt. Lookout, MD	07/28/64	Elmira, NY	CSR
					Elmira, NY	02/20/65	James R., VA Xc	CSR
Emanuel, William Pledger	Maj	4th SCVC	Louisa C.H., VA	06/11/64	Fts. Monroe, VA	06/23/64	Pt. Lookout, MD	CSR
					Pt. Lookout, MD	06/25/64	Ft. Delaware, DE	P113,P116,P120,ISH
					Ft. Delaware, DE	08/20/64	Hilton Head, SC	P42,CSR
					Hilton Head, SC	10/20/64	Ft. Pulaski, GA	CSR
					Ft. Pulaski, GA	11/19/64	Hilton Head, SC	CSR
					Hilton Head, SC		Charleston Harbor	CSR
					Charleston Harbor	12/15/64	Paroled to Xc	CSR
Embry, F.H.	Pvt	F 22nd SCVI	Petersburg, VA	03/25/65	Pt. Lookout, MD	06/26/65	Rlsd. G.O. #109	P114
Emens, Austin M.	Pvt	E Ham.Leg.	Fair Oaks, VA	05/31/62	Fts. Monroe, VA	07/05/62	Ft. Delaware, DE	CSR
					Ft. Delaware, DE	08/05/62	Aikens Ldg., VA Xc	CSR
Emery, J.B.	Pvt	F 1st SCVIH	Knoxville, TN	12/03/63	Louisville, KY	12/31/63	Rock Island, IL	P88,P89,P93,CSR
					Rock Island, IL	02/15/65	Tfd. for exchange	CSR
Emlyn, H.N.	Pvt	A 2nd SCVI	Cedar Creek, VA	10/20/64	Harpers Ferry, VA	10/23/64	Pt. Lookout, MD	CSR
					Pt. Lookout, MD	03/28/65	Aikens Ldg., VA Xc	SA2,H2,CSR
Emlyn, Horatio N.	Pvt	A 15th SCVI	Cedar Creek, VA	10/20/64	Pt. Lookout, MD	03/25/65	Aikens Ldg., MD Xc	P114,P121,P124,KEB
Emory, John P.	Pvt	G 27th SCVI	Town Creek, NC	02/20/65	Ft. Anderson, NC	02/28/65	Pt. Lookout, MD	CSR,HAG
					Pt. Lookout, MD	06/26/65	Rlsd. G.O. #109	P114,P117,P122,UD6
Emory, Russell	Pvt	I 15th SCVI	Hatchers Run, VA	03/31/65	City Pt., VA	04/02/65	Pt. Lookout, MD	CSR
					Pt. Lookout, MD	06/27/65	Rlsd. G.O. #109	CSR
Englert, John W.	Pvt	E 25th SCVI	Ft. Fisher, NC	01/15/65	New York, NY	01/30/65	Elmira, NY	CSR
					Elmira, NY	05/14/65	Released G.O. #85	P65,P66,HAG,CSR
English, John	Pvt	G 23rd SCVI	Bennettsville, SC	03/06/65	New Berne, NC	04/03/65	Pt. Lookout, MD	CSR
					Pt. Lookout, MD	05/18/65	Died, Lung Infl.	P6,P114,P119,FPH
English, R.J.W.	Pvt	K 23rd SCVI	Frederick, MD	09/13/62	Ft. Delaware, DE	10/02/62	Aikens Ldg., VA Xc	CSR
Enloe, Thomas A.	Pvt	G 18th SCVI	Drury's Bluff, VA	05/20/64	Pt. Lookout, MD	06/05/64	Died of wounds	P5,P116,FPH,YEB
Enlow, J.A.	Pvt	H Hol.Leg.	Petersburg, VA	10/27/64		03/20/65	Camp Lee, Prld POW	CSR
Enlow, Q.M.	Pvt	F 1st SCVIH	Richmond, VA Hos.	04/03/65	Libby Prison Rchmd.	04/23/65	Newport News, VA	CSR
					Newport News, VA	06/24/65	Rlsd. G.O. #109	P107,CSR
Enslen, David G.	Pvt	Wash'n LA	Montgomery, AL	05/15/65	Mongomery, AL	05/15/65	Paroled	CSR
Epperson, William H.	Pvt	I 23rd SCVI	Hatchers Run, VA	04/01/65	City Pt., VA	04/05/65	Pt. Lookout, MD	CSR
					Pt. Lookout, MD	06/11/65	Released	P114,P117,P122,CSR
Epps, Benjamin W.	Pvt	G 27th SCVI	Town Creek, NC	02/20/65	Ft. Anderson, NC	02/28/65	Pt. Lookout, MD	CSR,HAG
					Pt. Lookout, MD	06/26/65	Rlsd. G.O. #109	P114,P117,P122,CSR
Epps, Daniel E.	Pvt	Ferguson's	Salisbury, NC	04/12/65	Nashville, TN	04/29/65	Louisville, KY	P39,CSR
					Louisville, KY	05/02/65	Camp Chase, OH	P92,CSR
					Camp Chase, OH	06/13/65	Rlsd. G.O. #109	CSR
Epps, James Henry	Pvt	C 25th SCVI	Ft. Fisher, NC	01/15/65	New York, NY	01/30/65	Elmira, NY	CSR
					Elmira, NY	07/07/65	Rlsd. G.O. #109	P65,P66,CTA
Epps, W.J.	Pvt	F 14th SCVI	Farmville, VA	04/11/65	Farmville, VA	04/21/65	Paroled	CSR
Epps, William	2Lt	D 4th SCVC	Louisa C.H., VA	06/11/64	Fts. Monroe, VA	06/20/64	Pt. Lookout, MD	CSR
					Pt. Lookout, MD	06/23/64	Ft. Delaware, DE	P113,P116,P120,CSR
					Ft. Delaware, DE	08/20/64	Hilton Head, SC	CSR,P42,P44
					Hilton Head, SC	10/20/64	Ft. Pulaski, GA	CSR
					Ft. Pulaski, GA	11/19/64	Hilton Head, SC	CSR
					Hilton Head, SC	03/12/65	Ft. Delaware, DE	P2,CSR
					Ft. Delaware, DE	06/17/65	Rlsd. G.O. #109	P43,CSR

SOUTH CAROLINA SOLDIERS, SAILORS AND  CITIZENS HELD IN U.S. PRISONS 1861-1865

NAME	RANK	REGIMENT	CAPTURED AT	WHEN	PRISON	MOVED	DISPOSITION	SOURCES
Epting, G.M.	1Sg	I 5th SCVI	Deep Bottom, VA	08/14/64	Bermuda Hundred, VA	08/15/64	Fts. Monroe, VA	CSR
					Fts. Monroe, VA	08/16/64	Pt. Lookout, MD	CSR
					Pt. Lookout, MD	11/01/64	Venus Pt., GA Xc	P113,SA3,CSR
					Pt. Lookout, MD	03/14/65	Aikens Ldg., VA Xc	P116,P125
Epting, J.M.	Pvt	H 13th SCVI	Falling Waters, MD	07/14/63	Ft. McHenry, MD	08/08/63	Pt. Lookout, MD	P110,CSR
					Old Capitol, DC	08/23/63	Pt. Lookout, MD	CSR
					Pt. Lookout, MD	12/31/63	Hammond G.H., MD	P113,P121,P125,CSR
					Pt. Lookout, MD	01/07/64	Died, Ch. Diarrhea	P5,P116,FPH,CSR
Epting, T.	Pvt	G 3rd SCVABn	High Pt., NC	05/01/65	High Pt., NC	05/01/65	Paroled on oath	CSR
Erambert, Samuel C.	Pvt	B 15th SCVAB	Farmville, VA	04/23/65	Farmville, VA	04/23/65	Paroled	CSR
Erastus, J.A.	Pvt	F 1st SCVIG	Gettysburg, PA	07/05/63	Ft. Delaware, DE			P40,P42,CSR
Erichs, H.	Pvt	B German LA	Deserted/enemy					CSR
Erickson, Charles	Pvt	A Ham.Leg.MI	Westover Ch., VA	08/07/64	Bermuda Hundred, VA	08/22/64	Fts. Monroe, VA	CSR
					Fts. Monroe, VA	08/25/64	Pt. Lookout, MD	CSR
					Pt. Lookout, MD	10/15/64	Joined US Army	P113,P116,P122,P125
Erskine, J.C.	Pvt	B 37th VAVCB	Lynchburg, VA	06/18/64	Cumberland, MD	07/11/64	Wheeling, WV	CSR
					Wheeling, WV	07/12/64	Camp Chase, OH	CSR
					Camp Chase, OH	02/01/65	Died, Pneumonia	CSR
Ervin, L. Nelton	Pvt	I 25th SCVI	Ft. Fisher, NC	01/15/65	New York, NY	01/30/65	Elmira, NY	CSR,HAG
					Elmira, NY	07/11/65	Rlsd. G.O. #109	P65,P66,CSR
Erwin, Adolphus S.	Pvt	K Hol.Leg.	Stony Creek, VA	05/07/64	Fts. Monroe, VA	05/13/64	Pt. Lookout, MD	CSR
					Pt. Lookout, MD	08/15/64	Elmira, NY	P113
					Elmira, NY	10/29/64	Died, Pneumonia	P5,P12,FPH
Erwin, H.H.	Pvt	G 9th SCVIB	Williamsburg, VA	05/05/62	Fts. Monroe, VA			CSR
Erwin, T.D.	Pvt	D 22nd SCVI	Deserted/enemy	11/19/64	City Pt., VA	11/23/64	Washington, DC	CSR
					Washington, DC	11/25/64	Cincinnati, OH	CSR
Erwin, W.R.	Pvt	I 5th SCVI	Williamsburg, VA	05/05/62	Fts. Monroe, VA		(OR 12/31/61)	SA3,CSR
Erwin, W.Y.	Pvt	F 1st SCVA	Deserted/enemy	02/17/65	Charleston, SC	03/11/65	Taken oath & disch.	CSR
Esdorn, John	Pvt	A 24th SCVI	Jackson, MS	05/16/63	Jackson, MS	05/16/63	Paroled in Hos.	CSR
Esdra, A.A.	Pvt	C 3rd SCVABn	Citronelle, AL	05/04/65	Meridian, MS	05/16/64	Paroled	CSR
Eskew, G.W.	Pvt	19th SCVI	Deserted/enemy	12/15/64	Washington, DC P.M.	02/18/64	Philadelphia, PA	CSR
Eskew, Jacob	Msc	2nd SCVIRi			Washington, DC	04/10/65	Louisville, KY	CSR
Eskew, James B.	Pvt	I 1st SCVA	Morris Island, SC	07/10/63	Hilton Head, SC	07/14/63	Ft. Columbus, NY	CSR,SA1
					Ft. Columbus, NY	09/23/63	Took the oath	P1
					Ft. Columbus, NY	09/26/63	Pt. Lookout, MD	CSR
					Pt. Lookout, MD	02/15/64	Joined US Army	P113,P116,P125,CSR
Eskew, Samuel A.	Pvt	E Ham.Leg.	Warrenton, VA	09/29/62	Warrenton, VA	09/29/62	Paroled	CSR
Eskew, William R.	Pvt	F 2nd SCVIRi	High Bridge, VA	04/06/65	City Pt., VA	04/14/65	Newport News, VA	CSR
					Newport News, VA	06/24/65	Rlsd. G.O. #109	P107,CSR
Esters, William	Pvt	D 5th SCVI	Williamsburg, VA	05/05/62	Cliffburn GH, DC	06/18/62	Died of wounds	P6,SA3
Estes, Wiley	Pvt	L 2nd SCVIRi	Anderson, SC	05/08/65	Anderson, SC	05/08/65	Paroled	CSR
Estes, William	Pvt	F 18th SCVI	Five Forks, VA	04/01/65	City Pt., VA	04/05/65	Pt. Lookout, MD	CSR
					Pt. Lookout, MD	06/12/65	Released	P114,P117,P121,CSR
Etheredge, David	Pvt	D 14th SCVI	Gettysburg, PA	07/04/63	David's Island, NY	08/24/63	City Pt., VA Xc	P1,HOE,CSR
Etheredge, T.	Pvt	M 7th SCVI	N. Anna River, VA	05/24/64	Port Royal, VA	05/30/64	Pt. Lookout, MD	CSR
					Pt. Lookout, MD	03/14/65	Aikens Ldg., VA Xc	P113,P116,P124,CSR
Etheridge, Caleb	Pvt	B 14th SCVI	Petersburg, VA	04/03/65	City Pt., VA	04/11/65	Hart's Island, NY	CSR
					Hart's Island, NY	06/17/65	Rlsd. G.O. #109	P79,CSR,HOE
Etheridge, John B.	Pvt	I 2nd SCVC	Augusta, GA	06/02/65	Augusta, GA	06/02/65	Paroled on oath	CSR
Etheridge, Matthew A.	Pvt	5 10/19 SCVI	Missionary Ridge	11/25/63	Nashville, TN	12/07/63	Louisville, KY	P39,RAS,CSR
					Louisville, KY	12/09/63	Rock Island, IL	P88,P89,CSR
					Rock Island, IL	04/21/64	Released, Rjctd. US	P7,P131,CSR

E

SOUTH CAROLINA SOLDIERS, SAILORS AND CITIZENS HELD IN U.S. PRISONS 1861-1865

NAME	RANK	REGIMENT	CAPTURED AT	WHEN	PRISON	MOVED	DISPOSITION	SOURCES
Etheridge, William Wade	Pvt	F 24th SCVI	Nashville, TN	12/16/64	Nashville, TN	12/31/64	Louisville, KY	CSR
					Louisville, KY	01/05/65	Camp Douglas, IL	P92,P94,CSR
					Camp Chase, OH	06/12/65	Rlsd. G.O. #109	P22,CSR
Ethridge, John D.	Pvt	G 14th SCVI	Spotsylvania, VA	05/12/64	Belle Plain, VA	05/21/64	Ft. Delaware, DE	CSR
					Ft. Delaware, DE		Hos. 1/20-1/31/65	P47
					Ft. Delaware, DE		Hos. 3/1-3/6/65	P47
					Ft. Delaware, DE	06/16/65	Rlsd. G.O. #109	P41,P42,P45,CSR
Eubanks, Isaac	Pvt	I Hol.Leg.	Stony Creek, VA	05/07/65	Fts. Monroe, VA	05/13/64	Pt. Lookout, MD	CSR
					Pt. Lookout, MD	08/15/64	Elmira, NY	P113,P116
					Elmira, NY	03/02/65	James R., VA Xc	CSR
Eubanks, Thomas J.	Pvt	I 7th SCVC	New Kent C.H., VA	04/28/64	Fts. Monroe, VA	05/03/64	Pt. Lookout, MD	CSR
					Pt. Lookout, MD	05/17/64	Jd. U.S. Navy, rjctd.	P116,P125,CSR
					Pt. Lookout, MD	08/08/64	Elmira, NY	CSR
Eubanks, William J.	Pvt	I Hol.Leg.	Stony Creek, VA	05/07/64	Fts. Monroe, VA	05/13/64	Pt. Lookout, MD	CSR
					Pt. Lookout, MD	08/15/64	Elmira, NY	P113,P116
					Elmira, NY	10/11/64	Tfd. for exchange	P65
					Pt. Lookout, MD	10/29/64	Aikens Ldg., VA Xc	P114,P117,P123,CSR
Eubanks, William J.	Pvt	I Hol.Leg.	Five Forks, VA	04/01/65	Pt. Lookout, MD	06/08/65	Released	P117,P121,CSR
Evans, Alexander	Pvt	B 1st SCVIR	Cheraw, SC	03/04/65	New Berne, NC	04/10/65	Hart's Island, NY	CSR
					Hart's Island, NY	06/16/65	Rlsd. G.O. #109	SA1,P79,CSR
Evans, C.T.C.	Pvt	K 6th SCVC	Louisa C.H., VA	06/11/64	Pt. Lookout, MD	07/25/64	Elmira, NY	P113,P114,P120,CSR
					Elmira, NY	10/11/64	Venus Pt., GA Xc	P65,CSR
					Venus Pt., GA	11/15/64	Exchanged	CSR
Evans, G.	Pvt	D 22nd SCVI	Farmville, VA	04/06/65	Newport News, VA	06/14/65	Rlsd. G.O. #109	P107
Evans, George W.	Pvt	L Orr's Ri.	Salisbury, NC	04/12/65	Nashville, TN	04/29/65	Louisville, KY	P39,CDC,CSR
					Louisville, KY	05/02/65	Camp Chase, OH	P92,P94,CSR
					Camp Chase, OH	06/13/65	Released G.O.#109	P22,CSR
Evans, Ira	Pvt	D 22nd SCVI	Farmville, VA	04/06/65	City Pt., VA	04/14/65	Newport News, VA	CSR
					Newport News, VA	06/26/65	Rlsd. G.O. #109	CSR
Evans, J.	Pvt	G 21st SCVI	Weldon RR, VA	08/21/64	City Pt., VA	09/08/64	David's Island, NY	CSR
					David's Island, NY	09/09/64	Died of wounds	P1,P5,P12,FPH,CSR
Evans, J.H.	Pvt	I 25th SCVI	Ft. Fisher, NC	01/15/65	New York, NY	01/30/65	Elmira, NY	CSR,HAG
					Elmira, NY	07/13/65	Elmira, NY USGH	P65,P66,CSR
					Elmira, NY	07/21/65	Died	CSR
Evans, J.J.	Pvt	A 7th SCVC	Richmond, VA Hos.	04/03/65	Richmond, VA Hos.	04/21/65	Richmond, VA P.M.	CSR
					Richmond, VA P.M.	05/06/65	USS Thomas Powell	CSR
					USS Thomas Powell	05/06/65	Hammond G.H., MD	CSR
					Hammond G.H., MD	07/25/65	Rlsd. G.O. #109	CSR
Evans, J.W.	Pvt	K 4th SCVC	Old Church, VA	05/30/64	White House, VA	06/08/64	Pt. Lookout, MD	CSR
					Pt. Lookout, MD	03/15/65	Aikens Ldg., VA Xc	P113,P116,P124,CSR
Evans, James Chauncey	Cpl	B 1st SCVIG	Sutherland Stn., VA	04/02/65	City Pt. VA	04/13/65	Pt. Lookout, MD	CSR,SA1
					Pt. Lookout, MD	06/26/65	Rlsd. G.O. #109	P114,P117,P122,CSR
Evans, John A.	Cpt	B 26th SCVI	Crater, Pbg., VA	07/30/64	Old Capitol, DC	08/12/64	Ft. Delaware, DE	CSR
					Ft. Delaware, DE	06/17/65	Rlsd. G.O. #109	P42,P45,P46,CSR
Evans, John C.	Cpt	A 23rd SCVI	Dinwiddie CH, VA	04/01/65	Ft. McHenry, MD	04/09/65	Johnson's Isl., OH	P110,R48,CSR
					Johnson's Isl., OH	06/18/65	Rlsd. G.O. #109	P81,P82,P83,CSR
Evans, Joseph A.	Pvt	A 15th SCVI	Harpers Ferry, WV	08/26/64	Camp Chase, OH	05/14/65	Rlsd. G.O. #85	P22,P26,H15,CSR
Evans, Lewis B.	Pvt	A 5th SCVC	Stony Creek, VA	12/01/64	City Pt., VA	06/12/65	Pt. Lookout, MD	CSR
					Pt. Lookout, MD	06/12/65	Released	P114,CSR
Evans, Mitchell	Pvt	E 25th SCVI	Weldon RR, VA	08/21/64	McClellan GH Phila.	09/10/64	Died, Amputation	P1,P6,FPH,HAG,HMC
Evans, N. Jay	Pvt	L 21st SCVI	Weldon RR, VA	08/21/64	David's Island, NY	09/09/64	Died of wounds	P1,P12,HAG,HMC,FPH
Evans, Richard	Pvt	Ham.Leg.	Deserted/enemy	02/28/64	Chattanooga, TN	02/28/64	Released on oath	CSR

SOUTH CAROLINA SOLDIERS, SAILORS AND  CITIZENS HELD IN U.S. PRISONS 1861-1865

NAME	RANK	REGIMENT	CAPTURED AT	WHEN	PRISON	MOVED	DISPOSITION	SOURCES
Evans, Richard M.	Pvt	F 25th SCVI	Ft. Fisher, NC	01/15/65	New York, NY	01/30/65	Elmira, NY	CSR,HAG
					Elmira, NY	06/02/65	Died, Pneumonia	P6,P12,P65,P66,CSR
Evans, Solon	Pvt	H Orr's Ri.	Southside RR, VA	04/02/65	City Pt., VA	04/05/65	USS *State of Maine*	CSR,HMC
					USS *State of Maine*	04/06/65	Alexandria, VA Hos.	CSR
					Alexandria, VA Hos.	06/13/65	Lincoln G.H., D.C.	CSR
					Lincoln G.H., D.C.	06/06/65	Released	CSR
					Ft. McHenry, MD	06/13/65	Rlsd. G.O. #109	P110
Evans, Spry W.	Pvt	I 26th SCVI	Crater, Pbg., VA	07/30/64	City Pt., VA	08/03/64	Pt. Lookout, MD	CSR,CTA
					Pt. Lookout, MD	08/08/64	Elmira, NY	P113,P116,P120,CSR
					Elmira, NY	03/02/65	Tfd. for exchange	P65,CSR,CTA
Evans, T. Rush	Pvt	I 25th SCVI	Ft. Fisher, NC	01/15/65	New York, NY	01/30/65	Elmira, NY	CSR,HAG
					Elmira, NY	06/23/65	Rlsd. G.O. #109	P65,P66
Evans, W.W.	Pvt	E 2nd SCVA	Augusta, GA Hos.	06/26/65	Discharged	09/02/65		CSR
Evans, William D.	Pvt	B 7th SCVIBn	Poplar Spgs., SC	02/21/65	New Berne, NC	04/03/65	Pt. Lookout, MD	CSR
					Pt. Lookout, MD	06/26/65	Rlsd. G.O. #109	P114,P117,P122,CSR
Evans, William T.	Pvt	I 1st SCVIH	Frederick, MD	09/12/62	Ft. McHenry, MD	11/15/62	Paroled	CSR
Evatt, Adam	Pvt	D 2nd SCVI	Bentonville, NC	03/19/65	New Berne, NC	04/03/65	Pt. Lookout, MD	SA2,CSR,H2
					Pt. Lookout, MD	06/26/65	Rlsd. G.O. #109	P114,P117,P122,CSR
Evatt, Edward F.	Pvt	E 2nd SCVIRi	Lookout Mtn., TN	10/29/63	Bridgeport, AL Hos.	11/05/63	Nashville, TN USGH	P2,CSR
					Nashville, TN G.H.	04/27/64	Louisville, KY Hos.	P2,P39,CSR
					Louisville, KY	05/12/64	Camp Morton, OH	P91,P93
					Camp Morton, IN	03/15/65	Pt. Lookout, MD Xc	P101,CSR
Evatt, W.H.	Pvt	G 1st SCVIR	Wilkes Co., GA		Rlsd. on oath			SA1,CSR
Eveleigh, James E.	Pvt	G Ham.Leg.	Warrenton, VA	09/29/62	Warrenton, VA	09/29/62	Paroled	CSR
Everett, James	Pvt	A 1st SCVIR	Fayettville, NC	03/10/65	New Berne, NC	04/10/65	Hart's Island, NY	CSR
					Hart's Island, NY	06/18/65	Rlsd. G.O. #109	P79,CSR
Eye, William W.	Pvt	Brooks LA	Deep Bottom, VA	10/27/64	Pt. Lookout, MD	05/13/65	Released G.O. #85	P122
Ezell, Aaron C.	Pvt	E 13th SCVI	Deserted/enemy	02/24/65	City Pt., VA	02/26/65	Washington, DC	CSR
					Washington, DC	02/27/65	Springfield, IL	CSR
Ezell, John M.	Pvt	I 5th SCVI	Deep Bottom, VA	08/14/64	Bermuda Hundred, VA	08/22/64	Fts. Monroe, VA	CSR
					Fts. Monroe, VA	08/25/64	Pt. Lookout, MD	CSR
					Pt. Lookout, MD	03/14/65	Aikens Ldg., VA Xc	P113,P116,P124,SA3

SOUTH CAROLINA SOLDIERS, SAILORS AND **F** CITIZENS HELD IN U.S. PRISONS 1861-1865

NAME	RANK	REGIMENT	CAPTURED AT	WHEN	PRISON	MOVED	DISPOSITION	SOURCES
Fagan, J.H.	Pvt	H 25th SCVI	Petersburg, VA	05/09/64	Bermuda Hundred, VA	05/11/64	Fts. Monroe, VA	CSR,HAG
					Fts. Monroe, VA	05/13/64	Pt. Lookout, MD	CSR
					Pt. Lookout, MD	05/24/64	Jd. U.S. Army	CSR
Fail, H.C.	Pvt	H 17th SCVI	Richmond, VA Hos.	04/03/65	Libby Prison Rchmd.	04/23/65	Newport News, VA	CSR
					Newport News, VA	06/26/65	Rlsd. G.O. #109	P107,CSR
Fail, John	Pvt	I 17th SCVI	Kinston, NC	12/14/62	Kinston, NC	12/14/62	Paroled	CSR
Fail, William	Pvt	I 17th SCVI	Five Forks, VA	04/01/65	City Pt., VA	04/06/65	Pt. Lookout, MD	CSR,LAN
					Pt. Lookout, MD	06/26/65	Rlsd. G.O. #109	P114,P118,P122
Faile, John	Pvt	C 15th SCVAB	Cheraw, NC	03/05/65	New Berne, NC	04/10/65	Hart's Island, NY	CSR
					Hart's Island, NY	06/17/65	Rlsd. G.O. #109	P79,CSR
Faile, Nathan	Pvt	C 15th SCVAB	Cheraw, NC	03/05/65	New Berne, NC	04/25/65	Camp Hamilton, VA	CSR
					Camp Hamilton, VA	05/01/65	Newport News, VA	CSR
					Newport News, VA	06/15/65	Rlsd. G.O. #109	CSR
Faircloth, Andrew J.	Pvt	F 1st SCVIG	Petersburg, VA	04/02/65	Pt. Lookout, MD	06/26/65	Rlsd. G.O. #109	P114,P122,SA1,CSR
Faircloth, Isaac B.	Pvt	F 1st SCVIG	Petersburg, VA	04/02/65	Pt. Lookout, MD	06/26/65	Rlsd. G.O. #109	P114,P122,SA1,CSR
Fairey, E.A.	Pvt	G 4th SCVC	Deserted/enemy	11/05/64	P.M. 2nd US Cav. D	11/06/64	City Pt., VA	CSR
					City Point, VA	11/09/64	Washington, DC	P8,CSR
					Washington, DC	11/12/64	Phila., PA on oath	CSR
Fairey, Phillip W.	Sgt	G 4th SCVC	Hawe's Shop, VA	05/28/64	3rd Div. 5th A.C.	06/12/64	Stanton G.H., DC	CSR
					Stanton G.H., DC	10/14/64	Lincoln G.H., DC	CSR
					Lincoln G.H., DC	11/01/64	Old Capitol, DC	CSR
					Old Capitol, DC	12/15/64	Elmira, NY	CSR
					Ft. McHenry, MD	12/16/64	Elmira, NY	P110
					Elmira, NY	03/14/65	Tfd. for exchange	P65,CSR
					Richmond, VA Hos.	05/11/65	Escaped	CSR
Falkner, John	Smn	C.S. Navy	Deserted/enemy		Hilton Head, SC	10/04/64		P8
Fallon, J.A.	Pvt	K 13th SCVI	Southside RR, VA	04/02/65	Hart's Island, NY	06/16/65	Rlsd. G.O. #109	P79
Fallow, W.B.	Sgt	E 15th SCVI	Augusta, GA	05/22/65	Augusta, GA	05/22/65	Paroled	CSR,H15
Fanning, J.A.	Pvt	I 22nd SCVI			Provo.M.Army of P.	09/30/62	Paroled	CSR
Fanning, J.C.	1Sg	I 5th SCVC	Augusta, GA	05/25/65	Augusta, GA	05/25/65	Paroled	CSR
Fant, C.M.	Pvt	C 4th SCVC	Hawe's Shop, VA	05/28/64	White House, VA	06/08/64	Pt. Lookout, MD	CSR
					Pt. Lookout, MD	07/09/64	Elmira, NY	P113,P116,P120,CSR
					Elmira, NY	03/20/65	Died, Pneumonia	P6,P12,P65,FPH,CSR
Fant, E.W.	Pvt	K Ham.Leg.MI	Deserted/enemy	03/04/65	Bermuda Hundred, VA	03/05/64	City Pt., VA P.M.	CSR
					City Pt., VA P.M.	03/07/65	Washington, DC	CSR
					Washington, DC	03/08/64	Iowa City, Iowa	CSR
Fant, Jesse L.	Sgt	L Orr's Ri.	Petersburg, VA	04/02/65	City Pt., VA	04/07/65	Hart's Island, NY	CDC,CSR
					Hart's Island, NY	06/15/65	Rlsd. G.O. #109	P79,CSR
Fant, Napoleon	Pvt	D Hol.Leg.C	Talleyville, VA	07/03/63	Fts. Monroe, VA	07/16/63	Paroled	CSR
Faris, Harvey H.	Cpl	H 18th SCVI	Richmond, VA Hos.	04/09/65	Pt. Lookout, MD	06/26/65	Rlsd. G.O. #109	P119,YEB
Faris, James	Pvt	K 18th SCVI	Petersburg, VA	04/01/65	Lincoln G.H., DC	06/12/65	Rlsd. G.O. #109	CSR
Farman, James	Smn	Dis Boat	Morris Island, SC	09/07/63	Ft. Columbus, NY	10/09/63	Johnson's Isl., OH	P1
Farmer, A.B.	Pvt	A 3rd SCVABn	High Pt., NC	05/02/65	High Pt., NC	05/02/65	Paroled on oath	CSR
Farmer, Berry	Pvt	A 3rd SCVABn	High Pt., NC	05/02/65	High Pt., NC	05/02/65	Paroled on oath	CSR
Farmer, G.B.	Pvt	A 8th SCVI	Winchester, VA	09/13/64	Harpers Ferry, WV	09/19/64	Camp Chase, OH	CSR,KEB
					Camp Chase, OH	05/21/65	New Orleans, LA	P22,P26,CSR
					New Orleans, LA	05/12/65	Vicksburg, MS Xc	CSR
Farmer, Gaddis W.	Pvt	D Ham.Leg.	Lookout Mtn.,TN	10/29/63	Nashville, TN	02/24/64	Louisville, KY	CSR
					Louisville, KY	02/29/64	Ft. Delaware, DE	CSR
					Ft. Delaware, DE	09/18/64	Exchanged	CSR
Farmer, H.	Pvt	C SCVABN	Blakely, AL	04/09/65	Ship Island, MS	05/01/65	Vicksburg, MS Xc	P136

SOUTH CAROLINA SOLDIERS, SAILORS AND  CITIZENS HELD IN U.S. PRISONS 1861-1865

NAME	RANK	REGIMENT	CAPTURED AT	WHEN	PRISON	MOVED	DISPOSITION	SOURCES
Farmer, J.R.	Pvt	E 14th SCVI	Frederick, MD	09/12/62	Frederick, MD	10/02/62	Ft. Delaware, DE	CSR
					Ft. Delaware, DE	11/10/62	Aikens Ldg., VA Xc	CSR
Farmer, J.R.	Pvt	E 14th SCVI	Williamsport, MD	07/06/63	Ft. McHenry, MD	07/09/63	Ft. Delaware, DE	CSR
					Ft. Delaware, DE		Hos. 7/26-9/18/64	P47
Farmer, J.R.	Pvt	E 14th SCVI	Farmville, VA	04/11/65	Farmville, VA	04/21/65	Paroled	CSR
Farmer, James H.	Pvt	C 3rd SCVABn	Ft. Gaines, AL	08/08/64	New Orleans, LA	10/25/64	Ship Island, MS	P3,CSR
					Ship Island, MS	01/04/65	Exchanged	P136,CSR
Farmer, James H.	Pvt	C 3rd SCVABn	Augusta, GA	05/20/65	Augusta, GA	05/20/65	Paroled on oath	CSR
Farmer, Jasper	Pvt	B 27th SCVI	Town Creek, NC	02/20/65	Ft. Anderson, NC	02/28/65	Pt. Lookout, MD	CSR,HAG
					Pt. Lookout, MD	05/02/65	Died	P6,P114,P119,FPH
Farmer, Joel A.	Pvt	H 6th SCVC	Louisa C.H., VA	06/11/64	Fts. Monroe, VA	06/19/64	Pt. Lookout, MD	CSR
					Pt. Lookout, MD	07/25/64	Elmira, NY	P113,P116,P120,CSR
					Elmira, NY	07/03/65	Rlsd. G.O. #109	P65,CSR
Farmer, John L.	Pvt	D 1st SCVIR	Combahee Ferry, SC	01/29/65	New Berne, NC	04/10/65	Hart's Island, NY	CSR
					Hart's Island, NY	06/04/65	Died (Phlebitis)	P6,P12,P79,FPH,CSR
Farmer, Maxcy	Pvt	C 3rd SCVABn	Blakely, AL	04/09/65	Ship Island, MS	05/01/65	Vicksburg, MS Xc	P136,CSR
Farmer, N.O.	2Lt	D Ham.Leg.MI	Farmville, VA	04/11/65	Farmville, VA	04/11/65	Paroled	CSR
Farmer, R.	Pvt	D 2nd SCVA	Deserted/enemy	02/21/65	Charleston, SC		Released on oath	CSR
Farmer, R.C.	Pvt	C 3rd SCVABn	Augusta, GA	05/20/65	Augusta, GA	05/20/65	Paroled on oath	CSR
Farmer, Richard, Sr.	Pvt	C 3rd SCVABn	Blakely, AL	04/09/65	Ship Island, MS	05/01/65	Vicksburg, MS Xc	P136,CSR
Farmer, S.P.	Sgt	A 8th SCVI	Winchester, VA	09/13/64	Harpers Ferry, WV	09/19/64	Camp Chase, OH	CSR
					Camp Chase, OH	06/11/65	Rlsd. G.O. #109	P22,KEB,CSR
Farmer, W.A.	Cpl	C 3rd SCVABn	Ft. Gaines, AL	08/08/64	New Orleans, LA	09/06/64	St. Louis, MO USGH	CSR
					St. Louis, MO USGH	09/12/64	New Orleans, LA	CSR
					New Orleans, LA	10/25/64	Ship Island, MS	P3
					Ship Island, MS	01/04/65	Exchanged	P136,CSR
Farmer, W.R.	Pvt	C 2nd SCVIRi	Cold Harbor, VA	06/02/64	Elmira, NY	05/29/65	Released	P65
Farmer, William	Pvt	A 22nd SCVI	Deserted/enemy	06/04/64	Richmond, VA area			CSR
Farr, Anthony	Pvt	C 5th SCVI	Lookout Mtn., TN	11/25/63	Bridgeport, AL G.H.	12/13/63	Nashville, TN G.H.	P2,SA3,CSR
					Nashville, TN	02/15/64	Louisville, KY	P2,P39,CSR
					Louisvlle, KY	02/29/64	Ft. Delaware, DE	P88,P91,P92,CSR
					Ft. Delaware, DE		Hos. 6/12-7/2/64	P47,SA3
					Ft. Delaware, DE	06/10/65	Rlsd. G.O. #109	P41,P42,P45,CSR
Farr, F.M.	Pvt	F 15th SCVI	Gettysburg, PA	07/05/63	Gettysburg G.H.		Provost Marshal	P4,KEB,CSR
					David's Island, NY	09/23/63	City Pt., VA Xc	P1,CSR
Farr, James W.	Pvt	C 16th SCVI	Greenville, SC	05/08/65	Greenville, SC	05/08/65	Paroled on oath	CSR
Farr, Peter	Pvt	C 15th SCVAB	Charlottesville, VA	08/08/64	Old Capitol, DC	09/20/64	Ft. Delaware, DE	CSR
					Ft. Delaware, DE	05/03/65	Released Secy/war	P41,P42,P46,CSR
Farrell, Aaron	Pvt	H 7th SCVC	Lyttleton, VA	05/07/64	Elmira, NY	02/13/65	Tfd. for exchange	P65
Farrell, James B.	Pvt	B 25th SCVI	Richmond, VA	04/08/65	City Pt., VA	04/06/65	Newport News, VA	CSR
					Newport News, VA	06/18/65	Rlsd. G.O. #109	P107,CSR
Farrell, Joseph	Pvt	A 1st SCVA	Deserted/enemy	03/27/65	Charleston, SC	03/27/65	Released on oath	CSR
Farrell, Michael J.	Pvt	K 1st SCVIG	Fredericksburg, VA	12/13/62	Old Capitol, DC	12/31/62	City Pt., VA	CSR
					City Pt., VA	03/29/63	Exchanged	CSR
Farrell, William	Pvt	C 15th SCVI	Deserted/enemy	02/18/65	Charleston, SC	04/01/65	New York, NY P.M.	CSR
Farrington, O.J.	QSg	15th SCVAB	Raleigh, NC	04/15/65	Fts. Monroe, VA	04/24/65	Paroled	CSR
Farris, W.H.	Pvt	Lafayette A	Charlotte, NC Hos.	05/06/65	Charlotte, NC	05/06/65	Paroled	CSR
Faulk, Joseph E.	Pvt	L 7th SCVI	N. Anna River, VA	05/22/64	Port Royal, VA	05/30/64	Pt. Lookout, MD	CSR
					Pt. Lookout, MD	08/13/64	Died, Diarrhea	P5,P113,P116
Faulkenberry, John	Pvt	G 2nd SCVI	Gettysburg, PA	07/04/63	David's Island, NY	08/24/63	City Pt., VA Xc	SA2,P1,KEB,H2,CSR
Faulkenberry, Joseph W.	Pvt	G 2nd SCVI	Hedgesville, VA	07/23/63	Pt. Lookout, MD	01/18/65	Died	P6,P113,FPH,KEB

SOUTH CAROLINA SOLDIERS, SAILORS AND  CITIZENS HELD IN U.S. PRISONS 1861-1865

NAME	RANK	REGIMENT	CAPTURED AT	WHEN	PRISON	MOVED	DISPOSITION	SOURCES
Faulkner, John	Pvt	K 14th SCVI	Gettysburg, PA	07/05/63	Ft. Delaware, DE		Hos. 12/28/64-1/6/65	P47
					Ft. Delaware, DE	06/10/65	Released	P43,P45,UD2,CSR
Faulkner, Larkin L.	Pvt	B 14th SCVI	Petersburg, VA	07/29/64	Pt. Lookout, MD	08/08/64	Elmira, NY	P113,P117,P120,CSR
					Elmira, NY	10/11/64	Pt. Lookout, MD	P65,HOE,CSR
					Elmira, NY	10/11/64	Venus Pt., GA Xc	CSR
					Pt. Lookout, MD	10/29/64	Aikens Ldg., VA Xc	P114,P117,P123,HOE
Faulkner, Robert V.	Pvt	B 14th SCVI	Gettysburg, PA	07/05/63	Ft. McHenry, MD	07/09/63	Ft. Delaware, DE	CSR
					Ft. Delaware, DE		Jd US 3rd MD Cav.	P40,P44,HOE,CSR
Faulkner, S.J.V.	Pvt	I 17th SCVI	Crater, Pbg., VA	07/30/64	Pt. Lookout, MD	08/08/64	Elmira, NY	P113,P117,P120,LAN
					Elmira, NY	06/21/65	Rlsd. G.O. #109	P65,P113,P120,CSR
Faulkner, Thomas	Pvt	9 10/19 SCVI	Missionary Ridge, TN	11/25/63	Nashville, TN	12/07/63	Louisville, KY	P39,CSR
					Louisville, KY	12/09/63	Rock Island, IL	P88,P89,CSR
					Rock Island, IL	02/25/65	Pt. Lookout, MD Xc	P131,CSR
					Ft. Columbus, NY	03/06/65	Boulwares Wh. Xc	CSR
					Richmond, VA Hos.	03/08/65	Furloughed 30 days	CSR
Faulkner, W.L.	Pvt	I 17th SCVI	Petersburg, VA	07/30/64	City Pt., VA	08/05/64	Pt. Lookout, MD	CSR
					Pt. Lookout, MD	08/08/64	Elmira, NY	CSR
					Elmira, NY	09/17/64	Died, Typhoid	P5,P12,P65,FPH,CSR
Faulling, W.M.	Pvt	C 23rd SCVI	Deserted/enemy	04/04/65	Charleston, SC		North of Potomac R.	CSR
Faust, Sumpter	Pvt	G 24th SCVI	Missionary Ridge, TN	11/25/63	Bridgeport, AL G.H	12/28/63	Nashville, TN	P2,CSR
					Nashville, TN	12/07/63	Died, Dysentery	P6,P12,EFW
Fay, Daniel	Cit	Lexington			Pt. Lookout, MD	06/19/65	Released	P121
Feagin, J. Alford	Pvt	C 25th SCVI	Ft. Darling, VA	05/09/64	Pt. Lookout, MD	05/24/64	Vol. U.S. Army, Rjctd	P113,P116,P125
					Pt. Lookout, MD	08/18/64	Elmira, NY	P120,HAG,CTA
					Elmira, NY	03/14/65	Tfd. for exchange	P65,HAG,CTA
Feagin, R.M.	Pvt	A 23rd SCVI	Petersburg, VA	04/02/65	City Pt., VA	04/04/65	Pt. Lookout, MD	CSR,CTA
					Pt. Lookout, MD	06/27/65	Rlsd. G.O. #109	P114,P118,P121,CSR
Feagle, George	Pvt	I 15th SCVI	Gettysburg, PA	07/05/63	Gettysburg G.H.		Provost Marshal	P4,KEB,CSR
					Baltimore, MD	08/20/63	Pt. Lookout, MD	CSR
					Pt. Lookout, MD	07/27/64	Died, Lung Infl.	P12,FPH,CSR
Feamster, Elijah G.	Pvt	F 17th SCVI	Five Forks, VA	04/01/65	City Pt., VA	04/06/65	Pt. Lookout, MD	CSR
					Pt. Lookout, MD	06/27/65	Rlsd. G.O. #109	P114,P118,P121,CSR
Feaster, T.D.	Pvt	H 6th SCVI	Burkesville, VA	04/14/65	Burkesville, VA	04/17/65	Paroled	CSR
Featherstone, T.C.	Pvt	C P.S.S.	Seven Pines, VA	05/30/62	(Wwd & POW)			CSR
Feemster, Samuel M.	Pvt	K 17th SCVI	Petersburg, VA	03/25/65	City Pt., VA	03/25/65	Pt. Lookout, MD	CSR
					Pt. Lookout, MD	06/27/65	Rlsd. G.O. #109	P117,P121,CSR
Fehrenbach, H.H.	Pvt	B 5th SCVC	Stony Creek, VA	12/01/64	City Pt., VA	12/05/64	Pt. Lookout, MD	CSR
					Pt. Lookout, MD	02/16/65	Exchanged	P114,P124,CDC,CSR
Felder, Carson E.	Pvt	F 25th SCVI	Ft. Fisher, NC	01/15/65	New York, NY	01/30/65	Elmira, NY	CSR,HAG
					Elmira, NY	07/11/65	Rlsd. G.O. #109	P65,HAG
Felder, David	Pvt	I 11th SCVI	Drury's Bluff, VA	05/16/64	Bermuda Hundred, VA	05/17/64	Fts. Monroe, VA	CSR
					Fts. Monroe, VA	05/18/64	Pt. Lookout, MD	CSR
					Pt. Lookout, MD	08/15/64	Elmira, NY	P113,P116,P120,CSR
					Elmira, NY	02/13/65	Tfd. for exchange	P65,CSR
Felder, F.F.	Pvt	E 5th SCVC	Stony Creek, VA	12/01/64	City Pt., VA	12/05/64	Pt. Lookout, MD	CSR
					Pt. Lookout, MD	06/27/65	Rlsd. G.O. #109	P114,CDC,CSR
Felder, R.F.	2Lt	I 25th SCVI	Ft. Fisher, NC	01/15/65	Ft. Columbus, NY	03/01/65	City Pt., VA Xc	P2,HAG,CSR
Felker, Jacob W.	Pvt	G Hol.Leg.	Five Forks, VA	04/01/65	City Pt., VA	04/05/65	Pt. Lookout, MD	CSR,ANY
					Pt. Lookout, MD	06/27/65	Rlsd. G.O. #109	P114,P118,P121
Felker, Wiley H.	Pvt	E 18th SCVI	Appomattox R., VA	04/03/65	City Pt., VA	04/06/65	Hart's Island, NY	CSR
					Hart's Island, NY	06/16/65	Rlsd. G.O. #109	P79,HOS,CSR

NAME	RANK	REGIMENT	CAPTURED AT	WHEN	PRISON	MOVED	DISPOSITION	SOURCES
Felkman, Thomas C.	Pvt	G Hol.Leg.	Farmville, VA	04/06/65	City Pt., VA	04/14/65	Newport News, VA	CSR,ANY
					Newport News, VA	06/26/65	Rlsd. G.O. #109	P107,CSR
Fellers, Calvin	Pvt	F 5th SCVC	Augusta, GA	05/09/65	Augusta, GA	05/19/65	Paroled	CSR
Fellers, J.B.	1Lt	G 13th SCVI	Fredeicks, VA	05/10/62	Fts. Monroe, VA	06/21/62	Ft. Delaware, DE	CSR
					Ft. Delaware, DE	06/21/62	James R., VA Xc	BOS,CSR
Fellers, Jacob L.	Sgt	G 13th SCVI	Hewlitts Stn., VA	05/25/64	White house, VA	06/08/64	Pt. Lookout, MD	CSR
					Pt. Lookout, MD	08/16/64	Elmira, NY	P116,CSR
					Elmira, NY	06/19/65	Rlsd. G.O. #109	ANY,CSR
Fellers, Silas Hamilton	Pvt	C 3rd SCVI	Gettysburg, PA	07/02/63	Gettysburg, PA G.H.	09/10/63	Provost Marshal	P4,KEB,SA2,H3,CSR
					W. Bldg. Balt, MD	09/25/63	City Pt., VA Xc	P1,CSR
					Richmond, VA Hos.	10/03/63	Furloughed 30 days	CSR
Fellers, William L.	Pvt	G 13th SCVI	Fredericksburg, VA	05/11/62	Steamer Coatzacoal	07/05/62	Aikens LDg., VA Xc	CSR
					Aikens Ldg., VA	08/05/62	Exchanged	CSR
Felts, H.J.	Pvt	E 17th SCVI	South Mtn., MD	09/14/62	Ft. Delaware, DE	10/02/62	Aikens Ldg., VA Xc	CSR
Fender, J.W.	Pvt	A 19th SCVCB	Augusta, GA	05/26/65	Augusta, GA	05/26/65	Paroled on oath	CSR
Fender, Ransom	Pvt	K 11th SCVI	Petersburg, VA	06/15/64	Bermuda Hundred, VA	06/17/64	Fts. Monroe, VA	CSR,HAG
					Fts. Monroe, VA	06/18/64	Pt. Lookout, MD	CSR
					Pt. Lookout, MD	07/25/64	Elmira, NY	P116,CSR
					Elmira, NY	03/14/65	Aikens Ldg., VA Xc	CSR
Fendley, Charles B.	Pvt	C Orr's Ri.	Spotsylvania, VA	05/12/64	Belle Plain, VA	05/21/64	Ft. Delaware, DE	CSR
					Ft. Delaware, DE		Hos. 11/15-11/26/64	P47
					Ft. Delaware, DE		Hos. 3/11/65	P47
					Ft. Delaware, DE	05/18/65	Rlsd. G.O. #85	P41,P42,P45,CSR
Fendley, J.W.	Pvt	A Orr's Ri.	Petersburg, VA	04/03/65	City Pt., VA	04/10/65	Hart's Island, NY	CSR
					Hart's Island, NY	06/16/65	Rlsd. G.O. #109	P79,CDC
Fennel, W.J.	Pvt	I P.S.S.	Fair Oaks, VA	05/31/62	US Hos. Stmr.		Fts. Monroe, VA	CSR
					Fts. Monroe, VA	06/21/62	Aikens Ldg., VA Xc	CSR,TSE
					Aikens Ldg., VA	06/26/62	Exchanged	CSR
Fennell, G.M.	Pvt	B 5th SCVC	Augusta, GA	05/25/65	Augusta, GA	05/25/65	Paroled	CSR
Fennell, Robert H.	2Lt	K 24th SCVI	Chickamauga, TN	09/20/63	Nashville, TN	10/01/63	Louisville, KY	P38,EFW,HHC,CSR
					Louisville, KY	12/05/63	Johnson's Isl., OH	P88,P89,P93,CSR
					Johnson's Isl., OH	02/24/65	City Pt., VA Xc	P81,P82,CSR
Fennell, William A.	Pvt	D 11th SCVI	Weldon RR, VA	08/21/64	Pt. Lookout, MD	02/10/65	Aikens Ldg., VA Xc	P113,P117,P124,CSR
Fennell, William M.	Pvt	G 22nd SCVI	Kinston, NC	12/15/62	Kinston, NC	12/15/62	Paroled POW	CSR
Fennell, William M.	Pvt	G 22nd SCVI	Crater, Pbg., VA	07/30/64	City Pt., VA	08/05/64	Pt. Lookout, MD	CSR
					Pt. Lookout, MD	08/08/64	Elmira, NY	P117,P120,P125
					Elmira, NY	09/06/64	Died, Ch. Diarrhea	P5,P12,P65,FPH
Fenters, T.J.	Pvt	A 21st SCVI	Petersburg, VA	06/24/64	Pt. Lookout, MD	08/16/64	Elmira, NY	P120,HAG
					Elmira, NY	07/11/65	Rlsd. G.O. #109	P65
Feran, James	Pvt	A 1st SCVA	Morris Island, SC	09/07/63	Pt. Lookout, MD	09/18/64	Aikens Ldg., VA Xc	P113,P116,P123
Ferebee, John	Sgt	A 19th SCVCB	Augusta, GA	05/19/65	Augusta, GA	05/19/65	Paroled on oath	CSR
Ferguson, Christopher C.	Pvt	I 3rd SCVI	Knoxville, TN	12/05/63	Nashville, TN	02/11/64	Louisville, KY	P39,KEB,H3,CSR
					Louisville, KY	02/15/64	Rock Island, IL	P88,P91,P93,CSR
					Rock Island, IL	02/15/65	Pt. Lookout, MD Xc	P131
Ferguson, George S.	Sgt	A 17th SCVI	Petersburg, VA	07/30/64	City Pt., VA	08/05/64	Pt. Lookout, MD	CSR
					Pt. Lookout, MD	08/08/64	Elmira, NY	P113,P117,P120,CSR
					Elmira, NY	01/05/65	Died, Diarrhea	P6,P65,P12,FPH,CSR
Ferguson, J.	Pvt	A 17th SCVI	Petersburg, VA	07/30/64	City Pt., VA	08/05/64	Pt. Lookout, MD	CSR
					Pt. Lookout, MD	08/08/64	Elmira, NY	P113,P117,P120,CSR
					Elmira, NY	07/03/65	Rlsd. G.O. #109	P65,CSR

F

SOUTH CAROLINA SOLDIERS, SAILORS AND CITIZENS HELD IN U.S. PRISONS 1861-1865

NAME	RANK	REGIMENT	CAPTURED AT	WHEN	PRISON	MOVED	DISPOSITION	SOURCES
Ferguson, J.D.	Pvt	K 2nd SCVC	Gettysburg, PA	07/05/63	Ft. Delaware, DE		Hos. 2/9-3/5/64	P47
					Ft. Delaware, DE		Hos. 10/9-10/12/64	P47
					Ft. Delaware, DE	06/10/65	Rlsd. G.O. #109	P40,P43,P45,CSR
Ferguson, James T.	Pvt	H 12th SCVI	Warrenton, VA	09/29/62	Warrenton, VA	09/29/62	Paroled	CSR
Ferguson, John B.	Pvt	A 6th SCVI	Jetersville, VA	04/06/65	City Pt., VA	04/14/65	Newport News, VA	P107,HHC,CSR
					Newport News, VA	06/26/65	Rlsd. G.O. #109	P107
Ferguson, Judge H.	Pvt	C 4th SCVC	Blackwater R., VA	07/29/63	City Pt., VA US Hos.	08/01/63	Died of wounds	P12,CSR
Ferguson, P.J.	Pvt	A 6th SCVI	Charlotte, NC	05/18/65	Charlotte, NC	05/18/65	Paroled	CSR
Ferguson, Richard	Pvt	I 1st SCVA	Morris Island, SC	07/10/63	Hilton Head, SC	07/18/63	Ft. Columbus, NY	CSR
					Ft. Columbus, NY	09/23/63	Took the oath	P1,CSR
Ferguson, W.H.	Pvt	B 1st SCVC	Gettysburg, PA	07/05/63	Chester, PA G.H.	08/17/63	City Pt., VA Xc	P1
Ferguson, W.J.M.	Pvt	I P.S.S.	Richmond, VA area		Ft. Columbus, NY	07/31/62	Fts. Monroe, VA	CSR
					Aikens Ldg., VA	08/05/62	Exchanged	CSR
					Fts. Monroe, VA		Aikens Ldg., VA Xc	CSR
Ferguson, William	Pvt	H 12th SCVI	Petersburg, VA	04/02/65	City Pt., VA	04/04/65	Pt. Lookout, MD	CSR
					Pt. Lookout, MD	06/26/65	Rlsd. G.O. #109	P114,P117,P122,CSR
Fernell, W.A.	Pvt	B 3rd SCVABn	Ft. Tyler, GA	04/16/65	1st Div. Cavalry Co.	04/23/65	Macon, GA Prison	CSR
Feroben, J.	Pvt	F 3rd SCVABn	Memphis, TN	11/18/64	Memphis, TN	11/18/64	Took the oath	CSR
Ferrell, Charles E.	Pvt	E 24th SCVI	Jackson, MS	07/17/63	Snyders Bluff, MS	07/30/63	Camp Morton, IN	CSR
					Camp Morton, IN	09/22/63	Died, Ch. Diarrhea	P5,P12,P100,P101,FPH
Ferrell, H.C.	Pvt	A Ham.Leg.	Manassas, VA	07/15/61	Old Capitol, DC	11/12/61	Ft. McHenry, MD	CSR
					Ft. McHenry, MD	11/13/61	Fts. Monroe, VA Xc	CSR
					US 12th A.C. Hos.	10/29/63	Died of wounds	CSR
Ferrell, Robert	Pvt	F 12th SCVI	Wilderness, VA	05/05/64	Belle Plain, VA	05/21/64	Ft. Delaware, DE	CSR
					Ft. Delaware, DE		Hos. 2/9-2/27/65	P47
					Ft. Delaware, DE	02/27/65	City Pt., VA Xc	P41,P42,CSR
Ferrell, W.J.	1Sg	K 6th SCVI	Warrenton, VA	09/29/62	Warrenton, VA	09/29/62	Paroled	CSR
Ferring, James	Cit				Pt. Lookout, MD		Exchanged	P124
Ferris, Albert Gallatin		P. Savannah	Off Charleston	)6/03/61	Tombs Prison, NY	10/23/61	Turned states witness	OR,TCP
Ferris, John	Pvt	B 12th SCVI	Deep Bottom, VA	08/17/64	Pt. Lookout, MD	11/01/64	Aikens ldg., VA Xc	P113,P117,P124,CSR
Fersner, William F.	Sgt	F 25th SCVI	Ft. Fisher, NC	01/15/65	New York, NY	01/30/65	Elmira, NY	CSR,HAG
					Elmira, NY	07/07/65	Rlsd. G.O. #109	P65,HAG
Fertic, Charles	Pvt	F 25th SCVI	Weldon RR, VA	08/21/64	Alexandria, VA	08/26/64	DOW on transport	CSR,HAG
Fertic, John	Pvt	F 25th SCVI	Ft. Fisher, NC	01/15/65	New York, NY	01/30/65	Elmira, NY	CSR
					Elmira, NY	07/07/65	Rlsd. G.O. #109	P65,HAG
Fetner, David A.	Pvt	B Hol.Leg.C		12/13/63				CSR
Fetner, David A.	Pvt	D 7th SCVC	Winnsboro, SC	02/21/65	New Berne, NC	03/30/65	Pt. Lookout, MD	CSR
					Pt. Lookout, MD	05/03/65	Died, Lung Infl.	P6,P119,FPH,CSR
Fetter, George N.	Bug	B German LA	Deserted/enemy	03/15/65	Charleston, SC	03/15/65	Released on oath	CSR
Few, Francis Marion	Pvt	D 16th SCVI	Spring Hill, TN	12/15/64	Nashville, TN	12/31/64	Louisville, KY	CSR
					Louisville, KY	01/04/65	Camp Chase, OH	P92,P94,CSR
					Camp Chase, OH	06/12/64	Rlsd. G.O. #109	P22,16R,CSR
Few, James	Pvt	B 11th SCVI	Town Creek, NC	02/20/65	Ft. Anderson, NC	02/28/65	Pt. Lookout, MD	CSR
					Pt. Lookout, MD	06/26/65	Rlsd. G.O. #109	P122,CSR
Fewell, Alexander F.	Pvt	E 17th SCVI	Five Forks, VA	04/01/65	City Pt., VA	04/06/65	Pt. Lookout, MD	CSR,DEM,YEB
					Pt. Lookout, MD	06/27/65	Rlsd. G.O. #109	P114,P118,P121,CSR
Fewell, Uranus J.	Cpl	H 5th SCVI	Chattanooga, TN	10/29/63	Nashville, TN	11/07/63	Louisville, KY	P39,SA3,YEB,CSR
					Louisville, KY	11/09/63	Camp Morton, IN	P88,P89,CSR
					Camp Morton, IN	03/15/65	Cox's Wharf, VA Xc	CSR
Fewell, W. Alexander	Pvt	G P.S.S.	Seven Pines, VA	05/31/62	Fts. Monroe, VA	06/24/62	Died of wounds	P12,YEB,TSE,CNM

SOUTH CAROLINA SOLDIERS, SAILORS AND  CITIZENS HELD IN U.S. PRISONS 1861-1865

NAME	RANK	REGIMENT	CAPTURED AT	WHEN	PRISON	MOVED	DISPOSITION	SOURCES
Fickling, H.S.	Pvt	A 14th SCMil	Lynch's Creek, SC	02/25/65	New Berne, NC	04/10/65	Hart's Island, NY	CSR
					Hart's Island, NY	07/17/65	David's Island, NY	P79
					David's Island, NY	06/21/65	Rlsd. G.O. #109	P1,CSR
Fickling, William W.	Cpt	Brooks LA	Saylors Creek, VA	04/06/65	Ft. McHenry, MD	04/09/65	Johnson's Isl., OH	P110
					Old Capitol, DC	04/17/65	Johnson's Isl., OH	CSR
					Johnson's Isl., OH	06/18/65	Rlsd. G.O. #109	P81,R44,CSR
Fiddia, William B.	Pvt	F 3rd SCVABn	Deserted/enemy	02/26/65	Charleston, SC	03/02/65	Will take oath	CSR
Field, W.G.	Pvt	F 22nd SCVI	Kinston, NC	12/14/62	Kinston, NC	12/14/62	Paroled POW	CSR
Fielder, Thomas F.	Pvt	A Hol.Leg.	Five Forks, VA	04/01/65	City Pt., VA	04/05/65	Pt. Lookout, MD	CSR
					Pt. Lookout, MD	06/27/65	Rlsd. G.O. #109	P114,P118,HOS
Fielding, Isham	Pvt	H 7th SCVI	Leesburg, VA	09/18/62	Old Capitol, DC	09/27/62	Aikens Ldg., VA Xc	CSR
Fielding, J.B.	Pvt	D Ham.Leg.MI	Darbytown Rd., VA	01/25/65	Bermuda Hundred, VA	02/10/65	Pt. Lookout, MD	CSR
					Pt. Lookout, MD	06/11/65	Died, Ch. Diarrhea	P6,P114,P117,P119
Fields, Augustus A.	Pvt	A 14th SCVI	Burkesville, VA	04/14/65	Burkesville, VA	04/17/65	Paroled	CSR
Fields, J.A.	Pvt	E 6th SCVI	Bloomington, NC	04/28/65	Bloomington, NC	04/28/65	Paroled	CSR
Fields, Jacob	Pvt	D 1st SCVIR	Charleston Bar, SC	03/21/63	Ft. Delaware, DE	09/15/63	Jd. US 1st CN Cav.	P40,P42,SA1,OR,CSR
Fields, Jonas	Pvt	G 17th SCVI	Petersburg, VA	03/25/65	City Pt., VA	03/28/65	Pt. Lookout, MD	CSR
					Pt. Lookout, MD	06/26/65	Rlsd. G.O. #109	P114,P117,P121,CSR
Fields, Wesley	Pvt	B 21st SCVI	Petersburg, VA	06/24/64	Pt. Lookout, MD	08/16/64	Elmira, NY	P113,P117,P120,HAG
					Elmira, NY	07/03/65	Rlsd. G.O. #109	P65,HAG
Finch, John P.	Pvt	A Hol.Leg.	Five Forks, VA	04/01/65	City Pt., VA	04/05/65	Pt. Lookout, MD	CSR,HOS
					Pt. Lookout, MD	05/19/65	Died, Typhoid	P12,P114,P118,P119
Fincher, Silas A.	Pvt	E 22nd SCVI	Richmond, VA	04/03/65	Jackson Hos. Rchmd.	04/07/65	Died, Ch. Diarrhea	P6,P12,LAN
Findley, James W.	Pvt	C 7th SCVC	Petersburg, VA	06/15/64	Fts. Monroe, VA	06/23/64	Pt. Lookout, MD	CSR
					Pt. Lookout, MD	01/17/65	Aikens Ldg., VA Xc	P113,P117,CSR
Fink, George A.	Pvt	F 5th SCVC	Augusta, GA	05/20/65	Augusta, GA	05/20/65	Paroled	CSR
Finklea, Alfred	Pvt	H Orr's Ri.	Hatcher's Run, VA	03/03/65	City Pt., VA	04/02/65	Pt. Lookout, MD	CSR
					Pt. Lookout, MD	06/27/65	Rlsd. G.O. #109	P114,P117,P121,CDC
Finklea, George C.	2Lt	3 10/19 SCVI	Missionary Ridge, TN	11/25/63	Nashville, TN	12/04/63	Louisville, KY	CSR,RAS
					Louisville, KY	12/05/63	Johnson's Isl., OH	P39,P88,P89,CSR
					Johnson's Isl., OH	06/15/65	Rlsd. G.O. #109	P81,P82,P83,CSR
Finklea, Hardy	Pvt	H Orr's Ri.	Falling Waters, MD	07/14/63	Balltimore, MD	08/21/63	Pt. Lookout, MD	CSR
					Pt. Lookout, MD	03/17/64	City Pt., VA Xc	P113,P116,P123
Finklea, Hardy	Pvt	H Orr's Ri.	Hatchers Run, SC	03/31/65	Pt. Lookout, MD	06/27/65	Rlsd. G.O. #109	P114,P117,CDC,P121
Finklea, John L.	Pvt	H 8th SCVI	Winchester, VA	09/13/64	Harpers Ferry, WV	09/19/64	Camp Chase, OH	CSR
					Camp Chase, OH	05/02/65	New Orleans, LA	P22,P26,CSR
					New Orleans, LA	05/12/65	Vicksburg, MS Xc	CSR
Finklea, William E.	Pvt	3 10/19 SCVI	Missionary Ridge, TN	11/25/63	Bridgeport, AL G.H.	12/11/63	Nashville, TN	P2,RAS,CSR
					Nashville, TN	01/27/65	Louisville, KY	P2,P39,CSR
					Louisville, KY	01/30/64	Rock Island, IL	P88,P93,CSR
					Rock Island, IL	05/03/65	New Orleans, LA Xc	P131,CSR
					New Orleans, LA	05/23/65	Exchanged	CSR
Finley, James W.	Pvt	I 13th SCVI	Petersburg, VA	04/02/65	City Pt., VA	04/04/65	Pt. Lookout, MD	CSR
					Pt. Lookout, MD	06/26/65	Rlsd. G.O. #109	P114,P122,CSR
Finley, John Robert	Cpl	A 3rd SCVI	N. Anna River, VA	05/23/64	Port Royal, VA	05/30/64	Pt. Lookout, MD	CSR,KEB,H3
					Pt. Lookout, MD	01/17/65	Aikens Ldg., VA Xc	P113,P116,P124,CSR
Finley, Sidney J.	Pvt	B 3rd SCVIBn	Hanover Jctn., VA	05/23/64	Port Royal, VA	05/30/64	Pt. Lookout, MD	CSR
					Pt. Lookout, MD	02/08/65	Died, A. Diarrhea	P6,P113,P116,P119
Finley, William	Pvt	G 14th SCVI	Wilderness, VA	05/06/64	Belle Plain, VA	05/20/64	Ft. Delaware, DE	CSR
					Ft. Delaware, DE	05/07/65	Died, Lung Inflam.	P6,,P42,P45,P47,CSR

F

SOUTH CAROLINA SOLDIERS, SAILORS AND CITIZENS HELD IN U.S. PRISONS 1861-1865

NAME	RANK	REGIMENT	CAPTURED AT	WHEN	PRISON	MOVED	DISPOSITION	SOURCES
Finley, William M.	Pvt	B 12th SCVI	Malvern Hill, VA	07/28/64	City Pt., VA	08/05/64	Pt. Lookout, MD	CSR
					Pt. Lookout, MD	08/08/64	Elmira, NY	P113,P117,P120
					Elmira, NY	03/14/65	James R., VA Xc	P65,CSR
Finnerty, James	Pvt	D 1st SCVIR	Charleston Bar, SC	03/21/63	Ft. Lafayette, NY	06/29/63	Ft. Delaware, DE	P144,SA1
					Ft. Delaware, DE	07/30/64	City Pt., VA Xc	P40,P42,P44,CSR
Fishburn, L.N.	Pvt	K 2nd SCVC	Greensboro, NC	05/03/65	Greensboro, NC	05/03/65	Released on Parole	CSR
Fisher, Henry Newton	Pvt	D 16th SCVI	Missionary Ridge, TN	11/25/63	Nashville, TN	12/05/63	Louisville, KY	P39,16R,CSR
					Louisville, KY	12/08/63	Rock Island, IL	P88,P89,CSR
					Rock Island, IL	06/21/65	Rlsd. G.O. #109	P131
Fisher, J.M.	Pvt	I Ham.Leg.MI	Richmond, VA	04/03/65	Jackson Hos. Rchmd.	05/03/65	Died	P6,CSR
Fisher, James	Pvt	A German LA	Fayetteville, NC	03/10/65	New Berne, NC	03/30/65	Pt. Lookout, MD	CSR
					Pt. Lookout, MD	05/13/65	Washington, DC	CSR
Fisher, Samuel W.	Pvt	D 27th SCVI	Petersburg, VA	06/24/64	Fts. Monroe, VA	06/26/64	Pt. Lookout, MD	CSR,HAG
					Pt. Lookout, MD	08/16/64	Elmira, NY	P113,P117,P120,CSR
					Elmira, NY	10/11/64	Trfd. for exchange	HAG,CSR,P65
					Pt. Lookout, MD	10/29/64	Venus Pt., GA Xc	P114,P117,P123,CSR
Fisher, William A.	Pvt	G Orr's Ri.	Falling Waters, MD	07/14/63	Baltimore, MD	08/16/63	Pt. Lookout, MD	CSR,CDC
					Pt. Lookout, MD	08/16/64	Elmira, NY	P113,P120,P124
					Elmira, NY	03/10/65	Tfd. for exchange	P65,CSR
Fitts, Charles R.	Cpl	E 11th SCVI	Petersburg, VA	06/24/64	Bermuda Hundred, VA	06/25/64	Fts. Monroe, VA	CSR,HAG
					Fts. Monroe, VA	06/26/64	Pt. Lookout, MD	CSR
					Pt. Lookout, MD	03/17/65	Aikens Ldg., VA Xc	P113,P117,P124,CSR
Fitts, John A.	Sgt	E 11th SCVI	Petersburg, VA	06/24/64	Bermuda Hundred, VA	06/25/64	Fts. Monroe, VA	CSR,HAG
					Fts. Monroe, VA	06/26/64	Pt. Lookout, MD	CSR
					Pt. Lookout, MD	10/30/64	Aikens Ldg., VA Xc	P113,P117,P123,CSR
Fitzgerald, Robert	Pvt	I 1st SCVIH	Deserted/enemy	02/28/65	City Pt., VA	03/03/65	Washington, DC P.M.	CSR
					Washington, DC P.M.	03/06/65	Columbia, SC oath	CSR
Fitzpatrick, Thomas	Pvt	D 7th SCVIBn	Weldon RR, VA	08/21/64	City Pt., VA	08/24/64	Pt. Lookout, MD	CSR,HAG
					Pt. Lookout, MD	05/13/65	Released G.O. #85	P113,P117,P122
					Washington, DC P.M.	05/15/65	Camden, SC oath	CSR
Fitzsimmons, James	Cpl	C 1st SCVA	Deserted/enemy	02/20/65	Charleston, SC	03/22/65	Taken oath & disch.	CSR
Flake, J.W.	Pvt	K 1st SCVIG	Augusta, GA	05/23/65	Augusta, GA	05/23/65	Paroled	CSR
Flake, T.B.	Pvt	K 1st SCVIH	Farmville, VA	04/06/65	City Pt., VA	04/14/65	Newport News, VA	CSR
					Newport News, VA	07/06/65	Rlsd. G.O. #109	P107,SA1,CSR
Flanagan, R.H.	Cit	Fairfield Ds.		02/19/65	Pt. Lookout, MD	05/12/65	Released G.O. #85	P121
Flannagan, Patrick	Pvt	Macbeth LA	Asheville, NC	04/01/65	Knoxville, TN	04/14/65	Chattanooga, TN	CSR
					Louisville, KY	04/28/65	Baltimore, MD oath	CSR
Flannigan, Patrick	Pvt	H 27th SCVI	Weldon RR, VA	08/21/64	W. Bldg. Balt, MD	10/19/64	Ft. McHenry, MD	P1,HAG,CSR
					Ft. McHenry, MD	10/25/64	Pt. Lookout, MD	CSR,HAG
					Pt. Lookout, MD	10/30/64	Venus Pt., GA Xc	P114,P117,CSR
Flannigan, Patrick	Pvt	H 27th SCVI	Town Creek, NC	02/20/65	Ft. Anderson, NC	02/28/65	Pt. Lookout, MD	CSR
Fleiner, Victor	Pvt	B German LA	Fayetteville, NC	03/15/65	New Berne, NC	03/30/65	Pt. Lookout, MD	CSR
					Pt. Lookout, MD	06/12/65	Rlsd. G.O. #109	CSR
Fleming, Gainam	Pvt	B Hol.Leg.	Warrenton, VA	09/29/62	Warrenton, VA	09/29/62	Paroled/Hospital	CSR
Fleming, George M.	Pvt	F 24th SCVI	Taylors Ridge, GA	10/16/64	Louisville, KY	10/27/64	Camp Douglas, IL	P90,P91,P94
					Camp Douglas, IL	06/17/65	Rlsd. G.O. #109	P55,EFW
Fleming, Harvey L.B.	Pvt	I 25th SCVI	Morris Island, SC	09/07/63	Ft. Columbus, NY	09/26/63	Pt. Lookout, MD	CSR,HAG
					Pt. Lookout, MD	11/16/63	Hammond G.H., MD	P121,P125
					Pt. Lookout, MD	03/17/64	Exchanged	P121,HAG
Fleming, Harvey L.B.	Pvt	I 25th SCVI	Weldon RR, VA	08/21/64	Alexandria, VA	09/25/64	Died of wounds	P1,P5,P12,CSR
	Pvt	I 25th SCVI	Morris Island, SC	09/01/63	Pt. Lookout, MD	01/27/65	Aikens Ldg., VA Xc	P116,P124,HAG

SOUTH CAROLINA SOLDIERS, SAILORS AND  CITIZENS HELD IN U.S. PRISONS 1861-1865

NAME	RANK	REGIMENT	CAPTURED AT	WHEN	PRISON	MOVED	DISPOSITION	SOURCES
Fleming, Henry F.	Pvt	I 25th SCVI	Morris Island, SC	09/07/63	Ft. Columbus, NY	10/09/63	Johnson's Isl., OH	P1,HAG
					Pt. Lookout, MD	03/17/64	Exchanged	P123
Fleming, J.W.	Sgt	I 25th SCVI	Weldon RR, VA	08/21/64	Old Capitol, DC	12/16/64	Elmira, NY	CSR,HAG
					Ft. McHenry, MD	12/17/64	Elmira, NY	P110
					Elmira, NY	03/27/65	Tfd. for exchange	P65
Fleming, Newton	Pvt	B Hol.Leg.	Warrenton, VA	09/29/62	Warrenton, VA	09/29/62	Paroled/Hospital	CSR
Fleming, S.W.	Pvt	I 25th SCVI	Ft. Fisher, NC	01/15/65	New York, NY	01/30/65	Elmira, NY	CSR,HAG
					Elmira, NY	04/26/65	Died, Pneumonia	P6,P12,P65,FPH
Fleming, W.D.	Pvt	I 25th SCVI	Ft. Fisher, NC	01/15/65	New York, NY	01/30/65	Elmira, NY	CSR,HAG
					Elmira, NY	07/11/65	Rlsd. G.O. #109	P65
Flemming, John K.	Pvt	I 12th SCVI	N. Anna River, VA	05/23/64	Pt. Lookout, MD	02/13/65	Exchanged	P113,P124,LAN,CSR
Flemming, P.L.	Pvt	K 20th SCVI	N. Anna River, VA	05/23/64	Pt. Lookout, MD	02/13/65	Aikens Ldg., VA Xc	P121
Flemming, T.B.	Sgt	I 4th SCVI	Raleigh, NC	04/13/65	Raleigh, NC	04/20/65	Paroled	CSR
Fletcher, Abraham	Pvt	C 2nd SCVIRi	Frayser's Farm, VA	06/30/62	Harrisons Ldg., VA	07/03/62	Ft. Columbus, NY	CSR
					Ft. Columbus, NY	07/09/62	Ft. Delaware, DE	CSR
					Ft. Delaware, DE	08/05/62	Aikens Ldg., VA Xc	CSR
Fletcher, Croton	Pvt	F 1st SCVA	Deserted/enemy	05/11/64	Hilton Head, SC	07/25/64	New York, NY	CSR
Fletcher, J.D.	Pvt	C Ham.Leg.MI	Farmville, VA	04/11/65	Farmville, VA	04/11/65	Paroled	CSR
Fletcher, J.T.	Pvt	H Orr's Ri.	Petersburg, VA	04/03/65	City Pt., VA	04/10/65	Hart's Island, NY	CSR
					Hart's Island, NY	06/16/65	Rlsd. G.O. #109	P79,CSR
Fletcher, Thomas	Sgt	A 23rd SCVI	Five Forks, VA	04/01/65	City Pt., VA	04/05/65	Pt. Lookout, MD	CSR
					Pt. Lookout, MD	06/27/65	Rlsd. G.O. #109	P114,P118,P121,CSR
Flickenschildt, Henry N.	Pvt	K 12th SCVI	Deserted/enemy	02/23/65	City Pt., VA	02/24/65	Washington, DC	CSR
					Washington, DC	02/24/65	Oil City, PA oath	CSR
Flinn, Marion	Pvt	G Orr's Ri.	Falling Waters, MD	07/14/63	Pt. Lookout, MD	11/16/63	Hammond G.H., MD	P113,P121,P125,CDC
					Pt. Lookout, MD	11/24/63	Died, Ch. Diarrhea	P5,P12,P116,FPH,CSR
Flinn, R.H.	Pvt	C 3rd SCVABn	Blakely, AL	04/09/65	Ship Island, MS	05/01/65	Vicksburg, MS Xc	P136,CSR
					Augusta, GA	05/20/65	Paroled on oath	CSR
Florence, J.F.	Pvt	1st SCVIG	Petersburg, VA	04/02/65	Hart's Island, NY	04/14/65	Wants to take oath	CSR
Flotwell, R.	Pvt	E 25th SCVI	Ft. Fisher, NC	01/15/65	New York, NY	01/30/65	Elmira, NY	CSR
					Elmira, NY	05/29/65	Rlsd. on oath	P65,HAG
Flowers, Andrew	Pvt	B 21st SCVI	Petersburg, VA	06/18/64	City Pt., VA	06/24/64	Pt. Lookout, MD	CSR,HAG
					Pt. Lookout, MD	07/27/64	Elmira, NY	P113,P120
					Elmira, NY	03/29/65	Died, Ch. Diarrhea	P6,P12,P65,FPH
Flowers, Cyrus	Pvt	A 8th SCVI	Winchester, VA	09/13/64	Harpers Ferry, WV	09/19/64	Camp Chase, OH	CSR
					Camp Chase, OH	06/11/65	Released on oath	P22,KEB,CSR
Flowers, G.M.	Pvt	F 8th SCVI	Winchester, VA	09/13/64	Harpers Ferry, WV	09/19/64	Camp Chase, OH	CSR
					Camp Chase, OH	06/11/65	Rlsd. G.O. #109	P22,CSR
Flowers, Henry	Pvt	F 4th SCVC	Louisa C.H., VA	06/11/64	Fts. Monroe, VA	06/20/64	Pt. Lookout, MD	CSR,HMC
					Pt. Lookout, MD	07/25/64	Elmira, NY	P113,P116,P120,CSR
					Elmira, NY	09/22/64	Died, Rem. fever	P12,P65,CSR
Flowers, J.F.	Pvt	G 1st SCVIR	Averysboro, NC	03/16/65	New Berne, NC	04/10/65	Hart's Island, NY	CSR
					Hart's Island, NY	06/16/65	Rlsd. G.O. #109	SA1,P79,CSR
Flowers, J.Y.	Pvt	D 20th SCVI	Columbia, SC	02/14/65	New Berne, NC	04/10/65	Hart's Island, NY	CSR
					Hart's Island, NY	06/16/65	Rlsd. G.O. #109	P79,CSR
Flowers, Joel A.	Pvt	F 4th SCVC	Hawe's Shop, VA	05/28/64	White House, VA	06/08/64	Pt. Lookout, MD	CSR,HMC
					Pt. Lookout, MD	07/09/64	Elmira, NY	P113,P116,P120,CSR
					Elmira, NY	03/15/65	Died, Ch. Diarrhea	P12,P65,CSR
Flowers, John H.	Pvt	I 10th SCVI	Kentucky	09/15/62	Kentucky	11/15/62	Paroled for Xc	CSR
Flowers, Nathan	Pvt	5 10/19 SCVI	Missionary Ridge, TN	11/25/63	Nashville, TN	12/07/63	Louisville, KY	P39,RAS,CSR
					Louisville, KY	12/09/63	Rock Island, IL	P89,CSR
					Rock Island, IL	01/15/65	Died, Consumption	P6,P131,P132,FPH

SOUTH CAROLINA SOLDIERS, SAILORS AND  CITIZENS HELD IN U.S. PRISONS 1861-1865

NAME	RANK	REGIMENT	CAPTURED AT	WHEN	PRISON	MOVED	DISPOSITION	SOURCES
Flowers, R.N.	Pvt	C 26th SCVI	Deserted/enemy	01/27/65	City Pt., VA	01/29/65	Washington, DC	CSR
					Washington, DC	02/01/65	Phila., PA on oath	CSR
Flowers, T.D.	Pvt	G 21st SCVI	Ft. Fisher, NC	01/15/65	Elmira, NY	07/11/65	Rlsd. G.O. #109	P65
Flowers, William E.	Pvt	M 8th SCVI	Winchester, VA	09/13/64	Harpers Ferry, WV	09/19/64	Camp Chase, OH	CSR,KEB
					Camp Chase, OH	05/02/65	New Orleans, LA	P22,P26,CSR
					New Orleans, LA	05/12/65	Vicksburg, MS Xc	CSR
Floyd, Alexander	Pvt	I 26th SCVI	Five Forks, VA	04/02/65	City Pt., VA	04/07/65	Pt. Lookout, MD	CSR,CTA
					Pt. Lookout, MD	06/27/65	Rlsd. G.O. #109	P118,P121,CSR
Floyd, Averett	Pvt	B 1st SCVA	Goldsboro, NC	03/19/65	New Berne, NC	04/03/65	Pt. Lookout, MD	CSR
					Pt. Lookout, MD	05/05/65	Died, Pneumonia	P6,P117,FPH
Floyd, Charles P.	Pvt	B 1st SCVA	Fayetteville, NC	03/16/65	New Berne, NC	03/20/65	Pt. Lookout, MD	CSR
					Pt. Lookout, MD	06/27/65	Rlsd. G.O. #109	P114,P117,P121,CSR
Floyd, D.S.	Pvt	G 27th SCVI	Petersburg, VA	06/24/64	Bermuda Hundred, VA	06/25/64	Fts. Monroe, VA	CSR,HAG
					Fts. Monroe, VA	06/26/64	Pt. Lookout, MD	CSR
					Pt. Lookout, MD	08/16/64	Elmira, NY	P113,P117,P120,CSR
					Elmira, NY	02/20/65	Tfd. for exchange	P65,CSR
Floyd, David J.	Pvt	G 18th SCVI	Petersburg, VA	05/17/64	Pt. Lookout, MD	06/18/64	Joined US Army	P121,P125,CSR
Floyd, I.P.	Pvt	E 26th SCVI	Farmville, VA	04/06/65	City Pt., VA	04/14/65	Newport News, VA	CSR,CEN
					Newport News, VA	06/26/65	Rlsd. G.O. #109	P107,CSR
Floyd, J.C.	Pvt	H P.S.S.	Deserted/enemy	03/28/65	Bermuda Hundred, VA	03/28/65	Atheneum Prison	CSR
					Wheeling, VA		Washington, DC	CSR
Floyd, J.T.	Pvt	B 27th SCVI	Weldon RR, VA	08/21/64	Wdd & captured		No other data	CSR
Floyd, James A.	Pvt	D 11th SCVI	Town Creek, VA	02/20/65	Ft. Anderson, NC	06/27/65	Pt. Lookout, MD	CSR
					Pt. Lookout, MD	06/28/65	Rlsd. G.O. #109	P114,P121,P123,CSR
Floyd, James D.	Pvt	E 3rd SCVC	Deserted/enemy	02/03/65	Fts. Monroe, VA	04/02/65	Washington, DC	CSR
					Washington, DC	04/05/65	Savannah, GA oath	CSR
Floyd, John M.	Pvt	H 26th SCVI	Five Forks, VA	04/01/65	City Pt., VA	04/05/65	Pt. Lookout, MD	CSR
					Pt. Lookout, MD	06/27/65	Rlsd. G.O. #109	P118,P121,CSR
Floyd, L.A.	Pvt	L 1st SCVIG	Sutherland Stn., VA	04/03/65	Hart's Island, NY	06/16/65	Rlsd. G.O. #109	P79
Floyd, M.	Pvt	B 11th SCVI	Petersburg, VA	05/11/64	Bermuda Hundred, VA	05/21/64	Fts. Monroe, VA	CSR,HAG
					Fts. Monroe, VA	05/23/64	Pt. Lookout, MD	CSR
					Pt. Lookout, MD	09/18/64	Aikens Ldg., VA Xc	P113,P116,P123,CSR
Floyd, M.A.	Pvt	I 7th SCVI	Gettysburg, PA	07/05/63	David's Island, NY	09/12/63	City Pt., VA Xc	P1,P4,CSR
Floyd, Nathaniel	Pvt	H 26th SCVI	Deserted/enemy	03/01/65	City Pt., VA	03/03/65	Washington, DC	CSR
					Washington, DC	03/06/65	New York, NY oath	CSR
Floyd, P.T.	Pvt	H 26th SCVI	Swift Creek, VA	04/06/65	W. Bldg. Balt, MD	05/09/65	Ft. McHenry, MD	P1,P96,CSR
					Ft. McHenry, MD	06/09/65	Rlsd. G.O. #109	CSR
Floyd, S.P.	Pvt	I 26th SCVI	Deserted/enemy	01/20/65	City Pt., VA	01/23/65	Washington, DC	P8,CSR
					Washington, DC	01/24/65	Phila., PA on oath	CSR
Floyd, Stephen L.	Pvt	H 26th SCVI	Deserted/enemy	02/26/65	City Pt., VA	02/28/65	Washington, DC	CSR
					Washington, DC	03/01/65	Charleston, SC	CSR
Floyd, William H.	Pvt	F 27th SCVI	Town Creek, VA	02/20/65	Ft. Anderson, NC	02/28/65	Pt. Lookout, MD	CSR,HAG
					Pt. Lookout, MD	06/26/65	Rlsd. G.O. #109	P114,P121,CSR
Flynn, Charles H.	Pvt	B 25th SCVI	Not given					P7,HAG
Flynn, James	Pvt	H 27th SCVI	Deserted/enemy	07/12/64	Bermuda Hundred, VA	07/13/64	Fts. Monroe, VA	CSR,HAG
					Fts. Monroe, VA	07/17/64	New York, NY	P8,CSR
Flynn, John	Pvt	E 1st SCVA	Morris Island, SC	07/10/63	Hilton Head, SC	09/14/65	Ft. Columbus, NY	CSR,HAG
					Ft. Columbus, NY	09/23/63	Took the oath	P1,CSR
Flynn, John	Pvt	C 27th SCVI	Petersburg, VA	06/24/64	Bermuda Hundred, VA	06/25/64	Fts. Monroe, VA	CSR
					Fts. Monroe, VA	06/26/64	Pt. Lookout, MD	CSR
					Pt. Lookout, MD	07/25/64	Elmira, NY	P113,P117,P120,CSR
					Elmira, NY	08/15/64	Died, Ch. Diarrhea	P5,P12,FPH,P65,CSR

SOUTH CAROLINA SOLDIERS, SAILORS AND  CITIZENS HELD IN U.S. PRISONS 1861-1865

NAME	RANK	REGIMENT	CAPTURED AT	WHEN	PRISON	MOVED	DISPOSITION	SOURCES
Flynn, Michael F.	Pvt	E 1st SCVIR	Deserted/enemy	03/03/65	Ft. Monroe, VA	04/02/65	Washington DC	CSR
					Washington, DC	04/05/65	Memphis TN on oath	CSR
Flynn, Patrick	Sgt	H 1st SCVA	Smith Farm, NC	03/16/65	New Berne, NC	04/10/65	Hart's Island, NY	CSR
					Hart's Island, NY	06/17/65	Rlsd. G.O. #109	P79,CSR
Flynn, Thomas	Pvt	E 1st SCVA	Deserted/enemy	02/18/65	Charleston, SC	02/28/65	Will take oath	CSR
Flynn, Thomas G.	Pvt	D 1st SCVIH	South Mtn., MD	09/14/62	Ft. Delaware, DE	10/02/62	Aikens Ldg., VA Xc	CSR
Flynn, Thomas G.	Pvt	D 1st SCVIH	Mossy Creek, TN	01/22/64	Nashville, TN	02/01/64	Louisville, KY	P39,P131,CSR
					Louisville, KY	02/15/64	Rock Island, IL	P88,P91,P93,CSR
					Rock Island, IL	03/02/65	Pt.Lookout, MD Xc	P131,LAN,CSR
Fogarty, William	Sgt	E 1st SCVIR	Deserted/enemy	11/01/64	Hilton Head, SC	11/01/64	Working, QM oath	CSR
Fogle, Gabriel H.	Pvt	I 2nd SCVA	Fayetteville, NC	03/11/65	Pt. Lookout, MD	05/03/65	Died, Ch. Diarrhea	P6,P117,P119,CSR
Fogle, Thomas	Pvt	H Ham.Leg.MI	Edisto River, SC	02/10/65	Pt. Lookout, MD			P117
Fogle, W.C.	Pvt	H Ham.Leg.MI	Edisto R., SC	02/10/65	New Berne, NC	04/03/65	Pt. Lookout, MD	CSR
					Pt. Lookout, MD	06/19/65	Rlsd. G.O. #109	P114,CSR
Fogle, William C.	Cit	Orangeburg			Pt. Lookout, MD	06/27/65	Rlsd. G.O. #109	P121
Fogle, William J.	Pvt	F 25th SCVI	Ft. Fisher, NC	01/15/65	New York, NY	01/30/65	Elmira, NY	CSR
					Elmira, NY	03/16/65	Died, Diarrhea	P6,P65,FPH,HAG
Fogle, William J.	Cit	Orangeburg	Lynch's Creek, SC	02/23/65	Hart's Island, NY	06/02/65	Died, Ch. Diarrhea	P12,P79
Fogleburg, Louis	Pvt	A 25th SCVI	Morris Island, SC	09/07/63	Ft. Columbus, NY	10/09/63	Johnson's Isl., OH	P1
Foley, James	Pvt	E 1st SCVA	Deserted/enemy	02/20/65	Charleston, SC	03/02/65	Will take oath	CSR
Foley, James	Pvt	F 1st SCVA	Fayetteville, NC	03/10/65	Hart's Island, NY	06/14/65	Rlsd. G.O. #109	P79,CSR
Folk, Henry N.	Pvt	D 24th SCVI	Nashville, TN	12/16/64	Nashville, TN	12/31/64	Louisville, KY	CSR
					Louisville, KY	01/02/65	Camp Chase, OH	CSR
					Camp Chase	06/12/65	Rlsd. G.O. #109	P22,CSR
Folk, J.C.	Pvt	K 11th SCVI	Weldon RR, VA	08/21/64	City Pt., VA	08/24/64	Pt. Lookout, MD	CSR
					Pt. Lookout, MD	03/14/65	Aikens Ldg., VA Xc	P117,P123,P124,CSR
Folk, Jacob L.	1Lt	D 24th SCVI	Nashville, TN	12/16/64	Nashville, TN	12/18/64	Louisville, KY	CSR,EFW
					Louisville, KY	12/20/64	Johnson's Isl., OH	P90,P91,P93
					Johnson's Isl., OH	06/16/65	Rlsd. G.O. #109	P81,P82,P83
Folk, John J.	Pvt	G 4th SCVC	Stony Creek, VA	12/01/64	City Pt., VA	12/05/64	Pt. Lookout, MD	CSR
					Pt. Lookout, MD	06/27/65	Rlsd. G.O. #109	P114,P121,CSR
Folk, W. Calvin	Pvt	K 11th SCVI	Town Creek, NC	02/20/65	Ft. Anderson, NC	02/28/65	Pt. Lookout, MD	CSR
					Pt. Lookout, MD	06/26/64	Rlsd. G.O. #109	P114,P121,HAG,CSR
Follard, Michael	Smn	CS Chicora	Morris Island, SC	09/07/63	Pt. Lookout, MD	09/30/64	Ft. Warren, MA	P113,P116
					Ft. Warren, MA	10/01/64	Steamer Circasian	P2,P137
Fooshe, J.E.	Pvt	A 3rd SCVIBn	South Mtn., MD	09/11/62	Ft. Delaware, DE	10/02/62	Aikens Ldg., VA Xc	CSR
Fooshe, James D.	Pvt	A 3rd SCVIBn	Winchester, VA	09/14/62	Ft. McHenry, MD	10/13/62	Fts. Monroe, VA	CSR
					Fts. Monroe, VA	10/17/62	Aikens Ldg., VA Xc	CSR
Fooshe, John	Pvt	D 27th SCVI	Town Creek, NC	02/20/65	Ft. Anderson, NC	02/28/65	Pt. Lookout, MD	CSR,HAG
					Pt. Lookout, MD	06/27/65	Rlsd. G.O. #109	P114,CSR
Foot, A.H.	Pvt	I 27th SCVI	Town Creek, NC	02/20/65	Ft. Anderson, NC	02/28/65	Pt. Lookout, MD	CSR
					Pt. Lookout, MD	06/27/65	Rlsd. G.O. #109	CSR
Footman, John M.	1Sg	C 25th SCVI	Ft. Fisher, NC	01/15/65	Fts. Monroe, VA	02/01/65	Pt. Lookout, MD	CSR,CTA,HAG
					Pt. Lookout, MD	06/05/65	Released	P114
Footman, Richard M.	Pvt	K 6th SCVI	Seven Pines, VA	05/31/62	Fts. Monroe, VA	06/30/62	Died of wounds	P12,CTA,ROH,CSR
Foots, Mark	Pvt	B 13th SCVI	Deserted/enemy	07/29/63	On oath of alleg.			CSR
Forbes, J.R.	Pvt	G 14th SCVI	Richmond, VA Hos.	04/03/65	Provost Marshal	04/21/65	Libby Prison Rchmd.	CSR
					Libby Prison Rchmd.	04/23/65	Newport News, VA	CSR
					Newport News, VA	06/26/65	Rlsd. G.O. #109	P107,CSR
Force, Alexander W.	Cpl	B 25th SCVI	Weldon RR, VA	08/21/64	City Pt., VA	08/24/64	Pt. Lookout, MD	CSR,HAG
					Pt. Lookout, MD	03/14/65	Aikens Ldg., VA Xc	P117,P123,P124

SOUTH CAROLINA SOLDIERS, SAILORS AND  CITIZENS HELD IN U.S. PRISONS 1861-1865

NAME	RANK	REGIMENT	CAPTURED AT	WHEN	PRISON	MOVED	DISPOSITION	SOURCES
Force, George H.	Pvt	B 25th SCVI	Ft. Fisher, NC	01/15/65	New York, NY	01/30/65	Elmira, NY	CSR,HAG
					Elmira, NY	07/13/65	Transferred	P65
					Elmira, NY	08/07/65	Rlsd. G.O. #109	CSR
Ford, Benjamin	Cpl	D 2nd SCVI	Chesterfield, SC	02/28/65	Fts. Monroe, VA	04/02/65	Washington, DC	CSR
					Washington, DC	04/05/65	Charleston, SC	CSR
Ford, Charles P.	Pvt	E 1st SCVIG	Gettysburg, PA	07/04/63	Ft. Delaware, DE	10/07/63	Died	P5,P40,P47,FPH,SA1
Ford, Francis	Pvt	D 1st SCVIR	Morris Island, SC	07/10/63	Hilton Head, SC	07/24/63	Ft. Columbus, NY	P2,CSR
					Ft. Columbus, NY	09/23/63	Pt. Lookout, MD	P1,SA1,CSR
					Pt. Lookout, MD	01/21/64	Joined U.S. Army	P113,P116,P125,CSR
Ford, George W.	Pvt	E 1st SCVIG	Gettysburg, PA	07/05/63	Ft. Delaware, DE	11/29/63	Died, Abscess	P5,P40,P47,FPH,SA1
Ford, Henry A.	Pvt	I 27th SCVI	Town Creek, NC	02/20/65	Pt. Lookout, MD	06/27/65	Rlsd. G.O. #109	P114,P121,P123
Ford, Hiram	Pvt	D 12th SCVI	Richmond, VA	05/18/65	Richmond, VA	05/18/65	Paroled	CSR
Ford, J.W.	Cpl	F 7th SCVC	Deep Bottom, VA	08/16/64	City Pt., VA	08/22/64	Pt. Lookout, MD	CSR
					Pt. Lookout, MD	03/14/65	Aikens Ldg., VA Xc	P113,P124,CSR
Ford, Jacob	Pvt	C Ham.Leg.MI	Richmond, VA Hos.	04/03/65	Richmond, VA Hos.	04/14/65	Provost Marshal	CSR
					Libby Prison,Rchmd.	04/23/65	Newport News, VA	CSR
					Newport News, VA	06/26/65	Rlsd. G.O. #109	P107,CSR
Ford, John Long	Pvt	B 4th SCVC	Louisa C.H., VA	06/11/64	Fts. Monroe, VA	06/20/64	Pt. Lookout, MD	CSR,HHC
					Pt. Lookout, MD	07/25/64	Elmira, NY	P116,P117,P120
					Elmira, NY	10/11/64	Tfd. for exchange	P65,CSR
					Pt. Lookout, MD	10/29/64	Exchanged	P114,P123,CSR
Ford, Joseph	Pvt	H 14th SCVI	Gettysburg, PA	07/05/63	Ft. McHenry, MD	07/12/63	Ft. Delaware, DE	CSR
					Ft. Delaware, DE		Hos. 3/6-3/14/65	P47
					Ft. Delaware, DE	06/10/65	Released	P40,P44,P45,CSR
Ford, Lucius Milton	Pvt	E 4th SCVC	Louisa C.H., VA	06/11/64	Fts. Monroe, VA	06/20/64	Pt. Lookout, MD	CSR,HHC
					Pt. Lookout, MD	07/25/64	Elmira, NY	P113,P116,P120,CSR
					Elmira, NY	07/03/65	Released	P65
Ford, Nelson T.	Pvt	D 17th SCVI	Petersburg, VA	07/30/64	City Pt., VA	08/05/64	Pt. Lookout, MD	CSR,HHC
					Pt. Lookout, MD	08/08/64	Elmira, NY	P113,P117,P120,CSR
					Elmira, NY	07/07/65	Rlsd. G.O. #109	P65,CSR
Ford, Strother	Pvt	D 17th SCVI	Petersburg, VA	03/25/65	City Pt., VA	03/28/65	Pt. Lookout, MD	CSR,HFC
					Pt. Lookout, MD	06/27/65	Rlsd. G.O. #109	P114,P117,P121,CSR
Ford, Thomas	1Lt	A 21st SCVI	Weldon RR, VA	08/21/64	Ft. McHenry, MD	08/27/64	Ft. Delaware, DE	P110,HAG
					Ft. Delaware, DE	10/30/64	Pt. Lookout, MD	P43
					Pt. Lookout, MD	10/31/64	Aikens Ldg., VA Xc	P114,P116,P123
Ford, Thomas	Cpt	A 21st SCVI	Ft. Fisher, NC	01/15/65	Ft. Columbus, NY	03/01/65	City Pt., VA Xc	P2
Ford, W. Long	Pvt	D 17th SCVI	Petersburg, VA	07/30/64	City Pt., VA	08/05/64	Pt. Lookout, MD	CSR,HHC
					Pt. Lookout, MD	08/08/64	Elmira, NY	P117,P120,P125,CSR
					Elmira, NY	07/03/65	Rlsd. G.O. #109	P65,CSR
Fordson, William James	Pvt	B Ham.Leg.MI	Burkeville, VA	04/06/65	City Pt., VA	04/14/65	Pt. Lookout, MD	CSR
					Pt. Lookout, MD			P114,P119,CSR
Fore, Henry J.	Pvt	H 23rd SCVI	Five Forks, VA	04/01/65	City Pt., VA	04/06/65	Pt.Lookout, MD	CSR
					Pt. Lookout, MD	06/04/65	Released on oath	P114,P118,CSR
Fore, T.R.J.	Pvt	L 8th SCVI	Petersburg, VA	07/29/64	City Pt., VA	08/05/64	Pt. Lookout, MD	CSR
					Pt. Lookout, MD	08/08/64	Elmira, NY	P117,P125,P120,CSR
					Elmira, NY	07/03/65	Rlsd. G.O. #109	P65,CSR
Foreman, Jacob J.	Pvt	K 1st SCVC	Williamsport, MD	07/09/63	Hagerstown, MD USH	07/11/63	Died in enemy hand	CSR
Foreman, Jesse J.	Pvt	K 1st SCVC	Upperville, VA	06/21/63	Old Capitol, DC	06/25/63	Paroled	CSR
					Ft. McHenry, MD	06/27/63	City Pt., VA Xc	P110,P121
Foreman, Jesse J.	Pvt	K 1st SCVC	Mineral Springs, SC	03/05/65	New Berne, NC	04/03/65	Pt. Lookout MD	CSR
					Pt. Lookout, MD	06/27/65	Rlsd. G.O. #109	P114,P117,CSR

SOUTH CAROLINA SOLDIERS, SAILORS AND  CITIZENS HELD IN U.S. PRISONS 1861-1865

NAME	RANK	REGIMENT	CAPTURED AT	WHEN	PRISON	MOVED	DISPOSITION	SOURCES
Forester, Benjamin F.	Pvt	F Hol.Leg.	Five Forks, VA	04/01/65	City Pt., VA	04/05/65	Pt. Lookout, MD	CSR
					Pt. Lookout, MD	06/27/65	Rlsd. G.O. #109	P114,P118,CSR
Forester, J.P.	Pvt	A 3rd SCVABn	High Pt., NC	05/02/65	High Pt., NC	05/02/65	Paroled	CSR
Forester, John E.	Pvt	I 16th SCVI	Kennesaw Mtn., GA	06/19/64	Nashville, TN	06/24/64	Louisville, KY	P3,CSR
					Louisville, KY	06/27/64	Camp Morton, IN	P88,CSR
					Camp Morton, IN	03/19/65	Died, Infl. lungs	P6,P101,FPH
					Camp Morton, IN	06/12/65	Released on oath	P100
Forman, J.B.	Tmr	E 14th SCVI	Williamsport, MD	07/06/63	Ft. Delaware, DE	09/18/64	Aikens Ldg., VA Xc	P40,P42,P44
Forrest, William M.	Pvt	F 13th SCVI	Deserted/enemy	11/10/64	City Pt., VA	11/23/64	Washington, DC	CSR
					Washington, DC	11/27/64	Columbus, OH oath	HOS,CSR
Forrester, Henry	Pvt	D 6th SCVC	Stony Creek, VA	12/01/64	City Pt., VA	12/04/64	Pt. Lookout, MD	CSR
					Pt. Lookout, MD	06/27/65	Rlsd. G.O. #109	P114,P121,CDC,CSR
Forrester, L.M.	Pvt	F 22nd SCVI	Newton, NC	04/19/65	Newton, NC	04/19/65	Paroled	CSR
Forstall, A.	Pvt	1 18th SCVAB	Cheraw, SC	03/05/65	Cheraw, SC	03/05/65	Paroled	CSR
Fortner, William T.	Pvt	H 2nd SCVIRi	Fraysers Farm, VA	06/30/62	Harrisons Ldg., VA	07/03/62	Ft. Columbus, NY	CSR
					Ft. Columbus, VA	07/09/62	Ft. Delaware, DE	CSR
					Ft. Delaware, DE	08/05/62	Aikens Ldg., VA Xc	CSR
Fortune, Simon B.	Pvt	D 18th SCVI	Petersburg, VA	04/02/65	City Pt., VA	04/05/65	Pt. Lookout, MD	CSR
					Pt. Lookout, MD	06/26/65	Rlsd. G.O. #109	P114,P118,P122,CSR
Forty, Thomas	Pvt	H 3rd SCVC	Deserted/enemy	10/09/64	Hilton head, SC	02/18/65	New York, NY oath	CSR
Foster, Abner J.	Pvt	D P.S.S.	Richmond, VA	04/03/65	Libby Prison Richmd	04/08/65	Pt. Lookout, MD	CSR
					Pt. Lookout, MD	04/27/65	Died, Diarrhea	P6,P114,P119,FPH
Foster, Charles Bernard	Pvt	D 27th SCVI	Weldon RR, VA	08/21/64	Alexandria, VA	09/17/64	Died of wounds	P1,P5,HAG,CSR
Foster, Dean	Pvt	H 22nd SCVI	Petersburg, VA	07/29/64	Bermuda Hundred, VA	08/02/64	City Pt., VA	CSR
					City Pt., VA	08/05/64	Pt. Lookout, MD	CSR
					Pt. Lookout, MD	08/08/64	Elmira, NY	P113,P117,P120
					Elmira, NY	03/04/65	Died, Ch. Diarrhea	P6,P12,FPH,P65
Foster, E.D.	Pvt	D 22nd SCVI	Kinston, NC	12/15/62	Kinston, NC	12/15/62	Paroled POW	CSR
					Newton, NC	04/19/65	Paroled	CSR
Foster, Henry P.	Pvt	D 27th SCVI	Town Creek, NC	02/20/65	Ft. Anderson, NC	02/28/65	Pt. Lookout, MD	CSR,HAG
					Pt. Lookout, MD	06/12/65	Rlsd. G.O. #109	P114,P117,P121,CSR
Foster, J.W.	Pvt	I 5th SCVI	Deep Bottom, VA	08/14/64	Bermuda Hundred, VA	08/15/64	Fts. Monroe, VA	CSR
					Ft. Monroe, VA	08/16/64	Pt. Lookout, MD	CSR
					Pt. Lookout, MD	09/18/64	Aikens Ldg., VA Xc	CSR
Foster, James M.	Pvt	F Ham.Leg.MI	Burkeville, VA	04/06/65	Pt. Lookout, MD	06/20/65	Rlsd. G.O. #109	P114,P119
Foster, John	Pvt	B 17th SCVI	Farmville, VA	04/06/65	City Pt., VA	04/14/65	Newport News, VA	CSR
					Newport News, VA	06/26/65	Rlsd. G.O. #109	P107,CSR
Foster, John F.M.	Pvt	I 3rd SCVI	Knoxville, TN	12/05/63	Nashville, TN	01/24/64	Louisville, KY	P39,KEB,H3,CSR
					Louisville, KY	01/27/64	Rock Island, IL	P88,P93,CSR
					Rock Island, IL	06/20/65	Rlsd. G.O. #109	P131,CSR
Foster, John H.	Pvt	C 2nd SCVC	Greensboro, NC	05/01/65	Greensboro, NC	05/01/65	Paroled	CSR
Foster, John S.	Pvt	K 16th SCVI	Graysville, GA	11/27/63	Nashville, TN	12/09/63	Louisville, KY	P39,16R,CSR
					Louisville, KY	12/11/63	Rock Island, IL	P88,P89,CSR
					Rock Island, IL	06/19/65	Rlsd. G.O. #109	P131,CSR
Foster, John T.	2Lt	B 5th SCVC	Stony Creek, VA	12/01/63	Ft. McHenry, MD	12/18/63	Ft. Delaware, DE	P110
					Old Capitol, DC	12/16/64	Ft. Delaware, DE	CSR
					Ft. Delaware, DE	02/10/65	Dschd. Frm. Hos.	g5,P46,P47
					Ft. Delaware, DE	06/17/65	Rlsd. G.O. #109	P43,CSR
Foster, Josiah	Pvt	C Hol.Leg.C	New Kent Co., VA	01/23/64	Pt. Lookout, MD	05/03/64	Exchanged	P113

SOUTH CAROLINA SOLDIERS, SAILORS AND CITIZENS HELD IN U.S. PRISONS 1861-1865

NAME	RANK	REGIMENT	CAPTURED AT	WHEN	PRISON	MOVED	DISPOSITION	SOURCES
Foster, K.	Pvt	H 6th SCVC	Petersburg, VA	07/30/64	Pt. Lookout, MD	08/08/64	Elmira, NY	P113,P117,P120,CSR
					Elmira, NY	02/09/65	Pt. Lookout, MD	P65,CSR
					Pt. Lookout, MD	02/13/65	Cox's Wh., VA Xc	CSR
					Elmira, NY	02/13/65	Tfd. for exchange	P65,CSR
Foster, P.O.	Pvt	F 3rd SCVI	Sharpsburg, MD	09/19/62	Frederick, MD USGH	10/27/62	Baltimore, MD	CSR
					Ft. McHenry, MD	10/27/62	Fts. Monroe, VA Xc	CSR
					Fts. Monroe, VA	11/02/62	Aikens Ldg., VA Xc	CSR,H3
Foster, Ransom	Pvt	D 18th SCVI	Petersburg, VA	07/30/64	Pt. Lookout, MD	08/08/64	Elmira, NY	P113,P117,P120,CSR
					Elmira, NY	10/14/64	Pt. Lookout, MD	P65,UD2,CSR
					Pt. Lookout, MD	10/29/64	Venus Pt., GA Xc	P114,P117,P123,CSR
Foster, Robert	Pvt	D 23rd SCVI	Boonesboro, MD	09/15/62	Ft. Delaware, DE	10/02/62	Aikens LDg., VA Xc	CSR
Foster, Robert	Pvt	D 23rd SCVI	Appomattox R., VA	04/02/65	City Pt.,VA	04/06/65	Hart's Island, NY	CSR
					Hart's Island, NY	06/16/65	Rlsd. G.O. # 109	CSR
Foster, Robert J.	Pvt	B 5th SCVI	Burkeville, VA	04/17/65	Burkeville, VA	04/17/65	Paroled	CSR
Foster, Thomas J.	Sgt	A 3rd SCResB	Charlotte, NC	05/18/65	Charlotte, NC	05/18/65	Paroled	CSR
Foster, William H.	Pvt	F 13th SCVI	Deserted/enemy	02/24/65	City Pt., VA	02/26/65	Washington, DC	CSR
					Washington, DC	02/27/65	Springfield, OH	HOS,CSR
Foucher, J. Victor	Pvt	B 27th SCVI	Town Creek, NC	02/20/65	Ft. Anderson, NC	02/28/65	Pt. Lookout, MD	CSR,HAG
					Pt. Lookout, MD	05/18/65	Rlsd. G.O. #85	P114,P122,CSR
Foucher, R.F.	Pvt	27th SCVI			Pt. Lookout, MD	06/27/65	Rlsd. G.O. #109	P121
Fountain, Hugh E.C.	1Lt	E 6th SCVI	Richmond, VA	04/03/65	Hos.Str."Thomas Po	05/06/65	Pt. Lookout, MD Ge	CSR
					Pt. Lookout, MD	05/30/65	Col. Ingraham	P117
					Ft. McHenry, MD	05/31/65	Johnson's Isl., OH	P110,R46
					Old Capitol, DC	06/01/65	Johnson's Isl., OH	CSR
					Johnson's Isl., OH	06/14/65	Rlsd. G.O. #109	P81,CSR
Fountain, William A.	Sgt	B 21st SCVI	Morris Island, SC	07/10/63	Morris Island, SC	07/13/63	Hilton Head, SC	CSR
					Hilton Head, SC	07/28/63	Morris Isl., SC Xc	P2,HAG
Fountain, William J.	Pvt	B 21st SCVI	Town Creek, NC	02/20/65	Pt. Lookout, MD	06/26/65	Rlsd. G.O. #109	P114,P121,HAG
Fourcher, James	Pvt	L 1st SCVIG	Hatchers Run, VA	03/31/65	Pt. Lookout, MD	06/05/65	Released	P114,P117,SA1,CSR
Fowler, Andrew J.	Pvt	C 23rd SCVI	Five Forks, VA	04/01/65	City Pt., VA	04/04/65	Pt. Lookout, MD	CSR
					Pt. Lookout, MD	06/27/65	Rlsd. G.O. #109	P114,P118,P121,CSR
Fowler, B. Gadberry	Pvt	9 10/19 SCVI	Missionary Ridge, TN	11/25/63	Nashville, TN	12/07/63	Louisville, KY	P39,CSR
					Louisville, KY	12/09/63	Rock Island, IL	CSR,P88
					Louisville, KY	12/09/63	Rock Island, IL	P88,CSR
					Rock Island, IL	10/14/64	Enlstd. USA frntier	P131,CSR
Fowler, C.F.	Pvt	C 7th SCVIBn	Weldon RR, VA	08/14/64	Pt. Lookout, MD	02/18/65	Exchanged	P124
Fowler, C.J.	Pvt	H P.S.S.	Deserted/enemy	03/05/65	P.M. Army/Potomac	03/07/65	Washington, DC	CSR
					Washington, DC	03/08/65	Boston, MA oath	CSR
Fowler, Charles E.	Pvt	B 18th SCVI	Farmville, VA	04/11/65	Farmville, VA USH	04/30/65	Paroled	CSR
Fowler, Daniel M.	Pvt	F 1st SCVIG	Gettysburg, PA	07/05/63	Ft. Delaware, DE	12/27/63	Died, Ch. Diarrhea	P5,P40,P44,P47,FPH
Fowler, George R.	Pvt	I 16th SCVI	Ringgold Stn., GA	11/27/63	Bridgeport, AL G.H.	12/11/63	Nashville, TN	P2
					Nashville, TN G.H.	12/16/63	Died, Ch. Diarrhea	P12,CSR
Fowler, George W.	Pvt	K 26th SCVI	Farmville, VA	04/06/65	City Pt., VA	04/14/65	Newport News, VA	CSR
					Newport News, VA	06/13/65	Rlsd. G.O. #109	P107,CSR
Fowler, Harrison	Pvt	A 3rd SCVABn	High Pt., NC	05/02/65	High Pt., NC	05/02/65	Paroled	CSR
Fowler, Hosea	Pvt	K 27th SCVI	Petersburg, VA	06/24/64	Bermuda Hundred, VA	06/25/64	Fts. Monroe, VA	CSR,HAG
					Fts. Monroe, VA	06/26/64	Pt. Lookout, MD	CSR,HAG
					Pt. Lookout, MD	08/16/64	Elmira, NY	P113,P117,P120,CSR
					Elmira, NY	02/03/65	Died, Typhoid	P6,P12,P65,FPH,CSR
Fowler, Israel	Pvt	F 18th SCVI	Petersburg, VA	04/01/65	City Pt., VA	04/04/65	Pt. Lookout, MD	CSR
					Pt. Lookout, MD	06/26/65	Rlsd. G.O. #109	P114,P118,CSR
Fowler, J.J.	Pvt	E Ham.Leg.	Warrenton, VA	09/29/62	Warrenton, VA	09/29/62	Paroled	CSR

SOUTH CAROLINA SOLDIERS, SAILORS AND  CITIZENS HELD IN U.S. PRISONS 1861-1865

NAME	RANK	REGIMENT	CAPTURED AT	WHEN	PRISON	MOVED	DISPOSITION	SOURCES
Fowler, Jacob L.	Pvt	F 24th SCVI	Jackson, MS	05/16/63	Jackson, MS	05/16/63	Paroled in Hos.	CSR
Fowler, Jacob P.	Pvt	K 26th SCVI	Southside RR, VA	04/01/65	City Pt., VA	04/05/65	Pt. Lookout, MD	CSR
					Pt. Lookout, MD	06/27/65	Rlsd. G.O. #109	P118,P121,P122,CSR
Fowler, James F.	Pvt	L 21st SCVI	Town Creek, NC	02/20/65	Pt. Lookout, MD	06/26/65	Rlsd. G.O. #109	P114,P121,HAG
Fowler, Jesse	Pvt	D 16th SCVI	Franklin, TN	12/17/64	Nashville, TN	12/31/64	Louisville, KY	P92,P94,16R,CSR
					Louisville, KY	01/04/65	Camp Chase, OH	P92,P94,CSR
					Camp Chase, OH	06/13/64	Rlsd. G.O. #109	P22,CSR
Fowler, Jesse W.	Pvt	D Orr's Ri.	Petersburg, VA	04/03/65	City Pt., VA	04/10/65	Hart's Island, NY	CSR
					Hart's Island, NY	06/16/65	Rlsd. G.O. #109	P79,CSR
Fowler, John	Pvt	F 18th SCVI	Richmond, VA	04/03/65	Newport News, VA	05/25/65	Died, Lung Infl.	P12,P107,CSR
Fowler, John F.	Pvt	D 27th SCVI	Town Creek, NC	02/20/65	Ft. Anderson, NC	02/28/65	Pt. Lookout, MD	CSR,HAG
					Pt. Lookout, MD	06/26/65	Rlsd. G.O. #109	P122,CSR
Fowler, M.H.	Pvt	K Ham.Leg.MI	Newton, NC	04/19/65	Newton, NC	04/19/65	Paroled	CSR
Fowler, Marion	Pvt	H 15th SCVI	Charlestown, VA	08/16/64	Washington, DC	08/29/64	Camp Chase, OH	CSR
					Camp Chase, OH	03/18/65	Pt. Lookout, MD Xc	P22,P26,KEB,CSR
					Pt. Lookout, MD	03/27/65	Boulware's Wh. Xc	CSR
Fowler, Newton F.	Pvt	F 18th SCVI	Petersburg, VA	07/30/64	City Pt., VA	08/03/64	Pt. Lookout, MD	CSR
					Pt. Lookout, MD	08/08/64	Elmira, NY	P113,P117,P120,CSR
					Elmira, NY	08/31/64	Died, Typhoid	P5,P12,P65,FPH,CSR
Fowler, Valentine	Pvt	F 7th SCVC	Farmville, VA	04/06/65	City Pt., VA	04/15/65	Pt. Lookout, MD	CSR
					Pt. Lookout, MD	06/08/65	Rlsd. G.O. #109	CSR
Fowler, William P.	Pvt	6 10/19 SCVI	Missionary Ridge, TN	11/25/63	Nashville, TN	12/07/63	Louisville, KY	P39,CSR
					Louisville, KY	12/09/63	Rock Island, IL	P88,P89,RAS,CSR
					Rock Island, IL	10/14/64	Jd. US Army F.S.	P131,CSR
Fowler, William R.	Pvt	E 18th SCVI	Amelia C.H., VA	04/06/65	Pt. Lookout, MD	04/23/65	Died, Catarrh	P6,P114,P119,CSR
Fowler, Young A.	Pvt	E Hol.Leg.	Jarratts Stn., VA	05/08/64	Pt. Lookout, MD	08/15/64	Elmira, NY	P113,P116,P120,CSR
					Elmira, NY	10/11/64	Tfd. for exchange	P65,CSR
					Pt. Lookout, MD	10/29/64	Aikens Ldg., VA Xc	P114,P117,CSR
Fowler, Young A.	Pvt	E Hol.Leg.	Five Forks, VA	04/01/65	Fts. Monroe, VA	05/13/65	Pt. Lookout, MD	CSR
					Pt. Lookout, MD	06/27/65	Rlsd. G.O. #109	P114,P121
Fowles, John Newton	Pvt	I 2nd SCVC	Rappahannock R., VA	12/04/63	Pt. Lookout, MD	11/01/64	Aikens Ldg. Xc	P121,P123,P124,CSR
Fox, J.R.P.	Cpt	I 1st SCVC	Brandy Stn., VA	06/02/63	Old Capitol, DC	09/24/63	Ft. McHenry, MD	CSR
					Ft. McHenry, MD	09/25/63	Johnson's Isl., OH	P110,P144,CSR
					Johnson's Isl., OH	04/22/64	Pt. Lookout, MD	P80,P82,CSR
					Pt. Lookout, MD	05/03/64	City Pt., VA Xc	P116,CSR
Fox, John S.	Pvt	F P.S.S.	Loudon, TN	12/03/63	Chattanooga, TN G.H.			P1
					Nashville, TN	02/19/64	Louisville, KY	P39, CSR
					Louisville, KY	03/09/64	Camp Chase, OH	P88,P91,P93,CSR
					Camp Chase, OH	07/27/64	Enlstd. US Navy Rej.	P22,P25,CSR
					Camp Chase, OH	03/26/65	Pt. Lookout, MD	P26,CSR
					Pt. Lookout, MD	06/05/65	Released	P114,P119, CSR
Fox, William	2Sg	K 1st SCVIG	Gettysburg, PA	07/03/63	David's Island, NY	10/24/63	Escaped	P1,P7,SA1,CSR
Fox, William	Pvt	K 1st SCVA	Morris Island, SC	07/10/63	Hilton Head, SC	09/05/63	Ft. Columbus, NY	CSR
					Ft. Columbus, NY	09/23/63	Took the oath	P1,CSR
					Pt. Lookout, MD	09/30/63	Ft. Warren, MA	P113,P116
Fox, William	Smn	Ripleys DB	Morris Island, SC	09/07/63	Ft. Warren, MA	10/01/64	Steamer Circasian	P2,P137
Foxworth, Andrew B.	Pvt	6 10/19 SCVI	Missionary Ridge, TN	11/25/63	Nashville, TN	12/07/63	Louisville, KY	P39,RAS,CSR
					Louisville, KY	12/08/63	Rock Island, IL	P88,P89,CSR
					Rock Island, IL	06/20/65	Rlsd. G.O. #109	P131,CSR
Foxworth, Charles J.	Pvt	F 4th SCVC	Hawe's Shop, VA	05/28/64	Armory Sq. G.H., DC	06/18/64	Died of wounds	P6,P12,HMC,CSR
Foxworth, Charles W.	Cpl	H Orr's Ri.	Spotsylvania, VA	05/12/64	Belle Plain, VA	05/20/64	Ft. Delaware, DE	CSR
					Ft. Delaware, DE	06/11/65	Released	P41,P42,P45,CDC

SOUTH CAROLINA SOLDIERS, SAILORS AND **F** CITIZENS HELD IN U.S. PRISONS 1861-1865

NAME	RANK	REGIMENT	CAPTURED AT	WHEN	PRISON	MOVED	DISPOSITION	SOURCES
Foxworth, Samuel W.	Pvt	F 4th SCVC	Hawe's Shop, VA	05/28/64	White House, VA	06/08/64	Pt. Lookout, MD	CSR
					Pt. Lookout, MD	07/09/64	Elmira, NY	P113,P116,P120,CSR
					Elmira, NY	10/11/64	Tfd. for exchange	P65,CSR
					Pt. Lookout, MD	10/29/64	Venus Pt., GA Xc	P114,P117,P123,CSR
					Ocmulgee H. Macon	11/18/64	Cuthbert, GA Hos.	CSR
					Hood Hos. Cuhbert		Not stated	CSR
Foxworth, W.K.	Pvt	D 25th SCVI	Weldon RR, VA	08/21/64	City Pt., VA	08/26/64	Died of wounds	P12,CSR,HAG
Fracheur, Daniel N.	Pvt	K 12th SCVI	Deserted/enemy	12/06/64	City Pt., VA	12/06/64	Washington, DC	CSR
					Washington, DC	12/10/64	New York, NY oath	CSR
Fralic, William Joseph	Sgt	F 25th SCVI	Weldon RR, VA	08/27/64	Alexandria, VA	09/10/64	Died of wounds	P6,FPH,HAG
Francis, G.M.	Pvt	A 5th SCVI	Raleigh, NC	05/09/65	Raleigh, NC	05/09/65	Paroled	CSR
Francis, James	Pvt	C Ham.Leg.	Knoxville, TN	12/06/63	Knoxville, TN	12/15/63	Camp Chase, OH	P84,CSR
Franklin, Avery	Pvt	A 22nd SCVI	Bermuda Hundred, VA	06/02/64	Bermuda Hundred, VA	06/03/64	Fts. Monroe, VA	CSR
					Fts. Monroe, VA	06/06/64	Pt. Lookout, MD	CSR
					Pt. Lookout, MD	12/07/64	Died	P6,P113,P116,FPH
Franklin, C.E.	Pvt	B 1st SCVC	Gettysburg, PA	07/04/63	David's Island, NY	08/24/63	City Pt., VA Xc	P1,CSR
Franklin, M.	Pvt	E 6th SCResB	Augusta, GA	05/18/65	Augusta, GA	05/18/65	Paroled	CSR
Franklin, R.L.	Pvt	K 13th SCVI	Southside RR, VA	04/02/65	City Pt., VA	04/03/65	Hart's Island, NY	CSR
					Hart's Island, NY	06/23/65	Died, Typhoid fever	P12,P79,FPH
Franklin, William B.	Pvt	B 1st SCVIG	Gettysburg, PA	07/05/63	Gettysburg G.H.	07/13/63	Provost Marshal	P4,SA1,ANY,NCC
Franklow, Jacob A.	Pvt	K 13th SCVI	Southside RR, VA	04/02/65	City Pt., VA	04/07/65	Hart's Island, NY	P79,CSR
Franklow, Robert	Pvt	K 13th SCVI	Southside RR, VA	04/02/65	City Pt., VA	04/07/65	Hart's Island, NY	CSR
					Hart's Island, NY	06/22/65	Died, Typhoid fever	CSR
Franks, Benjamin	Coo	A 1st SCVIG	Petersburg, VA	04/03/65	City Pt., VA	04/04/65	Pt. Lookout, MD	CSR
					Pt. Lookout, MD	06/30/65	Rlsd. G.O. #109	P114,P117
Franks, Charles M.	Pvt	A 3rd SCVI	Knoxville, TN	12/05/63	Knoxville, TN	01/06/64	Hos. in country	P84,CSR
					Nashville, TN	02/11/64	Louisville, KY	P39,CSR
					Louisville, KY	02/15/64	Rock Island, IL	P88,P91,P93,CSR
					Rock Island, IL	02/15/65	Pt. Lookout, MD Xc	P131
Franks, John S.	Pvt	F 14th SCVI	Gettysburg, PA	07/03/63	David's Island, NY	10/22/63	Fts. Monroe, VA Xc	P1,CSR
Fraser, Benjamin B.	Pvt	A 7th SCVC	Farmville, VA	04/11/65	Farmville, VA	04/21/65	Paroled	CSR
Fraser, Daniel V.	Cpl	B 7th SCVIBn	Weldon RR, VA	08/21/64	City Pt., VA USFH	08/22/64	Fts. Monroe, VA GH	CSR,HAG,HFC
					Fts. Monroe, VA US	08/26/64	Alexandria, VA USGH	CSR
					Alexandria, VA USG	09/10/64	Died of wounds	P1,P6,CSR
Fraser, Samuel R.	Pvt	K 23rd SCVI	Five Forks, VA	04/01/65	City Pt., VA	04/06/65	Pt. Lookout, MD	CSR
					Pt. Lookout, MD	06/27/65	Rlsd. G.O. #109	P114,P118,P121,CSR
Frawley, John	Pvt	Gist Gd HA	Deserted/enemy	03/20/65	Charleston, SC	03/20/65	Released on oath	CSR
Frederick, R.E.	Pvt	22nd SCVI	Deserted/enemy		City Pt., VA	01/18/65		P8
Fredericks, Thomas M.	Pvt	C Orr's Ri.	Deserted/enemy	05/05/64	Knoxville, TN	03/06/65	Louisville, KY	P8,CSR
					Louisville, KY	03/21/65	Sent north on oath	P92,CDC,CSR
Free, David Belton	1Lt	F 18th SCVI	Crater, Pbg., VA	07/30/65	Ft. McHenry, MD	08/11/64	Ft. Delaware, DE	P45,P110,CSR
					Ft. Delaware, DE	06/17/64	Rlsd. G.O. #109	P43,CSR
Free, Joseph	Cpl	B 17th SCVI	Petersburg, VA	03/25/65	City Pt., VA	03/28/65	Pt. Lookout, MD	CSR
					Pt. Lookout, MD	06/26/65	Rlsd. G.O. #109	P114,P117,HFC,CSR
Free, Lewis M.	Pvt	K 14th SCVI	Appomattox R., VA	04/03/65	City Pt., VA	04/10/65	Hart's Island, NY	CSR
					Hart's Island, NY	06/16/65	Rlsd. G.O. #109	P79,HOE,CSR
Freeder, Francis	Pvt	Palmetto L	Richmond, VA	04/10/65	City Pt., VA	04/17/65	Washington, DC	CSR
					Washington, DC	04/17/65	Florence, SC oath	CSR
Freeman, Benjamin F.	Pvt	E 4th SCVC	Hanovertown, VA	06/03/64	Ft. McHenry, MD			P110
					Douglas G.H., DC	06/18/64	Died of wounds	P5,P12
Freeman, Chapman	Pvt	D 21st SCVI	Ft. Fisher, NC	01/15/65	Elmira, NY	07/11/65	Rlsd. G.O. #109	P65,HAG
Freeman, E.A.	Pvt	B 5th SCVC	Deserted/enemy	04/12/65	Savannah, GA		Beaufort, SC oath	CSR

SOUTH CAROLINA SOLDIERS, SAILORS AND CITIZENS HELD IN U.S. PRISONS 1861-1865

NAME	RANK	REGIMENT	CAPTURED AT	WHEN	PRISON	MOVED	DISPOSITION	SOURCES
Freeman, G.E.	Pvt	G Orr's Ri.	Deserted/enemy	04/06/65	City Pt., VA	04/12/65	Charleston, SC oath	CSR
Freeman, George	Pvt	D 25th SCVI	Ft. Fisher, NC	01/15/65	New York, NY	01/30/65	Elmira, NY	CSR
					Elmira, NY	02/25/65	Died, Pneumonia	P6,P12,P65,FPH
Freeman, Henry H.	Pvt	Ferguson's	Marrietta, GA	07/03/64	Chattanooga, GA	09/15/64	Rough & Ready, GA	CSR
					Rough & Ready, GA	09/19/64	Exchanged	CSR
Freeman, Henry H.	Pvt	Ferguson's	Salisbury, NC	04/12/65	Nashville, TN	04/29/65	Louisville, KY	P39,CSR
					Louisville, KY	05/02/65	Camp Chase, OH	P92,CSR
					Camp Chase, OH	06/13/65	Rlsd. G.O. #109	P23,CSR
Freeman, Irving	Pvt	F 8th SCVI	Winchester, VA	09/13/64	Harpers Ferry, WV	09/19/64	Camp Chase, OH	P22,CSR
					Camp Chase, OH	06/11/64	Released G.O. #109	P22,CSR
Freeman, Isaac	Pvt	D 12th SCVI	Malvern Hill, VA	08/18/64	Camp Hamilton, VA	12/23/64	Pt. Lookout, MD	CSR
					Pt. Lookout, MD	03/17/65	Aikens Ldg., VA Xc	P114,P121,CSR
					Richmond, VA Hos.	03/20/65	Prld. POW Camp Lee	CSR
Freeman, J.F.	Pvt	F 2nd SCVI	Salisbury, NC	05/02/00	Salisbury, NC	07/31/65	Paroled	CSR
Freeman, J.H.	Pvt	C 3rd SCVABn	Blakely, AL	04/09/65	Ship Island, MS	05/01/65	Vicksburg, MS Xc	CSR
Freeman, J.H.	Pvt	C 3rd SCVABn	Augusta, GA	05/20/65	Augusta, GA	05/20/65	Paroled on oath	CSR
Freeman, James	Pvt	E 2nd SCVI	Missionary Ridge, TN	11/25/63	Nashville, TN	12/04/63	Louisville, KY	P39,KEB,CSR
					Louisville, KY	12/06/63	Rock Island, IL	SA2,P89,H2,CSR
					Rock Island, IL	10/14/64	Jd. USA,Frtr. Ser.	P131,CSR
Freeman, James	Pvt	C 12th SCVI	Petersburg, VA	04/02/65	City Pt., VA	04/07/65	Hart's Island, NY	CSR
					Hart's Island, NY	06/16/65	Rlsd. G.O. #109	P79,UD2,CSR
Freeman, John	Pvt	E 21st SCVI	Petersburg, VA	06/18/64	Hampton, VA	06/21/64	Died of wounds	P12,HAG
Freeman, John	Pvt	Beaufort L	Deserted/enemy	02/12/65	Baltimore, MD	05/10/65	New York, NY oath	CSR
Freeman, John	Pvt	K 1st SCVIR	Bentonville, NC	03/22/65	New Berne, NC	04/10/65	Hart's Island, NY	CSR
					Hart's Island, NY	06/07/65	Died, Ch. Diarrhea	P6,P12,P79,FPH,CSR
Freeman, Lewis L.	Pvt	E 21st SCVI	Petersburg, VA	06/24/64	Pt. Lookout, MD	08/16/64	Elmira, NY	P113,P117,P120,HAG
					Elmira, NY	10/11/64	Tfd. for exchange	P65,HAG
					Pt. Lookout, MD	10/29/64	Aikens Ldg., VA Xc	P114,P117,P123
Freeman, Thadeus W.	Pvt	B Ham.Leg.MI	Deep Bottom, VA	09/29/64	Bermuda Hundred, VA	09/30/64	City Pt., VA P.M.	CSR
					City Pt., VA	10/05/64	Pt. Lookout, MD	CSR
					Pt. Lookout, VA	03/17/65	Aikens Ldg., VA Xc	P114,P117,P124,CSR
Freeman, W.C.	Pvt	Ham.Leg.MI	Albany, GA	05/20/65	Albany, GA	05/20/65	Paroled	CSR
Freeman, W.F.	Pvt	C 8th SCVI	Winchester, VA	09/13/64	Harpers Ferry, WV	09/19/64	Camp Chase, OH	CSR
					Camp Chase, OH	05/02/65	New Orleans, LA	P22,P26,KEB,CSR
					New Orleans, LA	05/12/65	Vicksburg, MS Xc	CSR
Freeman, W.J.	Pvt	K 7th SCVI	Anderson, SC	05/08/65	Anderson, SC	05/08/65	Paroled	CSR
Freeman, William	Pvt	E 21st SCVI	Morris Island, SC	07/10/63	Morris Island, SC	07/12/63	Hilton Head, SC	CSR,HAG
					Hilton Head G.H.	07/23/63	Morris Island, SC Xc	P2,CSR
Freeman, William	Pvt	E 21st SCVI	Petersburg, VA	06/24/64	Bermuda Hundred, VA	06/25/64	Fts. Monroe, VA	CSR
					Fts. Monroe, VA	06/26/64	Pt. Lookout, MD	CSR
					Pt. Lookout, MD	08/16/64	Elmira, NY	P113,P120
					Elmira, NY	10/11/64	Tfd. for exchange	P65
					Pt. Lookout, MD	10/29/64	Venus Pt., GA Xc	P114,P117,P123,CSR
					Venus Pt., GA	11/15/64	Macon, GA Hos.	CSR
Freeman, William Dixon	Pvt	D 24th SCVI	Nashville, TN	12/16/64	Nashville, TN	12/18/64	Louisville, KY	CSR
					Louisville, KY	12/20/64	Camp Douglas, IL	P91,P94,EFW
					Camp Douglas, IL	06/19/65	Rlsd. G.O. #109	P55
Freeman, William G.	Pvt	E 20th SCVI	Columbia, SC	02/14/65	New Berne, NC	04/10/65	Hart's Island, NY	CSR
					Hart's Island, NY	06/16/65	Rlsd. G.O. #109	P79,CSR
Frick, Elias D.	Pvt	C 20th SCVI	Cedar Creek, VA	10/19/64	Harpers Ferry, WV	10/23/64	Pt. Lookout, MD	CSR
					Pt. Lookout, MD	02/21/65	Died, Inflm. lungs	P6,P117,P119,CS

SOUTH CAROLINA SOLDIERS, SAILORS AND **F** CITIZENS HELD IN U.S. PRISONS 1861-1865

NAME	RANK	REGIMENT	CAPTURED AT	WHEN	PRISON	MOVED	DISPOSITION	SOURCES
Fricks, Jasper N.	Pvt	C Orr's Ri.	Petersburg, VA	04/03/65	City Pt., VA	04/07/65	Hart's Island, NY	CSR
					Hart's Island, NY	06/15/65	Rlsd. G.O. #109	P79,CDC,CSR
Fricks, John D.	Pvt	C Orr's Ri.	Gettysburg, PA	07/06/63	W. Bldg. Balt, MD	08/31/63	Died, Rem. fever	P1,P6,P12,FPH,CSR
Fricks, Joseph	Pvt	C 1st SCVC	Chilesburgh, VA	05/24/64	White House, VA	07/08/64	Pt. Lookout, MD	CSR
					Pt. Lookout, MD	07/09/64	Elmira, NY	P113,P116,P120,CSR
					Elmira, NY	06/30/65	Rlsd. G.O. #109	P65,CSR
Friday, James G.	Pvt	C 1st SCVIG	Fredericksburg, VA	05/03/63	Ft. McHenry, MD	05/07/63	Ft. Delaware, DE	P110,SA1
					Old Capitol, DC	05/07/63	Ft. Delaware, DE	CSR
Friday, James G.	Pvt	C 1st SCVIG	Hanover Jctn., VA	05/24/64	Pt. Lookout, MD	07/09/64	Elmira, NY	P113,P116,P120
					Elmira, NY	03/10/65	James R., VA Xc	P65,CSR
Friday, P.D.	Pvt	B 20th SCVI	Woodstock, VA	10/20/64	Harpers Ferry, WV	11/01/64	Pt. Lookout, MD	CSR
					Pt. Lookout, MD	01/17/65	Aikens Ldg., VA Xc	P114,P117,P124,CSR
Friday, William T.	2Lt	B 16th SCVI	Franklin, TN	12/17/64	Nashville, TN	01/08/65	Louisville, KY	P2,CSR,16R
					Louisville, KY	01/09/65	Ft. Delaware, DE	P92,P93,CSR
					Ft. Delaware, DE	02/27/65	City Pt., VA Xc	P43,P47,CSR
Friedman, Benjamin	Pvt	E 3rd SCVI	Chester, SC	05/05/65	Chester, SC	05/05/65	Paroled	CSR
Frierson, Augustus C.	Pvt	K 4th SCVC	Old Church, VA	05/30/64	Pt. Lookout, MD	07/30/64	Died	P6,P116,P119,CS
Frierson, James Mc.	Pvt	K 23rd SCVI	Petersburg, VA	06/15/64	Pt. Lookout, MD	07/25/64	Elmira, NY	P113,P116,P120,CSR
					Elmira, NY	06/24/65	Rlsd. G.O. #109	P65,UD3,CSR
Frierson, R. Adolphus	Pvt	K 23rd SCVI	Hatchers Run, VA	04/01/65	Pt. Lookout, MD	06/27/65	Rlsd. G.O. #109	P114,P118,P121,CSR
Frierson, William G.	Pvt	K 23rd SCVI	Petersburg, VA	04/02/65	Camp Hamilton, VA	05/04/65	Newport News, VA	CSR
					Newport News, VA	06/26/65	Rlsd. G.O. #109	K23,CSR
Fripp, B.E.	Cpl	B 4th SCVC	Chester, SC	05/05/65	Chester, SC	05/05/65	Paroled	CSR
Fripp, Charles E.	Pvt	Matthewes A	Averysboro, NC	03/17/65	Pt. Lookout, MD	06/27/65	Rlsd. G.O. #109	P123
Fripp, M.S.	Pvt	E 4th SCVC	Louisa C.H., VA	06/11/64	Fts. Monroe, VA	06/20/64	Pt. Lookout, MD	CSR
					Pt. Lookout, MD	07/25/64	Elmira, NY	CSR
					Elmira, NY	03/14/65	Tfd. for exchange	P65,CSR
Frohberg, H.F.	Pvt	G 25th SCVI	Deserted/enemy	12/24/64	Hilton Head, SC	02/18/65	Sent north on oath	CSR
Frohburg, H.C.	Pvt	C 1st SCVIH	Warrenton, VA	09/29/62	Warrenton, VA	09/29/62		CSR
Frost, Henry	Pvt	G 5th SCVC	Ream's Stn., VA	08/23/64	1st. Div. 2nd AC Hos.	08/26/64	Washington, DC G.H.	CSR
					Ft. McHenry, MD	08/27/64	Harewood Hos., DC	P110
					Harewood Hos. DC	08/27/64	Died of wounds	P5,P6,P12,CSR
Frost, Henry W.	1Lt	G 1st SCVA	Fayetteville, NC	03/10/65	New Berne, NC	04/03/65	Pt. Lookout, MD	CSR
					Pt. Lookout, MD	04/03/65	Washington, DC	P114,CSR
					Pt. Lookout, MD	04/03/65	Johnson's Isl., OH	P117,CSR
					Ft. McHenry, MD	04/09/65	Johnson's Isl., OH	P110
					Johnsons Isl., OH	06/17/65	Rlsd. G.O. #109	P81,P82,P83,CSR
Fry, Daniel	Pvt	D 15th SCMil	Lynch's Creek, SC	02/27/65	New Berne, NC P.M.	04/09/65	Pt. Lookout, MD	CSR
					Pt. Lookout, MD	06/19/65		P114,P117
Fry, J.R.	Pvt	A 20th SCVI	Deserted/enemy	02/18/65	Charleston, SC	02/18/65	Paroled on oath	CSR
Fry, Joseph Tyler	Pvt	H 20th SCVI	Winchester, VA	09/19/64	W. Bldg. Balt, MD	11/19/64	Ft. McHenry, MD	CSR
					Ft. McHenry, MD	01/01/65	Pt. Lookout, MD	P144,CSR,KEB
					Pt. Lookout, MD	03/19/65	Died Infl. lung	P6,P114,P119,FPH
Fullam, Richard J.	Pvt	B 1st SCVA	Deserted/enemy	04/18/65	Wilmington, NC	04/22/65	New York, NY	CSR
Fuller, Adolphus A.	1Lt	B 3rd SCVIBn	Gettysburg, PA	07/05/63	Letterman G.H. Gbg	07/15/63	Died of wounds	P1,KEB,ROH,GDR
Fuller, Adolphus M.	Sgt	B 3rd SCVIBN	South Mtn., MD	09/14/62	Ft. Delaware, DE	10/02/62	Aikens Ldg., VA Xc	CSR
Fuller, E.W.	Pvt	D 12th SCVI	Gettysburg, PA	09/14/62	Ft. McHenry, MD	07/07/63	Ft. Delaware, DE	CSR
					Ft. Delaware, DE	10/28/64	(Release denied)	P7
					Ft. Delaware, DE	01/02/65	Released on oath	P40,P47,P144,CSR
Fuller, Henry F.	Sgt	F 2nd SCVI	Gettysburg, PA	07/03/63	Letterman Hos. Gt	09/16/63	W. Bldg. Balt, MD	CSR
					W. Bldg. Balt, MD	09/25/63	City Pt., VA Xc	SA2,P1,KEB,H2,CSR
Fuller, Henry M.	Pvt	Beaufort L	Augusta, GA	05/22/65	Augusta, GA	05/22/65	Paroled	CSR

SOUTH CAROLINA SOLDIERS, SAILORS AND  CITIZENS HELD IN U.S. PRISONS 1861-1865

NAME	RANK	REGIMENT	CAPTURED AT	WHEN	PRISON	MOVED	DISPOSITION	SOURCES
Fuller, John	Pvt	C 14th SCVI	Appomattox R., VA	04/03/65	City Pt., VA	04/10/65	Hart's Island, NY	CSR
					Hart's Island, NY	06/20/65	Rlsd. G.O. #109	P79,CSR
Fuller, John N.	Pvt	G 3rd SCVI	N. Anna River, VA	05/24/64	Port Royal, VA	05/30/64	Pt. Lookout, MD	SA2,H3,CSR
					Pt. Lookout, MD	05/13/65	Rlsd. G.O. #85	CSR
Fuller, Robert	Pvt	H 7th SCVC	Lyttleton, VA	05/07/64	Pt. Lookout, MD	08/15/64	Elmira, NY	P120
					Elmira, NY	10/19/64	Died, Ch. Diarrhea	P12,P65
Fuller, S.P.	Pvt	F Orr's Ri.	Petersburg, VA	04/03/65	City Pt., VA	04/10/65	Hart's Island, NY	CSR
					Hart's Island, NY	06/16/65	Rlsd. G.O. #109	P79,CSR
Fuller, Silas M.	Pvt	C 3rd SCVIBn	Hanover Jctn., VA	05/24/64	Port Royal, VA	05/30/64	Pt. Lookout, MD	CSR,KEB
					Pt. Lookout, MD	03/14/65	Aikens Ldg., VA Xc	P113,P116,P124
					Pt. Lookout, MD	05/13/65	Released G.O. #85	P113,P122,CSR
Fullmore, J.R.	Pvt	I 22nd SCVI	Bermuda Hundred, VA	06/02/64	Pt. Lookout, MD	03/04/65	Aikens Ldg., VA Xc	P116,P123,P124,CSR
Fullwood, William	Pvt	E 26th SCVI	Five Forks, VA	04/02/65	City Pt., VA	04/07/65	Pt. Lookout, MD	CSR,CEN
					Pt. Lookout, MD	06/06/65	Released	P118,P121,CSR
Fulmer, G.C. Noah	Cpl	I 15th SCVI	Cedar Creek, VA	10/19/64	W. Bldg. Balt, MD	10/27/64	Pt. Lookout, MD	P1,KEB,H15,CSR
					Pt. Lookout, MD	10/29/64	Aikens Ldg., VA Xc	P114,P117,P123,H15
Fulmer, J.R.	Pvt	I 22nd SCVI	Bermuda Hundred, VA	06/02/64	Bermuda Hundred, VA	06/03/64	Fts. Monroe, VA	CSR
					Fts. Monroe, VA	06/04/64	Pt. Lookout, MD	CSR
Fulmer, John A.	Pvt	C 6th SCResB	Chesterfield, SC	02/28/65	New Berne, NC		Pt. Lookout, MD	CSR
					Pt. Lookout, MD	04/05/65	Died, Cong. fever	P6,P117,FPH
					Pt. Lookout, MD	04/05/65	Died, Lung Infl.	P12,FPH,CSR
Fulmer, Oliver P.	1Sg	H 3rd SCVI	Orangeburg, SC	02/13/65	New Berne, NC USGH	04/27/65	Returned to duty	H3,CSR
Fulmer, W.W.	Pvt	I 22nd SCVI	Five Forks, VA	04/01/65	City Pt., VA	04/05/65	Pt. Lookout, MD	CSR
					Pt. Lookout, MD	06/27/65	Rlsd. G.O. #109	P114,P118,P121
Fulmer, William E.C.	Pvt	F 3rd SCVIBn	Gettysburg, PA	07/04/63	Letterman G.H. Gbg	08/14/63	Died, GSW lung	P1,P5,P10,KEB,CSR
Fulton, J.C.	Pvt	G 14th SCVI	Appomattox R., VA	04/03/65	City Pt., VA	04/10/65	Hart's Island, NY	CSR
					Hart's Island, NY	06/16/65	Rlsd. G.O. #109	P79,CSR
Fulton, R.J.	Pvt	E 4th SCVC	Louisa C.H., VA	06/11/64	Fts. Monroe, VA	06/20/64	Pt. Lookout, MD	CSR
					Pt. Lookout, MD	07/25/64	Elmira, NY	P113,P116,P120,CSR
					Elmira, NY	06/19/65	Rlsd. G.O. #109	P65,CSR
Funderburg, J.N.	Pvt	I 22nd SCVI	Deep Bottom, VA	08/16/64	Pt. Lookout, MD	02/10/65	Exchanged	P113,P123
Funderburk, G.W.	3Lt	E 22nd SCVI	Kinston, NC	12/15/62	Kinston, NC	12/15/62	Paroled POW	CSR
Funderburk, G.W.	1Lt	E 22nd SCVI	US 24th AC Fld. H.	04/11/65	US 24th AC Fld. H.	04/14/65	US Gen. Hos.	CSR
Funderburk, G.W.	1Lt	E 22nd SCVI	Virginia	04/11/65	US Gen. Hos.	05/13/65	Prld. & released	CSR
Funderburk, H.W.	Pvt	B 8th SCVI	Charlotte, NC	05/16/65	Charlotte, NC	05/16/65	Paroled	KEB,CSR
Funderburk, J.M.	Pvt	E 22nd SCVI	Crater, Pbg., VA	07/30/64	US 9th AC Hos.	08/02/64	City Pt., VA P.M.	CSR
					City Pt., VA	08/05/65	Washington, DC	CSR,LAN
Funderburk, Jeremiah	Pvt	C 1st SCVA	Fayetteville, NC	03/10/65	New Berne, NC	03/30/65	Pt. Lookout, MD	CSR,LAN
					Pt. Lookout, MD	06/26/65	Rlsd. G.O. #109	P114,P117,P122,CSR
Funderburk, John	Pvt	C 5th SCResB	Chesterfield, SC	02/28/65	New Berne, NC	03/26/65	Pt. Lookout, MD	CSR
					Pt. Lookout, MD	06/26/65	Rlsd. G.O. #109	P114,P117,P122,CSR
Funderburk, Joshua C.	Pvt	A 1st SCVIR	Morris Island, SC	09/07/63	Hilton Head, SC	09/19/63	Ft. Columbus, NY	CSR,LAN
					Ft. Columbus, NY	10/06/63	Pt. Lookout, MD	CSR
					Pt. Lookout, MD	12/25/63	Exchanged	P113,P123,SA1,CSR
Funderburk, Laney N.	Pvt	E 22nd SCVI	Kinston, NC	12/15/62	Kinston, NC	12/15/62	Paroled POW	CSR
Funderburk, Laney N.	Pvt	E 22nd SCVI	Crater, Pbg., VA	07/30/64	City Pt., VA	08/05/64	Pt. Lookout, MD	CSR,LAN
					Pt. Lookout, MD	08/08/64	Elmira, NY	P113,P117,P120
					Elmira, NY	05/26/65	Died, Diarrhea	P65,LAN
Funderburk, William L.	Pvt	A 1st SCVIR	Morris Island, SC	09/01/63	Ft. Columbus, NY	10/09/63	Johnson's Isl., OH	P1
					Pt. Lookout, MD	12/25/34	City Pt., VA Xc	P113,P116,P123
Funderburk, William T.	Pvt	E 22nd SCVI	Petersburg, VA	04/02/65	City Pt., VA	04/04/65	Pt. Lookout, MD	CSR
					Pt. Lookout, MD	06/26/65	Rlsd. G.O. #109	P114,P118,P122

SOUTH CAROLINA SOLDIERS, SAILORS AND  CITIZENS HELD IN U.S. PRISONS 1861-1865

NAME	RANK	REGIMENT	CAPTURED AT	WHEN	PRISON	MOVED	DISPOSITION	SOURCES
Furman, S.	Pvt	A 3rd SCVABn	High Pt., NC	05/02/65	High Pt., NC	05/02/65	Paroled on oath	CSR
Furtick, E.	Pvt	D 20th SCVI	Cedar Creek, VA	10/19/64	Harpers Ferry, VA	10/24/64	Pt. Lookout, MD	CSR
					Pt. Lookout, MD	03/28/65	Aikens Ldg., VA Xc	P117,P121,P124,CSR
Futrill, John R.	Pvt	F 1st SCVIG	Petersburg, VA	04/02/65	City Pt., VA	04/07/65	Hart's Island, NY	CSR
					Hart's Island, NY	06/16/65	Rlsd. G.O. #109	P79,SA1,CSR

SOUTH CAROLINA SOLDIERS, SAILORS AND  CITIZENS HELD IN U.S. PRISONS 1861-1865

NAME	RANK	REGIMENT	CAPTURED AT	WHEN	PRISON	MOVED	DISPOSITION	SOURCES
Gable, Edwin E.	Pvt	H 20th SCVI	Salkahatchie, SC	02/10/65	Hilton Head, SC	03/12/65	Ft. Delaware, DE	CSR
					Ft. Delaware, DE	06/10/65	Released	P42,KEB,CSR
Gable, Godfrey E.	Cpl	H 20th SCVI	Savannah, GA	12/21/64	Ft. Delaware, DE			P45,KEB
Gable, Michael	Pvt	14th SCMil	Fayetteville, NC	02/24/65	Hart's Island, NY	06/16/65	Rlsd. G.O. #109	P79
Gaddy, John W.	Pvt	B 24th SCVI	Nashville, TN	12/16/64	Nashville, TN	12/18/64	Louisville, KY	CSR
					Louisville, KY	12/21/64	Camp Douglas, IL	P90,P91,P94
					Camp Douglas, IL	06/19/65	Rlsd. G.O. #109	P55
Gaddy, Tritcan C.	Pvt	H 23rd SCVI	Richmond, VA	04/03/65	Newport News, VA		Released	P107,HMC,CSR
Gadsden, Thomas	Sgt	A 27th SCVI	Petersburg, VA	06/24/64	Bermuda Hundred, VA	06/25/64	Fts. Monroe, VA	CSR,HAG
					Fts. Monroe, VA	06/26/64	Pt. Lookout, MD	CSR
					Pt. Lookout, MD	09/18/64	Aikens Ldg., VA Xc	P113,P117,P123
Gadsden, Thomas	Sgt	A 27th SCVI	Town Creek, NC	02/20/65	Pt. Lookout, MD	06/05/65	Rlsd. Instr. 5/30/65	P114,P122,CSR
Gaffney, Winfield S.	Pvt	F 15th SCMil	Darlington, SC	02/28/65	Pt. Lookout, MD	06/27/65	Rlsd. G.O. #109	P117,P121,P123,CSR
Gaillard, Hartwell S.	Pvt	G 20th SCVI	Cedar Creek, VA	10/19/64	Harpers Ferry, WV	10/24/64	Pt. Lookout, MD	CSR,KEB
					Pt. Lookout, MD	03/28/65	Aikens Ldg., VA Xc	P114,P121,P124,CSR
Gaillard, J.H.	QSg	H Ham.Leg.MI	Hartwell, GA	05/18/65	Hartwell, GA	05/18/65	Paroled	CSR
Gaillard, T. Edmund	Cpl	I 2nd SCVI	Gettysburg, PA	07/04/63	Letterman G.H. Gbg	10/11/63	Died of wounds	P1,P6,KEB,H2,CSR
Gaillard, Willis F.	Pvt	G 20th SCVI	Cedar Creek, VA	10/19/64	Pt. Lookout, MD			P117,KEB
Gaines, J.A.	Pvt	B 2nd SCVC	Fartwell, GA	05/19/65	Hartwell, GA	05/19/65	Released on parole	CSR
Gaines, J.P.	Pvt	A 22nd SCVI	Bermuda Hundred, VA	06/02/65	Bermuda Hundred, VA	06/03/64	Fts. Monroe, VA	CSR
					Fts. Monroe, VA	06/04/64	Pt. Lookout, MD	CSR
					Pt. Lookout, MD	02/12/65	Died, Ch. Diarrhea	P6,P113,P116,P119
Gaines, John F.	Pvt	F Hol.Leg.	Kinston, NC	12/15/62	Kinston, NC	12/15/62	Paroled POW	CSR
Gaines, John F.	Pvt	F Hol.Leg.	Petersburg, VA	11/06/64	City Pt., VA	11/11/64	Washington, DC	CSR
				11/06/64	Pt. Lookout, MD	06/27/65	Rlsd. G.O. #109	P114,P117,P121,CSR
Gaines, John H.	Pvt	K Orr's Ri.	Gaines' Mill, VA	06/29/62	Harisson's Ldg., VA		Ft. Columbus, NY	CSR
					Ft. Columbus, NY	07/09/62	Ft. Delaware, DE	CDC,CSR
Gaines, Perry G.	Sgt	K Orr's Ri.	Southside, RR	04/02/65	City Pt., VA	04/07/65	Hart's Island, NY	CSR
					Hart's Island, NY	06/25/65	Rlsd. G.O.#109	CDC,P79,CSR
Gaines, William H.	Pvt	I Hol.Leg.	Petersburg, VA	11/05/64	City Pt., VA	11/11/64	Washington, DC	CSR
					Pt. Lookout, MD	02/10/65	Aikens Ldg., VA Xc	P114,P117,CSR
					Richmd. Hospitals	02/21/65	Furloughed 60 days	CSR
Gainey, Charles J.	Pvt	Ch'fld LA	Deserted/enemy	03/15/65	Kinston, NC P.M.			CSR
Gainey, George W.	Pvt	E 21st SCVI	Petersburg, VA	06/18/64	Pt. Lookout, MD	07/25/64	Elmira, NY	P113,P117,P120,HAG
					Elmira, NY	09/04/64	Died, Ch. Diarrhea	P5,P12,P65,P66,FPH
Gainey, John A.	Pvt	E 6th SCVI	Burkeville, VA	04/21/65	Burkeville, VA	04/21/65	Paroled	CSR
Gainey, Lewis J.	Pvt	C 5th SCResB	Cheraw, SC	03/03/65	Pt. Lookout, MD	06/27/65	Rlsd. G.O. #109	P114,P117,P121,CSR
Gainey, Michael	Pvt	C 1st SCVA	Calhoun, GA	05/16/64	Louisville, KY	05/25/64	Rock Island, IL	P93
					Rock Island, IL	06/19/64	Joined US Navy	P131
Gainey, Thomas N.	Pvt	C 23rd SCVI	Five Forks, VA	04/01/65	City Pt., VA	04/04/65	Pt. Lookout, MD	CSR
					Pt. Lookout, MD	06/27/65	Rlsd. G.O. #109	P118,P121,P123,CSR
Gainey, Thomas W.	Pvt	G 21st SCVI	Ft. Fisher, NC	01/15/65	Elmira, NY	07/11/65	Rlsd. G.O. #109	P65,P66,HAG
Gaither, J.W.	Pvt	A 15th SCVI	Halltown, VA	08/26/64	Harpers Ferry, WV	09/02/64	Camp Chase, OH	P23,H3,CSR,KEB
					Camp Chase, OH	03/26/65	Pt. Lookout, MD Xc	P23,P26,P114,P117
Gallivan, Morris	Pvt	E 1st SCVIR	Deserted/enemy	02/22/65	Charleston, SC		Released on oath	SA1,CSR
Gallman, Henry G.	Pvt	C 3rd SCVI	Sharpsburg, MD	09/17/62	Died of wounds	09/17/62	Lavinia Groves Frm	P12,H3
Gallman, J.H.	Pvt	F 22nd SCVI	Burkeville, VA	04/14/65	Prov. Mar. US 9th AC	04/17/65	Prld. & released	CSR

SOUTH CAROLINA SOLDIERS, SAILORS AND  CITIZENS HELD IN U.S. PRISONS 1861-1865

NAME	RANK	REGIMENT	CAPTURED AT	WHEN	PRISON	MOVED	DISPOSITION	SOURCES
Gallman, Jehu J.	2Lt	H 5th SCVI	Spotsylvania, VA	05/10/64	Ft. Delaware, DE	08/20/64	Hilton Head, SC	P42,CSR,ISH
					Hilton Head, SC	10/16/64	Ft. Pulaski, GA	CSR
					Ft. Pulaski, GA	12/26/64	Hilton Head, SC	CSR
					Hilton Head, SC	03/12/65	Ft. Delaware, DE	CSR
					Ft. Delaware, DE	06/12/65	Rlsd. G.O. #109	P43,P44,P45,CSR
Gallman, John H.	2Lt	H 5th SCVI	Loudon, TN	11/14/63	Knoxville, TN	12/15/63	Louisville, KY	P84,CSR
					Louisville, KY	01/15/64	Camp Chase, OH	P88,P93,CSR
					Camp Chase, OH	03/25/64	Ft. Delaware, DE	P22,P26,CSR
					Ft. Delaware, DE	06/12/65	Released on oath	P42,P44,SA3,CSR
Galloway, Abram M.	Pvt	H 21st SCVI	Ft. Fisher, NC	01/15/65	Elmira, NY	07/13/65	Elmira, NY USGH	P65,HAG,CSR
					Elmira, NY	08/07/65	Rlsd. G.O. #109	P66,CSR
Galloway, James G.	Pvt	G 23rd SCVI	Petersburg, VA	04/02/65	Camp Hamilton, VA		Fts. Monroe, VA Hos.	CSR
					Fts. Monroe, VA		Newport News, VA	CSR
					Newport News, VA	06/26/65	Rlsd. G.O. #109	P107,CSR
Galloway, James M.	Pvt	A 12th SCVI	Gettysburg, PA	07/05/63	Ft. McHenry, MD	07/06/63	Ft. Delaware, DE	CSR,YEB
					Ft. Delaware, DE	08/10/63	Chester, PA G.H.	P40,P42,P44,CSR
					Chester, PA G.H.	10/03/63	Pt. Lookout, MD GH	P1,CSR
					Pt. Lookout, MD	03/17/64	City Pt., VA Xc	P116
					Pt. Lookout, MD	03/17/64	Exchanged	P121,P123,P124,CSR
Galloway, John	Pvt	B 3rd SCVI	Sharpsburg, MD	10/01/62	Ft. McHenry, MD	10/13/62	Fts. Monroe, VA Xc	P96,SA2,H3,CSR
Galloway, John	Pvt	I 1st SCVC	Deserted/enemy	03/06/65	Charleston, SC	03/06/65	Released on oath	CSR
Galloway, John C.	Pvt	G 23rd SCVI	Five Forks, VA	04/02/65	Pt. Lookout, MD	06/27/65	Rlsd. G.O. #109	P118,P121,HOM,CSR
Galloway, John H.	Pvt	C 10th SCVI	Ship's Gap, GA	05/08/64	Louisville, KY	05/21/64	Camp Morton, IN	P88,P93
Galloway, L.C.	Pvt	H 21st SCVI	Ft. Fisher, NC	01/15/65	Elmira, NY	04/25/65	Died, Ch. Diarrhea	P5,P65,P66,FPH,HAG
Galloway, Martin H.	Pvt	H 1st SCVIR	Fayetteville, NC	03/22/65	New Berne, NC	04/10/65	Hart's Island, NY	CSR
					Hart's Island, NY	06/19/65	Rlsd. G.O. #109	SA1,P79,CSR
Galloway, Moses P.	2Lt	G 23rd SCVI	Petersburg, VA	06/17/64	City Pt., VA	06/25/64	Ft. Delaware, DE	CSR
					Ft. Delaware, DE	08/20/64	Hilton Head, SC	P42,CSR
					Ft. Pulaski, GA			P4,ISH,CSR
					Ft. Delaware, DE	04/16/65	Discharged Hos.	P47
					Ft. Delaware, DE	06/16/65	Rlsd. G.O. #109	P43,P44,CSR
Galloway, Pipkin	Pvt	H 21st SCVI	Ft. Fisher, NC	01/15/65	Elmira, NY	03/07/65	Died, Hos. Gangrene	P5,P12,P65,P66,FPH,HAG
Galloway, Simon P.	Pvt	F 27th SCVI	Town Creek, NC	02/20/65	Ft. Anderson, NC	02/28/65	Pt. Lookout, MD	CSR,HAG
					Pt. Lookout, MD	06/27/65	Rlsd. G.O. #109	P117,P121,P123,CSR
Galloway, William A.	Pvt	G 23rd SCVI	Five Forks, VA	04/02/65	City Pt., VA	04/05/65	Pt. Lookout, MD	CSR,HOM
					Pt. Lookout, MD	06/27/65	Rlsd. G.O. #109	P114,P118,P121,CSR
Galloway, William M.	Pvt	H 14th SCVI	Augusta, GA	05/20/65	Augusta, GA	05/20/65	Paroled	CSR
Galloway, William T.	Pvt	F 27th SCVI	Town Creek, NC	02/20/65	Ft. Anderson, NC	02/28/65	Pt. Lookout, MD	CSR,HAG
					Pt. Lookout, MD	06/27/65	Rlsd. G.O. #109	P114,P117,P121,P123
Galman, J.A.	Pvt	F Hol.Leg.	Five Forks, VA	04/01/65	Pt. Lookout, MD	06/28/65	Rlsd. G.O. #109	P114
Galvin, Martin		P. Savannah	Off Charleston	06/03/61	Tombs Prison, NY	02/15/62	Ft. Lafayette, NY	OR,TCP
					Ft. Lafayette, NY	06/06/62	City Pt., VA Xc	OR,TCP
Gamble, George	Pvt	E 3rd SCMil	Lynch's Creek, SC	02/25/65	Hart's Island, NY	06/17/65	Rlsd. G.O. #109	P79
Gamble, J.F.	Pvt	H 26th SCVI	Crater, Pbg., VA	07/30/64	City Pt., VA	08/05/64	Pt. Lookout, MD	CSR
					Pt. Lookout, MD	08/08/64	Elmira, NY	P117,P120,P125,CSR
					Elmira, NY	03/12/65	Tfd. for exchange	P65,CSR
Gamble, J.M.	Pvt	C 25th SCVI	Ft. Fisher, NC	01/15/65	New York, NY	01/30/65	Elmira, NY	CSR
					Elmira, NY	07/03/65	Rlsd. G.O. #109	P65,P66
Gamble, James W.	Pvt	K 1st SCVIH	Richmond, VA Hos.	04/03/65	US Str. Mary Powel	05/12/65	Pt. Lookout, MD	CSR
					Pt. Lookout, MD	06/26/65	Rlsd. G.O. #109	CSR
Gamble, R.R.	Pvt	I 4th SCVC	Stony Creek, VA	12/01/65	City Pt., VA	12/05/64	Pt. Lookout, MD	CSR
					Pt. Lookout, MD	06/27/65	Rlsd. G.O. #109	P114,P123,CSR

SOUTH CAROLINA SOLDIERS, SAILORS AND  CITIZENS HELD IN U.S. PRISONS 1861-1865

NAME	RANK	REGIMENT	CAPTURED AT	WHEN	PRISON	MOVED	DISPOSITION	SOURCES
Gamble, Thomas E.	Pvt	I 25th SCVI	Ft. Fisher, NC	01/15/65	New York, NY	01/30/65	Elmira, NY	CSR,HAG
					Elmira, NY	04/07/65	Died, Ch. Diarrhea	P5,P12,P65,P66,FPH
Gambrell, H.J.	Pvt	L Orr's Ri.	Falling Waters, MD	07/14/63	Baltimore, MD	08/20/63	Pt. Lookout, MD	CSR
					Pt. Lookout, MD	03/17/64	City Pt., VA Xc	P113,P116,P123,CSR
Gambrell, J.M.	Pvt	D 18th SCVI	Farmville, VA	04/06/65	City Pt., VA	04/14/65	Newport News, VA	CSR
					Newport News, VA	06/13/65	Rlsd. G.O.#109	P107,UD2,CSR
Gambrell, John F.	Pvt	K Orr's Ri.	Petersburg, VA	04/03/65	City Pt., VA	04/11/65	Hart's Island, NY	CSR
					Hart's Island, NY	06/16/65	Rlsd G.O.#109	P79,CSR
Gammon, M.J.	Pvt	A 1st SCVC	Deserted/enemy	03/13/65	Charleston, SC	03/13/65	Released on oath	CSR
Gandor, A.R.	Pvt	B 6th SCVC	Bennett's Pt., SC	06/30/63	Pt. Lookout, MD	09/18/64	Exchanged	P123
Gandy, Elias	Pvt	D 8th SCVI	Winchester, VA	09/13/64	Harpers Ferry, WV	09/19/64	Camp Chase, OH	CSR
					Camp Chase, OH	04/22/65	Joined U.S. Army	P23,P26,KEB,CSR
Gandy, Ephraim	Pvt	B 21st SCVI	Petersburg, VA	06/18/64	City Pt., VA	06/24/64	Pt. Lookout, MD	CSR,HAG
					Pt. Lookout, MD	07/27/64	Elmira, NY	P113,P117,P120
					Elmira, NY	02/13/65	Tfd. for exchange	P65,CSR
					Boulwares Wharf, VA	02/22/65	Jackson Hos. Rchmd.	CSR
					Jackson Hos. Rchmd.	03/02/65	Camp Lee, VA	CSR
Gandy, Jackson	Pvt	F 26th SCVI	Petersburg, VA	04/02/65	City Pt., VA	04/07/65	Pt. Lookout, MD	CSR
					Pt. Lookout, MD	06/17/65	Rlsd. G.O. #109	P114,P118,P122,CSR
Gandy, John	Pvt	E 6th SCVI	Fair Oaks, VA	05/31/62	Fts. Monroe, VA	06/21/62	Ft. Delaware, DE	CSR
					Ft. Delaware, DE	08/05/62	Aikens Ldg., VA Xc	CSR
					Richmond, VA Hos.	09/12/62	Returned to duty	CSR
Gandy, John H.	Pvt	A 15th SCVI	Halltown, VA	08/26/64	Harpers Ferry, WV	09/02/64	Camp Chase, OH	CSR,KEB
					Camp Chase, OH	05/20/65	Pt. Lookout, MD	CSR
					Pt. Lookout, MD	06/27/65	Rlsd. G.O. #109	P114,P121,P123,CSR
Ganey, Barney	Pvt	C 1st SCVIR	Averysboro, NC	03/16/65	New Berne, NC	03/30/65	Pt. Lookout, MD	CSR,SA1
					Pt. Lookout, MD	06/27/65	Rlsd. G.O. #109	P117,P121,P123,CSR
Ganley, Michael	Pvt	H 1st SCVIR	Fayetteville, NC	03/22/65	New Berne, NC	04/10/65	Hart's Island, NY	CSR
					Hart's Island, NY	06/21/65	Rlsd. G.O. #109	P79,SA1,CSR
Gant, R.R.	Pvt	I 22nd SCVI	Deserted/enemy	02/27/65	City Pt., VA	03/01/65	Washington, DC	CSR
					Washington, DC	03/02/65	Charleston, SC	CSR
Gantt, Alfred	Pvt	I 20th SCVI	Cedar Creek, VA	10/19/64	Harpers Ferry, VA	10/24/64	Pt. Lookout, MD	CSR,KEB
					Pt. Lookout, MD	06/05/65	Released	P114,P117,P122,CSR
Gantt, C.	Pvt	D 20th SCVI	Cedar Creek, VA	10/19/64	Harpers Ferry, WV	10/24/64	Pt. Lookout, MD	CSR
					Pt. Lookout, MD	03/28/65	Aikens Ldg., VA Xc	P124,KEB,CSR
Gantt, Elias S.	Pvt	E 20th SCVI	Cedar Creek, VA	10/19/64	Harpers Ferry, WV	10/24/64	Pt. Lookout, MD	CSR
					Pt. Lookout, MD	03/28/65	Aikens Ldg., VA Xc	P117,P124,KEB,CSR
Gantt, Ulysses S.	Pvt	K 19th SCVI	Atlanta, GA	07/22/64	Nashville, TN		Louisville, KY	CSR,HOE
					Louisville, KY	07/30/64	Camp Chase, OH	P90,P91,CSR
					Camp Chase, OH	03/02/65	City Pt., VA Xc	CSR
					City Pt., VA	03/10/65	Boulwares Wh. Xc	CSR
					Camp Chase, OH	06/11/65	Released	P22,CSR
Gantt, Welmouth	Pvt	G 12th SCVI	Petersburg, VA	04/03/65	City Pt., VA	04/06/65	Pt. Lookout, MD	CSR
					Pt. Lookout, MD	06/27/65	Rlsd. G.O. #109	P118,P121,P123,CSR
Gantt, Zimri	Pvt	G 27th SCVI	Petersburg, VA	06/24/64	Camp Hamilton, VA	01/13/65	Fts. Monroe, VA	CSR,HAG
					Fts. Monroe, VA	01/14/65	Pt. Lookout, MD	CSR
					Pt. Lookout, MD	01/17/65	Exchanged	P114,P123,P124,CSR
Garden, J.W.	Pvt	I 6th SCVC	Petersburg, VA	07/30/64	City Pt., VA	08/04/64	Pt. Lookout, MD	CSR
					Pt. Lookout, MD	08/08/64	Elmira, NY	P113,CSR
					Elmira, NY	06/19/65	Rlsd. G.O. #109	P65,CSR
Gardner, C.D.	Cpl	A 8th SCVI	Winchester, VA	09/13/64	Harpers Ferry, WV	09/19/64	Camp Chase, OH	CSR
					Camp Chase, OH	06/11/65	Rlsd. G.O. #109	P23,KEB,CSR

SOUTH CAROLINA SOLDIERS, SAILORS AND  CITIZENS HELD IN U.S. PRISONS 1861-1865

NAME	RANK	REGIMENT	CAPTURED AT	WHEN	PRISON	MOVED	DISPOSITION	SOURCES
Gardner, Churchwell W.	1Sg	E 12th SCVI	Sutherland Stn., VA	04/03/65	City Pt., VA	04/07/65	Hart's Island, NY	CSR
					Hart's Island, NY	06/16/65	Rlsd. G.O. #109	P79,LAN
Gardner, D.F.	Pvt	E 12th SCVI	Spotsylvania, VA	05/12/64	Belle Plain, VA	05/21/64	Ft. Delaware, DE	CSR,LAN
					Ft. Delaware, DE	01/06/65	Hos. 1/6-1/12/65	P47
					Ft. Delaware, DE	06/25/64	Hos. 6/25-7/1/64	P47
					Ft. Delaware, DE	06/10/65	Released	P41,P42,P45,CSR
Gardner, Elijah T.	Pvt	E 2nd SCVI	Sharpsburg, MD	09/28/62	Ft. McHenry, MD	12/04/62	City Pt., VA Xc	SA2,H2,CSR
Gardner, Francis M.	Pvt	E 12th SCVI	Gettysburg, PA	07/05/63	David's Island, NY	07/23/63	Died of wounds	P6,P12,FPH,LAN,CSR
Gardner, George W.	1Sg	E 12th SCVI	Falling Waters, MD	07/14/63	Hagerstown, MD G.H	07/23/63	Baltimore, MD	CSR
					Frederick, MD USGH	08/07/63	Baltimore, MD USGH	CSR
					W. Bldg. Balt, MD	08/22/63	City Pt., VA Xc	P1,LAN,CSR
Gardner, Harville	Pvt	G 7th SCVIBn	Drury's Bluff, VA	05/16/64	Bermuda Hundred, VA	05/18/64	Fts. Monroe, VA	CSR,HAG
					Fts. Monroe, VA	05/19/64	Pt. Lookout, MD	CSR
					Pt. Lookout, MD	08/15/64	Elmira, NY	P113,P116,P120,CSR
					Elmira, NY	03/14/65	Pt. Lookout, MD Xc	P65,P66,CSR
Gardner, Ira	Pvt	B 6th SCResB	Augusta, GA	05/18/65	Augusta, GA	05/18/65	Paroled	CSR
Gardner, J.E.	Pvt	I 19th SCVCB	Augusta, GA	05/19/65	Augusta, GA	05/19/65	Paroled on oath	CSR
Gardner, James H.	Cpl	E 12th SCVI	Warrenton, VA	09/29/62	Warrenton, VA	09/29/62	Paroled	CSR
Gardner, James L.	Sgt	D 15th SCVI	Deep Bottom, VA	07/28/64	City Pt., VA USFH	07/31/64	Died of wounds	P12,HIC,KEB,CSR
Gardner, James W.	Pvt	E 12th SCVI	Gettysburg, PA	07/05/63	David's Island, NY	08/24/63	City Pt., VA Xc	P1,LAN
					Williamsburg, VA Hos.	09/09/63	Wdd. Furlough	CSR
Gardner, James W.	Cpl	E 12th SCVI	N. Anna River, VA	05/22/64	Pt. Lookout, MD	03/14/65	Aikens Ldg., VA Xc	P113,P116,P124,LAN
Gardner, James W.	2Lt	A 7th SCVIBn	Weldon RR, VA	08/21/64	City Pt., VA P.M.	08/23/64	Washington, DC	CSR,HAG
					Old Capitol, DC	08/27/64	Ft. Delaware, DE	CSR
					Ft. McHenry, MD	08/27/64	Ft. Delaware, DE	P110
					Ft. Delaware, DE	10/06/64	Pt. Lookout, MD Xc	P43,CSR
					Pt. Lookout, MD	10/11/64	Exchanged	P114,P123,CSR
Gardner, John B.	Pvt	H 21st SCVI	Petersburg, VA	06/18/64	Pt. Lookout, MD	07/09/64	Elmira, NY	P113,P117,P120,HAG
					Elmira, NY	10/11/64	Pt. Lookout, MD Xc	P65,HAG
					Pt. Lookout, MD	10/29/64	Aikens Ldg., VA Xc	P114,P117,P123
Gardner, John J.	Cpl	F 5th SCVI	Wilderness, VA	05/06/64	Belle Plain, VA	05/21/64	Ft. Delaware, DE	CSR
					Ft. Delaware, DE	11/07/64	Hos. 11/15-11/27/64	P47,SA3
					Ft. Delaware, DE		no release record	P41,P42,CSR
Gardner, Lewis	Pvt	D 15th SCVI	Cedar Creek, VA	10/19/64	Harpers Ferry, WV	10/23/64	Pt. Lookout, MD	CSR,KEB
					Pt. Lookout, MD	02/10/65	Aikens Ldg., VA Xc	P114,P121,P124,CSR
Gardner, M.G.	Pvt	E 6th SCResB	Raleigh, NC Hos.	04/13/65	Raleigh, NC Hos.	04/13/65	Paroled	CSR
Gardner, M.R.	Pvt	E 12th SCVI	Maryland		A. of the Potomac	09/27/62	Paroled	CSR
Gardner, Seab Caswell	Pvt	H 2nd SCVI	Sharpsburg, MD	09/17/62	A of P. Prov. Mar.	09/27/62	Ft. McHenry, MD	CSR
					Ft. McHenry, MD	10/18/62	Fts. Monroe, VA	CSR
					Fts. Monroe, VA	10/25/62	Aikens Ldg.,VA Xc	SA2,H2,CSR
Gardner, Thomas	Pvt	H Ham.Leg.MI	Farmville, VA	04/11/65	Farmville, VA	04/11/65	Paroled	CSR
Gardner, Thomas L.	Pvt	E 12th SCVI	Gettysburg, PA	07/05/63	David's Island, NY	09/12/63	City Pt., VA Xc	P1,CSR
					Williamsburg, VA Hos.	09/21/63	Wdd. Furlough	CSR
Gardner, William	Pvt	C 1st SCVA	Bentonville, NC	03/22/65	New Berne, NC	04/10/65	Hart's Island, NY	CSR
					Hart's Island, NY	06/17/65	Rlsd. G.O. #109	P79,CSR
Garey, Michael	Pvt	Ferguson's LA	Calhoun, GA	05/16/64	Nashville, TN	05/24/64	Louisville, KY	P2,CSR
					Louisville, KY	05/25/64	Rock Island, IL	CSR
					Rock Island, IL	06/10/64	Jd. U.S. Navy	CSR
Garland, Edward	Pvt	F 7th SCVC	Burkesville, VA	04/06/65	City Pt., VA	06/08/65	Pt. Lookout, MD	CSR
					Pt. Lookout, MD	05/21/65	Hammond G.H., MD	CSR
					Pt. Lookout, MD	05/31/65	Died, Diarrhea	P6,P118,P119,FPH
Garland, Leonidas H.	Pvt	I 1st SCVA	Morris Island, SC	07/13/63	Hilton Head, SC Hos.	07/23/63	Exchanged	P2,CSR

SOUTH CAROLINA SOLDIERS, SAILORS AND  CITIZENS HELD IN U.S. PRISONS 1861-1865

NAME	RANK	REGIMENT	CAPTURED AT	WHEN	PRISON	MOVED	DISPOSITION	SOURCES
Garner, Alexander	Pvt	B 21st SCVI	Morris Island, SC	07/10/63	Pt. Lookout, MD			P114,HAG
Garner, Columbus	Pvt	H 15th SCVI	Sharpsburg, MD	10/03/62	Ft. McHenry, MD	10/17/62	Fts. Monroe, VA Xc	CSR
Garner, Henry S.	Pvt	C 25th SCVI	Ft. Darling, VA	05/14/65	Bermuda Hundred, VA	05/16/64	Fts. Monroe, VA	CSR,HAG,CTA
					Fts. Monroe, VA	05/17/64	Pt. Lookout, MD	CSR
					Pt. Lookout, MD	08/15/64	Elmira, NY	P113,P116,P120,CSR
					Elmira, NY	10/11/64	Tfd. for exchange	P65,P66
					Pt. Lookout, MD	10/29/64	Aikens Ldg., VA Xc	P114,P117,P123,CSR
					Pt. Lookout, MD	11/12/64	Venus Pt., GA Xc	CSR
Garner, J.A.	Pvt	K 7th SCVC	Greensboro, NC	05/01/65	Greensboro, NC	05/01/65	Paroled	CSR
Garner, J.P.	Pvt	L 1st SCVIG	Petersburg, VA	04/03/65	City Pt., VA	04/11/65	Hart's Island, NY	CSR
					Hart's Island, NY	06/16/65	Rlsd. G.O. #109	P79,CSR
Garner, J.W.W.	Pvt	C 25th SCVI	Ft. Fisher, NC	01/15/65	New York, NY	01/30/65	Elmira, NY	CSR
					Elmira, NY	02/20/65	James R., VA Xc	P65,P66,CSR
					Howard Grove H., VA	03/09/65	Died	CSR
Garner, Jerry	Pvt	G 24th SCVI	Fayetteville, NC	03/17/65	New Berne, NC	03/30/65	Pt. Lookout, MD	CSR
					Pt. Lookout, MD	06/27/65	Rlsd. G.O. #109	P117,P121,P123,CSR
Garner, William W.	Pvt	G 23rd SCVI	Farmville, VA	04/06/65	Newport News, VA	06/13/65	Released	P107,HOM,CSR
Garrett, E.B.	Pvt	D 27th SCVI	Weldon RR, VA	08/21/64	City Pt., VA	08/24/64	Pt. Lookout, MD	CSR,HAG
					Pt. Lookout, MD	02/12/65	Died, Rheumatism	P12,P113,P119,FPH
Garrett, John W.	Sgt	C Hol.Leg.	Williamsport, MD	09/15/62	Ft. Delaware, DE	10/02/62	Aikens Ldg., VA Xc	CSR,HOS
Garrett, S.	Pvt	F 1st SCVIH	Loudon, TN		Pt. Lookout, MD	11/13/63	Died, Ch. Diarrhea	P12,SA1,JRH
Garrett, William	Pvt	H 1st SCVA	Deserted/enemy	05/11/63	Chattanooga, TN	02/14/64	Took oath	CSR
Garrett, William B.	Pvt	D 18th SCVI	Crater, Pbg., VA	07/30/64	City Pt., VA	08/05/64	Pt. Lookout MD	CSR,UD2
					Pt. Lookout, MD	08/08/64	Elmira, NY	P113,P117,P120,CSR
					Elmira, NY	10/11/64	Pt. Lookout, MD Xc	P65,P66
					W. Bldg. Balt. MD	10/13/64	Died, Ch. Diarrhea	P1,P5,P12,FPH,CSR
Garrett, William C.	Pvt	D 18th SCVI	Hatchers Run, VA	03/25/65	City Pt., VA	04/20/65	Pt. Lookout, MD	CSR,UD2
					Pt. Lookout, MD	06/27/65	Rlsd. G.O. #109	P117,P121,P123,CSR
Garrett, Zedok V.	Pvt	E 14th SCVI	Richmond, VA Hos.	04/03/65	Provost Marshal	05/02/65	Pt. Lookout, MD	CSR
					Pt. Lookout, MD	07/07/65	Rlsd. G.O. #109	P118,CSR
Garrick, J.A.	Pvt	H Ham.Leg.MI	Farmville, VA	04/11/65	Farmville, VA	04/11/65	Paroled	CSR
Garrick, J.P.	Pvt	F 2nd SCVA	James Island, SC	05/12/64	Port Royal Fy., SC	08/16/64	Exchanged	CSR
Garrick, John M.	Pvt	H Ham. Leg.	Ringgold, GA	11/27/63	Bridgeport, AL	12/11/63	Nashville, TN	P2,CSR
					Nashville, TN G.H.	03/23/64	Died	P2,P5,CSR
Garris, Elias	Pvt	McQueen LA	Petersburg, VA	04/02/65	City Pt., VA	04/04/65	Pt. Lookout, MD	CSR
					Pt. Lookout, MD	06/27/65	Rlsd. G.O. #109	CSR
Garris, F.M.	Pvt	D 1st SCVIH	Deserted/enemy	09/10/63	Chattanooga, TN	10/17/63	Louisville, KY	CSR
					Louisville, KY	10/20/63	North on oath	P88,SA1,CSR
Garrison, Elias B.	Pvt	H 18th SCVI	Petersburg, VA	03/25/65	City Pt., VA	03/28/65	Pt. Lookout, MD	CSR
					Pt. Lookout, MD	06/27/65	Rlsd. G.O. #109	P117,P121,YEB,CSR
Garrison, Isaac P.	Cpl	B 6th SCVI	Williamsburg, VA	05/05/62	Fts. Monroe, VA		Exchanged	CSR
Garrison, J. Thomas	Pvt	H 18th SCVI	Petersburg, VA	07/30/64	Pt. Lookout, MD	08/08/64	Elmira, NY	P113,P117,P120
					Elmira, NY	06/19/65	Rlsd. G.O. #109	P65,P66,YEB,UD5
Garrison, J.M.	Pvt	H 18th SCVI	Hatchers Run, VA	03/29/65	City Pt., VA	04/09/65	Hos. Steamer Maine	CSR
					Hos. Steamer Maine	04/10/65	Washington, DC Hos.	CSR
					Washington, DC Hos.	06/12/65	Rlsd. G.O. #109	P110,CSR
Garrison, J.T.	Pvt	H 18th SCVI	Petersburg, VA	07/30/64	City Pt., VA	08/05/64	Pt. Lookout, MD	CSR
					Pt. Lookout, MD	08/08/64	Elmira, NY	CSR
					Elmira, NY	06/19/65	Rlsd. G.O. #109	CSR
Garrison, John J.	Pvt	E 17th SCVI	Petersburg, VA	03/25/65	City Pt., VA	03/28/65	Pt. Lookout, MD	CSR,YEB
					Pt. Lookout, MD	06/22/65	Rlsd. G.O. #109	P117,P121,P122,CSR
Garrison, Levi N.	Pvt	D 2nd SCVIRi	Richmond, VA Hos.	04/03/65	Richmond, VA P.M.		Not given	CSR

SOUTH CAROLINA SOLDIERS, SAILORS AND  CITIZENS HELD IN U.S. PRISONS 1861-1865

NAME	RANK	REGIMENT	CAPTURED AT	WHEN	PRISON	MOVED	DISPOSITION	SOURCES
Garrison, Peter	Pvt	E 17th SCVI	Petersburg, VA	03/25/65	City Pt., VA	03/28/65	Pt. Lookout, MD	CSR,YEB
					Pt. Lookout, MD	06/22/65	Rlsd. G.O. #109	P114,P117,P121,CSR
Garrison, S.C.	Pvt	E 17th SCVI	Middleton, MD	09/21/62	Ft. McHenry, MD	10/02/62	Fts. Monroe, VA Xc	CSR
					Fts. Monroe, VA	10/03/62	Aikens Ldg., VA Xc	CSR
Garrison, W.F.	Pvt	E 17th SCVI	Stony Creek, VA	10/11/64	City Pt., VA	10/29/64	Pt. Lookout, MD	CSR,YEB
					Pt. Lookout, MD	01/17/65	Aikens Ldg., VA Xc	P117,P123,P124,CSR
Garrison, Zeneath A.W.	Cpl	E 17th SCVI	Five Forks, VA	04/02/65	City Pt., VA	04/06/65	Pt. Lookout, MD	CSR,YEB
					Pt. Lookout, MD	06/27/65	Rlsd. G.O. #109	P114,P118,P121,CSR
Garvin, C.H.	Pvt	C 1st SCVIH	Warrenton, VA	09/29/62	Warrenton, VA	09/29/62	Paroled	CSR
Garvin, Francis	Pvt	H 1st SCVIR	Charlotte, NC	05/04/65	Charlotte, NC	05/04/65	Paroled	CSR
Garvin, James E.	Pvt	I 20th SCVI	Orangeburg, SC	02/08/65	New Berne, NC	03/20/65	Pt. Lookout, MD	CSR,UD5
					Pt. Lookout, MD	06/27/65	Rlsd. G.O. #109	P114,P117,P121,CSR
Garvin, Thomas A.	Pvt	B 8th SCVI	Deserted/enemy	03/21/65	Charleston, SC	03/21/65	Released on oath	CSR
Garvin, W.T.	Pvt	I P.S.S.	Charlestowne, WV	10/16/62	Ft. McHenry, MD	10/25/62	Aikens Ldg., VA Xc	CSR,TSE
Garwood, Robert B.	Pvt	C 1st SCVIG	Tallahassee, FL	05/10/65	Tallahassee, FL	05/15/65	Paroled	SA1,CSR
Gary, James A.	Pvt	G Ham.Leg.MI	Richmond, VA Hos.	04/03/65	Richmond, VA Hos.	04/14/65	Provost Marshal	CSR
					Libby Prison, Rchmd.	04/23/65	Newport News, VA	CSR
					Newport News, VA	05/28/65	Died	P6,P107,PP
Gary, Jesse	Pvt	B 3rd SCVI	Sharpsburg, MD	09/17/62	Lavinia Groves Fm.	09/17/62	Died of wounds	P12,ROH,SA2,H3,CSR
Gasaway, Samuel	Pvt	D 22nd SCVI	Deserted/enemy	02/24/65	City Pt., VA	02/26/65	Washington, DC	CSR
					Washington, DC	02/27/65	Savannah, GA oath	CSR
Gaskin, John B.	Pvt	D 7th SCVIBn	Ft. Anderson, NC	02/19/65	Ft. Anderson, NC	02/28/65	Pt. Lookout, MD	CSR,HAG
					Pt. Lookout, MD	06/23/65	Rlsd. G.O. #109	P114,P117,HIC,CSR
Gaskins, M.	Pvt	Santee LA	Deserted/enemy	03/15/65	Charleston, SC	03/15/65	Released on oath	CSR
Gaskins, Robert E.	Pvt	I 26th SCVI	Five Forks, VA	04/01/65	City Pt., VA	04/05/65	Pt. Lookout, MD	CSR
					Pt. Lookout, MD	06/27/65	Rlsd. G.O. #109	P118,P121,P123,CSR
Gaskins, Sebastian	Pvt	G 1st SCVIR	Deserted/enemy	02/28/65	Ft. Monroe, VA	04/02/65	Washington, DC	CSR
					Washington, DC	04/05/65	Charleston SC oath	SA1,CSR
Gasque, Arna N.	1Sg	L 21st SCVI	Morris Island, SC	07/10/63	Morris Island, SC	07/13/63	Hilton Head, SC	CSR
					Hilton Head, SC	07/23/63	Morris Isl., SC Xc	P2,HAG,CSR
Gasque, C. Marion	Sgt	I 21st SCVI	Morris Island, SC	07/10/63	Morris Island, SC	07/13/63	Hilton Head, SC	CSR
					Hilton Head G.H.	07/23/63	Morris Isl., SC Xc	P2,HAG,CSR
Gasque, J. Martin	Cpl	L 21st SCVI	Ft. Fisher, NC	01/15/65	Elmira, NY	07/11/65	Rlsd. G.O. #109	P65,P66,HAG
Gasque, Samuel Oliver	Pvt	L 21st SCVI	Morris Island, SC	07/10/63	Elmira, NY		(Entry ruled out)	P65,HAG
					Ft. Columbus, NY	09/23/63	Took the oath	P1,HAG
					Pt. Lookout, MD	04/27/64	City Pt., VA Xc	P116,P123,P124,CSR
Gasque, Samuel Oliver	Pvt	L 21st SCVI	Ft. Fisher, NC	01/15/65	Elmira, NY	03/28/65	Died, Ch. Diarrhea	P5,P12,P65,P66,FPH
Gassaway, Thomas W.	Pvt	E 2nd SCVIRi	Chattanooga, TN	10/29/63	Nashville, TN	11/07/63	Louisville, KY	CSR
					Louisville, KY	11/09/63	Camp Morton, IN	P89,P93,CSR
					Camp Morton, IN	03/13/65	Pt. Lookout, MD Xc	CSR
Gaston, Albert	Pvt	C 1st SCVA	Wayne Co., NC	03/22/65	New Berne, NC	04/10/65	Hart's Island, NY	CSR
					Hart's Island, NY	06/19/65	Rlsd. G.O. #109	P79,CSR
Gaston, John T.	Pvt	K 2nd SCVC	Augusta, GA	05/18/65	Augusta, GA	05/18/65	Released on parole	CSR
Gaston, William C.	Pvt	D 17th SCVI	Petersburg, VA	03/25/65	City Pt., VA	03/28/65	Pt. Lookout, MD	CSR,HHC
					Pt. Lookout, MD	06/27/65	Rlsd. G.O. #109	P117,P121,P123
Gate, J.	Pvt	7th SCVC	Richmond, VA	04/21/65	Richmond, VA	04/21/65	Paroled	CSR
Gates, Thomas	Pvt	B 3rd SCVABn	Ft. Tyler, GA	04/16/65	1st Div. Cavalry C	04/23/65	Macon, GA prison	CSR
Gates, William B.	Cpl	E Hol.Leg.	Petersburg, VA	11/05/64	City Pt., VA	11/11/64	Washington, DC	CSR
					Pt. Lookout, MD	06/08/65	Rlsd. Instr. 5/30/65	P114,P117,P121,CSR
Gatley, John	Pvt	D 1st SCVA	Deserted/enemy	06/10/64	Morris Island, SC	09/01/64	Hilton Head, SC	CSR
Gaulden, J.D.	Pvt	H 18th SCVI	Farmville, VA	04/11/65	USF Hospital	04/13/65		CSR

SOUTH CAROLINA SOLDIERS, SAILORS AND  CITIZENS HELD IN U.S. PRISONS 1861-1865

NAME	RANK	REGIMENT	CAPTURED AT	WHEN	PRISON	MOVED	DISPOSITION	SOURCES
Gault, Henry C.	Pvt	H 15th SCVI	Gettysburg, PA	07/03/63	David's Island, NY	10/22/63	Fts. Monroe, VA	P1
					David's Island, NY	10/22/63	City Pt., VA Xc	P1,KEB,UD5,CSR
Gault, William H.	Pvt	H 5th SCVI	Richmond, VA Hos.	04/03/65	Not given		(Dtchd. to Hos.duty)	CSR
Gay, J.W.	Pvt	A 1st SCVIBn	James Island, SC	06/08/62	Ft. Columbus, NY	08/23/62	Ft. Delaware, DE	P37
Gay, L.B.	Pvt	G 3rd SCVABn	High Pt., NC	05/01/65	High Pt., NC	05/01/62	Paroled	CSR
Gay, Nathaniel	Sgt	E 12th SCVI	Sutherland Stn., VA	04/03/65	City Pt., VA	04/07/65	Hart's Island, NY	CSR
					Hart's Island, NY	06/16/65	Rlsd. G.O. #109	P79,LAN
Gay, P.W.	Pvt	F 21st SCVI	Ft. Fisher, NC	01/15/65	Elmira, NY	02/15/65	Died, Pneumonia	P5,P65,P66,FPH,HAG
Gayle, Thomas J.	Pvt	K 23rd SCVI	Southside RR, VA	04/02/65	City Pt., VA	06/12/65	Pt. Lookout, MD	CSR
					Pt. Lookout, MD	06/27/65	Rlsd. G.O. #109	P118,P121,CSR
Geddes, M.D.	Sgt	I 15th SCVI	Drury's Bluff, VA	05/16/64	Fts. Monroe, VA	05/23/64	Pt. Lookout, MD	CSR
					Pt. Lookout, MD	01/17/65	Exchanged	P113,P123,P124,CSR
Geddings, J.S.	Pvt	C 3rd SCVABn	Blakely, AL	04/09/65	Ship Island, MS	05/01/65	Vicksburg, MS Xc	P136,CSR
Geddings, Manning	Pvt	C 3rd SCVABn	Blakely, AL	04/09/65	Ship Island, MS	05/01/65	Vicksburg, MS Xc	P136,CSR
					Meridian, MS	05/10/65	Paroled	CSR
Geddings, Peter	Pvt	C 3rd SCVABn	Blakely, AL	04/09/65	Ship Island, MS	05/01/65	Vicksburg, MS Xc	P136,CSR
Geddings, Peter	Pvt	C 3rd SCVABn	Citronelle, AL	05/04/65	Meridian, MS	05/10/65	Paroled	CSR
Geddings, Thomas W.	Pvt	C 3rd SCVABn	Blakely, AL	04/09/65	Ship Island, MS	05/01/65	Vicksburg, MS Xc	P136,CSR
Geddings, Thomas W.	Pvt	C 3rd SCVABn	Citronelle, AL	05/04/65	Meridian, MS	05/15/65	Paroled	CSR
Gee, Edward	Pvt	9 10/19 SCVI	Missionary Ridge, TN	11/25/63	Nashville, TN	12/23/63	Louisville, KY	P39,CSR
					Louisville, KY	12/25/63	Sent north on oath	P88,P93,CSR
Gee, M.	Pvt	22nd SCVI	Crater, Pbg., VA	07/30/64	Pt. Lookout, MD	08/08/64	Elmira, NY	P113,P117,P120
Gehrs, John W.	Pvt	A German LA	Deserted/enemy	03/17/65	Charleston, SC	03/17/65	Released on oath	CSR
Geiger, George J.	Pvt	F 1st SCVA	Deserted/enemy	04/03/65	Philadelphia, PA	04/04/65	Released on oath	CSR
Geiger, R.B.	Pvt	B 1st SCVIH	Citronelle, AL	05/01/65	Gainesville, AL	06/30/65	Paroled	CSR
Geiger, William H.	Pvt	B 1st SCVIH	Citronelle, AL	05/01/65	Gainesville, AL	06/30/65	Paroled	CSR
Gelling, G.B.	Pvt	H Ham.Leg.	Sharpsburg, MD	09/17/62	Chester, PA	05/05/62	Ft. McHenry, MD	CSR
					Ft. McHenry, MD	05/11/62	Fts. Monroe Xc	CSR
Genobles, G.R.	Pvt	C 13th SCVI	Gettysburg, PA	07/05/63	David's Island, NY	09/05/63	City Pt., VA Xc	P1,CSR
Genobles, Rufus B.	Pvt	G 20th SCVI	Petersburg, VA	07/30/64	Pt. Lookout, MD	08/08/64	Elmira, NY	P117,P120,KEB,CSR
					Elmira, NY	09/08/64	Died, Typhoid pneu.	P5,P12,P65,P66,FPH
Gentry, John A.	Pvt	A Hol.Leg.	Kinston, NC	12/15/63	Kinston, NC	12/15/63	Paroled POW	CSR,HOS
Gentry, John A.	Sgt	A Hol.Leg.	Five Forks, VA	04/01/65	City Pt. VA	04/05/65	Pt. Lookout, MD	CSR
					Pt. Lookout, MD	06/27/65	Rlsd. G.O. #109	P118,P121,P123,CSR
Gentry, John A.	Pvt	F 24th SCVI	Taylors Ridge, GA	10/16/64	Nashville, TN	10/23/64	Louisville, KY	CSR
					Louisville, KY	10/27/64	Camp Douglas, IL	P90,P91,P94
					Camp Douglas, IL	06/17/86	Rlsd. G.O. #109	P55
Gentry, M.S.	Pvt	K 5th SCVI	Deserted/enemy	02/15/64	Knoxville, TN	02/29/64	Released on oath	CSR
Geochagan, David B.	Pvt	E 11th SCVI	Petersburg, VA	06/24/64	Bermuda Hundred, VA	06/25/64	Fts. Monroe, VA	CSR,HAG
					Fts. Monroe, VA	06/26/64	Pt. Lookout, MD	CSR
					Pt. Lookout, MD	08/16/64	Elmira, NY	P113,P117,P120,CSR
					Elmira, NY	06/16/65	Rlsd. G.O. #109	P65,P66,CSR
George, H.J.	Pvt	K 23rd SCVI	Richmond VA Hos.	04/03/65	Newport News, VA	06/14/65	Rlsd. G.O. #109	CSR
George, Henry	Pvt	E 24th SCVI	Nashville, TN	12/16/64	Nashville, TN	12/31/64	Louisville, KY	CSR
					Louisville, KY	01/05/65	Camp Chase, OH	P95
					Camp Chase, OH	06/12/65	Rlsd. G.O.#109	P23
George, J.A.	Pvt	G 3rd SCVABn	High Pt., NC	05/01/65	High Pt., NC	05/01/65	Paroled	CSR
George, J.B.	2Lt	1st SCVC	Deserted/enemy	02/19/65	Nashville, TN	02/19/65	Released on oath	CSR
George, Jacob L.	Pvt	E 24th SCVI	Resaca, GA	05/16/64	Nashville, TN	05/20/64	Louisville, KY	P39
					Louisville, KY	05/23/64	Alton, IL	P93,EFW
					Alton, IL	08/23/64	Camp Douglas, IL	P13,P14
					Camp Douglas, IL	12/24/64	Died, Pneumonia	P5,P12,FPH

G

SOUTH CAROLINA SOLDIERS, SAILORS AND CITIZENS HELD IN U.S. PRISONS 1861-1865

NAME	RANK	REGIMENT	CAPTURED AT	WHEN	PRISON	MOVED	DISPOSITION	SOURCES
George, W.J.	Pvt	H 23rd SCVI	Jarrats Stn., VA	04/02/65	City Pt., VA	04/07/65	Hart's Island, NY	CSR
					Hart's Island, NY	06/15/65	Rlsd. G.O. #109	P79,HMC,CSR
Gerald, Eli	Pvt	K 26th SCVI	Farmville, VA	04/06/65	City Pt., VA	04/14/65	Newport News, VA	CSR
					Newport News, VA	06/16/65	Rlsd. G.O. #109	P107,CSR
Gerald, Hugh	Pvt	K 26th SCVI	Farmville, VA	04/06/65	City Pt., VA	04/14/65	Newport News, VA	CSR,CEN
					Newport News, VA	06/26/65	Rlsd. G.O. #109	P107,CSR
Gerald, J.R.	Pvt	K 26th SCVI	Deserted/enemy	12/01/64	City Pt., VA	12/13/64	Washington, DC	P8,CSR
					Washington, DC	12/15/64	Released in DC	CSR
Gerald, John L.	Pvt	L 21st SCVI	Town Creek, NC	02/20/65	Pt. Lookout, MD	06/27/65	Rlsd. G.O. #109	P114,P117,P129,HAG
Gerald, Louis C.	Pvt	K 26th SCVI	Five Forks, VA	04/01/65	City Pt., VA	04/05/65	Pt. Lookout, MD	CSR,CEN
					Pt. Lookout, MD	06/27/65	Rlsd. G.O. #109	P118,P121,P123,CSR
Gerald, William	Pvt	K 26th SCVI	Petersburg, VA	03/22/65	City Pt., VA	03/25/65	Pt. Lookout, MD	CSR
					Pt. Lookout, MD	06/27/65	Rlsd. G.O. #109	P114,P121,CSR,CEN
Gerard, F.G.	Pvt	A German LA	Deserted/enemy	02/18/65	Hilton Head, SC	04/07/65	New York, NY P.M.	CSR
Gerhard, L.	Pvt	F 1st SCVA	Morris Island, SC	07/10/63	Stmr. Cosmopolitan	07/24/63	for exchange	CSR
Gerkin, E.F.H.	Msc	E 25th SCVI	Ft. Fisher, NC	01/15/65	New York, NY	01/30/65	Elmira, NY	CSR,HAG
					Elmira, NY	05/15/65	Rlsd. G.O. #85	P65,P66
Germany, W.J.	Pvt	F 12th SCVI	Gettysburg, PA	07/04/63	Ft. Delaware, DE	10/15/63	Exchanged	P40,P42,P44,CSR
Germany, W.J.	Pvt	F 12th SCVI	Spotsylvania, VA	05/12/64	Belle Plain, VA	05/21/64	Ft. Delaware, DE	CSR
					Ft. Delaware, DE	08/01/64	Hos. 8/1-9/18/64	P47
					Ft. Delaware, DE	09/18/64	Aikens Ldg., VA Xc	P41,P42,HFC
Germany, W.J.	Pvt	F 12th SCVI	Five Forks, VA	04/02/65	City Pt., VA	04/07/65	Hart's Island, NY	CSR
					Hart's Island, NY	06/23/65	Rlsd. G.O. #109	P79,CSR
Gerrocks, John H.	Pvt	K 26th SCVI	Crater, Pbg., VA	07/30/64	City Pt., VA	08/05/64	Pt. Lookout, MD	CSR,CEN
					Pt. Lookout, MD	08/08/64	Elmira, NY	P113,CSR
					Elmira, NY	10/11/64	Tfd. for exchange	P65,CSR
					Pt. Lookout, MD	10/29/64	Venus Pt., GA Xc	P114,P117,CSR
Gibbes, J. Perroneau	Pvt	A 27th SCVI	Petersburg, VA	06/24/64	Bermuda Hundred, VA	06/25/64	Fts. Monroe, VA	CSR,HAG
					Fts. Monroe, VA	06/26/64	Pt. Lookout, MD	CSR
					Pt. Lookout, MD	08/16/64	Elmira, NY	P113,P117,CSR
					Elmira, NY	10/11/64	Pt. Lookout, MD Xc	P65,P66,CSR
					Pt. Lookout, MD	10/29/64	Exchanged	P114,P123,CSR
Gibbons, J.C.	Pvt	F 27th SCVI	Weldon RR, VA	08/21/64	City Pt., VA	08/24/64	Pt. Lookout, MD	CSR,HAG
					Pt. Lookout, MD	03/15/65	Exchanged	P113,P124,CSR
Gibbons, Jesse P.	Sgt	F 27th SCVI	Town Creek, NC	02/20/65	Ft. Anderson, NC	02/28/65	Pt. Lookout, MD	CSR,HAG
					Pt. Lookout, MD	05/13/65	Rlsd. G.O. #85	P114,P117,P122,CSR
Gibbons, Thomas H.	Pvt	K 6th SCVI	Warrenton, VA	09/29/62	Warrenton, VA	09/29/62	Paroled	CSR
Gibbons, Thomas H.	Pvt	K 6th SCVI	Missionary Ridge TN	11/25/63	Bridgeport, AL G.H.	12/13/63	Nashville, TN G.H.	P2,CTA,CSR
					Nashville, TN G.H.	01/01/64	Died, Smallpox	P12,CSR
Gibbons, Thomas J.	Pvt	K 1st SCVIG	Petersburg, VA	04/02/65	Pt. Lookout, MD	06/27/65	Rlsd. G.O. #109	P117,P121,P123,SA1
Gibbs, George T.	Pvt	McQueen LA	Five Forks, VA	04/01/65	City Pt., VA	04/07/65	Hart's Island, NY	CSR
					Hart's Island, NY	04/11/65	Died, Anemia	P79,CSR
Gibbs, John R.	Pvt	B 1st SCVIBn	James Island, SC	06/16/62	Ft. Columbus, NY	08/23/63	Ft. Delaware, DE	P37
Gibson, A.	Pvt	B 5th SCVI	Williamsburg, VA	05/05/62	Fts. Monroe, VA		no more info	SA3,CSR
Gibson, Aaron C.	Pvt	F 26th SCVI	Five Forks, VA	04/01/65	City Pt., VA MD	04/05/65	Pt. Lookout, MD	CSR
					Pt. Lookout, MD	04/28/65	Died, Scurvy	P12,CSR
Gibson, Albert	Sgt	L 21st SCVI	Ft. Fisher, NC	01/15/65	Elmira, NY	07/11/65	Rlsd. G.O. #109	P65,P66,HAG,HMC
Gibson, Allan	Pvt	H 23rd SCVI	Petersburg, VA	03/25/65	City Pt., VA	03/28/65	Pt. Lookout, MD	CSR
					Pt. Lookout, MD	06/27/65	Rlsd. G.O. #109	P121,P123,HMC,CSR
Gibson, Ambrose	Cpl	B 14th SCVI	Richmond, VA Hos.	04/03/65	Provost Marshal	04/20/65		CSR
					Provost Marshal	07/30/65	Rlsd. on oath	CSR,HOE
Gibson, D.H.	Pvt	B 7th SCVI	Deserted/enemy	04/02/65	Washington, DC P.M.	04/05/65	Charleston, SC	CSR

SOUTH CAROLINA SOLDIERS, SAILORS AND  CITIZENS HELD IN U.S. PRISONS 1861-1865

NAME	RANK	REGIMENT	CAPTURED AT	WHEN	PRISON	MOVED	DISPOSITION	SOURCES
Gibson, Francis B.	Sgt	D 26th SCVI	Appomattox C.H., VA	04/09/65	Ft. McHenry, MD	06/12/65	Washington, DC	P110,HOM,CSR
					Lincoln G.H., DC	06/12/65	Rlsd. G.O. #109	CSR
Gibson, H.A.H.	Msc	2nd SCVIRi	Not Given		Washington, DC P.M.	04/12/65	Louisville, KY	CSR
Gibson, H.B.	Pvt	D 2nd SCVI	Gettysburg, PA	07/05/63	Letterman G.H. Gbg	09/10/63	Provost Marshal	P1,SA2,H2,CSR
					David's Island, NY	09/25/63	Paroled	P1,SA2,H2,CSR
Gibson, J.J.	Pvt	D 4th SCVC	Louisa C.H., VA	06/11/64	Fts. Monroe, VA	06/20/64	Pt. Lookout, MD	CSR
					Pt. Lookout, MD	07/23/64	Elmira, NY	P113,P120,CSR
					Elmira, NY	10/11/64	Tfd. for exchange	P65,CSR
					Pt. Lookout, MD	10/29/64	Aikens Ldg., VA Xc	P114,P117,P123,CSR
Gibson, J.L.	Pvt	I 5th SCVC	Augusta, GA	05/19/65	Augusta, GA	05/19/65	Paroled	CSR
Gibson, J.R.P.	Pvt	B 5th SCVI	Williamsburg, VA	05/05/62	Fts. Monroe, VA		no more info	SA3,CSR
Gibson, James D.	Sgt	G 24th SCVI	Nashville, TN	12/16/64	Nashville, TN	12/20/64	Louisville, KY	CSR
					Louisville, KY	01/04/65	Camp Chase, OH	P94
					Camp Chase, OH	05/02/65	New Orleans, LA Xc	P23,P26,EFW
Gibson, Jefferson C.	Pvt	F 26th SCVI	Hatchers Run, VA	04/05/65	City Pt., VA	05/01/65	Washington, DC	CSR
					Ft. McHenry, MD	06/12/65	Washington, DC	P110
					Washington, DC	06/14/65	Rlsd. G.O. #109	CSR
Gibson, Jesse L.	Pvt	H 23rd SCVI	Jarratts Stn., VA	04/02/65	City Pt., VA	04/04/65	Hart's Island, NY	CSR
					Hart's Island, NY	06/15/65	Rlsd. G.O. #109	P79,HMC,CSR
Gibson, John G.	Pvt	G Hol.Leg.	Hatchers Run, VA	03/25/65	City Pt., VA	04/01/65	Pt. Lookout, MD	CSR,ANY
					Pt. Lookout, MD	06/27/65	Rlsd. G.O. #109	P114,P117,P121,ANY,CSR
Gibson, John S.	Pvt	L 21st SCVI	Town Creek, NC	02/20/65	Pt. Lookout, MD	05/10/65	Died, Ch. Diarrhea	P6,P117,P119,FPH
Gibson, N.N.	Pvt	F 26th SCVI	Five Forks, VA	04/01/65	Pt. Lookout, MD	06/06/65	Rlsd. Instr. 5/30/65	P121
Gibson, Nathan W.	Pvt	F 7th SCVIBn	Weldon RR, VA	08/21/64	City Pt., VA	08/24/64	Pt. Lookout, MD	CSR,HAG,HIC
					Pt. Lookout, MD	09/18/64	Aikens Ldg., VA Xc	P113,P123,CSR
					Richmond, VA Hos.	09/26/64	Furloughed 30 days	CSR
Gibson, Nathan W.	Pvt	F 26th SCVI	Southside RR, VA	04/01/65	City Pt., VA	04/05/65	Pt. Lookout, MD	CSR
					Pt. Lookout, MD	04/29/65	Died, Scurvy	P6,P118,P119,FPH
Gibson, Nelson M.	2Lt	A 23rd SCVI	Dinwiddie C.H., VA	04/01/65	Ft. McHenry, MD	04/09/65	Johnson's Isl., OH	P110,CSR
Gibson, Nelson M.	2Lt	A 23rd SCVI	Five Forks, VA	04/01/65	Washington, DC	04/10/65	Johnson's Isl., OH	CSR
					Johnsons Isl., OH	06/18/65	Rlsd. G.O. #109	P81,P82,P83,CSR
Gibson, Oscar E.	Pvt	L 21st SCVI	Ft. Fisher, NC	01/15/65	Pt. Lookout, MD	02/02/65	Douglas G.H., DC	P114,HAG,HMC
					Pt. Lookout, MD	07/23/65	Washington, DC	P117,P121
					Douglas G.H., DC	08/24/65	Rlsd. G.O. #109	CSR
Gibson, P.D.	Pvt	G 15th SCMil	Flat Rock, SC	02/24/65	Hart's Island, NY	06/17/65	Rlsd. G.O. #109	P79
Gibson, Robert W.	Pvt	L 21st SCVI	Petersburg, VA	05/09/64	Pt. Lookout, MD			P113,P116
					Elmira, NY	10/11/64	Pt.Lookout, MD	P65,P66
					W. Bldg. Balt, MD	10/16/64	Died, Ch. Diarrhea	P1,P12,FPH,HMC,HAG
Gibson, T.D.	Pvt	E 15th SCVI	Gettysburg, PA	07/05/63	Letterman G.H. Gbg	10/14/63	Provost Marshal	P1,KEB
					Pt. Lookout, MD	12/25/63	Exchanged	P113,P123,CSR
Gibson, T.F.	Pvt	B 4th SCVC	Hawe's Shop, VA	05/28/64	White House, VA	06/08/64	Pt. Lookout, MD	CSR
					Pt. Lookout, MD	07/12/64	Elmira, NY	P113,CSR
					Elmira, NY	06/14/65	Rlsd. G.O. #109	P65,HHC,CSR
Gibson, Thomas P.	Pvt	E 4th SCVC	Louisa C.H., VA	06/11/64	Fts. Monroe, VA	06/20/64	Pt. Lookout, MD	CSR,HOM
					Pt. Lookout, MD	07/23/64	Elmira, NY	P113,P16,P120,CSR
					Elmira, NY	06/14/65	Rlsd. G.O. #109	P65,CSR
Gibson, W.H.	Pvt	E 2nd SCVI	Deserted/enemy	12/02/64	Bermuda Hundred, VA	01/07/65	Washington, DC	CSR
					Washington, DC	01/08/65	New York, NY oath	CSR
Gibson, W.J.	Pvt	F 12th SCVI	Sharpsburg, MD	09/17/62	Frederick, MD USGH	10/16/62	Ft. McHenry, MD GH	CSR
					Ft. McHenry, MD	10/18/62	Aikens Ldg., VA Xc	CSR
					Richmond, VA Hos.	11/12/62	Died of wounds	CSR
Gilbert, Allen A.	1Lt	G 3rd SCVABn	High Pt., NC	05/01/65	High Pt., NC	05/01/65	Paroled	CSR

SOUTH CAROLINA SOLDIERS, SAILORS AND  CITIZENS HELD IN U.S. PRISONS 1861-1865

NAME	RANK	REGIMENT	CAPTURED AT	WHEN	PRISON	MOVED	DISPOSITION	SOURCES
Gilbert, Richard	Pvt	A 1st SCVA	Greensboro, NC Hos.	04/26/65	Greensboro, NC	05/02/65	Paroled	CSR
Gilbert, Stephen Capers	1Lt	Brooks LA	Saylors Creek, VA	04/06/65	Old Capitol, DC	04/17/65	Johnson's Isl., OH	CSR
					Johnson's Isl., OH	06/18/65	Rlsd. G.O. #109	P81,P83,CSR
Gilchrist, Abram	Pvt	B 6th SCVC	Louisa C.H., VA	06/11/64	Fts. Monroe, VA	06/20/64	Pt. Lookout, MD	CSR
					Pt. Lookout, MD	07/23/64	Elmira, NY	P113,P116,P120,CSR
					Elmira, NY	02/13/65	Tfd. for exchange	P65,CSR
Gilchrist, Archibald E.	2Lt	F 4th SCVC	Stony Creek, VA	12/01/64	Hq. Army of Potomac	12/04/64	Washington, DC	CSR
					Old Capitol, DC	12/16/64	Ft. Delaware, DE	CSR
					Ft. Delaware, DE	02/26/65	Discharged frm Hos.	P47
					Ft. Delaware, DE	06/12/65	Rlsd. G.O. #109	P43,P45,P110,CSR
Gilder, Gifford A.	Pvt	B 14th SCVI	Gettysburg, PA	06/30/63	David's Island, NY	08/02/63	Died of wounds	P1,P6,FPH,HOE,CSR
Giles, Abraham J.	Pvt	5 10/19 SCVI	Missionary Ridge TN	11/25/63	Nashville, TN	12/07/63	Louisville, KY	P39,CSR
					Louisville, KY	12/09/63	Rock Island, IL	P88,P89,CSR
					Rock Island, IL	06/19/65	Rlsd. G.O. #109	CSR
Giles, Charles H.	SMj	15th SCVI	South Mtn., MD	09/15/62	Ft. McHenry, MD	10/17/63	Fts. Monroe, VA Xc	CSR
Giles, Leonard D.	Pvt	I 14th SCVI	Piedmont, VA	06/05/64	Staunton, VA	06/21/64	Camp Morton, IN	CSR
					Camp Morton, IN	02/26/65	City Pt., VA Xc	P100,CSR
					Aikens Ldg., VA Xc	03/11/65	Richmond, VA	CSR
Gilham, James	Pvt	C 1st SCVA	Fayetteville, NC	02/24/65	New Berne, NC	04/10/65	Hart's Island, NY	CSR
					Hart's Island, NY	06/16/65	Rlsd. G.O. #109	CSR
Gilland, A.	Sgt	C 15th SCVI	Jarratts Stn., VA	04/02/65	City Pt., VA	04/07/65	Hart's Island, NY	CSR
					Hart's Island, NY	06/15/65	Rlsd. G.O. #109	CSR
Gillespie, Frank S.	Cpl	F 7th SCVC	Farmville, VA	04/10/65	U.S. 24th A.C. Fld.	04/10/65	City Pt., VA USGH	CSR
					City Pt., VA USGH	04/21/65	Baltimore, MD	CSR
					U.S. Connecticutt	04/22/65	Baltimore, MD	CSR
					W. Bldg. Balt, MD	05/09/65	Ft. McHenry, MD	CSR
					Ft. McHenry, MD	05/31/65	Rlsd. on parole	P7,CSR
Gillespie, James	Pvt	E 1st SCVA	Morris Island, SC	07/25/64	Hilton Head, SC	08/18/64	New York, NY oath	CSR
Gillespie, John W.	Pvt	B 1st SCVA	Bentonville, NC	03/19/65	Pt. Lookout, MD	06/27/65	Rlsd. G.O. #109	P114,P117
Gillespie, Paul C.	Pvt	D 18th SCVI	Five Forks, VA	04/03/65	Pt. Lookout, MD	06/27/65	Rlsd. G.O. #109	P118,P121,P123
Gillfillan, John	Pvt	B Ham.Leg.MI	Deserted/enemy	09/30/64	Bermuda Hundred, VA	10/04/64	New York, NY oath	CSR
Gillham, James	Pvt	C 1st SCVA	Fayetteville, NC	02/24/65	Hart's Island, NY	06/16/65	Rlsd. G.O. #109	P79
Gilliam, B.B.	Pvt	G 27th SCVI	Weldon RR, VA	08/21/64	City Pt., VA	08/23/64	Pt. Lookout, MD	CSR,HAG
					Pt. Lookout, MD	03/14/65	Aikens Ldg., VA Xc	P113,P117,P124,CSR
Gilliam, J.R.	Pvt	Hol.Leg.	Petersburg, VA	11/06/64	Pt. Lookout, MD	02/18/65	Aikens Ldg., VA Xc	P117
Gilliam, John S.	Pvt	H 17th SCVI	Petersburg, VA	03/25/65	City Pt., VA	03/28/65	Pt. Lookout, MD	CSR
					Pt. Lookout, MD	06/27/65	Rlsd. G.O. #109	P121,P123,CSR
Gillian, J.M.	Pvt	A 1st SCVC	Johns Island, SC	07/02/64	Port Royal Fy., SC	08/16/64	Exchanged	CSR
Gilliland, Abner	Sgt	C 18th SCVI	Jarratts Stn., VA	04/02/65	Hart's Island, NY	06/15/65	Rlsd. G.O. #109	P79
					New York, NY Tr. Hos.	06/23/65	Died	P12,CSR,FPH
Gilliland, Arthur	Sgt	D 27th SCVI	Town Creek, NC	02/20/65	Ft. Anderson, NC	02/28/65	Pt. Lookout, MD	CSR,HAG
					Pt. Lookout, MD	06/27/65	Rlsd. G.O. #109	P117,P121,P123,CSR
Gilliland, E.	Pvt	K 1st SCVC	Mechanicstown, PA	06/30/63	Ft. Delaware, DE			P40
Gilliland, William M.	Sgt	E 3rd SCVIBn	Gettysburg, PA	07/03/63	Ft. Delaware, DE	03/24/64	Died, Ch. Diarrhea	P5,P40,P42,P47,FPH
Gillion, John R.	Pvt	B 14th SCVI	Gettysburg, PA	07/04/63	David's Island, NY	09/05/63	City Pt., VA Xc	P1,HOE,CSR
Gillion, John R.	Pvt	B 14th SCVI	Sutherland Stn., VA	04/03/65	City Pt., VA	04/13/65	Pt. Lookout, MD	CSR
					Pt. Lookout, MD	06/27/65	Rlsd. G.O. #109	P118,P121,P123,CSR
Gillion, William P.	Pvt	B 14th SCVI	Augusta, GA	05/31/65	Augusta, GA	05/31/65	Paroled	CSR
Gillyard, M.D.	Sgt	18th SCVAB	Hartwell, GA	05/18/65	Hartwell, GA	05/18/65	Paroled	CSR
Gilmer, J.A.	Pvt	F Hol.Leg.	Five Forks, VA	04/01/65	City Pt., VA	04/05/65	Pt. Lookout, MD	CSR
					Pt. Lookout, MD	06/27/65	Rlsd. G.O. #109	P118,P123,CSR

SOUTH CAROLINA SOLDIERS, SAILORS AND  CITIZENS HELD IN U.S. PRISONS 1861-1865

NAME	RANK	REGIMENT	CAPTURED AT	WHEN	PRISON	MOVED	DISPOSITION	SOURCES
Gilmer, William J.G.	Pvt	F 2nd SCVI	Halltown, VA	08/21/64	Harpers Ferry, WV	08/31/64	Camp Chase, OH	H2,CSR,KEB
					Camp Chase, OH	03/03/65	Died, Pneumonia	P23,P27,FPH,CSR
Gilreath, Larkin C.	Pvt	G 16th SCVI	Decatur, GA	07/22/64	Nashville, TN	10/27/64	Louisville, KY	CSR,16R
					Louisville, KY	10/29/64	Camp Douglas, IL	P90,P91,P94,CSR
					Camp Douglas, IL	06/12/65	Rlsd. G.O. #109	P53,P55,CSR
Gilreath, Lawrence P.	Pvt	B 2nd SCVI	Gettysburg, PA	07/05/63	Letterman G.H. Gbg	10/02/63	Died of wounds	P1,P6,P12,SA2,H2,CSR
Gilreath, W.H.	Pvt	A 3rd SCVABn	High Pt., NC	05/02/65	High Pt., NC	05/02/65	Paroled	CSR
Gilreath, William W.	Pvt	B 2nd SCVI	Gettysburg, PA	07/05/63	Letterman G.H. Gbg	10/15/63	Provost Marshal	P1,KEB,H2,CSR
					W. Bldg. Balt, MD	11/12/63	City Pt., VA Xc	SA2,P1,CSR
Ginn, Amos	Pvt	D 24th SCVI	Nashville, TN	12/16/64	Nashville, TN	01/05/65	Louisville, KY	CSR
					Louisville, KY	01/05/65	Camp Chase, OH	P95,CSR
					Camp Chase, OH	05/02/65	New Orleans, LA Xc	P23,P26,CSR
					Camp Chase, OH	06/13/65	Rlsd. G.O. #109	CSR
Girandeau, John L.	Chp	23rd SCVI	Saylors Creek, VA	04/06/65	Old Capitol, DC	05/01/65	Johnson's Isl., OH	P110,R48,CSR
					Johnson's Isl., OH	06/20/65	Rlsd. G.O. #109	P81,CSR
Giser, Thomas J.	1Lt	B 18th SCVI	Hatchers Run, VA	03/29/65	Old Capitol, DC	06/09/65	Released	P110
Gist, George W.	Pvt	C 25th SCVI	Ft. Fisher, NC	01/15/65	New Berne, NC	01/16/65	Pt. Lookout, MD	CSR,CTA,HAG
					Pt. Lookout, MD	06/05/65	Rlsd. Instr. 5/30/65	P114,P117,P122,CSR
Gitzy, J.G.	Pvt	Hol.Leg.	Petersburg, VA	04/03/65	Petersburg, VA Hos.	07/27/65	Died	CSR
Givens, David	Pvt	K 11th SCVI	Town Creek, NC	02/20/65	Ft. Anderson, NC	02/28/65	Pt. Lookout, MD	CSR
					Pt. Lookout, MD	06/27/65	Rlsd. G.O. #109	P117,P121,P123,CSR
Givens, J.C.	Pvt	Brooks LA	Appomattox C.H., VA	04/10/65	W. Bldg. Balt, MD	05/09/65	Provost Marshal	CSR
Givin, Josiah	Pvt	G 27th SCVI	Weldon RR, VA	08/21/64	City Pt., VA	08/23/64	Pt. Lookout, MD	CSR,HAG
					Pt. Lookout, MD	10/30/64	Venus Pt., GA Xc	P113,P123,P125,CSR
Givin, William P.	Pvt	G 27th SCVI	Town Creek, NC	02/20/65	Ft. Anderson, NC	02/28/65	Pt. Lookout, MD	CSR,HAG
					Pt. Lookout, MD	06/22/65	Rlsd. G.O. #109	P114,P117,P121,CSR
Gladden, Silas	Pvt	B 7th SCVIBn	Weldon RR, VA	08/21/64	City Pt., VA USFH	08/26/64	Washington, DC USG	P1,HAG,CSR
					Fts. Monroe, VA US	08/26/64	Alexandria, VA USG	CSR
					Alexandria, VA USG	08/28/64	Washington, DC USG	CSR
					Lincoln G.H., DC	09/21/64	Old Capitol, DC	CSR
					Elmira, NY	02/15/65	Died, Variola	P5,P65,P66,FPH,CSR
Gladden, William A.	Pvt	E 15th SCVI	Halltown, VA	08/26/64	Washington, DC.	08/29/64	Harpers Ferry, WV	CSR,KEB
					Harpers Ferry, WV	09/02/64	Camp Chase, OH	CSR
					Camp Chase, OH	11/11/64	Died, Smallpox	P23,P27,FPH,CSR
Gladden, William T.	Pvt	D 17th SCVI	Crater, Pbg., VA	07/30/64	City Pt., VA	08/05/65	Pt. Lookout, MD	CSR
					Pt. Lookout, MD	08/08/64	Elmira, NY	P113,P117,P120,CSR
					Elmira, NY	07/19/65	Rlsd. G.O. #109	P65,P66,CSR
Gladney, J.F.	Pvt	F 6th SCVC	Petersburg, VA	07/30/64	City Pt., VA	08/04/64	Elmira, NY	CSR
					Pt. Lookout, MD	08/08/64	Elmira, NY	P117,P120,P125,CSR
					Elmira, NY	06/19/65	Rlsd. G.O. #109	P65,CSR
Gladney, Samuel	Cpl	E 15th SCVI	Gettysburg, PA	07/04/63	David's Island, NY	08/24/63	City Pt., VA Xc	P1,KEB
Glanton, C.R.	Pvt	B 6th SCVC	Bennett's Pt., SC	06/30/63	Hilton Head, SC	09/18/63	Ft. Columbus, NY	CSR
					Ft. Columbus, NY	09/18/63	Pt. Lookout, MD	CSR
					Pt. Lookout, MD	09/18/64	Exchanged	P124,CSR
Glasgow, James N.	Pvt	G 14th SCVI	Petersburg, VA	04/03/65	City Pt., VA	04/11/65	Hart's Island, NY	CSR
					Hart's Island, NY	06/13/65	Died, Ch. Diarrhea	P6,P79,FPH,CSR
Glaskin, George W.	Lt	G 3rd SCVC	Deserted/enemy	12/10/64	Charleston, SC	02/25/65	New York, NY oath	CSR
Glaspy, Jeremiah M.	Pvt	D 18th SCVI	Five Forks, VA	04/01/65	City Pt., VA	04/04/65	Pt. Lookout, MD	CSR
					Pt. Lookout, MD	06/27/65	Rlsd. G.O. #109	P118,P121,P123,CSR
Glaspy, Paul	Pvt	D 18th SCVI	Sutherland Stn., VA	04/02/65	Pt. Lookout, MD	04/20/65	Pt. Lookout, MD	CSR
					Pt. Lookout, MD	06/27/65	Rlsd. G.O. #109	CSR

SOUTH CAROLINA SOLDIERS, SAILORS AND  G CITIZENS HELD IN U.S. PRISONS 1861-1865

NAME	RANK	REGIMENT	CAPTURED AT	WHEN	PRISON	MOVED	DISPOSITION	SOURCES
Glaspy, W.P.	Pvt	D 18th SCVI	Farmville, VA	04/06/65	City Pt., VA	04/14/65	Newport News, VA	CSR
					Newport News, VA	06/13/65	Rlsd. G.O. #109	P107,CSR
Glaspy, William Y.	Pvt	G 22nd SCVI	Farmville, VA	04/06/65	City Pt., VA	04/14/65	Newport News, VA	CSR
					Newport News, VA	06/26/65	Rlsd. G.O. #109	P107,UD3
Glass, John	Pvt	Brooks LA	Farmville, VA	04/06/65	Newport News, VA	07/02/65	Rlsd. G.O. #109	P107
Glauzier, Whitfield	Pvt	K 14th SCVI	Augusta, GA	05/19/65	Augusta, GA	05/19/65	Paroled	CSR
Glaze, John	Pvt	F 3rd SCVIBn	South Mtn., MD	09/14/62	Ft. Delaware, DE	10/02/62	Aikens Ldg., VA Xc	CSR
Glaze, Thomas J.	Cpl	K 19th SCVI	Augusta, GA	05/19/65	Augusta, GA	05/19/65	Paroled	CSR
Glazner, Samuel K.	Pvt	A 20th SCVI	Deserted/enemy	05/27/64		10/04/64	Knoxville, TN	CSR
					Knoxville, TN	10/05/64	Chattanooga, TN	CSR
					Chattanooga, TN	10/12/64	Louisville, KY	CSR
					Louisville, KY	10/14/64	North on oath	P8,P90,P92,CSR
Gleam, J.P.	Pvt	D Hol.Leg.	Frederick, MD	09/12/62	Ft. Delaware, DE	10/02/62	Aikens Ldg., VA Xc	CSR
Gleason, Frederick	Pvt	C 15th SCVAB	Smiths Ford, NC	03/16/65	New Berne, NC	04/03/65	Pt. Lookout, MD	CSR
					Pt. Lookout, MD	06/29/65	Rlsd. G.O. #109	P114,P117,CSR
Gleason, W.B.	Pvt	Wash'n LA	Charlotte, NC	05/23/65	Charlotte, NC	05/23/65	Paroled	CSR
Gleaton, Absolom E.	1Lt	22nd SCVI	Five Forks, VA	04/01/65	Old Capitol, DC	04/09/65	Johnson's Isl., OH	CSR
					Ft. McHenry, MD	04/09/65	Johnson's Isl., OH	P110
					Johnson's Isl., OH	06/17/65	Rlsd. G.O. #109	P81,P82,P83
Gleaton, D.T.	Pvt	I 22nd SCVI	Maryland		Frederick, MD Hos.	09/19/62	No other data	CSR
Gleaton, D.T.	Pvt	I 22nd SCVI	New Berne, NC	12/23/62	New Berne, NC	12/23/62	Paroled POW	CSR
Gleaton, David T.	Pvt	K 1st SCVIG	N. Anna River, VA	05/23/64	Pt. Lookout, MD	11/01/64	Aikens Ldg., VA Xc	P121,P123,CSR
Gleaton, H.H.	Cpl	I 22nd SCVI	Five Forks, VA	04/01/65	City Pt., VA	04/05/65	Pt. Lookout, MD	CSR
					Pt. Lookout, MD	06/05/65	Rlsd. Instr. 5/30/65	P114,P118,P122
Gleaton, Henry H.	Pvt	I 5th SCVC	Stony Creek, VA	12/01/64	City Pt., VA	12/05/64	Pt. Lookout, MD	CSR
Gleaton, J.P.	Pvt	A 1st SCVIH	Richmond, VA	04/03/65	Libby Prison Rchmd.	04/23/65	Newport News, VA	CSR
					Newport News, VA	06/26/65	Rlsd. G.O. #109	P107,CSR
Gleaton, J.W.	Pvt	I 5th SCVC	Augusta, GA	05/19/65	Augusta, GA	05/19/65	Paroled	CSR
Gleaton, M.L.	Pvt	I 5th SCVC	Augusta, GA	05/19/65	Augusta, GA	05/19/65	Paroled	CSR
Gleaton, R.S.	Pvt	I 5th SCVC	Augusta, GA	05/19/65	Augusta, GA	05/19/65	Paroled	CSR
Gleaton, William M.	Pvt	E 27th SCVI	Weldon RR, VA	08/21/64	City Pt., VA	08/23/64	Pt. Lookout, MD	CSR,HAG
					Pt. Lookout, MD	10/15/64	Joined U.S. Army	P117,P122,P125
Glenn, David J., Sr.	Pvt	H 18th SCVI	Appomattox C.H., VA	04/09/65	City Pt., VA	05/04/65	Newport News, VA	CSR
					Newport News, VA	06/14/65	Rlsd. G.O. #109	P107,YEB,CSR
Glenn, J.L.	Pvt	C 4th SCVC	Stony Creek, VA	12/01/64	City Pt., VA	12/05/64	Pt. Lookout, MD	CSR,CDC
					Pt. Lookout, MD	06/06/65	Rlsd. per Instr. 5/30	P114,P117,P121,CSR
Glenn, J.P.	Pvt	D Ham.Leg.	Frederick, MD	09/13/62	Frederick, MD USGH	10/22/62	Not stated	CSR
Glenn, James H.	Pvt	H 18th SCVI	Farmville, VA	04/07/65	Farmville, VA	06/08/65	Died of wounds	P6,P12,YEB,CSR
Glenn, John K.	Pvt	D Orr's Ri.	Malvern Hill, VA	07/28/64	Camp Chase, OH		Old Capital, DC	P23,CDC
					Old Capitol, DC	10/02/64	Elmira, NY	CSR
					Ft. McHenry, MD	10/24/64	Elmira, NY	P110
					Elmira, NY	02/13/65	Pt. Lookout, MD Xc	P65,P66,CSR
Glenn, Matthew T.	Pvt	G 2nd SCVIRi	Darbytown Rd., VA	10/07/64	Bermuda Hundred, VA	10/21/64	City Pt., VA P.M.	CSR
					City Pt., VA P.M.	10/29/64	Pt. Lookout, MD	CSR
					Pt. Lookout, MD	03/28/65	Aikens Ldg., VA Xc	P114,P124,CSR
Glenn, Michael	Pvt	C 27th SCVI	Petersburg, VA	06/24/64	Fts. Monroe, VA	06/26/64	Pt. Lookout, MD	CSR,HAG
					Pt. Lookout, MD	07/23/64	Elmira, NY	P113,P117,P120,CSR
					Elmira, NY	01/31/65	Died, Pneumonia	P5,P7,P65,P117,FPH
Glenn, P.A.	Cpl	A 3rd SCVABn	High Pt., NC	05/02/65	High Pt., NC	05/02/65	Paroled	CSR
Glenn, T.M.	Cpl	A 3rd SCVABn	High Pt., NC	05/02/65	High Pt., NC	05/02/65	Paroled	CSR
Glenn, Thomas A.	Cpl	L 1st SCVIG	Southside RR, VA	04/03/65	Petersburg, VA	06/27/65	Rlsd. G.O. #109	P118,P121,P123,SA1

SOUTH CAROLINA SOLDIERS, SAILORS AND  CITIZENS HELD IN U.S. PRISONS 1861-1865

NAME	RANK	REGIMENT	CAPTURED AT	WHEN	PRISON	MOVED	DISPOSITION	SOURCES
Glenn, Walker T.	Pvt	C 22nd SCVI	Crater, Pbg., VA	07/30/64	City Pt., VA	08/05/64	Pt. Lookout, MD	CSR
					Pt. Lookout, MD	08/08/64	Elmira, NY	P113,P117,P120,CSR
					Elmira, NY	07/03/65	Rlsd. G.O. #109	P65,CSR
Glines, Jacob	Pvt	I 1st SCVIR	Morris Island, SC	07/10/63	Hilton Head, SC	09/05/63	Ft. Columbus, NY	CSR
					Ft. Columbus, NY	09/23/63	Took the oath	P1,CSR
Glover, Christopher	Cpl	B 19th SCVI	Glasgow, KY		Glasgow, KY		Paroled in hospital	CSR
Glover, Colleton	Pvt	B 19th SCVI	Bardstown, KY	10/11/62	Bardstown, KY USA	11/15/62	Louisville, KY	CSR
					Louisville, KY	11/29/62	Vicksburg, MS Xc	P88,HOE,CSR
Glover, Colleton	Pvt	B 19th SCVI	Macon, GA	04/30/65	Macon, GA	04/30/65	Paroled	CSR
Glover, J.W.	Pvt	E 2nd SCVA	Charlotte, NC Hos.	05/07/65	Charlotte, NC	05/07/65	Paroled	CSR
Glover, John B.	Pvt	B 25th SCVI	Ft. Fisher, NC	01/15/65	New York, NY	01/30/65	Elmira, NY	CSR,HAG
					Elmira, NY	07/13/65	Elmira, NY USGH	P65
					Elmira, NY	07/26/65	Rlsd. G.O. #109	P66
Glover, John M.	Sgt	B Hol.Leg.	Burkeville, VA	04/04/65	City Pt., VA	04/13/65	Pt. Lookout, MD	CSR
					Pt. Lookout, MD	06/28/65	Rlsd. G.O. #109	P114,P118,P123,CSR
Glover, John R.	Pvt	C 1st SCVIG	Petersburg, VA	04/03/65	City Pt., VA	04/11/65	Hart's Island, NY	CSR
					Hart's Island, NY	05/25/65	Died, Pneumonia	P6,P79,FPH,SA1,CSR
Glover, L.H.	Pvt	F 27th SCVI	Petersburg, VA	06/24/64	Fts. Monroe, VA	06/26/64	Pt. Lookout, MD	CSR
					Pt. Lookout, MD	07/23/64	Elmira, NY	CSR
					Elmira, NY	10/11/64	Trfrd. for Xc	CSR
Glover, L.H.	Pvt	F 27th SCVI	Deserted/enemy	02/18/65	Columbia, SC		Fts. Monroe, VA	CSR
					Fts. Monroe, VA		Washington, DC	CSR
					Washington, DC	04/05/65	New York, NY oath	CSR
Glover, Mitchell O.	Pvt	I 2nd SCVC	Brandy Stn., VA	08/01/63	Ft. McHenry, MD			P110
					Old Capitol, DC	08/17/63	Pt. Lookout, MD	P110,CSR
					Pt. Lookout, MD	02/13/65	Aikens Ldg., VA Xc	P116,P121,P124,CSR
Goble, Julius	Pvt	E 3rd SCVC		02/20/64	Knoxville, TN	02/23/64	Camp Chase, OH	CSR
Godbolt, Asa	Pvt	F 7th SCVC	Fayetteville, NC	03/12/65	New Berne, NC	04/03/65	Pt. Lookout, MD	CSR
					Pt. Lookout, MD	06/27/65	Rlsd. G.O. #109	P114,P117,P121,CSR
Goddwyn, D.	Pvt	H 1st SCVIR	Morris Island, SC	07/10/63	Hilton Head, SC	09/05/63	Ft. Columbus, NY	CSR
					Ft. Columbus, NY	09/23/63	Took the oath	P1,CSR
Godfrey, Albert C.	Pvt	H 1st SCVIG	Petersburg, VA	03/25/65	City Pt., VA	03/27/65	Pt. Lookout, MD	CSR
					Pt. Lookout, MD	06/27/65	Rlsd. G.O. #109	P117,P121,P123,SA1
Godfrey, Jesse	Pvt	E Hol.Leg.	Boonesboro, MD	10/02/62	Frederick, MD Hos.	11/20/62	Ft. McHenry, MD	CSR
					Ft. McHenry, MD	12/08/62	Fts. Monroe, Xc	CSR
					Fts. Monroe, VA	12/16/62	Exchanged	CSR
					Petersburg, VA Hos.	12/19/62	Furloughed 90 days	CSR
Godfrey, John W.	Pvt	C Hol.Leg.	Petersburg, VA	11/05/64	City Pt., VA	11/11/64	Pt. Lookout, MD	CSR
					Pt. Lookout, MD	04/02/65	Died, Diarrhea	P6,P117,P119,FPH
Godfrey, Pinckney T.	Pvt	G 27th SCVI	Ft. Anderson, NC	02/19/65	Ft. Anderson, NC	02/28/65	Pt. Lookout, MD	CSR,HAG
					Pt. Lookout, MD	06/27/65	Rlsd. G.O. #109	P114,P121,P123,CSR
Godfrey, Samuel G.	1Lt	C 8th SCVI	Winchester, VA	09/13/64	Harpers Ferry, WV	09/19/64	Johnson's Isl., OH	CSR
					Johnson's Isl., OH	06/20/65	Rlsd. G.O. #109	P81,P82,P83,CSR
Godfrey, William	Pvt	E Hol.Leg.	Kinston, NC	12/15/62	Kinston, NC	12/15/62	Paroled POW	CSR
Godfrey, William H.	Pvt	H 1st SCVIG	N. Anna River, VA	05/23/64	Pt. Lookout, MD	03/14/65	Aikens Ldg., VA Xc	P116,P124,SA1,CSR
Godley, William B.	Pvt	E 11th SCVI	Petersburg, VA	06/24/64	Bermuda Hundred, VA	06/25/64	Fts. Monroe, VA	CSR
					Fts. Monroe, VA	06/26/64	Pt. Lookout, MD	CSR
					Pt. Lookout, MD	02/10/65	Aikens Ldg., VA Xc	P113,P117,HAG,CSR
Godley, William S.	Cpl	K 11th SCVI	Weldon RR, VA	08/21/64	Old Capitol, DC	08/24/64	Elmira, NY	CSR
					Ft. McHenry, MD	10/24/64	Elmira, NY	P65,HAG
					Elmira, NY	03/14/65	Pt. Lookout, MD Xc	P66

SOUTH CAROLINA SOLDIERS, SAILORS AND  CITIZENS HELD IN U.S. PRISONS 1861-1865

NAME	RANK	REGIMENT	CAPTURED AT	WHEN	PRISON	MOVED	DISPOSITION	SOURCES
Godwin, Henry Evander	Pvt	I 26th SCVI	Five Forks, VA	04/01/65	City Pt., VA	04/05/65	Pt. Lookout, MD	CSR,CTA
					Pt. Lookout, MD	06/27/65	Rlsd. G.O. #109	P118,P121,P123,CSR
Godwin, J.U.	Pvt	I 26th SCVI	Richmond, VA Hos.	04/03/65	Libby Prison Rchmd.	04/23/65	Newport News, VA	CSR
					Newport News, VA	06/26/65	Rlsd. G.O. #109	P10,CSR
Godwin, John A.	2Lt	I 26th SCVI	Dinwiddie C.H., VA	04/01/65	Old Capitol, DC	04/09/65	Johnson's Isl., OH	CSR,CTA
					Johnson's Isl., OH	06/18/65	Rlsd. G.O. #109	P81,P83
Godwin, Samuel F.R.	Cpl	H 10th SCVI	Murfreesboro, TN	12/31/62	Nashville, TN	01/07/63	Died of wounds	P12,P38,RAS,CSR
Goff, Henry M.	Pvt	H Orr's Ri.	Sutherland Stn., VA	04/02/65	City Pt., VA	04/07/65	Hart's Island, NY	CSR
					Hart's Island, NY	06/15/65	Rlsd. G.O. #109	P79,CDC,CSR
Goff, James E.	Pvt	G 14th SCVI	Richmond, VA Hos.	04/03/65	Provost Marshal	04/21/65	Libby Prison Rchmd.	CSR
					Libby Prison Rchmd.	04/23/65	Newport News, VA	CSR
					Newport News, VA	06/26/65	Rlsd. G.O. #109	P107,CSR
Goff, John	Cpl	G 3rd SCVABn	High Pt., NC	05/01/65	High Pt., NC	05/01/65	Paroled	CSR
Goff, W.C.	Pvt	D 6th SCResB	Augusta, GA	05/19/65	Augusta, GA	05/19/65	Paroled	CSR
Goings, E.B.	Pvt	A 3rd SCVI	Sharpsburg, MD	09/17/62	Lavinia Groves Fm.	09/17/62	Died of wounds	P12,H3,CSR
Goings, J.McF.	Cpl	C 7th SCVC	Columbia, VA	03/11/65	White House, VA	03/19/65	Fts. Monroe, VA	CSR
					Fts. Monroe, VA	03/25/65	Pt. Lookout, MD	CSR
					Pt. Lookout, MD	06/27/65	Rlsd. G.O. #109	P114,P117,P121,CSR
Goins, W.V.	Cpl	I Hol.Leg.	Warrenton, VA	09/29/62	Warrenton, VA	09/28/62	Paroled Hospital	CSR
Golden, Milton	Cpl	C 14th SCVI	Newton, NC	04/19/65	Newton, NC	04/19/65	Paroled	CSR
Golden, W.F.	Pvt	E 14th SCMil	Columbia, SC	02/17/65	Hart's Island, NY	06/15/65	Rlsd. G.O. #109	P79
Golding, John J.	Cpl	A 3rd SCVIBn	Gettysburg, PA	07/05/63	Letterman G.H. Gbg	07/17/63	Died of wounds	P1,P12,CSR
Golding, W.T.	Pvt	E 7th SCVC	Appomattox C.H., VA	04/09/65	U.S. 24th A.C., Fld	04/14/65	City Pt., VA USGH	CSR
					City Pt., VA USGU	04/21/65	USS Connecticut	CSR
					USS Connecticut	04/22/65	Baltimore, MD	CSR
					W. Bldg. Balt, MD	05/09/65	Ft. McHenry, MD	P1,P96
					Ft. McHenry, MD	05/09/65	Rlsd. on parole	ANY,CSR
Goleman, John	Pvt	C 19th SCVI	Danville, KY	10/13/62	Perryville, KY Hos.	01/06/63	Louisville, KY	CSR,HOE
					Louisville, KY	01/14/63	Vicksburg, MS	P88,CSR
					Camp Douglas, IL	03/18/63	City Pt., VA Xc	P54,CSR
					Petersburg, VA Hos.	04/18/63	Furloughed 40 days	CSR
Golson, James D.	Pvt	F 25th SCVI	Ft. Fisher, NC	01/16/65	Beaufort, NC	03/10/65	Died of wounds	P6,P12,CSR
Good, James K.	Pvt	G 18th SCVI	Farmville, VA	04/06/65	City Pt., VA	04/14/65	Newport News, VA	CSR,YEB
					Newport News, VA	06/15/65	Rlsd. G.O. #109	P107,CSR
Gooding, Eldred	Sgt	E 11th SCVI	Ft. Fisher, NC	01/15/65	Elmira, NY	03/02/65	Pt. Lookout, MD Xc	P65,P66,CSR
Gooding, Martin C.	Pvt	D 11th SCVI	Town Creek, NC	02/20/65	Ft. Anderson, NC	02/28/65	Pt. Lookout, MD	CSR
					Pt. Lookout, MD	06/27/65	Rlsd. G.O. #109	P114,P121,P123,CSR
Gooding, Perry	Pvt	F 11th SCVI	Swift Creek, VA	05/09/64	Hampton, VA	05/16/64	Died of wounds	P12,HAG,ROH
Gooding, Robert D.	Pvt	D 11th SCVI	Town Creek, NC	02/20/65	Ft. Anderson, NC	02/28/64	Pt. Lookout, MD	CSR
					Pt. Lookout, MD	06/27/65	Rlsd. G.O. #109	P117,P121,P123,CSR
Gooding, Thomas	Pvt	D 11th SCVI	Pocotaligo, SC	09/01/64	New Berne, NC	04/10/65	Hart' Island, NY	CSR
					Hart's Island, NY	04/23/65	Died, Dysentery	P6,P12,P79,FPH,CSR
Gooding, William L.	Pvt	D 11th SCVI	Town Creek, NC	02/20/65	Ft.Anderson, NC	02/28/64	Pt. Lookout, MD	CSR
					Pt. Lookout, MD	06/21/65	Rlsd. G.O. #109	P114,P117,P122,CSR
Goodlett, James H.	2Lt	K Ham.Leg.MI	Saylors Creek, VA	04/06/65	Old Capitol, DC	04/17/65	Johnson's Isl., OH	P110,CSR
					Johnsons Isl., OH	06/18/65	Rlsd. G.O. #109	P81,P82,P83,CSR
Goodlett, O.R.	Pvt	A 3rd SCVABn	High Pt., NC	05/02/65	High Pt., NC	05/02/65	Paroled	CSR
Goodman, John W.	Pvt	K 23rd SCVI	Five Forks, VA	04/01/65	City Pt., VA	04/05/65	Pt. Lookout, MD	CSR
					Pt. Lookout, MD	06/27/65	Rlsd. G.O. #109	P114,P118,P123,CSR
Goodman, Samuel J.	Pvt	I 26th SCVI	Petersburg, VA	03/25/65	Pt. Lookout, MD	06/27/65	Rlsd. G.O. #109	P114,P117

SOUTH CAROLINA SOLDIERS, SAILORS AND  CITIZENS HELD IN U.S. PRISONS 1861-1865

NAME	RANK	REGIMENT	CAPTURED AT	WHEN	PRISON	MOVED	DISPOSITION	SOURCES
Goodman, W.P.	Pvt	D 14th SCVI	Falling Waters, MD	07/14/63	Old Capitol, DC	08/08/63	Ft. McHenry, MD	CSR
					Ft. McHenry, MD	08/08/64	Pt. Lookout, MD	P110
					Pt. Lookout, MD	03/03/65	City Pt., VA Xc	P113,P116,P123,P124
Goodrich, Allan	Pvt	H 27th SCVI	Port Walthal Jctn. VA	05/07/65	Bermuda Hundred, VA	05/08/64	Camp Hamilton, VA	CSR,HAG
					Pt. Lookout, MD	05/28/64	Joined U.S. Army	CSR
					Camp Hamilton, VA	05/13/64	Pt. Lookout, MD	CSR
					Pt. Lookout, MD	05/28/64	Joined U.S. Army	P113,P116,P125,HAG
Goodson, A.L.	Pvt	H 8th SCVI	Winchester, VA	09/13/64	Harpers Ferry, WV	09/19/64	Camp Chase, OH	CSR
					Camp Chase, OH	06/11/65	Rlsd. G.O #109	CSR
Goodson, Allen J.	Pvt	F 1st SCVIG	Falling Waters, MD	07/14/63	Baltimore, MD	08/16/63	Pt. Lookout, MD	CSR,SA1
					Pt. Lookout, MD	08/16/64	Elmira, NY	P113,P116,P120,CSR
					Pt. Lookout, MD	08/18/64	Elmira, NY	CSR
					Elmira, NY	03/10/65	Pt. Lookout, MD Xc	P66,P65,CSR
Goodson, Henry M.	Pvt	G 17th SCVI	Petersburg, VA	03/25/65	City Pt., VA	03/28/65	Pt. Lookout, MD	CSR
					Pt. Lookout, MD	06/27/65	Rlsd. G.O. #109	P117,P121,P123,CSR
Goodson, Josiah T.	2Lt	A 8th SCVI	Winchester, VA	09/13/64	Harpers Ferry, WV	09/19/64	Johnson's Isl., OH	CSR
					Johnson's Isl., OH	06/20/65	Rlsd. G.O. #109	P81,P83,KEB,CSR
Goodson, Uzzell	Pvt	E 6th SCVI	Chattanooga, TN	10/29/63	Nashville, TN	11/07/63	Louisville, KY	CSR
					Louisville, KY	11/09/63	Camp Morton, IN	P88,P89,P93,CSR
					Camp Morton, IN	12/28/63	Died, Pneumonia	FPH,CSR
Goodson, William	Pvt	B 21st SCVI	Petersburg, VA	06/18/64	Pt. Lookout, MD	07/27/64	Elmira, NY	P113,P117,P120
					Elmira, NY	09/26/64	Died, Typhoid	P5,P12,P65,FPH
Goodwin, A.J.	Pvt	K 13th SCVI	Spotsylvania, VA	05/12/64	Belle Plain, VA	05/21/64	Ft. Delaware, DE	CSR
					Ft. Delaware, DE	05/26/64	Hos. 5/26-6/22/64	P47
					Ft. Delaware, DE	08/02/64	Hos. 8/2-8/15/64	Dd P47
					Ft. Delaware, DE	08/15/64	Died, Measles	P5,P41,P42,P42,P47
Goodwin, Alexander	Pvt	D 21st SCVI	Morris Island, SC	07/10/63	Ft. Columbus, NY	07/23/63	Took the oath	P1,HAG
					Pt. Lookout, MD	08/16/63	Elmira, NY	P113,P116,P120,HAG,FPH
					Elmira, NY	10/11/64	Pt. Lookout, MD Xc	P65,P66,P117,P124
					Pt. Lookout, MD	10/15/64	Died, Diarrhea	P12,P5,P119,P121,FPH
Goodwin, D.	Pvt	C 8th SCVI	Petersburg, VA	07/27/64	City Pt., VA	08/05/64	Pt. Lookout, MD	CSR,KEB
					Pt. Lookout, MD	08/08/64	Elmira, NY	P117,P120,CSR
					Elmira, NY	07/15/65	Rlsd. G.O. #109	P65,P66,CSR
					Elmira, NY	08/07/65	Rlsd. G.O. #109	P66,CSR
Goodwin, H.J.	Pvt	I 3rd SCVABn	Deserted/enemy	03/06/65	Fts. Monroe, VA	04/02/65	Washington, DC	CSR
					Washington, DC	04/05/65	Charleston, SC	CSR
Goodwin, Hilliard	Pvt	H SC Militia	Lexington, SC	02/16/65	New Berne, NC	03/30/65	Pt. Lookout, MD	CSR
					Pt. Lookout, MD	05/15/65	Rlsd. G.O. #85	P114,P117,CSR
Goodwin, Hiram J.	Pvt	F 14th SCVI	Cox Rd., Pbg, VA	04/03/65	City Pt., VA	04/07/65	Hart's Island, NY	CSR
					Hart's Island, NY	06/15/65	Rlsd. G.O. #109	P79,CSR
Goodwin, James G.	Pvt	Palmetto L	Deserted/enemy	03/06/65	Fts. Monroe, VA	04/02/65	Washington, DC	CSR
					Washington, DC	04/05/65	Newville, PA oath	CSR
Goodwin, P.	Pvt	F 22nd SCVI	Deserted/enemy	02/26/65	City Pt., VA	02/28/65	Washington, DC	CSR
					Washington, DC	03/01/65	Hilton Head, SC	CSR
Goodwin, Samuel	Pvt	D 21st SCVI	Morris Island, SC	07/10/63	Ft. Columbus, NY	09/26/63	Pt. Lookout, MD	P1,HAG,CSR
					Pt. Lookout, MD	08/16/64	Elmira, NY	P113,P116,P120
					Elmira, NY	03/10/65	Pt. Lookout, MD Xc	P65,P66
					Pt. Lookout, MD	03/15/65	Exchanged	P124,CSR
Goodwin, Samuel	Pvt	G 4th SCVC	Stony Creek, VA	12/01/64	City Pt., VA	12/05/64	Pt. Lookout, MD	CSR,CDC
					Pt. Lookout, MD	05/12/65	Rlsd. G.O. #85	P117,P121,CSR
Goodwin, William	Pvt	I 1st SCVA	Morris Island, SC	07/10/63	Hilton Head, SC	09/18/63	Ft. Columbus, NY	CSR
					Ft. Columbus, NY	09/23/63	Took the oath	P1

SOUTH CAROLINA SOLDIERS, SAILORS AND **G** CITIZENS HELD IN U.S. PRISONS 1861-1865

NAME	RANK	REGIMENT	CAPTURED AT	WHEN	PRISON	MOVED	DISPOSITION	SOURCES
Goodyear, John Emory	Pvt	E 1st SCVIG	Gettysburg, PA	07/05/63	Ft. Delaware, DE	08/25/63	Died	P5,P40,P42,P44,P47
Googe, W.H.	Pvt	A 19th SCVCB	Augusta, GA	05/20/65	Augusta, GA	05/19/65	Paroled on oath	CSR
Goost, G.H.	Pvt	B German LA	Deserted/enemy	10/01/64	Hilton Head, SC D.	10/13/64	New York, NY P.M.	P8,CSR
Gordon, A.B.	Pvt	K 4th SCVC	Louisa C.H., VA	06/11/64	Fts. Monroe, VA	06/20/64	Pt. Lookout, MD	CSR,CLD
					Pt. Lookout, MD	03/14/65	Aikens Ldg., VA Xc	P116,P124,CLD,CSR
Gordon, Charlton Henry	Pvt	G 15th SCVI	Gettysburg, PA	07/03/63	Ft. McHenry, MD	07/14/63	Ft. Delaware, DE	CSR
					Ft. Delaware, DE	10/19/64	Hos. 10/19-10/25/64	P47,KEB
					Ft. Delaware, DE	06/09/65	Died, Scurvy	P6,P40,P42,P45,P47
Gordon, David	Pvt	B 1st SCVA	Fayetteville, NC	03/16/65	New Berne, NC	03/30/65	Pt. Lookout, MD	CSR
					Pt. Lookout, MD	06/27/65	Rlsd. G.O. #109	P117,P121,CSR
Gordon, David E.	2Lt	I 4th SCVC	Louisa C.H., VA	06/11/64	Fts. Monroe, VA	06/20/64	Pt. Lookout, MD	CSR
					Pt. Lookout, MD	06/23/64	Ft. Delaware, DE	P113,P120,ISH,CSR
					Ft. Delaware, DE	08/20/64	Hilton Head, SC	P43,CSR
					Hilton Head, SC	10/20/64	Ft. Pulaski, GA	CSR
					Ft. Pulaski, GA	12/20/64	Hilton Head, SC	P4,CSR
					Hilton Head, SC	03/12/65	Ft. Delaware, DE	CSR
					Ft. Delaware, DE	06/17/65	Rlsd. G.O. #109	P43,P44,CTA,CSR
Gordon, J.E.	Pvt	I 17th SCVI	Deserted/enemy	02/26/65	P.M. 9th US A.C.	02/26/65	City Pt., VA	CSR
					City Pt., VA	02/28/65	Washington, DC	CSR
					Washington, DC	03/01/65	Danville, PA on oath	CSR
Gordon, J.M.	Pvt	D 6th SCVC	Petersburg, VA	07/30/64	Pt. Lookout, MD	08/08/64	Elmira, NY	P120,CSR
Gordon, John	Pvt	I 12th SCVI	Petersburg, VA	03/25/65	City Pt., VA	03/25/64	Pt. Lookout, MD	CSR
					Pt. Lookout, MD		Rlsd., date unknown	P114,P17,LAN,CSR
Gordon, Lee P.	Pvt	E 22nd SCVI	Sharpsburg, MD	09/14/62	Frederick, MD	09/30/62	Paroled	CSR
Gordon, Madison	Pvt	I 12th SCVI	Southside RR, VA	04/05/65	City Pt., VA	06/13/65	Pt. Lookout, MD	CSR,LAN
					Pt. Lookout, MD	06/21/65	Rlsd. G.O. #109	P114,P118,P122,CSR
Gordon, S.B.	Pvt	A 7th SCVC	Farmville, VA	04/11/65	Farmville, VA	04/21/65	Paroled	CSR
Gordon, Samuel	Pvt	B 1st SCVA	Fayetteville, NC	03/16/65	Pt. Lookout, MD	06/27/65	Rlsd. G.O. #109	P114
Gordon, Samuel M.	Pvt	I 12th SCVI	Deserted/enemy	02/28/65	City Pt., VA	03/01/65	Washington, DC	CSR
					Washington, DC	03/02/65	Frankfort, KY	CSR
Gordon, T.	Pvt	D 13th SCVI	Southside RR, VA	04/02/65	City Pt., VA	04/07/65	Hart's Island, NY	CSR
					Hart's Island, NY	06/14/65	Rlsd. G.O. #109	P79,CSR
Gordon, W.M.	Pvt	K 17th SCVI	Petersburg	03/25/65	City Pt., VA	03/28/65	Pt. Lookout, MD	CSR,YEB
					Pt. Lookout, MD	06/27/65	Rlsd. G.O. #109	P114,P117,P121,CSR
Gore, Jerry L.	Pvt	I Hol.Leg.	Kinston, NC	12/14/62	Kinston, NC	12/14/62	Paroled POW	CSR
Gore, Jerry L.	Pvt	I Hol.Leg.	Deserted/enemy	02/14/65	City Pt., VA	02/15/65	Washington, DC	CSR
					Washington, DC	02/21/65	Columbus, OH oath	CSR
Gore, John A.	Pvt	B Hol.Leg.	Five Forks, VA	04/01/65	City Pt., VA	04/05/65	Pt. Lookout, MD	CSR
					Pt. Lookout, MD	06/27/65	Rlsd. G.O. #109	P114,P118,P121,HOS
Gorman, Michael	Pvt	E 1st SCVA	Morris Island, SC	07/10/63	Hilton Head, SC	07/18/63	Ft. Columbus, NY	CSR
					Ft. Columbus, NY	09/23/63	Took the oath	P1,CSR
Gosnell, G.E.	Pvt	H 22nd SCVI	Deserted/enemy	02/25/65	City Pt., VA	03/01/65	Washington, DC	CSR
					Washington, DC	03/01/65	Oil City, PA oath	CSR
Gosnell, George W.	Pvt	H 22nd SCVI	Crater, Pbg., VA	07/30/64	City Pt., VA USH	08/02/64	Washington, DC	CSR
					Washington, DC	08/05/64	Pt. Lookout, MD	CSR
					Pt. Lookout, MD	08/08/64	Elmira, NY	P117,P120,P125
					Elmira, NY	05/15/65	Died, Ch. Diarrhea	P6,P12,P65,FPH,CSR
Gosnell, J.S.	Pvt	H 22nd SCVI	Deserted/enemy	02/25/65	City Pt., VA	03/01/65	Washington, DC	CSR
					Washington, DC	03/01/65	Oil City, PA oath	CSR
Gossett, John R.	2Lt	E 2nd SCVIRi	Hartwell, GA	05/15/65	Hartwell, GA	05/15/65	Paroled	CSR
Gossett, Samuel	Pvt	B Hol.Leg.	Deserted/enemy	03/01/65	City Pt., VA	03/02/65	Washington, DC	CSR
					Washington, DC	03/06/65	Cincinnatti, OH	CSR

SOUTH CAROLINA SOLDIERS, SAILORS AND  CITIZENS HELD IN U.S. PRISONS 1861-1865

NAME	RANK	REGIMENT	CAPTURED AT	WHEN	PRISON	MOVED	DISPOSITION	SOURCES
Gossett, W.A.	Pvt	G 27th SCVI	Petersburg, VA	06/24/64	Fts. Monroe, VA	06/25/64	Pt. Lookout, MD	CSR,HAG
					Pt. Lookout, MD	08/16/64	Elmira, NY	P113,P117
					Elmira, NY	10/11/64	Pt. Lookout to Xc	P65,P66
					Pt. Lookout, MD	10/29/64	Exchanged	P114,P123
Gossett, W.G.	Pvt	B Hol.Leg.	Deserted/enemy	02/14/65	City Pt., VA	02/16/64	Washington, DC	CSR
					Washington, DC	02/21/65	Columbus, OH oath	CSR
Gotti, Jacob	Pvt	D 1st SCVA	Rockingham, NC	03/09/65	New Berne, NC	04/10/65	Hart's Island, NY	CSR
					Hart's Island, NY	06/17/65	Rlsd. G.O. #109	P79,CSR
					New York, NY Tr. Hos.	06/28/65	Died	P12,CSR
Goude, Francis M.	Sgt	A 21st SCVI	Petersburg, VA	06/24/64	Bermuda Hundred, VA	08/16/64	Fts. Monroe, VA	CSR
					Fts. Monroe, VA	08/16/64	Pt. Lookout, MD	CSR
					Pt. Lookout, MD	08/16/64	Elmira, NY	P113,P120,CSR
					Elmira, NY	07/08/65	Rlsd. G.O. #109	P65,P66,CSR
Goude, John	Pvt	A 21st SCVI	Weldon RR, VA	08/21/64	City Pt., VA	08/24/64	Pt. Lookout, MD	CSR
					Pt. Lookout, MD		Ft. Delaware, DE	CSR
					Ft. Delaware, DE	09/23/64	Hos. 9/23-10/30/64	P47
					Ft. Delaware, DE	10/30/64	Venus Pt., GA Xc	CSR
					Ft. Delaware, DE	10/30/64	Aikens Ldg., VA Xc	CSR
					Camp Lee, Rchmd.	10/31/64	On roll	CSR
Goude, Joseph	Pvt	A 21st SCVI	Weldon RR, VA	08/21/64	City Pt., VA USFH	08/23/64	Alexandria, VA GH	CSR
					Alexandria, VA GH	08/27/64	Lincoln G.H., DC	CSR
					Lincoln G.H., DC	09/05/64	Old Capitol, DC	CSR
					Ft. McHenry, MD	09/19/64	Ft. Delaware, DE	P110
					Old Capitol, DC	09/19/64	Ft. Delaware, DE	CSR
					Ft. Delaware, DE	10/30/64	James R., VA Xc	CSR
					Pt. Lookout, MD	10/31/64	Exchanged	P123
Goude, Matthew	Pvt	A 21st SCVI	Petersburg, VA	06/24/64	Bermuda Hundred, VA	06/25/64	Fts. Monroe, VA	CSR
					Fts. Monroe, VA	06/26/64	Pt. Lookout, MD	CSR
					Pt. Lookout, MD	08/16/64	Elmira, NY	P113,P117,P120,CSR
					Elmira, NY	10/11/64	James R., VA Xc	P65,CSR
Goudelock, Joseph B.	Pvt	C 5th SCVI	Boonesboro, MD	09/15/62	Ft. Delaware, DE	10/02/62	Aikens Ldg., VA Xc	SA3,CSR
Goudelouck, Isaac	Pvt	F 18th SCVI	Petersburg, VA	03/25/65	Pt. Lookout, MD			P117
Gough, A.E.	Pvt	B 7th SCVC	Augusta, GA	05/18/65	Augusta, GA	05/18/65	Paroled	CSR
Gouvenier, Julius C.	Cpl	I 27th SCVI	Town Creek, NC	02/20/65	Ft. Anderson, NC	02/28/65	Pt. Lookout, MD	CSR,HAG
					Pt. Lookout, MD	06/27/65	Rlsd. G.O. #109	P121,CSR
Gowan, Peter, Jr.	Pvt	A 25th SCVI	Ft. Fisher, NC	01/15/65	New York, NY	01/30/64	Elmira, NY	CSR
					Elmira, NY	06/21/65	Rlsd. G.O. #109	P65,P66,HAG
Gowdy, J.E.	Pvt	H 26th SCVI	Deserted/enemy		City Pt., VA	04/21/65	Washington, DC	CSR
					Washington, DC		Charleston, SC	CSR
Gower, J.C.	Pvt	D Ham.Leg.	Warrenton, VA	09/29/62	Warrenton, VA	09/29/62	Paroled	CSR
Goza, J.L.	Pvt	C 12th SCVI	Sharpsburg, MD	10/01/62	Ft. McHenry, MD	10/18/62	Fts. Monroe, VA Xc	CSR
Graddick, Whitfield D.	Cpl	K 14th SCVI	Gettysburg, PA	07/04/63	Provost Marshal	07/17/63	David's Island, NY	CSR
					David's Island, NY	09/05/63	City Pt., VA Xc	P1,HOE,CSR
					City Pt., VA	09/09/63	Williamsburg Hos.	CSR
Graddick, Whitfield D.	Cpl	K 14th SCVI	Augusta, GA	05/18/65	Augusta, GA	05/18/65	Paroled	CSR
Gradeless, David	Pvt	A 21st SCVI	Petersburg, VA	06/24/64	Bermuda Hundred, VA	06/25/64	Fts. Monroe, VA	CSR,HAG
					Fts. Monroe, VA	06/26/64	Pt. Lookout, MD	CSR
					Pt. Lookout, MD	08/15/64	Elmira, NY	P113,P117,P120
					Elmira, NY	02/20/65	Pt. Lookout, MD Xc	P65,P66
Gradick, Edward W.	Pvt	I 27th SCVI	Town Creek, NC	02/20/65	Ft. Anderson, NC	02/28/65	Pt. Lookout, MD	CSR,HAG
					Pt. Lookout, MD	05/13/65	Rlsd. G.O. #85	P114,P117,P122,CSR
Grady, Henry C.	Pvt	K 2nd SCVC	Hartwell, GA	05/19/65	Hartwell, GA	05/19/65	Paroled	CSR

SOUTH CAROLINA SOLDIERS, SAILORS AND  CITIZENS HELD IN U.S. PRISONS 1861-1865

NAME	RANK	REGIMENT	CAPTURED AT	WHEN	PRISON	MOVED	DISPOSITION	SOURCES
Grady, James T.	Pvt	B 25th SCVI	Weldon RR, VA	08/21/64	City Pt., VA	08/24/64	Pt. Lookout, MD	CSR
					Pt. Lookout, MD	02/13/65	Aikens Ldg., VA Xc	P117,P121,P124,CSR
Grafford, John	Pvt	G 3rd SCVC	Deserted/enemy	03/05/65	Charleston, SC	03/15/65	Taken oath & disch.	CSR
Graffts, Charles N.	Sgt	D 21st SCVI	Cheraw, SC	03/02/65	Hart's Island, NY	06/17/65	Died, Ch. Diarrhea	P6,P12,P79,FPH,HAG
Graham, Balus B.	Pvt	D 2nd SCVIRi	Campbell Stn., TN	10/12/63	No US POW data			CSR
Graham, E.H.	2Lt	A 3rd SCVABn	High Pt., NC	05/02/65	High Pt., NC	05/02/65	Paroled	CSR
Graham, Evander M.	Sgt	K 6th SCVI	Warrenton, VA	09/29/62	Warrenton, VA	09/29/62	Paroled	CSR
Graham, Franklin	Pvt	A 2nd SCVI	Cedar Creek, VA	10/19/64	W. Bldg. Balt, MD	02/16/65	Ft. McHenry, MD Xc	P1,SA2,H2,CSR
Graham, George	Pvt	F 27th SCVI	Bentonville, NC	03/08/65	Pt. Lookout, MD	06/27/65	Rlsd. G.O. #109	P114,P117,HAG
Graham, J.M.	Pvt	G 15th SCVI	South Mtn., MD	09/14/62	Ft. Delaware, DE	10/02/62	Aikens Ldg., VA xc	CSR
Graham, J.W.	Pvt	A 19th SCVI	Augusta, GA	05/20/65	Augusta, GA	05/20/65	Paroled	CSR
Graham, James	Pvt	D 25th SCVI	Ft. Fisher, NY	01/15/65	New York, NY	01/30/65	Elmira, NY	CSR,HAG
					Elmira, NY	02/01/65	Died, Remit. fever	P5,P12,P65,FPH
Graham, John	Drm	E 1st SCVA	Fayetteville, NC	03/11/65	New Berne, NC	03/30/65	Pt. Lookout, MD	CSR
					Pt. Lookout, MD	05/13/65	Released G.O. #85	P114,P117,P122,CSR
Graham, John W.	Pvt	E 1st SCVC	Cherokee Co., AL	07/12/64	Louisville, KY	07/26/64	Camp Douglas, IL	P90,P91,P94
					Camp Douglas, IL	04/03/65	Joined US Army	P53,CSR
Graham, L.	Pvt	C 2nd SCRes	Charlotte, NC	05/12/65	Charlotte, NC	05/12/65	Paroled	CSR
Graham, Lewis Wills	Pvt	D 2nd SCVIRi	Farmville, VA	04/07/65	Farmville, VA		No relesase data	CSR
Graham, Nathaniel	Pvt	B 15th SCVAB	North Carolina	03/28/65	New Berne, NC USGH	04/04/65	Died, Consumption	P1,P6,P12,WAT,CSR
Graham, Neil F.	1Sg	K 6th SCVC	Stony Creek, VA	12/01/64	City Pt., VA	12/04/64	Pt. Lookout, MD	CSR
					Pt. Lookout, MD	05/12/65	Released G.O. #85	P114,P117,P121,CSR
Graham, S.J.	Pvt	I 26th SCVI	Petersburg, VA	03/25/65	City Pt., VA	03/27/65	Pt. Lookout, MD	CSR,CTA
					Pt. Lookout, MD	06/27/65	Rlsd. G.O. #109	P121,P123,CSR
Graham, Samuel R.H.	Pvt	E 22nd SCVI	Kinston, NC	12/15/62	Kinston, NC	12/15/62	Paroled POW	CSR
Graham, Thomas J.	Pvt	B 3rd SCVI	Gettysburg, PA	07/02/63	Ft. McHenry, MD	07/12/63	Ft. Delaware, DE	CSR
					Ft. Delaware, DE	07/10/65	Rlsd. G.O. #109	P42,P45,H3,ANY,CSR
Graham, William H.	Pvt	H 23rd SCVI	Five Forks, VA	04/01/65	City Pt., VA	04/06/65	Pt. Lookout, MD	CSR
					Pt. Lookout, MD	06/27/65	Rlsd. G.O. #109	P118,P121,P123,CSR
Graham, Windsor	Pvt	E 19th SCVCB	Bennettsville, SC	03/06/65	New Berne, NC	04/03/65	Pt. Lookout, MD	CSR
					Pt. Lookout, MD	06/27/65	Rlsd. G.O. #109	P117,P121,CSR
Grainger, Thomas W.	Pvt	K 26th SCVI	Petersburg, VA	04/02/65	City Pt., VA	04/05/65	Pt. Lookout, MD	CSR
					Pt. Lookout, MD	06/04/65	Released on oath	P114,P118,CSR
Grambling, A.M.	Cpl	B 20th SCVI	Strasburg, VA	10/23/64	Harpers Ferry, WV	10/23/64	Pt. Lookout, MD	CSR
					Pt. Lookout, MD	03/19/65	Died, Scurvy	P6,P12,P114,P117,P119,CS
Grambling, Frederick H.	Pvt	B 20th SCVI	Cedar Creek, VA	10/19/64	Harpers Ferry, WV	10/23/64	Pt. Lookout, MD	CSR
					Pt. Lookout, MD	06/27/65	Rlsd. G.O. #109	KEB,CSR
Grambling, Isaac H.	Pvt	B 20th SCVI	Cedar Creek, VA	10/19/64	Pt. Lookout, MD	06/27/65	Rlsd. G.O. #109	P121,KEB
Grambling, Martin Luther	Pvt	F 25th SCVI	Ft. Fisher, NC	01/15/65	New York, NY	01/30/65	Elmira, NY	CSR
					Elmira, NY	07/07/65	Rlsd. G.O. #109	P65,P66,HAG
Grandshig, Charles	SMj	1st SCVIR	Deserted/enemy	02/18/65	Charleston, SC		Released on oath	CSR
Granger, Samuel P.	Pvt	H 23rd SCVI	Deserted/enemy	03/05/65	City Pt. VA	03/08/65	Washington, DC	CSR
					Washington, DC	03/08/65	Mason City, Iowa	CSR
Grant, A.R.	Pvt	C 4th SCVC	Deserted/enemy	10/15/64	City Point, VA	10/22/64	Fts. Monroe, VA	P8,CSR
					Fts. Monroe, VA	11/14/64	Cincinnatti, OH	CSR
Grant, Barnabas	Pvt	E 4th SCVC	Louisa C.H., VA	06/11/64	Fts. Monroe, VA	06/20/64	Pt. Lookout, MD	CSR,HOM
					Pt. Lookout, MD	07/23/64	Elmira, NY	P116,P120,FPH,CSR
					Elmira, NY	01/31/65	Died, Diarhea	P5,P12,P65,FPH,CSR
Grant, Benjamin Andrew	Pvt	B 4th SCVC	Louisa C.H., VA	06/11/64	Fts. Monroe, VA	06/20/64	Pt. Lookout, MD	CSR,HHC
					Pt. Lookout, MD	07/25/64	Elmira, NY	P113,P116,P120,CSR
					Elmira, NY	06/14/65	Rlsd. G.O. #109	P65,CSR

SOUTH CAROLINA SOLDIERS, SAILORS AND  CITIZENS HELD IN U.S. PRISONS 1861-1865

NAME	RANK	REGIMENT	CAPTURED AT	WHEN	PRISON	MOVED	DISPOSITION	SOURCES
Grant, Bird C.	Pvt	D Orr's Ri.	Deserted/enemy	02/21/65	City Pt., VA	02/21/65	Washington, DC	CSR
					Washington D.C.	02/24/65	Burlington, Iowa	CSR
Grant, D.B.	Pvt	B 26th SCVI	Cheraw, SC	03/08/65	New Berne, NC	04/25/65	Hart's Island, NY	CSR
					Camp Hamilton, VA	05/01/65	Newport News, VA	CSR
					Newport, News, VA	06/16/65	Rlsd. G.O. #109	CSR
Grant, E.M.	Pvt	B 12th SCVI	Petersburg, VA	04/03/65	Hart's Island, NY	06/19/65	Rlsd. G.O. #109	P79
Grant, H.D.	Pvt	C 8th SCVI	Gettysburg, PA	07/03/63	Letterman G.H. Gbg	08/10/63	Balt & City Point	P1,KEB
					W. Bldg. Balt, MD	11/12/63	City Pt., VA Xc	P1,CSR
Grant, J.F.	Pvt	F 1st SCVIR	Cheraw, SC	03/05/65	City Pt., VA	04/11/65	Hart's Island, NY	CSR
					Hart's Island, NY	06/17/65	Rlsd. G.O. #109	P79,SA1,CSR
Grant, James T.	Sgt	D 26th SCVI	Cheraw, SC	03/05/65	New Berne, NC	04/10/65	Hart's Island, NY	CSR
					Hart's Island, NY	06/17/65	Rlsd. G.O. #109	P79,HOM
Grant, John	Pvt	B 4th SCVC	Louisa C.H., VA	06/11/64	Fts. Monroe, VA	06/20/64	Pt. Lookout, MD	CSR,HAG
					Pt. Lookout, MD	07/25/64	Elmira, NY	P113,P116,P120,CSR
					Elmira, NY	03/02/65	James R., VA Xc	P65,CSR
					Richmond, VA Hos.	03/09/65	Furloughed 30 days	CSR
Grant, Robert A.	Msc	1st SCVIR	Deserted/enemy	03/25/65	Charleston, SC	03/25/65	Released on oath	SA1,CSR
Grant, Samuel G.	Pvt	D 2nd SCVIRi	Burkeville, VA	04/14/65	Burkeville, VA	04/17/65	Paroled	CSR,OCS
Grant, Thomas	Pvt	D 21st SCVI	Petersburg, VA	06/27/64	Pt. Lookout, MD	02/10/65	Aikens Ldg., VA Xc	P114,P121,P124,HAG
Grant, W.G.	Pvt	K 2nd SCVIRi	Burkeville, VA	04/14/65	Burkeville, VA	04/17/65	Paroled	CSR
Grant, W.R.	Pvt	D 21st SCVI	Ft. Fisher, NC	01/15/65	Elmira, NY	03/02/65	Pt. Lookout to Xc	P65,P66,HAG
Grantham, R.W.	Pvt	H 21st SCVI	Ft. Fisher, NC	01/15/65	Elmira, NY	03/05/65	Died, Pneumonia	P5,P65,P66,HAG,FPH
Graser, George G.	Pvt	B 27th SCVI	Town Creek, NC	02/20/65	Ft. Anderson, NC	02/28/65	Pt. Lookout, MD	CSR,HAG
					Pt. Lookout, MD	05/13/65	Rlsd. G.O. #85	P114,P117,P122,CSR
Gratton, Daniel	Pvt	H 27th SCVI	Deserted/enemy	10/08/64	Bermuda Hundred, VA	10/09/64	City Pt., VA	CSR,HAG
					City Pt., VA	10/11/64	Washington, DC	CSR
					Washington, DC	10/12/64	New York, NY oath	CSR
Graver, Henry	Pvt	B German LA	Deserted/enemy	03/15/65	Charleston, SC	03/15/65	Released on oath	CSR
Graves, Bennett F.	Pvt	Ferguson's	Ringgold, GA	12/01/63	Nashville, TN	12/13/63	Louisville, KY	P39,CSR
					Louisville, KY	12/13/63	Rock Island, IL	P88,CSR
					Rock Island, IL	01/25/64	Joined US Navy	P131,CSR
Graves, G.C.	Pvt	G 1st SCVC	Raleigh, NC Hos.	04/13/65	U.S. Prov. Marshal	05/05/65	Paroled	CSR
Graves, Jacob S.	Pvt	F Hol.Leg.	Petersburg, VA	11/05/64	City Pt., VA	11/11/64	Washington, DC	CSR
					Pt. Lookout, MD	06/27/65	Rlsd. G.O. #109	P121,CSR
Graves, Joseph.	2Lt	G 25th SCVI	Ft. Fisher, NC	01/15/65	Ft. Columbus, NY	02/25/65	City Pt., VA Xc	P2,HAG,CSR
Graves, William W.	Pvt	C 27th SCVI	Town Creek, NC	02/20/65	Ft. Anderson, NC	02/28/65	Pt. Lookout, MD	CSR
					Pt. Lookout, MD	05/13/65	Rlsd. G.O. #85	P7,P114,P117,CSR
Gray, Alfred	Pvt	B 25th SCVI	Weldon RR, VA	08/20/64	Alexandria, VA Hos.	09/01/64	Died of wounds	P1,P6,P7,P12,HAG
Gray, Daniel A.	Pvt	K 21st SCVI	Wilmington, NC	02/20/65	Pt. Lookout, MD	06/27/65	Rlsd. G.O. #109	P114,P117,HAG
Gray, Jacob W.	Pvt	D 11th SCVI	Town Creek, NC	02/20/65	Ft. Anderson, NC	02/28/65	Pt. Lookout, MD	CSR,HAG
					Pt. Lookout, MD		No record found	P114,P117,CSR
Gray, James	Pvt	1st SCVIR	Cheraw, SC	03/05/65	Cheraw, SC	03/05/65	Paroled	CSR
Gray, James A.	1Lt	F 24th SCVI	Taylors Ridge, GA	10/15/64	Nashville, TN	10/23/64	Louisville, KY	CSR
					Louisville, KY	10/24/64	Johnson's Isl., OH	P91,P93,CSR
					Johnson's Isl., OH	06/16/65	Rlsd. G.O. #109	P81,P83,CSR
Gray, Joel	Pvt	H 7th SCVIBn	Ft. Darling, VA.	05/16/64	Bermuda Hundred, VA	05/17/64	Fts. Monre VA USG	CSR,HAG
					Fts. Monroe, VA	07/28/64	Pt. Lookout, MD	CSR
					Pt. Lookout, MD	02/10/65	Aikens Ldg., VA Xc	P113,P117,CSR
Gray, John T.	1Sg	D 14th SCVI	Sutherland Stn., VA	04/03/65	City Pt., VA	04/07/65	Hart's Island, NY	CSR
					Hart's Island, NY	06/16/65	Rlsd. G.O. #109	P79,CSR
Gray, Richard F.	Pvt	I 26th SCVI	Sayler's Creek, VA	04/06/65	City Pt., VA	04/19/65	Washington, DC	CSR
					Lincoln G.H., DC	06/12/65	Rlsd. G.O. #109	CSR

SOUTH CAROLINA SOLDIERS, SAILORS AND  CITIZENS HELD IN U.S. PRISONS 1861-1865

NAME	RANK	REGIMENT	CAPTURED AT	WHEN	PRISON	MOVED	DISPOSITION	SOURCES
Gray, Robert	Pvt	G 23rd SCVI	Five Forks, VA	04/01/65	City Pt., VA	04/06/65	Pt. Lookout, MD	CSR,HOM
					Pt. Lookout, MD	06/27/65	Rlsd. G.O. #109	P114,P118,P121,CSR
Gray, William	Pvt	G 23rd SCVI	Petersburg, VA	03/25/65	City Pt., VA	03/27/65	Pt. Lookout, MD	CSR,HOM
					Pt. Lookout, MD	06/27/65	Rlsd. G.O. #109	P114,P117,CSR
Gray, William H.	Pvt	K P.S.S.	Deserted/enemy	03/20/65	Bermuda Hundred, VA	03/24/65	Washington, DC	CSR
					Washington, DC	03/25/65	Memphis, TN oath	CSR,TSE
Gray, William S.	Pvt	B 1st SCVIR	Fayetteville, NC	03/10/65	New Berne, NC	04/03/65	Pt. Lookout, MD	CSR
					Pt. Lookout, MD	06/27/65	Rlsd. G.O. #109	P117,P121,P123,SA1
Graylish, Hugh	Pvt	E 18th SCVAB	Deserted/enemy	02/18/65	Charleston, SC	03/13/65	Released on oath	CSR
Grayson, Arthur B.	Cpl	E 24th SCVI	Nashville, TN	12/16/64	Nashville, TN	12/31/64	Louisville, KY	CSR
					Louisville, KY	01/05/65	Camp Chase, OH	P95,EFW
					Camp Chase, OH	06/13/65	Rlsd. G.O. #109	P23,CSR
Grayson, Edward H.	Cpl	D 24th SCVI	Nashville, TN	12/16/64	Nashville, TN	12/31/64	Louisville, KY	CSR
					Louisville, KY	01/05/65	Camp Chase, OH	P95,CSR
					Camp Chase, OH	06/12/65	Rlsd. G.O.#109	P23,CSR
Grayson, John M.	Pvt	C 25th SCVI	Ft. Fisher, NC	01/15/65	New York, NY	01/30/65	Pt. Lookout, MD	CSR,CTA,HAG
					Pt. Lookout, MD	02/22/65	Hammond G.H., MD	P114,P121
					Pt. Lookout, MD	06/26/65	Rlsd. G.O. #109	P117
Greason, John A.	Pvt	G 2nd SCVIRi	Burkesville, VA	04/14/65	Burkeville, VA	04/17/65		CSR
Green, B.Y.	Sgt	C 23rd SCVI	Five Forks, VA	04/02/65	City Pt., VA	04/04/65	Pt. Lookout, MD	CSR
					Pt. Lookout, MD	06/27/65	Rlsd. G.O. #109	CSR
Green, E.	Pvt	C 23rd SCVI	Spotsylvania, VA	05/12/64	Elmira, NY	05/04/65	Died	P6,FPH
Green, E.B.	Cpt	K 21st SCVI	Ft. Fisher, NC	01/15/65	Ft. Columbus, NY	03/01/65	City Pt., VA Xc	P2,HAG
Green, Henry	Sgt	F 1st SCVA	Fayetteville, NC	03/11/65	New Berne, NC	03/30/65	Pt. Lookout, MD	CSR
					Pt. Lookout, MD	05/13/65	Rlsd. G.O. #85	P114,P117,P122,CSR
Green, J.E.	Pvt	B 22nd SCVI	Crater, Pbg., VA	07/30/64	City Pt., VA	08/02/64	Washington, DC	CSR
Green, J.J.	Pvt	E 1st SCVIH	Augusta, GA	05/20/65	Augusta, GA	05/20/65	Paroled	CSR
Green, J.P.	Pvt	F 2nd SCVC	Hartwell, GA	05/19/65	Hartwell, GA	05/19/65	Paroled	CSR
Green, Jackson	Pvt	K 19th SCVI	Nashville, TN	12/16/64	Nashville, TN	12/21/64	Louisville, KY	CSR
					Louisville, KY	12/21/64	Camp Douglas, IL	P90,P94,CSR,HOE
					Camp Douglas, IL	06/19/65	Rlsd. G.O. #109	P55,CSR
Green, James	Pvt	K 19th SCVI	Augusta, GA	05/20/65	Augusta, GA	05/20/65	Paroled	CSR
Green, James Alexander	Pvt	B 22nd SCVI	Crater, Pbg., VA	07/30/64	City Pt., VA	08/05/64	Pt. Lookout, MD	CSR
					Pt. Lookout, MD	08/08/64	Elmira, NY	P113,P117,P120,FPH
					Elmira, NY	05/21/65	Died, Diarrhea	P6,P12,P65,FPH
Green, James J.	Pvt	D Hol.Leg.	Five Forks, VA	04/01/65	City Pt., VA	04/05/65	Pt. Lookout, MD	CSR
					Pt. Lookout, MD	06/22/65	Rlsd. G.O. #109	P118,P121,P123,CSR
Green, James W.	Pvt	A 3rd SCVABn	High Pt., NC	05/02/65	High Pt., NC	05/02/65	Paroled	CSR
Green, John	Pvt	K 19th SCVI	Glasgow, KY		Glasgow, KY		Paroled	CSR
Green, John J.	Cpl	Palmetto LA	Burkeville, VA	04/14/65	Burkeville, VA	04/16/65	City Pt., VA	CSR
					City Pt., VA		Fts. Monroe, VA	US CSR
					Fts. Monroe, VA US	05/06/65	Died, Erysipelas	CSR
Green, John T.	Pvt	K 5th SCVI	Deserted/enemy	02/28/65	City Pt., VA	03/03/65	Washington, DC	CSR
					Washington, DC P.M.	03/06/65	New York, NY oath	CSR
Green, Julian F.	Pvt	Ham.Leg.MI	Richmond, VA	04/11/65	Richmond, VA	04/11/65	Amnesty oath	CSR
Green, Louis V.	Pvt	D Ham.Leg.	Fair Oaks, VA	05/31/62	Fts. Monroe, VA	06/21/62	Died of wounds	P12,ROH,PP,CSR
Green, M.D.	2Lt	D 5th SCRes	Augusta, GA	05/20/65	Augusta, GA	05/20/65	Paroled	CSR
Green, M.V.	Cpl	A 1st SCVIG	Sharpsburg, MD	09/28/62	Ft. McHenry, MD	11/12/62	Paroled to Xc	SA1,CSR
Green, P.G.	Pvt	C 15th SCVI	Hartwell, GA	05/19/65	Hartwell, GA	05/19/65	Paroled	CSR
Green, Patrick M.	Pvt	B 1st SCVA	Fayetteville, NC	03/16/65	New Berne, NC	03/30/65	Pt. Lookout, MD	CSR
					Pt. Lookout, MD	05/13/65	Rlsd. G.O. #85	P114,P117,CSR
Green, R.R.	Pvt	G Ham.Leg.MI	Farmville, VA	04/11/65	Farmville, VA	04/11/65	Paroled	CSR

SOUTH CAROLINA SOLDIERS, SAILORS AND CITIZENS HELD IN U.S. PRISONS 1861-1865

NAME	RANK	REGIMENT	CAPTURED AT	WHEN	PRISON	MOVED	DISPOSITION	SOURCES
Green, S.H.	Pvt	K 2nd SCVC	Hartwell, GA	05/19/65	Hartwell, GA	05/19/65	Paroled	CSR
Green, S.M.	Pvt	B 1st SCVA	Bentonville, NC	03/25/65	Pt. Lookout, MD	05/13/65	Released G.O. #85	P122
Green, Samuel	Pvt	K 19th SCVI	Glasgow, KY	09/22/62	Glasgow, KY	09/22/62	Paroled	CSR
Green, Stephen M.	1Lt	D Hol.Leg.	Dinwiddie C.H., VA	04/01/65	City Pt., VA	04/05/65	Washington, DC	CSR
					Washington, DC	04/09/65	Johnson's Isl., OH	CSR
					Johnson's Isl., OH	06/18/65	Rlsd. G.O. #109	P81,P82,P83,CSR
Green, Thomas	Pvt	H 1st SCVIR	Morris Island, SC	07/10/63	Hilton Head, SC	07/21/63	Took oath	SA1,CSR
Green, W.M.	Pvt	F 6th SCVI	Williamsburg, VA	05/05/62	Fts. Monroe, VA	08/31/62	Aikens Ldg., VA Xc	CSR
Green, W.W.	Sgt	D Hol.Leg.	Five Forks, VA	04/01/65	City Pt., VA	04/05/65	Pt. Lookout, MD	CSR
					Pt. Lookout, MD	06/27/65	Rlsd. G.O. #109	P118,P121,P123,CSR
Green, William H.	Pvt	K 2nd SCVI	Winchester, VA	09/19/64	Pt. Lookout, MD	01/28/65	Hammond G.H., MD	P114,P121,KEB,CSR
					W. Bldg. Balt, MD	02/16/65	Ft. McHenry, MD	P1,CSR
					Pt. Lookout, MD	06/05/65	Rlsd. Instr. 5/30/65	SA2,P122,H2,CSR
Green, William R.	Pvt	K 16th SCVI	Graysville, GA	11/27/63	Nashville, TN	12/09/63	Louisville, KY	P39,16R,CSR
					Louisville, KY	12/11/63	Rock Island, IL	P88,P89,CSR
					Rock Island, IL	05/23/64	Joined US Navy	P131,CSR
Greenburg, Martin	Pvt	B 1st SCVA	NC or SC	04/01/65	New Berne, NC USGH	04/04/65	Died, Lung Infl.	P1,P6,P12,CSR
Greene, Bynum	Sgt	C 23rd SCVI	Five Forks, VA	04/01/65	Pt. Lookout, MD	06/26/65	Rlsd. G.O. #109	P114,P118,P121
Greenwood, Elly B.	Sgt	H 23rd SCVI	Five Forks, VA	04/01/65	City Pt., VA	04/05/65	Pt. Lookout, MD	CSR,HMC
					Pt. Lookout, MD	06/27/65	Rlsd. G.O. #109	P114,P118,P121,CSR
Greenwood, J.T.	Pvt	Ferguson's LA	Jackson, MS	07/17/63	Jackson, MS	07/30/63	Snyders Bluff, MS	CSR
					Snyders Bluff, MS	08/07/63	Camp Morton, IN	CSR
					Camp Morton, IN	05/20/65	Rlsd. G.O. #85	P100,CSR
Greenwood, James L.	Pvt	H 23rd SCVI	Five Forks, VA	04/01/65	City Pt., VA	04/05/65	Pt. Lookout, MD	CSR,HMC
					Pt. Lookout, MD	06/27/65	Rlsd. G.O. #109	P118,P121,CSR
Greer, David R.	2Lt	K Orr's Ri.	Appomattox R., VA	04/08/65	Ft. McHenry, MD	04/21/65	Johnson's Isl., OH	P110,CDC
					Old Capitol, DC	04/21/65	Johnson's Isl., OH	CSR
					Johnson's Isl., OH	06/17/65	Rlsd. G.O. #109	P82,P83,CSR
Greer, J.C.	Pvt	A 12th SCVI	Gettysburg, PA	07/03/63	David's Island, NY	10/22/63	Fts. Monroe, VA Xc	P1,CSR
Greer, J.N.	Pvt	F 2nd SCVC	Hartwell, GA	05/19/65	Hartwell, GA	05/19/65	Paroled	CSR
Greer, John F.	1Sg	A 2nd SCVIRi	Richmond, VA Hos.	04/03/65	Richmond, VA Hos.	04/20/65	Richmond, VA P.M.	CSR
Greer, John G.	Pvt	F 16th SCVI	Franklin, TN	12/18/64	Nashville, TN	01/04/65	Louisville, KY	P3,P39,16R,CSR
					Louisville, KY	01/09/65	Camp Chase, OH	P92,P94,CSR
					Camp Chase, OH	06/13/65	Rlsd. G.O. #109	P23,CSR
Greer, R.P.	Pvt	A 3rd SCVABn	High Pt., NC	05/02/65	High Pt., NC	05/02/65	Paroled	CSR
Greer, Robert A.	Pvt	K Orr's Ri.	Petersburg, VA	04/02/65	City Pt., VA	04/07/65	Hart's Island, NY	CSR
					Hart's Island, NY	06/15/65	Rlsd. G.O. #109	P79,CSR
Greer, Thomas J.	1Lt	B 18th SCVI	Hatchers Run, VA	03/29/65	City Pt., VA	04/09/65	US Hos. Stmr. *Maine*	CSR
					US Hos. Stmr. *Maine*	04/15/65	Washington, DC Hos.	CSR
					Washington, DC Hos.	06/06/65	Rlsd. G.O. #109	CSR
Greer, William Robert	Pvt	B 25th SCVI	Ft. Fisher, NC	01/15/65	New York, NY	01/30/65	Elmira, NY	CSR,HAG
					Elmira, NY	06/28/65	Rlsd. G.O. #109	P65,P66,CSR
Gregg, A. Stuart	Sgt	I 8th SCVI	Winchester, VA	09/13/64	Harpers Ferry, WV	09/19/64	Camp Chase, OH	CSR
					Camp Chase, OH	06/11/65	Rlsd. G.O. #109	P23,KEB,HMC,CSR
Gregg, A.M.	Sgt	K 21st SCVI	Ft. Fisher, NC	01/15/65	Elmira, NY	06/23/65	Rlsd. G.O. #109	P65,P66
Gregg, Alford E.	Pvt	L 10th SCVI	Nashville, TN	12/15/64	Louisville, KY	12/20/64	Camp Douglas, IL	P90,P91,P94,CSR
					Camp Douglas, IL	06/19/65	Rlsd. G.O. #109	P55,RAS,CSR
Gregg, H.W.	Pvt	C 1st SCVIR	Fayetteville, NC	03/16/65	New Berne, NC	04/10/65	Pt. Lookout, MD	CSR,SA1
					Pt. Lookout, MD	06/08/65	Rlsd. G.O. #109	P114,P117,121,CSR
Gregg, Henry Junius	Pvt	I 7th SCVC	Appomattox C.H., VA	04/08/65	U.S. 24th A.C. Fld.	04/13/65	Farmville, VA USGH	CSR
					Farmville, VA USGH	04/30/65	Died, of wounds	P6,P12,ROH,CSR

SOUTH CAROLINA SOLDIERS, SAILORS AND  CITIZENS HELD IN U.S. PRISONS 1861-1865

NAME	RANK	REGIMENT	CAPTURED AT	WHEN	PRISON	MOVED	DISPOSITION	SOURCES
Gregg, John W.	Pvt	H 8th SCVI	Winchester, VA	09/13/64	Harpers Ferry, WV	09/19/64	Camp Chase, OH	CSR,KEB,HMC
					Camp Chase, OH	04/09/65	Died, Ch. Diarrhea	P6,P12,P27,FPH
					Camp Chase, OH	06/11/65	Released	P23
Gregg, Robert L.	Pvt	C 3rd SCVABn	Blakely, AL	04/09/65	Ship Island, MS	05/01/65	New Orleans, LA	P136,CSR
					New Orleans, LA	05/04/65	Died, Ch. Diarrhea	CSR
Gregg, S.E.	Pvt	H 8th SCVI	Winchester, VA	09/13/64	Harpers Ferry, WV	09/19/64	Camp Chase, OH	CSR
					Camp Chase, OH	06/11/65	Rlsd. G.O.#109	P23,CSR
Gregg, Smiley E.	1Lt	McQueen LA	Petersburg, VA	04/03/65	City Pt., VA	04/04/65	Washington, DC	CSR
					Old Capitol, DC	06/03/65	Johnson's Isl., DC	CSR
					Johnson's Isl., OH	06/16/65	Rlsd. G.O. #109	CSR
Gregg, T.C.	Pvt	B 21st SCVI	Ft. Fisher, NC	01/15/65	Elmira, NY	06/23/65	Rlsd. G.O. #109	P65,P66
Gregg, W.W.	Pvt	I 21st SCVI	Ft. Fisher, NC	01/15/65	New York, NY	01/30/65	Elmira, NY	CSR
					Elmira, NY	02/20/65	Pt. Lookout, MD Xc	P65,P66
					Wayside Hos. Rchmd	03/03/65	Dead on arrival	CSR
Gregg, William M.	Pvt	5 10/19 SCVI	Missionary Ridge TN	11/25/63	Nashville, TN	12/07/63	Louisville, KY	P39,CSR
					Louisville, KY	12/09/63	Rock Island, IL	P88,P89,CSR
					Rock Island, IL	06/19/65	Rlsd. G.O. #109	CSR
Gregory, G. Sanford	Pvt	A 18th SCVI	Hatchers Run, VA	03/29/65	City Pt., VA	04/02/65	Pt. Lookout, MD	CSR
					Pt. Lookout, MD	06/27/65	Rlsd. G.O. #109	P114,P121,P122,CSR
Gregory, Isaac S.	Sgt	F 22nd SCVI	Petersburg, VA	03/25/65	City Pt., VA	03/28/65	Pt. Lookout, MD	CSR
					Pt. Lookout, MD	06/27/65	Rlsd. G.O. #109	P114,P117,CSR
Gregory, J.W.	Pvt	D 19th SCVI	Raleigh, NC Hos.	04/13/65	Raleigh, NC Hos.	04/13/65	Paroled	CSR
Gregory, John	Pvt	A 18th SCVI	Crater, Pbg., VA	07/30/64	City Pt., VA	08/05/65	Pt. Lookout, MD	CSR
					Pt. Lookout, MD	08/08/64	Elmira, NY	P117,P120,P125,UD5
					Elmira, NY	12/09/64	Died, Diarrhea	P5,P65,P66,FPH,CSR
Gregory, John B.	Pvt	C Hol.Leg.	Five Forks, VA	04/01/65	City Pt., VA	04/05/65	Pt. Lookout, MD	CSR
					Pt. Lookout, MD	06/27/65	Rlsd. G.O. #109	P118,P121,P123,CSR
Gregory, John G.A.	Pvt	H 20th SCVI	Lexington, SC	02/10/65	New Berne, NC	03/10/65	Pt. Lookout, MD	CSR,KEB
					Pt. Lookout, MD	06/27/65	Rlsd. G.O. #109	P114,P117,P121,CSR
Gregory, Oliver J.	Pvt	H Ham.Leg.	Knoxville, TN	12/05/63	Nashville, TN	01/24/64	Louisville, KY	P39,CSR
					Louisville, KY	01/27/64	Rock Island, IL	P88,P93,CSR
					Rock Island, IL	03/13/65	Pt. Lookout, MD Xc	P7,P131,CSR
Gregory, Owen	Pvt	I 1st SCVIH	Farmville, VA	04/11/65	Farmville, VA	04/21/85	Paroled	CSR
Gregory, Starks	Pvt	B 18th SCVI	Petersburg, VA	07/30/64	US Field Hosp. Pbg	08/02/64	City Pt., VA Hos.	CSR
Gregory, William H.	Pvt	D 1st SCVIH	Mossy Creek, TN	01/22/64	Nashville, TN	02/11/64	Louisville, KY	P39,SA1,CSR
					Louisville, KY	02/15/64	Rock Island, IL	P88,P91,P93,CSR
					Rock Island, IL	06/18/65	Rlsd. G.O. #109	P131,CSR
Gregory, William S.	Pvt	A 18th SCVI	Petersburg, VA	03/25/65	City Pt., VA	03/28/65	Pt. Lookout, MD	CSR,UD5
					Pt. Lookout, MD	06/27/65	Rlsd. G.O. #109	P114,P117,P121,CSR
Gresham, E.L.	Pvt	I 15th SCVI	Halltown, VA	08/26/64	Camp Chase, OH	03/26/65	Camp Lookout, MD	P26
					Pt. Lookout, MD	06/05/65	Released	P114,P118
Grey, Andrew	Pvt	B 20th SCVI	Cedar Creek, VA	10/19/64	Harpers Ferry, WV	10/23/64	Pt. Lookout, MD	CSR,KEB
					Pt. Lookout, MD	06/27/65	Rlsd. G.O. #109	P121,P123,CSR
Gribble, James H.	Pvt	B Ham.Leg.	Dandridge, TN	01/17/64	Nashville, TN	01/24/64	Louisville, KY	P39,CSR
					Louisville, KY	01/27/64	Rock Island, IL	P88,CSR
					Rock Island, IL	03/13/65	Pt. Lookout, MD Xch	P131
Grice, Frank	Pvt	G 27th SCVI	Petersburg, VA	06/24/64	Pt. Lookout, MD	08/15/64	Elmira, NY	P113,P117,P120,CSR
					Elmira, NY	10/11/64	Pt. Lookout, MD XC	P66,CSR
					Pt. Lookout, MD	10/29/64	Exchanged	P114,P123,HAG,CSR
Grice, Henry W.	Pvt	A 19th SCVI	Murfreesboro, TN	12/31/62	Murfreesboro Hos.	05/14/63	Died of wounds	P38,HOE,CSR

SOUTH CAROLINA SOLDIERS, SAILORS AND  CITIZENS HELD IN U.S. PRISONS 1861-1865

NAME	RANK	REGIMENT	CAPTURED AT	WHEN	PRISON	MOVED	DISPOSITION	SOURCES
Grice, John E.	Pvt	B 14th SCVI	Petersburg, VA	07/29/64	City Pt., VA	08/05/64	Pt. Lookout, MD	CSR,HOE
					Pt. Lookout, MD	08/08/64	Elmira, NY	P117,P120,P125,CSR
					Elmira, NY	10/11/64	Pt. Lookout, MD	P65,P66,CSR
					Pt. Lookout, MD	11/06/64	Died	P5,P119,FPH,CSR
Grice, M.	Pvt	A 7th SCVI	Knoxville, TN	12/03/63	Louisville, KY	12/31/63	Rock Island, IL	P89
					Louisville, KY	02/17/64	Died, Tuberculosis	P93,CNM,CSR
Grice, W.	Pvt	E 6th SCResB	Augusta, GA	05/18/65	Augusta, GA	05/18/65	Paroled	CSR
Grier, T. Coke	Pvt	A 21st SCVI	Ft. Fisher, NC	01/15/65	New York, NY	01/30/65	Elmira, NY	CSR
					Elmira, NY	03/02/65	Pt. Lookout, MD Xc	P65,P66,HAG,CSR
Grier, William S.	Pvt	A 21st SCVI	Ft. Fisher, NC	01/15/65	Elmira, NY	03/12/65	Died, Ch. Diarrhea	P5,P12,P65,P66,CSR
Grieshaber, G. Fritz	Pvt	A 15th SCVI	Halltown, VA	08/26/64	Harpers Ferry, WV	09/02/64	Camp Chase, OH	CSR,KEB
					Camp Chase, OH	03/26/65	Pt. Lookout, MD	P26,CSR
					Pt. Lookout, MD	06/27/65	Rlsd. G.O. #109	P114,P119,P121,CSR
Griffin, A. Brown	Pvt	F 25th SCVI	Ft. Fisher, NC	01/15/65	New York, NY	01/30/65	Elmira, NY	CSR,HAG
					Elmira, NY	05/06/65	Died, Diarrhea	P6,P12,P65,P66,FPH
Griffin, Benjamin F.	Pvt	B Hol.Leg.	Hatchers Run, VA	03/25/65	City Pt., VA	04/02/65	Pt. Lookout, MD	CSR
					Pt. Lookout, MD	06/27/65	Rlsd. G.O. #109	P121,CSR
Griffin, E. William	Pvt	A 5th SCVC	Pbg/Rchmd Pike, VA	05/12/64	Fts. Monroe, VA	05/15/64	Pt. Lookout, MD	CSR
					Pt. Lookout, MD	05/21/64	Joined U.S. Army	P113,P116,P125,CSR
Griffin, Elihu W.	Pvt	A 3rd SCVIBn	Frederick, MD	09/12/62	Ft. Delaware, DE	10/02/62	Aikens Ldg., VA Xc	CSR
Griffin, Elihu W.	Pvt	A 3rd SCVIBn	Knoxville, TN	12/18/63	Louisville, KY	01/23/64	Rock Island, IL	P88,P93,CSR
					Rock Island, IL	02/15/65	Pt. Lookout, MD Xc	P131,CSR
Griffin, George W.	Pvt	D 12th SCVI	Deserted/enemy	01/17/65	City Point, VA	01/19/65	Washington, DC	P8,CSR
					Washington, DC	01/20/65	Philadelphia, PA	CSR
Griffin, Henry	Pvt	I 1st SCVA	Morris Island, SC	07/10/63	Hilton Head G.H.	07/24/63	Paroled & Exchanged	P2,CSR
Griffin, Henry	Pvt	F 22nd SCVI	Petersburg, VA	03/25/65	City Pt., VA	03/28/65	Pt. Lookout, MD	CSR
					Pt. Lookout, MD	06/27/65	Rlsd. G.O. #109	P114,P117,P121,CSR
Griffin, Henry J.F.	Pvt	F 25th SCVI	Ft. Fisher, NC	01/15/65	New York, NY	01/30/65	Elmira, NY	CSR,HAG
					Elmira, NY	05/16/65	Died, Diarrhea	P6,P12,P65,P66,FPH
Griffin, J.F.	Pvt	G 2nd SCVC	Prince William Cty.	03/21/63	Old Capitol, DC	04/17/63	City Pt., VA Xc	CSR
Griffin, J.R.	Pvt	I 11th SCVI	Petersburg, VA	06/16/64	Bermuda Hundred VA	06/17/65	Fts. Monroe, VA	CSR
					Fts. Monroe, VA	06/18/64	Pt. Lookout, MD	CSR
					Pt. Lookout, MD	07/25/64	Elmira, NY	P113,P116,P120,CSR
					Elmira NY	02/09/65	Pt. Lookout for Xc	CSR
					Elmira, NY	02/13/65	Aikens Ldg., VA Xc	P65,P66,CSR
Griffin, John	Pvt	F 25th SCVI	Ft. Fisher, NC	01/15/65	Fts. Monroe, VA	02/01/65	Pt. Lookout, MD	CSR,HAG
					Pt. Lookout, MD	06/27/65	Rlsd. G.O. #109	P114,P121,HAG
Griffin, John Mc.	Pvt	B 13th SCVI	Sheppardstown, MD	07/28/62	Knoxville, MD	10/20/62	Ft. McHenry, MD	CSR
					Ft. McHenry, MD	10/25/62	Aikens Ldg., VA Xc	CSR
Griffin, Joseph H.	Pvt	C 13th SCVI	Petersburg, VA	04/02/65	City Pt., VA	04/07/65	Pt. Lookout, MD	CSR,HOS
					Pt. Lookout, MD	06/27/65	Rlsd. G.O. #109	P114,P118,P121,CSR
Griffin, Larkin A.	Sgt	B Orr's Ri.	Fredericksburg, VA	05/03/63	Washington, DC	05/10/63	City Pt., VA	CSR,CDC
					City Pt., VA	05/13/63	Exchanged	CSR
Griffin, Larkin A.	Sgt	B Orr's Ri.	Spotsylvania, VA	05/12/64	Fredericksburg, VA	05/23/64	Washington, DC Hos.	CSR
					Lincoln G.H., DC	06/08/64	Died of wounds	P1,P5,P12,P110,CSR
Griffin, Nolan	Pvt	K 27th SCVI	Petersburg, VA	05/10/64	Bermuda Hundred VA	05/11/64	Fts. Monroe, VA	CSR,HAG
					Fts. Monroe, VA	07/14/64	Pt. Lookout, MD	CSR
					Pt. Lookout, MD	08/16/64	Elmira, NY	CSR
					Elmira, NY	10/11/64	Pt. Lookout, MD Xc	P66,CSR
					Pt. Lookout, MD	10/29/64	Venus Pt., GA Xc	P114,P117,P123
Griffin, R.T.	Pvt	C 2nd SCVA	Deserted/enemy	03/05/65	Charleston, SC		Released on oath	CSR
Griffin, Robert C.	Pvt	F 5th SCVI	Sharpsburg, MD	09/17/62	Frederick, MD G.H.	09/30/62	Died, of wounds	P1,P6,FPH,SA3,CSR

SOUTH CAROLINA SOLDIERS, SAILORS AND  CITIZENS HELD IN U.S. PRISONS 1861-1865

NAME	RANK	REGIMENT	CAPTURED AT	WHEN	PRISON	MOVED	DISPOSITION	SOURCES
Griffin, Samuel N.	Pvt	E 6th SCVC	Petersburg, VA	07/30/64	City Pt., VA	08/04/64	Pt. Lookout, MD	CSR
					Pt. Lookout, MD	08/08/64	Elmira, NY	P117,P120,P125
					Elmira, NY	03/14/65	Tfd. for exchange	P65,CSR
Griffin, Silas	Pvt	A 14th SCMil	Lynch's Creek, SC	03/01/65	Hart's Island, NY	06/04/65	Died, Ch. Diarrhea	P6,P12,P79,FPH
Griffin, Silas D.	Pvt	F 25th SCVI	Ft. Fisher, NC	01/15/65	New York, NY	01/30/65	Elmira, NY	CSR,HAG
					Elmira, NY	07/11/65	Rlsd. G.O. #109	P65,P66,CSR
Griffin, Stephen	Pvt	D 15th SCVI	Gettysburg, PA	07/04/63	Letterman G.H. Gbg	10/15/63	Baltimore, MD	P1,CSR
					W. Bldg. Balt, MD	11/12/63	City Pt., VA Xc	P1,CSR
Griffin, T.J.	Pvt	B 15th SCVAB	Smithfield, NC	03/16/65	New Berne, NC	03/30/65	Pt. Lookout, MD	CSR
					Pt. Lookout, MD	06/27/65	Rlsd. G.O. #109	CSR
Griffin, Vincent	Pvt	G 2nd SCVC	Augusta, GA	05/24/65	Augusta, GA	05/24/65	Paroled	CSR
Griffin, W.A.	Pvt	B 18th SCVI	Deserted/enemy	02/25/65	Prov. Marshal	02/26/65	City Pt., VA	CSR
					City Pt., VA	02/26/65	Washington, DC	CSR
					Washington, DC	03/05/65	Baltimore, MD oath	CSR
Griffin, William	Pvt	K 11th SCVI	Town Creek, NC	02/20/65	Ft. Anderson, NC	02/28/64	Pt. Lookout, MD	CSR,HAG
					Pt. Lookout, MD	06/27/65	Rlsd. G.O. #109	P117,P121,P123,CSR
Griffin, William H.	Pvt	D 27th SCVI	Town Creek, NC	02/20/65	Ft. Anderson, NC	02/28/65	Pt. Lookout, MD	CSR,HAG
					Pt. Lookout, MD	06/27/65	Rlsd. G.O. #109	P114,P117,P121,CSR
Griffith, Aaron	Pvt	A 3rd SCVABn	High Pt., NC	05/02/65	High Pt., NC	05/02/65	Paroled	CSR
Griffith, George	Pvt	Ferguson's LA	Calhoun, GA	05/18/64	Nashville, TN	05/30/64	Louisville, KY	P2,CSR
					Louisville, KY	07/06/64	Camp Morton, IN	P91,P93,CSR
Griffith, Henry W.	Pvt	F 27th SCVI	Town Creek, NC	02/20/65	Ft. Anderson, NC	02/28/65	Pt. Lookout, MD	CSR,HAG
					Pt. Lookout, MD	06/27/65	Rlsd. G.O. #109	P117,P121,123,CSR
Griffith, James	Pvt	E 24th SCVI	Nashville, TN	12/16/64	Louisville, KY	01/04/65	Camp Chase, OH	P91,P92,EFW
					Camp Chase, OH	03/21/65	Died, Pneumonia	P6,P12,P23,P27,FPH
Griffith, Jesse G.	Pvt	C 27th SCVI	Town Creek, NC	02/20/65	Ft. Anderson, NC	02/28/65	Pt. Lookout, MD	CSR,HAG
					Pt. Lookout, MD	05/13/65	Rlsd. G.O. #85	P114,P117,CSR
Griffith, Robert J.	Pvt	B 26th SCVI	Amelia C.H., VA	04/03/65	City Pt., VA	04/07/65	Pt. Lookout, MD	CSR
					Pt. Lookout, MD	06/27/65	Rlsd. G.O. #109	P118,P121,P123,CSR
Griffith, William M.	Cpl	B 16th SCVI	Nashville, TN	12/16/64	Nashville, TN	12/19/64	Louisville, KY	CSR,16R
					Louisville, KY	12/21/64	Camp Douglas, IL	P90,P94,CSR
					Camp Douglas, IL	02/20/65	Pt. Lookout, MD Xc	P55,CSR
					Richmond, VA Hos.	03/01/65	Camp Lee, Prld POW	CSR
Griffiths, William B.	Pvt	D 14th SCVI	Gettysburg, PA	07/04/63	David's Island, NY	09/05/63	City Pt., VA Xc	P1,HOE,CSR
					Williamsburg, VA H	09/13/63	Furloughed	CSR
Griggs, Clement	Pvt	B 26th SCVI	Five Forks, VA	04/01/65	City Pt., VA	04/07/65	Pt. Lookout, MD	CSR
					Pt. Lookout, MD	06/27/65	Rlsd. G.O. #109	P118,P121,P123,CSR
Griggs, Henry	Pvt	Ch'fld LA	Lynchburg, VA	04/15/65	Lynchburg, VA	04/15/65	Paroled per SUR	CSR
Griggs, John W.	Pvt	B 26th SCVi	Crater, Pbg., VA	07/30/64	City Pt., VA	08/05/64	Pt. Lookout, MD	CSR
					Pt. Lookout, MD	08/08/64	Elmira, NY	P117,P120,P125,CSR
					Elmira, NY	10/11/64	Venus Pt., GA Xc	CSR,P65
Grimes, L.O.	Pvt	E 1st SCVC	Brandy Stn., VA	08/06/63	Ft. McHenry, MD		Pt. Lookout, MD	P110
					Old Capitol, DC	08/17/63	Pt. Lookout MD	CSR
					Pt. Lookout, MD	04/27/64	City Pt., VA Xc	P113,P116,P123,CSR
Grimsley, A.P.	Cpl	C 3rd SCVABn	Blakely, AL	04/09/65	Ship Island, MS	05/01/65	Vicksburg, MS Xc	P136,CSR
Griner, Jesse W.	Pvt	F 11th SCVI	Swift Creek, VA	05/09/64	Hampton, VA Hos.	06/17/64	Died of wounds	P12,ROH,CSR
Grist, John T.	Pvt	B 1st SCVA	Fayetteville, NC	03/16/65	New Berne, NC		Pt. Lookout, MD	CSR
					Pt. Lookout, MD	06/27/65	Rlsd. G.O. #109	P114,P117,CSR
Grogan, James Henry	Pvt	F 16th SCVI	Franklin, TN	12/18/64	Nashville, TN USGH	02/23/65	Died, Gangrene	P3,P5,P6,16R,CSR
Grogan, Robert	Pvt	B 2nd SCVIri	Deserted/enemy	03/03/65	Bermuda Hundred VA	03/03/64	City Pt., VA P.M.	CSR
					City Pt., VA P.M.	03/05/65	Washington, DC P.M.	CSR
					Washington, DC P.M	03/07/65	Bradford Cty., PA	CSR

SOUTH CAROLINA SOLDIERS, SAILORS AND **G** CITIZENS HELD IN U.S. PRISONS 1861-1865

NAME	RANK	REGIMENT	CAPTURED AT	WHEN	PRISON	MOVED	DISPOSITION	SOURCES
Groom, Charles D.	Pvt	G 5th SCVC	Trevillian Stn., VA	06/11/64	Fts. Monroe, VA	06/20/64	Pt. Lookout, MD	CSR
					Pt. Lookout, MD	11/01/64	Aikens Ldg., VA Xc	P123,P124
					Pt. Lookout, MD	11/01/64	Venus Pt., GA Xc	CSR
Groomes, R.E.	Pvt	B 11th SCVI	Darbytown Road, VA	09/30/64	Bermuda Hundred VA	10/08/64	City Pt., VA	CSR,HAG
					City Pt., VA	10/28/64	Pt. Lookout, MD	CSR
					Pt. Lookout, MD	06/03/65	Rlsd. Instr. 5/30/65	P114,P121,CSR
Grooms, Absalar	Pvt	A 24th SCVI	Deserted/enemy	04/01/65	Charleston, SC	04/01/65	Released on oath	CSR
Grooms, James	Cpl	C 11th SCVI	Town Creek, NC	02/20/65	Ft. Anderson, NC	02/28/65	Pt. Lookout, MD	CSR,HAG
					Pt. Lookout, MD	06/03/65	Rlsd. Instr. 5/30/65	P114,P117,P121,CSR
Grooms, Peter S.	Pvt	D 1st SCVIR	Deserted/enemy	02/18/65	Charleston, SC	03/02/65	Released on oath	SA1,CSR
Gross, John G.	Pvt	B 15th SCVI	Petersburg, VA	07/27/64	City Pt., VA	08/05/64	Pt. Lookout, MD	CSR,KEB
					Pt. Lookout, MD	08/08/64	Elmira, NY	P113,P120,CSR
					Elmira, NY	12/07/64	Died, Ch. Diarrhea	P5,P12,P66,FPH,CSR
Grove, Reuben H.	Sgt	F 1st SCVA	Bentonville, NC	03/22/65	New Berne, NC	04/10/65	Hart's Island, NY	CSR
					Hart's Island, NY	06/14/65	Rlsd. G.O. #109	P79,CSR
Grover, John H.	Pvt	I 27th SCVI	Petersburg, VA	06/24/64	Pt. Lookout, MD	07/23/64	Elmira, NY	P113,P120,HAG
					Elmira, NY	10/11/64	Tfd. for exchange	P65
					Pt. Lookout, MD	10/29/64	Aikens Ldg., VA Xc	P114,P117
Groves, Reginald N.	Cpl	I 14th SCVI	Hanover Jctn., VA	05/24/64	Pt. Lookout, MD	03/14/65	Aikens Ldg., VA Xc	P113,P116,P124,CSR
Grow, George	Pvt	D 1st SCVIG	Newton, VA	05/24/64	White House, VA	06/08/64	Pt. Lookout, MD	CSR
					Pt. Lookout, MD	07/09/64	Elmira, NY	CSR
					Elmira, NY	06/21/65	Rlsd. G.O. #109	CSR
Grubbs, A.J.	Pvt	E Hol.Leg.	Petersburg, VA	04/03/65	Petersburg Hos.	04/07/65	U.S. Gen. Hos.	CSR
					U.S. Gen. Hos.	04/08/65	Pt. of Rocks Hos.	CSR
Grubbs, Bardie	Pvt	E Hol.Leg.	Petersburg, VA	04/03/65	U.S. Gen. Hos. Pbg	04/07/65	Pt. of Rocks Hos.	CSR
Grubbs, J.	Pvt	C 1st SCVA	Smith's Ford, NC	03/16/65	New Berne, NC	04/03/65	Pt. Lookout, MD	CSR
					Pt. Lookout, MD	06/27/65	Rlsd. G.O. #109	P114,P117,P121,CSR
Grubbs, James M.	Pvt	E Hol.Leg.	Petersburg, VA	03/25/65	City Pt., VA	03/28/65	Pt. Lookout, MD	CSR
					Pt. Lookout, MD	06/27/65	Rlsd. G.O. #109	P117,P121,CSR
Grubbs, John	Pvt	D 17th SCVI	Crater, Pbg., VA	07/30/64	City Pt., VA	08/05/64	Pt. Lookout, MD	CSR
					Pt. Lookout, MD	08/08/64	Elmira, NY	P113,P117,P120,CSR
					Elmira, NY	07/07/65	Rlsd. G.O. #109	P65,P66,HHC,CSR
Grubbs, Joseph	Pvt	A 1st SCVIG	Gettysburg, PA	07/02/63	David's Island, NY	10/22/63	Fts. Monroe, VA Xc	P1,SA1,CSR
Grubbs, Samuel	Pvt	C 1st SCVA	Smith's Ford, NC	03/16/65	New Berne, NC	04/03/65	Pt. Lookout, MD	CSR
					Pt. Lookout, MD	06/27/65	Rlsd. G.O. #109	P114,P117,CSR
Grubbs, T.	Pvt	2nd SCVI	Cheraw, SC	03/05/65	Cheraw, SC	03/05/65	Paroled	CSR
Grubbs, Thomas	Pvt	C 1st SCVA	Smith's Ford, NC	03/16/65	Pt. Lookout, MD	06/15/65	Died, Diarrhea	P6,P117,P119,FPH
Gruber, Alexander	Pvt	B 23rd SCVI	Deserted/enemy	11/28/64	City Point, VA	12/05/64	Phila., PA on oath	P8,CSR
Gruber, Levi Henry	Pvt	C 3rd SCVI	Wilderness, VA	05/06/64	Belle Plain, VA	03/24/64	Ft. Delaware, DE	CSR
					Ft. Delaware, DE	07/28/64	Hos. 7/29-8/1/64	P47
					Ft. Delaware, DE	06/10/65	Released	P41,P42,P45,SA2,H2,ANY
Grumbles, George B.	Pvt	E 14th SCVI	Warrenton, VA	09/29/62	Warrenton, VA	09/29/62	Paroled	CSR
Grumbles, William W.	Pvt	E 3rd SCVIBn	Boonesboro, MD	09/15/62	Baltimore, MD Hosp	11/03/62	Aikens Ldg., VA Xc	CSR
Gruver, J.R.	Pvt	C Ham.Leg.MI	Deserted/enemy	01/07/65	Bermuda Hundred VA	01/08/65	Washington, DC	CSR
					Washington, DC	01/11/65	Baltimore, MD oath	CSR
Gubbins, John	Pvt	B 1st SCVA	Cape Fear R., NC	03/15/65	New Berne, NC	03/30/65	Pt. Lookout, MD	CSR
					Pt. Lookout, MD	05/13/65	Rlsd. G.O. #85	P114,P117,CSR
Gueast, Sidney B.	Pvt	G 2nd SCVIRi	Burkeville, VA	04/14/65	Burkeville, VA	04/17/65	Paroled	CSR

SOUTH CAROLINA SOLDIERS, SAILORS AND  CITIZENS HELD IN U.S. PRISONS 1861-1865

NAME	RANK	REGIMENT	CAPTURED AT	WHEN	PRISON	MOVED	DISPOSITION	SOURCES
Guerard, Jacob John	1Lt	C 11th SCVI	Petersburg, VA	05/09/64	Bermuda Hundred VA	05/11/64	Fts. Monroe, VA	CSR,HAG
					Fts. Monroe, Va	05/14/64	Pt. Lookout, MD	CSR
					Pt. Lookout, MD	06/23/64	Ft. Delaware, DE	P42,P116,P120,FPH
					Ft. Delaware, DE	07/17/64	Hos. 7/17/64-?	P47
					Ft. Delaware, DE	08/17/64		P47
					Ft. Delaware, DE	09/14/64	Died, Ch. Diarrhea	P5,P12,P47,FPH
Guerry, Elisha J.	Pvt	D 4th SCVC	Stony Creek, VA	12/01/64	City Pt., VA	12/05/64	Pt. Lookout, MD	CSR,CDC
					Pt. Lookout, MD	06/27/65	Rlsd. G.O. #109	P117,P12P2123
Guerry, John J.	Pvt	G 1st SCVA	Deserted/enemy	03/21/65	Charleston, SC		Released on oath	CSR
Guess, S.D.M.	Pvt	I 5th SCVC	Augusta, GA	05/18/65	Augusta, GA	05/18/65	Paroled	CSR
Guess, William	Pvt	C 25th SCVI	Ft. Anderson, NC	02/19/65	Ft. Anderson, NC	02/28/65	Pt. Lookout, MD	CSR,HAG,CTA
					Pt. Lookout, MD	06/27/65	Rlsd. G.O. #109	P114,P117,P121,CSR
Guilfoil, Michael	Pvt	B 1st SCVA	Natchez, MS	09/07/63	discharged on oath	09/10/63		CSR
Guin, Cater	Sgt	B 26th SCVI	Southside RR, VA	04/01/65	City Pt., VA	04/05/65	Pt. Lookout, MD	CSR
					Pt. Lookout, MD	06/27/65	Rlsd. G.O. #109	P118,P121,P123,CSR
Guin, John W.	Pvt	B 26th SCVI	Five Forks, VA	04/01/65	City Pt., VA	04/05/65	Pt. Lookout, MD	CSR
					Pt. Lookout, MD	06/27/65	Rlsd. G.O. #109	P118,P121,P123,CSR
Guinn, George	Pvt	F 21st SCVI	Bennettsville, SC	03/06/65	New Berne, NC	04/03/65	Pt. Lookout, MD	CSR
					Pt. Lookout, MD	06/27/65	Rlsd. G.O. #109	P121,HOM,CSR,HAG
Gunn, J.W.	Pvt	A 19th SCVI	Augusta, GA	05/19/65	Augusta, GA	05/19/65	Paroled	CSR
Gunnels, William M.	3Lt	D 3rd SCVIBn	Gettysburg, PA	07/02/63	Letterman G.H. Gbg	08/10/63	Provost Marshal	P1,KEB
					Letterman G.H. Gbg	08/10/63	Baltimore, MD	CSR
					Baltimore, MD	08/18/63	Ft. McHenry, MD	CSR
					Ft. McHenry, MD	09/28/63	Johnson's Isl., OH	P96,P144,CSR
					Johnson's Isl., OH	03/14/65	Pt. Lookout, MD	P80,P81,P82,CSR
					Pt. Lookout, MD	03/22/65	Cox's Wharf, VA Xc	CSR
Gunter, D. Jackson	Pvt	C 16th SCVI	Rome, GA	10/13/64	Camp Douglas, IL	02/01/65	Died, Typhoid	P6,FPH,CSR
Gunter, John G.	Pvt	K 8th SCVI	Winchester, VA	09/13/64	Harpers Ferry, WV	09/19/64	Camp Chase, OH	CSR
					Camp Chase, OH	06/11/65	Rlsd. G.O. #109	P23,KEB,CSR
Gunter, Joshua J.	Pvt	I 20th SCVI	Cedar Creek, VA	10/19/64	Baltimore, MD Hosp	10/28/64	Pt. Lookout, MD	CSR
					Pt. Lookout MD	10/29/64	Venus Pt., GA Xc	P114,P117,P123,CSR
Gunter, Tilman	Cpt	F P.S.S.	Hanging Rock, SC	02/25/65	Pt. Lookout, MD	04/03/65	Washington, DC	P114,P120
					Johnson's Isl., OH	06/17/65	Rlsd. G.O. #109	P81
Gunter, W.J.	Pvt	M 7th SCVI	Cedar Creek, VA	10/19/64	Harper's Ferry, WV	10/25/64	Pt. Lookout, MD	CSR
					Pt. Lookout, MD	12/27/64	Died, Ch. Diarrhea	P5,P114,P117,P119
Gunter, William H.	Pvt	I 20th SCVI	Cedar Creek, VA	10/19/64	Winchester, VA USH	10/29/64	Baltimore, MD	CSR,KEB
					Frederick, MD USGH	11/14/64	Baltimore, MD	P3,CSR
					W. Bldg. Balt, MD	01/07/65	Pt. Lookout, MD	P1
					Pt. Lookout, MD	01/28/65	Hammond G.H., MD	P114,P121
					Pt. Lookout, MD	02/13/65	Paroled for Xc	P114,P117,P124
					Hammond G.H., MD	04/07/65	Pt. Lookout, MD	CSR
					Pt. Lookout, MD	06/05/65	Rlsd. Instr. 5/30/65	P117,P121,P122
Gunther, John	Pvt	A 15th SCVI	Russellville, TN	04/26/64	Knoxville, TN	05/13/64	Nashville, TN	P1,P84
					Nashville, TN USGH	05/16/64	Louisville, KY	P2,KEB,CSR
					Louisville, KY	05/21/64	Camp Morton, IN	P88,P91,P93,CSR
					Camp Morton, IN	05/20/65	Released on oath	P100,CSR
Gunthorp, Osmund R.	1Lt	F 17th SCVI	Petersburg, VA	03/25/65	Old Capitol, DC	03/30/65	Ft. Delaware, DE	CSR
					Ft.McHenry, MD	03/30/65	Ft. Delaware, DE	P110
					Ft. Delaware, DE	06/17/65	Rlsd. G.O. #109	P43,P45,CSR
Guy, John W.	Sgt	I 27th SCVI	Town Creek, NC	02/20/65	Ft. Anderson, NC	02/28/65	Pt. Lookout, MD	CSR,HAG
					Pt. Lookout, MD	05/15/65	Rlsd. G.O. #85	P114,P117,P121,CSR

SOUTH CAROLINA SOLDIERS, SAILORS AND  CITIZENS HELD IN U.S. PRISONS 1861-1865

NAME	RANK	REGIMENT	CAPTURED AT	WHEN	PRISON	MOVED	DISPOSITION	SOURCES
Guyton, Aaron M.	2Lt	D Orr's Ri.	Appomattox R., VA	04/03/65	Army of Potomac	04/08/65	Old Capitol, DC	CSR
					Old Capitol, DC	04/21/65	Johnson's Isl., OH	CSR
					Ft.McHenry, MD	04/21/65	Johnson's Isl., OH	P110,CDC
					Johnson's Isl., OH	06/18/65	Rlsd. G.O. #109	P81,P82,P83,CSR
Guyton, James R.	Pvt	D Orr's Ri.	Petersburg, VA	04/03/65	City Pt., VA	04/11/65	Hart's Island, NY	CSR
					Hart's Island, NY	06/16/65	Rlsd. G.O. #109	P79,CSR
Guyton, John	Pvt	D 12th SCVI	Maryland		Aikens Ldg., VA Xc	09/27/62	Paroled & Exchange	CSR
Guyton, W.J.	Pvt	D Orr's Ri.	Petersburg, VA	04/03/65	City Pt., VA	04/11/65	Hart's Island, NY	CSR
					Hart's Island, NY	06/16/65	Rlsd. G.O. #109	P79,CSR
Gwin, James M.	Pvt	E 14th SCVI	Gettysburg, PA	07/03/63	Provost Marshal	07/17/63	David's Island, NY	CSR
					David's Island, NY	09/16/63	City Pt., VA Xc	CSR
					Williamsburg, VA H	09/24/63	Furloughed	CSR
Gwinn, Chesley D.	Pvt	G P.S.S.	Farmville, VA	04/06/65	City Pt., VA	04/14/65	Newport News, VA	CSR
					Newport News, VA	06/26/65	Rlsd. G.O. #109	P107,TSE,YEB
Gwinn, Jesse	Pvt	E 14th SCVI	Gettysburg, PA	07/03/63	David's Island, NY	10/22/63	Fts. Monroe, VA Xc	P1,CSR
Gwinn, Jesse	1Lt	E 14th SCVI	Appomattox, R., VA	04/03/65	Old Capitol, DC	04/17/65	Johnsons Isl., OH	P110,CSR
Gwinn, Jesse	1Lt	E 14th SCVI	Saylors Creek, VA	04/03/65	Johnsons Isl., OH	06/18/65	Rlsd. G.O. #109	P81,P83,CSR
Gwinn, Thomas	Pvt	G P.S.S.	Knoxville, TN	01/05/64	Nashville, TN	01/17/64	Louisville, KY	CSR
					Louisville, KY	01/27/64	Rock Island, IL	CSR
					Rock Island, IL	05/03/65	New Orleans, LA Xc	P131,CSR
					New Orleans, LA	05/23/65	Exchanged	P3,CSR
Gwinn, Thomas Murphy	Pvt	A 12th SCVI	Petersburg, VA	04/02/65	City Pt., VA	04/04/65	Pt. Lookout, MD	CSR
					Pt. Lookout, MD	06/27/65	Rlsd. G.O. #109	P117,P121,P123,CSR
Gwynne, Thomas A.	Pvt	C 1st SCVA	Raleigh, NC	04/20/65	Raleigh, NC		Paroled	CSR
Gyles, Frank E.	Sgt	B 25th SCVI	Ft. Fisher, NC	01/15/65	New York, NY	01/30/65	Elmira, NY	CSR,HAG
					Elmira, NY	03/14/65	James R., VA Xc	P65,P66,CSR

SOUTH CAROLINA SOLDIERS, SAILORS AND  CITIZENS HELD IN U.S. PRISONS 1861-1865

NAME	RANK	REGIMENT	CAPTURED AT	WHEN	PRISON	MOVED	DISPOSITION	SOURCES
Haas, H.	Pvt	G 2nd SCVI	Petersburg, VA	04/06/65	City Pt., VA	04/16/65	Newport News, VA	CSR
Habenicht, John D.	Pvt	A 18th SCVAB	Deserted/enemy	04/06/65	Charleston, SC	04/06/65	Taken oath & disch.	CSR
Hadden, A. Franklin	Pvt	G Orr's Ri.	Falling Waters, MD	07/14/63	Hagerstown, MD Hos.		Frederick, MD Hos.	P2,CSR
					Pt. Lookout, MD	02/10/65	Died, Typhoid	P6,P12,P113,FPH,CSR
					W. Bldg. Balt, MD	08/14/63	Ft. McHenry, MD	P1
					Baltimore, MD Hos.	08/21/63	Pt. Lookout, MD	CSR
Hadden, A. Franklin	Pvt	G Orr's Ri.	Falling Waters, MD	07/14/63	Frederick, MD USGH	08/07/65	Baltimore, MD Hos.	CSR
Hadden, James H.	Pvt	B 13th SCVI	Deserted/enemy	02/24/65	City Pt., VA	02/26/65	Washington, DC	CSR
					Washington, DC	02/27/65	Salem, OH on oath	HOS,CSR
Hadden, Michael D.	Pvt	B 13th SCVI	Deserted/enemy	02/24/65	City Pt., VA	02/26/65	Washington, DC	CSR
					Washington, DC	02/26/65	Salem, OH on oath	HOS,CSR
Haddon, Samuel P.	Cpl	D 7th SCVI	Knoxville, TN	12/05/63	Nashville, TN	02/11/64	Louisville, KY	P39,KEB,CSR
					Louisville, KY	02/15/64	Rock Island, IL	CSR
					Rock Island, IL	02/15/65	Trnfd for Xc	CSR
Haddy, John	Smn	CS Navy	Morris Island, SC	09/07/63	Pt. Lookout, MD	01/21/64	Joined U.S. Army	P125
Hadwin, John	Pvt	F 3rd SCVC	South Newport, GA	08/17/64	Philadelphia, PA	01/10/64	Ft. Delaware, DE	CSR
					Ft. Delaware, DE	05/18/65	Died, Ch. Diarrhea	P6,P41,P42,P43,P45
Hadwin, William	Pvt	A 19th SCVCB	Augusta, GA	06/02/65	Augusta, GA	06/02/65	Paroled on oath	CSR
Hagan, Edward	Pvt	F Hol.Leg.	Five Forks, VA	04/01/65	City Pt., VA	04/05/65	Pt. Lookout, MD	CSR
					Pt. Lookout, MD	06/27/65	Rlsd. G.O. #109	P114,CSR
Hagans, J.	Pvt	E 3rd SCVABn	Raleigh, NC	04/13/65	Pettigrew H. Raleigh	04/23/65	Paroled	CSR
Hagans, John C.	Pvt	Brooks LA	Gettysburg, PA	07/04/63	Ft. McHenry, MD	07/14/63	Ft. Delaware, DE	CSR
					Ft. Delaware, DE	07/30/63	Paroled for Xc	P40,P44,CSR
Hage, Arnold	Pvt	B German LA	Chambersburg, PA	07/02/63				CSR
Hagins, Robert J.	Pvt	I 12th SCVI	Gettysburg, PA	07/04/63	Ft. McHenry, MD	07/07/63	Ft. Delaware, DE	CSR,LAN
					Ft. Delaware, DE	06/10/65	Released	P42,P44,P45,CSR
Hagood, A.	Pvt	F 1st SCVIH	Warrenton, VA	09/29/62	Warrenton, VA	09/29/62	Paroled	CSR
Hagood, Jesse M.	Pvt	F 7th SCVIBn	Petersburg, VA	06/16/64	Bermuda Hundred, VA	06/17/64	Fts. Monroe, VA	CSR,HAG
					Fts. Monroe, VA	06/19/64	Pt. Lookout, MD	CSR
					Pt. Lookout, MD	07/25/64	Elmira, NY	P113,P120,CSR
					Elmira, NY	09/19/64	Died, Pneumonia	P5,P12,P65,P66,CSR
Hagood, Lemuel D.	Pvt	D 14th SCVI	Falling Waters, MD	07/14/63	Provost Marshal	07/23/63	Old Capitol, DC	CSR,HOE
					Old Capitol, DC	08/09/63	Pt. Lookout, MD	CSR
					Pt. Lookout, MD	11/12/63	Hammond G.H., MD	P113,CSR
					Hammond G.H., MD	03/17/64	Exchanged	P124,CSR
Hagood, R.M.	Pvt	G 3rd SCVIBn	South Mtn., MD	09/14/62	Ft. Delaware, DE	10/02/62	Aikens Ldg., VA Xc	CSR
Hagood, T.B.	Pvt	E 1st SCVIH	Warrenton, VA	09/29/62	Warrenton, VA	09/29/62	Paroled	CSR
Hagood, W.H.	Pvt	E 1st SCVIH	Warrenton, VA	09/29/62	Warrenton, VA	09/29/62	Paroled	CSR
Hahn, Christian	Pvt	B German LA	Fayetteville, NC	03/16/65	New Berne, NC	03/30/65	Pt. Lookout, MD	CSR
					Pt. Lookout, MD	06/21/65	Rlsd. G.O. #109	P114,CSR
Hahn, Henry	Cpl	A German LA	Deserted/enemy	03/15/65	Charleston, SC	03/15/65	Released on oath	CSR
Haig, A.R.	Pvt	A 18th SCVAB	James Island, SC	02/10/65	Beaufort, SC USGH	05/09/65	Hilton Head, SC	P1,CSR,STR
					Hilton Head, SC	05/10/65	Paroled & Released	STR
Haigler, D. Shadrick	Sgt	A 5th SCVC	Mt. Elen, SC	03/02/65	New Berne, NC	04/03/65	Pt. Lookout, MD	CSR
					Pt. Lookout, MD	06/27/65	Rlsd. G.O. #109	CSR
Haigler, Esan N.	Pvt	K 2nd SCVI	Gettysburg, PA	07/05/63	Gettysburg G.H.	07/20/63	Provost Marshal	P4,H2,CSR
					David's Island, NY	09/23/63	City Pt., VA Xc	SA2,P1,H2,CSR
Haigler, F.G.	Pvt	F 25th SCVI	Ft. Fisher, NC	01/15/65	New York, NY	01/30/65	Elmira, NY	CSR
					Elmira, NY	07/13/65	Rlsd. G.O. #109	P65,HAG
Haigler, William L.	Pvt	K 2nd SCVI	Sharpsburg, MD	09/18/62	Ft. McHenry, MD	10/13/62	Fts. Monroe, VA	CSR
					Fts. Monroe, VA	10/16/62	Aikens Ldg., VA Xc	CSR

SOUTH CAROLINA SOLDIERS, SAILORS AND **H** CITIZENS HELD IN U.S. PRISONS 1861-1865

NAME	RANK	REGIMENT	CAPTURED AT	WHEN	PRISON	MOVED	DISPOSITION	SOURCES
Haile, Benjamin F.	Pvt	E 22nd SCVI	Crater, Pbg., VA	07/30/64	US 9th AC Hos.	08/02/64	City Pt., VA P.M.	CSR,LAN
					City Pt., VA	08/05/64	Washington, DC	CSR
					Pt. Lookout, MD	11/01/64	Venus Pt., GA Xc	P113,P124,CSR
Haile, Columbus C.	1Lt	A 23rd SCVI	Dinwiddie C.H., VA	04/01/65	Washington, DC	04/11/65	Johnson's Isl., OH	CSR
					Johnson's Isl., OH	06/18/65	Rlsd. G.O. #109	CSR
Haile, H. Albert P.	Pvt	E 12th SCVI	Gettysburg, PA	07/05/63	David's Island, NY	08/24/63	Paroled	P1,LAN,CSR
Haile, H. Albert P.	Pvt	E 12th SCVI	Spotsylvania, VA	05/12/64	Belle Plain, VA	05/20/65	Ft. Delaware, DE	CSR
Haile, H. Albert P.	Pvt	E 12th SCVI	Spotsylvania, VA	05/12/64	Ft. Delaware, DE	05/31/64	Hos. 5/31-6/14/64	P47
					Ft. Delaware, DE	09/24/64	Hos. 9/24-9/29/64	P47
					Ft. Delaware, DE	12/17/64	Hos. 12/17/64-6/8/65	P47
					Ft. Delaware, DE	06/10/65	Released	P41,P43,P45,CSR
Haile, James S.	Pvt	B 12th SCVI	Petersburg, VA	04/02/65	City Pt., VA	04/04/65	Pt. Lookout, MD	CSR
					Pt. Lookout, MD	06/28/65	Rlsd. G.O. #109	CSR
Hailey, Jeramiah	Pvt	E 1st SCVA	Morris Island, SC	07/10/63	Hilton Head, SC	10/18/63	Ft. Columbus, NY	CSR
					Ft. Columbus, NY	09/23/63	Took the oath	P1
Hailey, William L.	Ldm	CS Navy	Rockingham, NC	03/07/65	Pt. Lookout, MD	06/15/65	Rlsd. G.O. #109	P114
Haines, William	Pvt	E 1st SCVA	Morris Island, SC	07/10/63	Ft. Columbus, NY	09/26/63	Pt. Lookout, MD	P124,CSR
					Pt. Lookout, MD	02/21/64	Joined US Army	P1,P113,P125,CSR
Hair, C.O.	Pvt	A 2nd SCVA	Charlotte, NC Hos.	05/07/65	Charlotte, NC	05/07/65	Paroled	CSR
Hair, D.J.	Pvt	I 5th SCVC	Augusta, GA	05/18/65	Augusta, GA	05/18/65	Paroled	CSR
Hair, John	Sgt	D 1st SCVIR				04/27/65	New Berne, NC Hos.	SA1,CSR
Hair, M.	Pvt	E 1st SCVIH	Augusta, GA	05/20/65	Augusta, GA	05/20/65	Paroled	CSR
Hair, W. Jennings	Pvt	I 1st SCVIG	Gettysburg, PA	07/03/63	David's Island, NY	09/14/63	Died	P1,P6,FPH,SA1,CSR
Hair, W.P.	Pvt	B 2nd SCVA	James Island, SC	06/16/62	Hilton Head, SC	07/31/62	Ft. Columbus, NY	CSR
					Ft. Columbus, NY	08/23/62	Ft. Delaware, DE	P37,CSR
					Ft. Delaware, DE	09/30/62	Aikens Ldg., VA Xc	CSR
					Aikens Ldg., VA	11/10/62	Exchanged	CSR
Hair, Wesley W.	Pvt	E P.S.S.	Richmond, VA Hos.	04/03/65	Libby Prison Richmd.		City Pt., VA	CSR
					City Pt., VA	04/14/65	Pt. Lookout, MD	CSR
Hair, Wesley W.	Pvt	E P.S.S.	Richmond, VA	04/03/65	Pt. Lookout, MD	06/27/65	Rlsd. G.O. #109	P114,TSE,CSR
Haithcock, Robert	Pvt	B 24th SCVI	Taylors Ridge, GA	10/16/64	Nashville, TN	10/23/64	Louisville, KY	CSR
					Louisville, KY	10/26/64	Camp Douglas, IL	CSR
					Camp Douglas, IL	04/25/65	Jd. 6th U.S. Vols.	CSR
Haithcock, S.H.	Pvt	G 23rd SCVI	Petersburg, VA Hos.	04/09/65	Point of Rocks Hos.	04/12/65	Fts. Monroe, VA	CSR
					Fts. Monroe, VA	05/30/65	Prov. Marshal	CSR
Hale, James	Pvt	E 26th SCVI	Petersburg, VA	04/02/65	Pt. Lookout, MD	06/28/65	Rlsd. G.O. #109	P114
Hale, John S.	Pvt	C 26th SCVI	Petersburg, VA	10/27/64	City Pt., VA	10/31/64	Pt. Lookout, MD	CSR
					Pt. Lookout, MD	03/28/65	Aikens Ldg., VA Xc	P114,P124,CSR
Haley, Archibald	Pvt	K 2nd SCVIRi	Darbytown Rd., VA	10/07/64	18th AC A.of J Hos.	10/31/64	Died of wounds	P12,CSR
Haley, F.W.	Pvt	I 25th SCVI	Town Creek, NC	02/20/65	Ft. Anderson, NC	02/28/65	Pt. Lookout, MD	CSR,HAG
					Pt. Lookout, MD	06/28/65	Rlsd. G.O. #109	P114
Haley, H.V.	Cpl	I 25th SCVI	Ft. Fisher, NC	01/15/65	New York, NY	01/30/65	Elmira, NY	CSR,HAG
					Elmira, NY	03/17/65	Died, Diarrhea	P65
Haley, James B.	Pvt	I 14th SCVI	Hanover C.H., VA	05/24/64	Port Royal, VA	05/30/64	Pt. Lookout, MD	CSR,HOL
					Pt. Lookout, MD	11/01/64	Venus Pt., GA Xc	P113,CSR
Hall, A.	Pvt	D 11th SCVI	Ft. Fisher, NC	01/15/65	Elmira, NY	04/02/65	Died, Rubeola	P65,P66,CSR
Hall, A.M.	Pvt	F 24th SCVI	Jackson, MS	05/14/63	Demopolis, AL	06/05/63	Paroled	CSR
Hall, A.O.	Pvt	G 7th SCVI	Salisbury, NC	05/02/65	Salisbury, NC	05/02/65	Paroled	CNM,CSR
Hall, Alexander	2Lt	D 26th SCVI	Petersburg, VA	03/25/65	Old Capitol, DC	03/30/65	Ft. Delaware, DE	CSR,HOM
					Ft. Delaware, DE	06/17/65	Rlsd. G.O. #109	P43,P45,CSR
Hall, Daniel	Pvt	G 21st SCVI	Ft. Fisher, NC	01/15/65	Elmira, NY	02/25/65	Died, Pneumonia	P6,P12,P65,FPH

H

SOUTH CAROLINA SOLDIERS, SAILORS AND CITIZENS HELD IN U.S. PRISONS 1861-1865

NAME	RANK	REGIMENT	CAPTURED AT	WHEN	PRISON	MOVED	DISPOSITION	SOURCES
Hall, Dudley	Pvt	F 13th SCVI	Richmond, VA Hos.	04/03/65	Libby Prison Rchmd.	04/23/65	Newport News, VA	CSR
					Newport News, VA	06/26/65	Rlsd. G.O. #109	CSR
Hall, Flemming	Pvt	I 14th SCVI	Deserted/enemy	08/30/64	Harrisburg, PA	09/19/63	Philadelphia, PA	CSR
					Ft. Miflin, PA	11/17/63	Released on oath	P2,CSR
Hall, George L.	Pvt	B 19th SCVI	Augusta, GA	05/18/65	Augusta, GA	05/18/65	Paroled	CSR
Hall, H.B.	Pvt	F 13th SCVI	Southside RR, VA	04/01/65	City Pt., VA	04/07/65	Hart's Island, NY	CSR,HOS
					Hart's Island, NY	06/16/65	Rlsd. G.O. #109	P79,CSR
Hall, Hilliard	Pvt	F 19th SCVI	Glasgow, KY		Glasgow, KY		Paroled	CSR
Hall, Irwin	Pvt	F 19th SCVI	Macon, GA	04/30/65	Macon, GA	04/30/65	Paroled	CSR
Hall, Isaac	Pvt	K 21st SCVI	Morris Island, SC	07/10/63	Ft. Columbus, NY	09/23/63	Took the oath	P1,HAG
					Pt. Lookout, MD	01/09/64	Died, Ch. Diarrhea	P5,P12,P113,FPH
Hall, J.	Pvt	F 1st SCVIH	Richmond, VA	04/03/65	Richmond, VA	05/05/65	Paroled	CSR
Hall, J.A.	Pvt	A 3rd SCVABn	High Pt., NC	05/02/65	High Pt., NC	05/02/65	Paroled	CSR
Hall, J.M.	Pvt	G 6th SCVC	Stony Creek, VA	12/01/64	City Pt., VA	12/04/64	Pt. Lookout, MD	CSR
					Pt. Lookout, MD	06/08/65	Released on oath	P114,CSR
Hall, J.N.	Pvt	K 22nd SCVI	Southside RR, VA	04/02/65	Hart's Island, NY	06/19/65	Rlsd. G.O. #109	P79
Hall, James	Pvt	D 2nd SCVI	Greencastle, PA	07/05/63	Harrisburg, PA G.H	07/23/63	Provost Marshal	P2,SA2,CSR,H2
					Ft. Delaware, DE	10/15/63	Pt. Lookout, MD	P42
					Pt. Lookout, MD	10/15/63	Hammond G.H., MD	P113,P125,CSR
					Pt. Lookout, MD	12/14/63	Died, Laryngitis	CSR,FPH
Hall, James H.	Pvt	K 21st SCVI	Ft. Fisher, NC	01/15/65	Elmira, NY	08/26/65	Died, Ch. Diarrhea	P6,P12,FPH,HAG
Hall, James M.	Pvt	C Orr's Ri.	Sutherland Stn., VA	04/02/65	City Pt., VA	04/07/65	Hart' Island, NY	CSR
					Hart's Island, NY	06/15/65	Rlsd. G.O. #109	P79,CSR
					Hart's Island, NY	04/05/65	David's Island, NY	CSR
					City Pt., VA	04/07/65	Hart's Island, NY	CSR
Hall, Jesse M.	Pvt	C Orr's Ri.	Sutherland Stn., VA	04/02/65	Hart's Island, NY	04/25/65	Died, Typhoid	P79,CDC,CSR
Hall, John Brannon	Pvt	G 2nd SCVI	Sharpsburg, MD	09/17/62	Frederick, MD USGH	10/01/62	Baltimore, MD	CSR,SA2,H2,KCE
					Baltimore, MD	04/27/63	Ft. McHenry, MD	CSR
					Ft. McHenry, MD	04/28/63	Paroled	CSR
Hall, John W.	Pvt	A 1st SCVIG	Richmond VA Hos.	04/03/65	Richmond, VA P.M.	05/12/65	Paroled	SA1,CSR
Hall, Marcus D.	Pvt	L 2nd SCVIRi	Burkeville, VA	04/14/65	Burkesville, VA	04/17/65	Paroled	CSR
Hall, Milledge M.		Mathewes A	Augusta, GA	05/18/65	Augusta, GA	05/18/65	Paroled	CSR
Hall, Nathan	Pvt	E 1st SCVIH	Augusta, GA	06/02/65	Augusta, GA	06/02/65	Paroled	CSR
Hall, P.	Pvt	A 19th SCVCB	Augusta, GA	05/19/65	Augusta, GA	05/19/65	Paroled on oath	CSR
Hall, Pennell P.	Pvt	K 12th SCVI	Gettysburg, PA	06/30/63	David's Island, NY	08/05/63	Died of wounds	P1,P6,P12,FPH
Hall, S.B.	Pvt	H 1st SCVC	Gettysburg, PA	07/06/63	David's Island, NY	08/24/63	City Pt., VA Xc	P1,CSR
Hall, S.B.	Pvt	K 7th SCVC	Kershaw Dist., SC	02/25/65	New Berne, NC	04/10/65	Hart's Island, NY	CSR
					Hart's Island, NY	06/17/65	Rlsd. G.O. #109	P79,CSR
Hall, S.D.	Sgt	F 1st SCVIH	Deep Bottom, VA	08/14/64	Bermuda Hundred, VA	08/15/64	Fts. Monroe, VA	CSR,SA1
					Fts. Monroe, VA	08/15/64	Pt. Lookout, MD	CSR
					Pt. Lookout, MD	06/28/65	Rlsd. G.O. #109	P113,CSR
Hall, Thomas J.	2Lt	E Orr's Ri.	Falling Waters, MD	07/14/62	Baltimore, MD	08/02/63	Johnson's Isl., OH	CSR
					Johnson's Isl., OH	06/11/65	Rlsd. G.O.#109	CSR
Hall, W.E.	Pvt	Beaufort L	Raleigh, NC Hos.	04/13/65	Raleigh, NC	04/13/65	Paroled	CSR
Hall, William	Pvt	B 37th VAVCB	Braxton Cty., WV	03/10/65	Wheeling, WV	03/29/65	Camp Chase, OH	37V,CSR
Hall, William D.	Pvt	H Ham.Leg.	Will's Valley, TN	10/29/63	Nashville, TN	11/07/63	Louisville, KY	P39,CSR
					Louisville, KY	11/09/63	Camp Morton, IN	CSR
					Camp Morton, IN	11/26/63	Died	P5,P12,FPH
Hall, Wyatt	Pvt	B 7th SCVC	Burkeville, VA	04/06/65	City Pt., VA	04/14/65	Pt. Lookout, MD	CSR
					Pt. Lookout, MD	06/27/65	Rlsd. G.O. #109	P114,CSR

H

SOUTH CAROLINA SOLDIERS, SAILORS AND CITIZENS HELD IN U.S. PRISONS 1861-1865

NAME	RANK	REGIMENT	CAPTURED AT	WHEN	PRISON	MOVED	DISPOSITION	SOURCES
Hallford, Jesse G.	2Lt	E 8th SCVI	Old Church, VA	05/30/64	White House, VA	06/08/64	Pt. Lookout, MD	CSR,KEB,ISH
					Pt. Lookout, MD	06/23/64	Ft. Delaware, DE	P113,P120,CSR
					Ft. Delaware, DE	08/20/64	Hilton Head, SC	P43,P45,CSR
					Ft. Pulaski, GA			P4
					Hilton Head, SC	03/12/65	Ft. Delaware, DE	P43,P45,CSR
					Ft. Delaware, DE	06/16/65	Rlsd. G.O. #109	P43,P44
Halliburton, John J.	Pvt	M 8th SCVI	Gettysburg, PA	07/05/63	Gettysburg G.H.	08/02/63	David's Island, NY	P4,KEB,CSR
					David's Island, NY	09/05/63	Died	P1,P12,P6,FPH
Hallifield, J.G.F.	Pvt	2nd SCVI	Deserted/enemy		City Pt., VA	04/21/65	Washington, DC	CSR
					Washington, DC	04/21/65	Nashville, TN oath	CSR
Hallman, Milledge	Pvt	F 19th SCVI	Augusta, GA	05/23/65	Augusta, GA	05/23/65	Paroled	CSR
Hallman, W.W.	Pvt	K 13th SCVI	Farmville, VA	04/11/65	Paroled	04/21/65	(DOW at Winchester)	CSR
Hallman, William	Pvt	E 15th SCVI	Augusta, GA	05/25/65	Augusta, GA	05/25/65	Paroled	H15,CSR
Hallman, William Burke	Pvt	C 15th SCVI	Knoxville, TN	12/03/63	Louisville, KY	01/27/64	Rock Island, IL	CSR
					Rock Island, IL	10/13/64	Vol. USA Front. Ser.	H15,CSR
Halon, W.	Pvt	I 1st SCVIG	Boonesborough, MD	09/13/62	Ft. Delaware, DE	10/02/62	Aikens Ldg. for Xc	CSR
Haltiwanger, J.L.	Pvt	H 3rd SCVI	Gettysburg, PA	07/05/63	Gettysburg G.H.	10/15/63	Provost Marshal	P4,KEB,SA2,H3,CSR
					W. Bldg. Balt, MD	11/12/63	City Pt., VA Xc	P1,CSR
Haltiwanger, J.L.	Pvt	H 3rd SCVI	Gettysburg, PA	07/05/63	Richmond, VA Hos.	11/20/63	Furloughed till Xc	CSR
Haltiwanger, Jacob S.	Sgt	H 3rd SCVI	Gettysburg, PA	07/05/63	Gettysburg G.H.	10/15/63	Provost Marshal	P4,KEB,SA2,H3,CSR
					W. Bldg. Balt, MD	11/12/63	City Pt., VA Xc	P1,KEB,SA2,H3,CSR
					Richmond, VA Hos.	11/21/63	Furloughed 30 days	CSR
Haltiwanger, John S.	Pvt	C 20th SCVI	Cedar Creek, VA	10/19/64	W. Bldg. Balt, MD	01/05/65	Ft. McHenry, MD	P1,KEB,CSR
					Ft. McHenry, MD	02/20/65	Pt. Lookout, MD Xc	CSR
Haltiwanger, John S.	Pvt	C 20th SCVI	Richmond, VA	04/03/65	Libby Prison Rchmd.	04/13/65	City Pt., VA	CSR
					City Pt., VA	04/14/65	Pt. Lookout, MD	CSR
					Pt. Lookout, MD	06/28/65	Rlsd. G.O. #109	P7,P114,CSR
Ham, H.H.	Pvt	C 3rd SCVABn	Blakely, AL	04/09/65	Ship Island, MS	05/01/65	Vicksburg, MS Prld.	CSR
Ham, H.H.	Pvt	C 3rd SCVABn	Augusta, GA	05/20/65	Augusta, GA	05/20/65	Paroled	CSR
Ham, Henry J.	2Lt	C 3rd SCVABn	Blakely, AL	04/09/65	Ship Island, MS	04/28/65	New Orleans, LA	CSR
					New Orleans, LA	05/01/65	Vicksburg, MS Xc	CSR
Ham, John	Pvt	B 7th SCVC	Wren's Mills, VA	04/14/64	Pt. Lookout, MD	03/06/65	Died	P6,P113,FPH
Ham, S.B.	Pvt	C 3rd SCVABn	Citronelle, AL	05/04/65	Meridian, MS	05/10/65	Paroled	CSR
Hambleton, Edward W.	Pvt	A 16th SCVI	Peachtree Crk., GA	07/20/64	Nashville, TN	07/29/64	Louisville, KY	CSR
					Louisville, KY	07/31/64	Camp Chase, OH	CSR
					Camp Chase, OH	02/06/65	Died, Pneumonia	P6,P23,P27,FPH,CSR
Hambrick, Drury H.	Pvt	G 8th SCVI	Winchester, VA	05/01/65	Winchester, VA	05/01/65	Paroled	CSR
Hambright, J.S.	Pvt	F 17th SCVI	Burkeville, VA	04/09/65	24th USAC Fld. Hos.	04/13/65	Depot Hos. Burkeville	CSR
					Depot Hos. Burkeville	04/16/65	City Pt., VA 2 ACH	CSR
					Depot Hos. 2nd AC	04/18/65	Lincoln G.H., DC	CSR
					Lincon G.H., DC	06/18/65	Released	CSR
Hambright, Phillip	Pvt	F 1st SCVA	Fayetteville, NC	03/13/65	New Berne, NC	03/30/65	Pt. Lookout, MD	CSR
					Pt. Lookout, MD	06/08/65	Rlsd. on oath	P114,CSR
Hamby, A.B.H.	Pvt	C 27th SCVI	Petersburg, VA	06/24/64	Fts. Monroe, VA	06/25/64	Pt. Lookout, MD	CSR,HAG
					Pt. Lookout, MD	08/19/64	Died, Ch. Diarrhea	P5,P113,FPH,CSR
Hamby, James W.	Pvt	I 3rd SCVI	Gettysburg, PA	07/05/63	Letterman G.H. Gbg	09/16/63	Provost Marshal	P1,P4,KEB,H3,CSR
					W. Bldg. Balt, MD	11/12/63	City Pt., VA Xc	P1,CSR
					Richmond, VA Hos.	12/03/63	Furloughed 30 days	CSR
Hamby, W.P.	Sgt	C 22nd SCVI	Sharpsburg, MD	09/17/62	Sharpsburg, MD	09/21/62	Prld. to Gen. Hos.	CSR
					Frederick, MD G.H.	10/27/62	Died of wounds	CSR
Hamby, William J.	Pvt	B 16th SCVI	Franklin, TN	12/18/64	Nashville, TN G.H.	03/20/65	Died of wounds	P4,P6,16R,CSR
Hamer, C.H.	Pvt	F 21st SCVI	Ft. Fisher, NC	01/15/65	Elmira, NY	02/06/65	Died, Pneumonia	P6,P65,FPH,HAG,HOM

H

SOUTH CAROLINA SOLDIERS, SAILORS AND CITIZENS HELD IN U.S. PRISONS 1861-1865

NAME	RANK	REGIMENT	CAPTURED AT	WHEN	PRISON	MOVED	DISPOSITION	SOURCES
Hamer, James C.	Pvt	F 21st SCVI	Ft. Fisher, NC	01/15/65	Elmira, NY	03/02/65	Died, Diarrhea	P6,P65,FPH,HAG,HOM
Hames, Franklin	Pvt	K 27th SCVI	Town Creek, NC	02/20/65	Ft. Anderson, NC	02/28/65	Pt. Lookout, MD	CSR
					Pt. Lookout, MD	06/27/65	Rlsd. G.O. #109	P114,CSR
Hames, Gadbury	Pvt	G 27th SCVI	Town Creek, NC	02/20/65	Ft. Anderson, NC	02/28/65	Pt. Lookout, MD	CSR,HAG
Hames, Gadbury	Pvt	G 27th SCVI	Florence, SC	03/11/65	Pt. Lookout, MD	04/09/65	Died	P6,P12,P114,FPH
Hames, L.B.	Pvt	K 27th SCVI	Weldon RR, VA	08/21/64	City Pt., VA	08/24/64	Pt. Lookout, MD	CSR,HAG
					Pt. Lookout, MD	04/04/65	Died, Scurvy	P6,P125,FPH
Hames, Zealous	Pvt	H 15th SCVI	Deep Bottom, VA	07/27/64	Pt. Lookout, MD	08/08/64	Elmira, NY	CSR
					Elmira, NY	10/14/64	Pt. Lookout, MD	P65,P66,P120,CSR
					W. Bldg. Balt, MD	11/11/64	Died, Ch. Diarrhea	P1,P5,P12,FPH,CSR
Hamilton, A.G.	Pvt	F 1st SCVA	Bentonville, NC	03/22/65	New Berne, NC	04/10/65	Hart's Island, NY	CSR
					Hart's Island, NY	06/16/65	Rlsd. G.O. #109	CSR
Hamilton, Evander	Pvt	H Orr's Ri.	Gettysburg, PA	07/04/63	Ft. Delaware, DE	07/27/63	Joined US Service	CSR
Hamilton, George W.	Pvt	B Ham.Leg.MI	Augusta, GA	05/30/65	Augusta, GA	05/30/65	Paroled	CSR
Hamilton, J.J.	Pvt	I 1st SCVIH	Richmond, VA	04/03/65	Richmond, VA		Paroled	CSR
Hamilton, James	Sgt	F 23rd SCVI	Farmville, VA	04/06/65	City Pt., VA	04/14/65	Newport News, VA	CSR
					Newport News, VA	06/26/65	Rlsd. G.O. #109	CSR
Hamilton, Joseph P.	Pvt	I 2nd SCVC	Augusta, GA	05/30/65	Augusta, GA	05/30/65	Paroled	CSR
Hamilton, R.B.	Sur	7th SCVIBn	Morris Island, SC	07/10/63	USHS "Cosmopolitan"		Charleston, SC Xc	CSR
Hamilton, Tobias	Pvt	H 23rd SCVI	Five Forks, VA	04/02/65	City Pt., VA	04/05/65	Pt. Lookout, MD	CSR
					Pt. Lookout, MD	06/28/65	Rlsd. G.O. #109	P114,HMC,CSR
Hamilton, Wiley M.	Cpt	K 23rd SCVI	Five Forks, VA	04/01/65	Washington, DC	04/09/65	Johnson's Isl., OH	CSR
					Johnson's Isl., OH	06/18/65	Rlsd. G.O. #109	CSR
Hamilton, William	Pvt	F 12th SCVI	Warrenton, VA	09/29/62	Warrenton, VA	09/29/62	Paroled	CSR
Hamilton, William	Pvt	F 12th SCVI	Petersburg, VA	04/02/65	City Pt., VA	04/04/65	Pt. Lookout, MD	CSR
					Pt. Lookout, MD	06/27/65	Rlsd. G.O. #109	P114
Hamilton, William M.	Pvt	C 19th SCVI	Atlanta, GA	07/22/64	Nashville, TN	07/29/64	Louisville, KY	CSR
					Louisville, KY	07/31/64	Camp Chase, OH	CSR
					Camp Chase, OH	01/23/65	Died, Pneumonia	P6,P12,P23,P27,FPH,HOE
Hamlin, J.R.	Sgt	F 1st SCVC	Upperville, VA	06/21/63	Old Capitol, DC	06/25/63	City Pt., VA Xc	CSR
Hammett, A.A.	Pvt	P.S.S.	Deserted/enemy	03/21/65	Bermuda Hundred, VA	03/24/65	City Pt., VA Hos.	CSR
					City Pt. Hospital	04/15/65	City Pt., VA P.M.	CSR
Hammett, Arthur G.	Pvt	L Orr's Ri.	Cox Road, VA	04/02/65	City Pt., VA	04/07/65	Hart's Island, NY	CSR
					Hart's Island, NY	06/15/65	Rlsd. G.O.#109	P79,CSR
Hammett, D.A.	Pvt	A 3rd SCVABn	High Pt., NC	05/02/65	High Pt., NC	05/02/65	Paroled	CSR
Hammett, H.C.	Pvt	A 3rd SCVABn	High Pt., NC	05/02/65	High Pt., NC	05/02/65	Paroled	CSR
Hammett, J.S.	Pvt	F 18th SCVI	Crater, Pbg., VA	07/30/64	City Pt., VA	08/08/64	Pt. Lookout, MD	P113,P120,CSR
					Pt. Lookout, MD	08/08/64	Elmira, NY	P113,P120,CSR
					Elmira, NY	07/03/65	Rlsd. G.O. #109	P65,P66,CSR
Hammett, Jesse M.	Pvt	A 3rd SCVABn	High Pt., NC	05/02/65	High Pt., NC	05/02/65	Paroled	CSR
Hammett, John J.	Pvt	I P.S.S.	Lookout Valley, TN	10/29/63	Chattanooga, TN	11/07/63	Nashville, TN	CSR
					Nashville, TN	11/07/63	Louisville, KY	P39,TSE,CSR
					Louisville, KY	11/09/63	Camp Morton, IN	CSR
					Camp Morton	06/12/65	Rlsd. G.O. #109	CSR
Hammett, Richard D.	Pvt	B Hol.Leg.	Farmville, VA	04/07/65	Farmville, VA	04/16/65	Burkeville, VA G.H.	CSR
Hammett, W.D.	Pvt	K P.S.S.	Deserted/enemy	03/21/65	Bermuda Hundred, VA	03/21/65	City Pt., VA	CSR
					City Pt., VA	03/24/65	Washington, DC	CSR
Hammond, Absolom	Pvt	D 26th SCVI	Farmville, VA	04/03/65	City Pt., VA	04/14/65	Newport News, VA	CSR
					Newport News, VA	06/26/65	Rlsd. G.O. #109	CSR
Hammond, Albert	Pvt	D 12th SCVI	Petersburg, VA	04/02/65	City Pt., VA	04/04/65	Pt. Lookout, MD	CSR
					Pt. Lookout, MD	06/27/65	Rlsd. G.O. #109	P114,CSR

SOUTH CAROLINA SOLDIERS, SAILORS AND  CITIZENS HELD IN U.S. PRISONS 1861-1865

NAME	RANK	REGIMENT	CAPTURED AT	WHEN	PRISON	MOVED	DISPOSITION	SOURCES
Hammond, Asa	Pvt	H 7th SCVIBn	Drury's Bluff, VA	05/16/64	Bermuda Hundred, VA	05/17/64	Fts. Monroe, VA	CSR,HAG
					Fts. Monroe, VA GH	06/09/64	Pt. Lookout, MD	CSR
					Pt. Lookout, MD	03/14/65	Aikens Ldg., VA Xc	P113,CSR
Hammond, Elisha H.	Pvt	A 16th SCVI	Yazoo City, MS	07/13/63	Yazoo City, MS	07/13/63	Paroled on oath	16R,CSR
Hammond, F.R.	Pvt	H 4th SCVC	Kershaw Dist., SC	02/23/65	New Berne, NC	04/10/65	Hart's Island, NY	CSR
					Hart's Island, NY	06/17/65	Rlsd. G.O. #109	P79,LAN,CSR
Hammond, Joel T.	Pvt	K 13th SCVI	Southside RR, VA	04/02/65	City Pt., VA	04/07/65	Hart's Island, NY	CSR
					Hart's Island, NY	06/16/65	Rlsd. G.O. #109	CSR
Hammond, S.B.	Pvt	H 4th SCVC	Hawe's Shop, VA	05/28/64	White House, VA	06/08/64	Pt. Lookout, MD	CSR,LAN
					Pt. Lookout, MD	07/09/64	Elmira, NY	P113,P120,CSR
					Elmira, NY	10/11/64	Tfd. for exchange	P65,CSR
					Pt. Lookout, MD	10/29/64	Exchanged	P114,CSR
Hammond, William H.	Cpl	B Orr's Ri.	Petersburg, VA	04/03/65	City Pt., VA	04/11/65	Hart's Island, NY	CSR
					Hart's Island, NY	06/16/65	Rlsd. G.O. #109	P79,CDC,CSR
Hammontry, Charles	Pvt	4 10/19 SCVI	Missionary Ridge, TN	11/25/63	Nashville, TN	12/07/63	Louisville, KY	P39,RAS,CSR
					Louisville, KY	12/09/63	Rock island, IL	CSR
					Rock Island, IL	12/19/65	Rlsd. G.O. #109	CSR
Hampton, J.A.	Pvt	H 22nd SCVI	Deserted/enemy	02/25/65	City Pt., VA	02/28/65	Washington, DC	CSR
					Washington, DC	03/01/65	Oil City, PA oath	CSR
Hampton, Thomas E.	2Cl	I 14th SCVI	Gettysburg, PA	07/02/63	Provost Marshal	07/17/63	David's Island, VA	CSR
					David's Island, NY	09/05/63	City Pt., VA Xc	P1,CSR
					Petersburg, VA Hos.	09/16/63	Furloughed 60 day	CSR
Hampton, William	Pvt	F 4th SCVC	Pocotaligo, SC	03/04/65	New Berne, NC	04/10/65	Hart's Island, NY	CSR
					Hart's Island, NY	06/16/65	Rlsd. G.O. #109	P79,HMC,CSR
Hanahan, Hobart D.	1Sg	I 2nd SCVI	Fair Oaks, VA	06/19/62	NYC US Hos 51st St	08/14/62	Ft. Columbus, NY	CSR,SA2,H2
					Ft. Columbus, NY	08/23/62	Ft. Delaware, DE	P37,CSR
					Ft. Delaware, DE	10/02/62	Aikens Ldg., VA Xc	CSR
Hanberry, W.A.	Pvt	I 5th SCVC	Deserted/enemy		Fts. Monroe, VA	04/02/65	Washington, DC	CSR
					Washington, DC		Baltimore on oath	CSR
Hancock, Ezekiel	Pvt	E 8th SCVI	Winchester, VA	09/13/64	Harpers Ferry, WV	09/19/64	Camp Chase, OH	CSR
					Camp Chase, OH	06/11/65	Rlsd. G.O. #109	P23,CSR
Hancock, George W.	Pvt	G 1st SCVIG	Hanover C.H., VA	05/28/64	White House, VA	06/08/64	Pt. Lookout, MD	CSR
					Pt. Lookout, MD	06/10/64	Joined U.S. Army	P125,SA1,CSR
Hancock, H.P.	Pvt	H 4th SCVC	Hawe's Shop, VA	05/28/64	3rd Div. 5th A.C.	05/28/64	Died of wounds	CSR
Hancock, James T.	Pvt	E Hol.Leg.C	Slatersville, VA	08/27/63	Ft. McGruder, VA	08/31/63	Ft. Norfolk, VA	CSR
					Ft. Norfolk, VA	09/22/63	Pt. Lookout, MD	CSR
					Pt. Lookout, MD	01/25/64	Joined U.S. Army	P113,P125,CSR
Hancock, John S.	Pvt	C 3rd SCVABn	Ft. Gaines, AL	08/08/64	New Orleans, LA	10/21/64	Ship Island, MS	P3,CSR
					Ship Island, MS	01/04/65	Exchanged	CSR
Hancock, John S.	Pvt	C 3rd SCVABn	Citronelle, AL	05/04/65	Meridian, MS	05/16/65	Paroled	CSR
Hancock, R.F.M.	Pvt	B 8th SCVI	Winchester, VA	09/13/64	Harpers Ferry, WV	09/19/64	Camp Chase, OH	CSR
					Camp Chase, OH	06/11/65	Rlsd. G.O. #109	P23,KEB,CSR
Hancock, W.H.	Pvt	G 2nd SCVC	Augusta, GA	05/18/65	Augusta, GA	05/18/65	Paroled	CSR
Hand, William	Pvt	B 3rd SCVIBn	Knoxville, TN	12/05/63	Nashville, TN	01/24/64	Louisville, KY	P39,KEB,CSR
					Louisville, KY	01/27/64	Rock Island, IL	CSR
					Rock Island, IL	02/25/65	Boulware's Wh., VA	CSR
Haney, A.J.	Pvt	H 15th SCVI	Cedar Creek, VA	10/19/64	Pt. Lookout, MD	06/27/65	Rlsd. G.O. #109	P114,KEB,UD5,CSR
Haney, James	Pvt	H 15th SCVI	Cedar Creek, VA	10/19/64	Harpers Ferry, WV	10/25/64	Pt. Lookout, MD	CSR
					Pt. Lookout, MD	06/27/65	Rlsd. G.O. #109	H15,CSR
Hankins, J.D.	Pvt	C 16th SCVI	Greenville, SC	05/18/65	Greenville, SC	05/18/65	Paroled on oath	CSR
Hankinson, A.H.	Pvt	I 7th SCVC	Augusta, GA	05/20/65	Augusta, GA	05/20/65	Paroled	CSR

SOUTH CAROLINA SOLDIERS, SAILORS AND  CITIZENS HELD IN U.S. PRISONS 1861-1865

NAME	RANK	REGIMENT	CAPTURED AT	WHEN	PRISON	MOVED	DISPOSITION	SOURCES
Hanna, George M.	Pvt	F 14th SCVI	Gettysburg, PA	07/03/63	David's Island, NY	09/12/63	City Pt., VA Xc	P1,CSR
					Williamsburg, VA Hos.	09/24/63	Furloughed	CSR
Hanna, George M.	Pvt	F 14th SCVI	Petersburg, VA	04/02/65	City Pt., VA	04/05/65	Pt. Lookout, MD	CSR
					Pt. Lookout, MD	06/27/65	Rlsd. G.O. #109	P114,CSR
Hanna, T.J.	Pvt	I 4th SCVC	Williamsburg Dist.,	04/06/65	P.M. Charleston			CSR
Hannah, D.P.	Pvt	F Hol.Leg.	Farmville, VA	04/06/65	City Pt., VA	04/14/65	Newport News, VA	CSR
					Newport News, VA	06/26/65	Rlsd. G.O. #109	CSR
Hannahan, Joseph S.	Cpt	B 25th SCVI	Town Creek, NC	02/20/65	Pt. Lookout, MD	02/28/65	Washington, DC	P114,P120,HAG
					Ft. Anderson, NC	02/28/65	Pt. Lookout, MD	CSR
					Old Capitol, DC	03/24/65	Ft. Delaware, DE	CSR
					Ft. Delaware, DE	06/17/65	Rlsd. G.O. #109	P43,P45,P46
Hannon, William	Pvt	B 1st SCVA	Fayetteville, NC	03/16/65	New Berne, NC	03/30/65	Pt. Lookout, MD	CSR
					Pt. Lookout, MD	06/13/65	Rlsd. HG.O. #109	P114,CSR
Hansford, Thomas	Pvt	C 1st SCVIR	Bentonville, NC	03/22/65	New Berne, NC	04/10/65	Hart's Island, NY	CSR
					Hart's Island, NY	06/16/65	Rlsd. G.O. #109	SA1,P79,CSR
Hanvey, George A.	Cpl	G 14th SCVI	Sutherland Stn., VA	04/02/65	City Pt., VA	04/07/65	Hart's Island, NY	CSR
					Hart's Island, NY	06/16/65	Rlsd. G.O. #109	P79,CSR
Hanvy, Wright J.	Pvt	B 3rd SCVIBn	Sharpsburg, MD	09/14/62	Ft. McHenry, MD	10/17/62	Fts. Monroe, VA Xc	CSR
Hanvy, Wright J.	Pvt	B 3rd SCVIBn	Gettysburg, PA	07/02/63	W. Bldg. Balt, MD	11/12/63	City Pt., VA Xc	CSR
Happerfield, Frank	Sgt	F 17th SCVI	Middletown, MD	09/13/62	Ft. Delaware, DE	10/02/62	Aikens Ldg., VA Xc	CSR
Happoldt, J.H.	Pvt	B 25th SCVI	Hartwell, GA	05/20/65	Hartwell, GA	05/20/65	Paroled on oath	CSR
Harbin, A.P.	Pvt	B P.S.S.	Greenville, SC	05/24/65	Greenville, SC	05/24/65	Paroled	CSR
Harbin, Harrison M.	Pvt	I Orr's Ri.	Spotsylvania, VA	05/12/64	Washington, D.C.	10/27/64	Elmira, NY	CSR
					Elmira, NY	02/20/65	James R., VA Xc	CSR
Harbin, John A.	Pvt	L P.S.S.	Lookout Mtn., TN	11/24/63	Nashville, TN	03/13/64	Louisville, KY	P39,TSE,CSR
Harbin, John A.	Pvt	L P.S.S.	Lookout Mtn., TN	09/24/63	Louisville, KY	03/24/64	Camp Chase, OH	CSR
					Camp Chase, OH	02/25/65	City Pt., VA Xc	CSR
Harbin, Robert D.A.	Pvt	F 1st SCVIH	Deserted/enemy	03/22/65	City Pt., VA P.M.	03/27/65	Washington, DC P.M.	CSR
					Washington, DC	03/27/65	Phila., PA on oath	CSR
Harbin, W.B.	Pvt	B 1st SCVIR	Smiths Ford, NC	03/16/65	New Berne, NC	04/23/65	Pt. Lookout, MD	CSR
					Pt. Lookout, MD	06/28/65	Rlsd. G.O. #109	P114,SA1,CSR
Harbin, W.J.	Pvt	F Orr's Ri.	Jarratts Stn., VA	04/03/65	City Pt., VA	04/07/65	Hart's Island, NY	CSR
					Hart's Island, NY	06/15/65	Rlsd. G.O. #109	P79,CDC,CSR
Harbin, W.J.	Pvt	G 7th SCVC	Farmville, VA	04/11/65	Farmville, VA	04/21/65	Paroled	CSR
Hardee, Calvin J.	Pvt	G 26th SCVI	Petersburg, VA	03/25/65	Washington, DC	03/30/65	Pt. Lookout, MD	CSR
					Pt. Lookout, MD	05/13/65	Rlsd. G.O. #85	CSR
Hardee, Isaac	Pvt	F 1st SCVIG	Sharpsburg, MD	10/01/62	Ft. McHenry, MD	10/13/62	Fts. Monroe, VA Xc	SA1,CSR
Hardee, Joel	Pvt	F 1st SCVIG	Gettysburg, PA	07/05/63	Ft. Delaware, DE	09/21/63	Died, Remit. fever	P5,P40,P42,P44,P47
Hardee, Joseph J.	Pvt	H 10th SCVI	Chattahootchie, GA	07/05/64	Camp Douglas, IL	05/13/65	Released GO #85	P55,CSR
Hardee, Michael W.	Pvt	C 10th SCVI			Vicksburg, MS	11/15/62	Exchanged	CSR,RAS
Hardee, R.C.	Pvt	H 10th SCVI	Chaplin Hills, KY	10/08/62	Danville, KY USGH	10/24/62	Died	CSR
Harden, Benson F.	Pvt	1st SCVIG	Deserted/enemy	01/13/65	City Pt., VA	01/14/65	Washington, DC	CSR,P8
					Washington, DC	01/14/65	Harrisburg, PA	CSR
Harden, J.B.	Pvt	B 14th SCMil	Lynch's Creek, SC	02/25/65	Hart's Island, NY	06/16/65	Rlsd. G.O. #109	P79
Harden, John L.	Pvt	H 5th SCVI	Cooke Co., TN	01/14/63	Nashville, TN	01/24/63	Louisville, KY	P39,SA3,CSR
					Louisville, KY	01/27/64	Rock Island, IL	CSR
					Rock Island, IL	05/03/65	New Orleans, LA	CSR
					New Orleans, LA	05/23/65	Exchanged	P4,CSR
Harden, Thomas	Smn	CS Chicora	Morris Island, SC	09/07/63	Pt. Lookout, MD	09/20/63	Ft. Warren, MA	P113,P124
Hardin, A.H.	Pvt	G 2nd SCVA	James Island, SC	02/10/65	Charleston, SC		Released on oath	CSR
Hardin, George	Cpl	G 5th SCVI	Middle Brook, TN	12/05/63	Knoxville, TN	12/05/63	Died of wounds	P1,P5,SA3,CSR

SOUTH CAROLINA SOLDIERS, SAILORS AND **H** CITIZENS HELD IN U.S. PRISONS 1861-1865

NAME	RANK	REGIMENT	CAPTURED AT	WHEN	PRISON	MOVED	DISPOSITION	SOURCES
Hardin, Martin	Pvt	C 15th SCVAB	Smith's Ford, NC	03/26/65	New Berne, NC	03/30/65	Pt. Lookout, MD	CSR
					Pt. Lookout, MD	06/08/65	Rlsd. on oath	P114,CSR
Hardin, Samuel	Pvt	C 15th SCVAB	Smith's Ford, NC	03/26/65	New Berne, NC	03/30/65	Pt. Lookout, MD	CSR
					Pt. Lookout, MD	06/05/65	Rlsd. on oath	P114,CSR
Hardin, William	Pvt	K 17th SCVI	Farmville, VA	04/11/65	Farmville, VA	04/21/65	Paroled	CSR
Hardin, William N.	Pvt	E 5th SCVI	Richmond, VA Hos.	04/03/65	Richmond, VA	04/20/65	Paroled	CSR
Harding, George	Cpl	C 2nd SCVA	Fayetteville, NC	03/12/65	Hart's Island, NY	06/16/65	Rlsd. G.O. #109	P79
Hardwick, S.P.	Pvt	A Ham.Leg.MI	Richmond, VA Hos.	04/03/65	Richmond, VA Hos.	04/21/65	Provost Marshal	CSR
					Libby Prison Rchmd.	04/23/65	Newport News, VA	CSR
					Newport News, VA	06/26/65	Rlsd. G.O. #109	CSR
Hardwick, William	Cpl	G 18th SCVI	Petersburg, VA	07/30/64	David's Island, NY	10/08/64	Elmira, NY	P1,CSR
					Elmira, NY	07/03/65	Rlsd. G.O. #109	P65,P66,CSR
Hardy, H.M.	Pvt	D 6th SCResB	Augusta, GA	05/24/65	Augusta, GA	05/24/65	Paroled	CSR
Hardy, John Y.	Pvt	C 14th SCVI	Jones Farm, VA	04/02/65	City Pt., VA	04/04/65	Pt. Lookout, MD	CSR
					Pt. Lookout, MD	06/27/65	Rlsd. G.O. #109	P114,CSR
Hardy, Miles J.	Sgt	I 1st SCVA	Mills Creek, NC	03/15/65	New Berne, NC	03/30/65	Pt. Lookout, MD	CSR
					Pt. Lookout, MD	06/28/65	Rlsd. G.O. #109	P114,CSR
Hardy, William A.	Pvt	B 14th SCVI	Petersburg, VA	07/29/64	City Pt., VA	08/05/64	Pt. Lookout, MD	P120,HOE
					Pt. Lookout, MD	08/08/64	Elmira, NY	P120,CSR
					Elmira, NY	05/19/65	Released G.O. #85	P65,P66,CSR
Hare, J.W.	Pvt	C 15th SCVI	Knoxville TN	12/05/63	Small pox Hospital	04/06/64	Louisville KY	CSR,KEB
					Camp Chase, OH	02/25/65	City Pt., VA Xc	P22,P26,CSR
					Richmond, VA Hos.	03/09/65	Furloughed 30 days	CSR
Hare, James	Pvt	B 14th SCVI	Petersburg, VA	04/03/65	City Pt., VA	04/13/65	Pt. Lookout, MD	CSR
					Pt. Lookout, MD	06/27/65	Rlsd. G.O. #109	P114,CSR
Hare, L.P.	Pvt	E 17th SCVI	Brandy Stn., VA	08/01/63	Old Capitol, DC		Baltimore, MD	CSR
					Baltimore, MD	08/23/63	Pt. Lookout, MD	CSR
Hare, L.P.	Pvt	E 17th SCVI	Brandy Stn., VA	08/01/63	Pt. Lookout, MD	03/15/65	Aikens Ldg., VA Xc	P113,P124,CSR
Hare, M.	Pvt	D 6th SCResB	Augusta, GA	05/24/65	Augusta, GA	05/24/65	Paroled	CSR
Hare, Thomas D.	Pvt	A 1st SCVIR	Morris Island, SC	09/07/63	Hilton Head, SC	09/19/63	Ft. Columbus, NY	CSR,SA1
					Ft. Columbus, NY	09/26/63	Pt. Lookout, MD	CSR
					Pt. Lookout, MD	11/15/63	Hammond G.H., MD	P113,P125
					Pt. Lookout, MD	01/11/64	Died, Ch. Diarrhea	P5,P12,FPH,CSR
Hare, William	Pvt	F 20th SCVI	Cedar Creek, VA	10/19/64	Harpers Ferry, WV	10/24/64	Pt. Lookout, MD	CSR
					Pt. Lookout, MD	03/28/65	Exchanged	P114,P124,CSR
Hargrove, D.T.	Pvt	K 8th SCVI	Gettysburg, PA	07/05/63	Gettysburg G.H.		Provost Marshal	P4,KEB
					David's Island, NY	10/26/63	Bedloes Island, NY	P1,CSR
					Bedloes Island, NY	01/06/64	Pt. Lookout, MD	CSR
					Pt.Lookout, MD	03/06/64	City Pt., VA Xc	CSR
Harken, James	Pvt	G 3rd SCVC	Deserted/enemy	02/19/65	Charleston, SC	03/02/65	Released	CSR
Harkins, James	Cpl	Ferguson's LA	Salisbury, NC	04/12/65	Nashville, TN	04/29/65	Louisville, KY	P39,CSR
					Louisville, KY	05/02/65	Camp Chase, OH	CSR
					Camp Chase, OH	06/13/65	Rlsd. G.O. #109	P23,CSR
Harleston, John	1Mt	P. *Savannah*	Off Charleston	06/06/61	Tombs Prison, NY	02/15/62	Ft. Lafayette, NY	OR,TCP
					Ft. Lafayette, NY	06/06/62	City Pt., VA Xc	OR,TCP,CDC
Harleston, John	1Lt	C 1st SCVA	Bentonville, NC	03/22/65	New Berne, NC	04/10/65	Hart's Island, NY	CSR
					Hart's Island, NY	04/15/65	Ft. Delaware, DE	P79,CSR
					Ft. Delaware, DE	06/16/65	Rlsd. G.O. #109	P43,P45,CSR
Harley, Calaway A.	Pvt	E 1st SCVC	Salisbury, NC	04/12/65	Nashville, TN	04/29/65	Louisville, KY	P39,CSR
					Camp Chase, OH	06/13/65	Rlsd. G.O. #109	P23,CSR
Harley, J.M.	Sgt	C 19th SCVCB	Augusta, GA	05/19/65	Augusta, GA	05/19/65	Paroled on oath	CSR

SOUTH CAROLINA SOLDIERS, SAILORS AND **H** CITIZENS HELD IN U.S. PRISONS 1861-1865

NAME	RANK	REGIMENT	CAPTURED AT	WHEN	PRISON	MOVED	DISPOSITION	SOURCES
Harley, James N.	Pvt	E 11th SCVI	Petersburg, VA	06/24/64	Bermuda Hundred, VA	06/24/64	Fts. Monroe, VA	CSR,HAG
					Fts. Monroe, VA	06/26/64	Pt. Lookout, MD	CSR
					Pt. Lookout, MD	08/16/64	Elmira, NY	P113,P120,CSR
					Elmira, NY	07/03/65	Rlsd. G.O. #109	P65,P66,CSR
Harley, Joseph M.	Pvt	I 2nd SCVI	Gettysburg, PA	07/04/63	Gettysburg G.H.	07/20/63	Provost Marshal	P4,KEB,CSR
					David's Island, NY	08/24/63	City Pt., VA Xc	SA2,P1,H2,CSR
Harley, Samuel R.	Pvt	A 1st SCVIG	Gettysburg, PA	07/05/63	Ft. Delaware, DE	06/10/65	Released	P43,P45,SA1,CSR
Harley, Thomas J.	Pvt	K 6th SCVC	Louisa C.H., VA	06/11/64	Fts. Monroe, VA	06/20/64	Pt. Lookout, MD	CSR
					Pt. Lookout, MD	07/25/64	Elmira, NY	P120
					Elmira, NY	03/14/65	Pt. Lookout, MD Xc	P65,P66,CSR
Harley, W.W.	Pvt	D 5th SCVC	Wilkinson Bridge, VA	12/01/64	City Pt., VA	12/05/64	Pt. Lookout, MD	CSR
					Pt. Lookout, MD	06/06/65	Released	P114,CSR
Harling, James	Pvt	K 14th SCVI	Gettysburg, PA	07/04/63	David's Island, NY	10/24/63	Bedloes Island, NY	CSR
					Bedloes Island, NY	01/07/64	Fts. Monroe, VA Xc	CSR,HOE
Harling, James F.	Cpl	G 1st SCVIG	Gettysburg, PA	07/03/63	Davids Island, NY	09/05/63	City Pt., VA Xc	P1,SA1,CSR
Harling, John M.	Pvt	B 15th SCVAB	Piney Grove, NC	03/18/65	New Berne, NC	04/03/65	Pt. Lookout, MD	CSR
					Pt. Lookout, MD	06/27/65	Rlsd. G.O. #109	P114,CSR
Harling, Lemuel	Cpl	K 14th SCVI	Spotsylvania, VA	05/12/64	Belle Plain, VA	05/21/64	Ft. Delaware, DE	CSR,HOE
					Ft. Delaware, DE	06/22/64	Hos. 6/22/64-?	P47
					Ft. Delaware, DE	08/22/64	Hos. 8/22-9/21/64	P47
					Ft. Delaware, DE	10/10/64	Hos. 10/10-10/30/64	P47
					Ft. Delaware, DE	10/30/64	Pt. Lookout, MD	P41,P43,CSR
					Pt. Lookout, MD	11/15/64	Venus Pt., GA Xc	P114,CSR
Harling, Rufus	Pvt	K 14th SCVI	Petersburg, VA	04/03/65	City Pt., VA	04/13/65	Pt. Lookout, MD	CSR
					Pt. Lookout, MD	06/27/65	Rlsd. G.O. #109	P114,HOE,CSR
Harmon, Duncan A.	Pvt	Brooks LA	Harpers Farm, VA	04/06/65	City Pt., VA	04/14/65	Pt. Lookout, MD	CSR
					Pt. Lookout, MD	06/28/65	Rlsd. G.O. #109	CSR
Harmon, Eliphus R.	Pvt	I 13th SCVI	Gettysburg, PA	07/04/63	Letterman G.H. Gbg	10/14/63	Provost Marshal	P1
					Letterman G.H. Gbg	10/14/63	Hammond USGH, MD	CSR
					Hammond G.H., MD	03/17/64	City Pt., VA Xc	P124,CSR
Harmon, Elisha	Pvt	B 26th SCVI	Deserted/enemy	02/14/65	City Pt., VA	02/17/65	Washington, DC	CSR
					Old Capitol, DC	02/20/65	Morris Island, SC	CSR
					Douglas G.H., DC	03/06/65	Died	P6,CSR
Harmon, Hugh T.	Pvt	B 3rd SCVI	Campbell Stn., TN	12/05/63	Nashville, TN	02/28/64	Louisville, KY	P39,SA2,ANY,CSR
					Loisville, KY	03/09/64	Camp Chase, OH	CSR,KEB
					Camp Chase, OH	07/23/64	Died, Dysntery	P6,P12,P22,P27,FPH
Harmon, James R.	Pvt	G 20th SCVI	Cedar Creek, VA	10/19/64	Harpers Ferry, WV	10/02/64	Pt. Lookout, MD	CSR
					Pt. Lookout, MD	03/28/65	Exchanged	P114,P124,KEB,CSR
Harmon, John H.	Pvt	G Hol.Leg.	Five Forks, VA	04/01/65	City Pt., VA	04/05/65	Pt. Lookout, MD	CSR
					Pt. Lookout, MD	06/28/65	Rlsd. G.O. #109	P114,ANY
Harmon, Monroe H.	1Lt	K 20th SCVI	Cedar Creek, VA	10/19/64	W. Bldg. Balt, MD	11/22/64	Pt. Lookout, MD	P1,KEB,CSR
					Ft. McHenry, MD	02/16/65	Pt. Lookout, MD	CSR
					Pt. Lookout, MD	02/16/65	James R., VA Xc	CSR
Harmon, Samuel	Pvt	I 13th SCVI	Gettysburg, PA	07/03/63	Ft. Delaware, DE	07/19/63	Chester, PA Hos.	P40,P42,HOS,CSR
					Chester, PA G.H.	07/28/63	Died, Ch. Diarrhea	P1,P6,P12,CSR
Harmon, T.C.	Cpl	I 13th SCVI	Falling Waters, MD	07/14/63	Pt. Lookout, MD	08/16/64	Elmira, NY	P113,P120,HOS,CSR
					Elmira, NY	10/11/64	Pt. Lookout, MD Xc	P65,P66,CSR
					Pt. Lookout, MD	10/29/64	Exchanged	P114,P124,CSR
Harmon, Wade	Pvt	B Hol.Leg.	Five Forks, VA	04/02/65	City Pt., VA	04/05/65	Pt. Lookout, MD	CSR
					Pt. Lookout, MD	06/28/65	Rlsd. G.O. #109	P114,CSR

SOUTH CAROLINA SOLDIERS, SAILORS AND **H** CITIZENS HELD IN U.S. PRISONS 1861-1865

NAME	RANK	REGIMENT	CAPTURED AT	WHEN	PRISON	MOVED	DISPOSITION	SOURCES
Harmon, William C.	Pvt	B 3rd SCVI	Knoxville, TN	12/05/63	Nashville, TN	02/28/64	Louisville, KY	P39,KEB,SA2,CSR,H3
					Louisville, KY	02/29/64	Ft. Delaware, DE	CSR
					Ft. Delaware, DE	07/14/64	Hos. 7/14-7/28/64	P47,KEB
					Ft. Delaware, DE	04/14/65	Hos. 4/14-5/11/65	P47,KEB
					Ft. Delaware, DE	06/10/65	Released	P41,P43,P45
Harmon, William Simpson	Sgt	H Hol.Leg.	Kinston, NC	12/15/62	Kinston, NC	12/15/62	Paroled POW	CSR,ANY
Harmon, William Simpson	Sgt	H Hol.Leg.	Five Forks, VA	04/01/65	City Pt., VA	04/05/65	Pt. Lookout, MD	CSR
					Pt. Lookout, MD	05/13/65	Died, Ac. Diarrhea	P6,P12,P114,FPH
Harner, Joseph	Pvt	Macbeth LA	Deserted/enemy		Knoxville, TN	02/27/65	Chattanooga, TN	CSR
					Louisville, KY	02/27/65	Sent north on oath	CSR
Haroldson, Edward F.	Pvt	B 1st SCVIG	Burkeville, VA	04/02/65	City Pt., VA	04/14/65	Pt. Lookout, MD	CSR
					Pt. Lookout, MD	06/23/65	Died, Ch. Diarrhea	P6,P114,FPH,CSR
Harp, John A.	Pvt	G Hol.Leg.	Hatchers Run, VA	03/25/65	City Pt., VA	04/02/65	Pt. Lookout, MD	CSR
					Pt. Lookout, MD	06/06/65	Released	P114,CSR
Harp, Player	Pvt	C 3rd SCVI	Black Creek, SC	03/01/65	New Berne, NC	04/03/65	Pt. Lookout, MD	CSR
					Pt. Lookout, MD	06/13/65	Rlsd. G.O. #109	P114,CSR
Harp, W.C.	Pvt	B 8th SCVI	Winchester, VA	09/13/64	Harpers Ferry, WV	09/19/64	Camp Chase, OH	CSR
					Camp Chase, OH	05/15/65	Rlsd. G.O.#85	P23,KEB,CSR
Harper, Henry Holcombe	Maj	14th SCVI	Deep Bottom, VA	07/28/64	Old Capitol, DC	08/04/64	Ft. Delaware, DE	CSR,LC
					Ft. Delaware, DE	07/24/65	Rlsd. G.O. #109	P43,P45,P46,CSR
Harper, J.K.	Pvt	K Orr's Ri.	Petersburg, VA	04/03/65	City Pt., VA	04/11/65	Hart's Island, NY	CSR
					Harts Island, NY	06/16/65	Rlsd. G.O. #109	P79,CSR
Harper, James W.	Pvt	L 2nd SCVIRi	Darbytown Rd., VA	12/10/64	Bermuda Hundred, VA	12/13/64	City Pt., VA P.M.	CSR
					City Pt., VA	12/15/64	Pt. Lookout, MD	CSR
					Pt. Lookout, MD	06/13/65	Rlsd. G.O. #109	P114,CSR
Harper, John H.	Pvt	A 15th SCVAB	Cheraw, SC	03/05/65	Cheraw, SC	03/05/65	Released on oath	CSR
Harper, John L.	Pvt	A 1st SCVA	Woodstock, VA	10/10/64	Pt. Lookout, MD	06/14/65	Rlsd. G.O. #109	CSR
Harrall, William	Pvt	D 1st CNREs	Cheraw, SC	03/05/65	Cheraw, SC	03/05/65	Paroled	CSR
Harrell, James A.	Sgt	A 14th SCVI	Petersburg, VA	04/02/65	City Pt., VA	04/04/65	Pt. Lookout, MD	CSR
					Pt. Lookout, MD	06/28/65	Rlsd. G.O. #109	P114,CSR
Harrell, Nathan	Pvt	H 21st SCVI	Morris Island, SC	07/10/64	Pt. Lookout, MD	08/16/64	Elmira, NY	P113,P120,P124,HAG
					Elmira, NY	10/11/64	Pt. Lookout, MD Xc	P65,P66
					Pt. Lookout, MD	10/29/64	Exchanged	P114
Harrell, Robert	Pvt	H 21st SCVI	Morris Island, SC	07/10/63	Morris Island, SC	07/13/63	Hilton Head, SC	CSR
					Hilton Head G.H.	07/13/63	Morris Island, SC Xc	P2,HAG,CSR
Harrell, W.T.	Pvt	H 8th SCVI	Maryland Hts., MD	09/13/62	Sandy Hook, MD USH	09/28/62	Died, Thigh amptd.	CSR
Harrelson, Elijah	Pvt	K 26th SCVI	Petersburg, VA	03/25/65	City Pt., VA	03/27/65	Pt. Lookout, MD	CSR
					Pt. Lookout, MD	06/13/65	Rlsd. G.O. #109	CSR
Harrelson, Frank H.	Pvt	A 21st SCVI	Morris Island, SC	07/10/63	Ft. Columbus, NY	09/23/63	Took the oath	P1,HAG
					Pt. Lookout, MD	02/18/65	Exchanged	P113,P124
Harrelson, J.	Pvt	I 8th SCVI	Winchester, VA	09/13/64	Harpers Ferry, WV	09/19/64	Camp Chase, OH	CSR
					Camp Chase, OH	05/02/65	New Orleans, LA	P23,P26,CSR
					New Orleans, LA	05/12/65	Vicksburg, MS Rls.	CSR
Harrelson, James	Pvt	C 26th SCVI	Petersburg, VA H	04/03/65	Camp Hamilton, VA	05/09/65	Newport News, VA	CSR
					Newport News, VA	06/26/65	Rlsd. G.O. #109	CSR
Harrelson, M. Jackson	Pvt	I 8th SCVI	Gettysburg, PA	07/03/63	Ft. Delaware, DE	06/10/65	Rlsd. G.O. #109	P40,P42,P44,CSR
Harrelson, Simeon	Pvt	C 26th SCVI	Five Forks, VA	04/01/65	City Pt., VA	04/03/65	Pt. Lookout, MD	CSR
					Pt. Lookout, MD	06/13/65	Rlsd. G.O. #109	P114,CSR
Harrelson, T.F.	Pvt	F 12th SCVI	Gettysburg, VA	07/04/63	Ft. Delaware, DE	06/10/65	Rlsd. G.O. #109	P42
Harrelson, William A.	Pvt	B Orr's Ri.	Devlins Bridge, VA	04/03/65	City Pt., VA	04/13/65	Pt. Lookout, MD	CSR
					Pt. Lookout, MD	06/27/65	Rlsd. G.O. #109	P114,CSR

H

SOUTH CAROLINA SOLDIERS, SAILORS AND CITIZENS HELD IN U.S. PRISONS 1861-1865

NAME	RANK	REGIMENT	CAPTURED AT	WHEN	PRISON	MOVED	DISPOSITION	SOURCES
Harrelson, William H.	Pvt	C 26th SCVI	Southside RR, VA	04/01/65	City Pt., VA	04/05/65	Pt. Lookout, MD	CSR
					Pt. Lookout, MD	06/13/65	Rlsd. G.O. #109	P114,CSR
Harrington, J.W.	1Sg	A 2nd SCVC	Stephensburg, VA	06/09/63	Old Capitol, DC	06/25/63	City Pt., VA Xc	CSR
Harrington, James T.	Pvt	A 24th SCVI	Kingston, GA	05/18/64	Nashville, TN	05/24/64	Louisville, KY	P3,EFW
					Louisville, KY	05/24/64	Rock Island, IL	CSR
Harrington, James T.	Pvt	A 24th SCVI	Kingston, GA	05/18/64	Rock Island, IL	06/10/64	Jd. U.S. Navy	CSR
Harrington, Patrick	Pvt	E 1st SCVIR	Morris Island, SC	09/07/64	Hilton Head, SC	10/03/64	Working at QM oath	SA1,CSR
Harriott, John	Pvt	B 5th SCVC	Augusta, GA	05/31/65	Augusta, GA	05/31/65	Pardoned	CSR
Harris, Alan	Sgt	A 24th SCVI	Oxford, GA	07/22/64	Camp Chase, OH	03/04/65	City Pt., VA Xc	P23
Harris, Alfred	2Lt	K 18th SCVI	Richmond, VA area		Ft. Delaware, DE	10/02/62	Aikens Ldg., VA Xc	CSR
Harris, Alfred	Pvt	F 6th SCVC	Stony Creek, VA	12/01/64	City Pt., VA	12/04/64	Pt. Lookout, MD	CSR
					Pt. Lookout, MD	05/15/65	Rlsd. G.O. #85	P114,CAG,CSR
Harris, Anderson K.	Pvt	A 18th SCVI	Petersburg, VA	07/30/64	City Pt., VA	08/05/64	Pt. Lookout, MD	CSR
					Pt. Lookout, MD	08/08/64	Elmira, NY	P113,P120,CSR
					Elmira, NY	07/07/65	Rlsd. G.O. #109	P65,P66,CSR
Harris, Arthur	Pvt	C Ham.Leg.MI	Richmond, VA	10/07/64	Pt. Lookout, MD	02/18/65	Exchanged	P114,P124
Harris, Edward J.	Pvt	D 6th SCResB	Smithfield, NC	03/19/65	New Berne, NC	04/10/65	Hart's Island, NY	CSR
					Hart's Island, NY	04/29/65	David's Island, NY	CSR
					David's Island, NY	06/03/65	Died, Ch. Diarrhea	P6,P12,P79,FPH,CSR
Harris, F.H.	Pvt	H 21st SCVI	Ft. Fisher, NC	01/15/65	Elmira, NY	07/11/65	Rlsd. G.O. #109	P65,HAG
Harris, Frank E.	Cpl	B 2nd SCVI	Cedar Creek, VA	10/23/64	Harpers Ferry, WV	10/25/64	Pt. Lookout, MD	CSR,SA2,KEB,H2
					Pt. Lookout, MD	03/28/65	Boulware's Wh. Xc	CSR
Harris, George P.	Pvt	C 7th SCVC	Deserted/enemy	11/10/64	Knoxville, TN P.M.	11/16/64	Chattanooga, TN	CSR
					Louisville, KY	11/25/64	Indiana on oath	CSR
Harris, George W.	Pvt	B 14th SCVI	Gettysburg, PA	07/04/63	David's Island, NY	08/24/63	City Pt., VA Xc	P1,HOE,CSR
Harris, H.L.	Pvt	B 2nd SCVC	Alexandria, VA	07/11/63	Old Capitol, DC	08/08/63	Pt. Lookout, MD	CSR
					Pt. Lookout, MD	10/30/64	Exchanged	P113,P124,CSR
Harris, James	Pvt	B 23rd SCVI	Frederick, MD	09/12/62	Ft. Delaware, DE	10/02/62	Aikens Ldg., VA Xc	CSR
Harris, James	Pvt	B 23rd SCVI	Deserted/enemy	02/09/65	City Pt., VA	02/22/65	New York, NY oath	CSR
Harris, James	Cpl	K Hol.Leg.	Stony Creek, VA	05/01/64	Fts. Monroe, VA	05/13/64	Pt. Lookout, MD	CSR
					Pt. Lookout, MD	08/15/64	Elmira, NY	P113,P120
					Elmira, NY	10/11/64	Pt. Lookout, MD Xc	P65,P66
					Pt. Lookout, MD	10/29/64	Exchanged	P114
Harris, James	Coo	H 12th SCVI	Charlotte, NC	05/16/65	Charlotte, NC	05/16/65	Paroled	CSR
Harris, John	Pvt	H 12th SCVI	Sharpsburg, MD	09/17/62	Frederick, MD USGH	05/16/63	Ft. McHenry, MD	CSR
					Ft. McHenry, MD	06/11/63	Fts. Monroe, VA Xc	CSR
					Petersburg, VA Hos.	06/12/63	Wdd Furlough 60 day	CSR
Harris, John	Pvt	B 15th SCVAB	Fayetteville, NC	03/16/65	New Berne, NC	03/30/65	Pt. Lookout MD	CSR
					Pt. Lookout, MD	05/15/65	Rlsd. G.O. #85	P114,CSR
Harris, John C.	Pvt	E 17th SCVI	Ft. Steadman, VA	03/25/65	City Pt., VA	03/27/65	Washington, DC	CSR,YEB
					Old Capital, DC	05/11/65	Elmira, NY	P7,CSR
					Elmira, NY	07/07/65	Rlsd. G.O. #109	P65,P66,CSR
Harris, John M.	Cpt	D 3rd SCVIBn	Gettysburg, PA	07/04/63	Ft. McHenry, MD	08/24/63	Johnson's Isl., OH	CSR
					Johnson's Isl., OH	09/16/64	Fts. Monroe, VA Xc	CSR
Harris, Laurence F.	Pvt	I 2nd SCVC	Rapidan R., VA	02/06/64	Old Capitol, DC	06/15/64	Ft. Delaware, DE	CSR,HOE
					Ft. Delaware, DE	02/25/65	Hos. 2/25-2/26/65	P45,P47
					Ft. Delaware, DE	06/10/65	Rlsd. G.O. #109	P41,P43,CSR
Harris, Martin	Pvt	K Hol.Leg.	Five Forks, VA	04/01/65	City Pt., VA	04/05/65	Pt. Lookout, MD	CSR
					Pt. Lookout, MD	05/25/65	Died, Ch. Diarrhea	P6,P12,P114,FPH
Harris, Morris	Sgt	A 24th SCVI	Stone Mtn., GA	07/24/64	Nashville, TN	07/25/64	Louisville, KY	CSR
					Louisville, KY	08/02/64	Camp Chase, OH	CSR
					Camp Chase, OH	03/04/65	City Pt., VA Xc	P26,CSR

SOUTH CAROLINA SOLDIERS, SAILORS AND  CITIZENS HELD IN U.S. PRISONS 1861-1865

NAME	RANK	REGIMENT	CAPTURED AT	WHEN	PRISON	MOVED	DISPOSITION	SOURCES
Harris, Oliver	Pvt	D 4th SCST	Greensboro, NC	05/09/65	Greensboro, NC	05/09/65	Paroled	CSR
Harris, Peter	Pvt	G 5th SCVI	Petersburg, VA	04/02/65	City Pt. VA	04/07/65	Hart's Island, NY	CSR
					Hart's Island, NY	06/16/65	Rlsd. G.O. #109	P79,YEB,CSR
Harris, Pinckney	Pvt	B 14th SCVI	Augusta, GA	05/19/65	Augusta, GA	05/19/65	Paroled	CSR
Harris, Samuel N.	Cpl	D 3rd SCVIBn	Gettysburg, PA	07/05/63	Letterman G.H. Gbg	09/16/63	Provost Marshal	P1,KEB,CSR
					W. Bldg. Balt, MD	09/25/63	City Pt., VA Xc	P1,CSR
Harris, T.H.	Pvt	A 14th SCVI	Sutherland Stn., VA	04/03/65	Hart's Island, NY	06/17/65	Rlsd. G.O. #109	P79
Harris, Thomas J.	Pvt	E 2nd SCVA	Goldsboro, NC	03/10/65	New Berne, NC	03/30/65	Pt. Lookout, MD	CSR
					Pt. Lookout, MD	04/28/65	Died, Pleurisy	P6,P114,FPH,CSR
Harris, Thomas Y.	Pvt	F 14th SCVI	Gettysburg, PA	07/04/63	David's Island, NY	09/05/63	City Pt., VA Xc	P1,CSR
					Petersburg, VA Hos.	09/15/63	Furloughed 30 days	CSR
Harris, Tillman E.	Pvt	A 22nd SCVI	Bermuda Hundred, VA	06/02/64	Bermuda Hundred, VA	06/03/64	Fts. Monroe, VA	CSR
					Fts. Monroe, VA	06/04/64	Pt. Lookout, MD	CSR
Harris, Tillman E.	Pvt	A 22nd SCVI	Bermuda Hundred, VA	06/02/64	Pt. Lookout, MD	03/11/65	Aikens Ldg., VA Xc	P113,P124,CSR
Harris, W.	Pvt	F 1st SCVIG	Richmond, VA area		Fts. Monroe, VA	09/07/62	Aikens Ldg., VA Xc	CSR
Harris, William	Pvt	K 14th SCVI	Petersburg, VA	04/03/65	City Pt., VA	04/07/65	Hart's Island, NY	CSR
					Hart's Island, NY	06/17/65	Rlsd. G.O. #109	P79,HOE,CSR
Harris, William M.	Pvt	K 18th SCVI	Five Forks, VA	04/01/65	Pt. Lookout, MD	06/13/65	Rlsd. G.O. #109	P114,CSR
Harrison, A.J.	2Lt	B 5th SCVC	Augusta, GA	05/20/65	Augusta, GA	05/20/65	Paroled	CSR
Harrison, A.M.	Pvt	H 1st SCVIH	Farmville, VA	04/06/65	City Pt., VA	04/14/65	Newport News, VA	CSR
					Newport News, VA	06/26/65	Rlsd. G.O. #109	CSR
Harrison, B.	Pvt	C 11th SCVI	Petersburg, VA	06/18/64	Pt. Lookout, MD	07/24/64	Elmira, NY	P113,P120,HAG,CSR
					Elmira, NY	09/18/64	Aikens Ldg., VA Xc	P65,P66,CSR
Harrison, B.L.	Pvt	C 14th SCVI	Sutherland Stn., VA	04/02/65	Hart's Island, NY	06/16/65	Rlsd. G.O. #109	P79
Harrison, C.W.	Pvt	K 1st SCVA	Deserted/enemy	03/25/65	Charleston, SC		Released on oath	CSR
Harrison, Daniel B.	Pvt	F 12th SCVI	Spotsylvania, VA	05/12/64	Belle Plain, VA	05/20/64	Ft. Delaware, DE	CSR,HFC
					Ft. Delaware, DE	06/10/65	Released	P41,P45,P43,CSR
Harrison, F.M.	Pvt	I 27th SCVI	Deserted/enemy	12/08/64	Bermuda Hundred, VA	12/14/64	Washington, DC	CSR
					Washington, DC	12/15/64	Cedar Falls, IA	CSR
Harrison, J.	Pvt	B 7th SCVI	Petersburg VA Hos.	04/03/65	Petersburg, VA P.M.	05/25/65	Paroled	CSR
Harrison, J.W.	Pvt	K 2nd SCVC	Raleigh, NC	04/13/65	Raleigh, NC	04/13/65	Released on parole	CSR
Harrison, John	Pvt	C 5th SCVI	Lookout Mtn., TN	11/24/63	Bridgeport, AL G.H	12/11/63	Nashville, TN	P2,CSR
Harrison, John D.	Pvt	F 12th SCVI	Spotsylvania, VA	05/12/64	Ft. Delaware, DE	12/29/64	Hos. 12/29-1/14/65	P47,HFC
					Ft. Delaware, DE	06/10/65	Released	P41,P43,P45
Harrison, John T.	Pvt	C Ham.Leg.	Missionary Ridge, TN	11/25/63	Nashville, TN	12/16/63	Louisville, KY	P39
					Louisville, KY	12/21/63	Rock Island, IL	CSR
					Rock Island, IL	05/26/65	Rlsd. G.O. 5/9/65	CSR
Harrison, Milton C.	Pvt	F 12th SCVI	Warrenton, VA	09/29/62	Warrenton, VA	09/29/62	Paroled	CSR
					Winder Hos. Rchmd.	10/18/62	Prld. POW Camp Lee	CSR
Harrison, P.H.	Pvt	K 7th SCVC	Augusta, GA	05/22/65	Augusta, GA	05/22/65	Paroled	CSR
Harrison, T.J.	Pvt	A 3rd SCVABn	High Pt., NC	05/02/65	High Pt., NC	05/02/65	Paroled	CSR
Harrison, Thomas F.	Pvt	F 12th SCVI	Gettysburg, PA	07/05/63	Ft. McHenry, MD	07/14/63	Ft. Delaware, DE	CSR,HFC
					Ft. Delaware, DE	06/10/65	Released	P40,P44,P45,CSR
Harrison, W.G.	HSd	G 17th SCVI	Amelia C.H., VA	04/06/65	Libby Prison Rchmd.		City Pt., VA	CSR
					City Pt., VA	04/14/65	Pt. Lookout, MD	CSR
					Pt. Lookout, MD	06/27/65	Rlsd. G.O. #109	P114,CSR
Harrison, Wilson S.	Pvt	K 1st SCVA	Smithville, NC	03/16/65	New Berne, NC	03/30/65	Pt. Lookout, MD	CSR
					Pt. Lookout, MD	04/14/65	Died, Pneumonia	P6,P114,FPH,CSR
Harrod, George M.	Pvt	C 1st SCVIH	Warrenton, VA	09/29/62	Warrenton, VA	09/29/62	Paroled	CSR
Harrod, George M.	Pvt	C 1st SCVIH	Chattanooga, TN	10/29/63	Nashville, TN	11/07/63	Louisville, KY	P39,SA1,CSR
					Louisville, KY	11/09/63	Camp Morton, IN	CSR
					Camp Morton, IN	03/04/65	City Pt., VA Xc	CSR

SOUTH CAROLINA SOLDIERS, SAILORS AND  CITIZENS HELD IN U.S. PRISONS 1861-1865

NAME	RANK	REGIMENT	CAPTURED AT	WHEN	PRISON	MOVED	DISPOSITION	SOURCES
Hart, Agnew R.	Pvt	G 27th SCVI	Town Creek, NC	02/20/65	Ft. Anderson, NC	02/28/65	Pt. Lookout, MD	CSR,HAG
					Pt. Lookout, MD	06/13/65	Released	P114
Hart, Capers H.	1Sg	F 25th SCVI	Weldon RR, VA	08/21/64	City Pt., VA	08/24/64	Pt. Lookout, MD	CSR,HAG
					Pt. Lookout, MD	03/14/65	Exchanged	P113,P124,P125
Hart, D.E.	Pvt	E 14th SCMil	Camden, SC	03/01/65	Hart's Island, NY	06/16/65	Rlsd. G.O. #109	P79
Hart, Harrison H.	Pvt	A 1st SCVIG	Gettysburg, PA	07/05/63	Ft. McHenry, MD	07/12/63	Ft. Delaware, DE	CSR,SA1
					Ft. Delaware, DE	03/04/64	Dis. Hos. 3/4/64	P47
					Ft. Delaware, DE	03/22/64	Hos. 3/22-9/18/64	P47
					Ft. Delaware, DE	09/14/64	Aikens Ldg., VA Xc	P40,P42,P44,CSR
Hart, Harvey L.	Pvt	H 12th SCVI	Spotsylvania, VA	05/12/64	Belle Plain, VA	05/20/64	Ft. Delaware, DE	CSR
					Ft. Delaware, DE	06/14/65	Released	CSR
Hart, Ira E.	Pvt	D 2nd SCVC	Charlotte, NC	05/23/65	Charlotte, NC	05/23/65	Released on Parole	CSR
Hart, J.M.	Pvt	H 22nd SCVI	Crater, Pbg., VA	07/30/64	City Pt., VA	08/05/64	Pt. Lookout, MD	CSR
					Pt. Lookout, MD	08/08/64	Elmira, NY	P113,P120
					Elmira, NY	10/11/64	Pt. Lookout to Xc	P65,P66
					Pt. Lookout, MD	10/29/64	Exchanged	P114
Hart, John L.	Pvt	H 12th SCVI	Spotsylvania, VA	05/12/64	Ft. Delaware, DE	12/21/64	Hos. 12/21/64-1/2/65	P47,CWC
					Ft. Delaware, DE	02/20/65	Hos. 2/20-2/24/65	P47
					Ft. Delaware, DE	03/17/65	Hos. 3/17-3/27/65	P47
					Ft. Delaware, DE	06/14/65	Released	P43,P45
Hart, Joseph S.	Pvt	D 2nd SCVC	Beverly Ford, VA	06/09/63	Old Capitol, DC	06/25/63	City Pt., VA Xc	CSR
Hart, Joseph W.	Pvt	H 16th SCVI	Chattahoochee, GA	07/03/64	Nashville, TN	07/12/64	Louisville, KY	CSR
					Louisville, KY	07/14/64	Camp Douglas, IL	CSR
					Camp Douglas, IL	05/13/65	Discharged on oath	P53,CSR
Hart, Thomas C.	1Sg	G 27th SCVI	Weldon RR, VA	08/21/64	City Pt., VA	08/23/64	Pt. Lookout, MD	CSR,HAG
					Pt. Lookout, MD	12/17/64	Died, Ac. Diarrhea	P5,P113,FPH,CSR
Harth, William E.	Pvt	Palmetto L	Appomattox C.H., VA	04/09/65	City Pt., VA	04/26/65	Washington, DC	CSR
					Lincoln G.H., DC	06/14/65	Released	CSR
Hartley,	Lt	C 3rd SCVABn	Blakely, AL	04/09/65	Provost Marshal	04/10/65		CSR
Hartley, Elmore F.	Pvt	F 19th SCVI	Augusta, GA	05/22/65	Augusta, GA	05/22/65	Paroled	CSR
Hartley, Gabriel	Pvt	H 1st SCVIH	Winchester, VA Hos.	12/04/62	Winchester, VA Hos.	12/04/62	Paroled	CSR
Hartley, James W.	Sgt	F 19th SCVI	Augusta, GA	05/22/65	Augusta, GA	05/22/65	Paroled	CSR
Hartman, Henry	Pvt	E Orr's Ri.	Ft.Whitworth, VA	04/02/65	City Pt., VA	04/05/65	Pt. Lookout, MD	CSR
					Pt. Lookout, MD	06/27/65	Rlsd. G.O. #109	P114,CDC,CSR
Hartman, J. Melvin	Pvt	C 3rd SCVI	Gettysburg, PA	07/05/63	Gettysburg, PA G.H.	07/21/63	Provost Marshal	P4,KEB,SA2,H3,CSR
					David's Island, NY	09/12/63	City Pt., VA Xc	P1,CSR
					Williamsburg, VA Hos.	09/21/63	Furloughed	CSR
Hartman, J.M.	Pvt	H Hol.Leg.	Kinston, NC	12/15/62	Kinston, NC	12/15/62	Paroled POW	CSR,ANY
Hartness, John R.	Pvt	C 17th SCVI	Crater, Pbg., VA	07/30/64	City Pt., VA	08/05/64	Pt. Lookout, MD	CSR,YEB
					Pt. lookout, MD	08/08/64	Elmira, NY	P113,P120
					Elmira, NY	03/02/65	Died, Diarrhea	P6,P65,P66,FPH,CSR
Hartnett, Michael	Pvt	C 1st SCVIH	Deserted/enemy	03/17/65	Washington, DC P.M.	03/30/65	New York, NY oath	CSR
					City Pt., VA P.M.	03/26/65	Washington, DC	CSR
Hartnett, Michael	Pvt	A 2nd SCVI	Salisbury, NC	04/12/65	Louisville, KY	04/29/65	Nashville, TN	CSR,SA2,KEB,H2
					Nashville, TN	04/29/65	Louisville, KY	P39,CSR
					Nashville, TN	07/06/65	Rlsd. on oath	SA2
Hartz, C.H.	Pvt	B German LA	Deserted/enemy	10/01/64	Hilton Head, SC D.	10/13/64	Str. Fulton to NY	CSR
Hartzog, Charles	Pvt	H 17th SCVI	Deserted/enemy	03/08/65	P.M. A. of Potomac	03/06/65	City Pt., VA P.M.	CSR
					City Pt., VA	03/07/65	Washington, DC	CSR
					Washington, DC	03/10/65	Charleston, SC oath	CSR

SOUTH CAROLINA SOLDIERS, SAILORS AND  CITIZENS HELD IN U.S. PRISONS 1861-1865

NAME	RANK	REGIMENT	CAPTURED AT	WHEN	PRISON	MOVED	DISPOSITION	SOURCES
Hartzog, Elias H.	Pvt	H 17th SCVI	Crater, Pbg., VA	07/30/64	City Pt., VA	08/05/64	Pt. Lookout, MD	CSR
					Pt. Lookout, MD	08/08/64	Elmira, NY	P113,P120,CSR
					Elmira, NY	10/11/64	Pt. Lookout, MD Xc	P65,P66,CSR
					Pt. Lookout, MD	10/29/64	Venus Pt., GA Xc	P114,CSR
					Pt. Lookout, MD	06/13/65	Rlsd. G.O. #109	P114,CSR
Harvel, Tristam	Pvt	K 8th SCVI	Petersburg, VA	07/29/64	Pt. Lookout, MD	08/11/64	Elmira, NY	P120,CSR,KEB
					Elmira, NY	10/11/64	Pt. Lookout, MD	P65,CSR
					Pt. Lookout, MD	10/29/64	Venus Pt., GA Xc	P114,CSR
Harvell, Daniel B.	Pvt	H 2nd SCVI	near Knoxville, TN	12/03/63	Knoxville, TN	12/15/63	Louisville, KY	CSR
					Louisville, KY	12/31/63	Rock Island, IL	CSR
					Rock Island, IL	02/05/64	Jd. U.S. Navy	H2,CSR
Harvely, Whitfield	Pvt	K 14th SCVI	Gettysburg, PA	07/04/63	David's Island, NY	09/08/63	City Pt., VA Xc	P1,CSR,HOE
Harvey, A.J.	Pvt	G 17th SCVI	Deserted/enemy	03/08/65	A of P. Prov. Mar.	03/08/65	City Pt., VA P.M.	CSR
					City Pt., VA	03/09/65	Washington, DC	CSR
					Washington, DC	03/10/65	Charleston, SC	CSR
Harvey, A.J.	Pvt	G 17th SCVI	Petersburg, VA	03/08/65	NY City Transit Hos.	03/25/65	Died	CSR,FPH
Harvey, George W.	Pvt	D 22nd SCVI	Kinston, NC	12/15/62	Kinston, NC	12/15/62	Paroled POW	CSR
Harvey, George W.	Pvt	D 22nd SCVI	Bermuda Hundred, VA	06/02/64	Fts. Monroe, VA	06/04/64	Pt. Lookout, MD	CSR
					Pt. Lookout, MD	04/01/65	Died, Scurvy	P6,P113,FPH,CSR
Harvey, J. Caswell	Pvt	B Hol.Leg.	Five Forks, VA	04/01/65	City Pt., VA	04/05/65	Pt. Lookout, MD	CSR
					Pt. Lookout, MD	06/28/65	Rlsd. G.O. #109	P114,HOS
Harvey, James R.	Pvt	F 12th SCVI	Gettysburg, PA	07/05/63	David's Island, NY	10/24/63	Bedloes Island, NY	P1,HFC
					Bedloes Island, NY	07/15/64	Ft. Delaware, DE	CSR
					Ft. Delaware, DE	09/14/64	Aikens Ldg., VA Xc	P41,P43,CSR
					Jackson Hos. Rchmd.	09/25/64	Wdd. Furlough 60 d.	CSR
Harvey, James W.	Cpl	D 16th SCVI	Marietta, GA	07/03/64	Nashville, TN	07/13/64	Louisville, KY	CSR
					Louisville, KY	07/16/64	Camp Douglas, IL	CSR
					Camp Douglas, IL	06/16/65	Rlsd. G.O. #109	P53,16R,CSR
Harvey, John	Pvt	B 18th SCVI	Burkeville, VA	04/03/65	City Pt., VA	04/13/63	Pt. Lookout, MD	P114,CSR
					Pt. Lookout, MD	06/28/65	Rlsd. G.O. #109	P114,CSR
Harvey, John	Pvt	C Hol.Leg.	Petersburg, VA	04/03/65	Petersburg F. Gds. Hos.	04/08/65	U.S. Gen. Hospital	CSR
Harvey, John	Pvt	B Hol.Leg.	Farmville, VA	04/06/65	City Pt., VA	04/14/65	Newport News, VA	CSR
					Newport News, VA	06/26/65	Rlsd. G.O. #109	CSR
Harvey, Joseph	Pvt	I Hol.Leg.	Petersburg, VA	04/03/65	Petersburg F. Gds. Hos.	04/07/65	U.S. Gen. Hospital	CSR
					U.S. Gen. Hospital	04/08/65	Pt. of Rocks Hos.	CSR
					Pt. of Rocks Hos.	04/12/65	Fts. Monroe G.H.	CSR
					Fts. Monroe G.H.	06/29/65	Released	CSR
Harvey, Samuel	Pvt	A 2nd SCVIRi	Missionary Ridge, TN	11/25/63	Bridgeport, AL Hos.	12/13/63	Nashville, TN	CSR,P2
Harvey, Thomas M.	Pvt	D 2nd SCVC	Madison C.H., VA	09/22/63	Old Capitol, DC	09/26/63	Elmira, NY	CSR
					Pt. Lookout, MD	08/16/64	Elmira, NY	P113,P120,P124,CSR
					Elmira, NY	03/10/65	Pt. Lookout to Xc	P65,P66,CSR
Harvin, Septimus Arthur	Pvt	C Ham.Leg.MI	Darbytown Rd., VA	10/07/64	Bermuda Hundred, VA	10/08/64	Provost Marshal	CSR
					Dutch Gap, VA	10/21/64	Pt. Lookout, MD	CSR
					Pt. Lookout, MD	02/18/65	Exchanged	CSR
Haselden, Edward A.	Pvt	C 26th SCVI	Five Forks, VA	04/01/65	Pt. Lookout, MD	06/28/65	Rlsd. G.O. #109	P114,HMC
					City Pt., VA	04/03/65	Pt. Lookout, MD	CSR
Haselden, Hugh G.	Pvt	F 4th SCVC	Hawe's Shop, VA	05/28/64	3rd Div. 5th A.C.	06/12/64	Washington, DC	CSR,HMC
					Douglas G.H., DC	06/27/64	Lincoln G.H., DC	CSR
					Lincoln, G.H., DC	08/17/64	Old Capitol, DC	CSR
					Old Capitol, DC	08/28/64	Elmira, NY	CSR
Haselden, Hugh G.	Pvt	F 4th SCVC	Hawe's Shop, VA	05/28/64	Elmira, NY	01/06/65	Died, Ch. Diarrhea	P5,P12,FPH,CSR

SOUTH CAROLINA SOLDIERS, SAILORS AND CITIZENS HELD IN U.S. PRISONS 1861-1865

NAME	RANK	REGIMENT	CAPTURED AT	WHEN	PRISON	MOVED	DISPOSITION	SOURCES
Hasell, Lewis	Sur	26th SCVI	Petersburg, VA	04/02/65	Washington, DC	05/13/65	Johnsons Isl., OH	CSR
					Johnsons Isl., OH	06/23/65	Rlsd. G.O. #109	CSR
Haskell, C.H.	Lt	CS Navy	Morris Island, SC	09/07/63	Ft. Columbus, NY	10/09/63	Johnson's Isl., OH	P1
Haskell, W.E.	Pvt	K 3rd SCVC	Pocotaligo, SC	01/18/65	Hilton Head, SC	03/12/65	Ft. Delaware, DE	CSR
					Ft. Delaware, DE	06/10/65	Released	P41,P43,P45,CSR
Haskell, William E., Jr.	Pvt	H 2nd SCVC	Kellys Ford, VA	03/17/63	Old Capitol, VA	03/29/63	City Pt., VA Xc	CSR
Haskins, Miles	Pvt	D 22nd SCVI	Boonesboro, MD	09/14/62	Gainesville, VA		Arlington, VA	CSR
					Arlington, VA	11/18/62	Old Capitol, DC	CSR,HOS
					Old Capitol, DC	12/27/62	Kalorama Hos., DC	CSR
					Kalorama Hos., DC	03/03/63	Died, Variola	P12,CSR
Haskins, William S.	Pvt	B 22nd SCVI	Gainesville, VA		Arlington, VA	11/17/62	Old Capitol, DC	CSR
					Old Capitol, DC	01/16/63	Died, Phtisis Pulm.	P12,CSR
Haste, John	Pvt	K 15th SCVI	Augusta, GA	05/18/65	Augusta, GA	05/18/65	Paroled on oath	H15,CSR
Hasting, William P.	Pvt	G 1st SCVIG	Petersburg, VA	04/02/65	City Pt., VA	04/04/65	Pt. Lookout, MD	CSR
					Pt. Lookout, MD	06/28/65	Rlsd. G.O. #109	P114,SA1,CSR
Hastings, John	Pvt	K 15th SCVI	Halltown, VA	08/26/64	Harpers Ferry, WV	08/31/64	Camp Chase, OH	CSR,KEB
					Camp Chase, OH	02/17/65	Pt. Lookout, MD	P23,P26,KEB,CSR
					Pt. Lookout, MD	03/27/65	Boulware's Wh. Xc	CSR
Hasty, James	Pvt	C 2nd SCVIRi	Richmond, VA Hos.	04/03/65	Libby Prison Rchmd.	04/23/65	Newport News, VA	CSR
					Newport News, VA	06/26/65	Rlsd. G.O. #109	CSR
Hatchel, F.	Pvt	C 3rd SCVABn	Ft. Gaines, AL	08/08/64	New Orleans, LA	10/25/64	Ship Island, MS	P3,CSR
Hatchel, F.	Pvt	C 3rd SCVABn	Blakely, AL	04/09/65	Ship Island, MS	05/01/65	Vicksburg, MS Xc	CSR
Hatchel, Thomas H.	Pvt	H 10th SCVI	Bardstown, KY USGH	10/14/62	Died, no record		Died per CTA	CSR,CTA
Hatchell, Calvin	Pvt	G 26th SCVI	Five Forks, VA	04/01/65	City Pt., VA	04/05/65	Pt. Lookout, MD	CSR
					Pt. Lookout, MD	06/28/65	Rlsd. G.O. #109	P114,CSR
Hatchell, Joel B.	Msc	C 3rd SCVABn	Blakely, AL	04/09/65	Ship Island, MS	05/01/65	Vicksburg, MS Xc	CSR
Hatchell, R.E.T.	Pvt	C 3rd SCVABn	Blakely, AL	04/09/65	Ship Island, IL	05/01/65	Vicksburg, MS Xc	CSR
Hatchell, R.E.T.	Pvt	C 3rd SCVABn	Augusta, GA	05/20/65	Augusta, GA	05/20/65	Paroled	CSR
Hatchell, R.F.	Pvt	C 3rd SCVABn	Ft. Gaines, AL	08/08/64	New Orleans, LA	10/25/64	Ship Island, MS	CSR
					Ship Island, MS	01/04/65	Exchanged	CSR
Hatchell, R.F.	Pvt	C 3rd SCVABn	Augusta, GA	05/20/65	Augusta, GA	05/20/65	Paroled	CSR
Hatchell, R.H.	Pvt	C 3rd SCVABn	Ft. Gaines, AL	08/08/64	New Orleans, LA	09/10/64	St. Louis, MO USGH	CSR
					New Orleans, LA	10/21/64	Ship Island, MS	P3
					St. Louis, MO USGH	11/13/64	Died, Remit. fever	P3,CSR
Hatchell, Spencer W.	Pvt	G 26th SCVI	Five Forks, VA	04/01/65	City Pt., VA	04/05/65	Pt. Lookout, MD	CSR
					Pt. Lookout, MD	06/28/65	Rlsd. G.O. #109	P114,CSR
Hatchell, Spias B.	Pvt	C 3rd SCVABn	Ft. Gaines, AL	08/08/64	New Orleans, LA	10/25/64	Ship Island, MS	CSR
					Ship Island, MS	12/05/64	Died, Dysentery	CSR
Hatchell, Theodore	Pvt	G 26th SCVI	Five Forks, VA	04/01/65	City Pt., VA	04/05/65	Pt. Lookout, MD	CSR
					Pt. Lookout, MD	06/28/65	Rlsd. G.O. #109	P114,CSR
Hatchell, W.G.	Pvt	C 3rd SCVABn	Blakely, AL	04/09/65	Ship Island, AL	05/01/65	Vicksburg, MS Xc	CSR
Hatchell, W.G.	Pvt	C 3rd SCVABn	Augusta, GA	05/20/65	Augusta, GA	05/20/65	Paroled	CSR
Hatchell, William H.	Pvt	D 21st SCVI	Ft. Fisher, NC	01/15/65	Elmira, NY	06/29/65	Died, Pneumonia	P6,P65,HAG,FPH
Hatcher, D.W.	Pvt	D 2nd SCVIRi	Farmville, VA	04/06/65	City Pt., VA	04/14/65	Newport News, VA	CSR
					Newport News, VA	06/26/65	Rlsd. G.O. #109	CSR
Hatcher, Francis M.	Pvt	B 15th SCVAB	Deserted/enemy		Louisville, KY	04/10/65	North of Ohio River	CSR
Hatcher, John	Pvt	I 2nd SCVI	Cedar Creek, VA	10/19/64	Harpers Ferry, WV	10/23/64	Pt. Lookout, MD	CSR,SA2,H2
					Pt. Lookout, MD	01/17/65	Exchanged 1/21/65	SA2,P114,P124,H2,CSR
Hatcher, William H.	Pvt	C 12th SCVI	Harpers Farm, VA	04/06/65	City Pt., VA	04/14/65	Pt. Lookout, MD	CSR
					Pt. Lookout, MD	06/27/65	Rlsd. G.O. #109	P114,HFC,CSR

SOUTH CAROLINA SOLDIERS, SAILORS AND  CITIZENS HELD IN U.S. PRISONS 1861-1865

NAME	RANK	REGIMENT	CAPTURED AT	WHEN	PRISON	MOVED	DISPOSITION	SOURCES
Hatfield, James W.	Pvt	E 7th SCVIBn	Weldon RR, VA	08/21/64	City Pt., VA USFH	08/23/64	Fts. Monroe, VA	CSR,HAG
					Fts. Monroe, VA	08/26/64	Alexandria, VA USG	CSR
					Alexandria, VA USG	10/04/64	Lincoln G.H., D C	P1,HAG,CSR
					Lincoln G.H., DC	10/14/64	Old Capitol, DC	CSR
					Old Capitol, DC	10/24/64	Elmira, NY	CSR
					Elmira, NY	04/29/65	Died, Ch. Diarrhea	P6,P65,P66,FPH,CSR
Hathaway, S.	Pvt	A 21st SCVI	Petersburg, VA	06/24/64	Pt. Lookout, MD	10/11/64	Exchanged	P113,HAG
Hathaway, Thomas B.	Pvt	Santee LA	Santee R., SC	10/15/64	Ft. Delaware, DE	03/09/65	Died, Diarrhea	P6,P41,P47,FPH,CSR
Hathcock, George W.	Pvt	C 12th SCVI	Amelia C.H., VA	04/05/65	City Pt., VA	04/13/65	Pt. Lookout, MD	CSR
					Pt. Lookout, MD	06/24/65	Rlsd. G.O. #109	P114,HFC,CSR
Hathcock, James W.	Pvt	C 12th SCVI	Sutherland Stn., VA	04/01/65	City Pt., VA	04/07/65	Hart's Island, NY	CSR
					Hart's Island, NY	06/16/65	Rlsd. G.O. #109	P79,HFC,CSR
Hattaway, Thomas	Pvt	5 10/19 SCVI	Missionary Ridge, TN	11/25/63	Nashville, TN	12/07/63	Louisville, KY	P39,RAS,CTA,CSR
					Louisville, KY	12/09/63	Rock Island, IL	CSR
					Rock Island, MS	06/19/65	Rlsd. G.O. #109	
Haverson, H.	Pvt	F 1st SCVIR	Deserted/enemy	02/20/65	Charleston, SC	04/01/65	Released on oath	CSR
Havird, J.O.	Pvt	K 2nd SCVA	Deserted/enemy		Hilton Head, SC	01/17/65	New York, NY	CSR
Havird, J.R.	Pvt	K 2nd SCVA	Salisbury, NC Hos.	05/02/65	Salisbury, NC	05/02/65	Paroled	CSR
Havird, William P.	Pvt	B 14th SCVI	Gettysburg, PA	07/05/63	David's Island, NY	10/22/63	Fts. Monroe, VA	P1,HOE
					Fts. Monroe, VA	10/28/63	City Pt., VA Xc	CSR
Havird, William P.	Pvt	1 14th SCVI	Appomattox R., VA	04/03/65	City Pt., VA	04/11/65	Hart's Island, NY	CSR
Havird, William P.	Pvt	B 14th SCVI	Appomattox R., VA	04/03/65	Hart's Island, NY	06/17/65	Rlsd. G.O. #109	P79,CSR
Hawkins, B.F.	Sgt	B 18th SCVI	Five Forks, VA	04/01/65	City Pt., VA	04/06/65	Pt. Lookout, MD	CSR
					Pt. Lookout, MD	06/28/65	Rlsd. G.O. #109	P114,CSR
Hawkins, Charles	Pvt	K 1st SCVIR	Deserted/enemy	04/12/65	Hilton Head, SC		New York, NY oath	CSR
Hawkins, Drayton P.	Pvt	H Hol.Leg.	Petersburg, VA	11/05/64	City Pt., VA	11/11/64	Washington, DC	CSR
					Pt. Lookout, MD	06/28/65	Rlsd. G.O. #109	P114,ANY
Hawkins, Edward Pressley	Sgt	H Hol.Leg.	Five Forks, VA	04/02/65	City Pt., VA	04/05/65	Pt. Lookout, MD	CSR
					Pt. Lookout, MD	06/28/65	Rlsd. G.O. #109	P114,ANY
Hawkins, H.E.	Pvt	B 18th SCVi	Farmville, VA	04/06/65	City Pt., VA	04/01/65	Newport News, VA	CSR
					Newport News, VA	06/25/65	Rlsd. G.O. #109	CSR
Hawkins, Henry	Pvt	F 10th SCVI	Naomi's Hill Ch., GA	06/07/64	Nashville, TN	06/07/64	Louisville, KY	P3,RAS,CSR
					Louisville, KY	06/22/64	Rock Island, IL	CSR
					Rock Island, IL	07/06/64	Joined US Navy	CSR
Hawkins, J.B.	Pvt	A 3rd SCVABn	High Pt., GA	05/02/65	High Pt., GA	05/02/65	Paroled	CSR
Hawkins, James M.	Pvt	K 16th SCVI	Ringgold, GA	11/27/63	Nashville, TN	12/11/63	Louisville, KY	P39,16R,CSR
					Louisville, KY	12/12/63	Rock Island, IL	CSR
					Rock Island	01/03/64	Died of Pneumonia	P5,FPH,CSR
Hawkins, John W.	Pvt	B 2nd SCVI	Sheppardstown, MD	10/16/62	Ft. McHenry, MD	10/25/62	Aikens Ldg., VA Xc	H2,CSR
Hawkins, Peter	Pvt	C 7th SCVIBn	Morris Island, SC	07/10/63	Hilton, Head, SC		Ft. Columbus, NY	CSR,HAG
					Ft. Columbus, Ny	09/26/63	Pt. Lookout, MD	P1,CSR
					Pt. Lookout, MD	08/16/64	Elmira, NY	P113,P120,P124,CSR
					Elmira, NY	03/10/65	James R., VA Xc	P65,P66,CSR
Hawkins, S.M.	Sgt	H 22nd SCVI	Crater, Pbg., VA	07/30/64	City Pt., VA	04/05/64	Pt. Lookout, MD	CSR
					Pt. Lookout, MD	08/08/64	Elmira, NY	P113,P120,CSR
					Elmira, NY	03/02/65	James R., VA Xc	P65,P66,CSR
					Richmond Hos.	03/08/65	Furloughed 30 days	CSR
Hawkins, Thomas	Pvt	B 1st SCVA	Rockingham, NC	03/08/65	New Berne, NC	03/30/65	Pt. Lookout, MD	CSR
					Pt. Lookout, MD	06/28/65	Rlsd. G.O. #109	P114,CSR
Hawkins, W.H.	Pvt	K 16th SCVI	Greenville, SC	05/23/65	Greenville, SC	05/23/65	Paroled on oath	CSR
Hawkins, W.J.	Pvt	B Hol.Leg.	Deserted/enemy	12/20/64	City Pt., VA	12/24/64	Washington, DC	CSR
					Washington, DC	12/27/64	Philadelphia, PA	CSR

SOUTH CAROLINA SOLDIERS, SAILORS AND  CITIZENS HELD IN U.S. PRISONS 1861-1865

NAME	RANK	REGIMENT	CAPTURED AT	WHEN	PRISON	MOVED	DISPOSITION	SOURCES
Hawley, Robert	Smn	CS *Chicora*	Morris Island, SC	09/07/63	Pt. Lookout, MD	09/20/63	Ft. Warren, MA	P113,P124
Hawlycke, John	Sgt	4th SCVC	Augusta, GA	05/20/65	Augusta, GA	05/20/65	Paroled	CSR
Hawthorn, Thomas M.	Pvt	G Orr's Ri.	Falling Waters, MD	07/14/63	Baltimore, MD	08/16/63	Pt. Lookout, MD	CSR,CDC
					Pt. Lookout, MD	10/15/63	Hammond G.H., MD	P113,P125
					Pt. Lookout, MD	03/16/64	Died, Ch. Diarrhea	P5,P12,FPH,CSR
Hawthorn, William B.	Sgt	G 2nd SCVC	Gettysburg, PA	07/05/63	Gettysburg, PA G.H.	07/13/65	Provost Marshal	P4
Hay, John	Pvt	B 14th SCVI	Greensboro, NC	05/03/65	Greensboro, NC	05/03/65	Paroled	CSR
Hay, W.A.	Pvt	B 14th SCMil	Lynch's Creek, SC	02/26/65	Hart's Island, NY	06/17/65	Rlsd. G.O. #109	P79
Hayden, S.C.	Pvt	I 2nd SCVA	Deserted/enemy	03/01/65	Charleston, SC		Released on oath	CSR
Hayden, Thomas	Pvt	H 27th SCVI	Weldon RR, VA	08/21/64	City Pt., VA	08/23/64	Pt. Lookout, MD	CSR,HAG
					Pt. Lookout, MD	10/15/64	Joined U.S. Army	P125
Hayes, B.R.	Pvt	I P.S.S.	Gaines' Mill, VA	06/09/64	City Pt., VA	06/24/64	Pt. Lookout, MD	CSR
					Pt. Lookout, MD	07/27/64	Elmira, NY	P113,P120,CSR
					Elmira, NY	07/03/65	Rlsd. G.O. #109	P65,P66,CSR,TSE
Hayes, Daniel S.	Pvt	C 26th SCVI	Farmville, VA	04/05/65	City Pt., VA	04/14/65	Newport News, VA	CSR,HMC
					Newport News, VA	06/15/65	Rlsd. G.O. #109	CSR
Hayes, E. Wilson	Pvt	F 4th SCVC	Cold Harbor, VA	05/30/64	White House, VA	06/08/64	Pt. Lookout, MD	CSR
					Pt. Lookout, MD	07/09/64	Elmira, NY	P120,CSR
					Elmira, NY	06/19/65	Rlsd. G.O. #109	P65,P66,CSR
Hayes, Hardy	Pvt	C 26th SCVI	Five Forks, VA	04/01/65	City Pt., VA	04/05/65	Pt. Lookout, MD	CSR,HMC
					Pt. Lookout, MD	06/25/65	Rlsd. G.O. #109	P114,CSR
Hayes, J.J.	Pvt	K 8th SCVI	Savage Stn., VA	06/27/62	Ft. Columbus, NY	08/05/62	Aikens Ldg., VA Xc	CSR,KEB,HOM
Hayes, J.J.	Pvt	K 8th SCVI	Gettysburg, PA	07/05/63	Ft. McHenry, MD	09/15/63	Pt. Lookout, MD	CSR
					Pt. Lookout, MD	02/18/65	Exchanged	P113,P124
Hayes, J.J.	Pvt	K 8th SCVI	Gettysburg, PA	07/05/63	Pt. Lookout, MD	02/20/65	Cox's Wh., VA Xc	CSR
Hayes, James A.	Pvt	Ch'fld LA	Petersburg, VA	09/22/64	City Pt., VA	10/05/64	Pt. Lookout, MD	CSR
					Pt. Lookout, MD	06/03/67	Released	P114,CSR
Hayes, John	Smn	CS *Chicora*	Morris Island, SC	09/07/63	Pt. Lookout, MD	11/15/63	Hammond G.H., MD	P113,P125
Hayes, Joseph D.	Cpl	E 23rd SCVI	Sharpsburg, MD	09/17/62	Ft. McHenry, MD	10/17/62	Fts. Monroe, VA Xc	HMC,CSR
Hayes, R.B.	Pvt	F Orr's Ri.	Petersburg, VA	04/03/65	City Pt., VA	04/11/65	Hart's Island, NY	CSR
					Hart's Island, NY	06/16/65	Rlsd. G.O. #109	P79,CSR
Hayes, Robert	Cpl	F 17th SCVI	Warrenton, VA	09/29/62	Warrenton, VA	09/29/62	Paroled	CSR
Hayes, Robert R.	Pvt	C 26th SCVI	Petersburg, VA Hos.	04/03/65	Fts. Monroe, VA	04/30/65	Died	CSR,HMC
Hayes, Robert W.	Pvt	K 8th SCVI	Winchester, VA	09/13/64	Harpers Ferry, WV	09/19/64	Camp Chase, OH	CSR
					Camp Chase, OH	06/11/65	Rlsd. G.O. #109	P23,KEB,HOM,CSR
Hayes, Thomas J.	Pvt	Brooks LA	Gettysburg, PA	07/04/63	Gettysburg, PA USH			CSR
					Richmond, VA Hos.	04/04/64	Rtd. to duty	CSR
Hayes, W.A.	Pvt	F 17th SCVI	Farmville, VA	04/06/65	City Pt., VA	04/14/65	Newport News, VA	CSR
					Newport News, VA	06/15/65	Rlsd. G.O. #109	CSR
Hayes, William	Pvt	E 23rd SCVI	North Carolina	05/14/65	Wilmington, NC USH	05/26/65		HMC,CSR
Haygood, J.L.	Pvt	B 7th SCVIBn	Deserted/enemy	04/02/65	Washington, DC P.M.	04/05/65	Charleston, SC oath	CSR
Hayne, N.A.	Pvt	F Hol.Leg.	Jarratts Stn., VA	05/08/64	Pt. Lookout, MD	08/15/64	Elmira, NY	P113,P120
					Elmira, NY	02/02/65	Pt. Lookout, MD Xc	P65,P66
					Richmond Hospitals	03/24/65	Furloughed 60 days	CSR
Hayne, Robert F.	Pvt	K Orr's Ri.	Petersburg, VA	04/03/65	City Pt., VA	04/11/65	Hart's Island, NY	CSR
					Hart's Island, NY	06/16/65	Rlsd. G.O. #109	P79,CDC
Haynes, E.M.	Pvt	B 7th SCVIBn	Fts. Monroe, VA	04/02/65	Deserted/enemy	04/05/65	Charleston, SC oath	CSR
Haynes, J.F.	Pvt	F 2nd SCVC	Greensboro, NC	04/29/65	Greensboro, NC	04/29/65	Paroled	CSR
					City Pt., VA	04/05/65	Pt. Lookout, MD	CSR
Haynes, J.H.	Pvt	B 22nd SCVI	Petersburg, VA	04/02/65	Pt. Lookout, MD	06/28/65	Rlsd. G.O. #109	P114,CSR
Hays, Austin G.	Sgt	D 25th SCVI	Town Creek, NC	02/20/65	Ft. Anderson, NC	02/28/65	Pt. Lookout, MD	CSR,HAG,HMC
					Pt. Lookout, MD	06/28/65	Rlsd. G.O. #109	P114

SOUTH CAROLINA SOLDIERS, SAILORS AND  CITIZENS HELD IN U.S. PRISONS 1861-1865

NAME	RANK	REGIMENT	CAPTURED AT	WHEN	PRISON	MOVED	DISPOSITION	SOURCES
Hays, C.F.	Pvt	D 25th SCVI	Ft. Fisher, NC	01/15/65	Elmira, NY	03/23/65	Died, Pneumonia	P6,P65,FPH,HAG,HFC
Hays, Erastus W.	Pvt	D 25th SCVI	Weldon RR, VA	08/21/64	City Pt., VA	08/24/64	Alexandria, VA	CSR,HAG
					Alexandria G.H.	09/14/64	Died of wounds	P1,P6,P12,P65,CSR
Hays, J.N.	Pvt	D 25th SCVI	Ft. Fisher, NC	01/15/65	New York, NY	01/30/65	Elmira, NY	CSR
					Elmira, NY	06/23/65	Rlsd. G.O. #109	CSR
Hays, Wesley	Pvt	G 27th SCVI	Town Creek, NC	02/20/65	Ft. Anderson, NC	02/28/65	Pt. Lookout, MD	CSR,HAG
					Pt. Lookout, MD	06/27/65	Rlsd. G.O. #109	P114,CSR
Haywood, Charles	Pvt	F 1st SCVIR	Deserted/enemy	02/18/65	Charleston, SC	03/22/65	Released on oath	CSR
Haywood, John	Pvt	I 1st SCVIR	Savannah, GA	04/18/65				CSR
Hazard, Patrick	Pvt	F 1st SCVC	P.M. Army/ Potomac	03/18/65	City Pt., VA	03/24/65	Pittsburg, PA oath	CSR
Hazard, William	Pvt	I 1st SCVIR	By navy off GA	09/01/64	Hilton Head, SC	10/03/64	New York, NY	P8,SA1,CSR
Hazel, G.	Pvt	B 3rd SCVIBn	Gettysburg, PA	07/05/63	Gettysburg G.H.	07/20/63	Provost Marshal	P4,KEB,CSR
					David's Island, NY	09/12/63	City Pt., VA Xc	P1,CSR
Hazel, G.	Pvt	B 3rd SCVIBn	Hanover C.H., VA	05/23/64	Port Royal, VA	05/30/64	Pt. Lookout, MD	CSR
					Pt. Lookout, MD	03/14/65	Exchanged	P113,P124,CSR
Head, Francis M.	Pvt	H 1st SCVA	Smith Farm, NC	03/16/65	New Berne, NC	04/10/65	Hart's Island, NY	CSR
					Hart's Island, NY	06/15/65	Rlsd. G.O. #109	P79,CSR
Head, Jeptha	Pvt	E Orr's Ri.	Petersburg, VA	04/03/65	City Pt., VA	04/11/65	Hart's Island, NY	CSR
					Hart's Island, NY	06/16/65	Rlsd. G.O. #109	P79,CSR
Head, Thomas R.W.	Pvt	C 3rd SCVABn	Citronelle, AL	05/04/65	Grenada, MS	05/18/65	Paroled	CSR
Healor, J.B.	Pvt	F 17th SCVI	Crater, Pbg., VA	07/30/64	City Pt., VA	08/05/64	Pt. Lookout, MD	CSR
					Pt. Lookout, MD	08/08/64	Elmira, NY	P113,P120,CSR
					Elmira, NY	09/11/64	Died, Ch. Diarrhea	P5,P12,P65,P66,CSR
Heap, B. S.amuel	Pvt	B 2nd SCVC	Martinsburg, VA	07/07/63	Baltimore, MD	09/15/63	Pt. Lookout, MD	CSR
					Ft. McHenry, MD	09/15/63	Pt. Lookout, MD	CSR
					Pt. Lookout, MD	10/15/63	Hammond G.H., MD	CSR
					Hammond G.H., MD	01/15/64	Pt. Lookout, MD	CSR
					Pt. Lookout, MD	02/10/65	Exchanged	P124,CSR
Heape, B.A.	Pvt	F 11th SCVI	Ft. Fisher, NC	01/15/65	Pt. Lookout, MD	06/28/65	Rlsd. G.O. #109	P114,HAG,CSR
Heape, D.	Pvt	C 19th SCVCB	Augusta, GA	05/26/65	Augusta, GA	05/26/65	Paroled on oath	CSR
Heape, W.H.	Pvt	C 5th SCVC	Augusta, GA	05/26/65	Augusta, GA	05/26/65	Paroled	CSR
Hearon, W.E.	Pvt	H 21st SCVI	Darlington, SC	02/25/65	Hart's Island, NY	06/16/65	Rlsd. G.O. #109	P79,HAG
Heartz, C.H.	Pvt	B German LA	Deserted/enemy		Hilton Head, SC	10/19/64		P8
Heath, Allen W.	2Lt	E 22nd SCVI	Bermuda Hundred, VA	08/02/64	Bermuda Hundred, VA	08/08/64	Old Capitol, DC	CSR,LAN
					Old Capitol, DC	08/11/64	Ft. Delaware, DE	CSR
					Ft. Delaware, DE	06/17/65	Rlsd. G.O. #109	P45,CSR
Heath, Andrew M.	Pvt	B 21st SCVI	Weldon RR, VA	08/21/64	City Pt., VA Hos.	08/29/64	Philadelphia, PA	CSR
Heath, Andrew M.	Pvt	B 21st SCVI	Weldon RR, VA	08/21/64	McClellan G.H. Phila.	11/06/64	Died of wounds	P6,P12,FPH
Heath, William D.	Pvt	I 17th SCVI	Charlotte, NC Hos.	05/03/65	Charlotte, NC	05/03/65	Paroled	CSR
Heaton Charles T.	Pvt	H 11th SCVI	Petersburg, VA	06/18/64	Bermuda Hundred, VA	06/21/64	Fts. Monroe, VA	CSR
					Fts. Monroe, VA	06/22/64	Pt. Lookout, MD	CSR
					Pt. Lookout, MD	12/05/64	Died	P5,P12,FPH,CSR
Heaton, Joseph Pennell	Pvt	I 14th SCVI	Petersburg, VA	07/29/64	Pt. Lookout, MD	08/08/64	Elmira, NY	P120,CSR
					Elmira, NY	02/09/65	Pt. Lookout, MD	P65,P66,CSR
					Pt. Lookout, MD	02/21/65	Boulware's Wh., VA	CSR
					Richmond, VA Hos.	02/27/65	Camp Lee, VA	CSR
Heckle, Andrew J.	Pvt	F 25th SCVI	Ft. Fisher, NC	01/15/65	New York, NY	01/30/65	Elmira, NY	CSR,HAG
					Elmira, NY	02/09/65	Died, Typhoid	P6,P12,P65,FPH
Heddin, Isaac	Pvt	A 20th SCVI	Deserted/enemy	08/10/63	Knoxville, TN	07/01/64	Louisville, KY	P8,KEB,CSR
					Louisville, KY	07/16/64	North on oath	CSR

SOUTH CAROLINA SOLDIERS, SAILORS AND  CITIZENS HELD IN U.S. PRISONS 1861-1865

NAME	RANK	REGIMENT	CAPTURED AT	WHEN	PRISON	MOVED	DISPOSITION	SOURCES
Hedrick, M.	Pvt	D 6th SCVI	Chattanooga, TN	10/29/63	Nashville, TN	11/07/63	Louisville, KY	P39,CSR
					Louisville, KY	11/09/63	Camp Morton, IN	CSR
					Camp Morton, IN	02/26/65	City Pt., VA Xc	CSR
Heffner, Marcus	Pvt	C 27th SCVI	Weldon RR, VA	08/21/64	City Pt., VA	08/23/64	Pt. Lookout, MD	CSR,HAG
					Pt. Lookout, MD	11/01/64	Exchanged	P113,P124,P125,CSR
Hefley, J.H.	Pvt	E 3rd SCResB	Not stated		New Berne, NC USGH	04/27/65	Rtd. to Prov. Mars	HHC,CSR
Hefley, Thomas	Pvt	B 4th SCVC	Cold Harbor, VA	05/20/64	U.S. Field Hos.	06/05/64	Lincoln G.H., DC	CSR
					Lincoln G.H., DC	07/14/64	Died of wounds	P5,P12,CSR
Heigh, Thomas P.	Pvt	C 27th SCVI	Town Creek, NC	02/20/65	Ft. Anderson, NC	02/28/65	Pt. Lookout, MD	CSR,HAG
					Pt. Lookout, MD	06/28/65	Rlsd. G.O. #109	P114,CSR
Heinisouth, A.	Pvt	C 23rd SCVI	Deserted/enemy	03/17/65	City Pt., VA	03/21/65	Washington, DC	CSR
Heins, Eibe	Msc	1st SCVA	Deserted/enemy	03/18/65	Charleston, SC		Released on oath	CSR
Heinsburg, Sydney	Sgt	E 1st SCVIR	Deserted/enemy	03/02/65	Charleston, SC		Released on oath	CSR
Heintz, Edward H.W.	Pvt	B German LA	Deserted/enemy	03/17/65	Charleston, SC	03/17/65	Released on oath	CSR
Helames, James H.	Pvt	D 27th SCVI	Town Creek, NC	02/20/65	Ft. Anderson, NC	02/28/65	Pt. Lookout, MD	CSR,HAG
					Pt. Lookout, MD	06/27/65	Rlsd. G.O. #109	P114,CSR
Helames, W.H.	Pvt	D 27th SCVI	Weldon RR, VA	08/21/64	City Pt., VA	08/23/64	Pt. Lookout, MD	CSR,HAG
					Pt. Lookout, MD	09/18/64	Aikens Ldg., VA Xc	CSR
Heldeman, Matthew	Msc	A 16th SCVI	Franklin, TN	12/17/64	Nashville, TN	12/31/64	Louisville, KY	P39,16R,CSR
					Louisville, KY	01/02/65	Camp Chase, OH	CSR
					Camp Chase, OH	03/21/65	Released on oath	P26,CSR
Hellams, John T.	Pvt	G 3rd SCVI	Beans Stn., TN	12/18/63	Louisville, KY	01/23/64	Rock Island, IL	CSR,SA2,H3
					Rock Island, IL	02/25/65	Tfd. for exchange	SA2
					Richmond, VA Hos.	03/09/65	Furloughed 30 days	CSR
Helton, Drayton	Pvt	A 12th SCVI	Sutherland Stn., VA	04/02/65	City Pt., VA	04/07/65	Hart's Island, NY	CSR,YEB
					Hart's Island, NY	06/16/65	Rlsd. G.O. #109	P79,CSR
Hembree, Bird	Pvt	A Hol.Leg.	Five Forks, VA	04/01/65	City Pt., VA	04/05/65	Pt. Lookout, MD	CSR
					Pt. Lookout, MD	06/08/65	Released, sick list	P114,P117,CSR
Hembree, Cornelius M.	Pvt	D 3rd SCVI	Lynch's Creek, SC	02/28/65	New Berne, NC	04/03/65	Pt. Lookout, MD	CSR,SA2,H3
					Pt. Lookout, MD	06/27/65	Rlsd. G.O. #109	CSR
Hembree, W.E.	Pvt	C 2nd SCVIRi	Deserted/enemy	03/04/65	Bermuda Hundred, VA	03/05/65	City Pt., VA P.M.	CSR
					City Pt., VA P.M.	03/07/65	Washington, DC P.M	CSR
					Washington, DC P.M.	03/08/65	Columbus, OH oath	CSR
Hembrey, Russell H.	Pvt	I 13th SCVI	Hatcher's Run, VA	03/31/65	Pt. Lookout, MD	06/27/65	Rlsd. G.O. #109	CSR
Heming, William	Msc	F 1st SCVA	Deserted/enemy	02/19/65	Charleston, SC		Released on oath	CSR
Heminnis, Mathew	Pvt	C 2nd SCVI	Knoxville, TN	12/04/63	Kentucky on oath		Left as nurse	SA2,H2,CSR
Hemmingway, Franklin G.	Pvt	B 10th SCVI	Atlanta, GA	07/22/64	Nashville, TN	07/29/64	Louisville, KY	CSR,RAS
					Louisville, KY	07/30/64	Camp Chase, OH	CSR
					Camp Chase, OH	03/02/65	City Pt., VA Xc	P23,P26
Hemphill, John L.	Pvt	G Orr's Ri.	Falling Waters, MD	07/14/63	Baltimore, MD	08/16/63	Pt. Lookout, MD	CSR
					Pt. Lookout, MD	08/16/64	Elmira, NY	P113,P120,P124,CSR
					Elmira, NY	02/25/65	Pt. Lookout, MD Xc	P65,P66,CSR
Hemphill, Robert R.	SMj	G Orr's Ri.	Falling Waters, MD	07/14/63	E. Bldg. Balt, MD			P1
					Baltimore, MD	08/23/63	City Pt., VA Xc	CSR,UD7
Hemphill, William M.	Pvt	G 18th SCVI	Five Forks, VA	04/01/65	City Pt., VA	04/06/64	Pt. Lookout, MD	CSR
					Pt. Lookout, MD	06/13/65	Rlsd. G.O. #109	P114,CSR
Henagan, A.B.	Cpl	I 2nd SCVC	Prince Wm. Co., VA	03/24/64	Ft. Delaware, DE			P43
Hencken, John L.	Pvt	K 12th SCVI	Southside RR, VA	04/02/65	City Pt., VA	04/07/65	Hart's Island, NY	CSR
					Hart's Island, NY	06/15/65	Rlsd. G.O. #109	P79,CSR
					New York Transit Hos.	06/23/65	Rtd. to Barracks	CSR

SOUTH CAROLINA SOLDIERS, SAILORS AND  CITIZENS HELD IN U.S. PRISONS 1861-1865

NAME	RANK	REGIMENT	CAPTURED AT	WHEN	PRISON	MOVED	DISPOSITION	SOURCES
Hencken, John M.	1Lt	K 12th SCVI	Petersburg, VA	04/02/65	City Pt., VA P.M.	04/05/65	Old Capitol, DC	CSR
					Old Capitol, DC	04/09/65	Johnson' Isl., OH	CSR
					Johnson's Isl., OH	05/12/65	Died, Pneumonia	P5,P6,P12,FPH,CSR
Henddrix, William N.	Pvt	K 13th SCVI	Appomattox R., VA	04/03/65	City Pt., VA	04/11/65	Hart's Island, NY	P79,CSR
Henderson, A.	Pvt	G 7th SCVC	Ft. Darling, VA	05/14/64	Bermuda Hundred, VA	05/16/64	Fts. Monroe, VA	CSR
					Fts. Monroe, VA	05/17/64	Pt. Lookout, MD	CSR
					Pt. Lookout, MD		No Release Data	CSR
Henderson, Andrew	Pvt	H 22nd SCVI	Crater, Pbg., VA	07/30/64	City Pt., VA	08/05/64	Pt. Lookout, MD	CSR
					Pt. Lookout, MD	08/08/64	Elmira, NY	P113,P120
					Elmira, NY	12/26/64	Died, Variola	P5,P12,FPH,P65,P66
Henderson, Burkett L.	Pvt	C 14th SCVI	Sutherland Stn., VA	04/02/65	City Pt., VA	04/07/65	Hart's Island, NY	CSR
					Hart's Island, NY	06/16/65	Rlsd. G.O. #109	P79,CSR
Henderson, Caloway K.	Sgt	F 7th SCVI	N. Anna River, VA	05/23/64	Port Royal, VA	05/30/64	Pt. Lookout, MD	CSR,KEB,HOE
					Pt. Lookout, MD	05/13/65	Rlsd. G.O. #85	P113,CSR
Henderson, D.A.	Pvt	D 1st SCVIR	Rockingham, NC	03/06/65	New Berne, NC	04/10/65	Hart's Island, NY	CSR,SA1
					Hart's Island, NY	06/16/65	Rlsd. G.O. #109	P79,CSR
Henderson, Daniel	Pvt	K 16th SCVI	Ringgold, GA	11/26/63	Nashville, TN	12/09/63	Louisville, KY	P39,CSR
					Louisville, KY	02/11/65	Rock Island, IL	CSR
					Rock Island, IL	02/15/65	Tfd. for exchange	CSR
Henderson, E.P.	Pvt	B 2nd SCVC	Augusta, GA	05/23/65	Augusta, GA	05/23/65	Paroled	CSR
Henderson, Eli	Pvt	B 16th SCVI	Nashville, TN	12/16/64	Nashville, TN USGH	04/05/65	Died of wounds	P3,P6,16R,CSR
Henderson, Elias	Pvt	F 13th SCVI	Deserted/enemy	02/24/65	City Pt., VA	02/26/65	Washington, DC	CSR,HOS
					Washington, DC	02/27/65	Springfield, IL	CSR
Henderson, Erasmus F.	Cpl	K 16th SCVI	Franklin, TN	12/17/64	Nashville, TN	02/08/65	Louisville, KY	P3,P39,16R,CSR
					Louisville, KY	02/15/65	Rock Island, IL	P3,CSR
					Rock Island, IL	03/13/65	Pt. Lookout, MD Xc	CSR
					Richmond, VA Hos.	03/25/65	Furloughed 60 days	CSR
Henderson, Esquire J.	Pvt	C 14th SCVI	Sutherland Stn., VA	04/02/65	City Pt., VA	04/07/65	Hart's Island, NY	CSR
					Hart's Island, NY	06/16/65	Rlsd. G.O. #109	P79,CSR
Henderson, George H.	Pvt	G 17th SCVI	Petersburg, VA	03/25/65	City Pt., VA	03/28/65	Pt. Lookout, MD	CSR
					Pt. Lookout, MD	06/27/65	Rlsd. G.O. #109	P114,CSR
Henderson, Henry	Pvt	L 1st SCVIG	Petersburg, VA	07/29/64	City Pt. VA	08/05/64	Pt. Lookout, MD	CSR,SA1
					Pt. Lookout, MD	08/08/64	Elmira, NY	P113,P120,CSR
					Elmira, NY	02/13/65	Pt. Lookout, MD Xc	P65,P66,CSR
Henderson, J.A.	Pvt	D 7th SCVC	Ft. Darling, VA	05/14/64	Fts. Monroe, VA	05/18/64	Pt. Lookout, MD	CSR
					Pt. Lookout, MD	02/10/65	Exchanged	P113,P124,CSR
Henderson, Jackson	Pvt	F 13th SCVI	Deserted/enemy	12/14/64	City Pt., VA	12/20/64	Columbus, OH oath	P8,CSR
Henderson, Jackson	Pvt	E 13th SCVI	Petersburg, VA	04/02/65	City Pt., VA	04/04/65	Pt. Lookout, MD	CSR,HOS
					Pt. Lookout, MD	06/27/65	Rlsd. G.O. #109	P114,CSR
Henderson, James R.	Pvt	B 19th SCVI	Atlanta, GA	08/12/64	Nashville, TN	08/30/64	Louisville, KY	CSR,HOE
					Louisville, KY	09/02/64	Camp Chase, OH	CSR
					Camp Chase, OH	03/31/65	Released on oath	P7,P23,CSR
Henderson, John T.	Pvt	K 7th SCVI	Williamsport, MD	07/14/63	Hagerstown, MD G.H.			P2,KEB,HOE
					Harrisburg, PA GH	09/14/63	Baltimore, MD	P2
					W. Bldg. Balt, MD	09/25/63	City Pt., VA Xc	P1,CNM,CSR
Henderson, Lewis T.	Pvt	A 13th SCVI	Gettysburg, PA	07/03/63	Ft. McHenry, MD	07/07/63	Ft. Delaware, DE	CSR
					Ft. Delaware, DE	10/15/63	Escaped Fm Grave Yd	P40,P42,P44,CSR
Henderson, M.L.	Pvt	C 14th SCVI	Sutherland Stn., VA	04/03/65	City Pt., VA	04/07/65	Hart's Island, NY	CSR
					Hart's Island, NY	06/16/65	Rlsd. G.O. #109	P79,CSR
Henderson, Robert	Pvt	D 3rd SCVC	Coosahatchie, SC	02/27/65	Hilton Head, SC	03/03/65	Wishes to take oath	CSR
Henderson, William	Pvt	I 5th SCVI	Chattanooga, TN	11/01/63	Bridgeport AL USGH	11/20/63	Died of wounds	P6,P12,CSR
Henderson, William P.	Pvt	I Ham.Leg.	Shell Mound, AL	10/28/63	Bridgeport, AL Fld.	11/20/63	Died of wounds	CSR

SOUTH CAROLINA SOLDIERS, SAILORS AND  CITIZENS HELD IN U.S. PRISONS 1861-1865

NAME	RANK	REGIMENT	CAPTURED AT	WHEN	PRISON	MOVED	DISPOSITION	SOURCES
Hendricks, G.P.	Pvt	G 1st SCVIG	Warrenton, VA	09/29/62	Warrenton, VA	09/29/62	Paroled	CSR
Hendricks, Henry B.	Pvt	C 22nd SCVI	Crater, Pbg., VA	07/30/64	City Pt., VA	08/05/64	Pt. Lookout, MD	CSR
					Pt. Lookout, MD	08/08/64	Elmira, NY	P113,P120,CSR
					Elmira, NY	03/28/65	Died, Diarrhea	P6,P65,P66,FPH,CSR
Hendricks, Henry W.	2Lt	C 27th SCVI	Weldon RR, VA	08/21/64	Old Capitol, DC	08/27/64	Ft. Delaware, DE	CSR,HAG
					Ft. Delaware, DE	10/06/64	Pt. Lookout, MD Xc	P43,P46,CSR
					Pt. Lookout, MD	10/11/64	Exchanged	P114,CSR
Hendricks, Henry W.	2Lt	C 27th SCVI	Town Creek, NC	02/20/65	Ft. Anderson, NC	02/28/65	Pt. Lookout, MD	CSR
					Pt. Lookout, MD	02/28/65	Washington, DC	P114,P120,CSR
					Old Capitol, DC	03/24/65	Ft. Delaware, DE	CSR
					Ft. Delaware, DE	05/30/65	Rlsd OO Gen. Grant	P43,CSR
Hendricks, J.H.	Pvt	G 3rd SCVABn	High Pt., NC	05/01/65	High Pt., NC	05/01/65	Paroled	CSR
Hendricks, Jesse S.	Cpl	C 12th SCVI	Gettysburg, PA	07/04/63	Ft. McHenry, MSD	07/07/63	Ft. Delaware, DE	CSR
					Ft. Delaware, DE	07/19/63	Chester, PA Hos.	P40,P42,P44
					Chester,PA USGH	07/29/63	Died, Ch. Diarrhea	P1,P6,P12,FPH,CSR
Hendricks, Mathew	Pvt	F 2nd SCVC	Salisbury, NC	05/03/65	Salisbury, NC	05/03/65	Paroled	CSR
Hendricks, Thomas M.	Pvt	K 27th SCVI	Petersburg, VA	06/24/64	Fts. Monroe, VA	06/26/64	Pt. Lookout, MD	CSR,HAG
					Pt. Lookout, MD	08/16/64	Elmira, NY	P113,P120
					Elmira, NY	11/14/64	Died, Pneumonia	P5,P65,P66,FPH,CSR
Hendricks, W.	Pvt	F 2nd SCVI	Salsbury, NC	05/11/65	Salsbury, NC	05/11/65	Paroled	CSR
Hendricks, W.W.	Pvt	C 22nd SCVI	Crater, Pbg., VA	07/30/64	City Pt., VA	08/05/64	Pt. Lookout, MD	CSR
					Pt. lookout, MD	08/08/64	Elmira, NY	P114,P120,P125,FPH
					Elmira, NY	10/11/64	Pt. Lookout, MD Xc	P65,P66
					Pt. Lookout, MD	10/27/64	Died	P5,P12,FPH,CSR
Hendrickson, J.S.	Pvt	K 13th SCVI	Gettysburg, PA	07/04/63	David's Island, NY	08/24/63	City Pt., VA Xc	P1,CSR
Hendrix, Daniel J.	Pvt	C 1st SCVIG	Petersburg, VA	07/29/64	City Pt., VA	08/05/64	Pt. Lookout, MD	CSR,SA1
					Pt. Lookout, MD	08/08/64	Elmira, NY	P120,P125,CSR
					Elmira, NY	07/03/65	Rlsd. G.O. #109	P65,P66,CSR
Hendrix, Franklin S.	Pvt	C 3rd SCVABn	Ft. Gaines, AL	08/08/64	New Orleans, LA	08/12/64	St. Louis, MO USGH	CSR
					St. Louis, MO USGH	09/15/64	New Orleans, LA	CSR
					New Orleans, LA	10/25/64	Ship Island, MS	P3,CSR
					Ship Island, MS	01/04/65	Exhanged	CSR
Hendrix, Robert	Pvt	B 1st SCVA	Bentonville, NC	03/22/65	New Berne, NC	04/10/65	Hart's island, NY	CSR
					Hart's Island, NY	06/16/65	Rlsd. G.O. #109	P79,CSR
Hendrix, William N.	Pvt	K 13th SCVI	Appomattox R., VA	04/03/65	City Pt., VA	04/11/65	Hart's Island, NY	P79,CSR
					Hart's Island, NY	06/14/65	Rlsd. G.O.#109	P79,CSR
Hendrix, William S.C.	Pvt	H 19th SCVI	Augusta, GA	05/29/65	Augusta, GA	05/29/65	Paroled	CSR
Henekin, J.C.	Pvt	G 6th SCVI	Charlotte, NC	05/24/65	Charlotte, NC	05/24/65	Paroled	CSR
Henley, Charles C.	Pvt	C 14th SCVI	Appomattox R., VA	04/03/65	City Pt., VA	04/11/65	Hart's Island, NY	CSR
					Hart's Island, NY	06/19/65	Died, Ch. Diarrhea	P6,P79,CSR
Hennaman, John A.	Pvt	B 1st SCVC	Deserted/enemy	02/18/65	Charleston, SC	03/29/65	Released on oath	CSR
Hennegan, Andrew Barnaba	Pvt	I 2nd SCVC	Prince Wm. Cty., VA	03/24/64	Old Capitol, DC	09/19/64	Ft. Delaware, DE	CSR
					Ft. Delaware, DE	05/31/65	Released	P7,P45,P46,CSR
Hennigan, John Williford	Col	8th SCVI	Winchester, VA	04/13/64	Harpers Ferry, WV	09/19/64	Johnson's Isl., OH	CSR
					Johnson's Isl., OH	04/26/65	Died	CSR
Henning, George W.	Pvt	B 15th SCVAB	Fayetteville, NC	03/13/65	New Berne, NC	04/03/65	Pt. Lookout, MD	CSR
					Pt. Lookout, MD	06/17/65	Died, Ch. Diarrhea	P6,P12,P114,FPH,CSR
Hennis, John H.	Pvt	B 5th SCVI	Williamsburg, VA	05/05/62	Fts. Monroe, VA		No more info	SA3,CSR
Henry, George R.	Pvt	I 6th SCVI	Sharpsburg, MD	09/20/62	Frederick, MD U.S.	02/09/63	Retd. to duty	CSR
					Baltimore, MD U.S.	02/13/63	Retd. to duty	CSR
					Ft. McHenry, MD	02/18/63	City Pt., VA Xc	CSR
					Petersburg, VA Hos.	03/31/63	Furloughed 60 days	CSR

H

SOUTH CAROLINA SOLDIERS, SAILORS AND CITIZENS HELD IN U.S. PRISONS 1861-1865

NAME	RANK	REGIMENT	CAPTURED AT	WHEN	PRISON	MOVED	DISPOSITION	SOURCES
Henry, J.N.	Pvt	H 12th SCVI	Sharpsburg, MD	09/17/62	Sharpsburg, MD	09/27/62	Paroled	CSR
Henry, James A.	Pvt	D 13th SCVI	Southside RR, VA	04/05/65	Hart's Island, NY	07/01/65	David's Island, NY	P79,ANY,CSR
					David's Island, NY	08/01/65	Released on oath	CSR
Henry, W.R.	Pvt	B 6th SCVI	Charlotte, NC	05/15/65	Charlotte, NC	05/15/65	Paroled	CSR
Hensley, James D.	Pvt	K P.S.S.	Richmond, VA	04/03/65	Libby Prison Rchmd.	04/08/65	Pt. Lookout, MD	CSR,HOS,TSE
					Pt. Lookout, MD	06/27/65	Rlsd. G.O. #109	P114,CSR
Henson, J.P.	Pvt	M 7th SCVI	Gettysburg, PA	07/02/63	Letterman G.H., PA	10/01/63	W. Bldg. Balt, MD	CSR
					W. Bldg. Balt, MD	11/12/63	City Point, VA Xc	CSR
Hepburn, C.C.	Pvt	I 6th SCVC	Ream's Stn., VA	08/23/64	City Pt., VA	09/07/64	Pt. Lookout, MD	CSR
					Pt. Lookout, MD	03/17/65	Exchanged	P113,P124,CSR
Herbert, J.Y.	Pvt	K 1st SCVC	Upperville VA	06/21/63	Old Capitol, DC	06/25/63	City Pt., VA Xc	CSR
Herbert, Joseph C.	Pvt	C 27th SCVI	Town Creek, NC	02/20/65	Ft. Anderson, NC	02/28/65	Pt. Lookout, MD	CSR,HAG
					Pt. Lookout, MD	05/13/65	Rlsd. G.O. #85	P114,CSR
Herbert, S.	Pvt	D 7th SCVIBn	Weldon RR, VA	08/21/64	Pt. Lookout, MD	10/15/64	Joined U.S. Army	P7,P125,HIC,CSR
Herd, W.E.	Pvt	B 2nd SCVIRi	Prob. Bulls Gap, TN	04/01/64			Escaped, went home	CSR
Heriott, William B.	Pvt	A 27th SCVI	Town Creek, NC	02/20/65	Ft. Anderson, NC	02/28/65	Pt. Lookout, MD	CSR,HAG
					Pt. Lookout, MD	06/28/65	Rlsd. G.O. #109	P114
Herlong, Nathan F.	Pvt	D 25th SCVI	Weldon RR, VA	08/21/64	City Pt., VA	08/24/64	Pt. Lookout, MD	CSR
					Pt. Lookout, MD	03/14/65	Exchanged	P113,P124,P125,CSR
Herman, Joseph	Pvt	K 1st SCV	Augusta, GA	05/24/65	Augusta GA	05/24/65	Paroled on oath	CSR
Hernandez, Benjamin	Msc	1st SCVIBn	Morris Island, SC	09/07/63	Ft. Columbus, NY	10/09/63	Johnson's Isl., OH	P1
					Pt. Lookout, MD	12/12/63	Escaped	P113
Herndon, H.G.	Cpl	I 11th SCVI	Petersburg, VA	06/24/64	Bermuda Hundred, VA	06/25/64	Fts. Monroe, VA	CSR,HAG
					Fts. Monroe, VA	06/26/64	Pt. Lookout, MD	CSR
					Pt. Lookout, MD	08/16/64	Elmira, NY	P113,P120,CSR
					Elmira, NY	03/14/65	Pt. Lookout, MD Xc	P65,P66,CSR
Herndon, H.G.	Cpl	I 11th SCVI	Petersburg, VA	06/24/64	Elmira NY	03/14/65	James R., VA Xc	CSR
Herndon, Josiah L.	Cpl	E 24th SCVI	Chickamauga, GA	09/20/63	Nashville, TN	10/05/63	Louisville, KY	P38,CSR
					Louisville, KY	10/07/63	Camp Douglas, IL	EFW,CSR
					Camp Douglas, IL	06/16/65	Rlsd. G.O. #109	P53,P55,P57,CSR
Herren, Stephen	Pvt	D 10th SCVI	Pulaski, TN	12/25/64	Nashville, TN	01/04/65	Louisville, KY	CSR
					Louisville, KY	01/06/65	Camp Chase, OH	CSR
					Camp Chase, OH	01/27/65	Died, Pneumonia	P6,P23,P27,FPH
Herricks, J.H.W.	Pvt	B German LA	Deserted/enemy		Hilton Head, SC	10/04/64		P8
Herrin, James P.	Pvt	D 10th SCVI			Holly Springs, MS		Died of disease	RAS,CSR
Herrin, James P.	Pvt	D 10th SCVI			Nashville, TN	02/07/65		P8
Herrin, Miles	Pvt	McQueen LA	Farmville, VA	04/11/65	Farmville, VA	04/21/65	Paroled	CSR
Herrin, William P.	Pvt	D 10th SCVI	Deserted/enemy		Chattanooga, TN	11/18/64	Released on oath	P8,RAS,HMC,CSR
Herring, D.W.	Pvt	A 26th SCVI	Farmville, VA	04/06/65	City Pt., VA	04/14/65	Newport News, VA	CSR
					Newport News, VA	06/15/65	Rlsd. G.O. #109	CSR
Herring, G.W.	Cpl	C 2nd SCVA	Fayettville, NC	03/15/65	New Berne, NC	04/10/65	Hart's Island, NY	CSR
					Hart's Island, NY	06/16/65	Released G.O. #10	CSR,P79
Herring, Marcus	Pvt	D 25th SCVI	Town Creek, NC	02/20/65	Ft. Anderson, NC	02/28/65	Pt. Lookout, MD	CSR,HAG
					Pt. Lookout, MD	06/28/65	Rlsd. G.O. #109	P114
Herring, Washington	Pvt	4 10/19 SCVI	Missionary Ridge, TN	11/25/63	Nashville, TN	12/07/63	Louisville, KY	P39,RAS,CSR
					Louisville, KY	12/09/63	Rock Island, IL	CSR
					Rock Island, IL	02/25/65	James R., VA Xc	CSR
					Richmond, VA Hos.	03/08/65	Furloughed 30 days	CSR
Herron, F.O.	Pvt	A Orr's Ri.	Petersburg, VA	04/03/65	City Pt., VA	04/11/65	Hart's Island, NY	CSR
					Hart's Island, NY	06/16/65	Rlsd. G.O. #109	CSR

SOUTH CAROLINA SOLDIERS, SAILORS AND  CITIZENS HELD IN U.S. PRISONS 1861-1865

NAME	RANK	REGIMENT	CAPTURED AT	WHEN	PRISON	MOVED	DISPOSITION	SOURCES
Herron, George S.	Pvt	F 7th SCVIBn	Weldon RR, VA	08/21/64	City Pt., VA USFH	08/23/64	Fts. Monroe, VA US	CSR
					Fts. Monroe, VA US	08/26/64	Alexandria, VA USG	CSR
					Alexandria, VA 2d	09/18/64	Died of wounds	P5,P12,CSR
Herron, Stanmore	Pvt	A 1st SCVA	Richmond Co., NC	03/04/65	New Berne, NC	03/30/65	Pt. Lookout, MD	CSR
					Pt. Lookout, MD	05/13/65	Rlsd. G.O. #85	P114,CSR
Hersey, George R.	Pvt	F 1st SCVA	Bennettsville, SC	03/06/65	New Berne NC	03/26/65	Pt. Lookout MD	CSR
					Pt. Lookout, MD	05/09/65	Died, Scurvy	P6,P114,FPH,CSR
Hersey, William	Pvt	E 23rd SCVI	Funkstown, MD	09/15/62	Ft. Delaware, DE	10/02/62	Aikens Ldg., VA Xc	CSR
Heustiss, George W.	Pvt	F 21st SCVI	Weldon RR, VA	08/21/64	Elmira, NY	03/09/65	Died, Diarrhea	P6,P65,HAG,HOM,FPH
Heuston, Charles G.	Pvt	I 1st SCVA	Fayettville, NC	03/14/65	New Berne, NC	03/30/65	Pt. Lookout, MD	CSR
					Pt. Lookout, MD	05/13/65	Rlsd. G.O. #85	P114,CSR
Hewett, Erwin	Pvt	E Hol.Leg.	Petersburg, VA	11/05/64	City Pt., VA	11/11/64	Washington, DC	CSR,HOS
					Pt. Lookout, MD	06/27/65	Rlsd. G.O. #109	P114
Hewett, Ransom H.	Pvt	I 13th SCVI	Wilderness, VA	05/05/64	Belle Plain, VA	05/21/64	Ft. Delaware, DE	CSR
					Ft. Delaware, DE	07/21/64	Hos. 7/21-8/5/64	P47
					Ft. Delaware, DE	04/10/64	Hos. 8/10-8/30/64	P47
					Ft. Delaware, DE	10/26/64	Hos. 10/26/64-2/9/65	P47
					Ft. Delaware, DE	06/08/65	Released GO #109	P43,CSR
Hewett, Robert	Pvt	E Hol.Leg.	Petersburg, VA	11/05/64	City Pt., VA	11/11/64	Washington, DC	CSR
					Pt. Lookout, MD	01/17/65	Exchanged	P114,P124,HOS
Hewin, J.M.	Pvt	G 2nd SCVIRi	Frederick, MD	10/27/62	Fredrick, MD USGH	11/12/62	Baltimore, MD USGH	CSR
					Baltimore, MD USGH	11/17/62	Ft. McHenry, MD Xc	CSR
Hewitt, William D.	Pvt	2 10/19 SCVI	Missionary Ridge, TN	11/25/63	Nashville, TN	12/07/63	Louisville, KY	P39,RAS,CSR
					Louisville, KY	12/09/63	Rock Island, IL	CSR
					Rock Island, IL	02/25/65	Boulware's Ldg. Xc	CSR
					Richmond, VA Hos.	03/08/65	Furloughed 30 days	CSR
Hewitt, William E.	Cpt	F 4th SCVC	Old Church, VA	05/20/64	3rd Div. 5th A.C.	06/05/64	Washington, DC	CSR
					Lincoln G.H., DC	06/19/64	Died of wounds	P6,P12,CSR
Heyward, F.W.	Pvt	Marion LA	Charlotte, NC	05/15/65	Charlotte, NC	05/15/55	Paroled	CSR
Heyward, Jacob Guerard	1Lt	G 1st SCVA	Morris Island, SC	07/10/63	Ft. Columbus, NY	10/09/63	Johnson's Isl., OH	P1,SCA,CSR
Heyward, Jacob Guerard	1Lt	G 1st SCVA	Morris Island, SC	07/09/63	Ft. Delaware, DE	06/12/65	Released	P43,P45,CSR
Heyward, William H.		1st MtdMil	Charlotte, NC	05/12/65	Charlotte, NC	05/12/65	Paroled	CSR
Hibbard, Samuel C.	Pvt	Brooks LA	Richmond, VA	04/03/65	Richmond, VA	04/21/65	Paroled	CSR
Hicklin, James H.	Pvt	A 6th SCVI	P.M.G. Army of Potom.	10/03/62	P.M.G. Army of Potom.	10/03/62	Paroled	CSR
Hickman, Charles	Pvt	F 6th SCVI	Jetersville, VA	04/06/65	City Pt., VA	04/14/65	Newport News, VA	CSR
					Newport News, VA	06/14/65	Rlsd. G.O. #109	CSR
Hickman, J. Medicus	Pvt	K 11th SCVI	Petersburg, VA	05/09/64	Bermuda Hundred, VA	05/11/64	Fts. Monroe, VA	CSR,HAG
					Fts. Monroe, VA	05/13/64	Pt. Lookout, MD	CSR
					Pt. Lookout VA	11/01/64	Venus Pt., GA Xc	CSR
					Pt. Lookout, MD	11/01/64	Exchanged	P113,P124
Hickman, W. Albert	2Lt	K 11th SCVI	Town Creek, NC	02/20/65	Ft. Anderson, NC	02/28/65	Washington, DC	P114,P120,CSR
					Pt. Lookout, MD	02/28/65	Washington, DC	P114,P120
					Old Capitol, DC	03/24/65	Ft. Delaware, DE	CSR
					Ft. Delaware, DE	06/17/65	Rlsd. G.O. #109	P43,CSR
Hicks, B.D.	Pvt	C Hol.Leg.	Petersburg, VA	11/05/65	City Pt., VA	11/11/64	Pt. Lookout, MD	CSR
					Pt. Lookout, MD	06/04/65	Rlsd. sick list	P114,CSR
Hicks, Bailey	Pvt	1st SCVIG	Deserted/enemy	02/25/65	Bermuda Hundred, VA	03/01/65	City Pt., VA	CSR
					Washington, DC	03/06/65	Phila., PA on oath	CSR
Hicks, J.A.	Pvt	B 8th SCVI	Winchester, VA	09/19/64	W. Bldg. Balt, MD	11/19/64	Ft. McHenry, MD	P1,CSR,KEB
					Ft. McHenry, MD	01/03/65	Pt. Lookout, MD	CSR
					Pt. Lookout, MD	03/17/65	Aikens Ldg., VA Xc	P114,P124,CSR
Hicks, J.A.	Pvt	B 8th SCVI	Charlotte, NC	05/16/65	Charlotte, NC	05/16/65	Paroled	CSR

SOUTH CAROLINA SOLDIERS, SAILORS AND **H** CITIZENS HELD IN U.S. PRISONS 1861-1865

NAME	RANK	REGIMENT	CAPTURED AT	WHEN	PRISON	MOVED	DISPOSITION	SOURCES
Hicks, J.W.	Pvt	H 26th SCVI	Deserted/enemy	02/23/65	City Pt., VA	02/25/65	Washington, DC	CSR
					Washington, DC	02/27/65	Dover, NH on oath	CSR
Hicks, John A.	Pvt	H 1st SCVA	Morris Island, SC	07/10/63	Hilton Head, SC	09/05/63	Ft. Columbus, NY	P1,CSR
					Ft. Columbus, NY	09/23/63	Took the oath	P1,CSR
Hicks, Josiah	Pvt	D 2nd SCVIRi	Farmville, VA	04/10/65	Farmville, VA	04/10/65	Paroled	CSR
Hickson, Simeon E.B.	Pvt	H 26th SCVI	Southside RR, VA	04/01/65	City Pt., VA	04/05/65	Pt. Lookout, MD	CSR
					Pt. Lookout, MD	06/28/65	Rlsd. G.O. #109	P114,CSR
Hickson, William L.	Pvt	H 26th SCVI	Crater, Pbg., VA	07/30/64	City Pt., VA	08/05/64	Pt. Lookout, MD	CSR
					Pt. Lookout, MD	08/08/64	Elmira, NY	P113,P120,CSR
					Elmira, NY	10/06/64	Died, Typhoid Pneum.	P5,P65,P66,FPH,CSR
Hiers, William J.	Pvt	K 11th SCVI	Town Creek, NC	02/20/65	Ft. Anderson, NC	02/28/65	Pt. Lookout, MD	P114,HAG,CSR
					Pt. Lookout, MD	03/22/65	Died	P6,FPH,CSR
Higgins, A.H.	Pvt	E 3rd SCVIBn	Williamsport, MD	09/15/62	Ft. Delaware, DE	10/02/62	Aikens Ldg., VA Xc	CSR
Higgins, Benjamin H.	Pvt	Ferguson's	Salisbury, NC	04/12/65	Nashville, TN	04/29/65	Louisville, KY	CSR
					Louisville, KY	05/02/65	Camp Chase, OH	CSR
					Camp Chase, OH	06/13/65	Rlsd. G.O. #109	P23,CSR
Higgins, J.T.	Pvt	A 3rd SCVABn	High Pt., NC	05/02/65	High Pt., NC	05/02/65	Paroled	CSR
Higgins, William B.	Pvt	I 11th SCVI	Petersburg, VA	06/18/64	Pt. Lookout, MD	07/27/64	Elmira, NY	CSR
					Elmira NY	10/11/64	Venus Pt., GA Xc	CSR
Higgs, John	Pvt	I 2nd SCVA	Coles Island, SC	08/05/64	Hilton Head, SC	08/18/64	New York, NY oath	CSR
High, M.M.	Pvt	C 13th SCVI	Appomattox R., VA	04/03/65	City Pt., VA	04/11/65	Hart's Island, NY	P79,CSR
					Hart's Island, NY	06/17/65	Rlsd. G.O. #109	P79,CSR
Highes, G.C.	Pvt	B 7th SCVC	Farmville, VA	04/11/65	Farmville, VA	04/11/65	Paroled	CSR
Highland, D.S.	Sgt	A 15th SCVI	Mount Allen, VA	03/02/65	Pt. Lookout, MD	06/27/65	Rlsd. G.O. #109	P114
Hightower, John	Pvt	D 6th SCVI	Augusta, GA	05/25/65	Augusta, GA	05/25/65	Paroled	CSR
Hightower, Martin H.	Pvt	Wash'n LA	Augusta, GA	05/25/65	Augusta, GA	05/25/65		CSR
Hightower, W.H.	Sgt	D 6th SCVI	Augusta, GA	05/19/65	Augusta, GA	05/19/65	Paroled	CSR
Hill, Alexander	Cpl	B 12th SCVI	Jarratts Stn., VA	04/02/65	City Pt., VA	04/07/65	Hart's Island, NY	CSR
					Hart's Island, NY	06/15/65	Rlsd. G.O. #109	P79,CSR
Hill, Alfred	Pvt	A Hol.Leg.	Farmville, VA	04/07/65	Farmville US G.H.	05/09/65	Sent home	CSR
Hill, B.F.	Pvt	F 3rd SCVIBn	Buckeytown, MD	09/26/62	Paroled		Found sick, left	CSR
Hill, B.M.	Pvt	D 3rd SCVI	Raleigh, NC Hos.	04/13/65	Raleigh, NC Hos.	04/13/65	Paroled	SA2,H3,CSR
Hill, Benjamin R.	Pvt	K 14th SCVI	Farmville, VA	04/11/65	Farmville, VA	04/21/65	Paroled	CSR
Hill, Brantley T.	Pvt	G 26th SCVI	Five Forks, VA	04/01/65	City Pt., VA	04/05/65	Pt. Lookout, MD	CSR
					Pt. Lookout, MD	06/05/65	Released on oath	P114,CSR
Hill, C.E.	Pvt	B 17th SCVI	Boonesboro, MD	09/14/62	Ft. Delaware, DE	10/02/62	Aikens Ldg., VA Xc	CSR
Hill, Calvin	Pvt	G 26th SCVI	Five Forks, VA	04/01/65	City Pt., VA	04/05/65	Pt. Lookout, MD	CSR
					Pt. Lookout, MD	06/27/65	Rlsd. G.O. #109	CSR
Hill, D.J.	Pvt	G 5th SCVC	Deserted/enemy	02/18/65	Charleston, SC	03/15/65	Released on oath	CSR
Hill, Eli	Pvt	B 21st SCVI	Ft. Fisher, NC	01/15/65	Elmira, NY	05/22/65	Died, Ch. Diarrhea	P6,P12,P65,FPH
Hill, George W.	Pvt	A Hol.Leg.	Five Forks, VA	04/01/65	City Pt., VA	04/05/65	Pt. Lookout, MD	CSR,HOS
					Pt. Lookout, MD	06/27/65	Rlsd. G.O. #109	P114
Hill, Harlan B.	Pvt	A 20th SCVI	DES, Jackson Hos.	07/06/64	Knoxville, TN	01/10/65	Chattanooga, TN	CSR
					Chattanooga, TN	01/27/65	Louisville, KY	CSR
					Louisville, KY	01/31/65	North on oath	CSR
Hill, Hezekiah	Pvt	E 8th SCVI	Winchester, VA	09/13/64	Harpers Ferry, WV	09/19/64	Camp Chase, OH	CSR,KEB
					Camp Chase, OH	06/11/65	Rlsd. G.O. #109	P23,CSR
Hill, J.E.	Pvt	G 26th SCVI	Richmond, VA Hos.	04/03/65	Jackson Hos. Rchmd.	05/03/65	Died of wounds	P6,CSR,HC
Hill, J.F.	Pvt	E 12th SCVI	Gettysburg, PA	07/05/63	David's Island, NY	09/23/63	City Pt., VA Xc	P1,LAN,CSR
Hill, J.H.	Pvt	C Orr's Ri.	Sutherland Stn., VA	04/02/65	David's Island, NY	04/28/65	Died of wounds	P6,FPH
Hill, J.M.	Pvt	I 14th SCVI	Gettysburg, PA	07/05/63	David's Island, NY	09/27/63	City Pt., PA Xc	P1,CSR
					Richmond, VA Hos.	10/03/63	Furloughed 30 days	CSR

H

SOUTH CAROLINA SOLDIERS, SAILORS AND  CITIZENS HELD IN U.S. PRISONS 1861-1865

NAME	RANK	REGIMENT	CAPTURED AT	WHEN	PRISON	MOVED	DISPOSITION	SOURCES
Hill, James	Cpl	B 7th SCVI	Knoxville, TN	12/05/63	Louisville, KY	12/31/63	Rock Island, IL	CSR
					Rock Island, IL	05/21/65	Released	CSR
Hill, James	Pvt	A Hol.Leg.	Five Forks, VA	04/01/65	City Pt., VA	04/05/65	Pt. Lookout, MD	CSR,HOS
					Pt. Lookout, MD	06/27/65	Rlsd. G.O. #109	P114
Hill, James C.	Sgt	F 3rd SCVI	Savage Stn., VA	06/28/62	Harrisons Ldg., VA	07/03/62	Ft. Columbus, NY	CSR,KEB,SA2,H3
					Ft. Columbus, NY	07/09/62	Ft. Delaware, DE	CSR
					Ft. Delaware, DE	08/05/62	Aikens Ldg., VA Xc	CSR
Hill, James E.	Pvt	E 1st SCVIG	Gettysburg, PA	07/04/63	David's Island, NY	08/24/63	City Pt., VA Xc	P1,SA1,CSR
Hill, James F.	Pvt	F 17th SCVI	Petersburg, VA	03/25/65	City Pt., VA	03/28/65	Pt. Lookout, MD	CSR,YEB
					Pt. Lookout, MD	06/27/65	Rlsd. G.O. #109	P114,CSR
Hill, James J.	Pvt	I 18th SCVI	Crater, Pbg., VA	07/30/64	City Pt., VA	08/05/64	Pt. Lookout, MD	CSR
					Pt. Lookout, MD	08/08/64	Elmira, NY	P113,P120,CSR
Hill, James J.	Pvt	I 18th SCVI	Crater, Pbg., VA	07/30/64	Elmira, NY	10/14/64	Died, Erysipalas	P5,P65,P66,FPH,CSR
Hill, John B.	Pvt	K 15th SCVI	Augusta, GA	05/19/65	Augusta, GA	05/19/65	Paroled on oath	H15,CSR
Hill, Nelson C.	Pvt	M 8th SCVI	Raleigh, NC	05/13/65	Raleigh, NC	05/13/65	Paroled	CSR
Hill, Nicholas	Pvt	A 3rd SCVIBn	Gettysburg, PA	07/02/63	Gettysburg, PA P.M.	08/03/63	Died of wounds	CSR
Hill, Peter	Pvt	B 3rd SCVIBn	Leesburg, VA	10/02/62	Leesburg, VA	10/02/62	Paroled	CSR
Hill, Simeon A.	Pvt	B 17th SCVI	Petersburg, VA	03/25/65	City Pt., VA	03/28/65	Pt. Lookout, MD	CSR
					Pt. Lookout, MD	06/27/65	Rlsd. G.O. #109	P114,CSR
Hill, T.F.C.	Cpl	D 3rd SCVI	Malvern Hill, VA	07/01/62	Harrisons Ldg., VA	07/12/62	Ft. Columbus, NY	CSR
					Ft. Columbus, NY	07/19/62	Ft. Delaware, DE	CSR
					Ft. Delaware, DE	08/05/62	Aikens Ldg., VA Xc	CSR
Hill, Thomas	Pvt	E 7th SCVC	Darbytown Rd., VA	10/07/64	City Pt., VA	10/29/64	Pt. Lookout, MD	CSR,ANY
					Pt. Lookout, MD		Dutch Gap Canal	CSR
					Dutch Gap Canal	10/21/62	Pt. Lookout, MD	CSR
					Pt. Lookout, MD	04/07/65	Died	P6,P114,FPH,CSR
Hill, W.E.	Pvt	A 1st SCVIH	Boonesboro, MD	09/14/62	Boonesboro, MD	09/25/62	Died, Typhoid	CSR
Hill, William	Sgt	C 2nd SCVI	Louden, TN	12/03/63	Nashville, TN P.M.	02/13/64	Louisville, KY	CSR,P39,SA2,H2,KEB
					Louisville, KY	02/29/64	Ft. Delaware, DE	CSR,P39
					Ft. Delaware, DE	06/10/65	Released on oath	P41,P43,P45,CSR
Hill, William C.	Pvt	K 19th SCVI	Glasgow, KY		Glasgow, KY		Paroled	CSR
Hill, William M.	Pvt	A 8th SCVI	Winchester, VA	09/13/64	Harpers Ferry, WV	09/19/64	Camp Chase, OH	P23,KEB,CSR
					Camp Chase, OH	06/11/65	Released	P23,CSR
Hiller, Samuel J.	Pvt	E 3rd SCVI	Cedar Creek, VA	10/19/64	Winchester, VA USF	12/10/64	Baltimore, MD USGH	CSR,KEB,SA2,H3,ANY
					W. Bldg. Balt, MD	01/08/65	Hammond G.H., MD	CSR
					Pt. Lookout, MD	01/28/65	Hammond G.H., MD	CSR
					Hammond G.H., MD	04/01/65	Pt. Lookout, MD	CSR
					Pt. Lookout, MD	06/05/65	Rlsd., sick list	CSR
Hilliard, Cornelius	Pvt	E 1st SCVA	Morris Island, SC	07/10/63	Hilton Head, SC	09/19/63	Ft. Columbus, NY	CSR
					Ft. Columbus, NY	09/23/63	Took the oath	P1,CSR
Hilliard, W.A.	Pvt	C 7th SCVC	Deserted/enemy	10/11/64	Fts. Monroe, VA	10/22/64	Newport News, VA	P8,CSR
Hilton, Joseph C.	Pvt	H 1st SCVIG	N. Anna River, VA	05/23/64	Front Royal, VA	05/30/64	Pt. Lookout, MD	CSR,SA1
					Pt. Lookout, MD	03/14/65	Aikens Ldg. for Xc	P113,P124,CSR
Hilton, Seburn J.	Cpl	D 1st SCVIH	Mossy Creek, TN	01/22/64	Nashville, TN	02/11/64	Louisville, KY	P39,SA1,LAN,CSR
					Louisville, KY	02/15/64	Rock Island, IL	CSR
					Rock Island, IL	06/20/65	Rlsd. G.O. #109	CSR
Hilton, Thomas F.	Pvt	D 1st SCVIH	Mossy Creek, TN	01/22/64	Nashville, TN	02/11/64	Louisville, KY	P39,SA1,LAN,CSR
					Louisville, KY	02/15/64	Rock Island, IL	CSR
					Rock Island, IL	03/01/64	Died, Rem. fever	CSR,FPH,CSR
Hilton, William B.	Pvt	C 15th SCVAB	Cheraw, SC	03/06/65	New Berne, NC	04/03/65	Pt. Lookout, MD	CSR
					Pt. Lookout, MD	06/27/65	Rlsd. G.O. #109	P114,CSR

SOUTH CAROLINA SOLDIERS, SAILORS AND  CITIZENS HELD IN U.S. PRISONS 1861-1865

NAME	RANK	REGIMENT	CAPTURED AT	WHEN	PRISON	MOVED	DISPOSITION	SOURCES
Hilton, William H.	Pvt	D 1st SCVIH	Mossy Creek, TN	01/22/64	Nashville, TN	02/11/64	Louisville, KY	P39,SA1,CSR
					Louisville, KY	02/15/64	Rock Island, IL	CSR
					Rock Island, IL	06/20/65	Rlsd. G.O. #109	CSR
Hinck, Henry	Pvt	B German LA	Martinsburg, VA	07/15/63				CSR
Hine, Michael	Pvt	A 1st SCVC	Johns Island, SC	07/02/64	Hilton Head, SC	10/25/64	Ft. Pulaski, GA	P2,CSR
Hines, Bynum	Pvt	K 5th SCVI	Amelia C.H., VA	04/06/65	City Pt., VA	04/14/65	Pt. Lookout, MD	CSR,SA3,HOS
					Pt. Lookout, MD	06/27/65	Rlsd. G.O. #109	P114,CSR
Hines, George W.	Pvt	A 3rd SCVIBn	Gettysburg, PA	07/03/63	Ft. McHenry, MD	07/06/63	Ft. Delaware, DE	CSR,KEB
Hines, George W.	Pvt	A 3rd SCVIBn	Knoxville, TN	02/29/64	Ft. Delaware, DE	06/05.64	Hos. 6/5-6/21/64	P47
Hines, George W.	Pvt	A 3rd SCVIBn	Gettysburg, PA	07/03/63	Ft. Delaware, DE	06/08/65	Released	P40,P42,P44
Hines, John	Pvt	C 27th SCVI	Petersburg, VA	06/16/64	Bermuda Hundred, VA	06/20/64	Fts. Monroe, VA	CSR,HAG
					Fts. Monroe, VA	06/22/64	Pt. Lookout, MD	CSR
					Pt. Lookout, MD	07/23/64	Elmira, NY	P113,P120
					Elmira, NY	05/17/65	Released	P7,P65
Hinkle, John C.	Pvt	I Ham.Leg.	Shell Mound, AL	10/28/63	Bridgeport, AL G.H.	12/10/63	Nashville, TN	P2,CSR
Hinkle, John C.	Pvt	I Ham.Leg.	Lookout Mtn., GA	10/28/63	Nashville, TN	07/26/64	Died of wounds	P2,P3,P6,P12,CSR
Hinkle, Silas	Cpl	G 12th SCVI	Falling Waters, MD	07/14/63	Old Capitol, DC		Baltimore, MD	CSR
					Lincoln G.H., DC	08/22/63	W. Bldg. Balt., MD	CSR
					Baltimore, MD	08/24/63	City Pt., VA Xc	CSR
					Williamsburg, VA Hos.	09/09/63	Wdd. Furlough	CSR
Hinnant, A.R.	Pvt	B 7th SCVIBn	Weldon RR, VA	08/21/64	City Pt., VA	08/24/64	Pt. Lookout, MD	CSR,HAG,HFC
					Pt. Lookout, MD	01/17/65	Exchanged	P113,P124,CSR
Hinnant, George S.	Pvt	A 12th SCVI	Sharpsburg, MD	09/17/62	Frederick, MD USGH	10/16/62	US General Hos.	CSR
					Richmond, VA Hos.	11/25/62	Wdd Furlough 25 day	CSR
Hinnant, George S.	Pvt	A 12th SCVI	Spotsylvania, VA	05/12/65	Judiciary Sq.H., D	06/11/64	Lincoln G.H., DC	CSR
					Lincoln G.H., DC	12/31/64	Amptd Rt. forearm	CSR
					Old Capitol, DC	03/27/65	Elmira, NY	CSR
					Elmira, NY	06/30/65	Rlsd. G.O. #109	P65,P66,CSR
Hinnant, Henry M.	Pvt	C 12th SCVI	Sharpsburg, MD	09/17/62	Frederick, MD USGH	10/16/62	US General Hos.	CSR
					Ft. McHenry, MD	10/18/62	Fts. Monroe, VA Xc	CSR
Hinnant, John A.	Cpt	C 12th SCVI	Gettysburg, PA	07/01/63	David's Island, NY	08/24/63	Bedloes Island, NY	CSR
					Bedloes Island, NY	10/29/63	Johnson's Isl., OH	P1,R47,CSR
					Johnson's Isl., OH		Pt. Lookout, MD	CSR
					Pt. Lookout, MD	04/24/64	City Pt., VA Xc	CSR
					Richmond, VA Hos.	05/05/64	CS Gen.Hos.	CSR
Hinrichs, J.H.W.	Pvt	B German LA	Deserted/enemy	10/01/64	Hilton Head, SC D.	10/13/64	Str. *Fulton* to NY	CSR
Hinson, Andrew Newton	Pvt	I 17th SCVI	Jackson, MS	07/16/63	Jackson, MS	07/16/63	Paroled	CSR,LAN
Hinson, Andrew Newton	Pvt	I 17th SCVI	Crater, Pbg., VA	07/30/64	City Pt., VA	08/05/64	Pt. Lookout, MD	CSR
					Pt. Lookout, MD	08/08/64	Elmira, NY	P113,P120,CSR
					Elmira, NY	10/11/64	Pt. Lookout, MD Xc	P65,P66,CSR
					Pt. Lookout, MD	10/29/64	Exchanged	P114,CSR
Hinson, Elijah	Pvt	H 2nd SCVI	Gettysburg, PA	07/05/63	G.H. Gettysburg	07/18/63	Died of wounds	P1,KEB,SA2,H2,CSR
Hinson, Erasmus	Pvt	C 15th SCVAB	Cheraw, NC	09/08/67	Camp Hamilton, VA	04/25/65	Newport News, VA	CSR
					Newport News, VA	06/15/65	Rlsd. G.O.#109	CSR
Hinson, J.M.	Pvt	I 17th SCVI	Kinston, NC	12/14/62	Kinston, NC	12/14/62	Paroled	CSR
Hinson, John	Pvt	A 21st SCVI	Ft. Fisher, NC	01/15/65	Elmira, NY	05/18/65	Died, Pneumonia	P6,P12,P65,FPH,HAG
Hinson, John S.	Pvt	E 12th SCVI	Wilderness, VA	05/05/64	Fredericksburg USGH			CSR
					Richmond, VA Hos.			CSR
Hinson, Lewis M.	Pvt	A 4th SCVC	Fayetteville, NC	03/14/65	New Berne, NC	03/30/65	Pt. Lookout, MD	CSR
					Pt. Lookout, MD	06/28/65	Rlsd. G.O. #109	P114,CSR

SOUTH CAROLINA SOLDIERS, SAILORS AND  CITIZENS HELD IN U.S. PRISONS 1861-1865

NAME	RANK	REGIMENT	CAPTURED AT	WHEN	PRISON	MOVED	DISPOSITION	SOURCES
Hiott, Joseph P.	Pvt	I 11th SCVI	Petersburg, VA	06/16/64	Bermuda Hundred, VA	06/17/64	Fts. Monroe, VA	CSR,HAG
					Fts. Monroe, VA	06/18/64	Pt. Lookout, MD	CSR
					Pt. Lookout, MD	07/25/64	Elmira, NY	P113,P120,CSR
					Elmira, NY	10/11/64	Pt. Lookout, MD Xc	P65,P66,CSR
					Elmira NY	10/11/64	Venus Pt., GA Xc	CSR
					Pt. Lookout, MD	10/29/64	Exchanged	P114
Hiott, Lawrence P.	Pvt	I 11th SCVI	Petersburg, VA	06/16/64	Bermuda Hundred, VA	06/17/64	Fts. Monroe, VA	CSR,HAG
					Fts. Monroe, VA	06/18/64	Pt. Lookout, MD	CSR
					Pt. Lookout, MD	07/25/64	Elmira, NY	P120,FPH,CSR
					Elmira, NY	10/26/64	Died, Ch. Diarrhea	P5,P12,P65,P66,CSR
Hipp, David	Cit		Lexington, SC	03/19/65	Pt. Lookout, MD	06/19/65	Rlsd. G.O. #109	P114
Hipp, Nathan L.	Sgt	G Hol.Leg.	Kinston, NC	12/15/62	Kinston, NC	12/15/62	Paroled POW	CSR
Hipp, Nathan L.	2Lt	G Hol.Leg.	Hatchers Run, VA	03/29/65	City Pt., VA	03/31/65	Old Capitol, VA	CSR
					Old Capitol, DC	04/09/65	Johnson's Isl., OH	CSR
					Johnson's Isl., OH	06/17/65	Rlsd. G.O. #109	CSR
Hires, J.C.	Pvt	H 17th SCVI	Augusta, GA	05/20/65	Augusta, GA	05/20/65	Paroled	CSR
Hires, O.M.	Pvt	H 17th SCVI	Augusta, GA	05/20/65	Augusta, GA	05/20/65	Paroled	CSR
Hirsch, Isaac W.	Pvt	B 2nd SCVI	Charlotte, NC	05/03/65	Charlotte, NC	05/03/65	Paroled	SA2,H2,CSR
Hite, William B.	Cpl	E 19th SCVI	Augusta, GA	05/19/65	Augusta, GA	05/19/65	Paroled	CSR
Hitt, Henry L.	Pvt	B 3rd SCVIBn	South Mtn., MD	09/14/62	Ft. Delaware, DE	10/02/62	Aikens Ldg., VA Xc	CSR
Hitt, Malcom C.	Pvt	B Ham.Leg.Ml	Augusta, GA	05/31/65	Augusta,GA	05/31/65	Paroled	CSR
Hix, Edward M.	SMj	3rd SCVI	Gettysburg, PA	07/05/63		09/22/63	City Pt., VA Xc	H3
Hix, Edward M.	SMj	3rd SCVI	Knoxville, TN	12/05/63	Nashville, TN	02/27/64	Louisville, KY	P39,CSR
					Louisville, KY	02/29/64	Ft. Delaware, DE	CSR
					Ft. Delaware, DE	04/05/64	Hos. 4/5-6/3/64	P47
					Ft. Delaware, DE	09/18/64	Aikens Ldg., VA X	P41,P43,CSR
					Richmond, VA Hos.	09/25/64	Furloughed 30 days	CSR
Hix, W.J.	Pvt	I Ham.Leg.Ml	Greenville, SC	05/24/65	Greenville, SC	05/24/65	Paroled	CSR
Hobbs, George W.	Pvt	K 12th SCVI	Gettysburg, PA	07/05/63	Ft. Delaware, DE	09/18/63	Died, Rem. fever	P5,P40,P42,P44,P47
Hockaday, Walter W.	Pvt	B Wash'n LA	Spotsylvania, VA		Bowling Green, KY	05/16/65	Paroled	CSR
Hocott, B.	Pvt	G 7th SCVIBn	Goldsboro, NC P.M.		Goldsboro, NC		Paroled, No date	CSR
Hocott, B.C.	Pvt	B 3rd SCVIBn	N. Anna River, VA	05/23/64	Port Royal, VA	05/30/64	Pt. Lookout, MD	CSR
					Pt. Lookout, MD	07/23/64	Elmira, NY	P120,CSR
					Elmira, NY	12/13/64	Escaped	P7,P65,P66,CSR
Hodge, Andrew Franklin	Cpl	E 15th SCVI	Knoxville, TN	12/05/63	Louisville, KY	01/27/64	Rock Island, IL	CSR
					Rock Island, IL	05/03/65	New Orleans, LA Xc	P4,CSR
Hodge, E.S.	Pvt	I 25th SCVI	Ft. Fisher, NC	01/15/65	New York, NY	01/30/65	Elmira, NY	CSR,HAG
					Elmira, NY	02/20/65	Tfd. for exchange	P65,CSR
					Richmond Rcvg. Hos.	03/04/65	Died	CSR
Hodge, Elihu J.	Pvt	C 3rd SCVABn	Blakely, AL	04/09/65	2nd Div. 16th A.C.	04/09/65	Head wound, flesh	CSR
					Ship Island, MS	05/01/65	Vicksburg, MS Xc	CSR
Hodge, Isaac B.	Pvt	D 2nd SCVI	Gettysburg, PA	07/02/63	Ft. Delaware, DE	06/14/65	Rlsd. G.O. #109	P40,P42,H2,SA2,CSR
Hodge, James A.	Pvt	K 23rd SCVI	Petersburg, VA	04/01/65	Pt. Lookout, MD	06/28/65	Rlsd. G.O. #109	P114
Hodge, James D.	Pvt	I 25th SCVI	Ft. Fisher, NC	01/15/65	New York, NY	01/30/65	Elmira, NY	CSR,HAG
					Elmira, NY	04/10/65	Died, Diarrhea	P6,P65,FPH
Hodge, Louis	Sgt	D 11th SCVI	Ft. Fisher, NC	01/15/65	Elmira, NY	07/13/65	Hospital	P65,HAG
					Elmira, NY	08/07/65	Rlsd. G.O. #109	P66,CSR
Hodge, R.J.	Sgt	I 23rd SCVI	Fair Gds GH Pbg.	04/03/65	Fair Gds G.H. Pbg.	04/15/65	Died	P6,HCL,CSR
Hodge, S.N.	Pvt	I 25th SCVI	Morris Island, SC	09/07/63	Hilton Head, SC	10/06/63	Ft. Columbus, NY	CSR,HAG
					Ft. Columbus, NY	10/09/63	Pt. Lookout, MD	P1
					Pt. Lookout, MD	05/03/64	Exchanged	P113,P124

SOUTH CAROLINA SOLDIERS, SAILORS AND  CITIZENS HELD IN U.S. PRISONS 1861-1865

NAME	RANK	REGIMENT	CAPTURED AT	WHEN	PRISON	MOVED	DISPOSITION	SOURCES
Hodge, S.N.	Pvt	I 25th SCVI	Ft. Fisher, NC	01/15/65	New York, NY	01/30/65	Elmira, NY	CSR
					Elmira, NY	02/11/65	Died, Diarrhea	P6,P65,CSR
Hodge, W.M.	Pvt	G 3rd SCVABn	High Pt., NC	05/01/65	High Pt., NC	05/01/65	Paroled	CSR
Hodge, William H.	2Cp	K 21st SCVI	Ft. Fisher, NC	01/15/65	Elmira, NY	03/07/65	Died, Diarrhea	P6,P65,FPH,HAG
Hodge. J.E.	Pvt	I 23rd SCVI	Petersburg, VA	04/01/65	City Pt., VA	04/05/65	Pt. Lookout, MD	CSR
					Pt. Lookout, MD	07/28/65	Rlsd. G.O. #109	CSR
Hodges, F.T.	Pvt	F Hol.Leg.	Jarratts Stn., VA	05/08/64	Fts. Monroe, VA	05/13/64	Pt. Lookout, MD	CSR
					Pt. Lookout, MD	08/15/64	Elmira, NY	P113,P120
					Elmira, NY	06/21/65	Rlsd. G.O. #109	P65,P66
Hodges, J.B.	Pvt	E 1st SCVIG	Gettysburg, PA	07/05/63	Ft. Delaware, DE	07/31/63	City Pt., VA Xc	P40,P42,SA1,CSR
Hodges, James A.	Cpl	D 10th SCVI	Danville, KY	09/15/62	Kentucky	11/15/62	Paroled	CSR,RAS
Hodges, James P.	Pvt	D 11th SCVI	Ft. Fisher, NC	01/15/65	Ft. Fisher, NC	02/01/65	Elmira, NY	CSR,HAG
					Elmira, NY	07/13/65	Elmira, NY USGH	P65,CSR
					Elmira, NY	08/07/65	Rlsd. G.O. #109	P66,CSR
Hodges, Joseph W.	Pvt	F 2nd SCVI	Cedar Creek, VA	10/19/64	Harpers Ferry, WV	10/23/64	Pt. Lookout, MD	CSR,KEB,SA2,H2
					Pt. Lookout, MD	03/28/65	Exchanged	P114,P124,CSR
Hodges, Joshua J.	Pvt	F 1st SCVIG	Petersburg, VA	04/02/65	City Pt. VA	04/04/65	Pt. Lookout, MD	CSR,SA1
					Pt. Lookout, MD	06/27/65	Rlsd. G.O. #109	P114,CSR
Hodges, Lewis	Pvt	D 11th SCVI	Ft. Fisher, NC	01/15/65	Ft. Fisher, NC	02/01/65	Elmira, NY	CSR
					Elmira, NY	07/13/65	Elmira, NY USGH	CSR
					Elmira, NY USGH	08/07/65	Rlsd. G.O.#109	CSR
Hodges, R.B.	Pvt	H 8th SCVI	Frederick, MD	09/12/62	Ft. Delaware, DE	10/02/62	Exchanged	CSR
Hodges, R.B.	Pvt	H 8th SCVI	Winchester, VA	09/13/64	Harpers Ferry, WV	09/19/64	Camp Chase, OH	CSR
					Camp Chase, OH	06/11/65	Rlsd. G.O. #109	P23,KEB,CSR
Hodges, Robert	Pvt	K 23rdSCVI	Deserted/enemy	03/05/65	City Pt., VA	03/05/65	Mason City, IL	CSR
Hodges, Samuel B.	Sgt	F Hol.Leg.	Jarratts Stn., VA	05/08/64	Fts. Monroe, VA	05/13/64	Pt. Lookout, MD	CSR,UD3
					Pt. lookout, MD	08/15/64	Elmira, NY	P113,P120
					Elmira, NY	06/14/65	Released	P65,P66
Hodgins, William B.	Pvt	C Orr's Ri.	Falling Waters, MD	07/14/63	Baltimore, MD	08/16/64	Pt. Lookout, MD	CSR,CDC
					Pt. Lookout, MD	08/16/64	Elmira, NY	P113,P120,CSR
					Elmira, NY	09/20/64	Died, Diarrhea	P5,P65,FPH,CSR
Hodgson, Peter P.	Pvt	H 25th SCVI	Deserted/enemy	04/22/65	Charleston, SC	04/22/65	Released on oath	CSR,HAG
Hoefer, Charles F.	Pvt	Brooks LA	Harpers Farm, VA	04/06/65	City Pt., VA	04/14/65	Pt. Lookout, MD	CSR
					Pt. Lookout, MD	06/27/65	Rlsd. G.O. #109	CSR
Hoffman, E. Julius	Cpl	A Orr's Ri.	Petersburg, VA	04/03/65	City Pt., VA	04/11/65	Hart's Island, NY	CSR
					Harts Island, NY	06/16/65	Rlsd. G.O. #109	P79,CSR
Hoffman, J.A.	Sgt	E 14th SCMil	Columbia, SC	02/19/65	Hart's Island, NY	06/17/65	Rlsd. G.O. #109	P79
Hoffman, Jacob M.	Pvt	K 10th SCVI	Glasgow, KY	09/10/62	Kentucky	11/15/62	Paroled	CSR
Hoffman, Michael	Pvt	B German LA	Desrted/enemy	10/17/64				CSR
Hoffman, Nicholas	Pvt	I 1st SCVA	Morris Island, SC	07/10/63	Hilton Head, SC			CSR
Hoffman, Richard	Pvt	C 5th SCVC	Deserted/enemy	06/10/64	Williamsburg, VA	06/13/64	Fts. Monroe, VA	CSR
					Fts. Monroe, VA	06/18/64	New York, NY oath	CSR
Hoffman, W.H.C.	Pvt	F 1st SCVIR	Deserted/enemy	02/18/65	Charleston, SC	03/15/65	Taken oath & disch.	CSR
Hogan, P.L.	Pvt	G 3rd SCVIBn	Petersburg, VA	07/30/64	Pt. Lookout, MD	08/08/64	Elmira, NY	P120,CSR
					Elmira NY	05/17/65	Rlsd. G.O. #85	P65,P66,P120,CSR
Hogan, Patrick R.	2Lt	H 27th SCVI	Weldon RR, VA	08/21/64	Old Capitol, DC	08/27/64	Ft. Delaware, DE	CSR,HAG
					Ft. Delaware, DE	06/17/65	Rlsd. G.O. #109	P43,P45,P46,CSR
Hogarth, Edmund A.	Pvt	D 24th SCVI	Nashville, TN	12/16/64	Nashville, TN	12/31/64	Louisville, KY	CSR
					Louisville, KY	01/02/65	Camp Chase, OH	CSR
					Camp Chase, OH	06/12/65	Rlsd. G.O. #109	P23,CSR
Hogg, J.C.	Sgt	H 1st SCVIG	Gettysburg, PA	07/04/63	David's Island, NY	08/24/63	City Pt., VA Xc	P1,SA1,CSR
Hogg, Thomas	Sgt	G Hol.Leg.	Warrenton, VA	09/29/62	Warrenton, VA	09/29/62	Paroled/ Hospital	CSR

H

SOUTH CAROLINA SOLDIERS, SAILORS AND CITIZENS HELD IN U.S. PRISONS 1861-1865

NAME	RANK	REGIMENT	CAPTURED AT	WHEN	PRISON	MOVED	DISPOSITION	SOURCES
Hogue, James A.	Pvt	E 17th SCVI	Amelia C.H., VA	04/03/65	City Pt., VA	04/13/65	Pt. Lookout, MD	CSR,YEB
					Pt. Lookout, MD	06/27/65	Rlsd. G.O. #109	P114,CSR
Hoke, John C.	Pvt	H 24th SCVI	Nashville, TN	12/16/64	Nashville, TN	12/19/64	Louisville, KY	CSR,HHC
					Louisville, KY	12/21/64	Camp Douglas, IL	CSR
					Camp Douglas, IL	06/19/65	Rlsd. G.O. #109	P55
Holbrooks, Elan H.	Pvt	A 12th SCVI	Gettysburg, PA	07/04/63	Chester, PA G.H.	08/17/63	City Pt., VA Xc	P1,YEB,CSR
Holcomb, Bennet	Pvt	H 1st SCVA	Deserted/enemy	05/15/64	Louisville, KY	05/27/64	Taken oath	CSR
Holcomb, T.J.	Pvt	A 3rd SCVABn	High Pt., NC	05/02/65	High Pt., NC	05/02/65	Paroled	CSR
Holcomb, William H.	Cpt	A Orr's Ri.	Appomattox R., VA	04/03/65	Old Capitol, DC	04/21/65	Johnson's Isl., OH	CSR
					Johnson's Isl., OH	06/18/65	Rlsd. G.O.#109	CSR
Holcombe, L.B.	Pvt	E 6th SCVC	Petersburg, VA	10/27/64	City Pt., VA	10/30/64	Pt. Lookout, MD	CSR
					Pt. Lookout, MD	02/18/65	Exchanged	P114,P124,CSR
Holden, Benjamin F.	Pvt	C Orr's Ri.	Falling Waters, MD	07/14/63	Baltimore, MD	08/16/63	Pt. Lookout, MD	CSR,CDC
					Pt. Lookout, MD	05/03/64	Exchanged	P113,P124,CSR
Holden, Benjamin F.	Pvt	C Orr's Ri.	Southside RR, VA	04/02/65	City Pt., VA	04/07/65	Hart's Island, NY	CSR
					Hart's Island, NY	06/15/65	Rlsd. G.O. #109	P79,CSR
Holden, Daniel	Pvt	A 22nd SCVI	Petersburg, VA	03/25/65	City Pt., VA	03/27/65	Pt. Lookout, MD	CSR
					Pt. Lookout, MD	06/28/65	Rlsd. G.O. #109	P114
Holder, Jacob	Pvt	G 7th SCVC	Buck Island, VA	05/06/64	Elmira, NY	10/11/64	Pt. Lookout, MD Xc	P66
					Pt. Lookout, MD	10/29/64	Exchanged	P114
Holladay, J.H.	Pvt	H 5th SCVC	Stony Creek, VA	12/01/64	City Pt., VA	12/05/64	Pt. Lookout, MD	CSR
					Pt. Lookout, MD	06/27/65	Rlsd. G.O. #109	CSR
Holland, A. Berry	Cpl	D 18th SCVI	Petersburg, VA	07/30/64	City Pt., VA	08/08/64	Pt. Lookout, MD	CSR
					Pt. Lookout, MD	08/08/64	Elmira, NY	P113,P120,CSR
					Elmira, NY	05/29/65	Rlsd. G.O. #85	P65,P66,CSR
Holland, Elijah M.	Pvt	L P.S.S.	Fair Oaks, VA	06/01/62	Fts. Monroe, VA	07/15/62	Ft. Delaware, DE	CSR,TSE
					Ft. Delaware, DE		Aikens Ldg., VA Xc	CSR
					Aikens Ldg., VA	08/05/62	Exchanged	CSR
Holland, Isaac F.	Sgt	G 3rd SCVABn	High Pt., NC	05/01/65	High Pt., NC	05/01/65	Paroled	CSR
Holland, J.S.	Pvt	H 8th SCVI	Gettysburg, PA	07/04/63	Gettysburg G.H.		Provost Marshal	P4,KEB
					David's Island, NY	08/24/63	City Pt., VA Xc	P1,CSR
Holland, J.W.	Pvt	B 2nd SCVI	Cheraw, SC	03/05/65	Cheraw, SC	03/05/65	Paroled	SA2,H2,CSR
Holland, James	Pvt	B 11th SCVI	Deserted/enemy		Washington, DC	04/17/65	Dedham, MA oath	CSR
Holland, James H.	Cpl	L Orr's Ri.	Spotsylvania, VA	05/12/64	Old Capitol, DC	06/15/64	Ft. Delaware, DE	CSR
					Ft. Delaware, DE	07/02/64	Hos. 7/2/64-?	P47
					Ft. Delaware, DE	11/07/64	Hos.11/7/64-1/23/65	P47
					Ft. Delaware, DE	02/08/65	Hos. 2/8-2/20/65	P47
					Ft. Delaware, DE	02/22/65	Died, Pleurisy	P5,P41,P43,P47,FPH
Holland, John	Pvt	D 7th SCVC	Deserted/enemy	10/13/64	Fts. Monroe, VA	10/22/64	New York, NY oath	P8,CSR
Holland, Robert	Pvt	8 10/19 SCVI	Missionary Ridge, TN	11/25/63	Nashville, TN	12/07/63	Louisville, KY	P39,CSR
					Louisville, KY	12/09/63	Rock Island, IL	CSR
					Rock Island, IL	06/19/65	Rlsd. G.O. #109	CSR
Holland, Robert	Pvt	G 7th SCVC	Farmville, VA	04/11/65	Farmville, VA	04/21/65	Paroled	CSR
Holland, W.E.	Pvt	K 22nd SCVI	Farmville, VA Hos.	04/27/65	Farmville, VA	04/27/65	Rlsd. on parole	CSR
Holland, William	Pvt	D Hol.Leg.	Augusta, GA	05/24/65	Augusta, GA	05/24/65	Paroled	CSR
Hollands, E.C.	Pvt	E 2nd SCVIRi	Hartwell, GA	05/20/65	Hartwell, GA	05/20/65	Paroled	CSR
Holleglad, J.H.	Pvt	22nd SCVI	Kinston, NC	12/15/62	Kinston, NC	12/15/62	Paroled POW	CSR
Holleman, Joseph W.	1Sg	G 12th SCVI	Spotsylvania, VA	05/12/64	Belle Plain, VA	05/20/64	Ft. Delaware, DE	CSR
					Ft. Delaware, DE	06/10/65	Released	P41,P43,P45,CSR
Hollen, John H.	Pvt	B German LA	Deserted/enemy	03/17/65	Charleston, SC	03/17/65	Released on oath	CSR
Holleran, J.	Pvt	B 11th SCVI	Richmond VA Hos.	04/03/65	Escaped	04/05/65		CSR
Holley, A.L.	2Lt	K 19th SCVI	Augusta, GA	05/18/65	Augusta, GA	05/18/65	Paroled	CSR

SOUTH CAROLINA SOLDIERS, SAILORS AND  CITIZENS HELD IN U.S. PRISONS 1861-1865

NAME	RANK	REGIMENT	CAPTURED AT	WHEN	PRISON	MOVED	DISPOSITION	SOURCES
Holley, Daniel	Pvt	F Orr's Ri.	Petersburg, VA	04/02/65	City Pt., VA	04/04/65	Pt. Lookout, MD	CSR,CDC
					Pt. Lookout, MD	06/28/65	Rlsd. G.O. #109	P114,CSR
Holley, G.W.	Pvt	C 6tth SCVI	Deserted/enemy	02/28/65	Bermuda Hundred, VA	03/01/65	City Pt., VA P.M.	gR
					City Pt., VA P.M.	03/03/65	Washington, DC P.M.	CSR
					Washington, DC P.M.	03/06/65	Boston, MA oath	CSR
Holley, G.W.	Pvt	C 6tth SCVI	Richmond, VA	07/03/65	Richmond, VA	07/05/65	Amnesty oath	CSR
Holliday, Henry	Pvt	A 21st SCVI	Morris Island, SC	07/10/63	Hilton Head, SC	07/14/63	Ft. Columbus, NY	CSR
					Ft. Columbus, NY	07/19/63	Pt. Lookout, MD	CSR,HAG
					Pt. Lookout, MD	06/28/64	Rlsd. G.O. #109	P113,P124,CSR
Holliday, Henry G.	Pvt	I 23rd SCVI	Petersburg, VA	04/01/65	City Pt., VA	04/05/65	Pt. Lookout, MD	CSR
					Pt. Lookout, MD	06/28/65	Rlsd. G.O. #109	P114,CSR
Holliday, James J.	Pvt	E 16th SCVI	Franklin, TN	11/30/64	Nashville, TN	12/02/64	Louisville, KY	CSR
					Louisville, KY	12/03/64	Camp Douglas, IL	CSR
					Camp Douglas, IL	04/14/65	Jd. 5th USVI	CSR
Holliday, William J.	Pvt	I 24th SCVI	Franklin, TN	12/18/64	Nashville, TN G.H.	03/17/65	Died	P6,EFW
Holliman, William	Pvt	I 18th SCVI	Hatchers Run, VA	04/01/65	City Pt., VA	04/04/65	Pt. Lookout, MD	CSR
					Pt. Lookout, MD	06/28/65	Rlsd. G.O. #109	P114,CSR
Hollingfield, Jacob	Pvt	G 1st SCVIR	Chester Stn., SC	04/03/65	Hart's Island, NY	05/08/65	Died, Ch. Diarrhea	P6,P79,FPH,SA1,CSR
Hollingsworth, John N.	Pvt	D Orr's Ri.	Deserted/enemy	02/21/65	City Pt., VA P.M.	02/24/65	Washington, DC	CSR
					Washington, DC	02/24/65	Burlington, Iowa	CDC,CSR
Hollingsworth, R.T.	Pvt	B 3rd SCVIBn	Gettysburg, PA	07/02/63	Gettysburg, PA G.H.	10/01/63	Provost Marshal	P4,CSR
					W. Bldg. Balt, MD	11/12/63	City Point, VA, Xc	P1,CSR
Hollingsworth, Thomas	Pvt	E 2nd SCVIRi	Hartwell, GA	05/20/65	Hartwell, GA	05/20/65	Paroled	CSR
Hollingsworth, William	Pvt	G 27th SCVI	Weldon RR, VA	08/21/64	Pt. Lookout, MD	10/30/64	Venus Pt., GA Xc	P113,P125,HAG,CSR
Hollins, M.J.	Pvt	D 1st SCVA	Deserted/enemy	02/26/65	Charleston, SC		Released on oath	CSR
Hollis, John L.	Pvt	C 12th SCVI	Wilderness, VA	05/06/64	Belle Plain, VA	05/20/64	Ft. Delaware, DE	CSR,HFC
					Ft. Delaware, DE	06/08/65	Released	P41,P43,P45,CSR
Hollis, Peter T.	Lt	H 24th SCVI	Nashville, TN	12/16/64	Nashville, TN	12/18/64	Louisville, KY	CSR
					Louisville, KY	12/20/64	Johnson's Isl., OH	CSR
					Johnson's Isl., OH	06/16/65	Rlsd. G.O. #109	CSR
Holloran, Patrick	Pvt	K 1st SCVIG	Malvern Hill, VA	07/04/62	Aikens Ldg., VA	08/05/62	Exchanged	CSR
Holloran, Patrick	Pvt	K 1st SCVIG	Sharpsburg, MD	09/30/62	Ft. McHenry, MD	03/13/63	Fts. Monroe, VA Xc	SA1,CSR
Holloran, Patrick	Pvt	K 1st SCVIG	Petersburg, VA	04/02/65	Pt. Lookout, MD	06/28/65	Rlsd. G.O. #109	P114,SA1,CSR
Holloway, D.W.	Cpl	B Ham.Leg.	Frederick, MD	09/12/62	Frederick, MD USGH	09/22/62	Ft. Delaware, DE	CSR
					Ft. Delaware, DE	10/02/62	Aikens Ldg., VA Xc	CSR
Holloway, D.W.	Pvt	K 2nd SCVC	Augusta, GA	05/31/65	Augusta, GA	05/31/65	Paroled	CSR
Holloway, E.P.	Pvt	F 4th SCResB	Augusta, GA	05/29/65	Augusta, GA	05/29/65	Paroled	CSR
Holloway, H.W.	Pvt	G 1st SCVIG	Gettysburg, PA	07/03/63	David's Island, NY	09/05/63	City Pt., VA Xc	P1,SA1,CSR
Holloway, O.A.	Pvt	G 1st SCVI	Deserted/enemy		Charleston, SC	03/01/65	Released on oath	CSR
Holloway, Thomas	Pvt	G 24th SCVI	Missionary Ridge, TN	11/25/63	Nashville, TN	12/02/63	Louisville, KY	P39
					Louisville, KY	12/13/63	Rock Island, IL	CSR
					Rock Island, IL	01/16/64	Died, Ch. Diarrhea	P5,FPH,CSR
Holly, Benjamin F.	Pvt	Brooks LA	Harpers Farm, VA	04/06/65	City Pt., VA	04/14/65	Pt. Lookout, MD	CSR
					Pt. Lookout, MD	06/28/65	Rlsd. G.O. #109	CSR
Hollywood, Thomas	Pvt	F 1st SCVA	Fayetteville, NC	03/11/65	New Berne, NC		Pt. Lookout, MD	CSR
					Pt. Lookout, MD			P114
Holman, Calvin	Pvt	F 19th SCVI	Nashville, TN	12/16/64	Nashville, TN	12/18/64	Louisville, KY	CSR
					Louisville, KY	12/20/64	Camp Douglas, IL	CSR
					Camp Douglas, IL	01/16/65	Died, Variola	P5,P55,P58,FPH,CSR
Holman, Daniel P.	Pvt	C 15th SCVI	Gettysburg, PA	07/05/63	Gettysburg, PA USH	07/20/63	David's Island, NY	P1,CSR,KEB
					David's Island, NY	08/24/63	City Pt., VA Xc	CSR

H

SOUTH CAROLINA SOLDIERS, SAILORS AND CITIZENS HELD IN U.S. PRISONS 1861-1865

NAME	RANK	REGIMENT	CAPTURED AT	WHEN	PRISON	MOVED	DISPOSITION	SOURCES
Holman, Daniel P.	Pvt	C 15th SCVI	Halltown, VA	08/26/64	Harpers Ferry, WV	08/26/64	Camp Chase, OH	P23,P26,CSR
					Camp Chase, OH	03/03/65	Died, Variola	P6,FPH,P27
Holman, Edward H.	Cpt	G 27th SCVI	Town Creek, NC	02/20/65	Ft. Anderson, NC	02/28/65	Pt. Lookout, MD	CSR,HAG
					Pt. Lookout, MD	02/28/65	Washington, DC	P114,P120,CSR
					Old Capitol, DC	03/26/65	Ft. Delaware, DE	CSR
					Ft. Delaware, DE	06/17/65	Rlsd. G.O. #109	P43,P45,CSR
Holman, James M.O.	Pvt	G 25th SCVI	Town Creek, NC	02/20/65	Ft. Anderson, NC	02/28/65	Pt. Lookout, MD	CSR,HAG
					Pt. Lookout, MD	06/27/65	Rlsd. G.O. #109	P114,CSR
Holman, Jesse	2Lt	B 15th SCMil			Foster G.H., Newbern	05/02/65	Died, Ac. Diarrhea	P5,P6,P12,WAT
Holmes, David H.	Pvt	A Ham.Leg.MI	Richmond, VA Hos.	04/03/65	Richmond, VA Hos.	04/14/65	Provost Marshal	CSR
					Libby Prison Rchmnd.	04/23/65	Newport News, VA	CSR
					Newport News, VA	06/26/65	Rlsd. G.O. #109	CSR
Holmes, Henry	Pvt	I 1st SCVA	Morris Island, SC	07/10/63	Hilton Head, SC	09/05/63	Ft. Columbus, NY	CSR
					Ft. Columbus, NY	09/23/63	Took the oath	P1
Holmes, Sharon	Sgt	I 7th SCVI	Chickamauga, GA	09/20/63	Nashville, TN	10/05/63	Louisville, KY	P38,KEB,CSR
					Camp Douglas, IL	06/16/65	Rlsd. G.O. #109	P55,P57,CSR
Holmes, William E.	Pvt	A 25th SCVI	Ft. Fisher, NC	01/15/65	New York, NY	01/30/65	Elmira, NY	CSR,HAG
					Elmira, NY	06/19/65	Rlsd. G.O. #109	P65,CSR
Holmes, Zebedee	Pvt	K 1st SCVA	Goldsboro, NC	03/16/65	New Berne, NC	03/30/65	Pt. Lookout, MD	CSR
					Pt. Lookout, MD	05/13/65	Rlsd. G.O. #85	P114,CSR
Holsenback, P.B.	Pvt	Col.Post G	Columbia, SC	02/19/65	Hart's Island, NY	06/20/65	Rlsd. G.O. #109	P79
Holsinger, Carl	Pvt	I 25th SCVI	Deserted/enemy	07/01/64	Knoxville, TN	07/01/64	Jeffersonville, IN	CSR
Holstein, Joseph A.	Pvt	G 25th SCVI	Ft. Fisher, NC	01/15/65	New York, NY	01/30/65	Elmira, NY	CSR,HAG
					Elmira, NY	03/07/65	Died, Diarrhea	P6,P65,FPH,CSR
Holston, W.W.	Sgt	B 14th SCVI	Sutherland Stn., VA	04/02/63	City Pt., VA	04/07/65	Hart's Island, NY	CSR
					Hart's Island, NY	06/16/65	Rlsd. G.O. #109	P79,CSR
Holton, John T.	Pvt	F 12th SCVI	Wilderness, VA	05/06/64	Belle Plain, VA	05/20/64	Ft. Delaware, DE	CSR
					Ft. Delaware, DE	06/10/65	Released	P41,P43,P45,CSR
Holtzclaw, George H.	Pvt	C 22nd SCVI	Farmville, VA	04/06/65	City Pt., VA	04/14/65	Newport News, VA	CSR
					Newport News, VA	05/09/65	Died, Ch. Diarrhea	P6,P12,PP,ROH
Holtzclaw, J. Pinckney	Pvt	C 22nd SCVI	Farmville, VA	04/06/65	City Pt., VA	04/14/65	Newport News, VA	CSR
					Newport News, VA	06/15/65	Rlsd. G.O. #109	CSR
					Fair Gds H. Pbg.	06/26/65	Died, Rem. fever	P6,P12,ROH
Holzhauer, Charles	Pvt	B Wash'n LA	Virginia	07/25/63	14th Penn. Cavalry		Taken oath	CSR
Holzhauer, Charles	Pvt	B Wash'n LA	Deserted/enemy	09/21/63	Ft. Mifflin, PA	09/22/63	Phila., PA oath	P2,CSR
Homlett, H.	Pvt	7th SCVC	Athens, GA	05/08/65	Athens, GA	05/08/65	Paroled	CSR
Honea, W.H.	Pvt	F Orr's Ri.	Southside RR, VA	04/02/65	City Pt., VA	04/07/65	Hart's Island, NY	CSR
					Hart's Island, NY	06/15/65	Rlsd. G.O. #109	P79,CSR
Honeycutt, W.A.	Pvt	C 4th SCVC	Hartwell, GA	05/20/65	Hartwell, GA	05/20/65	Paroled	CSR
Hood, C.W.A.J.	Pvt	I 5th SCVI	Fair Oaks, VA	05/31/62	Fts. Monroe, VA	06/05/62	Ft. Delaware, DE	CSR,SA3
					Ft. Delaware, DE	08/05/62	Aikens Ldg., VA Xc	CSR
Hood, George D.	Pvt	K 17th SCVI	Petersburg, VA	03/25/65	City Pt., VA	03/28/65	Pt. Lookout, MD	CSR,YEB
					Pt. Lookout, MD	06/27/65	Rlsd. G.O. #109	P114
Hood, H.B.	Pvt	C 15th SCVAB	Fayetteville, NC	03/15/65	New Berne, NC	04/03/65	Pt. Lookout, MD	CSR
					Pt. Lookout, MD	06/27/65	Rlsd. G.O. #109	CSR
Hood, Homer E.	Cpl	B 7th SCVIBn	Weldon RR, VA	08/21/64	City Pt., VA	08/24/64	Pt. Lookout, MD	CSR,HAG,HFC
					Pt. Lookout, MD	06/12/65	Rlsd. G.O. #85	P113,CSR
Hood, James W.	Pvt	I 12th SCVI	Farmville, VA	04/11/65	Farmville, VA	04/21/65	Paroled	CSR
Hood, John B.	Sgt	H 16th SCVI	Franklin, TN	12/17/64	Nashville, TN	03/24/65	Louisville, KY	P4,16R,CSR
					Louisville, KY	04/03/65	Camp Chase, OH	CSR
					Camp Chase, OH	06/11/65	Rlsd. G.O. #109	P23,16R,CSR

SOUTH CAROLINA SOLDIERS, SAILORS AND **H** CITIZENS HELD IN U.S. PRISONS 1861-1865

NAME	RANK	REGIMENT	CAPTURED AT	WHEN	PRISON	MOVED	DISPOSITION	SOURCES
Hood, John M.	1Sg	B 1st SCVIG	Hanover Jctn., VA	05/24/64	White House, VA	06/08/64	Pt. Lookout, MD	CSR,SA1
					Pt. Lookout, MD	07/09/64	Elmira, NY	P113,CSR
					Elmira, NY	03/10/65	Boulware's Wh., VA	P66,CSR
					Boulware's Wh., VA	03/15/65	Exchanged	CSR
Hood, S.C. Millan	Pvt	I 12th SCVI	Sutherland Stn., VA	04/03/65	City Pt., VA	04/07/65	Hart's Island, NY	CSR,LAN
					Hart's Island, NY	06/16/65	Rlsd. G.O. #109	P79,CSR
Hood, Samuel Y.	Pvt	D 6th SCVI	24th Corps A. of J	12/10/64	24th Corps A of J	12/11/64	Died of wounds	CSR
Hood, Thomas H.	Pvt	B 5th SCVC	Deserted/enemy	03/29/65	Charleston, SC	04/01/65	Released on oath	CSR
Hood, William	Sgt	E 3rd SCVI	Gettysburg, PA	07/05/63	Gettysburg, PA G.H.	07/20/63	Provost Marshal	P4,KEB,H3,CSR
					David's Island, NY	09/05/63	City Pt., VA Xc	P1,CSR
					Williamsburg, VA Hos.	09/13/63	Furloughed	CSR
Hook, D.M.	Pvt	F 5th SCVC	Stony Creek, VA	12/01/64	City Pt., VA	12/05/64	Pt. Lookout, MD	CSR,CDC
					Pt. Lookout, MD	06/26/65	Rlsd. G.O. #109	P114,CSR
Hook, John	Pvt	D 1st SCVIR	Charleston Hrbr.	03/21/63	Ft. Lafayette, NY	06/29/63	Ft. Delaware, DE	CSR,SA1
					Ft. Delaware, DE	11/02/64	Charleston, SC Xc	P40,P42,P44,CSR
Hook, Joseph	Pvt	D 15th SCVAB	SC or NC	03/28/65	New Berne, NC USGH	04/05/65	Died	P1,P6,WAT
Hook, Samuel P.	Pvt	G 25th SCVI	Ft. Fisher, NC	01/15/65	New York, NY	01/30/65	Elmira, NY	CSR,HAG
					Elmira, NY	03/08/65	Died, Pneumonia	P6,P65,FPH
Hook, Simon J.	Sgt	H 20th SCVI	Cedar Creek, VA	10/19/64	W. Bldg. Balt., MD	10/25/64	Pt. Lookout, MD	P1,CSR,KEB
					Pt. Lookout, MD	10/30/64	Venus Pt., GA Xc	P114,CSR
Hook, William	Pvt	D 15th SCMil	Lynch's Creek, SC	02/27/65	Pt. Lookout, MD	06/19/65	Rlsd. G.O. #109	P114,CSR
Hooker, James	Pvt	8 10/19 SCVI	Missionary Ridge, TN	11/25/63	Bridgeport, AL G.H.	12/11/63	Nashville, TN	P2,CSR
Hooks, James M.	Sgt	K 26th SCVI	Petersburg, VA	04/02/65	City Pt., VA	04/05/65	Pt. Lookout, MD	CSR
					Pt. Lookout, MD	06/28/65	Rlsd. G.O. #109	P114,CSR
Hoover, C.	Pvt	C 22nd SCVI	Petersburg, VA	04/02/65	Hart's Island, NY	06/19/65	Rlsd. G.O. #109	P79
Hoover, David M.	Cpl	G 17th SCVI	Ft. Steadman, VA	03/25/65	City Pt., VA USGH	03/29/65	H. Str. *Connecticut*	CSR
					H. Str. *Connecticut*	04/10/65	Lincoln G.H., DC	CSR
					Lincoln G.H., DC	05/01/65	Elmira, NY	CSR
					Elmira, NY	07/07/65	Rlsd. G.O. #109	P65,P66,CSR
Hoover, George H.	OSg	1st SCVIH	24th A.C. A. of J.	04/13/65	24th A/C. Fld. Hos.	04/14/65	U.S. Gen. Hospital	CSR
Hoover, George H.	OSg	1st SCVIH	Augusta, GA	05/31/65	Augusta, GA	05/31/65	Paroled	CSR
Hoover, H.E.	Pvt	A 15th SCMil	Flat Rock, SC	02/26/65	Hart's Island, NY	06/17/65	Rlsd. G.O. #109	P79
Hoover, Henry Lewis	Pvt	B 1st SCVIH	Mossy Creek, TN	01/22/64	Nashville, TN	02/11/64	Louisville, KY	P39,SA1
					Louisville, KY	02/15/64	Rock Island, IL	CSR
					Rock Island, IL	03/02/65	Tfd. for exchange	CSR
Hope, J.C.	Pvt	G 3rd SCVABn	High Pt., NC	05/01/65	High Pt., NC	05/01/65	Paroled	CSR
Hope, R.L.	Pvt	K 17th SCVI	Warrenton, VA	09/29/62	Warrenton, VA	09/29/62	Paroled	CSR
Hope, W.	Pvt	17th SCVI	Athens, GA	05/08/65	Athens, GA	05/08/65	Paroled	CSR
Hopkins, Charles M.	1Lt	D 27th SCVI	Town Creek, NC	02/20/65	Ft. Anderson, NC	02/28/65	Pt. Lookout, MD	CSR,HAG
					Pt. Lookout, MD	02/28/65	Washington, DC	P114,P120
					Old Capitol, DC	03/01/65	Fts. Monroe, VA	CSR
					Fts. Monroe, VA	03/14/65	Exhanged	CSR
Hopkins, J.H.	Pvt	A 22nd SCVI	Farmville, VA	04/06/65	City Pt., VA	04/14/65	Newport News, VA	CSR
					Newport News, VA	06/24/65	Died, Ch. Diarrhea	P12,CSR
Hopkins, James	Pvt	K 4th SCVC	Old Church, VA	05/30/64	White House, VA	06/08/64	Pt. Lookout, MD	CSR
					Pt. Lookout, MD	03/11/65	Exchanged	P113,CSR
Hopkins, M.	Pvt	F 7th SCVIBn	Raleigh, NC Hos.	04/13/65	Raleigh, NC	04/13/65	Paroled	CSR
Hopkins, Michael	Pvt	E 1st SCVIR	Deserted/enemy	02/24/65	Charleston, SC		Released on oath	CSR
Hopkins, W.M.	Pvt	C 2nd SCVIRi	Deserted/enemy	03/03/65	Bermuda Hundred, VA	03/04/65	City Pt., VA P.M.	CSR
					City Pt., VA P.M.	03/07/65	Washington, DC P.M.	CSR
					Washington, DC	03/08/65	Columbus, OH oath	CSR

H

SOUTH CAROLINA SOLDIERS, SAILORS AND CITIZENS HELD IN U.S. PRISONS 1861-1865

NAME	RANK	REGIMENT	CAPTURED AT	WHEN	PRISON	MOVED	DISPOSITION	SOURCES
Hopper, Anthony S.	Pvt	C 17th SCVI	Petersburg, VA	03/25/65	City Pt., VA	03/28/65	Pt. Lookout, MD	CSR
					Pt. Lookout, MD	06/28/65	Rlsd. G.O. #109	P114,CSR
Hopper, John S.	Pvt	C 17th SCVI	Hatchers Run, VA	03/29/65	City Pt., VA	04/02/65	Pt. Lookout, MD	CSR
					Pt. Lookout, MD	06/27/65	Rlsd. G.O. #109	P114,CSR
Horlbeck, Edward A.	Pvt	I 27th SCVI	Town Creek, NC	02/20/65	Ft. Anderson, NC	02/28/65	Pt. Lookout, MD	CSR,HAG
					Pt. Lookout, MD	06/27/65	Rlsd. G.O. #109	P7,P114,CSR
Horn, Ananeus	Pvt	I 5th SCVI	Boonesboro, MD	09/15/62	Ft. Delaware, DE	10/02/62	Aikens Ldg., VA Xc	SA3,CSR
Horn, Ananeus	Pvt	I 5th SCVI	Deserted/enemy	03/14/65	Bermuda Hundred, VA	03/15/65	City Pt., VA	CSR
					City Pt., VA	03/16/65	Washington DC Rlsd.	CSR
Horn, Christopher	Pvt	A 16th SCVI	Dalton, GA	01/24/64	Chattanooga, TN	02/07/64	Released on oath	P8,EFW,CSR
Horn, David M.	Sgt	C 24th SCVI	Franklin, TN	12/17/64	Nashville, TN	01/17/65	Louisville, KY	P3,P39,CSR
					Louisville, KY	01/18/65	Camp Chase, OH	CSR
					Camp Chase, OH	06/15/65	Rlsd. G.O.#109	P23,CSR
Horn, J.A.	Pvt	E 14th SCMil	Lynch's Creek, SC	02/25/65	Hart's Island, NY	04/28/65	Died	P6,P79,FPH
Horn, J.W.	Pvt	C 1st SCVIR	Charlotte, NC	05/07/65	Charlotte, NC	05/07/65	Paroled	SA1,CSR
Horn, James A.	Pvt	B 19th SCVI	Augusta, GA	05/20/65	Augusta, GA	05/20/65	Paroled	CSR
Horn, Joel	Pvt	A 2nd SCVI	Dept. of VA	12/26/64	Washington, DC	12/28/64	Cairo, IL on oath	SA2,H2,CSR
Horn, L.	Pvt	K 23rd SCVI	Petersburg, VA Hos.	04/02/65	Petersburg, VA Hos.	04/30/65	Not given	CSR
Horn, W.W.	Pvt	K 25th SCVI	Ft. Fisher, NC	01/15/65	New York, NY	01/30/65	Elmira, NY	CSR,HAG
					Elmira, NY	07/11/65	Rlsd. G.O. #109	P65,CSR
Horne, A.	Pvt	B 17th SCVI	Augusta, GA	05/27/65	Augusta, GA	05/27/65	Paroled	CSR
Horne, C.M.	Pvt	B 19th SCVI	Augusta, GA	06/03/65	Augusta, GA	06/03/65	Paroled	CSR
Horne, J.M.	Pvt	C 15th SCVI	Knoxville, TN	12/06/63	Camp Chase, OH	12/15/63	No further data Fd	CSR
Horne, Peter G.	Pvt	B 19th SCVI	Augusta, GA	05/20/65	Augusta, GA	05/20/65	Paroled	CSR
Horne, William	Pvt	B 19th SCVI	Munfordville, KY	09/23/62	Munfordville, KY	09/23/62	Paroled	CSR
Hornsby, S. Wyatt	Pvt	D 15th SCVI	Gettysburg, PA	07/02/63	W. Bldg. Balt, MD	09/25/63	City Pt., VA Xc	P1,KEB,CSR
Hornsby, William D.	Cpl	C 1st SCVIG	Chancellorsville	05/03/63	Old Capitol, DC	06/25/63	City Pt., VA Xc	SA1,CSR
Horsey, Wesley	Pvt	G 27th SCVI	Weldon RR, VA	08/21/64	City Pt., VA	11/16/64	Washington, DC	P1,HAG
					Old Capitol, DC	02/03/65	Elmira, NY	CSR
					Elmira, NY	02/13/65	Pt. Lookout, MD Xc	P66,CSR
Horst, William A.	Pvt	D Hol.Leg.	Augusta, GA	06/06/65	Augusta, GA	06/06/65	Paroled	CSR
Horton, Evan T.	Pvt	A 4th SCVC	Stony Creek, VA	12/01/64	City Pt., VA	12/05/64	Pt. Lookout, MD	CSR
					Pt. Lookout, MD	06/22/65	Rlsd. G.O. #109	P114,P122,CSR
Horton, Howell F.	Pvt	F 6th SCVC	Johns Island, SC	02/09/64	Hilton Head, SC	04/03/64	Ft. Lafayette, NY	CSR
					Ft. Lafayette, NY	04/03/64	Ft. Delaware, DE	CSR
					Ft. Delaware, DE	08/18/64	Hos. 8/18-10/30/64	P47
					Ft. Delaware, DE	10/30/64	Pt. Lookout, MD	P43,CSR
					Ft. Delaware, DE	10/30/64	Venus Pt., GA Xc	CSR
Horton, J.L.	Pvt	K 6th SCVC	Chesterfield, SC	03/02/65	New Bern, NC	03/30/65	Pt. Lookout, MD	CSR
					Pt. Lookout, MD	06/28/65	Rlsd. G.O. #109	P114,CSR
Horton, Job	Pvt	F 11th SCVI	Swift Creek, VA	05/09/64	Fts. Monroe, VA	11/02/64	Died of wounds	P12,CSR
Horton, Lewis	Pvt	K Hol.Leg.	Stony Creek, VA	05/07/64	Fts. Monroe, VA	05/13/64	Pt. Lookout, MD	CSR
					Pt. Lookout, MD	08/15/64	Elmira, NY	P113,P120,FPH
					Elmira, NY	02/20/65	Tfd. for exchange	P65,P66
					W. Bldg. Balt, MD	03/02/65	Died	CSR
Horton, Nimrod R.	Pvt	K Hol.Leg.	Stony Creek, VA	05/07/64	Fts. Monroe, VA	05/13/64	Pt. Lookout, MD	CSR
					Pt. Lookout, MD	08/15/64	Elmira, NY	P113,P120,CSR
					Elmira, NY	02/13/65	James R., VA Xc	P65,P66,CSR
Horton, R.A.	1Sg	H 25th SCVI	Town Creek, NC	02/20/65	Ft. Anderson, NC	02/28/65	Pt. Lookout, MD	CSR,HAG
					Pt. Lookout, MD	06/27/65	Rlsd. G.O. #109	P114
Horton, R.F.	Pvt	E 11th SCVI	Petersburg, VA	06/24/64	Fts. Monroe, VA	06/26/64	Pt. Lookout, MD	CSR
					Pt. Lookout, MD	09/18/64	Exchanged	P113,HAG,CSR

SOUTH CAROLINA SOLDIERS, SAILORS AND  CITIZENS HELD IN U.S. PRISONS 1861-1865

NAME	RANK	REGIMENT	CAPTURED AT	WHEN	PRISON	MOVED	DISPOSITION	SOURCES
Horton, Salathiel	Sgt	D 8th SCVI	Savage Stn., VA	06/28/62	Ft. Columbus, NY	07/09/62	Ft. Delaware, DE	CSR
					Ft. Delaware, DE	07/31/62	Aikens Ldg., VA Xc	CSR
Horton, Salathiel	Sgt	D 8th SCVI	Winchester, VA	09/13/64	Harpers Ferry, WV	09/19/64	Camp Chase, OH	CSR
					Camp Chase, OH	06/11/65	Rlsd. G.O. #109	P23,KEB,CSR
Horton, Solomon D.	Pvt	E 11th SCVI	Petersburg, VA	06/24/64	Bermuda Hundred, VA	06/26/64	Fts. Monroe, VA	CSR,HAG
					Fts. Monroe, VA	06/26/64	Pt. Lookout, MD	CSR
					Pt. Lookout, MD	08/16/64	Elmira, NY	P113,P120
					Elmira, NY	06/16/65	Rlsd. G.O. #109	P65,P66,CSR
Horton, Thomas	Pvt	F 7th SCVI	Marlboro Dist., SC	03/01/65	New Berne, NC	03/31/65	Hart's Island, NY	CSR
					Hart's Island, NY	06/17/65	Rlsd. G.O. #109	P79,CSR
Horton, Thomas C.	Cpl	D 7th SCVIBn	Weldon RR, VA	08/21/64	City Pt., VA	08/24/64	Pt. Lookout, MD	CSR,HIC,HAG
					Pt. Lookout, MD	03/17/65	Aikens Ldg., VA Xc	P113,P124,CSR
Horton, W.C.	Pvt	H 2nd SCVI	Gettysburg, PA	07/02/63	Gettysburg, PA G.H.	07/06/63	Died of wounds	P4,KEB,SA1,H2,CSR
Horton, W.S.	Pvt	C Ham.Leg.MI	Farmville, VA	04/11/65	Farmville, VA	04/11/65	Paroled	CSR
Horton, William H.	Cpl	G 14th SCVI	Petersburg, VA	04/04/65	City Pt., VA	04/13/65	Pt. Lookout, MD	CSR
					Pt. Lookout, MD	06/27/65	Rlsd. G.O. #109	P114,CSR
Horton, William Mc.	Pvt	H 2nd SCVI	Gettysburg, PA	07/03/63	Chester, PA G.H.	10/03/63	Pt. Lookout, MD	P1,KEB,CSR
					Gettysburg G.H.	10/04/63	Pt. Lookout, MD	P4
					Pt. Lookout, MD	03/03/64	City Pt., VA Xc	P4,KEB,SA2,H2,CSR
Horton, William Mc.	Pvt	H 2nd SCVI	Cedar Creek, VA	10/19/64	Harpers Ferry, WV	10/23/64	Pt. Lookout, MD	P114,P124,CSR
					Pt. Lookout, MD	03/28/65	Exchanged	P114,P124
Houck, Daniel D.S.	Pvt	F 25th SCVI	Petersburg, VA	06/16/64	City Pt., VA	06/24/64	Pt. Lookout, MD	CSR,HAG
					Pt. Lookout, MD	08/06/64	Died	P5,P113,FPH,CSR
Hough, Benjamin	Pvt	C 6th SCVI	Seven Pines, VA	05/31/62	Phila., PA U.S.G.H	09/10/62	Ft. Delaware, DE	CSR
					Ft. Delaware, DE	10/02/62	Aikens Ldg., VA Xc	CSR
					Richmond, VA Hos.	10/02/62	No release data	CSR
Hough, Joel	Pvt	G 2nd SCVI	Gettysburg, PA	07/05/63	Gettysburg G.H.	07/20/63	Provost Marshal	P4,CSR
					David's Island, VA	09/12/63	City Pt., VA Xc	P1,KEB,SA2,H2,CSR
Hough, Nathaniel	Cpl	G 2nd SCVI	Lynch's Creek, SC	02/27/65	New Berne, NC	04/24/65	Died	P6,KEB,SA2,H2,CSR
Hough, Nathaniel J.	Pvt	C 15th SCVAB	Cheraw, SC	03/06/65	New Berne, NC	04/05/65	Pt. Lookout, MD	CSR
					Pt. Lookout, MD	06/27/65	Rlsd. G.O. #109	P114,CSR
Hough, W.S.	Pvt	G 3rd SCVABn	High Pt., NC	05/02/65	High Pt., NC	05/02/65	Paroled	CSR
Hough, Wilson C.	Pvt	G 2nd SCVI	Charlotte, NC	05/26/65	Charlotte, NC	05/26/65	Paroled	SA2,H2,KCE,CSR
Houghey, G.P.	Pvt	F Hol.Leg.	Jarratts Stn., VA	05/08/64	Pt. Lookout, MD	08/15/64	Elmira, NY	P120
					Elmira, NY	07/07/65	Rlsd. G.O. #109	P65,P66
Houghton, R.H.	HSd	C 3rd SCVABn	Ft. Gaines, AL	08/08/64	Across the lines			CSR
Housen, J.J.	Pvt	K 26th SCVI	Deserted/enemy	01/14/65	City Pt., VA	01/19/65	Washington, DC	P8,CSR
					Washington, DC	01/20/65	Phila., PA on oath	CSR
Houston, Walter D.	Pvt	B Wash'n LA			Bowling Green, KY	05/05/65	Caroline Co., VA	CSR
Houston, William W.	Pvt	A 18th SCVAB	James Island, SC	02/10/65	Beaufort, SC USGH	05/09/65	Hilton Head, SC	P1,CSR,STR
					Hilton Head, SC	05/10/65	Paroled & released	STR
Howard, A.	Pvt	K 7th SCVi	Chester, SC	05/05/65	Chester, SC	05/05/65	Paroled	CSR
Howard, Abram	Pvt	C 11th SCVI	Deserted/enemy	02/18/65	Charleston, SC	03/13/65	Taken oath & disch.	HAG,CSR
Howard, Benjamin L.	Pvt	K 16th SCVI	Ringgold, GA	11/26/63	Nashville, TN	12/11/63	Louisville, KY	P39,CSR
					Louisville, KY	12/12/63	Rock Island, IL	CSR
					Rock Island, IL	04/24/64	Tfd. for exchange	P7,CSR
Howard, David A.	Pvt	B 2nd SCVA	Bentonville, NC	03/16/65	New Berne, NC	03/30/65	Pt. Lookout, MD	CSR,UD3
					Pt. Lookout, MD	06/27/65	Rlsd. G.O. #109	P114,CSR
Howard, G.W.R.	Pvt	D 18th SCVI	Crater, Pbg., VA	07/30/64	Pt. Lookout, MD	08/08/64	Elmira, NY	P113,P120,CSR
					Elmira, NY	01/19/65	Died, Variola	P65,P66,CSR
					Elmira, NY	03/14/65	Aikens Ldg., VA Xc	CSR
Howard, Gabriel	Pvt	C 11th SCVI	Deserted/enemy	02/18/65	Charleston, SC	03/13/65	Taken oath & disch.	HAG,CSR

SOUTH CAROLINA SOLDIERS, SAILORS AND  CITIZENS HELD IN U.S. PRISONS 1861-1865

NAME	RANK	REGIMENT	CAPTURED AT	WHEN	PRISON	MOVED	DISPOSITION	SOURCES
Howard, George	Pvt	B 19th SCVI	Glasgow, KY	09/12/62	Glasgow, KY	09/12/62	Paroled	CSR
Howard, Hampton H.	Pvt	F 7th SCVi	Sharpsburg, MD	09/17/62	Ft. Delaware, DE	12/15/62	Fts. Monroe, VA Xc	CSR
Howard, Henry Cashman		P. *Savannah*	Off Charleston	06/03/61	Tombs Prison, NY	02/15/62	Ft. Lafayette, NY	OR,TCP
					Ft. Lafayette, NY	06/06/62	City Pt., VA Xc	OR,TCP
Howard, J.A.	Pvt	C 1st SCVC	Madison C.H., VA	09/22/63	Old Capitol, DC	09/26/63	Pt. Lookout, MD	CSR
					Pt. Lookout, MD		Exchanged	P113,P124
Howard, J.A.	Pvt	D 19th SCVC	Wilmington, NC	05/26/65	Sherman U.S. G.H.	05/26/65	Sent home paroled	CSR
Howard, James B.	Pvt	D Hol.Leg.	Five Forks, VA	04/01/65	City Pt., VA	04/05/65	Pt. Lookout, MD	CSR
					Pt. Lookout, MD	06/27/65	Rlsd. G.O. #109	P114,CSR
Howard, Jason	Pvt	B 1st SCVIR	Fayetteville, NC	03/10/65	New Berne, NC	04/03/65	Pt. Lookout, MD	CSR,SA1
					Pt. Lookout, MD	06/13/65	Released	P114,CSR
Howard, John L.	Pvt	I 17th SCVI	Crater, Pbg., VA	07/30/64	City Pt., VA	08/05/64	Pt. Lookout, MD	CSR,LAN
					Pt. Lookout, MD	08/08/64	Elmira, NY	P66,P113,P120,CSR
					Elmira, NY	03/16/65	Died, Ch. Diarrhea	P6,P12,P65,FPH,CSR
Howard, Joseph A.	Pvt	A 21st SCVI	Morris Island, SC	07/10/63	Morris Island, SC	07/13/63	Hilton Head, SC	CSR
					Hilton Head, SC	07/23/63	Morris Island, SC Xc	P2,HAG,CSR
Howard, Joseph A.	Pvt	A 21st SCVI	Petersburg, VA	06/24/64	Bermuda Hundred, VA	06/25/64	Fts. Monroe, VA	CSR
					Fts. Monroe, VA	06/26/64	Pt. Lookout, MD	CSR
					Pt. Lookout, MD	08/16/64	Elmira, NY	P120
Howard, Joseph A.	Pvt	A 21st SCVI	Petersburg, VA	06/24/64	Elmira, NY	09/28/64	Died, Ch. Diarrhea	P5,P65,P66,FPH,CSR
Howard, L.H.	Pvt	K 16th SCVI	Greenville, SC	05/20/65	Greenville, SC	05/20/65	Paroled on oath	CSR
Howard, Michael	Pvt	A 19th SCVI	Augusta, GA	05/23/65	Augusta, GA	05/23/65	Paroled	CSR
Howard, Richard G.	Cpt	I 21st SCVI	Morris Island, SC	07/10/63	Ft. Columbus, NY	10/09/63	Johnson's Isl., OH	P1,HAG,HMC
Howard, Samuel A.	Pvt	5 10/19 SCVI	Missionary Ridge, TN	11/25/63	Nashville, TN	12/07/63	Louisville, KY	P39,RAS,CTA,CSR
					Louisville, KY	12/09/63	Rock Island, IL	CSR
					Rock Island, IL	02/15/65	Tfd. for Xc	CSR
Howard, W.	1Lt	G 2nd SCVI	Spotsylvania, VA	05/10/64	Belle Plain, VA	05/17/64	Fort Delaware, DE	CSR
					Ft. Delaware, DE	08/20/64	Hilton Head, SC	CSR
					Ft. Delaware, DE	11/23/64	Transferred	P7,P44,H2
					Ft. Delaware, DE	11/25/64	Rlsd. by O. Secy/W	P42,P47,CSR
Howard, W.T.	Pvt	H 22nd SCVI	Deserted/enemy	01/12/65	City Pt., VA	02/16/65	Old Capitol, DC	CSR
					Old Capitol, DC	02/17/65	Oil City, PA oath	CSR
Howard, Wilson	Pvt	H 22nd SCVI	Petersburg, VA	04/01/65	2nd D, 5th AC Hos.		No other data	CSR
Howe, Henry	Pvt	4th SCVI	Cheraw, SC	03/05/65	Cheraw, SC	03/05/65	Paroled	CSR
Howe, John T.	Pvt	G 18th SCVI	Crater, Pbg., VA	07/30/64	City Pt., VA	08/05/64	Pt. Lookout, MD	CSR
					Pt. Lookout, MD	08/08/64	Elmira, NY	P113,P120,CSR
					Elmira, NY	09/24/64	Died, Typhoid Pneum.	P5,P65,P66,FPH,CSR
Howe, Nathaniel L.	Pvt	B 22nd SCVI	Petersburg, VA	06/18/64	City Pt., VA	06/27/64	Pt. Lookout, MD	CSR
					Pt. Lookout, MD	07/27/64	Elmira, NY	P113,P120
					Elmira, NY	11/23/64	Died, Diarrhea	P5,P12,P65,P66,FPH
Howe, Robert T.	Pvt	G 18th SCVI	Five Forks, VA	04/01/65	City Pt., VA	04/06/65	Pt. Lookout, MD	CSR
					Pt. Lookout, MD		No other data Fd.	P114,CSR
Howea, Robert	Pvt	I 1st SCVIR	Deserted/enemy	03/27/65	Charleston, SC		Released on oath	CSR
Howell, Alexander	Pvt	H 21st SCVI	Morris Island, SC	07/10/63	Morris Island, SC	07/13/63	Hilton Head, SC	CSR,HAG
					Hilton Head G.H.	07/23/63	Morris Island, SC Xc	CSR
Howell, C.F.	Pvt	Ferguson's	Franklin, TN	12/17/64	Nashville, TN	12/18/64	Louisville, KY	CSR
					Louisville, KY	12/20/64	Camp Douglas, IL	CSR
					Camp Douglas, IL	04/06/65	Jd. 5th USVI	CSR
Howell, Daniel R.	Pvt	A 15th SCVI	Halltown, WV	08/06/64	Harpers Ferry, WV	09/02/64	Camp Chase, OH	CSR
					Camp Chase, OH	03/28/65	Pt. Lookout, MD	P23,P26,CSR
					Pt. Lookout, MD	06/27/65	Rlsd. G.O. #109	P114,KEB,CSR

SOUTH CAROLINA SOLDIERS, SAILORS AND **H** CITIZENS HELD IN U.S. PRISONS 1861-1865

NAME	RANK	REGIMENT	CAPTURED AT	WHEN	PRISON	MOVED	DISPOSITION	SOURCES
Howell, Darwin L.	Pvt	F 18th SCVI	Five Forks, VA	04/01/65	City Pt., VA	04/05/65	Pt. Lookout, MD	CSR
					Pt. Lookout, MD	06/28/65	Rlsd. G.O. #109	P114,YEB,CSR
Howell, Harvey R.	Cit		Lydia, SC		Hart's Island, NY	04/25/65	Died, Typhoid	P6,P79,FPH
Howell, J.M.	Pvt	K 4th SCVC	Old Church, VA	06/01/64	White House, VA	06/11/64	Pt. Lookout, MD	CSR
					Pt. Lookout, MD	11/01/64	Exchanged	P113,P124,CSR
Howell, James Barry	Pvt	H 21st SCVI	Morris Island, SC	07/10/63	Ft. Columbus, NY	09/23/63	Took the oath	P1,HAG
					Pt. Lookout, MD	08/16/64	Elmira, NY	P113,P120
					Elmira, NY	10/11/64	Tfd. for exchange	P65,P66
					Pt. Lookout, MD	10/29/64	Exchanged	P114,P124
Howell, John A.	Pvt	C 12th SCVI	Richmond, VA Hos.	04/03/65	Richmond, VA Hos.	04/21/65	US Provost Marshal	CSR
					Libby Prison Rchmd.	04/23/65	Newport News, VA	CSR
					Newport News, VA	06/26/65	Rlsd. G.O. #109	CSR
Howell, John H.	Pvt	I 12th SCVI	Falling Waters, MD	07/14/63	Old Capitol, DC	08/08/63	Pt. Lookout, MD	CSR,LAN
					Pt. Lookout, MD	08/16/64	Elmira, NY	P113,P120,CSR
					Elmira, NY	10/11/64	Venus Pt., GA Xc	P65,P66,CSR
					Pt. Lookout, MD	10/29/64	Exchanged	P114,CSR
Howell, John H.	Pvt	I 12th SCVI	Farmville, VA	04/11/65	Farmville, VA	04/21/65	Paroled	CSR
Howell, Josiah J.	Pvt	C 24th SCVI	Taylors Ridge, GA	10/16/64	Camp Douglas, IL	06/16/65	Rlsd. G.O. #109	P53,DRE
Howell, M.P.L.	Pvt	Gist Gd HA	Greenville, SC	05/23/65	Greenville, SC	05/23/65	Paroled	CSR
Howell, O.F.	Pvt	A 18th SCVI	Deserted/enemy	04/03/65	Charleston, SC	04/03/65	Columbia, SC oath	CSR
Howell, Orlando	Pvt	A 15th SCVI	Deserted/enemy	04/14/65	Charleston, SC	04/30/65	Released on oath	CSR
Howell, R.B.	Pvt	Palmetto LA	Richmond, VA	05/12/65	Richmond, VA	05/12/65	Paroled	CSR
Howell, Samuel M.	Pvt	B 7th SCVIBn	Charles City Rd., VA	10/27/64	Jones' Ldg, VA US	11/15/64	Died of wounds	P12,HAG,HFC,CSR
Howell, Thomas D.J.	Pvt	7 10/19 SCVI	Missionary Ridge, TN	11/25/63	Nashville, TN	12/25/63	Louisville, KY	P39
					Louisville, KY	12/29/63	Rock Island, IL	CSR
					Rock Island, IL	06/18/65	Rlsd. G.O. #109	CSR
Howell, W.B.	Sgt	A 14th SCVI	Hatchers Run, VA	04/02/65	City Pt., VA	04/07/65	Hart's Island, NY	CSR
					Hart's Island, NY	06/16/65	Rlsd. G.O. #109	CSR
Howell, W.P.	Pvt	F 1st SCVA	Bentonville, NC	03/22/65	New Berne, NC	04/10/65	Hart's Island, NY	CSR
					Hart's Island, NY	06/16/65	Rlsd. G.O. #109	P79,CSR
Howell, William M.	Pvt	A 16th SCVI	Jonesboro, GA	09/03/64	4th D,15th AC US A		Not given	CSR
Howerton, Thomas	Pvt	C 1st SCVIR	Deserted/enemy	03/28/65	Charleston, SC		Released on oath	CSR
Howie, W.H.	Cpl	H 4th SCVC	Stony Creek, VA	12/01/64	City Pt., VA	12/05/64	Pt. Lookout, MD	CSR,LAN
					Pt. Lookout, MD	06/03/65	Released	P114,CSR
Howle, Richard F.	Cpl	M 8th SCVI	Winchester, VA	09/13/64	Harpers Ferry, WV	09/19/64	Camp Chase, OH	CSR,KEB
					Camp Chase, OH	05/02/65	New Orleans, LA	P23,P26,CSR
Howle, Richard F.	Cpl	M 8th SCVI	Winchester, VA	09/13/64	New Orleans, LA	05/12/65	Vicksburg, MS Xc	CSR
Howle, William A.	Pvt	I 2ND SCVC	Warrenton, VA	11/16/62	Fredericksburg, VA	11/28/62	Old Capitol, DC	CSR
					Old Capitol, DC	03/29/63	City Pt., VA Xc	CSR
Howser, J.F.	Pvt	C 1st SCVIR	Charlotte, NC	05/06/65	Charlotte, NC	05/06/65	Paroled	SA1,CSR
Howze, John A.	Pvt	K 1st SCVA	Raleigh, NC Hos.	04/13/65	Raleigh, NC		Paroled	CSR
Hoyt, Charles	Smn	Charleston	Deserted/enemy		Hilton Head, SC	10/27/64		P8
Hubbard, A.A.	Sgt	D 22nd SCVI	Hartwell, GA	05/18/65	Hartwell, GA	05/18/65	Paroled on oath	CSR
Hubbard, Cydney G.	Pvt	B 1st SCVIR	Fayetteville, NC	03/16/65	New Berne, NC	03/30/65	Pt. Lookout, MD	CSR,SA1
					Pt. Lookout, MD			P114,CSR
Hubbard, J.B.	Pvt	H 25th SCVI	Ft. Fisher, NC	01/15/65	New York, NY	01/30/65	Elmira, NY	CSR
					Elmira, NY	07/14/65	Rlsd. G.O. #109	P65,CSR
Huckabee, James	Cpl	B 15th SCVI	Halltown, WV	08/26/64	Washington, DC	08/29/64	Camp Chase, OH	CSR,KEB
					Harpers Ferry, WV	09/02/64	Camp Chase, OH	CSR
					Camp Chase, OH	03/18/65	Pt. Lookout, MD	P23,P26
					Pt. Lookout, MD	03/27/65	Boulware's Wh. Xc	CSR

H

SOUTH CAROLINA SOLDIERS, SAILORS AND CITIZENS HELD IN U.S. PRISONS 1861-1865

NAME	RANK	REGIMENT	CAPTURED AT	WHEN	PRISON	MOVED	DISPOSITION	SOURCES
Huckabee, John J.	Pvt	G 8th SCVI	Gettysburg, PA	07/03/63	Ft. McHenry, MD	07/06/63	Ft. Delaware, DE	KEB,CSR
					Ft. Delaware, DE	07/30/63	City Pt., VA Xc	P40,P42,P44,CSR
Huckabee, John J.	Pvt	G 8th SCVI	Bennettsville, SC	03/06/65	New Berne, NC	04/03/65	Pt. Lookout, MD	CSR
					Pt. Lookout, MD	06/13/65	Rlsd. G.O. #109	P114,CSR
Huckabee, Oliver	Cpl	H 20th SCVI	Lexington, SC	02/14/65	Pt. Lookout, MD	06/05/65	Released	P114,KEB,CSR
Hucks, Henry K.	Cpt	D 11th SCVI	Ft. Fisher, NC	01/15/65	Fts. Monroe, VA	01/26/65	Ft. Columbus, NY	CSR
					Ft. Columbus, NY	02/25/65	City Pt., VA Xc	P2,HAG,CSR
Hucks, William D.	Pvt	F 1st SCVIG	Spotsylvania, VA	05/13/64	Belle Plain, VA	05/21/64	Ft. Delaware, DE	CSR,SA1
					Ft. Delaware, DE	09/20/64	Hos. 9/20-9/30/64	P47
					Ft. Delaware, DE	09/30/64	Aikens Ldg., VA Xc	P41,P43,CSR
Huddleston, T.J.	Pvt	H 18th SCVI	South Mtn., MD	09/14/62	Fts. Monroe, VA	07/17/62	City Pt., VA Xc	CSR
Hudgens, Cunningham	Cpl	C 3rd SCVIBn	Cedar Creek, VA	10/19/64	W. Bldg. Balt, MD	11/08/64	Died of wounds	P1,P5,FPH,KEB,CSR
Hudson, A.B.	Pvt	E 24th SCVI	Battery Isl., SC	05/21/62	Hilton Head, SC	08/14/62	Ft. Columbus, NY	CSR
					Ft. Columbus, NY	08/23/62	Ft. Delaware, DE	P37,CSR
					Ft. Delaware, DE	10/02/62	Aikens Ldg., VA Xc	CSR
					Hilton Head, SC	08/14/62	Ft. Columbus, NY	CSR
Hudson, B.C.	Pvt	E 24th SCVI	Battery Isl., SC	05/21/62	Hilton Head, SC	08/14/62	Ft. Columbus, NY	CSR
					Ft. Columbus, NY	08/23/63	Ft. Delaware, DE	P37
					Ft. Delaware, DE	09/04/63	Died	CSR
Hudson, E.	Pvt	A 3rd SCVC	Deserted/enemy	02/15/64	Hilton Head, SC	03/22/65	New York, NY P.M.	CSR
Hudson, E.A.	Pvt	A 3rd SCVABn	High Pt., NC	05/02/65	High Pt., NC	05/02/65	Paroled	CSR
Hudson, Edward G.	Sgt	C Orr's Ri.	Malvern Hill, VA	07/28/64	Old Capitol, DC	12/16/64	Elmira, NY	CSR
					Elmira, NY	02/26/65	Died, Variola	P65,P66,CSR
Hudson, J.C.	Pvt	A 3rd SCVABn	High Pt., NC	05/02/65	High Pt., NC	05/02/65	Paroled	CSR
Hudson, J.H.	Pvt	E 25th SCVI	Weldon RR, VA	08/21/64	Pt. Lookout, MD	10/30/64	Exchanged	P113,HAG
Hudson, J.P.	Pvt	A 3rd SCVABn	High Pt., NC	05/02/65	High Pt., NC	05/02/65	Paroled	CSR
Hudson, John M.	Pvt	C Orr's Ri.	Falling Waters, MD	07/14/63	Baltimore, MD	08/20/63	Pt. Lookout, MD	CSR
					Pt. Lookout, MD	02/18/65	Exchanged	P113,P124,CSR
Hudson, John W.	Pvt	C 3rd SCVABn	Blakely, AL	04/09/65	Ship Island, MS	05/01/65	Vicksburg, MS Xc	CSR
Hudson, L.J.	Pvt	A 3rd SCVABn	High Pt., NC	05/02/65	High Pt., NC	05/02/65	Paroled	CSR
Hudson, Thomas	Pvt	K 21st SCVI	Ft. Fisher, NC	01/15/65	Elmira, NY	06/30/65	Rlsd. G.O. #109	P65,HAG
Hudson, William A.	Cpl	B 2nd SCVI	Mechanicsville, VA	06/03/64	White House, VA	06/11/64	Pt. Lookout, MD	CSR,SA2,H2,KEB
					Pt. Lookout, MD	07/12/64	Elmira, NY	P113,P120,CSR
					Elmira, NY	09/09/64	Died, Diarhea	P5,P12,P65,P66,CSR
Huey, James	Sgt	I 1st SCVA	Bentonville, NC	03/16/65	New Berne, NC	03/30/65	Pt. Lookout, MD	CSR
					Pt. Lookout, MD	06/27/65	Rlsd. G.O. #109	P114,CSR
Huey, Simon H.	Sgt	I 12th SCVI	Gettysburg, PA	07/04/63	David's Island, NY	09/05/63	City Pt., VA Xc	P1,LAN,CSR
Huff, Philip W.	Pvt	B 2nd SCVI	Greencastle, PA	07/05/63	Harrisburg, PA	07/07/63	Philadelphia, PA	CSR,SA2,H2
					Ft. Delaware, DE	02/07/64	Died, Typhoid	P5,P12,P40,P44,P47,FPH
Huffman, Andrew	Pvt	F 25th SCVI	Ft. Fisher, NC	01/15/65	New York, NY	01/30/65	Elmira, NY	CSR
					Elmira, NY	04/06/65	Died, Diarrhea	P6,P65,FPH,CSR
Huffman, David J.	Pvt	F 25th SCVI	Ft. Fisher, NC	01/15/65	New York, NY	01/30/65	Elmira, NY	CSR,HAG
					Elmira, NY	06/11/65	Released	P65
Huffman, J.H.S.	Pvt	G 27th SCVI	Ft. Anderson, NC	02/19/65	Ft. Anderson, NC	02/28/65	Pt. Lookout, MD	CSR,HAG
					Pt. Lookout, MD	06/27/65	Rlsd. G.O. #109	P114,CSR
Huffman, Jacob	Pvt	B 1st SCVIH	Mossy Creek, TN	01/22/64	Nashville, TN	02/11/64	Louisville, KY	P39,SA1,CSR
					Louisville, KY	02/15/64	Rock Island, IL	CSR
					Rock Island, IL	06/17/65	Rlsd. G.O. #109	CSR
Huffman, W.R.	Pvt	F 25th SCVI	Petersburg, VA	06/16/64	City Pt., VA	06/24/64	Pt. Lookout, MD	CSR,HAG
					Pt. Lookout, MD	09/14/64	Died, Ac. Diarrhea	P6,P113,FPH,CSR

SOUTH CAROLINA SOLDIERS, SAILORS AND **H** CITIZENS HELD IN U.S. PRISONS 1861-1865

NAME	RANK	REGIMENT	CAPTURED AT	WHEN	PRISON	MOVED	DISPOSITION	SOURCES
Huffstiller, James S.	Cpl	C 12th SCVI	Wilderness, VA	05/06/64	Belle Plain, VA	05/20/64	Ft. Delaware, DE	CSR,HFC
					Ft. Delaware, DE	02/07/65	Hos. 2/7-2/11/65	P47
					Ft. Delaware, DE	03/23/65	Hos. 3/23-3/27/65	P47
					Ft. Delaware, DE	03/28/65	Hos. 3/28-3/30/65	P47
					Ft. Delaware, DE	04/07/65	Hos. 4/7-4/16/65	P47
					Ft. Delaware, DE	05/06/65	Hos. 5/6-5/29/65	P47,HFC
					Ft. Delaware, DE	06/10/65	Released	P41,P43,P45,CSR
Huger, Francis K.	2Lt	E 1st SCVIR	Fayetteville, NC	03/09/65	New Berne, NC	04/03/65	Pt. Lookout, MD	CSR
					Pt. Lookout, MD	04/03/65	Washington, DC	P120,SA1,CSR
					Washington, DC	04/09/65	Johnson's Isl., OH	CSR
					Johnson's Isl., OH	05/31/65	Rlsd. G.O. #109	SA1,CSR
Huggins, Charles	Pvt	5 10/19 SCVI	Missionary Ridge, TN	11/25/63	Nashville, TN	12/07/63	Louisville, KY	P39,CSR
					Louisville, KY	12/07/63	Rock Island, IL	CSR
Huggins, Christopher	Cpl	L 21st SCVI	Morris Island, SC	07/10/63	Morris Island, SC	07/13/63	Hilton Head, SC	CSR,HAG
					Hilton Head G.H.	07/23/63	Morris Island, SC Xc	P2,CSR
Huggins, Christopher	Sgt	L 21st SCVI	Ft. Fisher, NC	01/15/65	Ft. Fisher, NC	01/15/65	New York, NY	CSR
					New York, NY	01/30/65	Elmira, NY	CSR
					Elmira, NY	06/23/65	Rlsd. G.O. #109	P65,CSR
Huggins, G.S.B.	Pvt	K 6th SCVI	Warrenton, VA	09/29/62	Warrenton, VA	09/29/62	Paroled	CSR
Huggins, G.W.	Cpl	H 10th SCVI	Murfreesboro, TN	12/31/62	Nashville, TN		Louisville, KY	P38,RAS,CSR
					Louisville, KY	03/27/63	City Pt.,VA Xc	CSR
					Petersburg, VA G.H.	04/18/63	Furloughed 90 days	CSR
Huggins, Hillary L.	Pvt	A 14th SCVI	N. Anna River, VA	05/23/64	Port Royal, VA	05/30/64	Pt. Lookout, MD	CSR
					Pt. Lookout, MD	02/10/65	Exchanged	P113,P124,CSR
Huggins, J.D.	2Lt	C 23rd SCVI	Dinwiddie C.H., VA	04/01/65	Washington, DC	04/09/65	Johnson's Isl., OH	CSR
					Johnson's Isl., OH	06/18/65	Rlsd. G.O. #109	CSR
Huggins, J.H.	Pvt	K 23rd SCVI	Five Forks, VA	04/01/65	City Pt., VA	04/05/65	Pt. Lookout, VA	CSR,K23
					Pt. Lookout, MD	06/28/65	Rlsd. G.O. #109	P114,CSR
Huggins, John J.	Pvt	3 10/19 SCVI	Missionary Ridge, TN	11/25/63	Nashville, TN	12/07/63	Louisville, KY	P39,RAS,CSR
					Louisville, KY	12/09/63	Rock Island, IL	CSR
					Rock Island, IL	02/05/64	Jd. US Navy, Rlsd.	CSR
					Rock Island, IL	06/20/65	Rlsd. G.O. #109	CSR
Huggins, Moses	Pvt	A 8th SCVI	Winchester, VA	09/13/64	Harpers Ferry, WV	09/19/64	Camp Chase, OH	P23,CSR
					Camp Chase, VA	06/11/65	Rlsd. G.O.#109	P23,CSR
Huggins, Neal C.	Pvt	L 10th SCVI	Nashville, TN	12/15/64	Nashville, TN	01/13/65	Died of wounds	P3,P5,P12,RAS,CSR
Huggins, Robert J.	Sgt	H 26th SCVI	Five Forks, VA	04/02/65	City Pt., VA	04/05/65	Pt. Lookout, MD	CSR
					Pt. Lookout, MD	06/28/65	Rlsd. G.O. #109	P114,CSR
Huggins, Samuel	Pvt	E 6th SCVI	Burkeville, VA	04/14/65	Burkeville, VA	04/17/65	Paroled	CSR
Huggins, Samuel M.	Pvt	A 14th SCVI	Gettysburg, VA	07/05/63	Ft. McHenry, MD	07/12/63	Ft. Delaware, DE	CSR
					Ft. Delaware, DE	09/18/64	Aikens Ldg., VA Xc	P40,P42,P44,CSR
Huggins, Samuel M.	Pvt	A 14th SCVI	Petersburg, VA	04/03/65	City Pt., VA	04/07/65	Hart's Island, NY	CSR
					Hart's Island, NY	06/16/65	Rlsd. G.O. #109	P79,CSR
Huggins, T.N.	Pvt	D 5th SCVI	Boonesboro, MD	09/14/62	Ft. Delaware, DE	10/02/62	Aikens Ldg., VA Xc	CSR
					Richmond, VA Hos.	10/31/62	Furloughed 20 days	CSR
Huggins, W.J.	Pvt	I 21st SCVI	Petersburg, VA	06/24/64	Pt. Lookout, MD	08/16/64	Elmira, NY	P113,P120
					Elmira, NY	09/25/64	Died, Ch. Diarrhea	P5,P12,P66,FPH
Hugh, B.	Pvt	C 2nd SCVI	Fair Oaks, VA	06/19/62	New York, NY	10/06/62	Aikens Ldg. for Xc	CSR
Hughes, Edward	Pvt	Waccamaw A	Santee River, SC	02/27/63	Gunboat *Quaker Cit*	03/16/63	New York, NY P.M.	CSR
					Sandusky, OH	04/06/63	Fts. Monroe, VA Xc	CSR
Hughes, Edward T.	Pvt	A 27th SCVI	Petersburg, VA	06/24/64	Bermuda Hundred, VA	06/25/64	Fts. Monroe, VA	CSR,HAG
					Fts. Monroe, VA	06/26/64	Pt. Lookout, MD	CSR
					Pt. Lookout, MD	03/14/65	Exchanged	P113,P124,CSR

H

SOUTH CAROLINA SOLDIERS, SAILORS AND CITIZENS HELD IN U.S. PRISONS 1861-1865

NAME	RANK	REGIMENT	CAPTURED AT	WHEN	PRISON	MOVED	DISPOSITION	SOURCES
Hughes, Ephraim	Pvt	B 15th SCVI	Petersburg, VA	07/27/64	Pt. Lookout, MD	08/08/64	Elmira, NY	P120,P125,KEB,CSR
					Elmira, NY	07/03/65	Rlsd. G.O. #109	P65,P66,CSR
Hughes, F. Porcher	Pvt	A Ham.Leg.	Warrenton, VA	09/29/62	Warrenton, VA	09/29/62	Paroled	CSR
Hughes, George C.	Pvt	RMR & HA	Pocotaligo, SC	05/29/62	Richmond, VA	10/01/62	Rcd. paroled POW	CSR
Hughes, Henry	Pvt	B 1st SCVA	Fayetteville, NC	03/11/65	New Berne, NC	03/30/65	Pt. Lookout, MD	CSR
					Pt. Lookout, MD	04/19/65	Died, Ch. Diarrhea	P6,P12,P114,FPH,CSR
Hughes, Henry	Pvt	Ferguson's LA	Salisbury, NC	04/12/65	Nashville, TN	04/29/65	Louisville, KY	P39,CSR
					Louisville, KY	05/02/65	Camp Chase, OH	CSR
					Camp Chase, OH	06/13/65	Rlsd. G.O.#109	P23,CSR
Hughes, J.B.	Pvt	A 4th SCVC	Camden, SC	02/24/65	New Berne, NC	04/10/65	Hart's Island, NY	CSR
					Hart's Island, NY	06/17/65	Rlsd. G.O. #109	P79,CSR
Hughes, J.H.	Pvt	C 2nd SCVC	Gettysburg, PA	07/05/63	Ft. Delaware, DE	09/18/63	Died, Typhoid fever	P5,P42,P47,FPH,CSR
Hughes, John	Pvt	G 19th SCVI	Dalton, GA	05/13/64	Nashville G.H.	05/16/64	Louisville, KY	P2,P39,CSR
					Louisville, KY	05/21/64	Camp Morton, IN	P7,CSR
					Camp Morton, IN	05/22/65	Rlsd. G.O. #85	CSR
Hughes, John	Pvt	I 1st SCVA	Cheraw, SC	03/12/65	New Berne, NC	04/10/65	Pt. Lookout, MD	CSR
					Hart's Island, NY	06/16/65	Rlsd. G.O. #109	P79,CSR
Hughes, John	Pvt	I 1st SCVIG	Cox Rd., VA	04/02/65	City Pt., VA	04/07/65	Hart's Island, NY	SA1,CSR
					Hart's Island, NY	05/28/65	Died, Typhoid Pneum.	P6,P12,P79,FPH,CSR
Hughes, John H.	Pvt	B 3rd SCVIBn	Hagerstown, MD	07/02/63	Ft. Delaware, DE	09/20/63	Died, Scurvy	P5,P12,P40,P42,P44,P47
Hughes, Joseph S.	Pvt	C 19th SCVCB	Florence, SC	03/05/65	New Berne, NC	04/03/65	Pt. Lookout, MD	CSR
					Pt. Lookout, MD	04/25/65	Died, Lung Inflam.	P6,P12,P114,FPH,CSR
Hughes, Moses T.	Pvt	K Orr's Ri.	Petersburg, VA	04/02/65	City Pt., VA	04/04/65	Pt. Lookout, MD	CSR
					Pt. Lookout, MD	06/27/65	Rlsd. G.O. #109	P114,CSR
Hughes, Rapley H.	Cpl	F Hol.Leg.	Five Forks, VA	04/01/65	City Pt., VA	04/05/65	Pt. Lookout, MD	CSR
					Pt. Lookout, MD	06/27/65	Rlsd. G.O. #109	P114,CSR
Hughes, Saunders D.	Pvt	E 14th SCVI	Gettysburg, PA	07/05/63	David's Island, NY		Bedloes Island, NY	P1,CSR
					Bedloes Island, NY	10/24/63	Hammond G.H., MD	P2,CSR
					Hammond G.H., MD	02/16/64	Died of wounds	P5,P12,FPH,CSR
Hughes, Simeon J.	Pvt	C 22nd SCVI	Hatchers Run, VA	03/29/65	City Pt., VA	04/10/65	Lincoln G.H., DC	CSR
					Lincoln G. Hos., DC	05/01/65	Old Capitol, VA	CSR
					Old Capitol, DC	05/12/65	Elmira, NY	CSR
					Elmira, NY	07/11/65	Rlsd. G.O. #109	P65,P66,CSR
Hughes, T.S.	Pvt	F 17th SCVI	Crater, Pbg., VA	07/30/64	City Pt., VA	08/05/64	Pt. Lookout, MD	CSR
					Pt. Lookout, MD	08/08/64	Elmira, NY	P113,P120,CSR
					Elmira, NY	07/03/65	Rlsd. G.O. #109	P65,P66,CSR
Hughes, Thomas	Pvt	H 27th SCVI	Town Creek, NC	02/20/65	Ft. Anderson, NC	02/28/65	Pt. Lookout, MD	CSR,HAG
					Pt. Lookout, MD	05/13/65	Rlsd. G.O. #85	P114
Hughes, Thomas J.	Pvt	A 16th SCVI	Graysville, GA	11/27/63	Nashville, TN	12/09/63	Louisville, KY	P39,16R,CSR
					Louisville, KY	12/11/63	Rock Island, IL	CSR
					Rock Island, IL	06/19/65	Rlsd. G.O. #109	CSR
Hughes, Toliver H.	Pvt	L P.S.S.	Hartwell, GA	05/08/65	Hartwell, GA	05/08/65	Paroled	CSR,TSE
Hughes, W.W.	Sgt	C 22nd SCVI	Crater, Pbg., VA	07/30/64	City Pt., VA	08/05/64	Pt. Lookout, MD	CSR,HOS
					Pt. Lookout, MD	08/08/64	Elmira, NY	P113,P120
					Elmira, NY	07/03/65	Rlsd. G.O. #109	P65,P66,CSR
Hughes, William F.	Pvt	K 1st SCVIH	Warrenton, VA	09/29/62	Warrenton, VA	09/29/62	Paroled	CSR,WDC
Hughes, William J.	Pvt	H 1st SCVA	Morris Island, SC	07/10/63	Hilton Head, SC	08/31/63	Ft. Columbus, NY	CSR
					Ft. Columbus, NY	09/26/63	Pt. Lookout, MD	CSR
					Pt. Lookout, MD	05/03/64	Exchanged	P113,P124,CSR
Hughes, William J.	Cpl	C Orr's Ri.	Spotsylvania, VA	05/12/64	Old Capitol, DC	06/15/64	Ft. Delaware, DE	CSR
					Ft. Delaware, DE	06/10/65	Rlsd. G.O. #109	P41,P43,P45,CSR

SOUTH CAROLINA SOLDIERS, SAILORS AND **H** CITIZENS HELD IN U.S. PRISONS 1861-1865

NAME	RANK	REGIMENT	CAPTURED AT	WHEN	PRISON	MOVED	DISPOSITION	SOURCES
Hughey, G.P.	Pvt	F Hol.Leg.	Jarratts Stn., VA	05/08/64	Fts. Monroe, VA	05/13/64	Pt. Lookout, MD	CSR
					Pt. Lookout, MD	08/15/64	Elmira, NY	P113
					Elmira, NY	07/07/65	Rlsd. G.O. #109	CSR
Hughey, James H.	Pvt	K 1st SCVA	Smithfield, NC	03/16/65	New Berne, NC	03/30/65	Pt. Lookout, MD	CSR
					Pt. Lookout, MD	06/27/65	Rlsd. G.O. #109	P114,CSR
Hughey, Jesse R.	Pvt	F 22nd SCVI	Five Forks, VA	04/01/65	City Pt., VA	04/05/65	Pt. Lookout, MD	CSR
					Pt. Lookout, MD	06/27/65	Rlsd. G.O. #109	P114,CSR
Hughey, Silas D.	Pvt	K 1st SCVA	Goldsboro, NC	03/19/65	New Berne, NC	03/30/65	Pt. Lookout, MD	CSR
					Pt. Lookout, MD	06/06/65	Released	P114,CSR
Hughston, Thomas	Pvt	K P.S.S.	Fair Oaks, VA	06/19/62	US Hosp. Phila. PA	09/10/62	Ft. Delaware, DE	CSR,TSE
					Ft. Delaware, DE	10/02/62	Aikens Ldg., VA Xc	CSR
					Aikens Ldg., VA	10/06/62	Exchanged	CSR
Huguenin, Julius G.	1Lt	F 27th SCVI	Town Creek, NC	02/20/65	Ft. Anderson, NC	02/28/65	Pt. Lookout, MD	CSR,HAG
					Pt. Lookout, MD	02/28/65	Washington, DC	P114,P120
					Old Capitol, DC	03/24/65	Ft. Delaware, DE	CSR
					Ft. Delaware, DE	06/17/65	Rlsd. G.O. #109	P43,P45
Hulender, A.A.	Pvt	F 17th SCVI	Farmville, VA	04/06/65	City Pt., VA	04/14/65	Newport News, VA	CSR
					Newport News, VA	06/25/65	Rlsd. G.O. #109	CSR
Hulender, Nicholas	Pvt	F 17th SCVI	Petersburg, VA	03/25/65	City Pt., VA	03/28/65	Pt. Lookout, MD	CSR
					Pt. Lookout, MD	06/27/65	Rlsd. G.O. #109	P114,CSR
Hull, J.B.	Pvt	K 13th SCVI	Hatchers Run, VA	04/02/65	Hart's Island, NY	06/16/65	Rlsd. G.O. #109	P79
Hull, Samuel	Pvt	E 11th SCVI	Petersburg, VA	06/24/64	Bermuda Hundred, VA	06/25/64	Fts. Monroe, VA	CSR
					Fts. Monroe, VA	06/26/64	Pt. Lookout, MD	CSR
					Pt. Lookout, MD	08/16/64	Elmira, NY	P113,P120,CSR
					Elmira, NY	03/18/65	Died, Diarrhea	P6,P65,P66,FPH,HAG,CSR
Hull, William H.	Pvt	D 11th SCVI	Petersburg, VA	05/09/64	Fts. Monroe, VA	05/16/64	Died of wounds	P12,ROH,CSR
Hulon, Irvin	Pvt	F 27th SCVI	Town Creek, NC	02/20/65	Ft. Anderson, NC	02/28/65	Pt. Lookout, MD	CSR,HAG
					Pt. Lookout, MD	06/28/65	Rlsd. G.O. #109	P114,CSR
Humphreys, John L.	2Lt	G 2nd SCVIRi	Salisbury, NC	04/12/65	Nashville, TN	04/29/65	Louisville, KY	P39,CSR,UD5
					Louisville, KY	05/02/65	Camp Chase, OH	CSR
					Camp Chase, OH	06/14/65	Rlsd. G.O. #109	P23,CSR
Humphries, B.J.	Cpl	G 3rd SCVABn	High Pt., NC	05/01/65	High Pt., NC	05/01/65	Paroled	CSR
Humphries, Calvin	Pvt	Macbeth LA	Deserted/enemy		Knoxville, TN	02/27/65	Chattanooga, TN	CSR
					Louisville, KY	02/28/65	Sent north on oath	CSR
Humphries, Green B.	Pvt	K 18th SCVI	Petersburg, VA	03/25/65	City Pt., VA	04/06/65	Pt. Lookout, MD	CSR
					Pt. Lookout, MD	06/13/65	Rlsd. G.O. #109	P114,CSR
Humphries, J.H.	Pvt	A 3rd SCVABn	High Pt., NC	05/02/65	High Pt., NC	05/02/65	Paroled	CSR
Humphries, Jackson	Pvt	K 18th SCVI	Jackson, MS	07/14/63	Camp Morton, IN	01/01/64	Died, Pneumonia	P5,FPH,CSR
Humphries, John T.	Pvt	A 18th SCVAB	James Island, SC	02/10/65				CSR,STR
Humphries, Richard N.	Pvt	C 15th SCVAB	Morris Island, SC	09/07/63	Hilton Head, SC	09/11/63	Ft. Columbus, NY	CSR
					Ft. Columbus NY	09/15/63	Released on oath?	CSR
Humphries, S. Wesley	Pvt.	E 12th SCVI	Widerness, VA	05/06/64	Belle Plain, VA	05/20/64	Ft. Delaware, DE	CSR,LAN
					Ft. Delaware, DE		Hos. 9/24-9/27/64	P47
					Ft. Delaware, DE		Hos. 10/29-11/26/64	P47
					Ft. Delaware, DE		Hos. 1/28-2/4/65	P47
					Ft. Delaware, DE	06/10/65	Released	P43,P45,CSR
Humphries, Thomas H.D.	Pvt	C 3rd SCVABn	Blakely, AL	04/09/65	Ship Island, MS	05/01/65	Vicksburg, MS Xc	CSR
Humphries, W.L.	Pvt	E 27th SCVI	Petersburg, VA	06/24/64	Bermuda Hundred, VA	06/25/64	Fts. Monroe, VA	CSR,HAG
					Fts. Monroe, VA	06/26/64	Pt. Lookout, MD	CSR
					Pt. Lookout, MD	08/16/64	Elmira, NY	P113,P120
					Elmira, NY	10/01/64	Died, Diarrhea	P5,P66,FPH

H

SOUTH CAROLINA SOLDIERS, SAILORS AND CITIZENS HELD IN U.S. PRISONS 1861-1865

NAME	RANK	REGIMENT	CAPTURED AT	WHEN	PRISON	MOVED	DISPOSITION	SOURCES
Hungerpiller, Jacob J.	Pvt	G 27th SCVI	Petersburg, VA	06/24/64	Bermuda Hundred, VA	06/25/64	Fts. Monroe, VA	CSR,HAG
					Fts. Monroe, VA	06/27/64	Pt. Lookout, MD	CSR
					Pt. Lookout, MD	08/16/64	Elmira, NY	P113,P120,CSR
					Elmira, NY	02/13/65	Died, Peritonitis	P6,P12,P65,P66,FPH
Hungerpiller, T.N.	Pvt	B 20th SCVI	Cedar Creek, VA	10/19/64	Harpers Ferry, WV	10/23/64	Pt. Lookout, MD	CSR,KEB
					Pt. Lookout, MD	03/28/65	Exchanged	P114,P124,CDC
Hunnicut, William W.	Pvt	H 2nd SCVC	Putnam Cty., VA	07/17/63	Wheeling, WV	07/23/63	Camp Chase, OH	CSR
					Camp Chase, OH	09/19/63	Escaped in night	P22
					Camp Chase, OH	01/23/64	Rock Island, IL	P24,P26,CSR
					Rock Island, IL	06/16/65	Rlsd. G.O. #109	CSR
Hunnicutt, E.J.	Pvt	E Orr's Ri.	Petersurg, VA	04/03/65	City Pt., VA	04/11/65	Hart's Island, NY	CSR,CDC
					Hart's Island, NY	06/16/65	Rlsd. G.O. #109	P79,CSR
Hunnicutt, John T.	Cpl	C Orr's Ri.	Falling Waters, MD	07/14/63	Pt. Lookout, MD	08/16/64	Elmira, NY	P113,P120,CSR
					Elmira, NY	09/24/64	Died, Ch. Diarrhea	P5,P12,P65,FPH,CSR
Hunnicutt, John T.	Cpl	C Orr's Ri.	Falling Waters, MD	07/14/63	Baltimore, MD	07/16/63	Pt. Lookout, MD	CSR,CDC
Hunt, Absalom L.	Pvt	A Ham.Leg.MI	Deserted/enemy	05/21/65	Chattanooga, TN	05/21/65	Chattanooga, TN	CSR
Hunt, Britton	Pvt	C 24th SCVI	Cassville, GA	05/19/64	Nashville, TN	05/24/64	Louisville, KY	P3,EFW
					Louisville, KY	05/25/64	Rock Island, IL	CSR
					Rock Island, IL	06/10/64	Jd. U.S. Navy	CSR
Hunt, J. Eneas	Pvt	A 21st SCVI	Petersburg, VA	06/24/64	Bermuda Hundred, VA	06/25/64	Fts. Monroe, VA	CSR,HAG
					Fts. Monroe, VA	06/26/64	Pt. Lookout, MD	CSR
					Pt. Lookout, MD	08/16/64	Elmira, NY	P120,CSR
					Elmira, NY	03/02/65	James R., VA Xc	P65,P66,CSR
Hunt, L.S.	Pvt	E 3rd SCVIBn	Cedar Creek, VA	10/19/64	Harpers Ferry, WV	10/28/64	Pt. Lookout, MD	CSR,KEB
					Pt. Lookout, MD	05/26/65	Died, Scurvy	P6,P114,PH,CSR
Hunt, William	Pvt	K 19th SCVI	Franklin, TN	12/17/64	Camp Douglas, IL	06/19/65	Rlsd. G.O. #109	P55
Hunt, William Uriah	2Lt	K 16th SCVI	Missionary Ridge, TN	11/25/63	Nashville, TN	12/04/63	Louisville, KY	P39,16R,CSR
					Louisville, KY	12/05/64	Johnson's Isl., OH	CSR
					Johnson's Isl., OH	06/13/65	Rlsd. G.O. #109	CSR
Hunter, A.J.	Pvt	I 5th SCVC	Stony Creek, VA	12/01/64	City Pt., VA	12/05/64	Pt. Lookout, MD	CSR,CDC
					Pt. Lookout, MD	01/17/65	Exchanged	P114,P124,CSR
Hunter, H.C.	Pvt	G 21st SCVI	Morris Island, SC	07/10/63	Ft. Columbus, NY	09/22/63	Pt. Lookout, MD	P1,CSR
					Pt. Lookout, MD	08/16/64	Elmira, NY	P113,P120
					Elmira, NY	10/11/64	Pt. Lookout to Xc	P65,P66
					Pt. Lookout, MD	10/29/64	Venus Pt., GA Xc	P114,CSR
Hunter, Isaac K.	Pvt	B 1st SCVIG	Jarretts Stn., VA	04/03/65	Hart's Island, NY	06/14/65	Released	P79,SA1,CSR
Hunter, J.B.	Cpl	G 1st SCVIH	Warrenton, VA	09/29/62	Warrenton, VA	09/29/62	Paroled	CSR
Hunter, J.R.	Pvt	I 12th SCVI	Sutherland Stn., VA	04/03/65	City Pt., VA	04/07/65	Hart's Island, NY	CSR,LAN
					Hart's Island, NY	06/16/65	Rlsd. G.O. #109	P79,CSR
Hunter, J.W.	1Lt	F 22nd SCVI	Sharpsburg, MD	09/17/62	Frederick, MD Hos.	11/08/62	Aikens Ldg., VA Xc	CSR
Hunter, Jacob	Pvt	B 15th SCVAB	Averysboro, NC	03/16/65	New Berne, NC	03/30/65	Pt. Lookout, MD	CSR
					Pt. Lookout, MD	04/17/65	Died, Lung Inflam.	P6,P114,FPH,CSR
Hunter, James J.	Pvt	E Orr's Ri.	Petersburg, VA	04/03/65	City Pt., VA	04/11/65	Hart's Island, NY	CSR
					Hart's Island, NY	06/16/65	Rlsd. G.O. #109	CSR
Hunter, James T.	Pvt	G 14th SCVI	Gettysburg, PA	07/04/63	David's Island, NY	09/05/63	City Pt., VA Xc	P1,CSR
Hunter, James W.	1Lt	SC Reserve	Charlotte, NC	05/13/65	Richmond, VA	05/23/65	Rlsd. on oath	CSR
Hunter, John	Pvt	G 21st SCVI	Morris Island, SC	07/10/63	Hilton Head G.H.	07/23/63	Morris Island, SC Xc	P2,HAG,CSR
Hunter, John L.	Pvt	H Hol.Leg.	Five Forks, VA	04/01/65	City Pt., VA	04/05/65	Pt. Lookout, MD	CSR
					Pt. Lookout, MD	06/28/65	Rlsd. G.O. #109	P114,CSR
Hunter, Maurice W.	2Lt	I 18th SCVI	Appomattox C.H., VA	04/09/65	W. Bldg. Balt, MD	05/09/65	Ft. McHenry, MD	P1,CSR
					Ft. McHenry, MD	06/12/65	Rlsd. G.O. #109	CSR

SOUTH CAROLINA SOLDIERS, SAILORS AND  CITIZENS HELD IN U.S. PRISONS 1861-1865

NAME	RANK	REGIMENT	CAPTURED AT	WHEN	PRISON	MOVED	DISPOSITION	SOURCES
Hunter, R.T.C.	Pvt	H Hol.Leg.	Petersburg, VA	10/27/64	City Pt., VA	10/31/64	Pt. Lookout, MD	CSR,ANY
					Pt. Lookout, MD	03/28/65	Aikens Ldg., VA Xc	P114,P124,CSR
Hunter, Samuel A.	Pvt	H Hol.Leg.	Five Forks, VA	04/01/65	City Pt., VA	04/05/65	Pt. Lookout, MD	CSR,ANY
					Pt. Lookout, MD	06/28/65	Rlsd. G.O. #109	P114,CSR
Hunter, Silas J.	Pvt	E Orr's Ri.	Petersburg, VA	04/03/65	City Pt., VA	04/11/65	Hart's Island, NY	CSR,CDC
					Hart's Island, NY	06/16/65	Rlsd. G.O. #109	P79,CSR
Hunter, Thomas T.C.	Pvt	H Hol.Leg.	Five Forks, VA	04/01/65	City Pt., VA	04/05/65	Pt. Lookout, MD	CSR,ANY
					Pt. Lookout, MD	06/27/65	Rlsd. G.O. #109	P114,CSR
Hunter, W.F.	Pvt	B 26th SCVI	Crater, Pbg., VA	07/30/64	Pt. Lookout, MD	08/08/64	Elmira, NY	P113,P120,CSR
					Elmira, NY	10/11/64	Tfd. for exchange	P65,P66,CSR
					Pt. Lookout, MD	10/29/64	Exchanged	P114,CSR
Hunter, William John	Pvt	G 2nd SCVI	Cedar Creek, VA	10/19/64	Harpers Ferry, WV	10/24/64	Pt. Lookout, MD	CSR,SA2,KEB,H2
					Pt. Lookout, MD	06/03/65	Released	P114,CSR
Huntington, H.D.	Pvt	E 7th SCVC	Deserted/enemy	03/14/65	Camp Hamilton, VA	03/15/65	Bermuda Hundred, VA	CSR
					Bermuda Hundred, VA	03/18/65	City Pt., VA	CSR
					City Pt., VA	03/24/65	Washington, DC	CSR
					Washington, DC	03/24/65	Amboy, MI on oath	CSR
Hurley, Charles	Pvt	H 1st SCVIG	Warrenton, VA	09/29/62	Warrenton, VA	09/29/62	Paroled	SA1,CSR
Hurst, James M., Jr.	Pvt	A 1st SCVIBn			Beaufort, SC	07/26/63	Died of wounds	P10,PP
Hurst, James P.	Pvt	C 2nd SCVI	Cedar Creek, VA	10/19/64	Pt. Lookout, MD	01/17/65	Exchanged	SA2,P114,P124,CSR
Hurst, John E.	Pvt	A 14th SCVI	Deserted/enemy	03/23/65	City Pt., VA	03/27/65	Washington, DC	CSR
					Washington, DC	03/29/65	Springfield, OH	CSR
Hurst, Simeon A.	Pvt	A 14th SCVI	Deserted/enemy	03/23/65	City Pt., VA	03/27/65	Washington, DC	CSR
					Washington, DC	03/29/65	Springfield, OH	CSR
Hurt, Kindred	Pvt	C 1st SCVIG	Petersburg, VA	07/29/64	City Pt., VA	08/05/64	Pt. Lookout, MD	CSR,SA1
					Pt. Lookout, MD	08/08/64	Elmira, NY	P113,P120,CSR
					Elmira, NY	12/06/64	Died, Ch. Diarrhea	P5,P12,P65,P66,FPH
Huskamp, Henry	Pvt	C Orr's Ri.	Deserted,enemy	07/23/64	Bermuda Hundred, VA	07/26/64	Fts. Monroe, VA	CSR,CDC
					Fts. Monroe, VA	07/30/64	No other data Fd.	P8,CSR
Huskey, Joseph	Pvt	I 5th SCVI	Deep Bottom, VA	08/14/64	Bermuda Hundred, VA	08/15/64	Fts. Monroe, VA	SA3,CSR
					Fts. Monroe, VA	08/16/64	Pt. Lookout, MD	CSR
					Pt. Lookout, MD	03/14/65	Aikens Ldg., VA Xc	P125,CSR
Huskey, William A.	Pvt	F 6th SCVC	Stony Creek, VA	12/01/64	City Pt., VA	12/04/64	Pt. Lookout, MD	CSR
					Pt. Lookout, MD	06/14/65	Released G.O. #109	P114,CAG,CSR
Hussey, Simeon A.	Pvt	C 24th SCVI	Chickamauga, GA	09/20/63	Nashville, TN	09/30/63	Louisville, KY	P38,CSR
					Louisville, KY	10/02/63	Camp Douglas, IL	CSR
					Camp Douglas, IL	06/16/65	Rlsd. G.O. #109	P53,P55,P57,CSR
Hussey, W.J.	Pvt	H 11th SCVI	Weldon RR, VA	08/21/64	City Pt., VA	08/24/64	Pt. Lookout, MD	CSR,HAG
					Pt. Lookout, MD	02/10/65	Exchanged	P113,P124
Hutchings, D.A.	Pvt	F Ham.Leg.MI	Augusta, GA	05/28/65	Augusta, GA	05/28/65	Paroled	CSR
Hutchings, William P.	Pvt	K 16th SCVI	Jonesboro, GA	08/31/64	Rough & Ready, GA	09/19/64	Exchanged	CSR
Hutchins, B.F.	Pvt	D 2nd SCVIRi	Richmond, VA Hos.	04/03/65	Richmond, VA Hos.	04/14/65	Richmond, VA P.M.	CSR
					Libby Prison Rchmd.	04/23/65	Newport News, VA	CSR
					Newport News, VA	06/14/65	Rlsd. G.O. #109	CSR
Hutchins, Thomas M.	Pvt	K 2nd SCVIRi	Richmond, VA Hos.	04/03/65	Libby Prison Rchmd.	04/08/65	City Pt., VA	CSR
					City Pt., VA	04/13/65	Pt. Lookout, MD	CSR
					Pt. Lookout, MD	06/13/65	Rlsd. G.O. #109	P114,CSR
Hutchins, William	Pvt	15thSCMil	NC or SC	04/05/65	New Berne, NC USGH	04/12/65	Died	P1,P6,WAT
Hutchinson, Benjamin F.	Pvt	D 7th SCVI	Gettysburg, PA	07/04/63	David's Island, NY	09/05/63	City Pt., VA Xc	P1,P4,KEB,CSR
Hutchinson, George E.	Pvt	H 8th SCVI	Gettysburg, PA	07/05/63	W. Bldg. Balt. MD	07/30/63	Baltimore Jail	P1,KEB,CSR
Hutchinson, J.P.	Pvt	H 18th SCVI	Farmville, VA	04/06/65	City Pt., VA	04/14/65	Newport News, VA	CSR
					Newport News, VA	06/26/65	Rlsd. G.O. #109	CSR

SOUTH CAROLINA SOLDIERS, SAILORS AND  CITIZENS HELD IN U.S. PRISONS 1861-1865

NAME	RANK	REGIMENT	CAPTURED AT	WHEN	PRISON	MOVED	DISPOSITION	SOURCES
Hutchinson, James B.	Pvt	E 15th SCVI	Gettysburg, PA	07/04/63	Gettysburg G.H.	07/21/63	Provost Marshal	P4,KEB
					David's Island, NY	08/24/63	City Pt., VA Xc	P1,CSR
Hutchinson, John	Pvt	I 10th SCVI	Tyners, TN	08/20/62	Kentucky	11/15/62	Paroled	CSR,RAS
Hutchinson, John D.	Pvt	B 3rd SCVABn	Ft. Tyler, GA	04/16/65	1st Div. Cavalry C	04/23/65	Macon, GA Prison	
Hutchinson, Larry N.	Pvt	B 21st SCVI	Weldon RR, VA	08/21/64	Fts. Monroe, VA	08/25/64	Alexandria, VA	CSR
					Alexandria, VA	08/26/64	Lincoln G.H., DC	P1,CSR
					Lincoln G.H., DC	11/26/64	Old Capitol, DC	CSR
					Old Capitol, DC	12/16/64	Elmira, NY	CSR
					Elmira, NY	02/13/65	Pt. Lookout, MD Xc	P65,P66,CSR
Hutchinson, Milton T.	2Lt	I 14th SCVI	Deep Bottom, VA	07/28/64	City Pt., VA USFH	08/09/64	Lincoln G.H., DC	P23,CSR
					Lincoln G.H., DC	09/28/64	Old Capitol, DC	CSR
					Old Capitol, DC	10/21/64	Ft. Delaware, DE	CSR
Hutchinson, Milton T.	2Lt	I 14th SCVI	Deep Bottom, VA	07/28/64	Ft. Delaware, DE	10/30/64	Pt. Lookout, MD	P43
					Pt. Lookout, MD	10/31/64	Exchanged	P114
Hutchinson, R. Barney	Pvt	D 7th SCVI	Sharpsburg, MD	09/17/62	Frederick, MD	04/28/62	Ft. McHenry, MD	CSR
					Ft. McHenry, MD	04/30/62	Fts. Monroe, VA	CSR
					Fts. Monroe, VA	05/02/63	City Pt., VA Xc	CSR
Hutchinson, Samuel	Pvt	B 1st SCVA	Fayetteville, NC	03/16/65	New Berne, NC	03/30/65	Pt. Lookout, MD	CSR
					Pt. Lookout, MD	06/28/65	Rlsd. G.O. #109	P114,CSR
Hutchinson, T.	Pvt	A 1st SCVC	Deserted/enemy	02/16/65	Charleston, SC P.M.		Released on oath	CSR
Hutchison, Henry	Pvt	C 6th SCVC	Louisa C.H., VA	06/11/64	Fts. Monroe, VA	06/20/64	Pt. Lookout, MD	CSR
					Pt. Lookout, MD	01/09/65	Died, Ch. Diarrhea	P5,P12,FPH,CSR
Hutchison, James P.	Pvt	H 13th SCVI	Hatchers Run, VA	03/31/65	City Pt., VA	04/02/65	Pt. Lookout, MD	CSR
					Pt. Lookout, MD	06/27/65	Rlsd. G.O. #109	P114,CSR
Hutson, C.J.C.	LAd	H 1st SCVIG	Harpers Farm, VA	04/06/65	Washington, DC	04/13/65	Johnson's Isl., OH	SA1,CSR
					Johnson's Isl., OH	06/06/65	Rlsd. on oath	CSR
Hutson, Charles W.	Pvt	A Ham.Leg.	Fair Oaks, VA	05/31/62	Fts. Monroe, VA	06/05/62	Ft. Delaware, DE	CSR
					Ft. Delaware, DE	08/05/62	Aikens Ldg., VA Xc	CSR
Hutson, Evans	Pvt	A 14th SCVI	N. Anna River, VA	05/23/64	Port Royal, VA	05/30/64	Pt. Lookout, MD	P113,CSR
					Pt. Lookout, MD	09/18/64	Aikens Ldg., VA Xc	P113,CSR
Hutson, Evans	Pvt	A 14th SCVI	Petersburg, VA	04/02/65	City Pt., VA	04/05/65	Pt. Lookout, MD	P114,CSR
					Pt. Lookout, MD	06/28/65	Rlsd. G.O. #109	P114,CSR
Hutson, J.N.	Pvt	B 11th SCVI	Darbytown Rd., VA	10/07/64	Bermuda Hundred, VA	10/08/64	City Pt., VA	CSR,HAG
					City Pt., VA	10/29/64	Pt. Lookout, MD	CSR
					Pt. Lookout, MD	06/05/65	Released on oath	P114,CSR
Hutson, John H.	Pvt	E 25th SCVI	Weldon, RR, VA	08/21/64	City Pt., VA	08/24/64	Pt. Lookout, MD	CSR,HAG
					Pt. Lookout, MD	10/30/64	Exchanged	P125,CSR
Hutson, John H.	Pvt	E 25th SCVI	Deserted/enemy	03/15/65	Beaufort, SC	03/15/65	Released on oath	CSR
Hutson, L.M.	Pvt	B 22nd SCVI	Kinston, NC	12/14/62	Kinston, NC	12/14/62	Paroled POW	CSR
Hutson, Marion	Pvt	F 11th SCVI	Richmond, VA Hos.	04/03/65	Escaped 5/4/65			CSR
Hutson, Phillips	Pvt	C 13th SCVI	Deserted/enemy	02/18/65	Charleston, SC	02/18/65	Released on oath	CSR
Hutson, R.H.	Pvt	A 1st SCVA	Cheraw, SC	03/03/65	New Berne, NC	04/10/65	Hart's Island, NY	CSR
					Hart's Island, NY	06/16/65	Rlsd. G.O. #109	P79,CSR
Hutson, Thomas J.	Cpl	G 1st SCVA	Fayetteville, NC	03/10/65	New Berne, NC	03/30/65	Pt. Lookout, MD	CSR
					Pt. Lookout, MD	06/27/65	Rlsd. G.O. #109	P114,CSR
Hutto, Alonzo B.	Pvt	K 13th SCVI	Gettysburg, PA	07/05/63	Davids Island, NY	09/05/63	City Pt., VA Xc	P1,CSR
Hutto, Alonzo B.	Pvt	K 13th SCVI	Hatchers Run, VA	04/02/65	City Pt., VA	04/07/65	Hart's Island, NY	CSR
					Hart's Island, NY	06/16/65	Rlsd. G.O. #109	P79,CSR
Hutto, Andrew	Pvt	D 15th SCMil	South Carolina	03/29/65	New Berne, NC USGH	04/02/65	Died	P1,P6,WAT
Hutto, B.A.	Pvt	F P.S.S.	Richmond, VA	04/03/65	Pt. Lookout, MD	06/28/65	Rlsd. G.O. #109	P114,TSE
Hutto, B.R.	Pvt	H 17th SCVI	Augusta, GA	05/18/65	Augusta, GA	05/18/65	Paroled	CSR

SOUTH CAROLINA SOLDIERS, SAILORS AND **H** CITIZENS HELD IN U.S. PRISONS 1861-1865

NAME	RANK	REGIMENT	CAPTURED AT	WHEN	PRISON	MOVED	DISPOSITION	SOURCES
Hutto, Charles	Pvt	H 17th SCVI	Petersburg, VA	04/03/65	City Pt., VA	04/11/65	Hart's Island, NY	CSR
					Hart's Island, NY	06/14/65	Rlsd. G.O. #109	P79,CSR
					Transit H. NY City	06/23/65	Died	P12,CSR,FPH
Hutto, Daniel A.	Pvt	C 2nd SCVC	Augusta, GA	05/23/65	Augusta, GA	05/23/65	Paroled	CSR
Hutto, George W.	Pvt	H 17th SCVI	Petersburg, VA	03/25/65	City Pt., VA	03/28/65	Pt. Lookout, MD	CSR
					Pt. Lookout, MD	06/13/65	Rlsd. G.O. #109	P114,CSR
Hutto, H.D.	Pvt	H 17th SCVI	Deserted/enemy	03/08/65	P.M. A. of Potomac	03/08/65	City Pt., VA P.M.	CSR
					City Pt., VA P.M.	03/09/65	Washington, DC	CSR
					Washington, DC	03/10/65	Charleston, SC	CSR
Hutto, J. Murphy	Pvt	H 20th SCVI	Salkahatchie, SC	02/07/65	Hilton Head, SC	03/12/65	Ft. Delaware, DE	CSR
					Ft. Delaware, DE	03/13/65	Hos. 3/13-3/23/65	P47,KEB
					Ft. Delaware, DE	06/10/65	Released	P41,P45,CSR
Hutto, J.J.	Pvt	H Ham.Leg.	Warrenton, VA	09/29/62	Warrenton, VA	09/29/62	Paroled	CSR
Hutto, J.M.	Pvt	A 14th SCMil	Lynch's Creek, SC	02/25/65	Hart's Island, NY		David's Island, NY	P6,P79,CSR
					David's Island, NY	04/27/65	Died, Erysipelas	P6,FPH
Hutto, James E.	Pvt	K 13th SCVI	Hatchers Run, VA	04/02/65	Hart's Island, NY	06/16/65	Rlsd. G.O.#109	CSR
Hutto, Morgan B.	Pvt	K 1st SCVIH	Burkeville, VA	04/14/65	Ft. Delaware, DE	06/10/65	Released	CSR
Hutto, Starling	Pvt	H 17th SCVI	Deserted/enemy	03/08/65	P.M. A. of Potomac	03/08/65	City Pt., VA P.M.	CSR
					City Pt., VA P.M	03/09/65	Washington, DC	CSR
					Washington, DC	03/10/65	Charleston, SC oath	CSR
Hutto, W.M.	Pvt	H 17th SCVI	Deserted/enemy	03/08/65	P.M. A. of Potomac	03/08/65	City Pt., VA P.M.	CSR
					City Pt., VA P.M.	03/09/65	Washington, DC	CSR
					Washington, DC	03/10/65	Charleston, SC oath	CSR
Hutto, William C.	Pvt	H Ham.Leg.	Will's Valley, TN	10/29/63	Nashville, TN	11/07/63	Louisville, KY	P39,CSR
					Louisville, KY	11/09/63	Camp Morton, IN	CSR
					Camp Morton, IN	03/04/65	City Pt., VA Xc	CSR
Hux, Colin P.	Cpl	A 26th SCVI	Southside RR, VA	04/01/65	City Pt., VA	04/05/65	Pt. Lookout, MD	CSR
					Pt. Lookout, MD	06/28/65	Rlsd. G.O. #109	P114,CSR
Hux, James H.	Pvt	A 26th SCVI	Southside RR, VA	04/01/65	City Pt., VA	04/05/65	Pt. Lookout, MD	CSR
					Pt. Lookout, MD	06/28/65	Rlsd. G.O. #109	P114,CSR
Hyatt, Charles	Pvt	F 8th SCVI	Winchester, VA	09/13/64	Harpers Ferry, WV	09/19/64	Camp Chase, OH	CSR
					Camp Chase, OH	05/02/65	New Orleans, LA	P26,CSR
					New Orleans, LA	05/12/65	Vicksburg, MS Xc	CSR
Hyatt, George Thomas	Pvt	K 3rd SCVI	Lynch's Creek, SC	02/28/65	New Berne, NC	04/03/65	Pt. Lookout, MD	CSR,KEB,H3
					Pt. Lookout, MD	06/13/65	Rlsd. G.O. #109	P114,CSR
Hyatt, Isaac McF.	Sgt	A 17th SCVI	Petersburg, VA	04/02/65	City Pt., VA	04/04/65	Pt. Lookout, MD	CSR,HHC
					Pt. Lookout, MD	06/27/65	Rlsd. G.O. #109	P114,CSR
Hyatt, James	Pvt	I SC CoastGd	Columbia, SC	02/17/65	Hart's Island, NY	06/17/65	Rlsd. G.O. #109	P79
Hyde, James	Pvt	I 1st SCVA	Deserted/enemy	03/01/65	Charleston, SC	03/15/65	Released on oath	CSR
Hyde, Reuben H.	Sgt	C Orr's Ri.	Falling Waters, MD	07/14/63	Old Capitol, DC	08/08/63	Pt. Lookout, MD	CSR,CDC
					Pt. Lookout, MD	11/15/63	Hammond G.H., MD	P125
Hyde, Reuben H.	Sgt	C Orr's Ri.	Falling Waters, MD	07/14/63	Pt. Lookout, MD	12/09/63	Died, Ch. Diarrhea	P12,CSR
Hyers, Joseph McB.	Pvt	H 17th SCVI	Five Forks, VA	04/01/65	City Pt., VA	04/06/65	Pt. Lookout, MD	CSR
					Pt. Lookout, MD	06/13/65	Released	P114,CSR
Hyler, Henry L.	Pvt	C 15th SCVI	No capture in CSR		Camp Chase, OH	03/18/65	Camp Lookout, MD	P26,KEB
Hyman, C.	Pvt	D 7th SCResB	Cheraw, SC	03/05/65	Cheraw, SC	03/05/65	Paroled	CSR
Hyman, G.F.	Pvt	C 26th SCVI	Deserted/enemy	01/06/65	City Pt., VA	01/09/65	Washington, DC	CSR
					Washington, DC	01/14/65	Harrisburg, PA	CSR
Hyott, John	Pvt	I 1st SCVIH	South Mtn., MD	09/15/62	Ft. Delaware, DE	10/02/62	Aikens Ldg., VA Xc	CSR
Hyrne, Henry	Pvt	K 1st SCVIR	Fayetteville, NC	03/16/65	New Berne, NC	03/30/65	Pt. Lookout, MD	CSR,SA1
					Pt. Lookout, MD	06/27/65	Rlsd. G.O. #109	P114,CSR

I

SOUTH CAROLINA SOLDIERS, SAILORS AND CITIZENS HELD IN U.S. PRISONS 1861-1865

NAME	RANK	REGIMENT	CAPTURED AT	WHEN	PRISON	MOVED	DISPOSITION	SOURCES
Icault, Theodore	Pvt	K 1st SCVA	Bentonville, NC	03/19/65	New Berne, NC	03/30/65	Pt. Lookout, MD	CSR
					Pt. Lookout, MD	06/14/65	Rlsd. G.O. #109	CSR
Inabinet, A.	Pvt	A Cola P.Gd.	Columbia, SC	02/18/65	Hart's Island, NY	06/14/65	Released	P79
Inabinet, Ambrose B.	Pvt	B 14th SCVI	Gettysburg, PA	07/05/63	Provost Marshal	08/30/63	Ft. Delaware, DE	CSR
					Ft. Delaware, DE	09/22/63	Jd. US 3rd MD Cav.	P42,CSR
Inabinet, Archibald	Pvt	A 1st SCMil	Lynch's Creek, SC	02/23/65	Hart's Island, NY	05/29/65	Died, Ch. Diarrhea	P5,P12,P79,FPH
Inabinett, Andrew J.	Pvt	G 25th SCVI	Ft. Fisher, NC	01/15/65	New York, NY	01/30/65	Elmira, NY	CSR,HAG
					Elmira, NY	06/23/65	Released GO #109	P65,P66,CSR
					New York, NY	01/30/65	Elmira, NY	CSR,HAG
					Elmira, NY	07/07/65	Released GO #109	P65,P66
Inch, C.	Pvt	A 2nd SCVC	Augusta, GA	05/19/65	Augusta, GA	05/19/65	Paroled	CSR
Indgrove, G.C.	Pvt	B 15th SCVI	Warrenton, VA	09/29/62	Warrenton, VA	09/29/62	Paroled	H15,CSR
Infinger, Nathaniel	Cpl	B 11th SCVI	Town Creek, NC	02/20/65	Ft. Anderson, NC	02/28/65	Pt. Lookout, MD	CSR,HAG
					Pt. Lookout, MD	06/14/65	Released	P114,CSR
Ingram, Henry G.	Cpl	B 2nd SCVI	Gettysburg, PA	07/05/63	David's Island, NY	09/05/63	City Pt., VA Xc.	SA2,P1,KEB,H2,CSR
Ingram, Madison S.	Pvt	F 2nd SCVI	Gettysburg, PA	07/05/63	Letterman G.H. Gbg	09/29/63	Provost Marshal	P1,KEB,H2,SA2
					Letterman G.H. Gbg	09/29/63	W. Bldg. Balt, MD	CSR
					W. Bldg. Balt, MD	11/12/63	City Pt., VA Xc.	P1,CSR
Ingram, Russel A.	Pvt	E 12th SCVI	Gettysburg, PA	07/04/63	Chester, PA G.H.	08/17/63	City Pt., VA Xc.	P1,LAN
					Williamsburg, VA H	11/16/64	SC Hos. Petersburg	CSR
Ingram, Samuel B.	Pvt	E 12th SCVI	Gettysburg, PA	07/02/63	David's Island, NY	09/08/63	City Pt., VA Xc.	CSR
					Williamsburg, VA H	09/13/63	Wdd. Furlough	CSR
Ingram, William	Pvt	D Orr's Ri.	Gettysburg, PA	07/05/63	Ft. McHenry, MD	07/07/63	Ft. Delaware, DE	CSR
					Ft. Delaware, DE	01/07/65	Hos. 1/7-1/11/65	P47
					Ft. Delaware, DE	02/23/65	Hos. 2/23-3/5/65	P47
					Ft. Delaware, DE	06/10/65	Released	P40,P44,P45,CSR
Irby, M.D.	Pvt	F Orr's Ri.	Deserted/enemy	03/05/65	City Pt., VA	03/08/65	New York,NY/ oath	CSR
Irby, Sandford V.	Pvt	G 27th SCVI	Town Creek, NC	02/20/65	Pt. Lookout, MD	06/25/65	Rlsd. G.O. #109	P114,HAG
Irick, Alexander D.	Pvt	G 25th SCVI	Town Creek, NC	02/20/65	Ft. Anderson, NC	02/28/65	Pt. Lookout, MD	CSR,HAG
					Pt. Lookout, MD	06/28/65	Rlsd. G.O. #109	P114,CSR
Irick, Elliott H.	Pvt	G 25th SCVI	Ft. Fisher, NC	01/15/65	New York, NY	01/30/65	Elmira, NY	CSR,HAG
					Elmira, NY	02/20/65	Pt.Lookout, MD Xc.	P65,P66,CSR
Irick, Laban A.	Cpl	G 25th SCVI	Ft. Fisher, NC	01/15/65	New York, NY	01/30/65	Elmira, NY	CSR,HAG
					Elmira, NY	07/11/65	Rlsd. G.O. #109	P65,P66,CSR
Irick, William M.	Pvt	E 5th SCVC	Stony Creek, VA	12/01/64	City Pt., VA	12/05/64	Pt. Lookout, MD	CSR,CDC
					Pt. Lookout, MD	01/29/65	Died, Lung Inflam.	P5,P114,CDC,FPH,CSR
Irvin, James R.	Pvt	K 15th SCVI	Campbell Stn., TN	12/05/63	Nashville, TN	02/28/64	Louisville, KY	P39,KEB
					Louisville, KY	02/28/64	Camp Chase, OH	CSR
					Camp Chase, OH	02/25/65	City Pt., VA Xchg.	P26,CSR
Irvine, Daniel Pinckney	Pvt	B 2nd SCVI	Halltown, WV	08/06/64	Camp Chase, OH	03/26/65	Camp Lookout, MD	P22,P26,KEB,H2,CSR
					Pt. Lookout, MD	06/28/64	Rlsd. G.O. #109	SA2,KEB,CSR
Irwin, William J.	Pvt	B Ham.Leg.MI	Petersburg, VA	07/27/64	City Pt., VA	08/05/64	Pt. Lookout, MD	CSR,HHC
					Pt. Lookout, MD	08/08/64	Elmira, NY	P113,P125,CSR
					Elmira, NY	08/28/64	Died, Diarrhea	P5,P65,P66,CSR
Isbell, Benjamin M.	Pvt	K 22nd SCVI	Petersburg, VA	04/02/65	City Pt., VA	04/04/65	Pt. Lookout, MD	CSR
					Pt. Lookout, MD	06/14/65	Rlsd. G.O. #109	P114,CSR
Isbell, Henry Lawrence	1Lt	B 7th SCVIBn	Weldon RR, VA	08/21/64	City Pt., VA USFH	08/22/64	Washington, DC USG	HFC,CSR
					Ft. McHenry, MD	08/24/64	Washington, DC USG	P110
					Lincoln G.H., DC	08/26/65	Died of wounds	P5,P12,CSR
Isbell, Walter D.	Sgt	C 2nd SCVI	Gettysburg, PA	07/05/63	Letterman G.H. Gbg	07/10/63	Died of wounds	SA2,P12,KEB,H2,CSR
Isom, J.W.	Pvt	F 1st SCVIG	Spotsylvania, VA	05/13/64	Belle Plain, VA	05/21/64	Ft. Delaware, DE	CSR,SA1
					Ft. Delaware, DE	07/04/64	Died, Lung Inflam.	P5,P41,P42,P47

I

SOUTH CAROLINA SOLDIERS, SAILORS AND CITIZENS HELD IN U.S. PRISONS 1861-1865

NAME	RANK	REGIMENT	CAPTURED AT	WHEN	PRISON	MOVED	DISPOSITION	SOURCES
Isom, Thomas	Pvt	D Hol.Leg.C	Burnt Ordinary, VA	01/17/63	Ft. McHenry, MD	01/20/63	Paroled	CSR
Israel, Ancil	Pvt	C 26th SCVI	Five Forks, VA	04/01/65	City Pt., VA	04/05/65	Pt. Lookout, MD	CSR,HMC
					Pt. Lookout, MD	06/24/65	Rlsd. G.O. #109	P114,CSR
Ivey, C.P.	Pvt	C 3rd SCVABn	Augusta, GA	05/20/65	Augusta, GA	05/20/65	Paroled	CSR
Izlar, Adolphus Madison	Pvt	G 25th SCVI	Ft. Fisher, NC	01/15/65	New York, NY	01/30/65	Elmira, NY	CSR,HAG,EDR
					Elmira, NY	03/14/65	James R., VA Xc.	P66,CSR
Izlar, Benjamin Pou	1Sg	G 25th SCVI	Ft. Fisher, NC	01/15/65	New York, NY	01/30/65	Elmira, NY	CSR,HAG
					Elmira, NY	06/14/65	Rlsd. G.O. #109	P65,P66,CSR
Izlar, James Ferdinand	Cpt	G 25th SCVI	Ft. Fisher, NC	01/15/65	Ft. Columbus, NY	02/25/65	City Pt., VA Xc.	P2,HAG,EDR,CSR
Izlar, Lauriston T.	Pvt	G 25th SCVI	Town Creek, NC	02/20/65	Ft. Anderson, NC	02/28/65	Pt. Lookout, MD	CSR,HAG,EDR
					Pt. Lookout, MD	06/14/65	Rlsd. G.O. #109	P114,CSR
Izlar, William Valmore	Sgt	G 25th SCVI	Town Creek, NC	02/20/65	Ft. Anderson, NC	02/28/65	Pt. Lookout, MD	CSR,HAG,EDR
					Pt. Lookout, MD	06/14/65	Rlsd. G.O. #109	P114,CSR

J

SOUTH CAROLINA SOLDIERS, SAILORS AND CITIZENS HELD IN U.S. PRISONS 1861-1865

NAME	RANK	REGIMENT	CAPTURED AT	WHEN	PRISON	MOVED	DISPOSITION	SOURCES
Jackman, James	Pvt	D 1st SCVIR	Charleston Bar, SC	03/21/63	Ft. Lafayette, NY	06/29/63	Ft. Delaware, DE	CSR,SA1
					Ft. Delaware, DE	05/03/65	Rlsd O.O. Secy/War	P42,P7,P40,P44,CSR
Jacks, John J.	Pvt	A 13th SCVI	Gettysburg, PA	07/05/63	Bedloes Island, NY	01/06/64	City Pt., VA Xc	P2,CSR
Jacks, William Y.	Pvt	A 13th SCVI	Gettysburg, PA	07/05/63	David's Island, NY	10/24/63	Bedloes Island, NY	P1,CSR
					Bedloes Island, NY	12/26/63	Pt. Lookout, MD	CSR
					Pt. Lookout, MD	03/17/64	City Pt., VA Xc	P124,CSR
Jackson, A.J.	Pvt	E 23rd SCVI	Five Forks, VA	04/01/65	City Pt., VA	04/06/65	Pt. Lookout, MD	CSR
					Pt. Lookout, MD	06/28/65	Rlsd. G.O. #109	CSR
Jackson, Abner B.	Pvt	G 23rd SCVI	Five Forks, VA	04/01/65	City Pt., VA	04/05/65	Pt. Lookout, MD	CSR,HOM
					Pt. Lookout, MD	06/28/65	Rlsd. G.O. #109	P114,,CSR
Jackson, Allan M.	Sgt	C 27th SCVI	Town Creek, NC	02/20/65	Ft. Anderson, NC	02/28/65	Pt. Lookout, MD	CSR,HAG
					Pt. Lookout, MD	06/28/65	Rlsd. G.O. #109	P114,CSR
Jackson, Andrew K.	Pvt	H Orr's Ri.	Amelia C.H., VA	04/05/65	City Pt., VA	04/13/65	Pt. Lookout, MD	CSR,CDC,HMC
					Pt. Lookout, MD	06/16/65	Rlsd. G.O. #109	P114,CSR
Jackson, C.T.	Pvt	I 1st SCVIH	Burkeville, VA	04/14/65	Burkeville, VA	04/17/65	Paroled	CSR
Jackson, Charles	Pvt	E 4th SCVC	Hanover Jctn., VA	05/30/64	White House, VA	06/08/64	Pt. Lookout, MD	CSR,HOM
					Pt. Lookout, MD	07/08/64	Elmira, NY	P113,P120,CSR
					Elmira, NY	10/11/64	Pt. Lookout, MD Xc	P65,P66,CSR
					Pt. Lookout, MD	10/29/64	Exchanged	P114,CSR
Jackson, David S.	Pvt	C 1st SCVA	Smith Farm, NC	03/16/65	New Berne, NC	04/10/65	Hart's Island, NY	CSR
					Hart's Island, NY	06/16/65	Rlsd. G.O. #109	P79,CSR
Jackson, Douglas	Pvt	D 15th SCVI	Chickamauga, GA	09/20/63	Nashville, TN	10/01/63	Louisville, KY	P38,KEB,HIC,CSR
					Camp Douglas, IL		(Rcd 10/4/63)	P57
					Camp Douglas, IL	06/16/65	Rlsd. G.O. #109	P55,CSR
Jackson, Edward	Pvt	G 1st SCVA	Deserted/enemy	03/05/65	Charleston, SC	03/15/65	Taken oath & disch.	CSR
Jackson, Franklin M.	Pvt	E 23rd SCVI	Five Forks, VA	04/01/65	Pt. Lookout, MD	06/28/65	Rlsd. G.O. #109	P114,HMC,CSR
Jackson, G.J.	Pvt	C 6th SCVI	Deserted/enemy	10/07/64	Bermuda Hundred, VA	10/07/62	City Pt., VA P.M.G	CSR
					City Pt., VA P.M.G	10/21/64	Baltimore, MD oath	CSR
Jackson, H.B.	Pvt	B 22nd SCVI	Deserted/enemy	02/25/65	City Pt., VA	02/28/65	Washington, DC	CSR
					Washington, DC	03/01/65	Oil City, PA oath	CSR
Jackson, Howard	Pvt	Palmetto L	Gettysburg, PA	07/04/63	Baltimore, MD	07/30/63	Fts. Monroe, VA	CSR
					Fts. Monroe, VA	08/04/63	Paroled for Xc	CSR
Jackson, J.	Pvt	C 6th SCVI	Fair Oaks, VA	05/31/62	Fts. Monroe, VA	06/21/62	Ft. Delaware, DE	CSR
					Ft. Delaware, DE	08/05/62	Aikens Ldg., VA Xc	CSR
Jackson, J.	Pvt	C 6th SCVI	Deserted/enemy	02/28/65	Bermuda Hundred, VA	03/01/65	City Pt., VA P.M.	CSR
					City Pt., VA P.M.	03/03/65	Washington, DC P.M.	CSR
					Washington, DC P.M.	03/06/65	Troy, PA on oath	CSR
Jackson, J. Alexander	Pvt	B 1st SCVC	Gettysburg, PA	07/05/63	Letterman G.H. Gbg	08/22/63	Provost Marshal	P1,HOS,CSR
					Ft. McHenry, MD	09/15/63	Pt. Lookout, MD	CSR
					Pt. Lookout, MD	04/24/64	Died, Ch. Diarrhea	P5,P113,P124,FPH
Jackson, J. Lumpkin	Pvt	B 12th SCVI	Gettysburg, PA	07/04/63	Ft. McHenry, MD	07/07/63	Ft. Delaware, DE	CSR,YEB
					Ft. Delaware, DE	06/10/65	Released	P40,P44,P45,CSR
Jackson, J.F.	Pvt	K 19th SCVI	Augusta, GA	05/19/65	Augusta, GA	05/19/65	Paroled	CSR
Jackson, J.J.	Sgt	A 23rd SCVI	Petersburg, VA Hos.	04/03/65	Petersburg, VA USH	04/09/65	Fts. Monroe, VA Hos.	CSR
					Fts. Monroe, VA Hos.	07/17/65	Released	CSR
Jackson, James C.	Pvt	G 18th SCVI	Crater, Pbg., VA	07/30/64	City Pt., VA	08/04/64	Pt. Lookout, MD	CSR
					Pt. Lookout, MD	08/08/64	Elmira, NY	P113,P120,CSR
					Elmira, NY	10/11/64	Pt. Lookout, MD	P65,P66
					Elmira, NY	10/11/64	Venus Pt., GA Xc	CSR
					Pt. Lookout, MD	10/29/64	Exchanged	P114
Jackson, James F.	Pvt	C 3rd SCResB	Charlotte, NC	05/20/65	Charlotte, NC	05/20/65	Paroled	CSR
Jackson, James W.	Sgt	A 24th SCVI	Deserted/enemy	02/18/65	Charleston, SC	03/11/65	Released on oath	CSR,EFW

J

SOUTH CAROLINA SOLDIERS, SAILORS AND CITIZENS HELD IN U.S. PRISONS 1861-1865

NAME	RANK	REGIMENT	CAPTURED AT	WHEN	PRISON	MOVED	DISPOSITION	SOURCES
Jackson, John	Pvt	E 2nd SCVI	Norfolk, VA	08/03/64	Bermuda Hundred, VA		Deserted	SA2,H2,CSR
Jackson, John C.	Pvt	K 8th SCVI	Winchester, VA	09/13/64	Harpers Ferry, WV	09/19/64	Camp Chase, OH	CSR,KEB,HOM
					Camp Chase, OH	10/20/64	Died, Typhoid fever	P6,P22,P27,FPH,CSR
Jackson, John C.	Pvt	D 2nd SCVC	Washington, GA	05/29/65	Washington, GA	05/29/65	Released on parole	CSR
Jackson, John E.	Pvt	E Orr's Ri.	Deserted/enemy	02/21/65	City Pt., VA	02/21/65	Washington, D.C.	CSR
					Washington, DC	02/24/65	Burlington, Iowa	CSR
Jackson, John M.	Pvt	H 18th SCVI	Crater, Pbg., VA	07/30/64	Portsmouth, RI Hos.	10/24/64	Ft. Columbus, NY	P4,CSR,YEB
					Ft. Columbus, NY	12/04/64	Elmira, NY	P2,CSR
					Elmira, NY	02/20/65	James R., VA Xc	P65,P66,CSR
Jackson, Joseph C.	Pvt	E 4th SCVC	Louisa C.H., VA	06/11/64	Fts. Monroe, VA	06/20/64	Pt. Lookout, MD	CSR,HOM
					Pt. Lookout, MD	07/08/64	Elmira, NY	P113,P120,FPH,CSR
					Elmira, NY	08/12/64	Died, Rem. Fever	P5,P12,P65,P66,FPH,CSR
Jackson, Joseph H.	Pvt	I 23rd SCVI	Deserted/enemy	09/12/64	Washington, DC	09/21/64	Phila., PA on oath	CSR
Jackson, Lewis	Pvt	B 1st SCVA	Bentonville, NC	03/19/65	Pt. Lookout, MD	06/14/65	Released	P114
Jackson, Mathew	Pvt	F 8th SCVI	Bennettsville, SC	03/06/65	New Berne, NC	04/03/65	Pt. Lookout, MD	CSR
					Pt. Lookout, MD	06/28/65	Rlsd. G.O. #109	P114,CSR
Jackson, Pringle	Pvt	D 3rd SCVABn	Deserted/enemy	03/05/65	Charleston, SC	03/05/65	Released on oath	CSR
Jackson, S.R.	Sgt	I 18th SCVI	Hatchers Run, VA	04/01/65	City Pt., VA	04/04/65	Pt. Lookout, MD	CSR
					Pt. Lookout, MD	06/04/65	Released on oath	P114,CSR
Jackson, S.T.	1Sg	D 4th SCVC	Stony Creek, VA	12/01/64	City Pt., VA	12/05/64	Pt. Lookout, MD	CSR,CDC
					Pt. Lookout, MD	06/28/65	Rlsd. G.O. #109	P114,CSR
Jackson, Samuel E.	Pvt	A 12th SCVI	Spotsylvania, VA	05/12/64	Belle Plain, VA	05/20/64	Ft. Delaware, DE	CSR,YEB
					Ft. Delaware, DE	06/10/65	Released	P41,P42,P45,CSR
Jackson, T.F.	Pvt	C 6th SCVI	Boonesboro, MD	09/14/62	Frederick, MD	09/19/62	Ft. Delaware, DE	CSR
					Ft. Delaware, DE	10/02/62	Aikens Ldg., VA Xc	CSR
Jackson, T.F.	Pvt	C 6th SCVI	Deserted/enemy	10/07/64	Bermuda Hundred, VA	10/21/64	City Pt., VA P.M.	CSR
					City Pt., VA P.M.	10/23/64	Fts. Monroe, VA	CSR
					Fts. Monroe, VA	10/24/64	Baltimore, MD oath	CSR
Jackson, T.R.	Pvt	B 1st SCVC	Gettysburg, PA	07/06/63	Letterman G.H. Gbg	08/02/63	Died, Typhoid fever	P1,P12,CSR
Jackson, Thomas J.	Pvt	H 6th SCVI	Chaffins Farm, VA	10/01/64	Fts. Monroe, VA US	10/21/64	Died of wounds	P12,ROH,CSR
Jackson, William E.	Pvt	A 12th SCVI	Petersburg, VA	04/02/65	City Pt., VA	04/04/65	Pt. Lookout, MD	CSR
					Pt. Lookout, MD	06/28/65	Rlsd. G.O. #109	P114,YEB,CSR
Jackson, William F.	Pvt	C 2nd SCVC	Pocotaligo, SC	01/16/65	Beaufort, SC P.M.	02/24/65	Hilton Head, SC Hos.	CSR
					Hilton Head, SC Hos.	03/04/65	Provost Marshal	CSR
Jackson, William J.	Pvt	H 23rd SCVI	Five Forks, VA	04/01/65	Pt. Lookout MD	06/28/65	Rlsd. G.O. #109	CSR
Jackson, William P.	Pvt	C 27th SCVI	Town Creek, NC	02/20/65	Ft. Anderson, NC	02/28/65	Pt. Lookout, MD	CSR,HAG
					Pt. Lookout, MD	06/28/65	Rlsd. G.O. #109	P114
Jacobs, A.W.	Pvt	D 1st SCVIR	Marlboro, SC	03/06/65	New Berne, NC	04/10/65	Hart's Island, NY	CSR
					Hart's Island, NY	06/17/65	Rlsd. G.O. #109	CSR
Jacobs, Andrew Jackson	Pvt	A 21st SCVI	Petersburg, VA	06/24/64	Pt. Lookout, MD	08/16/64	Elmira, NY	P113,P120,HAG
					Elmira, NY	11/01/64	Died, Pneumonia	P6,P12,P65,P66,FPH
Jacobs, B.L.	Pvt	F 21st SCVI	Marlboro Dist., SC	03/06/65	Hart's Island, NY	06/23/65	Rlsd. G.O. #109	P79,HOM
Jacobs, C.W.	Pvt	C 3rd SCVABn	Blakely, AL	04/09/65	Ship Island, MS	05/01/65	Vicksburg, MS Xc	CSR
Jacobs, David	Pvt	E 4th SCVC	Not given		New Berne, NC	04/10/65	Hart's Island, NY	CSR
					Hart's Island, NY	04/15/65	David's Island, NY	CSR
					Davids Island, NY	05/25/65	Hart's Island, NY	CSR
					Hart's Island, NY	06/16/65	Rlsd. G.O. #109	P79,CSR

J

SOUTH CAROLINA SOLDIERS, SAILORS AND CITIZENS HELD IN U.S. PRISONS 1861-1865

NAME	RANK	REGIMENT	CAPTURED AT	WHEN	PRISON	MOVED	DISPOSITION	SOURCES
Jacobs, Hill	Pvt	D 12th SCVI	Wilderness, VA	05/06/64	Belle Plain, VA	05/21/64	Ft. Delaware, DE	CSR
					Ft. Delaware, DE	11/19/64	Hos. 11/19-12/17/64	P47
					Ft. Delaware, DE	12/24/64	Hos.12/24/64-1/16/65	P47
					Ft. Delaware, DE	01/23/65	Hos. 1/23-1/31/65	P47
					Ft. Delaware, DE	03/08/65	Hos. 3/8-3/21/65	P47
					Ft. Delaware, DE	06/10/65	Released G.O. #109	P41,P42,P45
Jacobs, John Christian	Pvt	Brooks LA	Harpers Farm, VA	04/06/65	City Pt., VA	04/14/65	Pt. Lookout, MD	CSR
					Pt. Lookout, MD	06/28/65	Rlsd. G.O. #109	CSR
Jacobs, John E.	Pvt	I 15th SCVI	South Mtn., MD	09/14/62	Frederick, MD USGH	10/02/62	Ft. Delaware, DE	CSR
					Ft. Delaware, DE	11/10/62	Aikens Ldg., VA Xc	CSR
Jacobs, Joseph	Pvt	C 20th SCVI	Deep Bottom, VA	07/28/64	US Cav. Corps Hos.	08/25/64	Died of wounds	P12,PP,KEB,CSR
Jacobs, Samuel	Pvt	G 6th SCVI	Norfolk, VA	08/03/64	Fts. Monroe, VA	08/14/64	Bermuda Hundred, VA	CSR
Jacobs, Snowden	Pvt	F 21st SCVI	Ft. Fisher, NC	01/15/65	Elmira, NY	07/07/65	Rlsd. G.O. #109	P65,HAG,P66,HOM
Jacobson, Martin L.	Pvt	A 6th SCVI	Centreville, VA	10/07/62	Centreville, VA	10/07/62	Paroled	CSR
Jager, Adolphus	Cpl	H 27th SCVI	Town Creek, NC	02/20/65	Ft. Anderson, NC	02/28/65	Pt. Lookout, MD	CSR,HAG
					Pt. Lookout, MD	05/13/65	Rlsd. G.O. #85	P114,CSR
James, Andrew F.	Pvt	B 13th SCVI	Spotsylvania, VA	05/13/64	Ft. McHenry, MD	08/28/64	Elmira, NY	P110,HOS,CSR
					Elmira, NY	10/11/64	Pt. Lookout, MD	P65,P66,CSR
					Pt. Lookout, MD	10/22/64	Died, Ch. Diarrhea	P6,P114,FPH,CSR
James, B.F.	Cpl	I 18th SCVI	Crater, Pbg., VA	07/30/64	City Pt., VA	08/05/64	Pt. Lookout, MD	CSR
					Pt. Lookout, MD	08/08/64	Elmira, NY	P120,CSR
					Elmira, NY	02/13/65	Elmira, NY USGH	P65,CSR
					Elmira, NY USGH	07/19/65	Rlsd. G.O. #109	P66,CSR
James, B.G.	Pvt	C 3rd SCVABn	Blakely, MS	04/09/65	Ship Island, MS	05/01/65	Vicksburg, MS Xc	CSR
James, F.P.	Pvt	H 27th SCVI	Weldon RR, VA	08/21/64	City Pt., VA	08/24/64	Pt. Lookout, MD	CSR
					Pt. Lookout, MD	02/18/65	Exchanged	P113,P124,CSR
James, G.	Pvt	A 26th SCVI	Hatchers Run, VA	03/25/65	City Pt., VA	03/26/65	Pt. Lookout, MD	CSR
					Pt. Lookout, MD	06/28/65	Rlsd. G.O. #109	P114
James, G.C.	Pvt	A Hol.Leg.	Five Forks, VA	04/01/65	City Pt., VA	04/05/65	Pt. Lookout, MD	CSR
					Pt. Lookout, MD	06/28/65	Rlsd. G.O. #109	P114,CSR
James, Galiban R.	Pvt	A Hol.Leg.	Keedysville, MD	09/20/62	Keedysville, MD	09/20/62	Paroled	CSR
James, Galiban R.	Cpl	A Hol.Leg.	Five Forks, VA	04/01/65	City Pt., VA	04/05/65	Pt. Lookout, MD	CSR
					Pt. Lookout, MD	06/28/65	Rlsd. G.O. #109	P114,CSR
James, H.V.	Pvt	H 25th SCVI	Ft. Fisher, NY	01/15/65	New York, NY	01/30/65	Elmira, NY	CSR,HAG
					Elmira, NY	07/19/65	Rlsd. G.O. #109	P65,P66,,CSR
James, Howard	Pvt	D Ham.Leg.MI	Deserted/enemy	09/06/64	Ft. Magruder, VA	09/06/64	Fts. Monroe, VA	CSR
					Fts. Monroe, VA	09/12/64	Took oath	CSR
James, J.	Pvt	C 3rd SCVABn	Blakely, AL	04/09/65	Ship Island, MS	05/01/65	Vicksburg, MS Xc	CSR
James, J.M.	Pvt	I 5th SCVI	Chattanooga, TN	10/29/63	Nashville, TN	11/07/63	Louisville, KY	P39,CSR,SA3
					Louisville, KY	11/09/63	Camp Morton, IN	CSR
					Camp Morton, IN	03/19/64	Ft. Delaware, DE	CSR
					Ft. Delaware, DE	06/10/65	Released	P41,P45,CSR
James, J.P.	Pvt	A 3rd SCVABn	High Pt., NC	05/02/65	High Pt., NC	05/02/65	Paroled	CSR
James, James N.	Pvt	I 5th SCVI	Farmville, VA	04/06/65	City Pt., VA	04/14/65	Newport News, VA	CSR
					Newport News, VA	06/26/65	Rlsd. G.O. #109	CSR,SA3
James, James V.	Cpl	I 21st SCVI	Petersburg, VA	06/24/64	Bermuda Hundred, VA	06/15/64	Fts. Monroe, VA	CSR,HAG,HMC
					Fts. Monroe, VA	06/26/64	Pt. Lookout, MD	CSR
					Pt. Lookout, MD	08/16/64	Elmira, NY	P113,P120
					Elmira, NY	03/14/65	Pt. Lookout, MD Xc	P65,P66,CSR
James, John F.	Cpl	F 1st SCVC	Culpepper, VA	09/19/63	Ft. McHenry, MD	09/26/63	Pt. Lookout, MD	P110
					Pt. Lookout, MD	08/16/64	Elmira, NY	P113,P120,CSR
					Elmira, NY	10/11/64	Pt. Lookout, MD Xc	P65,P66,CSR

SOUTH CAROLINA SOLDIERS, SAILORS AND **J** CITIZENS HELD IN U.S. PRISONS 1861-1865

NAME	RANK	REGIMENT	CAPTURED AT	WHEN	PRISON	MOVED	DISPOSITION	SOURCES
James, John F.	Pvt	F 26th SCVI	Deserted/enemy	01/22/65	City Pt., VA	01/24/65	Washington, DC	P8,CSR
					Washington, DC	01/30/65	Chicago, IL oath	CSR
James, Lemuel T.	Pvt	F 12th SCVI	Petersburg, VA	04/03/65	City Pt., VA	04/07/65	Hart's Island, NY	CSR
					Hart's Island, NY	06/16/65	Rlsd. G.O. #109	P79,CSR
James, Rufus	Pvt	G 27th SCVI	Town Creek, NC	02/20/65	Ft. Anderson, NC	02/28/65	Pt. Lookout, MD	CSR,HAG
					Pt. Lookout, MD	06/28/65	Rlsd. G.O. #109	P114,CSR
James, Samuel S.	Pvt	C 25th SCVI	Ft. Fisher, NC	01/15/65	Elmira, NY	07/13/65	Transferred	P65,HAG,CTA
James, Simon	Pvt	C 3rd SCVABn	Ft. Gaines, AL	08/08/64	New Orleans, LA	10/12/64	St. Louis, MO USGH	CSR
					St. Louis, MO USGH	10/22/64	New Orleans, LA	CSR
					New Orleans, LA	10/25/64	Ship Island, MS	P3,CSR
					Ship Island, MS	11/27/64	Died, Dysentery	CSR
James, W.	Pvt	A 3rd SCVABn	High Pt., NC	05/02/65	High Pt., NC	05/02/65	Paroled	CSR
James, W.A.	Pvt	B 3rd SCVI	Gettysburg, PA	07/03/63	Gettysburg, PA G.		Provost Marshal	P4,KEB,H3,CSR
					David's Island, NY	09/27/63	City Pt., VA Xc	CSR
					Richmond, VA Hos.	10/03/63	Furloughed 30 days	CSR
James, William	Pvt	2nd SCVI	Fairfax C.H., VA	07/22/61	Ft. McHenry, MD	11/14/64	Fts. Monroe, VA	CSR
James, William E.	1Lt	F 8th SCVI	Winchester, VA	09/13/64	Harpers Ferry, WV	09/19/64	Johnson's Isl., OH	CSR
					Johnsons Isl., OH	06/16/65	Rlsd. G.O. #109	P81,P82,R46,CSR
James, William H.	Pvt	M P.S.S.	Deserted/enemy	03/05/65	Bermuda Hundred, VA	03/07/65	Washington, DC	CSR,TSE
					Washington, DC	03/08/65	Nashville,TN oath	CSR
Jameson, J.H.	Pvt	C 1st SCVIR	Charlotte, NC	05/03/65	Charlotte, NC	05/03/65	Paroled	SA1,CSR
Jameson, James	Pvt	A 6th SCVI	Louisa, KY	04/14/64	Louisville, KY	04/22/64	Camp Morton, IN	CSR
					Camp Morton, IN	02/03/65	Released on oath	CSR
Jamison, A.R.	Pvt	G 5th SCVC	Hawe's Shop, VA	05/28/64	Pt. Lookout, MD	07/09/64	Elmira, NY	P113,P120,CSR
					Elmira, NY	10/11/64	Pt. Lookout to Xc	P65,P66,CSR
					Pt. Lookout, MD	10/29/64	Venus Pt., GA Xc	P114,CSR
Jamison, H.	Pvt	A 3rd SCVABn	High Pt., NC	05/02/65	High Pt., NC	05/02/65	Paroled	CSR
Jamison, J.F.	Sgt	G 18th SCVI	Crater, Pbg., VA	07/30/64	City Pt., VA	08/05/64	Pt. Lookout, MD	CSR
					Pt. Lookout, MD	08/08/64	Elmira, NY	P113,P120,P125,CSR
					Elmira, NY	07/03/65	Rlsd. G.O. #109	P65,P66,CSR
Janes, Moses	Pvt	F Orr's Ri.	Deserted/enemy	04/18/65	Washington, D.C.	04/21/65	Charleston, SC	CSR
Janes, Thomas A.Y.	Pvt	F Orr's Ri.	Petersburg, VA	04/03/65	City Pt., VA	04/11/65	Hart's Island, NY	CSR
					Hart's Island, NY	06/16/65	Rlsd. G.O. #109	P79,CSR
Jarcks, G.H.	Pvt	I 27th SCVI	Weldon RR, VA	08/21/64	City Pt., VA	08/24/64	Pt. Lookout, MD	CSR,HAG
					Pt. Lookout, MD	03/15/65	Exchanged	P113,P124,HAG,CSR
Jarrell, Richard H.	Pvt	E 11th SCVI	Petersburg, VA	06/24/64	Bermuda Hundred, VA	06/25/64	Fts. Monroe, VA	CSR,HAG
					Fts. Monroe, VA	06/26/64	Pt. Lookout, MD	CSR
					Pt. Lookout, MD	08/16/64	Elmira, NY	P113,P120,CSR
					Elmira, NY	10/11/64	Pt. Lookout, MD Xc	P65,P66
					Pt. Lookout, MD	10/29/64	Venus Pt., GA Xc	P114,CSR
Jarrett, J.A.	2Lt	K Hol.Leg.	Stony Creek, VA	05/07/64	Fts. Monroe, VA	05/13/64	Pt. Lookout, MD	CSR,ISH
					Pt. Lookout, MD	06/23/64	Ft. Delaware, DE	P113,P120
					Ft. Delaware, DE	08/20/64	Hilton Head, SC	P42,P44
					Hilton Head, SC		Ft. Pulaski, GA	CSR
					Ft. Pulaski, GA		Hilton Head, SC	P4,ISH
					Ft. Delaware, DE	06/16/65	Rlsd. G.O. #109	P43
Jarrot, Charles Edward	Pvt	A 2nd SCVC	Whitehall, NC	03/18/65	New Berne, NC	03/30/65	Pt. Lookout, MD	CSR
					Pt. Lookout, MD	06/28/65	Rlsd. G.O. #109	P114,CSR
Jayroe, John William	Pvt	C 25th SCVI	Drury's Bluff, VA	05/14/64	Ft. Monroe, VA	05/30/64	Died of wounds	P6,HAG,CTA,ROH,CSR
Jeannerette, E.N.	Cpl	A 1st SCVIBn	James Island, SC	06/08/62	Ft. Columbus, NY	08/23/62	Ft. Delaware, DE	P37
Jeannerette, E.N.	Sgt	I 27th SCVI	Weldon RR, VA	08/21/64	City Pt., VA	08/24/64	Pt. Lookout, MD	CSR,HAG
					Pt. Lookout, MD	03/14/65	Exchanged	P113,P124,CSR

SOUTH CAROLINA SOLDIERS, SAILORS AND  CITIZENS HELD IN U.S. PRISONS 1861-1865

NAME	RANK	REGIMENT	CAPTURED AT	WHEN	PRISON	MOVED	DISPOSITION	SOURCES
Jefcoat, Andrew	Pvt	B 1st SCVIH	Mossy Creek, TN	01/22/64	Nashville, TN	02/11/64	Louisville, KY	P39,CSR
					Louisville, KY	02/15/64	Rock Island, IL	CSR,SA1
					Rock Island, IL	06/17/65	Rlsd. G.O. #109	CSR
Jefcoat, D.J.	Pvt	I 6th SCVI	Deserted/enemy	10/07/64	Bermuda Hundred, VA	10/07/64	City Pt., VA P.M.G	CSR
					City Pt., VA P.M.G	10/21/64	New York, NY oath	CSR
Jefcoat, Henry E.	Pvt	B 1st SCVIH	Farmville, VA	04/06/65	City Pt., VA	04/14/65	Newport News, VA	CSR,SA1
					Newport News, VA	06/26/65	Rlsd. G.O. #109	P107,CSR
Jefcoat, J.M.	Cit	Lexington	Lynch's Creek, SC	02/23/65	Hart's Island, NY	06/20/65	Rlsd. G.O. #109	P79
Jeffcoat, A.D.	Pvt	A 15th SCMil	Flat Rock, SC	02/26/65	Hart's Island, NY	06/17/65	Rlsd. G.O. #109	P79
Jeffcoat, B.J.P.	Pvt	B 7th SCVC	Old Church, VA	05/30/64	White House, VA	06/08/64	Pt. Lookout, MD	CSR
					Pt. Lookout, MD	11/01/64	Listed to exchange	P113,P124
					Pt. Lookout, MD	11/01/64	Died at sea & buried	CSR
Jeffcoat, J.W.	Pvt	A 15th SCMil	Lynch's Creek, SC	02/25/65	Hart's Island, NY	06/16/65	Rlsd. G.O. #109	P79
Jeffers, A.	Pvt	C 6th SCVI	Deserted/enemy	03/01/65	Bermuda Hundred, VA	03/01/65	City Pt., VA P.M.	CSR
					City Pt., VA P.M.	03/03/65	Washington, DC P.M.	CSR
					Washington, DC	03/06/65	Bradford, PA oath	CSR
Jefferson, Thomas	Pvt	F 1st SCVA	Fayetteville, NC	03/16/65	New Berne, NC	03/30/65	Pt. Lookout, MD	CSR
					Pt. Lookout, MD	06/06/65	Released	P114,CSR
Jeffords, Daniel M.	Pvt	C 3rd SCVABn	Blakely, AL	04/09/65	Ship Island, MS	05/01/65	Vicksburg, MS Xc	CSR
Jeffords, Daniel M.	Pvt	C 3rd SCVABn	Augusta, GA	05/20/65	Augusta, GA	05/20/65	Paroled	CSR
Jeffords, E.G.	Sgt	C 3rd SCVABn	Ft. Gaines, AL	08/08/64	New Orleans, LA	10/25/64	Ship Island, MS	P3,CSR
					Ship Island, MS	01/04/65	Exchanged	CSR
Jeffords, Joseph B.	Pvt	K 21st SCVI	Ft. Fisher, NC	01/15/65	New York, NY	01/30/65	Elmira, NY	CSR,HAG
					Elmira, NY	07/03/65	Rlsd. G.O. #109	P65,P66,CSR
Jeffords, S.K.	Pvt	C 3rd SCVABn	Blakely, AL	04/09/65	Ship Island, MS	05/01/65	Vicksburg, MS Xc	CSR
Jeffords, T.J.	Pvt	E 11th SCVI	Petersburg, VA	06/24/64	City Pt., VA	06/30/64	Pt. Lookout, MD	CSR
					Pt. Lookout, MD	10/11/64	Coxes Wh., VA Xc	CSR
Jeffords, Thomas	Pvt	C 3rd SCVABn	Ft. Gaines, AL	08/08/64	New Orleans, LA	10/25/64	Ship Island, MS	P3,CSR
					Ship Island, MS	01/04/65	Exchanged	CSR
Jeffries, Andrew S.	Pvt	F 17th SCVI	Petersburg, VA Hos.	04/11/65	Petersburg, VA Hos.	05/08/65	Pt. O Rocks USGH	CSR
					Pt. O Rocks G.H.	05/17/65	Fts. Monroe, VA G.H.	CSR
					Fts. Monroe, VA G.H.	07/09/65	Died of wounds	CSR
Jeffries, Goodman	Cpt	F 18th SCVI	Petersburg, VA	03/25/65	Old Capitol, DC	03/30/65	Ft. Delaware, DE	CSR,UD3
					Ft. McHenry, MD	03/30/65	Ft. Delaware, DE	P110
					Ft. Delaware, DE	06/17/65	Rlsd. G.O. #109	P43,P45,CSR
Jenkins, Archibald E.	Pvt	F Orr's Ri.	Petersburg, VA	04/02/65	City Pt., VA	04/04/65	Pt. Lookout, MD	CSR
					Pt. Lookout, MD	06/28/65	Rlsd. G.O. #109	P114,CSR
Jenkins, B.W.	Pvt	F 3rd SCVC	South Newport, GA	08/17/64	Philadelphia, PA	01/10/65	Ft. Delaware, DE	CSR
					Ft. Delaware, DE	02/27/65	City Pt., VA Xc	P41,P42,p47,CSR
Jenkins, Benjamin O.	Pvt	G 18th SCVI	Crater, Pbg., VA	07/30/64	City Pt., VA	08/05/64	Pt. Lookout, MD	CSR
					Pt. Lookout, MD	08/08/64	Elmira, NY	CSR
					Elmira, NY	04/21/65	Died, Pneumonia	P66,FPH,CSR
Jenkins, Benjamin V.	Pvt	D 16th SCVI	Marietta, GA	06/17/64	Nashville, TN	06/24/64	Louisville, KY	P3,16R,CSR
					Louisville, KY	06/27/64	Camp Morton, IN	CSR
					Camp Morton, IN	03/15/65	Pt. Lookout, MD Xc	CSR
					Pt. Lookout, MD	03/23/65	Boulwares Wh., VA	CSR
Jenkins, C.B.	Pvt	I 3rd SCVC	Pocotaligo, SC	12/25/64	Hilton Head, SC G.H.	02/01/65	Pt. Lookout, MD	CSR
					Pt. Lookout, MD	03/15/65	Aikens Ldg. for Xc	P124,CSR
Jenkins, E.B.	Pvt	F 26th SCVI	Richmond, VA Hos.	04/03/65	Libby Prison, Rchmd.	04/21/65	Newport News, VA	CSR
					Newport News, VA	06/15/65	Rlsd. G.O. #109	P107,CSR

J

SOUTH CAROLINA SOLDIERS, SAILORS AND CITIZENS HELD IN U.S. PRISONS 1861-1865

NAME	RANK	REGIMENT	CAPTURED AT	WHEN	PRISON	MOVED	DISPOSITION	SOURCES
Jenkins, J.C.	Pvt	L 7th SCVI	Gettysburg, PA	07/03/63	Ft. Delaware, DE	06/15/64	Hos. 6/15-7/2/64	P47
					Ft. Delaware, DE	11/15/64	Hos. 11/15-21/64	P47
					Ft. Delaware, DE	07/10/65	Rlsd. G.O. #109	P42,P44,P45,CSR
Jenkins, James	Pvt	B 23rd SCVI	Deserted/enemy	02/15/65	City Pt., VA			CSR
Jenkins, James A.	Pvt	C 1st SCVIH	Warrenton, VA	09/29/62	Warrenton, VA	09/29/62	Paroled	CSR,SA1
Jenkins, James A.	Pvt	C 1st SCVIH	Chattanooga, TN	10/29/63	Nashville, TN	11/07/63	Louisville, KY	P39
					Louisville, KY	11/09/63	Camp Morton, IN	CSR
					Camp Morton, IN	03/04/65	City Pt., VA Xc	CSR
Jenkins, James A.	Pvt	C 1st SCVIH	Augusta, GA	06/03/65	Augusta, GA	06/03/65	Paroled	CSR
Jenkins, Kinnis	Pvt	B 26th SCVI	Five Forks, VA	04/01/65	City Pt., VA	04/05/65	Pt. Lookout, MD	CSR
					Pt. Lookout, MD	06/28/65	Rlsd. G.O. #109	P114,CSR
Jenkins, Lawson J.	Pvt	B 12th SCVI	2nd Manassas, VA	09/01/62	Washington, DC USH	09/27/62	Aikens Ldg., VA Xc	CSR
					Richmond, VA G.H.	10/08/62	Furloughed 25 days	CSR
Jenkins, Pleasant J.	Pvt	I 13th SCVI	Petersburg, VA	03/25/65	City Pt., VA	03/28/65	Pt. Lookout, MD	CSR
					Pt. Lookout, MD	06/28/65	Rlsd. G.O. #109	P114,HOS,CSR
Jenkins, R.S.	Pvt	B 17th SCVI	Five Forks, VA	04/01/65	City Pt., VA	04/06/65	Pt. Lookout, MD	CSR
					Pt. Lookout, MD	06/28/65	Rlsd. G.O. #109	CSR
Jenkins, R.W.	1Lt	I 6th SCVC	Raleigh, NC Hos.	04/13/65	Raleigh, NC	04/13/65	Paroled	CSR
Jenkins, Thomas M.	Pvt	F 22nd SCVI	Petersburg, VA	03/25/65	City Pt., VA	03/28/65	Pt. Lookout, MD	CSR
					Pt. Lookout, MD	06/06/65	Released	P114
Jenkins, W.H.H.	Pvt	F Orr's Ri.	Hanover Jctn., VA	05/22/64	Pt. Lookout, MD	06/06/65	Released	P113,CDC,CSR
Jenkins, W.K.	Pvt	F 3rd SCVC	South Newport, GA	08/17/64	Philadelphia, PA	01/10/65	Ft. Delaware, DE	CSR
					Ft. Delaware, DE	03/01/65	Died	P6,P41,P47,FPH,CSR
Jenkins, William B.	Pvt	K 2ndb SCVC	Greenville, SC	05/23/65	Greenville, SC	05/23/65	Paroled	CSR
Jenkins, Willis.	Pvt	A 1st SCVIR	Bentonville, NC	03/22/65	New Berne, NC	04/10/65	Hart's Island, NY	CSR,SA1
					Hart's Island, NY	06/16/65	Rlsd. G.O. #109	P79,CSR
Jennings, A.	Pvt	B 3rd SCVI	Sharpsburg, MD	09/17/62	P.M. A. of Potomac	09/30/62	Paroled	CSR
					Richmond, VA Hos.	10/23/62	Furloughed	CSR
Jennings, Alfred	Pvt	B Hol.Leg.	Kinston, NC	12/15/62	Kinston, NC	12/15/62	Paroled POW	CSR,HOS
Jennings, Alfred	Pvt	B Hol.Leg.	Five Forks, VA	04/01/65	City Pt., VA	04/05/65	Pt. Lookout, MD	CSR
					Pt. Lookout, MD	06/27/65	Rlsd. G.O. #109	P114
Jennings, Brown	Cpl	B 19th SCVI	Augusta, GA	05/19/65	Augusta, GA	05/19/65	Paroled	CSR
Jennings, C. Willis	Pvt	C 5th SCVI	Lookout Mtn., TN	10/29/63	Bridgeport, AL G.H.	11/06/63	Nashville, TN	CSR
					Nashville, TN	12/18/63	Died of wounds	P2,P6,P12,CSR
Jennings, Elihu E.	Pvt	B Hol.Leg.	Deserted/enemy	02/14/65	City Pt., VA	02/18/65	Washington, DC	CSR
					Washington, DC	02/21/65	Columbus, OH oath	CSR
Jennings, Henry J.	Pvt	B 14th SCVI	Gettysburg, PA	07/04/63	David's Island, NY	09/08/63	City Pt., VA Xc	P1,UD3,CSR
Jennings, Henry J.	Pvt	F 7th SCVI	Cheraw, SC	03/05/65	Cheraw, SC	03/05/65	Paroled	CSR
Jennings, Henry T.	Pvt	I 24th SCVI	Chickamauga, GA	09/20/63	Nashville, TN	09/30/63	Louisville, KY	P38
					Louisville, KY	10/02/63	Camp Douglas, IL	CSR
					Camp Douglas, IL	03/13/65	Pt. Lookout, MD Xc	P53,P55,P57,CSR
					Richmond Hospitals	03/27/65	Furloughed 60 days	CSR
Jennings, Henry T.	Pvt	I 24th SCVI	Augusta, GA	05/24/65	Augusta, GA	05/24/65	Paroled	CSR
Jennings, Isaac S.	Pvt	I 14th SCVI	Greensboro, NC	05/17/65	Greensboro, NC	05/17/65	Paroled	CSR
Jennings, John	Pvt	G 27th SCVI	Petersburg, VA	06/24/64	Bermuda Hundred, VA	06/25/64	Fts. Monroe, VA	CSR,HAG
					Fts. Monroe, VA	06/26/64	Pt. Lookout, MD	CSR
					Pt. Lookout, MD	08/15/64	Elmira, NY	P113,P120,CSR
					Elmira, NY	10/11/64	Pt. Lookout to Xc	P65,P66
					Pt. Lookout, MD	10/29/64	Venus Pt., GA Xc	P114,CSR
Jennings, Matthew W.	Pvt	B 14th SCVI	Port Royal, SC	12/17/62	Hilton Head, SC	02/09/62	Ft. Hamilton, NY	CSR,HOE
					Ft. Hamilton, NY	02/13/62	Ft. Lafayette, NY	CSR
					Ft. Lafayette, NY	03/11/62	Died	P85,FPH,CSR

SOUTH CAROLINA SOLDIERS, SAILORS AND CITIZENS HELD IN U.S. PRISONS 1861-1865

NAME	RANK	REGIMENT	CAPTURED AT	WHEN	PRISON	MOVED	DISPOSITION	SOURCES
Jennings, Patrick P.	Pvt	I 5th SCVC	Lee's Mills, VA	07/30/64	City Pt., VA	08/22/64	Pt. Lookout, MD	CSR
					Pt. Lookout, MD	09/18/64	Aikens Ldg., VA Xc	P113,CSR
					Richmond, VA Hos.	09/25/64	Furloughed 30 days	CSR
Jennings, R.H.	2Lt	G 3rd SCVIBn	Sharpsburg, MD	09/16/62	Ft. Delaware, DE	10/02/62	Aikens Ldg., VA Xc	CSR
Jennings, Richard	Pvt	C 3rd SCVABn	Blakely, AL	04/09/65	Ship Island, MS	05/01/65	Vicksburg, MS Xc	CSR
Jennings, S.D.	Pvt	E P.S.S.	Fair Oaks, VA	06/01/62	Fts. Monroe, VA	06/05/62	Ft. Delaware, DE	CSR,TSE
					Ft. Delaware, DE	08/05/62	Aikens Ldg., VA Xc	CSR,TSE
Jennings, William	Pvt	G 13th SCVI	Fredericksburg, VA	05/11/62	Steamer Coatzacoal	07/05/62	Aikens Ldg., VA	CSR
					Aikens Ldg., VA	08/05/62	Exchanged	CSR
Jennings, William H.	Pvt	A 3rd SCVI	N. Anna River, VA	05/22/64	Port Royal, VA	05/30/64	Pt. Lookout, MD	CSR,Sa2,H3
					Pt. Lookout, MD	09/15/64	Aikens Ldg., VA Xc	P113,CSR
					Richmond, VA Hos.	09/26/64	Furloughed 30 days	CSR
Jennings, Joseph H.	ASr	19th SCVI	Augusta, GA	05/18/65	Augusta, GA	05/18/65	Paroled	CSR
Jenrett, Wilson	Pvt	B 8th SCV	Fayettville, NC	03/11/65	New Berne, NC	03/30/65	Pt. Lookout, MD	CSR
Jenson, William F.	Pvt	L 1st SCVIG	Falling Waters, MD	07/14/63	Ft. McHenry, MD	08/08/63	Ft. Delaware, DE	P110
					Old Capitol, DC	08/08/63	Pt. Lookout, MD	CSR,SA1
					Pt. Lookout, MD	03/03/64	City Pt., VA Xc	P113,P124,CSR
Jenson, William F.	Pvt	L 1st SCVIG	Petersburg, VA	04/02/65	City Pt., VA	04/02/65	Pt. Lookout, MD	CSR
					Pt. Lookout, MD	06/28/65	Rlsd. G.O. #109	P114,CSR
Jernigan, James H.	Pvt	G 26th SCVI	Five Forks, VA	04/01/65	City Pt., VA	04/05/65	Pt. Lookout, MD	CSR
					Pt. Lookout, MD	06/28/65	Rlsd. G.O. #109	P114,CSR
Jernigan, Joseph	Pvt	K 1st SCVIH	Frederick, MD USGH		Frederick, MD	09/18/62	Transferred	CSR
Jerrold, W.E.	Pvt	G 10th SCVI	Munfordville, KY	09/23/62	Munfordville, KY	09/23/62	Paroled	CSR,RAS
Jervey, C.T.	Cit		Wilmington, NC	11/06/63	Ft. Warren, MA	06/15/65	Took the oath	P2
Jeter, C.	Pvt	G 3rd SCVABn	High Pt., NC	05/01/65	High Pt., NC	05/01/65	Paroled	CSR
Jeter, J.B.	Sgt	B 18th SCVI	Hatchers Run, VA	03/29/65	Pt. of Rocks, VA Hos.	04/12/65	Str. Hero of Jersey	CSR
					Str. Hero of Jersey	04/13/65	Fts. Monroe, VA Hos.	CSR
					Fts. Monroe, VA Hos.	06/29/65	Rlsd. G.O. #109	CSR
Jeter, J.L.	Pvt	A 18th SCVI	Richmond, VA Hos.	04/03/65	Capitol Bldg. Richmd.	05/12/65	Paroled	CSR
Jeter, W.L.	Pvt	A 25th SCVI	Swift Creek, VA	05/09/64	Bermuda Hundred, VA	05/10/64	Fts. Monroe, VA	CSR,HAG
					Pt. Lookout, MD	05/12/65	Released G.O. #85	P113,CSR
Jett, William E	Pvt	B Hol.Leg.	Deserted/enemy	02/14/65	City Pt., VA	02/18/65	Washington, DC	CSR
					Washington, DC	02/21/65	Columbus, OH oath	CSR
Jewel, W.J.	Pvt	A 3rd SCVABn	High Pt., NC	05/02/65	High Pt., NC	05/02/65	Paroled	CSR
Joel, George	Pvt	B 19th SCVI	Franklin, TN	12/18/64	Nashville, TN	01/17/65	Louisville, KY	P39,CSR
					Louisville, KY	01/18/65	Camp Chase, OH	CSR
					Camp Chase, OH	06/11/65	Rlsd. G.O. #109	P23,CSR
Joel, Julius	Pvt	E 1st SCVIH	Richmond, VA	04/03/65	No release data			SA1,CSR
Johns, J.E.	Pvt	E 15th SCVI	Winchester, VA	09/19/64	W. Bldg. Balt, MD	10/25/64	Pt. Lookout, MD	P1
					Pt. Lookout, MD	10/30/64	Exchanged	P114,CSR
Johns, S.K.	Pvt	H 22nd SCVI	Farmville, VA	04/06/65	City Pt., VA	04/14/65	Newport News, VA	CSR
					Newport News, VA	06/26/65	Rlsd. G.O. #109	P107,CSR
Johns, W.H.	Pvt	G 21st SCVI	Weldon RR, VA	08/21/64	City Pt., VA	08/24/64	Pt. Lookout, MD	CSR
					Pt. Lookout, MD	03/17/65	Exchanged	P113,P124
Johns, Wesley	Pvt	D 1st SCVIR	North Carolina		Hart's Island, SC	06/15/65	Rlsd. G.O. #109	SA1,CSR
Johnson, A.	Pvt	C 1st SCVA	Bennettsville, SC	03/08/65	Pt. Lookout, MD	06/28/65	Rlsd. G.O. #109	P114
Johnson, A. Cornelius	Pvt	G Orr's Ri.	Falling Waters, MD	07/14/63	Frederick, MD G.H.	08/10/63	W. Bldg. Balt, MD	P1,CDC
					W. Bldg. Balt, MD	08/22/63	City Pt., VA Xc	P1,CSR
Johnson, Alexander	Pvt	H 7th SCVC	Deep Bottom, VA	08/17/64	City Pt., VA	09/22/64	Pt. Lookout, MD	CSR
					Pt. Lookout, MD	03/14/65	Exchanged	P113,P124,P125,CSR

SOUTH CAROLINA SOLDIERS, SAILORS AND J CITIZENS HELD IN U.S. PRISONS 1861-1865

NAME	RANK	REGIMENT	CAPTURED AT	WHEN	PRISON	MOVED	DISPOSITION	SOURCES
Johnson, Alexander H.	Pvt	A 1st SCVIR	Morris Island, SC	09/07/63	Hilton Head, SC	10/06/63	Ft. Columbus, NY	CSR,SA1
					Ft. Columbus, NY	10/09/63	Pt. Lookout, MD	P1,CSR
					Pt. Lookout, MD	12/14/64	Died, Typhoid Fever	P6,P12,P113,FPH,CSR
Johnson, Amos	Wgn	H 7th SCVC	Littleton, NC	05/07/64	Elmira, NY	10/11/64	Pt. Lookout, MD Xc	P65,P66
					Pt. Lookout, MD	10/29/64	Exchanged	P114
Johnson, Anderson C.	Sgt	C 22nd SCVI	Crater, Pbg., VA	07/30/64	City Pt., VA	08/05/64	Pt. Lookout, MD	CSR,HOS
					Pt. Lookout, MD	08/08/64	Elmira, NY	P113,P120
					Elmira, NY	10/21/64	Died, Pneumonia	P6,P12,P65,P66,FPH
Johnson, Andrew	Pvt	E 24th SCVI	Nashville, TN	12/10/64	Nashville, TN	01/01/65	Louisville, KY	CSR,EFW
					Louisville, KY	01/04/65	Camp Chase, OH	CSR
					Camp Chase, OH	06/11/65	Rlsd. G.O. #109	P23
Johnson, B.R.	Pvt	I Ham.Leg.MI	Hartwell, GA	05/18/65	Hartwell, GA	05/18/65	Paroled	CSR
Johnson, Benjamin	Pvt	B 37th VAVCB	Gettysburg, PA	07/03/63	Pt. Lookout, MD	03/15/65	Boulwares Wh., VA	P124,CSR
Johnson, Blueford	Pvt	A 13th SCVI	Petersburg, VA	04/03/65	City Pt., VA	04/11/65	Hart's Island, NY	CSR
					Hart's Island, NY	06/15/65	Rlsd. G.O. #109	P79,CSR
Johnson, Capers T.	Pvt	B 27th SCVI	Town Creek, NC	02/20/65	Ft. Anderson, NC	02/28/65	Pt. Lookout, MD	CSR,HAG
					Pt. Lookout, MD	06/28/65	Rlsd. G.O. #109	CSR
Johnson, Charles P.	Pvt	A 15th SCVI	South Mtn., MD	09/14/62	Frederick, MD	01/17/63	Ft. McHenry, MD	KEB,CSR
					Ft. McHenry, MD	01/21/63	Fts. Monroe, VA	CSR
					Fts. Monroe, VA	01/26/63	City Pt., VA Xc	CSR
					Petersburg, VA Hos.	02/05/63	Furloughed 60 days	H15,CSR
Johnson, D.	Pvt	H 1st SCVA	Smith Farm, NC	03/15/65	Hart's Island, NY	06/16/65	Rlsd. G.O. #109	P79
Johnson, D.H.	Pvt	I 21st SCVI	Weldon RR, VA	08/21/64	City Pt., VA	08/24/64	Pt. Lookout, MD	CSR
					Pt. Lookout, MD	02/21/65	Exchanged	P113
Johnson, D.L.	Pvt	F 7th SCVI	Cedar Creek, VA	10/19/64	Harpers Ferry, WV	10/28/64	Pt. Lookout, MD	CSR
					Pt. Lookout, MD	05/18/65	Rlsd. G.O. #85	P114,CSR
Johnson, Daniel S.	Sgt	C 10th SCVI	Murfreesboro, TN	12/31/62	Nashville, TN		Louisville, KY	CSR
					Louisville, KY	03/22/63	City Pt., VA Xc	CSR
Johnson, Daniel W.	Pvt	E 10th SCVI	Nashville, TN USGH		(Smallpox Hos.)			CSR,RAS
Johnson, David	Pvt	A 1st SCVIR	Chesterfield, SC	03/03/65	New Berne, NC	04/01/65	Hart's Island, SC	CSR
					Hart's Island, NY	06/16/65	Rlsd. G.O. #109	SA1,P79,CSR
Johnson, Edward	Pvt	C 25th SCVI	Weldon RR, VA	08/21/64	City Pt., VA	08/24/64	Pt. Lookout, MD	CSR,HAG,CTA
					Pt. Lookout, MD	03/14/65	Exchanged	P113,P124,P125
Johnson, Elias R.	Pvt	F 5th SCVI	Spotsylvania, VA	05/13/64	Ft. Delaware, DE		Hos. 9/1-9/18/64	P47,SA3
					Belle Plain, VA	05/20/64	Ft. Delaware, DE	CSR
					Ft. Delaware, DE	09/18/64	Aikens Ldg., VA Xc	P41,P42,CSR
Johnson, Francis P.	Cpl	G 1st SCVIG	Petersburg, VA	04/03/65	City Pt., VA	04/13/65	Pt. Lookout, MD	CSR,SA1
					Pt. Lookout, MD	06/28/65	Rlsd. G.O. #109	P114,CSR
Johnson, Franklin A.	Pvt	C 13th SCVI	Hatchers Run, VA	03/30/65	City Pt., VA	04/28/65	Pt. Lookout, MD	CSR,HOS
					Pt. Lookout, MD	06/28/65	Rlsd. G.O. #109	P114,CSR
Johnson, Franklin P.	Pvt	F 2nd SCVI	Sharpsburg, MD	09/17/62	Sharpsburg, MD	09/17/62	Died of wounds	SA2,P12,H2,CSR
Johnson, G.A.T.	Pvt	B 11th SCVI	Town Creek, NC	02/20/65	Ft. Anderson, NC	02/28/65	Pt. Lookout, MD	CSR,HAG
					Pt. Lookout, MD	06/28/65	Rlsd. G.O. #109	P114,CSR
Johnson, G.W.	Pvt	E 20th SCVI	Cedar Creek, VA	10/19/64	Pt. Lookout, MD	03/28/65	Exchanged	P114,P124,UD5,CSR
Johnson, G.W.	Pvt	G 3rd SCVABn	High Pt., NC	05/02/65	High Pt., NC	05/02/65	Paroled	CSR
Johnson, George C.	Pvt	F 2nd SCVI	Winchester, VA	09/19/64	Winchester, VA USH	10/16/64	Baltimore, MD USGH	CSR,SA2,H2
					W. Bldg. Balt, MD	10/25/64	Pt. Lookout, MD	P1,CSR
					Pt. Lookout, MD	11/15/64	Venus Pt., GA Xc	CSR
Johnson, George L.	Pvt	A Hol.Leg.	Five Forks, VA	04/01/65	Pt. Lookout, MD	06/28/65	Rlsd. G.O. #109	P114
Johnson, George W.	Pvt	L 10th SCVI	Murfreesboro, TN	12/31/62	Nashville, TN	04/20/63	Louisville, KY	P38,CSR,RAS
					Louisville, KY	04/27/63	Baltimore, MD	CSR
					Ft. McHenry, MD	04/30/63	City Pt., VA Xc	CSR

J

SOUTH CAROLINA SOLDIERS, SAILORS AND CITIZENS HELD IN U.S. PRISONS 1861-1865

NAME	RANK	REGIMENT	CAPTURED AT	WHEN	PRISON	MOVED	DISPOSITION	SOURCES
Johnson, George W.	Pvt	G 1st SCVA	Fayetteville, NC	03/10/65	New Berne, NC	03/30/65	Pt. Lookout, MD	CSR
					Pt. Lookout, MD	06/28/65	Rlsd. G.O. #109	P114,CSR
Johnson, Hansford	Pvt	G 2nd SCVA	Cheraw, SC	03/05/65	Cheraw, SC	03/05/65	Paroled	CSR
Johnson, Harmon	Sgt	C 10th SCVI	Murfreesboro, TN	12/31/62	Murfreesboro, TN	01/26/63	Died of wounds	P12,P38,RAS,TOD
Johnson, Henry G.	Pvt	G 27th SCVI	Mt. Eden, SC	03/04/65	New Berne, NC		Camp Hamilton, VA	CSR,HAG
					Camp Hamilton, VA	04/25/65	Fts. Monroe, VA	CSR
					Fts. Monroe, VA	05/01/65	Newport News, VA	CSR
					Newport News, VA	06/26/65	Rlsd. G.O. #109	P107,HAG
Johnson, J. Bird	Pvt	C 25th SCVI	Ft. Fisher, NC	01/15/65	Fts. Monroe, VA		Pt. Lookout, MD	CSR,HAG,CTA
					Pt. Lookout, MD	02/02/65	U.S. Gen. Hos.	P114,CSR
					Pt. Lookout, MD	04/08/65	Died of wounds	P6,FPH,CSR
Johnson, J.B.	Pvt	G 6th SCVI	Richmond, VA	04/03/65	Newport News, VA	06/26/65	Rlsd. G.O. #109	P107
Johnson, J.C.	Pvt	B 20th SCVI	Cedar Creek, VA	10/19/64				CSR
Johnson, J.F.	Pvt	D 25th SCVI	Ft. Fisher, NC	01/15/65	New York, NY	01/30/65	Elmira, NY	CSR,HAG
					Elmira, NY	02/20/65	James R., VA Xc	P65,P66,CSR
Johnson, J.H.	Pvt	E Ham.Leg.MI	Richmond, VA Hos.	04/03/65	Richmond, VA Hos.	05/02/65	Pt. Lookout, MD	CSR
					Pt. Lookout, MD	05/10/65	Died	P6,FPH,CSR
Johnson, J.H.	Pvt	F 19th SCVI	Augusta, GA	06/06/65	Augusta, GA	06/06/65	Paroled	CSR
Johnson, J.J.	Pvt	D Hol.Leg.	Kinston, NC	12/15/62	Kinston, NC	12/15/62	Paroled POW	CSR
Johnson, J.J.	Pvt	K 6th SCVI	Burkeville, VA	04/11/65	Burkeville, VA	04/17/65	Paroled	CSR
Johnson, J.M.	Cpl	F P.S.S.	Augusta, GA	05/19/65	Augusta, GA	05/19/65	Paroled	CSR,TSE
Johnson, J.W.	Pvt	C 1st SCVIR	Darlington, SC	03/03/65	New Berne, NC	04/10/65	Hart's Island, NY	CSR
					Hart's Island, NY	06/16/65	Rlsd. G.O. #109	SA1,P79,CSR
Johnson, James	Pvt	H 14th SCVI	Gettysburg, PA	07/05/63	Ft. McHenry, MD	07/12/63	Ft. Delaware, DE	CSR,UD2
					Ft. Delaware, DE	10/31/64	Pt. Lookout, MD	P40,P44
					Pt. Lookout, MD	10/31/64	Venus Pt., GA Xc	P114,CSR
Johnson, James	Pvt	B 23rd SCVI	Big Sandy, KY	08/25/63	Camp Chase, OH	01/22/64	Rock Island, IL	P22,CSR no more info
Johnson, James	Pvt	I 22nd SCVI	Petersburg, VA	04/04/65	Prov. M. City Pt., VA	04/11/65	No further data	CSR
Johnson, James	Pvt	B 16th SCVI	Citronelle, AL	05/04/65	Meridian, MS	05/12/65	Paroled on oath	CSR
Johnson, James M.	Pvt	5 10/19 SCVI	Missionary Ridge, TN	11/25/63	Nashville, TN	12/07/63	Louisville, KY	P39,RAS,CSR,CTA
					Louisville, KY	12/09/63	Rock Island, IL	CSR
					Rock Island, IL	05/03/65	New Orleans, LA Xc	CSR
					New Orleans, LA	05/23/65	Exchanged	P3,CSR
Johnson, James W.	Pvt	G 2nd SCVIRi	Charlestown, VA	10/11/62	Harpers Ferry, WV	10/23/62	no other info	CSR
					Bolivar Hts., MD	10/24/62	Provost Marshal	CSR
					Ft. McHenry, MD	10/25/62	Aikens Ldg., VA Xc	CSR
Johnson, John	Pvt	G 16th SCVI	Franklin, TN	12/18/64	Nashville, TN	01/14/65	Louisville, KY	P3,P39,16R,CSR
					Louisville, KY	01/18/65	Camp Chase, OH	CSR
					Camp Chase, OH	05/02/65	New Orleans, LA Xc	CSR
					Camp Chase, OH	05/02/65	New Orleans, LA Xc	P26
					Vicksburg, MS USGH	05/31/65	Released on oath	CSR
Johnson, John	Sgt	G 1st SCVIR	Deserted/enemy	03/05/65	Fts. Monroe, VA	04/02/65	Washington, D.C.	CSR
					Washington, DC	04/05/65	New York, NY oath	SA1,CSR
Johnson, John A.	Pvt	B 1st SCVA	Fayetteville, NC	03/11/65	New Berne, NC	03/30/65	Pt. lookout, MD	CSR
					Pt. Lookout, MD	06/28/65	Rlsd. G.O. #109	P114,CSR
Johnson, John H.	Pvt	6 10/19 SCVI	Missionary Ridge, MD	11/25/63	Bridgeport, AL G.H	12/11/63	Nashville, TN	P2,RAS,CSR
					Nashville, TN	03/20/64	Louisville, KY	CSR
					Louisville, KY	03/24/64	Camp Chase, OH	CSR
					Camp Chase, OH	02/25/65	City Pt., VA Xc	P22,P26,CSR
					Richmond, VA Hos.	04/07/65	Escaped from Hos.	CSR

SOUTH CAROLINA SOLDIERS, SAILORS AND **J** CITIZENS HELD IN U.S. PRISONS 1861-1865

NAME	RANK	REGIMENT	CAPTURED AT	WHEN	PRISON	MOVED	DISPOSITION	SOURCES
Johnson, John J.	Pvt	C 22nd SCVI	Crater, Pbg., VA	07/30/64	City Pt., VA	08/05/64	Pt. Lookout, MD	CSR
					Pt. Lookout, MD	08/08/64	Elmira, NY	P113,P120,FPH,CSR
					Elmira, NY	10/11/64	Pt. Lookout, MD Xc	P65,P66,CSR
Johnson, John J.	Pvt	C 26th SCVI	Crater, Pbg., VA	07/30/64	Pt. Lookout, MD	10/29/65	Exchanged	P114
Johnson, John J.	Pvt	I 25th SCVI	Ft. Fisher, NC	01/15/65	New York, NY	01/30/65	Elmira, NY	CSR,HAG
					Elmira, NY	02/16/65	Died	P6,P66,FPH
Johnson, John L.	Pvt	A Hol.Leg.	Five Forks, VA	04/01/65	City Pt., VA	04/05/65	Pt. Lookout, MD	CSR
					Pt. Lookout, MD	06/28/65	Rlsd. G.O. #109	CSR
Johnson, John R.	Pvt	E 25th SCVI	Ft. Fisher, NC	01/15/65	New York, NY	01/30/65	Elmira, NY	CSR,HAG
					Elmira, NY	05/13/65	Pt. Lookout, MD Xc	P65,P66,CSR
Johnson, Joseph B.	Pvt	A 2nd SCVA	Salisbury, NC	04/12/65	Nashville, TN	04/29/65	Louisville, KY	P39,CSR
					Louisville, KY	05/02/65	Camp Chase, OH	CSR
					Camp Chase, OH	06/11/65	Released G.O. #109	P23,CSR
Johnson, Julius H.	Pvt	I 11th SCVI	Town Creek, NC	02/20/65	Ft. Anderson, NC	06/28/65	Pt. Lookout, MD	CSR,HAG
					Pt. Lookout, MD	06/28/65	Rlsd. G.O. #109	P114,CSR
Johnson, Lindsey M.	Pvt	H 1st SCVA	Smith's Farm, NC	03/16/65	New Berne, NC	04/10/65	Hart's Island, NY	CSR
					Hart's Island, NY	06/15/65	Rlsd. G.O. #109	CSR
Johnson, M. Pinckney	Pvt	I 25th SCVI	Ft. Fisher, NC	01/15/65	New York, NY	01/30/65	Elmira, NY	CSR,HAG
					Elmira, NY	03/23/65	Died, Variola	P6,P65,P66,FPH
Johnson, M.B.	Pvt	I 2nd SCVC	Beverly Ford, VA	06/09/63	Old Capitol, DC	06/25/63	City Pt., VA Xc	CSR,UD2
					Ft. McHenry, MD	06/25/63	City Pt., VA Xc	P110,CSR
Johnson, M.G.	Pvt	K 2nd SCVI	Deserted/enemy	03/15/65	Charleston, SC	03/15/65	Released on oath	CSR
Johnson, M.H.	Pvt	C 3rd SCVIBn	Spotsylvania, VA	05/09/64	Belle Plain, VA	05/21/64	Ft. Delaware, DE	CSR
					Ft. Delaware, DE	06/07/65	Released G.O. #109	P41,P42,P47,CSR
Johnson, M.H.J.	Pvt	B 18th SCVAB	Fayetteville, NC	03/11/65	Pt. Lookout, MD	06/28/65	Rlsd. G.O. #109	P114
Johnson, Milledge B.	ASr	2nd SCVC	Augusta, GA	05/25/65	Augusta, GA	05/25/65	Paroled	CSR
Johnson, Mishack	Pvt	B 8th SCResB	Fayetteville, NC	03/11/65	New Berne, NC	03/30/65	Pt. Lookout, MD	CSR
					Pt. Lookout, MD	06/28/65	Rlsd. G.O. #109	CSR
Johnson, Murdoch D.	Pvt	A 1st SCVIR	Darlington, SC	03/03/65	Hart's Island, NY	05/24/65	Died, Typhoid fever	P6,P79,FPH,SA1,CSR
Johnson, N.P.	Pvt	H 25th SCVI	Petersburg, VA	07/30/64	Pt. Lookout, MD	03/17/65	Exchanged	P114,P124
Johnson, Paul T.	Pvt	B 1st SCVIBn	James Island, SC	07/16/62	Ft. Columbus, NY	08/23/62	Ft. Delaware, DE	P37
Johnson, Peter	Pvt	A 8th SCVI	Winchester, VA	09/13/64	Harpers Ferry, WV	09/19/64	Camp Chase, OH	KEB,CSR
					Camp Chase, OH	06/11/65	Released G.O. #109	P22,CSR
Johnson, Peter	Pvt	I 13th SCVI	Deserted/enemy	02/26/65	City Pt., VA	02/28/65	Washington, DC	CSR,HOS
					Washington, D.C.	03/01/65	Savannah, GA oath	CSR
Johnson, Pleasant D.	Pvt	H 25th SCVI	Town Creek, NC	02/20/65	Ft. Anderson, NC	02/28/65	Pt. Lookout, MD	CSR
					Pt. Lookout, MD	06/28/64	Rlsd. G.O. #109	P114,CSR
Johnson, R.G.	Pvt	D 4th SCVC	Stony Creek, VA	12/01/64	City Pt., VA	03/05/65	Pt. Lookout, MD	CSR,CDC
					Pt. Lookout, MD	06/28/64	Rlsd. G.O. #109	P114,CSR
Johnson, Randolph S.	Pvt	C 1st SCVA	Bennettsville, SC	03/08/65	Kinston, NC	04/03/65	Pt. Lookout, MD	CSR
					Pt. Lookout, MD	06/28/65	Rlsd. G.O. #109	CSR
Johnson, Richard	Chp	C 1st SCVC	Bennettsville, SC	03/06/65	New Berne, NC			CSR
Johnson, Robert	Pvt	I 27th SCVI	Petersburg, VA	06/24/64	Bermuda Hundred, VA	06/25/64	Fts. Monroe, VA	CSR
					Fts. Monroe, VA	06/26/64	Pt. Lookout, MD	CSR
					Pt. Lookout, MD	08/16/64	Elmira, NY	P113,P120,CSR
					Elmira, NY	06/16/65	Rlsd. G.O. #109	P65,P66,CSR
Johnson, Robert	Pvt	G 4th SCVC	Stony Creek, VA	12/01/64	City Pt., VA	12/05/64	Pt. Lookout, MD	CSR
					Pt. Lookout, MD	06/28/65	Rlsd. G.O. #109	P1i4,CSR
Johnson, Robert C.	Sgt	C 27th SCVI	Town Creek, NC	02/20/65	Ft. Anderson, NC	02/28/65	Pt. Lookout, MD	CSR,HAG
					Pt. Lookout, MD		No other data	P114,CSR
Johnson, S.A.	Cpl	E 12th SCVI	Gettysburg, PA	07/04/63	David's Island, NY	10/22/63	Fts. Monroe, VA Xc	P1,LAN,CSR
					Richmond, VA G.H.	11/11/63	Died, Ch. Diarrhea	CSR

SOUTH CAROLINA SOLDIERS, SAILORS AND J CITIZENS HELD IN U.S. PRISONS 1861-1865

NAME	RANK	REGIMENT	CAPTURED AT	WHEN	PRISON	MOVED	DISPOSITION	SOURCES
Johnson, Simeon P.	Pvt	B 13th SCVI	Deep Bottom, VA	07/28/64	Ft. McHenry, MD	03/01/65	Elmira, NY	P110,HOS,CSR
					Elmira, NY	07/03/65	Rlsd. G.O. #109	P65,P66,CSR
Johnson, Simpson	Pvt	E 13th SCVI	Deserted/enemy	02/24/65	City Pt., VA	02/26/65	Washington, DC	CSR
					Washington, D.C.	02/27/65	New York, NY oath	CSR
Johnson, Thomas	Pvt	A 24th SCVI	Marietta, GA	07/03/64	Nashville, TN	07/13/64	Louisville, KY	CSR
					Louisville, KY	07/16/64	Camp Douglas, IL	CSR
					Camp Douglas, IL	02/21/85	Pt. Lookout, MD Xc	P55,CSR
					Pt. Lookout, MD	02/28/65	Exhanged	CSR
					Rchmnd. Rcvg. Hos.	03/01/65	Camp Lee, VA	CSR
Johnson, Thomas C.	Pvt	C 1st SCVIG	Richmond, VA Hos.	04/03/65	Escaped	05/11/65		SA1,CSR
Johnson, Thomas H.	Cpl	5 10/19 SCVI	Missionary Ridge, TN	11/25/63	Louisville, KY	12/20/63	Rock Island, IL	CSR
					Rock Island, IL	02/25/65	James R., VA Xc	CSR
					Richmond, VA Hos.	03/08/65	Furloughed 30 days	CSR
					Nashville, TN	12/07/63	Louisville, KY	P39,RAS,CSR
					Louisville, KY	12/09/63	Rock Island, IL	CSR
					Rock Island, IL	06/19/65	Rlsd. G.O. #109	CSR
Johnson, Thomas M.	Pvt	C 1st SCVA	Bennettsville, SC	03/08/65	New Berne, NC	04/03/65	Pt. Lookout, MD	CSR
					Pt. Lookout, MD	06/06/65	Released	P114,CSR
Johnson, Tyre H.	Pvt	H 16th SCVI	Deserted/enemy	05/24/64	Louisville, KY	05/27/64	Released on oath	CSR
Johnson, Tyre H.	Pvt	H 16th SCVI			Columbus, GA CSA H.	06/07/64	Issued clothing	CSR
Johnson, Tyre H.	Pvt	16/24 SCVI	Greensboro, NC	05/24/64	Greensboro, NC	05/01/65	SUR parole	CSR
Johnson, W. Ross	Pvt	B 3rd SCVI	Hanover Jctn., VA	05/25/64	White House, VA	06/08/64	Pt. Lookout, MD	CSR,KEB,SA2,H3
					Pt. Lookout, MD	07/08/64	Elmira, NY	P113,P120,CSR
					Elmira, NY	06/19/65	Rlsd. G.O. #109	P65,P66,CSR
Johnson, W.B.	Pvt	D 15th SCVI	Kershaw Dist., SC	02/04/65	New Berne, NC	04/10/65	Hart's Island, NY	CSR,KEB
					Hart's Island, NY	06/17/65	Rlsd. G.O. #109	P79,CSR
Johnson, W.D.	Pvt	F 22nd SCVI	Deserted/enemy	11/07/64	City Pt., VA	11/23/64	Washington, DC	CSR
					Washington, DC	11/25/64	New York, NY oath	CSR
Johnson, W.E.	2Lt	F 7th SCVC	Old Church, VA	05/30/64	White House, VA	06/08/64	Pt. Lookout, MD	CSR,ISH
					Pt. Lookout, MD	06/23/64	Ft. Delaware, DE	P113,P120,CSR
					Ft. Delaware, DE	08/20/64	Hilton Head, SC	P42,CSR
					Ft. Pulaski, GA			P4
					Hilton Head, SC	03/12/65	Ft. Delaware, DE	CSR
					Ft. Delaware, DE	06/16/65	Rlsd. G.O. #109	P43,P44,P45,CSR
Johnson, W.J.	Pvt	E 5th SCVC	Deserted/enemy	03/13/65	Charleston, SC	03/15/65	Released on oath	CSR
Johnson, W.N.	Cpl	C 22nd SCVI	Crater, Pbg., VA	07/30/64	City Pt., VA	08/05/64	Pt. Lookout, MD	CSR
					Pt. Lookout, MD	08/08/64	Elmira, NY	P113,P120,P125,CSR
					Elmira, NY	03/14/65	Pt. Lookout, MD Xc	P65,P66,CSR
Johnson, W.W.	Pvt	C 11th SCVI	Town Creek, NC	02/20/65	Ft. Anderson, NC	02/28/65	Pt. Lookout, MD	CSR
					Pt. Lookout, MD	06/28/65	Rlsd. G.O. #109	P114,CSR
Johnson, William	Pvt	Macbeth LA	Deserted/enemy		Knoxville, TN	02/27/65	Chattanooga, TN	CSR
					Louisville, KY	02/28/65	Sent north on oath	CSR
Johnson, William	Pvt	F 1st SCVIR	Fayetteville, NC	03/14/65	New Berne, NC	03/30/65	Pt. Lookout, MD	CSR,SA1
					Pt. Lookout, MD	06/06/65	Rlsd. on oath	CSR
Johnson, William	Pvt	F 18th SCVAB	Bentonville, NC	03/19/65	Pt. Lookout, MD	06/06/65	Rlsd. on oath	P114
Johnson, William	Pvt	G 26th SCVI	Five Forks, VA	04/01/65	City Pt., VA	04/05/65	Pt. Lookout, MD	CSR
					Pt. Lookout, MD	06/04/65	Released on oath	P114,CSR
Johnson, William A.	Pvt	F 2nd SCVI	Gettysburg, PA	07/03/63	Ft. Delaware, DE	08/13/64	Hos. 8/13-8/21/64	P47,SA2,H2
					Ft. Delaware, DE	09/16/64	Hos. 9/16-10/30/64	P47
					Ft. Delaware, DE	10/30/64	Pt. Lookout, MD	P40,P42,P44
					Ft. Delaware, DE	10/31/64	Venus Pt. GA Xc	SA2,H2,CSR
					Pt. Lookout, MD	10/31/64	Exchanged	P114,CSR

SOUTH CAROLINA SOLDIERS, SAILORS AND  CITIZENS HELD IN U.S. PRISONS 1861-1865

NAME	RANK	REGIMENT	CAPTURED AT	WHEN	PRISON	MOVED	DISPOSITION	SOURCES
Johnson, William D.	Pvt	E 26th SCVI	Five Forks, VA	04/01/65	City Pt., VA	04/05/65	Pt. Lookout, MD	CSR
					Pt. Lookout, MD	05/13/65	Died	P6,P114,FPH,CSR
Johnson, William H.	Pvt	A 15th SCVAB	NC or SC	03/28/65	New Berne, NC USGH	04/02/65	Died	P1,P6,CSR
Johnson, William L.	Cpl	K P.S.S.	Alexandria, VA	04/14/65	Alexandria, VA	04/14/65	Paroled	CSR,TSE
Johnson, William W.	Pvt	D 27th SCVI	Weldon RR, VA	08/21/64	City Pt., VA	08/24/64	Pt. Lookout, MD	CSR,HAG
					Pt. Lookout, MD	09/18/64	Exchanged	P113,CSR
					Richmond, VA Hos.	09/27/64	Died of wounds	CSR,HAG
Johnson, William W.	Pvt	I 2nd SCVC	Augusta, GA	05/25/65	Augusta, GA	05/25/00	Paroled	CSR
Johnson, Wyley	Pvt	A 1st SCVIR	Black Creek, NC	03/01/65	New Berne, NC	04/03/65	Pt. Lookout, MD	CSR,SA1
					Pt. Lookout, MD	06/28/65	Rlsd. G.O. #109	P114,CSR
Johnston, D.S.	Pvt	G Hol.Leg.	Petersburg, VA	04/04/65	Petersburg Hos.	04/09/65	Pt. of Rocks Hos.	CSR
					Pt. of Rocks Hos.	04/12/65	Fts. Monroe, VA	CSR
					Fts. Monroe, VA	07/16/65	Rlsd. G.O. #109	CSR
Johnston, H.F.	Cpl	B 6th SCVI	Stony Pt., VA	04/06/65	City Pt., VA	04/14/65	Newport News, VA	CSR
					Newport News, VA	06/26/65	Rlsd. G.O. #109	CSR
Johnston, J.F.	Pvt	E 17th SCVI	Tilla Town	09/17/62	New York, NY	10/06/62	Aikens Ldg., VA Xc	CSR
Johnston, Joseph E.	Pvt	6 10/19 SCVI	Missionary Ridge, TN	11/25/63	Nashville, TN	12/07/63	Louisville, KY	P39,CSR
					Louisville, KY	12/09/63	Rock Island, IL	CSR
					Rock Island, IL	06/19/65	Rlsd. G.O. #109	CSR
Johnston, S.R.	Pvt	G 6th SCVI	Richmond, VA Hos.	04/03/65	Libby Prison Rchmd.	04/23/65	Newport News, VA	CSR
					Newport News, VA	06/26/65	Rlsd. G.O. #109	CSR
Johnston, William A.	Pvt	A 27th SCVI	Town Creek, NC	02/20/65	Ft. Anderson, NC	02/28/65	Pt. Lookout, MD	CSR,HAG
					Pt. Lookout, MD	06/28/65	Rlsd. G.O. #109	P114
Johnston, William G.W.	Pvt	E 20th SCVI	Cedar Creek, VA	10/19/64	Harpers Ferry, WV	10/24/64	Pt. Lookout, MD	CSR
					Pt. Lookout MD	03/28/65	Aikens Ldg., VA Xc	CSR
Joiner, Edward	Pvt	H 17th SCVI	Richmond, VA Hos.	04/03/65	Richmobd, VA Hos.	04/15/65	Richmond, VA P.M.	CSR
					Libby Prison, Rchmd.	04/23/65	Newport News, VA	CSR
					Newport News, VA	06/26/65	Rlsd. G.O. #109	P107,CSR
Joiner, George W.	Sgt	E 22nd SCVI	Crater, Pbg., VA	07/30/64	City Pt., VA	08/05/64	Pt. Lookout, MD	CSR,LAN
					Pt. Lookout, MD	08/08/64	Elmira, NY	P113,P120,P125
					Elmira, NY	10/11/64	Venus Pt., GA Xc	CSR
					Elmira, NY	02/09/65	James R., VA Xc	CSR
Jolly, G. Wright	Pvt	H P.S.S.	Deserted/enemy	03/03/65	Bermuda Hundred, VA	03/04/65	Washington, DC	CSR
					Washington, DC	03/08/65	Boston, MA on oath	CSR
Jolly, Hugh H.	Cpl	B 10th SCVI	Atlanta, GA	07/28/64	Nashville, TN	08/30/64	Louisville, KY	CSR,RAS
					Louisville, KY	09/02/64	Camp Chase, OH	CSR
					Camp Chase, OH	06/11/65	Released G.O. #109	P22,CSR
Jolly, Joseph W.W.	Pvt	G 22nd SCVI	Petersburg, VA	03/25/65	City Pt., VA	03/28/65	Pt. Lookout, MD	CSR,UD3
					Pt. Lookout, MD	06/28/65	Rlsd. G.O. #109	P114
Jolly, Stephen	Cpl	K Hol.Leg.	Five Forks, VA	04/01/65	City Pt., VA	04/05/65	Pt. Lookout, MD	CSR
					Pt. Lookout, MD	06/28/65	Rlsd. G.O. #109	P114,CSR
Jones, A. Jackson	Pvt	I 6th SCVI	Augusta, GA	05/18/65	Augusta, GA	05/18/65	Paroled	CSR
Jones, Alfred N.	Cpl	F 3rd SCVABn	Augusta, GA	05/19/65	Augusta, GA	05/19/65	Paroled	CSR
Jones, Andrew P.	Pvt	F 3rd SCVABn	Augusta, GA	05/19/65	Augusta, GA	05/19/65	Paroled	CSR
Jones, B.B.	Pvt	H 2nd SCVI	Gettysburg, PA	07/03/63	W. Bldg. Balt, MD	07/30/63	Baltimore Jail	P1,SA2,H2
					W. Bldg. Balt, MD	08/20/63	Pt. Lookout, MD	CSR
					Pt. Lookout, MD	03/16/64	City Pt., VA Xc	P124,CSR
Jones, Benjamin A.	Sgt	D 14th SCVI	Sutherland Stn., VA	04/02/65	City Pt., VA	04/07/65	Hart's Island, NY	CSR,HOE
					Hart's Island, NY	06/16/65	Rlsd. G.O. #109	P79,CSR
Jones, Burrill	Pvt	22nd SCMil	Camden, SC	02/24/65	Hart's Island, NY	06/16/65	Rlsd. G.O. #109	P79

J

SOUTH CAROLINA SOLDIERS, SAILORS AND CITIZENS HELD IN U.S. PRISONS 1861-1865

NAME	RANK	REGIMENT	CAPTURED AT	WHEN	PRISON	MOVED	DISPOSITION	SOURCES
Jones, Caswell J.	Pvt	6 10/19 SCVI	Missionary Ridge, TN	11/25/63	Bridgeport, AL G.H.	12/11/63	Nashville, TN	P2,RAS,CSR
					Nashville, TN	12/16/63	Louisville, KY	P39,CSR
					Louisville, KY	12/21/63	Rock Island, IL	CSR
					Rock Island, IL	03/13/65	Tfd. to exchange	CSR
Jones, Chesley D.	Sgt	McQueen LA	Petersburg, VA	04/02/65	City Pt., VA	04/07/65	Pt. Lookout, MD	CSR
					Pt. Lookout, MD	06/28/65	Rlsd. G.O. #109	CSR
Jones, D. Henry	Sgt	A 25th SCVI	Ft. Fisher, NC	01/15/65	New York, NY	01/30/65	Elmira, NY	CSR,HAG
					Elmira, NY	06/17/65	Rlsd. G.O. #109	P65,P66,CSR
Jones, Daniel M.	Pvt	H 7th SCVIBn	Drury's Bluff, VA	05/16/64	Bermuda Hundred, VA	05/17/64	Fts. Monroe, VA	CSR,HAG
					Fts. Monroe, VA	05/19/64	Pt. Lookout, MD	CSR
					Pt. Lookout, MD	08/15/64	Elmira, NY	P113,P120,CSR
					Elmira, NY	10/10/64	Died, Ch. Diarrhea	P6,P65,P66,FPH,CSR
Jones, Dillon	Pvt	K 26th SCVI	Petersburg, VA	03/25/65	City Pt., VA	03/27/65	Pt. Lookout, MD	CSR
					Pt. Lookout, MD	06/28/65	Rlsd. G.O. #109	CSR
Jones, E.L.	Pvt	G 17th SCVI	Virginia	04/21/65	City Pt., VA	04/21/65	Washington, DC	CSR
					Washington, DC	04/21/65	Suffolk, VA	CSR
					Suffolk, VA	04/21/65	Released on oath	CSR
Jones, Edley	Sgt	H 2nd SCVIRi	Augusta, GA	05/27/65	Augusta, GA	05/27/65	Paroled	CSR
Jones, Edward J.	Pvt	E 18th SCVAB	Augusta, GA	05/23/65	Augusta, GA	05/23/65	Paroled	CSR
Jones, Elihu	Pvt	B 12th SCVI	Richmond, VA	04/02/65	Libby Prison, Rchmd.	04/10/65	Paroled	CSR
Jones, English	Pvt	K 1st SCVIR	Fayetteville, NC	03/09/65	New Berne, NC	03/30/65	Pt. Lookout, MD	CSR,SA1
					Pt. Lookout, MD	06/17/65	Rlsd. G.O. #109	P114,CSR
Jones, Evander	Sgt	H Orr's Ri.	Petersburg, VA	04/02/65	City Pt., VA	04/07/65	Hart's Island, NY	CSR,CDC
					Hart's Island, NY	07/18/65	David's Island, NY	P79,CSR
					David's Island, NY	07/21/65	Rlsd. G.O. #109	P1,CSR
Jones, George R.	Pvt	I 23rd SCVI	Petersburg, VA	03/25/65	City Pt., VA	03/26/65	Pt. Lookout, MD	CSR,HCL
					Pt. Lookout, MD	06/28/65	Rlsd. G.O. #109	P114,CSR
Jones, H.J.	Pvt	L 21st SCVI	Ft. Fisher, NC	01/15/65	Elmira, NY	06/19/65	Rlsd. G.O. #109	P66,CSR
Jones, H.N.	Pvt	H 17th SCVI	Crater, Pbg., VA	07/30/64	City Pt., VA	08/05/64	Pt. Lookout, MD	CSR
					Pt. Lookout, MD	08/08/64	Elmira, NY	P113,P120,CSR
					Elmira, NY	10/11/64	Prld. to exchange	CSR
					Pt. Lookout, MD	10/29/64	Venus Pt., GA Xc	P114,CSR
Jones, J. Quincy	Pvt	A Ham.Leg.	Richmond, VA	06/08/62	Fts. Monroe, VA G.H.	06/16/62	Died of wounds	CSR
Jones, J.C.P.	Pvt	Brooks LA	Harpers Farm, VA	04/06/65	City Pt., VA	04/14/65	Pt. Lookout, MD	CSR
					Pt. Lookout, MD	06/28/65	Rlsd. G.O. #109	CSR
Jones, J.E.	Sgt	G 7th SCVC	Burkeville, VA	04/14/65	Burkeville, VA	04/17/65	Paroled	CSR
Jones, J.F.	Pvt	G 17th SCVI	Augusta, GA	05/27/65	Augusta, GA	05/27/65	Paroled	CSR
Jones, J.H.	Pvt	G 26th SCVI	Deserted/enemy	02/25/65	City Pt., VA	02/28/65	Washington, DC	CSR
					Washington, DC	03/07/65	Phila., PA on oath	CSR
Jones, J.J.	Pvt	Ferguson's LA	Jackson, MS	07/15/63	Jackson, MS	07/30/63	Camp Morton, IN	CSR
					Snyder's Bluff, MS	08/07/63	Camp Morton, IN	CSR
					Camp Morton, IN	08/15/63	Jd. US 7th IN Cav.	CSR
Jones, J.T.	Pvt	L Orr's Ri.	Petersburg, VA	04/03/65	City Pt., VA	04/11/65	Hart's Island, NY	CSR
					Hart's Island, NY	06/16/65	Rlsd. G.O. #109	P79,CSR
Jones, J.W.	Sgt	A 14th SCVI	Spotsylvania, VA	05/10/64	Belle Plain, VA	05/20/64	Ft. Delaware, DE	CSR
					Ft. Delaware, DE	09/24/64	Hos. 9/24-10/11/64	P47
					Ft. Delaware, DE	11/01/64	Dis Hos. 1/21/65	P47
					Ft. Delaware, DE	06/10/65	Released G.O. #109	P41,P42,P45,CSR
Jones, Jack	Pvt	B 3rd SCVC	Deserted/enemy	02/18/65	Charleston, SC	03/15/65	Taken oath & disch.	CSR
Jones, James A.	Pvt	B 3rd SCVIBn	South Mtn., MD	09/14/62	Frederick, MD Hos.	12/13/62	Ft. McHenry, MD Xc	CSR
Jones, James A.	Pvt	L 21st SCVI	Ft. Fisher, NC	01/15/65	Elmira, NY	02/26/65	Died, Diarrhea	P6,P65,P66,FPH,HAG

J

SOUTH CAROLINA SOLDIERS, SAILORS AND CITIZENS HELD IN U.S. PRISONS 1861-1865

NAME	RANK	REGIMENT	CAPTURED AT	WHEN	PRISON	MOVED	DISPOSITION	SOURCES
Jones, James Ferdinand	Pvt	C 25th SCVI	Town Creek, NC	02/20/65	Ft. Anderson, NC	02/28/65	Pt. Lookout, MD	CSR,CTA,HAG
					Pt. Lookout, MD	06/28/65	Rlsd. G.O. #109	P114,CSR
Jones, James M.	Pvt	F Hol.Leg.	Jarratts Stn., VA	05/08/64	Fts. Monroe, VA	05/13/64	Pt. Lookout, MD	CSR
					Pt. Lookout, MD	06/25/64	Joined U.S. Army	P113,P125,CSR
Jones, James McD.	Pvt	Brooks LA	Harpers Farm, VA	04/06/65	City Pt., VA	04/14/65	Pt. Lookout, MD	CSR
					Pt. Lookout, MD	06/28/65	Rlsd. G.O. #109	CSR
Jones, James Robert	Cpl	F 2nd SCVI	Goldsboro, NC	03/19/65	New Berne, NC	03/30/65	Pt. Lookout, MD	CSR,SA2,H2
					Pt. Lookout, MD	06/28/65	Rlsd. G.O. #109	P114,CSR
Jones, James W.	Pvt	H P.S.S.	South Mtn., MD	09/14/62	Ft. Delaware, DE	10/02/62	Aikens Ldg., VA Xc	CSR
					Aikens Ldg., VA	11/10/62	Exchanged	CSR
Jones, John B.	Pvt	E 14th SCVI	Gettysburg, PA	07/05/63	David's Island, NY	10/22/63	Fts. Monroe, VA	P1,CSR
					Fts. Monroe, VA	10/28/63	City Pt., VA Xc	CSR
Jones, John C.	Pvt	G 2nd SCVI	Bentonville, NC	03/19/65	Pt. Lookout, MD	06/28/65	Rlsd. G.O. #109	P114,H2,CSR
Jones, John L.	Cpt	D 7th SCVIBn	Weldon RR, VA	08/21/64	Old Capitol, MD	08/27/64	Ft. Delaware, DE	P110,HAG,CSR
					Ft. McHenry, MD	08/27/64	Ft. Delaware, DE	P110
					Ft. Delaware, DE	05/30/65	Rlsd.O.O. G. Grant	P7,P42,P46,CSR
Jones, John L.	Pvt	C 10th SCVI	Macon, GA	04/29/65	Macon, GA	04/29/65	Paroled	CSR,RAS,CEN
Jones, John S.	Pvt	H 23rd SCVI	Deserted/enemy	12/04/64	City Pt., VA	12/13/64	Phila., PA on oath	P8,HMC,CSR
Jones, L.W.	Pvt	K 16th SCVI	Greenville, SC	05/23/65	Greenville, SC	05/23/65	Paroled on oath	CSR
Jones, Milton	Pvt	D 26th SCVI	Deserted/enemy	06/06/64	Fts. Monroe, VA	06/27/64	Release not given	P8,CSR
Jones, Newton B.	Pvt	Brooks LA	Harpers Farm, VA	04/06/65	City Pt., VA	04/14/65	Pt. Lookout, MD	CSR
					Pt. Lookout, MD	06/28/65	Rlsd. G.O. #109	CSR
Jones, O.T.	Pvt	H 2nd SCVIRi	Richmond, VA Hos.	04/03/65	Richmond, VA Hos.	04/09/65	Smallpox Hospital	CSR
					Richmond, VA Hos.	05/17/65	Released on oath	CSR
Jones, P.C.	Sgt	A 3rd SCVI	Sharpsburg, MD	09/17/62	Frederick, MD USGH	12/13/62	Baltimore, MD	CSR
					Ft. McHenry, MD	12/14/62	City Pt., VA Xc	CSR
Jones, Robert M.	Pvt	G 18th SCVI	Petersburg, VA	03/25/65	City Pt., VA	03/28/65	Pt. Lookout, MD	CSR
					Pt. Lookout, MD	06/28/65	Rlsd. G.O. #109	P114,CSR
Jones, Rufus G.	Cpl	C 3rd SCVABn	Augusta, GA	05/18/65	Augusta, GA	05/18/65	Paroled	CSR
Jones, Seaberry	Pvt	F 15th SCVI	Sharpsburg, MD	09/17/62	Ft. McHenry, MD	10/17/62	Fts. Monroe, VA	CSR
					Fts. Monroe, VA	10/19/62	Aikens Ldg., VA Xc	CSR
Jones, Sidney S.	Pvt	4 10/19 SCVI	Missionary Ridge, TN	11/25/63	Nashville, TN	12/07/63	Louisville, KY	P39,RAS,CSR
					Louisville, KY	12/09/63	Rock Island, IL	CSR
					Rock Island, IL	06/20/65	Rlsd. G.O. #109	CSR
Jones, Starke	Pvt	Brooks LA	Farmville, VA	04/11/65	Farmville, VSA	04/21/65	Paroled	CSR
Jones, Thomas	Pvt	I 27th SCVI	Weldon RR, VA	08/21/64	City Point, VA USH	08/21/64	Died of wounds	P12
Jones, Thomas	Pvt	F Hol.Leg.	Five Forks, VA	04/01/65	City Pt., VA	04/05/65	Pt. Lookout, MD	CSR
					Pt. Lookout, MD	06/28/65	Rlsd. G.O. #109	P114,CSR
Jones, Thomas S.	Pvt	H 1st SCVIG	Gettysburg, PA	07/04/63	Letterman Hos., PA	08/10/63	Died of wounds	P1,P5,P12,SA1,CSR
Jones, Thornton F.	Pvt	C 22nd SCVI	Boonesboro, MD	09/14/62	Frederick, MD P.M.	10/03/62	Baltimore, MD Prld	CSR
					Baltimore, MD	11/11/62	Died of wounds	CSR
Jones, W.N.	Pvt	A 16th SCVI	Greenville, SC	05/23/65	Greenville, SC	05/23/65	Paroled on oath	CSR
Jones, W.S.	Pvt	H 6th SCVI	Richmond, VA Hos.	04/03/65	Richmond, VA Hos.	05/06/65	Died of disease	P6,CSR
Jones, W.W.	Pvt	B 2nd SCVIRi	Gaines' Mill, VA	06/28/62	Ft. Columbus, NY	07/09/62	Ft. Delaware, DE	CSR
					Ft. Delaware, DE	08/05/62	Aikens Ldg., VA Xc	CSR
Jones, Wesley	Pvt	H Orr's Ri.	Hatcher's Run, VA	04/02/65	City Pt., VA	04/11/65	Hart's Island, NY	CSR
					Hart's Island, NY	04/15/65	David's Island, NY	CSR
					David's Island, NY	04/26/65	Hart's Island, NY	CSR
					Hart's Island, NY	06/15/65	Rlsd. G.O. #109	P79,CSR

SOUTH CAROLINA SOLDIERS, SAILORS AND  CITIZENS HELD IN U.S. PRISONS 1861-1865

NAME	RANK	REGIMENT	CAPTURED AT	WHEN	PRISON	MOVED	DISPOSITION	SOURCES
Jones, William	Pvt	B 23rd SCVI	Petersburg, VA	06/17/64	Pt. Lookout, MD	07/27/64	Elmira, NY	P113,P114,P120,CSR
					Elmira, NY	10/11/64	Pt. Lookout, MD Xc	P65,P66
					Pt. Lookout, MD	10/28/64	Died, Ch. Diarrhea	P6,P12,FPH,CSR
Jones, William	Pvt	D 26th SCVI	Hatchers Run, VA	03/29/65	City Pt., VA	04/05/65	Pt. Lookout, MD	CSR
					Pt. Lookout, MD	06/28/65	Rlsd. G.O. #109	P114,HOM,CSR
Jones, William H.	Pvt	H 7th SCVIBn	Drury's Bluff, VA	05/16/63	Bermuda Hundred, VA	05/16/64	Fts. Monroe, VA Hos.	CSR,HAG
					Fts. Monroe, VA Hos.	05/17/64	Aexandria, VA USGH	CSR
					Fts. Monroe, VA US	06/05/64	Died of wounds	P12,ROH,CSR
Jones, William Isaac	Pvt	E 17th SCVI	Petersburg, VA	03/25/65	City Pt., VA	03/28/65	Pt. Lookout, MD	CSR,YEB
					Pt. Lookout, MD	06/28/65	Rlsd. G.O. #109	P114,CSR
Jones, William N.	Pvt	K 11th SCVI	Town Creek, NC	02/20/65	Ft. Anderson, NC	02/28/65	Pt. Lookout, MD	CSR
					Pt. Lookout, MD	06/28/65	Rlsd. G.O. #109	P114,CSR
Jones, William S.	Pvt	F 24th SCVI	Missionary Ridge, TN	11/25/63	Nashville, TN	12/05/63	Louisville, KY	P39,CSR
					Louisville, KY	12/06/63	Rock Island, IL	CSR
					Rock Island, IL	04/02/64	Died, Erysipilas	P12,CSR
Jones, William T.	Pvt	F 24th SCVI	Missionary Ridge, TN	11/25/63	Nashville, TN	12/05/63	Louisville, KY	P39,EFW
					Louisville, KY	12/06/63	Rock Island, IL	CSR
					Rock Island, IL	03/07/65	Released on oath	CSR
Jones, Willis R.	Sgt	A 13th SCVI	Gettysburg, PA	07/04/63	David's Island, NY	08/24/63	City Pt., VA Xc	P1,CSR
Jones, Wilrick	Pvt	A Ham.Leg.	Warrenton, VA	09/29/62	Warrenton, VA	09/29/62	Paroled	CSR
Joniken, William	Pvt	H 14th SCVI	Petersburg, VA		Washington, DC	04/21/65	Ft. Powhatan, VA	CSR
Jordan, A.	Pvt	I 18th SCVI	Richmond VA Hos.	04/03/65	Provost Marshal	05/08/65	Paroled	CSR
Jordan, A.	Pvt	E 21st SCVI	Chesterfield, SC	03/03/65	Hart's Island, NY	06/16/65	Rlsd. G.O. #109	P79,HAG
Jordan, Andrew	Pvt	H 14th SCVI	Gettysburg, PA	07/05/63	Ft. McHenry, MD	07/12/63	Ft. Delaware, DE	CSR
					Ft. Delaware, DE	02/23/65	Hos. 2/23-4/15/65	P47
					Ft. Delaware, DE	06/17/65	Rlsd. G.O. #109	P44,P45,CSR
Jordan, Andrew Fuller	2Lt	H 14th SCVI	Gettysburg, PA	07/02/63	Chester, PA G.H.	08/31/63	Johnson's Isl., OH	P1,CSR
					Johnson's Isl., OH	03/14/65	Pt. Lookout, MD	P82
					Pt. Lookout, MD	03/14/65	City Pt., VA Xc	CSR
Jordan, Bryant	Pvt	A 26th SCVI	Hatchers Run, VA	03/29/65	City Pt., VA	04/02/65	Pt. Lookout, MD	CSR
					Pt. Lookout, MD	06/28/65	Rlsd. G.O. #109	P114,CSR
Jordan, Elijah	Pvt	H 1st SCVA	Morris Island, SC	07/10/63	Hilton Head, SC			CSR
Jordan, Ezekiel	Pvt	I 1st SCVA	Goldsboro, NC	03/10/65	New Berne, NC	03/30/65	Pt. Lookout, MD	CSR
					Pt. Lookout, MD	06/28/65	Rlsd. G.O. #109	P114,CSR
Jordan, George W.	Pvt	E 1st SCVIR	Kershaw, SC	03/01/65	New Berne, NC	03/30/65	Pt. Lookout, MD	CSR,SA1
					Pt. Lookout, MD	06/28/65	Rlsd. G.O. #109	P114,CSR
Jordan, Green B.	Pvt	E 16th SCVI	Nashville, TN	11/26/63	Nashville, TN	12/09/63	Louisville, KY	P39,16R,CSR
Jordan, Green B.	Pvt	E 16th SCVI	Ringgold, GA	11/26/63	Rock Island, IL	01/25/64	Jd. US Navy	CSR
					Louisville, KY	12/11/63	Rock Island, IL	CSR
Jordan, Henry	Pvt	G 27th SCVI	Petersburg, VA	06/18/64	City Pt., VA	06/24/64	Pt. Lookout, MD	CSR,HAG
					Pt. Lookout, MD	10/11/64	Exchanged	P113,CSR
Jordan, J.J.	Sgt	F 26th SCVI	Drury's Bluff, VA	05/20/64	Hammond GH Pt. LO	05/23/64	Died of wounds	P6,P12,FPH,CSR
Jordan, James	Pvt	Ferguson's LA	Ringgold, GA	11/26/63	Nashville, TN	12/11/63	Louisville, KY	P39,CSR
					Louisville, KY	12/11/63	Rock Island, IL	CSR
					Rock Island, IL	04/21/65	Rlsd. on oath	CSR
Jordan, John B.	Pvt	B 26th SCVI	Amelia C.H., VA	04/03/65	City Pt., VA	04/13/65	Pt. Lookout, MD	CSR
					Pt. Lookout, MD	06/06/65	Released on oath	P114,CSR
Jordan, John M.	Pvt	Palmetto LA	Amelia C.H., VA	04/05/65	City Pt., VA	04/08/65	Pt. Lookout, MD	CSR
					Pt. Lookout, MD	06/28/65	Rlsd. G.O. #109	CSR
Jordan, John Walker	Cpl	F 6th SCVC	Louisa C.H., VA	06/11/64	Pt. Lookout, MD	07/25/64	Elmira, NY	P120,CAG,CSR
					Elmira, NY	09/22/64	Died, Diarrhea	P6,P7,P12,P65,FPH

SOUTH CAROLINA SOLDIERS, SAILORS AND  CITIZENS HELD IN U.S. PRISONS 1861-1865

NAME	RANK	REGIMENT	CAPTURED AT	WHEN	PRISON	MOVED	DISPOSITION	SOURCES
Jordan, Lemuel B.	Pvt	A 17th SCVI	Petersburg, VA	03/25/65	City Pt., VA	03/28/65	Pt. Lookout, MD	CSR,HHC
					Pt. Lookout, MD	06/28/65	Rlsd. G.O. #109	P114,CSR
Jordan, Lovic A.	Pvt	A 6th SCVC	Stony Creek, VA	12/01/64	Pt. Lookout, MD	06/12/65	Released G.O. #85	P114,CSR
Jordan, Moses	Pvt	G 3rd SC	Florence, SC	03/05/65	New Berne, NC	04/03/65	Pt. Lookout, MD	CSR
					Pt. Lookout, MD	06/28/65	Rlsd. G.O. #109	P114,CSR
Jordan, Napoleon B.	Pvt	I 1st SCVA	Morris Island, SC	07/10/63	Hilton Head, SC	09/05/63	Ft. Columbus, NY	P1,CSR
					Ft. Columbus, NY	09/23/63	Took the oath	P1,CSR
Jordan, Nelson T.	Pvt	C 15th SCVAB	Cheraw, SC	03/06/65	New Berne, NC	04/03/65	Pt. Lookout, MD	CSR
					Pt. Lookout, MD	06/28/65	Rlsd. G.O. #109	P114,CSR
Jordan, Orin D.	Pvt	A 7th SCVI	Florence, SC	03/05/65	New Berne, NC	04/03/65	Pt. Lookout, MD	CSR
					Pt. Lookout, MD	06/28/65	Rlsd. G.O. #109	P114,CSR
Jordan, Seth A.	Sgt	G 19th SCVI	Murfreesboro, TN	12/31/62	CSA Hospital #2 Mf	04/17/63	Nashville, TN	CSR
					Nashville, TN	04/17/63	Louisville, KY	P38,CSR
					Louisville, KY	04/27/63	City Pt., VA Xc	CSR
					Ft. McHenry, MD	05/30/63	City Pt., VA Xc	CSR
Jordan, Thomas M.	Pvt	E 21st SCVI	Morris Island, SC	07/10/63	Morris Island, SC	07/13/63	Hilton Head, SC	CSR
					Hilton Head G.H.	07/23/63	Morris Island, SC Xc	P2,HAG,CSR
Jordan, Uriah	Pvt	A 17th SCVI	Petersburg, VA	04/02/65	City Pt., VA	04/04/65	Pt. Lookout, MD	CSR,HHC
					Pt. Lookout, MD	06/28/65	Rlsd. G.O. #109	P114,HHC,CSR
Jordan, W.J.	Pvt	B 26th SCVI	Petersburg, VA	06/24/64	City Pt., VA	06/30/64	Pt. Lookout, MD	CSR
					Pt. Lookout, MD	12/30/64	Died, Ac. Diarrhea	P6,P113,FPH,CSR
Jordan, William	Sgt	B 19th SCVI	Atlanta, GA	07/22/64	Marietta, GA P.M.	07/24/64	Nashville, TN	CSR
					Nashville, TN	07/29/64	Louisville, KY	CSR
					Louisville, KY	07/31/64	Camp Chase, OH	CSR
					Camp Chase, OH	03/04/65	City Pt., VA Xc	P22,P26,CSR
					Augusta, GA	05/24/65	Paroled on oath	CSR
Jordan, William King	Pvt	I 21st SCVI	Petersburg, VA	06/24/64	Pt. Lookout, MD	08/16/64	Elmira, NY	P113,P120,HAG
					Elmira, NY	09/16/64	Died, Ch. Diarrhea	P6,P12,P65,P66,FPH
Jordan, William T.	Cpl	6 10/19 SCVI	Missionary Ridge, TN	11/25/63	Nashville, TN	12/07/63	Louisville, KY	P39,RAS
					Louisville, KY	12/07/63	Rock Island, IL	CSR
					Rock Island, IL	05/03/65	New Orleans, LA Xc	CSR
					New Orleans, LA	05/23/65	Exchanged	P3
Jordan. James	Pvt	A SC Militia	Florence, SC	03/05/65	Pt. Lookout, MD	06/28/65	Rlsd. G.O. #109	P114
Jordon, Sidney M.	Pvt	A 9th SCVIBn	Secessionville, SC	06/16/62	Ft. Columbus, NY	08/23/62	Ft. Delaware, DE	P37,CSR
Jordon, W.D.	Pvt	B 3rd SCVC	Pocotaligo, SC	08/22/62	Hilton Head, SC	11/02/01	Ft. Columbus, NY	CSR
					Ft. Columbus, NY	11/21/62	Ft. Delaware, DE	CSR
					Ft. Delaware, DE	12/15/62	Fts. Monroe, VA Xc	CSR
Joseph, Alfred H.	Pvt	K 2nd SCVI	Harrisonburg, PA	09/25/64	Harpers Ferry, WV	10/01/64	Pt. Lookout, MD	CSR,SA2,H2
					Pt. Lookout, MD	10/14/64	Joined US Army	CSR
Josey, David Wilson	Pvt	K 23rd SCVI	Five Forks, VA	04/01/65	City Pt., VA	04/06/65	Pt. Lookout, MD	CSR
					Pt. Lookout, MD	06/28/65	Rlsd. G.O. #109	P114,K23,CSR
Josey, Elijah R.	Sgt	K 23rd SCVI	Five Forks, VA	04/01/65	City Pt., VA	04/05/65	Pt. Lookout, MD	CSR
					Pt. Lookout, MD	06/28/65	Rlsd. G.O. #109	P114,K23,CSR
Josey, Joshua J.	Sgt	H 1st SCVIG	Gettysburg, PA	07/05/63	Chester, PA G.H.	09/21/63	City Pt., VA Xc	P1,SA1,CSR
Josey, Joshua J.	Sgt	H 1st SCVIG	Sutherland Stn., VA	04/06/65	City Pt., VA	04/11/65	Pt. Lookout, MD	CSR
					Pt. Lookout, MD	06/28/65	Rlsd. G.O. #109	P114,CSR
Josey, Thomas J.	Pvt	K 23rd SCVI	Five Forks, VA	04/01/65	City Pt., VA	04/06/65	Pt. Lookout, MD	CSR
					Pt. Lookout, MD	06/28/65	Rlsd. G.O. #109	P114,K23,CSR
Joshua, W.B.	Pvt	K 16th SCVI	Greensboro, NC	05/03/65	Greensboro, NC	05/03/65	Paroled	CSR
Jowers, F.M.	Pvt	A 17th SCVI	Petersburg, VA	04/03/65	City Pt., VA, NY	04/07/65	Hart's Island, NY	CSR
					Hart's Island, NY	04/13/65	Died, Phthisis	P79,FPH,CSR

J

SOUTH CAROLINA SOLDIERS, SAILORS AND CITIZENS HELD IN U.S. PRISONS 1861-1865

NAME	RANK	REGIMENT	CAPTURED AT	WHEN	PRISON	MOVED	DISPOSITION	SOURCES
Jowers, J.W.	Pvt	A 23rd SCVI	Chesterfield, SC	02/25/65	New Berne, NC	04/08/65	Hart's Island, NY	CSR
					Hart's Island, SC	05/29/65	Died, Ch. Diarrhea	P6,P79,FPH,CSR
Jowers, Thomas	Pvt	H 1st SCVIR	Savannah, GA	12/21/64	Ft. Delaware, DE	05/05/65	Hos. 5/5/65-?	P47
					Ft. Delaware, DE	07/30/65	Died, Scurvy	P6,P41,P42,P47,FPH
Joy, L.W.	Sgt	K 23rd SCVI	Five Forks, VA	04/02/65	City Pt., VA	04/06/65	Pt. Lookout, MD	CSR
					Pt. Lookout, MD	06/28/65	Rlsd. G.O. #109	CSR
Joyce, James R.	Pvt	B Orr's Ri.	Fredericksburg, VA	05/03/63	Washington, DC	05/10/63	City Pt., VA Xc	CSR
					Ft. McHenry, MD	05/11/63	City Pt., VA Xc	P110
Joyner, Hiram G.	Pvt	I 17th SCVI	Petersburg, VA	03/25/65	City Pt., VA	03/28/65	Pt. Lookout, MD	CSR
					Pt. Lookout, MD	06/28/65	Rlsd. G.O. #109	P114,CSR
Joyner, J.A.	Pvt	Lafayette LA	Pocotaligo, SC	01/16/65	Hilton Head, SC	02/14/65	Pt. Lookout, MD	CSR
					Pt. Lookout, MD	06/28/65	Rlsd. G.O. #109	CSR
Joyner, Paul H.	Pvt	A 2nd SCVI	Gettysburg, PA	07/04/63	Gettysburg G.H.	07/20/63	Provost Marshal	P4,CSR,KEB,SA2,H2
					David's Island, NY	08/24/63	City Pt., VA Xc	P1,CSR
Joyner, Paul H.	Pvt	A 2nd SCVI	Cedar Creek, VA	10/19/64	Harpers Ferry, WV	10/23/64	Pt. Lookout, MD	CSR
					Pt. Lookout, MD	03/28/65	Exchanged	P114,P124
Judy, Jacob	Pvt	A 9th SCVIH	Hilton Head, SC	10/02/61	Str. *Coatzacoalcos*			CSR
Julien, John	Pvt	B 37th VAVCB	Rockbridge Co., VA	06/17/64	Wheeling, WV	07/11/64	Camp Chase, OH	CSR
					Camp Chase, OH	03/09/65	City Pt., VA	CSR
					City Pt., VA	03/09/65	Boulwares Wh., VA	CSR
Jumper, Daniel A.	Pvt	C 15th SCVI	Sharpsburg, MD	09/17/62	Ft. McHenry, MD	10/17/62	Fts. Monroe, VA	CSR
					Fts. Monroe, VA	10/19/62	Aikens Ldg., VA XC	CSR
Jumper, Daniel A.	Pvt	C 15th SCVI	Halltown, WV	08/26/64	Harpers Ferry, WV	08/29/64	Camp Chase, OH	CSR
					Camp Chase, OH	03/18/65	Pt. Lookout, MD Xc	P22,P26,KEB,CSR
					Pt. Lookout, MD	03/27/65	Boulware's Wh. Xc	CSR
Jumper, James Wade	Pvt	C 15th SCVI	South Mtn., MD	09/14/62	Frederick, MD USH		Ft. McHenry, MD	CSR
Jumper, James Wade	Pvt	C 15th SCVI	South Mtn., MD	10/03/62	Ft. McHenry, MD	11/12/62	Paroled to Xc	CSR,H15,CSR
Jumper, James Wade	1Sg	C 15th SCVI	Wilderness, VA	05/06/64			Exchanged	H15,KEB,CSR
Jumper, James.B.	Cit	Lexington	Lancaster Dist., SC	02/24/65	Hart's Island, NY	06/20/65	Rlsd. G.O. #109	P79
June, Adam H.	Pvt	G 15th SCVI	Gettysburg, PA	07/05/63	Ft. McHenry, MD	07/08/63	Ft. Delaware, DE	CSR,KEB,CTA
					Ft. Delaware, DE	10/11/63	Died, Typhoid	P5,P40,P44,P47,FPH
June, Samuel N.	Pvt	C 25th SCVI	Ft. Fisher, NC	01/15/65	New York, NY	01/30/65	Elmira, NY	CSR,HAG,CTA
					Elmira, NY	07/19/65	Rlsd. G.O. #109	P66
June, Theodore G.	Pvt	G 15th SCVI	Boonesboro, MD	09/15/62	Ft. Delaware, DE	10/02/62	Aikens Ldg., VA Xc	H15,CSR,KEB
Justi, William	Pvt	G 24th SCVI	Missionary Ridge, TN	11/28/63	Nashville, TN	12/02/63	Louisville, KY	P39,CSR
					Louisville, KY	12/03/63	Rock Island, IL	CSR
Justi, William	Pvt	F 24th SCVI	Missionary Ridge, TN	11/28/63	Rock Island, IL	05/16/65	Released on oath	CSR
Justice, Francis	Cpl	Waccamaw A	Santee R., SC	02/27/63	Gunboat Quaker Cit.	03/16/63	New York, NY P.M.	CSR
					Sandusky, OH	04/06/63	Fts. Monroe, VA Xc	CSR
Justus, J.F.	Pvt	D 22nd SCVI	Kinston, NC	12/15/62	Kinston, NC	12/15/62	Kinston, NC	CSR
Justus, J.F.	Pvt	D 22nd SCVI	Bermuda Hundred, VA	06/02/64	Bermuda Hundred, VA	06/03/64	Fts. Monroe, VA	CSR
					Fts. Monroe, VA	06/04/64	Pt. Lookout, MD	CSR
					Pt. Lookout, MD	08/27/64	Died, Dysentery	P5,P12,P113,FPH

SOUTH CAROLINA SOLDIERS, SAILORS AND  CITIZENS HELD IN U.S. PRISONS 1861-1865

NAME	RANK	REGIMENT	CAPTURED AT	WHEN	PRISON	MOVED	DISPOSITION	SOURCES
Kadle, James M.	Pvt	F 7th SCVI	Gettysburg, PA	07/03/63	Gettysburg G.H.		Provost Marshal	P4,HOE
					Ft. McHenry, MD	07/08/63	Ft. Delaware, DE	CSR
					Ft. Delaware, DE	11/05/63	Died, Scurvy	P5,P12,P40,P44,P47,FPH
Kail, Galley	Sgt	German Art	Deserted/enemy		Hilton Head, SC	12/18/64		P8
Kaler, James E.	Pvt	C 25th SCVI	Ft. Fisher, NC	01/15/65	New York, NY	01/30/65	Elmira, NY	CSR,HAG,CTA
					Elmira, NY	02/20/65	James R., VA Xc	P65,P66,WHR
Kanaday, T.F.	Pvt	F Orr's Ri.	Falling Waters, MD	07/14/63	Baltimore, MD	08/17/63	Pt. Lookout, MD	CSR,CDC
					Pt. Lookout, MD	08/16/64	Elmira, NY	P113,CSR
					Elmira, NY	03/10/65	Pt. Lookout, MD Xc	P65,P66,P124,CSR
Kanah, William	Pvt	C 1st SCVIR	Deserted/enemy		Charleston, SC		Released on oath	CSR
Kane, Lawrence	Cit		Bentsville, VA	04/06/65	W. Bldg. Balt, MD	05/09/65	Ft. McHenry, MD	P1
Kane, Thomas	Pvt	D 1st SCVA	Charlestown, WV	08/08/64	Ft. McHenry, MD	09/19/64	Ft. Delaware, DE	P110
					Old Capitol, DC	09/19/64	Ft. Delaware, DE	CSR
					Ft. Delaware, DE	04/27/65	Rlsd, oath/neutral	P42,P46,P47,CSR
Kaney, John	Pvt	F P.s.s.	Williamsburg, VA	05/05/62	Washington, DC Hos.	08/26/62	Old Capitol, DC	CSR
					Old Capitol, DC	09/01/62	Fts. Monroe, VA Xc	CSR
Karick, E.D.	Pvt	E 1st SCVC	Madison C.H., VA	09/22/63	Ft. McHenry, MD	09/23/63	Ft. Delaware, DE	P110
					Old Capitol, DC	09/26/63	Pt. Lookout, MD	CSR
					Pt. Lookout, MD	09/18/64	Exchanged	P113,P124,CSR
Karrigan, Ambrose	Pvt	B 27th SCVI	Ft. Anderson, NC	02/19/65	Ft. Anderson, NC	02/28/65	Pt. Lookout, MD	CSR
					Pt. Lookout, MD	05/13/65	Rlsd. G.O. #85	P114,CSR
Katon, John	Pvt	A 1st SCVIR	Smith's Ford, NC	03/16/65	Pt. Lookout, MD	06/28/65	Rlsd. G.O. #109	CSR
Kavanaugh, Thomas D.	Pvt	D 2nd SCVI	Bentonville, NC	03/19/65	New Berne, NC	04/03/64	Pt. Lookout, MD	CSR,SA2,KEB,H2
					Pt. Lookout, MD	06/28/65	Rlsd. G.O. #109	P114,CSR
Kay, George W.	Pvt	Ferguson's	Salisbury, NC	04/12/65	Nashville, TN	04/29/65	Louisville, KY	P39,CSR
					Louisville, KY	05/02/65	Camp Chase, OH	CSR
					Camp Chase, OH	06/13/65	Rlsd. G.O. #109	P23,CSR
Kay, Marcus	Cpl	L Orr's Ri.	Deserted/enemy	02/16/65	City Pt., VA	02/18/65	Washington, DC	CSR
					Washington, DC	02/21/65	White County, Il	CSR
Kay, Robert M.	Pvt	K Orr's Ri.	Petersburg, VA	04/03/65	City Pt., VA	04/11/65	Hart's Island, NY	CSR,CDC
					Hart's Island, NY	05/20/65	Died, Typhoid Pneum.	P6,P12,P79,FPH,CSR
Kay, W.R.	Pvt	E 20th SCVI	Cedar Creek, VA	10/19/64	W. Bldg. Balt, MD	10/27/64	Pt. Lookout, MD	P1,KEB,CSR
					Pt. Lookout, MD	10/29/64	Exchanged	P114,CSR
Kean, William L.	Pvt	B 5th SCVC	Wilson's Ldg., VA	06/06/64	Fts. Monroe, VA	06/12/64	Pt. Lookout, MD	CSR
					Pt. Lookout, MD	07/09/64	Elmira, NY	P113,P120,CSR
					Pt. Lookout, MD	10/29/64	Venus Pt., GA Xc	P114,CSR
Kearse, C.J.	Pvt	G 3rd SCVC	Augusta, GA	05/19/65	Augusta, GA	05/19/65	Paroled	CSR
Kearse, H.W.	Pvt	F 3rd SCVC	South Newport, GA	08/17/64	Philadelphia, PA	01/10/65	Ft. Delaware, DE	CSR
					Ft. Delaware, DE	01/22/65	Hos. 1/22-2/10/65	P47
					Ft. Delaware, DE	06/10/65	Rlsd. G.O. #109	P41,P42,45,CSR
Kearse, Oliver P.	Pvt	G 17th SCVI	Petersburg, VA	03/25/65	City Pt., VA	03/28/65	Pt. Lookout, MD	CSR
					Pt. Lookout, MD	06/28/65	Rlsd. G.O. #109	P114,CSR
Kearse, W.M.	2Lt	C 19th SCVCB	Augusta, GA	05/26/65	Augusta, GA	05/26/65	Paroled on oath	CSR
Kearse, William J.	Pvt	G 17th SCVI	Petersburg, VA	03/25/65	City Pt., VA	03/28/65	Pt. Lookout, MD	CSR
					Pt. Lookout, MD	06/28/65	Rlsd. G.O. #109	P114,CSR
Keasler, Henry C.	Pvt	L P.S.S.	Deserted/enemy	10/07/64	Bermuda Hundred, VA	10/22/64	City Pt., VA P.M.	CSR,TSE
					City Pt., VA	10/22/64	Illinois on oath	CSR
Keasler, William L.	Pvt	C Orr's Ri.	Falling Waters, MD	07/14/63	Frederick, MD G.H.	08/07/63	W. Bldg. Balt, MD	P1
					W. Bldg. Balt, MD	08/22/63	City Pt., VA Xc	P1,CSR
Keaton, James	Pvt	H 12th SCVI	Spotsylvania, VA	05/12/64	Belle Plain, VA	05/20/64	Ft. Delaware, DE	CSR
					Ft. Delaware, DE	02/27/65	City Pt., VA Xc	CSR
					Richmond, VA Hos.	03/16/65	Furloughed 60 days	CSR

SOUTH CAROLINA SOLDIERS, SAILORS AND  CITIZENS HELD IN U.S. PRISONS 1861-1865

NAME	RANK	REGIMENT	CAPTURED AT	WHEN	PRISON	MOVED	DISPOSITION	SOURCES
Keaton, John	Pvt	A 1st SCVIR	Smith's Ford, NC	03/16/65	New Berne, NC	04/03/65	Pt. Lookout, MD	CSR
					Pt. Lookout, MD	06/28/65	Rlsd. G.O. #109	CSR
Kee, R.R.	Pvt	I 17th SCVI	Petersburg, VA		Pt. Lookout, MD	08/08/64	Elmira, NY	P125
Kee, William L.	Pvt	A 17th SCVI	Crater, Pbg., VA	07/30/64	Elmira, NY	06/19/64	Pt. Lookout, MD Xc	P66,HHC
Kee, William L.	Pvt	A 17th SCVI	Petersburg, VA	03/25/65	City Pt., VA	03/28/65	Pt. Lookout, MD	CSR
					Pt. Lookout, MD	06/28/65	Rlsd. G.O. #109	P114,CSR
Keefe, Wellington	Pvt	Ferguson's LA	Ringgold, GA	11/27/63	Nashville, TN	12/22/63	Louisville, KY	P39,CSR
					Louisville, KY	12/24/63	Rock Island, IL	CSR
					Rock Island, IL	10/06/64	Jd. US Army/Rjctd.	CSR
Keeffe, Ervin H.	Pvt	McQueen LA			Hart's Island, NY	06/08/65	Died, Rmtnt. fever	CSR
Keel, C.W.S.	Pvt	A 1st SCVIG	Deep Bottom, VA	07/29/64	City Pt., VA	08/05/64	Pt. Lookout, MD	CSR,SA1
					Pt. Lookout, MD	08/08/64	Elmira, NY	P120,P113,P125,CSR
					Elmira, NY	07/03/65	Rlsd. G.O. #109	P65,P66,CSR
Keeler, Andrew T.	Pvt	A 3rd SCVABn	High Pt., NC	05/02/65	High Pt., NC	05/02/65	Paroled	CSR
Keels, B.A.	Cpl	E 1st SCVA	Bentonville, NC	03/22/65	New Berne, NC	04/10/65	Hart's Island, NY	CSR
					Hart's Island, NY	06/17/65	Rlsd. G.O. #109	P79,CSR
Keels, L.J.	Sgt	E 19th SCVI	Glasgow, KY	09/12/62	Glasgow, KY	09/12/62	Paroled	CSR
Keen, W.H.	Pvt	B 18th SCVI	Richmond, VA	04/03/65	Newport News, VA	06/30/65	Rlsd. G.O. #109	P107
Keenan, James	Pvt	A 24th SCVI	Marietta, GA	07/03/64	Nashville, TN	07/13/64	Louisville, KY	CSR,EFW,CDC
					Louisville, KY	07/16/64	Camp Douglas, IL	CSR
					Camp Douglas, IL	05/16/65	Released G.O. #85	P7,P53,P55
Keenan, Michael	Pvt	K 12th SCVI	Rappahanock R., VA	10/17/63	Old Capitol, DC		Ft. McHenry, MD	CSR
					Ft. McHenry, MD	12/19/63	Escaped	P110,CSR
Keenan, P.	Cpl	H 25th SCVI	Weldon RR, VA	08/21/64	City Pt., VA	08/24/64	Pt. Lookout, MD	CSR,HAG
					Pt. Lookout, MD	05/13/65	Rlsd. G.O. #85	P113
Keeney, John	Pvt	I 3rd SCVC	Cleveland, TN	04/10/65	Louisville, KY	04/28/65	Camp Chase, OH	CSR
					Camp Chase, OH	06/10/65	Rlsd. G.O.#109	P23,CSR
Keese, Benjamin F., Jr.	Pvt	D 2nd SCVIRi	Shell Mound, TN	10/28/63	Bridgeport, AL US	11/08/63	Died of wounds	P6,P12,CSR
Keese, D.T.	Pvt	K 22nd SCVI	Deserted/enemy	02/24/65	City Pt., VA	02/26/65	Washington, DC	CSR
					Washington, DC	02/27/65	Salem, IN on oath	CSR
Keever, Daniel A.	Sgt	D 25th SCVI	Weldon RR, VA	08/21/64	Alexandria, VA	08/28/64	Died, GSW arm/head	P1,P6,P12,HAG,HMC
Keggs, Jacob P.	Pvt	I 1st SCVC	Deserted/enemy		Charleston, SC	03/27/65	Released on oath	CSR
Keiff, W.S.	Pvt	F 26th SCVI	Petersburg, VA Hos.	04/03/65				CSR
Keisler, G.A.	Pvt	K 13th SCVI	Gettysburg, PA	06/30/63	David's Island, NY	07/28/63	Died, Bowel Hemo.	P6,P12,FPH,CSR
Keistler, S.G.	Pvt	H 12th SCVI	Warrenton, VA	09/29/62	Warrenton, VA	09/29/62	Paroled	CSR,YEB
Keistler, S.G.	Pvt	H 12th SCVI	Spotsylvania, VA	05/12/64	Ft. Delaware, DE	02/11/65	Hos. 2/11-2/27/65	P47
					Ft. Delaware, DE	02/27/65	City Pt., VA Xc	P41,P42
Keith, J.	Pvt	E 1st SCVIG	Southside RR, VA	04/02/65	City Pt., VA	04/07/65	Hart's Island, NY	CSR,HMC
					Hart's Island, NY	06/16/65	Rlsd. G.O. #109	P79,HMC,CSR
Keith, James H.	Pvt	E 8th SCVI	Winchester, VA	09/12/64	Harpers Ferry, WV	09/19/64	Camp Chase, OH	CSR
					Camp Chase, OH	05/14/65	Took the oath	P26
					Camp Chase, OH	05/15/65	Rlsd. G.O. #85	P22,KEB,CSR
Keith, M.W.	Pvt	H 2nd SCVC	Anderson, SC	05/03/65	Anderson, SC	05/03/65	Paroled	CSR
Keith, William C.	1Lt	A Orr's Ri.	Appomattox R., VA	04/03/65	Ft. McHenry, MD	04/11/65	Johnson's Isl., OH	P110
					Old Capitol, DC	04/21/65	Johnson's Isl., OH	CSR
					Johnson's Isl., OH	06/18/65	Rlsd. G.O. #109	P82,P83,CSR
Kell, J.D.	Pvt	B 12th SCVI	Gettysburg, PA	07/04/63	David's Island, NY	08/24/63	City Pt., VA Xc	CSR
					Chester, PA G.H.	08/24/63	City Pt., VA Xc	P1
					Williamsburg, VA	09/09/63	Furloughed	CSR
Kell, J.D.	Pvt	B 12th SCVI	Southside RR, VA	04/02/65	City Pt., VA	04/07/65	Hart's Island, NY	CSR
					Hart's Island, NY	06/16/65	Rlsd. G.O. #109	P79,CSR

SOUTH CAROLINA SOLDIERS, SAILORS AND  CITIZENS HELD IN U.S. PRISONS 1861-1865

NAME	RANK	REGIMENT	CAPTURED AT	WHEN	PRISON	MOVED	DISPOSITION	SOURCES
Kell, W.Z.	Pvt	B 5th SCVI	Wilderness, VA	05/06/64	Belle Plain, VA	05/20/64	Ft. Delaware, DE	CSR,YEB,SA3
					Ft. Delaware, DE	06/10/65	Released	P41,P42,P45,CSR
Keller, J.W.	Pvt	B 1st SCVC	Beverly Ford, VA	06/09/63	Ft. McHenry, MD	06/25/63	City Pt., VA Xc	P110,CSR
Keller, Thomas W.	Pvt	B 22nd SCVI	Deserted/enemy		Pt. Lookout, MD	05/12/65	Died, Scurvy	P12,HOS,CSR
Keller, William H.	Pvt	H Ham.Leg.	Frederick, MD	09/12/62	Frederick, MD		Ft. Delaware, DE	CSR
					Ft. Delaware, DE	10/02/62	Aikens Ldg., VA Xc	CSR
Keller, Y. Alexander	Cpl	B 22nd SCVI	Deep Bottom, VA	08/16/64	City Pt., VA	08/22/64	Pt. Lookout, MD	CSR
					Pt. Lookout, MD	04/13/65	Died	P6,P113,FPH,HOS
Keller, Y.E.	Cpl	B 22nd SCVI	Crater, Pbg., VA	07/30/64	City Pt., VA USFH	08/02/64	City Pt., VA P.M.	CSR
					City Pt., VA P.M.	08/05/64	Washington, DC	CSR
Kelley, B.E.	Pvt	I 1st SCVA	Bentonville, NC	03/22/65	New Berne, NC	04/10/65	Hart's Island, NY	CSR
					Hart's Island, NY	06/15/65	Rlsd. G.O. #109	P79,CSR
Kelley, C.M.	Pvt	C 7th SCVIBn	Weldon RR, VA	08/21/64	City Pt., VA USFH	08/22/74	Died of wounds	CSR
Kelley, Elisha	Pvt	E 2nd SCVIRi	Richmond, VA	04/03/65	Richmond, VA Hos.	04/14/65	Richmond, VA P.M.	CSR
					Libby Prison Rchmd.	04/23/65	Newport News, VA	CSR
					Newport News, VA	05/16/65	Died, Typhoid	P6,P12,P107,CSR
Kelley, Henry	Pvt	G 21st SCVI	Ft. Fisher, NC	01/15/65	Elmira, NY	06/14/65	Released	P65,P66
Kelley, J.A.	Pvt	K 15th SCVI	Halltown, VA	08/26/64	Camp Chase, OH	03/18/65	Pt. Lookout, MD	P22
Kelley, James	Sgt	B 21st SCVI	Ft. Fisher, NC	01/15/65	Elmira, NY	02/06/65	Died, Pneumonia	P5,P65,P66,FPH,HAG
Kelley, James	Pvt	C Orr's Ri.	Columbia, SC	02/17/65	New Bern, NC	04/10/65	Hart's Island, NY	CSR,CDC
					Hart's Island, NY	06/16/65	Rlsd. G.O. #109	P79,CSR
Kelley, Mansell	Pvt	G 16th SCVI	Stone Mtn., GA	09/30/64	Nashville, TN	10/27/64	Louisville, KY	CSR
					Louisville, KY	10/29/64	Camp Douglas, IL	CSR,16R
					Camp Douglas, IL	03/29/65	Joined 5th US Vol.	P53,P55,CSR
Kelley, Reuben D.	Pvt	F Orr's Ri.	Petersburg, VA	04/02/65	City Pt., VA	04/04/65	Pt. Lookout, MD	CDC,CSR
					Pt. Lookout, MD	06/28/65	Rlsd. G.O. #109	P114
Kelley, Simon H.	Pvt	G 21st SCVI	Ft. Fisher, NC	01/15/65	Elmira, NY	02/16/65	Died, Pneumonia	P5,P65,P66,FPH,HAG
Kelley, Thomas	Pvt	G 21st SCVI	Ft. Fisher, NC	01/15/65	Elmira, NY	07/03/65	Rlsd. G.O. #109	P65,P66,HAG
Kellongsworth, James M.	Pvt	G Orr's Ri.	Richmond, VA Hos.	04/03/65	Jackson Hos. Rchmd.	04/05/65	Died, Bronchitis	P10,CDC,CSR
Kelly, Asa D.	Sgt	C 7th SCVIBn	Weldon RR, VA	08/21/64	City Pt., VA	08/24/64	Pt. Lookout, MD	CSR,HAG
					Pt. Lookout, MD	03/14/65	Aikens Ldg., VA Xc	P113,P124
Kelly, Brooks B.	Pvt	H 3rd SCVI	N. Anna River, VA	05/23/64	Port Royal, VA	05/30/64	Pt. Lookout, MD	CSR
					Pt. Lookout, MD	11/03/85	Venus Pt., GA Xc	P113,P124,CSR
Kelly, Daniel J.	Pvt	H Orr's Ri.	Spotsylvania, VA	05/12/64	Belle Plain, VA	05/21/64	Ft. Delaware, DE	CSR,HMC,CDC
					Ft. Delaware, DE	06/22/65	Rlsd G.O. #109	P41,P42,P45
Kelly, David	Pvt	A 1st SCVA	Johnsonville, NC	03/12/65	New Berne, NC	04/10/65	Hart's Island, NY	CSR
					Hart's Island, NY	06/15/65	Rlsd. G.O. #109	P79,CSR
Kelly, Elbert J.	Pvt	C 25th SCVI	Weldon RR, VA	08/21/64	City Pt., VA Hos.	08/26/64	Philadelphia, PA	CSR,HAG,CTA
					Philadelphia G.H.	10/06/64	Died of wounds	P1,P5,P6,P12,FPH
Kelly, Fair	Pvt	C 7th SCVIBn	Weldon RR, VA	08/21/64	City Pt., VA	08/24/64	Pt. Lookout, MD	CSR,HAG
					Pt. Lookout, MD	03/14/65	Aikens Ldg., VA Xc	P113,CSR
Kelly, G.W.	Pvt	D 18th SCVI	Petersburg, VA Hos.	04/03/65	Jackson Hos.			CSR
Kelly, George	Pvt	A 15th SCVAB	Smithfield, NC	03/19/65	New Berne, NC	04/03/65	Pt. Lookout, MD	CSR
					Pt. Lookout, MD	06/05/65	Released on oath	P114,CSR
Kelly, Herbert	Pvt	D 7th SCVIBn	Ft. Anderson, NC	02/19/65	Ft. Anderson, NC	02/28/65	Pt. Lookout, MD	CSR
					Pt. Lookout, MD	06/28/67	Rlsd. G.O. # 109	CSR
Kelly, J.L.B.	Pvt	I 18th SCVI	Petersburg, VA	06/16/64	Bermuda Hundred, VA	06/18/64	Fts. Monroe, VA	CSR
					Fts. Monroe, VA	06/18/64	Pt. Lookout, MD	CSR
					Pt. Lookout, MD	07/25/64	Elmira, NY	P113,P120,CSR
					Elmira, NY	05/15/65	Rlsd. G.O. #85	P65,P66,CSR
Kelly, J.M.	Pvt	H 25th SCVI	Ft. Fisher, NC	01/15/65	New York, NY	01/30/65	Elmira, NY	CSR
					Elmira, NY	02/13/65	Died, Pneumonia	P5,P12,P65,FPH

K

SOUTH CAROLINA SOLDIERS, SAILORS AND CITIZENS HELD IN U.S. PRISONS 1861-1865

NAME	RANK	REGIMENT	CAPTURED AT	WHEN	PRISON	MOVED	DISPOSITION	SOURCES
Kelly, James	Pvt	C 7th SCVIBn	Weldon RR, VA	08/21/64	Pt. Lookout, MD	03/14/65	Exchanged	P124,HAG,CS
Kelly, James	Pvt	H 1st SCVA			Hart's Island, NY	06/16/65	Rlsd. G.O. #109	CSR
Kelly, James H.	Cpl	B 15th SCVI	Knoxville, TN	12/03/63	Nashville, TN	02/11/64	Louisville, KY	P39,CSR,KEB
					Louisville, KY	02/15/64	Rock Island, IL	CSR
					Rock Island, IL	03/02/65	Tfd. for Xc	CSR
Kelly, Jasper C.	Pvt	C 15th SCVI	Halltown, WV	08/26/64	Harpers Ferry, WV	09/02/64	Camp Chase, OH	CSR,KEB
					Camp Chase, OH	03/18/65	Pt. Lookout, MD Xc	P26,CSR
					Pt. Lookout, MD	03/27/65	Boulware's Wh. Xc	CSR
Kelly, John	Pvt	1st SCVA	Washington, DC	12/13/63	Took oath			CSR
Kelly, John	Pvt	C 27th SCVI	Weldon RR, VA	08/21/64	City Pt., VA	08/24/64	Pt. Lookout, MD	CSR,HAG
					Pt. Lookout, MD	10/17/64	Joined U.S. Army	P113,P125,CSR
Kelly, John	Pvt	C 23rd SCVI	Deserted/enemy	11/20/64	Hilton Head, SC	11/22/64	New York, NY oath	P8,CSR
Kelly, John C.	Pvt	H 25th SCVI	Morris Island, SC	09/07/63	Ft. Columbus, NY	10/09/63	Johnson's Isl., OH	P1,HAG
					Pt. Lookout, MD	04/27/64	Exchanged	P113,P124,CSR
Kelly, John C.	Pvt	H 25th SCVI	Ft. Fisher, NC	01/15/65	New York, NY	01/30/65	Elmira, NY	CSR
					Elmira, NY	02/28/65	Died, Variola	P5,P12,P65,P66,FPH
Kelly, John W.	Pvt	C 25th SCVI	Weldon RR, VA	08/21/64	City Pt., VA	08/24/64	Pt. Lookout, MD	CSR,HAG,CTA
					Pt. Lookout, MD	02/10/65	Exchanged	P113,P124
Kelly, Levi	Cit	Lexington	Flat Rock, SC	02/24/65	Hart's Island, NY	06/20/65	Rlsd. G.O.#109	P79
Kelly, Michael	Pvt	E 1st SCVA	Morris Island, SC	07/10/63	Hilton Head, SC	09/05/63	Ft. Columbus, NY	CSR
					Ft. Columbus, NY	09/23/63	Took the oath	P1,CSR
Kelly, Michael	Pvt	K 1st SCVA	Morris Island, SC	07/25/64	Hilton Head, SC	08/18/64	New York, NY oath	CSR
Kelly, Reuben B.	Sgt	G 2nd SCVIRi	Darbytown Rd., VA	10/07/64	Dutch Gap Canal	10/21/64	Pt. Lookout, MD	CSR
					City Pt., VA	10/29/64	Pt. Lookout, MD	CSR
					Pt. Lookout, MD	03/28/65	Aikens Ldg., VA Xc	P114,P124,CSR
Kelly, Rivers S.	Pvt	A 24th SCVI	Marietta, GA	07/03/64	Nashville, TN	07/13/64	Louisville, KY	CSR,EFW
					Louisville, KY	07/16/64	Camp Douglas, IL	CSR
					Camp Douglas, IL	05/19/65	Discharged on oath	P53
Kelly, Thomas	Pvt	F 1st SCVA	From the fleet	12/01/64	Hilton Head, SC	12/18/64		CSR
Kelly, Thomas	Pvt	C 23rd SCVI	Deserted/US Navy	11/10/64	Hilton Head, SC	12/22/64	New York, NY oath	P8,CSR
Kelly, W.D.	Pvt	A 3rd SCVABn	High Pt., NC	05/02/65	High Pt., NC	05/02/65	Paroled	CSR
Kelly, W.F.	Pvt	D 3rd SCVIBn	South Mtn., MD	09/14/62	Balt, MD Camden H	03/06/63	Ft. McHenry, MD	CSR
					Ft. McHenry, MD	03/13/63	Fts. Monroe, VA Xc	P96,CSR
Kelly, William	Pvt	D 1st SCVIR	Charleston Hrbr.	03/21/63	Ft. Delaware, DE	06/28/63	(Rcd. 06/28/63)	P40,P44,SA1,CSR
					Ft. Lafayette, NY	06/29/63	Ft. Delaware, DE	CSR
					Ft. Delaware, DE	02/27/65	Exchanged	CSR
Kelly, William	Pvt	B 1st SCVIG	Wilderness, VA	05/06/64	Belle Plain, VA	05/21/64	Ft. Delaware, DE	CSR
					Ft. Delaware, DE	09/16/64	Hos. 9/16-10/21/64	P47
					Ft. Delaware, DE	11/01/64	Hos. 11/1-12/11/64	P47
					Ft. Delaware, DE	02/11/65	Hos. 2/11-2/22/65	P47
					Ft. Delaware, DE	02/27/65	City Pt., VA Xc	P41,P42,SA1,CSR
Kelly, William D.	Pvt	B 7th SCVIBn	Weldon RR, VA	08/21/64	City Pt., VA	08/24/64	Pt. Lookout, MD	CSR,HAG
					Pt. Lookout, MD	10/18/64	Joined U.S. Army	P113,P125,CSR
Kelly, William J.	Pvt	G 12th SCVI	Gettysburg, PA	07/05/63	Ft. McHenry, MD	07/30/63	Chester, PA G.H.	CSR
					Chester, PA G.H.	08/10/63	Ft. Delaware, DE	P40,P44,P45,CSR
					Ft. Delaware, DE	05/27/64	Hos. 5/27-6/3/64	P47
Kelly, William J.	Pvt	G 12th SCVI	Gettysburg, PA	07/05/63	Ft. Delaware, DE	06/10/65	Released	CSR
Kelly, William P.	Pvt	I 1st SCVA	Fayetteville, NC	03/16/65	New Berne, NC	03/30/65	Pt. Lookout, MD	CSR
					Pt. Lookout, MD	06/28/65	Rlsd. G.O. #109	P114,CSR
Kemp, James	Pvt	A 6th SCVC	Lynch's Creek, SC	03/25/65	New Berne, NC	04/10/65	Hart's Island, NY	CSR
					Hart's Island, NY	05/05/65	Died, Ch. Diarrhea	P6,P12,P79,FPH,CSR

SOUTH CAROLINA SOLDIERS, SAILORS AND  CITIZENS HELD IN U.S. PRISONS 1861-1865

NAME	RANK	REGIMENT	CAPTURED AT	WHEN	PRISON	MOVED	DISPOSITION	SOURCES
Kemp, Jesse	2Lt	C 22nd SCVI	Crater, Pbg., VA	07/30/64	City Pt., VA P.M.	08/02/64	Washington, DC	CSR
					Old Capitol, DC	08/11/64	Ft. Delaware, DE	CSR
					Ft. Delaware, DE	03/12/65	Died, Ch. Diarrhea	P5,P42,P45,P47,FPH
Kemp, Wyatt H.	Pvt	C 22nd SCVI	Crater, Pbg., VA	07/30/64	City Pt., VA	08/05/64	Pt. Lookout, MD	CSR
					Pt. Lookout, MD	08/08/64	Elmira, NY	P113,P117,P120
					Elmira, NY	09/02/64	Died, Ch. Diarrhea	P5,P12,P65,P66,FPH
Kendrick, T.F.	Sgt	H 1st SCVIH	Knoxville, TN	12/03/63	Knoxville, TN	12/15/63	Camp Chase, OH	P84,CSR
Kennedy, Jerremiah C.	Pvt	Brooks LA	Falling Waters, MD	07/14/63	Provost Marshal, DC	08/01/63	Old Capitol, DC	CSR
					Old Capitol, DC	12/20/63	Sent north on oath	CSR
Kennedy, Joseph	Pvt	Brooks LA	Appomattox R., VA	04/05/65	City Pt., VA	04/07/65	Washington, DC	CSR
					Washington, DC	04/12/65	New York, NY oath	CSR
Kennedy, Michael F.	Pvt	A 8th SCResB	Deserted/enemy		Charleston, SC	03/21/65	Released on oath	CSR
Kennedy, Robert	Smn	CS Navy			Pt. Lookout, MD	04/24/65	Died, Ch. Diarrhea	P12,FPH
Kennedy, S.S.	Pvt	G 4th SCVC	Hawe's Shop, VA	05/28/64	US Field Hospital	05/29/64	Died of wounds	P12,ROH
Kennedy, Thomas	Pvt	C 17th SCVI	Deserted/enemy	03/01/65	P.M. 9th AC. A.of	03/02/65	City Pt., VA P.M.	CSR
					City Pt., VA P.M.	03/03/65	Washington, DC	CSR
					Washington, DC	03/15/65	Danville, PA oath	CSR
Kennedy, Thomas	Pvt	G 1st SCVIR	Bentonville, NC	03/19/65	New Berne, NC	04/18/65	Hart's Island, NY	CSR,SA1
					Hart's Island, NY	06/16/65	Rlsd. G.O. #109	P79,CSR
Kennedy, Thomas	Pvt	E Hol.Leg.	Petersburg, VA	03/25/65	City Pt., VA	03/28/65	Pt. Lookout, MD	CSR
					Pt. Lookout, MD	06/06/65	Rlsd. sick list	P114,CSR
Kennedy, W.A.	Pvt	H 2nd SCVC	Jerusalem Plk. Rd., VA	10/11/64	City Pt., VA	10/29/64	Pt. Lookout, MD	CSR
					Pt. Lookout, MD	02/13/65	Exchanged	P114,P124,CSR
Kennedy, W.P.	Pvt	C 7th SCVI	Sharpsburg, MD	10/01/62	Ft. McHenry, MD	10/13/62	Fts. Monroe, VA Xc	P96,KEB,CSR
Kennemore, Jacob	Pvt	D 18th SCVI	Crater, Pbg., VA	07/30/64	City Pt., VA	08/05/64	Pt. Lookout, MD	CSR
					Pt. Lookout, MD	08/08/64	Elmira, NY	P113,P120,CSR
					Elmira, NY	10/11/64	Pt. Lookout, MD	P65,P66
					Pt. Lookout, MD	10/29/64	Venus Pt., GA Xc	P114,CSR
Kennemore, Moses	Pvt	D 18th SCVI	Crater, Pbg., VA	07/30/64	City Pt., VA	08/05/64	Pt. Lookout, MD	CSR,UD2
					Pt. Lookout, MD	08/08/64	Elmira, NY	P113,P120,CSR
					Elmira, NY	09/29/64	Died, Diarrhea	P5,P65,P66,CSR
Kennemur, J.S.	Pvt	E Orr's Ri.	Deserted/enemy	02/21/65	City Pt., VA P.M.	02/22/65	Washington, DC	CSR,CDC
					Washington, DC	02/24/65	Burlington, IA	CSR
Kennerly, A.V.	Pvt	H Ham.Leg.	Sharpsburg, MD	09/17/62	Frederick, MD	12/15/62	Died of wounds	P12,CSR
Kennerly, L.D.	Pvt	H Ham.Leg.MI	Richmond, VA Hos.	04/03/65	Richmond, VA Hos.	05/25/65	Rlsd. on oath	CSR
Kenney, C	Pvt	K 1st SCVIR	Deserted/enemy		Hilton Head, SC	04/30/65	New York, NY oath	CSR
Kenney, Daniel	Pvt	C 3rd SCVABn	Blakely, AL	04/09/65	Ship Island, MS	05/01/65	Vicksburg, MS Xc	CSR
Kenney, Daniel	Pvt	C 3rd SCVABn	Augusta, GA	05/20/65	Augusta, GA	05/20/65	Paroled	CSR
Kenney, Enos	Pvt	K 1st SCVIR	Deserted/enemy		New York, NY	04/30/65	New York, NY oath	CSR
Kenney, J.	Pvt	C 15th SCVAB	Deserted/enemy	02/21/65	Charleston, SC	04/12/65	Rlsd. on oath	CSR
Kenney, John F.	Pvt	B 15th SCVAB	Smith's Ford, NC	03/16/65	New Berne, NC	04/10/65	Hart's Island, NY	CSR
					Hart's Island, NY	06/15/65	Rlsd. G.O. #109	P79,CSR
Kennington, A.	Pvt	G 3rd SCVABn	High Pt., NC	05/01/65	High Pt., NC	05/01/65	Paroled	CSR
Kennington, William W.	Pvt	E 12th SCVI	Petersburg, VA	04/02/65	City Pt., VA	04/04/65	Pt. Lookout, MD	CSR
					Pt. Lookout, MD	06/28/65	Rlsd. G.O. #109	CSR
Kenny, James	Pvt	D 1st SCVA	Deserted/enemy		Ft. McHenry, MD			P110
					Old Capitol, DC	12/19/63	Took the oath	CSR
Kenyon, William A.	Pvt	A Ham.Leg.	Chattanooga, TN	10/29/63	Nashville, TN	11/07/63	Louisville, KY	CSR
					Louisville, KY	11/09/63	Camp Morton, IN	CSR
					Camp Morton, IN	03/19/64	Ft. Delaware, DE	CSR
					Ft. Delaware, DE	06/10/65	Rlsd. G.O. #109	P45,CSR

K

SOUTH CAROLINA SOLDIERS, SAILORS AND CITIZENS HELD IN U.S. PRISONS 1861-1865

NAME	RANK	REGIMENT	CAPTURED AT	WHEN	PRISON	MOVED	DISPOSITION	SOURCES
Kerby, Redden	Sgt	B 1st SCVIR	Smith Ford, NC	03/16/65	New Berne, NC	04/03/65	Pt. Lookout, MD	CSR,SA1
					Pt. Lookout, MD	06/26/65	Rlsd. G.O. #109	P114,P123,SA1,CSR
Kernaghan, William G.	Pvt	G 1st SCVIG	N. Anna River, VA	05/23/64	Front Royal, VA	05/30/64	Pt. Lookout, MD	CSR,SA1
					Pt. Lookout, MD	08/17/64	Elmira, NY	P113,CSR
					Elmira, NY	02/13/65	Pt. Lookout, MD Xc	P65,P66,CSR
					Pt. Lookout, MD	02/13/65	Cox's Wharf, VA Xc	P65,P66,CSR
Kerney, Henry	Pvt	H 3rd SCVC	Deserted/enemy		Hilton Head, SC	02/18/65	New York, NY oath	CSR
Kerr, Robert M.	2Lt	H 12th SCVI	Sharpsburg, MD	09/17/62	Maryland	11/08/62	Aikens Ldg., VA Xc	CSR,YEB
Kerr, Robert M.	Cpt	H 12th SCVI	Appomattox C.H., VA	04/08/65	Ft. McHenry, MD	04/11/65	Johnson's Isl., OH	P110,CSR
					Johnson's Isl., OH	06/18/65	Rlsd. G.O. #109	P82,CSR
Kerr, W.J.	Pvt	D 17th SCVI	Crater, Pbg., VA	07/30/64	City Pt., VA	08/05/64	Pt. Lookout, MD	CSR,HHC
					Pt. Lookout, MD	08/08/64	Elmira, NY	P113,P120,CSR
					Elmira, NY	06/19/65	Rlsd. G.O. #109	P65,CSR
Kerrison, Charles, Jr.	Pvt	I 2nd SCVI	Gettysburg, PA	07/05/63	Gettysburg G.H.	07/10/63	Provost Marshal	P4
					Ft. Delaware, DE	07/19/63	Chester, PA Hos.	P40,P42,CSR
					Chester, PA G.H.	09/21/63	City Pt., VA Xc	P1,KEB,SA2,H2,CSR
Kersey, Ebin	Pvt	H 23rd SCVI	Deserted/enemy	02/10/64	City Pt., VA	11/10/64	Washington, DC	CSR
Kersey, Henry	Pvt	E 23rd SCVI	Deserted/enemy	01/28/65	City Pt., VA	01/01/65	Phila., PA on oath	P8,HMC,CSR
Kersey, James	Pvt	E 23rd SCVI	Deserted/enemy	01/28/65	City Pt., VA	02/01/65	Phila., PA on oath	P8,CSR
Kersey, William R.	Pvt	G Hol.Leg.	Jarratts Stn., VA	04/02/65	City Pt., VA	04/07/65	Hart's Island, NY	CSR,ANY
					Hart's Island, NY	06/21/65	Rlsd. G.O. #109	P79
Kesiah, John H.M.	Pvt	E 21st SCVI	Morris Island, SC	07/10/63	Ft. Columbus, NY	09/23/63	Paroled	P1
					Pt. Lookout, MD	02/03/64	Died, Ch. Diarrhea	P5,P12,P113,FPH
Kessler, H.	Pvt	B German LA	Deserted/enemy		Charleston, SC	03/15/65	Released on oath	CSR
Kesterson, W.	Pvt	C 3rd SCVABn	Blakely, AL	04/09/65	Ship Island, MS	05/01/65	Vicksburg, MS Xc	CSR
Key, B.P.	Pvt	B 26th SCVI	Petersburg, VA	04/02/65	City Pt., VA	04/05/65	Pt. Lookout, MD	CSR
					Pt. Lookout, MD	06/28/65	Rlsd. G.O. #109	P114,CSR
Key, David	Pvt	H 14th SCVI	Deep Bottom, VA	07/29/64	City Pt., VA	08/05/64	Pt. Lookout, MD	CSR
					Pt. Lookout, MD	08/08/64	Elmira, NY	P113,P120,CSR
					Elmira, NY	04/01/65	Died, Pneumonia	P6,P65,P66,FPH,CSR
Key, Hiram	Pvt	E 5th SCResB	Raleigh, NC	04/13/65	Raleigh, NC Hos.	04/13/65	Paroled	CSR
Key, John E.	Pvt	C 1st SCVIG	Gettysburg, PA	07/04/63	David's Island, NY	08/24/63	City Pt., VA Xc	CSR
Key, John E.	Pvt	C 1st SCVIG	Columbia, SC	02/16/65	New Berne, NC	04/10/65	Hart's Island, NY	P79,SA1,CSR
					Hart's Island, NY	06/16/65	Rlsd. G.O. #109	P79,SA1,CSR
Key, John J.	Pvt	E 8th SCVI	Gettysburg, PA	07/05/63	Letterman G.H. Gbg	09/28/63	W. Bldg. Balt, MD	P1,CSR
					W. Bldg. Balt, MD	11/12/63	City Pt, VA Xc	CSR
Key, Ransom R.	Cpl	I 17th SCVI	Crater, Pbg., VA	07/30/64	City Pt., VA	08/05/64	Pt. Lookout, MD	CSR
					Pt. Lookout, MD	08/08/64	Elmira, NY	P113,P120,LAN,CSR
					Elmira, NY	05/28/65	Died	P6,P65,P66,FPH,LAN
Keyser, Elias	Pvt	B 6th SCResB	Lexington, SC	02/13/65	New Berne, NC	03/30/65	Pt. Lookout, MD	CSR
					Pt. Lookout, MD	06/25/65	Rlsd. G.O. #109	P114,CSR
Keyser, Lewis	Pvt	F 3rd SCVABn	Cheraw, SC	03/05/65	Cheraw, SC	03/05/65	Paroled	CSR
Kibler, R. Calvin	Pvt	C 3rd SCVI	N. Anna River, VA	05/23/64	Port Royal, VA	05/30/64	Pt. Lookout, MD	CSR,H3,KEB,SA2,ANY
					Pt. Lookout, MD	03/14/65	Aikens Ldg., VA Xc	P113,P124,CSR
Kidd, William A.	Pvt	A 12th SCVI	Petersburg, VA	04/02/65	City Pt., VA	04/04/65	Pt. Lookout, MD	CSR
					Pt. Lookout, MD	06/28/65	Rlsd. G.O. #109	P114,YEB,CSR
Kiesler, Chesley S.	Pvt	K 20th SCVI	Cedar Creek, VA	10/19/64	Harpers Ferry, WV	10/24/64	Pt. Lookout, MD	KEB,CSR
					Pt. Lookout, MD	03/28/65	Exchanged	P114,P124,CSR
Kilby, J.S.	Pvt	H 7th SCVI	N. Anna River, VA	05/23/64	Pt. Lookout, MD	01/29/65	Died, Typhoid fever	P5,P113,FPH,CSR
Kilcrease, William E.	Pvt	B 6th SCVC	Fayetteville, NC	03/10/65	New Berne, NC	04/09/65	Hart's Island, NY	CSR
					Hart's Island, NY	06/17/65	Rlsd. G.O. #109	P79,CSR

SOUTH CAROLINA SOLDIERS, SAILORS AND  CITIZENS HELD IN U.S. PRISONS 1861-1865

NAME	RANK	REGIMENT	CAPTURED AT	WHEN	PRISON	MOVED	DISPOSITION	SOURCES
Kilgore, Robert F.	Cpl	D 17th SCVI	Petersburg, VA	03/25/65	City Pt., VA	03/28/65	Pt. Lookout, MD	CSR
					Pt. Lookout, MD	06/28/65	Rlsd. G.O. #109	P114,CSR
Kilgore, Thomas P.	Pvt	F 5th SCVI	Southside RR, VA	10/07/64	Pt. Lookout, MD	03/28/65	Aikens Ldg., VA Xc	P114,P124,SA3,CSR
Killian, Elbert L.	Sgt	K 12th SCVI	Spotsylvania, VA	05/12/64	Belle Plain, VA	05/20/64	Ft. Delaware, DE	CSR
					Ft. Delaware, DE	06/10/65	Released	P41,P42,P45,CSR
Kimbrell, J.	Pvt	H 1st SCVIH	Farmville, VA	04/11/65	Farmville, VA	04/21/65	Paroled	CSR
Kimbrell, J.H.	Pvt	C 3rd SCResB	Charlotte, NC	05/19/65	Charlotte, NC	05/19/65	Paroled	CSR
Kimbrell, John A.	Pvt	B 6th SCVI	Richmond, VA Hos.	04/04/65	Richmond, VA Hos.	04/08/65	City Pt., VA P.M.	CSR,YEB
					City Pt., VA	04/14/65	Pt. Lookout, MD	CSR
					Pt. Lookout, MD	06/28/65	Rlsd. G.O. #109	P114,CSR
Kimbrell, Martin	Pvt	B 6th SCVI	Richmond, VA Hos.	04/03/65	Libby Prison Rchmd.			CSR
Kimbrell, Robert W.	Pvt	B 22nd SCVI	Kinston, NC	12/15/62	Kinston, NC	12/15/62	Paroled POW	CSR,HOS
Kimby, Robert	Pvt	D 23rd SCVI	Deserted/enemy	02/11/65	City Pt., VA P.M.	02/12/65	Savannah, GA oath	CSR
Kimmey, Francis M.	Pvt	B 27th SCVI	Town Creek, NC	02/20/65	Ft. Anderson, NC	02/28/65	Pt. Lookout, MD	CSR,HAG
					Pt. Lookout, MD	05/13/65	Rlsd. G.O. #85	P114,CSR
Kinard, Alfred A.	Pvt	G 3rd SCVABn	Rivers Bridge, SC	02/05/65	New Berne, NC	04/25/65	Fts. Monroe, VA	CSR
					Fts. Monroe, VA	06/06/65	Newport News, VA	CSR
					Newport News, VA	06/30/65	Rlsd. G.O. #109	CSR
Kinard, George D.	Pvt	G 17th SCVI	Southside RR, VA	04/02/65	City Pt., VA	04/13/65	Pt. Lookout, MD	CSR
					Pt. Lookout, MD	06/28/65	Rlsd. G.O. #109	P114,CSR
Kinard, George F.	Pvt	G 17th SCVI	Petersburg, VA	03/25/65	City Pt., VA	03/28/65	Pt. Lookout, MD	CSR
					Pt. Lookout, MD	06/28/65	Rlsd. G.O. #109	P114,CSR
Kinard, George J.	Pvt	G 1st SCVIH	Loudon, TN	01/10/64	Nashville, TN	02/15/64	Louisville, KY	P39,SA1,CSR
					Louisville, KY	02/17/64	Rock Island, IL	CSR
					Rock Island, IL	02/11/65	Tfd. for exchange	CSR
Kinard, George W.	Pvt	B German LA	Augusta, GA	05/26/65	Augusta, GA	05/26/65	Paroled	CSR
Kinard, J.L.	Cit		Branchville, SC	03/06/65	Hart's Island, NY	06/20/65	Rlsd. G.O. #109	P79
Kinard, James P.	Pvt	D 13th SCVI	Gettysburg, PA	07/05/63	David's Island, NY	09/12/63	City Pt., VA Xc	P1,ANY,CSR
Kinard, William A.	Pvt	B German LA	Augusta, GA	05/26/65	Augusta, GA	05/26/65	Paroled	CSR
Kincaid, John A.	Pvt	B 12th SCVI	Farmville, VA	04/02/65	Farmville,VA USGH	04/12/65	Fts. Monroe G.H.	CSR
					Fts. Monroe, VA GH	05/18/65	Died, Exhaustion	CSR,P12
King, A.P.	Pvt	A 1st SCVC	Deserted/enemy		Hilton Head, SC		To work QM depot	P8,CSR
King, A.T.	Pvt	D 18th SCVAB	Raleigh, NC Hos.	04/13/65	Raleigh, NC	04/13/65	Paroled	CSR
King, Abner C.	Pvt	F 2nd SCVIRi	Burkesville, VA	04/14/65	Burkeville, VA	04/17/65	Paroled	CSR
King, Alexander A.	2Lt	A 3rd SCVIBn	Williamsport, MD	07/15/63	Hagerstown, MD Hos.	09/17/63	Chester, PA Hos.	CSR,P2,KEB
					Chester, PA G.H.	10/02/63	Pt. Lookout, MD	P1,CSR
					Pt. Lookout, MD	12/05/63	Johnson's Isl., OH	P1,CSR
					Johnsons Isl., OH	02/24/64	City Pt., VA Xc	P80,P81,P82,CSR
King, Alexander B.	Pvt	E 16th SCVI	Ringgold, GA	11/27/63	Nashville, TN	12/09/63	Louisville, KY	P39,16R,CSR
					Louisville, KY	12/11/63	Rock Island, IL	CSR
					Rock Island, IL	03/02/65	Trfd. for exchange	CSR
King, Calvin	Pvt	B 10th SCVI	Corinth, MS	05/03/62	Gratiot St., St. Lo	08/07/62	Alton, IL	CSR,RAS
					Alton, IL	09/23/62	Vicksburg, MS Xc	P14,CSR
					Vicksburg, MS	01/06/63	Died	CSR
King, Charles W.	Rfg		Hilton Head, SC		Hilton Head, SC	02/25/64	Died	P6
King, Edwin	Pvt	K 20th SCVI	Rockingham, NC	03/06/65	Pt. Lookout, MD	06/28/65	Rlsd. G.O. #109	P114,CSR,KEB
King, Ezekiel T.	Sgt	D 8th SCVI	Winchester, VA	09/13/64	Harpers Ferry, WV	09/19/64	Camp Chase, OH	P22,P26,KEB,CSR
					Camp Chase, OH	05/02/65	New Orleans, LA Xc	P22,P26,CSR
					New Orleans, LA	05/12/65	Vicksburg, MS Xc	P22,P26,CSR
King, H.	Pvt	C 3rd SCVABn	Blakely, AL	04/09/65	Ship Island, AL	05/01/65	Vicksburg, MS Xc	CSR
King, H.T.	2Lt	B 26th SCVI	Richmond, VA Hos.	04/03/65	Richmond, VA	05/06/65	Escaped	CSR
King, J.J.	Pvt	I 3rd SCVC	Fayetteville, NC	03/04/65	Pt. Lookout, MD	05/14/65	Rlsd. on oath	CSR

K

SOUTH CAROLINA SOLDIERS, SAILORS AND CITIZENS HELD IN U.S. PRISONS 1861-1865

NAME	RANK	REGIMENT	CAPTURED AT	WHEN	PRISON	MOVED	DISPOSITION	SOURCES
King, J.P.	Pvt	D 2nd SCVIRi	High Bridge, VA	04/06/65	City Pt., VA	04/14/65	Newport News, VA	CSR
					Newport News, VA	06/16/65	Rlsd. G.O. #109	P107,CSR
King, J.P.Z.	Sgt	B 21st SCVI	Ft. Fisher, NC	01/15/65	Elmira, NY	07/11/65	Rlsd. G.O. #109	P65,P66,HAG
King, James E.	1Lt	B 2nd SCVI	Salisbury, NC	04/12/65	Nashville, TN	05/01/65	Louisville, KY	P39,CSR
					Louisville, KY	05/02/65	Camp Chase, OH	CSR
					Camp Chase, OH	06/11/65	Rlsd. G.O. #109	P22,CSR
King, James R.	2Sg	F 1st SCVIG	Gettysburg, PA	07/05/63	Ft. Delaware, DE	10/15/63	Pt. Lookout, MD	P40,P44,P45,SA1
					Ft. Delaware, DE	06/10/65	Rlsd.	CSR
King, Jasper	Cpl	D 18th SCVI	Petersburg, VA	03/25/65	City Pt., VA	03/28/65	Pt. Lookout, MD	CSR
					Pt. Lookout, MD	06/28/65	Rlsd. G.O. #109	P114,CSR
King, Jehiel	Pvt	G 3rd SCVABn	Deserted/enemy		Charleston, SC	03/22/65	Released on oath	CSR
King, Joel J.	Pvt	A 3rd SCVIBn	Hanover Jctn., VA	05/23/64	Pt. Lookout, MD	04/24/65	Died	P6,P113,FPH,CSR
King, John	Pvt	F 5th SCVC	Deserted/enemy		Hilton Head, SC PM	04/07/65	P.M. New York, NY	CSR
King, John	Pvt	E 2nd SCVIRi	Burkeville, VA	05/08/65	Burkeville, VA	05/08/65	Paroled	CSR
King, John	Sgt	8th SCResB	Charlotte, NC	05/27/65	Charlotte, NC	05/27/65	Paroled	CSR
King, John W.	Pvt	F 1st SCVIG	Gettysburg, PA	07/05/63	Ft. Delaware, DE	06/30/63	City Pt., VA Xc	P44,SA1
					Ft. Delaware, DE	07/31/63	Exchanged	P40,CSR
King, Joseph	Pvt	I 1st SCVIG	N. Anna River, VA	05/23/64	Front Royal, VA	05/30/64	Pt. Lookout, MD	CSR,SA1
					Pt. Lookout, MD	07/23/64	Elmira, NY	P113,P120
					Elmira, NY	09/12/64	Died, Typhoid fever	P12,FPH,CSR
King, Judson	Pvt	E 16th SCVI	Ringgold, GA	11/26/63	Nashville, TN	12/09/63	Louisville, KY	P39,16R,CSR
					Louisville, KY	12/11/63	Rock Island, IL	CSR
					Rock Island, IL	06/18/65	Rlsd. G.O. #109	CSR
King, Martin M.	Pvt	A 7th SCVC	Pound Gap, VA	10/21/64	Camp Chase, OH	05/15/65	Rlsd. G.O. #85	P22,P26
King, Miles	Pvt	G 6th SCVI	Farmville, VA	04/11/65	Farmville, VA	04/21/65	Paroled	CSR
King, Mitchell C.	Cpt	H 1st SCVIR	Bentonville, NC	03/22/65	New Berne, NC	04/10/65	Hart's Island, NY	CSR
					Hart's Island, NY	04/15/65	Ft. Delaware, DE	P45,P79,CSR
					Ft. Delaware, DE	06/17/65	Rlsd. G.O. #109	SA1,CSR
King, Robert B.	Pvt	Macbeth LA	Jefferson Co., TN	10/28/64	Nashville, TN	11/21/64	Louisville, KY	CSR
					Louisville, KY	11/23/64	Camp Douglas, IL	CSR
					Camp Douglas, IL	06/17/65	Rlsd. G.O. #109	CSR
King, Sampson L.	Sgt	K 15th SCVI	Augusta, GA	05/18/65	Augusta, GA	05/18/65	Paroled on oath	H15,CSR
King, Sebastian S.	Pvt	G 13th SCVI	Gettysburg, PA	07/02/63	Chester, PA G.H.	10/03/63	Pt. Lookout, MD	P1,CSR
					Pt. Lookout, MD	03/16/64	Exchanged	P124,CSR
					Pt. Lookout, MD	03/16/64	City Pt., VA Xc	CSR
King, T.P.	Pvt	B 21st SCVI	Ft. Fisher, NC	01/15/65	Elmira, NY	07/11/65	Rlsd. G.O. #109	P65,P66,HAG
King, Tapley B.	Pvt	K 15th SCVI	Halltown, VA	08/26/64	Harper's Ferry, VA	09/02/64	Camp Chase, OH	CSR,KEB
					Camp Chase, OH	03/18/65	Pt. Lookout, MD Xc	CSR,P22,P26
					Camp Chase, OH	03/18/65	Pt. Lookout, MD	P22,P26
					Pt. Lookout, MD	03/27/65	Boulware's Wh. Xc	CSR
King, Thomas	Msc	1st SCVIBn	Morris Island, SC	09/07/63	Ft. Columbus, NY	09/23/63	Paroled	P1
King, W.	Pvt	E 7th SCResB	Darlington, SC	02/25/65	Hart's Island, NY	06/16/65	Rlsd. G.O. #109	P79
King, W.	Pvt	H 21st SCVI	Ft. Fisher, NC	01/15/65	Elmira, NY	06/23/65	Died, Diarrhea	P5,P6,P66,FPH,HAG
King, W.A.	Sgt	K 12th SCVI	Gettysburg, PA	07/04/63	Ft. Delaware, DE	06/10/65	Released	P44,P45,CSR
King, W.D.	Pvt	G 2nd SCVC	Upperville, VA	06/21/63	Old Capitol, DC	06/25/63	City Pt., VA Xc	CSR
					Ft. McHenry, MD	06/25/63	City Pt., VA Xc	P110
King, William A.	Pvt	D 2nd SCVIRi	Wauhatchie, TN	10/29/63	Bridgeport, AL G.H.	11/05/63	Nashville, TN USGH	P2,CSR
					Nashville, TN	12/13/63	Louisville, KY	P39,CSR
					Louisville, KY	12/16/63	Rock Island, IL	CSR
					Rock Island, IL	02/25/65	Tfd. for Exchange	CSR

SOUTH CAROLINA SOLDIERS, SAILORS AND **K** CITIZENS HELD IN U.S. PRISONS 1861-1865

NAME	RANK	REGIMENT	CAPTURED AT	WHEN	PRISON	MOVED	DISPOSITION	SOURCES
King, William A.	Pvt	K 2nd SCVIRi	Loudon, TN	12/03/63	Chattanooga, TN	01/26/64	Nashville, TN USGH	P1,CSR
					Nashville, TN USGH	02/20/64	Nashville, TN P.M	CSR
					Nashville, TN	02/20/64	Louisville, KY	P39,CSR
					Ft. Delaware, DE		Hos. 8/2-9/30/64	P47
					Louisville, KY	02/29/64	Ft. Delaware, DE	CSR
					Ft. Delaware, DE	09/30/64	Aikens Ldg., VA Xc	P41,CSR
King, William D.	Pvt	G 7th SCVI	Gaines' Mill, VA	06/03/64	Pt. Lookout, MD	06/27/64	Joined U.S. Army	P113,P125,KEB,CSR
King, William M.	Pvt	K 15th SCVI	Halltown, WV	08/26/64	Harper's Ferry, WV	09/02/64	Camp Chase, OH	CSR,KEB
					Camp Chase, OH	03/18/65	Camp Lookout, MD	P22,P26,CSR
					Pt. Lookout, MD	03/27/65	Boulware's Wh. Xc	CSR
King, Willy	Pvt	Waccamaw A	Darlington, SC	02/25/65	New Berne, NC	04/10/65	Hart's Island, NY	CSR
					Hart's Island, NY	06/06/65	Rlsd. G.O. #109	CSR
Kingman, John W.	Pvt	A 25th SCVI	Ft. Fisher, NC	01/15/65	New York, NY	01/30/65	Elmira, NY	CSR,HAG
					Elmira, NY	03/14/65	Pt. Lookout, MD Xc	P65,P66,CSR
Kingsey, William	Pvt	C 3rd SCVABn	Ft. Gaines, AL	08/08/64	New Orleans, LA	10/25/64	Ship Island, MS	P3
Kinlock, John M.	LtC	23rd SCI	Bennettsville, SC	03/06/65	Appomattox C.H., VA	04/09/65	Paroled	CSR
Kinney, Thomas	Cit				Fts. Monroe, VA	02/14/64		P8
Kinsey, Allen	Pvt	H 17th SCVI	Crater, Pbg., VA	07/30/64	City Pt., VA	08/05/64	Pt. Lookout, MD	CSR
					Pt. Lookout, MD	08/08/64	Elmira, NY	P113,P120,CSR
					Elmira, NY	10/11/64	Pt. Lookout, MD Xc	P65,P66,CSR
					Pt. Lookout, MD	10/29/64	Exchanged	P114,CSR
Kinsey, V.C.	Pvt	G 4th SCVC	Stony Creek, VA	12/01/64	City Pt., VA	12/05/64	Pt. Lookout, MD	CDC,CSR
					Pt. Lookout, MD	06/28/65	Rlsd. G.O. #109	P114,CSR
Kinsey, W.B.	Pvt	E 24th SCVI	Chickamauga, GA	09/20/63	Nashville, TN	10/01/63	Louisville, KY	P38,CSR
					Louisville, KY	10/09/63	Camp Morton, IN	CSR
					Camp Morton, IN	03/04/65	City Pt., VA Xc	CSR
Kirby, Absolom	Pvt	D 15th SCVI	Gettysburg, PA	07/05/63	Gettysburg G.H.		Provost Marshal	P4,KEB,CSR
					David's Island, NY	09/12/63	City Pt., VA Xc	P1,CSR
Kirby, Andrew H.	Pvt	C 2nd SCVC	Culpepper, VA	09/13/63	Pt. Lookout, MD	02/24/65	Exchanged	P113,P124
Kirby, Evander	Pvt	F 27th SCVI	Weldon RR, VA	08/21/64	City Pt., VA	08/24/64	Pt. Lookout, MD	CSR,HAG
					Pt. Lookout, MD	01/17/65	Exchanged	P113,P124
Kirby, Hezekiah	Pvt	D 25th SCVI	Ft. Fisher, NC	01/15/65	Hammond G.H., MD	05/13/65	Pt. Lookout, MD	CSR
					Pt. Lookout, MD	05/14/65	Rlsd. G.O. #85	P114,CSR
Kirby, J.W.	Pvt	D 15th SCVI	Gettysburg, PA	07/05/63	Ft. McHenry, MD	07/12/63	Ft. Delaware, DE	CSR,KEB,HIC
					Ft. Delaware, DE	11/20/63	Died, smallpox	P5,P40,P44,P47,FPH
Kirby, James M.	Pvt	B Hol.Leg.	Five Forks, VA	04/01/65	City Pt., VA	04/05/65	Pt. Lookout, MD	CSR
					Pt. Lookout, MD	06/28/65	Rlsd. G.O. #109	P114,HOS
Kirby, John M.	Cpl	C 3rd SCVABn	Blakely, AL	04/09/65	Ship Island, MS	05/02/65	Vicksburg, MS Xc	CSR
Kirby, John M.	Cpl	C 3rd SCVABn	Augusta, GA	05/20/65	Augusta, GA	05/20/65	Paroled	CSR
Kirby, Lafayette C.	Pvt	B 27th SCVI	Petersburg, VA	05/09/64	Fts. Monroe, VA	05/11/64	Pt. Lookout, MD	CSR,HAG
Kirby, Lafayette C.	Pvt	K 27th SCVI	Petersburg, VA	05/09/64	Pt. Lookout, MD	04/11/65	Died, Typhoid fever	P6,P113,FPH,CSR
Kirby, M.L.	Pvt	K 22nd SCVI			Pt. Lookout, MD	04/10/65	Died, Typhoid fever	P12
Kirby, Marshal	Pvt	I 13th SCVI	Petersburg, VA	04/02/65	City Pt., VA	04/04/65	Pt. Lookout, MD	CSR
					Pt. Lookout, MD	06/28/65	Rlsd. G.O. #109	P114,CSR
Kirby, R.B.M.	Pvt	B Hol.Leg.	Five Forks, VA	04/01/65	City Pt., VA	04/05/65	Pt. Lookout, MD	CSR
					Pt. Lookout, MD	06/28/65	Rlsd. G.O. #109	P114,HOS,CSR
Kirby, Ransom L.	Pvt	B Hol.Leg.	Five Forks, VA	04/01/65	City Pt., VA	04/05/65	Pt. Lookout, MD	CSR
					Pt. Lookout, MD	06/28/65	Rlsd. G.O. #109	P114,HOS
Kirby, Reuben W.	Pvt	H 10th SCVI	Murfreesboro, TN	12/31/62	Murfreesboro, TN	01/23/63	Died of wounds	P12,P38,RAS,CSR
Kirby, Samuel	Sgt	H 10th SCVI	Pulaski, TN	12/25/64	Nashville, TN	03/31/65	Louisville, KY	P3,P39,RAS,CTA,CSR
					Louisville, KY	04/04/65	Camp Chase, OH	CSR
					Camp Chase, OH	06/11/65	Released	CSR

SOUTH CAROLINA SOLDIERS, SAILORS AND **K** CITIZENS HELD IN U.S. PRISONS 1861-1865

NAME	RANK	REGIMENT	CAPTURED AT	WHEN	PRISON	MOVED	DISPOSITION	SOURCES
Kirby, Sylvester	Pvt	B Hol.Leg.	Charlotte, NC	05/15/65	Charlotte, NC Hos.	05/15/65	Paroled	CSR
Kirby, W.E.M.	Cpl	B Hol.Leg.	Petersburg, VA	03/25/65	City Pt., VA	03/28/65	Pt. Lookout, MD	CSR
					Pt. Lookout, MD	06/28/65	Rlsd. G.O. #109	CSR
Kirby, W.M.	Pvt	C 3rd SCVABn	Ft. Gaines, AL	08/08/64	New Orleans, LA	10/25/64	Ship Island, MS	P3,CSR
					Ship Island, MS	01/04/65	Exchanged	CSR
Kirby, William	Pvt	I 13th SCVI	Falling Waters, MD	07/14/63	Baltimore, MD	08/16/63	Pt. Lookout, MD	CSR,HOS
					Pt. Lookout, MD	01/26/64	Joined U.S. Army	P113,P125,CSR
Kirby, William	Pvt	C 3rd SCVABn	Blakely, AL	04/09/65	Ship Island, MS	05/01/65	Vicksburg, MS Xc	CSR
Kirby, William	Pvt	C 3rd SCVABn	Augusta, GA	05/20/65	Augusta, GA	05/20/65	Paroled	CSR
Kirby, William D.	Cpl	F 15th SCVI	Gettysburg, PA	07/04/63	Gettysburg, PA G.H.	07/21/63	Provost Marshal	P4,KEB,CSR,UD2,H15
					David's Island, NY	08/24/63	City Pt., VA Xc	P1,CSR
Kirby, William J.	Pvt	C 3rd SCVABn	Ft. Gaines, AL	08/08/64	New Orleans, LA	10/25/64	Ship Island, MS	P3,CSR
					Ship Island, MS	12/24/64	Died, Dysentery	CSR
Kirby, Reuben J.	Pvt	B 18th SCVI	Five Forks, VA	04/01/65	City Pt., VA	04/06/65	Pt. Lookout, MD	CSR
					Pt. Lookout, MD	06/28/65	Rlsd. G.O. #109	P114,CSR
Kirett, F.	Pvt	22nd SCVI	Wilderness, VA	05/06/64	Elmira, NY	03/16/65	Died	P5,FPH
Kirk, Charles E.	Lt	D 3rd SCVIBn	Sharpsburg, MD	09/16/62	David's Island, NY		Ft. Delaware, DE	CSR
					Ft. Delaware, DE	10/02/62	Aikens Ldg., VA Xc	CSR
Kirkland, John Murray	Pvt	F 6th SCVC	Petersburg, VA	07/30/64	City Pt., VA	08/04/64	Pt. Lookout, MD	CSR,CAG
					Elmira, NY	06/14/65	Released	P65,P66,CSR
					Pt. Lookout, MD	08/08/64	Elmira, NY	P113,P120,P125,CSR
Kirkland, Samuel	Pvt	K 7th SCVC	Darbytown Rd., VA	10/07/64	Dutch Gap Canal	10/21/64	City Pt., VA	CSR
					City Pt., VA	10/11/64	Pt. Lookout, MD	CSR
					Pt. Lookout, MD	02/13/65	Exchanged	P114,P124,CSR
Kirkland, William	Pvt	F P.S.S.	Deserted/enemy	08/25/64	Dept. of VA		No further record	CSR,TSE
Kirkland, William	Pvt	A 19th SCVI	Macon, GA	04/20/65	Macon, GA	04/21/65	Paroled	CSR
Kirkland, William	Pvt	E 6th SCResB	Augusta, GA	05/19/65	Augusta, GA	05/19/65	Paroled	CSR
Kirkley, Daniel M.	Cpl	G 2nd SCVI	Sharpsburg, MD	09/17/62	Frederick, MD	12/07/62	Died, Typhoid fever	P6,FPH,SA2,H2,CSR
Kirkley, E.P.H.	Sgt	E 6th SCResB	Augusta, GA	05/19/65	Augusta, GA	05/19/65	Paroled	CSR
Kirkley, James S.	1Lt	F 26th SCVI	Crater, Pbg., VA	07/30/64	Old Capitol, DC	08/05/64	Ft. Delaware, DE	CSR
					Ft. Delaware, DE	06/17/65	Rlsd. G.O. #109	P42,P45,CSR
Kirkley, Robert	Pvt	E 2nd SCVI	Gettysburg, PA	07/03/63	Ft. McHenry, MD	07/12/63	Ft. Delaware, DE	CSR,KEB,SA2,H2
					Ft. Delaware, DE	06/10/65	Rlsd. G.O. #109	P40,P43,P44,P45
Kirkley, William P.	Cpt	F 26th SCVI	Dinwiddie C.H., VA	04/01/65	Ft. McHenry, MD	04/09/65	Johnson's Isl., OH	P83,P110
					Old Capitol, DC	04/11/65	Johnson's Isl., OH	CSR
					Johnson's Isl., OH	06/18/65	Rlsd. G.O. #109	P81,CSR
Kirkpatrick, Elias F.	Pvt	A 14th SCVI	Burkeville, VA	04/14/65	Burkeville, VA	04/17/65	Paroled	CSR
Kirkpatrick, J.C.	Pvt	F 17th SCVI	Five Forks, VA	04/01/65	City Pt., VA	04/06/65	Pt. Lookout, MD	CSR
					Pt. Lookout, MD	06/28/65	Rlsd. G.O. #109	P114,CSR
Kirton, J.C.	Pvt	C 18th SCVAB	Cheraw, SC	03/08/65	Hart's Island, NY	06/14/65	Released	P79,CSR
Kirton, W.H.	Sgt	E 26th SCVI	Hatchers Run, VA	03/29/65	City Pt., VA	04/02/65	Pt. Lookout, MD	CSR
					Pt. Lookout, MD	06/24/65	Rlsd. G.O. #109	P114,CSR
Kissell, W.L.	Pvt	C 1st SCVC	Chilesburg, VA	05/24/64	White House, VA	06/08/64	Pt. Lookout, MD	CSR
					Pt. Lookout, MD	07/09/64	Elmira, NY	P113,P120,CSR
					Elmira, NY	06/30/65	Rlsd. G.O. #109	P65,P66,CSR
Kissick, Thomas R.	Pvt	E 27th SCVI	Florence, SC	03/05/65	New Berne, NC	04/03/65	Pt. Lookout, MD	CSR,HAG
					Pt. Lookout, MD		No other data	P114,CSR
Kitchens, Charles E	Pvt	G 23rd SCVI	Five Forks, VA	04/01/65	City Pt., VA	04/06/65	Pt. Lookout, MD	CSR
					Pt. Lookout, MD	06/28/65	Rlsd. G.O. #109	P114,CSR
Kitchens, James	Pvt	A 6th SCVI	Warrenton, VA	09/29/62	Warrenton, VA	09/29/62	Paroled	CSR
Kitchens, Smith	Sgt	A 17th SCVI	Farmville, VA	04/06/65	City Pt., VA	04/14/65	Newport News, VA	CSR
					Newport News, VA	06/25/65	Rlsd. G.O. #109	P107,HHC,CSR

SOUTH CAROLINA SOLDIERS, SAILORS AND **K** CITIZENS HELD IN U.S. PRISONS 1861-1865

NAME	RANK	REGIMENT	CAPTURED AT	WHEN	PRISON	MOVED	DISPOSITION	SOURCES
Kitchens, William	Pvt	A 17th SCVI	Petersburg, VA	03/25/65	City Pt., VA Hos.	03/28/65	US Str. *Connecticut*	CSR,HHC
					Hos. Str. *Connecticut*	03/29/65	Lincoln G.H., DC	CSR
					Lincoln G.H., DC	04/19/65	Died, Ch. Diarrhea	P6,P12,ROH,CSR
Kitchings, W.F.	Pvt	E 1st SCVIH	Augusta, GA	05/25/65	Augusta, GA	05/25/65	Paroled	CSR
Kitsinger, James	Pvt	D 2nd SCVIRi	Burkesville, VA	04/14/65	Burkesville, VA	04/17/65	Paroled	CSR
Kizer, C.J.	Pvt	A 6th SCVI	Chester, SC	05/05/65	Chester, SC	05/05/65	Paroled	CSR
Kizer, Pinckney C.	Cpl	C 24th SCVI	Nashville, TN	12/16/64	Nashville, TN	01/04/65	Louisville, KY	CSR
					Louisville, KY	01/06/65	Camp Chase, OH	CSR
					Camp Chase, OH	06/12/65	Released G.O. #109	P22,CSR
Kizer, Preston A.	Sgt	C 24th SCVI	Nashville, TN	12/16/64	Nashville, TN	01/04/65	Louisville, KY	CSR
					Louisville, KY	01/06/65	Camp Chase, OH	CSR
					Camp Chase, OH	06/12/65	Released G.O. #109	P22,EFW
Klaren, F.W.	Pvt	A German LA	Deserted/enemy	03/15/65	Charleston, SC	03/15/65	Released on oath	CSR
Kleckley, Thomas	Pvt	C 14th SCVCB	Cuthbert House, SC	10/22/62	Hilton Head, SC	11/02/62	Ft. Columbus, NY	CSR
					Ft. Columbus, NY	11/21/62	Ft. Delaware, DE	CSR
					Ft. Delaware, DE	12/15/62	Fts. Monroe, VA Xc	CSR
Kline, Joseph	Pvt	H 1st SCVA	Deserted/enemy		Charleston, SC	03/12/65	Taken oath & disch.	CSR
Klink, Theodore	1Lt	A Ham.Leg.	Fair Oaks, VA	06/08/62	Philadelphia, PA	06/11/62	Died of wounds	CSR
Klugh, Thomas H.	Pvt	F Hol.Leg.	Five Forks, VA	04/01/65	City Pt., VA	04/05/65	Pt. Lookout, MD	CSR
					Pt. Lookout, MD	06/28/65	Rlsd. G.O. #109	P114
Knee, Henry C.	Pvt	A German LA	Deserted/enemy		Chattanooga, TN	03/14/64	Took the oath	CSR
Kneuff, H.J.	Pvt	G 6th SCVC	Louisa C.H., VA	06/11/64	Fts. Monroe, VA	06/20/64	Pt. Lookout, MD	CSR
					Pt. Lookout, MD	07/20/64	Elmira, NY	P113,P120,CSR
					Elmira, NY	06/16/65	Rlsd. G.O.#109	P65,P66,CSR
Knight, A.L.	Pvt	A 3rd SCVABn	High Pt., NC	05/02/65	High Pt., NC	05/02/65	Paroled	CSR
Knight, Achilles H.	Pvt	H 1st SCVIR	Deserted/enemy		Ft. Monroe, VA	04/02/65	Washington DC	CSR
					Washington D.C.	04/04/65	Oberlin, OH oath	CSR
Knight, D.E.	Pvt	B 17th SCVI	Petersburg, VA Hos.	04/03/65	Washington St. Hos.	04/05/65	Petersburg, VA G.H.	CSR
					Petersburg, VA G.H.	06/21/65	Paroled	CSR
Knight, Elias	Pvt	F 26th SCVI	Southside RR, VA	04/01/65	City Pt., VA	04/05/65	Pt. Lookout, MD	CSR
					Pt. Lookout, MD	06/28/65	Rlsd. G.O. #109	P114,CSR
Knight, Elijah	Pvt	E 22nd SCVI	Five Forks, VA	04/01/65	City Pt., VA	04/05/65	Pt. Lookout, VA	CSR
					Pt. Lookout, MD	06/28/65	Rlsd. G.O. #109	P114,LAN
Knight, J.A.	Pvt	D 27th SCVI	Weldon RR, VA	08/21/64	City Pt., VA	08/24/64	Pt. Lookout, MD	CSR,HAG
					Pt. Lookout, MD	03/14/65	Exchanged	P113,P124,P125,CSR
Knight, J.C.	Pvt	Ch'fld LA	Charlotte, NC	05/23/65	Charlotte, NC	05/23/65	Paroled	CSR
Knight, J.F.	Pvt	G 21st SCVI	Petersburg, VA	06/17/64	Pt. Lookout, MD	07/27/64	Elmira, NY	P113,P120,HAG
					Elmira, NY	07/03/65	Rlsd. G.O. #109	P65,P66
Knight, John	Sgt	D 8th SCVI	Cedar Creek, VA	10/19/64	W. Bldg. Balt, MD	01/07/65	Pt. Lookout, MD	P1,KEB,CSR
					Pt. Lookout, MD	01/28/65	Hammond G.H., MD	P114,KEB
					Pt. Lookout, MD	06/05/65	Released	CSR
Knight, L.R.	Pvt	A 3rd SCVABn	High Pt., NC	05/02/65	High Pt., NC	05/02/65	Paroled	CSR
Knight, Richard	Pvt	C 14th SCVI	Sutherland Stn., VA	04/03/65	City Pt., VA	04/13/65	Pt. Lookout, MD	CSR
					Pt. Lookout, MD	06/28/65	Rlsd. G.O. #109	P114,CSR
Knight, Samuel	Pvt	H Ham.Leg.MI	Deserted/enemy	04/05/65	Bermuda Hundred, VA	04/05/65	City Pt., VA P.M.	CSR
					City Pt., VA	04/08/65	Washington, DC	CSR
					Washington, DC	04/12/65	Charleston, SC	CSR
Knight, Samuel T.	Pvt	G 22nd SCVI	Five Forks, VA	04/01/65	City Pt., VA	04/05/65	Pt. Lookout, MD	CSR,UD3
					Pt. Lookout, MD	06/28/65	Rlsd. G.O. #109	P114,CSR
Knight, Sydney T.	Pvt	C 15th SCVAB	Smith's Ford, NC	03/16/65	New Berne, NC	03/30/65	Pt. Lookout, MD	CSR
					Pt. Lookout, MD	06/28/65	Rlsd. G.O. #109	P114,CSR

SOUTH CAROLINA SOLDIERS, SAILORS AND  CITIZENS HELD IN U.S. PRISONS 1861-1865

NAME	RANK	REGIMENT	CAPTURED AT	WHEN	PRISON	MOVED	DISPOSITION	SOURCES
Knight, T. Jefferson	Pvt	D 8th SCVI	Winchester, VA	09/13/64	Harpers Ferry, WV	09/19/64	Camp Chase, OH	CSR
					Camp Chase, OH	05/02/65	New Orleans, LA	P22,P26,CSR
					New Orleans, LA	05/12/65	Vicksburg, MS	CSR
					Vicksburg, MS	05/15/65	Vicksburg US Hos.	CSR
					Vicksburg, MS USGH	05/22/65	Released	CSR
Knight, W.H.	Pvt	C 15th SCVAB	Smith's Ford, NC	03/16/65	New Berne, NC	03/30/65	Pt. Lookout, MD	CSR
					Pt. Lookout, MD	06/04/65	Released	P114,CSR
Knight, William W.	Pvt	C 8th SCVI	Gettysburg, PA	07/05/63	Baltimore, MD	08/20/63	Pt. Lookout, MD	CSR,KEB
					Pt. Lookout, MD	03/17/64	Exchanged	P113,P124,CSR
Knopf, Abraham	Pvt	A 22nd SCVI	Bermuda Hundred, VA	06/02/64	Bermuda Hundred, VA	06/03/64	Fts. Monroe, VA	CSR
					Fts. Monroe, VA	06/04/64	Pt. Lookout, MD	CSR
					Pt. Lookout, MD	02/13/65	Exchanged	P113,P124
Knowles, Madison	Pvt	G 20th SCVI	Cedar Creek, VA	10/19/64	Harpers Ferry, WV	10/24/64	Pt. Lookout, MD	CSR
					Pt. Lookout, MD	05/13/65	Rlsd. G.O. #85	P114,CSR
Knox, George J.	Pvt	F 5th SCVI	Chattanooga, TN	10/28/63	Nashville, TN	11/07/63	Louisville, KY	CSR
					Louisville, KY	11/09/63	Camp Morton, IN	CSR
					Camp Morton, IN	02/14/65	Died, Lung Inflam.	P6,P12,FPH,CSR
Knox, Morgan	Pvt	F 15th SCVI	South Mtn., MD	09/15/62	Ft. McHenry, MD	10/17/62	Fts. Monroe, VA	CSR
					Fts. Monroe, VA	10/19/62	Aikens Ldg., VA Xc	CSR
Koch, W.F.P.	Pvt	D 5th SCVC	Stony Creek, VA	12/01/64	City Pt., VA	12/05/64	Pt. Lookout, MD	CSR,MDM
					Pt. Lookout, MD	06/28/65	Rlsd. G.O. #109	P114,CSR
Koennecke, Albert	Pvt	I 27th SCVI	Town Creek, NC	02/20/65	Ft. Anderson, NC	02/28/65	Pt. Lookout, MD	CSR
					Pt. Lookout, MD	06/28/65	Rlsd. G.O. #109	P114,CSR
Koester, Louis	Pvt	A 12th SCVI	Sharpsburg, MD	09/17/62	Sharpsburg, MD	09/29/62	Paroled on oath	CSR
Kohler, J.H.	Sgt	D Ham.Leg.	Fair Oaks, VA	05/31/62	Fts. Monroe, VA	06/05/62	Ft. Delaware, DE	CSR
					Ft. Delaware, DE	08/05/62	Aikens Ldg., VA Xc	CSR
Kolb, B.T.	Pvt	C 3rd SCVABn	Blakely, AL	04/09/65	Ship Island, MS	05/01/65	Vicksburg, MS Xc	CSR
Konig, John H.	Pvt	B German LA	Deserted/enemy	07/13/63	Washington, DEC	12/13/63	Took the oath	CSR
Koon, George Elias	Cpl	I 15th SCVI	Halltown, VA	08/26/64	Harper's Ferry, VA	09/02/64	Camp Chase, OH	CSR,KEB
					Camp Chase, OH	03/14/65	Died, Typhoid	P6,P12,P27,FPH,KEB,CSR
Koon, H. William	Pvt	I 15th SCVI	South Mtn., MD	09/14/62	Ft. Delaware, DE	10/02/62	Aikens Ldg., VA Xc	CSR,KEB,H15
Koon, H. William	Pvt	I 15th SCVI	Gettysburg, PA	07/04/63	Gettysburg, PA USH		Provost Marshal	CSR
					Provost Marshal		David's Island, NY	CSR
					David's Island, NY	08/24/63	City Pt., VA Xc	CSR
Koon, Henry M.	Pvt	I 15th SCVI	Gettysburg, PA	07/04/63	Gettysburg G.H.		Provost Marshal	P4,KEB,H15
					David's Island, NY	08/24/63	City Pt., VA Xc	P1,KEB
Koon, Henry M.	Pvt	I 15th SCVI	Knoxville, TN	12/10/63	Took oath	12/15/63		CSR
Koon, Henry M.	Pvt	I 15th SCVI	Deserted/enemy		Dept. of Tenn.	12/18/63	Took oath & Rlsd.	P8
Koon, J.A.C.	Pvt	G 13th SCVI	Wilderness, VA	05/05/64	Belle Plain, VA	05/21/64	Ft. Delaware, DE	CSR,ANY
					Ft. Delaware, DE		Hos. 3/20-3/25/65	P41,P47,CSR
					Ft. Delaware, DE	06/10/65	Released, sick list	CSR
Koon, Jacob Franklin	Pvt	I 15th SCVI	Sharpsburg, MD	09/17/62	Frederick, MD USA	12/13/62	Paroled	CSR,KEB,H15
Koon, James F.	Pvt	I 15th SCVI	South Mtn., MD	09/14/62	Ft. McHenry, MD	12/14/62	City Pt., VA Xc	CSR,KEB,H15
Koon, James F.	Pvt	I 15th SCVI	Knoxville, TN	11/24/63	Knoxville, TN	01/10/64	Camp Chase, OH	P84,CSR
Koon, James F.	Pvt	I 15th SCVI	Knoxville, TN	01/05/64	Nashville, TN	01/17/64	Louisville, KY	P39,CSR
Koon, James F.	Pvt	I 15th SCVI	Knoxville, TN	01/05/64	New Orleans, LA	05/23/65	Exchanged	P4,CSR
Koon, John Wesley	Sgt	G Hol.Leg.	Five Forks, VA	04/01/65	City Pt., VA	04/05/65	Pt. Lookout, MD	CSR
					Pt. Lookout, MD	06/28/65	Rlsd. G.O. #109	P114,P118,ANY
Koon, Walter F.	Pvt	F 20th SCVI	Cedar Creek, VA	10/19/64	Harpers Ferry, WV	10/24/64	Pt. Lookout, MD	CSR,ANY,KEB
					Pt. Lookout, MD	02/13/65	Exchanged	P114,P124,CSR
Koon, Walter W.	Pvt	I 15th SCVI	Gettysburg, PA	07/05/63	Gettysburg, PA USH	07/10/63	Died of wounds	P4,KEB,CSR

SOUTH CAROLINA SOLDIERS, SAILORS AND  CITIZENS HELD IN U.S. PRISONS 1861-1865

NAME	RANK	REGIMENT	CAPTURED AT	WHEN	PRISON	MOVED	DISPOSITION	SOURCES
Koon, William H.	Pvt	B 18th SCVI	Richmond, VA Hos.	04/03/65	Provost Marshal V	04/15/65	Libby Prison, VA	CSR
					Libby Prison, VA	04/23/65	Newport News, VA	CSR
					Newport News, VA	06/26/65	Rlsd. G.O. #109	CSR
Koth, Henry C.	Pvt	D 4th SCVC	Salisbury, NC	04/12/65	Nashville, TN	04/29/65	Louisville, KY	P39,CSR
					Louisville, KY	05/02/65	Camp Chase, OH	CSR
					Camp Chase, OH	06/13/65	Rlsd. G.O. #109	P23,CSR
Krause, John W.	Pvt	D 1st SCVIR	Deserted/enemy		Charleston, SC		New York, NY oath	SA1,CSR
Kreps, Eugene S.	Pvt	A 19th SCVI	Kentucky	09/14/62	Kentucky	09/14/62	Paroled	CSR
Kruer, Henry	Pvt	A 24th SCVI	Deserted/enemy	07/02/64	Louisville, KY	07/16/64	Sent north on oath	CSR
Kruse, Frederick	Cpl	A German LA	Deserted/enemy		Hilton Head, SC	03/22/65	New York, NY P.M.	CSR
Kuck, George	Pvt	1st SCVIR	Deserted/enemy		Charleston, SC		Released on oath	CSR
Kyle, D.H.	Pvt	C 3rd SCVABn	Blakely, AL	04/09/65	Ship Island, MS	05/01/65	Vicksburg, MS Xc	CSR
Kyzer, Drury	Pvt	K 13th SCVI	Southside RR, VA	04/05/65	City Pt., VA	04/07/65	Hart's Island, NY	CSR
					Hart's Island, NY	06/14/65	Rlsd. G.O. #109	P79,CSR
Kyzer, H.P.	Pvt	C 1st SCVC	Pocotaligo, SC	10/22/62	Ft. Delaware, DE	12/15/62	Fts. Monroe, VA Xc	CSR
Kyzer, Henry Luther	Pvt	C 15th SCVI	Halltown, VA	08/26/64	Harper's Ferry, WV	08/29/64	Camp Chase, OH	CSR
					Camp Chase, OH	03/18/65	Pt. Lookout, MD	P22,H15,CSR
					Pt. Lookout, MD	03/27/65	Boulware's Wh., Xc	CSR
Kyzer, Henry Luther	Pvt	C 15th SCVI	Augusta, GA	05/24/65	Augusta, GA	05/24/65	Paroled on oath	H15
Kyzer, Jacob Shadrack	Pvt	C 15th SCVI	Lexington, SC	02/13/65	Pt. Lookout, MD	06/28/65	Rlsd. G.O. #109	P114,H15,KEB,CSR
Kyzer, John T.	Pvt	C 15th SCVI	Augusta, GA	05/24/65	Augusta, GA	05/24/65	Paroled on oath	KEB,H15,CSR
Kyzer, Joseph F.	Pvt	K 13th SCVI	Gettysburg, PA	07/05/63	Chester, PA G.H.	08/24/63	City Pt., VA Xc	P1
					David's Island, NY	08/24/63	City Pt., VA Xc	CSR
Kyzer, Karey P.	Pvt	C 14th SCVCB	Cuthbert House, SC	10/22/62	Hilton Head, SC	11/02/62	Ft. Columbus, NY	CSR
					Ft. Columbus, NY	11/21/62	Ft. Delaware, DE	CSR
Kyzer, S.B.	Pvt	C 15th SCVI	Augusta, GA	05/24/65	Augusta, GA	05/24/65	Paroled on oath	H15,CSR

L

SOUTH CAROLINA SOLDIERS, SAILORS AND CITIZENS HELD IN U.S. PRISONS 1861-1865

NAME	RANK	REGIMENT	CAPTURED AT	WHEN	PRISON	MOVED	DISPOSITION	SOURCES
LaBoone, Van L.	Pvt	H 7th SCVI	N. Anna River, VA	05/23/64	Pt. Lookout, MD	03/15/65	Exchanged	P113,P124,CSR
LaCoste, S.D.M.	Pvt	Palmetto LA	Burkesville, VA	04/15/65	Burkeville, VA	04/16/65	Released	CSR
Lackey, James D.	Pvt	F 23rd SCVI	Petersburg, VA	04/02/65	City Pt., VA	04/04/65	Pt. Lookout, MD	CSR,HHC
					Pt. Lookout, MD	06/28/65	Rlsd. G.O. #109	P114,CSR
Lackey, Russell G.	Pvt	F 23rd SCVI	Aberdeen Ch., VA	04/03/65	City Pt., VA	04/13/65	Pt. Lookout, MD	P114,HHC,CSR
					Pt. Lookout, MD	06/14/65	Rlsd. G.O. #109	P114,CSR
Lackey, William R.	Pvt	C 3rd SCVABn	Blakely, AL	04/09/65	Ship Island, MS	05/01/65	Vicksburg, MS Xc	CSR
Ladd, F.M.	Pvt	F Hol.Leg.	Stony Creek, VA	05/12/64	Elmira, NY	02/14/65	Died	P6,P10,FPH
Ladd, Pinckney B.	Pvt	H 2nd SCVIRi	New Market Hts., VA	08/03/64	U.S.H. Steamer	08/15/64	Died of wounds	CSR
Laderize, E.	Cit	Charleston	Columbia, SC	02/19/65	Hart's Island, NY	06/20/65	Rlsd. G.O. #109	P79
Lael, Adlai D.	Pvt	F 6th SCVI	Williamsburg, VA	05/05/62	Cliffburne G.H., DC	07/21/62	Old Capitol, DC	CSR
					Old Capitol, DC	08/01/62	Fts. Monroe, VA Xc	CSR
					Fts. Monroe, VA	08/05/62	Aikens Ldg., VA Xc	CSR
Lael, Adlai D.	Pvt	F 6th SCVI	Farmville, VA	04/06/65	City Pt., VA	04/14/65	Newport News, VA	CSR
					Newport News, VA	06/25/65	Rlsd. G.O. #109	HHC,CSR
Lael, Julius A.	Pvt	F 6th SCVI	Farmville, VA	04/06/65	Newport News, VA	06/25/65	Rlsd. G.O. #109	HHC,CSR
Lafoy, Isaac	Pvt	F 1st SCVIH	Deep Bottom, VA	08/14/64	Bermuda Hundred, VA	08/15/64	Fts. Monroe, VA	CSR,SA1
					Fts. Monroe, VA	08/17/64	Pt. Lookout, MD	CSR
					Pt. Lookout, MD	10/11/64	Exchanged	P113,CSR
					Libby Prison Rchmd.	04/24/65	Paroled	CSR
Lafoy, P.B.	Pvt	F 1st SCVIH	Richmond, VA Hos.	04/03/65	Richmond, VA P.M.	05/05/65	Paroled	CSR
Lafoy, W.E.	Pvt	F 1st SCVIH	Deep Bottom, VA	08/14/64	Bermuda Hundred, VA	08/15/64	Fts. Monroe, VA	CSR,SA1
					Fts. Monroe, VA	08/17/64	Pt. Lookout, MD	CSR
					Pt. Lookout, MD	06/06/65	Released	P113,CSR
Laile, James	Pvt	H 1st SCVA	Morris Island, SC	07/10/63	Hilton Head, SC	07/18/63	Ft. Columbus, NY	CSR
					Ft. Columbus, NY	09/25/63	Rlsd. on oath	P1,CSR
Lake, Enoch Jacob, Jr.	Pvt	E 3rd SCVI	Gettysburg, PA	07/05/63	Gettysburg, PA G.H.	07/21/63	Provost Marshal N	P4,ANY,CSR,H3,KEB
					David's Island, NY	10/22/63	Fts. Monroe, VA Xc	P1,CSR
Lake, George B.	1Lt	B 22nd SCVI	Crater, Pbg., VA	07/30/64	City Pt., VA P.M.	08/03/64	Washington, DC	CSR,HOS
					Ft. McHenry, MD	08/11/64	Ft. Delaware, DE	P110
					Old Capitol, DC	08/11/64	Ft. Delaware, DE	CSR
					Ft. Delaware, DE	06/17/65	Rlsd. G.O. #109	P43,P44
Lake, John B.	Pvt	D 13th SCVI	Spotsylvania, VA	05/12/64	Belle Plain, VA	05/21/64	Ft. Delaware, DE	CSR,ANY
					Ft. Delaware, DE	05/24/64	Hos. 5/24-6/13/64	P47
					Ft. Delaware, DE	09/19/64	Hos. 9/19-10/12/64	P47
					Ft. Delaware, DE	01/05/65	Hos. 1/5-1/12/65	P47
					Ft. Delaware, DE	06/10/65	Released G.O. #109	P41,P42,45,CSR
Lallie, D.D.	Lt	6th SCResB	Edisto River, SC	02/10/65	1st Div. 17th A.C.			CSR
Lamance, Erwin	Pvt	F 16th SCVI	Missionary Ridge, TN	11/25/63	Nashville, TN	12/05/63	Louisville, KY	P39,CSR
					Louisville, KY	12/06/63	Rock Island, IL	CSR
					Rock Island, IL	03/10/64	Died, Lung Infl.	P12,P5,FPH,CSR
Lamb, A.	Pvt	C 3rd SCVABn	Citronelle, AL	05/04/65	Meridian, MS	05/10/65	Paroled	CSR
Lamb, Andrew	Pvt	C 18th SCVI	Richmond, VA Hos.	04/03/65	Provost Marshal	04/20/65	Released	CSR
Lamb, Francis M.	Pvt	H P.S.S.	Williamsburg, VA	05/01/62	Fts. Monroe, VA		Aikens Ldg., VA Xc	CSR,TSE
					Aikens Ldg., VA	08/05/62	Exchanged	CSR
Lamb, John	Pvt	G 27th SCVI	Petersburg, VA	06/18/64	City Pt., VA	06/24/64	Pt. Lookout, MD	CSR,HAG
					Pt. Lookout, MD	07/27/64	Elmira, NY	P113,P120
					Elmira, NY	10/11/64	Pt. Lookout, MD	P65,P66
Lamb, John	Pvt	G 27th SCVI	Petersburg, VA	06/18/64	W. Bldg. Balt, MD	10/27/64	Pt. Lookout, MD	P1,P4
					Pt. Lookout, MD	10/29/64	Aikens Ldg., VA Xc	P114
					Fts. Monroe, VA	11/01/64	Died	CSR
Lamb, Robert	Cpl	B 15th SCVI	Sharpsburg, MD	09/17/62	Ft. McHenry, MD	10/17/62	Fts. Monroe, VA XC	CSR

L

SOUTH CAROLINA SOLDIERS, SAILORS AND CITIZENS HELD IN U.S. PRISONS 1861-1865

NAME	RANK	REGIMENT	CAPTURED AT	WHEN	PRISON	MOVED	DISPOSITION	SOURCES
Lamb, Robert	Cpl	H 25th SCVI	Petersburg, VA	05/09/64	Fts. Monroe, VA	07/27/64	Pt. Lookout, MD	CSR,HAG
					Pt. Lookout, MD	02/15/65	Died, Ch. Diarrhea	P12,P113,FPH,CSR
Lamb, Thomas	Pvt	I 22nd SCVI	Crater, Pbg., VA	07/30/64	City Pt., VA	08/05/64	Pt. Lookout, MD	CSR
					Pt. Lookout, MD	08/08/64	Elmira, NY	P113,P120
					Elmira, NY	03/14/65	James R., VA Xc	P65,P66,CSR
Lamb, William J.	Pvt	B 27th SCVI	Town Creek, NC	02/20/65	Ft. Anderson, NC	02/28/65	Pt. Lookout, MD	CSR,HAG
					Pt. Lookout, MD	06/29/65	Rlsd. G.O. #109	P114
Lambert, Charles	Pvt	A Ham.Leg.MI	Amelia C.H., VA	04/06/65	City Pt., VA P.M.	04/14/65	Pt. Lookout, MD	CSR
					Pt. Lookout, MD	06/06/65	Released on oath	CSR
Lambert, Daniel H.	Cpl	D 10th SCVI	Murfreesboro, TN	12/31/62	Nashville, TN	01/06/63	Died of wounds	P38,RAS,HMC,CSR
Lambert, John H.	Pvt	D 10th SCVI	Danville, KY	10/10/62	Louisville, KY	11/29/62	Vicksburg, MS Xc	CSR
Lammance, Jacob W.	Pvt	H 16th SCVI	Franklin, TN	11/30/64	Nashville, TN	12/03/64	Louisville, KY	CSR,16R
					Louisville, KY	12/04/64	Camp Douglas, IL	CSR
					Camp Douglas, IL	02/21/65	Pt. Lookout, MD Xc	P55,CSR
					Richmond, VA Hos.	03/17/65	Furloughed 60 days	CSR
Lammance, Jacob W.	Pvt	H 16th SCVI	Yazoo City, MS	07/13/65	Yazoo City, MS	07/13/65	Paroled	CSR
Lamny, William J.	Pvt	B 10th SCVI	Franklin, TN	12/18/64	Nashville, TN G.H.	03/07/65	Provost Marshal	P4
Lamothe, A.	Sgt	D 18th SCVAB	Greensboro, NC	05/03/65	Prld. New Orleans			CSR
Lamotte, John W.	Pvt	D 23rd SCVI	Petersburg, VA	04/01/65	City Pt., VA	04/04/65	Pt. Lookout, MD	CSR
					Pt. Lookout, MD	06/29/65	Rlsd. G.O. #109	P114,CSR
Lamson, John P.	Pvt	G 27th SCVI	Petersburg, VA	06/18/64	City Pt., VA	06/24/64	Pt. Lookout, MD	CSR,HAG
					Pt. Lookout, MD	07/08/64	Died	P112,P113,CSR
Lanaux, G.A.	Pvt	D 18th SCVAB	Raleigh, NC Hos.	04/07/65	Greensboro, NC	06/22/65	Paroled to LA	CSR
Lancaster, Calvin	Pvt	A Neale's Bn	Cheraw, SC	03/04/65	Pt. Lookout, MD	06/29/65	Rlsd. G.O. #109	P114
Lancaster, J.C.	Pvt	B 14th SCMil	Lynch's Creek, SC	03/22/65	Hart's Island, NY	06/14/65	Released GO #109	P79,CSR
Lancaster, L.L.	Pvt	B 14th SCMil	Lynch's Creek, SC	02/25/65	David's Island, NY	04/17/65	Died, Typhoid fever	P1,P6,P12,P79,FPH
Lancaster, William C.	Pvt	F 13th SCVI	Deserted/enemy	02/24/65	City Pt., VA	02/26/65	Washington, DC	CSR
					Washington, DC	02/27/65	Springfield, IL	CSR
Land, Francis	Pvt	B 7th SCVIBn	Weldon RR, VA	08/21/64	City Pt., VA	08/24/64	Pt. Lookout, MD	CSR,HAG
					Pt. Lookout, MD	10/18/64	Joined U.S. Army	P113,P125,CSR
Land, James J.	Pvt	D Hol.Leg.	Five Forks, VA	04/01/65	Pt. Lookout, MD	06/29/65	Rlsd. G.O. #109	P114
Land, William H.	Pvt	M P.S.S.	Cold Harbor, VA	06/01/64	White House, VA	06/05/64	Pt. Lookout, MD	CSR,TSE
					Pt. Lookout, MD	07/09/64	Elmira, NY	P113,P120,CSR
					Elmira, NY	06/14/65	Rlsd G.O. #109	P65,P66,CSR
Landis, William	Pvt	G 16th SCVI	Resaca, GA	10/11/64	Chattanooga, TN	10/21/64	Louisville, KY	CSR
					Louisville, KY	11/05/64	Sent north on oath	CSR
Landreth, P.	Pvt	B 27th SCVI	Petersburg, VA	06/24/64	Fts. Monroe, VA	06/26/64	Pt. Lookout, MD	CSR
					Pt. Lookout, MD	02/10/65	Exchanged	P113,P124,CSR
Landrum, Francis W.	Pvt	B Ham.Leg.	Deserted/enemy	07/24/63	Harrisburg, PA	08/08/63	Phila., PA oath	CSR
					Ft. Mifflin, PA	11/24/63	Released on oath	CSR,P2
					Ft. Mifflin, PA	11/24/63	Rlsd./ Gen. Cadwalder	P2
Landrum, L.D.	Pvt	F 19th SCVI	Augusta, GA	05/19/65	Augusta, GA	05/19/65	Paroled	CSR
Landrum, William M.	Pvt	A 22nd SCVI	Bermuda Hundred, VA	06/02/64	Bermuda Hundred, VA	06/03/64	Fts. Monroe, VA	CSR
					Fts. Monroe, VA	06/04/64	Pt. Lookout, MD	CSR
					Pt. Lookout, MD	02/13/65	Exchanged	P113,P124,CSR
Lane, Albert	Pvt	A 11th SCVI	Deserted/enemy	03/14/65	Hilton Head, SC	03/22/65	New York, NY oath	CSR
Lane, D.F.	Pvt	H 23rd SCVI	Frederick, MD Hos.	09/26/62	Ft. McHenry, MD	10/02/62	Fts. Monroe, VA Xc	CSR,HMC
Lane, D.F.	Cpl	H 23rd SCVI	Five Forks, VA	04/01/65	City Pt., VA	04/05/65	Pt. Lookout, MD	CSR
					Pt. Lookout, MD	06/29/65	Rlsd. G.O. #109	P114,CSR
Lane, David E.	Pvt	H Orr's Ri.	Petersburg, VA	04/03/65	Camp Hamilton, VA	06/05/65	Fts. Monroe, VA	CSR,CDC
					Fts. Monroe, VA	06/06/65	Newport News, VA	CSR
					Newport News, VA	06/25/65	Rlsd. G.O. #109	CSR

NAME	RANK	REGIMENT	CAPTURED AT	WHEN	PRISON	MOVED	DISPOSITION	SOURCES
Lane, Elisha	Pvt	1st SCVA	North Carolina	04/21/65	New Berne, NC USGH	04/26/65	Died, Tonsilitis	P1,P6,P12,WAT
Lane, James D.	Pvt	F 27th SCVI	Town Creek, NC	02/20/65	Pt. Lookout, MD	06/06/65	Released	P114,HAG
Lane, John	Sgt	H 17th SCVI	Farmville, VA	04/13/65	Farmville US Hos.	04/26/65	Died of wounds	P6,P12,CSR
Lane, Stephen D.	Pvt	D 25th SCVI	Town Creek, NC	02/20/65	Ft. Anderson, NC	02/28/65	Pt. Lookout, MD	CSR,HAG,HMC
					Pt. Lookout, MD	06/29/65	Rlsd. G.O. #109	P114,CSR
Lane, William	Pvt	B 10th SCVI	Murfreesboro, TN	12/30/62	Nashville, TN		Louisville, KY	P38,RAS,CSR
					Louisville, KY	03/20/63	Camp Butler, IL	CSR
					Camp Butler, IL	04/10/63	City Pt., VA Xc	P21
Lane, William	Pvt	B 10th SCVI	Murfreesboro, TN	12/30/62	Fts. Monroe, VA	04/14/63	Paroled & released	CSR
Lane, William	Pvt	B 10th SCVI	Murfreesboro, TN	12/30/62	Petersburg, VA Hos.	04/29/63	Furloughed, clothed	CSR
Laney, G.W.	Pvt	H 4th SCVC	Lancaster, SC	02/28/65	New Berne, NC	04/10/65	Pt. Lookout, MD	CS,LANR
					Pt. Lookout, MD	06/04/65	Released	P114,CSR
Laney, William	Pvt	E 10th SCVI	Lancaster, SC	02/28/65	Pt. Lookout, MD	06/04/65	Released on oath	P114,P121,CTA,CSR
Lanford, Daniel A.	Pvt	E Hol.Leg.	Five Forks, VA	04/01/65	City Pt., VA	04/05/65	Pt. Lookout, MD	CSR
					Pt. Lookout, MD	05/29/65	Died, Lung Infl.	P6,P114,FPH,CSR
Lanford, E.L.	Pvt	G 3rd SCVI	N. Anna River, VA	05/23/64	Port Royal, VA	05/30/64	Pt. Lookout, MD	CSR,KEB,SA2,H3
					Pt. Lookout, MD	03/14/65	Aikens Ldg., VA Xc	P113,P124,CSR
Lanford, G.W.	Pvt	E Hol.Leg.	Warrenton, VA	09/29/62	Warrenton, VA	09/29/62	Paroled/Hospital	CSR
Lanford, Greene L.	2Lt	E Hol.Leg.	Petersburg, VA	04/03/65	Petersburg, VA Hos.	04/07/65	Died of wounds	P5,P12,CSR
Lanford, Lewis Meredith	Pvt	E Hol.Leg.	Five Forks, VA	04/01/65	City Pt., VA	04/05/65	Pt. Lookout, MD	CSR,HOS
					Pt. Lookout, MD	06/29/65	Rlsd. G.O. #109	P114,CSR
Lanford, William L.	Pvt	E Hol.Leg.	Five Forks, VA	04/01/65	City Pt., VA	04/05/65	Pt. Lookout, MD	CSR,HOS
					Pt. Lookout, MD	06/04/65	Rlsd. sick list	P114,CSR
Lang, Henry	Pvt	C 1st SCVA	Gettysburg, PA	07/21/64	Harrisburg, PA	07/27/64	Ft. Delaware, DE	CSR
					Ft. Delaware, DE	05/10/65	Rlsd. G.O. #85	P42,P46,P47,CSR
Langballe, F.W.	Pvt	E 11th SCVI	Petersburg, VA	06/24/64	Bermuda Hundred, VA	06/25/64	Fts. Monroe, VA	CSR,HAG
					Fts. Monroe, VA	06/26/64	Pt. Lookout, MD	CSR
					Pt. Lookout, MD	08/16/64	Elmira, NY	P113,P120,CSR
					Elmira, NY	07/25/65	Rlsd. G.O. #109	P65,CSR
Langford, George Y.	Sgt	B 14th SCVI	Port Royal, SC	12/17/61	Hilton Head, SC	02/09/62	Ft. Lafayette, NY	CSR,HOE
					Ft. Lafayette, NY	07/11/62	Ft. Delaware, DE	P85,CSR
					Ft. Delaware, DE	08/05/62	Aikens Ldg., VA Xc	CSR
Langford, George Y.	Sgt	B 14th SCVI	Sutherland Stn., VA	04/02/65	City Pt., VA	04/07/65	Hart's Island, NY	CSR
					Hart's Island, NY	06/18/65	Rlsd. G.O. #109	P79
Langford, H.	Pvt	B 14th SCVI	Hilton Head, SC	10/07/61	Ft. Delaware, DE	08/05/62	Aikens Ldg., VA Xc	CSR
Langford, Lewis J.	Pvt	B 15th SCVI	Flat Rock, SC	02/10/65	New Berne, NC USGH	04/03/65	Fts. Monroe, VA	CSR,H15
					Fts. Monroe, VA	06/06/65	Newport News, VA	CSR
					Newport News, VA	06/15/65	Rlsd. G.O. #109	CSR
Langford, Lewis M.	Pvt	B 14th SCVI	Port Royal, SC	12/17/61	Hilton Head, SC	02/09/62	Ft. Lafayette, NY	CSR,HOE
					Ft. Lafayette, NY	07/11/62	Ft. Delaware, DE	P85
					Ft. Delaware, DE	08/05/62	Aikens Ldg., VA Xc	CSR
Langford, Patrick J.	Pvt	B 14th SCVI	Port Royal, SC	12/17/61	Hilton Head, SC	02/09/62	Ft. Lafayette, NY	CSR,HOE
					Ft. Lafayette, NY	07/11/62	Ft. Delaware, DE	P85,CSR
					Ft. Delaware, DE	08/05/62	Aikens Ldg., VA Xc	CSR
Langford, T.G.	Pvt	E 13th SCVI	Flat Rock, SC	02/10/65	Newport News, VA	06/13/65	Rlsd. G.O. #109	P107
Langford, William	Pvt	D 3rd SCVABn	Atlanta, GA	07/07/64	Etiwah, GA P.M.	08/13/64	Chattanooga, TN	CSR
					Chattanooga, TN	09/04/64	Louisville, KY	CSR
					Louisville, KY	09/26/64	Sent North of Ohio	CSR
Langley, James	Pvt	G 3rd SCVABn	High Pt., NC	05/02/65	High Pt., NC	05/02/65	Paroled	CSR,HIC
Langley, John B.	Pvt	I 12th SCVI	Gettysburg, PA	07/04/63	David's Island, NY	09/08/63	City Pt., VA Xc	P1,LAN,CSR
Langley, John H.	Cpl	G 14th SCVI	Petersburg, VA	04/04/65	City Pt., VA	04/13/65	Pt. Lookout, MD	CSR
					Pt. Lookout, MD	06/28/65	Rlsd. G.O. #109	P114,CSR

L

SOUTH CAROLINA SOLDIERS, SAILORS AND CITIZENS HELD IN U.S. PRISONS 1861-1865

NAME	RANK	REGIMENT	CAPTURED AT	WHEN	PRISON	MOVED	DISPOSITION	SOURCES
Langston, Ezra E.	Pvt	E 6th SCVI	Fair Oaks, VA	06/01/62	Fts. Monroe, VA	06/05/62	Ft. Delaware, DE	CSR
					Ft. Delaware, DE	08/05/62	Aikens Ldg., VA Xc	CSR
Langston, George McD.	Sgt	I 3rd SCVI	Gettysburg, PA	07/05/63	Letterman G.H. Gbg		Provost Marshal	P1,KEB,H3
					W. Bldg. Balt., MD	01/10/64	Hammond G.H., MD	P1,CSR
					Hammond G.H., MD	03/17/64	City Pt., VA Xc	CSR
Langston, Henry A.	Pvt	I 18th SCVI	Petersburg, VA	03/25/65	City Pt., VA	03/28/65	Pt. Lookout, MD	CSR
					Pt. Lookout, MD	06/29/65	Rlsd. G.O. #109	P114,CSR
Langston, Isaac J.	Pvt	E 2nd SCVIRi	Concord, TN	01/10/64	Nashville, TN	01/24/64	Louisville, KY	P39,CSR
					Louisville, KY	01/27/64	Rock Island, IL	CSR
					Rock Island, IL	05/22/65	Released on oath	CSR
Langston, J.W.	Pvt	H 26th SCVI	Farmville, VA	04/06/65	Farmville, VA	04/06/65	Paroled	CSR
Langston, Robert R.	Bug	C 3rd SCVABn	Ft. Gaines, AL	08/08/64	New Orleans, LA	10/25/64	Ship Island, MS	P4,CSR
					Ship Island, MS	01/04/65	Exchanged	CSR
Langtry, J.W.	Sgt	H 1st SCVA	Deserted/enemy	02/19/65	Charleston, SC		Released on oath	CSR
Lanier, Chesterfield	Pvt	H 18th SCVI	Five Forks, VA	04/01/65	City Pt., VA	04/05/65	Pt. Lookout, MD	CSR,YEB
					Pt. Lookout, MD	06/29/65	Rlsd. G.O. #109	P114,CSR
Lanier, Louis	Pvt	D 12th SCVI	Clover Hill, VA	04/04/65	Bermuda Hundred, VA	04/08/64	Hart's Island, NY	CSR
					City Pt., VA	04/11/65	Hart's Island, NY	CSR
					Hart's Island, NY	06/16/65	Rlsd. G.O. #109	P79,CSR
Lanier, Robert	Pvt	C 17th SCVI	Deserted/enemy	11/28/64	P.M. A. of Potomac	11/29/64	Washington, DC	CSR
					Washington, DC	12/01/64	Took the oath	CSR
Lanier, Thomas J.	Cpl	H Hol.Leg.	Five Forks, VA	04/01/65	Pt. Lookout, MD	06/14/65	Released	P114
Lanier, Virginius W.	Pvt	H Hol.Leg.	Five Forks, VA	04/02/65	Pt. Lookout, MD	06/14/65	Released	P114
Lanier, Richard	Pvt	G P.S.S.	Deserted/enemy	09/24/62	Sharpsburg, MD		Signed oath	CSR,TSE
Lanigan, Edward	Sgt	H 27th SCVI	Deserted/enemy	11/07/64	City Pt., VA	11/07/64	Washington, DC	CSR,HAG
					Washington, DC	11/08/64	Ft. Hudson, NY	CSR
Lankford, Martin V.B.	Sgt	G 1st SCVA	Fayetteville, NC	03/10/65	New Berne, NC	03/30/65	Pt. Lookout, MD	CSR
					Pt. Lookout, MD	06/28/65	Rlsd. G.O. #109	P114,CSR
Lanneau, B.M.	Pvt	K 2nd SCVC	Anderson, SC	05/05/65	Anderson, SC	05/05/65	Paroled	CSR
Lanneau, William S.	Pvt	A 25th SCVI	Ft. Fisher, NC	01/15/65	New York, NY	01/30/65	Elmira, NY	CSR,HAG
					Elmira, NY	06/14/65	Rlsd. G.O. #109	P65,P66
Lard, James J.	Pvt	D Hol.Leg.	Five Forks, VA	04/01/65	City Pt., VA	04/05/65	Pt. Lookout, MD	CSR
					Pt. Lookout, MD	06/29/65	Rlsd. G.O. #109	CSR
Lard, W.R.	Pvt	H 2nd SCVA	Raleigh, NC Hos.	04/13/65	Raleigh, NC	04/13/65	Paroled	CSR
Large, Francis M.	Pvt	A 14th SCVI	Jones Farm, VA	04/02/65	City Pt., VA	04/04/65	Pt. Lookout, MD	CSR
					Pt. Lookout, MD	06/28/65	Rlsd. G.O. #109	P114,CSR
Larisey, O.B.	Pvt	G 11th SCVI	Petersburg, VA	06/18/64	City Pt., VA	07/27/64	Pt. Lookout, MD	CSR,HAG
					Pt. Lookout, MD	07/27/64	Elmira, NY	P113,P120,CSR
					Elmira, NY	10/11/64	Pt. Lookout, MD Xc	P65,P66,CSR
					Pt. Lookout, MD	10/29/64	Exchanged	P114
Lark, C., Jr.	Pvt	A 3rd SCVABn	High Pt., NC	05/02/65	High Pt., NC	05/02/65	Paroled	CSR
Lark, Jacob R.	Pvt	I 17th SCVI	Boonesboro, MD	09/14/62	Ft. Delaware, DE	10/02/62	Aikens Ldg., VA Xc	LAN,CSR
Lark, William	Pvt	A 3rd SCVABn	High Pt., NC	05/02/65	High Pt., NC	05/02/65	Paroled	CSR
Larken, James	Cpl	H 1st SCVIG	Gettysburg, PA	07/04/63	David's Island, NY	08/24/63	City Pt., VA Xc	P1,SA1,CSR
Laroche, William	Pvt	A 1st SCVIR	Cheraw, SC	03/03/65	New Berne, NC	04/10/65	Hart's Island, NY	CSR
					Hart's Island, NY	06/07/65	Died	CSR
Lartigue, E.J.	Pvt	G 27th SCVI	Petersburg, VA	06/24/64	Fts. Monroe, VA	06/27/64	Pt. Lookout, MD	CSR,HAG
					Pt. Lookout, MD	08/16/64	Elmira, NY	P113,P120,CSR
					Elmira, NY	10/11/64	Pt. Lookout, MD Xc	P65,P66,CSR
					Pt. Lookout, MD	10/29/64	Venus Pt., GA Xc	P114,CSR
Latchicotte, P.R.	1Lt	Waccamaw A	Santee R., SC	02/27/63	Gunboat *Quaker Cit*	03/16/63	New York, NY P.M.	CSR
					Sandusky, OH	04/06/63	Fts. Monroe, VA Xc	CSR

L

SOUTH CAROLINA SOLDIERS, SAILORS AND CITIZENS HELD IN U.S. PRISONS 1861-1865

NAME	RANK	REGIMENT	CAPTURED AT	WHEN	PRISON	MOVED	DISPOSITION	SOURCES
Lateman, H.J.		I 1st SCVIR	Deserted, enemy	03/09/65	Charleston, SC		Released on oath	CSR
Latham, Andrew J.	Pvt	D Orr's Ri.	Appomattox R., VA	04/03/65	City Pt., VA	04/13/65	Pt. Lookout, MD	CSR
					Pt. Lookout, MD	06/20/65	Rlsd. G.O. #109	CSR
Latham, H.A.	SMj	7th SCVC	Hartwell, GA	05/18/65	Hartwell, GA	05/18/65	Paroled	CSR
Latham, James G.	Sgt	F 17th SCVI	Petersburg, VA	03/25/65	City Pt., VA	03/28/65	Pt. Lookout, MD	CSR
					Pt. Lookout, MD	06/28/65	Rlsd. G.O. #109	P114,CSR
Latham, S.B.	Pvt	D 17th SCVI	South Mtn., MD	09/14/62	Ft. McHenry, MD	12/29/62	Fts. Monroe, VA	P96,HHC,CSR
					Fts. Monroe, VA	01/05/63	Rlsd. on parole	CSR
					Petersburg, VA Hos.	01/26/63	Furloughed 30 days	CSR
Lathan, J.H.L.	Pvt	I 17th SCVI	Petersburg, VA	04/02/65	Pt. Lookout, MD	07/17/65	Died, Typhoid	P12,CSR
Lathan, John	Pvt	I 17th SCVI	Petersburg, VA	04/02/65	City Pt., VA	04/13/65	Pt. Lookout, MD	CSR,LAN
					Pt. Lookout, MD	06/28/65	Rlsd. G.O. #109	P114,CSR
Lathan, T.A.	Sgt	D 1st SCVIH	Deserted/enemy	03/01/65	Bermuda Hundred, VA	03/03/65	City Pt., VA P.M.	CSR,LAN
					City Pt., VA P.M.	03/05/65	Washington, DC P.M.	CSR
					Washington, DC P.M.	03/07/65	Phila., PA on oath	CSR
Lathrop, David George	Pvt	B 1st SCVIG	Farmville, VA	04/06/65	City Pt., VA	04/14/65	Newport News, VA	CSR,SA1
					Newport News, VA	06/26/65	Rlsd. G.O. #109	P107,CSR
Latimer, James S.	Pvt	G Orr's Ri	Falling Waters, MD	07/14/63	Old Capitol, DC	08/08/63	Pt. Lookout, MD	CSR,CDC
					Ft. McHenry, MD	08/08/63	Pt. Lookout, MD	P110
					Pt. Lookout, MD	04/27/64	Exchanged	P113,P124
Latta, Robert	Pvt	G 7th SCVIBn	Charlotte, NC	05/04/65	Charlotte, NC	05/04/65	Paroled	CSR
Lattimer, Thomas D.	Pvt	K 17th SCVI	Farmville, VA	04/06/65	City Pt., VA	04/14/65	Newport News, VA	CSR,YEB
					Newport News, VA	06/26/65	Rlsd. G.O. #109	P107,CSR
Laughlin, T.	Pvt	C 3rd SCVABn	Blakely, AL	04/09/65	Ship Island, MS	05/01/65	Vicksburg, MS Xc	CSR
Laveigne, D.P.	Pvt	B 2nd SCVC	Augusta, GA	05/22/65	Augusta, GA	05/22/65	Paroled	CSR
Lavell, Anthony J.	Pvt	Brooks LA	Harpers Farm, VA	04/06/65	City Pt., VA	04/12/65	Pt. Lookout, MD	CSR
					Pt. Lookout, MD	06/29/65	Rlsd. G.O. #109	CSR
Laviner, George W.	Pvt	G 8th SCVI	Gettysburg, PA	07/03/63	Gettysburg G.H.		Provost Marshal	P4,KEB,HOM
					David's Island, NY	09/05/63	City Pt., VA Xc	P1,CSR
Law, J. McD.	Pvt	A Hol.Leg.C	Burnt Ordinary, VA	01/19/63	Ft. McHenry, MD	01/20/63	Paroled	CSR
Law, J.W.	Pvt	K 4th SCVC	Old Church, VA	05/30/64	White House, VA	06/08/64	Pt. Lookout, MD	CSR
					Pt. Lookout, MD	10/30/64	Exchanged	P113,CSR
Law, R.W.	Pvt	E 11th SCVI	Deserted in VA		Fts. Monroe, VA	04/02/65	Washington, DC	CSR
					Washington, DC	04/05/65	To Savannah GA	CSR
Law, William A.	Pvt	I 6th SCVC	Raleigh NC Hos.	04/13/65	Raleigh, NC	04/13/65	Paroled	CSR
Lawhorn, Samuel J.	Pvt	G 26th SCVI	Petersburg, VA	04/01/65	City Pt., VA	04/01/65	Pt. Lookout, MD	CSR
					Pt. Lookout, MD	06/29/65	Rlsd. G.O. #109	P114,CSR
Lawless, Jordin J.	Pvt	L Orr's Ri.	Falling Waters, MD	07/14/63	Baltimore, MD	08/20/63	Pt. Lookout, MD	CSR,CDC
					Pt. Lookout, MD	03/17/64	Exchanged	P113
Lawless, Michael	Pvt	G 1st SCVA	Deserted/enemy	02/18/65	Charleston, SC	03/13/65	Taken oath & disch.	CSR
Lawrence, Alexander	Cit	Charleston	Wilmington, NC	11/06/63	Ft. Warren, MA	06/15/65	Rlsd. G.O. #109	P2,P137
Lawrence, G.J.	Pvt	I Hol.Leg.	Farmville, VA	04/11/65	Farmville, VA	04/21/65	Paroled	CSR
Lawrence, J.W.	Pvt	A 12th SCVI	Sharpsburg, MD	09/17/62	Frederick, MD USGH	10/27/62	Aikens Ldg., VA Xc	CSR
Lawrence, James J.	Pvt	C 13th SCVI	Petersburg, VA	04/03/65	City Pt., VA	04/11/65	Hart's Island, NY	CSR,HOS
					Hart's Island, NY	06/17/65	Rlsd. G.O. #109	P79,CSR
Lawrence, James P.	Pvt	C 3rd SCVABn	Blakely, AL	04/09/65	Ship Island, MS	05/01/65	Vicksburg, MS Xc	CSR
Lawrence, James P.	Pvt	C 3rd SCVABn	Citronelle, AL	05/11/65	Meridian, MS	05/14/65	Paroled	CSR
Lawrence, James W.	Pvt	E 2nd SCVI	Halltown, VA	08/26/64	Harpers Ferry, WV	09/02/64	Camp Chase, OH	CSR,SA2,H2
					Camp Chase, OH	03/18/65	Pt. Lookout, MD Xc	P22,P26,CSR
Lawrence, John A.	Sgt	C 3rd SCVABn	Ft. Gaines, AL	08/08/64	New Orleans, LA	10/25/64	Ship Island, MS	P4,CSR
					Ship Island, MS	01/04/65	Exchanged	CSR
Lawrence, John A.	Sgt	C 3rd SCVABn	Blakely, AL	04/09/65	Ship Island, MS	05/01/65	Vicksburg, MS Xc	CSR

SOUTH CAROLINA SOLDIERS, SAILORS AND **L** CITIZENS HELD IN U.S. PRISONS 1861-1865

NAME	RANK	REGIMENT	CAPTURED AT	WHEN	PRISON	MOVED	DISPOSITION	SOURCES
Lawrence, John A.	Sgt	C 3rd SCVABn	Citronelle, AL	05/11/65	Meridian, MS	05/14/65	Paroled	CSR
Lawrence, W.B.	Pvt	E Orr's Ri.	Spotsylvania, VA	05/12/64	Elmira, NY	03/04/65	Died, Ch. Diarrhea	P6,P12,FPH,CSR
Lawrence, W.M.	Pvt	I Hol.Leg.	Newton, NC	04/19/65	Newton, NC	04/19/65	Paroled	CSR
Lawson, Charles L.	Pvt	B 15th SCVI	Warrenton, VA	09/29/62	Warrenton, VA	09/29/62	Paroled on oath	H15,CSR,KEB
Lawson, Ephraim G.	Pvt	Ferguson's LA	Salisbury, NC	04/12/65	Nashville, TN	04/29/65	Louisville, KY	P39,CSR
					Louisville, KY	05/02/65	Camp Chase, OH	CSR
					Camp Chase, OH	06/13/65	Rlsd. G.O. #109	P23,CSR
Lawson, H.S.	Pvt	I P.S.S.	Richmond, VA Hos.	04/03/65	Libby Prison, VA	04/23/65	Newport News, VA	CSR,TSE
					Newport News, VA	06/26/65	Rlsd. G.O. #109	CSR
Lawson, J.L.	Pvt	I P.S.S.	Deserted/enemy	03/22/65	Bermuda Hundred, VA	03/22/65	Washington, DC	CSR, TSE
					Washington, DC	03/25/65	Nashville, TN oath	CSR,
Lawson, James H.	Pvt	B 15th SCVI	Halltown, VA	08/26/64	Harpers Ferry, WV	08/29/64	Camp Chase, OH	CSR,KEB,UD2,H15
					Camp Chase, OH	03/18/65	Pt. Lookout, MD	P22,CSR
					Pt. Lookout, MD	06/28/65	Rlsd. G.O. #109	P114,CSR
Lawson, Joseph T.	Pvt	H 21st SCVI	Morris Island, SC	07/10/62	Hilton Head, SC			P2,HAG
Lawson, W.R.S.	Pvt	H 21st SCVI	Morris Island, SC	07/10/63	Morris Island, SC	07/13/63	Hilton Head, SC	CSR,HAG
					Hilton Head, SC GH	07/23/63	Morris Island, SC Xc	P2,CSR
Lawson, W.R.S.	1Sg	H 21st SCVI	Ft. Fisher, NC	01/15/65	New York, NY	01/30/65	Elmira, NY	CSR
Lawson, W.R.S.	1Sg	H 21st SCVI	Ft. Fisher, NC	01/15/65	Elmira, NY	07/11/65	Rlsd. G.O. #109	P65,P66
Lawson, William	Pvt	K 13th SCVI	Gettysburg, PA	07/05/63	David's Island, NY	09/27/63	City Pt., VA Xc	CSR
Lawson, William	Pvt	K 13th SCVI	Southside RR, VA	04/06/65	City Pt., VA	04/16/65	Newport News, VA	CSR
					Newport News, VA	06/13/65	Released G.O. #109	P107,CSR
Lawton, Felix E.	Pvt	K 15th SCVI	Halltown, VA	08/26/64	Harper's Ferry, WV	08/29/64	Camp Chase, OH	CSR,KEB,H15
					Camp Chase, OH	03/18/65	Pt. Lookout, MD Xc	P22,P26,CSR
					Pt. Lookout, MD	03/26/65	Boulware's Wh. Xc	CSR
Lawton, J.M.	Pvt	K 4th SCVC	Louisa C.H., VA	06/11/64	Fts. Monroe, VA	06/20/64	Pt. Lookout, MD	CSR
					Pt. Lookout, MD	02/10/65	Exchanged	P113,P124,CSR
Lawton, Josiah	Pvt	B 5th SCVI	N. Anna River, VA	05/23/64	Port Royal, VA	05/30/64	Pt. Lookout, MD	CSR,SA3
					Pt. Lookout, MD	09/30/64	Exchanged	P113,CSR
Lawton, William M.	Pvt	I 2nd SCVI	Gettysburg, PA	07/04/63	W. Bldg. Balt., MD	09/25/63	City Pt., VA Xc	SA2,P1,KEB,H2,CSR
Lay, C.H.	Pvt	C 27th SCVI	Drury's Bluff, VA	05/16/64	Bermuda Hundred, VA	05/17/64	Fts. Monroe, VA	CSR,HAG
					Fts. Monroe, VA	05/19/64	Pt. Lookout, MD	CSR
					Pt. Lookout, MD	07/23/64	Elmira, NY	P120,CSR
					Elmira, NY	02/09/65	Released on oath	P65,P66,CSR
Layton, John M.	Pvt	H 1st SCVIG	Petersburg, VA	03/25/65	City Pt., VA	03/27/65	Pt. Lookout, MD	CSR,SA1
					Pt. Lookout, MD	04/20/65	Died, Interm. fever	P6,P114,FPH,CSR
Lazier, J.G.	Pvt	K 3rd SCVC	Pocotaligo, SC	01/16/65	Hilton Head, SC	02/01/65	Pt. Lookout, MD	CSR
					Pt. Lookout, MD	06/29/65	Rlsd. G.O. #109	P114,CSR
LeRoach, William T.	Pvt	A 1st SCMil	Cheraw, SC	03/03/65	New Berne, NC	04/10/65	Hart's Island, NY	CSR
					Hart's Island, NY	06/07/65	Died, Consumption	P12,P79,FPH,CSR
LeRoy, James H.	Sgt	A Orr's Ri.	Petersburg, VA	04/03/65	Hart's Island, NY	06/16/65	Rlsd. G.O. #109	P79,CDC
LeRoy, John B.	Pvt	A Orr's Ri.	Petersburg, VA	04/03/65	City Pt., VA	04/11/65	Hart's Island, NY	CSR
					Hart's Island, NY	06/16/65	Rlsd. G.O. #109	CSR
LeRoy, P.B.	Pvt	I 5th SCRes	Augusta, GA	05/29/65	Augusta, GA	05/29/65	Paroled	CSR
Leah, J.	Plt	Sr. *Memphis*	At sea	07/31/62	New York, NY P.M.	08/11/62	Ft. Lafayette, NY	CDC,LLC
Leach, Hosea	Pvt	G 1st SCVA	Raleigh, NC Hos.	04/13/65	Raleigh, NC Hos.	04/17/65	(clothing issued)	CSR

L

SOUTH CAROLINA SOLDIERS, SAILORS AND CITIZENS HELD IN U.S. PRISONS 1861-1865

NAME	RANK	REGIMENT	CAPTURED AT	WHEN	PRISON	MOVED	DISPOSITION	SOURCES
Leach, William F.	Pvt	E 7th SCVIBn	Weldon RR, VA	08/21/64	City Pt., VA USFH	08/23/64	Fts. Monroe, VA G.H.	CSR,HIC
					Fts. Monroe, VA G.H.	08/26/64	Alexandria, VA G.H.	P1,CSR
					Alexandria, VA G.H.	08/28/64	Washington, DC G.H.	CSR
					Lincoln G.H., DC	12/15/64	Old Capitol, DC	CSR
					Ft. McHenry, MD	12/16/64	Elmira, NY	P110
					Old Capitol, DC	12/16/64	Elmira, NY	CSR
					Elmira, NY	07/13/65	Released	P65,P66
					Elmira, NY	07/20/65	Died	FPH
League, William Plinny	Pvt	A 16th SCVI	Yazoo City, MS	07/13/65	Yazoo City, MS	07/13/65	Paroled on oath	CSR
Leaird, H.D.	Pvt	B 20th SCVI	Cedar Creek, VA	10/19/64	Harpers Ferry, WV	10/23/64	Pt. Lookout, MD	CSR,KEB
					Pt. Lookout, MD	03/28/65	Exchanged	P114,P124,CSR
Leaird, J.H.	Pvt	G 27th SCVI	Petersburg, VA	06/24/64	Pt. Lookout, MD	08/16/64	Elmira, NY	P113,P120,HAG
					Elmira, NY	07/11/65	Rlsd. G.O. #109	P66
Leaird, John J.	Pvt	G 27th SCVI	Town Creek, NC	02/20/65	Ft. Anderson, NC	02/28/65	Pt. Lookout, MD	CSR,HAG
					Pt. Lookout, MD	06/08/65	Released on oath	P114,CSR
Leaird, Rufus S.	Pvt	G 27th SCVI	Town Creek, NC	02/20/65	Ft. Anderson, NC	02/28/65	Pt. Lookout, MD	CSR,HAG
					Pt. Lookout, MD	06/28/65	Rlsd. G.O. #109	P114,CSR
Leaird, Thomas L.	Pvt	G 27th SCVI	Petersburg, VA	06/24/64	Fts. Monroe, VA	06/27/64	Pt. Lookout, MD	CSR,HAG
					Pt. Lookout, MD	08/16/64	Elmira, NY	CSR
Leaird, Thomas L.	Pvt	G 27th SCVI	Petersburg, VA	06/24/64	Elmira, NY	07/11/65	Rlsd. G.O. #109	CSR
Leaird, William	Cit		Lexington, SC	02/13/65	Pt. Lookout, MD	06/08/65	Released	P114
Leake, William G.	Pvt	F 22nd SCVI	Petersburg, VA	03/25/65	City Pt., VA	03/28/65	Pt. Lookout, MD	CSR
					Pt. Lookout, MD	05/24/65	Died, Brain Inflam.	P6,P12,P114,FPH
Leaphart, Franklin E.	Sgt	C 15th SCVI	Fishers Hill, VA	09/19/64	Winchester, VA USH	10/12/64	Died, Dysentery	H15,KEB,CSR
Leaphart, J.C.	Cpl	C 3rd SCVC	Cuthbert House, SC	08/22/62	Hilton Head, SC	11/02/62	Ft. Columbus, NY	CSR
					Ft. Columbus, NY	11/21/62	Ft. Delaware, DE	CSR
					Ft. Delaware, DE	12/15/62	Fts. Monroe, VA Xc	CSR
Leaphart, Jefferson G.	Cpl	C 14th SCVCB	Cuthbert House, SC	10/22/62	No U.S. data			CSR
Leaphart, John W.	Pvt	K 13th SCVI	Appomattox R., VA	04/05/65	City Pt., VA	04/14/65	Pt. Lookout, MD	CSR
					Pt. Lookout, MD	06/29/65	Rlsd. G.O. #109	P114,CSR
Leaphart, Joseph P.	Pvt	K 13th SCVI	Gettysburg, PA	07/05/63	David's Island, NY	09/05/63	City Pt., VA Xc	P1,CSR
Leaphart, R.H.	Pvt	C 23rd SCVI	Petersburg, VA	04/01/65	City Pt., VA	04/04/65	Pt. Lookout, MD	CSR
					Pt. Lookout, MD	06/29/65	Rlsd. G.O. #109	P114,CSR
Leaphart, Sherod Luther	Cpt	A 2nd SCVI	Gettysburg, PA	07/05/63	Letterman G.H. Gbg	08/21/63	Provost Marshal	P1,KEB,SA2,CSR,H2
					Letterman G.H. Gbg	08/21/63	Ft. McHenry, MD	CSR
					Ft. McHenry, MD	09/20/63	Johnson's Isl., OH	P96,CSR
					Johnson's Isl., OH	03/14/65	Pt. Lookout, MD	P80,CSR
					Pt. Lookout, MD	03/23/65	Coxes Wh., VA Xc	CSR
Leard, John B.	Pvt	G 14th SCVI	Richmond, VA	04/03/65	Jackson Hos. Rchmd.	05/07/65	Died of wounds	P6,P12,CSR
Lecluse, Leon	Pvt	Ferguson's LA	Mobile, AL	06/18/65	Mobile, AL	06/18/65	Paroled	CSR
Lecumtiguy, Victor	Pvt	Ferguson's LA	Jackson, MS	07/15/63	Jackson, MS	07/30/63	Snyder's Bluff, MS	CSR
					Snyder's Bluff, MS	08/07/63	Camp Morton, IN	CSR
					Camp Morton, IN	08/15/63	Jd. U.S. Forces	CSR
Ledingham, Thomas J.	Pvt	H 6th SCVI	Burkeville, VA	04/14/65	Burkeville, VA	04/17/65	Paroled	CSR
Lee, A.C.	Pvt	I 3rd SCVC	Edisto Island, SC	04/09/63	Ft. Norfolk, VA	06/29/63	Paroled	CSR
Lee, A.C.	Pvt	I 3rd SCVC	Pocotaligo, SC	12/21/64	Hilton Head, SC G.H.	02/01/64	Pt. Lookout, MD	P2,CSR
					Pt. Lookout, MD	03/17/65	Aikens Ldg., VA Xc	P124,CSR
Lee, A.C.	Pvt	I 3rd SCVC	Tallahassee, FL	05/19/65	Tallahassee, FL	05/19/65	Paroled	CSR
Lee, B.M.	Pvt	A 25th SCVI	Ft. Fisher, NC	01/15/65	New York, NY	01/30/65	Elmira, NY	CSR,HAG
					Elmira, NY	06/30/65	Rlsd. G.O. #109	P65,P66,HAG
Lee, Charles	Pvt	Gist Gd HA	Deserted/enemy	02/20/65	Charleston, SC	02/20/65	Released on parole	CSR

SOUTH CAROLINA SOLDIERS, SAILORS AND  L CITIZENS HELD IN U.S. PRISONS 1861-1865

NAME	RANK	REGIMENT	CAPTURED AT	WHEN	PRISON	MOVED	DISPOSITION	SOURCES
Lee, Elijah	Pvt	A 1st SCVIG	Hatchers Run, VA	03/31/65	City Pt., VA	04/02/65	Pt. Lookout, MD	CSR,SA1
					Pt. Lookout, MD	06/29/65	Rlsd. G.O. #109	P114,CSR
Lee, Eliphus H.	Sgt	I Hol.Leg.	Petersburg, VA	03/25/65	City Pt., VA	03/28/65	Pt. Lookout, MD	CSR,HOS
					Pt. Lookout, MD	06/28/65	Rlsd. G.O. #109	P114
Lee, Enoch W.	Pvt	K Orr's Ri.	Hatchers Run, VA	04/02/65	City Pt., VA	04/07/65	Hart's Island, NY	CSR
					Hart's Island, NY	06/15/65	Rlsd. G.O. #109	P79
Lee, Henry	Pvt	C 8th SCVI	Chesterfield, SC	03/08/65	New Berne, NC	03/30/65	Pt. Lookout, MD	CSR,KEB
					Pt. Lookout, MD	06/29/65	Rlsd. G.O. #109	P114,CSR
Lee, Isham	Pvt	A 2nd SCVI	Sharpsburg, MD	10/01/62	Ft. McHenry, MD	10/13/62	Fts. Monroe, VA	P96,CSR,KEB,SA2,H2
					Ft. Monroe, VA	10/17/62	Aikens Ldg., VA Xc	CSR
Lee, J.R.	Cpl	C 3rd SCVABn	Blakely, AL	04/09/65	Ship Island, MS	05/01/65	Vicksburg, MS Xc	CSR
Lee, J.R.	Cpl	C 3rd SCVABn	Augusta, GA	05/20/65	Augusta, GA	05/20/65	Paroled	CSR
Lee, J.T.	Pvt	G 1st SCVIR	Deserted/enemy	04/13/65	Charleston, SC		Released on oath	SA1,CSR
Lee, J.W.G.	Cpl	C 2nd SCVI	Cedar Creek, VA	10/23/64	Harpers Ferry, WV	10/23/64	Pt. Lookout, MD	SA2,CSR,KEB,H2
					Pt. Lookout, MD	03/28/65	Aikens Ldg., VA Xc	P114,P124,CSR
Lee, James L.	Pvt	3 10/19 SCVI	Missionary Ridge, TN	11/25/63	Nashville, TN	12/07/63	Louisville, KY	P39,RAS,CTA,CSR
					Louisville, KY	12/07/63	Rock Island, IL	CSR
					Rock Island, IL	05/03/65	New Orleans, LA Xc	CSR
					New Orleans, LA	05/23/65	Exchanged	P4,CSR
Lee, James W.	Pvt	F Hol.Leg.	Petersburg, VA	11/06/64	City Pt., VA	11/11/64	Washington, DC	CSR
					Pt. Lookout, MD	05/13/65	Rlsd. G.O. #85	P114,CSR
Lee, John	Sgt	B Hol.Leg.	Five Forks, VA	04/01/65	City Pt., VA	04/05/65	Pt. Lookout, MD	CSR,HOS
					Pt. Lookout, MD	06/29/65	Rlsd. G.O. #109	P114,CSR
Lee, John B.	Pvt	F 7th SCVC	Farmville, VA	04/06/65	City Pt., VA	04/15/65	Pt. Lookout, MD	CSR
					Pt. Lookout, MD	06/29/65	Rlsd. G.O. #109	CSR
Lee, John C.	Plt	Sr. Memphis	NC Coast	07/31/62	Ft. Delaware, DE			P47
Lee, John W.	Pvt	3 10/19 SCVI	Missionary Ridge, TN	11/25/63	Nashville, TN	01/08/64	Louisville, KY	P39,RAS,CTA,CSR
					Louisville, KY	02/03/64	Rock Island, IL	CSR
					Rock Island, IL	03/02/64	Died, Lung Inflam.	P5,P12,FPH,CSR
Lee, John W.	Pvt	D Ham.Leg.MI	Deserted/enemy	01/22/65	Bermuda Hundred, VA	01/23/65	City Pt., VA P.M.	CSR
					City Pt., VA	01/24/65	Washington, DC	CSR
					Washington, DC	01/24/65	Syracuse, NY oath	CSR
Lee, Josiah W.	Pvt	I 10th SCVI	Franklin, TN	12/18/64	Nashville, TN	05/06/65	Louisville, KY	P4,P39,RAS,CSR
					Louisville, KY	06/16/65	Rlsd. G.O. #109	CSR
Lee, Larkin S.	Cpl	B Hol.Leg.	Deserted/enemy	02/14/65	City Pt., VA	02/18/65	Washington, DC	CSR
					Washington, DC	02/21/65	Columbus, OH oath	CSR
Lee, Lecil	Pvt	B Hol.Leg.	Kinston, NC	12/15/62	Kinston, NC	12/15/62	Paroled POW	CSR
Lee, Marcus A.	Pvt	I 1st SCVA	Morris Island, SC	07/10/64	Pt. Lookout, MD			P113
					Hilton Head, SC	07/18/63	Ft. Columbus, NY	CSR
					Ft. Columbus, NY	09/23/63	Paroled	P1,CSR
Lee, Noah	Pvt	B 10th SCVI	Jonesboro, GA	09/12/64	Rough & Ready, GA	09/19/64	Exchanged	CSR,CEN
Lee, Patrick	Pvt	H 27th SCVI	Deserted/enemy	06/24/64	Bermuda Hundred, VA	06/26/64	Fts. Monroe, VA	CSR,HAG
					Fts. Monroe, VA	07/01/64	New York, NY oath	CSR
Lee, R.W.	Pvt	H 23rd SCVI	Middletown, MD	09/19/62	Ft. Delaware DE	10/02/62	Aikens Ldg., VA Xc	CSR
Lee, R.W.	Pvt	H 23rd SCVI	Farmville, VA	04/06/65	Newport News, VA	07/01/65	Rlsd. G.O. #109	P107,HMC,CSR
Lee, Robert	Pvt	F 1st SCEngs	Fayetteville, NC	03/11/65	Hart's Island, NY	06/16/65	Rlsd. G.O. #109	P79
Lee, Stephen D.	BGn	Post Arty.	Vicksburg, MS	07/04/63	Paroled on terms	07/ /63	Declared Exchanged	GIG,OR
Lee, Tilley S.	Pvt	6 10/19 SCVI	Missionary Ridge, TN	11/25/63	Nashville, TN	12/07/63	Louisville, KY	P39,RAS
					Louisville, KY	12/09/63	Rock Island, IL	CSR
					Rock Island, IL	06/20/65	Rlsd. G.O. #109	CSR

L

SOUTH CAROLINA SOLDIERS, SAILORS AND CITIZENS HELD IN U.S. PRISONS 1861-1865

NAME	RANK	REGIMENT	CAPTURED AT	WHEN	PRISON	MOVED	DISPOSITION	SOURCES
Lee, Tyre	Pvt	B 17th SCVI	Richmond, VA Hos.	04/03/65	Richmond, VA Hos.	04/21/65	P.M. Richmond	CSR
					Libby Prison, Rchmd.	04/23/65	Newport News, VA	CSR
					Newport News, VA	06/26/65	Rlsd. G.O. #109	P107,CSR
Lee, W.J.	Pvt	K 21st SCVI	Ft. Fisher, NC	01/15/65	Elmira, NY	07/11/65	Rlsd. G.O. #109	P65,P66,HAG
Lee, W.M.C.	Pvt	C 3rd SCVABn	Augusta, GA	05/20/65	Augusta, GA	05/20/65	Paroled	CSR
Lee, William	Pvt	C 3rd SCVABn	Blakely, AL	04/09/65	Ship Island, MS	05/01/65	Vicksburg, MS Xc	CSR
Lee, William A.	Pvt	7th SCVIBn	Cheraw, SC	03/02/65	Cheraw, SC	03/02/65	Paroled	CSR
Lee, William F.	Pvt	D Ham.Leg.MI	Farmville, VA	04/11/65	Farmville, VA	04/11/65	Paroled	CSR
Lee, William J.	Pvt	5th SCVC	Deserted/enemy	02/08/65	Fts. Monroe, VA	02/17/65	Baltimore, MD oath	P8,CSR
Lee, William M.	Pvt	B Hol.Leg.	Petersburg, VA	03/25/65	City Pt., VA	03/28/65	Pt. Lookout, MD	CSR
					Pt. Lookout, MD	06/29/65	Rlsd. G.O. #109	P114,HOS,CSR
Lee, William P.	QSg	E 3rd SCVI	Williamsport, MD	07/14/63	Wheeling, WV	07/30/63	Camp chase, OH	P1,SA2,H3,KEB
					Camp Chase, OH	01/10/64	Died, Ch. Diarrhea	P5,P24,P25,P27,FPH
Leech, Julius	Pvt	H 8th SCVI	Williamsburg, VA	05/06/62	Old Capitol, DC		Fts. Monroe, VA	CSR,KEB
					Fts. Monroe, VA	08/05/62	Exchanged	CSR
Legare, Solomon E.	Pvt	F 6th SCVC	Petersburg, VA	11/07/64	Pt. Lookout, MD	03/14/65	Exchanged	P114,CSR
Legg, C.W.	Pvt	A 7th SCVI	Pleasant Val., MD	09/14/62	Sandy Hook, MD	09/22/62	Knoxville, MD	CSR
					Knoxville, MD	10/20/62	Ft. McHenry, MD	CSR
					Ft. McHenry, MD	10/25/62	Aikens Ldg., VA Xc	KEB,CSR
Leggett, A.J.	Pvt	F 21st SCVI	Ft. Fisher, NC	01/15/65	Elmira, NY	06/14/65	Rlsd. G.O.#109	P65,P66,HAG,HOM
Leggett, James B.	2Lt	A 23rd SCVI	Saylors Creek, VA	04/06/65	Old Capitol, DC	04/17/65	Johnson's Isl., OH	P110,CSR
					Johnson's Isl., OH	06/19/65	Rlsd. G.O. #109	P81,P83,CSR
Legnon, A.H.	Pvt	Washn LA	Gettysburg, PA	07/04/63	Ft. Delaware, DE	03/18/64	Joined US Navy	P40
Legrand, Daniel J.	Pvt	D 12th SCVI	Harper Farm, VA	04/06/65	City Pt., VA	04/14/65	Pt. Lookout, MD	CSR
					Pt. Lookout, MD	06/29/65	Rlsd. G.O. #109	P114,CSR
Leitner, James J.	Pvt	C 2nd SCVC	Greensboro, NC	05/01/65	Greensboro, NC	05/01/65	Paroled	CSR
Leitner, John D.W.	Pvt	C 2nd SCVC	Greensboro, NC	05/01/65	Greensboro, NC	05/01/65	Paroled	CSR
Leitzey, J.G.	Pvt	Hol.Leg.	Petersburg, VA	04/03/65	Washington St. Hos.	07/27/65	Died of wounds	P6,CSR
Leitzey, Jacob	Pvt	G Hol.Leg.	Five Forks, VA	04/01/65	City Pt., VA	04/05/65	Pt. Lookout, MD	CSR,ANY
					Pt. Lookout, MD	06/28/65	Rlsd. G.O. #109	P114,CSR
Leitzey, Thomas B.	Pvt	B 1st SCVIG	Gettysburg, PA	07/05/63	Chester, PA G.H.	08/17/63	City Pt., VA Xc	P1,SA1,CSR
Lemacke, David P.	Pvt	C 5th SCVC	Deserted/enemy	03/22/65	Charleston, SC	03/22/65	Released on oath	CSR
Lemacke, Thomas	Pvt	C 5th SCVC	Deserted/enemy	03/28/65	Charleston, SC	03/28/65	Released on oath	CSR
Lemacks, Alfred A.	Pvt	G 11th SCVI	Deserted/enemy	04/07/65	Charleston, SC	04/07/65	Released on oath	CSR
Leman, L.B.	Pvt	G 11th SCVI	Ft. Fisher, NC	01/15/65	Pt. Lookout, MD	02/02/65	Hammond G.H., MD	P114,HAG,CSR
					Hammond G.H., MD	03/10/65	Died, Ch. Diarrhea	P12,CSR
Lemaster, Ralph	Pvt	C 13th SCVI	Southside RR, VA	04/02/65	City Pt., VA	04/07/65	Hart's Island, NY	CSR
					Hart's Island, NY	06/20/65	Rlsd. G.O. #109	P79,CSR
Lemaster, William E.	Pvt	A P.S.S.	Richmond, VA Hos.	04/03/65	Libby Prison, VA	04/23/65	Newport News, VA	CSR
					Newport News, VA	06/26/65	Rlsd. G.O. #109	P107,TSE,CSR
Lemen, F.	Sgt	E 8th SCVI	Gettysburg, PA	06/30/63	Gettysburg G.H.	10/15/63	Provost Marshal	P4,CSR
Lemmon, William O.	Pvt	F 27th SCVI	Town Creek, NC	02/20/65	Ft. Anderson, NC	02/28/65	Pt. Lookout, MD	CSR,HAG
					Pt. Lookout, MD	06/29/65	Rlsd. G.O. #109	P114
Lemon, R.E.	Pvt	G 3rd SCVABn	High Pt., NC	05/01/65	High Pt., NC	05/01/65	Paroled	CSR
Lemon, Samuel E.	Pvt	K 23rd SCVI	Farmville, VA	04/06/65	City Pt., VA	04/14/65	Newport News, VA	CSR
					Newport News, VA	06/13/65	Released	P107,K23,CSR
Lemon, W. Harvey	Pvt	A 17th SCVI	Petersburg, VA	03/25/65	City Pt., VA	03/28/65	Pt. Lookout, MD	CSR
					Pt. Lookout, MD	06/28/65	Rlsd. G.O. #109	P114,CSR
Lemons, William B.	Sgt	K 18th SCVI	Five Forks, VA	04/01/65	City Pt., VA	04/06/65	Pt. Lookout, MD	CSR
					Pt. Lookout, MD	06/28/65	Rlsd. G.O. #109	P114,CSR
Lenerieux, Francis M.	Pvt	G 15th SCVI	Gettysburg, PA	07/02/63	Gettysburg, PA USH	07/27/63	Died of wounds	P4,KEB,CTA,CSR
Lentz, George	Pvt	E 1st SCVIR	Deserted/enemy	02/21/65	Charleston, SC	03/02/65	Released on oath	CSR

SOUTH CAROLINA SOLDIERS, SAILORS AND  CITIZENS HELD IN U.S. PRISONS 1861-1865

NAME	RANK	REGIMENT	CAPTURED AT	WHEN	PRISON	MOVED	DISPOSITION	SOURCES
Leonard, J.D.	Pvt	B 13th SCVI	Gettysburg, PA	07/04/63	David's Island, NY	07/20/63	Died of wounds	P1,P12,FPH
Leonard, J.G.	Pvt	B 13th SCVI	Deserted/enemy	02/24/65	City Pt., VA	02/26/65	Washington, DC	CSR
					Washington, DC	02/27/65	Salem, OH on oath	HOS,CSR
Leonard, John	Pvt	C 2nd SCVI			Hilton Head, SC	04/30/65	New York, NY oath	CSR
Leonard, S.J.	Pvt	I 5th SCVI	Chattanooga, TN	10/29/63	Nashville, TN	11/07/63	Louisville, KY	P39,SA3,CSR
					Louisville, KY	11/09/63	Camp Morton, IN	CSR
					Camp Morton, IN	05/22/65	Rlsd. on oath	CSR
Leonard, William D.	Pvt	C Hol.Leg.	Five Forks, VA	04/01/65	City Pt., VA	04/05/65	Pt. Lookout, MD	CSR
					Pt. Lookout, MD	06/29/65	Rlsd. G.O. #109	CSR
Leopard, Alexander T.	Pvt	E 14th SCVI	Fords Depot, VA	04/08/65	City Pt., VA	04/14/65	Pt. Lookout, MD	CSR
					Pt. Lookout, MD	06/05/65	Released	P114,CSR
Lequeux, Marion B.	Pvt	I 27th SCVI	Petersburg, VA	06/24/64	Bermuda Hundred, VA	06/25/64	Fts. Monroe, VA	CSR,HAG
					Fts. Monroe, VA	06/29/64	Pt. Lookout, MD	CSR
					Pt. Lookout, MD	08/08/64	Elmira, NY	P66,P113,P120
					Elmira, NY	09/06/64	Died, Ch. Diarrhea	P5,P10,P12,FPH
Lesesne, Charles	1Lt	K 25th SCVI	Ft. Fisher, NC	01/15/65	Fts. Monroe, VA	02/11/65	Ft. Delaware, DE	CSR,HAG,CTA
					Ft. Delaware, DE	06/17/65	Rlsd. G.O. #109	P43,P45,P46,P47
Lesesne, William Cantey	Pvt	K 25th SCVI	Weldon RR, VA	08/21/64	City Pt., VA 15ACH	08/25/64	Died of wounds	P12,CTA
Lester, L.W.	Pvt	K 21st SCVI	Weldon RR, VA	08/21/64	City Pt., VA USFH	08/26/64	Died of wounds	P12
Lester, R.H.	Pvt	E 23rd SCVI	Funkstown, MD	09/16/62	Ft. Delaware, DE	10/02/62	Aikens Ldg., VA Xc	CSR
Lester, T.C.	Sgt	F 21st SCVI	Town Creek, NC	02/20/65	Pt. Lookout, MD	06/29/65	Rlsd. G.O. #109	P114,HAG,HOM
Lester, W.J.	Pvt	B 11th SCVI	Charleston, SC	02/18/65	Charleston, SC USH	05/20/65	Died of disease	P6,CSR
Lever, Jacob S.	Pvt	K 13th SCVI	Richmond, VA	04/03/65	Libby Prison Rchmd.	04/13/65	City Pt., VA	CSR
					City Pt., VA	04/13/65	Pt. Lookout, MD	CSR
					Pt. Lookout, MD	06/05/65	Released on oath	P114,CSR
Leverett, John B.	Pvt	F 24th SCVI	Taylors Ridge, GA	08/16/64	Nashville, TN	08/23/64	Louisville, KY	CSR
					Louisville, KY	08/27/64	Camp Douglas, IL	CSR
					Camp Douglas, IL	06/17/65	Rlsd. G.O. #109	P55,EFW
Levi, Moses	Pvt	I 23rd SCVI	Petersburg, VA	04/02/65	City Pt., VA	04/04/65	Pt. Lookout, MD	CSR,HCL
					Pt. Lookout, MD	06/11/65	Rlsd. G.O.#109	P114,CSR
Levin, Lewis C.	Pvt	C 2nd SCVC	Charlotte, NC	05/03/65	Charlotte, NC	05/03/65	Paroled	CSR
Levine, H.	Pvt	I 27th SCVI	Petersburg, VA	06/24/64	Bermuda Hundred, VA	06/25/64	Fts. Monroe, VA	CSR
					Fts. Monroe, VA	06/26/64	Pt. Lookout, MD	CSR
					Pt. Lookout, MD	02/13/65	Exchanged	P113,CSR
Leviner, Hiram	Pvt	D 26th SCVI	Deserted/enemy	01/28/65	City Point, VA	01/29/65	Washington, DC	P8,CSR
					Washington, DC	02/01/65	Savannah, GA oath	CSR
Leviner, Thomas	Pvt	B 1st SCVIH	Mossy Creek, TN	02/11/64	Nashville, TN	02/11/64	Louisville, KY	CSR
					Louisville, KY	02/15/64	Rock Island, IL	CSR
					Rock Island, IL	06/19/65	Rlsd. G.O. #109	CSR
Lewie, Frederick Sims	LtC	15th SCVI	Augusta, GA	05/27/65	Augusta, GA	05/27/65	Paroled on oath	H15,CSR
Lewie, J.M.	Pvt	F 5th SCVC	Stony Creek, VA	12/01/64	City Pt., VA	12/05/64	Pt. Lookout, MD	CSR,CDC
					Pt. Lookout, MD	06/29/65	Rlsd. G.O. #109	P114,CSR
Lewie, John Henry	Cpt	C 15th SCVI	Halltown, VA	08/26/64	Harpers Ferry, WV	09/01/64	Ft. Delaware, DE	CSR,KEB,H15
					Ft. Delaware, DE	06/17/65	Rlsd. G.O. #109	P43,P45,CSR
Lewis, Allen C.	Pvt	E 1st SCVIG	Gettysburg, PA	07/04/63	David's Island, NY	08/24/63	City Pt., VA Xc	P1,SA1,HMC,CSR
Lewis, Allen C.	Pvt	E 1st SCVIG	Garrett's Xing, VA	04/02/65	City Pt., VA	04/07/65	Hart's Island, NY	CSR
					Hart's Island, NY	06/16/65	Rlsd. G.O. #109	P79,CSR
Lewis, Archibald	Pvt	B Ham.Leg.MI	Amelia C.H., VA	04/04/65	City Pt., VA P.M.	04/14/65	Pt. Lookout, MD	CSR
					Pt. Lookout, MD	06/28/65	Rlsd. G.O. #109	P114,CSR
Lewis, B.R.	Pvt	A 19th SCVCB	Augusta, GA	05/22/65	Augusta, GA	05/22/65	Paroled on oath	CSR
Lewis, Charles	Pvt	1st SCVA	Deserted/enemy		Chattanooga, TN	05/13/65	Took the oath	P8,CSR

L

SOUTH CAROLINA SOLDIERS, SAILORS AND CITIZENS HELD IN U.S. PRISONS 1861-1865

NAME	RANK	REGIMENT	CAPTURED AT	WHEN	PRISON	MOVED	DISPOSITION	SOURCES
Lewis, Daniel M.	Pvt	A 21st SCVI	Petersburg, VA	06/24/64	Pt. Lookout, MD	08/16/64	Elmira, NY	P113,P120,FLR,HAG
					Elmira, NY	03/18/65	Died, Ch. Diarrhea	P6,P12,P65,P66,FPH
Lewis, E.H.	Pvt	I 5th SCVC	Lancaster, SC	02/26/65	New Berne, NC	03/30/65	Pt. Lookout, MD	CSR
					Pt. Lookout, MD	06/28/65	Rlsd. G.O. #109	P114,CSR
Lewis, Edward	Pvt	H Hol.Leg.	Five Forks, VA	04/01/65	Pt. Lookout, MD	06/14/65	Released	P114
Lewis, F.P.	Pvt	B 7th SCVC	Anderson, SC	05/05/65	Anderson, SC	05/05/65	Paroled	CSR
Lewis, G.A.	Cit	1st Mil?	Flat Rock, SC	02/24/65	Hart's Island, NY	06/20/65	Rlsd. G.O. #109	P79
Lewis, G.W.	Pvt	G 27th SCVI	Petersburg, VA	06/18/64	City Pt., VA	06/24/64	Pt. Lookout, MD	CSR,HAG
					Pt. Lookout, MD	07/27/64	Elmira, NY	P113,P120,HAG,CSR
					Elmira, NY	03/14/65	Pt. Lookout, MD Xc	P65,P66,CSR
Lewis, Goodey	Pvt	A 22nd SCVI	Five Forks, VA	04/01/65	Pt. Lookout, MD	06/28/65	Rlsd. G.O. #109	P114,CSR
Lewis, Henry	Pvt.	K 26th SCVI	Appomattox R., VA	04/03/65	City Pt., VA	04/09/65	Hart's Island, NY	CSR
					Hart's Island, NY	06/16/65	Rlsd. G.O. #109	P79,CSR
Lewis, J.D.	Pvt	Hol.Leg.	Deserted		City Pt., VA	04/10/65	Washington, DC	CSR
Lewis, J.O.	Pvt	B 7th SCVC	Dabney's Ferry, VA	05/27/64	White House, VA	06/08/64	Pt. Lookout, MD	CSR
					Pt. Lookout, MD	09/18/64	Exchanged	P113,CSR
Lewis, J.R.	Pvt	G 27th SCVI	Town Creek, NC	02/20/65	Ft. Anderson, NC	02/28/65	Pt. Lookout, MD	CSR,HAG
					Pt. Lookout, MD	06/28/65	Rlsd. G.O. #109	P114,CSR
Lewis, J.T.	Pvt	I 1st SCVIR	Bentonville, NC	03/22/65	New Berne, NC	04/10/65	Hart's Island, NY	CSR,SA1
					Hart's Island, NY	06/15/65	Rlsd. G.O. #109	CSR
Lewis, John	Pvt	C 2nd SCVC	Culpepper C.H., VA	09/13/63	Pt. Lookout, MD	02/24/65	Exchanged	P113
Louis, John D.	Pvt	C Hol. Leg.	Deserted/enemy		City Pt., VA	04/10/65	Washington, DC	HOS,CSR
Lewis, John T.	Pvt	A 22nd SCVI	Deep Creek, VA	04/03/65	City Pt., VA	04/13/65	Pt. Lookout, MD	CSR
					Pt. Lookout, MD	06/28/65	Rlsd. G.O. #109	CSR
Lewis, Joseph H.	Pvt	K 23rd SCVI	Frederick, MD	10/09/62	Ft. McHenry, MD	11/06/62	Paroled for Xc	CSR,K23
Lewis, Joseph H.	Pvt	K 23rd SCVI	Farmville, VA	04/06/65	City Pt., VA	04/14/65	Newport News, VA	CSR
					Newport News, VA	06/13/65	Rlsd. G.O. #109	P107,CSR
Lewis, Joseph H.	Pvt	B 17th SCVI	Five Forks, VA	04/01/65	City Pt., VA	04/06/65	Pt. Lookout, MD	CSR,HFC
					Pt. Lookout, MD	06/28/65	Rlsd. G.O. #109	P114,CSR
Lewis, Moses J.	Pvt	B 10th SCVI	Murfreesboro, TN	12/31/62	Nashville, TN	03/20/63	Louisville, KY	P38,RAS,CSR
					Louisville, KY	03/23/63	Camp Butler, IL	CSR
Lewis, Moses J.	Pvt	B 10th SCVI	Murfreesboro, TN	01/05/63	Camp Butler, IL	04/10/63	City Pt,. VA Xc	P21
Lewis, Moses J.	Pvt	B 10th SCVI	Murfreesboro, TN	12/31/62	Fts. Monroe, VA	04/14/63	Paroled to Xc	CSR
Lewis, Peter Charles	Pvt	A Ham.Leg.MI	Deserted/enemy	01/23/65	Bermuda Hundred, VA	02/01/65	City Pt., VA P.M.	CSR
					City Pt., VA	02/02/65	Washington, DC	CSR
					Washington, DC	02/04/65	Troy, NY on oath	CSR
Lewis, Poser	Pvt	K 27th SCVI	Petersburg, VA	05/24/64	Bermuda Hundred, VA	06/25/64	Fts. Monroe, VA	CSR,HAG
					Fts. Monroe, VA	06/26/64	Pt. Lookout, MD	CSR
					Pt. Lookout, MD	07/14/64	Died, Dysentery	P12,CSR
Lewis, R.S.	Pvt	H 4th SCVI	Williamsburg, VA	05/06/62	Old Capitol, DC	08/01/62	Fts. Monroe, VA Xc	CSR
					Fts. Monroe, VA	08/05/62	Aikens Ldg., VA Xc	CSR
Lewis, Richard	1Lt	B P.S.S.	Richmond, VA	10/07/64	Fts. Monroe, VA	05/08/65	Released on oath	CSR,TSE
Lewis, Robert O.	Pvt	B 4th SCVI	1st Manassas, VA	07/21/61	Ft. McHenry, MD	11/13/61	Fts. Monroe, VA Xc	CSR
Lewis, Stephen S.	Pvt	K 26th SCVI	Southside RR, VA	04/02/65	City Pt., VA	04/05/65	Pt. Lookout, MD	CSR
					Pt. Lookout, MD	06/29/65	Rlsd. G.O. #109	P114,CSR
Lewis, Thomas J.	Pvt	G 27th SCVI	Petersburg, VA	06/24/64	Bermuda Hundred, VA	06/25/64	Fts. Monroe, VA	CSR,HAG
					Fts. Monroe, VA	06/26/64	Pt. Lookout, MD	CSR,HAG
					Pt. Lookout, MD	08/16/64	Elmira, NY	P113,P120,HAG,CSR
					Elmira, NY	07/03/65	Rlsd. G.O. #109	P66,CSR
Lewis, W.	Pvt	E 19th SCVI	Augusta, GA	05/19/65	Augusta, GA	05/19/65	Paroled	CSR
Lewis, William E.	Pvt	A 12th SCVI	Wilderness, VA	05/06/64	Belle Plain, VA	05/20/64	Ft. Delaware, DE	CSR,YEB
					Ft. Delaware, DE	06/15/64	Died, Typhoid	P5,P41,P42,FPH,P47

SOUTH CAROLINA SOLDIERS, SAILORS AND  CITIZENS HELD IN U.S. PRISONS 1861-1865

NAME	RANK	REGIMENT	CAPTURED AT	WHEN	PRISON	MOVED	DISPOSITION	SOURCES
Lewis, Z.	Pvt	C Brown's A.	Southside RR, VA	04/02/65	Hart's Island, NY	06/16/65	Rlsd. G.O. #109	P79
Lide, D.F.	Sgt	C 3rd SCVABn	Blakely, AL	04/09/65	Ship Island, MS	05/01/65	Vicksburg, MS Xc	CSR
Lide, R.T.	Pvt	D 21st SCVI	Ft. Fisher, NC	01/15/65	Elmira, NY	07/07/65	Rlsd. G.O. #109	P65,P66,HAG
Lifrage, Theodore M.	Sgt	K 25th SCVI	Ft. Fisher, NC	01/15/65	New York, NY	01/31/65	Elmira, NY	CSR,HAG,CTA
					Elmira, NY	04/03/65	Died, Ch. Diarrhea	P6,P12,P65,P66,FPH
Lightsey, J.A.	Pvt	B 2nd SCVC	Augusta, GA	05/26/65	Augusta, GA	05/26/65	Paroled	CSR
Ligon, Edward F.	1Sg	K 16th SCVI	Graysville, GA	11/27/63	Nashville, TN	12/09/63	Louisville, KY	P39,16R,CSR
					Louisville, KY	12/11/63	Rock Island, IL	CSR,CSR
					Rock Island, IL	10/31/64	Rlsd. Vol.US Rjctd.	CSR
Ligon, George W.	SMj	3rd SCVIBn	South Mtn., MD	09/14/62	Ft. Delaware, DE	10/02/62	Aikens Ldg., VA Xc	CSR
Ligon, J. Nickolas	Pvt	E 15th SCVI	South Mtn., MD	09/14/62	Ft. Delaware, DE	10/02/62	Aikens Ldg., VA Xc	CSR
Ligon, J. Nickolas	Pvt	E 15th SCVI	Gettysburg, PA	07/03/63	Ft. McHenry, MD	07/12/63	Ft. Delaware, DE	CSR,KEB,H15
					Ft. Delaware, DE	03/24/64	Hos. 3/22-4/2/64	P47,KEB
					Ft. Delaware, DE	04/05/64	Hos. 4/5/64-?	P47,KEB
					Ft. Delaware, DE	06/10/65	Released G.O. #109	P40,P42,P44,CSR
Ligon, John J.	Pvt	K 2nd SCVC	Beverly Ford, VA	06/09/63	Old Capitol, DC	06/25/63	City Pt., VA Xc	CSR
					Ft. McHenry, MD	06/25/63	City Pt., VA Xc	P110
Liles, B.R.	Pvt	G 1st SCVIR	Bentonville, NC	03/22/65	New Berne, NC	04/10/65	Hart's Island, NY	CSR,SA1
					Hart's Island, NY	06/14/65	Rlsd. G.O. #109	CSR
					Hart's Island, NY	07/01/65	David's Island, NY	P79,CSR
Liles, H.I.	Pvt	C 2nd SCVIRi	Shell Mound, AL	10/29/63	Bridgeport, AL G.H.	11/05/63	Nashville, TN USGH	P2,CSR
Liles, H.I.	Pvt	C 2nd SCVIRi	Lookout Valley, TN	10/28/63	Nashville, TN USGH	11/17/63	Died of wounds	P12,CSR
Liles, J.W.	Pvt	B P.S.S.	Fair Oaks, VA	05/31/62	Fts. Monroe, VA	06/21/64	Ft. Delaware, DE	CSR,TSE
					Ft. Delaware, DE	04/09/65	Paroled	CSR,TSE
Limehouse, R.J.	Pvt	C 5th SCVC	Drury's Bluff, VA	05/13/64	Fts. Monroe, VA	05/16/64	Pt. Lookout, MD	CSR
					Pt. Lookout, MD	07/25/64	Elmira, NY	P113,P120,CSR
					Elmira, NY	06/19/65	Rlsd. G.O. #109	P65,P66,CSR
Lindall, J.M.	Cpl	H 2nd SCVC	Gettysburg, PA		Letterman G.H. Gbg	07/13/63	Died of wounds	P1,P12
Linder, Chambers	Pvt	A Hol.Leg.	Five Forks, VA	04/01/65	City Pt., VA	04/07/64	Died of wounds	P12,CSR
Linder, T.J.	Pvt	B 7th SCVC	Athens, GA	05/08/65	Athens, GA	05/08/65	Paroled	CSR
Lindler, Hezekiah M.	Pvt	B 14th SCVI	Augusta, GA	05/24/65	Augusta, GA	05/24/65	Paroled	CSR
Lindler, S.P.	Sgt	F 15th SCVI	Gettysburg, PA	07/04/63	Ft. McHenry, MD	07/15/63	Ft. Delaware, DE	CSR
					Ft. Delaware, DE	06/10/65	Rlsd. G.O. #109	P45,CSR
Lindon, Lewis	Pvt	C 27th SCVI	Weldon RR, VA	08/21/64	City Pt., VA	08/24/64	Pt. Lookout, MD	CSR,HAG
					Pt. Lookout, MD	03/15/65	Exchanged	P113,P124,P125,CSR
					Pt. Lookout, MD	03/15/65	Died, Scurvy	P6,P12,FPH
Lindsay, Charles T.	Pvt	B 27th SCVI	Town Creek, VA	02/20/65	Ft. Anderson, NC	02/28/65	Pt. Lookout, MD	CSR,HAG
					Pt. Lookout, MD	05/13/65	Rlsd. G.O. #85	P114,CSR
Lindsay, James	Pvt	E 3rd SCVI	Cedar Creek, VA	10/19/64	Harpers Ferry, WV	10/24/62	Pt. Lookout, MD	CSR,ANY,KEB,SA2,H3
					Pt. Lookout, MD	01/04/65	Died, Dysentery	P6,P12,P114,FPH
Lindsay, Oscar L.	Pvt	B 1st SCVC	Petersburg, VA	07/29/64	City Pt., VA	08/05/64	Pt. Lookout, MD	CSR,HOS
					Pt. Lookout, MD	08/08/64	Elmira, NY	P65,P66,CSR
					Elmira, NY	06/19/65	Rlsd. G.O. #109	P65,P66,CSR
Lindsey, Ebenezer E.	Pvt	G 3rd SCVI	Sharpsburg, MD	09/17/62	Sharpsburg, MD	09/20/62	Paroled	H3,SCR,KEB,SA2,H3
Lindsey, Ebenezer E.	Pvt	G 3rd SCVI	Chickamauga, GA	09/20/63	Nashville, TN	10/01/63	Louisville, KY	P38,CSR
					Louisville, KY	10/02/63	Camp Douglas, IL	CSR
					Camp Douglas, IL	05/04/65	Rlsd. President's O	P7,P53,P55,P57,P58
Lindsey, Peter N.	Sgt	K 22nd SCVI	Hartwell, GA	05/18/65	Hartwell, GA	05/18/65	Paroled	CSR

L

SOUTH CAROLINA SOLDIERS, SAILORS AND CITIZENS HELD IN U.S. PRISONS 1861-1865

NAME	RANK	REGIMENT	CAPTURED AT	WHEN	PRISON	MOVED	DISPOSITION	SOURCES
Lindsey, W.A.	Pvt	K 22nd SCVI	Deep Bottom, VA	08/16/64	City Pt., VA	08/22/64	Pt. Lookout, MD	CSR
					Pt. Lookout, MD	02/10/65	Exchanged	P113,CSR
					Richmond, VA	02/15/65	Jackson Hos. Rchmd.	CSR
					Jackson Hos. Rchmd.	03/17/65	Furlough, 60 days	CSR
Lindsey, William R.	Pvt	K 3rd SCVI	Sharpsburg, MD	09/17/62	Elias Grove's Farm	09/27/62	Died of wounds	P12,H3,CSR,SA2
Linguish, Matthew	Pvt	E 26th SCVI	Southside RR, VA	04/02/65	City Pt., VA	04/05/65	Pt. Lookout, MD	CSR
					Pt. Lookout, MD	06/29/65	Rlsd. G.O. #109	CSR
Link, Johnson	Pvt	G 14th SCVI	Appomattox R., VA	04/03/65	City Pt., VA	04/11/65	Hart's Island, NY	CSR
					Hart's Island, NY	06/16/65	Rlsd. G.O. #109	P79,CSR
Linning, John D.	Pvt	A 27th SCVI	Petersburg, VA	06/18/64	City Pt., VA	06/24/64	Pt. Lookout, MD	CSR
					Pt. Lookout, MD	07/24/64	Elmira, NY	P113,P120,CSR
					Elmira, NY	03/10/65	Trfd. for Xc	P65,P66,CSR
Linsey, John	Pvt	1st SCVC	Deserted/enemy	10/08/64	Kingston, TN	10/13/64	New York, NY oath	CSR
Linstedt, Henry	Pvt	B 27th SCVI	Town Creek, NC	02/20/65	Ft. Anderson, NC	02/28/65	Pt. Lookout, MD	CSR,HAG
					Pt. Lookout, MD	05/13/65	Rlsd. G.O. #85	P114,CSR
Linton, H.C.	Pvt	Chfld. LA	Chesterfield, SC	03/03/65	New Berne, NC	04/10/65	Hart's Island, NY	CSR
					Hart's Island, NY	06/17/65	Rlsd. G.O. #109	CSR
Lipford, William C.	Pvt	D Ham.Leg.MI	Richmond, VA Hos.	04/03/65	No further data			CSR
Lipscomb, J.M.	Pvt	F 18th SCVI	Five Forks, VA	04/01/65	City Pt., VA	04/05/65	Pt. Lookout, MD	CSR
					Pt. Lookout, MD	06/29/65	Rlsd. G.O. #109	P114,CSR
Lipscomb, John H.	Pvt	I 13th SCVI	Petersburg, VA	04/03/65	City Pt., VA	04/13/65	Pt. Lookout, MD	P114,HOS,CSR
					Pt. Lookout, MD	06/29/65	Rlsd. G.O. #109	P114,CSR
Lipscomb, Thomas J.	Pvt	G 2ND scvc	Goldsboro, NC	03/20/65	New Berne, NC	04/03/65	Pt. Lookout, MD	CSR
					Pt. Lookout, MD	06/28/65	Rlsd. G.O. #109	P114,CSR
Lipsey, John A.	Pvt	I 6th SCVI	Richmond, VA Hos.	04/15/65	Richmond, VA Hos.	04/21/65	Paroled	CSR
Liston, A.B.	Pvt	G 4th SCVC	Armstrongs Mills,	12/10/64	City Pt., VA	12/12/64	Pt. Lookout, MD	CSR
					Pt. Lookout, MD	06/05/65	Released	P114,CSR
Litchfield, G.T.	Cpt	L 7th SCVI	Cedar Creek, VA	10/19/64	Harpers Ferry, WV	10/25/64	Ft. Delaware, DE	CSR,KEB
					Ft. Delaware, DE	05/25/65	Rlsd O.O. Gen. Grant	P7,P43,P45,P46,CSR
Lites, James C.	Pvt	B Orr's Ri.	Falling Waters, MD	07/14/63	Baltimore, MD	08/16/63	Pt. Lookout, MD	CSR,CDC
					Pt. Lookout, MD	08/16/64	Elmira, NY	P113,P120
					Elmira, NY	03/10/65	Pt. Lookout, MD Xc	CSR
Lites, Joel W.	Pvt	B Orr's Ri	Petersburg, VA	04/03/65	City Pt., VA	04/11/65	Hart's Island, NY	CSR
					Hart's Island, NY	06/16/65	Rlsd. G.O. #109	P79,CSR
Little, George	Pvt	G 22nd SCVI	Deserted/enemy	06/02/64	Norfolk, VA	08/03/64	Fts. Monroe, VA	CSR
					Fts. Monroe, VA	08/04/64	No data	CSR
Little, Jacob	Pvt	K 26th SCVI	Appomattox R., VA	04/03/65	City Pt., VA	04/05/65	Hart's Island, NY	CSR
					Hart's Island, NY	04/10/65	Died, Typhoid fever	P79
Little, James B.	Pvt	B 5th SCVI	Sharpsburg, MD	09/17/62	Sharpsburg, MD	09/27/62	Paroled	CSR
Little, James L.	Pvt	I Ham.Leg.MI	Darbytown Rd., VA	01/25/65	Bermuda Hundred, VA	02/10/65	City Pt., VA P.M.	CSR
					City Pt., VA	02/10/65	Pt. Lookout, MD	CSR
					Pt. Lookout, MD	06/29/65	Rlsd. G.O. #109	P114,CSR
Little, Robert J.	Pvt	A 13th SCVI	Funkstown, MD	07/15/63	Hagerstown, MD G.H	08/15/63	No record found	P2,CSR
Little, Stephen	Pvt	H Orr's Ri.	Amelia C.H., VA	04/05/65	City Pt., VA	03/13/65	Pt. Lookout, MD	CSR
					Pt. Lookout, MD	06/29/65	Rlsd. G.O. #109	CSR
Littlejohn, B.S.	Pvt	B 27th SCVI	Ft. Anderson, NC	02/19/65	Ft. Anderson, NC	02/28/65	Pt. Lookout, MD	CSR
					Pt. Lookout, MD	06/24/65	Rlsd. G.O. #109	P114,CSR
Littlejohn, Calvin	Pvt	B Hol.Leg.	Deserted/enemy	03/14/65	City Pt., VA	03/15/65	Washington, DC	CSR
					Washington, DC	03/18/65	Newville, PA oath	CSR
Littlejohn, J.W.	Pvt	I 7th SCVI	Salisbury, NC	05/02/65	Salisbury, NC	05/02/65	Paroled	CSR
Littlejohn, Joseph	Pvt	Brooks LA	Burkeville, VA	04/14/65	Burkeville, VA	04/17/65	Paroled	CSR

SOUTH CAROLINA SOLDIERS, SAILORS AND **L** CITIZENS HELD IN U.S. PRISONS 1861-1865

NAME	RANK	REGIMENT	CAPTURED AT	WHEN	PRISON	MOVED	DISPOSITION	SOURCES
Littlejohn, Salathiel	Pvt	I 6th SCVC	Louisa C.H., VA	06/11/64	Fts. Monroe, VA	06/20/64	Pt. Lookout, MD	CSR
					Pt. Lookout, MD	07/25/64	Elmira, NY	P113,P120,CSR
					Elmira, NY	12/15/64	Died, Pneumonia	P6,P65,P66,FPH,CSR
Littlejohn, Thomas M.	Cpl	I 13th SCVI	Sutherland Stn., VA	04/03/65	City Pt., VA	04/07/65	Hart's Island, NY	CSR
					Hart's Island, NY	06/18/65	Rlsd. G.O. #109	P79,HOS,CSR
Littlejohn, W.E.S.	Pvt	B 27th SCVI	Petersburg, VA	06/24/64	Bermuda Hundred, VA	06/25/64	Fts. Monroe, VA	CSR
					Fts. Monroe, VA	06/26/64	Pt. Lookout, MD	CSR
					Pt. Lookout, MD	08/16/64	Elmira, NY	P113,P120,CSR
					Elmira, NY	02/20/65	Pt. Lookout, MD Xc	P66,CSR
					Richmond, VA Hos.	03/05/65	Died	CSR
Littleton, Asa	Pvt	A 20th SCVI	Cedar Creek, VA	10/19/64	Winchester, VA USH	11/17/64	Died of wounds/pne	CSR
Littleton, Daniel	Pvt	G 12th SCVI	Wilderness, VA	05/06/64	Belle Plain, VA	05/20/64	Ft. Delaware, DE	CSR
					Ft. Delaware, DE	01/20/62	Hos. 1/20-2/21/65	P47
					Ft. Delaware, DE	02/27/65	City Pt., VA Xc	P41,P42,CSR
Littleton, Jennings	Pvt	I 1st SCVA	Morris Island, SC	07/10/63	Morris Island, SC	07/24/63	Paroled	P2,CSR
Littleton, Thomas	Pvt	A 20th SCVI	Fishers Hill, VA	10/19/64	Winchester, VA Hos.	12/10/64	Baltimore, MD	CSR
					W. Bldg. Balt, MD	01/07/65	Pt. Lookout, MD	P4,CSR
					Pt. Lookout, MD	01/31/65	Hammond G.H., MD	CSR
					Hammond G.H., MD	04/01/65	Pt. Lookout, MD	CSR
					Pt. Lookout, MD	06/06/65	Released	CSR
Littleton, Thomas M.	Sgt	E 12th SCVI	Gettysburg, PA	07/04/63	Chester, PA G.H.	10/03/63	Pt. Lookout, MD	P1,CSR
					Pt. Lookout, MD	03/16/64	City Pt., VA Xc	CSR
Lively, Greenbury Jasper	Pvt	I Hol.Leg.	Stony Creek, VA	05/07/64	Fts. Monroe, VA	05/13/64	Pt. Lookout, MD	CSR
					Pt. Lookout, MD	08/15/64	Elmira, NY	P113,P120,FPH
Lively, Greenbury Jasper	Pvt	I Hol.Leg.	Stony Creek, VA	05/07/64	Elmira, NY	08/30/64	Died, Ch. Diarrhea	P5,P12,P65,P66,FPH
Lively, Robert Capers	Pvt	I 14th SCVI	Richmond, VA Hos.	04/03/65	Provost Marshal	04/21/65	Libby Prison Rchmd.	CSR
					Libby Prison Rchmd.	04/23/65	Newport News, VA	CSR
					Newport News, VA	06/13/65	Rlsd. G.O. #109	P107,CSR
Lively, Thomas	Pvt	F 13th SCVI	Deserted/enemy	02/24/65	City Pt., VA	02/26/65	Washington, DC	CSR,HOS
					Washington, DC	02/27/65	Springfield, IL	CSR
Livingston, Anthony T.	Pvt	E 1st SCVIH	Warrenton, VA	09/29/62	Warrenton, VA	09/29/62	Paroled	SA1,CSR
Livingston, Anthony T.	Pvt	E 1st SCVIH	Chattanooga, TN	11/26/63	Nashville, TN	12/16/63	Louisville, KY	P39
					Louisville, KY	12/21/63	Rock Island, IL	CSR
					Rock Island, IL	06/10/64	Joined U.S. Navy	CSR
Livingston, Emanuel	Pvt	B 3rd SCVI	Gettysburg, PA	07/02/63	Gettysburg, PA G.H.	09/01/63	Provost Marshal	P4,KEB,SA2,H3
					W. Bldg. Balt, MD	09/25/63	City Pt., VA Xc	P1,CSR
Livingston, Frederick	Pvt	A 15th SCVAB	Smith's Ford, NC	03/16/65	New Berne, NC	04/03/65	Pt. Lookout, MD	CSR
					Pt. Lookout, MD	06/29/65	Rlsd. G.O. #109	P114,CSR
Livingston, J.B.	Sgt	A 2nd SCVI	Gettysburg, PA	07/04/63	Gettysburg G.H.	07/20/63	Provost Marshal	P4,KEB,SA2,CSR,H2
					Ft. Delaware, DE	07/30/63	City Pt., VA Xc	P42,CSR
Livingston, John	Pvt	C 2nd SCVC	Greensboro, NC	05/01/65	Greensboro, NC	05/01/65	Paroled	CSR
Livingston, William D.	Pvt	H 3rd SCVC	Deserted/enemy	03/18/65	Charleston, SC		Released on oath	CSR
Llewellen, Benjamin F.	Pvt	I 6th SCVC	Louisa C.H., VA	06/11/64	Pt. Lookout, MD	07/25/64	Elmira, NY	P120,P113,CSR
					Elmira, NY	09/01/64	Died, Phthisis Pul.	P5,P10,P65,P66,FPH
Lloyd, G.F.	Pvt	C 3rd SCVABn	Blakely, AL	04/09/65	Ship Island, MS	05/01/65	Vicksburg, MS Xc	CSR
Lloyd, J.W.	Pvt	C 3rd SCVABn	Blakely, AL	04/09/65	Ship Island, MS	05/01/65	Vicksburg, MS Xc	CSR
Lloyd, James S.	Pvt	I 25th SCVI	Town Creek, NC	02/20/65	Ft. Anderson, NC	02/28/65	Pt. Lookout, MD	CSR
					Pt. Lookout, MD	06/05/65	Released	P114
Lloyd, John J.	1Sg	2 10/19 SCVI	Missionary Ridge	11/25/63	Bridgeport, AL G.H	12/06/63	Nashville, TN	P2,RAS,CSR
					Nashville, TN	12/13/63	Louisville, KY	P39,CSR
					Louisville, KY	12/16/63	Rock Island, IL	CSR
					Rock Island, IL	03/02/65	Tfd. for Xc	CSR

SOUTH CAROLINA SOLDIERS, SAILORS AND **L** CITIZENS HELD IN U.S. PRISONS 1861-1865

NAME	RANK	REGIMENT	CAPTURED AT	WHEN	PRISON	MOVED	DISPOSITION	SOURCES
Lloyd, Joseph	Pvt	K 6th SCVI	Frederick, MD	09/10/62	Ft. McHenry, MD	10/16/62	Died, Typhoid fever	P12,CSR
Lloyd, Lewis A.	Pvt	L 1st SCVIG	Sutherland Sta., VA	04/03/65	Hart's Island, NY		Hart's Island, NY	SA1,CSR
					City Pt., VA	06/16/65	Rlsd. G.O. #109	CSR
Lloyd, Thomas J.	Pvt	D 3rd SCVIBn	Sharpsburg, MD	09/14/62	Ft. McHenry, MD	10/17/62	Fts. Monroe, VA	CSR,KEB
					Fts. Monroe, VA	10/19/62	Aikens Ldg., VA Xc	CSR
Lloyd, Thomas J.	Pvt	D 3rd SCVIBn	Gettysburg, PA	07/05/63	Gettysburg G.H.		Provost Marshal	P4,KEB,CSR
					David's Island, NY	09/05/63	City Pt., VA Xc	P1,CSR
Lloyd, William G.	Sgt	C 3rd SCVABn	Ft. Gaines, AL	08/08/64	New Orleans, LA	10/25/64	Ship Island, MS	P4,CSR
					Ship Island, MS	01/05/65	Exchanged	CSR
Lochlier, Andrew	Pvt	G 24th SCVI	Franklin, TN	12/17/64	Nashville, TN	01/31/65	Louisville, KY	P4,P39,EFW
					Louisville, KY	02/01/65	Camp Chase, OH	CSR
					Camp Chase, OH	06/13/65	Rlsd. G.O. #109	P23
Lochlier, William N.	Pvt	H 11th SCVI	Darbytown Rd., VA	10/07/64	Bermuda Hundred, VA	10/08/64	City Pt., VA	HAG,CSR
					City Pt., VA	10/29/64	Pt. Lookout, MD	CSR
					Pt. Lookout, MD	06/29/65	Rlsd. G.O. #109	P114,CSR
Lockey, Benjamin B.	Pvt	E 1st SCVIG	Wilderness, VA	05/06/64	Belle Plain, VA	05/21/64	Ft. Delaware, DE	SA1,CSR
					Ft. Delaware, DE	03/23/65	Died, Diarrhea	P6,P41,P42,P47,FPH
Lockhard, Robert	Pvt	K 16th SCVI	Marietta, GA	06/20/64	Nashville, TN	06/28/64	Louisville, KY	P3,CSR
					Louisville, KY	06/30/64	Camp Morton, IN	CSR
					Camp Morton, IN	03/04/65	City Pt., VA Xc	CSR
					Richmond, VA Hos.	03/12/65	Camp Lee, Prld. PO	CSR
Lockhart, A.K.	Pvt	D 2nd SCVI	Wilderness, VA	05/06/64	Belle Plain, VA	05/24/64	Ft. Delaware, DE	CSR,SA2,H2
					Ft. Delaware, DE	04/21/65	Hos. 4/21-5/26/65	P47
					Ft. Delaware, DE	06/10/65	Released	P42,P45,CSR
Lockhart, Smith L.	Pvt	C 5th SCVI	Missionary Ridge	11/25/63	Bridgeport, AL G.H.	12/13/63	Nashville, TN	P2,SA3,CSR
					Nashville, TN G.H.	03/17/64	Louisville, KY	P2,P39,CSR
					Camp Chase, OH	02/25/65	City Pt., VA Xc	P22,P26,CSR
Locklier, John	Pvt	E 19th SCVI	Mumfordville, KY	09/19/62	Mumfordville, KY	09/19/62	Paroled	CSR
Lockwood, Henry A.	Pvt	H Ham.Leg.	Warrenton, VA	09/29/62	Warrenton, VA	09/29/62	Paroled	CSR
Lofton, Jerod J.	Pvt	K 10th SCVI	Deserted/enemy	03/13/65	Charleston, SC	03/13/65	Released on oath	CSR,RAS
Logan, Calhoun	Cpt	C 25th SCVI	Ft. Fisher, NC	01/15/65	Fts. Monroe, VA	01/26/65	Ft. Columbus, NY	CSR,HAG
					Ft. Columbus, NY	02/25/65	City Pt., VA Xc	P2
Logan, Francis	Pvt	F Hol.Leg.	Jarratts Stn., VA	05/08/64	Fts. Monroe, VA	05/13/64	Pt. Lookout, MD	CSR
					Pt. Lookout, MD	08/15/64	Elmira, NY	P113,P120
					Elmira, NY	03/03/65	Died, Pneumonia	P6,P12,P65,P66,FPH
Logan, John J.	Cpt	I 25th SCVI	Ft. Fisher, NC	01/15/65	Fts. Monroe, VA	02/09/65	Ft. Delaware, DE	CSR,HAG
					Ft. Delaware, DE	06/17/65	Rlsd. G.O. #109	P43,P45
Logan, Thomas H.	Pvt	G 14th SCVI	Petersburg, VA	04/02/65	City Pt., VA	04/07/65	Hart's Island, NY	CSR
					Hart's Island, NY	06/16/65	Rlsd. G.O. #109	P79,CSR
Logan, W. David	Pvt	C 25th SCVI	Weldon RR, VA	08/21/64	City Pt., VA	08/26/64	Washington, DC	P1,HAG,HOW,CTA
					Old Capitol, DC	10/17/64	Elmira, NY	CSR
					Ft. McHenry, MD	12/16/64	Elmira, NY	P110
					Elmira, NY	02/13/65	Elmira, NY USGH	P65,HAG
					Elmira, NY	07/26/65	Rlsd. G.O. #109	P66
Logan, William H.	Pvt	L 2nd SCVIRi	Sharpsburg, MD	10/01/62	Ft. McHenry, MD	10/20/62	Fts. Monroe, VA Xc	CSR
Logan, William R.	Pvt	F 1st SCVIR	Deserted/enemy		Chattanooga, TN	05/21/65	Took oath	P8,SA1
Logan, William S.	Pvt	G 14th SCVI	Wilderness, VA	05/06/64	Belle Plain, VA	05/21/64	Ft. Delaware, DE	CSR
					Ft. Delaware, DE	07/13/64	Hos. 7/13-7/15/64	P47
					Ft. Delaware, DE	03/19/65	Hos. 3/19-3/25/65	P47
					Ft. Delaware, DE	06/10/65	Rlsd. G.O. #109	P41,P42,P45,CSR
Lollis, J.T.T.	Pvt	L 8th SCVI			Pt. Lookout, MD		Exchanged	P124

SOUTH CAROLINA SOLDIERS, SAILORS AND  CITIZENS HELD IN U.S. PRISONS 1861-1865

NAME	RANK	REGIMENT	CAPTURED AT	WHEN	PRISON	MOVED	DISPOSITION	SOURCES
Lomas, William	Pvt	C 7th SCVIBn	Weldon RR, VA	08/21/64	City Pt., VA USFH	08/22/64	Alexandria, VA USG	CSR
					Alexandria, VA USG	09/12/64	Washington, DC USG	CSR
					Lincoln G.H., DC	02/11/65	Old Capitol, DC	CSR
					Old Capitol, VA	03/01/65	Elmira, NY	CSR
					Ft. McHenry, MD	03/01/65	Elmira, NY	P110
					Elmira, NY	03/28/65	Died, Hos. Gangrene	P1,P6,P66,FPH,CSR
Lominack, James J.	Pvt	C 15th SCVI	South Mtn., MD	09/14/62	Ft. McHenry, MD	09/29/62	Died of wounds	CSR,KEB,H15
Lonergan, J.D.	Pvt	K 2nd SCVI	Middletown, VA	09/25/62	Washington, DC Hos.	09/30/62	US Prison Hos.	SA2,H2,CSR,KEB
					Richmond, VA Hos.	10/13/62	Furloughed	H2,CSR
Long, Andrew	Pvt	K 12th SCVI	Petersburg, VA	04/03/65	City Pt., VA	04/13/65	Pt. Lookout, MD	CSR
					Pt. Lookout, MD	06/29/65	Rlsd. G.O. #109	P114,CSR
Long, Andrew Jackson	Pvt	C 3rd SCVI	Deserted/enemy	11/14/63	Knoxville, TN	12/16/63	Kentucky on oath	SA2,H3,CSR,KEB,ANY
Long, Charles R.	Pvt	D 7th SCVC	Old Church, VA	05/30/64	Lincoln G.H., DC	07/02/64	Old Capitol, DC	CSR
					Old Capitol, DC	07/23/64	Elmira, NY	CSR
					Ft. McHenry, MD	07/23/64	Elmira, NY	P110
					Elmira, NY	10/11/64	Venus Pt., GA Xc	P65,P66,CSR
					Elmira, NY	10/14/64	Pt. Lookout, MD	CSR
					Pt. Lookout, MD	10/29/64	Exchanged	P114
Long, D.S.	Pvt	H 3rd SCVI	Spotsylvania, VA	05/06/65	Belle Plain, VA	05/21/64	Ft. Delaware, DE	CSR,ANY,KEB,SA2,H3
					Ft. Delaware, DE	01/21/65	Died, Pneumonia	P6,P41,P42,P47,FPH
Long, Dock L.	Pvt	K 26th SCVI	Petersburg, VA	03/25/65	City Pt., VA	03/27/65	Pt. Lookout, MD	CSR
					Pt. Lookout, MD	06/28/65	Rlsd. G.O. #109	P114,CSR
Long, F.	Cpl	B 1st SCVA	Smiths Ford, NC	03/16/65	Pt. Lookout, MD	06/28/65	Rlsd. G.O. #109	P114
Long, Gabriel W.	Sgt	G Orr's Ri.	Falling Waters, MD	07/14/63	Pt. Lookout, MD	03/03/64	Exchanged	P113,P124,CDC
Long, George Frederick	Sgt	C 3rd SCVI	Knoxville, TN	12/04/63	Nashville, TN	01/17/64	Louisville, KY	P39,KEB,SA2,H3,ANY
					Louisville, KY	01/23/64	Rock Island, IL	CSR
					Rock Island, IL	03/20/65	Aikens Ldg., VA Xc	CSR
Long, H.C.	Pvt	G 3rd SCVABn	High Pt., NC	05/01/65	High Pt., NC	05/01/65	Paroled	CSR
Long, Henry	Pvt	K 12th SCVI	Deserted/enemy	02/23/65	City Pt., VA	02/24/64	Washington, DC	CSR
					Washington, DC	02/24/64	Oil City, PA oath	CSR
Long, J.O.	Pvt	F 24th SCVI	Jackson, MS Hos.	05/16/63	Jackson, MS	05/16/63	Paroled wdd POW	CSR
Long, J.W.	Pvt	K 15th SCVI	Halltown, VA	08/26/64	Camp Chase, OH	03/18/65	Pt. Lookout, MD	P22
					Pt. Lookout, MD	03/27/65	Boulware's Wharf X	CSR
Long, Jacob M.	Pvt	D 24th SCVI	Nashville, TN	12/16/64	Nashville, TN	12/31/64	Louisville, KY	CSR
					Louisville, KY	01/02/65	Camp Chase, OH	CSR
					Camp Chase, OH	06/12/65	Rlsd. G.O. #109	P23,CSR
Long, James A.	Pvt	C 15th SCVI	South Mtn., MD	09/14/62	Ft. Delaware, DE	11/10/62	Aikens Ldg.,VA Xc	CSR,KEB,H15
					Nashville, TN	01/17/64	Louisville, KY	P39
					Louisville, KY	01/23/64	Rock Island, IL	CSR
					Rock Island, IL	10/31/64	Jd. US Army Frtr. S	CSR
Long, James Wesley	Pvt	C 15th SCVI	Halltown, VA	08/26/64	Harpers Ferry, WV	08/29/64	Ft. Delaware, DE	CSR,KEB,H15
					Camp Chase, OH	03/18/65	Pt. Lookout, MD Xc	CSR
Long, John	Smn	CS Navy	Morris Island, SC	09/07/63	Pt. Lookout, MD	01/21/64	Joined U.S. Army	P125
Long, John	Pvt	D Orr's Ri.	Petersburg, VA	04/03/65	City Pt., VA	04/11/65	Hart's Island, NY	CSR,CDC
					Hart's Island, NY	06/16/65	Rlsd. G.O. #109	P79,CSR
Long, John A.	Pvt	G 13th SCVI	Petersburg, VA	04/02/65	City Pt., VA	04/04/65	Pt. Lookout, MD	CSR,ANY
					Pt. Lookout, MD	06/04/65	Released	P114,CSR
Long, John M.	Pvt	K 19th SCVI	Atlanta, GA	07/22/64	Nashville, TN	07/29/64	Louisville, KY	CSR,HOE
					Louisville, KY	07/31/64	Camp Chase, OH	CSR
					Camp Chase, OH	03/04/65	City Pt., VA Xc	P22,P26,CSR
					Richmond, VA Hos.	03/17/65	Furloughed 60 days	CSR

L

SOUTH CAROLINA SOLDIERS, SAILORS AND CITIZENS HELD IN U.S. PRISONS 1861-1865

NAME	RANK	REGIMENT	CAPTURED AT	WHEN	PRISON	MOVED	DISPOSITION	SOURCES
Long, John Wesley	Pvt	I 15th SCVI	Cedar Creek, VA	10/19/64	Harpers Ferry, WV	10/24/64	Pt. Lookout, MD	CSR,KEB,H15
					Pt. Lookout, MD	02/10/65	Exchanged	P114,P124,CSR
Long, Lattimer Wren	Pvt	C 3rd SCVI	Cedar Creek, VA	10/19/64	Harpers Ferry, WV	10/24/64	Pt. Lookout, MD	CSR,ANY,KEB,H3
					Pt. Lookout, MD	03/28/65	Aikens Ldg., VA Xc	P114,P124,CSR
Long, Leander	Pvt	G 13th SCVI	Sutherland Stn., VA	04/02/65	City Pt., VA	04/07/65	Hart's Island, NY	CSR
					Hart's Island, NY	06/20/65	Rlsd. G.O. #109	P79,ANY,CSR
Long, Levi W.	Pvt	C 15th SCVI	Gettysburg, PA	07/04/63	David's Island, NY	08/24/63	City Pt., VA Xc	P1,P4,KEB,CSR,H15
Long, Levi W.	Pvt	C 15th SCVI			Camp Chase, OH	03/18/65	Pt. Lookout, MD	P26
Long, Rowland	Pvt	K 12th SCVI	Deserted/enemy	02/23/65	City Pt., VA	02/24/65	Washington, DC	CSR
					Washington, DC	02/24/65	Oil City, PA oath	CSR
Long, Thomas D.	Pvt	F Orr's Ri.	Hatcher's Run, VA	04/03/65	City Pt., VA	04/13/65	Pt. Lookout, MD	CSR,CDC
					Pt. Lookout, MD	06/28/65	Rlsd. G.O. #109	CSR
Long, Thomas H.	Cpl	B 1st SCVIR	Smith's Ford, NC	03/16/65	New Berne, NC	04/03/65	Pt. Lookout, MD	CSR,SA1
					Pt. Lookout, MD	06/28/65	Rlsd. G.O. #109	CSR
Long, W.E.	Pvt	E P.S.S.	Petersburg, VA	04/03/65	Hart's Island, NY	06/16/65	Rlsd. G.O. #109	P79,TSE
Long, William A.	Pvt	C 15th SCVI	Halltown, WV	08/26/64	Harpers Ferry, WV	08/29/64	Camp Chase, OH	CSR,KEB,H15
					Camp Chase, OH	03/18/65	Pt. Lookout, MD	P22,P26,CSR
					Pt. Lookout, MD	06/29/65	Rlsd. G.O. #109	P114,CSR
Long, William H.	Pvt	F 6th SCVC	Johns Island, SC	02/09/64	Hilton Head, SC	03/31/64	Ft. Lafayette, NY	CSR
					Ft. Lafayette, NY	04/02/64	Ft. Delaware, DE	CSR
					Ft. Delaware, DE	01/05/65	Hos. 1/5-1/26/65	P47
					Ft. Delaware, DE	02/21/65	Hos. 2/21-4/7/65	P47
					Ft. Delaware, DE	06/10/65	Released	P41,P45,CSR
Longman, Charles	Smn	CS Chicora	Morris Island, SC	09/07/63	Pt. Lookout, MD	09/20/64	Ft. Warren, MA	P120,P124
					Ft. Warren, MA	10/01/64	Str. Circasian	P2
					Ft. Warren, MA	10/19/64		P137
Longshore, Euclydus C.	Pvt	B 3rd SCVI	Campbell Stn., TN	12/05/63	Nashville, TN	02/28/64	Louisville, KY	P39,KEB,SA2,H3,ANY
					Louisville, KY	03/09/64	Camp Chase, OH	CSR
					Camp Chase, OH	02/25/65	City Pt., VA Xc	P22,P26,CSR
Longshore, M.W.	Pvt	G Hol.Leg.	Warrenton, VA	09/29/62	Warrenton, VA	09/29/62	Paroled/Hospital	CSR
Longshore, William T.	Cpl	G Hol.Leg.	Five Forks, VA	04/01/65	City Pt., VA	04/05/65	Pt. Lookout, MD	CSR
					Pt. Lookout, MD	06/29/65	Rlsd. G.O. #109	P114,CSR
Longshore, Young	Pvt	G Hol.Leg.	Hatchers Run, VA	03/25/65	City Pt., VA	04/02/65	Pt. Lookout, MD	CSR,ANY
					Pt. Lookout, MD	06/28/65	Rlsd. G.O. #109	P114,CSR
Loomis, John	Pvt	C 2nd SCVC	Culpepper, VA	09/13/63	Lincoln G.H., DC	10/19/63	Old Capitol, DC	CSR
					Old Capitol, DC	10/28/63	Pt. Lookout, MD	CSR
					Pt. Lookout, MD	11/01/63	Aikens Ldg., VA Xc	P124,CSR
Loops, Frederick	Bug	Ch'fld LA	Kinston, NC	03/14/65	Kinston, NC		No release data	CSR
Loper, John	Pvt	B 3rd SCVC	Deserted/enemy	03/25/65	Charleston, SC		Released on oath	CSR
Lorick, J.D.	Pvt	C 20th SCVI	Cedar Creek, VA	10/19/64	Harpers Ferry, WV	10/23/64	Pt. Lookout, MD	CSR
					Pt. Lookout, MD	06/06/65	Released	P114,KEB,CSR
Loring, Alexander H.	Pvt	I 6th SCVI	Frederick, MD	09/12/62	Frederick, MD USGH	09/18/62	Ft. Delaware, DE	CSR
					Ft. Delaware, DE	10/02/62	Aikens Ldg., VA Xc	CSR
Lott, Arthur M.	Pvt	F 19th SCVI	Augusta, GA	05/20/65	Augusta, GA	05/20/65	Paroled	CSR
Lott, G.W.	Sgt	H 7th SCVI	Gettysburg, PA	07/04/63	Letterman G.H. Gbg	10/15/63	Balt. & City Pt.	CSR
					W. Bldg. Balt., MD	11/12/63	City Pt., VA Xc	P1,CSR
Lott, H.B.	Pvt	A 2nd SCVA	Raleigh, NC Hos.	04/13/65	Raleigh, NC	04/20/65	Released on oath	CSR
Lott, John Marshal	Sgt	B 14th SCVI	Petersburg, VA	07/29/64	City Pt., VA	08/05/64	Pt. Lookout, MD	CSR,HOE,UD3
					Pt. Lookout, MD	08/08/64	Elmira, NY	P113,P120,CSR
					Elmira, NY	06/16/65	Rlsd. G.O. #109	P65,P66,CSR
Lott, Lewis E.	Pvt	E 19th SCVI	Augusta, GA	05/23/65	Augusta, GA	05/23/65	Paroled	CSR

SOUTH CAROLINA SOLDIERS, SAILORS AND  CITIZENS HELD IN U.S. PRISONS 1861-1865

NAME	RANK	REGIMENT	CAPTURED AT	WHEN	PRISON	MOVED	DISPOSITION	SOURCES
Lott, Marshal	Pvt	D 14th SCVI	Petersburg, VA	04/03/65	City Pt., VA	04/13/65	Pt. Lookout, MD	CSR,HOE
					Pt. Lookout, MD	06/29/65	Rlsd. G.O. #109	P114,CSR
Lott, William A.	Pvt	B German LA	Deserted/enemy	03/30/65	Hilton Head, SC	04/04/65	P.M. New York, NY	CSR
Lott, William E.	Pvt	A 19th SCVI	Murfreesboro, TN	12/31/62	Murfreesboro, TN	01/05/63	Nashville, TN	CSR,HOE
					Nashville, TN	05/23/63	Louisville, KY	P38,CSR
					Louisville, KY	05/29/63	Ft. McHenry, MD	CSR
					Ft. McHenry, MD	06/03/63	Fts. Monroe, VA Xc	CSR
Lotts, James	Pvt	D 1st SCVIR	Bentonville, NC	03/22/65	New Berne, NC	04/10/65	Hart's Island, NY	CSR
					Hart's Island, NY	06/17/65	Rlsd. G.O. #109	SA1,CSR
Lotz, George M.	Pvt	E 1st SCVIR	Charleston, SC	02/18/65	Hilton Head, SC	03/22/65	To New York, NY	SA1,CSR
Lotzen, H.L.	Sgt	K 27th SCVI	Petersburg, VA	06/24/64	Fts. Monroe, VA	06/25/64	Pt. Lookout, MD	CSR,HAG
					Pt. Lookout, MD	07/23/64	Elmira, NY	P113,P120,CSR
					Elmira, NY	05/17/65	Rlsd. G.O. #85	P65,P66,CSR
Love, J.A.	Pvt	B 1st SCVIR	Charlotte, NC	05/15/65	Paroled			SA1,CSR
Love, James G.	Sgt	A 12th SCVI	Farmville, VA	04/11/65	Farmville, VA	04/21/65	Paroled	CSR
Love, Riley	Pvt	E 23rd SCVI	Deserted/enemy	12/05/64	City Pt., VA	12/08/64	Harrisburg, PA	P8,HMC,CSR
Love, Samuel M.	Sgt	K 17th SCVI	Five Forks, VA	04/01/65	City Pt., VA	04/06/65	Pt. Lookout, MD	CSR,YEB
					Pt. Lookout, MD	06/28/65	Rlsd. G.O. #109	P114,CSR
Love, W.A.	Pvt	K 17th SCVI	Five Forks, VA	04/01/65	City Pt., VA	04/06/65	Pt. Lookout, MD	CSR
					Pt. Lookout, MD	06/28/65	Rlsd. G.O. #109	CSR
Lovejoy, C.C.	Pvt	F 8th SCVI	PawPaw, WV	02/21/65	Cumberland, MD	02/23/65	Rlsd. on oath	P8,CSR
Loveless, Benjamin	Pvt	A 2nd SCVIRi	Sharpsburg, MD		Ft. McHenry, MD		Paroled & sent S.	CSR
Loveless, James H.	Pvt	7th SCVC	Washington, GA	06/07/65	Washington, GA	06/07/65	Paroled	CSR
Loveless, James Lewis	Pvt	A 2nd SCVIRi	Sharpsburg, MD		Provost Marshal A.	09/27/62	Paroled	CSR
Lovett, Frederick	Pvt	C 7th SCVIBn	Columbia, SC	02/20/65	New Berne, NC	04/10/65	Hart's Island, NY	CSR,HAG
					Hart's Island, NY	06/16/65	Rlsd. G.O. #109	P79,CSR
Lovett, Henry	Pvt	A 1st SCVA	Fayetteville, NC	03/16/65	New Berne, NC	04/10/65	Hart's Island, NY	CSR
					Hart's Island, NY	06/16/65	Rlsd. G.O. #109	P79,CSR
Lovett, Jacob	Pvt	A 1st SCVA	Bentonville, NC	03/13/65	New Berne, NC	03/30/65	Pt. Lookout, MD	CSR
					Pt. Lookout, MD	06/21/65	Rlsd. G.O. #109	CSR
Lovett, William J.	Pvt	C 6th SCVI	Williamsburg, VA	05/06/62	Cliffburne G.H.	07/11/62	Old Capitol, DC	CSR
					Old Capitol, DC	08/01/62	Fts. Monroe, VA	CSR
					Fts. Monroe, VA	08/05/62	Aikens Ldg., VA Xc	CSR
Lovick, A.J.	Pvt	F 5th SCVC	Stony Creek, VA	12/01/64	City Pt., VA	12/05/64	Pt. Lookout, MD	CSR,FDC
					Pt. Lookout, MD	06/28/65	Rlsd. G.O. #109	P114,CSR
Lovitt, Levin	Pvt	H Orr's Ri.	Petersburg, VA	04/02/65	Pt. Lookout, MD	06/21/65	Rlsd. G.O. #109	P114,CSR
Low, A.R.	Pvt	I 5th SCVI	Chattanooga, TN	10/29/63	Nashville, TN	11/07/63	Louisville, KY	P39,SA3
					Louisville, KY	11/09/63	Camp Morton, IN	CSR
					Camp Morton, IN	03/19/64	Ft. Delaware, DE	CSR
					Ft. Delaware, DE	04/18/64	Died	P47
Low, A.R.	Pvt	I 5th SCVI	Chattanooga, TN	10/29/63	Ft. Delaware, DE	04/18/64	Died, Lung Inflam.	P5,P41,P42,P47,FPH
Low, Ansell	Pvt	G 2nd SCVA	Cheraw, SC	03/04/65	New Berne, NC	03/30/65	Pt. Lookout, MD	CSR
					Pt. Lookout, MD	06/28/65	Rlsd. G.O. #109	P114,CSR
Low, James H.	Pvt	B Hol.Leg.	Kinston, NC	12/15/62	Kinston, NC	12/15/62	Paroled POW	CSR,HOS
Low, James H.	Pvt	B Hol.Leg.	Five Forks, VA	04/02/65	City Pt., VA	04/05/65	Pt. Lookout, MD	CSR
					Pt. Lookout, MD	06/07/65	Died, Ch. Diarrhea	P6,P12,P114,FPH
Low, L.H.	Pvt	C Hol.Leg.	Petersburg, VA	11/06/64	City Pt., VA	11/11/64	Washington, DC	CSR
					Pt. Lookout, MD	06/28/65	Rlsd. G.O. #109	P114
Low, Ransom L.	Pvt	G 2nd SCVA	Fayetteville, NC	03/19/65	New Berne, NC	03/30/65	Pt. Lookout, MD	P114,CSR
					Pt. Lookout, MD	06/28/65	Rlsd. G.O. #109	P114,CSR
Lowden, J.J.	Pvt	K 13th SCVI	Gettysburg, PA	07/05/63	David's Island, NY	09/12/63	City Pt., VA Xc	P1
Lowden, J.J.	Pvt	K 13th SCVI	Appomattox R., VA	04/05/65	Pt. Lookout, MD	06/29/65	Rlsd. G.O. #109	P114

L

SOUTH CAROLINA SOLDIERS, SAILORS AND CITIZENS HELD IN U.S. PRISONS 1861-1865

NAME	RANK	REGIMENT	CAPTURED AT	WHEN	PRISON	MOVED	DISPOSITION	SOURCES
Lowder, H.S.	Pvt	I 25th SCVI	Ft. Fisher, NC	01/15/65	New York, NY	01/31/65	Elmira, NY	CSR,HAG
					Elmira, NY	03/14/65	Pt. Lookout, MD Xc	P65,P66
					Jackson Hos. Rchmd.	03/24/65	Furloghed 60 days	CSR
Lowder, J.O.	Pvt	I 25th SCVI	Ft. Fisher, NC	01/15/65	New York, NY	01/31/65	Elmira, NY	CSR,HAG
					Elmira, NY	07/03/65	Rlsd. G.O. #109	P65,P66
Lowe, Elias J.W.	Cpl	C 13th SCVI	Petersburg, VA	04/03/65	City Pt., VA	04/13/65	Pt. Lookout, MD	CSR
					Pt. Lookout, MD	06/29/65	Rlsd. G.O. #109	P114,HOS,CSR
Lowe, J.D.	Pvt	K 25th SCVI	Ft. Fisher, NC	01/15/65				CSR
Lowe, Martin Van	Pvt	B 15th SCVI	Charlestowne, WV	08/25/64	Harpers Ferry, WV	08/29/64	Camp Chase, OH	CSR,H15
Lowe, Martin Van	Pvt	B 15th SCVI	Halltown, WV	08/25/64	Camp Chase, OH	03/18/65	Pt. Lookout, MD	P22,P26,CSR
					Pt. Lookout, MD	03/27/65	Boulware's Wh. Xc	CSR
Lowe, S.H.	Pvt	C 7th SCVC	Rchmd. &Pbg. Pike	05/11/64	Bermuda Hundred, VA	05/17/64	Fts. Monroe, VA	CSR
					Fts. Monroe, VA	05/18/64	Pt. Lookout, MD	CSR
					Pt. Lookout, MD	08/13/64	Elmira, NY	P113,P120
					Elmira, NY	10/11/64	Tfd. for exchange	P65,P66,CSR
					Pt. Lookout, MD	10/29/64	Venus Pt., GA Xc	P114
Lowe, Samuel	Pvt	D 6th SCVI	Deserted/enemy	03/20/65	Bermuda Hundred, VA	03/21/65	City Pt., VA P.M.	CSR
					City Pt., VA P.M.	03/24/65	Washington, DC P.M.	CSR
					Washington, DC P.M.	03/25/65	Harrisburg, PA oath	CSR
Lowe, William A.	Pvt	C 13th SCVI	Deserted/enemy	02/11/65	City Point, VA	03/15/65	Chicago, IL on oath	P8,HOS,CSR
Lowell, A.D.	Pvt	F 6th SCVI	Jetersville, VA	04/06/65	Newport News, VA		Released, date dim.	P107
Lowell, J.A.	Pvt	F 6th SCVI	Farmville, VA	04/06/65	Newport News, VA		Released, date dim.	P107
Lowell, J.A.	Pvt	F 6th SCVI	Farmville, VA	04/06/65	City Pt., VA	04/14/65	Newport News, VA	CSR
Lowery, Calvin	Cpl	K 6th SCVC	Louisa C.H., VA	06/11/64	Fts. Monroe, VA	06/20/64	Pt. Lookout, MD	CSR
					Pt. Lookout, MD	07/25/64	Elmira, NY	P113,P120,CSR
					Elmira, NY	08/30/64	Died, Diarrhea	P5,P65,P66,FPH,CSR
Lowery, Richard	Pvt	K 1st SCVIR	Bentonville, NC	03/22/65	New Berne, NC	04/10/65	Hart's Island, NY	CSR
					Hart's Island, NY	06/17/65	Rlsd. G.O. #109	P79,SA1,CSR
Lowery, Robert Y.H.	Sgt	C Orr's Ri.	Petersburg, VA	04/03/65	City Pt., VA	04/11/65	Hart's Island, NY	CSR,CDC
					Hart's Island, NY	06/16/65	Rlsd. G.O. #109	P79,CSR
Lowery, W.T.	Pvt	D 8th SCVI	Winchester, VA	09/13/64	Harpers Ferry, WV	09/19/64	Camp Chase, OH	CSR,KEB
					Camp Chase, OH	06/11/65	Rlsd. G.O. #109	P23,CSR
Lowery, Wesley W.	Pvt	H 2nd SCVI	Greencastle, PA	07/05/63	Ft. Delaware, DE	09/15/63	Jd. US 3rd MD Cav.	P40,P42,KEB,SA2,H2
Lowery, William A.	Pvt	E Orr's Ri.	Petersburg, VA	04/03/65	City Pt., VA	04/11/65	Hart's Island, NY	CSR
					Hart's Island, NY	06/16/65	Rlsd. G.O. #109	P79,CDC,CSR
Lowman, S.G.	Pvt	C 20th SCVI	Cedar Creek, VA	10/19/64	Harpers Ferry, WV	10/23/64	Pt. Lookout, MD	CSR,KEB
					Pt. Lookout, MD	03/28/65	Exchanged	P114,P124,CSR
Lown, J.J.	Pvt	K 13th SCVI	Gettysburg, PA	07/03/63	David's Island, NY		City Pt., VA Xc	CSR
Lown, J.J.	Pvt	K 13th SCVI	Appomattox R., VA	04/06/65	City Pt., VA	04/14/65	Pt. Lookout, MD	CSR
					Pt. Lookout, MD	06/29/65	Rlsd. G.O. #109	CSR
Lowrey, H.J.	Pvt	C 3rd SCVABn	Blakely, AL	04/09/65	Ship Island, MS	05/01/65	Vicksburg, MS Xc	CSR
Lowrimore, Hanson L.	Pvt	I 21st SCVI	Petersburg, VA	06/24/64	Pt. Lookout, MD	08/16/64	Elmira, NY	P113,P114,P120,HAG
					Elmira, NY	10/11/64	Pt. Lookout to Xc	P65,P66
					Pt. Lookout, MD	10/23/64	Died, Ch. Diarrhea	P5,P12,FPH,HMC
Lowrimore, John H.	Pvt	F 1st SCVIG	Ft. Harrison, VA	09/30/64	City Pt., VA	10/05/64	Pt. Lookout, MD	CSR,SA1
					Pt. Lookout, MD	03/17/65	Exchanged	P114,P124,CSR
Lowrimore, Robert W.	Sgt	A 26th SCVI	Southside RR, VA	04/01/65	City Pt., VA	04/05/65	Pt. Lookout, MD	CSR
					Pt. Lookout, MD	06/29/65	Rlsd. G.O. #109	P114,CSR
Lowrimore, William H.	Pvt	F 1st SCVIG	(Rcd. 10/5/64)		Pt. Lookout, MD			P125,SA1
Lowrimore, William H.	Pvt	A 10th SCVI	Murfreesboro, TN	12/28/62	Nashville, TN			P38,RAS,CSR
					Camp Douglas, IL	04/07/63	City Pt., VA Xc	P54

SOUTH CAROLINA SOLDIERS, SAILORS AND  **L** CITIZENS HELD IN U.S. PRISONS 1861-1865

NAME	RANK	REGIMENT	CAPTURED AT	WHEN	PRISON	MOVED	DISPOSITION	SOURCES
Lowry, John M.	Pvt	F 26th SCVI	Petersburg, VA	03/25/65	City Pt., VA	03/28/65	Pt. Lookout, MD	CSR
					Pt. Lookout, MD	06/28/65	Rlsd. G.O. #109	P114,CSR
Lowry, W.H.	Pvt	A 12th SCVI	Warrenton, VA	09/29/62	Warrenton, VA	09/29/62	Paroled	CSR
					Richmond, VA GH	10/24/62	Died	CSR
Lubben, Luer	Pvt	B German LA	Chambersburg, PA	07/04/63				CSR
Lubs, H.D.	Cpl	B German LA	Deserted/enemy	03/15/65	Charleston, SC	03/15/65	Released on oath	CSR
Lucas, Clarence	Pvt	A 3rd SCVABn	Cheraw, SC	03/07/65	Pt. Lookout, MD	06/28/65	Rlsd. G.O. #109	P114,CSR
Lucas, D.E.	Pvt	K 15th SCVI	N. Anna River, VA	05/24/64	Port Royal, VA	05/30/64	Pt. Lookout, MD	CSR
					Pt. Lookout, MD	03/14/65	Boulware's Wh. Xc	P113,P124,CSR
Lucas, David E.	Pvt	K 13th SCVI	Gettysburg, PA	07/05/63	David's Island, NY	09/12/63	City Pt., VA Xc	P1,CSR
					City Pt., VA Xc	09/27/63	Rcd. Camp Lee 9/29	CSR
Lucas, J.M.	Cit	Lexington	Flat Rock, SC	02/24/65	Hart's Island, NY	06/20/65	Rlsd. G.O. #109	P79
Lucas, J.N.	Pvt	K 15th SCVI	Augusta, GA	05/24/65	Augusta, GA	05/24/65	Paroled on oath	H15,CSR
Lucas, James	Pvt	K 13th SCVI	Gettysburg, PA	07/04/63	David's Island, NY	08/24/63	City Pt., VA Xc	P1,CSR
Lucas, Jerry R.	Pvt	H 2nd SCVI	Gettysburg, PA	07/02/63	Gettysburg, PA G.H	07/21/63	Provost Marshal	P4,KEB,SA2,H2
					David's Island, NY	08/24/63	City Pt., VA Xc	P1
Lucas, John	Pvt	C 12th SCVI	Falling Waters, MD	07/14/63	Pt. Lookout, MD	01/31/64	Died, Ch. Diarrhea	P5,P113,FPH,CSR
Lucas, Joseph	Pvt	A 14th SCVI	Sutherland Stn., VA	04/02/65	City Pt., VA	04/07/65	Hart's Island, NY	CSR,DEB
					Hart's Island, NY	06/16/65	Rlsd. G.O. #109	P79
Lucas, Joshua R.	Pvt	G 27th SCVI	Town Creek, NC	02/20/65	Ft. Anderson, NC	02/28/65	Pt. Lookout, MD	CSR,HAG
					Pt. Lookout, MD	06/29/65	Rlsd. G.O. #109	P114,HAG,CSR
Lucas, Moses L.	Pvt	H 2nd SCVI	Halltown, WV	08/26/64	Harpers Ferry, WV	08/29/64	Camp Chase, OH	CSR,KEB,SA2,H2
					Camp Chase, OH	03/26/65	Pt. Lookout, MD	P22,P26,CSR
					Pt. Lookout, MD	06/28/65	Rlsd. G.O. #109	P114CSR
Lucius, Joshua J.	Pvt	C 2nd SCVC	Greensboro, NC	05/01/65	Greensboro, NC	05/01/65	Paroled	CSR
Luck, Nathan B.	2Lt	G 12th SCVI	Spotsylvania, VA	05/10/64	Belle Plain, VA	05/17/64	Ft. Delaware, DE	CSR,ISH,R47
					Ft. Delaware, DE	08/20/64	Hilton Head, SC	P42
					Ft. Pulaski, GA			P4,CSR
					Ft. Delaware, DE	06/16/65	Rlsd. G.O. #109	P43,P44,P45
Luckey, William C.	Pvt	E 19th SCVI	Atlanta, GA	07/22/64	Nashville, TN	07/29/64	Louisville, KY	CSR
					Louisville, KY	08/01/64	Camp Chase, OH	CSR
					Camp Chase, OH	03/02/65	City Pt., VA Xc	P22,P26,CSR
					Richmond, VA Hos.	03/17/65	Furloughed 60 days	CSR
Luckie, J.C.	Pvt	I 1st SCVIR	Deserted/enemy	03/13/65	Charleston, SC		Released on oath	CSR
Luden, J.J.W.	Cpl	B German LA	Deserted/enemy	03/17/65	Charleston, SC	03/17/65	Released on oath	CSR
Lumpkin, Troy T.	Pvt	B 4th SCVC	Louisa C.H., VA	05/11/64	Fts. Monroe, VA	06/20/64	Pt. Lookout, MD	CSR,HHC
					Pt. Lookout, MD	07/25/64	Elmira, NY	P113,P120,CSR
					Elmira, NY	03/02/65	Pt. Lookout, MD Xc	P65,P66,CSR
Lumsden, D.L.	Pvt	H 2nd SCVC	Deserted/enemy	04/03/65	Charleston, SC	04/03/65	Released on oath	CSR
Lundy, Alfred	Pvt	B 1st SCVA	Rockingham, NC	03/07/65	New Berne, NC	03/30/65	Pt. Lookout, MD	CSR
					Pt. Lookout, MD	06/06/65	Released	P114,CSR
Lundy, James	Pvt	C 1st SCVA	Bentonville, NC	03/22/65	New Berne, NC	04/10/65	Hart's Island, NY	CSR
					Hart's Island, NY	06/15/65	Died, Ch. Diarrhea	P6,P12,P79,FPH,CSR
Lundy, Jesse	Pvt	D 1st SCVA	Rockingham, NC	03/07/65	New Berne, NC	03/30/65	Pt. Lookout, MD	CSR
					Pt. Lookout, MD	06/29/65	Rlsd. G.O. #109	P114,CSR
Lunn, Joshua T.	Pvt	B 21st SCVI	Town Creek, NC	02/20/65	Ft. Anderson, NC	02/28/65	Pt. Lookout, MD	CSR
					Pt. Lookout, MD	06/29/65	Rlsd. G.O. #109	P114,CSR
Luquire, Hugh	Pvt	B 1st SCVA	Cheraw, SC	03/06/65	New Berne, NC	04/10/65	Hart's Island, NY	CSR
					Hart's Island, NY	06/06/65	Rlsd. G.O. #109	CSR
Lybrand, Henry	Pvt	E 6th SCResB	Augusta, GA	05/18/65	Augusta,GA	05/18/65	Paroled	CSR

L

SOUTH CAROLINA SOLDIERS, SAILORS AND CITIZENS HELD IN U.S. PRISONS 1861-1865

NAME	RANK	REGIMENT	CAPTURED AT	WHEN	PRISON	MOVED	DISPOSITION	SOURCES
Lybrand, Samuel W.	Pvt	K 20th SCVI	Cedar Creek, VA	10/19/64	Harpers Ferry, WV	10/24/64	Pt. Lookout, MD	CSR
					Pt. Lookout, MD	06/28/65	Rlsd. G.O. #109	P114,KEB,CSR
Lyle, David	Pvt	A 17th SCVI	Petersburg, VA	03/25/65	City Pt., VA	03/28/65	Pt. Lookout, MD	CSR
					Pt. Lookout, MD	06/04/65	Released	P114,HHC,CSR
Lyle, James	Pvt	D 17th SCVI	Crater, Pbg., VA	07/30/64	City Pt., VA	08/05/64	Pt. Lookout, MD	CSR,HHC
Lyle, James	Pvt	D 17th SCVI	Crater, Pbg., VA	07/30/64	Pt. Lookout, MD	08/08/64	Elmira, NY	P113,P120,P125
					Elmira, NY	12/10/64	Died, Ch. Diarrhea	P6,P65,P66,FPH,CSR
Lyle, John	Pvt	A 17th SCVI	Petersburg, VA	03/25/65	City Pt., VA	03/28/65	Pt. Lookout, MD	CSR
					Pt. Lookout, MD	06/28/65	Rlsd. G.O. #109	P115,CSR
Lyles, Benjamin F.	Pvt	B 18th SCVI	Petersburg, MD	03/25/65	Ft. McHenry, MD	06/12/65	Rlsd. G.O. #109	P110,CSR
Lyles, D.A.	Pvt	E 22nd SCVI	Deserted/enemy		City Pt., VA	04/12/65	Washington, DC	CSR
					Washington, DC		Wilmington, NC	CSR
Lyles, Francis L.	Pvt	E 12th SCVI	Spotsylvania, VA	05/12/64	Old Capitol, DC	03/03/65	Elmira, NY	CSR,LAN
					Ft. McHenry, MD		Elmira, NY	P110
					Elmira, NY	06/30/65	Rlsd. G.O. #109	P65,P66,CSR
Lyles, J.L.	Pvt	G 3rd SCVABn	High Pt., NC	05/01/65	High Pt., NC	05/01/65	Paroled	CSR
Lyles, J.M.	Cpl	B 18th SCVI	Five Forks, VA	04/01/65	City Pt., VA	04/06/65	Pt. Lookout, MD	CSR
					Pt. Lookout, MD	06/29/65	Rlsd. G.O. #109	P114,CSR
Lyles, William	Pvt	B 15th SCVAB	Averysboro, NC	03/16/65	New Berne, NC	03/30/65	Pt. Lookout, MD	CSR
					Pt. Lookout, MD	04/04/65	Died, Interm. fever	P6,P114,FPH,CSR
Lynah, David	Pvt	H 2nd SCVC	Stephenburg, VA	06/09/63	Ft. McHenry, MD	06/25/63	City Pt., VA Xc	P110,CSR
					Old Capitol, DC	06/25/63	City Pt., VA Xc	CSR
Lynah, David	Pvt	H 2nd SCVC	Deserted/enemy		Fts. Monroe, VA	01/20/65	To work for U.S. G	P8,CSR
Lynch, Elias	Pvt	H 25th SCVI	Ft. Fisher, NC	01/15/65	Fts. Monroe, VA	02/01/65	Pt. Lookout, MD	CSR,HAG
					Pt. Lookout, MD	06/29/65	Rlsd. G.O. #109	P114
Lynch, F.L.	Pvt	I 27th SCVI	Petersburg, VA	06/24/64	Bermuda Hundred, VA	06/25/64	Fts. Monroe, VA	CSR,HAG
					Fts. Monroe, VA	06/26/64	Pt. Lookout, MD	CSR
					Pt. Lookout, MD	07/09/64	Elmira, NY	P113,P120,CSR
					Elmira, NY	10/11/64	Pt. Lookout, MD Xc	P65,P66,CSR
					Pt. Lookout, MD	10/29/64	Venus Pt., GA Xc	P114,CSR
Lynch, George W.	Pvt	I 26th SCVI	Crater, Pbg., VA	07/30/64	City Pt., VA	08/03/64	Pt. Lookout, MD	CSR,CTA
					Pt. Lookout, MD	08/04/64	Elmira, NY	P113,P120,CSR
					Elmira, NY	09/16/64	Died, Ch. Diarrhea	P5,P10,P65,P66,FPH
Lynch, John	Pvt	E 1st SCVA	Fayetteville, NC	03/16/65	New Berne, NC		Pt. Lookout, MD	CSR
					Pt. Lookout, MD			P114
Lynch, Joseph	Pvt	K 1st SCVA	Goldsboro, NC	03/24/65	New Berne, NC	04/26/65	Died, Ch. Diarrhea	P1,P12,CSR
Lynch, William H.	Pvt	H Orr's Ri.	Winchester, VA	12/02/62	Cumberland, MD	02/28/63	Wheeling, WV	CSR
					Wheeling, WV	03/03/63	Camp Chase, OH	CSR
					Camp Chase, OH	04/05/63	Died	P5,P22,P24,FPH
Lynes, Jesse C.	Pvt	G 1st SCVA	Bentonville, NC	03/19/65	New Berne, NC	04/10/65	Hart's Island, NY	CSR
					Hart's Island, NY	06/02/65	Rlsd. G.O. #109	P79,CSR
Lynes, P.L.	Pvt	C 19th SCVCB	Augusta, GA	05/19/65	Augusta, GA	05/19/65	Paroled on oath	CSR
Lynn, E.J.	Pvt	A 17th SCVI	Petersburg, VA	07/30/64	City Pt., VA	08/05/64	Pt. Lookout, MD	CSR
					Pt. Lookout, MD	08/08/64	Elmira, NY	P113,P120,CSR
					Elmira, NY	07/03/65	Rlsd. G.O. #109	P65,P66,CSR
Lynn, H.W.	Pvt	L 1st SCVIG	Caroline Co., VA	05/24/64	Old Capitol, DC	06/17/64	Ft. Delaware, DE	CSR,SA1
					Ft. McHenry, MD	06/22/64	Ft. Delaware, DE	P110
					Ft. Delaware, DE	09/18/64	Aikens Ldg., VA Xc	P41,P42,CSR
Lynn, H.W.	Pvt	L 1st SCVIG	Petersburg, VA	04/02/65	City Pt., VA	04/04/65	Pt. Lookout, MD	CSR
					Pt. Lookout, MD	06/08/65	Released on oath	P114,CSR
Lynn, Hugh	Pvt	Beaufort L	South Carolina	06/30/64	Louisville, KY	07/01/64	Jeffersonville, IN	P8,CSR

NAME	RANK	REGIMENT	CAPTURED AT	WHEN	PRISON	MOVED	DISPOSITION	SOURCES
Lynn, J.R.	Pvt	I 12th SCVI	Beaver Church, SC	02/23/65	New Berne, NC	04/10/65	Hart's Island, NY	CSR
					Hart's Island, NY	06/16/65	Rlsd. G.O. #109	P79,LAN,CSR
Lynn, Joseph W.	Pvt	B 15th SCVAB	Smithfield, NC	03/16/65	New Berne, NC	03/30/65	Pt. Lookout, MD	CSR
					Pt. Lookout, MD	06/29/65	Rlsd. G.O. #109	CSR
Lynn, Thomas K.	Pvt	F 5th SCVI	Lookout Mtn., TN	10/28/63	Nashville, TN	12/13/63	Louisville, KY	P39,CSR,YEB,SA3
					Louisville, KY	12/16/63	Rock Island, IL	CSR
					Rock Island, IL	02/15/65	Tfd. for Xc	CSR
					Camp Chase, OH	05/02/65	New Orleans, LA Xc	P26
Lyons, John	Pvt	D 1st SCVIR	Deserted/enemy	02/24/65	Hilton Head, SC	03/22/65	To New York, NY	CSR
Lyons, Newton J.	Pvt	E 14th SCVI	Wilderness, VA	05/06/64	Belle Plain, VA	05/21/64	Ft. Delaware, DE	CSR
					Ft. Delaware, DE	08/11/64	Hos. 8/11-8/21/64	P47
					Ft. Delaware, DE	11/17/64	Hos. 11/7-11/17/64	P47
					Ft. Delaware, DE	02/01/65	Hos. 2/1-2/27/65	P47
					Ft. Delaware, DE	02/27/65	City Pt., VA Xc	P41,P42,CSR
Lyons, P.	Smn	C 3rd SCVABn	Ft. Gaines, AL	08/08/64	New Orleans, LA			P4

SOUTH CAROLINA SOLDIERS, SAILORS AND CITIZENS HELD IN U.S. PRISONS 1861-1865

NAME	RANK	REGIMENT	CAPTURED AT	WHEN	PRISON	MOVED	DISPOSITION	SOURCES
Maberry, Samuel	Pvt	F 15th SCVI	Gettysburg, PA	07/04/63	Ft. McHenry, MD		Ft. Delaware, DE	P4,CSR,KEB
					Ft. Delaware, DE	07/19/63	Chester, PA Hos.	P40,P42,P44,CSR
					Chester, PA G.H.	09/21/63	City Pt., VA Xc	P1,CSR
Mabry, Foster	Pvt	B 18th SCVI	Crater, Pbg., VA	07/30/64	City Pt., VA	08/05/64	Pt. Lookout, MD	CSR
					Pt. Lookout, MD	08/08/64	Elmira, NY	P113,P117,P120,CSR
					Elmira, NY	10/11/64	Pt. Lookout, MD Xc	P65,P66,P118,CSR
					Pt. Lookout, MD	10/26/64	Died, Ch. Diarrhea	P5,P115,FPH,CSR
Mabry, Logan C.	Pvt	F 6th SCVC	Stony Creek, VA	12/01/64	City Pt., VA	12/05/64	Pt. Lookout, MD	CSR,CAG
					Pt. Lookout, MD	06/29/65	Rlsd. G.O. #109	P118
Macbeth, Charles J.	2Lt	G 27th SCVI	Weldon RR, VA	08/21/64	Old Capitol, DC	08/27/64	Ft. Delaware, DE	CSR,HAG
					Ft. Delaware, DE	10/06/64	Pt. Lookout, MD	CSR
					Pt. Lookout, MD	11/02/64	Washington, DC	P115,P117,CSR
					Old Capitol, DC	12/17/64	Ft. Delaware, DE	CSR
					Ft. Delaware, DE	02/27/65	City Pt., VA Xc	P43,CSR
Macbeth, James Ravanel	Cpt	E 1st SCVA	Morris Island, SC	07/10/63	Hilton Head, SC	10/06/63	Ft. Columbus, NY	CSR,SCA
					Ft. Columbus, NY	10/09/63	Johnson's Isl., OH	P1,SCA,CSR
					Johnson's Isl., OH	10/08/64	Fts. Monroe, VA	P80,P81,P82,SCA,CSR
					Fts. Monroe, VA	10/12/64	Forward for Xch.	CSR
Maccabee, N.P.	Pvt	C 27th SCVI	Town Creek, NC	02/20/65	Ft. Anderson, NC	02/28/65	Pt. Lookout, MD	CSR,HAG
					Pt. Lookout, MD	06/29/65	Rlsd. G.O. #109	P115,P118,CSR
Machray, William L.	Msc	F 14th SCVI	Burkeville, VA	04/14/65	Burkeville, VA	04/17/65	Paroled	CSR
Mack, Thomas	Pvt	1st SCVA	Fayetteville, NC	04/18/65	New York, NY	04/26/65		CSR
Mackey, D.	Pvt	H 4th SCVC	Hawe's Shop, VA	05/28/64	White House, VA	06/08/64	Pt. Lookout, MD	CSR
					Pt. Lookout, MD	03/14/65	Aikens Ldg., VA Xc	P117,P121,P124,CSR
Mackey, Francis H.	Pvt	A 5th SCVI	Manchester, VA	04/03/65	Libby Prison, VA	04/07/65	City Pt., VA	CSR
					City Pt., VA	04/14/65	Pt. Lookout, MD	CSR
					Pt. Lookout, MD		No release data	P115,P119
Macon, William H.	Cpl	B 17th SCVI	Petersburg, VA	03/25/65	City Pt., VA	03/28/65	Pt. Lookout, MD	CSR
					Pt. Lookout, MD	06/29/65	Rlsd. G.O. #109	P115,P118,P123,CSR
Madden, Charles D.	Pvt	C 12th SCVI	Sharpsburg, MD	09/17/62	Frederick, MD USGH	10/28/62	Died of wounds	P1,P6,P12,FPH,CSR
Madden, Charles T.	Pvt	D 3rd SCVIBn	Boonesboro, MD	09/14/62	Frederick, MD Hos.	10/28/62	Died of wound	CSR
Madden, Decatur	Pvt	D 3rd SCVIBn	South Mtn., MD	09/14/62	Ft. Delaware, DE	10/02/62	Aikens Ldg., VA Xc	CSR
Madden, James	Pvt	D 1st SCVA	Deserted/enemy	02/18/65	Charleston, SC	04/07/65	New York, NY/oath	CSR
Madden, N.M.	Pvt	F 1st SCVC	Rapidan R., VA	09/18/63	Ft. McHenry, MD	09/26/63	Pt. Lookout, MD	P110
					Old Capital, DC	02/03/64	Pt. Lookout, MD	P7,CSR
					Pt. Lookout, MD	02/24/65	Aikens Ldg., VA Xc	P113,P116,P124,CSR
Maddox, J.M.	Pvt	K 7th SCVI	Middletown, VA	09/14/62	Ft. Delaware, DE	10/02/62	Aikens Ldg., VA Xc	CSR,KEB
Maddox, J.M.	Pvt	F 7th SCVI	Williamsport, MD	07/14/63	Hagerstown, MD G.H.	09/17/63	Chester, PA Hos.	P2,CSR
					Pt. Lookout, MD	03/17/64	City Pt., VA Xc	P116,CSR
Maddox, John	Pvt	B 1st SCVA	Fayetteville, NC	03/12/65	New Berne, NC	03/30/65	Pt. Lookout, MD	CSR
					Pt. Lookout, MD	05/14/65	Rlsd. G.O. #85	P121,CSR
Maddox, M.	Pvt	F 7th SCVI	Williamsport, MD	07/14/63	Chester, PA G.H.	10/03/63	Pt. Lookout, MD Xc	P1,P124,KEB,CSR
Maddox, Samuel L.	Sgt	E 16th SCVI	Salisbury, NC	04/12/65	Nashville, TN	04/29/65	Louisville, KY	P39,16R,CSR
					Louisville, KY	05/02/65	Camp Chase, OH	P92,CSR
					Camp Chase, OH	06/13/65	Rlsd. G.O. #109	P23,CSR
Maddox, Thomas Pinckney	Pvt	G 22nd SCVI	Burkeville, VA	04/14/65	U.S. Field Hos.	04/15/65	City Pt., VA 9ACH	CSR
					City Pt., VA		Savannah, GA	CSR
					Savannah, GA G.H.	05/13/65	Died, consumption	P1,P6,P12,CSR
Maffett, George C.	Sgt	H Hol.Leg.	Kinston, NC	12/15/62	Kinston, NC	12/15/62	Paroled POW	CSR,ANY
Maffett, George C.	1Lt	H Hol.Leg.	Richmond, VA	04/03/65	Richmond, VA	04/24/65	Paroled	CSR
Maffett, Jacob Lamar	Pvt	H Hol.Leg.	Five Forks, VA	04/02/65	City Pt., VA	04/05/65	Pt. Lookout, MD	CSR,ANY
					Pt. Lookout, MD	05/01/65	Died, Ch. Diarrhea	P6,P115,P118,FPH

SOUTH CAROLINA SOLDIERS, SAILORS AND  CITIZENS HELD IN U.S. PRISONS 1861-1865

NAME	RANK	REGIMENT	CAPTURED AT	WHEN	PRISON	MOVED	DISPOSITION	SOURCES
Maffett, Robert Clayton	LtC	3rd SCVI	Halltown, VA	08/26/64	Harpers Ferry, WV	08/30/64	Ft. Delaware, DE	ANY,SA2,H3,KEB,LC
					Ft. Delaware, DE	02/15/65	Died, Ch. Diarrhea	P6,P43,P47,FPH,CSR
Magill, John G.	Sgt	A 17th SCVI	Richmond, VA Hos.	04/03/65	Richmond, VA Hos.	05/08/65	Released on parole	CSR
Magill, William	Pvt	G 1st SCVIG	Sharpsburg, MD	09/28/62	Ft. McHenry, MD	11/12/62	Paroled	CSR,SA1
Magill, William	Pvt	G 1st SCVIG	Gettysburg, PA	07/05/63	Ft. Delaware, DE	10/13/63	Pt. Lookout, MD	P40,P42,P44,CSR
					Pt. Lookout, MD	05/03/64	Exchanged	P113,P116,CSR
Magill, William	Pvt	G 1st SCVIG	Amelia C.H., VA	04/05/65	Pt. Lookout, MD	06/29/65	Rlsd. G.O. #109	P115,P119,P123
Magowdie, Edward	Smn	CS Navy	Harpers Farm, VA	04/06/65	Pt. Lookout, MD	06/29/65	Rlsd. G.O. #109	P123
Magwood, James J.	Pvt	B 23rd SCVI	Deserted/enemy	03/18/65	Charleston, SC	03/18/65	Rlsd. on oath	CSR
Mahaffey, J.T.	Pvt	K 7th SCVI	N. Anna River, VA	05/23/64	Port Royal, VA	05/30/64	Pt. Lookout, MD	CSR
					Pt. Lookout, MD	09/18/64	Aikens Ldg., VA Xc	P113,P117,CSR
Mahaffey, Josiah K.	Pvt	B 13th SCVI	Deserted/enemy	02/24/65	City Pt., VA	02/26/65	Washington, DC	CSR,HOS
					Washington, DC	02/27/65	Springfield, IL	CSR
Mahaffey, Louis H.	Cpl	C 14th SCVI	Petersburg, VA	04/03/65	City Pt., VA	04/11/65	Hart's Island, NY	P79,CSR
					Hart's Island, NY	06/17/65	Rlsd. G.O. #109	P79,CSR
Mahaffey, Roland	Pvt	I 16th SCVI	Marietta, GA	06/18/64	Nashville, TN	06/24/64	Louisville, KY	P3,16R,CSR
					Louisville, KY	06/27/64	Camp Morton, IN	P90,P91,P94,CSR
					Camp Morton, IN	03/15/65	City Pt., VA Xc	P100,P101,CSR
Maher, Edward	Pvt	Brooks LA	Gettysburg, PA	07/05/63	Chester, PA G.H.	10/02/63	Hammond G.H., MD	P1,P124,CSR
					Hammond G.H., MD	10/04/63	Pt. Lookout, MD	CSR
					Pt. Lookout, MD	03/02/64	Fts. Monroe, VA Xc	P121,CSR
					Fts. Monroe, VA	03/10/64	New York, NY oath	CSR
Mahon, Joseph	Pvt	C 8th SCVI	Deserted/enemy	01/06/62	New Bridge, VA	06/11/62	Baltimore, MD oath	KEB,CSR
Mahoney, James	Pvt	G 1st SCVA	Poplar Springs, SC	02/21/65	New Berne, NC	04/03/65	Pt. Lookout, MD	CSR
					Pt. Lookout, MD	06/29/65	Rlsd. G.O. #109	P115,P118,P121,CSR
Mahoney, Michael	Pvt	K 1st SCVIG	Fredericksburg, VA	12/13/62	Old Capitol, DC	03/29/63	City Pt, VA Xc	CSR,SA1
Mahoney, Michael	Pvt	K 1st SCVIG	Gettysburg, PA	07/06/63	Ft. McHenry, MD	07/10/63	Ft. Delaware, DE	CSR
					Ft. Delaware, DE	09/15/63	Jd. US 1st CN Cav.	P40,P42,P44,CSR
Mahoney, Michael	Pvt	D 27th SCVI	Town Creek, NC	02/20/65	Ft. Anderson, NC	02/28/65	Pt. Lookout, MD	CSR,HAG
					Pt. Lookout, MD	05/14/65	Rlsd. G.O. #85	P115,P118,P121,CSR
Mahuffer, D.P.	Pvt	K 12th SCVI	Gettysburg, PA	07/05/63	David's Island, NY	08/24/63	City Pt., VA Xc	P1,CSR
Mahuffer, D.P.	Pvt	K 12th SCVI	Deserted/enemy	02/23/65	City Pt., VA	02/14/65	Washington, DC	CSR
					Washington, DC	02/14/65	Oil City, PA on oath	CSR
Mainus, James	Pvt	B 6th SCVI	Frederick, MD	09/12/62	Frederick, MD USGH	09/19/62	Ft. Delaware, DE	CSR
					Ft. Delaware, DE	10/02/62	Aikens Ldg., VA Xc	CSR
Major, John C.	Pvt	C Orr's Ri.	Sutherland Stn., VA	04/02/65	City Pt., VA	04/07/65	Hart's Island, NY	CSR
					Hart's Island, NY	06/15/65	Rlsd. G.O. #109	P79,CDC,CSR
Major, John W.	Pvt	A 7th SCVI	Cedar Creek, VA	10/19/64	Harpers Ferry, WV	10/26/64	Pt. Lookout, MD	CSR
					Pt. Lookout, MD	05/14/65	Rlsd. G.O. #85	P115,P118,P121,CSR
Major, Joseph Marshal	Pvt	F 2nd SCVI	N. Anna River, VA	05/22/63	Ft. McHenry, MD	05/24/63	Fts. Monroe, VA Xc	P96,H2,CSR
Major, Thomas	Pvt	F 18th SCVI	Petersburg, VA	03/25/65	Pt. Lookout, MD	05/14/65	Rlsd. G.O. #85	P115
Major, Warren T.	Pvt	F 2nd SCVIRi	Warrenton, VA	09/29/62	Warrenton, VA	09/29/62	Paroled	CSR
Major, Warren T.	Pvt	F 2nd SCVIRi	Deserted/enemy	05/11/63	Knoxville, TN	05/12/63	Indiana on oath	CSR
Majors, H.W.	Pvt	B 1st SCVIR	Cheraw, SC	03/04/65	New Berne, NC	04/10/65	Hart's Island, NY	CSR,SA1
					Hart's Island, NY	06/16/65	Rlsd. G.O. #109	CSR
Mallard, A.H.	Pvt	H 11th SCVI	Petersburg, VA	06/18/64	City Pt., VA	06/24/64	Pt. Lookout, MD	HAG,CSR
					Pt. Lookout, MD	10/11/64	Aikens Ldg., VA Xc	P113,P117,P123,CSR
Malloy, John H.	Pvt	C 8th SCVI	Fayetteville, NC	03/11/65	Pt. Lookout, MD	06/29/65	Rlsd. G.O. #109	P115,P118,KEB,CSR
Malone, James M.	Pvt	H 27th SCVI	Town Creek, NC	02/20/65	Ft. Anderson, NC	02/28/65	Pt. Lookout, MD	CSR,HAG
					Pt. Lookout, MD	05/14/65	Rlsd. G.O. 85	P115,P118,P121,CSR
Malone, M.N.	Pvt	B Orr's Ri.	Petersburg, VA	04/03/65	City Pt., VA	04/11/65	Hart's Island, NY	CSR
					Hart's Island, NY	06/16/65	Rlsd. G.O. #109	P79,CSR

M

SOUTH CAROLINA SOLDIERS, SAILORS AND CITIZENS HELD IN U.S. PRISONS 1861-1865

NAME	RANK	REGIMENT	CAPTURED AT	WHEN	PRISON	MOVED	DISPOSITION	SOURCES
Malone, P.J.	Pvt	E 1st SCVC	Gettysburg, PA	07/05/63	David's Island, NY	09/12/63	City Pt., VA Xc	P1,P4,CSR
Malone, Patrick	Pvt	C 27th SCVI	Petersburg, VA	06/24/64	Bermuda Hundred, VA	06/24/64	Fts. Monroe, VA	CSR,HAG
					Fts. Monroe, VA	06/29/64	Pt. Lookout, MD	CSR
					Pt. Lookout, MD	07/23/64	Elmira, NY	P113,P117,P120,CSR
					Elmira, NY	11/20/64	Died, Ch. Diarrhea	P5,P12,P65,P66,FPH
Malone, Thomas	Pvt	H 27th SCVI	Weldon RR, VA	08/21/64	City Pt., VA	08/24/64	Pt. Lookout, MD	CSR,HAG
					Pt. Lookout, MD	10/17/64	Joined U.S. Army	P113,P122,P125
Maloney, James G.	Pvt	A 12th SCVI	Spotsylvania, VA	05/12/64	Belle Plain, VA	05/20/64	Ft. Delaware, DE	CSR,YEB
					Ft. Delaware, DE		Hos 7/23-9/7/64	P47
					Ft. Delaware, DE		Hos 12/29-1/21/65	P47
					Ft. Delaware, DE		Hos 1/26-1/31/65	P47
					Ft. Delaware, DE		Hos 2/7-2/21/65	P47
					Ft. Delaware, DE	02/27/65	City Pt., VA Xc	P41,P43,CSR
Maloney, John	Pvt	H 27th SCVI	Deserted/enemy	09/02/64	Hilton Head, SC	09/13/64	Sent North on oath	P8,HAG,CSR
Maloney, Joseph	Pvt	E 1st SCVA	Morris Island, SC	07/10/63	Hilton Head, SC	09/05/63	Took the oath	CSR
					Ft. Columbus, NY	09/23/63	Took the oath	P1,CSR
Maloney, Thomas	Pvt	D 3rd SCVC	Jonesboro, GA	09/01/64	Louisville, KY	10/28/64	Camp Douglas, IL	P95
Maloney, Thomas	Pvt	B 1st SCVA	Deserted/enemy	02/26/65	Charleston, SC	03/26/65	Taken oath & disch.	CSR
Manget, J.A.	2Lt	G 3rd SCVABn	Combahee Fy., SC	02/05/65	P.M. Hilton Hd., SC	02/06/65	Post Hospital	CSR
					Hilton Hd., SC USHos.	03/04/65	Hilton Hd., SC P.M.	CSR
					Hilton Hd., SC	03/12/65	Ft. Delaware, DE	CSR
					Ft. Delaware, DE	06/16/65	Rlsd. G.O. #109	CSR
Mangum, Andrew J.	Pvt	I Hol. Leg.	Kinston, NC	12/14/62	Kinston, NC	12/14/62	Paroled POW	CSR,HOS
Mangum, Andrew J.	Pvt	I Hol. Leg.	Stony Creek, VA	05/07/64	Fts. Monroe, VA	05/13/64	Pt. Lookout, MD	CSR
					Pt. Lookout, MD	03/17/65	Aikens Ldg., VA Xc	P113,P121,P124,CSR
Mangum, J.P.	Pvt	C Hol. Leg. C	Yorktown, VA	01/30/63	Yorktown, VA	01/30/63	Paroled	CSR
Mangum, Patrick T.	Pvt	H 1st SCVIR	Smith's Ford, NC	03/16/65	New Berne, NC	04/03/65	Pt. Lookout, MD	SA1, P115
					Pt. Lookout, MD	06/29/65	Rlsd. G.O. #109	P115,P118,P122,P123,SA1
Mangum, W.P.	Pvt	D 8th SCVI	Winchester, VA	09/13/64	Harpers Ferry, WV	09/19/64	Camp Chase, OH	CSR,KEB
					Camp Chase, OH	05/02/65	New Orleans, LA	P23,P25,CSR
					New Orleans, LA	05/12/65	Vicksburg, MS Xc	CSR
Manigault, Edward	Maj	18th SCVAB	James Island, SC	02/10/65	Beaufort, SC USGH	05/09/65	Hilton Head, SC	P1,CSR,STR
					Hilton Head, SC	05/10/65	Paroled & released	STR
Manigault, Gabriel E.	1Lt	K 4th SCVC	Louisa C.H., VA	06/11/64	Fts. Monroe, VA	06/20/64	Pt. Lookout, MD	CSR
					Pt. Lookout, MD	06/23/64	Ft. Delaware, DE	P44,P113,P117,CSR
					Ft. Delaware, DE	02/27/65	City Pt., VA Xc	CSR
Manion, James	Pvt	B 16th SCVI	Yazoo City, MS	07/13/63	Yazoo City, MS	07/13/63	Paroled Hos. Nurse	CSR
Manion, Patrick	Pvt	H 27th SCVI	Town Creek, NC	02/20/65	Ft. Anderson, NC	02/28/65	Pt. Lookout, MD	P7,P115,HAG,CSR
					Pt. Lookout, MD	05/14/65	Rlsd. G.O.#85	P115,P118,P121,CSR
Manker, Franklin	Pvt	K 10th SCVI	Memphis, TN	12/21/64	No other data			CSR,RAS
Manley, Robert	Pvt	F Orr's Ri.	Beaver Dam Stn., VA	06/08/64	White House, VA	07/09/64	Elmira, NY	CSR,CDC
					Pt. Lookout, MD	07/09/64	Elmira, NY	P113,P117,P120
					Elmira, NY	06/23/65	Rlsd. G.O. #109	P65,P66,CSR
Mann, D.N.	Pvt	G 6th SCVI	Richmond, VA Hos.	04/03/65	Libby Prison Rchmd.	04/23/65	Newport News, VA	CSR
					Newport News, VA	06/26/65	Rlsd. G.O. #109	CSR
Mann, John T.	Pvt	G 1st SCVA	Camden, SC	04/18/65	Camden, SC	05/18/65	Paroled	CSR
Mann, Samuel H.	Pvt	E 20th SCVI	Cedar Creek, VA	10/19/64	Harpers Ferry, WV	10/24/64	Pt. Lookout, MD	CSR
					Pt. Lookout, MD	02/21/65	Died, Ch. Diarrhea	P6,P115,P118,CSR
Manning, Brown	1Lt	AAG/Canby	Lynch's Creek, SC	02/27/65	Pt. Lookout, MD	04/03/65	Washington, DC	P118
Manning, Columbus M.	Pvt	H 2nd SCVIRi	Richmond, VA Hos.	04/03/65	Libby Prison Rchmd.	04/13/65	Pt. Lookout, MD	CSR
					Pt. Lookout, MD		No release data	P115,P119,CSR

SOUTH CAROLINA SOLDIERS, SAILORS AND  CITIZENS HELD IN U.S. PRISONS 1861-1865

NAME	RANK	REGIMENT	CAPTURED AT	WHEN	PRISON	MOVED	DISPOSITION	SOURCES
Manning, Eli	Sgt	D 8th SCVI	Maryland Hts., MD	09/16/62	Ft. McHenry, MD	12/08/62	Fts. Monroe, VA	P96,CSR
					Fts. Monroe, VA	12/10/62	City Pt., VA Xc	CSR
Manning, Franklin	Cpt	K 8th SCVI	Maryland Hts., MD	09/16/62	Ft. McHenry, MD	12/08/62	Fts. Monroe, VA	P96,HOM,CSR
					Ft. Monroe, VA	12/10/62	City Pt., VA Xc	CSR
Manning, John	Cpl	E 25th SCVI	Richmond, VA Hos.	05/13/65	Richmond, VA	05/13/65	Paroled on oath	CSR,HAG
Manning, Joseph J.	Pvt	F 24th SCVI	Taylors Ridge, GA	10/16/64	Nashville, TN	10/23/64	Louisville, KY	CSR
					Louisville, KY	10/26/64	Camp Douglas, IL	P90,P91,P95,CSR
					Camp Douglas, IL	06/17/65	Rlsd. G.O. #109	P55,CSR
Manning, Richard H.	Pvt	B 19th SCVI	Deserted/enemy	03/04/64		09/29/64	Atlanta, GA on oath	CSR
Manning, William C.	Pvt	B 12th SCVI	Sharpsburg, MD	09/17/62	Sharpsburg, MD	09/27/62	Paroled	CSR
Manor, Alexander	Pvt	D 12th SCVI	Warrenton, VA	09/29/62	Warrenton, VA	09/29/62	Paroled	CSR
Manor, John	Pvt	D 12th SCVI	Richmond, VA Hos.	04/03/65	Richmond, VA Hos.	05/04/65	Paroled	CSR
Manous, John L.	Pvt	I Hol.Leg.	Hatchers Run, VA	03/25/65	City Pt., VA	04/02/65	Pt. Lookout, MD	CSR,HOS
					Pt. Lookout, MD	06/29/65	Rlsd G.O. #109	P115,P118,P123
Manude, Jacob A.	Pvt	I 27th SCVI	Petersburg, VA	06/18/64	Bermuda Hundred, VA	06/24/64	Fts. Monroe, VA	CSR,HAG
					Fts. Monroe, VA	06/26/64	Pt. Lookout, MD	CSR
					Pt. Lookout, MD	09/10/64	Died, Dysentery	P12,P113,P117,P119
Manude, John A. Mc.	Cpl	I 27th SCVI	Petersburg, VA	06/24/64	Bermuda Hundred, VA	06/25/64	Fts. Monroe, VA	CSR,HAG
					Fts. Monroe, VA	07/14/64	Pt. Lookout, MD	CSR
					Pt. Lookout, MD	08/03/64	Elmira, NY	P113,CSR
					Elmira, NY	10/11/64	Tfd. for exchange	P65,CSR
					Pt. Lookout, MD	10/26/64	Died	P5,P115,P117,FPH
Manuel, John	Pvt	G 19th SCVI	Atlanta, GA	07/22/64	Nashville, TN	07/29/64	Louisville, KY	CSR,HOE
					Louisville, KY	07/31/64	Camp Chase, OH	P90,P91,P94,CSR
					Camp Chase, OH	06/05/65	Rlsd. G.O. #109	CSR
Manuel, Milford	Pvt	D 24th SCVI	Nashville, TN	12/16/64	Nashville, TN	12/18/64	Louisville, KY	CSR
					Louisville, KY	12/20/64	Camp Douglas, IL	P90,P91,P95,EFW
					Camp Douglas, IL	06/19/65	Rlsd. G.O. #109	CSR
Manuel, William	Pvt	A 19th SCVCB	Augusta, GA	05/20/65	Augusta, GA	05/20/65	Paroled on oath	CSR
Maples, C.W.	Pvt	F 26th SCVI	Deserted/enemy	01/02/65	City Point, VA	01/24/65	Washington, DC	P8,CSR
					Washington, DC	01/30/65	Chicago, IL, oath	CSR
Maples, J.W.	Pvt	F 26th SCVI	Deserted/enemy	01/02/65	City Point, VA	01/24/65	Washington, DC	P8,CSR
					Washington, DC	01/30/65	Chicago, IL oath	CSR
Maples, W.T.	Pvt	F 26th SCVI	Deserted/enemy	01/21/65	City Point, VA	01/24/65	Washington, DC	P8,CSR
					Washington, DC	01/30/65	Chicago, IL oath	CSR
Mappins, J.	Pvt	C 3rd SCVC			Hilton Head, SC	04/30/65	New York, NY oath	CSR
Marchbanks, F.M.	Pvt	A 3rd SCVABn	Bentonville, NC	03/21/65	New Berne, NC	04/10/65	Hart's Island, NY	CSR
					Hart's Island, NY	06/17/65	Rlsd. G.O. #109	P79
Marchbanks, J.T.	Pvt	A 3rd SCVABn	High Pt., NC	05/02/65	High Pt., NC	05/02/65	Paroled	CSR
Marchbanks, P.C.	Pvt	A 3rd SCVABn	High Pt., NC	05/02/65	High Pt., NC	05/02/65	Paroled	CSR
Marchbanks, S.S.	Pvt	A 3rd SCVABn	High Pt., NC	05/02/65	High Pt., NC	05/02/65	Paroled	CSR
Marion, J. Taylor	Pvt	B 4th SCVC	Old Church, VA	05/30/64	White House, VA	06/08/64	Pt. Lookout, MD	CSR,HHC
					Pt. Lookout, MD	07/09/64	Elmira, NY	P113,P117,P120,CSR
					Elmira, NY	06/21/65	Rlsd. G.O. #109	P65,P66,CSR
Markes, L.H.	Pvt	G 5th SCVC	Stony Creek, VA	12/01/64	City Pt., VA	12/05/64	Pt. Lookout, MD	CSR
					Pt. Lookout, MD	06/29/65	Rlsd. G.O. #109	P115,P118,CSR
Markey, Patrick	Pvt	H 1st SCVA	Morris Island, SC	07/10/63	Hilton Head, SC	09/19/65	Ft. Columbus, NY	CSR
					Ft. Columbus, NY	09/23/63	Took the oath	P1,CSR
Marler, John Ralston	Pvt	6 10/19 SCVI	Missionary Ridge, TN	11/25/63	Nashville, TN	12/07/63	Louisville, KY	P39,CSR,RAS
					Louisville, KY	12/09/63	Rock Island, IL	P88,P89,CSR
					Rock Island, IL	03/02/65	Pt. Lookout, MD Xc	P131,CSR
Marliam, T.M.	Pvt	F 14th SCVI	Warrenton, VA	09/29/62	Warrenton, VA	09/29/62	Paroled	CSR

SOUTH CAROLINA SOLDIERS, SAILORS AND M CITIZENS HELD IN U.S. PRISONS 1861-1865

NAME	RANK	REGIMENT	CAPTURED AT	WHEN	PRISON	MOVED	DISPOSITION	SOURCES
Marlow, Henry L.	Pvt	5 10/19 SCVI	Missionary Ridge, TN	11/25/63	Nashville, TN	12/07/63	Louisville, KY	P39,RAS,CTA,CSR
					Louisville, KY	12/09/63	Rock Island, IL	P88,RAS,CTA,CSR
					Rock Island, IL	06/20/65	Rlsd. G.O. #109	P131,CTA,CSR
Marlow, J.A.	Pvt	A 7th SCVC	Deep Bottom, VA	08/16/64	City Pt., VA	08/22/64	Pt. Lookout, MD	CSR
					Pt. Lookout, MD	12/12/64	Died, Dysentery	P5,P117,P119,FPH
Marlow, William E.	Pvt	I 1st SCVIG	Hatchers Run, VA	03/25/65	City Pt., VA	04/03/65	Pt. Lookout, MD	CSR,SA1
					Pt. Lookout, MD	06/29/65	Rlsd. G.O. #109	P115,CSR
					Richmond, VA	07/03/65	Died, Gangrene	P12,CSR
Maroney, Samuel S.	Pvt	A 18th SCVI	Crater, Pbg., VA	07/30/64	City Pt., VA	08/05/64	Pt. Lookout, MD	CSR
					Pt. Lookout, MD	08/08/64	Elmira, NY	P113,P117,P120,CSR
					Elmira, NY	03/02/65	Pt. Lookout, MD Xc	P65,P66,CSR
Mars, Nathan Renwick	Pvt	I 3rd SCVI	N. Anna River, VA	05/23/64	Port Royal, VA	05/30/64	Pt. Lookout, MD	CSR,KEB,SA2,H3
					Pt. Lookout, MD	09/18/64	Aikens Ldg., VA Xc	P113,P117,CSR
Marsengill, Finney	Pvt	H 1st SCVA	Smith's Farm, NC	03/16/65	New Berne, NC	04/10/65	Hart's Island, NY	CSR
					Hart's Island, NY	06/15/65	Rlsd. G.O. #109	P79
Marsh, A.J.	Pvt	G 15th SCVI	Cedar Creek, VA	10/19/64	Harpers Ferry, WV	10/21/64	Pt. Lookout, MD	CSR,KEB
					Pt. Lookout, MD	03/28/65	Aikens Ldg., VA Xc	P115,P118,P121,CSR
Marsh, Alfred	Pvt	G 3rd SCVABn	High Pt., NC	05/02/65	High Pt., NC	05/02/65	Paroled	CSR,KCE
Marsh, David C.	Pvt	A 25th SCVI	Ft. Fisher, NC	01/15/65	Fts. Monroe, VA	03/16/65	Pt. Lookout, MD	CSR,HAG
					Pt. Lookout, MD	06/29/65	Rlsd. G.O. #109	P118,CSR
Marsh, Jones A.	Pvt	H 2nd SCVI	Gettysburg, PA	07/03/63	Gettysburg G.H.	10/06/63	Provost Marshal	P4,SA2,KEB,H2
					W. Bldg. Balt., MD	11/12/63	City Pt., VA Xc	P1,CSR
Marsh, Jonothan	Pvt	C 7th SCVIBn	Weldon RR, VA	08/21/64	City Pt., VA	08/24/64	Pt. Lookout, MD	CSR,HAG
					Pt. Lookout, MD	03/15/65	Aikens Ldg., VA Xc	P113,P117,P123
Marshal, J.	Pvt	C 3rd SCVABn	Blakely, AL	04/09/65	Ship Island, MS	05/01/65	Vicksburg, MS Xc	P136,CSR
Marshal, Lawrence R.	Pvt	E 3rd SCVI	Gettysburg, PA	07/04/63	Letterman G.H. Gbg	09/25/63	Provost Marshal	P1,KEB,H3,SA2,ANY
					W. Bldg. Balt., MD	11/12/63	City Pt., VA Xc	P1,CSR
					Richmond, VA Hos.	11/20/63	Furloughed	CSR
Marshal, W.	Pvt	H 21st SCVI	Morris Island, SC	07/10/63	Ft. Columbus, NY	09/23/63	Took the oath	P1,HAG
					Pt. Lookout, MD	04/27/64	City Pt., VA Xc	P113,P116,P124
Marshal, Wiley S.	Pvt	K 7th SCVC	Kershaw Dis., SC	02/24/65	New Berne, NC	04/10/65	Hart's Island, NY	CSR,HIC
					Hart's Island, NY	06/17/65	Rlsd. G.O. #109	P79,CSR
Marshal, William	Pvt	Brooks LA	Shepherdstown, VA	11/25/62	Ft. McHenry, MD	01/31/63	Fts. Monroe, VA Xc	CSR
					Petersburg, VA Hos.	03/15/63	Furloughed 60 days	CSR
Marthis, Wesley	Pvt	C 6th SCVI	Burkesville, VA	04/14/65	Burkesville, VA	04/17/65	Paroled	CSR
Martin, Aaron M.	Pvt	I 21st SCVI	Town Creek, NC	02/20/65	Pt. Lookout, MD	06/04/65	Rlsd. Instr. 5/30/65	P115,P118,P121,HAG
Martin, Addison D.	Pvt	C 14th SCVI	Gettysburg, PA	07/03/63	Provost Marshal	07/17/63	David's Island, NY	CSR
					David's Island, NY	07/22/63	Fts. Monroe, VA	P1,CSR
					Fts. Monroe, VA	07/28/63	City Pt., VA Xc	CSR
Martin, Albert R.	Cpl	F Ham. Leg.	South Mtn., MD	09/14/62	Ft. Delaware, DE	10/02/62	Aikens Ldg., VA Xc	CSR
Martin, Allen T.	1Sg	K 1st SCVIH			24th A.C. A. of J.	04/14/65	U.S. Gen. Hos.	CSR
Martin, B.B.	Pvt	I 3rd SCVC	Deserted/enemy	03/05/65	Charleston, SC	03/15/65	Taken oath & disch.	CSR
Martin, Benjamin	Pvt	Ferguson's	Salisbury, NC	04/12/65	Nashville, TN	04/29/65	Louisville, KY	P39,CSR
					Louisville, KY	05/02/65	Camp Chase, OH	P92
					Camp Chase, OH	06/02/65	Died, Gv #2056	P23,P27,CSR,FPH
Martin, Benjamin F.	Pvt	E 14th SCVI	Petersburg, VA	07/29/64	City Pt., VA	08/05/64	Pt. Lookout, MD	CSR
					Pt. Lookout, MD	08/08/64	Elmira, NY	P113,P117,P120,CSR
					Elmira, NY	03/14/65	Pt. Lookout, MD Xc	P65,P66,CSR
					Richmond, VA Hos.	03/24/65	Furloughed 60 days	CSR
Martin, C.B.	Pvt	G Ham. Leg. MI	Richmond, VA	05/18/65	Richmond, VA	05/18/65	Paroled	CSR

SOUTH CAROLINA SOLDIERS, SAILORS AND  CITIZENS HELD IN U.S. PRISONS 1861-1865

NAME	RANK	REGIMENT	CAPTURED AT	WHEN	PRISON	MOVED	DISPOSITION	SOURCES
Martin, Daniel	Pvt	Santee LA	McIntosh Co., GA	10/15/64	Sapelo Sound, GA		Philadelphia, PA	CSR
					Philadelphia, PA	01/10/65	Ft. Delaware, DE	CSR
					Ft. Delaware, DE		Hos 3/20-4/6/65	P47
					Ft. Delaware, DE	06/10/65	Rlsd. G.O. #109	P41,P43,CSR
Martin, Daniel H.	Sgt	E 26th SCVI	Petersburg, VA	03/25/65	City Pt., VA	03/27/65	Pt. Lookout, MD	CSR
					Pt. Lookout, MD	06/29/65	Rlsd. G.O. #109	P118,P121,P123,CSR
Martin, Edward J.	Sgt	L 1st SCVIG	Richmond, VA Hos.	04/03/65	Paroled			SA1,CSR
Martin, Francis M.	Pvt	L 1st SCVIG	Spotsylvania, VA	05/12/64	Washington, DC	05/24/64	Died of wounds	P6,SA1,CSR
Martin, George E.	Pvt	B 7th SCVIBn	Weldon RR, VA	08/21/64	City Pt., VA	08/24/64	Pt. Lookout, MD	CSR,KEB
					Pt. Lookout, MD	03/14/65	Aikens Ldg., VA Xc	P117,P121,P124,HFC
Martin, George W.	Pvt	H 7th SCVI	N. Anna River, VA	05/23/64	Port Royal, VA	05/30/64	Pt. Lookout, MD	CNM,KEB,CSR
					Pt. Lookout, MD	09/14/64	Died	P6,P117,P119,FPH
Martin, Green H.	Pvt	M P.S.S.	Richmond, VA Hos.	04/03/65	Libby Prison Rchmd.	04/05/65	City Pt., VA	CSR
					City Pt., VA	04/18/65	Newport News, VA	CSR
					Newport News, VA	06/14/65	Rlsd. G.O. #109	CSR
Martin, Greenbury	Pvt	B 1st SCVA	Chesterfield, SC	02/28/65	New Berne, NC	04/01/65	Died, inflammation	CSR
Martin, Henry	Sgt	15th SCVAB	Deserted/enemy	12/21/64	Savannah, GA	12/27/64	Hilton Head, SC	P8,CSR
Martin, Irwin James	Pvt	C 25th SCVI	Town Creek, NC	02/20/62	Ft. Anderson, NC	02/28/65	Pt. Lookout, MD	CSR,HAG,CTA
					Pt. Lookout, MD	05/09/65	Died, Pneumonia	P6,P115,118,FPH
Martin, J.A.	Pvt	PeeDee LA	Augusta, GA	05/24/65	Augusta, GA	05/24/65	Paroled	CSR
Martin, J.M.	Pvt	PeeDee LA	Augusta, GA	05/24/65	Augusta, GA	05/24/65	Paroled	CSR
Martin, J.O.	Pvt	K Hol.Leg.	Stony Creek, VA	05/07/64	Fts. Monroe, VA	05/13/64	Pt. Lookout, MD	CSR
					Pt. Lookout, MD	08/20/64	Died inflam lungs	P5,P113,P119,FPH
Martin, J.O.	Pvt	I 23rd SCVI	Richmond, VA Hos.	04/03/65	Prov. Marshal	05/03/65	Paroled	CSR
Martin, J.R.	Pvt	E 3rd SCVIBn	Boonesboro, MD	10/03/62	Frederick, MD Hos.	12/05/62	Ft. McHenry, MD	CSR,KEB
					Ft. McHenry, MD	12/08/62	Fts. Monroe, VA	P96,CSR
					Fts. Monroe, VA	12/10/62	City Pt., VA Xc	CSR
Martin, J.W.	Pvt	H 6th SCVI	Sharpsburg, MD	10/01/62	Frederick, MD USGH	10/13/62	Baltimore, MD USGH	CSR
					Ft. McHenry, MD	10/14/62	Aikens Ldg., VA Xc	CSR
					Richmond, VA Hos.	10/20/62	Furloughed 60 days	CSR
Martin, J.W.	Pvt	B 7th SCVC	New Kent C.H., VA	04/28/64	Fts. Monroe, VA	07/31/64	Pt. Lookout, MD	CSR
					Pt. Lookout, MD	03/15/65	Aikens Ldg., VA Xc	P113,P124,CSR
Martin, Jacob Cooper	Sgt	D 18th SCVI	Five Forks, VA	04/01/65	City Pt., VA	04/05/65	Pt. Lookout, MD	CSR
					Pt. Lookout, MD	06/20/65	Rlsd. G.O. #109	P115,P118,CSR
Martin, James	Pvt	F 17th SCVI	Petersburg, VA	03/24/65	City Pt., VA	03/28/65	Pt. Lookout, MD	CSR
					Pt. Lookout, MD	06/29/65	Rlsd. G.O. #109	P118,P123,CSR
Martin, James	Pvt	D 12th SCVI	Sutherland Stn., VA	04/03/65	City Pt., VA	04/07/65	Hart's Island, NY	CSR
					Hart's Island, NY	06/16/65	Rlsd. G.O. #109	P79,CSR
Martin, James B.	Pvt	A 24th SCVI	Taylors Ridge, GA	10/16/64	Nashville, TN	10/23/64	Louisville, KY	CSR
					Louisville, KY	10/27/64	Camp Douglas, IL	P90,P91,P95
					Camp Douglas, IL	05/20/65	Released	P55
Martin, James F.	Pvt	K 2nd SCVI	Gettysburg, PA	07/04/63	Letterman G.H. Gbg	08/06/63	Died of wounds	SA2,P5,KEB,H2,CSR
Martin, James P.	Pvt	A Orr's Ri.	Petersburg, VA	04/03/65	City Pt., VA	04/11/65	Hart's Island, NY	CSR
					Hart's Island, NY	06/16/65	Rlsd. G.O. #109	P79,CSR
Martin, John	Pvt	E 25th SCVI	Ft. Fisher, NC	01/15/65	New York, NY	01/31/65	Elmira, NY	CSR,HAG
					Elmira, NY	05/17/65	Rlsd. G.O. #85	P65,P66
Martin, John C.	Pvt	C 7th SCVI	Gettysburg, PA	07/03/63	Gettysburg G.H.	07/20/63	David's Island, NY	P4,CSR
					David's Island, NY	09/12/63	City Pt., VA Xc	P1,CSR
Martin, John S.	Pvt	G 2nd SCVI	Gettysburg, PA	07/04/63	Gettysburg G.H.	11/03/63	Baltimore, MD G.H.	P1,KEB,CSR,SA2,U2
					W. Bldg. Balt., MD	11/12/63	City Pt., VA Xc	CSR
Martin, John W.	Pvt	C Orr's Ri.	Williamsport, MD	07/03/63	Baltimore, MD	07/18/63	Chester, PA USGH	CSR,CDC
					Chester, PA U.S.G.H.	09/23/63	City Pt., VA Xc	CSR

SOUTH CAROLINA SOLDIERS, SAILORS AND  CITIZENS HELD IN U.S. PRISONS 1861-1865

NAME	RANK	REGIMENT	CAPTURED AT	WHEN	PRISON	MOVED	DISPOSITION	SOURCES
Martin, John W.	Pvt	C Orr's Ri.	Petersburg, VA	04/03/65	Harts Island, NY	06/16/65	Rlsd. G.O. #109	P79,CSR
Martin, John, Jr.	Pvt	D 4th SCVC	Louisa C.H., VA	06/11/64	Fts. Monroe, VA	06/20/64	Pt. Lookout, MD	CSR
					Pt. Lookout, MD	07/25/64	Elmira, NY	P113,P117,P120,CSR
					Elmira, NY	07/03/65	Rlsd. G.O.#109	P65,P66,CSR
Martin, Joseph	QMr	6th SCVI	Warrenton, VA	09/29/62	Warrenton, VA	09/29/**62**	Paroled	CSR
Martin, K.M	Pvt	A 7th SCVC	Burkeville, VA	04/06/64	City Pt., VA	04/15/65	Pt. Lookout, MD	CSR
					Pt. Lookout, MD	06/29/65	Rlsd. G.O. #109	P119,CSR
Martin, M.H.	Pvt	A Orr's Ri.	Petersburg, VA	04/03/65	Hart's Island, NY	06/16/65	Rlsd. G.O. #109	P79
Martin, M.M.	Pvt	McQueen LA	Farmville, VA	04/11/65	Farmville, VA	04/21/65	Paroled	CSR
Martin, Madison P.	Pvt	G 3rd SCVI	Knoxville, TN	12/18/63	Louisville, KY	01/22/64	Rock Island, IL	P88,P94,H3,KEB,SA2
					Rock Island, IL	05/08/65	New Orleans, LA Xc	P131,CSR
Martin, Madison P.	Pvt	G 3rd SCVI	Knoxville, TN	12/18/63	New Orleans, LA	05/23/65	Exchanged	P4
Martin, Marion G.	Pvt	G 3rd SCVI	N. Anna River, VA	05/23/64	Port Royal, VA	05/30/64	Pt. Lookout, MD	CSR,KEB,SA2,H3
					Pt. Lookout, MD	02/24/65	Died, Ch. Diarrhea	P6,P117,P119,FPH
Martin, Moses	Pvt	G 11th SCVI	Darbytown Rd., VA	10/07/64	Bermuda Hundred, VA	10/08/64	City Pt., VA	CSR
					City Pt., VA	10/29/64	Pt. Lookout, MD	CSR
Martin, Moses	Pvt	G 11th SCVI	Darbytown Rd., VA	10/07/64	Pt. Lookout, MD	04/13/65	Died, Ch. Diarrhea	P6,P115,P118,FPH
Martin, Newton	Pvt	B 2nd SCVIRi	Buckytown, MD	09/26/62	Buckytown, MD	09/26/62	Paroled	CSR
Martin, Peter	Pvt	H 27th SCVI	Town Creek, NC	02/20/65	Ft. Anderson, NC	02/28/65	Pt. Lookout, MD	CSR,HAG
					Pt. Lookout, MD		No other data	P115,P118,CSR
Martin, Phillip	Pvt	G 7th SCVIBn	Drury's Bluff, VA	05/16/64	Bermuda Hundred, VA	05/17/64	Fts. Monroe, VA P.M.	CSR,HAG,HIC
					Fts. Monroe, VA	05/19/64	Pt. Lookout, MD	CSR
					Pt. Lookout, MD	08/15/64	Elmira, NY	P113,P117,P120,CSR
					Elmira, NY	06/21/65	Rlsd. G.O. #109	P65,P66,CSR
Martin, R.R.	Pvt	K 1st SCVIH	Frederick, MD	09/12/62	Frederick, MD USGH	10/22/62	Ft. Delaware, DE	CSR
					Ft. Delaware, DE	10/02/62	Aikens Ldg., VA Xc	CSR,SA1
Martin, R.R.	Sgt	K 1st SCVIH	Farmville, VA	04/11/65	Farmville, VA	04/21/65	Paroled	CSR
Martin, Robert L.	Pvt	B 12th SCVI	Hanover C.H., VA	05/24/64	Pt. Lookout, MD	06/20/64	Joined U.S. Army	P117,P125,YEB,CSR
					Pt. Lookout, MD	06/20/65	Rlsd. Instr. 5/30/65	P121
Martin, Samuel T.	Pvt	C 14th SCVI	Spotsylvania, VA	05/12/64	Belle Plain, VA	05/21/64	Ft. Delaware, DE	CSR
					Ft. Delaware, DE	06/10/65	Released	P45,CSR
Martin, Solomon	Pvt	I 11th SCVI	Weldon RR, VA	08/21/64	City Pt., VA	08/25/64	Pt. Lookout, MD	P125,HAG
					Pt. Lookout, MD	03/15/65	Aikens Ldg., VA Xc	P117,P123,P124
					Richmond, VA Hos.	03/25/65		CSR
Martin, Stephen W.	Pvt	McQueen LA	Farmville, VA	04/11/65	Farmville, VA	04/21/65	Paroled	CSR
Martin, Thomas	Pvt	Santee LA	Deserted/enemy	03/01/65	Charleston, SC	03/05/65	Released on oath	CSR
Martin, Thomas	Pvt	F 17th SCVI	Petersburg, VA	03/25/65	City Pt., VA	03/28/65	Pt. Lookout, MD	CSR
					Pt. Lookout, MD	06/29/65	Rlsd. G.O. #109	P115,P118,P123,CSR
Martin, Thomas B.	Cpt	I Hol. Leg.	Stony Creek, VA	05/07/64	Fts. Monroe, VA	05/13/64	Pt. Lookout, MD	CSR,HOS
					Pt. Lookout, MD	06/23/64	Ft. Delaware, DE	P113,P117,P120,ISH
					Ft. Delaware, DE	08/20/64	Hilton Head, SC	CSR
					Hilton Head, SC	03/12/65	Ft. Delaware, DE	CSR
Martin, Thomas W.A.	Cpl	H P.S.S.	Fair Oaks, VA	05/31/62	Ft. Delaware, DE	06/21/64	Aikens Ldg., VA Xc	CSR
Martin, W.A.	Pvt	C 7th SCVIBn	Weldon RR, VA	08/21/64	City Pt., VA	08/24/64	Pt. Lookout, MD	CSR
					Pt. Lookout, MD	01/17/65	Boulware's Wh., VA	P113,P117,P124,CSR
Martin, Warren J.	Pvt	G 22nd SCVI	Five Forks, VA	04/01/65	City Pt., VA	04/04/65	Pt. Lookout, MD	CSR
					Pt. Lookout, MD	06/29/65	Rlsd. G.O. #109	P118,P121,P123
Martin, William	Cpl	H 23rd SCVI	Petersburg, VA	06/17/64	City Pt., VA	06/24/64	Pt. Lookout, MD	CSR,HME
					Pt. Lookout, MD	07/27/64	Elmira, NY	P113,P117,P120,CSR
					Elmira, NY	06/19/65	Rlsd. G.O.#109	P65,P66

SOUTH CAROLINA SOLDIERS, SAILORS AND  CITIZENS HELD IN U.S. PRISONS 1861-1865

NAME	RANK	REGIMENT	CAPTURED AT	WHEN	PRISON	MOVED	DISPOSITION	SOURCES
Martin, William	Pvt	A 17th SCVI	Crater, Pbg., VA	07/30/64	City Pt., VA	08/05/64	Pt. Lookout, MD	CSR,HHC
					Pt. Lookout, MD	08/08/64	Elmira, NY	P117,P120,P125,CSR
					Elmira, NY	10/11/64	Pt. Lookout, MD Xc	P65,P66,CSR
Martin, William	Pvt	8th SCVI	Cheraw, SC	03/05/65	Cheraw, SC	03/05/65	Paroled	CSR
Martin, William	Pvt	A 15th SCVAB	Fayetteville, NC	03/10/65	Pt. Lookout, MD			P115,P118,CSR
Martin, William A.	Pvt	G 11th SCVI	Swift Creek, VA	05/09/64	Fts. Monroe, VA G.H.	08/01/64	Died of wounds	P12,HAG,CSR
Martin, William C.	Pvt	I 1st SCVIR	Smith's Ford, NC	03/16/65	New Berne, NC	04/10/65	Pt. Lookout, MD	CSR,SA1
					Pt. Lookout, MD	06/29/65	Rlsd. G.O. #109	P115,P121,P123,CSR
Mason, B.	Pvt	A 3rd SCVABn	High Pt., NC	05/02/65	High Pt., NC	05/02/65	Paroled	CSR
Mason, David A.	Pvt	D 11th SCVI	Town Creek, NC	02/20/65	Ft. Anderson, NC	02/28/65	Pt. Lookout, MD	CSR,HAG
					Pt. Lookout, MD	06/29/65	Rlsd. G.O. #109	P115,P118,P123
Mason, J.C.	Pvt	C 4th SCVC	Hartwell, GA	05/18/65	Hartwell, GA	05/18/65	Paroled	CSR
					Hartwell, GA	05/18/65	Paroled	CSR
Mason, James E.	Sgt	A Hol. Leg.	Five Forks, VA	04/01/65	City Pt., VA	04/05/65	Pt. Lookout, MD	CSR
					Pt. Lookout, MD	06/29/65	Rlsd. G.O.#109	P115,P118,P123
Mason, John K.	Cpl	K 22nd SCVI	South Mtn., MD	09/14/62	Frederick, MD USGH	10/11/62	Died of wounds	P12,CSR
Massay, Hohn W.	Smn	CSS Charleston	Charleston, SC	11/20/62	Ft. McHenry, MD	06/26/63	City Pt., VA Xc	P110
Massebeau, Joseph P.	Pvt	C 6th SCVI	Richmond, VA Hos.	04/03/65	Richmond, VA Hos.	04/29/65	Escaped	CSR
					Fts. Monroe, VA US	06/06/65	Fts. Monroe, VA	CSR
Massengill, Joseph	Pvt	B 37th VAVCB	Moorefield, VA	08/07/64	Wheeling, WV	08/11/64	Camp Chase, OH	CSR
					Camp Chase, OH	03/17/65	Died, Gv #1695	P6,P27,37V,FPH,CSR
Massey, James M.F.	Pvt	K Orr's Ri.	Deserted/enemy	02/21/65	City Pt., VA	02/22/65	Washington, DC	CDC,CSR
					Washington, D.C.	02/24/65	Rock Island, IL.	CSR
Massey, Samuel T.	Pvt	A 1st SCVIR	Bentonville, NC	03/22/65	New Berne, NC	04/10/65	Hart's Island, NY	CSR,SA1
					Hart's Island, NY	07/01/65	David's Island, NY	CSR
					David's Island, NY	08/01/65	Rlsd. G.O. #109	CSR
Masterman, Edwin J.	Sgt	B 27th SCVI	Town Creek, NC	02/20/65	Pt. Lookout, MD	05/14/65	Rlsd. G.O. #85	P7,P115,P118,HAG
Masters, J.D.	Pvt	H 7th SCVI	Boonesboro, MD	09/15/62	Ft. Delaware, DE	10/02/62	Aikens Ldg., VA Xc	CSR
Masters, W.S.	Msc	2nd SCVIRi	Petersburg, VA		City Pt., VA	04/12/65	Washington, DC P.M.	CSR
					Washington, DC	04/12/65	Louisville, KY	CSR
Mathes, Martin R.	Pvt	F 7th SCVI	Falmouth, VA	11/24/62	Paroled			KEB,CSR
Mathes, Morgan C.	Pvt	F 7th SCVI	Falmouth, VA	11/24/62	Paroled			CSR
Matheson, J.P.	Pvt	Marion LA	Augusta, GA	06/02/65	Augusta, GA	06/02/65	Paroled	CSR
Matheson, R.F.	Pvt	B 7th SCVC	Deserted/enemy	03/12/65	Bermuda Hundred, VA	03/13/65	City Pt., VA P.M.	CSR
					City Pt., VA P.M.			CSR
Mathewes, Edward	2Lt	I 1st SCVIR	Bentonville, NC	03/22/65	Hart's Island, NY	04/15/65	Ft. Delaware, DE	P79,CSR,SA1
					Ft. Delaware, DE	06/17/65	Rlsd. G.O. #109	P43,P45,CSR
Mathews, E. Franklin	Sgt	M 8th SCVI	Winchester, VA	09/13/64	Harpers Ferry, WV	09/19/64	Camp Chase, OH	P23,CSR
					Camp Chase, OH	06/11/65	Rlsd. G.O. #109	P23,CSR
Mathews, Richard	1Sg	K 1st SCVIG	Gettysburg, PA	07/05/63	Ft. Delaware, DE	08/12/63	Rlsd S.O. Sec. War	P40,P42,SA1,CSR
Mathews, W.M.	Pvt	K 18th SCVI	Crater, Pbg., VA	07/30/64	City Pt., VA	08/05/64	Pt. Lookout, MD	CSR
					Pt. Lookout, MD	08/08/64	Elmira, NY	P113,P117,120,CSR
					Elmira, NY	09/15/64	Died, Ch. Diarrhea	P5,P12,P65,P66,FPH,CSR
Mathews, William	Pvt	M 8th SCVI	Winchester, VA	09/13/64	Harpers Ferry, WV	09/19/64	Camp Chase, OH	KEB,CSR
					Camp Chase, OH	06/11/65	Rlsd. G.O. #109	P23,CSR
Mathias, J.E.	Sgt	F 5th SCVC	Lexington, SC	02/17/65	New Berne, NC	03/30/65	Pt. Lookout, MD	CSR
					Pt. Lookout, MD	06/29/65	Rlsd. G.O. #109	P115,P118,P123,CSR
Mathias, Jesse M.	Pvt	F 5th SCVC	Louisa C.H., VA	06/11/64	Fts. Monroe, VA	07/20/64	Pt. Lookout, MD	CSR
					Pt. Lookout, MD	07/25/64	Elmira, NY	P113,P117,P120
					Elmira, NY	03/02/65	James R., VA Xc	P65,P66,CSR
					Richmond, VA Hos.	03/17/65	Furloughed 60 days	CSR
Mathias, John T.	Pvt	C 1st SCVIG	Petersburg, VA	04/03/65	Fair Gds. Hos., Pbg.	04/14/65	Died of wounds	P6,P12,SA1,CSR

M

SOUTH CAROLINA SOLDIERS, SAILORS AND CITIZENS HELD IN U.S. PRISONS 1861-1865

NAME	RANK	REGIMENT	CAPTURED AT	WHEN	PRISON	MOVED	DISPOSITION	SOURCES
Mathis, Bird R.	Sgt	D 16th SCVI	Marietta, GA	06/17/64	Nashville, TN	06/24/64	Louisville, KY	P3,16R,CSR
					Louisville, KY	06/27/64	Camp Morton, IN	P90,P91,P94,CSR
					Camp Morton, IN	03/15/65	Pt. Lookout, MD Xc	P100,CSR
					Richmond, VA Hos.	03/28/65	Furloughed 60 days	CSR
Mathis, Columbus	Pvt	B Hol. Leg.	Deserted/Enemy	02/25/65	City Pt., VA	02/28/65	Washington, DC	CSR
Mathis, Holden D.	Pvt	B Hol. Leg.	Five Forks, VA	04/02/65	City Pt., VA	04/05/65	Pt. Lookout, MD	CSR,HOS
					Pt. Lookout, MD	06/29/65	Rlsd. G.O. #109	P118,P121,P123
Mathis, J.B.	Pvt	G 20th SCVI	Cedar Creek, VA	10/19/64	Pt. Lookout, MD	03/28/65	Aikens Ldg., VA Xc	CSR
Mathis, J.N.	Pvt	K 23rd SCVI	Middletown, MD	09/15/62	Ft. Delaware, DE	10/02/62	Aikens Ldg., VA Xc	CSR
Mathis, J.V.	Pvt	G 20th SCVI	Cedar Creek, VA	10/19/64	Harpers Ferry, WV	10/24/64	Pt. Lookout, MD	P115,CSR
					Pt. Lookout, MD	03/28/65	Washington D.C. P.M.	P7,P115,P118,CSR
					Washington, DC P.M.	04/02/65	Terre Haute, IN	CSR
Mathis, James C.	Pvt	H 19th SCVI	Missionary Ridge, TN	11/25/63	Nashville, TN	12/07/63	Louisville, KY	CSR
					Louisville, KY	12/21/63	Rock Island, IL	CSR
					Rock Island, IL	06/17/65	Rlsd. G.O. #109	CSR
Mathis, Jefferson	Pvt	I 12th SCVI	N. Anna River, VA	05/23/64	Pt. Lookout, MD	02/10/65	Listed for Xc	P124,CSR
					Pt. Lookout, MD	02/17/65	Died, Scurvy	P6,P117,P119,CS
Mathis, Jesse	Pvt	A Hol. Leg.	Five Forks, VA	04/01/65	City Pt., VA	04/05/65	Pt. Lookout, MD	CSR,HOS
					Pt. Lookout, MD	06/29/65	Rlsd. G.O. #109	P115
Mathis, John	Pvt	B Hol. Leg.	Deserted/Enemy	02/25/65	City Pt., VA	02/28/65	Washington, DC	CSR
					Washington, DC	03/01/65	Savannah, GA oath	CSR
Mathis, Thomas	Pvt	B Hol. Leg.	Deserted/Enemy	02/25/65	City Pt., VA	02/28/65	Washington, DC	CSR
					Washington, DC	03/01/65	Savannah, GA oath	CSR
Mathis, Thomas M.	Pvt	G 14th SCVI	Sutherland Stn., VA	04/02/65	City Pt., VA	04/07/64	Hart's Island, NY	CSR
					Hart's Island, NY	05/16/65	Died, Typhoid Fev.	P6,P12,P79,FPH,CSR
Mathis, W.H.	Pvt	E 18th SCVI	Farmville, VA	04/06/65	City Pt., VA	04/14/65	Newport News, VA	CSR
					Newport News, VA	06/26/65	Rlsd. G.O. #109	P107,UD2,CSR
Mathis, W.M.	Pvt	I 12th SCVI	Wilderness, VA	05/06/64	Belle Plain, VA	05/20/64	Ft. Delaware, DE	CSR,LAN
					Ft. Delaware, DE		Hos 11/11-11/14/64	P47
					Ft. Delaware, DE		Hos 4/12-4/17/65	P47
					Ft. Delaware, DE		Hos 1/6-1/12/65	P47
					Ft. Delaware, DE	06/10/65	Rlsd. G.O. #109	P41,P43,P45,CSR
Matthew, David	Pvt	E 12th SCVI	Petersburg, VA	04/02/65	Fts. Monroe, VA	07/10/65	Rlsd. G.O. #109	CSR
Matthewes, A.	Pvt	C 3rd SCVABn	Blakely, AL	04/09/65	Ship Island, MS	05/01/65	Vicksburg, MS Xc	P136,CSR
Matthewes, J.M.	Pvt	C 3rd SCVABn	Blakely, AL	04/09/65	Ship Island, MS	05/01/65	Vicksburg, MS Xc	P136,CSR
Matthewes, S.P.	Pvt	C 3rd SCVABn	Blakely, AL	04/09/65	Ship Island, MS	05/01/65	Vicksburg, MS Xc	P136,CSR
Matthews, B.C.W.	Pvt	M 7th SCVI	Cedar Creek, VA	10/19/64	W. Bldg. Balt., MD	10/27/64	Pt. Lookout, MD	P3,CSR
					Pt. Lookout, MD	10/29/64	Aikens Ldg., VA Xc	P115,P118,P123,CSR
Matthews, Bailey	Pvt	B 14th SCVI	Port Royal Fy., SC	12/18/61	Hilton Head, SC	02/09/62	Ft. Lafayette, NY	CSR,UD3
					Ft. Lafayette, NY	07/11/62	Ft. Delaware, DE	P85,CSR
					Ft. Delaware, DE	08/05/62	Aikens Ldg., VA Xc	CSR
Matthews, Bailey	Pvt	B 14th SCVI	Newton, NC	04/19/65	Newton, NC	04/19/65	Paroled	CSR
Matthews, Charles M.	Cpl	K 25th SCVI	Ft. Fisher, NC	01/15/65	New York, NY	01/31/65	Elmira, NY	CSR,HAG,CTA
					Elmira, NY	08/07/65	Rlsd. G.O. #109	P65,P66,CSR
Matthews, Elijah	Pvt	A 1st SCVIG	Gettysburg, PA	06/30/63	David's Island, NY	07/27/63	Died of wounds	P1,P6,FPH,SA1,CSR
Matthews, G.W.	Pvt	H 10th SCVI	Murfreesboro, TN	12/31/62	Nashville, TN	01/07/63	Died, of wounds	P12,P38,RAS,CSR
Matthews, Harvey	Pvt	3 10/19 SCVI	Missionary Ridge, TN	11/25/63	Nashville, TN	12/07/63	Louisville, KY	P39,CTA,CSR,RAS
					Louisville, KY	12/07/63	Rock Island, IL	P88,P89,CSR
					Rock Island, IL	03/02/65	Pt. Lookout, MD Xc	P131,CSR
Matthews, James	Pvt	E 13th SCVI	Gettysburg, PA	07/05/63	David's Island, NY	08/06/63	Died of wounds	P1,ROH,CDC

SOUTH CAROLINA SOLDIERS, SAILORS AND  CITIZENS HELD IN U.S. PRISONS 1861-1865

NAME	RANK	REGIMENT	CAPTURED AT	WHEN	PRISON	MOVED	DISPOSITION	SOURCES
Matthews, James C.	Pvt	8 10/19 SCVI	Missionary Ridge, TN	11/25/63	Nashville, TN	12/07/63	Louisville, KY	P39
					Louisville, KY	12/21/63	Rock Island, IL	P88,P89
					Rock Island, IL	06/17/65	Rlsd. G.O. #109	P131
Matthews, James M.	Pvt	H 10th SCVI	Murfreesboro, TN	12/31/62	Nashville, TN	01/07/63	Died, of wounds	P12,P38,CSR,RAS
Matthews, James M.	Pvt	C 25th SCVI	Ft. Fisher, NC	01/15/65	New York, NY	01/31/65	Elmira, NY	CSR,HAG
					Elmira, NY	07/11/65	Rlsd. G.O. #109	P65,P66,HAG,CTA
Matthews, John	Pvt	B 14th SCVI	Port Royal, SC	12/18/61	Hilton Head, SC	02/09/62	Ft. Lafayette, NY	CSR,UD3
					Ft. Lafayette, NY	07/11/62	Ft. Delaware, DE	P85,CSR
					Ft. Delaware, DE	08/05/62	Aikens Ldg., VA Xc	CSR
Matthews, John	Pvt	H Hol. Leg.	Petersburg, VA	11/05/64	City Pt., VA	11/11/64	Washington, DC	CSR,ANY
					Pt. Lookout, MD	06/29/65	Rlsd. G.O. #109	P118,P122,P123
Matthews, John A.	Pvt	H 18th SCVI	Crater, Pbg., VA	07/30/64	City Pt., VA	08/05/64	Pt. Lookout, MD	CSR,YEB
					Pt. Lookout, MD	08/08/64	Elmira, NY	P66,P125
					Elmira, NY	05/02/65	Died, Diarrhea	P6,P12,P65,P66,FPH
Matthews, Jonathan O.	Pvt	F 12th SCVI	Jarratts Stn., VA	04/04/65	City Pt., VA	04/07/65	Hart's Island, NY	CSR
					Hart's Island, NY	06/15/65	Rlsd. G.O. #109	P79,HFC,CSR
Matthews, Pleasant	Pvt	3 10/19 SCVI	Missionary Ridge, TN	11/25/63	Louisville, KY	12/07/63	Rock Island, IL	P89,RAS
Matthews, Robert N.	Pvt	D 11th SCVI	Petersburg, VA	06/16/64	Fts. Monroe, VA	07/08/64	Died of wounds	P12,HAG,CSR
Matthews, W.C.	Pvt	H 2nd SCVA	Salisbury, NC	06/21/65	Salisbury, NC	06/21/65	Released on oath	CSR
Matthews, W.J.	Pvt	H 25th SCVI	Ft. Fisher, NC	01/15/65	New York, NY	01/31/65	Elmira, NY	CSR,HAG
					Elmira, NY	04/07/65	Died, Variola	P6,P12,P65,P66,FPH
Matthews, William W.	Pvt	G 15th SCVI	Gettysburg, PA	07/05/63	Ft. McHenry, MD	07/14/63	Ft. Delaware, DE	CSR,KEB,CTA
					Ft. Delaware, DE	06/10/65	Released	P40,P42,P44,P45
Mattison, G.F.	Pvt	F 1st SCVIG	Hanover Jctn., VA	05/24/64	Front Royal, VA	05/30/64	Pt. Lookout, MD	CSR,SA1
					Pt. Lookout, MD	08/13/64	Died, Ch. Diarrhea	P5,P113,P117,FPH
Mattison, J.M.	Cpl	G Orr's Ri.	Petersburg, VA	04/03/65	City Pt., VA	04/11/65	Hart's Island, NY	CSR
					Hart's Island, NY	06/16/65	Rlsd. G.O. #109	P79,CDC
Mattison, Thomas S.	Pvt	E Ham. Leg.	Dandridge, TN	01/17/64	Nashville, TN	02/11/64	Louisville, KY	P39,CSR
					Louisville, KY	02/15/64	Rock Island, IL	P88,P91,P94,CSR
					Rock Island, IL	06/19/65	Rlsd. G.O. #109	CSR
Mattox, Daniel	Pvt	K 17th SCVI	Five Forks, VA	04/01/65	City Pt., VA	04/05/65	Pt. Lookout, MD	CSR
					Pt. Lookout, MD	06/29/65	Rlsd. G.O. #109	P115,P118,P122,CSR
Mattox, John	Pvt	B 1st SCVA	Fayetteville, NC	03/12/65	Pt. Lookout, MD	05/15/65	Rlsd. G.O. #85	P115,P118
Mattox, Samuel	Pvt	D 15th SCVI	Lynch's Creek, SC	02/27/65	New Berne, NC	03/26/65	Pt. Lookout, MD	CSR
					Pt. Lookout, MD	06/02/65	Died, Diarrhea	P6,P115,P118,FPH,KEB,HIC
Maul, C.N.	Pvt	G Ham. Leg. MI	Farmville, VA	04/11/65	Farmville, VA	04/11/65	Paroled	CSR
Mauldin, Archibald T.	Cpl	I 14th SCVI	Amelia C.H., VA	04/06/65	City Pt., VA	04/11/65	Pt. Lookout, MD	CSR
					Pt. Lookout, Md	06/29/65	Rlsd. G.O. #109	P115,P121,P123,CSR
Mauldin, James D.	Pvt	I 14th SCVI	Gettysburg, PA	07/05/63	Ft. McHenry, MD	07/07/63	Ft. Delaware, DE	CSR
					Ft. Delaware, DE	11/01/63	Died, Smallpox	P5,P40,P42,P44,P47
Mauldin, Rucker	Pvt	I P.S.S.	Richmond, VA Hos.	04/03/65	Libby Prison, VA	04/23/65	Newport News, VA	CSR
					Newport News, VA	07/03/65	Died, Diarrhea	P107,CSR,TSE
Mauldin, William	Pvt	K Ham. Leg. MI	Farmville, VA	04/11/65	Farmville, VA	04/11/65	Paroled	CSR
Mauldin, William P.	Pvt	F Orr's Ri.	Petersburg, VA	04/03/65	City Pt., VA	04/11/65	Hart's Island, NY	CSR
					Hart's Island, NY	06/16/65	Rlsd. G.O. #109	CSR
Maull, B.P.	Pvt	B 27th SCVI	Ft. Anderson, NC	02/19/65	Ft. Anderson, NC	02/28/65	Pt. Lookout, MD	CSR,HAG
					Pt. Lookout, MD	05/14/65	Rlsd. G.O. #85	P115,P121,CSR
Maurice, Sydney	Pvt	C 6th SCVI	Augusta, GA	05/25/65	Augusta, GA	05/25/65	Paroled	
Maxcy, George W.	Pvt	I 27th SCVI	Town Creek, NC	02/20/65	Ft. Anderson, NC	02/28/65	Pt. Lookout, MD	CSR,HAG
					Pt. Lookout, MD	05/14/65	Rlsd. G.O. #85	P115,P118,P121,CSR
Maxwell, B.A.	Pvt	H 2nd SCVC	Anderson, SC	05/19/65	Anderson, SC	05/19/65	Paroled	CSR
Maxwell, Barney	Pvt	B 1st SCVA	Deserted/enemy	03/24/65	Charleston, SC		Released on oath	CSR

SOUTH CAROLINA SOLDIERS, SAILORS AND  CITIZENS HELD IN U.S. PRISONS 1861-1865

NAME	RANK	REGIMENT	CAPTURED AT	WHEN	PRISON	MOVED	DISPOSITION	SOURCES
Maxwell, J.F.	Pvt	D 6th SCVC	Stony Creek, VA	12/01/64	City Pt., VA	12/05/64	Pt. Lookout, MD	CSR
					Pt. Lookout, MD	06/29/65	Rlsd. G.O. #109	P115,P118,CSR
Maxwell, Joseph	Pvt	H 1st SCVA	Morris Island, SC	07/10/63	Hilton Head, SC	09/19/63	Ft. Columbus, NY	P1,CSR
					Ft. Columbus, NY	09/23/63	Took the oath	P1
					Ft. Columbus, NY	09/26/63	Pt. Lookout, MD	CSR
					Pt. Lookout, MD	08/16/64	Elmira, NY	P113,P116,P120,CSR
					Elmira, NY	10/11/64	Tfd. for exchange	P65,CSR
					Pt. Lookout, MD		Exchanged	P124
May, Jacob	Pvt	E 10th SCVI	Stone Mtn., GA	07/25/64	Louisville, KY	08/13/64	Camp Chase, OH	P90,P91
					Camp Chase, OH	03/18/65	Pt. Lookout, MD Xc	P23,P26
May, John	Pvt	H 27th SCVI	Town Creek, NC	02/20/65	Ft. Anderson, NC	02/28/65	Pt. Lookout, MD	CSR,HAG
					Pt. Lookout, MD	05/14/65	Rlsd. G.O. #85	P115,P118,P121,CSR
May, Patrick F.	Sgt	E 25th SCVI	Ft. Fisher, NC	01/15/65	New York, NY	01/31/65	Elmira, NY	CSR,HAG
					Elmira, NY	05/17/65	Rlsd. G.O. #85	P65,P66
Maybank, David	Pvt	A 2nd SCVC	Augusta, GA	05/31/65	Augusta, GA	05/31/65	Paroled	CSR
Mayberry, D.Z.	Cpl	M P.S.S.	Cold Harbor, VA	06/01/64	Pt. Lookout, MD	07/09/64	Elmira, NY	P113,P117,P120,CSR
					Whitehouse, VA	06/11/64	Pt. Lookout, MD	CSR,TSE
					Elmira, NY	06/21/65	Rlsd. G.O. #109	P65,P66,CSR
Maybry, James G.	Pvt	I Hol. Leg.	Petersburg, VA	11/05/64	City Pt., VA	11/11/64	Washington, DC	CSR
					Pt. Lookout, MD	06/04/65	Rlsd. Sick list	P115,P118,CSR
Mayfield, L.W.	Pvt	C 22nd SCVI	Crater, Pbg., VA	07/30/64	Pt. Lookout, MD	08/08/64	Elmira, NY	P113,P117,P120,CSR
					Elmira, NY	03/14/65	James R., VA Xc	P65,P66,CSR
Mayfield, William N.	Pvt	D Ham. Leg.	Knoxville, TN	12/14/63	Nashville, TN	01/17/64	Louisville, KY	CSR
					Louisville, KY	01/23/64	Rock Island, IL	P91,P94,CSR
					Rock Island, IL	03/02/65	Pt.Lookout, MD Xc	P131,CSR
Mays, John A.	Pvt	I 24th SCVI	Marietta, GA	06/15/64	Nashville, TN	06/21/64	Louisville, KY	P3,CSR
					Louisville, KY	06/22/64	Rock Island, IL	P90,P91,P94,CSR
					Rock Island, IL	02/25/65	Pt.Lookout, MD Xc	P131,CSR
					Ft. Columbus, NY	03/05/65	Boulwares Wh., VA	CSR
					Rchmd. Hospitals	03/08/65	Furloughed 30 days	CSR
Mays, Samuel E.	Pvt	K 2nd SCVC	Hartwell, GA	05/18/65	Hartwell, GA	05/18/65	Paroled	CSR
Mayson, B.W.	Pvt	K 14th SCVI	Gettysburg, PA	07/05/63	David's Island, NY	09/12/63	City Pt., VA Xc	P1,CSR
					Williamsburg, VA Hos.	09/24/63	Furloughed	CSR
					City Pt., VA	08/05/64	Pt. Lookout, MD	CSR
					Pt. Lookout, MD	08/08/64	Elmira, NY	P113,P117,P120,CSR
					Elmira, NY	05/29/65	Rlsd. G.O. #85	P65,P66,CSR
Mayson, Robert C.	Pvt	K 15th SCVI	Halltown, VA	08/26/64	Harpers Ferry, WV	08/29/64	Camp Chase, OH	CSR,KEB
					Washington, DC	09/07/64	Camp Chase, OH	CSR
					Camp Chase, OH	03/18/65	Pt. Lookout, MD	P23,P26,CSR
					Pt. Lookout, MD	03/27/65	Boulwares Wh. Xc	CSR
Mayson, Robert C.	Pvt	K 15th SCVI	Augusta, GA	05/23/65	Augusta, GA	05/23/65	Paroled on oath	CSR
Mazeke, L.H.	Pvt	K P.S.S.	Deserted/enemy	02/25/64	East Tennessee		No further records	CSR
Mazyck, Nathaniel B.	Cpt	E 25th SCVI	Town Creek, NC	02/20/65	Pt. Lookout, MD	02/28/65	Washington, DC	P115,P118,P120,HAG
					Old Capitol, DC	03/06/65	Ft. Delaware, DE	P110,CSR
					Ft. Delaware, DE	06/17/65	Rlsd. G.O. #109	P43,P45,P46
McAbee, Alberry J.	Pvt	A 3rd SCVI	Loudon, TN	12/03/63	Chattanooga, TN			P1,KEB,SA2,H3
McAbee, Elisha	Pvt	I 13th SCVI	Petersburg, VA	04/01/65	Pt. Lookout, MD	06/29/65	Rlsd. G.O. #109	P118,P120,P121
McAbee, George W.	Pvt	C 5th SCVI	Point of Rocks, MD	09/20/62	City Pt., VA	09/24/62	Aikens Ldg., VA Xc	CSR,SA3
McAbee, George W.	Pvt	C 5th SCVI	Shell Mound, AL		Bridgeport, AL G.H.	11/15/63	Nashville TN G.H.	CSR
McAbee, George W.	Pvt	C 5th SCVI	Lookout Valley, TN	10/29/63	Nashville, TN	01/31/64	Louisville, KY	P39,CSR
					Louisville, KY	02/03/64	Rock Island, IL	P88,P94,CSR
					Rock Island, IL	10/11/64	Released on oath	P131,CSR

M

SOUTH CAROLINA SOLDIERS, SAILORS AND CITIZENS HELD IN U.S. PRISONS 1861-1865

NAME	RANK	REGIMENT	CAPTURED AT	WHEN	PRISON	MOVED	DISPOSITION	SOURCES
McAbee, Newport P.	Pvt	C 27th SCVI	Wilmington, NC	02/20/65	Pt. Lookout, MD	06/29/65	Rlsd. G.O. #109	P121,P123,HAG
McAdams, Samuel T.	Pvt	7 10/19 SCVI	Missionary Ridge, TN	11/25/63	Chattanooga, TN G.H.	12/18/63	Chattanooga, TN	CSR
					Nashville, TN	12/25/63	Louisville, KY	P39,CSR
					Louisville, KY	12/27/63	Rock Island, IL	P88,P89,P93,CSR
					Rock Island, IL	06/18/65	Rlsd. G.O. #109	P131,CSR
McAfee, R.	Pvt	C 3rd SCVABn	Blakely, AL	04/09/65	Ship Island, MS	05/01/65	Vicksburg, MS Xc	P136,CSR
					Vicksburg, MS	05/05/65	Exchanged	CSR
McAlheny, J.D.	Pvt	G 4th SCVI	Old Church, VA	05/28/64	Old Capitol, DC	10/26/64	Elmira, NY	P110,CSR
					Lincoln G.H., DC	10/26/64	Old Capitol, DC	CSR
					Elmira, NY	06/21/65	Rlsd. G.O. #109	P65,P66,CSR
McAlheny, William	Pvt	G 4th SCVC	Stony Creek, VA	12/01/64	City Pt., VA	12/05/64	Pt. Lookout, MD	CSR
					Pt. Lookout, MD	06/25/65	Rlsd. G.O. #109	P115,P123,CSR
McAlister, E.	Pvt	H 25th SCVI	Ft. Fisher, NC	01/15/65	New York, NY	01/30/65	Elmira, NY	CSR,HAG
					Elmira, NY	04/20/65	Died, Variola	P6,P12,FPH,CSR,HAG
McAlister, J.F.	Pvt	F 1st SCVIH	Deep Bottom, VA	08/14/64	Bermuda Hundred, VA	08/15/64	Fts. Monroe, VA	CSR,SA1
					Fts. Monroe, VA	08/16/64	Pt. Lookout, MD	CSR
					Pt. Lookout, MD	03/14/65	Aikens Ldg., VA Xc	P113,P117,P121,CSR
					Pt. Lookout, MD	04/03/65	Exchanged	P124
McAlister, Pleasant	Pvt	K 6th SCVI	Frederick, MD	09/12/62	Frederick, MD USGH	09/19/62	Ft. Delaware, DE	CSR
McAllister, F.B.	Pvt	D 26th SCVI	Deserted/enemy	02/24/65	City Pt., VA	02/25/65	Washington, DC	CSR
					Washington, DC	03/27/65	Savannah, GA oath	CSR
McAllister, George W.	Pvt	F 24th SCVI	Ringgold, GA	11/27/63	Nashville, TN	12/11/63	Louisville, KY	P39,EFW
					Louisville, KY	12/12/63	Rock Island, IL	P88,P89
					Rock Island, IL	02/01/64	Died, Variola	P5,P132,P12,FPH
McAllister, James A.	Pvt	G 22nd SCVI	Petersburg, VA	04/02/64	City Pt., VA	04/04/64	Pt. Lookout, MD	CSR
					Pt. Lookout, MD	06/29/65	Rlsd. G.O. #109	P118,P121,P123,CSR
McCallister, N.A.	Pvt	Wash'n LA	Ashland, VA	04/27/65	Ashland, VA	04/27/65	Paroled	CSR
McAllister, W.J.	Pvt	C 3rd SCVABn	Blakely, AL	04/09/65	Ship Island, MS	05/01/65	Vicksburg, MS Xc	P136,CSR
McAllister, W.J.	Pvt	C 3rd SCVABn	Augusta, GA	05/20/65	Augusta, GA	05/20/65	Paroled	CSR
McAndrews, William	Pvt	H 2nd SCVC	Hagerstown, MD	07/12/63	Baltimore, MD	08/20/63	Pt. Lookout, MD	CSR
					Pt. Lookout, MD	03/17/64	City Pt., VA Xc	P113,P116,P123,CSR
McArdle, Peter	Pvt	B 1st SCVA	Raleigh, NC Hos.	04/13/65	Raleigh, NC	04/13/65	Paroled	CSR
McArthur, William F.	Pvt	H P.S.S.	Williamsburg, VA	07/06/62	Old Capitol, DC	08/01/62	Fts. Monroe, VA	CSR,TSE
					Fts. Monroe, VA	08/05/62	Aikens Ldg., VA Xc	CSR
McAteer, John	Pvt	H 1st SCVA	Raleigh, NC Hos.	04/06/65	Raleigh, NC	04/26/65	Paroled	CSR
McAteer, William	Pvt	I 14th SCVI	Sutherland Stn., VA	04/03/65	City Pt., VA	04/07/65	Hart's Island, NY	CSR
					Hart's Island, NY	06/16/65	Rlsd. G.O. #109	P79,CSR
McBean, George B.	Pvt	Ham. Leg. MI	Deserted/enemy	04/14/65	City Pt., VA P.M.	11/03/65	Washington, DC	CSR
					Washington, VA	11/03/65	Cumberland, MD	CSR
McBrayer, John T.	Pvt	L 5th SCVI	Williamsburg, VA	05/05/62	Fts. Monroe, VA	08/05/62	Aikens Ldg., VA Xc	CSR,SA3
McBrayer, John T.	Pvt	L 5th SCVI	Sharpsburg, MD	09/17/62	Ft. McHenry, MD	10/17/62	Fts. Monroe, VA	CSR
					Fts. Monroe, VA	09/30/62	Aiken's Ldg., VA X	CSR
McBride, J.A.	Pvt	B 8th SCVI	Winchester, VA	09/13/64	Harpers Ferry, WV	09/19/64	Camp Chase, OH	KEB,CSR
					Camp Chase, OH	06/11/65	Rlsd. G.O. #109	P23,CSR
McBride, J.T.	Pvt	B Orr's Ri.	Spotsylvania, VA	05/12/64	Belle Plain, VA	05/21/64	Ft. Delaware, DE	CSR
					Ft. Delaware, DE	09/18/64	Hos 9/18-9/30/64	P47
					Ft. Delaware, DE	09/30/64	Aikens Ldg., VA Xc	P41,P43,CSR
McBride, John D.	Pvt	A 15th SCVAB	Silver Creek, NC	03/16/65	New Bern, NC	04/05/65	Pt. Lookout, MD	CSR
					Pt. Lookout, MD	06/29/65	Rlsd. G.O. #109	P115,P118,CSR

M

SOUTH CAROLINA SOLDIERS, SAILORS AND CITIZENS HELD IN U.S. PRISONS 1861-1865

NAME	RANK	REGIMENT	CAPTURED AT	WHEN	PRISON	MOVED	DISPOSITION	SOURCES
McBride, Samuel Stewart	Pvt	K 15th SCVI	Petersburg, VA	07/29/64	City Pt., VA	08/05/65	Pt. Lookout, MD	CSR
					Pt. Lookout, MD	08/08/64	Elmira, NY	P113,P117,P120,CSR
					Elmira, NY	10/11/64	Tfd. for exchange	P65,CSR
					Pt. Lookout, MD	10/29/64	Aikens Ldg., VA Xc	P66,P115,P118,P123
					Pt. Lookout MD	10/29/64	Venus Pt., GA Xc	CSR
McBride, Thomas M.	Pvt	I 13th SCVI	Amelia C.H., VA	04/05/65	City Pt.. VA	04/13/65	Pt. Lookout, MD	CSR
					Pt. Lookout, MD	06/29/65	Rlsd. G.O. #109	P119,P121,P123,CSR
McCabe, John Wesley	Pvt	A 25th SCVI	Weldon RR, VA	08/21/64	City Pt., VA	08/24/64	Pt. Lookout, MD	CSR,HAG
					Pt. Lookout, MD	12/19/64	Died, Diarrhea	P5,P117,P125,FPH
McCain, Henry H.	Sgt	I 17th SCVI	Petersburg, VA	03/25/65	City Pt., VA	03/28/65	Pt. Lookout, MD	CSR,LAN
					Pt. Lookout, MD	06/29/65	Rlsd. G.O. #109	P118,P121,P123,CSR
McCall, B.	Pvt	K 21st SCVI	Ft. Fisher, NC	01/15/65	Elmira, NY	06/07/65	Rlsd. G.O. #109	P65,P66
McCall, Duncan N.	Cpl	5 10/19 SCVI	Missionary Ridge	11/25/63	Nashville, TN	12/07/63	Louisville, KY	P39,RAS,CSR
					Louisville, KY	12/09/63	Rock Island, IL	P88,P89,CSR
					Rock Island, IL	06/20/65	Rlsd. G.O. #109	P131,CSR
McCall, G.M.	Pvt	I 17th SCVI	Deserted/enemy	03/09/65	P.M. A. of P.	03/10/65	City Pt., VA P.M.	CSR
					City Pt., VA P.M.	03/12/65	Washington, DC	CSR
					Washington, DC	03/13/65	Charleston, SC oath	CSR
McCall, Hugh S.	Pvt	E 4th SCVC	Hawe's Shop, VA	05/28/64	White House, VA	06/08/64	Pt. Lookout, MD	CSR,HOM
					Pt. Lookout, MD	07/09/64	Elmira, NY	P113,P117,P120,HOM,CSR
					Elmira, NY	10/10/64	Died, Pneumonia	P5,P65,FPH,P65,CSR
McCall, J.G.	Pvt	A 26th SCVI	Deserted/enemy	01/09/65	City Point, VA	01/13/65	Washington, DC	P8,CSR
					Washington, DC	01/14/65	Memphis, TN oath	CSR
McCall, John S.	Pvt	E 4th SCVC	Cheraw, SC	03/04/65	Cpt. Burns	03/26/64	New Berne, NC P.M.	CSR
					New Berne, NC	04/03/65	Pt. Lookout, MD	CSR
					Pt. Lookout, MD	06/29/65	Rlsd. G.O. #109	P118,P121,P123,CSR
McCall, John W.	Pvt	K 5th SCVI	Deserted/enemy	03/15/65	Washington, DC	03/18/65	Nashville, TN/oath	CSR
McCall, William A.	Pvt	I 1st SCVA	Sampson Co., NC	03/16/65	New Berne, NC	04/10/65	Hart's Island, NY	CSR
					Hart's Island, NY	06/16/65	Rlsd. G.O. #109	P79,CSR
McCallister, H.L.	Pvt	A Wash'n LA	Ashland, VA	04/27/65	Ashland, VA	04/27/65	Paroled	CSR
McCallister, N.A.	Pvt	B Wash'n LA	Ashland, VA	04/27/65	Ashland, VA	04/27/65	Paroled	CSR
McCallum, Hugh B.	Chp	15th SCVI	South Mtn., MD	09/14/62	Ft. McHenry, MD	10/14/62	Fts. Monroe, VA	CSR
					Fts. Monroe, VA	10/25/62	Aikens Ldg., VA Xc	CSR
McCane, James	Pvt	6 10/19 SCVI	Ringgold, GA	11/27/63	Nashville, TN	12/09/63	Louisville, KY	P39
McCants, David B.	Pvt	D 5th SCVI	Boonesboro, MD	09/15/62	Ft. Delaware, DE	10/02/62	Aikens Ldg., VA Xc	SA3,CSR
McCants, T.J.	2Lt	K 3rd SCVABn	Williamsburg D., SC	04/06/65	Charleston, SC		no release data	CSR
McCarter, Collins	2Lt	I Hol. Leg.	Kinston, NC	12/13/62	Kinston, NC	12/15/62	Paroled POW	CSR,HOS
McCarter, Collins	2Lt	I Hol. Leg.	Dinwiddie C.H., VA	04/01/65	City Pt., VA	04/04/65	Old Capitol, DC	CSR
					Old Capitol, DC	04/09/65	Johnson's Isl., OH	P110
					Johnson's Isl., OH	06/19/65	Rlsd. G.O. #109	P82
McCarter, Daniel T.	Cpl	G 18th SCVI	Southside RR, VA	04/01/65	City Pt., VA	04/05/65	Pt. Lookout, MD	CSR
					Pt. Lookout, MD	06/29/65	Rlsd. G.O. #109	P115,P118,CSR
McCarter, David B.	Pvt	G 18th SCVI	Petersburg, VA	03/25/65	City Pt., VA	03/28/65	Pt. Lookout, MD	CSR
					Pt. Lookout, MD	06/29/65	Rlsd. G.O. #109	P115,P118,CSR
McCarter, J.C.	Sgt	H 18th SCVI	Crater, Pbg., VA	07/30/64	City Pt., VA	08/05/64	Pt. Lookout, MD	CSR
McCarter, J.C.	Sgt	H 18th SCVI	Petersburg, VA	07/30/64	Pt. Lookout, MD	08/08/64	Elmira, NY	P113,P117,P120,CSR
					Elmira, NY	03/14/65	James R., VA Xchg.	P65,P66,CSR
McCarter, M.E.	Pvt	A 3rd SCVABn	High Pt., NC	05/02/65	High Pt., NC	05/02/65	Paroled	CSR
McCarter, Samuel	Pvt	H 6th SCVC	Deserted/enemy	12/04/64	City Point, VA	12/05/64	Baltimore on oath	P8,CSR
McCarter, T.P.	Pvt	A 3rd SCVABn	High Pt., NC	05/02/65	High Pt., NC	05/02/65	Paroled	CSR
McCarter, W.P.	Pvt	A 3rd SCVABn	High Pt., NC	05/02/65	High Pt., NC	05/02/65	Paroled	CSR
McCarthy, Jeremiah	Pvt	H 1st SCVIR	Deserted/enemy	02/23/65	Charleston, SC	03/02/65	Released on oath	SA1,CSR

SOUTH CAROLINA SOLDIERS, SAILORS AND  CITIZENS HELD IN U.S. PRISONS 1861-1865

NAME	RANK	REGIMENT	CAPTURED AT	WHEN	PRISON	MOVED	DISPOSITION	SOURCES
McCarthy, Jesse Y.	Pvt	K 13th SCVI	Petersburg, VA	04/02/65	City Pt., VA	04/04/65	Ft. Delaware, DE	CSR
					Ft. Delaware, DE	06/10/65	Rlsd. G.O. #109	P41,P43,P45,CSR
McCarthy, T.J.	Sgt	C 15th SCVAB	Deserted/enemy	02/21/65	Charleston, SC	02/21/65	Released on oath	CSR
McCarthy, Timothy	Pvt	Lafayette A	Columbia, SC	02/17/65	New Berne, NC	04/10/65	Hart's Island, NY	CSR
					Hart's Island, NY	06/16/65	Rlsd. G.O. #109	P79,CSR
McCarty, James	Pvt	F 1st SCVIG	Petersburg, VA	04/02/65	Pt. Lookout, MD	06/29/65	Rlsd. G.O. #109	P115,P119,SA1
McCarty, John T.	Pvt	C 15th SCVAB	Smith's Ford, NC	03/16/65	New Berne, NC	04/03/65	Pt. Lookout MD	CSR
					Pt. Lookout, MD	06/29/65	Rlsd. G.O. #109	P118,P121,P123,CSR
McCarty, William D.	Pvt	D 14th SCVI	Gettysburg, PA	07/05/63	W. Bldg. Balt., MD	07/30/63	Baltimore Jail	P1,HOE
					Pt. Lookout, MD	02/18/65	Aikens Ldg., VA Xc	P116,P123,P124,HOE
McCaskell, J.W.	Pvt	G 20th SCVI	Richmond, VA Hos.	04/03/65				CSR
McCaskill, C. Wesley	Pvt	F 7th SCVIBn	Weldon RR, VA	08/21/64	City Pt., VA	08/24/64	Pt. Lookout, MD	CSR
					Pt. Lookout, MD	03/14/65	Aikens Ldg., VA Xc	P117,P121,P124,CSR
McCaughrin, Samuel J.	Pvt	E 3rd SCVI	Loudon, TN	12/03/63	Nashville, TN	02/19/64	Louisville, KY	P39,KEB,H3,CSR,SA2
					Louisville, KY	03/02/64	Ft. Delaware, DE	P88,P91,P94
					Camp Chase, OH	09/13/64	Johnson's Isl., OH	P23,P26,CSR
					Johnson's Isl., OH	06/13/65	Rlsd. G.O. #109	P81,P82,P83,CSR
McCauley, Alexander	Pvt	H 16th SCVI	Franklin, TN	12/17/64	Nashville, TN	04/03/65	Louisville, KY	P39,16R,CSR
					Louisville, KY	04/11/65	Camp Chase, OH	CSR
					Camp Chase, TN	06/13/65	Rlsd. G.O. #109	CSR
McCauley, Lewis	Pvt	G 16th SCVI	Yazoo City, MS	07/13/63	Yazoo City, MS	07/13/63	Paroled on oath	CSR,16R
McCauley, Lewis	Pvt	G 16th SCVI	Franklin, TN	12/17/64	Nashville, TN	04/03/65	Louisville, KY	P39,CSR
					Louisville, KY	04/11/65	Camp Chase, OH	P92,P95,CSR
					Camp Chase, TN	06/13/65	Rlsd. G.O. #109	P23,CSR
McClain, Allen W.	Pvt	C 7th SCVIBn	Petersburg, VA	05/06/64	Bermuda Hundred, VA	05/08/64	Fts. Monroe, VA	CSR
					Fts. Monroe, VA	05/13/64	Pt. Lookout, MD	CSR
					Pt. Lookout, MD	05/23/64	Jd. U.S. Army	CSR,P113,P116,P125
McClain, David	Pvt	K 16th SCVI	Alpine, GA	10/19/64	Nashville, TN	10/29/64	Louisville, KY	CSR
					Louisville, KY	10/31/64	Camp Douglas, IL	P90,P91,P95,CSR
					Camp Douglas, IL	05/18/65	Released	P53,CSR
McClain, G.W.	Pvt	F 20th SCVI	Cedar Creek, VA	10/19/64	Harpers Ferry, WV	10/24/64	Pt. Lookout, MD	CSR
					Pt. Lookout, MD	02/10/65	Aikens Ldg., VA Xc	P124,CSR,P118
McClam, Samuel W.	Sgt	H 10th SCVI	Kentucky	09/15/62	Kentucky	11/15/62	Paroled	CSR,RAS
McClam, Thomas L.	Sgt	I 26th SCVI	Petersburg, VA	04/02/65	City Pt., VA	04/05/65	Pt. Lookout, MD	CSR,CTA
					Pt. Lookout, MD	06/29/65	Rlsd. G.O. #109	P115,P118,P121,CSR
McClanahan, F.M.	Pvt	K 6th SCVC	Ream's Stn., VA	08/24/64	Field Hos. USA			CSR
McClary, D.S.	Pvt	C 25th SCVI	Ft. Fisher, NC	01/15/65	New York, NY	01/30/65	Elmira, NY	CSR,CTA
					Elmira, NY	07/11/65	Rlsd. G.O. #109	P65,P66,CSR
McClary, John Calvin	Pvt	I 4th SCVC	Cypress Springs, VA	09/29/64	P.M. 5th A.C.	09/30/64	City Pt., VA	CSR
					City Pt., VA	10/03/64	Pt. Lookout, MD	CSR
					Pt. Lookout, MD	10/30/64	City Pt., VA Xc	P118,P121,P123,CSR
McClary, S.B.	Pvt	I 4th SCVC	Petersburg, VA	10/27/64	City Pt., VA	10/31/64	Pt. Lookout, MD	CSR
					Pt. Lookout, MD	01/17/65	Exchanged	P115,P124,CSR
McClary, S.J.	Pvt	I 4th SCVC	Petersburg, VA	10/27/64	City Pt., VA	10/31/64	Pt. Lookout, MD	CSR,CTA
					Pt. Lookout, MD	03/28/65	Aikens Ldg., VA Xc	P115,P121,P124,CSR
McClary, William David	Pvt	C 25th SCVI	Town Creek, NC	02/20/65	Ft. Anderson, NC	02/28/65	Pt. Lookout, MD	CSR,CTA,HAG
					Pt. Lookout, MD	06/29/65	Rlsd. G.O. #109	P1,P118,P121,P123
McCleery, Robert	Sgt	E 16th SCVI	Yazoo City, MS	07/13/63	Yazoo City, MS	07/13/63	Paroled on oath	CSR
McClellan, John Milton	Pvt	B P.S.S.	Knoxville, TN	11/24/63	Knoxville, TN	11/26/63	Died of wounds	P5,CSR,TSE
McClellan, John S.	Pvt	L 1st SCVIG	Warrenton, VA	09/29/62	Warrenton, VA	09/29/62	Paroled	CSR,SA1
McClellan, John T.	Sgt	L 2nd SCVIRi	Richmond, VA	04/05/65	Libby Prison Rchmd.	04/08/65	City Pt., VA P.M.	CSR
					City Pt., VA	04/13/65	Pt. Lookout, MD	CSR

SOUTH CAROLINA SOLDIERS, SAILORS AND  CITIZENS HELD IN U.S. PRISONS 1861-1865

NAME	RANK	REGIMENT	CAPTURED AT	WHEN	PRISON	MOVED	DISPOSITION	SOURCES
McClellan, John T.	Sgt	B 2nd SCVIRi	Richmond, VA	04/03/65	Pt. Lookout, MD	06/29/65	Rlsd. G.O. #109	P119,P122,P123,CSR
McClellan, P.C.	Pvt	I 21st SCVI	Ft. Fisher, NC	01/15/65	Elmira, NY	03/02/65	Died, Ch. Diarrhea	P6,P12,P65,P66,FPH
McClellan, T.P.	Pvt	F Hol. Leg.	Jarratts Stn., VA	05/08/64	Fts. Monroe, VA	05/13/64	Pt. Lookout, MD	CSR
					Pt. Lookout, MD	08/15/64	Elmira, NY	P113,P116,CSR
					Elmira, NY	03/02/65	James R., VA Xc	P65,P66,CSR
					Richmond, VA Hos.	03/09/65	Furloughed 30 days	CSR
McClellan, William P.	Sgt	F Hol. Leg.	Jarratts Stn., VA	05/08/64	Fts. Monroe, VA	05/13/64	Pt. Lookout, MD	CSR
					Pt. Lookout, MD	08/15/64	Elmira, NY	P113,P116
					Elmira, NY	10/11/64	Died, Typhoid Fev.	P5,P12,P65,P66,FPH
McClenaghan, George S.	Sgt	E 1st SCVIG	Hatchers Run, VA	04/02/65	City Pt., VA	04/07/65	Hart's Island, NY	CSR
					Hart's Island, NY	06/16/65	Rlsd. G.O. #109	P79,SA1,CSR
McClendon, F.P.	Pvt	A 22nd SCVI	Bermuda Hundred, VA	06/15/64	Bermuda Hundred, VA	06/15/64	Fts. Monroe, VA	CSR
					Fts. Monroe, VA	06/18/64	Pt. Lookout, MD	CSR
					Pt. Lookout, MD	07/09/64	Elmira, NY	P113,P117,P120,CSR
McClendon, F.P.	Pvt	A 22nd SCVI	Bermuda Hundred, VA	06/15/64	Elmira, NY	04/07/65	Died, Ch. Diarrhea	P6,P65,P66,FPH,CSR
McClendon, J.M.	Pvt	G 21st SCVI	Morris Island, SC	07/10/63	Hilton Head, SC	09/19/63	Ft. Columbus, NY	CSR,HAG
					Ft. Columbus, NY	09/26/63	Pt. Lookout, MD	P1,CSR
					Pt. Lookout, MD	01/25/64	Died, Ch. Diarrhea	P5,P116,P119,FPH
McClendon, L.L.	Pvt	I 5th SCVC	Augusta, GA	05/20/65	Augusta, GA	05/20/65	Paroled	CSR
McClimons, John P.	Pvt	F 1st SCVA	Smith's Ferry, NC	03/16/65	Pt. Lookout, MD	05/09/65	Died, Ch. Diarrhea	P6,P115,P118,FPH,CSR
McClintoch, Joseph	Pvt	H 24th SCVI	Nashville, TN	12/16/64	Nashville, TN	12/19/64	Louisville, KY	CSR
					Louisville, KY	12/24/64	Camp Douglas, IL	CSR
					Camp Douglas, IL	06/16/65	Rlsd. G.O. #109	CSR
McClintock, John H.	Cpl	H 24th SCVI	Franklin, TN	12/18/64	Nashville, TN	03/01/65	Louisville, KY	P4,P39,HHC
					Louisville, KY G.H.	03/07/65	Died, Smallpox	P6,P92,P95,CSR,FPH
McClintock, Joseph C.	Pvt	E 24th SCVI	Nashville, TN	12/16/64	Nashville, TN	01/01/65	Louisville, KY	P39,CSR,HHC
					Louisville, KY	01/04/65	Camp Chase, OH	P92,P95,CSR
					Camp Chase, OH	06/12/65	Rlsd. G.O. #109	P23,CSR
McCloud, D.J.	Pvt	B 5th SCResB	Camden, SC	04/18/65	Charleston, SC	04/27/65	Confined P.M.	CSR
McCluney, James	Pvt	D 3rd SCVIBn	South Mtn., MD	09/14/62	Provost Marshal	10/06/62	Ft. McHenry, MD	CSR
					Ft. McHenry, MD	10/13/62	Fts. Monroe, VA	CSR
McCluney, James	Pvt	D 3rd SCVIBn	South Mtn., MD	09/14/62	Fts. Monroe, VA	10/17/62	Aikens Ldg., VA Xc	CSR
McCluney, Thomas	Pvt	B 4th SCVC	Stony Creek, VA	12/01/64	City Pt., VA	12/05/64	Pt. Lookout, MD	CSR
					Pt. Lookout, MD	06/15/65	Rlsd. G.O. #109	P118,CSR
McClung, Charles	Cpl	G Hol. Leg.	Warrenton, VA	09/29/62	Warrenton, VA	09/29/62	Paroled/ Hospital	CSR
McClung, Charles	Cpl	G Hol. Leg.	Five Forks, VA	04/01/65	City Pt., VA	04/05/65	Pt. Lookout, MD	CSR
					Pt. Lookout, MD	06/29/65	Rlsd. G.O. #109	P118,CSR
McClung, Robert	Pvt	G Hol. Leg.	Five Forks, VA	04/01/65	City Pt., VA	04/05/65	Pt. Lookout, MD	CSR,ANY
					Pt. Lookout, MD	06/29/65	Rlsd. G.O. #109	P115,P118,P122,CSR
McCluny, J.L.	Pvt	E 5th SCVI	Williamsburg, VA	05/31/62	Fts. Monroe, VA			CSR
McClure, Charles D.	Pvt	F 13th SCVI	Richmond, VA Hos.	04/03/64	Pt. Lookout, MD	07/07/65	Rlsd. G.O. #109	P119,HOS,CSR
McClure, David	Pvt	F 13th SCVI	Southside RR, VA	04/02/65	City Pt., VA	04/07/65	Hart's Island, NY	CSR,HOS
					Hart's Island, NY	06/16/65	Rlsd. G.O. #109	P79,CSR
McClure, I.	Pvt	E 7th SCVI	Charlotte, NC	04/26/65	Charlotte, NC	04/26/65	Paroled	CSR
McClure, John	Pvt	G 2nd SCVI	Falling Waters, MD	07/14/63	Ft. McHenry, MD	07/08/63	Ft. Delaware, DE	P96,H2,SA2,KEB
					Ft. Delaware, DE	05/10/65	Released	P40,P42,P44,P46
McClure, John E.	Pvt	F 13th SCVI	Southside RR, VA	04/02/65	City Pt., VA	04/07/65	Hart's Island, NY	CSR,HOS
					Hart's Island, NY	06/16/65	Rlsd. G.O. #109	P79,CSR
McClure, John R.	Pvt	I 1st SCVIG	Gettysburg, PA	07/03/63	David's Island, NY	09/05/63	City Pt., VA Xc	P1,SA1,CSR
McClure, John R.	Pvt	I 1st SCVIG	Petersburg, VA	04/02/65	City Pt., VA	04/07/64	Pt. Lookout, MD	CSR
					Pt. Lookout, MD	06/29/65	Rlsd. G.O. #109	P115,P118,CSR
McClure, T.H.	Pvt	E 1st SCVA	Raleigh, NC Hos.	04/13/65	Raleigh, NC Hos.	04/13/65	Paroled	CSR

SOUTH CAROLINA SOLDIERS, SAILORS AND  CITIZENS HELD IN U.S. PRISONS 1861-1865

NAME	RANK	REGIMENT	CAPTURED AT	WHEN	PRISON	MOVED	DISPOSITION	SOURCES
McClure, Thomas J.	Pvt	D 2nd SCVIRi	Knoxville, TN	12/03/63	Louisville, KY	12/31/63	Rock Island, IL	P88,P89,P94,CSR
					Rock Island, IL	03/07/64	Died, Lung Inflam.	P12
McClusky, W.H.	Pvt	C 20th SCVI	Anderson, SC	05/19/65	Anderson, SC	05/19/65	Paroled	CSR
McColl, Alex	Pvt	K 8th SCVI	Richmond, VA Hos.	04/03/65	Richmond, VA		Paroled	CSR
McComb, J.A.	Pvt	F Hol. Leg.	Five Forks, VA	04/01/65	Pt. Lookout, MD	06/29/65	Rlsd. G.O. #109	P115
McCombs, Morgan C.	Pvt	K 18th SCVI	Petersburg, VA	07/30/64	City Pt., VA	08/05/64	Pt. Lookout, MD	CSR
					Pt. Lookout, MD	08/08/64	Elmira, NY	P113,P117,P120,CSR
					Elmira, NY	09/04/64	Died, Diarrhea	P5,P65,P66,FPH,CSR
McConnell, A.C.	Sgt	G 3rd SCVIBn	South Mtn., MD	09/14/62	Ft. Delaware, DE	10/02/62	Aikens Ldg., VA Xc	CSR
McConnell, A.C.	Sgt	G 3rd SCVIBn	Knoxville, TN	11/18/63	Knoxville, TN USGH	03/25/64	Died of wounds	P1,P5,P12,KEB,CSR
McConnell, James H.	Sgt	D Orr's Ri.	Petersburg, VA	04/03/65	City Pt., VA	04/11/65	Hart's Island, NY	CSR
					Hart's Island, NY	06/16/65	Rlsd. G.O. #109	P79,CSR
McCord, J.L.	Pvt	F Hol. Leg.	Jarratts Stn., VA	05/08/64	Fts. Monroe, VA	05/13/64	Pt. Lookout, MD	CSR
					Pt. Lookout, MD	08/15/64	Elmira, NY	P113,P116,CSR
					Elmira, NY	06/21/65	Rlsd. G.O. #109	P65,P66,CSR
McCord, James A.	Pvt	F Hol. Leg.	Petersburg, VA	11/06/64	City Pt., VA	11/11/64	Washington, DC	CSR
					Pt. Lookout, MD	06/29/65	Rlsd. G.O. #109	P115,P118,CSR
McCord, John Augustus	Pvt	F Hol. Leg.	Five Forks, VA	04/01/65	City Pt., VA	04/05/65	Pt. Lookout, MD	CSR
					Pt. Lookout, MD	06/29/65	Rlsd. G.O. #109	P118,CSR
McCord, S.B.	Cpl	C 3rd SCVABn	Blakely, AL	04/09/65	Ship Island, MS	05/01/65	Vicksburg, MS Xc	P136,CSR
McCorkle, J.F.	Pvt	D 25th SCVI	Ft. Fisher, NC	01/15/65	New York, NY	01/30/65	Elmira, NY	CSR,HMC,HAG
					Elmira, NY	07/07/65	Rlsd. G.O. #109	P65,P66,CSR
McCormack, E.	Pvt	D 3rd SCVABn	Deserted/enemy	03/15/65	Charleston, SC	03/15/65	Released on oath	CSR
McCormack, Henry J.	Pvt	L 1st SCVIG	Falling Waters, MD	07/14/63	Old Capitol, DC	08/08/63	Pt. Lookout, MD	CSR
					Ft. McHenry, MD	08/08/63	Pt. Lookout, MD	P110,SA1
					Pt. Lookout, MD	03/03/64	City Pt., VA Xc	P7,P113,P116,P123
McCormack, Henry J.	Pvt	L 1st SCVIG	Petersburg, VA	04/02/65	Pt. Lookout, MD	06/29/65	Rlsd. G.O. #109	P1,P115,P118,P121
McCormack, John E.	Pvt	E 24th SCVI	Nashville, TN	12/16/64	Nashville, TN	12/31/64	Louisville, KY	CSR
					Louisville, KY	01/02/65	Camp Chase, OH	CSR
					Camp Chase, OH	06/12/65	Rlsd. G.O. #109	P23,CSR
McCormack, Joseph W.	Pvt	E 24th SCVI	Franklin, TN	12/17/64	Nashville, TN	01/01/65	Louisville, KY	P4,P39,CSR
					Louisville, KY	01/09/65	Camp Chase, OH	P92,P95,COT,CSR
					Camp Chase, OH	06/13/65	Rlsd. G.O. #109	P23,CSR
McCormick, George	Pvt	A 1st SCVIH	Deserted/enemy	10/08/64	Bermuda Hundred, VA	10/09/64	City Pt., VA P.M.	CSR,SA1
					City Pt., VA P.M.	10/11/64	Washington, DC	CSR
					Washington, DC	10/12/64	Cincinnati, OH	CSR
McCormick, J.E.	Pvt	E 26th SCVI	Deserted/enemy	01/24/65	City Point, VA	01/25/65	Washington, DC	P8,CSR
					Washington, DC	01/30/65	Philadelphia, PA	CSR
McCormick, W.B.	Pvt	E 26th SCVI	Deserted/enemy	01/24/65	City Point, VA	01/25/65	Washington, DC	P8,CSR
					Washington, DC	01/30/65	Philadelphia, PA	CSR
McCorquodale, J.S.	Sgt	B 20th SCVI	Cedar Creek, VA	10/19/64	Harpers Ferry, WV	11/01/64	Pt. Lookout, MD	CSR,KEB
					Pt. Lookout, MD	03/17/65	Aikens Ldg., VA Xc	P118,P121,CSR
					Pt. Lookout, MD	03/28/65	Exchanged	P115,P124,CSR
McCosh, R.H.	Cpt	K 18th SCVI	Saylors Creek, VA	04/06/65	Old Capitol, DC	04/17/65	Johnson's Isl., OH	P110
					Johnson's Isl., OH	06/19/65	Rlsd. G.O. #109	P81,P82,CSR
McCowan, F.M.	Pvt	F 15th SCVI	South Mtn., MD	09/12/62	Frederick, MD USGH	09/21/62	Died of wounds	FPH,P6,BOD,KEB,H15,CSR
McCoy, Albert	Pvt	F 3rd SCVI	Cedar Creek, VA	10/19/64	Harpers Ferry, WV	10/25/64	Pt. Lookout, MD	CSR,KEB,SA2,H3
					Pt. Lookout, MD	03/28/65	Aikens Ldg., VA Xc	CSR
McCoy, Charles D.	Pvt	E 8th SCVI	Winchester, VA	09/13/64	Camp Chase, OH	02/25/65	Died, Pneumonia	P6,P23,P27,FPH,KEB
McCoy, Edwin C.	Pvt	B 1st SCVIG	Warrenton, VA	09/29/62	Warrenton, VA	09/29/62	Paroled	SA1,CSR
McCoy, Ira D.	Pvt	A 3rd SCVABn	High Pt., NC	05/02/65	High Pt., NC	05/02/65	Paroled on oath	CSR
McCoy, J.N.	Pvt	G 3rd SCVABn	High Pt., NC	05/02/65	High Pt., NC	05/02/65	Paroled on oath	CSR

SOUTH CAROLINA SOLDIERS, SAILORS AND  CITIZENS HELD IN U.S. PRISONS 1861-1865

NAME	RANK	REGIMENT	CAPTURED AT	WHEN	PRISON	MOVED	DISPOSITION	SOURCES
McCoy, Jacob M.	Pvt	E 8th SCVI	Spotsylvania, VA	05/08/64	Belle Plain, VA	05/21/64	Ft. Delaware, DE	CSR
					Ft. Delaware, DE	06/10/65	Released	CSR
McCoy, James F.	Pvt	K 6th SCVI	Richmond, VA Hos.	04/03/65	Libby Prison, Rchmd.	04/23/65	Newport News, VA	CSR
					Newport News, VA	05/15/65	Died, Heart Dis.	P6,P12,P107,PP,CSR
McCoy, Kelly C.	Pvt	L 2nd SCVIRi	Richmond, VA	06/28/62	Harrisons Ldg., VA	07/03/62	Ft. Columbus, NY	CSR
					Ft. Columbus, NY	07/09/62	Ft. Delaware, DE	CSR
					Ft. Delaware, DE	08/05/62	Aikens Ldg., VA Xc	CSR
McCoy, Samuel T.	Pvt	E 3rd SCVI	Sharpsburg, MD	09/17/62	Lavinia Groves Fm.	09/17/62	Died of wounds	P12,H3,ANY
McCoy, Thomas	Pvt	I 1st SCVIG	Gettysburg, PA	07/05/63	Ft. Delaware, DE	07/24/64	Hos 7/24-9/18/64	P47,SA1
					Ft. Delaware, DE	09/18/64	Aikens Ldg., VA Xc	P40,P42,P44,SA1,CSR
McCoy, William A.	Pvt	G 1st SCVA	Deserted/enemy	02/07/64	Charleston, SC		Released on oath	CSR
McCracken, Langdon C.	Pvt	C 3rd SCVI	Cedar Creek, VA	10/19/64	Harpers Ferry, WV	10/28/64	Pt. Lookout, MD	CSR,SA2,ANY,KEB,H3
					Pt. Lookout, MD	03/28/65	Aikens Ldg., VA Xc	P118,P121,P124,CSR
McCracken, R.Y. Hayne	Pvt	D 13th SCVI	Gettysburg, PA	07/05/63	Chester, PA G.H.	08/04/63	Died, 2nd Hemorrhage	P1,P6,P12,ANY,CSR
McCracken, William	Pvt	G 1st SCVA	Fayetteville, NC	03/10/65	New Berne, NC	04/05/65	Pt. Lookout MD	CSR
					Pt. Lookout, MD	06/26/65	Rlsd. G.O. #109	P115,P118,P123,CSR
McCracken, Wilson W.	Pvt	B 10th SCVI	Nashville, TN	12/16/64	Nashville, TN	12/31/64	Louisville, KY	CSR,RAS
					Louisville, KY	01/02/65	Camp Chase, OH	CSR
					Camp Chase, OH	02/21/65	Died, Pneumonia	P6,P12,P23,P27,FPH
McCrady, J.P.	Pvt	D 27th SCVI	Weldon RR, VA	08/21/64	City Pt., VA	08/24/64	Pt. Lookout, MD	CSR,HAG
					Pt. Lookout, MD	03/15/65	Aikens Ldg., VA Xc	P117,P123,P124,CSR
McCrady, James B.	Pvt	F Hol. Leg.	Petersburg, VA	11/05/64	City Pt., VA	11/11/64	Pt. Lookout, MD	CSR
					Pt. Lookout, MD	04/06/65	Died, Consumption	P6,P115P118,FPH
McCrary, Andrew M.	Pvt	F 2nd SCVIRi	Benton, TN	11/30/63	Nashville, TN	12/10/63	Louisville, KY	P39,CSR,UD5
					Louisville, KY	12/11/63	Rock Island, IL	P88,P89,CSR
					Rock Island, IL	05/03/65	New Orleans, LA Xc	CSR
					New Orleans, LA	05/23/65	Exchanged	P4,CSR
McCrary, James	Cpl	H 1st SCVA	Deserted/enemy		Chattanooga, TN	03/22/64	Took oath	CSR
McCravey, J.D.	Pvt	Brooks LA	Harpers Farm, VA	04/06/65	City Pt., VA	04/14/65	Pt. Lookout, MD	CSR
					Pt. Lookout, MD	06/29/65	Rlsd. G.O. #109	P123,CSR
McCrea, James Arthur	Pvt	I 4th SCVC	Louisa C.H., VA	06/11/64	Fts. Monroe, VA	06/20/64	Pt. Lookout, MD	CSR,CTA
					Pt. Lookout, MD	07/25/64	Elmira, NY	P113,P117,P120,CSR
					Elmira, NY	06/14/65	Rlsd. G.O. #109	P65,P66,CSR
McCrellers, Marion	Pvt	6th SCResB	Cheraw, SC	03/05/65	Cheraw, SC	03/05/65	Paroled	CSR
McCrory, J.L.	2Lt	B 4th SCVC	Old Church, VA	05/30/64	White House, VA	06/08/64	Pt. Lookout, MD	CSR,HHC
					Pt. Lookout, MD	06/23/64	Ft. Delaware, DE	P113,P117,P120,CSR
					Ft. Delaware, DE	08/21/64	Died, Lung Inflam.	P5,P43,P44,P47,FPH
McCue, David	Pvt	B 15th SCVAB	Smithfield, NC	03/16/65	New Berne, NC	04/03/65	Pt. Lookout, MD	CSR
					Pt. Lookout, MD	06/15/65	Rlsd. G.O. #109	P115,CSR
McCulloch, J.	Pvt	G 18th SCVI	Farmville, VA	04/06/65	City Pt., VA	04/14/65	Newport News, VA	CSR
					Newport News, VA	06/13/65	Rlsd. G.O. #109	P107,CSR
McCullough, James W.	Pvt	D 14th SCVI	Brandy Stn., VA	08/01/63	Old Capitol, DC	08/15/63	Baltimore, MD	CSR,HOE
					Ft. McHenry, MD	08/23/63	Pt. Lookout, MD	P110,CSR
					Pt. Lookout, MD	02/24/65	Aikens Ldg., VA Xc	P116,P123,P124,CSR
					Richmond, VA	03/05/65	Furloughed 30 days	CSR
McCullough, John	Pvt	B 4th SCVC	Louisa C.H., VA	06/11/64	Fts. Monroe, VA	06/20/64	Pt. Lookout, MD	HHC,CSR
					Pt. Lookout, MD	07/25/64	Elmira, NY	P113,P117,P120,CSR
					Elmira, NY	08/15/64	Died, Ch. Diarrhea	P5,P65,P66,FPH,HHC,CSR
McCullough, M.F.S.	Sgt	G 18th SCVI	Crater, Pbg., VA	07/30/64	City Pt., VA	08/05/64	Pt. Lookout, MD	CSR
McCullough, M.F.S.	Sgt	G 18th SCVI	Petersburg, VA	07/30/64	Pt. Lookout, MD	08/08/64	Elmira, NY	P113,P117,P120,CSR
					Elmira, NY	07/03/65	Rlsd. G.O. #109	P65,P66,CSR

M

SOUTH CAROLINA SOLDIERS, SAILORS AND CITIZENS HELD IN U.S. PRISONS 1861-1865

NAME	RANK	REGIMENT	CAPTURED AT	WHEN	PRISON	MOVED	DISPOSITION	SOURCES
McCullough, Samuel P.	Pvt	H 12th SCVI	Sutherland Stn. VA	04/03/65	City Pt., VA	04/13/65	Pt. Lookout, MD	CSR
					Pt. Lookout, MD	06/15/65	Rlsd. G.O. #109	P115,CSR,YEB
McCullough, Thomas	Cpl	B 4th SCVC	Louisa C.H., VA	06/11/64	Fts. Monroe, VA	06/20/64	Pt. Lookout, MD	CSR,HHC
					Pt. Lookout, MD	07/25/64	Elmira, NY	P113,P117,P120,CSR
					Elmira, NY	08/18/64	Died, Scurvy	P5,P65,P66,FPH,CSR
McCully, H.C.	Pvt	A 17th SCVI	Burkesville, VA	04/14/65	Burkesville, VA	04/17/65	Paroled	CSR
McCully, J.W.	Pvt	B 5th SCVI	Richmond, VA Hos.	04/03/65	Provost Marshal	04/20/65		CSR
McCully, N.A.	2Lt	C P.S.S.	Richmond, VA area	06/28/62	Ft. Columbus, NY	07/09/62	Ft. Delaware, DE	CSR,TSE
					Ft. Delaware, DE	08/05/62	Aikens Ldg., VA Xc	CSR
McCully, William M.	Pvt	A 12th SCVI	Warrenton, VA	09/29/62	Warrenton, VA	09/29/62	Paroled	CSR
McCurry, John S.	Pvt	I 14th SCVI	Gettysburg, PA	07/02/63	David's Island, NY	09/12/63	Died, Amp. L. thigh	P1,P6,P12,FPH,CSR
McCurry, John W.	Pvt	I 14th SCVI	Petersburg, MD	04/03/65	City Pt., VA	04/11/65	Hart's Island, NY	CSR
					Hart's Island, NY	06/16/65	Rlsd. G.O. #109	P79,CSR
McCutchen, T.J.	Pvt	I 4th SCVC	Louisa C.H., VA	06/11/64	Fts. Monroe, VA	06/20/64	Pt. Lookout, MD	CSR
					Pt. Lookout, MD	07/25/64	Elmira, NY	P113,P117,P120,CSR
					Elmira, NY	06/16/65	Rlsd. G.O. #109	P65,P66,CSR
McCutcheon, R.G.	Pvt	A Ham. Leg. MI	Petersburg, VA Hos.	04/03/65	Petersburg, VA Hos.	05/01/65	Pt. O Rocks, VA USG	CSR
McDaniel, E.C.	Pvt	15th SCVI			Ft. Delaware, DE	06/10/65		H15,CSR
McDaniel, J.J.	Pvt	D 2nd SCVIRi	Richmond, VA Hos.	04/03/65	Richmond, VA Hos.	04/09/65	Pt. Lookout, MD Hos.	CSR
					Pt. Lookout, MD	05/17/65	Died, Ch. Diarrhea	P12,P119,CSR
McDaniel, J.L.	Pvt	B 12th SCVI	Falling Waters, MD	07/14/63	Baltimore, MD	08/21/63	Pt. Lookout, MD	CSR
					Pt. Lookout, MD	04/27/64	City Pt., VA Xc	P113,P116,CSR
McDaniel, J.R.	Pvt	I 21st SCVI	Ft. Fisher, NC	01/15/65	Elmira, NY	06/11/65	Died, Pneumonia	P6,P12,P65,P66,FPH
McDaniel, James R.	Pvt	K 8th SCVI	Loudon, TN	12/03/63	Chattanooga, TN G.H.			P1,KEB,HOM
					Ft. Delaware, DE		Hos 4/29-5/16/65	P47
					Nashville, TN	02/19/64	Louisville, KY	P39,CSR
					Louisville, KY	03/01/64	Ft. Delaware, DE	P88,P91,P94,CSR
					Ft. Delaware, DE	06/08/65	Rlsd. G.O. #109	P41,P43,P45,CSR
McDaniel, Randall	Pvt	I 1st SCVIH	Chattanooga, TN	10/29/63	Nashville, TN	11/07/63	Louisville, KY	P39,CSR
					Louisville, KY	11/09/63	Camp Morton, IN	P88,P89,P93,CSR
					Camp Morton, IN	03/15/65	Pt. Lookout, MD Xc	P100,CSR
McDaniel, Samuel	Pvt	C 1st SCVA	Fayetteville, NC	03/16/65	New Berne, NC	03/30/65	Pt. Lookout, MD	CSR
					Pt. Lookout, MD	06/29/65	Rlsd. G.O. #109	P1,P118,P121,CSR
McDaniel, W.Y	Pvt	C 14th SCVI	Petersburg, VA	04/03/65	City Pt., VA	04/13/65	Pt. Lookout, MD	CSR
					Pt. Lookout, MD	06/05/65	Released G.O. #85	P115,P119,P121,CSR
McDavid, Peter A.	1Lt	L 2nd SCVIRi	Deep Bottom, VA	08/14/64	Fts. Monroe, VA Hos.	08/29/64	Exchanged	CSR
McDavitt, John M.	Pvt	C 27th SCVI	Deserted/enemy	05/08/64	Fts. Monroe, VA	06/02/64	Released on oath	P8,HAG,CSR
McDermott, James	Pvt	A 1st SCVA	Robeson County, NC	03/16/65	New Berne, NC	04/25/65	Camp Hamilton, VA	CSR
					Camp Hamilton, VA	05/01/65	Newport News, VA	CSR
					Newport News, VA	06/26/65	Rlsd. G.O. #109	CSR
McDill, W.W.	Pvt	F 2nd SCVIRi	Knoxville, TN	12/15/63	Knoxville, TN USGH	12/21/63	Died, Ch. Diarrhea	P1,P5,CSR
McDill, William Henry	Pvt	G Orr's Ri.	Petersburg, VA	04/03/65	City Pt., VA	04/11/65	Hart's Island, NY	CSR
					Hart's Island, NY	06/16/65	Rlsd. G.O. #109	P79,CSR
McDonald, A.A.	Pvt	C 27th SCVI	Petersburg, VA	06/24/64	Bermuda Hundred, VA	06/24/64	Fts. Monroe, VA	CSR,HAG
					Fts. Monroe, VA	06/27/64	Pt. Lookout, MD	CSR
					Pt. Lookout, MD	03/14/65	Exchanged	CSR
					Pt. Lookout, MD	04/22/65	Died	P113,P117,CSR
McDonald, A.M.	Sgt	C 2nd SCVIRi	Deserted/enemy	03/03/65	Bermuda Hundred, VA	03/04/65	City Pt., VA P.M.	CSR
					City Pt., VA P.M.	03/07/65	Washington, DC P.M.	CSR
					Washington, DC P.M.	03/08/65	Columbus, OH/ oath	CSR

M

SOUTH CAROLINA SOLDIERS, SAILORS AND CITIZENS HELD IN U.S. PRISONS 1861-1865

NAME	RANK	REGIMENT	CAPTURED AT	WHEN	PRISON	MOVED	DISPOSITION	SOURCES
McDonald, E.B.	Pvt	C 17th SCVI	Deserted/enemy	02/26/65	P.M. A. of P.	02/26/65	City Pt., VA	CSR
					City Pt., VA	02/28/65	Washington, DC	CSR
					Washingon, DC	03/01/65	Danville, PA oath	CSR
McDonald, George	Smn	Dis. Boat	Morris Island, SC	09/04/63	Ft. Delaware, DE	07/19/64	Hos 7/19-7/25/64	P47
					Ft. Lafayette, NY	04/19/64	Ft. Delaware, DE	P144
McDonald, Henry	Smn	Dis. Boat	Morris Island, SC	09/07/63	Ft. Columbus, NY	03/07/64	Ft. Lafayette, NY	P2
McDonald, James	Smn	CSS *Chicora*	Morris Island, SC	09/07/63	Pt. Lookout, MD	01/21/64	Joined U.S. Army	P113
McDonald, James	Pvt	K 1st SCVIG	Sutherland Stn., VA	04/03/65	City Pt., VA	04/13/65	Pt. Lookout, MD	CSR
					Pt. Lookout, MD	06/29/65	Rlsd. G.O. #109	P119,P121,P123,CSR
McDonald, Thomas W.	Cpl	K 23rd SCVI	Five Forks, VA	04/01/65	City Pt., VA	04/05/65	Pt. Lookout, MD	CSR,UD5
					Pt. Lookout, MD	06/29/65	Rlsd. G.O. #109	P115,P118,P122,CSR
McDonald, William	Pvt	B 21st SCVI	Petersburg, VA	06/24/64	Bermuda Hundred, VA	06/25/64	Fts. Monroe, VA	CSR,HAG
					Fts. Monroe, VA	06/26/64	Pt. Lookout, MD	CSR
					Pt. Lookout, MD	08/16/64	Elmira, NY	P113,P117,P120,CSR
					Elmira, NY	02/25/65	Pt. Lookout, MD Xc	P65,P66,CSR
McDougal, R.	Pvt	K 7th SCVI	Sharpsburg, MD	10/01/62	Ft. McHenry, MD	10/13/62	Fts. Monroe, VA Xc	CSR
McDow, H. Johnston	Pvt	I 17th SCVI	Boonesboro, MD	09/15/62	Frederick, MD	09/23/62	Died of wounds	P12,LAN,CSR
McDowell, Benjamin F.	Pvt	K 24th SCVI	Graysville, GA	11/27/63	Nashville, TN	12/11/63	Louisville, KY	P39,CSR
					Louisville, KY	12/12/63	Rock Island, IL	P88,P89,CSR
					Rock Island, IL	02/16/64	Died, Infirmity	P131,P132,CSR,FPH
McDowell, Charles J.	Pvt	A 2nd SCVC	Brandy Stn., VA	08/01/63	Ft. McHenry, MD	11/23/64	Ft. Delaware, DE	P110,HIC
					Old Capitol, DC	11/25/64	Ft. Delaware, DE	CSR
McDowell, Charles J.	Pvt	A 2nd SCVC	Brandy Stn., VA	08/01/63	Ft. Delaware, DE	06/10/65	Rlsd. G.O. #109	P41,P43,P45,CSR
McDowell, J.C.	Pvt	K 5th SCVI	Deserted/enemy	03/14/65	Bermuda Hundred, VA	03/24/65	Washington, DC P.M.	CSR
					Washington, DC	03/24/65	Cleveland, OH oath	CSR
McDowell, J.E.	Pvt	A 2nd SCVC	Cheraw, SC	03/05/65	Cheraw, SC	03/05/65	Paroled	CSR
McDowell, J.K.	Pvt	H 12th SCVI	Wilderness, VA	05/06/64	Belle Plain, VA	05/20/64	Ft. Delaware, DE	CSR,YEB
					Ft. Delaware, DE	05/08/65	Hos 5/4-6/4/65	P47
					Ft. Delaware, DE	02/17/65	Hos 2/17-3/7/65	P47
					Ft. Delaware, DE	06/10/65	Rlsd. G.O. #109	P41,P43,P45,CSR
McDowell, John E.C.	Sgt	G 2nd SCVI	Cedar Creek, VA	10/19/64	Harpers Ferry, WV	10/24/64	Pt. Lookout, MD	CSR,KEB,SA2,H2
					Pt. Lookout, MD	03/28/65	Aikens Ldg., VA Xc	P118,P121,P124,CSR
McDowell, Patrick H.	Pvt	B Orr's Ri.	Petersburg, VA	04/02/65	City Pt., VA	04/04/65	Old Capitol, DC	P6,P110,CDC,CSR
					Old Capitol, DC	04/14/65	Died of wounds	P6,P110,CSR
McDowell, R.J.	Pvt	B 15th SCVAB	Chester, SC	05/05/65	Chester, SC	05/05/65	Paroled	CSR
McDowell, Robert A.	Pvt	K Ham. Leg. MI	Westover Ch., VA	08/07/64	Fts. Monroe, VA	08/24/64	Pt. Lookout, MD	CSR
					Pt. Lookout, MD	03/15/65	Aikens Ldg., VA Xc	P1,P117,P121,P124
McDowell, W.J.	Pvt	K 5th SCVI	Sharpsburg, MD	09/17/62	Ft. McHenry, MD	10/14/62	Aikens Ldg., VA Xc	CSR,SA3
McDowell, William A.	Pvt	L 1st SCVIG	Falling Waters, MD	07/14/63	Old Capitol, DC	08/08/63	Pt. Lookout, MD	CSR,SA1
					Ft. McHenry, MD	08/08/63	Pt. Lookout, MD	P110
					Pt. Lookout, MD	03/03/64	City Pt., VA Xc	P116,P123,P124,CSR
McDrew, John	Pvt	E 1st SCVIR	Averysboro, NC	03/16/65	Pt. Lookout, MD	05/29/65	Died, Ch. Diarrhea	P6,P118,P119,FPH
McEachern, William C.	Pvt	G 20th SCVI	Cedar Creek, VA	10/19/64	Harpers Ferry, WV	10/24/64	Pt. Lookout, MD	CSR
					Pt. Lookout, MD	05/16/65	Rlsd. G.O. #85	P115,P118,P121,CSR
McElrath, John	Pvt	B 27th SCVI	Town Creek, NC	02/20/65	Ft. Anderson, NC	02/28/65	Pt. Lookout, MD	CSR
					Pt. Lookout, MD	06/06/65	Rlsd. Instr. 5/30/65	P115,P118,P121,CSR
McElrath, M.S.	Pvt	C 22nd SCVI	Sutherland Stn., VA	04/02/65	Fair Gds. Hos. Pbg.	04/17/65	Pt. of Rocks G.H.	CSR,HOS
					Pt. of Rocks G.H.	04/21/65	City Pt., VA	CSR
					City Pt., VA	04/23/65	Newport News, VA	CSR
					Newport News, VA	06/13/65	Rlsd. G.O. #109	P107
McElrath, Marion	Pvt	B 22nd SCVI	Deserted/Enemy	02/25/65	City Pt., VA	02/28/65	Washington, DC	CSR
					Washington, DC	03/01/65	Oil City, PA oath	CSR

SOUTH CAROLINA SOLDIERS, SAILORS AND  CITIZENS HELD IN U.S. PRISONS 1861-1865

NAME	RANK	REGIMENT	CAPTURED AT	WHEN	PRISON	MOVED	DISPOSITION	SOURCES
McElrath, Michael	Pvt	E 2nd SCVC	Bear Creek, NC	03/21/65	New Berne, NC	03/26/65	Pt. Lookout, MD	CSR
					Pt. Lookout, MD	06/29/65	Rlsd. G.O. #109	P118,P121,P123,CSR
McElveen, George G.	Cpl	K 6th SCVI	Darbytown Rd., VA	12/10/64	City Pt., VA	12/15/64	Pt. Lookout, MD	CSR,HOW,CTA
					Pt. Lookout, MD	06/05/65	Rlsd. Instr. 5/30/65	P115,P118,P121,CSR
McElveen, J.E.	Pvt	K 6th SCVI	Burkesville, VA	04/19/**65**	Burkesville, VA	04/19/65	Paroled	CSR
McElveen, J.F.	Pvt	H 26th SCVI	Crater, Pbg., VA	07/30/64	City Pt., VA	08/05/64	Pt. Lookout, MD	CSR
					Pt. Lookout, MD	08/08/64	Elmira, NY	P113,P117,CSR
McElveen, J.F.	Pvt	H 26th SCVI	Petersburg, VA	07/30/64	Elmira, NY	03/14/65	Pt. Lookout to Xc	P65,P66,CSR
McElveen, Joseph J.	Pvt	E 19th SCVI	Missionary Ridge, TN	11/25/63	Nashville, TN	12/07/63	Louisville, KY	CSR
					Louisville, KY	12/07/63	Rock Island, IL	CSR
					Rock Island, IL	05/03/65	New Orleans, LA Xc	CSR
					New Orleans, LA	05/23/65	Exchanged	CSR
McElveen, Major L.	Pvt	E P.S.S.	Petersburg, VA	04/03/65	Pt. Lookout, MD	06/05/65	Rlsd. Instr. 5/30/65	P115,P119,P121,TSE
McElway, R.	Pvt	K 1st SC Eng.	Richmond, VA	04/03/65	Newport News, VA		Died, date not given	P12,P107
McElwy, T.A.	Pvt	G 6th SCVI	Farmville, VA	04/06/65	Newport News, VA	06/26/65	Rlsd. G.O. #109	P107
McEureen, John	Pvt	B 1st SC Eng.	Richmond, VA	04/03/65	Newport News, VA	06/13/65	Rlsd. G.O. #109	P107
McEwen, Dwight F.	Pvt	A Ham. Leg. C	Williamsburg, VA	05/04/62	Ft. Delaware, DE	08/05/62	Aikens Ldg., VA Xc	CSR
McFadden, James H.	Pvt	A 17th SCVI	Petersburg, VA	03/25/65	City Pt., VA	03/28/65	Pt. Lookout, MD	CSR,YEB
					Pt. Lookout, MD	06/29/65	Rlsd. G.O. #109	P115,P118,P121,CSR
McFadden, Randolph M.	Cpl	A 17th SCVI	Crater, Pbg., VA	07/30/64	City Pt., VA	08/05/64	Pt. Lookout, MD	CSR,HHC
McFadden, Randolph M.	Cpl	A 17th SCVI	Petersburg, VA	07/30/64	Pt. Lookout, MD	08/08/64	Elmira, NY	P113,P117,P120,CSR
					Elmira, NY	06/16/65	Rlsd. G.O. #109	P65,P66,CSR
McFadden, Thomas S.	Pvt	D 1st SCVC	Berkeley Co., VA	07/19/63	Wheeling, WV	07/29/63	Camp Chase, OH	P1,HHC,CSR
					Camp Chase, OH	02/29/64	Ft. Delaware, DE	P22,P24,P25,CSR
					Ft. Delaware, DE	04/04/64	Died, Brain Inflam.	P5,P41,P43,P47,FPH
McFadden, W.D.	Sgt	K 6th SCVI	Frederick, MD	09/12/62	Baltimore, MD	10/11/62	Fts. Monroe, VA	CSR
					Fts. Monroe, VA	10/12/62	Aikens Ldg., VA Xc	CSR
McFall, James M.	Pvt	B 4th SCVI	Manassas, VA	07/21/61	Ft. McHenry, MD	11/13/62	Fts. Monroe, VA Xc	P145,SA2,CSR
McFarland, Archibald	Cpl	E 21st SCVI	Petersburg, VA	06/24/64	Pt. Lookout, MD	08/24/64	Died, Ch. Diarrhea	P5,P117,FPH,HAG
McFarland, Duncan	Pvt	E 21st SCVI	Black Creek, SC	03/01/65	New Berne, NC	04/03/65	Pt. Lookout, MD	CSR,HAG
					Pt. Lookout, MD	06/29/65	Rlsd. G.O. #109	P115,P118,P123,CSR
McFarland, Patrick	Pvt	D 1st SCVA	Smithville, NC	03/17/65	Pt. Lookout, MD	06/29/65	Rlsd. G.O. #109	P1,P118,P121,P123
McFeely, J.G.	Pvt	H 25th SCVI	Ft. Fisher, NC	01/15/65	New York, NY	01/30/65	Elmira, NY	CSR,HAG
					Elmira, NY	05/17/65	Rlsd. G.O. #85	P65,P66,CSR
McFeely, Thomas	Pvt	D 4th SCVC	Deserted/enemy	10/06/63	No Federal data			CSR
McFerrin, Robert	Pvt	E 26th SCVI	Richmond, VA Hos.	04/03/65	Libby Prison, Rchmd.	04/23/65	Newport News, VA	CSR
					Newport News, VA	06/26/65	Rlsd. G.O. #109	P107,CSR
McGaha, William	Pvt	K Orr's Ri.	Petersburg, VA	04/03/65	City Pt., VA	04/11/65	Hart's Island, NY	CSR
					Hart's Island, NY	06/16/65	Rlsd. G.O. #109	P79,CSR
McGahn, John William	Pvt	K 16th SCVI	Ringgold, GA	11/27/63	Nashville, TN	12/09/63	Louisville, KY	P39,CSR
					Louisville, KY	12/11/63	Rock Island, IL	P88,P89,CSR
					Rock Island, IL	05/23/64	Joined US Navy	P131,CSR
McGarity, David J.	Pvt	A 17th SCVI	Richmond, VA Hos.	04/03/65	Richmond, VA Hos.	04/14/65	Richmond, VA P.M.	CSR
					Libby Prison, Rchmd.	04/23/65	Newport News, VA	CSR
					Newport News, VA	06/14/65	Rlsd. G.O. #109	P107,CSR
					Newport News, VA	06/15/65	Fts. Monroe, VA	CSR
					Fts. Monroe, VA	06/21/65	Prob in Hos.	CSR
McGarity, H.M.	Pvt	A 17th SCVI	Deserted/enemy	02/25/65	P.M. A. of P.	02/26/65	City Pt., VA P.M.	CSR
					City Pt., VA	02/28/65	Washington, DC	CSR
					Washington, DC	03/01/65	Illinois on oath	CSR

SOUTH CAROLINA SOLDIERS, SAILORS AND  CITIZENS HELD IN U.S. PRISONS 1861-1865

NAME	RANK	REGIMENT	CAPTURED AT	WHEN	PRISON	MOVED	DISPOSITION	SOURCES
McGarity, Henderson S.	Sgt	H 24th SCVI	Nashville, TN	12/16/64	Nashville, TN	01/01/65	Louisville, KY	CSR,HHC
					Louisville, KY	01/05/65	Camp Chase, OH	P95,CSR
					Camp Chase, OH	03/11/65	Died, pneumonia	P6,P23,P27,FPH,CSR
McGarity, James	Pvt	H 24th SCVI	Nashville, TN	12/16/64	Nashville, TN	12/19/64	Louisville, KY	CSR
					Louisville, KY	12/25/64	Camp Douglas, IL	P95,HHC,EFW
					Camp Douglas, IL	06/10/65	Rlsd. G.O. #109	P55,HHC,EFW
McGarity, William A.	Pvt	A 17th SCVI	Petersburg, VA	03/25/65	City Pt., VA	03/28/65	Pt. Lookout, MD	CSR
					Pt. Lookout, MD	06/29/65	Rlsd. G.O. #109	P1,P118,P121,P123
McGarrity, William	Pvt	A 1st SCVA	Fayetteville, NC	03/12/65	New Berne, NC	04/10/65	Hart's Island, NY	CSR
					Hart's Island, NY	06/16/65	Rlsd. G.O. #109	P79,CSR
McGarty, William	Pvt	A 1st SCVIR	Goldsboro, NC	03/24/65	New Berne, NC			CSR
McGee, A.C.	Sgt	B 7th SCVI	Maryland Hts., MD	09/15/62	Ft. McHenry, MD	12/08/62	Fts. Monroe, VA	CSR,KEB,CNM
					Fts. Monroe, VA	12/10/65	City Pt., VA Xc	CSR
McGee, A.C.	Sgt	B 7th SCVI	Gettysburg, PA	07/04/63	David's Island, NY	08/24/63	City Pt., VA Xc	P1
McGee, A.C.	Sgt	B 7th SCVI	Cedar Creek, VA	10/19/64	Frederick, MD G.H.	12/30/64	Baltimore, MD	P3
					W. Bldg. Balt., MD	01/08/65	Pt. Lookout, MD	P4,CSR
					Pt. Lookout, MD	01/28/65	Hammond G.H., MD	P118,P121
					Pt. Lookout, MD	06/05/65	Rlsd. Ins. 5/30/65	P121,CSR
McGee, Elias	Pvt	D Orr's Ri.	Petersburg, VA	04/03/65	City Pt., VA	04/11/65	Hart's Island, NY	CSR,CDC
					Hart's Island, NY	06/16/65	Rlsd. G.O. #109	P79,CSR
McGee, G.G.	Pvt	I 26th SCVI	Crater, Pbg., VA	07/30/64	Elmira, NY	12/16/64	Released on oath	CSR,CTA
McGee, J.M.	Pvt	B 7th SCVI	Mayland Hts., MD	09/19/62	Ft. McHenry, MD	05/24/63	Fts. Monroe, VA	CSR,KEB
					Fts. Monroe, VA	05/26/63	City Pt., VA Xc	CSR
McGee, J.M.	Pvt	E 8th SCVI	Spotsylvania, VA	05/08/64	Ft. Delaware, DE	06/10/65	Rlsd. G.O. #109	KEB,P41,P43,P45
McGee, Judson	Pvt	I 22nd SCVI	Crater, Pbg., VA	07/30/64	City Pt., VA	08/05/64	Pt. Lookout, MD	CSR
					Pt. Lookout, MD	08/08/64	Elmira, NY	CSR
					Elmira, NY	05/19/65	Rlsd. G.O. #85	P65,P66,CSR
McGee, P.A.W.	Pvt	C 3rd SCVABn	Blakely, AL	04/09/65	Ship Island, MS	05/01/65	Vicksburg, MS Xc	P136,CSR
McGee, Pleasant	Pvt	3 10/19 SCVI	Missionary Ridge, TN	11/25/63	Nashville, TN	12/07/63	Louisville, KY	P39,RAS,CTA,CSR
					Louisville, KY	12/07/63	Rock Island, IL	P88,CSR
					Rock Island, IL	05/03/65	New Orleans, LA Xc	P131,CSR
					New Orleans, LA	05/23/65	Exchanged	P4
McGee, Sylvester W.	Pvt	F 24th SCVI	Taylors Ridge, GA	10/16/64	Nashville, TN	08/23/64	Louisville, KY	CSR
					Louisville, KY	10/27/64	Camp Douglas, IL	P90,P91,P95,CSR
					Camp Douglas, IL	01/30/65	Died, Scurvy	P5,P53,P55,P58,FPH
McGee, William D.	Pvt	D 14th SCVI	Sutherland Stn., VA	04/02/65	City Pt., VA	04/07/65	Hart's Island, NY	CSR
					Hart's Island, NY	06/16/65	Rlsd. G.O. #109	P79,CSR
McGill, Andrew J.	Pvt	G 1st SCVA	Fayetteville, NC	03/10/65	New Berne, NC	03/30/65	Pt. Lookout, MD	CSR
					Pt. Lookout, MD	06/29/65	Rlsd. G.O. #109	P115,CSR
McGill, Archibald	Pvt	11th SCVI	McPhersonville, SC	10/22/62	Hilton Head, SC		Ft. Columbus, NY	CSR
					Ft. Columbus, NY	11/21/64	Ft. Delaware, DE	CSR
McGill, Archibald	Pvt	E 27th SCVI	Petersburg, VA	05/10/64	Fts. Monroe, VA	05/13/64	Pt. Lookout, MD	CSR,HAG
					Pt. Lookout, MD	05/16/64	Joined U.S. Army	P116,P112,P125,CSR
McGill, Duncan	Cit		Columbia, SC	03/10/65	Pt. Lookout, MD			P118
McGill, Elias F.	Pvt	G 26th SCVI	Five Forks, VA	04/01/65	City Pt., VA	04/05/65	Pt. Lookout, MD	CSR
					Pt. Lookout, MD	06/29/65	Rlsd. G.O. #109	P118,P121,P123,CSR
McGill, J.F.	Pvt	E 20th SCVI	Charlotte, NC Hos.	05/05/65	Charlotte, NC	05/05/65	Paroled	CSR
McGill, James J.	Pvt	G 26th SCVI	Five Forks, VA	04/01/65	City Pt., VA	04/05/65	Pt. Lookout, MD	CSR
					Pt. Lookout, MD	06/29/65	Rlsd. G.O. #109	P118,P121,P123,CSR
McGill, John H.	Pvt	K 2nd SCVIRi	Boonesboro, MD	09/15/62	Ft. Delaware, DE	10/02/62	Aikens Ldg., VA Xc	CSR
McGill, W.T.	Pvt	L Orr's Ri.	Petersburg, VA	04/03/65	City Pt., VA	04/11/65	Hart's Island, NY	CSR,CDC
					Hart's Island, NY	06/16/65	Rlsd. G.O. #109	P79,CSR

SOUTH CAROLINA SOLDIERS, SAILORS AND  CITIZENS HELD IN U.S. PRISONS 1861-1865

NAME	RANK	REGIMENT	CAPTURED AT	WHEN	PRISON	MOVED	DISPOSITION	SOURCES
McGinnis, R.S.	Pvt	I Hol. Leg.	Deserted/Enemy	12/22/64	City Pt., VA	12/27/64	Washington, DC	CSR,HOS
					Washington, DC	12/30/64	Springfield, IL	CSR
McGinty, John	Pvt	B 15th SCVAB	Rockingham, NC	03/08/65	Pt. Lookout, MD	05/15/65	Rlsd. G.O. #85	P115,P121,CSR
McGougan, Angus	Pvt	F 7th SCVIBn	Richmond, VA Hos.	04/03/65	Richmond, VA P.M.	05/05/65	Pt. Lookout, MD US	CSR,HAG,HIC
					Hammond G.H., MD	07/25/65	Rlsd. G.O. #109	P119,CSR
McGougan, Archibald	Pvt	F 7th SCVIBn	Weldon RR, VA	08/21/64	City Pt., VA	08/24/64	Pt. lookout, MD	CSRHAG,HIC
					Pt. Lookout, MD	01/01/65	Died, Diarrhea	P5,P117,P119,CSR
McGoven, Peter	Pvt	A 17th SCVI	Danville, VA Hos.	04/29/65	Danville, VA	04/29/65	Paroled	CSR
McGovern, John	Pvt	K 16th SCVI	Franklin, TN	11/30/64	Nashville, TN	12/02/64	Louisville, KY	CSR
					Louisville, KY	12/03/64	Camp Douglas, IL	P90,P91,P95,CSR
					Camp Douglas, IL	06/18/65	Rlsd. G.O. #109	P55,CSR
McGowan, John	Pvt	G 3rd SCVABn	High Pt., NC	05/01/65	High Pt., NC	05/01/65	Paroled	CSR
McGowan, Owen W.	Pvt	C 7th SCVI	N. Anna River, VA	05/23/64	Port Royal, VA	05/30/64	Pt. Lookout, MD	CSR,KEB
					Pt. Lookout, MD	07/23/64	Elmira, NY	P113.P117,P120,CSR
					Elmira, NY	05/29/65	Rlsd. G.O. #85	P7,P65,P66,CSR
McGowan, R.	Pvt	G 3rd SCVABn	High Pt., NC	05/01/65	High Pt., NC	05/01/65	Paroled	CSR
McGregor, P.G.	Pvt	H 2nd SCVC	Charlotte, NC	05/06/65	Charlotte, NC	05/06/65	Paroled	CSR
McGuffin, J.H.	Cpl	D 22nd SCVI	Boonesboro, MD	09/14/62	Frederick, MD Hos.	09/19/62	Ft. Delaware, DE	CSR
					Ft. Delaware, DE	10/02/62	Aikens Ldg., VA Xc	CSR
McGuffin, J.H.	Pvt	F Orr's Ri.	Jarratts Stn., VA	04/03/65	City Pt., VA	04/07/65	Hart's Island, NY	CSR
					Hart's Island, NY	06/15/65	Rlsd. G.O. #109	P79, CSR
McGuinis, John	Pvt	E 4th SCVC	Deserted/enemy		Washington, DC	01/03/65	New Orleans, LA	CSR
McGuinnis, John	Pvt	C 2nd SCVC	Hagerstown, MD	07/12/63	Baltimore, MD	08/21/63	Pt. Lookout, MD	CSR
					Pt. Lookout, MD	03/17/64	City Pt., VA Xc	CSR
McGuinnis, John	Pvt	C 2nd SCVC	Greensboro, NC	05/01/65	Greensboro, NC	05/01/65	Paroled	CSR
McGuinnis, William M.	Pvt	H 2nd SCVC	Hedgesville, VA	07/17/63	Wheeling, WV	07/27/63	Camp Chase, OH	CSR
					Camp Chase, OH	02/29/64	Ft. Delaware, DE	P22,P25,P26,CSR
					Ft. Delaware, DE	03/29/64	Died, Lung Inflam.	P5,P41,P43,P47,FPH
McGuire, B.	Pvt	G 12th SCVI	Five Forks, VA	04/01/65	Pt. Lookout, MD	06/29/65	Rlsd. G.O. #109	P115
McGuire, John	Pvt	F 1st SCVIR	Deserted/enemy	02/20/65	Charleston, SC PM	03/01/65	Released on oath	SA1,CSR
McGuirt, J.	Pvt	G 1st SCVIR	Bentonville, NC	03/22/65	New Berne, NC	04/10/65	Hart's Island, NY	CSR
					Hart's Island, NY	06/16/65	Rlsd. G.O. #109	P79,CSR
McHenry, Michael T.	1Lt	D 14th SCVI	Appomattox R., VA	04/03/65	Old Capitol, DC	04/17/65	Johnson's Isl., OH	P110,CSR
					Johnson's Isl., OH	06/17/65	Rlsd. G.O. #109	P81,P82,P83,CSR
McHugh, J.H.	Pvt	22nd SCVI	Kinston, NC	12/15/62	Kinston, NC	12/15/62	Paroled POW	CSR
McIlroy, Joseph	Pvt	G 6th SCVI	Jetersville, VA	04/06/65	City Pt., VA	04/14/65	Newport News, VA	CSR,HHC
					Newport News, VA	06/26/65	Rlsd. G.O. #109	CSR
McIlvane, Joseph J.	Pvt	8 10/19 SCVI	Missionary Ridge, TN	11/25/63	Nashville, TN	12/07/63	Louisville, KY	P39,CSR
					Louisville, KY	12/07/63	Rock Island, IL	P88,P89,CSR
					Rock Island, IL	05/03/65	New Orleans, LA Xc	P131,CSR
					New Orleans, LA	05/23/65	Exchanged	P4,CSR
McIlveen, J.H.	Pvt	B 21st SCVI	Ft. Fisher, NC	01/15/65	Elmira, NY	07/07/65	Rlsd. G.O. #109	P65,P66,HAG
McIlwaine, Charles	Pvt	E 17th SCVI	Petersburg, VA	03/25/65	City Pt., VA	03/28/65	Pt. Lookout, MD	CSR,YEB
					Pt. Lookout, MD	06/06/65	Rlsd. Instr. 5/30/65	P115,P118,P121,CSR
McIlwaine, J.M.	Pvt	F Hol. Leg.	Jarratts Stn., VA	05/08/64	Fts. Monroe, VA	05/13/64	Pt. Lookout, MD	CSR
					Pt. Lookout, MD	08/15/64	Elmira, NY	P113,P116,CSR
					Elmira, NY	03/02/65	James R., VA Xc	P65,P66,CSR
McIlwaine, William M.	Pvt	F Hol. Leg.	Jarratts Stn., VA	05/08/64	Fts. Monroe, VA	05/13/64	Pt. Lookout, MD	CSR
					Pt. Lookout, MD	08/15/64	Elmira, NY	P113,CSR
					Elmira, NY	01/02/65	Died, Ch. Diarrhea	P5,P12,P65,P66,FPH
McInernay, Michael	Pvt	B 15th SCVAB	Deserted/enemy	03/22/65	Charleston, SC		Released on oath	CSR
McInis, John	Pvt	E 4th SCVC	Deserted/enemy		City Pt., VA	12/29/64		P8,CSR

SOUTH CAROLINA SOLDIERS, SAILORS AND  CITIZENS HELD IN U.S. PRISONS 1861-1865

NAME	RANK	REGIMENT	CAPTURED AT	WHEN	PRISON	MOVED	DISPOSITION	SOURCES
McInnis, Neil	Pvt	H Orr's Ri.	Petersburg, VA	04/03/65	City Pt., VA	04/11/65	Hart's Island, NY	CSR
					Hart's Island, NY	06/16/65	Rlsd. G.O. #109	P79,CSR
McIntosh, David A.	Sgt	I 27th SCVI	Town Creek, NC	02/20/65	Ft. Anderson, NC	02/28/65	Pt. Lookout, MD	CSR,HAG
					Pt. Lookout, MD	05/14/65	Rlsd. G.O. #85	P115,P118,CSR
McIntosh, J.E.	Pvt	C Ham. Leg. MI	Burkesville, VA	04/26/65	Burkesville, VA	04/26/65	Paroled	CSR
McIntosh, John F.	Pvt	I 25th SCVI	Morris Island, SC	09/07/63	Hilton Head, SC	10/06/63	Ft. Columbus, NY	CSR
					Ft. Columbus, NY	09/26/64	Pt. Lookout, MD	HAG,CSR
					Pt. Lookout, MD	10/11/64	Aikens Ldg., VA Xc	P113,P116,P123,P124,HAG
					Jackson Hos. Rchmd.	10/29/64	Died, Ch. Diarrhea	CSR
McIntyre, J.C.	Sgt	E 23rd SCVI	Petersburg, VA	04/02/65	Fts. Monroe, VA	06/06/65	Newport News, VA	CSR
					Newport News, VA	06/14/65	Rlsd. G.O. #109	P107,CSR
McIntyre, John T.	SMj	F 21st SCVI	Ft. Fisher, NC	01/15/65	Elmira, NY	03/05/65	Died, Ch. Diarrhea	P6,P12,P65,P66,FPH
McIntyre, Joseph J.	Sgt	D 25th SCVI	Weldon RR, VA	08/21/64	W. Bldg. Balt., MD	10/19/64	Ft. McHenry, MD	P3,HAG,CSR,HMC
					Ft. McHenry, MD	10/26/64	Pt. Lookout, MD	CSR
					Pt. Lookout, MD	02/13/65	Aikens Ldg., VA Xc	P118,P121,P124,CSR
McIver, David A.	Pvt	F 25th SCVI	Ft. Fisher, NC	01/15/65	New York, NY	01/30/65	Elmira, NY	CSR,HAG
					Elmira, NY	03/02/65	Pt.Lookout, MD Xc	P65,P66,CSR
McIver, David R.W.	1Lt	D 21st SCVI	Ft. Fisher, NC	01/15/65	Pt. Lookout, MD	02/02/65	Hammond G.H., MD	P115,P121,HAG
					Pt. Lookout, MD	05/30/65	Col. Ingraham, DC	P118
					Old Capitol, DC	05/30/65	Johnson's Isl., OH	P110
					Johnson's Isl., OH	06/16/65	Rlsd. G.O. #109	P81,P82
McIver, John Kalb	Cpt	F 8th SCVI	Williamsport, MD	07/14/63	Chester, PA G.H.	10/04/63	Pt. Lookout, MD	P1,KEB,CSR
					Pt. Lookout, MD	10/15/63	Died, of wounds	P5,FPH,CSR,P116
McKain, Hugh R.	Pvt	C 6th SCVI	Farmville, VA	04/07/65	Farmville, VA	04/21/65	Paroled	HIC,CSR
McKay, C.D.	Pvt	E 8th SCVI	Winchester, VA	09/13/64	Harpers Ferry, WV	09/19/64	Camp Chase, OH	CSR
					Camp Chase, OH	02/25/65	Died, pneumonia	CSR
McKay, George	Pvt	13th SCVI	Deserted/enemy	08/31/64				CSR
McKay, H.A.	Sgt	A 3rd SCVABn	High Pt., NC	05/02/65	High Pt., NC	05/02/65	Paroled	CSR
McKay, J.C.	Pvt	H 12th SCVI	Spotsylvania, VA	05/12/64	Belle Plain, VA	05/21/64	Ft. Delaware, DE	CSR
					Ft. Delaware, DE	09/18/64	Aikens Ldg., VA Xc	P41,P43,YEB,CSR
					Richmond, VA Hos.	09/25/64	Furloughed 30 days	CSR
McKay, John	Pvt	I 12th SCVI	Petersburg, VA Hos.	04/02/65	Petersburg, VA	07/05/65	Paroled	CSR
McKean, William	Pvt	A 2nd SCVC	Anderson, SC	05/19/65	Anderson, SC	05/19/65	Paroled	CSR
McKee, Aaron W.	Pvt	F 24th SCVI	Missionary Ridge, TN	11/25/63	Nashville, TN	12/09/63	Louisville, KY	CSR,EFW
					Louisville, KY	12/11/63	Rock Island, IL	P88,P89
					Rock Island, IL	02/25/65	Pt. Lookout to Xc	P131
					Ft. Columbus, NY	03/05/65	Boulwares Wh., VA	CSR
					Jackson H. Rchmd.	03/08/65	Furloughed 30 days	CSR
McKee, Alexander	Pvt	A 2nd SCVI	Gettysburg, PA	07/04/63	David's Island, NY	09/12/63	City Pt., VA Xc	SA2,P1,KEB,H2,CSR
McKee, Alexander	Pvt	A 2nd SCVI	Cedar Creek, VA	10/19/64	W. Bldg. Balt., MD	02/16/65	Ft. McHenry, MD Xc	P3,CSR
McKee, J.W.	Pvt	F 7th SCVI	Sharpsburg, MD	09/17/62	Frederick, MD	09/27/62	Ft. McHenry, MD	CSR,KEB
					Ft. McHenry, MD	10/25/62	Aikens Ldg., VA Xc	CSR
McKee, John O.	Pvt	F 24th SCVI	Taylors Ridge, GA	10/16/64	Nashville, TN	10/23/64	Louisville, KY	CSR,CDC
					Louisville, KY	10/26/64	Camp Douglas, IL	P90,P95,CSR
					Camp Douglas, IL	06/17/65	Rlsd. G.O. #109	P55,CSR
McKee, Joseph	Pvt	A 2nd SCVI	Sharpsburg, MD	10/01/62	Ft. McHenry, MD	10/13/62	Ft. Monroe, VA	CSR,SA2,H2
					Ft. Monroe, VA	10/17/62	Aikens Ldg., VA Xc	CSR
McKee, Robert	Pvt	E 1st SCVA	Marietta, GA	07/02/64	Louisville, KY	07/18/64	Camp Douglas, IL	P90,P91,P94,CSR
					Camp Douglas, IL	11/30/64	Died, Debility	P5,P53,P55,FPH,CSR
McKee, T.T.	Pvt	I 27th SCVI	Town Creek, NC	02/20/65	Ft. Anderson, NC	02/28/65	Pt. Lookout, MD	CSR
					Pt. Lookout, MD	05/14/65	Rlsd. G.O. #85	P121,CSR

SOUTH CAROLINA SOLDIERS, SAILORS AND  CITIZENS HELD IN U.S. PRISONS 1861-1865

NAME	RANK	REGIMENT	CAPTURED AT	WHEN	PRISON	MOVED	DISPOSITION	SOURCES
McKee, W.J.	Pvt	F Hol. Leg.	Petersburg, VA	11/06/64	City Pt., VA	11/11/64	Washington, DC	CSR
					Pt. Lookout, MD	06/29/65	Rlsd. G.O. #109	P115,P118,CSR
McKee, William L.	Pvt	F Hol. Leg.	Five Forks, VA	04/01/65	City Pt., VA	04/05/65	Pt. Lookout, MD	CSR
					Pt. Lookout, MD	06/06/65	Rlsd. Instr. 5/30/65	P115,P118,P121,CSR
McKelloy, H.A.	Pvt	K Hol. Leg.	Stony Creek, VA	05/07/64	Fts. Monroe, VA	05/13/64	Pt. Lookout, MD	CSR
					Pt. Lookout, MD	08/15/64	Elmira, NY	P113
					Elmira, NY	10/11/64	Venus Pt., GA Xc	P65,P66,CSR
					Pt. Lookout, MD	10/29/64	Exchanged	P115,P118
McKelloy, H.A.	Pvt	K Hol. Leg.	Savannah, GA	12/24/64	20th USGH	12/28/64	Died, Ch. Diarrhea	P1,P5,P12,CSR
McKenna, Edward	Pvt	I 1st SCVA	Morris Island, SC	07/10/63	Hilton Head, SC	09/05/63	Ft. Columbus, NY	CSR
					Ft. Columbus, NY	09/23/63	Took the oath	P1,CSR
					Ft. Columbus, NY		Rlsd. on oath	CSR
McKenna, Michael	Pvt	E 1st SCVIR	Morris Island, SC	07/10/63	Hilton Head, SC	09/05/63	Ft. Columbus, NY	CSR
McKenna, Patrick M.	Pvt	B 1st SCVA	Deserted/enemy	02/24/65	Charleston, SC		Released on oath	CSR
McKenzie, A.S.	Pvt	PeeDee LA	Darlington, SC	02/26/65	New Berne, NC	04/10/65	Hart's Island, NY	P79,CSR
					Hart's Island, NY	06/16/65	Rlsd. G.O. #109	CSR
McKenzie, Alfred M.	Pvt	H 23rd SCVI	Petersburg, VA	04/03/65	City Pt., VA	04/13/65	Pt. Lookout, MD	CSR
					Pt. Lookout, MD	06/29/65	Rlsd. G.O. #109	P115,P121,P123,CSR
McKenzie, Asa	Pvt	H 26th SCVI	Deserted/enemy	03/01/65	City Pt., VA	03/02/65	Washington, DC	CSR
					Washington, DC	03/06/65	Released on oath	CSR
McKenzie, Daniel S.	Pvt	I 26th SCVI	Petersburg, VA	04/03/65	City Pt., VA	04/11/65	Hart's Island, NY	CSR,CTA
					Hart's Island, NY	06/16/65	Rlsd. G.O. #109	P79
McKenzie, David	Pvt	Lafayette A	Anderson, SC	05/19/65	Anderson, SC	05/19/65	Paroled	CSR
McKenzie, Joseph C.	Pvt	F 21st SCVI	Bennettsville, SC	03/06/65	New Berne, NC	04/03/65	Pt. Lookout, MD	CSR,HAG
					Pt. Lookout, MD	06/29/65	Rlsd. G.O. #109	P118,P121,P123,CSR
McKenzie, W.D.	Sgt	H 26th SCVI	Five Forks, VA	04/01/65	City Pt., VA	04/05/65	Pt. Lookout, MD	CSR
					Pt. Lookout, MD	06/29/65	Rlsd. G.O. #109	P118,P121,P123,CSR
McKenzie, William M.	Pvt	H 17th SCVI	Crater, Pbg., VA	07/30/64	City Pt., VA	08/05/64	Pt. Lookout, MD	CSR
					Pt. Lookout, MD	08/08/64	Elmira, NY	P113,P117,P120,CSR
					Elmira, NY	10/11/64	Pt. Lookout, MD Xc	P65,P66,CSR
					Pt. Lookout, MD	10/29/64	Venus Pt., GA Xc	P115,P118,CSR
McKenzie, William M.	Pvt	H 17th SCVI	Five Forks, VA	04/01/65	City Pt., VA	04/06/65	Pt. Lookout, MD	CSR
					Pt. Lookout, MD	06/29/65	Rlsd. G.O. #109	P1,P121,P123,CSR
McKeown, F.M.	Pvt	F 15th SCVI	Frederick, MD	09/12/62	Frederick, MD USGH	09/21/62	Died of wounds	P1,P6,P12,KEB,UD2
McKeown, Samuel Scott	Pvt	D 17th SCVI	Crater, Pbg., VA	07/30/64	City Pt., VA	08/05/64	Pt. Lookout, MD	CSR,HHC
					Pt. Lookout, MD	08/08/64	Elmira, NY	P113,P117,CSR
					Elmira, NY	12/09/64	Died, Pneumonia	P5,P65,P66,FPH,CSR
McKeown, W.O.	Pvt	17th SCVI	Keedysville, MD	09/20/62	Keedysville, MD	09/20/62	Released on Parole	CSR
McKerrall, W.J.	Cpt	D 25th SCVI	Weldon RR, VA	08/21/64	Old Capitol, DC	08/21/64	Ft. Delaware, DE	P110,CSR,HMC,HAG
					Ft. Delaware, DE	10/06/64	Pt. Lookout, MD Xc	P43
					Pt. Lookout, MD	10/11/64	Aikens Ldg., VA Xc	P118,CSR
McKethan, J.A.	Pvt	L 1st SCVIG	Gettysburg, PA	07/02/63	David's Island, NY	08/03/63	Died	P1,P6,FPH,SA1,CSR
McKewn, James	Pvt	E 16th SCVI	Ringgold, GA	11/27/63	Nashville, TN	12/09/63	Louisville, KY	CSR,16R
					Louisville, KY	12/11/63	Rock Island, IL	P88,P89,CSR
					Rock Island, IL	06/19/65	Rlsd. G.O. #109	P131,CSR
McKinney, Daniel M.	1Lt	H 22nd SCVI	Crater, Pbg., VA	07/30/64	P.M. City Pt., VA	08/02/64	Washington, DC	CSR
					Washington, DC	08/11/64	Ft. Delaware, DE	CSR
					Ft. Delaware, DE	06/17/65	Rlsd. G.O. #109	P43,P45
McKinney, George	Pvt	I 5th SCVI	Deep Bottom, VA	08/14/64	Bermuda Hundred, VA	08/15/64	Fts. Monroe, VA	CSR
					Fts. Monroe, VA	08/16/64	Pt. Lookout, MD	CSR
					Pt. Lookout, MD	02/10/65	Exchanged	P113,P125,KEB
McKinney, George	Pvt	I 5th SCVI	Deep Bottom, VA	08/14/64	Pt. Lookout, MD	02/10/65	Coxes Ldg., VA Xc	SA3,CSR

M

SOUTH CAROLINA SOLDIERS, SAILORS AND CITIZENS HELD IN U.S. PRISONS 1861-1865

NAME	RANK	REGIMENT	CAPTURED AT	WHEN	PRISON	MOVED	DISPOSITION	SOURCES
McKinney, John	Pvt	K 15th SCVI	Halltown, VA	08/26/64	Harpers Ferry, WV	08/29/64	Camp Chase, OH	CSR,KEB,H5
					Camp Chase, OH	05/02/65	New Orleans, LA Xc	P23,P26,CSR
McKinney, William R.	Cpl	B Orr's Ri.	Petersburg, VA	04/02/65	City Pt., VA	04/07/65	Hart's Island, NY	CSR
					Hart's Island, NY	06/15/65	Rlsd. G.O. #109	P79,CDC,CSR
McKinnis, R.	Pvt	A 24th SCVI	Chattanooga, TN	11/24/63	Rock Island, IL	03/20/65	Pt. Lookout to Xc	P131
McKinnon, Cameron	Pvt	K 8th SCVI	Gettysburg, PA	07/02/63	Gettysburg G.H.		Provost M.	P4,KEB,HOM,CSR
					Baltimore, MD	08/16/63	Pt. Lookout, MD	CSR
					Pt. Lookout, MD	04/27/64	City Pt. VA Xc	P113,116,P124,CSR
McKnight, Hiram B.	Pvt	H 26th SCVI	Petersburg, VA	03/25/65	City Pt., VA	03/27/65	Pt. Lookout, MD	CSR
					Pt. Lookout, MD	06/29/65	Rlsd. G.O. #109	P115,P118,P121
McKnight, James L.	Pvt	I 26th SCVI	Richmond, VA Hos.	04/03/65	Libby Prison, Rchmd.	04/23/65	Newport News, VA	CSR
					Newport News, VA	06/14/65	Rlsd. G.O. #109	P107,CSR
McKnight, John	Pvt	3 10/19 SCV	Missionary Ridge, TN	11/25/63	Nashville, TN	12/07/63	Louisville, KY	P39,RAS,CSR
					Louisville, KY	12/09/63	Rock Island, IL	P88,RAS,CSR
					Rock Island, IL	05/23/64	Joined US Navy	P131,CSR
McKnight, John B.	Sgt	B 12th SCVI	Spotsylvania, VA	05/12/64	Belle Plain, VA	05/20/63	Ft. Delaware, DE	CSR,YEB
					Ft. Delaware, DE		Hos.3/28-4/4/65	P41,P45,P47
					Ft. Delaware, DE	06/10/65	Released	P43,CSR
McKnight, R.M.	Pvt	G 7th SCVC		04/11/65	24th A.C. US Fld. Hos.	04/14/65	Unknown U.S.G.H.	CSR
McKnight, Robert M.	Pvt	C Ham. Leg.	Fair Oaks, VA	05/31/62	Fts. Monroe, VA	06/05/62	Ft. Delaware, DE	CSR
					Ft. Delaware, DE	08/05/62	Aikens Ldg., VA Xc	CSR
McKnight, William E.	Pvt	E 5th SCVI	Wilderness, VA	05/06/64	Belle Plain, VA	05/21/64	Ft. Delaware, DE	CSR,SA3
					Ft. Delaware, DE	06/07/65	Released	P41,P43,P45,CSR
McKnight, William H.	Cpl	C 25th SCVI	Ft. Fisher, NC	01/15/65	New York, NY	01/30/65	Elmira, NY	CSR,CTA,HAG
					Elmira, NY	02/20/65	Pt. Lookout, MD Xc	P65,P66,CSR
					Richmond Hospital	03/25/65	Furloughed 60 days	CSR
McLain, A.B.	Pvt	H 12th SCVI	Gettysburg, PA	07/05/63	Ft. McHenry, MD	07/12/63	Ft. Delaware, DE	CSR
					Ft. Delaware, DE	09/18/64	Aikens Ldg., VA Xc	P40,P42,P44,CSR
McLain, Henry J.	Pvt	B 17th SCVI	Five Forks, VA	04/01/65	City Pt., VA	10/20/65	Pt. Lookout, MD	CSR
					Pt. Lookout, MD	06/06/65	Rlsd. G.O. #85	P115,P118,P121,CSR
McLain, John C.	Cpl	B 15th SCVAB	Averysboro, NC	03/16/65	New Berne, NC	03/30/65	Pt. Lookout, MD	CSR
					Pt. Lookout, MD	06/29/65	Rlsd. G.O. #109	P115,P121,P123,CSR
McLane, J.B.	Pvt	E 11th SCVI	Petersburg, VA	06/24/64	Bermuda Hundred, VA	06/25/64	Fts. Monroe, VA	CSR
					Fts. Monroe, VA	06/26/64	Pt. Lookout, MD	CSR
					Pt. Lookout, MD	08/15/64	Elmira, NY	P113,P117,P120,CSR
					Elmira, NY	05/10/65	Died, Diarrhea	P6,P65,P66,FPH,CSR
McLauchlin, D.H.	Pvt	D 8th SCVI	Winchester, VA	09/09/64	Harpers Ferry, WV	09/19/64	Camp Chase, OH	CSR,KEB
					Camp Chase, OH	06/10/65	Rlsd. G.O. #109	P23,CSR
McLaughlin, E.A.	Pvt	A 7th SCVIBn	Charleston, SC Hos.	02/18/65	No release record			CSR
McLaurin, Daniel W.	Cpl	G 23rd SCVI	Bennettsville, SC	03/05/65	New Berne, NC	03/26/65	Pt. Lookout, MD	CSR
					Pt. Lookout, MD	06/29/65	Rlsd. G.O. #109	P118,P121,P123,CSR
McLaurin, J.F.	Pvt	C Ham. Leg. MI	Bennettsville, SC	03/06/65	New Berne, NC	04/23/65	Pt. Lookout, MD	CSR
					Pt. Lookout, MD	06/29/65	Rlsd. G.O. #109	P115,P118,P123,CSR
McLaurin, James W.	Pvt	E 4th SCVC	Stony Creek, VA	12/01/64	City Pt., VA	12/05/64	Pt. Lookout, MD	CSR
					Pt. Lookout, MD	06/29/65	Rlsd. G.O. #109	P1,P118,P121,P123
McLaurin, Julius Colin	Sgt	D 2nd SCVI	Gettysburg, PA	07/05/63	Gettysburg, PA G.H.	07/21/63	Provost Marshal NY	P4,CSR,KEB,SA2,H2
					David's Island, NY	09/05/63	City Pt., VA Xc	P1,CSR
McLees, G.R.	Pvt	G 7th SCVC	Burkesville, VA	04/14/65	U.S. Sub Depot F.H.	04/16/65	City Pt., VA USGH	CSR
McLeish, John	Sgt	E 25th SCVI	Ft. Fisher, NC	01/15/65	New York, NY	01/30/65	Elmira, NY	CSR,HAG
					Elmira, NY	05/29/65	Rlsd. G.O. #85	P65,P66,HAG,CSR

SOUTH CAROLINA SOLDIERS, SAILORS AND  CITIZENS HELD IN U.S. PRISONS 1861-1865

NAME	RANK	REGIMENT	CAPTURED AT	WHEN	PRISON	MOVED	DISPOSITION	SOURCES
McLendon, Gillis	Pvt	F 7th SCVIBn	Weldon RR, VA	08/21/64	City Pt., VA U.S.G.H.	08/23/64	Baltimore, MD USGH	CSR,HAG,HIC
					Bristol, PA U.S.G.H.	09/09/64	Phila., PA USGH	CSR
					W. Bldg., Balt., M	10/18/64	Pt. Lookout, MD	P3,CSR
					Pt. Lookout, MD	10/30/64	Aikens Ldg., VA Xc	P115,P118,P123
McLendon, William	Pvt	F 7th SCVIBn	Weldon RR, VA	08/21/64	City Pt., VA	08/24/64	Pt. Lookout, MD	CSR,HAG,HIC
					Pt. Lookout, MD	09/18/64	Aikens Ldg., VA Xc	P113,P117,CSR
					Richmond, VA Hos.	09/26/64	Furloughed 30 days	CSR
					Danville, VA Hosp.	09/29/64	Died, Ch. Diarrhea	CSR
McLeod, A.S.	Pvt	K 6th SCVI	Seven Pines, VA	05/31/62	Fts. Monroe, VA	06/05/62	Ft. Delaware, DE	CSR
					Ft. Delaware, DE	08/05/62	Aikens Ldg., VA Xc	CSR
McLeod, R.T.	Pvt	C 3rd SCVABn	Blakely, AL	04/09/65	Vicksburg, MS	05/03/65	Exhanged	P136,CSR
McLeod, R.T.	Pvt	C 3rd SCVABn	Citronelle, AL	05/04/65	Meridian, MS	05/25/65	Paroled	CSR
McLeod, Robert A.	Sgt	B 25th SCVI	Weldon RR, VA	08/23/64	W. Bldg., Balt., MD	10/25/64	Pt. Lookout, MD	P3,HAG
McLeod, Robert A.	Sgt	B 25th SCVI	Weldon RR, VA	08/21/64	Baltimore, MD Hos.	10/29/64	Pt. Lookout, MD	CSR,HAG
McLeod, Robert A.	Sgt	B 25th SCVI	Weldon RR, VA	10/19/64	Pt. Lookout, MD	10/29/64	Venus Pt., GA Xc	P115,P118,HAG,CSR
McLintock, D.A.	Sgt	I 27th SCVI	Town Creek, NC	02/20/65	Pt. Lookout, MD	05/14/65	Rlsd. G.O. #85	P121
McMahan, Alexander H.	Pvt	F 24th SCVI	Ringgold, GA	11/25/63	Nashville, TN	12/05/63	Louisville, KY	P39,HOL,CSR
					Louisville, KY	12/06/63	Rock Island, IL	P89,CSR
					Rock Island, IL	01/27/64	Died, Diarrhea	P5,P132,CSR
McMahon, Daniel R.	Pvt	B 27th SCVI	Wilmington, NC	02/20/65	Pt. Lookout, MD	06/29/65	Rlsd. G.O. #109	P121,P123
McMahon, John	Pvt	H 27th SCVI	Deserted/enemy	05/30/64	Fts. Monroe, VA	06/06/64	New York, NY	CSR,HAG
					Philadelphia, PA	08/31/64	Ft. Miflin, PA	CSR
					Ft. Mifflin, PA	09/03/64	Released on oath	P2
McMahon, N.W.	Pvt	D Orr's Ri.	Petersburg, VA	04/03/65	City Pt., VA	04/11/65	Hart's Island, NY	CSR
					Hart's Island, NY	06/16/65	Rlsd. G.O. #109	P79,CSR
McMahon, R.D.	Pvt	B 27th SCVI			Pt. Lookout, MD	06/29/65	Rlsd. G.O. #109	CSR
McMakin, Jefferson B.	Pvt	H 6th SCVC	Deserted/enemy	05/19/64	Louisville, KY P.M.	05/21/64	N. of Ohio R. oath	P90,P94,CSR
McMakin, Peter	Pvt	B 22nd SCVI	Farmville, VA	04/06/65	City Pt., VA	04/14/65	Newport News, VA	CSR
					Newport News, VA	06/15/65	Rlsd. G.O. #109	P107,CSR
McMakin, William G.	Pvt	G 27th SCVI	Town Creek, NC	02/20/65	Ft. Anderson, NC	02/28/65	Pt. Lookout, MD	CSR,HAG
					Pt. Lookout, MD	06/29/65	Rlsd. G.O. #109	P1,P118,P121,P123
McManemin, Eugene	Pvt	A 1st SCVIR	Morris Island, SC	09/07/63	Hilton Head, SC		Ft. Columbus, NY	CSR
					Ft. Columbus, NY		Rlsd. on oath	P1,SAI,CSR
McManigal, James W.	Pvt	H 27th SCVI	Deserted/enemy	06/18/64	Bermuda Hundred, VA	06/21/64	Fts. Monroe, VA	CSR,HAG
					Fts. Monroe, VA	06/26/64	Phila., PA on oath	CSR
McManus, Abraham C.	Pvt	A 1st SCVIR	Morris Island, SC	09/07/63	Ft. Columbus, NY	10/09/63	Pt. Lookout, MD	CSR
					Pt. Lookout, MD	03/15/65	Aikens Ldg., VA Xc	P1,P116,P121,P124
McManus, Abraham C.	Pvt	A 1st SCVIR	Richmond, VA Hos.	04/03/65	Richmond, VA	05/08/65	Paroled	CSR
McManus, George B.	Pvt	H 2nd SCVI	Gettysburg, PA	07/04/63	Letterman G.H. Gbg.	09/16/63	Provost Marshal	P1,CSR,KEB,SA2,H2
					W. Bldg. Balt., MD	09/25/63	City Point, VA Xc	P1,LAN,CSR
McManus, John	Pvt	I 17th SCVI	Petersburg, VA	03/25/65	City Pt., VA	03/28/65	Pt. Lookout, MD	CSR,LAN
					Pt. Lookout, MD	06/15/65	Rlsd. G.O. #109	P115,P118,CSR
McManus, John Q.	SMj	1st SCVIR	Smiths Ford, NC	03/16/65	New Berne, NC	03/30/65	Pt. Lookout, MD	CSR,SA1
					Pt. Lookout, MD	05/14/65	Rlsd G.O. #85	P115,P118,P121,CSR
McManus, M.C.	Pvt	B 26th SCVI	Five Forks, VA	04/01/65	City Pt., VA	04/05/65	Pt. Lookout, MD	CSR
					Pt. Lookout, MD	06/29/65	Rlsd. G.O. #109	P118,P121,P123,CSR
McManus, Thomas	Pvt	9 10/19 SCVI	Missionary Ridge, TN	11/25/63	Nashville, TN	12/07/63	Louisville, KY	P39,CSR,HOE
					Louisville, KY	12/09/63	Rock Island, IL	P89,HOE,CSR
					Rock Island, IL	04/07/64	Died, Erysipelas	P5,P131,P132,FPH
McManus, William	Pvt	B 3rd SCVI	Fayetteville, NC	03/10/65	New Berne, NC	04/10/65	Hart's Island, NY	CSR
					Hart's Island, NY	06/14/65	Rlsd. G.O. #109	P79,CSR

SOUTH CAROLINA SOLDIERS, SAILORS AND  CITIZENS HELD IN U.S. PRISONS 1861-1865

NAME	RANK	REGIMENT	CAPTURED AT	WHEN	PRISON	MOVED	DISPOSITION	SOURCES
McManus, William H.	Pvt	H 2nd SCVI	Gettysburg, PA	07/04/63	Gettysburg G.H.	09/01/63	Provost Marshal	P4,CSR,KEB,SA2,H2
					W. Bldg. Balt., MD	09/25/63	City Point., VA Xc	P1,LAN,CSR
McMaster, Fitz William	Col	17th SCVI	Petersburg, VA	03/25/65	Old Capitol, DC	03/06/65	Ft. Delaware, DE	P110,CSR
					Ft. Delaware, DE	07/24/65	Rlsd. G.O. #109	P43,P45,LC,CSR
McMeekin, James A.	Pvt	F 12th SCVI	Sharpsburg, MD	09/17/62	Ft. McHenry, MD	10/13/62	Fts. Monroe, VA Xc	CSR,HFC
McMeekin, James A.	Pvt	F 12th SCVI	Deep Bottom, VA	08/17/64	Pt. Lookout, MD	03/15/65	Aikens Ldg., VA Xc	P113,P117,P124,CSR
McMeekin, Thomas	Pvt	F 12th SCVI	Spotsylvania, VA	05/12/64	5th US A.C. Hos.	05/17/64	Fredericksburg, VA	CSR
McMeekin, William B.	Pvt	F 12th SCVI	Deep Bottom, VA	08/17/64	City Pt., VA	08/22/64	Pt. Lookout, MD	CSR
					Pt. Lookout, MD	01/16/65	Died, Ch. Diarrhea	P5,P117,P119,CSR
McMelan, Richard	Pvt	B 27th SCVI	Town Creek, NC	02/20/65	Ft. Anderson, NC	02/28/65	Pt. Lookout, MD	CSR,HAG
					Pt. Lookout, MD	06/29/65	Rlsd. G.O. #109	P115,P118,CSR
McMichael, Paul Agabus	LtC	20th SCVI	Cedar Creek, VA	10/19/64	Harpers Ferry, WV	10/23/64	Ft. Delaware, DE	CSR,LC
					Ft. Delaware, DE	07/24/65	Rlsd. G.O. #109	P43,P45,P46,CSR
McMillan, J.R.	Pvt	I 5th SCVC	Stony Creek, VA	12/01/64	City Pt., VA	12/05/64	Pt. Lookout, MD	CSR
					Pt. Lookout, MD	06/29/65	Rlsd. G.O. #109	P118,P123,CSR
McMillin, J.H.	1Sg	A 3rd SCVABn	High Pt., NC	05/02/65	High Pt., NC	05/02/65	Paroled	CSR
McMorris, Jonathan M.	Pvt	G Hol.Leg.	Five Forks, VA	04/01/65	City Pt., VA	04/05/65	Pt. Lookout, MD	CSR
					Pt. Lookout, MD	06/29/65	Rlsd. G.O. #109	P118,P121,P123,CSR
McMurray, J.D.	Sgt	B 13th SCVI	Gettysburg, PA	07/04/63	David's Island, NY	09/27/63	City Pt., VA Xc	P1,CSR
McMurray, John M.	Pvt	A 1st SCVIR	Morris Island, SC	09/07/63	Hilton Head, SC		Pt. Lookout, MD	CSR,SA1,LAN
					Pt. Lookout, MD	09/18/64	Aikens Ldg., VA Xc	P113,P116,P124,CSR
McMurtry, G.R.	Pvt	D Orr's Ri.	Petersburg, VA	04/03/65	City Pt., VA	04/11/65	Hart's Island, NY	CSR
					Hart's Island, NY	06/16/65	Rlsd. G.O. #109	P79,CDC,CSR
McNab, Henry	Pvt	B 1st SCVA	Deserted/enemy	02/23/65	Charleston, SC		Rlsd. on oath	CSR
McNabb, John	Pvt	K 1st SCVIG	Gettysburg, PA	07/05/63	Ft. Delaware, DE	06/10/65	Rlsd. on oath	P40,P44,SA1,CSR
McNair, John D.	Pvt	F 26th SCVI	Five Forks, VA	04/01/65	City Pt., VA	04/05/65	Pt. Lookout, MD	CSR
					Pt. Lookout, MD	06/29/65	Rlsd. G.O. #109	P118,P121,P123,CSR
McNally, John R.	Pvt	Ferguson's LA	Marietta, GA	07/05/64	Nashville, TN	07/12/64	Louisville, KY	CSR
					Louisville, KY	07/14/64	Camp Douglas, IL	P94,CSR
					Camp Douglas, IL	03/13/65	Rlsd. on oath	CSR
McNamara, John	Pvt	I 1st SCVA	Morris Island, SC	07/10/63	Hilton Head, SC	09/05/63	Ft. Columbus, NY	CSR
					Ft. Columbus, NY	09/26/63	Rlsd. on oath	P1,CSR
McNamee, James Y.	2Lt	K 22nd SCVI	Appomattox R., VA	04/03/65	Old Capitol, DC	04/21/65	Johnson's Isl., OH	P83,P110,CSR
McNamee, James Y.	2Lt	K 22nd SCVI	Petersburg, VA	04/03/65	Johnson's Isl., OH	06/19/65	Rlsd. G.O. #109	P82,CSR
McNamee, John	Pvt	5 10/19 SCVI	Missionary Ridge, TN	11/25/63	Nashville, TN	12/07/63	Louisville, KY	P39,RAS,CSR
					Louisville, KY	12/09/63	Rock Island, IL	P88,CSR
					Rock Island, IL	06/20/65	Rlsd. G.O. #109	P7,P131,CSR
McNamee, Michael	Pvt	D 1st SCVIR	Deserted/enemy	03/15/65	Charleston, SC		Released on oath	SA1,CSR
McNeal, Daniel	Pvt	D 7th SCVIBn	Kershaw Dis., SC	02/24/65	New Berne, NC	04/10/65	Hart's Island, NY	CSR,HAG,HIC
					Hart's Island, NY	06/17/65	Rlsd. G.O. #109	P79,CSR
McNealy, John P.	Pvt	G 22nd SCVI	Kinston, NC	12/14/62	Kinston, NC	12/14/62	Paroled POW	CSR
McNeary, Levi C.	Pvt	H Hol.Leg.	Five Forks, VA	04/01/65	City Pt., VA	04/05/65	Pt. Lookout, MD	CSR
					Pt. Lookout, MD	06/29/65	Rlsd. G.O. #109	P115,P118,P122,CSR
McNeely, A.Y.	Sgt	C 3rd SCVI	Sharpsburg, MD	09/17/62	Elias Graves' Farm, MD	09/17/62	Died of wounds	P12,SA2,KEB,H2
McNeely, David	Pvt	G 1st SCVIR	Bentonville, NC	03/19/65	New Berne, NC	04/10/65	Hart's Island, NY	CSR,SA1
					Hart's Island, NY	06/16/65	Rlsd. G.O. #109	P79,CSR
McNeely, James H.	Cpl	K 16th SCVI	Graysville, GA	11/26/63	Nashville, TN	12/11/63	Louisville, KY	P39,16R,CSR
					Louisville, KY	12/12/63	Rock Island, IL	P88,P89,CSR
					Rock Island, IL	03/02/65	Pt. Lookout, MD Xc	P131,P132,CSR
McNeely, John P.	Pvt	G 22nd SCVI	Five Forks, VA	04/01/65	Pt. Lookout, MD	06/29/65	Rlsd. G.O. #109	P118,P121,P123,CSR
McNeely, Joseph O.	Pvt	E 3rd SCVIBn	South Mtn., MD	09/14/62	Ft. Delaware, DE	10/02/62	Aikens Ldg., VA Xc	CSR,KEB

SOUTH CAROLINA SOLDIERS, SAILORS AND **M** CITIZENS HELD IN U.S. PRISONS 1861-1865

NAME	RANK	REGIMENT	CAPTURED AT	WHEN	PRISON	MOVED	DISPOSITION	SOURCES
McNeil, Archibald D.	Pvt	H 26th SCVI	Five Forks, VA	04/01/65	City Pt., VA	04/05/65	Pt. Lookout, MD	CSR
					Pt. Lookout, MD	06/29/65	Rlsd. G.O. #109	P118,P121,P123,CSR
McNeil, G.S.	Pvt	A 22nd SCVI	Kinston, NC	12/15/62	Kinston, NC	12/15/62	Paroled POW	CSR
McNeil, Joel T.	Sgt	D 14th SCVI	Dinwiddie C.H., VA	04/04/65	City Pt., VA	04/13/65	Pt. Lookout, MD	CSR
					Pt. Lookout, MD	06/29/65	Rlsd. G.O. #109	P119,P121,P123,CSR
McNeil, John	Pvt	C 27th SCVI	Town Creek, NC	02/20/65	Ft. Anderson, NC	02/28/65	Pt. Lookout, MD	CSR,HAG
					Pt. Lookout, MD	05/15/65	Rlsd. G.O. #85	P115,P118,CSR
McNeil, M.D.	Pvt	I 1st SCVA	Ft. Fisher, NC	01/15/65	Pt. Lookout, MD	06/05/65	Rlsd. Instr. 5/30/65	P121
McNeil, Matthew	Pvt	Lafayette A	Deserted/enemy	03/29/65	Charleston, SC	03/29/65	Released on oath	CSR
McNeil, William M.	Pvt	I 4th SCVC	Stony Creek, VA	12/01/64	City Pt., VA	12/05/64	Pt. Lookout, MD	CSR
					Pt. Lookout, MD	01/17/65	Exchanged	P115,P118,P124,CSR
McNeily, John O.	Pvt	G Ham.Leg.	Deep Bottom, VA	08/17/64	City Pt., VA	08/22/64	Pt. Lookout, MD	CSR
					Pt. Lookout, MD	10/11/64	Aikens Ldg., VA Xc	P113,P117,CSR
McNelus, John	Pvt	C 3rd SCVI	Gettysburg, PA	07/05/63	Ft. Delaware, DE	07/18/64	Hos 7/18-7/29/64	P47,H3,ANY,SA2,KEB
					Ft. Delaware, DE	02/27/65	Rlsd oath Sec. War	P7,P40,P42,P44,CSR
McNewell, John	Pvt	B 14th SCVI	Augusta, GA	05/19/65	Augusta, GA	05/19/65	Paroled	CSR
McNichols, Daniel	Pvt	D 1st SCVA	Rockingham, NC	02/06/65	New Berne, NC	04/10/65	Hart's Island, NY	CSR
					Hart's Island, NY	06/21/65	Rlsd. G.O. #109	P79,CSR
McPherson, Charles Ervin	2Lt	H 8th SCVI	Winchester, VA	09/13/64	Johnson's Isl., OH	06/16/65	Rlsd. G.O. #109	P7,P81,P82,P83,KEB
McPherson, William	Pvt	Ham.Leg.MI	Deserted/enemy	03/02/65	Washington, DC	03/02/65	Chicago, IL oath	CSR
McPriest, P.F.	Pvt	H 7th SCVC	Burkesville, VA	04/14/65	Burkeville, VA	04/17/65	Paroled	CSR
McQuage, Angus	Pvt	D 26th SCVI	Five Forks, VA	04/01/65	City Pt., VA	04/05/65	Pt. Lookout, MD	CSR
					Pt. Lookout, MD	06/29/65	Rlsd. G.O. #109	P118,P121,P123,CSR
McQuaige, Farguar	Pvt	A 4th SCVC	Lynch's Creek, SC	02/25/65	New Berne, NC		Hart's Island, NY	CSR
					Hart's Island, NY	06/17/65	Rlsd. G.O. #109	P79,CSR
McQueen, J.	Pvt	G 8th SCVI	Winchester, VA	05/01/65	Winchester, VA	05/01/65	Paroled	KEB,CSR
McRae, Charles	Sgt	G 23rd SCVI	Petersburg, VA	06/17/64	City Pt., VA	06/24/64	Pt. Lookout, MD	CSR,HOM
					Pt. Lookout, MD	07/27/64	Elmira, NY	P113,P117,P120,CSR
					Elmira, NY	10/11/64	Pt. Lookout, MD Xc	P65,P66,CSR
					Pt. Lookout, MD	10/29/64	Venus Pt., GA Xc	P115,P118,CSR
McRae, Charles	Sgt	G 23rd SCVI	Five Forks, VA	04/01/65	Pt. Lookout, MD	06/29/65	Rlsd. G.O. #109	P118,P121,P123,CSR
McRae, Daniel D.	Pvt	H 7th SCVC	Old Church, VA	06/08/65	Lincoln, G.H., DC	06/14/64	Died of wounds	P5,P12,CSR
McRae, Virgil A.	Pvt	E 7th SCVC	Malvern Hill, VA	06/15/64	City Pt., VA	06/24/64	Pt. Lookout, MD	CSR
					Pt. Lookout, MD	07/27/64	Elmira, NY	P66,P113,P120,P117
					Elmira, NY	03/11/65	Died, pneumonia	P6,P12,P65,FPH,CSR
McRae, William J.	Pvt	B 24th SCVI	Chattanooga, TN	10/09/63	Louisville, KY	10/15/63	DTE, sent north	P88,P93,CSR
McRoy, W.H.	Cpl	C 3rd SCVABn	Ft. Gaines, AL	08/08/64	New Orleans, LA	08/21/64	St. Louis, MO USGH	CSR
					St. Louis, MO USGH	08/30/64	New Orleans, LA	CSR
					New Orleans, LA	09/03/64	St. Louis, MO USGH	CSR
					St. Louis, MO USGH	09/24/64	New Orleans, LA	CSR
					New Orleans, LA	09/26/64	St. Louis, MO USGH	CSR
					St. Louis, MO USGH	10/03/64	New Orleans, LA	CSR
					New Orleans, LA	10/09/64	St. Louis, MO USGH	CSR
					St. Louis, MO USGH	10/14/64	New Orleans, LA	CSR
					New Orleans, LA	10/25/64	Ship Island, MS	P136,CSR
					Ship Island, MS	01/04/65	Exchanged	CSR
McSwain, Eldridge T.	Pvt	K P.S.S.	Fair Oaks, VA	05/31/62	Fts. Monroe, VA	06/05/62	Ft. Delaware, DE	CSR,TSE
					Fts. Monroe, VA	07/10/62	City Pt., VA Xc	CSR
McTeer, Wiley W.	Pvt	B 2nd SCVC	Augusta, GA	05/19/65	Augusta, GA	05/26/65	Paroled	CSR
McVay, John D.	Pvt	B 13th SCVI	Gettysburg, PA	07/04/63	David's Island, NY	08/24/63	City Pt., VA Xc	P1,CSR

M

SOUTH CAROLINA SOLDIERS, SAILORS AND CITIZENS HELD IN U.S. PRISONS 1861-1865

NAME	RANK	REGIMENT	CAPTURED AT	WHEN	PRISON	MOVED	DISPOSITION	SOURCES
McVeigh, Joseph P.	Pvt	H 1st SCVIR	Morris Island, SC	07/10/63	Pt. Lookout, MD		Elmira, NY	CSR
					Elmira, NY	10/11/64	Pt. Lookout to Xc	P66,CSR
					Pt. Lookout, MD	10/29/64	Aikens Ldg., VA Xc	P115,P118,P123,CSR
McWaters, Ansil	Pvt	D 17th SCVI	Petersburg, VA	07/30/64	City Pt., VA	08/05/64	Pt. Lookout, MD	CSR,HHC
					Pt. Lookout, MD	08/08/64	Elmira, NY	P66,P117,P120,CSR
					Elmira, NY	02/20/65	Died, Variola	P65,P66,CSR
McWaters, Jesse	Pvt	D 17th SCVI	Petersburg, VA	07/30/64	City Pt., VA	08/05/64	Pt. Lookout, MD	CSR,HHC
					Pt. Lookout, MD	08/08/64	Elmira, NY	P113,P117,P120,CSR
					Elmira, NY	11/09/64	Died, Pneumonia	P5,P65,FPH,CSR
McWaters, John	Pvt	D 17th SCVI	Keedysville, MD	09/20/62	Keedysville, MD	09/20/62	Paroled as POW	CSR
McWaters, John	Pvt	D 17th SCVI	Crater, Pbg., VA	07/29/64	Pt. Lookout, MD	08/08/64	Elmira, NY	P117,P120,P125,CSR
					Elmira, NY	04/11/65	Died, Pneumonia	P6,P65,P66,FPH,CSR
McWaters, Sumter	Pvt	D 17th SCVI	Crater, Pbg., VA	07/30/64	City Pt., VA	08/05/64	Pt. Lookout, MD	CSR
					Pt. Lookout, MD	08/08/64	Elmira, NY	P117,P120,P125,CSR
					Elmira, NY	06/21/65	Rlsd. G.O. #109	P65,P66,CSR
McWaters, William	Pvt	D 17th SCVI	Crater, Pbg., VA	07/30/64	City Pt., VA	08/05/64	Pt. Lookout, MD	CSR,HHC
					Pt. Lookout, MD	08/08/64	Elmira, NY	CSR
					Elmira, NY	10/11/64	Pt. Lookout, MD Xc	P65,P66,CSR
					Pt. Lookout, MD	10/29/64	Venus Pt., GA Xc	P115,P118,P123,CSR
McWaters, William	Pvt	D 17th SCVI	Petersburg, VA	04/02/65	Washington St. Hos.	04/10/65	Petersburg US G.H.	CSR
					Petersburg G.H.	05/06/65	Camp Hamilton, VA	CSR
					Camp Hamilton, VA	05/09/65	Newport News, VA	CSR
					Newport News, VA	06/26/65	Rlsd. G.O. #109	P107
McWaters, William L.	Sgt	D 17th SCVI	Crater, Pbg., VA	07/30/64	City Pt., VA	08/05/64	Pt. Lookout, MD	CSR
					Pt. Lookout, MD	08/08/64	Elmira, NY	P113,P117,P120,CSR
					Elmira, NY	02/20/65	James R., VA Xc	P65,P66,CSR
McWhorter, D.	Pvt	C 4th SCVC	Stony Creek, VA	12/01/64	City Pt., VA	12/05/64	Pt. Lookout, MD	CSR
					Pt. Lookout, MD	06/29/65	Rlsd. G.O. #109	P115,CSR
McWhorter, John W.	Pvt	H 2nd SCVC	Martinsburg, VA	07/17/63	Wheeling, WV	07/22/63	Camp Chase, OH	P1,P25,CSR
					Camp Chase, OH	09/19/63	Escaped in night	P22,P26
					Cincinnati, OH	10/21/63	Camp Chase, OH	P2,P97,CSR
					Camp Chase, OH	01/14/64	Rock Island, IL	P22,P26,CSR
					Rock Island, IL	03/02/65	Tfd. for Exchange	CSR
McWhorter, John W.	Pvt	H 2nd SCVC	Charlotte, NC	05/22/65	Charlotte, NC	05/22/65	Paroled	CSR
McWilliams, J.R.	Pvt	K Orr's Ri.	Deserted/enemy	02/21/65	City Pt., VA	02/21/65	Washington, DC	CSR
					Washington, DC	02/24/65	Rock Island, IL	CSR
Meacham, Samuel B.	Cpt	E 5th SCVI	Wilderness, VA	05/10/64	Belle Plain, VA	05/17/64	Ft. Delaware, DE	P7,CSR,YEB,ISH
					Ft. Delaware, DE	08/20/64	Hilton Head, SC	P2,P43,P44,CSR
					Hilton Head, SC	10/20/64	Ft. Pulaski, GA	CSR
					Ft. Pulaski, GA	11/19/64	Hilton Head, SC	CSR
					Hilton Head, SC	03/12/65	Ft. Delaware, DE	CSR
					Ft. Delaware, DE	06/09/65	Released	P43,CSR
Meadows, John M.	Pvt	G 27th SCVI	Petersburg, VA	06/24/64	Bermuda Hundred, VA	06/25/64	Fts. Monroe, VA	CSR,HAG
					Fts. Monroe, VA	06/26/64	Pt. Lookout, MD	CSR
					Pt. Lookout, MD	08/16/64	Elmira, NY	P113,P117,P120,CSR
					Elmira, NY	06/19/65	Rlsd. G.O. #109	P65,P66,CSR
Meadows, William F.	Pvt	A Hol.Leg.	Five Forks, VA	04/01/65	City Pt., VA	04/05/65	Pt. Lookout, MD	CSR,HOS
					Pt. Lookout, MD	06/29/65	Rlsd G.O. #109	P118,P121,P123,CSR
Means, Samuel Clowney	2Lt	ACS 1st SCVIH		04/13/65	Washington, DC P.M			SA1,CSR
Means, Thomas B.	2Lt	G Orr's Ri.	Appomattox R., VA	04/03/65	Old Capitol, DC	04/17/65	Johnson's Isl., OH	P110,CSR,CDC
					Johnson's Isl., OH	06/19/65	Rlsd. G.O. #109	P81,P82,P83,CSR

SOUTH CAROLINA SOLDIERS, SAILORS AND  CITIZENS HELD IN U.S. PRISONS 1861-1865

NAME	RANK	REGIMENT	CAPTURED AT	WHEN	PRISON	MOVED	DISPOSITION	SOURCES
Mears, Wyatt T.	Pvt	E Ham.Leg.	Chattanooga, TN	10/29/63	Nashville, TN	11/07/63	Louisville, KY	CSR
					Louisville, KY	11/09/63	Camp Morton, IN	P88,P89,P93,CSR
					Camp Morton, IN	03/04/65	City Pt., VA Xc	P100,P101,CSR
Medlin, Allen	Pvt	D 12th SCVI	Wilderness, VA	05/06/64	Belle Plain, VA	05/20/64	Ft. Delaware, DE	CSR
					Ft. Delaware, DE		Hos 11/29-12/2/64	P47
					Ft. Delaware, DE	06/10/65	Rlsd. GO #109	P41,P43,P45,CSR
Medlin, Daniel	Cpl	C 7th SCVIBn	Weldon RR, VA	08/21/64	City Pt., VA U.S.G.H.	09/04/64	David's Island, NY	CSR,HAG
					David's Island, NY	10/09/64	Elmira, NY	CSR
					Elmira, NY	02/03/65	Died, Diarrhea	P6,P65,P66,FPH,CSR
Medlin, Elijah	Pvt	D 12th SCVI	Warrenton, VA	09/29/62	Warrenton, VA	09/29/62	Paroled	CSR
Medlin, Nicholas	Sgt	C 2nd SCVI	Cedar Creek, VA	10/19/64	Harpers Ferry, WV	10/23/64	Pt. Lookout, MD	CSR,KEB,SA2,H2
					Pt. Lookout, MD	03/28/65	Aikens Ldg., VA Xc	P118,P121,P124,CSR
Medlin, Samuel	Pvt	C 7th SCVIBn	Weldon RR, VA	08/21/64	City Pt., VA	08/24/64	Pt. Lookout, MD	CSR,HAG
					Pt. Lookout, MD	10/11/64	Aikens Ldg., VA Xc	P113,P117,P123,CSR
Medlock, A. Pickens	Pvt	B Ham.Leg.	Fair Oaks, VA	05/31/62	Fts. Monroe, VA G.H.	07/15/62	Ft. Delaware, DE	CSR
					Ft. Delaware, DE	08/05/62	Str. *Catskill* to Xc	CSR
					Richmond, VA Hos.	09/27/62	DIS, overage	CSR
Medlock, A. Pickens	Sgt	B Ham.Leg.MI	Augusta, GA	05/20/65	Augusta, GA	05/20/65	Paroled	CSR
Meek, J.R.	Sgt	A 27th SCVI	Town Creek, NC	02/20/65	Pt. Lookout, MD	06/03/65	Rlsd. Instr. 5/30/65	P121
Meek, Thomas F.	Pvt	K 17th SCVI	Petersburg, VA	03/25/65	City Pt., VA	03/28/65	Pt. Lookout, MD	CSR
					Pt. Lookout, MD	06/15/65	Rlsd. G.O. #109	CSR
Meetz, Orris T.	Pvt	I 15th SCVI	Halltown, WV	08/26/64	Harpers Ferry, WV	08/29/64	Camp Chase, OH	CSR,KEB
					Camp Chase, OH	03/26/65	Pt. Lookout, MD	P23,P26,CSR
					Pt. Lookout, MD	06/29/65	Rlsd. G.O. #109	P115,P121,P123,CSR
Mehrtens, R.	Pvt	A German LA	Deserted/enemy	03/15/65	Charleston, SC	03/15/65	Rlsd. on oath	CSR
Melchers, A.F.	Pvt	B German LA	Deserted/enemy	02/18/65	Hilton Head, SC	04/07/65	New York, NY oath	CSR
Melfi, Francis	Pvt	Lafayette A	Columbia, SC	02/17/65	New Berne, NC	04/10/65	Hart's Island, NY	CSR
					Hart's Island, NY	06/23/65	Rlsd. G.O. #109	P79,CSR
Mellett, Peter	Pvt	F 6th SCVC	Johns Island, SC	02/09/64	Hilton Head, SC	04/03/64	Ft. Lafayette, NY	CSR,CAG
					Ft. Lafayette, NY	04/19/64	Ft. Delaware, DE	P144,CSR
					Ft. Delaware, DE	01/24/65	Hos 1/24-1/30/65	P45,P47
					Ft. Delaware, DE	02/01/65	Hos 2/1-2/11/65	P47
					Ft. Delaware, DE	06/10/65	Rlsd. G.O. #109	P41,P43,CSR
Mellichamp, E.	Pvt	Engineers			Pt. Lookout, MD	05/25/65	Died, Bronchitis	P12,FPH
Mellichamp, James Manly	Pvt	A 25th SCVI	Ft. Fisher, NC	01/15/65	New York, NY	01/30/65	Elmira, NY	CSR,HAG
					Elmira, NY	02/12/65	Died, Pneumonia	P6,P12,P65,P66,FPH
Melton, Alexander	Pvt	F 26th SCVI	Deserted/enemy	12/29/64	City Pt., VA	01/02/65	Washington, DC	CSR
					Washington, DC	01/04/65	Phila., PA on oath	CSR
Melton, Jesse	Pvt	F 26th SCVI	Five Forks, VA	04/01/65	City Pt., VA	04/05/65	Pt. Lookout, MD	CSR
					Pt. Lookout, MD	06/29/65	Rlsd. G.O. #109	P118,P121,P123,CSR
Melton, John	Pvt	C 5th SCResB	Cheraw, SC	03/03/65	Pt. Lookout, MD		Not found, prob Rlsd.	P118
Melton, W.C.	Pvt	E 2nd SCVC	Goldsboro, NC	04/01/65	Pt. Lookout, MD	06/29/65	Rlsd. G.O. #109	P123
Melton, William D.M.	Pvt	G 21st SCVI	Petersburg, VA	06/18/64	Pt. Lookout, MD	07/27/64	Elmira, NY	P113,P117,P120
					Elmira, NY	10/10/64	Died, Pneumonia	P5,P12,P65,P66,FPH
Melton, William W.	Pvt	H 7th SCVI	N. Anna River, VA	05/23/64	Pt. Lookout, MD	06/29/65	Rlsd. G.O. #109	P121,P123,CSR
Mendanhall, Milton W.	Pvt	K 17th SCVI	Five Forks, VA	04/01/65	City Pt., VA	04/06/65	Pt. Lookout, MD	CSR,YEB
					Pt. Lookout, MD	06/29/65	Rlsd. G.O. #109	P115,P118,CSR
Merchant, Nicholas S.	Pvt	H Hol.Leg.	Kinston, NC	12/15/62	Kinston, NC	12/15/62	Paroled POW	CSR
Merchant, Nicholas S.	Pvt	H Hol.Leg.	Petersburg, VA	11/05/64	City Pt., VA	11/11/64	Pt. Lookout, MD	CSR
					Pt. Lookout, MD	06/29/65	Rlsd. G.O. #109	P118,P122,P123,CSR
Merchant, T.A.	Pvt	M 7th SCVI	Gettysburg, PA	07/04/63	Gettysburg G.H.	07/21/63	David's Island, NY	P4,KEB,CSR
					David's Island, NY	08/24/63	City Pt., VA Xc	P1,CSR

SOUTH CAROLINA SOLDIERS, SAILORS AND **M** CITIZENS HELD IN U.S. PRISONS 1861-1865

NAME	RANK	REGIMENT	CAPTURED AT	WHEN	PRISON	MOVED	DISPOSITION	SOURCES
Merck, Israel	Pvt	G 12th SCVI	Petersburg, VA	04/02/65	City Pt., VA	04/04/65	Pt. Lookout, MD	CSR
					Pt. Lookout, MD	06/29/65	Rlsd. G.O. #109	P115,P121,CSR
Merck, J. Daniel	Pvt	G 12th SCVI	Petersburg, VA	04/01/65	Pt. Lookout, MD	06/29/65	Rlsd. G.O. #109	P123
Merck, John M.	Pvt	G 12th SCVI	N. Anna River, VA	05/23/64	Pt. Royal, VA	05/30/64	Pt. Lookout, MD	CSR
					Pt. Lookout, MD	03/11/65	Aikens Ldg., VA Xc	P113,P117,P121,CSR
Meredith, G.P.	Pvt	A 2nd SCVA	Anderson, SC	05/19/65	Anderson, SC	05/19/65	Paroled	CSR
Merkel, Lewis.	Bug	7th SCVC	Petersburg, VA	06/16/64	Pt. Lookout, MD			P117
Meroney, T.A.	QSg	G 3rd SCVABn	High Pt., NC	05/01/65	High Pt., NC	05/01/65	Paroled	CSR
Merrett, N.	Pvt	G 7th SCVC	Greenville, SC	05/23/65	Greenville, SC	05/23/65	Paroled	CSR
Merrett, Thomas	Pvt	LafayetteA	Charlotte, NC Hos.	05/10/65	Charlotte, NC Hos.	05/10/65	Paroled	CSR
Merritt, John	Pvt	B 6th SCVI	Farmville, VA	04/06/65	City Pt., VA	04/14/65	Newport News, VA	CSR,YEB
					Newport News, VA	06/13/65	Rlsd. G.O. #109	P107,CSR
Merritt, Lewis R.	Pvt	C 2nd SCVI	Gettysburg, PA	07/05/63	Letterman G.H. Gbg.	07/09/63	Died, Tetanus	SA2,P1,P122,H2,CSR
Messer, Thomas	Pvt	F 18th SCVI	Petersburg, VA	03/25/65	Pt. Lookout, MD	05/14/65	Rlsd. G.O. #85	P118,P121,CSR
Messervey, P.H.	Pvt	G 7th SCVC	Augusta, GA	05/24/65	Augusta, GA	05/24/65	Paroled	CSR
Messervy, Thomas H.	Pvt	Stono Scts	Augusta, GA	05/24/65	Augusta, GA	05/24/65	Paroled on oath	CSR
Metts, Elijah C.	Pvt	C 20th SCVI	Cedar Creek, VA	10/19/64	W. Bldg. Balt., MD	11/22/64	Pt. Lookout, MD	P3,KEB,CSR
					Pt. Lookout, MD	01/28/65	Hammond G.H., MD	P115,P118,P121,CSR
					Pt. Lookout, MD	06/29/65	Rlsd. G.O. #109	P121,P123,CSR
Metts, John	Pvt	E 25th SCVI	Weldon RR, VA	08/21/64	City Pt., VA	08/24/64	Pt. Lookout, MD	CSR,HAG
					Pt. Lookout, MD	06/05/65	Rlsd. Instr. 5/30/65	P117,P121,P125
Metz, J.Y.	Pvt	K 4th SCVC	Charlotte, NC	05/04/65	Charlotte, NC	05/04/65	Paroled	CSR
Mew, Henry	Pvt	Beaufort L	Salkahatchie R., SC	02/01/65	Hilton Head, SC	03/12/65	Ft. Delaware, DE	CSR
					Ft. Delaware, DE	06/10/65	Rlsd. G.O. #109	CSR
Mew, J.E.	Sgt	A 19th SCVCB	Augusta, GA	05/23/65	Augusta, GA	05/23/65	Paroled on oath	CSR
Mew, John Rufus	Pvt	Beaufort L	Salkahatchie R., SC	02/01/65	Savannah, GA		Ft. Delaware, DE	P45,P47
					Hilton Head, SC	03/12/65	Ft. Delaware, DE	CSR
					Ft. Delaware, DE	06/10/65	Rlsd. G.O. #109	CSR
Meyer, Henry	Pvt	B German LA	Augusta, GA	06/05/65	Augusta, GA	06/05/65	Paroled	CSR
Meyer, Henry D.	Pvt	A German LA	Deserted/enemy	03/21/65	Charleston, SC	03/21/65	Rlsd. on oath	CSR
Meyer, John F.	Pvt	A German LA	Deserted/enemy	03/06/65	Charleston, SC	03/06/65	Rlsd. on oath	CSR
Meyer, Martin	Pvt	A German LA	Deserted/enemy	03/17/65	Charleston, SC	03/17/65	Rlsd. on oath	CSR
Meyers, C.D.	Pvt	B German LA	Deserted/enemy	10/01/64	Hilton Head, SC	10/13/64	Sent north on oath	CSR
Meyers, George	Pvt	B Wash. LA	Deserted/enemy	12/21/64	Hilton Head, SC	04/07/65	New York, NY P.M.	CSR
Meyers, John E.	Pvt	A German LA	Deserted/enemy	03/24/65	Charleston, SC	03/24/65	Released on oath	CSR
Meyers, John H.	Pvt	F 1st SCVA	Bentonville, NC	03/22/65	Hart's Island, NY	05/03/65	Died	P6,P79,FPH,CSR
Meyers, William	Pvt	G 6th SCVC	Deserted/enemy	10/01/64	St. Louis, MO P.M.			CSR
Michaelis, J.H.	Pvt	C 27th SCVI	Drury's Bluff, VA	05/18/64	Bermuda Hundred, VA	05/19/64	Fts. Monroe, VA	CSR,HAG
					Fts. Monroe, VA	05/20/64	Pt. Lookout, MD	CSR
					Pt. Lookout, MD	07/28/64	Elmira, NY	P113,P117,P120,CSR
					Elmira, NY	05/21/65	Rlsd. G.O. #85	P65,P66,CSR
Miche, W.H.	Pvt	H Ham. Leg.	South Mtn., MD	09/14/62	Ft. Delaware, DE	10/02/62	Aikens Ldg., VA Xc	CSR
Mickle, Robert R.	Pvt	I 6th SCVC	Louisa C.H., VA	06/11/64	Fts. Monroe, VA	06/20/64	Pt. Lookout, MD	CSR
					Pt. Lookout, MD	07/25/64	Elmira, NY	P113,P117,P120,CSR
					Elmira, NY	10/11/64	Pt. Lookout, MD Xc	P65,P66,CSR
					Pt. Lookout, MD	10/29/64	Aikens Ldg., VA Xc	P115,P118,P123,CSR
Mickle, Samuel T.	Pvt	A 17th SCVI	Crater, Pbg., VA	07/30/64	City Pt., VA	08/05/64	Pt. Lookout, MD	CSR,HHC
					Pt. Lookout, MD	08/08/64	Elmira, NY	P113,P117,P120,CSR
					Elmira, NY	06/24/65	Rlsd. G.O. #109	P65,P66,CSR
Middleton, Edwin B.	1Lt	K 1st SCVA	Averysboro, NC	03/16/65	Pt. Lookout, MD	04/03/65	Washington, DC	P115,P118
					Old Capitol, DC	04/09/65	Johnson's Isl., OH	P110,CSR
					Johnson's Isl., OH	06/17/65	Rlsd. G.O. #109	P81,P82,CSR

SOUTH CAROLINA SOLDIERS, SAILORS AND M CITIZENS HELD IN U.S. PRISONS 1861-1865

NAME	RANK	REGIMENT	CAPTURED AT	WHEN	PRISON	MOVED	DISPOSITION	SOURCES
Middleton, F.	Cit				Ft. Delaware, DE		Hos 9/15-9/30/64	P47
Middleton, Frank K.	Pvt	K 4th SCVC	Hawe's Shop, VA	05/28/64	3rd Div. 5th A.C. H	05/29/64	Died of wounds	P12,CLD,CSR
Middleton, J.F.	Pvt	D 1st SCVA	Raleigh, NC Hos.	04/13/65	Raleigh, NC Hos.	04/13/65	Paroled	CSR
Middleton, J.J.	Pvt	B 26th SCVI	Farmville, VA	04/06/65	City Pt., VA	04/14/65	Pt. Lookout, MD	CSR
					Newport News, VA	06/26/65	Rlsd. G.O. #109	P107,CSR
Middleton, Thomas A.	1Lt	F 1st SCVA	Bentonville, NC	03/22/65	Hart's Island, NY	04/15/65	Ft. Delaware, DE	P79,CSR
					Ft. Delaware, DE	06/17/65	Rlsd. G.O. #109	P43,P45,CSR
Mikell, Townsend	Sgt	I 3rd SCVC	Edisto Island, SC	04/09/63	Ft. Norfolk, VA	06/29/63	Paroled	CSR
Mikell, W.L.	Adj	19th SCVCB	Augusta, GA	05/24/65	Augusta, GA	05/24/65	Paroled on oath	CSR
Milam, W.H.	Pvt	F 22nd SCVI	Bermuda Hundred, VA	06/02/64	Bermuda Hundred, VA	06/03/64	Fts. Monroe, VA	CSR
					Fts. Monroe, VA	06/04/64	Pt. Lookout, MD	CSR
					Pt. Lookout, MD	02/23/65	Died, Ch. Diarrhea	P6,,P117,P119,FPH
Milam, William M.	Pvt	E 7th SCVC	Chickahominy R., VA	01/30/65	City Pt., VA	02/09/65	Pt. Lookout, MD	CSR,ANY
					Pt. Lookout, MD	02/13/65	Died, Pneumonia	P6,P115,FPH,CSR
Miles, Alexander	Pvt	C 24th SCVI	Nashville, TN	12/16/64	Nashville, TN	12/31/64	Louisville, KY	CSR
					Louisville, KY	01/05/65	Camp Chase, OH	P92,P95,CSR
					Camp Chase, OH	05/02/65	New Orleans Xchg.	P23,P26,CSR
					New Orleans, LA	05/12/65	Vicksburg, MS Xchg	CSR
Miles, Francis Alexander	Pvt	I 24th SCVI	Franklin, TN	12/17/64	Nashville, TN	01/01/65	Louisville, KY	P39,CSR
					Louisville, KY	01/14/65	Camp Chase, OH	P92,P95,CSR
					Camp Chase, OH	02/09/65	Died	P23,P27,CSR
Miles, J.J.	Pvt	H 4th SCVC	Stony Creek, VA	12/01/64	City Pt., VA	12/05/64	Pt. Lookout, MD	CSR
					Pt. Lookout, MD	06/29/65	Rlsd. G.O.#109	P118,P121,P123,CSR
Miles, Milton L.	Pvt	I 24th SCVI	Franklin, TN	12/17/64	Nashville, TN	02/08/65	Louisville, KY	P4,P39,CSR
					Louisville, KY	02/15/65	Rock Island, IL	P92,CSR
					Rock Island, IL	03/13/65	Pt.Lookout, MD Xch	P131,CSR
					Jackson H. Rchmd.	03/28/65	Furloughed 60 days	CSR
Miles, Silas	Pvt	C Ch'n Guard	Cheraw, SC	03/04/65	Pt. Lookout, MD	06/29/65	Rlsd. G.O.#109	P118,P121,P123
Miles, William A.	2Lt	A Orr's Ri.	Falling Waters, MD	07/14/63	Baltimore, MD	08/02/63	Johnson's Isl., OH	CSR,CDC
					Johnson's Isl., OH	06/19/65	Rlsd. G.O. #85	P80,P82,P83,CSR
Miley, H.	Pvt	A 19th SCVCB	Augusta, GA	05/19/65	Augusta, GA	05/19/65	Paroled on oath	CSR
Milford, Clayton B.	Pvt	G Orr's Ri	Petersburg, VA	04/03/65	City Pt., VA	04/11/65	Hart's Island, NY	CSR
Milford, Clayton D.	Pvt	G Orr's Ri	Petersburg, VA	04/03/65	Hart's Island, NY	06/16/65	Rlsd. G.O. #109	P79,CSR
Millard, J.P.	1Lt	ADC Rhett	Averysboro, NC	03/15/65	Hart's Island, NY	04/15/65	Ft. Delaware, DE	P79
Millard, J.P.	1Lt	1st SCVA	Averysboro, NC	03/15/65	Ft. Delaware, DE	06/17/65	Rlsd. G.O.#109	P43
Millen, Eli Harper	Sgt	H 24th SCVI	Franklin, TN	12/18/64	Nashville, TN	01/08/65	Louisville, KY	P4,P39,CSR,HHC
					Louisville, KY	01/14/65	Camp Chase, OH	P92,P95,CSR
					Camp Chase, OH	03/10/65	Took the oath	P26,CSR
					Camp Chase, OH	03/16/65	Rlsd. President O.	P23,CSR
Millen, G.A.	Pvt	A 17th SCVI	Crater, Pbg., VA	07/30/64	City Pt., VA	08/05/64	Pt. Lookout, MD	CSR,HHC
					Pt. Lookout, MD	08/08/64	Elmira, NY	P117,P120,P125,CSR
					Elmira, NY	06/30/65	Rlsd. G.O. #109	P65,P66,CSR
Millen, John A.	2Lt	H 24th SCVI	Franklin, TN	12/18/64	Nashville, TN	12/30/64	Died of wounds	P3,P6,P12,CSR,HHC
Miller, A.B.	Pvt	H 3rd SCVI	N. Anna River, VA	05/23/64	Port Royal, VA	05/30/64	Pt. Lookout, MD	CSR,SA2,KEB,H3
					Pt. Lookout, MD	01/27/65	Aikens Ldg., VA Xc	P113,P117,P124,CSR
Miller, A.J.	Pvt	C 15th SCVAB	Cheraw, SC	03/06/65	New Berne, NC	04/03/65	Pt. Lookout MD	CSR
					Pt. Lookout, MD	05/18/65	Died, Rmtnt.Fever	P6,P115,P118,FPH
Miller, C.W.	Pvt	I Ham.Leg.	Chattanooga, TN	10/29/63	Nashville, TN	11/07/63	Louisville, KY	P39,CSR
					Louisville, KY	11/09/63	Camp Morton, IN	P88,P89,P93,CSR
					Camp Morton, IN	12/07/63	Died	P5,P101,FPH,CSR
					Camp Morton, IN	03/04/65	Listed to Xchg.	P100,CSR
Miller, Clayton	Pvt	A 21st SCVI	Ft. Fisher, NC	01/15/65	Elmira, NY	02/20/65	Pt.Lookout, MD Xch	P65,P66,HAG

SOUTH CAROLINA SOLDIERS, SAILORS AND  CITIZENS HELD IN U.S. PRISONS 1861-1865

NAME	RANK	REGIMENT	CAPTURED AT	WHEN	PRISON	MOVED	DISPOSITION	SOURCES
Miller, D.B.	Cpt	F 3rd SCVIb	South Mtn., MD	09/13/62	Ft. Delaware, DE	10/02/62	Aikens Ldg., VA Xc	CSR
Miller, D.M.	Pvt	C 13th SCVI	Gettysburg, PA	07/05/63	Ft. Delaware, DE	06/10/65	Rlsd. G.O. #109	P42,P44,P45,CSR
Miller, Daniel	Pvt	A 21st SCVI	Ft. Fisher, NC	01/15/65	New York, NY	01/30/65	Elmira, NY	CSR
					Elmira, NY	02/20/65	Pt.Lookout, MD Xch	P65,P66,CSR
Miller, DeForest	Pvt	A 2nd SCVI	Deserted/enemy	12/27/64	Bermuda Hundred, VA	12/29/64	Washington, DC	CSR,SA2,H2
					Washington, DC	01/03/65	Indianapolis, IN	CSR
Miller, E.J.	Pvt	A 21st SCVI	Petersburg, VA	06/24/64	Bermuda Hundred, VA	06/25/64	Fts. Monroe, VA	CSR,HAG
					Fts. Monroe, VA	06/26/64	Pt. Lookout, MD	CSR
					Pt. Lookout, MD	08/16/64	Elmira, NY	P113,P117,P120,CSR
					Elmira, NY	07/30/65	Rlsd. G.O. #109	P65,P66,CSR
Miller, Frederick W.	Cpl	A 25th SCVI	Swift Creek, VA	05/09/64	Bermuda Hundred, VA	05/11/64	Fts. Monroe, VA	CSR,HAG
					Fts. Monroe, VA	05/13/64	Pt. Lookout, MD	CSR
					Pt. Lookout, MD	11/01/64	Aikens Ldg., VA Xc	P116,P121,P124
Miller, Frederick W.	Sgt	A 25th SCVI	Ft. Anderson, NC	02/19/65	Ft. Anderson, NC	02/28/65	Pt. Lookout, MD	CSR
					Pt. Lookout, MD	05/12/65	Rlsd G.O. #85	P118,P121,CSR
Miller, George McDuffie	Col	Orr's Ri.	Appomattox R., VA	04/03/65	Old Capitol, DC	04/21/65	Johnson's Isl., OH	P110,CDC,CSR
					Johnson's Isl., OH	07/25/65	Rlsd. G.O. #109	P82,P83,LC,CSR
Miller, Henry	Pvt	C 27th SCVI	Deserted/enemy	06/02/64	Knoxville, TN	06/02/64	Louisville, KY	CSR
					Louisville, KY	06/15/64	Took the oath	P90
Miller, Henry	Pvt	C 27th SCVI	Deserted/enemy	06/02/64	Louisville, KY	06/24/64	Jeffersonville, IN	P92,P94,CSR
Miller, Henry C.	Pvt	G 8th SCVI	Campbell Stn., TN	12/05/63	Nashville, TN		Louisville, KY	P39,KEB,CSR,HOM
					Louisville, KY	03/09/64	Camp Chase, OH	P88,P91,P94,CSR
					Camp Chase, OH	02/25/65	City Pt., VA Xc	P23,P26,CSR
Miller, Isaac N.	Pvt	C Orr's Ri.	Falling Waters, MD	07/14/63	Frederick, MD G.H.	08/07/63	W. Bldg. Balt., MD	P1,CDC,CSR
					Baltimore, MD	08/23/63	City Pt., VA Xc	P1,CSR
Miller, Isaac S.	Pvt	A Hol. Leg.	Five Forks, VA	04/01/65	City Pt., VA	04/05/65	Pt. Lookout, MD	CSR
					Pt. Lookout, MD	06/29/65	Rlsd. G.O. #109	P115,P118,P121,HOS
Miller, J. August	Pvt	F P.S.S.	Seven Pines, VA	05/31/62	Fts. Monroe, VA	07/17/62	Died of wounds	CSR
Miller, J.C.	Pvt	I 5th SCVC	Midway, SC	02/06/65	New Berne, NC	03/26/65	Died	CSR
Miller, J.G.	Pvt	G P.S.S.	Richmond, VA Hos.	04/03/65	Richmond, VA Hos.	04/14/65	Paroled	CSR
Miller, J.J.	Pvt	I 18th SCVI	Crater, Pbg., VA	07/30/64	City Pt., VA	08/05/64	Pt. Lookout, MD	CSR
					Pt. Lookout, MD	08/08/64	Elmira, NY	P113,P117,P120,CSR
					Elmira, NY	02/13/65	Pt.Lookout, MD Xc	P65,P66,CSR
Miller, J.S.	Pvt	D 11th SCVI	Wilmington, NC	02/20/65	Pt. Lookout, MD	06/29/65	Rlsd. G.O. #109	P123
Miller, J.T.	Sgt	E 8th SCVI	Winchester, VA	09/13/64	Harpers Ferry, WV	09/16/64	Camp Chase, OH	P23,KEB,CSR
					Camp Chase, OH	06/11/65	Rlsd. G.O. #109	P23,CSR
Miller, Jacob F.	Pvt	C 3rd SCVABn	Citronelle, AL	05/04/65	Meridian, MS	05/13/65	Paroled	CSR
Miller, James	Pvt	H 4th SCVC	Thompsons Bridge	03/04/65	New Berne, NC		Pt. Lookout, MD	CSR,LAN
					Pt. Lookout, MD	06/20/65	Rlsd. G.O. #109	P115,P118,P121,CSR
Miller, James	Pvt	B 3rd SCVC	Deserted/enemy	03/25/65	Charleston, SC	04/01/65	Taken oath & disch.	CSR
Miller, James M.	Pvt	C 5th SCResB	Chesterfield, SC	02/28/65	3rd Div. 17th A.C.	03/02/65	No release data	CSR
Miller, James M.	Pvt	H 7th SCVIBn	Augusta, GA	05/18/65	Augusta, GA	05/18/65		CSR,HAG
Miller, James P.	Pvt	B 1st SCVA	Bentonville, NC	03/19/65	New Berne, NC	03/30/65	Pt. Lookout, MD	CSR
					Pt. Lookout, MD	06/29/65	Rlsd.G.O.#109	P118,P121,P123,CSR
Miller, James R.	Pvt	F 5th SCVI	Williamsport, MD	09/15/62	Ft. Delaware, DE	10/02/62	Aikens Ldg., VA Xc	CSR
Miller, James R.	Pvt	K 5th SCVC	Stony Creek, VA	12/01/64	City Pt., VA	12/05/64	Pt. Lookout, MD	CSR
					Pt. Lookout, MD	06/29/65	Rlsd. G.O. #109	P118,CSR
Miller, Jesse F.	Pvt	L 1st SCVI	Warrenton, VA	09/30/62	Warrenton, VA	09/30/62	Paroled	SA1,CSR
Miller, Joel D.	Pvt	G 1st SCVA	Macon, NC	07/18/64	Louisville, KY	07/31/64	Knoxville, TN	P90,P95,CSR
Miller, Joel D.	Pvt	G 1st SCVA	Deserted/enemy	07/18/64	Knoxille, TN	08/01/64	Jeffersonville, IN	CSR

M

SOUTH CAROLINA SOLDIERS, SAILORS AND  CITIZENS HELD IN U.S. PRISONS 1861-1865

NAME	RANK	REGIMENT	CAPTURED AT	WHEN	PRISON	MOVED	DISPOSITION	SOURCES
Miller, John	Pvt	G 22nd SCVI	Ware Bottom Ch., VA	06/15/64	Bermuda Hundred, VA	06/18/64	Fts. Monroe, VA	CSR
					Fts. Monroe, VA	06/18/64	Pt. Lookout, MD	CSR
					Pt. Lookout, MD	07/23/64	Elmira, NY	P113,P117,P120,CSR
					Elmira, NY	01/27/65	Died, Pneumonia	P5,P65,P66,FPH,CSR
Miller, John A.	Pvt	D 1st SCVA	Deserted/enemy	02/18/65	Charleston, SC	03/13/65	Taken oath & disch.	CSR
Miller, John F.	Pvt	I 18th SCVI	Hatchers Run, VA	03/29/65	City Pt., VA	04/02/65	Pt. Lookout, MD	CSR
					Pt. Lookout, MD	06/29/65	Rlsd. G.O. #109	P118,P121,P123,CSR
Miller, John H.	Pvt	I 1st SCVC	Deserted/enemy	02/22/65	Charleston, SC	03/01/65	discharged on oath	CSR
Miller, John N.	Sgt	A Hol. Leg.	Five Forks, VA	04/01/65	City Pt., VA	04/05/65	Pt. Lookout, MD	CSR
					Pt. Lookout, MD	06/29/65	Rlsd. G.O. #109	P118,P121,P123,CSR
Miller, John W.	Pvt	E 3rd SCVI	Gettysburg, PA	07/05/63	Ft. McHenry, MD	07/20/63	Ft. Delaware, DE	CSR
					Ft. Delaware, DE		Chester, PA Hos.	P40,P44,KEB,SA2,H3
					Chester, PA G.H.	08/17/63	City Pt., VA Xc	P1,CSR
Miller, Jonathan	Pvt	F 16th SCVI	Franklin, TN	11/30/64	Nashville, TN	12/02/64	Louisville, KY	CSR
					Louisville, KY	12/03/64	Camp Douglas, IL	P90,P91,P95,CSR
					Camp Douglas, IL	06/18/65	Rlsd. G.O. #109	CSR
Miller, R.N.	Pvt	A 14th SC Mil	Lynch's Creek, SC	02/25/65	Hart's Island, NY	06/16/65	Rlsd. G.O. #109	P79,CSR
Miller, Robert A.	Pvt	K 5th SCVC	Stony Creek, VA	12/01/64	City Pt., VA	12/10/64	Pt. Lookout, MD	CSR,UD2
					Pt. Lookout, MD	02/13/65	Aikens Ldg., VA Xc	P118,P121,P124,CSR
Miller, S.C.	Pvt	A Hol. Leg.	Frederick, MD	09/12/62	Ft. Delaware, DE	10/02/62	Aikens Ldg., VA Xc	CSR
Miller, Simeon E.	Pvt	K 2nd SCVC	Warrenton Jctn., VA	05/03/63	Alexandria, VA USGH	05/21/63	Washington, DC	CSR
					Old Capitol, DC	06/10/63	City Pt., VA Xc	CSR
					Ft. McHenry, MD	06/10/63	City Pt., VA Xc	P110
Miller, T.J.	Pvt	D 8th SCVI	Gettysburg, PA		Gettysburg G.H.		Provost Marshal	P4,KEB
Miller, T.J.	Pvt	D 8th SCVI	Spotsylvania, VA	05/08/64	David's Island, NY	08/24/63	City Pt., Xc	P1,CSR
					Belle Plain, VA	05/20/64	Ft. Delaware, DE	P41,CSR
					Ft. Delaware, DE		(Rcd 5/20/64)	P41
					Ft. Delaware, DE	06/10/65	Released	P43,P45,CSR
Miller, Thomas H.	Pvt	B 14th SCVI	Gettysburg, PA	07/04/63	David's Island, NY	08/24/63	City Pt., VA. Xc	P1,CSR
Miller, W. Saxby	Pvt	B 2nd SCVI	Falling Waters, MD	07/04/63	Ft. McHenry, MD	07/08/63	Ft. Delaware, DE	P96,CSR
					Ft. Delaware, DE	03/03/64	Hos 3/3-4/1/64	P47
					Ft. Delaware, DE	01/06/65	Hos 1/6-1/12/65	P47,SA2,KEB,H2
					Ft. Delaware, DE	10/25/64	Hos 10/25/64- ?	P47
					Ft. Delaware, DE	06/10/65	Released	P40,P42,P44,P45
Miller, W.C.	Pvt	C 4th SCVC	Anderson, SC	05/19/65	Anderson, SC	05/19/65	Paroled	CSR
Miller, William W.	Pvt	C 1st SCVC	Petersburg, VA	11/15/64	City Pt., VA	11/24/64	Pt. Lookout, MD	CSR
					Pt. Lookout, MD	06/29/65	Rlsd. G.O. # 109	P118,P123,CSR
Miller, William W.	Pvt	I 17th SCVI	Petersburg, VA	03/25/65	City Pt., VA	03/28/65	Pt. Lookout, MD	CSR,LAN
					Pt. Lookout, MD	06/29/65	Rlsd. G.O. #109	P118,P121,P123,CSR
Miller, George	Pvt	C 1st SCVIR	Deserted/enemy	03/29/65	Wilmington, NC		New York, NY oath	CSR
Milligan, William	Pvt	B 1st SCVIG	Warrenton, VA	09/29/62	Warrenton, VA	09/29/62	Paroled	SA1,CSR
Milliken, Lawrence	Pvt	F 2nd SCVIRi	Farmville, VA	04/11/65	Farmville, VA	04/21/65	Paroled	CSR
Milling, George W.	Pvt	E 17th SCVI	Five Forks, VA	04/01/65	City Pt., VA	04/06/65	Pt. Lookout, MD	CSR,YEB
					Pt. Lookout, MD	06/29/65	Rlsd. G.O. #109	P115,P118,CSR
Milling, James	Pvt	A 15th SCVI	Halltown, VA	08/26/64	Harpers Ferry, WV	08/29/64	Camp Chase, OH	CSR
					Camp Chase, OH	03/26/65	Pt. Lookout, MD	P23,P26,KEB,CSR
					Pt. Lookout, MD	06/29/65	Rlsd. G.O. #109	P115,P121,P123,CSR
Milling, James S.	Pvt	H 18th SCVI	Deserted/enemy	01/27/65	City Point, VA	01/25/65	Illinois on oath	P8,CSR
Mills, Edward M.	Sgt	D 17th SCVI	Richmond, VA	04/03/65	Richmond, VA Hos.	04/14/65	Richmond, VA P.M.	CSR,HHC
					Libby Prison Rchmd.	04/23/65	Newport News, VA	CSR
					Newport News, VA	06/26/65	Rlsd. G.O. #109	P107,CSR
Mills, J.F.	Cit	Kingville	Augusta, GA	02/19/65	Hart's Island, NY	06/20/65	Rlsd. G.O. #109	P79

M

SOUTH CAROLINA SOLDIERS, SAILORS AND CITIZENS HELD IN U.S. PRISONS 1861-1865

NAME	RANK	REGIMENT	CAPTURED AT	WHEN	PRISON	MOVED	DISPOSITION	SOURCES
Mills, Jack A.	1Sg	H 20th SCVI	Lexington, SC	02/15/65	Pt. Lookout, MD	06/29/65	Rlsd. G.O. #109	P115,KEB,CSR
Mills, James B.	Msc	1st SCVIR	Cheraw, SC	03/05/65	Ft. Monroe, VA	04/02/65	Washington, D.C.	CSR
Mills, James B.	Msc	1st SCVIR	Deserted/enemy	03/05/65	Washington, DC	04/05/65	New York, NY oath	CSR
Mills, Julius	Cpt	F 23rd SCVI	Dinwiddie C.H., VA	04/01/65	Old Capitol, DC	04/09/65	Johnson's Isl., OH	P110,UD6,CSR
					Johnson's Isl., OH	06/19/65	Rlsd. G.O. #109	P81,P82,P83,CSR
Mills, Naseby	Pvt	E 5th SCVC	Armstrongs Mills, VA	12/10/64	City Pt., VA	12/12/64	Pt. Lookout, MD	CSR
					Pt. Lookout, MD	06/29/65	Rlsd. G.O. #109	P118,P121,P123,CSR
Mills, W.W.	Pvt	I 7th SCVC	Farmville, VA	04/11/65	Farmville, VA	04/21/65	Paroled	CSR
Millwee, James A.	Sgt	L P.S.S.	Deserted/enemy	03/05/65	Bermuda Hundred, VA	03/10/65	Washington, DC	CSR,TSE
					Washington, DC	03/10/63	New York, NY oath	CSR
Millwee, R.B.	Pvt	B 37th VAVCB	Opequan Creek, VA	09/13/64	Harpers Ferry, WV	09/16/64	Camp Chase, OH	CSR
					Camp Chase, OH	06/11/65	Rlsd. G.O. #109	CSR
Millwee, Theodore F.	Sgt	K Orr's Ri.	Petersburg, VA	04/03/65	City Pt., VA	04/11/65	Hart's Island, NY	CSR
					Hart's Island, NY	06/16/65	Rlsd. G.O. #109	P79,CSR
Millwood, J.C.	Pvt	F 15th SCVI	Gettysburg, PA	07/02/63	Gettysburg, PA U.S.H.	07/21/63	Provost Marshal	P4,KEB,CSR,H15
					David's Island, NY	08/24/63	City Pt., VA Xc	P1,CSR
Millwood, James Franklin	Pvt	B Hol. Leg.	Five Forks, VA	04/01/65	City Pt., VA	04/05/65	Pt. Lookout, MD	CSR,HOS
					Pt. Lookout, MD	06/29/65	Rlsd. G.O. #109	P118,P121,P123,CSR
Millwood, Joseph	Pvt	E 5th SCVI	Boonesboro, MD	09/14/62	Ft. Delaware, DE	10/02/62	Aikens Ldg., VA Xc	CSR,SA3
Millwood, Morgan	Pvt	F 15th SCVI	Gettysburg, PA	07/04/63	Gettysburg, PA U.S.H.	07/21/63	Provost Marshal	P4,KEB,CSR,H15
					David's Island, NY	08/24/63	City Pt., VA Xc	P1,CSR
Millwood, Richard	Pvt	B Hol. Leg.	Deserted/enemy	03/14/65	City Pt., VA	03/18/65	Washington, DC	CSR
					Washington, DC	03/18/65	Newville, PA/ oath	CSR
Mims, Alfred James	1Lt	E 25th SCVI	Ft. Fisher, NC	01/15/65	Ft. Columbus, NY	04/28/65	Ft. Delaware, DE	P2,P7,HAG,CSR
					Ft. Delaware, DE	05/15/65	Rlsd. G.O. #85	P43,P45,CSR
Mims, Cyrus Pascallus	Pvt	A 18th SCVI	Petersburg, VA	06/16/64	Bermuda Hundred, VA	06/18/64	Fts. Monroe, VA	CSR,UD5
					Fts. Monroe, VA	06/20/64	Pt. Lookout, MD	CSR
					Pt. Lookout, MD	09/10/64	Died, Diarrhea	P6,P117,FPH,CSR
Mims, Fletcher	Sgt	G 27th SCVI	Petersburg, VA	06/24/64	Bermuda Hundred, VA	06/25/64	Fts. Monroe, VA	CSR,HAG
					Fts. Monroe, VA	06/26/64	Pt. Lookout, MD	CSR
					Pt. Lookout, MD	08/16/64	Elmira, NY	P113,P117,P120,CSR
					Elmira, NY	06/18/65	Rlsd. G.O. #109	P65,P66,CSR
Mims, G.D.	Cpt	E 6th SCResB	Augusta, GA	03/24/65	Augusta, GA	03/24/65	Paroled	CSR
Mims, J.D.	Pvt	H 26th SCVI	Petersburg, VA	10/27/64	City Pt., VA	10/31/64	Pt. Lookout, MD	CSR
					Pt. Lookout, MD	05/14/65	Rlsd. G.O. #85	P115,P118,P121,CSR
Mims, J.T.	Pvt	H 11th SCVI	Darbytown Rd., VA	10/27/64	City Pt., VA	10/31/64	Pt. Lookout, MD	HAG,CSR
					Pt. Lookout, MD	03/28/65	Aikens Ldg., VA Xc	P118,P121,P124,CSR
Mims, Jacob N.W.	Pvt	K 21st SCVI	Town Creek, NC	02/20/65	Pt. Lookout, MD	06/29/65	Rlsd. G.O. #109	P115,P118,HAG
Mims, Robert	Sgt	I 5th SCVC	Augusta, GA	05/19/65	Augusta, GA	05/19/65	Paroled	CSR
Mims, Thomas J.	1Lt	Hol. Leg.	Dinwiddie C.H., VA	04/01/65	Old Capitol, DC	04/09/65	Johnson's Isl., OH	P110
					Johnson's Isl., OH	06/19/65	Rlsd. G.O. #109	P82
Mims, William W.	Pvt	A 14th SCVI	Gettysburg, PA	07/05/63	Chester, PA USGH	09/21/63	City Pt., VA Xc	P1,CSR
					Williamsburg, VA Hos.	09/28/63	Furloughed	CSR
Mincey, Patrick	Pvt	H 23rd SCVI	Petersburg, VA	06/17/64	City Pt., VA	06/24/64	Pt. Lookout, MD	CSR,HMC
					Pt. Lookout, MD	07/27/64	Elmira, NY	P113,P117,P120,CSR
					Elmira, NY	03/14/65	James R., VA Xc	P65,P66,CSR
Mincy, John D.	Pvt	F 1st SCVIG	Gettysburg, PA	07/05/63	Ft. Delaware, DE	07/30/63	City Pt., VA Xc	P40,P44,SA1,CSR
Miner, G.L.	Pvt	F 25th SCVI	Ft. Fisher, NC	01/15/65				CSR
Miner, James H.	Pvt	H 7th SCVIBn	Augusta, GA	05/20/65	Augusta, GA	05/20/65		CSR,HOE
Minick, Joel	Pvt	B 14th SCVI	Gettysburg, PA	07/04/63	David's Island, NY	08/24/63	City Pt., VA Xc	P1,CSR
Minick, Joel	Pvt	B 14th SCVI	N. Anna River, VA	05/24/64	Port Royal, VA	05/30/64	Pt. Lookout, MD	CSR
					Pt. Lookout, MD	03/14/65	Aikens Ldg., VA Xc	P117,P121,CSR

SOUTH CAROLINA SOLDIERS, SAILORS AND CITIZENS HELD IN U.S. PRISONS 1861-1865

NAME	RANK	REGIMENT	CAPTURED AT	WHEN	PRISON	MOVED	DISPOSITION	SOURCES
Minick, William T.	Pvt	B 14th SCVI	Sutherland Stn., VA	04/02/65	City Pt., VA	04/07/65	Hart's Island, NY	CSR,HOE
					Hart's Island, NY	06/16/65	Rlsd. G.O. #109	P79,CSR
Minor, Brantley L.	Pvt	G 1st SCVIG	Petersburg, VA	04/03/65	City Pt., VA	04/11/65	Hart's Island, NY	CSR,SA1
					Hart's Island, NY	06/14/65	Rlsd. G.O. #109	P79,CSR
Minor, John	Pvt	H 6th SCVI	Chattanooga, TN	11/26/63	Nashville, TN	12/03/63	Louisville, KY	P39
					Louisville, KY	12/06/63	Rock Island, IL	P88,P89,CSR
					Rock Island, IL	06/20/65	Rlsd. G.O. #109	P131,CSR
Mintz, John S.	Pvt	C 17th SCVI	Deserted/enemy	02/23/65	P.M. A. of P.	02/24/65	City Pt., VA P.M.	CSR
					City Pt., VA P.M.	02/24/65	Washington, DC	CSR
					Washington, DC	02/27/65	Jacksonville, FL	CSR
Minus, Isaac W.	Cpl	A 1st SCVI	Wilderness, VA	05/06/64	Belle Plain, VA	05/21/64	Ft. Delaware, DE	CSR
					Ft. Delaware, DE	06/10/65	Released	P41,P45,CSR
Minus, J.P.	2Lt	D 11th SCVI	Ft. Fisher, NC	01/15/65	Ft. Columbus, NY	02/25/65	City Pt., VA	CSR,HAG
					City Pt., VA	02/25/65	Boulwares Wh., VA	P2,CSR
Miot, John C.	Sgt	A 27th SCVI	Town Creek, NC	02/20/65	Ft. Anderson, NC	02/28/65	Pt. Lookout, MD	CSR,HAG
					Pt. Lookout, MD	06/03/65	Released	P115,P118,CSR
Mirk, B.	Pvt	C 4th SCVC	Hawe's Shop, VA	05/28/64	White House, VA	06/08/64	Pt. Lookout, MD	CSR
					Pt. Lookout, MD	07/09/64	Elmira, NY	P113,P117,P120,CSR
					Elmira, NY	06/30/65	Rlsd. G.O. #109	P65,P66,CSR
Mishoe, Jeremiah	Cpl	F 7th SCVC	Deep Bottom, VA	08/14/64	City Pt., VA	08/22/64	Pt. Lookout, MD	CSR
					Pt. Lookout, MD	03/15/65	Aikens Ldg., VA Xc	P117,P124,P125,CSR
Mishom, Thomas W.	Pvt	L 7th SCVI	Gettysburg, PA	07/03/63	Ft. Delaware, DE	06/10/65	Released	P40,P44,P43,KEB
Miskelly, James D.	Pvt	D 6th SCVI	Missionary Ridge, TN	11/23/63	Bridgeport, AL G.H	12/11/63	Nashville, TN G.H.	P2,CSR
					Nashville, TN U.S.G.H.	01/28/64	Nashville, TN pest	CSR
Miskelly, James D.	Pvt	D 6th SCVI	Lookout Mtn., TN	11/27/63	Nashville, TN U.S.G.H.	03/04/64	Died, Smallpox	P2,P5,P12,CSR
Mitchell, Andrew	Pvt	D Hol. Leg. C	Diaskin Creek, VA	11/22/62	Fts. Monroe, VA	11/29/62	Rlsd. till Xc	CSR
Mitchell, Benj. Newton	Pvt	I 19th SCVI	Cross Roads, KY	10/19/62	Louisville, KY	11/18/62	Cairo, IL	P88,CSR
					Cairo, IL	12/08/62	Vicksburg, MS Xc	CSR
Mitchell, Benj. Newton	Pvt	8 10/19 SCVI	Missionary Ridge, TN	11/25/63	Nashville, TN	12/07/63	Louisville, KY	P39,CSR
					Louisville, KY	12/09/63	Rock Island, IL	P88,P89
Mitchell, Benj. Newton	Pvt	I 19th SCVI	Missionary Ridge, TN	11/25/63	Rock Island, IL	02/25/65	Ft. Columbus, NY	CSR
					Ft. Columbus, NY	03/06/65	Boulwares Wh. Xc	CSR
					Jackson Hos. Rchmd.	03/08/65	Furloughed home 30	CSR
Mitchell, D.D.D.	Pvt	C 7th SCVIBn	Augusta, GA	05/20/65	Augusta, GA	05/20/65		CSR,HAG
Mitchell, Elias	Pvt	B 18th SCVI	Five Forks, VA	04/01/65	City Pt., VA	04/06/65	Pt. Lookout, MD	CSR
					Pt. Lookout, MD	06/29/65	Rlsd. G.O. #109	P118,P121,P123,CSR
Mitchell, George W.	Pvt	K Orr's Ri.	Hanover Jctn., VA	05/24/64	White House, VA	06/08/64	Pt. Lookout, MD	CSR,CDC
					Pt. Lookout, MD	07/09/64	Elmira, NY	P66,P113,P117,P120
					Elmira, NY	09/08/64	Died, Ch. Diarrhea	P5,P12,P65,FPH,CSR
Mitchell, Harrison M.	Pvt	C 3rd SCVIBn	Dandridge, TN	01/17/64	Louisville, KY	02/15/64	Rock Island, IL	P88,P91,P94,CSR
					Rock Island, IL	03/02/65	Pt.Lookout, MD Xc	P131,CSR
Mitchell, J.H.	Pvt	H 16th SCVI	Anderson, SC	05/19/65	Anderson, SC	05/19/65	Paroled on oath	CSR
Mitchell, J.W.	Pvt	B 37th VAVCB	Strasburg, VA	09/23/64	Harpers Ferry, WV	09/30/64	Pt. Lookout, MD	CSR
					Pt. Lookout, MD	10/18/64	Joined US Army	CSR
Mitchell, J.W.	Pvt	C 7th SCVC	Charlotte, NC	05/05/65	Charlotte, NC	05/05/65	Paroled	CSR
Mitchell, James M.	Pvt	D Orr's Ri.	Spotsylvania, VA	05/12/64	Belle Plain, VA	05/21/64	Ft. Delaware, DE	CSR,CDC
					Ft. Delaware, DE	12/13/64	Hos 12/13-12/29/64	P47
					Ft. Delaware, DE	01/29/65	Hos 1/29/65-?	P47
					Ft. Delaware, DE	02/09/65	Hos 2/9-2/21/65	P47
					Ft. Delaware, DE	02/25/65	Died, Pleurisy	P5,P12,P41,P43,P47,CDC

SOUTH CAROLINA SOLDIERS, SAILORS AND  CITIZENS HELD IN U.S. PRISONS 1861-1865

NAME	RANK	REGIMENT	CAPTURED AT	WHEN	PRISON	MOVED	DISPOSITION	SOURCES
Mitchell, John C.	Sgt	A 19th SCVI	Nashville, TN	12/15/64	Nashville, TN Hos.	01/05/65	Nashville, TN G.H.	CSR
					Nashville, TN	05/06/65	Louisville, KY	P4,P39
					Nashville, TN U.S.G.H.	05/06/65	Nashville, TN P.M.	CSR
					Louisville, KY	06/20/65	Releasd G.O. #109	P92,HOE,CSR
					Louisville, KY	07/02/65	Wdd & Paroled POW	CSR
Mitchell, Joseph L.	Pvt	A 2nd SCVC	Augusta, GA	05/20/65	Augusta, GA	05/20/65	Paroled	CSR
Mitchell, Nicholas	Pvt	6 10/19 SCVI	Missionary Ridge, TN	11/25/63	Nashville, TN	12/07/63	Louisville, KY	P39,RAS,CSR
					Louisville, KY	12/09/63	Rock Island, IL	P89,CSR
					Rock Island, IL	10/14/64	Jd. US Army F.S.	P131,CSR
Mitchell, Samuel	Pvt	B 18th SCVI	Deserted/enemy	02/24/65	City Pt., VA		Washington D.C.	CSR
					Washington D.C. oath	03/01/65	Baltimore MD	CSR
Mitchell, Thomas	Pvt	E 1st SCVA	Black River, NC	03/16/65	New Berne, NC	03/30/65	Pt. Lookout, MD	CSR
					Pt. Lookout, MD	06/29/65	Rlsd. G.O. #109	P115,P118,CSR
Mitchell, William	Pvt	E 1st SCVA	Deserted/enemy	02/06/65	Charleston, SC		Released on oath	CSR
Mitchell, William H.	Sgt	F 17th SCVI	Petersburg, VA	03/25/65	City Pt., VA	03/28/65	Pt. Lookout, MD	CSR
					Pt. Lookout, MD	06/29/65	Rlsd. G.O. #109	P115,P118,P123,CSR
Mitchum, John Sessions	Pvt	C 25th SCVI	Ft. Fisher, NC	01/15/65	New York, NY	01/30/65	Elmira, NY	CSR,HAG,CTA
					Elmira, NY	07/11/65	Rlsd. G.O. #109	P65,P66,CSR
Mitchum, Joseph G.	Pvt	D 1st SCVIR	Cheraw, SC	03/14/65	Hart's Island, NY	06/16/65	Rlsd. G.O. #109	P79,SA1,CSR
Mitchum, Sylvester S.	Sgt	C 25th SCVI	Ft. Fisher, NC	01/15/65	New York, NY	01/30/65	Elmira, NY	CSR,HAG,CTA
					Elmira, NY	02/20/65	Pt.Lookout, MD Xc	P65,P66
					Richmond, VA Hos.	03/06/65	Died	CSR
Mitchum, Theodore G.	Pvt	K 25th SCVI	Town Creek, NC	02/20/65	Ft. Anderson, NC	02/28/65	Pt. Lookout, MD	CSR,HAG,CTA
					Pt. Lookout, MD	06/29/65	Rlsd. G.O. #109	P115,P118,CSR
Mitchum, William E.	Cpl	K 25th SCVI	Ft. Fisher, NC	01/15/65	New York, NY	01/30/65	Elmira, NY	CSR,CTA,HAG
					Elmira, NY	07/07/65	Rlsd. G.O. #109	P65,P66,CSR
Mixon, Anthony W.	Pvt	I 25th SCVI	Ft. Fisher, NC	01/15/65	New York, NY	01/30/65	Elmira, NY	CSR,HAG
					Elmira, NY	02/14/65	Died, Ch. Diarrhea	P6,P12,P65,P66,FPH
Mixon, V.	Pvt	K 10th SCVI	Glasgow, KY	09/15/62	Kentucky	11/15/62	Paroled	CSR
Mixon, W.P.	SMj	H 21st SCVI	Ft. Fisher, NC	01/15/65	New York, NY	01/30/65	Elmira, NY	CSR
					Elmira, NY	02/20/65	Pt.Lookout, MD Xc	P65,P66,CSR
Mixon, William T.	Cpl	D 7th SCVIBn	Weldon RR, VA	08/21/64	Pt. Lookout, MD	03/14/65	Aikens Ldg., VA X	P117,P121,P124,HAG
Mixson, G.D.	Sgt	E 1st SCVIH	Chattanooga, TN	10/29/63	Nashville, TN	11/07/63	Louisville, KY	P39,SA1,CSR
					Louisville, KY	11/09/63	Camp Morton, IN	P88,P89,P93,CSR
					Camp Morton, IN	03/04/65	City Pt., VA Xc	P100,CSR
Mixson, W.T.	Cpl	D 11th SCVI	Weldon RR, VA	08/21/64	City Pt., VA	08/24/64	Pt. Lookout, MD	HAG,CSR
					Pt. Lookout, MD	03/14/65	Aikens Ldg., VA Xc	CSR
Mize, J.	Pvt	I 18th SCVI	Richmond, VA Hos.	04/03/65	Newport News, VA	06/13/65	Released	P107
Mize, Solomon M.	Pvt	A 18th SCVI	Richmond, VA Hos.	04/03/65	Libby Prison Rchmd.	04/23/65	Newport News, VA	CSR
					Newport News, VA	06/15/65	Rlsd. G.O. #109	CSR
Mobley, Robert B.	Cpl	B 17th SCVI	Five Forks, VA	04/01/65	City Pt., VA	04/06/65	Pt. Lookout, MD	CSR,HFC
					Pt. Lookout, MD	06/29/65	Rlsd. G.O. #109	P115,P118,P123,CSR
Mobly, P. John	Pvt	F 19th SCVI	Bainbridge, GA	05/20/65	Bainbridge, GA	05/20/65	Paroled	CSR
Mock, Alexander B.	Pvt	B 2nd SCVC	Deserted/enemy	06/23/63	Bloody Run, PA	07/03/63	Ft. Miflin, PA	P2
					Ft. Mifflin, PA	11/17/63	Released on oath	CSR
Mock, J.S.	Pvt	E 14th SCVI	Gettysburg, PA	07/03/63	Chester, PA G.H.	07/29/63	Died of wounds	P1,P6,P12,FPH
Mock, William Thomas	Pvt	D 24th SCVI	Franklin, TN	11/30/64	Nashville, TN	12/03/64	Louisville, KY	CSR,EFW
					Louisville, KY	12/05/64	Camp Douglas, IL	P90,P91,P95,CSR
					Camp Douglas, IL	06/18/65	Rlsd. G.O. #109	CSR
Modlin, J.T.	Pvt	I 1st SCVI	Deserted/enemy	03/18/65	City Pt., VA		Washington, DC	SA1,CSR
					Washington D.C.	03/24/65	Harper's Ferry, WV	CSR
					Washington D.C.	03/24/65	Atheneum Prison	CSR

M

SOUTH CAROLINA SOLDIERS, SAILORS AND CITIZENS HELD IN U.S. PRISONS 1861-1865

NAME	RANK	REGIMENT	CAPTURED AT	WHEN	PRISON	MOVED	DISPOSITION	SOURCES
Mollenhauer, William	Pvt	A German LA	Deserted/enemy	03/15/65	Charleston, SC	03/15/65	Rlsd. on oath	CSR
Molloy, Lawrence E.	Cpl	B 25th SCVI	Ft. Fisher, NC	01/15/65	New York, NY	01/30/65	Elmira, NY	CSR,HAG
					Elmira, NY	07/07/65	Rlsd. G.O. #109	P65,P66,CSR
Molloy, W.P.	Pvt	B 27th SCVI	Petersburg, VA	06/24/64	Bermuda Hundred, VA	06/25/64	Fts. Monroe, VA	CSR
					Fts. Monroe, VA	06/26/64	Pt. Lookout, MD	CSR
					Pt. Lookout, MD	08/16/64	Elmira, NY	P113,P117,P120,CSR
					Elmira, NY	10/11/64	Pt. Lookout, MD Xc	P65,P66,CSR
					Pt. Lookout, MD	10/29/64	Aikens Ldg., VA Xc	P115,P118
					Fts. Monroe, VA	11/01/64	Died & Bur. at sea	CSR
Monce, W.H.	Pvt	K 14th SCVI	Wilderness, VA	05/06/64	Belle Plain, VA	05/21/64	Ft. Delaware, DE	CSR,HOE
					Ft. Delaware, DE	01/05/65	Hos 1/5-2/22/65	P47
					Ft. Delaware, DE	02/27/65	City Pt., VA Xc	P41,P43,CSR
Monday, J.C.	Pvt	Mathewes A	Augusta, GA	05/25/65	Augusta, GA	05/25/65	Paroled	CSR
Monroe, Andrew Jackson	Cpt	E 16th SCVI	Graysville, GA	11/26/63	Nashville, TN	12/04/63	Louisville, KY	P39,16R,CSR
					Louisville, KY	12/05/63	Johnson's Isl., OH	P88,P89,CSR
					Johnson's Isl., OH	06/13/65	Rlsd. G.O. #109	P81,CSR
Monroe, George W.	Pvt	C Hol. Leg.C	New Kent C.H., VA	01/23/64	Norfolk, VA	02/27/64	Pt. Lookout, MD	CSR
					Pt. Lookout, MD	05/03/64	Exchanged	P113,P124,CSR
					Richmond, VA Hos.	05/21/64	Furloughed 30 days	CSR
Montague, Thomas	Pvt	C 15th SCVAB	Deserted/enemy	02/22/65	Charleston,SC	03/22/65	Taken oath & disch.	CSR
Montgomery, A.G.	Cpl	B 23rd SCVI	Petersburg, VA	04/01/65	Pt. Lookout, MD	06/29/65	Rlsd. G.O. #109	P118,P121,P123,CSR
Montgomery, Edward P.	Pvt	C 25th SCVI	Ft. Fisher, NC	01/15/65	New York, NY	01/30/65	Elmira, NY	CSR,HAG,CTA
					Elmira, NY	07/13/65	Elmira, NY USGH	P65,CSR
					Elmira, NY	08/07/65	Rlsd. G.O. #109	P66,CTA,CSR
Montgomery, G.W.	Pvt	C 25th SCVI	Weldon RR, VA	08/21/64	Alexandria, VA	08/29/64	Died of wounds	P6,CTA
Montgomery, Isaac	Sgt	C 25th SCVI	Ft. Fisher, NC	01/15/65	New York, NY	01/30/65	Elmira, NY	CSR,HAG,CTA
					Elmira, NY	07/13/65	Rlsd. G.O. #109	P65,P66,CSR
Montgomery, J. Franklin	Pvt	C 25th SCVI	Drury's Bluff, VA	05/16/64	Fts. Monroe, VA	07/13/64	Died of wounds	P12,CSR
Montgomery, J.A.	Pvt	C 25th SCVI	Ft. Fisher, NC	01/15/65	New York, NY	01/30/65	Elmira, NY	CSR,HAG
					Elmira, NY	07/26/65	Rlsd. G.O. #109	P65,P66,CSR
Montgomery, James Belton	Pvt	C 25th SCVI	Weldon RR, VA	08/21/64	Old Capitol, DC	10/24/64	Elmira, NY	P110,CTA,CSR,HAG
					Elmira, NY	02/13/65	Pt.Lookout, MD Xc	P65,P66,CSR
Montgomery, John	Pvt	K 17th SCVI	Petersburg, VA	03/25/65	City Pt., VA	03/28/65	Pt. Lookout, MD	CSR,YEB
					Pt. Lookout, MD	06/29/65	Rlsd G.O. #109	P115,P118,P122,CSR
Montgomery, John J.	Pvt	I 12th SCVI	Gettysburg, PA	07/05/63	David's Island, NY	09/12/63	City Pt., VA Xc	P1,LAN,CSR
					Williamsburg, VA Hos.	09/21/63	Furloughed	CSR
Montgomery, P.S.	Sgt	K 27th SCVI	Petersburg, VA	06/24/64	Bermuda Hundred, VA	06/25/64	Fts. Monroe, VA	CSR,HAG
					Fts. Monroe, VA	06/26/64	Pt. Lookoput, MD	CSR
Montgomery, P.S.	Sgt	K 27th SCVI	Petersburg, VA	06/24/64	Pt. Lookout, MD	08/16/64	Elmira, NY	P113,P117,P120,CSR
					Elmira, NY	10/11/64	Pt. Lookout, MD Xc	P65,P66,CSR
					Pt. Lookout, MD	10/29/64	Venus Pt., GA Xc	P115,P118,CSR
Montgomery, R.D.	Pvt	H 4th SCVC	Stony Creek, VA	12/01/64	City Pt., VA	12/05/64	Pt. Lookout, MD	CSR,LAN
					Pt. Lookout, MD	02/13/65	Aikens Ldg., VA Xc	P118,P121,P124,CSR
Montgomery, S. Edgar	Pvt	C 25th SCVI	Ft. Fisher, NC	01/15/65	New York, NY	01/30/65	Elmira, NY	CSR,HAG,CTA
					Elmira, NY	03/14/65	Pt.Lookout, MD Xc	P65,P66,CSR
Montgomery, Thomas	Pvt	B 1st SCVIG	Hagerstown, MD	09/26/62	New York, NY	10/06/62	Aikens Ldg., VA Xc	SA1,CSR
Montgomery, Thomas W.	Pvt	C 25th SCVI	Weldon RR, VA	08/21/64	City Pt., VA F.H.	08/23/64	Alexandria, VA GH	CSR,HAG,CTA
					Alexandria, VA G.H.	08/29/64	Died of wounds	P1,P6,P12,CSR
Montgomery, W.J.	Pvt	A 3rd SCVABn	High Pt., NC	05/02/65	High Pt., NC	05/02/65	Paroled	CSR
Monts, George Michael	Pvt	I 15th SCVI	South Mtn., MD	09/14/62	Ft. Delaware, DE	10/02/62	Aikens Ldg., VA Xc	CSR,ANY,KEB,H15

SOUTH CAROLINA SOLDIERS, SAILORS AND  CITIZENS HELD IN U.S. PRISONS 1861-1865

NAME	RANK	REGIMENT	CAPTURED AT	WHEN	PRISON	MOVED	DISPOSITION	SOURCES
Monts, George Michael	Pvt	I 15th SCVI	Halltown, VA	08/26/64	Harpers Ferry, WV	08/29/64	Camp Chase, OH	CSR
					Camp Chase, OH	03/26/65	Pt. Lookout, MD	P23,P26,KEB,CSR
					Pt. Lookout, MD	06/29/65	Rlsd G.O. #109	P115,P121,P123,CSR
Mood, Osgood A.	Sgt	C 1st SCVIG	Sutherland Stn., VA	04/03/65	City Pt. VA	04/13/65	Pt. Lookout, MD	CSR
					Pt. Lookout, MD	06/29/65	Rlsd. G.O. #109	P115,P119,SA1,CSR
Moody, Calvin C.	Pvt	E 1st SCVIG	Wilderness, VA	05/02/64	Belle Plain, VA	05/21/64	Ft. Delaware, DE	SA1,CSR
					Ft. Delaware, DE	08/02/64	Died	P5,P12,P47,FPH,P42
					Ft. Delaware, DE	08/02/64	Died	P41,P43,P47,CDC,FPH,SA1
Moody, Columbus J.L.	Sgt	E 12th SCVI	Wilderness, VA	05/06/64	Belle Plain, VA	05/20/64	Ft. Delaware, DE	CSR,LAN
					Ft. Delaware, DE	06/15/64	Hos 6/15-6/20/64	P47
					Ft. Delaware, DE	06/10/65	Rlsd. G.O. #109	P41,P43,P45,CSR
Moody, J.H.	Pvt	G 2nd SCVA	Cheraw, SC	03/05/65	Paroled			CSR
Moody, J.H.	Pvt	K 24th SCVI	Chattanooga, TN	11/24/63	Rock Island, IL	10/13/64	Jd.USA frontier S.	P131
Moody, John	Pvt	K 1st SCVA	Deserted/enemy	02/17/65	Charleston, SC		Rlsd. on oath	CSR
Moody, John H.	2Lt	H Orr's Ri.	Appomattox R., VA	04/03/65	Old Capitol, DC	04/21/65	Johnson's Isl., OH	P110,HMC,CSR
Moody, John H.	2Lt	H Orr's Ri.	Petersburg, VA	04/03/65	Johnson's Isl., OH	06/19/65	Rlsd. G.O. #109	P82,P83,CSR
Moody, Jonathan L.	Cpl	G 12th SCVI	Petersburg, VA	04/02/65	City Pt., VA	04/07/64	Hart's Island, NY	CSR
					Hart's Island, NY	06/15/65	Rlsd. G.O. #109	P79,CSR
Moody, Richard	Pvt	I 18th SCVI	Petersburg, VA	04/02/65	City Pt., VA	04/07/65	Hart's Island, NY	CSR
					Hart's Island, NY	06/16/65	Rlsd G.O. #109	P79,CSR
Moody, William A.	Cpl	D Hol. Leg.	Petersburg, VA	04/03/65	City Pt., VA	04/10/65	Pt. Lookout, MD	CSR
					Pt. Lookout, MD	06/29/65	Rlsd. G.O. #109	P121,P123
Moon, L.	Pvt	17th SCVI	Warrenton, VA	09/29/62	Warrenton, VA	09/29/62	Paroled	CSR
Moon, R.W.	Pvt	K Ham. Leg. MI	Newton, NC	04/19/65	Newton, NC	04/19/65	Paroled	CSR
Mooney, James	Pvt	G 3rd SCVC	Deserted/enemy	02/24/65	Charleston, SC	03/02/65	Will take oath	CSR
Mooney, Patrick	Pvt	A 1st SCVIR	Deserted/enemy	02/19/63	Hilton Head, SC		North on *Fulton*?	SA1,CSR
Mooneyham, John	Pvt	E 23rd SCVI	Deserted/enemy	03/14/65	City Pt., VA	03/14/65	Washington, DC	HMC,CSR
Mooneyham, Thomas C.	Pvt	E 23rd SCVI	Five Forks, VA	04/01/65	City Pt., VA	04/06/65	Pt. Lookout, MD	CSR,HMC
					Pt. Lookout, MD	06/29/65	Rlsd. G.O. #109	P118,P121,P123,CSR
Moore, A.W.	Pvt	D P.S.S.	Deserted/enemy	12/11/64	Bermuda Hundred, VA	12/12/64	City Pt., VA	CSR,TSE
					City Pt., VA	12/14/64	Washington, DC	CSR
					Washington, DC	12/15/64	Stay in DC on oath	CSR
Moore, Alfred	Pvt	D Naval Bn.	Fayetteville, NC	03/11/65	Hart's Island, NY	06/13/65	Released	P79
Moore, Alfred W.	Cpl	F 21st SCVI	Morris Island, SC	07/10/63	Hilton Head, SC	09/24/63	Ft. Columbus, NY	P124,HAG,CSR
					Ft. Columbus, NY	09/26/63	Pt. Lookout, MD	P1,CSR
					Pt. Lookout, MD	05/15/64	Joined U.S. Army	P113,P116,P125,CSR
Moore, B.F.	Pvt	B 21st SCVI	Ft. Fisher, NC	01/15/65	Elmira, NY	04/10/65	Died, Ch. Diarrhea	P6,P65,P66,FPH,HAG
Moore, Benjamin J.	Pvt	F 21st SCVI	Morris Island, SC	07/10/63	Pt. Lookout, MD	02/07/64	Died, Pneumonia	P5,P113,P119,FPH
Moore, Blaney J.	1Sg	H 8th SCVI	Winchester, VA	09/13/64	Harpers Ferry, WV	09/19/64	Camp Chase, OH	CSR,HMC,KEB
					Camp Chase, OH	01/29/65	Died	P6,P23,P27,FPH
Moore, Cornelius	Pvt	5 10/19 SCVI	Missionary Ridge, TN	11/25/63	Nashville, TN	12/07/63	Louisville, KY	P39,CSR,RAS
					Louisville, KY	12/09/63	Rock Island, IL	P88,P89,CSR
					Rock Island, IL	02/15/65	Transferred to Xc	P131,CSR
Moore, Cornelius M.	Pvt	C 1st SCVA	Bentonville, NC	03/21/65	New Berne, NC	04/10/65	Hart's Island, NY	CSR
					Hart's Island, NY	06/15/65	Rlsd. G.O. #109	P79,CSR
Moore, D.C.	Cpt	F Hol. Leg.	Jarratts Stn., VA	05/08/64	Fts. Monroe, VA	05/13/64	Pt. Lookout, MD	CSR,ISH
					Pt. Lookout, MD	06/23/64	Ft. Delaware, DE	P113,P117,P120
					Ft. Delaware, DE	08/20/64	Hilton Head, SC	CSR
					Hilton Head, SC	12/15/64	Charleston, SC Xc	CSR
Moore, David	Pvt	D 12th SCVI	Farmville, VA	04/23/65	Farmville, VA	04/30/65	Pt. O Rocks USGH	CSR
Moore, David L.	Pvt	D Orr's Ri	Appomattox R., VA	04/03/65	City Pt., VA	04/13/65	Pt. Lookout, MD	CSR
					Pt. Lookout, MD	06/29/65	Rlsd. G.O. #109	CSR

SOUTH CAROLINA SOLDIERS, SAILORS AND M CITIZENS HELD IN U.S. PRISONS 1861-1865

NAME	RANK	REGIMENT	CAPTURED AT	WHEN	PRISON	MOVED	DISPOSITION	SOURCES
Moore, E.P.	Pvt	Beaufort L	Charlotte, NC	05/04/65	Charlotte, NC	05/04/65	Paroled	CSR
Moore, Ebenezer	Pvt	A 21st SCVI	Morris Island, SC	07/10/63	Ft. Columbus, NY	09/23/63	Took the oath	P1,HAG
					Pt. Lookout, MD	01/25/64	Released on oath	P116
					Pt. Lookout, MD	01/25/64	Jd. U.S. Army/Rej.	P113,P125
Moore, Ebsanoh W.	Pvt	G 27th SCVI	Town Creek, NC	02/20/65	Ft. Anderson, NC	02/28/65	Pt. Lookout, MD	CSR,HAG
					Pt. Lookout, MD	06/29/65	Rlsd. G.O. #109	P118,P121,P123,CSR
Moore, Edward	Pvt	B 2nd SCVI	Knoxville, TN	12/03/63	Louisville, KY	12/31/63	Rock Island, IL	P89,P93,P94,SA2,H2
					Rock Island, IL	04/15/64	Died, heart dis.	P5,P131,P132,FPH
Moore, Edward B.	Pvt	B 26th SCVI	Five Forks, VA	04/01/65	City Pt., VA	04/05/65	Pt. Lookout, MD	CSR
					Pt. Lookout, MD	06/29/65	Rlsd G.O. #109	P118,P121,P125,CSR
Moore, Eli	Cpl	C 4th SCVC	Hawe's Shop, VA	05/28/64	3rd Div. 5th A.C.		Washington, DC	CSR
					Armory Sq. Hos., DC	07/19/64	Died of wounds	P6,P12,CSR
Moore, F.	Pvt	F 17th SCVI	Petersburg, VA	03/10/65	P.M. 9th A.C. USA	03/13/65	City Pt., VA P.M.	CSR
					City Pt., VA P.M.	03/23/65	Pt. Lookout, MD	CSR
					Pt. Lookout, MD	05/15/65	Rlsd. G.O. #85	P115,P118,CSR
Moore, G.W.	Sgt	A 3rd SCVIBn	Frederick, MD	09/12/62	Ft. Delaware, DE	10/02/62	Aiken's Ldg. VA Ex	CSR
Moore, G.W.	Pvt	A 3rd SCVABn	High Pt., NC	05/02/65	High Pt., NC	05/02/65	Paroled	CSR
Moore, G.W.	1Sg	F 11th SCVI	Ft. Fisher, NC	01/15/65	Pt. Lookout, MD	06/29/65	Rlsd. G.O. #109	P118,P121,P123,HAG
Moore, General M.	Pvt	F 17th SCVI	Petersburg, VA	03/25/65	City Pt., VA	03/28/65	Pt. Lookout, MD	CSR
					Pt. Lookout, MD	06/29/65	Rlsd. G.O. #109	P118,P123,CSR
Moore, George L.	Pvt	C 17th SCVI	Petersburg, VA	03/25/65	City Pt., VA	03/28/65	Pt. Lookout, MD	CSR,YEB
					Pt. Lookout, MD	06/29/65	Rlsd. G.O. #109	P115,P118,CSR
Moore, George S.	Pvt	G 13th SCVI	Gettysburg, PA	07/05/63	Chester, PA G.H.	08/17/63	City Pt., VA Xc	P1,CSR
Moore, George S.	Cpl	G 13th SCVI	Petersburg, VA	03/25/65	City Pt., VA	03/28/65	Pt. Lookout, MD	CSR
					Pt. Lookout, MD	06/29/65	Rlsd. G.O. #109	P115,P118,P123,CSR
Moore, H.F.	Pvt	F 24th SCVI	Jackson, MS	05/16/63	Jackson, MS	05/16/63	Paroled in Hos.	CSR
Moore, H.P.	Pvt	B 5th SCVC	Augusta, GA	05/24/65	Augusta, GA	05/24/65	Paroled	CSR
Moore, Isaac J.	Pvt	L 21st SCVI	Morris Island, SC	07/10/63	Ft. Columbus, NY		Pt. Lookout, MD	CSR
Moore, J.	Pvt	D Orr's Ri.	Gettysburg, PA	07/03/63	Chester, PA G.H.	08/11/63	Died of wounds	P1
Moore, J.	Pvt	E 6th SCVC	Raleigh, NC Hos.	04/13/65	Raleigh, NC	04/13/65	Paroled	CSR
Moore, J.A.	Pvt	A 17th SCVI	South Mtn., MD	09/14/62	Ft. Delaware, DE	10/02/62	Aikens Ldg., VA Xc	CSR
Moore, J.A.	Pvt	A 17th SCVI	Kinston, NC	12/15/62	Kinston, NC	12/15/62	Paroled	CSR
Moore, J.A.	Pvt	D 18th SCVI	Farmville, VA	04/06/65	City Pt., VA	04/14/65	Newport News, VA	CSR,UD2
					Newport News, VA	06/26/65	Rlsd. G.O. #109	P107,CSR
Moore, J.B.	Pvt	E 19th SCVCB	Bennettsville, SC	03/06/65	Pt. Lookout, MD	06/29/65	Rlsd. G.O. #109	P118,P121
Moore, J.E.	Sgt	D 12th SCVI	Petersburg, VA	04/03/65	Petersburg, VA	05/01/65	US General Hospital	CSR
Moore, J.F.	Pvt	B 21st SCVI	Ft. Fisher, NC	01/15/65	New York, NY	01/30/65	Elmira, NY	CSR,HAG
					Elmira, NY	07/13/65	Elmira, NY G.H.	P65
					Elmira, NY	08/07/65	Rlsd. G.O. #109	P66
Moore, J.J.	Pvt	A 21st SCVI	Petersburg, VA	06/24/64	Fts. Monroe, VA	06/25/64	Ft. Columbus, NY	CSR
					Ft. Columbus, NY	07/26/64	Pt. Lookout, MD	CSR
					Pt. Lookout, MD	08/16/64	Elmira, NY	P117, HAG
					Elmira, NY	02/17/65	Died, Ch. Diarrhea	P66,FPH,CSR
Moore, J.M.	Pvt	A 20th SCVI	Cedar Creek, VA	10/19/64	Harpers Ferry, WV	10/24/64	Pt. Lookout, MD	CSR
					Pt. Lookout, MD	03/28/65	Aikens Ldg., VA Xc	P118,P121,P124,CSR
Moore, J.R.	1Sg	F 21st SCVI	Ft. Fisher, NC	01/15/65	New York, NY	01/30/65	Elmira, NY	CSR,HAG,HOM
					Elmira, NY	07/13/65	Elmira, NY G.H.	P65,P66,CSR
					Elmira, G.H.	07/18/65	Died	CSR,FPH
Moore, James B.	Pvt	K 15th SCVI	Augusta, GA	05/18/65	Augusta, GA	05/18/65	Paroled on oath	H15,CSR
Moore, James C.	Pvt	H Hol. Leg.	Petersburg, VA	11/05/64	City Pt., VA	11/11/64	Pt. Lookout, MD	CSR,ANY
					Pt. Lookout, MD	06/29/65	Rlsd. G.O. #109	P118,P122,P123,CSR
Moore, James Lawrence	Pvt	F 17th SCVI	Petersburg, VA	03/10/65	Pt. Lookout, MD	05/14/65	Rlsd. G.O. #85	P121,CSR,YEB

SOUTH CAROLINA SOLDIERS, SAILORS AND **M** CITIZENS HELD IN U.S. PRISONS 1861-1865

NAME	RANK	REGIMENT	CAPTURED AT	WHEN	PRISON	MOVED	DISPOSITION	SOURCES
Moore, James T.	Pvt	F 1st SCVA	Bentonville, NC	03/22/65	New Berne, NC	04/10/65	Hart's Island, NY	CSR
					Hart's Island, NY	06/17/65	Rlsd. G.O. #109	CSR
Moore, James W.	LAd	2nd SCVC	Augusta, GA	05/24/65	Augusta, GA	05/24/65	Paroled	CSR
Moore, Jesse K.	Pvt	F 27th SCVI	Town Creek, NC	02/20/65	Ft. Anderson, NC	02/28/65	Pt. Lookout, MD	CSR,HAG
					Pt. Lookout, MD	06/29/65	Rlsd G.O. #109	P118,P121,P123,CSR
Moore, John	Pvt	K P.S.S.	Deserted/enemy	01/24/65	Bermuda Hundred, VA	01/25/65	City Pt., VA	CSR,TSE
					City Pt., VA	01/27/65	Washington, DC	CSR
					Washington, DC	01/30/65	New York, NY oath	CSR
Moore, John B.	Sgt	F 5th SCVI	Chattanooga, TN	10/29/63	Nashville, TN	11/07/63	Louisville, KY	P39,SA3,CSR
					Louisville, KY	11/09/63	Camp Morton, IN	P88,P89,P93,CSR
					Camp Morton, IN	03/15/65	Cox's Wf., VA Xc	P100,CSR
Moore, John H.	Pvt	D 27th SCVI	Town Creek, NC	02/20/65	Ft. Anderson, NC	02/28/65	Pt. Lookout, MD	CSR,HAG
					Pt. Lookout, MD	06/29/65	Rlsd. G.O. #109	P115,P118,CSR
Moore, John J.	Pvt	A 21st SCVI	Petersburg, VA	06/24/64	Fts. Monroe, VA	06/26/64	Pt. Lookout, MD	CSR,HAG
					Pt. Lookout, MD	08/16/64	Elmira, NY	P113,P120,CSR
					Elmira, NY	02/17/65	Died, Ch. Diarrhea	P6,P12,P65,FPH
Moore, John M.	Pvt	K 6th SCVC	Ream's Stn., VA	08/24/64	City Pt., VA	08/27/64	Washington, DC GH	CSR
					Washington, DC G.H.	11/26/64	Old Capitol, DC	CSR
Moore, John M.	Pvt	K 6th SCVC	Petersburg, VA	08/31/64	Old Capitol, DC	12/16/64	Elmira, NY	P110,CSR
					Elmira, NY	02/25/65	Tfd. for exchange	P65,P66,CSR
Moore, John W.	Pvt	C 26th SCVI	Five Forks, VA	04/01/65	City Pt., VA	04/05/65	Pt. Lookout, MD	CSR
					Pt. Lookout, MD	06/06/65	Released	P115,P118,P121,CSR
Moore, Nathan	Pvt	A 26th SCVI	Farmville, VA	04/06/65	Newport News, VA	06/26/65	Rlsd. G.O. #109	P107
Moore, Nathaniel	Pvt	H 18th SCVI	Farmville, VA	04/06/65	City Pt., VA	04/14/65	Newport News, VA	CSR
					Newport News, VA	06/26/**65**	Rlsd. G.O. #109	CSR
Moore, Peter A.	1Lt	B 8th SCVI	Winchester, VA	09/13/64	Harpers Ferry, WV	09/16/64	Johnson's Isl., OH	CSR,KEB
					Johnson's Isl., OH	06/16/65	Rlsd. G.O. #109	P81,P82,P83,CSR
Moore, R.L.	Pvt	B 7th SCVC	Charlotte, NC	05/23/65	Charlotte, NC	05/23/65	Paroled	CSR
Moore, Robert	Pvt	F 2nd SCVI	Cedar Creek, VA	10/19/64	Harpers Ferry, WV	10/23/64	Pt. Lookout, MD	CSR,SA2,H2,KEB
					Pt. Lookout, MD	03/30/65	Took the Oath	P119,P124,CSR,P118
Moore, Robert A.	Pvt	F 26th SCVI	Five Forks, VA	04/01/65	City Pt., VA	04/05/65	Pt. Lookout, MD	CSR
					Pt. Lookout, MD	06/29/65	Rlsd. G.O. #109	P118,P121,P123,CSR
Moore, S.M.	Pvt	B 2nd SCVC	Augusta, GA	05/18/65	Augusta, GA	05/18/65	Paroled	CSR
Moore, Samuel P.	Pvt	F 1st SCVIG	Sutherland Stn., VA	04/03/65	City Pt., VA	04/13/65	Pt. Lookout, MD	CSR,SA1
					Pt. Lookout, MD	06/29/65	Rlsd. G.O. #109	P115,P119,CSR
Moore, T.J.	Pvt	A 3rd SCVABn	High Pt., NC	05/02/65	High Pt., NC	05/02/65	Paroled	CSR
Moore, Thomas	Pvt	K 1st SCVA	Deserted/enemy	05/11/64	Hilton Head, SC	07/25/64	New York, NY oath	CSR
Moore, Thomas	Pvt	C 5th SCVC	Deserted/enemy	03/13/65	Charleston, SC	03/15/65	Released on oath	CSR
Moore, Thomas B.	Pvt	E 19th SCVCB	Bennettsville, SC	03/06/65	New Berne, NC	04/06/65	Pt. Lookout, MD	CSR
					Pt. Lookout, MD	06/29/65	Rlsd. G.O. #109	P115,P121,P123,CSR
Moore, Thomas J.	1Lt	A Hol. Leg.	Dinwiddie C.H., VA	04/02/65	City Pt., VA	04/05/65	Old Capitol, DC	CSR,HOS
					Old Capitol, DC	04/09/65	Johnson's Isl., OH	CSR
					Johnson's Isl., OH	06/19/65	Rlsd. G.O. #109	P81,P83,CSR
Moore, W.J.	Pvt	A 14th SCVI	Boonesboro, MD	09/14/62	Ft. Delaware, DE	10/02/62	Aikens Ldg., VA Xc	CSR
					Richmond, VA Hos.	10/31/62	Returned to duty	CSR
Moore, W.J.	Pvt	A 14th SCVI	Petersburg, VA	04/02/65	City Pt., VA	04/07/65	Hart's Island, NY	CSR
					Hart's Island, NY	06/16/65	Rlsd. G.O. #109	P79
Moore, W.R.	Pvt	K Orr's Ri.	Petersburg, VA	04/03/65	City Pt., VA	12/11/64	Hart's Island, NY	CSR
					Hart's Island, NY	06/16/65	Rlsd. G.O. #109	P79,CSR
Moore, Wesley	Pvt	H 21st SCVI	Darlington, SC	02/26/65	Hart's Island, NY	06/16/65	Rlsd. G.O. #109	P79,HAG
Moore, William	Pvt	A 21st SCVI	Morris Island, SC	07/10/63	Hilton Head G.H.	07/23/63	Morris Island Xc	P2,CSR

SOUTH CAROLINA SOLDIERS, SAILORS AND  CITIZENS HELD IN U.S. PRISONS 1861-1865

NAME	RANK	REGIMENT	CAPTURED AT	WHEN	PRISON	MOVED	DISPOSITION	SOURCES
Moore, William B.	Pvt	D 27th SCVI	Town Creek, NC	02/20/65	Ft. Anderson, NC	02/28/65	Pt. Lookout, MD	CSR,HAG
					Pt. Lookout, MD	06/29/65	Rlsd. G.O. #109	P115,P118,HAG,CSR
Moore, William H.	Pvt	A 4th SCVC	Anson Co., NC	03/02/65	New Berne, NC	03/04/65	Pt. Lookout, MD	CSR
					Pt. Lookout, MD	06/29/65	Rlsd. G.O. #109	P118,P121,P123,CSR
Moore, William S.	1Sg	A 16th SCVI	Nashville, TN	12/16/64	Nashville, TN	12/19/64	Louisville, KY	CSR
					Louisville, KY	12/21/64	Camp Douglas, IL	P90,P91,P95,CSR
					Camp Douglas, IL	06/20/65	Rlsd. G.O. #109	CSR
Moorehead, J.M.	Sgt	4th SCVC	Chester, SC	05/05/65	Chester, SC	05/05/65	Paroleed	CSR
Moorehead, John M.	Pvt	G 22nd SCVI	Kinston, NC	12/15/62	Kinston, NC	12/15/62	Paroled POW	CSR
Moorer, W.J.D.	Cpl	F 2nd SCVA	James Island, SC	05/12/64	Hilton Head, SC	08/01/64	Port Royal Fy., SC	CSR
					Port Royal Fy., SC	08/16/64	Exchanged	CSR
Moorhouse, George L.	Pvt	F 17th SCVI	Petersburg, VA	03/25/65	City Pt., VA	03/28/65	Pt. Lookout, MD	CSR
					Pt. Lookout, MD	06/15/65	Rlsd. G.O. #109	P115,P118,YEB,CSR
Morgan, E.A.	Pvt	K 18th SCVI	Warrenton, VA	09/29/62	Warrenton, VA	09/29/62	Paroled	CSR
Morgan, E.A.	Pvt	F 6th SCVC	Louisa C.H., VA	06/11/64	Fts. Monroe, VA	06/20/64	Pt. Lookout, MD	CSR,CAG
					Pt. Lookout, MD	07/25/64	Elmira, NY	P113,P117,P120,CSR
					Elmira, NY	03/02/65	Pt. Lookout, MD Xc	CSR,P65,P66
Morgan, Edward C.	Sgt	E 2nd SCVIRi	Campbell Stn., TN	01/10/64	Nashville, TN	02/28/64	Louisville, KY	P39,CSR
					Louisville, KY	03/09/64	Camp Chase, OH	P88,P91,P94,CSR
					Camp Chase, OH	02/25/65	City Pt., VA Xc	P23,P26,CSR
					Richmond, VA Hos.	03/17/65	Furloughed 60 days	CSR
Morgan, Evan G.	Pvt	I 2nd SCVC	Augusta, GA	05/24/65	Augusta, GA	05/24/65	Paroled	CSR
Morgan, Gilbert	Pvt	F Ham. Leg. MI	Washington, DC	04/26/65	Alexandria, VA	05/10/65	Paroled	CSR
Morgan, H.C.	Pvt	Beaufort LA	Port Royal, SC	09/24/62	New York, NY P.M.	11/06/62	Ft. Columbus, NY	CSR
					Ft. Columbus, NY	11/21/62	Ft. Delaware, DE	CSR
					Ft. Delaware, DE	12/15/62	Fts. Monroe, VA Xc	CSR
Morgan, Isaac J.	Pvt	E 14th SCVI	Gettysburg, PA	07/04/63	David's Island, NY	09/05/63	City Pt., VA Xc	P1,CSR
Morgan, Isaac J.	Pvt	E 14th SCVI	Sutherland Stn., VA	04/02/63	City Pt., VA	04/13/65	Pt. Lookout, MD	CSR
					Pt. Lookout, MD	06/29/65	Rlsd. G.O. #109	P115,P119,P121,P123
Morgan, J.C.	Pvt	F 3rd SCVI	Sharpsburg, MD	09/17/62	Elias Graves Farm	09/17/62	Died of wounds	P12,H3,CSR
Morgan, J.S.	Pvt	E 3rd SCVIBn	Sharpsburg, MD	09/17/62	Ft. McHenry, MD	10/17/62	Fts. Monroe, VA	CSR
					Fts. Monroe, VA	10/19/62	Aikens Ldg., VA Xc	CSR
Morgan, J.W.	Cpl	K 13th SCVI	Gettysburg, PA	07/03/63	David's Island, NY	09/05/63	City Pt., VA Xc	P1,CSR
Morgan, J.W.	Pvt	K 13th SCVI	Appomattox R., VA	04/03/65	City Pt., VA	04/11/65	Hart's Island, NY	CSR
					Hart's Island, NY	06/16/65	Rlsd. G.O. #109	P79,CSR
Morgan, James M.	Pvt	E Orr's Ri.	Petersburg, VA	04/03/65	City Pt., VA	04/11/65	Hart's Island, NY	CSR
					Hart's Island, NY	06/16/65	Rlsd. G.O. #109	P79,CSR
Morgan, John S.	Pvt	E Orr's Ri.	Hatchers Run, VA	03/31/65	City Pt., VA	04/02/65	Pt. Lookout, MD	CSR
					Pt. Lookout, MD	06/29/65	Rlsd. G.O. #109	P115,P121,P123,CSR
					Pt. Lookout, MD	07/22/65	Washington, DC	P118
Morgan, L.H.	Pvt	E 1st SCVIH	Warrenton, VA	09/29/**52**	Warrenton, VA	09/29/62	Paroled	CSR,SA1
Morgan, L.H.	Pvt	E 1st SCVIH	Jetersville, VA	04/06/65	City Pt., VA	04/14/65	Newport News, VA	CSR
					Newport News, VA	06/26/65	Rlsd. G.O. #109	P107,CSR
Morgan, Lewis W.	Pvt	Ferguson's	Franklin, TN	12/17/64	Nashville, TN	05/06/65	Louisville, KY	CSR
					Louisville, KY	06/16/65	Rlsd. G.O. #109	P92,CSR
Morgan, Lewis W.	Pvt	Ferguson's	Augusta, GA US	08/11/65	Augusta, GA US	08/22/65	Released	CSR
Morgan, P.	Pvt	H 2nd SCVC	Richmond, VA	04/03/65	Newport News, VA		Rlsd. G.O. #109	P107
Morgan, W.T.	Pvt	E 16th SCVI	Jonesboro, GA	09/01/64	Rough & Ready, GA	09/19/64	Exchanged	CSR
Morgan, William	Pvt	C 3rd SCVC	Tunnel Hill, GA	02/23/64	Louisville, KY	02/29/64	Ft. Delaware, DE	P88,P91,P94
					Ft. Delaware, DE			P41,P43
Morgan, William J.	Pvt	B 17th SCVI	Five Forks, VA	04/01/65	City Pt., VA	04/06/65	Pt. Lookout, MD	CSR
					Pt. Lookout, MD	06/29/65	Rlsd. G.O. #109	P118,P122,P123,CSR

M

SOUTH CAROLINA SOLDIERS, SAILORS AND CITIZENS HELD IN U.S. PRISONS 1861-1865

NAME	RANK	REGIMENT	CAPTURED AT	WHEN	PRISON	MOVED	DISPOSITION	SOURCES
Morgan, William P.	Pvt	H 16th SCVI	Franklin, TN	11/30/64	Nashville, TN	12/02/64	Louisville, KY	CSR
					Louisville, KY	12/04/64	Camp Douglas, IL	P90,P91,P95,CSR
					Camp Douglas, IL	06/18/65	Rlsd. G.O. #109	P55,CSR
Morgan, William P.	Pvt	I 3rd SCVABn	Fayetteville, NC	03/17/65	Pt. Lookout, MD	06/05/65	Released	P115,P118,CSR
Morrell, Hamilton M.	Pvt	C Hol. Leg.	Five Forks, VA	04/01/65	City Pt., VA	04/05/65	Pt. Lookout, MD	CSR
					Pt. Lookout, MD	06/14/65	Rlsd. G.O. #109	P115,P118,P121,CSR
Morrell, Harmon	Pvt	A 8th SCVI	Winchester, VA	09/13/64	Harpers Ferry, WV	09/19/64	Camp Chase, OH	CSR,KEB
					Camp Chase, OH	06/11/65	Rlsd. G.O. #109	CSR
Morris, Chauncey H.	Pvt	B Hol. Leg.	Petersburg, VA	11/05/64	City Pt., VA	11/11/64	Washington, DC	CSR
					Pt. Lookout, MD	04/08/65	Died, Erysipelas	P6,P118,P119,FPH
Morris, E.F.	Pvt	F 22nd SCVI	Hatchers Run, VA	03/25/65	Pt. Lookout, MD	06/29/65	Rlsd. G.O. #109	P115,P118
Morris, G.H.	Pvt	D 4th SCVC	Augusta, GA	05/20/65	Augusta, GA	05/20/65	Paroled	CSR
Morris, George H.	Pvt	H Hol. Leg.	Five Forks, VA	04/01/65	City Pt., VA	04/05/65	Pt. Lookout, MD	CSR
					Pt. Lookout, MD	06/29/65	Rlsd. G.O. #109	P118,P122,P123,CSR
Morris, H.	Pvt	D 4th SCVC	Augusta, GA	05/20/65	Augusta, GA	05/20/65	Paroled	CSR
Morris, Henry W.	Pvt	G 1st SCVIH	Concord, TN	01/10/64	Nashville, TN	01/24/64	Louisville, KY	P39,CSR,SA1
					Louisville, KY	01/27/64	Rock Island, IL	P88,P94,SR
					Rock Island, IL	05/03/65	New Orleans to Xc	P131,CSR
					New Orleans, LA	05/23/65	Exchanged	P4,SR
Morris, J.M.	Pvt	K 21st SCVI	Town Creek, NC	02/20/65	Ft. Anderson, NC	02/28/65	Pt. Lookout, MD	CSR
					Pt. Lookout, MD	06/29/65	Rlsd. G.O. #109	P121,P123,CSR
Morris, James	Pvt	H 17th SCVI	Richmond, VA	04/03/65	Libby Prison Rchmd.	04/23/65	Newport News, VA	CSR
					Newport News, VA	06/26/65	Rlsd. G.O. #109	P107,CSR
Morris, James M.	Pvt	D 7th SCVC	New Kent C.H., VA	04/28/64	Yorktown, VA	04/30/64	Fts. Monroe, VA	CSR
					Fts. Monroe, VA	05/02/64	Pt. Lookout, MD	CSR
					Pt. Lookout, MD	11/01/64	Aikens Ldg., VA Xc	P113,P121,P124,CSR
Morris, Jesse B.	Pvt	G 26th SCVI	Petersburg, VA	03/25/65	City Pt., VA	03/27/65	Pt. Lookout, MD	CSR
					Pt. Lookout, MD	06/29/65	Rlsd. G.O. #109	P118,P121,P123,CSR
Morris, John S.	Pvt	A 14th SCVI	Appomattox R., VA	04/03/65	Hart's Island, NY	04/15/65	David's Island, NY	P79
					David's Island, NY	04/20/65	Died, Typhoid fev.	P1,P6,P12,FPH
Morris, Joseph	Pvt	F Ham. Leg. MI	Richmond, VA Hos.	04/03/65	Richmond, VA Hos.	04/14/65	Provost Marshal	CSR
					Libby Prison Rchmd.	04/23/65	Newport News, VA	CSR
					Newport News, VA	06/26/65	Rlsd. G.O. #109	CSR
Morris, M.L.	Pvt	G 26th SCVI	Richmond, VA Hos.	04/03/65	Libby Prison Rchmd.	04/23/65	Newport News, VA	CSR
					Newport News, VA	06/13/65	Rlsd. G.O. #109	P107,CSR
Morris, Obediah	Pvt	A 14th SCVI	Amelia C.H., VA	04/03/65	City Pt., VA	04/13/65	Pt. Lookout, MD	CSR
					Pt. Lookout, MD	06/06/65	Released G.O.#85	P115,P119,P121,CSR
Morris, Patrick	Pvt	K 1st SCVIG	Deserted/enemy	01/30/65	City Pt., VA	02/01/65	Washington, D.C.	P8,SA1,CSR
					Washington, D.C.	02/04/65	Albany, NY on oath	CSR
Morris, Richard	Pvt	Wash'n LA	Cheraw, SC	03/05/65	Cheraw, SC	03/05/65	Paroled	CSR
Morris, Robert J.	Pvt	B Wash'n LA			Bowling Green, KY	05/16/65	Paroled	CSR
Morris, S.	Pvt	1st SCVIR	Deserted/enemy	04/12/64	Memphis, TN	04/21/64	Released on oath	CSR
Morris, Stanmore M.	Pvt	C 3rd SCVI	N. Anna River, VA	05/23/64	Port Royal, VA	05/30/64	Pt. Lookout, MD	CSR,ANY,SA2,KEB
					Pt. Lookout, MD	03/14/65	Aikens Ldg., VA Xc	P113,P117,P124,CSR
Morris, Thomas	Pvt	K 11th SCVI	Town Creek, NC	02/20/65	Ft. Anderson, NC	02/28/65	Pt. Lookout, MD	CSR,HAG
					Pt. Lookout, MD	06/29/65	Rlsd. G.O. #109	P115,P121,P123,CSR
Morris, Thomas	Pvt	H 17th SCVI	Augusta, GA	05/20/65	Augusta, GA	05/20/65	Paroled	CSR
\Morris, Thomas B.	Pvt	H Hol. Leg.	Five Forks, VA	04/02/65	Pt. Lookout, MD	06/29/65	Rlsd. G.O. #109	P115,P118,P123,ANY
Morris, William	Pvt	C 5th SCVI	Nashville, TN	05/07/65	Louisville, KY	05/09/65	paroled	CSR
Morris, William H.	Pvt	A SC Cadets	Fayetteville, NC	03/11/65	Pt. Lookout, MD	06/15/65	Rlsd. G.O. #109	P115,CSR
Morris, William R.	Pvt	H 17th SCVI	Petersburg, VA	03/25/65	City Pt., VA	03/28/65	Pt. Lookout, MD	CSR
					Pt. Lookout, MD	06/29/65	Rlsd. G.O. #109	P118,P121,P123,CSR

SOUTH CAROLINA SOLDIERS, SAILORS AND  CITIZENS HELD IN U.S. PRISONS 1861-1865

NAME	RANK	REGIMENT	CAPTURED AT	WHEN	PRISON	MOVED	DISPOSITION	SOURCES
Morris, William T.	Pvt	C 5th SCVI	Wilderness, VA	05/06/64	Pt. of Rocks, VA	11/10/64	Died of wounds	P12,SA3,ROH,JR,HHC
Morrison, Abram	Pvt	E 1st SCVIH	Richmond, VA Hos.	04/03/65	Richmond, VA Hos.	04/14/65	Richmond, VA P.M.	CSR,SA1
					Libby Prison Rchmd.	04/23/65	Newport News, VA	CSR
					Newport News, VA	06/26/65	Rlsd. G.O. #109	P107,CSR
Morrison, Angus	Pvt	A 1st SCVIR	Morris Island, SC	09/07/63	Hilton Head, SC	09/30/63	Ft. Columbus, NY	P1,SA1,CSR
					Ft. Columbus, NY	10/09/63	Pt. Lookout, MD	P1,CSR
					Pt. Lookout, MD	03/03/64	City Pt., VA Xc	P116,P123,P124,CSR
Morrison, Angus	Pvt	A 1st SCVIR	Columbia, SC	03/01/65	New Berne, NC	04/10/65	Hart's Island, NY	P6,P12,P79,FPH,CSR
Morrison, Angus	Pvt	A 1st SCVIR	Columbia, SC	02/14/65	Hart's Island, NY	05/13/65	Died, Ch. Diarrhea	P6,P12,FPH
Morrison, Charles A.	Msc	A 16th SCVI	Franklin, TN	12/11/64	Nashville, KY	12/31/64	Louisville, KY	CSR,16R
					Louisville, KY	01/02/65	Camp chase, OH	P92,P95,CSR
					Camp Chase, OH	03/21/65	Rlsd. on oath	P23,P26,CSR
Morrison, H.	Pvt	A German LA	Deserted/enemy	02/18/65	Hilton Head, SC	04/07/65	New York, NY P.M.	CSR
Morrison, J.R.	Pvt	E 17th SCVI	Petersburg, VA	01/28/65	City Pt., VA	02/01/65	Pt. Lookout, MD	CSR
					Pt. Lookout, MD	05/14/65	Rlsd. G.O. #85	P121,CSR
Morrison, James	Cpl	E 19th SCVI	Augusta, GA	05/22/65	Augusta, GA	05/22/65	Paroled	CSR
Morrison, John T.	1Lt	F 11th SCVI	Weldon RR, VA	08/21/64	Old Capitol, DC	08/27/64	Ft. Delaware, DE	CSR,HAG
					Ft. Delaware, DE	06/13/65	Released 6/10/64	P45,P46,P47,CSR
Morrow, Christopher C.	Pvt	A Hol. Leg.	Five Forks, VA	04/01/65	City Pt., VA	04/05/65	Pt. Lookout, MD	CSR
					Pt. Lookout, MD	06/29/65	Rlsd. G.O. #109	P118,P121,P123,CSR
Morrow, George A.	Pvt	G 14th SCVI	Petersburg, VA	04/02/65	City Pt., VA	04/04/65	Pt. Lookout, MD	CSR
					Pt. Lookout, MD	06/29/65	Rlsd. G.O. #109	P118,P121,P123,CSR
Morrow, J.A.	Pvt	G 2nd SCVC	Prince Wm. Cty., VA		Williamsburg, VA Hos.	08/28/63	Farmville, VA Hos.	CSR
					Farmville, VA	09/12/63	Furloughed 30 days	CSR
Morrow, Rufus G.	Pvt	B 11th SCVI	Town Creek, NC	02/20/65	Ft. Anderson, NC	02/28/65	Pt. Lookout, MD	CSR
					Pt. Lookout, MD	06/29/65	Rlsd. G.O. #109	P115,P118,P123,CSR
Morrow, William B.	Pvt	G 2nd SCVC	Accotink, VA	07/19/63	Alexandria, VA USGH	08/04/63	Washington, DC	P1,CSR
					Lincoln G.H., DC	08/22/63	Baltimore, MD GH	CSR
					Baltimore, MD	08/22/63	City Pt., VA Xc	CSR
					Ft. McHenry, MD	08/24/63	City Pt., VA Xc	P110,CSR
Morse, Albert A.	Chp	17th SCVI	Petersburg, VA	04/03/65	Old Capitol, DC	04/17/65	Johnson's Isl., OH	P110,CSR
					Johnson's Isl., OH	06/17/65	Rlsd G.O. #109	P81,P82,P83,CSR
Morse, J.A.	Pvt	G 2nd SCVC	Augusta, GA	05/31/65	Augusta,GA	05/31/65	Paroled	CSR
Morse, Richard	Pvt	F 23rd SCVI	Petersburg, VA	07/29/64	City Pt., VA	08/05/64	Pt. Lookout, MD	CSR
					Pt. Lookout, MD	08/08/64	Elmira, NY	P113,P117,P120,CSR
					Elmira, NY	01/09/65	New Haven, CN	P65,P66,CSR
Morse, S.D.	Pvt	A 23rd SCVI	Five Forks, VA	04/01/65	City Pt., VA	04/05/65	Pt. Lookout, MD	CSR
					Pt. Lookout, MD	06/15/65	Rlsd. G.O. # 109	P115,P118,CSR
Morton, J.W.	Pvt	C 12th SCVI	Gettysburg, PA	07/03/63	Chester, PA G.H.	09/21/63	City Pt., Xc	P1
Moseley, Samuel J.	Sgt	H 5th SCVI	Deep Bottom, VA	08/14/64	Bermuda Hundred, VA	08/15/64	Fts. Monroe, VA	SA3,CSR
					Fts. Monroe, VA	08/16/64	Pt. Lookout, MD	CSR
					Pt. Lookout, MD	03/14/65	Aikens Ldg., VA Xc	P113,P117,P124,CSR
Mosely, A.W.	Pvt	C 1st SCVC	Goldsboro, NC	03/31/65	New Berne, NC	04/10/65	Hart's Island, NY	CSR
					Hart's Island, NY	06/17/65	Rlsd. G.O. #109	P79,CSR
Mosely, Isaac	Pvt	A 7th SCVIBn	Weldon RR, VA	08/21/64	City Pt., VA U.S.G.H.	08/23/64	Alexandria, VA USGH	CSR,HAG,HIC
					Alexandria, VA G.H.	08/27/64	Washington, DC G H	P1,CSR
					Lincoln G.H., DC	09/05/64	Old Capitol, DC	CSR
					Old Capitol, DC	09/19/64	Ft. Delaware, DE	P110,CSR
					Ft. Delaware, DE	10/28/64	Hos 10/28-12/15/64	P47
					Ft. Delaware, DE	01/03/65	Hos 1/3-2/21/65	P47
					Ft. Delaware, DE	02/27/65	City Pt., VA Xc	P41,P43,CSR

SOUTH CAROLINA SOLDIERS, SAILORS AND CITIZENS HELD IN U.S. PRISONS 1861-1865

NAME	RANK	REGIMENT	CAPTURED AT	WHEN	PRISON	MOVED	DISPOSITION	SOURCES
Mosely, J.	Pvt	C 1st SCVC	Cheraw, SC	03/03/65	New Berne, NC	04/10/65	Hart's Island, NY	CSR
					Hart's Island, NY	06/17/65	Rlsd. G.O. #109	P79,CSR
Mosely, James H.	Pvt	E 13th SCVI	Deserted/enemy	02/24/65	City Pt., VA	02/26/65	Washington, DC	CSR
					Washington, DC	02/27/65	New York, NY oath	CSR
Moses, D.L.	Pvt	C 3rd SCVABn	Blakely, AL	04/09/65	Ship Island, MS	05/01/65	Vicksburg, MS Xc	P136,CSR
Moses, D.L.	Pvt	C 3rd SCVABn	Augusta, GA	05/20/65	Augusta, GA	05/20/65	Paroled	CSR
Moses, Edward L.	Pvt	D 27th SCVI	Salisbury, NC	04/12/65	Nashville, TN	04/29/65	Louisville, KY	P39,HAG,CSR
					Louisville, KY	05/02/65	Camp Chase, OH	P92,P95,CSR
					Camp Chase, OH	06/11/65	Died	P6,P12,P27,FPH,CSR
Moses, H.H.	QSg	C 3rd SCVABn	Blakely, AL	04/02/65				CSR
Moses, H.H.	QSg	C 3rd SCVABn	Augusta, GA	05/20/65	Augusta, GA	05/20/65	Paroled	CSR
Moses, Meyer B.	Pvt	D 2nd SCVI	Cedar Creek, VA	10/19/64	Harpers Ferry, WV	10/23/64	Pt. Lookout, MD	CSR,SA2,KEB,H2
					Pt. Lookout, MD	02/10/65	Aikens Ldg., VA Xc	P118,P123,P124,CSR
Mosley, John McGee	Cpl	B Orr's Ri.	Petersburg, VA	04/03/65	City Pt., VA	04/11/65	Hart's Island, NY	CSR,CDC
					Hart's Island, NY	06/16/65	Rlsd. G.O. #109	P79,CSR
Mosly, J.R.	Pvt	E 2nd SCVA	Cheraw, SC	03/03/65	New Berne, NC	03/31/65	Hart's Island, NY	CSR
					Hart's Island, NY	06/17/65	Rlsd. G.O. #109	P79,CSR
Moss, F.	Pvt	G 13th SCVI	Fredericksburg, VA	05/11/62	Aikens Ldg., VA Xc	08/05/62		CSR
Moss, John P.	Pvt	H 22nd SCVI	Crater, Pbg., VA	07/30/64	City Pt., VA	08/05/64	Pt. Lookout, MD	CSR
					Pt. Lookout, MD	08/08/64	Elmira, NY	P113,P117,P120,CSR
					Elmira, NY	09/02/64	Died, Typhoid Fev.	P5,P65,P66,FPH,CSR
Moss, Noah W.	Pvt	C 17th SCVI	Crater, Pbg., VA	07/30/64	City Pt., VA	08/05/64	Pt. Lookout, MD	CSR
					Pt. Lookout, MD	08/08/64	Elmira, NY	P113,P117,P125,CSR
					Elmira, NY	07/11/65	Rlsd. G.O. #109	P65,P66,CSR
Moss, R.H.	Pvt	C 17th SCVI	Crater, Pbg., VA	07/30/64	City Pt., VA	08/05/64	Pt. Lookout, MD	CSR
					Pt. Lookout, MD	08/08/64	Elmira, NY	P113,P117,CSR
					Elmira, NY	06/06/65	Released	CSR
Moss, Thomas	Pvt	C 17th SCVI	Richmond, VA Hos.	04/03/65	Richmond, VA Hos.	04/21/65	P.M. Richmond, VA	CSR
Moss, Warren W.	Sgt	E Orr's Ri.	Petersburg, VA	04/03/65	City Pt., VA	04/11/65	Hart's Island, NY	CSR
					Hart's Island, NY	06/23/65	Rlsd. G.O. #109	P79,CSR
Moss, William V.	Pvt	F 17th SCVI	Petersburg, VA	03/25/65	City Pt., VA	03/28/65	Pt. Lookout, MD	CSR
					Pt. Lookout, MD	06/29/65	Rlsd. G.O. #109	P115,P118,CSR
Moss, Willis	Pvt	B 27th SCVI	Town Creek, NC	02/20/65	Ft. Anderson, NC	02/28/65	Pt. Lookout, MD	CSR,HAG
					Pt. Lookout, MD	06/29/65	Rlsd. G.O. #109	P115,P118,P123,CSR
Mosteller, Phillip H.	Pvt	B 11th SCVI	Town Creek, NC	02/20/65	Ft. Anderson, NC	02/28/65	Pt. Lookout, MD	CSR
					Pt. Lookout, MD	06/29/65	Rlsd. G.O. #109	P115,P118,P123,CSR
Motes, John B.	Pvt	C 19th SCVI	Nashville, TN	12/16/64	Nashville, TN	12/18/64	Louisville, KY	CSR,HOE
					Louisville, KY	12/20/64	Camp Douglas, IL	P90,P91,P95,CSR
					Camp Douglas, IL	06/12/65	Rlsd. G.O. #109	P55,CSR
Mothershed, E.	Pvt	G 3rd SCVABn	High Pt., NC	05/01/65	High Pt., NC	05/01/65	Paroled	CSR
Mott, John	Pvt	C 1st SCVIG	Deserted/enemy	11/28/64	City Pt., VA	11/30/64	Washington, DC	SA1,CSR
					Washington, D.C.	12/01/64	New York, NY oath	CSR
Mounell, John	Pvt	K 19th SCVI	Atlanta, GA	07/22/64	Camp Chase, OH	06/11/65	Rlsd. G.O. #109	P23
Mouzon, Samuel Ruffin	Pvt	I 4th SCVC	Louisa C.H., VA	06/11/64	Fts. Monroe, VA	06/20/64	Pt. Lookout, MD	CSR,CTA
					Pt. Lookout, MD	07/25/64	Elmira, NY	P113,P117,P120,CSR
					Elmira, NY	10/11/64	Pt. Lookout, MD Xc	P65,P66,CSR
					Pt. Lookout, MD	10/29/64	Aikens Ldg., VA Xc	P115,P118,P123,CSR
Mouzon, William R.	Pvt	A 18th SCVAB	James Island, SC	02/10/65	Beaufort, SC USGH	05/09/65	Hilton Head, SC	P1,CSR,STR
					Hilton Head, SC	05/10/65	Paroled & released	STR
Moye, J.A.	Pvt	PeeDee LA	Danville, VA	06/19/65	Danville, VA	06/19/65	Paroled	CSR

M

SOUTH CAROLINA SOLDIERS, SAILORS AND CITIZENS HELD IN U.S. PRISONS 1861-1865

NAME	RANK	REGIMENT	CAPTURED AT	WHEN	PRISON	MOVED	DISPOSITION	SOURCES
Moyer, Daniel	Sgt	B 19th SCVI	Atlanta, GA	07/22/64	1st Div. 15th AC Hos.	08/02/64	Chattanooga, TN G.	CSR,HOE
					Chattanooga,TN GH	11/02/64	Nashville, TN	CSR
					Nashville, TN	11/21/64	Louisville, KY	CSR
					Louisville, KY	11/24/64	Camp Douglas, IL	P90,P95,CSR
					Camp Douglas, IL	12/30/64	Died, Remttnt Fvr.	P5,P12,P58,FPH,CSR
Moyer, L.	Pvt	E 6th SCResB	Augusta, GA	05/18/65	Augusta, GA	05/18/65	Paroled	CSR
Moyers, David	Pvt	E 1st SCVC	Deserted/enemy	03/22/65	Charleston, SC	03/22/65	Released on oath	CSR
Moyers, Stephen	Msc	D Hol. Leg.	Five Forks, VA	04/01/65	City Pt., VA	04/05/65	Pt. Lookout, MD	CSR
					Pt. Lookout, MD	06/29/65	Rlsd. G.O. #109	P115,P118,P121,CSR
Muckenfuss, Allen W.	2Lt	B 27th SCVI	Weldon RR, VA	08/21/64	Old Capitol, DC	08/21/64	Ft. Delaware, DE	P110,HAG
					Ft. Delaware, DE	10/06/64	Pt. Lookout, MD	P43,P47,CSR
					Pt. Lookout, MD	10/11/64	Aikens Ldg., VA Xc	P115,P117,P123,CSR
Muckenfuss, William M.	1Sg	A 25th SCVI	Town Creek, NC	02/20/65	Ft. Anderson, NC	02/28/65	Pt. Lookout, MD	CSR,HAG
					Pt. Lookout, MD	06/29/65	Rlsd. G.O. #109	P118,P121,P123,CSR
Mudd, T.G.	Pvt	Hol. Leg.	Kinston, NC	12/15/62	Kinston, NC	12/15/62	Paroled POW	CSR
Mulholland, Robert	Pvt	F 17th SCVI	Deserted/enemy	01/12/65	City Point, VA	01/04/65	Washington, DC	P8,CSR
					Washington, DC	01/06/65	Pittsburg, PA/oath	CSR
Mulkey, Hiram Newton	Pvt	G 12th SCVI	Petersburg, VA	04/03/65	City Pt., VA	04/13/65	Pt. Lookout, MD	CSR
					Pt. Lookout, MD	06/29/65	Rlsd. G.O. #109	P115,P119,P123,CSR
Mulkey, John H.	Pvt	F 1st SCVIH	Deep Bottom, VA	08/14/64	Bermuda Hundred, VA	08/15/64	Fts. Monroe, VA	CSR,SA1
					Fts. Monroe, VA	08/16/64	Pt. Lookout, MD	CSR
					Pt. Lookout, MD	06/29/65	Rlsd. G.O. #109	P117,P121,P123,CSR
Mullen, John	Pvt	1st SCVIBn	Morris Island, SC	09/07/63	Ft. Columbus, NY	10/09/63	Johnson's Isl., OH	P1
Mullen, John	Smn	CS Navy	Morris Island, SC	09/02/63	Pt. Lookout, MD	01/21/64	Joined U.S. Army	P125
Mulligan, A. Gideon	Pvt	E 11th SCVI	Petersburg, VA	06/24/64	Bermuda Hundred, VA	06/25/64	Fts. Monroe, VA	HAG,CSR
					Fts. Monroe, VA	06/26/64	Pt. Lookout, MD	CSR
					Pt. Lookout, MD	08/15/64	Elmira, NY	P113,P117,P120,CSR
Mulligan, F.J.	Sgt	B 5th SCVC	Charlotte, NC	05/06/65	Charlotte, NC	05/06/65	Paroled	CSR
Mulligan, Felix R.	3Lt	B Hol. Leg.	Kinston, NC	12/15/62	Kinston, NC	12/15/62	Paroled POW	CSR,HOS
Mulligan, Felix R.	2Lt	B Hol. Leg.	Petersburg, VA	04/02/65	City Pt., VA	04/13/65	Old Capitol, DC	CSR
Mulligan, Felix R.	2Lt	B Hol. Leg.	Appomattox R., VA	04/02/65	Old Capitol, DC	04/17/65	Johnson's Isl., OH	P110
Mulligan, Felix R.	2Lt	B Hol. Leg.	Petersburg, VA	04/02/65	Johnson's Isl., OH	06/19/65	Rlsd. G.O. #109	P81,P82,P83,CSR
Mulligan, George H.	Pvt	E 11th SCVI	Petersburg, VA	06/24/64	Bermuda Hundred, VA	06/25/64	Fts. Monroe, VA	HAG,CSR
					Fts. Monroe, VA	06/26/64	Pt. Lookout, MD	CSR
					Pt. Lookout, MD	08/16/64	Elmira, NY	P113,P117,P120,CSR
					Elmira, NY	02/20/65	James R., VA Xc	P65,P66,CSR
Mulligan, George H.	Pvt	E 11th SCVI	Richmond, VA Hos.	04/03/65	Provost Marshal	04/14/65	Libby Prison	CSR
					Libby Prison	04/24/65	Paroled	CSR
Mulligan, M.H.	Pvt	K 22nd SCVI	Kinston, NC	12/15/62	Kinston, NC	12/15/62	Paroled POW	CSR
Mulligan, P.	Pvt	C 19th SCVCB	Augusta, GA	05/31/65	Augusta, GA	05/31/65	Paroled on oath	CSR
Mulligan, William H.	Pvt	E 11th SCVI	Petersburg, VA	06/24/64	Bermuda Hundred, VA	06/25/64	Fts. Monroe, VA	HAG,CSR
					Fts. Monroe, VA	06/26/64	Pt. Lookout, MD	CSR
					Pt. Lookout, MD	08/16/64	Elmira, NY	P113,P117,P120,CSR
					Elmira, NY	01/27/65	Died, Pneumonia	P5,P65,P66,FPH,CSR
Mullikin, John W.	Pvt	G 22nd SCVI	Boonesboro, MD	09/14/62			On POW roll 9/21/62	CSR
Mullinax, A.J., Jr.	Pvt	F 18th SCVI	Five Forks, VA	04/01/65	City Pt., VA	04/04/65	Pt. Lookout, MD	CSR
					Pt. Lookout, Md	06/27/65	Rlsd. G.O. #109	P123,CSR
Mullinax, A.L.	Pvt	A 12th SCVI	Warrenton, VA	09/29/62	Warrenton, VA	09/29/62	Paroled	CSR
Mullinax, Andrew	Pvt	C 1st SCVA	Deserted/enemy	02/26/65	Charleston, SC		Released on oath	CSR
Mullinax, F.M.	Pvt	I P.S.S.	Deserted/enemy	03/18/65	Bermuda Hundred, VA	03/22/65	City Pt., VA	CSR,TSE
					City Pt., VA	03/25/65	Washington, DC	CSR
					Washington, DC	03/25/65	Nashville,TN oath	CSR

SOUTH CAROLINA SOLDIERS, SAILORS AND  CITIZENS HELD IN U.S. PRISONS 1861-1865

NAME	RANK	REGIMENT	CAPTURED AT	WHEN	PRISON	MOVED	DISPOSITION	SOURCES
Mullinax, Felix H.	2Lt	E 5th SCVI	Lookout Valley, TN	10/29/63	Bridgeport, AL G.H.	11/05/63	Nashville, TN	P2,SA3
					Nashville, TN	01/10/64	Louisville, KY	P39,CSR
					Louisville, KY	01/15/64	Camp Chase, OH	P88,P94,CSR
					Camp Chase, OH	03/25/64	Ft. Delaware, DE	P23
					Ft. Delaware, DE	10/06/64	Pt. Lookout, MD	CSR
					Pt. Lookout, MD	10/11/64	Aikens Ldg., VA Xc	P115,P117,P123,CSR
Mullinax, James	Pvt	I 1st SCVIR	Morris Island, SC	07/10/63	Hilton Head, SC Hos.	07/24/63	Exchanged	P2,SA1,CSR
Mullinax, James L.	Pvt	G 5th SCVI	Chattanooga, TN	10/17/63	Nashville, TN	11/04/63	Louisville, KY	P39,SA3,CSR,TSE
					Louisville, KY	11/05/63	Camp Morton, IN	P88,P89,P93,CSR
					Camp Morton, IN	02/12/64	Died	P5,P100,P101,FPH
Mullinax, James L.	Pvt	G 5th SCVI	Chattanooga, TN	10/29/63	Camp Morton, IN	05/22/65	Released on oath	P100
Mullinax, John	Pvt	H 16th SCVI	Nashville, TN	12/15/64	Nashville, TN	01/12/65	Died, Pneumonia	P4,P12,16R,CSR
Mullinax, W.B.	Pvt	I Ham. Leg. MI	Petersburg, VA	07/29/64	City Pt, VA	08/05/64	Pt. Lookout, MD	CSR
					Pt. Lookout, MD	08/08/64	Elmira, NY	P117,P120,P125,CSR
					Elmira, NY	03/14/65	Pt. Lookout, MD Xc	P65,P66,CSR
Mullinax, W.W.	Pvt	B 12th SCVI	Warrenton, VA	09/29/62	Warrenton, VA	09/29/62	Paroled	CSR
Mullins, John	Sgt	E 1st SCVIR	Deserted/enemy	10/31/64	Hilton Head, SC	11/01/64	Jd. US Navy	P8,SA1,CSR
Mullins, Dudley	Pvt	I 13th SCVI	Petersburg, VA	04/02/65	City Pt., VA	04/04/65	Pt. Lookout, MD	CSR
					Pt. Lookout, MD	06/29/65	Rlsd. G.O. #109	P115,P118,P121,CSR
Mullins, John	Pvt	G Hol. Leg.	Petersburg, VA	03/25/65	City Pt., VA	03/28/65	Old Capitol, DC	CSR
					Old Capitol, DC	05/17/65	Elmira, NY	P110
					Old Capitol, DC	06/12/65	Lincoln G.H., DC	CSR
Mullins, Uriah	Pvt	E 13th SCVI	Deserted/enemy	02/09/65	City Pt., VA	02/12/65	Washington, DC	P8,CSR
Mullins, W.	Pvt	I 13th SCVI	Petersburg, VA	04/01/65	Pt. Lookout, MD	06/29/65	Rlsd. G.O. #109	P123
Mullins, William	Pvt	C 27th SCVI	Petersburg, VA	06/24/64	Fts. Monroe, VA	06/26/64	Pt. Lookout, MD	CSR,HAG
					Pt. Lookout, MD	07/25/64	Elmira, NY	P113,P117,P120,CSR
					Elmira, NY	05/19/65	Released	P7,P65,CSR
Mulloy, Thomas F.	3Lt	C 8th SCVI	Sharpsburg, MD	09/17/62	Ft. McHenry, MD		Fts. Monroe, VA	CSR
					Fts. Monroe, VA	11/08/62	Aikens Ldg., VA Xc	CSR
Mulrooney, Barney	Pvt	E 1st SCVA	Morris Island, SC	07/10/63	Ft. Columbus, NY	09/23/63	Took the oath	P1,CSR
Mulvaney, James M.	Cpt	H 27th SCVI	Petersburg, VA	06/24/64	Bermuda Hundred, VA	06/25/64	Fts. Monroe, VA	CSR,HAG,ISH
					Fts. Monroe, VA	06/26/64	Pt. Lookout, MD	CSR
					Pt. Lookout, MD	06/29/64	Washington, DC	P113,P117,P120,CSR
					Old Capitol, DC	07/22/64	Ft. Delaware, DE	CSR
					Ft. Delaware, DE	08/20/64	Hilton Head, SC	P43,P44,P46,CSR
					Hilton Head, SC	10/20/64	Ft. Pulaski, GA	CSR
					Ft. Pulaski, GA		(Took the oath)	P4,CSR
Mulvaney, Nicholas	Pvt	E 18th SCVAB	Charlotte, NC	05/03/65	Charlotte, NC	05/03/65	Paroled	CSR
Mundle, John D.	Pvt	B 7th SCVIBn	Deserted/enemy	04/02/65	Washington, DC P.M.	04/05/65	Charleston, SC oath	CSR
Mundle, W.W.	Pvt	F 12th SCVI	Hagerstown, MD	09/14/62	Ft. Delaware, DE	11/10/62	Aikens Ldg., VA Xc	CSR
Mundy, James C.	Pvt	F Hol. Leg.	Jarratts Stn., VA	05/08/64	Pt. Lookout, MD	08/15/64	Elmira, NY	P113,P116,P118,CSR
					Elmira, NY	10/11/64	Pt.Lookout to Xc	P65,P66,CSR
Mundy, James C.	Pvt	F Hol. Leg.	Jarratts Stn., VA	05/08/64	Pt. Lookout, MD	10/29/64	Venus Pt., GA Xc	P115,CSR
Mungo, E.M.	Pvt	K 6th SCVC	Louisa C.H., VA	06/11/64	Pt. Lookout, MD	07/25/64	Elmira, NY	P113,P117,P120,CSR
					Elmira, NY	10/11/64	Pt. Lookout, MD Xc	P65,P66
					W. Bldg. Balt, MD	10/22/64	Died, Ch. Diarrhea	P12,CSR
Munn, Daniel M.	Pvt	D 7th SCVIBn	Kershaw Dis., SC	02/24/65	New Berne, NC	04/10/65	Hart's Island, NY	CSR,HAG,HIC
					Hart's Island, NY	06/17/65	Rlsd. G.O. #109	P79,CSR
Munnerlyn, Charles T.	2Lt	G 8th SCVI	Knoxville, TN	11/29/63	Louisville, KY	01/15/64	Camp Chase, OH	P88,P94,KEB,CSR
					Camp Chase, OH	03/25/64	Ft. Delaware, DE	P23,P26,CSR
					Ft. Delaware, DE	06/12/65	Rlsd. G.O. #109	P43,P44,P45,CSR

M

SOUTH CAROLINA SOLDIERS, SAILORS AND CITIZENS HELD IN U.S. PRISONS 1861-1865

NAME	RANK	REGIMENT	CAPTURED AT	WHEN	PRISON	MOVED	DISPOSITION	SOURCES
Munroe, John P.	Cpl	E 2nd SCVI	Halltown, VA	08/26/64	Harpers Ferry, WV	04/02/64	Camp Chase, OH	CSR
					Camp Chase, OH	02/20/65	Died, Pneumonia	P6,P23,P27,FPH,CSR
Muns, Robert	Pvt	D Hol. Leg.	Petersburg, VA	03/25/65	City Pt., VA	03/29/65	Pt. Lookout, MD	CSR
					Pt. Lookout, MD	06/29/65	Rlsd. G.O. #109	P118,P121,P123,CSR
Murdoch, Stephen G.	Pvt	E 20th SCVI	Columbia, SC	02/14/65	Hart's Island, NY	06/16/65	Rlsd. G.O. #109	P79,CSR
Murdock, James	Pvt	E 26th SCVI	Five Forks, VA	04/01/65	City Pt., VA	04/05/65	Pt. Lookout, MD	CSR
					Pt. Lookout, MD	06/15/65	Rlsd. G.O. #109	P115,P118,CSR
Murphree, J.N.	Pvt	A Orr's Ri.	Petersburg, VA	04/03/65	City Pt., VA	04/11/65	Hart's Island, NY	CSR,CDC
					Hart's Island, NY	06/16/65	Rlsd. G.O. #109	P79,CSR
Murphy, Daniel	Pvt	I 1st SCVA	Raleigh, NC	04/20/65	Raleigh, NC	04/20/65	Paroled	CSR
Murphy, David F.	Pvt	G 25th SCVI	Ft. Fisher, NC	01/15/65	New York, NY	01/30/65	Elmira, NY	CSR,HAG
					Elmira, NY	03/02/65	Pt. Lookout, MD Xc	P66,CSR
Murphy, Emanuel	Pvt	G 25th SCVI	Town Creek, NC	02/20/65	Ft. Anderson, NC	02/28/65	Pt. Lookout, MD	CSR,HAG
					Pt. Lookout, MD	06/29/65	Rlsd. G.O. #109	P118,P121,P123,CSR
Murphy, Enoch E.	Pvt	E 15th SCVI	Gettysburg, PA	07/02/63	David's Island, SC	09/20/63	Died, Pyemia	P1,P6,FPH,KEB,CSR
Murphy, Evans J.	Pvt	F 18th SCVI	Hatchers Run, VA	03/25/65	City Pt., VA	04/02/65	Pt. Lookout, MD	CSR
					Pt. Lookout, MD	06/29/65	Rlsd.G.O. #109	P115,P118,P122,CSR
Murphy, Henry	Pvt	B Orr's Ri.	Deserted/enemy	04/04/65	City Pt., VA	04/24/65	Petersburg, VA	CSR
Murphy, James	Pvt	A 1st SCVIA	Richmond, VA	04/21/65	Took oath			SA1,CSR
Murphy, James Calvin	Pvt	C 25th SCVI	Ft. Fisher, NC	01/15/65	New York, NY	01/30/65	Elmira, NY	CSR,HAG,CTA
					Elmira, NY	07/11/65	Rlsd. G.O. #109	P65,P66,CSR
Murphy, John	Pvt	F 22nd SCVI	Kinston, NC	12/14/62	Kinston, NC	12/14/62	Paroled POW	CSR
Murphy, John	Cit	Charleston	Charleston, SC	04/09/63	Ft. McHenry, MD	05/07/63	Ft. Lafayette	P110
Murphy, John	Pvt	E 1st SCVA	Morris Island, SC	07/10/63	Ft. Columbus, NY	09/23/63	Took the oath	P1,CSR
Murphy, John	Pvt	C 15th SCVAB	Deserted/enemy	02/17/65	Charleston, SC	03/22/65	New York, NY oath	CSR
Murphy, John		P. Savannah	Off Charleston	06/03/61	Tombs Prison, NY	02/15/62	Ft. Lafayette, NY	OR,TCP
					Ft. Lafayette, NY	06/06/62	City Pt., VA Xc	OR,TCP
Murphy, John R.	Pvt	H 1st SCVIH	Petersburg, VA	04/03/65	City Pt., VA	04/13/65	Pt. Lookout, MD	CSR
					Pt. Lookout, MD	06/29/65	Rlsd. G.O. #109	CSR
					Pt. Lookout, MD	06/29/65	Rlsd. G.O. #109	P115,P119
					Washington, DC P.M.	06/30/65	Yazoo City, MS oath	CSR
Murphy, Joseph B.	Pvt	5 10/19 SCVI	Missionary Ridge, TN	11/25/63	Nashville, TN	12/07/63	Louisville, KY	P39,RAS,HMC,CSR
					Louisville, KY	12/09/63	Rock Island, IL	P88,P89,CSR
					Rock Island, IL	06/20/65	Rlsd. G.O. #109	P131,CSR
Murphy, Joshua M.	Pvt	F 15th SCVI	Cedar Creek, VA	10/19/64	Pt. Lookout, MD	12/08/64	Died, Ch. Diarrhea	P5,P118,P119
Murphy, Lorenzo D.	Pvt	H 25th SCVI	Petersburg, VA	05/29/64	Fts. Monroe, VA	05/18/64	Pt.Lookout, MD	CSR,HAG
					Pt. Lookout, MD	08/15/64	Elmira, NY	P113,P116,CSR
Murphy, Lorenzo D.	Pvt	H 25th SCVI	Ft. Fisher, NC	01/15/65	Elmira, NY	02/28/65	Died, Ch. Diarrhea	P6,P12,FPH
Murphy, Neil C.	2Lt	F 10th SCVI	Nashville, TN	12/16/64	Louisville, KY	12/20/64	Johnson's Isl., OH	P90,P91,P95,CSR
					Johnson's Isl., OH	06/19/65	Rlsd. G.O. #109	P81,P83,HMC,CSR
Murphy, Robert	Pvt	B 2nd SC	Cheraw, SC	03/03/65	Fts. Monroe, VA	04/02/65	Washington, DC	CSR
Murphy, T.W.	Cpl	D 20th SCVI	Cedar Creek, VA	10/19/64	Harpers Ferry, WV	10/24/64	Pt. Lookout, MD	CSR,KEB
					Pt. Lookout, MD	03/28/65	Aikens Ldg., VA Xc	P124,P121,P123,CSR
Murphy, W.R.	Pvt	B 17th SCVI	Farmville, VA	04/06/65	City Pt., VA	04/14/65	Newport News, VA	CSR
					Newport News, VA	06/26/65	Rlsd. G.O. #109	P107,CSR
Murphy, William	Pvt	F 22nd SCVI	Kinston, NC	12/14/62	Kinston, NC	12/14/62	Paroled POW	CSR
Murphy, William E.	Pvt	E 15th SCVI	Gettysburg, PA	07/04/63	Gettysburg, PA G.H.	07/21/63	Provost Marshal	P4,CSR,KEB,H15
					David's Island, NY	09/05/63	City Pt., VA Xc	P1,CSR
Murphy, William L.	Sgt	H 1st SCVA	Fayetteville, NC	03/08/65	Pt. Lookout, MD	06/29/65	Rlsd. G.O. #109	P115,P118,P122,CSR
Murrah, E.F.	Pvt	H 7th SCVC	Dabneys Ferry, VA	05/27/64	White House, VA	06/08/64	Elmira, NY	CSR
					Pt. Lookout, MD	07/09/64	Elmira, NY	P113,P117,P120,CSR
					Elmira, NY	06/19/65	Rlsd. G.O. #109	P65,P66,CSR

SOUTH CAROLINA SOLDIERS, SAILORS AND  CITIZENS HELD IN U.S. PRISONS 1861-1865

NAME	RANK	REGIMENT	CAPTURED AT	WHEN	PRISON	MOVED	DISPOSITION	SOURCES
Murray, A.D.	Pvt	H 11th SCVI	Petersburg, VA	06/18/64	City Pt., VA	06/24/64	Pt. Lookout, MD	HAG,CSR
					Pt. Lookout, MD	07/27/64	Elmira, NY	P113,P117,P120,CSR
					Elmira, NY	07/07/65	Rlsd. G.O. #109	P65,P66,CSR
Murray, Henry F.C.	Pvt	H 11th SCVI	Petersburg, VA	06/18/64	City Pt., VA	06/24/64	Pt. Lookout, MD	HAG,CSR
					Pt. Lookout, MD	07/27/64	Elmira, NY	P113,P117,P120,CSR
					Elmira, NY	02/02/65	Died, Variola	P6,P65,P66,FPH,CSR
Murray, J.G.	Pvt	H 11th SCVI	Petersburg, VA	06/18/64	Pt. Lookout, MD	07/27/64	Elmira, NY	P113,P117,P120,CSR
					Elmira, NY	03/14/65	James R. for Xc	P65,HAG,P66,CSR
Murray, James E.	Pvt	A 7th SCVC	Old Church, VA	05/30/64	Lincoln G.H., DC	11/20/64	Old Capitol, DC	CSR
					Old Capitol, DC	12/16/64	Elmira, NY	P110
					Elmira, NY	03/02/65	James R., VA Xc	P66,CSR
					Richmond, VA Hos.	03/14/65	Furloughed 60 days	CSR
Murray, John	Cit	Sr. *Memphis*	NC Coast	07/31/62	Ft. Delaware, DE			P47
Murray, Joseph J.	Sur	23rd SCVI	Petersburg, VA	04/02/65	Old Capitol, DC	05/11/65	Johnson's Isl., OH	P110,CSR
					Johnson's Isl., OH	06/23/65	Rlsd. G.O. #109	P81,CSR
Murray, Murdock W.	Pvt	B 1st SCVA	Bentonsville, NC	03/19/65	Pt. Lookout, MD	06/29/65	Rlsd. G.O. #109	P115,P118
Murray, T.	Plt	Str. *Memphis*	At sea	07/31/62	New York, NY P.M.	08/11/62	Ft. Lafayette, NY	CDC,LLC
Murray, T.A.	Pvt	F 12th SCVI	Deserted/enemy	02/18/65	Charleston, SC	03/15/65	Released on oath	CSR
Murray, Thomas	Pvt	B 27th SCVI	Weldon RR, VA	08/21/64	City Pt., VA	08/24/64	Pt. Lookout, MD	CSR,HAG
					Pt. Lookout, MD	02/18/65	Aikens Ldg., VA Xc	P113,P117,P124,CSR
Murray, W.S.	Pvt	I 3rd SCVC	Edisto Island, SC	04/09/63	Ft. Norfolk, VA	06/29/63	paroled	CSR
Murray, Warren W.	Pvt	Ferguson's LA	Salisbury, NC	04/12/65	Nashville, TN	04/29/65	Louisville, KY	CSR
					Louisville, KY	05/02/65	Camp Chase, OH	CSR
					Camp Chase, OH	06/13/65	Rlsd. G.O. #109	CSR
Murray, William B.	Sgt	G 7th SCVIBn	Morris Island, SC	07/10/63	Morris Island, SC	07/14/63	Hilton Head, SC PM	CSR,HAG,HIC
					Hilton Head, SC US	07/23/63	USHS 'Cosmopolitan	P2,CSR
Murray, William O.	Pvt	H 11th SCVI	Town Creek, NC	02/20/65	Ft. Anderson, NC	02/28/65	Pt. Lookout, MD	CSR,HAG
					Pt. Lookout, MD	06/29/65	Rlsd. G.O. #109	P115,CSR
Murrell, Benjamin L.	Pvt	F 27th SCVI	Town Creek, NC	02/20/65	Ft. Anderson, NC	02/28/65	Pt. Lookout, MD	CSR,HAG
					Pt. Lookout, MD	06/29/65	Rlsd. G.O. #109	P118,P121,P123,CSR
Murrell, F.A.	Pvt	D 14th SCVI	Augusta, GA	05/20/65	Augusta, GA	05/20/65	Paroled	CSR
Murtishaw, Samuel W.	Pvt	E 3rd SCVI	Cedar Creek, VA	10/19/64	Harpers Ferry, WV	10/28/64	Pt. Lookout, MD	CSR,ANY,KEB,SA2,H3
					Pt. Lookout, MD	03/28/65	Aikens Ldg., VA Xc	P118,P123,P124,CSR
Music, J.M.	Pvt	A 7th SCVC	Deep Bottom, VA	08/19/64	Pt. Lookout, MD	09/08/64	Died	P113,FPH
Mustard, Robert W.	Pvt	A Ham. Leg.	Fair Oaks, VA	05/31/62	Philadelphia, PA	07/30/62	Ft. Delaware, DE	CSR
					Ft. Delaware, DE	08/05/62	Aikens Ldg., VA Xc	CSR
Myer, John	Pvt	F 1st SCVA	Morris Island, SC	07/10/63	Hilton Head, SC	09/25/63	Rlsd on oath	P1,CSR
Myer, John	Pvt	F 1st SCVA	Bentonsville, NC	03/22/65	New Berne, NC	04/10/65	Hart's Island, NY	CSR
					Hart's Island, NY	06/17/65	Rlsd. G.O. #109	P79,CSR
Myer, W.M.	Pvt	F 7th SCVI	N. Anna River, VA	05/24/64	Pt. Lookout, MD	03/11/65	Aikens Ldg., VA Xc	P113,P117,P124,CSR
Myers, F.A.	Pvt	I 24th SCVI	Franklin, TN	12/17/64	Camp Chase, OH	02/09/65	Died pneumonia	P6,P12,P27,FPH
Myers, Frederick	Pvt	G 25th SCVI	Ft. Fisher, NC	01/15/65	New York, NY	01/30/65	Elmira, NY	CSR,HAG
					Elmira, NY	06/23/65	Rlsd. G.O. #109	P65,P66,CSR
Myers, G.H.	Pvt	I 10th SCVI	Danville, KY	09/15/62	Kentucky	11/15/62	Paroled	CSR
Myers, George M.	Pvt	G 3rd SCVC	Deserted/enemy	03/18/65	Charleston, SC	04/01/65	Taken oath & disch.	CSR
Myers, James	Pvt	D 4th SCVC	Stony Creek, VA	12/01/64	City Pt., VA	12/05/64	Pt. Lookout, MD	CSR
					Pt. Lookout, MD	02/15/65	Aikens Ldg., VA Xc	P118
					Pt. Lookout, MD	02/18/65	Exchanged	P115,P124,CSR
Myers, John	Pvt	E 25th SCVI	James Island, SC	07/16/63	Folly Island, SC	07/18/63	Hilton Head, SC	CSR,HAG
Myers, John	Pvt	E 25th SCVI	Deserted/enemy	07/16/63	Hilton Head, SC	09/05/63	Took the oath	CSR
Myers, John H.	Pvt	F 1st SCVA	Bentonsville, NC	03/22/65	New Berne, NC	04/10/65	Hart's Island, NY	CSR
					Hart's Island, NY	05/03/65	Died, phlebitis	CSR

SOUTH CAROLINA SOLDIERS, SAILORS AND  CITIZENS HELD IN U.S. PRISONS 1861-1865

NAME	RANK	REGIMENT	CAPTURED AT	WHEN	PRISON	MOVED	DISPOSITION	SOURCES
Myers, John W.	Pvt	SC Marines	Peen's Bridge, SC	02/11/65	Pt. Lookout, MD	05/02/65	Took the Oath	P115,P124
Myers, Joseph	Pvt	D 8th SCVI	Winchester, VA	09/13/64	Harpers Ferry, WV	09/16/64	Camp Chase, OH	CSR,KEB
					Camp Chase, OH	03/07/65	Died Gv #1589	P6,P23,P27,FPH,KEB,P12
Myers, Luther	Pvt	G 25th SCVI	Ft. Fisher, NC	01/15/65	New York, NY	01/30/65	Elmira, NY	CSR,HAG
					Elmira, NY	07/07/65	Rlsd. G.O. #109	P65,P66,HAG,CSR
Myers, Nicholas	Pvt	D 21st SCVI	Morris Island, SC	07/10/63	Ft. Columbus, NY	09/23/63	Took the oath	P1,HAG
					Pt. Lookout, MD	01/25/64	Joined U.S. Army	P113,P116,P125
Myers, Richard Canty	Pvt	D 2nd SCVI	Halltown, VA	08/26/64	Harpers Ferry, WV	09/02/64	Camp Chase, OH	CSR,KEB,SA2,H2
					Camp Chase, OH	03/26/65	Pt. Lookout, MD	P7,P23,P26,CSR
					Pt. Lookout, MD	06/29/65	Rlsd. G.O. #109	P121,P123,CSR
Myers, Richard T.	Sgt	A 23rd SCVI	Petersburg, VA	04/02/65	City Pt., VA	04/04/65	Pt. Lookout, MD	CSR
Myers, Richard T.	Sgt	A 23rd SCVI	Five Forks, VA	04/02/65	Pt. Lookout, MD	06/29/65	Rlsd. G.O. #109	P115,P118,P121,P123,CSR

SOUTH CAROLINA SOLDIERS, SAILORS AND **N** CITIZENS HELD IN U.S. PRISONS 1861-1865

NAME	RANK	REGIMENT	CAPTURED AT	WHEN	PRISON	MOVED	DISPOSITION	SOURCES
Nabers, Austin	Pvt	G 2nd SCVC	Gettysburg, PA	07/05/63	Letterman G.H. Gbg	09/05/63	Died of wounds	P1,P5,P12,CSR
Nagle, Luke	Pvt	C 27th SCVI	Weldon RR, VA	08/21/64	City Pt., VA	08/24/64	Pt. Lookout, MD	CSR,HAG
					Pt. Lookout, MD	05/14/65	Washington, DC	P113,P116,P122,CSR
					Washington, DC	05/16/65	Chicago, IL oath	CSR
Nance, J.D.	Pvt	D Hol.Leg.C	Williamsburg, VA	11/22/62	Fts. Monroe, VA	11/29/62	City Pt., VA Xc	CSR
Nance, Marshal H.	Pvt	D 2nd SCVI	Raleigh, NC Hos.	04/13/65	Raleigh, NC Hos.	04/13/65	Paroled	SA2,H2,CSR
Napper, Joseph W.	Pvt	B 19th SCVI	Nashville, TN	12/16/64	Nashville, TN	12/19/64	Louisville, KY	CSR,HOE
					Louisville, KY	12/21/64	Camp Douglas, IL	P90,P93,CSR
					Camp Douglas, IL	06/06/65	Rlsd. G.O. #109	CSR
Nash, J.T. Franklin	Pvt	C 8th SCVI	Winchester, VA	09/13/64	Harpers Ferry, WV	09/19/64	Camp Chase, OH	CSR,KEB
					Camp Chase, OH	11/16/64	Died, Pneumonia	P12,P22,P27,CSR
Nates, George H.	Pvt	G 13th SCVI	Hatchers Run, VA	03/31/65	City Pt., VA	05/21/64	Pt. Lookout, MD	CSR,ANY
					Pt. Lookout, MD	06/22/65	Rlsd. G.O. #109	P115,P117,P121,CSR
Neal, Benjamin	Pvt	B 15th SCVAB	Thomasville, NC Hos.	05/01/65	Thomasville, NC	05/01/65	Paroled	CSR
Neal, H.R.	Pvt	G P.S.S.	Fair Oaks, VA	06/05/62	Fts. Monroe, VA	08/03/62	Aikens Ldg., VA Xc	CSR,TSE
					Aikens Ldg., VA	09/01/62	Exchanged	CSR
Neal, John B.	Pvt	G 16th SCVI	Missionary Ridge, TN	11/25/63	Nashville, TN USGH	12/13/63	Died in transit	P6,16R,CSR
Neal, Leon T.	Pvt	1 10/19 SCVI	Missionary Ridge, TN	11/25/63	Bridgeport, AL G.H.	10/11/63	Nashville, TN	P2,CSR
Neal, S.M.	Cpl	I P.S.S.	Deserted/enemy	03/18/65	Bermuda Hundred, VA	03/22/65	Washington, DC	CSR,TSE
					Washington, DC	03/22/65	Franklin Cty., IN	CSR
Neal, Samuel	Pvt	A Orr's Ri.	Hannover C.H., VA	05/23/64	Port Royal, VA	05/30/64	Pt. Lookout, MD	CDC,CSR
Neal, Sion T.	Pvt	G 16th SCVI	Chattanooga, TN	11/26/63	(No US POW data)			16R,CSR
Neal, W.C.	Pvt	D 17th SCVI	Sharpsburg, MD		Sharpsburg, MD P.M.	09/21/62	Paroled	CSR,HHC
					City Pt., VA	08/05/65	Pt. Lookout, MD	CSR
Neal, W.C.	Pvt	D 17th SCVI	Crater, Pbg., VA	07/30/64	Pt. Lookout, MD	08/08/64	Elmira, NY	P113,P116,P120,CSR
					Elmira, NY	04/23/65	Died, Variola	P6,P65,P66,FPH,CSR
Neal, William M.	Pvt	A Orr's Ri.	Gettysburg, PA	07/04/63	Ft. Delaware, DE			P40,P44,P144
					Ft. Delaware, DE	02/16/64	Died, Lung Inflam.	P5,P12,P40,P47,FPH
Neelands, John	Pvt	F 17th SCVI	Five Forks, VA	04/01/65	City Pt., VA	04/06/65	Pt. Lookout, MD	CSR,YEB
					Pt. Lookout, MD	06/29/65	Rlsd. G.O.#109	P115,P117,P122,CSR
Neeley, W.J.	Pvt	H 12th SCVI	Spotsylvania, VA	05/12/64	Belle Plain, VA	05/21/64	Ft. Delaware, DE	CSR
					Ft. Delaware, DE	01/20/65	Fts. Monroe, VA Xc	P41,P42,CSR
					Fts. Monroe, VA	02/02/65	Flag of truce boat	CSR
Neely, Hiram S.	Pvt	C 16th SCVI	Cassville, GA	05/20/64	Nashville, G.H.	05/27/64	Louisville, KY	P2,P39,16R
					Louisville, KY	05/30/64	Rock Island, IL	P88,P91,P93,CSR
					Rock Island, IL	06/19/64	Joined US Navy	P131,CSR
Neely, Isaiah	Sgt	C 12th SCVI	Burkeville, VA	04/05/65	City Pt., VA	04/14/65	Pt. Lookout, MD	CSR
					Pt. Lookout, MD	06/29/65	Rlsd. G.O. #109	P115,P117,P122,CSR
Neely, Willis W.	2Lt	A 17th SCVI	Petersburg, VA	03/25/65	Old Capitol, DC	03/30/65	Ft. Delaware, DE	CSR,HHC
					Ft. McHenry, VA	03/30/65	Ft. Delaware, DE	P110,R47
					Ft. Delaware, DE	06/17/65	Rlsd. G.O. #109	P43,P45,CSR
Neese, Godfrey	Pvt	G 27th SCVI	Petersburg, VA	06/18/64	Fts. Monroe, VA	06/22/64	Pt. Lookout, MD	CSR,HAG,UD6
					Pt. Lookout, MD	03/14/65	Died, Scurvy	P12,CSR
Neighbors, Joseph	Pvt	G 27th SCVI	Petersburg, VA	06/24/64	Fts. Monroe, VA	07/25/64	Died of wounds	P12,HAG
Neighbors, William	Pvt	G 27th SCVI	Petersburg, VA	06/24/64	Bermuda Hundred, VA	06/25/64	Fts. Monroe, VA	CSR
					Fts. Monroe, VA	06/26/64	Pt. Lookout, MD	CSR
					Pt. Lookout, MD	08/16/64	Elmira, NY	P113,P120,CSR
					Elmira, NY	10/03/64	Died, Ch. Diarrhea	P12,P65,FPH
Neil, James A.	Pvt	E 5th SCVI	Charlotte, NC Hos.	05/11/65	Charlotte, NC	05/11/65	Paroled	CSR
Neil, Joseph W.	2Lt	K 17th SCVI	Dinwiddie C.H., VA	04/02/65	Ft. McHenry, MD	04/09/65	Johnson's Isl., OH	P110,YEB
					Old Capitol, DC	04/09/65	Johnson's Isl., OH	P110,CSR
					Johnson's Isl., OH	06/19/65	Rlsd. G.O. #109	P81,P82,P83,CSR

SOUTH CAROLINA SOLDIERS, SAILORS AND  CITIZENS HELD IN U.S. PRISONS 1861-1865

NAME	RANK	REGIMENT	CAPTURED AT	WHEN	PRISON	MOVED	DISPOSITION	SOURCES
Neil, W.M.	Pvt	I 17th SCVI	Petersburg, VA	03/25/65	City Pt., VA	03/28/65	Pt. Lookout, MD	CSR
					Pt. Lookout, MD	06/29/65	Rlsd. G.O. #109	P115,P117,P122,CSR
Neill, John P.	Pvt	G 14th SCVI	Petersburg, VA	04/02/65	Pt. O Rocks, VA USH	04/04/65	Fts. Monroe, VA	CSR
					Fts. Monroe, VA	04/20/65	Died, GS Wd ankle	CSR
Neill, S.A.	Pvt	A 1st SCVIR	Bentonville, NC	03/22/65	New Berne, NC	04/10/65	Hart's Island, NY	CSR,SA1,LAN
					Hart's Island, NY	06/21/65	Rlsd. G.O.#109	P79,CSR
Neison, Solomon	Pvt	27th SCVI			Pt. Lookout, MD	06/29/65	Rlsd. G.O. #109	P122
Nelson, Andrew	Pvt	H 1st SCVIR	Cheraw, SC	03/05/65	Cheraw, SC	03/05/65	Paroled	CSR
Nelson, Columbus	Pvt	G 7th SCVIBn	Charlotte, NC	05/04/65	Charlotte, NC	05/04/65	Paroled	CSR,HAG,HIC
Nelson, Erwin	Pvt	F 21st SCVI	Morris Island, SC	07/10/63	Ft. Columbus, NY	09/23/63	Took the oath	P1,HAG
					Ft. Columbus, NY	09/26/63	Pt. Lookout, MD	CSR
					Pt. Lookout, MD	11/21/63	Died	FPH
Nelson, Foster	Pvt	C 3rd SCVIBn	Hanover Jctn., VA	05/24/64	Port Royal, VA	05/30/64	Pt. Lookout, MD	CSR,KEB
					Pt. Lookout, MD	06/29/65	Rlsd. G.O. #109	P113,P116,CSR
Nelson, J.K.	Pvt	A 3rd SCVIBn	Cedar Creek, VA	10/19/64	Pt. Lookout, MD	03/28/65	Exchanged	P124
Nelson, J.M.	Pvt	8th SCVI			Pt. Lookout, MD	06/29/65	Rlsd. G.O. #109	P122
Nelson, James F.	Pvt	B 3rd SCVIBn	South Mtn., MD	09/14/62	Ft. Delaware, DE	10/02/62	Aikens Ldg., VA Xc	CSR
Nelson, James M.	Pvt	A 3rd SCVIBn	South Mtn., MD	09/14/62	Ft. Delaware, DE	10/02/62	Aikens Ldg., VA Xc	CSR,KEB
Nelson, James M.	Pvt	A 3rd SCVIBn	N. Anna River, VA	05/24/64	Port Royal, VA	05/30/64	Pt. Lookout, MD	CSR
					Pt. Lookout, MD	03/15/65	Aikens Ldg., VA Xc	P113,P116,P121,CSR
Nelson, John A.	Pvt	D 19th SCVI	Murfreesboro, TN	12/31/62	Nashville, TN		Louisville, KY	P38,CSR,HOE
Nelson, John A.	Pvt	D 19th SCVI	Murfreesboro, TN	01/09/63	Louisville, KY	02/27/63	Camp Morton, IN	P88,CSR
					Cincinnatti, OH	02/27/63	Camp Morton, IN	P37,CSR
Nelson, John A.	Pvt	D 19th SCVI	Murfreesboro, TN	12/31/62	City Pt., VA	04/12/63	Exchanged	CSR
					Williamsburg, VA Hos.	04/18/63	Furloughed home	CSR
Nelson, John W.	Cpl	C Hol.Leg.	Richmond, VA Hos.	04/08/65	City Pt., VA	04/14/65	Pt. Lookout, MD	CSR,HOS
					Pt. Lookout, MD	06/29/65	Rlsd. G.O. #109	P115,P117,P122,CSR
Nelson, Joseph	Pvt	F 1st SCVIH	Knoxville, TN	12/18/63	Louisville, KY	01/23/64	Rock Island, IL	P88,P93,SA1,CSR
					Rock Island, IL	05/03/65	New Orleans Xc	P131,CSR
					New Orleans, LA	05/23/65	Exchanged	CSR
Nelson, Joseph H.	Pvt	G 24th SCVI	Nashville, TN	12/16/64	Nashville, TN	12/31/64	Louisville, KY	CSR
					Louisville, KY	01/05/65	Camp Chase, OH	P92,P93,EFW
					Camp Chase, OH	06/12/65	Released	P22,CSR
Nelson, N. Tillman	Pvt	G 27th SCVI	Petersburg, VA	06/24/64	Bermuda Hundred, VA	06/25/64	Fts. Monroe, VA	CSR,HAG
					Fts. Monroe, VA	06/26/64	Pt. Lookout, MD	CSR
					Pt. Lookout, MD	08/16/64	Elmira, NY	P113,P120,CSR
					Elmira, NY	02/25/65	Tfd. for exchange	P65,CSR
					Pt. Lookout, MD	06/29/65	Rlsd. G.O. #109	CSR
Nelson, Thomas J.	Pvt	K 7th SCVC	Burkeville, VA	04/06/65	City Pt., VA	04/15/65	Pt. Lookout, MD	HIC,CSR
					Pt. Lookout, MD	05/20/65	Died, Dysentery	P6,P115,P117,P119
Nelson, Wallace	Pvt	L Orr's Ri.	Spotsylvania, VA	05/12/64	Belle Plain, VA	05/21/64	Ft. McHenry, MD.	P41,CSR,CDC
					Ft. McHenry, MD	06/15/64	Ft. Delaware, DE	P41,P110
					Old Capitol, DC	06/16/64	Ft. Delaware, DE	P42,P45,CSR
					Ft. Delaware, DE	11/07/64	Hos. 11/7-12/23/64	P47
					Ft. Delaware, DE	06/10/65	Released	P42,P45,CSR
Nelson, William A.	Pvt	A 3rd SCVIBn	Hanover Jctn., VA	05/24/64	Pt. Lookout, MD	06/29/65	Rlsd G.O. #109	P113,P116,KEB,CSR
Nelson, William A.	Pvt	F 3rd SCVI	Hanover C.H., VA	05/26/64	Port Royal, VA	05/30/64	Pt. Lookout, MD	CSR
					Pt. Lookout, MD	06/29/65	Rlsd. G.O. #109	H3,CSR,P122
Nesbit, M.C.	Pvt	Palmetto L	Hagerstown, MD	07/06/63	Baltimore, MD	08/20/63	Pt. Lookout, MD	CSR
					Pt. Lookout, MD	03/16/64	City Pt., VA Xc	P124,CSR
Nesbit, S.E.	Pvt	C 3rd SCVABn	Blakely, AL	04/09/65	Ship Island, MS	05/01/65	Vicksburg, MS Xc	CSR

N

SOUTH CAROLINA SOLDIERS, SAILORS AND CITIZENS HELD IN U.S. PRISONS 1861-1865

NAME	RANK	REGIMENT	CAPTURED AT	WHEN	PRISON	MOVED	DISPOSITION	SOURCES
Nesbitt, G.G.	Pvt	A 5th SCVI	Richmond, VA Hos.	04/03/65	Libby Prison, Richmd.	04/23/65	Newport News, VA	CSR
					Newport News, VA	06/26/65	Rlsd. G.O. #109	P107,CSR
Nesbitt, J.J.	Pvt	E 2nd SCVC	Cheraw, SC	03/05/65	Cheraw, SC	03/05/65	Paroled	CSR
Nesley, John	Pvt	B 1st SCVIG	Petersburg, VA	04/02/65	City Pt., VA	04/02/63	Pt. Lookout, MD	CSR,SA1
					Pt. Lookout, MD	06/29/65	Rlsd. G.O. #109	P115,P117,P122,CSR
Nesmith, Nathaniel	Pvt	E 10th SCVI	Kentucky	09/15/62	Kentucky	11/15/62	Paroled	CSR
Nesmith, Samuel	Pvt	A 7th SCVC	Farmville, VA	04/06/65	City Pt., VA	04/15/65	Pt. Lookout, MD	CSR
					Pt. Lookout, MD	05/16/65	Died, Diarrhea	P6,P117,P119,FPH
Nettles, C.B.	Pvt	G Ham.Leg.MI	Farmville, VA	04/11/65	Farmville, VA	04/11/65	Paroled	CSR
Nettles, F.L.	Sgt	E 8th SCVI	Gettysburg, PA	07/04/63	Letterman G.H. Gbg	08/18/63	Died of wounds	P1,P5,P12,KEB,CSR
Nettles, Henry	Pvt	B 3rd SCVC	Deserted/enemy	03/10/65	Hilton Head, SC	03/22/65	New York, NY oath	CSR
Nettles, J.C.	Pvt	K 11th SCVI	Weldon RR, VA	08/21/64	City Pt., VA	08/24/64	Pt. Lookout, MD	CSR
					Pt. Lookout, MD	03/14/65	Exchanged	P113,P124,CSR
Nettles, James C.	Pvt	I 26th SCVI	Southside RR, VA	04/01/65	City Pt., VA	04/05/65	Pt. Lookout, MD	CSR
					Pt. Lookout, MD	06/29/65	Rlsd. G.O.#109	P115,P117,P122,CTA,CSR
Nettles, John R.	Cpt	H 10th SCVI	Murfreesboro, TN	12/31/62	Nashville, TN	01/14/63	Died of wounds	P38,RAS,CTA,CSR
Nettles, Samuel J.	1Sg	E 6th SCVI	Chattanooga, TN	11/24/63	Nashville, TN	04/20/64	Paroled,Chattanooga	P39,CSR
					Nashville, TN	05/10/64	Louisville, KY	CSR
					Louisville, KY	05/20/64	Ft. McHenry, MD	P88,P93,CSR
					Fts. Monroe, VA	07/13/64	Truce boat Xc	CSR
Nettles, W. Wyatt	Pvt	G 21st SCVI	Morris Island, SC	07/10/63	Ft. Columbus, NY	09/23/63	Took the oath	P1,HAG
					Ft. Columbus, NY	09/26/63	Pt. Lookout, MD	CSR
					Pt. Lookout, MD	08/16/64	Elmira, NY	P113,P120
					Elmira, NY	03/10/65	James R., VA Xc	P65,P66,P124
Neugas, Max	Pvt	PeeDee LA	Cashtown, PA	07/05/63	Ft. McHenry, MD	07/22/63	Ft. Delaware, DE	CSR
					Ft. Delaware, DE	05/10/65	Released on oath	CSR
Neves, J.P.	Pvt	A 3rd SCVABn	High Pt., NC	05/02/65	High Pt., NC	05/02/65	Paroled	CSR
New, Joseph	Pvt	G 10/19 SCVI	Missionary Ridge, TN	11/25/63	Nashville, TN	12/07/63	Louisville, KY	P39,CSR,HOE
					Louisville, KY	12/09/63	Rock Island, IL	P88,P89,CSR
					Rock Island, IL	02/25/65	Pt. Lookout, MD Xc	P131,CSR
					Boulwares Wh., VA	03/05/65	Received & Xc	CSR
New, Joseph	Pvt	K 19th SCVI	Augusta, GA	05/22/65	Augusta, GA	05/22/65	Paroled	CSR
New, Pickens	Pvt	C 24th SCVI	Nashville, TN	12/16/64	Nashville, TN	12/31/64	Louisville, KY	CSR,HOE
New, Pickens	Pvt	K 24th SCVI	Nashville, TN	12/16/64	Louisville, KY	01/02/65	Camp Chase, OH	P92,P93,CSR
					Camp Chase, OH	06/12/65	Released	P22,CSR
Newby, Franklin P.	1Lt	F 1st SCVIH	Deep Bottom, VA	08/14/64	Bermuda Hundred, VA	08/15/64	Fts. Monroe, VA	CSR,SA1
					Fts. Monroe, VA	08/16/64	Pt. Lookout, MD	CSR
					Pt. Lookout, MD	08/18/64	Washington, DC	P113,P120,P125,CSR
					Old Capitol, DC	08/27/64	Ft. Delaware, DE	CSR
					Ft. Delaware, DE	08/17/65	Rlsd. G.O. #109	P45,P46,P47
Newell, Isaiah J.	Pvt	F 24th SCVI	Taylors Ridge, GA	10/16/64	Nashville, TN	10/23/64	Louisville, KY	CSR
					Louisville, KY	10/28/64	Camp Douglas, IL	P90,P91,P93,CSR
					Camp Douglas, IL	06/17/65	Rlsd. G.O. #109	P55,CSR
Newman, B.S.	Sgt	A 7th SCVIBn	Weldon RR, VA	08/21/64	City Pt., VA	08/24/64	Pt. Lookout, MD	CSR,HAG,HIC
					Pt. Lookout, MD	03/15/65	Exchanged	P113,P116,P124,CSR
Newman, J.J.	Pvt	F 13th SCVI	Spotsylvania, VA	05/13/64	Belle Plain, VA	05/21/64	Ft. Delaware, DE	CSR,HOS
					Ft. Delaware, DE	10/17/64	Hos. 10/17-2/27/65	P47
					Ft. Delaware, DE	02/27/65	Exchanged	P41,P42,CSR
Newman, John W.	Pvt	C 3rd SCVABn	Blakely, AL	04/09/65	Ship Island, MS	05/01/65	Vicksburg, MS Xc	CSR
Newman, Lewis Phillip	Pvt	F 3rd SCVABn	Deserted/enemy	03/22/65	Charleston, SC	03/22/65	Released on oath	CSR
Newman, Roland T.	Cpl	E 14th SCVI	Cox Rd., Pbg. VA	04/02/65	City Pt., VA	04/07/65	Hart's Island, NY	CSR
					Hart's Island, NY	06/15/65	Rlsd. G.O. #109	P79,CSR

SOUTH CAROLINA SOLDIERS, SAILORS AND  CITIZENS HELD IN U.S. PRISONS 1861-1865

NAME	RANK	REGIMENT	CAPTURED AT	WHEN	PRISON	MOVED	DISPOSITION	SOURCES
Newman, S. James	Pvt	B 2nd SCVI	Charlotte, NC	05/03/65	Charlotte, NC	05/03/65	Paroled	SA2,H2,CSR
Newman, Samuel N.	Pvt	B 26th SCVI	Petersburg, VA	03/25/65	City Pt., VA	04/02/65	Pt. Lookout, MD	CSR
Newman, Samuel N.	Pvt	B 26th SCVI	Hatchers Run, VA	03/25/65	Pt. Lookout, MD	06/29/65	Rlsd. G.O. #109	P115,P117,P122,CSR
Newton, Cornelius D.	Pvt	E 4th SCVC	Stony Creek, VA	12/01/64	City Pt., VA	12/05/64	Pt. Lookout, MD	CSR,HOM
					Pt. Lookout, MD	06/29/65	Rlsd. G.O. #109	P117,P122,CSR
Newton, David D.	Cpl	F 21st SCVI	Ft. Fisher, NC	01/15/65	Elmira, NY	07/11/65	Rlsd. G.O. #109	P65,P66,HAG,HOM
Newton, E.C.	Pvt	Brooks LA	Gettysburg, PA	07/04/63	Ft. McHenry, MD	07/12/63	Ft. Delaware, DE	CSR
					Ft. Delaware, DE	01/07/64	Died, Bronchitis	P40,P44,CSR,FPH
Newton, E.D.	Mte	CS Navy		09/12/63	Pt. Lookout, MD	09/20/63	Ft. Warren, MA	P120
Newton, J.D.	Sgt	E 26th SCVI	Farmville, VA	04/06/65	City Pt., VA	04/14/65	Newport News, VA	CSR
					Newport News, VA	06/26/65	Rlsd. G.O. #109	P107,CSR
Newton, Joel B.	Pvt	A Orr's Ri.	Sutherland Stn., VA	04/02/65	City Pt., VA	04/07/65	Hart's Island, NY	CSR
					Hart's Island, NY	06/16/65	Rlsd. G.O. #109	P79,CSR
Newton, John	Pvt	I 2nd SCVC	Bristoe Stn., VA	12/13/63	Pt. Lookout, MD		Exchanged	P113,P116,P124
					Ft. McHenry, MD	02/03/64	Pt. Lookout, MD	P110
					Old Capitol, DC	02/03/64	Pt. Lookout, MD	CSR
Newton, John Thomas	Pvt	A Orr's Ri.	Falling Waters, MD	07/14/63	Baltimore, MD	08/16/63	Pt. Lookout, MD	CSR
					Pt. Lookout, MD	08/16/64	Elmira, NY	P113,P120,CSR
					Elmira, NY	10/11/64	Pt.Lookout, MD Xc	P65,P66,CSR
					Pt. Lookout, MD	10/29/64	Aikens Ldg., VA Xc	P115,P116
					Pt. Lookout, MD	10/29/64	Venus Pt., GA Xc	CSR
Newton, William W.	Pvt	A 26th SCVI	Petersburg, VA	03/25/65	City Pt., VA	04/02/65	Pt. Lookout, MD	CSR
Newton, William W.	Pvt	A 26th SCVI	Hatchers Run, VA	03/29/65	Pt. Lookout, MD	06/29/65	Rlsd. G.O.#109	P115,P117,P122,CSR
Nicholls, James W.	Cpl	C 3rd SCVABn	Ft. Gaines, AL	08/08/64	New Orleans, LA	10/21/64	Ship Island, MS	P3,CSR
					Ship Island, MS	01/04/65	Exchanged	P136,CSR
Nicholls, W.R.	Pvt	I 1st SCVA	Morris Island,SC	07/10/63	Ft. Columbus, NY	09/23/63	Took the oath	P1,CSR
Nichols, Henry B.	Pvt	F Hol.Leg.	Petersburg, VA	11/06/64	City Pt., VA	11/11/64	Pt. Lookout, MD	CSR
					Pt. Lookout, MD	12/13/64	Died, Ch. Diarrhea	P115.P119,FPH,CSR
Nichols, Isaac	Pvt	A 7th SCVIBn	Weldon RR, VA	08/21/64	City Pt., VA USFH	08/25/64	Alexandria, VA USG	CSR,HAG,HIC
					Alexandria, VA USG	10/05/64	Lincoln G.H., DC	P1,CSR
					Ft. McHenry, MD	12/10/64	Elmira, NY	P110
					Old Capitol, DC	12/10/64	Elmira, NY	CSR
					Elmira, NY	07/20/65	Died, Pneumonia	P5,P65,P66,FPH,CSR
Nichols, Isaac M.	Pvt	K 2nd SCVC	Greensboro, NC	05/01/65	Greensboro, NC	05/01/65	Paroled	CSR
Nichols, J. Alonzo	Pvt	B 12th SCVI	Gettysburg, PA	07/05/63	David's Island, NY	09/12/63	City Pt., VA Xc	P1,YEB,CSR
Nichols, James A.	Pvt	E P.S.S.	Big Springs, TN	12/17/63	Louisville, KY	01/09/64	DTE sent north	P92,P93,TSE,CSR
Nichols, James H.	Sgt	F Hol.Leg.	Five Forks, VA	04/01/65	City Pt., VA	04/05/65	Pt. Lookout, MD	CSR
					Pt. Lookout, MD	06/29/65	Rlsd. G.O. #109	P115,P117,P122,CSR
Nichols, James W.	Pvt	C Hol.Leg.C	James Gate, VA	11/22/62	Fts. Monroe, VA	11/29/62	City Pt., VA Xc	CSR
Nichols, John H.	Pvt	A 3rd SCVIBn	Frederick, MD	09/12/62	Philadelphia, PA H	11/28/62	Ft. Delaware, DE	CSR,KEB
					Ft. Delaware, DE	12/15/62	Fts. Monroe, VA	CSR
					Fts. Monroe, VA	12/18/62	City Pt., VA Xc	CSR
Nichols, John H.	Pvt	A 3rd SCVIBn	Cedar Creek, VA	10/19/64	Harpers Ferry, VA	10/23/64	Pt. Lookout, MD	P115,CSR
					Pt. Lookout, MD	06/29/65	Rlsd. G.O. #109	P115,P122,CSR
Nichols, John H.	Pvt	I Hol.Leg.	Petersburg, VA	11/06/64	City Pt., VA	11/11/64	Washington, DC	CSR,HOS
					Pt. Lookout, MD	05/14/65	Rlsd. G.O. #85	P115,CSR
Nichols, Minor R.	Pvt	B 12th SCVI	Amelia C.H., VA	04/05/65	City Pt., VA	04/13/65	Pt. Lookout, MD	CSR,YEB
					Pt. Lookout, MD	06/15/65	Rlsd. G.O. #109	P115,P117,YEB,CSR
Nichols, Noah	Pvt	G 20th SCVI	Cedar Creek, VA	10/19/64	Harpers Ferry, WV	10/24/64	Pt. Lookout, MD	CSR,HHC
					Pt. Lookout, MD	12/02/64	Released on oath	P119,P124,CSR

N

SOUTH CAROLINA SOLDIERS, SAILORS AND CITIZENS HELD IN U.S. PRISONS 1861-1865

NAME	RANK	REGIMENT	CAPTURED AT	WHEN	PRISON	MOVED	DISPOSITION	SOURCES
Nichols, R.S.	Pvt	B 4th SCVC.	Hawe's Shop, VA	05/28/64	White House, VA	06/08/64	Pt. Lookout, MD	CSR,HHC
					Pt. Lookout, MD	07/09/64	Elmira, NY	P113,P120,CSR
					Elmira, NY	10/11/64	Tfd. for exchange	P65,P66,CSR
					Pt. Lookout, MD	10/29/64	Aikens Ldg., VA Xc	P116,P123,HHC
Nichols, Richard Gus.	Pvt	B 10th SCVI	Danville, KY	10/13/62	Louisville, KY	11/29/62	Vicksburg, MS Xc	P88,RAS,CSR
Nichols, W.P.	Pvt	E P.S.S.	Deserted/enemy	12/17/63	Chattanooga, TN	01/22/64	Louisville, KY	CSR
					Louisville, KY	01/09/64	DTE sent north	P88,CSR
Nichols, W.W.	Pvt	I 23rd SCVI	Deserted/enemy	02/28/65	Washington, DC	02/28/65	Washington, DC	CSR
Nichols, William Austin	Pvt	G 20th SCVI	Cedar Creek, VA	10/19/64	Pt. Lookout, MD	12/02/64	Took the oath	P115,KEB,CSR
					Pt. Lookout, MD	05/12/65	Released G.O. #85	P121
Nicholson, Benjamin E.	Col	Ham.Leg.MI	Augusta, GA	05/23/65	Augusta, GA	05/23/64	Paroled	LC
Nicholson, Duncan	Pvt	B 21st SCVI	Darlington, SC	03/03/65	Hart's Island, NY	06/21/65	Rlsd. G.O.#109	P79,CSR
Nicholson, George S.	Pvt	K 12th SCVI	Petersburg, VA	04/02/65	Pt. Lookout, MD	06/08/65	Rlsd. instr. 5/30/65	P115,P117,P121,CSR
Nicholson, Hugh	Pvt	F 26th SCVI	Five Forks, VA	04/01/65	City Pt., VA	04/05/65	Pt. Lookout, VA	CSR
					Pt. Lookout, MD	06/29/65	Rlsd. G.O. #109	P115,P117,P122,CSR
Nickoll, James	Pvt	A 3rd SCVABn	High Pt., NC	05/02/65	High Pt., NC	05/02/65	Paroled	CSR
Nimmons, J.H.	Pvt	H 17th SCVI	Richmond, VA Hos.	04/03/65	Richmond, VA Hos.	04/14/65	P.M. Richmond, VA	CSR
					Libby Prison Rchmd.	04/23/65	Newport News, VA	CSR
					Newport News, VA	06/26/65	Rlsd. G.O. #109	P107,CSR
Nimmons, William A.J.	Pvt	A 1st SCVIG	Farmville, VA	04/07/65	USGH Farmville, VA	05/01/65	Died	P6,P12,SA1
Nipson, John A.	Pvt	B 5th SCVC	Deserted/enemy	03/22/65	Charleston, SC	03/22/65	Released on oath	CSR
Nix, A.J.	Pvt	B 14th SCMil	Lynch's Creek, SC	02/25/65	Hart's Island, NY	06/16/65	Rlsd. G.O. #109	P79
Nix, David M.	Pvt	F 22nd SCVI	Hatchers Run, VA	03/29/64	City Pt., VA	04/02/65	Pt. Lookout, MD	CSR
					Pt. Lookout, MD	06/29/65	Rlsd. G.O. #109	P115,P117,P122,CSR
Nix, Henry	Sgt	C 1st SCVA	Raleigh, NC Hos.	04/17/65	Raleigh, NC	04/20/65	Paroled	CSR
Nix, J.C.	Pvt	Mathewes A	Salisbury, NC	05/13/65	Salisbury, NC	05/13/65	Paroled	CSR
Nix, J.F.	Pvt	B 14th SCMil	Lynch's Creek, SC	02/25/65	Hart's Island, NY	06/16/65	Rlsd. G.O. #109	P79
Nix, Jesse	Pvt	B 18th SCVI	Petersburg, VA	07/29/64	City Pt., VA	08/05/64	Pt. Lookout, MD	CSR
					Pt. Lookout, MD	08/08/64	Elmira, NY	P113,P116,P120,CSR
					Elmira, NY	03/02/65	James R., VA Xc	P65,P66,CSR
Nix, Lewis V.	Pvt	D 3rd SCVABn	Deserted/enemy	02/23/65	Charleston, SC	02/26/65	Released on oath	CSR
Nix, R.J.	Cpl	F 22nd SCVI	Kinston, NC	12/15/62	Kinston, NC	12/15/62	Paroled POW	CSR
Nix, R.W.	Pvt	B 2nd SCVA	Charlotte, NC Hos.	05/26/65	Charlotte, NC	05/26/65	Paroled	CSR
Noble, A.R.	Pvt	E 14th SCVI	Boonesboro, MD	09/14/62	Ft. Delaware, DE	10/02/62	Aikens Ldg., VA Xc	CSR
Noble, John W.	Pvt	B 6th SCVC	Louisa C.H., VA	06/11/64	Pt. Lookout, MD	07/25/64	Elmira, NY	P113,P116,P120,CSR
					Elmira, NY	10/11/64	Pt. Lookout, MD Xc	P65,P66,P123
					Pt. Lookout, MD	10/29/64	Aikens Ldg., VA Xc	P115,P116,CSR
Nobles, James R.	Pvt	E 5th SCVC	Deserted/enemy	03/31/65	Charleston, SC	03/31/65	Released on oath	CSR
Nobles, John	Pvt	? Orr's Ri.	Deserted/enemy	03/31/65	Bermuda Hundred, VA		City Pt., VA	CSR
					City Pt., VA	04/05/65	Washington, DC	CSR
					Washington, DC	04/06/65	New York, NY oath	CSR
Nobles, Lewis	Pvt	C 9th SCVI	Hilton Head, SC	11/07/61	Ft. Lafayete, NY	07/11/62	Ft. Delaware, DE	CSR
					Ft. Delaware, DE	08/05/62	Aikens Ldg., VA Xc	CSR
Nobles, Needham	Pvt	D 10th SCVI	Nashville, TN	12/16/64	Nashville, TN	01/01/65	Louisville, KY	P39,RAS,HMC,CSR
					Louisville, KY	01/02/65	Camp Chase, OH	CSR
					Camp Chase, OH	03/20/65	Chicago, IL	P26,CSR
					Camp Chase, OH	03/20/65	Enlisted U.S. Army	P22
Nobles, William	Pvt	C 9th SCVI	Hilton Head, SC	11/07/61	Ft. Lafayette, NY	07/11/62	Ft. Delaware, DE	CSR
					Ft. Delaware, DE	07/29/62	Died	CSR
Nobles, William F.	Pvt	G 13th SCVI	Hatchers Run, VA	03/31/65	City Pt., VA	04/02/65	Pt. Lookout, MD	P115,ANY,CSR
					Pt. Lookout, MD	06/25/65	Died, Measles	P6,P117,FPH,CSR
					Pt. Lookout, MD	06/29/65	Rlsd. G.O. #109	P115,CSR

SOUTH CAROLINA SOLDIERS, SAILORS AND **N** CITIZENS HELD IN U.S. PRISONS 1861-1865

NAME	RANK	REGIMENT	CAPTURED AT	WHEN	PRISON	MOVED	DISPOSITION	SOURCES
Nolan, Thomas	Mtr	Dis. Boat	Morris Island, SC	09/07/63	Pt. Lookout, MD	09/20/64	Ft. Warren, MA	P113,P120
Nolan, Thomas	Mtr	Ripleys DB	Morris Island, SC	09/07/63	Ft. Warren, MA	10/01/64	Str. Circasian	P2,P137
Noland, George S.	2Lt	B 18th SCVI	Dinwiddie C.H., VA	04/01/65	Ft. McHenry, MD	04/09/65	Johnson's Isl., OH	P110,CSR
					Johnson's Isl., OH	06/19/65	Rlsd. G.O. #109	P81,P82,P83,CSR
Noll, Charles	Pvt	Brooks LA	Gettysburg, PA	07/04/63	Ft. Delaware, DE			P40,CSR
					Ft. McHenry, MD	07/12/63	Ft. Delaware, DE	CSR
					Petersburg, VA Hos.	08/20/63	Returned to duty	CSR
Noll, Charles	Pvt	Brooks LA	Harpers Farm, VA	04/06/65	City Pt., VA	04/14/65	Pt. Lookout, MD	CSR
					Pt. Lookout, MD	06/15/65	Rlsd. G.O. #109	CSR
Nolte, John O.	Pvt	I 27th SCVI	Town Creek, NC	02/20/65	Ft. Anderson, NC	02/28/65	Pt. Lookout, MD	CSR,HAG
					Pt. Lookout, MD	06/22/65	Rlsd. G.O.#109	P115,P117,P121,CSR
Norman, Jesse	Pvt	C 18th SCVI	Petersburg, VA Hos.	04/03/65	Pt. of Rocks Hos.			CSR
Normands, P.F.	Pvt	H 22nd SCVI	Deserted/enemy	02/25/65	City Pt., VA	02/26/65	No other data	CSR
Norris, Andrew O.	Pvt	A 1st SCVA	Bentonville, NC	03/22/65	New Berne, NC	04/10/65	Hart's Island, NY	CSR
					Hart's Island, NY	06/16/65	Rlsd. G.O. #109	P79,CSR
Norris, D.C.	Pvt	A 19th SCVCB	Augusta, GA	05/25/65	Augusta, GA	05/25/65	Paroled on oath	CSR
Norris, Edward J.	2Lt	E 25th SCVI	Ft. Fisher, NC	01/15/65	Ft. Columbus, NY	04/28/65	Ft. Delaware, DE	P1,P7,HAG,CSR
					Ft. Delaware, DE	05/15/65	Rlsd. G.O. #85	P43,P45,CSR
Norris, Elzey F.	Pvt	F 22nd SCVI	Kinston, NC	12/14/62	Kinston, NC	12/14/62	Paroled POW	CSR
Norris, Elzey F.	Pvt	F 22nd SCVI	Hatchers Run, VA	03/29/65	City Pt., VA	04/03/65	Pt. Lookout, MD	CSR
					Pt. Lookout, MD	05/20/65	Rlsd. G.O. #109	P122,CSR
Norris, G.M.	2Lt	F 2nd SCVI	Charlotte, NC	05/23/65	Charlotte, NC	05/23/65	Paroled	CSR
Norris, Harvey T.	Pvt	F 1st SCVIH	Deep Bottom, VA	08/14/64	Bermuda Hundred, VA	08/15/64	Fts. Monroe, VA	CSR,SA1
					Fts. Monroe, VA	08/17/64	Pt. Lookout, MD	CSR
					Pt. Lookout, MD	06/29/65	Rlsd. G.O. #109	P113,122,P125,CSR
Norris, Hubert	Pvt	F 7th SCVIBn	Weldon RR, VA	08/21/64	City Pt., VA USFH	08/23/64	Bristol, PA USGH	CSR
					Bristol, PA	12/23/64	Philadelphia, PA	CSR
					Phila., PA USGH	12/24/64	Baltimore, MD USGH	CSR
					W. Bldg. Balt, MD	02/16/65	Ft. McHenry, MD Xc	P1,HAG,HIC
Norris, Hubert	Pvt	F 7th SCVIBn	Richmond, VA Hos.	04/03/65	Richmond, VA Hos.	05/09/65	Pt. Lookout, MD US	CSR
					Pt. Lookout, MD US	07/07/65	Rlsd. G.O. #109	CSR
Norris, James	Pvt	C 27th SCVI	Deserted/enemy		New Orleans, LA		Knoxville, TN	CSR
					Knoxville, TN	06/21/64	Louisville, KY	CSR
					Louisville, KY	06/30/64	Jeffersonville, IN	CSR
					Louisville, KY	07/07/64	New Orleans, LA	P88,P92
Norris, T.L.	Pvt	F 22nd SCVI	Crater, Pbg., VA	07/30/64	City Pt., VA	08/05/64	Pt. Lookout, MD	CSR
					Pt. Lookout, MD	08/08/64	Elmira, NY	P113,P116,P120
					Elmira, NY	10/11/64	Venus Pt., GA Xc	P65,P66,P115,CSR
Norris, T.L.	Pvt	F 22nd SCVI	Farmville, VA	04/06/65	City Pt., VA	04/14/65	Newport News, VA	CSR
					Newport News, VA	06/26/65	Rlsd. G.O. #109	P107,CSR
North, John F. McD.	Cpl	D 20th SCVI	Cedar Creek, VA	10/19/64	Harpers Ferry, WV	10/24/65	Pt. Lookout, MD	CSR,KEB
North, John F. McD.	Cpl	D 20th SCVI	Cedar Creek, VA	10/19/64	Pt. Lookout, MD	06/25/65	Rlsd. G.O. #109	P115,P122,CSR
Northcutt, A.N.	Pvt	B 21st SCVI	Petersburg, VA	06/24/64	Pt. Lookout, MD	08/16/64	Elmira, NY	P113,P120,HAG
					Elmira, NY	10/11/64	Tfd. for exchange	P65
					Pt. Lookout, MD	10/29/64	Aikens Ldg., VA Xc	P115,P116
Northcutt, John W.	Cpl	B 21st SCVI	Ft. Fisher, NC	01/15/65	New York, NY	01/30/65	Elmira, NY	CSR,HAG
					Elmira, NY	03/02/65	Pt. Lookout, MD Xc	P65,P66,CSR
Northcutt, S. Travis	Pvt	B 21st SCVI	Ft. Fisher, NC	01/15/65	Elmira, NY	07/19/65	Rlsd. G.O. #109	P65,P66,HAG
Northrop, L.C.	Pvt	PeeDee LA		10/16/63	Ft. McHenry, MD		Fts. Monroe, VA Xc	CSR
Norton, H.L.	Pvt	I 21st SCVI	Ft. Fisher, NC	01/15/65	Elmira, NY	07/11/65	Rlsd. G.O. #109	P65,P66,CSR

SOUTH CAROLINA SOLDIERS, SAILORS AND  CITIZENS HELD IN U.S. PRISONS 1861-1865

NAME	RANK	REGIMENT	CAPTURED AT	WHEN	PRISON	MOVED	DISPOSITION	SOURCES
Norton, J.A.	Pvt	I 7th SCVI	Sharpsburg, MD	09/17/62	Frederick, MD	10/17/62	Ft. McHenry, MD	CSR
					Ft. McHenry, MD	10/20/62	Fts. Monroe, VA	CSR
					Fts. Monroe, VA	10/22/62	Aikens Ldg., VA Xc	CSR
Norton, James	Cpl	E 1st SCVIG	Petersburg, VA	04/02/65	Pt. Lookout, MD	06/15/65	Rlsd. G.O. #109	P115,SA1,CSR
Norton, John Wesley	Pvt	E 1st SCVIG	Sutherland Stn., VA	04/03/65	City Pt., VA	04/13/65	Pt. Lookout, MD	CSR,SA1
					Pt. Lookout, MD	06/29/65	Rlsd. G.O. #109	P115,P117,P122,CSR
Norton, Patrick	Smn	CS *Chicora*	Morris Island, SC	09/07/63	Pt. Lookout, MD	07/20/64	Elmira, NY	P113,P120,P124
					Elmira, NY	03/06/65	Released	P65,P66
Norton, W.B.	Pvt	C 3rd SCVABn	Blakely, AL	04/02/65				CSR
Norwood, William Tully	2Lt	E 6th SCVI	Chattanooga, TN	10/19/63	Nashville, TN	11/07/63	Louisville, KY	CSR
					Louisville, KY	11/09/63	Camp Chase, OH	P89,CSR
					Camp Chase, OH	11/14/63	Johnson's Isl., OH	CSR
					Johnson's isl., OH	01/11/64	Died of Dysentery	CSR
Nott, Henry Junius	Sur	2nd SCVI	Gettysburg, PA	08/11/63	Ft. McHenry, MD	07/08/63	City Pt., VA Xc	SA2,P96,KEB,H2,CSR
Nott, Henry Junius	Sur	2nd SCVI	Gettysburg, PA	07/05/63	Letterman G.H. Gbg	09/10/63	Provost Marshal	P1,CSR
Nowell, Lionel C.	1Lt	K 4th SCVC	Old Church, VA	05/30/64	White House, VA	06/08/64	Pt. Lookout, MD	CSR
					Pt. Lookout, MD	06/23/64	Ft. Delaware, DE	P116,P120,CSR
					Ft. Delaware, DE	02/26/65	Discharged Hos.	P47
					Ft. Delaware, DE	06/13/65	Rlsd. G.O.#109	P42,P44,P45,CSR
Nowell, Thomas Wigfall	Cpl	A 2nd SCVC	White Hall, NC	03/18/65	New Berne, NC	03/30/65	Pt. Lookout, MD	CSR
					Pt. Lookout, MD	06/29/65	Rlsd. G.O.#109	P115,P117,P122,CSR
Nugas, Max	Pvt	Pee Dee LA	Cashtown, PA	07/05/63	Ft. Delaware, DE		Detail at hospital	P40,P44,P47
Nunn, L.D.	Pvt	15th SCVAB	Bentonville, NC	03/19/65	Savannah, GA USH	03/23/65	Died of wounds	P1,P6,CSR
Nunnery, Amos L.	Sgt	A 17th SCVI	Crater, Pbg., VA	07/30/64	City Pt., VA	08/05/64	Pt. Lookout, MD	CSR,HHC
					Pt. Lookout, MD	08/08/64	Elmira, NY	P116,P120,P125,CSR
					Elmira, NY	06/14/65	Released	P65,CSR

SOUTH CAROLINA SOLDIERS, SAILORS AND  CITIZENS HELD IN U.S. PRISONS 1861-1865

NAME	RANK	REGIMENT	CAPTURED AT	WHEN	PRISON	MOVED	DISPOSITION	SOURCES
O'Bannon, William	Pvt	H 14th SCVI	Appomattox R., VA	04/03/65	City Pt., VA	04/11/65	Hart's Island, NY	CSR
					Hart's Island, NY	06/17/65	Rlsd. G.O. #109	P79,CSR
O'Brien, George	Cit				Ft. Delaware, DE	05/10/64		P7,P47
O'Brien, H.G.	Sgt	A 1st SCVA	Deserted/enemy		Charleston, SC	04/01/65	New York, NY oath	CSR
O'Brien, John	Pvt	Ferguson's LA	Ringgold, GA	11/26/63	Nashville, TN	12/11/63	Louisville, KY	P39,CSR
					Louisville, KY	12/12/63	Rock Island, IL	P89,CSR
					Rock Island, IL	04/21/64	Rlsd. on oath	P131,CSR
O'Brien, Mortimer C.	Pvt	F 1st SCVIBn	Morris Island, SC	09/07/63	Ft. Columbus, NY	10/09/63	Johnson's Island	P1
					Pt. Lookout, MD	02/24/64	Exchanged	P113,P124
O'Brien, Mortimer C.	Pvt	C 27th SCVI	Town Creek, NC	02/20/65	Ft. Anderson, NC	02/25/65	Pt. Lookout, MD	CSR
					Pt. Lookout, MD	05/14/65	Rlsd. G.O. #85	P115,P117,P122
O'Brien, Patrick	Pvt	E 1st SCVA	Deserted/enemy	02/18/64	Hilton Head, SC	08/18/64	Took oath & release	CSR
O'Brien, Thomas	Pvt	B 1st SCVA	Fayetteville, NC	03/16/65	Pt. Lookout, MD	06/29/65	Rlsd. G.O. #109	P115,P118,P122,CSR
O'Brien, Timothy	Pvt	K 4th SCVC	Charlotte, NC	05/03/65	Charlotte, NC	05/03/65	Paroled	CSR
O'Bryan, Henry	Pvt	A 3rd SCVC	Florence, SC	03/05/65	New Berne, NC	04/03/65	Pt. Lookout, MD	P115,P118,P121,CSR
					Pt. Lookout, MD	06/30/65	Rlsd. G.O. #109	P115,P118,P121
O'Connell, Edward	Pvt	C 15th SCVAB			Camp Morton, IN	12/05/64	Died	FPH,CSR
O'Connell, James	Cit	Columbia	Columbia, SC	02/17/65	Hart's Island, NY	06/20/65	Rlsd. G.O. #109	P79
O'Donnell, James	Sgt	A 15th SCVAB	Deserted/enemy	02/18/65	Charleston, SC	03/22/65	New York, NY oath	CSR
O'Dwyer, Thomas O.	Cpl	K 2nd SCVIRi	Chattanooga, TN	11/29/63	Nashville, TN	11/07/63	Louisville, KY	CSR
					Louisville, KY	11/09/63	Camp Morton, IN	CSR
					Camp Morton, IN	03/04/65	City Pt., VA Xc	CSR
O'Farrell, G.H.	Pvt	G P.S.S.	Fair Oaks, VA	03/01/62	Fts. Monroe, VA	06/21/62	Ft. Delaware, DE	CSR
					Ft. Delaware, DE	08/03/62	Aikens Ldg., VA Xc	CSR
O'Harry, P.M.	Sgt	G 4th SCVC	Richmond, VA Hos.	04/03/65	Richmond, VA	05/28/65	Prob. paroled	CSR
O'Kelly, Benjamin F.	Pvt	K 22nd SCVI	Sharpsburg, MD	09/17/62	Ft. McHenry, MD	10/17/62	Fts. Monroe, VA Xc	CSR
					Fts. Monroe, VA	10/23/62	Richmond, VA Hos.	CSR
					Richmond, VA Hos.	11/07/62	Furloughed 30 days	CSR
O'Meally, Alexander	Pvt	I 1st SCVA	Morris Island, SC	07/10/63	Ft. Columbus, NY	09/23/63	Took the oath	P1,CSR
O'Nails, Wiley D.	Pvt	G 21st SCVI	Ft. Fisher, NC	01/15/65	New York, NY	01/30/65	Elmira, NY	CSR
					Elmira, NY	07/11/65	Rlsd. G.O. #109	P65,P66,CSR
O'Neal, John B.	1Lt	F 3rd SCVI	Williamsport, MD	07/14/63	Hagerstown, MD G.H.	07/15/63	Died of wounds	P2,KEB,SA2,H3,CSR
O'Neal, Joseph	Pvt	K 1st SCVIR	Bentonville, NC	03/06/65	New Berne, NC	03/30/65	Pt. Lookout, MD	CSR,SA1
					Pt. Lookout, MD	06/29/65	Rlsd. G.O. #109	P115,P118,P122,CSR
O'Neil, Edmund F.	2Lt	Brooks LA	Cashtown, PA	07/05/63	Chester, PA G.H.	10/03/63	Pt. Lookout, MD	P1,CSR
					Hammond G.H., MD	12/05/63	Johnson's Isl., OH	P116,CSR
					Johnson's Isl., OH	03/14/65	Pt. Lookout, MD Xc	P82,CSR
O,Neil, J.J.	Pvt	K 4th SCVC	Charlotte, NC	05/03/65	Charlotte, NC	05/03/65	Paroled	CSR
O'Neil, John	Pvt	1st SCVA	Deserted/enemy		Hilton Head, SC	12/18/64		P8
O'Neil, Patrick	Pvt	B 1st SCVA	Fayetteville, NC	03/10/65	New Berne, NC	04/10/65	Hart's Island, NY	CSR
					Hart's Island, NY	06/21/65	Rlsd. G.O. #109	P79,CSR
O'Neil, William J.	Pvt	D 2nd SCVI	Halltown, VA	08/29/64	Harpers Ferry, WV	09/02/64	Camp Chase, OH	CSR,KEB,SA2,H2
					Camp Chase, OH	03/26/65	Pt. Lookout, MD	P26,CSR
					Pt. Lookout, MD	06/29/65	Rlsd. G.O. #109	P118,P122,CSR
O'Quinn, James H.	Pvt	K 11th SCVI	Town Creek, NC	02/20/65	Ft. Anderson, NC	02/28/65	Pt. Lookout, MD	CSR,HAG
					Pt. Lookout, MD	06/29/65	Rlsd. G.O. #109	P115,P117,P122,CSR
O'Shields, John	Pvt	G 27th SCVI	Petersburg, VA	06/24/64	Bermuda Hundred, VA	06/25/64	Fts. Monroe, VA	CSR,HAG
					Fts. Monroe, VA	06/26/64	Pt. Lookout, MD	CSR
					Pt. Lookout, MD	08/16/64	Elmira, NY	P113,P117,P120
					Elmira, NY	10/11/64	Tfd. for exchange	P65
					Pt. Lookout, MD	10/29/64	Venus Pt., GA Xc	P115,P117,P123,CSR

SOUTH CAROLINA SOLDIERS, SAILORS AND  CITIZENS HELD IN U.S. PRISONS 1861-1865

NAME	RANK	REGIMENT	CAPTURED AT	WHEN	PRISON	MOVED	DISPOSITION	SOURCES
O'Shields, William D.	1Lt	F 13th SCVI	Appomattox R., VA	04/03/65	Ft. McHenry, MD	04/21/65	Johnson's Isl., OH	P10,HOS
					Old Capitol, DC	04/21/65	Johnson's Isl., OH	CSR
					Johnson's Isl., OH	06/19/65	Rlsd. G.O. #109	P82,P83,CSR
O'Sullivan, Michael A.	Pvt	D 27th SCVI	Town Creek, NC	02/20/65	Pt. Lookout, MD	06/20/65	Rlsd. G.O. #109	P115,HAG
Oakley, Daniel L.	Pvt	C 26th SCVI	Farmville, VA	04/06/65	City t., VA	04/14/65	Newport News, VA	CSR
					Newport News, VA	06/13/65	Rlsd. G.O. #109	P107,CSR
Oakley, Robert N.	Pvt	H Orr's Ri.	Petersburg, VA	04/02/65	City Pt., VA	04/04/65	Pt. Lookout, MD	CSR,CDC
					Pt. Lookout, MD	06/04/65	Rlsd. G.O. #85	P115,P118,P121,CSR
Oates, J.P.	Pvt	B 21st SCVI	Ft. Fisher, NC	01/15/65	Elmira, NY	07/07/65	Rlsd. G.O. #109	P65,P66,HAG
Odell, Jackson M.	Pvt	F 22nd SCVI	Petersburg, VA	03/25/65	City Pt., VA	03/28/65	Pt. Lookout, MD	CSR
					Pt. Lookout, MD	06/29/65	Rlsd. G.O. #109	P115,P118,P122,CSR
Odena, Peter	Pvt	B 23rd SCVI	Fayetteville, NC	03/12/65	New Berne, NC	04/07/65	Hart's Island, NY	CSR
					Hart's Island, NY	06/16/65	Rlsd. G.O. #109	P79,CSR
Odom, B.F.	Pvt	C 1st SCVIR	Raleigh, NC Hos.	04/13/65	Raleigh, NC	04/13/65	Paroled	SA1,CSR
Odom, J.S.	Pvt	D 6th SCVC	Trevillian Stn., VA	06/11/64			No U.S. data	CSR
Odom, James Leonard	Pvt	B 24th SCVI	Nashville, TN	12/16/64	Nashville, TN	12/19/64	Louisville, KY	CSR
					Louisville, KY	12/21/64	Camp Douglas, IL	P90,P91,P95,CSR
					Camp Douglas, IL	04/02/65	Jd. US 6th Vol.I.	P55,CSR
Odom, Joel	1Sg	H 21st SCVI	Weldon RR, VA	08/20/64	Philadelphia, PA	09/13/64	Died of wounds	P5,P6,P12,FPH,CSR
Odom, John J.	Pvt	D 12th SCVI	Wilderness, VA	05/06/65	Old Capitol, DC	06/15/64	Ft. Delaware, DE	CSR
					Ft. McHenry, MD	06/18/64	Ft. Delaware, DE	P110
					Ft. Delaware, DE	07/13/64	Died, Lung Inflam.	P5,P43,P47,FPH,CSR
Odom, Leander	Pvt	D 24th SCVI	Jonesboro, GA	09/04/64	Rough & Ready, GA	09/23/64	Exchanged	CSR
Odom, Peter	Pvt	I 18th SCVI	Petersburg, VA	03/25/65	City Pt., VA	03/28/65	Pt. Lookout, MD	CSR
					Pt. Lookout, MD	06/29/65	Rlsd. G.O. #109	P115,P118,P122,CSR
Odom, W.B.	Sgt	F 21st SCVI	Ft. Fisher, NC	01/15/65	Elmira, NY	07/26/65	Rlsd. G.O. #109	P66,HOM,HAG
Odom, William	Pvt	E 21st SCVI	Morris Island, SC	07/10/63	Morris Island, SC	07/13/63	Hilton Head, SC	CSR,HAG
					Hilton Head, SC GH	07/23/63	Morris Island, SC Xc	P2,CSR
Odom, William	Cpt	A 8th SCVI	Winchester, VA	09/13/64	Harpers Ferry, WV	09/16/64	Johnson's Isl., OH	CSR,KEB
					Johnson's Isl., OH	06/16/65	Rlsd. G.O. #109	P81,P82,P83,CSR
Odom, William C.	Pvt	D 26th SCVI	Amelia C.H., VA	04/06/65	City Pt., VA	04/13/65	Pt. Lookout, MD	CSR
					Pt. Lookout, MD	06/29/65	Rlsd. G.O. #109	CSR
Odom, William J.	Pvt	H 17th SCVI	Petersburg VA	03/25/65	City Pt., VA	03/28/65	Pt. Lookout, MD	CSR
					Pt. Lookout, MD	06/29/65	Rlsd. G.O. #109	P118,P122,CSR
Odom, William W.	Cpl	I 26th SCVI	Five Forks, VA	04/02/65	City Pt., VA	04/05/65	Pt. Lookout, MD	CSR,CTA
					Pt. Lookout, MD	06/29/65	Rlsd. G.O. #109	P109,P118,P122
Ogburn, L.D.	Pvt	D 8th SCVI	Winchester, VA	09/13/64	Harpers Ferry, WV	09/16/64	Camp Chase, OH	CSR,KEB
					Camp Chase, OH	05/02/65	New Orleans, LA	P26,CSR
					New Orleans, LA	05/12/65	Vicksburg, MS Xc	CSR
Ogden, D.S.	Cpl	E 1st SCVIH	Chaffin's Farm, VA	09/30/64	Str. Hero of Jersey	10/21/64	U.S. Gen. Hospital	CSR,SA1
					Fts. Monroe, VA	01/13/65	Pt. Lookout, MD	CSR
					Pt. Lookout, MD	05/28/65	Died, Diarrhea	P6,P115,P119,FPH
Oglesby, William	Pvt	A 23rd SCVI	Farmville, VA	04/06/65	City Pt., VA	04/14/65	Newport News, VA	CSR
					Newport News, VA	06/26/65	Rlsd. G.O. #109	P107,CSR
Olandt, J.E.	Pvt	B German LA	Deserted/enemy	10/01/64	Hilton Head, SC	10/31/64	At work in Q.M.	P8,CSR
Oledman, G.	Pvt	L 1st SCVIG	Warrenton, VA	09/29/62	Warrenton, VA	09/29/62	Paroled	CSR
Oliphant, Marcut	Pvt	E Hol.Leg.	Boonesboro, MD	09/14/62	Ft. Delaware, DE	10/02/62	Aikens Ldg., VA Xc	CSR
Oliver, Alexander	Pvt	F 26th SCVI	Williamson Dpt., VA	04/06/65	City Pt., VA	04/07/65	Pt. Lookout, MD	CSR
					Pt. Lookout, MD	06/29/65	Rlsd. G.O. #109	P115,P118,P122,CSR
Oliver, Alexander R.	Pvt	E 1st SCVIG	Petersburg, VA	04/02/65	City Pt., VA	04/04/65	Pt. Lookout, MD	CSR,SA1
					Pt. Lookout, MD	06/29/65	Rlsd. G.O. #109	P115,P122,CSR
Oliver, H.C.	Pvt	F 15th SCMil	Chesterfield, SC	02/16/65	Pt. Lookout, MD	05/07/65	Died, Pneumonia	P6,P118,P119,FPH

SOUTH CAROLINA SOLDIERS, SAILORS AND  CITIZENS HELD IN U.S. PRISONS 1861-1865

NAME	RANK	REGIMENT	CAPTURED AT	WHEN	PRISON	MOVED	DISPOSITION	SOURCES
Oliver, Ishmael	Pvt	I Hol.Leg.	Newton, NC	04/19/65	Newton, NC	04/19/65	Paroled	CSR
Oliver, J.H.	Pvt	C 3rd SCVABn	Ft. Gaines, AL	08/08/64	New Orleans, LA	10/25/64	Ship Island, MS	P3,CSR
					Ship Island, MS	01/04/65	Exchanged	P136,CSR
Oliver, Jackson	Pvt	E 13th SCVI	Falling Waters, MD	07/14/63	Old Capitol, DC	08/08/62	Pt. Lookout, MD	P110,CSR,HOS
					Ft. McHenry, MD	08/08/62	Pt. Lookout, MD	P110
					Pt. Lookout, MD	03/03/64	City Pt., VA Xc	P113,P116,P124,CSR
Oliver, Jackson	Pvt	E 13th SCVI	Deserted/enemy	02/24/65	City Pt., VA	02/26/65	Washington, DC	CSR
					Washington, DC	02/27/65	New York, NY oath	CSR
Oliver, Joseph	Pvt	I 27th SCVI	Town Creek, NC	02/20/65	Ft. Anderson, NC	02/28/65	Pt. Lookout, MD	CSR,HAG
					Pt. Lookout, MD	05/04/65	Rlsd. G.O. #85	P115,P117,CSR
Oliver, Nelson T.	Pvt	G 26th SCVI	Five Forks, VA	04/01/65	City Pt., VA	04/05/65	Pt. Lookout, MD	CSR
					Pt. Lookout, MD	06/29/65	Rlsd. G.O. #109	P115,P118,P122,CSR
Oliver, P. Erastus	Pvt	D 7th SCVI	Sharpsburg, MD	09/17/62	Ft. McHenry, MD	10/13/62	Fts. Monroe VA	CSR
					Fts. Monroe, VA	11/10/63	Aikens Ldg., VA Xc	CSR
Oliver, Samuel A.	Sgt	B 14th SCVI	Petersburg, VA	04/02/65	City Pt., VA	04/07/65	Hart's Island, NY	CSR
					Hart's Island, NY	06/15/65	Rlsd. G.O. #109	P79,CSR
Olivet, Edwin A.	Pvt	H 1st SCVA	Deserted/enemy		Chattanooga, TN	02/07/64		P8,CSR
Opdebeck, Francis	Cit	*Charleston*	At sea	02/13/63	Ft. Lafayette, NY	07/02/63	Ft. Warren, MA	P144
					Ft. Warren, MA	12/06/64	Took the oath	P2
Opry, E.G.	Pvt	C 3rd SCVABn	Ft. Gaines, AL	08/08/64	New Orleans, LA	09/05/64	St. Louis, MO USGH	CSR
					St. Louis, MO USGH	09/19/64	New Orleans, LA	CSR
					New Orleans, LA	10/25/64	Ship Island, MS	P3,CSR
					Ship Island, MS	12/04/64	Died, Dysentery	CSR
					Ship Island, MS	01/04/65	Exchanged	P136,CSR
Orander, Lewis	Pvt	I 2nd SCVI	Gettysburg, PA	07/05/63	Gettysburg G.H.	07/28/63	Died of wounds	SA2,P4,H2,CSR
Orr, James M.	Pvt	A 17th SCVI	Petersburg, VA	04/02/65	City Pt., VA	04/04/65	Pt. Lookout, MD	CSR,HHC
					Pt. Lookout, MD	06/29/65	Rlsd. G.O. #109	P115,P118,P122,CSR
Orton, George	Pvt	H 1st SCVA	Deserted/enemy		Chattanooga, TN	01/10/64		P8,CSR
Osborn, John W.	Pvt	H 26th SCVI	Crater, Pbg., VA	07/30/64	City Pt., VA	08/05/64	Pt. Lookout, MD	CSR
					Pt. Lookout, MD	08/08/64	Elmira, NY	P113,P117,P120,CSR
					Elmira, NY	05/13/65	Released	P65,P66,CSR
Osborn, Lewis A.	Pvt	F Hol.Leg.	Five Forks, VA	04/01/65	City Pt., VA	04/05/65	Pt. Lookout, MD	CSR
					Pt. Lookout, MD	06/29/65	Rlsd. G.O. #109	P115,P118,CSR
Osborne, Elisha C.	Pvt	2 10/19 SCVI	Missionary Ridge, TN	11/25/63	Nashville, TN	12/07/63	Louisville, KY	P39,CSR,RAS
					Louisville, KY	12/09/63	Rock Island, IL	P88,P89,CSR
					Rock Island, IL	06/20/65	Rlsd. G.O. #109	P131,CSR
Osborne, James P.	Pvt	L Orr's Ri.	Deserted/enemy	03/05/65	City Pt., VA	03/07/65	Washington, DC	CSR
					Washington D.C.	03/08/65	New York, NY oath	CDC,CSR
Osmet, John R.	Pvt	C 2nd SCVI	Gettysburg, PA	07/04/63	David's Island, NY	08/24/63	Paroled	SA2,P1,CSR,H2
Osteen, John M.	Pvt	C 3rd SCVABn	Ft. Gaines, AL	08/08/64	New Orleans, LA	10/25/64	Ship Island, MS	P3,CSR
					Ship Island, MS	01/04/65	Exchanged	P136,CSR
Oswalt, Daniel Wilson	Pvt	C 15th SCVI	Boonesboro, MD	09/14/62	Ft. McHenry, MD	10/17/62	Fts. Monroe, VA Xc	H15,CSR
Oswalt, Daniel Wilson	Pvt	C 15th SCVI	Gettysburg, PA	07/02/63	Gettysburg, PA USH	07/04/63	Died, of wounds	CSR
Oswalt, Simeon O.	Pvt	C 15th SCVI	Gettysburg, PA	07/02/63	Gettysburg, PA USH	07/20/63	Provost Marshal	P4,CSR,H15
					David's Island, NY	07/31/63	Died, Typhoid	P6,FPH,CSR
Otis, John	Sgt	A 1st SCVIR	Morris Island, SC	09/07/63	Hilton Head, SC	09/19/63	Ft. Columbus, NY	P1,CSR
					Ft. Columbus, NY	09/23/63	Took the oath	P1,CSR
Ott, John David	Pvt	G 25th SCVI	Weldon RR, VA	08/21/64	Alexandria, VA G.H.	08/26/64	Washington, DC	P1,HAG
					Old Capitol, DC	10/24/64	Elmira, NY	P110,CSR
					Elmira, NY	02/20/65	Tfd. for exchange	P65
Ott, Samuel H.	Pvt	E 25th SCVI	Ft. Fisher, NC	01/15/65	New York, NY	01/30/65	Elmira, NY	CSR,HAG
					Elmira, NY	07/14/65	Rlsd. G.O. #109	P65,P66,CSR

SOUTH CAROLINA SOLDIERS, SAILORS AND  CITIZENS HELD IN U.S. PRISONS 1861-1865

NAME	RANK	REGIMENT	CAPTURED AT	WHEN	PRISON	MOVED	DISPOSITION	SOURCES
Ott, William Elmore	Pvt	G 25th SCVI	Ft. Fisher, NC	01/15/65	New York, NY	01/30/65	Elmira, NY	CSR,HAG
					Elmira, NY	03/05/65	Died, Pneumonia	P6,P12,P65,P66,FPH
Otts, Martin	Cpl	A 3rd SCResB	Cheraw, SC	03/07/65	Hart's Island, NY	06/09/65	Died, Ch. Diarrhea	P6,P79,FPH,CSR
Otts, R.M.	Pvt	I 5th SCVI	Deep Bottom, VA	08/14/64	Bermuda Hundred, VA	08/15/64	Fts. Monroe, VA	SA3,CSR
					Fts. Monroe, VA	08/16/64	Pt. Lookout, MD	CSR,P125
Outen, Daniel	Pvt	C 7th SCVIBn	Clinton, NC	03/20/65	New Berne, NC	04/10/65	Hart's Island, NY	CSR
					Hart's Island, NY	06/17/65	Rlsd. G.O. #109	P79,CSR
Outen, Joel	Cpl	A 1st SCVIR	Morris Island, SC	09/07/63	Ft. Columbus, NY	10/09/63	Pt. Lookout, MD	P1,SA1,CSR
					Pt. Lookout, MD	02/24/65	Aikens Ldg., VA Xc	P113,P116,P124,CSR
Outen, L. Berry	Pvt	E 12th SCVI	Spotsylvania, VA	05/12/64	Belle Plain, VA	05/21/64	Ft. Delaware, DE	CSR,LAN
					Ft. Delaware, DE	09/27/64	Hos. 9/27-10/21/64	P47
					Ft. Delaware, DE	10/25/64	Hos. 10/25-10/30/64	P47
					Ft. Delaware, DE	10/30/64	Pt. Lookout, MD	P43,CSR
					Ft. Delaware, DE	10/31/64	Venus Pt., GA Xc	CSR
					Pt. Lookout, MD	10/31/64	Aikens Ldg., VA Xc	P115,P117
Outland, Burrill T.	Pvt	E 10th SCVI	Goldsboro, NC	05/04/65	Goldsboro, NC	05/04/65	Paroled	CSR
Outlaw, Bentley	Pvt	G 7th SCVIBn	Drury's Bluff, VA	05/16/64	Pt. Lookout, MD	08/15/64	Elmira, NY	P113,HAG,HIC,KCE
					Elmira, NY	10/11/64	Tfd. for exchange	P65
Outlaw, Drury	Pvt	Ch'fld LA	Petersburg, VA Hos.	04/03/65	Fts. Monroe, VA G.	06/11/65	Rlsd. G.O. #109	CSR
Outlaw, Edward W.	Pvt	D 21st SCVI	Morris Island, SC	07/10/63	Ft. Columbus, NY	09/23/63	Took the oath	P1,HAG
					Ft. Columbus, NY	09/26/63	Pt. Lookout, MD	CSR
					Pt. Lookout, MD	05/03/64	City Pt., VA Xc	P116,P123,CSR
Outlaw, John	Pvt	A 8th SCVI	Winchester, VA	09/13/64	Harpers Ferry, WV	09/16/64	Camp Chase, OH	CSR,KEB
					Camp Chase	06/10/65	Rlsd. G.O. #109	P22,CSR
Outlaw, Richard	Pvt	G 7th SCVIBn	Drury's Bluff, VA	05/16/64	Bermuda Hundred, VA	05/17/64	Fts. Monroe, VA	CSR,HAG,HIC
					Fts. Monroe, VA	05/18/64	Pt. Lookout, MD	CSR
					Pt. Lookout, MD	08/15/64	Elmira, NY	P117,CSR
Outlaw, Richard	Pvt	G 7th SCVIBn	Kershaw Dist., SC	02/25/65	New Berne, NC	04/10/65	Hart's Island, NY	CSR
					Hart's Island, NY	06/17/65	Rlsd. G.O. #109	P79,HIC,CSR
Outler, Stephen	Pvt	H 1st SCVA	Deserted/enemy	02/20/65	Charleston, SC		Released on oath	CSR
Ouzts, Caleb Pinckney	Pvt	B Ham.Leg.MI	Augusta, GA	05/30/65	Augusta, GA	05/30/65	Paroled	CSR
Ouzts, J.A.	Pvt	B 2nd SCVC	Charlotte, NC	05/06/65	Charlotte, NC	05/06/65	Paroled	CSR
Ouzts, James	Pvt	K 14th SCVI	Greencastle, PA	07/02/63	Ft. Miflin, PA	11/17/63	Ft. Delaware, DE	UD6,CSR
Ouzts, Marion	Pvt	K 14th SCVI	Hagerstown, MD	07/06/63	Provost Marshal	07/07/63	Ft. Delaware, DE	UD6,CSR
Ouzts, Marion	Pvt	K 14th SCVI	Gettysburg, PA	07/05/63	Ft. Delaware, DE	08/30/63	Jd. US 1st CN Cav.	P40,P44,CSR
					David's Island, NY	09/08/63	City Pt., VA Xc	UD6,P1,CSR
Ouzts, Peter D.	Pvt	C 19th SCVI	Atlanta, GA	07/22/64	Nashville, TN	07/29/64	Louisville, KY	CSR
					Louisville, KY	07/31/64	Camp Chase, OH	P88,P91,P94,CSR
					Camp Chase, OH	03/04/65	City Pt., VA Xc	P22,P26,CSR
Ouzts, W.H.	Cpl	K 17th SCVI	Augusta, GA	05/30/65	Augusta, GA	05/30/65	Paroled	CSR
Overstreet, G.W.	Pvt	G 14th SCVI	Gettysburg, PA	07/05/63	Chester, PA G.H.	09/21/63	City Pt., VA Xc	P1,CSR
Overstreet, Laban	Pvt	D 24th SCVI	Nashville, TN	12/16/64	Nashville, TN	12/31/64	Louisville, KY	CSR
					Louisville, KY	01/02/65	Camp Chase, OH	CSR
					Camp Chase, OH	03/05/65	Died, Pneumonia	P6,P12,P27,FPH,CSR
Overstreet, Samuel	Pvt	D 14th SCVI	Gettysburg, PA	07/05/63	Chester, PA G.H.	09/23/63	City Pt., VA Xc	CSR
Owen, D.T.	Cpl	F 22nd SCVI	Petersburg, VA	03/25/65	Pt. Lookout, MD			P118
Owens, Abner	Pvt	E 14th SCVI	Appomattox R., VA	04/02/65	City Pt., VA	04/11/65	Hart's Island, NY	CSR
					Hart's Island, NY	06/17/65	Rlsd. G.O. #109	P79,CSR
Owens, Albert P.	Cpl	E 1st SCVIG	Gettysburg, PA	07/05/63	David's Island, NY	08/06/63	Died of wounds	P6,SA1,FPH,CSR
Owens, Andrew	Pvt	1st SCVR	Deserted/enemy	02/18/65	Hilton Head, SC	04/07/65	New York, NY oath	SA1,CSR
Owens, Archibald	Cpl	A 23rd SCVI	Petersburg, VA	04/02/65	City Pt., VA	04/04/65	Pt. Lookout, MD	CSR
					Pt. Lookout, MD	06/29/65	Rlsd. G.O. #109	P115,P118,P122,CSR

SOUTH CAROLINA SOLDIERS, SAILORS AND CITIZENS HELD IN U.S. PRISONS 1861-1865

NAME	RANK	REGIMENT	CAPTURED AT	WHEN	PRISON	MOVED	DISPOSITION	SOURCES
Owens, Benjamin	Pvt	D Hol.Leg.	Five Forks, VA	04/01/65	City Pt., VA	04/05/65	Pt. Lookout, MD	CSR
					Pt. Lookout, MD	06/30/65	Rlsd. G.O. #109	P115,P118,P121,CSR
Owens, Calvin	Pvt	A 1st SCVIG	Petersburg, VA	04/02/65	City Pt. VA	04/04/65	Pt. Lookout, MD	SA1,CSR
					Pt. Lookout, MD	06/29/64	Rlsd. G.O. #109	P115,P118,P122,CSR
Owens, David F.	Cpl	E 23rd SCVI	Petersburg, VA	03/25/65	City Pt., VA	04/02/65	Pt. Lookout, MD	CSR,HMC
					Pt. Lookout, MD	06/29/65	Rlsd. G.O. #109	P115,P122,CSR
Owens, Dempsey	Pvt	A 5th SCVC	Petersburg, VA	07/29/64	City Pt., VA	08/05/64	Pt. Lookout, MD	CSR
					Pt. Lookout, MD	08/08/64	Elmira, NY	P113,P117,P120,CSR
					Elmira, NY	09/12/64	Died, Diarrhea	P5,P65,P66,FPH,CSR
Owens, E.B.	Sgt	F 4th SCVC	Louisa C.H., VA	06/11/64	Fts. Monroe, VA	06/20/64	Pt. Lookout, MD	CSR,HMC
					Pt. Lookout, MD	07/25/64	Elmira, NY	P113,P117,P120,CSR
					Elmira, NY	10/11/64	Pt. Lookout, MD Xc	P65,P66,CSR
					Pt. Lookout, MD	10/29/64	Aikens Ldg., VA Xc	P115,P117,P123,CSR
Owens, G.H.	Pvt	B 22nd SCVI	Deserted/enemy	02/25/65	City Pt., VA	02/28/65	Washington, DC	CSR
					Washington, DC	03/01/65	Oil City, PA oath	CSR
Owens, H.C.	Pvt	G 1st SCVIR	Bentonville, NC	03/22/65	New Berne, NC	04/10/65	Hart's Island, NY	CSR,SA1
					Hart's Island, NY	06/17/65	Rlsd. G.O. #109	P79,CSR
Owens, Henry	Pvt	C 22nd SCVI	Kinston, NC	12/15/62	Kinston, NC	12/15/62	Paroled POW	CSR,HOS
Owens, Henry	Pvt	C 22nd SCVI	Crater, Pbg., VA	07/30/64	City Pt., VA	08/05/64	Pt. Lookout, MD	CSR
					Pt. Lookout, MD	08/08/64	Elmira, NY	P113,P117,P120
					Elmira, NY	01/07/65	Died, Typhoid fever	P6,P12,P65,P66,FPH
Owens, J. Marion	Pvt	C 25th SCVI	Ft. Darling, VA	05/14/65	Fts. Monroe, VA	05/17/64	Pt. Lookout, MD Xc	CSR,HAG,CTA
					Pt. Lookout, MD	11/01/64	Venus Pt., GA Xc	P113,P117,P121,CSR
Owens, J.A.	Pvt	E 27th SCVI	Petersburg, VA	06/24/64	Bermuda Hundred, VA	06/25/64	Fts. Monroe, VA	CSR,HAG
					Fts. Monroe, VA	06/26/64	Pt. Lookout, MD	CSR
					Pt. Lookout, MD	08/16/64	Elmira, NY	P113,P117,P120,CSR
					Elmira, NY	03/02/65	Tfd. for exchange	P65,CSR
Owens, J.L.	Pvt	E 27th SCVI	Petersburg, VA	06/24/64	Bermuda Hundred, VA	06/25/64	Fts. Monroe, VA	CSR,HAG
					Fts. Monroe, VA	06/26/64	Pt. Lookout, MD	CSR
					Pt. Lookout, MD	08/16/64	Elmira, NY	P113,P117,P120,CSR
					Elmira, NY	06/06/65	Rlsd. G.O. #109	P65,CSR
Owens, J.W.	Pvt	E 23rd SCVI	Deserted/enemy	11/15/64	City Pt., VA	11/20/64	Washington, DC	CSR
					Washington, DC	11/25/64	Phila., PA on oath	CSR
Owens, James D.	Cpl	B Hol.Leg.	Deserted/enemy	03/14/65	City Pt., VA	03/14/65	Washington, DC	CSR
					Washington, DC	03/18/65	Newville, PA oath	CSR
Owens, John	Pvt	F 21st SCVI	Morris Island, SC	07/10/63	Hilton Head, SC	07/13/63	Ft. Columbus, NY	CSR,HAG,HOM
					Ft. Columbus, NY	10/06/63	Pt. Lookout, MD	P1
					Pt. Lookout, MD	02/25/64	Joined U.S. Army	P113,P116,P125
Owens, John	Pvt	D 11th SCVI	Midway, SC	02/06/65	New Berne, NC	04/03/65	Pt. Lookout, MD	CSR
					Pt. Lookout, MD	06/29/65	Rlsd. G.O. #109	P115,P118,P122,CSR
Owens, John A.	Pvt	G 15th SCVI	South Mtn., MD	09/14/62	Ft. Delaware, DE	10/02/62	Aikens Ldg., VA Xc	CSR
Owens, John I.	Pvt	E 1st SCVIH	Chattanooga, TN	10/29/63	Nashville, TN	11/07/63	Louisville, KY	CSR,SA1
					Louisville, KY	11/09/63	Camp Morton, IN	P88,P89,P93,CSR
					Camp Morton, IN	01/21/65	Died, Typhoid fever	P6,P100,P101,FPH
Owens, John W.	Pvt	C Hol.Leg.	Petersburg, VA	11/06/64	City Pt., VA	11/11/64	Washington, DC	CSR,HOS
					Pt. Lookout, MD	01/17/65	Aikens Ldg., VA Xc	P115,P117,P124,CSR
Owens, John W.	Pvt	C Hol.Leg.	Five Forks, VA	04/01/65	City Pt., VA	04/05/65	Pt. Lookout, MD	CSR
					Pt. Lookout, MD	06/29/65	Rlsd. G.O. #109	P115,P118,P122
Owens, Jonathan W.	Pvt	D 18th SCVI	Farmville, VA	04/06/65	City Pt., VA	04/14/65	Newport News, VA	CSR,UD5
					Newport News, VA	06/26/65	Rlsd. G.O. #109	P107,CSR
Owens, L.C.	Pvt	D 1st SCVA	Bentonville, NC	03/22/65	Hart's Island, NY	06/17/65	Rlsd. G.O. #109	P79
Owens, M.	Pvt	E 3rd SCVIBn	South Mtn., MD	09/14/62	Ft. Delaware, DE	10/02/62	Aikens Ldg., VA Xc	CSR

SOUTH CAROLINA SOLDIERS, SAILORS AND  CITIZENS HELD IN U.S. PRISONS 1861-1865

NAME	RANK	REGIMENT	CAPTURED AT	WHEN	PRISON	MOVED	DISPOSITION	SOURCES
Owens, M.L.	Pvt	K 4th SCVI	Charlotte, NC	05/13/65	Charlotte, NC	05/13/65	Paroled	CSR
Owens, O.E.	Pvt	D Hol.Leg.	Warrenton, VA	09/29/62	Warrenton, VA	09/29/62	Paroled/Hospital	CSR
Owens, Peter E.	Pvt	C 2nd SCVI	Columbia, TN	02/19/64	Louisville, KY	03/15/64	North on oath	SA2,P92,P94,H2,CSR
Owens, R.L.	Pvt	D 3rd SCVIBn	South Mtn., MD	09/14/62	Ft. McHenry, MD	10/11/62	Fts. Monroe, VA	CSR
					Fts. Monroe, VA	04/22/65	Aikens Ldg., VA Xc	CSR
Owens, Richard L.	Pvt	B 7th SCVC	Richmond, VA Hos.	04/03/65	Richmond, VA Hos.	07/22/06	Richmond, VA P.M.	CSR
					Libby Prison Rchmd.	04/23/65	Newport News, VA	CSR
					Newport News, VA	06/26/65	Rlsd. G.O. #109	CSR
Owens, Robert D.	Pvt	K P.S.S.	Charlotte, NC	05/13/65	Charlotte, NC	05/13/65	Paroled	CSR
Owens, S.H.	Pvt	B 7th SCVC	White Oak Swamp VA	01/30/65	Bermuda Hundred, VA	02/01/65	City Pt., VA P.M.	CSR
					City Pt., VA	02/09/65	Pt. Lookout, MD	CSR
					Pt. Lookout, MD	06/29/65	Rlsd. G.O. #109	P115,P117,CSR
Owens, S.O.	Pvt	F 2nd SCVIRi	Buekeville, VA	04/14/65	Burkeville, VA	04/17/65	Paroled	CSR
Owens, Samuel	Pvt	A 21st SCVI	Ft. Fisher, NC	01/15/65	Elmira, NY	02/21/65	Died, Lung fever	P6,P65,P66,FPH,HAG
Owens, Sherod Harvey	Pvt	F 6th SCVC	Louisa C.H., VA	06/11/64	Pt. Lookout, MD	03/17/65	Aikens Ldg., VA Xc	P113,P124,CSR
					Aikens Ldg., VA	03/19/65	Camp Lee, VA P. camp	CSR
Owens, Thomas A.	Pvt	C 22nd SCVI	Crater, Pbg., VA	07/30/64	City Pt., VA	08/05/64	Pt. Lookout, MD	CSR,HOS
					Pt. Lookout, MD	08/05/64	Elmira, NY	P113,P117,P120,CSR
					Elmira, NY	10/10/64	Died, Ch. Diarrhea	P6,P12,P65,P66,FPH
Owens, Virgil	Pvt	B 7th SCVI	Charlestown, WV	10/16/62	Ft. McHenry, MD	10/25/62	Aikens Ldg., VA Xc	KEB,CSR
Owens, W.H.	Pvt	K 25th SCVI	Ft. Fisher, NC	01/15/65	New York, NY	01/30/65	Elmira, NY	CSR
					Elmira, NY	03/21/65	Died, Catarrh	P6,P12,P65,P66,FPH
Owens, W.K.	Pvt	B 15th SCVAB	Fayetteville, NC	03/07/65	New Berne, NC	04/03/65	Pt. Lookout, MD	CSR
					Pt. Lookout, MD	05/15/65	Rlsd. G.O. #85	P115,P118,P121,CSR
Owens, William	Pvt	C 22nd SCVI	Crater, Pbg., VA	07/30/64	City Pt., VA	08/05/64	Pt. Lookout, MD	CSR,HOS
					Pt. Lookout, MD	08/08/64	Elmira, NY	P113,P117
					Elmira, NY	11/29/64	Died, Diarrhea	P6,P65,FPH
Owens, William	Pvt	A 21st SCVI	Ft. Fisher, NC	01/15/65	Elmira, NY	04/26/65	Died, Ch. Diarrhea	P6,P65,P66,FPH,HAG
Owens, William R.	Pvt	H 23rd SCVI	Five Forks, VA	04/01/65	City Pt., VA	04/02/65	Pt. Lookout, MD	CSR,HMC
					Pt. Lookout, MD	06/29/65	Rlsd. G.O. #109	P115,P118,P122,CSR
Owens, Y.J.D.	Pvt	B 1st SCVC	Morris Island, SC	10/12/64	Hilton Head, SC	10/12/64	Took oath	P8,CSR
Owens, Andrew	Pvt	I 1st SCVIR	Deserted/enemy	02/18/65	Hilton Head SC	04/07/65	New York, NY oath	SA1,CSR
Oxendine, Manning	Pvt	G 26th SCVI	Piney Grove, NC	03/19/65	New Berne, NC	04/03/65	Pt. Lookout, MD	CSR
					Pt. Lookout, MD	06/29/65	Rlsd. G.O. #109	P122,CSR
Oxner, John P.	Pvt	G Hol.Leg.	Five Forks, VA	04/01/65	City Pt., VA	04/05/65	Pt. Lookout, MD	CSR,ANY
					Pt. Lookout, MD	06/29/65	Rlsd. G.O. #109	P115,P118,CSR

SOUTH CAROLINA SOLDIERS, SAILORS AND  CITIZENS HELD IN U.S. PRISONS 1861-1865

NAME	RANK	REGIMENT	CAPTURED AT	WHEN	PRISON	MOVED	DISPOSITION	SOURCES
Pace, Columbus S.	Cpl	D 16th SCVI	Macon, GA	04/30/65	Macon, GA	04/30/65	Paroled on oath	CSR
Pace, James A.	Pvt	I 21st SCVI	Morris Island, SC	07/10/63	Ft. Columbus, NY	09/23/63	Took the oath	P1,HMC,HAG
					Pt. Lookout, MD	12/23/63	Died, Ch. Diarrhea	P5,P12,FPH
Pace, W.T.	Pvt	F Hol.Leg.	Jarratts Stn., VA	05/08/64	Fts. Monroe, VA	05/13/64	Pt. Lookout, MD	CSR
					Pt. Lookout, MD	08/15/64	Elmira, NY	P113,P116,P120,CSR
					Elmira, NY	06/21/65	Rlsd G.O. #109	P65,P66,CSR
Pack, Bartemeus W.	Pvt	G 2nd SCVIRi	Amelia C.H., VA	04/06/65	City Pt., VA	04/13/65	Pt. Lookout, MD	CSR
					Pt. Lookout, MD	06/17/65	Rlsd. G.O. #109	P115,P119,P122,CSR
Pack, Morgan	Pvt	I 1st SCVIR	Bentonville, NC	03/22/65	New Berne, NC	04/10/65	Hart's Island, NY	CSR,SA1
					Hart's Island, NY	06/16/65	Rlsd. G.O. #109	P79,CSR
Packer, John K.	Pvt	C 26th SCVI	Five Forks, VA	04/01/65	City Pt., VA	04/05/65	Pt. Lookout, MD	CSR
					Pt. Lookout, MD	06/16/65	Rlsd. G.O. #109	P115,P119,P122,CSR
Paden, B.M.	Pvt	7th SCVI	Deserted/enemy	05/12/62	Bermuda Hundred, VA	05/17/62	Baltimore, MD	P8,CSR
					Fts. Monroe, VA	05/17/62		P8,CSR
Padgett, Abraham	Pvt	K 11th SCVI	Town Creek, NC	02/20/65	Ft. Anderson, NC	02/28/65	Pt. Lookout, MD	CSR,HAG
					Pt. Lookout, MD	06/17/65	Rlsd. G.O. #109	P115,P118,CSR
Padgett, Albert M.	Cpl	M 7th SCVI	Sharpsburg, MD	09/17/62	Frederick, MD	01/03/63	Died of wounds	P12,BOD,UD3,CSR
Padgett, Arenton R.	Pvt	A 19th SCVI	Murfreesboro, TN	01/05/63	Murfreesboro, TN Hos.	04/17/63	Nashville, TN	CSR
					Nashville, TN	04/21/63	Louisville, KY	CSR
					Louisville, KY	04/27/63	City Pt., VA Xc	CSR
					Ft. McHenry, MD	05/02/63	City Pt., VA Xc	CSR
					Lynchburg, VA	05/22/63	Died of wounds	CSR
Padgett, Daniel A., Jr.	Pvt	K 11th SCVI	Weldon RR, VA	08/21/64	City Pt., VA	08/24/64	Pt. Lookout, MD	HAG,CSR
					Pt. Lookout, MD	03/15/65	Died, Lung Infl.	P6,P113,P117,P119
Padgett, Dryden	Pvt	A 19th SCVI	Augusta, GA	05/19/65	Augusta, GA	05/19/65	Paroled	CSR
Padgett, F.V.	Pvt	C 5th SCVC	Deserted/enemy	03/28/65	Charleston, SC	03/28/65	Released on oath	CSR
Padgett, Frank	Pvt	K 11th SCVI	Weldon RR, VA	08/21/64	City Pt., VA	08/24/64	Pt. Lookout, MD	HAG,CSR
					Pt. Lookout, MD	12/28/64	Died, Dysentery	P6,P117,P119,CS
Padgett, Henry H.	Pvt	B 18th SCVI	Sutherland Stn., VA	04/03/65	City Pt., VA	04/13/65	Pt. Lookout, MD	CSR
					Pt. Lookout, MD	06/17/65	Rlsd. G.O. #109	CSR
Padgett, Henry W.	Pvt	K 11th SCVI	Town Creek, NC	02/20/65	Ft. Anderson, NC	02/28/65	Pt. Lookout, MD	CSR,HAG
					Pt. Lookout, MD	06/17/65	Rlsd. G.O. #109	P115,P118,P122,CSR
Padgett, Irvington R.	Sgt	A 19th SCVI	Murfreesboro, TN	01/05/63	Murfreesboro, TN Hos.	04/17/63	Nashville, TN	CSR
					Nashville, TN	04/21/63	Louisville, TN	CSR
					Louisville, KY	04/27/63	City Pt., VA	CSR
					Ft. McHenry, MD	05/02/63	City Pt., VA Xc	CSR
Padgett, Joel	Pvt	K 11th SCVI	Town Creek, NC	02/20/65	Ft. Anderson, NC	02/28/65	Pt. Lookout, MD	CSR,HAG
					Pt. Lookout, MD	06/16/65	Rlsd. G.O. #109	P115,P118,P122,CSR
Padgett, Josiah N.	Pvt	B 14th SCVI	Gettysburg, PA	07/05/63	Ft. Delaware, DE	06/10/65	Released	CSR
Padgett, Martin	Pvt	K 11th SCVI	Weldon RR, VA	08/21/64		08/28/64	Washington, DC	P1,HAG
					Old Capitol, DC	08/24/64	Elmira NY	CSR
					Ft. McHenry, MD	10/24/64	Elmira, NY	P110
					Elmira, NY	03/10/65	Pt. Lookout, MD Xc	P65,P66,HAG,CSR
Padgett, Thomas	Pvt	E 24th SCVI	Chickamauga, GA	09/20/63	Nashville, TN	10/05/63	Louisville, KY	P38,CSR
					Louisville, KY	10/07/63	Camp Douglas, IL	P88,P89,CSR
					Camp Douglas, IL	11/01/64	Died, Smallpox	P5,P53,P55,P57,FPH
Padgett, W.	Pvt	D 6th SCResB	Augusta, GA	05/18/65	Augusta, GA	05/18/65	Paroled	CSR
Padjett, Josiah	Pvt	B 8th SCVI	Deserted/enemy	03/21/65	Charleston, SC		Released on oath	CSR
Page, Abraham	Pvt	L 10th SCVI	Resaca, GA	05/16/64	Chattanooga, TN G.H.	06/17/64	Nashville, TN	CSR,RAS,HMC
					Nashville, TN	07/17/64	Louisville, KY	P4,CSR
					Louisville, KY	07/18/64	Camp Douglas, IL	P90,P91,P94,CSR
					Camp Douglas, IL	06/16/65	Rlsd. G.O. #109	P53,CSR

P

SOUTH CAROLINA SOLDIERS, SAILORS AND CITIZENS HELD IN U.S. PRISONS 1861-1865

NAME	RANK	REGIMENT	CAPTURED AT	WHEN	PRISON	MOVED	DISPOSITION	SOURCES
Page, Benjamin F.	Pvt	B 19th SCVI	Nashville, TN	05/19/65	Nashville, TN USGH	05/22/65	Nashville, TN P.M.	CSR
Page, John C.	Pvt	K 27th SCVI	Town Creek, NC	02/20/65	Ft. Anderson, NC	02/28/65	Pt. Lookout, MD	CSR
					Pt. Lookout, MD	06/16/65	Rlsd. G.O. #109	P115,P122,CSR
Page, Minor W.	Pvt	B 1st SCVA	Fayetteville, NC	03/16/65	New Berne, NC	03/30/65	Pt. Lookout, MD	CSR
					Pt. Lookout, MD	06/16/65	Rlsd. G.O. #109	P118,P122,CSR
Page, Randolph	Pvt	E 6th SCVC	Stony Creek, VA	12/01/64	Pt. Lookout, MD	06/16/65	Rlsd. G.O. #109	P115,P118,P122,CSR
					City Pt., VA	12/02/64	Pt. Lookout, MD	CSR
Page, William	Pvt	F 1st SCVIG	Petersburg, VA	06/22/64	City Pt., VA	06/30/64	Pt. Lookout, MD	CSR
					Pt. Lookout, MD	11/01/64	Aikens Ldg., VA Xc	P117,P121,P124
Page, William B.	Pvt	A Ham.Leg	Cass County, GA	01/10/64	Knoxville, TN	01/31/64	Chattanooga, TN	CSR
					Chattanooga, TN	08/01/64	Louisville, KY	CSR
Page, William B.	Pvt	A Ham.Leg	Deserted/enemy	01/10/64	Louisville, KY	08/05/64	North on oath	CSR
Page, William C.	2Lt	B 27th SCVI	Lexington, MS	01/21/65	Memphis, TN G.H.	01/12/65	Johnson's Isl., OH	P2,CSR
					Johnson's Isl., OH	02/24/65	City Pt., VA Xc	P81,P82,CSR
Pagett, W.E.	Sgt	L Orr's Ri.	Petersburg, VA	04/02/65	City Pt., VA	04/07/65	Hart's Island, NY	CSR,CDC
					Hart's Island, NY	06/15/65	Rlsd. G.O. #109	P79,CSR
Painter, Spain	Pvt	C Hol.Leg.	Prov. Mars. A. of P.	09/30/62	MD or VA	09/30/62	Paroled	CSR
Painter, Spain	Pvt	C Hol.Leg.	Deserted/enemy	11/25/64	City Pt., VA	11/27/64	Washington, DC	CSR
					Washington, DC	11/28/65	Phila., PA oath	CSR
Palmer, E.	Pvt	D 22nd SCVI	Deserted/enemy	02/24/65	City Pt., VA	02/26/65	Washington, DC	CSR
					Washington, DC	02/27/65	Salem, IL oath	CSR
Palmer, Edwin C.	Pvt	C 10th SCVI	Calhoun, GA	05/18/64	Nashville, TN	05/22/64	Louisville, KY	P2,P39,RAS,CSR
					Louisville, KY	05/23/64	Alton, IL	P91,P93,CSR
					Alton, IL	01/02/65	Died, Pneumonia	P6,P12,P14,FPH,CSR
Palmer, George Pierce	Pvt	B Ham.Leg.MI	Deep Bottom, VA	09/29/64	Bermuda Hundred, VA	09/30/64	City Pt., VA P.M.	CSR
					City Pt., VA	10/05/64	Pt. Lookout, MD	CSR
					Pt. Lookout, MD	11/21/64	Died, Acute Dysent	CSR,P12,FPH
Palmer, Horlbeck C.	Pvt	L 1st SCVIG	Warrenton, VA	09/29/62	Warrenton, VA	09/29/62	Paroled	CSR,SA1
Palmer, Horlbeck C.	Pvt	L 1st SCVIG	Petersburg, VA	04/09/65	City Pt., VA	04/13/65	Pt. Lookout, MD	CSR
					Pt. Lookout, MD	06/16/65	Rlsd. G.O. #109	P115,P119,P122,CSR
Palmer, J.L.	Sgt	A 7th SCVC	Richmond, VA Hos.	04/03/65	Richmond, VA Hos.	04/19/65	Richmond, VA P.M.	CSR
					Libby Prsn. Rchmd.	04/23/65	Newport News, VA	CSR
					Newport News, VA	06/15/65	Rlsd. G.O. #109	CSR
Palmer, J.W.	Pvt	D 6th SCVC	Armstrong's Mill	12/10/64	City Pt., VA	12/12/64	Pt. Lookout, MD	CSR
					Pt. Lookout, MD	06/07/65	Died, Lung Inflam.	P6,P118,P119,FPH
Palmer, Jackson P.	Pvt	H 15th SCVI	Spotsylvania, VA	05/08/64	Belle Plain, VA	05/20/64	Ft. Delaware, DE	H15,CSR,KEB
					Ft. Delaware, DE	06/10/65	Rlsd. G.O. #109	P41,P42,P45,CSR
Palmer, James	Pvt	H 2nd SCVI	Richmond, VA	04/03/65	Pt. Lookout, MD	06/16/65	Rlsd. G.O. #109	CSR
Palmer, John	Pvt	K 2nd SCVC	Gettysburg, PA	07/04/63	Ft. McHenry, MD	07/12/63	Ft. Delaware, DE	CSR
					Ft. Delaware, DE	07/15/63	Jd. US Forces	P40,P42,P44,CSR
Palmer, K.L.	Pvt	G 2nd SCVC	Urbanna, VA	10/13/67	Frederick, MD	10/14/62	Aikens Ldg., VA Xc	CSR
Palmer, M.J.	Pvt	E 6th SCResB	Augusta, GA	05/19/65	Augusta, GA	05/19/65	Paroled	CSR
Palmer, Nicholas Hodges	2Lt	C 7th SCVI	Gettysburg, PA	07/03/63	Ft. McHenry, MD	07/07/63	Ft. Delaware, DE	CSR,KEB,CNM
					Ft. Delaware, DE	07/18/63	Johnson's Isl., OH	P44,P144,CSR
					Johnson's Isl., OH	03/14/65	Pt. Lookout, MD	P80,P81,P82,CSR
					Pt. Lookout, MD	03/22/65	Cox's Wh., VA Xc	CSR
Palmer, Thomas	Pvt	L 1st SCVIG	Petersburg, VA	04/02/65	City Pt., VA	04/04/65	Pt. Lookout, MD	CSR,SA1
					Pt. Lookout, MD	06/16/65	Rlsd. G.O. #109	P115,P118,P122,CSR
Palmer, William R.	Pvt	C 2nd SCVI	Cold Harbor, VA	06/02/64	White House, VA	06/11/64	Pt. Lookout, MD	CSR,KEB,H2,SA2
					Pt. Lookout, MD	07/12/64	Elmira, NY	P113,P117,P120
					Elmira, NY	05/29/65	Rlsd. G.O. #85	P66,CSR

SOUTH CAROLINA SOLDIERS, SAILORS AND **P** CITIZENS HELD IN U.S. PRISONS 1861-1865

NAME	RANK	REGIMENT	CAPTURED AT	WHEN	PRISON	MOVED	DISPOSITION	SOURCES
Pannel, William	Pvt	F 23rd SCVI	Petersburg, VA	04/02/65	City Pt., VA	04/04/65	Pt. Lookout, MD	CSR
					Pt. Lookout, MD	06/06/65	Rlsd. G.O. #109	CSR,HAG
Paramore, Allen	Pvt	C 11th SCVI	Weldon RR, VA	08/21/64	City Pt., VA	08/24/64	Pt. Lookout, MD	CSR
					Pt. Lookout, MD	02/10/65	Aikens Ldg., VA Xc	P117,P123,P124
Pardue, George W.	Pvt	A 22nd SCVI	Bermuda Hundred, VA	06/15/64	Bermuda Hundred, VA	06/16/64	Fts. Monroe, VA	CSR
					Fts. Monroe, VA	06/18/64	Pt. Lookout, MD	CSR
					Pt. Lookout, MD	07/08/64	Elmira, NY	P113,P117,P120
					Elmira, NY	05/29/65	Rlsd. G.O. #85	P65,P66,CSR
Pardue, J.M.	Pvt	B 4th SCVC	Stony Creek, VA	12/01/64	City Pt., VA	12/05/64	Pt. Lookout, MD	CSR,HHC
					Pt. Lookout, MD	01/17/65	Aikens Ldg., VA Xc	P115,P118,P124,CSR
Parham, A.R.	Pvt	E 19th SCVCB	Camden, SC	04/18/65	Charleston, SC		No data	CSR
Parham, Robert	Cpl	A 23rd SCVI	Five Forks, VA	04/01/65	City Pt., VA	04/05/65	Pt. Lookout, MD	CSR
					Pt. Lookout, MD	06/17/65	Rlsd. G.O. #109	CSR
Paris, Moses J.	Pvt	K 16th SCVI	Cassville, GA	05/20/64	Nashville, TN	05/27/64	Louisville, KY	CSR
					Louisville, KY	05/30/64	Rock Island, IL	P88,P91,P93,CSR
					Rock Island, IL	06/10/64	Jd, US Navy & Tfd.	CSR
Paris, Reuben J.	Pvt	K 16th SCVI	Cassville, GA	05/20/64	Nashville, TN	05/27/64	Louisville, KY	P3,P39,CSR
					Louisville, KY	05/30/64	Rock Island, IL	CSR
					Rock Island, IL	06/10/64	Jd. US Navy & Tfd.	P131,CSR
Parish, Gilliam D.	Pvt	D 19th SCVI	Franklin, TN	12/18/64	Nashville, TN	12/31/64	Louisville, KY	CSR
					Nashville, TN	01/01/65	Escaped en route	CSR
					Camp Chase, OH	06/12/65	Rlsd. G.O. #109	CSR
Parish, John L.	Pvt	B 1st SCVIG	Hatchers Run, VA	04/02/65	City Pt., VA	04/11/65	Pt. Lookout, MD	CSR,ANY,SA1
					Pt. Lookout, MD	06/16/65	Rlsd. G.O. #109	P115,P122,CSR
Park, James M.	Pvt	F 14th SCVI	Petersburg, VA	04/02/65	City Pt., VA	04/04/65	Pt. Lookout, MD	CSR
					Pt. Lookout, MD	06/17/65	Rlsd. G.O. #109	CSR
Parker, A.D.	Pvt	L 7th SCVI	Falling Waters, MD	07/04/63	Ft. McHenry, MD	07/08/63	Fts. Monroe, VA	CSR,KEB
					Ft. McHenry, MD	07/12/63	Ft. Delaware, DE	P96,CSR
					Ft. Delaware, DE	06/10/65	Rlsd.	P40,P44,P45,CSR
Parker, Alexander P.	Pvt	K 16th SCVI	Chickamauga, TN	09/20/63	Nashville, TN	12/09/63	Louisville, KY	P39,16R,CSR
Parker, Alexander P.	Pvt	K 16th SCVI	Chickamauga, GA	09/20/63	Louisville, KY	12/11/63	Rock Island, IL	P88,P89,CSR
					Rock Island, IL	10/31/64	Jd. USA, Frontier S	P131,CSR
Parker, Anderson	Pvt	D 26th SCVI	Cheraw, SC	03/05/65	New Berne, NC	04/10/65	Hart's Island, NY	CSR
					Hart's Island, NY	06/17/65	Rlsd. G.O. #109	P79,CSR
Parker, B.W.	Pvt	G 3rd SCVABn	High Pt., NC	05/01/65	High Pt., NC	05/01/65	Paroled	CSR
Parker, Badgegood B.	Sgt	E 21st SCVI	Ft. Fisher, NC	01/15/65	Elmira, NY	07/12/65	Died, Ch. Diarrhea	P6,P65,P66,HAG,FPH
Parker, Britton	Pvt	G 2nd SCVI	Gettysburg, PA	07/03/63	Letterman G.H. Gbg	10/06/63	Provost Marshal	P1,KEB,SA2,H2
					David's Island, NY	11/12/63	City Pt., VA Xc	CSR
Parker, C. Rutledge	Pvt	B 23rd SCVI	Boonesboro, MD	09/15/62	Ft. Delaware, DE	10/02/62	Aikens Ldg., VA Xc	CSR
Parker, Calvin	Pvt	D 21st SCVI	Morris Island, SC	07/10/63	Ft. Columbus, NY	09/23/63	Took the oath	P1,HAG
					Pt. Lookout, MD	05/03/64	City Pt., VA Xc	P116,P123,P124
					Pt. Lookout, MD	04/21/65	Died, Paralysis	P6,P118,P119,FPH
Parker, E.	Pvt	K 5th SCVC	Bentonville, NC	03/22/65	New Berne, NC	04/10/65	Hart's Island, NY	CSR
					Hart's Island, NY	06/16/65	Rlsd. G.O. #109	P79,CSR
Parker, Elijah	Pvt	E 4th SCVC	Cheraw, SC	03/06/65	New Berne, NC	04/10/65	Hart's Island, NY	CSR
					Hart's Island, NY	06/17/65	Rlsd. G.O. #109	P79,CSR
Parker, Ervin M.	Pvt	F 4th SCVC	Louisa C.H., VA	06/11/64	Pt. Lookout, MD	07/25/64	Elmira, NY	P113,P117,CSR
					Elmira, NY	02/21/65	Died, Pneumonia	P6,P65,P66,FPH,CSR
					Fts. Monroe, VA	06/20/64	Pt. Lookout, MD	CSR
Parker, George A.	Pvt	D 6th SCVC	Chesterfield, SC	03/04/65	New Berne, NC	03/30/65	Pt. Lookout, MD	CSR
					Pt. Lookout, MD	06/17/65	Rlsd. G.O. #109	P118,CSR
Parker, J.P.	Sgt	E 20th SCVI	Deserted/enemy		Washington, DC PM	04/28/65	Phila., PA on oath	CSR

SOUTH CAROLINA SOLDIERS, SAILORS AND **P** CITIZENS HELD IN U.S. PRISONS 1861-1865

NAME	RANK	REGIMENT	CAPTURED AT	WHEN	PRISON	MOVED	DISPOSITION	SOURCES
Parker, James	Cpl	D 19th SCVI	Atlanta, GA	07/22/64	Nashville, TN	07/29/64	Louisville, KY	CSR
					Louisville, KY	07/31/64	Camp Chase, OH	CSR
					Camp Chase, OH	12/27/64	Died, Variola	CSR,P6,P12,FPH
Parker, James	Pvt	F 1st SCVIR	Cheraw, SC	03/06/65	New Berne, NC	04/10/65	Hart's Island, NY	CSR,SA1
					Harts Island, NY	05/15/65	Died, Typhoid pneum.	P6,P12,P79,FPH,CSR
Parker, James W.	Pvt	A 12th SCVI	Hatchers Run, VA	03/31/65	City Pt., VA	04/02/65	Pt. Lookout, MD	CSR
					Pt. Lookout, MD	06/30/65	Rlsd. G.O. #109	CSR
					Pt. Lookout, MD	07/02/65	Hammond G.H., MD	CSR
					Hammond G.H., MD	07/06/65	Rlsd. G.O. #109	CSR
Parker, John	Pvt	F 2nd SCVIRi	Warrenton, VA	09/29/62	Warrenton, VA	09/29/62	Paroled	CSR
Parker, John W.	Pvt	G P.S.S.	Richmond, VA Hos.	04/03/65	Richmond, VA Hos.	05/10/65	Died of pneumonia	CSR
Parker, Joseph	Pvt	L 1st SCVIG	Wilderness, VA	05/06/64	Ft. Delaware, DE	01/24/65	Hos. 1/24-2/27/65	P47
					Belle Plain, VA	05/21/64	Ft. Delaware, DE	CSR,SA1
					Ft. Delaware, DE	02/27/65	City Pt., VA Xc	P41,P42,CSR
Parker, Peter	Sgt	D 26th SCVI	Hatchers Run, VA	03/21/65	City Pt., VA	04/02/65	Pt. Lookout, MD	CSR,HOM
					Pt. Lookout, MD	06/16/65	Rlsd. G.O. #109	P115,P118,P122,CSR
Parker, Robert G.	Pvt	F 17th SCVI	Petersburg, VA	03/25/65	City Pt., VA	03/28/65	Pt. Lookout, MD	CSR
					Pt. Lookout, MD	05/15/65	Rlsd. G.O. #85	P115,CSR
Parker, Samuel	Pvt	C 18th SCVI	Petersburg, VA	04/03/65	Fairgrounds Hos.	05/06/65	Camp Hamilton, VA	CSR
Parker, Samuel	Pvt	A Ham.Leg.MI	Charlotte, NC	05/11/65	Charlotte, NC	05/11/65	Paroled	CSR
Parker, Samuel	Pvt	C 18th SCVI	Petersburg, VA	04/03/65	Camp Hamilton, VA	05/18/65	Newport News, VA	CSR
					Newport News, VA	06/14/65	Rlsd. G.O. #109	CSR
Parker, Samuel F.	Pvt	6 10/19 SCVI	Missionary Ridge, TN	11/25/63	Nashville, TN	12/07/63	Louisville, KY	P39,RAS,HMC,CSR
					Louisville, KY	12/07/63	Rock Island, IL	P88,P89,CSR
					Rock Island, IL	06/22/65	Rlsd. G.O. #109	P131,CSR
Parker, T.F.	Sgt	G 21st SCVI	Petersburg, VA	06/18/64	Pt. Lookout, MD	07/27/64	Elmira, NY	P113,P117,P120,HAG
					Elmira, NY	07/03/65	Rlsd. G.O. #109	P65,P66
Parker, Thomas	Pvt	I 21st SCVI	Morris Island, SC	07/10/63	Ft. Columbus, NY	09/23/63	Took the oath	P1,P124,HAG,HMC
					Pt. Lookout, MD	02/27/64	Joined U.S. Army	P113,P116,P125
Parker, Thomas J.	Pvt	C 14th SCVI	Deserted/enemy	04/12/65	Washington, DC	04/12/65	Dunkirk, NY oath	CSR
					City Pt., VA	04/12/65	Washington, DC	CSR
Parker, W.L.	Pvt	I 2nd SCVC	Augusta, GA	05/22/65	Augusta, GA	05/22/65	Paroled	CSR
Parker, William E.	Pvt	A 15th SCVI	Shenandoah Co., VA	05/23/64	Wheeling, WV	06/10/64	Camp Chase, OH	P1,KEB,CSR
					Camp Chase, OH	03/02/65	City Pt., VA Xc	P22,P26,CSR
Parker, William H.	Pvt	F 1st SCVIH	Petersburg, VA	06/22/64	City Pt., VA	06/30/64	Pt. Lookout, MD	CSR
					Pt. Lookout, MD	03/14/65	Exchanged	P113,P117,P124,CSR
					Pt. Lookout, MD	03/14/65	Aikens Ldg., VA Xc	P121,SA1,CSR
Parkins, Charles A.	Cpt	B 16th SCVI	Graysville, GA	11/25/63	Nashville, TN	12/04/63	Louisville, KY	P39,16R,CSR
					Louisville, KY	12/05/63	Johnson's Isl., OH	P88,P89,P93,CSR
					Johnson's Isl., OH	06/13/65	Rlsd. G.O. #109	P80,P82,P83,H16,CSR
Parkman, James	Pvt	G 1st SCVIG	Petersburg, VA	03/25/65	City Pt. VA	03/29/65	Pt. Lookout, MD	CSR
					Pt. Lookout, MD	06/16/65	Rlsd. G.O. #109	P115,P118,SA1,CSR
Parkman, James M.	Pvt	A 22nd SCVI	Petersburg, VA	03/25/65	City Pt., VA	03/27/65	Pt. Lookout, MD	CSR
					Pt. Lookout, MD	06/16/65	Rlsd. G.O. #109	P115,P118
Parks, Edmund B.	Pvt	C 2nd SCVC	Williamsport, MD	07/04/63	Harrisburg, PA	08/15/63	Ft. Delaware, DE	CSR
					Ft. Delaware, DE	01/02/64	Died, Diarrhea	P5,P42,P47,FPH,CSR
Parks, Thomas J.	Pvt	H 6th SCVI	Dranesville, VA	12/20/61	McCall's Div. F.H.	02/23/62	Old Capitol, DC	CSR
Parks, William Drayton	Pvt	B 5th SCVI	Kelly's Ford, TN	09/25/63	Chattanooga, TN H.	11/19/63	Murfreesboro, TN H	CSR
					Murfreesboro, TN H	01/25/64	Nashville,TN	CSR
					Nashville, TN	01/27/64	Louisville, KY	P39,CSR
					Louisville, KY	01/29/64	Rock Island, IL	P88,P93,CSR
					Rock Island, IL	05/03/65	New Orleans, LA Xc	P3,P131,CSR

SOUTH CAROLINA SOLDIERS, SAILORS AND  CITIZENS HELD IN U.S. PRISONS 1861-1865

NAME	RANK	REGIMENT	CAPTURED AT	WHEN	PRISON	MOVED	DISPOSITION	SOURCES
Parks, William T.	Pvt	H 2nd SCVC	Wilmington Rd., NC	03/08/65	New Berne, NC	03/30/65	Pt. Lookout, MD	CSR
					Pt. Lookout, MD	06/16/65	Rlsd. G.O. #109	P118,CSR
Parlor, Edwin	Pvt	D 4th SCVC	Louisa C.H., VA	06/11/64	Fts. Monroe, VA	06/20/64	Pt. Lookout, MD	CSR
					Pt. Lookout, MD	07/25/64	Elmira, NY	P113,P120,CSR
					Elmira, NY	10/05/64	Died, Ch. Diarrhea	P5,P65,P66,FPH,CSR
Parnell, F.M.	Pvt	B 21st SCVI	Morris Island, SC	07/10/63	Pt. Lookout, MD	05/03/64	City Pt., VA Xc	P113,P116
Parnell, George W.	Pvt	A 14th SCVI	Petersburg, VA	04/02/65	City Pt., VA	04/07/65	Hart's Island, NY	CSR
					Hart's Island, NY	06/16/65	Rlsd. G.O. #109	CSR
Parnell, H.W.	Pvt	F 3rd SCVC	South Newport, GA	08/17/64	Philadelphia, PA	01/10/65	Ft. Delaware, DE	CSR
					Ft. Delaware, DE	03/28/65	Died	P47,FPH,P6,P12
Parnell, Harmon G.	Pvt	A 14th SCVI	Petersburg, VA	03/25/65	City Pt., VA	03/27/65	Pt. Lookout, MD	CSR
					Pt. Lookout, MD	06/16/65	Rlsd. G.O. #109	CSR
Parnell, J.H.	Pvt	G 3rd SCVIBn	Gettysburg, PA	07/02/63	Ft. Delaware, DE	07/16/64	Hos. 7/16-7/25/64	P47
					Ft. Delaware, DE	10/30/64	Pt. Lookout, MD	P42,P47,CSR
					Pt. Lookout, MD	10/31/64	Exchanged	P115,P123,CSR
Parnell, J.M.	Pvt	B 21st SCVI	Morris Island, SC	07/10/63	Ft. Columbus, NY	09/23/63	Paroled on oath	P1
					Ft. Columbus, NY	09/23/63	Pt. Lookout, MD	CSR
					Pt. Lookout, MD	05/03/64	Aikens Ldg., VA Xc	CSR
Parnell, Jerry H.	Pvt	H 1st SCVIG	Petersburg, VA	04/01/65	City Pt., VA	04/04/65	Pt. Lookout, MD	CSR,SA1
					Pt. Lookout, MD	06/16/65	Rlsd. G.O. #109	P115,P119,CSR
Parnell, John R.	Pvt	A 14th SCVI	Petersburg, VA	04/03/65	City Pt., VA	04/13/65	Pt. Lookout, MD	CSR
					Pt. Lookout, MD	06/16/65	Rlsd. G.O. #109	CSR
Parnell, Robert M.	Pvt	B 21st SCVI	Petersburg, VA	06/24/64	Bermuda Hundred, VA	06/25/64	Fts. Monroe, VA	CSR,HAG
					Fts. Monroe, VA	06/26/64	Pt. Lookout, MD	CSR
					Pt. Lookout, MD	08/16/64	Elmira, NY	P113,P117,P120
					Elmira, NY	03/02/65	Pt. Lookout, MD Xc	P65,P66
Parnell, T. Joshua	Pvt	H 21st SCVI	Ft. Fisher, NC	01/14/65	Elmira, NY	06/14/65	Rlsd. G.O. #109	P65,P66,HAG
Parnell, Thomas N.	Pvt	B 21st SCVI	Morris Island, SC	07/10/63	Pt. Lookout, MD	05/03/64	Exchanged	P123,P124,HAG
Parnell, Thomas N.	Pvt	B 21st SCVI	Ft. Fisher, NC	01/15/65	Elmira, NY	03/14/65	Tfd. for exchange	P65,P66
Parnell, William C.	Pvt	A 14th SCVI	Petersburg, VA	04/02/65	City Pt., VA	04/07/65	Pt. Lookout, MD	CSR
					Pt. Lookout, MD	06/16/65	Rlsd. G.O. #109	CSR
Parr, Richard	Sgt	H 15th SCVI	Gettysburg, PA	07/03/63	Gettysburg, PA USH	07/21/63	Provost Marshal	P4,KEB,UD5,CSR
					David's Island, NY	09/12/63	City Pt., VA Xc	P1,CSR
Parris, J.C.	Pvt	I 5th SCVI	Chattanooga, TN	10/29/63	Nashville, TN	11/07/63	Louisville, KY	P39,SA3,CSR
					Louisville, KY	11/09/63	Camp Morton, IN	P88,P89,P93,CSR
					Camp Morton, IN	02/26/65	City Pt., VA Xc	P100,P101,CSR
Parris, P.G.	Pvt	A P.S.S.	Darbytown Rd., VA	10/02/64	Bermuda Hundred, VA	10/07/64	City Pt., VA	CSR
					City Pt., VA	10/21/64	Pt. Lookout, MD	CSR
					Pt. Lookout, MD	05/15/65	Rlsd. G.O. #85	CSR
Parris, W.B.	Pvt	K 27th SCVI	Petersburg, VA	06/24/64	Bermuda Hundred, VA	06/25/64	Fts. Monroe, VA	CSR,HAG
					Fts. Monroe, VA	06/26/64	Pt. Lookout, MD	CSR
					Pt. Lookout, MD	08/16/64	Elmira, NY	P113,P117,P120,CSR
					Elmira, NY	10/11/64	Pt. Lookout, MD Xc	P65,P66,CSR
					Pt. Lookout, MD	10/29/64	Venus Pt., GA Xc	P117,P225,CSR
Parris, William	Pvt	K Hol.Leg.	Hatchers Run, VA	03/29/65	City Pt., VA	04/02/65	Old Capitol, DC	CSR
					Old Capitol, DC	06/07/65	Rlsd.& sent home	CSR
Parrish, Doctor F.	Pvt	G P.S.S.	Chattanooga, TN	10/29/63	Nashville, TN	11/07/63	Louisville, KY	CSR,SA3
					Louisville, KY	11/09/63	Camp Morton, IN	CSR
Parrish, Doctor F.	Pvt	G P.S.S.	Chattanooga, TN	10/29/63	Camp Morton, IN	08/06/64	Died	P5,FPH,CSR,P12
Parrish, James H.	Pvt	G 23rd SCVI	Petersburg, VA	03/22/65	City Pt., VA	03/27/65	Pt. Lookout, MD	CSR
					Pt. Lookout, MD	06/16/65	Rlsd. G.O. #109	CSR

P

SOUTH CAROLINA SOLDIERS, SAILORS AND CITIZENS HELD IN U.S. PRISONS 1861-1865

NAME	RANK	REGIMENT	CAPTURED AT	WHEN	PRISON	MOVED	DISPOSITION	SOURCES
Parrot, Robert L.	Pvt	E 15th SCVI	Sharpsburg, MD	09/17/62	Provost Marshal	09/27/62	Ft. McHenry, MD	CSR,KEB,H15
					Ft. McHenry, MD	10/18/62	Fts. Monroe, VA Xc	CSR
Parrott, James M.	Sgt	B 21st SCVI	Ft. Fisher, NC	01/15/65	Elmira, NY	07/13/65	Transferred	P65,P66,HAG
Parrott, James W.	Pvt	E 4th SCVC	Stony Creek, VA	12/01/64	City Pt., VA	12/05/64	Pt. Lookout, MD	CSR
					Pt. Lookout, MD	06/17/65	Rlsd. G.O. #109	P115,P118,CSR
Parsons, Andrew Jackson	HSd	C 25th SCVI	Ft. Fisher, NC	01/15/65	Pt. Lookout, MD	06/16/65	Rlsd. G.O. #109	P115,HAG,CTA,CSR
Parsons, F.C.	2Lt	F 22nd SCVI	Kinston, NC	12/15/62	Kinston, NC	12/15/62	Paroled POW	CSR
Parsons, T.B.	Pvt	K 7th SCVI	Gettysburg, PA	07/03/63	Ft. Delaware, DE			P42
Parsons, William B.	Cpl	E 14th SCVI	Gettysburg, PA	07/04/63	Davids Island, NY	09/08/63	City Pt., VA Xc	CSR
Partin, John W.	Pvt	G 20th SCVI	Cold Harbor, VA	06/01/64	White House, VA	06/11/64	Pt. Lookout, MD	CSR
					Pt. Lookout, MD	06/12/64	Elmira, NY	CSR
					Elmira, NY	02/20/65	James R., VA Xc	CSR
Patat, Lewis P.	Pvt	A 24th SCVI	Marietta, GA	07/03/64	Nashville, TN	07/13/64	Louisville, KY	CSR
					Louisville, KY	07/16/64	Camp Douglas, IL	P90,P91,P94,CSR
					Camp Douglas, IL	06/16/65	Rlsd. G.O. #109	P53,P55,CSR
Pate, Benjamin T.	Pvt	19th SCVI	Franklin, TN	12/17/64	Nashville, TN	05/22/65	Rlsd. G.O. #85	CSR
Patrick, E.D.	Pvt	F 2nd SCVA	Raleigh, NC Hos.	04/13/65	Raleigh, NC	04/13/65	Paroled	CSR
Patrick, Emanuel M.	Pvt	I 1st SCVA	Bentonville, NC	03/22/65	New Berne, NC	03/31/65	Hart's Island, NY	CSR
					Hart's Island, NY	06/16/65	Rlsd. G.O. #109	P79,CSR
Patrick, James B.	Pvt	G 5th SCVC	Ream's Stn., VA	08/25/64	City Pt., VA	09/08/64	Pt. Lookout, MD	CSR
					Pt. Lookout, MD	11/01/64	Aikens Ldg., VA Xc	P113,P121,P124,CSR
Patrick, James B.	Pvt	G 5th SCVC	Orangeburg, SC	02/13/65	New Berne, NC	04/03/65	Pt. Lookout, MD	CSR
					Pt. Lookout, MD		No release data	P115,P118,CSR
Patrick, Jasper C.	Cpl	F 18th SCVI	Petersburg, VA	07/30/64	City Pt., VA	08/08/64	Pt. Lookout, MD	CSR
					Pt. Lookout, MD	08/08/64	Elmira NY	CSR
					Elmira, NY	06/21/65	Rlsd. G.O. #109	CSR
Patrick, John	Pvt	F P.S.S.	Boonesboro, MD	09/15/62	Ft. Delaware, DE	10/02/62	Aikens Ldg., VA Xc	CSR
					Aikens Ldg., VA	11/10/62	Exchanged	CSR
Patrick, Robert C.	Pvt	F 18th SCVI	Crater, Pbg., VA	07/30/64	Portsmouth, RI Hos.	10/24/64	Ft. Columbus, NY	CSR
					Ft. Columbus, NY	12/04/64	Elmira, NY	CSR
					Elmira, NY	02/05/65	Died, Diarrhea	CSR,P6,P12,FPH
Patrick, Thomas	Sgt	F 18th SCVI	Deep Bottom, VA	08/16/64	City Pt., VA	08/22/64	Pt. Lookout, MD	CSR
					Pt. Lookout, MD	03/16/65	Aikens Ldg., VA Xc	CSR
Patterson, Darling P.	Pvt	B Wash'n LA	Augusta, GA	05/19/65	Augusta, GA	05/19/65	Paroled	CSR
Patterson, E.L.	Pvt	B 5th SCVC	Deserted/enemy	03/29/65	Charleston, SC	03/29/65	Released on oath	CSR
Patterson, J.A.	Pvt	B 6th SCVI	Charlotte, NC	05/18/65	Charlotte, NC	05/18/65	Paroled	CSR
Patterson, J.L.	Pvt	B P.S.S.	Anderson, SC	05/19/65	Anderson, SC	05/19/65	Paroled	CSR
Patterson, J.W.	Pvt	Beaufort LA	Augusta, GA	05/19/65	Augusta, GA	05/19/65	Paroled	CSR
Patterson, John	Pvt	Ferguson's LA	Ringgold, GA	11/26/63	Nashville, TN	12/11/63	Louisville, KY	P39,CSR
					Louisville, KY	12/12/63	Rock Island, IL	P88,P89,CSR
					Rock Island, IL	04/22/64	Jd. US Navy/Rjctd.	P131,CSR
Patterson, John B.	Pvt	I 14th SCVI	Hanover Jctn., VA	05/24/64	Port Royal, VA	05/30/64	Pt. Lookout, MD	CSR
					Pt. Lookout, MD	11/01/64	Venus Pt., GA Xc	CSR
Patterson, John B.	Pvt	I 14th SCVI	Southside RR, VA	04/02/65	City Pt., VA	04/07/65	Hart's Island, NY	CSR
					Hart's Island, NY	06/16/65	Rlsd. G.O. #109	CSR
Patterson, Samuel L.	Pvt	I 17th SCVI	Five Forks, VA	04/01/65	City Pt., VA	04/06/65	Pt. Lookout, MD	CSR
					Pt. Lookout, MD	06/16/65	Rlsd. G.O. #109	P115,CSR
Patterson, Thomas A.	Pvt	K 22nd SCVI	Crater, Pbg., VA	07/30/64	3Div. 9AC Fld. Hos.	08/02/64	HQ Army of Potomac	CSR
					HQ Army of Potomac	08/05/64	City Pt., VA	CSR
					City Pt., VA	08/22/64	Pt. Lookout, MD	CSR
					Pt. Lookout, MD	05/14/65	Rlsd. G.O. #85	P122
Patterson, W.H.	Pvt	K 7th SCVI	Gettysburg, PA	07/04/63	David's Island, NY	08/24/63	City Pt., VA Xc	P1

SOUTH CAROLINA SOLDIERS, SAILORS AND  CITIZENS HELD IN U.S. PRISONS 1861-1865

NAME	RANK	REGIMENT	CAPTURED AT	WHEN	PRISON	MOVED	DISPOSITION	SOURCES
Patterson, W.P.	Pvt	E 3rd SCVIBn	South Mtn., MD	09/14/62	Frederick, MD	01/17/63	Ft. McHenry, MD	CSR
					Ft. McHenry, MD	11/27/63	Fts. Monroe, VA	CSR
					Fts. Monroe, VA	01/23/64	City Pt., VA Xc	CSR
Patton, S.W.	Pvt	C 2nd SCVIRi	Gaines' Mill, VA	06/28/62	Harrisons Ldg., VA	07/03/62	Ft. Columbus, NY	CSR
					Ft. Columbus, NY	07/09/62	Ft. Delaware, DE	CSR
					Ft. Delaware, DE	08/05/62	Aikens Ldg., VA Xc	CSR
Patton, Tagliaferro P.	Pvt	F 14th SCVI	Petersburg, VA	04/03/65	City Pt., VA	04/13/65	Pt. Lookout, MD	CSR
					Pt. Lookout, MD	06/16/65	Rlsd. G.O. #109	CSR
Patton, W.W.	Pvt	H 12th SCVI	Petersburg, VA	07/29/64	City Pt., VA	08/05/64	Pt. Lookout, MD	CSR
					Pt. Lookout, MD	08/08/64	Elmira, NY	CSR
					Elmira, NY	06/21/65	Rlsd. G.O. #109	CSR
Paul, J.F.	Cpl	B 3rd SCVIBn	South Mtn., MD	09/12/62	Ft. McHenry, MD	10/13/62	Fts. Monroe, VA	CSR
					Fts. Monroe, VA	10/17/62	Aikens Ldg., VA Xc	CSR
Paul, James A.	Cpl	D 14th SCVI	Brandy Stn., VA	08/01/63	Old Capitol, DC	08/17/63	Pt. Lookout, MD	CSR
					Pt. Lookout, MD	02/24/65	Aikens Ldg., VA Xc	CSR
Paul, Joseph W.	Pvt	C 12th SCVI	Hatchers Run, VA	03/31/65	City Pt., VA	04/02/65	Pt. Lookout, MD	CSR
					Pt. Lookout, MD	06/16/65	Rlsd. G.O. #109	CSR
Pauley, P.C.	Pvt	C 26th SCVI	Deserted/enemy	01/27/65	City Pt., VA	01/28/65	Washington, DC	CSR
					Washington, DC	02/01/65	Released on oath	CSR
Paxton, J.R.	Pvt	Pee Dee LA	Fountaindale, PA	06/28/63	Ft. Delaware, DE	06/14/64	Died	P5,FPH
Paysinger, Henry M.	Sgt	C 3rd SCVI	Gettysburg, PA	07/04/63	Letterman G.H. Gbg	09/05/63	Died of wounds	P1,KEB,SA2,H3,CSR
Paysinger, Thomas M.	Pvt	C 3rd SCVI	Gettysburg, PA	07/05/63	Letterman G.H. Gbg	09/29/63	Escaped	P1,KEB,SA2,H3,CSR
Peach, Daniel	Pvt	D 7th SCVIBn	Weldon RR, VA	08/21/64	City Pt., VA	08/24/64	Pt. Lookout, MD	CSR,HAG,HIC
					Pt. Lookout, MD	03/14/65	Aikens Ldg., VA Xc	P113,P121,P124,CSR
Peagler, Jacob W.	Pvt	C 11th SCVI	Petersburg, VA	06/16/64	Bermuda Hundred, VA	06/17/64	Fts. Monroe, VA	CSR
					Fts. Monroe, VA	06/18/64	Pt. Lookout, MD	CSR
					Pt. Lookout, MD	07/25/64	Elmira, NY	P113,P118,P120,CSR
					Elmira, NY	10/03/64	Baltimore, MD USGH	P66,CSR
					Baltimore, MD USGH	01/08/65	Pt. Lookout, MD	P115,P121,CSR
					Pt. Lookout, MD	01/31/65	Hammond G.H., MD	CSR
					Hammond G.H., MD	05/14/65	Rlsd. G.O. #85	P121,P122,CSR
Peagler, Thomas H.	Pvt	H 1st SCVIG	Wilderness, VA	05/06/64	Belle Plain, VA	05/21/64	Ft. Delaware, DE	CSR,SA1
					Ft. Delaware, DE	08/30/64	Hos. 8/30-9/2/64	P47
					Ft. Delaware, DE	09/25/64	Died	P41,P42,CSR
Peake, Samuel L.	Pvt	G 24th SCVI	Nashville, TN	12/16/64	Nashville, TN	01/01/65	Louisville, KY	P39,CSR,EFW
					Louisville, KY	01/02/65	Camp Douglas, IL	P92,CSR
					Camp Chase, OH	02/14/65	Died, Variola	P6,P12,P23,P27,FPH
Peal, Asa D.	Pvt	D 5th SCVI	N. Anna River, VA	05/23/64	Port Royal, VA	05/30/64	Pt. Lookout, MD	CSR,SA3
					Pt. Lookout, MD	07/23/64	Elmira, NY	P113,P117,P120
					Elmira, NY	09/20/64	Died, Diarrhea	P5,P65,P66,FPH,CSR
Pearce, Benjamin McCoy	Pvt	G 3rd SCVABn	High Pt., NC	05/01/65	High Pt., NC	05/01/65	Paroled	CSR,HIC
Pearce, James F.	Sur	8th SCVI	Gettysburg, PA	07/05/63	Letterman G.H. Gbg		Provost Marshal	P1,KEB
					Ft. McHenry, MD	11/21/63	City Pt., VA Xc	P96,P114,CSR
Pearson, Anthony Jackson	Pvt	C 22nd SCVI	Crater, Pbg., VA	07/30/64	City Pt., VA	08/05/64	Pt. Lookout, MD	CSR
					Pt. Lookout, MD	08/08/64	Elmira	P113,P117
					Elmira, NY	10/16/64	Died, Diarrhea	P5,P12,P65,P66,FPH
Pearson, C.	Pvt	I 2nd SCVC	Gettysburg, PA	07/05/63	Chester, PA	08/17/63	City Pt., VA Xc	P1
Pearson, David	Pvt	C 22nd SCVI	Petersburg, MD	06/18/64	City Pt., VA	06/24/64	Pt. Lookout, MD	CSR
					Pt. Lookout, MD	06/25/64	Elmira, NY	P113,P117,P120,CSR
					Elmira, NY	05/29/65	Rlsd. G.O. #85	P65,P66,CSR

P

SOUTH CAROLINA SOLDIERS, SAILORS AND CITIZENS HELD IN U.S. PRISONS 1861-1865

NAME	RANK	REGIMENT	CAPTURED AT	WHEN	PRISON	MOVED	DISPOSITION	SOURCES
Pearson, F.W.	Pvt	K Ham.Leg.MI	Picketts Farm, VA	07/22/64	Bermuda Hundred, VA	07/24/64	Fts. Monroe, VA	CSR
					Camp Hamilton, VA	07/27/64	Pt. Lookout, MD	CSR
					Pt. Lookout, MD	03/14/65	Aikens Ldg., VA Xc	CSR
Pearson, G.L.	Pvt	K 27th SCVI	Petersburg, VA	06/24/64	Bermuda Hundred, VA	06/25/64	Fts. Monroe, VA	CSR,HAG
					Fts. Monroe, VA	06/26/64	Pt. Lookout, MD	CSR
					Pt. Lookout, MD	08/16/64	Elmira, NY	P117,P120
					Elmira, NY	10/11/64	Pt. Lookout, MD Xc	P65,P66
					Pt. Lookout, MD	10/29/64	Venus Pt., GA Xc	P115,P117,CSR
Pearson, George Butler	Pvt	E 15th SCVI	South Mtn., MD	09/14/62	Ft. Delaware, DE	10/02/62	Aikens LDg., VA Xc	CSR,KEB,H15
Pearson, George W.	Pvt	A 12th SCVI	Sutherland Stn., VA	04/03/65	City Pt., VA	04/07/65	Hart's Island, NY	CSR
					Hart's Island, NY	06/16/65	Rlsd. G.O. #109	CSR
Pearson, Ira M.	Pvt	C 22nd SCVI	Bermuda Hundred, VA	06/02/64	Bermuda Hundred, VA	06/03/64	Fts. Monroe, VA	CSR
					Fts. Monroe, VA	06/04/64	Pt. Lookout, MD	CSR
					Pt. Lookout, MD	09/18/64	Aikens Ldg., VA Xc	P113,P117,CSR
					Richmond Hospital	09/25/64	Furloughed 30 days	CSR
Pearson, Irvin	Pvt	22nd SCVI	Kinston, NC	12/15/62	Kinston, NC	12/15/62	Paroled POW	CSR
Pearson, J.P.	Pvt	I Hol.Leg.	Petersburg, VA Hos.	04/03/65	Fair Gds. Hos. Pbg	04/23/65	Died of wounds	P6,P12,CSR
Pearson, J.W.	Pvt	K 3rd SCVI	Sharpsburg, MD	09/19/62	Sharpsburg, MD	09/27/62	Paroled	CSR,KEB,SA3
Pearson, J.W.	Pvt	H 25th SCVI	Ft. Fisher, NC	01/15/65	New York, NY	01/30/65	Elmira, NY	CSR, HAG
					Elmira, NY	07/11/65	Rlsd. G.O. #109	P65,P66
Pearson, John R.	Sgt	K 23rd SCVI	Five Forks, VA	04/02/65	City Pt., VA	04/04/65	Pt. Lookout, MD	CSR
					Pt. Lookout, MD	06/17/65	Rlsd. G.O. #109	CSR
Pearson, Robert Raiford	Pvt	C 2nd SCVI	Gettysburg, PA	07/05/63	Gettysburg, PA Hos.	07/23/63	Died of wounds	SA2,H2,CSR,KEB
Pearson, S. Jefferson	Pvt	C 22nd SCVI	Crater, Pbg., VA	07/30/64	City Pt., VA	08/05/64	Pt. Lookout, MD	CSR,HOS
					Pt. Lookout, MD	08/08/64	Elmira, NY	P113,P117,P120,CSR
					Elmira, NY	09/24/64	Died, Hos. Gangrene	P5,P65,P66,FPH,CSR
Pearson, W.S.	Pvt	A 13th SCVI	Petersburg, VA	04/03/65	City Pt., VA	04/07/65	Hart's Island, NY	CSR
					Hart's Island, NY	06/16/65	Rlsd. G.O. #109	CSR
Pease, John	Pvt	D 3rd SCVIBn	Gettysburg, PA	07/02/63	David's Island, NY	07/24/63	Died of wounds	CSR,P1,KEB,FPH
Peavey, Malcomb	Pvt	D 26th SCVI	Hatchers Run, VA	03/29/65	City Pt., VA	04/02/65	Pt. Lookout, MD	CSR
					Pt. Lookout, MD	05/14/65	Rlsd. G.O.#85	P115,P118,CSR
Peden, R.E.	Pvt	E Ham.Leg.MI	Farmville, VA	04/11/65	Farmville, VA	04/11/65	Paroled	CSR
Peebles, William D.	Sgt	M 8th SCVI	Winchester, VA	09/13/64	Harpers Ferry, WV	09/19/64	Camp Chase, OH	CSR,KEB
					Camp Chase, OH	05/02/65	New Orleans, LA	P23,CSR
					New Orleans, LA	05/12/65	Vicksburg, MS Xc	CSR
Peel, Freeman	Pvt	B 24th SCVI	Nashville, TN	12/16/64	Nashville, TN	12/19/64	Louisville, KY	CSR,HOM,EFW
					Louisville, KY	12/21/64	Camp Douglas, IL	P90,P91,P94
					Camp Douglas, IL	06/10/65	Rlsd. G.O. #109	P55,CSR
Peeler, David S.	Pvt	F 1st SCVA	Fayetteville, NC	03/16/65	New Berne, NC	03/30/65	Pt. Lookout, MD	CSR
					Pt. Lookout, MD	06/16/65	Rlsd. G.O. #109	P115,P122,CSR
Peeples, Thomas N.	Pvt	Stono Scts	Deserted/enemy	03/05/65	Charleston, SC	03/05/65	Released on oath	CSR
Peets, John	Smn	CS Chicora	Morris Island, SC	09/07/63	Pt. Lookout, MD	09/20/64	Ft. Warren, MA	P113
					Ft. Warren, MA	10/01/64	Str. Circasian	P2,P137
Pelfrey, Joseph M.	Pvt	A 2nd SCVI	Gettysburg, PA	07/05/63	Letterman G.H. Gbg		Provost Marshal	P1,KEB,SA2,H2
					David's Island, NY	09/05/63	City Pt., VA Xc	P1,CSR
Pelham, James E.	Cpl	I 11th SCVI	Town Creek, NC	02/20/65	Ft. Anderson, NC	02/28/65	Pt. Lookout, MD	CSR,HAG
					Pt. Lookout, MD	06/17/65	Rlsd. G.O. #109	P115,P118,CSR
Pelham, James F.	Pvt	G 17th SCVI	Petersburg, VA	03/25/65	City Pt., VA	03/28/65	Pt. Lookout, MD	CSR
					Pt. Lookout, MD	06/17/65	Rlsd. G.O. #109	CSR
Pelletier, L.L.	Pvt	D 21st SCVI	Ft. Fisher, NC	01/15/65	Elmira, NY	07/07/65	Rlsd. G.O. #109	P65,P66,HAG
Pelot, J.M.	Sur	CS Navy	Morris Island, SC	09/07/63	Ft. Columbus, NY	10/09/63	Johnson's Isl., OH	P1

SOUTH CAROLINA SOLDIERS, SAILORS AND  CITIZENS HELD IN U.S. PRISONS 1861-1865

NAME	RANK	REGIMENT	CAPTURED AT	WHEN	PRISON	MOVED	DISPOSITION	SOURCES
Pendarvis, Jacob P.	Pvt	C 24th SCVI	Franklin, TN	12/17/64	Nashville, TN	01/17/65	Louisville, KY	P3,P39
					Louisville, KY	01/18/65	Camp Chase, OH	P92,P95,CSR
					Camp Chase, OH	06/13/65	Rlsd. G.O. #109	CSR
Pendarvis, James O.A.	Pvt	D 3rd SCVABn	1st Brgd., 2nd Cav.	04/30/65	Macon, GA		No released data	CSR
Pendarvis, Wright J.	Pvt	B 11th SCVI	Town Creek, NC	02/20/65	Ft. Anderson, NC	02/28/65	Pt. Lookout, MD	CSR,HAG
					Pt. Lookout, MD	05/15/65	Rlsd. G.O. #85	P115,P118,P121,CSR
Pender, R.	Pvt	K 11th SCVI	Petersburg, VA	06/16/64	Pt. Lookout, MD	07/25/64	Elmira, NY	P113,P120
					Elmira, NY	03/14/65	Trfd for exchange	P65
Pendergrass, John M.	1Lt	C 25th SCVI	Ft. Fisher, NC	01/15/65	Fts. Monroe, VA	01/26/65	Ft. Columbus, NY	CSR,HAG
					Ft. Columbus, NY	02/25/65	City Pt., VA Xc	CSR
					Ft. Columbus, NY	04/08/65	Ft. Delaware, DE	P2
Pendergrass, Joseph	Pvt	D 7th SCVIBn	Smithfield, NC	01/18/65	Ft. Fisher, NC	02/04/65	Pt. Lookout, MD	CSR,HAG,HIC
					Pt. Lookout, MD	02/18/65	Aikens Ldg., VA Xc	P115,P118,P123,CSR
Pendleton, J.	Pvt	1st SCVIG	Fredericksburg, VA	05/03/63	Washington, DC	05/10/63	City Pt., VA Xc	CSR
Pendley, Andrew J.	Pvt	A Orr's Ri.	Falling Waters, MD	07/14/63	Pt. Lookout, MD	08/16/64	Elmira, NY	P116,CDC
Pendley, Andrew J.	Sgt	A Orr's Ri.	Petersburg, VA	04/03/65	City Pt., VA	04/07/65	Hart's Island, NY	CSR
					Hart's Island, NY	06/16/65	Rlsd. G.O. #109	P79
Pennell, John A.	Cpl	D Hol.Leg.	Five Forks, VA	04/01/65	City Pt., VA	04/05/65	Pt. Lookout, MD	CSR
					Pt. Lookout, MD	06/16/65	Rlsd. G.O. #109	P115,P119,P122,CSR
Penney, J.H.	Pvt	A 1st SCVC	Culpepper, VA	09/14/63	Ft. McHenry, MD	09/20/63	Pt. Lookout, MD	P110
					Old Capitol, DC	09/26/63	Pt. Lookout, MD	CSR
					Pt. Lookout, MD	11/15/63	Hammond G.H., MD	P113,CSR
					Pt. Lookout, MD	04/27/64	City Pt., VA Xc	P116,CSR
Pennington, J.M.	Pvt	H 4th SCVC	Charlotte, NC	05/04/65	Charlotte, NC	05/04/65	Paroled	CSR
Penton, John	Pvt	D 1st SCVIR	Deserted/enemy	02/10/65	Hilton Head, SC		New York, NY oath	CSR
Pepper, Henry	Pvt	Brooks LA	Harpers Farm, VA	04/06/65	City Pt., VA	04/14/65	Pt. Lookout, MD	CSR
					Pt. Lookout, MD	06/17/65	Rlsd. G.O. #109	CSR
Pepper, Robert H.	Pvt	A German LA	Deserted/enemy	03/24/65	Charleston, SC	03/24/65	Released on oath	CSR
Percival, E.S.	2Lt	F 3rd SCVIBn	Gettysburg, PA	07/04/63			No release found	CSR
Perdieux, Colleton	Pvt	E 21st SCVI	Ft. Fisher, NC	01/15/65	Elmira, NY	06/21/65	Died, Pneumonia	P6,P65,P66,FPH,HAG
Perkins, A.G.	Pvt	F Orr's Ri.	Southside RR, VA	04/02/65	City Pt., VA	04/07/65	Hart's Island, NY	CSR
					Hart's Island, NY	06/15/65	Rlsd. G.O. #109	P79,CSR
Perkins, Josiah	Pvt	F Orr's Ri.	Petersburg, VA	04/03/65	City Pt., VA	04/11/65	Hart's Island, NY	CSR,CDC
					Hart's Island, NY	06/16/65	Rlsd. G.O. #109	P79,CSR
Perkins, T.C.	Pvt	G 27th SCVI	Weldon RR, VA	08/21/64	City Pt., VA	08/24/64	Pt. Lookout, MD	CSR,HAG
					Pt. Lookout, MD	03/14/65	Aikens Ldg., VA Xc	P113,P117,P121
Perkins, William	Pvt	D 26th SCVI	Amelia C.H., VA	04/03/65	City Pt., VA	04/13/65	Pt. Lookout, MD	CSR
					Pt. Lookout, MD	06/06/65	Rlsd. Instr. 5/30/65	P115,P119,P121,HOM
Perrin, Lewis Wardlaw	Cpt	A 1st SCVIR	Bentonville, NC	03/22/65	New Berne, NC	04/10/65	Hart's Island, NY	CSR,SA1
					Hart's Island, NY	04/15/65	Ft. Delaware, DE	P79,CSR
					Ft. Delaware, DE	06/17/65	Rlsd. G.O. #109	P43,P45,CSR
Perritt, S.B.	Pvt	F 3rd SCVC	South Newport, GA	08/17/64	Philadelphia, PA	01/10/65	Ft. Delaware, DE	CSR
					Ft. Delaware, DE	06/08/65	Released	CSR
Perry, Alexander	Pvt	K 1st SCVA	Columbia, SC	02/18/65	Camp Hamilton, VA	04/02/65	Washington, D.C.	CSR
					New Berne NC	04/02/65	Camp Hamilton, VA	CSR
					Camp Hamilton, VA	05/04/65	Military prison	CSR
Perry, Andrew J.	Sgt	K 18th SCVI	Petersburg, VA	03/20/64	City Pt., VA	03/28/64	Pt. Lookout, MD	CSR
					Pt. Lookout, MD	06/16/65	Rlsd. G.O. #109	CSR

P

SOUTH CAROLINA SOLDIERS, SAILORS AND CITIZENS HELD IN U.S. PRISONS 1861-1865

NAME	RANK	REGIMENT	CAPTURED AT	WHEN	PRISON	MOVED	DISPOSITION	SOURCES
Perry, Isaac	Pvt	B 7th SCVIBn	Weldon RR, VA	08/21/64	City Pt., VA USFH	08/24/64	Alexandria, VA USG	CSR,HAG,HFC
					Alexandria, VA USG	11/19/64	Washington, DC USG	P1,CSR
					Lincoln G.H., DC	11/23/64	Elmira, NY	CSR
					Ft. McHenry, MD	12/16/64	Elmira, NY	P110
					Elmira, NY	06/14/65	Rlsd. G.O. #109	P66,CSR
Perry, J.W.	Pvt	C 13th SCVI	Deserted/enemy	02/24/65	City Pt., VA	02/26/65	Washington, DC	CSR
					Washington, DC	02/27/65	Philadelphia, oath	CSR
Perry, James B.	Pvt	B 1st SCVIG	Gettysburg, PA	07/05/63	Ft. Delaware, DE	06/10/65	Rlsd. G.O. #109	P42,P45,SA1,CSR
Perry, John	Smn	CS Chicora	Morris Island, SC	09/07/63	Pt. Lookout, MD	02/12/64	Joined U.S. Army	P113,P125
Perry, John	Pvt	D 2nd SCVC	Deserted/enemy	02/27/65	Charleston, SC	03/01/65	To take oath	CSR
Perry, Lawrence T.	Pvt	B 14th SCVI	Gettysburg, PA	07/04/63	David's Island, NY	09/08/63	City Pt., VA Xc	CSR
Perry, Matthew	Pvt	C 11th SCVI	Town Creek, NC	02/20/65	Ft. Anderson, NC	02/28/65	Pt. Lookout, MD	CSR
					Pt. Lookout, MD	06/17/65	Rlsd. G.O. #109	CSR
Perry, Pressley	Pvt	E 22nd SCVI	Petersburg, VA	06/17/64	City Pt., VA	06/24/64	Pt. Lookout, MD	CSR,LAN
					Pt. Lookout, MD	07/27/64	Elmira, NY	P113,P117,P120
					Elmira, NY	08/09/64	Died, Ch. Diarrhea	P5,P12,P65,P66,FPH
Perry, R.N.	Pvt	I 17th SCVI	Petersburg, VA	03/25/65	City Pt., VA	03/27/65	Pt. Lookout, MD	CSR
					Pt. Lookout, MD	06/16/65	Rlsd. G.O. #109	P115,CSR
Perry, Richard S.	Pvt	I 12th SCVI	Wilderness, VA	05/06/64	Belle Plain, VA	05/20/64	Ft. Delaware, DE	CSR
					Ft. Delaware, DE	06/10/65	Released	CSR
Perry, S.A.	Pvt	I P.S.S.	Deserted/enemy	03/22/65	Bermuda Hundred, VA	03/22/65	Washington, DC	CSR,TSE
					Washington, DC	03/25/65	Nashville, TN oath	CSR
Perry, Silas R.	Pvt	C 12th SCVI	Sharpsburg, MD	09/18/62	Sharpsburg, MD	09/21/62	Paroled	CSR
Perry, Silas R.	Pvt	C 12th SCVI	Petersburg, VA	04/03/65	City Pt., VA	04/07/65	Hart's Island, NY	CSR
					Harts Island, NY	06/16/65	Rlsd. G.O. #109	CSR
Perry, William	Plt	Charleston	Wassau Sound, NC	12/23/63	Ft. Lafayette, NY	07/02/63	Ft. Warren, MA	P144
				02/23/63	Ft. Warren, MA	03/18/65		P2,P7
Perry, William	Pvt	C 11th SCVI	Town Creek, NC	02/20/65	Pt. Lookout, MD	06/16/65	Rlsd. G.O. #109	P115,HAG
Persons, J.A.	Pvt	17th SCVI	Athens, GA	05/08/65	Athens, GA	05/08/65	Paroled	CSR
Pervis, James N.	Cpl	C 3rd SCVABn	Blakely, AL	04/09/65	Ship Island, MS	05/01/65	Vicksburg, MS Xc	P136,CSR
					Vicksburg, MS	05/03/65	Exchanged	CSR
Petch, Emmanuel M.	Pvt	B 27th SCVI	Town Creek, NC	02/20/65	Ft. Anderson, NC	02/28/65	Pt. Lookout, MD	CSR,HAG
					Pt. Lookout, MD	06/16/65	Rlsd. G.O. #109	P115,P118,P122,CSR
Petch, Julius	Pvt	B 27th SCVI	Town Creek, NC	02/20/65	Ft. Anderson, NC	02/28/65	Pt. Lookout, MD	CSR
					Pt. Lookout, MD	06/16/65	Rlsd. G.O. #109	P115,P118,P122,CSR
Peters, J. Albert	Cpl	K 11th SCVI	Weldon RR, VA	08/21/64	City Pt., VA	08/24/64	Pt. Lookout, MD	HAG,CSR
					Pt. Lookout, MD	03/14/65	Aikens Ldg., VA Xc	P113,P117,P121
Peterson, Bazil	2Lt	D 19th SCVI	Augusta, GA	05/18/65	Augusta, GA	05/18/65	Paroled	CSR
Peterson, Benjamin	Pvt	F 18th SCVI	Petersburg, VA	04/02/65	City Pt., VA	04/07/65	Hart's Island, NY	CSR
					Hart's Island, NY	06/15/65	Rlsd. G.O. #109	CSR
Petree, Pink C.	Sgt	I 13th SCVI	Falling Waters, MD	07/14/63	Baltimore, MD	08/16/63	Pt. Lookout, MD	CSR
					Pt. Lookout, MD	08/16/64	Elmira, NY	CSR
					Elmira, NY	03/10/65	James R., VA Xc	CSR
Pettis, J.F.	Sgt	I 7th SCVI	Gettysburg, PA	07/04/63	Gettysburg, PA G.H.	09/14/63	W. Bldg. Balt, MD	P4,CSR
Pettis, J.M.	Pvt	I 7th SCVI	Gettysburg, PA	07/05/63	David's Island, NY	09/25/63	City Pt., VA Xc	P1,CSR
Pettit, Benjamin F.	Pvt	K 3rd SCVI	Lynch's Creek, SC	02/28/65	New Berne, NC	04/03/65	Pt. Lookout, MD	H3,KEB,SA2,CSR
					Pt. Lookout, MD	06/17/65	Rlsd. G.O. #109	P115,P122
Pettit, David	Pvt	F 1st SCVIR	Marlboro, SC	04/06/65	New Berne, NC	04/02/65	Camp Hamilton, VA	CSR
					Camp Hamilton, VA	04/03/65	Newport News, VA	CSR
					Newport News, VA	06/13/65	Rlsd. G.O. #109	P107,CSR
Pettit, Nathan L.	Sgt	A Hol.Leg.	Petersburg, VA	03/25/65	City Pt., VA	03/28/65	Pt. Lookout, MD	CSR,HOS
					Pt. Lookout, MD	06/16/65	Rlsd. G.O. #109	P115,P118,P122,CSR

SOUTH CAROLINA SOLDIERS, SAILORS AND  CITIZENS HELD IN U.S. PRISONS 1861-1865

NAME	RANK	REGIMENT	CAPTURED AT	WHEN	PRISON	MOVED	DISPOSITION	SOURCES
Pettus, R.R.	Pvt	D Hol.Leg.	Hatchers Run, VA	03/25/65	City Pt., VA	04/02/65	Pt. Lookout, MD	CSR
					Pt. Lookout, MD	06/17/65	Rlsd. G.O. #109	P115,P118,CSR
Petty, M.T.	Pvt	E P.S.S.	Athens, GA	05/08/65	Athens, GA	05/08/65	Paroled	CSR,TSE
Petty, Pinckney M.	Pvt	K 3rd SCVI	Lynch's Creek, SC	02/28/65	New Berne, NC	04/03/65	Pt. Lookout, MD	CSR,KEB,SA2
					Pt. Lookout, MD	06/05/65	Released sick list	P115,P118,CSR
Petty, Thomas M.	Pvt	K 3rd SCVI	Lynch's Creek, SC	02/28/65	New Berne, NC	04/03/65	Pt. Lookout, MD	CSR,KEB,SA2,H3
					Pt. Lookout, MD	06/30/65	Rlsd. G.O. #109	P115,P121,CSR
Phelps, Francis B.	Pvt	F 2nd SCMil	Chesterfield, SC	02/28/65	Pt. Lookout, MD	06/16/65	Rlsd. G.O. #109	P115,P118,P122
Phillips, A.B.	Pvt	K 4th SCVC	Charlotte, NC	05/04/65	Charlotte, NC	05/04/65	Paroled	CSR
Phillips, Aaron	Pvt	F 26th SCVI	Southside RR, VA	04/06/65	City Pt., VA	04/12/65	Pt. Lookout, MD	CSR
					Pt. Lookout, MD	06/04/65	Rlsd. Instr. 5/30/65	P115,P119,P121,CSR
Phillips, B.	Pvt	C 3rd SCVABn	Blakely, AL	04/09/65	Ship Island, MS	05/01/65	Vicksburg, MS Xc	P136,CSR
Phillips, Chapman P.	Cpl	D 8th SCVI	Winchester, VA	09/13/64	Harpers Ferry, WV	09/19/64	Camp Chase, OH	CSR,KEB
					Camp Chase, OH	06/11/65	Rlsd. G.O. #109	P23,CSR
Phillips, E.	Pvt	E Orr's Ri.	Petersburg, VA	04/03/65	City Pt., VA	04/11/65	Hart's Island, NY	CSR
					Hart's Island, NY	06/16/65	Rlsd. G.O. #109	P79,CSR
Phillips, E.D.	Pvt	G 7th SCVIBn	Weldon RR, VA	08/21/64	City Pt., VA	08/24/64	Pt. Lookout, MD	HIC,CSR,HAG
					Pt. Lookout, MD	03/14/65	Aikens Ldg., VA Xc	P113,P117,P121
Phillips, Eli	Pvt	A 21st SCVI	Ft. Fisher, NC	01/15/65	Elmira, NY	02/20/65	Died, Diarrhea	P6,P65,P66,FPH,HAG
Phillips, G.W.	Pvt	F 7th SCVIBn	Marlboro Dist., SC	03/07/65	New Berne, NC	04/10/65	Hart's Island, NY	CSR,HAG,HIC
					Hart's Island, NY	06/17/65	Rlsd. G.O. #109	P79,CSR
Phillips, George W.	Pvt	A 4th SCVC			Hart's Island, NY	06/17/65	Rlsd. G.O. #109	CSR
Phillips, H.	Pvt	E Orr's Ri.	Petersburg, VA	04/03/65	City Pt., VA	04/11/65	Hart's Island, NY	CSR
					Hart's Island, NY	06/16/65	Rlsd. G.O. #109	P79,CSR
Phillips, Isidore	Pvt	B German LA	Cheraw, SC	05/05/65	Cheraw, SC	05/05/65	Paroled	CSR
Phillips, J.G.	Pvt	G 22nd SCVI	Virginia	04/11/65	24C, Army o/t James	04/14/65	U.S. General Hos.	CSR
Phillips, J.J.	Pvt	I 17th SCVI	Petersburg, VA	03/25/65	City Pt., VA	03/27/65	Pt. Lookout, MD	CSR
					Pt. Lookout, MD			P115,CSR
Phillips, J.R.	Cpl	E 8th SCVI	Chickahominy R., VA	05/30/64	White House, VA	06/08/64	Pt. Lookout, MD	CSR,KEB
					Pt. Lookout, MD	07/09/64	Elmira, NY	P113,P117,P120,CSR
					Elmira, NY	06/19/65	Rlsd. G.O. #109	P65,KEB,CSR
Phillips, J.W.	Pvt	I 5th SCVC	Augusta, GA	05/25/65	Augusta, GA	05/25/65	Paroled	CSR
Phillips, James B.	Pvt	C 2nd SCVIRi	Deserted/enemy	03/03/65	Bermuda Hundred, VA	03/05/65	City Pt., VA P.M.	CSR
					City Pt., VA	03/07/65	Washington, DC P.M.	CSR
					Washington, DC	03/08/65	Columbus, OH oath	CSR
Phillips, James P.	Pvt	I 6th SCVI	Richmond, VA	04/03/65	City Pt., VA	04/14/65	Pt. Lookout, MD	CSR,HIC
					Pt. Lookout, MD	06/16/65	Rlsd. G.O. #109	P115,P119,CSR
Phillips, James S.	Sgt	F 18th SCVI	Five Forks, VA	04/01/65	City Pt., VA	04/05/65	Pt. Lookout, MD	CSR
					Pt. Lookout, MD	06/17/65	Rlsd. G.O. #109	CSR
Phillips, James T.	Pvt	E 22nd SCVI	Deserted/enemy	02/17/65	City Pt., VA	02/19/65	Washington, DC	CSR
					Washington, DC		No further data	CSR
Phillips, John	Pvt	H 17th SCVI	Crater, Pbg., VA	07/30/64	City Pt., VA	08/05/65	Pt. Lookout, MD	P125,CSR
					Pt. Lookout, MD	08/08/64	Elmira, NY	P113,P120,CSR
					Elmira, NY	05/13/65	Released on oath	P65,P66,CSR
Phillips, John	Pvt	A 21st SCVI	Ft. Fisher, NC	01/15/65	Elmira, NY	02/06/65	Died, Ch. Diarrhea	P6,P65,P66,FPH,HAG
Phillips, Mitchell A.	Pvt	B German LA	Port Royal Fy., SC	10/16/64	Hilton Head, SC PM	10/25/64	Ft. Pulaski, GA	P2,CSR
					Charleston Hrbr., SC	12/15/64	Paroled	CSR
Phillips, O.N.	Pvt	I 3rd SCVI	Lookout Valley, TN	03/13/64	Louisville, KY	04/02/64	Camp Chase, OH	SA2,P91,P93,H3,CSR
Phillips, Peter	Pvt	E Orr's Ri.	Falling Waters, MD	07/14/63	Baltimore, MD	08/20/63	Pt. Lookout, MD	CSR
					Pt. Lookout, MD	12/21/63	Hammond G.H., MD	P113,P121,P125,CSR
					Hammond G.H., MD	01/01/64	Died, Ch. Diarrhea	P116,CSR,P12,FPH

P

SOUTH CAROLINA SOLDIERS, SAILORS AND CITIZENS HELD IN U.S. PRISONS 1861-1865

NAME	RANK	REGIMENT	CAPTURED AT	WHEN	PRISON	MOVED	DISPOSITION	SOURCES
Phillips, Robert J.	Pvt	F 7th SCVIBn	Cheraw, SC	03/07/65	New Berne, NC	04/10/65	Hart's Island, NY	CSR,HAG,HIC
					Hart's Island, NY	06/17/65	Rlsd. G.O. #109	P79,CSR
Phillips, S.Y.	Pvt	D 17th SCVI	Crater, Pbg., VA	07/30/64	City Pt., VA	08/05/64	Pt. Lookout, MD	CSR
					Pt. Lookout, MD	08/08/64	Elmira, NY	P113,P120,CSR
					Elmira, NY	10/11/64	Paroled for exchange	P65,P66,CSR
					Venus Pt., GA Xc	11/15/64	Exchanged	P115,CSR
Phillips, Thornberry P.	Pvt	F 2nd SCVC	Hartwell, GA	05/18/65	Hartwell, GA	05/18/65	Paroled	CSR
Phillips, W.R.	Pvt	A 3rd SCVABn	High Pt., NC	05/02/65	High Pt., NC	05/02/65	Paroled	CSR
Phillips, Wade H.	Pvt	C 14th SCVI	Gettysburg, PA	07/04/63	David's Island, NY	10/15/63	Bedloes Island, NY	CSR
					Bedloes Island, NY	07/15/64	Ft. Delaware, DE	CSR
					Ft. Delaware, DE	09/14/64	Aikens Ldg., VA Xc	CSR
Phillips, Warren	Pvt	D 4th SCVC	Greenville, SC	05/28/65	Greenville, SC	05/28/65	Paroled	CSR
Phillips, William D.	Pvt	E 22nd SCVI	Kinston, NC	12/15/62	Kinston, NC	12/15/62	Paroled POW	CSR
Phillips, William H.	Pvt	C 2nd SCVIRi	Deserted/enemy	03/03/65	Bermuda Hundred, VA	03/05/65	City Pt., VA P.M.	CSR
					City Pt., VA P.M.	03/07/65	Washington, DC P.M.	CSR
					Washington, DC P.M.	03/08/65	Columbus, OH oath	CSR
Phipps, W.E.	HSd	3rd SCVABn	Hartwell, GA	05/17/65	Hartwell, GA	05/17/65	Paroled	CSR
Pickens, James M.	Cpt	G 22nd SCVI	Kinston, NC	12/15/62	Kinston, NC	12/15/62	Paroled POW	CSR
Pickerel, W.R.	Pvt	K Ham.Leg.MI	Deserted/enemy	03/04/65	Bermuda Hundred, VA	03/05/65	City Pt., VA P.M.	CSR
					City Pt., VA	03/08/65	Washington, DC	CSR
					Washington, DC	03/08/65	Iowa City, IA oath	CSR
Pickett, Evander	Pvt	I 26th SCVI	Crater, Pbg., VA	07/30/64	City Pt., VA	08/05/64	Pt. Lookout, MD	CSR,CTA,HOW
					Pt. Lookout, MD	08/08/64	Elmira, NY	P113,P117,P120
					Elmira, NY	10/11/64	Pt. Lookout, MD Xc	P65,P66
					Pt. Lookout, MD	10/29/64	Aikens Ldg., VA Xc	P115,P117
Pickett, John R.	Pvt	K 7th SCVC	Farmville, VA	04/06/65	City Pt., VA	04/13/65	Pt. Lookout, MD	CSR,HIC
					Pt. Lookout, MD	06/06/65	Rlsd. Instr. 5/30/65	P115,P121,CSR
Pickrell, J.A.	Pvt	I 1st SCVIR	Cheraw, SC	03/05/65	Cheraw, SC	03/05/65	Paroled	CSR,SA1
Pickren, James M.	Pvt	B Col.Ars.Bn	Ft. McAlister, GA	12/13/64	Pt. Lookout, MD	02/18/65	Exchanged	P124
Pieper, H.W.	Pvt	A German LA	Macon, GA	04/30/65	Macon, GA	04/30/65	Paroled	CSR
Pierce, J.H.	Sgt	K 1st SCVC	Morrisville, VA	03/02/64	Ft. Delaware, DE	03/24/64	Kalorama Hos., DC	CSR
					Kalorama Hos., DC	04/16/64	Washington, DC G.H.	CSR
					Washington, DC G.H.	04/22/64	Ft. Delaware, DE	CSR
					Old Capitol, DC	06/10/64	Ft. Delaware, DE	CSR
					Ft. McHenry, MD	06/15/64	Ft. Delaware, DE	P110
					Ft. Delaware, DE	07/24/63	Hos. 7/24-7/31/64	P47
					Ft. Delaware, DE	06/10/65	Rlsd. G.O. #109	P41,P42,P45,CSR
Pierce, J.M.	Pvt	C 13th SCVI	Southside RR, VA	04/02/65	City Pt., VA	04/07/65	Hart's Island, NY	CSR,HOS
					Hart's Island, NY	06/16/65	Rlsd. G.O. #109	CSR
Pierce, John Albert	Pvt	C 15th SCVAB	Smith Ford, NC	03/16/65	New Berne, NC	04/03/65	Pt. Lookout, MD	CSR
					Pt. Lookout, MD	06/16/65	Rlsd. G.O. #109	P115,P122,CSR
Pierce, Joseph	Pvt	H 6th SCVC	Deserted/enemy	05/20/64	Louisville, KY	05/31/64	N. of Ohio R. oath	P88,P92,P94,CSR
Pierce, L.	Pvt	E 17th SCVI	Petersburg, VA	03/25/65	City Pt., VA	03/28/65	Pt. Lookout, MD	CSR
					Pt. Lookout, MD	06/16/65	Rlsd. G.O. #109	CSR
Pierce, L.M.	Pvt	H 22nd SCVI	Deserted/enemy	01/15/65	City Pt., VA	02/18/65	Washington, DC	CSR
					Washington, DC	02/21/65	Ducktown, TN oath	CSR
Pierce, Levi	Pvt	B Hol.Leg.	Petersburg, VA	10/27/64	City Pt., VA	10/31/64	Pt. Lookout, MD	CSR,HOS
					Pt. Lookout, MD	06/17/65	Rlsd. G.O. #109	P115,P122,CSR
Pierce, Mathias P.	Pvt	H 6th SCVC	Deserted/enemy	05/20/64	Louisville, KY	05/31/64	N. of Ohio R. oath	P88,P92,P94,CSR
Pierce, William	Pvt	D 6th SCVI	Warrenton, VA	09/29/62	Warrenton, VA	09/29/62	Paroled	CSR
Pierce, William J.	Pvt	B 26th SCVI	Petersburg, VA	04/02/65	City Pt., VA	04/05/65	Pt. Lookout, MD	CSR
					Pt. Lookout, MD	06/16/65	Rlsd. G.O. #109	P115,P119,P122,CSR

SOUTH CAROLINA SOLDIERS, SAILORS AND  CITIZENS HELD IN U.S. PRISONS 1861-1865

NAME	RANK	REGIMENT	CAPTURED AT	WHEN	PRISON	MOVED	DISPOSITION	SOURCES
Pierson, C.	Pvt	I 2nd SCVI	Gettysburg, PA	07/04/63	Chester, PA Hos.	08/17/63	City Pt., VA Xc	CSR
Pierson, D.W.	Pvt	C 27th SCVI	Petersburg, VA	06/24/64	Hampton, VA G.H.	06/27/64	Died of wounds	P12,HAG
Pigg, William P.	Pvt	B 26th SCVI	Five Forks, VA	04/01/65	City Pt., VA	04/05/65	Pt. Lookout, MD	CSR
					Pt. Lookout, MD	06/19/65	Died, Scurvy	P6,P115,P119,FPH
Pinckham, Emory	Pvt	C 8th SCVI	Deserted/enemy	06/06/62	Baltimore, MD	06/11/62	DTE, sent north	KEB,CSR
Pinckney, E.B.	Pvt	D 5th SCVC	Petersburg, VA	09/29/64	City Pt., VA	10/02/64	Pt. Lookout, MD	CSR
					Pt. Lookout, MD	10/30/64	Aikens Ldg., VA Xc	P115,P117,CSR
Pinckney, Roger	Pvt	K 4th SCVI	Mannasas, VA	07/21/61	Ft. McHenry, MD	11/13/62	Fts. Monroe, VA Xc	P145,SA2,CSR
Pinckney, Thomas	Cpt	D 4th SCVC	Hawe's Shop, VA	05/28/64	White House, VA	06/08/64	Pt. Lookout, MD	CSR
					Pt. Lookout, MD	06/23/64	Ft. Delaware, DE	P113,P116,P120,CSR
					Hilton Head, SC	08/20/64	Ft. Pulaski, GA	CSR
					Ft. Delaware, DE	08/20/64	Hilton Head, SC	P42,P44,CSR
					Ft. Pulaski, GA	12/15/64	Charleston for Xc	CSR
Pinson, Amanette	Pvt	F 2nd SCVI	Loudon, TN	12/03/63	Nashville, TN	02/19/64	Louisville, KY	P39,KEB,SA2,CSR,H2
					Louisville, KY	02/29/64	Ft. Delaware, DE	P91
					Ft. Delaware, DE	09/30/64	Aikens Ldg., VA Xc	P41,P42,CSR
Pinson, Cornelius F.	Pvt	A 3rd SCVIBn	N. Anna River, VA	05/23/64	Port Royal, VA	05/30/64	Pt. Lookout, MD	CSR,KEB
					Pt. Lookout, MD	05/14/65	Died, Diarrhea	P6,P117,P119,FPH
Pinson, Eber	Pvt	A Hol.Leg.	Five Forks, VA	04/01/65	City Pt., VA	04/05/65	Pt. Lookout, MD	CSR,HOS
					Pt. Lookout, MD	06/17/76	Rlsd. G.O. #109	P115,P119,CSR
Pinson, Jesse	Cpl	A Hol.Leg.	Kinston, NC	12/15/62	Kinston, NC	12/15/62	Paroled POW	CSR,HOS
Pinson, John R.	Pvt	E 7th SCVI	Gettysburg, PA	07/03/63	David's Island, NY	10/24/63	Bedloes Island, NY	P1,HOE,CSR,KEB
					Bedloes Island, NY	01/06/64	City Pt., VA Xc	P2,CSR
					Pt. Lookout, MD	02/28/64	Exchanged	P124,CSR
Pinson, Martin	Pvt	Brooks LA	Petersburg, VA	04/03/65	Bermuda Hundred, VA	04/08/65	New York Harbor	CSR
					Hart's Island, NY	06/16/65	Rlsd. G.O. #109	P79,CSR
Pinson, Randolph P.	Pvt	K 19th SCVI	Atlanta, GA	07/22/64	Nashville, TN	07/29/64	Louisville, KY	CSR
					Louisville, KY	07/31/64	Camp Chase, OH	CSR
					Camp Chase, OH	03/04/65	City Pt., VA Xc	CSR
Pinson, W.V.	Pvt	I 1st SCVA	Mills Creek, NC	03/19/65	Pt. Lookout, MD	06/16/65	Rlsd. G.O. #109	P115,CSR
					New Berne, NC	04/10/65	Hart's Island, NY	CSR
Pirle, H.H.	Pvt	B 1st SCVIR	Cheraw, SC	03/04/65	Hart's Island, NY	06/16/65	Rlsd. G.O. #109	SA1,CSR
Pitjens, Henry	Pvt	C 1st SCVA	Deserted/enemy	02/03/65	Hilton Head, SC	02/18/65	New York, NY oath	CSR
Pitman, Amos O.	Pvt	A 17th SCVI	Petersburg, VA	04/02/65	City Pt., VA	04/04/65	Pt. Lookout, MD	CSR
					Pt. Lookout, MD	06/16/65	Rlsd. G.O. #109	P115,CSR
Pitman, Jethro	Pvt	D 1st SCVIH	Deserted/enemy	03/01/65	City Pt., VA P.M.	03/05/65	Washington, DC P.M.	CSR
					Washington, DC	03/07/65	Phila., PA on oath	CSR
Pittman, David G.	Pvt	F 4th SCVC	Stony Creek, VA	12/01/64	City Pt., VA	12/05/64	Pt. Lookout, MD	CSR,HMC
					Pt. Lookout, MD	01/17/65	Boulwares Wh., VA	P115,P124,CSR
Pittman, David T.	Pvt	F 14th SCVI	Petersburg, VA	04/02/65	City Pt., VA	04/04/65	Pt. Lookout, MD	CSR
					Pt. Lookout, MD	06/16/65	Rlsd. G.O. #109	CSR
Pittman, W.L.	Pvt	B 5th SCVI	Farmville, VA	04/06/65	City Pt., VA	04/14/65	Newport News, VA	CSR
					Newport News, VA	06/15/65	Rlsd. G.O. #109	CSR
Pittman, William J.	Pvt	D 6th SCVC	Cheraw, SC	03/14/65	New Berne, NC	03/30/65	Pt. Lookout, MD	CSR
					Pt. Lookout, MD	06/17/65	Rlsd.G.O. #109	P118,CSR
Pitts, Charles	Pvt	B Orr's Ri.	Appomattox R., VA	04/03/65	City Pt., VA	04/11/65	Hart's Island, NY	CSR
					Hart's Island, NY	06/16/65	Rlsd. G.O. #109	P79
Pitts, D.S.	Pvt	C Hol.Leg.C	Bottoms Bridge, VA	08/27/63	Ft. Magruder, VA	08/30/63	Fts. Monroe, VA	CSR
					Fts. Monroe, VA	08/31/63	Ft. Norfolk, VA	CSR
					Ft. Norfolk, VA		Pt. Lookout, MD	CSR
					Pt. Lookout, MD	05/03/64	Exchanged	CSR

SOUTH CAROLINA SOLDIERS, SAILORS AND  CITIZENS HELD IN U.S. PRISONS 1861-1865

NAME	RANK	REGIMENT	CAPTURED AT	WHEN	PRISON	MOVED	DISPOSITION	SOURCES
Pitts, D.Y.	Sgt	A 6th SCVC	Louisa C.H., VA	06/11/64	Pt. Lookout, MD	07/08/64	Elmira, NY	P113,P117,P120,CSR
					Elmira, NY	05/29/65	Rlsd. G.O. #85	P65,P66,CSR
Pitts, David	Pvt	B 3rd SCVI	Wilderness, VA	05/06/64	Belle Plain, VA	05/21/64	Ft. Delaware, DE	CSR,KEB,SA2,H3
					Ft. Delaware, DE	05/04/65	Hos. 5/4-5/17/65	P47
					Ft. Delaware, DE	12/10/64	Hos. 12/10/64-2/4/65	P47
					Ft. Delaware, DE	06/10/65	Released	P41,P42,P45,CSR
Pitts, G.W.	Pvt	B 3rd SCVIBn	Cedar Creek, VA	10/19/64	Harpers Ferry, WV	10/23/64	Pt. Lookout, MD	CSR,KEB
					Pt. Lookout, MD	05/14/65	Rlsd. G.O. #85	P115,P117,P121,CSR
Pitts, J.	Smn	CS *Chicora*			Pt. Lookout, MD		Exchanged	P124
Pitts, J.B.	Pvt	D 13th SCVI	Gettysburg, PA	07/05/63	Chester, PA Hos.	09/17/63	City Pt., VA Xc	CSR
Pitts, J.P.	Pvt	C 13th SCVI	Deserted/enemy	02/24/65	City Pt., VA	02/26/65	Washington, DC	CSR
					Washington, DC	02/27/65	Philadelphia oath	CSR
Pitts, James Y.	Pvt	D 27th SCVI	Petersburg, VA	06/24/64	Bermuda Hundred, VA	06/25/64	Fts. Monroe, VA	CSR,HAG
					Fts. Monroe, VA	06/26/64	Pt. Lookout, MD	CSR
					Pt. Lookout, MD	08/16/64	Elmira, NY	P113,P117,P120
					Elmira, NY	06/14/65	Rlsd. G.O. #109	P65,P66
Pitts, John S.	Pvt	G Hol.Leg.	Five Forks, VA	04/01/65	City Pt., VA	04/05/65	Pt. Lookout, MD	CSR,ANY
					Pt. Lookout, MD	06/17/65	Rlsd. G.O. #109	P115,P119,CSR
Pitts, Joseph	Pvt	G Hol.Leg.	Petersburg, VA	04/02/65	City Pt., VA	04/05/65	Pt. Lookout, MD	CSR,ANY
					Pt. Lookout, MD	06/17/65	Rlsd. G.O. #109	CSR
Pitts, W.M.	Pvt	K Ham.Leg.MI	Deep Bottom, VA	08/17/64	City Pt., VA	08/22/64	Pt. Lookout, MD	CSR
					Pt. Lookout, MD	10/11/64	James R., VA Xc	CSR
					Richmond, VA Hos.	10/21/64	Furlough 30 days	CSR
Pitts, William C.	Cpl	G 12th SCVI	Appomattox R., VA	04/03/65	City Pt., VA	04/11/65	Hart's Island, NY	CSR
					Hart's Island, NY	06/16/65	Rlsd. G.O. #109	CSR
Pitts, Young J.H.	Pvt	D 19th SCVI	Chickamauga, GA	11/27/63	USA Hos. Bridgepor	11/30/63	P.M. Nashville, TN	CSR
					Nashville, TN USGH	01/05/64	Nashville, TN P.M.	CSR
					Nashville, TN	01/06/64	Louisville, KY	CSR
					Louisville, KY	01/17/64	Rock Island, IL	CSR
					Rock Island, IL	03/02/65	Tfd. for Xc	CSR
Platt, D.B.	Pvt	I 3rd SCVC	Deserted/enemy	03/06/65	Charleston, SC	03/15/65	Taken oath & disch.	CSR
Platt, D.H.	Pvt	F 6th SCVC	Deserted/enemy	03/06/65	Charleston, SC		Released on oath	CSR
Platt, Harmon B.	Pvt	I 3rd SCVC	Deserted/enemy	03/05/65	Charleston, SC	03/15/65	Taken oath & disch.	CSR
Platt, J.D.	Pvt	C 26th SCVI	Richmond, VA Hos.	04/03/65	Pt. Lookout, MD	07/07/65	Rlsd. G.O. #109	CSR,HMC
Platt, John	Sgt	B 11th SCVI	Deserted/enemy	03/18/65	Charleston, SC	03/18/65	Released on oath	HAG,CSR
Platt, John B.	Pvt	I 3rd SCVC	Deserted/enemy	03/05/65	Charleston, SC	03/01/65	Taken oath & disch.	CSR
Platt, John H.	Pvt	B 11th SCVI	Deserted/enemy	03/18/65	Charleston, SC	03/18/65	Taken oath & disch.	HAG,CSR
Platt, William M.	Pvt	C 5th SCVC	McDaniels House, VA	10/01/64	2nd Cav. Div. Hos.	10/02/64	City Pt., VA USFH	CSR
					City Pt., VA	10/26/64	Died of wounds	P12,ROH,CSR
Platts, D.H.	2Lt	F 3rd SCVC	South Newport, GA	08/17/64	Philadelphia, PA	01/10/65	Ft. Delaware, DE	CSR
					Ft. Delaware, DE	04/13/65	Dschgd. Frm. Hos.	P47
					Ft. Delaware, DE	06/17/65	Rlsd. G.O. #109	P43,P45,P46
Plaxico, James H.	Pvt	C 3rd SCResB	Charlotte, NC	05/13/65	Charlotte, NC	05/13/65	Paroled	CSR
Plaxico, James M.	Pvt	F 17th SCVI	Petersburg, VA	03/25/65	City Pt., VA	03/28/65	Pt. Lookout, MD	CSR
					Pt. Lookout, MD	06/16/65	Rlsd. G.O. #109	P115,CSR
Plaxico, Joseph L.	Pvt	F 17th SCVI	Petersburg, VA	03/25/65	City Pt., VA	03/28/65	Pt. Lookout, MD	CSR
					Pt. Lookout, MD	06/16/65	Rlsd. G.O. #109	P115,CSR
Plaxico, Robert M.	Sgt	A 12th SCVI	Sutherland Stn., VA	04/03/65	City Pt., VA	04/07/65	Hart's Island, NY	CSR
					Hart's Island, NY	06/16/65	Rlsd. G.O. #109	CSR
Player, E.J.	Pvt	K 23rd SCVI	Five Forks, VA	04/01/65	City Pt., VA	04/03/65	Pt. Lookout, MD	CSR
					Pt. Lookout, MD	06/06/65	Rlsd. G.O. #109	CSR

SOUTH CAROLINA SOLDIERS, SAILORS AND  CITIZENS HELD IN U.S. PRISONS 1861-1865

NAME	RANK	REGIMENT	CAPTURED AT	WHEN	PRISON	MOVED	DISPOSITION	SOURCES
Player, H.C.	Pvt	D 13th SCVI	Deserted/enemy	02/24/65	City Pt., VA	02/26/65	Washington, DC	CSR
					Washington, DC	02/27/65	Philadelphia oath	CSR
Plowden, John C.	Pvt	I 25th SCVI	Ft. Fisher, NC	01/15/65	New York, NY	01/30/65	Elmira, NY	CSR,HAG
					Elmira, NY	05/03/65	Died, Ch. Diarrhea	P6,P12,P65,P66,FPH
Plummer, Charles H.	Pvt	E 8th SCVI	Gettysburg, PA	07/05/63	Ft. Delaware, DE	10/05/63	Died, Ch. Diarrhea	P5,P40,P42,P47,CSR
Plummer, James M.	Sgt	B 1st SCVIG	Gettysburg, PA	07/05/63	Chester, PA USGH	09/04/63	Died, 2ndry Hemo.	P1,P12,P6,SA1,CSR
Plummer, John	Sgt	14th SCMil	Lynch's Creek, SC	02/26/65	Hart's Island, NY	06/17/65	Rlsd. G.O. #109	P79
Plummer, M.	Sgt	B 14th SCMil	Lynch's Creek SC	02/26/65	Hart's Island, NY	06/17/65	Rlsd. G.O. #109	P79
Plunkett, John T.	Pvt	H 14th SCVI	Gettysburg, PA	07/03/63	Chester, PA	08/17/63	City Pt., VA Xc	CSR
Plunkett, William B.	Cpl	H 14th SCVI	Gettysburg, PA	07/05/63	Chester, PA	08/17/63	City Pt., VA Xc	CSR
					Williamsburg, VA	08/28/63	Farmville, VA Hos.	CSR
					Farmville, VA	09/07/63	Camp Lee, Richmond	CSR
Plyler, Ellis K.	Pvt	I 12th SCVI	Gettysburg, PA	07/03/63	Ft. McHenry, MD	07/12/63	Ft. Delaware, DE	CSR
					Ft. Delaware, DE	06/10/65	Released	CSR
Plyler, Felt P.	Pvt	A 4th SCVC	Old Church, VA	06/30/64	White House, VA	06/08/64	Pt. Lookout, MD	CSR
					Pt. Lookout, MD	09/18/64	Died, Ch. Diarrhea	P6,P117,P119,FPH
Plyler, G. Harrison	Pvt	E 22nd SCVI	Petersburg, VA	03/25/65	City Pt., VA	03/27/65	Pt. Lookout, MD	CSR
					Pt. Lookout, MD	06/17/65	Rlsd. G.O. #109	P115,P118,CSR
Plyler, Jacob	Pvt	G 3rd SCVABn	High Pt., NC	05/01/65	High Pt., NC	05/01/65	Paroled	CSR
Plyler, Jonas R.	Pvt	I 12th SCVI	S. Anna River, VA	05/23/64	Port Royal, VA	05/30/64	Pt. Lookout, MD	CSR
					Pt. Lookout, MD	06/17/65	Rlsd. G.O. #109	CSR
Plyler, Peter L.	Sgt	B 26th SCVI	Southside RR, VA	04/01/65	City Pt., VA	04/02/65	Pt. Lookout, MD	CSR
					Pt. Lookout, MD	06/16/65	Rlsd. G.O. #109	P115,P119,CSR
Plymale, Jasper	Pvt	K 13th SCVI	Gettysburg, PA	07/05/63	David's Island, NY	10/24/63	Bedloes Island, NY	CSR
					Bedloes Island, NY	12/17/63	Pt. Lookout, MD	CSR
					Pt. Lookout, MD	01/23/64	Joined US Service	CSR
Poag, James M.	Pvt	E 17th SCVI	Maryland	09/30/62	P.M. A.of Potomac	09/30/62	Paroled	CSR
Poag, James M.	Pvt	E 17th SCVI	Deserted/enemy	03/03/65	P.M. A.of Potomac	03/06/65	City Pt., VA P.M.	CSR
					City Pt., VA P.M.	03/07/65	Washington, DC	CSR
					Washington, DC	03/07/65	Chattanooga, TN oath	CSR
Poag, Samuel G.	Cpl	E 17th SCVI	Petersburg, VA	03/25/65	City Pt., VA USFH	04/09/65	Died of wounds	P6,P12,CSR
Poag, W.H.C.	Pvt	E 17th SCVI	Hatchers Run, VA	03/30/65	City Pt., VA	04/01/65	Pt. Lookout, MD	CSR
					Pt. Lookout, MD	06/16/65	Rlsd. G.O. #109	P115,CSR
Pointer, John	Pvt	G 12th SCVI	Sharpsburg, MD	09/17/62	Ft. McHenry, MD	10/17/62	Fts. Monroe, VA Xc	CSR
Pointer, John	Pvt	G 12th SCVI	Deep Bottom, VA	08/16/64	City Pt., VA	08/22/64	Pt. Lookout, MD	CSR
					Pt. Lookout, MD	10/30/64	Venus Pt., GA Xc	CSR
Polan, George	Pvt	E 14th SCMil	Lynch's Creek, SC	03/01/65	New Berne, NC	04/10/65	Hart's Island, NY	CSR
					Hart's Island, NY	06/17/65	Rlsd. G.O. #109	P79,CSR
Poland, Charles W.	Cit	Charleston	Wilmington, NC	01/23/63	Ft. McHenry, MD	05/07/63	Ft. Lafayette	P110
Polatty, James M.	Pvt	C 19th SCVI	Atlanta, GA	07/22/64	Nashville, OH	07/24/64	Louisville, KY	CSR
					Louisville, KY	07/31/64	Camp Chase, OH	CSR
					Camp Chase, OH	12/06/64	Died, Pneumonia	FPH,CSR
Polk, J.C.	Pvt	K 21st SCVI	Ft. Fisher, NC	01/14/65	Elmira, NY	07/07/65	Rlsd. G.O. #109	P65,P66
Polk, Jacob T.	Cpl	K 11th SCVI	Town Creek, NC	02/20/65	Ft. Anderson, NC	02/28/65	Pt. Lookout, MD	CSR,HAG
					Pt. Lookout, MD	06/17/65	Rlsd. G.O. #109	P115,P118,P122,CSR
Polk, James	Pvt	E 21st SCVI	Chesterfield, SC	03/03/65	Hart's Island, NY	06/17/65	Rlsd. G.O. #109	P79,HAG
Polk, James K.	Pvt	C 19th SCVCB	Florence, SC	03/05/65	New Berne, NC	04/06/65	Pt. Lookout, MD	CSR
					Pt. Lookout, MD	06/16/65	Rlsd. G.O. #109	P115,P118,P122,CSR
Polk, John B.	Pvt	D 21st SCVI	Weldon RR, VA	08/21/64	Pt. Lookout, MD	10/11/64	Exchanged	P113,P123,HAG
Polk, Robert	Pvt	E 21st SCVI	Chesterfield, SC	03/03/65	Hart's Island, NY	06/17/65	Rlsd. G.O. #109	P79,HAG
Pollard, B.F.	Pvt	A 3rd SCVABn	High Pt., NC	05/02/65	High Pt., NC	05/02/65	Paroled	CSR

SOUTH CAROLINA SOLDIERS, SAILORS AND **P** CITIZENS HELD IN U.S. PRISONS 1861-1865

NAME	RANK	REGIMENT	CAPTURED AT	WHEN	PRISON	MOVED	DISPOSITION	SOURCES
Pollard, John	Pvt	B 22nd SCVI	Deserted/enemy	10/20/64	City Point, VA	10/22/64	Camp Hamilton, VA	P8,CSR,HOS
					Camp Hamilton, VA	11/12/64	Ogden, IL oath	CSR
Pollard, W.P.	Pvt	A 3rd SCVABn	High Pt., NC	05/02/65	High Pt., NC	05/02/65	Paroled	CSR
Pollard, W.R.	Pvt	K 5th SCVI	Wilderness, VA	05/06/64	Belle Plain, VA	05/21/64	Ft. Delaware, DE	CSR,SA3
					Ft. Delaware, DE	06/07/65	Rlsd. G.O. #109	P41,P42,P45,CSR
					Ft. Delaware, DE	12/15/64	H.12/15/64-1/11/65	P47
Pollard, William	Pvt	B 16th SCVI	Franklin, TN	12/17/64	Nashville, TN	12/18/64	Camp Douglas, IL	CSR,16R
					Louisville, KY	12/20/64	Camp Douglas, IL	P90,P91,P94,CSR
					Camp Douglas, IL	03/26/65	Jd. US 6th Vol.I.	P55,CSR
Polson, Alex	Pvt	G 23rd SCVI	Black Creek, SC	03/01/65	17th Army Corps US	03/08/65	Paroled	CSR
Polson, James H.	Pvt	D 21st SCVI	Morris Island, SC	07/10/63	Ft. Columbus, NY	09/23/63	Took the oath	P1,HAG
					Pt. Lookout, MD	01/09/64	Died, Dysentery	P5,P113,P116,FPH
Polson, John	Pvt	E 21st SCVI	Chesterfield, SC	02/28/65	Pt. Lookout, MD	06/17/65	Rlsd. G.O. #109	P115,P118,P122,HAG
Ponder, George B.	Pvt	I 4th SCVI	Williamsport, MD	09/15/62	Ft. Delaware, DE	10/02/62	Aikens Ldg., VA Xc	CSR
Ponder, George R.	Pvt	H 6th SCVC	White House, VA	06/21/64	Fts. Monroe, VA	06/26/64	Pt. Lookout, MD	CSR
					Pt. Lookout, MD	08/08/64	Elmira, NY	P113,P117,CSR
					Elmira, NY	07/03/65	Rlsd. G.O. #109	P65,P66,CSR
Pool, Ephraim M.	Pvt	G 22nd SCVI	Kinston, NC	12/14/65	Kinston, NC	12/14/65	Paroled POW	CSR
Pool, H.P.	Pvt	A 3rd SCVABn	High Pt., NC	05/02/65	High Pt., NC	05/02/65	Paroled	CSR
Pool, I.P.	Pvt	B 2nd SCVIRi	Knoxville, TN	12/05/63	Knoxville, TN	12/18/63	Knoxville, TN USGH	P84,CSR
					Knoxville, TN USGH	12/24/64	Died, Typhoid	P1,P5,CSR
Pool, J.C.	3Lt	C 14th SCVI	Gettysburg, PA	07/04/63	US Field Hospital	07/14/63	US General Hospital	CSR
					US General Hospital	07/16/63	Died of wounds	CSR
Pool, M.B.	Pvt	E 5th SCBI	Boonesboro, MD	09/15/62	Ft. Delaware, DE	10/02/62	Aikens Ldg., VA Xc	CSR
Pool, Martin S.	Pvt	E 5th SCBI	Boonesboro, MD	09/15/62	Ft. Delaware, DE	10/02/62	Aikens Ldg., VA Xc	CSR,SA3
Pool, Martin S.	Pvt	E 5th SCVI	Lookout Valley, TN	10/28/63	Chattanooga, TN	10/29/63	Nashville, TN	CSR
					Nashville, TN	11/07/63	Louisville, KY	P39,CSR
					Louisville, KY	11/09/63	Camp Morton, IN	P88,CSR
					Camp Morton, IN	02/26/65	Tfd. for Xc	P7,P100,P101
					Camp Morton, IN	05/10/65	Rlsd. on oath	CSR
Pool, Robert J.	Sgt	D Orr's Ri	Petersburg, VA	04/02/65	City Pt., VA	04/04/65	Pt. Lookout, MD	CSR
					Pt. Lookout, MD	06/17/65	Rlsd. G.O. #109	CSR
Pool, Walter	Pvt	K 13th SCVI	Deserted/enemy	03/23/65	P.M. 6th A.C.	03/23/65	City Pt., VA P.M.	CSR
					City Pt., VA	03/27/65	Washington, DC	CSR
					Washington, DC	03/29/65	Springfield, IL	CSR
Pool, William M.	Pvt	B 15th SCVI	Halltown, VA	08/26/64	Harpers Ferry, WV	08/29/64	Camp Chase, OH	CSR,KEB,H15
					Camp Chase, OH	03/18/85	Pt. Lookout, MD	P22,P26,CSR
					Pt. Lookout, MD	03/27/65	Boulware's Wh., VA	CSR
Poole, Franklin S.	Cpl	D 27th SCVI	Town Creek, NC	02/20/65	Ft. Anderson, NC	02/28/65	Pt. Lookout, MD	CSR,HAG
					Pt. Lookout, MD	06/30/65	Rlsd. G.O. #109	P115,P118,P121,CSR
Poole, G.B.	Pvt	H 1st SCVIH	Farmville, VA	04/11/65	Farmville, VA	04/21/65	Paroled	CSR
Poole, J.T.	Pvt	A 3rd SCVABn	High Pt., NC	07/02/64	High Pt., NC	05/02/65	Paroled	CSR
Poole, J.W.F.	Pvt	E Orr's Ri.	Petersburg, VA	04/03/65	City Pt., VA	04/11/65	Hart's Island, NY	P79,CDC,CSR
					Hart's Island, NY	06/16/65	Rlsd. G.O. #109	P79,CSR
Poole, John	Pvt	A 3rd SCVCBn	Deserted/enemy	02/25/65	Hilton Head, SC	04/07/65	P.M. New York, NY	CSR
Poole, William D.D.	Pvt	I 5th SCVI	Campbell Stn., TN	11/16/64	Knoxville, TN	02/11/64	Hospital	P84,SA3
Poole, William D.D.	Sgt	I 5th SCVI	Campbell Stn., TN	11/16/63	Chattanooga, TN Hos.	11/28/64	Nashville, TN	CSR
					Nashville, TN	12/06/64	Louisville, KY	P3,CSR
					Louisville, KY	12/08/64	Camp Douglas, IL	P3,P90,P91,P94,CSR
					Camp Douglas, IL	02/24/65	Died, Remitnt. fever	P6,P12,P58,FPH,CSR
Poole, William G	Pvt	D 17th SCVI	Petersburg, VA	03/25/65	City Pt., VA	03/28/65	Pt. Lookout, MD	CSR
					Pt. Lookout, MD	06/30/65	Rlsd. G.O. #109	P115,CSR

SOUTH CAROLINA SOLDIERS, SAILORS AND  CITIZENS HELD IN U.S. PRISONS 1861-1865

NAME	RANK	REGIMENT	CAPTURED AT	WHEN	PRISON	MOVED	DISPOSITION	SOURCES
Poor, J.J.	Cpl	K Orr's Ri.	Spotsylvania, VA	05/12/64	Belle Plain, VA	05/20/64	Ft. Delaware, DE	CSR
					Ft. Delaware, DE		Hos. 9/17-10/15/64	P47
					Ft. Delaware, DE	06/10/65	Released	P41,P42,CSR
Poor, John W.	Pvt	G 1st SCVA	Bentonville, NC	03/22/65	New Berne, NC	04/10/65	Hart's Island, NY	CSR
					Hart's Island, NY	06/18/65	Died Ch. Diarrhea	P6,P12,P79,FPH,CSR
Pooser, Elisha W.	Sgt	I 27th SCVI	Town Creek, NC	02/20/65	Ft. Anderson, NC	02/28/65	Pt. Lookout, MD	CSR,HAG
					Pt. Lookout, MD	06/17/65	Rlsd. G.O. #109	P115,P118,P122
Pooser, Emanuel L.	Pvt	F 15th SCMil	Lynch's Creek, SC		New Berne, NC USGH	04/30/65	Died, Piles	P1,P6,P12
Poovey, Duncan M.	Pvt	K 17th SCVI	Five Forks, VA	04/01/65	City Pt., VA	04/06/65	Pt. Lookout, MD	CSR
					Pt. Lookout, MD	06/16/65	Rlsd. G.O. #109	P115,CSR
Poovey, William P.	Pvt	K 17th SCVI	Five Forks, VA	04/01/65	City Pt., VA	04/06/65	Pt. Lookout, MD	CSR
					Pt. Lookout, MD	06/16/65	Rlsd. G.O. #109	P115,CSR
Pope, David E.	Cpl	I Hol.Leg.	Stony Creek, VA	05/07/64	Fts. Monroe, VA	05/13/64	Pt. Lookout, MD	CSR
					Pt. Lookout, MD	08/13/64	Elmira, NY	P113,P116,P120,CSR
					Elmira, NY	10/11/64	Pt. Lookout, MD Xc	P65,P66,CSR
					W.Bldg. Balt, MD	10/13/64	(Dead on arrival)	P1,P5,P10,FPH,CSR
Pope, Elijah L.	Pvt	F 13th SCVI	Deserted/enemy	02/24/65	City Pt., VA	02/26/65	Washington, DC	CSR,HOS
					Washington, DC	02/27/65	Springfield, IL	CSR
Pope, Iranus	Pvt	I 6th SCVI	Richmond, VA Hos.	04/03/65	Libby Prison Rchmd.	04/08/65	City Pt., VA P.M.	CSR
					City Pt., VA	04/14/65	Pt. Lookout, MD	CSR,HHC
					Pt. Lookout, MD	06/16/65	Rlsd. G.O. #109	P115,P119,P122,CSR
Pope, John	Pvt	F 22nd SCVI	Petersburg, VA	04/01/65	City Pt., VA	04/05/65	Pt. Lookout, MD	CSR
					Pt. Lookout, MD	06/16/65	Rlsd. G.O. #109	P115
Pope, Thomas W.	Pvt	E 2nd SCVI	Morristown, TN	01/11/64	Nashville, TN	01/24/64	Louisville, KY	P39,KEB,SA2,H2
					Louisville, KY	01/27/64	Rock Island, IL	P88,P92,CSR
					Rock Island, IL	05/03/65	New Orleans Xc	P131,CSR
					New Orleans, LA	05/23/65	Released	P3
Porcher, A.M.	Pvt	B 7th SCVC	Old Church, VA	06/30/64	White House, VA	06/08/64	Pt. Lookout, MD	CSR
					Pt. Lookout, MD	10/30/64	Aikens Ldg., VA Xc	P113,P117,CSR
Pore, J.G.	Pvt	A 4th SCVC	Stony Creek, VA	12/01/64	City Pt., VA	12/05/64	Pt. Lookout, MD	CSR,CDC
					Pt. Lookout, MD	06/16/65	Rlsd. G.O. #109	P115,P118,P122,CSR
Port, L.C.	Pvt	D 10th SCVI	Chaplin Hills, KY	10/05/62	Harrodsburg, KY US	11/13/62	Died	CSR
Porte, Jehu	Pvt	D 10th SCVI	Resaca, GA	05/01/64	Camp Douglas, IL	06/16/65	Rlsd. G.O. #109	P55,CSR
Porter, Carter C.	Pvt	Ferguson's LA	Salisbury, NC	04/12/65	Nashville, TN	04/29/65	Louisville, KY	CSR
					Louisville, KY	05/02/65	Camp Chase, OH	P92,CSR
					Camp Chase, OH	06/13/65	Rlsd. G.O. #109	P23,CSR
Porter, J.M.	Pvt	K 1st SCVC	Upperville, VA	06/21/63	Ft. McHenry, MD	06/25/63	City Pt., VA Xc	P110,CSR
Porter, J.T.	Pvt	F 22nd SCVI	Farmville, VA	04/06/65	City Pt., VA	04/14/65	Newport News, VA	CSR
					Newport News, VA	06/26/65	Rlsd. G.O. #109	P107,CSR
Porter, James W.	Pvt	H 19th SCVI	Munfordville, KY	09/15/62	Munfordville, KY	09/15/62	Paroled	CSR
Porter, James W.	Pvt	H 19th SCVI	Franklin, TN	12/17/64	Nashville, TN	01/04/65	Louisville, KY	CSR
					Louisville, KY	01/09/65	Camp Chase, OH	CSR
Porter, James W.	Pvt	H 19th SCVI	Franklin, TN	12/17/64	Camp Chase, OH	04/09/65	Died	CSR,P6,P12,P23,FPH
Porter, James W.	Pvt	I 12th SCVI	Richmond, VA	04/03/65	Richmond, VA	05/02/65	Pt. Lookout, MD	CSR
					Pt. Lookout, MD	06/26/65	Rlsd. G.O. #109	CSR
Porter, Joseph H.	Pvt	D 27th SCVI	Town Creek, NC	02/20/65	Ft. Anderson, NC	02/28/65	Pt. Lookout, MD	CSR,HAG
Porter, Joseph H.	Cpl	D 27th SCVI	Town Creek, NC	02/20/65	Pt. Lookout, MD	06/17/65	Rlsd. G.O. #109	P115,P118,CSR
Porter, N.	Pvt	I Ham.Leg.Ml	Augusta, GA	05/25/65	Augusta, GA	05/25/65	Paroled	CSR
Porter, Patrick	Pvt	B Wash'n LA	Raleigh, NC	04/22/65	Raleigh, NC	04/22/65	Paroled	CSR
Porter, Perry W.	Pvt	Ferguson's LA	Nashville, TN	12/16/64	Nashville, TN	12/19/64	Louisville, KY	CSR
					Louisville, KY	12/21/64	Camp Douglas, IL	P94,CSR
					Camp Douglas, IL	06/22/65	Rlsd. G.O. #109	P55,CSR

SOUTH CAROLINA SOLDIERS, SAILORS AND  CITIZENS HELD IN U.S. PRISONS 1861-1865

NAME	RANK	REGIMENT	CAPTURED AT	WHEN	PRISON	MOVED	DISPOSITION	SOURCES
Porter, Samuel	Cpl	F 18th SCVI	Petersburg, VA	07/30/64	City Pt., VA	08/05/64	Pt. Lookout, MD	CSR
					Pt. Lookout, MD	08/08/64	Elmira, NY	CSR
					Elmira, NY	07/03/65	Rlsd. G.O. #109	CSR
Porter, Walter S.	Cpl	A 10th SCVI	Lafayette, GA	12/12/63	Nashville, TN	12/18/63	Louisville, KY	CSR,RAS
					Louisville, KY	12/21/63	Rock Island, IL	P88,P89,P93,CSR
					Rock Island, IL	05/22/65	Rlsd. Instr. 5/9/65	CSR
Porter, William C.	Pvt	Ferguson's	Salisbury, NC	04/12/65	Nashville, TN	04/29/65	Louisville, KY	CSR
					Louisville, KY	05/02/65	Camp Chase, OH	P92,P95,CSR
					Camp Chase, OH	06/13/65	Rlsd. G.O. #109	P23,CSR
Posey, B.M.	Pvt	I 22nd SCVI	Farmville, VA	04/06/65	City Pt., VA	04/14/65	Newport News, VA	CSR
					Newport News, VA	06/26/65	Rlsd. G.O. #109	P107,CSR
Posey, M.A.	Pvt	I 22nd SCVI	Williamsport, MD	09/15/62	Ft. Delaware, DE	10/12/62	Aikens Ldg., VA Xc	CSR
Posey, Marshal	Pvt	K 19th SCVI	Augusta, GA	05/20/65	Augusta, GA	05/20/65	Paroled	CSR
Posey, William N.	Pvt	E 2nd SCVIRi	Shell Mound, TN	10/28/63	Bridgeport, AL G.H	11/11/63	Died of wounds	P2,P6,P12
Posey, William Newton	Pvt	E Ham.Leg.	Lookout Valley, TN	10/28/63	Bridgeport, AL USF	11/11/63	Died of wounds	CSR
Postell, Daniel	Pvt	C 5th SCVC	Deserted/enemy	02/18/65	Charleston, SC	03/11/65	Released on oath	CSR
Postell, George	Pvt	C 5th SCVC	Deserted/enemy	02/18/65	Charleston, SC	03/11/65	Released on oath	CSR
Postell, Willis	Pvt	C 5th SCVC	Deserted/enemy	02/18/65	Charleston, SC	03/11/65	Released on oath	CSR
Poston, Andrew	1Lt	I 10th SCVI	Kentucky	09/15/62	Kentucky	11/15/62	Paroled	CSR
Poston, Ezra	Pvt	G 26th SCVI	Five Forks, VA	04/01/65	City Pt., VA	04/05/65	Pt. Lookout, MD	CSR
					Pt. Lookout, MD	06/16/65	Rlsd. G.O. #109	P115,P119,CSR
Poston, H.A.	Pvt	G 15th SCVI	South Mtn., MD	09/14/62	Ft. Delaware, DE	10/02/62	Aikens Ldg., VA Xc	CSR
Poston, Hugh	Pvt	H 1st SCVIR	Cheraw, SC	03/05/65	Cheraw, SC	03/05/65	Paroled	CSR
Poston, Simon	Pvt	McQueen LA	Farmville, VA	04/11/65	Farmville, VA	04/21/65	Paroled	CSR
Potter, Abraham	Pvt	E 13th SCVI	Deserted/enemy	02/24/65	City Pt., VA	02/26/65	Washington, DC	CSR,HOS
					Washington, DC	02/27/65	Springfield, IL	CSR
Potter, Charles	Pvt	I 1st SCVA	Deserted/enemy	02/18/65	Charleston, SC		Released on oath	CSR
Potter, Doctor	Pvt	E 13th SCVI	Deserted/enemy	02/24/65	City Pt., VA	02/26/65	Washington, DC	CSR,HOS
					Washington, DC	02/27/65	Springfield, IL	CSR
Potter, Ephraim	Pvt	E 13th SCVI	Richmond VA Hosp.	04/03/65	Richmond, VA P.M.	04/26/65	Paroled	CSR
Potter, John R.	Pvt	M P.S.S.	Darbytown Rd., VA	10/07/64	Bermuda Hundred, VA	10/21/64	City Pt., VA	CSR,TSE
					City Pt., VA	10/29/64	Pt. Lookout, MD	CSR
					Pt. Lookout, MD	02/18/65	Boulware's Wh., VA	CSR
Potter, Solomon L.	Pvt	G 2nd SCVC	Culpepper, VA	09/13/63	Old Capitol, DC	09/26/63	Pt. Lookout, MD	CSR
					Ft. McHenry, MD	09/26/63	Pt. Lookout, MD	P110
					Pt. Lookout, MD	01/24/64	Joined U.S. Army	P113,P125,CSR
					Pt. Lookout, MD	05/24/64	Released	P116
Potter, T.B.	Pvt	D 22nd SCVI	Kinston, NC	12/15/62	Kinston, NC	12/15/62	Paroled POW	CSR
Potts, Milton	Pvt	H 22nd SCVI	Kinston, NC	12/15/62	Kinston, NC	12/15/62	Paroled POW	CSR
Pouncey, James A.	Pvt	G 15th SCVI	Lawrence Mills, TN	12/25/63	Nashville, TN	01/17/64	Louisville, KY	P39,KEB,CSR
					Louisville, KY	01/23/64	Rock Island, IL	P88,P91,P93,CSR
					Rock Island, IL	02/25/64	Tfd. to Xc	CSR
					Unknown Trsfer Pt.	03/05/65	Boulware's Wh. Xc	CSR
Pound, James H.	Pvt	A 2nd SCVC	Lexington, SC	02/14/65	New Berne, NC	03/30/65	Pt. Lookout, MD	CSR
					Pt. Lookout, MD	06/06/65	Rlsd. Instr. 5/30/65	P115,P121
Powe, Ellerbe F.	Pvt	D 21st SCVI	Ft. Fisher, NC	01/15/65	Elmira, NY	07/07/65	Rlsd. G.O. #109	P65,HAG
Powe, James F.	Pvt	D 21st SCVI	Ft. Fisher, NC	01/15/65	Elmira, NY	05/15/65	Died, Pneumonia	P6,P12,P65,FPH,HAG
Powe, Joseph E.	Cpl	D 21st SCVI	Ft. Fisher, NC	01/15/65	Elmira, NY	03/08/65	Died, Pneumonia	P65,P66,HAG
Powe, N.	Pvt	D 21st SCVI	Weldon RR, VA	08/21/64	Pt. Lookout, MD	11/01/64	Aikens Ldg., VA Xc	P121
Powe, Thomas E.	Cpt	C 8th SCVI	Gettysburg, PA		Letterman G.H. Gbg		Provost Marshal	P1,KEB

SOUTH CAROLINA SOLDIERS, SAILORS AND  CITIZENS HELD IN U.S. PRISONS 1861-1865

NAME	RANK	REGIMENT	CAPTURED AT	WHEN	PRISON	MOVED	DISPOSITION	SOURCES
Powell, A. Edgar	QSg	C 1st SCVIG	Gettysburg, PA	07/05/63	Ft. Delaware, DE	02/05/64	Dis. Hos. 2/5/64	P47,SA1
					Ft. Delaware, DE	06/27/64	Hos. 6/27-7/1/64	P47
					Ft. Delaware, DE	09/30/64	Aikens Ldg., VA Xc	P40,P42,P44,CSR
Powell, A. Lewis	Pvt	C 22nd SCVI	Crater, Pbg., VA	07/30/64	Pt. Lookout, MD	08/08/64	Elmira, NY	P117,P120,P223,CSR
					Elmira, NY	08/14/64	Died, Pneumonia	P5,P65,P66,FPH,CSR
Powell, C.	Pvt	H 25th SCVI	Ft. Fisher, NC	01/15/65	New York, NY	01/30/65	Elmira, NY	CSR,HAG
					Elmira, NY	03/02/65	James R., VA Xc	P65,P66,CSR
Powell, C.F.	Pvt	C 22nd SCVI	Petersburg, VA	06/16/64	Elmira, NY	03/10/65	Pt. Lookout, MD Xc	P66
Powell, Corma	Pvt	C 1st SCVIR	Deserted/enemy		Louisville, KY	10/15/64	DTE, sent north	P90,P92,SA1,CSR
Powell, David	Pvt	H 25th SCVI	Ft. Fisher, NC	01/15/65	New York, NY	01/30/65	Elmira, NY	CSR,HAG
					Elmira, NY	02/20/65	James R., VA Xc	P65,P66,CSR
Powell, E.	Pvt	H 25th SCVI	Ft. Fisher, NC	01/15/65	New York, NY	01/30/65	Elmira, NY	CSR,HAG
					Elmira, NY	06/23/65	Died, Lung Inflam.	P6,P12,P65,P66,FPH
Powell, Foster	Pvt	H Orr's Ri.	Gettysburg, PA	07/05/63	Ft. McHenry, MD	07/11/63	Ft. Delaware, DE	CDC,CSR
					Ft. Delaware, DE	08/30/63	Joined US service	P40,P42,P44,CSR
Powell, Freeman	Pvt	D 6th SCVI	Augusta, GA	06/06/65	Augusta, GA	06/06/65	Paroled	CSR
Powell, J.	Pvt	E 6th SCResB	Augusta, GA	05/19/65	Augusta, GA	05/19/65	Paroled	CSR
Powell, J. Addison	Pvt	I 3rd SCVI	N. Anna River, VA	05/23/64	Port Royal, VA	05/30/64	Pt. Lookout, MD	CSR,KEB,SA2,H3
					Pt. Lookout, MD	08/13/64	Died, Scurvy	P5,P117,P119,FPH
Powell, James M.	Pvt	C 26th SCVI	Five Forks, VA	04/01/65	Pt. Lookout, MD	06/16/65	Rlsd. G.O. #109	P115,P119,HMC
Powell, James T.	Pvt	I 1st SCVA	Grants Mills, SC	03/07/65	New Berne, NC	04/10/65	Hart's Island, NY	CSR
					Hart's Island, NY	06/16/65	Rlsd. G.O. #109	P79,CSR
Powell, Joseph	Pvt	E 1st SCVA	Deserted/enemy	07/25/64	Hilton Head, SC	08/18/64	New York, NY oath	CSR
Powell, Joseph W.	Pvt	G 6th SCVI	Seven Pines, VA	05/31/62	Fts. Monroe, VA US	08/31/62	Aikens Ldg., VA Xc	CSR
Powell, M.M.	Pvt	C 26th SCVI	Five Forks, VA	04/01/65	City Pt., VA	04/05/65	Pt. Lookout, MD	CSR
					Pt. Lookout, MD	06/16/65	Rlsd. G.O. #109	CSR
Powell, R.U.	Pvt	E Orr's Ri.	Petersburg, VA	04/03/65	City Pt., VA	04/11/65	Hart's Island, NY	CSR
					Hart's Island, NY	06/16/65	Rlsd. G.O. #109	P79,CSR
Powell, Richard T.	Cpt	A 8th SCVI	Winchester, VA	09/13/64	Harpers Ferry, WV	09/24/64	Johnson's Isl., OH	CSR,KEB
					Johnson's Isl., OH	06/16/65	Rlsd. G.O. #109	P81,P83,CSR
Powell, Samuel C.	Pvt	3 10/19 SCVI	Missionary Ridge, TN	11/25/63	Nashville, TN	12/07/63	Louisville, KY	P39,RAS,CSR
					Louisville, KY	12/07/63	Rock Island, IL	P88,P89,CSR
					Rock Island, IL	02/25/65	Pt. Lookout, MD Xc	P131,CSR
Powell, T.J.	1Lt	B 15th SCVI	Halltown, VA	08/26/64	Harpers Ferry, WV	08/30/64	Ft. Delaware DE	CSR
					Ft. Delaware, DE	06/17/65	Rlsd. G.O. #109	P43,R47,CSR
Powell, Thomas	Pvt	C 11th SCVI	Petersburg, VA	06/16/64	Bermuda Hundred, VA	06/17/64	Fts. Monroe, VA	CSR,HAG
					Fts. Monroe, VA	06/18/64	Pt. Lookout, MD	CSR
					Pt. Lookout, MD	07/09/64	Elmira, NY	P113,P117,P120,CSR
					Elmira, NY	03/10/65	Tfd. for exchange	CSR
Powell, Thomas S.	Pvt	E 15th SCVAB	Fayetteville, NC	03/13/65	New Berne, NC	04/10/65	Hart's Island, NY	CSR
					Hart's Island, NY	06/17/65	Rlsd. G.O. #109	P79,CSR
Powell, Thomas W.	Pvt	C 26th SCVI	Five Forks, VA	04/01/65	City Pt., VA	04/05/65	Pt. Lookout, MD	CSR
					Pt. Lookout, MD	06/16/65	Rlsd. G.O. #109	P115,P119,P122,CSR
Powell, W.L.	Pvt	G Ham.Leg.MI	Farmville, VA	04/11/65	Farmville, VA	04/11/65	Paroled	CSR
Powell, William	Pvt	1st SCVIG	Deserted/enemy		Washington, DC PM	04/13/65	New York, NY oath	CSR
Powell, William H.	Pvt	I 3rd SCVI	Sharpsburg, MD	09/17/62	Frederick, MD USGH	05/02/63	Died of wounds	P1,P6,FPH,SA2,H3
Powell, William T.	Pvt	Ch'fld LA	Lynchburg, VA	04/13/65	Lynchburg, VA	04/13/65	Paroled	CSR
Powell, William W.	Pvt	C 26th SCVI	Five Forks, VA	04/01/65	City Pt., VA	04/05/65	Pt. Lookout, MD	CSR
					Pt. Lookout, MD	06/16/65	Rlsd. G.O. #109	P115,P119,CSR
Power, James M.	Pvt	E 14th SCVI	Boonesboro, MD	09/14/62	Ft. Delaware, DE	11/10/62	Aikens Ldg., VA Xc	CSR

SOUTH CAROLINA SOLDIERS, SAILORS AND **P** CITIZENS HELD IN U.S. PRISONS 1861-1865

NAME	RANK	REGIMENT	CAPTURED AT	WHEN	PRISON	MOVED	DISPOSITION	SOURCES
Power, James W.	Pvt	A Orr's Ri.	Spotsylvania, VA	05/12/64	Belle Plain, VA	05/21/64	Ft. Delaware, DE	CSR
					Ft. Delaware, DE		Hos. 11/14-12/5/64	P47
					Ft. Delaware, DE	06/10/65	Rlsd. G.O. #109	P41,P42,P45,CSR
Powers, A.W.	Pvt	B 1st SCVA	Bentonville, NC	03/19/65	Pt. Lookout, MD	06/14/65	Rlsd. G.O. #109	P115
Powers, Allen	Pvt	L 1st SCVIG	Southside RR, VA	04/03/65	City Pt., VA	04/07/65	Hart's Island, NY	CSR,SA1
					Hart's Island, NY	06/16/65	Rlsd. G.O. #109	P79,CSR
Powers, Barfield	Pvt	A 21st SCVI	James Island, SC	06/14/62	Hilton Head, SC	08/14/62	Ft. Columbus, NY	CSR,HAG
					Ft. Columbus, NY	08/23/62	Ft. Delaware, DE	P37,CSR
					Ft. Delaware, DE	10/02/62	Aikens Ldg., VA Xc	CSR
Powers, George	Pvt	G 27th SCVI	Petersburg, VA	06/24/64	Bermuda Hundred, VA	06/25/64	Fts. Monroe, VA	CSR
					Fts. Monroe, VA	06/26/64	Pt. Lookout, MD	CSR,HAG
					Pt. Lookout, MD	08/16/64	Elmira, NY	P113,P117,P120,CSR
					Elmira, NY	04/12/65	Died, Ch. Diarrhea	P6,P65,P66,FPH,CSR
Powers, J.A.	Pvt	I 15th SCVI	Sharpsburg, MD	09/17/62	Frederick, MD USGH	10/10/62	Died, Typhoid	P1,P6,P12,CSR
Powers, James J.	Pvt	A 21st SCVI	Petersburg, VA	06/24/64	Fts. Monroe, VA	06/26/64	Pt. Lookout, MD	CSR,HAG
					Pt. Lookout, MD	01/27/65	U.S. Gen. Hospital	P115,P121
					Pt. Lookout, MD	06/05/65	Rlsd. per Instr.	P121,P122
Powers, Kincher T.	Pvt	B 1st SCVA	Bentonville, NC	03/19/65	Pt. Lookout, MD			P118
Powers, L.F.	Pvt	B 1st SCVA	Bentonville, NC	03/19/65	Pt. Lookout, MD	06/16/65	Rlsd. G.O. #109	P115
Powers, Lawrence	Pvt	B 7th SCVIBn	Drury's Bluff, VA	05/16/64	Bermuda Hundred, VA	05/17/64	Fts. Monroe, VA	CSR,HAG
					Fts. Monroe, VA	05/19/64	Pt. Lookout, MD	CSR
					Pt. Lookout, MD	08/15/64	Elmira, NY	P113,P117,P120,CSR
					Elmira, NY	02/20/65	James R., VA Xc	P65,P66,CSR
					Richmond, VA Hos.	03/24/65	Furloughed 60 days	CSR
Powers, Levi B.	Pvt	A 21st SCVI	Petersburg, VA	06/24/64	Bermuda Hundred, VA	06/25/64	Fts. Monroe, VA	CSR
					Fts. Monroe, VA	06/26/64	Pt. Lookout, MD	CSR
					Pt. Lookout, MD	08/16/64	Elmira, NY	P113,P117,P120,HAG,CSR
					Elmira, NY	07/11/65	Rlsd. G.O. #109	P65,P66,CSR
Powers, N.W.	Pvt	B 1st SCVA	Bentonville, NC	03/19/65	Pt. Lookout, MD			P118
Powers, Nathaniel	Pvt	I 1st SCVC	Deserted/enemy	03/06/65	Charleston, SC	03/06/65	Released on oath	CSR
Powers, Tilman B.	Pvt	A Orr's Ri.	Falling Waters, MD	07/14/63	Old Capitol, DC	08/08/63	Pt. Lookout, MD	CSR
					Ft. McHenry, MD	08/08/63	Pt. Lookout, MD	P110
					Pt. Lookout, MD	03/03/64	City Pt., VA Xc	P113,P116,P123,CDC,CSR
					Hart's Island, NY	05/17/65	Died, Ch. Diarrhea	P6,P79,FPH
Powers, W.S.	Pvt	I 1st SCVA	Mills Creek, NC	03/19/65	Pt. Lookout, MD			P118
Powers, William C.	Sgt	E 14th SCVI	Sutherland Stn., VA	04/03/65	City Pt., VA	04/13/65	Pt. Lookout, MD	CSR
					Pt. Lookout, MD	06/08/65	Rlsd. on sick list	CSR
Powers, Winston W.	Pvt	H 22nd SCVI	Petersburg, VA	04/02/65	Pt. Lookout, MD	06/16/65	Rlsd. G.O. #109	P115
Pownell, John W.	Pvt	E 1st SCVA	Deserted/enemy		Hilton Head, SC	01/17/65	New York, NY oath	CSR
Prall, Thomas	Pvt	LafayetteA	Deserted/enemy	03/24/65	Savannah, GA	03/24/65	Released on oath	CSR
Prater, Presley M.	Pvt	D 14th SCVI	Petersburg, VA	07/29/64	City Pt., VA	08/05/64	Pt. Lookout, MD	CSR
					Pt. Lookout, MD	08/08/64	Elmira, NY	CSR
					Elmira, NY	12/18/64	Died, Typhoid pneum.	CSR
Prater, W.D.	Pvt	B 14th SCVI	Augusta, GA	05/23/65	Augusta, GA	05/23/65	Paroled	CSR
Prather, Holly W.	Pvt	A 13th SCVI	Gettysburg, PA	07/05/63	Ft. McHenry, MD	07/12/63	Ft. Delaware, DE	CSR
					Ft. Delaware, DE	07/31/63	Exchanged	CSR
Prather, Thomas Y.	Pvt	A 13th SCVI	Spotsylvania C.H.	05/13/64	Belle Plain, VA	03/20/64	Ft. Delaware, DE	CSR
Prather, Thomas Y.	Pvt	A 13th SCVI	Spotsylvania, VA	05/13/64	Ft. Delaware, DE	09/14/64	Aikens Ldg., VA Xc	CSR
Pratt, Robert R.	Pvt	G Hol.Leg.	Dinwiddie C.H. VA	04/01/65	US 5th AC Hos.	04/03/65	City Pt., VA	CSR
					City Pt., VA	04/08/65	Hart's Island, NY	CSR
					Hart's Island, NY	06/17/65	Rlsd. G.O. #109	P79,CSR

SOUTH CAROLINA SOLDIERS, SAILORS AND  CITIZENS HELD IN U.S. PRISONS 1861-1865

NAME	RANK	REGIMENT	CAPTURED AT	WHEN	PRISON	MOVED	DISPOSITION	SOURCES
Preacher, William E.	Pvt	E 24th SCVI	Nashville, TN	12/16/64	Nashville, TN	01/02/65	Louisville, KY	CSR
					Louisville, KY	01/03/65	Camp Douglas, IL	P92,P94,CSR
					Camp Chase, OH	02/17/65	Died, Variola	P6,P23,P27,FPH,CSR
Prentis, F.J.	Sgt	A Orr's Ri	Gettysburg, PA		David's Island, NY	07/28/63	Died	P1
Prentis, William F.	Pvt	G 3rd SCVC	Gillisonville, SC	12/30/64	Hilton Head, SC	02/01/65	Pt. Lookout, MD	CSR
					Pt. Lookout, MD	06/16/65	Rlsd. G.O. #109	P115,P122,CSR
Presley, C.A.	Cpl	B 18th SCVI	Farmville, VA	04/02/65	City Pt., VA	04/14/65	Newport News, VA	CSR
					Newport News, VA	06/28/65	Rlsd. G.O. #109	CSR
Presley, Ira	Sgt	F 23rd SCVI	Petersburg, VA	04/02/65	City Pt., VA	04/07/65	Pt. Lookout, MD	CSR
					Pt. Lookout, MD	07/17/65	Rlsd. G.O. #109	P114,P118,CSR
Pressley, Hugh M.	Pvt	C 25th SCVI	Ft. Fisher, NC	01/15/65	New York, VA	01/30/65	Elmira, NY	CSR,HAG,CTA
					Elmira, NY	03/02/65	James R., VA Xc	P65,P66,CSR
Preston, John F.	2Lt	H 27th SCVI	Town Creek, NC	02/20/65	Ft. Anderson, NC	02/28/65	Pt. Lookout, MD	CSR,HAG
					Pt. Lookout, MD	02/28/65	Washington, DC	P115,P117,P120
					Ft. McHenry, MD	03/21/65	Ft. Delaware, DE	P110
					Ft. Delaware, DE	06/17/65	Rlsd. G.O. #109	P43,P45,CSR
Preston, W.	Pvt	2nd SCVI	Gettysburg, PA	07/03/63	Ft. Delaware, DE			P40,P44,CSR
Prevost, Clarence	Pvt	A 25th SCVI	Ft. Fisher, NC	01/15/65	New York, NY	01/30/65	Elmira, NY	CSR,HAG
					Elmira, NY	06/19/65	Rlsd. G.O. #109	P65,P66,CSR
Prevost, J.W.	Cpl	D 5th SCVC	Stony Creek, VA	12/01/64	City Pt., VA	12/05/64	Pt. Lookout, MD	CSR,CDC
					Pt. Lookout, MD	06/17/65	Rlsd. G.O. #109	P115,P118,P122,CSR
Prewitt, Edwin	Pvt	E 18th SCVI	Appomattox CH., VA	04/09/65	Lincoln G.H., DC	08/07/65	Rlsd. G.O. #109	CSR
Prewitt, Talliafero	Pvt	D 1st SCVIR	Averysboro, NC	03/24/65	New Berne, NC	04/10/65	Hart's Islalnd, NY	CSR,SA1
					Hart's Island, NY	06/16/65	Rlsd. G.O. #109	P79,CSR
Price, Alexander	Pvt	F 1st SCVIG	Petersburg, VA	04/02/65	City Pt., VA	04/04/65	Pt. Lookout, MD	CSR,SA1
					Pt. Lookout, MD	06/16/65	Rlsd. G.O. #109	P115,P118,CSR
Price, Calvin	Pvt	K 13th SCVI	Petersburg, VA	04/02/65	City Pt., VA	04/04/65	Ft. Delaware, DE	CSR
					Ft. Delaware, DE	06/10/65	Rlsd. on oath	CSR
Price, Daniel	Pvt	C 15th SCVI	Halltown, VA	08/26/64	Harpers Ferry, WV	08/29/64	Camp Chase, OH	CSR,KEB,H15
					Camp Chase, OH	10/07/64	Died, Diarrhea	P5,P22,P27,FPH,CSR
Price, Daniel W.	Pvt	D 12th SCVI	Petersburg, VA	04/02/65	City Pt., VA	04/04/65	Pt. Lookout, MD	CSR
					Pt. Lookout, MD	06/17/65	Rlsd. G.O. #109	CSR
Price, David W.	Pvt	C 15th SCVI	Halltown, VA	08/26/64	Harpers Ferry, WV	08/29/64	Camp Chase, OH	CSR,KEB,H15
					Camp Chase, OH	03/18/65	Pt. Lookout, MD	CSR
					Pt. Lookout, MD	03/27/65	Boulwares Wh. Xc	CSR
Price, Edmund	Pvt	C 12th SCVI	Gettysburg, PA	07/04/63	David's Island, NY	09/08/63	City Pt., VA Xc	CSR
					Williamsburg, VA Hos.	09/13/63	Furloughed	CSR
Price, Edward C.	Pvt	A 12th SCVI	Sutherland Stn., VA	04/03/65	City Pt., VA	04/07/65	Hart's Island, NY	CSR
					Hart's Island, NY	06/16/65	Rlsd. G.O. #109	CSR
Price, G.W.	Pvt	C 15th SCVI	Halltown, VA	08/26/64	Camp Chase	03/18/65	Pt. Lookout, MD	P22,P26,KEB,CSR
Price, George S.	Pvt	C 15th SCVI	Sharpsburg, MD	09/17/62	Sharpsburg, MD	09/28/62	Ft. McHenry, MD	CSR,H15
					Ft. McHenry, MD	10/11/62	Fts. Monroe, VA Xc	CSR
Price, Henry L.	Sgt	C 15th SCVI	Gettysburg, PA	07/05/63	Letterman G.H. Gbg	07/21/63	Provost Marshal	P1,KEB,CSR,H15
					David's Island, NY	09/12/63	City Pt., VA Xc	P1,CSR
Price, Hugh	Pvt	C 7th SCVIBn	Morris Island, SC	07/10/63	Hilton Head, SC	09/22/63	Ft. Columbus, NY	CSR,HAG
					Ft. Columbus, NY	09/26/63	Pt. Lookout, MD	CSR
					Pt. Lookout, MD	02/25/64	Joined U.S. Army	P116,P124,P125
Price, J.H.	Pvt	F Orr's Ri.	Southside RR, VA	04/02/65	City Pt., VA	04/07/65	Hart's Island, NY	CSR
					Hart's Island, NY	06/15/65	Rlsd. G.O. #109	P79,CSR
Price, Jacob, Jr.	Pvt	C 15th SCVI	Halltown, VA	08/26/64	Harpers Ferry, WV	08/29/64	Camp Chase, OH	CSR,KEB,H15
					Camp Chase, OH	03/18/65	Pt. Lookout, MD	P22,P26,CSR
					Pt. Lookout, MD	03/27/65	Boulware's Wh. Xc	CSR

SOUTH CAROLINA SOLDIERS, SAILORS AND P CITIZENS HELD IN U.S. PRISONS 1861-1865

NAME	RANK	REGIMENT	CAPTURED AT	WHEN	PRISON	MOVED	DISPOSITION	SOURCES
Price, Jesse C.	Pvt	5 10/19 SCVI	Missionary Ridge, TN	11/25/63	Nashville, TN	12/07/63	Louisville, KY	P39,RAS,HMC,CSR
					Louisville, KY	12/07/63	Rock Island, IL	P88,P89,CSR
					Rock Island, IL	06/20/65	Rlsd. G.O. #109	P131,CSR
Price, Jesse N.	Pvt	B 26th SCVI	Five Forks, VA	04/01/65	City Pt., VA	04/05/65	Pt. Lookout, MD	CSR
					Pt. Lookout, MD	06/16/65	Rlsd. G.O. #109	P115,P119,P122,CSR
Price, John	Pvt	K 18th SCVI	Petersburg, VA	12/30/63	City Pt., VA	08/03/64	Pt. Lookout, MD	CSR
					Pt. Lookout, MD	08/08/64	Elmira, NY	CSR
					Elmira, NY	09/18/64	Died, Ch. Diarrhea	CSR
Price, John M.	Pvt	C 7th SCVIBn	Weldon RR, VA	08/21/64	City Pt., VA	08/24/64	Pt. Lookout, MD	CSR
					Pt. Lookout, MD	03/14/65	Aikens Ldg., VA Xc	P117,P121,P124,CSR
Price, Joseph	Pvt	C 23rd SCVI	Hatchers Run, VA	04/02/65	City Pt., VA	04/04/65	Pt. Lookout, VA	CSR
					Pt. Lookout, VA	06/30/65	Rlsd. G.O. #109	CSR
Price, Paul	Pvt	15th SCMil			New Berne, NC USGH	05/12/65	Died, Ch. Diarrhea	P6,P12
Price, Quincy J.	Pvt	H 14th SCVI	Gettysburg, PA	07/05/63	Chester, PA	10/04/63	Pt. Lookout, MD	CSR
					Pt. Lookout, MD	03/06/64	City Pt., VA Xc	CSR
Price, Quincy J.	Pvt	H 14th SCVI	Augusta, GA	05/18/65	Augusta, GA	05/18/65	Paroled	CSR
Price, R.	Pvt	A 2nd SCVA	Raleigh, NC Hos.	04/13/65	Raleigh, NC	04/20/65	Paroled	CSR
Price, Robert E.	Pvt	C 15th SCVI	Halltown, VA	08/26/64	Harpers Ferry, WV	08/29/64	Camp Chase, OH	CSR,KEB,H15
					Camp Chase, OH	01/30/65	Died, Pneumonia	P6,P22,P27,FPH,CSR
Price, T.J.	Pvt	C 17th SCVI	Deserted/enemy	02/26/65	P.M. A. of Potomac	02/26/65	City Pt., VA P.M.	CSR
					City Pt., VA P.M.	02/28/65	Washington, DC	CSR
					Washington, DC	03/01/65	Ithica, NY on oath	CSR
Price, Thomas	Pvt	I 26th SCVI	Fayetteville, NC	03/06/65	New Berne, NC	04/10/65	Hart's Island, NY	CSR
					Hart's Island, NY	06/17/65	Rlsd. G.O. #109	P79,CSR
Price, Thomas K.	Pvt	F 1st SCVIH	Deep Bottom, VA	08/14/64	Pt. Lookout, MD	02/24/65	Died	P6,P117,CDC,FPH
Price, W.A.	Pvt	K 1st SCVIR	Deserted/enemy	02/23/65	Charleston SC	03/02/65	Will take oath	SA1
Prichard, James	Pvt	A Hol.Leg.	Frederick, MD	09/12/62	Ft. Delaware, DE	10/02/62	Aikens Ldg., VA Xc	CSR,HOS
Prickett, James H.	Sgt	H 25th SCVI	Ft. Fisher, NC	01/15/65	New York, NY	01/30/65	Elmira, NY	CSR,HAG
					Elmira, NY	06/15/65	Died, Ch. Diarrhea	P6,P12,P65,P66,CSR
Priester, Andrew H.	Pvt	D 24th SCVI	Franklin, TN	12/17/64	Nashville, TN	12/31/64	Louisville, KY	CSR,EFW
					Louisville, KY	01/02/65	Camp Douglas, IL	P92,P94
					Camp Chase, OH	05/02/65	New Orleans Xc	P23,P26
					Vicksburg, MS Hos.	05/31/65	Released	CSR
Priester, F.B.	Pvt	F 3rd SCVC	South Newport, GA	08/17/64	Philadelphia, PA	01/10/65	Ft. Delaware, DE	CSR
					Ft. Delaware, DE	02/06/65	Hos. 2/8-2/21/65	P47
					Ft. Delaware, DE	02/27/65	City Pt., VA Xc	P41,P42,CSR
Priester, Hezekiah	Pvt	H 17th SCVI	Farmville, VA	04/06/65	City Pt., VA	04/14/65	Newport News, VA	CSR
					Newport News, VA	06/15/65	Rlsd. G.O. #109	CSR
Priester, Miles	Pvt	F 3rd SCVC	South Newport, GA	08/17/64	Hilton Head, SC GH	09/07/64	Port Royal, SC Xc	P2,CSR
Prince, Berryman	Pvt	B 2nd SCVIRi	Mechanicsville, VA	06/03/64	White House, VA	06/11/64	Pt. Lookout, MD	CSR
					Pt. Lookout, MD	07/12/64	Elmira, NY	P113,P117,P120,CSR
					Elmira, NY	04/25/65	Died, Ch. Diarrhea	P6,P12,P65,FPH,CSR
Prince, Cornelius J.	Cpl	K 26th SCVI	Petersburg, VA	04/02/65	City Pt., VA	04/05/65	Pt. Lookout, MD	CSR
					Pt. Lookout, MD	06/16/65	Rlsd. G.O. #109	P115,P119,CSR
Prince, J. Edward	Pvt	B 3rd SCVC	Rockingham Ferry	12/09/64	Hilton Head, SC	02/10/65	New York, NY oath	CSR
Prince, Jefferson	Pvt	C 18th SCVI	Crater, Pbg., VA	07/30/64	City Pt., VA	08/05/64	Pt. Lookout, MD	CSR
					Pt. Lookout, MD	08/08/64	Elmira, NY	CSR
					Elmira, NY	07/05/65	Rlsd. G.O. #109	CSR
Prince, John E.	2Lt	E 25th SCVI	Ft. Fisher, NC	01/15/65	Ft. Columbus, NY	04/28/65	Ft. Delaware, DE	CSR,HAG
					Ft. Delaware, DE	05/15/65	Rlsd. G.O.#85	P43,P45,CSR

SOUTH CAROLINA SOLDIERS, SAILORS AND  CITIZENS HELD IN U.S. PRISONS 1861-1865

NAME	RANK	REGIMENT	CAPTURED AT	WHEN	PRISON	MOVED	DISPOSITION	SOURCES
Prince, John F.	Pvt	Ferguson's LA	Ringgold, GA	11/26/63	Nashville, TN	12/11/63	Louisville, KY	P39,CSR
					Louisville, KY	12/12/63	Rock Island, IL	P88,P89,CSR
					Rock Island, IL	01/09/64	Died	P5,P131,P132,FPH
Prince, John T.	Pvt	G 8th SCVI	Bennettsville, SC	03/06/65	New Berne, NC	03/26/65	Pt. Lookout, MD	CSR,KEB,HOM
					Pt. Lookout, MD	06/17/65	Rlsd. G.O. #109	P115,P118,P122
Prince, Joseph	Pvt	H 1st SCVA	Morris Island, SC	07/10/63	Hilton Head, SC		Sick in H.H. Hos.	CSR
Prince, L.F.	Pvt	B 15th SCVI	Halltown, VA	08/26/64	Harpers Ferry, WV	08/29/64	Camp Chase, OH	CSR,KEB,H15
					Camp Chase, OH	03/18/65	Pt. Lookout, MD	P22,CSR
					Pt. Lookout, MD	06/17/65	Rlsd. G.O. #109	P115,P119,CSR
Prince, Samuel W.	Pvt	I 24th SCVI	Franklin, TN	12/17/64	Nashville, TN	06/27/65	Rlsd. G.O. #109	P3,CSR
					Nashville, TN	08/31/65	In hospital	P3,CSR
Prince, Williamson	Pvt	H 4th SCVI	Nashville, TN	01/21/65	Louisville, KY	01/31/65	Paroled N. of Ohio	CSR
Pringle, M. Brewton	Pvt	K 4th SCVC	Charlotte, NC	05/03/65	Charlotte, NC	05/03/65	Paroled	CSR
Prior, George T.	Pvt	A Ham.Leg.A	Augusta, GA	05/25/65	Augusta, GA	05/25/65	Paroled	CSR
Pritchard, S.C.	Pvt	D 4th SCVC	Hartwell, GA	05/18/65	Hartwell, GA	05/18/65	Paroled	CSR
Privett, J. Hamilton	Pvt	M 8th SCVI	Winchester, VA	09/13/64	Harpers Ferry, WV	09/19/64	Camp Chase, OH	CSR,KEB
					Camp Chase, OH	05/02/65	New Orleans, LA	CSR
					New Orleans, LA	05/12/65	Vicksburg, MS Xc	CSR
Privett, James H., Sr.	Pvt	F 8th SCVI	Winchester, VA	09/13/64	Harpers Ferry, WV	09/19/64	Camp Chase, OH	CSR
					Camp Chase, OH	05/02/65	New Orleans, LA	CSR
					New Orleans, LA	05/12/65	Vicksburg, MS	CSR
					Vicksburg, MS	05/27/65	Vicksburg, MS USGH	CSR
					Vicksburg, MS USGH	05/31/65	Exchanged	CSR
Probst, Jacob	Pvt	K 1st SCVA	Deserted/enemy		Fayetteville, NC	04/18/65	New York, NY oath	CSR
Procter, S.M.	Pvt	17th SCVI	Athens, GA	05/08/65	Athens, GA	05/08/65	Paroled	CSR
Proctor, Henry G.	Pvt	A 25th SCVI	Weldon RR, VA	08/22/64	Alexandria, VA USH	09/18/64	Died of wounds	P1,P5,P12,HAG,CSR
Proctor, M.L.B.	Pvt	A 17th SCVI	Five Forks, VA	04/01/65	2nd D 5th AC USHH		US Gen. Hos.	HHC,CB,CSR
Proctor, S.A.	Pvt	F 12th SCVI	Gettysburg, PA	07/03/63	David's Island, NY	09/16/63	City Pt., VA Xc	CSR
					Williamsburg, VA Hos.	09/21/63	Furloughed	CSR
Proctor, S.J.	Pvt	H 11th SCVI	Darbytown Rd., VA	10/02/64	City Pt., VA	10/31/64	Pt. Lookout, MD	CSR,HAG
					Pt. Lookout, MD	02/18/65	Aikens Ldg., VA Xc	P118,P123,P124
Proctor, Stephen R.	1Lt	E 27th SCVI	Town Creek, NC	02/20/65	Pt. Lookout, MD	02/28/65	Washington, DC	P115,P117,P120,HAG
					Ft. Anderson, NC	02/28/65	Pt. Lookout, MD	CSR,HAG
					Ft. McHenry, MD	03/21/65	Ft. Delaware, DE	P110
					Old Capitol, DC	03/21/65	Ft. Delaware, DE	CSR,HAG
					Ft. Delaware, DE	06/04/65	Rlsd OO Gen. Grant	P43,P45,CSR
Prosser, Timothy	Pvt	G 26th SCVI	Five Forks, VA	04/01/65	City Pt., VA	05/05/65	Pt. Lookout, MD	CSR
					Pt. Lookout, MD	06/16/65	Rlsd. G.O. #109	P115,P119,CSR
Provan, George W.	Pvt	D 1st SCVA	Fayetteville, NC	03/19/65	New Berne, NC	03/30/65	Pt. Lookout, MD	CSR
					Pt. Lookout, MD	06/05/65	Rlsd. G.O. #109	P115,P122,CSR
Pruitt, Benjamin F.	Pvt	K 3rd SCMil	Lynch's Creek, SC	02/28/65	Pt. Lookout, MD			P118
Pruitt, Eli	Pvt	K 16th SCV	Macon, GA	04/30/65	Macon, GA	04/30/65	Paroled on oath	CSR
Pruitt, John Marion	Pvt	G Orr's Ri.	Petersburg, VA	04/03/65	City Pt., VA	04/11/65	Hart's Island, NY	CSR
					Hart's Island, NY	06/16/65	Rlsd. G.O. #109	P79,CSR
Pruitt, S.B.	Pvt	F 3rd SCVC	South Newport, GA	08/17/64	Ft. Delaware, DE	03/12/65	To Hos. 3/12/65	P47
					Ft. Delaware, DE	06/08/65	Rlsd. G.O. #109	P41,P42,P45
Pry, John C.	Pvt	D 2nd SCVI	Knoxville, TN	03/07/64	Knoxville, TN	03/10/64	Released on oath	SA2,P84,H2,CSR
Pryor, Kincher R.	Cpl	D Hol.Leg.	Hatchers Run, VA	03/29/65	City Pt., VA	04/01/65	Pt. Lookout, MD	CSR
					Pt. Lookout, MD	06/16/65	Rlsd. G.O. #109	P115,P118,P122,CSR
Puckett, F.R.	Pvt	B Orr's Ri.	Spotsylvania, VA	05/12/64	Belle Plain, VA	05/21/64	Ft. Delaware, DE	CSR
					Ft. Delaware, DE	12/18/64	Ft. Del. Hospital	P47
					Ft. Delaware, DE	06/10/65	Rlsd. G.O. #109	P41,P42,P45,CSR

SOUTH CAROLINA SOLDIERS, SAILORS AND  CITIZENS HELD IN U.S. PRISONS 1861-1865

NAME	RANK	REGIMENT	CAPTURED AT	WHEN	PRISON	MOVED	DISPOSITION	SOURCES
Puckett, Samuel D.	Pvt	A 3rd SCVIBn	South Mtn., MD	09/14/62	Ft. Delaware, DE	10/02/62	Aikens Ldg., VA Xc	CSR,KEB
Puckett, Samuel D.	Pvt	A 3rd SCVIBn	Falling Waters, MD	07/14/63	Pt. Lookout, MD	02/13/65	Aikens Ldg., VA Xc	P116,P121,P124
Puckhaber, F.	Pvt	F 25th SCVI	Deserted/enemy	03/17/65	Charleston, SC	03/17/65	Released on oath	CSR,HAG
Pugh, H.P.	Pvt	G 15th SCMil	Flat Rock, SC	02/24/65	Hart's Island, NY	06/17/65	Rlsd. G.O. #109	P79
Puler, David S.A.	Pvt	F 1st SCVA	Fayetteville, NC	03/16/65	Pt. Lookout, MD			P118
Pulley, J.T.	Pvt	12th SCVI	Deserted/enemy	04/04/65	Washington, DC	04/06/65	Norfolk, VA oath	CSR
					Bermuda Hundred, VA	04/06/65	Washington, DC	CSR
Pullig, Samuel W.	2Lt	B 3rd SCVI	Cedar Creek, VA	10/19/64	Winchester, VA USF	11/19/64	Baltimore, MD USGH	CSR,KEB,SA2,H3
					W. Bldg. Balt, MD	12/09/64	Ft. Delaware, DE	CSR
					Ft. McHenry, MD	01/01/65	Ft. Delaware, DE	P144,CSR
					Ft. Delaware, DE H	01/10/65	Dschgd. Frm. Hos.	P47
					Ft. Delaware, DE	06/16/65	Rlsd. G.O. #109	P43,P45,CSR
Purcell, Michael	Pvt	F 1st SCVA	Deserted/enemy	12/01/64	U.S. Fleet		Hilton Head, SC	P8,CSR
Purdy, S.A.	Pvt	G Orr's Ri.	Falling Waters, MD	07/14/63	Baltimore, MD	08/16/63	Pt. Lookout, MD	CSR,CDC
					Pt. Lookout, MD	08/16/64	Elmira, NY	P113,P120,CSR
					Elmira, NY	02/13/65	Pt. Lookout, MD Xc	P65,P66,CSR
Purkerson, W.H.	Pvt	B Orr's Ri.	Greencastle, PA	07/05/63	Chester, PA USGH	08/17/63	City Pt., VA Xc	CSR
Purse, Edward L.	OSg	Brooks LA	Sharpsburg, MD		P.M. Army of Potomac	09/30/62	Paroled	CSR
Pursley, J.A.	Pvt	G 18th SCVI	Farmville, VA	04/02/65	City Pt., VA	04/14/65	Newport News, VA	CSR
					Newport News, VA	01/12/66	Rlsd. G.O. #109	CSR
Pursley, P.L.	Pvt	G 18th SCVI	Crater, Pbg., VA	07/30/64	City Pt., VA	08/05/64	Pt. Lookout, MD	CSR
					Pt. Lookout, MD	08/08/64	Elmira, NY	CSR
					Elmira, NY	07/03/65	Rlsd. G.O. #109	CSR
Pursley, Willis A.	Pvt	G 16th SCVI	Ringgold, GA	11/27/63	Nashville, TN	12/09/63	Louisville, KY	P39,16R,CSR
					Louisville, KY	12/11/63	Rock Island, IL	P89,16R,CSR
					Rock Island, IL	10/06/64	Jd. US Army Frontr	CSR
Purvis, J. Henry	Pvt	K 21st SCVI	Ft. Fisher, NC	01/15/65	Elmira, NY	02/12/65	Died, Diarrhea	P6,P65,P66,FPH,HAG
Purvis, R.N.	Pvt	C 3rd SCVABn	Ft. Gaines, AL	08/08/64	New Orleans, LA	10/25/64	Ship Island, MS	P3,CSR
					Ship Island, MS	01/04/65	Exchanged	P136,CSR
Purvis, R.N.	Pvt	C 3rd SCVABn	Blakely, AL	04/09/65	Ship Island, MS	05/01/65	Vicksburg, MS Xc	P136,CSR
Purvis, William	Pvt	E 21st SCVI	Weldon RR, VA	08/21/64	Pt. Lookout, MD	11/02/64	Exchanged	P113,P117,P124,HAG
Putman, Bluford	Pvt	E 14th SCVI	Appomattox R., VA	04/03/65	City Pt., VA	04/11/65	Hart's Island, NY	CSR
					Hart's Island, NY	06/17/65	Rlsd. G.O. #109	CSR
Putnam, J.H.	Pvt	D 22nd SCVI	Deserted/enemy	02/01/65	City Pt., VA	02/05/65	Washington, DC	CSR
					Washington, DC	02/08/65	Chambersburg, PA	CSR
Pyles, Newton M.	Pvt	G 27th SCVI	Petersburg, VA	06/24/64	Bermuda Hundred, VA	06/25/64	Fts. Monroe, VA	CSR,HAG
					Fts. Monroe, VA	06/26/64	Pt. Lookout, MD	CSR,HAG
					Pt. Lookout, MD	07/30/64	Died, Typhoid fever	P6,P117,P119,FPH

SOUTH CAROLINA SOLDIERS, SAILORS AND  CITIZENS HELD IN U.S. PRISONS 1861-1865

NAME	RANK	REGIMENT	CAPTURED AT	WHEN	PRISON	MOVED	DISPOSITION	SOURCES
Qualls, Benjamin	Pvt	D 22nd SCVI	Kinston, NC	12/15/62	Kinston, NC	12/15/62	Paroled POW	CSR
Qualls, Benjamin	Pvt	D 22nd SCVI	Five Forks, VA	04/01/65	City Pt., VA	04/05/65	Pt. Lookout, MD	CSR
					Pt. Lookout, MD	06/17/65	Rlsd. G.O. #109	P115,P117
Qualls, W.H.	Pvt	D 22nd SCVI	Kinston, NC	12/15/62	Kinston, NC	12/15/62	Paroled POW	CSR
Qualls, W.H.	Pvt	D 22nd SCVI	Five Forks, VA	04/01/65	City Pt., VA	04/05/65	Pt. Lookout, MD	CSR
					Pt. Lookout, MD	06/17/65	Rlsd. G.O. #109	P115
Quarles, David	Pvt	E Orr's Ri.	Falling Waters, MD	07/14/63	Baltimore, MD	08/20/63	Pt. Lookout, MD	CSR
					Pt. Lookout, MD	03/17/64	Exchanged	P113,P123,P124,CSR
Quarles, David	Pvt	E Orr's Ri.	Petersburg, VA	04/02/65	Hart's Island, NY	06/16/65	Rlsd. G.O. #109	P79
Quarles, Thomas P.	Sgt	C 7th SCVI	Gettysburg, PA	07/04/63	Chester, PA G.H.	08/24/63	City Pt., VA Xc	P1,CNM,KEB
Quattlebaum, Giles J.	Pvt	G 13th SCVI	Southside RR, VA	04/02/65	City Pt. VA	04/07/65	Hart's Island, NY	CSR,ANY
					Hart's Island, NY	06/21/65	Rlsd. G.O.#109	P79,CSR
Quattlebaum, J.P.	Pvt	E 6th SCResB	Augusta, GA	05/18/65	Augusta, GA	05/18/65	Paroled	CSR
Quattlebaum, James J.	Pvt	B 1st SCVIH	Mossy Creek, TN	01/22/64	Nashville, TN	02/11/64	Louisville, KY	P38,SA1,CSR
					Louisville, KY	02/15/64	Rock Island, IL	P88,P91,P93,CSR
					Rock Island, IL	02/15/65	Pt. Lookout to Xc	P131,CSR
Quattlebaum, Joseph E.	Pvt	G 13th SCVI	Southside RR, VA	04/02/65	City Pt., VA	12/04/64	Hart's Island, NY	CSR,ANY
					Hart's Island, NY	06/16/65	Rlsd. G.O. #109	P79,CSR
Quattlebaum, R.W.	Pvt	M 6th SCVC	Stony Creek, VA	12/01/65	City Pt., VA	12/04/64	Pt. Lookout, MD	CSR
					Pt. Lookout, MD	06/17/65	Rlsd. G.O. #109	P115,P122,CSR
Quattlebaum, T.	Pvt	C 6th SCResB	Augusta, GA	05/19/65	Augusta, GA	05/19/65	Paroled	CSR
Quick, Aaron F.	Pvt	D 26th SCVI	Bennettsville, SC	03/06/65	New Berne, NC	03/26/65	Pt. Lookout, MD	CSR
					Pt. Lookout, MD	06/17/65	Rlsd. G.O. #109	P115,P117,CSR
Quick, Alfred	Pvt	G 23rd SCVI	Five Forks, VA	04/01/65	City Pt., MD	04/02/65	Pt. Lookout, MD	CSR,HOM
					Pt. Lookout, MD	06/17/65	Rlsd. G.O. #109	P115,P117,CSR
Quick, Allie	Pvt	D 26th SCVI	Amelia C.H., VA	04/01/65	City Pt., VA	04/04/65	Pt. Lookout, MD	CSR
					Pt. Lookout, MD	06/17/65	Rlsd. G.O. #109	CSR
Quick, Angus	Pvt	F 21st SCVI	Ft. Fisher, NC	01/15/65	Elmira, NY	03/02/65	Pt. Lookout, MD Xc	P65,P66,HAG,HOM
Quick, Giles	Pvt	G 23rd SCVI	Five Forks, VA	04/01/65	City Pt., VA	04/05/65	Pt. Lookout, MD	HOM,CSR
					Pt. Lookout, MD	06/17/65	Rlsd. G.O. #109	P115,P117,CSR
Quick, Henry	Pvt	F 1st SCVIR	Morris Island, SC	07/10/63	Hilton Head, SC	09/19/65	Ft. Columbus, NY	CSR,HAG,HOM
					Ft. Columbus, NY		Released on oath	CSR
					Ft. Columbus, NY	09/23/63	Paroled on oath	P1,CSR
Quick, James H.	Pvt	G 23rd SCVI	Five Forks, VA	04/01/65	Fts. Monroe, VA	06/21/65	Rlsd. G.O. #109	CSR
Quick, John B.	Pvt	F 21st SCVI	Ft. Fisher, NC	01/15/65	Pt. Lookout, MD	02/02/65	Hammond G.H., MD	P121,HOM,HAG
					Hammond G.H., MD	03/10/65	Died of wounds	P12,P115,P116
Quick, Leggett	Pvt	E 4th SCVC	Louisa C.H., VA	06/11/64	Pt. Lookout, MD	07/23/64	Elmira, NY	P113,P116,P120,CSR
					Elmira, NY	10/11/64	Pt. Lookout, MD Xc	P65,P66,HOM,CSR
					W. Bldg. Balt, MD	02/16/65	Prld. to Ft. McHenry	P3,CSR
					Richmond, VA Hos.	03/06/65	Furloughed 30 days	CSR
Quick, M.C.	Pvt	C 7th SCResB	Bennettsville, SC	03/06/65	Pt. Lookout, MD	06/17/65	Rlsd. G.O. #109	P115,P117
Quick, Madison	Pvt	D 26th SCVI	Deserted/enemy	02/26/65	City Pt., VA	03/01/65	Washington, DC	CSR
					Washington, DC	03/01/65	Savannah, GA oath	CSR
Quick, Robert W.	Sgt	D 26th SCVI	Five Forks, VA	04/01/65	Pt. Lookout, MD	06/17/65	Rlsd. G.O. #109	P115,P117,HOM,CSR
Quinlan, George	Pvt	G 7th SCVC	High Point, NC	05/01/65	High Point, NC	05/01/65	Paroled	CSR
Quinn, J.F.	Pvt	H P.S.S.	Deserted/enemy	03/03/65	Bermuda Hundred, VA	03/07/65	Washington, DC	CSR
					Washington, DC	03/08/65	Nashville, TN oath	CSR
Quinn, John	Pvt	E 1st SCVIR	Deserted/enemy	03/27/65	Charleston, SC	03/27/65	Released on oath	SA1,CSR
Quinn, John F.	1Sg	Ferguson's LA	Nashville, TN	12/16/64	Nashville, TN	12/19/64	Louisville, KY	CSR
					Louisville, KY	12/21/64	Camp Douglas, IL	CSR
					Camp Douglas, IL	05/12/65	Rlsd. G.O. #85	CSR
Quinn, Michael	Pvt	B Wash'n LA	Gettysburg, PA	07/03/63	Ft. Delaware, DE	07/12/63	Jd. 1st Conn. Cav.	P40,CSR

SOUTH CAROLINA SOLDIERS, SAILORS AND  CITIZENS HELD IN U.S. PRISONS 1861-1865

NAME	RANK	REGIMENT	CAPTURED AT	WHEN	PRISON	MOVED	DISPOSITION	SOURCES
Quinn, Patrick	Smn	CS *Chicora*	Morris Island, SC	09/07/63	Pt. Lookout, MD	09/20/64	Ft Warren, MA	P113,P116,P120
					Ft. Warren, MA	10/01/64	Str. Circasian	P2
Quinn, Thomas	Pvt	G P.S.S.	Knoxville, TN	01/05/64	Nashville, TN	01/17/64	Louisville, KY	P38
					Louisville, KY	01/27/64	Rock Island, IL	P88,P91,P93
Quinn, William	Pvt	Ferguson's LA	Calhoun, GA	05/16/64	Louisville, KY	05/25/64	Rock Island, IL	P7,P88,P91,P93
					Rock Island, IL	06/19/64	Joined US Navy	P131
Quinton, James	Pvt	G 5th SCVC	Louisa C.H., VA	06/11/64	Pt. Lookout, MD	07/25/64	Elmira, NY	P113,P116,P120,CSR
					Elmira, NY	03/10/65	Released per S.O.	P65,P66,CSR

SOUTH CAROLINA SOLDIERS, SAILORS AND  CITIZENS HELD IN U.S. PRISONS 1861-1865

NAME	RANK	REGIMENT	CAPTURED AT	WHEN	PRISON	MOVED	DISPOSITION	SOURCES
Rabb, Charles	Pvt	F 12th SCVI	Petersburg, VA	04/02/65	City Pt., VA	04/04/65	Pt. Lookout, MD	CSR
					Pt. Lookout, MD	06/17/65	Rlsd. G.O. #109	P115,P118,CSR
Rabb, James W.	Pvt	E 15th SCVI	Gettysburg, PA	07/05/63	Gettysburg, PA USH		Provost Marshal	P4,KEB,CSR
					Pt. Lookout, MD	02/18/65	Aikens Ldg., VA Xc	P113,P116,P124,CSR
Rabon, Daniel	Pvt	D 12th SCVI	Amelia C.H., VA	04/05/65	City Pt., VA	04/13/65	Pt. Lookout, MD	CSR
					Pt. Lookout, MD	06/17/65	Rlsd. G.O. #109	P115,P118,CSR
Rabon, David	Cpl	E 7th SCVI	Sharpsburg, MD	09/17/62	Ft. McHenry, MD	10/13/62	Fts. Monroe, VA	CSR
					Fts. Monroe, VA	11/17/62	Aikens Ldg., VA Xc	CSR
Rabon, John	Pvt	G 24th SCVI	Nashville, TN	12/16/64	Nashville, TN	01/01/65	Louisville, KY	P39,EFW
					Louisville, KY	01/02/65	Camp Douglas, IL	P92
					Louisville, KY	01/05/65	Camp Chase, OH	P94,EFW
					Camp Chase, OH	01/24/65	Died, Pneumonia	P6,P23,P127,FPH
Raborn, William M.	Pvt	D 19th SCVI	Murfreesboro, TN	12/31/62	Murfreesboro, TN	01/07/63	Died of wounds	P12,P38,HOE,CSR
Raburn, Joel H.	Pvt	Santee LA	McIntosh Co., GA	10/15/64	Atl. Blockade Fleet	01/03/65	Philadelphia, PA	CSR,UD5
					Philadelphia, PA	01/10/65	Ft. Delaware, DE	CSR
					Ft. Delaware, DE	04/19/65	Hos. 4/19-5/25/65	P47
					Ft. Delaware, DE	03/09/65	Hos. 3/9-4/13/65	P47
					Ft. Delaware, DE	06/08/65	Rlsd. G.O. #109	P41,P42,CSR
Rackley, J.S.	Pvt	K Orr's Ri.	Burkesville, VA	04/16/65	Burkesville, VA	04/16/65	Paroled	CSR
Rackley, William B.	Pvt	B P.S.S.	Knoxville, TN	11/14/63	Louisville, KY	01/29/64	Rock Island, IL	P88,P89,P93,TSE
					Rock Island, IL	10/27/64	Released on oath	P131,CSR
Radcliffe, A.	Pvt	B 5th SCVC	Augusta, GA	05/18/65	Augusta, GA	'05/18/65	Paroled	CSR
Radcliffe, O.R.	Pvt	B 5th SCVC	Augusta, GA	05/18/65	Augusta, GA	05/18/65	Paroled	CSR
Radford, L.F.	Pvt	H 7th SCVI	Port Republic, VA	10/04/64	Harpers Ferry, WV	10/16/64	Pt. Lookout, MD	CSR
					Pt. Lookout, MD	02/14/65	Coxes Ldg., VA Xc	P115,P117,CSR
Rady, James	Pvt	B Wash'n LA	Gettysburg, PA	07/04/63	Ft. McHenry, MD	07/07/63	Ft. Delaware, DE	CSR
					Ft. Delaware, DE	06/10/65	Released on oath	CSR
Rae, Thomas	Pvt	D 6th SCVC	Burgess Mills, VA	10/27/64	City Pt., VA	10/30/64	Pt. Lookout, MD	CSR
					Pt. Lookout, MD	05/14/65	Rlsd. G.O. #85	P115,SR
Raemboll, C.	Pvt	G 3rd SCVC	Deserted/enemy	03/27/65	Charleston, SC	04/01/65	Taken oath & disch.	CSR
Raffield, Harvey J.	Pvt	K 23rd SCVI	Five Forks, VA	04/01/65	City Pt., VA	04/05/65	Pt. Lookout, MD	CSR,K23
					Pt. Lookout, MD	06/08/65	Rlsd. G.O. #85	P115,P118,CSR
Ragan, Calvin	Pvt	H 6th SCVC	Stony Creek, VA	12/01/64	City Pt., VA	12/04/64	Pt. Lookout, MD	CSR
					Pt. Lookout, MD	06/17/65	Rlsd. G.O. #109	P117,CSR,P115
Ragin, G.H.	Pvt	C 25th SCVI	Ft. Darling, VA	05/14/64	Bermuda Hundred, VA	05/16/64	Fts. Monroe, VA	CSR
					Fts. Monroe, VA	05/17/64	Pt. Lookout, MD	CSR
					Pt. Lookout, MD	08/15/64	Elmira, NY	P116,CSR
					Elmira, NY	03/14/65	Pt. Lookout, MD Xc	P66,CSR
Ragsdale, John S.	Pvt	K Orr's Ri.	Petersburg, VA	04/03/65	City Pt., VA	04/11/65	Hart's Island, NY	CSR
					Hart's Island, NY	06/16/65	Rlsd. G.O. #109	P79,CSR
Railey, Benjamin A	Pvt	G 2nd SCVI	Petersburg, VA	07/29/64	Pt. Lookout, MD	08/08/64	Elmira, NY	CSR
					Elmira, NY	07/03/65	Rlsd. G.O. #109	SA2,H2,CSR,P65,P66
Raimey, Nathan P.	Pvt	D 14th SCVI	Sutherland Stn., VA	04/02/65	City Pt. VA	04/07/65	Hart's Island, NY	CSR,HOE
					Hart's Island, NY	06/16/65	Rlsd. G.O. #109	P79,CSR
Raines, J.H.	Pvt	A 3rd SCVABn	High Pt., NC	05/02/65	High Pt., NC	05/02/65	Paroled	CSR
Raines, L.B.	Pvt	A 3rd SCVABn	High Pt., NC	05/02/65	High Pt., NC	05/02/65	Paroled	CSR
Raines, Warren A.	Pvt	F 16th SCVI	Franklin, TN	11/30/64	Nashville, TN	11/30/64	Louisville, KY	CSR,16R
					Louisville, KY	12/03/64	Camp Douglas, IL	P90,P91,P94,CSR
					Camp Douglas, IL	02/21/65	Pt. Lookout, MD Xc	P55,P58,CSR
Rainey, Jonas Mc.	Pvt	H 12th SCVI	Gettysburg, PA	07/05/63	David's Island, NY	09/12/63	City Pt., VA Xc	P1,YEB

SOUTH CAROLINA SOLDIERS, SAILORS AND  CITIZENS HELD IN U.S. PRISONS 1861-1865

NAME	RANK	REGIMENT	CAPTURED AT	WHEN	PRISON	MOVED	DISPOSITION	SOURCES
Rainey, Jonas Mc.	Pvt	H 12th SCVI	Spotsylvania, VA	05/12/64	Belle Plain, VA	05/20/64	Ft. Delaware, DE	CSR
					Ft. Delaware, DE	01/15/65	Hos. 1/15-2/22/65	P47
					Ft. Delaware, DE	02/27/65	City Pt., VA Xc	P41,P42,CSR
Rainey, Jonas Mc.	Pvt	H 12th SCVI	Jackson H. Rchmd.	04/03/65	Jackson H. Rchmd.	04/13/65	Died, Ch. Diarrhea	P12,CSR
Rainey, Michael	Pvt	B 27th SCVI	Petersburg, VA	09/14/64	Pt. Lookout, MD	10/14/64	Joined US Army	P122
Rainey, Simeon	Pvt	I 1st SCVA	Morris Island, SC	07/10/63	Hilton Head, SC	09/01/63	Ft. Columbus, NY	CSR
					Ft. Columbus, NY	09/26/63	Pt. Lookout, MD	CSR
					Pt. Lookout, MD	05/03/64	Aikens Ldg., VA Xc	P113,P123,CSR
Rainwater, J.P.	Pvt	G 27th SCVI	Petersburg, VA	06/24/64	Bermuda Hundred, VA	06/25/64	Fts. Monroe, VA	CSR,HAG
					Fts. Monroe, VA	06/26/64	Pt. Lookout, MD	CSR
					Pt. Lookout, MD	07/19/64	Died, Dysentery	P6,P117,P119,FPH
Rainwaters, Joshua W.	Pvt	E 4th SCVC	Louisa C.H., VA	06/11/64	Fts. Monroe, VA	06/20/64	Pt. Lookout, MD	CSR,HMC
					Pt. Lookout, MD	07/23/64	Elmira, NY	P116,P120,CSR
					Elmira, NY	10/21/64	Died, Ch. Diarrhea	P6,P113,P65,FPH
Raleigh, Benjamin W.	Pvt	2nd SCVIRi	Petersburg, VA	07/29/64	Pt. Lookout, MD	08/08/64	Elmira, NY	P113,P117,P120
					Elmira, NY	07/03/65	Rlsd. G.O. #109	P65,P66
Raleigh, G.W.	Pvt	B 1st SCVI	Cheraw, SC	03/06/65	New Berne, NC	04/10/65	Hart's Island, NY	CSR
					Hart's Island, NY	06/16/65	Rlsd. G.O. #109	P79,CSR
Raleigh, John	Pvt	A 15th SCVI	Deserted/enemy	04/03/65	Charleston, SC	04/14/65	Rlsd. on oath	CSR
Ramage, J.F.	Sgt	D 3rd SCVIBn	Gettysburg, PA	07/02/63	Ft. McHenry, MD	07/07/63	Ft. Delaware, DE	CSR
					Ft. Delaware, DE	06/10/65	Released	P42,P45,CSR
Ramage, James H.	Pvt	A 13th SCVI	Spotsylvania, VA	05/12/64	Fredericksburg, VA	05/27/64	Lincoln G.H., DC	P1,CSR
					Old Capitol, DC	07/23/64	Elmira, NY	CSR
					Ft. McHenry, MD	07/23/64	Elmira, NY	P110
					Elmira, NY	06/27/65	Rlsd. G.O. #109	P65,P66,CSR
Rambo, John	Pvt	C 19th SCVI	Egypt Stn., MS	12/28/64	Memphis, TN	01/15/65	Alton, IL	CSR,HOE
					Alton, IL	02/28/65	Pt. Lookout, MD Xc	P13,P14,CSR
					Richmond, VA Hos.	03/09/65	Furloughed 30 days	CSR
Rambo, John	Pvt	C 19th SCVI	Augusta, GA	05/31/65	Augusta, GA	05/31/65	Paroled	CSR
Ramey, David	Pvt	K 12th SCVI	Deserted/enemy	12/05/62	City Pt., VA	12/09/64	Washington, DC	CSR
					Washington, DC	12/10/64	New York, NY oath	CSR
Ramey, J.W.	Pvt	K 12th SCVI	Deserted/enemy	02/23/65	City Pt., VA	02/24/65	Washington, DC	CSR
					Washington, DC	02/24/65	Oil City, PA oath	CSR
Rampey, J.R.	Pvt	F Hol.Leg.	Kinston, NC	12/15/62	Kinston, NC	12/15/62	Paroled POW	CSR
Rampey, J.R.	Pvt	F Hol.Leg.	Jarratts Stn., VA	05/08/64	Fts. Monroe, VA	05/13/64	Pt. Lookout, MD	CSR
					Pt. Lookout, MD	07/29/64	Died, Remitnt fever	P6,P113,P116,P119
Rampey, John P.	Pvt	I 14th SCVI	Brandy Stn., VA	08/01/63	Old Capitol, DC		Baltimore, MD	CSR
					Baltimore, MD	08/23/63	Pt. Lookout, MD	CSR
					Pt. Lookout, MD	01/13/65	Died, Typhoid fever	P6,P113,FPH,CSR
Rampey, Joseph M.	Pvt	A 3rd SCVIBn	South Mtn., MD	09/14/62	Ft. Delaware, DE	12/15/62	Fts. Monroe, VA	CSR,KEB
					Fts. Monroe, VA	12/18/62	City Pt., VA Xc	CSR
Rampey, Samuel D.	Pvt	F 2nd SCVI	Cedar Creek, VA	10/19/64	Winchester, VA Hos.	10/31/64	Baltimore, MD USGH	P1,CSR
Rampey, Samuel D.	Pvt	F 2nd SCVI	Winchester, VA	09/19/64	W. Bldg. Balt, MD	11/22/64	Pt. Lookout, MD	P1,KEB,SA2,H2
Rampey, Samuel D.	Pvt	F 2nd SCVI	Cedar Creek, VA	10/19/64	Pt. Lookout, MD	01/25/65	Hammond G.H., MD	P115,P121
Rampey, Samuel D.	Pvt	F 2nd SCVI	Winchester, VA	09/19/64	Hammond G.H., MD	02/07/65	Pt. Lookout, MD	P10
Rampey, Samuel D.	Pvt	F 2nd SCVI	Cedar Creek, VA	10/19/64	Pt. Lookout, MD	02/10/65	Cox's Ldg., VA Xc	P121,P124,CSR
Ramsay, James	Pvt	C 2nd SCVI	Gettysburg, PA	07/04/63	Gettysburg G.H.	07/20/63	Provost Marshal	P4,CSR,KEB,SA2,H2
					David's Island, NY	08/24/63	City Pt., VA Xc	P1,CSR
Ramsey, David	Pvt	A Hol.Leg.	Deserted/enemy	11/27/64	Washington, DC	11/30/64	Rlsd. on oath	CSR
					City Pt., VA	11/30/64	Washington, DC	CSR
Ramsey, David	Pvt	F 18th SCVI	Petersburg, VA	03/25/65	City Pt., VA	03/28/65	Pt. Lookout, MD	CSR
					Pt. Lookout, MD	06/17/65	Rlsd. G.O. #109	P115,P117,CSR

SOUTH CAROLINA SOLDIERS, SAILORS AND  CITIZENS HELD IN U.S. PRISONS 1861-1865

NAME	RANK	REGIMENT	CAPTURED AT	WHEN	PRISON	MOVED	DISPOSITION	SOURCES
Ramsey, Elias	Pvt	C 17th SCVI	Hatchers Run, VA	04/01/65	City Pt., VA	04/05/65	Pt. Lookout, MD	CSR,YEB
					Pt. Lookout, MD	06/17/65	Rlsd. G.O. #109	P115,P118,YEB,CSR
Ramsey, J.A.	Pvt	F 7th SCVI	Maryland		PM Army of Potomac	09/24/62	Paroled	KEB,CSR
Ramsey, James	Pvt	A 3rd SCVIBn	South Mtn., MD	09/14/62	Ft. Delaware, DE	12/15/62	Fts. Monroe, VA	CSR
					Fts. Monroe, VA	12/18/62	City Pt., VA Xc	CSR
Ramsey, Lucius B.	Sgt	B Orr's Ri.	Petersburg, VA	04/03/65	City Pt., VA	04/11/65	Hart's Island, NY	CSR
					Hart's Island, NY	06/18/65	Rlsd. G.O. #109	P79,CSR
Ramsey, Whitier	Pvt	F 18th SCVI	Petersburg, VA	03/25/65	City Pt., VA	03/28/65	Pt. Lookout, MD	CSR
					Pt. Lookout, MD	06/17/65	Rlsd. G.O. #109	P115,P117,CSR
Randall, C.W.	2Lt	K 19th SCVI	Augusta, GA	05/19/65	Augusta, GA	05/19/65	Paroled	CSR
Randall, Ezekiel	Cpt	C Walkers Bn	Augusta, GA	05/18/65	Augusta, GA	05/18/65	Paroled	CSR
Randall, H.G.	Pvt	D 5th SCVC	Augusta, GA	05/25/65	Augusta, GA	05/25/65	Paroled	CSR
Randall, M.L.	Sgt	F 17th SCVI	Farmville, VA	04/06/65	City Pt., VA	04/14/65	Newport News, VA	CSR
					Newport News, VA	06/25/65	Rlsd. G.O. #109	P107,CSR
Randall, Robert S.	Pvt	F 17th SCVI	Hatchers Run, VA	04/01/65	City Pt., VA	04/05/65	Pt. Lookout, MD	CSR
					Pt. Lookout, MD	06/17/65	Rlsd. G.O. #109	P115,P118,P122,CSR
Randall, William	Pvt	K 19th SCVI	Snake Creek Gap, GA	10/15/64	Nashville, TN	12/09/64	Louisville, KY	P3,HOE,CSR
Randall, William	Pvt	K 19th SCVI	Snake Creek Gap, GA	10/13/64	Louisville, KY	12/15/64	Camp Douglas, IL	P90,P94,CSR
					Camp Douglas, IL	01/30/65	Died, Smallpox	P6,F12,P55,P58,FPH
Raney, William	Pvt	D 2nd SCVA	Deserted/enemy	02/25/65	Charleston, SC		Released on oath	CSR
Rankin, A.J.	Pvt	G 13th SCVI	Fredericksburg, VA	05/11/62	Steamer Coatzacoal			CSR
Rankin, A.J.	Pvt	G 13th SCVI	Port Royal, VA	05/30/62	Aikens Ldg., VA Xc	08/05/62	Exchanged	CSR
Rankin, George F.	Pvt	A 27th SCVI	Ft. Anderson, NC	02/19/65	Ft. Anderson, NC	02/28/65	Pt. Lookout, MD	CSR,HAG
					Pt. Lookout, MD	03/22/65	Released on oath	P7,P119,P122,P114
Rankin, George W.	Pvt	H Hol.Leg.	Five Forks, VA	04/01/65	City Pt., VA	04/05/65	Pt. Lookout, MD	CSR
					Pt. Lookout, MD	04/23/65	Died, Ch. Diarrhea	P6,P115,P118,P119
Rankin, H.C.	Pvt	G 13th SCVI	Fredericksburg, VA	05/11/62	Steamer Coatzacoal			CSR
Rankin, H.C.	Pvt	G 13th SCVI	Port Royal, VA	05/30/62	Aikens Ldg., VA Xc	08/05/62	Exchanged	CSR
Rankin, William	Pvt	E Orr's Ri.	Petersburg, VA	07/29/64	Pt. Lookout, MD	08/08/64	Elmira, NY	P117,P120,P125,CSR
					Elmira, NY	01/30/65	Died, Remitnt. fever	P6,P65,P66,FPH,CSR
Ransom, J.C.	Pvt	K Orr's Ri.	Spotsylvania, VA	05/12/64	White House, VA	06/08/64	Pt. Lookout, MD	CSR
					Pt. Lookout, MD	07/09/64	Elmira, NY	P113,P117,P120,CSR
					Elmira, NY	06/21/65	Rlsd. G.O. #109	P65,P66
Ransom, William N.	Pvt	C Orr's Ri.	Charlesburgh, VA	05/24/64	White House, VA	06/08/64	Pt. Lookout, MD	CSR,CDC
					Pt. Lookout, MD	07/09/64	Elmira, NY	P113,P117,P120,CSR
					Elmira, NY	06/21/65	Rlsd. G.O. #109	CSR
Rantin, C.C.	Pvt	I 27th SCVI	Petersburg, VA	05/07/64	Bermuda Hundred, VA	05/08/64	Fts. Monroe, VA	CSR
					Fts. Monroe, VA	05/08/64	Pt. Lookout, MD	CSR
					Pt. Lookout, MD	05/27/64	Joined U.S. Army	P113,P116,P125,CSR
Rantin, F.C.	Pvt	Marion LA	Charlotte, NC	05/15/65	Charlotte, NC	05/15/65	Paroled	CSR
Rants, S.	Pvt	18th SCVI	Deserted/enemy	01/30/65	Washington, DC P.M.	01/30/65	Springfield, IL	CSR
Rascoe, Alexander H.	Pvt	F 21st SCVI	Ft. Fisher, NC	01/15/65	Elmira, NY	03/14/65	Pt. Lookout, MD Xc	P65,HAG,HOM,P66
Rast, Frederick M.	Pvt	G 25th SCVI	Town Creek, NC	02/20/65	Ft. Anderson, NC	02/28/65	Pt. Lookout, MD	CSR,HAG
					Pt. Lookout, MD	06/17/65	Rlsd. G.O. #109	P115,P117,P122,CSR
Rast, Pinckney D.	Pvt	LafayetteA	Raleigh, NC	04/13/65	Raleigh, NC	04/24/65	Paroled	CSR
Rast, Thomas F.	Pvt	B 20th SCVI	Cedar Creek, VA	10/19/64	Harpers Ferry, WV	10/23/64	Pt. Lookout, MD	P1,KEB,CSR
Rast, Thomas F.	Pvt	B 20th SCVI	Winchester, VA USH	09/19/64	W. Bldg. Balt, MD	11/19/64	Pt. Lookout, MD	P1
Rast, Thomas F.	Pvt	B 20th SCVI	Cedar Creek, VA	10/19/64	Pt. Lookout, MD	02/23/65	Died, Lung Infl.	P1,P6,P12,P115,CSR
Rast, William R.	Pvt	C 14th SCMil	Lynch's Creek, SC	02/28/65	Hart's Island, NY	05/13/65	Died, Pneumonia	P6,P12,P79,FPH
Rateree, John	Pvt	B 5th SCVI	Richmond, VA Hos.	04/03/65	Libby Prison, VA	04/23/65	Newport News, VA	CSR
					Newport News, VA	06/26/65	Rlsd. G.O. #109	CSR

R

SOUTH CAROLINA SOLDIERS, SAILORS AND CITIZENS HELD IN U.S. PRISONS 1861-1865

NAME	RANK	REGIMENT	CAPTURED AT	WHEN	PRISON	MOVED	DISPOSITION	SOURCES
Ratteree, Joseph	Pvt	D 17th SCVI	Deserted/enemy	02/25/65	P.M. A. of Potomac	02/26/65	City Pt., VA P.M.	CSR
					City Pt., VA P.M.	02/28/65	Washington, DC	CSR
					Washington, DC	03/01/65	Savannah, GA oath	CSR
Ratteree, Robert	Pvt	D 17th SCVI	Deserted/enemy	02/26/65	P.M. A. of Potomac	02/28/65	City Pt., VA P.M.	CSR
					City Pt., VA P.M.	02/28/65	Washington, DC	CSR
					Washington, DC	03/01/65	Savannah, GA	CSR
Rauch, Henry J., Jr.	3Lt	B 14th SCVI	Gettysburg, PA	07/05/63	Died of wounds			CSR,HOE
Rauch, Samuel N.	Pvt	B 14th SCVI	Gettysburg, PA	07/04/63	David's Island, NY	08/24/63	City Pt., VA Xc	P1,HOE,CSR
Rauch, Samuel N.	Cpl	B 14th SCVI	Amelia C.H., VA	04/03/65	City Pt., VA	04/13/65	Pt. Lookout, MD	CSR
					Pt. Lookout, MD	06/17/65	Rlsd. G.O. #109	P115,P118,CSR
Rauch, Wallace W.	Pvt	C 20th SCVI	Cedar Creek, VA	10/19/64	W. Bldg. Balt, MD	11/05/64	Died of wounds	P1,P6,FPH,KEB,CSR
Rauls, F.	Pvt	C 15th SCMil	Bentonville, NC	03/22/65	Hart's Island, NY	06/16/65	Rlsd. G.O. #109	P79
Ravan, J.	Pvt	I 7th SCVI	Spotsylvania, VA	05/07/64	Belle Plain, VA	05/21/65	Ft. Delaware, DE	CSR
					Ft. Delaware, DE	10/12/64	Hos. 10/12-10/21/64	P47
					Ft. Delaware, DE	03/31/65	Hos. 3/31-4/12/65	P47
					Ft. Delaware, DE	04/29/65	Hos. 4/29/65-?	P47
					Ft. Delaware, DE	06/16/65	Died, Scurvy	P6,P42,P45,P47,FPH
Rawch, J.	Pvt	E 1st SCVA	Barnwell, SC	02/06/65	Hart's Island, NY	06/16/65	Rlsd. G.O. #109	P79
Rawl, Franklin	Pvt	C 15th SCVI	Bentonville, NC	03/29/65	New Berne, NC	04/10/65	Hart's Island, NY	CSR,KEB,H15
					Hart's Island, NY	06/16/65	Rlsd. G.O. #109	CSR
Rawl, James E.	Cpl	K 13th SCVI	Petersburg, VA	04/03/65	City Pt., VA	04/11/65	Hart's Island, NY	CSR
					Hart's Island, NY	06/16/65	Rlsd. G.O. #109	P79,CSR
Rawl, Lewis	Pvt	C 15th SCVI	Halltown, VA	08/26/64	Harpers Ferry, WV	08/29/64	Camp Chase, OH	CSR,KEB,H15
					Camp Chase, OH	03/18/65	Pt. Lookout, MD	P26,P23,CSR
					Pt. Lookout, MD	03/27/65	Boulware's Wh. Xc	CSR
Rawl, O.D.	Pvt	C 15th SCVI	Halltown, VA	08/26/64	Harpers Ferry, WV	08/29/64	Camp Chase, OH	CSR,KEB,H15
					Washington, DC	08/29/64	Camp Chase, OH	CSR
					Camp Chase, OH	03/18/65	Pt. Lookout, MD	P23,P26,CSR
					Pt. Lookout, MD	03/27/65	Boulware's Wh. Xc	CSR
Rawl, O.D.	Pvt	A 7th SCVI	Augusta, GA	05/27/65	Augusta, GA	05/27/65	Paroled on oath	CSR
Rawl, Phillip J.	Pvt	K 20th SCVI	Cedar Creek, VA	10/19/64	Harpers Ferry, WV	10/24/64	Pt. Lookout, MD	CSR,KEB
					Pt. Lookout, MD	06/17/65	Rlsd. G.O. #109	P115,P117,P122,CSR
Rawlings, Lewis P.	Pvt	G 24th SCVI	Missionary Ridge, TN	11/25/63	Nashville, TN	12/09/63	Louisville, KY	P39
					Rock Island, IL	12/24/63	Died, Typhoid fever	P131,P132,FPH
Rawls, J.B.	Sgt	C 5th SCVI	Burkesville, VA	04/04/65	City Pt., VA	04/21/65	W. Bldg. Balt, MD	CSR,SA3,YEB
					W. Bldg. Balt, MD	05/09/65	Ft. McHenry, MD	P3,CSR
					Ft. McHenry, MD	06/06/65	Rlsd. G.O. #109	P96,CSR
Rawls, J.B.D.	Pvt	K 21st SCVI	Ft. Fisher, NC	01/15/65	Elmira, NY	03/14/65	Pt. Lookout, MD Xc	P65,P66
Rawls, J.W.	Pvt	B 21st SCVI	Morris Island, SC	07/10/63	Pt. Lookout, MD			P113,P116
					Ft. Columbus, NY	09/23/63	Paroled on oath	P1
Rawls, James L.	Pvt	A 21st SCVI	Ft. Fisher, NC	01/15/65	Elmira, NY	04/05/65	Died, Diarrhea	P6,P65,P66,HAG,FPH
Ray, A.	Pvt	B 20th SCVI	Cedar Creek, VA	10/19/64	Pt. Lookout, MD			P115,P117
Ray, Andrew C.	Pvt	K Hol.Leg.	Petersburg, VA	03/25/65	City Pt., VA	03/28/65	Pt. Lookout, MD	CSR
					Pt. Lookout, MD	06/17/65	Rlsd. G.O. #109	P115,P117,P122,CSR
Ray, Charles K.	Pvt	B Wash'n LA	Spotsylvania, VA	05/09/64	Bermuda Hundred, VA	05/15/64	Fts. Monroe, VA	CSR
					Fts. Monroe, VA	05/16/64	Pt. Lookout, MD	CSR
					Pt. Lookout, MD	08/18/64	Elmira, NY	P120,CSR
					Elmira, NY	03/02/65	James R., VA Xc	CSR
					Richmond, VA Hos.	03/11/65	Furloughed 30 days	CSR
Ray, Elijah	Sgt	A P.S.S.	Fair Oaks, VA	05/31/62	Phila., PA Hos.	07/18/62	Died of wounds	CSR
Ray, H.W.F.	Cit	Orangeburg	Columbia, SC	02/17/65	Hart's Island, NY	06/20/65	Rlsd. G.O. #109	P79
Ray, J.C.	Pvt	A 13th SCVI	Falling Waters, MD	07/14/63	Pt. Lookout, MD	09/28/63	Died, Typhoid fever	P6,P116,P119,FPH

SOUTH CAROLINA SOLDIERS, SAILORS AND  CITIZENS HELD IN U.S. PRISONS 1861-1865

NAME	RANK	REGIMENT	CAPTURED AT	WHEN	PRISON	MOVED	DISPOSITION	SOURCES
Ray, J.H.	Pvt	B 15th SCVI	Halltown, VA	08/26/64	Harpers Ferry, WV	08/29/63	Camp Chase, OH	CSR,KEB
					Camp Chase, OH	03/26/65	Pt. Lookout, MD	P23,P26,CSR
					Pt. Lookout, MD	06/17/65	Rlsd. G.O. #109	P115,P119,P122,CSR
Ray, James F.	Pvt	A Hol.Leg.	Petersburg, VA	03/25/65	City Pt., VA	03/28/65	Pt. Lookout, MD	CSR
					Pt. Lookout, MD	06/17/65	Rlsd. G.O. #109	P115,P117,P122,CSR
Ray, John W.	Pvt	B 13th SCVI	Petersburg, VA	03/25/65	Pt. Lookout MD	06/17/65	Rlsd. G.O. #109	CSR
Ray, Joseph C.	Pvt	A 13th SCVI	Falling Waters, MD	07/14/63	Old Capitol, DC	08/08/63	Pt. Lookout, MD	CSR
					Pt. Lookout, MD	09/28/63	Died	CSR,P6,P113,FPH,CSR
Ray, Middleton	Pvt	H 6th SCVC	Deserted/enemy	05/20/64	Louisville, KY	05/31/64	N. of Ohio R. oath	P88,P92,P93,CSR
Ray, Samuel J.	1Lt	C 18th SCVI	Crater, Pbg., VA	07/30/64	Old Capitol, DC	08/11/64	Ft. Delaware, DE	CSR
					Ft. McHenry, MD	08/11/64	Ft. Delaware, DE	P110
					Ft. Delaware, DE	06/17/65	Rlsd. G.O. #109	P43,P45,CSR
Ray, Simon	Pvt	C 10th SCVI	Atlanta, GA	07/22/64	Nashville, TN	07/29/64	Louisville, KY	CSR,RAS,CEN
					Louisville, KY	07/30/64	Camp Chase, OH	P90,P91,P94,CSR
					Camp Chase, OH	06/11/65	Released	P22,CSR
Ray, Thomas W.	Pvt	E Hol.Leg.	Williamsport, MD	09/15/62	Ft. Delaware, DE	10/02/62	Aikens Ldg., VA Xc	CSR,HOS
Ray, W.J.	Pvt	E 1st SCVIH	Warrenton, VA	09/29/62	Warrenton, VA	09/29/62	Paroled	CSR
Ray, William H.	Pvt	A 3rd SCVABn	High Pt., NC	05/02/65	High Pt., NC	05/02/65	Paroled	CSR
Ray, Willis T.	Pvt	B 13th SCVI	Petersburg, VA	03/25/65	Pt. Lookout, MD	06/17/65	Rlsd. G.O. #109	P115,P117,P122,HOS,CSR
Raymond, H.H.	Pvt	4TH SCVC	Anderson, SC	05/03/65	Anderson, SC	05/03/65	Paroled	CSR
Raymond, O.G.	Pvt	F 3rd SCVC	South Newport, GA	08/17/64	Philadelphia, PA	01/10/65	Ft. Delaware, DE	CSR
					Ft. Delaware, DE	06/10/65	Rlsd. G.O.#109	P41,P42,P45,CSR
Raysor, James M.	Pvt	B R.M.R.& HA	Hilton Head, SC	11/10/63	Hilton Head, SC	01/13/64	Ft. Columbus, NY	CSR,UD7
					Ft. Columbus, NY	02/11/64	Ft. McHenry, MD	CSR
					Balt, MD Marine H	10/10/64	Ft. McHenry, MD	CSR
					Ft. McHenry, MD	10/25/64	Pt. Lookout, MD	CSR
					Pt. Lookout, MD	12/25/64	Died, Typhoid fever	P5,P12,121,FPH,CSR
Raysor, Thomas E.	Cpt	H 11th SCVI	Petersburg, VA	06/24/64	Bermuda Hundred, VA	06/25/64	Fts. Monroe, VA	CSR,HAG
					Fts. Monroe, VA	06/27/64	Pt. Lookout, MD	CSR
					Pt. Lookout, MD	06/29/64	Washington, DC	P116,P120,CSR
					Old Capitol, DC	07/22/64	Ft. Delaware, DE	CSR
					Ft. Delaware, DE	06/17/65	Rlsd. G.O. #109	P43,P44,P46
Reader, J.B.	Pvt	F 26th SCVI	Crater, Pbg., VA	07/30/64	City Pt. VA	08/05/64	Pt. Lookout, MD	CSR
					Pt. Lookout, MD	08/04/64	Elmira, NY	P117,P120,P125,CSR
					Elmira, NY	03/14/65	Pt. Lookout to Xc	P65,P66,CSR
Ready, W.J.	1Lt	14th SCVI	Augusta, GA	05/18/65	Augusta, GA	05/18/65	Paroled	CSR
Ready, William	Pvt	D Hol.Leg.	Five Forks, VA	04/01/65	City Pt., VA	04/05/65	Pt. Lookout, MD	CSR
					Pt. Lookout, MD	06/08/65	Rlsd. G.O. #85	P115,P118
Reagin, Thomas Edward	Pvt	I 4th SCVC	Hawe's Shop, VA	05/28/64	3rd Div. 5th A.C.	06/12/64	Washington, DC	CSR,CTA
					Armory Sq. G.H., D	10/05/64	Lincoln G.H., DC	CSR
					Lincoln G.H., DC	10/05/64	Old Capitol, DC	CSR
					Old Capitol, DC	10/24/64	Elmira, NY	CSR
					Elmira, NY	02/13/65	Pt. Lookout, MD Xc	P65,P66,CSR
					W. Bldg. Balt, MD	05/09/65	Ft. McHenry, MD	P3,CSR
					Ft. McHenry, MD	06/10/65	Rlsd. S.O. #114	P96,P110,CSR
Reardon, Robert	Pvt	D 2nd SCVI	Cedar Creek, VA	10/19/64	Pt. Lookout, MD	06/17/65	Rlsd. G.O. #109	H2,CSR
Reaves, Burrel F.	Pvt	H P.S.S.	Deserted/enemy	03/05/65	Bermuda Hundred, VA	03/05/65	City Pt., VA	CSR
					City Pt., VA	03/08/65	Washington, DC	CSR
					Washington, DC	03/08/65	Boston, MA oath	CSR
Reaves, J.H.	Pvt	M 8th SCVI	Winchester, VA	09/13/64	Harpers Ferry, WV	09/19/64	Camp Chase, OH	CSR
					Camp Chase, OH	06/11/65	Rlsd. G.O. #109	P23,CSR

SOUTH CAROLINA SOLDIERS, SAILORS AND  CITIZENS HELD IN U.S. PRISONS 1861-1865

NAME	RANK	REGIMENT	CAPTURED AT	WHEN	PRISON	MOVED	DISPOSITION	SOURCES
Reaves, Joseph L.	2Lt	F 4th SCVC	Old Church, VA	05/28/64	3rd Div. 5th A.C.	06/05/64	Lincoln G.H., DC	CSR,HMC
					Lincoln G.H., DC	06/20/64	Died of wounds	P5,P6,P12,CSR
Reaves, W.A.	Pvt	C 14th SCVI	Richmond, VA Hos.	04/03/65	Richmond, VA	05/01/65	Paroled	CSR
Reaves, W.L.	Pvt	F 22nd SCVI	Kinston, NC	12/14/62	Kinston, NC	12/14/62	Paroled POW	CSR
Reaves, W.L.	Pvt	F 22nd SCVI	Petersburg, VA	06/17/64	City Pt., VA		Pt. Lookout, MD	CSR
					Pt. Lookout, MD	07/27/64	Elmira, NY	P113,P117,P120
					Elmira, NY	12/13/64	Died, Pneumonia	P6,P12,P65,P66,FPH
Reaves, W.R.	Pvt	I 13th SCVI	Gettysburg, PA	07/04/63	David's Island, NY	08/24/63	City Pt., VA Xc	P1,CSR
Recel, Jacob	Pvt	G 19th SCVI	Missionary Ridge, TN	11/25/63	Bridgeport, AL USAH	12/13/63	Nashville, TN	CSR,P2
Rector, David L.	Pvt	D 16th SCVI	Missionary Ridge, TN	11/27/63	Nashville, TN	12/17/63	Louisville, KY	P39,16R,CSR
					Louisville, KY	12/21/63	Rock Island, IL	P88,P89,P93,CSR
					Rock Island, IL	01/29/64	Died, Variola	P5,P132,FPH,CSR
Rector, J.P.	Pvt	A 3rd SCVABn	High Pt., NC	05/02/65	High Pt., NC	05/02/65	Paroled	CSR
Rector, N.G.	Pvt	B 11th SCVI	Town Creek, NC	02/20/65	Ft. Anderson, NC	02/28/65	Pt. Lookout, MD	CSR
					Pt. Lookout, MD	06/17/65	Rlsd. G.O. #109	P115,P117,P122,HAG,CSR
Reddick, Hymbrick	Pvt	B 1st SCVIH	Richmond, VA Hos.	04/03/65	Richmond, VA Hos.	04/14/65	Richmond, VA P.M.	CSR
					Libby Prison Rchmd.	04/23/65	Newport News, VA	CSR
					Newport News, VA	06/14/65	Rlsd. G.O. #109	P107,CSR
Reddick, J.E.	Pvt	C 3rd SCVABn	Blakely, AL	04/09/65	Ship Island, MS	05/01/65	Vicksburg, MS Xc	P136,CSR
Redding, James	Pvt	K 10th SCVI	Murfreesboro, TN	12/31/62	Nashville, TN		St. Louis, MO	P38,RAS
Redding, James	Pvt	K 10th SCVI	Murfreesboro, TN	01/05/63	St.Louis, MO	02/13/63	Rlsd. on oath	P72,CSR,CSR
Redish, D.S.	Pvt	G 4th SCVC	Black Creek, SC	03/01/65	Cpt. Burns	03/26/65	New Berne, NC P.M.	CSR
					New Berne, NC		Pt. Lookout, MD	CSR
					Pt. Lookout, MD	06/05/65	Released	CSR
Redman, Allan	Pvt	D 20th SCVI	Cedar Creek, VA	10/19/64	Harpers Ferry, WV	10/24/64	Pt. Lookout, MD	CSR,KEB
					Pt. Lookout, MD	06/17/65	Rlsd. G.O. #109	P115,P117,P122,CSR
Redman, Jacob W.	Pvt	D 25th SCVI	Weldon RR, VA	08/21/64	Alexandria G.H., VA	09/03/64	Died, GSW L. foot	P1,P6,HAG,HMC,CSR
Redmond, J.W.D.	Pvt	A 14th SCVI	Kellys Bridge, SC	02/25/65	New Berne, NC	04/25/65	Camp Hamilton, VA	CSR
					Camp Hamilton, VA	05/01/65	Newport News, VA	CSR
					Newport News, VA	06/26/65	Rlsd. G.O. #109	CSR
Redmond, Peter	Pvt	B 15th SCVAB	Bentonville, NC	03/19/65	New Berne, NC	03/30/65	Pt. Lookout, MD	CSR
					Pt. Lookout, MD	06/17/65	Rlsd. G.O. #109	P115,P117,P122,CSR
Reece, Robert M.	Sgt	B 22nd SCVI	Crater, Pbg., VA	07/30/64	City Pt., VA	08/05/64	Pt. Lookout, MD	CSR
					Pt. Lookout, MD	08/30/64	Elmira, NY	P113,P120,HOS
					Elmira, NY	10/11/64	Pt. Lookout, MD Xc	P65,P66,HOS
					Elmira, NY	10/11/64	Venus Pt., GA Xc	CSR
					Pt. Lookout, MD	10/29/64	Aikens Ldg., VA Xc	P115,P117,P123
Reed, C.H.	Pvt	D 27th SCVI	Weldon RR, VA	08/21/64	W. Bldg. Balt, MD	01/07/65	Pt. Lookout, MD	P3,HAG,CSR
					Pt. Lookout, MD	01/28/65	Hammond G.H., MD	P115,P121,CSR
					Pt. Lookout, MD	06/05/65	Released	P121,CSR
Reed, J.J.	Pvt	C 4th SCVC	Louisa C.H., VA	06/11/64	Fts. Monroe, VA	06/20/64	Pt. Lookout, MD	CSR
					Pt. Lookout, MD	07/23/64	Elmira, NY	P113,P116,P120,CSR
					Elmira, NY	08/30/64	Died, Pneumonia	P5,P65,P66,FPH,CSR
Reed, J.N.	Pvt	D 20th SCVI	Cedar Creek, VA	10/19/64	Harpers Ferry, WV	10/24/64	Pt. Lookout, MD	CSR
					Pt. Lookout, MD	06/17/65	Rlsd. G.O. #109	P115,P117,KEB,CSR
Reed, James R.	Pvt	E 11th SCVI	Petersburg, VA	06/24/64	Bermuda Hundred, VA	06/25/64	Fts. Monroe, VA	CSR,HAG
					Fts. Monroe, VA	06/26/64	Pt. Lookout, MD	CSR
					Pt. Lookout, MD	08/16/64	Elmira, NY	P113,P117,P120,CSR
					Elmira, NY	06/30/65	Rlsd. G.O. #109	P65,P66,CSR
Reed, James R.	Pvt	H 25th SCVI	Ft. Fisher, NC	01/19/65	New York, NY	01/30/65	Elmira, NY	CSR,HAG
					Elmira, NY	03/13/65	Died, Variola	P6,P12,P65,P66,FPH
Reed, W.W.	Pvt	F 2nd SCVI	Thomasville, GA H.	05/01/65	Thomasville, GA	05/01/65	Paroled	CSR

SOUTH CAROLINA SOLDIERS, SAILORS AND  CITIZENS HELD IN U.S. PRISONS 1861-1865

NAME	RANK	REGIMENT	CAPTURED AT	WHEN	PRISON	MOVED	DISPOSITION	SOURCES
Reeder, James J.	2Lt	G Hol.Leg.	Hatchers Run, VA	03/29/65	U.S. Field Hos.	03/30/65	City Pt., VA 5AC H	CSR,ANY
					City Pt., VA Hos.	05/01/65	"State of Maine" SS	CSR
					"State of Maine" SS	05/02/65	Armory Sq. Hos., DC	CSR
					Old Capitol, DC	06/25/65	Rlsd. G.O. #109	P110
					Armory Sq. Hos., DC	08/17/65	Douglas G.H., DC	CSR
					Douglas G.H., DC	09/21/65	Home in Newberry	CSR
Reeder, John H.	Pvt	G Hol.Leg.	Five Forks, VA	04/01/65	Pt. Lookout, MD	06/17/65	Rlsd. G.O. #109	P115,P118,P122
Reeder, Lewis T.	1Lt	F Orr's Ri.	Appomattox R., VA	04/03/65	Old Capitol, DC	04/21/65	Johnson's Isl., OH	P110,CDC,CSR
					Johnson's Isl., OH	06/19/65	Rlsd. G.O. #109	P81,P82,P83,CSR
Rees, B.F.	Pvt	C 27th SCVI	Richmond, VA Hos.	04/03/65	Jackson H. Rchmd.	07/17/64	Died of wounds	P12,HAG,CSR
Reese, G.	Pvt	G 27th SCVI	Petersburg, VA	06/18/64	Pt. Lookout, MD	03/14/65	Died, Scurvy	P6,P117,P119,FPH
Reese, John A.	Pvt	L Orr's Ri.	Falling Waters, MD	07/14/63	Ft. McHenry, MD	08/08/63	Pt. Lookout, MD	P110
					Old Capitol, DC	08/08/63	Pt. Lookout, MD	CSR
					Pt. Lookout, MD	03/03/64	City Pt., VA Xc	P116,P123,P124,CSR
Reese, John A.	Pvt	L Orr's Ri.	Southside RR, VA	04/02/65	City Pt., VA	04/07/65	Hart's Island, NY	CSR
					Hart's Island, NY	06/06/65	Rlsd. G.O. #109	P79,CSR
Reese, John B.	Pvt	K Orr's Ri.	Petersburg, VA	04/03/65	City Pt., VA	04/11/65	Hart's Island, NY	CSR
					Hart's Island, NY	06/16/65	Rlsd. G.O. #109	P79,CSR
Reeves, C.B.	Pvt	G 17th SCVI	Jarratts Stn., VA	04/02/65	City Pt., VA	04/07/65	Harts Island, NY	CSR
					Hart's Island, NY	06/14/65	Rlsd. G.O. #109	P79,CSR
Reeves, Daniel E.	Sgt	B 25th SCVI	Weldon RR, VA	08/21/64	Alexandria, VA G.H.	08/28/64	Died of wounds	P1,P6
Reeves, Morgan	Pvt	I 13th SCVI	Hanover Jctn., VA	05/24/64	Pt. Lookout, MD	03/17/65	Aikens Ldg., VA Xc	CSR
Register, James	Pvt	B 21st SCVI	Petersburg, VA	06/24/64	Bermuda Hundred, VA	06/25/64	Fts. Monroe, VA	CSR,HAG
					Fts. Monroe, VA	06/26/64	Pt. Lookout, MD	CSR
					Pt. Lookout, MD	08/16/64	Elmira, NY	P113,P117,P120,CSR
					Elmira, NY	07/03/65	Rlsd. G.O. #109	P65,P66,CSR
Rehse, John	Pvt	B Wash'n LA	Deserted/enemy		Memphis, TN	11/05/64	Taken the oath	CSR
Reid, A.C.	Pvt	A 3rd SCVABn	High Pt., NC	05/02/65	High Pt., NC	05/02/65	Paroled	CSR
Reid, Daniel G.	Pvt	B 7th SCVIBn	Weldon RR, VA	08/21/64	City Pt., VA USFH	08/24/64	Alexandria, VA USG	P1,HAG,HFC,CSR
					Alexandria, VA USG	08/26/64	Washington, DC USG	P1,CSR
					Lincoln G.H., DC	02/05/65	Old Capitol, DC	CSR
					Old Capitol, DC	03/01/65	Elmira, NY	CSR
					Ft. McHenry, MD	03/01/65	Elmira, NY	P110
					Elmira, NY	07/03/65	Rlsd. G.O. #109	P65,P66,CSR
Reid, David C.	Pvt	C Orr's Ri.	Petersburg, VA	04/02/65	City Pt., VA	04/04/65	Pt. Lookout, MD	CSR,CDC
					Pt. Lookout, MD	06/17/65	Rlsd. G.O. #109	P115,P118
Reid, G.N.	Pvt	C 1st SCVIR	Raleigh, NC Hos.	04/13/65	Raleigh, NC	04/13/65	Paroled	SA1,CSR
Reid, J.	Pvt	A 3rd SCVABn	High Pt., NC	05/02/65	High Pt., NC	05/02/65	Paroled	CSR
Reid, Jacob P.	Pvt	C P.S.S.	Lookout Mtn., TN	11/25/63	Nashville G.H.	01/12/64	Louisville, KY	P2,P39,TSE
					Louisville, KY	01/17/64	Rock Island, IL	P88,P93
					Rock Island, IL	03/02/65	Pt. Lookout to Xc	P131
Reid, James	Pvt	A 6th SCVI	Warrenton, VA	09/29/62	Warrenton, VA	09/29/62	Paroled	CSR
Reid, John	Pvt	G 7th SCVC	Deserted/enemy	03/18/65	Charleston, SC	03/18/65	Released on oath	CSR
Reid, John	Pvt	C Orr's Ri.	Petersburg, VA	04/02/65	Ft. Delaware, DE	06/10/65	Rlsd. on oath	P41,CSR
Reid, John W.	Sgt	B Orr's Ri.	Gravel Hill, VA	07/28/64	City Pt., VA	10/27/64	Died of wounds	P12,CSR
Reid, M.	Pvt	F 3rd SCVI	Sharpsburg, MD	09/17/62	P.M. Army of Patomac	09/30/62	Paroled for Xc	CSR
					Ft. Mchenry, MD	10/13/62	Fts. Monroe, VA Xc	CSR
Reid, Nathan W.	Pvt	A 20th SCVI	Desrted/enemy	08/10/63	Knoxville, TN	07/01/64	Louisville, KY	P8,CSR
					Louisville, KY	07/16/64	Jeffersonville, IN	P90,P94,CSR
Reid, S.H.	Pvt	F 26th SCVI	Petersburg, VA	03/25/65	City Pt., VA	03/27/65	Pt. Lookout, MD	CSR
					Pt. Lookout, MD	06/30/65	Rlsd. G.O. #109	P117,P121,P123,CSR

SOUTH CAROLINA SOLDIERS, SAILORS AND **R** CITIZENS HELD IN U.S. PRISONS 1861-1865

NAME	RANK	REGIMENT	CAPTURED AT	WHEN	PRISON	MOVED	DISPOSITION	SOURCES
Reid, Samuel M.	Cpl	B 18th SCVI	Richmond, VA Hos.	04/03/65	Libby Prison Rchmd.	04/23/65	Newport News, VA	CSR
					Newport News, VA	06/26/65	Rlsd. G.O. #109	CSR
Reid, Samuel Newton	Pvt	C 3rd SCVI	N. Anna River, VA	05/23/64	Port Royal, VA	05/30/64	Pt. Lookout, MD	CSR,ANY,KEB,SA2,H2
					Pt. Lookout, MD	03/14/65	Aikens Ldg., VA Xc	P116,P121,P124,CSR
Reid, Thomas B.	Pvt	D 16th SCVI	Franklin, TN	12/17/64	Nashville, TN	02/24/65	Louisville, KY	P3,P39,16R,CSR
					Louisville, KY	03/03/65	Camp Chase, OH	P92,P95,CSR
					Camp Chase, OH	03/25/65	Pt. Lookout, MD	P23,P26,CSR
					Pt. Lookout, MD	06/17/65	Rlsd. G.O. #109	P115,P119,CSR
Reid, Thomas W.	Pvt	G 13th SCVI	Richmond, VA	04/03/65	Newport News, VA	05/27/65	Died	P107,ANY,CSR
Reid, W.	Pvt	A 3rd SCVABn	High Pt., NC	05/02/65	High Pt., NC	05/02/65	Paroled	CSR
Reid, W.	Pvt	A 3rd SCVABn	Augusta, GA	05/20/65	Augusta, GA	05/20/65	Paroled	CSR
Reid, W.C.	Pvt	A 6th SCVI	Charlotte, NC	05/23/65	Charlotte, NC	05/23/65	Paroled	CSR
Reighley, D.H.	Pvt	B 4th SCVC	Louisa C.H., VA	06/11/64	Fts. Monroe, VA	06/20/64	Pt. Lookout, MD	CSR
					Pt. Lookout, MD	07/25/64	Elmira, NY	P113,P116,P120,CSR
					Elmira, NY	03/14/65	Pt. Lookout, MD Xc	P65,P66,CSR
					Elmira, NY	06/19/65	Rlsd. G.O. #109	P65,P66,CSR
Reighley, William	Pvt	F 23rd SCVI	Hatchers Run, VA	03/29/65	Pt. Lookout, MD	06/17/65	Rlsd. G.O. #109	P117,P122,HHC,CSR
Reighly, Meredith	Pvt	B 4th SCVC	Stony creek, VA	12/01/64	City Pt., VA	12/05/64	Pt. Lookout, MD	CSR
					Pt. Lookout, MD	06/17/65	Rlsd. G.O. #109	P115,P122,HHC,CSR
Reilley, William	Pvt	I 17th SCVI	Deserted/enemy	03/10/65	P.M. A. of Potomac	03/11/65	City Pt., VA P.M.	CSR
					City Pt., VA P.M.	03/12/65	Washington, DC	CSR
					Washington, DC	03/13/65	Charleston, SC oath	CSR
Reilly, Jeremiah	Pvt	K 1st SCVIG	Warrenton, VA	09/29/62	City Pt., VA	11/18/62	Rlsd. on parole	CSR,SA1
Rembert, John	Pvt	F 3rd SCVIBn	South Mtn., MD	09/12/62	Ft. McHenry, MD	10/17/62	Fts. Monroe, VA	CSR,KEB
					Fts. Monroe, VA	10/19/62	Aikens Ldg., VA Xc	CSR
Rembert, Lawrence M.	Cpl	D 2nd SCVI	Cedar Creek, VA	09/30/64	W. Bldg. Balt, MD	10/09/64	Ft. McHenry, MD	P1,SA2,H2,CSR
					Ft. McHenry, MD	01/02/65	Pt. Lookout, MD	CSR
Rembert, Lawrence M.	Cpl	D 2nd SCVI	Cedar Creek, VA	10/19/64	Pt. Lookout, MD	06/17/65	Rlsd. G.O. #109	P115,P117,CSR
Rembert, Stephen	Pvt	B German LA	Deserted/enemy	03/02/65	Charleston, SC	03/02/65	Released on oath	CSR
Renew, John P.	Pvt	Mathewes A	Augusta, GA	05/25/65	Augusta, GA	05/25/65	Paroled	CSR
Renneker, F.W.	Pvt	B 25th SCVI	Ft. Fisher, NC	01/15/65	New York, NY	01/30/65	Elmira, NY	CSR,HAG
					Elmira, NY	03/14/65	James R., VA Xc	P65,P66,CSR
Renneker, J.H.	Pvt	B 25th SCVI	Ft. Fisher, NC	01/15/65	New York, NY	01/30/65	Elmira, NY	CSR,HAG
					Elmira, NY	06/23/65	Rlsd. G.O. #109	P65,P66,CSR
Renno, John A.	Pvt	C 1st SCVIG	Petersburg, VA	04/03/65	City Pt., VA	04/07/65	Hart's Island, NY	CSR
					Hart's Island, NY	06/16/65	Rlsd. G.O. #109	P79,SA1,CSR
Rentiers, J.G.	Pvt	A 2nd SCVI	Gettysburg, PA	07/03/63	Letterman G.H. Gbg			P1,KEB,SA2
					Gettysburg G.H.	09/01/63	Provost Marshal	P4,KEB,SA2,H2
					Ft. McHenry, MD	09/12/63	Pt. Lookout, MD	P96,P144,CSR
					Pt. Lookout, MD	05/03/64	City Pt., VA Xc	P116,P123,P124,CSR
Rentz, George W.	Sgt	K 11th SCVI	Weldon RR, VA	08/21/64	Old Capitol, DC	10/24/64	Elmira, NY	HAG,CSR
					Ft. McHenry, MD	10/24/64	Elmira, NY	P110
					Elmira, NY	12/29/64	Died, Pneumonia	P6,P65,P66,FPH,CSR
Rentz, J.	Pvt	K 11th SCVI	Deep Bottom, VA	08/14/64	Pt. Lookout, MD	10/30/64	Aikens Ldg., VA Xc	P113,P117,HAG
Rentz, J.W.	Pvt	F 22nd SCVI	Deserted/enemy	02/26/65	City Pt., VA	02/28/65	Washington, DC	CSR
					Washington, DC	03/01/65	Hilton Head, SC	CSR
Rentz, Jacob	Pvt	K 11th SCVI	Weldon RR, VA	08/21/64	City Pt., VA	08/24/64	Pt. Lookout, MD	CSR
					Pt. Lookout, MD	10/30/64	Venus Pt., GA Xc	CSR
Rentz, William A.	Pvt	C 15th SCVAB	Cheraw, SC	03/06/65	New Berne, NC	04/03/65	Pt. Lookout, MD	CSR
					Pt. Lookout, MD	06/17/65	Rlsd. G.O. #109	P115,P117,CSR
Rentze, J.C.	Pvt	E 8th SCResB	Barnwell, SC	02/06/65	New Berne, NC	04/10/65	Hart's Island, NY	CSR
					Hart's Island, NY	06/16/65	Rlsd. G.O. #109	CSR

SOUTH CAROLINA SOLDIERS, SAILORS AND  CITIZENS HELD IN U.S. PRISONS 1861-1865

NAME	RANK	REGIMENT	CAPTURED AT	WHEN	PRISON	MOVED	DISPOSITION	SOURCES
Resinger, Thomas	Pvt	C 15th SCVI	Salibury, NC	04/12/65	Nashville, TN	04/29/65	Louisville, KY	P39,CSR
					Louisville, KY	05/02/65	Camp Chase, OH	P92,P95,CSR
					Camp Chase, OH	06/19/65	Rlsd. G.O. #109	P23,P26,CSR
Revel, G.W.	Sgt	G 26th SCVI	Farmville, VA	04/06/65	City Pt., VA	04/14/65	Newport News, VA	CSR
					Newport News, VA	06/26/65	Rlsd. G.O. #109	P107,CSR
Revel, William M.	Pvt	G 26th SCVI	Five Forks, VA	04/01/65	City Pt., VA	04/05/65	Pt. Lookout, MD	CSR
					Pt. Lookout, MD	06/16/65	Rlsd. G.O. #109	P115,P118,CSR
Revell, M.H.	Pvt	C 1st SCVC	Goldsboro, NC	03/31/65	New Berne, NC	03/31/10	Hart's Island, NY	CSR
					Hart's Island, NY	06/17/65	Rlsd. G.O. #109	CSR
Revels, John J.	Pvt	G 18th SCVI	Petersburg, VA	03/25/65	City Pt., VA	03/28/65	Pt. Lookout, MD	CSR
					Pt. Lookout, MD	05/26/65	Died, Measles	P6,P117,P119,FPH
Revels, Stephen	Pvt	G 18th SCVI	Deserted/enemy	01/22/65	City Pt., VA	01/24/65	Washington, DC P.M.	CSR
Reynolds, Benjamin F.	Pvt	C 22nd SCVI	Crater, Pbg., VA	07/30/64	City Pt., VA	08/05/64	Pt. Lookout, MD	CSR
					Pt. Lookout, MD	08/08/64	Elmira, NY	113,P117,P120,CSR
					Elmira, NY	11/14/64	Died, Scurvy	P6,P65,P66,FPH,CSR
Reynolds, E.F.	Sgt	H 16th SCVI	Jonesboro, GA	09/01/64	Rough & Ready, GA	09/19/64	Exchanged	CSR
Reynolds, E.W.	Pvt	K 7th SCVI	Sharpsburg, MD	09/17/62	Ft. McHenry, MD	10/14/02	Aikens Ldg., VA Xc	KEB,CSR
Reynolds, F.M.	Pvt	I 5th SCVI	Deserted/enemy	03/14/65	Bermuda Hundred, VA	03/15/65	City Pt., VA	CSR
					City Pt., VA	03/16/65	Washington, DC	CSR
					Washington, DC	03/18/65	Nashville, TN oath	CSR
Reynolds, Fowler W.	Pvt	A Hol.Leg.	Kinston, NC	12/15/62	Kinston, NC	12/15/62	Paroled POW	CSR
Reynolds, James C.	2Lt	F 1st SCVA	Charlotte, NC	05/03/65	Washington, DC			CSR
Reynolds, John	Pvt	C 15th SCVAB	Deserted/enemy	10/09/64	Hilton Head, SC	10/21/64	North on oath	P8,CSR
Reynolds, John H.	Pvt	A 15th SCVI	Sharpsburg, MD	09/17/62	Provost Marshal	09/27/62	Sent north on oath	CSR,KEB,H15
Reynolds, P.G.	Pvt	H 26th SCVI	Petersburg, VA	04/02/65	City Pt., VA	04/05/65	Pt. Lookout, MD	CSR
					Pt. Lookout, MD	06/17/65	Rlsd. G.O. #109	P115,P118,P122,CSR
Reynolds, Wiley C.	3Lt	H 8th SCVI	Greencastle, PA	07/05/63	Ft. Delaware, DE	07/18/63	Johnson's Isl., OH	P42,P44,P144,KEB
					Johnson's Isl., OH	03/14/65	Pt. Lookout, MD Xc	P80,P81,CSR
Rhame, John E.	Pvt	A 2nd SCVC	Stephenburg, VA	06/09/63	Old Capitol, DC	06/25/63	City Pt., VA Xc	CSR
					Ft. McHenry, MD	06/25/63	City Pt., VA Xc	P110
					Petersburg, VA Hos.	07/08/63	Returned to duty	CSR
Rhames, Nathaniel	Pvt	A 21st SCVI	Ft. Fisher, NC	01/15/65	Elmira, NY	06/10/65	Died, Ch. Diarrhea	P6,P65,P66,HAG,FPH
Rhea, Robert A.	Pvt	A 12th SCVI	Gettysburg, PA	07/02/63	Chester, PA G.H.	09/23/63	City Pt., VA Xc	P1,CSR
					Williamsburg, VA H	09/28/63	Furloughed	CSR
Rhett, Alfred	Col	1st SCVA	Averysborough, NC	03/15/65	New Berne, NC	04/10/65	Hart's Island, NY	CSR
					Hart's Island, NY	04/15/65	Ft. Delaware, DE	P79,CSR
					Ft. Delaware, DE	07/24/65	Rlsd. by president	P7,P43,P45,CSR
Rhett, Benjamin S.	Pvt	K 4th SCVC	Wakefield, NC	04/20/65	Wakefield, NC	04/20/65	Paroled	CSR
Rhode, W.J.	Sgt	I 1st SCVC	Beverly Ford, VA	06/09/63	Old Capitol, DC	06/25/63	City Pt., VA Xc	CSR
					Ft. McHenry, MD	06/25/63	City Pt., VA Xc	P110
Rhoden, C.J.	Pvt	B 19th SCVI	Augusta, GA	05/21/65	Augusta, GA	05/21/65	Paroled	CSR
Rhoden, Thomas A.	Sgt	G 17th SCVI	Petersburg, VA	03/25/65	City Pt., VA	03/28/65	Pt. Lookout, MD	CSR
					Pt. Lookout, MD	06/17/65	Rlsd. G.O. #109	P115,P117,P122,CSR
Rhodes, Eldred J.	Pvt	G 1st SCVIG	Hatchers Run, VA	04/02/65	City Pt., VA	04/07/65	Hart's Island, NY	CSR
					Hart's Island, NY	06/16/65	Rlsd. G.O. #109	P79,SA1,CSR
Rhodes, George D.	Pvt	I 27th SCVI	Petersburg, VA	06/24/64	Bermuda Hundred, VA	06/25/64	Fts. Monroe, VA	CSR,HAG
					Fts. Monroe, VA	06/26/64	Pt. Lookout, MD	CSR
					Pt. Lookout, MD	08/16/64	Elmira, NY	P113,P120,CSR
					Elmira, NY		Trfd. for Xc	CSR
					Pt. Lookout, MD	10/30/64	Venus Pt., GA Xc	P117,CSR
Rhodes, H. Ashton	Pvt	B 21st SCVI	Ft. Fisher, NC	01/15/65	Elmira, NY	07/07/65	Rlsd. G.O. #109	P65,P66,HAG
Rhodes, J. Burt	Pvt	B 21st SCVI	Petersburg, VA	05/09/64	Pt. Lookout, MD	08/18/64	Elmira, NY	P120,HAG

SOUTH CAROLINA SOLDIERS, SAILORS AND **R** CITIZENS HELD IN U.S. PRISONS 1861-1865

NAME	RANK	REGIMENT	CAPTURED AT	WHEN	PRISON	MOVED	DISPOSITION	SOURCES
Rhodes, James S.	Pvt	I 27th SCVI	Deserted/enemy	02/20/65	Wilmington, NC	02/20/65	Ft. Anderson, NC	CSR,HAG
					Ft. Anderson, NC	02/28/65	Pt. Lookout, MD	CSR
					Pt. Lookout, MD	05/15/65	Washington, DC oath	P115,P117,CSR
Rhodes, James T.	2Lt	F 8th SCVI	Winchester, VA	09/13/64	Harpers Ferry, WV	09/24/64	Johnson's Isl., OH	CSR,KEB
					Johnson's Isl., OH	06/16/65	Rlsd. G.O. #109	P82,P83,CSR
Rhodes, John B.	Pvt	M 8th SCVI	Winchester, VA	09/13/64	Harpers Ferry, WV	09/16/64	Camp Chase, OH	CSR
					Camp Chase, OH	05/02/65	New Orleans, LA	P23,P26,CSR
					New Orleans, LA	05/12/65	Vicksburg, MS Xc	CSR
Rice, H.F.	Pvt	C P.S.S.	Seven Pines, VA	05/31/62	Harrisons Ldg., VA	08/05/62	Aikens Ldg., VA Xc	CSR
Rice, Henry W.	Pvt	G 27th SCVI	Petersburg, VA	06/24/64	Fts. Monroe, VA	07/13/64	Ctrct. nurse at G.H.	P8,HAG,CSR
					Fts. Monroe, VA G.H.	07/13/65	Died of disease	CSR
Rice, James H.	Pvt	E 16th SCVI	Ringgold, GA	11/26/63	Bridgeport, AL G.H	12/11/63	Nashville, TN	P2,16R,CSR
Rice, Larkin	Pvt	K 14th SCVI	Augusta, GA	05/31/65	Augusta, GA	05/31/65	Paroled	CSR
Rice, Ulysses	Pvt	G 1st SCVIG	Gettysburg, PA	07/05/63	Ft. Delaware, DE	07/30/63	City Pt., VA Xc	P42,P44,CSR,SA1
Rice, Ulysses	Pvt	H 1st SCVIG	Sutherland Stn., VA	04/03/65	City Pt., VA	04/14/65	Pt. Lookout, MD	CSR
					Pt. Lookout, MD	06/17/65	Rlsd. G.O. #109	P115,P118,P122,CSR
Rice, William R.	Pvt	F 24th SCVI	Taylors Ridge, GA	10/16/64	Nashville, TN	10/23/64	Louisville, KY	CSR,EFW
					Louisville, KY	10/27/64	Camp Douglas, IL	P90,P91,P94,CSR
					Camp Douglas, IL	12/10/64	Died, Smallpox	P5,P12,P53,P55,FPH
Richard, Meyer	Sgt	D 25th SCVI	Ft. Fisher, NC	01/15/65	New York, NY	01/30/65	Elmira, NY	CSR,HAG
					Elmira, NY	02/28/65	Released on oath	P7,P65,P66,CSR
Richards, Daniel M.	Pvt	I 13th SCVI	Petersburg, VA	03/25/65	City Pt., VA	03/28/65	Pt. Lookout, MD	CSR,HOS
					Pt. Lookout, MD	06/17/65	Rlsd. G.O. #109	P115,P117,CSR
Richards, G.G.	Cpl	L 18th SCVAB	Hartwell, GA	05/17/65	Hartwell, GA	05/17/65	Paroled	CSR
Richards, John M.	Pvt	B 22nd SCVI	Kinston, NC	12/15/62	Kinston, NC	12/15/62	Paroled POW	CSR
Richards, Levi	Pvt	B 22nd SCVI	Kinston, NC	12/15/62	Kinston, NC	12/15/62	Paroled POW	CSR
Richardson, David	Pvt	C 3rd SCVI	Richmond, VA Hos.	04/03/65	Richmond, VA Hos.	04/18/65	Paroled Nurse	CSR
Richardson, George W.	3Lt	A 16th SCVI	Nashville, TN	12/16/64	Nashville, TN	12/18/64	Louisville, KY	CSR
					Louisville, KY	12/20/64	Johnson's Isl., OH	P90,P91,P94,CSR
					Johnson's Isl., OH	06/17/65	Rlsd. G.O. #109	P81,P82,CSR
Richardson, Griffin	Pvt	C 15th SCVAB	Cheraw, SC	03/06/65	New Berne, NC	04/03/65	Pt. Lookout, MD	CSR
					Pt. Lookout, MD	06/17/65	Rlsd. G.O. #109	P115,P117
Richardson, H.W.	Pvt	K 4th SCVC	Old Church, VA	05/30/64	White House, VA	06/08/64	Pt. Lookout, MD	CSR,CLD
					Pt. Lookout, MD	03/14/65	Aikens Ldg., VA Xc	P117,P121,P124
Richardson, J.D.	Pvt	E 15th SCVI	Halltown, VA	08/06/64	Pt. Lookout, MD	06/17/65	Rlsd. G.O. #109	P115,KEB,CSR
Richardson, J.G.	Pvt	L 10th SCVI	Danville, KY	09/20/62	Louisville, KY	11/12/62	Vicksburg, MS	P88,HMC,RAS,CSR
					Vicksburg, MS	12/04/62	Exchanged	CSR
Richardson, J.S.	Pvt	I 21st SCVI	Ft. Fisher, NC	01/15/65	Elmira, NY	07/13/65	Elmira, NY G.H.	P65,HAG
					Elmira, NY	08/07/65	Rlsd. G.O. #109	P66
Richardson, James W.	Msc	1st SCVIBn	Morris Island, SC	09/07/63	Ft. Columbus, NY	09/23/63	Took the oath	P1
Richardson, John	Pvt	C 12th SCVI	Wilderness, VA	05/06/64	Belle Plain, VA	05/20/64	Ft. Delaware, DE	CSR
					Ft. Delaware, DE	06/30/64	Died, Typhoid fever	P5,P41,P42,P47,FPH
Richardson, John D.	Pvt	E 15th SCVI	Halltown, VA	08/26/64	Harpers Ferry, WV	08/29/64	Camp Chase, OH	CSR,KEB,H15
					Camp Chase, OH	03/26/65	Pt. Lookout, MD	P23,P26,P119
Richardson, John H.	Pvt	G 1st SCVIG	Petersburg, VA	03/25/65	City Pt., VA	03/29/65	Pt. Lookout, MD	CSR,SA1
					Pt. Lookout, MD	05/14/65	Rlsd. G.O. #85	P115,P117,P122,CSR
Richardson, Joseph J.	Pvt	I 10/19 SCVI	Missionary Ridge, TN	11/25/63	Nashville, TN	12/07/63	Louisville, KY	P39,RAS,CSR
					Louisville, KY	12/09/63	Rock Island, IL	P88,P89,CSR
					Rock Island, IL	10/15/64	Jd. US Army F.S.	P131,CSR

SOUTH CAROLINA SOLDIERS, SAILORS AND  CITIZENS HELD IN U.S. PRISONS 1861-1865

NAME	RANK	REGIMENT	CAPTURED AT	WHEN	PRISON	MOVED	DISPOSITION	SOURCES
Richardson, Joseph M.	Pvt	I 12th SCVI	Spotsylvania, VA	05/12/64	Belle Plain, VA	05/21/64	Ft. Delaware, DE	CSR
					Ft. Delaware, DE	09/15/64	Hos. 9/15-9/20/64	P47,LAN
					Ft. Delaware, DE	02/22/65	Hos. 2/22-2/26/65	P47
					Ft. Delaware, DE	06/10/65	Released	P41,P42,P45
Richardson, Pinckney G.	Pvt	I 21st SCVI	Ft. Fisher, NC	01/15/65	Elmira, NY	07/11/65	Rlsd. G.O. #109	P65,P66,HAG,HMC
Richardson, R.W.	Pvt	F 3rd SCVC	South Newport, GA	08/17/64	Ft. Delaware, DE	02/01/65	Hos. 2/1-2/10/65	P47
					Philadelphia, PA	01/10/65	Ft. Delaware, DE	CSR
					Ft. Delaware, DE	06/10/65	Released	P41,P42,P45,CSR
Richardson, Robert L.	Pvt	G 2nd SCVIRi	Richmond, VA Hos.	04/03/65	Richmond, VA Hos.	04/25/65	Paroled	CSR
Richardson, Robert P.	Pvt	D Orr's Ri.	Hatchers Run, VA	03/31/65	City Pt., VA	04/02/65	Pt. Lookout, MD	CSR
					Pt. Lookout, MD	06/17/65	Rlsd. G.O. #109	P115,P117,P122,CDC,CSR
Richardson, Samuel F.	Pvt	A 3rd SCVI	N. Anna River, VA	05/23/64	Port Royal, VA	05/30/64		KEB,SA2,CSR,H3
					Pt. Lookout, MD	07/20/64	Died, Dysentery	P6,P116,P119,H3,FPH
Richardson, Samuel M.	Pvt	G Orr's Ri.	Petersburg, VA	04/03/65	City Pt., VA	04/11/65	Hart's Island, NY	CSR
					Hart's Island, NY	06/16/65	Rlsd. G.O. #109	P79,CSR
Richardson, T.W.	Pvt	D P.S.S.	Richmond, VA Hos.	04/03/65	Newport News, VA	06/26/65	Rlsd. G.O. #109	P107,TSE,CSR
Richardson, Thomas L.	Pvt	C 12th SCVI	Sharpsburg, MD	10/01/62	Frederieck, MD USG	10/11/62	Ft. McHenry, MD	CSR
					Ft. McHenry, MD	10/13/62	Exchanged	CSR
Richardson, William	Pvt	C 12th SCVI	Hatchers Run, VA	03/31/65	3rd A.C. Hospital	03/31/65	Died of wounds	P12,CSR
Richardson, William	Pvt	McQueen LA	Petersburg, VA	04/02/65	City Pt., VA	04/04/65	Pt. Lookout, MD	CSR
					Pt. Lookout, MD	04/21/65	Died	CSR
Richbourg, A.J.	SMj	23rd SCVI	Farmville, VA	04/06/65	City Pt., VA	04/14/65	Newport News, VA	CSR
					Newport News, VA	06/26/65	Rlsd. G.O. #109	P107,HCL,CSR
Richburg, B.D.	Pvt	I 25th SCVI	Ft. Fisher, NC	01/15/65	New York, NY	01/30/65	Elmira, NY	CSR,HAG
					Elmira, NY	04/24/65	Died, Pneumonia	P6,P65,P66,FPH,CSR
Richburg, Joseph E.	Pvt	I 25th SCVI	Ft. Fisher, NC	01/15/65	New York, NY	01/30/65	Elmira, NY	CSR,HAG
					Elmira, NY	06/23/65	Rlsd. G.O. #109	P65,P66,CSR
Richburg, L.F.	Pvt	C 6th SCVI	Appomattox R., VA	04/03/65	City Pt., VA	04/11/65	Hart's Island, NY	CSR
					Hart's Island, NY	06/17/65	Rlsd. G.O. #109	P79,CSR
Richey, J.J.	Pvt	F Hol.Leg.	Jarratts Stn., VA	05/08/64	Pt. Lookout, MD	08/18/64	Elmira, NY	P113,P116,P120
					Elmira, NY	03/02/65	Pt. Lookout, MD Xc	P65,P66
Richey, J.M.	Pvt	K 12th SCVI	Sharpsburg, MD	09/17/62	P.M. Army of Patomac	09/27/62	Exchanged	CSR
Richey, James W.	Pvt	A 2nd SCVIRi	Richmond, VA	04/03/65	Richmond, VA Hos.	04/08/65	City Pt., VA P.M.	CSR
					City Pt., VA P.M.	04/13/65	Pt. Lookout, MD	CSR
					Pt. Lookout, MD	06/17/65	Rlsd. G.O. #109	P115,P118,CSR
Richie, J.S.	Pvt	I 1st SCVIR	Cheraw, SC	03/05/65	Cheraw, SC	03/05/65	Paroled	SA1,CSR
Richter, Jacob J.	Pvt	D 7th SCVC	Lexington, SC	02/14/65	New Berne, NC	03/30/65	Pt. Lookout, MD	CSR
					Pt. Lookout, MD	06/08/65	Rlsd. Inst. 5/30/65	P115,P121,CSR
Rickenbacker, Nicholas	Pvt	F 25th SCVI	Town Creek, NC	02/20/65	Ft. Anderson, NC	02/28/65	Pt. Lookout, MD	CSR,HAG
					Pt. Lookout, MD	06/17/65	Rlsd. G.O. #109	P115,P117
Rickenbacker, T.E.	1Lt	B 1st SCVIH	24th U.S.A.C. FH	04/14/65	U.S. Gen. Hospital			CSR,SA1,
Ricketts, James E.	Pvt	A 4th SCVC	Louisa C.H., VA	06/11/64	Fts. Monroe, VA	06/20/64	Pt. Lookout, MD	CSR
					Pt. Lookout, MD	07/25/64	Elmira, NY	P113,P116,P120,CSR
					Elmira, NY	07/26/65	Rlsd. G.O. #109	P65,CSR,P66
Ricks, Edward T.	Pvt	E 26th SCVI	Southside RR, VA	04/01/65	City Pt., VA	04/05/65	Pt. Lookout, MD	CSR
					Pt. Lookout, MD	06/17/65	Rlsd. G.O. #109	P115,P118,CSR
Riddle, J.	Sgt	E 3rd SCVIBn	Maryland	09/12/62	Frederick, MD Hos	09/19/62	Prov. Marshal	CSR,KEB
					A of P Prov. Mar.	09/27/62	Paroled	CSR
Riddle, Martin	Pvt	E 3rd SCVIBn	South Mtn., MD	09/14/62	Ft. Delaware, DE	10/02/62	Aikens Ldg., VA Xc	CSR,KEB

R

SOUTH CAROLINA SOLDIERS, SAILORS AND CITIZENS HELD IN U.S. PRISONS 1861-1865

NAME	RANK	REGIMENT	CAPTURED AT	WHEN	PRISON	MOVED	DISPOSITION	SOURCES
Riddle, S.T.	Pvt	G 27th SCVI	Petersburg, VA	06/24/64	Bermuda Hundred, VA	06/25/64	Fts. Monroe, VA	CSR,HAG
					Fts. Monroe, VA	06/26/64	Pt. Lookout, MD	CSR
					Pt. Lookout, MD	08/16/64	Elmira, NY	P113,P117,P120,CSR
					Elmira, NY	03/02/65	Pt. Lookout, MD Xc	P65,P66,CSR
					Jackson Hos. Rchmd.	03/08/65	Furloughed 60 days	CSR
Riddle, Thomas R.	Pvt	K 1st SCVIG	Petersburg, VA	04/02/65	City Pt., VA	04/04/65	Pt. Lookout, MD	CSR,SA1
					Pt. Lookout, MD	06/30/65	Rlsd. G.O. #109	P115,P118,P121,CSR
Riddle, William S.	Pvt	G 27th SCVI	Petersburg, VA	06/24/64	Bermuda Hundred, VA	06/25/64	Fts. Monroe, VA	CSR,HAG
					Fts. Monroe, VA	06/26/64	Pt. Lookout, MD	CSR
					Pt. Lookout, MD	08/16/64	Elmira, NY	P113,117,P120,CSR
					Elmira, NY	07/03/65	Rlsd. G.O. #109	P65,P66,CSR
Ridge, John H.	Pvt	G 14th SCVI	Petersburg, VA	04/03/65	City Pt., VA	04/07/65	Hart's Island, NY	CSR
					Hart's Island, NY	06/16/65	Rlsd. G.O. #109	P79,CSR
Ridgell, Daniel W.	Pvt	E 7th SCVI	Winchester, VA	10/19/64	Frederick, MD G.H.	12/30/64	Baltimore, MD	P3,HOE,KEB,CSR
Ridgell, Daniel W.	Pvt	E 7th SCVI	Winchester, VA	09/19/64	W. Bldg. Balt, MD	01/05/65	Ft. McHenry, MD	P3,CSR
					Ft. McHenry, MD	02/20/65	Pt. Lookout, MD	P144,CSR
Ridgell, Pulaski H.	Pvt	I 23rd SCVI	Petersburg, VA	04/01/65	City Pt., VA	04/05/65	Pt. Lookout, MD	P115,P118,CSR
					Pt. Lookout, MD	06/17/65	Rlsd. G.O. #109	P115,P118,CSR
Ridgell, Tudor T.	Pvt	D 14th SCVI	Gettysburg, PA	07/04/63	Chester, PA G.H.	09/21/63	City Pt., VA Xc	P1,CSR
Ridgeway, J.N.	Pvt	I 25th SCVI	Ft. Fisher, NC	01/15/65	New York, NY	01/30/65	Elmira, NY	CSR,HAG
					Elmira, NY	03/14/65	James R., VA Xc	P65,P66,CSR
Ridgeway, John J.	Pvt	E 16th SCVI	Ringgold, GA	11/27/63	Nashville, TN	12/09/63	Louisville, KY	P39,16R,CSR
					Louisville, KY	12/11/63	Rock Island, IL	P88,P89,CSR
					Rock Island, IL	06/20/65	Rlsd. G.O. #109	P131,CSR
Ridgeway, John M.	Pvt	I 25th SCVI	Ft. Fisher, NC	01/15/65	New York, NY	01/30/65	Elmira, NY	CSR,HAG
					Elmira, NY	04/06/65	Died, Pneumonia	P6,P12,P65,P66,FPH,CSR
Ridgeway, Reuben F.	Sgt	I 25th SCVI	Ft. Fisher, NC	01/15/65	New York, NY	01/30/65	Elmira, NY	HAG,CSR
					Elmira, NY	02/20/65	James R., VA Xc	P65,P66,CSR
Ridley, C.M.	Sgt	K 12th SCVI	Gettysburg, PA	07/04/63	Williamsburg, VA H	09/09/62	Furloughed	CSR
					David's Island, NY	08/23/63	City Pt., VA Xc	P1,CSR
Riemann, Emile	Pvt	B Wash'n LA	Stony Creek, VA	12/01/64	City Pt., VA	12/05/64	Pt. Lookout, MD	CSR
					Pt. Lookout, MD	02/10/65	Exchanged	P115,CSR
Rigby, Edward L.	Pvt	C 24th SCVI	Chickamauga, GA	09/20/63	Nashville, TN	09/30/63	Louisville, KY	P38,CSR
					Louisville, KY	10/02/63	Camp Douglas, IL	P88,P89,HOA,CSR
					Camp Douglas, IL	06/16/65	Rlsd. G.O. #109	P53,P55,P57,CSR
Rigdon, Benjamin H.	Pvt	Ferguson's LA	Brandon, MS	07/18/63	Jackson, MS	07/30/63	Snyder's Bluff, MS	CSR
					Snyders Bluff, MS	07/30/63	Camp Morton, IN	CSR
					Camp Morton, IN	05/16/65	Released on oath	P100,P101,CSR
Rigdon, J.M.	Pvt	B 2nd SCVIRi	Knoxville, TN	12/03/63	St. Louis, MO	04/02/64	Allens Pt., VA Xc	CSR
Riggins, Allen	Pvt	B 2nd SCVIRi	Knoxville, TN	12/03/63	Louisville, KY	12/31/63	Rock Island, IL	P89,CSR
					Louisville, KY	02/04/64	Died, Typhoid fever	P5,P12,P93,FPH,CSR
Riggins, William	Pvt	F 22nd SCVI	Deserted/enemy	01/07/65	Knoxville, TN	01/10/65	Chattanooga, TN	CSR
					Chattanooga, TN	01/27/65	Louisville, KY	CSR
					Louisville, KY	01/31/65	Rlsd. on oath	P92,CSR
Riggs, Benjamin H.	Pvt	C 15th SCVAB	Deserted/enemy	04/07/65	Cumberland, MD	05/01/65	North of PA line	CSR
Riggs, Benjamin S.	Pvt	C 1st SCVIG	Petersburg, VA	07/29/64	Pt. Lookout, MD	08/08/64	Elmira, NY	P113,P117,P120,CSR
					City Pt., VA	08/05/64	Pt. Lookout, MD	CSR,SA1
					Elmira, NY	05/29/65	Released	P65,P66,CSR
Rikard, James P.	Pvt	D 13th SCVI	Deep Bottom, VA	07/21/64	Bermuda Hundred, VA	07/26/64	Camp Hamilton, VA	CSR,ANY
					Camp Hamilton, VA	08/11/64	Pt. Lookout, MD	CSR
					Pt. Lookout, MD	08/16/64	Elmira, NY	P117,P120,CSR
					Elmira, NY	07/03/65	Rlsd. G.O. #109	P65,P66,CSR

SOUTH CAROLINA SOLDIERS, SAILORS AND  CITIZENS HELD IN U.S. PRISONS 1861-1865

NAME	RANK	REGIMENT	CAPTURED AT	WHEN	PRISON	MOVED	DISPOSITION	SOURCES
Rikard, John Glenn	Cpl	D 13th SCVI	Petersburg, VA	04/02/65	City Pt., VA	04/04/65	Pt. Lookout, MD	CSR,ANY
					Pt. Lookout, MD	06/17/65	Rlsd. G.O. #109	P115,P118,CSR
Riley, J.	Pvt	C 27th SCVI	Petersburg, VA	06/24/64	Bermuda Hundred, VA	06/25/64	Fts. Monroe, VA	CSR,HAG
					Fts. Monroe, VA	06/26/64	Pt. Lookout, MD	CSR
					Pt. Lookout, MD	07/23/64	Elmira, NY	P113,P117,P120,CSR
					Elmira, NY	05/29/65	Rlsd. G.O. #109	P65,P66,CSR
Riley, J.M.	Pvt	C 7th SCVI	Cedar Creek, VA	10/19/64	Harpers Ferry, WV	10/23/64	Pt. Lookout, MD	CSR
Riley, J.O.	Pvt	B 2nd SCVIRi	Burkesville, VA	04/14/65	Burkesville, VA	04/17/65	Paroled	CSR
Riley, James	1Sg	C 27th SCVI	Weldon RR, VA	08/21/64	Pt. Lookout, MD	05/14/65	Rlsd. G.O. #85	P117,P125,HAG,CSR
Riley, Jerry	Pvt	1st SCVIH	Warrenton, VA	09/03/62	Warrenton, VA	09/03/62	Released to North	CSR
Riley, John	Pvt	D Ham.Leg.MI	Petersburg, VA	07/28/64	City Pt., VA P.M.	08/05/64	Pt. Lookout, MD	CSR
					Pt. Lookout, MD	08/08/64	Elmira, NY	P117,P120,P125,CSR
					Elmira, NY	06/21/65	Rlsd. G.O. #109	P66,CSR
Riley, Robert R.	Pvt	B Orr's Ri.	Spotsylvania, VA	05/12/64	Ft. McHenry, MD	06/13/64	Ft. Delaware, DE	P110,CDC
					Old Capitol, DC	06/15/64	Ft. Delaware, DE	CSR
					Ft. Delaware, DE	06/22/65	Rlsd. G.O. #109	P41,P42,CSR
Riley, T.F.	Pvt	B Orr's Ri.	Petersburg, VA	04/03/65	City Pt., VA	04/11/65	Hart's Island, NY	CSR
					Hart's Island, NY	06/16/65	Rlsd. G.O. #109	P79,CSR
Riley, Thomas J.	Pvt	F 3rd SCVC	South Newport, GA	08/17/64	Philadelphia, PA	01/10/65	Ft. Delaware, DE	CSR
					Ft. Delaware, DE		Hos. 3/1-4/2/65	P7,P45,P47
					Ft. Delaware, DE	06/15/65	Rlsd. oath War Dpt.	P41,P42,CSR
Riley, W.H.	Pvt	A 4th SCVC	Kershaw Dist., SC	02/21/65	New Berne, NC	04/10/65	Hart's Island, NY	CSR
					Hart's Island, NY	06/13/65	Released	P79,CSR
Ringold, Ernest	Pvt	C 15th SCVAB	Deserted/enemy		Hilton Head, SC	05/30/64	New York, NY oath	CSR
Riser, George Canter	Pvt	E 3rd SCVI	Cedar Creek, VA	10/19/64	W. Bldg. Balt, MD	11/22/64	Pt. Lookout, MD	P1,SA2,H3,ANY,CSR
					Pt. Lookout, MD	01/25/65	Hammond G.H., MD	P115,P121
					Pt. Lookout, MD	02/10/65	Exchanged	P121,CSR
					Richmond, VA	02/21/65	Furloughed 60 days	CSR
Risser, Henry H.	Pvt	H Hol.Leg.	Petersburg, VA	03/25/65	Pt. Lookout, MD	06/17/65	Rlsd. G.O. #109	P115,P117
Rissland, Albion	Pvt	H 1st SCVIR	Deserted/enemy	02/24/65	Charleston, SC		Released on oath	SA1,CSR
Rister, John A.	Pvt	K 13th SCVI	Petersburg, VA	04/02/65	City Pt., VA	04/04/65	Pt. Lookout, MD	CSR
					Pt. Lookout, MD	06/17/65	Rlsd. G.O. #109	P115,P118,CSR
Ritchie, John	Pvt	F 1st SCVA	Black River, NC	03/16/65	New Berne, NC	03/30/65	Pt. Lookout, MD	CSR
					Pt. Lookout, MD	06/17/65	Rlsd. G.O. #109	P115,P117,CSR
Ritchie, William M.	Pvt	D 17th SCVI	Kinston, NC	12/17/62	Kinston, NC	12/17/62	Paroled	CSR
Ritter, Henry R.	Cpl	E 24th SCVI	Chickamauga, GA	09/19/63	Nashville, TN	10/01/63	Louisville, KY	P38,CSR
					Louisville, KY	10/07/63	Camp Douglas, IL	P88,P89,CSR
					Camp Douglas, IL	06/16/65	Rlsd. G.O. #109	P53,P55,P57,CSR
Ritter, John F.	Pvt	F 1st SCVA	Bentonville, NC	03/22/65	New Berne, NC	04/10/65	Hart's Island, NY	CSR
					Hart's Island, NY	06/16/65	Rlsd. G.O. #109	P79,CSR
Ritter, Rudolph	Pvt	I 11th SCVI	Pocotaligo, SC	10/22/62	Hilton Head, SC	11/02/62	Ft. Columbus, NY	CSR
					Ft. Columbus, NY	11/21/62	Ft. Delaware, DE	CSR
					Ft. Delaware, DE	12/15/62	Fts. Monroe, VA	CSR
					Fts. Monroe, VA	12/15/62	City Pt., VA Xc	CSR
Ritz, Thomas	Pvt	D 11th SCVI	Town Creek, NC	02/20/65	Ft. Anderson, NC	02/28/65	Pt. Lookout, MD	CSR
					Pt. Lookout, MD	06/17/65	Rlsd. G.O. #109	P115,P117,CSR
Rivers, C.H.	Pvt	C 15th SCVAB	Cheraw, SC	03/05/65	Cheraw, SC	03/05/65	Paroled	CSR
Rivers, C.M.	Pvt	C 19th SCVCB	Augusta, GA	05/23/65	Augusta, GA	05/23/65	Paroled on oath	CSR
Rivers, D.S.	Pvt	D 23rd SCVI	Farmville VA Hos.	04/07/65	Farmville, VA	04/07/65	Paroled	CSR
Rivers, David T.	Pvt	H 7th SCVC	Deep Bottom, VA	08/14/64	City Pt., VA	08/22/64	Pt. Lookout, MD	CSR
					Pt. Lookout, MD	10/30/64	Aikens Ldg., VA Xc	P113,P117,HIC,CSR
Rivers, Drew	Cit	CD Dist.	Chesterfield, SC	02/24/65	Pt. Lookout, MD	05/08/65	Died, Ch. Diarrhea	P6,P117,P119,FPH

SOUTH CAROLINA SOLDIERS, SAILORS AND  CITIZENS HELD IN U.S. PRISONS 1861-1865

NAME	RANK	REGIMENT	CAPTURED AT	WHEN	PRISON	MOVED	DISPOSITION	SOURCES
Rivers, F.F.	Pvt	D 6th SCVC	Stony Creek, VA	12/01/64	City Pt., VA	12/04/64	Pt. Lookout, MD	CSR
					Pt. Lookout, MD	06/17/65	Rlsd. G.O. #109	P115,P117,CSR
Rivers, Franklin D.	Pvt	D 11th SCVI	Town Creek, NC	02/20/65	Ft. Anderson, NC	02/28/65	Pt. Lookout, MD	CSR,HAG
					Pt. Lookout, MD	06/17/65	Rlsd. G.O. #109	P115,P117,CSR
Rivers, Frederick	2Lt	E 21st SCVI	Ft. Fisher, NC	01/15/65	Ft. Columbus, NY	03/01/65	City Pt., VA Xc	P2,HAG
Rivers, J.M.	Pvt	D 11th SCVI	Ft. Fisher, NC	01/15/65	New York, NY	02/01/65	Elmira, NY	CSR
					Elmira, NY	03/02/65	James R., VA for Xc	P65,P66,HAG,CSR
Rivers, James	Pvt	A 2nd SCVC	Augusta, GA	05/29/65	Augusta, GA	05/29/65	Paroled	CSR
Rivers, L.J.	Pvt	B 26th SCVI	Crater, Pbg., VA	07/30/64	City Pt., VA	08/05/64	Pt. Lookout, MD	CSR
					Pt. Lookout, MD	08/08/64	Elmira, NY	P117,P120,P125,CSR
					Elmira, NY	10/11/64	Venus Pt., GA Xc	P65,P66,CSR
					Pt. Lookout, MD	10/29/64	Aikens Ldg., VA Xc	P115,P117,P123,CSR
Rivers, M.J.	Cpl	B 26th SCVI	Crater, Pbg., VA	07/30/64	Pt. Lookout, MD	08/05/64	Pt. Lookout, MD	CSR
					Pt. Lookout, MD	08/08/64	Elmira, NY	P117,P120,P125,CSR
					Elmira, NY	03/14/65	Tfd. for exchange	P65,CSR
Rivers, P.H.	Pvt	I 1st SCVC	Deserted/enemy	03/06/65	Charleston, SC	03/06/65	Released on oath	CSR
Rivers, Phillip	Pvt	B 26th SCVI	Richmond, VA Hos.	04/03/65	Libby Prison Rchmd.	04/23/65	Newport News, VA	CSR
					Newport News, VA	06/14/65	Rlsd. G.O. #109	CSR
Rivers, Thomas	Pvt	B 26th SCVI	Richmond, VA	04/03/65	Newport News, VA	06/14/65	Released	P107
Rivers, W.W.	Pvt	I 14th SCVI	Augusta, GA	05/23/65	Augusta, GA	05/23/65	Paroled	CSR
Rives, Wade H.	1Lt	D 12th SCVI	Cox Rd., VA	04/02/65	City Pt., VA Hos.	05/01/65	Washington, DC	CSR
					Old Capitol, DC	05/05/65	Johnson's Isl., OH	P110,CSR
					Johnson's Isl., OH	06/14/65	Released	P81,P82,P83,CSR
Rives, William C.	Pvt	G 25th SCVI	Ft. Fisher, NC	01/15/65	New York, NY	01/30/65	Elmira, NY	CSR,HAG
					Elmira, NY	06/16/65	Rlsd. G.O. #109	P65,P66,CSR
Rivett, Benjamin J.	Pvt	K 1st SCVIG	Gettysburg, PA	07/05/63	Ft. Delaware, DE		Hos. 4/27-5/10/64	P47,SA1
					Ft. Delaware, DE	03/25/65	Released Secy/War	P7,P40,P42,CSR
Roach, Baxter	Pvt	D 22nd SCVI	Deserted/enemy	02/24/65	City Pt., VA	02/28/65	Washington, DC	CSR
					Washington, DC	02/28/65	Salem, IL on oath	CSR
Roach, Charles A.	2Lt	C 2nd SCVC	Greensboro, NC	05/01/65	Greensboro, NC	05/01/65	Paroled	CSR
Roach, Henry	Pvt	D 22nd SCVI	Deserted/enemy	02/01/65	City Pt., VA	02/05/65	Washington, DC	CSR
					Washington, DC	02/08/65	Chambersburg, PA	CSR
Roach, Miles	Pvt	D 22nd SCVI	Deserted/enemy	02/24/65	City Pt., VA	02/26/65	Washington, DC	CSR
Roach, Napoleon B.	Pvt	A 12th SCVI	Sutherland Stn., VA	04/03/65	City Pt., VA	04/07/65	Hart's Island, NY	CSR
					Hart's Island, NY	06/16/65	Rlsd. G.O. #109	P79,YEB,CSR
Roach, Thomas J.	Pvt	H 12th SCVI	Warrenton, VA	09/29/62	Warrenton, VA	09/29/62	Paroled	CSR
Roach, W.F.	2Lt	Paymstr CS	Columbia, SC	02/17/65	Hart's Island, NY	04/15/65	Ft. Delaware, DE	P79
Roach, W.L.	HSd	H 12th SCVI	Richmond, VA	04/03/65	Richmond, VA	04/16/65	Paroled	CSR
Roach, William	Pvt	H 1st SCVA	Smith Farm, NC	03/16/65	New Berne, NC	04/10/65	Hart's Island, NY	CSR
					Hart's Island, NY	06/15/65	Rlsd. G.O. #109	P79,CSR
Robbins, Henry	Pvt	D 1st SCVIR	Morris Island, SC	07/10/63	Hilton Head, SC	09/19/63	Ft. Columbus, NY	CSR
					Ft. Columbus, NY	09/25/63	Rlsd. on oath	P1,CSR
Robbins, James H.	2Lt	C Orr's Ri.	Saylors Ck., VA	04/03/65	Old Capitol, DC	04/09/65	Johnson's Isl., OH	P110,CDC
					Johnson's Isl., OH	06/19/65	Rlsd. G.O. #109	P81,P82
Robbins, James S.	Pvt	H P.S.S.	Richmond, VA	04/03/65	Libby Prison, VA	04/13/65	City Pt., VA	CSR
					City Pt., VA	04/14/65	Pt. Lookout, MD	CSR
					Pt. Lookout, MD	06/07/65	Died, Lung Inflam.	P6,P118,P119,FPH
Robbins, Obediah	1Lt	E 13th SCVI	Petersburg, VA	04/02/65	Old Capitol, DC	04/09/65	Johnson's Isl., OH	P110,HOS,CSR
					Johnson's Isl., OH	06/19/65	Rlsd. G.O. #109	P81,P82,P83,CSR
Roberson, John	Pvt	A 15th SCVAB	Deserted/enemy	02/18/65	Charleston, SC	03/02/65	Released on oath	CSR
Roberts, A.J.	Pvt	K 17th SCVI	Lynchburg, VA Hos.	04/13/65	Lynchburg, VA	04/13/65	Paroled	CSR

SOUTH CAROLINA SOLDIERS, SAILORS AND **R** CITIZENS HELD IN U.S. PRISONS 1861-1865

NAME	RANK	REGIMENT	CAPTURED AT	WHEN	PRISON	MOVED	DISPOSITION	SOURCES
Roberts, Alexander	Pvt	B 17th SCVI	Petersburg, VA	03/25/65	City Pt., VA	03/28/65	Pt. Lookout, MD	CSR,HFC
					Pt. Lookout, MD	06/17/65	Rlsd. G.O. #109	P115,P117,CSR
Roberts, B.F.	Bug	A 3rd SCVABn	High Pt., NC	05/02/65	High Pt., NC	05/02/65	Paroled	CSR
Roberts, Darius	Pvt	K 16th SCVI	Chattahootchee, GA	07/05/64	Nashville, TN	07/12/64	Louisville, KY	CSR
					Louisville, KY	07/17/64	Camp Douglas, IL	P90,P91,CSR
					Camp Douglas, IL	06/16/65	Rlsd. G.O. #109	P53,P55,CSR
Roberts, Elias E.	Pvt	K 16th SCVI	Chickamauga, GA	11/26/63	Nashville, TN	12/11/63	Louisville, KY	P39,16R,CSR
					Louisville, KY	12/12/63	Rock Island, IL	P88,P89,CSR
					Rock Island, IL	05/03/65	New Orleans, LA Xc	P131,CSR
					New Orleans, LA	05/23/65	Exchanged	CSR
Roberts, G.W.	Pvt	B 23rd SCVI	Farmville, VA	04/06/65	City Pt., VA	04/14/65	Newport News, VA	CSR
					Newport News, VA	06/26/65	Rlsd. G.O. #109	CSR
Roberts, J.C.	Pvt	C 4th SCVC	Stony Creek, VA	12/01/64	City Pt., VA	12/05/64	Pt. Lookout, MD	CSR
					Pt. Lookout, MD	06/30/65	Rlsd. G.O. #109	P115,P121,P123,CSR
Roberts, J.M.	Bug	A 3rd SCVABn	High Pt., NC	05/02/65	High Pt., NC	05/02/65	Paroled	CSR
Roberts, J.T.	Pvt	B 3rd SCVIBn	Charlotte, NC Hos.	05/10/65	Charlotte, NC Hos.	05/10/65	Paroled	CSR,KEB
Roberts, James M.	1Lt.	C 16th SCVI	Franklin, TN	12/18/64	Nashville, TN	01/29/65	Died, Erysipelas	P3,P5,P12,16R,CSR
Roberts, John	Msc	1st SCVA	Deserted/enemy	02/18/65	Charleston, SC		Released on oath	CSR
Roberts, John J.	Pvt	B 5th SCVC	Augusta, GA	05/23/65	Augusta, GA	05/23/65	Paroled	CSR
Roberts, Josiah	Pvt	C 16th SCVI	Cassville, GA	05/20/64	Nashville, TN	05/27/64	Louisville, KY	P3,16R,CSR
					Louisville, KY	05/30/64	Rock Island, IL	P88,P91,CSR
					Rock Island, IL	06/10/64	Joined US Navy	P131,CSR
Roberts, Leroy	Pvt	F 23rd SCVI	Chester Stn., VA	04/04/65	City Pt., VA	04/07/65	Hart's Island, NY	CSR,HHC
					Hart's Island, NY	06/16/65	Rlsd. G.O. #109	P79,CSR
Roberts, Thomas J.	Pvt	G 14th SCVI	Petersburg, VA	04/03/65	City Pt., VA	04/07/65	Hart's Island, NY	CSR
					Hart's Island, NY	06/16/65	Rlsd. G.O. #109	P79,CSR
Roberts, W.	Pvt	B 23rd SCVI	Farmville, VA	04/06/65	Newport News, VA	06/26/65	Rlsd. G.O. #109	P107
Roberts, W. Francis	Pvt	B 18th SCVAB	Deserted/enemy	03/24/65	Charleston, SC		Released on oath	CSR
Roberts, W.T.	Pvt	F 23rd SCVI	Petersburg, VA	04/02/65	City Pt., VA	04/04/65	Pt. Lookout, MD	CSR,HAG,HHC
					Pt. Lookout, MD	06/17/65	Rlsd. G.O. #109	P115,P118,CSR
Roberts, William	Pvt	K 1st SCVA	Fayetteville, NC	03/16/65	New Berne, NC	03/30/65	Pt. Lookout, MD	CSR
					Pt. Lookout, MD			P115,P117,CSR
Roberts, William A.	Pvt	E 26th SCVI	Hatchers Run, VA	03/29/65	City Pt., VA	04/02/65	Pt. Lookout, MD	CSR
					Pt. Lookout, MD	06/17/65	Rlsd. G.O. #109	P79,P115,CSR
Roberts, William C.	Cpl	E 12th SCVI	Spotsylvania, VA	05/12/64	Fredericksburg, VA	05/23/64	Hos. 05/23/64	P1,LAN,CSR
					Ft. McHenry, MD			P110
Roberts, William C.	Cpl	E 12th SCVI	Spotsylvania, VA	05/12/64	Old Capitol, DC	08/12/64	Elmira, NY	CSR
					Elmira, NY	10/11/64	Tfd. for exchange	P65,P66
					Pt. Lookout, MD	10/29/64	Aikens Ldg., VA Xc	P117,P123,LAN
Roberts, William C.	Pvt	H 7th SCVIBn	Drury's Bluff, VA	05/16/64	Bermuda Hundred, VA	05/17/64	Fts. Monroe, VA	CSR,HAG
					Fts. Monroe, VA	05/18/64	Pt. Lookout, MD	CSR
					Pt. Lookout, MD	08/19/64	Elmira, NY	P113,CSR
					Elmira, NY	10/11/64	Pt. Lookout, MD Xc	P65,CSR
					Pt. Lookout, MD	10/29/64	Aikens Ldg., VA Xc	P115,P117,P123,CSR
Roberts, William R.	Pvt	B 2nd SCVIRi	Richmond, VA Hos.	04/03/65	Richmond, VA Hos.	04/14/65	Richmond, VA P.M.	CSR
Roberts, William R.	Pvt	B 2nd SCVIRi	Richmond, VA	04/03/65	Libby Prison Rchmd.	04/23/65	Newport News, VA	CSR
					Newport News, VA	06/26/65	Rlsd. G.O. #109	P107,CSR
Roberts, William W.	Pvt	E 26th SCVI	Five Forks, VA	04/01/65	City Pt., VA	04/07/65	Pt. Lookout, MD	CSR
					Pt. Lookout, MD	06/16/65	Rlsd. G.O. #109	CSR
Roberts, Wilson A.	Pvt	F 11th SCVI	Ft. Fisher, NC	01/15/65	Pt. Lookout, MD	06/04/65	Died, Consumption	P6,P12,HAG,FPH,CSR
Robertson, Abraham	Pvt	F 1st SCVA	Bentonville, NC	03/22/65	New Berne, NC	04/10/65	Hart's Island, NY	CSR
					Hart's Island, NY	06/16/65	Rlsd. G.O. #109	P79,CSR

SOUTH CAROLINA SOLDIERS, SAILORS AND  CITIZENS HELD IN U.S. PRISONS 1861-1865

NAME	RANK	REGIMENT	CAPTURED AT	WHEN	PRISON	MOVED	DISPOSITION	SOURCES
Robertson, Benjamin W.	Pvt	C 14th SCVI	Richmond, VA	04/27/65	Richmond, VA	04/27/65	Paroled	CSR
Robertson, George W.T.	Pvt	I 16th SCVI	Marietta, GA	06/19/64	Nashville, TN	06/24/64	Louisville, KY	P3,CSR
					Louisville, KY	06/27/64	Camp Morton, IN	P88,P91,CSR
					Camp Morton, IN	02/26/65	City Pt., VA Xc	P100,P101,CSR
					Richmond, VA Hos.	03/31/65	Furloughed 60 days	CSR
Robertson, H.C.	Pvt	C 3rd SCVABn	Blakely, AL	04/09/65	Ship Island, MS	05/01/65	Vicksburg, MS Xc	P136,CSR
Robertson, H.C.	Pvt	C 3rd SCVABn	Citronelle, AL	05/04/65	Meridian, MS	05/10/65	Paroled	CSR
Robertson, Henry	Pvt	K 15th SCVI	Augusta, GA	05/29/65	Augusta, GA	05/29/65	Paroled on oath	H15
Robertson, J.A.	Pvt	C 12th SCVI	Gettysburg, PA	07/05/63	Chester, PA USGH	09/23/63	City Pt., VA Xc	CSR
					Williamsburg, VA H	09/28/63	Furloughed	CSR
Robertson, J.H.	Pvt	I 12th SCVI	Appomattox R., VA	04/03/65	City Pt., VA	04/11/65	Hart's Island, NY	CSR
					Hart's Island, NY	06/17/65	Rlsd. G.O. #109	P79,CSR
Robertson, James W.	Pvt	C 19th SCVI	Pulaski, TN	12/25/64	Nashville, TN	02/14/65	Louisville, KY	P3,P39,CSR,HOE
					Louisville, KY	02/17/65	Camp Chase, IL	P92,P95,CSR
					Camp Chase, OH	04/22/65	Joined U.S. Forces	P23,CSR
Robertson, Levi D.	Pvt	G 2nd SCVI	Gettysburg, PA	07/04/63	Gettysburg G.H.		Provost Marshal	P4,KEB,SA2,H2,CSR
					David's Island, NY	10/22/63	Fts. Monroe, VA Xc	P1,CSR
Robertson, Lucien K.	Pvt	G Orr's Ri.	Petersburg, VA	04/03/65	City Pt., VA	04/11/65	Hart's Island, NY	CSR
					Hart's Island, NY	06/16/65	Rlsd. G.O. #109	P79,CSR
Robertson, M.K.	Sgt	H 16th SCVI	Jonesboro, GA	09/01/64	Rough & Ready, GA	09/19/64	Exchanged	CSR
Robertson, Thomas L.	Sgt	E Orr's Ri.	Petersburg, VA	04/03/65	City Pt., VA	04/11/65	Hart's Island, NY	CSR
					Hart's Island, NY	06/18/65	Rlsd. G.O. #109	P79,CSR
Robertson, Thomas M.	Pvt	F 12th SCVI	Richmond, VA Hos.	04/03/65	Richmond, VA Hos.	04/26/65	Paroled	CSR
Robertson, Thomas P.	Pvt	I 24th SCVI	Calhoun, GA	05/16/64	Nashville, TN	05/24/64	Louisville, KY	P2,EFW
					Louisville, KY	05/25/64	Rock Island, IL	P88,P91,P93
					Rock Island, IL	10/16/64	Joined US Army	P131
					Rock Island, IL	02/05/65	Tfd. for Exchange	CSR
					Ft. Columbus, NY	03/06/65	Boulwares Wh., VA	CSR
					Jackson H. Rchmd.	03/08/65	Furloughed 30 days	CSR
Robertson, W. Ladell	Pvt	I 24th SCVI	Chickamauga, GA	09/20/63	Nashville, TN	09/30/63	Louisville, KY	P38,EFW
					Louisville, KY	10/02/63	Camp Douglas, IL	P88,P89
					Camp Douglas, IL	03/13/65	Pt. Lookout, MD	P53,P55,P57
					Pt. Lookout, MD	03/18/65	Boulwares Wh., VA	CSR
					Jackson H. Rchmd.	03/27/65	Furloughed 60 days	CSR
Robertson, W.M.	Pvt	B 7th SCVC	Augusta, GA	05/19/65	Augusta, GA	05/19/65	Paroled	CSR
Robier, Phillip	Pvt	Ferguson's LA	Ringgold, GA	11/26/63	Nashville, TN	12/09/63	Louisville, KY	P39,CSR
					Louisville, KY	12/11/63	Rock Island, IL	P89,CSR
					Rock Island, IL	01/25/64	Joined US Navy	P131,CSR
Robins, James H.	2Lt	C Orr's Ri.	Appomattox R., VA	04/03/65	Old Capitol, DC	04/07/65	Johnson's Isl., OH	CSR
					Johnson's Isl., OH	06/19/65	Rlsd. G.O. #109	CSR
Robins, Obediah C.	Pvt	I 6th SCVI	Darbytown Rd., VA	10/07/64	Bernuda Hundred, VA	10/21/64	City Pt., VA	CSR
					City Pt., VA	10/29/64	Pt. Lookout, MD	CSR
					Pt. Lookout, MD	02/10/65	Aikens Ldg., VA Xc	P117,CSR
					Richmond, VA Hos.	02/25/65	Furloughed 60 days	CSR
Robinson, Allen J.	Pvt	I 17th SCVI	Crater, Pbg., VA	07/30/64	City Pt., VA	08/05/64	Pt. Lookout, MD	CSR,LAN
					Pt. Lookout, MD	08/08/64	Elmira, NY	P113,P117,P120,CSR
					Elmira, NY	11/08/64	Died, Ch. Diarrhea	P6,P65,P66,FPH,CSR
Robinson, Benjamin E.	Pvt	A 24th SCVI	Jackson, MS	05/14/63	Demopolis, AL	06/05/63	Paroled	EFW
Robinson, Benjamin E.	2Lt	A 24th SCVI	Nashville, TN	12/16/64	Louisville, KY	12/20/64	Johnson's Isl.	OH P90,P91,P94,CSR
					Johnson's Isl., OH	06/17/65	Rlsd. G.O. #109	P81,P82,CSR
Robinson, Charles S.D.	Pvt	B 1st SCVIH	Warrenton, VA	09/29/62	Warrenton, VA	09/29/62	Paroled	CSR

SOUTH CAROLINA SOLDIERS, SAILORS AND  CITIZENS HELD IN U.S. PRISONS 1861-1865

NAME	RANK	REGIMENT	CAPTURED AT	WHEN	PRISON	MOVED	DISPOSITION	SOURCES
Robinson, Ellison	Sgt	H 26th SCVI	Southside RR, VA	04/01/65	City Pt., VA	04/05/65	Pt. Lookout, MD	CSR
					Pt. Lookout, MD	06/17/65	Rlsd. G.O. #109	P115,P118,CSR
Robinson, Frank	Pvt	G 18th SCVI	Crater, Pbg., VA	07/30/64	City Pt., VA	08/05/64	Pt. Lookout, MD	CSR
					Pt. Lookout, MD	08/08/64	Elmira, NY	P113,P117,P120,CSR
					Elmira, NY	07/03/65	Rlsd. G.O. #109	P65,P66,CSR
Robinson, G.F.	Pvt	A 7th SCVI	Cedar Creek, VA	10/19/64	Harpers Ferry, WV	10/25/64	Pt. Lookout, MD	CSR
					Pt. Lookout, MD	06/17/65	Rlsd. G.O. #109	P115,P117,CSR
Robinson, G.M.B.	Pvt	E 20th SCVI	Cedar Creek, VA	10/19/64	Harpers Ferry, WV	10/24/64	Pt. Lookout, MD	CSR,KEB
					Pt. Lookout, MD	06/17/65	Rlsd. G.O. #109	P115,P117,CSR
Robinson, Hugh	2Lt	G 22nd SCVI	Petersburg, VA	04/03/65	City Pt., VA	04/08/65	Old Capitol, DC	CSR
					Old Capitol, DC	04/21/65	Johnson's Isl., OH	P110,CSR
					Johnson's Isl., OH	06/20/65	Rlsd. G.O. #109	P81,P82,P83,R48
Robinson, Isaac	Pvt	I 19th SCVI	Nashville, TN	12/15/64	Nashville, TN	12/18/64	Louisville, KY	CSR
					Louisville, KY	12/20/64	Camp Douglas, IL	P90,P94,CSR
					Camp Douglas, IL	06/20/65	Rlsd. G.O. #109	P55,CSR
Robinson, Isom E.	Pvt	C 22nd SCVI	Crater, Pbg., VA	07/30/64	Pt. Lookout, MD	08/08/64	Elmira, NY	P113,P117,P120
					Elmira, NY	10/01/64	Died, Diarrhea	P6,P12,P65,FPH
Robinson, J.A.	Pvt	G 22nd SCVI	Crater, Pbg., VA	07/30/64	City Pt., VA	08/05/64	Pt. Lookout, MD	CSR
					Pt. Lookout, MD	08/08/64	Elmira, NY	CSR
					Elmira, NY		No Release/SUR Apx	CSR
Robinson, J.M.	Pvt	K Orr's Ri.	Warrenton, VA	09/29/62	Warrenton, VA	09/29/62	Paroled	CSR
Robinson, J.W.	Pvt	A 1st SCVC	Culpepper, VA	09/14/63	Old Capitol, DC	09/26/63	Pt. Lookout, MD	CSR
					Ft. McHenry, MD	09/26/63	Pt. Lookout, MD	P110
					Pt. Lookout, MD	09/18/64	Aikens Ldg., VA Xc	P113,P116,P124,CSR
Robinson, James	Pvt	H Ham.Leg.	Frederick, MD	09/12/62	Ft. Delaware, DE	10/02/62	Aikens Ldg., VA Xc	CSR
Robinson, Jesse	Pvt	E 20th SCVI	Columbia, SC	02/14/65	New Berne, NC	04/10/65	Hart's Island, NY	CSR,KEB
					Hart's Island, NY	06/16/65	Rlsd. G.O. #109	P79,CSR
Robinson, John	Pvt	A 1st SCVIR	Deserted/enemy		Charleston, SC	03/24/65	Released on oath	CSR
Robinson, John	Pvt	D 1st SCVIR	Fayetteville, NC	03/12/65	New Berne, NC	04/10/65	Hart's Island, NY	CSR
					Hart's Island, NY	07/07/65	Escaped Frm Gd.Hou	P79,CSR
Robinson, John A.	Pvt	I 1st SCVIG	Petersburg, VA	04/03/65	City Pt., VA	04/13/65	Pt. Lookout, MD	CSR,SA1
					Pt. Lookout, MD	06/06/65	Rlsd. Instr. 5/30/65	P115,P118,P121,CSR
Robinson, Joseph T.	Sgt	B 1st SCVIH	Warrenton, VA	09/29/62	Warrenton, VA	09/29/62	Paroled	CSR
Robinson, Murray	Pvt	G 25th SCVI	Town Creek, NC	02/20/65	Ft. Anderson, NC	02/28/65	Pt. Lookout, MD	CSR,HAG
					Pt. Lookout, MD	06/17/65	Rlsd. G.O. #109	P115,P117,CSR
Robinson, P.J.	Pvt	C 7th SCVI	Sharpsburg, MD	09/17/62	P.M. Army of Potomac	09/27/62	Paroled	CSR
Robinson, R.B.	Pvt	E 20th SCVI	Columbia, SC	02/14/65	New Berne, NC	04/10/65	Hart's Island, NY	CSR,KEB
					Hart's Island, NY	06/16/65	Rlsd. G.O. #109	P79,CSR
Robinson, Robert W.	Pvt	A 21st SCVI	Petersburg, VA	03/25/65	Pt. Lookout, MD	06/17/65	Rlsd. G.O. #109	P115
Robinson, S.B.	Pvt	D Hol.Leg.	Warrenton, VA	09/29/62	Warrenton, VA	08/29/62	Paroled in Hos.	CSR
Robinson, Samuel	2Lt	I 2nd SCVI	Sharpsburg, MD	09/17/62	Shepherdstown, MD	09/17/62	Died of wounds	SA2,P12,H2,CSR
Robinson, Samuel N.	Pvt	E 12th SCVI	Gettysburg, PA	07/05/63	Ft. Delaware, DE	10/30/64	Pt. Lookout, MD	P42,P44,LAN
					Pt. Lookout, MD	10/31/64	Exchanged	P40,P115
Robinson, Samuel N.	Pvt	E 12th SCVI	Petersburg, VA	04/02/65	City Pt., VA	04/11/65	Hart's Island, NY	CSR
					Hart's Island, NY	06/16/65	Rlsd. G.O. #109	P79,CSR
Robinson, W.H.	Pvt	G 3rd SCVIBn	Sharpsburg, MD	09/17/62	Ft. McHenry, MD	10/17/62	Fts. Monroe, VA	CSR
					Fts. Monroe, VA	10/19/62	Aikens Ldg., VA Xc	CSR
Robinson, W.M.	Pvt	E 12th SCVI	Sharpsburg, MD	09/17/62	Frederick, MD USGH	10/16/62	Ft. McHenry, MD	CSR
					Ft. McHenry, MD	10/18/62	Fts. Monroe, VA Xc	CSR
					Richmond, VA Hos.	01/30/63	Furloughed 50 days	CSR
Robinson, Wiley R.	Pvt	E 5th SCResB	Bentonville, NC	03/19/65	Pt. Lookout, MD	06/17/65	Rlsd. G.O. #109	CSR

SOUTH CAROLINA SOLDIERS, SAILORS AND  CITIZENS HELD IN U.S. PRISONS 1861-1865

NAME	RANK	REGIMENT	CAPTURED AT	WHEN	PRISON	MOVED	DISPOSITION	SOURCES
Robinson, William	Pvt	H Ham.Leg.	Chattanooga, TN	10/29/63	Nashville, TN	11/07/63	Louisville, KY	P39,CSR
					Louisville, KY	11/09/63	Camp Morton, IN	P88,P89,P93,CSR
					Camp Morton, IN	01/16/64	Died, Pneumonia	P12,P100,FPH,CSR
Robinson, William S.B.	Pvt	A 18th SCVI	Crater, Pbg., VA	07/30/64	City Pt., VA	08/05/64	Pt. Lookout, MD	CSR,UD2
					Pt. Lookout, MD	08/08/64	Elmira, NY	P113,P117,P120,P125,CSR
					Elmira, NY	10/11/64	Pt. Lookout, MD Xc	P65,P66,CSR
					Pt. Lookout, MD	10/28/64	Died, Ch. Diarrhea	P5,P119,FPH,CSR
					Pt. Lookout, MD	10/29/64	Venus Pt., GA Xc	P115,P117,CSR
Roche, T.W.	Pvt	I 22nd SCVI	Deserted/enemy	01/02/65	City Pt., VA	01/05/65	Washington, DC	CSR
					Washington, DC	01/06/65	Vicksburg, MS oath	CSR
Rochester, H.D.	Pvt	C 2nd SCVIRi	Burkesville, VA	04/14/65	Burkesville, VA	04/17/65	Paroled	CSR
Rochester, John	Pvt	H 22nd SCVI	Deserted/enemy	01/15/65	City Pt., VA	02/18/65	Washington, DC	CSR
					Washington, DC	02/27/65	Ducktown, TN oath	CSR
Rochester, William	Pvt	K 16th SCVI	Ringgold, GA	11/26/63	Nashville, TN	12/11/63	Louisville, KY	P39,CSR
					Louisville, KY	12/12/63	Rock Island, IL	P88,P89,CSR
					Rock Island, IL	09/12/64	Died, Consumption	P5,P12,P131,P132,FPH
Rockwell, J.H.	Pvt	F Hol.Leg.	Jarratts Stn., VA	05/08/64	Pt. Lookout, MD	06/15/64	Died, Lung Inflam.	P6,P116,P119,FPH
Roddey, William Lyle	Cpt	H 24th SCVI	Taylors Ridge, GA	10/16/64	Nashville, TN	10/23/64	Louisville, KY	CSR,HHC
					Louisville, KY	10/28/64	Johnson's Isl., OH	P90,P91,P94,CSR
					Johnson's Isl., OH	06/16/65	Rlsd. G.O. #109	P81,CSR
Roddy, David	Pvt	A 6th SCVI	Deep Bottom, VA	08/14/64	Bermuda Hundred, VA	08/15/64	City Pt., VA P.M.	CSR,HHC
					Fts. Monroe, VA	08/17/64	Pt. Lookout, MD	CSR
					Pt. Lookout, MD	11/02/64	Exchanged	P121,P124,P125
Roddy, W.T.	Pvt	A 17th SCVI	Deserted/enemy	02/25/65	P.M. A. of Potomac	02/26/65	Pt. Lookout, VA	CSR
					City Pt., VA P.M.	02/28/65	Washington, DC	CSR
					Washington, DC	03/01/65	Savannah, GA oath	CSR
Roden, John D.	Pvt	B 5th SCVI	Chattanooga, TN	09/25/63	Chattanooga, TN	10/15/63	Died of wounds	P12,SA3,HHC,CSR
Rodgers, A.H.	Pvt	F 2nd SCVIRi	Warrenton, VA	09/29/62	Warrenton, VS	09/29/62	Paroled	CSR
Rodgers, A.M.	Pvt	G 27th SCVI	Petersburg, VA	06/24/64	Bermuda Hundred, VA	06/25/64	Fts. Monroe, VA	CSR,HAG
					Fts. Monroe, VA	06/26/64	Pt. Lookout, MD	CSR
					Pt. Lookout, MD	08/16/64	Elmira, NY	P113,P117,P120,CSR
					Elmira, NY	02/20/65	James R., VA Xc	P65,P66,CSR
					Elmira, NY Trnspt.	02/20/65	Died on the boat	CSR
Rodgers, Cambyses	Pvt	H 8th SCVI	Gettysburg, PA	07/05/63	Gettysburg G.H.		Provost Marshal	P4,KEB,HMC
Rodgers, Ephraim A.	Pvt	G 6th SCVC	Fairfield, SC	02/21/65	New Berne, NC	03/29/65	Pt. Lookout, MD	CSR
					Pt. Lookout, MD	06/17/65	Rlsd. G.O. #109	P115,P117,CSR
Rodgers, Francis E.	Pvt	A 7th SCVC	Burkesville, SC	04/06/65	City Pt., VA	04/15/65	Pt. Lookout, MD	CSR
					Pt. Lookout, MD	06/17/65	Rlsd. G.O. #109	CSR
Rodgers, H.	HSd	14th SCVI	Gettysburg, PA	07/02/63	Chester, PA G.H.	08/17/63	City Pt., VA Xc	P1,CSR
Rodgers, Hugh	Pvt	F 20th SCVI	Cedar Creek, VA	10/19/64	Harpers Ferry, WV	10/24/64	Pt. Lookout, MD	CSR
					Pt. Lookout, MD	06/14/65	Rlsd. G.O. #109	P115,P117,P122,CSR
Rodgers, J.D.	Pvt	G 20th SCVI	Cedar Creek, VA	10/19/64	Pt. Lookout, MD	05/15/65	Rlsd. G.O. #85	P115,P117,P121,KEB
Rodgers, James L.	Pvt	G 20th SCVI	Cedar Creek, VA	10/19/64	Harpers Ferry, WV	10/24/64	Pt. Lookout, MD	CSR
					Pt. Lookout, MD	05/15/65	Released on oath	CSR
Rodgers, John	Pvt	F 26th SCVI	Petersburg, VA	03/25/65	City Pt., VA	03/28/65	Pt. Lookout, MD	CSR
					Pt. Lookout, MD	06/17/65	Rlsd. G.O. #109	CSR
Rodgers, John C.	Pvt	B 37th VAVCB	Greenbrier Co., VA	10/08/63	Wheeling, WV	10/23/63	Camp Chase, OH	CSR
					Camp Chase, OH	01/22/64	Rock Island, IL	CSR
					Rock Island, IL	03/02/65	Transferred to Xc	CSR
Rodgers, Josiah	Pvt	K 1st SCVIH	Richmond, VA Hos.	04/03/65	Richmond, VA Hos.	04/05/65	Libby Prison Rchmd.	CSR
Rodgers, Josiah	Pvt	K 1st SCVIH	Richmond, VA	04/03/65	City Pt., VA	04/14/65	Pt. Lookout, MD	CSR
					Pt. Lookout, MD	06/21/65	Died, Brain Inflam.	P6,P12,P115,P118,P119,CS

R

SOUTH CAROLINA SOLDIERS, SAILORS AND CITIZENS HELD IN U.S. PRISONS 1861-1865

NAME	RANK	REGIMENT	CAPTURED AT	WHEN	PRISON	MOVED	DISPOSITION	SOURCES
Rodgers, L.P.	Pvt	G 27th SCVI	Petersburg, VA	06/24/64	Bermuda Hundred, VA	06/25/64	Fts. Monroe, VA	CSR,HAG
					Fts. Monroe, VA	06/26/64	Pt. Lookout, MD	CSR
					Pt. Lookout, MD	08/16/64	Elmira, NY	P113,P117,P120
					Elmira, NY	03/02/65	Pt. Lookout, MD Xc	P65,P66,CSR
Rodgers, M.	Pvt	H 23rd SCVI	Deserted/enemy	03/14/65	City Pt., VA	03/14/65	Washington, DC	CSR
					Washington, DC	03/18/65	Harrisburg, PA	CSR
Rodgers, Marion D.	Pvt	H 12th SCVI	Sutherland Stn., VA	04/03/65	City Pt., VA	04/07/65	Hart's Island, VA	CSR,YEB
					Hart's Island, NY	06/16/65	Rlsd. G.O. #109	P79,CSR
Rodgers, William	Pvt	B Ham.Leg.MI	Augusta, GA	05/23/65	Augusta, GA	05/23/65	Paroled	CSR
Rodgers, Willis	Pvt	H 23rd SCVI	Jackson, MS	07/11/63	Camp Morton, IN	03/15/65	Tfd. for Xc	P100,HMC,CSR
Rodley, Edward S.	Pvt	C 15th SCVAB	Staunton, VA	06/08/64	Wheeling, WV	07/15/64		CSR
Rodman, Alexander K.	Pvt	H 24th SCVI	Jackson, MS	05/14/63	Demopolis, AL	06/05/63	Paroled	EFW,HHC
Rodman, Alexander K.	Pvt	H 24th SCVI	Missionary Ridge, TN	11/25/63	Bridgeport, AL G.H	12/23/63	Nashville, TN	P2,CSR
					Nashville, TN	01/02/64	Died, Ch. Diarrhea	P6,CSR
Rodt, M.H.	Pvt	E 1st SCVIR	Goldsboro, NC	03/31/65	Hart's Island, NY	06/17/65	Rlsd. G.O. #109	P79,SA1
Rodt, Martin H.	1Lt	G 17th SCVI	Petersburg, VA	03/25/65	Old Capitol, DC	03/30/65	Ft. Delaware, DE	P110,CSR
					Ft. Delaware, DE	06/17/65	Rlsd. G.O. #109	P43,P45,CSR
Roe, Carter	Pvt	E 2nd SCVIRi	Burkesville, VA	04/14/65	Burkesville, VA	04/17/65	Paroled	CSR
Roe, John	Pvt	G 2nd SCVI	Gettysburg, PA	07/03/63	Gettysburg G.H.	07/21/63	Provost Marshal	P4,KEB,SA2,H2,CSR
					David's Island, NY	10/22/63	Fts. Monroe, VA	P1,CSR
					Fts. Monroe, VA	10/28/63	City Pt., VA Xc	CSR
Roebuck, Benjamin F.	Pvt	K 3rd SCVI	Amelia C.H., VA	04/05/65	City Pt., VA	04/14/65	Pt. Lookout, MD	CSR,HOS,KEB,SA2,H3
					Pt. Lookout, MD	06/17/65	Rlsd. G.O. #109	P115,CSR
Roebuck, J.H.	Pvt	E Hol.Leg.	Warrenton, VA	09/29/62	Warrenton, VA	09/29/62	Paroled in Hos.	CSR
Roebuck, John P.	Sgt	K 3rd SCVI	Sharpsburg, MD	09/17/62	P.M. Army of Patomac	09/30/62	Paroled	CSR,KEB,SA2,H3
Roebuck, John P.	Cpt	K 3rd SCVI	Loudon, TN	12/03/63	Nashville, TN	04/27/64	Louisville, KY	P2,P39,CSR
					Louisville, KY	05/12/64	Johnson's Isl., OH	P88,P91,P93,CSR
					Johnson's Isl., OH	06/13/65	Rlsd. G.O. #109	CSR
Roett, J. (?)	Pvt	B 1st SCVA	Bentonville, NC	03/22/65	Hart's Island, NY	06/16/65	Rlsd. G.O. #109	P79
Rogers, A.D.	Pvt	McQueen LA	Farmville, VA	04/11/65	Farmville, VA	04/21/65	Paroled	CSR
Rogers, Andrew M.	Cpl	G 3rd SCVI	Wilderness, VA	05/06/64	Belle Plain, VA	05/21/64	Ft. Delaware, DE	CSR,KEB,SA2,H3
					Ft. Delaware, DE	04/01/65	Hos. 4/11-4/16/65	P47
					Ft. Delaware, DE	06/17/65	Hos. 6/17-6/21/64	P47
					Ft. Delaware, DE	10/10/64	Hos. 10/10-10/17/64	P47,KEB
					Ft. Delaware, DE	06/10/65	Rlsd. G.O. #109	P41,P42,P45,CSR
Rogers, Anson	Pvt	H Orr's Ri.	Falling Waters, MD	07/14/63	Baltimore, MD	08/20/63	Pt. Lookout, MD	CSR
					Pt. Lookout, MD	03/17/64	City Pt., VA Xc	P113,P116,P124,CDC,HMC
Rogers, Daniel R.	Pvt	E 1st SCVC	Malvern Hill, VA	05/23/64	City Pt., VA	08/10/64	Alexandria, VA USH	CSR
					Alexandria, VA USH	08/22/64	Died of wounds	CSR
Rogers, Dennis B.	Pvt	E 1st SCVIG	N. Anna River, VA	05/23/64	Pt. Lookout, MD	06/10/64	Joined U.S. Army	P116,P122,P125,SA1
Rogers, Enoch	Pvt	F 4th SCVC	Louisa C.H., VA	06/11/64	Fts. Monroe, VA	06/20/64	Pt. Lookout, MD	CSR
					Pt. Lookout, MD	07/25/64	Elmira, NY	P113,P116,P120,HMC,CSR
Rogers, Enoch	Pvt	F 4th SCVC	Louisa C.H., VA	06/11/64	Elmira, NY	06/14/65	Rlsd. G.O. #109	P65,P66,HMC,CSR
Rogers, Frank A.	Pvt	K 8th SCVI	Winchester, VA	09/13/64	Harpers Ferry, WV	09/19/64	Camp Chase, OH	CSR,HOM,KEB
					Camp Chase, OH	06/11/65	Rlsd. G.O. #109	P23,CSR
Rogers, Henry A.	Pvt	H 5th SCVC	Columbia, SC	02/16/65	New Berne, NC	04/10/65	Hart's Island, NY	CSR
					Hart's Island, NY	06/17/65	Rlsd. G.O. #109	P79,CSR
Rogers, J. Benjamin	Pvt	I 21st SCVI	Petersburg, VA	05/09/64	Pt. Lookout, MD	08/15/64	Elmira, NY	P113,P116,HMC,HAG
					Pt. Lookout, MD	09/18/64	Aikens Ldg., VA Xc	P121
Rogers, John	Pvt	McQueen LA	Petersburg, VA	04/02/65	City Pt., VA	04/04/65	Pt. Lookout, MD	CSR
					Pt. Lookout, MD	06/17/65	Rlsd. G.O. #109	CSR

SOUTH CAROLINA SOLDIERS, SAILORS AND  CITIZENS HELD IN U.S. PRISONS 1861-1865

NAME	RANK	REGIMENT	CAPTURED AT	WHEN	PRISON	MOVED	DISPOSITION	SOURCES
Rogers, John A.	Pvt	C 22nd SCVI	Crater, Pbg., VA	07/30/64	City Pt., VA	08/05/64	Pt. Lookout, MD	CSR,HOS
					Pt. Lookout, MD	08/08/64	Elmira, NY	P113,P117,P120,CSR
					Elmira, NY	06/14/65	Rlsd. G.O. #109	P65,P66,CSR
Rogers, John Dew	Pvt	E 1st SCVIG	Petersburg, VA	07/29/64	Pt. Lookout, MD	08/08/64	Elmira, NY	P113,P117,HMC,SA1
					Elmira, NY	07/03/65	Rlsd. G.O. #109	P65,P66,CSR
Rogers, John Green	Pvt	K 3rd SCVI	Lynch's Creek, SC	02/28/65	New Berne, NC	03/26/65	Pt. Lookout, MD	CSR
					Pt. Lookout, MD	06/17/65	Rlsd. G.O. #109	H3,KEB,CSR
Rogers, John W.	Sgt	H Orr's Rl.	Richmond, VA area	05/31/62	Ft. Columbus, NY			CDC,CSR
Rogers, L.B.	Pvt	L 8th SCVI	Winchester, VA	09/13/64	Harpers Ferry, WV	09/19/64	Camp Chase, OH	CSR,KEB,HMC
					Camp Chase, OH	05/02/65	New Orleans, LA	P23,P26,CSR
					New Orleans, LA	05/12/65	Vicksburg, MS Xc	CSR
Rogers, Leonard P.	Cpt	C Orr's Ri.	Wilderness, VA	05/10/64	Belle Plain, VA	05/17/64	Ft. Delaware, DE	P42, CSR
Rogers, Leonard P.	Cpt	C Orr's Ri.	Spotsylvania, VA	05/12/64	Ft. Delaware, DE		Hos. 5/21-5/28/64	P47
					Ft. Delaware, DE	06/16/65	Rlsd. G.O. #109	P42,P44, CSR
Rogers, Lindsay L.	Pvt	H Orr's Ri.	Deserted/enemy	03/14/65	City Pt., VA	03/16/65	Washington, DC	CSR
					Washington, DC	03/18/65	Harrisburg, PA	CSR
Rogers, Millington R.J.	Pvt	H 8th SCVI	Gettysburg, PA	07/05/63	Pt. Lookout, MD	03/16/65	City Pt., VA Xc	P113,P124,KEB,CSR
Rogers, Millington R.J.	Pvt	H 8th SCVI	Winchester, VA	09/13/64	Harpers Ferry, WV	09/19/64	Camp Chase, OH	CSR,HMC
					Camp Chase, OH	06/11/65	Rlsd. G.O. #109	P23,CSR
Rogers, Owen M.	Pvt	L 21st SCVI	Morris Island, SC	07/10/63	Hilton Head G.H.	07/23/63	Morris Island, SC Xc	P2,HMC,CSR,HAG
Rogers, Peter A.	Pvt	K 15th SCVI	Halltown, VA	08/26/64	Harpers Ferry, WV	08/29/64	Camp Chase, OH	CSR,KEB,H15
					Camp Chase, OH	03/18/65	Pt. Lookout, MD	P23,P26,CSR
					Pt. Lookout, MD	03/27/65	Boulware's Wh. Xc	CSR
Rogers, Peter A.	Pvt	K 15th SCVI	Augusta, GA	05/24/65	Augusta, GA	05/24/65	Paroled on oath	CSR
Rogers, Pinckney	Pvt	B 8th SCVI	Gettysburg, PA	07/03/63	Ft. Delaware, DE	06/08/65	Rlsd. G.O. #109	P42,P45,KEB,CSR
Rogers, Robert W.	Pvt	D 1st SCVIR	Bentonville, NC	03/22/65	New Berne, NC	04/10/65	Hart's Island, NY	CSR
					Hart's Island, NY	06/19/65	Rlsd. G.O. #109	SA1,P79,CSR
Rogers, S.P.	Pvt	F 2nd SCVI	Gettysburg, PA	07/05/63	Letterman G.H. Gbg	10/15/63	Provost Marshal	CSR
Rogers, Sanford V.	Pvt	C 22nd SCVI	Crater, Pbg., VA	07/30/64	City Pt., VA	08/05/64	Pt. Lookout, MD	CSR,HOS
					Pt. Lookout, MD	08/08/64	Elmira, NY	P66,P113,P117,P120
					Elmira, NY	10/31/64	Died, Ch. Diarrhea	P6,P12,P65,FPH
Rogers, Thomas G.	Pvt	I 21st SCVI	Ft. Fisher, NC	01/15/65	Elmira, NY	02/16/65	Died, Ch. Diarrhea	P6,P65,P66,FPH,HAG
Rogers, Thomas J.	Pvt	H Orr's Ri.	Deserted/enemy	03/14/65	City Pt., VA	03/15/65	Washington, DC	CSR
					Washington, DC	03/16/65	Harrisburg, PA	CSR
Rogers, W.J.	Pvt	D 4th SCVC	Stony Creek, VA	12/01/64	City Pt., VA	12/05/64	Pt. Lookout, MD	CSR
					Pt. Lookout, MD	06/17/65	Rlsd. G.O. #109	P115,CSR
Rogers, W.R.	Pvt	K 3rd SCVI	Sharpsburg, MD	09/17/62	P.M. Army of Potomac	09/27/62	Paroled	CSR,KEB,SA2,H3
Rogers, William H.	Pvt	5 10/19 SCVI	Missionary Ridge, TN	11/25/63	Nashville, TN	12/07/63	Louisville, KY	P39,RAS,CSR
					Louisville, KY	12/07/63	Rock Island, IL	P88,P89,CSR
					Rock Island, IL	05/03/65	New Orleans, LA Xc	P131,CSR
					New Orleans, LA	05/23/65	Exchanged	P3,CSR
Rogers, William T.	2Lt	K 8th SCVI	Winchester, VA	09/13/64	Harpers Ferry, WV	09/24/64	Johnson's Isl., OH	CSR,HOM,KEB
					Johnson's Isl., OH	06/16/65	Rlsd. G.O. #109	P81,P82,P83,CSR
Rogerson, H.C.	Cpl	Waccamaw A	Deserted/enemy	03/20/65	Hilton Head, SC	04/07/65	New York, NY P.M.	CSR
Rohleter, Joseph	Pvt	A 20th SCVI	Fayetteville, NC	03/17/65	Pt. Lookout, MD	06/17/65	Rlsd. G.O. #109	P115,CSR
Roland, Jeremiah M.	Pvt	D 18th SCVI	Petersburg, VA	04/01/65	City Pt., VA	04/04/65	Pt. Lookout, MD	CSR,UD5
					Pt. Lookout, MD	06/17/65	Rlsd. G.O. #109	P115,P118,CSR
Roland, T.	Pvt	C 1st SCEng.	Bentonville, NC	03/20/65	Hart's Island, NY	06/16/65	Rlsd. G.O. #109	P79
Rollins, Benjamin F.	Pvt	D 8th SCVI	Gettysburg, PA	07/04/63	Ft. McHenry, MD	07/09/63	Ft. Delaware, DE	CSR,KEB
					Ft. Delaware, DE	09/15/63	Jd. US 1st CN Cav.	P40,P42,P44,CSR
Rollins, David	Pvt	A 1st SCVIR	Morris Island, SC	09/07/63	Ft. Delaware, DE	09/26/63	Pt. Lookout, MD	CSR
					Pt. Lookout, MD	02/12/64	Joined U.S. Army	P113,P116,P125,SA1,CSR

SOUTH CAROLINA SOLDIERS, SAILORS AND  CITIZENS HELD IN U.S. PRISONS 1861-1865

NAME	RANK	REGIMENT	CAPTURED AT	WHEN	PRISON	MOVED	DISPOSITION	SOURCES
Rollins, G.T.	Pvt	G 26th SCVI	Richmond, VA Hos.	04/03/65	Libby Prison, Rchmd.	04/23/65	Newport News, VA	CSR
					Newport News, VA	06/26/65	Rlsd. G.O. #109	P107,CSR
Rollins, Lewis P.	Pvt	G 24th SCVI	Missionary Ridge, TN	11/25/63	Nashville, TN	12/09/63	Louisville, KY	CSR
					Louisville, KY	12/11/63	Rock Island, IL	P88,P89,CSR
					Rock Island, IL	12/24/63	Died	P5,FPH,CSR
Rollins, Offa	Pvt	I 18th SCVI	Crater, Pbg., VA	07/30/64	City Pt., VA	08/05/64	Pt. Lookout, MD	CSR
					Pt. Lookout, MD	08/08/64	Elmira, NY	P113,P117,CSR
					Elmira, NY	09/01/64	Died, Ch. Diarrhea	P5,P12,P65,FPH,CSR
Rollins, R.J.	Pvt	C 3rd SCVABn	Blakely, AL	04/09/65	Ship Island, MS	05/01/65	Vicksburg, MS Xc	P136,CSR
Rollins, Thomas	Pvt	C 1st SCVIR			New York, NY	06/23/65	Died	P12,FPH,SA1,CSR
Rollins, W.L.D.	Pvt	K P.S.S.	Deserted/enemy	01/24/65	City Pt., VA	01/27/65	Washington, DC	CSR,TSE
					Washington, DC	01/30/65	New York, NY oath	CSR
Rollins, William P.	Pvt	K 18th SCVI	Petersburg, VA	03/25/65	City Pt., VA	03/28/65	Pt. Lookout, MD	CSR
					Pt. Lookout, MD	06/17/65	Rlsd. G.O. #109	P115,P117,CSR
Ronan, Michael	Pvt	H 13th SCVI	Gettysburg, PA	07/03/63	Ft. McHenry, MD	07/07/63	Ft. Delaware, DE	CSR
					Ft. Delaware, DE	09/27/63	Jd. US 3rd MD Cav.	CSR
Ronan, Patrick	Pvt	D 1st SCVA	Charleston, SC	05/08/64	Washington, DC	04/14/65	Oath taken	CSR
Roof, John	Pvt	F 5th SCVC	Augusta, GA	05/24/65	Augusta, GA	05/24/65	Paroled	CSR
Roof, John N.	Cpl	I 22nd SCVI	Kinston, NC	12/14/62	Kinston, NC	12/14/62	Paroled POW	CSR
Roof, John N.	Cpl	I 22nd SCVI	Deserted/enemy	02/27/65	City Pt., VA	02/28/65	Washington, DC	CSR
					Washington, DC	03/02/65	Charleston, SC	CSR
Rook, Permain	Pvt	K 20th SCVI	Middletown, MD	07/12/64	Elmira, NY	04/03/65	Died, Ch. Diarrhea	P6,P12,FPH
Rook, Samuel L.	Pvt	A 27th SCVI	Weldon RR, VA	08/21/64	Davids Island, NY	10/08/64	Elmira, NY	P1,P66,FPH,CSR
					Elmira, NY	01/16/65	Died, Bronchitis	P6,P12,P65,FPH,CSR
Rook, Thomas J.	Pvt	F 20th SCVI	Cedar Creek, VA	10/19/64	Harpers Ferry, WV	10/24/64	Pt. Lookout, MD	CSR,ANY,KEB
					Pt. Lookout, MD	01/17/65	Aikens Ldg., VA Xc	P115,P124,CSR
Rook, Thomas P.	Pvt	A 13th SCVI	Petersburg, VA	03/25/65	City Pt., VA	03/26/65	Pt. Lookout, MD	CSR
					Pt. Lookout, MD	06/17/65	Rlsd. G.O. #109	P115,P122,CSR
Rooke, E.C.	Pvt	F 25th SCVI	Ft. Fisher, NC	01/15/65	New York, NY	01/30/65	Elmira, NY	CSR,HAG
					Elmira, NY	03/02/65	James R., VA Xc	P65,P66,CSR
Roon, J.H.	Pvt	F Ham.Leg.MI	Anderson, SC	05/03/65	Anderson, SC	05/03/65	Paroled	CSR
Rooney, Michael	Pvt	B 27th SCVI	Petersburg, VA	09/10/64	Pt. Lookout, MD	10/14/64	Joined U.S. Army	P113,P117,P125
Rooper, T.L.	Pvt	B 37th VAVCB	Strasburg, VA	09/23/64	Pt. Lookout, MD	03/01/65	Died, Ch. Diarrhea	P6,37V,CSR,FPH
Rosamond, William H.	Pvt	F Ham.Leg.MI	Newton, NC	04/19/65	Newton, NC	04/19/65	Paroled	CSR
Rosborough, J.A.	Sgt	C 12th SCVI	Petersburg, VA	04/03/65	City Pt., VA	04/07/65	Hart's Island, NY	CSR,HFC,UD2
					Hart's Island, NY	06/16/65	Rlsd. G.O. #109	P79,CSR
Roscoe, John R.	Pvt	G 8th SCVI	Cedar Creek, VA	10/19/64	Harpers Ferry, WV	10/25/64	Pt. Lookout, MD	CSR,HOM,KEB
					Pt. Lookout, MD	06/17/65	Rlsd. G.O. #109	P115,P117,CSR
Roscoe, Joseph F.	Pvt	E 21st SCVI	Petersburg, VA	06/24/64	Pt. Lookout, MD	08/16/64	Elmira, NY	P113,P117,P120,HAG
					Elmira, NY	03/14/65	Pt. Lookout, MD Xc	P65,P66
Rose, Augustus	Pvt	E 25th SCVI	Town Creek, NC	02/20/65	Ft. Anderson, NC	02/28/65	Pt. Lookout, MD	CSR,HAG
					Pt. Lookout, MD	06/17/65	Rlsd. G.O. #109	P115,P117,CSR
Rose, Jesse C.	Pvt	A 2nd SCVI	Columbia, SC	02/21/65	New Berne, NC	04/10/65	Hart's Island, NY	CSR,KEB,SA2,H2
					Hart's Island, NY	06/17/65	Rlsd. G.O. #109	P79,CSR
Rose, William	Pvt	E 27th SCVI	Town Creek, NC	02/20/65	Ft. Anderson, NC	02/28/65	Pt. Lookout, MD	CSR
					Pt. Lookout, MD	05/15/65	Rlsd. G.O. #85	P115,P117,CSR
Rose, William A.	Pvt	C 12th SCVI	Virginia	04/03/65	City Pt., VA Hos.	04/04/65	Old Capitol, DC G.H.	CSR
					Old Capitol, DC	06/07/65	Columbia, SC oath	CSR
Rose, Wyatt W.	Sgt	C 2nd SCVC	Greensboro, NC	05/01/65	Greensboro, NC	05/01/65	Paroled	CSR
Rosier, Robert A.	Pvt	F 11th SCVI	Swift Creek, VA	05/09/64	Hampton, VA G.H.	09/15/64	Died, Hos. Gangrene	P12,HAG,CSR
Ross, A.A.	Pvt	H 1st SCVC	Gettysburg, PA	07/03/63	Gettysburg G.H.	09/14/63	Provost Marshal	P4
					W. Bldg. Balt, MD	09/25/63	City Pt., VA Xc	P1,CSR

SOUTH CAROLINA SOLDIERS, SAILORS AND  CITIZENS HELD IN U.S. PRISONS 1861-1865

NAME	RANK	REGIMENT	CAPTURED AT	WHEN	PRISON	MOVED	DISPOSITION	SOURCES
Ross, Alexander A.	Pvt	C 3rd SCVIBn	Knoxville, TN	12/05/63	Nashville, TN	02/11/64	Louisville, KY	P39,CSR
					Louisville, KY	02/15/64	Rock Island, IL	P88,P91,P93,CSR
					Rock Island, IL	02/15/65	Pt. Lookout, MD Xc	P131,CSR,KEB
Ross, Charles C.	Sgt	C 15th SCVAB	Smith's Ford, NC	03/16/65	New Berne, NC	04/03/65	Pt. Lookout, MD	CSR
					Pt. Lookout, MD	06/30/65	Rlsd. G.O. #109	P115,P117,P121,CSR
Ross, James H.	Pvt	A Ham.Leg.C	Virginia			09/27/62	Aikens Ldg., VA Xc	CSR
Ross, Jonathan	Pvt	F 2nd SCVI	Gettysburg, PA	07/05/63	Letterman G.H. Gbg	10/06/63	Provost Marshal	P1,CSR,KEB,SA2,H2
					W. Bldg. Balt, MD	11/12/63	City Pt., VA Xc	CSR
Ross, Thomas	Pvt	F 3rd SCVIBn	Gettysburg, PA	07/06/63	Ft. Delaware, DE	05/03/65	Released Secy/War	P7,P40,P42,KEB,CSR
Ross, William M.G.	Pvt	I 27th SCVI	Town Creek, NC	02/20/65	Ft. Anderson, NC	02/28/65	Pt. Lookout, MD	CSR
					Pt. Lookout, MD	06/17/65	Rlsd. G.O. #109	P115,P117,CSR
Rossa, S.A.	Pvt	G 3rd SCVABn	High Pt., NC	05/01/65	High Pt., NC	05/01/65	Paroled	CSR
Rosser, William	Pvt	K 1st SCVA	Hartwell, GA	05/18/65	Hartwell, GA	05/18/65	Paroled on oath	CSR
Rothrock, J.H.	Pvt	F Hol.Leg.	Jarratts Stn., VA	05/08/64	Fts. Monroe, VA	05/13/64	Pt. Lookout, MD	CSR
					Pt. Lookout, MD	06/14/64	Died	CSR
Rotton, Frank L.	Pvt	A 22nd SCVI	Petersburg, VA	03/25/65	City Pt., VA	03/27/65	Pt. Lookout, MD	CSR
					Pt. Lookout, MD	06/17/65	Rlsd. G.O. #109	P115,P117,CSR
Rotton, Henry P.	Pvt	A 22nd SCVI	Petersburg, VA	03/25/65	City Pt., VA	03/27/65	Pt. Lookout, MD	CSR
					Pt. Lookout, MD	06/17/65	Rlsd. G.O. #109	P115,P117
Roundtree, M.E.	Pvt	G 8th SCVI	Chesterfield, SC	03/03/65	New Berne, NC	04/10/65	Hart's Island, NY	CSR,KEB
					Hart's Island, NY	06/17/65	Rlsd. G.O. #109	P79,CSR
Roundtree, Thomas J.	Pvt	K 7th SCVI	Sharpsburg, MD	09/17/62	Frederick, MD USGH	12/08/62	Died	P6,P12,CSR,KEB
Rourke, Artemus V.	Pvt	G 27th SCVI	Petersburg, VA	06/24/64	Bermuda Hundred, VA	06/25/64	Fts. Monroe, VA	CSR,HAG
					Fts. Monroe, VA	06/26/64	Pt. Lookout, MD	CSR
					Pt. Lookout, MD	08/16/64	Elmira, NY	P113,P117,P120,CSR
					Elmira, NY	02/20/65	Pt. Lookout, MD Xc	P65,P66,CSR
					Richmond, VA Hos.	03/28/65	Furloughed 60 days	CSR
Rouse, John J.	1Lt	A 8th SCVI	Winchester, VA	09/13/64	Harpers Ferry, WV	09/24/64	Johnson's Isl., OH	CSR,KEB
					Johnson's Isl., OH	06/16/65	Rlsd. G.O. #109	P81,P82,P83,CSR
Rouse, Oliver P.	Sgt	I 1st SCVIG	Petersburg, VA	04/02/65	City Pt., VA	04/04/65	Pt. Lookout, MD	CSR,SA1
					Pt. Lookout, MD	06/17/65	Rlsd. G.O. #109	P115,P118,CSR
Rouse, William R.	Pvt	E 11th SCVI	Petersburg, VA	06/24/64	Fts. Monroe, VA	08/27/64	Baltimore, MD	P8,HAG,CSR
Rouse, William R.	Pvt	E 11th SCVI	Petersburg, VA	06/24/64	Baltimore, MD	09/23/64	Rlsd. on oath	CSR
Rovett, W.S.	Pvt	7th SCVC	Athens, GA	05/08/65	Athens, GA	05/08/65	Paroled	CSR
Rowan, Samuel W.	Cpl	A 2nd SCVI	Sharpsburg, MD	10/01/62	Frederick, MD	11/26/62	Ft. McHenry, MD	CSR
					Ft. McHenry, MD	11/26/62	City Pt., VA Xc	SA2,H2,CSR
Rowand, Charles E.	Pvt	A 25th SCVI	Town Creek, NC	02/20/65	Ft. Anderson, NC	02/28/65	Pt. Lookout, MD	CSR,HAG
					Pt. Lookout, MD	06/17/65	Rlsd. G.O. #109	P115,P117,CSR
Rowand, Robert	Sgt	I 27th SCVI	Town Creek, NC	02/20/65	Ft. Anderson, NC	02/28/65	Pt. Lookout, MD	CSR,HAG
					Pt. Lookout, MD	06/17/65	Rlsd. G.O. #109	P115,P117,CSR
Rowe, Amos B.	Cpl	E 26th SCVI	Southside RR, VA	04/01/65	City Pt., VA	04/05/65	Pt. Lookout, MD	CSR
					Pt. Lookout, MD	06/17/65	Rlsd. G.O. #109	P115,P118,CSR
Rowe, Irving M.	Pvt	B 13th SCVI	Amelia C.H., VA	04/05/65	City Pt., VA	04/13/65	Pt. Lookout, MD	CSR,HOS
					Pt. Lookout, MD	06/06/65	Rlsd. Instr. 5/30/65	P115,CSR
Rowe, James N.	Pvt	A 10th SCVI	Murfreesboro, TN	12/31/62	Nashville, TN		Louisville, KY	P38,RAS,CSR
					Louisville, KY	03/20/63	Camp Butler, IL	P88,CSR
					Camp Butler, IL	04/10/63	City Pt., VA Xc	P21,CSR
					Fts. Monroe, VA	04/14/63	Paroled & Xc	CSR
Rowe, John	Pvt	F 1st SCVC	Gettysburg, PA	07/04/63	W. Bldg. Balt, MD	11/12/63	City Pt., VA Xc	P1
Rowe, Martin A.	Pvt	B 14th SCVI	Augusta, GA	05/19/65	Augusta, GA	05/19/65	Paroled	CSR
Rowe, Nathaniel	Pvt	A 7th SCVC	Charlotte, NC	05/11/65	Charlotte, NC	05/11/65	Paroled	CSR

SOUTH CAROLINA SOLDIERS, SAILORS AND  CITIZENS HELD IN U.S. PRISONS 1861-1865

NAME	RANK	REGIMENT	CAPTURED AT	WHEN	PRISON	MOVED	DISPOSITION	SOURCES
Rowe, Thomas N.	Pvt	E 26th SCVI	Hatchers Run, VA	03/29/65	City Pt., VA	04/02/65	Pt. Lookout, MD	CSR
					Pt. Lookout, MD	06/06/65	Rlsd. Instr. 5/30/65	P115,P121,CSR
Rowell, James V.	Pvt	H 23rd SCVI	Petersburg, VA	06/17/64	City Pt., VA	06/24/64	Pt. Lookout, MD	CSR
					Pt. Lookout, MD	07/27/64	Elmira, NY	P113,P117,P120,CSR
					Elmira, NY	12/20/64	Died, Pneumonia	P5,P65,P66,FPH,CSR
Rowell, James V.	Sgt	D 1st SCVA	Smithfield, NC	03/16/65	New Berne, NC	03/30/65	Pt. Lookout, MD	CSR
					Pt. Lookout, MD	06/17/65	Rlsd. G.O. #109	P115,P117,P122,CSR
Rowell, James W.	Pvt	I 21st SCVI	Morris Island, SC	07/10/63	Morris Island, SC	07/13/63	Hilton Head, SC	CSR,HMC,HAG
					Hilton Head G.H.	07/23/63	Morris Island, SC Xc	P2,CSR
Rowell, William	Pvt	E 22nd SCVI	Hatchers Run, VA	03/28/65	City Pt., VA 5AC H	04/09/65	Lincoln G.H., DC	CSR,LAN
					Lincoln G.H., DC	04/18/65	Died of wounds	P6,P12,P110
Rowell, William J.	Pvt	D 24th SCVI	Nashville, TN	12/16/64	Nashville, TN	12/31/64	Louisville, KY	CSR
					Louisville, KY	01/02/65	Camp Chase, OH	P94,CSR
					Camp Chase, OH	06/12/65	Rlsd. G.O. #109	P23,CSR
Rowland, John W.	Pvt	F 2nd SCVIRi	Deserted/enemy	02/28/65	Bermuda Hundred, VA	03/01/65	City Pt., VA P.M.	CSR
					City Pt., VA	03/03/65	Washington, DC P.M.	CSR
					Washington, DC P.M.	03/06/65	Boston, MA on oath	CSR
Rowland, W.F.	Pvt	A 1st SCVA	Cheraw, SC	03/05/65	Cheraw, SC	03/05/65	Released on oath	CSR
Rowland, W.R.	Pvt	G 22nd SCVI	Crater, Pbg., VA	07/30/64	City Pt., VA	08/05/64	Pt. Lookout, VA	CSR,UD3
					Pt. Lookout, MD	08/08/64	Elmira, NY	P113,P117,P120
					Elmira, NY	05/19/65	Released	P65,P66
Rowley, Elbert F.S.	Pvt	B 2nd SCVI	Cedar Creek, VA	10/19/64	Harpers Ferry, WV	10/23/64	Pt. Lookout, MD	CSR,KEB,SA2,H2
					Pt. Lookout, MD	02/13/65	Exchanged	P117,P121,P124
Rowlinski, William	Pvt	A 24th SCVI	Jackson, MS	05/14/63	Demopolis, AL	06/05/63	Paroled	CSR
Rowlinski, William	Pvt	A 24th SCVI	Atlanta, GA	07/19/64	Nashville, TN	07/27/64	Louisville, KY	CSR
					Louisville, KY	07/30/64	Camp Douglas, IL	P90,P91,P94,CSR
					Camp Douglas, IL	05/13/65	Released G.O. #85	P53,P55,CSR,CDC
Royals, William W.	Pvt	A 26th SCVI	Southside RR, VA	04/01/65	City Pt., VA	04/05/65	Pt. Lookout, MD	CSR
					Pt. Lookout, MD	06/17/65	Rlsd. G.O. #109	P115,P118,CSR
Royles, Asa	Pvt	F 7th SCVC	Farmville, VA	04/06/64	City Pt., VA	04/15/65	Pt. Lookout, MD	CSR
					Pt. Lookout, MD	06/17/65	Rlsd. G.O. #109	P119,CSR
Rubens, Joseph	Pvt	B 1st SCA	Raleigh, NC Hos.	04/13/65	Wilmington, NC	05/11/65	Released on oath	CSR
Rucker, Henry L.	Pvt	B 1st SCVIH	Mossy Creek, TN	01/22/64	Nashville, TN	02/11/64	Louisville, KY	P39,SA1,CSR
					Louisville, KY	02/15/64	Rock Island, IL	P88,P91,P93,CSR
					Rock Island, IL	03/07/64	Died, Lung Inflam.	P5,P131,132,FPH
Rucker, W.A.	Pvt	D 20th SCVI	Cedar Creek, VA	10/19/64	Harpers Ferry, WV	10/24/64	Pt. Lookout, MD	CSR,KEB
					Pt. Lookout, MD	06/17/65	Rlsd. G.O. #109	P115,P117,CSR
Rudisill, G. Alexander	Cpl	H 6th SCVC	Louisa C.H., VA	06/11/64	Pt. Lookout, MD	07/23/64	Elmira, NY	P113,P116,P120
					Elmira, NY	08/19/64	Died, Remitnt fever	P5,P65,P66,FPH,CSR
Rudisill, Wylie V.	Pvt	D 17th SCVI	Crater, Pbg., VA	07/30/64	City Pt., VA	08/05/64	Pt. Lookout, MD	CSR,HHC
					Pt. Lookout, MD	08/08/64	Elmira, NY	P113,P117,P120,CSR
					Elmira, NY	05/28/65	Died, Ch. Diarrhea	P6,P12,P65,P66,FPH,HHC
Rudolph, Lucien A.	Pvt	Brooks LA	Gettysburg, PA	07/05/63	Baltimore, MD	08/17/63	Pt. Lookout, MD	CSR
					Pt. Lookout, MD	01/21/64	Joined U.S. Army	P125,CSR
Ruer, Daniel	Pvt	C 3rd SCVABn	Ft. Gaines, AL	08/08/64	New Orleans, LA	08/18/64	St. Louis, MO USGH	CSR
					St. Louis, MO USGH	08/22/64	New Orleans, LA	CSR
					New Orleans, LA	10/25/64	Ship Island, MS	P3
					New Orleans, LA	10/31/64	Elmira, NY	CSR
					Ship Island, MS	04/04/65	Exchanged	CSR
					Elmira, NY	05/29/65	Released	CSR
Ruff, Benjamin Franklin	Pvt	G 24th SCVI	Jackson, MS	05/16/63	Jackson, MS	05/16/64	Paroled	CSR
Ruff, D.	Cit	Lexington	Flat Rock, SC	02/24/65	Hart's Island, NY	06/20/65	Rlsd. G.O. #109	P79

SOUTH CAROLINA SOLDIERS, SAILORS AND  CITIZENS HELD IN U.S. PRISONS 1861-1865

NAME	RANK	REGIMENT	CAPTURED AT	WHEN	PRISON	MOVED	DISPOSITION	SOURCES
Ruff, John A.	Pvt	H 2nd SCVC	Montgomery, AL	06/16/65	Montgomery, AL	06/16/65	Paroled	CSR
Ruff, S.W.	Pvt	F 12th SCVI	Sharpsburg, MD	09/17/62	Ft. McHenry, MD	10/27/62	Fts. Monroe, VA Xc	CSR
Ruff, S.W.	Pvt	F 12th SCVI	Petersburg, VA	04/03/65	City Pt., VA	04/07/65	Hart's Island, NY	CSR
					Hart's Island, NY	06/16/65	Rlsd. G.O. #109	P79,CSR
Ruff, Samuel M.	Cpt	H 20th SCVI	Cedar Creek, VA	10/19/64	Winchester, VA USH	11/19/64	W. Bldg. Balt, M	CSR
					W. Bldg. Balt, MD	12/09/64	Ft. McHenry, MD	P1,KEB,CSR
					Ft. McHenry, MD	01/11/65	Ft. Delaware, DE	P144,CSR
					Ft. Delaware, DE	06/14/65	Released	P43,P45,CSR
Ruff, William W.	Pvt	E 3rd SCVI	Sharpsburg, MD	09/17/62	P.M. Army of Potomac	09/27/62	Paroled for Xc	CSR
					Ft. McHenry, MD	10/13/62	Fts. Monroe, VA Xc	CSR
Rumff, David J.	Col	15th SCMil	Chesterfield, SC	02/28/65	Pt. Lookout, MD	04/03/65	Washington, DC	P115,P117,P120
					Old Capitol, DC	04/09/65	Johnson's Isl., OH	P110
					Johnson's Isl., OH	07/25/65	Rlsd. G.O. #109	P81
Rummels, Jordan	Pvt	C 18th SCVI	Boonesboro, MD	09/14/62	Ft. Delaware DE	10/02/62	Aikens Ldg., VA Xc	CSR
Rumph, D.A.	Sgt	B 11th SCVI	Deserted/enemy	03/12/65	Charleston, SC	03/12/65	Released on oath	CSR
Rumph, George	Pvt	G 6th SCVC	Stony Creek, VA	12/01/64	City Pt., VA	12/04/64	Pt. Lookout, MD	CSR
					Pt. Lookout, MD	02/13/65	Aikens Ldg., VA Xc	P117,P121,P124,CSR
Runions, J.E.	Pvt	K 1st SCVA	Charlotte, NC Hos.	04/21/65	Charlotte, NC	05/06/65	Paroled	CSR
Runnells, S.	Pvt	D 6th SCResB	Cheraw, SC	03/05/65	Cheraw, SC	03/05/65	Paroled	CSR
Runyan, Andrew M.	Pvt	B 37th VAVCB	Fishers Hill, VA	09/22/64	Harpers Ferry, WV	10/01/64	Pt. Lookout, MD	CSR
					Pt. Lookout, MD	02/13/65	Cox's Wh., VA Xc	CSR
Ruppe, J.D.B.	Pvt	K Hol.Leg.	Stony Creek, VA	05/07/64	Pt. Lookout, MD	08/13/64	Elmira, NY	P113,P116
					Elmira, NY	02/20/65	Pt. Lookout, MD Xc	P66
Ruppe, Ward M.	Cpl	K Hol.Leg.	Stony Creek, VA	05/07/64	Elmira, NY	09/09/64	Died, Remitnt. fever	P5,P12,P65,FPH
Rusch, Leopold	Msc	1st SCVA	Deserted/enemy	02/18/65	Charleston, SC		Released on oath	CSR
Rush, Andrew J.	Pvt	A 1st SCVIR	Morris Island, SC	09/07/63	Ft. Delaware, DE	10/26/63	Pt. Lookout, MD	CSR
					Hilton Head, SC	10/09/63	Ft. Delaware, DE	P1,SA1,CSR
					Pt. Lookout, MD	01/13/64	Died, Ch. Diarrhea	P5,P116,P119,FPH
Rush, David	Pvt	E 6th SCResB	Augusta, SC	05/20/65	Augusta, GA	05/20/65	Paroled	CSR
Rush, E.W.	2Lt	H 25th SCVI	Ft. Fisher, NC	01/15/65	New York, NY	01/30/65	Elmira, NY	CSR,HAG
					Ft. Columbus, NY	03/01/65	City Pt., VA Xc	P2,CSR
Rush, Sem H.	Pvt	G 17th SCVI	Petersburg, VA	03/25/65	3rd Div, 9th AC H.	03/26/65	City Pt., VA Hos.	CSR
					9th AC Depot Hos.	03/29/65	Washington, DC G.H.	CSR
					Lincoln G.H., DC	05/27/65	Died, Pyaemia	P6,P12,CSR
Rush, William H.	Pvt	C 7th SCVIBn	Columbia, SC	02/19/65	New Berne, NC USGH	04/17/65	Died acute diarrhea	P1,P6,P12,HAG,CSR
Rushing, Albert R.	Pvt	E 11th SCVI	Petersburg, VA	06/24/64	Pt. Lookout, MD	02/10/65	Aikens Ldg., VA Xc	P117,P124,HAG,CSR
					Bermuda Hundred, VA	06/25/64	Fts. Monroe, VA	CSR,HAG
					Fts. Monroe, VA	06/26/64	Pt. Lookout, MD	CSR
Rushing, J.H.	Pvt	E 11th SCVI	Weldon RR, VA	08/21/64	City Pt., VA	08/24/64	Pt. Lookout, MD	CSR,HAG
					Pt. Lookout, MD	09/18/64	Aikens Ldg., VA Xc	CSR,P113,P117
					Varina, VA	09/22/64	Richmond VA Conf H	CSR
Rushing, James B.	Pvt	D 25th SCVI	Ft. Fisher, NC	01/15/65	New York, NY	01/30/65	Elmira, NY	CSR,HAG,HMC
					Elmira, NY	02/20/65	James R., VA Xc	P65,P66,CSR
Rushing, John P.	Sgt	B 8th SCVI	Black Creek, SC	03/01/65	New Berne, NC	04/03/65	Pt. Lookout, MD	CSR
					Pt. Lookout, MD	06/04/65	Released on oath	P121,KEB,CSR
Rushing, Matthew	Pvt	C 3rd SCVI	Chesterfield, SC	03/04/65	Pt. Lookout, MD			P115,P117
Rushton, James	Pvt	7 10/19 SCVI	Missionary Ridge, TN	11/25/63	Nashville, TN	12/07/63	Louisville, KY	P39,HOE
					Louisville, KY	12/07/63	Rock Island, IL	P88,P89
					Rock Island, IL	10/13/64	Jd. US Army F.S.	P131,CSR
Rushton, John	Pvt	D 19th SCVI	Missionary Ridge, TN	11/25/63	Nashville, TN	12/06/63	Louisville, KY	CSR
					Louisville, KY	12/07/63	Rock Island, IL	CSR
					Rock Island, IL	10/13/64	Jd. USA Frontier S	CSR

SOUTH CAROLINA SOLDIERS, SAILORS AND  CITIZENS HELD IN U.S. PRISONS 1861-1865

NAME	RANK	REGIMENT	CAPTURED AT	WHEN	PRISON	MOVED	DISPOSITION	SOURCES
Rusin, J.F.	Pvt	H 2nd SCVIRi	Warrenton, VA	09/29/62	Warrenton, VA	09/29/62	Paroled	CSR
Russ, Isham	Pvt	D 6th SCVC	Louisa C.H., VA	06/11/64	Fts. Monroe, VA	06/15/64	Pt. Lookout, MD	CSR
					Pt. Lookout, MD	07/25/64	Elmira, NY	P113,P116,P120,CSR
					Elmira, NY	03/14/65	Pt. Lookout, MD Xc	P65,P116,P120,CSR
Russ, Joseph B.	Pvt	E 10th SCVI	Murfreesboro, TN	12/31/62	Nashville, TN	01/03/63	Died, of wounds	P38,RAS,CTA,CSR
Russ, William	Pvt	A 9th SCVIBn	Secessionville, SC	06/16/62	Ft. Columbus, NY	08/23/62	Ft. Delaware, DE	P37
					Ft. Delaware, DE	10/22/62	Aikens Ldg., VA xC	CSR
Russ, Zachariah	Pvt	H Orr's Ri.	Spotsylvania, VA	05/12/64	Old Capitol, DC	06/10/64	Ft. Delaware, DE	CDC,CSR
					Ft. McHenry, MD	06/13/64	Ft. Delaware, DE	P110
					Ft. Delaware, DE	06/10/65	Released	P41,P42,P45,CSR
Russell, Charles	Pvt	K 17th SCVI	Petersburg, VA	03/25/65	EM 2nd Div 9th AC	03/27/65	Died of wounds	P12,YEB,CSR
Russell, H.D.	Pvt	A 1st SCVC	Gettysburg, PA	07/04/63	David's Island, NY	09/27/63	City Pt., VA Xc	CSR
					Gen'l Hosp. Gettys	08/02/63	David's Island, NY	CSR
Russell, J.S.	Pvt	C P.S.S.	Deserted/enemy	03/04/65	Bermuda Hundred, VA	03/05/65	City Pt., VA	CSR
					City Pt., VA	03/07/65	Washington, DC	CSR
					Washington, DC	03/08/65	Pittsburgh, PA	CSR
Russell, James B.	Pvt	A Orr's Ri.	Falling Waters, MD	07/14/63	Baltimore, MD	08/16/64	Pt. Lookout, MD	CSR
					Pt. Lookout, MD	08/18/64	Elmira, NY	P113,P116,P120,CSR
					Elmira, NY	09/13/64	Died, Ch. Diarrhea	P5,P65,P66,FPH,CSR
Russell, M.B.	Pvt	F 12th SCVI	Warrenton, VA	09/29/62	Warrenton, VA	09/29/62	Paroled	CSR
Russell, M.B.	Pvt	F 12th SCVI	Gettysburg, PA	07/05/63	W. Bldg. Balt, MD	07/30/63	Died of wounds	CSR,FPH
Russell, Robert G.	Pvt	G 14th SCVI	Sutherland Stn., VA	04/03/65	City Pt., VA	04/13/65	Pt. Lookout, MD	CSR
					Pt. Lookout, MD	06/17/65	Rlsd G.O. #109	P115,P118,CSR
Russell, S.L.	Pvt	A 1st SCVC	Gettysburg, PA	07/02/63	Ft. Delaware, DE		Hos. 6/22/64-?	P47
					Ft. Delaware, DE	06/10/65	Rlsd. G.O. #109	P42,CSR
Russell, S.R.	3Lt	1st SCVI	Gettysburg, PA	07/03/63	Ft. Delaware, DE	05/28/65	Rlsd. on oath	P44,CSR
Russell, Squire H.	Pvt	E Orr's Ri.	Hatchers Run, VA	04/03/65	City Pt., VA	04/13/65	Pt. Lookout, MD	CSR
					Pt. Lookout, MD	06/17/65	Rlsd. G.O. #109	P115,P118,CSR
Russell, Timothy	Pvt	G 14th SCVI	Gettysburg, PA	07/05/63	Ft. McHenry, MD	07/12/63	Ft. Delaware, DE	CSR
					Ft. Delaware, DE	09/06/63	Died, Typhoid	P5,P40,P42,FPH,CSR
Russell, W.W.	Pvt	F 1st SCVC	Proctors XRds., VA	10/11/64	City Pt., VA	10/29/64	Pt. Lookout, MD	CSR
					Pt. Lookout, MD	03/15/65	Aikens Ldg., VA Xc	P117,P121,P124,CSR
Ruth, A.J.	Pvt	E 11th SCVI	Petersburg, VA	06/24/64	Bermuda Hundred, VA	06/25/64	Fts. Monroe, VA	CSR
					Fts. Monroe, VA	06/26/64	Pt. Lookout, MD	CSR
					Pt. Lookout, MD	08/16/64	Elmira, NY	P113,P117,P120,HAG,CSR
					Pt. Lookout, MD Xc	03/02/65	Richmond CSR Hos.	CSR
					Elmira, NY	03/02/65	Pt. Lookout, MD Xc	P65,P66,HAG,CSR
Ruth, A.M.	Cpt	B 2nd SCVC	Augusta, GA	05/29/65	Augusta, GA	05/29/65	Paroled	CSR
Ruth, R.G.	Pvt	B 5th SCVC	Augusta, GA	05/25/65	Augusta, GA	05/25/65		CSR
Rutherford, Alexander	Pvt	I 2nd SCVC	Greensboro, NC	04/29/65	Greensboro, NC	04/29/65	Paroled	CSR
Rutherford, James F.	Pvt	B 14th SCVI	Gettysburg, PA	07/05/63	David's Island, NY	10/24/63	Bedloes Island, NY	P1,HOE,CSR
					Bedloes Island, NY	10/28/63	Pt. Lookout, MD	CSR
					Pt. Lookout, MD	03/03/64	City Pt., VA Xc	P116,CSR
Rutherford, William D.	LtC	3rd SCVI	South Mtn., MD	09/13/62	Baltimore, MD	10/11/62	Fts. Monroe, VA Xc	CSR,ANY,KEB,SA2,H3
					Fts. Monroe, VA	10/12/62	Aikens Ldg., VA Xc	CSR
Rutland, H.	Pvt	B 14th SCMil	Lynch's Creek, SC	02/25/65	Hart's Island, NY	06/16/65	Rlsd. G.O. #109	P79
Rutledge, Robert S.	SMj	Hol.Leg.	Petersburg, VA	04/03/65	Petersburg F.G. Hos.	04/04/65	Pt. of Rocks G.H.	CSR
					Pt. of Rocks G.H.	05/04/65	Sent home	CSR
Rutledge, W.F.	Pvt	F 7th SCVIBn	Anderson, SC	05/03/65	Anderson, SC	05/03/65	Paroled	CSR
Ryan, Edward C.	Pvt	F 1st SCVA	Deserted to US Fleet	12/01/64	Hilton Head, SC	12/25/64		P8,CSR

SOUTH CAROLINA SOLDIERS, SAILORS AND  CITIZENS HELD IN U.S. PRISONS 1861-1865

NAME	RANK	REGIMENT	CAPTURED AT	WHEN	PRISON	MOVED	DISPOSITION	SOURCES
Ryan, George K.	2Lt	I 11th SCVI	Town Creek, NC	02/20/65	Ft. Anderson, NC	02/28/65	Pt. Lookout, MD	CSR
					Pt. Lookout, MD	02/28/65	Washington, DC	P115,P117,P120,CSR
					Old Capitol, DC	03/21/65	Ft. Delaware, DE	P110,CSR
					Ft. Delaware, DE	06/17/65	Rlsd. G.O. #109	CSR
Ryan, J.H.	Pvt	A 2nd SCVIRi	Richmond, VA Hos.	04/03/65	Richmond, VA Hos.	04/21/65	Richmond, VA P.M.	CSR
					Libby Prison Rchmd.	04/23/65	Newport News, VA	CSR
					Newport News, VA	06/26/65	Rlsd. G.O. #109	P107,CSR
Ryan, John	Pvt	I 27th SCVI	Petersburg, VA	06/24/64	Bermuda Hundred, VA	06/25/64	Fts. Monroe, VA	CSR,HAG
					Fts. Monroe, VA	06/26/64	Pt. Lookout, MD	CSR
					Pt. Lookout, MD	08/16/64	Elmira, NY	P113,P120,CSR
					Elmira, NY	03/14/65	Pt. Lookout, MD Xc	P65,P66,CSR
Ryan, John	Pvt	B 1st SCVA	Fayetteville, NC	03/16/65	New Berne, NC	03/30/65	Pt. Lookout, MD	CSR
					Pt. Lookout, MD	06/17/65	Rlsd. G.O. #109	P115,CSR
					New Berne, NC	04/10/65	Hart's Island, NY	CSR
Ryan, John	Cpl	H 1st SCVA	Fayettville, NC	03/16/65	Hart's Island, NY	06/17/65	Rlsd. G.O. #109	P79,CSR
Ryan, John T.	Pvt	L 1st SCVIG	Falling Waters, MD	07/14/63	Old Capitol, DC	08/08/63	Pt. Lookout, MD	CSR,SA1
					Ft. McHenry, MD	08/08/63	Pt. Lookout, MD	P110
					Pt. Lookout, MD	03/03/64	City Pt., VA Xc	P116,123,P124
Ryan, P.H.	Cpl	E 2nd SCVI	Petersburg, VA	07/29/64	City Pt., VA	08/05/64	Pt. Lookout, MD	CSR,KEB,SA2
					Pt. Lookout, MD	08/08/64	Elmira, NY	P113,P120,CSR
					Elmira, NY	03/14/65	Pt. Lookout, MD Xc	P65,P66,CSR
Ryan, Peter	Pvt	F 1st SCVA	Deserted	12/01/64	Hilton Head, SC	12/25/64	No release date CS	P8,CSR
Ryan, Stamman B.	Pvt	D 5th SCVC	Killans Mill, SC	02/18/65	New Berne, NC	04/10/65	Pt. Lookout, MD	CSR
					Hart's Island, NY	06/16/65	Rlsd. G.O. #109	P79,CSR
Ryan, Thomas	Pvt	E 18th SCVAB	Deserted/enemy	03/28/65	Charleston, SC	03/28/65	Released on oath	CSR
Ryan, Thomas P.	Cpt	C 23rd SCVI	Richmond, VA Hos.	04/03/65	Richmond, VA P.M.	05/02/65	Paroled	CSR
Ryan, William P.	Pvt	D 14th SCVI	Falling Waters, MD	07/14/63	Old Capitol, DC	08/08/64	Pt. Lookout, MD	CSR,HOE
					Ft. McHenry, MD	08/19/63	Pt. Lookout, MD	P110,CSR
					Pt. Lookout, MD	03/03/64	City Pt., VA Xc	P113,P116,P124
Rye, J.E.	Pvt	E 14th SCVI	Gettysburg, PA	07/05/63	Ft. Delaware, DE		No other data	P40,P42,CSR
Rykard, Frederick	Pvt	Coast Gd.	Lexington, SC	02/15/65	Pt. Lookout, MD			P117
Rykard, John H.	Pvt	C 6th SCVC	Louisa C.H., VA	06/11/64	Pt. Lookout, MD	07/25/64	Elmira, NY	P113,P116,P120,CSR
					Elmira, NY	09/06/64	Died, Typhoid	P5,P65,P66,FPH,CSR
Ryles, H.E.	Pvt	G 26th SCVI	Farmville, VA	04/06/65	City Pt., VA	04/14/65	Pt. Lookout, MD	CSR
					Pt. Lookout, MD	06/26/65	Rlsd. G.O. #109	CSR

SOUTH CAROLINA SOLDIERS, SAILORS AND  CITIZENS HELD IN U.S. PRISONS 1861-1865

NAME	RANK	REGIMENT	CAPTURED AT	WHEN	PRISON	MOVED	DISPOSITION	SOURCES
Sabry, Rufus	Pvt	I 17th SCVI	Deserted/enemy	11/15/64	P.M. A. of Potomac	11/17/64	City Pt., VA P.M.	CSR
					City Pt., VA P.M.	11/23/64	Washington, DC	CSR
Sabry, Rufus	Pvt	I 17th SCVI	Deserted/enemy	11/15/64	Washington, DC	11/25/64	Released on oath	CSR
Saddler, Isaac	Pvt	E 20th SCVI	Petersburg, VA	07/29/64	City Pt., VA	08/05/64	Pt. Lookout, MD	CSR,KEB,UD5
					Pt. Lookout, MD	08/08/64	Elmira, NY	P113,P117,P120
					Elmira, NY	02/20/65	James R., VA Xc	P65,P66,CSR
Saddler, John S.	Pvt	K 5th SCVC	Stony Creek, VA	12/01/64	City Pt., VA	12/05/64	Pt. Lookout, MD	CSR
					Pt. Lookout, MD	02/18/65	Aikens Ldg., VA Xc	P115,P118,P124,CSR
Saddler, William	Pvt	E 20th SCVI	Petersburg, VA	07/30/64	City Pt., VA	08/08/64	Elmira, NY	KEB,CSR
					Elmira, NY	01/19/65	Died, Ch. Diarrhea	P5,P65,P66,FPH,CSR
Sadler, George M.	Pvt	F 3rd SCVI	Loudon, TN	12/03/63	Nashville, TN	02/19/64	Louisville, KY	P39,CSR,KEB,SA2,H3
					Louisville, KY	02/29/64	Ft. Delaware, DE	P88,P91,P94,CSR
					Ft. Delaware, DE		Hos. 6/17-7/11/64	P47
					Ft. Delaware, DE	09/18/64	Aikens Ldg., VA Xc	P41,P43,CSR
					Richmond, VA Hos.	09/25/64	Furloughed 30 days	CSR
Sadler, J.M.	Pvt	G 6th SCVI	Chester, SC	05/05/65	Chester, SC	05/05/65	Paroled	CSR
Sadler, Oscar W.	Pvt	K 17th SCVI	Southside RR, VA	04/02/65	City Pt., VA	04/07/65	Hart's Island, NY	CSR,YEB
					Hart's Island, NY	06/16/65	Rlsd. G.O. #109	P79,CSR
Sageman, P.	Pvt	14th SCVI	Winchester, VA	12/04/62	Winchester, VA	12/04/62	Paroled/ hospital	CSR
Sahlman, L.	Pvt	D 5th SCVC	Charleston, SC	04/11/65	Charleston, SC	04/11/65	Released on oath	CSR
Sale, William Augustus	Pvt	G 1st SCVIG	Gettysburg, PA	06/30/63	David's Island, NY	10/23/63	Died of wounds	P1,P6,FPH,SA1,CSR
Salisbury, T.W.	Pvt	D 5th SCVC	Deserted/enemy	02/18/65	Charleston, SC	03/10/65	Released on oath	CSR
Salmons, F.Y.	Pvt	K 2nd SCVC	Charlotte, NC	05/12/65	Charlotte, NC	05/12/65	Paroled	CSR
Salter, J.M.	Pvt	E 2nd SCVA	Cheraw, SC	03/04/65	New Berne, NC	03/30/65	Pt. Lookout, MD	CSR
					Pt. Lookout, MD	06/19/65	Rlsd. G.O. #109	P115,P118,CSR
Salter, J.P.	Pvt	E 7th SCVI	Gettysburg, PA	07/05/63	David's Island, NY	10/22/63	Fts. Monroe, VA Xc	P1,KEB,HOE,CSR
Salter, J.P.	Pvt	E 7th SCVI	Wilderness, VA	05/07/64	Ft. Delaware, DE		Hos. 5/31-6/30/64	P47
					Ft. Delaware, DE		Hos. 9/15-9/26/64	P47
					Ft. Delaware, DE	09/30/64	Aikens Ldg., VA Xc	P41,P43,CSR
Salter, S.J.	Pvt	D 17th SCVI	Augusta, GA	05/29/65	Augusta, GA	05/29/65	Paroled	CSR
Salters, J.C.	1Lt	I 27th SCVI	Petersburg, VA	06/17/64	City Pt., VA	06/25/64	Ft. Delaware, DE	CSR,HAG
					Ft. Delaware, DE	06/17/65	Rlsd. G.O. #109	P45,P47,CSR
Salters, Phillip	Msc	25th SCVI	Deserted/enemy	03/24/65	Washington, DC		Charleston, SC	CSR
Salters, William	2Lt	K 25th SCVI	Ft. Fisher, NC	01/15/65	Ft. Columbus, NY	02/25/65	City Pt., VA Xc	CSR,HAG,CTA
Sample, John B.	2Lt	F Hol.Leg.	Petersburg, VA	11/05/64	City Pt., VA	12/04/64	Washington, DC	CSR
					Old Capitol, DC	12/17/64	Ft. Delaware, DE	P110,CSR
					Ft. Delaware, DE	06/17/65	Rlsd. G.O. #109	P43,P45,CSR
Sample, Samuel W.	Pvt	B 1st SCVIG	Petersburg, VA	04/14/65	City Pt., VA	04/16/65	Newport News, VA	CSR,ANY,SA1
					Newport News, VA	06/26/65	Rlsd. G.O. #109	P107,CSR
Sams, T.C.	Pvt	Beaufort A	Salisbury, NC	04/12/65	Camp Chase, OH	06/13/65	Released	P23
Samson, Abraham J.	Pvt	L 1st SCVIG	Falling Waters, MD	07/14/63	Ft. McHenry, MD	08/08/63	Pt. Lookout, MD	P110,SA1
					Old Capitol, DC	08/08/63	Pt. Lookout, MD	CSR
					Pt. Lookout, MD	03/03/64	City Pt., VA Xc	P113,P116,P124,CSR
					City Pt., VA	03/06/64	Exchanged	CSR
Samson, W.H.	Pvt	K 13th SCVI	Gettysburg, PA	07/05/63	David's Island, NY	08/24/63	City Pt., VA Xc	P1
Samuel, George	Pvt	B 19th SCVI	Augusta, GA	06/06/65	Augusta, GA	06/06/65	Paroled	CSR
Samuels, E.R.	Pvt	A 22nd SCVI	Deserted/enemy	02/27/65	City Pt., VA	03/01/65	Washington, DC	CSR
					Washington, DC	03/02/65	Savannah, GA	CSR
Sanders, Augustus A.	Cpl	B 26th SCVI	Five Forks, VA	04/01/65	City Pt., VA	04/05/65	Pt. Lookout, MD	CSR
					Pt. Lookout, MD	06/19/65	Rlsd. G.O. #109	P115,P119,P122,CSR
Sanders, Benjamin H.	Pvt	G 25th SCVI	Ft. Fisher, NC	01/15/65	New York, NY	01/30/65	Elmira, NY	CSR,HAG
					Elmira, NY	07/07/65	Rlsd. G.O. #109	P65,P66,CSR

SOUTH CAROLINA SOLDIERS, SAILORS AND  CITIZENS HELD IN U.S. PRISONS 1861-1865

NAME	RANK	REGIMENT	CAPTURED AT	WHEN	PRISON	MOVED	DISPOSITION	SOURCES
Sanders, C.W.	Pvt	B 4th SCVC	Mechanicsville, VA	05/30/64	Stanton Hos. D.C.	06/11/64	Died of wounds	P5,P12,P110,CSR
Sanders, J.C.	Pvt	H 7th SCVC	Farmville, VA	04/11/65	Farmville, VA	04/21/65	Paroled	CSR
Sanders, James A.	Sgt	E 5th SCVI	Seven Pines, VA	05/31/62	Fts. Monroe, VA G.H.	06/16/62	Ft. Delaware, DE	CSR,SA3
Sanders, James A.	Cpl	E 7th SCVIBn	Weldon RR, VA	08/21/64	City Pt., VA USFH	08/29/64	Alexandria, VA USG	CSR,HAG
					Alexandria, VA USG	10/29/64	Washington, DC USG	CSR
					Lincoln G.H., DC	12/30/64	Old Capitol, DC	CSR
					Old Capitol, DC	03/01/65	Elmira, NY	P110,CSR
					Elmira, NY	03/14/65	James R., VA Xc	P65,P66,CSR
Sanders, James Wade	Pvt	B 1st SCVIG	Petersburg, VA	04/14/65	City Pt., VA	04/15/65	Newport News, VA	CSRANY,SA1
					Newport News, VA	06/13/65	Rlsd. G.O. #109	P107,CSR
Sanders, John C.	2Lt	C 17th SCVI	Petersburg, VA	03/25/65	Old Capitol, DC	03/30/65	Ft. Delaware, DE	P110,YEB,CSR
					Ft. Delaware, DE	06/17/65	Rlsd. G.O. #109	P43,P45,CSR
Sanders, John M., Jr.	Pvt	D 22nd SCVI	Petersburg, VA	03/25/65	City Pt., VA	03/28/65	Pt. Lookout, MD	CSR
					Pt. Lookout, MD	06/19/65	Rlsd. G.O. #109	P122
Sanders, John M., Sr.	Pvt	D 22nd SCVI	Deserted/enemy	02/25/65	City Pt., VA MD	02/28/65	Washington, DC	CSR
					Washington, DC	03/01/65	Salem, IL on oath	CSR
Sanders, John R.	Pvt	C 6th SCVC	Petersburg, VA	11/11/64	City Pt., VA	11/23/64	Pt. Lookout, MD	P115,CSR
					Pt. Lookout MD	02/24/65	Aikens Ldg., VA Xc	P115,CSR
Sanders, John W.	Pvt	K 24th SCVI	Franklin, TN	12/15/64	Camp Douglas, IL	06/20/65	Rlsd. G.O. #109	P55
Sanders, Joseph T.	Sgt	E 25th SCVI	Ft. Fisher, NC	01/15/65	New York, NY	01/30/65	Elmira, NY	CSR,HAG
					Elmira, NY	02/20/65	James R., VA Xc	P65
Sanders, Joseph W.	Sgt	I 11th SCVI	Town Creek, NC	02/20/65	Ft. Anderson, NC	02/28/65	Pt. Lookout, MD	CSR
					Pt. Lookout, MD	06/19/65	Rlsd. G.O. #109	P115,P118,P122,CSR
Sanders, M.V.	Pvt	F 3rd SCVC	South Newport, GA	08/17/64	Philadelphia, PA	01/10/65	Ft. Delaware, DE	CSR
					Ft. Delaware, DE	04/11/65	Died, Measles	P6,P41,P43,P45,P47
Sanders, Reid	Maj	CSA	Off Charleston, SC	01/04/63	Ft. Lafayette, NY	07/02/63	Ft. Warren, MA	P144
Sanders, Reid	Maj	Staff	Off Charleston, SC	01/05/63	Ft. Warren, MA	09/03/63	Died	P2
Sanders, Samuel D.	1Lt	D 21st SCVI	Ft. Fisher, NC	01/15/65	Ft. Columbus, NY	03/01/65	City Pt., VA Xc	P2,HAG
Sanders, Simpson	Pvt	I 13th SCVI	Petersburg, VA	03/25/65	City Pt., VA	03/28/65	Pt. Lookout, MD	CSR,HOS
					Pt. Lookout, MD	06/19/65	Rlsd. G.O. #109	P115,P118,HOS,CSR
Sanders, T.N.	Pvt	B 1st SCVIR	Deserted/enemy	02/21/65	Charleston, SC	03/02/65	Will take oath	SA1,CSR
Sanders, Theodore A.	2Lt	A 2nd SCVC	Martinsburg, VA	07/17/63	Wheeling, WV	07/22/63	Camp Chase, OH	P1,CSR
					Camp Chase, OH	10/10/63	Johnson's Isl., OH	P25,P26,P22,CSR
Sanders, Theodore A.	2Lt	A 2nd SCVC	Martinsburg, VA	07/17/63	Johnson's Isl., OH	06/11/65	Rlsd. G.O. #109	P80,P83,CSR
Sanders, W.E.	Pvt	K 17th SCVI	Warrenton, VA	09/29/62	Warrenton, VA	09/29/62	Paroled	CSR
Sanders, William E.	Pvt	C 17th SCVI	Five Forks, VA	04/01/65	City Pt., VA	04/06/65	Pt. Lookout, MD	CSR
					Pt. Lookout, MD	06/19/65	Rlsd. G.O. #109	P115,P119,P122,CSR
Sanders, William F.	Sgt	C 15th SCVI	Halltown, VA	08/26/64	Harpers Ferry, WV	08/29/64	Camp Chase, Oh	CSR
					Camp Chase, OH	12/18/64	Died, Ch. Diarrhea	P6,P23,P27,FPH,KEB
Sanderson, Solomon A.	Pvt	E 1st SCVIG	Warrenton, VA	09/29/62	Warrenton, VA	09/29/62	Paroled	SA1,CSR
Sandlin, Dempsey M.	Pvt	F 16th SCVI	Kingston, GA	11/27/63	Nashville, TN		Louisville, KY	CSR,16R
					Louisville, KY		Rock Island, IL	CSR
					Rock Island, IL	02/02/64	Died, Ch. Diarrhea	P5,P131,P132,FPH
Sanford, H.H.	Pvt	I 5th SCVC	Stony Creek, VA	12/01/64	City Pt., VA	12/05/64	Pt. Lookout, MD	CSR
					Pt. Lookout, MD	06/19/65	Rlsd. G.O. #109	P115,P118,CSR
Sanford, Jesse	Pvt	G 25th SCVI	Ft. Fisher, NC	01/15/65	New York, NY	01/30/65	Elmira, NY	CSR,HAG
					Elmira, NY	03/20/65	Died, Ch. Diarrhea	P65,P66,FPH,CSR
Sanford, T.W.	Cpl	D 22nd SCVI	Kinston, NC	12/15/62	Kinston, NC	12/15/62	Paroled POW	CSR
Sanford, T.W.	Cpl	D 22nd SCVI	Deserted/enemy	02/24/65	City Pt., VA	02/26/65	Washington, DC	CSR
					Washington, DC	02/27/65	Salem, IL on oath	CSR
Sanford, William D.	Pvt	G 12th SCVI	Hatchers Run, VA	03/31/65	City Pt., VA	04/02/65	Pt. Lookout, MD	P118,CSR
					Pt. Lookout, MD	06/19/65	Rlsd. G.O. #109	P115,P122,CSR

SOUTH CAROLINA SOLDIERS, SAILORS AND  CITIZENS HELD IN U.S. PRISONS 1861-1865

NAME	RANK	REGIMENT	CAPTURED AT	WHEN	PRISON	MOVED	DISPOSITION	SOURCES
Sansbury, James L.	2Lt	G 26th SCVI	Dinwiddie C.H., VA	04/01/65	Old Capitol, DC	04/09/65	Johnson's Isl., OH	P110,CSR
					Johnson's Isl., OH	06/20/65	Rlsd. G.O. #109	P81,P82,CSR
Sansbury, Thomas J.	Sgt	G 26th SCVI	Five Forks, VA	04/01/65	City Pt., VA	04/05/65	Pt. Lookout, MD	CSR
					Pt. Lookout, MD	06/19/65	Rlsd. G.O. #109	P115,P119,CSR
Sansbury, William W.	Pvt	G 26th SCVI	Petersburg, VA	03/25/65	City Pt., VA	03/27/65	Pt. Lookout, MD	CSR
					Pt. Lookout, MD	06/19/65	Rlsd. G.O. #109	P115,P118,P122,CSR
Sargent, Jesse H.	Pvt	Ferguson's LA	Salisbury, NC	04/12/65	Nashville, TN	04/29/65	Louisville, KY	P39,CSR
					Louisville, KY	05/02/65	Camp Chase, OH	P92,P95,CSR
					Camp Chase, OH	06/13/65	Rlsd. G.O. #109	CSR
Sargent, William H.	Sgt	Ferguson's LA	Salisbury, NC	04/12/65	Nashville, TN	04/29/65	Louisville, KY	CSR
					Louisville, KY	05/02/65	Camp Chase, OH	P92,P95,CSR
					Camp Chase, OH	06/13/65	Rlsd. G.O. #109	P23,CSR
Sarratt, A.A.	2Lt	K Hol.Leg.	Stony Creek, VA	05/07/64	Pt. Lookout, MD	06/23/64	Ft. Delaware, DE	P117,P120
					Ft. Delaware, DE	06/17/65	Rlsd. G.O. #109	P43,P44,P45,P46
Sarratt, H.J.	Pvt	G P.S.S.	Fair Oaks, VA	05/31/65	Fts. Monroe, VA	06/21/62	Ft. Delaware, DE	CSR,TSE
					Ft. Delaware, DE		No further info	CSR
Sarratt, Iverson G.	Pvt	F 6th SCVC	Louisa C.H., VA	05/11/64	Fts. Monroe, VA	06/19/64	Pt. Lookout, MD	CSR,CAG,SA3
					Pt. Lookout, MD	07/23/64	Elmira, NY	P113,P117,P120,CSR
					Elmira, NY	03/02/65	Pt. Lookout, MD Xc	P65,P66,CSR
Sarvis, Samuel S.	2Lt	A 9th SCVIBn	Secessionville, SC	06/16/62	Hilton Head, SC		Ft. Columbus, NY	IRQ
					Ft. Columbus, NY	08/23/62	Ft. Delaware, DE	SARVIS REM IRQ
					Ft. Delaware, DE	10/06/62	Aikens Ldg., VA Xc	CSR
Satterfield, A.B.	Pvt	K Ham.Leg.MI	Richmond, VA Hos.	04/03/65	Richmond, VA Hos.	04/21/65	Provost Marshal	CSR
					Libby Prison Rchmd.	04/23/65	Newport News, VA	CSR
					Newport News, VA	06/26/65	Rlsd. G.O. #109	CSR
Satterfield, Alphor B.	Pvt	K 16th SCVI	Jonesboro, GA	09/01/64	Rough & Ready, GA	09/19/64	Exchanged	CSR
Satterfield, Alphor B.	Pvt	K 16th SCVI	Alpine, GA	10/19/64	Louisville, KY	10/31/64	Camp Douglas, IL	P90,P95,CSR
					Nashville, TN	10/30/64	Louisville, KY	CSR
					Camp Douglas, IL	04/02/65	Jd. Co.I, 6th USVI	CSR
Satterfield, John B.O.	Pvt	E Ham.Leg.MI	Nine Mile Rd., VA	10/27/64	City Pt., VA	11/01/64	Pt. Lookout, MD	CSR
					Pt. Lookout, MD	06/19/65	Rlsd. G.O. #109	P115,CSR
Sattlemeyer, J.W.	Sgt	D 12th SCVI	Sutherland Stn., VA	04/03/65	Hart's Island, NY	06/17/65	Rlsd. G.O. #109	P79
Sauls, H.M.	Pvt	A 19th SCVCB	Augusta, GA	05/25/65	Augusta, GA	05/25/65	Paroled on oath	CSR
Sauls, Isaiah H.	Pvt	I 26th SCVI	Petersburg, VA	04/02/65	Camp Hamilton, VA	05/09/65	Newport News, VA	CSR,CTA
					Newport News, VA	06/26/65	Rlsd. G.O. #109	P107,CSR
Sauls, James N.	Pvt	K 6th SCVI	Warrenton, VA	09/29/62	Warrenton, VA	09/29/62	Paroled	CSR
Sauls, James N.	Pvt	K 6th SCVI	Knoxville, TN	12/03/63	Louisville, KY	12/31/63	Rock Island, IL	P88,P89,P94,CSR
					Rock Island, IL	03/02/65	Pt. Lookout, MD Xc	P131,CSR
Sauls, James W.	Pvt	E 10th SCVI	Stone Mtn., GA	07/23/64	Louisville, KY	08/13/64	Camp Chase, OH	P90,RAS,CTA
Sauls, James W.	Pvt	E 10th SCVI	Stone Mtn., GA	08/05/64	Louisville, KY	08/13/64	Camp Chase, OH	P91,CTA
Sauls, James W.	Pvt	E 10th SCVI	Stone Mtn., GA	07/26/64	Camp Chase, OH	03/18/65	Pt. Lookout, MD	P23,P26,CSR,CTA
Sauls, Josiah	Pvt	D 24th SCVI	Jonesboro, GA	08/31/64	Rough & Ready, GA	09/19/64	Exchanged	CSR
Sauls, Josiah	Pvt	D 24th SCVI	Nashville, TN	12/16/64	Nashville, TN	12/31/64	Louisville, KY	CSR
					Louisville, KY	01/05/65	Camp Chase, OH	P92,P95,CSR
					Camp Chase, OH	06/12/65	Rlsd. G.O. #109	P23,CSR
Saunders, A.	Cpl	16th SCVI	Greenville, SC	05/07/65	Greenville, SC	05/07/65	Paroled on oath	CSR
Saunders, D.W.	Pvt	B 2nd SCVC	Charlotte, NC	05/06/65	Charlotte, NC	05/06/65	Paroled	CSR
Saunders, George	Pvt	B Wash'n LA	Raleigh, NC Hos.	04/22/65	Raleigh, NC	04/22/65	Paroled	CSR
Saunders, M.T.	Pvt	F 7th SCVC	Richmond, VA Hos.	04/03/65	Richmond, VA Hos.	04/14/65	P.M. Richmond, VA	CSR
					Libby Prison Rchmd.	04/23/65	Newport News, VA	CSR
					Newport News, VA	06/26/65	Rlsd. G.O. #109	CSR

SOUTH CAROLINA SOLDIERS, SAILORS AND CITIZENS HELD IN U.S. PRISONS 1861-1865

NAME	RANK	REGIMENT	CAPTURED AT	WHEN	PRISON	MOVED	DISPOSITION	SOURCES
Saunders, P.A.	Pvt	Ham.Leg.	Deserted/enemy	02/27/65	City Pt., VA P.M.	03/01/65	Washington, DC	CSR
					Washington, DC	03/02/65	Iowa City, IA oath	CSR,KEB,H15
Savage, Abram	Pvt	H 15th SCVI	Deserted/enemy	12/29/63	Knoxville, TN	12/23/63	Released on oath	CSR
Savage, George	Pvt	C 3rd SCVC	Spanish Wells, SC	11/10/63	Ft. Columbus, NY	02/11/64	Ft. McHenry, MD	P2,P113
					Ft. McHenry, MD	07/26/64	Pt. Lookout, MD	P144,P96,CSR
					Pt. Lookout, MD	10/18/64	Aikens Ldg., VA Xc	P117,P123,CSR
Sawyer, George	Pvt	F 1st SCVA	Bentonville, NC	03/21/65	New Berne, NC	04/10/65	Hart's Island, NY	CSR
					Hart's Island, NY	06/17/65	Rlsd. G.O. #109	P79,CSR
Sawyer, George C.	Pvt	C 2nd SCVC	Deserted/enemy	11/09/63	Old Capitol, DC	03/18/64	Phila., PA on oath	CSR
Sawyer, J.W.	Pvt	F 5th SCVC	Bentonville, NC	03/21/65	New Berne, NC	04/10/65	Hart's Island, NY	CSR
					Hart's Island, NY	06/17/65	Rlsd. G.O. #109	P79,CSR
Sawyer, Joel	Pvt	G 23rd SCVI	Five Forks, VA	04/01/65	City Pt., VA	04/05/65	Pt. Lookout, MD	CSR
					Pt. Lookout, MD	06/19/65	Rlsd. G.O. #109	P122,CSR
Sawyer, John	Sgt	H 23rd SCVI	Five Forks, VA	04/01/65	City Pt., VA	04/06/65	Pt. Lookout, MD	HMC,CSR
					Pt. Lookout, MD	06/19/65	Rlsd. G.O. #109	P115,P119,P122,CSR
Sawyer, Ptolmy S.	Pvt	I 20th SCVI	Cedar Creek, VA	10/19/64	Harpers Ferry, WV	10/24/64	Pt. Lookout, MD	
					Pt. Lookout, MD	06/19/65	Rlsd. G.O. #109	P115,P118,KEB,CSR
Sawyer, W.J.	Pvt	F 3rd SCVC	Bentonville, NC	03/21/65	Hart's Island, NY	06/17/65	Rlsd. G.O. #109	P79
Saxon, J.F.	Pvt	D 27th SCVI	Pt. Walthal Jctn.	05/07/64	Bermuda Hundred, VA	05/08/64	Fts. Monroe, VA	CSR,HAG
					Fts. Monroe, VA	05/13/64	Pt. Lookout, MD	CSR
					Pt. Lookout, MD	03/17/65	Aikens Ldg., VA Xc	P117,P121,P124
Saxon, William P.	Pvt	7 10/19 SCVI	Missionary Ridge, TN	11/25/63	Nashville, TN	01/10/64	Louisville, KY	P39,CSR
					Louisville, KY	01/17/64	Rock Island, IL	P88,P89,P94,CSR
					Rock Island, IL	04/05/64	Died, Smallpox	P5,P132,FPH,CSR
Sayle, J.N.	Sgt	B 2nd SCRes	Raleigh, NC Hos.	04/13/65	Raleigh, NC Hos.	04/13/65	Paroled	CSR
Saylor, Jacob J.	Sgt	D 27th SCVI	Town Creek, NC	02/20/65	Ft. Anderson, NC	02/28/65	Pt. Lookout, MD	CSR,HAG
					Pt. Lookout, MD	06/19/65	Rlsd. G.O. #109	P115,P118,P122,CSR
Saylors, David W.	Pvt	A 12th SCVI	Amelia C.H., VA	04/03/65	City Pt., VA	04/04/65	Pt. Lookout, MD	CSR
					Pt. Lookout, MD	06/06/65	Rlsd. Inst. 5/30/65	P115,P119,P121,CSR
Saylors, William J.	Pvt	A 12th SCVI	Sutherland Stn., VA	04/02/65	City Pt., VA	04/07/65	Hart's Island, NY	CSR
					Hart's Island, NY	06/16/65	Rlsd. G.O. #109	P79,CSR
Sayron, A.H.	Pvt	Wash'n. LA	Gettysburg, PA	07/05/63	Ft. Delaware, DE		Released	P42
Scaff, Henry	Pvt	G 16th SCVI	Hartwell, GA	05/17/65	Hartwell, GA	05/17/65	Paroled on oath	CSR
Scaff, Matthew	Pvt	K 21st SCVI	Weldon RR, VA	08/21/64	City Pt., VA USFH	08/21/64	Died of wounds	P12,HAG,CSR
Scaff, Samuel	Pvt	K 21st SCVI	Morris Island, SC	07/10/63	Ft. Columbus, NY	10/09/63	Pt. Lookout, MD	P1,HAG
					Pt. Lookout, MD	02/26/64	Joined U.S. Army	P113,P117,P125
Scaff, W.H.	Pvt	I 27th SCVI	Weldon RR, VA	10/01/64	Pt. Lookout, MD	06/03/65	Rlsd. Instr. 5/30/65	P121
Scaif, W.J.	OSg	A 5th SCVI	Fair Oaks, VA	05/31/62	Fts. Monroe, VA	06/05/62	Ft. Delaware, DE	CSR
					Ft. Delaware, DE	08/09/62	Fts. Monroe, VA	CSR
					Fts. Monroe, VA	08/26/62	Aikens Ldg., VA Xc	CSR
Scarborough, Edward R.	Pvt	K 23rd SCVI	Five Forks, VA	04/01/65	City Pt., VA	04/05/65	Pt. Lookout, MD	CSR,UD3
					Pt. Lookout, MD	06/19/65	Rlsd. G.O. #109	P115,P122,CSR
Scarborough, Frank G.	Pvt	E 3rd SCVABn	Fayetteville, NC	03/16/65	New Berne, NC	03/20/65	Pt. Lookout, MD	CSR
					Pt. Lookout, MD	06/21/65	Washington, DC	CSR
					Pt. Lookout, MD	06/20/65	Rlsd. G.O. #109	P115,P118,P121
					Washington, DC	06/21/65	Donaldsville, LA oath	CSR
Scarborough, George P.	Pvt	A 14th SCVI	Appomattox C.H., VA	04/09/65	Appomattox C.H., VA	04/17/65	City Pt., VA	CSR
					City Pt., VA	04/23/65	Lincoln G.H., DC	CSR
					Lincoln G.H., DC	06/14/65	Rlsd. G.O. #109	CSR
Scarborough, H.G.	Cpl	Palmetto LA	Not given		City Pt., VA USGH	04/15/65	Not given	CSR
Scarborough, W.H.	Pvt	I 7th SCVC	Old Church, VA	05/30/64	White House, VA	01/03/64	Pt. Lookout, MD	CSR
					Pt. Lookout, MD	09/18/64	Aikens Ldg., VA Xc	P117,P123,CSR

SOUTH CAROLINA SOLDIERS, SAILORS AND  CITIZENS HELD IN U.S. PRISONS 1861-1865

NAME	RANK	REGIMENT	CAPTURED AT	WHEN	PRISON	MOVED	DISPOSITION	SOURCES
Scarborough, William M.	ASr	14th SCVI	Gettysburg, PA	07/04/63	Gettysburg, PA	07/14/63	Ft. McHenry, MD	CSR
					Ft. McHenry, MD	07/18/63	Ft. Delaware, DE	CSR
					Ft. Delaware, DE	11/17/63	City Pt., VA Xc	P44,P144,CSR
Scarborough, William S.	Pvt	E 3rd SCVABn	Fayetteville, NC	03/16/65	New Berne, NC	03/30/65	Pt. Lookout, MD	CSR
					Pt. Lookout, MD	06/19/65	Rlsd. G.O. #109	P115,P118,P122,CSR
Schaft, Alexander	Pvt	Macbeth LA	Leesburg, VA Hos.	10/02/62	Leesburg, VA	10/02/62	Paroled	CSR
Schenk, John M.	Pvt	9 10/19 SCVI	Missionary Ridge, TN	11/25/63	Nashville, TN	12/07/63	Louisville, KY	P39,HOE,CSR
					Louisville, KY	12/09/63	Rock Island, IL	P88,P89,CSR
					Rock Island, IL	08/10/64	Died, Dysntery	P12,P131,P132,FPH
Scheper, F.W.	Pvt	B German LA	Deserted/enemy	10/01/64	Hilton Head, SC	10/31/64	At work in Q.M.	CSR
Scherer, John	Cpl	B 25th SCVI	Ft. Fisher, NC	01/15/65	New York, NY	01/30/65	Elmira, NY	CSR,HAG
					Elmira, NY	05/29/65	Rlsd. G.O. #85	P7,P65,P66,CSR
Schipman, Herman G.	Pvt	F 6th SCVC	Stony Creek, VA	12/01/64	City Pt., VA	12/02/64	Pt. Lookout, MD	CSR,CAG
					Pt. Lookout, MD	06/05/65	Rlsd. Instr. 5/30/65	P115,P118,P121,CSR
Schlimmermeyer, Dietere	Sgt	B German LA	Deserted/enemy	03/15/65	Charleston, SC	03/15/65	Released on oath	CSR
Schmidt, Hermann	Pvt	B German LA	Deserted/enemy	10/22/64				CSR
Schneider, A. Henry	Pvt	A 15th SCVI	Halltown, VA	08/26/64	Harpers Ferry, WV	08/29/64	Camp Chase, OH	CSR,KEB,H15
					Camp Chase, VA	05/15/65	Rlsd. G.O. #85	P23,P25,CSR
Schnibble, Charles	Smn	Dis. Boat	Morris Island, SC	09/07/63	Pt. Lookout, MD	09/20/64	Ft. Warren, MA	P113
					Ft. Warren, MA	10/01/64	Str. Circasian	P2,P137
Schnibble, J.S.	Smn	Dis. Boat	Morris Island, SC	09/07/63	Pt. Lookout, MD	09/20/64	Ft. Warren, MA	P113
					Ft. Warren, MA	10/02/64	Str. Circasian	P2,P137
Schnible, C.	Pvt	A German LA	Deserted/enemy	02/18/65	Hilton Head, SC	04/04/65	New York, NY P.M.	CSR
Schroeder, Henry	Pvt	C 27th SCVI	Petersburg, VA	06/24/64	Bermuda Hundred, VA	06/25/64	Fts. Monroe, VA	CSR
					Fts. Monroe, VA	06/26/64	Pt. Lookout, MD	CSR,HAG
					Pt. Lookout, MD	08/16/64	Elmira, NY	P113,P117,P120
					Elmira, NY	03/04/65	Died, Pneumonia	P6,P12,P65,P66,FPH
Schroeder, Nicholas	Pvt	B German LA	Deserted/enemy	07/13/63	Washington, DC	03/15/64	Released on oath	CSR
Schroeder, William	Pvt	B German LA	Deserted/enemy	03/21/65	Charleston, SC	03/21/65	Released on oath	CSR
Schulte, J. Herman	Pvt	B 25th SCVI	Ft. Fisher, NC	01/15/65	New York, NY	01/30/65	Elmira, NY	CSR,HAG
					Elmira, NY	06/16/65	Rlsd. G.O. #109	P66,CSR
Schultheiss, John	Cpl	C 27th SCVI	Town Creek, NC	02/20/65	Ft. Anderson, NC	02/28/65	Pt. Lookout, MD	CSR
					Pt. Lookout, MD	05/14/65	Rlsd. G.O. #85	P118,P121,CSR
Schultz, Will	Pvt	B German LA	Deserted/enemy	07/13/63	Maryland			CSR
Schumpert, Daniel P.	Pvt	H 20th SCVI	Lexington, SC	02/05/65	New Berne, NC	03/20/65	Pt. lookout, MD	CSR,KEB
					Pt. Lookout, MD	06/30/65	Rlsd. G.O. #109	P115,P118,P121,CSR
Schumpert, Osborne Lamar	Pvt	B 3rd SCVI	Virginia		Harrisonburg, VA	05/02/65	Paroled	H3,CSR
Schwartz, George H.	Pvt	H 3rd SCVI	N. Anna River, VA	05/23/64	Port Royal, VA	05/30/64	Pt. Lookout, MD	CSR,KEB,SA2,H3
					Pt. Lookout, MD	03/14/65	Aikens Ldg., VA Xc	117,P121,P124,CSR
Schwartz, Godfrey W.	Pvt	H 13th SCVI	Sharpsburg, MD	09/17/62	Paroled			CSR
Schwartz, Godfrey W.	Pvt	H 13th SCVI	Gettysburg, PA	07/03/63	Ft. Delaware, DE		Hos. 3/13-5/13/64	P47
					Ft. Delaware, DE		Hos. 7/30-?	P47
					Ft. McHenry, MD	07/07/63	Ft. Delaware, DE	CSR
					Ft. Delaware, DE	08/07/64	Died, Typhoid fever	P5,P12,P40,P42,P47,FPH
Schwartz, Jacob A.	Pvt	C 12th SCVI	Sutherland Stn., VA	04/03/65	City Pt., VA	04/07/65	Hart's Island, NY	CSR,HFC
					Hart's Island, NY	06/16/65	Rlsd. G.O. #109	P79,CSR
Scott, A.Q.	Pvt	E 1st SCVIG	Warrenton, VA	09/29/62	Warrenton, VA	09/29/62	Paroled	SA1,CSR
Scott, Absolom Winfield	Pvt	G 15th SCVI	Cedar Creek, VA	10/19/64	Harpers Ferry, WV	10/24/64	Pt. Lookout, MD	CSR,KEB,H15,CTA
					Pt. Lookout, MD	02/13/65	Aikens Ldg., VA Xc	P115,P118,P121,P124
Scott, Allen	Pvt	C 26th SCVI	Petersburg, VA H	04/03/65	Fts. Monroe, VA G.H.	07/05/65	Released	CSR

SOUTH CAROLINA SOLDIERS, SAILORS AND  CITIZENS HELD IN U.S. PRISONS 1861-1865

NAME	RANK	REGIMENT	CAPTURED AT	WHEN	PRISON	MOVED	DISPOSITION	SOURCES
Scott, Andrew D.	Pvt	E 1st SCVIG	Petersburg, VA	07/29/64	City Pt., VA	08/05/64	Pt. Lookout, MD	CSR,SA1,HMC
					Pt. Lookout, MD	08/08/64	Elmira, NY	P113,P117,P120,CSR
					Elmira, NY	07/03/65	Rlsd. G.O. #109	P65,P66,CSR
Scott, Archibald	Pvt	D 6th SCVC	Stony Creek, VA	12/01/64	City Pt., VA	12/04/64	Pt. Lookout, MD	CSR
					Pt. Lookout, MD	06/19/65	Rlsd. G.O. #109	P115,P118,P122,CSR
Scott, Berry B.	Pvt	M P.S.S.	Loudon, TN	12/03/63	Nashville, TN	12/30/63	Louisville, KY	P39,TSE,CSR
					Louisville, KY	12/31/63	Rock Island, IL	P88,P89,P94,CSR
					Rock Island, IL	02/14/64	Died, Variola	P5,P131,P132,FPH
Scott, Edward M.	Pvt	G 5th SCVC	James Island, SC	03/02/64	Ft. Delaware, DE	06/10/65	Rlsd. G.O.#109	P41,P43,P45,CSR
					Ft. Lafayette, NY	04/19/64	Ft. Delaware, DE	P144,CSR
					Ft. Delaware, DE	04/25/65	Hos. 4/25-5/19/65	P47
					Hilton Head, SC	04/03/64	Ft. Lafayette, NY	CSR
Scott, Frederick J.	Pvt	F 3rd SCVIBn	Knoxville, TN	11/29/63	Nashville, TN	01/17/64	Louisville, KY	P39,KEB,CSR
Scott, Frederick J.	Pvt	F 3rd SCVIBn	Knoxville, TN	01/05/64	Louisville, KY	01/23/64	Rock Island, IL	P88,P94,CSR
					Rock Island, IL	05/11/65	Released, Sp. Order	P131,CSR
Scott, G.W.	Pvt	I Hol.Leg.	Stony Creek, VA	05/07/64	Fts. Monroe, VA	05/13/64	Pt. Lookout, MD	CSR
					Pt. Lookout, MD	06/25/64	Died, Measles	P6,P119,P121,FPH
Scott, G.W.	Cpl	B 5th SCVC	Stony Creek, VA	12/01/64	City Pt., VA	12/05/64	Pt. Lookout, MD	CSR
					Pt. Lookout, MD	05/14/65	Rlsd. G.O.#85	P115,P118,P122,CSR
Scott, George W.	Pvt	A 7th SCVI	Gettysburg, PA		Gettysburg G.H.	10/15/63	Provost Marshal	P4,CSR
Scott, George W.	Pvt	E 7th SCVIBn	Weldon RR, VA	08/21/64	Pt. Lookout, MD	04/14/65	Died	P6,P113,P119,FPH
Scott, H.W.	Pvt	G 5th SCVC	James Island, SC	03/02/64	Hilton Head, DC	04/03/64	Ft. Lafayette, NY	CSR
					Ft. Lafayette, NY	04/19/64	Ft. Delaware, DE	P144,CSR
					Ft. Delaware, DE	09/29/64	Hos. 9/29-10/17/64	P47
					Ft. Delaware, DE	03/20/65	Hos. 3/20-4/8/65	P47
					Ft. Delaware, DE	06/08/65	Rlsd. G.O. #109	P41,P43,P45,CSR
Scott, J.M.	Pvt	B 27th SCVI	Petersburg, VA	06/24/64	Fts. Monroe, VA	08/01/64	Died of wounds	CSR,TOD
Scott, J.R.	Sgt	A 3rd SCVABn	High Pt., NC	05/02/65	High Pt., NC	05/02/65	Paroled	CSR
Scott, J.T.	Pvt	B 7th SCVIBn	Deserted/enemy		Fts. Monroe, VA	04/02/65	Washington, DC	CSR,HAG
					Washington, DC	04/06/65	Charleston, SC oath	CSR
Scott, James Madison	Pvt	H 1st SCVIG	Sutherland Stn., VA	04/06/65	City Pt., VA	04/14/65	Pt. Lookout, MD	CSR,SA1
					Pt. Lookout, MD	06/19/65	Rlsd. G.O. #109	P115,P119,CSR
Scott, James R.	Pvt	A 24th SCVI	Nashville, TN	12/16/64	Camp Chase, OH	03/20/65	Jd. US Service	CSR,EFW
Scott, John E.	Pvt	A 24th SCVI	Nashville, TN	12/16/64	Nashville, TN	12/20/64	Louisville, KY	CSR,EFW
					Louisville, KY	01/04/65	Camp Chase, OH	P92,P95,CSR
					Camp Chase, OH	03/21/65	Chicago, IL	P23,P26
Scott, John M.	Pvt	A 15th SCVI	Columbia, SC	02/19/65	New Berne, NC	03/26/65	Pt. Lookout, MD	CSR,KEB,H15
					Pt. Lookout, MD	06/19/65	Rlsd. G.O. #109	P115,P118,CSR
Scott, Junius E.	2Lt	C 25th SCVI	Weldon RR, VA	08/21/64	Old Capitol, DC	08/27/64	Ft. Delaware, DE	P110,CSR,HAG,CTA
					Ft. Delaware, DE	10/06/64	Pt. Lookout, MD Xc	P43,CSR
					Pt. Lookout, MD	10/11/64	Coxe's Ldg. Xc	P117,P115,P123
Scott, Junius E.	2Lt	C 25th SCVI	Ft. Fisher, NC	01/15/65	New York, NY	01/30/65	Elmira, NY	CSR
					Elmira, NY	06/30/65	Rlsd. G.O. #109	P65,CSR
Scott, Junius L.	Pvt	G 25th SCVI	Ft. Fisher, NC	01/15/65	New York, NY	01/30/65	Elmira, NY	CSR,HAG
					Elmira, NY	07/11/65	Rlsd. G.O. #109	P65,P66,CSR
Scott, Langford J.	Pvt	L Orr's Ri.	Hatchers Run, VA	03/31/65	City Pt., VA	04/02/65	Pt. Lookout, MD	CSR,CDC
					Pt. Lookout, MD	06/19/65	Rlsd. G.O. #109	P115,P118,CSR
Scott, Samuel M.	Cpl	A 12th SCVI	Southside RR, VA	04/03/65	City Pt., VA	04/07/65	Hart's Island, NY	CSR,YEB
					Hart's Island, NY	06/16/65	Rlsd. G.O. #109	P79,CSR
Scott, Thomas A.	Pvt	H 7th SCVIBn	Drury's Bluff, VA	05/16/64	Fts. Monroe, VA	02/02/65	Pt. Lookout, MD	HAG,CSR
					Pt. Lookout, MD	02/13/65	Aikens Ldg., VA Xc	P118,121,P124,CSR

SOUTH CAROLINA SOLDIERS, SAILORS AND  CITIZENS HELD IN U.S. PRISONS 1861-1865

NAME	RANK	REGIMENT	CAPTURED AT	WHEN	PRISON	MOVED	DISPOSITION	SOURCES
Scott, Thomas C.	Pvt	K P.S.S.	Deserted/enemy	02/25/65	Bermuda Hundred, VA	02/27/65	City Pt., VA	CSR,TSE
					City Pt., VA	03/02/65	Washington, DC	CSR
					Washington, DC	03/02/65	New York, NY oath	CSR
Scott, W.	Pvt	E 7th SCVIBn	Weldon RR, VA	08/21/64	City Pt., VA	08/24/64	Pt. Lookout, MD	CSR
					Pt. Lookout, MD	04/14/65	Died	CSR,FPH
Scott, W.B.	Pvt	A 2nd SCVI	Raleigh, NC	04/20/65	Raleigh, NC	04/20/65	Paroled	CSR
Scott, W.H.	Pvt	Palmetto L	Burkesville, VA	04/14/65	City Pt., VA USGH	04/15/65	Not given	CSR
Scott, W.R.	1Eng	Huntress	Off Charleston	01/18/63	Ft. Lafayette, NY	06/10/63	Washington, DC	P144
Scott, Wade	Pvt	B 1st SCVIR	Fayetteville, NC	03/16/65	New Berne, NC	03/30/65	Pt. Lookout, MD	CSR,SA1
					Pt. Lookout, MD	05/07/65	Died, Dysentery	P118,CSR
Scott, Wade	Pvt	B 1st SCVIR	Fayetteville, NC	03/16/65	Pt. Lookout, MD	06/19/65	Rlsd. G.O. #109	P115,CSR
Scott, William	Pvt	I 27th SCVI	Deserted/enemy	08/06/64	Unstated prison		Barnegat, NJ oath	CSR
Scott, William H.	Cpl	A 15th SCVI	Fredericksburg, VA	05/03/63	Washington, DC	05/10/63	City Pt. VA.	CSR,H15
					Ft. McHenry, MD	05/11/63	City Pt., VA Xc	P110
Scott, William P.	Pvt	H 10th SCVI	Murfreesboro, TN	01/05/63	Nashville, TN		Louisville, KY	P38,CTA,CSR,HOW
					Louisville, KY	03/27/63	City Pt., VA Xc	P88,CSR
Scott, William T.	1Sg	G 1st SCVIG	Gettysburg, PA	07/03/63	David's Island, NY	09/12/63	City Pt., VA Xc	P1,SA1,CSR
Scott, William W.	Pvt	F 21st SCVI	Bennettsville, SC	03/08/65	Pt. Lookout, MD	06/19/65	Rlsd. G.O. #109	P118,P122,HAG,HOM
Scruggs, B.O.	Pvt	K Hol.Leg.	Stony Creek, VA	05/07/64	Fts. Monroe, VA	05/13/64	Pt. Lookout, MD	CSR
					Pt. Lookout, MD	08/15/64	Elmira, NY	P113,P117,P120
					Elmira, NY	02/20/65	Aikens Ldg., VA Xc	P65,CSR
Scruggs, D.S.	Pvt	K Hol.Leg.	Petersburg, VA	10/27/64	Pt. Lookout, MD	01/12/65	Aikens Ldg., VA Xc	P114,P118,P124,CSR
					Pt. Lookout, MD	01/17/65	Exchanged	P115,P124
Scruggs, J.P.	Pvt	K Hol.Leg.	Kinston, NC	12/15/62	Kinston, NC	12/15/62	Paroled POW	CSR
Scruggs, J.P.	Sgt	K Hol.Leg.	Stony Creek, VA	05/07/64	Fts. Monroe, VA	05/13/64	Pt. Lookout, MD	CSR
					Pt. Lookout, MD	08/15/64	Elmira, NY	P113,P117
					Elmira, NY	10/07/64	Escaped by tunnel	P65,P66,CSR
Scruggs, J.P.	Sgt	A 3rd SCVABn	High Pt., NC	05/02/65	High Pt., NC	05/02/65	Paroled	CSR
Scruggs, J.W.	Pvt	K Hol.Leg.	Stony Creek, VA	05/07/64	Fts. Monroe, VA	05/13/64	Pt. Lookout, MD	CSR
					Pt. Lookout, MD	08/15/64	Elmira, NY	P113,P117,P120,CSR
					Elmira, NY	02/20/65	James R., VA Xc	P65,P66,CSR
Scruggs, John J.	Pvt	A 3rd SCVABn	High Pt., NC	05/02/65	High Pt., NC	05/02/65	Paroled	CSR
Scruggs, Lemuel D.	Sgt	K Hol.Leg.	Five Forks, VA	04/01/65	City Pt., VA	04/05/65	Pt. Lookout, MD	CSR
					Pt. Lookout, MD	06/19/65	Rlsd. G.O. #109	P115,P119,P122,CSR
Scruggs, R.A.	Pvt	K Hol.Leg.	Stony Creek, VA	05/07/64	Fts. Monroe, VA	05/13/64	Pt. Lookout, MD	CSR
					Pt. Lookout, MD	08/15/64	Elmira, NY	CSR
					Elmira, NY	02/20/65	Pt. Lookout, MD Xc	P66
Scruggs, R.M.	Pvt	D 1st SCVIR	Deserted/enemy	02/26/65	Charleston, SC	03/12/65	Taken oath & disch.	SA1,CSR
Scruggs, Richard M.	Cpt	K Hol.Leg.	Stony Creek, VA	05/07/64	Fts. Monroe, VA	05/13/64	Pt. Lookout, MD	CSR
					Pt. Lookout, MD	06/25/64	Ft. Delaware, DE	P116,P120,CSR
					Ft. Delaware, DE	06/16/65	Rlsd. G.O. #109	P43,P45,P46,CSR
Scruggs, W.W.	Pvt	K Hol.Leg.	Kinston, NC	12/15/62	Kinston, NC	12/15/62	Paroled POW	CSR
Scruggs, W.W.	Pvt	K Hol.Leg.	Stony Creek, VA	05/07/64	Fts. Monroe, VA	05/13/64	Pt. Lookout, MD	CSR
					Pt. Lookout, MD	08/15/64	Elmira, NY	P113,P117,P120
					Elmira, NY	02/20/65	Pt. Lookout, MD Xc	P65,P66
Scurry, John J.	Pvt	C 3rd SCVABn	Blakely, AL	04/09/65	Ship Island, MS	05/01/65	Vicksburg, MS Xc	P136,CSR
					Vicksburg, MS	05/03/65		CSR
Scurry, John J.	Pvt	C 3rd SCVABn	Citronelle, AL	05/04/65	Meridian, MS	05/15/65	Paroled	CSR
Seabrook, E.B.	Pvt	B 1st SCVA	St. Paul's parish	03/10/65				CSR
Seabrook, P.	Pvt	G 1st SCVC	Bacons Bridge, SC	04/10/65				CSR
Seabrook, R.F.	Pvt	I 3rd SCVC	Edisto Island, SC	04/09/63				CSR
Seabrook, Whitmarsh H.	1Lt	H 25th SCVI	Swift Creek, VA	05/09/64	Fts. Monroe, VA GH	05/21/64	Died of wounds	P12,HAG,CSR

SOUTH CAROLINA SOLDIERS, SAILORS AND  CITIZENS HELD IN U.S. PRISONS 1861-1865

NAME	RANK	REGIMENT	CAPTURED AT	WHEN	PRISON	MOVED	DISPOSITION	SOURCES
Seal, Thomas C.	Pvt	A 2nd SCVIRi	Wilderness, VA	05/06/65	Belle Plain, VA	05/21/64	Ft. Delaware, DE	CSR
					Ft. Delaware, DE		Hos. 9/15-10/1/64	P47
					Ft. Delaware, DE		Hos. 2/1-2/11/65	P47
					Ft. Delaware, DE		Hos. 2/13-2/19/65	P47
					Ft. Delaware, DE	02/27/65	Aikens Ldg., VA Xc	P43,CSR
					Richmond, VA Hos.		Not given	CSR
Searcey, John H.	Pvt	I 1st SCVA	Morris Island, SC	07/10/63	Hilton Head, SC	09/19/63	Ft. Columbus, NY	CSR
					Ft. Columbus, NY	09/23/63	Took the oath	P1,CSR
Searle, R.H.	Pvt	E 11th SCVI	Petersburg, VA	06/24/64	Bermuda Hundred VA	06/25/64	Fts. Monroe, VA	CSR
					Fts. Monroe, VA.	06/26/64	Pt. Lookout, MD	P121,CSR
					Pt. Lookout, MD	12/01/64	Venus Pt., GA Xc	P113,P117,P124,CSR
Sears, E.	Pvt	Eng. Corps			Farmville, VA	04/26/65	Died	P12
Sears, Thomas G.	Pvt	Ferguson's LA	Salisbury, NC	04/12/65	Nashville, TN	04/29/65	Louisville, KY	P39,CSR
					Louisville, KY	05/02/65	Camp Chase, OH	P92,P95
					Camp Chase, OH	06/13/65	Rlsd. G.O. #109	CSR
Sease, A. Noah	Pvt	C 3rd SCVI	Gettysburg, PA	07/05/63	Gettysburg, G.H.	09/28/63	Provost Marshal	P4,KEB,SA2,CSR,H3
					Letterman G.H. Gbg	10/01/63	Baltimore, MD	P1,CSR
					W. Bldg. Balt, MD	11/12/63	City Pt., VA Xc	CSR
Sease, A. Noah	Pvt	C 3rd SCVI	Gettysburg, PA	07/05/63	Richmond, VA Hos.	11/21/63	Furloughed 30 days	CSR
Sease, Daniel Isaiah	Pvt	C 15th SCVI	Halltown, VA	08/26/64	Harpers Ferry, WV	08/29/64	Camp Chase, OH	CSR,KEB,H15
					Camp Chase, OH	03/18/65	Died, Pneumonia	P23,P27,FPH,CSR
Sease, J.C.	Pvt	C 1st SCVA	Cheraw, NC	03/07/65	New Berne, NC	04/10/65	Hart's Island, NY	CSR
					Hart's Island, NY	06/16/65	Rlsd. G.O. #109	CSR,P79
Sease, J.D.	Pvt	G 1st SCVIH	Warrenton, VA	09/29/62	Warrenton, VA	09/29/62	Paroled	CSR
Sease, J.R.	Sgt	K 20th SCVI	Cedar Creek, VA	10/19/64	Harpers Ferry, WV	10/24/64	Pt. Lookout, MD	CSR
					Pt. Lookout, MD	06/19/65	Rlsd. G.O. #109	P115,118,KEB,CSR
Seats, A.	Pvt	D 2nd SCVC	Augusta, GA	06/02/65	Augusta, GA	06/02/65	Paroled	CSR
Seawright, Enoch W.	Pvt	Ferguson's LA	Salisbury, NC	04/12/65	Nashville, TN	04/29/65	Louisville, KY	P39,CSR
					Louisville, KY	05/02/65	Camp Chase, OH	P92,P95,CSR
					Camp Chase, OH	06/13/65	Rlsd. G.O. #109	CSR
Seay, Allen B.	Pvt	C Hol.Leg.	Five Forks, VA	04/01/65	City Pt., VA	04/05/65	Pt. Lookout, MD	CSR
					Pt. Lookout, MD	06/08/65	Rlsd. Instr. 5/30/65	P115,P119,P121,CSR
Seay, Daniel E.	Pvt	F 5th SCVC	Hawe's Shop, VA	05/28/64	White House, VA	06/09/64	Pt. Lookout, MD	CSR
					Pt. Lookout, MD	07/09/64	Elmira, NY	P66,P117,P120,CSR
					Elmira, NY	01/30/65	Died, Variola	P6,P12,P65,FPH,CSR
Seay, H. Harley	1Lt	B 15th SCMil			New Berne, NC	04/29/65	Died	P6
Seay, Irvin	Pvt	I 6th SCVI	Richmond, VA Hos.	04/03/65	Libby Prison Rchmd	04/08/65	City Pt., VA P.M.	CSR
					City Pt., VA	04/14/65	Pt. Lookout, MD	CSR
					Pt. Lookout, MD	06/19/65	Rlsd. G.O. #109	CSR
Seay, J.K.	Pvt	E 13th SCVI	Spotsylvania, VA	05/12/64	Belle Plain, VA	05/21/64	Ft. Delaware, DE	CSR
					Ft. Delaware, DE	11/29/64	Hos. 11/29-12/14/64	P47
					Ft. Delaware, DE	02/01/65	Hos. 2/1-2/4/65	P47
					Ft. Delaware, DE	02/04/65	Hos. 2/24-4/2/65	P47
					Ft. Delaware, DE	06/10/65	Released	P41,P43,P45,CSR
Seay, John	Pvt	I 1st SCVIH	Farmville, VA	04/11/65	Farmville, VA	04/21/65	Paroled	CSR,SA1
Seay, John C.	Cpl	K 13th SCVI	Petersburg, VA	04/03/65	City Pt., VA	04/11/65	Hart's Island, NY	CSR
					Hart's Island, NY	06/16/65	Rlsd. G.O. #109	P79,CSR
Seay, William F.	Pvt	H 7th SCVIBn	Gaines' Mill, VA	06/01/64	Pt. Lookout, MD	07/04/64	Elmira, NY	P113,P117,P120,CSR
					Elmira, NY	10/11/64	Pt. Lookout, MD	P65,P66,CSR
					Pt. Lookout, MD	10/29/64	Aikens Ldg., VA Xc	P115,P118,P123,CSR

SOUTH CAROLINA SOLDIERS, SAILORS AND  CITIZENS HELD IN U.S. PRISONS 1861-1865

NAME	RANK	REGIMENT	CAPTURED AT	WHEN	PRISON	MOVED	DISPOSITION	SOURCES
Sechrist, A.J.	Pvt	B 4th SCVC	Louisa C.H., VA	06/11/54	Fts. Monroe, VA	06/20/64	Pt. Lookout, MD	CSR
					Pt. Lookout, MD	07/23/64	Elmira, NY	P113,P117,P120,CSR
					Elmira, NY	10/11/64	Pt. Lookout to Xc	P66,CSR
					Pt. Lookout, MD	10/29/64	Aikens Ldg., VA Xc	P118,P123
					Elmira, NY	05/29/65	Released GO #85	P65,P66,CSR
Seebeck, C.	Cpl	B German LA	Deserted/enemy	03/15/65	Charleston, SC	03/15/65	Released on oath	CSR
Sego, Leonidas	Pvt	B 19th SCVI	Glasgow, KY	09/12/62	Glasgow, KY	09/12/62	Paroled on oath	HOE,CSR
Segrist, William D.	Pvt	I 5th SCVC	Hawe's Shop, VA	05/28/64	3rd Div.5th A.C. H		Washington, DC G.H.	CSR
					Lincoln G.H., DC	06/16/64	Died of wounds	P6,P12,P110,CSR
Seightler, William A.	Pvt	H 20th SCVI	Columbia, SC	02/16/65	Pt. Lookout, MD	06/19/65	Rlsd. G.O. #109	P115,KEB
Self, William	Pvt	E 7th SCVIBn	Tedgeworth, VA	10/02/64	Louisville, KY	10/24/64	Camp Chse, OH	CSR
					Camp Chase, OH	04/22/65	Jd. U.S. Army	CSR
Sell, Andrew	Pvt	K 21st SCVI	Harpers Ferry, WV	07/08/64	Elmira, NY	02/16/65	Died	P6,FPH
Sellers, Andrew W.	Pvt	A 4th SCVC	Stony Creek, VA	12/01/64	City Pt., VA	12/05/64	Pt. Lookout, MD	CSR
					Pt. Lookout, MD	06/19/65	Rlsd. G.O. #109	P115,P118,P122,CSR
Sellers, Phillip	1Lt	B 8th SCVI	Winchester, VA	09/13/64	Harpers Ferry, WV	09/24/64	Johnson's Isl., OH	CSR,KEB
					Johnson's Isl., OH	06/16/65	Rlsd. G.O. #109	P81,P82,P83,CSR
Sellers, Richard C.	Pvt	D 6th SCVC	Hamey, NC	03/17/65	New Berne, NC	03/29/65	Pt. Lookout, MD	CSR
					Pt. Lookout, MD	06/19/65	Rlsd. G.O. #109	P115,CSR
Sellers, W. Riley	Pvt	A 4th SCVC	Hawe's Shop, VA	05/28/64	White House, VA	06/05/64	Pt. Lookout, MD	CSR
					Pt. Lookout, MD	07/09/64	Elmira, NY	P113,P117,P120,CSR
					Elmira, NY	03/23/65	Died, Pneumonia	P6,P65,P66,FPH,CSR
Sellers, W.P.	Pvt	D 6th SCVC	Petersburg, VA	07/30/64	City Pt., VA	08/05/64	Pt. Lookout, MD	CSR
					Elmira, NY	06/19/65	Rlsd. G.O. #109	P65,P66,CSR
Sellers, William B.	Cpl	D 6th SCVC	Armstrongs Mill, VA	12/10/64	City Pt., VA	12/11/64	Pt. Lookout, MD	CSR
					Pt. Lookout, MD	06/19/65	Rlsd. G.O. #109	P115,P118,P122,CSR
Senn, James P.	Pvt	D 13th SCVI	Gettysburg, PA	07/05/63	Ft. McHenry, MD	07/30/63	Ft. Delaware, DE	CSR,ANY
					Ft. Delaware, DE	12/12/64	Died, Lung Inflam.	P5,P40,P42,P47,FPH
Senn, John P.	Pvt	D 13th SCVI	Hatchers Run, VA	03/31/65	City Pt.,VA	04/02/65	Pt. Lookout, MD	CSR,ANY
					Pt. Lookout, MD	06/06/65	Rlsd. per Inst. 5/3	P115,P118,P121,CSR
Senn, M.A.	Pvt	K Ham.Leg.MI	Deserted/enemy	03/04/65	Bermuda Hundred VA	03/05/65	City Pt., VA P.M.	CSR
					City Pt., VA	03/07/65	Washington, DC	CSR
					Washington, DC	03/08/65	Iowa City, IA oath	CSR
Senn, Samuel	Pvt	G 3rd SCVI	Augusta, GA	05/23/65	Augusta, GA	05/23/65	Paroled	H3,CSR
Sentell, J.R.	Pvt	G 7th SCVI	Gettysburg, PA	07/02/63	Johnson's Isl., OH	03/14/65	Pt. Lookout, MD	CSR
Sepaugh, Phillip	Pvt	F 17th SCVI	Burkesville, VA	04/14/65	Burkesville, VA	04/17/65	Paroled	CSR
Sepoch, Joseph	Pvt	F 17th SCVI	Petersburg, VA	03/25/65	City Pt., VA	03/28/65	Pt. Lookout, MD	CSR
					Pt. Lookout, MD	06/19/65	Rlsd. G.O. #109	P114,CSR
Sessions, J.D.	Pvt	F 7th SCVC	Farmville, VA	04/11/65	Farmville, VA	04/21/65	Paroled	CSR
Sessions, John G.	Pvt	C 6th SCVI	Darbytown Rd., VA	10/07/64	Bermuda Hundred VA	10/07/64	Dutch Gap Canal	CSR,HIC
					Dutch Gap Canal	10/24/64	Pt. Lookout, MD	CSR
					Pt. Lookout, MD	01/27/65	Aikens Ldg. Xc	P115,P118,P124,CSR
Sessions, L.S.	Pvt	F 7th SCVC	Lynchburg, VA	04/14/65	Lynchburg, VA	04/14/65	Paroled	CSR
Sessions, Loraine T.	Pvt	6 10/19 SCVI	Missionary Ridge, TN	11/25/63	Nashville, TN	12/07/63	Louisville, KY	P39,RAS,CSR
					Louisville, KY	12/09/63	Rock Island, IL	P88,P89,CSR
					Rock Island, IL	02/15/65	Pt. Lookout, MD Xc	P131,CSR
Sessions, Philander C.	Cpl	K 26th SCVI	Southside RR, VA	04/02/65	City Pt., VA	04/05/65	Pt. Lookout, MD	CSR
					Pt. Lookout, MD	06/06/65	Released	P115,P119,P121,CSR
Settlemeyer, M.E.	Pvt	D P.S.S.	Fair Oaks, VA	05/31/62	Fts. Monroe, VA	06/05/62	Ft. Delaware, DE	CSR
					Ft. Delaware, DE	08/05/62	Aikens Ldg., VA Xc	CSR
Setzler, Jacob Thomas	Pvt	H 3rd SCVI	Salisbury, NC	05/02/65	Salisbury, NC G.H.	05/02/65	Paroled	SA2,H3,CSR,KEB
Sever, Charles	Pvt	F 1st SCVIR	Prob. Balt, MD		Ft. McHenry, MD	08/08/62	Rlsd.on oath S.O.	P145,SA1,CSR

SOUTH CAROLINA SOLDIERS, SAILORS AND  CITIZENS HELD IN U.S. PRISONS 1861-1865

NAME	RANK	REGIMENT	CAPTURED AT	WHEN	PRISON	MOVED	DISPOSITION	SOURCES
Severance, Joseph J.	Pvt	A 14th SCVI	Gettysburg, PA	07/04/63	Davids Island, NY	09/05/63	City Pt., VA Xc	P1,CSR
Severance, Thomas G.	Pvt	C 3rd SCVABn	Ft. Gaines, AL	08/08/64	St. Louis, MO USGH	10/13/64	New Orleans, LA	CSR
					New Orleans, LA	10/24/64	Ship Island, MS	P3,CSR
					Ship Island, MS	12/27/64	Died, Dysentery	P136,CSR
Seyle, Samuel H.	Pvt	A 25th SCVI	Town Creek, NC	02/20/65	Ft. Anderson, NC	02/28/65	Pt. Lookout, MD	CSR,HAG
					Pt. Lookout, MD	06/08/65	Rlsd. G.O. #85	P115,P118,CSR
Shackleford, Bushrod M.	Pvt	E 26th SCVI	Ft. Stedman, VA	03/25/65	City Pt., VA	04/09/65	Lincon G.H., DC	CSR
					Lincoln G.H., DC	06/14/65	Released	P110,CSR
Shackleford, Jonathan C.	Pvt	E 18th SCVI	Crater, Pbg., VA	07/30/64	City Pt., VA	08/05/64	Elmira, NY	CSR
					Pt. Lookout, MD	08/08/64	Elmira, NY	P117,P120,P125,CSR
					Elmira, NY	10/11/64	Pt. Lookout to Xc	P65,P66
					Pt. Lookout, MD	10/29/64	Venus Pt., GA Xc	P115,P123,CSR
Shackleford, T.C.	Pvt	B 10th SCVI	Estelle Spgs.,TN	07/02/63	Nashville, TN	12/14/63	Nashville, sick	P38,RAS,CSR
					Nashville, TN		Died	CSR
ShadracH, John B.	Pvt	F 2nd SCVI	Gettysburg, PA	07/04/63	Gettysburg G.H.	07/24/63	Provost Marshal	P4,SA2,CSR,H2
					David's Island, NY	08/24/63	City Pt., VA Xc	P1,CSR
Shadrach, John B.	Pvt	F 2nd SCVI	Bentonville, NC	03/19/65	New Berne, NC	03/30/65	Pt. Lookout, MD	CSR
					Pt. Lookout, MD	06/19/65	Rlsd. G.O. #109	P115,P118,P122,SA2
Shafenberger, C.H.	Pvt	F 1st SCVIR	Deserted/enemy	02/21/65	Charleston, SC	03/01/65	Will take oath	SA1,CSR
Shaffer, John	Pvt	C 15th SCVAB	Deserted/enemy	03/05/65	Charleston, SC	03/05/65	Baltimore, MD	CSR
Shaffer, R. Randolph	Cpl	B 25th SCVI	Ft. Fisher, NC	01/15/65	New York, NY	01/30/65	Elmira, NY	CSR,HAG
					Elmira, NY	07/10/65	Rlsd. G.O. #109	P65,P66,CSR
Shaffer, William H.	Pvt	B 25th SCVI	Deserted/enemy	02/18/65	Charleston, SC	02/18/65	Released on oath	CSR,HAG
Shairuss, G.L.	Pvt	C 1st SCVIG	Warrenton, VA	09/29/62	Warrenton, VA	09/29/62	Paroled	CSR
Shands, R.C.	Pvt	D P.S.S.	Williamsport, MD	09/17/62	Ft. Delaware, DE	10/02/62	Aikens Ldg., VA Xc	CSR
					Aikens Ldg., VA	11/10/62	Exchanged	CSR
Shands, R.C.	Pvt	D P.S.S.	Jetersville, VA	04/06/65	City Pt., VA	04/14/65	Newport News, VA	CSR
					Newport News, VA	06/26/65	Rlsd. G.O. #109	CSR
Shannon, Benjamin	Pvt	G 3rd SCVABn	Camden, SC	02/24/65	New Berne, NC	04/10/65	Hart's Island, NY	CSR
					Hart's Island, NY	06/17/65	Rlsd. G.O. #109	CSR
Shannon, Charles J.	Pvt	A 2nd SCVC	Camden, SC	02/24/65	New Berne, NC	04/10/65	Hart's Island, NY	CSR,HIC
					Hart's Island, NY	06/17/65	Rlsd. G.O. #109	P79,CSR
Shannon, James	Pvt	C 15th SCVAB	Cheraw, SC	03/06/65	New Berne, NC	04/03/65	Pt. Lookout, MD	CSR
					Pt. Lookout, MD	06/08/65	Released	P115,P118,P121,CSR
Shannon, Kirkland	2Lt	K 7th SCVC	Saylors Creek, VA	04/06/65	City Pt., VA US Ho	04/18/65	US Str. *St. of Maine*	CSR,HIC
					US Str. *St. of Maine*	04/19/65	Washington, DC	CSR
					Lincoln G.H., DC	06/06/65	Old Capitol, DC	CSR
					Old Capitol, DC	06/09/65	Rlsd. G.O.#109	P110,CSR
Shannon, Terry	Pvt	G Orr's Ri.	Falling Waters, MD	07/14/63	Frederick, MD G.H.	08/10/63	W. Bldg. Balt, MD	P1,CDC,CSR
					W. Bldg. Balt, MD	08/23/63	City Pt., VA Xc	P1,CSR
Sharp, C.C.	Pvt	H 15th SCVI	Gettysburg, PA	07/05/63	Ft. Delaware, DE	12/04/63	Died, Ch. Diarrhea	P5,P42,P44,P47,FPH
Sharp, Calvin R.	Pvt	H 20th SCVI	Lexington, SC	02/13/65	Pt. Lookout, MD	05/13/65	Rlsd. G.O. #85	P115,P118,KEB,CSR
Sharp, Felix	Pvt	H 20th SCVI	Lexington, SC	02/14/65	Pt. Lookout, MD	05/14/65	Rlsd. G.O. #85	P118,P121,KEB,CSR
Sharp, Francis F.	Pvt	C Orr's Ri.	Petersburg, VA	04/02/65	City Pt., VA	04/05/65	Pt. Lookout, MD	CSR
					Pt. Lookout, MD	06/19/65	Rlsd. G.O. #109	P115,P119,P122,CSR
Sharp, J.D.	Pvt	G 3rd SCVABn	High Pt., NC	05/01/65	High Pt., NC	05/01/65	Paroled	CSR
Sharp, Jacob	Pvt	H 20th SCVI	Lexington, SC	02/14/65	New Berne, NC	03/30/65	Pt. Lookout, MD	CSR,KEB
					Pt. Lookout, MD	06/19/65	Rlsd. G.O. #109	P115,P118,CSR
Sharp, John P.	Pvt	G 3rd SCVABn	High Pt., NC	05/01/65	High Pt., NC	05/01/65	Paroled	CSR

SOUTH CAROLINA SOLDIERS, SAILORS AND  CITIZENS HELD IN U.S. PRISONS 1861-1865

NAME	RANK	REGIMENT	CAPTURED AT	WHEN	PRISON	MOVED	DISPOSITION	SOURCES
Sharp, Miller R.	1Lt	D 12th SCVI	Gettysburg, PA	07/05/63	David's Island, NY	10/24/63	Bedloes Island, NY	P1,CSR
					Bedloes Island, NY	02/10/64	Ft. McHenry, MD	P2,CSR
					Ft. McHenry, MD	06/15/64	Ft. Delaware, DE	P96,P144,CSR
					Ft. Delaware, DE	09/18/64	Aikens Ldg., VA Xc	P43,P44,CSR
Sharp, Paul A.	Pvt	K 1st SCVIH	Concord, TN	01/10/64	Nashville, TN	01/24/64	Louisville, KY	P39,SA1,CSR
					Louisville, KY	01/27/64	Rock Island, IL	P88,P94,CSR
					Rock Island, IL	02/15/65	Pt. Lookout to Xc	P131,CSR
Sharp, Phillip M.	Pvt	H 20th SCVI	Lexington, SC	02/14/65	New Berne, NC	03/30/65	Pt. Lookout, MD	CSR,KEB
					Pt. Lookout, MD	06/19/65	Rlsd. G.O. #109	P115,P118,P122,KEB
Sharp, R.	Pvt	G 3rd SCVABn	High Pt., NC	05/01/65	High Pt., NC	05/01/65	Paroled	CSR
Sharp, Reuben	Pvt	H 20th SCVI	Lexington, SC	02/13/65	New Berne, NC	03/30/65	Pt. Lookout, MD	CSR,KEB
					Pt. Lookout, MD	05/15/65	Rlsd. G.O. #85	P115,P118,P121,CSR
Sharp, Uriah	Pvt	H 20th SCVI	Lexington, SC	02/04/65	New Berne, NC	03/30/65	Pt. Lookout, MD	P118,CSR,KEB
					Pt. Lookout, MD	06/19/65	Rlsd. G.O. #109	P115,P118,CSR
Sharpe, E.P.	Pvt	G 15th SCVI	South Mtn., MD	09/14/62	Ft. Delaware, DE	10/02/62	Aikens Ldg., VA Xc	CSR,H15
Sharpton, Benjamin F.	1Lt	I 7th SCVI	Gettysburg, PA	07/03/63	Ft. Delaware, DE	07/18/63	Johnson's Isl., OH	P44,KEB,HOE,CSR
					Johnson's Isl., OH	03/14/65	Pt. Lookout, MD	CSR
					Pt. Lookout, MD	03/22/65	Cox's Ldg., VA Xc	CSR
Shaver, William	Cit	Columbia	Lynch's Creek, SC	02/25/65	Hart's Island, NY	05/13/65	Died, Ch Diarrhea	P6,P12,P79,FPH
Shaw, A.	Pvt	H 12th SCVI	Charlotte, NC	05/16/65	Charlotte, NC	05/16/65	Paroled	CSR
Shaw, Benjamin A.	Pvt	L 21st SCVI	Morris Island, SC	07/10/63	Hilton Head, SC GH			P2,HMC,HAG
					Pt. Lookout, MD	10/15/63	Hammond G.H., MD	P113,P121
					Hammond G.H., MD	11/02/63	Died, Ch. Diarrhea	P5,P12,P116,FPH
Shaw, H. David	Pvt	C 25th SCVI	Ft. Fisher, NC	01/15/65	New York, NY	01/30/65	Elmira, NY	CSR,HAG,CTA
					Elmira, NY	07/11/65	Rlsd. G.O. #109	P65,P66,CSR
Shaw, Henry Y.	2Lt	M 10th SCVI	Atlanta, GA	07/28/64	Nashville, TN	08/08/64	Louisville, KY	CSR,RAS
					Louisville, KY	08/10/64	Johnson's Isl., OH	P91,P94,CSR
					Johnson's Isl., OH	10/06/64	Fts. Monroe, VA	P81,CSR
					Pt. Lookout, MD	10/11/64	Exchanged	P115,P123,CSR
Shaw, James J.	Pvt	B 5th SCVI	N. Anna River, VA	05/22/64	Port Royal, VA	05/30/64	Pt. Lookout, MD	CSR,YEB,SA3
					Pt. Lookout, MD	02/13/65	Cox's Ldg., VA Xc	P113,P117,CSR
Shaw, John C.	2Lt	E 19th SCVI	Decatur, GA	07/22/64	Marietta, GA	07/24/64	Louisville, KY	CSR
					Louisville, KY	07/30/64	Johnson's Isl., OH	P90,P91,P94,CSR
					Johnson's Isl., OH	06/15/65	Rlsd. G.O. #109	P80,P81,P83,CSR
Shaw, John D.	Pvt	F 7th SCVIBn	Kershaw Dist., SC	02/25/65	New Berne, NC	04/25/65	Fts. Monroe, VA	CSR,HAG,HIC
					Fts. Monroe, VA	05/01/65	Newport News, VA	CSR
					Newport News, VA	06/15/65	Rlsd. G.O. #109	CSR
Shaw, John W.	Pvt	I 1st SCVA	Bentonville, NC	03/19/65	New Berne, NC	03/30/65	Pt. Lookout, MD	CSR
					Pt. Lookout, MD	06/19/65	Rlsd. G.O. #109	P115,P118,P122,CSR
Shaw, L.	Pvt	C 5th SCVC	Deserted/enemy	03/06/65	Charleston, SC	03/06/65	Released on oath	CSR
Shaw, Theodore M.	ASr	22nd SCVI	Saylors Creek, VA	04/06/65	City Pt., VA	04/13/65	Old Capitol, DC	CSR
					Old Capitol, DC	05/11/65	Johnson's Isl., OH	P110
					Johnson's Isl., OH	06/20/65	Rlsd. G.O. #109	P82,P83,CSR
Shaw, Thomas P.B.	Col	19th SCVI	Franklin, TN	12/17/64	Nashville, TN	03/07/65	Louisville, KY	P2,P39,HOE,CSR
					Louisville, KY	03/10/65	Camp Chase, OH	P92,P95
					Camp Chase, OH	03/18/65	Pt. Lookout, MD Xc	P23,P26,CSR
					Richmond, VA Hos	03/29/65	Furloughed 30 days	CSR
Shay, Patrick	Pvt	E 1st SCVA	Deserted/enemy	02/18/65	Charleston, SC	03/23/65	Taken oath & disch.	CSR
Shaylor, C.H.	Pvt	D 15th SCVI	Cedar Creek, VA	10/19/64	Harpers Ferry, WV	10/23/64	Pt. Lookout, MD	H15,CSR,KEB,HIC
					Pt. Lookout, MD	06/19/65	Rlsd. G.O. #109	P115,P118,CSR
Sheahan, Thomas	Pvt	H 27th SCVI	Weldon RR, VA	08/21/64	Pt. Lookout, MD	10/30/64	Aikens Ldg., VA Xc	P113,P117,HAG

SOUTH CAROLINA SOLDIERS, SAILORS AND  CITIZENS HELD IN U.S. PRISONS 1861-1865

NAME	RANK	REGIMENT	CAPTURED AT	WHEN	PRISON	MOVED	DISPOSITION	SOURCES
Shealey, Melvin	Pvt	I 20th SCVI	Cedar Creek, VA	10/19/64	Harpers Ferry, WV	10/24/64	Pt. Lookout, MD	CSR,UD6,KEB
					Pt. Lookout MD	06/19/65	Rlsd. G.O. #109	P115,P118,P122,CSR
Shealey, W. Riley	Pvt	K 20th SCVI	Cedar Creek, VA	10/19/64	Harpers Ferry, WV	10/24/64	Pt. Lookout, MD	CSR,KEB
					Pt. Lookout, MD	11/19/64	Died of disease	P118,CSR,P12,FPH
Shseally, W.E.	Pvt	D 5th SCVC	Augusta, GA	05/23/65	Augusta, GA	05/23/65	Paroled	CSR
Shealy, George M.	Pvt	I 15th SCVI	South Mtn., MD	09/15/62	Ft. McHenry, MD	10/13/62	Fts. Monroe, VA Xc	CSR,KEB,H15
Shealy, Littleton	Pvt	C 15th SCVI	Halltown, VA	08/26/64	Harpers Ferry, WV	08/29/64	Camp Chase, OH	CSR,KEB,H15
					Camp Chase, OH	12/23/64	Died, Typhoid fever	P23,P27,CSR,FPH
Shealy, W.A.	Pvt	H Hol.Leg.	Petersburg, VA	11/05/64	City Pt., VA	11/11/64	Washington, DC	CSR
					Pt. Lookout, MD	06/19/65	Rlsd. G.O. #109	P115,P118,CSR
Shealy, Wiley	Pvt	C 15th SCVI	Gettysburg, PA	07/03/63	Ft. Delaware, DE	07/15/63	Chester, PA G.H.	P42,CSR
					Ft. Delaware, DE	07/31/63	Chester, PA Hos.	P40,KEB,CSR
					Ft. Delaware, DE	08/19/63	Died, Ac. Diarrhea	P5,P12,FPH,H15,CSR
Shearer, Benjamin H.	Pvt	G 7th SCVC	Old Church, VA	05/30/64	White House, VA	06/08/64	Pt. Lookout, MD	CSR
					Pt. Lookout, MD	07/09/64	Elmira, NY	P113,117,P120,CSR
					Elmira, NY	08/10/64	Died, Ch. Diarrhea	P5,P12,P65,P66,FPH
Sheckles, R.H.	Pvt	C 15th SCVAB	Deserted/enemy	02/18/65	Charleston, SC	03/22/65	North, Str. *Argo*	CSR
Sheeley, Yerby	Pvt	C 2nd SCVI	Brandy Stn., VA	08/01/63	Old Capitol, DC	08/23/63	Pt. Lookout, MD	CSR,SA2,H2
					Pt. Lookout, MD	01/26/65	Died	P6,P113,FPH,P12
Sheely, James B.	Sgt	H 13th SCVI	Gettysburg, PA	07/05/63	David' Island, NY	09/08/63	City Pt., VA Xc	P1,CSR
Shehane, Alfred C.	Pvt	A 5th SCVI	Williamsburg, VA	05/05/62	Fts. Monroe, VA	08/31/62	Aikens Ldg., VA Xc	CSR
Shehorn, John	Pvt	D 5th SCResB	Kershaw District	02/25/65	New Berne, NC	03/30/65	Pt. Lookout, MD	FPH,CSR,HIC
					Pt. Lookout, MD	06/10/65	Died, Ac. Diarrhea	P6,P12,P115,FPH
Shelby, Benjamin	Smn	CS *Chicora*	Morris Island, SC	09/07/64	Pt. Lookout, MD	10/02/64	Escaped	P113
Shelley, W.D.	Pvt	D 10th SCVI	Munfordville, KY H	09/23/62	Munfordville, KY H	09/23/62	Paroled	CSR
Shelly, David	2Lt	I 21st SCVI	Petersburg, VA	05/09/64	Pt. Lookout, MD	10/04/64	Died, Typhoid fever	P5,P117,P119,FPH
Shelly, Isaac	Pvt	2 10/19 SCVI	Missionary Ridge, TN	11/25/63	Nashville, TN	12/07/63	Louisville, KY	P39,RAS,CSR
					New Orleans, LA	05/23/65	Exchanged	P4,CSR
Shelly, James T.	Pvt	5 10/19 SCVI	Missionary Ridge, TN	11/25/63	Louisville, KY	12/07/63	Rock Island, IL	P88,P89,RAS,CSR
					Rock Island, IL	05/03/65	New Orleans, LA Xc	P131,CSR
					New Orleans, LA	05/23/65	Exchanged	CSR
Shelor, J.W.	Pvt	G 7th SCVC	Dabney Ferry, VA	05/27/64	White House, VA	06/08/64	Pt. Lookout, MD	CSR
					Pt. Lookout, MD	03/14/65	Aikens Ldg., VA Xc	P117,P121,P124,CSR
Sheon, Michael	Pvt	C 15th SCVAB	Staunton, VA	06/08/64	Wheeling, WV			CSR
Shepard, D.T.	Pvt	D 23rd SCVI	Petersburg, VA	06/17/64	Bermuda Hundred VA	06/21/64	Fts. Monroe, VA	CSR
					Fts. Monroe, VA	09/29/64	Pt. Lookout, MD	CSR
					Pt. Lookout, MD	03/17/65	Aikens Ldg., VA Xc	P117,P121.P124,CSR
Sheppard, Elihu Y.	Pvt	F 2nd SCVI	Gettysburg, PA	07/06/63	Gettysburg G.H.		Provost Marshal	P4,KEB,SA2,H2
					Ft. Delaware, DE	07/31/63	City Pt., VA, Ex	P40,P44,P144,CSR
Sheppard, Henry	Pvt	D 18th SCVI	Deserted/enemy	04/02/65	Cumberland, MD	04/24/65	North on oath	P8,CSR
Sheppard, James A.	Pvt	F 1st SCVC	Upperville, VA	06/21/63	Ft.McHenry, MD	05/07/63	Ft. Delaware, DE	P110
					Old Capitol, DC	06/25/63	City Pt., VA Xc	CSR
Sheppard, Samuel C.	Pvt	H Hol.Leg.	Hatchers Run, VA	03/29/65	City Pt., VA	04/01/65	Pt. Lookout, MD	CSR,ANY
					Pt. Lookout, MD	06/19/65	Rlsd. G.O. #109	P115,P118,CSR
Sheppard, W.G.	Pvt	I 1st SCVC	Ely's Ford, VA	02/29/64	Old Capitol, DC	06/13/64	Ft. Delaware, DE	P110,CSR
					Pt. Lookout, MD	10/31/64	Aikens Ldg.,VA Xc	P41,P43,P118,CSR
Sherard, Samuel W.	Cpt	F 24th SCVI	Taylors Ridge, GA	10/16/64	Nashville, TN	10/25/64	Louisville, KY	CSR
					Louisville, KY	10/28/64	Johnson's Isl., OH	P90,P91,P94,CSR
					Johnson's Isl., OH	06/16/65	Rlsd. G.O. #109	P81,P82,CSR
Sherbutt, A.M.	Pvt	E 18th SCVI	Petersburg, VA	07/30/64	City Pt., VA	08/12/64	Pt. Lookout, MD	CSR
					Pt. Lookout, MD	08/08/64	Elmira, NY	P113,P117,P120,CSR
					Elmira, NY	05/29/65	Rlsd. G.O. #85	P65,P66,CSR

SOUTH CAROLINA SOLDIERS, SAILORS AND  CITIZENS HELD IN U.S. PRISONS 1861-1865

NAME	RANK	REGIMENT	CAPTURED AT	WHEN	PRISON	MOVED	DISPOSITION	SOURCES
Sherbutt, B.W.	Pvt	I Hol.Leg.	Stony Creek, VA	05/07/64	Fts. Monroe, VA	05/13/64	Pt. Lookout, MD	CSR
					Pt. Lookout, MD	08/15/64	Elmira, NY	P113,P117,P120,CSR
					Elmira, NY	07/19/65	Rlsd. G.O. #109	P65,P66,CSR
Sherer, James N.	Pvt	C 17th SCVI	Farmville, VA	04/06/65	City Pt., VA	04/14/65	Newport News, VA	CSR,HHC
					Newport News, VA	06/25/65	Rlsd. G.O.#109	P107,CSR
Sherer, John M.	Cpl	C 27th SCVI	Town Creek, NC	02/20/65	Pt. Lookout, MD	05/15/65	Rlsd. G.O. #85	P115,HAG
Sheriff, A.	Pvt	F 1st SCVA	Bentonville, NC	03/22/65	New Berne, NC	04/10/65	Hart's Island, NY	CSR
					Hart's Island, NY	06/17/65	Rlsd. G.O. #109	P79,CSR
Sheriff, Exodus	Pvt	F 1st SCVA	Bentonville, NC	03/22/65	New Berne, NC	04/10/65	Hart's Island, NY	CSR
					Hart's Island, NY	06/17/65	Rlsd. G.O. #109	P79,CSR
Sherrer, Andrew Franklin	Pvt	G 2nd SCVIRi	Amelia C.H., VA	04/05/65	City Pt., VA	04/13/65	Pt. Lookout, MD	CSR,UD5
					Pt. Lookout, MD	06/19/65	Rlsd. G.O. #109	P115,P119,P122,CSR
Sherrer, William A.	Pvt	B 12th SCVI	Southside RR, VA	04/03/65	City Pt., VA	04/07/65	Hart's Island, NY	CSR,YEB
					Hart's Island, NY	06/16/65	Rlsd. G.O. #109	P79,CSR
Sherriff, William M.	Pvt	C 4th SCVC	Louisa C.H., VA	06/11/64	White House, VA	06/20/64	Pt. Lookout, MD	CSR
					Pt. Lookout, MD	07/23/64	Elmira, NY	P113,P117,P120,CSR
					Elmira, NY	02/16/65	Died, Variola	P6,P12,P65,P66,FPH,CSR
Sherrill, Thomas F.	Sgt	F 26th SCVI	Southside RR, VA	04/01/65	City Pt., VA	04/05/65	Pt. Lookout, MD	CSR
					Pt. Lookout, MD	06/19/65	Rlsd. G.O. #109	P115,P119,P122,CSR
Sherry, M.C.	Pvt	D 15th SCMil	Lynch's Creek, SC	02/27/65	Pt. Lookout, MD	06/19/65	Rlsd. G.O. #109	P115,P118,P122
Sherson, Lewis A.	Pvt	D 2nd SCVC	Williamsport, MD	07/14/63	Washington, DC	07/31/63	Pt. Lookout, MD	CSR
					Pt. Lookout, MD	01/27/65	Hammond G.H., DC	P121,CSR
					Pt. Lookout, MD	03/06/65	Died, Ch. Diarrhea	P12,CSR,P113,P116
Shetley, William	Pvt	C 1st SCVA	Deserted/enemy	02/20/65	Charleston, SC	03/11/65	Taken oath & disch.	CSR
Shields, T.M.	Pvt	D 3rd SCVI	Cheraw, SC	03/05/65	Cheraw, SC	03/05/65	Paroled	CSR
Shields, W.H.	1Lt	I Hol.Leg.	Stony Creek, VA	05/07/64	Fts. Monroe, VA	05/13/64	Pt. Lookout, MD	CSR
					Pt. Lookout, MD	07/16/64	Washington, DC	P117
					Old Capitol, DC	07/22/64	Ft. Delaware, DE	CSR
					Ft. Delaware, DE	05/06/65	Discharged	P46,P47
Shillinglaw, John	Pvt	H 12th SCVI	Gettysburg, PA	07/04/63	Davids Island, NY	08/24/63	City Pt., VA Xc	P1,YEB,CSR
Shinall, George W.	Pvt	H 7th SCVIBn	Ft. Anderson, NC	02/19/65	Ft. Anderson, NC	02/28/65	Pt. Lookout, MD	CSR,HAG
					Pt. Lookout, MD		No release record	P115,P118,CSR
Shinall, John	Pvt	H 7th SCVIBn	Ft. Anderson, NC	02/19/65	Ft. Anderson, NC	02/28/65	Pt. Lookout, MD	CSR,HAG
					Pt. Lookout, MD		No release record	P118,CSR
Shinall, Pleasant	Pvt	G 1st SCVIG	Petersburg, VA	03/25/65	City Pt., VA	03/27/65	Pt. Lookout, MD	CSR,SA1
					Pt. Lookout, MD	05/14/65	Rlsd. G.O. #85	P115,P118,P121,CSR
Shine, Richard	Pvt	I 1st SCVA	Morris Island, SC	07/10/63	Hilton Head, SC	09/19/63	Ft. Columbus, NY	CSR
					Ft. Columbus, NY	09/23/63	Took the oath	P1,CSR
Shipes, J.W.	Pvt	A 19th SCVCB	Augusta, GA	05/24/65	Augusta, GA	05/24/65	Paroled on oath	CSR
Shipes, Jacob J.	Pvt	B 11th SCVI	Petersburg, VA	06/16/64	Bermuda Hundred VA	06/17/64	Fts. Monroe, VA	CSR
					Fts. Monroe, VA	06/18/64	Pt. Lookout, MD	CSR
					Pt. Lookout, MD	06/19/64	Elmira, NY	P117,P120,CSR
					Elmira, NY	12/08/64	Died, Ch. Diarrhea	P5,P65,P66,FPH,CSR
Shipes, James P.	Cpl	D 11th SCVI	Town Creek, NC	02/20/65	Pt. Lookout, MD	06/19/65	Rlsd. G.O. #109	P118,P122,HAG
Shipes, John Phillips	Pvt	D 11th SCVI	Town Creek, NC	02/20/65	Ft. Anderson, NC	02/28/65	Pt. Lookout, MD	CSR,HAG
					Pt. Lookout, MD	06/19/65	Rlsd. G.O. #109	P115,CSR
Shipes, William D.	Cpl	D 11th SCVI	Town Creek, NC	02/20/65	Ft. Anderson, NC	02/28/64	Pt. Lookout, MD	CSR,HAG
					Pt. Lookout, MD	06/19/65	Rlsd. G.O. #109	P115,P118,P122,CSR
Shipp, Thomas A.	Cpl	C 22nd SCVI	Deserted/enemy	02/18/65	City Pt., VA	02/20/65	Washington, DC	CSR
					Washington, DC		No further data	CSR
Shippey, Johnson J.	Pvt	C 5th SCVI	Wilderness, VA	05/06/64	Belle Plain, VA	05/21/64	Ft. Delaware, DE	CSR,SA3
					Ft. Delaware, DE	09/30/64	Aikens Ldg., VA Xc	P41,P43,CSR

S

SOUTH CAROLINA SOLDIERS, SAILORS AND CITIZENS HELD IN U.S. PRISONS 1861-1865

NAME	RANK	REGIMENT	CAPTURED AT	WHEN	PRISON	MOVED	DISPOSITION	SOURCES
Shirer, Henry W.	Pvt	F 25th SCVI	Ft. Fisher, NC	01/15/65	New York, NY	01/30/65	Elmira, NY	CSR,HAG
					Elmira, NY	06/30/65	Died, Variola	P6,P12,P65,P66,FPH
Shirer, Jesse R.	Pvt	K 2nd SCVI	Sharpsburg, MD	09/02/62	Ft. McHenry, MD	11/12/62	City Pt., VA Xc	SA2,H2,CSR
Shirer, W.D.	Pvt	E 1st SCVC	Gettysburg, PA	07/05/63	Letterman G.H. Gbg	08/15/63	Died of wounds	P1,P12,CSR
Shirey, M.C.	Pvt	D 15th SCVI	Lynch's Creek, SC	02/27/65	Point Lookout, MD	06/19/65	Rlsd. G.O.#109	CSR
Shirey, Simeon W.	Pvt	E 27th SCVI	Florence, SC	03/05/65	New Berne, NC	04/03/65	Pt. Lookout, MD	CSR,HAG
					Pt. Lookout, MD	06/19/65	Rlsd. G.O. #109	P115,P118,CSR
Shirley, A.T.	Cpl	E 19th SCVI	Sumter Dist., SC	02/26/65	Hart's Island, NY	06/17/65	Rlsd. G.O. #109	P79
Shirley, Aaron Y.	Pvt	L Orr's Ri.	Petersburg, VA	04/03/65	City Pt., VA	04/11/65	Hart's Island, NY	CSR
					Hart's Island, NY	06/16/65	Rlsd. G.O. #109	CSR
Shirley, Amaziah N.	Pvt	K Orr's Ri.	Petersburg, VA	04/02/65	City Pt., VA	04/07/65	Hart's Island, NY	CSR
					Hart's Island, NY	06/15/65	Rlsd. G.O. #109	P79,CSR
Shirley, Hampton	Pvt	G 24th SCVI	Nashville, TN	12/16/64	Nashville, TN	12/31/64	Louisville, KY	CSR,EFW
					Louisville, KY	01/02/65	Camp Chase, OH	P92,P95
					Camp Chase, OH	02/26/65	Died, Variola	P6,P23,P27,FPH,CSR
Shirley, James	Pvt	8 10/19 SCVI	Missionary Ridge, TN	11/25/63	Nashville, TN	12/07/63	Louisville, KY	P39,CSR
					Louisville, KY	12/09/63	Rock Island, IL	P88,P89
					Rock Island, IL	02/14/64	Died, Pneumonia	P5,P131,P132,FPH
Shirley, James M.	Pvt	E 20th SCVI	Cedar Creek, VA	10/19/64	Harpers Ferry, WV	10/24/64	Pt. Lookout, MD	CSR
					Pt. Lookout, MD	06/19/65	Rlsd. G.O. #109	P115,P118,KEB,CSR
Shirley, W.B.	Pvt	K 20th SCVI	Cedar Creek, VA	10/19/64	Pt. Lookout, MD	11/18/64	Died, Typhoid fever	P5,P115,P119,FPH
Shiver, Robert C.	2Lt	A 2nd SCVC	Kinston, NC	03/18/65	Kinston, NC	04/02/65	New Berne, NC G.H.	CSR
					New Berne, NC USGH	05/04/65	Returned to duty	CSR
Shiver, Zack	Sgt	C 6th SCVI	Camden, SC	02/24/65	New Berne, NC	04/10/65	Hart's Island, NY	CSR
					Hart's Island, NY	06/17/65	Rlsd. G.O. #109	P79,CSR
Shluter, Christian	Pvt	K 12th SCVI	Sharpsburg, MD	09/17/62	Frederick, MD USGH	10/16/62	Ft. McHenry, MD	CSR
					Ft. McHenry, MD	10/18/62	Fts. Monroe, VA Xc	CSR
Shluter, Christian	Pvt	K 12th SCVI	Richmond, VA Hos.	04/03/65	Richmond, VA Hos.	05/04/65	Paroled	CSR
Shockley, John	Pvt	C 1st SCVA	Bentonville, NC	03/22/65	New Berne, NC	04/10/65	Hart's Island, NY	CSR
					Hart's Island, NY	06/17/65	Rlsd. G.O. #109	P79,CSR
Shockley, W.T.	Pvt	F 1st SCVIH	Richmond, VA Hos.	04/03/65	Richmond, VA Hos.	05/02/65	Paroled & escaped	CSR
Shoemaker, Ira T.	Sgt	G 25th SCVI	Ft. Fisher, NC	01/15/65	New York, NY	01/30/65	Elmira, NY	CSR,HAG
					Elmira, NY	06/14/65	Rlsd. G.O.#109	P65,P66,CSR
Shoemaker, Warren	Pvt	D 2nd SCVA	Darlington, SC	02/27/65	New Berne, NC	04/10/65	Hart's Island, NY	CSR
					Hart's Island, NY	06/17/65	Rlsd. G.O. #109	P79,CSR
Shoolbred, J. Stanyard	Pvt	B 2nd SCVC	Catletts Stn., VA	03/30/63	P.M. Army of Patomac	04/03/63	Washington, DC	CSR
					Old Capitol, DC	04/13/63	City Pt., VA Xc	CSR
					Ft.McHenry, MD	04/13/63	City Pt., VA Xc	P110
Shorter, William J.	Pvt	I 23rd SCVI	Petersburg, VA	04/02/65	City Pt., VA	04/04/65	Pt. Lookout, MD	CSR
					Pt. Lookout, MD	06/19/65	Rlsd. G.O. #109	P115,P119,P122,CSR
Shotwell, John L.	Cpl	C 1st SCVIG	Petersburg, VA	07/29/64	City Pt., VA	08/05/64	Pt. Lookout, MD	CSR,SA1
					Pt. Lookout, MD	08/08/64	Elmira, NY	P113,P117,P120,CSR
					Elmira, NY	12/20/64	Released per S.O.	P7,P65,P66,CSR
Shrimp, George	Sgt	B 1st SCVIG	Warrenton, VA	09/29/62	Warrenton, VA	09/29/62	Paroled	CSR
Shuler, Bennett	Pvt	A SC Militia	Columbia, SC	03/01/65	Pt. Lookout, MD	06/03/65	Died, Ch. diarrhea	P6,P118,P119,FPH
Shuler, Daniel M.	Pvt	C 14th SCMil	Camden, SC	03/01/65	Hart's Island, NY	05/05/65	Died, Ch. Diarrhea	P6,P12,P79,FPH
Shuler, David G.B.	Pvt	F 25th SCVI	Town Creek, NC	02/20/65	Ft. Anderson, NC	02/28/65	Pt. Lookout, MD	CSR,HAG
					Pt. Lookout, MD	06/19/65	Rlsd. G.O. #109	P115,P118,CSR
Shuler, Erastus V.	Pvt	F 25th SCVI	Town Creek, NC	02/20/65	Ft. Anderson, NC	02/28/65	Pt. Lookout, MD	CSR,HAG
					Pt. Lookout, MD	06/19/65	Rlsd. G.O. #109	P115,P118,P122,CSR
Shuler, F. Pinckney H.	Pvt	F 25th SCVI	Ft. Fisher, NC	01/15/65	New York, NY	01/30/65	Elmira, NY	CSR,HAG
					Elmira, NY	03/02/65	Tfd. for exchange	P65,P66,HAG,CSR

SOUTH CAROLINA SOLDIERS, SAILORS AND  CITIZENS HELD IN U.S. PRISONS 1861-1865

NAME	RANK	REGIMENT	CAPTURED AT	WHEN	PRISON	MOVED	DISPOSITION	SOURCES
Shuler, F. Pinckney H.	Pvt	F 25th SCVI	Jackson H. Rchmd.	04/03/65	Jackson Hos. Rchmd	04/07/65	Died, Ch.Bronchitis	P6,P12,CSR
Shuler, George L.V.S.	Pvt	F 25th SCVI	Ft. Fisher, NC	01/15/65	New York, NY	01/30/65	Elmira, NY	CSR,HAG
					Elmira, NY	03/02/65	James R., VA Xc	P65,P66,CSR
Shuler, Marion J.	Pvt	I 3rd SCVI	Sharpsburg, MD	09/17/62	Elias Graves' Farm	09/17/62	Died of wounds	P12,H3,CSR
Shuler, Peter H.B.	1Lt	A 2nd SCVI	Gettysburg, PA	07/06/63	Letterman G.H. Gbg	08/26/63	Provost Marshal	P1,KEB,SA2,H2
					Newton U. Balt,MD			P1
					Ft. McHenry, MD	09/28/63	Johnson's Isl., OH	P144,CSR
					Johnson's Isl., OH	04/22/64	Pt. Lookout, MD	P80,P82,CSR
					Pt. Lookout, MD	05/03/64	City Pt., VA Xc	P116,CSR
Shuler, Peter L.	Pvt	C 20th SCVI	Cedar Creek, VA	10/19/64	Harpers Ferry, WV	10/23/64	Pt. Lookout, MD	CSR,KEB
					Pt. Lookout, MD	02/12/65	Died, Lung Inflam.	P6,P118,P119,FPH
Shull, William	Pvt	D 15th SCMil	Lynch's Creek, SC	02/27/65	Pt. Lookout, MD	06/19/65	Rlsd. G.O. #109	P115,118,P121
Shulte, J.H.	Pvt	B 25th SCVI	Ft. Fisher, NC	01/15/65	Elmira, NY	06/16/65	Rlsd. G.O. #109	P65,HAG
Shuman, W.S.	Pvt	E 11th SCVI	Petersburg, VA	06/16/64	Bermuda Hundred VA	06/17/64	Fts. Monroe, VA	CSR,HAG
					Fts. Monroe, VA	06/18/64	Pt. Lookout, MD	CSR
					Pt. Lookout VA	07/25/64	Elmira NY	P113,P117,P120,CSR
					Elmira NY	03/14/65	Tfd. for exchange	CSR
Shumate, John Lewis	Pvt	B 2nd SCVI	Cedar Creek, VA	10/19/64	Harpers Ferry, WV	10/23/64	Pt. Lookout, MD	CSR,KEB,H2
					Pt. Lookout, MD	02/13/65	Exchanged	P121,P123,P129
Shumpert, Jacob	Pvt	K 13th SCVI	Petersburg, VA	04/03/65	City Pt., VA	04/11/65	Hart's Island, NY	CSR
					Hart's Island, NY	06/16/65	Rlsd. G.O. #109	P79,CSR
Shurbert, Sidney S.	Pvt	B 1st SCVIR	Cumberland Co., NC	03/16/65	Pt. Lookout, MD	06/20/65	Rlsd. G.O. #109	P121,CSR
Shuttleworth, J.A.	Pvt	Ferguson's	Citronelle, AL	05/04/65	Meridian, MS	05/12/65	Paroled	CSR
Shuttleworth, Jackson B.	Pvt	Ferguson's LA	Yazoo City, MS	07/13/63	Yazoo City, MS	07/13/63	Paroled	CSR
Shuttleworth, Jackson B.	Pvt	Ferguson's LA	Salisbury, NC	04/12/65	Nashville, TN	04/29/65	Louisville, KY	CSR
					Louisville, KY	05/02/65	Camp Chase, OH	CSR
					Camp Chase, OH	06/13/65	Rlsd. G.O. #109	CSR
Sibley, W.S.	Pvt	B 1st SCVA	Chester, SC	05/05/65	Chester, SC	05/05/65	Paroled	CSR
Sielaff, Charles W.	Cpl	A 2nd SCVI	Gettysburg, PA	07/03/63	Letterman G.H. Gbg	07/21/63	Provost M. NY	P1,CSR,KEB,SA2,H2
					David's Island, NY	09/12/63	City Pt., VA Xc	P1,CSR
Sielken, H.	Pvt	G 3rd SCVC	Deserted/enemy	02/19/65	Charleston,SC	03/01/65	Released on oath	CSR
Sightler, W.S.	Pvt	K 1st SCVIH	Boonesboro, MD	09/14/62	A of P. Pro. Marsh	09/25/62		SA1,CSR
Sightler, William A.	Pvt	H 20th SCVI	Columbia, SC	02/16/65	New Berne NC	04/03/65	Pt. Lookout, MD	CSR,KEB
					Pt. Lookout, MD	06/17/65	Rlsd. G.O. #109	P118,KEB,CSR
Sikes, C.B.	Pvt	B 18th SCVI	Hatchers Run, VA	04/02/65	Hart's Island, NY	06/16/65	Rlsd. G.O. #109	P79
Silbert, F.	Pvt	E 14th SCVI	Sharpsburg, MD	09/17/62	Deserted/enemy	09/17/62	Rlsd. to go north	CSR
Silks, James W.	Pvt	F 2nd SCVI	Centreville, VA	07/20/61	Fts. Monroe, VA	11/29/61	Exchanged	SA2,H2,CSR
Siloff, Charles	Pvt	K 5th SCVI	Deserted/enemy	03/09/65	Charleston, SC	03/16/65	Released on oath	CSR
Simmons, A.J.	Pvt	F 11th SCVI	Swift Creek, VA	05/07/64	Fts. Monroe, VA		Pt. Lookout, MD	P115,HAG,CSR
					Pt.Lookout, MD	09/15/64	Hammond G.H., MD	CSR
					Hammond G.H., MD	11/24/64	Pt. Lookout, MD	CSR
					Pt. Lookout, MD	02/10/65	Aikens Ldg., VA Xc	P118,CSR
					Pt. Lookout MD		Rcd. Coxs Ldg 2/14	CSR
Simmons, A.J.	Pvt	F 11th SCVI	Augusta, GA	05/23/65	Augusta, GA	05/23/65	Paroled on oath	CSR
Simmons, Asa	Pvt	F 3rd SCVC	South Newport, GA	08/17/64				CSR
Simmons, Charles H.	Pvt	L Orr's Ri.	Petersburg, VA	04/03/65	City Pt., VA	04/11/65	Hart's Island, NY	CSR
					Hart's Island, NY	06/16/65	Rlsd. G.O. #109	P79,CSR
Simmons, D.G.	Sgt	B 5th SCVC	Augusta, GA	05/23/65	Augusta, GA	05/23/65	Paroled	CSR
Simmons, Drewry T.	Pvt	D Orr's Ri.	Ft. Gregg, VA	04/01/65	City Pt., VA	04/05/65	Pt. Lookout, MD	CSR
					Pt. Lookout, MD	06/19/65	Rlsd. G.O. #109	P115,P119,CSR
Simmons, E.B.	Pvt	B 5th SCVC	Augusta, GA	05/23/65	Augusta, GA	05/23/65	Paroled	CSR

SOUTH CAROLINA SOLDIERS, SAILORS AND S CITIZENS HELD IN U.S. PRISONS 1861-1865

NAME	RANK	REGIMENT	CAPTURED AT	WHEN	PRISON	MOVED	DISPOSITION	SOURCES
Simmons, Francis M.	Pvt	I 27th SCVI	Town Creek, NC	02/20/65	Ft. Anderson, NC	02/28/65	Pt. Lookout, MD	CSR
					Pt. Lookout, MD	05/14/65	Rlsd. G.O. #85	P115,P118,P121
Simmons, Isaac T.	Cpl	D Orr's Ri.	Deserted/enemy	02/21/65	City Pt., VA	02/21/65	Washington, DC	CSR
					Washington D.C.	02/24/65	Burlington, IA	CSR
Simmons, J.B.	Pvt	D 3rd SCVIBn	Cedar Creek, VA	10/19/64	W. Bldg. Balt, MD	10/27/64	Pt. Lookout, MD	P4,KEB,CSR
					Pt. Lookout, MD	11/15/64	Venus Pt., GA Xc	CSR
Simmons, J.P.	Pvt	D Orr's Ri.	Deserted/enemy	02/21/65	City Pt., VA	02/22/65	Washington, DC	CSR
					Washington D.C.	02/24/65	Burlington, Iowa	CSR
Simmons, J.S.	Pvt	B 11th SCVI	Deserted/enemy	02/14/64	Charleston SC	03/06/65	Taken oath & disch.	HAG,CSR
Simmons, John	Pvt	H 2nd SCVA	Bentonville, NC	03/19/65	New Berne, NC	04/10/65	Hart's Island, NY	CSR
					Hart's Island NY	06/16/65	Released G.O. #109	CSR
Simmons, M.	Pvt	B 5th SCVC	Augusta, GA	05/23/65	Augusta, GA	05/23/65	Paroled	CSR
Simmons, Richard L.	2Lt	B 12th SCVI	Petersburg, VA	04/02/65	Old Capitol, DC	04/09/65	Johnson's Isl., OH	P110,YEB,CSR
					Johnson's Isl., OH	06/20/65	Rlsd. G.O. #109	P81,P83,CSR
Simmons, Washington	Pvt	A 19th SCVCB	Deserted/enemy	02/13/65	Charleston, SC		Fts. Monroe, VA	CSR
					Fts. Monroe, VA	04/02/65	Washington, DC	CSR
Simmons, William	Pvt	D 24th SCVI	Taylor's Ridge, GA	10/16/64	Nashville, TN	10/23/64	Louisville, KY	CSR
					Louisville, KY	10/27/64	Camp Douglas, IL	P58,P90,P91,CSR
					Camp Douglas, IL	12/01/64	Died, Smallpox	P5,P12,P53,FPH
Simons, A.D.	1Lt	27th SCVI	Town Creek, NC	02/20/65	Ft. Anderson, NC	02/28/65	Pt. Lookout, MD	CSR,HAG
					Pt. Lookout, MD	02/28/65	Washington, DC	P115,P120,HAG
					Old Capitol, DC	02/28/65	Ft. Delaware, DE	CSR,HAG
					Ft. Delaware, DE	06/17/65	Rlsd. G.O. #109	P43,P45,P46,HAG
Simons, Charles	Sgt	L Orr's Ri.	Deserted/enemy	02/16/65	City Pt., VA	02/16/65	Washington, DC	CSR
					Washington D.C.	02/18/65	White County, IL	CSR
Simons, J.	Pvt	I 2nd SCVA	Deserted/enemy	02/27/65	Charleston, SC		Released on oath	CSR
Simons, Samuel M.	Pvt	D 2nd SCVC	Augusta, GA	05/20/65	Augusta, GA	05/20/65	Paroled	CSR
Simons, W. Lucas	Pvt	B 25th SCVI	Ft. Fisher, NC	01/15/65	New York, NY	01/30/65	Elmira, NY	CSR,HAG
					Elmira, NY	03/10/65	James R., VA Xc	P65,P66,CSR
Simonton, Charles H.	Col	25th SCVI	Town Creek, NC	02/20/65	Pt. Lookout, MD	02/28/65	Washington, DC	P115,P118,P120,LC
					Ft. Anderson, NC	02/28/65	Pt. Lookout, MD	CSR,HAG
					Old Capitol, DC.	03/24/65	Ft. Delaware, DE	CSR
					Ft. Delaware, DE	07/24/65	Rlsd. G.O. #109	P43,P45,CSR
Simonton, W Boyce	Pvt	H 6th SCVI	Seven Pines, VA	05/31/62	Fts. Monroe, VA US	06/14/62	Died of wounds	P12,CSR
Simpson, Carolus Adams	Pvt	A 3rd SCVI	Sharpsburg, MD	09/17/62	Frederick, MD USFH	10/31/62	Baltimore, MD USGH	H3,CSR,SA2
					Richmond, VA Hos	11/10/62	Furloughed 20 days	CSR
Simpson, David F.	Cpl	H 12th SCVI	Gettysburg, PA	07/03/63	David's Island, NY	09/05/63	City Pt., VA Xc	P1,YEB
					Williamsburg, VA H	09/13/63	Furloughed	CSR
Simpson, George	Pvt	E 14th SCVI	Gettysburg, PA	07/04/63	Gettysburg, PA	07/17/63	David's Island, NY	CSR
					David's Island, NY	08/28/63	City Pt., VA Xc	CSR
Simpson, J.R.	Pvt	B 1st SCVIR	Raleigh, NC Hos.	04/13/65	Raleigh, NC	04/13/65	Paroled	SA1,CSR
Simpson, J.W.	Pvt	G 6th SCVI	Burkesville, VA	04/14/65	Burkesville, VA	04/17/65	Paroled	CSR
Simpson, James M.	Pvt	I 3rd SCVI	Winchester, VA	09/19/64	W. Bldg. Balt, MD	11/22/64	Pt. Lookout, MD	P4,KEB,SA2,H3
					Pt. Lookout, MD	01/27/65	Hammond G.H., MD	P115,P121,CSR
					Hammond G.H., MD	02/09/65	Pt. Lookout, MD	CSR
					Pt. Lookout, MD	02/14/65	Coxe's Ldg., VA Xc	CSR
Simpson, James M.	Pvt	I 3rd SCVI	Richmond, VA Hos.	04/03/65	Richmond, VA Hos.	04/14/65	P.M. Richmond, VA	CSR
					Libby Prison Rchmd	04/24/65	Paroled	CSR
Simpson, James W.	Pvt	D Orr's Ri.	Petersburg, VA	04/03/65	City Pt., VA	04/11/65	Hart's Island, NY	CSR
					Hart's Island, NY	06/16/65	Rlsd. G.O. #109	P79,CSR

SOUTH CAROLINA SOLDIERS, SAILORS AND  CITIZENS HELD IN U.S. PRISONS 1861-1865

NAME	RANK	REGIMENT	CAPTURED AT	WHEN	PRISON	MOVED	DISPOSITION	SOURCES
Simpson, John B.	ASr	1st SCVC	Petersburg, VA	10/27/64	Old Capitol, DC	11/08/64	Ft. Delaware, DE	P110,CSR
					Ft. Delaware, DE	12/05/64	Fts. Monroe, VA Xc	P43,CSR
					Fts. Monroe, VA	12/06/65	Camp Hamilton, VA	CSR
					Camp Hamilton, VA	01/06/65	Exchanged	CSR
Simpson, John F.	Pvt	F Hol.Leg.	Jarratts Stn., VA	05/08/65	Fts. Monroe, VA	05/13/64	Pt. Lookout, MD	CSR
					Pt. Lookout, MD	08/15/64	Elmira, NY	P117,P120,CSR
					Elmira, NY	01/19/65	Died, Variola	P12,P65,P66,FPH
Simpson, S.N.	Pvt	Ham.Leg.	Winchester, VA	10/04/62	Winchester, VA	10/04/62	Paroled	CSR
Simpson, Washington	Pvt	19th SCVI	Fts. Monroe, VA		Washington, DC	04/05/65	Charleston, SC oath	CSR
Simpson, William	Pvt	H 1st SCVA	Chester, SC	05/05/65	Chester, SC	05/05/65	Paroled	CSR
Sims, Farley C.	Pvt	A 3rd SCVIBn	Gettysburg, PA	07/05/63	Gettysburg, PA USH	07/20/63	David's Island, NY	P4,CSR
					David's Island, NY	09/05/63	City Pt., VA Xc	P1,CSR
Sims, George M.	Pvt	H 12th SCVI	Richmond, VA Hos.	04/27/65	Richmond, VA	04/27/65	Paroled	CSR
Sims, James E.	Pvt	C 3rd SCVABn	Ft. Gaines, AL	08/08/64	New Orleans, LA	10/24/64	Ship Island, MS	P3,CSR
					Ship Island, MS	01/04/65	Exchanged	P136,CSR
Sims, Jefferson	Pvt	E 12th SCVI	Spotsylvania, VA	05/12/64	Old Capitol, DC	06/15/64	Ft. Delaware, DE	P110,CSR
					Ft. Delaware, DE	05/05/65	Hos. 5/5-5/23/65	P47
					Ft. Delaware, DE	06/10/65	Rlsd. G.O.#109	P41,P43,P45,CSR
Sims, M.P.	Sgt	C 3rd SCVABn	Blakely, AL	04/09/65	Ship Island, MS	05/01/65	Vicksburg, MS Xc	P136,CSR
Sims, R.A.	Pvt	B Wash'n LA	Ashland, VA	04/27/65	Ashland, VA	04/27/65	Paroled	CSR
Sims, William	Sgt	D 22nd SCVI	Kinston, NC	12/15/62	Kinston, NC	12/15/62	Paroled POW	CSR
Sineath, F.R.M.	2Lt	C 11th SCVI	Bermuda Hundred, VA	05/23/64	Fts. Monroe, VA	05/27/64	Pt. Lookout, MD	CSR
					Ft. Delaware, DE	07/26/64	Hos. 7/26-?	P47,HAG
					Pt. Lookout, MD	06/23/64	Ft. Delaware, DE	P113,P117,P120,HAG
					Ft. Delaware, DE	08/06/64	Pt. Lookout, MD Xc	P43,P44,P47,HAG
					Pt. Lookout, MD	10/31/64	Aikens Ldg., VA Xc	P115,P118,HAG
Sineath, Joseph A.	Pvt	B 27th SCVI	Petersburg, VA	06/24/64	Fts. Monroe, VA	07/05/64	Died of wounds	P12,HAG,CSR
Singletary, S.M.	Pvt	I 4th SCVC	Armstrong Mills, VA	12/10/64	City Pt., VA	12/12/64	Pt. Lookout, MD	CSR,CTA
					Pt. Lookout, MD	06/19/65	Rlsd. G.O. #109	P115,P118,CSR
Singleton, B.J.	Pvt	F 7th SCVI	Farmville, VA	04/21/65	Farmville, VA	04/21/65	Paroled	CSR
Singleton, Benjamin F.	Pvt	E 26th SCVI	Burkesville, VA	04/06/65	City Pt., VA	04/18/65	Lincoln G.H., DC	CSR
					Old Capitol, DC	06/12/65	Rlsd. G.O. #109	P110,CSR
Singleton, G.W.	Pvt	B P.S.S.	Chafins Farm, VA	10/07/64	Bermuda Hundred VA	10/07/64	Fts. Monroe, VA	CSR,TSE
					Fts. Monroe, VA	04/14/65	Camp Hamilton, VA	CSR
					Camp Hamilton, VA	05/31/65	Released	CSR
Singleton, Richard B.	Pvt	E 26th SCVI	Southside RR, VA	04/01/65	City Pt., VA	04/05/65	Pt. Lookout, MD	CSR
					Pt. Lookout, MD	06/20/65	Rlsd. G.O. #109	P115,P119,P121,CSR
Singleton, Thomas A.	Pvt	E 26th SCVI	Amelia C.H., VA	04/04/65	City Pt., VA	04/13/65	Pt. Lookout, MD	CSR
					Pt. Lookout, MD	06/19/65	Rlsd. G.O. #109	P115,P119
Singleton, W.F.	Pvt	D 7th SCVI	Maryland Hts., MD	09/15/62	Ft. McHenry, MD	12/08/62	Fts. Monroe, VA	P96,CSR
					Fts. Monroe, VA	12/10/62	City Pt., VA Xc	CSR
Singley, Henry Middleton	Pvt	H Hol.Leg.	Five Forks, VA	04/01/65	City Pt., VA	04/05/65	Pt. Lookout, MD	CSR,ANY
					Pt. Lookout, MD	06/19/65	Rlsd. G.O. #109	P115,P119,P122
Singley, Miles S.	Pvt	H 13th SCVI	Gettysburg, PA	07/03/63	Ft. McHenry, MD	07/07/63	Ft. Delaware, DE	ANY,CSR
					Ft. Delaware, DE	03/03/64	Died, Ch. Diarrhea	P40,P43,P47,P144
Sings, William C.	Sgt	D 1st SCVIH	Mossy Creek, TN	01/22/64	Nashville, TN	02/11/64	Louisville, KY	P39,SA1,LAN,CSR
					Louisville, KY	02/15/64	Rock Island, IL	P88,P91,P94,CSR
					Rock Island, IL	03/02/65	Tfd. for exchange	CSR
Sipple, Henry	Pvt	A 18th SCVI	Petersburg, VA	07/30/64	City Pt., VA	08/05/64	Ft. Schuyler, NY H	CSR
Sipple, Henry	Pvt	A 18th SCVI	Crater, Pbg., VA	07/30/64	Ft. Schuyler, NY H	09/15/64	Disch. on oath	CSR

SOUTH CAROLINA SOLDIERS, SAILORS AND  CITIZENS HELD IN U.S. PRISONS 1861-1865

NAME	RANK	REGIMENT	CAPTURED AT	WHEN	PRISON	MOVED	DISPOSITION	SOURCES
Sistare, W.T.	Pvt	I 12th SCVI	Spotsylvania, VA	05/12/64	Ft. Delaware, DE	06/08/65	Rlsd. G.O.#109	P41,P43,LAN,CSR
					Ft. Delaware, DE	06/18/64	Hos. 6/18-6/23/64	P47
					Ft. Delaware, DE	08/25/64	Hos. 8/25-9/9/64	P47
					Ft. Delaware, DE	10/15/64	Hos. 10/15-10/25/64	P47
					Ft. Delaware, DE	10/31/64	Hos. 10/31-11/14/64	P47
					Ft. Delaware, DE	12/02/64	Hos. 12/2-12/24/64	P47
					Ft. Delaware, DE	02/19/65	Hos. 2/19-3/7/65	P47
					Belle Plain, VA	05/20/64	Ft. Delaware, DE	CSR
Sistrunk, G.L.	Pvt	D 15th SCMil	Orangeburg, SC	02/13/65	Hart's Island, NY	06/16/65	Rlsd. G.O. #109	P79
Sistrunk, W.A.J.	Pvt	D 2nd SCVC	Raleigh, NC	04/13/65	Raleigh, NC	04/13/65	Paroled	CSR
Sisum, David O.	Pvt	H 1st SCVA	Morris Island, SC	07/10/63	Hilton Head, SC	09/19/63	Ft. Columbus, NY	CSR
					Ft. Columbus, NY	09/23/63	Took the oath	P1
Sizemore, D.S.	Pvt	K 8th SCVI			Camp Chase, OH	11/20/64	Died, Gv #499	P27,FPH
Sizemore, Edward D.	Pvt	C 22nd SCVI	Kinston, NC	12/15/62	Kinston, NC	12/15/62	Paroled POW	CSR,HOS
Sizemore, Edward D.	Pvt	C 22nd SCVI	Crater, Pbg., VA	07/30/64	City Pt., VA	08/05/64	Pt. Lookout, MD	CSR,HOS
					Pt. Lookout, MD	08/08/64	Elmira, NY	P113,P117,P120
					Elmira, NY	11/19/64	Died, Diarrhea	P5,P65,P66,FPH
Sizemore, Ephraim	Pvt	K Orr's Ri.	Southside RR, VA	04/02/65	City Pt., VA	04/07/65	Hart's Island, NY	CSR
					Hart's Island, NY	06/15/65	Rlsd. G.O. #109	P79,CSR
Sizemore, J.T.	Sgt	C 22nd SCVI	Crater, Pbg., VA	07/30/64	City Pt., VA	08/05/64	Pt. Lookout, MD	CSR,HOS
					Pt. Lookout, MD	08/08/64	Elmira, NY	P113,P117,P120
					Elmira, NY	02/20/65	Pt. Lookout, MD Xc	P66
					Jackson Hos. Rchmd	03/16/65	Furloughd 60 days	CSR
Sizemore, Powell	Pvt	H 14th SCVI	Gettysburg, PA	07/05/63	Ft. McHenry, MD	07/12/63	Ft. Delaware, DE	CSR
					Ft. Delaware, Hos.	02/11/64	Ft. Delaware, DE	P47
					Ft. Delaware, DE	06/01/64	Rlsd. Hos. 6/9/64	P47
					Ft. Delaware, DE	06/15/64	Hospital	P47
					Ft. Delaware, DE	07/15/64	Hospital	P47
					Ft. Delaware, DE	07/28/64	Died, Typhoid	P5,P40,P144,FPH
Sizemore, R.P.	Pvt	C 22nd SCVI	Crater, Pbg., VA	07/30/64	City Pt., VA	08/05/64	Pt. Lookout, MD	CSR
					Pt. Lookout, MD	08/08/64	Elmira, NY	P113,P117,P120
					Elmira, NY	07/03/65	Rlsd. G.O. #109	P65,P66
Sizemore, W.M.	Pvt	C 22nd SCVI	Kinston, NC	12/15/62	Kinston, NC	12/15/62	Paroled POW	CSR
Sizemore, William	Pvt	Ferguson's LA	Ringgold, GA	11/27/63	Nashville, TN	12/09/63	Louisville, KY	CSR
					Louisville, KY	12/11/63	Rock Island, IL	P88,P89,CSR
					Rock Island, IL	10/06/64	Vol. US Frontier s	CSR
Sizemore, William	Pvt	Ferguson's LA	Salisbury, NC	04/12/65	Camp Chase, OH	06/13/65	Rlsd. G.O.#109	P23
Sizemore, William	Pvt	H 3rd SCVABn	High Pt., NC	05/02/65	High Pt., NC	05/02/65	Paroled	CSR
Skelton, Andrew J.	Pvt	B 15th SCVAB	Averysboro, NC	03/16/65	New Berne, NC	03/30/65	Pt. Lookout, MD	CSR
					Pt. Lookout, MD	05/07/65	Died, Ch. Dysntery	P6,P115,P118,FPH
Skelton, W.T.	Pvt	C P.S.S.	Sharpsburg, MD	10/01/62	Ft. McHenry, MD	10/14/62	Aikens Ldg., VA Xc	CSR
Skinner, B.	Pvt	M 8th SCVI	Spotsylvania, VA	05/08/64	Belle Plain, VA	05/21/64	Ft. Delaware, DE	P41,KEB,CSR
					Ft. Delaware, DE	06/16/65	Rlsd. G.O. #109	P41,P43,CSR
Skinner, Franklin	Pvt	H 21st SCVI	Ft. Fisher, NC	01/15/65	Elmira, NY	04/09/65	Died, Ch. Diarrhea	P6,P65,P66,FPH,HAG
Skipper, E.M.	Pvt	K 1st SCVA	Charleston, SC Hos.	02/18/65	Charleston, SC	03/27/65	Released on oath	CSR
Skipper, James T.	Pvt	G 21st SCVI	Town Creek, NC	02/20/65	Pt. Lookout, MD	06/19/65	Rlsd. G.O. #109	P115,P118
Skipper, John W.	Pvt	Prvost Grd	Fayetteville, NC	03/10/65	Pt. Lookout, MD	06/19/65	Rlsd. G.O. #109	P115,P118
Skipper, Samuel	Pvt	G 21st SCVI	Deserted/enemy	08/22/64	Washington, DC	08/30/64	Provost Marshal	CSR
Skipper, Samuel T.	Pvt	A 21st SCVI	Morris Island, SC	07/10/63	Morris Island, SC	07/13/63	Hilton Head, SC	CSR,HAG
					Hilton Head, SC	07/22/63	Ft. Columbus, NY	CSR
					Ft. Columbus, NY	07/26/63	Pt. Lookout, MD	CSR
					Pt. Lookout, MD	07/27/64	Died, Ch. Diarrhea	P6,P116,P119,FPH

SOUTH CAROLINA SOLDIERS, SAILORS AND  CITIZENS HELD IN U.S. PRISONS 1861-1865

NAME	RANK	REGIMENT	CAPTURED AT	WHEN	PRISON	MOVED	DISPOSITION	SOURCES
Skipper, Stephen	Pvt	G 21st SCVI	Town Creek, NC	02/20/65	Pt. Lookout, MD	06/19/65	Rlsd. G.O. #109	P115,P118
Slagle, W.F.	Pvt	A 15th SCVI	Williamsburg, VA	05/06/62	Old Capitol, DC	08/01/62	Fts. Monroe, VA	CSR
					Fts. Monroe, VA	08/05/62	Aikens Ldg., VA Xc	CSR
Slagle, W.T.	Pvt	A 5th SCVI	Williamsburg, VA	05/06/62	Washington, DC Hos	07/21/62	Old Capitol, DC	SA3,CSR
Slater, John R.	Pvt	K 3rd SCVI	Lynch's Creek, SC	02/28/65	New Berne, NC	04/03/65	Pt. Lookout, MD	CSR,KEB,SA2,H3
					Pt. Lookout, MD	06/19/65	Rlsd. G.O. #109	P115,P118
Slaton, J.R.	Pvt	D Ham.Leg.MI	Deserted/enemy	01/24/65	Hqs. Army of Potomac	01/30/65	Washington, DC	CSR
					Washington, DC	01/30/65	Philadelphia, PA	CSR
Slaven, Robert C.	Pvt	I 13th SCVI	Spotsylvania, VA	05/12/64	Belle Plain, VA	05/21/64	Ft. Delaware, DE	CSR
					Ft. Delaware, DE	04/27/65	Rlsd. OO War Dept.	P41,P43,CSR
Slice, Samuel N.	Pvt	H 13th SCVI	Gettysburg, PA	07/03/63	David's Island, NY	09/12/63	City Pt. VA for Xc	CSR
Sligh, Thomas W.	2Lt	G 7th SCVIBn	Weldon RR, VA	08/21/64	City Pt., VA P.M.	08/23/64	Washington, DC P.M.	CSR
					Old Capitol, DC	08/27/64	Ft. Delaware, DE	P110,HAG,HIC,CSR
					Ft. Delaware, DE	06/17/65	Rlsd. G.O. #109	P43,P45,P46,CSR
Sloan, Calvin W.	Pvt	F 12th SCVI	Sharpsburg, MD	09/17/62	Sharpsburg, MD	09/27/62	Paroled	CSR
Sloan, D.N.	Pvt	B 7th SCVC	Augusta, GA	05/19/65	Augusta, GA	05/19/65	Paroled	CSR
Sloan, David H.	Pvt	B Hol.Leg.	Five Forks, VA	04/01/65	City Pt., VA	04/05/65	Pt. Lookout, MD	CSR,HOS
					Pt. Lookout, MD	06/19/65	Rlsd. G.O. #109	P115,P119,P122
Sloan, James P.	2Lt	F 14th SCVI	Gettysburg, PA	07/03/63	Gettysburg Fld.Hos	07/14/63	Chester, PA G.H.	CSR
					Chester, PA G.H.	08/30/63	Johnson's Isl., OH	P1,CSR
					Johnson's Isl., OH	03/14/65	Pt. Lookout, MD Xc	P80,CSR
					Pt. Lookout, MD	03/22/65	Boulwares Wh., VA	CSR
Sloan, James R.	Pvt	F 12th SCVI	Hatchers Run, VA	03/31/65	City Pt., VA	04/02/65	Pt. Lookout, MD	CSR
					Pt. Lookout, MD	06/19/65	Rlsd. G.O. #109	P115,P122,CSR
Sloan, Timothy S.	Pvt	B Hol.Leg.	Five Forks, VA	04/01/65	City Pt., VA	04/05/65	Pt. Lookout, MD	CSR,HOS
					Pt. Lookout, MD	06/19/65	Rlsd. G.O. #109	P115,P119,P122
Sloan, William H.	Pvt	F 20th SCVI	Cedar Creek, VA	10/19/64	Harpers Ferry, WV	10/24/64	Pt. Lookout, MD	CSR
					Pt. Lookout, MD	06/19/65	Rlsd. G.O. #109	P115,P118,CSR
Small, Amos C.	Pvt	K 26th SCVI	Crater, Pbg., VA	07/30/64	City Pt., VA	08/05/64	Pt. Lookout, MD	CSR,CEN
					Pt. Lookout, MD	08/08/64	Elmira, NY	P113,P117,P120
					Elmira, NY	12/07/64	Died, Ch. Diarrhea	P5,P65,P66,FPH,CSR
Small, C.	Pvt	F 21st SCVI	Petersburg, VA	06/18/54	Elmira, NY	03/02/65	Pt. Lookout, MD Xc	P66
Small, James M.	Cpl	H 2nd SCVI	Gettysburg, PA	07/03/63	Gettysburg, PA Hos	07/13/63	Died of wounds	SA2,H2,CSR,KEB
Small, John D.	Pvt	E 12th SCVI	Warrenton, VA	09/29/62	Warrenton, VA	09/29/62	Paroled	CSR
Small, Robert F.	Cpl	Palmetto L	Gettysburg, PA	07/04/63	Gettysburg, PA	07/07/63	Died of wounds	CSR
Smalley, Joshua	Pvt	I 1st SCVIR	Chattanooga, TN	11/24/64	Took oath			SA1,CSR
Smart, C.	Pvt	I 7th SCVC	Augusta, GA	06/02/65	Augusta, GA	06/02/62	Paroled	CSR
Smike, E.S.	Pvt	A 1st SCVIG	Warrenton, VA	09/29/62	Warrenton, VA	09/29/62	Paroled	CSR
Smiley, James	Pvt	H 26th SCVI	Deserted/enemy	02/27/65	City Pt., VA	02/28/65	Washington, DC	CSR
					Washington, DC	03/02/65	Charleston, SC	CSR
Smith, A.J.	Pvt	A 7th SCVC	Richmond, VA Hos.	04/03/65	No other data			CSR
Smith, A.K.	Pvt	I 1st SCVC	Deserted/enemy	03/22/65	Charleston, SC	03/22/65	Released on oath	CSR
Smith, A.R.	Pvt	H 22nd SCVI	Deserted/enemy	02/24/65	City Pt., VA	02/28/65	Washington, DC	CSR
					Washington, DC	03/01/65	Savannah, GA oath	CSR
Smith, A.W.	Pvt	I 25th SCVI	Ft. Fisher, NC	01/15/65	Fts. Monroe, VA			CSR
Smith, Adolphus G.	Pvt	C 17th SCVI	Petersburg, VA	03/25/65	City Pt., VA	03/28/65	Pt. Lookout, MD	CSR,YEB
					Pt. Lookout, MD	06/19/65	Rlsd. G.O. #109	P115,P118,P122,CSR
Smith, Allen N.	Pvt	5 10/19 SCVI	Missionary Ridge, TN	11/25/63	Nashville, TN	12/07/63	Louisville, KY	P39,CSR,RAS,HMC
					Louisville, KY	12/07/63	Rock Island, IL	P88,P89,CSR
					Rock Island, IL	06/20/65	Rlsd. G.O. #109	P131,CSR

SOUTH CAROLINA SOLDIERS, SAILORS AND S CITIZENS HELD IN U.S. PRISONS 1861-1865

NAME	RANK	REGIMENT	CAPTURED AT	WHEN	PRISON	MOVED	DISPOSITION	SOURCES
Smith, Ambrose R.	Pvt	F 16th SCVI	Franklin, TN	12/17/64	Nashville, TN	02/27/65	Louisville, KY	P4,P39,16R,CSR
					Louisville, KY	03/28/65	Hospital, G.S. Wd.	P95
					Louisville, KY	04/03/65	Camp Chase, OH	P92,P95,CSR
					Camp Chase, OH	06/10/65	Rlsd. G.O. #109	P23,CSR
Smith, Anderson A.	Pvt	G 22nd SCVI	Sutherland Stn., VA	04/03/65	City Pt., VA	04/03/65	Pt. Lookout, MD	CSR,UD3
					Pt. Lookout, MD	04/29/65	Died of wounds	P6,P115,P119,FPH
Smith, Andrew H.	Pvt	E 11th SCVI	Petersburg, VA	06/16/64	Bermuda Hundred VA	06/17/64	Fts. Monroe, VA	CSR
					Fts. Monroe, VA	06/18/64	Pt. Lookout, MD	CSR
					Pt. Lookout, MD	07/25/64	Elmira, NY	P113,P117,HAG
					Elmira, NY	03/02/65	James R., VA Xc	CSR
					Elmira, NY	07/11/65	Rlsd. G.O. #109	P65,P66,HAG
Smith, Andrew Jackson	Pvt	F Hol.Leg.	Jarratts Stn., VA	05/08/64	Fts. Monroe, VA	05/13/64	Pt. Lookout, MD	CSR
					Pt. Lookout, MD	08/15/64	Elmira, NY	P113,P117,P120,CSR
					Elmira, NY	09/05/64	Died, Scurvy	P5,P12,P65,P66,FPH
Smith, B.F.	Pvt	K 7th SCVC	Raleigh, NC Hos.	04/13/65	No further data			CSR
Smith, Benjamin	Pvt	E 18th SCVI	Petersburg, VA	06/16/64	Fts. Monroe, VA	06/20/64	Pt. Lookout, MD	CSR,HOS
					Pt. Lookout, MD	06/25/64	Joined U.S. Forces	P117,P121,P125
Smith, Benjamin	Pvt	E 18th SCVI	Petersburg, VA	04/03/65	City Pt., VA	04/07/65	Hart's Island, NY	P79,CSR
					Hart's Island, NY	06/16/65	Rlsd. G.O. #109	CSR
Smith, Benjamin F.	Pvt	E 11th SCVI	Petersburg, VA	06/24/64	Bermuda Hundred, VA	06/24/64	Fts. Monroe, VA	CSR,HAG
					Fts. Monroe, VA	08/15/64	Elmira, NY	CSR
					Pt. Lookout, MD	08/16/64	Elmira, NY	P66,P117,P120
					Elmira, NY	05/03/65	Died, Ch. Diarrhea	P6,P12,P65,FPH,P66
Smith, Benjamin P.	Pvt	E 16th SCVI	Franklin, TN	11/30/64	Nashville, TN	12/03/64	Louisville, KY	CSR,16R
					Louisville, KY	12/04/64	Camp Douglas, IL	P90,P91,CSR
					Camp Douglas, IL	06/18/65	Rlsd. G.O. #109	CSR
Smith, Charles E.	Pvt	C 1st SCVIH	Libby Prison, Rchmd.	04/10/65	Not given			SA1,CSR
Smith, Charles S.	Pvt	I 11th SCVI	CSA Hospital		Jackson H. Rchmd	06/15/64	Died of wounds	P12,HAG
Smith, Cholson	Pvt	F 21st SCVI	Petersburg, VA	06/18/64	City Pt., VA		Pt. Lookout, MD	CSR,HAG
					Pt. Lookout, MD	07/27/64	Elmira, NY	P113,P117,P120
					Elmira, NY	03/02/65	Pt. Lookout, MD Xc	P65,P66
Smith, David H.	Pvt	F 18th SCVI	Petersburg, VA	07/30/64	Old Capitol, DC	10/26/64	Elmira, NY	P110,CSR
					Elmira, NY	06/21/65	Rlsd. G.O. #109	P65,P66,CSR
Smith, E.	Pvt	B 15th SCVAB	Bentonville, NC	03/20/65	New Berne, NC	04/05/65	Hart's Island, NY	CSR
					Hart's Island, NY	06/15/65	Rlsd. G.O. #109	P79,CSR
Smith, E.A.	Pvt	I 1st SCVA			Pt. Lookout, MD		Joined U.S. Army	P125
Smith, E.B.	Pvt	D 21st SCVI	Ft. Fisher, NC	01/15/65	New York, NY	01/30/65	Elmira, NY	CSR
					Elmira, NY	03/02/65	Pt. Lookout to Xc	P66
					Elmira, NY	03/02/65	Died, Ch. Diarrhea	P65,CSR
Smith, E.B.	ASr	21st SCVI	Town Creek, NC	02/20/65	Pt. Lookout, MD	02/28/65	Old Capitol, DC	P120,HAG,CSR
					Old Capitol, DC	03/26/65	Camp Hamilton, VA	CSR
					Camp Hamilton, VA	03/28/65	Pt. Lookout, MD	CSR
					Pt. Lookout, MD	03/28/65	Aikens Ldg., VA Xc	CSR
Smith, E.E.	Pvt	K 3rd SCVI	Appomattox C.H., VA	04/09/65	Appomattox C.H., VA	04/09/65	Paroled	CSR,SA2,H3
Smith, E.L.	Cpl	E 27th SCVI	Florence, SC	03/05/65	New Berne, NC	04/03/65	Pt. Lookout, MD	CSR,HAG
					Pt. Lookout, MD	06/19/65	Rlsd. G.O. #109	P115,P118
Smith, E.S.	Pvt	A 3rd SCVABn	In the field	03/21/65	New Berne, NC		No further data	CSR
Smith, E.S.	Pvt	A 3rd SCVABn	High Pt., NC	05/02/65	High Pt., NC	05/02/65	Paroled	CSR
Smith, E.T.	Pvt	K 1st SCVC	Gettysburg, PA	07/04/63	David's Island, NY	08/24/63	City Pt., VA Xc	P1,CSR
Smith, E.T.	Pvt	K 1st SCVC	Rapidan R., VA	02/29/64	Old Capitol, DC	06/15/64	Ft. Delaware, DE	P110
					Ft. Delaware, DE	06/08/65	Rlsd. G.O.#109	P41,P43,P45,CSR
Smith, Edward R.	Pvt	D 18th SCVI	Deserted/enemy	12/26/64	City Point, VA	12/27/64	Phila., PA oath	P8,CSR

SOUTH CAROLINA SOLDIERS, SAILORS AND  CITIZENS HELD IN U.S. PRISONS 1861-1865

NAME	RANK	REGIMENT	CAPTURED AT	WHEN	PRISON	MOVED	DISPOSITION	SOURCES
Smith, Elihu P.	Pvt	E 6th SCVC	Petersburg, VA	07/30/64	City Pt., VA	08/02/64	Pt. Lookout, MD	CSR
					Pt. Lookout, MD	08/08/64	Elmira, NY	P117,P120,P125,CSR
					Elmira, NY	02/20/65	Died, Ch. Diarrhea	P6,P65,P66,FPH,CSR
Smith, F.H.	Pvt	A 1st SCVIR	Deserted/enemy	02/18/65	Charleston, SC	03/22/65	New York, NY oath	CSR
Smith, Francis H.	Pvt	I 26th SCVI	Southside RR, VA	04/01/65	City Pt., VA	04/05/65	Pt. Lookout, MD	CSR,CTA
					Pt. Lookout, MD	06/19/65	Rlsd. G.O. #109	P115,P119,P122,CSR
Smith, G.S.	Pvt	E 7th SCVC	Albany, GA	05/29/65	Albany, GA	05/29/65	Paroled	CSR
Smith, George H.	Pvt	C 12th SCVI	Sutherland Stn., VA	04/02/65	City Pt., VA	04/07/65	Hart's Island, NY	CSR
					Hart's Island, NY	06/16/65	Rlsd. G.O. #109	P79,CSR
Smith, George H.	Pvt	E 2nd SCVI	Charlotte, NC Hos.	05/02/65	Charlotte, NC Hos.	05/02/65	Paroled	SA2,H2,CSR
Smith, George H.	Pvt	C 6th SCVI	Augusta, GA	05/24/65	Augusta, GA	05/24/61	Paroled	CSR
					Augusta, GA	06/03/65	Paroled	CSR
Smith, Gustav	Pvt	C 15th SCVI	Deserted/enemy	02/18/65	Charleston, SC	03/17/65	N. on Str. "Fulton"	CSR
Smith, H.A.	Pvt	C 1st SCVIR	Spartanburg, SC	03/26/65	Knoxville, Tn	04/17/65	Chattanooga, TN	CSR
					Chattanooga TN	04/17/65	Louisville, KY	CSR
					Louisville, KY	04/25/65	Rlsd. on oath	P8,P92,CSR
Smith, H.B.	Pvt	H 26th SCVI	Deserted/enemy	01/09/65	City Point, VA	01/13/65	Washington, DC	P8,CSR
					Washington, DC	01/16/65	Released on oath	CSR
Smith, H.B.	Pvt	A 3rd SCVABn	High Pt., NC	05/02/65	High Pt., NC	05/02/65	Paroled	CSR
Smith, H.E.	Pvt	F 18th SCVI	Southside RR, VA	04/02/65	City Pt., VA	04/07/65	Hart's Island, NY	CSR
					Hart's Island, NY	06/16/65	Rlsd. G.O. #109	P79,CSR
Smith, Hammond	Cpl	A German LA	Port Royal Fy., SC	10/16/64	Hilton Head, SC	10/25/64	Ft. Pulaski, GA	CSR
Smith, Hannon	Pvt	I Hol.Leg.	Petersburg, VA	11/05/64	City Pt., VA	11/11/64	Washington, DC	CSR,HOS
					Pt. Lookout, MD	05/14/65	Rlsd. G.O.#85	P115,P118,P122
Smith, Henry	Pvt	E 24th SCVI	Nashville, TN	12/16/64	Nashville, TN	12/18/64	Louisville, KY	CSR
					Louisville, KY	12/20/64	Camp Douglas, IL	P90,P91,P95
Smith, Henry	Pvt	E 24th SCVI	Nashville, TN	12/17/64	Camp Douglas, IL	06/20/65	Rlsd. G.O. #109	P55
Smith, Henry H.	Pvt	C 7th SCVIBn	Weldon RR, VA	08/21/64	City Pt., VA	08/24/64	Pt. Lookout, MD	CSR
					Pt. Lookout, MD	01/27/65	Aikens Ldg., VA Xc	P113,P117,P124,CSR
Smith, Henson L.	Pvt	E 16th SCVI	Franklin, TN	11/30/64	Nashville, TN	12/02/64	Louisville, KY	CSR
					Louisville, KY	12/03/64	Camp Douglas, IL	P90,CSR
Smith, Henson L.	Pvt	B 16th SCVI	Franklin, TN	11/30/64	Camp Douglas, IL	01/19/65	Died, Typhoid fever	P5,P55,P58,FPH,CSR
Smith, Herbert M.	Pvt	E 4th SCVC	Louisa C.H., VA	06/11/64	Fts. Monroe, VA	06/20/64	Pt. Lookout, MD	CSR
					Pt. Lookout, MD	07/23/64	Elmira, NY	P113,P117,P120,CSR
Smith, Herbert M.	Pvt	E 4th SCVC	Louisa C.H., VA	06/11/64	Elmira, NY	09/16/64	Died, Diarrhea	P5,P12,P65,P66,FPH
Smith, Hugh G.	Pvt	H 23rd SCVI	Five Forks, VA	04/02/65	City Pt., VA	04/05/65	Pt. Lookout, MD	CSR,HMC
					Pt. Lookout, MD	06/19/65	Rlsd. G.O. #109	P115,P119,P122,CSR
Smith, J.A.	Pvt	F Hol.Leg.	Jarratts Stn., VA	05/08/64	Fts. Monroe, VA	05/13/64	Pt. Lookout, MD	CSR
					Pt. Lookout, MD	08/15/64	Elmira, NY	P113,P117,P120,CSR
					Elmira, NY	06/14/65	Rlsd. G.O.#109	P65,P66,CSR
Smith, J.A.	Pvt	I 5th SCVC	Hawe's Shop, VA	05/28/64	Lincoln G.H., DC	06/19/64	Died of wounds	P12
Smith, J.C.	Cit	Charleston			Pt. Lookout, MD		Exchanged	P124
Smith, J.C.	Pvt	I 3rd SCVI	N. Anna River, VA	05/23/64	Port Royal, VA	05/30/64	Pt. Lookout, MD	CSR,KEB,SA2,H3
					Pt. Lookout, MD	03/14/65	Aikens Ldg., VA Xc	P117,P121,P124,CSR
Smith, J.F.	Pvt	I 2nd SCVC	Augusta, GA	05/24/65	Augusta, GA	05/24/65	Paroled	CSR
Smith, J.G.	Pvt	Ham.Leg.MI	Deserted/enemy	03/08/65	Bermuda Hundred VA	03/10/65	City Pt., VA P.M.	CSR
					City Pt., VA	03/11/65	Washington, DC	CSR
					Washington, DC	03/13/65	Norfolk, VA oath	CSR
Smith, J.H.	Pvt	B 12th SCVI	Centreville, VA	10/07/62	Centreville, VA	10/07/62	Paroled	CSR
Smith, J.H.	Pvt	B 12th SCVI	Gettysburg, PA	06/30/63	David's Island, NY	08/02/63	Died	P1,P6,P12,FPH,CSR

SOUTH CAROLINA SOLDIERS, SAILORS AND  CITIZENS HELD IN U.S. PRISONS 1861-1865

NAME	RANK	REGIMENT	CAPTURED AT	WHEN	PRISON	MOVED	DISPOSITION	SOURCES
Smith, J.P.	Pvt	K 27th SCVI	Petersburg, VA	06/24/64	Bermuda Hundred VA	06/25/64	Fts. Monroe, VA	CSR,HAG
					Fts. Monroe, VA	06/26/64	Pt. Lookout, MD	CSR
					Pt. Lookout, MD	08/16/64	Elmira, NY	P113,P117,P120
Smith, J.P.	Pvt	K 27th SCVI	Petersburg, VA	06/24/64	Elmira, NY	06/16/65	Rlsd. G.O. #109	P65,P66
Smith, J.R.	Pvt	A 3rd SCVABn	High Pt., NC	05/02/65	High Pt., NC	05/02/65	Paroled	CSR
Smith, J.T.	Pvt	A 20th SCVI	Cedar Creek, VA	10/19/64	W. Bldg. Balt, MD	11/22/64	Pt. Lookout, MD	P4,CSR
					Pt. Lookout, MD	01/28/65	Hammond G.H., MD	P115,P118,P121,CSR
Smith, J.T.	Pvt	K 1st SCVIH	Augusta, GA	05/24/65	Augusta, GA	05/24/65	Paroled	CSR
Smith, J.T.	Pvt	A 20th SCVI	Cedar Creek, VA	10/19/64	Hammond G.H., MD	06/19/65	Rlsd. G.O. #109	CSR
Smith, J.W.	1Sg	K 8th SCVI	Richmond, VA Hos.	04/03/65	Richmond, VA		Paroled	CSR
Smith, J.W.	Pvt	C 12th SCVI	Spotsylvania, VA	05/12/64	Ft. Delaware, DE	02/27/65	City Pt., VA Xc	P41,P43,HFC
Smith, James	Pvt	A Hol.Leg.	Frederick, MD	09/12/62	Ft. Delaware, DE	10/02/62	Aikens Ldg., VA Xc	CSR
Smith, James	Pvt	I 1st SCVA	Morris Island, SC	07/10/63	Hilton Head, SC	09/05/63	Ft. Columbus, NY	P1,CSR
					Ft. Columbus, NY	09/23/63	Took the oath	P1,CSR
Smith, James	Pvt	A 4th SCVC	Stony Creek, VA	12/01/64	City Pt., VA	12/05/64	Pt. Lookout, MD	CSR
					Pt. Lookout, MD	06/19/65	Rlsd. G.O. #109	P115,P122,CSR
Smith, James	Pvt	E 16th SCVI	Franklin, TN	12/17/64	Nashville, TN	03/27/65	Louisville, KY	P23,P39,16R,CSR
					Louisville, KY	04/03/65	Camp Chase, OH	P92,P95,CSR
					Camp Chase, OH	06/11/65	Rlsd. G.O. #109	CSR
Smith, James	Pvt	A Hol.Leg.	Five Forks, VA	04/01/65	City Pt., VA	04/05/65	Pt. Lookout, MD	CSR,HOS
					Pt. Lookout, MD	06/16/65	Died, Ac. Diarrhea	P6,P12,P115,P119,HOS
Smith, James	Pvt	A 3rd SCVABn	High Pt., NC	05/01/65	High Pt., NC	05/01/65	Paroled	CSR
Smith, James E.	Pvt	A 27th SCVI	Town Creek, NC	02/20/64	Ft. Anderson, NC	02/28/64	Pt. Lookout, MD	CSR,HAG
					Pt. Lookout, MD	06/19/65	Rlsd. G.O. #109	P115,P118,CSR
Smith, James F.	Pvt	I 1st SCVA	Morris Island, SC	07/10/63	Hilton Head, SC	09/19/63	Ft. Columbus, NY	P1,CSR
					Ft. Columbus, NY	09/23/63	Took the oath	P1,CSR
Smith, James F.	Pvt	I 25th SCVI	Ft. Fisher, NC	01/15/65	Elmira, NY	03/16/65	Died, Ch. Diarrhea	P6,P12,FPH
Smith, James H.	Pvt	5 10/19 SCVI	Chattanooga, TN	11/23/63	Chattanooga, TN	03/26/63	Died of wounds	P12,CSR,RAS
Smith, James L.	Pvt	K 12th SCVI	Sharpsburg, MD	09/17/62	Balimore, MD USGH	11/05/62	Fts. Monroe, VA Xc	CSR
					Richmond, VA Hos.B	11/25/62	Furloughed 30 days	CSR
Smith, James P.	Pvt	B 10th SCVI	Atlanta, GA	07/22/64	Nashville, TN	07/26/64	Louisville, KY	CSR,RAS
					Louisville, KY	07/30/64	Camp Chase, OH	P90,P91
					Camp Chase, OH	03/02/65	City Pt., VA Xc	P26
Smith, James R.	Pvt	F 13th SCVI	Deserted/enemy	02/24/65	City Pt., VA	02/26/65	Washington, DC	CSR
					Washington, DC	02/27/65	Springfield, IL	CSR
Smith, James R.	Cpl	C 12th SCVI	Petersburg, VA	04/02/65	City Pt., VA	04/07/65	Hart's Island, NY	CSR
					Hart's Island, NY	06/16/65	Rlsd. G.O. #109	P79,CSR
Smith, James T.	Pvt	E 16th SCVI	Franklin, TN	12/16/64	Nashville, TN US G	01/26/65	Died of wounds	CSR,P12
Smith, James T.	Pvt	B Ham.Leg.MI	Burkeville, VA	04/06/65	City Pt., VA P.M.	06/14/65	Pt. Lookout, MD	CSR
					Pt. Lookout, MD	06/19/65	Rlsd. G.O. #109	P115,P119,P122,CSR
Smith, James W.	Pvt	E 11th SCVI	Weldon RR, VA	08/21/64	Pt. Lookout, MD	10/30/64	Exchanged	P123,HAG,CSR
Smith, Jasper S.	Pvt	H 16th SCVI	Anderson, SC	05/03/65	Anderson, SC	05/03/65	Paroled on oath	CSR
Smith, Jesse C.	Pvt	K 6th SCVC	Chesterfield, SC	03/04/65	New Berne, NC	03/30/65	Pt. Lookout, MD	CSR
					Pt. Lookout, MD	06/19/65	Rlsd. G.O. #109	P115,P118,P122,CSR
Smith, Jesse L.	Pvt	F 2nd SCVIRi	Knoxville, TN	12/03/63	Louisville, KY	12/31/63	Rock Island, IL	P88,P94,CSR
					Rock Island, IL	02/15/64	Died, Variola	P5,P131,P132,FPH
Smith, Joel	Pvt	K Orr's Ri.	Petersburg, VA	04/03/65	City Pt., VA	04/11/65	Hart's Island, NY	CSR
					Hart's Island, NY	06/16/65	Rlsd. G.O. #109	P79,CSR
Smith, Joel R.	Pvt	C 17th SCVI	Deserted/enemy	11/28/64	P.M 15th AC	11/29/64	City Pt., VA P.M.	CSR
					Washington, DC	12/01/64	Alexandria, VA	CSR
Smith, John	Pvt	D 18th SCVI	Crater, Pbg., VA	07/30/64	Pt. Lookout, MD	08/08/64	Elmira, NY	P117,P113,P120,CSR
					Elmira, NY		No other data	P65

SOUTH CAROLINA SOLDIERS, SAILORS AND CITIZENS HELD IN U.S. PRISONS 1861-1865

NAME	RANK	REGIMENT	CAPTURED AT	WHEN	PRISON	MOVED	DISPOSITION	SOURCES
Smith, John	Pvt	F 22nd SCVI	Deserted/enemy	02/20/65	Charleston, SC	02/20/65	Hilton Head, SC	CSR
					Hilton head, SC	03/22/65	New York, NY oath	CSR
Smith, John	Pvt	F 5th SCVI	Farmville, VA	04/25/65	Farmville, VA	04/25/65	Paroled	CSR,SA3
Smith, John	Pvt	A 3rd SCVABn	High Pt., NC	05/01/65	High Pt., NC	05/01/65	Paroled	CSR
Smith, John	Cpl	C 5th SCVI	Hartwell, GA	05/18/65	Hartwell, GA	05/18/65	Paroled	CSR
Smith, John E.	Pvt	K 22nd SCVI	Deserted/enemy		Norfolk, VA	08/03/64	Fts. Monroe, VA	CSR
					Fts. Monroe, VA	08/04/64	Bermuda Hundred, VA	CSR
Smith, John F.	Pvt	Ferguson's LA	Salisbury, NC	04/12/65	Nashville, TN	04/29/65	Louisville, KY	CSR
					Louisville, KY	05/02/65	Camp Chase, OH	CSR
					Camp Chase, OH	06/13/65	Rlsd. G.O. #109	CSR
Smith, John J.	Cpl	C Orr's Ri.	Petersburg, VA	04/03/65	City Pt., VA	04/11/65	Hart's Island, NY	CSR
					Hart's Island, NY	06/16/65	Rlsd. G.O. #109	P79,CSR
Smith, John M.	Pvt	C 12th SCVI	Spotsylvania, VA	05/12/64	Belle Plain, VA	05/20/64	Ft. Delaware, DE	CSR
					Ft. Delaware, DE	10/28/64	Camp Hospital	P47
					Ft. Delaware, DE	02/27/65	City Pt., VA Xc	CSR
Smith, John N.	Pvt	C 4th SCVC	Stony Creek, VA	12/01/64	City Pt., VA	12/05/64	Pt. Lookout, MD	CSR
					Pt. Lookout, MD	06/19/65	Rlsd. G.O. #109	P115,P118,P122,CSR
Smith, John O.	Pvt	D 24th SCVI	Nashville, TN	12/16/64	Nashville, TN	12/31/64	Louisville, KY	CSR,EFW
					Louisville, KY	01/02/65	Camp Chase, OH	P92,P95
					Camp Chase, OH	02/16/65	Died, Variola	P6,P23,P27,FPH,CSR
Smith, John R.	Pvt	C 14th SCVI	Gettysburg, PA	07/04/63	David's Island, NY	04/19/64	Ft. Delaware, DE	P1,CSR
					Ft. Delaware, DE	09/18/64	Aikens Ldg., VA Xc	P41,P43,CSR
Smith, John W.	Pvt	B 26th SCVI	Five Forks, VA	04/01/65	City Pt., VA	04/05/65	Pt. Lookout, MD	CSR
					Pt. Lookout, MD	06/19/65	Rlsd. G.O. #109	P115,P119,P122,CSR
Smith, Jordan	Pvt	A 21st SCVI	Petersburg, VA	06/24/64	Bermuda Hundred VA	06/25/64	Fts. Monroe, VA	CSR
					Fts. Monroe, VA	06/26/64	Pt. Lookout, MD	CSR
					Pt. Lookout, MD	08/16/64	Elmira, NY	P113,P117,HAG
					Elmira, NY	03/14/65	Pt. Lookout, MD Xc	P65,P66,HAG
Smith, Joseph W.	Pvt	C 17th SCVI	Kinston, NC	12/17/62	Kinston, NC	12/17/62	Paroled	CSR
Smith, Joseph W.	Pvt	F Hol.Leg.	Jarratts Stn., VA	05/08/64	Fts. Monroe, VA	05/13/64	Pt. Lookout, MD	CSR
					Pt. Lookout, MD	08/15/64	Elmira, NY	P113,P117,P120,CSR
					Elmira, NY	02/08/65	Died, Ch. Diarrhea	P6,P65,P66,FPH,CSR
Smith, Joseph W.	Pvt	C 17th SCVI	Crater, Pbg., VA	07/30/64	City Pt., VA	08/05/64	Pt. Lookout, MD	CSR
					Pt. Lookout, MD	08/08/64	Elmira, NY	P113,P117,P120,CSR
					Elmira, NY	01/09/65	Died, Pneumonia	P5,P12,P65,CSR
Smith, Joseph W.	Pvt	E 25th SCVI	Ft. Fisher, VA	01/15/65	New York, NY	01/30/65	Elmira, NY	CSR,HAG
Smith, Joseph W.	Pvt	E 25th SCVI	Ft. Fisher, NC	01/15/65	Elmira, NY	07/11/65	Rlsd. G.O. #109	P65,P66
Smith, L.R.	Pvt	B 1st SCVIH	Warrenton, VA	09/29/62	Warrenton, VA	09/29/62	Paroled	CSR,SA1
Smith, L.R.	Pvt	B 1st SCVIH	Richmond, VA Hos.	04/03/65	Libby Prison Rchmd	04/13/65	Pt. Lookout, MD	CSR
					City Pt., VA P.M.	04/14/65	Pt. Lookout, MD	CSR
Smith, L.R.	Pvt	B 1st SCVIH	Richmond, VA Hos.	04/03/65	Pt. Lookout, MD	06/05/65	Released	CSR
Smith, Lewis B.	Pvt	G 14th SCVI	Petersburg, VA	04/03/65	City Pt., VA	04/07/65	Hart's Island, NY	CSR
					Hart's Island, NY	06/16/65	Rlsd. G.O. #109	P79,CSR
Smith, Lewis R.	Pvt	B 2nd SCVI	Gettysburg, PA	07/05/63	Gettysburg G.H.	08/07/63	Died of wounds	SA2,P4,KEB,H2,CSR
Smith, Lovett R.	Pvt	B Orr's Ri.	Richmond, VA	04/03/65	Pt. Lookout, MD	06/08/65	Rlsd. Instr 5/30/65	P115,P119,P121
Smith, M.	Pvt	E 16th SCVI	Franklin, TN	11/30/64	Louisville, KY	12/03/64	Camp Douglas, IL	P91,16R
Smith, M.E.A.	Pvt	F Ham.Leg.MI	Anderson, SC	05/03/65	Anderson, SC	05/03/65	Paroled	CSR
					Anderson, SC	05/03/65	Paroled	CSR
Smith, Marcus	Pvt	G 12th SCVI	Petersburg, VA	03/25/65	City Pt., VA	03/28/65	Pt. Lookout, MD	CSR
					Pt. Lookout, MD	06/19/65	Rlsd. G.O. #109	P115,P118,P122,CSR
Smith, Mark	Pvt	G 1st SCVIG	Hatchers Run, VA	03/31/65	City Pt., VA	04/02/65	Pt. Lookout, MD	CSR,SA1
					Pt. Lookout, MD	06/19/65	Rlsd. G.O. #109	P115,P118,CSR

SOUTH CAROLINA SOLDIERS, SAILORS AND  CITIZENS HELD IN U.S. PRISONS 1861-1865

NAME	RANK	REGIMENT	CAPTURED AT	WHEN	PRISON	MOVED	DISPOSITION	SOURCES
Smith, Martin H.	Pvt	K 11th SCVI	Town Creek, NC	02/20/65	Pt. Lookout, MD	06/19/65	Rlsd. G.O. #109	P115,P118,HAG,CSR
Smith, Matthew S.	Pvt	E 27th SCVI	Florence, SC	03/05/65	New Berne, NC	04/03/65	Pt. Lookout, MD	CSR
					Pt. Lookout, MD	06/19/65	Rlsd. G.O. #109	P115,P118,CSR
Smith, Nathaniel	Pvt	H 1st SCVIG	Warrenton, VA	09/29/62	Warrenton, VA	09/29/62	Paroled	CSR
Smith, O.H.C.	Sgt	Brooks LA	Gettysburg, PA	07/05/63	Letterman G.H. Gbg	10/15/63	Provost Marshal	P1,CSR
					W. Bldg. Balt, MD	11/25/63		CSR
					Richmond, VA Hos.	11/25/63	Furloughed 30 days	CSR
Smith, P.F.	Pvt	A 3rd SCVABn	High Pt., NC	05/02/65	High Pt., NC	05/02/65	Paroled	CSR
Smith, Patrick	Smn	CS Chicora	Morris Island, SC	09/07/63	Ft. Warren, MA	10/01/64	Str. Circasian	P2,P137
					Pt. Lookout, MD	09/20/64	Ft. Warren, MA	P113
					Pt. Lookout, MD		Exchanged	P124
Smith, Phillip D.	Pvt	H 21st SCVI	Ft. Fisher, NC	01/15/65	Elmira, NY	07/11/65	Rlsd. G.O. #109	P65,P[66,HAG
Smith, R.E.	Pvt	5th SCResB	Chesterfield, SC	02/28/65	Pt. Lookout, MD	06/19/65	Rlsd. G.O. #109	P115,P118
Smith, R.S.	Pvt	I P.S.S.	Richmond, VA Hos.	04/03/65	Oibby Prison, VA	04/23/65	Newport News, VA	CSR
					Newport News, VA	06/26/65	Rlsd. G.O. #109	P107,TSE,CSR
Smith, Reddick K.	Pvt	A 14th SCVI	Hatchers Run, VA	04/02/65	City Pt., VA	04/07/65	Hart's Island, NY	CSR
					Hart's Island, NY	06/16/65	Rlsd. G.O. #109	P79,CSR
Smith, Richard W.	Pvt	B 14th SCVI	Gettysburg, PA	07/03/63	Harrisburg, PA	07/07/63	Ft. Delaware, DE	CSR
					Ft. Delaware, DE	11/18/63	Died, Ch. Diarrhea	P5,P12,P40,P42,P47,FPH
Smith, Riley W.	Pvt	C 5th SCResB	Cheraw, SC	03/04/65	New Berne, NC	03/30/65	Pt. Lookout, MD	CSR
					Pt. Lookout, MD	06/19/65	Rlsd. G.O. #109	P115,P118,P122,CSR
Smith, Robert E.	Pvt	C 5th SCResB	Chesterfield, SC	02/28/65	New Berne, NC	04/03/65	Pt. Lookout, MD	CSR
					Pt. Lookout, MD	06/19/65	Rlsd. G.O. #109	CSR
Smith, Robert J.	Pvt	F 25th SCVI	Ft. Fisher, NC	01/15/65	New York, NY	01/30/65	Elmira, NY	CSR,HAG
					Elmira, NY	02/27/65	Died, Ch. Diarrhea	P6,P12,P65,P66,FPH
Smith, Robert J.	Pvt	I 1st SCVIG	Petersburg, VA	04/02/65	City Pt., VA	04/04/65	Pt. Lookout, MD	CSR,SA1
					Pt. Lookout, MD	06/30/65	Rlsd. G.O. #109	P115,P118,P121,CSR
Smith, Robert M.	Pvt	B 4th SCVC	Louisa C.H., VA	06/11/64	Fts. Monroe, VA	06/20/64	Pt. Lookout, MD	CSR,HHC
					Pt. Lookout, MD	07/25/64	Elmira, NY	P113,P117,P120,CSR
					Elmira, NY	11/16/64	Died, Diarrhea	P5,P65,P66,FPH
Smith, Robert W.	Pvt	D 22nd SCVI	Petersburg, VA		City Pt., VA	04/12/64	Washington, DC	CSR
Smith, S. Calhoun	Pvt	K 2nd SCVC	Brandy Stn., VA	08/01/63	Old Capitol, DC	08/17/63	Pt. Lookout, MD	CSR
					Baltimore, MD	08/23/63	Pt. Lookout, MD	CSR
					Pt. Lookout, MD	12/25/63	Exchanged	P110,P113,P123,CSR
Smith, S.E.	Pvt	H 26th SCVI	Deserted/enemy	02/24/65	City Pt., VA	02/25/65	Washington, DC	CSR
					Washington, DC	02/25/65	Dover, NH on oath	CSR
Smith, S.M.	HSd	F 27th SCVI	Richmond, VA Hos.	04/03/65	Richmond, VA	05/04/65	Escaped	CSR
Smith, Samuel J.	Pvt	D 5th SCVC	Charleston, SC	03/31/65	Charleston, SC	03/31/65	Released on oath	CSR
Smith, Samuel W.	Pvt	F 4th SCVC	Stony Creek, VA	12/01/64	City Pt., VA	12/05/64	Pt. Lookout, MD	CSR
					Pt. Lookout, MD	06/19/65	Rlsd. G.O. #109	CSR
Smith, Steven B.	1Sg	K 15th SCVI	Halltown, VA	08/26/64	Harpers Ferry, WV	08/29/64	Camp Chase, OH	CSR
					Camp Chase, OH	03/18/65	Pt. Lookout, MD	P23,P26,KEB
					Pt. Lookout, MD	03/27/65	Boulware's Wh. Xc	CSR
Smith, T.F.	Cit	Marlboro	New Bern, NC	02/17/65	Hart's Island, NY	06/20/65	Rlsd. G.O. #109	P79
Smith, T.J.	Pvt	D 6th SCVI	Deserted/enemy	10/07/64	Bermuda Hundred VA	10/09/64	City Pt., VA P.M.	CSR
					City Pt., VA P.M.	10/12/64	Washington, DC P.M.	CSR
					Washington, DC P.M	10/12/64	Pittsburg, PA oath	CSR
Smith, Thomas	Smn	Dis. Boat	Morris Island, SC	09/07/63	Pt. Lookout, MD	01/23/64	Joined U.S. Forces	P113,P125
Smith, Thomas	Pvt	I 26th SCVI	Cheraw, SC	03/06/65	New Berne, NC	04/10/65	Hart's Island, NY	CSR
					Hart's Island, NY	06/17/65	Rlsd. G.O. #109	P79,CSR

SOUTH CAROLINA SOLDIERS, SAILORS AND  CITIZENS HELD IN U.S. PRISONS 1861-1865

NAME	RANK	REGIMENT	CAPTURED AT	WHEN	PRISON	MOVED	DISPOSITION	SOURCES
Smith, Thomas C.	Pvt	H 20th SCVI	Cedar Creek, VA	10/19/64	W. Bldg. Balt, MD	01/07/65	Pt. Lookout, MD	P4,KEB,CSR
					Pt. Lookout, MD	01/28/65	Hammond G.H., MD	P115,P118,P121,CSR
					Winchester, VA USH	02/08/65	Pt. Lookout, MD	CSR
					Pt. Lookout, MD	06/05/65	Rlsd. Instr. 5/30/65	P121,CSR
Smith, Thomas H.	Pvt	E 11th SCVI	Petersburg, VA	06/16/64	Bermuda Hundred VA	06/17/64	Fts. Monroe, VA	CSR,HAG
					Fts. Monroe, VA	06/18/64	Pt. Lookout, MD	CSR
					Pt. Lookout, MD	07/28/64	Elmira, NY	P113,P117,P120,CSR
					Elmira, NY	03/02/65	Pt. Lookout, MD	P65,P66
Smith, Thomas H.	Pvt	E 11th SCVI	Petersburg, VA	06/16/64	Elmira NY	07/11/65	Rlsd. G.O. #109	CSR
Smith, Thomas H.	Pvt	E 11th SCVI	Petersburg, VA	06/16/64	Pt. Lookout, MD	07/11/65	Rlsd. G.O. #109	CSR
Smith, W.	Pvt	A 19th SCVCB	Augusta, GA	05/26/65	Augusta, GA	05/26/65	Paroled on oath	CSR
Smith, W. Bryant	Pvt	M 8th SCVI	Cedar Creek, VA	10/19/64	W. Bldg. Balt, MD	11/05/64	Died of wounds	P4,P5,P12,FPH,CSR
Smith, W.A.	Pvt	G 19th SCVI	Petersburg, VA Hos.	04/03/65	Petersburg, VA Hos	04/09/65	US Gen. Hos.	CSR
Smith, W.B.	Pvt	D 18th SCVI	Farmville, VA	04/06/65	Newport News, VA	06/26/65	Rlsd. G.O. #109	P107,UD2,CSR
Smith, W.C.	Pvt	C 4th SCVC	Hawes Shop, VA	05/28/64	White House, VA	06/05/64	Pt. Lookout, MD	CSR
					Pt. Lookout, MD	08/29/64	Died, Typhoid fever	P5,P113,P119,FPH
Smith, W.G.	Pvt	C P.S.S.	Fair Oaks, VA	06/01/62	Phila. PA Hosp.	09/11/62	Ft. Delaware, DE	CSR
					Ft. Delaware, DE	10/02/62	Aikens Ldg., VA Xc	CSR
					Aikens Ldg., VA	11/10/62	Exchanged	CSR
Smith, W.H.	1Sg	C 17th SCVI	Kinston, NC	12/17/62	Kinston, NC	12/17/62	Paroled	CSR
Smith, W.M.	Pvt	F 18th SCVI	Crater, Pbg., VA	07/30/64	City Pt., VA	08/05/64	Pt. Lookout, MD	P113,P120,CSR
					Pt. Lookout, MD	08/08/64	Elmira, NY	P113,P120,CSR
					Elmira, NY	10/11/64	Pt. Lookout, MD Xc	P65,P66,CSR
					Pt. Lookout, MD	10/29/64	Venus Pt., GA Xc	P115,P118
Smith, W.N.	Pvt	B 2nd SCVIRi	Deserted/enemy	03/03/65	Bermuda Hundred VA	04/05/65	City Pt., VA P.M.	CSR
					City Pt., VA P.M.	04/07/65	Washington, DC P.M.	CSR
					Washington, DC P.M	04/08/65	Columbus, OH oath	CSR
Smith, W.P.	Sgt	C 8th SCVI	Cheraw, SC	03/06/65	New Berne, NC	04/10/65	Hart's Island, NY	CSR,KEB
					Hart's Island, NY	06/16/65	Rlsd. G.O. #109	P79,CSR
Smith, W.R.	Pvt	B 5th SCVC	Charleston, SC	03/29/65	Charleston, SC	03/29/65	Released on oath	CSR
Smith, W.T.	Pvt	F 7th SCVC	Farmville, VA	04/11/65	Farmville, VA	04/21/65	Paroled	CSR
Smith, Warren K.	Pvt	F 19th SCVI	Augusta, GA	05/19/65	Augusta, GA	05/19/65	Paroled	CSR
Smith, Wiley	Pvt	D 7th SCVIBn	Deserted/enemy	07/06/64	Bermuda Hundred VA	07/08/64	Fts. Monroe, VA	HAG,CSR
					Fts. Monroe, VA PM	07/15/64	Phila., PA on oath	P8,CSR
Smith, Wiley Alexander	1Lt	K 15th SCVI	Halltown, VA	08/26/64	Harpers Ferry, WV	09/01/64	Ft. Delaware, DE	CSR,KEB,H15
					Ft. Delaware, DE	06/17/65	Rlsd. G.O. #109	P43,P45,CSR
Smith, Wiliam H.	Pvt	C 12th SCVI	Sharpsburg, MD	09/17/62	Frederick, MD USGH	10/16/62	Ft. McHenry, MD	CSR
					Ft. McHenry, MD	10/18/62	Fts. Monroe, VA Xc	CSR
					Richmond, VA Hos.	11/06/62	Furloughed 25 days	CSR
Smith, William	Pvt	B 15th SCVI	Deep Bottom, VA	07/27/64	City Pt., VA	08/05/64	Pt. Lookout, MD	CSR,KEB,H15
					Pt. Lookout, MD	08/08/64	Elmira, NY	P113,P117,P120,CSR
					Elmira, NY	06/19/65	Rlsd. G.O. #109	P65,P66,CSR
Smith, William	Pvt	Ham.Leg.MI	Deserted/enemy	08/15/64	Washington, DC	08/18/64	Philadelphia, PA	CSR
Smith, William D.	Sgt	I 1st SCVA	Morris Island, SC	07/10/63	Hilton Head, SC	09/19/63	Ft. Columbus, NY	CSR
					Ft. Columbus, NY	09/23/63	Took the oath	P1,CSR
					Pt. Lookout, MD	02/08/64	Jd. U.S. Army	P116,CSR
					Pt. Lookout, MD	08/16/64	Elmira, NY	P113,P120,P121,CSR
Smith, William D.	Sgt	I 1st SCVA	Morris Island, SC	07/27/63	Elmira, NY	03/10/65	Pt. Lookout, MD Xc	P65,P66,P124
Smith, William L.	Pvt	G 7th SCVIBn	Swift Creek, VA	05/06/64	Bermuda Hundred VA	05/12/64	Fts. Monroe, VA	CSR,HAG,HIC
					Fts. Monroe, VA	05/13/64	Pt. Lookout, MD	CSR
Smith, William L.	Pvt	G 7th SCVIBn	Swift Creek, VA	05/06/64	Pt. Lookout, MD	05/18/64	Joined U.S. Army	P113,P122,P125,CSR

SOUTH CAROLINA SOLDIERS, SAILORS AND  CITIZENS HELD IN U.S. PRISONS 1861-1865

NAME	RANK	REGIMENT	CAPTURED AT	WHEN	PRISON	MOVED	DISPOSITION	SOURCES
Smith, William M.	Pvt	B 16th SCVI	Graysville, GA	11/27/63	Nashville, TN	12/09/63	Louisville, KY	P39,CSR
					Louisville, KY	12/11/63	Rock Island, IL	P88,P89,16R,CSR
Smith, William M.	Pvt	B 16th SCVI	Graysville, GA	11/27/63	Rock Island, IL	10/15/64	Jd. USA Frontier S	P131,CSR
Smith, William M.	Pvt	H 1st SCVIG	Spotsylvania, VA	05/12/64	Belle Plain, VA	05/21/64	Ft. Delaware, DE	CSR,SA1
					Ft. Delaware, DE	10/26/64	Hos. 10/26-10/30/64	P47
					Ft. Delaware, DE	10/30/64	Pt. Lookout, MD	P41,P43,CSR
					Pt. Lookout, MD	10/31/64	Aikens Ldg. for Xc	P115,P118,P123,CSR
Smith, William Robert	Pvt	E 1st SCVIR			New Berne, NC	05/09/65	Died	P12,CSR
Smitheart, J.A.	Pvt	K 1st SCVIH	Burkesville, VA Hos.	04/14/65	Burkesville, VA Ho	04/17/65	Paroled	CSR
Smithson, D.E.	Pvt	G 7th SCVC	White Oak Swamp, VA	02/06/65	Bermuda Hundred VA	02/09/65	City Pt., VA P.M.	CSR
					City Pt., VA	02/10/65	Pt. Lookout, MD	CSR
					Pt. Lookout, MD	06/19/65	Rlsd. G.O. #109	P115,P118,P122,CSR
Smithson, M.T.	Sgt	C 2nd SCVIRi	Darbytown Rd., VA	12/12/64	Bermuda Hundred VA	12/10/64	City Pt., VA	CSR
					City Pt., VA	12/15/64	Pt. Lookout, MD	CSR
					Pt. Lookout, MD	06/19/65	Rlsd. G.O. #109	P115,P118,CSR
Smoak, Anderson A.	Pvt	F 25th SCVI	Weldon RR, VA	08/21/64	City Pt., VA Hos.	08/26/64	Alexandria, VA G.H.	CSR,HAG
					McClellan GH Phila	09/19/64	Died of wounds	P6,P12,HAG,CSR
Smoak, David	Pvt	A 1st SCVIH	Deserted/enemy	03/23/65	Bermuda Hundred	04/24/65	City Pt., VA P.M.	CSR
					City Pt., VA P.M.	04/27/65	Washington, DC P.M.	CSR
Smoak, David	Pvt	A 1st SCVIH	Deserted/enemy	03/23/65	Washington, DC P.M	04/29/65	Charleston, SC oath	CSR
Smoak, H.E.	Pvt	H 25th SCVI	Ft. Fisher, NC	01/15/65	New York, NY	01/30/65	Elmira, NY	CSR,HAG
					Elmira, NY	02/21/65	Died, Ch. Diarrhea	P6,P12,P65,FPH,CSR
Smoak, J.M.	Pvt	A 1st SCVIH	Warrenton, VA	09/29/65	Warrenton, VA	09/29/65	Paroled	CSR
Smoak, Robert	Pvt	A 1st SCVIH	Deserted/enemy	03/23/65	Bermuda Hundred, VA	03/24/65	City Pt., VA P.M.	CSR
					City Pt., VA P.M.	03/27/65	Washington, DC P.M	CSR
					Washington, DC P.M	03/29/65	Charleston, SC oath	CSR
Smoke, Daniel	Pvt	G 4th SCVC	Hawes Shop, VA	05/28/64	3rd Div. 5th A.C.	06/04/64	Died of wounds	P12,CSR
Smoke, Henry L.	Pvt	I 11th SCVI	Town Creek, NC	02/20/65	Ft. Anderson, NC	02/28/65	Pt. Lookout, MD	CSR
					Pt. Lookout, MD	06/19/65	Rlsd. G.O. #109	P115,P118,P122,HAG,CSR
Smoke, James	Pvt	G 4th SCVC	Armstrong's Mill, VA	12/10/64	City Pt., VA	12/12/64	Pt. Lookout, MD	CSR
					Pt. Lookout, MD	06/05/65	Released	P115,P118,P121,CSR
Smoke, Wiley	Pvt	H 17th SCVI	Crater, Pbg., VA	07/30/64	City Pt., VA	08/05/64	Pt. Lookout, MD	CSR
					Pt. Lookout, MD	08/08/64	Elmira, NY	P113,P117,P120,CSR
					Elmira, NY	10/11/64	Tfd. for exchange	P65,P66,CSR
					Pt. Lookout, MD	10/29/64	Exchanged	P115,P123,CSR
Smoot, Calvin	Pvt	I 18th SCVI	Crater, Pbg., VA	07/30/64	City Pt., VA	08/05/64	Pt. Lookout, MD	CSR
					Pt. Lookout, MD	08/08/64	Elmira, NY	P113,P120,P125,CSR
					Elmira, NY	07/11/65	Rlsd. G.O. #109	P65,P66
Smothers, Henry	Pvt	F 26th SCVI	Crater, Pbg., VA	07/30/64	City Pt., VA	08/05/64	Pt. Lookout, MD	CSR
					Pt. Lookout, MD	08/08/64	Elmira, NY	P113,P117,P120,CSR
					Elmira, NY	07/03/65	Rlsd. G.O. #109	P65,P66,CSR
Smothers, J.A.	Pvt	F 26th SCVI	Petersburg, VA H	04/03/65	Fair Gds. Hos. Pbg	04/09/65	Camp Hamilton, VA	CSR
					Camp Hamilton, VA	06/08/65	Released on oath	CSR
Smothers, J.M.	Pvt	E 6th SCVI	Burkeville, VA	04/14/65	Burkeville, VA	04/17/65	Paroled	CSR
Smothers, Simon	Pvt	G 21st SCVI	Ft. Fisher, NC	01/15/65	New York, NY	01/30/65	Elmira, NY	CSR
					Elmira, NY	02/20/65	Pt. Lookout, MD Xc	P65,P66
Smothers, William	Pvt	G 21st SCVI	Town Creek, NC	02/20/65	Pt. Lookout, MD	06/19/65	Rlsd. G.O. #109	P115,P118
Smyer, G.F.	3Lt	K 5th SCVI	Wilderness, VA	05/06/64	Belle Plain, VA	05/17/64	Ft. Delaware, DE	CSR,SA3
					Ft. Delaware, DE	06/16/65	Rlsd. G.O. #109	P43,P44,P45,CSR
Smyley, John	Pvt	G 4th SCVC	Thompsons Brdg., SC	03/04/65	New Berne, NC	03/30/65	Pt. Lookout, MD	CSR
					Pt. Lookout, MD	06/25/65	Died, Ch. Diarrhea	P6,P115,P118,FPH
Smyth, Isaac	Cit	Sr.Memphis	NC Coast	07/31/62	Ft. Delaware, DE			P47

SOUTH CAROLINA SOLDIERS, SAILORS AND  CITIZENS HELD IN U.S. PRISONS 1861-1865

NAME	RANK	REGIMENT	CAPTURED AT	WHEN	PRISON	MOVED	DISPOSITION	SOURCES
Snead, Nathaniel C.V.	Pvt	F 14th SCVI	Gettysburg, PA	07/04/63	Ft. McHenry, MD	07/07/63	Ft. Delaware, DE	CSR
					Ft. Delaware, DE	07/30/63	City Pt., VA Xc	P42,CSR
Snead, Nathaniel C.V.	Pvt	F 14th SCVI	Petersburg, VA	04/03/65	City Pt., VA	04/13/65	Pt. Lookout, MD	CSR
					Pt. Lookout, MD	06/19/65	Rlsd. G.O. #109	P115,P119,CSR
Snelgrove, Carey P.	Pvt	K 20th SCVI	Cedar Creek, VA	10/19/64	Harpers Ferry, WV	10/24/64	Pt. Lookout, MD	CSR,KEB
					Pt. Lookout, MD			P115,P118,CSR
Snelgrove, F.M.	Pvt	B 14th SCVI	Gettysburg, PA	07/05/63	Gettysburg, PA	07/08/63	Died of wounds	CSR
Snelgrove, Henry	Pvt	M 7th SCVI	Sharpsburg, MD	09/17/62	Fredrick, MD USGH	10/22/62	Ft. McHenry, MD	CSR
					Ft. McHenry, MD	10/25/62	Aikens Ldg., VA Xc	CSR
Snelgrove, Luther	Pvt	B 14th SCVI	Petersburg, VA	04/03/65	City Pt., VA	04/11/65	Hart's Island, NY	CSR
					Hart's Island, NY	06/17/65	Rlsd. G.O. #109	P79,CSR
Snell, Horatio S.	Pvt	B 1st SCVIG	Gettysburg, PA	07/05/63	David's Island, NY	10/24/63	Bedloes Island, NY	P1,SA1,CSR,ANY
					Bedloes Island, NY	01/06/64	Pt. Lookout, MD Xc	P2,CSR
					Pt. Lookout, MD	03/03/64	City Pt., VA Xc	P117,CSR
Snell, Horatio S.	Pvt	B 1st SCVIG	N. Anna River, VA	05/23/64	Front Royal, VA	05/31/64	Pt. Lookout, MD	CSR
					Pt. Lookout, MD	03/14/65	Aikens Ldg., VA Xc	P113,P121,P124
Snelling, William	Pvt	I 17th SCVI	Augusta, GA	06/03/65	Augusta, GA	06/03/65	Paroled	CSR
Snibble, H.	Plt	*Huntress*	Off Charleston	01/18/63	Ft. Lafayette, NY	04/15/63	Ft. Delaware, DE	P144
Snider, George E.	Pvt	D 24th SCVI	Nashville, TN	12/16/64	Nashville, TN	12/31/64	Louisville, KY	CSR
					Louisville, KY	01/05/65	Camp Chase, OH	P92,P95,CSR
					Camp Chase, OH	06/11/65	Rlsd. G.O. #109	P23,CSR
Snider, H.J.	Pvt	A 19th SCVCB	Augusta, GA	05/25/65	Augusta, GA	05/25/65	Paroled on oath	CSR
Snider, W. Perry	Cpl	G 17th SCVI	Deserted/enemy	02/21/65	P.M. A. of P.	02/23/65	City Pt., VA P.M.	CSR
					City Pt., VA P.M.	02/24/65	Washington, DC	CSR
					Washington, DC	02/24/65	Savannah, GA oath	CSR
Snipes, Daniel	Pvt	McQueen LA	Southside RR, VA	04/02/65	City Pt., VA	04/07/65	Hart's Island, NY	CSR
					Hart's Island, NY	06/14/65	Rlsd. G.O. #109	CSR
Snipes, John	Pvt	I 17th SCVI	Petersburg, VA	03/25/65	City Pt., VA	03/27/65	Pt. Lookout, MD	CSR,LAN
					Pt. Lookout, MD	06/19/65	Rlsd. G.O. #109	P118,P122,CSR
Snipes, Nathan	Pvt	A 1st SCVIR	Morris Island, SC	09/07/63	Hilton Head, SC	10/06/63	Ft. Columbus, NY	CSR,SA1
					Ft. Columbus, NY	10/09/63	Pt. Lookout, MD	CSR
					Pt. Lookout, MD	02/15/64	Joined U.S. Army	P113,P124,P125,CSR
Snipes, Robert	Pvt	I 17th SCVI	Petersburg, VA	03/25/65	City Pt., VA	03/27/65	Pt. Lookout, MD	CSR,LAN
					Pt. Lookout, MD	06/19/65	Rlsd. G.O. #109	P115,P118,P122,CSR
Snoddy, John Crawford	Pvt	C 22nd SCVI	Petersburg, VA	06/18/64	City Pt., VA	06/24/64	Pt. Lookout,MD	CSR
					Pt. Lookout, MD	07/25/64	Elmira, NY	P113,P117,P120,FPH
					Elmira, NY	10/28/64	Died, Ch. Diarrhea	P6,P65,P66,FPH,P12
Snow, Jesse L.	Pvt	L 1st SCVIG	Southside RR, VA	04/02/65	City Pt., VA	04/07/65	Hart's Island, NY	CSR,SA1
					Hart's Island, NY	05/10/65	Died, Dbl. Pneum.	P6,P12,P79,FPH,CSR
Snyder, A.J.	Pvt	A 3rd SCVABn	High Pt., NC	05/02/65	High Pt., NC	05/02/65	Paroled	CSR
Snyder, C.A.	Pvt	A 3rd SCVABn	High Pt., NC	05/02/65	High Pt., NC	05/02/65	Paroled	CSR
Snyder, P.C.	Pvt	A 3rd SCVABn	High Pt., NC	05/02/65	High Pt., NC	05/02/65	Paroled	CSR
Soatman, John	Pvt	F 1st SCVIR	Deserted/enemy	02/20/65	Charleston, SC		Released on oath	SA1,CSR
Sompayrac, Theodore	Sgt	A 23rd SCVI	Farmville, VA	04/06/65	City Pt., VA	04/14/65	Newport News, VA	P107,CSR
					Newport News, VA	06/26/65	Rlsd. G.O. #109	P107,CSR
Son, J.D.	Pvt	H 25th SCVI	Ft. Fisher, NC	01/15/65	Pt. Lookout, MD	01/28/65	Hammond G.H., MD	P121,CSR
					Pt. Lookout, MD	06/06/65	Rlsd. Istr. 5/30/65	P121,CSR
Soseby, John H.	Pvt	D 27th SCVI	Town Creek, NC	02/20/64	Ft. Anderson, NC	02/28/65	Pt. Lookout, MD	CSR
					Pt. Lookout, MD	06/19/65	Rlsd. G.O. #109	P115,P118,CSR
Soujourner, D.E.	Pvt	I 5th SCVC	Stony Creek, VA	12/01/64	City Pt., VA	12/05/64	Pt. Lookout, MD	CSR
					Pt. Lookout, MD	06/19/65	Rlsd. G.O. #109	P115,P118,CSR
Souter, H.G.	Cpl	G 24th SCVI	Jackson, MS	05/16/63	Jackson, MS	05/16/63	Paroled	CSR

SOUTH CAROLINA SOLDIERS, SAILORS AND **S** CITIZENS HELD IN U.S. PRISONS 1861-1865

NAME	RANK	REGIMENT	CAPTURED AT	WHEN	PRISON	MOVED	DISPOSITION	SOURCES
Southerland, J.W.	Pvt	C 4th SCVC	Stony Creek, VA	12/01/64	City Pt., VA	12/05/64	Pt. Lookout, MD	CSR,CDC
					Pt. Lookout, MD	01/17/65	Aikens Ldg., VA Xc	P115,P118,P124,CSR
Southerland, M.T.	Pvt	K 2nd SCVIRi	Deserted/enemy	03/03/65	Bermuda Hundred VA	03/03/65	City Pt., VA P.M.	CSR
					City Pt., VA P.M.	03/05/65	Washington, DC P.M.	CSR
					Washington, DC	03/07/65	Bradford, PA oath	CSR
Sowell, G.R.	Pvt	B 26th SCVI	Farmville, VA	04/06/65	City Pt., VA	04/14/65	Newport News, VA	CSR
					Newport News, VA	06/26/65	Rlsd. G.O. #109	CSR
Sowell, George R.	Pvt	A 4th SCVC	Stony Creek, VA	12/01/64	City Pt., VA	12/05/64	Pt. Lookout, MD	CSR
					Pt. Lookout, MD	06/30/65	Rlsd. G.O. #109	P115,P121,CSR
Sowell, John A.	Cpl	G 2nd SCVI	Gettysburg, PA	07/05/63	Gettysburg G.H.		Provost Marshal	P4,KEB,SA2,H2
Sowell, John A.	Cpl	G 2nd SCVI	Gettysburg, PA	07/04/63	David's Island, NY	08/24/63	City Pt., VA Xc	P1,CSR
Sowell, William H.	Sgt	D 8th SCVI	Charlotte, NC	05/06/65	Charlotte, NC	05/06/65	Paroled	CSR
Sowls, John B.	Pvt	G 10th SCVI	Naomis Hill Ch., GA	06/07/64	Nashville, TN	06/17/64	Louisville, KY	P3,CSR
					Louisville, KY	06/22/64	Rock Island, IL	P90,P91,P94,CSR
					Rock Island, IL	01/24/65	Died, Pleurisy	P131,P132,FPH,CSR
Sox, Samuel	Pvt	D 15th SCMil	Lynch's Creek, SC	02/27/65	Pt. Lookout, MD			P115,P118
Spady, Southey G.	Cpl	A 27th SCVI	Weldon RR, VA	08/21/64	City Pt., VA	08/24/64	Pt. Lookout, MD	CSR,HAG
					Pt. Lookout, MD	12/08/64	Died, Ac. Diarrhea	P5,P113,P119,FPH
Spann, Henry Asbury	Pvt	F 6th SCVC	Johns Island, SC	02/09/64	Hilton Head, SC	02/28/64	Ft. Lafayette, NY	CSR,CAG
					Ft. Lafayette, NY	04/19/64	Ft. Delaware, DE	P144,CSR
					Ft. Delaware, DE	06/08/65	Released	P41,P43,P45,CSR
Sparkman, E.H.	Pvt	A 7th SCVC	Deep Bottom, VA	08/16/64	City Pt., VA	08/22/64	Pt. Lookout, MD	CSR
					Pt. Lookout, MD	03/15/65	Aikens Ldg., VA Xc	P113,P121,P124
Sparks, D.P.	Pvt	K 2nd SCVC	Catletts Stn., VA	03/30/63	Old Capitol, DC	04/13/63	City Pt., VA	CSR
					Ft.McHenry, MD	04/13/63	City Pt., VA Xc	P110
Sparks, D.P.	Pvt	K 2nd SCVC	Montgomery, AL	05/19/65	Montgomery, AL	05/19/65	Paroled	CSR
Sparks, G.C.	Pvt	A 19th SCVCB	Augusta, GA	05/22/65	Augusta, GA	05/22/65	Paroled on oath	CSR
Sparks, J.C.	Pvt	H 12th SCVI	Charlotte, NC	05/16/65	Charlotte, NC	05/16/65	Paroled	CSR
Spatcher, Robert	Plt	Huntress	Off Charleston	01/18/63	Ft. Lafayette, NY	05/23/63	Released	P144
Speake, J.L.	Pvt	D 3rd SCVIBn	Sharpsburg, MD	09/17/62	Ft. McHenry, MD	10/17/62	Fts. Monroe, VA	CSR,KEB
					Fts Monroe, VA	10/19/62	Aikens Ldg., VA Xc	CSR
Spear, B.E.	Pvt	A 3rd SCVABn	High Pt., NC	05/02/65	High Pt., NC	05/02/65	Paroled	CSR
Spear, D.R.	Pvt	A 3rd SCVABn	High Pt., NC	05/02/65	High Pt., NC	05/02/65	Paroled	CSR
Spears, Andrew S.	Cpl	B 3rd SCVI	Knoxville, TN	12/18/63	Louisville, KY	01/23/64	Rock Island, IL	P88,P94,H3,ANY,CSR
					Rock Island, IL	05/03/65	New Orleans, LA Xc	P131,H3,CSR,SA2
					New Orleans, LA	05/23/65	Exchanged	P4,CSR
Spears, George S.	Pvt	F 15th SCVI	Cedar Creek, VA	10/19/64	Harpers Ferry, WV	10/23/64	Pt. Lookout, MD	CSR,KEB,H15
					Pt. Lookout, MD	01/27/65	Hammond G.H., MD	P115,P118,P121
					Hammond G.H., MD	02/04/65	Died, Ch. Diarrhea	P6,P12,FPH,CSR
Spears, Robert S.	Pvt	D 3rd SCVIBn	South Mtn., MD	09/14/62	David's Island, NY	10/06/62	Aikens Ldg., VA Xc	CSR,KEB
Spears, William	Pvt	G 23rd SCVI	Farmville, VA	04/03/65	City Pt., VA	04/14/65	Newport News, VA	CSR
					Newport News, VA	06/26/65	Rlsd. G.O. #109	CSR
Specketer, C.	Pvt	B German LA	Deserted/enemy	10/01/64	Hilton Head, SC	10/31/64	New York, NY P.M.	CSR
Speers, E.H.	Pvt	D 7th SCVI	Gettysburg, PA	07/03/63	Ft. McHenry, MD	06/30/63	Ft. Delaware, DE	CSR,KEB
					Ft. Delaware, DE		Hos. 11/17-12/2/64	P47
					Ft. Delaware, DE		Hos. 1/20-1/30/65	P47
					Ft. Delaware, DE	06/10/65	Released	P40,P44,P45,CSR
Speers, James	Pvt	F 20th SCVI	Richmond, VA Hos.	04/03/65	Provost Marshal R	05/03/65	Paroled	CSR
Speigner, Edward	Pvt	F 25th SCVI	Ft. Fisher, NC	01/15/65	New York, NY	01/30/65	Elmira, NY	CSR,HAG
					Elmira, NY	07/07/65	Rlsd. G.O. #109	P65,P66,CSR
Speigner, Joel	Pvt	E 1st SCVC	Orangeburg, SC	02/13/65	New Berne, NC	04/03/65	Pt. Lookout, MD	CSR
					Pt. Lookout, MD	06/19/65	Rlsd. G.O. #109	P115,P118,P122,CSR

SOUTH CAROLINA SOLDIERS, SAILORS AND  CITIZENS HELD IN U.S. PRISONS 1861-1865

NAME	RANK	REGIMENT	CAPTURED AT	WHEN	PRISON	MOVED	DISPOSITION	SOURCES
Speissigger, Charles A.	Cpl	I 27th SCVI	Weldon RR, VA	08/21/64	City Pt., VA	08/24/64	Pt. Lookout, MD	CSR,HAG
					Pt. Lookout, MD	09/30/64	City Pt., VA Xc	P7,P113,P123,P125
Speissigger, Charles A.	Cpl	I 27th SCVI	Town Creek, NC	02/20/95	Ft. Anderson, NC	02/28/65	Pt. Lookout, MD	CSR
					Pt. Lookout, MD	05/14/65	Rlsd. G.O. #85	P115,P118,P122
Speissigger, W.T.	Cit	Charleston	Columbia, SC	02/17/65	Hart's Island, NY	06/20/65	Rlsd. G.O. #109	P79
Spell, Eldred	Sgt	I 11th SCVI	Petersburg, VA	06/24/64	Bermuda Hundred VA	06/25/64	Fts. Monroe, VA	CSR,HAG
					Fts. Monroe, VA	06/26/64	Pt. Lookout, MD	CSR
					Pt. Lookout, MD	08/16/64	Elmira, NY	P113,P120,CSR
					Elmira, NY	03/14/65	James R., VA Xc	P65,P66,CSR
Spell, James E.F.	Pvt	E 24th SCVI	Marietta, GA	07/03/64	Nashville, TN	07/13/64	Louisville, KY	CSR
					Louisville, KY	07/16/64	Camp Douglas, IL	P55,P90,P91,CSR
					Camp Douglas, IL	10/07/64	Died, Smallpox	P5,P12,P53,FPH,CSR
Spell, William	Pvt	I 11th SCVI	Petersburg, VA	06/16/64	Pt. Lookout, MD	09/11/64	Aikens Ldg., VA Xc	P117,CSR,HAG
					Pt. Lookout, MD	09/18/64	Exchanged	P113,P123,CSR
Spellman, Dominick	Sgt	K 1st SCVIG	Warrenton, VA	09/29/65	Warrenton, VA	09/29/62	Paroled	SA1,CSR
Spellman, Dominick	Sgt	K 1st SCVIG	Petersburg, VA	07/29/64	City Pt., VA	08/05/64	Pt. Lookout, MD	CSR
					Pt. Lookout, MD	08/08/64	Elmira, NY	P113,P117,P120,CSR
					Elmira, NY	05/17/65	Rlsd. G.O. #85	P65,P66,CSR
Spells, H.T.	Pvt	B 3rd SCVC	Adams Run, SC	04/19/65	Charleston, SC			CSR
Spelts, Robert J.	Pvt	E 3rd SCVIBn	Gettysburg, PA	07/05/63	Gettysburg, PA USH	07/20/63	Provost Marshal	P4,KEB
					David's Island, NY	09/12/63	City Pt., VA Xc	P1,CSR
Spence, James M.	Pvt	F 20th SCVI	Cedar Creek, VA	10/19/64	W. Bldg. Balt, MD	10/25/64	Pt. Lookout, MD	P4,ANY,KEB,CSR
					Pt. Lookout, MD	10/29/64	Aikens Ldg., VA Xc	P115,P118,P123
Spence, James M.	Pvt	F 20th SCVI	Cedar Creek, VA	10/19/64	Pt. Lookout, MD	10/29/64	Venus Pt., GA Xc	CSR
Spence, John D.	Pvt	C 3rd SCVI	Cedar Creek, VA	10/19/64	Winchester, VA USF	12/23/64	Frederick, MD	CSR,ANY,KEB,SA2,H3
					Frederick, MD USFH	12/30/64	Baltimore, MD	P3
					W. Bldg. Balt, MD	01/07/65	Pt. Lookout, MD	P4
					Pt. Lookout, MD	01/28/65	Hammond G.H., MD	P115,P121,CSR
					Hammond G.H., MD	03/31/65	Pt. Lookout, MD	CSR
					Pt. Lookout, MD	06/05/65	Rlsd. Instr. 5/30/65	P118,P121,CSR
Spencer, A.J.	ASr	C 3rd SCVABn	Blakely, AL	04/09/65	Ship Island, MS	04/28/65	New Orleans, LA	P136,CSR
Spencer, A.J.	ASr	C 3rd SCVABn	Blakely, AL	08/09/64	New Orleans, LA	05/01/65	Vicksburg, MS Xc	P3,CSR
Spencer, G.W.	Pvt	I 27th SCVI	Petersburg, VA	05/12/64	Pt. Lookout, MD			P117
Spencer, Jasper M.	Pvt	G 18th SCVI	Petersburg, VA	06/16/64	Bermuda Hundred VA	06/18/64	Fts. Monroe, VA	CSR
					Fts. Monroe, VA	06/20/64	Pt. Lookout, MD	CSR
					Pt. Lookout, MD	07/25/64	Elmira, NY	P113,P117,P120
					Elmira, NY	11/28/64	Died, Diarrhea	P6,P65,P66,FPH
Spencer, Jasper M.	Pvt	G 18th SCVI	Petersburg, VA	06/16/64	Pt. Lookout, MD	06/19/65	Rlsd. G.O. #109	P122,CSR
Spencer, John R.	Cpl	C 16th SCVI	Franklin, TN	12/18/64	Nashville, TN	01/11/65	Louisville, KY	P4,P39,16R,CSR
					Louisville, KY	01/14/65	Camp Chase, OH	P92,P95,CSR
					Camp Chase, OH	06/11/65	Rlsd. G.O. #109	P23,CSR
Spencer, Robert	Pvt	C 2nd SCVIRi	Warrenton, VA	09/29/62	Warrenton, VA	09/29/62	Paroled	CSR
Spencer, S.H.	Pvt	A 4th SCVC	Raleigh, NC	04/13/65	Raleigh, NC	04/13/64	Paroled	CSR
Spencer, Spencer G.	Pvt	Ham.Leg.MI	Deserted/enemy	03/08/65	Bermuda Hundred VA	03/10/65	City Pt., VA	CSR
					City Pt., VA	03/13/65	Washington, DC	CSR
Spencer, Thomas M.	Pvt	B 12th SCVI	Wilderness, VA	05/05/64	Belle Plain, VA	05/20/64	Ft. Delaware, DE	CSR,YEB
					Ft. Delaware, DE		Hos. 7/23-?	P47
					Ft. Delaware, DE	06/10/65	Released	P41,P43,P45,CSR
Spencer, William T.	Pvt	C 16th SCVI	Nashville, TN	12/16/64	Nashville, TN	12/19/64	Louisville, TN	CSR,16R
					Louisville, KY	12/21/64	Camp Douglas, IL	P95,CSR
					Camp Douglas, IL	03/24/65	Jd. 6th US Vols.	CSR
Spenken, H.	Pvt	B German LA	Deserted/enemy	10/01/64	Hilton Head, SC	10/31/64	New York, NY P.M.	CSR

SOUTH CAROLINA SOLDIERS, SAILORS AND  CITIZENS HELD IN U.S. PRISONS 1861-1865

NAME	RANK	REGIMENT	CAPTURED AT	WHEN	PRISON	MOVED	DISPOSITION	SOURCES
Sperry, D.A.	Pvt	Waccanaw A	Santee River, SC	02/27/63	Ft. McHenry, MD			P145
					Gunboat *Quaker Cit*	03/16/63	New York, NY P.M.	CSR
					Sandusky, OH	04/06/63	Fts. Monroe, VA Xc	CSR
Spicer, James	Pvt	D 19th SCVI	Selma, AL	06/15/65	Selma, AL	06/15/65	Paroled	CSR
Spiers, Simpson	Pvt	G 26th SCVI	Petersburg, VA	03/25/65	City Pt., VA	03/27/65	Pt. Lookout, MD	CSR
					Pt. Lookout, MD	06/19/65	Rlsd. G.O. #109	P115,P118,P122,CSR
Spillers, William F.	Pvt	K 2nd SCVI	Loudon, TN	12/03/63	Chattanooga, TN Hosp.	02/15/64	Nashville, TN	P1,KEB,SA2,H2
Spillers, William F.	Pvt	K 2nd SCVI	Loudon, TN	10/23/63	Nashville, TN	02/20/64	Louisville, KY	P39,CSR
					Louisville, KY	03/09/64	Camp Chase, OH	P88,P94,CSR
Spillers, William F.	Pvt	K 2nd SCVI	Loudon, TN	12/03/63	Camp Chase, OH	03/14/64	Ft. Delaware, DE	P22,P26,CSR
					Ft. Delaware, DE	04/30/64	Died, Lung Inflam.	P5,P41,P42,P47,FPH
Spinks, J.M.	Pvt	C 3rd SCVABn	Blakely, AL	04/09/65	Ship Island, MS	05/01/65	Vicksburg, MS Xc	P136,CSR
Spires, James H.	Pvt	H 20th SCVI	Lexington, SC	02/14/65	New Berne, NC	03/30/65	Pt. Lookout, MD	CSR,KEB
					Pt. Lookout, MD	05/13/65	Rlsd. G.O. #85	P115,CSR
Spires, William A.	Pvt	H 20th SCVI	Lexington, SC	02/14/65	New Berne, NC	03/03/65	Pt. Lookout MD	CSR,KEB
					Pt. Lookout, MD	05/15/65	Released G.O.#85	P115,P121,CSR
Spivey, W.L.	Pvt	D Ham.Leg.MI	Deserted/enemy	04/12/65	City Pt., VA P.M.	04/12/65	Washington, DC	CSR
					Washington, DC	04/12/65	Philadelphia, PA	CSR
Spradley, Benjamin F.	Pvt	F P.S.S.	Knoxville, TN	12/05/63	Nashville, TN	01/24/64	Louisville, KY	P39,TSE,CSR
					Louisville, KY	01/27/64	Rock Island, IL	P88,P94,CSR
					Rock Island, IL	03/14/64	Died, Variola	P5,P131,P132,FPH
Sprague, Henry	Pvt	K 6th SCVC	Deserted/enemy	03/06/65	Hilton Head, SC	03/06/65	Str. *Fulton* to NY	CSR
Spraler, Edward C.	Pvt	H 20th SCVI	Lexington, SC	02/14/65	New Berne, NC	03/30/65	Pt. Lookout, MD	CSR,KEB
Spraler, Edward E.	Pvt	H 20th SCVI	Lexington, SC	02/14/65	Pt. Lookout, MD	06/19/65	Rlsd. G.O. #109	P115,P122,CSR
Spraler, John J.	Pvt	H 20th SCVI	Lexington, SC	02/24/65	New Berne, NC	03/30/65	Pt. Lookout, MD	CSR
					Pt. Lookout, MD	06/19/65	Rlsd. G.O. #109	P115,KEB,CSR
Sprawls, J.H.	Pvt	H 2nd SCVC	Augusta, GA	05/19/65	Augusta, GA	05/19/65	Paroled	CSR
Sprawls, John F.	Sgt	A 1st SCVIG	Gettysburg, PA	07/01/63	David's Island, NY	07/25/63	Died of wounds	P1,P6,FPH,SA1,CSR
Spriggs, W.L.	Pvt	A 2nd SCVIRi	Charlestown, VA	10/16/62	Ft. McHenry, MD	10/25/62	Aikens Ldg., VA Xc	CSR
					Harpers Ferry, WV	10/26/62	Not given	CSR
Springer, Rudolph	Sgt	D 15th SCVI	Barnsville, MD	09/10/62	Washington, DC PM	09/27/62	Aikens Ldg., VA Xc	H15,CSR,KEB
Springs, William	Pvt	A 21st SCVI	Ft. Fisher, NC	01/15/65	Elmira, NY	02/19/65	Died, Ch. Diarrhea	P6,P12,P65,P66,FPH
Sprouse, Anderson	Pvt	I 5th SCVI	Deep Bottom, VA	08/14/64	Camp Hamilton, VA	11/13/64	Took oath	SA3,CSR
					Fts. Monroe, VA GH	11/23/64	Camp Hamilton, VA	P8,CSR
Sprouse, H.H.	Pvt	A 6th SCVC	Stony Creek, VA	12/01/64	Pt. Lookout, MD	04/15/65	Died, Ch. Diarrhea	P6,P115,P118,FPH
Sprouse, John	Pvt	C 17th SCVI	Deserted/enemy	02/23/65	P.M. 9th A.C A.of	02/23/65	City Pt., VA P.M.	CSR
					City Pt., VA P.M.	02/24/65	Washington, DC	CSR
					Washington, DC	02/24/65	Danville, PA oath	CSR
Sprouse, W.F.	Pvt	K Ham.Leg.MI	Deserted/enemy	02/27/65	Bermuda Hundred VA	02/28/65	City Pt., VA P.M.	CSR
					City Pt., VA	03/01/65	Washington, DC	CSR
					Washington, DC	03/02/65	Springfield, IL	CSR
Squier, John C.	Pvt	C 1st SCVIG	Sutherland Stn., VA	04/03/65	Pt. Lookout, MD	06/08/65	Rlsd. on oath	P119,P121,SA1,CSR
Stabler, D.V.	Pvt	D 20th SCVI	Cedar Creek, VA	10/19/64	Pt. Lookout, MD	01/20/65	Died, Interm. fever	P6,P12,P115,P118,FPH
					Harpers Ferry, WV	10/24/64	Pt. Lookout, MD	CSR
Stabler, Madison	Pvt	D 20th SCVI	Cedar Creek, VA	10/19/64	W. Bldg. Balt, MD	10/27/64	Pt. Lookout, MD	P4,P123,KEB,CSR
					Pt. Lookout, MD	10/29/64	Aikens Ldg., VA Xc	P115,P118,P123,CSR
Stacey, James Franklin	Pvt	F 6th SCVC	Ream's Stn., VA	08/23/64	City Pt., VA	08/26/64	Harewood Hos., DC	CSR
					Harewood Hos., DC	10/25/64	Lincoln G.H., DC	CSR
					Lincoln G.H., DC	03/01/65	Old Capitol, DC	CSR
					Old Capitol, DC	08/23/65	Elmira, NY	P110,CSR
					Elmira, NY	06/21/65	Rlsd. G.O. #109	P65,P66,CSR

SOUTH CAROLINA SOLDIERS, SAILORS AND  CITIZENS HELD IN U.S. PRISONS 1861-1865

NAME	RANK	REGIMENT	CAPTURED AT	WHEN	PRISON	MOVED	DISPOSITION	SOURCES
Stacey, R.M.	Pvt	K 18th SCVI	Crater, Pbg., VA	07/30/64	City Pt., VA	08/05/64	Pt. Lookout, MD	CSR
					Pt. Lookout, MD	08/08/64	Elmira, NY	P113,P117,P120
					Elmira, NY	10/11/64	Pt. Lookout, MD Xc	P65,P66
					Pt. Lookout, MD	11/10/64	Died, Ch. Diarrhea	P5,P12,P115,FPH
Stack, James	Pvt	C 27th SCVI	Deserted/enemy	07/10/64	Bermuda Hundred VA	07/11/64	Fts. Monroe, VA	CSR,HAG
					Fts. Monroe, VA	07/17/64	Washington, DC	P8,HAG
Stack, Samuel	Pvt	A 18th SCVI	Petersburg, VA	03/25/65	City Pt., VA	03/28/65	Pt. Lookout, MD	CSR,UD5
					Pt. Lookout, MD	06/19/65	Rlsd. G.O. #109	P115,P118,CSR
Stack, William H.	1Lt	C 2nd SCVC	Hedgeville, VA	10/20/62	Ft. McHenry, MD	10/25/62	Aikens Ldg., VA Xc	CSR
Stackhouse, John W.	Pvt	E 4th SCVC	Louisa C.H., VA	06/11/64	Fts. Monroe, VA	06/20/64	Pt. Lookout, MD	CSR,HOM
					Pt. Lookout, MD	07/08/64	Elmira, NY	P111,P120,CSR
					Elmira, NY	09/19/64	Died, Diarrhea	P5,P65,P66,FPH,CSR
Stacy, D.H.	Pvt	F Hol.Leg.	Jarratts Stn., VA	05/08/64	Fts. Monroe, VA	05/13/64	Pt. Lookout, MD	CSR
					Pt. Lookout, MD	08/15/64	Elmira, NY	P113,P117,P120
					Elmira, NY	02/20/65	James R., VA Xc	P65,P66,CSR
Stacy, D.H.	Pvt	F Hol.Leg.	Jarratts Stn., VA	05/08/64	Richmond, VA Hos.	02/28/65	No disposition Fd.	CSR
Stacy, Samuel	1Sg	K 18th SCVI	Burkesville, VA	04/06/65	City Pt., VA		Baltimore, MD	CSR
					W. Bldg. Balt, MD	05/09/65	Ft. McHenry, MD	P4,CSR
					Ft. McHenry, MD	06/10/65	Rlsd. G.O. #109	P96,CSR
Stacy, W.R.	Pvt	K 18th SCVI	Crater, Pbg., VA	07/30/64	City Pt., VA	08/05/64	Pt. Lookout, MD	CSR
					Pt. Lookout, MD	08/08/64	Elmira, NY	P113,P117,P120,CSR
					Elmira, NY	03/07/65	Died, Variola	P6,P12,P65,CSR
Staggs, William Jackson	Sgt	F 13th SCVI	Hatchers Run, VA	03/31/65	City Pt., VA	04/02/65	Pt. Lookout, VA	CSR,HOS
					Pt. Lookout, MD	06/19/65	Rlsd. G.O. #109	P115,P118,CSR
Staley, D.N.	Pvt	H Ham.Leg.MI	Harpers Farm, VA	04/06/65	City Pt., VA	04/23/65	Newport News, VA	CSR
					Newport News, VA	06/26/65	Rlsd. G.O. #109	CSR
Staley, J.H.	Sgt	H Ham.Leg.MI	Deserted/enemy	03/25/65	Bermuda Hundred VA	03/27/65	City Pt., VA P.M.	CSR
					City Pt., VA	03/29/65	Washington, DC	CSR
					Washington, DC	03/30/65	Philadelphia, PA	CSR
Staley, John L.	Pvt	Ham.Leg.MI		04/22/65	Newport News, VA		Oath not given	CSR
Stallings, Silas	Pvt	D Hol.Leg.	Winchester, VA	10/04/62	Winchester, VA	10/04/62	Paroled in Hos.	CSR
Stallins, W.F.	Pvt	E 18th SCVAB	Rockingham, NC	03/08/65	New Berne, NC	04/10/65	Hart's Island, NY	CSR
					Hart's Island, NY	06/16/65	Rlsd. G.O. #109	CSR
Stalnaker, Benjamin F.	Pvt	H 7th SCVIBn	Drury's Bluff, VA	05/16/64	Bermuda Hundred VA	05/17/64	Fts. Monroe, VA	CSR,HAG
					Fts. Monroe, VA	05/18/64	Pt. Lookout, MD	CSR
					Pt. Lookout, MD	09/15/64	Elmira, NY	P113,P117,P120,CSR
					Elmira, NY	10/09/64	Died, Diarrhea	P5,P12,P65,P66,FPH
Stalnaker, J.W.	Pvt	K 7th SCVI	Sharpsburg, MD	09/17/62	Fredrick, MD USGH	10/13/62	Ft. McHenry, MD	CSR
					Ft. McHenry, MD	10/14/62	Aikens Ldg., VA Xc	CSR
Stalnaker, R.	Pvt	H 7th SCVIBn	Drury's Bluff, VA	05/16/64	Bermuda Hundred VA	05/17/64	Fts. Monroe, VA	CSR,HAG
					Fts. Monroe, VA	05/18/64	Pt. Lookout, MD	CSR
					Pt. Lookout, MD	06/04/64	Died	P6,P113,P117,P119
Stalvey, A.	Pvt	F 7th SCVC	Richmond, VA Hos.	04/03/65	Richmond, VA Hos.	04/14/65	Richmond, VA P.M.	CSR
					Libby Prsn., Rchmd	04/23/65	Newport News, VA	CSR
					Newport News, VA	05/30/65	Died, Ch. Diarrhea	P6,CSR
Stalvey, A.J.	Pvt	E 26th SCVI	Deserted/enemy	01/24/65	City Point, VA	02/07/65	Washington, DC	P8,CSR
					Washington, DC	02/10/65	Pittsburg, PA oath	CSR
Stancel, Eli	Pvt	Ferguson's LA	Salisbury, NC	04/12/65	Nashville, TN	04/29/65	Louisville, KY	P39,CSR
					Louisville, KY	05/02/65	Camp Chase, OH	P92,P95,CSR
					Camp Chase, OH	06/13/65	Rlsd. G.O.#109	P23,CSR
Stancel, James E.	Pvt	Ferguson's LA	Ringgold, GA	11/27/63	Nashville, TN	12/09/63	Louisville, KY	P39,CSR
					Louisville, KY	12/11/63	Rock Island, IL	P89

SOUTH CAROLINA SOLDIERS, SAILORS AND  CITIZENS HELD IN U.S. PRISONS 1861-1865

NAME	RANK	REGIMENT	CAPTURED AT	WHEN	PRISON	MOVED	DISPOSITION	SOURCES
Stancel, Joseph A.	Pvt	Ferguson's LA	Ringgold, GA	11/27/63	Nashville, TN	12/09/63	Louisville, KY	CSR
					Louisville, KY	12/11/63	Rock Island, IL	P88,CSR
					Rock Island, IL	12/19/63	Died, Pneumonia	P5,P131,P132,FPH
Stancell, John G.	Pvt	1st SCMil.	North Carolina	04/25/65	Foster G.H.NewBern	04/30/65	Died, Lung Inflam.	P1,P6,P12,WAT
Stancil, J.	Sgt	C 8th SCVI	Gettysburg, PA	07/04/63	Letterman G.H. Gbg	07/17/63	Died resctd. L. shld.	P1,P12,KEB,CSR
Stancil, L.M.	Pvt	F 22nd SCVI	Kinston, NC	12/15/62	Kinston, NC	12/15/62	Paroled POW	CSR
Stancil, L.M.	Pvt	F 22nd SCVI	Bermuda Hundred, VA	06/02/64	Bermuda Hundred VA	06/03/64	Fts. Monroe, VA	CSR
					Fts. Monroe, VA	06/04/64	Pt. Lookout, MD	CSR
					Pt. Lookout, MD	02/06/65	Died acute diarhea	P6,P113,P119,FPH
Stancil, W.H.	Pvt	H 12th SCVI	Sharpsburg, MD	07/30/62	Ft. McHenry, MD	10/27/62	Fts. Monroe, VA Xc	CSR
Stanley, Benjamin J.	Pvt	D 11th SCVI	Town Creek, NC	02/20/65	Ft. Anderson, NC	02/28/65	Pt. Lookout, MD	CSR,HAG
					Pt. Lookout, MD	06/06/65	Rlsd. Inst. 5/30/65	P115,P118,P122
Stanley, George E.	Pvt	D 11th SCVI	Town Creek, NC	02/20/65	Ft. Anderson, NC	02/28/65	Pt. Lookout, MD	CSR,HAG
					Pt. Lookout, MD	06/19/65	Rlsd. G.O. #109	P115,P118,CSR
Stanley, James H.	Pvt	C 11th SCVI	Town Creek, NC	02/20/65	Ft. Anderson, NC	02/28/65	Pt. Lookout, MD	CSR
					Pt. Lookout, MD	06/12/65	Released	P115,P121,P122,HAG
Stanley, James J.	Pvt	B 15th SCVAB	Fayetteville, NC	03/16/65	New Berne, NC	03/30/65	Pt. Lookout, MD	CSR
					Pt. Lookout, MD	06/19/65	Rlsd. G.O. #109	P115,P118,CSR
Stanley, Joseph	Pvt	D 11th SCVI	Town Creek, NC	02/20/65	Ft. Anderson, NC	02/28/65	Pt. Lookout, MD	CSR
					Pt. Lookout, MD	06/19/65	Rlsd. G.O. #109	P115,P118,P122,CSR
Stanley, Thomas	Pvt	D 11th SCVI	Town Creek, NC	02/20/65	Ft. Anderson, NC	02/28/65	Pt. Lookout, MD	CSR,HAG
					Pt. Lookout, MD	06/19/65	Rlsd. G.O. #109	P115,P118,CSR
Stanridge, Samuel	Pvt	G 12th SCVI	Petersburg, VA	04/02/65	City Pt., VA	04/04/65	Pt. Lookout, MD	CSR,HAG
					Pt. Lookout, MD	06/19/65	Rlsd. G.O. #109	P115,P118,P122,CSR
Stanton, Andrew	Pvt	C 27th SCVI	Town Creek, NC	02/20/65	Ft. Anderson, NC	02/28/65	Pt. Lookout, MD	CSR,HAG
					Pt. Lookout, MD	05/14/65	Washington, DC	P115,P118,P122,CSR
					Old Capitol, DC	05/16/65	Memphis, TN oath	CSR
Stanton, Milton B.	Pvt	B 24th SCVI	Franklin, TN	12/18/64	Nashville, TN	01/17/65	Louisville, KY	P4,P39,HOM,CSR
					Louisville, KY	01/18/65	Camp Chase, OH	P92,P95,CSR
					Camp Chase, OH	06/13/65	Died, Diarrhea	P6,P12,P23,P17,FPH
Stanton, Noah	Pvt	B 24th SCVI	Jonesboro, GA	09/01/64	Rough & Ready, GA	09/19/64	Exchanged	CSR
Stanton, R.E.	2Lt	G 17th SCVI	Warrenton, VA	09/29/62	Warrenton, VA	09/29/62	Paroled	CSR
Stark, T. Lamar	Pvt	I 2nd SCVC	Fredericksburg, VA	05/03/63	Old Capitol, VA	05/07/63	Ft. Delaware, DE	CSR
					Ft. Delaware, DE	05/23/64	City Pt., VA Xc	CSR
Starnes, J.G.	Sgt	C 17th SCVI	Crater, Pbg., VA	07/30/64	City Pt., VA	08/05/64	Pt. Lookout, MD	CSR
					Pt. Lookout, MD	08/08/64	Elmira, NY	P113,P117,P120,CSR
					Elmira, NY	10/11/64	Pt. Lookout, MD Xc	P65,P66,CSR
					W. Bldg. Balt, MD	01/07/65	Pt. Lookout, MD	P4
					Pt. Lookout, MD	01/28/65	Hammond G.H., MD	P115,P118,P121,CSR
					Pt. Lookout, MD	06/05/65	Rlsd. Instr. 5/30/65	CSR
Starr, William S.	Pvt	A 17th SCVI	Hatchers Run, VA	03/25/65	City Pt., VA	03/28/65	Pt. Lookout, MD	CSR,P118
					Pt. Lookout, MD	06/20/65	Rlsd. G.O. #109	P115,P121,CSR
Staton, William	Pvt	F 13th SCVI	Deserted/enemy	02/24/65	City Pt., VA	02/26/65	Washington, DC	CSR
					Washington, DC	02/27/65	Springfield IL	CSR
Stay, W.P.	Pvt	E 25th SCVI	Ft. Fisher, NC	01/15/65	New York, NY	01/30/65	Elmira, NY	CSR,HAG
					Elmira, NY	07/13/65	Rlsd. G.O. #109	P65,P66,CSR
Steading, G.F.	Cpl	D P.S.S.	Richmond, VA area	10/07/64	Point O Rocks Hos.	10/15/64	Died of wound	CSR
Steadman, Edward	Pvt	A 17th SCVI	Petersburg, VA	03/25/65	City Pt., VA	03/28/65	Pt. Lookout, MD	CSR,HHC
					Pt. Lookout, MD	06/19/65	Rlsd. G.O. #109	P115,P118,P122,CSR
Steadman, J.T.	Pvt	A 17th SCVI	Richmond, VA Hos.	04/03/65	Richmond, VA P.M.	04/29/65	Paroled	CSR
					Richmond, VA P.M.	05/04/65	Escaped from hos.	CSR
Steadman, L.B.	Pvt	H 4th SCVI	Chester, SC	05/05/65	Chester, SC	05/05/65	Paroled	CSR

SOUTH CAROLINA SOLDIERS, SAILORS AND  CITIZENS HELD IN U.S. PRISONS 1861-1865

NAME	RANK	REGIMENT	CAPTURED AT	WHEN	PRISON	MOVED	DISPOSITION	SOURCES
Steedman, James B.	Sgt	L 1st SCVIG	Gettysburg, PA	07/05/63	Ft. Delaware, DE	12/18/63	Died, Apoplexy	P40,P47,P144,FPH
Steedman, Jonathan E.	1Lt	H 14th SCVI	Appomattox R., VA	04/03/65	Old Capitol, DC	04/21/65	Johnson's Isl., OH	CSR
					Johnsons Isl, OH	06/20/65	Rlsd. G.O. #109	P81,P82,P83
Steel, Isaiah	Pvt	K 13th SCVI	Petersburg, VA	04/02/65	City Pt., VA	04/04/65	Ft. Delaware, DE	CSR
					Ft. Delaware, DE	06/10/65	Rlsd. G.O.#109	P41,P43,P45,CSR
Steele, J.F.	Cpt	D 17th SCVI	Virginia	04/11/65	Field Hos. 24th AC	04/13/65	US Gen. Hos.	CSR
Steele, J.J.	Pvt	A 23rd SCVI	Richmond, VA Hos.	04/09/65	Pt. Lookout, MD	07/19/65	Rlsd. G.O. #109	P119,P121,CSR
Steele, John G.	Pvt	H 1st SCVC	Beverly Ford, VA	06/09/63	Ft.McHenry, MD	06/25/63	City Pt., VA Xc	P110,YEB,CSR
Steele, John M.	Cpl	H 12th SCVI	Sutherland Stn., VA	04/03/65	City Pt., VA	04/13/65	Pt. Lookout, MD	CSR
					Pt. Lookout, MD	06/19/65	Rlsd. G.O. #109	CSR
Steele, Joseph N.	SMj	12th SCVI	Charlotte, NC	05/16/65	Charlotte, NC	05/16/65	Paroled	CSR
Steele, W.M.	Cpl	H 12th SCVI	Sutherland Stn., VA	04/03/65	Pt. Lookout, MD	06/19/65	Rlsd. G.O. #109	P115,P119,YEB
Steele, William A.	Sgt	H 12th SCVI	Sutherland Stn., VA	04/03/65	City Pt., VA	04/13/65	Pt. Lookout, MD	CSR,YEB
					Pt. Lookout, MD	06/19/65	Rlsd. G.O. #109	P115,P119,CSR
Steen, Allen	Pvt	F 21st SCVI	Ft. Fisher, NC	01/15/65	Elmira, NY	02/17/65	Died, Pneumonia	P6,P12,P65,P66,FPH
Steen, F. Pinckney	Pvt	F 26th SCVI	Petersburg, VA	03/25/65	City Pt., VA	03/28/65	Pt. Lookout, MD	CSR
					Pt. Lookout, MD	06/19/65	Rlsd. G.O. #109	P115,P118,P122,CSR
Steen, James B.	Pvt	H Orr's Ri.	Spotsylvania, VA	05/12/64	Old Capitol, DC	06/15/64	Ft. Delaware, DE	CSR,HMC,CDC
					Ft. Delaware, DE	01/20/65	Hos. 1/20-1/24/65	P45,P47
					Ft. Delaware, DE	06/10/65	Released	P41,P43,CSR
Steen, John	Pvt	Post Gd.	Chesterfield, SC	02/21/65	Pt. Lookout, MD	06/19/65	Rlsd. G.O. #109	P115,P121
Steen, John E.	Pvt	F 26th SCVI	Petersburg, VA	03/25/65	City Pt., VA	03/28/65	Pt. Lookout, MD	CSR
					Pt. Lookout, MD	06/19/65	Rlsd. G.O. #109	P115,P118,P122,CSR
Steers, Thomas	Mct	Huntress	Off Charleston	01/18/63	Ft. Lafayette, NY	04/29/63	Released on oath	P144
Stegall, G.W.	Pvt	D 6th SCVC	Stony Creek, VA	12/01/64	City Pt., VA	12/04/64	Pt. Lookout, MD	CSR
					Pt. Lookout, MD	06/19/65	Rlsd. G.O. #109	P115,P118,CSR
Stegin, J.H.	Sgt	D 27th SCVI	Weldon RR, VA	08/21/64	City Pt., VA	08/24/64	Pt. Lookout, MD	CSR,HAG
					Pt. Lookout, MD	03/15/65	Aikens Ldg., VA Xc	P113,P121,P124
Steinke, F.	Pvt	A German LA	Deserted/enemy	03/31/65	Savannah, GA	03/31/65	Charleston on oath	CSR
Steinmeyer, A.B.	Pvt	Brooks LA	Harpers Farm, VA	04/06/65	City Pt., VA	04/14/65	Pt. Lookout, MD	CSR
					Pt. Lookout, MD	06/19/65	Rlsd. G.O. #109	CSR
Steinmeyer, John H., Jr.	Cpt	A 24th SCVI	Taylors Ridge, GA	10/16/64	Nashville, TN	10/23/64	Louisville, KY	CSR
					Louisville, KY	10/26/64	Johnson's Isl., OH	P90,P91,P94,CSR
					Johnson's Isl., OH	06/16/65	Rlsd. G.O. #109	P81,P82,CSR
Stephens, A.C.	Pvt	D Ham.Leg.MI	Farmville, VA	04/11/65	Farmville, VA	04/11/65	Paroled	CSR
Stephens, Enoch	Pvt	A Hol.Leg.	Warrenton, VA	09/29/62	Warrenton, VA	09/29/62	Paroled in Hos.	CSR,HOS
Stephens, George	Pvt	B 7th SCVI	Deserted/enemy	09/08/64	Chambersburg, PA	09/23/64	Ft. Mifflin, PA	CSR
					Ft. Mifflin, PA	10/31/64	Rlsd. on oath	P2,CSR
Stephens, James E.	Pvt	F 21st SCVI	Ft. Fisher, NC	01/15/65	New York, NY	01/30/65	Elmira, NY	P65,P66,HAG,HOM
					Elmira, NY	02/23/65	Died, Pneumonia	P6,P12,P65,P66,FPH
Stephens, John Asa	Pvt	K 14th SCVI	Spotsylvania, VA	05/12/64	Belle Plain, VA	05/21/64	Ft. Delaware, DE	CSR,HOE
					Ft. Delaware, DE	06/21/65	Rlsd. G.O. #109	P41,P43,P45,CSR
Stephens, Reuben	Pvt	F 21st SCVI	Morris Island, SC	07/10/63	Pt. Lookout, MD	11/15/63	Hammond G.H., MD	P113,P121,HAG
					Hammond G.H., MD	02/23/64	Died, Pneumonia	P5,P12,FPH
Stephens, S. Perry	Pvt	G 27th SCVI	Petersburg, VA	06/24/64	Bermuda Hundred VA	06/25/64	Fts. Monroe, VA	CSR
					Fts. Monroe, VA	06/26/64	Pt. Lookout, MD	CSR
					Pt. Lookout, MD	08/16/64	Elmira, NY	P113,P117,P120,CSR
					Elmira, NY	02/19/65	Died, Edema	P6,P12,P65,P66,FPH
Stepp, John	Pvt	I 16th SCVI	Ringgold, GA	11/26/63	Nashville, TN	12/09/63	Louisville, KY	P39,CSR
					Louisville, KY	12/11/63	Rock Island, IL	P88,P89,CSR
					Rock Island, IL	02/04/64	Died, Ch. Diarrhea	P5,P131,P132,FPH
Stepp, John C.	Pvt	I 5th SCVC	Deserted/enemy		Chattanooga	04/02/64		P8,CSR

SOUTH CAROLINA SOLDIERS, SAILORS AND  CITIZENS HELD IN U.S. PRISONS 1861-1865

NAME	RANK	REGIMENT	CAPTURED AT	WHEN	PRISON	MOVED	DISPOSITION	SOURCES
Sterling, G. Pinckney	Pvt	B 3rd SCVI	Hanover Jctn., VA	05/25/64	White House, VA	06/08/64	Pt. Lookout, MD	CSR,ANY,KEB,SA2,H3
					Pt. Lookout, MD	07/08/64	Elmira, NY	P17,P113,P120
					Elmira, NY	03/11/65	Died, Pneumonia	P6,P12,P65,P66FPH
Stevens, A.S.	Pvt	D 7th SCVC	Columbia, VA	03/11/65	White House, VA	03/19/65	Fts. Monroe, VA	CSR
					Fts. Monroe, VA	03/25/65	Pt. Lookout, MD	CSR
					Pt. Lookout, MD	06/19/65	Rlsd. G.O. #109	P115,P122,CSR
Stevens, H.H.	2Lt	Jenkins St			Ft. Delaware, DE	03/08/65	Discharged	P47
Stevens, Joseph W.	Pvt	C 3rd SCVABn	Blakely, AL	04/09/65	Ship Island, MS	05/01/65	Vicksburg, MS Xc	P136,CSR
Stevens, Reuben	Pvt	A 1st SCVIR	Morris Island, SC	07/10/63	Ft. Columbus NY	09/23/63	Rlsd. on oath	P1,CSR
Stevens, Simeon	Pvt	I Hol.Leg.	Petersburg, VA	11/05/64	City Pt., VA	11/11/64	Washington, DC	CSR
					Pt. Lookout, MD	12/04/64	Died	P5,P12,P115,P119,FPH
Stevens, W.H.	Pvt	F 2nd SCVIRi	Burkeville, VA	04/14/65	Burkeville, VA	04/17/65	Paroled	CSR
Stevens, Wesley C.	Pvt	SC Militia N.	Carolina	03/29/65	New Berne, NC USGH	04/01/65	Died Ch. Diarrhea	P1,P6,P12,WAT
Stevens, William	Pvt	I 1st SCVA	Morris Island, SC	07/10/63	Hilton Head, SC	09/19/63	Ft. Columbus, NY	P1,CSR
					Ft. Columbus, NY	09/23/63	Took the oath	P1,CSR
					Pt. Lookout, MD	01/25/64	Joined U.S. Army	P113,CSR
Stevens, William	Pvt	H 8th SCVI	Bermuda Hundred, VA	05/19/64	Fts. Monroe, VA	06/02/64	Oath of amnesty	P8,CSR
Stevenson, Andrew T.	Pvt	F 24th SCVI	Ringgold, GA	11/26/63	Nashville, TN	12/11/63	Louisville, KY	P39,CSR,EFW
					Louisville, KY	12/12/63	Rock Island, IL	P89,CSR
					Rock Island, IL	01/07/64	Died	P5,P131,P132,FPH
Stevenson, H.T.	Pvt	C Hol.Leg.	Deserted/enemy	11/27/64	City Pt., VA	11/28/64	Washington, DC	CSR
					Washington, DC	12/01/64	Alexandria, VA	CSR
Stevenson, Hugh	Pvt	D 12th SCVI	Southside RR, VA	04/02/65	City Pt., VA	04/07/65	Hart's Island, NY	CSR
					Hart's Island, NY	06/15/65	Rlsd. G.O. #109	P79,CSR
Stevenson, J.E.	Pvt	F Hol.Leg.	Jarratts Stn., VA	05/08/64	Fts. Monroe, VA	05/13/64	Pt. Lookout, MD	CSR
					Pt. Lookout, MD	08/15/64	Elmira, NY	P113,P117,P120,CSR
Stevenson, J.E.	Pvt	F Hol.Leg.	Jarratts Stn., VA	05/08/64	Elmira, NY	02/28/65	Died, Ch. Diarrhea	P6,P12,P65,P66,FPH
Stevenson, James C.	Pvt	I 2nd SCVA	Cheraw, SC	03/02/65	New Berne, NC	04/03/65	Pt. Lookout, MD	CSR
					Pt. Lookout, MD	06/19/65	Rlsd. G.O. #109	P115,P118,CSR
Stevenson, James E.	Pvt	K 7th SCVC	Farmville, VA	04/06/65	City Pt., VA	04/15/65	Pt. Lookout, MD	CSR,HIC
					Pt. Lookout, MD	06/19/65	Rlsd. G.O. #109	P119,CSR
Stevenson, James W.	Pvt	D Orr's Ri.	Warrenton, VA	09/29/62	Warrenton, VA	09/29/62	Paroled	CSR
Stevenson, James W.	Pvt	D Orr's Ri.	Petersburg, VA	04/03/65	City Pt., VA	04/11/65	Hart's Island, NY	CSR
					Hart's Island, NY	06/16/65	Rlsd. G.O. #109	P79,CSR
Stevenson, John A.	Pvt	F 24th SCVI	Nashville, TN	12/16/64	Nashville, TN	12/31/64	Louisville, KY	CSR
					Louisville, KY	01/02/65	Camp Douglas, IL	P92,P95,CSR
					Camp Chase, OH	06/12/65	Rlsd. G.O. #109	P23,CSR
Stevenson, Thomas A.	Pvt	F 24th SCVI	Nashville, TN	12/16/64	Nashville, TN	12/31/64	Louisville, KY	CSR
					Louisville, KY	01/02/65	Camp Douglas, IL	P92,P95,CSR
					Camp Chase, OH	06/12/65	Rlsd. G.O. #109	P23,CSR
Stevenson, Thomas Dean	Pvt	F 24th SCVI	Taylors Ridge, GA	10/14/64	Nashville, TN	10/23/64	Louisville, KY	CSR
					Louisville, KY	10/27/64	Camp Douglas, IL	P90,P91,CSR
					Camp Douglas, IL	06/17/65	Rlsd. G.O. #109	P53,CSR
Stevenson, W.G.	Cpt	I 17th SCVI	Virginia	04/11/65	Field Hos. 24th AC	04/13/65	US Gen. Hos.	CSR
Steward, J.W.	Cpl	E 6th SCResB	Augusta, SC	05/20/65	Augusta, GA	05/20/65	Paroled	CSR
Steward, William N.	Pvt	H 18th SCVI	Petersburg, VA	04/02/65	Newport News, VA	06/13/65	Released	P107,YEB
Stewart, A.	Pvt	F 22nd SCVI	Deserted/enemy	01/07/65	Knoxville, TN	01/10/65	Chattanooga, TN	CSR
Stewart, Alexander	CSg	E 1st SCVIR	Smiths Ford, NC	03/16/65	New Berne, NC	04/03/65	Pt. Lookout, MD	CSR,SA1
					Pt. Lookout, MD	06/20/65	Rlsd. G.O. #109	P115,P118,P121,CSR
Stewart, David	Pvt	K 1st SCVIH	Richmond, VA Hos.	04/03/65	Libby Prison Rchmd	04/13/65	City Pt., VA P.M.	CSR,SA1
					City Pt., VA	04/14/65	Pt. Lookout, MD	CSR
					Pt. Lookout, MD	06/19/65	Rlsd. G.O. #109	P115,P119,CSR

SOUTH CAROLINA SOLDIERS, SAILORS AND CITIZENS HELD IN U.S. PRISONS 1861-1865

NAME	RANK	REGIMENT	CAPTURED AT	WHEN	PRISON	MOVED	DISPOSITION	SOURCES
Stewart, E.W.	Pvt	C P.S.S.	Fair Oaks, VA	07/01/62	Phila., PA Hosp.	07/30/62	Ft. Delaware, DE	CSR,TSE
					Ft. Delaware, DE	08/05/62	Aikens Ldg., VA Xc	CSR
Stewart, J.V.	Pvt	F 22nd SCVI	Bermuda Hundred, VA	06/02/64	Bermuda Hundred VA	06/03/64	Fts. Monroe, VA	CSR
					Fts. Monroe, VA	06/04/64	Pt. Lookout, MD	CSR
					Pt. Lookout, MD	03/14/65	Aikens Ldg., VA Xc	P117,P121,P124,CSR
Stewart, J.W.	Pvt	B 25th SCVI			Elmira, NY	04/24/65	Died	P6,FPH
Stewart, James	Pvt	E 7th SCVI	Gettysburg, PA	07/05/63	Ft. Delaware, DE	07/15/63	Jd. US Forces	P40,P42,P44,CSR
Stewart, John P.	Pvt	B 3rd SCVI	Knoxville, TN	12/05/63	Nashville, TN	02/11/64	Louisville, KY	P39,KEB,SA2,CSR,H3
					Louisville, KY	02/15/64	Rock Island, IL	P88,P91,P94,CSR
					Rock Island, IL	03/02/64	Died, Variola	P5,P131,P132,FPH
Stewart, John T.	Pvt	F 22nd SCVI	Deserted/enemy	01/07/65	Knoxville, TN	01/22/65	Chattanooga, TN	CSR
					Chattanooga, TN	02/21/65	Died, Infl. Pleura	P12,CSR
Stewart, L.G.	Pvt	F 24th SCVI	Jackson, MS	05/16/64	Jackson, MS	05/16/64	Paroled	CSR
Stewart, R.	Pvt	D 2nd SCVI	Cedar Creek, VA	10/19/64	Harpers Ferry, WV	10/24/64	Pt. Lookout, MD	CSR no more info
					Pt. Lookout, MD			P115,P118
Stewart, Richard U.	Pvt	F 22nd SCVI	Petersburg, VA	03/25/65	City Pt., VA	03/28/65	Pt. Lookout, MD	CSR
					Pt. Lookout, MD	06/19/65	Rlsd. G.O. #109	P115,P118,P122,CSR
Stewart, Robert	Pvt	D 17th SCVI	Petersburg, VA	03/25/65	City Pt., VA	03/28/65	Pt. Lookout, MD	CSR,HHC
					Pt. Lookout, MD	06/19/65	Rlsd. G.O. #109	P115,P118,CSR
Stewart, Robert S.	Pvt	H 13th SCVI	Petersburg, VA	04/02/65	City Pt., VA	04/07/65	Hart's Island, NY	CSR
					Hart's Island, NY	06/16/65	Rlsd. G.O. #109	P79,CSR
Stewart, Samuel C.	Pvt	B 21st SCVI	Ft. Fisher, NC	01/15/65	Elmira, NY	04/04/65	Died, Diarrhea	P6,P65,P66,HAG,FPH
Stewart, Thomas B.	Pvt	D 17th SCVI	Petersburg, VA	03/25/65	City Pt., VA	03/28/65	Pt. Lookout, MD	CSR,HHC
					Pt. Lookout, MD	06/19/65	Rlsd. G.O. #109	P115,P118,CSR
Stewart, W.	Pvt	K 1st SCVIH	Richmond, VA Hos.	04/03/65	Richmond, VA Hos.	05/28/65	On Hos. roll	CSR
Stewart, W.M.	Pvt	H 18th SCVI	Petersburg, VA Hos.	04/03/65	City Pt., VA	05/17/65	Newport News, VA	CSR
					Newport News, VA	06/15/65	Rlsd. G.O. #109	CSR
Stewart, W.S.	Pvt	F 20th SCVI	Richmond, VA Hos.	04/03/65	Jackson Hos Rchmd	05/06/65	Died, Consumption	P6,HC,CSR
Stewart, Warren	Pvt	G 4th SCVC	Brandy Stn., VA	11/23/63	Old Capitol, DC	01/08/64	Released on oath	P7,CSR
Stewart, William	Pvt	C 6th SCVI	Seven Pines, VA	05/31/62	Fts. Monroe, VA	06/21/62	Ft. Delaware, DE	CSR
					Ft. Delaware, DE	08/05/62	Aikens Ldg., VA Xc	CSR
Stewart, William	Pvt	H 1st SCVA	Morris Island, SC	07/10/63	Hilton Head, SC	09/19/63	Ft. Columbus, NY	CSR
					Ft. Columbus, NY	09/23/63	Took the oath	P1,CSR
					Ft. Columbus, NY	09/26/63	Pt. Lookout, MD	P113,P116,P124,CSR
					Pt. Lookout, MD	03/03/64	City Pt., VA Xc	P113,P116,P124,CSR
Stewart, William G.	Cpt	A 5th SCVI	Wilderness, VA	05/06/64	Belle Plain, VA	05/17/64	Ft. Delaware, DE	CSR,LAN,SA3
					Ft. Delaware, DE	01/20/65	Fts. Monroe, VA Xc	P43,P44,CSR
Stewart, William J.	Pvt	F 22nd SCVI	Deserted/enemy	01/07/65	Knoxville, TN	01/10/65	Chattanooga, TN	CSR
					Chattanooga, TN	01/27/65	Louisville, KY	CSR
					Louisville, ky	01/31/65	Sent north on oath	P92,CSR
Stewart, William T.	Pvt	D 17th SCVI	Petersburg, VA	03/25/65	City Pt., VA	03/28/65	Pt. Lookout, MD	CSR,HHC
					Pt. Lookout, MD	06/19/65	Rlsd. G.O. #109	P115,P118,CSR
Stiles, William	Pvt	C 1st SCVIG	Columbia, SC	02/17/65	New Berne, NC	04/18/65	Hart's Island, NY	CSR,SA1
					Hart's Island, NY	07/01/65	David's Island, NY	P79
					David's Island, NY	07/22/65	Rlsd. G.O. #109	P1,CSR
Still, Barnard M.	Pvt	H 17th SCVI	Petersburg, MD	03/25/65	City Pt., VA	03/28/65	Pt. Lookout, MD	CSR
					Pt. Lookout, MD	06/19/65	Rlsd. G.O. #109	P118,CSR
Still, H.W.	Pvt	H 17th SCVI	Crater, Pbg., VA	07/30/64	Pt. Lookout, MD	08/08/64	Elmira, NY	P113
Still, Hansford	Pvt	G 2nd SCVA	Deserted/enemy	02/20/65	Charleston, SC		Released on oath	CSR
Still, Isaac	Pvt	A 14th SCMil	Lynch's Creek, SC	02/25/65	Hart's Island, NY	05/16/65	Died	P6,P12,P79,FPH
Still, J.B.	Pvt	B 14th SCMil	Lynch's Creek, SC	02/25/65	Hart's Island, NY	06/17/65	Rlsd. G.O. #109	P79

SOUTH CAROLINA SOLDIERS, SAILORS AND  CITIZENS HELD IN U.S. PRISONS 1861-1865

NAME	RANK	REGIMENT	CAPTURED AT	WHEN	PRISON	MOVED	DISPOSITION	SOURCES
Still, James T.	Pvt	H 17th SCVI	Petersburg, VA	07/30/64	City Pt., VA	08/05/64	Pt. Lookout, MD	CSR
					Pt. Lookout, MD	08/08/64	Elmira, NY	P113,P117,P120,CSR
					Elmira, NY	01/06/64	Died, Pneumonia	P5,P12,P65,FPH,CSR
Still, Judson S.	Pvt	H 17th SCVI	Petersburg, VA	03/25/65	City Pt., VA	03/28/65	Pt. Lookout, MD	CSR
					Pt. Lookout, MD	06/19/65	Rlsd. G.O. #109	P115,P118,P122,CSR
Still, Robert M.	Pvt	H 17th SCVI	Petersburg, VA	03/25/65	Pt. Lookout, MD	06/19/65	Rlsd. G.O. #109	P115,P122
Still, Thomas E.	Pvt	B 14th SCMil	Lynch's Creek, SC	02/25/65	Hart's Island, NY	04/28/65	Died	P6,P12,P79,FPH
Still, William	Pvt	H 17th SCVI	Crater, Pbg., VA	07/30/64	City Pt., VA	08/05/64	Pt. Lookout, MD	CSR
					Pt. Lookout, MD	08/08/64	Elmira, NY	P117,P120,P125,CSR
					Elmira, NY	10/11/64	Pt. Lookout, MD Xc	P65,P66,CSR
					Pt. Lookout, MD	10/29/64	Venus Pt., GA Xc	P115,P123,CSR
Still, William	Pvt	H 17th SCVI	Deserted/enemy	03/09/65	P.M. 9th AC	03/09/65	City Pt., VA P.M.	CSR
					City Pt., VA P.M.	03/11/65	Washington, DC	CSR
					Washington, DC	03/13/65	Charleston, SC oath	CSR
Still, William L.	Pvt	G 22nd SCVI	South Mtn., MD	10/07/62	Ft. McHenry, MD	02/14/63	Fts. Monroe, VA Xc	P145
Stillin, Charles	Pvt	Ferguson's	Salisbury, NC	04/12/65	Nashville, TN	04/29/65	Louisville, KY	P39,CSR
					Louisville, KY	05/02/65	Camp Chase, OH	P92,P95,CSR
Stillin, Charles	Pvt	Ferguson's LA	Salisbury, NC	04/12/65	Camp Chase, OH	06/13/65	Rlsd. G.O. #109	P23,CSR
Stillwell, Harmon S.	Pvt	E Orr's Ri.	Spotsylvania, VA	05/12/64	Belle Plain, VA	05/20/64	Ft. Delaware, DE	CSR,CDC
					Ft. Delaware, DE	06/10/65	Rlsd. G.O. #109	P41,P43,P45,CSR
Stillwell, James Thomas	Pvt	B 3rd SCVI	Sharpsburg, MD	09/18/62	P.M. Army of Potomac	09/27/62	Paroled	SA2,H3,CSR
					Frederick, MD USFH	10/25/62	Baltimore, MD USGH	CSR
					Ft. McHenry, MD	10/25/62	Aikens Ldg., VA Xc	CSR
Stinnyre, C.F.	Cit		Liberty Hill, SC	02/24/65	Hart's Island, NY	06/20/65	Rlsd. G.O. #109	P79
Stocker, Samuel H.	1Sg	A Ham.Leg.MI	Appomattox C.H., VA	04/09/65	City Pt., VA USGH	05/13/65	Lincoln G.H., DC	CSR
					Lincoln G.H., DC	06/14/65	Rlsd. G.O. #109	CSR
Stockman, J.Q.A.	Pvt	C 3rd SCVI	Charlotte, NC	05/27/65	Charlotte, NC	05/27/65	Paroled	SA2,H3,CSR,KEB
Stocton, R.C.	Pvt	C 16th SCVI	Citronelle, AL	05/04/65	Meridian, MS	05/17/65	Paroled on oath	CSR
Stoddard, Alexander R.	Pvt	G 3rd SCVI	Sharpsburg, MD	09/18/62	Shepherdstown, VA	09/30/62	Paroled	SA2,H3,CSR,KEB
Stoddard, J.M.	Pvt	G 26th SCVI	Five Forks, VA	04/01/65	Pt. Lookout, MD	06/19/65	Rlsd. G.O. #109	P115
Stoddard, Robert J.	Sgt	E 14th SCVI	Petersburg, VA	04/02/65	City Pt., VA	04/05/65	Pt. Lookout, MD	CSR
					Pt. Lookout, MD	06/19/65	Rlsd. G.O. #109	P115,P119,P122,CSR
Stogner, A.J.	Pvt	D 6th SCVC	Louisa C.H., VA	06/11/64	Fts. Monroe, VA	06/20/64	Pt. Lookout, MD	CSR
					Pt. Lookout, MD	07/25/64	Elmira, NY	P113,P117,P120,CSR
					Elmira, NY	03/14/64	Pt. Lookout to Xc	P65,P66
					Boulwares Wh., VA	03/18/65	Exchanged	CSR
Stogner, S.H.	Pvt	H 4th SCVC	Petersburg, VA	10/27/64	City Pt., VA	10/31/64	Pt. Lookout, MD	CSR,LAN
					Pt. Lookout, MD	06/04/65	Rlsd. Instr. 5/30/65	P115,P121,CSR
Stogner, Thomas	Pvt	F 21st SCVI	Morris Island, SC	07/10/63	Ft. Columbus, NY	09/23/63	Took the oath	P1,HAG,HOM
					Pt. Lookout, MD	03/26/64	Died, Diarrhea	P5,P12,P113,P116
Stogner, William	Pvt	G 23rd SCVI	Five Forks, VA	04/01/65	City Pt., VA	04/05/65	Pt. Lookout, MD	CSR,HOM
					Pt. Lookout, MD	06/19/65	Rlsd. G.O. #109	P115,P119,P122,CSR
Stokes, David P.	Pvt	I Ham.Leg.MI	Amelia C.H., VA	04/05/65	City Pt., VA	04/13/65	Pt. Lookout, MD	CSR
					Pt. Lookout, MD	06/30/65	Rlsd. G.O. #109	P115,P121,P229,CSR
Stokes, Elwood R.	Pvt	B 3rd SCVIBn	Sharpsburg, MD	09/17/62	Ft. McHenry, MD	10/17/62	Fts. Monroe, VA	CSR
					Fts. Monroe, VA	10/19/62	Aikens Ldg., VA Xc	CSR
Stokes, Greenberry	Sgt	D 5th SCVI	Dade Cty., GA	09/03/62	Rock Island, IL	10/31/64	Jd. U.S. Army F.S.	CSR
Stokes, J.B.	Pvt	B 5th SCVI	Farmville, VA	04/06/65	City Pt., VA	04/14/65	Newport News, VA	CSR
					Newport News, VA	06/26/65	Rlsd. G.O. #109	CSR
Stokes, J.R.	Pvt	H 11th SCVI	Darbytown Rd., VA	10/27/64	Pt. Lookout, MD	06/19/65	Rlsd.G.O. #109	CSR,P115,P122,P118
Stokes, T.M.	Pvt	H 11th SCVI	Deserted/enemy	03/12/65	Charleston, SC	03/12/65	Released on oath	HAG,CSR

SOUTH CAROLINA SOLDIERS, SAILORS AND  CITIZENS HELD IN U.S. PRISONS 1861-1865

NAME	RANK	REGIMENT	CAPTURED AT	WHEN	PRISON	MOVED	DISPOSITION	SOURCES
Stokes, Thomas H.	Pvt	I 3rd SCVI	Falling Waters, MD	07/14/63	Old Capitol, DC	08/08/63	Pt. Lookout, MD	CSR,KEB,SA2,H3
					Ft.McHenry, MD	08/08/63	Pt. Lookout, MD	P110
					Pt. Lookout, MD	03/03/64	City Pt., VA Xc	P113,P116,P123,CSR
Stokes, Thomas H.	Pvt	I 3rd SCVI	Hanover Jctn., VA	05/24/64	White House, VA	06/08/64	Pt. Lookout, MD	CSR
					Pt. Lookout, MD	07/09/64	Elmira, NY	P113,P120,P124,KEB
					Elmira, NY	05/29/65	Rlsd. G.O. #85	P65,P66,CSR
Stokes, W.E.	Pvt	I 5th SCVC	Louisa C.H., VA	06/11/64	Pt. Lookout, MD	07/23/64	Elmira, NY	P113,P117,P120,CSR
					Elmira, NY	03/02/65	James R., VA Xc	P65,P66,CSR
					Richmond, VA Hos.	03/17/65	Furloughed 60 days	CSR
Stokes, W.J.C.	Pvt	D 7th SCVIBn	Weldon RR, VA	08/21/64	City Pt., VA	08/24/64	Pt. Lookout, MD	CSR,HAG,HIC
					Pt. Lookout, MD	06/06/65	Rlsd. instr. 5/30/65	P113,P117,P121,CSR
Stokes, W.R.	Pvt	E 3rd SCVABn	Sumter, SC	02/26/65	New Berne, NC	04/10/65	Hart's Island, NY	CSR
					Hart's Island, NY	06/21/65	Rlsd. G.O. #109	P79,CSR
Stokes, William H.	Pvt	I 3rd SCVI	Charlotte, NC	05/15/65	Charlotte, NC	05/15/65	Paroled	CSR,KEB,SA2,H3
Stone, Bannister	Pvt	D 2nd SCVIRi	Leesburg, VA	10/02/62	Leesburg, VA	10/02/62	Paroled	CSR
Stone, Francis Marion	Pvt	B Ham.Leg.MI	Richmond, VA Hos.	04/03/65	Richmond, VA Hos.	04/14/65	Provost Marshal	CSR
					Libby Prsn. Rchmd.	04/23/65	Newport News, VA	CSR
					Newport, News, VA	06/13/65	Died, Ch. Diarrhea	CSR
Stone, H. Caldwell	Pvt	B 15th SCVI	Halltown, VA	08/26/64	Harpers Ferry, WV	08/29/64	Camp Chase, OH	CSR,KEB,H15
					Camp Chase, OH	03/25/65	Pt. Lookout, MD	P23,KEB,CSR
					Pt. Lookout, MD	06/19/65	Rlsd. G.O. #109	P115,P119,CSR
Stone, Henry	Cpl	B Ham.Leg.MI	Augusta, GA	05/19/65	Augusta, GA	05/19/65	Paroled	CSR
Stone, Isaac M.	Cpl	B 2nd SCVIRi	Deserted/enemy	03/03/65	Bermuda Hundred VA	03/04/65	City Pt., VA P.M.	CSR
					City Pt., VA P.M.	03/05/65	Washington, DC P.M.	CSR
					Washington, DC P.M	03/08/65	Columbus, OH oath	CSR
Stone, J.B.	3Lt	E 6th SCResB	Augusta, GA	05/20/65	Augusta, GA	05/20/65	Paroled	CSR
Stone, James	Cpl	E Orr's Ri.	Gaines' Mills, VA	07/26/62	City Pt., VA USGH	07/29/62	Died of wounds	CSR
Stone, James	Pvt	H 1st SCVA	Morris Island, SC	07/10/63	Hilton Head, SC	09/23/63	Ft. Columbus, NY	CSR
					Ft. Columbus, NY	09/23/63	Took the oath	P1,CSR
					Pt. Lookout, MD	03/08/64	Died, Chr. diarrhea	P5,P113,P116,FPH
Stone, Jesse	Pvt	B Ham.Leg.MI	Augusta, GA	05/19/65	Augusta, GA	05/19/65	Paroled	CSR
Stone, John F.	1Lt	D 18th SCVI	Petersburg, VA	07/20/64	Ft. Delaware, DE	06/14/65	Rlsd. G.O. #109	P43,P45,UD2,CSR
Stone, John Thaddeus	Pvt	D 18th SCVI	Farmville, VA	04/06/65	City Pt., VA	04/14/65	Newport News, VA	CSR
					Newport News, VA	06/26/65	Rlsd. G.O. #109	P107,CSR
Stone, R.P.	Pvt	B 7th SCVI	Charlotte, NC Hos.	05/06/65	Charlotte, NC	05/06/65	Paroled	CNM,CSR,KEB
Stone, Reuben C.	Pvt	K 12th SCVI	Gettysburg, PA	07/06/63	Ft. Delaware, DE	09/14/63	Died, Ch. Diarrhea	P5,P12,P40,P47,FPH
Stone, Stephen H.	Cpl	K Orr's Ri.	Spotsylvania, VA	05/12/64	Belle Plain, Va	05/21/64	Ft. Delaware, DE	CSR
					Ft. Delaware, DE	03/25/65	Hos. 3/25-4/6/65	P47
					Ft. Delaware, DE	06/10/65	Rlsd. G.O. #109	P41,P43,P45,CSR
Stone, W.A.	Pvt	G 27th SCVI	Petersburg, VA	06/24/64	Bermuda Hundred VA	06/25/64	Fts. Monroe, VA	CSR,HAG
					Fts. Monroe, VA	06/26/64	Pt. Lookout, MD	CSR
					Pt. Lookout, MD	08/06/64	Died, Ch. Diarrhea	P5,P12,P113,FPH
Stone, W.A.	Pvt	B 5th SCVC	Augusta, GA	05/19/65	Augusta, GA	05/19/65	Paroled	CSR
Stone, William	Pvt	K 1st SCVC	Williamsport, MD	07/14/63	Lincoln G.H., DC	07/17/63	Died of wounds	P6,P12,CSR
Stone, William B.	Pvt	L 1st SCVIG	Petersburg, VA	03/25/65	City Pt. VA	03/27/65	Pt. Lookout, MD	CSR,SA1
					Pt. Lookout, MD	06/19/65	Rlsd. G.O. #109	P115,P118,CSR
Stone, William H.	Pvt	B 14th SCVI	Petersburg, VA	04/03/65	City Pt., VA	04/13/65	Pt. Lookout, MD	CSR,HOE
					Pt. Lookout, MD	06/19/65	Rlsd. G.O. #109	P115,P119
Stone, William J.	Pvt	F 4th SCVC	Chester, SC	05/05/65	Chester, SC	05/05/65	Paroled	CSR
Stone, William N.	Pvt	B 2nd SCVIRi	Deserted/enemy	03/03/65	Bermuda Hundred VA	03/04/65	City PT., VA P.M.	CSR
					City Pt., VA P.M.	03/05/65	Washington, DC P.M.	CSR
					Washington, DC P.M	03/08/65	Columbus, OH oath	CSR

SOUTH CAROLINA SOLDIERS, SAILORS AND  CITIZENS HELD IN U.S. PRISONS 1861-1865

NAME	RANK	REGIMENT	CAPTURED AT	WHEN	PRISON	MOVED	DISPOSITION	SOURCES
Stone, William T.	Pvt	D 24th SCVI	Taylors Ridge, GA	10/16/64	Nashville, TN	10/23/64	Louisville, KY	CSR
					Louisville, KY	10/27/64	Camp Douglas, IL	P90,P91,P95,CSR
					Camp Douglas, IL	06/17/65	Rlsd. G.O. #109	P53,P55,CSR
Storey, Jesse	Pvt	C 22nd SCVI	Petersburg, VA	06/17/64	No other POW data			CSR
Storey, Thomas P.	Pvt	A 18th SCVI	Sutherland Stn., VA	04/04/65	Pt. Lookout, MD	06/19/65	Rlsd. G.O. #109	P115,P119,CSR
Stork, John J.	Pvt	A 15th SCVI	Wilderness, VA	05/06/64	Belle Plain, VA	05/15/64	Pt. Lookout, MD	KEB,CSR,H15
					Pt. Lookout, MD	08/15/64	Elmira, NY	P113,P117,P120,CSR
					Elmira, NY	03/21/65	Pt. Lookout, MD Xc	P7,P65,P66,CSR
					Richmond, VA Hos.	03/24/65	Furloughed 60 days	CSR
Story, N.J.	Pvt	E 17th SCVI	Deserted/enemy	03/05/65	P.M. A. of P.	03/05/65	City Pt., VA P.M.	CSR
					City Pt., VA P.M.	03/05/65	Washington, DC	CSR
					Washington, DC	03/08/65	Philadelphia oath	CSR
Story, William	Pvt	A 19th SCVI	Augusta, GA	05/19/65	Augusta, GA	05/19/65	Paroled	CSR
Stoudemire, Elias	Pvt	C 6th SCResB	Camden, SC	03/01/65	New Berne, NC	04/25/65	Fts. Monroe, VA	CSR
					Fts. Monroe, VA	05/01/65	Newport News, VA	CSR
					Newport News, VA	06/26/65	Rlsd. G.O. #109	P107,CSR
Stoudemire, John A.W.	Pvt	H 3rd SCVI	Wilderness, VA	05/06/64	Ft. Delaware, DE	06/04/64	Hos. 6/4-6/12/64	P47,KEB,SA2,H3
					Ft. Delaware, DE	10/31/64	Exchanged	P41,CSR
Stoudemire, John A.W.	Cpl	H 3rd SCVI	Orangeburg, SC	02/13/65	New Berne, NC	04/03/65	Pt. Lookout, MD	CSR
					Pt. Lookout, MD	06/19/65	Rlsd. G.O. #109	P115,P118,CSR
Stoutamire, T.J.	Pvt	G 5th SCVC	Old Church, VA	05/30/64	Hos. 3rd Div 5 A.C	05/31/64	Died of wounds	P12,CSR
Stover, Thomas B.	Pvt	E 4th SCVC	Old Church, VA	05/30/64	Hos. 3rd Div 5 A.C	05/31/64	Died of wounds	P12,CSR
Stover, William J.	1Lt	I 12th SCVI	Sharpsburg, MD	09/17/62	Ft. McHenry, MD	10/27/62	Fts. Monroe, VA Xc	CSR
Stover, William J.	Cpt	I 12th SCVI	Appomattox R., VA	04/03/65	Old Capitol, DC	04/21/65	Johnson's Isl., OH	P110,LAN,CSR
					Johnson's Isl., OH	06/20/65	Rlsd. G.O. #109	P82,P83,LAN,CSR
Stowe, Robert S.	Pvt	K 1st SCVC	Upperville, VA	06/21/63	Old Capitol DC	06/25/63	City Pt., VA Xc	CSR
Stowe, Robert S.	Pvt	K 1st SCVC	Pocotaligo, SC	12/13/64	Hilton Head, SC GH	12/30/64	Died of wounds	P2,P6,P12,BNC,CSR
Strain, William W.	Pvt	D 1st SCVIH	Deserted/enemy	03/01/65	City Pt., VA P.M.	03/05/65	Washington, DC P.M.	CSR,SA1
					Washington, DC P.M	03/07/65	Phila., PA on oath	CSR
Strait, George W.	Pvt	A 17th SCVI	Petersburg, VA	03/25/65	City Pt., VA	03/26/65	Died of wounds	P12,HHC,CB,CSR
Strait, William L.	Pvt	A 17th SCVI	Petersburg Hos.	04/03/65	Fair Gds, Hos Pbg	04/04/65	Died, GSW lung	P6,P12,HHC,CSR
Strand, Richard	Pvt	C 23rd SCVI	Five Forks, VA	04/01/65	Pt. Lookout, MD	06/19/65	Rlsd. G.O. #109	P115,P118,P122
Strange, J.A.W.	Pvt	D 27th SCVI	Weldon RR, VA	08/21/64	City Pt., VA	08/24/64	Pt. Lookout, MD	CSR,HAG
					Pt. Lookout, MD	10/30/64	Venus Pt., GA Xc	P113,P117,P123,CSR
Strange, W.T.	Pvt	I 7th SCVC	Richmond, VA	05/18/65	Richmond, VA	05/18/65	Paroled	CSR
Strange, William	Sgt	A P.S.S.	Darbytown Rd., VA	10/07/64	Bermuda Hundred VA	10/21/64	City Pt., VA	CSR,TSE
					City Pt., VA	10/29/64	Pt. Lookout, MD	CSR
					Pt. Lookout, MD	05/14/65	Rlsd. G.O. #85	P122,CSR
Strauss, George F.	Pvt	A 17th SCVCB	Deserted/enemy	03/21/65	Charleston, SC	03/21/65	Released on oath	CSR
Strawhorn, J.T.	Pvt	F Hol.Leg.	Jarratts Stn., VA	05/08/64	Fts. Monroe, VA	05/13/64	Pt. Lookout, MD	CSR
					Pt. Lookout, MD	08/15/64	Elmira, NY	P113,P117,P120
					Elmira, NY	02/13/65	James R., VA Xc	P65,P66,CSR
Street, George W.	Cpl	G 1st SCVIG	Petersburg, VA	07/29/64	City Pt., VA	08/05/64	Pt. Lookout, MD	CSR,SA1
					Pt. Lookout, MD	08/08/64	Elmira, NY	P113,P117,P120,CSR
					Elmira, NY	07/03/65	Rlsd. G.O. #109	P65,CSR
Street, S.R.	Cpl	K 2nd SCVC	Rappahannock R., VA	11/07/63	Pt. Lookout, MD	10/30/64	Exchanged	P123
Striblin, Casswell	Pvt	F 14th SCVI	Gettysburg, PA	07/02/63	Chester, PA G.H.	10/02/63	Pt. Lookout, MD	P1,CSR
					Hammond G.H., MD	01/15/64	Pt. Lookout, MD	CSR
					Pt. Lookout, MD	10/30/64	Venus Pt., GA Xc	P116,P121,P124,CSR
Stribling, J.C.	Pvt	G 7th SCVC	Raleigh, NC	05/29/65	Raleigh, NC	05/29/65	Paroled	CSR
Stribling, L.D.	Pvt	G 7th SCVC	Deep Bottom, VA	08/16/64	City Pt., VA	08/22/64	Pt. Lookout, MD	CSR
					Pt. Lookout, MD	11/01/64	Exchanged	P113,P124,P125,CSR

SOUTH CAROLINA SOLDIERS, SAILORS AND  CITIZENS HELD IN U.S. PRISONS 1861-1865

NAME	RANK	REGIMENT	CAPTURED AT	WHEN	PRISON	MOVED	DISPOSITION	SOURCES
Strickland, D.O.	Pvt	G 6th SCVC	Stony Creek, VA	12/01/64	City Pt., Va	12/04/64	Pt. Lookout, MD	CSR
					Pt. Lookout, MD	05/31/65	Died, Ch. Diarrhea	P6,P115,P119,FPH
Strickland, Henry	Pvt	G 4th SCVC	Stony Creek, VA	12/01/64	City Pt., VA	12/05/64	Pt. Lookout, MD	CSR
					Pt. Lookout, MD	02/13/65	Aikens Ldg., VA Xc	P115,P118,P121,P123
Strickland, Henry	Pvt	I 11th SCVI	Town Creek, NC	02/20/65	Ft. Anderson, NC	02/28/65	Pt. Lookout, MD	CSR,HAG
					Pt. Lookout, MD	06/19/65	Rlsd. G.O. #109	P115,P118,P122,CSR
Strickland, Henry	Pvt	D 26th SCVI	Petersburg, VA H	04/03/65	City Pt., VA	04/07/65	David's Island, NY	CSR
					David's Island, NY	06/14/65	Died, Ch. Diarrhea	P12,P79,HOM,CSR
Strickland, J. Madison	Pvt	G 26th SCVI	Five Forks, VA	04/01/65	City Pt., VA	04/05/65	Pt. Lookout, MD	CSR
					Pt. Lookout, MD	06/19/65	Rlsd. G.O. #109	P119,P122,CSR
Strickland, John C.	Pvt	D 11th SCVI	Town Creek, NC	02/20/65	Ft. Anderson, NC	02/28/65	Pt. Lookout, MD	CSR,HAG
					Pt. Lookout, MD	06/19/65	Rlsd. G.O. #109	P115,P118,CSR
Strickland, P.C.	Pvt	17th SCVI	Athens, GA	05/08/65	Athens, GA	03/08/65	Paroled	CSR
Strickland, Yancey L.	Pvt	I 1st SCVIR	New Berne, NC	03/31/65	New Berne, NC USGH	04/13/65	Died, Ch. Diarrhea	P1,P6,P12,SA1,CSR
Stringfellow, Lemuel	Pvt	A 1st SCVIG	Spotsylvania, VA	05/12/64	Belle Plain, VA	05/21/64	Ft. Delaware, DE	CSR,SA1
					Ft. Delaware, DE		Hos. 5/27-6/14/64	P47
					Ft. Delaware, DE	06/16/64	Hos. 6/17-7/23/64	P47
					Ft. Delaware, DE	12/21/64	Hos.12/21/64-1/12/	P47
					Ft. Delaware, DE	01/27/65	Hos. 1/27-2/27/65	P47
					Ft. Delaware, DE	02/27/64	City Pt., VA Xc	P41,P43,CSR
Striplin, A.C.	Pvt	K 3rd SCVI	Petersburg, VA	07/29/64	City Pt., VA	08/05/64	Pt. Lookout, MD	KEB,SA2,H3,CSR
					Pt. Lookout, MD	08/08/64	Elmira, NY	P113,P120,P125,CSR
					Elmira, NY	06/19/65	Rlsd. G.O. #109	P65,P66,CSR
Striplin, John	Pvt	K 3rd SCVI	Cedar Creek, VA	10/19/64	Harpers Ferry, WV	10/25/64	Pt. Lookout, MD	CSR,KEB,SA2,H3
					Pt. Lookout, MD	05/14/65	Released	P115,P118,P122
Strobhart, William	Pvt	B 2nd SCVC	Occaquam, VA	10/09/62	Old Capitol, DC			CSR
Strock, E.B.	Pvt	F 25th SCVI	Ft. Fisher, NC	01/15/65	New York, NY	01/30/65	Elmira, NY	CSR,HAG
					Elmira, NY	02/20/65	James R., VA Xc	P65,P66,CSR
Strom, George B.	Pvt	D 14th SCVI	Petersburg, VA	04/03/65	City Pt., VA	04/07/65	Hart's Island, NY	CSR
					Hart's Island, NY	05/17/65	Died, Ch. Diarrhea	P6,P12,P79,FPH,CSR
Strom, H.A.	Pvt	D 14th SCVI	N. Anna River, VA	05/22/64	Alexandria, VA	05/30/64	Died of wounds	P1,P5,P12,HOE
Strom, Thadeus C.	Pvt	D 14th SCVI	Sutherland Stn., VA	04/02/65	City Pt., VA	04/07/65	Hart's Island, NY	CSR,HOE
					Hart's Island, NY	06/16/65	Rlsd. G.O. #109	P79,CSR
Strom, William H.	Pvt	K 24th SCVI	Nashville, TN	12/16/64	Nashville, TN	12/31/64	Louisville, KY	CSR
					Louisville, KY	01/02/65	Camp Chase, OH	CSR
					Camp Chase, OH	04/22/65	Jd. U.S. Army	P23,CSR
Stroman, Absalom	Pvt	E 14th SCMil	Lynch's Creek, SC	03/01/65	New Berne, NC	04/10/65	Hart's Island, NY	CSR
					Hart's Island, NY	04/29/65	Died, Ch. Diarrhea	P6,P79,FPH
Stroman, Charles	Pvt	F 25th SCVI	Ft. Fisher, NC	01/15/65	New York, NY	01/30/65	Elmira, NY	CSR,HAG
					Elmira, NY	05/10/65	Died, Variola	P6,P12,P65,P66,FPH
Stroman, Emanuel	Pvt	F 25th SCVI	Petersburg, VA	06/18/64	Fts. Monroe, VA	06/22/64	Pt. Lookout, MD	CSR,HAG
					Pt. Lookout, MD	02/13/65	Aikens Ldg., VA Xc	P113,P121,P124,CSR
Stroman, H.	Pvt	D 12th SCVI	Southside RR, VA	04/02/65	Hart's Island, NY	06/15/65	Rlsd. G.O. #109	P79
Strong, Andrew	Pvt	D 17th SCVI	Crater, Pbg., VA	07/30/64	City Pt., VA	08/05/64	Pt. Lookout, MD	CSR,HHC
					Pt. Lookout, MD	08/08/64	Elmira, NY	P113,P120,P125
					Elmira, NY	10/30/64	Died, Typhoid fever	P6,P12,P65,P66,FPH
Strong, J.M.	Pvt	E 1st SCVIR	Deserted/enemy	03/08/65	Charleston, SC	03/15/65	Released on oath	SA1,CSR
Strong, M.J.	Pvt	A P.S.S.	Knoxville, TN	11/19/63	Knoxville, TN	12/15/63	Louiseville, KY	CSR,TSE
					Louisville, KY	12/31/63	Rock Island, IL	P88,P89,P94,CSR
Strong, M.J.	Pvt	A P.S.S.	Knoxville, TN	12/03/63	Rock Island, IL	03/02/65	Pt. Lookout, MD Xc	P131
Strong, M.J.	Pvt	A P.S.S.	Salisbury, NC	05/03/65	Salisbury, MD	05/03/65	Paroled	CSR

SOUTH CAROLINA SOLDIERS, SAILORS AND  CITIZENS HELD IN U.S. PRISONS 1861-1865

NAME	RANK	REGIMENT	CAPTURED AT	WHEN	PRISON	MOVED	DISPOSITION	SOURCES
Strother, Allen B.	Cpl	E 1st SCVA	Morris Island, SC	07/10/63	Hilton Head, SC	09/05/63	Ft. Columbus, NY	P1,CSR
					Ft. Columbus, NY	09/23/63	Took the oath	P1,CSR
Strother, D.P.	Pvt	F 7th SCVC	Old Church, VA	05/30/64	Lincoln G.H., DC	09/05/64	Old Capitol, DC	CSR
					Ft. Delaware, DE		Hos. 9/24-10/30/64	P47
					Old Capitol, DC	09/19/64	Ft. Delaware, DE	P110,CSR
					Ft. Delaware, DE	10/30/64	Pt. Lookout, MD	P43,CSR
					Pt. Lookout, MD	10/31/64	Exchanged	P41,P115,P123,CSR
Strother, John C.	Pvt	K 23rd SCVI	Five Forks, VA	04/01/65	City Pt., VA	04/05/65	Pt. Lookout, MD	CSR
					Pt. Lookout, MD	06/19/65	Rlsd. G.O. #109	P115,P119,P122,CSR
Stroup, M.A.	Pvt	K 18th SCVI	Crater, Pbg., VA	07/30/64	City Pt., VA	08/05/64	Pt. Lookout, MD	CSR
					Pt. Lookout, MD	08/08/64	Elmira, NY	P113,P117,P120
					Elmira, NY	12/09/64	Died, Pneumonia	P5,P12,P65,P66,FPH
Strouse, James	Pvt	D 23rd SCVI	Deserted/enemy	02/21/65	City Pt., VA	02/25/65	Washington, DC	CSR
					Washington, DC	02/27/65	New York, NY oath	CSR
Stuart, George F.	Pvt	B 7th SCVC	Darbytown Rd., VA	10/11/64	Bermuda Hundred, VA	10/18/64	City Pt., VA P.M.	CSR
					Dutch Gap Canal	10/21/64	Pt. Lookout, MD	CSR
					City Pt., VA	10/29/64	Pt. Lookout, MD	CSR
					Pt. Lookout, MD	12/26/64	Died, Typhoid fever	P5,P115,P118,FPH
Stuart, Richard	Pvt	C 23rd SCVi	Five Forks, VA	04/01/65	City Pt., VA	04/04/65	Pt. Lookout, MD	CSR
					Pt. Lookout, MD	06/19/65	Rlsd. G.O. #109	CSR
Stubblefield, W.	Pvt	G 14th SCVI	Richmond, VA	04/03/65	Newport News, VA	06/30/65	Rlsd. G.O. #109	P107
Stubblefield, William H.	Pvt	C 2nd SCVI	Cold Harbor, VA	06/02/64	Old Capitol, DC	06/12/65	Rlsd. G.O. #109	P110,H2,CSR
Stubbs, David D.	Cpl	F 21st SCVI	Ft. Fisher, NC	01/15/65	Elmira, NY	07/11/65	Rlsd. G.O. #109	P65,P66,HAG,HOM
Stubbs, John B.	Pvt	F 21st SCVI	Petersburg, VA	06/18/64	City Pt., VA	06/21/64	Pt. Lookout, MD	CSR,HAG,HOM
					Pt. Lookout, MD	07/27/64	Elmira, NY	P113,P117,P120
					Elmira, NY	03/02/65	Pt. Lookout, MD Xc	P65,P66
Stubbs, Samuel F.	Pvt	F 21st SCVI	Ft. Fisher, NC	01/15/65	Elmira, NY	02/11/65	Died, Typhoid fever	P6,P65,FPH,HAG,HOM
Stubbs, William G.	Pvt	A 2nd SCVI	Henrico, VA	07/20/65	Rlsd. on oath			H2,CSR,KEB,SA2
Stuck, C.M.	Pvt	G 3rd SCVABn	High Pt., NC	05/01/65	High Pt., NC	05/01/65	Paroled	CSR
Stuckey, A. Furman	Cpl	E 19th SCVI	Sumter, SC	02/26/65	New Berne, NC	03/01/65	Hart's Island, NY	CSR
					Hart's Island, NY	06/16/65	Rlsd. G.O. #109	P79,CSR
Stuckey, David A.	Pvt	H 20th SCVI	Lexington, SC	02/14/65	Pt. Lookout, MD	05/15/65	Rlsd. G.O. #85	P115,P121,KEB,CSR
Stuckey, E.W.	Pvt	B 21st SCVI	Petersburg, VA	06/24/64	Pt. Lookout, MD	08/16/64	Elmira, NY	P113,P117
					Elmira, NY	07/03/65	Rlsd. G.O. #109	P65,P66
Stuckey, Howell G.	Pvt	H 21st SCVI	Morris Island, SC	07/10/63	Morris Island, SC	07/13/64	Hilton Head, SC	CSR,HAG
					Hilton Head G.H.	07/23/63	Fts. Monroe, VA	P2,CSR
					Fts. Monroe, VA	07/13/64	Died, Amptd. thigh	P12,CSR
Stuckey, James Thomas	Pvt	D 14th SCVI	Petersburg, VA	04/03/65	City Pt., VA	04/11/65	Hart's Island, NY	CSR
					Hart's Island, NY	06/16/65	Rlsd. G.O. #109	CSR
Stuckey, Jasper E.	Sgt	E 19th SCVI	Atlanta, GA	07/22/64	Nashville, TN	07/29/64	Louisville, KY	CSR
					Louisville, KY	07/31/64	Camp Chase, OH	P90,P94,CSR
					Camp Chase, OH	03/04/65	City Pt., VA Xc	CSR
					Camp Chase, OH	03/04/65	Died, Pneumonia	P6,P12,P23,P27,FPH
Stuckey, John W.	Pvt	A 14th SCVI	Gettysburg, PA	07/03/63	Chester, PA G.H.	09/25/63	City Pt., VA Xc	P1,CSR
Stuckey, John W.	Pvt	A 14th SCVI	Hatchers Run, VA	04/02/65	City Pt., VA	04/07/65	Hart's Island, NY	CSR
					Hart's Island, NY	06/16/65	Rlsd. G.O. #109	P79,CSR
Stuckey, Wiley D.	Pvt	H 21st SCVI	Petersburg, VA	05/09/64	Pt. Lookout, MD	01/22/65	Died, Ac. Dysntery	P6,P113,P117,FPH
Stukes, Alfred M.	Pvt	D 4th SCVC	Louisa C.H., VA	06/11/64	Fts. Monroe, VA	06/20/64	Pt. Lookout, MD	CSR
					Pt. Lookout, MD	07/25/64	Elmira, NY	P113,P120,CSR
					Elmira, NY	09/02/64	Died, Ch.Bronchitis	P5,P12,P65,P66,FPH
Stukes, C.W.	Pvt	I 23rd SCVI	Five Forks, VA	04/01/65	City Pt., VA	04/05/65	Hart's Island, NY	CSR,HCL
					Hart's Island, NY	06/16/65	Rlsd. G.O. #109	P79,CSR

SOUTH CAROLINA SOLDIERS, SAILORS AND  CITIZENS HELD IN U.S. PRISONS 1861-1865

NAME	RANK	REGIMENT	CAPTURED AT	WHEN	PRISON	MOVED	DISPOSITION	SOURCES
Stumps, Charles	Pvt	K 6th SCVC	Deserted/enemy		Hilton Head, SC	03/06/65	Str." Fulton"to NY	CSR
Sturgeon, Richard D.	Pvt	H 7th SCVIBn	Drury's Bluff, VA	05/16/64	Bermuda Hundred, VA	05/17/64	Fts. Monroe, VA	CSR,HAG
					Fts. Monroe, VA	05/18/64	Pt. Lookout, MD	CSR
					Pt. Lookout, MD	08/15/64	Elmira, NY	P113,P117,P120,CSR
					Elmira, NY	12/10/64	Died, Diarrhea	P5,P12,P65,FPH,CSR
Sturgis, William T.	Cpl	H 12th SCVI	Gettysburg, PA	07/03/63	David's Island, NY	09/05/63	City Pt., VA Xc	P1,YEB,CSR
Sturkey, Marion B.	Pvt	B Ham.Leg.MI	Augusta, GA	05/24/65	Augusta, GA	05/24/65	Paroled	CSR
Sturkey, Thomas J.	Pvt	B Ham.Leg.MI	Farmville, VA	04/11/65	Farmville, VA	04/11/65	Paroled	CSR
Sturkey, W.O.	Pvt	F Ham.Leg.MI	St. Mary's Ch., VA	06/14/64	City Pt., VA	06/24/64	Pt. Lookout, MD	CSR
					Pt. Lookout, MD	07/27/64	Elmira, NY	P113,P117,P120,CSR
Sturkey, W.O.	Pvt	B Ham.Leg.MI	St. Mary's Ch., VA	06/14/54	Elmira, NY	07/03/65	Rlsd. G.O. #109	P65,P66,CSR
Stutts, George H.	Sgt	B 11th SCVI	Town Creek, NC	02/20/65	Ft. Anderson, NC	02/28/65	Pt. Lookout, MD	CSR,HAG
					Pt. Lookout, MD	06/19/65	Rlsd. G.O. #109	P115,P118,P122,CSR
Stutts, Madison M.	Pvt	B 27th SCVI	Town Creek, NC	02/20/65	Ft. Anderson, NC	02/28/65	Pt. Lookout, MD	CSR,HAG
					Pt. Lookout, MD	05/14/65	Rlsd. G.O. #85	P7,P115,P118,P122
Stutts, Richard R.	1Sg	B 11th SCVI	Town Creek, NC	02/20/65	Ft. Anderson, NC	02/28/65	Pt. Lookout, MD	CSR,HAG
					Pt. Lookout, MD	06/19/65	Rlsd. G.O. #109	P115,P118,P122,CSR
Suber, David F.	Pvt	G Hol.Leg.	Five Forks, VA	04/01/65	City Pt., VA	04/05/65	Pt. Lookout, MD	CSR,ANY
					Pt. Lookout, MD	06/19/65	Rlsd. G.O. #109	P115,P119
Suber, James A.	Pvt	F 1st SCVA	Bentonville, NC	03/22/65	New Berne, NC	04/10/65	Hart's Island, NY	CSR
					Hart's Island, NY	06/19/65	Rlsd. G.O. #109	CSR
Sudduth, John W.	Pvt	B 11th SCVI	Town Creek, NC	02/20/65	Ft. Anderson, NC	02/28/65	Pt. Lookout, MD	CSR
					Pt. Lookout, MD	06/19/65	Rlsd. G.O. #109	P115,P118,P122,CSR
Suggs, Robert R.	Pvt	M 8th SCVI	Gettysburg, PA	07/05/63	Letterman Hos. PA	10/06/63	W. Bldg. Balt, MD	P1,CSR,KEB
					W. Bldg. Balt, MD	11/12/63	City Pt., VA Xc	P1,CSR
Sullivan, C.R.	Pvt	D 4th SCVC	Louisa C.H., VA	06/11/64	Fts. Monroe, VA	06/20/64	Pt. Lookout, MD	CSR
Sullivan, Charles B.	Pvt	Ferguson's LA	Nashville, TN	12/16/64	Nashville, TN	12/19/64	Louisville, KY	CSR
					Louisville, KY	12/21/64	Camp Douglas, IL	CSR
					Camp Douglas, IL	01/17/65	Took the oath	CSR
Sullivan, Daniel	Pvt	B 1st SCVIG	Sharpsburg, MD	09/17/62	Baltimore, MD Hos.	11/03/62	Fts. Monroe, VA	CSR,SA1
					Baltimore, MD Hos.	11/03/62	Aikens Ldg., VA Xc	CSR
Sullivan, Daniel	Pvt	B 1st SCVIG	Deserted/enemy	02/28/65	City Pt., VA	02/28/65	Washington, DC	CSR
					Washington, DC	03/02/65	Charleston, SC	CSR
Sullivan, Dennis	Pvt	F 1st SCVA	Deserted/enemy	03/23/65	Charleston, SC		Released on oath	CSR
Sullivan, Elias	Pvt	F 26th SCVI	Petersburg, VA	04/02/65	City Pt., VA	04/05/65	Pt. Lookout, MD	CSR
					Pt. Lookout, MD	06/19/65	Rlsd. G.O. #109	P115,P119,P122,CSR
Sullivan, J.M.	Pvt	D 1st SCVIG	Winchester, VA	12/02/62	Winchester, VA	12/04/62	Paroled	CSR
Sullivan, James M.	Smn	CSN	Off Charleston	10/05/63	Ft. Lafayette, NY	09/19/64	Ft. Warren, MA	P144
Sullivan, Jerry	Sgt	E 1st SCVA	Deserted/enemy	02/18/65	Charleston,SC	03/23/65	Taken oath & disch.	CSR
Sullivan, John	Pvt	H 22nd SCVI	Crater, Pbg., VA	07/30/64	City Pt., VA	08/05/64	Pt. Lookout, MD	CSR
					Pt. Lookout, MD	08/08/64	Elmira, NY	P113,P117,P120,P125
					Elmira, NY	06/14/65	Rlsd. G.O.#109	P65,P66,CSR
Sullivan, John	Pvt	E 1st SCVIR	Charleston, SC	02/18/65	Hilton Head, SC	09/05/65	Ft. Columbus, NY	CSR
Sullivan, M.R.	Pvt	D 4th SCVC	Louisa C.H., VA	06/11/64	Pt. Lookout, MD	07/25/64	Elmira, NY	P113,P117,P120,CSR
					Elmira, NY	10/11/64	Pt. Lookout, MD Xc	P65,P66,CSR
					W. Bldg. Balt, MD	11/20/64	Died, Ch. Diarrhea	P4,P5,P12,FPH,CSR
Sullivan, Martin J.	Pvt	H 27th SCVI	Weldon RR, VA	08/21/64	City Pt., VA	08/24/64	Pt. Lookout, MD	CSR,HAG
					Pt. Lookout, MD	02/13/65	Aikens Ldg., VA Xc	P113,P121,P124,CSR
Sullivan, Michael	Pvt	K 1st SCVIG	Wilderness, VA	05/06/64	Old Capitol, DC	06/15/64	Ft. Delaware, DE	CSR
					Ft. Delaware, DE	12/10/64	Hos. 12/10-12/13/64	P47
					Ft. Delaware, DE	12/19/64	Hos.12/19/64-1/6/6	P47
					Ft. Delaware, DE	05/08/65	Rlsd. OO War Dept.	P41,P43,CSR

SOUTH CAROLINA SOLDIERS, SAILORS AND  CITIZENS HELD IN U.S. PRISONS 1861-1865

NAME	RANK	REGIMENT	CAPTURED AT	WHEN	PRISON	MOVED	DISPOSITION	SOURCES
Sullivan, Michael A.	Pvt	D 27th SCVI	Town Creek, NC	02/20/65	Ft. Anderson, NC	02/28/65	Pt. Lookout, MD	CSR
					Pt. Lookout, MD	06/20/65	Rlsd. G.O. #109	P121,CSR
Sullivan, Nimrod K.	1Lt	C Orr's Ri.	Falling Waters, MD	07/14/63	Baltimore, MD	08/02/63	Johnson's Isl., OH	CSR
					Johnson's Isl., OH	06/18/65	Rlsd. G.O. #109	P80,P81,P82,CSR
Sullivan, R.M.	Pvt	D 1st SCVIH	Winchester, VA	12/04/62	Cumberland, MD	02/28/63	Wheeling, WV	CSR,SA1
					Wheeling, WV	03/03/63	Camp Chase, OH	CSR
					Camp Chase, OH	03/28/63	City Pt., VA Xc	P24,CSR
Sullivan, R.M.	Pvt	D 1st SCVIH	Deserted/enemy	03/01/65	Bermuda Hundred, VA	03/03/65	City Pt., VA P.M.	CSR
					City Pt., VA P.M.	03/05/65	Washington, DC P.M.	CSR
Sullivan, R.M.	Pvt	D 1st SCVIH	Deserted/enemy	03/01/65	Washington, DC	03/07/65	Phila., PA on oath	CSR
Sullivan, Samuel	Pvt	H 1st SCVIR	Smith's Ford, NC	03/16/65	New Berne, NC	04/03/65	Pt. Lookout, MD	P115,P118,SA1,CSR
					Pt. Lookout, MD			P115,P118,CSR
Sullivan, Ulysses	Pvt	D Hol.Leg.	Petersburg, VA	04/03/65	Fair Gds. Hos., Pbg	04/09/65	U.S. Gen. Hos. Pbg	CSR
					U.S. Gen. Hos., Pbg.	04/11/65	Pt. of Rocks H., VA	CSR
					Pt.of Rocks H., VA	04/14/65	U.S. Gen. Hos., VA	CSR
					U.S. Gen. Hos., VA	05/25/65	Camp Hamilton, VA	CSR
					Camp Hamilton, VA	05/31/65	Paroled	CSR
Sullivan, W.J.	Pvt	B 27th SCVI	Petersburg, VA	06/24/64	Bermuda Hundred, VA	06/25/64	Fts. Monroe, VA	CSR,HAG
					Fts. Monroe, VA	06/26/64	Pt. Lookout, MD	CSR
					Pt. Lookout, MD	07/23/64	Elmira, NY	P117,P120
					Elmira, NY	03/04/65	Died, Ch. Diarrhea	P12,P65,P66,FPH,CSR
Sullivan, Wilson S.	Pvt	D 4th SCVC	Stony Creek, VA	12/01/64	City Pt., VA	12/05/64	Pt. Lookout, MD	CSR
					Pt. Lookout, MD	06/19/65	Rlsd. G.O. #109	P115,P118,CSR
Summer, Edwin D.	Pvt	E 6th SCVI	Deep Bottom, VA	08/14/64	Bermuda Hundred, VA	08/15/64	Fts. Monroe, VA	CSR
					Fts. Monroe, VA	08/16/64	Pt. Lookout, MD	CSR
					Pt. Lookout, MD	03/14/65	Aikens Ldg. Xc	P113,P121,P124,P125
Summer, Martin B.	HSd	F 13th SCVI	Gettysburg, PA	07/05/63	Ft. McHenry, MD	07/30/63	Ft. Delaware, DE	CSR
					Ft. Delaware, DE	09/13/63	Died, Ch. Diarrhea	P5,P12,P40,P42,FPH
Summerall, Pleasant M.	Pvt	Ferguson's LA	Salisbury, NC	04/12/65	Nashville, TN	04/29/65	Louisville, KY	P39,CSR
					Louisville, KY	05/02/65	Camp Chase, OH	P92,P95,CSR
					Camp Chase, OH	06/13/65	Rlsd. G.O. #109	CSR
Summerall, T.	Cpl	E 3rd SCVIBn	South Mtn., MD	09/14/62	Frederick, MD Hos.	10/08/62	Ft. McHenry, MD	CSR,KEB
					Ft. McHenry, MD	10/13/62	Fts. Monroe, VA	CSR
					Fts. Monroe, VA	10/27/62	Aikens Ldg., VA Xc	CSR
Summerall, W. F.	Pvt	C 3rd SCVIBn	Charlotte, NC	05/06/65	Charlotte, NC	05/06/65	Paroled	CSR
Summerall, W.W.	Pvt	E 3rd SCVIBn	Frederick, MD	09/12/62	USGH Frederick, MD	09/19/62	Died of wounds	P1,P6,FPH,KEB,CSR
Summerall, William H.	Sgt	B 27th SCVI	Town Creek, NC	02/20/65	Ft. Anderson, NC	02/28/65	Pt. Lookout, MD	CSR,HAG
					Pt. Lookout, MD	06/19/65	Rlsd. G.O. #109	P115,P118,P122,HAG,CSR
Summerford, James T.	2Lt	K 17th SCVI	Petersburg, VA	03/25/65	P.M. A.of P.	03/26/65	City Pt., VA P.M.	CSR
					Old Capitol, DC	03/30/65	Ft. Delaware, DE	P110,YEB,CSR
					Ft. Delaware, DE	06/17/65	Rlsd. G.O. #109	P43,P45,YEB,CSR
Summerford, Noah	Pvt	I 18th SCVI	Five Forks, VA	04/01/65	City Pt., VA	04/04/65	Pt. Lookout, MD	CSR
					Pt. Lookout, MD	06/19/65	Rlsd. G.O. #109	P115,P122,CSR
Summerford, William	Pvt	L 21st SCVI	Morris Island, SC	07/10/63	Hilton Head, SC G.H.	07/23/63	Morris Island, SC Xc	P2,HAG,HMC,CSR
Summers, Drayton P.	Sgt	B 1st SCVIG	Southside RR, VA	04/02/65	City Pt., VA	04/07/65	Hart's Island, NY	SA1,CSR,ANY
					Hart's Island, NY	06/15/65	Rlsd. G.O. #109	P79,CSR
Summers, Larkin J.	Pvt	B 1st SCVIG	Farmville, VA	04/06/65	City Pt., VA	04/14/65	Newport News, VA	CSR
					Newport News, VA	06/25/65	Rlsd. G.O. #109	SA1,CSR
Summers, William A.	Pvt	C 6th SCResB	Chesterfield, SC	02/28/65	New Berne, NC	04/03/65	Pt. Lookout, MD	CSR
					Pt. Lookout, MD	05/11/65	Died, Erysipelas	P6,P12,P115,FPH
Summerville, T.N.	Pvt	G 6th SCVI	Burkeville, VA	04/14/65	Burkeville, VA	04/17/65	Paroled	CSR

SOUTH CAROLINA SOLDIERS, SAILORS AND CITIZENS HELD IN U.S. PRISONS 1861-1865

NAME	RANK	REGIMENT	CAPTURED AT	WHEN	PRISON	MOVED	DISPOSITION	SOURCES
Summey, Peter	Pvt	L P.S.S.	Fair Oaks, VA	06/01/62	Fts. Monroe, VA	08/31/62	Aikens Ldg., VA Xc	CSR
					Aikens Ldg., VA	09/21/62	Exchanged	CSR
Suneath, C.M.	Pvt	Ferguson's	Salisbury, NC	04/12/65	Camp Chase, OH	06/13/65	Rlsd. G.O. #109	P23
Suraw, John	Pvt	C 15th SCVAB	Fayetteville, NC	03/17/65	New Berne, NC	04/03/65	Pt. Lookout, MD	CSR
					Pt. Lookout, MD	06/20/65	Rlsd. G.O. #109	P115,P118,P121,CSR
Sureau, W.F.	Pvt	I 27th SCVI	Weldon RR, VA	08/21/64	City Pt., VA	08/24/64	Pt. Lookout, MD	CSR
					Pt. Lookout, MD	03/15/65	Aikens Ldg., VA Xc	P121,P124,CSR
Surles, E.	Pvt	F 7th SCVIBn	Cheraw, SC	03/03/65	Cheraw, SC	03/03/65	Paroled	CSR
Sutherland, A.B.	Pvt	K Ham.Leg.MI	Richmond, VA Hos.	04/03/65	Newport News, VA	06/26/65	Rlsd. G.O. #109	P107
Sutherland, Leitner N.	Pvt	K 5th SCVI	Chattanooga, TN	10/29/63	Nashville, TN	11/07/63	Louisville, KY	P39,SA3,CSR
					Louisville, KY	11/09/63	Camp Morton, IN	P89,CSR
					Camp Morton, IN	02/26/65	City Pt. VA for Xc	P100,CSR
Sutherland, Marcus L.	Pvt	C 13th SCVI	Wilderness, VA	05/05/64	Belle Plain, VA	05/21/64	Ft. Delaware, DE	CSR,HOS
					Ft. Delaware, DE	08/15/64	Hos. 8/15-8/18/64	P47
					Ft. Delaware, DE	05/11/65	Released on oath	P41,P43,P46,CSR
Suttlemeyer, J.W.	Sgt	D 12th SCVI	Sutherland Stn. VA	04/03/65	City Pt., VA	04/07/65	Hart's Island, NY	CSR
					Hart's Island, NY	06/18/65	Rlsd. G.O. #109	CSR
Sutton, B.F.	Pvt	H 2nd SCVI	Cedar Creek, VA	10/19/64	Harpers Ferry, WV	10/23/64	Pt. Lookout, MD	CSR,LAN,SA2,H2
					Pt. Lookout, MD	06/19/65	Rlsd. G.O. #109	P115,P118,P122
Sutton, John D.	Pvt	B 6th SCVI	Campbell Stn., TN	11/16/63	Nashville, TN	02/11/64	Louisville, KY	P39,CSR
					Louisville, KY	02/15/64	Rock Island, IL	P88,P91,P94,CSR
					Rock Island, IL	02/15/65	Pt. Lookout, MD XC	P131,CSR
					Richmond, VA Hos.	03/16/65	Furloughed 60 days	CSR
Sutton, William M.	Pvt	B 6th SCVI	Richmond, VA Hos.	04/03/65	Richmond VA Hos.	04/14/65	Richmond, VA U.S.P.	CSR
					Libby Prison Rchmd.	04/23/65	Newport News, VA	CSR
					Newport News, VA	06/16/65	Rlsd. G.O. #109	CSR
Swafford, Henry	Pvt	B 1st SCVIR	Deserted/enemy	02/28/65	Charleston, SC		Released on oath	SA1,CSR
Swafford, James	Pvt	E 13th SCVI	N. Anna River, VA	05/23/64	Port Royal, VA	05/30/64	Pt. Lookout, MD	CSR
					Pt. Lookout, MD	03/14/65	Aikens Ldg., VA Xc	P113,P121,P124,CSR
Swaford, James	Pvt	D 22nd SCVI	Deserted/enemy	02/01/65	City Point, VA	02/05/65	Washington, DC	P8,CSR
					Washington, DC	02/08/65	Chambersburg, PA	CSR
Swails, Morgan E.	Pvt	C 3rd SCVABn	Blakely, AL	04/09/65	Ship Island, MS	05/01/65	Vicksburg, MS Xc	P136,CSR
Swails, W. Taylor	Pvt	C 3rd SCVABn	Blakely, AL	04/09/65	Ship Island, MS	05/01/65	Vicksburg, MS Xc	P136,CSR
Sweat, Capers	Pvt	E 1st SCVIH	Warrenton, VA	09/29/62	Warrenton, VA	09/29/62	Paroled	SA1,CSR
Sweat, J.A.	Pvt	F 23rd SCVI	Deserted/enemy	03/31/65	City Pt., VA	04/10/65	Washington, DC	CSR
					Washington, DC	04/10/65	Wilmington, NC	CSR
Sweat, Thomas	Pvt	C 11th SCVI	Town Creek, NC	02/20/65	Ft. Anderson, NC	02/28/65	Pt. Lookout, MD	CSR
					Pt. Lookout, MD	06/19/65	Rlsd. G.O. #109	P115,CSR
Sweat, W.W.	Pvt	I 1st SCVA	Marlboro, SC	03/06/65	New Berne, NC	04/10/65	Hart's Island, NY	CSR
					Hart's Island, NY	06/16/65	Rlsd. G.O. #109	P79,CSR
Sweat, William	Pvt	B 4th SCVC	Salem Church, VA	05/28/64	3rd Div. 5th A.C.	06/05/64	Washington, DC	CSR,HHC
					Lincoln G.H., DC	08/11/64	Died, Pneumonia	P6,P12,P110,CSR
Sweatman, George W.	Pvt	C 12th SCVI	Amelia C.H., VA	04/05/65	City Pt., VA	04/13/65	Pt. Lookout, MD	CSR,HFC
					Pt. Lookout, MD	06/19/65	Rlsd. G.O. #109	P115,P119,P122,CSR
Sweatt, Steven S.	Pvt	B 8th SCVI	Petersburg, VA	07/29/64	City Point, VA	08/05/64	Pt. Lookout, MD	CSR,KEB
					Pt. Lookout, MD	08/08/64	Elmira, NY	P113,P117,P120,CSR
					Elmira, NY	02/20/65	James R., VA Xc	P65,P66,CSR
Sweeney, William	Pvt	D 1st SCVC	Deserted/enemy	03/13/65	Charleston, SC	03/13/65	Released on oath	CSR
Sweeny, Calvin	Pvt	G 1st SCVA	Greensboro, NC		Greensboro, NC	06/30/65	Died of wounds	P12
Swenson, August	Pvt	D 2nd SCVI	Charlotte, NC	05/15/65	Charlotte, NC	05/15/65	Paroled	CSR
Swett, J.W.	Pvt	B 1st SCVIR	Deserted/enemy	02/18/65	Charleston, SC		Released on oath	SA1,CSR

NAME	RANK	REGIMENT	CAPTURED AT	WHEN	PRISON	MOVED	DISPOSITION	SOURCES
Swett, William E.	Pvt	A 1st SCVIR	Morris Island, SC	09/07/63	Hilton Head, SC	10/06/63	Pt. Lookout, MD	CSR,LAN,SA1
					Pt. Lookout, MD	02/27/64	Joined U.S. Army	P113,P117,P125
Swindler, S.	Sgt	I 15th SCVI	Gettysburg, PA	07/03/63	Ft. Delaware, DE	06/10/65	Released	P42
Swinton, E.C.	Pvt	I 3rd SCVC	Pocotaligo, SC	12/21/64	Hilton Head, SC	02/01/65	Pt. Lookout, MD	CSR
					Pt. Lookout, MD	02/18/65	Aikens Ldg., VA Xc	P2,P115,P118,CSR
Swinton, H.R.	Pvt	A 27th SCVI	Weldon RR, VA	08/21/64	City Pt., VA Pt. Lo	08/24/64	Pt. Lookout, MD Xc	CSR,HAG
					Pt. Lookout, MD	02/18/65	Aikens Ldg., VA Xc	P113,P123,P124,CSR
Swinton, Thomas L.	Cpt	B 23rd SCVI	Dinwiddie C.H., VA	04/01/65	Old Capitol, DC	04/09/65	Johnson's Isl., OH	P110,CSR
					Johnson's Isl., OH	06/19/65	Rlsd. G.O. #109	P81,P82,P83,CSR
Switzer, L. Oscar	Pvt	D 27th SCVI	Town Creek, NC	02/20/65	Ft. Anderson, NC	02/28/65	Pt. Lookout, MD	CSR,HAG
					Pt. Lookout, MD	06/19/65	Rlsd. G.O. #109	P115,P118,CSR
Sylvanus, J.	Smn	Dis. Boat	Morris Island, SC	09/07/63	Pt. Lookout, MD	09/20/64	Ft. Warren, MA	P113
					Ft. Warren, MA	10/01/64	Str. Circasian	P2,P137
Syphrett, Obadiah J.	Pvt	G 25th SCVI	Ft. Fisher, NC	01/15/65	New York, NY	01/30/65	Elmira, NY	CSR,HAG
					Elmira, NY	06/23/65	Rlsd. G.O. #109	P65,P66,HAG

SOUTH CAROLINA SOLDIERS, SAILORS AND  CITIZENS HELD IN U.S. PRISONS 1861-1865

NAME	RANK	REGIMENT	CAPTURED AT	WHEN	PRISON	MOVED	DISPOSITION	SOURCES
Tabler, Charles	Bug	A 10th SCVI	Booneville, MS	06/03/62	No further data		Missing	RAS,CSR
Tadlock, W.T.	Pvt	I 26th SCVI	Richmond, VA	04/03/65	Newport News, VA	06/13/65	Rlsd. G.O. #109	P107
Taggart, Patrick	Pvt	K 15th SCVI	Cumberland Gap, TN	02/04/64	Louisville, KY	02/09/64	Rock Island, IL	P88,P93,KEB,H15
					Rock Island, IL	10/14/64	Jd.USA Frontier S.	P131,CSR
Taggert, Alexander	Pvt	B 1st SCVA		06/27/65	Paroled			CSR
Talbert, C.L.	Pvt	F 26th SCVI	Richmond, VA Hos.	04/03/65	Richmond, VA Hos.	05/12/65	Rlsd. on parole	CSR
Talbert, James Franklin	Pvt	G 19th SCVI	Atlanta, GA	08/13/64	Nashville, TN	08/30/64	Louisville, KY	CSR
					Louisville, KY	09/02/64	Camp Chase, OH	P90,P93,CSR
					Camp Chase, OH	01/27/65	Died, Gen. Debility	P6,P22,P27,FPH,CSR
Talbert, Joseph W.	Pvt	I 15th SCVI	Spotsylvania, VA	05/08/64	Frdereicksburg, VA	05/12/64	Alexandria, VA USH	CSR,KEB,H15
					Alexandria, VA USH	05/16/64	Lincoln G.H., DC	CSR
					Lincoln G.H., VA	05/27/64	Old Capitol, DC	CSR
					Old Capitol, DC	06/15/64	Ft. Delaware, DE	CSR
					Ft. McHenry, MD	06/15/64	Ft. Delaware, DE	P110,CSR
					Ft. Delaware, DE	09/20/64	Hos. 9/20-9/27/64	P47,CSR
					Ft. Delaware, DE	09/30/64	Aikens Ldg., VA Xc	P41,P42,CSR
Talbert, Thomas B.	Sgt	G 14th SCVI	Petersburg, VA	04/04/65	City Pt., VA	04/13/65	Pt. Lookout, MD	CSR
					Pt. Lookout, MD	06/20/65	Rlsd. G.O. #109	P115,P119,P121,CSR
Tallevast, Alexander	Pvt	B 21st SCVI	Ft. Fisher, NC	01/15/65	New York, NY	01/30/65	Elmira, NY	CSR
					Elmira, NY	04/04/65	Died, Diarrhea	P5,P12,P65,P66,FPH
Talley, Evan	Pvt	A 20th SCVI	Deserted/enemy	08/10/63	Knoxville, TN	07/14/64	Louisville, KY	P8,CSR
					Louisville, KY	07/31/64	Sent north on oath	P90,P92,CSR
Talley, W.D.	Pvt	A 3rd SCVABn	High Pt., NC	05/02/65	High Pt., NC	05/02/65	Paroled	CSR
Tankersley, John	Pvt	H 22nd SCVI	Deserted/enemy	03/18/65	Knoxville, TN	03/21/65	Louisville, KY	P8,CSR
					Louisville, KY	03/21/65	Sent north on oath	P8,P92,CSR
Tanner, Alonzo	Pvt	C 13th SCVI	Appomattox R., VA	04/03/65	City Pt., VA	04/13/65	Pt. Lookout, MD	CSR,HOS
					Pt. Lookout, MD	06/20/65	Rlsd. G.O. #109	P115,P119,P121,CSR
Tanner, James Robert	Pvt	G 15th SCVI	Charleston, SC Hos.	02/18/65	Charleston, SC	03/27/65	Paroled on oath	H15,KEB
Tanner, John	Pvt	H 1st SCVA	Morris Island, SC	07/10/63	Hilton Head, SC			CSR
Tanner, W.T.	Pvt	A 3rd SCVABn	High Pt., NC	05/02/65	High Pt., NC	05/02/65	Paroled	CSR
Tannery, J.A.	Pvt	F Orr's Ri.	Falling Waters, MD	07/14/63	Baltimore, MD	08/21/63	Pt. Lookout, MD	CSR
					Pt. Lookout, MD	03/17/64	City Pt., VA Xc	P113,P116,P123,CSR
Tant, L.O.	Pvt	I 11th SCVI	Barnwell Dist., SC	02/07/65	New Berne, NC	04/10/65	Hart's Island, NY	CSR,HAG
					Hart's Island, NY	06/17/65	Rlsd. G.O. #109	P79, CSR
Tant, Spartan G.	Pvt	I 11th SCVI	Town Creek, NC	02/20/65	Ft. Anderson, NC	02/28/65	Pt. Lookout, MD	CSR,HAG
					Pt. Lookout MD	06/05/65	Rlsd. On oath	CSR
Tarlton, Andrew J.	Pvt	E 21st SCVI	Ft. Fisher, NC	01/15/65	New York, NY	01/30/65	Elmira, NY	CSR,HAG
					Elmira, NY	07/05/65	Rlsd. G.O. #109	P65,P66
Tarrant, W.W.	Cpl	F Ham.Leg,MI	Newton, NC	04/19/65	Newton, NC	04/19/65	Paroled	CSR
Tart, Henry H.	Pvt	McQueen LA	Petersburg, VA	04/02/65	City Pt., VA	04/04/65	Pt. Lookout, MD	CSR
					Pt. Lookout, MD	06/20/65	Rlsd. G.O. #109	CSR
Tart, John M.	Pvt	McQueen LA	Farmville, VA	04/11/65	Farmville, VA	04/21/65	Paroled	CSR
Tart, L.C.	Pvt	D 10th SCVI	Chaplin Hill, KY	10/05/62	Harrodsburg, KY H.	11/13/62	Died	P12,RAS,HMC
Tate, James B.	Sgt	H 18th SCVI	Crater, Pbg., VA	07/30/64	City Pt., VA	08/05/64	Pt. Lookout, MD	CSR,YEB
					Pt. Lookout, MD	08/08/64	Elmira, NY	P116,P117,P125,CSR
					Elmira, NY	10/11/64	Pt. Lookout, MD Xc	P65,P66,CSR
					Pt. Lookout, MD	10/29/64	Exchanged	P115,CSR
Tate, James T.	Pvt	E 13th SCVI	Petersburg, VA	04/02/65	Pt. Lookout, MD	06/21/65	Rlsd. G.O. #109	P115
Tate, W.B.	Cpl	D Orr's Ri.	Petersburg, VA	04/03/65	City Pt., VA	04/11/65	Hart's Island, NY	CSR,CDC
					Hart's Island, NY	06/16/65	Rlsd. G.O. #109	P79,CSR
Tatum, John H.	Pvt	A 18th SCVI	Richmond, VA	04/03/65	Newport News, VA	06/30/65	Rlsd. G.O. #109	P107

T

SOUTH CAROLINA SOLDIERS, SAILORS AND CITIZENS HELD IN U.S. PRISONS 1861-1865

NAME	RANK	REGIMENT	CAPTURED AT	WHEN	PRISON	MOVED	DISPOSITION	SOURCES
Tatum, R.J.	Pvt	G 8th SCVI	New Creek, VA	07/13/63	Wheeling, WV	07/22/63	Camp Chase, OH	P1,HOM,CSR,KEB
					Ft. Delaware, DE	12/02/64	Hos. 12/2-12/15/64	P47
					Camp Chase, OH	02/27/64	Ft. Delaware, DE	P22,P25,P26,CSR
					Ft. Delaware, DE	06/10/65	Released	P41,P42,P45,CSR
Taulman, F.A.	Pvt	C 3rd SCVABn	Blakely, AL	04/09/65	Ship Island, MS	05/01/65	Vicksburg, MS Xc	CSR
Taylor, A.J.	Pvt	D 1st SCVIH	Knoxville, TN	01/25/64	Knoxville, TN	01/25/64	Released on oath	P84,SA1,LAN,CSR
					Knoxville, TN	03/18/64	Died, Smallpox	P12
Taylor, Aaron	Pvt	K 13th SCVI	Petersburg, VA	04/02/65	City Pt., VA	04/04/65	Ft. Delaware, DE	CSR
					Ft. Delaware, DE	06/10/65	Rlsd. G.O. #109	P41,P42,P45,CSR
Taylor, Benjamin B.	Pvt	H 23rd SCVI	Five Forks, VA	04/01/65	City Pt., VA	04/06/65	Pt. Lookout, MD	CSR,HMC
					Pt. Lookout, MD	06/28/65	Died, Ch. Dysentery	P6,P12,P119,FPH
Taylor, David	Pvt	E 1st SCVIG	Winchester, VA	12/02/62	Winchester, VA	12/04/64	Paroled	SA1,CSR
Taylor, E.G.	Pvt	D 27th SCVI	Weldon RR, VA	08/21/64	City Pt., VA	08/24/64	Pt. Lookout, MD	CSR,HAG
					Pt. Lookout, MD	02/13/65	Aikens Ldg., VA Xc	P113,P116,P121
Taylor, G.W.	Pvt	K 1st SCVC	Upperville, VA	06/21/63	Ft. McHenry, MD	06/25/63	City Pt., VA Xc	P110,CSR
Taylor, George	Pvt	G 2nd SCVC	Augusta, GA	05/28/65	Augusta, GA	05/28/64	Paroled	CSR
Taylor, George B.	Pvt	C 7th SCVIBn	Ft. Motte, SC	02/15/65	New Berne, NC	04/03/65	Pt. Lookout, MD	CSR
					Pt. Lookout, MD	06/21/65	Rlsd. G.O. #109	P115,P117,CSR
Taylor, Henry B.	Pvt	F 27th SCVI	Ft. Anderson, NC	02/19/65	Ft. Anderson, NC	02/28/65	Pt. Lookout, MD	CSR,HAG
					Pt. Lookout, MD	06/30/65	Rlsd. G.O. #109	P115,P117,CSR
Taylor, Henry S.	Pvt	F 14th SCVI	Gettysburg, PA	07/05/63	Harrisburg, PA	07/07/63	Ft. Delaware, DE	CSR
					Ft. Delaware, DE	06/10/65	Released	P40,P42,P44,CSR
					Ft. Delaware, DE	04/11/64	Dis. Hos. 4/11/64	P47
Taylor, Hiram	Pvt	C 27th SCVI	Town Creek, NC	02/20/65	Ft. Anderson, NC	02/28/65	Pt. Lookout, MD	CSR,HAG
					Pt. Lookout, MD	06/30/65	Rlsd. G.O. #109	P115,P117,HAG,CSR
Taylor, J.C.	Pvt	I 7th SCVI	Sharpsburg, MD	09/28/62	Ft. McHenry, MD	11/12/62	City Pt., VA Xc	CSR
Taylor, J.H.	Pvt	E 5th SCVC	Stony Creek, VA	12/01/64	City Pt., VA	12/05/64	Pt. Lookout, MD	CSR
					Pt. Lookout, MD	06/06/65	Rlsd. Instr. 5/30/65	P115,P117,P121,CSR
Taylor, J.H.	Pvt	H 6th SCVI	Columbia, SC	02/20/65	New Berne, NC	04/10/65	Hart's Island, NY	CSR
					Hart's Island, NY	06/16/65	Rlsd. G.O. #109	P79,CSR
Taylor, J.M.	Pvt	H 4th SCVC	Stony Creek, VA	12/01/64	City Pt., VA	12/05/64	Pt. Lookout, MD	CSR
					Pt. Lookout, MD	06/21/65	Rlsd. G.O. #109	P115,P117,CSR
Taylor, J.P.	Pvt	I Ham.Leg.MI	Farmville, VA	04/11/65	Farmville, VA	04/11/65	Paroled	CSR
Taylor, J.S.	Pvt	C 3rd SCVABn	Blakely, AL	04/09/65	Ship Island, MS	05/01/65	Vicksburg, MS Xc	P136,CSR
					Vicksburg, MS	05/03/65	Exchanged	CSR
Taylor, J.W.	Pvt	G 25th SCVI	Ft. Fisher, NC	01/15/65	Fts. Monroe, VA			CSR
Taylor, James	Pvt	Ferguson's LA	Macon, GA	04/20/65	Macon, GA		No release data	CSR
Taylor, James M.	Pvt.	I 12th SCVI	Petersburg, VA	04/02/65	City Pt., VA	04/04/65	Pt. Lookout, MD	CSR
					Pt. Lookout, MD	06/21/65	Rlsd. G.O. #109	P115,P117,CSR
Taylor, James O.	Pvt	I 1st SCVIG	Petersburg, VA	04/03/65	City Pt., VA	04/13/65	Pt. Lookout, MD	CSR,SA1
					Pt. Lookout, MD	06/21/65	Rlsd. G.O. #109	P115,P119,CSR
Taylor, James Rediford	Pvt	D 1st SCVIH	Mossy Creek, TN	10/29/63	Nashville, TN	02/11/64	Louisville, KY	P39,SA1,CSR,LAN
Taylor, James Rediford	Pvt	D 1st SCVIH	Mossy Creek, TN	01/22/64	Louisville, KY	02/15/64	Rock Island, IL	P88,P91,P93,CSR
					Rock Island, IL	03/02/65	Pt. Lookout to Xc	P131,CSR
Taylor, James T.	Pvt	E 18th SCVI	Farmville, VA	04/06/65	City Pt., VA	04/14/65	Newport News, VA	CSR,HOS
					Newport News, VA	06/26/65	Rlsd. G.O. #109	P107,CSR
Taylor, Jefferson M.	Pvt	G 13th SCVI	Petersburg, VA	03/25/65	City Pt., VA	03/28/65	Pt. Lookout, MD	CSR,ANY
					Pt. Lookout, MD	06/20/65	Rlsd. G.O. #109	P115,P117,P121,CSR
Taylor, Jesse	Pvt	F 16th SCVI	Nashville, TN	12/18/64	Nashville, TN	01/04/65	Louisville, KY	P3,P39,16R
Taylor, Jesse	Pvt	F 16th SCVI	Franklin, TN	12/17/64	Louisville, KY	01/09/65	Camp Chase, OH	P92,P94,CSR
					Camp Chase, OH	03/26/65	Pt. Lookout, MD	P23,P26,CSR
					Pt. Lookout, MD	06/20/65	Rlsd. G.O. #109	P115,P119,P121,CSR

SOUTH CAROLINA SOLDIERS, SAILORS AND  CITIZENS HELD IN U.S. PRISONS 1861-1865

NAME	RANK	REGIMENT	CAPTURED AT	WHEN	PRISON	MOVED	DISPOSITION	SOURCES
Taylor, John	2Lt	B Hol.Leg.C.	White House, VA	07/03/63	Ft. Delaware, DE	07/18/63	Johnson's Isl., OH	P44,P144,CSR
					Johnson's Isl., OH	03/14/65	Pt. Lookout, MD Xc	P80,P81,CSR
Taylor, John G.	Pvt	B 17th SCVI	Amelia C.H., VA	04/03/65	City Pt., VA	04/13/65	Pt. Lookout, MD	CSR,HFC
					Pt. Lookout, MD	06/04/65	Rlsd. Instr. 5/30/65	P115,P119,P121,CSR
Taylor, Joseph R.	Pvt	E 23rd SCVI	Deserted/enemy	04/06/65	Washington, DC	04/06/65	Rlsd. on oath	CSR
Taylor, M.	Pvt.	B 1st SC Eng	Richmond, VA	04/03/65	Newport News, VA	06/30/65	Rlsd. G.O. #109	P107
Taylor, Marshal	Pvt	K 13th SCVI	Gettysburg, PA	07/03/63	David's Island, NY	09/05/63	City Pt., VA Xc	P1,CSR
Taylor, Martin L.	Sgt	K 20th SCVI	Cedar Creek, VA	10/19/64	Harpers Ferry, WV	03/24/64	Pt. Lookout, MD	CSR
					Pt. Lookout, MD	06/20/65	Rlsd. G.O. #109	P115,P117,P121,KEB,CSR
Taylor, Middleton E.	Pvt	F 25th SCVI	Ft. Fisher, NC	01/15/65	New York, NY	01/30/65	Elmira, NY	CSR
					Elmira, NY	02/20/65	James R., VA Xc	P65,P66,HAG,CSR
					Richmond Hospital	03/15/65	Died	CSR
Taylor, Pinckney H.	Pvt	F 25th SCVI	Ft. Fisher, NC	01/15/65	New York, NY	01/30/65	Elmira, NY	CSR,HAG
					Elmira, NY	07/07/65	Rlsd. G.O. #109	P65,P66,CSR
Taylor, Preston	Pvt	E 1st SCVIH	Frederick, MD	10/12/62	Frederick, MD USGH	10/13/62	U.S. Gen. Hospital	CSR,SA1
					Ft. McHenry, MD	10/14/62	Aikens Ldg., VA Xc	CSR
Taylor, Preston	Pvt	E 1st SCVIH	Frederick, MD	10/12/62	Richmond, VA Hos.	11/12/62	FUR 60 days	CSR
Taylor, R.	Pvt	Brooks LA	South Mtn., PA	07/05/63	Ft. Delaware, DE	07/30/63	City Pt., VA Xc	P42
Taylor, S.H.	Pvt	F 22nd SCVI	Bermuda Hundred, VA	06/02/64	Bermuda Hundred, VA	06/03/64	Fts. Monroe, VA	CSR
					Fts. Monroe, VA	06/04/54	Pt. Lookout, MD	CSR
					Pt. Lookout, MD	02/18/65	Aikens Ldg., VA Xc	P113,P116,P123
					Jackson Hos. Rchmd.	02/27/65	Camp Lee, VA	CSR
Taylor, Samuel	Pvt	McQueen LA	Farmville, VA	04/11/65	Farmville, VA	04/21/65	Paroled	CSR
Taylor, Samuel H.	Pvt	F 24th SCVI	Chickamauga, TN	11/26/63	Nashville, TN	12/27/63	Louisville, KY	P39,CSR
					Louisville, KY	12/29/63	Rock Island, IL	P88,P89,P93,CSR
					Rock Island, IL	05/23/64	Joined US Navy	P131,CSR
Taylor, Thompson Y.	Sgt	E 14th SCVI	Amelia C.H., VA	04/05/65	City Pt., VA	04/14/65	Pt. Lookout, MD	CSR
					Pt. Lookout, MD	06/21/65	Rlsd. G.O. #109	P115,P119,P122
Taylor, W.E.	Pvt	C 3rd SCVABn	Blakely, AL	04/09/65	Ship Island, MS	05/01/65	Vicksburg, MS	P136,CSR
					Vicksburg, MS	05/03/65	Exchanged	CSR
Taylor, W.P.	Pvt	I Ham.Leg.MI	Farmville, VA	04/07/65	USGH Farmville, VA	05/02/65	Died	P6,CSR
Taylor, William B.F.	Pvt	F 24th SCVI	Ringgold, GA	11/27/63	Nashville, TN	12/11/63	Louisville, KY	P39,CSR
					Louisville, KY	12/12/63	Rock Island, IL	P88,P89,CSR
					Rock Island, IL	03/02/65	Pt. Lookout, MD Xc	P131,CSR
Taylor, William E.	Pvt	C 12th SCVI	Spotsylvania, VA	05/12/64	Belle Plain, VA	05/20/64	Ft. Delaware, DE	CSR,HFC,UD2
					Ft. Delaware, DE	06/10/65	Rlsd. G.O. #109	P41,P42,CSR
Taylor, William H.	Pvt	B 27th SCVI	Town Creek, NC	02/20/65	Ft. Anderson, NC	02/28/65	Pt. Lookout, MD	CSR,HAG
					Pt. Lookout, MD	05/15/65	Rlsd. G.O. #85	P115,P117,P121,CSR
Taylor, William W.	Pvt	G 25th SCVI	Weldon RR, VA	08/21/64	Fts. Monroe, VA	08/26/64	Alexandria, VA G.H.	CSR,HAG
					Alexandria G.H.	09/11/64	Died of wounds	P1,CSR
Teabout, Thomas	Pvt	I 25th SCVI	Ft. Fisher, NC	01/15/65	Fts. Monroe, VA			CSR
Teague, Henry	Pvt	I 5th SCVI	Seven Pines, VA	05/31/62	Chesapeake G.H. VA	06/09/62	Died, Suicide	P12,SA3,HOS,CSR
Teague, William C.	Pvt	E 6th SCVC	Petersburg, VA	07/30/64	City Pt., VA	08/04/64	Pt. Lookout, MD	CSR
					Pt. Lookout, MD	08/08/64	Elmira, NY	P116,P120,P125,CSR
					Elmira, NY	02/01/65	Died, Ch. Diarrhea	P5,P12,P65,FPH,CSR
Teal, David R.	Pvt	E 21st SCVI	Chesterfield, SC	03/04/65	New Berne, NC	03/30/65	Pt. Lookout, MD	CSR,HAG
					Pt. Lookout, MD	06/21/65	Rlsd. G.O. #109	P115,P117,P122
Teal, Duncan	Pvt	K 6th SCVC	Stony Creek, VA	12/01/64	City Pt., VA	12/04/64	Pt. Lookout, MD	CSR
					Pt. Lookout, MD	06/20/65	Rlsd. G.O. #109	P117,P121,CSR
Teal, George Washington	Pvt	D 21st SCVI	Ft. Fisher, NC	01/15/65	New York, NY	01/30/65	Elmira, NY	CSR,HAG
					Elmira, NY	04/07/65	Died, Pneumonia	P5,P65,P66,FPH

SOUTH CAROLINA SOLDIERS, SAILORS AND **T** CITIZENS HELD IN U.S. PRISONS 1861-1865

NAME	RANK	REGIMENT	CAPTURED AT	WHEN	PRISON	MOVED	DISPOSITION	SOURCES
Teal, Harrison	Pvt	C 15th SCVAB	Cheraw, SC	03/06/65	New Berne, NC	04/03/65	Pt. Lookout, MD	CSR
					Pt. Lookout, MD	06/20/65	Rlsd. G.O. #109	P115,CSR
Teal, J.C.	Pvt	L 1st SCVIG	Petersburg, VA	04/02/65	City Pt. VA	04/07/65	Hart's Island, NY	CSR,SA1
					Hart's Island, NY	06/16/65	Rlsd. G.O. #109	P79,CSR
Tedder, Daniel M.	Pvt	C 1st SCVIR	Bentonville, NC	03/22/65	New Berne, NC	04/10/65	Hart's Island, NY	CSR,SA1
					Hart's Island, NY	06/17/65	Rlsd. G.O. #109	P79,CSR
Tedder, Richard F.	Pvt	C 3rd SCVABn	Blakely, AL	04/09/65	Ship Island, MS	05/01/65	Vicksburg, MS	P136,CSR
					Vicksburg, MS	05/03/65	Exchanged	CSR
Tedder, Stephen	Pvt	G 3rd SCVC	Darlington Dist.	03/03/65	New Berne, NC	04/10/65	Hart's Island, NY	P6,CSR
					Hart's Island, NY	05/10/65	Died, Typhoid	P6,P79,CSR
Tedder, Wyley	Pvt	I 18th SCVI	Petersburg, VA	04/02/65	City Pt., VA	04/04/65	Pt. Lookout, MD	CSR
					Pt. Lookout, MD	06/21/65	Rlsd. G.O. #109	P115,P117,CSR
Teichman, Herman	Pvt	B German LA	Gettysburg, VA	07/04/63	Ft. Delaware, DE	05/10/65	Rlsd. G.O. #85	P40,P42,P44
Telford, R.C.	Sgt	K Orr's Ri.	Petersburg, VA	04/03/65	City Pt., VA	04/11/65	Hart's Island, NY	CSR
					Hart's Island, NY	06/19/65	Rlsd. G.O. #109	P79,CSR
Telford, W.B.	Pvt	L P.S.S.	Darbytown Rd., VA	10/07/64	Bermuda Hundred, VA	10/21/64	City Pt., VA	CSR
					City Pt., VA	10/29/64	Pt. Lookout, MD	CSR
					Pt. Lookout, MD	05/14/65	Released G.O. #85	P115,TSE,CSR
Templeton, H.B.	Pvt	B 14th SCMil	Lynch's Creek, SC	02/25/65	Hart's Island, NY	06/01/65	Died, Ch. Diarrhea	P6,P12,P79,FPH
Templeton, H.T.	Pvt	A 3rd SCVI	Knoxville, TN	12/03/63	Knoxville, TN	12/29/63	Louisville, KY	CSR,SA2,H3
					Louisville, KY	12/31/63	Rock Island, IL	P88,P89,P93,SCR
					Rock Island, IL	06/22/65	Rlsd. G.O. #109	P131,CSR
Templeton, J.W.	Pvt	B 12th SCVI	Warrenton, VA	09/29/62	Warrenton, VA	09/29/62	Paroled	CSR
Templeton, John A.	Pvt	B 15th SCVI	Halltown, VA	08/26/64	Harpers Ferry, WV	08/29/64	Camp Chase, OH	CSR,KEB,UD5
					Camp Chase, OH	03/25/65	Pt. Lookout, MD	P22,CSR
					Pt. Lookout, MD	06/21/65	Rlsd. G.O. #109	P115,P119,CSR
Templeton, Samuel	Pvt	F 14th SCVI	Amelia C.H., VA	04/05/65	City Pt., VA	04/13/65	Pt. Lookout, MD	CSR
					Pt. Lookout, MD	06/20/65	Rlsd. G.O. #109	P115,P119,P121
Templeton, W.C.	Pvt	F 22nd SCVI	Bermuda Hundred, VA	06/02/64	Bermuda Hundred, VA	06/03/64	Fts. Monroe, VA	CSR
					Fts. Monroe, VA	06/04/64	Pt. Lookout, MD	CSR
					Pt. Lookout, MD	09/18/64	Aikens Ldg., VA Xc	P113,P116,CSR
					Jackson Hos. Rchmd.	09/26/64	Scurvy, Furl. 40 days	CSR
Templeton, William C.	Pvt	F 14th SCVI	Appomattox R., VA	04/03/65	City Pt., VA	04/11/65	Hart's Island, NY	CSR
					Hart's Island, NY	06/17/65	Rlsd. G.O. #109	P79,CSR
Tennant, William	Pvt	K Ham.Leg.MI	Richmond, VA Hos.	04/03/65	Richmond, VA Hos.	04/14/65	Provost Marshal	CSR
					Libby Prison Rchmd.	04/23/65	Newport News, VA	CSR
					Newport News, VA	06/26/65	Rlsd. G.O. #109	CSR
Tennent, T.G.	Pvt	I 7th SCVI	Sharpsburg, MD	09/17/62	Ft. McHenry, MD	10/17/62	Aikens Ldg., VA Xc	CSR
Terrell, A.N.	Pvt	H 4th SCVC	Louisa C.H., VA	06/11/64	Fts. Monroe, VA	06/20/64	Pt. Lookout, MD	CSR
					Pt. Lookout, MD	07/25/64	Elmira, NY	P113,P116,P120,CSR
					Elmira, NY	03/14/65	Pt. Lookout, MD Xc	P65,P66,CSR
Terrell, H.C.	Pvt	Ham.Leg.			Ft. McHenry, MD	11/13/62	Fts. Monroe, VA	P145
Terrell, James B.	Pvt	B 5th SCVI	Shell Mound, TN		Bridgeport, AL G.H.	11/26/63	Died, G.S. L lung	P2,P6,P12,SA3,CSR
Terry, E.L.	Cpl	D 27th SCVI	Weldon RR, VA	08/21/64	City Pt., VA	08/24/64	Pt. Lookout, MD	CSR,HAG
					Pt. Lookout, MD	03/14/65	Aikens Ldg., VA Xc	P113,P116,P121
Terry, G.W.	Cpl	B 2nd SCVC	Augusta, GA	05/29/65	Augusta, GA	05/29/65	Paroled	CSR
Terry, George W.	Cpl	K 25th SCVI	Ft. Fisher, NC	01/15/65	New York, NY	01/30/65	Elmira, NY	CSR,CTA,HAG
					Elmira, NY	07/11/65	Rlsd. G.O. #109	P65,P66
Terry, J.M.	Pvt	B 2nd SCVC	Augusta, GA	05/25/65	Augusta, GA	05/25/65	Paroled	CSR
Terry, James B.	Pvt	Ferguson's	Salisbury, NC	04/12/65	Nashville, TN	04/29/65	Louisville, KY	CSR
					Louisville, KY	05/02/65	Camp Chase, OH	P92,P94,CSR
					Camp Chase, OH	06/13/65	Rlsd. G.O. #109	CSR

SOUTH CAROLINA SOLDIERS, SAILORS AND  CITIZENS HELD IN U.S. PRISONS 1861-1865

NAME	RANK	REGIMENT	CAPTURED AT	WHEN	PRISON	MOVED	DISPOSITION	SOURCES
Terry, Thomas W.	Pvt	Palmetto A	Paynesville, VA	04/05/65	City Pt., VA	04/13/65	Pt. Lookout, MD	CSR
					Pt. Lookout, MD	06/03/65	Released on oath	P119,CSR
Terry, William H.	Pvt	C 14th SCVI	Falling Waters, MD	07/14/63	Baltimore, MD	08/16/63	Pt. Lookout, MD	CSR
					Pt. Lookout, MD	03/03/64	City Pt., VA Xc	P113,P116,P123,CSR
Terry, William H.	Pvt	C 14th SCVI	Petersburg, VA	04/03/65	City Pt., VA	04/11/65	Hart's Island, NY	CSR
					Hart's Island, NY	06/17/65	Rlsd. G.O. #109	P79,CSR
Terry, William P.	Pvt	D 24th SCVI	Nashville, TN	12/16/64	Nashville, TN	12/31/64	Louisville, KY	P39,CSR
					Louisville, KY	01/02/65	Camp chase, OH	P92,P94,CSR
					Camp Chase, OH	01/09/65	Died, Pneumonia	P5,P12,P22,P27,FPH
Thacker, J.P.	Pvt	D 22nd SCVI	Deserted/enemy	02/24/65	P.M. City Pt., VA	02/26/65	Washington, DC	CSR
					Washington, DC	02/27/65	Savannah, GA	CSR
Thackston, James M..	Pvt	F Ham.Leg.MI	Burkesville, VA	04/06/65	City Pt., VA P.M.	04/14/65	Pt. Lookout, MD	CSR
					Pt. Lookout, MD	06/20/65	Rlsd. G.O. #109	P121,CSR
Thackston, John	Cpl	C 16th SCVI	Hartwell, GA	05/18/65	Hartwell, GA	05/16/65	Paroled on oath	CSR
Thackston, William P.	Pvt	F Ham.Leg.	Fair Oaks, VA	05/31/62	Fts. Monroe, VA	06/05/62	Ft. Delaware, DE	CSR
					Ft. Delaware, DE	08/05/62	Aikens Ldg., VA Xc	CSR
Thames, Francis	Pvt	D 11th SCVI	Town Creek, NC	02/20/65	USHS Spaulding	02/28/65	Wilmington, NC USH	CSR
					Wilmington, NC USH	04/23/65	Smithville, NC USH	CSR
Thames, Robert J.,Jr.	Pvt	I 23rd SCVI	Deserted/enemy	03/03/65	Washington, DC	03/07/65	Charleston, SC	CSR
Thames, Robert J.,Sr.	Pvt	I 23rd SCVI	Petersburg, VA	04/02/65	City Pt. VA	04/05/65	Pt. Lookout, MD	CSR,HCL
					Pt. Lookout, MD	06/21/65	Rlsd. G.O. #109	P115,P118,P122,CSR
Thames, Rufus R.	Pvt	D 4th SCVC	Louisa C.H., VA	06/11/64	Fts. Monroe, VA	06/20/64	Pt. Lookout, MD	CSR
					Pt. Lookout, MD	10/11/64	Aikens Ldg., VA Xc	P113,P116,P123,CSR
Thames, S.J.	Pvt	I 23rd SCVI	Deserted/enemy	04/04/65	Washington, DC			CSR
Thames, T.W.	Pvt	I 23rd SCVI	Deserted/enemy	02/25/65	City Pt., VA	02/28/65	Washington, DC	CSR
					Washington, DC	03/01/65	Trenton, N.J. oath	CSR
Tharin, Manley R.	2Lt	L 1st SCVIG	Saylors Creek, VA	04/03/65	Old Capitol, DC	04/24/65	Johnson's Isl., OH	P110,SA1,CSR
					Johnson's Isl., OH	06/20/65	Rlsd. G.O. #109	P81,P83,CSR
Tharp, Wesley	Pvt	M 10th SCVI	Kentucky	09/15/62	Kentucky	11/15/62	Paroled	CSR,RAS
Thees, H.	Pvt	G 3rd SCVC	Deserted/enemy	03/17/65	Charleston, SC	04/01/65	Taken oath & disch.	CSR
Them, James	Pvt	B 26th SCVI	Petersburg, VA	04/01/65	Pt. Lookout, MD	06/21/65	Rlsd. G.O. #109	P115
Therrell, James	Pvt	H 1st SCVIR	Charlotte, NC Hos.	05/15/65	Charlotte, NC	05/15/65	Paroled	SA1,CSR
Thiele, Phillip	Pvt	A German LA	Deserted/enemy	03/31/65	Savannah, GA	03/31/65	Charleston, SC	CSR
Thigpen, Jackson	Pvt	A 15th SCVAB	Thomasville, NC Hos.	05/01/65	Thomasville, NC	05/01/65	Paroled	CSR
Thomas, Alfred E.	Pvt	D 2nd SCVC	Beverly Ford, VA	06/09/63	Old Capitol, DC	06/25/63	City Pt., VA Xc	CSR
					Ft. McHenry, MD	06/25/63	City Pt., VA Xc	P110
Thomas, Alfred E.	Pvt	D 2nd SCVC	Deserted/enemy	04/26/65	Charleston,SC	04/28/65	Released on oath	CSR
Thomas, Amos B.	Pvt	C 19th SCVCB	Florence, SC	03/05/65	Pt. Lookout, MD	06/21/65	Rlsd. G.O. #109	P115,P117
Thomas, Angus P.	Pvt	C 19th SCVCB	Florence, SC	03/05/65	New Berne, NC	04/03/65	Pt. Lookout, MD	CSR
					Pt. Lookout, MD	06/21/65	Rlsd. G.O. #109	P115,P117,P122,CSR
					Pt. Lookout, MD	06/21/65	Rlsd. G.O. #109	P115,P117,CSR
Thomas, D.	Pvt	E 1st SCVIG	Richmond VA Hos.	04/03/65	Escaped from Hos.	05/04/65		CSR
Thomas, D.J.	Pvt	I 5th SCVC	Augusta, GA	05/19/65	Augusta, GA	05/19/65	Paroled	CSR
Thomas, Daniel Y.	Pvt	F 3rd SCVABn	Deserted/enemy	02/18/65	Charleston, SC	03/27/65	Released on oath	CSR
Thomas, David L.	Pvt	McQueen LA	Petersburg, VA	04/02/65	City Pt., VA	04/04/65	Pt. Lookout, MD	CSR
					Pt. Lookout, MD	06/10/65	Died, Acute Diarrh.	P6,P115,P119,FPH
Thomas, David W.	Pvt	D 14th SCVI	Petersburg, VA	07/29/64	City Pt., VA	08/05/64	Pt. Lookout, MD	CSR,HOE
					Pt. Lookout, MD	08/08/64	Elmira, NY	P113,P116,P120,CSR
					Elmira, NY	06/16/65	Rlsd. G.O. #109	P65,P66,CSR
Thomas, Elisha	Pvt	G 27th SCVI	Weldon RR, VA	08/21/64	City Pt., VA	08/24/64	Pt. Lookout, MD	CSR,HAG
					Pt. Lookout, MD	03/14/65	Aikens Ldg., VA Xc	P113,P116,P121

T

SOUTH CAROLINA SOLDIERS, SAILORS AND CITIZENS HELD IN U.S. PRISONS 1861-1865

NAME	RANK	REGIMENT	CAPTURED AT	WHEN	PRISON	MOVED	DISPOSITION	SOURCES
Thomas, Elliot O.	Sgt	E 14th SCVI	Gettysburg, PA	07/05/63	Chester, PA G.H.	10/04/63	Pt. Lookout, MD	P1,CSR
					Pt. Lookout, MD	03/16/64	City Pt., VA Xc	P116,P124,CSR
Thomas, Emile	Pvt	F 15th SCVI	Deserted/enemy	04/03/65	Charleston, SC	04/03/65	Released on oath	CSR
Thomas, H.L.	Cpl	Santee LA	McIntosh Co., GA	10/15/64	Ft. Delaware, DE		Hos. 2/24-4/17/65	P47,UD5
					Ft. Delaware, DE			P41,P45,UD5,CSR
Thomas, Henry B.	Pvt	I 26th SCVI	Southside RR, VA	04/01/65	City Pt., VA	04/05/65	Pt. Lookout, MD	CSR,CTA
					Pt. Lookout, MD	06/20/65	Rlsd. G.O. #109	P115,P119,P121,CSR
Thomas, J.N.	Pvt	A Hol.Leg.	Richmond, VA Hos.	04/03/65	Pro. Marshal Rchmd.	05/12/65	Paroled	CSR
Thomas, J.W.	Pvt	A Orr's Ri.	Petersburg, VA	04/03/65	City Pt., VA	04/11/65	Hart's Island, NY	CSR
					Hart's Island, NY	06/16/65	Rlsd. G.O. #109	P79,CSR
Thomas, James A.	Pvt	D 12th SCVI	Hagerstown, MD	09/17/62	New York, NY	10/06/62	Aikens Ldg., VA Xc	CSR
Thomas, James A.	Pvt	D 12th SCVI	Farmville, VA	04/11/65	Farmville, VA	04/21/65	Paroled	CSR
Thomas, James H.	Pvt	D 21st SCVI	Ft. Fisher, NC	01/15/65	New York, NY	01/30/65	Elmira, NY	CSR,HAG
					Elmira, NY	07/07/65	Rlsd. G.O. #109	P65,P66
Thomas, James M.	Pvt	M 8th SCVI	Winchester, VA	09/13/64	Harpers Ferry, WV	09/19/64	Camp Chase, OH	CSR,KEB
					Camp Chase, OH	01/29/65	Died, Pneumonia	P6,P12,P22,P27,FPH
Thomas, Jesse	Pvt	I 26th SCVI	Five Forks, VA	04/01/65	City Pt., VA	04/05/65	Pt. Lookout, MD	CSR
					Pt. Lookout, MD	06/20/65	Rlsd. G.O. #109	P115,P119,P121,CSR
Thomas, John	Sgt	A 26th SCVI	Southside RR, VA	04/01/65	Pt. Lookout, MD	06/21/65	Rlsd. G.O. #109	P115,P119,P122,CSR
					City Pt., VA	04/05/65	Pt. Lookout, MD	CSR
Thomas, John	Pvt	C 7th SCVC	Farmville, VA	04/11/65	Farmville, VA	04/21/65	Paroled	CSR
Thomas, John	Pvt	M 7th SCVI	Gettysburg, PA	07/02/63	Ft. Delaware, DE	09/15/63	Jd. US 3rd MD Cav.	P40,P42,P44,CSR
Thomas, John A.	Pvt	K 17th SCVI	Five Forks, VA	04/01/65	City Pt., VA	04/06/65	Pt. Lookout, MD	CSR
					Pt. Lookout, MD	06/20/65	Rlsd. G.O. #109	P115,P119,P121,CSR
Thomas, John B.	Pvt	I 10/19 SCVI	Missionary Ridge, TN	11/25/63	Nashville, TN	12/07/63	Louisville, KY	P39,CSR,RAS
					Louisville, KY	12/09/63	Rock Island, IL	CSR
					Rock Island, IL	03/02/65	Pt. Lookout, MD Xc	P131
Thomas, John M.	Pvt	E Hol.Leg.	Five Forks, VA	04/01/65	City Pt., VA	04/05/65	Pt. Lookout, MD	CSR,HOS
					Pt. Lookout, MD	06/21/65	Rlsd. G.O. #109	P115,P118,CSR
Thomas, John R.	Pvt	B 17th SCVI	Five Forks, VA	04/01/65	City Pt., VA	04/06/65	Pt. Lookout, MD	CSR,HFC
					Pt. Lookout, MD	06/16/65	Rlsd. G.O. #109	P115,P119,P122,CSR
Thomas, John R.	Cpt	C 12th SCVI	Petersburg, VA	04/02/65	Old Capitol, DC	04/10/65	Johnson's Isl., OH	CSR,HFC
					Ft. McHenry, MD	04/09/65	Johnson's Isl., OH	P110
					Johnson's Isl., OH	06/20/65	Rlsd. G.O. #109	P81,P83,CSR
Thomas, Joseph	Pvt	H Orr's Ri.	Richmond, VA Hos.	04/03/65	Jackson H. Rchmd.	06/03/64	Died, G.S. Rt. hip	P12,CDC,HMC
Thomas, Oliver F.	Pvt	F 27th SCVI	Weldon RR, VA	08/21/64	City Pt., VA	08/24/64	Pt. Lookout, MD	CSR,HAG
					Pt. Lookout, MD	02/05/65	Died, Ch. Diarrhea	P5,P12,P113,FPH
Thomas, Peter C.	Pvt	H 2nd SCVC	Jacksonville, NC	03/08/65	New Berne, NC	03/30/65	Pt. Lookout, MD	CSR
					Pt. Lookout, MD	06/21/65	Rlsd. G.O. #109	P115,P117,CSR
Thomas, Phillip	Sgt	D 24th SCVI	Jackson, MS	05/14/63		06/05/63	Demopolis, Prl. cmp.	CSR,EFW
						08/09/63	Xchd	EFW
Thomas, Phillip	Sgt	D 24th SCVI	Nashville, TN	12/16/64	Nashville, TN	12/31/64	Louisville, KY	P39,CSR
					Louisville, KY	01/05/65	Camp Chase, OH	P92,P94,CSR
					Camp Chase, OH	06/12/65	Rlsd. G.O. #109	P22,CSR
Thomas, Phillip	Pvt	E 5th SCVC	Drury's Bluff, VA	05/16/64	Fts. Monroe, VA	05/21/64	Pt. Lookout, MD	CSR
					Pt. Lookout, MD	07/25/64	Elmira, NY	P113,P116,P120,CSR
					Elmira, NY	10/01/64	Died, Typhoid fever	P5,P12,P65,P66,FPH
Thomas, Phillip T.	Pvt	G 23rd SCVI	Five Forks, VA	04/01/65	City Pt. VA	04/05/65	Pt. Lookout, MD	CSR,HOM
					Pt. Lookout, MD	06/20/65	Rlsd. G.O. #109	P115,P121,CSR

SOUTH CAROLINA SOLDIERS, SAILORS AND  CITIZENS HELD IN U.S. PRISONS 1861-1865

NAME	RANK	REGIMENT	CAPTURED AT	WHEN	PRISON	MOVED	DISPOSITION	SOURCES
Thomas, Ransom	Pvt	C 11th SCVI	Drury's Bluff, VA	05/16/64	Bermuda Hundred, VA	05/17/64	Fts. Monroe, VA	CSR,HAG
					Fts. Monroe, VA	05/18/64	Pt. Lookout, MD	CSR
					Pt. Lookout, MD	08/15/64	Elmira, NY	P113,P116,P120
					Elmira, NY	03/02/65	Tfd. for exchange	P65,P66
Thomas, Redden	Pvt	D 11th SCVI	Town Creek, NC	02/20/65	Ft. Anderson, NC	02/28/65	Pt. Lookout, MD	CSR
					Pt. Lookout, MD	06/21/65	Rlsd. G.O. #109	P115,P117,CSR
Thomas, Robert M.	Pvt	E 18th SCVI	Crater, Pbg., VA	07/30/64	City Pt., VA	08/08/64	Pt. Lookout, MD	CSR,HOS
					Pt. Lookout, MD	08/08/64	Elmira, NY	P113,P116,P125,CSR
					Elmira, NY	06/11/65	Rlsd. G.O. #109	P65,P66,CSR
Thomas, Samuel	Pvt	D 22nd SCVI	Boonesboro, MD	09/14/62	Frederick, MD G.H.	10/20/62	Ft. McHenry, MD	CSR
					Ft. McHenry, MD		Fts. Monroe, VA Xc	CSR
Thomas, T.C.	Cpl	G 18th SCVI	Petersburg, VA Hos.	03/25/65	Point of Rocks, VA	04/12/65	Fts. Monroe, VA	CSR
Thomas, Thomas Seborn	Pvt	K 3rd SCVI	Cedar Creek, VA	10/19/64	Harpers Ferry, WV	10/24/64	Pt. Lookout, MD	CSR,KEB,SA2,H3
					Pt. Lookout, MD	05/14/65	Rlsd. G.O. #85	P115,P117,CSR
Thomas, Vincent J.	Pvt	D 11th SCVI	Midway, SC	02/06/65	Fts. Monroe, VA	04/02/65	Washington, DC	HAG,CSR
					Washington, DC	04/05/65	Took oath	CSR
Thomas, W.	Pvt	B 1st SCVIG	Warrenton, VA	09/29/62	Warrenton, VA	09/29/62	Paroled	CSR
Thomas, Wiley B.	Pvt	B 5th SCVC	Augusta, GA	05/23/65	Augusta, GA	05/23/65	Paroled	CSR
Thomas, William	Pvt	D 1st SCVIR	Cheraw, SC	03/06/65	Hart's Island, NY	06/17/65	Rlsd. G.O. #109	P79
Thomas, William F.	Cpl	K 17th SCVI	Petersburg, VA	03/25/65	City Pt., VA	03/28/65	Pt. Lookout, MD	CSR
					Pt. Lookout, MD	06/20/65	Rlsd. G.O. #109	P115,P117,P121,CSR
Thomas, William Kelly	Sgt	D Hol.Leg.C	Williamsburg, VA	11/22/62	Fts. Monroe, VA	11/29/62	Exchanged	CSR
Thomas, William T.	Pvt	D 1st SCVA	Cheraw, SC	03/06/65	New Berne, NC	04/10/65	Hart's Island, NY	CSR
					Hart's Island, NY	06/17/65	Rlsd. G.O. #109	CSR
Thomason, Churchwell S.	Pvt	F Ham.Leg.	Warrenton, VA	09/29/62	Warrenton, VA	09/29/62	Paroled	CSR
Thomason, Francis	Pvt	H 18th SCVI	Five Forks, VA	04/01/65	City Pt., VA	04/04/65	Pt. Lookout, MD	CSR
					Pt. Lookout, MD	06/30/65	Rlsd. G.O. #109	P115,P118,P121,CSR
Thomason, James G.	Pvt	A 12th SCVI	Sutherland Stn., VA	04/02/65	City Pt., VA	04/07/65	Hart's Island, NY	CSR,YEB
					Hart's Island, NY	06/14/65	Rlsd. G.O. #109	P79,CSR
Thomason, James P.	Pvt	F Ham.Leg.MI	Burkeville, VA	04/06/65	City Pt., VA	04/14/65	Pt. Lookout, MD	CSR
					Pt. Lookout, MD	05/30/65	Died, Typhoid fever	P6,P12,P115,FPH
Thomason, John G.	Pvt	C 11th SCVI	Town Creek, NC	02/20/65	Ft. Anderson, NC	02/28/65	Pt. Lookout, MD	CSR,HAG
					Pt. Lookout, MD	06/21/65	Rlsd. G.O. #109	P115,P117,P122,CSR
Thomason, William P.	1Sg	C 14th SCVI	Petersburg, VA	04/03/65	City Pt., VA	04/11/65	Hart's Island, NY	CSR
					Hart's Island, NY	06/17/65	Rlsd. G.O. #109	P79,CSR
Thomasson, John M.	Pvt	A 12th SCVI	Spotsylvania, VA	05/12/64	Belle Plain, VA	05/20/64	Ft. Delaware, DE	CSR,YEB
					Ft. Delaware, DE	07/28/64	Hos. 7/28- 8/11/64	P47
					Ft. Delaware, DE	09/18/64	Aikens Ldg., VA Xc	P41,P42,CSR
Thomlinson, F.F.	Pvt	F 8th SCVI	N. Anna River, VA	05/23/64	Port Royal, VA	05/30/64	Pt. Lookout, MD	KEB,CSR
Thomlinson, Frederick F.	Pvt	L 1st SCVIG	Charlestown, WV	10/16/62	Ft. McHenry, MD	10/25/62	Aikens Ldg. for Xc	SA1,CSR
Thompsn, S.P.M.	Pvt	K 12th SCVI	Warrenton, VA	09/29/62	Warrenton, VA	09/29/62	Paroled	CSR
Thompson, A.	Pvt	H 25th SCVI	Petersburg, VA	05/09/64	Bermuda Hundred, VA	05/11/64	Fts. Monroe, VA	CSR,HAG
					Pt. Lookout, MD	07/25/64	Elmira, NY	P113,P116,P120,CSR
					Elmira, NY	05/19/65	Rlsd. G.O. #85	P65,P66,CSR
Thompson, Alexander	Msc	1st SCVIBn	Morris Island, SC	09/07/63	Ft. Columbus, NY	09/23/63	Took the oath	P1
Thompson, B.S.	Pvt	A 7th SCVC	Farmville, VA	04/11/65	Farmville, VA	04/21/65	Paroled	CSR
Thompson, Benjamin V.	2Lt	E 16th SCVI	Franklin, TN	12/17/64	Nashville, TN	01/04/65	Louisville, KY	P2,P39,16R,CSR
					Louisville, KY	01/09/65	Ft. Delaware, DE	P92,P94,CSR
					Ft. Delaware, DE		Not stated	P43,P47,CSR
Thompson, D.V.	Pvt	F 25th SCVI	Ft. Fisher, NC	01/15/65	Elmira, NY	07/11/65	Rlsd. G.O. #109	P65,P66,CSR
					New York, NY	01/30/65	Elmira, NY	CSR,HAG

T

SOUTH CAROLINA SOLDIERS, SAILORS AND CITIZENS HELD IN U.S. PRISONS 1861-1865

NAME	RANK	REGIMENT	CAPTURED AT	WHEN	PRISON	MOVED	DISPOSITION	SOURCES
Thompson, H.H.	Lt	K P.S.S.	Sharpsburg, MD	09/16/62	Baltimore, MD Hos.	11/03/62	Fts. Monroe, VA	CSR,TSE
					Fts. Monroe, VA	11/05/62	Aikens Ldg., VA Xc	CSR
					Aikens Ldg., VA	11/08/62	Exchanged	CSR
Thompson, Henry	Pvt	G 23rd SCVI	Petersburg, VA	06/17/64	City Pt., VA	06/27/64	Pt. Lookout, MD	CSR
					Pt. Lookout, MD	07/27/64	Elmira, NY	P113,P116,P120
					Elmira, NY	10/21/64	Died, Pneumonia	P5,P12,P65,P66,FPH
Thompson, Henry J.	Pvt	F 7th SCVIBn	Weldon RR, VA	08/21/64	City Pt., VA	08/24/64	Pt. Lookout, MD	HAG,HIC,LAN,CSR
					Pt. Lookout, MD	02/18/65	Aikens Ldg, VA Xc	P113,P116,P123,CSR
					Richmond, VA Hos.	03/06/65	Furloughed 30 days	CSR
Thompson, J.A.	Pvt	A Ham.Leg.MI	Anderson, SC	05/03/65	Anderson, SC	05/03/65	Paroled	CSR
Thompson, J.C.	Pvt	I 26th SCVI	Crater, Pbg., VA	07/30/64	Bermuda Hundred, VA	06/25/64	Fts. Monroe, VA	CSR
					Fts. Monroe, VA	06/26/64	Pt. Lookout, MD	CSR
					Pt. Lookout, MD	08/16/64	Elmira, NY	P113,P116,P120,CSR
Thompson, J.C.	Pvt	B 27th SCVI	Petersburg, VA	06/24/64	Elmira, NY	07/11/65	Rlsd. G.O. #109	P65,P66,CSR
Thompson, J.C.	Pvt	I 26th SCVI	Crater, Pbg., VA	07/30/64	City Pt., VA	08/05/64	Pt. Lookout, MD	CSR
					Pt. Lookout, MD	08/08/64	Elmira, NY	P113,P116,CSR
					Elmira, NY	09/13/64	Died	P5,P65,FPH,CSR
Thompson, J.Wellington	Pvt	I 27th SCVI	Town Creek, NC	02/20/65	Ft. Anderson, NC	02/28/65	Pt. Lookout, MD	CSR,HAG
					Pt. Lookout, MD	05/14/65	Rlsd. G.O. #85	P115,P117
Thompson, James	Pvt	B 11th SCVI	Deserted/enemy	03/08/65	Charleston, SC		Released on oath	CSR
Thompson, John C.	Pvt	I 17th SCVI	Crater, Pbg., VA	07/30/64	Pt. Lookout, MD	08/08/64	Elmira, NY	P120,LAN,CSR
					Elmira, NY	09/13/64	Died, Diarrhea	P12,CSR
Thompson, John J.	Pvt	D 16th SCVI	Missionary Ridge, TN	11/25/63	Nashville, TN	12/07/63	Louisville, KY	P39,16R,CSR
					Louisville, KY	12/08/63	Rock Island, IL	P88,P89,CSR
					Rock Island, IL	05/02/64	Died, Typhoid fever	P5,P131,P132,FPH
Thompson, Jonathan	Pvt	I 12th SCVI	Gettysburg, PA	07/06/63	Ft. Delaware, DE	10/16/64	Hos. 10/16-10/30/64	P47,LAN
					Ft. Delaware, DE	10/20/64	Pt. Lookout, MD	P43,CSR
					Ft. Delaware, DE	10/30/64	Venus Pt., GA Xc	CSR
Thompson, Jonathan	Pvt	I 12th SCVI	Petersburg, VA	04/02/65	Pt. Lookout, MD	10/31/64	Aikens Ldg., VA Xc	P115,P117,CSR
					Pt. Lookout, MD	06/21/65	Rlsd. G.O. #109	P115,P117,P122,CSR
Thompson, Joseph M.	Pvt	A 26th SCVI	Southside RR, VA	04/01/65	City Pt., VA	06/05/65	Pt. Lookout, MD	CSR
					Pt. Lookout, MD	06/21/65	Rlsd. G.O. #109	P115,P119,P122,CSR
Thompson, Manassa	Cpl	A 26th SCVI	Southside RR, VA	04/01/65	City Pt., VA	04/05/65	Pt. Lookout, MD	CSR
					Pt. Lookout, MD	06/21/65	Rlsd. G.O. #109	P115,P119,CSR
Thompson, Michael T.	Pvt	I 13th SCVI	Appomattox R., VA	04/03/65	City Pt., VA	04/11/65	Hart's Island, NY	CSR
					Hart's Island, NY	06/21/65	Rlsd. G.O. #109	P79,HOS,CSR
Thompson, Raymond	Sgt	G 6th SCVI			City Pt., VA	04/11/65	Hart's Island, NY	CSR
					Hart's Island, NY	06/17/65	Rlsd. G.O. #109	P79,CSR
Thompson, Samuel D.	Pvt	D 21st SCVI	Morris Island, SC	07/10/63	Ft. Columbus, NY	09/23/63	Paroled on oath	P1,HAG,FPH
					Ft. Columbus, NY	09/26/63	Pt. Lookout, MD	CSR
					Pt. Lookout, MD	11/05/63	Died, Typhoid fever	P6,P12,P113,FPH
Thompson, Thomas R.	Pvt	C 13th SCVI	Deserted/enemy	01/19/65	City Pt., VA	01/24/65	Washington, DC	CSR,P8
					Washington, DC	01/26/65	Savannah, GA oath	CSR
Thompson, Thomas W.	Pvt	B 11th SCVI	Deserted/enemy	03/08/65	Charleston, SC		Released on oath	HAG,CSR
Thompson, Wallace	Pvt	E Hol.Leg.	Five Forks, VA	04/01/65	City Pt., VA	04/05/65	Pt. Lookout, MD	CSR,HOS
					Pt. Lookout, MD	06/21/65	Rlsd. G.O. #109	P115,P118,CSR
Thompson, William A.	Pvt	D 16th SCVI	Nashville, TN	12/16/64	Nashville, TN	12/19/64	Louisville, KY	CSR
					Louisville, KY	12/21/64	Camp Douglas, IL	P90,P91,P94,CSR
					Camp Douglas, IL	04/02/65	Jd. 6th USVI	CSR
Thompson, William B.	Pvt	I 17th SCVI	Five Forks, VA	04/01/65	City Pt., VA	04/06/65	Pt. Lookout, MD	CSR,LAN
					Pt. Lookout, MD	06/20/65	Rlsd. G.O. #109	P115,P119,P121,CSR

SOUTH CAROLINA SOLDIERS, SAILORS AND **T** CITIZENS HELD IN U.S. PRISONS 1861-1865

NAME	RANK	REGIMENT	CAPTURED AT	WHEN	PRISON	MOVED	DISPOSITION	SOURCES
Thompson, William F.	Pvt	B 21st SCVI	Ft. Fisher, NC	01/15/65	New York, NY	01/30/65	Elmira, NY	CSR
					Elmira, NY	02/17/65	Died, Ch. Diarrhea	P5,P12,P65,P66,FPH
Thompson, William J.	Pvt	G 26th SCVI	Five Forks, VA	04/01/65	City Pt., VA	04/05/65	Pt. Lookout, MD	P121,CSR
					Pt. Lookout, MD	06/20/65	Rlsd. G.O. #109	P115,P118,CSR
Thompson, William K.	Cpl	B Hol.Leg.	Five Forks, VA	04/01/65	City Pt., VA	04/05/65	Pt. Lookout, MD	CSR,HOS
					Pt. Lookout, MD	06/29/65	Rlsd. G.O. #109	P115,P118,P121
Thompson, William T.	Pvt	I 13th SCVI	Howlett House, VA	03/03/65	Hart's Island, NY	06/21/65	Rlsd. G.O. #109	P79,HOS
Thomson, John W.	Pvt	G Orr's Ri.	Falling Waters, MD	07/14/63	Baltimore, MD	08/17/63	Pt. Lookout, MD	CSR,CDC
					Pt. Lookout, MD	08/16/64	Elmira, NY	P113,P116,P120,CSR
					Elmira, NY	06/16/65	Rlsd. G.O. #109	P65,P66,CSR
Thorne, William Ross	Pvt	B 6th SCVI	Richmond, VA	04/03/65	Libby Prison Rchmd.	04/08/65	City Pt., VA P.M.	CSR,YEB
					City Pt. VA	04/16/65	Pt. Lookout, MD	CSR
					Pt. Lookout, MD	06/21/65	Rlsd. G.O. #109	P115,P119,CSR
Thornhill, John C.	Pvt	K 21st SCVI	Weldon RR, VA	08/21/64	Pt. Lookout, MD	03/14/65	Aikens Ldg., VA Xc	P113,P116,P121
Thornwell, Gillespie	Pvt	H 2nd SCVC	Warrenton Jtn., VA	05/02/63	Alexandria, VA USG	05/04/63	Died of wounds	P12,CSR
Threat, B.R.	Pvt	I 17th SCVI	Kinston, NC	12/14/62	Kinston, NC	12/14/62	Paroled	CSR
Threat, J.S.	Cpl	D 8th SCVI	Gettysburg, PA	07/05/63	Gettysburg G.H.		Provost Marshal	P4,KEB
					David's Island, NY	09/12/63	City Pt., VA Xc	P1
Threatt, James	Pvt	B 26th SCVI	Five Forks, VA	04/01/65	City Pt., VA	04/05/65	Pt. Lookout, MD	CSR
					Pt. Lookout, MD	06/21/65	Rlsd. G.O. #109	P119,CSR
Threatt, Jeremiah	Pvt	H 1st SCVIR	James Island, SC	07/16/63	Hilton Head, SC	09/22/63	Ft. Columbus, NY	CSR,SA1
					Ft. Columbus, NY	09/26/63	Elmira, NY	CSR
					Pt. Lookout, MD	08/18/64	Elmira, NY	P113,CSR
Threatt, Jeremiah	Pvt	H 1st SCVIR	Morris Island, SC	07/18/63	Elmira, NY	03/10/65	Pt. Lookout, MD Xc	P65,P66,P124,CSR
Threatt, Jeremiah	Pvt	H 1st SCVIR	Charlotte, NC	05/25/65	Charlotte, NC	05/25/65	Paroled	CSR
Threatt, John W.	Pvt	B 8th SCVI	Winchester, VA	09/13/64	Harpers Ferry, WV	09/19/64	Camp Chase, OH	CSR,KEB
					Camp Chase	06/11/65	Rlsd. G.O.#109	P22,CSR
Threatt, John W.	Sgt	F 26th SCVI	Southside RR, VA	04/01/65	City Pt., VA	04/05/65	Pt. Lookout, MD	CSR
					Pt. Lookout, MD	06/21/65	Rlsd. G.O. #109	P118,CSR
Threatt, Joseph	Cpl	D 8th SCVI	Gettysburg, PA	07/04/63	Gettysburg, PA Hos.	07/21/63	David's Island, NY	CSR,KEB
					David's Island, NY	08/31/63	City Pt., VA Xc	CSR
Threatt, Miles	Pvt	F 26th SCVI	Farmville, VA	04/06/65	City Pt., VA	04/14/65	Newport News, VA	CSR
					Newport News, VA	06/26/65	Rlsd. G.O. #109	P107,CSR
Threatt, Peter L.	Pvt	K 1st SCVIR	Bentonville, NC	03/19/65	New Berne, NC	04/10/65	Hart's Island, NY	CSR,SA1
					Hart's Island, NY	06/17/65	Rlsd. G.O. #109	P79,CSR
Threatt, William	Pvt	B 8th SCVI	Winchester, VA	09/13/64	Harpers Ferry, WV	09/19/64	Camp Chase, OH	CSR,KEB
					Camp Chase, OH	06/11/65	Rlsd. G.O. #109	P22,CSR
Thrift, Allen	Pvt	M P.S.S.	Amelia C.H., VA	04/05/65	City Pt., VA	04/13/65	Pt. Lookout, MD	CSR,TSE
					Pt. Lookout, MD	06/21/65	Rlsd. G.O. #109	P115,P119,CSR
Thrift, R.	Pvt	F 3rd SCVIBn	South Mtn., MD	09/14/62	David's Island, NY		Ft. Delaware, DE	CSR,KEB
					Ft. Delaware, DE	10/02/62	Aikens Ldg., VA Xc	CSR
Thurmond, George W.	Pvt	K 24th SCVI	Columbia, TN	12/22/64	Nashville, TN	01/31/65	Louisville, KY	P39,HOE,CSR
					Louisville, KY	02/01/65	Camp Chase, OH	P92,P94,CSR
					Camp Chase, OH	03/26/65	Pt. Lookout, MD	P23,CSR
					Pt. Lookout, MD	06/04/65	Rlsd.I nstr. 5/30/65	P115,P119,P121,CSR
Thurston, J.	1Lt	CS Marines	Atlanta, GA	06/27/63	Ft. Lafayette, NY	07/03/63	Ft. Warren, MA	P144
Thurston, James R.	Sgt	K 10th SCVI	Somerville, GA	10/19/64	Nashville, TN	10/24/64	Louisville, KY	CSR,RAS
					Louisville, KY	10/31/64	Camp Douglas, IL	P90,P91,CSR
					Camp Douglas, IL	06/17/65	Rlsd. G.O. #109	CSR
Thurston, John B.	Pvt	H 16th SCVI	Nashville, TN	12/17/64	Nashville, TN	01/01/65	Louisville, KY	CSR
					Louisville, KY	01/04/65	Camp Chase, OH	P92,P94,CSR

SOUTH CAROLINA SOLDIERS, SAILORS AND  CITIZENS HELD IN U.S. PRISONS 1861-1865

NAME	RANK	REGIMENT	CAPTURED AT	WHEN	PRISON	MOVED	DISPOSITION	SOURCES
Thurston, John B.	Pvt	H 16th SCVI	Nashville, TN	12/16/64	Camp Chase, OH	05/14/65	Took the oath	P26,16R,CSR
					Camp Chase, OH	06/12/65	Rlsd. G.O. #85	P22,16R
Thurston, John W.	Pvt	D 4th SCVC	Louisa C.H., VA	06/11/64	Fts. Monroe, VA	06/20/64	Pt. Lookout, MD	CSR
Thurston, John W.	Pvt	D 4th SCVC	Louisa C.H., VA	06/11/64	Pt. Lookout, MD	07/23/64	Elmira, NY	P113,P116,P120,CSR
Thurston, John W.	Pvt	D 4th SCVC	Louisa C.H., VA	06/11/64	Elmira, NY	02/17/65	Died, Aneurism/Hrt.	P5,P12,P65,P66,FPH
Tice, George M.	Pvt	I Hol.Leg.	Five Forks, VA	04/01/65	City Pt., VA	04/01/65	Pt. Lookout, MD	CSR,HOS
					Pt. Lookout, MD	06/20/65	Rlsd. G.O. #109	CSR
Tidwell, Charles L.	Pvt	B 7th SCVIBn	Weldon RR, VA	08/21/64	City Pt., VA	08/24/64	Pt. Lookout, MD	CSR,HAG,HFC
					Pt. Lookout, MD	09/18/64	Aikens Ldg., VA Xc	P113,P116,CSR
Tidwell, J. Clark	Pvt	E 18th SCVAB	Bentonville, NC	03/22/65	Hart's Island, NY	05/11/65	Died, Brain Infl.	P6,P79,LAN,CSR
Tiencken, D.	Pvt	A German LA	Deserted/enemy	03/31/65	Savannah, GA	03/31/65	Charleston on oath	CSR
Tiernan, Miles	Pvt	E 1st SCVA	Deserted/enemy	02/18/65	Hilton Head, SC	04/04/65	New York, NY oath	CSR
Tiller, Henry A.	Pvt	G 7th SCVIBn	Weldon RR, VA	08/21/64	City Pt., VA	08/24/64	Pt. Lookout, MD	CSR,HAG
					Pt. Lookout, MD	03/14/65	Aikens Ldg., VA Xc	P113,P116,P121
Tillotson, Cicero B.	3Lt	I Hol.Leg.	Stony Creek, VA	05/07/64	Fts. Monroe, VA	05/13/64	Pt. Lookout, MD	CSR,HOS
					Pt. Lookout, MD	06/23/64	Ft. Delaware, DE	P113,P116,P120
					Ft. Delaware, DE	06/16/65	Rlsd. G.O. #109	P43,P44,P46
Tillotson, John J.	Pvt	C Hol.Leg.	Five Forks, VA	04/01/65	City Pt., VA	04/05/65	Pt. Lookout, MD	CSR,HOS
					Pt. Lookout, MD	06/06/65	Died, Rmt. fvr/diarh.	P6,P12,P115,FPH
Tillotson, Richard	Pvt	C Hol.Leg.	Five Forks, VA	04/01/65	City Pt., VA	04/05/65	Pt. Lookout, MD	CSR,HOS
					Pt. Lookout, MD	06/06/65	Rlsd. Instr. 5/30/65	P115,P118,P121,CSR
Tilly, William	Pvt	D 14th SCMil	Lynch's Creek, SC	02/25/65	Hart's Island, NY		David's Island, NY	P5,P79
					David's Island, NY	04/23/65	Died, Ch. Diarrhea	P12,FPH
Timme, George W.	Pvt	I 6th SCVI	Richmond, VA	04/23/65	Richmond, VA	05/13/65	Paroled	CSR
Timme, W.O.	Pvt	I 6th SCVI	Richmond, VA	04/03/65	Richmond, VA	05/13/65	Paroled	CSR
Timmerman, Andrew J.	Cpl	K 14th SCVI	Gettysburg, PA	07/05/63	Ft. Delaware, DE	06/10/65	Rlsd. G.O.#109	P44,P45,HOE,CSR
Timmerman, Benjamin M.	Pvt	K 14th SCVI	Gettysburg, PA	07/05/63	Ft. Delaware, DE	01/25/64	Died, Erysipelas	P5,P42,FPH,HOE,CSR
Timmerman, Edward	Pvt	K 14th SCVI	Gettysburg, PA	07/05/63	Ft. Delaware, DE	07/30/63	City Pt., VA Xc	P40,P42,P44,HOE
Timmerman, Edward	Pvt	K 14th SCVI	Petersburg, VA	04/03/65	City Pt., VA	04/11/65	Hart's Island, NY	CSR
					Hart's Island, NY	06/16/65	Rlsd. G.O. #109	P79
Timmerman, Frank A.	Pvt	K 24th SCVI	Chickamauga, GA	09/20/63	Nashville, TN	09/30/63	Louisville, KY	P38,HOE,CSR
					Louisville, KY	10/02/63	Camp Douglas, IL	P88,P89,CSR
					Camp Douglas, IL		(Rcd. 10/4/63)	P55,P57
Timmerman, Frank A.	Pvt	K 24th SCVI	Chickamauga, GA	09/19/63	Camp Douglas, IL	01/30/64	Died, Typhoid fever	P12,P5,FPH,CSR
Timmerman, J.F.	Pvt	K 14th SCVI	Gettysburg, PA	07/05/63	Ft. Delaware, DE	09/19/63	Died, Ch. Diarrhea	P5,P12,P40,HOE,FPH
Timmerman, Jacob B.	Pvt	G 1st SCVIG	Petersburg, VA	04/03/65	City Pt., VA	04/13/65	Pt. Lookout, MD	CSR,SA1
					Pt. Lookout, MD	06/06/65	Rlsd. Instr. 5/30/65	P121,CSR
Timmerman, N. Douglas	Pvt	I 2nd SCVC	Augusta, GA	05/24/65	Augusta, GA	05/24/65	Paroled	CSR
Timmerman, William E.	Pvt	K 14th SCVI	Spotsylvania, VA	05/13/64	Belle Plain, VA	05/21/64	Ft. Delaware, DE	CSR,HOE
					Ft. Delaware, DE	06/10/65	Rlsd. G.O. #109	P41,P42,CSR
Timmons, Alfred J.	Pvt	B 27th SCVI	Town Creek, NC	02/20/65	Ft. Anderson, NC	02/28/65	Pt. Lookout, MD	CSR
					Pt. Lookout, MD	06/20/65	Rlsd. G.O. #109	P115,P117,P121,CSR
Timmons, Isaac John	Pvt	D 8th SCVI	Spotsylvania, VA	05/08/64	Belle Plain, VA	05/21/64	Ft. Delaware, DE	CSR
					Ft. Delaware, DE	04/27/65	Rlsd. by O. Sec./W	P7,P41,P42,P46,SCR
Timmons, Isaac T.	Pvt	F 26th SCVI	Five Forks, VA	04/02/65	City Pt., VA	04/05/65	Pt. Lookout, MD	CSR
					Pt. Lookout, MD	06/21/65	Rlsd. G.O. #109	P115,P119,P122,CSR
Timmons, J.A.	Pvt	I 25th SCVI	Weldon RR, VA	08/21/64	1 Div 5 A.C. Hos.	08/21/64	Died of wounds	P12,HAG,CSR
Timmons, John M.	Pvt	I 18th SCVI	Crater, Pbg., VA	07/30/64	City Pt., VA	08/05/64	Pt. Lookout, MD	CSR
					Pt. Lookout, MD	08/08/64	Elmira, NY	P116,P125,CSR
					Elmira, NY	12/16/64	Died, Pneumonia	P65,P66,CSR

SOUTH CAROLINA SOLDIERS, SAILORS AND T CITIZENS HELD IN U.S. PRISONS 1861-1865

NAME	RANK	REGIMENT	CAPTURED AT	WHEN	PRISON	MOVED	DISPOSITION	SOURCES
Timmons, William J.	Pvt	I 25th SCVI	Morris Island, SC	09/07/63	Ft. Columbus, NY	10/09/63	Johnson's Isl., OH	P1,HAG
					Pt. Lookout, MD	10/15/63	Hammond G.H., MD	P113,P121,P125,HAG,CSR
					Pt. Lookout, MD	11/19/63	Died, Erysipelas	P5,P12,P116,FPH
Timms, Andrew M.	Pvt	F 12th SCVI	Falling Waters, MD	07/14/63	W. Bldg. Balt, MD	08/14/63	Ft. McHenry, MD	P1,HFC,CSR
Timms, Andrew M.	Pvt	F 12th SCVI	Falling Waters, MD	07/14/63	Ft. McHenry, MD	08/22/63	City Pt., VA Xc	P144,CSR
					City Pt., VA	08/23/64	Pt. Lookout, MD	CSR
					Pt. Lookout, MD	03/16/64	City Pt., VA Xc	P113,P123,P124,CSR
Timms, Andrew M.	Pvt	F 12th SCVI	Sutherland Stn., VA	04/02/65	City Pt., VA	04/07/65	Hart's Island, NY	CSR
					Hart's Island, NY	06/16/65	Rlsd. G.O. #109	P79,CSR
Timms, Garrison	Pvt	D Ham.Leg.				09/25/62	Paroled	CSR
Timms, James A.	Pvt	H 12th SCVI	Charlotte, NC	05/16/65	Charlotte, NC	05/16/65	Paroled	CSR
Timms, James T.	Pvt	F 12th SCVI	Sutherland Stn., VA	04/02/65	City Pt., VA	04/07/65	Hart's Island, NY	CSR,HFC
					Hart's Island, NY	06/16/65	Rlsd. G.O. #109	P79,CSR
Tindal, Henry F.	Pvt	I 5th SCVC	Barnwell Dist. SC	02/10/65	New Berne, NC	04/10/65	Hart's Island, NY	CSR
					Hart's Island, NY	05/02/65	Died, Ch. Diarrhea	P5,P12,CSR
Tindal, John	Pvt	A 26th SCVI	Five Forks, VA	04/01/65	City Pt., VA	04/05/65	Pt. Lookout, MD	CSR
					Pt. Lookout, MD	06/21/65	Rlsd. G.O. #109	P114,CSR
Tindall, Emanuel	Cpl	I 21st SCVI	Petersburg, VA	06/24/64	Bermuda Hundred, VA	06/25/64	Fts. Monroe, VA	CSR
					Fts. Monroe, VA	06/26/64	Pt. Lookout, MD	CSR
					Pt. Lookout, MD	08/15/64	Elmira, NY	P113,P116,P120,HAG
					Elmira, NY	07/11/65	Rlsd. G.O. #109	P65,P66,HAG,HMC
Tindall, L.R.	Cpl	B 7th SCVC	Farmville, VA	04/06/65	Pt. Lookout, MD	06/20/65	Rlsd. G.O. #109	P115,P119,P121,CSR
					City Pt., VA	04/15/65	Pt. Lookout, MD	CSR
Tiner, John G.	Pvt	G 21st SCVI	Morris Island, SC	07/10/63	Pt. Lookout, MD	01/09/64	Died, Ch. Diarrhea	P5,P12,P113,FPH
					Hilton Head, SC	09/22/63	Ft. Columbus, NY	CSR,HAG
					Ft. Columbus, OH	09/26/63	Pt. Lookout, MD	CSR
Tinkler, George S.	Pvt	G 3rd SCVIBn	South Mtn., MD	09/14/62	Aikens Ldg., VA Xc	09/27/62		KEB,CSR
Tinkler, L.D.	Pvt	H 7th SCVIBn	Drury's Bluff, VA	05/16/64	Bermuda Hundred, VA	05/17/64	Fts. Monroe, VA	CSR
					Fts. Monroe, VA	05/18/64	Pt. Lookout, MD	CSR
					Pt. Lookout, MD	08/15/64	Elmira, NY	P113,P116,P120,HAG,CSR
					Elmira, NY	03/02/65	James R., VA Xc	P65,P66,HAG,CSR
Tinslely, Charles	Pvt	G 1st SCVA	Bentonville, NC	03/22/65	New Berne, NC	04/10/65	Hart's Island, NY	CSR
					Hart's Island, NY	06/19/65	Rlsd. G.O. #109	CSR,P79
Tinsley, Brackin A.	Cpl	G 16th SCVI	Nashville, TN	12/18/64	Nashville Gen. Hos.	02/06/65	Died of wounds	P5,P12,CSR
Tinsley, Calvin	Pvt	F 13th SCVI	Petersburg, VA	03/25/65	City Pt., VA	03/28/65	Pt. Lookout, MD	CSR,HOS
					Pt. Lookout, MD	06/21/65	Rlsd. G.O. #109	P115,P117,P122,CSR
Tinsley, E.	Pvt	D 1st SCVA	Combahee Ferry, SC	01/28/65	New Berne, NC	04/10/65	Hart's Island, NY	CSR
					Hart's Island, NY	06/17/65	Rlsd. G.O. #109	P79,CSR
Tinsley, James K.P.	Pvt	C Hol.Leg.	Deserted/enemy	12/31/64	City Point, VA	01/01/65	Washington, DC	P8,HOS
					Washington, DC	01/04/65	Phila., PA oath	CSR
Tinsley, John B.	Pvt	C Hol.Leg.	Petersburg, VA	03/25/65	City Pt., VA	03/28/65	Pt. Lookout, MD	CSR
					Pt. Lookout, MD	06/21/65	Rlsd. G.O. #109	P115,P117
Tippins, T.S.	Pvt	F 17th SCVI	Crater, Pbg., VA	07/30/64	Pt. Lookout, MD	08/08/64	Elmira, NY	P113,P116,CSR
					City Pt., VA	08/05/64	Pt. Lookout, MD	CSR
					Elmira, NY	05/09/65	Died, Pneumonia	P66,P12,P65, CSR
Tisdale, James G.	Pvt	G 3rd SCVABn	High Pt., NC	05/01/65	High Pt., NC	05/01/65	Paroled	CSR
Tisdale, Thomas J.	Pvt	G 3rd SCVABn	High Pt., NC	05/01/65	High Pt., NC	05/01/65	Paroled	CSR
Tisdale, William W.	Pvt	C 25th SCVI	Ft. Fisher, NC	01/15/65	New York, NY	01/30/65	Elmira, NY	CSR,HAG,CTA
					Elmira, NY	06/30/65	Rlsd. G.O. #109	P65,P66,CSR
Tobias, Isaac N.	Pvt	I 25th SCVI	Town Creek, NC	02/20/65	Ft. Anderson, NC	02/28/65	Pt. Lookout, MD	CSR,HAG
					Pt. Lookout, MD	06/20/65	Rlsd. G.O. #109	P115,P117,P121,CSR

SOUTH CAROLINA SOLDIERS, SAILORS AND  CITIZENS HELD IN U.S. PRISONS 1861-1865

NAME	RANK	REGIMENT	CAPTURED AT	WHEN	PRISON	MOVED	DISPOSITION	SOURCES
Tobias, John S.	Pvt	I 25th SCVI	Ft. Fisher, NC	01/15/65	New York, NY	01/30/65	Elmira, NY	CSR
					Elmira, NY	02/23/65	Died, Pneumonia	P5,P12,P65,P66,FPH
Todd, Drury	Pvt	B 1st SCVIG	Farmville, VA	04/06/65	City Pt., VA	04/14/65	Newport News, VA	CSR,ANY,SA1
					Newport News, VA	06/26/65	Rlsd. G.O. #109	P107,CSR
Todd, James M.	Pvt	G 10th SCVI	Kentucky	09/15/62	Kentucky	11/15/62	Paroled	CSR
Todd, Joseph	Pvt	6 10/19 SCVI	Missionary Ridge, TN	11/25/63	Louisville, KY	12/27/63	Rock Island, IL	P88,P89,P93,CSR
					Nashville, TN	12/25/63	Louisville, KY	P39,RAS,CSR
					Rock Island, IL	06/19/65	Rlsd. G.O. #109	P131,CSR
Todd, Joseph	Pvt	K 26th SCVI	Petersburg, VA	04/02/65	Pt. Lookout, MD	06/21/65	Rlsd. G.O. #109	P115,P122,CSR
					City Pt., VA	04/05/65	Pt. Lookout, MD	CSR
Todd, Joseph T.	Pvt	F 14th SCVI	Deep Bottom, VA	07/28/64	US Cav. Corps Hos.	11/30/64	City Pt., VA P.M.	CSR
					P.M.A.of P. City Pt.	12/03/64	Pt. Lookout, MD	CSR
Todd, Joseph T.	Pvt	F 14th SCVI	Deep Bottom, VA	07/28/64	Pt. Lookout, MD	02/01/65	Died, Diarrhea	P5,P12,P117,FPH
Todd, R.J.	Pvt	E 3rd SCVIBn	South Mtn., MD	09/14/62	Ft. Delaware, DE	10/02/62	Aikens Ldg., VA Xc	KEB,CSR
Todd, William M.	Pvt	H 2nd SCVI	Halltown, VA	08/26/64	Harpers Ferry, WV	08/28/64	Camp Chase, OH	CSR,SA2,H2
Todd, William M.	Pvt	H 2nd SCVI	Halltown, VA	08/06/64	Camp Chase, OH	03/26/65	Pt. Lookout, MD	P26,CSR
					Pt. Lookout, MD	06/20/65	Rlsd. G.O. #109	P115,P119,P121
Todd, William Washington	Pvt	F 1st SCVIG	Petersburg, VA	04/02/65	City Pt., VA	04/04/65	Pt. Lookout, MD	CSR,SA1
					Pt. Lookout, MD	06/20/65	Rlsd. G.O. #109	P115,P119,P121,CSR
Toland, Robert	Pvt	E 5th SCVC	Cheraw, SC	03/05/65	Cheraw, SC	03/05/65	Paroled	CSR
Tolbert, J.R.	2Lt	I 2nd SCVC	Augusta, GA	05/24/65	Augusta, GA	05/24/65	Paroled	CSR
Tolbert, Samuel	Pvt	E 22nd SCVI	Deep Bottom, VA	08/17/64	City Pt., VA	08/22/64	Pt. Lookout, MD	CSR,LAN
					Pt. Lookout, MD	09/17/64	Died, Ch. Diarrhea	P6,P12,P113,FPH
Tolbert, Thomas J.	Pvt	E 12th SCVI	Gettysburg, PA	07/04/63	Davids Island, NY	09/08/63	City Pt., VA Xc	P1,CSR,LAN,CSR
Tolbert, Thomas J.	Pvt	E 12th SCVI	Spotsylvania, VA	05/12/64	Fredericksburg G.H.		(In Hos. 05/23/64)	P1,CSR,CSR
Tolleson, Alfred J.	Pvt	C Hol.Leg.	Kinston, NC	12/15/62	Kinston, NC	12/15/62	Paroled	CSR,HOS
Tolleson, Daniel	Pvt	E 16th SCVI	Kingston, GA	11/27/63	Nashville, TN	12/11/63	Louisville, KY	P39,16R,CSR
					Louisville, KY	12/12/63	Rock Island, IL	P88,P89,CSR
					Rock Island, IL	03/06/64	Died, Variola	P5,P131,P132,FPH
Tolleson, J.D.	Pvt	I 3rd SCVI	N. Anna River, VA	05/23/64	Port Royal, VA	05/30/64	Pt. Lookout, MD	CSR,KEB,H3
					Pt. Lookout, MD	10/14/64	Jnd. U.S. Army FS	P113,P122,P123
Tolleson, J.W.	OSg	Hol.Leg.	Richmond, VA	04/03/65	P.M. Richmond, VA	04/29/65	Paroled in Hos.	CSR,HOS
					Jackson H. Rchmd.	05/03/65	Died	P6
Tolleson, James A.	Cpt	C Hol.Leg.	Dinwiddie C.H., VA	04/01/65	Ft. McHenry, MD	04/09/65	Johnson's Isl., VA	P110,HOS
					Johnson's Isl., OH	06/20/65	Rlsd. G.O. #109	P81
Tolliard, Michael	Smn	CS Chicora			Pt. Lookout, MD		Took the Oath	P124
Tolly, George F.	Pvt	C P.S.S.	Lookout Mtn., TN	11/24/63	Nashville, TN	02/06/64	Louisville, KY	P39,TSE
					Louisville, KY	02/09/64	Rock Island, IL	P88,P91,P93
					Pt. Lookout, MD	05/03/65		CSR
Tolson, George W.	Pvt	McQueen LA	Petersburg, VA	04/03/65	City Pt., VA	04/11/65	Hart's Island, NY	CSR
					Hart's Island, NY	06/17/65	Rlsd. G.O. #109	CSR
Tomkins, William M.	Pvt	K 15th SCVI	Halltown, VA	08/26/64	Harpers Ferry, WV	08/29/64	Camp Chase, OH	CSR
					Camp Chase, OH	03/18/65	Pt. Lookout, MD	P22,P26,KEB
					Pt. Lookout, MD	03/27/65	Boulware's Wh. Xc	CSR
Tomkins, William M.	Pvt	K 15th SCVI	Augusta, GA	06/05/65	Augusta, GA	06/06/65	Paroled on oath	H15,CSR
Tomlinson, F.	Pvt	H 18th SCVI	Five Forks, VA	04/01/65	Pt. Lookout, MD	06/30/65	Rlsd. G.O. #109	P123
Tomlinson, Reece	Cpt	H 26th SCVI	Petersburg, VA	03/25/65	Old Capitol, DC	03/30/65	Ft. Delaware, DE	CSR
					Ft. McHenry, MD	03/30/65	Ft. Delaware, DE	P110
					Ft. Delaware, DE	06/17/65	Rlsd. G.O. #109	P43,P45,CSR
Tompkins, Henry C.	Pvt	I 1st SCVIR	Chattanooga, TN	11/04/64	Took oath		Des. 8/30/64	SA1,CSR

SOUTH CAROLINA SOLDIERS, SAILORS AND  CITIZENS HELD IN U.S. PRISONS 1861-1865

NAME	RANK	REGIMENT	CAPTURED AT	WHEN	PRISON	MOVED	DISPOSITION	SOURCES
Tompkins, James	Cpl	C 10th SCVI	Murfreesboro, TN	12/31/62	Nashville, TN		Louisville, KY	P38,RAS,CSR
					Louisville, KY	03/11/63	Camp Butler, IL	P88,CSR
					Camp Butler, IL	04/10/63	City Pt., VA Xc	P21,CSR
Tompkins, James W.	Pvt	K 16th SCVI	Alpine, GA	10/19/64	Nashville, TN	10/29/64	Louisville, KY	CSR
					Louisville, KY	10/31/64	Camp Douglas, IL	P90,P91,P94CSR
					Camp Douglas, IL	03/14/65	Pt. Lookout Xc	CSR
					Pt. Lookout, MD	03/18/65	Boulwares Wh., VA	CSR
					Richmond, VA Hos.	03/28/65	Furloughed 60 days	CSR
Tompkins, John	Pvt	E 26th SCVI	Petersburg, VA	04/02/65	City Pt., VA	04/05/65	Pt. Lookout, MD	CSR
					Pt. Lookout, MD	06/21/65	Rlsd. G.O. #109	P115,P119,P122,CSR
Tompkins, John S.	Cpl	C 10th SCVI	Atlanta, GA	07/22/64	Nashville, TN	07/29/64	Louisville, KY	CSR,RAS
					Louisville, KY	07/30/64	Camp Chase, OH	P90,P91,CSR
					Camp Chase, OH	03/04/65	City Pt., VA Xc	P22,CSR
Tompkins, John W.	Pvt	B Ham.Leg.	Fair Oaks, VA	05/31/62	Fts. Monroe, VA	06/05/62	Ft. Delaware, DE	CSR
					Ft. Delaware, DE	08/05/62	Aikens Ldg., VA Xc	CSR
Tompkins, K.M.	Pvt	2 10/19 SCVI	Missionary Ridge, TN	11/25/63	Nashville, TN	12/07/63	Louisville, KY	P39,RAS,CSR
					Louisville, KY	12/09/63	Rock Island, IL	P88,P89,CSR
					Rock Island, IL	06/21/65	Rlsd. G.O. #109	P131,CSR
Tompkins, Samuel	Pvt	B Ham.Leg.MI	Augusta, GA	06/06/65	Augusta, GA	06/06/65	Paroled	CSR
Tompkins, Turner C.	Sgt	G 1st SCVIG	N. Anna River, VA	05/23/64	Front Royal, VA	05/30/64	Pt. Lookout, MD	CSR,SA1
					Pt. Lookout, MD	07/09/64	Elmira, NY	P113,P116,CSR
					Elmira, NY	05/13/65	Rlsd. G.O.#109	P65,P66,CSR
Tompkins, William W.	Pvt	M 10th SCVI	Pulaski, TN	12/23/64	Nashville, TN	02/14/65	Louisville, KY	P3,P39,CSR
					Louisville, KY	02/17/65	Camp Chase, OH	P92,P94,CSR
					Camp Chase, OH	08/16/65	Rlsd. G.O. #109	P23,CSR
Toney, George F.	Pvt	D 14th SCVI	Jones Farm, VA	04/02/65	City Pt., VA	04/04/65	Pt. Lookout, MD	CSR,HOE
					Pt. Lookout, MD	06/30/65	Rlsd. G.O. #109	P115,P117,P121
Toole, Julius L.	Pvt	A 1st SCVIG	Burkeville, VA	04/05/65	City Pt., VA	04/13/65	Pt. Lookout, MD	CSR,SA1
					Pt. Lookout, MD	06/21/65	Rlsd. G.O. #109	P115,P119,CSR
Toole, R.J. Manning	Pvt	H 14th SCVI	Gettysburg, PA	07/03/63	Chester, PA G.H.	08/17/63	City Pt., VA Xc	P1,CSR
Toole, Stephen	Pvt	D Hol.Leg.	Hatchers Run, VA	03/25/65	City Pt., VA	04/02/65	Pt. Lookout, MD	CSR
					Pt. Lookout, MD	06/20/65	Rlsd. G.O. #109	P115,P117,P121,CSR
Torbitt, U.S.	Pvt	D 2nd SCVC	Augusta, GA	05/24/65	Augusta, GA	05/24/65	Paroled	CSR
Touchberry, Joseph E.	Pvt	C Ham.Leg.MI	Richmond, VA Hos.	04/03/65	Richmond, VA Hos.	04/04/65	Paroled	CSR
Touchberry, William T.	Pvt	D 4th SCVC	Stony Creek, VA	12/01/64	City Pt., VA	12/05/64	Pt. Lookout, MD	CSR
					Pt. Lookout, MD	06/20/65	Rlsd. G.O. #109	P115,P117,P121,CSR
Tow, Joseph	Pvt	F 1st SCVIH	Deep Bottom, VA	08/14/64	Bermuda Hundred, VA	08/15/64	Fts. Monroe, VA	CSR,SA1
					Fts. Monroe, VA	08/17/64	Pt. Lookout, MD	CSR
					Pt. Lookout, MD	01/31/65	Died	P125,CSR
Towles, Ralph S.	Pvt	K 14th SCVI	Gettysburg, PA	07/05/63	Bedloes Island, NY	01/06/64	City Pt., VA	P2,UD2,HOE
					Hammond G.H., MD	03/17/64	City Pt., VA Xc	P116,HOE
Townsend, Green B.	Sgt	4 10/19 SCVI	Missionary Ridge, TN	11/25/63	Nashville, TN	12/07/63	Louisville, KY	P39,RAS,CSR
					Louisville, KY	12/09/63	Rock Island, IL	P88,P89,CSR
					Rock Island, IL	05/24/65	Rlsd. G.O. #85	P131,CSR
Townsend, Joshua M.	Cpt	A 3rd SCVIBn	Maryland		Frederick, MD Hos.	09/19/62	Ft. Delaware, DE	CSR,KEB
					Ft. Delaware, DE	10/02/62	Aikens Ldg., VA Xc	CSR
Townsend, W.T.	Pvt	G 19th SCVI	Kentucky		Kentucky		Paroled	CSR
Townsend, Walter S.	Pvt	D 26th SCVI	Amelia C.H., VA	04/03/65	City Pt., VA	04/13/65	Pt. Lookout, MD	CSR,HOM
					Pt. Lookout, MD	06/20/65	Rlsd. G.O. #109	P115,P119,P121
Tracy, William	Sgt	K 1st SCVIG	Sutherland Stn., VA	04/03/65	City Pt., VA	04/13/65	Pt. Lookout, MD	CSR,SA1
					Pt. Lookout, MD	06/20/65	Rlsd. G.O. #109	P115,P119,P121,CSR

SOUTH CAROLINA SOLDIERS, SAILORS AND T CITIZENS HELD IN U.S. PRISONS 1861-1865

NAME	RANK	REGIMENT	CAPTURED AT	WHEN	PRISON	MOVED	DISPOSITION	SOURCES
Tradewell, Allister	Sgt	B Hol.Leg.C.	12 Mile Ordinary	02/18/64	Fts. Monroe, VA	02/25/64	Pt. Lookout, MD	CSR
					Pt. Lookout, MD	11/01/64	Aikens Ldg., VA Xc	P113,P116,P121,CSR
Trail, George P.	Pvt	A Hol.Leg.	Five Forks, VA	04/01/65	City Pt., VA	04/05/65	Pt. Lookout, MD	CSR
					Pt. Lookout, MD	06/30/65	Rlsd. G.O. #109	P115,P118,P121,CSR
Trammel, William H.	Pvt	H 1st SCVIG	Petersburg, VA	04/04/65	City Pt., VA	04/14/65	Pt. Lookout, MD	SA1,CSR
Trammell, B.F.	Pvt	F 1st SCVIH	Deep Bottom, VA	08/14/64	Bermuda Hundred, VA	08/15/64	Fts. Monroe, VA	CSR,SA1
					Fts. Monroe, VA	08/17/64	Pt. Lookout, MD	CSR
					Pt. Lookout, MD	03/14/65	Aikens Ldg. Xc	P113,P121,P123
Trammell, B.P.	Cpl	H 22nd SCVI	Crater, Pbg., VA	07/30/64	City Pt., VA	08/05/64	Pt. Lookout, MD	CSR
					Pt. Lookout, MD	08/08/64	Elmira, NY	P116,P120,P125
					Elmira, NY	06/14/65	Rlsd. G.O. #109	P65,P66
Trammell, William C.	Pvt	K Ham.Leg.MI	Deserted/enemy	03/04/65	Bermuda Hundred, VA	03/05/65	City Pt., VA P.M.	CSR
					City Pt., VA	03/07/65	Washington, DC	CSR
					Washington, DC	03/08/65	Iowa City, Iowa	CSR
Trapier, T.D.	Pvt	Marion LA			New Berne, NC USGH			CSR
Trapp, L.H.	Sgt	G 3rd SCVIBn	South Mtn., MD	09/14/62	Ft. Delaware, DE	10/02/62	Aikens Ldg., VA Xc	CSR
Travers, John	Pvt	B 1st SCVA	New Salem, NC	04/19/65	Wilmington, NC	04/26/65	New York, NY oath	CSR
Traylor, A.A.	Pvt	C 7th SCVI	Gettysburg, PA	07/04/63	David's Island, NY	08/24/63	City Pt., VA Xc	P1,KEB,CSR
Traylor, W.H.	Pvt	H 6th SCVI	Burkeville, VA	04/14/65	Burkeville, VA	04/14/65	Paroled	CSR
Traylor, Winfield S.	Sgt	B 5th SCVI	Wilderness, VA	05/06/64	Belle Plain, VA	05/21/64	Ft. Delaware, DE	CSR
					Ft. Delaware, DE	06/10/65	Released	P41,P42,SA3,CSR
Traynham, James H.	1Lt	F 16th SCVI	Franklin, TN	12/17/64	Nashville, TN	01/08/65	Louisville, KY	P2,P39,16R,CSR
					Louisville, KY	01/09/65	Ft. Delaware, DE	P92,P94,CSR
					Ft. Delaware, DE	04/29/65	Camp Hospital	P47
					Ft. Delaware, DE	06/14/65	Rlsd. G.O. #109	P43,P45,CSR
Traynham, John	Pvt	E 16th SCVI	Jonesboro, GA	09/02/64	Rough & Ready, GA	09/19/64	Exchanged	CSR
Traynham, Nimrod	Pvt	E 16th SCVI	Missionary Ridge, TN	11/26/63	Nashville, TN	12/09/63	Louisville, KY	P39,16R
					Louisville, KY	12/11/63	Rock Island, IL	P89,CSR
					Rock Island, IL	06/21/65	Rlsd. G.O. #109	CSR
Trevett, Joseph W.	Pvt	G 24th SCVI	Franklin, TN	12/17/64	Nashville, TN	01/04/65	Louisville, KY	P3,CSR,EFW
					Louisville, KY	01/09/65	Camp Chase, OH	P92,P94,CSR
					Camp Chase, OH	06/13/65	Rlsd. G.O. #109	P23,CSR
Treville, Jasper	Pvt	D Hol.Leg.	Petersburg, VA	04/04/65	6th A.C. Hos.	05/09/65	Died of wounds	P12,CSR
Trexler, John J.	Pvt	A 18th SCMil	Lynch's Creek, SC	03/03/65	Hart's Island, NY	05/02/65	Died, Ch. Diarrhea	P6,P12,FPH
Tribble, A.K.	Pvt	E 7th SCVC	Farmville, VA	04/11/65	Farmville, VA	04/21/65	Paroled	CSR
Trimnall, Joseph B.	Cpl	E 19th SCVI	Franklin, TN	12/17/64	Nashville, TN	03/27/65	Louisville, KY	P3,P39,CSR
					Louisville, KY	03/28/65	Hospital, GS wound	P95
					Louisville, KY	04/03/65	Camp Chase, OH	P92,P94,CSR
					Camp Chase, OH	05/02/65	New Orleans, LA Xc	CSR
					New Orleans, LA	05/02/65	Vicksburg, MS Xc	CSR
					Camp Chase, OH	06/13/65	Rlsd. G.O. #109	P23,CSR
Trimnall, Robert J.	Pvt	8 10/19 SCVI	Missionary Ridge, TN	11/25/63	Nashville, TN	12/07/63	Louisville, KY	P39,CSR
					Louisville, KY	12/09/63	Rock Island, IL	P88,P89,CSR
					Rock Island, IL	05/18/65	Rlsd. G.O. #85	P131,CSR
Tripp, Charles E.	Pvt	White's Bn	Fayetteville, NC	03/17/65	Pt. Lookout, MD			P117
Tripp, J.B.	Pvt	A 3rd SCVABn	High Pt., NC	05/02/65	High Pt., NC	05/02/65	Paroled	CSR
Tripp, R.R.	Pvt	A 3rd SCVABn	High Pt., NC	05/02/65	High Pt., NC	05/02/65	Paroled	CSR
Troh, G.	Pvt	D 1st SCVC	Newton, VA	05/24/64	Pt. Lookout, MD	07/09/64	Elmira, NY	P116,P120
					Elmira, NY	06/21/65	Rlsd. G.O. #109	P65,P66
Trotter, J.S.	Pvt	B 37th VAVCB	Opequan Creek, VA	09/13/64	Harpers Ferry, WV	09/19/64	Camp Chase, OH	CSR
					Camp Chase, OH	06/11/65	Rlsd.G.O. #109	CSR,37V

SOUTH CAROLINA SOLDIERS, SAILORS AND CITIZENS HELD IN U.S. PRISONS 1861-1865

NAME	RANK	REGIMENT	CAPTURED AT	WHEN	PRISON	MOVED	DISPOSITION	SOURCES
Trotter, P.L.	Pvt	C 4th SCVC	Deserted/enemy	10/15/64	City Pt., VA	10/22/64	Fts. Monroe, VA G.H.	P8,CSR
					Fts. Monroe, VA G.	11/09/64	Died, Typhoid fever	CSR
Trotter, Thomas J.	Pvt	G 1st SCVA	Deserted/enemy	03/23/65	Charleston, SC	03/23/65	Taken oath & disch.	CSR
Trotti, Frank B.	Pvt	Mathewes A	Augusta, GA	05/18/65	Augusta, GA	05/18/65	Paroled	CSR
Trowell, J.	Pvt	F 3rd SCVC	South Newport, GA	08/17/64	Hilton Head, SC G.H.	09/07/64	Pt. Royal Fy. Xc	P2,CSR
True, James H.	Sgt	C 12th SCVI	Petersburg, VA	04/03/65	City Pt., VA	04/07/65	Hart's Island, NY	CSR
					Hart's Island, NY	06/16/65	Rlsd. G.O. #109	P79,CSR
Truesdell, D.B.	Sgt	B 23rd SCVI	Five Forks, VA	04/01/65	City Pt., VA	04/04/65	Pt. Lookout, MD	CSR
					Pt. Lookout, MD	06/21/65	Rlsd. G.O. #109	P115,P118,CSR
Truitt, James A.F.	Pvt	A 14th SCVI	Gettysburg, PA	07/03/63	Chester, PA G.H.	08/17/63	City Pt., VA Xc	P1,CSR
Truitt, W.M.	Pvt	G 26th SCVI	High Bridge, VA	04/04/65	City Pt., VA	04/23/65	Newport News, VA	CSR
					Newport News, VA	06/15/65	Rlsd. G.O. #109	P107,CSR
Truluck, J.T.	Pvt	H 26th SCVI	Farmville, VA	04/06/65	City Pt., VA	04/14/65	Newport News, VA	CSR
					Newport News, VA	06/26/65	Rlsd. G.O. #109	P107,CSR
Tryon, William T.	Pvt	C 11th SCVI			Hampton, VA G.H.	06/29/64	Died, Peritonitis	P12
Tubba, John W..	Pvt	B German LA	Alexandria, VA	05/31/65	Alexandria, VA	05/31/65	Oath of amnesty	CSR
Tuck, Thomas M.	Pvt	C Hol.Leg.	Sharpsburg, MD	09/17/62	USGH Frederick, MD	09/30/62	Died of wounds	P1,P6,P12,FPH,HOS
Tuck, William J.	Pvt	C Hol.Leg.	Five Forks, VA	04/01/65	City Pt., VA	04/05/65	Pt. Lookout, MD	CSR,HOS
					Pt. Lookout, MD	06/21/65	Rlsd. G.O. #109	P115,P118,CSR
Tucker, A.J.	Pvt	B 5th SCVC	Augusta, GA	05/19/65	Augusta, GA	05/19/65	Paroled	CSR
Tucker, J.B.	Pvt	E P.S.S.	Sharpsburg, MD	10/01/62	Ft. McHenry, MD	10/14/62	Aikens Ldg., VA Xc	CSR
					Aikens Ldg., VA	11/10/62	Exchanged	CSR
Tucker, James A.	Pvt	I Hol.Leg.	Stony Creek, VA	05/07/64	Fts. Monroe, VA	05/13/64	Pt. Lookout, MD	CSR,HOS
					Pt. Lookout, MD	08/15/64	Elmira, NY	P113,P120,CSR
					Elmira, NY	02/20/65	James R., VA Xc	P65,P66,CSR
Tucker, Joel T.	Pvt	H Ham.Leg.MI	Deep Bottom, VA	08/16/64	Pt. Lookout, MD	02/13/65	Aikens Ldg., VA Xc	P113,P116,P121,P124
Tucker, Joel T.	Pvt	H Ham.Leg.MI	Charleston, SC	04/03/65	Charleston, SC	04/03/65	Paroled	CSR
Tullis, E.M.	Pvt	A 1st SCVA	Bentonville, NC	03/22/65	New Berne, NC	04/10/65	Hart's Island, NY	CSR
					Hart's Island, NY	06/21/65	Rlsd. G.O. #109	P79,CSR
Tully, Lovat A.	1Lt	B Ham.Leg.MI	Augusta, GA	05/24/65	Augusta, GA	05/24/65	Paroled	CSR
Tully, William J.	Pvt	B Ham.Leg.MI	Augusta, GA	06/02/65	Augusta, GA	06/02/65	Paroled	CSR
Tumbleston, Josiah J.	Pvt	I 1st SCVC	Deserted/enemy	03/22/65	Charleston, SC	03/22/65	Released on oath	CSR
Tumbleston, Nathaniel	Pvt	I 1st SCVC	Deserted/enemy	03/22/65	Charleston, SC	03/22/65	Released on oath	CSR
Tumbleston, R.R.	Pvt	I 1st SCVC	Deserted/enemy	03/22/65	Charleston, SC	03/22/65	Released on oath	CSR
Tumbleston, William M.	Pvt	I 1st SCVC	Charleston, SC	03/22/65	Charleston, SC	03/22/65	Released on oath	CSR
Tumblin, James M.	Pvt	E 14th SCVI	Petersburg, VA	04/02/65	City Pt., VA	04/04/65	Pt. Lookout, MD	CSR
					Pt. Lookout, MD	06/21/65	Rlsd. G.O. #109	P115,P117,CSR
Tumblin, Silas J.	Cpl	E 14th SCVI	Sutherland Stn., VA	04/03/65	City Pt., VA	04/13/65	Pt. Lookout, MD	CSR
					Pt. Lookout, MD	06/21/65	Rlsd. G.O. #109	P115,P119,P122,CSR
Tupper, James	1Lt	D 27th SCVI	Town Creek, NC	02/20/65	Ft. Anderson, NC	02/28/65	Pt. Lookout, MD	CSR
					Pt. Lookout, MD	02/28/65	Washington, DC	P115,P120,CSR
Tupper, James	1Lt	G 27th SCVI	Town Creek, NC	02/20/85	Old Capitol, DC	03/24/65	Ft. Delaware, DE	CSR
					Ft. Delaware, DE	06/17/65	Rlsd. G.O. #109	P43,P45,P46,CSR
Turbeville, Pickett	Sgt	D 25th SCVI	Town Creek, NC	02/20/65	Ft. Anderson, NC	02/28/65	Pt. Lookout, MD	CSR
					Pt. Lookout, MD	06/20/65	Rlsd. G.O. #109	P115,P117,P121,CSR
Turbeville, Ransom	Sgt	3 10/19 SCVI	Missionary Ridge, TN	11/25/63	Nashville, TN	12/07/63	Louisville, KY	P39,RAS,CSR,HMC
					Louisville, KY	12/07/63	Rock Island, IL	P88,P89,CSR
					Rock Island, IL	05/03/65	New Orleans, LA Xc	P3,P131,CSR
					New Orleans, LA	05/23/65	Exchanged	CSR
Turbeville, Solomon	Pvt	E 1st SCVIG	Sharpsburg, MD	09/17/62	USGH Frederick, MD	10/01/62	Died	P1,P6,FPH,SA1,CSR
Turnage, D.	Pvt	B 8th SCVI	Winchester, VA	09/13/64	Harpers Ferry, WV	09/19/64	Camp Chase, OH	CSR,KEB
					Camp Chase, OH	06/11/65	Rlsd. G.O. #109	P22,CSR

SOUTH CAROLINA SOLDIERS, SAILORS AND T CITIZENS HELD IN U.S. PRISONS 1861-1865

NAME	RANK	REGIMENT	CAPTURED AT	WHEN	PRISON	MOVED	DISPOSITION	SOURCES
Turnage, Luke	Pvt	F 21st SCVI	Ft. Fisher, NC	01/15/65	New York, NY	01/30/65	Elmira, NY	CSR,HOM,HAG
					Elmira, NY	07/03/65	Rlsd. G.O. #109	P65,P66
Turnage, William A.	Pvt	K 21st SCVI	Black Creek, SC	03/02/65	New Berne, NC	04/03/65	Pt. Lookout, MD	CSR,HAG
Turnage, William A.	Pvt	D 21st SCVI	Black Creek, SC	03/02/65	Pt. Lookout, MD	06/21/65	Rlsd. G.O. #109	P115,P117,P122
Turner, C.J.	Pvt	P.S.S.	Deserted/enemy	03/03/65	Bermuda Hundred, VA	03/05/65	City Pt., VA	CSR,TSE
Turner, Claude C.	2Lt	I 5th SCVI	Spotsylvania, VA	05/10/64	Belle Plain, VA	05/17/64	Ft. Delaware, DE	CSR,SA3
					Ft. Delaware, DE	06/16/65	Rlsd. G.O. #109	P42,P44,P45,CSR
Turner, Daniel	Pvt	B 24th SCVI	Jonesboro, GA	09/01/64	Rough & Ready, GA	09/19/64	Exchanged	CSR,EFW
Turner, E.J.	Pvt	C 3rd SCVABn	Blakely, AL	04/09/65	Ship Island, MS	05/01/65	Vicksburg, MS	P136,CSR
					Vicksburg, MS	05/03/65		CSR
Turner, G.W.	Pvt	G 2nd SCVC	Augusta, GA	05/26/65	Augusta, GA	05/26/65	Paroled	CSR
Turner, George D.	Pvt	H 18th SCVI	Five Forks, VA	04/02/65	Pt. Lookout, MD	06/16/65	Rlsd. G.O. #109	P115,P118,YEB,CSR
Turner, George W.	Msc	B 27th SCVI	Town Creek, NC	02/20/65	Ft. Anderson, NC	02/28/65	Pt. Lookout, MD	CSR,HAG
					Pt. Lookout, MD	06/20/65	Rlsd. G.O. #109	P115,P117,P121
Turner, H.P.	Pvt	F 1st SCVA	Bentonville, NC	03/22/65	Hart's Island, NY	06/16/65	Rlsd. G.O. #109	P79
Turner, Hiram	Pvt	D Ham.Leg.MI	Deserted/enemy	01/22/65	Bermuda Hundred, VA	01/23/65	City Pt., VA P.M.	CSR
					City Pt., VA	01/24/65	Washington, DC	CSR
					Washington, DC	01/26/65	Syracuse, NY oath	CSR
Turner, Ira	Pvt	G 7th SCVI	Deserted/enemy	09/06/64	Harpers Ferry, WV	09/14/64	Washington, DC P.M.	CNM,CSR
					Washington, DC	09/15/64	Philadelphia, PA	CSR
Turner, J.	Pvt	F Hol.Leg.	Petersburg, VA	11/06/64	Pt. Lookout, MD	06/21/65	Rlsd. G.O. #109	P115
Turner, J.	Pvt	C 3rd SCVABn	Blakely, AL	04/09/65	Ship Island, MS	05/01/65	Vicksburg, MS	P136,CSR
					Vicksburg, MS	05/03/65	Exchanged	CSR
Turner, J.B.	Pvt	D Ham.Leg.MI	Deserted/enemy	01/22/65	Bermuda Hundred, VA	01/23/65	City Pt., VA P.M.	CSR
Turner, J.B.	Pvt	D Ham.Leg.MI	Deserted/enemy	01/22/65	City Pt., VA	01/23/65	Washington, DC	CSR
					Washington, DC	01/26/65	Syracuse, NY oath	CSR
Turner, J.H.	Cpl	A Hol.Leg.	Kinston, NC	12/15/62	Kinston, NC	12/15/62	Paroled POW	CSR
Turner, J.H.	Cpl	A Hol.Leg.	Petersburg, VA	11/06/64	Pt. Lookout, MD		No other data	P115,CSR
					City Pt., VA	11/11/64	Washington, DC	CSR
Turner, J.M.	Sgt	B 19th SCVI	Augusta, GA	05/19/65	Augusta, GA	05/19/65	Paroled	CSR
Turner, J.S.	Pvt	G 2nd SCVC	Stephenburg, VA	06/09/63	Old Capitol, DC	06/25/63	City Pt., VA Xc	CSR
					Ft. McHenry, MD	06/25/63	City Pt., VA Xc	P110
Turner, J.W.	Cpt	F 19th SCVI	Thompkinsville, KY		Thompkinsville, KY		Paroled	CSR
Turner, J.W.	Cpt	F 19th SCVI	Macon, GA	04/30/65	Macon, GA	04/30/64	Paroled	CSR
Turner, James J.	Pvt	McQueen LA	Farmville, VA	04/11/65	Farmville, VA	04/21/65	Paroled	CSR
Turner, James Leonard	Pvt	G 1st SCVIG	Gettysburg, PA	07/05/63	Pt. Lookout, MD	03/05/64	City Pt., VA Xc	P116,CSR
					Bedloe's Island, NY	01/06/64	City Pt., VA Xc	P2
					David's Island, NY	10/24/63	Bedloe's Island, NY	P1,SA1,CSR
Turner, James M.	Pvt	F 13th SCVI	Hatchers Run, VA	03/31/65	City Pt., VA	04/02/65	Pt. Lookout, MD	CSR,HOS
					Pt. Lookout, MD	06/20/65	Rlsd. G.O. #109	P115,P117,P121,CSR
Turner, James P.	Pvt	F 17th SCVI	Petersburg, VA	03/25/65	City Pt., VA	03/28/65	Pt. Lookout, MD	CSR
					Pt. Lookout, MD	06/17/65	Died, Scurvy	P6,P12,P115,FPH
Turner, John	Pvt	H 1st SCVA	Morris Island, SC	07/10/63	Hilton Head, SC	09/19/63	Ft. Columbus, NY	CSR
					Ft. Columbus, NY	09/23/63	Took the oath	P1,P113
					Ft. Columbus, NY	09/26/63	Pt. Lookout, MD	CSR
Turner, John	Pvt	H 1st SCVIR	Augusta, GA	05/13/65	Augusta, GA	05/13/65	Paroled	CSR
Turner, John D.	Pvt	F 19th SCVI	Franklin, TN	12/17/64	Nashville, TN	01/01/65	Louisville, KY	P39
					Louisville, KY	01/05/65	Camp Chase, OH	P92,P94,CSR
					Camp Chase, OH	01/14/65	Died, Pneumonia	P5,P12,P22,P27,FPH
Turner, John F.	Pvt	D 15th SCVI	In Reb hospital	11/30/63	Knoxville, TN		In hospital	P84,HIC,CSR,KEB
Turner, John F.	Pvt	D 15th SCVI	Knoxville, TN	12/05/64	Louisville, KY	06/16/65	Rlsd. G.O. #109	P92,P94

SOUTH CAROLINA SOLDIERS, SAILORS AND  CITIZENS HELD IN U.S. PRISONS 1861-1865

NAME	RANK	REGIMENT	CAPTURED AT	WHEN	PRISON	MOVED	DISPOSITION	SOURCES
Turner, John H.	Sgt	B 26th SCVI	Petersburg, VA	03/25/65	City Pt., VA	03/27/65	Pt. Lookout, MD	CSR
					Pt. Lookout, MD	06/20/65	Rlsd. G.O. #109	P115,P117,P121,CSR
Turner, John K.	Pvt	C 26th SCVI	Southside RR, VA	04/01/65	City Pt., VA	04/05/65	Pt. Lookout, MD	CSR
					Pt. Lookout, MD	06/21/65	Rlsd. G.O. #109	P115,P119,HMC,CSR
Turner, Joseph B.	Pvt	I Hol.Leg.	Stony Creek, VA	05/07/64	Fts. Monroe, VA	05/13/64	Pt. Lookout, MD	CSR,HOS
					Pt. Lookout, MD	08/15/64	Elmira, NY	P113,P120
					Elmira, NY	02/20/65	James R., VA Xc	P65,P66,CSR
Turner, Joseph B.	Pvt	I Hol.Leg.	Stony Creek, VA	05/07/64	Richmond, VA Hos.	03/13/65	Died	CSR
Turner, Joshua	Pvt	F Hol.Leg.	Petersburg, VA	11/06/64	City Pt., VA	11/11/64	Washington, DC	CSR
					Pt. Lookout, MD	06/21/66	Rlsd. G.O. #109	P122,CSR
Turner, Levi	Pvt	B 24th SCVI	Nashville, TN	12/16/64	Nashville, TN	12/19/64	Louisville, KY	CSR,HOM
					Louisville, KY	12/21/64	Camp Douglas, IL	P90,P91,P94,CSR
					Camp Douglas, IL	06/20/65	Rlsd. G.O. #109	P55,HOM,CSR
Turner, R.A.	Pvt	H 1st SCVA	Deserted/enemy	02/19/65	Charleston, SC	02/19/65	Will take oath	CSR
Turner, R.B.	Pvt	I 15th SCVI	Gettysburg, PA	07/02/63	Ft. McHenry, MD	07/06/63	Ft. Delaware, DE	CSR
					Ft. Delaware, DE	06/10/65	Released	P45,KEB,H15,CSR
Turner, R.J.	Pvt	C 3rd SCVABn	Ft. Gaines, AL	08/08/64	New Orleans, LA	10/24/64	Ship Island, MS	P3,CSR
					Ship Island, MS	01/04/65	Exchanged	P136,CSR
Turner, Robert D.	Pvt	C 26th SCVI	Deserted/enemy	01/09/65	City Point, VA	01/10/65	Harrisburg, PA	P8,HMC,CSR
Turner, Stringfellow	Pvt	A 18th SCVAB	Washington, GA	06/13/65	Washington, GA	06/13/65	Paroled	CSR
Turner, T.J.	Pvt	G 22nd SCVI	Gettysburg, PA	07/04/63	Gettysburg, PA	08/09/63	Died of wounds	P1,P5,P12
Turner, T.J.	Pvt	K 5th SCVI	Richmond, VA Hos.	04/03/65	Pt. Lookout, MD	05/09/65	No more info	CSR,HOS,SA3
Turner, Thomas A.	Pvt	C 3rd SCVABn	Ft. Gaines, AL	08/08/64	New Orleans, LA	10/24/64	Ship Island, MS	P3,CSR
					Ship Island, MS	01/04/65	Exchanged	P136,CSR
Turner, Thomas A.	Pvt	C 3rd SCVABn	Citronelle, AL	05/04/65	Meridian, MS	05/10/65	Paroled	CSR
Turner, Thomas D.	Pvt	F 10th SCVI	Nashville, TN	12/15/64	Louisville, KY	12/20/64	Camp Douglas, IL	P91,P94,RAS,HMC,CSR
					Camp Douglas, IL	04/05/65	Died, Pneumonia	P6,P12,P58,FPH
Turner, W.P.	Pvt	F 1st SCVA	Bentonville, NC	03/22/65	New Berne, NC	04/10/65	Hart's Island, NY	CSR
					Hart's Island, NY	06/16/65	Rlsd. G.O. #109	CSR
Turner, William	Pvt	G 3rd SCVABn	Greene Springs	06/04/63	Pt. Lookout, MD	12/25/63	Exchanged	P123
Turner, William	Pvt	A Orr's Ri.	Gettysburg, PA	07/03/63	Ft. Delaware, DE	09/15/63	Jd. US 1st CN Cav.	P42
Turner, William	Pvt	L Orr's Ri.	Spotsylvania, VA	05/12/64	Belle Plain, VA	05/21/64	Ft. Delaware, DE	CSR,CDC
					Ft. Delaware, DE	10/22/64	Hos. 10/22-12/12/64	P47
					Ft. Delaware, DE	05/07/65	Rlsd., Secy. of War	P41,P42,P45,CSR
					Ft. Delaware, DE	04/08/65	Hos. 4/8-4/13/65	P47
Turner, William	Pvt	I Hol.Leg.	Deserted/enemy	01/03/65	City Point, VA	01/09/65	Washington, SC	P8,CSR
					Washington, DC	01/11/65	Toffeton, NH oath	CSR
Turner, William H.	Pvt	C 6th SCVC	Jerusalem Plk. Rd.	11/29/64	City Pt., VA	12/03/64	Pt. Lookout, MD	CSR
					Pt. Lookout, MD	02/18/65	Aikens Ldg., VA Xc	P115,P117,P123,CSR
Turner, William T.	Cpl	K 19th SCVI	Murfreesboro, TN	12/31/62	Murfreesboro, TN	02/18/63	Died of wounds	P12,HOE,CSR
Turnipseed, James Owens	Pvt	E 3rd SCVI	High Bridge, VA	04/06/65	City Pt., VA	04/14/65	Pt. Lookout, MD	CSR,KEB,ANY,SA2,H3
					Pt. Lookout, MD	06/20/65	Rlsd. G.O. #109	P115,P119,P121
Tuten, J.G.	Pvt	F 3rd SCVC	South Newport, GA	08/17/64	Hilton Head, SC G.H.	09/07/64	Pt. Royal Fy. Xc	P2
Tuten, J.H.	Pvt	B 19th SCVCB	Augusta, GA	05/19/65	Augusta, GA	05/19/65	Paroled on oath	CSR
Tuten, J.S.	Pvt	E 3rd SCVC	Deserted/enemy	03/31/65	Savannah, GA	03/31/65	Released on oath	CSR
Tuten, J.T.	Pvt	F 3rd SCVC	South Newport, GA	08/17/64	Port Royal Fy., SC	09/07/64	Exchanged	CSR
Tuten, Joseph J.	Sgt	D 24th SCVI	Macon, GA	04/30/65	Macon, GA	04/30/65	Paroled on oath	CSR,EFW
Tuten, Thomas	Pvt	C 3rd SCVC	Deserted/enemy	03/05/65	Charleston, SC	03/15/65	Taken oath & disch.	CSR
Tuten, Thomas S.	2Lt	E 11th SCVI	Weldon RR, VA	08/21/64	Old Capitol, DE	08/27/64	Ft. Delaware, DE	CSR,HAG
					Ft. McHenry, MD	08/27/64	Ft. Delaware, DE	P46,P110
					Ft. Delaware, DE	06/17/65	Rlsd. G.O. #109	P43,P45,CSR
Tuten, W.H.	Pvt	B 19th SCVCB	Augusta, GA	05/19/65	Augusta, GA	05/19/65	Paroled on oath	CSR

SOUTH CAROLINA SOLDIERS, SAILORS AND  CITIZENS HELD IN U.S. PRISONS 1861-1865

NAME	RANK	REGIMENT	CAPTURED AT	WHEN	PRISON	MOVED	DISPOSITION	SOURCES
Tuten, William H.	Pvt	E 3rd SCVC	Deserted/enemy	03/30/65	Savannah, GA	03/31/65	Took oath, stayed	CSR
Twachtman, Herman	Pvt	B German LA	Gettysburg, PA	07/29/63	Harrisburg, PA	08/08/63	Philadelphia, PA	CSR
Twachtman, Herman	Pvt	B German LA	Gettysburg, PA	07/29/63	Harrisburg, PA	08/30/63	Ft. Delaware, DE	CSR
					Ft. Delaware, DE	05/10/65	Rlsd. G.O. #85	CSR
Twitty, P.B.	Pvt	G 3rd SCVABn	High Pt., NC	05/01/65	High Pt., NC	05/01/65	Paroled	CSR
Twitty, W.B.	Sgt	I 12th SCVI	Spotsylvania, VA	05/12/64	Belle Plain, VA	05/20/64	Ft. Delaware, DE	CSR,LAN
					Ft. Delaware, DE	05/11/65	Released	P41,P42,P45,CSR
Tyce, George M.	Pvt	I Hol.Leg.	Five Forks, VA	04/01/65	Pt. Lookout, MD	06/20/65	Rlsd. G.O. #109	P115,P118,P121
Tylee, William C.	Pvt	D 1st SCVIR	Morris Island, SC	07/10/63	Hilton Head, SC	09/24/63	Ft. Columbus, NY	CSR
					Ft. Columbus, NY	09/25/63	Rlsd. on oath	P1,CSR
Tyler, Hugh	Pvt	F 1st SCVIG	Gettysburg, PA	07/05/63	Ft. Delaware, DE	11/04/63	Died, Ch. Diarrhea	P5,P12,P40,P42,FPH
Tyler, James W.	Pvt	A 1st SCVIG	Petersburg, VA	04/02/65	City Pt., VA	04/04/65	Pt. Lookout, MD	SA1,CSR
					Pt. Lookout, MD	06/21/65	Rlsd. G.O. #109	CSR

U

SOUTH CAROLINA SOLDIERS, SAILORS AND CITIZENS HELD IN U.S. PRISONS 1861-1865

NAME	RANK	REGIMENT	CAPTURED AT	WHEN	PRISON	MOVED	DISPOSITION	SOURCES
Ulmer, Frederick F.	Pvt	F 25th SCVI	Ft. Anderson, NC	02/19/65	Ft. Anderson, NC	02/28/65	Pt. Lookout, MD	CSR,HAG
					Pt. Lookout, MD	06/21/65	Rlsd. G.O. #109	P115,P116,P122,CSR
Ulmer, G.L.	Pvt	F 25th SCVI	Ft. Fisher, NC	01/15/65	New York, NY	01/30/65	Elmira, NY	CSR,HAG
					Elmira, NY	07/11/65	Rlsd. G.O. #109	P65,P66,CSR
Ulmer, Henry M.	Cpt	H 17th SCVI	Petersburg, VA	03/25/65	Old Capitol, DC	03/30/65	Ft. Delaware, DE	CSR
					Ft. McHenry, MD	03/31/65	Ft. Delaware, DE	P110
					Ft. Delaware, DE	06/17/65	Rlsd. G.O. #109	P42,P45,CSR
Ulmer, J.B.	Pvt	K 17th SCVI	Augusta, GA	05/31/65	Augusta, GA	05/31/65	Paroled	CSR
Ulmer, James M.	Cpl	H 17th SCVI	Petersburg, VA	03/25/65	City Pt., VA	03/28/65	Pt. Lookout, MD	CSR
					Pt. Lookout, MD	06/21/65	Rlsd. G.O. #109	P115,P116,P122,CSR
Ulmer, Thomas W.	Cpl	F 25th SCVI	Town Creek, NC	02/20/65	Ft. Anderson, NC	02/28/65	Pt. Lookout, MD	CSR,HAG
					Pt. Lookout, MD	06/21/65	Rlsd. G.O. #109	P115,P116
Underwood, Elbert	Pvt	A 15th SCVAB	Smith's Ford, NC	03/16/65				CSR
Unfug, Casper	Pvt	E 18th SCVAB	Deserted/enemy		Charleston, SC	02/18/65	Released on oath	CSR
Ussery, J.M.	Pvt	A 1st SCVIG	N. Anna River, VA	05/23/64	Front Royal, VA	05/30/64	Pt. Lookout, MD	CSR
					Pt. Lookout, MD	10/30/64	Aikens Ldg., VA Xc	P113,P116,P123,SA1,CSR
Utes, John	Pvt	I 1st SCVIG	Falling Waters, MD	07/14/63	Ft. McHenry, MD			P110
					Old Capitol, DC		Pt. Lookout, MD	CSR
					Baltimore, MD	08/23/63	Pt. Lookout, MD	CSR
					Pt. Lookout, MD	01/21/65	Aikens Ldg., VA Xc	P116,CSR
					Pt. Lookout, MD	01/17/65	Exchanged	P113,P123,P124,CSR

SOUTH CAROLINA SOLDIERS, SAILORS AND  CITIZENS HELD IN U.S. PRISONS 1861-1865

NAME	RANK	REGIMENT	CAPTURED AT	WHEN	PRISON	MOVED	DISPOSITION	SOURCES
Valentine, L.W.	Pvt	A 1st SCVIH	Deserted/enemy	03/23/65	Fts. Monroe, VA	03/24/65	Washington, DC	CSR
					Washington, DC P.M.	03/29/65	Charleston, SC	CSR
Van Horne, Arnold A.	Pvt	I 14th SCVI	Petersburg, VA	07/29/64	City Pt., VA	08/05/64	Pt. Lookout, MD	CSR
					Pt. Lookout, MD	08/08/64	Elmira, NY	P113,P120,CSR
					Elmira, NY	10/11/64	Pt. Lookout, MD Xc	P65,P66,CSR
					Pt. Lookout, MD	10/29/64	To exchange	P115,CSR
					Fts. Monroe, VA	11/05/64	Died	CSR
Van Horne, John G.	Pvt	I 14th SCVI	Gettysburg, PA	07/04/63	David's Island, NY	09/05/63	City Pt., VA Xc	P1,CSR
Van Horne, Joseph E.	Pvt	I 14th SCVI	Petersburg, VA	04/03/65	City Pt., VA	04/11/65	Hart's Island, NY	CSR
					Hart's Island, NY	06/14/65	Rlsd. G.O. #109	P79,CSR
Van Patton, Adam E.	Pvt	E 14th SCVI	Warrenton, VA	09/29/62	Warrenton, VA	09/29/62	Paroled	CSR
Van Ripper, Henry W.	Pvt	B 27th SCVI	Town Creek, NC	02/20/65	Ft. Anderson, NC	02/28/65	Pt. Lookout, MD	CSR,HAG
					Pt. Lookout, MD	05/14/65	Rlsd. G.O. #85	P115,P117,P121,CSR
VanTassel, James	Sgt	C 2nd SCVA	Deserted/enemy		Charleston, SC		Released on oath	CSR
Vance, G.W.	Pvt	A 7th SCVI	Cedar Creek, VA	10/19/64	Pt. Lookout, MD	06/21/65	Rlsd. G.O. #109	P115,P117,P122,CSR
Vance, Samuel G.	Pvt	E 16th SCVI	Jonesboro, GA	09/02/64	Rough & Ready, GA	09/19/64	Exchanged	CSR
Vanderford, Hampton	Pvt	C 15th SCVI	South Mtn., MD	09/14/62	Ft. McHenry, MD	10/06/62	Aikens Ldg., VA Xc	CSR
Vanderford, Hampton	Pvt	H 15th SCVI	Gettysburg, PA	07/05/63	Letterman G.H. Gbg	07/12/63	Died of wounds	P1,P12,CSR
Vandiver, Henry C.	Pvt	B Hol.Leg.	Petersburg, VA	03/25/66	City Pt., VA	03/28/65	Pt. Lookout, MD	CSR,HOS
					Pt. Lookout, MD	06/21/65	Rlsd. G.O. #109	P115,P117,CSR
Vandiver, John B.	Pvt	H 7th SCVIBn	Weldon RR, VA	08/21/64	City Pt., VA USFH	08/23/64	Fts. Monroe, VA US	CSR,HAG
					Fts. Monroe, VA G.H.	08/26/64	Alexandria, VA G.H.	CSR
					Alexandria, VA G.H.	09/09/64	Washington, SC G.H.	CSR
					Lincoln G.H., DC	10/26/64	Old Capitol, DC	CSR
					Ft. McHenry, MD	12/16/64	Elmira, NY	P110
					Old Capitol, DC	12/16/64	Elmira, NY	CSR
					Elmira, NY	03/02/65	James R., VA Xc	P65,P66,CSR
					Richmond, VA Hos.	03/09/65	Furloughed 30 days	CSR
Vanlandingham, William	Pvt	H 4th SCVC	Hawe's Shop, VA	05/28/64	3rd Div. 5th A.C.	10/17/64	Lincoln G.H., DC	CSR,LAN
					Lincoln G.H., DC	10/23/64	Old Capitol, DC	CSR
					Old Capitol, DC	10/24/64	Elmira, NY	CSR
					Ft. McHenry, MD	10/24/64	Elmira, NY	P110
					Elmira, NY	02/13/65	Pt. Lookout, MD Xc	P65,P66,CSR
					Richmond, VA Hos.	03/07/65	Camp Lee, VA wait	CSR
Vanpatten, Veela V.	Pvt	D 23rd SCVI	Petersburg, VA	04/01/65	City Pt., VA	04/04/65	Pt. Lookout, MD	CSR
					Pt. Lookout, MD	06/21/65	Rlsd. G.O. #109	P115,P117,P122,CSR
Vansant, Addison	Pvt	C 15th SCVI	Leesburg, VA	10/02/62	Leesburg, VA	10/02/62	Paroled	H15
Varn, Carson W.	Pvt	G 17th SCVI	Deserted/enemy	04/14/65	Washington, DC P.M.	04/14/65	Charleston, SC oath	CSR
Varn, Hangford D.	Pvt	K 14th SCMil	Lynch's Creek, SC	02/25/65	Hart's Island, NY	05/11/65	Died, Ch. Diarrhea	P6,P79,FPH
Varn, John W.	Pvt	G 17th SCVI	Burkeville, VA	04/14/65	Burkeville, VA	04/14/65	Paroled	CSR
Varn, P.M.	Pvt	C 19th SCVCB	Augusta, GA	05/20/65	Augusta, GA	05/20/65	Paroled on oath	CSR
Varn, William D.L.	Pvt	A 1st SCVIG	Hatchers Run, VA	04/02/65	City Pt., VA	04/07/65	Hart's Island, NY	CSR,SA1
					Hart's Island, NY	06/16/65	Rlsd. G.O. #109	P79,CSR
Vaughan, D.T.	2Lt	A 22nd SCVI	Bermuda Hundred, VA	06/02/64	Fts. Monroe, VA	06/04/64	Pt. Lookout, MD	CSR
					Pt. Lookout, MD	06/23/64	Ft. Delaware, DE	P113,P116,P120
					Ft. Delaware, DE	06/17/65	Rlsd. G.O. #109	P42,P44,P45,P46
Vaughan, F.H.	Pvt	E Ham.Leg.	Fredericksburg, VA	05/02/63	Ft. McHenry, MD	05/11/63	Fts. Monroe, VA Xc	P96,CSR
Vaughan, James B.	Pvt	D 3rd SCVI	Gettysburg, PA	07/04/63	Letterman G.H. Gbg	10/14/63	Provost Marshal	P1,SA2,H3,KEB
					W. Bldg. Balt, MD	11/12/63	City Pt., VA Xc	P1,CSR
					Richmond, VA Hos.	11/21/63	Furloughed 30 days	CSR

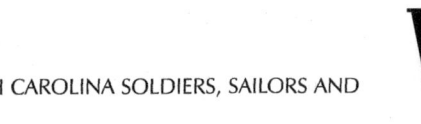

SOUTH CAROLINA SOLDIERS, SAILORS AND V CITIZENS HELD IN U.S. PRISONS 1861-1865

NAME	RANK	REGIMENT	CAPTURED AT	WHEN	PRISON	MOVED	DISPOSITION	SOURCES
Vaughan, Jesse A.	Cpl	E 16th SCVI	Franklin, TN	12/18/64	Nashville, TN	01/31/65	Louisville, KY	P3,P39,16R,CSR
					Louisville, KY	02/01/65	Camp Chase, OH	P92,P94,16R,CSR
					Camp Chase, OH	03/03/65	Died, Consumption	P6,P22,P27,FPH,16R
Vaughan, M.P.	Pvt	G 4th SCVC	Deserted/enemy	03/27/65	Hilton Head, SC	04/07/65	New York, NY P.M.	CSR
Vaughan, Samuel	Pvt	F Ham.Leg.MI	Ft. Harrison, VA	09/29/64	Bermuda Hundred, VA	09/30/64	City Pt., VA	CSR
					City Pt., VA	10/05/64	Pt. Lookout, MD	CSR
					Pt. Lookout, MD	03/17/65	Aikens Ldg., VA Xc	P115,P117,P121
Vaughan, W.C.	Pvt	F 18th SCVI	Crater, Pbg., VA	07/30/64	City Pt., VA	08/04/64	Pt. Lookout, MD	CSR
					Pt. Lookout, MD	08/08/64	Elmira, NY	P113,P116,P120,CSR
					Elmira, NY	07/03/65	Rlsd. G.O. #109	P65,P66,CSR
Vaughn, D.K.	Pvt	K 15th SCVI	Spotsylvania, VA	05/08/64	Belle Plain, VA	05/20/64	Ft. Delaware, DE	CSR,KEB,H15
					Ft. Delaware, DE	06/10/65	Rlsd. G.O. #109	P41,P42,CSR
Vaughn, David	Pvt	F Ham.Leg.MI	Burkeville, VA	04/06/65	Pt. Lookout, MD	06/30/65	Died, Ch. Diarrhea	P6,P115,P118,FPH
Vaughn, H.W.	Pvt	G 4th SCVC	Stony Creek, VA	12/01/64	City Pt., VA	12/05/64	Pt. Lookout, MD	CSR
Vaughn, H.W.	Pvt	G 4th SCVC	Stony Creek, VA	12/01/64	Pt. Lookout, MD	06/21/65	Rlsd. G.O. #109	P115,CSR
Vaughn, James A.	Pvt	E 16th SCVI	Franklin, TN	12/17/64	Camp Chase, OH	03/03/65	Died, Consumption	P12,CSR,FPH
Vaughn, James P.	Pvt	K 15th SCVI	Halltown, VA	08/26/64	Harpers Ferry, WV	08/29/64	Camp Chase, OH	CSR,KEB,H15
					Camp Chase, OH	03/18/65	Pt. Lookout, MD	P22,P26
					Pt. Lookout, MD	03/27/65	Boulware's Wh. Xc	CSR
Vaughn, Marshal	Pvt	F Ham.Leg.	Warrenton, VA	09/29/62	Warrenton, VA	09/29/62	Paroled	CSR
Vaughn, William P.	Pvt	A Orr's Ri.	Wilderness, VA	05/05/64	Belle Plain VA	05/21/64	Ft. Delaware, DE	CSR,CDC
					Ft. Delaware, DE	05/26/64	Hos. 5/26-6/3/64	P47
					Ft. Delaware, DE	06/10/65	Rlsd. G.O. #109	P41,P42
Vaught, Mathias	Pvt	Waccamaw A	Stmr. Wave Queen	02/27/63	Ft. McHenry, MD			P145
					Gunboat Quaker Cit	03/16/63	New York, NY P.M.	CSR
Vaught, Mathias	Pvt	Waccamaw A	N. Santee R., SC	02/27/63	Sandusky, OH	04/06/63	Fts. Monroe, VA Xc	CSR
Vaught, S.W.	Pvt	L 7th SCVI	Sharpsburg, MD	09/28/62	Ft. McHenry, MD	11/16/62	Aikens Ldg., VA Xc	CSR
Vausse, Admiran E.	Pvt	F 27th SCVI	Town Creek, NC	02/20/65	Ft. Anderson, DE	02/28/65	Pt. Lookout, MD	CSR,HAG
					Pt. Lookout, MD	06/21/65	Rlsd. G.O. #109	P115,P117,P122,CSR
Veal, John Malcomb	Cpl	A 15th SCVI	Wilderness, VA	05/06/64	Pt. Lookout, MD	09/18/64	Aikens LDg., VA Xc	P116,CSR,KEB,H15
					Richmond, VA Hos.	09/25/64	Furloughed 30 days	CSR
Vehorn, Elias	Pvt	F 13th SCVI	Gettysburg, PA	07/05/63	W. Bldg. Balt, MD	09/17/63	Chester, PA USGH	P1,CSR,HOS
					Chester, PA USGH	10/13/63	Died of wounds	P1,P6,P12,CSR
Vehorn, William L.	Pvt	F 2nd SCVIRi	Knoxville, TN	12/05/63	Knoxville, TN	12/29/63	Took the oath	CSR
Venters, A.J.	Pvt	G 15th SCVI	Petersburg, VA Hos.	04/02/65	Petersburg, VA	04/27/65	Died of wounds	P12
Venters, James L.	Pvt	G 15th SCVI	Gettysburg, PA	07/05/63	Gettysburg, PA USH	07/21/63	Provost Marshal	P4,KEB,CTA,CSR
					David's Island, NY	09/23/63	City Pt., VA Xc	P1,CSR
Vereen, B.F.	Pvt	Waccamaw A	N. Santee R., SC	02/27/63	Ft. McHenry, MD			P145
					Gunboat Quaker Cit	03/16/63	New York, NY P.M.	CSR
					Ft. Lafayette, NY	04/07/63	Fts. Monroe, VA Xc	P144
Vereen, J.D.	Pvt	E 26th SCVI	Hatchers Run, VA	03/29/65	City Pt., VA	04/02/65	Pt. Lookout, MD	CSR
					Pt. Lookout, MD	06/21/65	Rlsd. G.O. #109	P115,P117,CSR
Vermillion, W.T.	Pvt	F 1st SCVIH	Deep Bottom, VA	08/14/64	Bermuda Hundred, VA	08/15/64	Fts. Monroe, VA	CSR,SA1
					Fts. Monroe, VA	08/16/64	Pt. Lookout, MD	CSR
					Pt. Lookout, MD	06/21/65	Rlsd. G.O. #109	P113,P116,P125,CSR
Vernon, J.M.	Mct	Huntress	Off Charleston	01/18/63	Ft. Lafayette, NY	07/02/63	Ft. Warren, MA	P144
Verrelle, William C.	Pvt	F Hol.Leg.	Five Forks, VA	04/01/65	City Pt., VA	04/05/65	Pt. Lookout, MD	CSR
					Pt. Lookout, MD		No other data	P115,P117,CSR
Vestz, W.	Pvt	C 3rd SCVABn	Blakely, AL	04/09/65	Ship Island, MS	05/01/65	Vicksburg, MS	P136,CSR
					Vicksburg, MS	05/04/65	Exchanged	CSR
Vickers, A.B.	QSg	A 3rd SCVABn	High Pt., NC	05/02/65	High Pt., NC	05/02/65	Paroled	CSR

SOUTH CAROLINA SOLDIERS, SAILORS AND **V** CITIZENS HELD IN U.S. PRISONS 1861-1865

NAME	RANK	REGIMENT	CAPTURED AT	WHEN	PRISON	MOVED	DISPOSITION	SOURCES
Villepigue, C.L.	Pvt	A 7th SCVC	Lytleton, VA	05/07/64	Pt. Lookout, MD	08/10/64	Elmira, NY	P120
					Elmira, NY	02/04/65	Died, Variola	P6,P12,P65,P66,FPH
Villepigue, John T.	Pvt	G 7th SCVIBn	Drury's Bluff, VA	05/16/64	Bermuda Hundred, VA	05/17/64	Fts. Monroe, VA	CSR
					Fts. Monroe, VA	05/18/64	Pt. Lookout, MD	CSR
					Pt. Lookout, MD	08/15/64	Elmira, NY	P116
					Pt. Lookout, MD	02/13/65	Aikens Ldg., VA Xc	P113,P121,P124,CSR
Vilt, Henry	Pvt	G 1st SCVIR	Deserted/enemy		Charleston, SC		Released on oath	CSR
Vincent, Daniel B.	Cpt	Str. Emily	Bulls Bay, SC	07/07/62	Ft. Delaware, DE			P47,OR
Vincent, J. Tillman	Pvt	I 12th SCVI	Gettysburg, PA	07/05/63	David's Island, NY	09/05/63	City Pt., VA Xc	P1,LAN,CSR
Vincent, J. Tillman	Pvt	I 12th SCVI	Farmville, VA	04/11/65	Farmville, VA	04/21/65	Paroled	CSR
Vincent, John	Pvt	F 1st SCVA	Smiths Ford, NC	03/16/65	New Berne, NC	04/03/65	Pt. Lookout, MD	CSR
					Pt. Lookout, MD	06/21/65	Rlsd. G.O. #109	P115,P117,CSR
Vincent, Josiah	Pvt	D 7th SCVIBn	Petersburg, VA	04/11/65	U.S. Field Hos.	04/13/65	U.S. Gen. Hos.	CSR,HAG,HIC
Vincente, John H.	Pvt	G 1st SCVIR	Charlotte, NC	11/27/64	Old Capitol, DC	12/16/64	Elmira, NY	CSR,SA1
					Elmira, NY	06/23/65	Rlsd. G.O. #109	P7,P65,P66,CSR
Vinson, D.D.	Pvt	1st SCVIG	Fredericksburg, VA	05/05/63	Washington, DC	05/10/63	City Pt., VA Xc	CSR
Vocelle, Augustus	Pvt	E 25th SCVI	Ft. Fisher, NC	01/15/65	New York, NY	01/30/65	Elmira, NY	CSR,HAG
					Elmira, NY	03/21/65	Died, Pneumonia	P6,P12,P65,P66,FPH
Vogelburg, Louis	Pvt	A 25th SCVI	Morris Island, SC	09/07/63	Hilton Head, SC	10/06/63	Ft. Columbus, NY	CSR
					Ft. Columbus, NY	10/09/63	Pt. Lookout, MD	CSR
					Pt. Lookout, MD	01/17/65	Transf. for Xc	P124,CSR
Voght, Adam N.	Pvt	H 1st SCVIG	N. Anna River, VA	05/23/64	Pt. Lookout, MD	10/11/64	Aikens Ldg., VA Xc	P113,P116,P123,SA1
Voght, Adam N.	Pvt	H 1st SCVIG	Hatchers Run, VA	03/31/65	Front Royal, VA	05/25/65	Pt. Lookout, MD	CSR
					Pt. Lookout, MD	06/21/65	Rlsd. G.O. #109	P115,P117,CSR
Vogt, L.C.	Pvt	F 25th SCVI	Town Creek, NC	02/20/65	Ft. Anderson, NC	02/28/65	Pt. Lookout, MD	CSR,HAG
					Pt. Lookout, MD	06/21/65	Rlsd. G.O. #109	P115,P117,HAG,CSR
Von Kohlnitz, G.F.	Pvt	D 5th SCVC	Sussex C.H., VA	12/12/64	City Pt., VA	12/15/64	Pt. Lookout, MD	CSR
					Pt. Lookout, MD	05/15/65	Rlsd. G.O. #85	P115,P117,CSR
Von Lehe, J.C.	Pvt	F 1st SCVIG	Southside RR, VA	04/03/65	City Pt., VA	04/03/65	Hart's Island, NY	CSR,SA1
					Hart's Island, NY	06/15/65	Rlsd. G.O. #109	SA1,P79,CSR

W

SOUTH CAROLINA SOLDIERS, SAILORS AND  CITIZENS HELD IN U.S. PRISONS 1861-1865

NAME	RANK	REGIMENT	CAPTURED AT	WHEN	PRISON	MOVED	DISPOSITION	SOURCES
Waddell, Ellison S.	Pvt	B 13th SCVI	Deserted/enemy	02/24/65	City Pt., VA	02/26/65	Washington, DC	CSR
					Washington, DC	02/27/65	Springfield, IL	CSR
Waddell, George W.	Pvt	E 14th SCVI	N. Anna River, VA	05/24/64	Port Royal, VA	05/30/64	Pt. Lookout, MD	CSR, HOS
					Pt. Lookout, MD	01/27/65	Hammond G.H., MD	P113,P117,P122,CSR
					Hammond G.H., MD	02/04/65	Died, Ch. Diarrhea	P12,CSR
Waddell, J.J.	Pvt	E Hol.Leg.	Warrenton, VA	09/29/62	Warrenton, VA	09/29/62	Paroled in Hos.	CSR
Waddell, R.B.	1Lt	B 3rd SCVABn	Ft. Tyler, GA	04/16/65	2nd Bgd. 1st Div.	04/23/65	Macon, GA Prison	CSR
Waddell, Thomas P.	Pvt	E 14th SCVI	Gettysburg, PA	07/05/63	Harrisburg, PA	07/07/63	Ft. Delaware, DE	CSR
					Ft. Delaware, DE	07/31/63	City Pt., VA Xc	P40,P44,CSR
Waddell, W.R.	Pvt	E 14th SCVI	Richmond, VA Hos.	04/09/65	Hammond G.H., MD	06/26/65	Rlsd. G.O. #109	P119,HOS,CSR
Waddell, William R.	Pvt	E Hol.Leg.	Warrenton, VA	09/29/62	Warrenton, VA	09/29/62	Paroled in Hos.	CSR,HOS
Waddle, E.S.	Pvt	C 22nd SCVI	Frederick, MD	09/12/62	Ft. Delaware, DE	10/12/62	Aikens Ldg., VA Xc	CSR,HOS
Waddle, Jesse T.	Pvt	G 3rd SCVI	Knoxville, TN	12/05/63	Nashville, TN	01/24/64	Louisville, KY	P39,KEB,SA2,CSR,H3
					Louisville, KY	01/29/64	Rock Island, IL	P88,P93, CSr
					Rock Island, IL	05/03/65	New Orleans, LA Xc	CSR
					New Orleans, LA	05/23/65	Exchanged	P4,CSR
Wade, E.T.	Pvt	D 1st SCVC	John's Island, SC	06/07/63	Hilton Head, SC	08/01/62	Ft. Columbus, NY	P37,CSR
					Ft. Columbus, NY	08/23/62	Ft. Delaware, DE	P37,CSR
					Ft. Delaware, DE	10/02/62	Aikens Ldg.,VA Xch	CSR
Wade, James	Pvt	B 2nd SCVC	Salisbury, NC	05/15/65	Salisbury, NC	05/15/65	Paroled	CSR
Wade, O.J.	Pvt	D 1st SCVCBn	John's Island, SC	06/07/62	Ft. Columbus, NY	08/23/62	Ft. Delaware, DE	P37
Wade, Richard J.	Sgt	H 14th SCVI	Gettysburg, PA	07/04/63	David's Island, NY	09/08/63	City Pt., VA Xchg.	P1,CSR
Wadford, W.H.	Pvt	K 21st SCVI	Ft. Fisher, NC	01/15/65	No other data			CSR
Wadkins, J.T.	Pvt	B 2nd SCVIRi	Deserted/enemy	03/03/65	Bermuda Hundred, VA	03/05/65	City Pt., VA P.M.	CSR
					City Pt., VA P.M.	03/07/65	Washington, DC P.M	CSR
					Washington, DC P.M.	03/08/65	Columbus, OH, oath	CSR
Wadle, John R.	Pvt	B 27th SCVI	Ft. Anderson, NC	02/19/65	Ft. Anderson, NC	02/28/65	Pt. Lookout, MD	CSR
					Pt. Lookout, MD	06/22/65	Rlsd. G.O. #109	P115,P118,P121,CSR
Wafford, J.T.	Pvt	B 13th SCVI	Williamsport, MD	09/16/62	New York, NY		Aikens Ldg., VA Xc	CSR
Wages, John	Pvt	B 14th SCVI	Petersburg, VA	04/02/65	2AC Hos.City Pt.VA	04/09/65	Lincoln G.H., DC	CSR
					Lincoln G.H., DC	04/19/65	Died, Pyaemia	P6,P12,CSR
Wages, Romeo	Pvt	B 3rd SCVABn	Ft. Tyler, GA	04/16/65	2nd Bgd. 1st Div.	04/23/65	Macon, GA Armory p	CSR
Wages, Wade	Pvt	F 3rd SCVIBn	Fisher's Hill, VA	09/22/64	Harpers Ferry, WV	10/01/64	Pt. Lookout, MD	CSR
					Pt. Lookout, MD	05/14/65	Rlsd. G.O. #85	P115,P117,CSR
Wagner, C.	Pvt	B 7th SCVC	Farmville, VA	04/11/65	Farmville, VA	04/21/65	Paroled	CSR
Wainwright, William T.H.	Pvt	8 10/19 SCVI	Missionary Ridge ,TN	11/25/63	Nashville, TN	12/07/63	Louisville, KY	P39,CSR
					Louisville, KY	12/09/63	Rock Island, IL	P88,P89,CSR
					Rock Island, IL	10/06/64	Jd. US Army F.S.	P131,CSR
Wait, W.	Pvt	6th SCResB	Cheraw, SC	03/05/65	Cheraw, SC	03/05/65	Paroled	CSR
Waits, Buford	Pvt	H Hol.Leg.	Five Forks, VA	04/01/65	City Pt., VA	04/05/65	Pt. Lookout, MD	CSR,ANY
					Pt. Lookout, MD	06/22/65	Rlsd. G.O. #109	P115,CSR
Waits, Drayton	Pvt	H Hol.Leg.	Five Forks, VA	04/01/65	City Pt., VA	04/05/65	Pt. Lookout, MD	CSR,ANY
					Pt. Lookout, MD	04/24/65	Died, Ch. Diarrhea	P6,P115,P118,FPH
Wakefield, Lafayette	Pvt	I 15th SCVI	Frederick, MD	09/13/62	Ft. Delaware, DE	12/15/62	Fts. Monroe, VA Xc	CSR,H15
Walden, Robert A.	Pvt	C Hol.Leg.	Five Forks, VA	04/01/65	City Pt., VA	04/05/65	Pt. Lookout, MD	CSR
Walden, Robert A.	Pvt	C Hol.Leg.	Five Forks, VA	04/01/65	Pt. Lookout, MD		No other data	P115,P118,CSR
Walden, Robert A.	Pvt	C Hol.Leg.	Kinston, NC	12/15/62	Kinston, NC	12/15/62	Paroled POW	CSR
Walden, W.A.	Pvt	K P.S.S.	Tunketstown, VA	09/15/62	Ft. Delaware, DE	10/02/62	Aikens Ldg., VA Xc	CSR
Walden, W.A.	Pvt	K P.S.S.	Tunketstown, VA	09/15/62	Aikens Ldg., VA	11/10/62	Exchanged	CSR
Waldrip, M.C.	Pvt	G 16th SCVI	Gainesville, AL	05/10/65	Gainesville, AL	05/10/65	Paroled on oath	CSR

W

SOUTH CAROLINA SOLDIERS, SAILORS AND CITIZENS HELD IN U.S. PRISONS 1861-1865

NAME	RANK	REGIMENT	CAPTURED AT	WHEN	PRISON	MOVED	DISPOSITION	SOURCES
Waldrip, William M.	Pvt	B 15th SCVI	Halltown, VA	08/26/64	Harpers Ferry, WV	08/29/64	Camp Chase, OH	CSR,KEB,H15
					Camp Chase, OH	03/18/65	Pt. Lookout, MD	P22,CSR
					Pt. Lookout, MD	06/21/65	Rlsd. G.O. #109	P115,P119,P122,CSR
Waldrop, A.B.	Pvt	H 22nd SCVI	Deserted/enemy	02/13/65	P.M. City Pt., VA	02/15/65	Washington, DC	CSR
Waldrop, J.W.	Pvt	H 22nd SCVI	Deserted/enemy	02/14/65	Old Capitol, DC	02/16/65	Ducktown, TN oath	CSR
Waldrop, William H.	Pvt	C 18th SCVI	Five Forks, VA	04/01/65	City Pt., VA	04/06/65	Pt. Lookout, MD	CSR
					Pt. Lookout, MD	06/22/65	Rlsd. G.O. #109	P115,P118,CSR
Waldrop, Wilson W.	Sgt	G Hol.Leg.	Five Forks, VA	04/01/65	City Pt., VA	04/05/65	Pt. Lookout, MD	CSR
					Pt. Lookout, MD	06/22/65	Rlsd. G.O. #109	P115,P118,P121,P122,CSR
Waldrup, P.A.	Pvt	B 11th SCVI	Deserted Richmond	10/14/64	Chattanooga, TN	11/11/64	Indiana--on oath	P8,CSR
Walker, A. Jackson	Pvt	A 17th SCVI	Five Forks, VA	04/01/65	Pt. Lookout, MD	06/22/65	Rlsd. G.O. #109	P115,P118,HHC
Walker, A.E.	Pvt	K 11th SCVI	Weldon RR, VA	08/21/64	City Pt., VA	08/24/64	Pt. Lookout, MD	HAG,CSR
					Pt. Lookout, MD	03/14/65	Aikens Ldg., VA Xc	P113,P117,P121
Walker, Albert R.	Pvt	1 10/19 SCVI	Missionary Ridge,TN	11/25/63	Nashville, TN	12/07/63	Louisville, KY	P39,RAS,CSR
					Louisville, KY	12/09/63	Rock Island, IL	P88,P89,FLR,CSR
					Rock Island, IL	06/18/65	Rlsd. G.O. #109	P131,CSR
Walker, Alexander M.	Pvt	K 11th SCVI			Pt. Lookout, MD	06/21/65	Rlsd. G.O. #109	HAG,CSR
Walker, Alexander S.	HSd	A 14th SCVI	Gettysburg, PA	07/05/63	Ft. McHenry, MD	07/07/63	Ft. Delaware, DE	CSR
					Ft. Delaware, DE	10/10/64	Hos 10/10-10/30/64	P47
					Ft. Delaware, DE	10/30/64	Pt. Lookout, MD	P43,P44,P144
					Pt. Lookout, MD	10/31/64	Venus Pt., GA Xchg	CSR
Walker, Andrew J.	Pvt	A 17th SCVI	Five Forks, VA	04/01/65	City Pt., VA	04/04/65	Pt. Lookout, MD	CSR,HHC
					Pt. Lookout, MD	06/22/65	Rlsd. G.O. #109	P121,CSR
Walker, B.C.	Pvt	B 7th SCVC	Augusta, GA	05/29/65	Augusta, GA	05/29/65	Paroled	CSR
Walker, Bryan T.	Pvt	F 19th SCVI	Augusta, GA	05/23/65	Augusta, GA	05/23/65	Paroled	CSR
Walker, C.W.	Pvt	D 6th SCResB	Augusta, GA	05/18/65	Augusta, GA	05/18/65	Paroled	CSR
Walker, Chesley B.	Pvt	K 15th SCVI	Halltown, VA	08/26/64	Harpers Ferry, WV	08/29/64	Camp Chase, OH	CSR,KEB,H15
					Camp Chase, OH	03/18/65	Pt. Lookout, MD	P22,P26
					Pt. Lookout, MD	03/27/65	Boulware's Wh. Xch	CSR
Walker, David L.	2Lt	B 7th SCVC	Albany, GA	05/16/65	Albany, GA	05/16/65	Paroled	CSR
Walker, Felix	Pvt	A Hol.Leg.	Stony Creek, VA	05/07/64	No U.S. records			CSR
Walker, Felix P.	Pvt	I 2nd SCVC	Augusta, GA	05/29/65	Augusta, GA	05/29/65	Paroled	CSR
Walker, Francis M.	Cpl	D 3rd SCVIBn	South Mtn., MD	09/14/62	Ft. Delaware, DE	10/02/62	Aikens Ldg., VA Xc	CSR,KEB
Walker, Francis M.	Cpl	D 3rd SCVIBn	Hanover Jctn., VA	05/23/64	Port Royal, VA	05/30/64	Pt. Lookout, MD	CSR
					Pt. Lookout, MD	10/29/64	Died,Ac. Diarrhea	P5,P113,P117,FPH
Walker, Fredrick A	Pvt	H 1st SCVIR	Charleston, SC	08/01/63	Louisville, KY	11/05/64	Knoxville, TN	CSR
					Knoxville, TN	11/14/63	Pass to Indiana	P8,P92,CSR
Walker, George	Pvt	F Ham.Leg.MI	Burkeville, VA	04/06/65	City Pt., VA	04/14/65	Pt. Lookout, MD	CSR
					Pt. Lookout, MD	06/22/65	Rlsd. G.O. #109	P115,P119,P121,CSR
					Washington, DC	06/23/65	Knoxville, TN	CSR
Walker, Henry	Pvt	A 1st SCVIR	Deserted/enemy	03/21/65	Charleston, SC		Released on oath	SA1,CSR
Walker, Henry	Pvt	F 1st SCVIBn			Hilton Head, SC	07/02/62	Died of wounds	P12
Walker, Henry A.	Pvt	F Ham.Leg.	Warrenton, VA	09/29/62	Warrenton, VA	09/29/62	Paroled	CSR
Walker, J.D.	Pvt	Ferguson's LA	Macon, GA	04/20/65	Macon, GA		No release data	CSR
Walker, J.M.	Pvt	C 3rd SCVIBn	South Mtn., MD	09/14/62	Ft. McHenry, MD	10/02/62	Fts. Monroe, VA	CSR
					Fts. Monroe, VA	10/03/62	Aikens Ldg., VA Xc	CSR
Walker, J.M.	Pvt	B 3rd SCVABn	Ft. Tyler, GA	04/16/65	2nd Bgd. 1st Div.	04/23/65	Macon, GA Armory p	CSR
Walker, Jacob C.	Cpl	C 2nd SCVIR	Deserted/enemy	03/03/65	Bermuda Hundred, VA	03/05/65	City Pt., VA P.M.	CSR
					City Pt., VA P.M.	03/07/65	Washington, DC P.M	CSR
					Washington, DC P.M.	03/08/65	Columbus, OH oath	CSR
Walker, James	Pvt	I 6th SCVI	Seven Pines, VA	05/31/62	Fts. Monroe, VA	07/01/62	Died of wounds	P12,CSR
Walker, James	Pvt	F Ham.Leg.MI	Burkeville, VA	04/06/65	Lincoln G.H., DC	06/27/65	Rlsd. G.O. #109	P110,CSR

SOUTH CAROLINA SOLDIERS, SAILORS AND **W** CITIZENS HELD IN U.S. PRISONS 1861-1865

NAME	RANK	REGIMENT	CAPTURED AT	WHEN	PRISON	MOVED	DISPOSITION	SOURCES
Walker, James D.	Pvt	E 24th SCVI	Chickamauga, GA	09/20/63	Nashville, TN	10/05/63	Louisville, KY	P38,CSR
					Louisville, KY	10/07/63	Camp Douglas, IL	P88,P89,CSR,P55,P58
					Camp Douglas, IL	12/11/64	Died, Smallpox	P5,P12,P53,FPH,P55
Walker, John E.	Pvt	K 11th SCVI	Weldon RR, VA	08/21/64	3rd Div 5A.C. Hos.	08/21/64	Died of wounds	P12,HAG,CSR
Walker, John H.	2Lt	E 16th SCVI	Egypt Stn., MS	12/28/64	Johnson's Isl., OH	05/13/65	Rlsd. G.O. #85	P82,CSR,16R
Walker, L.J.	Cpt	B 7th SCVC	Farmville, VA	04/09/65	U.S. 24th A.C. Fld.	04/10/65	U.S. G.H.	CSR
Walker, M.C.	Pvt	F 1st SCVA	Bentonville, NC	03/22/65	New Berne, NC	04/10/65	Hart's Island, NY	CSR
					Hart's Island, NY	06/16/65	Rlsd. G.O. #109	P79,CSR
Walker, Milton S.	Pvt	D 14th SCVI	Petersburg, VA	07/29/64	Pt. Lookout, MD	08/08/64	Elmira, NY	P117,P120,CSR
					Elmira, NY	07/11/65	Rlsd. G.O. #109	P65,P66,CSR
Walker, S.M.	Pvt	D 18th SCVI	Southside RR, VA	04/03/65	Hart's Island, NY	06/16/65	Rlsd. G.O. #109	P79
Walker, Samuel	Pvt	D 15th SCVI	Deserted/enemy		P.M. S. of Potomac	12/29/62	Old Capitol, DC	CSR
Walker, Samuel A.	Sgt	G 14th SCVI	Spotsylvania, VA	05/12/64	Belle Plain, VA	05/20/64	Ft. Delaware, DE	CSR
					Ft. Delaware, DE	06/08/65	Released	P41,P43
Walker, W.	Pvt	G 3rd SCVABn	High Pt., NC	05/01/65	High Pt., NC	05/01/65	Paroled	CSR
Walker, W.G.	Pvt	C 15th SCMil	Cheraw, SC	03/06/65	Pt. Lookout, MD	04/18/65	Died diarrhea	P6,P115,P118,P119,FPH
Walker, W.Y.	Pvt	C 15th SCVAB	Cheraw, SC	03/06/65	New Berne, NC	04/03/65	Pt. Lookout, MD	P165,P118,P119,FPH
					Pt. Lookout, MD	04/18/65	Died, Ch. Diarrhea	CSR
Walker, William	Pvt	8th SCVI	Deserted/enemy		Washington, DC P.M.	05/15/65	New York, NY oath	CSR
Walker, William F.	Pvt	K Hol.Leg.	Stony Creek, VA	05/07/64	Fts. Monroe, VA	05/13/64	Pt. Lookout, MD	CSR
					Pt. Lookout, MD	08/15/64	Elmira, NY	P113,P116,P120,CSR
					Elmira, NY	04/19/65	Died, Ch. Diarrhea	P6,P12,P65,P66,FPH
Walker, William F.	Pvt	A 2nd SCVIRi	Farmville, VA	04/11/65	Farmville, VA	04/21/65	Paroled	CSR
Walkup, J.M.	Pvt	I 1st SCVIR	Cheraw, SC	03/05/65	Cheraw, SC	03/15/65	Released on oath	SA1,CSR
Wall, Alexander C.	Pvt	H 14th SCVI	Gettysburg, PA	07/05/63	Ft. McHenry, MD	07/07/63	Ft. Delaware, DE	CSR
					Ft. Delaware, DE		To Rebel Barracks	P46
					Ft. Delaware, DE	06/10/65	Rlsd. G.O. #109	P40,P42,P44,P45
Wall, D.	Pvt	G 23rd SCVI	Richmond, VA	04/03/65	Newport News, VA	06/26/65	Rlsd. G.O. #109	P107
Wall, J.R.P.	Pvt	D 1st SCVC	Johns Island, SC	06/07/62	Hilton Head, SC	08/14/62	Ft. Columbus, NY	CSR
					Ft. Columbus, NY	08/23/62	Ft. Delaware, DE	CSR
					Ft. Delaware, DE	10/02/62	Aikens Ldg., VA Xc	CSR
Wall, James	Pvt	H 14th SCVI	Southside RR, VA	04/02/65	City Pt., VA	04/07/65	Hart's Island, NY	CSR,UD2
					Hart's Island, NY	06/16/65	Rlsd. G.O. #109	P79
Wall, Samuel J.	Pvt	F 11th SCVI	Swift Creek, VA	05/09/64	Fts. Monroe, VA	05/28/64	Died of wounds	P6,P12,HAG,ROH,CSR
Wall, W.D.	Cpl	F 4th SCVC	Hawe's Shop, VA	05/28/64	White House, VA	06/08/64	Pt. Lookout, MD	CSR
					Pt. Lookout, MD	09/06/64	Died	P6,P113,P119,FPH
Wallace, Alexander L.	Pvt	B 12th SCVI	Maryland		Ft. McHenry, MD	09/07/62	Aikens Ldg., VA Xc	CSR
Wallace, Alexander L.	Sgt	B 12th SCVI	Spotsylvania, VA	05/12/64	Belle Plain, VA	05/12/64	Ft. Delaware, DE	P47,CSR
					Ft. Delaware, DE	06/10/65	Rlsd. G.O.#109	P41,P43,P45,CSR
Wallace, Andrew Jackson	Pvt	Ch'fld LA	Richmond, VA Hos.	04/03/65	Richmond, VA Hos.	04/20/65	P.M. Richmond, VA	CSR
Wallace, Beaty	Pvt	D 17th SCVI	Deserted/enemy	02/26/65	9th A.C., A. of P.	02/26/65	City Pt., VA P.M.	CSR
					City Pt., VA P.M.	02/28/65	Washington, DC	CSR
					Washington, DC	03/01/65	Savannah, GA oath	CSR
					Savannah, GA P.M.	03/13/65	Released on oath	CSR
Wallace, Benjamin	Sgt	E 2nd SCVC	Beverly Ford, VA	06/09/63	Old Capitol, DC	06/25/63	City Pt., VA Xc	CSR
					Ft. McHenry, MD	06/25/63	City Pt., VA Xc	P110
Wallace, D.C.	Pvt	I 17th SCVI	Warrenton, VA	09/29/62	Warrenton, VA	09/29/62	Paroled	CSR
Wallace, D.C.	Pvt	I 17th SCVI	Deserted/enemy	11/16/64	P.M. 22nd AC AOP	11/17/64	City Pt., VA P.M.	CSR
					City Pt., VA P.M.	11/23/64	Washington, DC	CSR
					Washington, DC	11/25/64	Released on oath	CSR
Wallace, Enoch	Pvt	B 3rd SCVABn	Ft. Tyler, GA	04/16/65	2nd Bgd. 1st Div.	04/23/65	Macon, GA Armory p	CSR
Wallace, Franklin	Pvt	G 18th SCVI	Deserted/enemy	03/01/65	City Pt., VA P.M.	03/06/65	Oil City, PA oath	CSR

SOUTH CAROLINA SOLDIERS, SAILORS AND W CITIZENS HELD IN U.S. PRISONS 1861-1865

NAME	RANK	REGIMENT	CAPTURED AT	WHEN	PRISON	MOVED	DISPOSITION	SOURCES
Wallace, Hugh K.	Pvt	H 24th SCVI	Nashville, TN	12/16/64	Nashville, TN	12/21/64	Louisville, KY	HHC,CSR
					Louisville, KY	12/21/64	Camp Douglas, IL	P90,P95,CSR,EFW
					Camp Douglas, IL	01/22/65	Died, Pleurisy	P6,P12,P58,FPH,CSR
Wallace, J.A.	Pvt	F 17th SCVI	Petersburg, VA	03/25/65	City Pt., VA	03/28/65	Pt. Lookout, MD	CSR,YEB
					Pt. Lookout, MD	06/22/65	Rlsd. G.O. #109	P115,P118,P121,CSR
Wallace, James	Pvt	G P.S.S.	Knoxville, TN Hos.	01/15/64	Knoxville, TN G.H.	02/19/64	Died, Pneumonia	P1,P12,TSE,CSR
Wallace, James	Pvt	D 17th SCVI	Deserted/enemy	02/25/65	P.M. 9th A.C. AOP	02/25/65	City Pt., VA P.M.	CSR
					City Pt., VA P.M.	02/28/65	Washington, DC	CSR
					Washington, DC	03/01/65	Savannah, GA on oath	CSR
					Savannah, GA P.M.	03/13/65	Released	CSR
Wallace, James	Sgt	C 15th SCVAB	Smiths Ford, NC	03/16/65	New Berne, NC	04/03/65	Pt. Lookout, MD	CSR
Wallace, James	Pvt	H 7th SCVI	Deserted/enemy	03/28/65	Charleston, SC	04/01/65	Released on oath	CSR
					Pt. Lookout, MD	06/22/65	Rlsd. G.O. #109	P115,P118,CSR
Wallace, John	Pvt	B 3rd SCVABn	Ft. Tyler, GA	04/16/65	2nd Bgd. 1st Div.	04/23/65	Macon, GA Armory p	CSR
					Macon, GA Prison	04/23/65	Paroled	CSR
Wallace, John J.	Pvt	G 18th SCVI	Boonesboro, MD	09/14/62	Frederick, MD	10/13/62	Died of wounds	P12,FPH,CSR
Wallace, Julius L.	Pvt	Brooks LA	Harpers Farm, VA	04/06/65	City Pt., VA	04/14/65	Pt. Lookout, MD	CSR
					Pt. Lookout, MD	06/22/65	Rlsd. G.O. #109	CSR
Wallace, Morell W.	1Lt	B 37th VAVCB	Moorefield, VA	08/07/64	Wheeling, WV	08/11/64	Camp Chase, OH	CSR
					Camp Chase, OH	03/02/65	City Pt., VA	CSR
					City Pt. VA	03/10/65	James R., VA Xc	CSR
Wallace, Peter	Pvt	B 3rd SCVABn	Ft. Tyler, GA	04/16/65	2nd Bgd. 1st Div.	04/23/65	Macon, GA Armory p.	CSR
					Macon, GA Prison	04/23/65	Paroled	CSR
Wallace, R.D.	Pvt	I 17th SCVI	Kinston, NC	12/14/62	Kinston, NC	12/14/62	Paroled	CSR
Wallace, Samuel W.	Sgt	E 17th SCVI	Farmville, VA	04/06/65	City Pt., VA	04/14/65	Newport News, VA	CSR,YEB
					Newport News, VA	06/25/65	Rlsd. G.O. #109	P107,CSR
Wallace, Thomas A.	Pvt	4 10/19 SCVI	Missionary Ridge,TN	11/25/63	Nashville, TN	12/07/63	Louisville, KY	P39,RAS,CSR
					Louisville, KY	12/09/63	Rock Island, IL	P88,P89,CSR
					Rock Island, IL	10/14/64	Jd. US Army F.S.	P131,CSR
Wallace, Thomas N.	Pvt	B 16th SCVI	Franklin, TN	11/30/64	Nashville, TN	12/03/64	Louisville, KY	CSR
					Louisville, KY	12/04/64	Camp Douglas, IL	P90,P91,P94
Wallace, Thomas N.	Pvt	B 16th SCVI	Franklin, TN	11/30/64	Camp Douglas, IL	06/18/65	Rlsd. G.O. #109	P55,CSR
Wallace, William	Pvt	G 23rd SCVI	Deserted/enemy	03/04/65	City Pt., VA	03/06/65	Washington, DC	CSR
					Washington, DC	03/06/65	New York, NY oath	CSR
Wallace, William	Pvt	Ch'fld LA	Farmville, VA	04/11/65	Farmville, VA	04/21/65	Paroled	CSR
Wallace, William J.	Pvt	5 10/19 SCVI	Missionary Ridge,TN	11/25/63	Nashville, TN	12/07/63	Louisville, KY Xc	P39,CSR,RAS
					Louisville, KY	12/09/63	Rock Island, IL	P88,P89,CSR
					Rock Island, IL	10/31/64	Jd. US Army F.S.	P131,CSR
Wallace, Wilson	Pvt	I 17th SCVI	Petersburg, VA	07/30/64	City Pt., VA	08/05/64	Pt. Lookout, MD	CSR
					Pt. Lookout, MD	08/08/64	Elmira, NY	P113,P117,P120,CSR
					Elmira, NY	06/19/65	Rlsd. G.O. #109	P65,CSR
Wallen, M.	Pvt	F 1st SCVIR	Cheraw, SC	02/28/65	To Provost Marshal			CSR
Waller, James	Sgt	PalmettoLA			Pt. Lookout, MD	06/22/65	Rlsd. G.O. #109	P121
Waller, R.B.	Pvt	C 21st SCVI			Hampton, VA G.H.	06/06/64	Died of wounds	P6,P12
Waller, William J.	Pvt	E 26th SCVI	Amelia C.H., VA	04/04/65	City Pt., VA	04/13/65	Pt. Lookout, MD	CSR
					Pt. Lookout, MD	06/22/65	Rlsd. G.O. #109	P115,P119,P122,CSR
Walling, Joseph A.	Pvt	F 25th SCVI	Ft. Fisher, NC	01/15/65	New York, NY	01/30/65	Elmira, NY	CSR,HAG
					Elmira, NY	07/07/65	Rlsd. G.O. #109	P65,P66,CSR
Walls, E.B.	Pvt	B Hol.Leg.C	Deserted/enemy	05/04/63	Fts. Monroe, VA		No other data	CSR
Walls, John W.	Pvt	H 22nd SCVI	Deserted/enemy	02/13/65	P.M. City Pt., VA	02/16/65	Washington, DC	CSR
Walser, Richard	Pvt	F 1st SCVIR	Deserted/enemy	02/18/65	Charleston, SC		Released on oath	CSR

SOUTH CAROLINA SOLDIERS, SAILORS AND  CITIZENS HELD IN U.S. PRISONS 1861-1865

NAME	RANK	REGIMENT	CAPTURED AT	WHEN	PRISON	MOVED	DISPOSITION	SOURCES
Walsh, James	Pvt	H 27th SCVI	Weldon RR, VA	08/21/64	City Pt., VA	08/24/64	Pt. Lookout, MD	CSR,HAG
					Pt. Lookout, MD	01/17/65	Aikens Ldg., VA Xc	P113,P124,P125
Walsh, James B.	Pvt	H 23rd SCVI	Jackson, MS	07/14/63	Camp Morton, IN	03/19/64	Ft. Delaware, DE	P100,CSR,HMC
					Ft. Delaware, DE	09/08/64	Hos. 9/8-9/21/64	P47
					Ft. Delaware, DE	06/10/65	Released	P41,P42,P45,CSR
Walsh, Richard	Pvt	I 17th SCVI	Appomattox C.H., VA	04/09/65	Old Capitol, DC	06/12/65	Rlsd. G.O.#109	P110
Walters, A.T.	Sgt	E 22nd SCVI	Deep Bottom, VA	08/16/64	Pt. Lookout, MD	02/13/65	Aikens Ldg., VA Xc	P121,P124,LAN,CSR
Walters, Evan S.	Pvt	Ch'fld LA	Charlotte, NC	05/30/65	Charlotte, NC	05/30/65	Paroled	CSR
Walters, F. Jasper	Pvt	H 21st SCVI	Morris Island, SC	07/10/63	Morris Island, SC	07/13/63	Hilton Head, SC	CSR
					Hilton Head, SC G.H.	07/23/63	Morris Island, SC Xc	P2,CSR
Walters, Isaac P.	Pvt	K 25th SCVI	Town Creek, NC	02/20/65	Ft. Anderson, NC	02/28/65	Pt. Lookout, MD	CSR,HAG,CTA
					Pt. Lookout, MD	06/14/65	Rlsd. G.O. #109	P115,P118,P121,CSR
Walters, John Amanuel	Sgt	C 24th SCVI	Chickamauga, GA	09/20/63	Nashville, TN	09/30/63	Louisville, KY	P38,CSR,EFW
					Louisville, KY	10/02/63	Camp Douglas, IL	P88,P89,CSR
					Camp Douglas, IL	06/16/65	Rlsd. G.O. #109	P53,CSR,P57
Walters, Landon	Sgt	C 18th SCVI	Five Forks, VA	04/01/65	Pt. Lookout, MD	06/22/65	Rlsd. G.O. #109	P115,P121,CSR
Walters, Phillip	Pvt	K 1st SCVIR	Charlotte, NC	05/30/65	Charlotte, NC	05/30/65	Paroled	SA1,
Walters, R.B.	Pvt	C 25th SCVI	Drurys Bluff, VA	05/14/64	Fts. Monroe, VA	06/02/64	Died of wounds	CSR,CTA
Walters, Stephen S.	Pvt	H Ham.Leg.MI	Burkeville, VA	04/06/65	City Pt., VA	04/14/65	Pt. Lookout, MD	CSR
					Pt. Lookout, MD	06/21/65	Rlsd. G.O. #109	P115,P119,CSR
Walters, William E.	Chp	A 2nd SCVIRi	Benton, TN	11/03/63	Nashville, TN	12/10/63	Louisville, KY	P39,CSR
					Louisville, KY	12/13/63	Johnson's Isl., OH	P88,P89,P93,CSR
					Johnson's Isl., OH	01/15/64	Fts. Monroe, VA Xc	P82,CSR
					Fts. Monroe, VA	01/27/64	City Pt., VA Xc	CSR
Walther, Richard	Pvt	A 11th SCVI	Deserted/enemy	12/21/64	Savannah, GA	12/21/64	Hilton Head, SC	CSR
					Hilton Head, SC	04/04/65	Released on oath	CSR
Walton, John Frank	Pvt	H 7th SCVIBn	Drury's Bluff, VA	05/16/64	Bermuda Hundred, VA	05/17/64	Fts. Monroe, VA	CSR,HAG
					Fts. Monroe, VA	05/18/64	Pt. Lookout, MD	CSR
					Pt. Lookout, MD	09/18/64	Aikens Ldg., VA Xc	P113,P117,CSR
					Richmond, VA Hos.	09/26/64	Furloughed 30 days	CSR
Walton, S.M.	Pvt	B Ham.Leg.MI	Augusta, GA	05/20/65	Augusta, GA	05/20/65	Paroled	CSR
Walton, William T.	Pvt	B Ham.Leg.MI	Farmville, VA	04/11/65	Farmville, VA	04/11/65	Paroled	CSR
Wambach, John	Pvt	G 3rd SCVC	St. Catherine, SC	11/18/64	Hilton Head, SC	01/17/65	New York, NY oath	CSR
Wannamaker, Irvin W.	Sgt	F 25th SCVI	Weldon RR, VA	08/21/64	Lincoln G.H., DC	08/26/64	Died, leg amp. Xc	P6,P12,HAG,CSR
Wannamaker, Jacob G.	1Lt	15th SCMil	Chesterfield, SC	02/28/65	Pt. Lookout, MD	04/03/65	Washington, DC	P115,P118,P120
					Old Capitol, DC	04/09/65	Johnson's Isl., OH	P110
					Johnson's Isl., OH	06/20/65	Rlsd. G.O. #109	P81,P82
Wannamaker, William S.	Cit	15th SCMil	Lynch's Creek, SC	02/23/65	Hart's Island, NY	05/11/65	Died, Ch. Diarrhea	P6,P12
Ward, Andrew Jackson	Pvt	G 27th SCVI	Petersburg, VA	06/24/64	Bermuda Hundred, VA	06/25/64	Fts. Monroe, VA	CSR,HAG
					Fts. Monroe, VA	06/26/64	Pt. Lookout, MD	CSR
					Pt. Lookout, MD	08/16/64	Elmira, NY	P113,P117,P120
					Elmira, NY	10/02/64	Died, Diarrhea	P5,P12,P65,P66,FPH
Ward, Charles W.	Pvt	H 6th SCVI	Ft. Harrison, VA	09/30/64	Pt. O Rocks, VA FH	10/09/64	Died of wounds	P12,CSR
Ward, Daniel	Sgt	H 27th SCVI	Weldon RR, VA	08/21/64	City Pt., VA	08/24/64	Pt. Lookout, MD	CSR,HAG
					Pt. Lookout, MD	10/14/64	Joined US Army	P113,P117,P122
Ward, George W.	Sgt	L 7th SCVI	Cedar Creek, VA	10/19/64	Harpers Ferry, WV	10/28/64	Pt. Lookout, MD	CSR,KEB
					Pt. Lookout, MD	06/22/65	Rlsd. G.O. #109	P115,P121,CSR
Ward, Henry	Pvt	A 3rd SCVABn	High Pt., NC	05/02/65	High Pt., NC	05/02/65	Paroled	CSR
Ward, J.E.	Cpl	C 3rd SCVABn	Blakely, AL	04/09/65	Ship Island, MS	05/01/65	Vicksburg, MS	P136,CSR
					Vicksburg, MS	05/04/65	Exchanged	CSR
Ward, J.E.	Cpl	C 3rd SCVABn	Augusta, GA	05/20/65	Augusta, GA	05/20/65	Paroled	CSR

SOUTH CAROLINA SOLDIERS, SAILORS AND W CITIZENS HELD IN U.S. PRISONS 1861-1865

NAME	RANK	REGIMENT	CAPTURED AT	WHEN	PRISON	MOVED	DISPOSITION	SOURCES
Ward, James Decatur	Pvt	G 1st SCVA	Fayetteville, NC	03/10/65	New Berne, NC	03/30/65	Pt. Lookout, MD	CSR
					Pt. Lookout, MD	06/21/65	Rlsd. G.O. #109	P118,CSR
Ward, James L.	Pvt	A 10th SCVI	Citronelle, MS	05/04/65	Jackson, MS	05/19/65	Paroled	CSR,HCL
Ward, John A.	Pvt	I 23rd SCVI	Petersburg, VA	04/01/65	City Pt., VA	04/05/65	Pt. Lookout, MD	CSR
					Pt. Lookout, MD	06/22/65	Rlsd. G.O. #109	P115,P118,P122,CSR
Ward, John H.	Pvt	H 5th SCVI	Williamsport, MD	09/24/62	Ft. Delaware, DE	10/02/62	Aikens Ldg., VA Xc	SA3,CSR
Ward, John H.	Pvt	D 6th SCVI	Burkesville, VA	04/14/65	Burkesville, VA	04/14/65	Paroled	CSR
Ward, Joseph	Pvt	E 2nd SCVC	Goldsboro, NC	03/21/65	New Berne, NC	04/03/65	Pt. Lookout, MD	CSR
					Pt. Lookout, MD		No release data	P115,P118
Ward, L.T.	Pvt	H 22nd SCVI	Kinston, NC	12/15/62	Kinston, NC	12/15/62	Paroled POW	CSR
Ward, Napoleon B.	Pvt	I 5th SCVI	Campbell's Stn., TN	11/16/63	Nashville, TN	01/24/64	Louisville, KY	P39,SA3,CSR
					Louisville, KY	01/27/64	Rock Island, IL	P88,P93,CSR
					Rock Island, IL	03/02/65	Pt. Lookout, MD Xc	P131,CSR
Ward, Phillip	Pvt	I 23rd SCVI	Petersburg, VA	04/02/65	City Pt., VA	04/05/65	Pt. Lookout, MD	CSR,HCL
					Pt. Lookout, MD	06/22/65	Rlsd. G.O. #109	P118,P122,CSR
Ward, R.H.	Sgt	E 8th SCVI	Winchester, VA	09/13/64	Harpers Ferry, WV	09/19/64	Camp Chase, OH	P23,CSR
					Camp Chase, OH	06/11/65	Rlsd. G.O. #109	P23,KEB,CSR
Ward, Rowan C.	Pvt	C 3rd SC Eng	Marion, AL	01/01/65	Louisville, KY	01/16/65	Camp Chase, OH	P95
Ward, William	Pvt	F 22nd SCVI	Deserted/enemy	02/20/65	Charleston, SC	02/20/65	Hilton Head, SC	CSR
					Hilton Head, SC	03/22/65	New York, NY	CSR
Ward, William	Pvt	C 3rd SCVABn	Blakely, AL	04/09/65	Ship Island, MS	05/01/65	Vicksburg, MS	P136,CSR
					Vicksburg, MS	05/04/65	Exhanged	CSR
Ward, William	Pvt	C 3rd SCVABn	Augusta, GA	05/20/65	Augusta, GA	05/20/65	Paroled	CSR
Warden, J.C.	Pvt	G 23rd SCVI	Deserted/enemy	11/16/64	City Pt. VA	11/23/64	Washington, DC	CSR
					Washington DC	11/25/64	Chicago, IL on oath	CSR
Wardlaw, E.M.	Pvt	H 7th SCVI	Sharpsburg, MD	09/19/62	Frederick, MD	10/27/62	Ft. McHenry, MD	CSR
					Ft. McHenry, MD	10/28/62	Fts. Monroe, VA	CSR
					Fts. Monroe, VA	10/30/62	Aikens Ldg., VA Xc	CSR
Wardlaw, James L.	Pvt	L 2nd SCVIRi	Warrenton, VA	09/29/62	Warrenton, VA	09/29/62	Paroled	CSR
Ware, Henry L.	Pvt	F 7th SCVIBn	Cheraw, SC	03/07/65	New Berne, NC	04/10/65	Hart's Island, NY	CSR,HIC,HAG
					Hart's Island, NY	06/17/65	Rlsd. G.O. #109	P79,CSR
Ware, Samuel M.	Pvt	H 12th SCVI	N. Anna River, VA	05/22/64	Pt. Lookout, MD	09/18/64	Aikens Ldg., VA Xc	P113,P117,YEB,CSR
Ware, Samuel M.	Pvt	H 12th SCVI	Charlotte, NC	05/14/65	Charlotte, NC	05/14/65	Paroled	CSR
Waring, John B.	Pvt	A 27th SCVI	Petersburg, VA	06/24/64	Bermuda Hundred, VA	06/25/64	Fts. Monroe, VA	CSR,HAG
					Fts. Monroe, VA	06/26/64	Pt. Lookout, MD	CSR
					Pt. Lookout, MD	09/18/64	Aikens Ldg., VA Xc	P113,P117,P121,CSR
Waring, T.M.	Pvt	A 18th SCVAB	Cheraw, SC	03/05/65	Cheraw, SC	03/05/65	Paroled	CSR
Warley, F.F.	Maj	2nd SCVA	Charleston Hrbr.	09/04/63	Steamer *Cosmopolit*	09/18/63	Hilton Head, SC	CSR
					Hilton Head, SC	09/18/63	Beaufort, SC	CSR
					Hilton Head, SC	12/04/64	Ft. Columbus, NY	CSR
					Ft.Columbus, NY	02/11/64	Ft. McHenry, MD	CSR
					Ft. McHenry, MD	06/15/64	Ft. Delaware DE	CSR,P144
					Ft. Delaware, DE	06/25/64	Hilton Head, SC	P43,P44,CSR
					Hilton Head, SC	08/03/64	Exchanged	CSR
Warner, H.W.	Pvt	G 7th SCVC	Cypress Bridge, VA	05/07/64	Elmira, NY	06/23/65	Rlsd. G.O. #109	P65,P66
Warner, Henry	Pvt	I 11th SCVI	Drury's Bluff, VA	05/16/64	Monroe, VA	05/18/64	Pt. Lookout, MD	CSR,HAG
					Pt. Lookout, MD	07/25/64	Elmira, NY	P113,P117,P120,CSR
					Elmira, NY	05/29/65	Released on oath	P65,P66,CSR
Warnick, J.F.	Pvt	C 15th SCVAB	Augusta, GA	05/20/65	Augusta, GA	05/20/65	Took oath, paroled	CSR
Warren, B.A.	Pvt	B 5th SCResB	Greensboro, NC Hos.	05/02/65	Greensboro, NC Hos.	05/02/65	Paroled	CSR
Warren, Benjamin	Cit	Horry Ds., SC		04/21/64	Unknown Prison	03/13/65	Ft. Warren, MS	P145
					Ft. Warren, MA	06/20/65	Rlsd. on oath	P2

W

SOUTH CAROLINA SOLDIERS, SAILORS AND CITIZENS HELD IN U.S. PRISONS 1861-1865

NAME	RANK	REGIMENT	CAPTURED AT	WHEN	PRISON	MOVED	DISPOSITION	SOURCES
Warren, Franklin M.	Pvt	B Ham.Leg.MI	Farmville, VA	04/11/65	Farmville, VA	04/11/65	Paroled	CSR
Warren, G.S.	Pvt	I 11th SCVI	Petersburg, VA	06/24/64	Bermuda Hundred, VA	06/25/64	Fts. Monroe, VA	CSR
					Fts. Monroe, VA	06/26/64	Pt. Lookout, MD	CSR
					Pt. Lookout, MD	08/16/64	Elmira, NY	P113,P117,P120,CSR
					Elmira, NY	10/11/64	Baltimore, MD USGH	CSR
					W. Bldg. Balt. MD	12/11/64	Died, Ch. Diarrhea	P3,P5,P12,FPH
Warren, Joseph H.	Pvt	I 11th SCVI	Town Creek, NC	02/20/65	Ft. Anderson, NC	02/28/64	Pt. Lookout, MD	CSR,HAG
					Pt. Lookout, MD	06/22/65	Rlsd. G.O. #109	P115,P118,P121,CSR
Warren, Robert S.	Pvt	B 6th SCVI	Richmond, VA	04/03/65	Richmond, VA P.M.	04/23/65	Newport News, VA	CSR
					Newport News, VA	06/26/65	Rlsd. G.O. #109	P107,CSR
Warren, Thomas R.	Pvt	D 11th SCVI	Town Creek, NC	02/20/65	Ft. Anderson, NC	02/28/64	Pt. Lookout, MD	CSR,HAG
					Pt. Lookout, MD	06/21/65	Rlsd. G.O. #109	P115,P118,P122,CSR
Washburn, J.	Pvt	D 12th SCVI	Maryland		Fts. Monroe, VA	09/07/62	Aikens Ldg., VA Xc	CSR
Wate, Thomas A.	Pvt	G 1st SCVIG	Petersburg, VA	04/03/65	City Pt., VA	04/13/65	Pt. Lookout, MD	CSR,SA1
					Pt. Lookout, MD	06/22/65	Rlsd. G.O. #109	P115,P118,P121,CSR
Waters, Abner	Pvt	I 13th SCVI	Petersburg, VA	04/02/65	City Pt., VA	04/04/65	Pt. Lookout, MD	CSR,HOS
					Pt. Lookout, MD	06/21/65	Rlsd. G.O. #109	P115,P118,P121,CSR
Waters, Armsted J.	Pvt	I 14th SCVI	Falling Waters, MD	07/14/63	Baltimore, MD	08/16/63	Pt. Lookout, MD	CSR
					Pt. Lookout, MD	02/02/64	Joined U.S. Army	P113,P116,P125
Waters, David P.	Pvt	A 17th SCVI	Five Forks, VA	04/01/65	City Pt., VA	04/04/65	Pt. Lookout, MD	HHC,CSR
					Pt. Lookout, MD	06/22/65	Rlsd. G.O. #109	P115,P118,P121,CSR
Waters, Landon C.	Sgt	E 18th SCVI	Five Forks, VA	04/01/65	City Pt., VA	04/06/65	Pt. Lookout, MD	CSR,HOS
					Pt. Lookout, MD	06/22/65	Rlsd. G.O. #109	P118,CSR
Waters, Moses	Pvt	A 1st SCVIR	Morris Island, SC	09/07/63	Hilton Head, SC	10/06/63	Ft. Columbus, NY	SA1,CSR
					Pt. Lookout, MD	04/27/64	City Pt., VA Xc	P113,P116,P123,CSR
Waters, Moses	Pvt	A 1st SCVIR	Cheraw, SC	03/02/65	New Berne, NC	04/03/65	Pt. Lookout, MD	CSR
					Pt. Lookout, MD	06/21/65	Rlsd. G.O. #109	P115,P118,P122,CSR
Waters, Nathan	Pvt	H 1st SCVA	Marlboro, SC	03/06/65	New Berne, NC	04/10/63	Hart's Island, NY	CSR
					Hart's Island, NY	06/17/65	Rlsd. G.O. #109	P79,CSR
Waters, William	Sgt	I 13th SCVI	Hatchers Run, VA	03/31/65	City Pt., VA	04/02/65	Pt. Lookout, MD	CSR,HOS
					Pt. Lookout, MD	06/22/65	Rlsd. G.O. #109	P115,P118,P121,CSR
Waters, William L.	Pvt	F 14th SCVI	Wilderness, VA	05/06/64	Belle Plain, VA	05/21/64	Ft. Delaware, DE	CSR
					Ft. Delaware, DE	08/03/64	Hos. 8/3-8/5/64	P47
					Ft. Delaware, DE	12/19/64	Hos. 12/19-12/23/64	P47
					Ft. Delaware, DE	06/10/65	Rlsd. G.O.#109	P41,P43,P45
Watford, Joret N.	Pvt.	G 26th SCVI	Five Forks, VA	04/01/65	City Pt., VA	04/05/65	Pt. Lookout, MD	CSR
					Pt. Lookout, MD	06/22/65	Rlsd. G.O. #109	P115,P118,P121,CSR
Waties, J.R.	Cpl	A 3rd SCVABn	High Pt., NC	05/02/65	High Pt., NC	05/02/65	Paroled	CSR
Waties, Thomas	2Lt	B 3rd SCVABn	Franklin, TN	11/30/64	Nashville, TN	12/18/64	Louisville, KY	CSR
					Louisville, KY	12/20/64	Johnson's Isl., OH	CSR
					Johnson's Isl., OH	06/17/65	Rlsd. G.O. #109	CSR
Watkins, Albert	Pvt	Brooks LA	Harpers Farm, VA	04/06/65	City Pt., VA	04/14/65	Pt. Lookout, MD	CSR
					Pt. Lookout, MD	06/22/65	Rlsd. G.O. #109	CSR
Watkins, David O.	Pvt	G 22nd SCVI	Petersburg, VA	04/01/65	City Pt., VA	04/04/65	Pt. Lookout, MD	CSR
					Pt. Lookout, MD	06/21/65	Rlsd. G.O. #109	P115,P118,P122
Watkins, E.H.	Pvt	B 37th VAVCB	Middletown, VA	07/10/64	Frederick, MD Hos.	07/25/64	Baltimore MD Hos.	CSR
					Baltimore, MD Hos.	10/26/64	Pt. Lookout, MD	CSR
					Pt. Lookout, MD	10/30/64	Venus Pt. for Xc	CSR
Watkins, Ephraim	Pvt	B Ham.Leg.MI	Newton, NC	04/19/65	Newton, NC	04/19/65	Paroled	CSR
Watkins, Thomas C.	LtC	22nd SCVI	South Mtn., MD	09/14/62	Frederick, MD	09/25/62	Died of wounds	P12,LC

W

SOUTH CAROLINA SOLDIERS, SAILORS AND CITIZENS HELD IN U.S. PRISONS 1861-1865

NAME	RANK	REGIMENT	CAPTURED AT	WHEN	PRISON	MOVED	DISPOSITION	SOURCES
Watkins, William E.	Pvt	8 10/19 SCVI	Missionary Ridge, TN	11/25/63	Nashville, TN	12/25/63	Louisville, KY	P39,CSR
					Louisville, KY	12/27/63	Rock Island, IL	P88,P89,P93,CSR
					Rock Island, IL	11/11/64	Died, Pneumonia	P5,P12,P132,FPH
Watkins, William T.	Pvt	G 12th SCVI	Sharpsburg, MD	09/17/62	Ft. McHenry, MD	10/13/62	Fts. Monroe, VA Xc	CSR
					Richmond, VA Hos.	11/04/62	Furloughed 40 days	CSR
Watson, A.O.	3Lt	F Hol.Leg.	Jarratts Stn., VA	05/08/64	Fts. Monroe, VA	05/15/64	Pt. Lookout, MD	CSR
					Pt. Lookout, MD	06/23/64	Ft. Delaware, DE	P117,P120
					Ft. Delaware, DE	06/16/65	Rlsd. G.O. #109	P43,P44,P45,P46
Watson, Allen M.	Pvt	K 19th SCVI	Atlanta, GA	07/22/64	Nashville, TN	07/29/64	Louisville, KY	CSR
					Louisville, KY	07/30/64	Camp Chase, OH	P90,P91,P94,CSR
					Camp Chase, OH	09/18/64	Died, Variola	P5,P12,P22,FPH,CSR
Watson, Charles	Pvt	Ferguson's LA	Salisbury, NC	04/12/65	Nashville, TN	04/29/65	Louisville, KY	P39,CSR
					Louisville, KY	05/02/65	Camp Chase, OH	P92
					Camp Chase, OH	06/13/65	Rlsd. G.O. #109	CSR
Watson, Charles H.	Pvt	A 4th SCVC	Stony Creek, VA	12/01/64	City Pt., VA	12/05/64	Pt. Lookout, MD	CSR
					Pt. Lookout, MD	06/22/65	Rlsd. G.O. #109	P115,P118,P121,CSR
Watson, David	Pvt	D 21st SCVI	Morris Island, SC	07/10/63	Morris Island, SC	07/13/63	Hilton Head, SC	CSR,HAG
					Hilton Head G.H.	07/24/63	Morris Island, SC Xc	P2,HAG,CSR
Watson, Edward W.	Pvt	G 14th SCVI	Petersburg, VA	04/03/65	City Pt., VA	04/07/65	Hart's Island, NY	CSR
					Hart's Island, NY	06/16/65	Rlsd. G.O. #109	P79,CSR
Watson, Francis M.	Pvt	D 16th SCVI	Ringgold, GA	11/25/63	Nashville, TN	12/05/63	Louisville, KY	P39,16R,CSR
					Louisville, KY	12/06/63	Rock Island, IL	P88,P89,CSR
					Rock Island, IL	03/17/64	Died, Consumption	P5,P12,P132,FPH
Watson, Francis Marion	Pvt	F Hol.Leg.	Five Forks, VA	04/01/65	City Pt., VA	04/05/65	Pt. Lookout, MD	CSR
					Pt. Lookout, MD	06/05/65	Released	P115,P118,CSR
Watson, H.B.	Pvt	B 5th SCVC	Augusta, GA	05/31/65	Augusta, GA	05/31/65	Paroled	CSR
Watson, J.M.	Pvt	D 18th SCVI	Farmville, VA	04/06/65	City Pt., VA	04/14/65	Newport News, VA	CSR
					Newport News, VA	06/26/65	Rlsd. G.O. #109	P107,CSR
Watson, James A.	1Lt	A 12th SCVI	Saylors Creek, VA	04/03/65	Old Capitol, DC	04/21/65	Johnson's Isl., OH	CSR,YEB
					Johnson's Isl., OH	06/20/65	Rlsd. G.O. #109	P81,P82,P83,CSR
Watson, James E.	Pvt	C 3rd SCVIBn	South Mtn., MD	09/14/62	Aikens Ldg., VA	10/06/62	Exchanged	CSR
Watson, James J.	Pvt	H P.S.S.	Sutherland Stn., VA	04/03/65	Pt. Lookout, MD	06/21/65	Rlsd. G.O. #109	P115,P119,TSE,CSR
Watson, James T.	Pvt	G 20th SCVI	Cedar Creek, VA	10/19/64	Harpers Ferry, WV	10/24/64	Pt. Lookout, MD	CSR,KEB
					Pt. Lookout, MD	05/14/65	Rlsd. G.O. #85	P115,P117,P122,CSR
Watson, Levon A.	Pvt	D 1st SCVIH	Deserted/enemy	03/01/65	Bermuda Hundred, VA	03/03/65	City Pt., VA P.M.	CSR,SA1
					City Pt., VA P.M.	03/05/65	Washington, DC P.M.	CSR
					Washington, DC P.M.	03/07/65	Phila., PA on oath	CSR
Watson, M.	Pvt	D 8th SCVI	Winchester, VA	09/13/64	Harpers Ferry, WV	09/19/64	Camp Chase, OH	CSR
					Camp Chase, OH	06/10/65	Rlsd. G.O. #109	CSR
Watson, Marion P.	Pvt	A 13th SCVI	Hatchers Run, VA	04/03/65	City Pt., VA	04/03/65	Hart's Island, NY	CSR
					Hart's Island, NY	06/16/65	Rlsd. G.O. #109	P79,CSR
Watson, Michael J.	Pvt	B 14th SCVI	Sutherland Stn., VA	04/03/65	City Pt., VA	04/13/65	Pt. Lookout, MD	CSR,HOE
					Pt. Lookout, MD	06/22/65	Rlsd. G.O. #109	P115,P119,P121
Watson, S.M.	Pvt	D 18th SCVI	Southside RR, VA	04/02/65	City Pt., VA	04/07/65	Hart's Island, NY	CSR
					Hart's Island, NY	06/16/65	Rlsd. G.O. #109	P79,CSR
Watson, Solomon	Pvt	B 26th SCVI	Southside RR, VA	04/01/65	City Pt., VA	04/05/65	Pt. Lookout, MD	CSR
					Pt. Lookout, MD	06/22/65	Rlsd. G.O. #109	P115,P118,P121,CSR
Watson, Stanmore	Pvt	B Ham.Leg.MI	Newton, NC	04/19/65	Newton, NC	04/19/65	Paroled	CSR
Watson, Thomas A.	1Sg	H 19th SCVI	Murfreesboro, TN	12/31/62	Murfreesboro, TN	01/05/63	Nashville, TN	CSR
					Nashville, TN	04/21/63	Louisville, KY	CSR
Watson, Thomas A.	1Sg	H 19th SCVI	Murfreesboro, TN	01/05/63	Louisville, KY	04/27/63	City Pt., VA Xc	P88,P89,P93,CSR
Watson, Thomas A.	1Sg	H 19th SCVI	Murfreesboro, TN	12/31/62	Ft. McHenry, MD	04/30/63	Paroled for Xc	CSR

SOUTH CAROLINA SOLDIERS, SAILORS AND **W** CITIZENS HELD IN U.S. PRISONS 1861-1865

NAME	RANK	REGIMENT	CAPTURED AT	WHEN	PRISON	MOVED	DISPOSITION	SOURCES
Watson, Thomas B.	Pvt	K 16th SCVI	Hartwell, GA	05/23/65	Hartwell, GA	05/23/65	Paroled on oath	CSR
Watson, W.W.	Pvt	D 15th SCVI	South Mtn., MD	09/14/63	Ft. Delaware, DE	10/02/62	Aikens Ldg., VA Xc	CSR
Watson, William	Pvt	F 5th SCVI	Shell Mound, TN		Bridgeport, AL G.H.	11/15/63	Murfreesboro, TN	P2
					Nashville, TN	01/09/64	Died of wounds	P6,SA3,YEB,CSR,P12
Watson, William	Pvt	B Ham.Leg.MI	Augusta, GA	05/24/65	Augusta, GA	05/24/65	Paroled	CSR
Watson, William H.	Pvt	F Ham.Leg.	Burkeville, VA	04/06/65	City Pt., VA	04/14/65	Pt. Lookout, MD	CSR
					Pt. Lookout, MD	06/21/65	Rlsd. G.O. #109	P115,P119,CSR
Watt, Andrew J.	Pvt	F 24th SCVI	Jackson, MS	05/16/63	Jackson, MS	05/16/63	Paroled	CSR,EFW
Watt, B.F.	Sgt	G 3rd SCVIBn	South Mtn., MD	09/14/62	Ft. Delaware, DE	10/02/62	Aikens Ldg., VA Xc	CSR
Watt, Jennings G.	Pvt	F 24th SCVI	Jackson, MS	05/14/63	Jackson, MS	05/14/63	Paroled on oath	EFW,CSR
Watt, Jennings G.	Pvt	F 24th SCVI	Nashville, TN	12/16/64	Nashville, TN	12/31/64	Louisville, KY	CSR
					Louisville, KY	01/05/65	Camp Chase, OH	P92,P95,CSR
					Camp Chase, OH	06/12/65	Rlsd. G.O. #109	P23,CSR
Watt, William B.	Pvt	C Orr's Ri.	Falling Waters, MD	07/14/63	Frederick, MD USGH	08/08/63	Died of wounds	P1,P6,P12,CDC,FPH
Watt, William H.	Pvt	F 2nd SCVIRi	Burkeville, VA	04/14/65	Burkeville, VA	04/17/65	Paroled	CSR
Watters, J.W.	Pvt	F 19th SCVI	Thomasville, NC	05/01/65	Thomasville, NC	05/01/65	Paroled	CSR
Watts, James	Pvt	K 26th SCVI	Petersburg, VA	04/03/65	City Pt., VA	04/11/65	Harts Island, NY	CSR
					Hart's Island, NY	06/17/65	Rlsd. G.O. #109	P79,CSR
Watts, Joel J.	Pvt	B 8th SCVI	Charlotte, NC	05/03/65	Charlotte, NC	05/03/65	Paroled	CSR,KEB
Watts, Lewis W.	Pvt	C 6th SCVC	Darbytown Rd., VA	10/07/64	Bermuda Hundred, VA	10/07/64	City Pt., VA	CSR
					City Pt. VA oath	10/24/64	Orange County, FL	CSR
Watts, Lewis W.	Pvt	C 6th SCVC	Petersburg, VA	10/27/64	Pt. Lookout, MD	05/13/65	Rlsd. G.O. #85	P115,CSR
Watts, Thomas M.	Pvt	A 15th SCVAB	Fayetteville, NC	03/10/65	New Berne, NC	03/30/65	Pt. Lookout MD	CSR
					Pt. Lookout, MD	06/22/65	Rlsd. G.O. #109	P115,P118,CSR
Watts, W.D.	Pvt	Brooks LA	Gettysburg, PA	07/05/63	David's Island, NY	09/12/63	City Pt., VA Xc	P1,CSR
Watts, W.R.	Pvt	C 6th SCVI	Deserted/enemy	02/28/65	Bermuda Hundred, VA	03/01/65	City Pt., VA P.M.	CSR
					City Pt., VA P.M.	03/03/65	Washington, DC	CSR
					Washington, DC	03/06/65	Troy, PA on oath	CSR
Waugh, B.A.	Pvt	D 4th SCVI	Salisbury, NC	05/29/65	Salisbury, NC	05/29/65	Paroled	CSR
Way, A.H.	Sgt	B 20th SCVI	Deep Bottom, VA	07/27/64	City Pt., VA	07/29/64	Died, of wounds	P12,KEB,CSR
Way, David A.	Cpl	F 25th SCVI	Weldon RR, VA	08/21/64	Alexandria, VA G.H.	10/13/64	Lincoln G.H., DC	P1,HAG
					Old Capitol, DC	12/16/64	Elmira, NY	CSR
					Elmira, NY	02/20/65	James R., VA Xc	P65,P66,CSR
Way, George W.	Pvt	I 11th SCVI	Petersburg, VA	06/24/64	Bermuda Hundred, VA	06/25/64	Fts. Monroe, VA	CSR,HAG
					Fts. Monroe, VA	06/26/64	Pt. Lookout, MD	CSR
					Pt. Lookout, MD	08/16/64	Elmira, NY	P113,P117,P120,CSR
					Elmira, NY	10/11/64	Tfd. for exchange	P65
					Pt. Lookout, MD	10/29/64	Exchanged	P115,CSR
Way, W.B.	Pvt	F 25th SCVI	Ft. Fisher, NC	01/15/65	New York, NY	01/30/65	Elmira, NY	CSR,HAG
					Elmira, NY	07/26/65	Rlsd. G.O. #109	P65,P66,CSR
Wayne, Francis Asbury Jr	Pvt	L 1st SCVIG	Southside RR, VA	04/02/65	City Pt., VA	04/07/65	Hart's Island, NY	CSR,SA1
					Hart's Island, SC	05/11/65	Died dbl pneumonia	P6,P12,P79,FPH,SA1,CSR
Wayne, John	Pvt	K 8th SCVI	Harpers Ferry, MD	07/13/63	Ft. McHenry, MD		Ft Delaware, DE	P40,P42,P44,CSR
Wear, George	Cpl	A Ham.Leg.C	White House, VA	07/01/63	Fts. Monroe, VA	07/06/63	Exchanged	CSR
Wear, George	Cpl	A Ham.Leg.MI	Ashland, VA	05/03/65	Ashland, VA	05/03/65	Paroled	CSR
Weatherford, H.	Pvt	H 1st SCVIG	Warrenton, VA	09/29/62	Warrenton, VA	09/29/62	Paroled	SA1,CSR
Weatherford, Henry H.	Pvt	F 13th SCVI	Southside RR, VA	04/04/65	City Pt., VA	04/07/65	Hart's Island, NY	CSR
					Hart's Island, NY	06/16/65	Rlsd. G.O. #109	P79,CSR
Weatherford, James	Pvt	I Hol.Leg.	Boonesboro, MD	09/14/62	Ft. Delaware, DE	10/02/62	Aikens Ldg., VA Xc	CSR,HOS
Weatherford, Lemuel J.	Pvt	C 11th SCVI	Town Creek, NC	02/20/65	Ft. Anderson, NC	02/28/65	Pt. Lookout, MD	CSR,HAG
					Pt. Lookout, MD	06/17/65	Died, Lung Inflam.	P6,P12,P115,FPH

W

SOUTH CAROLINA SOLDIERS, SAILORS AND CITIZENS HELD IN U.S. PRISONS 1861-1865

NAME	RANK	REGIMENT	CAPTURED AT	WHEN	PRISON	MOVED	DISPOSITION	SOURCES
Weatherford, Watson J.	Sgt	C 11th SCVI	Town Creek, NC	02/20/65	Ft. Anderson, NC	02/28/65	Pt. Lookout, MD	CSR,HAG
					Pt. Lookout, MD	06/21/65	Rlsd. G.O. #109	P115,P118,CSR
Weatherford, William	Pvt	F 3rd SCVABn	Cheraw, SC	03/05/65	Cheraw, SC	03/05/65	Paroled	CSR
Weathern, W.	Pvt	B 18th SCVI	Deserted/enemy	02/25/65	City Pt., VA	02/26/65	Washington DC P.M.	CSR
					Washington, DC	03/24/65	Baltimore, MD oath	CSR
Weathers, H.A.	Pvt	C 14th SCVI	Spotsylvania, VA	05/13/64	Ft. Delaware, DE	01/19/65	Hos. 1/19-1/21/65	P47
					Ft. Delaware, DE	06/10/65	Released	P41,P43
Weathers, J.W.W.	Pvt	G 11th SCVI	Town Creek NC	02/20/65	Ft. Anderson, NC	02/28/65	Pt. Lookout MD	CSR,HAG
					Pt. Lookout, MD	06/21/65	Rlsd. G.O. #109	P115,P118,CSR
Weathers, Lacey	Pvt	C Hol.Leg.	Warrenton, VA	09/29/62	Warrenton, VA	09/29/62	Paroled POW	CSR
Weathers, Thomas	Pvt	C Hol.Leg.	Petersburg, VA	10/27/64	City Pt., VA	10/31/64	Pt. Lookout, MD	CSR
					Pt. Lookout, MD	06/23/65	Rlsd. G.O. #109	P115,P117,P121,CSR
Weathers, Thomas	Pvt	B Hol.Leg.	Deserted/enemy	02/25/65	City Pt., VA	02/28/65	Washington, DC	CSR
					Washington, DC	03/01/65	Savannah, GA oath	CSR,HOS
Weathersbee, C.	Pvt	D Hol.Leg.	Warrenton, VA	09/29/62	Warrenton, VA	09/29/62	Paroled POW	CSR
Weathersbee, J. Alfred	Pvt	E 2nd SCVI	Deserted/enemy		Knoxville	02/17/64	Released on oath	P8,KEB,SA2,H2,CSR
Weathersbee, J.B.	Pvt	A 1st SCVIG	Gettysburg, PA	07/05/63	David's Island, NY	08/11/63	Died, Pyaemia	P1,P6,FPH,SA1,CSR
Weathersbee, Tully F.S.	Pvt	A 1st SCVIG	Gettysburg, PA	07/05/62	David's Island, NY	09/23/63	City Pt., VA Xc	P1,SA1,CTA,CSR
Weathersby, Hamilton H.	Pvt	D Hol.Leg.	Five Forks, VA	04/01/65	City Pt., VA	04/05/65	Pt. Lookout, MD	CSR
					Pt. Lookout, MD	06/22/65	Rlsd. G.O. #109	P115,P118,CSR
Weaver, James	Pvt	A 15th SCVAB	Fayetteville, NC	03/16/65	New Berne, NC	03/30/65	Pt. Lookout, MD	CSR,YEB
					Pt. Lookout, MD	06/21/65	Rlsd. G.O. #109	P115,P118,CSR
Weaver, Oscar F.	Pvt	F 27th SCVI	Town Creek, NC	02/20/65	Ft. Anderson, NC	02/28/65	Pt. Lookout, MD	CSR,HAG
					Pt. Lookout, MD	06/21/65	Rlsd. G.O. #109	P115,P118,CSR
Weaver, W.T.	Sgt	D 19th SCVI	Marietta, GA	10/13/64	Atlanta, GA USGH	10/31/64	North to Hospital	P3,CSR
Webb, Benjamin F.	Pvt	G 22nd SCVI	Richmond Hos. VA	04/03/65	Richmond, VA Hos.	04/09/65	Pt. Lookout, MD	P119,CSR
					Pt. Lookout, MD	04/09/65	Arnory Sq. Hos. DC	CSR
					Armory Sq. Hos., DC	08/17/65	Douglas G.H., DC	CSR
Webb, D.	Pvt	G 23rd SCVI	Richmond, VA Hos.	05/03/65	Newport News, VA	06/26/65	Rlsd. G.O. #109	CSR
Webb, E.	Pvt	E 14th SCVI	Greencastle, PA	07/05/63	Ft. Delaware, DE	07/30/63	City Pt., VA Xc	P42
Webb, John	Pvt	B 17th SCVI	Augusta, GA	05/14/65	Augusta, GA	05/14/65	Paroled	CSR
Webb, John H.	Pvt	B 19th SCVI	Augusta, GA	05/19/65	Augusta, GA	05/19/65	Paroled	CSR
Webb, John T.	Pvt	A 1st SCVIG	Gettysburg, PA	07/05/63	Harrisburg, PA	07/07/63	Philadelphia, PA	SA1,CSR
					Philadelphia, PA	07/30/63	Ft. Delaware, DE	CSR
					Ft. Delaware, DE	07/30/63	Paroled	CSR
Webb, Paul H.W.	Pvt	A 27th SCVI	Petersburg, VA	06/24/64	Bermuda Hundred, VA	06/25/64	Fts. Monroe, VA	CSR,HAG
					Fts. Monroe, VA	06/26/64	Pt. Lookout, MD	CSR,HAG
					Pt. Lookout, MD	03/14/65	Aikens Ldg., VA Xc	P113,P121,P123
Webb, Thomas J.	Pvt	G 5th SCVC	Deserted/enemy	03/15/65	Charleston, SC	03/15/65	Released on oath	CSR
Webber, Drury D.	Pvt	A Hol.Leg.	Williamsport, MD	09/15/62	Ft. Delaware, DE	10/02/62	Aikens Ldg., VA Xc	CSR,HOS
Webber, John	Pvt	H 2nd SCVC	Martinsburg, VA	07/17/63	Camp Chase, OH	02/29/64	Ft. Delaware, DE	P22,P25
Webster, George	Pvt	E 19th SCVCB	Mineral Spgs., SC	03/05/65	New Berne, NC	04/03/65	Pt. Lookout, MD	CSR
					Pt. Lookout, MD	06/22/65	Rlsd. G.O. #109	P115,P118,P121,CSR
Webster, Henry D.	Pvt	G 8th SCVI	Bennettsville, SC	03/06/65	New Berne, NC	03/26/65	Pt. Lookout, MD	CSR,HOM,KEB
					Pt. Lookout, MD	06/22/65	Rlsd. G.O. #109	P115,P118,P122
Webster, J.R.	Pvt	K 5th SCVC	Stony Creek, VA	12/01/64	City Pt., VA	12/05/64	Pt. Lookout, MD	CSR
					Pt. Lookout, MD	02/13/65	Aikens Ldg., VA Xc	P115,P121,P124,UD5
Webster, Thomas M.	Pvt	G 8th SCVI	Gettysburg, PA	07/02/63	Gettysburg G.H.		Provost Marshal	P4,KEB,HOM,CSR
					Pt. Lookout, MD	08/16/64	Elmira, NY	P113,P116,P120,CSR
					Elmira, NY	10/11/64	Pt. Lookout, MD Xc	P65,P66,CSR
					Pt. Lookout, MD	10/29/64	Exchanged	P115,P124,CSR

W

SOUTH CAROLINA SOLDIERS, SAILORS AND CITIZENS HELD IN U.S. PRISONS 1861-1865

NAME	RANK	REGIMENT	CAPTURED AT	WHEN	PRISON	MOVED	DISPOSITION	SOURCES
Webster, Thomas M.	Pvt	G 8th SCVI	Bennettsville, SC	03/06/65	New Berne, NC	03/26/65	Pt. Lookout, MD	CSR
					Pt. Lookout, MD	06/22/65	Rlsd. G.O. #109	P115,P118,P124
Weed, J.T.	Pvt	H 3rd SCVI	Cedar Creek, VA	10/19/64	Harpers Ferry, WV	10/23/64	Pt. Lookout, MD	CSR,SA2,H3
					Pt. Lookout, MD	02/18/65	Aikens Ldg., VA Xc	P117,P124,CSR
Weed, Reuben	Pvt	G 14th SCVI	Spotsylvania, VA	05/12/64	Ft. Delaware, DE	06/10/65	Released	P41,P43
Weekley, G.W.	Pvt	F 3rd SCVC	South Newport, GA	08/17/64	Philadelphia, PA	01/10/65	Ft. Delaware, DE	CSR
					Ft. Delaware, DE	03/19/65	Hos. 3/19-4/16/65	P47
					Ft. Delaware, DE	02/26/65	Hos. 2/26-3/6/65	P47
					Ft. Delaware, DE	06/10/65	Released	P43,P45,CSR
Weekly, T.J.	Pvt	A 19th SCVCB	Augusta, GA	05/25/65	Augusta, GA	05/25/65	Paroled on oath	CSR
Weeks, Augustus	Pvt	C 3rd SCVABn	Blakely, AL	04/09/65	Ship Island, MS	05/01/65	Vicksburg, MS	P136,CSR
					Vicksburg, MS	05/04/65	Exchanged	CSR
Weeks, G.W.	Pvt	D 4th SCVC	Stony Creek, VA	12/01/64	City Pt., VA	12/05/64	Pt. Lookout, MD	CSR
					Pt. Lookout, MD	06/21/65	Rlsd. G.O. #109	P115,P118,CSR
Weeks, J.D.	Cpl	D 4th SCVC	Louisa C.H., VA	06/11/64	Fts. Monroe, VA	06/20/64	Pt. Lookout, MD	CSR
					Pt. Lookout, MD	07/24/64	Died, Ch. Diarrhea	P6,P12,P113,FPH
Weeks, J.W.	Pvt	I 1st SCVA	Deserted/enemy	02/18/65	Charleston, SC	03/13/65	Taken oath & disch.	CSR
Weeks, J.W.	Cpl	G 1st SCVIR	Fayetteville, NC	03/16/65	New Berne, NC	04/10/65	Hart's Island, NY	CSR,SA1
					Hart's Island, NY	06/18/65	Rlsd. G.O. #109	P79,CSR
Weeks, Thomas	Pvt	G 1st SCVIG	Gettysburg, PA	07/04/63	Letterman G.H. Gbg	09/14/63	Provost Marshal	P1,SA1,HOE
					W. Bldg. Balt, MD	09/25/63	City Pt., VA Xc	P1,CSR
Weems, J.	Pvt	A Orr's Ri.	Falling Waters, MD	07/14/63	Baltimore, MD	08/16/63	Pt. Lookout, MD	CSR
					Pt. Lookout, MD	10/15/63	Hammond G.H., MD	P121,P125
					Pt. Lookout, MD	01/27/64	Died, Ch. Diarrhea	P5,P12,FPH,CSR
Weibins, F.	Cpl	K 12th SCVI	Warrenton, VA	09/29/62	Warrenton, VA	09/29/62	Paroled	CSR
Weicking, Frederick	Pvt	L 1st SCVIG	Petersburg, VA	07/29/64	City Pt. VA	08/05/64	Pt. Lookout, MD	CSR,SA1
					Pt. Lookout, MD	08/08/64	Elmira, NY	P113,P117,P120
					Elmira, NY	10/01/64	Died, Diarrhea	P5,P12,P65,P66,FPH
Weicking, Herman R.	Pvt	L 1st SCVIG	Gettysburg, PA	07/05/63	David's Island, NY		City Pt. VA, Xc	SA1,CSR
Weimer, Daniel	Pvt	I 2nd SCVI	Bentonville, NC	03/19/65	New Berne, NC	03/30/65	Pt. Lookout, MD	CSR,SA2,H2
					Pt. Lookout, MD	06/21/65	Rlsd. G.O. #109	P115,P118,CSR
Weir, David T.	Pvt	H 6th SCVI	Richmond, VA	04/03/65	Richmond, VA Hos.	04/03/65	Libby Prison Rchmd.	CSR
					Richmond, VA P.M.	04/23/65	City Pt., VA P.M.	CSR
					City Pt., VA	04/23/65	Newport News, VA	CSR
					Newport News, VA	06/26/65	Rlsd. G.O. #109	P107,CSR
Welborn, James	Pvt	D 18th SCVI	Five Forks, VA	04/01/65	City Pt., VA	04/04/65	Pt. Lookout, MD	CSR
					Pt. Lookout, MD	06/21/65	Rlsd. G.O. #109	P115,P118,CSR
Welborn, Thomas Martin	1Lt	G 1st SCVIG	Appomattox R., VA	04/03/65	Old Capitol, DC	04/24/65	Johnson's Isl., OH	CSR,SA1,UD2,F110
					Johnson's Isl., OH	06/20/65	Rlsd. G.O. #109	P81,P82,P83,CSR
Welch, Francis M.	1Lt	D 1st SCVIH	Warrenton, VA	09/29/62	Warrenton, VA	09/29/62	Paroled	CSR,SA1,LAN
Welch, Francis M.	1Lt	D 1st SCVIH	French Broad R.,TN	01/02/64	Nashville, TN	02/11/64	Louisville, KY	P39,CSR
					Louisville, KY	02/13/64	Camp Chase, OH	P88,P93,CSR
					Camp Chase, OH	03/25/64	Ft. Delaware, DE	P23,P26,CSR
					Ft. Delaware, DE	06/12/65	Rlsd. G.O.#109	P42,P44,P45,CSR
Welch, J.W.	Pvt	F 27th SCVI	Weldon RR, VA	08/21/64	City Pt., VA	08/24/64	Pt. Lookout, MD	CSR
					Pt. Lookout, MD	03/14/65	Exchanged	CSR
Welch, James	Pvt	H 27th SCVI	Deserted/enemy	07/11/64	Bermuda Hundred, VA	07/18/64	Roundout, NY oath	CSR
Welch, James	Pvt	H 26th SCVI	Farmville, VA	04/06/65	City Pt., VA	04/14/65	Newport News, VA	CSR
					Newport News, VA	06/26/65	Rlsd. G.O. #109	P107,CSR
Welch, Jefferson J.	Pvt	C 7th SCVIBn	Weldon RR, VA	08/21/64	Pt. Lookout, MD	03/14/65	Exchanged	P123
Welch, Jefferson J.	Pvt	C 7th SCVIBn	Clinton, NC	03/26/65	New Berne, NC	04/10/65	Hart's Island, NY	P79,CSR
					Hart's Island, NY	06/17/65	Rlsd. G.O. #109	P79,CSR

SOUTH CAROLINA SOLDIERS, SAILORS AND **W** CITIZENS HELD IN U.S. PRISONS 1861-1865

NAME	RANK	REGIMENT	CAPTURED AT	WHEN	PRISON	MOVED	DISPOSITION	SOURCES
Welch, John F.	Pvt	H Ham.Leg.	Cumberland Gap, TN	01/12/64	Louisville, KY	02/11/64	Rock Island, IL	P88,P93,CSR
					Rock Island, IL	02/13/65	Pt. Lookout, MD Xc	P131,CSR
Welch, L.R.	Pvt	B 6th SCVI	Richmond, VA	04/03/65	Libby Prison Rchmd.	04/23/65	Newport News, VA	CSR
					Newport News, VA	06/26/65	Rlsd. G.O.#109	P107,CSR
Welch, Maurice C.	Pvt	K 1st SCVIG	Deserted/enemy	03/21/65	Charleston, SC	03/21/65	Released on oath	SA1,CSR
Welch, Nicholas	Pvt	I 17th SCVI	Appomattox C.H., VA	04/09/65	Burkeville, VA G.H.	04/16/65	City Pt., VA	CSR
					City Pt., VA 5th A	04/19/65	City Pt., VA Depot	CSR
					City Pt., VA Depot	05/01/65	Lincoln G.H., DC	CSR
					Lincoln G.H., DC	06/12/65	Paroled	CSR
Welch, Richard	Pvt	A 14th SCVI	Gettysburg, PA	07/05/63	David's Island, NY	10/24/63	Bedloes Island, NY	P1,CSR
					Bedloes Island, NY	12/17/63	Pt. Lookout, MD	P2
					Pt. Lookout, MD	01/22/64	Joined U.S. Army	P113,P125
					Pt. Lookout, MD	01/27/64	Released on oath	P116
Welch, Samuel W.	Pvt	F 27th SCVI	Weldon RR, VA	08/21/64	Pt. Lookout, MD	03/14/65	Aikens Ldg., VA Xc	P113,P121,P124,HAG
Welch, W.H.	Pvt	G 7th SCVC	Darbytown Rd., VA	10/07/64	Bermuda Hundred, VA	10/21/64	City Pt., VA P.M.	CSR
					City Pt., VA	10/29/64	Pt. Lookout, MD	CSR
					Pt. Lookout, MD	02/10/65	Exchanged	P115,P124,CSR
Welch, William E.	Pvt	D 13th SCVI	Petersburg, VA	03/25/65	City Pt., VA	03/28/65	Pt. Lookout, MD	CSR,ANY
					Pt. Lookout, MD	06/21/65	Rlsd. G.O. #109	P115,P118,CSR
Welch, William T.	Pvt	I 1st SCVA	Morris Island, SC	07/10/63	Ft. Columbus, NY	09/23/63	Took the oath	P1,P124
					Pt. Lookout, MD	07/27/64	Jd. U.S. Army	P116,P125,CSR
Wells, Aaron	Pvt	E 7th SCVC	Chickahominy R., VA	01/30/65	Bermuda Hundred, VA	02/09/65	City Pt., VA P.M.	CSR
					City Pt., VA	02/10/65	Pt. Lookout, MD	CSR,ANY
					Pt. Lookout, MD	06/22/65	Rlsd. G.O. #109	P115,P118,P121,CSR
Wells, Barney W.	Pvt	D 24th SCVI	Marietta, GA	06/17/64	Nashville, TN	06/24/64	Louisville, KY	P3,CSR
					Louisville, KY	06/29/64	Camp Morton, IN	P90,P91,P94,CSR
					Camp Morton, IN	02/19/65	Pt. Lookout, MD Xc	P100,P101,CSR
Wells, David A.	Pvt	L P.S.S.	Chattanooga, TN	10/29/63	Nashville, TN	11/07/63	Louisville KY	CSR,TSE
					Louisville, KY	11/09/63	Camp Morton, IN	P88,P89,P93,CSR
					Camp Morton, IN	03/19/64	Ft. Delaware, DE	P100,P101,CSR
					Ft. Delaware, DE	06/16/64	Hos. 6/16/64-?	P47
					Ft. Delaware, DE	10/25/64	Hos. 10/25-11/28/64	P47
					Ft. Delaware, DE	11/29/64	Hos. 11/29-12/4/64	P47
					Ft. Delaware, DE	03/09/65	Hos. 3/9/65-?	P47
					Ft. Delaware, DE	05/10/65	Rlsd. G.O. #85	P42,P45,CSR
Wells, Elby M.	1Sg	G 21st SCVI	Ft. Fisher, NC	01/15/65	Ft. Fisher, NC	01/31/65	Pt. Lookout, MD	CSR,HAG
					Pt. Lookout, MD	02/02/65	Hammond G.H., MD	P115,P121
					Pt. Lookout, MD	06/03/65	Rlsd. Instr. 5/30/65	P118,P121,P122
Wells, Eldred	Pvt	D 24th SCVI	Marietta, GA	06/17/64	Nashville, TN	06/24/64	Louisville, KY	P3,CSR
					Louisville, KY	06/27/64	Camp Morton, IN	P90,P91,P94,CSR
					Camp Morton, IN	03/04/65	City Pt., VA Xc	P100,P101,CSR
Wells, F.C.	Pvt	E 17th SCVI	Deserted/enemy	03/03/65	P.M. 9th A.C. A. o	03/03/65	City Pt., VA P.M.	CSR
					City Pt., VA P.M.	03/05/65	Washington, DC	CSR
					Washington, DC	03/05/65	Chattanooga, TN oath	CSR
Wells, F.P.	Pvt	B Ham.Leg.MI	Augusta, GA	05/19/65	Augusta, GA	05/19/65	Paroled	CSR
Wells, Gansey H.	Pvt	D 24th SCVI	Nashville, TN	12/16/64	Nashville, TN	12/31/64	Louisville, KY	CSR
					Louisville, KY	01/20/65	Died, Pneumonia	P92,EFW,FPH
Wells, James	Pvt	D 7th SCVC	Haw River, NC	05/15/64	Pt. Lookout, MD	01/30/65	Died, Ch. Diarrhea	P6,P12,FPH

SOUTH CAROLINA SOLDIERS, SAILORS AND CITIZENS HELD IN U.S. PRISONS 1861-1865

NAME	RANK	REGIMENT	CAPTURED AT	WHEN	PRISON	MOVED	DISPOSITION	SOURCES
Wells, James T.	Cpl	A 2nd SCVI	Gettysburg, PA	07/06/63	Letterman G.H. Gbg	08/21/63	Provost Marshal	P1,CSR,KEB,SA2,H2
					Seminary Hos. PA	08/24/63	Baltimore, MD P.M.	CSR
					Newton U., Balt.			P1
					Baltimore, MD P.M.	08/24/63	Ft. McHenry, MD	CSR
					Ft. McHenry, MD	09/15/63	Pt. Lookout, MD	P96,P144,CSR
					Pt. Lookout, MD	02/13/65	Aikens Ldg., VA Xc	P113,P121,P124
Wells, Samuel P.	2Lt	I 23rd SCVI	Dinwiddie C.H., VA	04/01/65	Old Capitol, DC	04/12/65	Johnson's Isl., OH	CSR,HCL
					Johnson's Isl., OH	06/20/65	Rlsd. G.O. #109	P81,P82,CSR
Wells, Thomas	Pvt	I 20th SCVI	Cedar Creek, VA	10/19/64	Harpers Ferry, WV	10/24/64	Pt. Lookout, MD	CSR,KEB
					Pt. Lookout, MD	06/22/65	Rlsd. G.O. #109	P117,P121,CSR
Welsh, Edward	Pvt	C 1st SCVIG	Falling Waters, MD	07/14/63	Pt. Lookout, MD	02/13/65	Aikens Ldg., VA Xc	P116,P121,P124,CSR
Welsh, James V.	Pvt	D 1st SCVIH	Mossy Creek, TN	01/22/64	Nashville, TN	02/11/64	Louisville, KY	P39,SA1,CSR,LAN
					Louisville, KY	02/15/64	Rock Island, IL	P88,P91,P93,CSR
					Rock Island, VA	06/18/65	Rlsd. G.O. #109	CSR
Welsh, Sebra	Sgt	D 8th SCVI	Winchester, VA	09/13/64	Harpers Ferry, WV	09/19/64	Camp Chase, OH	P23,KEB,CSR
					Camp Chase, OH	06/11/65	Rlsd. G.O. #109	CSR
Welsh, Thomas J.	Cpl	D 1st SCVIH	Mossy Creek, TN	01/22/64	Nashville, TN	02/11/64	Louisville, KY	P39,CSR,SA1,LAN
					Louisville, KY	02/15/64	Rock Island, IL	P88,P91,P93,CSR
					Rock Island, IL	02/15/65	Tfd. for exchange	CSR
Wendelkin, Carson	Pvt	K 12th SCVI	Spotsylvania, VA	05/12/64	Belle Plain, VA	05/20/64	Ft. Delaware, DE	CSR
					Ft. Delaware, DE	06/10/65	Rlsd. G.O.#109	P41,P43,P45,CSR
Werts, Andrew C.	Pvt	K 14th SCVI	Sutherland Stn., VA	04/02/65	City Pt., VA	04/07/65	Hart's Island, NY	CSR,HOE
					Hart's Island, NY	06/16/65	Rlsd. G.O. #109	P79,CSR
Werts, Andrew S.	Pvt	C 3rd SCVI	Gettysburg, PA	07/04/63	Letterman G.H. Gbg	09/10/63	Provost Marshal	P1,ANY,CSR,SA2,H3
					W. Bldg. Balt, MD	09/25/63	City Pt., VA Xc	P1,H3,CSR
					Richmond, VA Hos.	10/03/63	Furloughed 30 days	CSR
Werts, Daniel Hilliard	Pvt	H Hol.Leg.	Hatchers Run, VA	03/29/65	City Pt.VA 5ac Hos.	04/02/65	Lincoln G.H., DC	CSR,ANY
					Lincoln G.H., DC	06/14/65	Rlsd. G.O. #109	CSR
Werts, Henry Middleton	Pvt	H Hol.Leg.	Five Forks, VA	04/01/65	City Pt., VA	04/05/65	Pt. Lookout, MD	CSR,ANY
					Pt. Lookout, MD	05/16/65	Died, Typhoid fever	P6,P115,P118,FPH
Werts, J.M.	Pvt	G 13th SCVI	Petersburg, VA Hos.	04/03/65	Pt. Rocks, VA USH	05/10/65	Released	CSR
Werts, James N.	Sgt	K 14th SCVI	Spotsylvania, VA	05/12/64	Ft. Delaware, DE	06/10/65	Rlsd. G.O.#109	P41,P43,HOE,CSR
Werts, O.S.	Pvt	G 13th SCVI	Petersburg, VA	04/03/65	City Pt., VA	04/13/65	Pt. Lookout, MD	CSR,ANY
					Pt. Lookout, MD	06/06/65	Rlsd. on oath	CSR
Wescoat, J.J.	Pvt	I 3rd SCVC	Edisto Island, SC	04/09/63	Ft. Norfolk, VA	06/29/63	Paroled	CSR
Wescoat, St.Julian D.	Pvt	H 25th SCVI	Ft. Fisher, NC	01/15/65	New York, NY	01/30/65	Elmira, NY	CSR,HAG
					Elmira, NY	02/20/65	James R., VA Xc	P65,P66,HAG,CSR
Wescoat, W. Preston	Sgt	I 2nd SCVI	Gettysburg, PA	07/04/63	Gettysburg G.H.	07/21/63	Provost Marshal	P4,CSR,KEB,SA2,H2
					David's Island, NY	08/24/63	City Pt., VA Xc	P1,KEB,SA2,H2,CSR
Wessinger, E.	Cit	Lexington	Flat Rock, SC	02/24/65	Hart's Island, NY	06/20/65	Rlsd. G.O. #109	P79
Wessinger, J.L.	Pvt	F 5th SCVC	Stony Creek, VA	12/01/64	City Pt., VA	12/05/64	Pt. Lookout, MD	CSR
					Pt. Lookout, MD	06/21/65	Rlsd. G.O. #109	P115,P118,CSR
Wessinger, John N.	Cpl	I 15th SCVI	Gettysburg, PA	07/05/63	Gettysburg, PA USH	07/21/63	Provost Marshal	P4,KEB,CSR,H15
					David's Island, NY	10/22/63	Paroled	P1,CSR
					Richmond, VA Hos.	11/14/63	Died, Ch. Diarrhea	CSR
Wessinger, Joseph R.	Cpl	K 13th SCVI	Gettysburg, PA	07/05/63	David's Island, NY	09/16/63	City Pt., VA Xc	P1,CSR
					David's Island, NY	10/22/63	Fts. Monroe, VA	P1,CSR
West, Andrew J.	Pvt	C 27th SCVI	Town Creek, NC	02/20/65	Ft. Anderson, NC	02/28/65	Pt. Lookout, MD	CSR,HAG
					Pt. Lookout, MD	06/22/65	Rlsd. G.O. #109	P115,P118,P121,CSR
West, Archibald	Pvt	E 1st SCVIR	NC or SC		Foster GH New Bern	04/01/65	Died, Ac. Diarrhea	P1,P6,WAT,CSR,SA1
West, Benjamin	Cpl	F 14th SCVI	Sutherland Stn., VA	04/02/65	City Pt., VA	04/07/65	Hart's Island, NY	CSR
					Pt. Lookout, MD	06/22/65	Rlsd. G.O. #109	P115,P118,P122

W

SOUTH CAROLINA SOLDIERS, SAILORS AND CITIZENS HELD IN U.S. PRISONS 1861-1865

NAME	RANK	REGIMENT	CAPTURED AT	WHEN	PRISON	MOVED	DISPOSITION	SOURCES
West, Benjamin F.	Pvt	C Hol.Leg.	Five Forks, VA	04/01/65	City Pt., VA	04/05/65	Pt. Lookout, MD	CSR,HOS
					Pt. Lookout, MD	06/04/65	Rlsd. on sick list	P115,P118,CSR
West, D.F.	Pvt	Ham.Leg.MI	Turkey Bend, VA	07/22/64	Bermuda Hundred, VA	07/27/64	Fts. Monroe, VA	CSR
					Fts. Monroe, VA	07/28/64	Baltimore on oath	P8,CSR
West, F.A.	Sgt	F 13th SCVI	Gettysburg, PA	07/05/63	Chester, PA USGH	08/17/63	City Pt., VA Xc	P1,HOS,CSR
West, G.H.	Pvt	H Ham.Leg.MI	Farmville, VA	04/07/65	Farmville, VA	04/07/65	Paroled	CSR
West, Henry H.	Pvt	Ch'fld LA	Charlotte, NC	05/16/65	Charlotte, NC	05/16/65	Paroled	CSR
West, Isaac S.	Pvrt	B 8th SCVI	Winchester, VA	09/13/64	Harpers Ferry, WV	09/19/64	Camp Chase, OH	CSR
					Camp Chase, OH	06/10/65	Rlsd. G.O. #109	CSR
West, John P.	Pvt	B 15th SCVI	Warrenton, VA	09/29/62	Warrenton, VA	09/29/62	Paroled	H15,KEB
West, John P.	Pvt	B 15th SCVI	Halltown, VA	08/26/64	Harpers Ferry, WV	08/29/64	Camp Chase, OH	CSR
					Camp Chase, OH	03/18/65	Pt. Lookout, MD	P22,CSR
					Pt. Lookout, MD	06/21/65	Rlsd. G.O. #109	P115,P119,P122,CSR
West, Joseph	Pvt	I Hol.Leg.	Stony Creek, VA	05/07/64	Fts. Monroe, VA	05/13/64	Pt. Lookout, MD	CSR,HOS
					Pt. Lookout, MD	08/15/64	Elmira, NY	P113,P116,P120
					Elmira, NY	04/03/65	Died, Variola	P6,P12,P65,P66,FPH
West, Joseph D.	Pvt	A 10th SCVI	Atlanta, GA	07/22/64	Nashville, TN	08/08/64	Louisville, KY	CSR,RAS
					Louisville, KY	08/10/64	Camp Chase, OH	P90,P91,P94
					Camp Chase, OH	03/04/65	City Pt., VA Xc	P22,P26,CSR
West, M.	Pvt	F Hol.Leg.	Deserted/enemy	12/03/64	City Pt., VA	12/05/64	Rlsd. on oath	CSR
West, Solomon W.	Pvt	A 3rd SCVI	N. Anna River, VA	05/22/64	Port Royal, VA	05/30/64	Pt. Lookout, MD	KEB,SA2,CSR
					Pt. Lookout, MD	06/24/64	Died, Ch. Diarrhea	P6,P12,P113,FPH
West, Thomas George	Sgt	G 2nd SCVI	Cedar Creek, VA	10/19/64	Harpers Ferry, WV	10/24/64	Pt. Lookout, MD	CSR,KEB,SA2,H2
					Pt. Lookout, MD	06/22/65	Rlsd. G.O. #109	P115,P121,CSR
West, William	Pvt	F Hol.Leg.	Deserted/enemy	12/03/64	City Pt., VA	12/05/64	Washington, DC	CSR
					Washington, DC	12/07/64	Baltimore, MD oath	CSR
West, William M.	Pvt	G 2nd SCVI	Gettysburg, PA	07/02/63	Gettysburg G.H.		New York, NY P.M.	P4,CSR
					David's Island, NY	07/20/63	Died of wounds	SA2,H2,CSR
Westberry, James P.	Pvt	C 6th SCVI			Nashville, TN G.H.	01/15/64	Died	P2,HIC
Westbrook, J.R.	Pvt	H 12th SCVI	Warrenton, VA	09/29/62	Warrenton, VA	09/29/62	Paroled	CSR
Westbrook, J.R.	Pvt	H 12th SCVI	Farmville, VA	04/11/65	Farmville, VA	04/21/65	Paroled, Rlsd. 6/12	CSR
Westbrook, James A.	Pvt	H 12th SCVI	Warrenton, VA	09/29/62	Warrenton, VA	09/29/62	Paroled	CSR
Westbury, Thomas B	Pvt	B 23rd SCVI	Deserted/enemy	02/23/65	Washington, DC	02/26/65	Charleston, SC	CSR
Westbury, William M.	Pvt	Santee LA	McIntosh Co., GA	10/15/64	Sapelo Sound, GA	01/03/65	Philadelphia, PA	CSR
					Philadelphia, PA	01/12/65	Ft. Delaware, DE	CSR
					Ft. Delaware, DE	03/12/65	Hos. 3/12-3/15/65	P47
					Ft. Delaware, DE	06/10/65	Rlsd. G.O. #109	P41,P45,CSR
Westcoat, Julius J.	Cpt	B 11th SCVI	Town Creek, NC	02/20/65	Ft. Anderson, NC	02/28/65	Washington, DC	CSR
					Pt. Lookout, MD	02/28/65	Washington, DC	P115,P120,CSR
					Old Capitol, DC	03/24/65	Ft. Delaware, DE	P110,CSR
					Ft. Delaware, DE	06/17/65	Rlsd. G.O. #109	P43,P45,P47,CSR
Westendorf, Charles H.	Pvt	B 25th SCVI	Town Creek, NC	02/20/65	Ft. Anderson, NC	02/28/65	Pt. Lookout, MD	CSR,HAG
					Pt. Lookout, MD	06/22/65	Rlsd. G.O. #109	P115,P118,P121,CSR
Westendorff, Charles	Pvt	A 27th SCVI	Ft. Anderson, NC	02/19/65	Ft. Anderson, NC	02/28/65	Pt. Lookout, MD	CSR,HAG
					Pt. Lookout, MD	04/04/65	Died, Erysipelas	P6,P115,P118,FPH
Westfall, George H.	Sgt	G 15th SCVAB	Charlotte, NC	05/09/65	Baltimore, MD oath			CSR
Westmoreland, J.R.	Pvt	E 6th SCVC	Fayetteville, NC	03/16/65	New Berne, NC	04/10/65	Hart's Island, NY	CSR
					Hart's Island, NY	06/17/65	Rlsd. G.O. #109	P79,CSR
Westmoreland, James G.	Pvt	I Hol.Leg.	Stony Creek, VA	05/07/64	Fts. Monroe, VA	05/13/64	Pt. Lookout, MD	CSR,HOS
					Pt. Lookout, MD	08/15/64	Elmira, NY	P113,P116,P120,CSR
					Elmira, NY	12/10/64	Died, Ch. Diarrhea	P5,P65,P66,FPH,CSR

SOUTH CAROLINA SOLDIERS, SAILORS AND CITIZENS HELD IN U.S. PRISONS 1861-1865

NAME	RANK	REGIMENT	CAPTURED AT	WHEN	PRISON	MOVED	DISPOSITION	SOURCES
Westmoreland, John A.	Pvt	E 6th SCVC	Ream's Stn., VA	08/23/64	City Pt. VA	09/07/64	Pt. Lookout, MD	CSR
					Pt. Lookout, MD	02/18/65	Aikens Ldg., VA Xc	P113,P117,P124,CSR
Westmoreland, Lorenzo D.	Pvt	I Hol.Leg.	Jackson, MS	07/06/63	Vicksburg, MS	07/07/63	Snyders Bluff, MS	CSR,HOS
					Snyders Bluff, MS	07/08/63	Camp Morton, IN	CSR
					Camp Morton, IN	07/19/64	Died, Pth. Pneum.	P6,P100,FPH,CSR
Westmoreland, Oliver P.	Pvt	E Hol.Leg.	Petersburg, VA	03/25/65	City Pt., VA	03/28/65	Pt. Lookout, MD	CSR,HOS
					Pt. Lookout, MD	06/22/65	Rlsd. G.O. #109	P115,P118,CSR
Westmoreland, William T.	Pvt	E 14th SCVI	Hanover Jctn., VA	05/24/64	White House, VA	06/08/64	Pt. Lookout, MD	CSR
					Pt. Lookout, MD	11/01/64	Aikens Ldg., VA Xc	P113,P121,P124
					Pt. lookout, MD	11/01/64	Venus Pt., GA Xc	CSR
Weston, Bentley	Pvt	A 7th SCVC	Deep Bottom, VA	08/16/64	City Pt., VA	08/22/64	Pt. Lookout, MD	CSR
					Pt. Lookout, MD	03/14/65	Aikens Ldg., VA Xc	P113,P121,P124,CSR
Weston, R.A.	Pvt	K 4th SCVC	Augusta, GA	05/22/65	Augusta, GA	05/22/64	Paroled	CSR
Wethersbee, A.J.	Cpl	1st MtdMil	Augusta, GA	05/18/65	Augusta, GA	05/18/65	Paroled	
Wetherton, W.	Cit	Charleston	Margaret and Jessie	11/03/63	Ft. Lafayette, NY	02/08/64	Released Sp. Order	P144
Wetterhorn, S.	Pvt	E 25th SCVI	Weldon RR, VA	08/21/64	City Pt., VA	08/24/64	Pt. Lookout, MD	CSR
					Pt. Lookout, MD	02/18/65	Aikens Ldg., VA Xc	P117,P118,P124,CSR
Wever, Lafayette B.	Cpt	I 24th SCVI	Augusta, GA	05/18/65	Augusta, GA	05/18/65	Paroled on oath	CSR,EFW
Whaley, Benjamin J.	Pvt	C 27th SCVI	Weldon RR, VA	08/21/64	City Pt., VA	08/24/64	Pt. Lookout, MD	CSR
					Pt. Lookout, MD	02/13/65	Aikens Ldg. Xc	P113,P121,P124,CSR
Whaley, W.B.	Pvt	I 3rd SCVC	Edisto Island, SC	04/09/63	Ft. Norfolk, VA	06/29/63	Paroled	CSR
Whaley, Walter C.	Pvt	D 2nd SCVC	Charleston, SC	04/07/65	Charleston, SC		Confined, Wdd NC	CSR
Wham, Joseph	Pvt	E 2nd SCVC	Goldsboro Rd., NC	03/21/65	New Berne, NC	03/26/65	Pt. Lookout, MD	CSR
					Pt. Lookout, MD	06/22/65	Rlsd. G.O. #109	P121,CSR
Wheatley, Joseph	Pvt	C 15th SCVAB	Fayetteville, NC	04/18/65	Wilmington, NC	04/24/65	Paroled on oath	CSR
Wheeler, A.H.	Sgt	G 13th SCVI	Warrenton, VA	09/29/62	Warrenton, VA	09/29/62	Paroled	CSR,ANY
Wheeler, A.H.	Sgt	G 13th SCVI	Gettysburg, PA	07/05/63	Ft. McHenry, MD	07/07/63	Ft. Delaware, DE	CSR
Wheeler, A.H.	Pvt	G 13th SCVI	Gettysburg, PA	07/05/63	Ft. Delaware, DE	03/11/64	Hos. 3/11/64	P47
					Ft. Delaware, DE	06/10/65	Released	P40,P42,P45,CSR
Wheeler, Charles D.	Pvt	D 2nd SCVI	Gettysburg, PA	07/04/63	Gettysburg G.H.	07/21/63	Pro. Mar. New York	P4,CSR,KEB,SA2,H2
					David's Island, NY	08/24/63	City Pt., VA Xc	P1,CSR
Wheeler, J.B.	Pvt	I 26th SCVI	Deserted/enemy	02/25/65	City Pt., VA	02/26/65	Washington, DC	CSR
					Washington, DC	03/01/65	Philadelphia, PA	CSR
Wheeler, Jacob Wiley	Pvt	I 15th SCVI	Cedar Creek, VA	10/19/64	Harpers Ferry, WV	10/24/64	Pt. Lookout, MD	CSR,KEB,H15
					Pt. Lookout, MD	06/08/65	Rlsd. Instr. 5/30/65	P115,P117,P121,CSR
					Pt. Lookout, MD	07/14/65	Died, Typhoid	P12
Wheeler, James	Pvt	B 18th SCVAB	Deserted/enemy	03/01/65	Charleston, SC		Released on oath	CSR
Wheeler, Timothy	Pvt	D 1st SCVA	Hartwell, GA	05/19/65	Hartwell, GA	05/19/65		CSR
Whelan, Rhody	Pvt	H 27th SCVI	Petersburg, VA	06/18/64	City Pt., VA	06/24/64	Pt. Lookout, MD	CSR,HAG
					Pt. Lookout, MD	07/25/64	Elmira, NY	P113,P117,P120
					Elmira, NY	10/05/64	Died, Ch. Diarrhea	P5,P65,P66,FPH
Wherry, James A.	Pvt	H 12th SCVI	Gettysburg, PA	06/30/63	David's Island, NY	07/22/63	Died	P1,P6,FPH,YEB,CSR
Whetstone, William	1Sg	B Wash'n LA	Stephensburg, VA	09/19/63	Ft. McHenry, MD	10/03/63	Pt. Lookout, MD	P110,CSR
					Lincoln G.H., DC	10/27/63	Old Capitol, DC	CSR
					Old Capitol, DC	10/27/63	Pt. Lookout, MD	CSR
					Pt. Lookout, MD	11/25/63	Died, Smallpox	P113,P116,P6,FPH
Whidby, William T.	Pvt	I 1st SCVA	Morris Island, SC	07/10/63	Hilton Head, SC	09/19/63	Ft. Columbus, NY	CSR
					Ft. Columbus, NY	09/23/63	Took the oath	P1,CSR
Whisenant, Alexander	Msc	B 2nd SCVI	Gettysburg, PA	07/05/63	Gettysburg G.H.		Provost Marshal	P4,KEB,SA2,H2
					Ft. Delaware, DE	07/17/63	Chester, PA Hos.	P40,P42,P44,CSR
					Chester, PA G.H.	08/17/63	City Pt., VA Xc	P1,CSR

W

SOUTH CAROLINA SOLDIERS, SAILORS AND CITIZENS HELD IN U.S. PRISONS 1861-1865

NAME	RANK	REGIMENT	CAPTURED AT	WHEN	PRISON	MOVED	DISPOSITION	SOURCES
Whisenant, John	Pvt	K 17th SCVI	Petersburg, VA	03/25/65	3rd Div. 9th AC H	03/27/65	Washington, DC	CSR
					Lincoln G.H., DC	06/14/65	Rlsd. G.O. #109	CSR
Whisenant, John Brown	Cpl	B 12th SCVI	Petersburg, VA	04/03/65	City Pt., VA	04/07/65	Hart's Island, NY	CSR,YEB
					Hart's Island, NY	06/16/65	Rlsd. G.O. #109	CSR
Whisenant, Thomas P.	Pvt	B 12th SCVI	Petersburg, VA	04/02/65	City Pt., VA	04/04/65	Pt. Lookout, MD	P115,P118,CSR
Whisenant, Thomas P.	Pvt	B 12th SCVI	Petersburg, VA	04/04/65	Pt. Lookout, MD	06/22/65	Rlsd. G.O. #109	P115,P118,P121,CSR
Whit, Richard J.	Cpl	B 13th SCVI	Appomattox R., VA	04/03/65	City Pt., VA	04/11/65	Hart's Island, NY	CSR
					Hart's Island, NY	06/17/65	Rlsd. G.O. #109	P79,CSR
Whitaker, Benjamin F.	Pvt	I 17th SCVI	Petersburg, VA	07/30/64	City Pt., VA	08/05/64	Pt. Lookout, MD	CSR,LAN
					Pt. Lookout, MD	08/08/64	Elmira, NY	P113,P117,P120,CSR
					Elmira, NY	09/11/64	Died, Ch. Diarrhea	P5,P12,P65,FPH,CSR
Whitaker, William	Pvt	H 7th SCVC	Burkeville, VA	04/06/65	City Pt., VA	04/15/65	Pt. Lookout, MD	CSR,P125
Whitaker, William	Sgt	H 7th SCVC	Burkeville, VA	04/06/65	Pt. Lookout, MD	06/22/65	Rlsd. G.O. #109	P115,P119,P121,CSR
Whitby, George	Pvt	Gist Gd HA	Deserted/enemy	02/22/65	Charleston, SC	02/22/65	Released on oath	CSR
White, A.	Pvt	17th SCVI	Athens, GA	05/08/65	Athens, GA	05/08/65	Paroled	CSR
White, Abbott B.	2Lt	G 27th SCVI	Petersburg, VA	06/24/64	Bermuda Hundred, VA	06/25/64	Fts. Monroe, VA	CSR,HAG
					Fts. Monroe, VA	06/26/64	Pt. Lookout, MD	CSR
					Old Capitol, DC	06/30/64	Ft. Delaware, DE	CSR
					Ft. Delaware, DE	10/30/64	Venus Pt., GA Xc	P43,P44,P115,CSR
White, Abbott B.	2Lt	G 27th SCVI	Town Creek, NC	02/20/65	Pt. Lookout, MD	02/28/65	Washington, DC	P115,P117,P120
					Ft. Anderson, NC	02/28/65	Pt. Lookout, MD	CSR
					Old Capitol, DC	03/24/65	Ft. Delaware, DE	P110
					Ft. Delaware, DE	05/25/65	Rlsd OO Gen. Grant	P43,P45,P46
White, Augustus J.	Pvt	I 2nd SCVC	Augusta, GA	05/19/65	Augusta, GA	05/19/65	Paroled	CSR
White, Augustus K.	Cpl	L 21st SCVI	Morris Island, SC	07/10/63	Morris Island, SC	07/13/63	Hilton Head, SC	CSR
					Hilton Head G.H.	07/23/63	Morris Island, SC Xc	P2
White, B.S.	Sgt	C 8th SCVI	Gettysburg, PA	07/05/63	Gettysburg G.H.		Provost Marshal	P4,KEB,CSR
					Ft. McHenry, MD	07/12/63	Ft. Delaware, DE	CSR
					Ft. Delaware, DE	02/20/64	Hos. 2/20-3/3/64	P47
					Ft. Delaware, DE	01/20/65	Hos. 1/20-1/23/65	P47
					Ft. Delaware, DE	03/03/65	Hos. 3/3-3/6/65	P47
					Ft. Delaware, DE	06/10/65	Rlsd. G.O. #109	P40,P42,P45,CSR
White, Benjamin F.	Cpl	K 17th SCVI	Petersburg, VA	03/25/65	City Pt., VA	03/28/65	Pt. Lookout, MD	CSR
					Pt. Lookout, MD	06/22/65	Rlsd. G.O. #109	P115,P118,CSR
White, Calvin J.	Pvt	K 18th SCVI	Crater, Pbg., VA	07/30/64	City Pt., VA	08/05/64	Pt. Lookout, MD	CSR
					Pt. Lookout, MD	08/08/64	Elmira, NY	P113,P117,P120,CSR
					Elmira, NY	09/01/64	Died, Ch. Diarrhea	P5,P12,P65,P66,FPH,CSR
White, D.	Pvt	Mathewes A	Str. Memphis	07/31/62	New York, NY		Deserter	CSR
White, Daniel J.	Pvt	H 1st SCVIH	Sharpsburg, MD	09/18/62	Ft. McHenry, MD		No release record	CSR
White, Daniel J.	Pvt	H 1st SCVIH	Knoxville, TN	12/03/63	Louisville, KY	01/27/64	Rock Island, IL	P88,P89,P93,CSR
					Rock Island, IL	10/15/64	Jd. USA Frontier S.	P131,CSR
White, Edwin R.	Cpt	D 23rd SCVI	Dinwiddie C.H., VA	04/01/65	Old Capitol, DC		Elmira, NY	P110,CSR
					Johnson's Isl., OH	06/20/65	Rlsd. G.O. #109	P81,P82,P83,CSR
White, Elihu	Sgt	E 13th SCVI	Gettysburg, PA	06/30/63	David's Island, NY	07/20/63	Died of wounds	P1,P6,P12,FPH,HOS
White, George	Pvt	K 12th SCVI	Deserted/enemy	02/23/65	City Pt., VA	02/24/65	Washington, DC	CSR
					Washington, DC	02/24/65	Oil City, PA on oath	CSR
White, George	Sgt	B Orr's Ri.	Petersburg, VA	04/03/65	City Pt., VA	04/11/65	Hart's Island, NY	CSR,CDC
					Hart's Island, NY	06/22/65	Rlsd. G.O. #109	P79,CSR
White, George A.	Sgt	F 3rd SCVIBn	Knoxville, TN	12/04/63	Louisville, KY	01/23/64	Rock Island, IL	P88,P91,P93,CSR
					Rock Island, IL	03/20/65	Boulwares Wh., VA	P131,CSR
White, George W.	Pvt	B P.S.S.	Knoxville, TN	12/04/63	Knoxville TN	12/06/63	Louisville, KY	CSR,TSE

SOUTH CAROLINA SOLDIERS, SAILORS AND CITIZENS HELD IN U.S. PRISONS 1861-1865

NAME	RANK	REGIMENT	CAPTURED AT	WHEN	PRISON	MOVED	DISPOSITION	SOURCES
White, George W.	Pvt	B P.S.S.	Knoxville, TN	12/06/63	Louisville, KY	01/27/64	Rock Island, IL	P88,P93,CSR
					Rock Island, IL	03/20/65	Pt. Lookout, MD Xc	P131,CSR
White, George W.	Pvt	B P.S.S.	Knoxville, TN	12/04/63	Pt. Lookout, MD	03/27/65	Boulwares Wh., VA	CSR
White, Henry C.	Pvt	B 14th SCVI	Sutherland Stn., VA	04/03/65	City Pt., VA	04/13/65	Pt. Lookout, MD	CSR,HOE
					Pt. Lookout, MD	06/22/65	Rlsd. G.O. #109	P115,P119,P121
White, Hugh	Sgt	D 17th SCVI	Crater, Pbg., VA	07/30/64	City Pt., VA	08/05/64	Pt. Lookout, MD	CSR,HHC
					Pt. Lookout, MD	08/08/64	Elmira, NY	P113,P120,P125,CSR
					Elmira, NY	06/30/65	Rlsd. G.O. #109	P65,P66,CSR
White, Hugh B.	2Lt	G 21st SCVI	Ft. Fisher, NC	01/15/65	Ft. Columbus, NY	02/25/65	City Pt., VA Xc	P2,CSR
White, Isaac B.	Cpl	I 25th SCVI	Ft. Fisher, NC	01/15/65	New York, NY	01/30/65	Elmira, NY	CSR,HAG
					Elmira, NY	06/23/65	Rlsd. G.O. #109	P65,P66,CSR
White, J.A.	Pvt	K 12th SCVI	Deep Bottom, VA	08/17/64	Pt. Lookout, MD	10/30/64	Aikens Ldg., VA Xc	P117
White, J.M.	Pvt	K 21st SCVI	Ft. Fisher, NC	01/15/65	Elmira, NY	03/02/65	Pt. Lookout, MD Xc	P65,P66,HAG
White, James G.	Pvt	C 3rd SCVABn	Ft. Gaines, AL	08/08/64	New Orleans, LA	10/25/64	Ship Island, MS	P3,CSR
					Ship Island, MS	01/04/65	Vicksburg, MS Xc	P136,CSR
White, James G.	Sgt	K 23rd SCVI	Petersburg, VA	03/25/65	City Pt., VA	03/27/65	Pt. Lookout, MD	CSR
					Pt. Lookout, MD	06/22/65	Rlsd. G.O. #109	P115,P118,P122,CSR
White, John	Pvt	B 17th SCVI	Deserted/enemy	12/05/64	P.M. US 9th A.C.	12/05/64	City Pt., VA P.M.	CSR
					City Point, VA	12/06/64	Washington, DC	CSR,P8
					Washington, DC	12/07/64	Phila., PA oath	P8,CSR
White, John C.	Pvt	D 6th SCVC	Deserted/enemy	08/23/64	City Pt., VA	09/10/64	Washington, DC	CSR
					Washington, DC	09/10/64	St. Louis, MO oath	CSR
White, John G	Cpl	I 12th SCVI	Petersburg, PA	03/25/65	Pt. Lookout, MD	06/22/65	Rlsd. G.O. #109	P121,CSR
White, Julius	Pvt	A Ham.Leg.MI	Deserted/enemy	01/23/65	Bermuda Hundred, VA	01/31/64	City Pt., VA P.M.	CSR
					City Pt., VA	02/01/65	Washington, DC	CSR
					Washington, DC	02/04/65	Troy, NY on oath	CSR
White, Legrand M.	Sgt	K 12th SCVI	Petersburg, VA	04/03/65	City Pt., VA	04/13/65	Pt. Lookout, MD	CSR
					Pt. Lookout, MD	06/21/65	Rlsd. G.O. #109	P118,CSR
White, Mathew J.	Pvt	L Orr's Ri.	Deserted/enemy	02/16/65	City Pt., VA	02/18/65	Washington, DC	CSR
					Washington DC	02/18/65	White County, IL	CSR
White, Nelson J.	Pvt	E 1st SCVIG	Petersburg, VA	04/02/65	City Pt., VA	04/04/65	Pt. Lookout, MD	CSR,SA1
					Pt. Lookout, MD	06/21/65	Rlsd. G.O. #109	P115,CSR
White, O.P.	Pvt	K 5th SCVI	Knoxville, TN	11/26/63	Chattanooga, TN	12/29/63	Died, Typhoid pneum.	P1,P5,P12,SA3,CSR
White, Patrick	Smn	CS Chicora	Morris Island, SC	09/07/63	Pt. Lookout, MD	09/20/63	Ft. Warren, MA	P113,P116,P120
					Ft. Warren, MA	10/01/64	Str. Circasian	P2,P137
White, Patrick.	Smn	CS Chicora			Pt. Lookout, MD		Exchanged	P124
White, Robert J.	Sgt	B Orr's Ri.	Petersburg, VA	04/03/65	City Pt., VA	04/11/65	Hart's Island, NY	CSR,CDC
					Hart's Island, NY	06/23/65	Rlsd. G.O. #109	P79,CSR
White, Samuel C.	Pvt	E 24th SCVI	Battery Isl., SC	05/21/62	Hilton Head, SC	08/14/62	Ft. Columbus, NY	CSR,EFW
					Ft. Columbus, NY	08/23/62	Ft. Delaware, DE	P37,CSR
					Ft. Delaware, DE	10/02/62	Aikens Ldg., VA Xc	CSR
White, T.M.	Pvt	A 17th SCVI	Deserted/enemy	02/25/65	P.M. 9th A.C. A. of	02/26/65	City Pt., VA P.M.	CSR
					City Pt., VA P.M.	02/28/65	Washington, DC	CSR
					Washington, DC	03/01/65	Savannah, GA oath	CSR
White, Theodore A.	Pvt	K 12th SCVI	Deep Bottom, VA	08/16/64	City Pt., VA	08/22/64	Pt. Lookout, MD	CSR
					Pt. Lookout, MD	10/30/64	Exchanged	P113,P123,CSR
White, Thomas	Pvt	I 1st SCVA	Morris Island, SC	07/10/63	Hilton Head, SC	09/19/63	Fort Columbus, NY	CSR
					Ft. Columbus, NY	09/23/63	Took the oath	P1
White, W.F.	Pvt	LafayetteA	Deserted/enemy	03/27/65	Charleston, SC	03/27/65	Released on oath	CSR
White, W.J.	Pvt	H 4th SCVC	Stony Creek, VA	12/01/64	City Pt., VA	12/05/64	Pt. Lookout, MD	CSR,LAN
					Pt. Lookout, MD	06/03/65	Rlsd. Instr. 5/30/	P115,P118,P122,CSR

SOUTH CAROLINA SOLDIERS, SAILORS AND **W** CITIZENS HELD IN U.S. PRISONS 1861-1865

NAME	RANK	REGIMENT	CAPTURED AT	WHEN	PRISON	MOVED	DISPOSITION	SOURCES
White, W.R.	Pvt	D P.S.S.	Sharpsburg, MD	10/07/62	Frederick, MD USGH	01/17/62	Ft. McHenry, MD	CSR
					Ft. McHenry, MD	01/20/62	City Pt., VA	CSR
					City Pt., VA	01/26/62	Exchanged	CSR
White, Wesley B.	2Lt	G 12th SCVI	Southside RR, VA	04/02/65	City Pt, VA	04/12/65	Washington, DC	CSR
					Old Capitol, DC	06/09/65	Rlsd. G.O. #109	P110,CSR
White, William	Cit	CD Distr.	Chesterfield, SC	03/04/65	Pt. Lookout, MD	06/19/65	Rlsd. G.O. #109	P115,P118
White, William F.	Pvt	D 3rd SCVI	Knoxville, TN	12/03/63	Louisville, KY	12/31/63	Rock Island, IL	P89,H3,CSR,SA2
					Louisville, KY	01/15/64	Gnl. Hospital	P89,P93,CSR
					Rock Island, IL	04/10/64	Died, Pneumonia	P12,P131,P132,CSR
White, William H.	Pvt	B 12th SCVI	Charlotte, NC	05/06/65	Charlotte, NC	05/06/65	Paroled	CSR
White, William J.	Pvt	H 5th SCVI	Richmond, VA	06/30/62	Ft. Columbus, NY	07/09/62	Ft. Delaware, DE	CSR
					Ft. Delaware, DE	07/12/62	Harrisons Ldg., VA	CSR
					Harrisons Ldg., VA	07/12/62	Aikens Ldg., VA Xc	CSR
					City Pt., VA	03/24/65	Washington, DC	CSR
					Bermuda Hundred, VA	03/16/65	City Pt., VA	CSR
					Washington, DC	03/24/65	Cleveland, OH oath	CSR
White, William J.	Pvt	B 18th SCVI	Crater, Pbg., VA	07/30/64	City Pt., VA	08/04/64	Pt. Lookout, MD	CSR
					Pt. Lookout, MD	08/08/64	Elmira, NY	P113,P117.P120,CSR
					Elmira, NY	10/05/64	Died, Diarrhea	P5,P65,FPH,CSR
White, William R.	Cpl	I 25th SCVI	Ft. Fisher, NC	01/15/65	New York, NY	01/30/65	Elmira, NY	CSR,HAG
					Elmira, NY	06/27/65	Rlsd. G.O. #109	P65,P66,HAG
White, William R.	Cpt	I 14th SCVI	Southside RR, VA	04/02/65	Old Capitol, DC	04/30/65	Johnson's Isl., OH	CSR
					Johnson's Isl., OH	06/20/65	Rlsd. G.O. #109	P81,P82,P83
White, William W.	Pvt	K 4th SCVC	Hawe's Shop, VA	05/28/64	3rd Div. 5th A.C.	06/09/64	Alexandria, VA G.H.	CSR
					Alexandria, VA G.H.	06/10/64	Washington, DC	P1,CSR
					Lincoln G.H., DC		Elmira, NY	CSR
					Ft. McHenry, MD	08/13/64	Elmira, NY	P110
					Elmira, NY	02/25/65	Pt. Lookout, MD Xc	P65,P66,CSR
White, William W.	Sgt	B 12th SCVI	Sutherland Stn., VA	04/02/65	City Pt., VA	04/07/65	Hart's Island, NY	CSR,YEB
					Hart's Island, NY	06/16/65	Rlsd. G.O. #109	P79,CSR
White, Willis	Pvt	F 17th SCVI	Petersburg, VA	03/25/64	3rd Div. 9th AC Hos.	03/26/65	City Pt., VA US Hos.	CSR
					City Pt., VA US Hos.	04/09/65	Lincoln G.H., DC	CSR
					Lincoln G.H., DC	08/07/65	Rlsd. G.O. #109	P110,CSR
Whitehead, James S.	Pvt	F 1st SCVA	Bentonville, NC	03/22/65	New Berne, NC	04/10/65	Hart's Island, NY	CSR
					Hart's Island, NY	06/16/65	Rlsd. G.O. #109	P79,CSR
Whitehead, John W.	Pvt	D 4th SCVC	Deserted/enemy	01/19/65	Old Capitol, DC	03/02/65	Ft.Warren, MA	CSR
					Ft. McHenry, MD		Ft. Warren, MA	P110
					Ft. Warren, MA	06/16/65	Rlsd. on oath	P2,CSR
Whitehead, W.B.	Pvt	D 7th SCVC	Deep Bottom, VA	08/19/64	Pt. Lookout, MD	02/10/65	Exchanged	P123
Whitehead, W.H.	Pvt	B 7th SCVC	Farmville, VA	04/11/65	Farmville, VA	04/21/65	Paroled	CSR
Whitehead, William	Pvt	D 6th SCVI	Darbytown Rd., VA	12/12/64	Bermuda Hundred, VA	12/13/64	City Pt., VA P.M.	CSR
					City Pt., VA	12/15/64	Pt. Lookout, MD	CSR
					Pt. Lookout, MD	01/17/65	Exchanged	P115,P118,P124,CSR
Whites, U.B.	1Lt	H 3rd SCVI	Cedar Creek, VA	10/19/64	Ft. Delaware, DE	06/17/65	Rlsd. G.O. #109	P45,P46,KEB,H3,CSR
Whiteside, William	Pvt	E 1st SCVA	Deserted/enemy	02/18/65	Charleston, SC	03/12/65	Taken oath & disch.	CSR
Whitesides, J.T.	Pvt	G 1st SCVA	Bentonville, NC	03/22/65	New Berne, NC	04/10/63	Hart's Island, NY	CSR
					Hart's Island, NY	06/17/65	Rlsd. G.O. #109	P79,CSR
Whitesides, James M.	Pvt	B 12th SCVI	Southside RR, VA	04/03/65	City Pt., VA	04/07/65	Hart's Island, NY	CSR
					Hart's Island, NY	06/16/65	Rlsd. G.O. #109	P79,YEB,CSR
Whitesides, R.N.	Pvt	A 12th SCVI	Sharpsburg, MD	09/17/62	Frederick, MD USGH	10/11/62	Ft. McHenry, MD	CSR
					Ft. McHenry, MD	10/13/62	Fts. Monroe, VA Xc	CSR
					Richmond, VA Hos.	11/16/62	Died of wounds	CSR

SOUTH CAROLINA SOLDIERS, SAILORS AND  CITIZENS HELD IN U.S. PRISONS 1861-1865

NAME	RANK	REGIMENT	CAPTURED AT	WHEN	PRISON	MOVED	DISPOSITION	SOURCES
Whitesides, Rufus G.	Sgt	B 12th SCVI	Southside RR, VA	04/03/65	City Pt., VA	04/07/65	Hart's Island, NY	CSR
					Hart's Island, NY	06/16/65	Rlsd. G.O. #109	P79,YEB,CSR
Whitesides, W.R.	Cpl	F 17th SCVI	Petersburg, VA	03/11/65	P.M.9th A.C. A.of P	03/13/65	City Pt., VA P.M.	CSR
					City Pt., VA P.M.	03/16/65	Pt. Lookout, MD	CSR
					Pt. Lookout, MD	05/15/65	Rlsd. G.O. #85	P115,P118,P122,CSR
Whitesides, William C.	Cpl	K 17th SCVI	Warrenton, VA	09/29/62	Warrenton, VA	09/29/62	Paroled	CSR
Whitesides, William C.	Cpl	K 17th SCVI	Petersburg, VA	03/25/65	City Pt., VA	03/28/65	Pt. Lookout, MD	CSR
					Pt. Lookout, MD	06/22/65	Rlsd. G.O. #109	P115,P118,P121,CSR
Whitfield, Benjamin	Pvt	I 2nd SCVC	Hartwell, GA	05/19/65	Hartwell, GA	05/19/65	Paroled	CSR
Whitfield, Doctor B.	Pvt	K 12th SCVI	Deserted/enemy	02/23/65	City Pt., VA	02/24/65	Washington, DC	CSR
					Washington, DC	02/24/65	Oil City, PA on oath	CSR
Whitfield, Sylvester	Pvt	4 10/19 SCVI	Missionary Ridge,TN	11/25/63	Nashville, TN	12/05/63	Louisville, KY	P39,RAS
					Louisville, KY	12/20/63	Died, Typhoid fever	P5,P89,P93,FPH,CSR
Whitlock, Calvin M.	Cpl	C 7th SCVC	Farmville, VA	04/11/65	Farmville, VA	04/30/65	Burkeville, VA G.H.	CSR
Whitlock, Calvin M.	Cpl	C 7th SCVC	Petersburg, VA Hos.	04/03/65	Fair Gds.H.Pbg. VA	05/01/65	Pt. O Rocks, VA	CSR
					Pt. O Rocks, VA G.H.	05/10/65	Released	CSR
Whitlock, Drury	Pvt	E Ham.Leg.MI	Deep Bottom, VA	08/17/64	City Pt., VA	08/22/64	Pt. Lookout, MD	CSR
					Pt. Lookout, MD	09/18/64	Aikens Ldg., VA Xc	P117,P125,CSR
Whitlock, J.C.	Pvt	A 22nd SCVI	Boonesboro, MD	09/14/62	P.M. Frederick, MD	09/23/62	Ft. McHenry, MD	CSR
					Ft. McHenry, MD	10/20/62	Fts. Monroe, VA	CSR
					Fts. Monroe, VA	10/22/62	Aikens Ldg., VA Xc	CSR
Whitlock, John	Pvt	B 27th SCVI		03/10/65	Camp Hamilton, VA	03/08/65	Pt. Lookout, MD	CSR
Whitlock, Martin C.	Pvt	H 14th SCVI	Gettysburg, PA	07/05/63	Chester, PA G.H.	10/03/63	Pt. Lookout, MD	P1,UD2
					Pt. Lookout, MD	04/27/64	City Pt., VA Xc	P116,UD2
Whitlock, Robert	Pvt	E Ham.Leg.MI	Richmond, VA Hos.	04/03/65	Libby Prison Rchmd.	04/13/65	City Pt., VA	CSR
					City Pt., VA	04/14/65	Pt. Lookout, MD	CSR
					Pt. Lookout, MD	06/21/65	Rlsd. G.O. #109	P115,P119,P122
Whitman, John B.	Pvt	C 13th SCVI	Spotylvania, VA	05/23/64	Port Royal, VA	05/30/64	Pt. Lookout, MD	CSR
					Pt. Lookout, MD	07/03/64	Died, Remitnt fever	P12,P113,P119,CSR
Whitman, T.J.	Pvt	D 13th SCVI	Gettysburg, PA	07/05/63	David's Island, NY	09/05/63	City Pt., VA Xc	P1,CSR
Whitmire, George S.	Pvt	K 16th SCVI	Graysville, GA	11/27/63	Nashville, TN	12/16/63	Louisville, KY	P39,16R,CSR
					Louisville, KY	12/21/63	Rock Island, IL	P88,P89,P93,CSR
					Rock Island, IL	01/23/64	Joined US Navy	P131
Whitmire, J.B.	Pvt	G 27th SCVI	Petersburg, VA	06/24/64	Bermuda Hundred, VA	06/25/64	Fts. Monroe, VA	CSR,HAG
					Fts. Monroe, VA	06/26/64	Pt. Lookout, MD	CSR
					Pt. Lookout, MD	09/18/64	Aikens Ldg. Xc	P113,P117,CSR
					Richmond, VA Hos.	09/26/64	Died of disease	CSR
Whitmire, N.P.	Pvt	A 3rd SCVABn	High Pt., NC	05/02/65	High Pt., NC	05/02/65	Paroled	CSR
Whitmire, W.H.	Pvt	A 3rd SCVABn	High Pt., NC	05/02/65	High Pt., NC	05/02/65	Paroled	CSR
Whitner, James H.	Cpt	D 22nd SCVI	Jackson H., Rchmd.	04/03/65	P.M. Richmond, VA	05/03/65	Rlsd. on parole	CSR
Whitney, E.G.	Cit	Charleston	Wilmington, NC	11/06/63	Ft. Lafayette, NY	12/17/64	Ft. Warren, MS	P144
Whitney, Eli	Cit	Charleston	Wilmington, NC	11/06/63	Ft. Warren, MA	04/17/65	Released	P137
Whitt, J.V.	Pvt	I Ham.Leg.MI	Farmville, VA	04/11/65	Farmville, VA	04/11/65	Paroled	CSR
Whitt, Merritt	Pvt	LafayetteA	Gillisonville, SC	01/16/65	Hilton Head, SC	02/01/65	Pt. Lookout, MD	CSR
					Pt. Lookout, MD	06/22/65	Rlsd. G.O. #109	CSR
Whittaker, C.	Pvt	E 1st SCVIR	Deserted/enemy	02/21/65	Charleston, SC		Released on oath	CSR
Whitten, A.	Pvt	G 27th SCVI	Petersburg, VA	06/24/64	Bermuda Hundred, VA	06/25/64	Fts. Monroe, VA	CSR,HAG
					Ft. Monroe, VA	06/26/64	Pt. Lookout, MD	CSR
					Pt. Lookout, MD	08/16/64	Elmira, NY	P113,P117,P120
					Elmira, NY	03/14/65	Pt. Lookout to Xc	P65,P66,CSR
					Pt. Lookout, MD	03/18/65	Boulwares Wh., VA	CSR

SOUTH CAROLINA SOLDIERS, SAILORS AND **W** CITIZENS HELD IN U.S. PRISONS 1861-1865

NAME	RANK	REGIMENT	CAPTURED AT	WHEN	PRISON	MOVED	DISPOSITION	SOURCES
Whitten, Henry P.	Pvt	C 18th SCVI	Crater, Pbg., VA	07/30/64	City Pt., VA	08/05/64	Pt. Lookout, MD	CSR
					Pt. Lookout, MD	08/08/64	Elmira, NY	P113,P117,P120,CSR
					Elmira, NY	07/03/65	Rlsd. G.O. #109	P65,P66,CSR
Whitten, John B.	Pvt	B P.S.S.	Knoxville, TN	11/14/63	Knoxville, TN	12/03/63	Louisville, KY	CSR,TSE
Whitten, John B.	Pvt	B P.S.S.	Knoxville, TN	12/03/63	Louisville, KY	12/31/63	Rock Island, IL	P89,P93,CSR
					Rock Island, IL	10/13/64	Jd. USA Frontier S	P131,CSR
Whitten, L.P.	Pvt	A Ham.Leg.	Knoxville, TN	12/03/63	Louisville, KY	12/31/63	Rock Island, IL	P88,P89,P93,CSR
					Rock Island, IL	01/29/64	Died, Typhoid fever	P5,P131,P132,FPH
Whitten, M.B.	Pvt	G 27th SCVI	Petersburg, VA	06/24/64	Bermuda Hundred, VA	06/25/64	Fts. Monroe, VA	CSR,HAG
					Pt. Lookout, MD	08/16/64	Elmira, NY	P113,P117,P120,HAG,CSR
					Elmira, NY	07/11/65	Rlsd. G.O. #109	P65,P66,HAG,CSR
Whittier, Christian	Pvt	E 1st SCVIR	Deserted/enemy	02/21/65	Charleston, SC	02/21/65	Hilton Head, SC P.M.	CSR
					Hilton Head, SC	03/22/65	NY City, NY oath	CSR
Whittington, Eli	Pvt	A 4th SCVC	Stony Creek, VA	12/01/64	City Pt., VA	12/05/64	Pt. Lookout, MD	CSR
					Pt. Lookout, MD	02/13/65	Aikens Ldg., VA Xc	P121,P123,P124,CSR
					Pt. Lookout, MD	06/22/65	Rlsd. G.O. #109	P115,P118,CSR
Whittington, John G.	Pvt	E 23rd SCVI	Hatchers Run, VA	04/02/65	City Pt., VA	04/06/65	Pt. Lookout, MD	CSR,HMC
					Pt. Lookout, MD	06/22/65	Rlsd. G.O. #109	P115,P118,P122,CSR
Whittington, W.G.	Pvt	D 25th SCVI	Weldon RR, VA	08/21/64	City Pt., VA	08/24/64	Pt. Lookout, MD	CSR,HAG,HMC
					Pt. Lookout, MD	03/14/65	Aikens Ldg., VA Xc	P113,P121,P124
Whittle, D.	Pvt	B 14th SCVI	Gettysburg, PA	07/05/63	David's Island, NY	08/24/63	City Pt., VA Xc	P1
Whittle, Hezekiah K.	Pvt	B 14th SCVI	Falling Waters, MD	07/14/63	Baltimore, MD	08/23/63	Pt. Lookout, MD	CSR,HOE
					Pt. Lookout, MD	03/07/64	Smallpox Hospital	CSR
					Smallpox Hospital	05/02/64	Pt. Lookout, MD	CSR
					Pt. Lookout, MD	11/01/64	Aikens Ldg., VA Xc	P113,P121,P124
					Pt. Lookout, MD	11/01/64	Venus Pt., GA Xc	CSR
Whittle, Jacob W.	Pvt	B 14th SCVI	Petersburg, VA	04/03/65	Pt. Lookout, MD	06/22/65	Rlsd. G.O. #109	P115,P118,P121,HOE
Whittle, James E.	Pvt	B 14th SCVI	Falling Waters, MD	07/14/63	Ft. McHenry, MD			P110
Whittle, Joel M.	Pvt	B 14th SCVI	Gettysburg, PA	07/05/63	Ft. McHenry, MD	07/07/63	Ft. Delaware, DE	CSR,HOE
					Ft. Delaware, DE	08/10/63	Chester, PA Hos.	P40,P44,P144,
					USGH Chester, PA	08/19/63	Died, Peritonitis	P1,P6,P12,FPH
Whittle, John	Pvt	D 14th SCVI	Petersburg, VA	04/02/65	City Pt., VA	04/04/65	Pt. Lookout, MD	CSR
					Pt. Lookout, MD	06/22/65	Rlsd. G.O. #109	P115,P118,P121,HOE
Whittle, Malachi	Pvt	B 14th SCVI	Falling Waters, MD	07/14/63	Old Capitol, DC		Pt. Lookout, MD	CSR,HOE
					Ft. McHenry, MD		Pt. Lookout, MD	P110
					Pt. Lookout, MD	02/18/65	Aikens Ldg., VA Xc	P113,P123,P124
Whittle, Oratio	Pvt	B Ham.Leg.MI	Richmond, VA Hos.	04/03/65	Richmond, VA Hos.	04/14/65	Provost Marshal	CSR
					Libby Prison Rchmd.	04/23/65	Newport News, VA	CSR
					Newport News, VA	06/13/65	Rlsd. G.O. #109	P107,CSR
Whitton, Chapil T.	Cpl	K 15th SCVI	Gettysburg, PA	07/04/63	Gettysburg G.H.	07/15/63	Provost Marshal	P4,CSR,KEB,H15
					Chester, PA G.H.	10/03/63	Pt. Lookout, MD	P1
					Pt. Lookout, MD	04/27/64	City Pt., VA Xc	P121,P123,P124,CSR
					Richmond, VA Hos.	05/08/64	Furloughed 60 days	CSR
Whitworth, P.H.	Pvt	C 3rd SCVABn	Blakely, AL	04/09/65	Ship Island, MS	05/01/65	Vicksburg, MS	P136,CSR
					Vicksburg, MS	05/04/65	Exchanged	CSR
Wicker, Samuel	Pvt	G Hol.Leg.	Kinston, NC	12/15/62	Kinston, NC	12/15/62	Paroled POW	CSR,ANY
Wickler, Carnes	Pvt	Brook's LA	South Mtn., PA	07/04/63	Ft. Delaware, DE			P42
Wicks, William R.	Pvt	B 1st SCVC	Martinsburg, WV	07/19/63	Wheeling, WV	08/12/63	Camp Chase, OH	CSR
					Camp Chase, OH	02/29/64	Ft. Delaware, DE	CSR
					Ft. Delaware, DE	05/31/65	Released on oath	CSR

SOUTH CAROLINA SOLDIERS, SAILORS AND  CITIZENS HELD IN U.S. PRISONS 1861-1865

NAME	RANK	REGIMENT	CAPTURED AT	WHEN	PRISON	MOVED	DISPOSITION	SOURCES
Wideman, Francis B.	Pvt	G 14th SCVI	Sutherland Stn., VA	04/02/65	Hart's Island, NY	06/16/65	Rlsd. G.O. #109	P79
					Hart's Island, NY	06/20/65	NY City Transit Hos.	CSR
					NYCity Transit Hos.	06/22/65	Rlsd. sent south	CSR
Widener, Abraham	Pvt	G 2nd SCVA	Cheraw, SC	03/04/65	New Berne, NC	03/30/65	Pt. Lookout, MD	CSR
					Pt. Lookout, MD	06/08/65	Rlsd. G.O. #109	P115,P118,CSR
Wiedner, John P.	Pvt	C 15th SCVAB	Deserted/enemy	02/14/65	Charleston, SC	02/18/65	Taken oath & disch.	CSR
Wieland, David W.	Sgt	I 1st SCVA	Morris Island, SC	07/10/63	Ft. Columbus, NY	09/23/63	Took the oath	P1,CSR
Wiers, B.	Pvt	G 3rd SCVC	Deserted/enemy	02/19/65	Charleston, SC	03/02/65	Will take oath	CSR
Wiggington, Robert A.	Pvt	A Orr's Ri.	Falling Waters, MD	07/14/63	Baltimore, MD	08/16/63	Pt. Lookout, MD	CSR,CDC
					Pt. Lookout, MD	07/09/64	Elmira, NY	P113,P116,P120,CSR
					Elmira, NY	12/24/64	Died, Pneumonia	P5,P12,P65,P66,FPH
Wiggins, Baker	Pvt	H Orr's Ri.	Deep Bottom, VA	07/28/64	City Pt., VA	08/09/64	Lincoln G.H., DC	CSR,CDC,HMC
					Lincoln G.H., D.C.	11/23/64	Old Capitol, DC	CSR
					Old Capitol, DC	12/16/64	Elmira, NY	CSR
					Ft. McHenry, MD	12/16/64	Elmira, NY	P110
					Elmira, NY	02/13/65	W. Bldg. Balt, MD	CSR
					W. Bldg. Balt, MD	05/09/65	Ft. McHenry, MD	P3,CSR
					Ft. McHenry, MD H.	05/11/65	Died, Tuberculosis	P6,P12,P96,FPH,HMC,CDC
Wiggins, Benjamin W.	Pvt	E 11th SCVI	Town Creek, NC	02/20/65	Ft. Anderson, NC	02/28/65	Pt. Lookout, MD	CSR,HAG
					Pt. Lookout, MD	06/21/65	Rlsd. G.O. #109	P115,P118,P122,CSR
Wiggins, Elijah	Pvt	I 1st SCVA	Morris Island, SC	07/10/63	Ft. Columbus, NY	09/23/63	Took the oath	P1,CSR
Wiggins, H.	Pvt	F 4th SCVC	Hawe's Shop, VA	05/28/64	3rd Div. 5th A.C.	05/28/65	Died of wounds	CSR
Wiggins, Thomas	Pvt	E 5th SCVC	Stony Creek, VA	12/01/64	City Pt., VA	12/05/64	Pt. Lookout, MD	CSR
					Pt. Lookout, MD	06/22/65	Rlsd. G.O. #109	P115,P121,CSR
Wiggins, William	Pvt	I 11th SCVI	Petersburg, VA	06/18/64	Pt. Lookout, MD	07/27/64	Elmira, NY	P113,P117,P120,HAG
					Elmira, NY	10/11/64	Pt. Lookout to Xc	P65,P66
Wightman, William S.	Pvt	F 27th SCVI	Town Creek, NC	02/20/65	Ft. Anderson, NC	02/28/65	Pt. Lookout, MD	CSR,HAG,HOE
					Pt. Lookout, MD	06/20/65	Rlsd. G.O. #109	P115,P118,CSR
Wilbank, E.W.	Pvt	K 12th SCVI	Southside RR, VA	04/03/65	City Pt., VA	04/07/65	Hart's Island, NY	CSR
					Hart's Island, NY	04/19/65	Died, Typhoid fever	P6,P79,CSR
Wilbourn, John	Pvt	H 2nd SCVC	Martinsburg, WV	07/17/63	Wheeling, WV	07/22/63	Camp Chase, OH	P1,CSR
					Camp Chase, OH	02/29/64	Ft. Delaware, DE	P26,CSR
					Ft. Delaware, DE	06/10/65	Rlsd. G.O. #109	P41,P45,CSR
Wilbur, John L.	Pvt	G 2nd SCVC	Upperville, VA	06/21/63	Old Capitol, DC	06/24/63	City Pt., VA Xc	CSR
					Ft. McHenry, MD	06/25/63	City Pt., VA Xc	P110
Wilcox, Richard B.	Pvt	27th SCVI	Deserted/enemy	07/05/64	Jamestown Isl., VA	07/15/64	Fts. Monroe, VA	P8,CSR
					Fts. Monroe, VA	07/15/64	New York, NY oath	CSR
Wilder, Arhur	Pvt	H 26th SCVI	Petersburg, VA	04/02/65	City Pt., VA	04/05/65	Pt. Lookout, MD	CSR
					Pt. Lookout, MD	06/22/65	Rlsd. G.O. #109	P115,P118,P121,CSR
Wilder, Benjamin K.	Pvt	K 25th SCVI	Charleston, SC	09/02/63	Pt. Lookout, MD	11/07/63	Hammond G.H., MD	P121,CTA,HAG
Wilder, Benjamin K.	Pvt	K 25th SCVI	Ft. Fisher, NC	01/15/65	New York, NY	01/30/65	Elmira, NY	CSR
					Elmira, NY	03/16/65	Died, Pneumonia	P6,P12,P65,P66,FPH
Wilder, J.T.	Pvt	A 14th SCVI	Deserted/enemy	12/18/64	City Point, VA	12/20/64	Columbus, OH oath	P8,CSR
Wilder, L.	Pvt	K 25th SCVI	Ft. Fisher, NC	01/15/65	New York, NY	01/30/65	Elmira, NY	CTA,CSR,HAG
					Elmira, NY	04/02/65	Died Intrmitnt fever	P6,P12,P65,P66,FPH
Wilder, Peter E.	Pvt	G 27th SCVI	Petersburg, VA	06/24/64	Fts. Monroe, VA	07/09/64	Died of wounds	P12
Wilder, Samuel T.	Pvt	K 25th SCVI	Morris Island, SC	09/07/63	Ft. Columbus, NY	10/09/63	Johnson's Isl., OH	P1,HAG,CTA
Wilder, Samuel T.	Pvt	K 25th SCVI	Morris Island, SC	09/07/64	Pt. Lookout, MD	11/15/63	Hammond G.H., MD	P113
					Pt. Lookout, MD	03/17/64	City Pt., VA Xc	P116,CSR

W

SOUTH CAROLINA SOLDIERS, SAILORS AND CITIZENS HELD IN U.S. PRISONS 1861-1865

NAME	RANK	REGIMENT	CAPTURED AT	WHEN	PRISON	MOVED	DISPOSITION	SOURCES
Wilds, Samuel Hugh	Maj	21st SCVI	Town Creek, NC	02/20/65	Ft. Anderson, NC	02/28/65	Pt. Lookout, MD	CSR,HAG,LC
					Pt. Lookout, MD	02/28/65	Washington, DC	P115,P120
					Old Capitol, DC	03/24/65	Ft. Delaware, DE	P110
					Ft. Delaware, DE	07/24/65	Rlsd. G.O. #109	P43,P45,P46
Wiles, G.A.	Pvt	F 25th SCVI	Weldon RR, VA	08/21/64	City Pt., VA	08/26/64	Phila., PA USGH	CSR,HAG
					Phila., PA USGH	09/01/64	Died of wounds	P5,P6,P12,FPH,CSR
Wiles, V.P.	Pvt	F 25th SCVI	Ft. Fisher, NC	01/15/65	New York, NY	01/30/65	Elmira, NY	CSR
					Elmira, NY	02/20/65	James R., VA Xc	P65,P66,HAG
Wiles, William	Pvt	F 25th SCVI	Ft. Fisher, NC	01/15/65	New York, NY	01/30/65	Elmira, NY	CSR,HAG
					Elmira, NY	05/11/65	Died acute diarrhea	P6,P12,P65,P66,FPH
Wiley, Jacob S.	Sgt	K 18th SCVI	Petersburg, VA	03/25/65	City Pt., VA	03/28/65	Pt. Lookout, MD	CSR
					Pt. Lookout, MD	06/21/65	Rlsd. G.O. #109	P115,P118,P122,CSR
Wiley, Lewis B.	Pvt	A 15th SCVAB	Farmville, VA	04/06/65	Camp Hamilton, VA	05/03/65	Newport News, VA	CSR
					Newport News, VA	06/26/65	Rlsd. G.O. #109	CSR
Wiley, Thomas	Pvt	F Orr's Ri.	Petersburg, VA	04/03/65	City Pt., VA	04/11/65	Hart's Island, NY	CSR,CDC
					Hart's Island, NY	06/17/65	Rlsd. G.O. #109	P79
Wiley, William	Pvt	K 17th SCVI	South Mtn., MD	09/14/62	Ft. Delaware, DE	10/02/62	Aikens Ldg., VA Xc	CSR
Wilkerson, William	Pvt	B 11th SCVI	Deserted/enemy	03/14/65	Charleston, SC	03/14/65	Released on oath	CSR
Wilkes, Alexander M.	Sgt	E 21st SCVI	Weldon RR, VA	08/21/64	City Pt., VA	08/24/64	Pt. Lookout, MD	CSR,HAG
					Pt. Lookout, MD	09/18/64	Aikens Ldg., VA Xc	P113,P117,P125
Wilkes, Daniel M.	Pvt	E 21st SCVI	Morris Island, SC	07/10/63	Morris Island, SC	07/15/63	Hilton Head, SC	CSR,HAG
					Hilton Head G.H.	07/23/63	Morris Island, SC Xc	P2,CSR
Wilkes, James	Pvt	D 25th SCVI	Weldon RR, VA	08/21/64	City Pt., VA	08/24/64	Pt. Lookout, MD	CSR,HMC,HAG
					Pt. Lookout, MD	03/14/65	Aikens Ldg., VA Xc	P113,P117,P125,CSR
Wilkes, John W. M.	Sgt	F 8th SCVI	Winchester, VA	09/13/64	Harpers Ferry, WV	09/17/64	Camp Chase, OH	CSR,KEB
					Camp Chase, OH	12/19/64	Died, Pneumonia	P12,P23,P27,FPH
Wilkes, Joseph T.	Pvt	D 21st SCVI	Ft. Fisher, NC	01/15/65	New York, NY	01/30/65	Elmira, NY	CSR,HAG
					Elmira, NY	03/02/65	Pt. Lookout, MD Xc	P65,P66,HAG,CSR
Wilkes, L.M.	Pvt	C 26th SCVI	Deserted/enemy	02/25/65	City Pt., VA	02/26/65	Washington, DC	CSR
					Washington, DC	03/01/65	Phila., PA oath	CSR
Wilkes, William F.	Pvt	I 18th SCVI	Petersburg, VA	03/25/65	City Pt., VA	03/27/65	Pt. Lookout, MD	CSR
					Pt. Lookout, MD	06/06/65	Released	P115,P118,CSR
Wilkes, William R.	Pvt	D 1st SCVC	Martinsburg, WV	07/19/63	Wheeling, WV			P1,HHC,CSR
				08/13/63	Camp Chase, OH			P24
Wilkes, William R.	Pvt	D 1st SCVC	Martinsburg, WV		Ft. Delaware, DE	06/10/65	Rlsd. G.O. #109	P41,P42,P45,HHC,CSR
Wilkins, John C.	Pvt	K 5th SCVI	Richmond, VA Hos.	04/03/65	Richmond, VA	04/03/65	Paroled	CSR
Wilkins, Robert	Pvt	D Ham.Leg.MI	Deserted/enemy	09/06/64	Fts. Monroe, VA	09/12/64	Released on oath	CSR
Wilkins, Robert S.	Pvt	F 15th SCVI	Chancellorsville, VA	05/02/63	Alexandria, VA G.H.	06/14/63	Old Capitol, DC	CSR,KEB,H15
					Ft. McHenry, MD	08/23/63	Pt. Lookout, MD	P110
					Pt. Lookout, MD	11/06/63	Hammond G.H., MD	P113,P121
Wilkins, Robert S.	Pvt	F 15th SCVI	Chancellorsville, VA	07/12/63	Pt. Lookout, MD	03/17/64	City Pt., VA Xc	P116,P124,CSR
Wilkins, Robert S.	Pvt	F 15th SCVI	Chancellorsville, VA	05/02/63	Richmond, VA Hos.	03/26/64	Furloughed 30 days	CSR
Wilkins, Robert Y.	Pvt	A Hol.Leg.	Five Forks, VA	04/01/65	City Pt., VA	04/05/65	Pt. Lookout, MD	CSR
					Pt. Lookout, MD	05/21/65	Died, Ch. Diarrhea	P6,P12,P118,FPH
Wilkins, Toliver	Pvt	D 27th SCVI	Ft. Anderson, NC	02/19/65	Pt. Lookout, MD	06/22/65	Rlsd. G.O. #109	P115,P118
Wilkins, William Davis	Sgt	F 15th SCVI	Gettysburg, PA	07/05/63	Gettysburg, PA G.H.	07/20/63	Provost Marshal	P4,KEB,CSR,H15
					David's Island, NY	09/23/63	City Pt., VA Xc	P1,CSR
Wilkinson, James	Pvt	D 25th SCVI	Ft. Fisher, NC	01/15/65	New York, NY	01/30/65	Elmira, NY	CSR,HAG,HMC
					Elmira, NY	07/07/65	Rlsd. G.O. #109	P65,P66
Wilkinson, L.D.	Pvt	I 17th SCVI	Richmond, VA Hos.	04/03/65	Richmond, VA Hos.	06/27/65	Released on oath	CSR
Wilks, H.A.	Pvt	1st SCVC	Martinsburg, WV	07/19/63	Camp Chase, OH	02/29/64	Ft. Delaware, DE	P22,CSR
Willaford, William H.	Pvt	H 12th SCVI	Spotsylvania, VA	05/12/64	Fredericksburg, VA		Hos. 05/21/64	P1,CSR

SOUTH CAROLINA SOLDIERS, SAILORS AND W CITIZENS HELD IN U.S. PRISONS 1861-1865

NAME	RANK	REGIMENT	CAPTURED AT	WHEN	PRISON	MOVED	DISPOSITION	SOURCES
Willard, Christopher Y.	Sgt	A 18th SCVI	Crater, Pbg., VA	07/30/64	City Pt., VA		Portsmouth Gr., RI	CSR
					Portsmouth Grove H	10/20/64	Ft. Columbus, NY	P4,CSR
					Ft. Columbus, NY	12/04/64	Elmira, NY	P2,CSR
					Elmira, NY	07/11/65	Rlsd. G.O. #109	CSR
Willard, Francis M.	Pvt	F 14th SCVI	Cox Rd. Pbg., VA	04/03/65	City Pt., VA	04/07/65	Hart's Island, NY	CSR
					Hart's Island, NY	06/13/65	Rlsd. G.O.#109	P79,CSR
Wille, Herman	Pvt	B German LA	Falling Waters, MD	07/14/63	Old Capitol, DC	12/20/63	Sent North on oath	CSR
Willhalf, Charles H.	Pvt	I 1st SCVA	Bentonville, NC	03/22/65	New Berne, NC	04/10/65	Hart's Island, NY	P79,CSR
					Hart's Island, NY	06/16/65	Rlsd. G.O. #109	P79,CSR
Williaman, V.N.	Pvt	A 3rd SCVABn	Hartwell, GA	05/23/65	Hartwell, GA	05/23/65	Paroled	CSR
Williams, A.C.	Pvt	K 2nd SCVC	Brandy Stn., VA	08/01/63	Old Capitol, DC	11/23/63	Ft. Delaware, DE	CSR
					Ft. Delaware, DE	06/10/65	Rlsd. G.O. #109	P41,P43,CSR
Williams, A.H.	Pvt	B 15th SCVAB	Cheraw, SC	03/06/65	New Berne, NC	04/10/65	Hart's Island, NY	CSR
					Hart's Island, NY	06/16/65	Rlsd. G.O. #109	P79,CSR
Williams, Alexander	Pvt	M P.S.S.	Deserted/enemy	03/05/65	Bermuda Hundred, VA	03/05/65	Washington, DC	CSR,TSE
					Washington, DC	03/08/65	Nashville, TN oath	CSR
Williams, Alexander H.	Pvt	D 21st SCVI	Ft. Fisher, NC	01/15/65	New York, NY	01/30/65	Elmira, NY	HAG,CSR
					Elmira, NY	04/20/65	Died, Ac. Diarrhea	P6,P12,P65,P66,FPH
Williams, Ambrose	Pvt	D 16th SCVI	Citronelle, AL	05/04/65	Columbus, MS	05/16/65	Paroled on oath	CSR
Williams, B.J.	Pvt	D 21st SCVI	Morris Island, SC	07/10/63	Pt. Lookout, MD			P116
Williams, Budd	Pvt	C 1st SCVIR	Bentonville, NC	03/22/65	New Berne, NC	04/10/65	Hart's Island, NY	CSR,SA1
					Hart's Island, NY	06/16/65	Rlsd. G.O. #109	CSR
Williams, C.H.	Pvt	I 3rd SCVC	Grenada, MS	05/22/65	Surrendered			CSR
Williams, C.J.	1Lt	21st SCVI	Ft. Fisher, NC	01/15/65	Ft. Delaware, DE	06/17/65	Rlsd. G.O. #109	P43
Williams, C.M.	Pvt	D 3rd SCVI	Thomasville, NC	05/01/65	Thomasville, NC	05/01/65	Paroled	CSR
Williams, C.T.	Pvt	D 7th SCVIBn	Morris Island, SC	07/10/63	Hilton Head, SC	07/18/63	Hilton Head, SC P.	CSR
Williams, D.M.	Pvt	C 17th SCVI	Appomattox R., VA	04/03/65	City Pt., VA	04/11/65	Hart's Island, NY	CSR
					Hart's Island, NY	06/19/65	Rlsd. G.O. #109	P79,CSR
Williams, D.W.	Pvt	F 5th SCVC	Augusta, GA	05/22/65	Augusta, GA	05/22/65	Paroled	CSR
Williams, David A.	Sgt	H 2nd SCVI	Gettysburg, PA	07/04/63	Gettysburg G.H.	07/21/63	Pro. Mar. New York	P4,KEB,SA2,H2
					David's Island, NY	10/22/63	Fts. Monroe, VA Xc	P1
					David's Island, NY	10/22/63	City Pt., VA Xc	CSR
Williams, David O.	2Lt	A 20th SCVI	Deserted/enemy	08/21/64	Chattanooga, TN	07/01/64	Took oath	P8,KEB,CSR
Williams, E.M.	Pvt	A 3rd SCVABn	High Pt., NC	05/02/65	High Pt., NC	05/02/65	Paroled	CSR
Williams, E.P.	Pvt	17th SCVI	(Not given)	08/16/65	Washington, DC P.M.	08/16/65	Barnwell, SC	CSR
Williams, Evan L.M.	Pvt	I 12th SCVI	Gettysburg, PA	07/05/63	David's Island, NY	09/05/63	City Pt., VA Xc	P1,LAN,CSR
Williams, F.A.	Pvt	Santee LA	Deserted/enemy	03/05/65	Charleston, SC	03/05/65	Released on oath	CSR
Williams, G.B.	Pvt	K 2nd SCVC	Hartwell, GA	05/23/65	Hartwell,GA	05/23/65	Paroled	CSR
Williams, G.W.	Pvt	G 17th SCVI	Deserted/enemy	02/22/65	P.M. 9th A.C. AOP	02/22/65	City Pt., VA P.M.	CSR
					City Pt., VA P.M.	02/23/65	Washington, DC	CSR
					Washington, DC		(No release data)	CSR
Williams, George P.	Pvt	G 17th SCVI	Petersburg, VA	03/25/65	City Pt., VA	03/28/65	Pt. Lookout, MD	CSR
					Pt. Lookout, MD	06/30/65	Rlsd. G.O. #109	P115,P118,CSR
					Pt. Lookout, MD	07/13/65	US Hos. Str. Conn.	CSR
					Hos. Str. Connecticut	07/24/65	Armory Sq. G.H., DC	CSR
					Armory Sq. G.H., DC	08/16/65	Rlsd. on oath	CSR
Williams, Gordon	Cpl	B 15th SCVI	Halltown, VA	08/26/64	Harpers Ferry, WV	08/29/64	Camp Chase, OH	CSR,KEB
					Camp Chase, OH	03/18/65	Pt. Lookout, MD	P22,P26,CSR
					Pt. Lookout, MD	03/27/65	Boulwares Wh., VA	CSR
Williams, Henry D.	Pvt	F 21st SCVI	Petersburg, VA	06/18/64	Bermuda Hundred, VA	06/22/64	Fts. Monroe, VA	CSR,HAG
					Fts. Monroe, VA	06/23/64	Pt. Lookout, MD	CSR
					Pt. Lookout, MD	01/17/65	Aikens Ldg., VA Xc	P113,P123,P124

SOUTH CAROLINA SOLDIERS, SAILORS AND CITIZENS HELD IN U.S. PRISONS 1861-1865

NAME	RANK	REGIMENT	CAPTURED AT	WHEN	PRISON	MOVED	DISPOSITION	SOURCES
Williams, J.	Pvt	B 1st SCVIG	Warrenton, VA	09/29/62	Warrenton, VA	09/29/62	Paroled	CSR
Williams, J.	Pvt	A 1st SCVIG	Petersburg, VA	04/03/65	Hart's Island, NY	06/16/65	Rlsd. G.O. #109	P79
Williams, J. Renwick	Pvt	K 17th SCVI	Farmville, VA	04/07/65	Farmville, VA	04/27/65	Released on oath	CSR
Williams, J.B.	Cpl	L 19th SCVCB	Hartwell, GA	05/18/65	Hartwell, GA	05/18/65	Paroled on oath	CSR
Williams, J.C.	Pvt	E 22nd SCVI	Petersburg, VA	06/17/64	Pt. Lookout, MD	07/27/64	Elmira, NY	P113,LAN
Williams, J.C.	Pvt	A 2nd SCVA	Raleigh, NC Hos.	04/13/63	Took oath	04/20/65		CSR
Williams, J.D.	Pvt	C 1st SCVIH	Warrenton, VA	09/29/62	Warrenton, VA	09/29/62	Paroled	CSR,SA1
Williams, J.D.	Pvt	C 1st SCVIH	Deep Bottom, VA	08/14/64	Bermuda Hundred, VA	08/15/64	Fts. Monroe, VA	CSR
					Fts. Monroe, VA	08/17/64	Pt. Lookout, MD	CSR
					Pt. Lookout, MD	02/10/65	Aikens Ldg., VA Xc	P113,P123,P124
Williams, J.D.	Pvt	C 1st SCVIH	Augusta, GA	05/22/65	Augusta, GA	05/22/65	Paroled	CSR
Williams, J.F.	Pvt	F 1st SCVIH	Charlotte, NC Hos.	05/15/65	Charlotte, NC Hos.	05/15/65	Paroled	SA1,CSR
Williams, J.F.	Pvt	G 1st SCVIG	Petersburg, VA	04/02/65	Hart's Island, NY	06/15/65	Rlsd. G.O. #109	P79
Williams, J.G.	Pvt	I 21st SCVI	Petersburg, VA	06/24/64	Bermuda Hundred, VA	06/25/64	Fts. Monroe, VA	CSR
					Fts. Monroe, VA	06/26/64	Pt. Lookout, MD	CSR
					Pt. Lookout, MD	08/16/64	Elmira, NY	P113,P117,P120
					Elmira, NY	03/14/65	Pt. Lookout, MD Xc	P65,P66
Williams, J.H.	Pvt	G 1st SCVIR	Deserted/enemy	03/20/65	Charleston, SC		Released on oath	CSR
Williams, J.K.	Pvt	B 27th SCVI	Deserted/enemy	06/01/64	Bermuda Hundred, VA	06/06/64	Fts. Monroe, VA	CSR
					Fts. Monroe, VA	06/11/64	New York, NY oath	P8,CSR
Williams, J.L.	Pvt	C 17th SCVI	Petersburg, VA	07/30/64	City Pt., VA	08/05/64	Pt. Lookout, MD	CSR
					Pt. Lookout, MD	08/08/64	Elmira, NY	P113,P120,P125,CSR
					Elmira, NY	07/03/65	Rlsd. G.O. #109	P65,CSR
Williams, J.O.	Pvt	E 22nd SCVI	Spotsylvania, VA	05/12/64	Pt. Lookout, MD	08/10/64	Died	P5,P119,FPH
Williams, J.R.	Pvt	I 20th SCVI	Cedar Creek, VA	10/19/64	Harpers Ferry, WV	10/24/64	Pt. Lookout, MD	CSR
					Pt. Lookout, MD	05/13/65	Rlsd. G.O. #85	CSR
Williams, J.R.	Sgt	F 23rd SCVI	Petersburg, VA Hos.	04/03/65	Fair Gds H. Pbg VA	05/01/65	Died of wounds	P6,ROH,HHC,CSR
Williams, J.R.	Pvt	D 19th SCVCB	Augusta, GA	05/20/65	Augusta, GA	05/20/65	Paroled on oath	CSR
Williams, J.T.	Pvt	G Orr's Ri.	Petersburg, VA	04/02/65	City Pt., VA	04/11/65	Hart's Island, NY	CSR
					Hart's Island, NY	06/15/65	Rlsd. G.O. #109	CSR
Williams, J.W.	Pvt	G 17th SCVI	Deserted/enemy	02/21/65	Washington, DC	02/24/65	Savannah, GA oath	CSR
Williams, Jack	Pvt	K P.S.S.	Deserted/enemy	03/26/65	Bermuda Hundred, VA	03/26/65	Washington, DC	CSR,TSE
					Washington, DC	03/28/65	Phila., PA oath	CSR
Williams, James A.	Pvt	B 13th SCVI	Warrenton, VA	09/29/62	Warrenton, VA	09/29/62	Paroled	HOS,CSR
Williams, James A.	Pvt	B 13th SCVI	Gettysburg, PA	07/05/63	Ft. Delaware, DE	02/09/64	Died, Consumption	P5,P12,P40,P42,FPH
Williams, James Berry	Pvt	D Ham.Leg.	Warrenton, VA	09/29/62	Warrenton, VA	09/29/62	Paroled	CSR
Williams, James F.	Pvt	I 22nd SCVI	Five Forks, VA	04/01/65	City Pt., VA	04/05/65	Pt. Lookout, MD	CSR
					Pt. Lookout, MD	06/22/65	Rlsd. G.O. #109	P115,P121,CSR
Williams, James H.	1Lt	F 14th SCVI	Gettysburg, PA	07/05/63	Letterman G.H. Gbg	09/10/63	Provost Marshal	P1
					W. Bldg. Balt, MD	09/28/63	Johnson's Isl., OH	P1,CSR
					Johnsons Isl., OH	04/22/64	Pt. Lookout, MD	P81
					Pt. Lookout, MD	04/22/64	Hammond, G.H., MD	CSR
					Hammond G.H., MD	04/27/64	City Pt., VA Xc	P116
Williams, James H.	Pvt	D 24th SCVI	Nashville, TN	12/16/64	Nashville, TN	12/31/64	Louisville, KY	CSR,EFW
					Louisville, KY	01/02/65	Camp Douglas, IL	P92,EFW
					Camp Chase, OH	06/12/65	Rlsd. G.O. #109	P23,CSR,EFW
Williams, John	Pvt	G 2nd SCVI	Gettysburg, PA	07/05/63	Baltimore, MD	08/16/63	Pt. Lookout, MD	CSR,KEB,SA2,H2
					Pt. Lookout, MD	12/24/63	City Pt. VA Xc	CSR,P113,P115
Williams, John	Pvt	F 21st SCVI	Petersburg, VA	06/18/64	City Pt., VA	06/24/64	Pt. Lookout, MD	CSR,HOM
					Pt. Lookout, MD	07/27/64	Elmira, NY	P113,P120,CSR
					Elmira, NY	10/11/64	Pt. Lookout, MD Xc	P65,P66,P115
					Pt. Lookout, MD	10/29/64	Aikens Ldg., VA Xc	P66,P115,P117,P123

W

SOUTH CAROLINA SOLDIERS, SAILORS AND CITIZENS HELD IN U.S. PRISONS 1861-1865

NAME	RANK	REGIMENT	CAPTURED AT	WHEN	PRISON	MOVED	DISPOSITION	SOURCES
Williams, John	Pvt	F 21st SCVI	Ft. Fisher, NC	01/15/65	Elmira, NY	07/11/65	Rlsd. G.O. #109	P65,P66
Williams, John	Pvt	B 1st SCVA	Fayetteville, NC	03/15/65	New Berne, NC	04/03/65	Pt. Lookout, MD	CSR,LAN
					Pt. Lookout, MD	06/22/65	Rlsd. G.O. #109	P115,P118,CSR
Williams, John	Sgt	D Hol.Leg.	Five Forks, VA	04/01/65	City Pt., VA	04/05/65	Pt. Lookout, MD	CSR
					Pt. Lookout, MD	06/22/65	Rlsd. G.O. #109	P115,P118,P121,CSR
Williams, John	Pvt	C Hol.Leg.	Petersburg, MD	03/25/65	Lincoln G.H., DC	06/14/65	Rlsd. G.O. #109	CSR,HOS
Williams, John B.	Pvt	E 12th SCVI	Petersburg, VA	04/02/65	City Pt., VA	04/04/65	Pt. Lookout, MD	CSR
					Pt. Lookout, MD	06/21/65	Rlsd. G.O. #109	P115,P118,CSR
Williams, John C.	Pvt	D 27th SCVI	Town Creek, NC	02/20/65	Ft. Anderson, NC	02/28/65	Pt. Lookout, MD	CSR,HAG
					Pt. Lookout, MD	06/17/65	Rlsd. G.O. #109	P115,CSR
Williams, John C.P.	Pvt	K 7th SCVC	Burkeville, VA	04/06/65	City Pt., VA	04/15/65	Pt. Lookout, MD	CSR,HIC
					Pt. Lookout, MD	06/22/65	Rlsd. G.O. #109	P115,P119,P121,CSR
Williams, John D.	Pvt	K 1st SCVIG	Hatchers Run, VA	03/31/65	City Pt., VA	04/02/65	Pt. Lookout, MD	CSR
					Pt. Lookout, MD	06/22/65	Rlsd. G.O. #109	P115,P118,P121,CSR
Williams, John N.	Pvt	4 10/19 SCVI	Missionary Ridge,TN	11/25/63	Nashville, TN	12/07/63	Louisville, KY	P39,CSR,RAS
					Louisville, KY	12/08/63	Rock Island, IL	P88,P89,CSR
					Rock Island, IL	06/18/65	Rlsd. G.O. #109	P131,CSR
Williams, John R.	2Lt	L Orr's Ri.	Richmond, VA Hos.	04/03/65	Richmond, VA P.M.	08/07/65	Released on oath	CSR
Williams, Joseph F.	Pvt	C 3rd SC Eng	Marion, AL	01/01/65	Louisville, KY	01/16/65	Camp Chase, OH	P95
Williams, Lawrence O.	Pvt	K Orr's Ri.	Spotsylvania, VA	05/12/64	Ft. McHenry, MD		Ft. Delaware, DE	P110,CDC,AR
					Old Capitol, DC	05/09/64	Ft. Delaware, DE	CSR
					Ft. Delaware, DE	09/18/64	Aikens Ldg., VA Xc	P41,P43,CSR
Williams, Leroy R.	Sgt	E 17th SCVI	Petersburg, VA	03/25/65	City Pt., VA	03/28/65	Pt. Lookout, MD	CSR,YEB
					Pt. Lookout, MD	06/22/65	Rlsd. G.O. #109	P115,P121,P118,CSR
Williams, Lewis T.	Pvt	H 17th SCVI	Salisbury, NC	04/12/65	Nashville, TN	04/29/65	Louisville, KY	CSR
					Louisville, KY	05/02/65	Camp Chase, OH	P92,P95,CSR
					Camp Chase, OH	06/13/65	Released	P23,CSR
Williams, Luke G.	Pvt	C 19th SCVI	Augusta, GA	05/18/65	Augusta, GA	05/18/65	Paroled	CSR
Williams, M.P.	Pvt	I 22nd SCVI	Kinston, NC	12/14/62	Kinston, NC	12/14/62	Paroled POW	CSR
Williams, M.P.	Pvt	I 22nd SCVI	Bermuda Hundred, VA	06/02/64	Bermuda Hundred, VA	06/03/64	Fts. Monroe, VA	CSR
					Fts. Monroe, VA	06/04/64	Pt. Lookout, MD	CSR
					Pt. Lookout, MD	02/13/65	Aikens Ldg., MD Xc	P113,P121,P124,CSR
Williams, P.L.	Pvt	F 3rd SCVC	South Newport, GA	08/17/64	Hilton Head, SC G.H.	09/07/64	Pt. Royal Fy. Xc	P2,CSR
Williams, Pinckney H.	Pvt	Brooks LA	Gettysburg, PA	07/05/63	Chester, PA USGH	08/17/63	City Pt., VA Xc	CSR
					Williamsburg, VA H	09/09/63	Returned to duty	CSR
Williams, R.F.	Pvt	K 5th SCVI	Deserted/enemy	03/14/65	Bermuda Hundred, VA	03/15/65	City Pt., VA	CSR
					City Pt., VA	03/18/65	Washington, DC	CSR
					Washington, DC	03/18/65	Nashville, TN oath	CSR
Williams, R.H.	Pvt	F 3rd SCVC	South Newport, GA	08/17/64	Philadelphia, PA	01/10/65	Ft. Delaware, DE	CSR
					Ft. Delaware, DE	02/01/65	Hos. 2/1-2/13/65	P47
					Ft. Delaware, DE	04/06/65	Died, Ac. Diarrhea	P6,P12,P43,P47,FPH
Williams, Robert	Pvt	Ham.Leg.MI	Deserted/enemy	09/23/64	Fts. Monroe, VA	09/23/64	Released on oath	CSR
Williams, S.B.	Pvt	C 26th SCVI	Deserted/enemy	01/27/65	City Point, VA	01/29/65	Washington, DC	P8,CSR
					Washington, DC	02/01/65	Phila., PA oath	CSR
Williams, S.L.	Pvt	K 6th SCVI	Burkeville, VA	04/14/65	Burkeville, VA	04/17/65	Paroled	CSR
Williams, Samuel M.	Pvt	D 14th SCVI	Winchester, VA	07/30/63	Winchester, VA G.H.	07/30/63	Paroled	P2,CSR,HOE
Williams, Samuel M.	Pvt	D 14th SCVI	Appomattox R., VA	04/03/65	City Pt., VA	04/11/65	Hart's Island, NY	CSR
					Hart's Island, NY	06/17/65	Rlsd. G.O. #109	P79,CSR
Williams, Samuel R.	Pvt	K Orr's Ri.	Falling Waters, MD	07/14/63	Baltimore, MD	08/20/63	Pt. Lookout, MD	CSR
Williams, Samuel R.	Pvt	K Orr's Ri.	Falling Waters, MD	07/14/64	Pt. Lookout, MD	03/16/64	Exchanged	P113,CSR
Williams, Samuel R.	Pvt	K Orr's Ri.	Petersburg, VA	04/03/65	City Pt., VA	04/11/65	Hart's Island, NY	CSR

SOUTH CAROLINA SOLDIERS, SAILORS AND **W** CITIZENS HELD IN U.S. PRISONS 1861-1865

NAME	RANK	REGIMENT	CAPTURED AT	WHEN	PRISON	MOVED	DISPOSITION	SOURCES
Williams, Samuel W.	Pvt	D 11th SCVI	Town Creek, NC	02/20/65	Ft. Anderson, NC	02/28/65	Pt. Lookout, MD	CSR,HAG
					Pt. Lookout, MD	06/22/65	Rlsd. G.O. #109	P115,P118,P122,CSR
Williams, Seth	Pvt	E 7th SCVC	Burkeville, VA	04/14/65	Burkeville, VA	04/17/65	Paroled	CSR
Williams, T.G.	Cpl	C Orr's Ri.	Petersburg, VA	04/03/65	Harts Island, NY	06/17/65	Rlsd. G.O. #109	P79
Williams, T.H.	Pvt	A 14th SCVI	Gettysburg, PA	07/04/63	Chester, PA G.H.	08/17/63	City Pt., VA Xc	P1,CSR
Williams, T.J.	Pvt	B 22nd SCVI	Boonesboro, MD	09/14/62	Ft. Delaware, DE	10/02/62	Aikens Ldg., VA Xc	CSR
Williams, T.J.	Pvt	B 22nd SCVI	Deserted/enemy	02/23/65	City Pt., VA	02/24/65	Washington, DC	CSR
					Washington, DC	02/24/65	Charleston, SC	CSR
Williams, Thomas	Pvt	B 5th SCVC	Stony Creek, VA	12/01/64	Pt. Lookout, MD	06/21/65	Released	P115,P118
Williams, Thomas J.	Pvt	A 19th SCVI	Franklin, TN	12/17/64	Nashville, TN	01/04/65	Louisville, KY	CSR
					Louisville, KY	01/09/65	Camp Chase, OH	CSR
					Camp Chase, OH	06/13/65	Rlsd. G.O. #109	CSR
Williams, Thomas L.	Pvt	A 1st SCVIR	Savannah, GA	05/03/65	Savannah, GA	05/16/65	Remains in city	CSR
Williams, W.B.	Pvt	E 5th SCVI	Deserted/enemy	04/14/65	Washington, DC	04/21/65	New York, NY oath	CSR
Williams, W.H.	Pvt	G 6th SCVI	Charlotte, NC	05/16/65	Charlotte, NC	05/16/65	Paroled	CSR
Williams, W.W.	Pvt	I 22nd SCVI	Deserted/enemy	02/23/65	P.M. City Pt., VA	02/24/65	Washington, DC	CSR
					Washington, DC	02/24/65	Charleston, SC	CSR
Williams, Wallace T.	Pvt	H 1st SCVIG	Spotsylvania, VA	05/13/64	Ft. Delaware, DE	06/09/64	Died, Lung Inflam.	P5,P12,P43,P47,FPH
Williams, William W.	Sgt	A 1st SCVIG	N. Anna River, VA	05/23/64	Front Royal, VA	05/30/64	Pt. Lookout, MD	CSR,SA1
					Elmira, NY	03/02/65	Pt. Lookout, MD Xc	P65,P66,P113
Williams, Winthrop	SMj	27th SCVI	Weldon RR, VA	08/21/64	City Pt., VA	08/24/64	Pt. Lookout, MD	HAG,CSR
					Pt. Lookout, MD	03/14/65	Aikens Ldg., VA Xc	P113,P121,P125
Williamson, Bright J.	Pvt	L 21st SCVI	Morris Island, SC	07/10/63	Morris Island, SC	07/13/63	Hilton Head, SC	CSR,HAG
					Hilton Head, SC	09/22/63	Ft. Columbus, NY	CSR
					Ft. Columbus, NY	09/23/63	Paroled on oath	P1
					Pt. Lookout, MD	10/15/63	Hammond G.H., MD	P113,P121,P125
Williamson, J.D.	Pvt	B 1st SCVIR	Deserted/enemy	03/06/65	Charleston, SC		Released on oath	CSR
Williamson, J.H.	Pvt	A 3rd SCVABn	High Pt., NC	05/02/65	High Pt., NC	05/02/65	Paroled	CSR
Williamson, James B.	Pvt	2 10/19 SCVI	Missionary Ridge,TN	11/25/63	Nashville, TN	12/07/63	Louisville, KY	P39,RAS,HMC
					Louisville, KY	12/09/63	Rock Island, IL	P88,P89,CSR
					Rock Island, IL	06/21/65	Rlsd. G.O. #109	P131,CSR
Williamson, James R.	Pvt	B 17th SCVI	Petersburg, VA	07/30/64	City Pt., VA	03/28/65	Pt. Lookout, MD	CSR
Williamson, James R.	Pvt	B 17th SCVI	Petersburg, VA	03/25/65	Pt. Lookout, MD	06/22/65	Rlsd. G.O. #109	P115,P118,P121,CSR
Williamson, James W.	Pvt	C 12th SCVI	Gettysburg, PA	07/03/63	David's Island, NY	09/05/63	City Pt., VA Xc	P1,HFC,CSR
					Petersburg, VA G.H.	09/16/63	Furloughed 40 days	CSR
Williamson, James Wilds	Sgt	B 21st SCVI	Ft. Fisher, NC	01/15/65	New York, NY	01/30/65	Elmira, NY	CSR,HAG
					Elmira, NY	03/15/65	Died, Pneumonia	P6,P12,P65,P66,FPH
Williamson, John	Pvt	K 17th SCVI	Petersburg, VA	03/28/65	Ft. McHenry, MD	06/12/65	Rlsd. G.O. #109	P110
Williamson, John P.	Pvt	C 12th SCVI	Amelia C.H., VA	04/05/65	City Pt., VA	04/13/65	Pt. Lookout, MD	CSR
					Pt. Lookout, MD	06/22/65	Rlsd. G.O. #109	P115,P118,P121,CSR
Williamson, Joseph T.	Pvt	F 3rd SCVIBn	Gettysburg, PA	07/05/63	Ft. Delaware, DE	12/11/63	Died, Smallpox	P5,P12,P40,P42,FPH
Williamson, Lucius V.	Pvt	D Hol.Leg.	Petersburg, VA	11/08/64	City Pt., VA	11/11/64	Washington, DC	CSR
Williamson, Lucius V.	Pvt	D Hol.Leg.	Petersburg, VA	11/06/64	Pt. Lookout, MD	01/17/65	Exchanged	P115,P124,CSR
Williamson, Samuel	Pvt	I 22nd SCVI	Leesburg, VA	10/02/62	Prld. in Hospital			CSR
Williamson, Thomas J.	Pvt	A 19th SCVI	Franklin, TN	12/18/64	Nashville, TN	01/04/65	Louisville, KY	P3,P39,CSR,HOE
Williamson, Thomas J.	Pvt	A 19th SCVI	Franklin, TN	12/17/64	Louisville, KY	01/09/65	Camp Chase, OH	P92,P95,CSR
					Camp Chase, OH	06/13/65	Rlsd. G.O. #109	P23,CSR
Williamson, W.	Pvt	17th SCVI	Athens, GA	05/08/65	Athens, GA	05/08/65	Paroled	CSR
Williamson, W.H.	Pvt	C 20th SCVI	Cedar Creek, VA	10/19/64	Harpers Ferry, WV	10/23/64	Pt. Lookout, MD	CSR,KEB
					Pt. Lookout, MD	06/21/65	Rlsd. G.O. #109	P115,P117,CSR

SOUTH CAROLINA SOLDIERS, SAILORS AND **W** CITIZENS HELD IN U.S. PRISONS 1861-1865

NAME	RANK	REGIMENT	CAPTURED AT	WHEN	PRISON	MOVED	DISPOSITION	SOURCES
Williamson, W.W.	Pvt	A 8th SCVI	Winchester, VA	09/13/64	Harpers Ferry, WV	09/19/64	Camp Chase, OH	CSR
					Camp Chase, OH	06/10/65	Rlsd. G.O. #109	P23,CSR
Williamson, Wade	Cpl	C 20th SCVI	Cedar Creek, VA	10/19/64	Harpers Ferry, WV	10/23/64	Pt. Lookout, MD	CSR,KEB
					Pt. Lookout, MD	02/10/65	Aikens Ldg., VA Xc	P115,P123,P124
Williman, R.P.	Pvt	K 2nd SCVC	Hartwell, GA	05/23/65	Hartwell, GA	05/25/65	Paroled	CSR
Willingham, Edward G.	Pvt	C Ham.Leg.C	Albany, GA	05/24/65	Albany, GA	05/24/65	Paroled	CSR
Willingham, W.E.	1Sg	F 12th SCVI	Sharpsburg, MD	09/17/62	David Smith's Farm	09/28/62	Died of wounds	P12,HFC,CSR
Willingham, Walker	Pvt	G Hol.Leg.	Five Forks, VA	04/01/65	City Pt., VA	04/05/65	Pt. Lookout, MD	CSR,ANY
					Pt. Lookout, MD	06/22/65	Rlsd. G.O. #109	P115,P118,CSR
Willis, Abraham W.	Sgt	I 13th SCVI	Petersburg, VA	03/25/65	City Pt., VA	03/28/65	Pt. Lookout, MD	CSR,HOS
					Pt. Lookout, MD	06/22/65	Rlsd. G.O. #109	P115,P118,P121,CSR
Willis, C.A.	Sgt	A 1st SCVIG	Gettysburg, PA	07/03/63	Chester, PA G.H.	09/21/63	City Pt., VA Xc	P1,SA1,CSR
Willis, David	Pvt	E 13th SCVI	Gettysburg, PA	07/05/63	Davids Island, NY	09/05/63	City Pt., VA Xc	P1,HOS,CSR
Willis, David	Pvt	E 13th SCVI	Deserted/enemy	02/24/65	City Pt., VA	02/26/65	Washington, DC	CSR
					Washington, DC	02/27/65	Columbus, OH oath	CSR
Willis, E.	Pvt	B 6th SCResB	Augusta, GA	05/24/65	Augusta, GA	05/24/65	Paroled	CSR
Willis, E.R.	Pvt	H 2nd SCVC	Augusta, GA	05/18/65	Augusta, GA	05/18/65	Paroled	CSR
Willis, Francis M.	Pvt	E 13th SCVI	Gettysburg, PA	07/03/63	Ft. McHenry, MD	07/30/63	Ft. Delaware, DE	CSR,HOS
					Ft. Delaware, DE	06/10/65	Rlsd. G.O. #109	P42,P44,P45,CSR
Willis, G.T.	Pvt	E Ham.Leg.	Chattanooga, TN	10/29/63	Louisville, KY	11/09/63	Camp Morton, IN	P88,P89,CSR
					Camp Morton, IN	11/14/64	Escaped	P100,P101,CSR
Willis, J.W.	Pvt	I 11th SCVI	Bentonville, NC	03/20/65	Newberne, NC	04/10/65	Hart's Island, NY	CSR
					Hart's Island, NY	06/16/65	Rlsd. G.O. #109	P79
Willis, John P.	Pvt	C Hol.Leg.	Kinston, NC	12/15/62	Kinston, NC	12/15/62	Paroled POW	CSR
Willis, John P.	Pvt	C Hol.Leg.	Petersburg, VA	02/01/64	City Pt., VA	02/10/64	Pt. Lookout, MD	CSR,HOS
					Pt. Lookout, MD		No other data	CSR
Willis, Milton H.	Pvt	L 1st SCVIG	Gettysburg, PA	07/05/63	Harrisburg, PA	07/07/63	Philadelphia, PA	CSR
					Philadelphia, PA	07/22/63	Ft. Delaware, DE	CSR,SA1
					Ft. Delaware, DE	09/02/63	Died, Erysipelas	P5,P12,P40,P47,FPH
Willis, Rufus S.	Pvt	A Hol.Leg.	Warrenton, VA	09/29/62	Warrenton, VA	09/29/62	Paroled in Hos.	CSR,HOS
Willis, Thomas	Pvt	E 13th SCVI	Gettysburg, PA	07/05/63	David's Island, NY	09/08/63	City Pt., VA Xc	CSR
					David's Island, NY	09/05/63	Paroled	P1,HOS
Willis, Thomas	Pvt	E 13th SCVI	Deserted/enemy	11/14/64	City Pt., VA	11/23/64	Washington, DC	CSR
Willis, W.P.	Sgt	I Hol.Leg.	Maryland	09/25/62	P.M. Army of Potomac			CSR
Willis, W.P.	Sgt	I Hol.Leg.	Petersburg, VA	04/02/65	City Pt., VA	04/20/65	Ft. Powhattan, VA	CSR
Willis, W.W.	Lt	D 2nd SCVI	Charlotte, NC	05/03/65	Charlotte, NC	05/03/65	Paroled	CSR
Willis, William W.	Pvt	C 7th SCVI	Gettysburg, PA	07/05/63	David's Island, NY	09/12/63	City Pt., VA Xc	P1,KEB,CSR
Willis, William W.	Pvt	C 7th SCVI	Bentonville, NC	03/19/65	Pt. Lookout, MD	06/22/65	Rlsd. G.O. #109	P115,P118,P121,CSR
Willman, Fred.W.	Pvt	B German LA	Franklin, PA	07/27/63	Chambersburg, PA	07/28/63	Harrisburg, PA	CSR
					Harrisburg, PA	07/29/63	Philadelphia, PA	CSR
					Ft. Delaware, DE	09/05/63	Joined U.S. Army	P40,CSR
Willoughby, J.P.	Pvt	C Ham.Leg.MI	Farmville, VA	04/06/65	Newport News, VA	05/07/65	Died	P107,PP
Wilson, Albert	Pvt	H 17th SCVI	Petersburg, VA	03/25/65	City Pt., VA	03/28/65	Pt. Lookout, MD	CSR
					Pt. Lookout, MD	06/21/65	Rlsd. G.O. #109	P115,P118,CSR
Wilson, Andrew O.	Pvt	H 3rd SCVI	Knoxville, TN	12/05/63	Nashville, TN	02/11/64	Louisville, KY	P39,KEB,H3,CSR,SA2
					Louisville, KY	02/15/64	Rock Island, IL	P88,P91,P93,CSR
					Rock Island, IL	02/15/65	Trfd. for exchange	CSR
					Richmond, VA Hos.	03/02/65	Paid sick parolees	CSR
Wilson, Benjamin F.	2Lt	A 7th SCVC	Farmville, VA	04/11/65	Farmville, VA	04/21/65	Paroled	CSR
Wilson, Benjamin T.	Pvt	A 7th SCVC	Richmond, VA Hos.	04/03/65	Libby Prison Rchmd.	04/08/65	City Pt., VA	CSR
Wilson, Benjamin T.	Pvt	A 7th SCVC	Richmond, VA	04/03/65	City Pt., VA	04/14/65	Pt. Lookout, MD	CSR
					Pt. Lookout, MD	06/21/65	Rlsd. G.O. #109	P115,P119,P122,CSR

SOUTH CAROLINA SOLDIERS, SAILORS AND W CITIZENS HELD IN U.S. PRISONS 1861-1865

NAME	RANK	REGIMENT	CAPTURED AT	WHEN	PRISON	MOVED	DISPOSITION	SOURCES
Wilson, Bird	Pvt	H 24th SCVI	Jonesboro, GA	09/02/64	Nashville, TN	10/27/64	Louisville, KY	CSR,EFW,HHC
					Louisville, KY	10/29/64	Camp Douglas, IL	P90,P91,P94,CSR
					Camp Douglas, IL	06/12/65	Rlsd. G.O. #109	CSR
Wilson, Calvin P.	Pvt	E 24th SCVI	Battery Isl., SC	05/21/62	Hilton Head, SC	08/14/62	Ft. Columbus, NY	CSR
					Ft. Columbus, NY	08/23/62	Ft. Delaware, DE	P37,CSR,EFW
					Ft. Delaware, DE	11/02/62	Aikens Ldg., VA Xc	CSR
Wilson, Charles	Pvt	G 13th SCVI	Gettysburg, PA	07/03/63	Ft. Delaware, DE	10/29/63	Died, Ch. Diarrhea	P5,P12,P40,P42,FPH
Wilson, Charles L.	Pvt	H 12th SCVI	Sutherland Stn., VA	04/03/65	City Pt., VA	04/13/65	Pt. Lookout, MD	CSR,YEB
					Pt. Lookout, MD	06/30/65	Rlsd. G.O. #109	P115,P122,CSR
Wilson, Conrad	Pvt	D 12th SCVI	Petersburg, VA	04/02/65	City Pt., VA	04/07/65	Hart's Island, NY	CSR
					Hart's Island, NY	06/15/65	Rlsd. G.O. #109	P79,CSR
Wilson, David	Pvt	B 7th SCVIBn	Weldon RR, VA	08/21/64	City Pt., VA	08/24/64	Alexandria, VA USG	CSR
					Alexandria, VA USGH	08/26/64	Washington, DC G.H.	P1,CSR
					Lincoln G.H., DC	09/19/64	Old Capitol, DC	CSR
					Old Capitol, DC	10/24/64	Elmira, NY	HAG,CSR
					Ft. McHenry, MD	10/24/64	Elmira, NY	P110
					Elmira, NY	12/09/64	Died, Ch. Diarrhea	P5,P12,P65,P66,FPH
Wilson, E.W.	Pvt	D Hol.Leg.	Petersburg, VA	04/03/65	City Pt., VA	04/11/65	Hart's Island, NY	CSR
					Hart's Island, NY	06/17/65	Rlsd. G.O. #109	P79
Wilson, Erving	Pvt	F 21st SCVI	Morris Island, SC	07/10/63	Pt. Lookout, MD			P113,P116
Wilson, Franklin N.	Pvt	C 12th SCVI	Richmond, VA Hos.	04/03/65	Richmond, VA Hos.	05/02/65	Escaped	CSR
Wilson, G.	Pvt	B 8th SCVI	Fayetteville, NC	03/11/65	Pt. Lookout, MD	04/18/65	Died, Lung Inflam.	P6,P12,P119,FPH
Wilson, G.B	Pvt	H 2nd SCVI	Sharpsburg, MD	09/17/62	Ft. McHenry, MD	10/18/62	Aikens Ldg., VA Xc	SA2,H2,CSR,KEB
Wilson, G.J.	Pvt	G 18th SCVI	Petersburg, VA	04/03/65	City Pt., VA	04/11/63	Hart's Island, NY	CSR
					Hart's Island, NY	06/17/65	Rlsd. G.O. #109	P79,CSR
Wilson, George A.	Pvt	B 37th VAVCB	Greenbrier, VA	10/08/63	Wheeling, WV	10/23/63	Camp Chase, OH	CSR,37V
					Camp Chase, OH	01/22/64	Rock Island, IL	CSR
					Rock Island, IL	10/13/64	Joined US Army	CSR
Wilson, George W.	Pvt	C 15th SCVAB	Morris Island, SC	09/07/63	Ft. Columbus, NY	10/09/63	Pt. Lookout, MD	P1,CSR
					Pt. Lookout, MD	12/12/63	Escaped	P116,CSR
Wilson, George W.	Pvt	F 17th SCVI	Five Forks, VA	04/02/65	City Pt., VA	04/05/65	Pt. Lookout, MD	CSR,YEB
					Pt. Lookout, MD	06/22/65	Rlsd. G.O. #109	P115,P118,P121,CSR
Wilson, H. Carter	Pvt	F 20th SCVI	Cedar Creek, VA	10/19/64	Harpers Ferry, WV	10/24/64	Pt. Lookout, MD	KEB,CSR
					Pt. Lookout, MD	01/17/65	Aikens Ldg., VA Xc	P115,P123,P124,CSR
Wilson, H.A.	Pvt	H 20th SCVI	Deserted/enemy	02/18/65	Charleston, SC	03/01/65	Released on oath	CSR
Wilson, Harvey	2Lt	H 21st SCVI	Ft. Fisher, NC	01/15/65	Ft. Columbus, NY	03/01/65	City Pt., VA Xc	P2,HAG,CSR
Wilson, Henry G.	Pvt	I 17th SCVI	Petersburg, VA	03/25/65	City Pt., VA	03/28/65	Pt. Lookout, MD	CSR,LAN
					Pt. Lookout, MD	06/22/65	Rlsd. G.O. #109	P115,P118,P121,CSR
Wilson, J.	Pvt	A 3rd SCVABn	High Pt., NC	05/02/65	High Pt., NC	05/02/65	Paroled	CSR
Wilson, J.D.	Sgt	F 8th SCVI	Gettysburg, PA	07/03/63	Gettysburg, PA G.H.	10/14/63	Provost Marshal	P4,KEB,CSR
					W. Bldg. Balt, MD	11/12/63	City Pt., VA Xc	P1,CSR
Wilson, J.E.	Pvt	I 1st SCVIR	Goldsboro, NC	03/22/65	New Berne, NC	04/10/65	Hart's Island, NY	CSR,SA1
					Hart's Island, NY	06/16/65	Rlsd. G.O. #109	CSR
Wilson, J.M.	Pvt	H 1st SCVA	Smith Farm, NC	03/16/65	New Berne, NC	04/10/65	Hart's Island, NY	CSR
					Hart's Island, NY	06/16/65	Rlsd. G.O. #109	P79,CSR
Wilson, J.N.	Pvt	C 3rd SCVIBn	South Mtn., MD	09/14/62	Frederick, MD	11/24/62	Ft. McHenry, MD	CSR
					Ft. McHenry, MD	12/04/62	City Pt., VA Xc	CSR
Wilson, J.N.	Pvt	C 3rd SCVIBn	N. Anna River, VA	05/22/64	Pt. Lookout, MD	06/05/65	Released	P113,CSR
Wilson, J.W.	Pvt	C 12th SCVI	Sutherland Stn., VA	04/02/65	City Pt., VA	04/07/65	Hart's Island, NY	CSR
					Hart's Island, NY	06/16/65	Rlsd. G.O. #109	P79,CSR

SOUTH CAROLINA SOLDIERS, SAILORS AND **W** CITIZENS HELD IN U.S. PRISONS 1861-1865

NAME	RANK	REGIMENT	CAPTURED AT	WHEN	PRISON	MOVED	DISPOSITION	SOURCES
Wilson, James B.	Sgt	K Hol.Leg.	Stony Creek, VA	05/07/64	Fts. Monroe, VA	05/13/64	Pt. Lookout, MD	CSR
					Pt. Lookout, MD	08/15/64	Elmira, NY	P113,P116,P120,CSR
					Elmira, NY	01/23/65	Died, Ch. Diarrhea	P6,P12,P65,FPH,CSR
Wilson, James C.	Pvt	B 1st SCVIG	Hanover Jctn., VA	05/24/64	Front Royal, VA	05/30/64	Pt. Lookout, MD	CSR,SA1
					Pt. Lookout, MD	08/08/64	Elmira, NY	P113,P117,SA1
					Aikens Ldg., VA Xc	09/07/64	Xc 9/21/64	CSR
					Elmira, NY	05/29/65	Took oath	CSR
Wilson, James C.	Pvt	C 24th SCVI	Nashville, TN	12/16/64	Nashville, TN	12/31/64	Louisville, KY	CSR
					Louisville, KY	01/02/65	Camp Chase, OH	CSR
					Camp Chase, OH	01/28/65	Died, Pneumonia	P6,P12,P23,P27,FPH
Wilson, James F.	Pvt	D 18th SCVI	South Mtn., MD	09/10/62	Ft. Delaware, DE	10/02/62	Aikens Ldg., VA Xc	CSR
Wilson, James J.	Pvt	K 12th SCVI	Warrenton, VA	09/29/62	Warrenton, VA	09/29/62	Paroled	CSR
Wilson, James J.	Pvt	K 12th SCVI	Charlotte, NC	05/16/65	Charlotte, NC	05/16/65	Paroled	CSR
Wilson, James L.	Pvt	B 37th VAVCB	Winchester, VA	09/13/64	Harpers Ferry, WV	09/19/64	Camp Chase, OH	CSR,37V
					Camp Chase, OH	06/11/65	Released	P23,CSR
Wilson, James R.	Pvt	E 17th SCVI	Petersburg, VA	03/25/65	City Pt., VA	03/28/65	Pt. Lookout, MD	CSR
					Pt. Lookout, MD	06/22/65	Rlsd. G.O. #109	P115,P118,P121,CSR
Wilson, John	Pvt	K 1st SCVIG	Falling Waters, MD	07/14/63	Old Capital, DC	12/13/63	New York, NY oath	P7,SA1,CSR
					Ft. McHenry, MD	12/13/63	Released on oath	P110
Wilson, John	Pvt	C 7th SCVIBn	Weldon RR, VA	08/21/64	City Pt., VA USFH	08/23/64	Washington, DC USG	CSR,HAG
					Lincoln G.H., DC	03/28/65	Old Capitol, DC	CSR
					Old Capitol, DC	05/01/65	Elmira, NY	CSR
					Ft. McHenry, MD	05/01/65	Elmira, NY	P110
					Elmira, NY	07/11/65	Rlsd. G.O. #109	P66,CSR
Wilson, John	Pvt	E 1st SCVA	Deserted/enemy	03/01/65	Charleston, SC	03/01/65	Hilton Head, SC	CSR
					Hilton Head, SC	04/04/65	New York, NY oath	CSR
Wilson, John B.	Sgt	H 1st SCVIG	Gettysburg, PA	07/03/63	David's Island, NY	09/05/63	City Pt., VA Xc	P1,SA1,CSR
Wilson, John B.	Sgt	H 1st SCVIG	Petersburg, VA	04/06/65	City Pt., VA	04/14/65	Pt. Lookout, MD	CSR
					Pt. Lookout, MD	06/22/65	Rlsd. G.O. #109	P115,P119,P121,CSR
Wilson, John C.	Pvt	C 1st SCVA	Deserted/enemy	02/25/65	Charleston, SC	03/02/65	Released on oath	CSR
Wilson, John D.	Pvt	G 22nd SCVI	Deserted/enemy	12/20/64	City Point, VA	12/23/64	Washington, DC	P8,CSR
					Washington, DC	12/27/64	Indianapolis, IN	CSR
Wilson, John H.	Sgt	G 14th SCVI	Gettysburg, PA	07/05/63	Ft. McHenry, MD	07/07/63	Ft. Delaware, DE	CSR
					Ft. Delaware, DE	03/13/64	Hos. 3/13-4/11/64	P47
					Ft. Delaware, DE	09/13/64	Hos. 9/13-9/21/64	P47
					Ft. Delaware, DE	12/28/64	Hos.12/28/64-1/12/65	P47
					Ft. Delaware, DE	03/18/65	Died, Lung Inflam.	P6,P12,P40,P42,FPH
Wilson, Joseph C.	Pvt	C Ham.Leg.MI	Richmond, VA Hos.	04/03/65	Richmond, VA	04/18/65	Paroled	CSR
Wilson, Joseph S.	Pvt	K 7th SCVC	Farmville, VA	04/06/65	City Pt., VA	04/15/65	Pt. Lookout, MD	CSR
					Pt. Lookout, MD	06/22/65	Rlsd. G.O. #109	P115,P119,P122,CSR
Wilson, Judge	Pvt	G 3rd SCVABn	High Pt., NC	05/01/65	High Pt., NC	05/01/65	Paroled	CSR
Wilson, M.G.	Pvt	C 22nd SCVI	Crater, Pbg., VA	07/30/64	City Pt., VA	04/05/64	Pt. Lookout, MD	CSR
					Pt. Lookout, MD	08/08/64	Elmira, NY	P113,P117,CSR
					Elmira, NY	10/11/64	Venus Pt., GA Xc	CSR
Wilson, M.W. Nathaniel	Pvt	D 12th SCVI	Wilderness, VA	05/06/64	Belle Plain, VA	05/20/64	Ft. Delaware, DE	CSR
					Ft. Delaware, DE	01/07/65	Hos. 1/7-2/27/65	P47
					Ft. Delaware, DE	02/27/65	City Pt., VA Xc	P41,P43,CSR
Wilson, Malachi H.	Pvt	C Orr's Ri.	Falling Waters, MD	07/14/63	Baltimore, MD	08/17/63	Pt. Lookout, MD	CSR,CDC
					Pt. Lookout, MD	02/24/65	Aikens Ldg., VA Xc	P113,P116,P124,CSR
Wilson, Peter	Pvt	PeeDee LA	Gettysburg, PA	07/04/63	Ft. Delaware, DE	10/18/63	Pt. Lookout, MD	CSR
					Pt. Lookout, MD	05/02/64	Exchanged	CSR
Wilson, Robert	Pvt	G 15th SCVI	Hartwell, GA	05/23/65	Hartwell, GA	05/23/65	Paroled on oath	H15

W

SOUTH CAROLINA SOLDIERS, SAILORS AND  CITIZENS HELD IN U.S. PRISONS 1861-1865

NAME	RANK	REGIMENT	CAPTURED AT	WHEN	PRISON	MOVED	DISPOSITION	SOURCES
Wilson, S.B.	Pvt	Wash'n. LA	Chattanooga, TN	09/12/63	Louisville, KY	09/27/63	Took oath	P88
Wilson, T.J.	Cpl	A 3rd SCVI	Cedar Creek, VA	10/19/64	Harpers Ferry, WV	10/24/64		SA2,KEB,CSR,H3
					Pt. Lookout, MD	06/04/65	Rlsd. Instr. 5/30/6	P115,P122,CSR
Wilson, Thomas J.	Pvt	C 3rd SCVIBn	N. Anna River, VA	05/22/64	Port Royal, VA	05/30/64	Pt. Lookout, MD	CSR
Wilson, Thomas J.	Cpl	H 19th SCVI	Columbia, TN	12/18/64	Nashville, TN	01/03/65	Louisville, KY	P39,CSR
					Louisville, KY	01/09/65	Camp Chase, OH	P92,P95,CSR
					Camp Chase, OH	06/12/65	Rlsd. G.O. #109	P23,CSR
Wilson, W.C.	Pvt	H 4th SCVC	Richmond, VA Hos.	04/03/65	Richmond, VA Hos.	05/09/65	Pt. Lookout, MD	CSR
					Hammond G.H., MD	07/23/65	USH. Stm Connecticut	CSR
					USH Stmr. Connecticut	07/24/65	Armory Sq. G.H., DC	CSR
					Armory Sq. G.H., D	08/17/65	Douglas G.H., DC	CSR
					Douglas G.H., DC	11/02/65	Harwood G.H., DC	CSR
					Harwood G.H., DC	01/16/66	Home to Lancaster	CSR
Wilson, W.G.	1Lt	H 11th SCVI	Town Creek, NC	02/20/65	Ft. Anderson, NC	02/28/64	Pt. Lookout, MD	CSR,HAG
					Pt. Lookout, MD	02/28/65	Washington, DC	P115,P120,CSR
					Old Capitol, DC	03/24/65	Ft. Delaware, DE	P110,CSR
					Ft. Delaware, DE	06/17/65	Rlsd. G.O. #109	P43,P45,CSR
Wilson, W.H.	Pvt	H 24th SCVI	Egypt Stn., MS	12/28/64	Memphis, TN	01/17/65	Alton, IL	CSR,EFW
					Alton, IL	02/21/65	Pt. Lookout, MD Xc	P13,P14,CSR
					Richmond, VA Hos.	03/06/65	No further Disp.	CSR
Wilson, William	Pvt	C 1st SCVIG	Wilderness, VA	05/06/64	Belle Plain, VA	05/21/64	Ft. Delaware, DE	CSR,SA1
					Ft. Delaware, DE	01/26/65	Hos. 1/26-1/31/65	P47
					Ft. Delaware, DE	03/11/65	Hos. 3/11-3/15/65	P47
					Ft. Delaware, DE	06/09/65	Released	P41,P43,P45,CSR
Wilson, William C.	Pvt	K 21st SCVI	Drury's Bluff, VA	05/16/64	Pt. Lookout, MD	08/15/64	Elmira, NY	P113,P117,HAG
					Elmira, NY	03/14/65	Pt. Lookout., MD	P66
					Elmira, NY	03/24/65	Died, Interm. fever	P6,P12,P65,FPH
Wilson, William E.	Pvt	C 22nd SCVI	Kinston, NC	12/15/62	Kinston, NC	12/15/62	Paroled POW	CSR,HOS
Wilson, William E.	Pvt	C 22nd SCVI	Crater, Pbg., VA	07/30/64	City Pt., VA	08/05/64	Pt. Lookout, MD	CSR
					Pt. Lookout, MD	08/08/64	Elmira, NY	P120
					Elmira, NY	10/11/64	Pt. Lookout, MD Xc	P65,P66
					W. Bldg. Balt, MD	11/12/64	Died, Ch. Diarrhea	P3,P5,P12,FPH,HOS
Wilson, William E.	Pvt	I 17th SCVI	Petersburg, VA	03/25/65	City Pt., VA	03/27/65	Pt. Lookout, MD	CSR,LAN
					Pt. Lookout, MD	06/22/65	Rlsd. G.O. #109	P115,P118,P121,CSR
Wilson, William H.	Pvt	K 23rd SCVI	Hatchers Run, VA	04/01/65	City Pt., VA	04/05/65	Pt. Lookout, MD	CSR
					Pt. Lookout, MD	06/21/65	Rlsd. G.O. #109	P115,P118,CSR
Windham, Calvin M.	Pvt	A 14th SCVI	Boonesboro, MD	09/15/62	Ft. Delaware, DE	10/06/62	Aikens Ldg., VA Xc	CSR,DEB
Windham, Calvin M.	Pvt	A 14th SCVI	Hatchers Run, VA	03/31/65	Pt. Lookout, MD	06/22/65	Rlsd. G.O. #109	P115,P118
Windham, Flinn M.	Pvt	I 25th SCVI	Ft. Fisher, NC	01/15/65	New York, NY	01/30/65	Elmira, NY	CSR,HAG
					Elmira, NY	07/11/65	Rlsd. G.O. #109	P65,P66,CSR
Windham, John	Pvt	K 25th SCVI	Ft. Fisher, NC	01/15/65	New York, NY	01/30/65	Elmira, NY	CSR,HAG
					Elmira, NY	02/20/65	James R., VA Xc	P65,P66,CSR
Windham, John M.	Pvt	E 5th SCVC	Deserted/enemy	03/31/65	Charleston, SC	03/31/65	Released on oath	CSR
Windham, S.L.	Pvt	K 23rd SCVI	South Mtn., MD	09/14/62	Baltimore, MD Hos.	10/03/62	Fts. Monroe, VA	CSR
					Fts. Monroe, VA	11/05/62	Aikens Ldg., VA Xc	CSR
Windham, W.J.	Pvt	K 21st SCVI	Ft. Fisher, NC	01/15/65	Pt. Lookout, MD	02/02/65	Hammond G.H., MD	P115,P118,P121,HAG
					Pt. Lookout, MD	06/04/65	Rlsd. Instr. 5/30/65	P121,P122
Wineburg, Andrew	Pvt	Ferguson's LA	Ringgold, GA	11/26/63	Nashville, TN	12/09/63	Louisville, KY	P39,CSR
					Louisville, KY	12/11/63	Rock Island, IL	P88,CSR
					Rock Island, IL	04/21/64	Jd. US Navy / Rjctd.	P131,CSR
Winfrey, J.L.	Pvt	F 14th SCVI	Petersburg, VA	04/03/65	Hart's Island, NY	06/21/65	Rlsd. G.O. #109	P79

SOUTH CAROLINA SOLDIERS, SAILORS AND  CITIZENS HELD IN U.S. PRISONS 1861-1865

NAME	RANK	REGIMENT	CAPTURED AT	WHEN	PRISON	MOVED	DISPOSITION	SOURCES
Wingard, Henry S.	Pvt	E 3rd SCVI	Loudon, TN	12/03/63	Chattanooga G.H.			P1,KEB,SA2,H3
					Nashville, TN U.S.	04/27/64	Louisville, KY	P2,P39,CSR
					Louisville, KY	05/12/64	Camp Morton, IN	P91,P93,CSR
					Camp Morton, IN	02/26/65	City Pt., VA Xc	P100,CSR
					Camp Morton, IN	05/23/65	Rlsd. G.O. #85	P101
Wingard, Job F.	Pvt	F 5th SCVC	Louisa C.H., VA	06/11/64	Fts. Monroe, VA	06/20/64	Pt. Lookout, MD	CSR
					Pt. Lookout, MD	07/25/64	Elmira, NY	P113,P117,P120,CSR
					Elmira, NY	03/10/65	James R., VA Xc	P65,P66,CSR
Wingard, Thomas J.	Pvt	K 20th SCVI	Cedar Creek, VA	10/19/64	W. Bldg. Balt, MD		Ft. McHenry, MD	CSR,KEB
					Ft. McHenry, MD	04/06/65	James R., VA Xc	CSR
Wingate, T.	Pvt	Waccamaw A	Deserted/enemy	07/21/62				CSR
Wingo, Andrew J.	Cpl	C 13th SCVI	Southside RR, VA	04/02/65	City Pt., VA	04/07/65	Hart's Island, NY	CSR,HOS
					Hart's Island, NY	06/16/65	Rlsd. G.O. #109	P79,HOS,CSR
Wingo, G.W.	Pvt	C 13th SCVI	Gettysburg, PA	07/03/63	Ft. Delaware, DE	09/02/63	Died, Kidney Infect	P5,P12,P42,FPH,CSR
Wingo, Ransom F.	Pvt	C 13th SCVI	Falling Waters, MD	07/14/63	Pt. Lookout, MD	01/25/64	Joined U.S. Army	P113,P116,P125,CSR
Wingo, Ransom F.	Pvt	C 13th SCVI	Hatchers Run, VA	04/02/65	Ft. Monroe, VA	05/03/65	Died of wound	P12,CSR
Wingo, Robert	Cpl	C 13th SCVI	Southside RR, VA	04/02/65	City Pt., VA	04/07/65	Hart's Island, NY	CSR
					Hart's Island, NY	06/16/65	Rlsd. G.O. #109	CSR
Winn, Allison	Pvt	G 3rd SCVC	Society Hill, SC	03/02/65	New Berne, NC	03/26/65	Pt. Lookout, MD	CSR
					Pt. Lookout, MD	06/22/65	Rlsd. G.O. #109	CSR
Winn, Barney B.	Pvt	E 11th SCVI	Petersburg, VA	06/16/64	Bermuda Hundred, VA	06/17/64	Fts. Monroe, VA	CSR
					Fts. Monroe, VA	06/18/64	Pt. Lookout, MD	CSR
					Pt. Lookout, MD	07/25/64	Elmira, NY	P113,P120,CSR
					Elmira, NY	05/29/65	Rlsd. G.O. #85	P65,CSR
Winn, C.	Pvt	A 3rd SCVABn	High Pt., NC	05/02/65	High Pt., NC	05/02/65	Paroled	CSR
Winn, Charles w.	Sgt	I 2nd SCVC	Augusta, GA	05/19/65	Augusta, GA	05/19/65	Paroled	CSR
Winn, Edward Frank	Pvt	C 11th SCVI	Town Creek, NC	02/20/65	Ft. Anderson, NC	02/28/65	Pt. Lookout, MD	CSR
					Pt. Lookout, MD	06/09/65	Rlsd. G.O. #109	P118,CSR
Winn, George W.	Pvt	B 17th SCVI	Crater, Pbg., VA	07/30/64	Pt. Lookout, MD	08/08/64	Elmira, NY	P117
Winn, George W.	Pvt	B 17th SCVI	Five Forks, VA	04/01/65	City Pt., VA	04/06/65	Pt. Lookout, MD	CSR
					Pt. Lookout, MD	06/24/65	Rlsd. G.O. #109	P115,CSR
Winn, H.	Pvt	D 1st SCVC	Newton, VA	05/24/64	White House, VA	06/08/64	Pt. Lookout, MD	CSR
					Pt. Lookout, MD	07/09/64	Elmira, NY	P113,P117,P120,CSR
					Elmira, NY	09/29/64	Died, Diarhea	P5,P65,P66,FPH,CSR
Winn, R.C.	Pvt	E 11th SCVI	Petersburg, VA	06/16/64	Bermuda Hundred, VA	06/17/64	Fts. Monroe, VA	CSR,HAG
					Fts. Monroe, VA	06/18/64	Pt. Lookout, MD	CSR
					Pt. Lookout, MD	07/25/64	Elmira, NY	P113,P117,P120,CSR
					Elmira, NY	05/29/65	Rlsd. G.O. #85	P65,P66,CSR
Winn, William F.	Pvt	8th SCResB	Deserted/enemy	03/28/65	Charleston, SC	03/28/65	Released on oath	CSR
Winn, William T.	Pvt	C 11th SCVI	Deserted/enemy	03/21/65	Charleston, SC	03/21/65	Taken oath & disch.	CSR
Winningham, Daniel Y.	Pvt	C 11th SCVI	Town Creek, NC	02/20/65	Ft. Anderson, NC	02/28/65	Pt. Lookout, MD	CSR,HAG
					Pt. Lookout, MD	06/21/65	Rlsd. G.O. #109	P118,CSR
Winningham, J.W.	Cpl	B Wash'n LA	Raleigh, NC	04/13/65	Raleigh, NC Hos.	05/05/65	Paroled	CSR
Winston, D.C.	Pvt	E 15th SCVAB	Charleston, SC	07/10/63	Pt. Lookout, MD	11/07/63	Hammond G.H., MD	P121
Winters, James H.	Cpl	G 2nd SCVIRi	Amelia C.H., VA	04/05/65	City Pt., VA	04/13/65	Pt. Lookout, MD	CSR
					Pt. Lookout, MD	06/22/65	Rlsd. G.O. #109	P115,P119,P121,CSR
Winters, John G.	Pvt	A 2nd SCVC	Whitehall, NC	03/18/65	New Berne, NC	03/20/65	Pt. Lookout, MD	CSR
					Pt. Lookout, MD	06/21/65	Rlsd. G.O. #109	P118,CSR
Wireighy, Philip	Pvt	C 20th SCVI	Winchester, VA	05/03/65	Winchester, VA	05/03/65	Paroled	CSR
Wise, A.J.	Pvt	B 1st SCVIH	Warrenton, VA	09/29/62	Warrenton, VA	09/29/62	Paroled	CSR
Wise, Adam S.	Sgt	M 7th SCVI	Gettysburg, PA	07/05/63	Gettysburg G.H.		Provost Marshal	P4
					David's Island, NY	09/05/63	City Pt., VA Xc	P1,CSR

SOUTH CAROLINA SOLDIERS, SAILORS AND W CITIZENS HELD IN U.S. PRISONS 1861-1865

NAME	RANK	REGIMENT	CAPTURED AT	WHEN	PRISON	MOVED	DISPOSITION	SOURCES
Wise, Evander C.	Pvt	E 23rd SCVI	Hatchers Run, VA	04/02/65	City Pt., VA	04/06/65	Pt. Lookout, MD	CSRHMC
					Pt. Lookout, MD	06/22/65	Rlsd. G.O. #109	P115,P118,P122,CSR
Wise, J.	Pvt	F 5TH SCVC	Augusta, GA	05/22/65	Augusta, GA	05/22/65	Paroled	CSR
Wise, James F.	Pvt	H 20th SCVI	Cedar Creek, VA	10/19/64	Pt. Lookout, MD	10/30/64	Aikens Ldg., VA Xc	P115,P117,KEB,CSR
					W. Bldg. Balt., MD	02/16/65	Ft. McHenry, MD	P3,CSR
Wise, Thomas H.	Pvt	H 27th SCVI	Pt. Walthal Jctn.	05/07/64	Bermuda Hundred, VA	05/08/64	Fts. Monroe, VA	CSR
					Fts. Monroe, VA	05/13/64	Pt. Lookout, MD	CSR
					Pt. Lookout, MD	05/27/64	Joined U.S. Army	P113,P116,P125,CSR
Wise, Wade W.	2Lt	F 25th SCVI	Ft. Fisher, NC	01/15/65	Ft. Columbus, NY	03/01/65	City Pt., VA Xc	P2,HAG,CSR
Wise, William H.	2Lt	F 23rd SCVI	Dinwiddie C.H., VA	04/01/65	Old Capitol, DC		Johnson's Isl., OH	CSR,HHC
					Johnson's Isl., OH	06/20/65	Rlsd. G.O. #109	P81,P82,P83,CSR
Wiseman, James M.	Pvt	9 10/19 SCVI	Missionary Ridge,TN	11/25/63	Nashville, TN	12/07/63	Louisville, KY	P39,CSR
					Louisville, KY	12/09/63	Rock Island, IL	P88,P89,CSR
					Rock Island, IL	02/03/64	Died, Variola	P5,P12,P131,FPH
Wisenhart, J.B.	Cpl	B 12th SCVI	Petersburg, VA	04/03/65	Hart's Island, NY	06/16/65	Rlsd. G.O. #109	P79
Wisher, Joseph A.	Pvt	C 17th SCVI	Crater, Pbg., VA	07/30/64	City Pt., VA	08/05/64	Pt. Lookout, MD	CSR,YEB
					Pt. Lookout, MD	08/08/64	Elmira, NY	CSR
					Elmira, NY	05/19/65	Died, Pneumonia	P6,P12,P65,FPH,CSR
Wisner, Adam	Pvt	A 2nd SCVC	Fairfax C.H., VA	05/12/65	Fairfax C.H., VA	05/12/65	Paroled	CSR
Withers, Harrison H.	Pvt	C 14th SCVI	Spotsylvania, VA	05/13/64	Belle Plain, VA	05/20/64	Ft. Delaware, DE	CSR
					Ft. Delaware, DE	06/10/65	Released	CSR
Withers, Lawrence L.	Pvt	C 17th SCVI	Ft. Stedman, VA	03/25/65	City Pt., VA	04/09/65	Washington, DC G.H.	CSR
					Lincoln G.H., DC	05/01/65	Old Capitol, DC	CSR
					Ft. McHenry, MD	05/11/65	Elmira, NY	P110
					Old Capitol, DC	05/14/65	Elmira, NY	CSR
					Elmira, NY	07/11/65	Rlsd. G.O. #109	P66,CSR
Withers, Richard J.	Cpl	F 17th SCVI	Petersburg, VA	03/25/65	City Pt., VA	03/28/65	Pt. Lookout, MD	CSR,YEB
					Washington, DC	06/21/65	Philadelphia, PA	CSR
					Pt. Lookout, MD	06/21/65	Rlsd. G.O. #109	P115,P118,P122,CSR
Withers, Tobias R.	Pvt	D 27th SCVI	Ft. Anderson, NC	02/19/65	Ft. Anderson, NC	02/28/65	Pt. Lookout, MD	CSR,HAG
					Pt. Lookout, MD	06/22/65	Rlsd. G.O. #109	P121,CSR
Witherspoon, Bartlett J.	Cpt	C 1st SCVIR	Charlotte, NC	05/03/65	Paroled			SA1,CSR
Witherspoon, Charles L.	Pvt	C Ham.Leg.	Richmond area	06/08/62	Fts. Monroe, VA G.H.	07/15/62	Ft. Delaware, DE	CSR
Wittkowski, A.	Pvt	C 6th SCVI	Williamsburg, VA	05/05/62	Cliffbourne GH, DC	08/26/62	Old Capitol, DC	CSR
					Str. *Junata Aiken*	09/01/62	Paroled to Xc	CSR
					Richmond, VA Hos.	09/22/62	Furloughed 40 days	CSR
Wix, J.T.	Pvt	A 5th SCVI	Deserted/enemy	10/26/64	City Pt., VA	11/01/64	Fts. Monroe, VA	CSR
					Fts. Monroe, VA	11/14/64	Chicago, IL oath	CSR
Wofford, Isaac	Pvt	B 1st SCVA	Fayetteville, NC	03/16/65	New Berne, NC	03/30/65	Pt. Lookout, MD	CSR
					Pt. Lookout, MD	06/22/65	Rlsd. G.O. #109	P115,P118,P121,CSR
Wofford, Joseph W.	Pvt	E 18th SCVI	Petersburg, VA	04/03/65	City Pt., VA	04/13/65	Pt. Lookout, MD	CSR
					Pt. Lookout, MD	05/25/65	Died, Diarrhea	P6,P115,P118,FPH
Wofford, Thomas C.	Pvt	F 13th SCVI	Gettysburg, PA	07/03/63	Chester, PA USGH	09/30/63	Pt. Lookout, MD	HOS,CSR
Wofford, Thomas C.	Pvt	F 13th SCVI	Gettysburg, PA	07/05/63	Hammond G.H., MD	10/04/63	Pt. Lookout, MD	P116,CSR
					Pt. Lookout, MD	11/07/63	Hammond G.H., MD	P121
Wofford, Thomas C.	Pvt	F 13th SCVI	Gettysburg, PA	07/04/63	Pt. Lookout, MD	03/17/64	City Pt., VA Xc	P116,P124,CSR
Wofford, Thomas C.	Pvt	F 13th SCVI	Petersburg, VA	07/29/64	Elmira, NY	03/17/65	Died, Pneumonia	P6,P12,FPH,CSR
Wolf, Lewis	Pvt	F 15th SCMil	Chesterfield, SC	02/28/65	Pt. Lookout, MD			P115
Wolfe, C.O.	Pvt	7th SCVC	Charleston, SC	05/13/65	Charleston, SC	05/13/65	New York, NY oath	CSR
Wolfe, D.W.	Pvt	G 25th SCVI	Ft. Fisher, NC	01/15/65	New York, NY	01/30/65	Elmira, NY	CSR
					Elmira, NY	03/01/65	Died, Diarrhea	P6,P12,P65,P66,FPH
Wolfe, David	Pvt	F 15th SCMil	Lancaster, SC	02/23/65	Pt. Lookout, MD	04/17/65	Died, Scurvy	P6,P12,P118,FPH

SOUTH CAROLINA SOLDIERS, SAILORS AND  CITIZENS HELD IN U.S. PRISONS 1861-1865

NAME	RANK	REGIMENT	CAPTURED AT	WHEN	PRISON	MOVED	DISPOSITION	SOURCES
Wolfe, J.A.	Cpl	H 25th SCVI	Ft. Fisher, NC	01/15/65	New York, NY	01/30/65	Elmira, NY	CSR,HAG
					Elmira, NY	07/07/65	Rlsd. G.O. #109	P65,P66,HAG,CSR
Womack, J.W.	SMj	5th SCVC	White House, VA	06/20/64	Fts. Monroe, VA	06/23/64	Pt. Lookout, MD	CSR
					Pt. Lookout, MD	07/25/64	Elmira, NY	P113,P117,P120,CSR
					Elmira, NY	10/27/64	Escaped	P65,P66,CSR
Wood, Allen W.	Pvt	C 1st SCVIH	Boonesboro, MD	09/14/62	Army of Potomac P.M.	09/25/62	Paroled	CSR,SA1
Wood, Allen W.	Pvt	C 1st SCVIH	Warrenton, VA	09/29/62	Warrenton, VA	09/29/62	Paroled	CSR
Wood, Arthur S.	Pvt	C 14th SCVI	Petersburg, VA	04/03/65	City Pt., VA	04/13/65	Pt. Lookout, MD	CSR
					Pt. Lookout, MD	06/21/65	Rlsd. G.O. #109	P115,P119,P122,CSR
Wood, Benjamin	Pvt	B 3rd SCResB	Black Creek, SC	03/01/65	New Berne, NC	04/10/65	Hart's Island, NY	CSR
					Hart's Island, NY	06/16/65	Rlsd. G.O. #109	P79
Wood, D.M.	Pvt	C 22nd SCVI	Petersburg, VA	04/03/65	City Pt., VA	04/14/65	Pt. Lookout, MD	CSR,HOS
					Pt. Lookout, MD	05/02/65	Died, Dysentery	P6,P12,P115,P119,FPH
Wood, Decatur	Pvt	G 1st SCVA	Fayetteville, NC	03/10/65	Pt. Lookout, MD	06/21/65	Rlsd. G.O. #109	P115
Wood, Frank	Pvt	E 27th SCVI	Town Creek, NC	02/20/65	Ft. Anderson, NC	02/28/65	Pt. Lookout, MD	CSR,HAG
					Pt. Lookout, MD	05/13/65	Rlsd. G.O. #85	P115,P118,CSR
Wood, George T.	Pvt	C 7th SCVC	Columbia, VA	03/11/65	White House, VA	03/19/65	Fts. Monroe, VA	CSR
					Fts. Monroe, VA	03/25/65	Pt. Lookout, MD	CSR
					Pt. Lookout, MD	06/22/65	Rlsd. G.O. #109	P115,P118,P121,CSR
Wood, George W.	Pvt	I 22nd SCVI	Hatchers Run, VA	03/30/65	City Pt., VA	04/02/65	Pt. Lookout, MD	CSR
Wood, George W.	Pvt	I 22nd SCVI	Hatchers Run, VA	03/25/65	Pt. Lookout, MD	06/22/65	Rlsd. G.O. #109	P115,P118,P121
Wood, J.J.	Pvt	A 3rd SCVABn	High Pt., NC	05/02/65	High Pt., NC	05/02/65	Paroled	CSR
Wood, J.N.	Pvt	G 16th SCVI	Hartwell, GA	05/23/65	Hartwell, GA	05/23/65	Paroled on oath	CSR
Wood, James	Pvt	G 2nd SCVA	Cheraw, SC	03/04/65	New Berne, NC	03/30/65	Pt. Lookout, MD	FPH,CSR
					Pt. Lookout, MD	05/30/65	Died, Lung Inflam.	P6,P12,P115,P118,P119,CS
Wood, James C.	Pvt	B 19th SCVI	Augusta, GA	05/18/65	Augusta, GA	05/18/65	Paroled	CSR
Wood, Jesse	Pvt	E 27th SCVI	Petersburg, VA	06/24/64	Bermuda Hundred, VA	06/25/64	Fts. Monroe, VA	CSR,HAG
					Fts. Monroe, VA	06/26/64	Pt. Lookout, MD	CSR
					Pt. Lookout, MD	08/16/64	Elmira, NY	P113,P117,P120
					Elmira, NY	02/13/65	Pt. Lookout, MD Xc	P65,P66,CSR
Wood, John P.	Pvt	C 22nd SCVI	Hatchers Run, VA	03/25/65	City Pt., VA	04/02/65	Pt. Lookout, MD	CSR,HOS
					Pt. Lookout, MD	06/22/65	Rlsd. G.O. #109	P115,P118,CSR
Wood, Joseph L.	Pvt	B 12th SCVI	Petersburg, VA	04/02/65	City Pt., VA	04/04/65	Pt. Lookout, MD	CSR
					Pt. Lookout, MD	06/22/65	Rlsd. G.O. #109	P115,P118,P121,CSR
Wood, Joseph W.	Pvt	F 1st SCVA	Deserted/enemy	03/17/65	Charleston, SC		Released on oath	CSR
Wood, M.V.	Pvt	A 3rd SCVABn	High Pt., NC	05/02/65	High Pt., NC	05/02/65	Paroled	CSR
Wood, Manning A.	Pvt	C 22nd SCVI	New Bern, NC	05/06/64	Pt. Lookout, MD	08/15/64	Elmira, NY	P113,P116,P120,FPH
					Elmira, NY	12/26/64	Died, Typhoid Pneum.	P5,P12,P65,FPH,HOS
Wood, Nicholas A.	Smn	CS Chicora	Morris Island, SC	12/06/63	Pt. Lookout, MD	01/21/64	Joined U.S. Forces	P113,P116,P125
Wood, O.P.	Sgt	C 22nd SCVI	Crater, Pbg., VA	07/30/64	City Pt., VA	08/05/64	Pt. Lookout, MD	CSR,HOS
					Pt. Lookout, MD	08/08/64	Elmira, NY	P113,P117,P120
					Elmira, NY	03/14/65	Pt. Lookout, MD Xc	P65,P66
					Wayside H. Rchmd.	03/28/65	Furloughed 60 days	CSR
Wood, Oliver	Pvt	I 13th SCVI	Hatchers Run, VA	03/31/65	City Pt., VA	04/02/65	Pt. Lookout, MD	CSR
					Pt. Lookout, MD	06/10/65	Died, Ch. Diarrhea	P6,P12,P118,FPH
Wood, Robert J.	Pvt	C 5th SCVI	Deserted/enemy	04/10/65	Washington, DC	04/10/65	Portsmouth, VA	CSR
Wood, Robert M.	Pvt	B 27th SCVI	Town Creek, NC	02/20/65	Ft. Anderson, NC	02/28/65	Pt. Lookout, MD	CSR,HAG
					Pt. Lookout, MD	06/21/65	Rlsd. G.O. #109	P115,P118,P122,CSR
Wood, S.A.	Sgt	D 15th SCMil	Chesterfield, SC	03/28/65	Pt. Lookout, MD			P118
Wood, Samuel A.	Pvt	2nd SCVI			Pt. Lookout, MD	06/22/65	Rlsd. G.O. #109	P121,CSR
					Washington, DC	07/17/65	Transport. to SC	CSR
Wood, T.J.	Pvt	A 3rd SCVABn	High Pt., NC	05/02/65	High Pt., NC	05/02/65	Paroled	CSR

W

SOUTH CAROLINA SOLDIERS, SAILORS AND CITIZENS HELD IN U.S. PRISONS 1861-1865

NAME	RANK	REGIMENT	CAPTURED AT	WHEN	PRISON	MOVED	DISPOSITION	SOURCES
Wood, Turner R.L.	Pvt	E 16th SCVI	Salisbury, NC	04/12/65	Nashville, TN	04/29/65	Louisville, KY	P39,16R,CSR
					Louisville, KY	05/02/65	Camp Chase, OH	P92,P95,CSR
					Camp Chase, OH	06/13/65	Released	P23,CSR
Wood, William C.	HSd	2nd SCVC	Maryland	07/13/63	Camp Chase, OH	02/29/64	Ft. Delaware, DE	P22
Wood, William C.	Sgt	C 27th SCVI	Town Creek, NC	02/20/65	Ft. Anderson, NC	02/28/65	Pt. Lookout, MD	CSR,HAG
					Pt. Lookout, MD	06/22/65	Rlsd. G.O. #109	P115,P118,P122,CSR
Wood, William J.	Pvt	A Hol.Leg.	Warrenton, VA	09/29/62	Warrenton, VA	09/29/62	Paroled in Hos.	CSR
Woodall, J.J.	Pvt	D Orr's Ri.	Petersburg, VA	04/02/65	City Pt., VA	04/11/65	Hart's Island, NY	CSR
					Hart's Island, NY	06/16/65	Rlsd. G.O. #109	P79,CSR
Woodard, J.R.	Pvt	E 2nd SCVA	Cheraw, NC	03/03/65	New Berne, NC	04/10/65	Hart's Island, NY	CSR
					Hart's Island, NY	06/17/65	Released G.O. #109	CSR
Woodberry, J.B.	Pvt	K 7th SCVC	Lynchburg, VA	04/14/65	Lynchburg, VA	04/14/65	Paroled	CSR
Woodberry, William D.	1Lt	L 21st SCVI	Ft. Fisher, NC	01/15/65	Ft. Columbus, NY	03/01/65	City Pt., VA Xc	P2,HAG,HMC,CSR
Woodle, Edward	Pvt	B 24th SCVI	Peachtree Ck., GA	07/20/64	Nashville, TN	11/25/64	Louisville, KY	P3,CSR,EFW,HOM
					Louisville, KY	11/30/64	Camp Douglas, IL	P90,P91,P94,CSR
					Camp Douglas, IL	03/13/65	Pt. Lookout, MD Xc	P55,CSR
					Richmond, VA Hos.	03/28/65	Furloughed 60 days	CSR
Woodrow, John E.	Sgt	I 8th SCVI	Gettysburg, PA	07/04/63	Gettysburg G.H.		Provost Marshal	P4,KEB
					David's Island, NY	08/24/63	City Pt., VA Xc	P1,CSR
Woodruff, Andrew B.	Cpt	E Hol.Leg.	Dinwiddie C.H., VA	04/01/65	City Pt., VA	04/05/65	Old Capitol, DC	CSR
					Old Capitol, DC	04/09/65	Johnson's Isl., OH	P110
					Johnson's Isl., OH	06/20/65	Rlsd. G.O. #109	P81,P83
Woodruff, Archibald G.	Pvt	D 14th SCVI	Sutherland Stn., VA	04/02/65	City Pt., VA	04/07/65	Hart's Island, NY	CSR,HOE
					Hart's Island, NY	06/16/65	Rlsd. G.O. #109	P79,CSR
Woodruff, J.D.	Pvt	E Hol.Leg.	Petersburg, VA	11/06/64	City Pt., VA	11/11/64	Washington, DC	CSR,HOS
					Pt. Lookout, MD	02/10/65	Exchanged	P115,P123,P124,CSR
					Richmond, VA Hos.	02/21/65	Furloughed 60 days	CSR,HOS
Woodruff, James A.	Cpl	E Hol.Leg.	Petersburg, VA	11/05/64	City Pt., VA	11/11/64	Washington, DC	CSR
					Pt. Lookout, MD	06/22/65	Rlsd. G.O. #109	P121
Woodruff, Samuel P.	Sgt	L Orr's Ri.	Petersburg, VA	04/02/65	City Pt., VA	04/07/65	Hart's Island, NY	CSR,CDC
					Hart's Island, NY	06/15/65	Rlsd. G.O. #109	P79
Woods, H.J.	Pvt	E 1st SCVIR	Smiths Ford, NC	03/16/65	New Berne, NC	04/03/65	Pt. Lookout, MD	CSR
					Pt. Lookout, MD	06/22/65	Rlsd. G.O. #109	P115,P118,SA1,CSR
Woods, J.	Pvt	B 6th SCVI	Augusta, GA	05/22/65	Augusta, GA	05/22/65	Paroled	CSR
Woods, John D.	Pvt	E 7th SCVI	Gettysburg, PA	07/03/63	Harrisburg, PA	07/04/63	Philadelphia, PA	CSR
					Ft. Delaware, DE	10/28/63	Died, Smallpox	P5,P12,P40,P42
Woods, John T.	Pvt	A 17th SCVI	Petersburg, VA	03/25/65	Washington, DC	03/30/65	Pt. Lookout, MD	CSR
					Pt. Lookout, MD	05/14/65	Rlsd. G.O. #85	P115,P118,P122,CSR
Woods, Joshua	Pvt	C 3rd SCVC	Pocotaligo, SC	01/19/65	Dept. Hdqtrs.	01/28/65		CSR
Woods, P.E.	Pvt	K 7th SCVC	Richmond, VA	10/07/64	Dutch Gap Canal	10/21/64	Pt. Lookout, MD	CSR,HIC
					City Pt., VA	10/29/64	Pt. Lookout, MD	CSR
					Pt. Lookout, MD	01/17/65	Exchanged	P115,P124,CSR
Woods, Robert J.	Pvt	E 3rd SCVC	Pocotaligo, SC	01/19/65	Dept. Hdqtrs.	01/28/65		CSR
Woods, Spencer	Pvt	E 14th SCVI	Gettysburg, PA	07/04/63	David's Island, NY	08/28/63	City Pt., VA Xc	P1,CSR
Woods, William	Msc	1st SCVIR	Deserted/enemy	03/25/65	Charleston, SC		Released on oath	SA1,CSR
Woodson, Azariah	Pvt	E Ham.Leg.	Warrenton, VA	09/29/62	Warrenton, VA	09/29/62	Paroled	CSR
Woodson, J.A.	Pvt	A 3rd SCVABn	High Pt., NC	05/02/65	High Pt., NC	05/02/65	Paroled	CSR
Woodson, W.T.	Pvt	A 3rd SCVABn	High Pt., NC	05/02/65	High Pt., NC	05/02/65	Paroled	CSR
Woodson, William A.	Pvt	D 26th SCVI	Amelia C.H., VA	04/06/65	Pt. Lookout, MD	06/22/65	Rlsd. G.O. #109	P115,P118
Woodsworth, Henry	Pvt	Brooks LA	Gettysburg, PA	07/03/63	Chester, PA G.H.	08/17/63	City Pt., VA Xc	P1,CSR
					Williamsburg, VA H	08/28/63	Farmville, VA CSGH	CSR
Woodward, A.P.	Pvt	D Hol.Leg.	Kinston, NC	12/15/62	Kinston, NC	12/15/62	Paroled POW	CSR

W

SOUTH CAROLINA SOLDIERS, SAILORS AND CITIZENS HELD IN U.S. PRISONS 1861-1865

NAME	RANK	REGIMENT	CAPTURED AT	WHEN	PRISON	MOVED	DISPOSITION	SOURCES
Woodward, J.A.	Pvt	E 1st SCVIH	Augusta, GA	05/19/65	Augusta, GA	05/19/65	Paroled	CSR
Woodward, James M.	2Lt	G 21st SCVI	Morris Island, SC	07/10/63	Hilton Head, SC	10/06/63	Ft. Columbus, NY	CSR,HAG
					Ft. Columbus, NY	10/09/63	Johnson's Isl., OH	P1
					Johnson's Isl., OH	06/11/65	Released	P81,P83
Woodward, Thomas J.	Pvt	G 27th SCVI	Petersburg, VA	06/24/64	Bermuda Hundred, VA	06/25/64	Fts. Monroe, VA	CSR,HAG
					Fts. Monroe, VA	06/26/64	Pt. Lookout, MD	CSR
					Pt. Lookout, MD	08/16/64	Elmira, NY	P113,P117,P120,FPH
Woodward, Thomas J.	Pvt	G 27th SCVI	Petersburg, VA	06/24/64	Elmira, NY	09/19/64	Died, Ch. Diarrhea	P5,P12,P65,P66,FPH
Woodward, W.A.	Sgt	Waccamaw A	N. Santee R., SC	02/27/63	Ft. McHenry, MD			P145
					Gunboat Quaker Cit.	03/16/63	New York, NY P.M.	CSR
					Ft. Lafayette, NY	04/07/63	Fts. Monroe, VA Xc	P144
Woodward, W.W.	Pvt	E 1st SCVIH	Augusta, GA	05/20/65	Augusta, GA	05/20/65	Paroled	CSR
Woodward, William J.	Pvt	B 17th SCVI	Five Forks, VA	04/01/65	City Pt., VA	04/06/65	Pt. Lookout, MD	CSR
					Pt. Lookout, MD	06/22/65	Rlsd. G.O. #109	P115,P118,P121,CSR
Woody, Edward T.	Pvt	Brooks LA	Falling Waters, MD	07/14/63	Baltimore, MD	08/16/63	Pt. Lookout, MD	CSR
					Pt. Lookout, MD	12/25/63	City Pt., VA Xc	P116,CSR
Wooley, Miner W.	Pvt	A 1st SCVIG	Gettysburg, PA	07/05/63	David's Island, NY	09/12/63	City Pt., VA Xc	P1,SA1,CSR
Wooten, Daniel	Pvt	C 7th SCVIBn	Bentonville, NC	03/22/65	New Berne, NC	04/10/66	Hart's Island, NY	CSR,HAG
					Hart's Island, NY	06/16/65	Rlsd. G.O. #109	P79,CSR
Wooten, James J.	Pvt	F 3rd SCVC	South Newport, GA	08/17/64	Ft. Delaware, DE	01/30/65	Hos. 1/30-2/21/65	P47
					Ft. Delaware, DE	02/27/65	City Pt., VA Xc	P43,CSR
Wooten, Thomas	Pvt	B 7th SCVIBn	Weldon RR, VA	08/21/64	City Pt., VA	08/24/64	Pt. Lookout, MD	CSR,HAG
					Pt. Lookout, MD	10/11/64	Aikens Ldg., VA Xc	P113,P117,P123,CSR
Wooten, W.R.	Pvt	I P.S.S.	Deserted/enemy	03/18/65	Bermuda Hundred, VA	03/22/65	Washington, DC	CSR,TSE
					Washington, DC	03/24/65	Nashville, TN oath	CSR
Wooten, William J.	Pvt	C Hol.Leg.	Five Forks, VA	04/01/65	City Pt., VA	04/05/65	Pt. Lookout, MD	CSR,HOS
					Pt. Lookout, MD	06/21/65	Rlsd. G.O. #109	P115,P118,CSR
Wooton, M.J.	Pvt	C Ham.Leg.	Warrenton, VA	09/29/62	Warrenton, VA	09/29/62	Paroled	CSR
Workman, Harrison	Pvt	D 3rd SCVI	Richmond, VA Hos.	04/03/65	Richmond, VA Hos.	04/29/65	Paroled	CSR
Workman, Hugh H.	Pvt	F 14th SCVI	Appomattox R., VA	04/03/65	City Pt., VA	04/13/65	Pt. Lookout, MD	CSR
					Pt. Lookout, MD	06/22/65	Rlsd. G.O. #109	P115,P118,P122,CSR
Workman, William Clark	Pvt	K 7th SCVC	Lynchburg, VA Hos.	04/14/65	Lynchburg, VA Hos.	04/14/65	Paroled	CSR
Worsham, Joseph R.	Pvt	I 25th SCVI	Ft. Fisher, NC	01/15/65	New York, NY	01/30/65	Elmira, NY	CSR
					Elmira, NY	02/24/65	Died, Pneumonia	P6,P12,P65,FPH
Worth, D.M.	Pvt	H 12th SCVI	Warrenton, VA	09/29/62	Warrenton, VA	09/29/62	Paroled	CSR
Worthy, Thomas C.	Sgt	B 4th SCVC	Old Church, VA	05/30/64	White House, VA	06/08/64	Pt. Lookout, MD	CSR,HHC
					Pt. Lookout, MD	07/09/64	Elmira, NY	P113,P117,P120,CSR
					Elmira, NY	03/02/65	Pt. Lookout, MD Xc	P65,P66,CSR
					Richmond, VA Hos	03/07/65	Camp Lee, VA	CSR,HHC
Wrenn, Thomas N.	Pvt	A 17th SCVI	Petersburg, VA	07/30/64	City Pt., VA	08/05/64	Pt. Lookout, MD	CSR
					Pt. Lookout, MD	08/08/64	Elmira, NY	P113,P120,P125,FPH
					Elmira, NY	11/18/64	Died, Ch Diarrhea	P5,P12,P65,P66,FPH
Wright, Benjamin H.	Pvt	E 18th SCVAB	Salisbury, NC	04/12/65	Nashville, TN	04/29/65	Louisville, KY	CSR
					Louisville, KY	05/02/65	Camp Chase, OH	CSR
					Camp Chase, OH	06/13/65	Rlsd. G.O. #109	P92,CSR
Wright, Daniel	Pvt	H 22nd SCVI	Kinston, NC	12/14/62	Kinston, NC	12/14/62	Paroled POW	CSR
Wright, Daniel	Pvt	H 22nd SCVI	Deserted/enemy	02/16/65	P.M. City Pt., VA	02/18/65	Washington, DC	CSR
					Washington, DC	02/21/65	Ducktown, TN	CSR
Wright, Drury A.	Pvt	B 1st SCVIG	Falling Waters, MD	07/14/63	Baltimore, MD	08/16/63	Pt. Lookout, MD	SA1,CSR
					Pt. Lookout, MD	08/18/64	Elmira, NY	P113,P120,P124,CSR
					Elmira, NY	02/25/65	James R., VA Xc	SA1,P65,P66,CSR

W

SOUTH CAROLINA SOLDIERS, SAILORS AND CITIZENS HELD IN U.S. PRISONS 1861-1865

NAME	RANK	REGIMENT	CAPTURED AT	WHEN	PRISON	MOVED	DISPOSITION	SOURCES
Wright, E.C.	Pvt	H 7th SCVIBn	Drury's Bluff, VA	05/16/64	Bermuda Hundred, VA	05/17/64	Fts. Monroe, VA	CSR,HAG,HHC
					Fts. Monroe, VA	05/18/64	Pt. Lookout, MD	CSR
					Pt. Lookout, MD	08/15/64	Elmira, NY	P113,P117,P120
					Pt. Lookout, MD	10/29/64	Died, Ch. Diarrhea	P5,P12,P119,FPH
Wright, Elias	Pvt	A 14th SCVI	Gettysburg, PA	07/04/63	David's Island, NY	09/08/63	City Pt., VA Xc	P1,CSR,DEB
Wright, Elias	Pvt	A 14th SCVI	Hatchers Run, VA	04/03/65	City Pt., VA	04/07/65	Hart's Island, NY	CSR
					Hart's Island, NY	06/16/65	Rlsd. G.O. #109	P79,CSR
Wright, George W.	Pvt	G 24th SCVI	Jackson, MS	05/14/63	Demopolis Prl. Camp	06/05/63		CSR,EFW
Wright, George W.	Pvt	6 10/19 SCVI	Missionary Ridge,TN	11/25/63	Nashville, TN	12/07/63	Louisville, KY	P39,CSR
					Louisville, KY	12/09/63	Rock Island, IL	P88,P89,CSR
					Rock Island, IL	03/02/65	Pt. Lookout, MD Xc	P131,CSR
					Charlotte, NC Hos.	04/26/65	Tfd. to other hos.	CSR
Wright, J.	Pvt	G 20th SCVI	Richmond VA Hos.	04/03/65				CSR
Wright, J.B.C.	Pvt	G 26th SCVI	Richmond, VA Hos	04/03/65	Libby Prsn., Rchmd	04/23/65	Newport News, VA	CSR
					Newport News, VA	06/14/65	Rlsd. G.O. #109	CSR
Wright, J.E.	Pvt	A 22nd SCVI	Kinston, NC	12/14/62	Kinston, NC	12/14/62	Paroled POW	CSR
Wright, J.M.	Pvt	H 18th SCVI	Crater, Pbg., VA	07/30/64	City Pt., VA	08/05/64	Pt. Lookout, MD	CSR
					Pt. Lookout, MD	08/08/64	Elmira, NY	P113,P120,P125
					Elmira, NY	10/20/64	Died, Variola	P5,P12,P60,P65,FPH
Wright, J.P.	Pvt	H 22nd SCVI	Crater, Pbg., VA	07/30/64	City Pt., VA	08/05/64	Pt. Lookout, MD	CSR
					Pt. Lookout, MD	08/08/64	Elmira, NY	P113,P117,P120,FPH
					Elmira, NY	04/09/65	Died, Variola	P6,P12,P66,FPH
Wright, J.S.	Cpl	G 26th SCVI	Deserted/enemy	02/20/65	City Pt., VA	02/26/65	Washington, DC	CSR
					Washington, DC	03/01/65	Phila., PA on oath	CSR
Wright, James	Pvt	Gist Gd HA	Deserted/enemy	03/20/65	Charleston, SC	03/20/65	Released on oath	CSR
Wright, James B.	Cpl	E Hol.Leg.	New Berne, NC	12/17/62	New Berne, NC	12/17/62	Paroled POW	CSR
Wright, James C.	Pvt	K Orr's Ri.	Gettysburg, PA	07/03/63	Harrisburg, PA	07/07/63	Philadelphia, PA	CSR
					Ft. Delaware, DE	02/06/64	Died, Ch. Diarrhea	P5,P40,P42,P47,FPH
Wright, James D.	Sgt	B 27th SCVI	Petersburg, VA	06/24/64	Bermuda Hundred, VA	06/25/64	Fts. Monroe, VA	CSR,HAG
					Fts. Monroe, VA	06/26/64	Pt. Lookout, MD	CSR
					Pt. Lookout, MD	08/16/64	Elmira, NY	P113,P117,P120,CSR
					Elmira, NY	10/11/64	Pt. Lookout, MD Xc	P65,P66,CSR
					Pt. Lookout, MD	10/29/64	Venus Pt., GA Xc	P115,P117,CSR
Wright, John	Pvt	B 1st SCVIR	Fayetteville, NC	03/16/65	New Berne, NC	03/30/65	Pt. Lookout, MD	CSR,LAN
					Pt. Lookout, MD	06/06/65	Released on oath	P115,P118,SA1,CSR
Wright, John D.	Cpl	B 17th SCVI	Boonesboro, MD	09/15/62	Ft. Delaware, DE	10/02/62	Aikens Ldg.,VA Xc	CSR,HFC
Wright, John D.	Sgt	B 17th SCVI	Petersburg, VA	03/25/65	City Pt., VA	03/28/65	Pt. Lookout, MD	CSR
					Pt. Lookout, MD	06/22/65	Rlsd. G.O. #109	P115,P118,P121,CSR
Wright, John W.	Pvt	A 14th SCVI	Gettysburg, PA	06/30/63	Ft. Delaware, DE	06/08/65	Released	P43,P45,CSR,DEB
Wright, Jonathan	Pvt	B 27th SCVI	Town Creek, NC	02/20/65	Ft. Anderson, NC	02/28/65	Pt. Lookout, MD	CSR
					Pt. Lookout, MD	06/21/65	Rlsd. G.O. #109	P115,P118,CSR
Wright, Joseph H.	Pvt	F 18th SCVI	Richmond, VA Hos.	04/03/65	P. M. Richmond, VA	05/05/65	Released	CSR
Wright, McPherson	1Lt	K 22nd SCVI	Kinston, NC	12/15/62	Kinston, NC	12/15/62	Paroled POW	CSR
Wright, McPherson	Cpt	K 22nd SCVI	Southside RR, VA	04/02/65	City Pt., VA	04/05/65	Old Capitol, DC	CSR
					Old Capitol, DC	04/19/65	Johnson's Isl., OH	CSR
					Johnson's Isl., OH	06/20/65	Rlsd. G.O. #109	P81,P82,P83,CSR
Wright, N.D.	Pvt	G 26th SCVI	Richmond, VA Hos.	04/03/65	Libby Prison Rchmd	04/23/65	Newport News, VA	CSR
Wright, N.D.	Pvt	G 26th SCVI	Richmond, VA	04/03/65	Newport News, VA	06/14/65	Rlsd. G.O. #109	P107,CSR
Wright, Samuel	Pvt	I 21st SCVI	Bentonville, NC	03/20/65	Hart's Island, NY	06/21/65	Rlsd. G.O. #109	P79,CSR
Wright, Thomas L.	Sgt	A 5th SCVI	Fair Oaks, VA	06/03/62	Ft. Delaware, DE	08/05/62	Aikens Ldg., VA Xc	CSR,SA3
Wulbern, H.	Cpl	A German LA	Deserted/enemy	03/17/65	Charleston, SC	03/17/65	Released on oath	CSR

SOUTH CAROLINA SOLDIERS, SAILORS AND W CITIZENS HELD IN U.S. PRISONS 1861-1865

NAME	RANK	REGIMENT	CAPTURED AT	WHEN	PRISON	MOVED	DISPOSITION	SOURCES
Wyatt, H.D.	Pvt	G 27th SCVI	Petersburg, VA	06/24/64	Bermuda Hundred, VA	06/25/64	Fts. Monroe, VA	CSR
					Fts. Monroe, VA	09/11/64	Pt. Lookout, MD	CSR
					Pt. Lookout, MD	05/14/65	Rlsd. G.O. #85	P115,P117,P122,CSR
Wyatt, Henry M.	Pvt	K P.S.S.	Loudon, TN	12/03/63	Nashville, TN	12/30/63	Louisville, KY	P39,TSE,CSR
					Louisville, KY	12/31/63	Rock Island, IL	P88,P89,P93,CSR
					Rock Island, IL	02/03/64	Died, Pneumonia	P5,P131,P132,FPH
Wyatt, John	Pvt	F 22nd SCVI	Hatchers Run, VA	03/29/65	City Pt., VA	04/02/65	Pt. Lookout, MD	CSR
					Pt. Lookout, MD	06/22/65	Rlsd. G.O. #109	P118,P115,P121,CSR
Wyatt, Samuel T.	Pvt	C 4th SCVC	Stony Creek, VA	12/01/64	City Pt., VA	12/05/64	Pt. Lookout, MD	CSR
					Pt. Lookout, MD	06/22/65	Rlsd. G.O. #109	P115,P118,P122,CSR
Wyatt, W.F.	Pvt	F 7th SCVI	Charlestowne, WV	10/16/62	Harpers Ferry, WV	10/22/62	Ft. McHenry, MD	CSR
					Ft. McHenry, MD	10/30/62	Aikens Ldg., VA Xc	CSR
Wyler, Harvey	Pvt	H 12th SCVI	Farmville, VA	04/11/65	Farmville, VA	04/21/65	Paroled	CSR
Wyles, H.S.	Pvt	H 12th SCVI	Spotsylvania, VA	05/12/64	Ft. Delaware, DE			P41,CWC,YEB
Wyley, Joseph M.	Pvt	K 17th SCVI	Five Forks, VA	04/01/65	City Pt., VA	04/06/65	Pt. Lookout, MD	CSR
					Pt. Lookout, MD	06/22/65	Rlsd. G.O. #109	P118,CSR
Wyley, Starnes	Pvt	C 17th SCVI	Five Forks, VA	04/01/65	City Pt., VA	04/06/65	Pt. Lookout, MD	CSR
					Pt. Lookout, MD	06/22/65	Rlsd. G.O. #109	P115,P118,P121,CSR
Wyley, Thomas	Pvt	F Orr's Ri.	Petersburg, VA	04/03/65	Hart's Island, NY	06/17/65	Rlsd. G.O. #109	CSR
Wyley, Thomas S.	Cpl	D 17th SCVI	Crater, Pbg., VA	07/30/64	City Pt., VA	08/05/64	Pt. Lookout, MD	CSR
					Pt. Lookout, MD	08/08/64	Elmira, NY	P113,P117,P120,CSR
					Elmira, NY	11/30/64	Died, Ch. Diarrhea	P5,P12,P65,P66,FPH
Wylie, Hugh M.	Pvt	A 17th SCVI	Petersburg, VA	03/25/65	2nd Div. 9th A.C.	04/03/65	1st Div, Hos.	CSR
Wylie, Joseph M..	Pvt	K 17th SCVI	Five Forks, VA	04/01/65	City Pt., VA	04/06/65	Pt. Lookout, MD	CSR
					Pt. Lookout, MD	06/22/65	Rlsd. G.O. #109	P121,CSR
Wylie, Newton I.	Sgt	H 24th SCVI	Jackson, MS	05/14/63	Jackson, MS	05/14/63	Paroled in Hos.	CSR,EFW
Wylie, Samuel Moffatt	1Lt	K 17th SCVI	Petersburg, VA	03/25/65	City Pt., VA P.M.	03/26/65	Washington, DC	CSR,YEB
					Old Capitol, DC	03/30/65	Ft. Delaware, DE	P110,CSR
					Ft. Delaware, DE	06/17/65	Rlsd. G.O. #109	P43,P45,CSR
Wylie, William	Sgt	G 5th SCVI	Lookout Valley, TN	11/28/63	Bridgeport, AL G.H.	12/05/63	Nashville, TN	P2,SA3,CSR,YEB
					Nashville, TN	12/13/63	Louisville, KY	P39,CSR
Wylie, William	Pvt	G 5th SCVI	Lookout Valley, TN	11/28/63	Louisville, KY	12/16/63	Rock Island, IL	P88,P89,CSR
					Rock Island, IL	11/10/64	Died, Consumption	P5,P12,P132,FPH
Wynn, J.F.	Pvt	A 3rd SCVABn	High Pt., NC	05/02/65	High Pt., NC	05/02/65	Paroled	CSR
					High Pt., NC	05/02/65	Paroled	CSR
Wynne, Charles G.	1Lt	E Orr's Ri.	Saylors Creek, VA	04/03/65	Old Capitol, DC	04/09/65	Johnson's Isl., OH	CSR,CDC
					Johnson's Isl., OH	06/20/65	Rlsd. G.O. #109	P81,P82,P83,CSR
Wynne, J.H.	Pvt	A Orr's Ri.	Falling Waters, MD	07/14/63	Pt. Lookout, MD	10/15/63	Hammond G.H., MD	P113
					Pt. Lookout, MD	01/27/64	Died	P116
Wyrick, Laban V.	Pvt	H 7th SCVIBn	Drury's Bluff, VA	05/16/64	Bermuda Hundred, VA	05/17/64	Fts. Monroe, VA	CSR
					Fts. Monroe, VA	05/18/64	Pt. Lookout, MD	CSR,HAG
					Pt. Lookout, MD	08/15/64	Elmira, NY	P113,P117,CSR
					Elmira, NY	06/27/65	Rlsd. G.O. #109	P65,P66,CSR
Wyrick, W.P.	Pvt	C 12th SCVI	Gettysburg, PA	06/30/63	David's Island, NY	07/26/63	Died, Pyaemia	P1,P6,P12,FPH,HFC,CSR

SOUTH CAROLINA SOLDIERS, SAILORS AND  CITIZENS HELD IN U.S. PRISONS 1861-1865

NAME	RANK	REGIMENT	CAPTURED AT	WHEN	PRISON	MOVED	DISPOSITION	SOURCES
Yarberry, O.L.	Pvt	K 22nd SCVI	Jackson, MS	07/30/63	Camp Morton, IN	11/12/63	Died, Pneumonia	P5,P12,P100,FPH
Yarborough, J.W.	Pvt	H 26th SCVI	Deserted/enemy	01/21/65	City Pt., VA	01/22/65	Washington, DC	CSR
					Washington, DC	01/26/65	Savannah, GA oath	CSR
Yarborough, James M.	Pvt	A 1st SCVIR	Morris Island, SC	09/07/63	Hilton Head, SC	10/06/63	Ft. Columbus, NY	CSR,SA1
					Ft. Columbus, NY	10/09/63	Pt. Lookout, MD	CSR
					Pt. Lookout, MD	01/09/64	Died, Typhoid fever	P12,P116,P119,FPH
Yarborough, John E.	Pvt	H 26th SCVI	Southside RR, VA	04/01/65	City Pt., VA	04/05/65	Pt. Lookout, MD	CSR
					Pt. Lookout, MD	06/22/65	Rlsd. G.O. #109	P115,P117,P121,CSR
Yarborough, Lewis	Pvt	C 18th SCVI	Five Forks, VA	04/01/65	City Pt., VA	04/06/65	Pt. Lookout, MD	CSR
					Pt. Lookout, MD	06/22/65	Rlsd. G.O. #109	P115,P117,P121,CSR
Yarborough, Moses C.	Pvt	D 21st SCVI	Ft. Fisher, NC	01/15/65	New York, NY	01/30/65	Elmira, NY	CSR,HAG
					Elmira, NY	07/13/65	Rlsd. G.O. #109	P65,P66,CSR
Yarborough, T.J.M.	Sgt	I 17th SCVI	Petersburg, VA	03/25/65	City Pt., VA	03/27/65	Pt. Lookout, MD	CSR,LAN
					Pt. Lookout, MD	06/30/65	Rlsd. G.O.#109	P115,P121,P122,CSR
Yarborough, Thomas L.	Pvt	B 21st SCVI	Ft. Fisher, NC	01/15/65	New York, NY	01/30/65	Elmira, NY	CSR,HAG
					Elmira, NY	04/28/65	Died, Pneumonia	P5,P12,P65,FPH
Yates, Joseph	ASr	1st SCVC	Gettysburg, PA	07/04/63	Ft. McHenry, MD	11/21/63	Fts. Monroe, VA	CSR
					Ft. McHenry, MD	11/21/63	City Pt., VA Xc	P144,CSR
Yeargan, Rufus	Pvt	F 24th SCVI	Taylor's Ridge, GA	10/16/64	Nashville, TN	10/23/64	Louisville, KY	P39,CSR,EFW
					Louisville, KY	10/27/64	Camp Douglas, IL	P88,P91,P93,CSR
					Camp Douglas, IL	06/17/65	Rlsd. G.O. #109	P53,P55,CSR
Yeldell, W.H.	Pvt	K 7th SCVI	Sharpsburg, MD	10/01/62	Ft. McHenry, MD	10/13/62	Fts. Monroe, VA	CSR
					Fts. Monroe, VA	10/17/62	Aikens Ldg., VA Xc	KEB,CNM,CSR
Yewley, James C.	Pvt	I 11th SCVI	Petersburg, VA	06/24/64	Bermuda Hundred, VA	06/25/64	Fts. Monroe, VA	CSR,HAG
					Fts. Monroe, VA	06/26/64	Pt. Lookout, MD	CSR
					Pt. Lookout, MD	08/16/64	Elmira, NY	P113,P116,P120
					Elmira, NY	03/14/65	James R., VA Xc	P65,P66,CSR
Yon, D.P.	Cpl	I 22nd SCVI	Kinston, NC	12/14/62	Kinston, NC	12/14/62	Paroled POW	CSR
Yon, J.C.	Sgt	I 22nd SCVI	Richmond, VA Hos.	04/03/65	P.M. Libby Prison	04/23/65	Newport News, VA	CSR
					Newport News, VA	05/12/65	Died, Typhoid fever	P12,P107,CSR
Yon, M.J.	Cpl	I 22nd SCVI	Kinston, NC	12/14/62	Kinston, NC	12/14/62	Paroled POW	CSR
Yon, M.J.	Cpl	I 22nd SCVI	Five Forks, VA	04/01/65	City Pt., VA	04/05/65	Pt. Lookout, MD	CSR
					Pt. Lookout, MD	06/22/65	Rlsd. G.O. #109	P115,P117,P121
Yon, W.P.	Pvt	I 22nd SCVI	Deserted/enemy	02/23/65	P.M. City Pt., VA	02/23/65	Washington, DC	CSR
					Washington, DC	02/24/65	Charleston, SC	CSR
Youmans, E.C.	Pvt	F 3rd SCVC	South Newport, GA	08/17/64	Morris Island, SC	01/15/65	Died of disease	CSR
Youmans, J.A.	Pvt	B 5th SCVC	Augusta, GA	05/31/65	Augusta, GA	05/31/65	Paroled	CSR
Youmans, J.J.	Sgt	B 5th SCVC	Augusta, GA	05/31/65	Augusta, GA	05/31/65	Paroled	CSR
Youmans, W.	Pvt	D 2nd SCVI	Hagerstown, MD	07/12/63	Baltimore, MD	08/20/63	Pt. Lookout, MD	CSR
					Pt. Lookout, MD	03/17/64	Exchanged	CSR
Youmans, William R.	Pvt	B 2nd SCVC	Hagerstown, MD	07/12/63	Pt. Lookout, MD	03/16/64	City Pt., VA Xc	P113,P121,P124,CSR
Young, A.C.	Pvt	A 13th SCVI	Falling Waters, MD	07/14/63	Ft. McHenry, MD			P110
					Pt. Lookout, MD	02/15/65	Aikens Ldg., VA Xc	P113,P123,CSR
Young, A.J.	Pvt	K 18th SCVI	Crater, Pbg., VA	07/30/64	City Pt., VA	08/05/64	Pt. Lookout, MD	CSR
					Pt. Lookout, MD	08/08/64	Elmira, NY	P113,P116,P120,P125,CSR
					Elmira, NY	10/11/64	Pt. Lookout, MD Xc	P65,P66,CSR
					Pt. Lookout, MD	10/29/64	Venus Pt., GA Xc	P115,P116,P123,CSR
Young, Abner M.	Pvt	Ferguson's	Decatur, AL	10/30/64	Nashville, TN	11/07/64	Louisville, KY	CSR
					Louisville, KY	11/11/64	Camp Douglas, IL	P93,CSR
					Camp Douglas, IL	04/15/65	Joined 5th US Vol.	P53,P55,CSR

SOUTH CAROLINA SOLDIERS, SAILORS AND  CITIZENS HELD IN U.S. PRISONS 1861-1865

NAME	RANK	REGIMENT	CAPTURED AT	WHEN	PRISON	MOVED	DISPOSITION	SOURCES
Young, Andrew	Pvt	D 1st SCVA	Salisbury, NC	04/12/65	Nashville, TN	04/29/65	Louisville, KY	P39,CSR
					Louisville, KY	05/02/65	Camp Chase, OH	P92,P93,CSR
					Camp Chase, OH	06/13/65	Rlsd. G.O. #109	P22,CSR
Young, Archibald M.	Pvt	Ferguson's LA	Ringgold, GA	11/26/63	Nashville, TN	03/02/64	Died of wounds	P2,P5,P12,CSR
Young, Charles T.	Cpl	I 18th SCVI	Petersburg, VA	04/02/65	City Pt., VA	04/04/65	Pt. Lookout, MD	CSR
					Pt. Lookout, MD	06/22/65	Rlsd. G.O. #109	P115,P117,P121,CSR
Young, David Wesley	Pvt	I 19th SCVI	Murfreesboro, TN	12/31/62	Murfreesboro, TN	02/07/63	Died of wounds	P12,P38,CSR
Young, Eugene A.	1Lt	D 7th SCVIBn	Weldon RR, VA	08/21/64	Old Capitol, DC	08/30/64	Ft. Delaware, DE	CSR
					Ft. Delaware, DE	10/06/64	Pt. Lookout, MD	P42,CSR
					Pt. Lookout, MD	11/02/64	Washington, DC	P115,P116,P120
					Ft. Delaware, DC	02/27/65	City Pt., VA Xc	CSR
					Pt. Lookout, MD	02/27/65	City Pt., VA Xc	P42
Young, Francis M.	Pvt	B 15th SCVI	Cedar Creek, VA	10/19/64	Harpers Ferry, WV	10/23/64	Pt. Lookout, MD	CSR
					Pt. Lookout, MD	12/09/64	Died, Remitnt fever	P5,P115,P116,FPH
Young, George	Pvt	B 2nd SCVIRi	Chattanooga, TN	10/29/63	Ft. Delaware, DE	11/25/64	Hos.11/25/64-4/12/65	P47
					Nashville, TN	11/07/63	Louisville, KY	P38,CSR
					Louisville, KY	11/09/63	Camp Morton, IN	P88,P89,P93,CSR
					Camp Morton, IN	03/19/64	Ft. Delaware, DE	P100,CSR
					Ft. Delaware, DE	06/10/65	Released	P41,P45,CSR
Young, George G.	Pvt	A 2nd SCVC	Kinston, NC	03/28/65	New Berne, NC	04/23/65	Fts. Monroe, VA	CSR
					Fts. Monroe, VA	05/01/65	Newport News, VA	CSR
					Newport News, VA	06/26/65	Rlsd. G.O. #109	CSR
Young, George M.	Pvt	G 14th SCVI	Wilderness, VA	05/06/64	Belle Plain, VA	05/21/64	Ft. Delaware, DE	CSR
					Ft. Delaware, DE	07/01/64	Hos. 7/1-7/9/64	P47
					Ft. Delaware, DE	08/26/64	Hos. 8/26-9/30/64	P47
					Ft. Delaware, DE	09/30/64	Aikens Ldg., VA Xc	P41,P42,CSR
Young, H.C.	Pvt	D 17th SCVI	Petersburg, VA Hos.	04/03/65	Petersburg, VA Hos.	04/12/65	Str. Hero of Jersey	CSR
					US General Hos.	05/30/65	Camp Hamilton, VA	CSR
					Camp Hamilton, VA	05/31/65	Released	CSR
Young, Henry	Pvt	I 27th SCVI	Town Creek, NC	02/20/65	Ft. Anderson, NC	02/28/65	Pt. Lookout, MD	CSR
					Pt. Lookout, MD	06/22/65	Rlsd. G.O. #109	P115,HAG
Young, Henry B.	Pvt	17th SCVI			Pt. Lookout, MD	06/22/65	Released G.O. #109	P121
Young, J.A.	Cpl	C 12th SCVI	Cox Rd., VA	04/02/65	Hart's Island, NY	06/16/65	Rlsd. G.O. #109	P79,HFC,CSR
Young, J.B.	Pvt	E Hol.Leg.	Deserted/enemy	12/17/64	City Pt., VA	12/20/64	Washington, DC	CSR
					Washington, DC	12/21/64	Albany, NY oath	CSR
Young, James A.B.	Pvt	G Orr's Ri.	Falling Waters, MD	07/14/63	Baltimore, MD	08/16/63	Pt. Lookout, MD	CSR,CDC
					Pt. Lookout, MD	08/16/63	Elmira, NY	P113,FPH,CSR
					Elmira, NY	08/15/64	Died, Typhoid fever	P5,P12,P65,P66,FPH
Young, James Hugh	Pvt	C 25th SCVI	Ft. Fisher, NC	01/15/65	New York, NY	01/30/65	Elmira, NY	CSR,HAG,CTA
					Elmira, NY	03/02/65	James R., VA Xc	P65,P66,CSR
Young, James V.	Pvt	B 7th SCVI	Gettysburg, PA	07/04/63	Ft. McHenry, MD	07/30/63	Ft. Delaware, DE	CSR,KEB
					Ft. Delaware, DE	03/27/64	Hos. 3/27-4/4/64	P47
					Ft. Delaware, DE	06/24/64	Hos. 6/24-7/1/64	P47
					Ft. Delaware, DE	07/27/64	Hos. 7/27-8/1/64	P47
					Ft. Delaware, DE	06/10/65	Released	P40,P44,P45,P144
Young, John	Cit	Charleston	Columbia, SC	02/19/65	Hart's Island, NY	06/21/65	Rlsd. G.O. #109	P79
Young, John Henry	Pvt	B 15th SCVI	Bentonville, NC	03/22/65	Hart's Island, NY	06/17/65	Rlsd. G.O. #109	P79,CSR
Young, Joseph	Pvt	B 4th SCVC	Louisa C.H., VA	06/11/64	Fts. Monroe, VA	06/20/64	Pt. Lookout, MD	CSR,HHC
					Pt. Lookout, MD	07/25/64	Elmira, NY	P116,P120
					Pt. Lookout, MD	07/26/64	Died, Lung Inflam.	P6,P12,P121,FPH
Young, Joseph	Pvt	B 4th SCVC	Louisa C.H., VA	06/11/64	Elmira, NY	03/02/65	Pt. Lookout, MD Xc	P66

SOUTH CAROLINA SOLDIERS, SAILORS AND CITIZENS HELD IN U.S. PRISONS 1861-1865

NAME	RANK	REGIMENT	CAPTURED AT	WHEN	PRISON	MOVED	DISPOSITION	SOURCES
Young, Levi E.	Pvt	C 25th SCVI	Town Creek, NC	02/20/65	Ft. Anderson, NC	02/28/65	Pt. Lookout, MD	CSR,HAG,CTA
					Pt. Lookout, MD	05/14/65	Rlsd. G.O. #85	CSR
Young, R.D.	Pvt	B 18th SCVI	N. Anna River, VA	05/23/64	Pt. Lookout, MD	09/18/64	Aikens Ldg., VA Xc	P121,P123
Young, Richard	Pvt	B 2nd SCVIRi	Knoxville, TN	12/05/63	Nashville, TN	01/24/64	Louisville, KY	P39,CSR
					Louisville, KY	01/29/64	Rock Island, IL	P88,P93,CSR
					Rock Island, IL	03/29/64	Died, Inflam. Lung	P5,P131,P132,FPH
Young, Robert H.	Pvt	F 24th SCVI	Jackson, MS	05/14/63	Jackson, MS	05/14/63	Paroled in Hos.	CSR,EFW
Young, S.R.	Pvt	G 1st SCVC	Piedmont, VA	06/05/64	Camp Morton, IN	03/04/65	City Pt., VA Xc	P101,CSR
Young, Samuel R.	Pvt	G Orr's Ri.	Staunton, VA	06/05/64	Camp Morton, IN	03/04/65	City Pt., VA Xc	CSR
					City Pt., VA	03/10/65	Boulware's Wh., VA	CSR
Young, Thomas A.	Pvt	K 21st SCVI	Morris Island, SC	07/10/63	Pt. Lookout, MD	08/16/64	Elmira, NY	P113,P116,P120,HAG
					Elmira, NY	10/11/64	Pt. Lookout, MD Xc	P65,P66
					Pt. Lookout, MD	10/29/64	Aikens Ldg., VA Xc	P115,P123,P124
Young, Thomas J.	Pvt	B 15th SCVI	Gettysburg, PA	07/05/63	Ft. McHenry, MD	07/09/63	Ft. Delaware, DE	CSR,KEB,H15
					Ft. Delaware, DE	06/10/65	Rlsd. G.O. #109	P40,P44,P45,P144
Young, William	Pvt	I 14th SCVI	Gettysburg, PA	07/05/63	Ft. Delaware, DE	11/13/63	Died, Pneumonia	P12,P40,P47,FPH
Young, William H.	Cpl	K 21st SCVI	Weldon RR, VA	08/21/64	David's Island, NY	10/08/64	Elmira, NY	P1,HAG
					Elmira, NY	03/02/65	James R., VA Xc	P65,CSR
Young, William J.	Pvt	Ferguson's LA	Salisbury, NC	04/12/65	Nashville, TN	04/29/65	Louisville, KY	P39,CSR
					Louisville, KY	05/02/65	Camp Chase, OH	P92,CSR
					Camp Chase	06/13/65	Rlsd. G.O. #109	P22,CSR
Young, William W.	Pvt	G 24th SCVI	Jackson, MS	05/14/63	Jackson, MS	05/14/63	Paroled	CSR,EFW
Youngblood, Ira A.	Pvt	D 14th SCVI	N. Anna River, VA	05/24/64	Pt. Lookout, MD	08/17/64	Elmira, NY	P116,CSR,HOE
					Elmira, NY	03/08/65	Died, Pneumonia	P12,HOE,CSR,FPH
Youngblood, James	Pvt	F 22nd SCVI	Kinston, NC	12/14/62	Kinston, NC	12/14/62	Paroled/enemy	CSR
Youngblood, James M.	Cpl	D 14th SCVI	Gettysburg, PA	07/04/63	David's Island, NY	09/05/63	City Pt., VA Xc	P1,HOE,CSR
Youngblood, O.C.	Pvt	A 3rd SCVABn	High Pt., NC	05/02/65	High Pt., NC	05/02/65	Paroled	CSR
Younginer, George W.	Pvt	H 3rd SCVI	Wilderness, VA	05/06/64	Belle Plain, VA	05/21/64	Ft. Delaware, DE	CSR,KEB,SA2,H3
					Ft. Delaware, DE	09/19/64	Hos. 9/19-10/17/64	P47
					Ft. Delaware, DE	10/20/64	Hos. 10/20-10/30/64	P47
					Ft. Delaware, DE	06/30/64	Hos. 6/30-8/22/64	P47
					Ft. Delaware, DE	10/30/64	Pt. Lookout, MD	P42
					Ft. Delaware, DE	10/31/64	Pt. Lookout, MD Xc	CSR
					Pt. Lookout, MD	10/31/64	Venus Pt., GA 11/1	P115,P116,P123,H3,CSR
Younginger, J.	Pvt	H 15th SCMil			Hart's Island, NY	04/29/65	Died, Typhoid fever	P6,P12,FPH

SOUTH CAROLINA SOLDIERS, SAILORS AND  CITIZENS HELD IN U.S. PRISONS 1861-1865

NAME	RANK	REGIMENT	CAPTURED AT	WHEN	PRISON	MOVED	DISPOSITION	SOURCES
Zahler, J.M.	Pvt	D 4th SCVC	Stony Creek, VA	12/01/64	City Pt., VA	12/05/64	Pt. Lookout, MD	CSR
					Pt. Lookout, MD	06/04/65	Died, Ch. Dysentery	P6,P115,P116,FPH
Ze, J.M.	Pvt	E Ham.Leg.MI	Chester, SC	05/05/65	Chester, SC	05/05/65	Paroled	CSR
Zedica, J.	Pvt	A 18th SCVI	Petersburg, VA	07/30/64	City Pt., VA	08/05/64	Pt. Lookout, MD	CSR
					Pt. Lookout, MD	08/08/64	Elmira, NY	P113,P120,CSR
					Elmira, NY	05/17/65	Rlsd. G.O. #85	P65,P66,CSR
Zehe, John H.	Pvt	E 11th SCVI	Petersburg, VA	06/16/64	Bermuda Hundred, VA	06/17/64	Fts. Monroe, VA	CSR,HAG
					Fts. Monroe, VA	06/19/64	Pt. Lookout, MD	CSR
					Pt. Lookout, MD	07/25/64	Elmira, NY	P113,P116,P120,CSR
Zehe, John H.	Pvt	E 11th SCVI	Petersburg, VA	06/16/64	Elmira, NY	10/24/64	Died, Diarrhea	P5,P65,CSR
Zeigler, E.H.	Pvt	B German LA	Deserted/enemy	03/15/65	Charleston, SC	03/15/65	Released on oath	CSR
Zeigler, J.G.T.	Pvt	K 1st SCVIH	Warrenton, VA	09/29/62	Warrenton, VA	09/29/62	Paroled	CSR
Zeigler, J.J.	Pvt	G 1st SCVIH	Petersburg, VA	04/03/65	Petersburg, VA	07/12/65	Released on oath	CSR
Zeigler, John M.	Sgt	H 17th SCVI	Petersburg, VA	03/25/65	City Pt., VA	03/28/65	Pt. Lookout, MD	CSR
					Pt. Lookout, MD	06/22/65	Rlsd. G.O. #109	P115,P116,P122,CSR
Zeigler, Martin Govan	Maj	Hol.Leg.	Stony Creek, VA	05/07/64	Pt. Lookout, MD	06/23/64	Ft. Delaware, DE	P113,P120,ISH,LC
					Ft. Delaware, DE	08/20/64	Hilton Head, SC	CSR
					Ft. Pulaski, GA		Hilton Head, SC	P4
					Hilton Head, SC	03/12/65	Ft. Delaware, DE	CSR
					Ft. Delaware, DE	07/24/65	Rlsd. G.O. #109	P42,P44,P45,P116
Zeigler, Washington P.	Pvt	B Wash'n LA	Gettysburg, PA	07/04/63	Ft. Delaware, DE	06/30/64	Hos. 6/30-7/5/64	P47
					Ft. Delaware, DE	05/11/65	Released	P46,CSR
Zeikle, Aaron	Pvt	G 27th SCVI	Petersburg, VA	06/24/64	Bermuda Hundred, VA	06/25/64	Fts. Monroe, VA	CSR,HAG
					Fts. Monroe, VA	06/26/64	Pt. Lookout, MD	CSR
					Pt. Lookout, MD	08/16/64	Elmira, NY	P113,P120
					Elmira, NY	03/14/65	Tfd. for exchange	P65,CSR
Zimmerman, D.R.	Pvt	C 7th SCVI	Near Knoxville, TN	12/18/63	Louisville, KY	01/23/64	Rock Island, IL	P88,P93,KEB,CSR
					Rock Island, IL	04/10/64	Died, Laryngitis	P5,P131,P132
Zimmerman, T. Dargan	2Lt	B 21st SCVI	Ft. Fisher, NC	01/15/65	Ft. Columbus, NY	03/01/65	City Pt., VA Xc	P2,CSR,HAG
Zimmerman, William	Pvt	C 14th SCMil	Lynch's Creek, SC	02/28/65	Hart's Island, NY	06/14/65	Released	P79
Zobel, Julius	Pvt	E 3rd SCVI	Campbells Stn., TN	12/05/63	Nashville, TN	02/28/64	Louisville, KY	P38,KEB,SA2,ANY,H3
					Louisville, KY	03/09/64	Camp Chase, OH	P88,P91,P93,CSR
					Camp Chase, OH	02/25/65	City Pt., VA Xc	P22,P26,CSR
Zollers, R.D.	Sgt	D 5th SCVC	Louisa C.H., VA	06/11/64	Fts. Monroe, VA	06/20/64	Pt. Lookout, MD	CSR
					Pt. Lookout, MD	07/25/64	Elmira, NY	P113,P120,CSR
					Elmira, NY	10/11/64	Venus Pt. GA Xc	CSR
					Pt. Lookout, MD	10/29/64	Aikens Ldg., VA Xc	P65,P115,P123,CSR
Zorn, H.J.	Pvt	E 1st SCVIH	Jetersville, VA	04/06/65	City Pt., VA	04/14/65	Newport News, VA	CSR,SA1
					Newport News, VA	06/26/65	Rlsd. G.O. #109	P107,CSR
Zorn, S.S.	Pvt	G 1st sCVIH	Sharpsburg, MD	09/17/62	Frederick, MD USGH		Ft. Mchenry, MD	CSR,SA1
					Ft. McHenry, MD	10/14/62	Aikens Ldg., VA Xc	CSR

APPENDICES

Source Codes and Abbreviations

ACC   R. Wayne Bratcher, *Anderson County Cemeteries*, Volume 1 (Greenville, S.C.: A Press, 1985) R. Wayne Bratcher, *Anderson County Cemeteries*, Volume 2 (Greenville, S.C.: A Press, 1986) Anne Sheriff, *Anderson County Cemeteries*, Volume 3 (Greenville, S.C.: A Press, 19)

ACH   Undated manuscript prepared by The Albemarle County Historical Society, Charlottesville, Va. Volume now in the collections of the South Carolina Historical Society.

ACL   Mary D. Robertson, ed., *A Confederate Lady Comes of Age: The Journal of Pauline DeCaradeuc Heyward, 1863-1888* (Columbia, SC: University of South Carolina Press, 1992)

AHB   Richard Manning Boykin, *Capt. Alexander Hamilton Boykin* (New York: Privately printed, 1942)

ALH   Louise Haskell Daly, Alexander Cheves Haskell, *Portrait of a Man* (Norwood, Mass.: Plimpton Press, 1934; repr., Wilmington, N.C.: Broadfoot Publishing Co., 1989)

ANY   John Belton O'Neall and John A. Chapman, *Annals of Newberry* (Newberry, S.C.: n.p., 1892; repr., Baltimore, Md.: Genealogical Publishing Co., 1974)

AOA   E. Prioleau Henderson, *Autobiography of Arab* (Self-published, 1901; repr., Camden, S.C.: J.J. Fox, 1991)

APC   Ernest McPherson Lander, Jr., *The Life and Times of Ella Louton, a Pendleton, SC Confederate* (Clemson, SC: Clemson Printers, 1996)

AR   R. A. Brock, "The Appomattox Roster," *Southern Historical Society Papers*, Volume V (1887, repr., New York: Antiquarian Press, Ltd., 1962)
William G. Nines and Ronald G. Wilson, *The Appomattox Paroles, April 9-15, 1865* (Lynchburg, Va.: H. E. Howard, 1989)

ARL   Philip Katcher, *The Army of Robert E. Lee* (London: Arms and Armour Press, 1994)

BBC   Berry Benson, *Berry Benson's Civil War Book, Memoirs of a Confederate Scout and Sharpshooter* (Athens: University of Georgia Press, 1962; repr., Frances Benson Thompson, ed., Athens: University of Georgia Press, 1991)

BBW   Lucy Harrison, Miller Baber and Evelyn Lee Moore, *Behind the Old Brick Wall* (Lynchburg, Va.: The Lynchburg Committee of The National Society of The Colonial Dames of America in the Commonwealth of Virginia, 1968)

BCI   *Berkeley County Cemetery Inscriptions* (Charleston Chapter, S.C. Genealogical Society, 1985)

BFC   Janet B. Hewett, ed. *South Carolina Confederate Soldiers, 1861-1865* (Vol. 1, Name Roster, Vol. 2, Unit Roster) (Wilmington, N.C.: Broadfoot Publishing Company, 1998)

BGA   James Thomas Woodward, "South Carolina Confederate Soldiers Buried in Georgia." (Undated typed manuscript in the S.C. Department of Archives and History, Columbia, S.C.)

BHC   U.R. Brooks, *Butler and His Cavalry in the War of Secession* (Columbia, S.C.: The State Co., 1909)

BIG   Mamie Yeary, *Reminiscences of the Boys In Gray* (Dallas, Tex.: Smith & Lamar, 1912)

BLC   "Known South Carolina dead buried in Blandford Church Cemetery." (A list provided by John R. Davis, Jr., chief of interpretation, Petersburg National Battlefield, National Park Service, 1990. List is based upon City of Petersburg records of deaths in hospitals and a record of the dead of Elliott's Brigade at the Crater. This manuscript is in the collections of the South Carolina Historical Society.)

BLM   "Blandford Church Memorial, erected by the State of South Carolina to the memory of her sons who lost their lives in the defence of their country at the Battle of the Crater, July 30, 1864, Elliott's Brigade." (Virginia Historical Inventory, Dinwiddie County, 1936-1937, by the Works Progress Administration. Copy provided by the National Park Service and now in the collections of the South Carolina Historical Society.)

BNC   "Individuals from southern states who died during the Civil War and are buried in the Beaufort National Cemetery, 1601 Boundary Street, Beaufort, South Carolina." (Typed list is in the collections of the South Carolina Historical Society.)

BOD   Steven R. Stotelmeyer, "The Bivouacs of the Dead: The Story of Those Who Died at Antietam and South Mountain With Histories and Rosters of Antietam, Washington, Mt. Olivet and Elmwood Cemeteries" (Baltimore, Md.: Toomey Press, 1992)

BOS   J.F.J. Caldwell, *The History of a Brigade of South Carolinians First Known as Gregg's and Subsequently as McGowan's Brigade* (Philadelphia, Pa.: King and Baird Printers, 1866; repr., Dayton, Ohio: Morningside Press, 1992)

CCA   Stewart Sifakis, *Compendium of the Confederate Armies, South Carolina and Georgia* (New York: Facts on File, Inc., 1995)

CAE   R. Wayne Bratcher, *Cemetery Records of Abbeville County, S.C.* (Greenville, S.C.: A Press, 1982)

CAG   Gary R. Baker, *Cadets in Gray* (Columbia, S.C.: Palmetto Bookworks, 1989)

CB   Robert J. Stevens, *Captain Bill, Book One: The Records and Writings of Captain William Henry Edwards (and others), Company A, 17th Regiment, South Carolina Volunteers, Confederate States of America* (Richburg, S.C.: Chester District Genealogical Society, 1985) Robert J. Stevens, *Captain Bill, Book Two: The Records and Writings of Captain William Henry Edwards (and others), Company A, 17th Regiment, South Carolina Volunteers, Confederate States of America* (Richburg, S.C.: Chester District Genealogical Society, 1985) Robert J. Stevens, *Captain Bill, Book Three: A Genealogy of the Catawba River Valley of South Carolina, Chester-York-Lancaster Counties Edwards, Culp, McFadden families* (Darlington, S.C.: Self-published, 1990)

CBC   Theodore P. Savas, ed., *Charleston Battles and Seacoast Operations in South Carolina* (Campbell, Calif.: Regimental Studies Inc., 1996)

CC   William H. Krause, *The Story of Camp Chase* (Nashville, Tenn.: Publishing House of the Methodist Episcopal Church, South, 1906)

CCM   Larry O. Blair and Thomas E. Lyle, *Confederate Veterans Interred in the Confederate Cemetery, Marietta, Ga.* (Maryville, Tenn.: Printed by Byron's Graphic Arts, 1991)

CCP   Ron Chepesiuk, *Chester County, A Pictorial History* (Norfolk, Va.: The Donning Co., 1984)

CD   *Confederate Soldiers, Sailors and Civilians Who Died as Prisoners of War at Camp Douglas, Chicago, Ill., 1862-1865* (Kalamazoo, Mich.: Edgar Gray Publications, n.d.)

CDC   *Charleston Daily Courier* (Various issues 1860-1865. Microfilm in the Charleston County Library)

CDG   *The Bulletin of the Chester District Genealogical Society, Volume XVII, No. 2* (June 1993)

CDN   Brent Holcombe, *Marriage and Death Notices From Camden, S.C. Newspapers, 1816-1865* (Easley, S.C.: Southern Historical Press, 1978)

CEN   1860 Census schedules, M653 series Microfilm rolls, National Archives, Washington, D.C.

CGB   Richard Lewis, *Camp Life of a Confederate Boy of Bratton's Brigade, Longstreet's Corps, C.S.A.* (Charleston, S.C.: News and Courier Book Presses, 1883; repr., Gaithersburg, Md.: The Butternut Press, n.d.)

CGH   Robert A. Hodge, *A Death Roster of the Confederate General Hospital at Culpepper, Virginia* (Fredericksburg, Va.: Robert A. Hodge, 1977)

CGS   Varina D. Brown, *A Colonel at Gettysburg and Spotsylvania* (Columbia, S.C.: The State Co., 1931; repr., Baltimore, Md.: Butternut and Blue, n.d.)

CGW   R. Lockwood Tower, ed., *A Carolinian Goes to War: The Civil War Narrative of Arthur Middleton Manigault, Brigadier General, C.S.A.* (Columbia, S.C.: Published for the Charleston Library Society by the University of South Carolina Press, 1983)

CIG   Larry J. Daniel, *Cannoneers in Gray: The Field Artillery of the Army of Tennessee, 1861-1865* (Tuscaloosa, Ala: University of Alabama Press, 1984)

CKB   Charles Kelly Barrow, "Letter list of South Carolina dead buried in Forsyth, Milner, Barnesville & Thomaston, Ga." Sent to the author, 1991.

CLD   Edward L. Wells, *A Sketch of the Charleston Light Dragoons from the Earliest Formation of the Corps* (Charleston, S.C.: Lucas, Richardson & Co., 1888)

CMH5 Ellison Capers, *South Carolina, Volume V of Confederate Military History* (Atlanta, Ga.: Confederate Publishing Co., 1899; repr., n.p.:Blue & Grey Press, n.d.)

CML   W.J. Tancig, *Confederate Military Land Units, 1861-1865* (Cranbury, N.J.: Thomas Yoseloff, 1967)

CMO   Chester CSA Memorial Monument, erected May 7, 1938, in Richburg, S.C., by the Lafayette Strait Chapter, United Daughters of the Confederacy.

CNM   *Charleston Mercury* (Various issues, 1860-1865. (Microfilm held by the Charleston County Library.)

COF   William A. Albaugh III, *Confederate Faces: A Pictorial Review of the Individuals in the Confederate Armed Forces* (Solana Beach, Calif.: Wm. A. Albaugh III and Verde Publishers; repr., Wilmington, N.C.: Broadfoot Publishing Co., 1993)

COL   Confederate Letters and Diaries by Walbrook D. Swank, Colonel, USAF Ret. 1988 Route 2, Box 433, Mineral, VA 23117. Printed by Papercraft Printing and Design Co., Charlottesville, Va.

COT   Colleton County Township and County Confederate Enrollment books. Original and microfilm in Colleton County Clerk of Court office. Transcription manuscript by William Syfrett, Walterboro, S.C. Copy held by R.W. Kirkland, Hagood, S.C.

CRD   Eleanor D. McSwain, ed., *Crumbling Defences or Memoirs and Reminiscences of John Logan Black, Colonel, C.S.A.* (Macon, Ga.: The J.W. Burke Co., 1960)

CRM   "Chester Militia Roll" (A partial list of men who

APPENDICES

had gone into Confederate service from Beat No. 5, Western Battalion, 27th Regiment, South Carolina Militia, Chester District. Original document consisted of several hand-written pages from a larger ledger. The pages were purchased as memorabilia by R.W. Kirkland, transcribed, and the original document sent to a dealer for resale; it was lost in the mail. A copy of the transcription is in the collections of the South Carolina Historical Society.

CSR   Compiled Service Records of Confederate Soldiers Who Served in Organizations From the State of South Carolina. National Archives microfilm Series M267 in 392 rolls.

CSC   Fairfax Press, *The Confederate Soldier in the Civil War*. Imprint Society, Crown Publishers Inc. L.O.C. card # 77- 21259.

CSL   Spencer Glasgow Welch, *A Confederate Surgeon's Letters to his Wife* (New York: Neale Publishing Company, 1911; repr., Marietta, Ga.: Continental Book Co., 1954)

CSO   Joseph H. Crute, Jr., *Confederate Staff Officers, 1861-1865* (Powhatan, Va.: Derwent Books, 1982)

CSP   *Carolina Spartan*, Spartanburg, SC newspaper Dec. 19, 1861.- Dec.8, 1864. Microfilmed for the Wofford College Library Spartanburg, S.C. by Micro Photo, Inc. Cleveland, Ohio.

CTA   Danny H. Smith, *The Call to Arms* (Hemingway, S.C.: Three Rivers Historical Society, n.d.)

CUC   E.M.F. Bryan and G.H. Bryan, *Cemeteries of Upper Colleton County, S.C.* (Jacksonville, Fla.: Florentine Press, 1974)

CUS   J. Roderick Heller III & Carolynn Ayres Heller, *The Confederacy is on Her Way Up the Spout: Letters to South Carolina,1861-1864* (Athens: University of Georgia Press, 1992)

CV   Louis H. Manarin, ed., *Cumulative Index, The Confederate Veteran Magazine, 1893-1932* (Wilmington, N.C.: Broadfoot Publishing Co., 1990). See index for references to names of deceased soldiers, events, and places.

CVGA Charles Kelly Barrow, "List of S.C. CSA soldiers buried in Oakland Cemetery, Atlanta & Glenwood Cemetery, Thomaston, Ga.," *Palmetto Partisan* (Winter 1992)

CWC   Douglas Summers Brown, *City Without Cobwebs (A History of Rock Hill, S.C.)* (Spartanburg, S.C.: Reprint Co., 1975)

CWP   Robert E. Denney, *Civil War Prisons and Escapes* (New York, N.Y.: Sterling Publishing Co., Inc., 1993)

D14   "Roll of Honor, Co. D, 14th Regiment, S.C. Volunteers" (Edgefield, S.C.: Advertiser Office, 1866)

DAR   Eliza Cowan Ervin and Horace Fraser Rudisill, *Darlingtoniana: A History of People, Places and Events in Darlington County, S.C.* (Columbia, S.C.: R.L. Bryan Co., 1964)

DCH   Brent H. Holcomb, *Ancestors and Descendants of Charles Humphries of Union District, SC* (Columbia, S.C.: Brent H. Holcombe, 1985)

DEB   Bessie Mell Lane, ed., *Dear Bet, The Carter Letters, 1861-1865, The Letters of Lieutenant Sidney Carter, Company A, 14th Regiment, South Carolina Volunteers, Gregg's- McGowan's Brigade, CSA to Ellen Timmons Carter* (Clemson, S.C.: Self-published, 1978)

DEM   Robert Harley Mackintosh, Jr., ed., *"Dear Martha..." The Confederate War Letters of a South Carolina Soldier Alexander Faulkner Fewell* (Columbia, S.C.: R.L. Bryan Co., 1976)

DOC   John Johnson, *The Defense of Charleston Harbor including Fort Sumter and the Adjacent Islands, 1861-1865* (Charleston, S.C.: Walker, Evans & Cogswell, 1890; repr., Freeport, N.Y.: Books For Libraries Press, 1970)

DRE   "Dorchester County & Township CSA Enrollment Book." (A ledger manuscript in the collections of the South Carolina Historical Society)

EA   *Edgefield Advertiser*, Edgefield, S.C. newspaper Dec. 21, 1859-April 22, 1868. University Microfilms International, 300 N. Zeeb Rd., Ann Arbor, Mich. 48106

EDN   Carlee J. McClendon, *Edgefield Death Notices and Cemetery Records* (Columbia, S.C.: The Hive Press, 1977)

EDR   William Valmore Izlar, *A Sketch of the War Record of the Edisto Rifles, 1861-1865* (Columbia, S.C.: The State Co., 1914; repr., Camden, S.C.: J.J. Fox, 1990)

EFW   Eugene W. Jones, Jr., *Enlisted For the War, The Struggles of the Gallant 24th Regiment, South Carolina Volunteers, Infantry, 1861-1865* (Hightstown, N.J.: Longstreet House,1997)

ELM   C.W. Holmes, *Elmira Prison Camp* (New York: G. P. Putnam's Sons, 1912)

EMC   William A. Turner, *Even More Confederate Faces* (Orange, Va.: Moss Publications, 1983)

ETT   Eleanor Boland Owens, *Sketches of Private E.T. Tollison, C.S.A.* (Bamberg, S.C.: Kilgus Printing Co., Inc., 1992)

ETW   Walbrook Davis Swank, *Eyewitness to War, 1861-1865, Vol. 1: Memoirs of Men Who Fought in the Battle of Trevillian Station 11-12 June 1864* (Charlottesville, Va.: USAFRET Papercraft Printing & Design Co., Inc., 1990)

FAF   "Farr and Near Farr," Pamphlet self published by Eugene Farr, 1997.

FBG Robert K. Krick, *Roster of the Confederate Dead in the Fredericksburg Confederate Cemetery* (Fredericksburg, Va.: n.p., 1974)

FCP Brent H. Holcomb and Elmer O. Parker, *Early Records of Fishing Creek Presbyterian Church, Chester County, SC, 1799-1859* (Greenville, S.C.: A Press, 1980)

FIP Fisher Papers, a manuscript selection of research notes on South Carolina Cofederate soldier service records and other material chiefly concerning the Florence, SC area and Darlington County. South Carolina Historical Society files.

FLR The Arthur Manigault Chapter of the United Daughters of the Confederacy, Georgetown, S.C. *For Love of a Rebel* (Charleston, S.C.: Walker, Evans & Cogswell, 1964; Revised ed., 1974)

FPH Frances Ingmire and Carolyn Ericson, *Confederate P.O.W.'s Soldiers & Sailors Who Died in Federal Prisons & Military Hospitals in the North*. Compiled in the Office of the Commissioner for Marking Ground of Confederate Dead, War Department, 1912. (n.p., 1984)

FRB John M. Carroll, *List of Field Officers, Regiments & Battalions in the Confederate States Army 1861-1865* (Mattituck, N.Y.: J.M. Carroll & Co., 1983)

FSC National Park Service, Ft. Sumter National Monument, A list of casualties incurred in the defense of Ft. Sumter 1861-1865 compiled and maintained by the historian. Copy in South Carolina Historical Society files.

GAO Judith N. Arthur and Orville Vernon Burton, *A Gentleman and an Officer, A Military and Social History of James B. Griffin's Civil War*, (New York: Oxford University Press, 1996).

GAY D. Alexander Brown, *The Galvanized Yankees* (Urbana: University of Illinois Press, 1963)

GDR Robert W. Krick, *Gettysburg Death Roster* (Dayton, Ohio: Press of Morningside Book-shop, 1981)

GEC Greenville Chapter, S.C. Genealogical Society, *Greenville County Cemetery Survey*, Vols. 1-5 (Greenville, S.C.: A Press, 1977-1983)

GEE Beverly T. Whitmore, ed., *The Presence of the Past: Epitaphs of 18th and 19th Century Pioneers in Greenville County, South Carolina, and Their Descendants* ...(Baltimore, Md.: Published for the Greenville County Historical Society by Gateway Press, 1976)

GIG Ezra J. Warner, *Generals in Gray: Lives of the Confederate Commanders* (Baton Rouge: Louisiana State University Press, 1983)

GLS William Francis Strait III, ed., *Gilbert Matier Lafayette Strait, His Letters and His Times, 1851-1863* (Self-published, 1988)

GMJ *General Micah Jenkins and the Palmetto Sharpshooters*. South Carolina Regimental Series. (Germantown, Tenn.: Guild Bindery Press, Inc., 1994)

GNG *Georgetown County, S.C. Tombstone Inscriptions* (Georgetown: Georgetown County Historical Society and the Georgetown Committee of the National Society of Colonial Dames of America in the State of South Carolina, 1980)

GOR "Gordonsville, Va. Receiving Hospital Death Roster." (Manuscript held by the City of Gordonsville, copy in the collections of the South Carolina Historical Society.)

GRG Sol Emanuel, "An Historical Sketch of The Georgetown Rifle Guards and as Co. A of the Tenth Regiment S.C. Volunteers ..." (n.p., n.d. [1909?])

GRS J.L. Mauldin, "Minutes of the Meeting of the Gist Rifles Survivors Association, Company D, Hampton Legion, C.S.A. at Williamston, S.C., August 15,1883 and Company Muster Roll, From 1st Manassas to Appomattox 1861-1865." (n.p., n.d.)

GSR "Greensboro Surrender Paroles." National Archives Microfilm #418, held by R.W. Kirkland, Hagood, S.C.

H2 Mac Wyckoff, *A History of the 2nd South Carolina Infantry,1861-65* (Fredericksburg, Va.: Sergeant Kirkand's Museum and Historical Society, 1994)

H3 Mac Wyckoff, *A History of the 3rd South Carolina Infantry, 1861-1865* (Fredericksburg, Va.: Sergeant Kirkland's Museum and Historical Society, 1995)

H15 Robert B. Wilkinson, Jr., "A Brief History & Roster of the Fifteenth South Carolina Volunteer Infantry, Confederate States Army, Company C and Company I in the War Between the States, 1861-1865." (Unpublished manuscript in the Newberry/Saluda Regional Library, July 1987)

HAG Johnson Hagood, *Memoirs of the War of Secession* (Columbia, S.C.: The State Company, 1910; repr., Camden, S.C.: J.J. Fox, 1989)

HC Hollywood Memorial Association, *Register of Confederate Dead Interred in Hollywood Cemetery, Richmond, Va.* (Richmond,Va.: Gary, Clemmitt & Jones, 1869)

HCD Edward McCrady, *Heroes of the Old Camden District, South Carolina, 1776-1861...* (Richmond, Va.: Wm. Ellis Jones, Printer, 1888)

HCL Virginia K.G. Orvin, *History of Clarendon County,1700-1961* (n.p., n.d.)

HFC Fitz Hugh McMaster, *History of Fairfield County, South Carolina From Before The White Man Came to 1942* (Columbia, S.C.: The State Co., 1946)

APPENDICES

HGC George C. Rogers, Jr., *The History of Georgetown County, South Carolina* (Columbia: University of South Carolina Press, 1970)

HHC Anne Pickens Collins, *Heritage History of Chester County, South Carolina* (Chester, S.C.: Self-published, 1982)

HHS *History of the Hibernian Society in Charleston, S.C., 1799-1981* (Charleston: Self-published, 1981)

HIC Thomas J. Kirkland and Robert M. Kennedy, *Historic Camden, Part One: Colonial and Revolutionary* (Columbia, S.C.: The State Co., 1905; repr., Camden, S.C.: Kershaw County Historical Society, 1963) Thomas J. Kirkland and Robert M. Kennedy, *Historic Camden, Part Two: Nineteenth Century* (Columbia, S.C.: The State Co.,1926; repr., Camden, S.C.: The Kershaw County Historical Society, 1963)

HLS "Minutes of the Proceedings of The Reunion of the Hampton Legion Survivors Held in Columbia, S.C. on the 21st Day of July, A.D. 1875" (Charleston, S.C.: Walker, Evans & Cogswell, Printers, 1875)

HMA John Peyre Thomas, *History of the South Carolina Military Academy* (Charleston, S.C.: Walker, Evans and Cogswell Printers, 1893)

HMC W.W. Sellers, *History Of Marion County, S.C., From Its Earliest Times to the Present* (Columbia, S.C.: R.L. Bryan Co., 1902; repr., Marion, S.C.: Marion Public Library, 1956)

HOA J. Gavin Appleby, M.D. "A History of Appleby's Church." An unpublished manuscript including a roster of Company C, 24th SCVI Walterboro, SC 1987. South Carolina Historical Society files.

HOE John A. Chapman, *History of Edgefield County From the Earliest Settlements to 1897* (Newberry, S.C.: Elbert H. Aull, 1897; repr., Easley, S.C.: Southern Historical Press, 1976)

HOF J. W. Reid, *History of the Fourth Regiment of S.C. Volunteers From the Commencement of the War Until Lee's Surrender ...* (n.p., 1891; repr., Dayton, Ohio: Press of Morningside Bookshop, 1975)

HOL H.A. Carlisle, *History of Lowndesville* (Danielsville, Ga.: Heritage Papers, 1987)

HOM J.A.W. Thomas, *A History of Marlboro County, With Traditions and Sketches of Numerous Families* (Atlanta, 1897; repr., Baltimore, Md.: Regional Publishing Co., 1971)

HOS Dr. T.B.D. Landrum, *History of Spartanburg County* (1900; repr., Spartanburg, S.C.: Reprint Co., 1960)

HOW William Willis Bodie, *History of Williamsburg* (Columbia, S.C.: The State Co. 1923; repr., Spartanburg, S.C.: Reprint Co., 1980)

HSF South Carolina Historical Society miscellaneous genealogical files containing data on Confederate soldiers submitted by individuals.

HSU Anne King Gregorie, *History of Sumter County* (Sumter, S.C.: Library Board of Sumter County, 1954)

IRQ *The Independant Republic Quarterly*, a journal published quarterly by the Horry County Historical Society, P.O. Box 2025 Conway, S.C. 29528.

ISH James R. Hagood, *The Immortal Six Hundred: A Story of Cruelty to Confederate Prisoners of War* (Winchester, Va.: The Eddy Press Corp., 1905; repr., Little Rock, Ark.: Eagle Press, 1986)

JES C. Foster Smith, *Jeremiah Smith and The Confederate War* (Spartanburg, S.C.: Reprint Co., 1993)

JLC James Lide Coker, *History of Company G, 9th S.C. Regiment, Infantry, S.C. Army and of Company E, Sixth S.C. Regiment, Infantry, S.C. Army* (Charleston, S.C.: Walker, Evans & Cogswell, 1899; repr., Greenwood, S.C.: Attic Press, Inc., 1979)

JMB Ruth Barr McDaniel, *Confederate War Correspondence of James Michael Barr & Wife Rebecca Ann Dowling Barr* (n.p., 1963)

JR A partial list of South Carolina Confederate dead prepared by William B. Johnston under the direction of the South Carolina legislature. This work was superseded by "The Roll of the Dead" by Professor William Rivers. The manuscript ledger is in the S.C. Department of Archives and History, Columbia.

JRH Col. James R. Hagood, "Memoirs of the 1st SCVI in the Confederate War for Independence from April 12, 1861 to April 10, 1865." (Manuscript in the South Caroliniana Library, Columbia, S.C.)

K23 W.J. Andrews, *Sketch of Company K, 23rd South Carolina Volunteers, in the Civil War, From 1862-1865* (Richmond, Va.: Whittet & Shepperson, 1909; repr., Suffolk, Va.: Robert Hardy Publications, 1986)

KCE The 1850 Kershaw Co. South Carolina Census, Compiled by the Catawba-Wateree Chapter of the South Carolina Genealogical Society 1997.

KCS Kershaw County Cemetery Survey Project, Kershaw County, South Carolina, Cemetery Survey, 3 Volumes (Camden, S.C.: Kershaw County Historical Society, 1991)

KEB D. Augustus Dickert, *History of Kershaw's Brigade...* (Newberry, S.C.: Albert H. Aull Co., 1899; repr., Dayton, Ohio: The Press of Morningside Bookshop, 1976)

LAN	Frances Reeves Jeffcoat, Confederate Records, Lancaster District, S.C., gleaned from S.C. Department of Archives and History and the Lancaster Ledger, 1986 (Columbia, S.C.: Self-published, 1986)
LC	Robert W. Krick, ed., Lee's Colonels: A Biographical Register of the Field Officers of the Army of Northern Virginia (3rd ed., Dayton, Ohio: Press of Morningside House, Inc., 1991)
LCA	Arthur P. Ford and Marion Johnstone Ford, Life in the Confederate Army and Some Experiences and Sketches of Southern Life (New York: The Neale Publishing Co., 1905)
LCD	Confederate Burials, a series of booklets compiled by the Lauderdale County Department of Archives and History, Mississippi. Based upon the research of Raymond W. Watkins of Falls Church, Va.
LED	A. Toomer Porter, Led On! Step By Step ... (New York: G.P. Putnam's Sons, The Knickerbocker Press, 1898; repr. New York: Arno Press, 1967)
LGS	"Lexington County Genealogical Survey," in Lexington County Genealogical Association Exchange Jane Anderson Seay, Silent Cities: A Tombstone Registry of Old Lexington District, S.C.(Self-published, 1984)
LSC	James Leland Bolt and Margaret Eltinge Bolt, Church and Family Cemeteries, Laurens County, S.C. (Greenville, S.C.: A Press, 1983)
LSS	W.S. Dunlop, Lee's Sharpshooters or The Forefront of Battle... (Little Rock, Ark., 1899; repr., Dayton, Ohio: Press of Morningside Bookshop, 1982)
MAC	The Magazine of Albemarle County, Va. History 22 (1963-1964, Civil War issue) (Charlottesville, Va.: The Michie Co., 1964)
MAG	A Brief History of the Ladies Memorial Association of Charleston, S.C. ...Together With A Roster of the Confederate Dead, Interred At Magnolia and the Various City Church Yards (Charleston, S.C.: H.P. Cooke & Co., 1880)
MCC	McCormick County Historical Society, McCormick County Cemeteries (McCormick County, S.C.: Dick Moon Printing, Inc., 1987)
MCF	William A. Albaugh III, More Confederate Faces: A Pictorial Review (Washington, D.C.: ABS Printers, Inc., 1972; repr., Wilmington, N.C.: Broadfoot Publishing Co., 1993)
MCG	Betty Couch Wiltshire, Mississippi Confederate Graves Registration (Bowie, Md.: Heritage Books, Inc., 1991)
MDM	Olin Fulmer Hutchinson, Jr., ed., "My Dear Mother & Sisters," Civil War Letters of Capt. A.B. Mulligan, Co. B, 5th South Carolina Cavalry-Butler's Division-Hampton's Corps 1861-1865 (Spartanburg, S.C.: Reprint Co., 1992)
MIG	Thomas M. Spratt, Men in Gray, a set of 15 volumes listing Confederate soldier burials in Virginia (Athens, Ga.: Iberian Publishing Company Athens, Ga.)
MJL	Diary, J.L. McCrorey, 2nd Lieut., Co. B, 4th South Carolina Cavalry, 1864. Typescript in The South Caroliniana Library, Columbia, S.C.
MP	The Wade Hampton Chapter, United Daughters of the Confederacy, Columbia, S.C., Memorial Pamphlet: "Confederate Soldiers Who Died in the Service of Their Country and are Buried in Columbia, South Carolina 1861-1865" (n.p., n.d.)
MSF	Daniel E. Huger Smith, Alice R. Huger Smith, and Arney R. Childs, eds., Mason Smith Family Letters, 1860-1868 (Columbia: University of South Carolina Press, 1950)
NCC	George Carter Abrams, ed., Newberry County, South Carolina Cemeteries: Volumes One and Two (Newberry, S.C.: Newberry Publishing Co. for The Newberry County Historical Society, 1982)
NHU	Alan D. Charles, Narrative History of Union County, S.C. (Spartanburg, S.C.: Reprint Co., 1987)
NPS	Confederate casualties at Ft. Sumter, S.C., a listing compiled by Richard Hatcher, Historian National Park Service. Fort Sumter National Park.
NYH	Newberry Herald, Issue of August 7, 1867 in which appeared a letter to the editor by J. Hawkins listing South Carolina soldiers buried in the Gordonsville, VA Confederate Cemetery, copied for the South Carolina Historical Society by Christopher S. Prince.
OCS	B.W. Roach and Sarah Roach, Oconee County, South Carolina Cemetery Survey: Volumes One and Two (Greenville, S.C.: A Press for The Pendleton Chapter of the South Carolina Genealogical Society, 1983-1984)
OWC	Oakwood Cemetery, Richmond, Va., a typed manuscript list of Confederate soldiers buried there provided by Keith C. Morgan, Chief of Interpretation National Park Service, Richmond National Battlefield Park. This copy is now in the files of the South Carolina Historical Society.
Px	National Archives Selected Records of the War Department Relating to Confederate Prisoners of War, 1861-1865 (145 microfilm rolls, series M598.) In this volume the particular roll sourced is identified by "P" followed by a number identifying the specific microfilm roll of the 145 in the National Archives catalogue.
PCS	Pendleton Chapter of the South Carolina Genealogical Society, Pickens County, South Carolina Cemetery Survey Volumes One and Two (Greenville, S.C.: A Press, n.d.)

APPENDICES

PDL   Joseph Woods Brunson, ed., *Pee Dee Light Artillery of Maxcy Gregg's (Later Samuel McGowan's) Brigade First South Carolina Volunteers (Infantry) C.S.A ...* (Winston-Salem, N.C.: Stewart Printers, 1927; repr., William Stanley Hoole, ed., Dayton, Ohio: Morningside House, 1983)

PL   E. W. Beitzell, *Point Lookout Prison Camp* (n.p., n.d.)

PMC   Manuscript list of camps occupied by South Carolina units during the Civil War compiled by Patrick McCawley, S.C. Dept. of Archives and History from various unidentified sources. Copy in South Carolina Historical Society files.

PP   *Paths to the Past*, Confederate death and burial lists compiled in a number of bound pamphlets by the Lauderdale County (Mississippi) Department of Archives and History. These are largely based on the Watkins compilations, with added material derived from local research. Copies in the collections of the South Carolina Historical Society.

Rx   National Archives Compiled Records Showing Service of Military Units in Confederate Organizations, 74 microfilm rolls, series M861. In this volume the particular microfilm roll sourced is identified by an R followed by the number of the specific roll.

RAP   Frank M. Mixson, *Reminiscences of a Private* (Columbia, S.C.: The State Co., 1910; repr., Camden, S.C.: J.J. Fox, 1990)

RAS   C. I. Walker, *Rolls and Historical Sketch of the Tenth Regiment So. Ca. ...* (Charleston, S.C.: Walker, Evans & Cogswell, 1881; repr., Alexandria, Va.: Stonewall House, 1985)

RCD   June Wells, ed., "Roster of Confederate Dead." A manuscript compiled by Agatha Aimar Simmons in 1957 with a list prepared by Yates Snowden in 1880. Includes material collected by M.C. Meigs, tombstone inscriptions by W.P.A., and private data. Copy is in the collections of the South Carolina Historical Society.

RCO   Rome *Courier* (July 17,1866, Rome, Georgia). A list of S.C. soldiers buried in Myrtle Hill Cemetery, Rome, Georgia.

RHL   "Roll of Honor, Confederate Dead in Laurens Cemetery." A copy of a 1918 pamphlet in The South Caroliniana Library, Columbia, S.C.

RME   Richard L. Beach, ed., *Remember Me: The Civil War Letters of Lt. George Robinson and His Son Sgt. James Robinson of "The Glenn" Hamburg, South Carolina, 1861-1862* (Bowie, Md.: Heritage Books, Inc., 1991)

ROD   Records of Deaths in Columbia, SC and Elsewhere as Recorded by John Glass 1859-1877 by Brent Holcombe.

ROH   National Archives microfilm list of South Carolina CSA dead, 1861-1865. This microfilm, made from Professor Rivers's "Roll of Honor" which had been deposited in the National Archives in 1947 after being discovered in the vaults of a bank in Charleston, S.C. The original document was returned to the S.C. Department of Archives and History in 1994.

ROP   Alan Thigpen, *The Illustrated Recollections of Potter's Raid* (Columbia, S.C.: Gamecock City Printing, Inc. 1998)

RRT   "Rivers' Raising of Troops for Confederate Service," included in *The Report of the Historian of the Confederate Records to the General Assembly of South Carolina For the Year 1899* (Columbia, S.C.: R. L. Bryan Co., 1900)

RSP   Samuel N. Thomas, Jr. and Jason H. Silverman, eds., *A Rising Star of Promise, The Civil War Odyssey of David Jackson Logan, 17th SCVI* (Campbell, Calif.: Savas Publishing Co., 1998)

16R   John S. Taylor, *Sixteenth South Carolina Regiment CSA From Greenville County, S.C.* (n.p., 1964)

SA1   A.S. Salley, Jr., *South Carolina Troops in Confederate Service, Volume 1* (Columbia, S.C.: R.L. Bryan Co. 1913)

SA2   A.S. Salley, Jr., *South Carolina Troops in Confederate Service, Volume II* (Columbia, S.C.: The State Co., 1914)

SA3   A.S. Salley, Jr., *South Carolina Troops in Confederate Service, Volume III* (Columbia, S.C.: The State Co., 1930)

SAS   Carol Bleser, ed., *Secret and Sacred: The Diaries of James Henry Hammond, a Southern Slaveholder* (New York: Oxford University Press, 1988)

SCA   Charles Inglesby, *Historical Sketch of the 1st Regiment of South Carolina Artillery* (Regulars) (Charleston, S.C.: n.p., n.d.)

SCC   The Pinckney Chapter, South Carolina Genealogical Society, *Spartanburg County, S.C. Cemetery Survey* (n.p., n.d.)

SCH   "Register of men buried in Confederate Cemetery, Spotsylvania Court House, Va.," (repr., Confederate Cemetery Association, 1966)

SCL   Allen H. Stokes, Jr., *A Guide to the Manuscript Collection of the South Caroliniana Library* (Columbia: South Caroliniana Library, 1982)

SCS   John Amasa May and John Reynolds Faunt, *South Carolina Secedes ...* (Columbia: University of South Carolina Press, 1960)

SEW   John Michael Priest, *Stephen Elliott Welch of the*

	Hampton Legion (Shippensburg, Pa.: Burd Street Press, 1994)
SHS	James I. Robertson, ed., *Index-Guide to The Southern Historical Society Papers, 1876-1959* (Wilmington, N.C.: The Broadfoot Publishing Co., 1992). See index for references to specific names and battles.
SMC	Domenick A. Serrano, *Still More Confederate Faces* (Bayside, N.Y.: Metropolitan Co., 1992)
SOB	Glenn Dedmont, *Southern Bronze, Capt. Garden's (S.C.) Artillery Company During the War Between the States* (Columbia, S.C.: Palmetto Bookworks, 1993)
SOC	E. Milby Burton, *The Siege of Charleston, 1861-1865* (Columbia: University of South Carolina Press, 1970)
SRG	Walter Brian Cisco, *States Rights Gist: A South Carolina General of the Civil War* (Shippensburg, Pa.: White Mane Publishing Co., 1991)
SSC	Joseph R. Gainey, ed., *Some Spartanburg County Cemeteries* (Spartanburg, S.C.: Piedmont Historical Society, 1983)
SSO	Lloyd Halliburton, *Saddle Soldiers: The Civil War Correspondence of General William Stokes of the 4th South Carolina Cavalry* (Orangeburg, S.C.: Sandlapper Publishing Co., 1993)
STC	U.R. Brooks, ed., *Stories of the Confederacy* (Columbia, S.C.: The State Co., 1912)
STR	Warren Ripley, ed., *Siege Train: The Journal of a Confederate Artilleryman in the Defense of Charleston* (Columbia: Published for the Charleston Library Society by the University of South Carolina Press, 1986)
37V	J.L. Scott, *36th and 37th Battalions Virginia Cavalry* (Lynchburg, Va.: H.E. Howard, Inc., 1986)
3RC	Three Rivers Historical Society, *Survey of Cemeteries in Williamsburg, Florence and Georgetown Counties* (n.p., n.d.)
TCC	Bobby G. Moss and Dennis R. Amos, *Tombstones & Cemeteries of Cherokee County, S.C., Vols.1-4* (Greenville, S.C.: A Press, 1984)
TCP	William Morrison Robinson, Jr., *The Confederate Privateers* (New Haven, Ct.: Yale University Press 1928; reprinted Columbia, S.C.: University of South Carolina Press 1990)
THL	Ron Field with William B. Bynam and Howard Michael Madaus, *The Hampton Legion* (Lower Swell, Gloucestershire, UK: Design Folio, 1994)
TOD	Manuscript research records on the CSA service of the Todd and Amick families of South Carolina plus research into the records of Companies I and C of the 15th SCVI. This collection includes a number of Confederate graveyard lists from varous places in Virginia, North Carolina, Georgia, etc., and has been completed through 1994. Copy in the collections of the South Carolina Historical Society.
TRR	John K. McIver Chapter, United Daughters of the Confederacy, *Treasured Reminiscences Including accounts of the 1st, 6th, 8th, 9th, and 21st Regiments, South Carolina Volunteer Infantry, The 6th South Carolina Cavalry Regiment, and the 1st, 15th and Pee Dee Volunteer Artillery Battalions, Confederate States Army, 1861-1865* (Columbia, S.C.: The State Co., 1911)
TSC	Natalie Jenkins Bond and Osman Latrobe Coward, eds., *The South Carolinians: Colonel Asbury Coward's Memoirs* (New York: Vantage Press, 1968)
TSE	James J. Baldwin, III, *The Struck Eagle, A Biography of Brigadier General Micah Jenkins, and a History of the Fifth South Carolina Volunteers and the Palmetto Sharpshooters* (Shippenburg, Pa.: Burd Street Press, 1996)
TYL	James Lee Conrad, *The Young Lions: Confederate Cadets at War* (Mechanicsburg, Pa.: Stackpole Books,1997).
UCH	Union County Heritage, 1981
UCS	Joseph H. Croute, Jr., *Units of the Confederate States Army* (Midlothian, Va.: Derwent Books, 1987)
UD1	*Recollections and Reminiscences,1861-1865 Through World War I, Volume One* (n.p.: The South Carolina Division of the United Daughters of the Confederacy, 1990)
UD2	*Recollections and Reminiscences, 1861-1865 Through World War I, Volume Two* (n.p.: The South Carolina Division of the United Daughters of the Confederacy, 1991)
UD3	*Recollections and Reminiscences, 1861-1865 Through World War I, Volume Three* (n.p.: The South Carolina Division of the United Daughters of the Confederacy, 1992)
UD4	*Recollections and Reminiscences 1861-1865 Through World War I, Volume Four* (n.p.: The South Carolina Division of the United Daughters of the Confederacy, 1993)
UD5	*Recollections and Reminscences, 1861-1865 Through World War I, Volume Five* (n.p.: The South Carolina Division of the United Daughters of the Confederacy, 1994)
UD6	*Recollections and Reminiscences, 1861-1865 Through World War I, Volume Six* (n.p.: The South Carolina Division of the United Daughters of the Confederacy, 1995)
UD7	*Recollections and Reminiscences, 1861-1865 Through World War I, Volume Seven* (n.p.: The South Carolina Division of the United Daughters

APPENDICES

UD8   of the Confederacy, 1997)
Recollections and Reminiscences, 1861-1865 Through World War I, Volume Eight (n.p.: The South Carolina Division of the United Daughters of the Confederacy, 1998)

UNC   Mrs. E.D. Whaley, Sr., *Union County Cemeteries: Epitaphs of 18th and 19th Century Settlers in Union County, S.C. and Their Descendants* (Greenville, S.C.: A Press, 1976)

V1G   Ron Field, *1st South Carolina Volunteers (Gregg's)* (Lower Swell, Gloucestershire, U.K:. Design Folio, 1991)

V4   Ron Field, *4th South Carolina Volunteers (Sloan's)* (Lower Swell, Gloucestershire, U.K.: Design Folio, 1992) (A pamphlet publication in a series describing S.C. regiments and battalions)

WAT   The Watkins S.C. Confederate Burial Papers, four folders with various unbound reports of South Carolina CSA graves around the country. Researched and reported by Mr. Raymond F. Watkins, Springfield, Va. Copies held in S.C. Department of Archives and History, Columbia.

WCT   "Williamson County Confederate Cemetery, Tennessee." (An extract list of South Carolina dead in cemetery sections 83, 84, 85, and 86. The original is lost but page 17 of a larger list survives; it probably was prepared by a Williamson County research group. Copy in the collections of the South Carolina Historical Society.

WDB   James Richmond Boulware, "The War Diary of Dr. J.R. Boulware, C. S. Army Assistant Surgeon 6th South Carolina Volunteer Infantry." (Unpublished typed manuscript in the South Caroliniana Library, Columbia, S.C.)

WDC   "In the Name of the Fallen: A list of the Names of the Dead Confederate Soldiers Buried in the Confederate Mound at Warrenton, VA." A circular prepared by the Black Horse Chapter, UDC for support of a memorial Black Horse Chapter, UDC, P.O. Box 1006, Warrenton, Va. 20188.

WHR   Wayside (1st Louisiana) Confederate Hospital, Charleston, S.C. Patient Register. A manuscript transcript from records in the S.C. Dept. of Archives and History compiled by Lewis F. Knudsen, Jr., 301 Timberhill Court, Columbia, S.C. 29212. Copy in South Carolina Historical Society files.

WIN   Lucy Fitzhugh Kurtz and Benny Ritter, *A Roster of Confederate Soldiers Buried in Stonewall Cemetery, Winchester, Virginia* (Winchester, Va.: Published through the courtesy of the Farmers & Merchants National Bank, 1962)

WLI   Washington Light Infantry Monument list of Confederate dead in Washington Park, Charleston, S.C.

WV   Gregory A. Coco, *Wasted Valor: The Confederate Dead at Gettysburg* (Gettysburg, Pa.: Thomas Publications, 1990)

YE   *Yorkville Enquirer,* 1861-1866, University Microfilms International 300 N. Zeeb Rd., Ann Arbor, Mich. 48106-1346.

YEB   Jo Robert Owens and Ruth Dickson Thomas, *Confederate Veterans Enrollment Book of York County, S.C. 1902* (Glover, S.C.: Westmoreland Printers, Inc., 1983)

YMD   Brent H. Holcomb, *York, South Carolina, Newspapers Marriage and Death Notices, 1823-1865* (Spartanburg, S.C.: Reprint Co., 1981)

Place Name Conventions

Appomattox, VA

Averysboro, NC (3/16/65)

Armstrong Mills, VA (12/10/64, Cavalry skirmish)

Battery Isl., SC (5/21/62, Skirmish, 24th SCVI)

Bean's Stn., TN (12/14/63)

Bentonville, NC (3/19-21/65)

Blackwater, VA

Blandford Church Pbg., VA (Burial site in Petersburg, Va.)

Boonesboro, MD (AKA South Mountain, Md., 1862 Campaign)

Brandy St., VA (8/1/63, Cavalry battle, 2nd SCVC)

Brown's Ferry, VA

Bty. Wagner, SC (8/17-26/64, 9/1-6/64)

Bull's Gap, TN (3/15/64, skirmish)

Burgess Mills, VA (10/27/64, 6th SCVC)

Burke's Stn., VA (10/28/63, 2nd SCVC)

Campbell Stn., TN (12/05/63, P.S.S.)

Centreville, VA

Chaffin's Farm, VA (9/29-10/02/64, 6th SCVC)

Chancellorsville, VA (5/5-6/63)

Culpepper Gen. Hos. (Culpepper, Va. General Hospital)

Chattanooga, TN

Charlottesville (VA.)

Clay's Farm, VA (5/20/64)

Cold Harbour, VA (6/1-3/64)

Crater Pbg., VA (Petersburg, Va., 7/30/64)

Darbytown Rd., VA (Richmond, Va. front)

Deep Bottom, VA (Richmond, Va. front, 7/27/64)

Dranesville, VA (12/20/61)

Drury's Bluff, VA (5/12/64)

Enterprise, MS

Fairfax, VA (Fairfax Court House, Va.)

Five Forks, VA (4/1/65)

Frayser's Farm (Richmond, Va. front, 6/30/62)

Fredericksburg (Fredericksburg, Va., 12/13/62)

Ft. Anderson, NC (2/19/65)

Ft. Fisher, NC (1/15/65)

Ft. Gaines, AL (Mobile Bay Culpepper's Battery, 8/8/64)

Ft. Harrison, VA (Richmond, Va. front, 9/20-30/64)

Fts. Monroe, VA (Fortress Monroe, Va.)

Ft. Sanders, TN (11/29/63)

Ft. Stedman, VA (3/25/65 Hol. Leg.)

Fussell's Mill, VA (8/16/64)

Gaines' Mill, VA (Richmond, Va. front, 6/27/62)

Gettysburg, PA (7/1-2-3/63)

Globe Tavern, VA (8/21/64, Hagood's Bgd.)

Gordonsville, VA

Germantown, VA

Hatcher's Run, VA (10/27/64, 2/5-7/65)

Hawes Shop, VA (5/28/64, 4th SCVC and 5th SCVC)

Jackson, MS (5/14/63, 24th SCVI - 7/16/63, 22nd SCVI)

James Island, SC (Various events and units)

Jarratt's Stn., VA (Jarratt's Depot or Station, 5/8/64)

Jericho Ford, VA (North Anna River, 5/23/64)

Jerusalem, VA

Kennesaw Mtn., GA (6/27-28/64)

Kinston, NC (12/14/62, Evan's Brigade 17th SCVI, 18th SCVI, 22nd SCVI, 23rd SCVI, 26th SCVI, Hol. Leg.)

Lee's Mill, VA (6/30/64, 6th SCVC)

Lenoir's Stn. (6/19/63)

Lookout Mtn., TN (11/24/63)

Lookout Valley, TN (10/28/63)

Louisa C.H., VA (Louisa Court House, Va., 5/2/64)

Lovejoy's St., GA (Lovejoy's Station, Ga., 7/29/64)

Lynchburg, VA

1st Manassas, VA (7/21/61)

2nd Manassas, VA (8/29-30/62)

Manassas Jnctn. (Mannassas Junction, Va.)

Manchester, VA (Suburb of Richmond, Va., hospital site)

N. Anna River, VA (North Anna River, Va. AKA Jericho Ford, Va., 5/23/64)

New Hope Ch., GA (New Hope Church, Ga., 5/27/64)

New Kent C.H., VA (New Kent Court House, Va., 8/27/63)

APPENDICES

New Market, VA

Noel Station, VA (5/23/64)

Orange, VA (Orange Court House, Va.)

Ox Hill, VA (AKA Chantilly, Va., 9/1/62)

Peebles Farm, VA (9/29/64)

Petersburg, VA

Pickett's Fm., VA (7/21/64, 18th SCVI)

Rappahanock Stn. (Rappahanock Station, Va.)

Ream's Stn., VA (On the Weldon Railroad, Petersburg, Va., 8/21/64 & 8/25/64, Richmond, Va.)

Sappony Ch., VA (Sappony Church, Va., 7/1/64)

Savage Stn., VA (Richmond, Va. front, 6/29/62)

Secessionville (Secessionville, James Island, S.C., 6/16/64)

Sharpsburg, MD (9/17/62)

Smith's Crnr., NC (Smith's Corner, N.C. AKA Averysboro & Smith's Ford, 3/15/65)

S. Newport, GA (South Newport, Ga. skirmish, 8/17/64)

Spotsylvania, VA (5/8-19/64)

Springplace, GA (2/27/64, 3rd SCVC)

Stony Creek, VA (4/2/64)

Sullivans I., SC (Sullivan's Island, S.C.)

Sutherland Stn., VA (4/2/65)

Swift Creek, VA (5/7/64)

Town Creek, NC (2/20/65)

Trevillian Stn., Va. (6/11-12/64)

Walthall Jctn. (Port Walthall Junction, Va., 5/6/64)

Warrenton, VA

Wauhatchie, TN (AKA Racoon Mtn., 10/28/63)

Weldon RR, VA (8/18-22/64)

Whites Bridge, VA (11/26/63, skirmish, 2nd SCVC)

Wildcat Mtn., TN

Wills Valley, TN (8/31/63)

Winchester, VA

Wilderness, VA (5/5-6/64)

Williamsburg, VA (5/5/62)

Williamsburg Rd. (Richmond, Va. front, 10/27/64)

Wyatt's Farm, VA (9/29/64, 5th SCVC)

Unit Abbreviations

Ham. Leg. Hampton Legion

Hol. Leg. Holcombe Legion

Orr's Ri. Orr's Rifles, AKA 1st Regiment of Rifles

P.S.S. Palmetto Sharpshooter Regiment

1st SCVIG First South Carolina Volunteer Infantry Regiment (Gregg's)

1st SCVIH First South Carolina Volunteer Infantry Regiment (Hagood's)

1st SCVIR First South Carolina Volunteer Infantry Regiment (Regulars, converted to Heavy Artillery)

2nd SCVIRi. 2nd South Carolina Rifle Regiment

9th SCVIH 9th South Carolina Volunteer Infantry Regiment (Col. Heyward)

9th SCVIB 9th South Carolina Volunteer Infantry Regiment (Col. Blanding)

2nd SCVI-27th SCVI
Line infantry regiments with no identity complications

1st -3rd SCVA
Line artillery regiments. Note that the Ist SCVIR regiment served as fortification troops and is sometimes referred to as the First Atillery.

1st SCVIBn The First South Carolina Infantry Battalion, AKA as the Charleston Battalion

3rd SCVIBn The Third South Carolina Infantry Battalion, AKA the James Battalion.

4th SCVIBn The Forth South Carolina Infantry Battalion, AKA the Mattison Battalion.

7th SCVIBn The Seventh South Carolina Infantry Battalion, AKA the Enfield Rifles.

1st SCVC-7th SCVC
The seven line cavalry regiments. Note that these were formed by combining various older battalions and independant companies. The tracing of these earlier units is confusing but it should be recognized that many captures attributed to the final regimental

structure occured in one of the earlier smaller units.

SCRes There is no established listing of the various reserve orginizations called up from time to time. In some cases these are referred to as State Troops. The reserves called up late in the war seem to have been formed into battalions best known by their commander. An example is Gill's Battalion, a unit formed to guard prisoners at the Florence stockade. In this compilation an attempt has been made to assign official number identities to these units using the numbers cited in the National Archive M861 series of microfilm rolls of Confederate Units.

Rank Abbreviations

Pvt-Private
Cpl-Corporal
CCp-Color Corporal
2Cp-Second Corporal
Sgt-Sergeant
1Sg- First Sergeant
2Sg-Second Sergeant
QSg-Quartermaster Sergeant
OSg-Ordnance Sergeant
CSg-Color Sergeant
1Lt-First Lieutenant
2Lt-Second Lieutenant
3Lt-Third Lieutenant
Lt-Lieutenant
Adj-Adjutant
1Ad-First Lieutenant Adjutant
Cpt-Captain
Cap-Captain (Vessel)
Maj-Major
LtC-Lieutenant Colonel
Col-Colonel
BGn-Brigadier General
PMr-Paymaster
Sur-Surgeon
ASr-Assistant Surgeon
HSd-Hospital Steward
Bug-Buglar
Tsr-Teamster
Drm-Drummer
Msc-Musician
1Mt-First Mate
2Of-Second Officer
QMr-Quarter master
Smn-Seaman
Mte-Mate
Mct-Merchant
Plt-Pilot
Pgr-Passenger
1En-First Engineer
AEn-Assistant Engineer
Mtr-Master
Chp-Chaplain
Coo-Cook
Wgr-Wagoneer
Cit-Citizen
CiO-Civil Official
Rfg-Refugee

Extracts from the *Official Records* Concerning Prisoners of War

SERIES II AND SERIES M598 MICROFILM RECORDS RELATING TO CONFEDERATE PRISONERS OF WAR

RESOLUTION ADOPTED BY THE HOUSE OF REPRESENTATIVES – July 8, 1861

Resolved, That the Secretary of War be directed to instruct the officers of the Army of the United States taking prisoners and releasing them upon their oath of allegiance to the United States to report their name and residence to him that they may be recorded in his Department.

* * * *

JOINT RESOLUTION ADOPTED BY THE HOUSE OF REPRESENTATIVES – December 11, 1861

Whereas, the exchange of prisoners in the present rebellion has already been practiced indirectly, and as such exchange would not only increase the enlistment and vigor of our Army but subserve the highest interests of humanity and such exchange does not involve a recognition of the rebels as a government; therefore; Resolved, by the Senate and House of Representatives of the United States of America in Congress assembled, That the President of the United States be requested to inaugurate systematic measures for the exchange of prisoners in the present rebellion.

* * * *

**GENERAL ORDERS
HDQRS DEPARTMENT OF THE OHIO
NO. 17** – Louisville, Ky., December 17, 1861

The following extracts from the Army Regulations concerning duties in campaign are published for the information of the troops. They will be carefully studied by every officer:

ARTICLE XXXVI.

745. Prisoners of war will be disarmed and sent to the rear and reported as soon as practicable to the headquarters. The return of prisoners from the Headquarters of the Army to the War Department will specify the number, rank and corps.

746. The private property of prisoners will be duly respected and each shall be treated with the regard due to his rank. They are to obey the necessary orders given them. They receive for subsistence one ration each without regard to rank, and the wounded are to be treated with the same care as the wounded of the Army. Other allowances to them will depend on conventions with the enemy. Prisoners' horses will be taken for the army.

747. Exchanges of prisoners and release of officers on parole depend on the orders of the general commanding-in-chief under the instructions of the government.

By command of Brigadier-General Buell
James B. Fry
Assistant Adjutant General Chief of Staff

* * * *

**OFFICE COMMISSARY-GENERAL
OF PRISONERS** – New York, December 7, 1861

General L. Thomas
Adjutant-General U.S. Army, Washington D.C.
General: The office and duties of commissary-general of prisoners are not familiar to the service and I therefore respectfully request in order to avoid embarrassment that those who are in charge of prisoners of war, civil or military, may be notified that I have been appointed to that office and that any directions I may give in relation to prisoners may be complied with.

Very respectfully, your obedient servant,
W. Hoffman
*Lieut. Col. Eighth Infantry
Commissary-General of Prisoners*

* * * *

**GENERAL ORDERS
HEADQUARTERS ARMY OF THE POTOMAC
NO. 60** – Washington, February 21, 1862

I. Brig. Gen. Andrew Porter is announced as provost-marshal-general of the Army of the Potomac and will be obeyed and respected accordingly.

II. A provost-marshal for each division will be appointed by its commander. The division provost marshal will obey the orders of the division commander in all matters affecting interior police, but will be responsible to the provost marshal-general and be guided by such instructions as he may from time to time give. A sufficient guard will be detailed by the division commandeer for duty under the orders of the provost-marshal.

IX. All prisoners captured from the enemy will be turned over to the provost-marshal of division, who will send them at the earliest practicable moment with complete descriptive list and information as to where, when and how they were captured to the provost marshal-general.

By command of Major-General McClellan
S. Williams
Assistant Adjutant General

* * * *

**GENERAL ORDERS
WAR DEPT., ADJT. GENERAL'S OFFICE
NO. 60** – Washington, June 6, 1862

IV. The principle being recognized that medical officers should not be held as prisoners of war it is hereby directed that all medical officers so held by the United States shall be immediately and unconditionally discharged.

By order of the Secretary of War
L. Thomas
Adjutant-General

* * * *

**GENERAL ORDERS
WAR DEPT., ADJT. GENERAL'S OFFICE
NO. 67** – Washington, June 17, 1862

The supervision of prisoners of war sent by generals commanding in the field to posts or camps prepared for their reception is placed entirely under Col. William Hoffman, Third Infantry, commissary-general of prisoners, who is subject only to the orders of the War Department. All matters in relation to prisoners will pass through him. He will establish regulations for issuing clothing to prisoners, and will direct the manner in which all funds arising from the saving of rations at prison hospitals or otherwise shall be accounted for and disbursed by the regular disbursing officers of the departments in providing under existing regulations such articles as may be absolutely necessary for the welfare of the prisoners.

He will select positions for camps for prisoners (or prison camps) and will cause plans and estimates for necessary buildings to be prepared and submitted to the Quartermaster-General upon whose approval they will be erected by the officers of the Quartermaster's Department.

He will if practicable visit the several prison camps once a month. Loyal citizens who may be found among the prisoners of war confined on false accusations or through mistake may lay their cases before the commissary-general of prisoners, who will submit them to the Adjutant-General.

The commissary-general of prisoners is authorized to grant paroles to prisoners on the recommendation of the medical officer attending the prison in case of extreme illness but under no other circumstances.

By order of the Secretary of War
L. Thomas
Adjutant-General

* * * *

**OFFICE COMMISSARY-GENERAL
OF PRISONERS** – Detroit, Mich; July 7, 1862

The following regulations will be observed at all stations where prisoners of war are held:

1. The commanding officer at each station is held accountable for the discipline and good order of his command and for the security of the prisoners, and will take such measures as will best secure these results. He will divide the prisoners into companies, and will cause written reports to be made to him of their condition every morning showing the changes made during the preceding twenty-four hours, giving the names of the "joined", "transferred", "deaths",

&c. At the end of every month commanders will send to the commissary-general of prisoners a return of prisoners, giving names and details to explain alterations. Where rolls of "joined" or "transferred" have been forwarded during the month it will be sufficient to refer to them on the return.

2. On the arrival of prisoners at any station a careful comparison of them with rolls that accompany them will be made and all errors on the rolls will be corrected. When no roll accompanies the prisoners one will be immediately made out containing all the information required as correct as can be from the statements of the prisoners themselves. When the prisoners are citizens the town, county and State from which they come will be given on the rolls under the heads, rank, regiment and company. At the same time they will be required to give up all arms and weapons of every description and all moneys which they have in their possession, for which the commanding officer will give receipts.

3. The hospital will be under the immediate charge of the senior surgeon who will be held responsible to the commanding officer for its good order and the condition of the sick. "The fund" of this hospital will be kept separate from the fund of the hospital for the troops and will be disbursed for the sole benefit of the sick prisoners on the requisition of the surgeon approved by the commanding officer. When the fund is sufficiently large there will be bought with it besides the articles usually purchased all articles of table furniture, kitchen utensils, articles for policing, shirts and drawers for the sick, the expense of washing, and all articles that may be indispensably necessary to promote the sanitary condition of the hospital.

4. The commanding officer will cause requisitions to be made by his quartermaster on the nearest depot for such clothing as may be absolutely necessary for the prisoners, which requisition will be approved by him after a careful inquiry as to the necessity and submitted for the approval of the commissary-general of prisoners. The clothing will be issued by the quartermaster to the prisoners with the assistance and under the supervision of an officer detailed for the purpose, whose certificate that the issue has been made in his presence will be the quartermaster's voucher for the clothing issued. From the 30th of April to the 1st of October neither drawers nor socks will be allowed except to the sick.

5. A general fund for the benefit of the prisoners will be made by withholding from their rations all that can be spared without inconvenience to them, and selling this surplus under existing regulations to the commissary, who will hold the funds in his hands and be accountable for them subject to the commanding officer's order to cover purchases. The purchases with the fund will be made by or through the quartermaster with the approval or order of the commanding officer, the bills being paid by the commissary, who will keep an account book in which will be carefully entered all receipts and disbursements, which account will be forwarded to the commissary-general of prisoners with the remarks of the commanding officer. With this fund will be purchased all such articles as may be necessary for the health and comfort of the prisoners and which would otherwise have to be purchased by the Government. Among these articles are all table furniture and cooking utensils, articles for policing purposes, bedticks and straw, the means of improving or enlarging the barrack accommodations, extra pay to clerks who have charge of the camp post-office, and who keep the accounts of moneys deposited with the commanding officer, &c., &c.

6. The sutler is entirely under the control of the commanding officer who will see that he furnishes proper articles and at reasonable rates. For his privilege the sutler will be taxed a small amount by the commanding officer according to the amount of his trade, which tax will make a part of the general fund.

7. Prisoners will not be permitted to hold or receive money. All moneys in possession or received will be taken charge of by the commanding officer who will give receipts for it to those to whom it belongs. They will purchase from the sutler such articles as they may wish, which are not prohibited, and on the bill of the articles they will give an order on the commanding officer for the amount and this will be kept as a voucher with the individual's account. The commanding officer will keep a book in which the accounts of all those who have money deposited with him will be kept, and this book with the vouchers must be always ready for the inspection of the commissary-general of prisoners.

8. All articles contributed by friends for the prisoners in whatever shape they come if proper to be received will be carefully distributed as the donors may request; such articles as are intended for the sick passing through the hands of the surgeon who will be responsible for their proper use. Contributions must be received by an officer who must be held responsible that they are delivered to the persons for whom they are intended.

9. Visitors to these stations out of mere curiosity will in no case be permitted. Persons having business with the commanding officer or quartermaster may with the permission of the commanding officer enter the camp to remain only long enough to transact their business. When prisoners are seriously ill their nearest relatives, parents, wives, brothers or sisters if they are loyal people may be permitted to make them short visits; but under no other circumstances will visitors be allowed to see them without the approval of the commissary-general of prisoners.

10. Prisoners will not be permitted to write letters of more than one page of common letter paper, the matter to be strictly of a private nature, or the letter must be destroyed.

11. Prisoners will be paroled or released only by the authority of the War Department, or by direction of the commissary-general of prisoners.

W. Hoffman

Colonel Third Infantry, Commissary-General of Prisoners

* * * *

THE EXCHANGE CARTEL OF JULY 22, 1862
Haxall's Landing, on James River, VA.

The undersigned having been commissioned by the authorities they respectively represent to make arrangements for a general exchange of prisoners of war have agreed to the following articles:

Article 1. It is hereby agreed and stipulated that all prisoners of war held by either party including those taken on private armed vessels known as privateers shall be discharged upon the conditions and terms following: Prisoners to be exchanged man for man and officer for officer, privateers to be placed upon the footing of officers and men of the navy. Men and officers of lower grades may be exchanged for officers of a higher grade, and men and officers of different services may be exchanged according to the following scale of equivalents:

A general commanding-in-chief or an admiral shall be exchanged for officers of equal rank, or for forty privates or common seamen.

A flag-officer or major-general shall be exchanged for officers of equal rank, or for forty privates or common seamen.

A commodore carrying a broad pennant or a brigadier-general shall be exchanged for officers of equal rank, or twenty privates or common seamen.

A captain of the navy or a colonel shall be exchanged for officers of equal rank or for fifteen privates or common seamen.

A lieutenant colonel or a commander in the navy shall be exchanged for for officers of equal rank, or ten privates or common seamen.

A lieutenant commander or a major shall be exchanged for officers of equal rank, or eight privates or common seamen.

A lieutenant or a master in the navy or a captain in the army or marines shall be exchanged for officers of equal rank, or six privates or common seamen.

Masters mates in the navy, or lieutenants and ensigns in the army, shall be exchanged for officers of equal rank, or four privates or common seamen.

Midshipmen, warrant officers in the navy, masters of merchant vessels and commanders of privateers shall be exchanged for officers of equal rank, or three privates or common seamen.

Second captains, lieutenants or mates of merchant vessels or privateers, and all petty officers in the navy and all non-commissioned officers in the army or marines shall be severally exchanged for persons of equal rank, or for two privates or common seamen; and private soldiers or common seamen shall be exchanged for each other, man for man.

Article 2. Local State, civil and militia rank held by persons not in actual military service will not be recognized, the basis of exchange being the grade actually held in the naval and military service of the respective parties.

Article 3. If citizens, held by either party on charges of disloyalty or any alleged civil offense are exchanged it shall only be for citizens. Captured sutlers, teamsters and all civilians in the actual service of either party to be exchanged for persons in similar positions.

Article 4. All prisoners of war to be discharged on parole in ten days after their capture, and the prisoners now held and those hereafter taken to be transported to the points mutually agreed upon at the expense of the capturing party. The surplus prisoners not exchanged shall not be permitted to take up arms again, nor to serve as military police or constabulary force in any fort, garrison or field work held by either of the respective parties, nor as guards of prisons, depots or stores, nor to discharge any duty usually performed by soldiers, until exchanged under the provision of this cartel. The exchange is not to be considered complete until the officer or soldier exchanged for has been actually restored to the lines to which he belongs.

Article 5. Each party upon the discharge of prisoners of the other party is authorized to discharge an equal number of their own officers or men, from parole, furnishing at the same time to the other party a list of their prisoners discharged and of their own officers and men relieved from parole, thus enabling each party to to relieve from parole such of their own officers and men as the party may choose. The list thus mutually furnished will keep both parties advised of the true condition of the exchange of prisoners.

Article 6. The stipulations and provisions above mentioned to be of binding during the continuance of the war, it matters not which party may have the surplus of prisoners, the great principles involved being, first, an equitable exchange of prisoners, man for man, officer for officer, or officers of higher grade exchanged for officers of lower grade or for privates, according to the scale of equivalents; second, that privateers and officers and men of different services may be exchanged according to the same scale of equivalents; third, that all prisoners, of whatever arm of service, are to be exchanged or paroled in ten days from the time of their capture, if it be practicable to transfer them to their own lines in that time; if not, as soon thereafter as practicable; fourth, that no officer, soldier or employee, in the service of either party, is to be considered as exchanged and absolved from his parole until his equivalent has actually reached the lines of his friends; fifth, that the parole forbids the performance of field, garrison, police, or guard, or constabulary duty.

D.H. Hill
Major General C. S. Army

John A. Dix
Major General

Supplementary Articles
Article 7. All prisoners of war now held on either side and all prisoners hereafter taken shall be sent with all reasonable dispatch to A.M. Aiken's, below Dutch Gap, on the James River, Va., or to Vicksburg, on the Mississippi River, in the state of Mississippi, and there exchanged or paroled until such exchange can be effected, notice being previously given by each party of the number of prisoners it will send and the time when they will be delivered at these points respectively; and in case the vicissitudes of war shall change the military relations of the places designated in this article to the contending parties so as to render the same inconvenient for the delivery and exchange of prisoners, other places bearing as nearly as may be the present local relations of said places to the lines of said parties shall be by mutual agreement substituted. But nothing in this article contained shall prevent the commanders of two opposing armies from exchanging prisoners or releasing them on parole from other points mutually agreed on by said commanders.

Article 8. For the purpose of carrying into effect the foregoing articles of agreement each party will appoint two agents, to be called agents for the exchange of prisoners of war, whose duty it shall be to communicate with each other by correspondence and otherwise, to prepare the lists of prisoners, to attend to the delivery of the prisoners at the places agreed on and to carry out promptly, effectually, and in good faith all the details and provisions of the said articles of agreement.

Article 9. And in case any misunderstanding shall arise in regard to any clause or stipulation in the foregoing articles it is mutually agreed that such misunderstanding shall not interrupt the release of prisoners on parole, as herein provided, but shall be made the subject of friendly explanations in order that the object of this agreement may neither be defeated nor postponed.

D.H. Hill
Major General C. S. Army

John A. Dix
Major General

* * * *

GENERAL ORDERS
WAR DEPT., ADJT GENERAL'S OFFICE
NO. 90 – Washington, July 26, 1862

I. The principal being recognized that chaplains

should not be held as prisoners of war it is hereby ordered that all chaplains so held by the United States shall be immediately and unconditionally discharged.

By order of the Secretary of War
L. Thomas
Adjutant-General

* * * *

OFFICE OF COMMISSARY-GENERAL OF PRISONERS
Washington, D.C., December 3, 1862

Capt. S. E. Jones
Headquarters Western District, Louisville, Ky.

Captain: Your letter of the 22d ultimo is received and I have to reply that deserters from the rebel army cannot be considered prisoners of war but to insure their loyalty they should be required to take the oath of allegiance with the penalty of death for its violation.

If professed deserters come within our lines they may be spies and every commander should judge of each case after careful inquiries according to the circumstances. All soldiers taken in arms, whether recruits or conscripts, are prisoners of war, and if they desire not to be exchanged but to be released on bond a special report should be made in each case with a recommendation for or against. All civilians who took part with the rebels during their recent inroad into Kentucky should be sent to the depot at Johnson's Island, Sandusky, with a clear statement of the charges in each case. Doubtful cases may be sent to Camp Chase.

Very respectfully, your obedient servant,
W. Hoffman
Colonel Third Infantry, Commissary-General of Prisoners

* * * *

FORT MONROE
December 27, 1862

Col. W. Hoffman
Commissary-General of Prisoners

No Confederate prisoners who have taken the oath of allegiance should be sent South against their will. They would be immediately impressed into the Confederate military service. It is best to set them at liberty.

WM. H. Ludlow
Lieutenant-Colonel and Agent for the Exchange of Prisoners

* * * *

TEXT OF THE OATH ACCEPTED AND SIGNED BY PRISONERS OF WAR WHO WILLINGLY ABANDONED CONFEDERATE SERVICE (From M598 series Microfilm)

We, the undersigned, desire to take and have taken the Oath of Allegiance and Parole hereunto annexed, to return to our homes within the lines of the United States Army, and to suffer the penalty of Death, if willingly found South, beyond those lines, during the War.

* * * *

OATH AND PAROLE

"I do solemnly swear, in the presence of Almighty God, that I will henceforth faithfully support, protect and defend the Constitution of the United States, and the Union of the States there under; and that I will in like manner abide by and faithfully support all acts of Congress passed during the existing rebellion with reference to slaves, so long and so far as not repealed, modified or held void by Congress, or by decision of the Supreme Court: and that I will in like manner abide by and faithfully support all proclamations of the President made during the existing rebellion, having reference to slaves, so long and so far as not modified or declared void by decision of the Supreme Court. So help me God: and we give our solemn parole of honor (to be enforced according to military law) that we will hold no correspondence with, or afford aid or comfort to any enemies or opposers of the United States, save as an act of humanity, to administer to the necessities of individuals, who are in sickness or distress; and we solemnly declare that this Oath and Parole are taken and given freely and willingly, without any mental reservation or evasion whatever, and with full intention to keep the same."

* * * *

FORT MONROE
December 28, 1862

Hon. E.M. Stanton
Secretary of War

In view of the recent proclamation of Jeff. Davis directing that no commissioned officer of the United States taken prisoner shall be released on parole before exchange until General Butler is punished shall not all Confederate commissioned officers taken prisoners be detained instead of being forwarded as usual for exchange? I shall go to City Point to meet Mr. Ould immediately after the 1st of January. Do you wish to see me at Washington before I go?

WM. H. Ludlow
Lieutenant Colonel and Agent for Exchange of Prisoners

* * * *

WASHINGTON
December 28, 1862

Colonel Ludlow:

You will not make any exchange of commissioned officers until further instructions and come to Washington previous to going to City Point.

Edwin M. Stanton
Secretary of War

* * * *

OFFICE COMMISSARY-GENERAL OF PRISONERS
Washington, D.C., February 17, 1863

Capt. E. L. Webber,
Commanding Camp Chase Prison, Columbus, Ohio

Captain: Your letter of the 11th instant is received. General Orders, Nos. 60 and 90, of 1862, are still in force and all medical officers and chaplains received among the prisoners of war should be discharged and sent beyond our lines. Send them on their parole to report to General Wright at Cincinnati and write a letter to the general requesting him to forward them by such points in our lines as he may deem proper. None can be recognized as holding the place of a medical officer or chaplain but those who are so designated on the rolls.

I am not yet prepared to say that "contract surgeons" can be classed with medical officers.

It will be determined in a few days whether rebel officers can be permitted to take the oath of allegiance.

You are not at liberty to grant paroles to rebel officers under any circumstances without the authority of the Secretary of War except in case of illness which is provided for by the circular of regulations.

Very respectfully, your obedient servant,
W. Hoffman
Colonel Third Infantry, Commissary of Prisoners

* * * *

OFFICE COMMISSARY-GENERAL OF PRISONERS
Washington D.C., February 18, 1863

Brig. Gen. Jacob Ammen
Commanding Camp Douglas, Chicago, Ill.

General: Pursuant to instructions from the General-in-Chief you are authorized to release all prisoners of war belonging to the Confederate Army not officers on their taking the oath of allegiance in good faith. A careful examination will be made in each case to ascertain the sincerity of the applicant, and it will be explained that by taking the oath of allegiance he becomes liable to be called on for military service as any other loyal citizen. Whenever there is a doubt the application must be rejected. The oath will be taken in duplicate, one copy for the person to whom it is administered and one with roll of all so discharged to be sent to this office. This permission does not extend to guerrillas or other irregular organizations. None of these will be released except on special report in each case, approved at this office. The

above instructions will cover the several applications made by individuals to be released on taking the oath of allegiance.

WM. Hoffman
Colonel Third Infantry, Commissary-General of Prisoners

(Same to commandants of all other important prison posts.)

* * * *

FORT MONROE
April 7, 1863

Hon. E. M. Stanton

Shall such Confederate prisoners as arrive here en route to City Point who desire to take the oath of allegiance and enter our military service be permitted to do so?

WM. H. Ludlow
Lieutenant Colonel and Agent for Exchange of Prisoners

* * * *

WAR DEPARTMENT
April 7, 1863

Col. W.H. Ludlow
Fort Monroe

The rule is not to permit Confederate prisoners to join our Army. But in any case in which you are satisfied a prisoner is sincerely desirous of renouncing all connections with the rebels you may on his taking the oath of allegiance send him to Fort Delaware, to be released there after further investigation as to his sincerity and sent North to reside.

P. H. Watson
Assistant Secretary of War

* * * *

HDQRS. DEPT. OF VIRGINIA AND NORTH CAROLINA
Fort Monroe, January 9, 1864

Brig. Gen. G. Marston

You will cause every prisoner at Point Lookout to answer one of the following questions, taking his answer, after he has heard them all:

First. Do you desire to be sent South as a prisoner of war for exchange?

Second. Do you desire to take the oath of allegiance and go to your home within the lines of the U. S. Army, under like penalty if found South beyond those lines during the war?

Third. Do you desire to take the oath and parole and be sent North to work on public works, under penalty of death if found in the South before the end of the war?

Fourth. Do you desire to take the oath of allegiance and go to your home within the lines of the U.S. Army, under like penalty if found South beyond those lines during the war?

You will adopt the form set forth in this book, and let each signature be witnessed, causing the oath and parole to be read to each man, the questions to be propounded to these men alone and apart from any other rebel prisoner.

The book mentioned herein will be forwarded in a few days.

Truly, yours,
Benj. F. Butler
Major-General and Chief of Staff

* * * *

HEADQUARTERS OF THE ARMY
Washington, September 6, 1864

Major-General CANBY
New Orleans

General: I presume that General Grant's order to make no more exchanges of prisoners was based on the fact that they gave us only such men as they have utterly broken down by starvation, receiving in return from us men fit for duty. Every exchange, therefore, gives them strength, without a corresponding advantage to us. Not so, however, with exchanges made on the battle-field or immediately after an engagement. Exchanges of this kind, made man for man, as provided for under the cartel, General Grant did not intend to prohibit. You and the officers under your command are therefore at liberty to continue the exchanges in the field, as provided for in last clause of article 7 of the cartel of July 22, 1862.

Very respectfully, your obedient servant,
H.W. Halleck
Major-General and Chief of Staff

* * * *

SPECIAL ORDERS HDQRS. ARMIES OF THE UNITED STATES
NO. 44 – City Point, Va., March 4, 1865

The following order relating to deserters, with additional provision allowing payment to them for arms and other property, together with Circular Orders, No. 31, of date of August 31, 1864, from the office of the Provost-Marshal General, War Department, exempting them from conscription into the service of the United States, are republished for the information and guidance of all concerned.

* * * *

SPECIAL ORDERS, HEADQUARTERS ARMIES OF THE UNITED STATES NO. 3 – In the Field, Va, January 4, 1865

Hereafter deserters from the Confederate Army who deliver themselves up to the U.S. forces will, on taking an oath that they will not again take up arms during the present rebellion, be furnished subsistence and free transportation to any point in the Northern States.

All deserters who take the oath of allegiance will, if they desire it, be given employment in the Quartermaster's and other departments of the Army, and the same remuneration paid them as given to civilian employees for similar services.

Military duty, or service endangering them to capture by the Confederate forces, will not abe exacted from such as give themselves up to the U.S. Military Authorities. Deserters who bring arms, horses mules or other property into our lines with them, will, on delivering the same to the Quartermaster's department, receive in money the highest price such arms, horses, mules and other property are worth.

Railroad employees, telegraph operators, mechanics and other civilians employed by the Confederate authorities who desert from their present employment and come into the Federal lines will be entitled to all the benefits and immunities of this order.

By command of Lieutenant-General Grant
T. S. Bowers
Assistant Adjutant-General

* * * *

CIRCULAR
WAR DEPARTMENT, PROVOST-MARSHAL-GENERAL'S OFFICE
NO. 31 – Washington, August 31, 1864

Deserters from the rebel army are not subject to enrollment or draft, nor are they acceptable as substitutes or recruits.

James B. Fry
Provost-Marshall General

By command of Lieutenant-General Grant
T. S. Bowers
Assistant Adjutant-General

* * * *

CITY POINT, VA
March 7, 1865

Brig. Gen. W. Hoffman
Commissary-General of Prisoners

The enemy are putting all their returned prisoners into the ranks of the Eastern army without regard to the organization to which they belong. As the men returned to us are unfit for duty, I want all of the same class in our hands returned before any well men are sent back.

U.S. Grant
Lieutenant-General

* * * *

WASHINGTON
March 7, 1865

Brig. Gen. W. P. Richardson
Commanding Camp Chase, Ohio, Columbus, Ohio

I hear that you give transportation to released prisoners. It is not authorized.

W. Hoffman
Commissary-General of Prisoners

* * * *

**GENERAL ORDERS
WAR DEPT., ADJT. GENERAL'S OFFICE
NO. 85** – Washington, May 8, 1865

Ordered, That all prisoners of war, except officers above the rank of colonel, who before the capture of Richmond signified their desire to take the oath of allegiance to the United States and their unwillingness to be exchanged be forthwith released upon their taking the said oath, and transportation furnished them to their respective homes. In respect to all other prisoners of war further orders will be issued.

The Commissary-General of Prisoners will issue the necessary regulations for preserving the requisite record of the prisoners of war to be released under this order, the record to set forth the name of the prisoner, his place of residence, the organization to which he belonged, the time and place of capture, &c. The oaths of allegiance will be administered by the commanding officers of the prison camps and forts, who will send by telegraph daily reports of the prisoners released to the Commissary-General of Prisoners. These reports will be consolidated for each day and transmitted to the Secretary of War.

By order of the Secretary of War
E. D. Townsend
Assistant Adjutant-General

* * * *

**GENERAL ORDERS,
WAR DEPT., ADJUT. GENERAL'S OFFICE
NO. 109** – Washington, June 6, 1865

Order for the discharge of certain prisoners of war.

The prisoners of war at the several depots in the North will be discharged under the following regulations and restrictions:

I. All enlisted men of the rebel Army and petty officers and seamen of the rebel Navy will be discharged upon taking the oath of allegiance.

II. Officers of the rebel Army not above the grade of captain, and of the rebel Navy not above the grade of lieutenant, except such as have graduated at the U.S. Military or Naval Academies, and such as held a commission in either the U.S. Army or Navy at the beginning of the rebellion, may be discharged upon taking the oath of allegiance.

III. When the discharges hereby ordered are completed, regulations will be issued in respect to the discharge of officers having higher rank than captain in the Army or lieutenant in the Navy.

IV. The several commanders of prison stations will discharge each day as many of the prisoners hereby authorized to be discharged as proper rolls can be prepared for, beginning with those who have been longest in prison and from the most remote points of the country; and certified rolls will be forwarded daily to the Commissary-General of Prisoners of those so discharged. The oath of allegiance only will be administered, but notice will be given that all who desire will be permitted to take the oath of amnesty after their release, in accordance with the regulations of the Department of State respecting the amnesty.

V. The Quartermaster's Department will furnish transportation to all released prisoners to the nearest accessible point to their homes by rail or by steam boat.

By order of the President of the United States:
E. D. Townsend
Assistant Adjutant-General

CIRCULAR
DEPARTMENT OF STATE
Washington, May 29, 1865

Sir: A copy of the President's amnesty proclamation of this date is herewith appended. By a clause in the instrument the Secretary of State is directed to establish rules and regulations for administering and recording the amnesty oath, so as to insure its benefits to the people and guard the Government against fraud. Pursuant to this injunction you are informed that the oath prescribed in the proclamation may be taken and subscribed before any commissioned officer, civil, military or naval, in the service of the United States, or any civil or military officer of a loyal State or Territory, who by the laws thereof may be qualified for administering oaths. All officers who receive such oaths are hereby authorized to give certified copies thereof to the persons respectively by whom they were made. And such officers are hereby required to transmit the original of such oaths at as early a day as may be convenient to this Department, where they will be deposited and remain in the archives of the Government. A register thereof will be kept in the Department and on application in proper cases certificates will be issued of such records in the customary form of official certificates.

I am, sir, your obedient servant,

William H. Seward

Inclosure

By the President of the United States of America:

A PROCLAMATION

Whereas, the President of the United States, on the 8th day of December, A. D. 1863, and on the 26th day of March, A. D. 1864, did, with the object to suppress the existing rebellion, to induce all persons to return to their loyalty and to restore the authority of the United States, issue proclamations offering amnesty and pardon to certain persons who had directly or by implication participated in the said rebellion: and whereas many persons who had so engaged in said rebellion have since the issuance of said proclamations failed or neglected to take the benefits offered thereby; and whereas, many persons who have been justly deprived of all claim to amnesty and pardon thereunder, by reason of their participation directly or by implication in said rebellion and continued hostility to the Government of the United States since the date of said proclamation, now desire to apply for and obtain amnesty and pardon:

To the end, therefore, that the authority of the Government of the United States may be restored, and that peace, order and freedom may be established, I, Andrew Johnson, President of the United States, do proclaim and declare that I hereby grant to all persons who have, directly or indirectly, participated in the existing rebellion, except as hereinafter excepted, amnesty and pardon, with restoration of all rights of property, except as to slaves, and except in cases where legal proceedings, under the laws of the United States providing for the confiscation of property of persons engaged in rebellion, have been instituted; but upon the condition, nevertheless, that every such person shall take and subscribe the following oath (or affirmation), and thenceforward keep and maintain said oath inviolate; and which oath shall be registered for permanent preservation, and shall be of the tenor and effect following, to wit:

I,_____, do solemnly swear (or affirm), in the presence of Almighty God, that I will henceforth faithfully support, protect and defend the Constitution of the United States, and the Union of the States thereunder; and that I will, in like manner, abide by and faithfully support all laws and proclamations which have been made during the existing rebellion with reference to the emancipation of slaves: So help me God. The following classes of persons are excepted from the benefits of this proclamation: First, all who are or shall have been pretended civil or diplomatic officers or otherwise domestic or foreign agents of the pretended Confederate Government; second, all who left judicial stations under the United States to aid the rebellion; third, all who shall have been military or naval officers of said pretended Confederate Government above the rank of colonel in the Army or lieutenant in the Navy; fourth, all who left seats in the Congress of the United States to aid the rebellion; fifth, all who resigned or tendered resignations of their commissions in the Army or Navy of the United States to evade duty in resisting the rebellion; sixth, all who have engaged in any way in treating otherwise than lawfully as prisoners of war persons found in the U.S. service, as officers, soldiers, seamen, or in other capacities; seventh, all persons who have been or are absentees from the United States for the purpose of aiding the rebellion; eighth, all military and naval officers in the rebel service who were educated by the Government in the Military Academy at West Point or the U.S. Naval Academy; ninth, all persons who held the pretended offices of Governors of States in insurrection against the United States; tenth, all persons who left their homes within the jurisdiction and protection of the United States and passed beyond the Federal military lines into the pretended Confederate States for the purpose of aid the rebellion; eleventh, all persons who have been engaged in the destruction of the commerce of the United States upon the high seas, and all persons who have made raids into the United States from Canada, or been engaged in destroying the commerce of the United States upon the lakes and rivers that separate the British Provinces from the United States; twelfth, all persons who, at the time when they seek to obtain the benefits hereof by taking the oath herein prescribed, are in military, naval or civil confinement or custody, or under bonds of the civil, military or naval authorities, or agents of the United States, as prisoners of war, or persons detained for offenses of any kind, either before or after conviction; thirteenth, all persons who have voluntarily participated in said rebellion, and the estimated value of whose taxable property is over $20,000; fourteenth, all persons who have taken the oath of amnesty as prescribed in the President's proclamation, and who have not thenceforward kept and maintained the same inviolate.

Provided, That special application may be made to the President for pardon by any person belonging to the excepted classes; and such clemency will be liberally extended as may be consistent with the facts of the case and the peace and dignity of the United States.

The Secretary of State will establish rules and regulations for administering and recording the said amnesty oath, so as to insure its benefit to the people and guard the Government against fraud.

In testimony whereof I have hereunto set my hand and caused the seal of the United States to be affixed.

Done at the city of Washington the twenty-ninth day of May in the year of our Lord one thousand eight hundred and sixty-five, and of the Independence of the United States the eighty-ninth.

By the President
Andrew Johnson
William H. Seward
Secretary of State

WAR DEPARTMENT, ADJUTANT-GENERAL'S OFFICE – Washington, May 29, 1865

The Secretary of War directs that you send a list of names of the prisoners who would be discharged under the following order to this office immediately, giving number of order promulgating sentence, and that the prisoners be not discharged until you receive further instructions from here.

**GENERAL ORDERS
WAR DEPARTMENT, ADJUTANT-GENERAL'S OFFICE, NO. 98** – Washington, May 29, 1865

Ordered, that in all cases of sentences by military tribunals of imprisonment during the war the sentence be remitted and that the prisoners be discharged. The Adjutant-General will issue immediately the necessary instructions to carry this order into effect.

By order of the President of the United States
E. D. Townsend
Assistant Adjutant-General
Acknowledge receipt

E. D. Townsend
Assistant Adjutant-General

Statistical Summaries

A preliminary review of those held captive by disposition and regiment produces a few interesting statistics.

TOTAL BY DISPOSITION

Died in Prison/Conditions	1,687
Deserters to Enemy	1,213
Paroled in Field	418
Entered US Ser./Released on Oath	334
Captured/ Gettysburg	619
Died of Wounds/Disease on or before capture	406
Captured Twice	328
Captured Three Times	6
Died of exposure	2
Captured after March 31, 1865	2,049

CATEGORIES OF CAPTURE

A simple listing of the names and prison history of the men who appear in the Union and Confederate records does not adequately explain the variations in prisoner experience. The manner or condition of capture was the first and most important consideration of this study and will be examined later in this summary.

The names of 11,238 South Carolina civilians, soldiers and sailors have been identified on Federal prison records and or field capture or parole reports. This total count can be broken down into categories as follows:

Normal prisoners-of-war	8,867
Paroled in the field	418
Deserters to the enemy	1,213
Deserted after capture	334
Died of wounds or disease	406
Total	11,238

Normal prisoners-of-war

These were healthy men who were made prisoners, unwounded or not dangerously wounded. These men went through the Union prison system and were exchanged, died of disease, escaped or released at the end or by special orders.

Paroled in the field

These men were paroled and released in the field when captured and did not enter the prison system unless later exchanged and recaptured. The men of Evan's Brigade, captured at the engagement at Kinston, NC in 1862, were paroled in the field and either furloughed home or held in a camp for paroled prisoners until formally exchanged and returned to duty. The men in Confederate hospitals taken by Union patrols were likewise paroled in place. On September 29, 1862, 173 South Carolina wounded from Second Manassas were captured by a Federal cavalry unit and paroled at hospitals in Warrenton, VA.

Deserters to the enemy

These were men who willingly crossed the lines and surrendered to the Federal army. These men were examined for sincerity, given the oath of allegiance and swiftly sent north, given menial jobs in the prisons or, later in the war, sent home through Charleston or Savannah.

Deserted after capture

These were men who voluntarily took the oath of allegiance while in prison and were released, or who were recruited to join the Federal army or Navy. Some of the men who volunteered for Federal service were rejected and released. Many of the men were recruited for service on the frontier to protect settlers from Indian attacks. Of the 334 South Carolinians who elected to take the oath of allegiance 188 joined the U.S. Army, 30 joined the U.S. Navy, and 9 were rejected and released. A total of 116 took the oath and were released or given jobs in the prisons or quarter-master depots.

Died of wounds or diseases

These were men who were mortally wounded or seriously ill when captured. The records show that the Federal Medical Service provided excellent care for sick and wounded Confederate prisoners. These men have been set apart from the prisoners who went on into the prison camps so that their deaths will not be attributed to prison conditions.

THE PRISON EXPERIENCE

The 8,867 South Carolina normal prisoners of war endured a hard and depressing existence. Food was indifferent and meager, The camps were crowded and bleak, and 1,687 South Carolina prisoners died of disease, malnutrition and exposure. This is a death rate of 19%. The overall death rate for Federal prisons has been calculated at just over 12%.

There is nothing in the prison records to suggest that there were extreme variations in the treatment of prisoners at any camp. No prison camp was located on prime real estate. The prisons in the upper north were certain to be very cold in the winter. Camp Douglas, near Chicago, had a death rate of 12% in February 1863. This was the highest monthly death rate of any prison North or South. Ft. Delaware was low and swampy. The most deadly prisons for South Carolinians were:

```
Elmira, NY . . . . . . . . . . . . . . . . . . . . . . . . . . . 408
Pt. Lookout, MD . . . . . . . . . . . . . . . . . . . . . . 321
Ft. Delaware, DE . . . . . . . . . . . . . . . . . . . . . . . 92
Camp Chase, OH . . . . . . . . . . . . . . . . . . . . . . . 79
Rock Island, IL . . . . . . . . . . . . . . . . . . . . . . . . . 59
```

DIED OF WOUNDS AND DISEASES

There were many prisoners of war who were picked up on the battlefield very seriously wounded. In some instances the Confederate army left very sick men behind when on the march. These men would be left with surgeons and nurses to care for them, but they became prisoners when the Federal army occupied the location. Many men were thus left in Frederick, MD during the Maryland campaign in 1862. Many of these sick and wounded died in Federal hands, but their death should not be charged to the Federal prison system. The deaths following the battle of Gettysburg are a unique example. At Gettysburg, 728 South Carolina soldiers were captured. The great majority were sick and wounded who were left behind on the night of July 5th, 1862. Of these, 81 died in Federal hospitals in Gettysburg, Chester, Philadelphia and Davids Island, NY.

EXCHANGES AND RECAPTURES

Exchanges of prisoners occurred throughout the war. General Grant stopped such exchanges for a time in 1864 but resumed them under public pressure. In all cases, North and South, the weakest and most severely crippled prisoners were selected for exchange.

Exchanged Confederate prisoners were usually examined in a hospital and either hospitalized, sent to a parole camp, returned to duty or given furloughs home. A considerable number were unfit for further field service, but 328 South Carolina soldiers were captured a second time and a paltry 6 were caught a third time.

ESCAPES

The Federal prison records note very few successful escapes. Only 14 South Carolinians are logged as having escaped from established prisons. It is known from personal diaries and reminisceces that many escaped soon after capture. The best known escape involving South Carolinians is the escape from Elmira prison on 10/07/64 of nine prisoners that included Sgt. Berry Benson, 1st SCVIG and Sgt. J.P. Scruggs, Holcombe Legion. They tunneled out and returned safely to their units.

PLACES AND TIMES

There were certain engagements that involved the capture of large numbers of Confederate soldiers. Gettysburg, PA, Kinston, NC and Warrenton, VA have been cited. Other noteworthy examples include:

```
Falling Waters, MD 7/14/63 . . . . . . . . . . . . . . . . 114
Missionary Ridge, TN 11/25/63 . . . . . . . . . . . . 158
The Crater, Pbg., VA 7/30/64 . . . . . . . . . . . . . . 174
Weldon RR, VA 08/21/64 . . . . . . . . . . . . . . . . 258
Cedar Creek, VA 10/19/64 . . . . . . . . . . . . . . . 203
Spotsylvania, VA 5/12/64 . . . . . . . . . . . . . . . . 141
Town Creek, NC 2/20/65 . . . . . . . . . . . . . . . . 344
```

REGIMENTAL RECORDS

There is wide disparity in the number of men captured or surrendered to the enemy by South Carolina units. Artillery and cavalry organizations generally lost fewer men than the infantry. Garrison units in South Carolina also lost fewer men from enemy action. Some South Carolina regiments lost more prisoners than others because they were involved in difficult or disastrous battles. The regiments of the Kershaw Brigade lost heavily at Cedar Creek, VA. Hagood's Brigade lost heavily in the defense of the Weldon RR, VA and Town Creek, NC. The five regiments losing the most prisoners were:

```
Holcombe Legion . . . . . . . . . . . . . . . . . . . . . . . 527
27th SCVI . . . . . . . . . . . . . . . . . . . . . . . . . . . . 452
17th SCVI . . . . . . . . . . . . . . . . . . . . . . . . . . . . 456
25th SCVI . . . . . . . . . . . . . . . . . . . . . . . . . . . . 433
21st SCVI . . . . . . . . . . . . . . . . . . . . . . . . . . . . 422
```

Note that the 21st SCVI, 25th SCVI and the 27th SCVI were in Hagood's Brigade.

The regimental records for desertions to the enemy merit some study. The desertion rate of a unit is considered a prime indicator of unit morale and efficiency. The 5 units with the worst and the best desertion to the enemy rate were:

Worst

1st SCVA	124
1st SCVIR	100
22nd SCVI	72
13th SCVI	57
P.S.S.	46

Best

3rd SCVI	2
16th SCVI	2
10th SCVI	3
19th SCVI	3
24th SCVI	4

The 1st SCVA and the 1st SCVIR were in the Charleston garrison and most of their desertions to the enemy were passive in that the deserters simply hunkered down in Charleston and refused to go with their units when Charleston was evacuated. The 1st SCVIR was also a state regular regiment raised from all over the state and lacked the cohesiveness provided by neighborhood volunteer companies. The P.S.S. was also a unit raised from other regiments during the 1862 reorganization and its companies lacked neighborhood backgrounds. The case of the 22nd SCVI is not clear but it is worth noting that its first Colonel, Joseph Abney, was dropped at the reorganization and the second Colonel, Spartan D. Goodlett, was cashiered by court martial in 1864, and the third and fourth colonels were killed in action. The 3rd SCVI was a strong unit with solid locally raised companies and good leadership. It is interesting to note that the 10th SCVI, 16th SCVI and the 24th SCVI were all units that served in the west and did not enjoy the battlefield successes of the Army of Northern Virginia.